WEST'S
BUSINESS LAW

Text
Cases
Legal Environment

FOURTH EDITION

WEST'S BUSINESS LAW

Text
Cases
Legal Environment

FOURTH EDITION

KENNETH W. CLARKSON
Director, Law and Economics Center
University of Miami

ROGER LeROY MILLER
Center for Policy Studies
Clemson University
and
School of Law
University of Miami

GAYLORD A. JENTZ
Herbert D. Kelleher
Professor in Business Law
MSIS Department
University of Texas at Austin

FRANK B. CROSS
MSIS Department
and
Associate Director, Center for Legal and Regulatory Studies
University of Texas at Austin

WEST PUBLISHING COMPANY
St. Paul   New York   Los Angeles   San Francisco

A study guide has been developed to assist you in mastering the concepts presented in the text. The study guide includes a "Things to Keep in Mind" section, a list of key terms, an outline of each chapter, a set of fill-in questions (a type of programmed learning device), a set of multiple-choice questions, the answers to the fill-in and multiple choice questions, and a new section entitled Uniform CPA Business Law Examination Information. This workbook is available from your local bookstore under the title *Study Guide to Accompany West's Business Law: Text, Cases, Legal Environment, Fourth Edition,* prepared by Barbara Behr of Bloomsburg University of Pennsylvania.

Composition: Parkwood Composition
Copy Editing: Beverly Peavler, Naples Editing Services
Artwork: Rolin Graphics

Library of Congress Cataloging-in-Publication Data

West's business law: text and cases/Kenneth W. Clarkson . . . [et al.].—4th ed.
    p. cm.
    Rev. ed. of: West's business law/Kenneth W. Clarkson. 3rd ed. 1986.
    Includes index.
    ISBN 0-314-47214-2
    1. Commercial law—United States—Cases.
    2. Business law—United States.
    I. Clarkson, Kenneth W.
    II. Clarkson, Kenneth W. West's business law.
    KF888.C55 1989
    346.73'07—dc19
    [347.3067]

CONTENTS IN BRIEF

v

CONTENTS

APPENDICES

PREFACE

The first course in business law is often an exciting adventure for the student preparing for a career in business, accounting, government, law, and most other careers in today's world. Now, more than ever before, a basic knowledge of business law is an important part of a student's general education, for the law touches on just about every individual at one time or another. All you need to do to confirm this statement is glance through some of the case excerpts contained within the following pages. You will see how the litigation represented by these cases involves many different types of individuals and situations and how the law and the legal process affects people from all walks of life. It is no exaggeration to say that the law provides an all-encompassing framework in our society.

It is with this universal applicability of the law in mind that we have fashioned this text. The result is, we believe, a useful "tool for living" and a text that should satisfy the demands of students preparing for future careers. (The text also includes all areas covered by the CPA exam.)

In this preface we would like to point out not only the changes that have been made in the Fourth Edition, but also the numerous pedagogical devices that aid the student-reader in systematically learning business law.

MAJOR CHANGES IN THE FOURTH EDITION

We have made substantial changes to the Fourth Edition in order to maintain the absolute accuracy, currency, and teachability of our presentation of business law. To accomplish these changes, we have both added some new chapters and completely rewritten others.

New Chapters in the Fourth Edition

The first three editions of this text included a number of unique chapters that were necessary to keep pace with contemporary legal trends. We have retained these chapters on special partnerships, private franchises, business torts, and other topics, with appropriate revisions to reflect current legislation and recent court rulings. In addition, three completely new chapters have been added to the Fourth Edition. They are:

- Electronic Fund Transfers (Chapter 28)
- Landlord-Tenant Relationships (Chapter 53)
- Computers and the Law (Chapter 55)

Important Chapter Revisions

The entire first unit of the text on the Legal Environment of Business has been thoroughly revised. Additionally, all of the following chapters in Unit Seven on Government Regulation have been completely rewritten:

- Introduction and Administrative Law (Chapter 45)
- Consumer Protection (Chapter 46)
- Environmental Protection (Chapter 47)
- Antitrust (Chapter 48)
- Employment and Labor Relations Law (Chapter 49)

In addition, Chapter 58 (The Effect of International Law in a Global Economy) has been completely rewritten with new cases.

Other Significant Changes

- Chapter 1 (Introduction to Law and Legal Reasoning) now has a section on Legal Reasoning.
- Chapter 2 (Courts and Civil Dispute Resolution) has an expanded discussion of arbitration and mediation as an alternative to court settlement of disputes.
- Chapter 12 (Writing and Form) includes a new section on the interpretation of contracts.
- Chapter 16 (Introduction to Sales Contracts and Their Formation) includes a section on leases under new Article 2A of the Uniform Commercial Code.
- Chapter 30 (Rights of Debtors and Creditors) has a major section on suretyship.
- Chapter 31 (Bankruptcy and Reorganization) has been simplified, and a new section on Chapter 12 of the Bankruptcy Code has been added.
- Chapter 42 (Corporations/Merger, Consolidation, and Termination) has sections on corporate takeovers, golden parachutes, and poison pills.
- Chapter 43 (Corporations/Financial Regulation and Investor Protection) contains an expanded discussion of exemptions from securities regulations.
- Chapter 54 (Insurance) has been rewritten to conform more closely to the requirements for the CPA exam.

- Chapter 56 (Wills, Trusts, and Estates) now includes a discussion of principal and income allocation, plus sections on estate planning.

CONCEPT SUMMARIES

Whenever key areas of the law need explicit repetition, we provide a *Concept Summary*. These summaries have proved to be such popular pedagogical tools that we increased their number in this edition. In the third edition, there were twenty-one *Concept Summaries;* in the Fourth Edition, there are almost thirty. Some examples are:

- Valid Business Contracts under the Statute of Frauds (Chapter 12)
- Discharge of Contracts (Chapter 14)
- Seller's Remedies for Buyer's Breach (Chapter 19)
- Rules and Requirements for Status of a Holder in Due Course (Chapter 25)

CASES, CASE CITATIONS, AND CASE EXCERPTS

Learning how to read case citations and case excerpts is a major part of understanding business law. We have made a significant advance in the Fourth Edition toward our goal of helping the student in these areas.

Expanded Section on How to Find Case Law

In Chapter 1 we use a unique format to explain case citations. In addition to our explanatory text, we offer an exhibit in four-color graphics to lead the student to a full understanding of how to read and understand case citations in this text and in other legal references.

Case Presentation

Our cases are fully integrated into the surrounding text. That is to say, they directly follow and illustrate the points of law that are being discussed within the text. Each case also has a unique format. First, the full case citation is presented in the margin. Then, we summarize the *Background and Facts* of the case in our own words. Following the summary, an excerpt from the actual court opinion is presented in different type size to differentiate it from the surrounding textual material. The case presentation concludes with a *Decision and Remedy* section and, in many instances, a *Comments* section.

We have examined virtually every word of every case excerpt in this edition to make sure that the terminology used by the court will be comprehensible to the student-reader. Whenever a difficult term does appear in the case opinion, it is briefly explained in brackets.

New Cases

Approximately one-third of the cases in the Fourth Edition are new. Of those one-third, the majority are from the 1980s with special emphasis on cases from 1987 and 1988.

FOCUS ON ETHICS

The teaching of ethics as an integral part of an introductory course in business law is becoming a common practice throughout the United States. Additionally, accreditation committees usually require the inclusion of a minimum of ethical considerations in an introductory business law course. To satisfy this requirement and the increased interest in ethical questions, we have expanded these sections and have updated them to include current ethical problems and controversies. These specially prepared sections are found at the end of each of the nine units in the text, and each *Focus on Ethics* addresses aspects of the law discussed in the preceding unit. These sections are not intended as a course in ethics; rather, they are designed to elicit comments and discussion from the student-readers. For this reason, each *Focus* ends with a set of discussion questions. Brief suggested answers to these questions can be found in the *Instructor's Manual*.

APPENDICES

Since most students keep their business law text as a future reference source, we have included a full set of appendices. They are as follows:

A The United States Constitution
B The Uniform Commercial Code, fully updated, including Article 2A on leases

C The Uniform Partnership Act
D The Uniform Limited Partnership Act
E The Revised Uniform Limited Partnership Act (including the 1985 Amendments)
F The Model Business Corporation Act
G Selected Provisions of the Revised Model Business Corporation Act
H Spanish Equivalents for Important Legal Terms in English

IMPROVED VOCABULARY EXPLANATIONS

One of the major stumbling blocks in the study of business law is legal vocabulary. This edition has been completely reedited to ensure that every important legal term is fully defined when it is first introduced. The number of boldfaced terms for which definitions are included in the glossary at the end of the text has been increased by over twenty-five percent.

EXPANDED QUESTIONS AND CASE PROBLEMS

Every edition of *West's Business Law* has had numerous end-of-chapter hypothetical questions and actual case problems. Complete answers are found in a booklet entitled *Answers to Questions and Case Problems*. In this edition, through the use of extensive student and user reviews, these problems have become even better suited to today's user. Specifically, ambiguous problems have been replaced by those that are classroom-tested. We have also increased the number of problems by twenty percent. And, finally, we have included numerous additional problems based on cases that can be found in their entirety in the LEGAL CLERK Research Software System (see below). The *Answers to Questions and Case Problems* is free to adopters and can be placed on reserve in the library if desired.

GREATLY EXPANDED SUPPLEMENTS PACKAGE

Most business law instructors face a difficult task in finding the time to teach all of the materials they wish to cover during each term. We have therefore developed, in conjunction with a number of our colleagues, supplementary teaching materials that, we believe, are the best available today. For this edition we have greatly expanded the supplements package.

LEGAL CLERK—A Software Package for Research and Learning

New to this edition is the highly acclaimed West Publishing LEGAL CLERK Research Software System. LEGAL CLERK is a user-friendly, interactive software package that simultaneously introduces students to the rudiments of computer-aided legal research and reinforces the underlying concepts of business law. LEGAL CLERK provides a valuable learning tool to help your school meet AACSB recommendations for using microcomputers in business law courses.

LEGAL CLERK enables students with access to IBM-PC and compatible personal computers to retrieve specific cases found in *West's Business Law: Text, Cases, Legal Environment, Fourth Edition* for extensive study.

THREE VERSIONS AVAILABLE To provide instructors with maximum flexibility LEGAL CLERK covers three major subject areas of business law and legal environment—UCC Article 2 Sales; Government Regulation and the Legal Environment of Business; and Contracts. Instructors may select one version or all three versions for their classes. Cases appearing in LEGAL CLERK are clearly identified in the text with a computer logo. The logos are color coded to help users easily identify which version of LEGAL CLERK contains specific cases.

> *Uniform Commercial Code Article 2 Sales-Version 1.0*

> *Government Regulation and The Legal Environment of Business-Version 1.0*

> *Contracts-Version 1.0*

SEVERAL CASES ARE INCLUDED ON MORE THAN ONE VERSION OF LEGAL CLERK The following cases are on both the *Uniform Commercial Code Article 2 Sales* and *Government Regulation and The Legal Environment of Business* versions of LEGAL CLERK:

- Continental T.V., Inc. v. GTE Sylvania, Inc.
- Cote v. Wadel
- Thompson Medical Co. Inc. v. Federal Trade Commission
- United States v. Faulkner

The following cases appear on both the *Uniform Commercial Code Article 2 Sales* and *Contracts* versions of LEGAL CLERK:

- Application of Gaynor-Stafford Industries, Inc. by Mafco Textured Fibers
- Butkovich & Sons, Inc. v. State Bank of St. Charles
- Dunn v. General Equities of Iowa, Ltd.
- Fischer v. Division West Chinchilla Ranch
- Haydocy Pontiac, Inc. v. Lee
- Hunter v. Hayes
- Illinois Bell Telephone Co. v. Reuben H. Donnelley Corp.
- Lefkowitz v. Great Minneapolis Surplus Store, Inc.
- Lewis v. Mobil Oil Corporation
- Marchiondo v. Scheck
- McLouth Steel Corp. v. Jewell Coal and Coke Co.

A site license for all three versions of LEGAL CLERK is free to qualified adopters. Each version is accompanied by an *Instructor's Resource Guide* and, for student purchase, a *Student User's Guide*.

West's Book of Forms

A *Book of Forms* containing approximately forty sample business forms is available.

Expanded Transparency Masters

The supplements package now contains additional transparency masters for overhead projection in the classroom. Included in this package are key actual business forms.

West's Business Law on Tape

Completely new to the Fourth Edition is a packet of four sixty-minute audiocassettes containing chapter summaries. The high points of every single chapter in the text are reviewed orally on the tapes in language that the student-user will easily understand. This packet is available free to adopters.

Case Booklet

Most of the cases in the main body of the text have been reprinted in their entirety and published in a separate booklet, the *West's Business Law Case Printout,* which is available free to adopters. This booklet provides adopters with readily accessible and complete information on any cases selected for detailed discussion in the classroom.

Instructor's Manual

In this edition there is a fully revised *Instructor's Manual* prepared by Lorne H. Seidman of the University of Nevada, Las Vegas, and Lawrence Bradley of the University of Notre Dame. The *Instructor's Manual* contains the following materials:

■ Chapter outlines
■ Major chapter concepts with notes for classroom lectures
■ Practical teaching suggestions
■ Questions for the student that are designed to stimulate classroom discussion
■ Full notes on all cases excerpted within each chapter, including potential classroom discussion questions
■ A new section on ethics to assist instructors in discussing the *Focus on Ethics* sections that end each unit within the text

Improved Test Bank

Within the *Instructor's Manual* is an improved *Test Bank* that has been student tested and extensively reviewed by adopters to make sure that there are no ambiguous questions. There are approximately 2,500 multiple-choice questions with answers and approximately 1,600 true/false questions with answers.

The *Test Bank* is available on WESTEST, which offers computerized testing for IBM-PC and compatible microcomputers or the Apple II family of microcomputers (requires 128K). WESTEST allows instructors to create new tests, modify existing tests, change the questions from West's original *Test Bank,* and print tests in a variety of formats. Instructors can add questions of their own to the *Test Bank.* Instructors should contact their West sales representative to inquire about acquiring WESTEST.

Study Guide to Accompany *WEST'S BUSINESS LAW,* Fourth Edition

Professor Barbara E. Behr of Bloomsburg University of Pennsylvania has put together the most comprehensive, informative, and useful Study Guide ever produced for business law students. She allows the student to comprehend not only "black letter" law, but also some of the subtleties behind the legal process. The *Study Guide* contains:

1. A "Things to Keep in Mind" section.
2. A list of key terms.
3. An outline of the chapter.
4. A set of fill-in questions (a type of programmed learning device).
5. A set of multiple-choice questions.
6. The answers to the fill-in and multiple choice questions.
7. A section entitled "Uniform C.P.A. Business Law Examination Information."

ACKNOWLEDGMENTS FOR THE FIRST EDITION

Barbara E. Behr, Bloomsburg University of Pennsylvania; Robert Staaf, Daniel E. Murray, Richard A. Hausler, Irwin Stotsky, Patrick O. Gudridge, all of the University of Miami School of Law; William Auslen, San Francisco City College; Donald Cantwell, University of Texas at Arlington; Frank S. Forbes, University of Nebraska; Bob Garrett, American River College-California; Thomas Gossman, Western Michigan University; Charles Hartman, Wright State University-Ohio; Telford Hollman, University of Northern Iowa; Robert Jesperson, University of Houston; Susan Liebeler, Loyola University; Robert D. McNutt, California State University-Northridge; Roger E. Meiners, Texas A&M University; Gerald S. Meisel, Bergen Community College-New Jersey; James E. Moon, Meyer, Johnson & Moon-Minneapolis; Bob Morgan, Eastern Michigan University; Arthur Southwick, University of Michigan; Raymond Mason Taylor, North Carolina State; Edwin Tucker, University of Connecticut; Gary Victor, Eastern Michigan University; Gary Watson, California State University, Los Angeles.

ACKNOWLEDGMENTS FOR THE SECOND EDITION

Robert Staaf, Kenneth Burns, Judith Kenney, Thomas Crane, all of the University of Miami; Sylvia A. Spade, David A. Escamilla, Peyton J. Paxson, and JoAnn W. Hammer, all of the University of Texas at Austin.

Frank S. Forbes of the University of Nebraska-Omaha, Jeffrey E. Allen, University of Miami; Raymond August, Washington State University; David L. Baumer, North Carolina State; Barbara E. Behr, Bloomsburg University of Pennsylvania; William J. Burke, University of Lowell-Massachusetts; Robert Chatov, State University of New York-Buffalo; Larry R. Curtis, Iowa State University; Gerard Halpern, University of Arkansas; June A. Horrigan, California State University-Sacramento; John P. Huggard, North Carolina State University; John W. McGee, Southwest Texas State University; Robert D. McNutt, California State University-Northridge; Thomas E. Maher, California State University-Fullerton; David Minars, Brooklyn College-New York; Joan Ann Mrava, Los Angeles Southwest College; Thomas L. Palmer, Northern Arizona University; Charles M. Patten, University of Wisconsin-Oshkosh; Arthur D. Wolfe, Michigan State University.

ACKNOWLEDGMENTS FOR THE THIRD EDITION

Kristi K. Brown, Kenneth S. Culotta, Michele A. Dunkerley, Karen Kay Matson, Melinda Ann Mora, Dana Blair Smith, Marshall Wilkerson, Elizabeth Anene Wolfe, all from the University of Texas at Austin; Tamra Kempf, University of Miami; Janine S. Hiller, Virginia Polytechnic Institute and State College; Margaret Jones, Southwest Missouri State College; Carol D. Rasnic, Virginia Commonwealth University; Lorne H. Seidman, Larry Strate, and Cotton Meagher of the University of Nevada, Las Vegas; Thomas M. Apke, California State University, Fullerton; John J. Balek, Morton College, Illinois; Joseph E. Cantrell, DeAnza College, California; Frank S. Forbes, University of Nebraska, Omaha; Chris L. Hamilton, Golden West College, California; Woodrow

J. Maxwell, Hudson Valley Community College, New York; David Minars, City University of New York, Brooklyn; Rick F. Orsinger, College of DuPage, Illinois; Ralph L. Quinones, University of Wisconsin, Oshkosh; Jesse C. Trentadue, University of North Dakota; Robert J. Walter, University of Texas, El Paso.

ACKNOWLEDGMENTS FOR THE FOURTH EDITION

We greatly benefited from the useful criticisms, comments, and suggestions received from the following professors: Lawrence J. Bradley, University of Notre Dame; Robert J. Enders, California State Polytechnic University, Pomona; Frank Forbes, University of Nebraska at Omaha; James M. Haine, University of Wisconsin, Stevens Point, Wisconsin; Christopher L. Hamilton, Golden West College; Harry E. Hicks, Butler University, Indianapolis; Janine S. Hiller, Virginia Polytechnic Institute and State University; June A. Horrigan, California State University, Sacramento; Terry Hutchins, Pembroke State University, North Carolina; Carey Kirk, University of Northern Iowa; Nancy P. Klintworth, University of Central Florida; Kathleen M. Knutson, College of St. Catherine, St. Paul, Minnesota; Gene A. Marsh, University of Alabama; Richard Mills, Cypress College; Alan Moggio, Illinois Central College; Violet E. Molnar, Riverside City College; Dwight D. Murphey, Wichita State University; Paula C. Murray, Univesity of Texas; John M. Norwood, University of Arkansas; Michael J. O'Hara, University of Nebraska at Omaha; Peyton Paxson, Mesa College; S. Alan Schlact, Kennesaw College, Georgia; Lorne H. Seidman, University of Nevada at Las Vegas; Bennett D. Shulman, Lancing Community College; David Vyncke, Scott Community College.

We wish to thank Lavina Leed Miller for her extensive editorial services on this project. Additional legal research was masterfully accomplished by Eric Hollowell. We also wish to thank our copyeditor, Beverly Peavler, for smoothing out the rough spots in the original manuscript; Eric Hollowell, for providing proofreading services on both galleys and page proofs; and Rosemary Porter, whose weekend endeavors kept materials flowing through Austin. As always, our editor, Clyde Perlee, Jr., has served as an inspiration and faithful arbitrator during the several years of preparation that went into this edition. Our production manager and designer at West, John Orr, has given us everything we needed and more—and ahead of schedule!

As always, any remaining errors in the text are solely our own responsibility. We have always welcomed and continue to welcome comments from all users of this text. It is by incorporating those comments that we continue to write a business law text that is right for students and instructors alike.

DEDICATION

R. L. M. dedicates this edition to the memory of his father, Vern Leslie Miller, a great fisherman and an even better storyteller.

Gaylord A. Jentz dedicates this book to his wife, JoAnn; his children, Kathy, Gary, Lori, and Rory; and all his former, present, and future students.

Frank B. Cross dedicates this book to his parents and sisters.

WEST'S
BUSINESS LAW

Text
Cases
Legal Environment

FOURTH EDITION

Unit One

THE LEGAL
ENVIRONMENT
OF BUSINESS

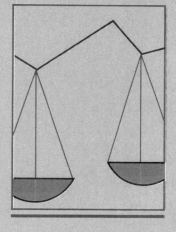

Introduction to Law and Legal Reasoning

Law has developed because individuals and society need certain standards to govern relationships among individuals and between the people and their government. Law works within a social order that contains numerous activities, among which are business activities. The rules, or laws, to be described exist as an expression of the compulsory standards set by society.

WHAT IS LAW?

There have been and will continue to be different definitions of law. Aristotle saw law as a rule of conduct. Plato believed law was a form of social control. Cicero contended that law was the agreement of reason and nature, the distinction between the just and the unjust. The British jurist Sir William Blackstone described law as "a rule of civil conduct prescribed by the supreme power in a state, commanding what is right, and prohibiting what is wrong." In America, the eminent jurist Oliver Wendell Holmes contended that law was a set of rules that allowed one to predict how a court would resolve a particular dispute—"the prophecies of what the courts will do in fact, and nothing more pretentious, are what I mean by the law."

Although these definitions vary in their particulars, note that all are based on the following general observation: *Law consists of enforceable rules governing relationships among individuals and between individuals and their society.* In the study of law, often referred to as **jurisprudence,** this very broad statement concerning the nature of law is the point of departure for all legal scholars and philosophers.

SCHOOLS OF LEGAL, OR JURISPRUDENTIAL, THOUGHT

All legal philosophers agree that custom, history, logic, and ideals have influenced the development of law in some way. These philosophers disagree, however, on the importance that each of these influences should have in shaping law, and their disagreements have produced different schools, or philosophies, of jurisprudence. For our purposes, these schools may be simplified and divided into two approaches—the historical school, or traditional approach, and the realistic school, or sociological approach.

The Traditional Approach

Concentrating on the legal system's origin and history, the historical school emphasizes the evolutionary process of law. This school looks to the past to discover what the principles of contemporary law should be. The legal principles that have withstood the passage of time—those that have worked in the past—are deemed best suited for shaping present laws. Law is seen as deriving its legitimacy and authority from adhering to the principles that historical development has shown to be workable. Followers, or adherents, of the historical school are likely to follow strictly decisions that have been presented in past cases.

The traditional approach sees law as a body of principles and rules that courts apply in deciding disputes, and the study of law as the study of these rules and the general principles of right and wrong on which the rules are based. The traditional approach is based on the idea that the principles of right and wrong change, if at all, only very slowly and over a long period of time. Hence, this approach fulfills one of the important functions of law—to provide stability, predictability, and continuity so that individuals can be sure of how to order their affairs.

The Sociological Approach

Legal realism is based on the idea that social forces and needs shape law and, hence, that law may be viewed as an instrument of social control. In addition to stressing the pragmatic and empirical sides of law, legal realists perceive law as a means to a social end, and so they seek to predict and influence lawmaking. They believe that, despite historical principles, the same conclusion need not always follow from the same set of facts. One particular court, therefore, may view facts differently from another court. For the legal realist, how well law and legal institutions serve the needs of society is the measure of their legitimacy.

For our purposes, this may be termed the sociological approach to law. According to this approach, law is a social institution and only one part of the total environment of society. In this view, the purpose of law is to create a legal system with the proper incentives to provide and promote justice and stability. The term **justice,** however, is subject to great controversy. Justice has different meanings to different people; thus, conflicting ideas arise as to how the law should be structured.

Most people, for example, agree that the law should protect individuals from being injured or killed. People also look upon crimes against the government, such as treason and sedition, with disfavor, and consequently, we have laws that prohibit these types of crimes. Laws also protect the public health, safety, and morals. Questions frequently arise, however, as to how the public health, safety, and morals can best be protected, and the social environment exercises much influence over what decisions are made. As society changes, its laws must also change. Scientific and technological advances in our culture have often created situations in which there is no existing law to rely upon, and hence new principles of law have had to be developed. Moreover, people's ideas of right and wrong change over time. Thus, law is often perceived as an instrument by which society can go about rectifying social wrongs through the orderly process provided by the legal system.

Most of the material in this book takes the traditional approach. It presents the rules of law that apply to the business world and the principles on which they are based. Remember, however, that *outside forces in the environment do shape the rules.*

HISTORY AND SOURCES OF AMERICAN LAW

Because of our colonial heritage, much of American law is based on the English legal system. Without a knowledge of this legal heritage, one cannot understand the nature of our legal system today.

Common Law

In 1066 the Normans conquered England, and William the Conqueror and his successors began the process of unifying the country under their rule. One of the means they used to this end was the establishment of the king's court. Before the conquest, disputes had been settled according to local custom. The king's court sought to establish a common or uniform set of customs for the whole country. The body of rules that evolved under the king's court, called the *Curia Regis,* was the beginning of the **common law**—law that was common for the entire realm. As the number of courts and cases increased, the more important decisions of each year were gathered together and recorded in year books. Judges, settling disputes similar to ones that had been decided before, used decisions recorded in the year books as the basis for their decisions. If a case was unique, judges had to create new laws, but they based their decisions on the general principles suggested by earlier cases. The body of judge-made law that developed under this system is still used today and is known as the common law.

Today, in the United States, common law includes the *statutory* and *case-law* background of England and of the American colonies prior to the American Revolution, and the case law of the United States since the American Revolution. Case law consists of the rules of law announced in court decisions. Some case law consists of court interpretations of statutes, regulations, and provisions in constitutions. Each interpretation becomes part of the authoritative law on the subject and serves as a *precedent* in the particular jurisdiction. A prior case that is similar in legal principles or in facts to a case under consideration is referred to as a **precedent.** The practice of deciding new cases with reference to former decisions is called the doctrine of *stare decisis,* discussed in the next section.

Common law must be distinguished from **statutory law,** which, generally, consists of those laws enacted by state legislatures and, at the federal level, by Congress. Where common law does not conflict with a statute, it generally has the same force as statutory law, since most states have adopted much common law by legislative decree.

Thus, in areas where legislation has not covered the relevant issue, courts still refer to the common law. The history and circumstances of the various states differ, and this has given rise to differences among the courts' decisions and thus in the common law among states. Even where legislation has been substituted for common law principles, courts often rely on common law to interpret the legislation, on the theory that the people who drafted the statute intended to codify an existing common-law rule.

Stare Decisis

The practice of deciding new cases with reference to former decisions eventually became a cornerstone of the English and American judicial systems. As noted, it forms the doctrine of *stare decisis* ("to stand on decided cases").

The doctrine of *stare decisis* performs many useful functions. First, it helps the courts to be more efficient. It would be very time-consuming if each judge had to reason out the policies for deciding what the law should be for each case brought before the court. If other courts have confronted the same issue and reasoned through the case carefully, their opinions can serve as guides.

Second, *stare decisis* creates a more just and uniform system. The rule of precedent tends to neutralize the prejudices of individual judges. If judges feel pressure to use precedent as the basis for their decisions, they will be less influenced by any personal prejudices. Different states and regions, however, often follow different precedents, and hence variations in rules of law occur.

Third, *stare decisis* makes the law more stable and predictable. If the law on a given subject is well settled, someone bringing a case to court can usually rely upon the court to make a decision based on what the law has been.

Finally, *stare decisis* reflects the experience of the past and is based on the wisdom of the past. Sometimes a court departs from the rule of precedent because it has decided that the precedent is incorrect. For example, if changes in technology, business practice, or society's attitudes necessitate a change in the law, courts may depart from precedent. Judges are reluctant to overrule precedent, however, and whether they do so depends on the subject of the case, the number and prestige of prior decisions, the degree of social change that has occurred, and the identity of the deciding court.

Sometimes there is no precedent on which to base a decision, or there are conflicting precedents. In these situations, a court will: (1) refer to past decisions that may be similar to the current case and decide the case by reasoning through analogy; (2) look at social factors—changes in the status of women, for example—that might influence the issues involved; and (3) consider what the fairest result would be.

Cases that overturn precedent often receive a great deal of publicity. In *Brown v. Board of Education*,[1] for example, the U.S. Supreme Court expressly overturned precedent when it concluded that separate educational facilities for whites and blacks are inherently unequal. Previously, in *Plessy v. Ferguson*,[2] as well as in numerous other cases, the Court had upheld as constitutional the provision of separate but equal accommodations. The Supreme Court's departure from precedent in *Brown* received a tremendous amount of publicity as people began to realize the ramifications of this change in the law. Irrespective of the publicity that is typically generated when cases overturn precedent, in reality the majority of cases are decided according to precedent because of the application of the doctrine of *stare decisis*.

Legal Reasoning

When applying, overruling, or creating precedent, judges use many forms of reasoning. Generally, a judge writes an opinion in the form of a **syllogism**—that is, deductive reasoning consisting of a major premise, a minor premise, and a conclusion. For example, a judge might point out in a particular case that "under the common law, an individual must be aware of a threat of danger for the threat to constitute civil assault" (major premise), "the plaintiff in this case was unaware of the threat complained of at the time it occurred" (minor premise), and "therefore, the circumstances do not amount to a civil assault" (conclusion).

A second important form of reasoning commonly employed in considering a set of circumstances and applying legal principles to them might be thought of as a section of knotted rope, with each knot tying together separate pieces of rope to form a tight length. As a whole, the rope represents a logical progression of connected points, and the last knot represents the conclusion.

For example, imagine that a tenant in an apartment building sues the landlord for damages for an injury resulting from an allegedly dimly lit stairway. The landlord, who was on the premises the evening the injury occurred, testifies that none of the other nine tenants who used the stairway that night complained about the lights. The court concludes that the tenant is not entitled to compensation on the basis of the stairway's lighting. The "pieces of rope" might be stated as follows:

1. The landlord testifies that none of the tenants who used the stairs on the evening in question complained about the lights.
2. The fact that none of the tenants complained is the same as if they had said the lighting was sufficient.
3. That there were no complaints does *not* prove that the lighting was sufficient but proves that the landlord had no reason to believe that it was not.
4. The landlord's belief was reasonable, considering that no one complained.
5. Therefore, the landlord acted reasonably and was not negligent in providing adequate lighting.

In the majority of cases, these two methods of reasoning predominate, and it is unnecessary to look beyond them. There are, however, two other important forms of reasoning that judges use in deciding cases: reasoning by analogy and the process of determining which rules and policies to apply.

To reason by analogy is to compare the facts in the case at hand to the facts in other cases and, to the extent the patterns are similar, apply the same rule to both. To the extent the facts are unique, or "distinguishable," different rules may apply. For example, in case A, it is held that a driver who crosses a highway's center line is negligent. In case B, a driver crosses the line to avoid hitting a child. In determining whether case A's rule applies in case B, a judge would consider what the reasons were for the decision in A and whether B is sufficiently similar for those reasons to apply. If the judge holds that B's driver is not liable, he or she must pinpoint a policy and explain a rule that is not inconsistent with A's holding.

---

1. 347 U.S. 483, 74 S.Ct. 686, 98 L.Ed. 873 (1954).
2. 163 U.S. 537, 16 S.Ct. 1138, 41 L.Ed. 256 (1896).

Simply put, a judge must harmonize a decision with decisions that have been made before. Of course, judges have a seemingly infinite array of precedential decisions from which to choose. In sum, when determining which rules and policies to apply in a given case, and in applying them, a judge may examine:

1. Previous case law and the legal principles and policies behind the decisions, as well as their historical setting.
2. Statutes and the policies—legal, historical, and social—underlying the legislature's decision to enact a particular statute.
3. Society's values (for example, fairness).
4. Custom (for example, when a controversial business transaction involves a contract, a judge might ask what the participants expected, based on the usual and customary practices within their trade).
5. Other sources, including the fields of economics, psychology, sociology, and philosophy.

MORE RECENT SOURCES OF LAW

Much law has been made since the officials of the king's court made decisions with reference to the year books. Today, courts have sources other than case-law precedent to consider when making their decisions.

Constitutions

The federal government and the states have separate constitutions that set forth the general organization, powers, and limits of their respective governments. The U.S. Constitution[3] is the supreme law of the land. A law in violation of the Constitution, no matter what its source, will be declared unconstitutional and will not be enforced. Similarly, unless it conflicts with the U.S. Constitution, each state constitution is supreme within the state's borders.

The U.S. Constitution defines the powers and limitations of the federal government. The Tenth Amendment reserves all powers not granted to the federal government to the states or the people. The Constitution, for example, gives the federal government the power to regulate *interstate* commerce (commerce between or among states), and thus states retain the power to regulate *intrastate* commerce (commerce within a state). The Constitution further delineates how federal powers are divided among the three governmental branches, establishing a system of checks and balances. Article I vests the legislative power (power to make laws) in the Congress; Article II vests the executive power (power to see that laws are carried out) in the president; and Article III vests the judicial power (power to determine what the law is and whether laws are valid) in the courts.[4]

Codified Law: Statutes and Ordinances

Statutes enacted by the Congress and the various state legislative bodies comprise another source of law, which is generally referred to as *statutory law*. The statutory law of the United States further consists of the ordinances passed by cities, counties, and other political subdivisions. None of these laws can violate the U.S. Constitution or the relevant state constitution. Today, legislative bodies and regulatory agencies have assumed an ever-increasing share of lawmaking. Much of the work of modern courts consists of interpreting what the rulemaker meant when the law was passed and applying it to a present set of facts.

Administrative Agency Regulations

An administrative agency is created when the executive or legislative branch of the government delegates some of its authority to an appropriate group of persons usually called an agency or a commission. Administrative agencies exercise legislative, executive, and judicial power. In their rulemaking, they use legislative power; in their regulation and supervision, they use executive

---

3. See Appendix A for the complete text of the U.S. Constitution.

4. State governments are generally organized in the same way as the federal government.

power; and in their adjudication procedures, they use judicial power. Unlike legislators, presidents, governors, and many judges, administrative agency personnel are rarely chosen by popular elections, and many do not serve fixed terms. As a result, great power is given to people who may not be responsive to the public.

Administrative law is the branch of public law concerned with the executive power and actions of administrative agencies, their officials, and their workers.[5] When an individual has a dispute with such an agency, administrative law applies. The scope of administrative law has expanded enormously in recent years, and the scope of administrative agencies has increased so much that their activities have come to be called **administrative process,** in contrast to **judicial process.** Administrative process involves the administration of law by nonjudicial agencies, such as the Federal Trade Commission, whereas judicial process is the administration of law by judicial bodies (the courts).

SOURCES OF COMMERCIAL (OR BUSINESS) LAW

The body of law that pertains to commercial dealings is commonly referred to as commercial, or business, law. It includes most of the topics in this text—contracts, partnerships, and corporations, for example. For business students, the most important codification of commercial law is the Uniform Commercial Code (UCC). Since the UCC forms the basis of many chapters in this book, its origins will be briefly discussed here.

Codification of Commercial Law

In the interests of uniformity and reform, in the late nineteenth century the legal profession suggested that comprehensive codes of laws concerning specific subject areas be adopted by the states. (When adopted by a state, these codes of laws become statutory law.)

The National Conference of Commissioners on Uniform State Laws first started to meet in the late 1800s in order to draft uniform statutes. Once these uniform codes had been drawn up, the commissioners urged each state legislature to adopt them. Adoption of uniform codes is a state matter, and a state may reject all or part of a code or rewrite it as the state's legislature sees fit. Hence, even when a proposed code is said to have been adopted in many states, those states' laws may not be entirely "uniform."

The first uniform code, or act, was the Uniform Negotiable Instruments Law, which was finally approved in 1896 and was adopted in every state by the early 1920s (though not all states used exactly the same wording). Afterwards, other acts were drawn up in a similar manner; they included the Uniform Sales Act, the Uniform Warehouse Receipts Act, the Uniform Bills of Lading Act, the Uniform Partnership Act, the Model Business Corporation Act (drafted by the American Bar Association), and the Uniform Stock Transfer Act. More recently, a Uniform Probate Code was prepared. The most ambitious uniform act of all, however, was the Uniform Commercial Code.

The Uniform Commercial Code (UCC)

The National Conference of Commissioners on Uniform State Laws and the American Law Institute sponsored and directed the preparation of the Uniform Commercial Code. These two organizations were assisted by literally hundreds of law professors, businesspersons, judges, and lawyers. The complete text of the Code can be found in Appendix B in this book. The District of Columbia, the Virgin Islands, and forty-nine states have adopted all Articles of the Uniform Commercial Code.[6]

The UCC is designed to assist the legal relationship of parties involved in modern commercial transactions by helping to determine the intentions of the parties to a commercial contract and by giving force and effect to their agreement. Moreover, the Code is meant to encourage business transactions by assuring businesspersons that

---

5. See Chapter 45 for a more extensive discussion of administrative law.

6. Louisiana has adopted only Articles 1, 3, 4, and 5.

their contracts, if validly entered into, will be uniformly enforced.

CLASSIFICATION OF LAW

The body of·law is huge. In order to study it, one must break it down by some means of classification. No single system of classification can cover such a large mass of information; consequently, those systems that have been devised tend to overlap. Moreover, they are, of necessity, arbitrary in some respects. A discussion of the best-known systems follows.

Substantive versus Procedural Law

Substantive law includes all laws that define, describe, regulate, and create legal rights and obligations. For example, a rule stating that promises are enforced only when each party has received something of value from the other party is part of substantive law. So, too, is a rule stating that a person who has injured another through negligence must pay damages.

Procedural law (or adjective law) establishes the methods of enforcing the rights established by substantive law. Questions about how a lawsuit should begin, what papers need to be filed, to which court the suit should go, which witnesses can be called, and so on are all questions of procedural law. In brief, substantive law tells us our rights; procedural law tells us how to exercise them.

Exhibit 1-1 classifies law in terms of its subject matter, dividing it into law covering substantive issues and law covering procedural issues. Most of this text concerns substantive law.

Public versus Private Law

Public law addresses the relationship between persons and their government, whereas **private law** addresses direct dealings between persons.

Criminal law and constitutional law, for example, are generally classified as public law because they deal with persons and their relation-

ships to government. Criminal acts, though they may involve only one victim, are seen as offenses against society as a whole and are prohibited by governments in order to protect the public. Constitutional law is frequently classified as public law, since it involves questions of whether the government—federal, state, or local—has the power to act in a particular fashion; often the issue is whether a law, duly passed, exceeds the limits set on the government. See Exhibit 1-2 for examples of private and public law.

Exhibit 1-1 Subject Matter Divided into Substantive and Procedural Laws[a]

SUBSTANTIVE	PROCEDURAL
Administrative law	Administrative procedure
Agency	Appellate procedure
Bailments	Civil procedure
Commercial paper	Criminal procedure
Constitutional law	Evidence
Contracts	
Corporation law	
Criminal law	
Insurance	
Partnerships	
Personal property	
Real property	
Sales	
Taxation	
Torts	
Trusts and Wills	

a. The importance of this distinction is more than academic: The *result* of a case may well depend upon the determination that a rule is substantive rather than procedural.

Exhibit 1-2 Examples of Public and Private Laws

PUBLIC LAW	PRIVATE LAW
Administrative law	Agency
Civil, criminal, and appellate procedure	Commercial paper
	Contracts
Constitutional law	Corporation law
Criminal law	Partnerships
Evidence	Personal property
Taxation	Real property
	Sales
	Torts
	Trusts and Wills

Civil versus Criminal Law

Civil law spells out the duties that exist between persons or between citizens and their governments, excluding the duty not to commit crimes. Contract law, for example, is part of civil law. The whole body of *tort law*, which has to do with the infringement by one person of the legally recognized rights of another, is an area of civil law.[7]

Criminal law, in contrast to civil law, is concerned with wrongs committed against the public as a whole.[8] Criminal acts are prohibited by local, state, or federal government statutes. Criminal law is always public law, whereas civil law is sometimes public and sometimes private. In a criminal case, the government seeks to impose a penalty on an allegedly guilty person. In a civil case, one party (sometimes the government) tries to make the other party comply with a duty or pay for the damage caused by failure to so comply.

REMEDIES AT LAW VERSUS REMEDIES IN EQUITY

The distinction between law and equity courts is primarily of historical interest, but it has special relevance to students of business law, because legal and equitable **remedies** differ. (*Remedies* are the legal means to recover a right or redress a wrong.) To seek the proper remedy for a wrong, one must know what remedies are available. In the early king's courts, the kinds of remedies that the courts could grant were severely restricted. If one person wronged another in some way, the king's court could award as compensation one or more of the following: (1) land, (2) items of value, or (3) money. The courts that awarded these compensations became known as **courts of law** and the three remedies were called **remedies at law.** Even though the system introduced uniformity in the settling of disputes, when *plaintiffs* (parties suing) wanted a remedy other than economic compensation, the courts of law could do nothing, so "no remedy, no right."

---

7. Tort law is treated in Chapters 4 and 5.
8. Chapter 6 addresses criminal law in greater detail.

Equity Courts: Going to the King for Relief

When individuals could not obtain an adequate remedy in a court of law because of strict technicalities, they petitioned the king for relief. Most of these petitions were decided by an adviser to the king, called a **chancellor.** The chancellor was said to be the "keeper of the king's conscience." When the chancellor thought that the claim was a fair one, new and unique remedies were granted. In this way, a new body of rules and remedies came into being, and eventually formal chancery courts were established. These became known as **courts of equity.**

Equity is that branch of law, founded on what might be described as notions of justice and fair dealing, that seeks to supply a remedy when there is no adequate remedy available at law. Thus, two distinct systems were created, each having a different set of judges. Two bodies of rules and remedies existed at the same time, remedies at law and **remedies in equity.** Plaintiffs had to specify whether they were bringing an "action at law" or an "action in equity," and they chose their courts accordingly. Only one remedy could be granted for a particular wrong, and even in equity the wrong had to be of a type the court could recognize as remediable.

Courts of equity had the responsibility of using discretion in supplementing the common law. Even today, when the same court can award both legal and equitable remedies, such discretion is often guided by so-called **equitable principles and maxims.** Maxims are propositions or general statements of rules of law that courts often invoke. Listed below are a few of the various maxims of equity.

1. Whoever seeks equity must do equity. (Anyone who wishes to be treated fairly must treat others fairly.)
2. Where there is equal equity, the law must prevail. (The law will determine the outcome of a controversy in which the merits of both sides are equal.)
3. One seeking the aid of an equity court must come to the court with clean hands. (Plaintiffs must have acted fairly and honestly.)

4. Equity will not suffer a right to exist without a remedy. (Equitable relief will be awarded when there is a right to relief and there is no adequate remedy at law.)

5. Equity regards substance rather than form. (Equity is more concerned with fairness and justice than with legal technicalities.)

6. Equity aids the vigilant, not those who rest on their rights. (Individuals who fail to look out for their rights until after a reasonable period of time has passed will not be helped.)

The last maxim is worthy of discussion. It has become known as the equitable doctrine of **laches,** and it can be used as a **defense** (an argument raised by the defendant to defeat the plaintiff's cause of action or recovery). The doctrine arose to encourage people to bring lawsuits while the evidence was fresh. What constitutes a reasonable time, of course, varies according to the circumstances of the case. Time periods for different types of cases are now usually fixed by **statutes of limitations.** After the time allowed under a statute of limitations has expired, no action can be brought, no matter how strong the case was originally.

Equitable Relief

A number of equitable remedies are available. Three of them—specific performance, injunctions, and rescission—are briefly discussed here. These and other equitable remedies are discussed in more detail at appropriate points in the chapters that follow.

DECREES OF SPECIFIC PERFORMANCE Previously, courts of law and equity were separate. Hence, a plaintiff might come into a court of equity asking it to order a defendant to perform within the terms of a contract. A court of law could not issue such an order because its remedies were limited to payment of money or property as compensation for damages. A court of equity, however, could issue a **decree of specific performance**—an order to perform what was promised. This remedy was, and still is, only available when the dispute before the court involves a *contractual* transaction.

INJUNCTIONS If a person wanted to prevent the occurrence of a certain activity, he or she would have to go the chancellor in equity to ask that the person doing the wrongful act be ordered to stop. The order was called an injunction. An **injunction** is usually an order to a specific person, directing that person to do or to refrain from doing a particular act.

RESCISSION Often the legal remedy of the payment of money for damages is unavailable or inadequate when disputes occur over agreements among persons. In such cases, the equitable remedy of rescission is frequently given. **Rescission** is an action to undo an agreement—to return the parties to their *status quo* prior to the agreement. If rescission is granted, all duties created by the agreement are abolished. If, for example, a sales agreement is made because a seller misrepresents the quality of goods but the fraud is discovered before any money changes hands, the buyer might want merely to rescind the agreement.

The Merging of Law and Equity

Today, generally, the courts of law and equity are merged. A plaintiff or a petitioner in equity (the person bringing the action) may now request both legal and equitable remedies in the same action, and the trial court judge may grant either or both forms of relief.

Despite the merging of the courts, it is still important to distinguish between actions at law and actions in equity. As already mentioned, the primary importance is in the remedy sought. Vestiges of the procedures used when the courts were separate still exist. Today, differences in procedure depend on whether the civil lawsuit involves an action in equity or an action at law. Exhibit 1-3 is illustrative and applies to most states.

The major practical difference between law and equity today is the right to demand a jury trial in actions at law. In the old courts of equity, the chancellor heard both sides of an issue and decided what should be done. Juries were considered inappropriate. In actions at law, however, juries heard evidence and made determinations regarding questions of fact, including the amount of damages to be awarded. Today, in a case involving equi-

Exhibit 1-3 Procedural Differences between an Action at Law and an Action in Equity

PROCEDURE	ACTION AT LAW	ACTION IN EQUITY
Initiation of law suit	By filing of a complaint	By filing of a petition
Decision	By jury or judge	By judge (no jury)
Result	Judgment	Decree
Remedy	Monetary damages	Injunction, decree of specific performance, or rescission

table rights, a judge may impanel a jury to serve in an advisory capacity.

HOW TO FIND CASE LAW

Laws pertaining to business consist of case law as well as statutory law. A substantial number of cases are presented in this text to provide you with concise, real-life illustrations of the interpretation and application of the law by the courts. Many other court decisions have been referenced in footnotes throughout the text. Because of the importance of knowing how to find these and other court opinions, this section offers a brief introduction to the case reporting system and to the legal "shorthand" employed in referencing court cases.

State Court Decisions

Most state trial court decisions are not published. Except in New York and a few other states that publish selected opinions of their trial courts, decisions from the state trial courts are merely filed in the office of the clerk of the court, where they are available for public inspection.

Written decisions of the appellate courts, however, are published and distributed. The reported appellate decisions are published in volumes called *Reports*, which are numbered consecutively. State appellate court decisions are found in the state reports of that particular state.

Additionally, state court opinions appear in regional units of the *National Reporter System*, published by West Publishing Company. Most lawyers and libraries have the West reporters because they report cases more quickly and are distributed more widely than the state-published re-

ports. In fact, many states have eliminated their own reports in favor of West's National Reporter System. The National Reporter System divides the states into the following geographical areas: Atlantic (A. or A.2d), Southeastern (S.E. or S.E.2d), Southwestern (S.W. or S.W.2d), Northwestern (N.W. or N.W.2d), Northeastern (N.E. or N.E.2d), Southern (So. or So.2d), and Pacific (P. or P.2d). The states included in each of these regional divisions are indicated in Exhibit 1-4, which illustrates West's National Reporter System.

After appellate decisions have been published, they are normally referred to (cited) by the name of the case; the volume, name, and page of the state's official report (if different from West's National Reporter System); the volume, unit, and page number of the *National Reporter;* and the volume, name, and page number of any other selected reporter. This information comprises what is called the **citation.** For example, consider the following case: Quality Motors, Inc. v. Hays, 216 Ark. 264, 225 S.W.2d 326 (1949). We see that the opinion in this case may be found in volume 216 of the official *Arkansas Reports* on page 264 and in Volume 225 of the *Southwestern Reporter*, Second Series, on page 326. When two or more citations are given for the same case, they are called *parallel citations*. In reprinting appellate opinions in this text, in addition to the citation, we give the name of the court hearing the case and the year of the court decision.

A few of the states—including those with intermediate appellate courts, such as California, Illinois, and New York—have more than one report for opinions given by courts within their states. Sample citations from these courts, as well as others, are listed and explained in Exhibit 1-5.

Exhibit 1-4 **National Reporter System—Regional/Federal**

Regional Reporters	Coverage Beginning	Coverage
Atlantic Reporter	1885	Connecticut, Delaware, Maine, Maryland, New Hampshire, New Jersey, Pennsylvania, Rhode Island, Vermont, and District of Columbia.
North Eastern Reporter	1885	Illinois, Indiana, Massachusetts, New York and Ohio.
North Western Reporter	1879	Iowa, Michigan, Minnesota, Nebraska, North Dakota, South Dakota, and Wisconsin.
Pacific Reporter	1883	Alaska, Arizona, California, Colorado, Hawaii, Idaho, Kansas, Montana, Nevada, New Mexico, Oklahoma, Oregon, Utah, Washington and Wyoming.
South Eastern Reporter	1887	Georgia, North Carolina, South Carolina, Virginia and West Virginia.
South Western Reporter	1886	Arkansas, Kentucky, Missouri, Tennessee, and Texas.
Southern Reporter	1887	Alabama, Florida, Louisiana and Mississippi.
Federal Reporters		
Federal Reporter	1880	U.S. Circuit Court from 1880 to 1912; U.S. Commerce Court from 1911 to 1913; U.S. District Courts from 1880 to 1932; U.S. Court of Claims from 1929 to 1932 and since 1960; U.S. Court of Appeals since 1891; U.S. Court of Customs and Patent Appeals since 1929; U.S. Emergency Court of Appeals since 1943.
Federal Supplement	1932	U.S. Court of Claims from 1932 to 1960; U.S. District Courts since 1932; U.S. Customs Court since 1956.
Federal Rules Decisions	1939	U.S. District Courts involving the Federal Rules of Civil Procedure since 1939 and Federal Rules of Criminal Procedure since 1946.
Supreme Court Reporter	1882	U.S. Supreme Court since the October term of 1882.
Bankruptcy Reporter	1980	Bankruptcy decisions of U.S. Bankruptcy Courts, U.S. District Courts, U.S. Courts of Appeals, and U.S. Supreme Court.
Military Justice Reporter	1978	U.S. Court of Military Appeals and Courts of Military Review for the Army, Navy, Air Force, and Coast Guard.

NATIONAL REPORTER SYSTEM MAP

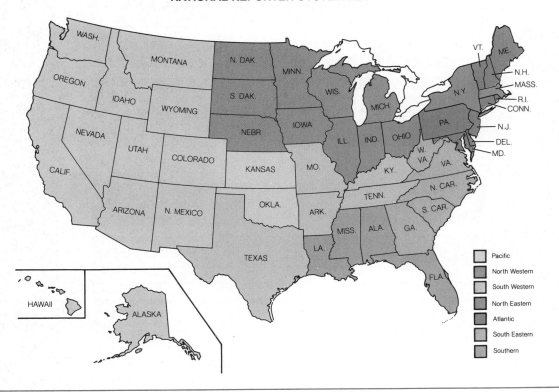

Exhibit 1-5 **Sample Court Citations**[a]

State Courts

398 Mass. 254, 496 N.E.2d 827 (1986)

> *N.E.* is the abbreviation for West's publication of state court decisions rendered in the northeastern region of the National Reporter System. *2d* indicates that this case was included in the second series of those reports.

> *Mass.* is an abbreviation for *Massachusetts Reports,* Massachusetts's official reports of the decisions of its highest court, the supreme judicial court, which is comparable to other states' supreme courts.

> The numbers 398 and 496 refer to reporters' volumes. The numbers 254 and 827 refer to the first pages in those volumes on which this case can be found.

59 Cal. 2d 428, 380 P.2d 644, 30 Cal. Rptr. 4 (1963)

> *Cal. Rptr.* is the abbreviation for West's unofficial reports—titled *California Reporter*—of the decisions of California courts.

113 Misc. 2d 1017, 450 N.Y.S.2d 957 (N.Y. City Crim. Ct. 1982)

> *N.Y. City Crim. Ct.* is an abbreviation indicating that this case was decided in a criminal court in New York City.

> *N.Y.S.* is the abbreviation for West's unofficial reports—titled *New York Supplement*—of the decisions of New York courts.

> There is no parallel citation to N.E.2d, because West did not report this case in its regional reporter.

> *Misc.* is the abbreviation for *New York Miscellaneous Reports,* New York's official reports of the decisions of its courts other than the court of appeals and the appellate division of the supreme courts. (New York's court of appeals is the state's highest court, comparable to other states' supreme courts. In New York, a supreme court is a trial court.)

531 S.W.2d 55 (Mo. App. 1981)

> *Mo. App.* is an abbreviation denoting Missouri's court of appeals. Including the abbreviation in the citation to West's regional reporter makes it clear that this case was decided in Missouri at the appellate level.

> There is no parallel citation to a state reporter, because Missouri discontinued its publication of the decisions of its courts in the 1950s.

---

a. The case names have been deleted from these citations to emphasize the publications. It should be kept in mind, however, that the name of a case is as important as the specific page numbers in the volumes in which it is found. If a citation is incorrect, the correct citation may be found in a publication's index of case names. The date of a case is also important, both to provide a check on error in citations and because the value of a recent case as an authority is likely to be greater than that of earlier cases.

Exhibit 1-5 Sample Court Citations (Continued)

Federal Courts

792 F.2d 1423 (9th Cir. 1986)

> *9th Cir.* is an abbreviation denoting that this case was decided in one of the United States Courts of Appeals for the Ninth Circuit.

352 F. Supp. 1105 (S.D.N.Y. 1972)

> *S.D.N.Y.* is an abbreviation indicating that the United States District Court for the Southern District of New York decided this case.

Old Decisions

100 Mass. 63, 97 Am. Dec. 76 (1868)

> *Am. Dec.* is an abbreviation for *American Decisions,* a series of unofficial reports of selected cases. *American Decisions* was one of the "Trinity Series" (the others were *American Reports* and *American State Reports*), which ceased publication in 1911.[b]

> There is no parallel citation to a West regional reporter, because West did not begin publishing its reports until 1879.

18 Johns. 145, 9 Am. Dec. 191 (N.Y. 1820)

> *N.Y.* denotes that this case was decided in the Court for the Correction of Errors, the former name of a New York court that had jurisdiction to hear cases by appeal or writ of error.

> *Johns.* is an abbreviation for *Johnson's Reports,* a series of reports of cases decided in certain New York courts between 1806 and 1823.

English Courts

9 Exch. 341, 156 Eng. Rep. 145 (1854)

> *Eng. Rep.* is an abbreviation for *English Reports, Full Reprint,* a series of reports containing selected decisions made in English courts between 1378 and 1865.

> *Exch.* is an abbreviation for *English Exchequer Reports,* which included the original reports of cases decided in England's Court of Exchequer.

---

b. In the nineteenth century, there were more than two hundred reporters with which an American lawyer had to be familiar. With the advent of West's National Reporter System, legal research became more efficient and could be conducted more quickly and more thoroughly.

Federal Court Decisions

Federal trial court decisions are published unofficially in West's *Federal Supplement* (F.Supp.), and opinions from the circuit courts of appeal are reported unofficially in West's *Federal Reporter* (F. or F.2d). Cases concerning federal bankruptcy law are published unofficially in West's *Bankruptcy Reporter* (B.R.). Opinions from the United States Supreme Court are reported in West's *Supreme Court Reporter* (S.Ct.), the *United States Reports* (U.S.), the *Lawyers' Edition of the Supreme Court Reports* (L.Ed.), and other publications.

The *United States Reports* is the official edition of all decisions of the United States Supreme Court for which there are written opinions. Published by the federal government, the series includes reports of Supreme Court cases dating from the August term of 1791, although originally many of the decisions were not reported in the early volumes.

The Lawyers Cooperative Publishing Company of Rochester, New York, publishes the *Lawyers' Edition of the Supreme Court Reports,* which is an unofficial edition of the entire series of the Supreme Court reports and contains many of the decisions not reported in the early official volumes. Also, among other editorial features, the *Lawyers' Edition,* in its second series, precedes the report of each case with a full summary, includes excerpts from briefs of counsel, and discusses in detail selected cases of special interest to the legal profession.

West's *Supreme Court Reporter* is an unofficial edition dating from the Court's term in October 1882. Preceding each of its case reports are a summary of the case and *headnotes* (brief editorial statements of the law involved in the case, numbered to correspond to numbers in the report). The headnotes are also given classification numbers that serve to cross-reference each headnote to other headnotes on similar points throughout the National Reporter System and other West publications to facilitate research of all relevant cases on a given point. This is important because, as may be evident from the discussion of *stare decisis,* a lawyer's goal in undertaking legal research is to find an authority that cannot be factually distinguished from his or her case.

Sample citations for federal court decisions are listed and explained in Exhibit 1-5.

Old Case Law

On a few occasions, the opinions cited in this text are from old, classic cases dating to the nineteenth century or earlier; some of these are from the English courts. The citations to these cases appear not to conform to the descriptions given above because the reports in which they were published have since been replaced. Sample citations from this group have also been included in Exhibit 1-5.

HOW TO ANALYZE CASE LAW

The cases presented in this text have already been analyzed and edited by the authors. For each case presented, the authors have provided a "Background and Facts" section so that the student may quickly perceive the issue or issues before the court. These sections are strictly the authors' own summaries—in their own words—of information given in the full written opinion of the court. The authors conclude each case presentation with the court's "Decision and Remedy"—again, in the authors' own words—and, occasionally, with a "Comments" section.

For those wishing to review court cases for future research projects or to gain additional legal information, the following sections will provide useful insights into how to read and understand case law.

Case Titles

In the title of a case, such as *Adams v. Jones,* the *v.* or *vs.* stands for versus, which means against. (This is also called the *style* of the case, or the names of the parties in the lawsuit.) In the trial court, Adams was the plaintiff—the person who filed the suit. Jones was the defendant. If the case is appealed, however, the appellate court will sometimes place the name of the party appealing the decision first, so that the case may be called *Jones v. Adams.* Since some appellate courts retain the trial court order of names, it is often impossible to distinguish the plaintiff from the defendant in the title of a reported appellate court decision. The student must carefully read the facts of each case in order to identify each party. Otherwise, the discussion by the appellate court will be difficult to understand.

Terminology

The following terms and phrases are frequently encountered in court opinions and legal publications. Because it is important to understand what is meant by these terms and phrases, we define and discuss them here.

DECISIONS AND OPINIONS Most decisions reached by reviewing, or appellate, courts are explained in writing. A decision contains the opinion (the court's reasons for its decision), the rules of law that apply, and the judgment. There are four possible types of written opinions for any particular case decided by an appellate court. When all judges or justices unanimously agree on an opinion, the opinion is written for the entire court and can be deemed a **unanimous opinion.** When there is not a unanimous opinion, a **majority opinion** is written, outlining the views of the majority of the judges or justices deciding the case. Often a judge or justice who feels strongly about making or emphasizing a point that was not made or emphasized in the unanimous or majority opinion will write a **concurring opinion.** That means the judge or justice agrees (concurs) with the judgment given in the unanimous or majority opinion, but for different reasons. In other than unanimous opinions, a **dissenting opinion** is usually written by a judge or justice who does not agree with the majority. The dissenting opinion is important because it may form the basis of the arguments used years later in overruling the precedential majority opinion.

JUDGES AND JUSTICES The terms *judge* and *justice* are usually synonymous and represent two designations given to judges in various courts. All members of the U.S. Supreme Court, for example, are referred to as justices. And justice is the formal title usually given to judges of appellate courts, although this is not always the case. In New York, a justice is a trial judge of the trial court (which is called the Supreme Court), and a member of the Court of Appeals (the state's highest court) is called a judge. The term *justice* is commonly abbreviated to J., and *justices* to JJ. A Supreme Court case might refer to Justice Kennedy as Kennedy, J.; or to Chief Justice Rehnquist as Rehnquist, C. J.

APPELLANTS AND APPELLEES The **appellant** is the party who appeals a case to another court or jurisdiction from the court or jurisdiction in which the case was originally brought. Sometimes, an appellant who appeals from a judgment is referred to as the **petitioner** (which is also the term used to refer to a party who initiates a proceeding in equity, as previously mentioned). The **appellee** is the party against whom the appeal is taken. Sometimes, an appellee is referred to as the **respondent.**

A Supreme Court Case

To illustrate how to read and analyze a court opinion, we have annotated an actual case that was heard by the U.S. Supreme Court in 1988. The lawsuit was initiated by students of Hazelwood High School who claimed that their First Amendment rights to free speech had been violated by school authorities when the principal refused to allow the publication of certain articles in the school newspaper.

You will note that triple asterisks (* * *) and quadruple asterisks (* * * *) frequently appear within the opinion. The triple asterisks indicate that the authors have deleted a few words or sentences from the opinion for the sake of readability or brevity. Quadruple asterisks mean that an entire paragraph (or more) has been omitted. Also, where the opinion cited another case or legal source, the citation to the referenced cases or sources has been omitted to save space and to improve the flow of the text. These editorial practices are continued in the other court opinions presented in this text. In addition, the authors have occasionally added a bracketed comment to clarify a term or a passage of the opinion or to replace a section of the opinion with a briefer, paraphrased version.

HAZELWOOD SCHOOL DISTRICT v. KUHLMEIER

1 — Supreme Court of the United States, 1988.
___U.S. ___ , 108 S.Ct. 562, 98 L.Ed.2d 592.

2 — JUSTICE WHITE delivered the opinion of the Court.

3 — This case concerns the extent to which educators may exercise editorial control over the contents of a high school newspaper produced as part of the school's journalism curriculum.

4 — Petitioners are the Hazelwood School District in St. Louis County, Missouri, * * * the principal of Hazelwood East High School, and Howard Emerson, a teacher in the school district. Respondents are three former Hazelwood East students [one of whom is Cathy Kuhlmeier] who were staff members of Spectrum, the school newspaper. They contend that school officials violated their First Amendment rights, by deleting two pages of articles from the May 13, 1983 issue of Spectrum.

5 — Spectrum was written and edited by the Journalism II class at Hazelwood East. The newspaper was published every three weeks or so during the 1982–1983 school year. * * *

The Board of Education allocated funds from its annual budget for the printing of Spectrum. * * *
* * * *

The practice at Hazelwood East during the spring 1983 semester was for the journalism teacher to submit page proofs of each Spectrum issue to Principal Reynolds for his review prior to publication.

6 — On May 10, Emerson delivered the proofs of the May 13 edition to Reynolds, who objected to two of the articles scheduled to appear in that edition. One of the stories described three Hazelwood East students' experiences with pregnancy; the other discussed the impact of divorce on students at the school.

Reynolds was concerned that, although the pregnancy story used false names "to keep the identity of these girls a secret," the pregnant students still might be identifiable from the text. He also believed that the article's references to sexual activity and birth control were inappropriate for some of the younger students at the school.
* * * *

* * * He concluded that his only options under the circumstances were to publish a four-page newspaper instead of the planned six-page newspaper, eliminating the two pages on which the offending stories appeared, or to publish no newspaper at all. Accordingly, he directed Emerson to withhold from publication the two pages containing the stories on pregnancy and divorce. He informed his superiors of the decision, and they concurred.

7 —

Respondents subsequently commenced this action in the United States District Court for the Eastern District of Missouri seeking a declaration that their First Amendment rights had been violated, injunctive relief, and monetary damages. After a bench trial, the District Court denied an injunction, holding that no First Amendment violation had occurred. ＊ ＊ ＊

The District Court concluded that school officials may impose restraints on students' speech in activities that are " 'an integral part of the school's educational function' "—including the publication of a school-sponsored newspaper by a journalism class—so long as their decision has " 'a substantial and reasonable basis.' "

8 —

The Court of Appeals for the Eighth Circuit reversed. The court held at outset that Spectrum was not only "a part of the school adopted curriculum," but also a public forum, because the newspaper was "intended to be and operated as a conduit for student viewpoint." The court then concluded that Spectrum's status as a public forum precluded school officials from censoring its contents except when " 'necessary to avoid material and substantial interference with school work or discipline . . . or the rights of others.' " ＊ ＊ ＊
＊ ＊ ＊ ＊

＊ ＊ ＊ Accordingly, the court held that school officials had violated respondent's First Amendment rights by deleting the two pages of the newspaper.

9 —

We granted certiorari, 479 U.S. ___ (1987), ＊ ＊ ＊.

10 —

Students in the public schools do not "shed their constitutional rights to freedom of speech or expression at the schoolhouse gate." They cannot be punished merely for expressing their personal views on the school premises—whether "in the cafeteria, or on the playing field, or on the campus during the authorized hours," unless school authorities have reason to believe that such expression will "substantially interfere with the work of the school or impinge upon the rights of other students."
＊ ＊ ＊

We have nonetheless recognized that the First Amendment rights of students in the public schools "are not automatically coextensive with the rights of adults in other settings," and must be "applied in light of the special characteristics of the school environment." A school need not tolerate student speech that is inconsistent with its "basic educational mission," even though the government could not censor similar speech outside the school. ＊ ＊ ＊

We deal first with the question whether Spectrum may appropriately be characterized as a forum for public expression. The public schools do not possess all of the attributes of streets, parks, and other traditional public forums that "time out of

11 —

mind, have been used for purposes of assembly, communicating thoughts between citizens, and discussing public questions." Hence, school facilities may be deemed to be public forums only if school authorities have "by policy or by practice" opened those facilities "for indiscriminate use by the general public," * * * or by some segment of the public, such as student organizations. If the facilities have instead been reserved for other intended purposes, "communicative or otherwise," then no public forum has been created, and school officials may impose reasonable restrictions on the speech of students, teachers, and other members of the school community.
* * * *

12 —

The question whether the First Amendment requires a school to tolerate particular student speech is different from the question whether the First Amendment requires a school affirmatively to promote particular student speech. The former question addresses educators' ability to silence a student's personal expression that happens to occur on the school premises. The latter question concerns educators' authority over school-sponsored publications, theatrical productions, and other expressive activities that students, parents, and members of the public might reasonably perceive to bear the imprimatur of the school.
* * *

Educators are entitled to exercise greater control over this second form of student expression to assure that participants learn whatever lessons the activity is designed to teach, that readers or listeners are not exposed to material that may be inappropriate for their level of maturity, and that the views of the individual speaker are not erroneously attributed to the school. Hence, a school may in its capacity as publisher of a school newspaper or producer of a school play "disassociate itself," * * * not only from speech that would "substantially interfere with [its] work . . . or impinge upon the rights of other students," * * * but also from speech that is, for example, ungrammatical, poorly written, inadequately researched, biased or prejudiced, vulgar or profane, or unsuitable for immature audiences. * * *
* * * *

13 —

* * * [W]e hold that educators do not offend the First Amendment by exercising editorial control over the style and content of student speech in school-sponsored expressive activities so long as their actions are reasonably related to legitimate pedagogical concerns.
* * * *

We also conclude that Principal Reynolds acted reasonably in requiring the deletion from the May 13 issue of Spectrum of the pregnancy article, the divorce article, and the remaining articles that were to appear on the same pages of the newspaper.
* * * *

14 — ⌈ The judgment of the Court of Appeals for the Eighth Circuit
  ⌊ is therefore reversed.

15 — ⌈ JUSTICE BRENNAN, with whom JUSTICE MARSHALL
  ⌊ and JUSTICE BLACKMUN join, dissenting.

REVIEW OF CASE

1. The first line informs us that the name of the case is *Hazelwood School District v. Kuhlmeier.* The second line indicates that the case was decided by the United States Supreme Court in 1988. Parallel citations for the case are given on the third line. The citation to the *United States Supreme Court Reports* (abbreviated to "U.S." in the first citation) is obviously incomplete. That is because this is a recent opinion and has not yet been published in the *Reports.* The second citation is to the *Supreme Court Reporter* (abbreviated to "S.Ct." in the citation) and indicates that this case can be found in volume 108 of that reporter, on page 562. The third citation is to the *Lawyers' Edition of the Supreme Court Reports* (abbreviated to "L.Ed." in the citation) and indicates that this case can be found in volume 98 of the second series of that reporter, on page 592.

2. Justice White of the Supreme Court delivered the opinion for the majority of the Court.

3. This sentence simply states the issue or dispute to be decided by the Court. An *issue* is a disputed point of fact or law (such as a constitutional right).

4. This paragraph states who the parties are and further defines the conflict between the parties. The school district, principal, and teacher are the petitioners (persons appealing a lower court's decision), and the students are the respondents (persons defending the appeal). Although the citation lists only the school district and one of the students as the parties to the action, there are frequently other plaintiffs and defendants, which can only be learned from a reading of the actual decision.

5. These paragraphs state the general setting and practices for the publication of the school newspaper. They set forth the background for the controversy.

6. These paragraphs describe the events that created the issue before the Court.

7. These sentences indicate that the initial action was commenced by the students in a federal district court in Missouri. The plaintiffs (students) claimed that their First Amendment rights had been violated. The passage indicates that the school district, principal, and teacher were defendants. It further states that the district court held for the defendants and stated the court's reasoning for its decision.

8. These paragraphs indicate that the students appealed the district court's decision to the United States Court of Appeals for the Eighth Circuit. The Court of Appeals reversed the district court's decision, stating its reasons for holding that the students' First Amendment rights had been violated.

9. This sentence states that the school district petitioned the United States Supreme Court to *hear* its appeal of the U.S. Court of Appeals decision and that the petition was granted in 1987, as published in volume 479 of the *United States Supreme Court Reports.* The petition is by a *writ of certiorari.* When the writ is granted, the lower court is required (ordered) to produce a certified record of the case for the appellate court that has used its discretion to hear the appeal. If, however, the writ is denied, this denial indicates that the appellate court has refused to hear the appeal, and thus the judgment of the lower court remains unchanged. The Supreme Court probably granted certiorari because of the apparent constitutional importance of the lower courts' decisions.

10. These paragraphs set forth the general boundaries of the First Amendment rights as applied to students attending public schools. It does not address the specific facts or issue before the Court but serves as a foundation for its decision.

11. This paragraph establishes that the student newspaper is the type of activity that permits reasonable restrictions to be imposed on a student's freedom of expression.

12. These paragraphs set forth the Court's legal reasoning for its final decision. They present an analysis of why educators have a right to control student expression in pursuit of a school's basic educational mission.

13. These paragraphs represent the final conclusions of the Court.

14. The Supreme Court reversed the Court of Appeals decision, holding that limited censorship of student newspapers is not a violation of the First Amendment to the United States Constitution.

15. The opinion of the Court was not unanimous; and three justices (Brennan, Marshall, and Blackmun) dissented. It is not uncommon for dissenting judges to write their own opinions. In this case the dissenting opinion was written by Justice Brennan, who was joined in the dissent (without separate opinions) by Justices Marshall and Blackmun. Each justice could have written his own opinion (reasons) for his dissent. Dissenting opinions are frequently important and used as a basis for changing or modifying the law in future decisions.

QUESTIONS AND CASE PROBLEMS

1. What is the difference between common law and statutory law? Should judges have the same authority to overrule statutory law as they have to overrule common law?

2. What is substantive law? What is procedural, or adjective, law? Are there reasons for the two to exist side by side?

3. The concept of *equity* was mentioned in this chapter. Courts of equity tend to follow general rules or maxims rather than common law or *stare decisis* as courts of law do. Some of those maxims are: whoever seeks equity must do equity; one seeking the aid of an equity court must come to the court with clean hands; and equity aids the vigilant, not those who rest on their rights. (The last maxim is the equitable doctrine of laches, and it refers to those who do not pursue a remedy within a reasonable time.) Why would equity courts give more credence to such maxims than to a hard-and-fast body of law?

4. Law is constantly changing to reflect the attitudes and beliefs of society. Therefore, a society ultimately determines what rules govern the conduct of persons within that society. Briefly discuss how social attitudes and beliefs—and, consequently, the law—concerning the following topics has changed over time.

(a) The shooting of a trespasser.

(b) Laws governing minors.

5. A student is interested in reading the entire court opinion in the case of *U.S. v. Sun and Sand Imports, Ltd., Inc.,* 725 F.2d 184 (2d Cir. 1984). The case deals with the transportation, via interstate commerce, of flammable sleepwear for children in violation of the Flammable Fabrics Act. Explain specifically where the student would locate the court's opinion.

6. The equitable principle "Equity aids the vigilant, not those who rest on their rights" means that courts will not aid those who do not pursue a cause of action while the evidence is fresh and while the true facts surrounding the issue can be discovered. The statute of limitations, discussed in Section 2-725 of the Uniform Commercial Code (see Appendix B), is based on this principle. Under the statute of limitations, the period of time within which a party can bring an action for breach of a contract covering the sale of goods is four years—although the parties (the seller and the buyer) can reduce this period by agreement to only one year. As a practical matter, discuss which party would benefit more by a one-year period and which would benefit more by a four-year period.

7. Most states hold that a manufacturer who sells a defective product that causes harm to a person is strictly liable for damages, even though the manufacturer used reasonable care in the production and sale of the product and was unaware of the defect. Most state constitutions and statutes do not provide for such liability. Where, then, does such a law come from, and on what basis can such liability be imposed?

8. Briefly discuss whether an action at law or an action in equity is more appropriate in the following situations:

(a) Divorce.

(b) Automobile accident.

(c) Preventing future trespass on your property by a neighbor.

(d) Bankruptcy.

(e) Libel or slander (defaming a person's reputation).

9. In the text of this chapter, we stated that the doctrine of *stare decisis* "became a cornerstone of the English and American judicial systems." What does *stare decisis* mean, and why has this doctrine been so fundamental to the development of our legal tradition?

10. Different courts sometimes reach opposite conclusions when deciding cases involving similar, if not identical, issues. Assuming the laws and case precedents pertaining to the issues are identical in the jurisdictions in question, how can such differences in legal reasoning and consequent decisions be accounted for?

11. What is the difference between a concurring opinion and a majority opinion? Between a concurring opinion and a dissenting opinion? Why do judges and justices write concurring and dissenting opinions, since they will not affect the outcome of the case at hand—which has already been decided by majority vote?

Chapter 2

Courts and Civil Dispute Resolution

Today in the United States there are fifty-two separate court systems. Each of the fifty states, in addition to the District of Columbia, has its own fully developed, independent system of courts. Additionally, there is a separate federal court system. It is important to understand that the federal courts—the system taken as a whole—are not necessarily superior to the state courts. They are simply an independent system authorized by Article III, Section 2, of the United States Constitution. The federal courts were set up to handle matters of particular federal interest. As we shall see, the United States Supreme Court is the final controlling voice over all these fifty-two systems, at least when questions of U.S. constitutional law are involved.

In this chapter both the state and the federal court systems will be examined. Then a typical case will be followed through the courts. Remember that an important step in the use of the courts or in the process of adjudication is *determining which rules apply to the facts in the case*. These rules can be *substantive* or *procedural*. They may come from several sources and can cover several areas of the law.

In studying the courts and their procedures, the first question should be which courts have the power to decide a particular case—that is, which courts have jurisdiction.

JURISDICTION

Juris means "law"; *diction* means "to speak." Thus, the power to speak the law is the literal meaning of the term **jurisdiction.** Before any court can hear a case, it must have jurisdiction—that is, the power to hear and decide the case. Without jurisdiction, a court cannot exercise any authority in the case. Thus, in order for a court to exercise valid authority, it must have jurisdiction over both the person against whom the suit is brought or the property involved in the suit and the subject matter of the case.

In personam, In rem, and *Quasi in rem* Jurisdiction

In order to consider a case, a court must have power over the *person* or the *property* involved in the action. Generally, a court's power is limited to the territorial boundaries of the state in which it is located. Thus, a court has jurisdiction over the person of anyone who can be served with a summons within those boundaries. Additionally, if a person is a resident of the state or does business within the state, the court will have jurisdiction over that person. Finally, in some cases in which an individual has committed a wrong, such as an automobile injury or the sale of defective goods within the state, a court can exercise jurisdiction using the authority of a *long arm statute*, even if the individual is outside the state. A **long arm statute** is a state law permitting courts to obtain jurisdiction over nonresident defendants. A court can further exercise jurisdiction over a corporation in the state where it is incorporated, in the state where it has its main plant or office, and in any state where it does business.[1]

Power over the person is often referred to as *in personam* **jurisdiction.** *In personam* jurisdiction is required before a court can enter a personal judgment against a party to the action. This type of jurisdiction may be contrasted with **in rem jurisdiction.** An *in rem* proceeding is one that is taken directly against property. In an *in rem* proceeding, for example, a court may use property within a state to help satisfy a general debt.

A third type of jurisdiction—**quasi in rem jurisdiction**—is based on a person's interest in property within the court's jurisdiction. Because the action is brought against the party personally, it is not an *in rem* proceeding. This type of jurisdiction is used when *in personam* jurisdiction is not possible, but there must be a minimum connection between the property and the subject matter of the action for the court to use it. For example, a non-resident person's boat may serve as the basis for *quasi in rem* jurisdiction in a dispute over the boat's rental.

In all cases in which a court exercises jurisdiction, the parties must be served either with actual notice that they are involved in a suit (usually by service of a summons) or, when the parties cannot be located, by publication of notice in a newspaper or in some other manner if permitted by statute.

---

1. For an example of the minimum contacts required for a court to exercise jurisdiction over a corporation that is not based within its state, see International Shoe Co. v. Washington, 326 U.S. 310, 66 S.Ct. 154, 90 L.Ed. 95 (1945).

Subject Matter Jurisdiction

Subject matter jurisdiction involves a limitation on types of cases a court can hear. For example, probate courts—courts that handle only matters relating to wills and estates—offer a common example of limited subject matter jurisdiction. The subject matter jurisdiction of a court is usually defined in the statute or constitution that created the court. A court's subject matter jurisdiction can be limited not only by the subject of the lawsuit but also by the amount of money in controversy, by whether a case is a felony or a misdemeanor, or by whether the proceeding is a trial or an appeal.

GENERAL JURISDICTION AND SPECIAL, OR LIMITED, JURISDICTION The distinction between courts of general jurisdiction and courts of special, or limited, jurisdiction lies in the subject matter of cases heard. A court of general jurisdiction can decide virtually any type of case. Every state has one level of such courts, which may be called county courts, circuit courts, district courts, or some other name. On the other hand, at both federal and state levels there are courts that hear only cases of specialized, or limited, subject matter. For example, one court may handle only cases dealing with divorce or child custody. Another may handle disputes over relatively small amounts of money (a small claims court). Courts of general jurisdiction will not handle cases that are appropriate for these courts of special, or limited, jurisdiction.

Original and Appellate Jurisdiction

The distinction between courts of original jurisdiction and courts of appellate jurisdiction normally lies in whether the case is being heard for the first time. Courts having original jurisdiction are those of the first instance. In other words, they are where the trial of a case begins. In contrast, courts having appellate jurisdiction act as reviewing courts. In general, cases can be brought to them only on appeal from an order or a judgment of a lower court.

VENUE

Jurisdiction is concerned with whether a court has authority over a specific subject matter or individual. **Venue,** in contrast, is concerned with the particular geographic area within a judicial district where a suit should be brought. It is a question that arises after a determination of jurisdiction. A particular court may have jurisdiction but not venue.

Basically, the concept of venue reflects the policy that a court trying a suit should be in the geographic neighborhood where the incident leading to the suit occurred or where the parties involved in the suit reside. That neighborhood is usually the county where the incident occurred or where the parties live. Pretrial publicity or other factors may, however, require a change of venue to another community, especially in criminal cases, if the defendant's right to a fair and impartial jury is impaired.

The proper venue for a suit is defined by statute. Sometimes the parties by contract will designate the venue should a future contractual dispute arise. Improper venue does not deprive the court of power to hear a case, but a party can request a change of venue if venue is not proper.

A TYPICAL STATE COURT SYSTEM

Most state court systems are based on a three-tiered model. Any person who is a party to a lawsuit typically has the opportunity to plead the case before a trial court and then, if he or she loses, before two levels of appellate courts. Therefore, in most states a case may proceed first through a trial court, with an automatic right to review by a state appellate court, and then, if accepted, to the state supreme court. Finally, if a federal constitutional issue is involved in the decision of the state supreme court, that decision may be appealed to the United States Supreme Court.

Consider the typical state court system represented in Exhibit 2-1. It has three main tiers: (1) the state trial court of general or limited juris-

diction, (2) the state appellate court, and (3) the state supreme court.

One can view the typical state system as being made up of trial courts and of appellate courts, or courts of appeal and review. Trial courts are exactly what their name implies—courts in which trials are held and testimony is taken. Trial courts may be courts of record, where a written record is taken, or courts not of record. Today, most are courts of record. Most states have trial courts of both limited and general jurisdiction.

Limited-Jurisdiction Trial Courts

Every state has trial courts that have original jurisdiction. Those with limited jurisdiction as to subject matter are often called special inferior trial courts or minor judiciary courts. Some typical courts of limited jurisdiction are domestic relations courts, which handle only divorce actions and child custody cases; local municipal courts, which handle mainly traffic cases; probate courts, which handle the administration of wills and estate settlement problems; and small claims and justice of the peace courts. Typically, the minor judiciary courts do not keep complete written records of trial proceedings.

General-Jurisdiction Trial Courts

Trial courts that have general jurisdiction as to subject matter may be called county, district, superior, or circuit courts.[2] General-jurisdiction trial courts have authority to hear and decide cases of nearly every subject matter. These courts of general jurisdiction may be supplemented by the courts of limited jurisdiction or the minor judiciary courts discussed above.

At the trial level, the parties to a controversy may dispute the particular facts, what law should be applied to those facts, and how that law should be applied. Generally, with some exceptions, as discussed below, it may be said that judges decide questions of law and juries decide questions of fact. If a party is entitled to and requests a trial

---

2. The name in Ohio is Court of Common Pleas; the name in New York is Supreme Court; the name in Massachusetts is Trial Court.

Exhibit 2-1 A Typical State Court System

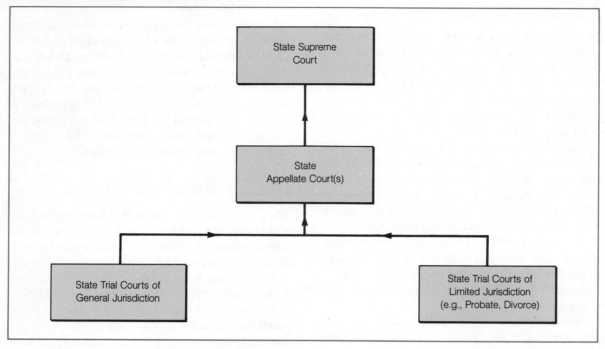

by jury, the appropriate issues will be tried before a jury at the trial level, not on appeal. In an appeal, what is at issue is the initial tribunal's legal procedures and application of the law to the facts.

Appellate Courts, or Courts of Appeal and Review

Although, in some states, trial courts of general jurisdiction also have limited jurisdiction to hear appeals from the minor judiciary—for example, small claims and traffic cases—when one discusses courts of review, or appellate courts, one usually means courts that are not trial courts. With this in mind, it may be said that generally most, if not all, appellate courts have multijudge panels.

Every state has at least one court of review, or appellate court. The subject matter jurisdiction of these courts is substantially limited to hearing appeals. Many states have intermediate reviewing courts and one supreme court. The intermediate

appellate, or review, court is often called the court of appeals. The highest court of the state is normally called the supreme court.[3] Appellate courts try few cases. They examine the record of the case on appeal and determine whether the trial court committed an error. They look at questions of law and procedure, not questions of fact.[4] The decisions of each state's highest court in all questions of state law are final. It is only when questions of federal law are involved that a state's highest court can be overruled by the United States Supreme Court.

---

3. In New York, Maryland, and the District of Columbia, it is called the Court of Appeals. In Maine and Massachusetts, it is called the Supreme Judicial Court. In West Virginia, it is called the Supreme Court of Appeals.

4. The only times an appellate court tampers with a trial court's findings of fact are when the finding is clearly erroneous (that is, when it is contrary to the evidence presented at trial) or when there is no evidence to support the finding.

THE FEDERAL COURT SYSTEM

The federal court system is similar in many ways to most state court systems. It is also a three-tiered model consisting of: (1) trial courts, (2) intermediate courts of appeal, and (3) the Supreme Court. Exhibit 2–2 shows the organization of the federal court system in some detail.

District Courts

At the federal level, the equivalent of a state trial court of general jurisdiction is the district court. There is at least one federal district court in every state. The number of judicial districts can vary over time, primarily due to population changes and corresponding case loads. Thus, a state can comprise a single district or be divided into several districts. United States district courts are often referred to as federal trial courts. Most federal cases originate in these courts. When there are two or more district courts within a state, the geographical jurisdiction in each court is limited. The state of Florida, for example, has district courts for northern, middle, and southern Florida.

In the Bankruptcy Amendments and Federal Judgeship Act of 1984, Congress took the opportunity to increase the total number of federal judgeships in the United States. These judges are appointed by the president, with the advice and consent of the Senate. The law provides for 563

Exhibit 2–2 The Organization of the Federal Court System

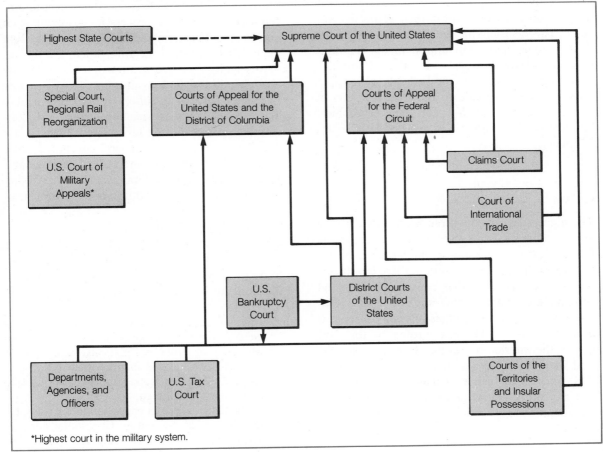

*Highest court in the military system.

district court judgeships within the ninety-six judicial districts.[5]

U.S. district courts have original jurisdiction in federal matters. In other words, district courts are where federal cases originate. There are other trial courts with original, albeit special (or limited), jurisdiction, in federal matters. These include the U.S. Tax Court, the U.S. Bankruptcy Court, and the U.S. Claims Court. Certain administrative agencies and departments having judicial power also have original jurisdiction.

U.S. Courts of Appeal

Congress has established twelve judicial circuits. Each of the fifty states, the District of Columbia, and the territories are assigned to one of these circuits. There is also a thirteenth circuit, the Federal Circuit, which has national jurisdiction limited by subject matter. The circuit courts, or United States Courts of Appeal, hear appeals from the district courts located within their respective circuits. The decisions of the courts of appeal are final in most cases, but appeal to the Supreme Court is possible. Appeals from federal administrative agencies, such as the Federal Trade Commission, are also made to the federal courts of appeal. See Exhibit 2–3 for the geographical boundaries of U.S. district courts and U.S. courts of appeal.

The Supreme Court of the United States

The highest level of the three-tiered model of the federal court system is the Supreme Court of the United States. According to the language of Article III of the U.S. Constitution, there is only one Supreme Court. All other courts in the federal system are considered "inferior." Congress is empowered to create such other inferior courts as it deems necessary. Thus, according to this language, the inferior courts that Congress has created include the second tier in our model—the U.S. courts of appeal, as well as the district courts and any other courts of limited, or specialized, jurisdiction.

---

5. See Sections 44(a) and 133 of Title 28 of the United States Code.

The Supreme Court of the United States consists of nine justices; these justices are nominated by the president of the United States and confirmed by the Senate. They receive lifetime appointments (since under Article III they "hold their offices during Good Behavior"). The Supreme Court was created by the U.S. Constitution. Although it has original, or trial, jurisdiction in rare instances, set forth in Article III, Section 2, most of its work is as an appeals court. The Supreme Court can review any case decided by any of the federal courts of appeal, and it also has appellate authority over some cases decided in the state courts.

JUDICIAL REVIEW

The problem often arises as to whether a law is contrary to the mandates of the Constitution. **Judicial review** is the process for resolving such a problem. The term *judicial review* means that the judicial branch of the government has the authority and power to determine if a particular law is in violation of the Constitution. Thus, any state or federal court may refuse to enforce a statute that it concludes is in violation of the U.S. Constitution. Assuming the jurisdictional criteria are satisfied, both state and federal courts may rule on the validity of state and federal statutes and executive acts. Also, federal courts may rule that provisions of state constitutions are unconstitutional.

The power of judicial review was first established in *Marbury v. Madison.* In determining that the United States Supreme Court had the power to decide that a law passed by Congress violated the Constitution, the Court stated:

> It is emphatically the province and duty of the Judicial Department to say what the law is. Those who apply the rule to a particular case, must of necessity expound and interpret that rule. If two laws conflict with each other, the courts must decide on the operation of each.
>
> So if the law be in opposition to the Constitution, if both the law and the Constitution apply to a particular case, so that the court must either decide that case conformably to the law, disregarding the Constitution; or conformably to the Constitution,

Exhibit 2–3 United States Courts of Appeal and United States District Courts

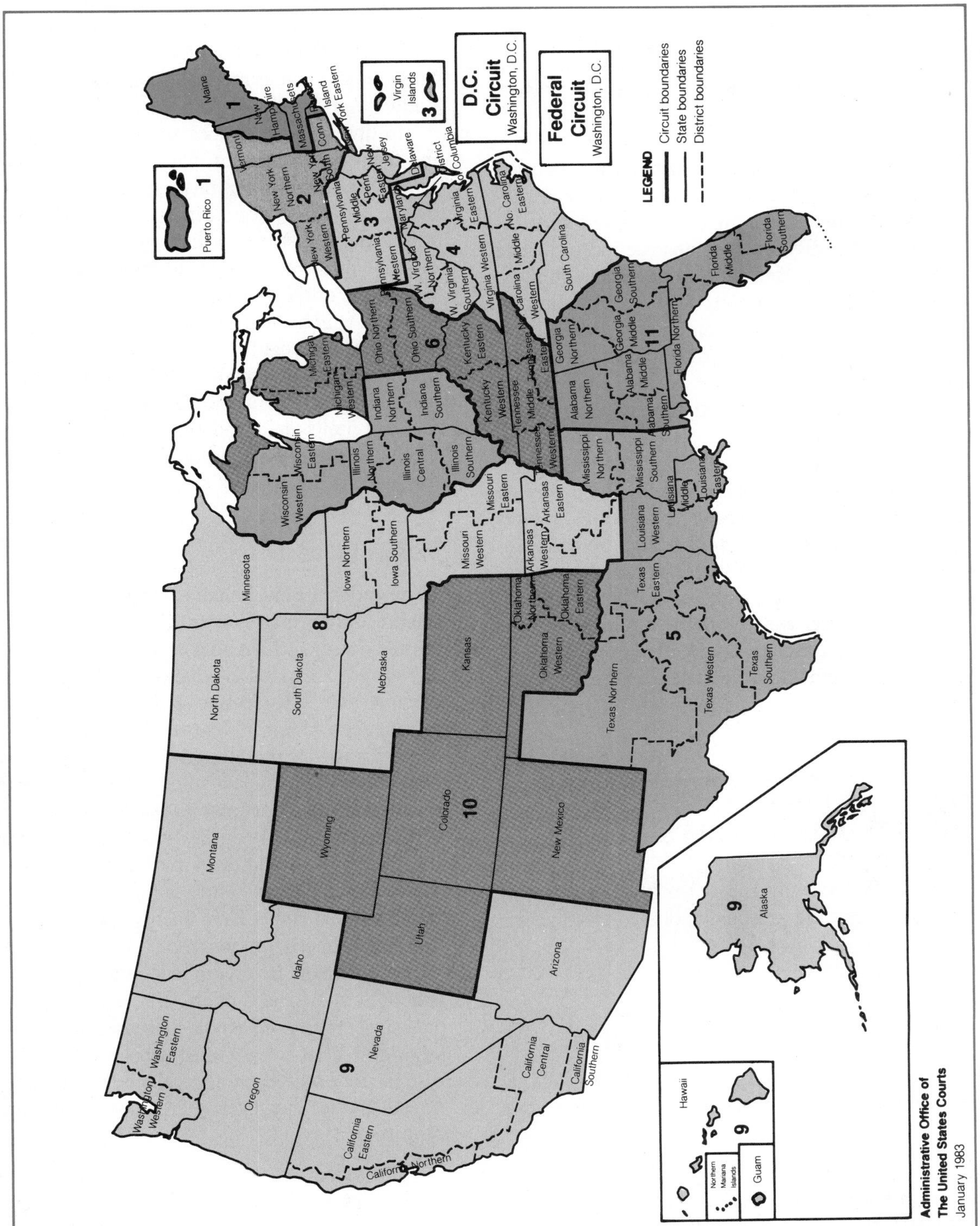

LEGEND
Circuit boundaries
State boundaries
District boundaries

D.C. Circuit
Washington, D.C.

Federal Circuit
Washington, D.C.

Administrative Office of
The United States Courts
January 1983

disregarding the law; the court must determine which of these conflicting rules governs the case. This is of the very essence of judicial duty.

If, then, the courts were to regard the Constitution and the Constitution is superior to any ordinary Act of the Legislature, the Constitution, and not such ordinary Act, must govern the case to which they both apply.[6]

In another famous case, *United States v. Nixon*,[7] the Supreme Court established its power over actions of the president. In 1974 a grand jury indicted seven individuals for obstruction of justice and conspiracy to defraud (among other things). President Nixon was ordered by the special prosecutor to produce tapes, memoranda, papers, and transcripts. The president attempted to avoid the subpoena on the ground of "executive privilege," but this ground was denied him by the district court.

The president's view of the privilege was broad, and he claimed the courts lacked the power to demand the records sought. The United States Supreme Court subsequently heard the case, denied the claim of executive privilege that was at the heart of the controversy, and affirmed the order of the district court. Among other things, the Court balanced the president's claim against the needs of the defendants and the courts to have the records.

JURISDICTION OF FEDERAL COURTS

Since the federal government is a government of limited powers, the jurisdiction of the federal courts is limited.

Constitutional Boundaries of Federal Judicial Power

Section 1 of Article III states that "The judicial Power of the United States shall be vested in one

---

6. 5 U.S. (1 Cranch) 137, 2 L.Ed. 60 (1803).

7. 418 U.S. 683, 94 S.Ct. 3090, 41 L.Ed.2d 1039 (1974), certiorari denied 431 U.S. 933, 97 S.Ct. 2641, 53 L.Ed.2d 250 (1977), rehearing denied 433 U.S. 916, 97 S.Ct. 2992, 53 L.Ed.2d 1103 (1977).

supreme Court and in such inferior Courts as the Congress may from time to time ordain and establish." Section 2 states that "The judicial Power shall extend to all Cases in Law and Equity arising under this Constitution, the Laws of the United States, and Treaties made, or which shall be made, under their Authority."

In line with the checks and balances system of the federal government, Congress has the power to control the number and kind of inferior courts in the federal system. Except in those cases in which the Constitution gives the Supreme Court original jurisdiction ("In all cases affecting Ambassadors, other public Ministers and Consuls and those in which the State shall be a Party"), Congress can also regulate the jurisdiction of the Supreme Court. Although the Constitution sets the outer limits of federal judicial power, Congress can set other limits on federal jurisdiction. Furthermore, the courts themselves can promulgate rules that further narrow the types of cases they will hear.

Federal Questions

"The Judicial Power shall extend to all cases * * * arising under this Constitution, the laws of the United States and Treaties made * * * under their authority." Thus, federal-question jurisdiction arises from Article III, Section 2 of the Constitution. Whenever a plaintiff's cause of action is based, at least in part, on the United States Constitution, a treaty, or a federal law, then a **federal question** arises, and the case comes under the judicial power of federal courts. People whose claims are based on rights granted by an act of Congress can sue in a federal court. People who claim that their constitutional rights have been violated can begin their suits in federal court.

Any lawsuit involving a federal question can originate in a federal court. In lawsuits involving *diversity of citizenship* (to be discussed shortly), the amount in controversy must exceed $50,000 if the case is to proceed in federal court. In federal-question cases, however, there is no dollar-amount requirement.

Diversity of Citizenship

Article III, Section 2 of the Constitution establishes another basis for federal district court jurisdiction: **diversity of citizenship.** Diversity of citizenship cases are those arising between (1) citizens of different states, (2) a foreign country and citizens of a state or different states, and (3) citizens of a state and citizens or subjects of a foreign country. As indicated above, under Title 28 of the United States Code, Section 1332, the amount in controversy must be more than $50,000 before a federal district court can take jurisdiction. For purposes of diversity of citizenship jurisdiction, a corporation is a citizen of the state where it is incorporated and of the state where it has its principal place of business. Cases involving diversity of citizenship can commence in the appropriate federal court or, if they have started in a state court, can sometimes be transferred to federal court.

Diversity jurisdiction originated in 1789. The authors of the Constitution felt that a state court might be biased toward its own citizens. Hence, the option of using the federal courts provided by the principle of diversity of citizenship is a means of protecting the out-of-state party. A large percentage of the more than 70,000 cases filed in federal courts each year are based on diversity of citizenship.

Consider an example. Ortega is driving from his home state, New York, to Florida. In Georgia he runs into a car owned by Flanders, a citizen of Georgia. Flanders's new Mercedes is demolished, and, as a result of the personal injuries she sustains in the accident, Flanders is unable to work for six months. Thus, the case in question involves more than $10,000 worth of damages. Flanders can therefore bring suit in a federal district court on the basis of diversity of citizenship.

Concurrent versus Exclusive Jurisdiction

When both federal and state courts have the power to hear a case, as when there is diversity of citizenship of the parties, **concurrent jurisdiction** exists. In contrast, when cases can be tried only in federal courts or only in state courts, **exclusive jurisdiction** exists. Federal courts have exclusive jurisdiction in cases involving federal crimes, bankruptcy, patents, and copyrights; in suits against the United States; and in some areas of admiralty (maritime) law. States have exclusive jurisdiction

in certain subject matters also—for example, in divorce and in adoptions. The concepts of concurrent and exclusive jurisdiction are illustrated in Exhibit 2–4.

Standing to Sue

Standing is a jurisdictional issue that affects the power of courts to hear and decide cases. A party that has *standing to sue* has a sufficient "stake" in a controversy to seek judicial resolution of it. In other words, a party must have a legally protectible and tangible interest at stake in the litigation to have standing. The party must have been injured or be threatened with injury by the action complained of.

The question is whether the **litigant** is the proper party to fight the suit, not whether the matter at issue is **justiciable.** (A *justiciable* controversy is real and substantial, as opposed to hypothetical or academic.) To illustrate: a conservation organi-

Exhibit 2–4 Exclusive and Concurrent Jurisdiction

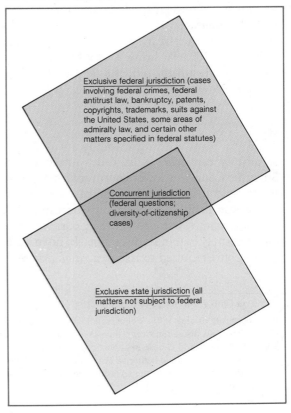

Exclusive federal jurisdiction (cases involving federal crimes, federal antitrust law, bankruptcy, patents, copyrights, trademarks, suits against the United States, some areas of admiralty law, and certain other matters specified in federal statutes)

Concurrent jurisdiction (federal questions; diversity-of-citizenship cases)

Exclusive state jurisdiction (all matters not subject to federal jurisdiction)

zation wanted to challenge a government agency's approval of locating a ski complex near a national wilderness area. Before the court would consider whether the challenge involved justiciable issues, the organization needed to show that it was a proper party to bring the suit. To show that it was a proper party—that is, to show that it had standing—the organization alleged that some of its members used, hiked in, and enjoyed the wilderness area that the development threatened. The organization also alleged that the ski complex compromised these members' enjoyment of the area.[8]

WHICH CASES REACH THE SUPREME COURT?

Many people are surprised to learn that in a typical case there is no absolute right of appeal to the United States Supreme Court. The Supreme Court is given original, or trial court, jurisdiction in a small number of situations. In all other cases, its jurisdiction is appellate "with such Exceptions, and under such Regulations as the Congress shall make." Thousands of cases are filed with the Supreme Court each year; yet it hears, on average, only about 200. To bring a case before the Supreme Court, a party requests the Court to issue a *writ of certiorari.*[9]

Writ of Certiorari

A *writ of certiorari* is an order issued by the Supreme Court to a lower court requiring the latter to send it the record of the case for review. Parties can petition the Supreme Court to issue a *writ of certiorari*, but whether the Court will issue one is entirely within its discretion. In no instance is the Court required to issue a *writ of certiorari.*

---

8. Sierra Club v. Morton, 348 F.Supp. 219 (N.D.Cal. 1972).

9. Between 1790 and 1891, Congress allowed the Supreme Court almost no discretion over which cases to decide. After 1925, the Court could choose in almost ninety-five percent of appealed cases to decide whether to hear arguments and issue an opinion. Beginning with the term in October, 1988, mandatory review was eliminated altogether.

Below are some of the situations in which the Supreme Court may issue a *writ of certiorari:*

1.　When a state court has decided a substantial federal question that has not been determined by the Supreme Court or when a state court has decided such a question in a way that is probably in disagreement with the trend of the Supreme Court's decisions.
2.　When two or more federal courts of appeal are in disagreement with each other.
3.　When a federal court of appeals has decided an important state question in conflict with state law, has decided an important federal question not yet addressed by the Court but which should be decided by the Court, has decided a federal question in conflict with applicable decisions of the Court, or has departed from the accepted and usual course of judicial proceedings.
4.　When a federal court of appeals holds that a state statute is invalid because it violates federal law.
5.　When the highest state court of appeals holds a federal law invalid or upholds a state law that has been challenged as violating federal law.
6.　When a federal court holds an act of Congress unconstitutional and the federal government or one of its employees is a party.

Most petitions for *writs of certiorari* are denied. A denial is not a decision on the merits of a case, nor does it indicate agreement with the lower court's opinion. Denial of the writ also has no value as a precedent.[10] The Court will not issue a writ unless at least four justices approve of it. This is called the "rule of four." Typically, only the petitions that raise the possibility of important constitutional questions are granted.

JUDICIAL PROCEDURES: FOLLOWING A CASE THROUGH THE COURTS

American and English courts follow the *adversary system of justice.* The judge's role is viewed as non-

---

10. Singleton v. Commissioner of Internal Revenue, 439 U.S. 940, 99 S.Ct. 335, 58 L.Ed.2d 335 (1978).

biased and mostly passive. The lawyer functions as the client's advocate, presenting the client's version of the facts in order to convince the judge or the jury (or both) that this version is true. Judges do not have to be entirely passive. They are responsible for the appropriate application of the law. They do not have to accept the legal reasoning of the attorneys. They can base a ruling and a decision on a personal study of the law. Judges sometimes ask questions of witnesses and even suggest types of evidence to be presented. For example, if an indigent defendant chooses to act as his or her own counsel, the judge will often play a role more like that of an advocate, intervening during the trial proceedings to help the defendant.[11]

Rules of Procedure

Procedure involves the way in which disputes are handled in the courts. A large body of law, procedural law, establishes the rules and standards for determining disputes in courts. The rules are very complex, and they vary from court to court. There is a set of federal *rules of procedure,* and there are various sets of procedural rules in the state courts. Rules of procedure differ in criminal and civil cases.

We will now present a hypothetical civil case. The case involves an automobile accident in which John Jones, driving a Cadillac, struck Jane Adams, driving a Ford. The accident occurred at an intersection in New York City. Adams suffered personal injuries, incurring medical and hospital expenses as well as lost wages for four months. Jones and Adams are unable to agree on a settlement, and Adams sues Jones. Adams is the *plaintiff,* and Jones is the *defendant.* Both are represented by lawyers.

The Pleadings

The complaint and answer (and the counterclaim and reply)—all of which are discussed below—taken together are called the **pleadings.** The pleadings inform each party of the claims of the other and specify the issues (disputed questions) involved in the case. Pleadings remove the element of surprise from a case. They allow lawyers to gather the most persuasive evidence and to prepare better arguments, thus increasing the probability that a just and true result will be forthcoming from the trial.

COMPLAINT AND SUMMONS   Adams's suit, or action, against Jones will commence when her lawyer files a *complaint* (sometimes called a petition or declaration) with the clerk of the trial court in the appropriate geographic area (the proper venue). In most states it will be a court having general jurisdiction; in others it may be a court having special jurisdiction with regard to subject matter. The complaint will contain: (1) a statement alleging the facts necessary for the court to take jurisdiction, (2) a short statement of the facts necessary to show that the plaintiff is entitled to a remedy, and (3) a statement of the remedy the plaintiff is seeking. A typical complaint is shown in Exhibit 2–5.

The complaint will state that Adams was driving her Ford through a green light at the specified intersection, exercising good driving habits and reasonable care, when Jones negligently drove his Cadillac through a red light and into the intersection from a cross street, striking Adams and causing serious personal injury and property damage. The complaint will go on to state that she is entitled to $85,000 to cover medical bills, $10,000 to cover lost wages, and $5,000 to cover property damage to the car.

After the complaint has been filed, the sheriff or a deputy of the county will serve a *summons* and a copy of the complaint on the defendant, Jones. The summons notifies Jones that he is required to prepare an answer to the complaint and to file a copy of his answer with both the court and the plaintiff's attorney within a specified time period (usually twenty to thirty days after the summons has been served). The summons also informs Jones that failure to answer will result in a judgment by default for the plaintiff—the plaintiff would be awarded the damages alleged in her complaint. A typical summons is shown in Exhibit 2–6.

Rules governing the service of a summons vary, but usually *service* is made by handing the sum-

---

11. See Faretta v. California, 422 U.S. 806, 95 S.Ct. 2525, 45 L.Ed.2d 562 (1975).

Exhibit 2–5 **Example of a Typical Complaint**

IN THE UNITED STATES DISTRICT COURT
FOR THE ___Southern___ DISTRICT OF ___New York___

CIVIL NO. 9–1047

_____Jane Adams_____ ,
Plaintiff

vs.   COMPLAINT

_____John Jones_____ ,
Defendant.

Comes now the plaintiff and for his cause of action against the defendant alleges and states as follows:

1. This action is between plaintiff, who is a resident of the State of New York, and defendant, who is a resident of the State of New Jersey. There is diversity of citizenship between parties.
2. The amount in controversy, exclusive of interest and costs, exceeds the sum of $50,000.
3. On September 10th, 1989 plaintiff, Jane Adams, was exercising good driving habits and reasonable care in driving her car through the intersection of Broadwalk and Pennsylvania Ave. when defendant, John Jones, negligently drove his vehicle through a red light at the intersection and collided with plaintiff's vehicle.
4. As a result of the collision plaintiff suffered severe physical injury, that prevented her from working, and property damage to her car. The cost she incurred included: $85,000 in medical bills, $10,000 in lost wages, $5,000 automobile repair.

WHEREFORE, plaintiff demands judgment against the defendant for the sum of $100,000 plus interest at the maximum legal rate and the costs of this action.

By   _____

Joseph Roe
Attorney for Plaintiff
100 Main Street
New York, New York

1/2/90

Exhibit 2–6 A Typical Summons

SUMMONS IN A CIVIL ACTION

United States District Court

FOR THE ___Southern___ DISTRICT OF: New York

CIVIL ACTION FILE No. _91047_

Jane Adams

Plaintiff

v.

John Jones

Defendant

SUMMONS

To the above named Defendant:

You are hereby summoned and required to serve upon   Joseph Roe

plaintiff's attorney, whose address is   100 Main Street
New York, New York

an answer to the complaint which is herewith served upon you, within 20* days after service of this summons upon you, exclusive of the day of service. If you fail to do so, judgment by default will be taken against you for the relief demanded in the complaint.

_____Tom Smith_____
Clerk of Court

_____Mary Doakes_____
Deputy Clerk.

Date: 1/10/90

[Seal of Court]

NOTE:—This summons is issued pursuant to Rule 4 of the Federal Rules of Civil Procedure.

mons to the defendant personally or by leaving it at the defendant's residence or place of business. In a few states a summons can be served by mail. When the defendant cannot be reached, special rules sometimes permit serving the summons by leaving it with a designated person, such as the secretary of state.

CHOICES AVAILABLE AFTER RECEIPT OF THE SUMMONS AND COMPLAINT   Once the defendant has been served with a copy of the summons and complaint, the defendant may simply **default**—that is, fail to respond—and the court may enter a judgment against him or her. If the defendant chooses to respond, he or she must file a *motion to dismiss* or an *answer*.

Motion to Dismiss   If the defendant challenges the sufficiency of the plaintiff's complaint, the defendant can present to the court a **motion to dismiss** for failure to state a claim on which relief can be granted, or **demurrer.** (The rules of civil procedure in many states do not use the term *demurrer;* they use only *motion to dismiss.*) The motion to dismiss for failure to state a claim on which relief can be granted is an allegation that even if the facts presented in the complaint are true, their legal consequences are such that there is no reason to go further with the suit and no need for the defendant to present an answer. It is a contention that the defendant is not legally liable even if the facts are as the plaintiff alleges. If, for example, Adams's complaint alleges facts that exclude the possibility of negligence on Jones's part, Jones can move to dismiss, and he will not be required to answer if his motion is granted. If the court denies the motion to dsmiss, the judge is indicating that the plaintiff has stated a recognized cause of action, and the defendant is given an extension of time to file a further pleading. If the defendant does not do so, a judgment will normally be entered for the plaintiff.

In addition to a plaintiff's failure to state a claim on which relief can be granted, a defendant's pre-answer motion to dismiss may be based on the court's lack of subject matter or personal jurisdiction, improper venue, and other specific reasons. The motion to dismiss is often used for purposes of delay.

If Adams wishes to discontinue the suit be-

cause, for example, an out-of-court settlement has been reached, she can likewise move for dismissal. The court can also dismiss on its own motion. If the court grants the motion to dismiss for failure to state a claim on which relief can be granted, the judge is saying that the plaintiff has failed to state a recognized cause of action. The plaintiff generally is given time to file an amended complaint. If the plaintiff does not file this amended complaint, a judgment will be entered against the plaintiff solely on the basis of the pleadings, and the plaintiff will not be allowed to bring suit on the matter again.

Answer and Counterclaim   If the defendant has not chosen to file a motion to dismiss or has filed a motion to dismiss that has been denied, then an **answer** must be filed with the court. This document either admits the statements or allegations set out in the complaint or denies them and sets out any defenses that the defendant may have. If Jones admits to all of Adams's allegations in his answer, a judgment will be entered for Adams. If Jones denies Adams's allegations, the matter will proceed to trial.

Jones can deny Adams's allegations and set forth his own claim that Adams was in fact negligent and therefore owes Jones money for damages to the Cadillac. This is appropriately called a **counterclaim,** or a **cross-complaint.** If Jones files a counterclaim, Adams will have to answer it with a pleading, normally called a *reply*, that has the same characteristics as an answer.

Answer and Affirmative Defenses   Jones can also admit the truth of Adams's complaint but raise new facts that will result in dismissal of the action. This is called raising an **affirmative defense.** For example, Jones could admit that he was negligent but plead that the time period for raising the claim has passed and that Adams's complaint must therefore be dismissed because it is barred by the statute of limitations (a statutory limit on the time during which one can raise a claim).

Dismissals and Judgments before Trial

Many actions for which pleadings have been filed never come to trial. There are numerous procedural avenues for disposing of a case without a trial. Many of them involve one or the other party's attempts to get the case dismissed through the use of **pretrial motions.** We have already mentioned the motion to dismiss, or the demurrer. Another equally important motion is the motion for a judgment on the pleadings.

MOTION FOR JUDGMENT ON THE PLEADINGS After the pleadings are closed—after the complaint, answer, and any counterclaim and reply have been filed—either of the parties can file a *motion for judgment on the pleadings.* This motion may be used when no facts are disputed and, thus, only questions of law are at issue. The difference between this motion and a motion for summary judgment, discussed below, is that the party requesting the motion may support a motion for summary judgment with sworn statements, or **affidavits,** and other materials; but on a motion for a judgment on the pleadings, a court may consider only those facts pleaded.

MOTION FOR SUMMARY JUDGMENT A lawsuit can be shortened or a trial can be avoided if there are no disagreements about the facts in a case and the only question is which laws apply to those facts. Both sides can agree to the facts and ask the judge to apply the law to them. In this situation, it is appropriate for either party to move for **summary judgment.** Summary judgment will be granted when there are no genuine issues of fact in a case and the only question is one of law. When the court considers a motion for summary judgment, it can take into account evidence outside the pleadings. This distinguishes the motion for summary judgment from the motion to dismiss and, as noted, from the motion for a judgment on the pleadings. In a pretrial setting, one party can bring in a sworn statement, or affidavit, that refutes the other party's claim. Unless the second party brings in affidavits of conflicting facts, the first party will normally receive summary judgment.

Jones, for example, can bring in the sworn statement of a witness that Jones was in California at the time of the accident. Unless Adams can bring in other statements raising the possibility that Jones was at the scene of the accident, Jones will normally be granted his motion for summary judgment. Motions for summary judgment can be made before or during a trial, but they will be granted only if it is clear that there are no factual disputes.

Discovery

Before a trial begins, the parties can use a number of procedural devices in order to obtain information and gather evidence about the case. Adams, for example, will want to know how fast Jones was driving, whether or not he had been drinking, whether he saw the red light, and so on. The process of obtaining information from the opposing party or from other witnesses is known as **discovery.**

Discovery serves several purposes. It preserves evidence from witnesses who might not be available at the time of the trial or whose memories will fade as time passes. It can pave the way for summary judgment if it is found that both parties agree on all facts. It can lead to an out-of-court settlement if one party decides that the opponent's case is too strong to challenge. (A civil case can normally be settled at any time, often without the court's permission.) Even if the case does go to trial, discovery prevents surprises by giving parties access to evidence that might otherwise be hidden, and it serves to narrow the issues so that trial time is spent on the main questions in the case. In addition, discovery procedures may serve to establish a witness's testimony so that the witness's credibility can be attacked at trial if that testimony is changed.

The federal rules of civil procedure and similar rules in the states set down the guidelines for discovery activity. Discovery includes gaining access to witnesses, documents, records, and other types of evidence.

DEPOSITIONS AND INTERROGATORIES Discovery can involve the use of depositions or interrogatories, or both. **Depositions** are sworn testimony by either party or any witness, recorded by a court official. The person deposed appears before a court officer and is sworn. That person then answers questions asked by the attorneys from both sides. The questions and answers are taken down, sworn to, and signed. These answers will, of course, help the attorneys prepare their cases. They can also be used in court to dispute a party or a witness who changes testimony at the trial. Finally, they can be used as testimony if the witness is not available at trial. Depositions can also be taken with written questions from both sides prepared ahead of time.

Interrogatories are series of written questions for which written answers are prepared and then signed under oath. The main difference between interrogatories and depositions with written questions is that interrogatories are directed only to a party, not to a witness, and the party can prepare answers with the aid of an attorney. The scope of interrogatories is broader, because parties are obligated to answer questions even if the answer requires disclosing information from their records and files. Interrogatories are also usually less expensive than depositions.

REQUEST FOR ADMISSIONS   A party can serve a written request to the other party for an admission of the truth of matters relating to the trial. Any matter admitted under such a request is conclusively established for the trial. For example, Adams can ask Jones to admit that he was driving at a speed of forty-five miles an hour. A request for admission saves time at trial because parties will not have to spend time proving facts on which they already agree.

DOCUMENTS, OBJECTS, AND ENTRY UPON LAND   A party can gain access to documents and other items not in his or her possession in order to inspect and examine them. Likewise, a party can gain "entry upon land" to inspect the premises. Jones, for example, can gain permission to inspect and duplicate Adams's medical records and repair bills.

PHYSICAL AND MENTAL EXAMINATION Where the physical or mental condition of one party is in question, the opposing party can ask the court to order a physical or mental examination. If the court is willing to make the order, the opposing party can obtain the results of the examination. It is important to note that the court will make such an order only when the need for the information outweighs the right to privacy of the person to be examined.

The rules governing discovery are designed to make sure that a witness or party is not unduly harassed, that privileged material is safeguarded, and that only matters relevant to the case at hand are discoverable.

Pretrial Hearing

Either party or the court can request a pretrial conference or hearing. Usually the hearing consists of an informal discussion between the judge and the opposing attorneys after discovery has taken place. The purpose of the hearing is to identify the matters that are in dispute and to plan the course of the trial. The pretrial hearing is not intended to compel the parties to settle their case before trial, although judges may encourage them to settle out of court if circumstances suggest that a trial would be a waste of time.

Jury Trials

A trial can be held with or without a jury. If there is no jury, the judge determines the truth of the facts alleged in the case. The Seventh Amendment to the U.S. Constitution guarantees the right to a jury trial in federal courts in all "suits of common law" when the amount in controversy exceeds $20. Most states have similar guarantees in their own constitutions, although many states put a higher minimum dollar restriction on the guarantee. For example, Iowa requires the dollar amount of damages to be at least $1,000 before there is a right to a jury trial. If this threshold requirement is met, either party may normally request that the trial be by jury.

The right to a trial by jury does not have to be exercised, and many cases are tried without one. In most states and in federal courts, one of the parties must request a jury or the right is presumed to be waived.

Jury Selection

In the case between Adams and Jones, both parties want a jury trial. The examination that the judge and both attorneys make of prospective jurors to ensure that their judgment will be impartial is called *voir dire,* a French phrase meaning "to speak the truth." In most jurisdictions, *voir dire* consists of oral questions that attorneys for the plaintiff and the defendant ask a group of prospective jurors (one at a time) in order to determine whether a potential jury member is biased or has any connection with a party to the action or with a prospective witness. During *voir dire,* a party may challenge a certain number of prospective jurors peremptorily—that is, without providing any reason—and ask that these individuals not be sworn in as jurors. Alternatively, a party may challenge a prospective juror for cause—that is, provide a reason why this individual should not be sworn in as a juror. If the judge grants the challenge, the individual is asked to step down. After the jurors have been selected, they are impaneled and sworn in, and the trial is ready to begin.

Note that there are two types of juries: the ordinary ("petit," or small) jury and the grand jury. The latter is called "grand" because it consists of a greater number of jurors than the ordinary trial jury. A grand jury does not determine the guilt or innocence of an accused party; rather, its function is to determine, after hearing the state's evidence, whether probable (reasonable) cause exists for supposing that a crime has been committed and whether a trial ought to be held. If the jury finds probable cause, it will return a "bill of indictment"; if no probable cause is found, it will return "no bill."

The Trial

Both attorneys are allowed to make *opening statements* concerning the facts that they expect to prove during the trial. Since Adams is the plaintiff and has the burden of proving that her case is correct, Adams's attorney begins the case by calling the first witness for the plaintiff and examining (questioning) the witness. (For both attorneys, the type of question and the manner of asking are governed by the rules of evidence.) This examination is called *direct examination.* After Adams's attorney is finished, the witness will be questioned by Jones's attorney on *cross-examination.* After that, Adams's attorney has another opportunity to question the witness in *redirect examination,* and Jones's attorney can then follow with *recross-examination.* When both attorneys have finished with the first witness, Adams's attorney will call the succeeding witnesses in the plaintiff's case, each of whom is subject to cross-examination (and redirect and recross, if necessary).

The plaintiff must prove her case through a preponderance of the evidence. That is, she need not provide indisputable proof that she is entitled to a judgment. She needs to show only that her factual claim is more likely truer than the defendant's.

At the conclusion of the plaintiff's case in a jury trial, the defendant's attorney has the opportunity to ask the judge to direct a verdict for the defendant on the ground that the plaintiff has failed to present a **prima facie** case for jury consideration and, thus, there can be only one verdict as a matter of law—a verdict in the defendant's favor. This is called a *motion for a directed verdict.* In considering the motion, the judge will look at the evidence that is favorable to the plaintiff and the unquestionable evidence that is favorable to the defendant and will grant the motion only if he or she believes that a reasonable jury could not find for the plaintiff. (Motions for directed verdicts at this stage of trial are seldom granted.)

The defendant's attorney will then present the evidence and witnesses for the defendant's case. Witnesses are called and examined. The plaintiff's attorney has a right to cross-examine them, and there is a redirect and recross-examination if necessary. At the end of the defendant's case, either attorney can again move for a directed verdict, and the test will again be whether the jury could, under any reasonable interpretation of the evidence, find for the party against whom the motion is made.

After the defendant's attorney has finished presenting evidence, the plaintiff's attorney can present additional evidence to refute the defendant's case in a **rebuttal.** The defendant's attorney can meet that evidence in a **rejoinder.** After both sides have rested their cases, the attorneys each present a **closing argument,** urging a verdict in favor of their respective clients. The judge instructs the jury (assuming it is a jury trial) in the law that applies to the case. The instructions to the jury are often called *charges.* Then the jury retires to the jury room to deliberate a verdict. In the *Adams v. Jones* case the jury will not only decide for the plaintiff or for the defendant but, if it finds for the plaintiff, will also decide on the amount of money to be paid to her. Let us assume that the jury does decide for Adams, the plaintiff.

MOTION FOR NEW TRIAL   At the end of the trial, a motion can be made to set aside an adverse verdict and to hold a new trial. The motion will be granted if the judge is convinced, after looking at all the evidence, that the jury was in error. A new trial can also be granted on the grounds of newly discovered evidence, misconduct by the participants during the trial, or error by the judge.

JUDGMENT N.O.V. (NOTWITHSTANDING THE VERDICT)   If Jones's attorney previously moved for a directed verdict, this attorney can now make a motion for a **judgment n.o.v.** (from the Latin *non obstante veredicto*, or notwithstanding the verdict). In other words, Jones can state that even if

the evidence is viewed in the light most favorable to Adams, a reasonable jury should not have found a verdict in Adams's favor. If the judge finds this contention to be correct or decides that the law requires the opposite result, the motion will be granted. The standards for granting a judgment n.o.v. are the same as those for granting a motion to dismiss or a motion for a directed verdict. Assume here that this motion is made and denied and that Jones appeals the case. (If Adams had received a smaller money award than she sought, she could have appealed also.) These events are illustrated in Exhibit 2–7.

The Appeal

A notice of appeal must be filed with the clerk of the trial court within the prescribed time. Jones

Exhibit 2–7 A Typical Lawsuit

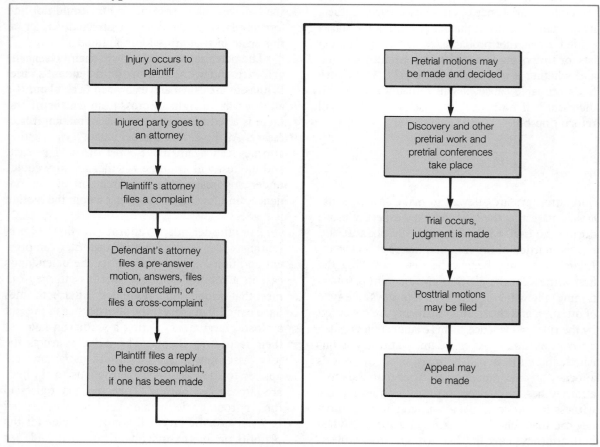

then becomes the *appellant*. His attorney files in the reviewing court (usually an intermediate court of appeals) the record on appeal, which contains the following: (1) the pleadings, (2) a transcript of the trial testimony and copies of the exhibits, (3) the judge's rulings on motions made by the parties, (4) the arguments of counsel, (5) the instructions to the jury, (6) the verdict, (7) the post-trial motions, and (8) the judgment order from which the appeal is taken. Jones may also be required to post a bond for the appeal.

In some courts, Jones's attorney will be required to prepare a condensation of the record, known as an *abstract*. The abstract and a brief are filed with the reviewing court. Generally, an appellant's **brief** contains (1) a short statement of the facts, (2) a statement of the issues, (3) the rulings by the trial court that the appellant contends are erroneous and prejudicial, (4) the grounds for reversal of the judgment, (5) a statement of the applicable law, and (6) arguments on the appellant's behalf, citing applicable statutes and relevant cases as precedent. The attorney for the *appellee*, or *respondent*, Adams, must now file an answering brief and argument. Jones's attorney can file a reply (although this is not required). The reviewing court then considers the case.

NO EVIDENCE HEARD   Appeals courts do not hear any evidence. An appeals court's decision concerning a case is based upon the abstracts, the record, and the briefs. The attorneys can present oral arguments, after which the case is taken under advisement. After the court reaches a decision, the decision is usually written. It contains the opinion (the court's reasons for its decision), the rules of law that apply, and the court's ultimate decision. In general, appellate courts do not reverse findings of fact unless the findings are unsupported or contradicted by the evidence. Rather, they review the record for errors of law. If the reviewing court believes that a reversible error was committed during the trial or that the jury was improperly instructed, the judgment will be reversed. Sometimes the case will be *remanded* (sent back to the court that originally heard the case) for a new trial. In many cases the decision of the lower court is *affirmed*, resulting in the enforcement of that court's judgment or decree.

HIGHER APPEALS COURTS   If the reviewing court is an intermediate appellate court, the losing party (in that court) may seek a reversal of its decision by filing within the prescribed time period a petition for leave to appeal to a higher court.[12] Such a petition corresponds to a petition for a *writ of certiorari* in the United States Supreme Court. The winning party in the intermediate appellate court can file an answer to the petition for leave to appeal. If the petition is granted, the complete record is certified and forwarded to the higher court. New briefs must be filed before the state supreme court and the attorneys may be allowed or requested to present oral arguments. Whenever the state supreme court concludes that the judgment of the intermediate appellate court is correct, it affirms. If it decides otherwise, it reverses the appellate court's decision and enters an appropriate order of remand. At this point, unless a federal question is at issue or there is some other jurisdictional ground for an appeal to a federal court, the case has reached its end. If a new trial is ordered, it will start again at the court of origin.

It is important to know that the vast majority of disputes are settled out of court, mainly because of the time and expense of trying a case. Furthermore, of those cases that go to trial, about 97 percent are finally resolved at the trial level, as relatively few trial court decisions are changed on appeal.

ALTERNATIVE DISPUTE RESOLUTION

Businesspersons and other individuals increasingly are turning to **alternative dispute resolution (ADR)** as an alternative to civil lawsuits. Since trials are often characterized by extensive court delays, going to trial is both costly and time-consuming. ADR offers a less formal way of settling claims. With the assistance of expert arbitrators, disputes can be settled quickly and satisfactorily, without the expense and publicity of court trials. One form of ADR is **mediation,** which involves a third party called the mediator. The

---

12. In most states, the appeal from the court of original jurisdiction up to the state supreme court is a matter of right.

mediator's function is to listen to all sides of a dispute, analyze each party's contentions, communicate with each party, and then help the parties settle the matter. A more formal method of ADR is **arbitration,** in which the dispute is formally submitted to a third person (not part of the judiciary), who renders a legally binding decision.

Mediation

In the mediation process, the parties themselves must reach the agreement. The mediator is often a volunteer from the community, and not necessarily a lawyer. The mediator talks face to face with the parties and allows them to discuss their disagreement in an informal atmosphere, such as a community center, church, or neighbor's home. There are fewer procedural rules than in a courtroom. In fact, most mediation programs discourage lawyers from participating, and thus legal terminology is frequently avoided. Mediation often results in disputes being settled quickly. Initial meetings between the parties and the mediator often occur within several weeks after a voluntary request to mediate has been made by one or both of the parties.

Mediation is not free. The mediator charges an hourly rate that is similar to what an attorney would charge, but the parties split the cost.

Arbitration

With arbitration, the arbitrator makes a *legally binding decision* by which both parties must abide. The arbitrator becomes a private judge, but he or she does not have to be a lawyer, even though many are. Arbitrators decide on their own pro-

cedural rules as well as their own rules of evidence. The decision of the arbitrator is called the **award.** A losing party may appeal an arbitrator's decision to a court, but, except in cases of evident error, courts are reluctant to overturn decisions arrived at through arbitration.

Virtually any commercial matter can be submitted to arbitration. Parties can agree, when a dispute arises, to settle their differences informally through arbitration rather than formally through the court system. Frequently, disputes are arbitrated because of an **arbitration clause** in a contract entered into before the dispute arose. An arbitration clause provides that any disputes arising under the contract will be resolved by arbitration. Most states have statutes (often based in part on the Uniform Arbitration Act of 1955) under which arbitration clauses will be enforced, and some state statutes compel arbitration of certain types of disputes, such as those involving public employees. At the federal level, the Federal Arbitration Act, enacted in 1925, enforces arbitration clauses in contracts involving maritime activity or interstate commerce and can preempt state coverage in these areas in the event of conflict between a state statute and the federal act.

It is important to note that, if parties agree in their contract to arbitrate subsequent disputes arising thereunder, they will very likely be compelled to do so by state or federal statute—providing the dispute is arbitrable. The arbitrability of a dispute involving an alleged violation of the Securities Exchange Act of 1934[13] is at issue in the following case.

---

13. See Chapter 43 for a detailed discussion of this act.

CONCEPT SUMMARY: Courts and Procedures	
Types of Jurisdiction	1. *Jurisdiction over persons/property*—Power of a court over the defendant or the defendant's property; generally limited by territorial boundaries.
	2. *Jurisdiction over subject matter*—Restriction on the types of cases a court can hear.
	a. Limited jurisdiction—Exists when a court is limited to specific subject matter, such as probate or divorce.
	b. General jurisdiction—Exists when a court can hear any kind of case.

CONCEPT SUMMARY: Courts and Procedures (Continued)

Types of Jurisdiction (Continued)	3. *Original jurisdiction*—Exists with courts that have authority to hear a case first (trial courts).
	
	4. *Appellate jurisdiction*—Exists with courts of appeal and review; generally, appellate courts do not have original jurisdiction.
	
	5. *Federal jurisdiction*—Arises in the following situations:
	  a. When a federal question is involved (when the plaintiff's cause of action is based at least in part on the U.S. Constitution, a treaty, or a federal law).
	  b. In diversity-of-citizenship cases between (1) citizens of different states; (2) a foreign country and citizens of a state or different states; or (3) citizens of a state and citizens or subjects of a foreign country. The amount in controversy must exceed $10,000.
	
	6. *Concurrent jurisdiction*—Exists when two different courts have authority to hear the same case.
	
	7. *Exclusive jurisdiction*—Exists when only one court has authority to hear a case.

Types of Courts	1. *Trial courts*—Courts of original jurisdiction, where an action is initiated.
	  a. State—Courts of general jurisdiction can hear any case; courts of limited jurisdiction include divorce courts, probate courts, traffic courts, small claims courts, etc.
	  b. Federal—The federal district court is the equivalent of the state trial court. Federal courts of limited jurisdiction include the U.S. Tax Court, the U.S. Bankruptcy Court, and the U.S. Claims Court.
	
	2. *Intermediate appellate courts*—Courts of appeal and review, generally without original jurisdiction. Many states have an intermediate appellate court; in the federal court system, the U.S. circuit courts of appeal are the intermediate appellate courts.
	
	3. *Supreme court*—The highest court. Each state has a supreme court, although it may be called by some other name, from which appeal to the U.S. Supreme Court is only possible if a federal question is involved. The U.S. Supreme Court is the highest court in the federal court system and the final arbiter of the Constitution and federal law.

Rules of Procedure	Procedural laws that prescribe how disputes are handled in the courts. Rules differ from court to court, and separate sets of rules exist for federal and state courts, as well as for criminal and civil cases. A sample civil court procedure in a state court involves the following steps:
	
	1. *The pleadings:*
	  a. Complaint or petition—A statement of the cause of action and parties involved, filed with the court by the plaintiff's attorney. After the filing, a summons is delivered to the defendant.
	  b. Pre-answer motion, such as a motion to dismiss for failure to state a claim on which relief can be granted.
	  c. Answer—Can take the form of (1) an admission; (2) an affirmative defense; (3) a counterclaim; or (4) an answer denying some or all of the allegations, which may also contain an admission, an affirmative defense, and a counterclaim.

(Continued on the next page)

CONCEPT SUMMARY: Courts and Procedures (Continued)

Rules of Procedure (Continued)	2. *Dismissal/judgment before trial:*
	  a. Motion for judgment on the pleadings—May be made by either party; will be granted if no cause of action exists or if the defendant fails to answer.
	  b. Motion for summary judgment—May be made by either party; will be granted if the parties agree on the facts. Judge applies law in rendering judgment.
	
	3. *Discovery*—The process of gathering evidence concerning the case; involves *depositions* (sworn testimony by either party or any witness) and *interrogatories* (in which parties to the action write answers to questions with the aid of their attorneys).
	
	4. *Pretrial hearing*—Either party or the court can request a pretrial hearing to identify the matters in dispute after discovery has taken place and to plan the course of the trial.
	
	5. *Trial*—Involves opening statements from both parties' attorneys and then:
	  a. Plaintiff's introduction and direct examination of witnesses and cross-examination by defendant's attorney; possible redirect by plaintiff's attorney and recross-examination by defendant's attorney.
	  b. Defendant's introduction and direct examination of witnesses and cross-examination by plaintiff's attorney; possible redirect by defendant's attorney and recross-examination by plaintiff's attorney.
	  c. Possible rebuttal of defendant's argument by plaintiff's attorney, who presents more evidence.
	  d. Possible rejoinder by defendant's attorney to meet that evidence.
	  e. Closing arguments by both plaintiff's and defendant's attorneys in favor of their respective clients.
	  f. Judge's instructions to the jury.
	  g. Jury verdict.
	
	6. *Posttrial options:*
	  a. Motion for a new trial—Will be granted if the judge is convinced that the jury was in error.
	  b. Motion for judgment n.o.v. (notwithstanding the verdict)—Movant (party making the motion) must have filed a motion for a directed verdict at the close of all the evidence during the trial; motion will be granted if the judge is convinced that the jury was in error.
	  c. Motion for judgment (made by winner of case).
	  d. Motion for relief from judgment or order—May be granted for such reasons as (1) mistake or excusable neglect, if not due to negligence of movant; (2) newly discovered evidence that by due diligence could not have been discovered in time to move for a new trial; (3) fraud; or (4) the judgment's being void or having been satisfied, released, or discharged.
	  e. Appeal—Either party can appeal the trial court's judgment to an appropriate court of appeals. After posting of bond(s), briefs are filed, a hearing is held, and the court renders a written opinion.
	  f. Independent action at equity—Relief may be granted if the statute of limitations has run at the time for filing a motion for a new trial or a motion for relief from the judgment and for such reasons as (1) mistake or excusable neglect, if not due to negligence of petitioner; (2) fraud; or (3) the judgment's being void.

BACKGROUND AND FACTS   *Between 1980 and 1982, respondents Eugene and Julia McMahon, individually and as trustees for various pension and profit-sharing plans, were customers of petitioner Shearson/American Express, Inc., a brokerage firm registered with the Securities and Exchange Commission. Two customer agreements signed by Julia McMahon provided for arbitration of any controversy relating to the accounts the McMahons maintained with Shearson. The arbitration provision provided in relevant part as follows:*

> *Unless unenforceable due to federal or state law, any controversy arising out of or relating to my accounts, to transactions with you for me or to this agreement or the breach thereof, shall be settled by arbitration in accordance with the rules, then in effect, of the National Association of Securities Dealers, Inc. or the Boards of Directors of the New York Stock Exchange, Inc. and/or the American Stock Exchange, Inc. as I may elect.*

In October 1984, the McMahons filed a complaint against Shearson and petitioner Mary Ann McNulty, the registered representative (stockbroker) who handled their accounts, in the United States District Court for the Southern District of New York. The complaint alleged that McNulty, with Shearson's knowledge, had violated Section 10(b) of the Securities Exchange Act of 1934 by engaging in fraudulent excessive trading on respondents' accounts and by making false statements.

The complaint also alleged a violation under the Racketeer Influenced and Corrupt Organizations Act (RICO).[1]

Relying on the customer agreement, petitioners (McNulty and Shearson) moved to compel arbitration of the McMahons' claims pursuant to the Federal Arbitration Act. The district court found that the McMahons' Section 10(b) claims were arbitrable under the terms of the agreement but that their RICO claim was not arbitrable "because of the important federal policies inherent in the enforcement of RICO by federal courts."

The court of appeals affirmed the district court on the RICO claim but reversed the decision on the Section 10(b) Securities Exchange Act claims. The U.S. Supreme Court granted certiorari *to resolve the conflicting court opinions regarding the arbitrability of Section 10(b) and RICO claims.*

 Case 2.1

SHEARSON/ AMERICAN EXPRESS, INC., AND McNULTY v. McMAHON
Supreme Court of the United States, 1987.
482 U.S. ___, 107 S.Ct. 2332, 96 L.Ed.2d 185.

O'CONNOR, Justice.

This case presents two questions regarding the enforceability of predispute arbitration agreements between brokerage firms and their customers. The first is whether a claim brought under ∫ [Section] 10(b) of the Securities Exchange Act of 1934 (Exchange Act) must be sent to arbitration in accordance with the terms of an arbitration agreement. The second is whether a claim brought under the Racketeer Influenced and Corrupt Organizations Act (RICO) must be arbitrated in accordance with the terms of such an agreement.

The Federal Arbitration Act provides the starting point for answering the questions raised in this case. * * * The Arbitration Act provid[es] that arbitration agreements "shall be valid, irrevocable, and enforceable, save upon such grounds as exist at law or in equity for the revocation of any contract." The Act also provides that a court must stay its proceedings if it is satisfied that an issue before it is arbitrable under the agreement, and it authorizes a federal district court to issue an order compelling ar-

---

1. RICO is discussed in Chapters 5 and 6.

bitration if there has been a "failure, neglect, or refusal" to comply with the arbitration agreement, *   *   *.

The Arbitration Act thus establishes a "federal policy favoring arbitration." *   *   *

The Arbitration Act mandates enforcement of agreements to arbitrate statutory claims. Like any statutory directive, the Arbitration Act's mandate may be overriden by a contrary congressional command. The burden is on the party opposing arbitration, however, to show that Congress intended to preclude a waiver of judicial remedies for the statutory rights at issue. *   *   *

To defeat application of the Arbitration Act in this case, therefore, the McMahons must demonstrate that Congress intended to make an exception to the Arbitration Act for claims arising under RICO and the Exchange Act, an intention discernible from the text, history, or purposes of the statute. *   *   *

*   *   *   *

Congress did not intend *   *   * to bar enforcement of all predispute arbitration agreements. In this case, where the SEC has sufficient statutory authority to ensure that arbitration is adequate to vindicate Exchange Act rights, enforcement does not effect a waiver of "compliance with any provision" of the Exchange Act. *   *   * Accordingly, we hold the McMahons' agreements to arbitrate Exchange Act claims "enforce[able] *   *   * in accord with the explicit provisions of the Arbitration Act."

Unlike the Exchange Act, there is nothing in the text of the RICO statute that even arguably evinces congressional intent to exclude civil RICO claims from the dictates of the Arbitration Act. This silence in the text is matched by silence in the statute's legislative history. [RICO's] private treble-damages provision *   *   * was added to the House version of the bill after the bill had been passed by the Senate, and it received only abbreviated discussion in either House. There is no hint in these legislative debates that Congress intended for RICO treble-damages claims to be excluded from the ambit of the Arbitration Act.

*   *   *   *

[W]e find no basis for concluding that Congress intended to prevent enforcement of agreements to arbitrate RICO claims. The McMahons may effectively vindicate their RICO claim in an arbitral forum, and therefore there is no inherent conflict between arbitration and the purposes underlying [the treble-damages provision]. Moreover, nothing in RICO's text or legislative history otherwise demonstrates congressional intent to make an exception to the Arbitration Act for RICO claims. Accordingly, the McMahons, "having made the bargain to arbitrate," will be held to their bargain. Their RICO claim is arbitrable under the terms of the Arbitration Act.

*   *   *   *

DECISION AND REMEDY   *The Supreme Court reversed the judgment of the court of appeals. The Court held that both the Section 10(b) Securities Exchange Act claims and the RICO claim should be sent to arbitration pursuant to the parties' agreement in their contract to have any disputes concerning the accounts arbitrated.*

ARBITRATION SERVICES   Arbitration services are provided by both government agencies and private organizations. The major source of private arbitration services is the **American Arbitration Association (AAA).** The majority of the largest law firms in the nation are members of this association. Founded in 1926, the AAA now settles more than 50,000 disputes a year in its thirty-one offices throughout the country. Settlements usu-

ally are effected quickly and, at times, in informal settings, such as a conference room or even a hotel room. Cases brought before the AAA are heard by an expert or a panel of experts—about half of whom are usually lawyers—in the area relating to the dispute.

To cover its costs, the nonprofit organization charges a fee, paid by the party filing the claim. In addition, each party to the dispute pays a price for each hearing day, as well as a special additional fee in cases involving personal injuries or property loss.

THE TREND TOWARD ARBITRATION

The federal and state arbitration statutes referred to previously were adopted with the intention of encouraging arbitration. Many industries now have arbitration programs to facilitate timely and inexpensive settlement of disputes. The insurance industry, for example, established the Insurance Alternative Dispute Resolution Program, which allows insurance companies and policyholders to choose either mediation or binding arbitration of their disputes.

In recent years, programs have been initiated in the court system to ease the burden of the courts by referring cases for arbitration. The U.S. District Court for the Southern District of New York, for example, has adopted a case-referral project. Under this project, participating judges may order the parties to meet within thirty days with the director of the AAA's New York Regional Office. During this meeting, available nonjudicial methods for resolving disputes are discussed. Of the cases referred to the AAA, more than half have resulted in an agreement to use some method of alternative dispute resolution.

South Carolina has become the first state to institute a voluntary arbitration program at the *appellate court level*. Appealing a case is very costly and time-consuming and, hence, arbitration at this level is designed to reduce the time and expense of having an appeal decided. Litigants, under the South Carolina system, must waive the court hearing when requesting arbitration. Moreover, all decisions by the arbitrators are final.

QUESTIONS AND CASE PROBLEMS

1. The American system of government is unique in that it has essentially two sets of governments—state and federal. This is called the dual, or federal, system. One problem that arises in a federal system is that each government tends to duplicate the other's efforts. Can you see any way to avoid such problems of duplication?

2. When a person commits an act that violates both state and federal law, quite often both the federal and the state government have jurisdiction. What problems do you see here?

3. (a) Before two parties go to trial, there is an involved process called pleadings and discovery. Until recently, the rules of discovery were very formal, and trials often turned on elements of surprise. For example, a plaintiff would not necessarily know until the trial what the defendant's defense was going to be. Does this seem like a fair way to conduct a trial?

(b) Within the last twenty years, new rules of discovery have substantially changed all this. Now each attorney can discover practically all the evidence that the other will be presenting at trial. However, certain information is still not available to the parties—namely, each attorney's work product. *Work product* is not a clear concept. Basically, it includes all the attorney's thoughts on the case. Can you see any reason why such information should not be made available to the opposing attorney?

4. Quite often, trials are concluded before they are begun. If the parties do not disagree on the facts, they simply relate those facts to the judge, and then, through a motion for judgment on the pleadings, they ask the judge to decide what the law is and how it applies to this set of facts. How is it possible that two parties can agree on the facts yet disagree as to which party is liable?

5. If a judge enters judgment on the pleadings, the losing party can usually appeal but cannot present evidence to the appellate court. Does this seem fair? Explain.

6. Once a case is appealed, most appellate courts do not have the power to enter judgment or to award damages to a party who should have received them at trial. Consequently, if the appellate court disagrees with the trial court's decision, it will reverse and remand—in effect, ordering the trial court judge to change the judgment. Why should an appellate court not take a judge's word as final?

7. Sometimes on appeal there are questions of whether the facts presented in a trial support the conclusion reached by the judge or the jury. The appellate court will reverse on the basis of the facts only when no reasonable person, from the evidence presented at trial, could have reached the conclusion that the judge or jury reached. Appellate courts normally defer to a judge's decision with regard to the facts. Can you see any reason for this?

8. Martin (plaintiff) brought a civil rights action against his employer, the New York Department of Mental Hygiene (defendant) when it failed to promote him on several occasions. His complaint stated only that the defendant had discriminated against him on the basis of race by denying him "the authority, salary, and privileges commensurate with his position." The defendant made a motion to dismiss the claim for failure to state a cause of

action. Discuss whether the defendant could be successful. [Martin v. New York State Dept. of Mental Hygiene, 588 F.2d 371 (2d Cir. 1978)]

9. On June 16, 1986, the director of the Administrative Office of the U.S. Courts notified the ninety-four federal district courts that no civil jury trials could be initiated until the end of the fiscal year (September 30) due to lack of funds with which to pay the jurors. The petitioners in this case (Armster) claimed that the consequent delay (of three and a half months) in scheduling a jury trial violated the Seventh Amendment right to a civil jury trial. The Justice Department maintained that unlike the Sixth Amendment, which guarantees a speedy *criminal* jury trial, the Seventh Amendment does not guarantee a speedy *civil* jury trial. The Justice Department further noted that district courts have postponed civil jury trials before, although for other reasons—such as court-calendar congestion, lack of a sufficient number of judges, and the priority accorded to trying criminal cases before civil actions. Discuss whether the suspension of civil jury trials for a period of three and a half months due to lack of funds to pay jurors violates the constitutional right to a trial by jury. Are people always entitled to a jury trial in civil law suits? [Armster v. United States District Court for the Central District of California, 792 F.2d 1423 (9th Cir. 1986)]

10. In January of 1983, Colleen Cote, a Wisconsin resident, hired a Michigan lawyer, Peter Wadel, to represent her in a medical malpractice action in a Michigan state court. Wadel filed an appearance for her on February 10, 1983, and sent her a bill for $118.25 for court costs that he had paid on her behalf. She paid him the following month. In July she learned from the defendant's lawyer that the court had dismissed her case in April for lack of prosecution. On checking with Wadel's office, she was told that settlement negotiations were under way with the defendant's insurer—which Cote knew to be untrue, since the defendant was uninsured. She then contacted another lawyer to look into the matter, but the lawyer could obtain no information from Wadel or his law firm concerning the issue. Cote then brought suit in a Wisconsin federal court (there is at least one federal trial court in each state) against Wadel, alleging malpractice in handling her case. Under Wisconsin's long arm statute, jurisdiction is conferred on Wisconsin state and federal courts over nonresident defendants "in any action claiming injury to person or property within or without this state arising out of an act or omission within this state by the defendant." The federal district court in Wisconsin dismissed Cote's suit for lack of personal jurisdiction over the defendant, whose business and residence were in Michigan. Cote appealed, claiming that Wisconsin's long arm statute gave her jurisdiction or that, if it did not, the district should have transferred her case to a court with jurisdiction. Discuss her claims. [Cote v. Wadel, 796 F.2d 981 (7th Cir. 1986)]

Chapter 3

Constitutional Authority to Regulate Business

The United States Constitution is the supreme law in this country.[1] Neither Congress nor any state may pass a law that conflicts with the Constitution. Laws that govern business have their origin in the lawmaking authority granted by this document.

Before the Constitution was written, a *confederal* form of government existed. The Articles of Confederation, ratified in 1778, established a confederation of independent states and a national government of very limited powers. The central government could handle only those matters of common concern expressly delegated to it by the member states, and the national congress had no ability to make laws directly applicable to individuals unless the member states explicitly supported such laws. In short, the *sovereign power*[2] to govern rested essentially with the states. The Articles of Confederation clearly reflected the central tenet of the American Revolution—that a government should not have unlimited power.

After the Revolutionary War, however, the states began to pass laws that hampered national commerce and foreign trade by preventing the free movement of goods and services. Consequently, in 1787, the Constitutional Convention convened to amend the Articles of Confederation to give the national government the power to address the country's commercial problems. Instead of amending the Articles of Confederation, the Convention created the Constitution and a completely new type of federal government, which they believed was much better equipped than its predecessor to resolve the problems of the nation.

BASIC CONSTITUTIONAL CONCEPTS

The U.S. Constitution delineates the structure and powers of the government, as well as the limitations on those powers.

---

1. The U.S. Constitution has been included as Appendix A in this text.

2. *Sovereign power* refers to that supreme power to which no other person or authority is superior or equal.

Federalism

Federalism is the basic structure of the government in the United States. A *federal* form of government is one in which the states form a union and the sovereign power is divided between a central governing authority and the member states. The Constitution reserves certain powers for the federal government, and the states retain all powers not delegated to the federal government. Neither government is superior to the other except within the particular area of authority granted to it under the Constitution. Hence, the concept of federalism recognizes that society may be best served by a distribution of functions among local governments and the national government on the basis of which government is better equipped to perform these functions. The Constitution reflects the Federalist belief that a national government can handle certain problems better than individual state governments can.

Conflicts frequently arise regarding the question of which government—federal or state—should be exercising power in a particular area. The United States Supreme Court, as the arbiter of the Constitution, resolves such conflicts by deciding which governmental system is empowered to act under the Constitution.

Delegated Powers

The Constitutional Convention created a federal government in which the states delegated certain enumerated powers to the federal government and reserved all other powers to themselves. Thus, the federal government has no powers apart from those delegated to it by the states. The federal government is also frequently referred to as one holding only *enumerated powers*, since it has no inherent powers (except in dealings with other nations) and can only exercise those powers that have been granted to it or that are necessary and proper for carrying out those powers.

The Bill of Rights

For various reasons, proposals related to the rights of individuals made during the Constitutional Convention of 1787 were rejected. Yet the importance of a written declaration of the rights of individuals eventually caused the first Congress to submit ten amendments to the Constitution for the approval of the states. These amendments, commonly known as the **Bill of Rights,** were adopted in 1791 and embody a series of protections for the individual against various types of interference by the federal government. Among the guarantees provided for by the Bill of Rights are the First Amendment protection of the freedom of religion, speech, and assembly; the Fourth Amendment provisions regarding arrest, search, and seizure; and the Sixth Amendment rights to counsel, confrontation, and cross-examination in criminal prosecutions. Furthermore, through the Fourteenth Amendment, passed after the Civil War, most of these guarantees have been held to be so fundamental as to be applicable at the state level as well.

Separation of Powers

The federal government is divided into three branches—the executive branch, which enforces the laws; the legislative branch, which makes the laws; and the judicial branch, which interprets the laws. Article I of the Constitution provides for the legislative branch. The duties of the executive branch and the method of electing the president are set forth in Article II. The federal judicial system was created by Article III.

Deriving its power from the Constitution, each branch performs a separate function, and no branch may exercise the authority of another branch. Each branch, however, has some power to *limit* the actions of the other branches. In each article of the Constitution that grants specific powers to one of the three branches of the government, there is also a provision for the limitation of that power by another branch. Congress, for example, has power over spending and commerce, but the president can veto that legislation. The executive branch is responsible for foreign affairs, but treaties with foreign governments require the advice and consent of the members of the Senate. Under Article III, Congress determines the jurisdiction of the federal courts, but the Supreme Court has the power to hold acts of the other branches of the federal government unconstitutional.[3] Thus, with this system of **checks and balances,** no one branch of government can accumulate too much power.

---

3. See Marbury v. Madison, 5 U.S. (1 Cranch) 137, 2 L.Ed. 60 (1803).

The Commerce Clause

Article I, Section 8, of the United States Constitution grants Congress the power "[t]o regulate Commerce with foreign Nations, and among the several States, and with the Indian tribes." It is important to note that this clause has had a greater impact on business than any other provision in the Constitution. Theoretically, the power over commerce authorizes the federal government to regulate every commercial enterprise in the United States. This power was delegated to the federal government to ensure the uniformity of rules governing the movement of goods through the states.

Traditionally, the commerce power was interpreted as applying only to interstate, not to intrastate, commerce. The Supreme Court, however, now recognizes that Congress has the power to regulate any activity, interstate or intrastate, that "affects" interstate commerce. Wheat production of an individual farmer intended wholly for consumption on his or her own farm, for example, was held to be subject to federal regulation, since such home consumption reduces the demand for wheat and thus may have a substantial economic effect on interstate commerce.[4]

The following case, *Heart of Atlanta Motel v. United States*, illustrates this doctrine. The case specifically demonstrates the Supreme Court's use of the commerce clause to affirm the power of Congress to pass the Civil Rights Act of 1964. The breadth of the commerce clause permits the national government to legislate in areas in which there is no explicit grant of power to Congress.

---

4. See Wickard v. Filburn, 317 U.S. 111, 63 S.Ct. 82, 87 L.Ed. 122 (1942).

BACKGROUND AND FACTS   *The owner of a motel, who refused to rent rooms to blacks despite the Civil Rights Act of 1964, brought an action to have the Civil Rights Act of 1964 declared unconstitutional. The motel owner alleged that Congress, in passing the act, had exceeded its power to regulate commerce.*

Mr. Justice CLARK delivered the opinion of the Court.
* * * *

This is a declaratory judgment action * * * attacking the constitutionality of Title II of the Civil Rights Act of 1964 * * *. Appellant owns and operates the Heart of Atlanta Motel which has 216 rooms available to transient guests. * * * It is readily accessible to interstate highways 75 and 85 and state highways 23 and 41. Appellant solicits patronage from outside the State of Georgia through various national advertising media, including magazines of national circulation; it maintains over 50 billboards and highway signs within the State, soliciting patronage for the motel; it accepts convention trade from outside Georgia and approximately 75 percent of its registered guests are from out of State. Prior to passage of the Act the motel had followed a practice of refusing to rent rooms to Negroes, and it alleged that it intended to continue to do so. In an effort to perpetuate that policy this suit was filed. [The District Court sustained the Act.] * * *

The sole question posed is, therefore, the constitutionality of the Civil Rights Act of 1964 as applied to these facts. The legislative history of the Act indicates that Congress based the Act on ∫ [section] 5 and the Equal Protection Clause of the Fourteenth Amendment as well as its power to regulate interstate commerce under Art. I, ∫ 8, cl. [clause] 3 [the commerce clause] of the Constitution.

The Senate Commerce Committee made it quite clear that the fundamental object of Title II was to vindicate "the deprivation of personal dignity that surely accompanies denials of equal access to public establishments." At the same time, however, it noted that such an objective has been and could be readily achieved "by congressional action based on the commerce power of the Constitution." Our study of the legislative record, made in the light of prior cases, has brought us to the conclusion that Congress possessed ample power in this regard, and we have therefore not considered the other grounds relied upon. * * *

While the Act as adopted carried no congressional findings, the record of its passage through each house is replete with evidence of the burdens that discrimination by race

 Case 3.1

HEART OF ATLANTA MOTEL v. UNITED STATES

Supreme Court of the United States, 1964.
379 U.S. 241, 85 S.Ct. 348, 13 L.Ed. 2d 258.

or color places upon interstate commerce *   *   *. This testimony included the fact that our people have become increasingly mobile with millions of all races traveling from State to State; that Negroes in particular have been the subject of discrimination in transient accommodations, having to travel great distances to secure the same; that often they have been unable to obtain accommodations and have had to call upon friends to put them up overnight. *   *   * These exclusionary practices were found to be nationwide, the Under Secretary of Commerce testifying that there is "no question that this discrimination in the North still exists to a large degree" and in the West and Midwest as well *   *   *. This testimony indicated a qualitative as well as quantitative effect on interstate travel by Negroes. The former was the obvious impairment of the Negro traveler's pleasure and convenience that resulted when he continually was uncertain of finding lodging. As for the latter, there was evidence that this uncertainty stemming from racial discrimination had the effect of discouraging travel on the part of a substantial portion of the Negro community *   *   *. We shall not burden this opinion with further details since the voluminous testimony presents overwhelming evidence that discrimination by hotels and motels impedes interstate travel *   *   *.

The power of Congress to deal with these obstructions depends on the meaning of the Commerce Clause. *   *   * [T]he determinative test of the exercise of power by the Congress under the Commerce Clause is simply whether the activity sought to be regulated is "commerce which concerns more States than one" and has a real and substantial relation to the national interest *   *   *

*   *   *   *

That Congress was legislating against moral wrongs in many of these areas rendered its enactments no less valid. In framing Title II of this Act Congress was also dealing with what it considered a moral problem. But that fact does not detract from the overwhelming evidence of the disruptive effect that racial discrimination has had on commercial intercourse. *   *   *

It is said that the operation of the motel here is of a purely local character. But, assuming this to be true, "if it is interstate commerce that feels the pinch, it does not matter how local the operation that applies the squeeze." Thus the power of Congress to promote interstate commerce also includes the power to regulate the local incidents thereof, including local activities in both the States of origin and destination, which might have a substantial and harmful effect upon that commerce. *   *   *

We, therefore, conclude that the action of the Congress in the adoption of the Act as applied here to a motel which concededly serves interstate travelers is within the power granted it by the Commerce Clause of the Constitution, as interpreted by this Court for 140 years *   *   *

DECISION AND REMEDY   *The Court upheld the constitutionality of the Civil Rights Act of 1964. The power of Congress to regulate interstate commerce permitted the enactment of legislation that could halt local discriminatory practices.*

SINCE HEART OF ATLANTA Actions are still brought to determine whether a local activity "substantially affects" interstate commerce and is thus subject to regulation by Congress. In *McLain v. Real Estate Board of New Orleans, Inc.,*[5] the Supreme Court held that local real estate brokers, who were licensed to perform their function only in Louisiana, substantially affected financial transactions and title insurance that were clearly inter-state in nature. Thus, the brokers' activities sufficiently affected interstate commerce to be regulated by federal laws. The Court acknowledged that the commerce clause has "long been interpreted to extend beyond activities actually in interstate commerce to reach other activities, while wholly local in nature, which nevertheless substantially affect interstate commerce."[6]

---

5. 444 U.S. 232, 100 S.Ct. 502, 62 L.Ed.2d 441 (1980).

6. 444 U.S. 232, 241, 100 S.Ct. 502, 508, 62 L.Ed.2d 441, 449 (1980).

THE POWER OF STATES TO REGULATE Another problem that frequently arises under the commerce clause concerns a state's ability to regulate matters within its own borders. There is no doubt that states have a strong interest in regulating activities within their borders. As part of their inherent sovereignty, states possess **police powers.** In exercising police powers, states may regulate private activities to protect or to promote the public health, safety, morals, or general welfare of their citizens. States, for example, have a strong interest in keeping their local roads and highways safe for their residents. Most state regulations in this area place some burden on interstate commerce, however, and when state regulations impinge upon interstate commerce, courts must balance the state's interest in the merits and purposes of the regulation against the burden placed on interstate commerce.[7] In *Raymond Motor Transportation, Inc. v. Rice,*[8] for example, the Supreme Court invalidated Wisconsin administrative regulations limiting the length of trucks traveling on its highways. The Court weighed the burden on interstate commerce against the benefits of the regulations and concluded that the challenged regulations "place a substantial burden on interstate commerce and they cannot be said to make more than the most speculative contribution to highway safety."[9]

Because courts balance the interests involved, it is extremely difficult to predict the outcome in a particular case. State laws enacted pursuant to a state's police powers and affecting the health, safety, and welfare of local citizens do carry a strong presumption of validity. This is clearly illustrated in the following case.

---

7. See Southern Pacific Co. v. Arizona, 325 U.S. 761, 65 S.Ct. 1515, 89 L.Ed. 1915 (1945).

8. 434 U.S. 429, 98 S.Ct. 787, 54 L.Ed.2d 664 (1978).

9. 434 U.S. 429, 447, 98 S.Ct. 787, 797, 54 L.Ed.2d 664, 679 (1978).

BACKGROUND AND FACTS *Taylor owned a bait business in Maine and arranged to have live baitfish imported into the state, which violated a Maine statute. Taylor was indicted under a federal statute that makes it a federal crime to transport fish in interstate commerce in violation of state law. Taylor moved to dismiss the indictment on the ground that the Maine statute unconstitutionally burdened interstate commerce. Maine intervened to defend the validity of its statute, arguing that the law legitimately protected the state's fisheries from parasites and non-native species that might be included in shipments of live baitfish. Taylor's motion to dismiss the indictment was denied by the federal district court, but the U.S. Court of Appeals for the First Circuit reversed the district court's ruling. The state of Maine appealed to the Supreme Court of the United States.*

 Case 3.2

MAINE v. TAYLOR
United States Supreme Court, 1986.
477 U.S. 131, 106 S.Ct. 2440, 91 L.Ed.2d 110.

Justice BLACKMUN delivered the opinion of the Court.

Once again, a little fish has caused a commotion. * * * The fish in this case is the golden shiner, a species of minnow commonly used as live bait in sport fishing.
* * * *

The Commerce Clause of the Constitution grants Congress the power "[t]o regulate Commerce with foreign Nations, and among the several States, and with the Indian tribes." * * * Although the Clause thus speaks in terms of powers bestowed upon Congress, the Court long has recognized that it also limits the power of the States to erect barriers against interstate trade. * * * Maine's statute restricts interstate trade in the most direct manner possible, blocking all inward shipments of live baitfish at the State's border. Still, as both the District Court and the Court of Appeals recognized, this fact alone does not render the law unconstitutional. The limitation imposed by the Commerce Clause on state regulatory power "is by no means absolute," and "the States retain authority under their general police powers to regulate matters of 'legitimate local concern,' even though interstate commerce may be affected." * * *
* * * *

* * * The Court explained in *Hughes v. Oklahoma* * * * that once a state law is shown to discriminate against interstate commerce "either on its face or in practical effect," the burden falls on the State to demonstrate both that the statute "serves a legitimate local purpose," and that this purpose could not be served as well by available nondiscriminatory means. * * *

* * * *

The District Court found after an evidentiary hearing that both parts of the *Hughes* test were satisfied, but the Court of Appeals disagreed. We conclude that the Court of Appeals erred in setting aside the findings of the District Court. To explain why, we need to discuss the proceedings below in some detail.

* * * The prosecution experts testified that live baitfish imported into the State posed two significant threats to Maine's unique and fragile fisheries. First, Maine's population of wild fish—including its own indigenous golden shiners—would be placed at risk by three types of parasites prevalent in out-of-state baitfish, but not common to wild fish in Maine. * * * Second, non-native species inadvertently included in shipments of live baitfish could disturb Maine's aquatic ecology to an unpredictable extent by competing with native fish for food or habitat, by preying on native species, or by disrupting the environment in more subtle ways. * * *

The prosecution experts further testified that there was no satisfactory way to inspect shipments of live baitfish for parasites or commingled species. * * *

Appellee's expert denied that any scientific justification supported Maine's total ban on the importation of baitfish. * * * He testified that none of the three parasites discussed by the prosecution witnesses posed any significant threat to fish in the wild, * * * and that sampling techniques had not been developed for baitfish precisely because there was no need for them. * * * He further testified that professional baitfish farmers raise their fish in ponds that have been freshly drained to insure that no other species is inadvertently collected. * * *

* * * *

* * * After reviewing the expert testimony, * * * we cannot say that the District Court clearly erred in finding that substantial scientific uncertainty surrounds the effect that baitfish parasites and non-native species could have on Maine's fisheries. Moreover, we agree with the District Court that Maine has a legitimate interest in guarding against imperfectly understood environmental risks, despite the possibility that they may ultimately prove to be negligible. * * *

* * * *

The Commerce Clause significantly limits the ability of States and localities to regulate or otherwise burden the flow of interstate commerce, but it does not elevate free trade above all other values. As long as a State does not needlessly obstruct interstate trade or attempt to "place itself in a position of economic isolation," * * * it retains broad regulatory authority to protect the health and safety of its citizens and the integrity of its natural resources. The evidence in this case amply supports the District Court's findings that Maine's ban on the importation of live baitfish serves legitimate local purposes that could not adequately be served by available nondiscriminatory alternatives.

DECISION   *The Court reversed the decision of the court of appeals and held the Maine*
AND REMEDY   *statute to be constitutional.*

The Supremacy Clause

Article VI of the Constitution provides that the Constitution, laws, and treaties of the United States are "the supreme Law of the Land. . . ." This article, the supremacy clause, is important in the ordering of state and federal relationships. When there is a direct conflict between a federal law and a state law, the state law is rendered invalid. But because some powers are shared by the federal government and the states—because they are concurrent powers—it is necessary to determine which law governs in a particular circumstance.

When concurrent federal and state powers are involved, a state law that conflicts with a federal law is prohibited. A federal action pursuant to a power specifically delegated to it by the Constitution always has the capacity to override a state law on the same matter. A federal regulatory scheme will supersede state law whenever there is an outright conflict between the two or when the state regulation interferes with federal objectives.

When Congress chooses to act exclusively in a concurrent area, it is said to have *preempted* the area. In this circumstance, a valid federal statute or regulation precludes even a nonconflicting state or local law or regulation on the same general subject. Congress, however, rarely makes clear its intent to preempt an entire subject area against state regulation, and consequently, the courts must determine whether Congress intended to exercise exclusive dominion over a given area. Consider-

ation of supersession or preemption often occurs in the commerce clause context.

Before declaring that federal law supersedes or preempts a state statute, courts must first determine Congress's intent. If the federal law is not explicit on whether a state regulation should be deemed superseded because of a conflict or preempted because of federal occupation of the entire field, no single factor is decisive as to whether a court will find supersession or preemption. Generally, congressional intent to preempt will be found if the federal law is so pervasive, comprehensive, or detailed that the states have no room to supplement it. Also, when a federal statute creates an agency—such as the National Labor Relations Board—to enforce the law, matters that may come within the agency's jurisdiction will likely preempt state laws.

In the following case, the Supreme Court had to determine whether various federal laws preempted a city ordinance.

BACKGROUND AND FACTS *The city council of Burbank, California, passed an ordinance making it unlawful for jet aircraft to take off from the Hollywood-Burbank Airport between 11:00 P.M. and 7:00 A.M. Lockheed Air Terminal sought an injunction against enforcement of the ordinance. The district court found the ordinance to be unconstitutional on both supremacy clause and commerce clause grounds. The court of appeals affirmed on the grounds of the supremacy clause.*

 Case 3.3

BURBANK v. LOCKHEED AIR TERMINAL

Supreme Court of the United States, 1973.
411 U.S. 624, 93 S.Ct. 1854, 36 L.Ed.2d 547.

Mr. Justice DOUGLAS delivered the opinion of the Court.
*   *   *   *

The Federal Aviation Act of 1958, as amended by the Noise Control Act of 1972 and the regulations under it, are central to the question of preemption.

Section 1108(a) of the Federal Aviation Act provides in part, "The United States of America is declared to possess and exercise complete and exclusive national sovereignty in the airspace of the United States *   *   *." By §§ [sections] 307(a), (c) of the Act, the Administrator of the Federal Aviation Administration (FAA) has been given broad authority to regulate the use of the navigable airspace, "in order to insure the safety of aircraft and the efficient utilization of such airspace" and "for the protection of persons and property on the ground *   *   *."
*   *   *   *

The original complaint was filed on May 14, 1970; the District Court entered its judgment November 30, 1970; and the Court of Appeals announced its judgment and opinion March 22, 1972—all before the Noise Control Act of 1972 was approved by the President on October 27, 1972. That Act reaffirms and reinforces the conclusion that FAA, now in conjunction with EPA [Environmental Protection Agency], has full control over aircraft noise, preempting state and local control.

There is, to be sure, no express provision of preemption in the 1972 Act. That, however, is not decisive. As we stated in *Rice v. Santa Fe Elevator Corp.*, 331 U.S. 218, 230:

"Congress legislated here in a field which the States have traditionally occupied

* * *. So we start with the assumption that the historic police powers of the States were not to be superseded by the Federal Act unless that was the clear and manifest purpose of Congress * * *. Such a purpose may be evidenced in several ways. The scheme of federal regulation may be so pervasive as to make reasonable the inference that Congress left no room for the States to supplement it * * *. Or the Act of Congress may touch a field in which the federal interest is so dominant that the federal system will be assumed to preclude enforcement of state laws on the same subject * * *. Likewise, the object sought to be obtained by the federal law and the character of obligations imposed by it may reveal the same purpose * * *. Or the state policy may produce a result inconsistent with the objective of the federal statute."

It is the pervasive nature of the scheme of federal regulation of aircraft noise that leads us to conclude that there is preemption. As Mr. Justice Jackson stated, concurring in *Northwest Airlines, Inc. v. Minnesota*, 322 U.S. 292, 303:

"Federal control is intensive and exclusive. Planes do not wander about in the sky like vagrant clouds. They move only by federal permission, subject to federal inspection, in the hands of federally certified personnel, and under an intricate system of federal commands. The moment a ship taxis onto a runway it is caught up in an elaborate and detailed system of controls."

* * * *

If we were to uphold the Burbank ordinance and a significant number of municipalities followed suit, it is obvious that fractionalized control of the timing of takeoffs and landings would severely limit the flexibility of FAA in controlling air traffic flow. The difficulties of scheduling flights to avoid congestion and the concomitant decrease in safety would be compounded. In 1960 FAA rejected a proposed restriction on jet operations at the Los Angeles airport between 10:00 P.M. and 7:00 A.M. because such restrictions could "create critically serious problems to all transportation patterns." The complete FAA statement said:

"The proposed restriction on the use of the airport by jet aircraft between the hours of 10:00 P.M. and 7:00 A.M. under certain surface wind conditions has also been reevaluated and this provision has been omitted from the rule. The practice of prohibiting the use of various airports during certain specific hours could create critically serious problems to all air transportation patterns. The network of airports throughout the United States and the constant availability of these airports are essential to the maintenance of a sound air transportation system. The continuing growth of public acceptance of aviation as a major force in passenger transportation and the increasingly significant role of commercial aviation in the nation's economy are accomplishments which cannot be inhibited if the best interest of the public is to be served. It was concluded therefore that the extent of relief from the noise problem which this provision might have achieved would not have compensated the degree of restriction it would have imposed on domestic and foreign Air Commerce."

This decision, announced in 1960, remains peculiarly within the competence of FAA, supplemented now by the input of EPA. We are not at liberty to diffuse the powers given by Congress to FAA and EPA by letting the States or municipalities in on the planning. If that change is to be made, Congress alone must do it.

DECISION   *The Supreme Court declared the Burbank ordinance to be unconstitutional.*
AND REMEDY   *Federal regulation of the airspace preempted the local law.*

The Taxing Power

Article I, Section 8, further provides that Congress has the "Power to lay and collect Taxes, Duties, Imposts, and Excises . . . but all Duties, Imposts and Excises shall be uniform throughout the United States." The requirement of uniformity refers to geographic uniformity among the states, and thus Congress may not tax some states while exempting others. Traditionally, in reviewing cases the courts have examined whether Congress was actually attempting to regulate indirectly, by taxation, an area in which it had no authority to regulate directly. If the regulatory effect was one that could have been achieved directly by Congress, then the tax would not be stricken as an invalid, disguised regulation. If Congress was attempting to regulate an area over which it had no authority, however, then such a regulation would be invalidated.

In recent cases, though, the Supreme Court has focused less on the motives of Congress and more on whether the tax can be sustained as a valid exercise of federal regulation. The Court has upheld taxes on dealers in firearms,[10] on the transfer of marijuana,[11] and on persons engaged in the business of accepting wagers.[12] If Congress does not have the power to regulate the activity being taxed, the tax will be upheld only if it is a valid revenue-raising measure. If a tax measure bears some reasonable relationship to revenue production, it is generally held to be within the national taxing power. Moreover, the expansive interpretation of the commerce clause almost always provides a basis for sustaining a federal tax.

The Spending Power

Under Article I, Section 8, Congress has the power "to pay the Debts and provide for the common Defence and general welfare of the United States. . . ." Through the spending power, Congress disposes of the revenues accumulated from the taxing power, and thus this power necessarily involves policy choices. The requirement of *standing to sue* (discussed in Chapter 2) makes it difficult for taxpayers to use the judicial system to object to government spending, and consequently, the spending power is seldom challenged. The doctrine of standing to sue requires a litigant to demonstrate *a direct and immediate personal injury* due to the challenged action.[13] Thus, a litigant must show that the injury suffered can be fairly traced to the challenged action and will be re-

dressed by the judicial relief sought.[14] Communicating directly with members of Congress has proved to be a more efficient route to curbing or increasing federal allocations.

The spending power exists separately from all other powers delegated to the federal government. Therefore, Congress can spend revenues not only to carry out its enumerated powers but also to promote any objective it deems worthwhile, so long as it does not violate the Bill of Rights. For example, Congress could not condition welfare payments on the recipients' agreements not to criticize government policies.

THE BILL OF RIGHTS IN A BUSINESS CONTEXT

A business consists of one or more persons operating under their own names, a common name, or a fictitious name. Some business entities, such as corporations, exist as separate legal entities and enjoy the same rights and privileges as *natural* persons. A corporation is generally identified as an artificial person, or legal entity under law. The Bill of Rights guarantees citizens certain protections, and some constitutional protections apply to business entities as well.

Specific actions of the federal government are prohibited by the first ten amendments, and the Fourteenth Amendment further prohibits most of the same actions by state governments. The due process clause of the Fourteenth Amendment makes certain rights guaranteed by the first ten amendments applicable to the states. Under the doctrine of *selective incorporation*, only those guarantees of individual liberty that are fundamental to the American system of law must be protected by the states.

Freedom of Speech

All of the First Amendment freedoms of religion, speech, press, assembly, and petition have been applied to the states through the due process clause of the Fourteenth Amendment. None of these freedoms, however, confers an absolute right. It is unclear what types of speech the First Amend-

---

10. Sonzinsky v. United States, 300 U.S. 506, 57 S.Ct. 554, 81 L.Ed. 772 (1937).

11. United States v. Sanchez, 340 U.S. 42, 71 S.Ct. 108, 95 L.Ed. 47 (1950).

12. United States v. Kahriger, 345 U.S. 22, 73 S.Ct. 510, 97 L.Ed. 754 (1953).

13. Sierra Club v. Morton, 405 U.S. 727, 92 S.Ct. 1361, 31 L.Ed.2d 636 (1972).

14. Simon v. Eastern Kentucky Welfare Rights Organization, 426 U.S. 26, 96 S.Ct. 1917, 48 L.Ed.2d 450 (1976).

ment was designed to protect, but constitutional protection has never been afforded to certain classes of speech. In 1942, for example, the U.S. Supreme Court concluded:

> There are certain well-defined and narrowly limited classes of speech, the prevention and punishment of which have never been thought to raise any Constitutional problem. These include the lewd and obscene, the profane, the libelous, and the insulting or "fighting" words—those which by their very utterance inflict injury or tend to incite an immediate breach of the peace. It has been well observed that such utterances are no essential part of any exposition of ideas, and are of such slight social value as a step to truth that any benefit that may be derived from them is clearly outweighed by the social interest in order and morality.[15]

Although the Supreme Court initially took the view that language treated as defamatory under state law was not entitled to First Amendment protection, it subsequently concluded that the First Amendment requires that a defense for honest error be allowed where statements are made about *public officials* relating to their *official conduct.* In

---

15. Chaplinsky v. New Hampshire, 315 U.S. 568, 62 S.Ct. 766, 86 L.Ed. 1031 (1942).

the well-known case of *New York Times v. Sullivan*,[16] the Court articulated a formal rule in stating that the First Amendment prohibits public officials from recovering damages for defamatory falsehoods relating to their official conduct unless they prove that the statements were made with "actual malice." Actual malice means that a statement must be made *with knowledge that it was false* or *with reckless disregard of whether it was false or not.*

Freedom-of-speech cases generally distinguish between commercial and noncommercial messages. Commercial advertising is not completely outside the First Amendment. As stated in *First National Bank of Boston v. Bellotti*,[17] speech that otherwise would be within the protection of the First Amendment does not lose that protection simply because its source is a corporation.

Although commercial speech is protected by the First Amendment, its protection is not as extensive as that afforded noncommercial speech. The greater protection to noncommercial speech offered by the First Amendment is stressed in the following case.

---

16. 376 U.S. 254, 84 S.Ct. 710, 11 L.Ed.2d 686 (1964).

17. 435 U.S. 765, 98 S.Ct. 1407, 55 L.Ed.2d 707 (1978).

Case 3.4

METROMEDIA, INC. v. CITY OF SAN DIEGO

Supreme Court of the United States, 1981.
453 U.S. 490, 101 S.Ct. 2882, 69 L.Ed.2d 800.

BACKGROUND AND FACTS *The city of San Diego enacted an ordinance that imposed substantial prohibitions on the erection of outdoor advertising displays within the city. The stated purpose of the ordinance was "to eliminate hazards to pedestrians and motorists brought about by distracting sign displays" and "to preserve and improve the appearance of the City." The ordinance permitted on-site commercial advertising (defined as a sign advertising goods or services available on the property where the sign was located) but forbade other commercial advertising and noncommercial advertising using fixed-structure signs. The ordinance did provide for exceptions, such as temporary political campaign signs. Companies that were engaged in the outdoor-advertising business in the city when the ordinance was passed brought suit in state court to enjoin enforcement of the ordinance. The trial court held that the ordinance was an unconstitutional exercise of the city's police power and an abridgment of the companies' First Amendment rights. The California Court of Appeal affirmed the decision, but the California Supreme Court reversed, holding that the ordinance was not invalid under the First Amendment. The companies appealed.*

Justice WHITE delivered the opinion of the Court.
*   *   *   *

This Court has often faced the problem of applying the broad principles of the First Amendment to unique forums of expression. [The Court cited numerous cases

ranging from billing-envelope inserts to picketing in residential areas to advertising on city-owned transit systems.] Even a cursory reading of these opinions reveals that at times First Amendment values must yield to other societal interests. *   *   *
*   *   *   *

Appellants' principal submission is that enforcement of the ordinance will eliminate the outdoor advertising business in San Diego and that the First and Fourteenth Amendments prohibit the elimination of this medium of communication. Appellants contend that the city may bar neither all offsite commercial signs nor all noncommercial advertisements and that even if it may bar the former, it may not bar the latter. *   *   *
Because our cases have consistently distinguished between the constitutional protection afforded commercial as opposed to noncommercial speech, in evaluating appellants' contention we consider separately the effect of the ordinance on commercial and noncommercial speech.

The extension of the First Amendment protections to purely commercial speech is a relatively recent development in First Amendment jurisprudence. Prior to 1975, purely commercial advertisements of services or goods for sale were considered to be outside the protection of the First Amendment. That construction of the First Amendment was severely cut back in *Bigelow* v. *Virginia*, supra. In *Virginia Pharmacy Board* v. *Virginia Citizens Consumer Council*, 425 U.S. 748 (1976), we plainly held that speech proposing no more than commercial transaction enjoys a substantial degree of First Amendment protection: A State may not completely suppress the dissemination of truthful information about an entirely lawful activity merely because it is fearful of that information's effect upon its disseminators and its recipients. That decision, however, did not equate commercial and noncommercial speech for First Amendment purposes; indeed, it expressly indicated the contrary.

*   *   * [W]e continued to observe the distinction between commercial and noncommercial speech, indicating that the former could be forbidden and regulated in situations where the latter could not be. *   *   * In the course of doing so, we again recognized the common-sense and legal distinction between speech proposing a commercial transaction and other varieties of speech: "*   *   * [W]e have afforded commercial speech a limited measure of protection, commensurate with its subordinate position in the scale of First Amendment values, while allowing modes of regulation that might be impermissible in the realm of noncommercial expression."
*   *   *   *

*   *   *The protection available for a particular commercial expression turns on the nature both of the expression and of the governmental interests served by its regulation." We [have] adopted a four-part test for determining the validity of government restrictions on commercial speech as distinguished from more fully protected speech. (1) The First Amendment protects commercial speech only if that speech concerns lawful activity and is not misleading. A restriction on otherwise protected commercial speech is valid only if it (2) seeks to implement a substantial governmental interest, (3) directly advances that interest, and (4) reaches no further than necessary to accomplish the given objective.
*   *   *   *

There can be little controversy over the application of the first, second, and fourth criteria. There is no suggestion that the commercial advertising at issue here involves unlawful activity or is misleading. Nor can there be substantial doubt that the twin goals that the ordinance seeks to further—traffic safety and the appearance of the city— are substantial governmental goals. *   *   * [As to the fourth criterion, the] city has gone no further than necessary in seeking to meet its ends. Indeed, it has stopped short of fully accomplishing its ends: It has not prohibited all billboards, but allows onsite advertising and some other specifically exempted signs.

The more serious question, then, concerns the third of the *   *   * criteria: Does the ordinance "directly advance" governmental interests in traffic safety and in the appearance of the city? It is asserted that the record is inadequate to show any connection between billboards and traffic safety. The California Supreme Court noted the meager

record on this point but held "as a matter of law that an ordinance which eliminates billboards designed to be viewed from streets and highways reasonably relates to traffic safety." Noting that "[b]illboards are intended to, and undoubtedly do, divert a driver's attention from the roadway, and that whether the distracting effect contributes to traffic accidents invokes an issue of continuing controversy," the California Supreme Court agreed with many other courts that a legislative judgment that billboards are traffic hazards is not manifestly unreasonable and should not be set aside. We likewise hesitate to disagree with the accumulated, common-sense judgments of local lawmakers and of the many reviewing courts that billboards are real and substantial hazards to traffic safety. There is nothing here to suggest that these judgments are unreasonable. *   *   *
*   *   *   *

It does not follow, however, that San Diego's general ban on signs carrying non-commercial advertising is also valid under the First and Fourteenth Amendments. The fact that the city may value commercial messages relating to onsite goods and services more than it values commercial communications relating to offsite goods and services does not justify prohibiting an occupant from displaying its own ideas or those of others.

As indicated above, our recent commercial speech cases have consistently accorded noncommercial speech a greater degree of protection than commercial speech. San Diego effectively inverts this judgment, by affording a greater degree of protection to commercial than to noncommercial speech. There is a broad exception for onsite commercial advertisements, but there is no similar exception for noncommercial speech. The use of onsite billboards to carry commercial messages related to the commercial use of the premises is freely permitted, but the use of otherwise identical billboards to carry noncommercial messages is generally prohibited. The city does not explain how or why noncommercial billboards located in places where commercial billboards are permitted would be more threatening to safe driving or would detract more from the beauty of the city. Insofar as the city tolerates billboards at all, it cannot choose to limit their content to commercial messages; the city may not conclude that the communication of commercial information concerning goods and services connected with a particular site is of greater value than the communication of noncommercial messages.

Furthermore, the ordinance contains exceptions that permit various kinds of non-commercial signs, whether on property where goods and services are offered or not, that would otherwise be within the general ban. A fixed sign may be used to identify any piece of property and its owner. Any piece of property may carry or display religious symbols, commemorative plaques of recognized historical societies and organizations, signs carrying news items or telling the time or temperature, signs erected in discharge of any governmental function, or temporary political campaign signs. No other non-commercial or ideological signs meeting the structural definition are permitted, re-gardless of their effect on traffic safety or esthetics.

Although the city may distinguish between the relative value of different categories of commercial speech, the city does not have the same range of choice in the area of noncommercial speech to evaluate the strength of, or distinguish between, various communicative interests.

With respect to noncommercial speech, the city may not choose the appropriate subjects for public discourse: "To allow a government the choice of permissible subjects for public debate would be to allow that government control over the search for political truth." Because some noncommercial messages may be conveyed on billboards through-out the commercial and industrial zones, San Diego must similarly allow billboards conveying other noncommercial messages throughout those zones.

DECISION AND REMEDY   *The Supreme Court concluded that the ordinance was unconstitutional on its face because it reached too far into the realm of protected (noncommercial) speech. The judgment of the California Supreme Court was reversed, and the case was remanded to that court.*

Freedom of Religion

The First Amendment requires that the government neither establish any religion nor prohibit the free exercise of religious practices. Government action, both federal and state, must be neutral toward religion. However, regulation that does not promote, or place a significant burden on, religion is constitutional even if it has some impact on religion. "Sunday closing laws," for example, make some commercial activities illegal if performed on Sunday. These statutes, also known as "blue laws," have been upheld on the ground that it is a legitimate function of government to provide a day of rest. The Supreme Court has held that the closing laws, although originally of a religious character, have taken on the secular purpose of promoting the health and welfare of workers.[18] Even though closing laws admittedly make it easier for Christians to attend religious services, the Court has viewed this effect as an incidental, not a primary, purpose of Sunday closing laws.

Another freedom of religion involves the accommodation that businesses must make for the religious beliefs of their employees. Title VII of the Civil Rights Act of 1964 prohibits government, and private employers and unions, from discriminating against persons because of their religion. The U.S. Supreme Court recently addressed this issue in *Estate of Thornton, et al. v. Caldor, Inc.*[19] In this case, the Court held that a Connecticut statute granting employees the absolute right not to work on their Sabbath had the effect of advancing religious practices in violation of the establishment clause of the First Amendment. The Court felt that such a statute discriminated against employees who might want a weekend day off for secular reasons.

Search and Seizure

The Fourth Amendment protects the "right of the people to be secure in their persons, houses, papers, and effects. . . ." Federal, state, and local governments must obtain search warrants. There are exceptions, though, as when there is *probable cause* to believe that the items sought will be removed before a warrant can be obtained. Probable cause requires law enforcement officials to have trustworthy evidence that would convince a reasonable person that it is more likely than not that the proposed search or seizure is justified. Thus, to obtain a warrant, law enforcement officers must convince a judge that they have probable cause to believe a search will reveal a specific illegality.

The Fourth Amendment prohibits general warrants and requires a particular description of that which is to be searched or seized. General searches through a person's belongings are impermissible. Nothing is left to the discretion of the officer executing a search warrant; the search cannot extend beyond what is described in the warrant.

Constitutional protection against searches and seizures is extremely important to businesses and professionals. With increased federal and state regulation of commercial activities, frequent and unannounced government inspection to ensure compliance with the law would be extremely disruptive. In *Marshall v. Barlow's, Inc.*,[20] the Supreme Court held that government inspectors do not have the right to enter business premises without a warrant, although the standard of probable cause is not the same as that required in nonbusiness contexts. A general and neutral enforcement plan will justify issuance of the warrant. Lawyers and accountants are frequently in possession of the business records of their clients, and inspecting these documents while they are out of the hands of their true owners also requires a warrant.

On the other hand, no warrant is required for seizures of spoiled or contaminated food. Nor are warrants required for searches of businesses in such highly regulated industries as liquor, guns, and strip mining. General manufacturing is not considered to be one of these highly regulated industries.

Self-Incrimination

The Fifth Amendment guarantees that no person "shall be compelled in any criminal case to be a witness against himself." Thus, in any federal proceeding, an accused person cannot be compelled to give evidence of a testimonial or communicative nature that might subject him or her to any criminal prosecution. An accused person cannot be forced to testify against himself or herself in state

---

18. McGowan v. Maryland, 366 U.S. 420, 81 S.Ct. 1101, 6 L.Ed.2d 393 (1961).

19. 472 U.S. 703, 105 S.Ct. 2914, 86 L.Ed.2d 557 (1985).

20. 436 U.S. 307, 98 S.Ct. 1816, 56 L.Ed.2d 305 (1978).

courts either, because the Fourteenth Amendment due process clause incorporates the Fifth Amendment provision against self-incrimination.

The Fifth Amendment's guarantee against self-incrimination extends only to natural persons. Since a corporation is a legal entity and not a natural person, the privilege against self-incrimination is inapplicable to it. Similarly, the business records of a partnership do not receive Fifth Amendment protection.[21] No artificial organization may utilize

the personal privilege against compulsory self-incrimination. When it is required that records of these organizations be produced, the information must be given even if it incriminates the persons who comprise the business entity.

Sole proprietors and sole practitioners who have not incorporated cannot be compelled to produce their business records. These individuals have the full protection against self-incrimination because they function in only one capacity: There is no separate business entity.

In the following case, the sole stockholder in a corporation attempted to assert his Fifth Amendment privilege to avoid having to produce his corporation's records.

---

21. The privilege has been applied to some small family partnerships. See United States v. Slutsky, 352 F.Supp. 1105 (S.D.N.Y. 1972).

Case 3.5

WILD v. BREWER

United States Court of Appeals,
Ninth Circuit, 1964.
329 F.2d 924.

BACKGROUND AND FACTS *Brewer, an IRS agent, served Wild with a summons requiring Wild to appear and testify about the tax liability of "Albert J. Wild, President, Air Conditioning Supply Company." The corporation was wholly owned by Wild, and all books and records requested were those of the corporation. Wild appeared but refused to produce the records on the ground that they might tend to incriminate him and hence were protected by the Fifth Amendment. When Wild was cited for contempt, he appealed. The majority of the appellate court affirmed, ordering Wild to produce the corporate books and records. One judge, however, found support for Wild's position.*

MADDEN, Judge [dissenting].
* * * *

The privilege guaranteed by the Fifth Amendment, against the Government of the United States, "in any criminal case" not to be compelled to be a witness against one's self, is available not only to defendants in criminal trials but to witnesses in any kind of official proceeding under the auspices of the United States. It applies not only to the giving of oral testimony, but to the production from one's possession of incriminating documents or objects.
* * * *

There is without question a general doctrine that an officer of a corporation who, as such officer, has custody of its records may not successfully refuse to produce those records in response to a subpoena [court-ordered summons] issued to the corporation and served upon him as custodian, on the ground that the records contain material which would incriminate him. * * *

A corporation does not have the Constitutional privilege against self-incrimination. It therefore cannot, if its records are subpoenaed, assert the Fifth Amendment privilege.
* * *

* * * [But Wild] did not claim the privilege for the corporation, and could not have done so. He claims it for himself, and says that he, and not any artificial legal entity, will be the one to suffer the punishment if he is obliged to furnish to the Government the evidence which will bring about his conviction. * * *

Wild says that since he is the sole owner of his corporation, the corporation does embody the "purely private or personal interests of its [only] constituent(s)," who is Wild himself.

[The dissenting judge was sympathetic to Wild's position. However, only the majority decision was binding. A corporation does not enjoy the Fifth Amendment privilege against self-incrimination, even when it is claimed for the benefit of the sole owner.]

The trial court's ruling of contempt was affirmed. Wild was unable to invoke the Fifth Amendment to protect company records. He was required to produce the records in response to the IRS subpoena.

DECISION AND REMEDY

A corporation is a legal fiction; that is, it is considered to be a person for most purposes under the law. An unsettled area of corporation law has to do with the criminal acts of a corporation. It is obvious that a corporation cannot be sent to prison even though, under law, it is a person. Most courts hold a corporation that has violated the criminal statutes liable for fines. Where criminal conduct can be attributed to corporate officers or agents, those individuals, as natural persons, are held liable and can be imprisoned for their acts.

COMMENTS

OTHER CONSTITUTIONAL GUARANTEES

Two other constitutional guarantees of great significance to Americans are mandated by the due process clauses of the Fifth and Fourteenth Amendments and the equal protection clause of the Fourteenth Amendment.

Due Process

Both the Fifth and the Fourteenth Amendments provide that no person shall be deprived "of life, liberty, or property, without due process of law." The due process clauses have two aspects: procedural and substantive. Procedural due process requires that any government decision to take life, liberty, or property must be made fairly, and thus there must be fairness in the procedures used to determine that a person will be subjected to punishment or have some burden imposed on him or her. Fair procedure has been interpreted as requiring at least an opportunity to present objections to a proposed action to a fair, neutral decision maker (which need not be a judge). Thus, for example, if a driver's license is construed as a "property" interest, some sort of opportunity to object to suspension or termination must be provided to an individual whose license the state wants to suspend or terminate.

Substantive due process focuses on the content, or substance, of legislation. Unless a law is compatible with the Constitution, it is a violation of substantive due process. If a law or other gov-

ernmental action limits a *fundamental right*, the law or action must be necessary to promote a *compelling or overriding interest*. Fundamental rights include interstate travel, privacy, voting, and all First Amendment rights. Compelling interests could include, for example, the public's safety. Thus, laws designating speed limits may be upheld, even though they affect interstate travel, if they are shown to reduce highway fatalities, because the state has a compelling interest in protecting the lives of its citizens.

In all other cases, a law or action does not violate substantive due process if it rationally relates to any legitimate governmental end. It is almost impossible for a law or action to fail the "rationality" test. Under this test, virtually any business regulation will be upheld as reasonable—the Supreme Court has sustained insurance regulations, price and wage controls, banking controls, and controls of unfair competition and trade practices against substantive due process challenges.

To illustrate: If a state legislature enacted a law imposing a fifteen-year term of imprisonment without allowing a trial on all businesspersons who appeared in their own television commercials, the law would be unconstitutional on both substantive and procedural grounds. Substantive review would invalidate the legislation because it abridges freedom of speech. Procedurally, the law is unfair because it imposes the penalty without giving the accused a chance to defend his or her actions. The lack of procedural due process will cause a court to invalidate any statute or prior court decision.

Similarly, a denial of substantive due process requires courts to overrule any state or federal law that violates the Constitution.

Equal Protection

Under the Fourteenth Amendment, a state may not "deny to any person within its jurisdiction the equal protection of the laws." The Supreme Court has used the due process clause of the Fifth Amendment to make the equal protection guarantee applicable to the federal government. Equal protection means that the government must treat similarly situated individuals in a similar manner.

Both substantive due process and equal protection require review of the substance of the law or other governmental action rather than the procedures used. When a law or action limits the liberty of all persons to do something, it may violate substantive due process; when a law or action limits the liberty of some persons but not others, it may violate the equal protection clause. Thus, for example, if a law prohibits all persons from buying contraceptive devices, it raises a substantive due process question; if it prohibits only unmarried persons from buying the same devices, it raises an equal protection issue.

Basically, in determining whether a law or action violates the equal protection clause, a court will consider questions similar to those previously noted as applicable in a substantive due process review. Under an equal protection inquiry, when a law or action distinguishes between or among individuals, the basis for the distinction—that is, the *classification*—is examined. If the law or action inhibits some persons' exercise of a fundamental right, the classification must be necessary to promote a compelling interest. Also, if the classification is based on a *suspect* trait, it must be necessary to promote a compelling interest. A classification is suspect if it is based on race, national origin, or citizenship status.

In matters of economic or social welfare, the classification will be considered valid if there is any conceivable rational basis on which the classification might relate to any legitimate government interest. It is almost impossible for a law or action to fail this test. Thus, for example, a city ordinance that in effect prohibits all pushcart vendors except a specific few from operating in a particular area of the city will be upheld, if the city proffers a rational basis—perhaps regulation and reduction of traffic in the particular area—for the ordinance. On the other hand, a law that provides unemployment benefits only to people over six feet tall would violate the guarantee of equal protection. There is no rational basis for determining the distribution of unemployment compensation on the basis of height. Such a distinction could not further any legitimate government objective.

QUESTIONS AND CASE PROBLEMS

1. The U.S. Constitution is a document in which the people of the United States give the government the "power to govern." Yet the Constitution was written by a handful of men who represented the aristocracy of the time. Surprisingly, this group of aristocrats wrote a document giving more freedoms to common people than any other constitution in existence. Look at Appendix A. Name some of the basic guarantees found in the Constitution.

2. Suppose that in 1973 the Public Service Commission of the State of Illinois ordered that all "promotional advertising" by electric utilities cease. Assume that this order was based upon the Commission's finding that the state in all likelihood did not have sufficient fuel for the upcoming winter. If the Public Service Commission sought to enforce its ban in 1977, when the fuel shortage had eased, would such enforcement be a regulation of commercial speech in violation of the First Amendment? Assume that the Commission's interest in conservation could not have been adequately protected by a less restrictive alternative.

3. Suppose that the Ohio legislature passed a statute prohibiting the issuance of a liquor license to any establishment located within 600 feet of a church if the church objects in writing to the issuance of such a license. Would this statute be valid under the establishment clause (of religion) of the First Amendment?

4. A Georgia statute requires the use of contoured rear-fender mudguards on trucks and trailers operating within its state lines. The statute further makes it illegal for trucks and trailers to use straight mudguards. In approximately 35 other states, straight mudguards are legal. Moreover, in Florida, straight mudguards are explicitly required by law. There is some evidence that suggests that contoured mudguards might be a little safer than straight mudguards. Does this Georgia statute violate any constitutional provisions?

5. A mayoral election is about to be held in a large U.S. city. One of the candidates is Gregory Schumann, and his campaign supporters wish to post campaign signs on lamp

posts and utility posts throughout the city. A city ordinance, however, prohibits the posting of any signs on public property. Schumann's supporters contend that the city ordinance is unconstitutional because it violates their rights to free speech. Do you agree? In your answer, discuss what factors a court might consider in determining the constitutionality of the ordinance.

6. Florida Lime & Avocado Growers, Inc., is engaged in the business of growing and packing Florida avocados and marketing them via interstate commerce. Section 792 of the California Agricultural Code requires that avocados contain no less than 8 percent of oil by weight before they may be transported or sold within California. Under the Federal Agricultural Marketing Agreement Act of 1937, Florida avocados may be certified as mature and yet not satisfy the standards prescribed by the California Code. The federal standards attribute no significance to oil content. Should this California statute, as applied, be held unconstitutional under the supremacy clause? Is the California statute displaced by the Federal Agricultural Marketing Agreement Act of 1937? [Florida Lime and Avocado Growers v. Paul, 373 U.S. 132, 83 S.Ct. 1210, 10 L.Ed.2d 248 (1963)]

7. New Jersey enacted a law prohibiting the importation of most wastes into the state. Some of the landfill operators in New Jersey, however, had agreements with out-of-state residents to dispose of their solid and liquid waste. Philadelphia brought an action claiming that this statute violated the commerce clause by discriminating against interstate commerce. New Jersey asserted that its statute was justified since its landfills were inadequate to dispose of its own waste and importation had a significant and adverse potential effect on the environment. Is this state regulation of interstate commerce permissible? [Philadelphia v. New Jersey, 437 U.S. 617, 98 S.Ct. 2531, 57 L.Ed.2d 475 (1978)]

8. The plaintiffs, Americans United for Separation of Church and State, Inc., *as taxpayers,* brought an action to challenge a conveyance of land from the Department of Health, Education, and Welfare (HEW) to Valley Forge Christian College, the defendant. The plaintiffs alleged that such a conveyance violated the establishment clause of the First Amendment to the Constitution. The district court dismissed the complaint on the ground that the plaintiffs lacked "standing." What was the result on appeal? [Valley Forge Christian College v. Americans United, 454 U.S. 464, 102 S.Ct. 752, 70 L.Ed.2d 700 (1982)]

9. The California Fair Employment and Housing Act requires employers to provide leave and reinstatement to employees disabled by pregnancy. Title VII of the Civil Rights Act of 1964, which prohibits employment discrimination on the basis of sex, was amended by the Pregnancy Discrimination Act (PDA) in 1978. The PDA specifies that sex discrimination includes discrimination on the basis of pregnancy. (The PDA does not, though, require employers to provide pregnancy leave and reinstatement of employment.) A woman employed as a receptionist by California Federal Savings and Loan Association (Cal Fed) took a pregnancy disability leave in 1982. When she notified Cal Fed that she was able to return to work, she was told that her job had been filled and that there were no similar positions available. She then filed a complaint with the California Department of Fair Employment and Housing, which charged Cal Fed with violating the Fair Employment and Housing Act. Before a hearing was held on the complaint, Cal Fed, joined by other employers, brought an action in federal court seeking a declaration that the California Fair Employment and Housing Act is inconsistent with and is preempted by Title VII of the Civil Rights Act, as amended, and that thus, Cal Fed is entitled to an injunction against its enforcement. How should the court rule? [California Federal Savings and Loan Association v. Guerra, 479 U.S. 272, 107 S.Ct. 683, 93 L.Ed.2d 613 (1987)]

10. Eligibility and benefit levels in the Federal Food Stamp Program are determined on a household rather than an individual basis. The statutory definition of the term *household* was amended in 1981 and 1982 so that parents, children, and siblings who live together were to be generally treated as a single household but more distant relatives or groups of unrelated persons living together were not to be treated as households unless they also customarily purchased food and prepared meals together. Families that generally bought food and prepared meals as separate economic units, and not as a family, would either lose benefits or have their food stamp allotments decreased as a result of the 1981 and 1982 amendments. Several of these families brought suit, claiming the statutory definition of the term *household* was unconstitutional. Did the statutory distinction between parents, children, and siblings, on the one hand, and all other groups of individuals, on the other, violate the guarantee of equal treatment in the due process clause of the Fifth Amendment? [Lyng v. Castillo, 477 U.S. 635, 106 S.Ct. 2727, 91 L.Ed.2d 527 (1986)]

11. In 1982, Philip Zauderer, an attorney practicing in Columbus, Ohio, placed a series of newspaper ads directed at women who had used the Dalkon Shield intrauterine device (IUD). In his ads, Zauderer included a drawing of the Dalkon Shield and informed women that they could still sue for any injuries or other harm to their health sustained by its use, even though the IUD was no longer being marketed. As a result of these ads, Zauderer filed lawsuits for 106 women. The Ohio Supreme Court deemed such advertisements unethical, and Zauderer was reprimanded by the court for his actions. He was further reprimanded for not having disclosed in his ads that, although his clients would owe no legal fees if they lost, they might still be faced with other costs involved in litigation. Zauderer appealed, claiming the ads were protected under the First Amendment as "commercial speech" and that failure to disclose other costs was not deceptive. Discuss the probable success of Zauderer's appeal. [Zauderer v. Office of Disciplinary Counsel, 471 U.S. 626, 105 S.Ct. 2265, 85 L.Ed.2d 652 (1985)]

Chapter 4

Torts

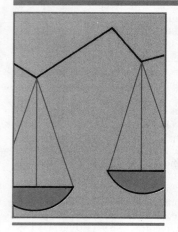

Part of doing business today and, indeed, part of everyday life is the risk of being involved in a lawsuit. A normal and ever-increasing business operating cost is that of liability insurance to protect against lawsuits. The list of circumstances in which business people can be sued is long and varied. An employee injured on the job may attempt to sue the employer because of an unsafe working environment. The consumer who is injured while using a product may attempt to sue the manufacturer because of a defect in the product. The issue in all of these examples is alleged wrongful conduct by one person that causes injury to another. Such wrongful conduct is covered by the law of **torts.** (The word *tort* is French for "wrong.")

Tort law covers a broad variety of injuries. Society recognizes an interest in personal physical safety, and tort law provides a remedy for acts causing physical injury or interfering with physical security and freedom of movement. Society recognizes an interest in protecting property, and tort law provides a remedy for acts causing destruction or damage to property. Society recognizes other, more intangible interests in such things as personal privacy, family relations, reputation, and dignity. Tort law provides a remedy for invasion of protected interests in these areas.

Tort law is constantly changing and growing with society. Although many torts have their origin in the old common law, new torts are recognized in order to protect new interests that develop with social change. For example, until recently, because of old notions of family structure, it was not a legally recognizable tort for a husband to negligently injure his wife or child. But today minors, as well as spouses, receive much more protection. Traditionally, one could not recover **damages** for psychological injury unless one had personally risked physical harm. That rule is changing, with more and more courts allowing recovery for emotional damage to those who witness traumatic injury to another.

TORT LAW VERSUS CRIMINAL LAW

Two notions serve as the basis of all torts: wrongs and compensation. Tort law recognizes that some acts are wrong because they cause injuries to persons. Those who commit the acts are to blame, or bear the fault for these injuries. Of course, torts are not the only type of wrongs that exist in the law; crimes involve wrongs also. In fact, most crimes involve torts. The commission of a tort, however, is not always a crime. A crime is an act so reprehensible that it is considered to be a wrong against the state or against society as a whole, as well as against the individual victim. Therefore, the *state* prosecutes the criminal. A tort action, in contrast, is a *civil* action in which one person brings a suit of a personal nature against another. The state is not a party to the suit. Thus, for example, an assault could be the basis for a criminal prosecution as well as the basis of an action in tort.[1] In such a case the same act can be a criminal wrong *and* a civil wrong.

The function of tort law is to provide the injured party with some remedy. The law of torts is used to decide when victims must bear the loss themselves and when the responsibility belongs to someone else. A typical tort action involves an intentional or a negligent act of one party that causes personal or property damage to another.

KINDS OF TORTS

Determining whether an injury resulting from some action is compensable under tort law involves, to some degree, a decision on how losses are allocated in our society. Thus, the many factors that make up social policy are weighed against one another. Torts are traditionally divided into three categories:

1. Intentional torts.
2. Negligence.
3. Strict liability.

Intentional torts involve acts that were intended to bring about the consequences that are the basis of the tort. Negligence involves matters of risk—sometimes a negligent actor is unaware of the results that will follow from his or her act, and sometimes he or she considers the consequences carefully before acting, but in neither case are the consequences intended. Strict liability rules require someone to compensate the injured party without regard to fault.

INTENTIONAL TORTS: WRONGS AGAINST THE PERSON

An **intentional tort** arises from an act that the defendant consciously desired to perform, either in order to harm another or knowing with substantial certainty that injury to another could result. Note that it is the *intent* to bring about the consequences of an act that is important. The nature of the damage ultimately caused is irrelevant in determining whether there was intent. If Johnson intentionally pushes Adams and Adams falls to the ground and breaks her arm, it does not matter that Johnson never wished to break Adams's arm. Johnson did intend to bring about harmful or offensive contact to Adams; Johnson is liable for the consequences, including injury to Adams's arm.

Because intent is a subjective concept, the law generally assumes that one intends the normal consequences of his or her actions. Thus, a push is an intentional tort because the object of the push can ordinarily be expected to go flying; however, a playful pat on the shoulder is not an intentional tort even though, in drawing away suddenly, the person touched may be injured. The injured person must normally prove real harm has occurred in order to recover damages.

Assault

Any intentional, unexcused act that creates in another person a reasonable apprehension or fear of immediate harmful or offensive contact is an **assault.** Apprehension is not the same as fear. If the contact is such that a reasonable person would want to avoid it, and if there is a reasonable basis for believing the contact is coming, then the plaintiff suffers apprehension whether or not he or she is afraid. For example, the *threat* of forceful delivery of an unwanted kiss may constitute an assault.

The interest protected by tort law concerning assault is the freedom from having to expect harmful or offensive contact. The arousal of apprehension is enough to justify compensation. Of course, the *completion* of the act that caused the apprehension, if it results in harm to the plaintiff, is a battery, discussed next. For example, Jones brings a gun along to an interview with Smith. There is

---

1. An assault may be described as any word or action intended to cause the person to whom it is directed to expect immediate physical harm.

no assault unless she threatens Smith with it, perhaps by pointing it at him and showing that all she has to do to use it is to cock it. If she fires the gun, and the bullet hits Smith, she has committed a *battery*.

Battery

A **battery** is an unexcused, harmful, or offensive physical contact intentionally performed. If Jones intentionally punches Smith in the nose, it is a battery. The interest tort law protects in this case is the right to personal security and safety. The contact can be harmful, or it can be merely offensive (such as an unwelcome kiss). Physical injury does not have to occur. The contact can be to any part of the body or anything attached to it—for example, a hat or other clothing, a purse, a chair, or an automobile in which one is sitting. Whether the contact is offensive or not is determined by whether it would be considered harmful or offensive by a *reasonable person* with ordinary sensibilities.[2] The contact can be made by the defendant or by some force that the defendant sets in motion—for example, a rock thrown, food poisoned, or a stick swung.

If the plaintiff shows that there was a contact, and the jury agrees that the contact was offensive, that is enough to establish a right to some compensation. Furthermore, there is no need to show that the defendant acted out of malice. The person could have been joking or playing or could even have had some benevolent motive. The underlying motive does not matter, only the intent to bring about the harmful or offensive contact to the plaintiff's person. In fact, proving a motive is never necessary (but is sometimes relevant). Damages from a battery can be for emotional harm or loss of reputation as well as for physical harm.

Defenses to Assault and Battery

A number of legally recognized defenses can be raised by a defendant who is sued for assault or battery, or both. The defenses to be discussed here are (1) **consent,** (2) **self-defense,** (3) **defense of others,** and (4) **defense of property.**

CONSENT   When a person consents to the act that harms him or her, there is no liability for the damage done. A person who voluntarily signs up for a touch football team implicitly consents to the *normal* physical punishment that takes place during such activities. This defense is good only so long as the defendant remains within the boundaries of the consent given—that is, plays football by the normal rules.

SELF-DEFENSE   An individual who is defending his or her life or physical well-being may use the defense of self-defense. A person is privileged to use whatever force is *reasonably* necessary to prevent harmful contact. This defense extends not only to *real* danger, but also to *apparent* danger. Reasonable grounds must exist for believing the danger is real, however. Also, force cannot be used once the danger has passed, and revenge is always prohibited.

DEFENSE OF OTHERS   An individual can act in a reasonable manner to protect others who are in real or apparent danger.

DEFENSE OF PROPERTY   Individuals who use reasonable force in attempting to remove intruders from their homes can use defense of property to counter tort lawsuits for assault or battery, or both. The law does value life, though, more than it values property. In principle, force that is likely to cause death or great bodily injury may never be used just to protect property. Setting a mechanical device that fires a gun if an intruder enters an empty house is not considered reasonable by most courts.

False Imprisonment

False imprisonment is defined as the intentional confinement or restraint of another person without justification. It involves interference with the freedom to move without restraint. The confinement can be accomplished through the use of physical barriers, physical restraint, or threats of physical force. Moral pressure or future threats are not restraints sufficient to constitute false imprisonment. It is essential that the person being restrained not comply with the restraint willingly.

Business people are often confronted with suits for false imprisonment after they have attempted to confine a suspected shoplifter for questioning. Consider, for example, the case in which a store

---

2. The *reasonable person standard* is an objective test of how a reasonable (normal) person would have acted under the same circumstances. See page 79 under "Breach of Duty of Care."

detective locks an alleged shoplifter in one of the store's offices. If the customer can prove that the detention was totally unreasonable, the store can be sued for false imprisonment.

The loss to business from shoplifting is estimated to exceed 15 billion dollars a year. Almost all states have adopted so-called merchant-protection legislation, which allows a merchant to detain any suspected shoplifter, provided that there is reasonable cause for suspicion and provided that the confinement is carried out in a reasonable way. Because the risk of real injury to an innocent person is great, however, educational programs are often offered to all employees; these programs explain the exact procedures to be followed when a

customer is suspected of shoplifting and help to prevent unlawful detentions and consequent lawsuits. Harm to reputation and mental distress caused by wrongful imprisonment are believed by the law to be so real that damages are presumed and need not be proved to make a case.

Under the privilege to detain granted to merchants in some states, a merchant can use the defense of *probable cause* to justify delaying a suspected shoplifter. Probable cause exists when there is more evidence for the belief that a person is guilty than against it. The detention, however, must be conducted in a *reasonable* manner and for only a *reasonable* length of time. The following case provides a good example.

BACKGROUND AND FACTS *Deborah Johnson, the plaintiff, went to the defendant's store in Madison one evening in September of 1976. She took her small child with her, carrying the child in an infant seat that she had purchased at K-Mart two or three weeks before. After purchasing some diapers and children's clothes, she attempted to leave the store. The store's security officer stopped the plaintiff and asked her to come back into the store because a K-Mart employee reported that she had seen plaintiff steal the infant seat. To show ownership, the plaintiff pointed to cat hair, food crumbs, and various stains on the seat. After a twenty-minute delay, the security officer apologized and let the plaintiff leave. The trial court dismissed Johnson's action for false imprisonment, and Johnson appealed.*

DYKMAN, Judge.

* * * *

 Case 4.1

JOHNSON v. K-MART ENTERPRISES, INC.
Court of Appeals of Wisconsin, 1980.
98 Wis.2d 533, 297 N.W.2d 74.

Probable Cause

* * * *

Because defendant is a corporation, it must transact business through its officers and employees. Section 943.50(3), Stats., permits a merchant (here K-Mart) to detain a shopper if certain conditions are met, one of which is that the merchant has probable cause for believing that the shopper stole the merchant's goods. Plaintiff's deposition shows that defendant's security officer believed that plaintiff stole the infant seat because another K-Mart employee told him that she saw plaintiff steal it. There is no conflicting evidence on this point. The question is whether the employee who said she saw plaintiff steal the infant seat was fabricating her story. Our inquiry is whether there is an issue of material fact in dispute as to whether the K-Mart employee who detained the plaintiff had probable cause for believing that plaintiff stole the infant seat.

We find no material facts in dispute, nor reasonable alternative inferences to be drawn from the facts. The merchant received word, through one of its employees, that plaintiff removed an infant seat from the shelf, put her child in it, and left the store without paying for the seat. We hold as a matter of law that the merchant, through its security guard, had probable cause based on this report to believe that plaintiff had shoplifted.

Reasonable Manner of Detention

Plaintiff argues that her deposition shows that the place of detention made the detention unreasonable, or at least would permit an inference from which a jury could find that the manner of detention was unreasonable.

Few innocent persons who are detained because they are suspected of shoplifting will feel that their detention was accomplished in a reasonable manner. Plaintiff's complaint is that the place she was detained was public. Yet, plaintiff's deposition shows that defendant's only actions were to stop plaintiff, ask her to return to the store, inform her that she was suspected of shoplifting, produce the witness who allegedly saw plaintiff steal the infant seat, apologize to plaintiff for the detention and release her. There is no suggestion in plaintiff's complaint or deposition that she asked to go to a more private place. Defendant's actions do not permit an inference that the detention was accomplished in an unreasonable manner.

Length of Time Detained

In plaintiff's deposition, she testified that she was detained for 20 minutes. An inference that could be drawn from the entire deposition is that most of this time was spent in obtaining the presence of the K-Mart employee who said she saw plaintiff steal the infant seat. Plaintiff suggests that the employee was not produced more quickly because she was afraid of confronting the person she had falsely accused.

* * * In determining whether a 20-minute detention is reasonable as a matter of law, we must weigh the customer's important liberty interests against a merchant's need for protection against shoplifters. Such a balancing is evident in the language of the statute which gives merchants the power to detain suspected shoplifters while at the same time safeguarding the customer's rights. We hold that a merchant's interest in detaining suspected shoplifters is such that a 20-minute detention is reasonable.

* * * *

DECISION AND REMEDY *The appellate court upheld the trial court's dismissal of Johnson's claim. The security officer acted reasonably and with probable cause.*

Infliction of Mental Distress

Recently the courts have begun to recognize an interest in freedom from mental distress as well as an interest in physical security. The tort of *infliction of mental distress* can be defined as an intentional act that amounts to extreme and outrageous conduct resulting in severe emotional distress to another.[3] For example, a prankster telephones an individual and says that the individual's spouse has just been in a horrible accident. As a result, the individual suffers intense mental pain or anxiety. This is deemed to be extreme and outrageous conduct that exceeds the bounds of decency accepted by society and is therefore actionable.

As this is a relatively new tort, it poses some problems. One major problem is that it could flood the courts with lawsuits asserting this basis of recovery. A society in which individuals are rewarded if they are unable to endure the normal mental stresses of day-to-day living is obviously undesirable. Therefore, the law usually focuses on the nature of the acts that come under this tort.

Indignity or annoyance alone are usually not enough to support a lawsuit based on intentional infliction of emotional distress. Many times, however, repeated annoyances, coupled with threats, are enough. In a business context, for example, the repeated use of extreme methods to collect a delinquent account may be actionable. Also, an unusually severe emotional reaction, such as the extreme distress of a woman incorrectly informed that her husband and two sons have been killed, may be actionable. Because it is difficult to prove the existence of mental suffering, a few states require that the mental disturbance be evidenced by some physical illness.

Defamation

The protection of a person's body is involved in the torts of assault, battery, and false imprisonment. **Defamation** of character involves wrongfully hurting a person's good reputation. The law has imposed a general duty on all persons to refrain from making false, defamatory statements about others. Breaching this duty orally involves the tort of **slander;** breaching it in writing or in any form of communication that has "the poten-

---

3. Restatement, Second, Torts, Section 46, Comment d.

tially harmful qualities characteristic of written or printed words"[4] involves the tort of **libel.** Courts have held that the forms of libelous communication include pictures, signs, statues, and films.

The basis of the tort is the *publication* of a statement or statements that hold an individual up to contempt, ridicule, or hatred. *Publication* here means that the defamatory statements are made to or within the hearing of persons other than the defamed party. If Thompson writes Andrews a private letter accusing him of embezzling funds, that does not constitute libel. If Peters calls Gordon dishonest, unattractive, and incompetent when no one else is around, that does not constitute slander. In neither case was the message communicated to a third party. Interestingly, the courts have generally held that dictating a letter to a secretary constitutes publication. Moreover, if a third party overhears defamatory statements by chance, the courts have generally held that this also constitutes publication. Note further that any individual who republishes or repeats defamatory statements is liable even if that person reveals the source of such statements. Most radio stations have instituted seven-second delays for live broadcasts, such as talk shows, to avoid this kind of liability.

The common law has defined four types of false utterances that are considered slander *per se,* or on their face. That means that no proof of damages is required before these false utterances become actionable. They are:

1. *A statement that another has a loathsome communicable disease.* Courts have generally limited this tort to imputations that an individual has a venereal disease.

2. *A statement that another has committed improprieties while engaging in a profession or trade.* For example, it is actionable to say of an attorney that he or she is unethical, of a merchant that his or her credit is bad, or of a person holding public office that he or she has accepted a bribe. But statements alleging that a clerk has consorted with prostitutes or is a homosexual, that a physician has committed adultery, or that a stenographer's credit is bad have not been held to be actionable— since the clerk, the physician, and the stenographer may still be competent at their work.

3. *A statement that another has committed or has been imprisoned for a serious crime.* Courts generally agree that the crime referred to in the statement must involve "moral turpitude," which has been defined as "inherent baseness or vileness of principle in the human heart." Beating children, for example, involves moral turpitude, while other forms of battery may not.

4. *A statement that an unmarried woman is unchaste.*

DEFENSES TO DEFAMATION Truth is normally an *absolute* defense against a defamation charge. But the statement at issue must be true in whole, not in part, and if the statement is specific, the truth must be the same. For instance, if the accusation is that Tony stole a stereo from Sam, it is insufficient to show that Tony is known as a bad character or that Tony stole stereos from Simon. On the other hand, if the statement is substantially true, it is not necessary to prove every detail. For example, saying a politician has wasted $80,000 of the taxpayers' money has been held justified when it was proved that he wasted $17,500.

Also, there may be a **privilege,** or immunity, involved. For example, statements made by attorneys and judges during a trial are *absolutely privileged* and therefore cannot be the basis for a defamation charge. Members of Congress making statements on the floor of Congress have an absolute privilege. Legislators have complete immunity from liability for false statements made in debate, even if they make such statements maliciously—that is, knowing them to be untrue. In general, false and defamatory statements that concern public figures and are published in the press are privileged if they are made without malice.[5] Under this rule of privilege, public figures are defined as those who "thrust" themselves into the forefront of public controversy.

Privileged communications are of two types, absolute and qualified. Only in limited cases, such as in judicial proceedings and legislative proceedings, mentioned above, is absolute privilege granted. Qualified or conditional privilege is a common law concept based on the philosophy that the right to know or speak is of equal importance with the right not to be defamed. If the communication is conditionally privileged, the plaintiff must show that the privilege was abused in order to recover.

---

4. Restatement, Second, Torts, Section 568.

5. New York Times Co. v. Sullivan, 376 U.S. 254, 84 S.Ct. 710, 11 L.Ed.2d 686 (1964).

An example of a qualified privilege is found in letters of recommendation and in written evaluations of employees. This privilege allows for some latitude in making mistakes in the communication without defamation liability. Generally, if the communication statements are made in good faith and the publication is limited to those who have a legitimate interest in the communication, the statement falls within the qualified privilege.

In order to prove malice, a plaintiff must show that the defendant acted with either actual knowledge of falsity or a reckless disregard of the truth. The balance between free speech and the torts of slander and libel is delicate. The following case illustrates a libel case involving a public figure and the extent of liability when malice is proved.

Case 4.2
BURNETT v. NATIONAL ENQUIRER

California Court of Appeal, Second District, 1983. 144 Cal.App.3d 991, 193 Cal.Rptr. 206.

BACKGROUND AND FACTS   *Plaintiff Carol Burnett, the comedienne, believed she had been libeled by an article in* The National Enquirer, *which stated that Burnett was intoxicated and involved in a "row" with Henry Kissinger in a Washington, D.C., restaurant. She sued the* Enquirer *and the jury awarded her $300,000 in general damages and $1,300,000 in punitive damages. The National Enquirer* moved for judgment notwithstanding the verdict and a new trial, claiming that (a) there was no actual malice on its part, (b) it is a news publication and protected from false statements that it has neither time nor opportunity to ascertain, (c) the jury was tainted because three members heard a Johnny Carson "tirade" against the* Enquirer, and (d) the damages were excessive. The trial court judge reduced the general damages to $50,000 and the punitive damages to $760,000. The National Enquirer appealed.*

ROTH, Presiding Justice.
*   *   *   *

The National Enquirer is a publication whose masthead claims the "Largest Circulation Of Any Paper in America." It is a member of the American Newspaper Publishers Association. It subscribes to the Reuters News Service. Its staff call themselves newspaper reporters. It describes its business as "newspaper" in its filings with the Los Angeles County Assessor and in its applications for insurance. A State Revenue Department has ruled it qualifies as a newspaper and is thus exempt from sales and use tax. The United States Department of Labor describes it as "belonging to establishments primarily engaged in publishing or printing and publishing newspapers."

By the same token the National Enquirer is designated as a magazine or periodical in eight mass media directories and upon the request and written representation of its general manager in 1960 that "In view of the feature content and general appearance [of the publication], which differ markedly from those of a newspaper * * *," its classification as a newspaper was changed to that of magazine by the Audit Bureau of Circulation. It does not subscribe to the Associated Press or United Press International news services. According to a statement by its Senior Editor it is not a newspaper and its content is based on a consistent formula of "how to" stories, celebrity or medical or personal improvement stories, gossip items and TV column items, together with material from certain other subjects. It provides little or no current coverage of subjects such as politics, sports or crime, does not attribute content to wire services, and in general does not make reference to time. Normal "lead time" for its subject matter is one to three weeks. Its owner allowed it did not generate stories "day to day as a daily newspaper does."
*   *   *   *

*   *   * [While the trial court] took into account the indicia relating to status detailed above, it relied upon the most fundamental of those considerations which have been deemed sufficient to justify the designation of that particular class [newspapers and radio stations] as the beneficiary of the protection afforded by the statute, namely, that newspapers by virtue of the manner in which they are obliged to operate are not

generally in a position adequately to guard against the publication of material which is untrue, such that:

In view of the complex and far-flung activities of the news services upon which newspapers and radio stations must largely rely and the necessity of publishing news while it is new, newspapers and radio stations may in good faith publicize items that are untrue but whose falsity they have neither the time nor the opportunity to ascertain.

* * * *

* * * [We are] satisfied to conclude without extensive recitation of the evidence that the trial court consistently with the foregoing rationale correctly determined the National Enquirer should not be deemed a newspaper for the purposes of the instant litigation.

* * * *

Nearly twenty years ago, it was announced in *New York Times Co. v. Sullivan* that:

The constitutional guarantees [relating to protected speech] require, we think, a federal rule that prohibits a public official from recovering damages for a defamatory falsehood relating to his official conduct unless he proves that the statement was made with 'actual malice'—that is, with knowledge that it was false or with reckless disregard of whether it was false or not.

The constitutional privilege thus defined was extended three years later in *Curtis Publishing Co. v. Butts* to include within its protection not only public officials but also "public figures," such that:

Those who, by reason of the notoriety of their achievements or the vigor and success with which they seek the public's attention, are properly classed as public figures and those who hold governmental office may recover for injury to reputation only on clear and convincing proof that the defamatory falsehood was made with knowledge of its falsity or with reckless disregard for the truth.

* * * *

The matter herein was tried upon the premise respondent is a "public figure" and there was employed in establishing the liability of appellant the *New York Times* standard, expressed in the trial court's instruction to the jury that:

In addition, plaintiff must prove by clear and convincing evidence that defendant published the item complained of with actual malice—that is, that the defendant published the item either knowing that it was false or with reckless disregard for whether it was true or false.

* * * *

* * * As can be ascertained from what we have set out above, the "actual malice" required by *New York Times* to be established by "clear and convincing evidence" refers to that aspect of malice, properly denominated malice in law, necessary to find liability for libel and not to malice in fact, essential to the recovery of punitive damages, which under the cases discussed may be arrived at on the basis of applicable state standards, here on the basis of a preponderance of the evidence. [The court concluded that malice was proved at the trial by a preponderance of the evidence.]

* * * *

It is next contended, however, that regardless of what we have just said, the punitive damages assessed herein are still legally unsupportable. More specifically it is urged (a) the amount of those damages was grossly excessive; (b) such damages were impermissibly disproportionate to the compensatory damages awarded; (c) that the trial court erred in revising the ratio between punitive and compensatory damages on its remittitur [the process by which a jury damages verdict is reduced]; and (d) that insufficient evidence was present which would show appellant ratified the acts of its employees, so as to justify its liability for punitive damages. * * *

* * * *

Viewing the record in the light of these principles, and assuming, as we will hereinafter decide, that the award of compensatory damages was proper, we are of the opinion the award to respondent of $750,000 in order to punish and deter appellant was not justified.

*   *   *   *

In the second incident referred to, at least a number of the jurors became aware of a verbal denunciation of the National Enquirer by television star Johnny Carson on his program "The Tonight Show," wherein he asserted essentially that the publication was composed of fabrications authored by liars. After examining each juror concerning the effect of the tirade on the juror's ability to participate in a fair and impartial trial and being satisfied in the premises, the trial court excused two of the triers of fact, seated the only available alternate, and proceeded with a panel of eleven, from which it was agreed nine could determine the cause. No more was required.

The judgment is affirmed except that the punitive damage award herein is vacated and the matter is remanded for a new trial on that issue only, provided that if respondent shall, within 30 days from the date of our remittitur, file with the clerk of this court and serve upon appellant a written consent to a reduction of the punitive damage award to the sum of $150,000, the judgment will be modified to award respondent punitive damages in that amount, and as so modified affirmed in its entirety.   *   *   *

DECISION AND REMEDY	*The appellate court affirmed the trial court's denial of* The National Enquirer's *motions for judgment notwithstanding the verdict and a new trial on basically the same grounds. The court upheld the general damage reduction to $50,000 but lowered punitive damages from $750,000 to $150,000.*

Slander of Title, Disparagement of Goods, and Defamation by Computer

There are three torts, typically called business torts, that involve defamation. Defamation arising from a false statement made about a person's product, business, or title to property is called *slander of title* or *disparagement of goods*, depending on the case. Erroneous information from a computer about a person's credit standing or business reputation can impair that person's ability to obtain further credit and is called *defamation by computer*. These torts are treated in more detail in the following chapter.

Invasion of the Right to Privacy

A person's right to solitude and freedom from prying public eyes is the interest protected by the tort of invasion of privacy. Four different acts qualify as an invasion of privacy:

1. *The use of a person's name, picture, or other likeness for commercial purposes without permission.* For example, using without permission someone's picture to advertise a product or someone's name to enhance a company name invades the person's privacy.

2. *Intrusion upon an individual's affairs or seclusion.* For example, invading someone's home or illegally searching someone's briefcase is an in-

vasion of privacy. This tort has been held to extend to eavesdropping by wiretap, unauthorized scanning of a bank account, compulsory blood testing, and window peeping.

3. *Publication of information that places a person in a false light.* This could be a story attributing to a person ideas not held or actions not taken by that person. (Publishing such a story could involve the tort of defamation as well.)

4. *Public disclosure of private facts about an individual that an ordinary person would find objectionable.* A newspaper account of a private citizen's sex life could be an actionable invasion of privacy. An example of what would *not* constitute this form of invasion of privacy is an article publicizing what a one-time child star is doing today, as long as nothing is revealed that the community would regard as highly objectionable (unless the objectionable information is truthful and contained in official records open to public inspection).

Misrepresentation (Fraud, Deceit)

The tort of misrepresentation involves the use of fraud and deceit for personal gain. It includes several elements:

1. Misrepresentation of facts or conditions with knowledge that they are false or with reckless disregard for the truth.

2. Intent to induce another to rely on the misrepresentation.
3. Justifiable reliance by the deceived party.
4. Damages suffered as a result of reliance.
5. Causal connection between the misrepresentation and the injury suffered.

In general, the reliance must be upon a statement of fact. Reliance on a statement of opinion is not justified unless the person making the statement has a superior knowledge of the subject matter. A lawyer's opinion of the law, for instance, is an example of superior knowledge, and reliance on that opinion will be regarded as reliance upon a statement of fact.

In order for fraud to occur, more than mere *seller's talk*, or **puffing,** must be involved. Fraud exists only when a person represents as a material fact something he or she knows is untrue. For example, it is fraud to claim that a building does not leak when one knows it does. Facts are objectively ascertainable, whereas seller's talk is not. "I'm the best lawyer in town," is seller's talk. The speaker is not trying to represent something as fact, because "best" is a subjective, not an objective, term. (The topic of fraud in contracts is discussed in Chapter 10.)

INTENTIONAL TORTS: WRONGS AGAINST PROPERTY

Wrongs against property include (1) trespass to land and to personal property, (2) conversion, and (3) nuisance. The wrong is against the individual who has legally recognized rights with regard to real or personal property. The law distinguishes real property from personal property. *Real property* is land and things permanently attached thereto. *Personal property* includes things that are basically movable. Thus, a house and lot are real property, whereas the furniture inside a house is personal property. Money and securities are also personal property.

Trespass to Land

Any time a person, without permission, enters onto land that is owned by another, or causes anything to enter onto the land, or remains on the land, or permits anything to remain on it, such action constitutes the civil tort called a **trespass to land.** Note that actual harm to the land is not an essential element of this tort, because tort law in respect to trespass is designed to protect the right of an owner to exclusive possession. If no harm is done, usually only nominal—in name only, not significant—damages (such as $1) can be recovered by the landowner. Examples of common types of trespass to land include walking or driving on the land, shooting across it with a gun, throwing rocks or spraying water on a building in the possession of another, building a dam across a river that causes water to back up on someone else's land, and placing part of one's building on the adjoining landowner's property.

In the past, the right to land gave exclusive possession of a space that extended from "the center of the earth to the heavens," but this rule has been relaxed. Today, reasonable intrusions are permitted. Thus, aircraft can normally fly over privately owned land. The temporary invasion of the air space over such land is, in effect, considered privileged as to the aircraft owner. Society's interest in air transportation preempts the individual's interest in the air space.

TRESPASS CRITERIA, RIGHTS, AND DUTIES Before a person can be a trespasser, the real property owner (the person who legally controls the realty) must expressly or impliedly establish that person as a trespasser. For example, "posted" trespass signs expressly establish a person as a trespasser when that person ignores these signs and enters upon the property. A guest in your home, however, is not a trespasser. Should the guest become unruly, you could *ask* your guest to leave and at that moment establish your guest as a trespasser. Any person who enters upon another's property to commit an illegal act (such as a thief entering a lumberyard at night to steal lumber) is impliedly established as a trespasser without verbal establishment or posted signs.

Once a person is established as a trespasser, certain rights and duties are applied to both the owner of the realty and to the trespasser. Some of these rights and duties are as follows:

1. A trespasser is liable for any damage caused to the property. The owner does not have to prove negligence.
2. A trespasser assumes the risks of the premises and cannot hold the owner liable for injuries sustained. This rule does not permit the owner to lay traps with the intent to injure a trespasser. Under

the "attractive nuisance" doctrine, infants or young persons do not assume the risks of the premises if they are attracted to the premises. Under some circumstances an owner may even have a duty to warn of dangers on the property, such as guard dogs.

3. As previously discussed, a trespasser can be removed from the premises through the use of reasonable force without the owner being liable

for assault and battery. This same basic concept allows an owner to remove, without liability, another's property, the presence of which constitutes a trespass, if the removal is accomplished by the exercise of reasonable care.

In the following case, the court points out that a trespasser is liable for damages even when a trespass is not willful.

Case 4.3
ROSSI v. VENTRESCA BROS. CONST. CO., INC.
City Court of the City of White Plains, Westchester County, New York. Small Claims Part, 1978.
94 Misc.2d 756, 405 N.Y.S.2d 375.

BACKGROUND AND FACTS   *During a severe snowstorm the plaintiff, Ronald Rossi, parked his car in the privately owned parking lot of a shopping center. The car was towed from the lot. Rossi sued the shopping center owners, Ventresca Bros. Const. Co., Inc., and the towing company to recover the $113.40 he paid to retrieve his car.*

BLAUSTEIN, Judge.
*   *   *   *

This Court reluctantly finds that the plaintiff was trespassing in parking on private property and the snowstorm does not justify the trespass. Further, the owner of the shopping center has the corollary right to remove any car so parked. The rule is stated in 87 C.J.S. [*Corpus Juris Secundum* (C.J.S. is a legal reference encyclopedia published by West Publishing Company.)] Trespass § 45a:
> "He [the owner] may remove chattels which are wrongfully on his land, if he uses due care in the removal. The removal should be effected with as little injury to the chattels removed as is possible, and without the exercise of excessive force."

*   *   *   *

While plaintiff here is not a willful trespasser considering the severity of the storm, still, he was violating the owner's property and is liable for damages incurred. Even the most innocent of trespassers is liable for nominal damages as a minimum. (87 C.J.S. Trespass § 117).

DECISION AND REMEDY   *Plaintiff was allowed to recover $27 of the towing charge. The court held that the towing and storage charges constituted Ventresca's damages. But the court found $113.40 to be an excessive amount.*

DEFENSES TO TRESPASS TO LAND   Trespass to land involves wrongful interference with another person's real property rights. But if one can show that the trespass was warranted, as when a trespasser enters to assist someone in danger, a complete defense exists. Another defense is to show that the purported owner did not actually have the right to possess the land in question.

In some situations, courts can easily assess damages for trespass to land, especially when the trespasser damages or wrongfully destroys items of value on the land. For example, land purchasers can recover the value of destroyed trees when

avoidable errors caused construction crews to knock them down.

Trespass to Personal Property

Whenever any individual unlawfully harms the personal property of another or otherwise interferes with the personal property owner's right to exclusive possession and enjoyment of that property, **trespass to personalty, or personal property,** occurs. Trespass to personal property involves interference with a person's right to possess his or her property and, thus, may entail acts of damage, dispossession, or both. For example, if a student takes another student's business law book as a practical joke and hides it so that the owner is unable to find it for several days prior to the final examination, the student has engaged in a trespass to personal property.

If it can be shown that trespass to personal property was warranted, then a complete defense has been made. Many states, for example, allow automobile repair shops to hold a customer's car when he or she has refused to pay for repairs rendered (under what is called an artisan's, or possessory, lien).

Conversion

Whenever personal property is taken from its rightful owner or possessor and placed in the service of another or whenever the rightful owner of personal property is otherwise deprived of its use (due to vandalism, for example), the act of **conversion** occurs. A store clerk who steals merchandise from the store commits a crime and the tort of conversion at the same time. Of course, when conversion occurs, the lesser offense of trespass to personal property usually occurs as well. If the initial taking of the property was unlawful, there is trespass. Retention of the property is conversion. Even if the initial taking of the property was permitted by the owner or, for some other reason, is not a trespass, failure to return it may constitute conversion.

Even if a person mistakenly believed that he or she was entitled to the goods, a tort of conversion may take place. In other words, good intentions are not a defense against a charge of conversion, and conversion can be an entirely innocent act. To illustrate: ABC Hardware allowed Samuels to take a lawn mower home to try it out. Samuels used the lawn mower once. He then lent it to his neighbor, Nichols. A thief stole the lawn mower from Nichols. When ABC Hardware learned what had happened to the mower, it demanded that Samuels pay for it. Samuels is guilty of conversion because he had no right to lend the mower to Nichols. His misuse of the mower renders him liable. He obviously did not intend for the mower to be stolen, but he intentionally took the mower from ABC and intentionally and knowingly lent it to his neighbor.

Whoever suffers a conversion is generally entitled to recover the reasonable value of the lost goods. If Henries deliberately smashes a vase that Arts, Inc., exhibits for sale in its store, Henries is liable for the value of the vase. Deliberate destruction of the personal property of another is conversion. Henries treated the vase as if he owned it when he asserted a right to destroy it. (When the goods are not destroyed, the owner can either try to get them back through a lawsuit or ask for damages for conversion. The court will not give the owner full value for the goods and return the property as well.)

The following case illustrates the concept of the tort of conversion.

BACKGROUND AND FACTS *Plaintiff Rouse was negotiating a new car purchase with the defendant's salespersons. Rouse gave the salespersons the keys to the car he then owned, which was to be traded for the new automobile. When Rouse decided not to purchase a new car, the sales representative said they had lost the keys. Rouse summoned police, and when they arrived, the salespersons produced the missing keys and stated that they "just wanted to see him cry a while."*

 Case 4.4

RUSSELL-VAUGHN FORD, INC. v. ROUSE

Supreme Court of Alabama, 1968.

281 Ala. 567, 206 So.2d 371.

SIMPSON, Justice.

*   *   *   *

*   *   * Initially it is argued that the facts of this case do not make out a case of conversion. It is argued that the conversion if at all, is a conversion of the keys to the automobile, not of the automobile itself. It is further contended that there was not under the case here presented a conversion at all. We are not persuaded that the law of Alabama supports this proposition. As noted in [a previous case],

It has been held by this court that the fact of conversion does not necessarily import an acquisition of property in the defendant. The conversion may consist, not only in an appropriation of the property to one's own use, but in its destruction, *or in exercising dominion* [complete retention of control] *over it in exclusion or defiance of plaintiff's right.* *   *   *

It is not contended that the plaintiff here had no right to demand the return of the keys to his automobile. Rather, the appellants seem to be arguing that there was no conversion which the law will recognize under the facts of this case because the defendants did not commit sufficient acts to amount to a conversion. We cannot agree.

We see nothing in our cases which requires in a conversion case that the plaintiff prove that the defendant appropriated the property to his own use: rather, as noted in the cases referred to above, it is enough that he show that the defendant exercised dominion over it in exclusion or defiance of the right of the plaintiff. *   *   *

Further, appellants argue that there was no conversion since the plaintiff could have called his wife at home, who had another set of keys and thereby gained the ability to move his automobile. We find nothing in our cases which would require the plaintiff to exhaust all possible means of gaining possession of a chattel [an article of personal property] which is withheld from him by the defendant, after demanding its return. On the contrary, it is the refusal, without legal excuse, to deliver a chattel, which constitutes a conversion.

We find unconvincing the appellants contention that if there were a conversion at all, it was the conversion of the automobile keys, and not of the automobile. In *Compton v. Sims,* supra, this court sustained a finding that there had been a conversion of cotton where the defendant refused to deliver to the plaintiff "warehouse tickets" which would have enabled him to gain possession of the cotton. The court spoke of the warehouse tickets as a symbol of the cotton and found that the retention of them amounted to a conversion of the cotton. So here, we think that the withholding from the plaintiff after demand of the keys to his automobile, without which he could not move it, amounted to a conversion of the automobile.

It is next argued by appellants that the amount of the verdict is excessive. It is not denied that punitive damages are recoverable here in the discretion of the jury. [In a previous case, we held that:]

If the conversion was committed in known violation of the law and of plaintiff's rights with circumstances of insult, or contumely, or malice, punitive damages were recoverable in the discretion of the jury.

We think that the evidence justifies the jury's conclusion that these circumstances existed in this case.

DECISION AND REMEDY   *The jury verdict for Rouse was upheld. The jury had awarded Rouse $5,000 in damages for the conversion of his property, and the Alabama supreme court ruled that this amount was not excessive.*

STOLEN GOODS   Here again, intent to engage in a wrongdoing is not necessary for conversion to exist. Rather, it is the intent to exercise control over property when such control is inconsistent with the plaintiff's rights that constitutes conversion. Therefore, someone who buys stolen goods is guilty of conversion even if he or she did not know the goods were stolen. If the true owner brings a tort action against the buyer, the buyer must pay the owner the full value of the property, despite having already paid some money to the thief.

DEFENSES TO CONVERSION   A successful defense against the charge of conversion is that the purported owner has no title, or right to possess, superior to the holder's rights.

Necessity is another possible defense against conversion. If Abrams takes Stephens's cat, Abrams is guilty of conversion. If Stephens sues Abrams, Abrams must return the cat and pay damages. If, however, the cat has rabies and Abrams took the cat to protect the public, Abrams has a valid defense—necessity (and perhaps even self-defense if he can prove that he was in danger from the cat).

Nuisance

It is possible to commit a tort and be liable because of unreasonable uses you make of your own property. A **nuisance** is an improper activity that interferes with another's enjoyment or use of his or her property. Nuisances can be either *public* or *private*. A public nuisance disturbs or interferes with the public in general, such as burning leaves thereby causing smoke to pollute an entire neighborhood. A private nuisance interferes with the property interest of a limited number of individuals, such as leaving a trash pile next to a neighbor's property thereby creating an attraction for rodents. Reasonable limitations are placed on the use of property in all situations. Such limitations prevent the owner from unreasonably interfering with the health and comfort of neighbors or with their right to enjoy their own private property. The usual remedy is damages for one who suffers as a result of a nuisance. Where damages are unavailable or inadequate, one can have the nuisance stopped by seeking an injunction in the courts. An injunction is an equitable remedy. The court, if it grants the injunction, will prohibit the continuation of the undesirable activity.

Nuisances can also involve indecent, improper, or unlawful personal conduct. Obviously, there is an extremely subjective element in any definition of nuisance, particularly when it involves personal conduct. Moreover, a nuisance may be a crime as well as a tort, and the dividing line is difficult to ascertain. Finally, nuisances may result from intentional types of conduct as well as from negligent (careless) conduct. The defendant may even be held liable on the ground of strict liability (discussed at the end of this chapter). The difficulties in applying the nuisance doctrine are apparent.

UNINTENTIONAL TORTS: NEGLIGENCE

Intentional torts normally involve an actor's intent to bring about the consequences that are the basis of the tort. In negligence, however, the actor neither wishes to bring about the consequences of the act nor believes that they will occur. The actor's conduct merely creates a *risk* of such consequences. Without the creation of a risk, there can be no negligence. Moreover, the risk must be foreseeable; that is, it must be such that a reasonable person would anticipate it and guard against it. In determining what is reasonable conduct, courts consider the nature of the possible harm. A very slight risk of a dangerous explosion might be unreasonable, whereas a distinct possibility of burning one's fingers on a stove might be reasonable.

Many of the actions discussed in the preceding section on intentional torts would constitute negligence if they were done carelessly but without intent. For instance, carelessly bumping into someone who falls and breaks an arm constitutes negligence. Likewise, carelessly, as opposed to intentionally, flooding someone's land constitutes negligence. In a sense, negligence is a *way of committing* a tort rather than a distinct *category* of torts.

Negligence has been committed when someone has suffered injury caused by the failure of another to live up to a required duty of care. Generally, the tort of negligence requires the presence of the following four elements:

1. The defendant owed a duty of care to the plaintiff.
2. The defendant breached that duty.
3. The plaintiff suffered a legally recognizable injury.
4. The defendant's breach of the duty of care caused the plaintiff's injury.

Each of these elements is examined below.

Breach of Duty of Care

The first two elements in establishing a case for negligence can be rephrased as a two-part question:

1. Is there a duty of care?
2. Did the defendant's action breach (fail to live up to) that duty?

DUTY OF CARE Basically, the concept of duty arises from the notion that if we are to live in society with other people, some actions can be tolerated and some cannot, some actions are right and some are wrong, and some actions are reasonable and some are not. The basic rule of duty is that people are free to act as they please so long as their actions do not infringe upon the interests of others.

Tort law measures duty by a standard of reasonableness—the *reasonable person standard*. In determining whether a tort has been committed, the courts ask how a reasonable person would have acted in the same circumstances. The reasonable person standard is said to be (though in an absolute sense it cannot be) objective. It is not necessarily how a particular person would act. It is society's judgment on how people should act. If the so-called reasonable person existed, he or she would be careful, conscientious, even-tempered, and honest. This hypothetical "reasonable person" is frequently used in discussions of law.

If an individual has knowledge, skill, or intelligence superior to that of an ordinary person, the individual's conduct must be consistent with it. In other words, that individual has a higher standard of care—his or her duty is that which is reasonable in light of his or her capabilities. Further, professionals (doctors, dentists, psychiatrists, architects, engineers, accountants, lawyers, and so on) are required to have a standard minimum level of special knowledge and ability.

BREACH OF DUTY   When someone either intentionally harms another or fails to comply with the duty of exercising reasonable care, a potentially tortious act may have been committed (but not necessarily a completed tort, since that will depend on whether damage and causation exist). Failure to live up to the standard of care may be an act (setting fire to a building) or an omission (neglecting to put out a fire). It may be an intentional act, a careless act, or a carefully performed but nevertheless dangerous act that results in injury.

Whether or not a person's act or failure to act is unreasonable depends on the interaction of a number of factors. One factor is the nature of the act. Some actions—shooting off a gun in a crowd, for instance—are so outrageous and certain other acts, like blasting with dynamite, are so dangerous that any damage caused should be paid for. Another factor in determining whether damages should be awarded is the manner in which an act is performed. Nearly all human acts carry some risk of harm, and individuals are expected to pay attention to their conduct and surroundings when undertaking to do something rather than to proceed heedlessly. A third factor is the nature of the injury—whether it is serious or slight, extraordinary or simply part of everyday life. Another factor to be considered is whether the activity causing the injury was socially useful. For example, a person may be justified in darting into the path of an

oncoming train to save a child, but not to save a hat. Yet another factor to consider is how easily the injury could have been guarded against. Could, for example, a simple, inexpensive warning sign have prevented the injury?

Injury

In order for a tort to have been committed, there must be a *legally* recognizable injury to the plaintiff. The plaintiff must have suffered some loss, harm, wrong, or invasion of a protected interest to recover damages (that is, to receive compensation). The reason for the requirement of injury is obvious. Without an injury of some kind, there is nothing to "recover." Essentially, the purpose of tort law is to compensate for legally recognized injuries resulting from wrongful acts, not to punish people for these acts. For some torts, however, the injured person may be given extra compensation as punitive damages, because society tries to discourage these acts. But few negligent acts are so reprehensible that punitive damages are available.[7]

Causation

The fourth element necessary to a tort is causation. If a person fails in a duty of care and someone suffers injury, the wrongful activity must have caused the harm for a tort to have been committed. In deciding whether there is causation, the court must actually address two questions:

1. Is there *causation in fact?*
2. Was the act the *proximate cause* of the injury?

CAUSATION IN FACT   Did the injury occur because of the defendant's act, or would it have occurred anyway? If an injury would not have occurred without the defendant's act, then there is **causation in fact.** If Johnson carelessly leaves a campfire burning and the fire burns down the forest, there is causation in fact. If Johnson carelessly leaves a campfire burning, but it burns out, and then lightning causes a fire that burns down the forest, there is no causation in fact. In both cases there is a wrongful act and damage. In the second case, however, there is no causal connection and thus no liability. Causation in fact can usually be

---

7. Although punitive damages may be awarded in tort actions, they are usually *not* available in breach of contract actions.

determined by use of the *but for* test: But for the wrongful act, the injury would not have occurred.

In some cases, causation in fact is difficult to determine. What if Johnson's campfire did spread, but at the same time lightning also started a fire? In this type of situation, the courts apply the *substantial factor* test: If Johnson's conduct was a substantial factor in bringing about the damage, Johnson will be held liable.

Determining causation in fact entails examining the facts portrayed in evidence at a trial. The plaintiff has the burden of proving causation in fact as well as other elements, such as damages. The plaintiff must prove the case by a *preponderance of the evidence* in a civil suit.

PROXIMATE CAUSE   How far should a defendant's liability extend for a wrongful act that was a substantial factor in causing injury? For example, suppose Johnson's fire not only burns down the forest but also sets off an explosion in a nearby chemical plant that spills chemicals into a river, killing all the fish for a hundred miles downstream and ruining the economy of a tourist resort. Should Johnson be liable to the resort owners? To the tourists whose vacations were ruined? These are questions about the limitation of liability, which

is the second element in the general issue of causation. The courts use the term **proximate cause** (or sometimes *legal cause*) to describe this element. Proximate cause is a question not of fact but of law and policy. The question is whether the connection between an act and an injury is strong enough to justify imposing liability.

There is probably nothing in the field of law that has caused more disagreement than the subject of proximate cause. The term is somewhat misleading, because the question is not primarily one of causation and does not arise until causation has been established. Instead, the question concerns a fundamental policy of law: should a negligent defendant's responsibility extend to consequences that could in no way have been anticipated?

The most discussed and debated of all tort cases, the *Palsgraf* case, which follows, involves what may be called, instead of unforeseeable consequences, the unforeseeable plaintiff. The question before the court is: Does the defendant's duty of care extend only to those who may be injured as a result of a foreseeable risk, or does it extend also to a person who is outside the zone of danger and whose injury could not reasonably have been foreseen?

BACKGROUND AND FACTS   *The plaintiff, Palsgraf, was waiting for a train on a station platform. A man carrying a package was rushing to catch a train that was already moving. As the man attempted to jump aboard the moving train, he seemed unsteady and about to fall. A railroad guard on the car reached forward to grab him, and another guard on the platform pushed him from behind to help him on the train. The man's package, which contained fireworks, fell on the railroad tracks and exploded. There was nothing about the package to indicate its contents. The explosion caused scales located at the other end of the platform to fall upon Palsgraf, causing injuries for which she sued the railroad company. At the trial, the jury found that the railroad guards were negligent in their conduct toward the plaintiff, and Palsgraf was awarded damages. The railroad company appealed.*

Case 4.5
PALSGRAF v. LONG ISLAND R.R. CO.
Court of Appeals of New York, 1928.
248 N.Y. 339, 162 N.E. 99.

CARDOZO, Chief Justice.
*   *   *   *

The conduct of the defendant's guard, if a wrong in its relation to the holder of the package, was not a wrong in its relation to the plaintiff, standing far away. Relatively to her it was not negligence at all. Nothing in the situation gave notice that the falling package had in it the potency of peril to persons thus removed. *Negligence is not actionable unless it involves the invasion of a legally protected interest, the violation of a right.* "Proof of negligence in the air, so to speak, will not do." [Emphasis added.]
*   *   * If no hazard was apparent to the eye of ordinary vigilance, an act innocent and harmless, at least to outward seeming, with reference to her, did not take to itself

the quality of a tort because it happened to be a wrong, though apparently not one involving the risk of bodily insecurity, with reference to someone else. "In every instance, before *negligence* can be predicated of a given act, *back of the act must be sought and found a duty to the individual complaining*, the observance of which would have averted or avoided the injury." [Emphasis added.]

* * * One who jostles one's neighbor in a crowd does not invade the rights of others standing at the outer fringe when the unintended contact casts a bomb upon the ground. The wrongdoer as to them is the man who carries the bomb, not the one who explodes it without suspicion of the danger. Life will have to be made over, and human nature transformed, before prevision so extravagant can be accepted as the norm of conduct, the customary standard to which behavior must conform.

* * * What the plaintiff must show is "a wrong" to herself; i.e., a violation of her own right, and not merely a wrong to some one else, nor conduct "wrongful" because unsocial, but not "a wrong" to any one. * * * The risk reasonably to be perceived defines the duty to be obeyed[.] * * * Here, by concession, there was nothing in the situation to suggest to the most cautious mind that the parcel wrapped in newspaper would spread wreckage through the station. If the guard had thrown it down knowingly and willfully, he would not have threatened the plaintiff's safety, so far as appearances could warn him. His conduct would not have involved, even then, an unreasonable probability of invasion of her bodily security. Liability can be no greater where the act is inadvertent.

* * * One who seeks redress at law does not make out a cause of action by showing without more that there has been damage to his person. *If the harm was not willful, he must show that the act as to him had possibilities of danger so many and apparent as to entitle him to be protected against the doing of it though the harm was unintended.* [Emphasis added.] * * * The victim does not sue derivatively, or by right of subrogation, to vindicate an interest invaded in the person of another. * * * He sues for breach of a duty owing to himself.

* * * [To rule otherwise] would entail liability for any and all consequences, however novel or extraordinary.

DECISION AND REMEDY   *Palsgraf's complaint was dismissed. The railroad was not negligent toward her because injury to her was not foreseeable. Had the owner of the fireworks been harmed, there could well be a different result if he filed suit. Judge Cardozo indicated that while the conduct of the defendant's guards may have been a wrong against the holder of the package, it was not a wrong in relation to the plaintiff who was standing far away.*

FORESEEABILITY   Since the decision in the *Palsgraf* case, the courts have used *foreseeability* as the test for proximate cause. The railroad guards were negligent, but the railroad's duty of care did not extend to Palsgraf because she was an unforeseeable plaintiff. According to this view, a defendant's duty of care does not extend to a victim who is not located within a foreseeable zone of danger. Thus, a victim can recover damages only on proving that a reasonable person would have foreseen in the circumstances a risk of injury to him or her.

SUPERSEDING INTERVENING FORCES   A superseding intervening force may break the con-

nection between a wrongful act and injury to another. If so, it cancels out the wrongful act. For example, keeping a can of gasoline in the trunk of one's car creates a foreseeable risk and is thus a negligent act. If lightning strikes the car, exploding the gas tank *and* can, injuring passing pedestrians, the lightning supersedes the original negligence as a cause of the damage, since it was not foreseeable. This example illustrates that the doctrine of superseding intervening forces is also a matter of proximate cause and legal duty.

In other situations, the intervention of a force may not relieve one of liability. If medical maltreatment of an injury aggravates the injury, the person whose negligence originally caused the injury is not relieved of liability. If subsequent disease or a subsequent accident is proximately caused by the original injury, the person who caused the original injury will be liable for the injury caused by the subsequent disease or accident. When negligence endangers property and the owner is injured in an attempt to protect the property, the negligent party will be liable for the injury.

In negligence cases, the negligent party will often attempt to show that some act has intervened after his or her action and that this second act was the proximate cause of injury. Typically, in cases where an individual takes a defensive action, such as attempting to escape by swerving or leaping from a vehicle, the original wrongdoer will not be relieved of liability even if the injury actually resulted from the escape attempt. The same is true under the "danger invites rescue" doctrine. Under this doctrine, if Smith commits an act that endangers Jones, and Brown sustains an injury trying to protect Jones, then Smith will be liable for Brown's injury, as well as for any injuries Jones may sustain. Rescuers can injure themselves, or the person rescued, or even a stranger, but the original wrongdoer will still be liable. The following case illustrates this doctrine.

BACKGROUND AND FACTS *This case arose out of an accident that killed three men and seriously injured five others. All were sewage treatment workers. After they had corrected a water leakage problem in a New York City sewer, one of the workers, Rooney, was fatally stricken by lethal gas present in the sewer when the protective mask he was wearing failed to operate properly. A co-worker attempted to drag Rooney from the sewer tunnel, but finding himself having difficulty breathing, he released Rooney, ripped off his own mask, and yelled for help. Stephen P. Guarino and another co-worker were fatally stricken by the lethal gas present in the sewer when they left their posts in the sewer shaft and entered the sewer tunnel without masks in response to the call for help. Mary Guarino (plaintiff), the wife of Stephen P. Guarino, filed suit individually and as administrator of her husband's estate against the manufacturer of the oxygen masks (defendant). The trial court held for the plaintiff, and the manufacturer appealed.*

 Case 4.6

GUARINO v. MINE SAFETY APPLIANCE CO.

Court of Appeals of New York, 1969.

25 N.Y.2d 460, 306 N.Y.S.2d 942, 255 N.E.2d 173.

JASEN, Judge.

* * * *

This appeal presents for our review the "danger invites rescue" doctrine.

* * * *

Here the defendant committed a culpable act against the decedent Rooney, by manufacturing and distributing a defective oxygen-producing mask * * *. By virtue of this defendant's culpable act, Rooney was placed in peril, thus inviting his rescue by the plaintiffs who were all members of Rooney's sewage treatment crew. There was no time for reflection when it became known that Rooney was in need of immediate assistance in the dark tunnel some 30 to 40 feet below the street level. These plaintiffs responded to the cries for help in a manner which was reasonable and consistent with their concern for each other as members of a crew. To require that a rescuer answering the cry for help make inquiry as to the nature of the culpable act that imperils someone's life would defy all logic.

As Judge Cardozo so eloquently stated in *Wagner v. International Ry. Co.*: "Danger invites rescue. The cry of distress is the summons to relief. * * * The wrong that imperils life is a wrong to the imperilled victim; it is a wrong also to his rescuer."

* * * *

We conclude that a person who by his culpable act, whether it stems from negligence or breach of warranty, places another person in a position of imminent peril, may be held liable for any damages sustained by a rescuer in his attempt to aid the imperilled victim.

DECISION
AND REMEDY

The manufacturer of the malfunctioning oxygen mask was held liable for damages sustained by the co-workers who sought to rescue the worker overcome by sewer gas when the mask failed.

Defenses to Negligence

Basic defenses in negligence cases include assumption of risk, contributory negligence, comparative negligence, and the last-clear-chance doctrine.

ASSUMPTION OF RISK   A plaintiff who voluntarily enters into a risky situation, knowing the risk involved, will not be allowed to recover damages. This is the defense of **assumption of risk.** For example, a driver who enters a race knows that there is a risk of being killed or injured in a crash. By entering the race, the driver has thus assumed the risk of injury. The two requirements of this defense are: (1) knowledge of the risk and (2) voluntary assumption of the risk.

The risk can be assumed by express agreement, or the assumption of risk can be implied by the plaintiff's knowledge of the risk and subsequent conduct. Of course, the plaintiff does not assume a risk different from or greater than the risk normally carried by the activity. In our example, the race driver assumes the risk of being injured in the race but not the risk that the banking in the curves of the racetrack will give way during the race because of a construction defect.

Risks are not deemed to be assumed in situations involving emergencies. Neither are they assumed where a statute protects a class of people from harm and a member of the class is injured by the harm. For example, courts have generally held that an employee cannot assume the risk of an employer's violation of safety statutes passed for the benefit of employees.

CONTRIBUTORY NEGLIGENCE   All individuals are expected to exercise a reasonable degree of care in looking out for themselves. In some jurisdictions, recovery for injury resulting from negligence is prevented by failure of the injured person to have exercised such care. This is the defense of **contributory negligence,** according to which both parties have been negligent and their negligence has combined to cause the injury. When one party sues the other in tort for damages for negligence,

the defendant can claim contributory negligence, which is a complete defense under common law rules. (Contributory negligence is not, however, a defense to intentional torts or to suits based on strict liability, a topic that will be covered later.) Over the last century, the contributory negligence doctrine has been eroded considerably.

COMPARATIVE NEGLIGENCE   The modern trend is toward narrowing the scope of the defense of contributory negligence. Instead of allowing contributory negligence to negate a cause of action completely, an increasing number of states allow recovery based on the doctrine of **comparative negligence.**[8] This doctrine permits computation of both the plaintiff's and the defendant's negligence. The plaintiff's damages are reduced by a percentage that represents the degree of his or her contributing fault. In an extreme case, if the plaintiff's negligence is found to be greater than the defendant's, the plaintiff may receive nothing. Indeed, the plaintiff may be subject to counterclaim by the defendant. In jurisdictions that follow the contributory negligence doctrine, negligence on the part of the plaintiff will bar any recovery of damages. Where the comparative negligence doctrine is used, however, the plaintiff will be able to recover the percentage of damages that was due to the defendant's negligence.

LAST CLEAR CHANCE   **Last clear chance** is a doctrine that can excuse the effect of a plaintiff's contributory negligence. If applicable, the last-clear-chance rule allows the plaintiff to recover full damages despite failure to exercise care. This rule operates when, through his or her own negligence, the plaintiff is endangered (or his or her property is endangered) by a defendant who has the last clear chance to avoid the event that causes the damage. For example, if Murphy walks across the street against the light and Lewis, a motorist, sees her in time to avoid hitting her but hits her anyway, Lewis (the defendant) is not permitted to

---

8. The comparative negligence doctrine has been adopted in approximately forty-one states.

use Murphy's (the plaintiff's) prior negligence as a defense. The defendant negligently missed the opportunity to avoid injuring the plaintiff. The adoption of the comparative negligence rule has effectively abolished the last-clear-chance doctrine in some jurisdictions.

The last-clear-chance doctrine is not easy to apply. Court decisions in which it appears are often in conflict. Its correct application requires knowledge of the nature and time span of the negligence of two or more persons, as well as knowledge of split-second sequences of events and perceptions. The principal variables for last-clear-chance cases are (1) the nature of the plaintiff's

predicament and (2) the degree of the defendant's attentiveness to the plaintiff's peril. The classic last-clear-chance situation involves a helpless plaintiff and an observant defendant. In any event, the defendant's ability to have prevented the injury must be proved. It is the existence of this last clear chance that allows a plaintiff to recover damages for injury despite his or her negligence.

The following case briefly summarizes a court's consideration of the elements required for a successful negligence action, including the establishment of an act as superseding and intervening and the defenses of contributory negligence and assumption of risk.

BACKGROUND AND FACTS   *Donald Dalton (plaintiff) lived in an area that was predominantly a poultry-farming community. The Habersham Electric Membership Corporation (defendant) was aware of this and, in particular, knew that the Dalton farm was being used as a chicken farm. Furthermore, the power company knew that the chicken houses and feed bins used by the Daltons in their chicken-farming operation were constructed in proximity to its power lines. When the plaintiff's father decided that it would be necessary to build his chicken houses under the two power lines that traversed his farm at that time, he contacted the general manager of the power company, Mr. Cook. When the plaintiff's father requested that the lines be moved, Mr. Cook responded that the power company could not do this, despite the fact that Mr. Dalton offered to pay one-half the relocation cost. Three additional electric wires were installed below the original two after the feed bin in question had been installed. The installation of the wires did not meet the clearance requirement of the National Electric Safety Code. On or about October 30, 1979, Dalton, while on top of a chicken feed bin, suffered electrical burns when a tool he was using to clean the bin touched overhead high-voltage power lines owned by the defendant. He filed suit against the power company, contending that it had maintained, constructed, and inspected the lines that traversed the Dalton farm in a negligent manner and that this negligence was the proximate cause of his injury. Habersham filed a motion for a directed verdict, claiming that as a matter of law Dalton's contributory negligence caused his own injury. At the trial court, the motion for a directed verdict was denied, and the jury awarded damages to the plaintiff. The defendant appealed. On appeal, the appellate court briefly discussed contributory negligence and assumption of risk as defenses to a suit based on negligence.*

Case 4.7

HABERSHAM ELEC. MEMBERSHIP CORP. v. DALTON

Court of Appeals of Georgia, 1984.
170 Ga.App. 483, 317 S.E.2d 312.

McMURRAY, Chief Judge.

*   *   *   *

The power company owed a duty to maintain the lines "in such a manner and at such a location as not to injure persons who might be reasonably expected to come in contact with such lines." *   *   * [As an earlier court stated,] "[t]he causal connection between an original act of negligence and injury to another is not broken by the 'intervening' act *   *   * if the nature of such intervening act was such that it could reasonably have been anticipated or foreseen by the original wrongdoer." The court further added that "the foreseeability of [an intervening agency] is for the jury [to decide] where reasonable minds might differ."

In light of the evidence presented, we decline to hold that plaintiff's act [of sticking the conduit pipe handle into the overhead high-voltage power lines while cleaning the feed bin in question] was unforeseeable as a matter of law. The evidence was sufficient for the jury to find that the defendant power company should have anticipated that someone in the ordinary and usual course of farming operations, either lawfully or negligently, might strike its alleged negligently maintained wire. Similarly, we cannot conclude as a matter of law that the plaintiff's own negligence was the proximate cause of his injury, nor can we conclude that the plaintiff assumed the risk. [In a previous case, it was stated that "o]nly in plain and palpable cases will assumption of risk or contributory negligence issues be decided by the court as a matter of law." The general grounds are without merit, and the trial court did not err in denying defendant's motion for a directed verdict.

DECISION AND REMEDY   *The appellate court denied Habersham's appeal and upheld the verdict for Dalton reached by the trial court.*

STRICT LIABILITY

The final category of torts is called **strict liability,** or *liability without fault.* Intentional or negligent torts involve acts that depart from a reasonable standard of care and cause an injury. Under the doctrine of strict liability, liability for injury is imposed for reasons other than fault.

Abnormally Dangerous Activities

Strict liability for damages proximately caused by abnormally dangerous activities is one application of this doctrine. Abnormally dangerous activities have three characteristics:

1. The activity involves potential harm, of a serious nature, to persons or property.
2. The activity involves a high degree of risk that cannot be completely guarded against by the exercise of reasonable care.

3. The activity is not commonly performed in the community or area.

Strict liability is applied because of the extreme risk of the activity. Although an activity such as blasting with dynamite is performed with all reasonable care, there is still a risk of injury. Balancing that risk against the potential for harm, it is fair to ask the person engaged in the activity to pay for injury caused by the activity. Although there is no fault, there is still responsibility because of the nature of the activity. In other words, it is reasonable to require the person engaged in the activity to carry the necessary insurance or otherwise stand prepared to compensate anyone who suffers.

The following case illustrates a type of abnormally dangerous activity.

Case 4.8

YOMMER v. McKENZIE

Court of Appeals of Maryland, 1969.
255 Md. 220, 257 A.2d 138.

BACKGROUND AND FACTS   *The Yommers operated a gasoline station. In December 1967 their neighbors, the McKenzies, noticed a smell in their well water, which proved to be caused by gasoline in the well water. McKenzie complained to the Yommers, who arranged to have one of their underground storage tanks replaced. Nevertheless, the McKenzies were unable to use their water for cooking or bathing until they had a filter and water softener installed. At the time of the trial, in December 1968, they were still bringing in drinking water from an outside source.*

The McKenzies sued the Yommers for nuisance and recovered damages of
$3,500. The Yommers appealed the verdict on the grounds that the McKenzies
had not proved that there was any negligence and that a gas station is not a
nuisance.

SINGLEY, Judge.
*   *   *   *

We have previously held that the establishment of a gasoline filling station does
not constitute a nuisance *per se*, but that it may become a nuisance because of its
location or manner in which it is operated.

The argument that the McKenzies must prove negligence in order to recover fails
to take into account the doctrine of strict liability imposed by the rule of *Rylands v.*
Fletcher which has been adopted by our prior decisions.
*   *   *   *

The black letter of [Section 520 of Restatement, Second, Torts] sets out the definition:

"520. *Abnormally Dangerous Activities*

In determining whether an activity is abnormally dangerous, the following factors
are to be considered.

(a) Whether the activity involves a high degree of risk of some harm to the person,
land or chattels of others;

(b) Whether the gravity of the harm which may result from it is likely to be great;

(c) Whether the risk cannot be eliminated by the exercise of reasonable care;

(d) Whether the activity is not a matter of common usage;

(e) Whether the activity is inappropriate to the place where it is carried on; and

(f) The value of the activity to the community."

We believe that the present case is clearly within the ambit [limits] of this definition.
Although the operation of a gasoline station does not of itself involve "a high degree
of risk of some harm to the person, land or chattels of others," the placing of a large
underground gasoline tank in close proximity to the appellees' residence and well does
involve such a risk, since it is not a matter of common usage.* The harm caused to
the appellees was a serious one, and it may well have been worse if the contamination
had not been detected promptly.

Although there is no evidence of negligence on the part of the Yommers (indeed
such a showing is not required as will be discussed below), it is proper to surmise that
this risk cannot [be], or at least was not, eliminated by the exercise of reasonable care.

The fifth and perhaps most crucial factor *   *   * as applied to this case is the
appropriateness of the activity in the particular place where it is being carried on. No
one would deny that gasoline stations as a rule do not present any particular danger to
the community. However, when the operation of such activity involves the placing of
a large tank adjacent to a well from which a family must draw its water for drinking,
bathing and laundry, at least that aspect of the activity is inappropriate to the locale,
even when equated to the value of the activity.
*   *   *   *

We accept the test of appropriateness as the proper one: that the unusual, the
excessive, the extravagant, the bizarre are likely to be non-natural uses which lead to
strict liability.
*   *   *   *

It is apparent to us that the storage of large quantities of gasoline immediately
adjacent to a private residence comes within this rule and relieved the McKenzies of
the necessity of proving negligence. *   *   *

---

* "An activity is a matter of common usage if it is customarily carried on by the great mass of mankind, or by
many people in the community. *   *   * Gas and electricity in household pipes and wires [are examples of
common usage], as contrasted with large gas storage tanks or high tension power lines." Restatement, Torts 2d,
[Section 520,] comment on clause (d) at 65–66.

DECISION AND REMEDY *The Yommers lost on appeal; the judgment for the McKenzies was upheld. There was no need to prove negligence in the case because the nature of the activity and the location of the tank caused the Yommers to be held strictly liable for the gasoline seepage.*

Other Applications of Strict Liability

There are other applications of the strict liability principle, notably in the workers' compensation acts and in the area of product liability. Liability here is a matter of social policy, and it is based on two factors: (1) the ability of the employer and manufacturer to better bear the cost of injury by spreading it out to society through an increase in the cost of goods and services and (2) the fact that the employer and manufacturer are making a profit from their activities and therefore should bear the cost of injury as an operating expense. Product liability will be considered in depth in Chapter 21.

CONCEPT SUMMARY: Common Basic Torts

KINDS	DEFINITIONS AND RULES
1. Intentional torts against a person	
a. Assault and battery	Unexcused and intentional act that creates in another apprehension or fear of immediate harm is assault and, if it results in physical contact, battery.
b. False imprisonment	Intentional confinement or restraint of another person's movement without consent or justification.
c. Libel or slander	False statement of fact, not made under privilege, which is communicated to a third person and which causes damage to a person's reputation or disparagement of a product. For public figures, the plaintiff must also prove malice.
d. Invasion of privacy	1. Use of a person's name, picture, or other likeness for commercial purposes without permission. 2. Intrusion into an individual's affairs or seclusion.
e. Misrepresentation	Misrepresentation of facts or conditions made with knowledge of their falsity or reckless disregard for their truth. Elements also include intent to induce another to rely on the misrepresentation, the other's justifiable reliance on the misrepresentation, and damages caused by the misrepresentation.
2. Intentional torts against property a. Trespass to land	Invasion onto another's real property without consent or privilege. Rights and duties apply once a person is established expressly or impliedly as a trespasser. Rights and Duties 1. Trespassers are liable for damages they cause to the property. 2. Trespassers assume the risks of the premises unless the premises are held to be an "attractive nuisance." 3. Owner cannot lay traps and may have a duty to warn of dangers on the property. 4. Trespassers can be removed through use of reasonable force without owner being liable for assault and battery.

CONCEPT SUMMARY: Common Basic Torts (Continued)

KINDS	DEFINITIONS AND RULES
b. Trespass to personal property or conversion	Unlawfully damaging or interfering with the owner's right to use, possess, or enjoy his or her personal property. When personal property of the owner is wrongfully converted to the use of the trespasser, conversion occurs.
3. Unintentional torts a. Negligence	Careless performance of or failure to perform a legally required act. A legal duty must exist, the defendant must have breached that duty, and the breach must have caused damage or injury.
b. Strict liability	Liability for damages or injuries caused by a product or activity regardless of fault. This includes liability for defective products and abnormally dangerous activities.

QUESTIONS AND CASE PROBLEMS

1. Richards is an employee of the Dun Construction Corporation. While delivering materials to a construction site, he carelessly runs Dun's truck into a passenger vehicle driven by Green. This is Richard's second accident in six months. When Dun learns of this latest accident, a heated discussion ensues, and Dun fires Richards. Dun is so angry that he immediately writes a letter to the union of which Richards is a member and to all other construction outfits in the community, stating that Richards is the "worst driver in the city" and that "anyone who hires him is asking for legal liability." Richards files suit against Dun, alleging libel on the basis of the statements made in the letters. Discuss the results.

2. It is a cold, wintry day. Ken needs to do some shopping on his way home from work. He is running late and is in a hurry. He stops at a drugstore to buy a tube of toothpaste on sale. He sticks the toothpaste in his overcoat pocket, laying the correct amount of change for the purchase on the counter. He is proceeding home when he suddenly remembers his wife's request that he pick up some much-needed groceries. He stops at a grocery store and rushes through the store picking up the groceries. He checks out and in a slow trot starts to leave the store when the checkout clerk sees the toothpaste in his overcoat pocket. Believing Ken is attempting to leave the store without declaring the item, the clerk yells, "Stop, thief!" Two bagboys grab Ken and haul him, struggling and protesting, to a small, dark back room, where he is locked in. One hour later, the store manager gets back from dinner, learns of the events, and, after questioning a distraught Ken, lets him go. Ken starts having nightmares, acquires backaches, and becomes extremely nervous when friends and neighbors look at him.

Discuss fully whether any torts have been committed against Ken.

3. Frank is a former employee of ABC Auto Repair Company. He enters the property of ABC, claiming the company owes him $150 in back wages. An argument ensues, and the ABC general manager, Steward, orders Frank off the property. Frank refuses to leave, and Steward orders two mechanics to throw him off the property. Frank runs to his truck, but on the way he grabs some tools valued at $150. Frank gets into his truck and, in his haste to drive away, destroys a gatepost. Frank refuses to return the tools.

(a) Discuss whether Frank has committed any torts.

(b) If the mechanics had thrown Frank off the property, would ABC be guilty of assault and battery? Explain.

4. John is a delivery employee for Crystal Glass, Inc. He is making a delivery when, at an intersection, his van and the passenger car of Jane collide. Jane wants to hold both John and Crystal Glass liable for the damages she has sustained. John claims that Jane was also at fault, at least as much at fault as he, and therefore neither he nor Crystal should be liable. Discuss fully these claims.

5. Ruth carelessly parks her car on a steep hill, leaving the car in neutral and failing to engage the parking brake. The car rolls down the hill, knocking down an electric line. The sparks from the broken line ignite a grass fire. The fire spreads until it reaches a barn one mile away. The barn has dynamite inside, and the burning barn explodes, causing part of the roof to fall upon and injure a passing motorist, Jim. Can Jim recover from Ruth? Why or why not?

6. Professor Ronald R. Hutchinson received federal funding for animal (monkey) studies on aggression. United States Senator William Proxmire bestowed his Golden Fleece of the Month Award on the federal agency that funded Hutchinson's research. The purpose of the award was to publicize wasteful government spending. Senator Proxmire announced the award in a speech prepared for and given to the Senate. The speech was reprinted in a press release

mailed to 275 members of the news media and in a newsletter sent to 100,000 people. Proxmire described the federal grants for Hutchinson's research, among other critical comments, as "monkey business." Hutchinson sued Proxmire for defamation. The U.S. district court and court of appeals confirmed Senator Proxmire's claims that his communication was privileged and that Professor Hutchinson was a public figure who had not proved there was malice. Is either of Senator Proxmire's claims a valid defense? [Hutchinson v. Proxmire, 443 U.S. 111, 99 S.Ct. 2675, 61 L.Ed.2d 411 (1979)]

7. H. E. Butt Grocery Company (H.E.B.) has numerous retail grocery stores scattered throughout the state of Texas. Hawkins went to grocery shop at one of the H.E.B. stores. A heavy rainstorm and north wind had caused water to be tracked into the store by customers and water to be blown through the door each time it was opened. As Hawkins entered through the automatically opened door, she slipped and fell in approximately one-half inch of rain water that had accumulated on the floor. The manager knew of the weather conditions and had employees mop the floor on numerous occasions. There was no sign posted warning customers of the water hazard. Can Hawkins recover from H.E.B. for injuries sustained from slipping on the water-covered floor? [H. E. Butt Grocery Co. v. Hawkins, 594 S.W.2d 187 (Tex.Civ.App. 1980)]

8. O'Neill was injured when he was struck in the eye by a softball thrown by Daniels, a teammate, during warm-up activities before an amateur softball game. O'Neill claimed Daniels was negligent and filed suit. Discuss the probable success of O'Neill's suit in light of the fact that the injury occurred during the warm-up activities. [O'Neill v. Daniels, 135 A.D.2d 1076, 523 N.Y.S.2d 264 (1987)]

9. The Merritts (plaintiffs) purchased a 1984 Mercury from Bernie Hughes Lincoln Mercury (defendants). The plaintiffs subsequently had numerous problems with the automobile. One problem concerned damage to the tires caused by defective construction of the automobile. Ford Motor Company granted the plaintiffs a rebate, which was reflected in the dealership records as being held on a parts account in the name of the Merritts. The money was never paid to the plaintiffs. There is conflicting testimony as to whether or not the plaintiffs made a demand for the money that had been credited to their account. The plaintiffs sued for conversion of their account. What is the result? [Bernie Hughes Lincoln Mercury v. Merritt, 523 So.2d 441 (Ala.Civ.App. 1988)]

10. Dun & Bradstreet, the well-known credit-reporting agency, included false information concerning Greenmoss Builders in a computerized letter sent to several of its subscribers. The false information was that Greenmoss had filed for bankruptcy, when, in fact, it had not. The erroneous report resulted in a loss of business and income for Greenmoss, and, because of these damages, Greenmoss sued Dun & Bradstreet for defamation. The trial court held for Greenmoss and awarded substantial damages. Dun & Bradstreet appealed. Discuss whether a showing of malice is required on the part of Dun & Bradstreet before Greenmoss can recover damages for defamation. [Dun & Bradstreet, Inc. v. Greenmoss Builders, Inc., 464 U.S. 959, 104 S.Ct. 389, 78 L.Ed.2d 334 (1983)]

11. Friedman Steel Sales, Inc., owns several flatbed trucks, which it uses in connection with its business of buying and selling steel. A. J. Hendrix, a driver for Friedman, returned from a delivery in one of the trucks, parked it in the Friedman yard, and gave the keys to the warehouse supervisor. The supervisor later parked the truck in the parking lot across the street, removed the keys, and placed them in the office; he locked the office before going home. After locking the truck, he placed the chains used to secure steel during transport on the barrier ("headache" rack) between the cab and trailer bed of the truck. The chains were not locked down. That night, the truck and trailer were stolen from the parking lot. They were later discovered at the scene of an accident in which Raymond Combs, the father of the plaintiff, was killed. The death occurred when Combs, traveling north on Highway 59, collided with the flatbed trailer. The trailer had been abandoned, without lights, on the highway, blocking both northbound lanes. An accident investigation revealed that the headache rack had been torn from the truck when the cargo chains fell and tangled in the wheels of the truck, severing the airbrake hose and bringing the truck to a stop on the highway. The trial court jury held that the defendant, Friedman Steel Sales, Inc., was negligent in failing to lock down the chains on the cargo rack and that this was the proximate cause of Combs's injuries and subsequent death. Damages were set at $334,649. Friedman moved for a judgment notwithstanding the verdict, which the trial court granted. The plaintiff appealed. What will result? [Wolf v. Friedman Steel Sales, Inc., 717 S.W.2d 669 (Tex.App.—Texarkana 1986)]

Chapter 5

Torts Related to Business

Our economic system of free enterprise is predicated on the ability of individuals, acting either as individuals or as business firms, to compete for customers and for sales. Unfettered competitive behavior has been shown to lead to economic efficiency and economic progress. On the other hand, overly enthusiastic competitive efforts sometimes fall into the realm of intentional torts and crimes. Businesses may, generally speaking, engage in whatever is *reasonably* necessary to obtain a fair share of a market or to recapture a share that has been lost. But they are not allowed to use the motive of completely eliminating competition to justify certain business activities. Thus, an entire area of what is called business torts has arisen. **Business torts** are defined as wrongful interference with another's business rights. Included in business torts are such vaguely worded concepts as *unfair competition* and *interfering with the business relations of others*. Because the field is so broad, it is necessary to restrict this discussion to the following causes of action, which are presented in terms of general categories:

1. Wrongful interference with a contractual relationship.
2. Wrongful interference with a business relationship.
3. Wrongfully entering into business.
4. Infringement of trademarks, trade names, patents, and copyrights.
5. Disparagement of property or reputation.

Following our discussion of these torts, we consider the application of the Racketeer Influenced and Corrupt Organizations Act (known more popularly as RICO) to fraudulent business activities.

WRONGFUL INTERFERENCE WITH A CONTRACTUAL RELATIONSHIP

The body of tort law relating to *intentional interference with a contractual relationship* has increased greatly in recent years. A landmark case in this area involved an opera singer, Joanna Wagner, who was under contract to sing for a man named Lumley for a specified period of years.[1] A man named Gye, who knew of this contract, nonetheless "enticed" Wagner to refuse

---

1. Lumley v. Gye, 118 Eng.Rep. 749 (1853).

to carry out the agreement, and Wagner began to sing for Gye. Gye's action constituted a tort because it interfered with the contractual relationship between Wagner and Lumley. (Wagner's refusal to carry out the agreement also entitled Lumley to sue for breach of contract.)

In principle, any lawful contract can be the basis for an action of this type. The plaintiff must prove that the defendant actually induced the breach of a contractual relationship, not merely that the defendant reaped the benefits of a broken contract. If Jones has a contract with Smith that calls for Smith to mow Jones's lawn every week for a year at a specified price, Jones cannot sue Miller when Smith breaches the contract merely because Miller now receives gardening services from Smith.

Three basic elements are necessary to the existence of wrongful interference with a contractual relationship:

1. A valid, enforceable contract must exist between two parties.
2. A third party must *know* that this contract exists.

3. This third party must *intentionally* cause either of the two parties to the contract to break the contract. Whether this third party acts in bad faith or with malice is immaterial to establishing this tort, even though in most cases malice or bad faith is in evidence. The interference, however, must be for the purpose of advancing the economic or pecuniary interest of the inducer.

The contract may be between a firm and its employees or a firm and its customers. Sometimes a competitor of a firm may attempt to draw away a key employee, even to the extent of paying the damages for breach of contract. If the original employer can show that the competitor induced the breach—that is, that the employee would not normally have broken the contract—damages can be recovered.

The following, highly publicized case illustrates the requirements for the tort of wrongful interference with a contractual relationship.

Case 5.1

TEXACO, INC. v. PENNZOIL CO.

Court of Appeals of Texas, First District, 1987.
729 S.W.2d 768.

BACKGROUND AND FACTS *Pennzoil had made an offer to buy control of Getty Oil and had negotiated the offer with the major stockholders, Gordon Getty and the Getty Museum. A Memorandum of Agreement was made subject to the agreement of Getty's board of directors. The board declined to approve the arrangement and made a counteroffer; the board also began looking for other potential bidders. Although some details of the agreement remained unsettled, Pennzoil eventually accepted one of Getty's offers. The news was announced by both companies and reported widely in newspapers, including the Wall Street Journal, on January 5, 1984. While the lawyers from each company were negotiating a formal and specific written document, Getty's investment banker continued to look for another bidder. Texaco made a bid that Getty's board promptly accepted on January 6. Pennzoil subsequently sued Texaco, alleging tortious interference with its contract with Getty Oil.*

The trial court jury found that (1) Getty had agreed to Pennzoil's offer to purchase its stock; (2) Texaco knowingly interfered with this agreement; (3) as a result of Texaco's interference, Pennzoil suffered damages of $7.53 billion; (4) Texaco's actions were intentional, willful, and in wanton disregard of Pennzoil's rights; and (5) Pennzoil was entitled to punitive damages of $3 billion. Texaco appealed. Among a number of points of error claimed by Texaco, the appellate court examined (1) whether Pennzoil and Getty actually had a contract, (2) whether Texaco knew that a contract existed between Getty and Pennzoil, and (3) whether Texaco acted to interfere with this contract.

WARREN, Justice.

*   *   *   *

Texaco contends that under controlling principles of *   *   * law, there was insufficient evidence to support the jury's finding that at the end of the Getty Oil board meeting *   *   *, the Getty entities intended to bind themselves to an agreement with Pennzoil.

*   *   *   *

Under [applicable principles of] law, if *   *   * there is no understanding that a signed writing is necessary before the parties will be bound, and the parties have agreed upon all substantial terms, then an informal agreement can be binding, even though the parties contemplate evidencing their agreement in a formal document later.

*   *   *   *

The record as a whole demonstrates that there was legally and factually sufficient evidence to support the jury's finding *   *   * that the Trust, the Museum, and the Company intended to bind themselves to an agreement with Pennzoil at the end of the Getty Oil board meeting *   *   *.

*   *   *   *

Texaco's next points of error concern the jury's finding *   *   * that Texaco knowingly interfered with the agreement, if so found, between Pennzoil and the Getty entities. Texaco contends that the evidence is legally and factually insufficient to show that Texaco had actual knowledge of any agreement, that it actively induced breach of the alleged contract, and that the alleged contract was valid and capable of being interfered with.

[T]he commentary to the Restatement (Second) of Torts describes the knowledge requirement as follows:

> *Actor's knowledge of other's contract.* To be subject to liability . . . the actor must have knowledge of the contract with which he is interfering. . . . [I]t is not necessary that the actor appreciate the legal significance of the facts giving rise to the contractual duty. . . . If he knows those facts, he is subject to liability even though he is mistaken as to their legal significance and believes that the agreement is not legally binding. . . .

[The court considered points in Texaco's arguments and then turned to Pennzoil's counterarguments.]

Pennzoil responds that *   *   * the jury could reasonably infer that Texaco knew about the Pennzoil deal from the evidence of (1) how Texaco carefully mapped its strategy to defeat Pennzoil's deal by acting to "stop the train" or "stop the signing"; (2) the notice of a contract given by a January 5 Wall Street Journal article reporting on the Pennzoil agreement—an article that Texaco denied anyone at Texaco had seen; (3) the knowledge of an agreement that would arise from comparing the Memorandum of Agreement with the Getty press release; (4) the demands made by the Museum and the Trust for full indemnity from Texaco against any claims by Pennzoil arising out of the Memorandum of Agreement; and (5) the Museum's demand that, even if the Texaco deal fell through, the Museum would be guaranteed the price Pennzoil had agreed to pay for the Museum's shares. *   *   *

*   *   *   *

The jury was not required to accept Texaco's version of events in this case, and this Court may not substitute its own interpretation of the evidence for the decision of the trier of fact. There was legally and factually sufficient evidence to support an inference by the jury that Texaco had the required knowledge of an agreement. *   *   *

*   *   *   *

A necessary element of the plaintiff's cause of action is a showing that the defendant took an active part in persuading a party to a contract to breach it. Merely entering into a contract with a party with the knowledge of that party's contractual obligations to someone else is not the same as inducing a breach. It is necessary that there be some act of interference or of persuading a party to breach, for example by offering better terms or other incentives, for tort liability to arise. The issue of whether a defendant affirmatively took steps to induce the breach of an existing contract is a question of fact for the jury.

* * * Texaco argues that it merely responded to a campaign of active solicitation by Getty Oil and the Museum, who were dissatisfied by the terms of Pennzoil's offer.

[The court reviewed the events and testimony concerning whether Texaco actively induced the breach or whether Getty's actions induced the Texaco offer. The court concluded as follows:]

Texaco argues that its testimony shows that Getty Oil and the Museum were the real moving forces that eventually led to the Texaco contract. However, we find that there is legally and factually sufficient evidence in the record to support the jury's finding that Texaco actively induced the breach of the Getty entities' agreement with Pennzoil.

DECISION AND REMEDY

Although the facts in the case were disputed, the appellate court accepted the findings of the jury and affirmed the lower court's decision. The Supreme Court of Texas later found no reversible errors in this decision. Other federal issues in the case were appealed as high as the U.S. Supreme Court.

WRONGFUL INTERFERENCE WITH A BUSINESS RELATIONSHIP

Individuals devise countless schemes to attract business, but they are forbidden by the courts to interfere unreasonably with another's business in their attempts to gain a share of the market. There is a difference between *competition* and *predatory behavior*. The distinction usually depends on whether a business is attempting to attract customers in general or to solicit only those customers who have already shown an interest in the similar product or service of a specific competitor. If a shopping center contains two shoe stores, an employee of Store A cannot be positioned at the entrance of Store B for the purpose of diverting customers to Store A. This type of activity constitutes the tort of wrongful interference with a business relationship, often referred to as interference with a prospective economic advantage, and is commonly considered to be an unfair trade practice. If this type of activity were permitted, Store A would reap the benefits of Store B's advertising.

A salesperson cannot follow another company's salesperson through the city, soliciting the same prospective customers. Even though the people contacted may have purchased nothing from the first salesperson, that salesperson still has a business relationship with them. Courts will issue injunctions against this kind of behavior and will award damages when the business alleging interference can prove it suffered a monetary loss. In the following case a salesperson's activities exceeded the bounds of fair competition.

Case 5.2

AZAR v. LEHIGH CORP.

District Court of Appeal of Florida, Second District, 1978. 364 So.2d 860.

BACKGROUND AND FACTS *Lehigh Corporation, a developer of real estate, obtained a restraining order (which is similar to an injunction) against one of its former sales representatives, Leroy Azar. Lehigh brought prospective customers to its development, Lehigh Acres, and provided accommodations at its company-owned motel. Azar pursued a practice of following Lehigh purchasers and persuading them to rescind (cancel) their contracts with Lehigh and purchase less expensive property from him.*

The circuit court issued the following order:

IT IS HEREBY ORDERED AND ADJUDGED that the Defendant, Leroy Azar, is hereby restrained and enjoined from directly or indirectly contacting or soliciting the Plaintiff's perspective [sic] or actual customers on the premises of the Lehigh Resort Motel or at the sales offices of the Plaintiffs if such purchasers are in Lee County as guests of the Plaintiffs. "Guests" of the Plaintiffs shall mean persons who have been invited by the Plaintiffs, either directly or indirectly, to view the Lehigh Acres community and real estate situate therein. "Invited" shall mean those persons who have come to the Lehigh Acres community as a result of any promotional activities of the Plaintiffs wherein some incentive of value has been given or offered to said persons. The "Defendant," Leroy Azar, shall include any person or entity acting in the Defendant's behalf or at the urging of the Defendant, Leroy Azar.

Azar contended that Lehigh's customers had a right under federal law to rescind their contracts within three days and that he was merely providing them with an opportunity to be relieved of their contracts and to obtain comparable property for lower prices. Lehigh asserted that Azar was tortiously interfering with the advantageous business relationship between Lehigh and its customers.

GRIMES, Chief Justice.
*   *   *   *
[T]he elements of [the tort of interference with business are] as follows:
    (1) the existence of a business relationship under which the plaintiff has legal rights, (2) an intentional and unjustified interference with that relationship by the defendant, and (3) damage to the plaintiff as a result of the breach of the business relationship. *   *   *
It is not essential, however, that the business relationship be founded upon an enforceable contract. *   *   *

There is a narrow line between what constitutes vigorous competition in a free enterprise society and malicious interference with a favorable business relationship. Under the heading of "Interference with prospective advantage," Prosser states:
    Though trade warfare may be waged to the bitter end, there are certain rules of combat which must be observed. . . . W. Prosser, Law of Torts (4th ed. 1971) at 956.

He goes on to say that the courts have generally prohibited such activities as defamation of the competitor, disparagement of his goods and his business methods, and intimidation, harassment and annoyance of his customers. In the final analysis, the issue seems to turn upon whether the subject conduct is considered to be "unfair" according to contemporary business standards.

Keeping in mind the trial judge's broad discretion to enter temporary restraining orders, we believe there is sufficient evidence in this record to support the court's decision. Moreover, we believe the terms of the order are precise enough for the appellant to understand what he cannot do. Considering appellant's knowledge of Lehigh's operation, we are confident that he will have no difficulty in ascertaining which of the motel patrons constitute appellees' guests as defined in the temporary restraining order.

The restraining order against Azar was allowed to stand. Azar remained under court order not to solicit business from those customers brought to Lehigh Acres by Lehigh Corporation.

DECISION AND REMEDY

Defenses to Wrongful Interference with a Contractual or Business Relationship

Justification is the defense used most often against the accusation of the tort of wrongful interference with a contractual or business relationship. For example, bona fide competitive behavior is a privileged interference even if it results in the breaking of a contract. If Jones Meats advertises so effectively that it induces Sam's Restaurant Chain to break its contract with Paul's Meat Company, Paul's Meat Company will be unable to recover against Jones Meats on a wrongful interference theory. After all, the public policy that favors free competition in advertising definitely outweighs any possible instability that such competitive activity might cause in contractual relations.

Permissive Interferences

Permissive interferences are interfering actions that the courts have not held to be tortious interferences. For example, luring customers away from a competitor through aggressive marketing and advertising strategies obviously interferes with the competitor's relationship with his or her customers, but such activity is permitted by the courts. Also, so long as there is no associated illegal activity, a businessperson will not incur tort liability for negotiating secretly behind a rival's back, refusing to do business with a competitor, or refusing to deal with third parties until they stop doing business with a rival.

WRONGFULLY ENTERING INTO BUSINESS

In a freely competitive society it is usually true that any person can enter into any business in order to compete for the customers of existing businesses. Two situations in which this general notion of free competition does not hold, however, are (1) when entering into a business is in violation of law and (2) when competitive behavior is predatory in nature.

Entering a Business in Violation of the Law

Although we live in a free enterprise system, government at all levels—local, state, and federal—restricts who may enter certain businesses. Indeed, there exists a whole area of regulated economic activities in which people cannot engage unless they first obtain permission from a regulatory agency or commission. Although the trend is toward increasing deregulation, the number of businesses under such regulation is still large. For example, a group of people could not simply agree among themselves to start a business competitive with their local electric company or natural gas company. First they would have to gain approval from the public utility, or service, commission in their state—approval that the commission would be highly unlikely to grant. As another example, one cannot simply put up a radio or television transmitter and start transmitting on some frequency believed to be open. A license is necessary. The Federal Communications Commission grants all licenses for both television and radio, and these allow operation only on designated frequencies.

Many occupations require licenses in the United States. Not only are lawyers, physicians, and dentists licensed, but so are palm readers and astrologers. In many states the licensed member of a profession is allowed to bring action on behalf of the entire profession in order to prevent an unlicensed individual from practicing that occupation.

Predatory Competitive Activities

Any business or profession not subject to regulatory agencies or occupational licensing standards is open to an individual; however, no one can open a business for the sole purpose of driving another firm out of business. Such a predatory motive for opening a business is considered to constitute *simulated competition*.

What the courts consider normal competitive activity is not always easy to ascertain. One might ask when the normal desire to compete and obtain profits ends and when a tortious action begins. The courts often emphasize parties' bad motives, but the cases often involve conduct that would be objectionable anyway—for example, efforts that are directed toward driving a competitor out of business are objectionable for the same reasons that led to the enactment of antitrust laws (see Chapter 48). The landmark case that follows illustrates how a Minnesota court grappled with the question of malicious injury to business.

BACKGROUND AND FACTS *The plaintiff, Edward Tuttle, filed suit against the defendant, Cassius Buck, for malicious interference with his barbershop in the small village of Howard Lake, Minnesota. The plaintiff had owned and operated the shop for the previous ten years and had been able to maintain himself and his family comfortably from the income of the business. The defendant was a banker in the same community who "maliciously" established a competitive barbershop. The defendant employed a barber to carry on the business and used his personal influence to attract customers from the plaintiff's barbershop. Apparently, the defendant circulated false and malicious reports and accusations about the plaintiff and personally solicited and persuaded many of the plaintiff's patrons to stop using the plaintiff's services; indeed, the defendant used his personal power as the town's banker to threaten some customers in order to force them to use the defendant's shop instead. The plaintiff charged that the defendant undertook this entire plan with the sole design of injuring the plaintiff and destroying his business, not for serving any legitimate business interest. The trial court's decision for the plaintiff was affirmed by the appellate court, and the defendant appealed.*

 Case 5.3

TUTTLE v. BUCK
Supreme Court of Minnesota, 1909.
107 Minn. 145, 119 N.W. 946.

ELLIOTT, Justice.

*   *   *   *

*   *   * It is not at all correct to say that the motive with which an act is done is always immaterial, providing the act itself is not unlawful. *   *   *

*   *   * For generations there has been a practical agreement upon the proposition that competition in trade and business is desirable, and this idea has found expression in the decisions of the courts as well as in statutes. But it has led to grievous and manifold wrongs to individuals, and many courts have manifested an earnest desire to protect the individuals from the evils which result from unrestrained business competition. The problem has been to so adjust matters as to preserve the principle of competition and yet guard against its abuse to the unnecessary injury to the individual. So the principle that man may use his own property according to his own needs and desires, while true in the abstract, is subject to many limitations in the concrete. Men cannot always, in civilized society, be allowed to use their own property as their interests or desires may dictate without reference to the fact that they have neighbors whose rights are as sacred as their own. The existence and well-being of society requires that each and every person shall conduct himself consistently with the fact that he is a social and reasonable person. The purpose for which a man is using his own property may thus sometimes determine his rights. "If there exists, then, a positive duty to avoid harm, much more, then, exists the negative duty of not doing willful harm, subject, as all general duties must be subject, to the necessary exceptions. The three main heads of duty with which the law of torts is concerned, namely, to abstain from willful injury, to respect the property of others, and to use due diligence to avoid causing harm to others, are all alike of a comprehensive nature." Pollock, Torts, (8th Ed.) p. 21.

*   *   * To divert to one's self the customers of a business rival by the offer of goods at lower prices is in general a legitimate mode of serving one's own interest, and justifiable as fair competition. But when a man starts an opposition place of business, not for the sake of profit to himself, but regardless of loss to himself, and for the sole purpose of driving his competitor out of business, and with the intention of himself retiring upon the accomplishment of his malevolent purpose, he is guilty of a wanton wrong and an actionable tort. In such a case he would not be exercising his legal right, or doing an act which can be judged separately from the motive which actuated him. To call such conduct competition is a perversion of terms. It is simply the application of force without legal justification, which in its moral quality may be no better than highway robbery.

DECISION   *The plaintiff's cause of action was recognized under Minnesota law. The Supreme*
AND REMEDY   *Court of Minnesota concluded that modern business requires certain protection*
against abusive business practices. Minnesota recognized a cause of action for
tortious interference with business relations.

INFRINGEMENT OF TRADEMARKS, TRADE NAMES, PATENTS, AND COPYRIGHTS

Perhaps the central tort in unfair competition at common law is what is known as *passing off*, which is falsely inducing buyers to believe that one product is another, usually because the other product is well-known or has a reputation for quality. Recent examples abound—jeans, perfume, cameras, and a variety of other consumer goods have been passed off through reputable merchants. It has been estimated that $10 billion in goods are passed off each year; in at least one instance, it was estimated that as much as 17 percent of the amount purportedly representing a product's sales did not represent sales of the actual product.

Commonly, passing off constitutes infringement of a trademark, a trade name, a patent, or a copyright. The basic question is whether the ordinary customer, paying the usual amount of attention, would be deceived.

Infringement of Trademarks and Service Marks

A **trademark** is a distinctive mark, motto, device, or emblem that a manufacturer stamps, prints, or otherwise affixes to the goods it produces, so that they may be distinguished from the goods of other manufacturers and merchants. At common law, the person who used a symbol or mark to identify a business or product was protected in the use of that trademark. Clearly, if one used the trademark of another, one would mislead consumers into believing that one's goods were made by the other. The law seeks to avoid the kind of confusion that would result if trademarks were not protected. Normally, personal names, words, or places that are descriptive of an article or its use cannot be trademarked; they are available to anyone. Words

that are used as part of a design or device, however, or words that are uncommon or fanciful may be trademarked.

Consider an example. *English Leather* may not be trademarked to describe leather processed in England. On the other hand, *English Leather* may be, and is, trademarked as a name for after-shave lotion, since this constitutes a *fanciful* use of the words. Consider also that even the common name of an individual may be trademarked if that name is accompanied by a picture or some fanciful design that allows for easy identification of the product—for example, Smith Brothers' Cough Drops.

A **service mark** is similar to a trademark but is used to distinguish the services of one person from those of another. For example, each airline has a particular mark or symbol associated with its name. Titles or character names used in radio and television are frequently registered as service marks.

WHEN INFRINGEMENT OCCURS   Once a trademark has been registered, a firm is entitled to its exclusive use for marketing purposes. Whenever that trademark is copied to a substantial degree or used in its entirety by another, intentionally or unintentionally, the trademark has been infringed. The trademark need not be registered with the state or with the federal government in order to obtain protection from the tort of trademark infringement, but registration does furnish proof of the date of inception of its use. Moreover, registration may prolong the life of the trademark. Registration is renewable between the fifth and sixth years after the initial registration and every twenty years thereafter, so long as the mark remains distinctive and is used. Service marks are registered in the same manner as trademarks.

The defendant firm in the following case was liable for trademark infringement even though it did not manufacture the article.

BACKGROUND AND FACTS *The plaintiff, Vuitton et Fils, S.A., is a French corporation that manufactures expensive handbags and distributes them through an exclusive retail network in the United States. (S.A. stands for* société anonyme, *which is the French equivalent of a corporation.) The handbags are of high quality and bear the Vuitton registered trademark, the firm's initials and a* fleur de lis. *Robert Cullen was employed by Vuitton as a private investigator and by chance passed the defendant's shop window, where two handbags bearing the Vuitton trademark were hanging. The defendant, Crown Handbags, was not a retail outlet for Vuitton handbags. The defendant offered to sell Cullen six handbags in a bulk transaction. At the trial, the handbags were shown to be cheap imitations of Vuitton's product. Vuitton sued Crown Handbags for infringement of its registered trademark.*

 Case 5.4

VUITTON ET FILS, S.A. v. CROWN HANDBAGS

District Court, Southern District of New York, 1979.
492 F.Supp. 1071.

BRIEANT, District Judge.

*   *   *   *

The goal of the framers of the Lanham Trade-Mark Act [of 1946] was to secure to the owner of a trademark the goodwill of his business, and at the same time protect the buying public against spurious and falsely marked goods. The Vuitton trademark has been used in connection with the advertising and sale of goods in commerce for over 46 years since its entry upon the Principal Trademark Register of the United States Patent Office in 1932. The trademark, #297,594, specifically refers to "handbags and pocketbooks" as items to which the mark would be affixed. Defendant makes no effort to challenge the validity or ownership of the Vuitton mark.

It remains to be determined whether defendant's actions in offering for sale copies of genuine Vuitton handbags was an infringement of plaintiff's registered mark within the meaning of 15 U.S.C. ₰ 1114 which provides in pertinent part:

"1) Any person who shall, without the consent of the registrant—

(a) use in commerce any reproduction, counterfeit copy, or colorable imitation of a registered mark in connection with the sale, offering for sale, distribution, or advertising of any goods or services on or in connection with which such use is likely to cause confusion, or to cause mistake, or to deceive . . . shall be liable in a civil action by the registrant for the remedies hereinafter provided."

Where an alleged infringing mark is used in connection with the sale of similar goods, the long standing rule in this Circuit has been that the second comer to the marketplace "has a duty to so name and dress his product as to avoid all likelihood of consumers confusing it with the product of the first comer." The second comer has no right to trade upon the good will of the first comer developed over a period of time and at considerable expense. As our Court of Appeals in this Circuit ruled many years ago:

"It is so easy for the honest business man, who wishes to sell his goods upon their merits, to select from the entire material universe, which is before him, symbols, marks and coverings which by no possibility can cause confusion between his goods and those of his competitors, that the courts look with suspicion upon one who, in dressing his goods for the market, approaches so near to his successful rival that the public may fail to distinguish between them."

The great weight of the evidence in the case leads to the conclusion that the Vuitton trademark is a strong mark, and as such is entitled to broad protection. The strength of the mark stems from its conspicuously distinctive nature. It is unique in its design and color, and during the more than 46 years of its continuous use in this country it has come to represent a source of product of perceived quality and prestige. *   *   *

It would be impossible for one engaged in the same trade as plaintiff is, and defendant is so engaged, to be unaware of the presence of the counterfeits in the trade.

Nor could such a person be unaware of the plaintiff's rights to its valued mark. I find that defendant was a willful violator.

* * * *

Both Vuitton and consumers in general would suffer by the purchase of counterfeit bags of inferior quality. Vuitton would soon lose its reputation for quality and exclusivity, and consumers would be deceived into believing they were getting something they were not.

Defendant clearly infringed upon plaintiff's registered trademark in violation of 15 U.S.C. § 1114, by offering for sale a combination of product and trademark which exactly mimics that of plaintiff, resulting in the type of confusion and deception which the Lanham Act was designed to prevent. In doing so, defendant acted willfully and with knowledge of the fact that these handbags which it offered for sale infringed upon the trademark rights of plaintiff. Defendant was in the business of manufacturing leather handbags in New York. As noted earlier, logic dictates that it must be charged with actual as well as constructive knowledge of plaintiff's mark and merchandise. The counterfeit bags were manufactured with the intention to trade upon the plaintiff's established reputation for quality merchandise. Although defendant apparently did not itself manufacture the infringing articles, it took an active part in their distribution and sale, making use of plaintiff's trademark in the process.

DECISION AND REMEDY   *Vuitton was granted permanent injunctive relief from Crown Handbag's commercial practices that violated Vuitton's trademark rights. Crown had to pay damages amounting to the sales price of the six handbags offered to Vuitton's investigator. Crown also had to pay Vuitton's attorneys' fees.*

CERTIFICATION AND COLLECTIVE MARKS   A certification mark is used by one or more persons, other than the owner, to certify the region, materials, mode of manufacture, quality, or accuracy of the owner's goods or services. When used by members of a cooperative, association, or other organization, it is referred to as a collective mark. Examples of certification marks are the "Good Housekeeping Seal of Approval" and "UL Tested." Collective marks appear at the ends of the credits of movies to indicate the various associations and organizations that participated in the making of the movies. The union marks found on the tags of certain products are also collective marks. The same policies and restrictions that apply to trade and service marks normally apply to certification and collective marks.

Infringement of Trade Names

The term **trade name** is used to indicate part or all of a business's name, whether that business be a sole proprietorship, a partnership, or a corporation. Generally, a trade name is directly related to a business and to its goodwill. As with trademarks, words must be unusual or fancifully used in order to be protected as trade names. The word *Safeway* was held by the courts to be sufficiently fanciful to obtain protection as a trade name.[2] The decisions of the courts do not give entirely clear guidelines as to when the name of a corporation can be regarded as a trade name. A particularly thorny problem arises when a trade name acquires generic use. Originally, *aspirin* and *thermos* were used only as trade names, but they are now used to refer to those products generally. Similarly, other trade names—for example, Frigidaire, Scotch Tape, Xerox, and Kleenex—have acquired secondary meanings and are close to becoming generic terms. Even so, the courts will not allow another firm to use those names in such a way as to deceive a potential consumer. Consider, for example, the following famous case concerning Coca-Cola, decided by the Supreme Court.

---

2. Safeway Stores v. Suburban Foods, 130 F.Supp. 249 (E.D.Va. 1955).

BACKGROUND AND FACTS

to enjoin other beverage companies from using the words "Koke" or "Dope" for their products. The defendants, The Koke Co. of America, et al., contended that the Coca-Cola trademark was a fraudulent representation and that Coca-Cola was therefore not entitled to any help from the courts. The defendants alleged that the Coca-Cola Company, by its use of the Coca-Cola name, represented that the beverage contained cocaine (from coca leaves).

MR. JUSTICE HOLMES delivered the opinion of the court.

This is a bill in equity brought by the Coca-Cola Company to prevent the infringement of its trade-mark Coca-Cola and unfair competition with it in its business of making and selling the beverage for which the trade-mark is used. The District Court gave the plaintiff a decree [an injunction]. This was reversed by the Circuit Court of Appeals. Subsequently a writ of certiorari was granted by this Court.

* * * *

Of course a man is not to be protected in the use of a device the very purpose and effect of which is to swindle the public. But the defects of a plaintiff do not offer a very broad ground for allowing another to swindle him. The defense relied on here should be scrutinized with a critical eye. The main point is this: Before 1900 the beginning of the good will was more or less helped by the presence of cocaine, a drug that, like alcohol or caffein or opium, may be described as a deadly poison or as a valuable item of the pharmacopœa according to the rhetorical purposes in view. The amount seems to have been very small, but it may have been enough to begin a bad habit and after the Food and Drug Act of June 30, 1906, if not earlier, long before this suit was brought, it was eliminated from the plaintiff's compound. Coca leaves still are used, to be sure, but after they have been subjected to a drastic process that removes from them every characteristic substance except a little tannin and still less chlorophyl. The cola nut, at best, on its side furnishes but a very small portion of the caffein, which now is the only element that has appreciable effect. That comes mainly from other sources. It is argued that the continued use of the name imports a representation that has ceased to be true and that the representation is reinforced by a picture of coca leaves and cola nuts upon the label and by advertisements, which however were many years before this suit was brought, that the drink is an "ideal nerve tonic and stimulant," * * * and that thus the very thing sought to be protected is used as a fraud.

The argument does not satisfy us. We are dealing here with a popular drink not with a medicine, and although what has been said might suggest that its attraction lay in producing the expectation of a toxic effect the facts point to a different conclusion. Since 1900 the sales have increased at a very great rate corresponding to a like increase in advertising. The name now characterizes a beverage to be had at almost any soda fountain. It means a single thing coming from a single source, and well known to the community. It hardly would be too much to say that the drink characterizes the name as much as the name the drink. In other words Coca-Cola probably means to most persons the plaintiff's familiar product to be had everywhere rather than a compound of particular substances. The coca leaves and whatever of cola nut is employed may be used to justify the continuance of the name or they may affect the flavor as the plaintiff contends, but before this suit was brought the plaintiff had advertised to the public that it must not expect and would not find cocaine, and had eliminated everything tending to suggest cocaine effects except the name and the picture of the leaves and nuts, which probably conveyed little or nothing to most who saw it. It appears to us that it would be going too far to deny the plaintiff relief against a palpable fraud because possibly here and there an ignorant person might call for the drink with the hope for incipient cocaine intoxication. The plaintiff's position must be judged by the facts as

 Case 5.5

THE COCA-COLA CO. v. THE KOKE CO. OF AMERICA ET AL.

Supreme Court of the United States, 1920.
254 U.S. 143, 41 S.Ct. 113, 65 L.Ed. 189.

they were when the suit was begun, not by the facts of a different condition and an earlier time.

The decree of the District Court restrains the defendant from using the word Dope. The plaintiff illustrated in a very striking way the fact that the word is one of the most featureless known even to the language of those who are incapable of discriminating speech. In some places it would be used to call for Coca-Cola. It equally would have been used to call for anything else having about it a faint aureole of poison. It does not suggest Coca-Cola by similarity and whatever objections there may be to its use, objections which the plaintiff equally makes to its application to Coca-Cola, we see no ground on which the plaintiff can claim a personal right to exclude the defendant from using it.

The product including the coloring matter is free to all who can make it if no extrinsic deceiving element is present.

DECISION AND REMEDY   *The competing beverage companies were enjoined from calling their products "Koke," but the Court would not prevent them from calling their products "Dope."*

Infringement of Patents

A **patent** is a grant from the government that conveys and secures to an inventor the exclusive right to make, use, and sell an invention for a period of seventeen years. Patents for a lesser period are given for designs, as opposed to inventions. For either a regular patent or a design patent, the applicant must demonstrate to the satisfaction of the patent office that the invention, discovery, or design is genuine, novel, useful, and not obvious in the light of the technology of the time. A patent holder gives notice to all that an article or design is patented by placing on it the word "Patent" or "Pat.," plus the patent number.

If a firm makes, uses, or sells another's patented invention, device, or design, without the patent owner's permission, the tort of patent infringement exists. Patent infringement may exist even though not all features or parts of an invention are copied. (With respect to a patented process, however, all steps or their equivalent must be copied in order for infringement to exist.) Often, litigation for patent infringement is so costly that the patent holder will instead offer to sell to the infringer a license to use the patented design, product, or process. Indeed, in many cases the costs of detection, prosecution, and monitoring are so high that patents are valueless to their owners, since they cannot afford to protect them.

Infringement of Copyright

A **copyright** is an intangible right granted by statute to the author or originator of certain literary or artistic productions. Works created after January 1, 1978, are automatically given statutory copyright protection for the life of the author plus fifty years, or, in the case of a corporation, for a total of seventy-five years. Note that it is not possible to copyright an idea. What is copyrightable is the particular way in which an idea is expressed.

Recent legislation permits the copyrighting of computer programs. The problem arises, however, as to how trade secrets may be protected once a program is registered. This issue will be discussed further in Chapter 55.

Under the "fair use" doctrine, the reproduction of copyrighted material is permitted without the payment of royalties under certain circumstances. Section 107 of the Copyright Act provides:

Nothwithstanding the provisions of section 106, the fair use of a copyrighted work, including such use by reproduction in copies or phonorecords or by any other means specified by that section, for purposes such as criticism, comment, news reporting, teaching (including multiple copies for classroom use), scholarship, or research, is not an infringement of copyright. In determining whether the use made of a work in any particular case is a fair use the factors to be considered shall include—

(1) the purpose and character of the use, including whether such use is of a commercial nature or is for nonprofit educational purposes;

(2) the nature of the copyrighted work;

(3) the amount and substantiality of the portion used in relation to the copyrighted work as a whole; and

(4) the effect of the use upon the potential market for or value of the copyrighted work.

Unfortunately the act does not *clearly* define this doctrine, and any reproduction can still make the producer thereof subject to a violation.

The act does provide that a copyright owner no longer needs to place a © or P on the work to have the work protected against infringement.

Chances are that if somebody created it, somebody owns it.

Whenever the form of expression of an idea is copied, an infringement of copyright has occurred. The reproduction does not have to be exactly the same as the original; nor does it have to reproduce the original in its entirety. If a substantial part of the original is reproduced, a copyright infringement exists.

Penalties or remedies can be imposed on those who infringe copyrights. These range from actual damages or statutory damages ($250–$10,000) imposed at the discretion of the court, to criminal proceedings for willful violations, which may result in fines and/or imprisonment.

The following case discusses whether recording television broadcasts on home videotape recorders constitutes a copyright infringement.

BACKGROUND AND FACTS   *Universal City Studios, respondents, own the copyrights on some of the television programs broadcast on the public airways. Sony Corporation, petitioners, manufacture and sell home videotape recorders. Universal alleged that members of the general public used Betamax videotape recorders (VTRs) to record some broadcasts of Universal's copyrighted works, thereby infringing Universal's copyrights. Universal then maintained that Sony was liable for these copyright infringements because Sony marketed the Betamax VTRs. Universal sought money damages, an accounting for profits, and an injunction against the manufacture and marketing of Betamax VTRs. The district court denied Universal any relief, but the court of appeals held Sony liable for contributory infringement. The United States Supreme Court took up the case.*

Case 5.6
SONY CORP. v. UNIVERSAL CITY STUDIOS
Supreme Court of the United States, 1984.
464 U.S. 417, 104 S.Ct. 774, 78 L.Ed.2d 574.

STEVENS, Justice.
*   *   *   *

Copyright protection "subsists . . . in original works of authorship fixed in any tangible medium of expression." This protection has never accorded the copyright owner complete control over all possible uses of his work. Rather, the Copyright Act grants the copyright holder "exclusive" rights to use and to authorize the use of his work in five qualified ways, including reproduction of the copyrighted work in copies. All reproductions of the work, however, are not within the exclusive domain of the copyright owner; some are in the public domain. Any individual may reproduce a copyrighted work for a "fair use"; the copyright owner does not possess the exclusive right to such a use.

"Anyone who violates any of the exclusive rights of the copyright owner," that is, anyone who trespasses into his exclusive domain by using or authorizing the use of the copyrighted work in one of the five ways set forth in the statute, "is an infringer of the copyright." Conversely, anyone who is authorized by the copyright owner to use the copyrighted work in a way specified in the statute or who makes a fair use of the work is not an infringer of the copyright with respect to such use.
*   *   *   *

The two respondents in this case do not seek relief against the Betamax users who have allegedly infringed their copyrights. Moreover, this is not [an] action on behalf of all copyright owners who license their works for television broadcast, and respondents have no right to invoke whatever rights other copyright holders may have to bring infringement actions based on Betamax copying of their works. As was made clear by their own evidence, the copying of the respondent's programs represents a small portion of the total use of VTRs. It is, however, the taping of respondents' own copyrighted programs that provides them with standing to charge Sony with contributory infringement. To prevail, they have the burden of proving that users of the Betamax have infringed their copyrights and that Sony should be held responsible for that infringement.

*   *   *   *

If vicarious liability is to be imposed on petitioners in this case, it must rest on the fact that they have sold equipment with constructive knowledge of the fact that their customers may use that equipment to make unauthorized copies of copyrighted material. There is no precedent in the law of copyright for the imposition of vicarious liability on such a theory. *   *   *

*   *   *   *

*   *   * Accordingly, the sale of copying equipment, like the sale of other articles of commerce, does not constitute contributory infringement if the product is widely used for legitimate, unobjectionable purposes. Indeed, it need merely be capable of substantial noninfringing uses.

*   *   *   *

Even unauthorized uses of a copyrighted work are not necessarily infringing. An unlicensed use of the copyright is not an infringement unless it conflicts with one of the specific exclusive rights conferred by the copyright statute. *   *   * Moreover, the definition of exclusive rights in § 106 of the present Act is prefaced by the words "subject to sections 107 through 118." Those sections describe a variety of uses of copyrighted material that "are not infringements of copyright notwithstanding the provisions of § 106." The most pertinent in this case is § 107, the legislative endorsement of the doctrine of "fair use."

*   *   *   *

*   *   * A challenge to a noncommercial use of a copyrighted work [requires] proof either that the particular use is harmful, or that if it should become widespread, it would adversely affect the potential market for the copyrighted work.

*   *   *   *

When these factors are all weighted in the "equitable rule of reason" balance, we must conclude that this record amply supports the District Court's conclusion that home time-shifting is fair use. In light of the findings of the District Court regarding the state of the empirical data, it is clear that the Court of Appeals erred in holding that the statute as presently written bars such conduct.

DECISION AND REMEDY   *The Supreme Court concluded (1) that a substantial number of television broadcast copyright holders would not object to having their broadcasts recorded and (2) that Universal failed to demonstrate that the recordings would cause more than minimal harm to the market for, or value of, their copyrighted works. Therefore, the Betamax VTR is capable of noninfringing uses, and Sony was not liable for contributory infringement.*

Theft of Trade Secrets

Some processes or items of information that are not patented, or not patentable, are nevertheless protected by law against appropriation by a competitor. Businesses that have *trade secrets* generally protect themselves by having all employees who use the process or information agree in their contracts never to divulge it. Thus, if a salesperson tries to solicit the company's customers for non-company business, or if an employee copies the employer's unique method of manufacture, he or she has appropriated a trade secret and has also broken a contract, two separate wrongs. Theft of confidential data by industrial espionage, as when a business taps into a competitor's computer, is a theft of trade secrets without any contractual violations and is actionable in itself.

Appropriation

The use of one person's name or likeness by another, without permission and for the benefit of the user, constitutes the tort of **appropriation.** Under the law, an individual's right to privacy includes the right to the exclusive use of his or her identity. Recently, a number of cases have arisen concerning the use of a famous person's name for the benefit of the user. One case involved the use of "Here's Johnny"—the opening line of the Johnny Carson show. A Michigan corporation that rented and sold portable toilets advertised them as "Here's Johnny" toilets. Carson brought suit, claiming that the Michigan corporation had violated his right to privacy by publicly appropriating his celebrity status for the corporation's commercial benefit. Even though the corporation had not used Carson's name or picture, the court held that the use of "Here's Johnny" was an appropriation of Carson's identity because the phrase was so strongly associated with Carson's public personality.[3] Other cases have involved the unauthorized use of Muhammad Ali's appellation "The Greatest" to describe a nude male model[4] and Elroy Hirsch's moniker "Crazylegs" as the name of a shaving gel.[5]

DISPARAGEMENT OF PROPERTY OR REPUTATION

Business firms are encouraged to compete in our society, but they have the right to be reasonably free from disparagement of their products and their reputations.

Disparagement of Product

Some torts involve economically injurious falsehoods but not personal defamation. These include the torts referred to as disparagement of product or, more generally, disparagement of property, which in turn include the torts of *slander of quality* and *slander of title*. Unprivileged publication of false information about another's product, alleging it is not what its seller claims, constitutes a tort of slander of quality. This tort has also been given the name *trade libel*. Actual damages must be proved by the plaintiff to have proximately resulted from the slander of quality. It must be shown that a third person refrained from dealing with the plaintiff because of the improper publication. It is possible for an improper publication to be both a slander of quality and a defamation. For example, a statement that disparages the quality of an article may also, by implication, disparage the character of the person who would sell such a product.

When a publication denies or casts doubt upon another's legal ownership of any property, and when this results in financial loss to that property's owner, the tort of slander of title may exist. Usually this is an intentional tort in which someone knowingly publishes an untrue statement about property with the intent of discouraging a third person from dealing with the person slandered. For example, it would be difficult for a car dealer to attract customers after competitors put out a notice that the dealer's stock consisted of stolen autos.

Disparagement of Reputation

In Chapter 4 we divided defamation into its component parts of libel in written or printed form and slander in oral form. Defamation becomes a business tort when the defamatory matter injures someone in a profession, business, or trade or when it adversely affects a business entity in its credit rating and other dealings.

RICO

In 1970 Congress passed the Organized Crime Control Act. It included the Racketeer Influenced and Corrupt Organizations Act, otherwise known

---

3. Carson v. Here's Johnny Portable Toilets, 698 F.2d 831 (6th Cir. 1983).

4. Ali v. Playgirl, Inc., 447 F.Supp. 723 (S.D.N.Y. 1978).

5. Hirsch v. S. C. Johnson & Son, Inc., 90 Wis.2d 379, 280 N.W.2d 129 (1979).

as RICO.[6] The purpose of the act was to curb the apparently increasing entry of organized crime into the legitimate business world. Under RICO, it is a federal crime (1) to use income obtained from racketeering activity to purchase any interest in an enterprise, (2) to acquire or maintain an interest in an enterprise through racketeering activity, (3) to conduct or participate in the affairs of an enterprise through racketeering activity, or (4) to conspire to do any of the preceding.

Racketeering activity is not a new type of substantive crime created by RICO; rather, RICO incorporates by reference twenty-six separate types of federal crime and nine types of state felonies[7] and states that if a person commits two of these offenses, he or she is guilty of "racketeering activity." Recently, the statute has been rigorously enforced, and the penalties for violations are harsh. The act provides for both criminal liability (to be discussed in the following chapter) and civil liability.

In the event of a violation, the RICO statute permits the government to seek civil penalties,

6. 18 U.S.C. Sec. 1961–1968 (1976).
7. See 18 U.S.C. Sec. 1961(1)(A).

including the divestiture of a defendant's interest in a business or the dissolution of the business. Perhaps the most controversial section of RICO is section 1964(c), under which, in some cases, private individuals are allowed to recover three times their actual loss (treble damages), plus attorneys' fees, for business injuries caused by a violation of the statute.

The broad language of RICO has allowed it to be applied in cases that have little or nothing to do with organized crime, and an aggressive prosecuting attorney may attempt to show that any business fraud constitutes "racketeering activity." Plaintiffs have used the RICO statute in numerous commercial fraud cases because of the inviting prospect of being awarded triple damages if they win. The most frequent targets of civil RICO lawsuits are insurance companies, employment agencies, commercial banks, and stock brokerage firms.

In the case presented below, a plaintiff brought suit against a business firm, claiming that the firm's fraudulent business activities violated RICO. By interpreting RICO provisions very broadly, the U.S. Supreme Court set a significant precedent for subsequent applications of RICO.

Case 5.7
**SEDIMA, S.P.R.L. v.
IMREX CO., INC.**
Supreme Court of the United
States, 1985.
473 U.S. 479, 105 S.Ct. 3275,
87 L.Ed.2d 346.

BACKGROUND AND FACTS *In 1979 a Belgian corporation, Sedima, entered into a contract with another Belgian firm to supply the latter with electronic components. Sedima also formed a joint venture with a U.S. firm, Imrex Company, whereby Imrex would ship the components to Europe and share the proceeds jointly with Sedima. Approximately $8 million in orders had been shipped by Imrex when Sedima concluded that Imrex was fraudulently claiming extra expenses and inflating its bills accordingly—in order to get more than its fair portion of the proceeds. Sedima brought suit against Imrex, alleging, in part, that Imrex had violated section 1962(c) of RICO. Section 1962(c) requires that a private suit under RICO must be based on an injury brought about by the (1) conduct (2) of an enterprise (3) through a pattern (4) of racketeering activity. Sedima claimed an injury of at least $175,000 (the amount of alleged overbilling) and asked for treble damages, as allowed by section 1964(c). Sedima's RICO claims were dismissed by the district court on the ground that Sedima failed to demonstrate it had suffered any "racketeering injury." The appellate court affirmed, and Sedima appealed to the U.S. Supreme Court.*

WHITE, Justice.

The Racketeer Influenced and Corrupt Organizations Act (RICO) provides a private civil action to recover treble damages for injury "by reason of a violation of" its substantive provisions. The initial dormancy of this provision and its recent greatly increased utilization are now familiar history. In response to what it perceived to be misuse of civil RICO by private plaintiffs, the court below construed § 1964(c) to permit private actions only against defendants who had been convicted on criminal charges, and only where there had occurred a "racketeering injury." While we understand the court's concern over the consequences of an unbridled reading of the statute, we reject * * * its holdings.

* * * *

[W]e can find no support in the statute's history, its language, or considerations of policy for a requirement that a private treble-damages action under ∫ 1964(c) can proceed only against a defendant who has already been criminally convicted. To the contrary, every indication is that no such requirement exists. Accordingly, the fact that Imrex and the individual defendants have not been convicted under RICO or the federal mail and wire fraud statutes does not bar Sedima's action.

* * * *

Underlying the Court of Appeals' holding was its distress at the "extraordinary, if not outrageous," uses to which civil RICO has been put. Instead of being used against mobsters and organized criminals, it has become a tool for everyday fraud cases brought against "respected and legitimate 'enterprises.' " Yet Congress wanted to reach both "legitimate" and "illegitimate" enterprises. The former enjoy neither an inherent incapacity for criminal activity nor immunity from its consequences. The fact that ∫ 1964(c) is used against respected businesses allegedly engaged in a pattern of specifically identified criminal conduct is hardly a sufficient reason for assuming that the provision is being misconstrued. Nor does it reveal the "ambiguity" discovered by the court below. "[T]he fact that RICO has been applied in situations not expressly anticipated by Congress does not demonstrate ambiguity. It demonstrates breadth."

It is true that private civil actions under the statute are being brought almost solely against such defendants, rather than against the archetypal, intimidating mobster. Yet this defect—if defect it is—is inherent in the statute as written, and its correction must lie with Congress. It is not for the judiciary to eliminate the private action in situations where Congress has provided it simply because plaintiffs are not taking advantage of it in its more difficult applications.

We nonetheless recognize that, in its private civil version, RICO is evolving into something quite different from the original conception of its enactors. Though sharing the doubts of the Court of Appeals about this increasing divergence, we cannot agree with either its diagnosis or its remedy. The "extraordinary" uses to which civil RICO has been put appear to be primarily the result of the breadth of the predicate offenses, in particular the inclusion of wire, mail, and securities fraud, and the failure of Congress and the courts to develop a meaningful concept of "pattern." We do not believe that the amorphous standing requirement imposed by the Second Circuit effectively responds to these problems, or that it is a form of statutory amendment appropriately undertaken by the courts.

The Supreme Court reversed the decision of the appellate court. The Court held that section 1964(c) merely states that anyone injured may recover if he or she meets the requirements under any of the provisions of the RICO statute.

DECISION AND REMEDY

QUESTIONS AND CASE PROBLEMS

1. Stevens owns a bakery. He has been trying to obtain a long-term contract with the owner of Martha's Tea Salons for some time. Stevens starts a local advertising campaign on radio and television and in the newspaper. This advertising campaign is so persuasive that Martha decides to break the contract she has had with Hank's Bakery so that she can patronize Stevens's bakery. Is Stevens liable to Hank's Bakery for the tort of wrongful interference with contractual relations? Is Martha liable for this tort? For anything?

2. Professor Wise is teaching a summer seminar in business torts at State University. Several times during the course, he makes copies of relevant sections from business law texts and distributes them to his students. Unbeknownst to Wise, the daughter of one of the textbook authors is a member of his seminar. She tells her father about Wise's copying activities, which have been done without her father's permission. Her father sues Wise for copyright infringement. Wise claims protection under the "fair use" doctrine. Who will prevail? Explain.

3. An Atlanta theater group produced a musical entitled "Scarlett Fever." The production opened with Shady Charlotte O'Mara at her plantation, Tiara, and moved through the major episodes of the film *Gone With The Wind*. This was not a parody or a farce, but another play. The play also utilized backdrops reminiscent of the settings in the film. Original songs and dances were performed. Did this production infringe copyright interests in the film and the novel *Gone With The Wind*? [Metro-Goldwyn-Mayer, Inc. v. Showcase Atlanta Coop. Productions, Inc., 479 F.Supp. 351 (N.D.Ga. 1979)]

4. Franchisees of a T.G.I. Friday's restaurant in Jackson, Mississippi, opened a restaurant in Baton Rouge, Louisiana. They named the new restaurant E.L. Saturday's, or Ever Lovin' Saturday's. The Baton Rouge restaurant was physically similar to T.G.I. Friday's, in Jackson. Both used a turn-of-the-century motif. "T.G.I. Friday's" is registered as a trademark with the United States patent office. Was the opening of the Baton Rouge restaurant a trademark infringement? [T.G.I. Friday's, Inc. v. International Restaurant Group, Inc., 569 F.2d 895 (5th Cir. 1978)]

5. Southard was stranded in Hawaii as the result of an airline strike. He had purchased a round-trip ticket before leaving his home in Denver. He sued the union for tortious interference with his contract with the airline and sought to recover the additional expense he incurred on another airline. Was the union liable to Mr. Southard? [International Ass'n of Machinists v. Southard, 170 Colo. 119, 459 P.2d 570 (1969)]

6. Roto-Rooter was granted a federal registration in 1954 for its service mark "Roto-Rooter" for sewer, pipe, and drain cleaning services. In 1973 O'Neal opened a business with the name Rotary D-Routing. Roto-Rooter sued for damages for trademark infringement. Could O'Neal continue using the name Rotary D-Routing? [Roto-Rooter Corp. v. O'Neal, 513 F.2d 44 (5th Cir. 1975)]

7. In the early 1960s Schenck employees Klaus Federn, Heinrick Geiss, and Alfred Seibert discovered a hard-bearing device for balancing rotors. This invention was registered with the patent office, but it was never used as an automobile wheel balancer. Nortron produced an automobile wheel balancer that used a hard-bearing device with a support plate similar to Schenck's. Is Schenck's patent not infringed, since its device was not used for automobile wheel balancing? [Schenck v. Nortron Corporation, 570 F.Supp. 810 (M.D.Tenn. 1982)].

8. Duggin entered into a contract to purchase certain land from Williams. The contract specified that if the property was not rezoned by June 15, 1981, either party could cancel. Duggin invested a great deal of time and money for engineering studies and surveys that increased the value of the property. Before the June 15 rezoning deadline, Duggin made an agreement to assign the contract to Centennial Development Corp. at a profit. The land was not rezoned as of June 15, but Centennial was prepared to purchase the land without the rezoning. Williams's attorney, Adams, learned of Duggin's deal and convinced Williams to cancel on July 30, 1981, in accordance with the provision in the agreement. Adams also convinced Williams to transfer the property to Adams, after which he sold the land to Centennial. Adams claimed that he was merely working on behalf of his client, Williams. Does Duggin have a claim against Adams for intentional interference with contract rights even though Williams had the right to terminate the contract at will? [Duggin v. Adams, 234 Va. 221, 360 S.E.2d 832 (1987)]

9. Dierdorff was the president of Sun Savings and Loan Association. Sun Savings claimed that over a period of time Dierdorff had received kickbacks from several of Sun's larger loan customers. In relation to the fraudulent kickback scheme, Dierdorff had written letters to four entities—the Internal Revenue Service, the Federal Home Loan Bank Board, the California Savings and Loan commissioner, and the accounting firm of Arthur Young. Sun filed a civil suit alleging that Dierdorff had violated the federal Racketeering Influenced and Corrupt Organizations Act (RICO). The federal district court decided in favor of Dierdorff, holding that the plaintiff, Sun, had failed to allege a "pattern of racketeering activity" and that the acts had not been conducted by an "enterprise." On appeal, how should the appellate court rule on the decision of the district court? [Sun Savings and Loan Association v. Dierdorff, 825 F.2d 187 (9th Cir. 1987)]

10. Original Appalachian Artworks, Inc. (OAA) makes and distributes the very successful product called Cabbage Patch Kids—soft, sculptured dolls that were in great demand in the early 1980s. The dolls are unique in appearance, and the name is registered as a trademark to OAA. The design, too, is protected under a copyright registration. The testimony at trial indicated that in 1986 Topps Chewing Gum, Inc., had an artist copy many of the features of the dolls for Topps's new product—stickers that depicted obnoxious cartoon characters called Garbage Pail Kids. The stickers, and the other product line that Topps developed, proved very lucrative; in fact, Topps expanded the product line to include T-shirts, balloons, and school notebooks.

(a) Did Topps infringe upon OAA's trademark and copyrighted product?

(b) Topps claimed that its product was actually a satire of OAA's product and therefore a fair use of a protected work. Would this amount to a fair use?

[Original Appalachian Artworks, Inc. v. Topps Chewing Gum, Inc., 642 F.Supp. 1031 (N.D.Ga. 1986)]

Chapter 6

Criminal Law

Previously in this text we referred to a **crime** as a wrong defined by society and perpetrated against society. A discussion of criminal law is appropriate to a study of business law because the prevention of crime and the effort of capturing and prosecuting those accused of crimes are time-consuming and costly activities. Consequently, it is important that we understand the nature and extent of such activities and their impact on businesses.

The sanctions used to bring about a peaceful society, in which individuals engaging in business can compete and flourish, include those imposed by the civil law, such as damages for various types of tortious conduct (as discussed in the preceding chapters) and damages for breach of contract (to be discussed in Chapter 15). Chapter 1 also pointed out that courts of equity may restrain certain unlawful conduct or require that things done unlawfully or having certain unlawful effects be undone by issuing injunctions.

These remedies have not been sufficient deterrents in some instances. Consequently, additional sanctions have been developed for particular undesirable activities. As a result, a *criminal law element* exists within the legal environment of business. The prerequisites of *fault* or *guilt* in this area are different from those in the civil law, as are the sanctions and penalties.

A *Concept Summary* showing which types of offenses are classified as criminal law and which are classified as civil law can be found on pages 124 and 125, near the end of this chapter.

THE NATURE OF CRIME

Crimes can be distinguished from other wrongful acts in that they are *offenses against society as a whole*. Criminal defendants are prosecuted by a public official, not by their victims. In addition, those who have committed crimes are punished. Tort remedies—remedies for civil wrongs—are generally intended to compensate the injured (except when damages of a punitive nature are assessed), but criminal law is directly concerned with punishing (and, ideally, rehabilitating) the wrongdoer.

A final factor distinguishing criminal sanctions from tort remedies is that the source of criminal law is primarily statutory. Both the acts that constitute crimes and the resulting punishments are formally and very specifically set out in statutes. A crime can thus be defined as a wrong against society proclaimed in a statute and, if intentionally committed, punishable by society.

Classifications of Crimes

Crimes are classified as felonies or misdemeanors according to their seriousness.

FELONIES **Felonies** are more serious than misdemeanors and are punishable by death or by imprisonment in a federal or state penitentiary for more than a year. Felonies can also be divided by degree of seriousness. The Model Penal Code,[1] for example, provides for four degrees of felony: capital offenses for which the maximum penalty is death, first degree felonies punishable by a maximum penalty of life imprisonment, second degree felonies punishable by a maximum of ten years' imprisonment, and third degree felonies punishable by up to five years' imprisonment. (It is important to note that these are maximum penalties. The actual sentence served can be less than the maximum.)

When death occurs during or as the result of a felonious crime, many states have laws whereby the individual accused of the crime is charged with **felony murder** in addition to the crime that was intended. State legislatures determine which crimes can lead to felony murder charges. Many states do not impose the death penalty in felony murder cases but choose instead to impose a life sentence.

MISDEMEANORS **Misdemeanors** are crimes punishable by a fine or by confinement for up to a year. Misdemeanors are also sometimes defined as offenses punishable by incarceration in a local jail instead of a penitentiary. In practice, the jail confinement usually lasts no more than a year. Disorderly conduct and trespass are common misdemeanors. Some states have different classes of misdemeanors. For example, in Illinois there are Class A misdemeanors (confinement for up to a year), Class B (not more than six months), and Class C (not more than thirty days). A case concerning a crime classified as a misdemeanor may be tried before a justice of the peace, a police court judge, or some other official with limited judicial authority.

PETTY OFFENSES Another kind of wrong is termed a *petty offense* and often is not classified as a crime. Petty offenses include many traffic violations and violations of building codes. Even for petty offenses, a guilty party may be put in jail for a few days, or fined, or both.

ATTEMPTS AND CONSPIRACIES An *attempt to commit a crime* is conduct intended to lead to the commission of a crime. It is more than mere preparation, but it falls short of actual commission of the intended offense. *Intent* to commit a crime is not the same as an *attempt* to commit a crime. Intent, discussed later in this chapter, is a mental quality that implies a purpose, whereas an attempt implies an effort to carry that purpose or intent into execution. Generally, an attempt to commit a crime is a misdemeanor, regardless of whether the attempted crime is a misdemeanor or a felony, but an attempt may be classified as a felony in a statute.

A *conspiracy* is an agreement between two or more persons to engage in an unlawful act or an act innocent in itself that becomes unlawful when done by the persons' *combined* efforts. Conspiracy is a crime distinct from the act contemplated. The parties' agreement is its essence; a single person acting alone cannot be guilty of the offense. Also, to support a criminal prosecution, some statutes require that an act be accomplished in furtherance of the conspiracy.

FEDERAL AND STATE CRIMES Criminal law is primarily the province of the states, but the federal government also has a criminal code. Federal crimes relate to federal government functions or involve federal personnel or institutions. Counterfeiting, unlawful immigration, spying, robbing a federally insured bank, and assaulting a federal officer are examples of federal crimes. In other instances, the federal government can use its general regulatory powers to aid state law enforcement agencies in combating crimes that have a national impact. Transportation of stolen vehicles across state lines, kidnapping, and civil rights violations are areas that fall under federal criminal law.

CLASSIFICATION BY NATURE Crimes can be classified according to their nature. For example, there are crimes against property (theft, burglary, arson), crimes against the person (murder, assault, rape), and crimes against the government (perjury, bribery). These classifications are used to group crimes within a statutory code.

---

1. American Law Institute Model Penal Code, official draft, 1962. This code contains four parts relating to general provisions, definitions of specific crimes, treatment and correction, and organization of correction.

THE ESSENTIALS OF CRIMINAL LIABILITY

Two elements are necessary for a person to be convicted of a crime: (1) the performance of a prohibited act and (2) a specified state of mind or intent on the part of the actor.

Performance of Prohibited Acts

Every criminal statute prohibits certain behavior. Most crimes require an act of *commission;* that is, a person must *do* something in order to be accused of a crime.[2] In some cases an act of *omission* can be a crime, but only if what is omitted is a legal duty. Failure to file a tax return is an example of an omission that is a crime.

The *guilty act* requirement is based on one of the premises of criminal law—that a person is punished for *harm done* to society. Thinking about killing someone or about stealing a car may be wrong, but these thoughts in themselves do no harm until they are translated into action. Of course, a person can be punished for attempting murder or robbery, but normally only if substantial steps toward the criminal objective have been taken.

Even a completed act that harms society is not legally a crime unless the court finds that the required state of mind was present.

State of Mind or Intent

A wrongful mental state[3] is as necessary as a wrongful act to establish criminal liability. What constitutes such a mental state varies according to the wrongful action. Thus, for murder, the *actus reus* (act) is the taking of a life, and the *mens rea* (mental state) is the intent to take life. For theft, the *actus reus* is the taking of another person's property, and the *mens rea* involves both the knowledge that the property belongs to another and the intent to deprive the owner of it. Without the mental state required by law for a particular crime, there can be no crime.

The *mens rea* in which a particular act is committed can vary in the degree of its wrongfulness. The same act—shooting someone—can result from varying mental states. It can be done coldly, after

premeditation, as in murder in the first degree. It can be done in the heat of passion, as in voluntary manslaughter. Or it can be done as the result of negligence, as in involuntary manslaughter. In each of these situations, the law recognizes a different degree of wrongfulness, and the harshness of the punishment depends on the degree of intent.

DEFENSES TO CRIMINAL LIABILITY

The law recognizes certain conditions that will relieve a defendant of criminal liability. These conditions are called defenses, and among the important ones are infancy, intoxication, insanity, mistake, consent, duress, justifiable use of force, entrapment, and statutes of limitations. The burden of proving one or more of these defenses lies on the defendant. A criminal defendant can also be given immunity from prosecution.

Infancy

In the common law, children up to seven years of age were considered incapable of committing a crime because they did not have the moral sense to understand that they were doing wrong. Children between the ages of seven and fourteen were presumed to be incapable of committing a crime, but this presumption could be rebutted by a demonstration that the child understood the wrongful nature of the act. (See Exhibit 6–1.)

Today, states vary in their approaches, but all retain the defense of infancy as a bar to criminal liability. Most states retain the common law approach, although age limits vary from state to state. Other states have rejected the rebuttable pre-

Exhibit 6–1 Responsibility of Infants for Criminal Acts under the Common Law

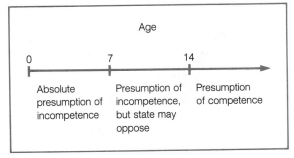

---

2. Called the *actus reus*, or guilty act.

3. Called the *mens rea*, or evil intent.

sumption and simply set a minimum age required for criminal responsibility. All states have juvenile court systems that handle children below the age of criminal responsibility who commit delinquent acts. Their aim is allegedly to reform rather than to punish. In states that retain the rebuttable presumption approach, children who are beyond the minimum age but are still juveniles can be turned over to the criminal courts if the juvenile court determines that they should be treated as adults.

Intoxication

The law recognizes two types of intoxication, whether from drugs or alcohol: *involuntary* and *voluntary*. Involuntary intoxication occurs when a person is physically forced to ingest or inject an intoxicating substance, is unaware that a substance contains drugs or alcohol, or takes an intoxicating substance under medical advice. Involuntary intoxication is a defense to crime if its effect was to make a person either incapable of understanding that the act committed was wrong or incapable of obeying the law.

Voluntary intoxication can also be used as a defense if intoxication precludes having the required *mens rea*. Thus, if Johnson shoots Peters while too drunk to know what she is doing, she cannot be convicted of *murder* because she did not have the required *intent* to kill when she shot Peters.

Voluntary intoxication, however, does not serve as a defense for crimes of recklessness or negligence. The law requires that people understand that intoxication can prevent the intoxicated from behaving as a reasonable person. Therefore, becoming intoxicated and committing a reckless or negligent act is a crime. In the example above, Johnson could be convicted of the lesser crime of *manslaughter*.

Insanity

Just as a child is judged incapable of having the state of mind required to commit a crime, so also is someone suffering from mental illness. Thus, insanity is a defense to a criminal charge. The courts have had difficulty deciding what the test for legal insanity should be, and psychiatrists, as well as lawyers, are critical of the tests used. Al-

most all federal courts and some states use the standard in the Model Penal Code:

> A person is not responsible for criminal conduct if at the time of such conduct as a result of mental disease or defect he lacks substantial capacity either to appreciate the wrongfulness of his conduct or to conform his conduct to the requirements of the law.

Other states use the *M'Naghten* test, also known as the "right from wrong" test, which excuses a criminal act if a mental defect makes a person incapable of either appreciating the nature of the act or knowing that it was wrong.[4] Some states have also adopted the irresistible impulse test. A person operating under an irresistible impulse may know that an act is wrong but may still be unable to keep from doing it. Even if a mental illness is not grave enough to serve as a complete defense, it may render a person legally incapable of certain crimes if the illness precludes the possibility of the required *mens rea*. The *Durham* rule is still another alternative. In *Durham*, the District of Columbia court held that the proper solution is to discard all tests of insanity.[5] Instead, the *jury* should determine whether the defendant was sane or insane at the time of the alleged crime, and if he or she was insane, whether the harmful act was the product of the defendant's insanity. A crime is considered a product of insanity if it would not have been committed *but for* the disease. Even though the *Durham* rule has received favorable reactions from commentators, it has received little support from the courts.

Mistake

Everyone has heard the saying "ignorance of the law is no excuse." It may seem harsh to presume that everyone knows or should know the law, but the result of a different rule would be unmanageable. Ordinarily, ignorance of the law or a mistaken idea about what the law requires is not a valid defense. In some states, however, that rule has been modified. A person who claims that he or she honestly did not know that a law was being broken may have a valid defense if: (1) the law was not published or reasonably made known to

---

4. M'Naghten's Case, 8 Eng.Rep. 718 (1843).

5. Durham v. United States, 214 F.2d 862 (D.C.Cir. 1954).

the public, or (2) the person relied on an official statement of the law that was erroneous. An official statement is a statute, judicial opinion, administrative order, or statement by someone responsible for administering, interpreting, or enforcing the law. Statements in newspapers or textbooks are not official statements.

A *mistake of fact,* as opposed to a *mistake of law,* will operate as a defense if it negates the required *mens rea.* If, for example, Jones mistakenly drives off in Thompson's car because he thinks that it is his, there is no theft. Theft requires knowledge that the property belongs to another. (Of course, this has no bearing on a civil action for the tort of conversion, discussed in Chapter 4.)

Consent

What if a victim consents to a crime or even encourages the person intending a criminal act to commit it? The law will allow consent as a defense if the consent cancels the harm that the law is designed to prevent. In each case, the question is whether the law forbids an act against the victim's will or forbids the act without regard to the victim's wish. The law forbids murder, prostitution, and drug use whether the victim consents to it or not. Consent operates as a defense most successfully in crimes against property, since one can always give away one's property. Of course, if the act operates to harm a third person who has not consented, there will be no escape from criminal liability. Consent or forgiveness given after a crime has been committed is not really a defense, though it can affect the likelihood of prosecution.

Duress

A person who is asked or instructed to commit a crime is not excused from criminal liability, but committing a crime, other than homicide, under *duress* is a valid defense. Duress exists when the *wrongful threat* of one person induces another person to perform an act that he or she would not otherwise perform. In such a situation, duress is said to negate the *mens rea* necessary to commit a crime.

The courts use a number of requirements to determine whether duress exists. First, the threat must be of serious bodily harm or death. A person who was threatened with failing a course or losing

a job cannot plead duress as a defense. Second, the harm that is threatened must be greater than the harm that will be caused by the crime. A threat to shoot a woman's husband unless she robs a bank would be sufficient; a threat to hit her might not be. The third requirement is that the threat must be immediate and inescapable. Finally, people who plead duress as a defense must have been involved in the situation through no fault of their own. If, for example, a person committing a burglary forces an accomplice to kill someone, the accomplice cannot use duress as an excuse. The act of participating in the burglary carries with it the possibility of being forced to commit a greater crime.

Justifiable Use of Force

Probably the most well-known defense to criminal liability is *self-defense.* But there are other situations that justify the use of force: the defense of one's dwelling, the defense of other property, and the prevention of a crime. In all of these situations, it is important to distinguish between the use of deadly and nondeadly force. Deadly force is likely to result in death or serious bodily harm. Nondeadly force is force that reasonably appears necessary to prevent the imminent use of criminal force.

Generally speaking, people can use the amount of nondeadly force that seems necessary to protect themselves, their dwellings, or other property or to prevent the commission of a crime. Deadly force can be used in self-defense if there is a *reasonable belief* that imminent death or grievous bodily harm will otherwise result, if the attacker is using unlawful force (an example of lawful force is that exerted by a police officer), and if the person has not initiated or provoked the attack. Deadly force can be used to defend a dwelling only if the person believes that deadly force is necessary to prevent imminent death or great bodily harm or—in some jurisdictions—if the person believes deadly force is necessary to prevent the commission of a felony in the dwelling.

In defense of other property, the use of nondeadly force is justified to prevent or to end a criminal attempt to take away or otherwise interfere with the property. Deadly force usually is justifiable only when used in self-defense.

Force reasonably necessary to prevent a serious crime is permissible but, in the majority view, deadly force can be used to prevent only crimes that involve a substantial risk of death or great bodily harm.

Entrapment

Entrapment is a defense designed to prevent the police or other government agents from encouraging criminal acts in order to apprehend persons wanted for criminal acts. In the typical entrapment case, an undercover agent *suggests* that a crime be committed and somehow pressures or induces an individual to commit it. The agent then arrests the individual for the crime. Both the suggestion and the inducement must take place. The defense is not intended to prevent the police from setting a trap for an unwary criminal. It is intended to prevent them from pushing the suspected wrongdoer into it. The crucial issue is whether a person who committed a crime was *predisposed* to commit the crime or committed the crime because the agent induced it. This is often a question of fact, as illustrated by the following case.

Case 6.1

UNITED STATES v. BOWER

United States Court of Appeals,
Fifth Circuit, 1978.
575 F.2d 499.

BACKGROUND AND FACTS *This case involves a cocaine transaction that resulted in conviction of the defendant, Bower, for selling the narcotic to a government Drug Enforcement Administration (DEA) agent, Sylvestri. An informer, Clegg, initiated a relationship with the defendant. The informer encouraged the defendant to supply a quantity of cocaine to an out-of-town buyer. The defendant agreed to meet the buyer and make the exchange. After the defendant delivered the cocaine to the agent, the agent arrested him. The trial court found the defendant guilty on various charges, including possession and distribution of cocaine. The defendant claimed entrapment on the part of the government agents and appealed his conviction.*

RONEY, Circuit Judge.

*   *   *   *

Defendant contends the evidence established an entrapment as a matter of law. In support of this claim, defendant relies primarily on his own trial testimony that he had agreed to participate in the criminal enterprise in a moment of extreme depression. Defendant had recently turned 30 and, reflecting upon an uneventful past and contemplating a similar future, had decided to return to college and finish his education. Unfortunately, a year of voluntary unemployment had so depleted his personal finances that he could not return to school without working at least part time. Having hoped to be able to focus his undivided attention on his studies, defendant began to recognize Clegg's proposals as an opportunity to finance his schooling. His depression at this time was heightened by the fact that he and his girlfriend had recently severed their long-standing relationship. Consequently, although he had repeatedly rejected Clegg's earlier entreaties, he could no longer resist the temptation of the promised "exorbitant gains" to be reaped from a single cocaine sale.

Since Clegg did not testify at trial, defendant's account of Clegg's repeated attempts to persuade defendant to procure narcotics is uncontradicted. The record nevertheless contains evidence weighing against the contention that defendant was "an innocent seduced by a government agent." Defendant admitted that he saw the sale as a source of "easy money" and that he expected to make a $1,000 profit on the transaction. He purchased the cocaine from a nongovernment source who trusted defendant enough to defer payment until defendant had resold the drug. Indeed, while negotiating the actual exchange, defendant assured DEA agent Sylvestri that he could handle Sylvestri's future cocaine needs if the amounts were not too large. Both agent Sylvestri and defendant testified that during the transaction, defendant received a telephone call from his source. Defendant interrupted his telephone conversation to ask Sylvestri if he was interested in buying another four ounces of cocaine. When the DEA agent expressed interest, defendant requested his source "not to lock up the other four" and offered to produce the additional cocaine for Sylvestri in 30 minutes.

On this evidence, the trial court did not err in submitting the entrapment issue to the jury. The crucial issue in entrapment cases is whether the defendant was predisposed to commit the crime. The Government's provisions of aid, incentive, and opportunity for commission of the crime amounts to an entrapment only if it appears that the defendant has done that which he would never have done were it not for the inducement of Government operatives. Although the record contains evidence upon which a jury might conclude that defendant was induced by a Government informer to commit a crime that he was not otherwise predisposed to commit, the evidence was not "so overwhelming that it was 'patently clear' or 'obvious' that [defendant] was entrapped as a matter of law."

The appellate court affirmed the defendant's convictions. The evidence supported the jury's verdict that the defendant, Bower, was predisposed to commit the crime.

DECISION AND REMEDY

Statutes of Limitations

An individual can be excused from criminal liability by a statute of limitations. Such statutes provide that the state has only a certain amount of time within which to prosecute a crime. If the state does not do so within the allotted time, it has lost its opportunity, and the suspect is free from prosecution. The idea behind these statutes is to prevent stale or false claims from arising. If prosecution is delayed for too long, it becomes difficult to find out what the truth is because witnesses die or disappear and evidence is destroyed.

Time limits vary from state to state. Felonies usually have longer statutes of limitations than misdemeanors, and there is no time limitation placed on murder. For all other crimes, the time limit runs from the time the crime is committed, unless it is a crime that is difficult to discover. In those cases, the time begins to run when the crime is discovered. A time limitation will be suspended, however, if the suspect leaves the state or cannot be found. Normally, statutes will provide for subtraction of time if the suspect is not available to stand trial.

Immunity

At times, the state may wish to obtain information from a person accused of a crime. Such accused persons are understandably reluctant to give information, which under the Fifth Amendment they can refuse to provide on the ground of self-incrimination, if it will be used to prosecute them. In these cases, the state can grant immunity from prosecution or agree to prosecute for a less serious offense in exchange for the information. Once immunity is given, the person can no longer refuse to testify on Fifth Amendment grounds, since he or she now has an absolute privilege against self-incrimination. Often a grant of immunity from prosecution for a serious crime is part of the **plea-bargaining** negotiations between defense and prosecution. The defendant may still be convicted of a lesser offense, but the state uses his or her testimony to prosecute accomplices for serious crimes carrying heavy penalties.

CRIMINAL PROCEDURE

Our criminal justice system operates on the premise that it is far worse for an innocent person to be punished than for a guilty person to go free. A person is innocent until proved guilty, and guilt must be proved beyond a reasonable doubt. The procedure of the criminal legal system is designed to protect the rights of the individual and to preserve the presumption of innocence.

Constitutional Safeguards

Criminal law brings the weighty force of the state, with all its resources, to bear against the individual. Specific safeguards are provided in the Constitution for those accused of crimes. The Supreme Court has ruled that most of these safeguards apply not only in federal but also in state courts by virtue of the due process clause of the Fourteenth Amendment. The safeguards include:

1. Fourth Amendment protection from unreasonable searches and seizures.
2. The Fourth Amendment requirement that no warrants for a search or an arrest can be issued without probable cause.

3. The Fifth Amendment requirement that no one can be deprived of "life, liberty, or property without due process of law."

4. Fifth Amendment prohibition against double jeopardy (trying someone twice for the same criminal offense).

5. Sixth Amendment guarantees of a speedy trial, trial by jury, a public trial, the right to confront witnesses, and the right to a lawyer at various stages in some proceedings.

6. Eighth Amendment prohibitions against excessive bails and fines and cruel and unusual punishment.[6]

In recent years the Supreme Court has been active in interpreting these rights. Some of the cases are widely known. The *Miranda* decision, for example, established the rule that individuals who are arrested must be informed of their right to remain silent, of the fact that anything they say can be used against them in court, of their right to have a lawyer present, and of the duty of the state to provide lawyers for individuals who cannot pay for them.[7]

Criminal Process

A criminal prosecution differs significantly from a civil case in several respects. These differences reflect the desire to safeguard the rights of the individual against the state.

ARREST Before a warrant for arrest can be issued, probable cause must exist for believing that the individual in question has committed a crime. **Probable cause** can be defined as a substantial likelihood that the individual has committed or is about to commit a crime. Note that probable cause involves a likelihood, not just a possibility. Arrests may sometimes be made without a warrant when there is no time to get one, but the action of the arresting officer is still judged by the standard of probable cause.

INDICTMENT Individuals must be formally charged with having committed specific crimes before they can be brought to trial. This charge is called an **indictment** if issued by a grand jury and an **information** if issued by a magistrate. Be-

fore a charge can be issued, the grand jury or the magistrate must determine that there is sufficient evidence to justify bringing the individual to trial. The standard used to make this determination varies from jurisdiction to jurisdiction. Some courts use the probable cause standard. Others use the *preponderance of evidence* standard, which requires the evidence as a whole to show that it is more likely than not that the individual committed the crime. Still another standard is the *prima facie* case standard, which is a belief based only on the prosecution's evidence that the individual is guilty.

TRIAL At the trial the accused person does not have to prove anything. The entire burden of proof is on the prosecution (the state). Guilt must be established **beyond a reasonable doubt.** The prosecution must show that, based on all the evidence, the defendant's guilt is clear and unquestionable. Note that a verdict of "not guilty" is not the same as a statement that the defendant is innocent. It merely means that not enough evidence was properly presented to the court to prove guilt beyond all reasonable doubt. Courts have complex rules about what types of evidence may be presented and how the evidence may be brought out, especially in jury trials. These rules are designed to ensure that evidence in trials is relevant, reliable, and not unfairly prejudicial to the defendant. The defense attorney will cross-examine the witnesses who present evidence against his or her client in an attempt to show that their evidence is not reliable. Of course, the state may also cross-examine any witnesses presented by the defendant.

CRIMES AFFECTING BUSINESS

Numerous forms of crime occur in a business context. In this section, we focus on some of the more important crimes affecting business.

Forgery

The fraudulent making or alteration of any writing that changes the legal liability of another is **forgery.** If Samson signs Brewster's name without authorization to the back of a check made out to Brewster, Samson has committed forgery. Forgery also includes changing trademarks, falsifying public records, counterfeiting, and altering any legal document.

---

6. See the U.S. Constitution in Appendix A.

7. *Miranda v. Arizona*, 384 U.S. 436, 86 S.Ct. 1602, 16 L.Ed.2d 694 (1966).

CONCEPT SUMMARY: Criminal versus Civil Law

ISSUE	CRIMINAL LAW	CIVIL LAW
Who initiates the legal action?	The government, on behalf of the people.	The plaintiff or petitioner.
Reason for the legal action.	Punishment, deterrence, rehabilitation.	Compensation for wrongful act and/or deterrence.
Burden of proof.	Beyond reasonable doubt.	Preponderance of the evidence.
Major sanctions available.	Fines, incarceration, capital punishment.	Various equitable remedies (injunction, specific performance, etc.) and/or monetary damages.
Result of trial.	Conviction/acquittal.	Judgment or decree/dismissal.
Trial by jury.	Yes.	Yes in actions at law; no for actions in equity.

Most states have a special statute, often called a *credit card statute*, to cover the illegal use of credit cards. Thus, the state attorney can prosecute a person who misuses a credit card for violating either the forgery statute or the special credit card statute.

In the following case, the court examines the elements that are necessary to the crime of forgery.

 Case 6.2

PEOPLE v. BOKUNIEWICZ

Appellate Court of Illinois, Second District, 1987.
160 Ill.App.3d 270, 111 Ill.Dec. 892, 513 N.E.2d 138.

BACKGROUND AND FACTS   *Bokuniewicz was a practicing attorney. In the spring of 1983, he was hired by Rose Harnett to handle the sale of her home in Bellwood, Illinois. After the house had been sold, Harnett gave Bokuniewicz the money realized from the sale, as well as money from her savings account, to invest for her. In June 1985, Harnett's daughter, Ellen Mangano, noticed that her mother's resources were being depleted. She questioned Bokuniewicz about this but did not receive a satisfactory answer—although Bokuniewicz did give her a check for $5,600, representing a portion of her mother's funds. She thereafter hired attorney Edward Dean to do what he could to recoup her mother's money.*

Dean arranged a meeting with Bokuniewicz on June 22, 1985, at Dean's office. Dean demanded that Bokuniewicz either turn over Harnett's funds or provide an accounting for them. Bokuniewicz told Dean that he had all of Harnett's funds but was having trouble liquidating them. He gave Dean a cashier's check drawn on the Bank of Wheaton for $176,000. Bokuniewicz told Dean not to cash the check, stating that he had obtained it only to show Harnett that he had her money and could produce it as soon as he could liquidate her assets. Bokuniewicz did not indorse the check.

It was later discovered that the check had originally been made out by Barbara Bibbiano, an employee of the Bank of Wheaton, to Bokuniewicz for $176, not $176,000. Bokuniewicz was later arrested and charged with forgery. At trial, he was convicted. Bokuniewicz appealed, claiming that he did not commit the forgery and that there was no intent to defraud.

DUNN, Justice.
*   *   *   *

The elements of the offense of forgery *   *   * [are] as follows:
"(1) a document apparently capable of defrauding another; (2) a making or altering

of such document by one person in such manner that it purports to have been made by another; (3) knowledge by defendant that it has been thus made; (4) knowing delivery of the document; and (5) intent to defraud."

Defendant concedes that the cashier's check was altered by someone, but claims that the State failed to prove that it was defendant who altered it, or that defendant passed the check knowing it had been altered.

The drawer of the check was Barbara Bibbiano. Defendant postulates that it is at least as likely that Bibbiano altered the check as defendant. This argument is patently without merit.

David Ellis, vice-president of the Bank of Wheaton, testified about the bank's procedure for issuing a cashier's check. When a teller receives a cashier's check requisition and payment therefor, the teller prepares the check, and it is then signed by either a teller or a supervisor, depending on the amount of the check. It is apparent that Barbara Bibbiano was the Bank of Wheaton employee who prepared the check. A carbon copy of the check in the amount of $176 was introduced into evidence. Defendant does not even speculate as to a possible motive, much less an opportunity, for Bibbiano to alter the amount of the check after it had been thus prepared.

Further, it is undisputed that defendant purchased the check in the amount of $176 and later gave the check to Dean showing an amount of $176,000. Thus, defendant must have known that the check had been altered by someone. It is not necessary that defendant himself had altered the check, only that he knew of the alteration.

Defendant next contends that the State failed to prove that he possessed the intent to defraud. Defendant points out that he informed Dean that the check represented defendant's own funds rather than Harnett's and told Dean not to cash it. This, according to defendant, vitiated any intent to defraud.

Generally, if a defendant passes a forged document, intent to defraud is presumed. Defendant's statements to Dean do not overcome this presumption. At the June meeting, defendant gave Mangano a check for $5,600 and told her he needed more time to obtain the rest of the money. He later gave Dean the $176,000 check. Although defendant did not tell Dean that the money represented Mrs. Harnett's funds, he did imply that the check represented sufficient collateral for those funds. The obvious motive was to buy himself more time until his "inevitable arrest." Although defendant correctly points out that he did not receive value for the check, he did cause Harnett to delay, at least for a few days, or forego entirely, possible legal remedies which she might have had.

*   *   *   *

*   *   *   There is no requirement that someone be actually defrauded.

*   *   *   *

Defendant in the instant case intended that Dean, Mangano and Harnett treat the check as genuine in order to avoid possible legal consequences of his actions. Although he did not intend the check as repayment of the funds, he did intend it as "false security" for his debt to Harnett.

Defendant also argues that the check was not an instrument "apparently capable of defrauding another" because Dean could not have cashed the check absent defendant's endorsement and because he told Dean not to cash it. The capacity of the forged instrument to defraud need only be apparent, not actual. The test is whether a reasonable or ordinary person might be deceived into accepting the document as genuine. *   *   * [It] is generally held that the payee's endorsement is not necessary to make the instrument capable of defrauding.

*   *   *   *

In addition, we have already determined that defendant intended to defraud Dean and Harnett by offering the check as false security for Harnett's funds. Under such circumstances, defendant's endorsement was not required to achieve the desired result. For the same reason, defendant's warning to Dean not to cash the check did not render the document incapable of defrauding.

The lower court's decision was affirmed. The defendant's conviction and sentence were upheld.

Bokuniewicz also argued that his five-year sentence was too harsh, but, in light of the fact that he had squandered the life savings of a woman in her eighties, the court was not sympathetic.

Robbery

At common law, **robbery** was the taking of another's personal property, from his or her person or immediate presence, by force or intimidation. The use of force or fear is this crime's distinguishing characteristic. Thus, picking pockets is not robbery because the action is unknown to the victim. Typically, states have more severe penalties for *aggravated* robbery—robbery by use of a deadly weapon.

Burglary

At common law, **burglary** was defined as breaking and entering the dwelling of another at night with the intent to commit a felony. Originally, the definition was aimed at protecting an individual's home and its occupants. Most state statutes have eliminated some of the requirements found in the common law definition. Thus, the time at which the breaking and entering occurs is usually immaterial. State statutes frequently omit the element of breaking and do not restrict all degrees of the crime to dwellings, but include all buildings. Aggravated burglary, which is defined as burglary with the use of a deadly weapon, and burglary of a dwelling incur greater penalties.

Larceny

The wrongful or fraudulent taking and carrying away by any person of the personal property of another is **larceny.** It includes the fraudulent intent to permanently deprive an owner of property. Many business-related larcenies entail fraudulent conduct.

The place from which physical property is taken is generally immaterial. Statutes usually prescribe a stiffer sentence, however, when property is taken from buildings such as banks or warehouses. Larceny is differentiated from robbery by the fact that robbery involves force or fear and larceny does not. Therefore, picking another's pockets is larceny, not robbery.

As society has become more complex, the question has often arisen as to what is property. In most states, the definition of the property that is subject to larceny statutes has been expanded. Stealing computer programs may constitute larceny even though the programs consist of magnetic impulses. Trade secrets can be subject to larceny statutes. Stealing the use of telephone wires by the device known as a "blue box" is subject to larceny statutes. So, too, is the theft of natural gas.

There is a common law distinction between grand and petit larceny that depends on the value of the property taken. Many states have abolished this distinction, but in those that have not, grand larceny is a felony and petit larceny is a misdemeanor.

Obtaining Goods by False Pretenses

It is a criminal act to obtain goods by means of false pretenses—that is, to represent as true some fact or circumstance that is not true, with the intent of deceiving and with the result of defrauding an individual into relinquishing property without adequate compensation. For example, buying groceries with a check knowing that one has insufficient funds to cover it is obtaining goods by false pretenses. Statutes covering such illegal activities vary widely from state to state.

Receiving Stolen Goods

It is a crime to receive stolen goods. The recipient of such goods need not know the true identity of the owner or of the thief. All that is necessary is that the recipient knows or should have known that the goods are stolen, which implies an intent to deprive the owner of those goods.

Embezzlement

The fraudulent conversion of property or money owned by one person but *entrusted* to another is **embezzlement.** Typically, it involves an employee who fraudulently appropriates money. Banks face this problem, and so do a number of businesses in which corporate officers or accountants "jimmy" the books to cover up the fraudulent conversion of money for their own benefit. Embezzlement is not larceny because to commit embezzlement the wrongdoer does not need to carry away the property from the possession of another. In fact, embezzlement involves the conversion of property by a person *in lawful possession* of that property, whereas larceny involves the taking and carrying away of another's property, usually without any right to possession at all. (For example, Stevenson's taking his office typewriter home is embezzlement. If he gets caught and fired for it and, on the way out, takes the office calculator, he commits larceny.)

Embezzlement is not robbery because there is no taking by use of force or fear.

It does not matter whether the accused takes the money from the victim or from a third person. If, as the comptroller of a large corporation, Saunders pockets a certain number of checks from third parties that were given to her to deposit into the account of another company, she has committed embezzlement.

Often the owner of property will remit money to a contractor specifically for the contractor to pay various persons who worked on the owner's building. The contractor who does not use the money for this purpose commits a special form of embezzlement called *misapplication of trust funds.* The funds were entrusted to the contractor for a specific purpose, and that trust has been violated.

An embezzler who returns what has been taken will not ordinarily be prosecuted, because the owner usually will not take the time to make a complaint, give depositions, and appear in court. The fact that the accused intended eventually to return the embezzled property, however, does not constitute a sufficient defense to the crime of embezzlement. This point is made clear in the following case.

Case 6.3

STATE v. SLEMMER
Court of Appeals of Washington,
Division 1, 1987.
48 Wash.App. 48, 738 P.2d 281.

BACKGROUND AND FACTS   *Slemmer, who had been a successful options trader, gave lectures to small groups about stock options. Several persons who attended his lectures decided to invest in stock options and have Slemmer advise them. They formed an investment club called Profit Design Group (PDG).*

Slemmer set up an account for PDG with a brokerage firm. Slemmer had control of the PDG account and could make decisions on which stock options to buy or sell. He was not authorized to withdraw money from the account for his own benefit. Nonetheless, he withdrew money from the PDG account to make payments on real estate he owned.

Slemmer made false representations to the members of PDG, and he eventually lost all the money in their account. A jury found him guilty of first degree theft by embezzlement. Slemmer objected to the trial court's failure to instruct the jury that an intent to permanently deprive was an element of the crime charged.

RINGOLD, Acting Chief Judge.
* * * *

Slemmer was PDG's agent. He was authorized by agreement to make investment decisions with the money in the PDG account. Slemmer was not authorized to withdraw money from the account for any other purpose than investing in stock options. Slemmer, however, used money from PDG's account to make payments on investment property he owned and to make his house payments.

The facts demonstrate embezzlement. Slemmer had control of PDG's account as their agent, and was authorized to control the account by agreement. Thus, when he appropriated the funds in the account to his own use he was [embezzling].

The crime of theft by embezzlement does not require a finding of intent to permanently deprive. The trial court correctly refused to instruct the jury that such an element was required.

The court of appeals affirmed the trial court's ruling that proof of intent to permanently deprive is not a necessary element for the crime of embezzlement.

**DECISION
AND REMEDY**

Arson

The willful and malicious burning of a building or some other structure (and in some states personal property) owned by another is the crime of **arson.** At common law, arson applied only to burning down the house of another. Such law was designed to protect human life. Today, arson statutes apply to other kinds of structures as well. Also, if someone is killed as a result of arson, the act is murder under the felony murder rule.

BURNING TO DEFRAUD INSURERS   Every state has a special statute that covers burning a building in order to collect insurance. If Allison owns an insured apartment building that is falling apart and burns it himself or pays someone else to set fire to it, Allison is guilty of burning to defraud insurers. Of course, the insurer need not pay the claim when insurance fraud is proved.

Use of the Mails to Defraud

It is a federal crime to use the mails to defraud the public. Illegal use of the mails must involve (1) mailing or causing someone else to mail a writing for the purpose of executing a scheme to defraud and (2) a contemplated or organized scheme to defraud by false pretenses. If, for example, Johnson advertises the sale of a cure for cancer that he knows to be fraudulent because it has no medical validity, he can be prosecuted for fraudulent use of the mails. Federal law also makes it a crime to use a telegram to defraud.

WHITE-COLLAR CRIME

Although no official definition exists for **white-collar crime,** the term is popularly used to mean

an illegal act or series of acts committed by an individual or corporation using some nonviolent means to obtain a personal or business advantage. Usually, this kind of crime is committed in the course of a legitimate occupation. The cost to the public of so-called white-collar crimes ranges between $50 billion and $120 billion a year.

Since it is impossible to cover the vast range of what are considered to be white-collar crimes, the efforts in this chapter will center on four areas: (1) bribery, (2) bankruptcy fraud, (3) corporate crimes, and (4) criminal RICO violations. Computer crime, a white-collar crime of growing significance in the business world, will be discussed in Chapter 55.

Bribery

Basically, three types of actions called bribery are considered crimes. They involve: (1) bribery of foreign officials, (2) bribery of public officials, and (3) commercial bribery.

BRIBERY OF FOREIGN OFFICIALS   Until the 1970s, bribery of foreign officials to obtain business contracts was rarely, if ever, discussed. Indeed, giving payments in cash or in-kind benefits to foreign government officials for such purposes is often considered normal practice. This is not to say that the practice is legal. In order to reduce the amount of such bribes given to foreign government officials by representatives of U.S. corporations, Congress passed the Foreign Corrupt Practices Act in 1977.[8]

The act is divided into two major parts. The first part, which applies to all U.S. companies and their directors, officers, shareholders, employees,

---

8. 15 U.S.C.A. Section 78 *et seq.*

and agents, prohibits bribery of most foreign government officials if the purpose is to obtain or retain business for the U.S. company.

The second part is directed toward accountants because, prior to the passage of the act, bribes were often concealed in corporate financial records. The act requires all companies to keep detailed records that "accurately and fairly" reflect the company's financial activities and to have an accounting system that provides "reasonable assurance" that all transactions entered into by the company are accounted for and legal. Although broad in scope, these requirements should assist in detecting illegal foreign bribes.

The act further prohibits any person in the company from making false statements to accountants and prohibits any person from making any false entry in any record or account. Violation of the act results in fines of up to $1 million and the incarceration of officers or directors of convicted companies for a maximum of five years. Those officers and directors can also be fined up to $10,000, and the fine cannot be paid by the company.

Notice that the act does not prohibit payment of substantial sums to minor officials, as long as their duties are ministerial, or clerical. Such payments are often referred to as "grease," or facilitating, payments. They are meant to ensure that customary services that might be performed at a rather slow pace are speeded up.

BRIBERY OF PUBLIC OFFICIALS   The attempt to influence a public official to act in a way that serves a private interest is a crime. As an element of this crime, *intent* must be present and proved. The bribe that is offered can be anything that the recipient of the offer considers valuable. *The commission of the crime of bribery occurs when the bribe is tendered* (offered or given). The recipient does not have to agree to perform whatever action is desired by the person tendering the bribe; nor does the recipient have to accept the bribe.

COMMERCIAL BRIBERY   In some states, so-called kickbacks and payoffs from an individual working for one company to another individual or individuals working for another company are crimes. No public official need be involved. Such commercial bribes are typically given with the intent of obtaining proprietary information, covering up an inferior product, or securing new business. Industrial espionage sometimes involves this kind of

activity—for example, a payoff of some type to an employee in a competing firm in exchange for trade secrets and pricing schedules.

Bankruptcy Fraud

When a business finds itself with an oppressive amount of debt, its creditors may seek to have the court adjudge it a bankrupt company. Alternatively, the individual or business entity may seek voluntary bankruptcy. Today, individuals and businesses can be relieved of oppressive debt by federal law under the Bankruptcy Reform Act of 1978, as amended by the Bankruptcy Amendments and Federal Judgeship Act of 1984 and by the Bankruptcy Judges, United States Trustees, and Family Farmer Bankruptcy Act of 1986 (see Chapter 31). The act requires that the debtor disclose all assets. The assets are then taken into possession by a trustee, unless they are exempt. The trustee must follow certain rules in distributing those assets to creditors. We discuss below some examples of the numerous white-collar crimes that can be perpetrated throughout the many phases of a bankruptcy proceeding.

FALSE CLAIMS OF CREDITORS   Creditors are required to file their individual claims against the debtor who is in bankruptcy proceedings. A creditor who files a false claim commits a crime.

TRANSFER OF PROPERTY   Obviously, a debtor, knowing that he or she will be in bankruptcy proceedings, has an incentive to transfer assets to favored parties before or after the petition for bankruptcy is filed. For example, a company-owned automobile can be "sold" at a bargain price to a trusted friend or relative. Closely related to the crime of fraudulent transfer of property is fraudulent concealment of property, such as hiding of gold coins. The number of ways in which debtors have fraudulently concealed assets would require several books to outline.

SCAM BANKRUPTCIES   The term *scam bankruptcy* has been used to indicate a swindle in which a bankruptcy is planned in advance. The perpetrators purchase a legitimate business that sells highly liquid goods, such as jewelry or electronic home entertainment equipment. Numerous items are purchased on credit by the new owners. The creditors are paid off within a relatively short period of time. This activity continues until the creditors are willing to offer larger and larger amounts of credit to the new owners. Finally, the new owners order a very large amount of merchandise on credit, sell it at whatever price is necessary to unload it quickly for cash, and then close down the business. Of course, creditors file an involuntary petition in bankruptcy against the business. The amount that those creditors will recover, however, is typically very small. And the scam operators are nowhere to be found.

Corporate Crimes

Corporations are "artificial" persons created by law. Clearly, they cannot harbor the criminal intent that is required for conviction of a crime, but their officers can. The modern tendency is to hold corporations criminally responsible for their acts or omissions if the assigned penalty is a fine and if intent either is not an element of the crime or can be implied.

Obviously, a crime such as perjury cannot be committed by a corporation but can be committed by a natural person, such as an officer of the corporation. Furthermore, a corporation cannot be convicted of a crime punishable by imprisonment. When a statute allows a fine in addition to, or in place of, these penalties, however, a corporation can be convicted of that crime. If, for example, a statute requires that adequate safety equipment be installed on machines, and a corporation fails to do so—and if the result is the death of a worker—the corporation can be fined for committing criminal manslaughter. In addition, the corporate officers who were in a position to prevent the wrong can be prosecuted under specific federal and state statutes.

Criminal RICO Violations

The passage and essential provisions of the Racketeer Influenced and Corrupt Organizations (RICO) Act were discussed in the preceding chapter. Essentially, the act was passed in an attempt to prevent the use of legitimate business enterprises as shields for racketeering activity and to prohibit the purchase of any legitimate business interest with illegally obtained funds.

Most of the criminal RICO offenses have little, if anything, to do with normal business activities, for they involve gambling, arson, and extortion. But securities fraud (involving the sale of stocks and bonds) and mail fraud are also criminal RICO violations, and RICO has become an effective tool in attacking these white-collar crimes in recent years. Under criminal provisions of RICO, any individual found guilty of a violation is subject to a fine of up to $25,000 per violation or imprisonment for up to twenty years—or both.

In the following case, the owner of a motel was charged with criminal RICO violations because the person to whom he leased the motel operated it as a place of prostitution. The owner-defendant was considered by the court to be sufficiently involved in the illegal operation to warrant conviction under criminal RICO.

BACKGROUND AND FACTS *In 1967 Tunnell purchased the Pines Motel at Kilgore, Texas. For over three decades, the motel had been known as a place of prostitution. When Tunnell was imprisoned for tax evasion in 1974, he leased the motel to Odessa Mae (Mildred) French for one year. Following two successive annual renewals, a five-year lease was executed in 1977. In each instance, the lease payment was $1,500 per month.*

The government maintained that Tunnell and French jointly operated the Pines Motel as a place of prostitution and that they bribed law enforcement officials, specifically King Russell, a justice of the peace, and Dwight Watson, a local constable, to permit their operations. Russell testified that he had an arrangement with Tunnell by which Tunnell reimbursed the sums Russell paid the prostitutes at the motel. The testimony of several witnesses—including prostitutes, motel employees, and law-enforcement officials—linked Tunnell to the prostitution activities and to the corruption of the constable and the justice of the peace. Tunnell admitted knowing Russell and Watson and acknowledged the long-standing reputation of the motel, but he denied knowledge of any bribes and of the reimbursement scheme.

 Case 6.4

UNITED STATES v. TUNNELL

United States Court of Appeals, Fifth Circuit, 1982.
667 F.2d 1182.

Tunnell was indicted for a RICO substantive offense (prostitution) and a RICO conspiracy offense, together with French (the madam) and King Russell. Prior to trial Russell pleaded guilty to a lesser charge. The jury found Tunnell and French guilty on both counts. Tunnell appealed his conviction, claiming there was no bribery or conspiracy.

POLITZ, Circuit Judge.
* * * *

We * * * reject Tunnell's contention that French's action in furnishing the services of a prostitute free of charge to the peace officers does not constitute the predicate crime of bribery. Tunnell would limit the term "benefit" to pecuniary gain. * * *

The evidence in the record establishes the economic value of the services of a prostitute. These services were provided at no cost. This constitutes the bestowing of an economic gain, a benefit, upon the recipient public official. The argument to the contrary is not convincing.
* * * *

Tunnell challenges the sufficiency of the evidence relating to his aiding and abetting French in her acts of bribery. Specifically, Tunnell argues that the mere act of leasing his motel to French, even with knowledge that she intended to conduct a prostitution operation on the premises, is not enough to link him to the bribery of public officials as a principal. * * * While simple presence at the scene of a crime is insufficient to convict one of aiding and abetting, the record establishes that Tunnell played an active role in the prostitution business and in the corruption of local officials. He obviously was more involved than he was prepared to admit.

Testimony received at trial demonstrated that Tunnell often ran the prostitution business, even though French had leased the motel. He personally passed approval on new prostitutes, bribed the local justice of the peace and constable, told others about the operation, and bragged that if it "wasn't for his politicking * * * Mildred [French] and Watson wouldn't have a job." In short, the record is replete with evidence that Tunnell possessed active knowledge of the racketeering operations conducted on the motel premises and involved himself in these activities.

DECISION AND REMEDY   *The appellate court affirmed Tunnell's conviction under RICO's criminal statute provisions.*

CONCEPT SUMMARY: Classifications of Law	
LAW CLASSIFICATIONS	**TYPES OF OFFENSE**

Criminal law is concerned with acts against society for which society seeks redress in the form of punishment.	1. Felony
	  a. Homicide
	  b. Manslaughter
	  c. Robbery
	  d. Burglary
	  e. Larceny (grand)
	  f. Bribery
	  g. Arson

CONCEPT SUMMARY: Classifications of Law (Continued)	
LAW CLASSIFICATIONS	**TYPES OF OFFENSE**

Criminal Law (Continued)	2. Misdemeanor
	  a. Public intoxication
	  b. Vagrancy
	  c. Prostitution
	  d. Larceny (petit)
	  e. Trespass
	  f. Disturbing the peace
	  g. Assault and Battery

Civil law is concerned with acts against a person for which the injured party seeks redress in the form of compensation or other relief.	1. Contract Breach
	  a. Real estate
	  b. Insurance
	  c. Sales
	  d. Business organization formation
	  e. Services
	  f. Commercial paper obligations
	  g. Commercial bailments
	2. Tort
	  a. Defamation
	  b. Invasion of privacy
	  c. Assault and battery
	  d. Negligence
	  e. Strict liability
	  f. Trespass
	  g. Fraud

QUESTIONS AND CASE PROBLEMS

1. Civil trials and criminal trials are conducted under essentially the same format. There are, however, several important differences. In criminal trials, the defendant must be proved guilty beyond reasonable doubt, whereas in civil trials, the defendant need only be proved guilty by a preponderance of the evidence. Can you see any reason for this difference?

2. Crimes are classified as either felonies or misdemeanors. Determine from the facts below what type of crime has been committed and whether the crime is a felony or a misdemeanor.

(a) Allen and George become involved in a shouting argument. Allen knocks George down, causing a serious head injury to George.

(b) Darrell continually crosses Mary's backyard without permission, despite Mary's notice to Darrell to get off her land.

(c) Harold walks into a camera shop. Without force and without the owner noticing, Harold walks out of the store with a camera.

3. The following fact situations are similar (the theft of Jean's television set); yet three different crimes are described. Identify the three crimes, noting the differences among them.

(a) While passing Jean's house one night, Sam sees a portable television set left unattended on Jean's lawn. Sam takes the television set, carries it home, and tells everyone he owns it.

(b) While passing Jean's house one night, Sam sees Jean outside with a portable television set. Holding Jean at gunpoint, Sam forces her to give up the set. Then Sam runs away with it.

(c) While passing Jean's house one night, Sam sees a portable television set in a window. Sam breaks the front door lock, enters, and leaves with the set.

4. Jack, an undercover police officer, stops Patricia on a busy street and offers to sell her an expensive wristwatch for a fraction of its value. After some questioning, Jack admits that the watch is stolen property, although he says that he was not the thief. Patricia pays for and receives the wristwatch and is immediately arrested by Jack for receiv-

ing stolen property. At trial, Patricia contends she was a victim of entrapment. What is the result of the trial?

5. Two basic elements are needed for a person to be convicted of a crime. The first element is called *actus reus*, and the second is called *mens rea*. Explain what these terms mean, and discuss how each is applied to the following:

    (a) Murder or manslaughter.

    (b) Forgery.   (c) Arson.

6. Faulkner was a seaman on the ship Zemindar. One night while on duty, Faulkner went in search of the rum that he knew the ship was carrying. He found it and opened one of the kegs, but because he was holding a match at the time, he inadvertently ignited the rum and set fire to the ship. Faulkner was criminally prosecuted for setting the fire. At the trial, it was determined that even though he had not intended to set fire to the rum, he had been engaged in the unlawful act of stealing it. Does Faulkner's theft of the rum make him criminally liable for setting fire to the ship? [Regina v. Faulkner, 13 Cox C.C. 550 (1877)]

7. In 1965 Rybicki failed to pay the complete amount of income tax he owed the federal government. Attempts by the IRS to collect the tax proved fruitless. Therefore, the IRS, through lawful means, obtained a tax lien on Rybicki's personal property, which included his truck. In February 1967 Rybicki's wife, upon hearing the motor of the truck, awoke her sleeping husband. Wielding a shotgun, Rybicki went to his front door and told the two men who were attempting to take his truck to stop. Rybicki claimed that he did not know that the two men were IRS agents. Subsequently, the federal government indicted Rybicki for obstructing justice. Can Rybicki be held criminally liable if he did not know that the men were IRS agents performing their duty? [United States v. Rybicki, 403 F.2d 599 (6th Cir. 1968)]

8. Pivowar agreed to lend Mills approximately $9,000. Mills agreed to repay the loan and further agreed that the loan would be secured by two houses that he owned. Mills showed Pivowar the two houses but falsely represented that Pivowar was to get a first mortgage on the houses. Pivowar later learned that the mortgages he held were not on the two houses but on two vacant lots and, further, that the mortgages were second mortgages and not first mortgages as Mills had promised. Can Mills be prosecuted criminally for false pretenses if he contends that he intended to pay back the loan and that Pivowar never demanded payment on the note? [State v. Mills, 96 Ariz. 377, 396 P.2d 5 (1964)]

9. Gomez, an informant for the police, approached Saldana and, in order to gain his trust, told him he was an ex-convict. Gomez urged Saldana on several occasions to sell cocaine in order to make money, but Saldana, although he used cocaine, did not wish to sell any. Finally, in order to get Gomez to stop pestering him, Saldana agreed to sell some cocaine to one Castello, who turned out to be a police officer. May Saldana successfully claim an entrapment defense? [Saldana v. State, 732 S.W.2d 701 (Tex.App.—Corpus Christi 1987)]

10. Britt was convicted of second-degree homicide for the shooting death of his neighbor, Cavell. The victim was killed by a .44 caliber revolver that was part of a trap set by Britt to prevent forcible entry into his home from the back door. The booby trap was set to discharge if the door was opened a distance of two to four inches. The relevant Louisiana law reads: "A homicide is justifiable . . . when committed by a person lawfully inside a dwelling against a person who is attempting to make an unlawful entry into the dwelling or who has made an unlawful entry into the dwelling and the person committing the homicide reasonably believes that the use of deadly force is necessary to prevent the entry or to compel the intruder to leave the premises. The homicide shall be justifiable even though the person committing the homicide does not retreat from the encounter." Britt argues on appeal that the shooting of Cavell was justified because, had he been present, he would have been authorized to use deadly force and to use a mechanical contrivance. Will Britt's appeal be successful? [State v. Britt, 510 So.2d 670 (La.App. 1st Cir. 1987)]

11. Patterson was charged with first degree robbery for pointing a loaded gun at a man and demanding money from him. At trial, Patterson did not contest the state's proof that she committed these acts but instead relied on the defense of insanity. She claimed she was unable, as a result of mental disease or defect, to appreciate the nature and quality of her conduct. The superior court instructed the jury that in order to find Patterson not guilty by reason of insanity, it had to find that, because of a mental disease or defect, she did not understand that she was performing the physical acts that comprise the elements of the crime with which she was charged. In other words, the superior court read the insanity defense statute as incorporating only the first prong of the traditional *M'Naghten* insanity defense—that the defendant did not understand the basic nature and quality of his or her conduct. The jury found Patterson did not come within this interpretation. The court of appeals, however, ruled that the trial court had interpreted the insanity defense too narrowly. It held that the correct interpretation of the insanity defense included *both* prongs of the *M'Naghten* test—that the defendant could be found not guilty by reason of insanity if the defendant *either* was not aware of the physical acts he or she was performing *or* did not understand the wrongfulness of those acts. Is the appellate court right? [State v. Patterson, 740 P.2d 944 (Alaska 1987)]

12. The defendant (Faulkner), a truck driver, was hauling a load of refrigerators from San Diego to New York for the trucking company that employed him. He departed from his assigned route and stopped in Las Vegas, where he attempted to display and sell some of the refrigerators to a firm. Although the refrigerators never left the truck, in order to display them he had to break the truck's seals, enter the cargo department, and open two refrigerator cartons. The store owner refused to purchase the appliances, and when Faulkner left the store, he was arrested. He was later convicted under federal law for the embezzlement of an interstate shipment. Faulkner appealed, claiming that there were no grounds for the charge, since he had never removed any equipment from the truck. Discuss whether the charge of embezzlement applies when the property has not been physically removed from the owner's possession. [United States v. Faulkner, 638 F.2d 129 (9th Cir. 1981)]

Focus on Ethics

The Central Problem: Defining Business Ethics

Every day, people in all walks of life face ethical questions—questions such as, What is fair? What is just? What is the right thing to do in this particular situation? Essentially, any question involving the fairness, justice, rightness, or wrongness of an action is an ethical question. It goes without saying that business people are not exempt from the task of making ethical decisions. Indeed, ethical decision making in the business context frequently takes on added significance because of the number of people—employees, shareholders, consumers, competitors, and so on—who may be affected by the outcome.

Since many decisions faced by businesspersons are complicated by ethical dimensions, it is important for anyone embarking on a career in business today to be able to both recognize and deal effectively with ethical issues. Although no textbook can provide all the answers, the *Focus on Ethics* sections that conclude each unit in this text provide useful insights into the ethical dimensions of business transactions and business law. A knowledge of how and why ethical issues have arisen in the past and how they have been

dealt with is the first step toward handling them effectively in the future.

As a point of departure in our exploration of ethical issues, it is important to recognize the distinction between ethics and the law.

THE DISTINCTION BETWEEN ETHICS AND THE LAW

In all societies, ethics and the law go hand in hand—to a certain extent. That is to say, the law reflects a society's customs and values and is intended to enforce principles of behavior that society deems right and just. *Good faith, honesty, reasonability,* and similar terms frequently encountered in business law ultimately rest on ethical premises—that is, on collectively held opinions as to what constitutes right or wrong behavior. In a sense, then, many ethical decisions are made for us—by our laws, in which many of our ethical values are codified.

Nonetheless, simply obeying the law does not fulfill all ethical obligations. In the interest of preserving personal freedom, as well as for practical reasons, the law does not, and cannot, codify all ethical requirements. No law says, for example, that it is

illegal to lie to one's family, but it may be *unethical* to do so. Likewise, in the business world, numerous actions might be unethical but not necessarily illegal. And even though it may be convenient for business persons to satisfy themselves with legal compliance, such an approach may not always yield ethical outcomes.

Consider the following example. The U.S. federal government has discovered that a child's toy is dangerous and has caused the death of some children. Consequently, the government has banned sales of the toy, leaving the manufacturer with a large unsold inventory. Although sales of the product are banned in the United States, it may be perfectly legal to export this purportedly dangerous toy to nations that have little consumer protection legislation. But would it be ethical?

Consider a similar situation. A corporate executive needs to decide whether to continue manufacturing a product that, although very popular, has injured some consumer-users in the past several years. Because the corporation has complied with all government requirements to warn consumers of the product's potential dangers if not used as intended, the company has so far escaped liability for these injuries. To continue manufacturing the product would therefore not be illegal; but again, it might not be ethical.

The answers to ethical questions such as these are not always simple, because the context in which they arise often involves not one but many ethical considerations.

WHY DO ETHICAL ISSUES ARISE?

For business people, ethical issues arise because of competing interests in the business world among buyers, sellers, owners, managers, nonmanagerial personnel, and other groups. In the hypothetical situations described in the preceding section, for example, most people would agree that the producers have an ethical obligation to protect consumers from hazardous products. But they also have ethical obligations to act in the best interests of their corporate shareholders—which means running the business profitably. They have a further ethical obligation toward corporate employees and their families. If the products were discontinued, some employees might be laid off or receive reduced salaries or benefits because of the consequent reduction in profits. In short, ethical issues frequently arise in the business context because of conflicting obligations. Often, there is no single completely "right" solution to an ethical problem. Rather, ethical business judgments usually involve balancing the interests and welfare of one group against those of another.

Ethical problems may also arise when there is a conflict between the goals of different departments of the same company. It is frequently difficult in a company to determine who has the responsibility to voice concern over the quality or safety of a product being manufactured. It is often middle management that has the knowledge upon which an ethical dilemma turns. All too often the manager in such a case is in a no-win situation. He or she must be concerned with the reaction of upper-management personnel as well as with the reactions of fellow employees. A middle manager most likely has also developed a loyalty to the reputation of the company and its long-run interests. Thus, disclosing or not disclosing quality problems places a great deal of pressure on the middle manager. How do you decide whether it is your ethical responsibility to disclose quality problems? What if the situation is clearly under someone else's control and that person obviously is content to ignore what you personally perceive to be unethical conduct?

CONFRONTING ETHICAL DILEMMAS

The case of *Geary* v. *United States Steel Corporation* [456 Pa. 171, 319 A.2d 174 (1974)] illustrates some possible consequences of an ethical dilemma. George Geary was employed by the United States Steel Corporation to sell tubular products to the oil and gas industry. Geary alleged that he believed that one of the company's new products, a tubular casing, had not been adequately tested and constituted a serious danger to anyone who used it. Even though Geary at all times performed his duties to the best of his ability, he continued to express his reservations with respect to the company's new product. Geary alleged that because of the above events, he was summarily discharged without notice.

This case reached the Supreme Court of Pennsylvania, which ruled against Geary as a matter of law. The court noted that Geary was not a safety expert and had bypassed ordinary company procedures in his complaints. Most significant, though, was the court's fear that permitting such cases would embroil our legal system in too many internal company disputes. Thus, the company acted lawfully, but did it act ethically?

To make a reliable ethical analysis of this case would require more facts about company policies and other issues. Suppose you were a manager and Geary raised the matter with you. How would you act and what ethical factors would influence your decision? If you were a shareholder in the company, how would you want your managers to respond to this situation? As a member of society, how would you want managers to respond to the situation? And what about Geary's ethics? What are his duties relative to his employer and to society?

Clearly, there are conflicting interests to which our laws must address themselves. On the one hand, our legal system serves to encourage individuals to acknowledge their ethical responsibilities. Yet, on the other hand, our laws must be structured in such a way as to discourage frivolous suits that unnecessarily disrupt business.

WHITE-COLLAR CRIME

White-collar crime is composed of numerous categories of behavior that society considers to be unethical. The term *white-collar crime* generally refers to nonviolent crimes committed by corporations and individuals. Theft, fraud, and embezzlement are examples of white-collar crime.

Increasingly, ethical dilemmas are facing men and women in their careers. What if fraud is being committed by your boss? How will you know if the entire company is involved in a fraudulent conspiracy? In this situation, complaining to top management will be of little avail. Furthermore, what if the behavior you regard as unethical is in fact behavior that you have misinterpreted or behavior that is actually quite legal and ethical? If you have simply made a mistake, the company shouldn't worry. Yet all too often companies see inquiries concerning their ethics as a lack of company loyalty. These types of ethical dilemmas are not easy to resolve and indeed can be quite stressful.

WHITE-COLLAR SENTENCING

Ethical issues also arise with respect to the sentencing of those convicted of white-collar crimes. Should they be subject to the traditional penalties—such as imprisonment and fines—or are different modes of punishment more appropriate? In 1974, Judge Renfrew of the Northern District of California imposed suspended jail sentences on five corporate executives convicted of conspiring to fix prices in the paper label industry.* The suspension of these jail sentences was conditional upon each of the five defendants

*Charles B. Renfrew, "The Paper Label Sentences: An Evaluation," 86 *Yale Law Journal* 590 (1977).

making an oral presentation before twelve business, civic, or other groups concerning the circumstances of the case and each defendant's participation therein. The defendants were further required to submit a written report giving the details of each presentation, the composition of the group, and the response of the group.

Even though Judge Renfrew's sentencing is unusual, there is a tendency for judges to impose fines, as opposed to criminal sanctions, upon those who have committed white-collar crimes. Do you think this tendency is justified or desirable? Should white-collar offenders, who otherwise are charitable and law-abiding citizens, be given sentences other than the traditional forms of punishment? The defense counsel generally argues that "they have suffered enough." Have they? Or is this not the point?

WHISTLE-BLOWING

What happens to employees who blow the whistle on dangerous or improper business behavior? In the past, employees who exposed illegal activities frequently found themselves disciplined or even fired by their employers. The states, however, are slowly beginning to extend protection to whistle-blowers.

California, Connecticut, Maine, Michigan, and New York have passed special laws with respect to workers and whistle-blowing. Yet many states uphold the "fire at will" doctrine. Furthermore, companies may use subtle techniques, such as transferring a whistle-blower to a less desirable location or otherwise making his or her work hours miserable.

Many who sympathize with whistle-blowers are attempting to change business attitudes toward this type of activity. These sympathizers are attempting to impress upon companies that they can benefit in various ways by avoiding improper and dangerous practices. Costly liability actions by injured workers or consumers can often be avoided when dangerous business practices are eliminated.

Regardless of the movement for greater protection of whistle-blowers, the dilemma remains. How many working men or women with children to feed and to send through school are willing to risk their jobs, or at the least face subtle types of punishment, in order to expose business behavior that they know is unethical and often dangerous? Even though whistle-blowing is more often than not in the public interest, too often the pressure upon individuals to tolerate or ignore unethical behavior deters workers from blowing the whistle.

THE COMPLEXITY OF ETHICS

Ethical decision making is not always an easy matter. Individuals are often tempted to go with their own "gut impulse" about ethics. Indeed, such impulses may often be well founded. In other cases, however, ethics may require greater reflection upon the issues.

Business ethics presents all the great ethical difficulties, problems with which philosophers have grappled for centuries. For example, is the practice of lying to others always wrong? Or does it depend upon circumstances?

May lying be ethically acceptable in support of a higher moral objective? Does a business person have special or different ethical responsibilities because of that person's role in society? Or should such a business person simply behave as he or she would in a nonbusiness setting? All of these positions have their advocates and detractors. Perhaps each individual should approach these issues independently and in line with his or her personal ethical beliefs.

DISCUSSION QUESTIONS

1. Should businesses be concerned with ethics? In other words, should companies have social or ethical goals in addition to profit-making goals?

2. If companies should have goals other than making profits, who in the company should set those goals?

3. Should the choice of who will set the goals depend on the type of business conducted by the company or on the current political and social climate?

4. Should ethics be a concern of top management alone, or should it be a shared concern of all employees, distributors, suppliers, and so on?

5. If ethics is a concern shared throughout the company, how would you design corporate policy to reflect ethical considerations?

Unit Two

CONTRACTS

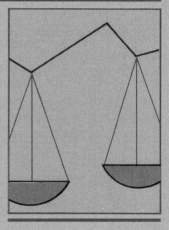

Chapter 7

Nature and Terminology

In the legal environment of business, contracts is one of the most significant bodies of law. Contract law shows to what extent our society allows people to make promises or commitments that are legally binding. It shows what excuses our society will accept for the breaking of such promises. And it shows what kinds of promises will be considered as being against public policy and therefore legally void.

A **contract** may be defined as a promise enforceable at law directly or indirectly.[1] A **promise** is an undertaking that something will or will not happen in the future. Thus, a contract may be formed when two or more parties each promise to perform or to refrain from performing some act now or in the future. On the contract's **breach** (that is, if a contractual promise is not fulfilled), the breaching party may be subject to legal or equitable sanctions. These sanctions may include a payment of money to the nonbreaching party for the *failure to perform*. Under some circumstances, the breaching party may be required to render **specific performance** (that is, to fulfill the promise).

As general rule, a promise will be enforced by a court (or damages will be imposed for breaking the promise) as long as it was made knowingly and voluntarily. Sometimes, however, enforcing a promise will transgress an important public policy. If the promise is against the interests of society as a whole, it may be invalidated. Also, if it was made by a child, or by an insane person, or on the basis of false information, a question will be raised about whether it should be enforced. Resolving such questions is the essence of contract law.

The use of contract principles to govern the relationships of those who make promises to one another dates back thousands of years. Very early in history the importance of contracts was recognized and given legal effect. The following chapters will explain how contracts are formed, how they are discharged, and what happens when they are not performed. The rules relating to the formation, discharge, and breach of enforceable promises are called the *law of contracts*.

Society's need of contracts is obvious. The foundation for almost all commercial activity is the contract. The purchase of goods, such as auto-

---

1. The American Law Institute defines a *contract* as "a promise or set of promises for the breach of which the law gives a remedy, or the performance of which the law in some way recognizes as a duty." Restatement, Second, Contracts, Section 1.

mobiles, is governed by a sales contract; the hiring of people to work for us or to make repairs, by service contracts; the sharing of risks on our property, by insurance contracts. In short, we could not order our daily activities without contracts.[2] Contract law helps us predict the future because it looks to the future.

Although from state to state the laws concerning certain aspects of contract law may vary, much of the law is based on the common law. In 1932, the American Law Institute compiled the Restatement of the Law of Contracts. This work is a nonstatutory, authoritative exposition of the present law on the subject of contracts. The Restatement is presently in its second edition and will be referred to throughout the following contract chapters.

THE FUNCTION OF CONTRACTS

Contract law assures the parties to private agreements that the promises they make will be enforced. Not all promises or obligations are enforceable. Sometimes the promises exchanged create *moral* rather than *legal* obligations. Failure to perform a moral obligation such as a sweetheart's promise to be faithful forever, does not create a legal liability. Nonperformance of a contract generally does. The promise of a father to pay for the college education of his daughter may involve a legal, as well as a moral, question.

Clearly, many promises are kept because of a sense of duty, or because keeping them is in the mutual self-interest of the parties involved, not because the **promisor** (the person making the promise) or the **promisee** (the person to whom the promise is made) is conscious of the rules of contract law. Nevertheless, the rules of contract law are often followed in business agreements so that potential problems may be avoided.

By providing procedures for enforcing private agreements, contract law provides an essential condition for the existence of a market economy. Without a legal framework for reasonably assured expectations within which to plan and venture, businesspersons would be able to rely only on the good faith of others. Duty and good faith are usually sufficient, but when price changes or adverse economic factors make it costly to comply with a promise, these elements may not be enough. Contract law is necessary to ensure compliance with a promise or to entitle a nonbreaching party to some form of relief.

Understanding the law concerning contracts is one of the keys to understanding the U.S. legal system. Contract law provides a major part of the foundation on which more specialized areas of the law have been built. A basic understanding of the principles governing contracts facilitates an understanding of the principles involved in: sales of goods (Chapters 16–21); negotiation and transfer of funds by check, draft, note, or electronic means (Chapters 22–28); secured transactions (Chapter 29); relations between debtors and creditors (Chapters 30 and 31); relations among employers, employees, and agents (Chapters 32–33); creation, operation, and termination of partnerships and corporations (Chapters 34–43); regulation of trade and monopolies (Chapter 48); and transfers of property other than goods or by means other than sales or between parties who are not merchants (Chapters 50–53).

FREEDOM OF CONTRACT AND FREEDOM FROM CONTRACT

As a general rule, the law recognizes everyone's ability to enter freely into contractual arrangements. This recognition is called *freedom of contract*, a freedom protected by the U.S. Constitution in Article I, Section 10. But as the character of institutions and society changes, the functions of contract law and its enforcement must also change. Such change can be perceived today in the fact that certain types of agreements are no longer considered valid. For example, illegal bargains, agreements unreasonably in restraint of trade,

---

2. The Soviet Union attempted to eliminate the need for contracts by dispensing with the private ordering of activities. The state required everyone to engage in certain specified activities—work, education, recreation—in the hope of redistributing wealth according to administrative standards and norms. The experiment failed, and Lenin explicitly recognized this when he wrote in 1921, "The private market proved to be stronger than we [thought]. * * * We ended up with ordinary * * * trade." Ultimately, contracts were reintroduced, and contract law was codified along traditional lines. See Loeber, *"Plan and Contract Performance in Soviet Law,"* reprinted in *Law in the Soviet Society,* ed. Wayne R. LaFave (Urbana: University of Illinois Press, 1965).

and certain unfair contracts made between one party with an inordinate amount of bargaining power and another with little power are generally not enforced. In addition, certain contracts with consumers, as well as certain clauses within those contracts, are not enforceable under the rationale of public policy, fairness, and justice (see Chapter 11 for details). The law of contracts is broadening to include new controls on the manner of contracting and on the allowable terms of agreements. These controls are meant to provide freedom *from* contract for certain members of society who heretofore may have been forced into making contracts unfavorable to themselves.

THE BASIC REQUIREMENTS OF A CONTRACT

The many topics that will be discussed in this unit on contracts require an understanding of the basic requirements of a contract and the processes by which one is created. The following list gives a brief description of these requirements. They will be explained more fully in subsequent chapters.

1. **Agreement.** An agreement includes an offer and an acceptance. One party must offer to enter into a legal agreement, and another party must accept the terms of the offer.
2. **Consideration.** Generally, consideration is the inducement (reason, cause, motive, or price) to a contract. Any promises made by the parties must be supported by legally sufficient and bargained-for consideration.
3. **Contractual capacity.** Both parties entering into the contract must have the contractual capacity to do so; they must be recognized by the law as possessing characteristics that qualify them as competent parties.
4. **Legality.** The contract must be made to accomplish some goal that is legal and not against public policy.

These four requirements constitute what are formally known as the elements of a contract. Also important are possible *defenses* (that is, reasons why a party should not be awarded what he or she seeks in an action or suit) to the formation or enforcement of a contract. These include:

1. **Reality of assent.** Apparent consent of both parties must be genuine.

2. **Form.** The contract must be in whatever form the law requires, such as in writing.

TYPES OF CONTRACTS EXPLAINED

Contracts are divided into various categories. In studying these categories, it is important to remember that each signifies a legal distinction regarding a contract's formation, performance, or enforceability (see the *Concept Summary* at the end of this chapter).

Bilateral versus Unilateral Contracts

Every contract involves at least two parties. The **offeror** is the party making the offer, and the **offeree** is the party to whom the offer is made. The offeror always promises to do or not to do something and thus is also a promisor. Whether the contract is classified as *unilateral* or *bilateral* depends on what the offeree must do to accept the offer and to bind the offeror to a contract. If the offer requires as acceptance only that the offeree promise to perform, the contract formed is called a **bilateral contract.** Hence, a bilateral contract is a promise for a promise. The exchange of mutual promises (called mutuality of obligation) is the basis of the consideration for the contract and the heart of the formation of a bilateral contract. If the offer is phrased so that the offeree can accept only by complete performance, the contract formed by completion of the act (performance) is called a **unilateral contract.** Hence, a unilateral contract is a promise for an act.

A problem arises in unilateral contracts when the promisor attempts to revoke the offer after the promisee has begun performance but before performance has been completed. Offers are normally revocable until accepted, and in the case of unilateral contracts, the traditional view was that acceptance could occur only on full performance. The modern view, however, is that the offer becomes irrevocable once performance has begun. This does not act as an acceptance but prohibits the offeror from revoking the offer for a reasonable period of time.

Suppose Ann offers to buy John's sailboat, moored in San Diego, upon delivery to Ann's dock in Newport Beach. John rigs the boat and sets sail. Shortly before his arrival at Newport Beach, John receives a radio message from Ann withdrawing her offer. Ann's offer is for a unilateral contract, and only John's delivery of the sailboat at her dock is an acceptance. Under the traditional view, her revocation would terminate the offer, but since substantial performance has been completed by John, under the modern-day view her offer is irrevocable. John can deliver the boat and bind Ann to the contract.

The classic illustration of a unilateral contract is that in which Alan says to Barbara, "If you walk across the Brooklyn Bridge, I'll give you $10." Alan promises to pay only if Barbara walks the entire span of the bridge. Only upon Barbara's

complete crossing does she accept Alan's offer to pay $10. If she chooses not to walk at all, there are no legal consequences.

Under a unilateral contract, only one party is obligated to perform—the promisor (because the promisee has already performed his or her part of the bargain, or the contract would not have come into existence). In contrast, under a bilateral contract, both parties are obligated to perform, because the contract reflects only the *promises* of the parties to do (or refrain from doing) some act in the future. In the following case, the court discusses this fundamental difference between bilateral and unilateral contracts.

Case 7.1

GREENE v. OLIVER REALTY, INC.

Superior Court of Pennsylvania, 1987.
363 Pa.Super. 534, 526 A.2d 1192.

BACKGROUND AND FACTS   *William Greene, plaintiff and appellant, began working for Grant Building, Inc., in 1959. Greene allegedly agreed to work at a pay rate below union scale in exchange for a promise that Grant would employ him "for life." In 1975, appellee Oliver Realty, Inc., took over management of Grant Building. Oliver's president assured former Grant employees that existing employment contracts would be honored. During that same year Greene explained the terms of his agreement to an Oliver Realty supervisor. The supervisor stated that he would look into the matter but never got back to Greene. After twenty-four years of service, Greene was fired by the new owners of the business. Greene brought suit for breach of a unilateral contract against defendant Oliver Realty, Inc. The lower court gave summary judgment for Oliver, and Greene appealed.*

CIRILLO, President Judge.
*   *   *   *

Traditional contract law distinguished between contracts involving two promises which were called bilateral and contracts involving only one promise which were called unilateral. A bilateral contract is created when one party promises to do or forbear from doing something in exchange for the other party's promise to do or forbear from doing something else. In a unilateral contract there is only one promise. It is formed when one party makes a promise in exchange for the other person's act or performance. Mutuality of obligation means that both parties are under an obligation to perform their promises. It is often stated that a contract is unenforceable if there is no such mutuality but this principle is inapplicable to unilateral contracts. If A promises B $100 if B walks across the Brooklyn Bridge, a unilateral contract will be formed if B does as A requests. It is a unilateral contract because it consists of a promise in exchange for a performance. However, the contract is not formed until B walks across the bridge. At that time, A owes B $100 even though B no longer has any obligation to A. A unilateral contract is formed by the very act which constitutes the offeree's performance. Therefore, mutuality of obligation will never exist in such a situation. By the time the contract is formed, only the offeror will remain obligated. The offeree will already have performed. This is why the Restatement provides that: "If the requirement of consideration [something of value given] is met, there is no additional requirement of . . . (c) 'mutuality of obligation.' "
*   *   *   *

*   *   * An employer is free to promise lifetime employment to someone in exchange for that person coming to work for the employer. Once that person accepts and starts work, the employer has received exactly what he bargained for. The employee has performed the desired act. That act is the consideration for the employer's promise and their agreement is a unilateral contract. It is irrelevant that the employee's services are also consideration for his salary. Modern contract law recognizes that consideration may be a single act exchanged for several promises. Therefore, an employee is free to sell his services in exchange for wages *and* a promise of lifetime employment.

Once the employee begins work, the employer may be the only party obligated, but that is standard in situations involving a unilateral contract. The promisor has requested a performance as the price of his promise. Once he receives that performance, it would defy all notions of equity to allow him to avoid his obligation by claiming that the promisee is no longer obligated. He is no longer obligated because he has already performed the agreed upon acts. As previously discussed, this is the reason that mutuality of obligation is inapplicable to unilateral contracts.

*   *   *   *

The reviewing court held that the trial court erred in granting summary judgment in favor of Oliver. The appellate court thus reversed the lower court's decision and remanded the case for a trial.

DECISION AND REMEDY

Express versus Implied Contracts

An **express contract** is one in which the terms of the agreement are fully and explicitly stated in words, oral or written. A signed agreement to buy a house is an express written contract. If a classmate calls you on the phone and agrees to buy your textbooks from last semester for $50, an express oral contract has been made.

A contract that is implied from the conduct of the parties is called an **implied-in-fact contract,** or an implied contract. Implied-in-fact contracts differ from express contracts in that the *conduct* of the parties, rather than their words, reveals that they *intended* to form a contract and creates and defines the terms of the contract. For example, suppose you need a tax consultant or an accountant to fill out your tax return this year. You look through the phone book and find both an accountant and a tax consultant at an office in your neighborhood, so you drop by to see them. You go into the office and explain your problem, and they tell you what their fees are. The next day you return, giving the secretary all of the necessary information, such as cancelled checks, W-2 copies, and so on. You say nothing expressly to the secretary; rather, you walk out the door. Nonetheless, you have entered into an implied-in-fact contract to pay the tax consultant and accountant the usual and reasonable fees for their services. The contract is implied by your conduct and by the consultants' conduct. They expect to be paid for preparing your tax return. By bringing in all of the records that will allow them to do so, you have implied an intent to pay them for their work.

SUMMARY OF STEPS NECESSARY FOR AN IMPLIED-IN-FACT CONTRACT The following three steps establish an implied-in-fact contract:

1. The plaintiff furnished some service or property.
2. The plaintiff expected to be paid for that service or property and the defendant knew or should have known that payment was expected (by using the objective theory of contracts test, described below).
3. The defendant had a chance to reject the services or property and did not.

OBJECTIVE THEORY OF CONTRACTS The intent or apparent intent to enter into a contract is of prime importance in the formation of the contract. This intent is determined by what is called the **objective theory of contracts,** not by the personal or subjective intent, or belief, of a party. The theory is that a party's intention to enter into a contract is judged by outward, objective facts as interpreted by a **reasonable offeree** (one to whom the offer is being made), rather than by the party's own secret, subjective intentions. Objective facts include: (1) what the party said when entering into the contract, (2) how the party acted or appeared,

and (3) the circumstances surrounding the transaction.

Courts need verifiable evidence in order to determine whether a contract has been made, so they
usually rely only on objective factors when passing
judgment on a contract dispute. In other words,
courts examine all the objective facts, conduct,
and circumstances surrounding a particular trans-

action in order to determine if the parties have
made a contract and, if so, what its terms are.

The following case illustrates a court's use of
the objective theory of contracts to review the conduct and circumstances surrounding a transaction
in order to determine whether a contract exists,
and what its terms might be.

Case 7.2

**COMPUTER
NETWORK, LTD. v.
PURCELL TIRE &
RUBBER COMPANY,
E.D.**
Missouri Court of Appeals,
1988.
747 S.W.2d 669.

BACKGROUND AND FACTS   *Purcell Tire and Rubber Company operated fifteen motor-vehicle stores in Missouri. In 1983 Purcell discussed purchasing personal computers through Computer Network (CN), the plaintiff.
On February 23, Harry Chapman, an agent of Purcell, signed a memo prepared
by CN verifying some of the information that had been discussed in a prior
meeting. The memo referred to twenty-one personal computers, a description of
the equipment, and what its price would be. In 1984 nine computers were
delivered to Purcell. Purcell paid for them but refused to accept any more.
Chapman claimed that the memorandum did not constitute a contract and
that "there had only been conversations regarding the possible transactions."
He also stated at trial that he had only wanted to verify a price-and-equipment
configuration and that he had intended eventually to purchase only fifteen
personal computers, one for each store. CN claimed that the memo signed by
Chapman was a contract and filed suit. The trial court gave a judgment for
CN, and Purcell appealed.*
SIMEONE, Senior Judge.
*   *   *   *
[The court quotes from a previous case:]
"Practical business people cannot be expected to govern their actions with reference
to nice legal formalisms. Thus, when there is basic agreement, . . . failure to
articulate that agreement in the precise language of a lawyer with every difficulty
and contingency considered and resolved, will not prevent formation of a contract."

The core issue here, under the evidence, is whether the parties intended a legally
binding contract to arise from the February 23 letter and if the parties intended no
binding agreement or contract, the rules of construction and interpretation will not
establish one. If no intent is found, the inquiry is put to an end. If the expressions in
the agreement are clear, the court determines the intent from a reading of the writing.
If the intent is not clearly expressed, then surrounding circumstances may be considered—the subsequent actions of the parties and the practical construction of the contract. But the question whether there is an "intent to contract" is a question of fact to
be determined by the trier of fact. The formation of a contract does not require that
all terms be settled. One or more of the terms may be left open and the agreement
will not fail for indefiniteness; but the parties must intend to make a contract. If the
parties act in a way which recognizes the existence of a contract, one may exist even
though the writing does not otherwise establish a contract. "Sellers usually do not ship
and buyers do not receive goods unless they think they have struck a deal."

Courts do not favor the destruction of agreements, but will, if feasible, construe
agreements so as to carry into effect the reasonable intention of the parties.

The main thrust of the appellant's contention is that the trial court failed to consider
that there was no "mutual assent" and that Harry Chapman did not "intend" to enter
into a binding agreement for the purchase of twenty-one computers. But the trial court
held otherwise, and recognized that there was mutual assent.

The essential elements of an enforceable contract are parties competent to contract,
a proper subject matter, legal consideration, mutuality of agreement and obligation.
"For at least a century the objective theory of contracts has been dominant." The

"subjective" theory of intent is now regarded as irrelevant. "The objective theory lays stress on the outward manifestation of assent made to the other party in contrast to the older idea that a contract was a true meeting of the minds." What a person may have intended subjectively is not controlling. *   *   *

As stated by Professor Immel: " *   *   * The intent with which we are concerned is the objective manifestation of intent by the parties, that is, what a reasonably prudent person would be led to believe from the actions and words of the parties. This is a question to be resolved by the (trier of fact)."
*   *   *   *

Tested by these principles, there was, under the circumstances here, "mutual assent" to purchase twenty-one computers. Regardless of Chapman's intent to purchase a lesser number, the letter of February 23 explicitly contained that number. Although the trial court admitted testimony of Chapman *   *   * that Purcell did not intend to purchase twenty-one computers, because it had only fifteen stores, the trial court found mutual assent and that the contract called for the sale of twenty-one computers. Chapman acknowledged that he signed the letter containing that number; presumably he must have read the letter when it was presented to him. Having signed the letter, he is charged with knowledge of its contents. He admitted he signed the letter; he admitted that he could have changed the letter if he desired to do so but did not. A mere change could have effected a lesser number.

[The essentials] to formation of a contract may not be found or determined on the undisclosed assumption or secret surmise of either party but must be gathered from the intention of the parties as expressed or manifested by their words or acts.

Under these circumstances, the objective manifestation of mutual assent is present; the trial court so concluded and in this respect the court did not err.

The court of appeals affirmed the lower court's decision that a contract existed.   **DECISION AND REMEDY**

Quasi-Contracts, or Contracts Implied in Law

Quasi-contracts, or **contracts implied in law,** arise in order to achieve justice rather than from a mutual agreement between the parties. A quasi-contract is imposed on the parties in order to avoid *unjust enrichment.* The doctrine of unjust enrichment holds that people should not be allowed to profit or enrich themselves inequitably at the expense of others. The doctrine is equitable rather than contractual in nature.

The quasi-contract is, in essence, a legal fiction. It is based neither on an expressed promise by the defendant to pay for the benefit received nor on conduct of the defendant implying such a promise. Indeed, the recipient of such a benefit (the defendant) not only has not solicited it but often may be unaware that it has been conferred. The doctrine under which the court implies such a contract is called **quantum meruit,** an expression that means "as much as he deserves." *Quantum meruit* essentially describes the extent of liability on a contract implied-in-law.

EXAMPLES OF QUASI-CONTRACTS Suppose Steve enters into an oral agreement with Diane, agreeing to work with Diane for two years to develop a noise reduction turbine for fixed-wing commercial jets. Diane agrees to pay Steve a "fair share of the profit" derived from the sale of the device. After they have worked six months on the project and made considerable headway, Diane tells Steve she will not pay him anything because the terms of the contract are too indefinite. Diane claims that there is no way to "objectively" determine "fair share of the profit." Assuming Diane is correct, Steve cannot sue on the contract itself, since there is no contract. Instead Steve sues on the theory of quasi-contract for the reasonable value of his services. Obviously, it would be unfair to allow Diane to pay nothing for Steve's work, so the court will impose a quasi-contract. Thus, Diane will be required to pay Steve a fair wage for the six months of work.

In another example, a doctor is driving down the highway on vacation and comes upon Smith lying on the side of the road unconscious. The doctor renders medical aid that saves Smith's life. Although the injured, unconscious Smith has not solicited the medical aid and is not aware that the aid has been rendered, Smith has received a valuable benefit, and the requirements for a quasi-contract have been fulfilled.

A LIMITATION ON THE QUASI-CONTRACT   The principle underlying quasi-contractual obligations is based on the notion of "unjust enrichment." Nonetheless, there are situations in which the party obtaining the "unjust enrichment" is not liable. Basically, the quasi-contractual principle cannot be invoked by the party who has conferred a benefit on someone else unnecessarily or as a result of misconduct or negligence. Consider the following example. You take your car to the local car wash and ask to have it run through the washer and to have the gas tank filled. While it is being washed, you go to a nearby shopping center for two hours. In the meantime, one of the workers at the car wash has mistakenly hand waxed your car. When you come back, you are presented with a bill for a full tank of gas, a wash job, and a hand wax. Clearly, a benefit has been conferred on you. But this benefit has been conferred because of a mistake by the car wash employee. You have not received an *unjust* benefit under these circumstances. People cannot normally be forced to pay for benefits "thrust" upon them.

Also, the doctrine of quasi-contract cannot normally be used when there is a contract that covers the area in controversy. For example, Gonzales contracts with Mott to deliver a furnace to a building project owned by Mitchell. Mott goes out of business without paying Gonzales. Gonzales cannot collect from Mitchell in quasi-contract, because Gonzales had an existing contract with Mott.

The following case illustrates the philosophy behind the creation and enforcement of a quasi-contract and the limitation on its use when there is an express contract covering the subject matter on which the quasi-contractual claim rests.

Case 7.3

INDUSTRIAL LIFT TRUCK v. MITSUBISHI INTERNATIONAL CORPORATION

Appellate Court of Illinois, First District, Fourth Division, 1982. 104 Ill.App.3d 357, 60 Ill. Dec. 100, 432 N.E.2d 999.

BACKGROUND AND FACTS   *Industrial Lift Truck, the plaintiff, sells and services fork-lift trucks. The defendant, Mitsubishi International Corporation, is a United States distributor of fork-lift trucks. In 1973 Industrial entered into a deal with Mitsubishi whereby the plaintiff would purchase fork-lift trucks from the defendant and use its best efforts to sell the trucks. Under the dealership agreement, the plaintiff was required to service the trucks it sold. In 1976, the original agreement was terminated and replaced by a new agreement, which stated that the plaintiff would use its best efforts to service and sell the defendant's product. A pertinent part of the agreement allowed the defendant to terminate the agreement without just cause by giving ninety days' notice.*

From 1973 to 1977, the plaintiff allegedly became the nation's largest dealer in the product. The plaintiff's success was attributed to its "great expenditures of time, effort, and money," among which were expenditures that went toward design changes in the defendant's product. These changes were made in order to adapt the Japanese product to the American market. The defendant did not request these changes, but it did eventually incorporate the changes into the products it sold to other dealers.

In 1978, the defendant terminated the dealership agreement with the plaintiff. The plaintiff tried to recover for the benefits conferred upon the defendant by the plaintiff's design changes under quasi-contract principles. The plaintiff's action in quasi-contract was dismissed at trial.

LINN, Justice.
*   *   *   *

A contract implied in law, or a quasi-contract, is fictitious and arises by implication of law wholly apart from the usual rules relating to contract. *   *   * Quasi-contractual claims involving services usually arise when there is no contract, either express or implied, between the parties. One party performs a service that benefits another. The benefiting party has not requested the service but accepts the benefit. Circumstances indicate that the services were not intended to be gratuitous. As a result, the law will sometimes impose a duty on the benefiting party to pay for the services rendered despite the lack of a contract. *   *   *

Difficulties arise with quasi-contractual claims when there is an express contract between the parties. The general rule is that no quasi-contractual claim can arise when a contract exists between the parties concerning the same subject matter on which the quasi-contractual claim rests.

*   *   *   *

In the present case, plaintiff obviously made the design changes with a view to being compensated pursuant to the contract terms. By its own admission, the design changes allowed plaintiff to become one of the nation's largest dealers in defendant's product. When the changes were made, plaintiff knew the risk involved. It knew the contract could be terminated as it was terminated, and thus knew when it made the changes that it might not be compensated under the contract to the extent it hoped to be compensated. Now that a situation plaintiff knew could occur has occurred, plaintiff seeks to shift a risk it assumed in light of the contract to defendant. In essence, plaintiff is seeking to use quasi-contract as a means to circumvent the realities of a contract it freely entered into.

*   *   *   *

The contract defined the entire relationship of the parties with respect to its general subject matter—the sale and servicing of defendant's products. Plaintiff's attempt here to bring a quasi-contract action is nothing more than an attempt to unilaterally amend the agreement in a manner prohibited by the agreement. In such circumstances, the benefit received by defendant can hardly be considered unjust. *   *   * Defendant had a right to assume that the contract defined the entire relationship of the parties with respect to all matters related to defendant's product. Defendant had a right to assume, absent a valid amendment to the agreement, that it should not have to compensate plaintiff for any acts done in relation to the subject matter of the contract except pursuant to the contract terms.

The existence of the specific contract barred the plaintiff's action in quasi-contract, and the reviewing court held that the plaintiff's action in quasi-contract was properly dismissed.

DECISION AND REMEDY

Formal versus Informal Contracts

Formal contracts are contracts that require a special form or method of creation (formation) to be enforceable. They include: (1) contracts under seal, (2) recognizances, (3) negotiable instruments, and (4) letters of credit.[3] **Contracts under seal** are formalized writings with a special seal attached.[4] The significance of the seal has eroded, although about ten states require no consideration when a contract is under seal. (See Chapter 9 for details.) A **recognizance** is an acknowledgment in court by a person that he or she will pay a certain sum if a certain event occurs. A common form of recognizance is the criminal recognizance bond. Negotiable instruments and letters of credit are special methods of payment that are designed for use in many commercial settings. **Negotiable instruments** include checks, notes, drafts, and certificates of deposit. **Letters of credit** are agreements to pay, contingent on the purchaser's receipt of invoices and bills of lading. Negotiable instruments and letters of credit are discussed at length in subsequent chapters.

Informal contracts include all other contracts. (Such contracts are also called *simple contracts*.) No special form is required (except for certain types of contracts that must be in writing), as the contracts are usually based on their substance rather than on their form.

---

3. Restatement, Second, Contracts, Section 6.

4. A seal may be actual (made of wax or some other durable substance) or impressed on the paper or indicated simply by the word *seal* or the letters *L.S.* at the end of the document. *L.S.* stands for *locus sigilli* and means "the place for the seal."

Executed versus Executory Contracts

Contracts are also classified according to their stage of performance. A contract that has been fully performed on both sides is called an **executed contract.** A contract that has not been fully performed on both sides is called an **executory contract.** If one party has fully performed but the other has not, the contract is said to be executed on the one side and executory on the other, but the contract is still classified as executory. For example, assume you have agreed to buy ten tons of coal from the Wheeling Coal Company. Further assume that Wheeling has delivered the coal to your steel mill, where it is now being burned, but that you have not yet paid for it. At this point, the contract is executed on the part of Wheeling and executory on your part. After you pay Wheeling for the coal, the contract will be executed on both sides.

Valid versus Void, Voidable, and Unenforceable Contracts

A **valid contract** is one with the elements necessary to entitle at least one of the parties to enforce it in court. Those elements consist of an offer and an acceptance, supported by legally sufficient consideration, for a legal purpose, and made by parties who have the legal capacity to enter into the contract. Each element is discussed in detail in the following chapters.

A **void contract** is no contract at all. The terms *void* and *contract* are contradictory. A void contract produces no legal obligations on the part of any of the parties. For example, a contract can be void because one of the parties was adjudged by a court to be legally insane or because the purpose of the contract was illegal.

A **voidable contract** is a *valid* contract in which one or both of the parties has the option of avoiding his or her legal obligations. The party having this option can elect to avoid any duty to perform or can elect to *ratify* the contract. If the contract is avoided, both parties are released from it. If it is ratified, both parties must fully perform their legal obligations.

As a general rule, but subject to exceptions, contracts made by minors are voidable at the option of the minor. (See Chapter 10 for details.) Contracts entered into under fraudulent conditions are voidable at the option of the defrauded party. (These are also discussed in Chapter 10.) In addition, some contracts entered into because of mistakes and all contracts entered into under legally defined duress or undue influence are voidable.

An **unenforceable contract** is a valid contract that cannot be enforced because of certain legal defenses against it. It is not unenforceable because it fails to satisfy any of the legal requirements of a contract; rather, it is a valid contract rendered unenforceable by some statute or law. For example, a valid contract barred by a statute of limitations is an unenforceable contract.[5] Some oral contracts under the Statute of Frauds are also unenforceable. (See Chapter 12 for details.)

---

5. A *statute of limitations* prevents a party from suing on a contract after a certain period of time has elapsed.

CONCEPT SUMMARY: Classification of Contracts	
CLASSIFICATION	**TYPES AND DEFINITIONS**
Formation	1. Bilateral—A promise for a promise.
	2. Unilateral—A promise for an act (acceptance is completed by performance of the act).
	3. Express—Formed by words (oral, written, or a combination).
	4. Implied-in-fact—Formed by conduct of the parties.
	5. Implied-in-law (Quasi-contract)—Imposed by law to prevent unjust enrichment.
	6. Formal—Requires a special form for creation.
	7. Informal—Requires no special form for creation.

CONCEPT SUMMARY: Classification of Contracts (Continued)	
CLASSIFICATION	**TYPES AND DEFINITIONS**
Enforceability	1. Valid—It has the necessary contractual elements of offer and acceptance, consideration, parties with capacity, and legal purpose.
	2. Voidable—One party has the option of avoiding or enforcing the contractual obligation.
	3. Void—No contract exists or there is a contract without legal obligations.
	4. Unenforceable—A contract exists, but it cannot be enforced because of a legal defense.
Performance	1. Executed—A fully performed contract.
	2. Executory—A contract not fully performed.

QUESTIONS AND CASE PROBLEMS

1. Suppose Felix, a local businessman, is a good friend of Miller, the owner of a local candy store. Every day at his lunch hour Felix goes into Miller's candy store and usually spends about five minutes looking at the candy. After examining Miller's candy and talking with Miller, Felix usually buys one or two candy bars. One afternoon, Felix goes into Miller's candy shop, looks at the candy, picks up a $1 candy bar and, seeing that Miller is very busy at the time, waves the candy bar at Miller without saying a word and walks out. Is there a contract? If so, classify it within the categories presented in this chapter.

2. Mary is a minor, age sixteen. By letter, Mary offers to buy John's bicycle for $100. John, an adult, accepts by telegram. Mary pays John $100, and John delivers the bicycle to Mary. How would this contract be classified, and what is the legal effect on Mary?

3. James is confined to his bed. He calls a friend who lives across the street and offers to sell her his watch next week for $100. If his friend wishes to accept, she is to put a red piece of paper in her front window. The next morning, she places a red piece of paper in her front window. Is the contract formed bilateral or unilateral? Explain.

4. Air Advertising employed Red, a World War II flying ace, to fly its advertisements above Long Island Sound beaches. Burger Baby restaurants engaged Air Advertising to fly an advertisement above the Connecticut beaches. The advertisement offered $1,000 to any person who could swim from the Connecticut beaches to Long Island across Long Island Sound in less than a day. On Saturday, October 10, at 10:00 A.M., Red flew a sign above the Connecticut beaches that read: "Swim across the Sound and Burger Baby pays $1,000." Upon seeing the sign, Davison dived in. About four hours later, when he was about halfway across the Sound, Red flew another sign over the Sound that read: "Burger Baby revokes." Is there a contract between Davison and Burger Baby? Can Davison recover anything?

5. Susan contacts Joe and makes the following offer: "When you finish mowing my yard, I'll pay you $25." Joe responds by saying, "I accept your offer." Is there a contract? Is it a bilateral or unilateral contract? What is the legal significance of the distinction?

6. Sosa Crisan, an eighty-seven-year-old widow of Romanian origin, collapsed while shopping at a local grocery store. The Detroit police took her to the Detroit city hospital. She was admitted, and she remained there fourteen days. Then she was transferred to another hospital, where she died some eleven months later. Crisan had never regained consciousness after her collapse at the local grocery store. After she died, the city of Detroit sued her estate to recover the expenses of both the ambulance that took her to the hospital and the expenses of her hospital stay. Is there a contract between Sosa Crisan and the hospital? If so, how much can the Detroit hospital recover? [In re Estate of Crisan, 362 Mich. 569, 107 N.W.2d 907 (1961)]

7. On April 1, 1969, McLouth Steel Corporation entered into a contract with Jewell Coal and Coke Company under which Jewell agreed to supply all McLouth's coal requirements for the next thirty years. The contract mentioned no specific quantities. The price was set at $14.25 a ton for the first six months and was subject to an escalation clause whereby in each subsequent six months the original price would be increased by the cost increases encountered by Jewell. Ten years later Jewell found that even with those cost increases, the price it could charge McLouth was far less than the price it could receive in the open market. Jewell therefore stopped shipping coal. Is the contract enforceable or unenforceable, or does it fail on the ground of indefiniteness? [McLouth Steel Corp. v. Jewell Coal and Coke Co., 570 F.2d 594 (6th Cir. 1978)]

8. Josephine Wideman was an elderly woman who moved

in with her daughter and son-in-law so that they could provide care for her. Until that time each of Wideman's children had periodically lived with her in her own home. While Wideman lived with her daughter, other members of Wideman's family would come and care for her while the daughter was at work. Wideman had always paid her family members for these services, and the evidence at trial supported the proposition that Wideman intended that everyone who cared for her should be paid. The daughter had never received any such remuneration. When Wideman died, her daughter sued the estate for the reasonable value of her services and rent. Discuss whether the daughter can state a claim and specify the theory on which such a claim would be based. [Sturgeon v. Estate of Wideman, 631 S.W.2d 55 (Mo.App. 1981)]

9. Nichols is the principal owner of Samuel Nichols, Inc., a real estate firm. Nichols signed an exclusive brokerage agreement with Molway to find a purchaser for Molway's property within ninety days. This type of agreement entitles the broker to a commission if the property is sold to any purchaser to whom the property is shown during the ninety-day period. Molway tried to cancel the brokerage agreement before the ninety-day term had expired. Nichols had already advertised the property, put up a "for sale" sign, and shown the property to prospective buyers. Molway claimed that the brokerage contract was unilateral and that she could cancel at any time before Nichols found a buyer. Nichols claimed the contract was bilateral and that Molway's cancellation breached the contract. Discuss who should prevail at trial. [Samuel Nichols, Inc. v. Molway, 25 Mass.App. 913, 515 N.E.2d 598 (1987)]

10. Engelcke Manufacturing, Inc., planned to design and manufacture Whizball, an electronic parlor game. Engelcke asked Eaton to design the electronic schematic for it. Engelcke told Eaton that he would be paid for the reasonable value of his services upon the project's completion, but no written contract was signed. The specific amount and terms were also not discussed. Eaton had produced a plan that represented 90 percent of the finished design when Engelcke terminated his employment. Eaton sued Engelcke for breach of an implied-in-fact contract. Engelcke claimed that they had an express contract. Why did Engelcke claim an express contract rather than an implied-in-fact contract? [Eaton v. Engelcke Mfg., Inc., 37 Wash.App. 677, 681 P.2d 1312 (1984)]

Chapter 8

Agreement

Essential to any contract is an **agreement;** that is, an offer must be made by one party and accepted or assented to by the other party. The agreement does not necessarily have to be in writing. Both parties, however, must exhibit what is called a manifestation of assent to the same bargain.[1] If the agreement is supported by legally sufficient consideration,[2] is not illegal,[3] and is entered into freely by parties with contractual capacity,[4] a valid contract is formed, generally creating enforceable rights and duties between the parties.

A contract must include the following terms, either expressed in the agreement or capable of being reasonably inferred from it:

1. Identification of the parties.
2. Identification of the object or subject matter of the contract (also quantity, where appropriate), with specific identification of such items as goods, services, and land.
3. The consideration to be paid.
4. The time of performance.

If these terms are expressly stated in the agreement, the contract is definite. Although terms and intent are equally important in both the offer and the acceptance, for simplicity's sake we will discuss the relevant laws only in terms of the offer.

MUTUAL ASSENT

Ordinarily, mutual assent is evidenced by an *offer* and an *acceptance*. One party offers a certain bargain to another party, who then accepts that bargain. The parties are required to manifest to each other their **mutual assent** to

---

1. Under early English and American law, many contracts were not enforced unless they complied with rigid legal standards requiring a writing and in many cases a seal or impression made on wax, which was firmly affixed to the writing. Today, some contracts must still be in writing (see Chapter 12). The seal has been almost entirely done away with. [UCC 2–203]
2. See Chapter 9.
3. See Chapter 11.
4. See Chapter 10.

the same bargain.[5] Because words often fail to convey the precise meaning intended, the law of contracts generally adheres to the objective theory of contracts, as discussed in Chapter 7. Under this theory, a party's words and conduct are held to mean whatever a reasonable person in the offeree's position would think they meant. The court will give words their usual meaning even if "it were proved by twenty bishops that [the] party ★ ★ ★ intended something else."[6]

REQUIREMENTS OF THE OFFER

The parties to a contract are the **offeror,** the one who makes an offer or proposal to another party, and the **offeree,** the one to whom the offer or proposal is made. An **offer** is a promise or commitment to do or refrain from doing some specified thing in the future. Three elements are necessary for an offer to be effective:

1. There must be a *serious and objective intention* by the offeror to become bound by the offer.
2. The terms of the offer must be reasonably *certain*, or *definite*, so that the parties and the court can ascertain the terms of the contract.
3. The offer must be communicated to the offeree.

Once an effective offer has been made, the offeree has the power to accept the offer. If the offeree accepts, the offer is translated into an agreement (and thus into a contract if other essential elements are present).

Intention

The first element for an effective offer to exist is a serious and objective intent on the part of the offeror. But serious intent is not determined by the *subjective* intentions of the offeror. It is determined instead by whether the offer created a *reasonable* impression in the mind of the offeree. Objective intent is therefore inferred from the words and actions of the parties as interpreted by a reasonable person. Offers made in obvious anger, jest, or undue excitement do not meet the serious and objective intent test. Since these offers are not effective, an offeree's acceptance would not create an agreement. For example, suppose you and three classmates ride to school each day in Jane's new automobile, which has a market value of $18,000. One cold morning the four of you get into the car, but Jane cannot get the car started. She yells in anger, "I'll sell this car to anyone for $500!" You drop $500 in her lap. Given these facts, a reasonable person, taking into consideration Jane's frustration and the obvious difference in value between the car and the purchase price, would declare that her offer was not made with serious and objective intent and that you do not have an agreement.

The concept of intention can be further explained by distinctions between offers and various kinds of non-offers. Consider the following:

1. Expressions of opinion.
2. Statements of intention.
3. Preliminary negotiations.
4. Certain kinds of advertisements, catalogues, and circulars.

In each of these cases, an offer (as legally defined) probably does not exist, because the legal requirement of intention has probably not been met.

EXPRESSIONS OF OPINION   An expression of opinion is not an offer. It does not evidence an intention to enter into a binding agreement. Hawkins took his son to McGee, a doctor, and asked McGee to operate on the son's hand. McGee said the boy would be in the hospital three or four days and that the hand would *probably* heal within a few days afterward. The son's hand did not heal for a month, but the father did not win a suit for breach of contract. The court held that McGee did not make an offer to heal the son's hand in three or four days. He merely expressed an opinion as to when the hand would heal.[7]

STATEMENTS OF INTENTION   If Henry says "I *plan* to sell my stock in Ryder Systems for $150 per share," a contract will not be created if Fred "accepts" and tenders the $150 per share for the stock. Henry has merely expressed his intention

---

5. Restatement, Second, Contracts, Section 22.

6. Learned Hand in Hotchkiss v. National City Bank of N.Y., 200 F. 287 (2d Cir. 1911), aff'd 231 U.S. 50, 34 S.Ct. 20, 58 L.Ed. 115 (1913). [The term *aff'd* is an abbreviation for *affirmed;* an appellate court can affirm a lower court's judgment, decree, or order, thereby declaring that it is proper and must stand as rendered.]

---

7. Hawkins v. McGee, 84 N.H. 114, 146 A. 641 (1929).

to enter into a future contract for the sale of the stock. No contract is formed, because a reasonable person would conclude that Henry was only *thinking* about selling his stock, not promising to sell, even if Fred accepts and tenders the $150 per share. Henry is stating a future contractual intent, not a present one.

PRELIMINARY NEGOTIATIONS   A request or invitation to negotiate is not an offer. It only expresses a willingness to discuss the possibility of entering into a contract. Included are statements such as "Will you sell Blythe Estate?" or "I wouldn't sell my car for less than $1,000." A reasonable

person in the offeree's position would not conclude that these statements evidenced an intention to enter into a binding obligation. Likewise, when construction work is done for the government and private firms, contractors are invited to submit bids. The *invitation* to submit bids is not an offer, and a contractor does not bind the government or private firm by submitting a bid. (The bids that the contractors submit *are* offers, however, and the government or private firm can bind the contractor by accepting the bid.)

Consider whether the court was dealing with preliminary negotiations or an actual offer in the following case.

BACKGROUND AND FACTS   *Oliver and Southworth were ranchers in Grant County, Oregon. Oliver, the defendant, decided to sell his Bear Valley ranch and, on May 20, 1976, stopped by Southworth's ranch to ask if Southworth was interested in buying it. Southworth said that he was "very interested" in the land. No price or terms were discussed, and the conversation terminated with the understanding that whenever the Olivers got information about the sale together, they would send it to Southworth and the other neighbors and give them first chance at buying the ranch. On June 17, 1976, Oliver sent to Southworth and the other neighbors the following letter:*

Case 8.1

SOUTHWORTH v. OLIVER

Supreme Court of Oregon, 1978.
284 Or. 361, 587 P.2d 994.

> Enclosed please find the information about the ranch sales that I had discussed with you previously.
>
>   *   *   *   *
>
>   Please contact me if there are any questions.

There were two enclosures with that letter. The first was as follows:

> JOSEPH C. and ARLENE G. OLIVER
> 200 Ford Road
> John Day, OR 97845
>
> Selling approximately 2933 Acres in Grant County in
>   T. 16 S., R. 31 E., W. M.
> near Seneca, Oregon at the assessed market value of:
>   LAND $306,409
>   IMPROVEMENTS   18,010
>   Total $324,419
>   Terms available—29% down—balance over 5 years at 8% interest. Negotiate sale date for December 1, 1976 or January 1, 1977.
>   Available after hay is harvested and arrangements made for removal of hay, equipment and supplies.

*On June 21, after receiving the letter, Southworth responded, "I accept your offer." Oliver responded on June 24, "You have misconstrued our prior negotiations   *   *   *. That was not made as or intended to be a firm offer of sale.   *   *   * The memorandum of ours was for informational purposes only and as* *a starting point for further negotiation between us and you and the others also interested in the properties." Southworth filed suit for specific performance of the contract. The trial court held for the plaintiff and granted specific performance. Oliver appealed.*

TONGUE, Justice.

*   *   *   *

The difficulty in determining whether an offer has been made is particularly acute in cases involving price quotations, as in this case. It is recognized that although a price quotation, standing alone, is not an offer, there may be circumstances under which a price quotation, when considered together with facts and circumstances, may constitute an offer which, if accepted, will result in a binding contract. It is also recognized that such an offer may be made to more than one person. Thus, the fact that a price quotation is sent to more than one person does not, of itself, require a holding that such a price quotation is not an offer.

We agree with the analysis of this problem as stated in Murray on Contracts 37–40, § 24 (1977), as follows:

> If A says to B, 'I am going to sell my car for $500,' and B replies, 'All right, here is $500, I will take it,' no contract results, assuming that A's statement is taken at its face value. A's statement does not involve any promise, commitment or undertaking; it is at most a statement of A's *present intention.* *   *   *

*   *   *   *

> *   *   * However, a price quotation or advertisement may contain sufficient indication of willingness to enter a bargain so that the party to whom it is addressed would be justified in believing that his assent would conclude the bargain. *   *   *

*   *   *   *

> *   *   * The basic problem is found in the expressions of the parties. People very seldom express themselves either accurately or in complete detail. Thus, difficulty is encountered in determining the correct interpretation of the expression in question. Over the years, some more or less trustworthy guides to interpretation have been developed.

*   *   *   *

Upon application of these tests to the facts of this case we are of the opinion that defendants' letter to plaintiff dated June 17, 1976, was an offer to sell the ranch lands. We believe that the "surrounding circumstances" under which this letter was prepared by defendants and sent by them to plaintiff were such as to have led a reasonable person to believe that defendants were making an offer to sell to plaintiff the lands described in the letter's enclosure and upon the terms as there stated.

That letter did not come to plaintiff "out of the blue," as in some of the cases involving advertisements or price quotations. Neither was this a price quotation resulting from an inquiry by plaintiff. According to what we believe to be the most credible testimony, defendants decided to sell the lands in question and defendant Joseph Oliver then sought out the plaintiff who owned adjacent lands. Defendant Oliver told plaintiff that defendants were interested in selling that land, inquired whether plaintiff was interested, and was told by plaintiff that he was "very interested in the land," after which they discussed the particular lands to be sold. That conversation was terminated with the understanding that Mr. Oliver would "determine" the value and price of that land, i.e., "what he wanted for the land," and that plaintiff would undertake to arrange financing for the purchase of that land. In addition to that initial conversation, there was a further telephone conversation in which plaintiff called Mr. Oliver "to ask him if his plans for selling *   *   * continued to be in force" and was told "yes"; that there had been some delay in getting information from the assessor, as needed to establish the value of the land; and that plaintiff then told Mr. Oliver that "everything was in order" and that "he had the money available and everything was ready to go."

Under these facts and circumstances, we agree with the finding and conclusion by the trial court, in its written opinion, that when plaintiff received the letter of June 17th, with enclosures, which stated a price of $324,419 for the 2,933 acres * * * and stating "terms" of 29 percent down—balance over five years at eight percent interest—with a "sale date" of either December 1, 1976, or January 1, 1977, a reasonable person in the position of the plaintiff would have believed that defendants were making an offer to sell those lands to him.

The Supreme Court of Oregon held that Oliver's letter dated June 17, 1976, was an offer that was accepted by Southworth on June 21, 1976. The court upheld the trial court's decision to award Southworth specific performance.

DECISION AND REMEDY

ADVERTISEMENTS, CATALOGUES, AND CIRCULARS   In general, advertisements, mail order catalogues, price lists, and circular letters are treated not as *offers* to contract but as *invitations to negotiate*. Suppose Loeser & Co. advertises a used paving machine. The ad is mailed to hundreds of firms and reads, "Used Case Construction Co. paving machine. Builds curbs and finishes cement work all in one process. Price $11,250." If Star Paving calls Loeser and says, "We accept your offer," no contract is formed. Any reasonable person would conclude that Loeser was not promising to sell the paving machine but rather that it was soliciting offers to buy it.

The same result occurs when a new car dealership advertises, "New Lincoln Continentals; loaded with options; now only $13,899." The ad is intended to draw customers who will make offers. If Bill Weinberg goes to the dealership with a check for $13,899, the dealership is not legally bound to sell the Lincoln. (Note, however, that federal and state statutes prohibit "false and misleading advertising" that is intended solely to draw customers to the retail outlet.)

Most advertisements are not offers, because the seller never has an unlimited supply of goods. If advertisements were offers, then everyone who "accepted" after the retailer's supply was exhausted could sue for breach of contract. Suppose you put an ad in the classified section of your local newspaper offering to sell a guitar for $75. Suppose further that seven people called and "accepted" your "offer" before you could remove the ad from the newspaper. If the ad were truly an offer, you would be bound on seven contracts to sell your guitar. But since initial advertisements are treated as *invitations* to make offers, rather than

as offers, you would have seven offers to choose from, and you could accept the best one without incurring any liability for the six you rejected.

Price lists are another form of invitation to negotiate or trade. The price list of the seller is not an offer to sell at that price. It merely invites the buyer to offer to buy at that price. As further evidence of the lack of intent to offer to sell at the listed prices, the words "prices subject to change" are usually printed somewhere on the price list.

Although most advertisements and the like are treated as invitations to negotiate, this does not mean that an advertisement can never be an offer. If the advertisement makes a promise so definite in character that it is apparent that the offeror is binding himself or herself to the conditions stated, the advertisement is treated as an offer. This is particularly true when the advertisement solicits performance—for example, by offering a reward for the capture of a criminal or for the return of a lost article.

Suppose an advertisement states, "To the first five persons in our store at 8:00 A.M. on May 1, we offer to sell Singer Sewing Machines, Model X, at $50." This statement invites an acceptance of terms stated rather than an offer to buy. If you were one of the first five in the store at the time specified, your acceptance would create a contract. Another example is a reward offered in a newspaper for the return of a lost dog. The finder's return of the dog in response to the advertisement creates a unilateral contract, as the reward obviously invited an acceptance, not an offer, from the offeree.

In the following case, the court had to decide whether a newspaper advertisement announcing a "special sale" in a department store should be construed as an offer, the acceptance of which would complete a contract. (Today, the Federal Trade Commission has a set of rules governing such ads.)

Case 8.2

LEFKOWITZ v. GREAT MINNEAPOLIS SURPLUS STORE, INC.

Supreme Court of Minnesota, 1957.
251 Minn. 188, 86 N.W.2d 689.

BACKGROUND AND FACTS *Plaintiff Lefkowitz read a newspaper advertisement offering certain items of merchandise for sale on a first come-first served basis. Plaintiff went to the store twice and was the first person to demand the merchandise and indicate a readiness to pay the sale price. On both occasions, the defendant department store refused to sell the merchandise to the plaintiff, saying that the offer was intended for women only, even though the advertisement was directed to the general public. The plaintiff sued the store for breach of contract, and the trial court awarded him damages.*

MURPHY, Justice.
*   *   *   *

This case grows out of the alleged refusal of the defendant to sell to the plaintiff a certain fur piece which it had offered for sale in a newspaper advertisement. It appears from the record that on April 6, 1956, the defendant published the following advertisement in a Minneapolis newspaper:

"Saturday 9 A.M. Sharp
3 Brand New
Fur
Coats
Worth to $100.00
First Come
First Served
$1 Each"

On April 13, the defendant again published an advertisement in the same newspaper as follows:

"Saturday 9 A.M.
2 Brand New Pastel
Mink 3-Skin Scarfs
Selling for $89.50
Out they go
Saturday. Each . . . $1.00
1 Black Lapin Stole
Beautiful,
worth $139.50 . . . $1.00
First Come
First Served"

The record supports the findings of the court that on each of the Saturdays following the publication of the above-described ads the plaintiff was the first to present himself at the appropriate counter in the defendant's store and on each occasion demanded the coat and the stole so advertised and indicated his readiness to pay the sale price of $1. On both occasions, the defendant refused to sell the merchandise to the plaintiff, stating on the first occasion that by a "house rule" the offer was intended for women only and sales would not be made to men, and on the second visit that plaintiff knew defendant's house rules.
*   *   *   *

The defendant contends that a newspaper advertisement offering items of merchandise for sale at a named price is a "unilateral offer" which may be withdrawn without notice. He relies upon authorities which hold that, where an advertiser publishes in a newspaper that he has a certain quantity or quality of goods which he wants to dispose of at certain prices and on certain terms, such advertisements are not offers which become contracts as soon as any person to whose notice they may come signifies his acceptance by notifying the other that he will take a certain quantity of them. Such advertisements have been construed as an invitation for an offer of sale on the terms stated, which offer, when received, may be accepted or rejected and which therefore does not become a contract of sale until accepted by the seller; and until a contract has been so made, the seller may modify or revoke such prices or terms.

*   *   *   *

[However,] *   *   * [t]here are numerous authorities which hold that a particular advertisement in a newspaper or circular letter relating to a sale of articles may be construed by the court as constituting an offer, acceptance of which would complete a contract.

The test of whether a binding obligation may originate in advertisements addressed to the general public is "whether the facts show that some performance was promised in positive terms in return for something requested."

The authorities above cited emphasize that, where the offer is clear, definite, and explicit, and leaves nothing open for negotiation, it constitutes an offer, acceptance of which will complete the contract. *   *   *

Whether in any individual instance a newspaper advertisement is an offer rather than an invitation to make an offer depends on the legal intention of the parties and the surrounding circumstances. We are of the view on the facts before us that the offer by the defendant of the sale of the Lapin fur was clear, definite, and explicit, and left nothing open for negotiation. The plaintiff having successfully managed to be the first one to appear at the seller's place of business to be served, as requested by the advertisement, and having offered the stated purchase price of the article, he was entitled to performance on the part of the defendant. We think the trial court was correct in holding that there was in the conduct of the parties a sufficient mutuality of obligation to constitute a contract of sale.

The defendant contends that the offer was modified by a "house rule" to the effect that only women were qualified to receive the bargains advertised. The advertisement contained no such restriction. This objection may be disposed of briefly by stating that, while an advertiser has the right at any time before acceptance to modify his offer, he does not have the right, after acceptance, to impose new or arbitrary conditions not contained in the published offer.

DECISION AND REMEDY

The Supreme Court of Minnesota affirmed the trial court's judgment, awarding the plaintiff the sum of $138.50 ($139.50 for the Lapin stole less the $1 purchase price) in damages for breach of contract against the defendant department store.

COMMENTS

Although Lefkowitz recovered for his visit in response to the second advertisement (April 13), he did not recover for the earlier visit. The trial court disallowed the plaintiff's claim for the value of the fur coats in the first ad, since the value of those articles was speculative and uncertain. The only evidence of value was the advertisement's statement that the coats were "worth to $100.00"—a statement too indefinite to serve as a basis for recovery.

OTHER NON-OFFER SITUATIONS Sometimes what appears to be an offer is not sufficient to serve as the basis for formation of a contract.

Auctions In an auction, a seller "offers" goods for sale through an auctioneer. This is not, however, an offer for purposes of contract. The seller is really only expressing a willingness to sell. Unless the terms of the auction are explicitly stated to be *without reserve*, the seller (through the auctioneer) may withdraw the goods at any time before the auctioneer closes the sale by announcement or by fall of the hammer. The seller's right to withdraw goods characterizes an auction *with reserve;* all auctions are assumed to be of this type unless a clear statement to the contrary is made.[8] At auctions "without reserve," the goods cannot be withdrawn and must be sold to the highest bidder.

In an auction with reserve, there is no obligation to sell, and the seller may refuse the highest bid. The bidder is actually the offeror. Before the auctioneer strikes the hammer, which constitutes acceptance of the bid, a bidder may revoke his or her bid, or the auctioneer may reject that bid or all bids. Typically, an auctioneer will reject a bid that is below the price the seller is willing to accept. When the auctioneer accepts a higher bid, he or she rejects all previous bids. Because rejection terminates an offer (as will be pointed out below), if the highest bidder withdraws his or her bid before the hammer falls, none of the previous bids are reinstated. If the bid is not withdrawn or rejected, the contract is formed when the auctioneer announces "Going once, going twice, sold" (or something similar) and lets the hammer fall.

Agreements to Agree Agreements to agree are not contracts and cannot be enforced. Suppose Zahn Consulting gets together with Leon Construction Company to discuss plans for designing a shopping mall. Zahn and Leon agree further to meet in a month and work out the terms of the contract. The agreement to agree, or make a contract at a future time, is not enforceable. There is nothing to enforce in an agreement to agree, because the terms have not yet been agreed upon.

Sham Transactions A sham transaction is entered into by two parties in order to deceive a third person and is unenforceable. For example, a sham transaction might involve the alleged sale or transfer of a house to make one party's net worth appear larger that it really is. Suppose that Sneed is trying to get a loan to buy a new BMW. In order to increase his unimpressive net worth on paper, he agrees in a personal letter to a close friend to sell his power boat for $50,000 (it's actually worth only about $25,000), and his friend agrees in a letter to pay that much. In filling out his net worth statement, Sneed claims that his boat is worth $50,000, and, if questioned, he can produce a personal letter from his friend to show that that is the price at which it will be sold. Sneed and his friend entered into the sham transaction knowing that they were not actually going to perform their respective obligations. Sneed cannot attempt now to enforce that transaction by requesting payment of $50,000 for his boat.

Definiteness

The second element for an effective offer is the definiteness of its terms. An offer must have reasonably definite terms so that a court can determine if a breach has occurred and can give an appropriate remedy.[9] An offer may invite an acceptance to be worded in such specific terms that the contract is made definite. For example, assume D'Onfro contacts your corporation and offers to sell "from one to ten sheet metal presses for $1,750 each" and further specifies that your company should "state number desired in acceptance." Your corporation agrees to buy two presses. If the quantity had not been specified in the acceptance, the contract would have been unenforceable, because the terms of the contract would have been indefinite. But since the acceptance states that your corporation wants two presses, the contract is definite and can be enforced.

Is an employment contract that provides for a salary plus "a share of the profits" too vague and indefinite for a court to enforce? The following case tells the plight of a plaintiff, Victor Petersen, who worked first as construction supervisor and then as manager for the Pilgrim Village Company, the defendant.

---

8. See UCC 2–328.

9. Restatement, Second, Contracts, Section 33.

Case 8.3

PETERSEN v. PILGRIM VILLAGE

Supreme Court of Wisconsin, 1950.

256 Wis. 621, 42 N.W.2d 273.

BACKGROUND AND FACTS   *Petersen was employed by Pilgrim Village for nearly ten years. His contract of employment provided that he was to be paid a stated salary. Petersen claimed that Pilgrim told him when he began work that he would share in the profits of the corporation and promised him repeatedly throughout the term of his employment that he would share in the profits.*

When Petersen left Pilgrim Village, Pilgrim paid him all but $666.67 of his salary for the time he had worked the previous year.

Petersen sued Pilgrim for the back salary of $666.67 and for $20,000, which he declared was his "reasonable" share of corporate profits. Pilgrim agreed to pay Petersen the salary but objected to paying any amount based on Petersen's claim that he was entitled to "a share of the profits." The trial court instructed the jury to award Petersen whatever part of the $20,000 they thought corresponded to "the reasonable value of services" Petersen had rendered to Pilgrim. The jury decided on $8,000. Pilgrim appealed, arguing that the parties had never come to any definite agreement as to what, if any, the percentage of profits was to be. The Supreme Court of Wisconsin reviewed Pilgrim's arguments.

FRITZ, Chief Justice.

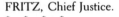

As stated in Restatement of the Law on Contracts, sec. 32, pp. 40, 41, "An offer must be so definite in its terms, or require such definite terms in the acceptance, that the promises and performances to be rendered by each party are reasonably certain."

*   *   *   *

As stated in 12 Am.Jur. [American Jurisprudence] sec. 70, p. 561, "The general rule is that price is an essential ingredient of every contract for the transfer of property or rights therein or for the rendering of services. Accordingly, an agreement must be definite as to compensation. In order that an executory agreement may be valid, it is generally necessary that the price must be certain or capable of being ascertained from the agreement itself. By this is not meant that the exact amount in figures must be stated in the agreement; however, where that is not the case, the price must, by the terms of the agreement, be capable of being definitely ascertained. An agreement leaving the price for future determination is not binding. *   *   * (p. 562) Although there is some authority to the contrary, a promise to pay a reasonable sum for goods or services is generally held valid. *   *   * On the other hand, a promise to pay a fair share of profits has been held too indefinite to be valid."

In *Varney v. Ditmars*, the employer promised to pay plaintiff $40 a week and "the first of January next year I will close my books and give you a fair share of my profits." The court said:

"The statement alleged to have been made by the defendant about giving the plaintiff and said designer a fair share of his profits is vague, indefinite, and uncertain, and the amount cannot be computed from anything that was said by the parties or by reference to any document, paper, or other transaction. The minds of the parties never met upon any particular share of the defendant's profits to be given the employees or upon any plan by which such share could be computed or determined. The contract so far as it related to the special promise or inducement was never consummated. It was left subject to the will of the defendant or for further negotiation. It is urged that the defendant by the use of the word 'fair,' in referring to a share of his profits, was as certain and definite as people are in the purchase and sale of a chattel [an item of personal property] when the price is not expressly agreed upon, and that if the agreement in question is declared to be too indefinite and uncertain to be enforced, a similar conclusion must

be reached in every case where a chattel is sold without expressly fixing the price therefor. The question whether the words 'fair' and 'reasonable' have a definite and enforceable meaning when used in business transactions is dependent upon the intention of the parties in the use of such words and upon the subject-matter to which they refer. In cases of merchandising and in the purchase and sale of chattels the parties may use the words 'fair and reasonable value' as synonymous with 'market value.'
* * *

"The contract in question, so far as it relates to a share of the defendant's profits, is not only uncertain, but it is necessarily affected by so many other facts that are in themselves indefinite and uncertain that the intention of the parties is pure conjecture. * * * The courts cannot aid parties in such a case when they are unable or unwilling to agree upon the terms of their own proposed contract."
* * * *

Consequently, * * * plaintiff's [claim] * * * was merely that he was to be paid "some share of the profits," and as the parties never came to any definite agreement as to what that percentage of the profits was to be, the [trial] court erred.

DECISION AND REMEDY   *Petersen left the appellate court without any of the $8,000 in "reasonable profits" the trial court jury had awarded him originally. Even assuming Petersen had been offered some share of the profits, the parties never showed that they had come to any definite agreement as to what that percentage of the profits ought to be. The appellate court did, however, allow Petersen a new trial to establish sufficient evidence that he was entitled to payment of "the reasonable value" of any additional services he had rendered to Pilgrim over and above what he had been paid in his actual salary. Petersen's recovery could be based on a quasi-contractual theory.*

COMMENTS   *Courts are sometimes willing to supply a missing term in a contract when the parties have clearly manifested an intent to form a contract. If, on the other hand, the parties have attempted to deal with a particular term of the contract but their expression of intent is too vague or uncertain to be given any precise meaning, the court will not supply a "reasonable" term, since to do so might conflict with the intent of the parties. In other words, the court will not rewrite the contract. Thus, when Petersen's employer promised that Petersen would share in the profits of the corporation, the promise was too indefinite to comprise an enforceable contract. Article 2 of the UCC has different rules relating to the requisite definiteness of an offer for the sale of goods. In essence, Article 2 modifies general contract law on offers by requiring less specificity. (See Chapter 16.)*

Communication

A third element for an effective offer is communication, resulting in the offeree's knowledge of the offer. One cannot agree to a bargain without knowing that the bargain exists. Suppose Emerman advertises a reward for the return of her lost dog. Baldwin, not knowing of the reward, finds the dog and returns it to Emerman. Baldwin can-

not recover the reward because he did not know it had been offered.[10]

A reward can be accepted only by complete performance. Thus, the contract formed by com-

---

10. A few states will allow recovery of the reward, but not on contract principles. Since Emerman wanted her dog returned, and Baldwin returned it, these few states would allow Baldwin to recover on the basis that it would be unfair to deny him the reward just because he did not know about it.

pletion of the act for which the reward was offered is *unilateral,* as explained in Chapter 7. An essential element in the reward contract is that the one who claims the reward must have known that it was offered. This rule follows because it is im-

possible to have an acceptance under contract law unless the offeree knows that the offer exists. The following case is one of the classic reward cases in the common law dealing with the requirement of communication of the offer.

BACKGROUND AND FACTS   *The Jewish War Veterans of the United States offered a reward of $500 in a newspaper "to the person or persons furnishing information resulting in the apprehension and conviction of the persons guilty of the murder of Maurice L. Bernstein." A day or so after the notice appeared, one of the men suspected in the crime was arrested, and the police received information that the other murderer was the "boyfriend" of a daughter of Mary Glover, the plaintiff and claimant in the present case. That evening, the police visited Mary Glover. She provided names and addresses and possible locations where her daughter and the suspect might be found. The suspect was arrested at one of the places suggested by Glover, and all suspects were subsequently convicted of the crime.*

Glover claimed the $500 reward from the Jewish War Veterans, the defendants, arguing that the information she gave to the police officers led to the arrest and conviction of the murderers. But there was some question as to whether she was entitled to the reward. At the time she gave the information to the police officers, she did not know that any reward had been offered for information leading to the arrest and conviction of the guilty persons. In fact, she did not learn about the reward until several days afterward. The trial court denied Glover the $500 reward, and Glover appealed. The appellate court reviewed the law of contracts concerning rewards.

Case 8.4
GLOVER v. JEWISH WAR VETERANS OF THE UNITED STATES, POST NO. 58
Municipal Court of Appeals for the District of Columbia, 1949. 68 A.2d 233.

CLAGETT, Associate Judge.

*   *   *   *

The issue determinative of this appeal is whether a person giving information leading to the arrest of a murderer without any knowledge that a reward has been offered for such information by a nongovernmental organization is entitled to collect the reward. The trial court decided the question in the negative and instructed the jury to return a verdict for defendant.

*   *   *   *

We have concluded that the trial court correctly instructed the jury to return a verdict for defendant. While there is some conflict in the decided cases on the subject of rewards, most of such conflict has to do with rewards offered by governmental officers and agencies. So far as rewards offered by private individuals and organizations are concerned, there is little conflict on the rule that questions regarding such rewards are to be based upon the law of contracts.

Since it is clear that the question is one of contract law, it follows that, at least so far as private rewards are concerned, *there can be no contract unless the claimant when giving the desired information knew of the offer of the reward and acted with the intention of accepting such offer* [emphasis added]; otherwise the claimant gives the information not in the expectation of receiving a reward but rather out of a sense of public duty or other motive unconnected with the reward. "In the nature of the case," according to Professor Williston, "it is impossible for an offeree actually to assent to an offer unless he knows of its existence." After stating that courts in some jurisdictions have decided to the contrary, Williston adds, "It is impossible, however, to find in such a case [that is, in a case holding to the contrary] the elements generally held in England and

America necessary for the formation of a contract. If it is clear the offeror intended to pay for the services, it is equally certain that the person rendering the service performed it voluntarily and not in return for a promise to pay. If one person expects to buy, and the other to give, there can hardly be found mutual assent. These views are supported by the great weight of authority, and in most jurisdictions a plaintiff in the sort of case under discussion is denied recovery."

The American Law Institute in its Restatement of the Law of Contracts follows the same rule, thus: "It is impossible that there should be an acceptance unless the offeree knows of the existence of the offer." The Restatement gives the following illustration of the rule just stated: "A offers a reward for information leading to the arrest and conviction of a criminal. B, in ignorance of the offer, gives information leading to his arrest and later, with knowledge of the offer and intent to accept it, gives other information necessary for conviction. There is no contract."

We have considered the reasoning in state decisions following the contrary rule. Mostly, as we have said, they involve rewards offered by governmental bodies and in general are based upon the theory that the government is benefited equally whether or not the claimant gives the information with knowledge of the reward and that therefore the government should pay in any event. We believe that the rule adopted by Professor Williston and the Restatement and in the majority of the cases is the better reasoned rule and therefore we adopt it. We believe furthermore that this rule is particularly applicable in the present case since the claimant did not herself contact the authorities and volunteer information but gave information only upon questioning by the police officers and did not claim any knowledge of the guilt or innocence of the criminal but only knew where he probably could be located.

DECISION AND REMEDY   *The trial court judgment was affirmed. The Jewish War Veterans did not have to pay the reward to Glover. No contract existed, because Glover's performance was not induced by the offer, of which she had had no knowledge.*

COMMENTS   *In this case, the court indicated that there is some conflict concerning rewards offered by government officers and agencies. Some courts provide a remedy when a government body offers a reward on the theory that the government is benefited equally whether or not the claimant gave it the information while knowing about the reward. The public good is served regardless. Another rationale is that knowledge of government actions may be imputed. Whichever theory the courts use, the result is the same—the government pays the reward.*

TERMINATION OF THE OFFER

The communication of an effective offer to an offeree creates a power in the offeree to transform the offer into a binding, legal obligation—a contract. This power of acceptance, however, does not continue forever. It can be terminated by either *action of the parties* or *operation of law*.

Termination by Action of the Parties

The power of the offeree to transform the offer into a binding, legal obligation can usually be terminated by any of the following actions:

1. Revocation of the offer by the offeror.
2. Rejection of the offer by the offeree.
3. Counteroffer by the offeree.

REVOCATION OF THE OFFER BY THE OFFEROR. **Revocation** is the withdrawal of the offer by the offeror. An offer may be revoked by the offeror, even if the offeror has promised to keep it open, if a revocation is communicated to the offeree before he or she accepts. Revocation may be accomplished by express repudiation of the offer (such as "I withdraw my previous offer of October 17") or by acts inconsistent with the existence of the offer that are made known to the offeree.

The revocation must be communicated to the offeree before acceptance, or it will be ineffective, and a valid contract can be formed. The general rule followed by most states is that a revocation is effective only upon actual receipt of the revocation by the offeree or offeree's agent. Therefore, a letter of revocation that is mailed on April 1 and is delivered at the offeree's residence or place of business on April 3 becomes effective on April 3.

Alternatively, communication to the offeree exists if the offeree indirectly discovers that the offer has been revoked. This indirect discovery may occur when a third person tells the offeree that the offer has been revoked prior to the offeree's acceptance, when the offeree learns that the subject matter of the contract has been sold to a third party, or when the offeree learns that the offeror is no longer willing or able to fulfill the promise made in the offer.

Revocation of offers made to the general public must be communicated in the same manner in which the offer was originally communicated. For example, suppose Macy's offers a $10,000 reward for anyone giving information leading to the apprehension of the persons who burglarized Macy's downtown store. The offer is published in three local papers and in four papers in neighboring communities. In order to revoke the offer, Macy's must publish the revocation in all seven papers for the same number of days as it published the offer. The revocation will then be accessible to the general public, even if some particular offeree does not learn about it.

IRREVOCABLE OFFERS Although most offers are revocable, certain offers can be made irrevocable. Three such types of **irrevocable offers** deserve discussion. They are:

1. Option contracts.
2. Firm offers under the UCC.
3. Offeree's detrimental reliance on the offer (promissory estoppel).

Option Contracts As a general rule, offerors may revoke their offers even if they expressly agreed to hold them open for a specified period of time. When an offeror promises to hold an offer open for a specified period of time, however, and the offeree pays for the promise (gives consideration), an **option contract** is created. An option contract is a *separate* contract that takes away the offeror's

power to revoke the offer for the period of time specified in the option. If no time is specified, then a reasonable period of time is implied.

For example, suppose Brennan offers to sell one hundred shares of stock in Texas Instruments to Columbus for $189 per share. Brennan promises to keep the offer open for thirty days. After fourteen days Brennan calls Columbus on the telephone and says that the offer is revoked. If Columbus has not given any consideration (say $25 in cash) for the option (to keep the offer open) up to this time, Brennan may revoke the offer despite his promise to keep it open for thirty days. But if Columbus has given some consideration for the option, Brennan must hold the offer open for the stated thirty days. This particular option contract (for the purchase of common stock) is becoming increasingly popular, and similar options are traded publicly on numerous exchanges.

Death or incompetency of the offeror does not terminate an offer under an option contract, unless the offeror's personal performance is essential to the fulfillment of the contract.[11] For example, assume Vendrick executes an option to Carney entitling Carney to purchase Vendrick's hundred-acre ranch in Costa Rica. Carney pays $750 for the option, but before she can exercise it, Vendrick dies. Carney can still exercise the option against Vendrick's estate, since Vendrick is not required to perform the act of conveying the ranch to Carney personally. In sum, option contract rights and duties are not discharged by the death of either party unless the performance is of a personal nature—that is, consists of personal services.

Firm Offers Under the UCC, certain offers may be irrevocable even if no consideration is given. These are called **firm offers.**[12] If a merchant[13] makes a written, signed offer to buy or sell goods and states that the offer will be held open, the offer cannot be revoked regardless of the lack of consideration. The offer will remain open for the period of time specified in the offer or, if no time is specified, for a reasonable period; but the period

---

11. Restatement, Second, Contracts, Section 37.
12. UCC 2-205.
13. Generally, under the UCC, a *merchant* is a person who deals in goods of the kind involved in the transaction or otherwise by his or her occupation holds himself or herself out as having knowledge or skill peculiar to the practices or goods involved [see Chapter 16 and UCC 2-104(1)].

of irrevocability without consideration cannot exceed three months. Note the various elements necessary for a firm offer:

1. The offer must be for the purchase or sale of goods.
2. The offer must be made by a merchant dealing in those goods.
3. The offer must be written and signed by the merchant.
4. The offer must give assurance that it will be held open.

Detrimental Reliance   Increasingly, courts are refusing to allow an offeror to revoke an offer when the offeree has changed position in justifiable reliance on the offer. In such cases, revocation is considered unjust to the offeree. Consider an example. Feinberg has rented commercial property from Pfeiffer for thirty-three years under a series of five-year leases. Under business conditions existing as their seventh lease nears its end, the rental property market is more favorable for tenants than landlords. Feinberg tells Pfeiffer that she is going to look at other, less expensive properties as possible sites for her business. Wanting Feinberg to remain a tenant, Pfeiffer promises to reduce the rent in their next lease. In reliance on the promise, Feinberg does not look at other sites but continues to occupy and do business on Pfeiffer's property. When they sit down to negotiate a new lease, Pfeiffer says he has changed his mind and will increase the rent. Can he effectively revoke his promise?

The argument is that he will not be able to do so because Feinberg has been relying on his promise to reduce the rent. Had the promise not been made, she would have relocated her business. This is a case of detrimental reliance on a promise, which therefore cannot be revoked. The situation is normally called **promissory estoppel.** To **estop** means to bar or impede or to preclude. Thus, promissory estoppel means that the promisor (the offeror) is barred or prevented from revoking the offer, in this case because the offeree has already changed her actions in reliance on the offer. We will cover the doctrine of promissory estoppel again in Chapter 9.

Another situation causing detrimental reliance on the part of the offeree involves *partial performance* by the offeree in response to an offer looking toward formulation of a *unilateral* contract. The offer invites acceptance only by full performance; merely promising to perform does not constitute acceptance. Obviously, injustice can result if an offeree expends time and money in partial performance, and then the offeror revokes the offer before performance is complete. Consequently, many courts will not allow the offeror to revoke after the offeree has performed some substantial part of his or her duties.[14] In effect, partial performance renders the offer irrevocable, giving the original offeree reasonable time to complete performance. Of course, when performance is complete, a unilateral contract exists.

The following case clearly illustrates the principle that partial performance by the offeree in response to a unilateral offer can make the offer irrevocable. This case has often been cited by courts in more recent decisions concerning the issue.

---

14. Restatement, Second, Contracts, Section 25.

Case 8.5

MARCHIONDO v. SCHECK

Supreme Court of New Mexico, 1967.
78 N.M. 440, 432 P.2d 405.

BACKGROUND AND FACTS   *Scheck, the defendant, had a prospective buyer for some real estate he wished to sell. Scheck offered in writing to pay Marchiondo, the plaintiff, a commission (a percentage of the sales price) as a broker if the purchase was accepted by the prospective buyer within a six-day limit. Just before the six-day period for the purchaser's acceptance had lapsed, Scheck, in writing, sent Marchiondo a notice of revocation. Marchiondo received the revocation on the morning of the sixth day. Later that day, Marchiondo obtained the acceptance of the purchaser. Marchiondo claimed he had spent time and money in attempting to get the purchaser to agree to Scheck's offer. Scheck refused to pay Marchiondo a commission, and Marchiondo filed suit. The trial court dismissed the complaint on the basis that the offer had been revoked prior to the acceptance (which occurred when the purchaser agreed to purchase Scheck's property). Marchiondo appealed.*

WOOD, Judge.

* * * *

We are not concerned with the revocation of the offer as between the offeror and the prospective purchaser. With certain exceptions, * * * the right of a broker to the agreed compensation, or damages measured thereby, is not defeated by the refusal of the principal to complete or consummate a transaction.

* * * *

When defendant made his offer to pay a commission upon sale of the property, he offered to enter a unilateral contract; the offer was for an act to be performed, a sale.

Many courts hold that the principal has the right to revoke the broker's agency at any time before the broker has actually procured a purchaser. The reason given is that until there is performance, the offeror has not received that contemplated by his offer, and there is no contract. Further, the offeror may never receive the requested performance because the offeree is not obligated to perform. Until the offeror receives the requested performance, no consideration has passed from the offeree to the offeror. Thus, until the performance is received, the offeror may withdraw the offer.

* * * *

* * * "A greater number of courts, however, hold that part performance of the consideration may make such an offer irrevocable and that where the offeree or broker manifests his assent to the offer by entering upon performance and spending time and money in his efforts to perform, then the offer becomes irrevocable during the time stated and binding upon the principal according to its terms. * * * "

* * * *

* * * It is the action taken by the offeree which deprives the offeror of that right. Until there is action by the offeree—a partial performance pursuant to the offer— the offeror may revoke even if his offer is of an exclusive agency or an exclusive right to sell.

Once partial performance is begun pursuant to the offer made, a contract results. This contract has been termed a contract with conditions or an option contract. This terminology is illustrated as follows:

> "If an offer for a unilateral contract is made, and part of the consideration requested in the offer is given or tendered by the offeree in response thereto, the offeror is bound by a contract, the duty of immediate performance of which is conditional on the full consideration being given or tendered within the time stated in the offer, or, if no time is stated therein, within a reasonable time."

* * * *

The reason for finding such a contract is stated * * * as follows:
This rule avoids hardship to the offeree, and yet does not hold the offeror beyond the terms of his promise. It is true by such terms he was to be bound only if the requested act was done; but this implies that he will let it be done, that he will keep his offer open till the offeree who has begun can finish doing it. At least this is so where the doing of it will necessarily require time and expense. In such a case it is but just to hold that the offeree's part performance furnishes the 'acceptance' and the 'consideration' for a binding subsidiary promise not to revoke the offer, or turns the offer into a presently binding contract conditional upon the offeree's full performance.

We hold that part performance by the offeree of an offer of a unilateral contract results in a contract with a condition. The condition is full performance by the offeree. Here, if plaintiff-offeree partially performed prior to receipt of defendant's revocation, such a contract was formed. Thereafter, upon performance being completed by plaintiff, upon defendant's failure to recognize the contract, liability for breach of contract would arise. Thus, defendant's right to revoke his offer depends upon whether plaintiff had partially performed before he received defendant's revocation.

DECISION AND REMEDY	*The case was remanded to the trial court for findings on the issue of the plaintiff's partial performance of the offer prior to its revocation.*
COMMENTS	*If the offer makes it clear that acceptance can occur only through performance, and not by a promise, substantial performance by the offeree creates the equivalent of an option contract. That is, once the offeree starts to perform, the offer becomes irrevocable.*

REJECTION OF THE OFFER BY THE OFFEREE The offer may be rejected by the offeree, in which case the offer is terminated. Any subsequent attempt by the offeree to accept will be construed as a new offer, giving the original offeror (now the offeree) the power of acceptance. A rejection is ordinarily accomplished by words or conduct evidencing an intent not to accept the offer.

As in the case of revocation of the offer, rejection is effective only when actually received by the offeror or the offeror's agent.

Suppose you offer to sell Procter & Gamble twenty-five tons of linseed oil at 35 cents per gallon. Procter & Gamble could reject your offer by writing or telephoning you, expressly rejecting the offer (perhaps by saying, "We are sufficiently stocked in linseed oil and do not need any more"). Alternatively, the company could mail your offer back to you, evidencing an intent to reject the offer. Or it could offer to buy the oil at 20.3 cents per gallon, which would operate as a counteroffer, necessarily rejecting the original offer.

Merely inquiring about the offer does not constitute rejection. For example, a friend offers to buy your bicycle for $75. If you respond, "Is this your best offer?" or "Will you pay me $100 for it?" a reasonable person would conclude that you did not reject the offer but merely made an inquiry for further consideration of the offer. You can still accept and bind your friend to the $75 purchase price. When the offeree merely inquires as to the firmness of the offer, there is no reason to presume that he or she intends to reject it.

Some responses are borderline in nature. For example, if you respond to your friend's offer with, "The price seems low. I'll bet you can do better than that," it could be argued that you are inquiring about the offer or that you are rejecting it.

COUNTEROFFER BY THE OFFEREE A counteroffer is usually a rejection of the original offer and the simultaneous making of a new offer. Suppose Stewart offers to sell his home to Twardy for $70,000. Twardy responds, "Your price is too high. I'll offer to purchase your house for $65,000." Twardy's response is termed a counteroffer, since it terminates Stewart's offer to sell at $70,000 and creates a new offer by Twardy to purchase at $65,000. At common law, the **mirror image rule** requires the offeree's acceptance to match the offeror's offer exactly—to mirror the offer. Any material change in, or addition to, the terms of the original offer automatically terminates that offer and substitutes the counteroffer, which, of course, need not be accepted. The original offeror can, however, accept the terms of the counteroffer and create a valid contract.

Variance in terms between the offer and the offeree's acceptance, violating the mirror image rule, has caused considerable problems in commercial transactions. This is particularly true when, in the sale of goods, the seller and buyer exchange different standardized purchase forms in the process of offer and acceptance. Seldom do the terms of both purchase forms match exactly. This phenomenon has been called the "battle of the forms" because of the problem of whose form will prevail.

Dealing with contracts for the sale of goods, the UCC in Section 2-207 has addressed this problem by providing that a contract is formed if the offeree makes a definite expression of acceptance, even though the terms of the acceptance modify or add to the terms of the original offer.[15] *Between merchants,* the new terms become part of the contract automatically unless:

1. The original offer expressly required acceptance of its terms.
2. The new or changed terms materially alter the contract.

---

15. For example, Sylvestre v. Minnesota, 289 Minn. 142, 214 N.W.2d 658 (1973).

3. The offeror rejects the new or changed terms within a reasonable period of time.

The Code further provides that if one or both parties are nonmerchants, the contract is formed according to the terms of the offer, not according to the additional terms of the acceptance.

It is possible for an offeree to make a new offer without intending to reject the original offer. In such a case two offers exist, each capable of being accepted. To illustrate, suppose Frank offers to sell his bicycle for $100. Irene's response is, "I do not have $100 but will try to raise that sum. I do have $75 and will offer to purchase your bicycle for that price." Since the offeree did not reject the $100 offer, that offer remains effective. But the offeree did offer to purchase the bicycle for $75. Thus, two offers exist, and the first to be accepted binds the parties to a contract for that amount.

Termination by Operation of Law

The power in the offeree to transform the offer into a binding, legal obligation can be terminated by operation of the law through the following:

1. Lapse of time.
2. Destruction of the subject matter of the contract.
3. Death or incompetency of the offeror or the offeree.
4. Supervening illegality of the proposed contract.

LAPSE OF TIME An offer terminates automatically when the period of time specified in the offer has passed. For example, suppose Anna offers to sell her boat to Bob if he accepts within twenty days. Bob must accept within the twenty-day period or the offer will lapse (terminate). The period of time specified in an offer begins to run when the offer is actually received by the offeree, not when it is sent or drawn up. When the offer has been delayed, the period begins to run from the date the offeree would have received the offer, but only if the offeree knows or should know the offer was delayed.[16] For example, if Anna used improper postage when mailing the offer to Bob, but Bob knew Anna used improper postage, the offer would lapse twenty days after the day Bob would

ordinarily have received the offer had Anna used proper postage.

If no time for acceptance is specified in the offer, the offer terminates at the end of a *reasonable* period of time. A reasonable period is determined by the subject matter of the contract, business and market conditions, and other relevant circumstances. An offer to sell farm produce, for example, will terminate sooner than an offer to sell farm equipment because farm produce is perishable and subject to greater fluctuations in market value.

DESTRUCTION OF THE SUBJECT MATTER An offer is automatically terminated if the specific subject matter of the offer is destroyed before the offer is accepted.[17] For example, if Watts offers to sell her race horse to Teagle but the horse dies before Teagle can accept, the offer is automatically terminated.

DEATH OR INCOMPETENCY OF THE OFFEROR OR OFFEREE An offeree's power of acceptance is terminated when the offeror or offeree dies or is deprived of legal capacity to enter into the proposed contract.[18] An offer is personal to both parties and cannot pass to the decedent's heirs, guardian, or estate. Furthermore, this rule applies whether or not the other party had notice of the death or incompetency. For example, on June 4, Manne offers to sell Clark a rowboat for $300, telling Clark that he, Manne, needs the answer by June 20. On June 10, Manne dies. On June 18, Clark informs the executor of Manne's estate that he has accepted the offer. The executor can refuse to sell the rowboat because the death of the offeror has terminated the offer.

There is an exception to the rule that the death of either the offeror or the offeree before acceptance terminates an offer. The exception applies to *irrevocable offers*—offers that legally cannot be withdrawn by the offeror once made. As previously discussed, an *option* is an example of an irrevocable offer. Although some disagree, many legal scholars believe that the exception also applies to *firm offers* (irrevocable under the UCC).

SUPERVENING ILLEGALITY OF THE PROPOSED CONTRACT A statute or court decision that makes

---

16. Restatement, Second, Contracts, Section 49.

---

17. Restatement, Second, Contracts, Section 36.
18. Restatement, Second, Contracts, Section 48.

CONCEPT SUMMARY: Methods by Which an Offer Can Be Terminated	

METHODS OF TERMINATION	BASIC RULES
By Acts of the Parties:	
1. Revocation	1. An offer can be revoked at any time before acceptance without liability unless the offer is irrevocable. 2. Option contracts, firm offers under UCC 2-205, and the promissory estoppel theory render some offers irrevocable. 3. Except for public offers, revocation is not effective until *known* by the offeree or the offeree's authorized agent.
2. Rejection	1. Rejection of an offer is accomplished by words or actions that demonstrate a clear intent not to accept or consider the offer further. Inquiries about an offer do not constitute a rejection. 2. A rejection is not effective until *known* by the offeror or an authorized agent of the offeror.
3. Counteroffer	1. A counteroffer is a rejection of the original offer and the making of a new offer. Inquiries are not rejections. 2. Under UCC 2-207, a definite acceptance of an offer is not a counteroffer, even if the acceptance terms modify the terms of the offer.
By Operation of Law:	
1. Lapse of Time	1. If a time period for acceptance is stated in the offer, the offer ends at the stated time. 2. If no time period for acceptance is stated, the offer terminates at the end of a reasonable period.
2. Destruction	Destruction of the specific subject matter of the offer terminates the offer.
3. Death or Incompetence	Death or incompetence of either offeror or offeree terminates an offer, unless the offer is irrevocable.
4. Illegality	Supervening illegality terminates an offer.

an offer illegal will automatically terminate the offer.[19] If Barker offers to loan Jackson $20,000 at 15 percent annually and a law is enacted prohibiting loans at interest rates greater than 14 percent before Jackson can accept, the offer is automatically terminated. (If, in this hypothetical case, the law had been passed after Jackson accepted the offer, a valid contract would have been formed, but the contract might have been unenforceable.)

---

19. Restatement, Second, Contracts, Section 36.

ACCEPTANCE

Acceptance is a voluntary act (either words or conduct) by the offeree that shows assent (agreement) to the terms of an offer. The acceptance must be unequivocal and communicated to the offeror.

Who Can Accept?

Generally, a third person cannot interpose himself or herself as a substitute for the offeree and effectively accept the offer. After all, the identity of the offeree is as much a condition of a bargaining offer as any other term contained therein. Thus, except in certain special circumstances to be discussed, only the person to whom the offer is made can accept the offer and create a binding contract. For example, Jones makes an offer to Hanley. Hanley is not interested, but Hanley's friend, Smith, accepts the offer. No contract is formed.

EXCEPTIONS The special circumstances in which a third party can accept an offer in place of the offeree are as follows:

1. If the offer is an option contract, the right to exercise the option is generally considered a contract right. As such, it is assignable or transferable to third persons (with exceptions—see Chapter 13).
2. If the offeree is an agent for a principal, the acceptance may be made by the principal, and a contract will be formed between the principal and the offeror (see Chapter 33).

WHEN THE OFFER IS MADE TO TWO OR MORE PERSONS If an offer is made to two or more persons, it must be accepted by all of them. If individual offers are made to two or more persons individually, then contracts are created only with those persons who accept the offer.

Unequivocal Acceptance

In order to exercise the power of acceptance effectively, the offeree must accept unequivocally. This is the *mirror image rule* previously discussed. If the acceptance is subject to new conditions, or if the terms of the acceptance materially change the original offer, the acceptance may be considered a counteroffer that implicitly rejects the original offer. An acceptance may be unequivocal even though the offeree expresses dissatisfaction with the contract. For example, "I accept the goods, but I wish I could have gotten a better price" will operate as an effective acceptance. So, too, will "I accept, but can you shave the price?" On the other hand, the statement "I accept the goods, but only if I can pay on ninety days' credit" is not an unequivocal acceptance and operates as a counteroffer, rejecting the original offer.

Certain conditions, when added to an acceptance, do not qualify the acceptance sufficiently to make it a rejection of the offer. Suppose Childs offers to sell her sixty-five-acre cotton farm to Sharif. Sharif replies, "I accept your offer to sell the farm, provided you can supply good title." This condition (providing a good title) does not make the acceptance equivocal. A warranty of good title is normally implied in every offer for the sale of land, so the condition does not add any new or different terms to the offer.

Or suppose that in response to an offer to sell a motorcycle, the offeree replies, "I accept; please send written contract." The offeree has requested a written contract but has not made it a condition for acceptance. Therefore, the acceptance is effective without the written contract. If, however, the offeree replies "I accept if you send a written contract," the acceptance is expressly conditioned on the request for a writing, and the statement is not an acceptance but a counteroffer. (Notice how important *each* word is!) As noted above, under the UCC, an acceptance is still valid even if terms are added. The additional terms are simply treated as proposals for additions to the contract.[20]

Silence as Acceptance

Ordinarily, silence cannot be acceptance, even if the offeror states, "By your silence and inaction you will be deemed to have accepted this offer." This general rule applies because an offeree should not be put under a burden or liability to act affirmatively in order to reject an offer when no consideration has passed to the offeree to impose such a liability.

On the other hand, silence can operate as an acceptance when an offeree takes the benefit of offered services even though he or she had an opportunity to reject them and knew that they were offered with the expectation of compensation. Suppose Holmes watches while her daughter is given piano lessons. The piano instructor has not been requested to give the daughter lessons but plans to give a series of fifteen. Holmes knows the instructor expects to be paid but lets the lessons continue nonetheless. Here, her silence constitutes an acceptance, and a contract is created. She is bound to pay a reasonable value for the

---

20. Restatement, Second, Contracts, Section 61 and UCC 2-207.

lessons. This rule applies only to services and goods from which the offeree has received a benefit.

Silence can also operate as acceptance when the parties have had prior dealings in which the offeree has led the offeror reasonably to understand that the offeree will accept all offers unless the offeree sends notice to the contrary. For example, Brodsky, a sales agent, has previously received shipments of goods from Morales and paid without notifying Morales of his acceptance. Brodsky sells the goods and simply sends Morales a check. Only if the goods are defective does he notify Morales. The last shipment has been neither paid for nor rejected. Nonetheless, Brodsky is bound on a contract and must pay Morales for this last shipment of goods.[21]

In the past, at common law, silence could constitute acceptance in the following situation: Books or magazines are sent to an individual through the mails. The individual did not order the books or magazines and is under no duty to reship them to the seller. If, however, the individual uses the books or magazines, acceptance is established, and he or she must pay reasonable value for them. Note that silence does not constitute an acceptance unless the receiver exercises control over the goods. This common law rule of contract law has been changed by statute. The Postal Reorganization Act of 1970 provides that *unsolicited* merchandise sent by U.S. mail may be retained, used, discarded, or disposed of in any manner deemed appropriate, without the individual incurring any obligation to the sender.[22] In addition, the mailing of unordered merchandise (except for free samples) constitutes an unfair trade practice and is not permitted. (Exceptions include mailings by charitable agencies.)

Another situation in which silence creates an acceptance occurs when the offeree solicits the offer. In such a case the offeree has a *duty to speak*, if he or she wishes to reject. Failure to reject operates as acceptance by silence. For example, Melrose tells Levine that she is interested in purchasing a complete textbook on business law for approximately $45. Levine responds that he has just the book Melrose is looking for, published by West and costing $42. Levine further informs Melrose that he has sent the book to Melrose and

unless he hears from Melrose to the contrary in thirty days, he will bill Melrose. Since Melrose solicited Levine's offer, Melrose has a duty to reject, and her failure to do so during the thirty-day period will constitute an acceptance.

A similar situation occurs with such organizations as the Book-of-the-Month Club. Once an individual has agreed that his or her failure to respond will constitute acceptance, merchandise is shipped periodically (usually every month) unless the customer sends a card indicating that he or she does not want the merchandise. Failure to reject the offered merchandise in this manner operates as acceptance by silence.

Communication of Acceptance

Whether the offeror must be notified of the acceptance depends on the nature of the contract. In a unilateral contract, no notification or communication is generally necessary. Since a unilateral contract calls for the performance of some act, acceptance is not complete until the act has been substantially performed. Therefore, notice of acceptance is usually unnecessary. To illustrate: Beta offers to pay Gamma $150 to paint Beta's garage. Gamma can accept only by painting the garage. Once the garage is completely painted (and hence the acceptance is complete), notification of the acceptance is superfluous. Exceptions do exist. When the offeror requests notice of acceptance or has no adequate means of determining whether the requested act has been performed, or when the law requires such notice of acceptance, then notice is necessary.[23]

In a bilateral contract, *communication* of acceptance is necessary because acceptance is in the form of a promise (not performance), and the contract is formed when the promise is made (rather than when the act is performed). The offeree must use reasonable efforts to communicate the acceptance to the offeror. In a bilateral contract, however, *notification* of acceptance is not necessary if the offer dispenses with the requirement. In addition, if the offer can be accepted by silence, no communication or notification is necessary.

Under the UCC, an order or other offer to buy goods for prompt shipment may be treated as either

21. Restatement, Second, Contracts, Section 72.

22. 39 U.S.C.A., Section 3009.

23. UCC 2-206(2).

a bilateral or a unilateral offer and can be accepted by a promise to ship or by actual shipment.[24]

Consider an example. Peters receives a telegram that he is to ship certain goods to Johnson. The UCC provides that Peters can accept by either promptly shipping the goods or sending a telegram to Johnson saying that he is going to ship the goods. (If the shipment will take a considerable amount of time, Peters would be wise to telegraph Johnson that the goods are in transit.)

Mode and Timeliness of Acceptance in Bilateral Contracts

The general rule is that an acceptance is timely if it is effective within the duration of the offer. Problems arise, however, when the parties involved are not dealing face to face. In such cases, the offeree may use an authorized mode of communication. Acceptance takes effect, thus completing formation of the contract, at the time that communication is sent by the mode expressly or impliedly authorized by the offeror. This is the so-called acceptance-upon-dispatch rule (**mailbox rule**), which the majority of courts uphold. (Note that this is an exception to the normal rule of bilateral contracts that acceptance requires a completed communication.) What becomes an issue is the *authorized* means of communicating the acceptance. Authorized means can be either expressly stated in the offer or impliedly authorized by facts or by law. In any case, the acceptance becomes effective at the time that it is sent by an authorized means of communication, whether or not the offeror receives that communication.[25]

When an offeror specifies an exclusive means by which acceptance should be sent (for example, by first-class mail or by telegram), *express authorization* is said to exist, and the contract is not formed unless the offeree uses that specified means of acceptance. Moreover, both offeror and offeree are bound in contract the moment such means of acceptance are employed. If telegraph is expressly authorized as the means for acceptance, a contract is established as soon as the offeree gives his or her message to Western Union. Even if Western Union for some reason fails to deliver the message, the contract still exists.

Most offerors do not specify expressly the means by which the offeree is to accept. Thus, the common law and statutes recognize what are called *implied authorized means of acceptance*. In the absence of expressly authorized means, three implied authorized means have been designated, as follows:

1. The means chosen by the offeror to make the offer implies that the offeree is authorized to use the *same* or a *faster* means for acceptance.
2. When two parties are at a distance, unless otherwise inferred, *mailing* is impliedly authorized.[26]
3. Under the UCC, acceptance of an offer for sale of goods can be made by any *medium* that is *reasonable* under the circumstances.[27]

An acceptance sent by means not expressly or impliedly authorized is often not effective until it is received by the offeror.[28]

To illustrate authorized means of acceptance, note the following cases:

1. On January 1, Jones makes an offer to sell Smith his motorcycle for $450, stipulating that Smith should send acceptance by telegram. On January 2, Jones mails Smith a letter of revocation

---

24. UCC 2-206(1)(b).

25. Restatement, Second, Contracts, Section 30 provides that an offer invites acceptance "by any medium reasonable in the circumstances," unless the offer is specific about the means of acceptance. Under Section 65, a medium is reasonable if it is one used by the offeror or one customary in similar transactions, unless the offeree knows of circumstances that would argue against the reasonableness of a particular medium (e.g., the need for speed because of rapid price changes). Acceptance by mail is ordinarily reasonable where the parties are negotiating at a distance, even though the offer was transmitted by telephone or telegraph. Care must be taken, however, to ensure a safe transmission. Under Section 66, "[a]n acceptance by mail or otherwise from a distance is not operative when dispatched, unless it is properly addressed and such other precautions taken as are ordinarily observed to insure safe transmission of similar messages." See also UCC 2-206(1)(a).

26. Adams v. Lindsell, 106 Eng.Rep. 250 (K.B. 1818).

27. UCC 2-206(1)(a) changes the common law rule from "authorized means" to "a reasonable medium."

28. An exception to this rule is given in Restatement, Second, Contracts, Section 67. Under the Restatement, an acceptance is effective upon dispatch even though the means of transmission is improper or the offeree fails to use care in ensuring safe transmission (e.g., wrong address or postage) if (1) the acceptance sent is timely and (2) the offeror receives the communication within the same period of time as that in which a properly transmitted acceptance would have arrived.

that is received by Smith at noon on January 4. On January 3, Smith delivers to Western Union his telegram of acceptance. The telegram is incorrectly sent and is not received by Jones until January 5. Are Jones and Smith bound in contract? The answer is yes. Telegram was the expressly stated means of acceptance in the offer; therefore, acceptance is effective the moment Smith delivers his acceptance to Western Union on January 3. A revocation is not effective until it is received by the offeree, in this case on January 4. This is subsequent to the acceptance, and the revocation is ineffective.

2. On January 1, Jones by telegram offers to sell Smith his motorcycle for $450. The offer contains no expressly stated means for Smith to make his acceptance. The telegram is received by Smith the same day it is sent. On January 2, Smith delivers his acceptance to Western Union. The telegram is lost and is never received by Jones. Jones sells the motorcycle to Green on January 20, believing Smith was not interested in his offer. Can Smith hold Jones liable for breach of contract? The answer is yes. Although the offer did not expressly state a means for Smith's acceptance, telegraph was impliedly authorized. The court here could use either the common law "same or faster means" rule of implied authorization or the UCC "reasonable medium" rule dealing with the sale of goods. Either way, Smith formed a contract with Jones on January 2.

There are three basic exceptions to the rule that a contract is formed when acceptance is sent by authorized means:

1. If the acceptance is not properly dispatched, in most states it will not be effective until it is received by the offeror.[29] For example, if mail is the authorized means for acceptance, the offeree's letter must be properly addressed and have the correct postage.

2. The offeror can specifically condition his or her offer on receipt of acceptance by a certain time. For example, an offer may be worded as follows: "Acceptance is not binding unless received by the offeror in her office by 5:00 P.M. on May 1." In this case it is immaterial how the offeree sends acceptance, as the acceptance is effective only when received.

3. Sometimes an offeree sends a rejection first, then later changes his or her mind and sends an acceptance. Obviously, this chain of events could cause confusion and even detriment to the offeror, depending on whether the rejection or the acceptance arrived first. Because of this, the law cancels the rule of acceptance upon dispatch in such situations, and the first communication to be received by the offeror determines whether a contract is formed. If the rejection is received first, there is no contract.[30]

---

29. But see exception in footnote 28.
30. Restatement, Second, Contracts, Section 40.

 ## QUESTIONS AND CASE PROBLEMS

---

1. As a bank officer, you have been given the responsibility of purchasing word processing equipment. On May 6, the ABC Manufacturing Corporation sends you a letter offering to sell your bank some word processing equipment at a price of $10,000, to be shipped via LM Truck Lines. The letter states that the offer is to remain open until May 20. On May 12, you write ABC a letter stating, "Offer appears a little high; I am sure you can do better. I'll need presidential approval for the $10,000 offer. I have authority to purchase word processing equipment for $8,500 and will buy your products at that price." ABC receives this letter on May 16. On May 15, the president of your bank approves the $10,000 purchase. On the same date, ABC sends you

a letter revoking its offer. The letter of revocation is received at your bank at 11:00 A.M. on May 19. On May 19 at 11:15 A.M. you send ABC the following telegram: "Accept your offer for $10,000." Because of a delay by the telegraph company, this message is not delivered until May 21.

(a) Discuss the legal effect of ABC's revocation sent on May 15.
(b) Discuss fully the legal effect of your response sent on May 12.
(c) Discuss whether your bank has a contract in light of the fact that the telegram was not delivered until May 21.

2. Ball writes Sullivan and inquires how much Sullivan is asking for a specific forty-acre tract of land Sullivan owns. In a letter received by Ball, Sullivan states "I will not take less than $60,000 for the forty-acre tract as specified." Ball immediately sends Sullivan a telegram stating, "I accept your offer for $60,000." Discuss whether Ball can hold Sullivan to a contract for sale of the land.

3. Smith, operating a sole proprietorship, has a large piece of used equipment for sale. He offers to sell the equipment to Barry for $10,000. Discuss the legal effect of the following events on the offer.

(a) Smith dies prior to Barry's acceptance, and at the time Barry accepts, she is unaware of Smith's death.

(b) The night before Barry accepts, fire destroys the equipment.

(c) Barry pays $100 for a thirty-day option to purchase the equipment. During this period Smith dies, and later Barry accepts the offer, knowing of Smith's death.

(d) Barry pays $100 for a thirty-day option to purchase the equipment. During this period Barry dies, and Barry's estate accepts Smith's offer within the stipulated time period.

4. Perez sees an advertisement in the newspaper that the ABC Corporation has for sale a two-volume set of *How to Make Repairs around the House* for $12.95. All Perez has to do is send in a card requesting delivery of the books for a thirty-day trial period of examination. If he does not ship the books back within thirty days of delivery, ABC will bill him for $12.95. Discuss whether or not Perez and ABC have a contract under either of the following circumstances.

(a) Perez sends in the card and receives the books in the U.S. mail. He uses the books to make repairs and fails to return them within thirty days.

(b) Perez does not send in the card, but ABC sends him the books anyway through the U.S. mail. Perez uses the books and fails to return them within thirty days.

5. [image] A plaintiff is attempting to recover death benefits under a life insurance policy. The policy contained a provision that allowed the policy's owner to terminate the policy and receive its cash value. All that the company required was a written request received at the home office. The owner of the policy died after having sent a letter requesting the cash value of the policy (which was much less than the face value). The letter was received *after* the policyowner died. The representative of the deceased owner contended that the estate was entitled to the death benefits of the life insurance policy. What was the result? [Franklin Life Ins. Co. v. Winney, 469 S.W.2d 21 (Tex.Civ.App. 1971)]

6. John H. Surratt was one of John Wilkes Booth's alleged accomplices in the murder of President Lincoln. On April 20, 1865, the secretary of war issued and caused to be published in newspapers the following proclamation: "$25,000 reward for the apprehension of John H. Surratt and liberal rewards for any information that leads to the arrest of John H. Surratt." On November 24, 1865, President Johnson revoked the reward and published the revocation in the newspapers. Henry B. St. Marie learned of the reward but left for Rome prior to its revocation. In Rome, St. Marie discovered Surratt's whereabouts; and, in April of 1866, unaware that the reward had been revoked, he reported this information to United States officials. Pursuant to receiving this information, the officials were able to arrest Surratt. Should St. Marie have received the reward? If so, was he entitled to the full $25,000? [Shuey v. United States, 92 U.S. (2 Otto) 73, 23 L.Ed. 697 (1875)]

7. Dodds signed and delivered to Dickinson the following memorandum on Wednesday, June 10:

"I hereby agree to sell to Mr. George Dickinson the whole of the dwelling houses, garden ground, stabling, and outbuildings these to belonging, situated at Croft, belonging to me, for the sum of £800. As witness my hand this tenth day of June, 1874."

"£800 [signed] John Dodds."

"P.S. this offer to be left over until Friday, 9 o'clock A.M. 12th June, 1874."

[Signed] J. Dodds."

The next afternoon (Thursday) Dickinson's agent told Dickinson that Dodds had decided to sell the property to a man named Allan and was negotiating with Allan for that purpose. That evening Dickinson went to the house of Dodd's mother-in-law and left her a written acceptance. This document never reached Dodds. The next morning, at 7 A.M., Dickinson's agent gave Dodds a copy of the acceptance. Dodds replied that it was too late, as he had already sold the property. Did Dickinson's knowledge that Dodds was negotiating to sell the property to Allan revoke Dodd's offer to Dickinson? Explain. [Dickinson v. Dodds, 2 Ch.D 463 (1876)]

8. Central Properties entered into a contract with Robbinson and Westside, a real estate development company, whereby Central Properties purchased 60 acres of land. The contract included a "right of first refusal" to purchase the water and sewage system on the remaining property of Westside. Westside wanted to sell the sewage system and over the course of three months exchanged letters with Central asking whether it wished to exercise its "right." Central Properties never affirmatively accepted in any of its responses but requested different terms, price, and so on. Central now wishes to hold Westside to a contract for the system. Westside states no contract was formed. Discuss who is right. [Central Properties, Inc. v. Robbinson, 450 So.2d 277 (Fla.App. 1 Dist. 1984)]

9. [image] Anderson Chevrolet/Olds, the plaintiff, leased a truck to Higgins, the defendant. The lease agreement provided that the "lessee shall pay for all maintenance and repairs to keep the vehicle in good working order and condition." A little over a year later, Higgins had the truck towed by Anderson to Anderson's garage, as it had stopped running. After inspecting the vehicle, Anderson determined that it would be necessary to disassemble the engine to ascertain the damage and repairs needed. Anderson did so and informed Higgins of the needed repairs and estimated costs. Higgins sent some employees to confirm the damage. Twenty-two days later, without hearing from Higgins, Anderson made the repairs and sent Higgins a bill for $1,407 (approximately equal to the estimate). Higgins sent employees to pick up the truck, but Anderson would not release the truck without payment. When Higgins refused to pay, Anderson filed suit. Higgins claimed that there was no contract for the truck repairs. Discuss fully whether Anderson had a contract to repair the truck even though Higgins never expressly accepted Anderson's offer of repair. [Anderson Chevrolet/Olds, Inc. v. Higgins, 57 N.C.App. 650, 292 S.E.2d 159 (1982)]

10. Deeco, Inc., owned a campground and had made a three-year lease with 3-M Company in 1976 for advertising Deeco's campsite on a billboard. The lease was renewed in 1979. The billboard was destroyed by a hurricane shortly thereafter, and 3-M wanted to form another contract because the wrong form had been used in 1976. The new 1980 form, which stated that it would not be a binding contract until signed by 3-M, was signed by Deeco but never signed by 3-M, although the 3-M representative told Deeco's president that 3-M would have the new billboard up in sixty days. The billboard was never erected. 3-M did, however, send Deeco monthly bills from January until April 1981 for advertising services on the nonexistent billboard, and delinquent payment notices were also sent to Deeco. Deeco sued for breach of contract. 3-M held that no contract existed because it had not signed (accepted) the contract offered by Deeco in 1980. Deeco argued that 3-M had indicated acceptance by its subsequent conduct—especially by the monthly bills sent by 3-M to Deeco. Discuss fully whether there is a contract between Deeco and 3-M. [Deeco, Inc. v. 3-M Co., 435 So.2d 1260 (Ala. 1983)]

11. In April 1974, Mafco Textured Fabrics began to purchase yarn from Gaynor-Stafford Industries using the following procedure: Mafco would place an oral order, Gaynor would send a written acknowledgment, and then Mafco would send a written and signed purchase order. In November 1974, Mafco refused to pay for a shipment of yarn that it claimed did not include "dyeable yarn" as asked for. Gaynor's acknowledgments contained the statement, "The acceptance of this order is conditional on the assent by the buyer to all of the conditions and terms on the reverse side * * * assent will be assumed unless you notify us to the contrary upon receipt of this acknowledgment or * * * accept delivery * * * of goods." The reverse side of each acknowledgment included a statement requiring all disputes relating to the contract to be settled by arbitration. The written purchase order form used by Mafco did not contain an arbitration clause, and Mafco did not object to the arbitration clause in Gaynor's acknowledgment. Discuss whether there is an agreement to arbitrate between the two parties. [Application of Gaynor-Stafford Industries, Inc. by Mafco Textured Fibers, 52 A.D.2d 481, 384 N.Y.S.2d 788 (N.Y.App.Div. 1976)]

12. On July 31, 1966, Lee Calan Imports (the defendant) advertised a 1964 Volvo Station Wagon for sale in the Chicago *Sun Times*. The defendant had instructed the newspaper to advertise the price of the automobile at $1,795. Through an error of the newspaper, however, and without fault on part of the defendant, the newspaper inserted a price of $1,095 for the automobile in the advertisement. Christopher O'Brien (the plaintiff) visited the defendant's place of business, examined the automobile, and stated that he wished to purchase it for $1,095. One of the defendant's sales agents at first agreed, but then refused to sell the car for the erroneous price listed in the advertisement. O'Brien sued Lee Calan Imports for breach of contract, claiming the ad constituted an offer that had been accepted by O'Brien. O'Brien died before the trial, and his administrator (O'Keefe) continued the suit. Discuss whether there is a contract. [O'Keefe v. Lee Calan Imports, Inc., 128 Ill.App.2d 410, 262 N.E.2d 758 (1970)]

Chapter 9

Consideration

The fact that a promise has been made does not mean the promise can or will be enforced. Therefore, it is important to consider what makes promises enforceable. Under Roman law, a promise was not enforceable without some sort of *causa*—that is, a reason for making the promise that was also deemed to be a sufficient reason for enforcing it. Since the beginning of the common law tradition in England, good reasons for enforcing informal[1] promises have been held to include the following: something given as an agreed exchange, a benefit that the promisor received, a detriment that the promisee incurred, and an action that the promisee took in reasonable reliance. Over time, these reasons came to be grouped under the single heading "consideration."

Thus, for centuries, it has been said that no informal promise is enforceable without consideration. **Consideration** may be defined as the *value* given in return for a promise. In other words, consideration is something that is exchanged for something else. A contract cannot be formed without legally sufficient consideration.

Often, consideration is broken into two elements: (1) something of *legal* value must be given in exchange for the promise, and (2) there must be a *bargained-for* exchange. The "something of legal value" may consist of a return promise that is bargained for. If it consists of performance, that performance may consist of:

1. An act (other than a promise).
2. A forbearance.
3. The creation, modification, or destruction of a legal relation.[2]

For example, Earl says to his son, "Upon completion of your mowing my yard, I promise to pay you $25." Earl's son mows the yard. The act of mowing the yard is the consideration that creates the contractual obligation of Earl to pay his son $25. Suppose, however, that Earl says to his son,

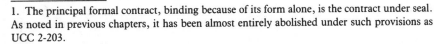

1. The principal formal contract, binding because of its form alone, is the contract under seal. As noted in previous chapters, it has been almost entirely abolished under such provisions as UCC 2-203.

2. Restatement, Second, Contracts, Section 71.

"In consideration of the fact that you are not as wealthy as your brothers, I will pay you $500." This promise is not enforceable because Earl's son has not given any consideration for the $500 promised.[3] Earl has simply stated his *motive* for giving his son a gift. The fact that the word *consideration* is used does not, alone, mean that consideration has been given.

LEGAL SUFFICIENCY OF CONSIDERATION

In order to create a binding contract, the elements of consideration must not only exist but must be legally sufficient. To be *legally sufficient,* consideration for a promise must be either legally *detrimental to the promisee*—the one receiving the promise—or legally *beneficial to the promisor*—the one making the promise—or both. Legal detriment occurs when one does or promises to do something that there was no prior legal duty to do. It also includes a forbearance, a refraining or promising to refrain from doing something that

---

3. Fink v. Cox, 18 Johns. 145, 9 Am.Dec. 191 (N.Y.1820).

there was no prior legal duty to refrain from doing. Conversely, legal benefit is obtaining something that there was no prior legal right to obtain. *Legal* detriment or benefit is not synonymous with *actual* (economic) detriment or benefit. In most cases, the promisor's legal benefit is the same as the promisee's legal detriment. The existence of *either* a legal detriment to the promisee *or* a legal benefit to the promisor, however, constitutes legally sufficient consideration.

Suppose Myers owns a brickhouse that causes considerable air pollution in and around his property. Bernard, his neighbor, is sick of the smoke and pollution and offers Myers $1,500 to stop making bricks (and thus stop the smoke). Myers agrees. The consideration flowing from Myers to Bernard is the promise to refrain from doing an act that Myers is legally entitled to do—that is, to earn a living by making bricks. The consideration flowing from Bernard to Myers is the promise to pay a sum of money that is not otherwise legally required to be paid.

In the following case, one of the classics of contract law, the court found that refraining from certain behavior at the request of another was sufficient consideration to support a promise to pay a sum of money.

Case 9.1
HAMER v. SIDWAY
Court of Appeals of New York,
Second Division, 1891.
124 N.Y. 538, 27 N.E. 256.

BACKGROUND AND FACTS *William E. Story, Sr., was the uncle of William E. Story II. In the presence of family members and guests invited to a family gathering, Story, Sr., promised to pay his nephew $5,000 if he would refrain from drinking, using tobacco, swearing, and playing cards or billiards for money until he became twenty-one. (Note that in 1869, when this contract was formed, it was legal in New York to drink and play cards for money prior to the age of twenty-one.) The nephew agreed and fully performed his part of the bargain. When he reached twenty-one, he wrote and told his uncle that he had kept his part of the agreement and was therefore entitled to $5,000. The uncle replied that he was pleased with his nephew's performance, writing, "I have no doubt but you have, for which you shall have five thousand dollars, as I promised you. I had the money in the bank the day you was twenty-one years old that I intend for you, and you shall have the money certain. * * * P.S. You can consider this money on interest."*

The nephew received his uncle's letter and thereafter consented that the money should remain with his uncle according to the terms and conditions of the letter. The uncle died about twelve years later without having paid his nephew any part of the $5,000 and interest. The executor of the uncle's estate (Sidway, the defendant in this action) did not want to pay the $5,000 (with interest) to Hamer, a third party to whom the nephew had assigned the note, claiming that there had been no valid consideration for the promise.

The court disagreed with the executor and reviewed the doctrine of detriment-benefit as valid consideration under the law.

PARKER, Justice.

*   *   *   *

The defendant contends that the contract was without consideration to support it, and therefore invalid. He asserts that the promisee, by refraining from the use of liquor and tobacco, was not harmed, but benefited; that that which he did was best for him to do, independently of his uncle's promise,—and insists that it follows that, unless the promisor was benefited, the contract was without consideration,—a contention which, if well founded, would seem to leave open for controversy in many cases whether that which the promisee did or omitted to do was in fact of such benefit to him as to leave no consideration to support the enforcement of the promisor's agreement. Such a rule could not be tolerated, and is without foundation in the law. The exchequer chamber in 1875 defined "consideration" as follows: "A valuable consideration, in the sense of the law, may consist either in some right, interest, profit, or benefit accruing to the one party, or some forbearance, detriment, loss, or responsibility given, suffered, or undertaken by the other." Courts "will not ask whether the thing which forms the consideration does in fact benefit the promisee or a third party, or is of any substantial value to any one. It is enough that something is promised, done, forborne, or suffered by the party to whom the promise is made as consideration for the promise made to him. In general a waiver of any legal right at the request of another party is a sufficient consideration for a promise. Any damage, or suspension, or forbearance of a right will be sufficient to sustain a promise." *   *   * Now, applying this rule to the facts before us, the promisee used tobacco, occasionally drank liquor, and he had a legal right to do so. That right he abandoned for a period of years upon the strength of the promise of the testator that for such forbearance he would give him $5,000. We need not speculate on the effort which may have been required to give up the use of those stimulants. It is sufficient that he restricted his lawful freedom of action within certain prescribed limits upon the faith of his uncle's agreement, and now, having fully performed the conditions imposed, it is of no moment whether such performance actually proved a benefit to the promisor, and the court will not inquire into it; but, were it a proper subject of inquiry, we see nothing in this record that would permit a determination that the uncle was not benefited in a legal sense.

The court ruled that the nephew had provided legally sufficient consideration by giving up smoking, drinking, swearing, and playing cards or billiards for money until he became twenty-one and was therefore entitled to the money.

DECISION AND REMEDY

The Hamer v. Sidway case is a good illustration of the distinction between benefits to the promisor and detriment to the promisee. Here the court did not inquire as to whether a benefit flowed to the promisor but required only that there was a legally sufficient detriment to the promisee.

COMMENTS

ADEQUACY OF CONSIDERATION

Adequacy of consideration refers to the fairness of the bargain. On the surface, when the values of the items that are exchanged are unequal, fairness would appear to be an issue. If Bryant and Kowalewski make an agreement by which Bryant is to pay $1 for Kowalewski's car (which has a market value of $1,000), is the agreement supported by consideration? There is no question that $1 is legal value and that Kowalewski is giving up her legal title to the car. Thus, it appears that the requirements of legal value, bargained-for exchange, and legally sufficient consideration have been met. The consideration is far from adequate, however, since Kowalewski does not appear to be getting a fair bargain. Does this unfairness negate the bargain?

In general, a court of law will not question the adequacy of consideration if the consideration is legally sufficient. Under the doctrine of freedom of contract, parties are normally free to bargain as they wish. If people could sue merely because they entered into an unwise contract, the courts would be overloaded with frivolous suits. In extreme cases, a court of law may consider the adequacy of consideration in terms of its amount or worth, because inadequate consideration may indicate fraud, duress, or undue influence. It may also reflect a party's incompetency (for example, an individual might have been too intoxicated, insane, or simply too young to make a contract). Suppose Lansky has a house worth $100,000, and he sells it for $50,000. A $50,000 sale could indicate that the buyer unduly pressured Lansky into selling or that Lansky was defrauded into selling the house at far below market value.

In an equity suit, courts will more likely question the adequacy of consideration. (Remember from Chapter 1 that actions at law allow for remedies that consist of some form of compensation. Actions in equity allow for remedies that involve specific performance, injunction, or rescission.) The parties in an equity suit must show that the transaction was not **unconscionable**—that is, generally speaking, so one-sided under the circumstances as to be unfair—and that consideration was exchanged. For example, a suit to compel specific performance is equitable and requires the losing party to perform the contract duties rather than pay damages for breach of contract. Assume McMichael agrees to sell land worth $45,000 to Price for only $7,500. After signing the contract, McMichael refuses to deliver possession, and Price sues for specific performance. The court may now look at the relative amounts or worth of what was to be exchanged in light of the circumstances and refuse to allow specific performance on the ground that the consideration is inadequate.

As a general principle of contract law, the courts will not ordinarily attempt to evaluate the adequacy of the consideration in an agreed-upon exchange, unless the consideration is so grossly inadequate as to "shock the conscience" of the court. This principle is stressed in the following case.

Case 9.2

FINEMAN v. CITICORP USA, INC.

Appellate Court of Illinois, First District, 1985.
137 Ill.App.3d 3055, 92 Ill.Dec. 780, 485 N.E.2d 591.

BACKGROUND AND FACTS *Plaintiffs Ellen and Gabriel Fineman held MasterCards issued by the defendant Citibank. Holders of these credit cards paid an annual $15 fee. The issuance and use of the cards was governed by a retail installment credit agreement. In the agreement was the following statement: "We can change this Agreement including the finance charge and the annual percentage rate at any time." The agreement did provide for thirty days' notice of any such changes, and the cardholder had a right to reject the changes in writing and return the credit card. Two months before the expiration of their cards, Citibank notified the Finemans that it was increasing its annual fee to $20; however, Citibank was also providing its cardholders with extra services and benefits, such as "$100,000 common carrier travel insurance." The Finemans did not object in writing, nor did they return the cards. Citibank added 83 cents to the Finemans' next bill, the prorated portion of the increase for the two months remaining on their cards. Fineman filed suit (a class-action lawsuit on behalf of all cardholders) to recover the increased charges. Among other claims, the Finemans argued that the modification failed because there was no consideration for the modification. The trial court dismissed the plaintiffs' complaint, and the Finemans appealed.*

WHITE, Presiding Justice.
    First, plaintiffs argue that there was no consideration for the modification because defendants did not promise to do anything more than they were obliged to do under the original agreement. Plaintiffs contend that the "10 valuable extra services" cannot

be construed as consideration because nine of the services are only sales solicitations. The only service whose availability was clearly contingent on payment of the increased fee was the provision of $100,000 insurance for travel on common carriers. Plaintiffs argue that the insurance is not adequate consideration for the modification because plaintiffs never received any benefits from the insurance, and the cost to defendants of the insurance was negligible.

"The adequacy of consideration must be determined as of the time a contract is agreed upon, not from the hindsight of how the parties fare under it." Insurance has value to those insured even if the events on which the payments of benefits is conditioned do not occur. The absence of any paid benefits from the insurance does not render the insurance inadequate consideration for the modification.

Plaintiffs also argue that the insurance was not adequate consideration for the five dollar increase in the annual fee because the cost to defendants of the insurance was negligible. Defendants paid only 10½ cents per year per cardholder for the common carrier insurance. However, "[i]t is not the function of either the circuit court or this court to review the amount of the consideration which passed to decide whether either party made a bad bargain unless the amount is so grossly inadequate as to shock the conscience of the court." We cannot say that our conscience is shocked by the exchange of two months of $100,000 of common carrier travel insurance coverage, for plaintiffs' 83 cents. Therefore, we find that there was adequate consideration for the proposed modification of the credit agreement.

The appellate court affirmed the trial court's dismissal of the Finemans' action, holding that there was adequate (legally sufficient) consideration for the modification of the annual credit card fee.	**DECISION AND REMEDY**

PREEXISTING DUTY RULE

Under most circumstances, a promise to do what one already has a legal duty to do is not legally sufficient consideration, because no legal detriment or benefit has been incurred or received.[4] The preexisting legal duty may arise out of a previous contract or may be imposed by law. A sheriff cannot collect a reward for information leading to the capture of a criminal if the criminal's capture is one of the sheriff's official duties. Similarly, assume Healey agrees to hire Brewster for one year at $350 per week. Brewster begins working. After two months, Healey agrees orally to increase the wages to $400 per week. Healey's promise falls under the preexisting duty rule and is generally held to be unenforceable unless the promise is supported by legally sufficient consideration. Brewster was under a preexisting contractual duty to work for one year, and the performance of that duty cannot serve as consideration for the wage increase.

The harshness of the preexisting duty rule is evident. In the examples above, the sheriff is denied a reward that anyone else could have received, and Brewster, the employee, can be denied his pay raise. Therefore, the courts are alert to finding any legal detriment or benefit that may exist, no matter how small or insignificant it may be, so that the promise will be enforceable. Hence, if Brewster was required to perform any extra duties, the promise modifying his employment contract would be enforceable.[5]

The law recognizes some basic exceptions to the preexisting duty rule. They are:

1. Rescission and new contract.
2. Sale of goods—modification of contract without consideration.
3. Unforeseen difficulties.

Rescission and New Contract

The law recognizes that two parties can mutually agree to rescind (nullify) their contract, at least to

---

4. Foakes v. Beer, 9 App.Cas. 605 (1884).

5. Note, however, that in the example of the sheriff, the person taking the job as sheriff knows ahead of time that he or she will not be allowed to take rewards.

the extent that it is executory (not yet performed). For example, suppose Jerry contracts with Anna to purchase Anna's watch for $100. Later Jerry tells Anna that he would prefer not to purchase the watch. As it happens, Anna no longer desires to sell it, so they call off the deal. This is called **rescission,** defined as the unmaking of a contract, in which the parties to it are returned to their status quo prior to the making of the contract.

Suppose one day later Jerry decides he really wants the watch and offers to purchase it once again. Anna is willing to sell, but this time for a price of $125. Jerry agrees, and a new contract is formed. Similarly, in the Healey-Brewster example above, to arrange a raise for Brewster before the contract expires, the parties need to rescind the first contract and agree to a new one that includes the wage increase.

When rescission and the making of the contract take place at the same time, the courts are frequently given a choice of using the preexisting duty rule (not enforcing the new promise) or rescission and new contract. To illustrate, suppose Bauman-Bache, Inc., begins construction on a seven-floor office building and after three months says that if it is not paid an extra $75,000 on its contract it will stop working. The owner of the land, having no one else to complete construction, agrees to pay the extra $75,000. The agreement is not enforceable, because it is not supported by legally sufficient consideration; Bauman-Bache was under a preexisting duty to complete the building. Some courts, however, have held such a modifying agreement to be enforceable by holding that the original contract was rescinded and replaced with the new agreement.[6] Some courts even hold that the original considerations carry over into the new agreement.[7] The conflicting policies are: (1) people should be able to modify their legal relations when circumstances make it equitable to do so; and (2) modification in some cases resembles duress, as in the Bauman-Bache example.

Sale of Goods—Modification

The UCC deals with the problem of preexisting duty or modification of an existing contract very

simply: "[A]n agreement modifying a contract within this Article needs no consideration to be binding."[8]

To illustrate, Sachs and Jacobsen have entered into a one-year contract whereby Sachs is to supply Jacobsen with all the flour she needs for her bakery at $50 per barrel. Subsequently, the price of wheat to Sachs increases so sharply that the cost of producing a barrel of flour is $56. Sachs tells Jacobsen he will not ship her any more flour unless she agrees to pay $58 per barrel. Jacobsen agrees. This modification of an existing sales contract is enforceable under the UCC even though Sachs was under a preexisting duty to supply flour at $50 per barrel. Jones must pay the additional $8 per barrel. The UCC simply eliminates the consideration requirement when both parties in good faith agree to a modification.

Unforeseen Difficulties

Sometimes a party to a contract runs into unforeseen and substantial difficulties that could not have been anticipated at the time the contract was entered into. If the parties later agree to pay extra compensation for overcoming these unforeseen difficulties, the court may enforce the agreement. It should be noted that these unforeseen difficulties do not include the types of risks ordinarily assumed in business. For example, the increase in the price of wheat in the preceding example would not normally be deemed an unforeseen hardship or difficulty.

Suppose you contract with Carvelli to dig a basement on your vacant lot for $1,000. Carvelli starts to dig the basement and unexpectedly encounters a concrete slab reinforced with steel. He will now require special equipment and additional time to finish digging the basement. He asks for an additional $200 to dig the basement, and you agree. Many courts will enforce the modification, under the unforeseen difficulty exception.

MORAL OBLIGATIONS

Promises based on moral duty or obligation are not enforceable because a moral obligation is not held to be legally sufficient consideration. Suppose

---

6. See, for example, Armour & Co. v. Celic, 294 F.2d 432 (2d Cir. 1961).

7. See, for example, Holly v. First Nat'l Bank, 218 Wis. 259, 260 N.W. 429 (1935).

8. UCC 2-209(1).

your friend is injured in a distant city and a grocer takes care of him during his injury. Thereafter, feeling a moral obligation to help your friend and aid the grocer, you promise the grocer to pay for your friend's expenses. The promise is unenforceable, since it is supported only by your moral obligation, and a moral obligation cannot be legally sufficient consideration.

Sometimes people feel a moral obligation to make promises to loved ones. A father may promise to pay $10,000 to his daughter "in consideration of the love and affection that I have for you." An employer may promise to give a sum of money to a trusted employee "in consideration of your many acts of kindness and thoughtfulness over the years." Frequently, promises to pay for acts already performed (called past consideration, as will be discussed) are premised upon moral obligations or on natural duty and affection. These are not legally sufficient consideration, however and promises made in exchange for them are unenforceable.

Another example of a promise made out of a moral obligation is a promise to pay the debts of one's parents or a promise to pay for the care rendered to relatives one was under no duty to support. A minority of states enforce such promises supported only by a moral obligation—but only to the extent of the actual obligation or of the services or care rendered. For an example, see California Civil Code, Section 1606.

PAST CONSIDERATION

Promises made with respect to events that have already taken place are unenforceable. These promises lack consideration in that the element of bargained-for exchange is missing. In short, you can bargain for something to take place now or in the future, but not for something that has already taken place. Therefore, **past consideration** is no consideration.

Suppose a father tells his son, "In consideration of the fact that you named your son after me when he was born, I promise to pay you $1,000." The promise relates to an event that has already taken place, so it is unenforceable. A similar example is a promise to pay for "past love and affection given." Although there may be strong moral obligations to fulfill those promises, there is no legal obligation to do so.

Suppose instead that the father tells his son, "In consideration of your promise to name your next child after me, I promise to pay you $1,000." The son names his next child after his father. Here is a bargained-for exchange with legally sufficient consideration; so the father is bound to pay.

In the following case, we see an illustration of how "past" and "moral" issues can be involved in consideration.

BACKGROUND AND FACTS *The plaintiff was born on December 17, 1925, and two days later was named August Dwayne Lanfier after his grandfather August Schultz. Over three months later, Schultz orally agreed with the plaintiff's mother to give the plaintiff certain real estate if the plaintiff's mother would name the plaintiff (his grandson) after him. He also agreed to reserve to the plaintiff's parents a life estate (possession and use during their lives) in that same real estate. The plaintiff's parents accepted the proposal, since they had already named the plaintiff after Schultz. Schultz neglected to perform his oral contract and never arranged for title to the property to pass to plaintiff. He did, however, deliver possession of the real estate to plaintiff's parents, who held possession for about twelve years. Schultz died without a will, and the plaintiff (a minor) through his father filed suit to have the court adjudge him the absolute owner of the real estate. The administrator of Schultz's estate and the other beneficiaries challenged the plaintiff's right to the property. The trial court awarded the property to the plaintiff based on the alleged oral contract between the decedent and the plaintiff's mother, and the estate appealed.*

 Case 9.3

LANFIER v. LANFIER
Supreme Court of Iowa, 1939.
227 Iowa 258, 288 N.W. 104.

MILLER, Judge.

*   *   *   *

"The general principle of the law of contracts, that to be valid and legally enforce-able, as between the parties thereto an agreement or undertaking of any kind must be supported by a consideration, is too elementary to call for citation of authorities."

Under the record herein, there is a total absence of any evidence of a legal consideration to support the alleged contract plaintiff seeks to enforce. The evidence is undisputed that plaintiff was born on December 17, 1925, and, two days later, December 19, 1925, he was named August Dwayne Lanfier. He was named August after his grandfather, the decedent herein. *   *   * There is no evidence of any request on the part of the decedent that plaintiff be named after him until the latter part of March, 1926, over three months after plaintiff had been named. There are several witnesses who testified to conversations between plaintiff's mother and the decedent at that time, the substance of which was that, if plaintiff's mother would name plaintiff after the decedent, decedent would make a will and would thereby devise to plaintiff the real estate in question, subject to a life estate in plaintiff's parents. At the time these conversations were had, plaintiff and his parents were already in possession of the property, as tenants of the decedent. *   *   *

Counsel for plaintiff assert that the contract was supported by sufficient consideration, in that the prior naming of the plaintiff for the decedent constituted a past or moral consideration, and further that the contract should be supported on the basis of love and affection being good consideration. The contentions of counsel are without merit.

This court has repeatedly held that past or moral consideration is not sufficient to support an executory contract. *   *   * If the services are gratuitous, no obligation, either moral or legal, is incurred by the recipient. No one is bound to pay for that which is a gratuity. No moral obligation is assumed by a person who receives a gift. Suppose the plaintiff had given the defendant a horse, was he morally bound to pay what the horse was reasonably worth? We think not. In such case there never was any liability to pay, and therefore a subsequent promise would be without any consideration to support it.

*   *   *   *

The contentions of counsel to the effect that love and affection constitute sufficient consideration to support the contract here asserted are likewise without merit. No such consideration is expressed in the contract, and we seriously doubt that the record supports any claim that such might have been consideration for the alleged contract. However, in any event, the proposition of law contended for by counsel has no support in the decisions of this court or in the courts generally.

*   *   *   *

"Although love and affection is a 'good' consideration, it is not a sufficient consideration for a promise. Promises or contracts made on the basis of mere love and affection, unsupported by a pecuniary or material benefit, create at most bare moral obligations, and a breach thereof presents no cause for redress by the court."

DECISION AND REMEDY   *The plaintiff was not awarded title to the property, because the consideration was insufficient to support the contract. The court determined that the consideration created no detriment to the promisee because it was an event that had happened in the past. The plaintiff was named after his grandfather several months before the oral contract was made. The court stated that "past or moral consideration is not sufficient to support an executory contract." The plaintiff argued that love and affection constituted sufficient consideration to support the contract, but the court held that a promise made on this basis created "at most bare moral obligations."*

PROBLEM AREAS IN BUSINESS CONCERNING CONSIDERATION

Because of the difficulty in clearly defining the requirements for consideration, numerous exceptions have been created in order to enforce contracts without consideration or to emphasize the intent of the parties to contract with one another, rather than to emphasize the existence or nonexistence of consideration.

Businesses face a great deal of uncertainty (risk) in the form of changing market conditions. This uncertainty makes it difficult to define the future rights and duties of parties who contract today. As a result, some output and requirements contracts may not call for any performance in the future under certain market considerations. Yet this does not mean that the contracts fail for lack of consideration. Problems concerning the issue of consideration usually fall into one of the following categories:

1. Promises exchanged for which total performance by the parties is uncertain.
2. Settlement of claims.
3. Certain promises enforceable without consideration.

The court's solutions to these types of problems offer insights into how the law views the complex concept of consideration.

Uncertain Performance— Illusory versus Non-Illusory Promises

If the terms of the contract express such uncertainty of performance that the promisor has not actually promised to do anything, the promise is said to be *illusory*—without consideration and unenforceable. For example, suppose the president and sole owner of ABC Corporation says to his employees: "All of you have worked hard, and if profits remain high, you will be given a 10 percent bonus at the end of the year—if management thinks it is warranted." The employees continue to work hard, and profits remain high, but no bonus is given. This is an illusory promise, or no promise at all, because performance depends solely on the discretion of the president. There is no bargained-for consideration. The statement declares merely that the president may or may not do something in the future. The president is not obligated (incurs no detriment) now or in the future.

The following four types of business contracts have a degree of uncertainty as to the amount of performance legally required:

1. Requirements contracts.
2. Output contracts.
3. Exclusive dealing contracts.
4. Option to cancel clauses.

Frequently, the determination of whether the promise is illusory or non-illusory depends on all the surrounding facts, not just on the terms of the agreement.

REQUIREMENTS CONTRACTS   A **requirements contract** is a contract in which the buyer agrees to purchase from the seller exclusively all of the goods of a designated type the buyer *needs* or *requires*. If the contract terms permit the buyer to purchase only if the buyer *wishes or desires* to do so, or if the buyer reserves the right to buy the goods from someone other than the seller, the promise is illusory (without consideration), and the agreement is unenforceable.

For example, a manufacturer uses coal to operate and to heat his plant. The manufacturer agrees to purchase from a coal producer all the coal that the manufacturer will require or need to heat and to run his plant for one year at a set price per ton. Since the agreement is based on the *established* needs of the buyer, and since the contract requires the buyer to purchase the goods to fill those needs from this seller, the contract is non-illusory (with consideration) and enforceable, even though the exact amount of coal tonnage to be purchased is unknown. If the agreement had stated that the buyer had to buy only the coal he wanted or wished or desired, however, or if the buyer had reserved the right to purchase from any seller whose delivery price was lowest, there would have been no contract, because the buyer would not have been obligated to buy any coal from this seller and would thus have incurred no legal detriment.

But, one might ask, is there not a possibility that the manufacturer will go out of business and thus have no requirements? Where, then, is the detriment, or consideration? The detriment is that the buyer gives up the opportunity (legal right) to purchase from other sellers and the seller gives up the opportunity (legal right) to sell to other buyers (who do not have requirements contracts) until he or she has satisfied the obligation under the requirements contract.

OUTPUT CONTRACTS An **output contract** is a contract in which the seller agrees to sell to the buyer exclusively all of what the seller produces.

For example, if U.S. Steel agrees to sell to Boeing Aircraft all I-beams it produces during the month of March at an agreed-upon price per beam, a binding, non-illusory promise will be made. The criteria for a non-illusory output contract are basically the same as for a requirements contract, except that the criteria are applied to the seller's obligation to produce rather than to the buyer's obligation to purchase.

Under the common law of contracts, a court may compel performance according to what it believes the implied obligation of good faith and fair dealing requires. Thus, the buyer may be liable if in bad faith he or she goes out of business or changes methods of doing business so as to lessen requirements. The UCC also imposes a *good faith limitation* on output and requirements contracts. The quantity under such contracts is the amount of output or the amount of requirements that occur during a *normal* production year. The actual quantity sold or purchased cannot be unreasonably disproportionate to normal or comparable prior output or requirements.[9]

EXCLUSIVE DEALING CONTRACTS—"BEST EF-FORTS" RULE An **exclusive dealing contract** gives a party the sole right to deal in or with the product of the other party. For example, an exclusive dealing contract may require a buyer to carry only products made by the seller. Wood agrees to market only the fabrics, millinery, and dresses upon which Lady Duff-Gordon places her endorsement. Lady Duff-Gordon receives no promise that Wood will market any dresses, but she gives Wood an exclusive right to market whatever number of items Wood deems appropriate. At first glance, Wood's promise appears illusory. He has not agreed to sell anything. As in the output and the requirements contracts, however, Wood is under a duty to use his "best efforts" to market the dresses.[10] This duty, or obligation, is consideration for the promise to either supply or sell.

Consider another example. A real estate broker obtains a thirty-day *exclusive* contract from the seller of a house. The broker has the duty to perform his or her best efforts in selling the house within thirty days and in dealing with potential buyers. The seller's detriment is the loss of the opportunity (legal right) to hire another broker and a duty to pay the agent if the agent finds a satisfactory buyer for the house. In return for this detriment, the law imposes a legal obligation on the broker to perform according to his or her best efforts.

OPTION TO CANCEL CLAUSES A term, or time, contract may include a clause in which one or both parties reserve the right to cancel the contract before the stated period has elapsed. For example, consider a three-year lease (a term contract) in which the tenant reserves the right to cancel, with notice, at any time after one year's occupancy. The uncertainty of performance is that the contract may or may not last for the entire three-year period.

The basic rule of law is that the contract with an option to cancel will be enforced if the party having the option has given up an opportunity (legal right). The loss of the opportunity is a detriment and thus constitutes consideration. This point will become clearer as we look at two more examples.

Suppose I contract to hire you for one year at $4,000 per month, reserving the right to cancel the contract at any time. Upon close examination of these words, you can see that I have not actually agreed to hire you, as I could cancel without liability before you start performance. I have not given up the opportunity of hiring someone else. This contract, therefore, is illusory.

Now suppose I contract to hire you for one year at $4,000 per month, reserving the right to cancel the contract at any time after you begin performance by giving you thirty days' notice. By saying that I will give you thirty days' notice, I am relinquishing the opportunity (legal right) to hire someone else instead of you for a thirty-day period. Therefore, if you work for one month, at the end of which I give you thirty days' notice, you will be entitled to enforce the contract for $8,000 in salary.

Settlement of Claims

An understanding of the enforceability of agreements to settle claims or discharge debts is im-

---

9. UCC 2-306.
10. *Wood v. Lucy, Lady Duff-Gordon*, 222 N.Y. 88, 118 N.E. 214 (1917). See UCC 2-306(2).

portant in the business world. The following agreements are the most frequent:

1. Accord and satisfaction.
2. Creditors' composition agreements.
3. Release or covenant not to sue.

ACCORD AND SATISFACTION The concept of **accord and satisfaction** deals with a debtor's offer of payment and a creditor's acceptance of a lesser amount than the debt the creditor originally purported to be owed. The accord is defined as the agreement whereby one of the parties undertakes to give or perform, and the other to accept, in satisfaction of a claim, something other than that which was originally agreed upon. Satisfaction takes place when the accord is executed. Accord and satisfaction deal with an attempt by the obligor to extinguish an obligation. A basic rule is that there can be no satisfaction unless there is first an accord.

Liquidated Debt There is a situation in which accord and satisfaction does not apply: when a debtor pays a part of an already overdue debt, the amount owed of which is already well determined. In that case, he or she is doing no more than performing part of an already existing legal duty to the creditor, and thus, the partial payment is held not to operate as satisfaction of the whole. The debt must be *liquidated* (that is, ascertained, fixed, agreed-on, settled, well determined); and in some states, the creditor must not have agreed to discharge the entire debt on a partial payment. As an example, if Baker signs an installment loan contract with her banker in which she agrees to pay a specified rate of interest on a specified sum of borrowed money at timely monthly intervals in the form of $100-per-month payments for two years, that is a liquidated debt. Reasonable persons will not differ over the amount owed.

In the majority of states, acceptance of a lesser sum than the entire amount of a liquidated debt

is not satisfaction, and the balance of the debt is still legally owed. The rationale for this rule is that no consideration is given by the debtor to satisfy the obligation of paying the balance to the creditor, since the debtor has a preexisting legal obligation to pay the entire debt.

To illustrate, suppose a debtor, by agreement, borrows $100, payable at the end of one year at 10 percent interest. At the end of the year, the debtor sends the creditor a check for $100 (not $110), marked clearly "payment in full." The creditor, under the majority rule, could cash the check and still legally sue for the balance of $10.

Unliquidated Debt The opposite of a liquidated debt is an *unliquidated debt*. Here reasonable persons may differ over the amount owed. It is not settled, fixed, agreed-upon, ascertained, or determined. In these circumstances, acceptance of payment of the lesser sum operates as a satisfaction, or discharge, of the debt. Suppose that Devereaux goes to the dentist's office. The dentist tells him that he needs three special types of gold inlays. The price is not discussed, and there is no standard fee for this type of work. Devereaux leaves the office. At the end of the month, the dentist sends him a bill for $3,000. Devereaux, believing that this amount is grossly out of proportion with what a reasonable person would believe to be the debt owed, sends a check for $2,000. On the back of the check he writes "payment in full for three gold inlays." The dentist cashes the check. Since we are dealing with an unliquidated debt—the amount has not been agreed upon—partial payment accepted by the dentist will eradicate the debt. One argument to support this rule is that the parties give up a legal right to contest the amount in dispute, and thus consideration passes. The use of a payment-in-full check to discharge an unliquidated (disputed) debt is illustrated by the following case.

BACKGROUND AND FACTS *PLM, Inc., orally contracted with Quaintance Associates, Inc., an executive recruiting firm, for Quaintance to undertake a search for a new controller for PLM. Quaintance, after a four-month search during which it had not located a controller, billed PLM for search expenses of $808.61 plus a fee of $9,000 for its services. Quaintance alleged that the contract stipulated that PLM would pay a fee plus expenses regardless of whether a successful candidate for the controller position was found. PLM argued that it had agreed to pay a fee only if Quaintance succeeded in*

 Case 9.4

QUAINTANCE ASSOCIATES, INC. v. PLM, INC.

Appellate Court of Illinois, 1981.
95 Ill.App.3d 818, 51 Ill.Dec.
153, 420 N.E.2d 567.

finding a controller for PLM. To settle the dispute, PLM sent Quaintance a check for $6,060.48 (a "reasonable fee" of $5,400 plus "reasonable" expenses of $660.48) with a letter stating, in part: "I don't know any other way to handle the situation but I do believe this is fair. I consider this the end of the matter but certainly would be prepared to discuss it if you so desire." PLM wrote on the back of the check: "In full payment of any claims Mr. Simpler [Quaintance's agent] has against PLM, Inc." Quaintance cashed the check, but a company official wrote on the check that "negotiation does not release claim of payee against PLM, Inc." When Quaintance sued PLM for the remainder of the alleged debt, PLM argued that the cashing of the check by Quaintance constituted an accord and satisfaction. The trial court held for PLM, and Quaintance appealed.

MEJDA, Justice.
*   *   *   *

An accord is an agreement or settlement of an existing dispute, controversy or demand which presupposes a disagreement as to the amount due. However, the partial payment of a fixed and certain demand which is due and not in dispute is no satisfaction of the whole debt even where the creditor agrees to receive a part for the whole and gives a receipt for the whole demand. But, where there is a bona fide dispute as to the amount due, it makes no difference that the creditor protests or states that he does not accept the amount proffered in full satisfaction. The creditor must either accept what is offered with the condition upon which it is offered or refuse it. The acceptance of the check given in full satisfaction of a disputed claim is an accord and satisfaction if the creditor took the check with notice of the condition upon which the check was tendered. A creditor has no right to cash the check and thereby obtain the benefit of such offer without its accompanying burden of compromise. Where there is substantially no dispute as to the facts upon which the claim of accord and satisfaction is based, the question of the creditor's assent is one of law to be determined by the court.
*   *   *   *

*   *   * Defendant placed the following legend on the back of this check: "In full payment of any claims Mr. Simpler has against PLM, Inc." Plaintiff admits in its reply that prior to negotiating the check it placed on the check the words "negotiation does not release claim of payee against PLM, Inc." without the knowledge or authority of defendant. The act of negotiating a check that is offered in compromise of a disputed debt constitutes acceptance notwithstanding that the creditor added, without the debtor's knowledge or authority, words indicating a refusal to accept the offer.
*   *   *   *

*   *   * Plaintiff accepted and cashed the proffered check. There is no allegation that plaintiff did not understand that the proffered check was offered as a compromise and settlement. The correspondence between the parties indicates that terms of the oral contract and the amount of fees due pursuant to this contract were fairly in dispute. Accordingly, plaintiff was required to accept the amount proffered in full satisfaction or refuse it. Plaintiff had no right to cash the check and thereby obtain the benefit of such offer without its corresponding burden of compromise.

DECISION AND REMEDY   *The decision of the trial court was affirmed. The cashing of the check by Quaintance was held to constitute an accord and satisfaction.*

COMMENTS   *This case illustrates four important concepts of the law concerning accord and satisfaction. First, it is important that the creditor receiving the tendered payment have notice that the payment is intended to satisfy the purported debt. Second,* *the recipient of the notice cannot negate it by scratching it off or altering it. Third, acceptance of the payment by the creditor constitutes accord. Fourth, if the debt is genuinely in dispute, accord will discharge (satisfy) the debt.*

CREDITORS' COMPOSITION AGREEMENTS   A **creditors' composition agreement** is similar to an accord. The difference is that, whereas an accord is an agreement between a debtor and a single creditor, a creditors' composition agreement is an agreement between a debtor and two or more creditors acting together to liquidate their claims. Under this arrangement, an insolvent or financially troubled debtor's creditors agree to accept either a specified amount or a percentage of the full amount owed.

As in the case of any contract, to be enforceable the creditors' composition agreement must be supported by consideration. Each creditor's promise to accept a proportionate share of the debtor's partial payment in lieu of full payment of whatever amount is outstanding is his or her consideration for the agreement. Surrender of the right to file a petition for bankruptcy is the debtor's consideration.

RELEASE OR COVENANT NOT TO SUE   A **release** serves to bar any further recovery beyond the terms stated in the release. For example, suppose you are involved in an automobile accident caused by the negligence of Jean. Jean offers you $500 if you will release her from any further liability resulting from the accident. You believe that the damages to your car will not exceed $400. You agree to the release. Later you discover that the damage to your car is $600. Can you collect the balance? The answer is no; you are limited to the $500 in the release. Therefore, it is important to know the extent of injuries or damages before signing a release.

Generally, releases are binding if three criteria are proved:

1.   The release is secured and given in good faith— that is, in the absence of fraud and the like.
2.   In many states, the release must be in a signed writing.
3.   Consideration for the release is given.

Consideration in the above case is Jean's promised payment of $500 in return for your promise not to bring an action for a larger amount. Under the UCC, a written, signed waiver or renunciation by an aggrieved party discharges any further liability for a breach, even without consideration.[11]

A **covenant not to sue,** unlike a release, does not always bar further recovery. The parties simply substitute a contractual obligation for some other type of action. For example, assume that in the accident just described, you say that you are going to sue the negligent party, Jean, in tort (negligence) for your damages. Jean and you agree that if you will refrain from bringing a tort action, she will pay for all damages to your car. Therefore, a contract is substituted for the tort action. If Jean fails to pay for your damages as agreed, your action is for breach of contract (you do not have to prove negligence). This does not prevent you from bringing a tort-negligence suit; but if you do so, you have breached your contract. The three criteria required for a binding release are also required for a valid covenant not to sue.

Promises Enforceable Without Consideration

There are exceptions to the rule that only promises supported by consideration are enforceable. Other circumstances in which promises will be enforced despite the lack of what one normally considers legal consideration are as follows:

1.   Promises to pay debts barred by a statute of limitations.
2.   Promises to pay debts barred by discharge in bankruptcy. (Since 1984, the enforcement of these promises has been severely restricted. See Chapter 31.)
3.   Detrimental reliance, or promissory estoppel.
4.   Charitable subscriptions.

PROMISES TO PAY DEBTS BARRED BY A STATUTE OF LIMITATIONS   Statutes of limitations in all states require a creditor to sue within a specified period to recover debts. If the creditor fails to sue in time, recovery of the debt is barred by the statute of limitations. A debtor who promises to

---

11. UCC 1-107.

pay a previous debt barred by the statute of limitations makes an enforceable promise. *The promise needs no consideration.* (Some states, however, require that it be in writing.) In effect, the promise extends the limitations period, and the creditor can sue to recover the entire debt, or at least the amount promised. The promise can be implied if the debtor acknowledges the barred debt by making a partial payment.

Suppose you borrow $5,000 from First National Bank of San Jose. The loan is due in November 1990. You fail to pay, and the bank does not sue you until December 1995. If California's statute of limitations for this debt is five years, recovery of the debt is barred. If you then agree to pay off the loan, First National Bank can sue for the entire amount. This is an example of an express promise, which extends the limitations period. Likewise, you can make a monthly payment and implicitly acknowledge the existence of the debt. Again First National Bank can sue you for the entire debt. This is an example of acknowledgment. Suppose instead that you expressly promise First National Bank to pay it $2,500. In most states, this promise is enforceable only to the extent of $2,500 (and usually must be in writing).

PROMISES TO PAY DEBTS BARRED BY DISCHARGE IN BANKRUPTCY

A promise to pay a debt discharged in bankruptcy (called a reaffirmation) may be enforceable despite the absence of consideration for the promise, which nevertheless must be clear and explicit.

The Bankruptcy Reform Act of 1978, as amended by the Bankruptcy Amendments and Federal Judgeship Act of 1984, has made substantial changes in the law concerning reaffirmations of debts barred by a discharge in bankruptcy. Prior to the enactment of the law, a former debtor could make a promise in writing to repay a debt totally discharged by a bankruptcy decree, and that promise would be enforced without consideration. Currently, the law severely restricts such reaffirmations, which must be made before the debts are discharged in bankruptcy. (See Chapter 31 for a detailed discussion of these restrictions.)

DETRIMENTAL RELIANCE, OR THE DOCTRINE OF PROMISSORY ESTOPPEL

The doctrine of detrimental reliance, or **promissory estoppel,** involves a promise given by one party that induces another party to rely on that promise to his or her detriment. When the promisor can reasonably expect the promisee to act on the promise, and injustice cannot be avoided any other way, the promise will be enforced.[12] Additionally, the promisee must act with justifiable reliance on the promise—that is, must be justified in relying on it—and the act must be of a substantial nature.

The promise is enforced by refusal to allow the promisor to set up the defense of lack of consideration. The promisor is estopped (prevented) from asserting the lack of consideration. The estoppel arises from the promise, and hence *promissory estoppel* is the term used. (This doctrine is not used in some jurisdictions.)

Imagine that your grandfather tells you, "I'll pay you $350 per week so you won't have to work anymore." Then you quit your job, and your grandfather refuses to pay. You may be able to enforce the promise, since you have justifiably relied on it to your detriment.[13]

Traditionally, promissory estoppel has been applied only to gratuitous promises—that is, when the parties are not bargaining in a commercial setting. The trend, however, is to apply it in any situation if justice so requires. The following classic case illustrates this point.

---

12. Restatement, Second, Contracts, Section 90 provides: "A promise which the promisor should reasonably expect to induce action or forbearance on the part of the promisee or a third person and which does induce such action or forbearance is binding if injustice can be avoided only by enforcement of the promise."

13. Ricketts v. Scothorn, 57 Neb. 51, 77 N.W. 365 (1898).

Case 9.5

HOFFMAN v. RED OWL STORES, INC.

Supreme Court of Wisconsin, 1965.
26 Wis.2d 683, 133 N.W.2d 267.

BACKGROUND AND FACTS *Red Owl Stores, Inc. (defendant), induced the Hoffmans (plaintiffs) to give up their current business and run a Red Owl franchise. The Hoffmans relied on the representations of Red Owl, and when the deal ultimately fell through because of Red Owl's failure to keep its promise concerning the operation of the franchise agency store, the Hoffmans brought this suit to recover their losses, and the trial court found in their favor. Red Owl appealed.*

CURRIE, Chief Justice.
*   *   *   *

Recognition of a Cause of Action Grounded on Promissory Estoppel.

Sec. 90 of Restatement, 1 Contracts, provides (at p. 110):

"A promise which the promisor should reasonably expect to induce action or forbearance of a definite and substantial character on the part of the promisee and which does induce such action or forbearance is binding if injustice can be avoided only by enforcement of the promise."

*   *   *   *

Because we deem the doctrine of promissory estoppel, as stated in sec. 90 of Restatement, 1 Contracts, as one which supplies a needed tool which courts may employ in a proper case to prevent injustice, we endorse and adopt it.

Applicability of Doctrine to Facts of this Case.

The record here discloses a number of promises and assurances given to Hoffman by Lukowitz in behalf of Red Owl upon which plaintiffs relied and acted upon to their detriment.

Foremost were the promises that for the sum of $18,000 Red Owl would establish Hoffman in a store. After Hoffman had sold his grocery store and paid the $1,000 on the Chilton lot, the $18,000 figure was changed to $24,100. Then in November, 1961, Hoffman was assured that if the $24,100 figure were increased by $2,000 the deal would go through. Hoffman was induced to sell his grocery store fixtures and inventory in June, 1961, on the promise that he would be in his new store by fall. In November, plaintiffs sold their bakery building on the urging of defendants and on the assurance that this was the last step necessary to have the deal with Red Owl go through.

We determine that there was ample evidence to sustain the answers of the jury to the questions of the verdict with respect to the promissory representations made by Red Owl, Hoffman's reliance thereon in the exercise of ordinary care, and his fulfillment of the conditions required of him by the terms of the negotiations had with Red Owl.

There remains for consideration the question of law raised by defendants that agreement was never reached on essential factors necessary to establish a contract between Hoffman and Red Owl. Among these were the size, cost, design, and layout of the store building; and the terms of the lease with respect to rent, maintenance, renewal, and purchase options. This poses *the question of whether the promise necessary to sustain a cause of action for promissory estoppel must embrace all essential details of a proposed transaction* between promisor and promisee so as to be the equivalent of an offer that would result in a binding contract between the parties if the promisee were to accept the same. [Emphasis added.]

Originally the doctrine of promissory estoppel was invoked as a substitute for consideration rendering a gratuitous promise enforceable as a contract. In other words, the acts of reliance by the promisee to his detriment provided a substitute for consideration. If promissory estoppel were to be limited to only those situations where the promise giving rise to the cause of action must be so definite with respect to all details that a contract would result were the promise supported by consideration, then the defendants' instant promises to Hoffman would not meet this test. However, sec. 90 of Restatement, 1 Contracts, does not impose the requirement that the promise giving rise to the cause of action must be so comprehensive in scope as to meet the requirements of an offer that would ripen into a contract if accepted by the promisee. Rather the conditions imposed are:

(1) Was the promise one which the promisor should reasonably expect to induce action or forbearance of a definite and substantial character on the part of the promisee?

(2) Did the promise induce such action or forbearance?

(3) Can injustice be avoided only by enforcement of the promise?

We deem it would be a mistake to regard an action grounded on promissory estoppel as the equivalent of a breach of contract action. As Dean Boyer points out, it is desirable that fluidity in the application of the concept be maintained. While the first two of the above listed three requirements of promissory estoppel present issues of fact which ordinarily will be resolved by a jury, the third requirement, that the remedy can only be invoked where necessary to avoid injustice, is one that involves a policy decision by the court. Such a policy decision necessarily embraces an element of discretion.

We conclude that injustice would result here if plaintiffs were not granted some relief because of the failure of defendants to keep their promises which induced plaintiffs to act to their detriment.

DECISION AND REMEDY

The trial court's judgment was affirmed. Hoffman was entitled to damages, the exact amount to be determined when the case was returned to the trial court.

COMMENTS

Promissory estoppel does not mean that each and every gratuitous promise will be binding merely because the promisee has changed position. Liability is created only when there is "justifiable reliance on the promise." The promisor must have known or had reason to believe that the promisee would likely be induced to change position as a result of the promise.

CHARITABLE SUBSCRIPTIONS Subscriptions to religious, educational, and charitable institutions are promises to make gifts and are unenforceable on traditional contract grounds because they are not supported by legally sufficient consideration. A gift is the opposite of bargained-for consideration. The modern view, however, is to enforce these promises under the doctrine of promissory estoppel or to find consideration simply as a matter of public policy.

The premise for enforcement is that a promise is made and an institution changes its position because of reliance on that promise. For example, suppose a church solicits and receives donative subscriptions to build a new church. On the basis of these pledges, the church purchases land, employs architects, and makes other contracts that change its position. Courts may enforce the pledges under promissory estoppel or find consideration in the fact that each promise is made in reliance on the other promises of support or that the trustees, by accepting the subscription, impliedly promise to complete the proposed undertaking. Such cases represent exceptions to the general rule that consideration must exist for the formation of a contract. And these exceptions come about as a result of public policy.

 QUESTIONS AND CASE PROBLEMS

1. D'Albergo is the owner of a large bakery. She contracts to purchase from XYZ Flour, Inc., all the flour she might desire for a one-year period at $30 per barrel. Payment terms call for a billing at the end of each month for shipments made, with a 3 percent discount for payment within twenty days of the billing date. During the first month D'Albergo orders and XYZ delivers 1,000 barrels of flour. On the third day of the next month, XYZ sends D'Albergo a bill for $30,000 dated that same day. A dispute develops between the two parties. XYZ refuses to ship any more flour to D'Albergo, and on the thirtieth day of the month, D'Albergo sends XYZ a check for $29,100 marked clearly, "payment in full." Discuss whether XYZ's refusal to ship any more flour places it in breach of contract. Also, if XYZ cashes D'Albergo's check, can XYZ recover in a lawsuit the balance of $900?

2. Tabor is the buyer of widgits manufactured by Martin. Martin's contract with Tabor calls for delivery of 10,000 widgits at $1 per widgit in ten equal installments. After delivery of two installments, Martin informs Tabor that because of inflation, Martin is losing money and will promise to deliver the remaining 8,000 widgits only if Tabor will pay $1.20 per widgit. Tabor agrees in writing. Discuss whether Martin can legally collect the additional $200 upon delivery to Tabor of the next installment of 1,000 widgits.

3. Star Furniture Company manufactures summer lawn furniture. Its sole product consists of webbed aluminum

frame furniture used mainly on outdoor patios and on beaches. As of October 1, Star Furniture was heavily indebted to its three main suppliers—Aluminum Pole, Inc.; Plastic Webbing, Ltd.; and The Little Steel Rivet Company. Star owed each of these suppliers approximately $10,000. Star's president met with the presidents of the three suppliers to work out some arrangement whereby the company could avoid declaring bankruptcy. Since all the parties desired that Star Furniture not go bankrupt, an agreement was made among the four parties that Star would pay each supplier $7,000, which would be accepted as full payment of all outstanding debts as of October 1. Discuss whether this agreement is enforceable.

4. Bernstein owns a lot and wants to build a house according to a specific set of plans and specifications. She solicits bids from building contractors and receives three bids: one from Carlton for $60,000, one from Friend for $58,000, and one from Shade for $53,000. She accepts Shade's bid. One month after construction of the house has begun, Shade contacts Bernstein and informs her that because of inflation and a recent price hike in materials, he will not finish the house unless Bernstein agrees to pay an extra $3,000. Bernstein reluctantly agrees to pay the additional sum. After the house is finished, however, Bernstein refuses to pay the additional $3,000. Discuss whether Bernstein is legally required to pay this additional amount.

5. Daniel, a recent college graduate, is on his way home for the Christmas holidays from his new job. Daniel gets caught in a snowstorm and is taken in by an elderly couple, who provide him with food and shelter. After the snowplows have cleared the road, Daniel proceeds home. Daniel's father, Fred, is most appreciative of the elderly couple's action and in a letter promises to pay them $500. The elderly couple, in need of money, accept Fred's offer. Because of a dispute between Daniel and Fred, Fred refuses to pay the elderly couple the $500. Discuss whether they can hold Fred in contract for the services rendered to Daniel.

6. Martino was a police officer in Atlantic City. Gray, who lost a significant amount of her jewelry during a burglary of her home, offered a reward for the recovery of the property. Incident to his job, Martino possessed certain knowledge concerning the theft of Gray's jewelry. When Martino informed Gray of his knowledge of the theft, Gray offered Martino $500 to help her recover her jewelry. As a result of Martino's police work, the jewelry was recovered and returned to Gray. Martino sued Gray for the reward he claimed she promised him. Was there a valid contract between Gray and Martino? [Gray v. Martino, 91 N.J.L. 462, 103 A. 24 (1918)]

7. Kowalsky, a contractor, was required to make periodic payments to a union pension fund administered by Kelly, trustee for the union. Kowalsky and Kelly disagreed over the amount of money Kowalsky owed the union. After a number of heated discussions Kowalsky sent Kelly four checks totaling $8,500 and enclosed them in a letter saying: "These checks are tendered with the understanding that they are full payment of all claims against Kowalsky." Immediately after receiving the checks, Kelly called Kowalsky

and told him the checks were not going to be cashed but would simply be held and that Kowalsky still owed Kelly money because the $8,500 did not cover late charges on the deposited payments. Kowalsky did not ask for the return of the checks or stop payment. Kelly retained, but did not cash, the checks and sued Kowalsky for the late charges. Kowalsky claimed that retention of the checks constituted full accord and satisfaction of the debt. Who won, and why? [Kelly v. Kowalsky, 186 Conn. 618, 442 A.2d 1355 (1982)]

8. Hurst was a general partner in a limited partnership (a special type of business organization). The limited partnership owned a tract of land it wanted badly to sell. In 1973, Hurst contacted Breedlove, a real estate appraiser, and put him in contact with Hillman, a prospective purchaser. Hillman contracted with Breedlove for two appraisals of the property for a total fee of $8,500, paying $1,000 as a retainer. Breedlove gave the appraisals to Hillman, but Hillman made no further payment. In early 1974, some of the limited partners contemplated leaving the partnership, partially because of the failure to sell the land. Hurst, to prevent their leaving, contacted Breedlove and requested copies of the appraisals. Breedlove made Hurst agree, in acknowledgment of receiving the appraisal copies, to guaranty payment of $7,500 (the balance Hillman owed) plus 8 percent interest. Hurst did pay the copying charges for the appraisal reports. The sale to Hillman was never completed. When Hillman failed to pay the $7,500 owed to Breedlove, Breedlove filed suit against Hurst. The trial court denied Breedlove's claim because Hurst had not received any consideration for the guaranty he signed with Breedlove. Breedlove appealed. Discuss whether there was sufficient consideration to sustain a contract. [Breedlove v. Hurst, 181 Ga.App. 4, 351 S.E.2d 212 (1986)]

9. In 1972, Thomas L. Weinsaft signed a written agreement with his son, Nicholas L. Weinsaft. Thomas agreed that during his lifetime he would not transfer any interest in his 765 shares of stock of Crane Manufacturing Company unless he first gave Nicholas an opportunity to purchase it, and upon Thomas's death, Nicholas would have the "option and right to purchase all of the stock" from the estate. The agreement stated that it was entered into "In consideration of $10.00 and other good and valuable consideration, including the inducement of Second Party [Nicholas] to remain the chief executive officer of said company." Thomas died in 1980. Nicholas gave notice that he intended to buy the stock, but one of the beneficiaries under Thomas's will objected, contending that there was no consideration for Thomas's promises. Nicholas sued to force the estate to transfer the shares. Discuss whether this contract is supported by consideration. [In re Estate of Weinsaft, 647 S.W.2d 179 (Mo.App. 1983)]

10. Patricia Woodbury applied to Libertyville Township for welfare benefits. The welfare director had discretion in determining which applications would be approved. Before Woodbury could get the welfare benefits, she had to sign a form stating that she promised to repay the township the aid it gave her. She signed the form and received $1,090.26 in welfare payments between February 1, 1980, and March

18, 1981. On or about April 30, 1981, Woodbury sold her house for $42,000. She received $15,705.49 after paying the mortgage. Libertyville Township sued for her promise to repay the amount she had received in welfare payments. Woodbury argued that Libertyville Township had given her no consideration for her promise to repay. She claimed that the township had a preexisting legal duty to pay her welfare. Therefore, her promise to repay the township was unenforceable. Discuss fully whether the welfare payments and her promise to pay constituted consideration. [Libertyville Township v. Woodbury, 121 Ill.App.3d 587, 77 Ill.Dec. 207, 460 N.E.2d 66 (2 Dist. 1984)]

11. Gordon Hayes and Winslow Construction Company (Hayes) promised to hire Kathleen Hunter as a flag girl on a construction job beginning June 14, 1971. Relying on the offer, Hunter left her position with the telephone company, as Hayes had asked her to do. When Hayes failed to hire her, she was unemployed for two months—in spite of her efforts to find another job. Hunter sued Hayes for damages in the amount of $700, which she would have earned during the two months had she not left the telephone company, where she had been earning $350 a month. The trial court ruled for Hunter, awarding her $700 in damages. Hayes appealed, contending he should not be liable since no valid employment contract existed between the plaintiff and the defendants. Discuss whether Hunter should be allowed to recover damages incurred by her reliance on Hayes's offer of employment, even in the absence of a valid employment contract. [Hunter v. Hayes, 533 P.2d 952 (Colo.App. 1975)]

Chapter 10

Capacity and Genuineness of Assent

Although the parties to a contract must assume certain risks, the law indicates that neither party should be allowed to benefit from the other party's lack of **contractual capacity**—the legal ability to enter into a contractual relationship. Contractual capacity will not exist if a person is legally incompetent because of youth, intoxication, or some mental impairment. The law also will not allow parties to benefit from contracts resulting from deceit, undue influence, duress, or certain types of mistakes. In such contracts, **genuineness of assent** to the contract is lacking. Therefore, certain contracts are **voidable.** A *voidable contract* may be either validated or avoided (cancelled) at the option of the incapable or wronged party. Other contracts may be **void.** A *void contract* lacks an essential element for the formation of a legal contract, and thus, either party may ignore it.

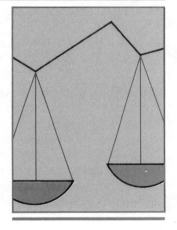

The first part of this chapter will discuss the element of capacity. The second part will focus on situations in which parties with full legal capacity have entered into an agreement, supported by consideration and for a legal purpose, in which genuineness of assent is lacking because of misrepresentation, mistake, duress, or undue influence.

CAPACITY

Historically, the law has concerned itself with the relative strength of the bargaining power of each contracting party. Thus, special protection is afforded those who bargain with the inexperience of youth or those who lack the degree of mental competency required by law.

Full competence exists when both parties have full legal capacity to enter into a contract and to have the contract enforced against them. *No competence* exists when one or both the parties have been adjudged by a court to be mentally incompetent and therefore have no legal capacity to contract. In this event, an essential element for a valid contract is missing, and the contract is void. *Limited competence* exists when one or both parties are minors, intoxicated, or mentally incompetent (but not yet adjudicated officially as such). These parties have full and legal capacity to enter into a contract; but if they so wish, they can avoid liability under the contract, which is thus voidable.

187

Minors

At common law, a minor was defined as a male who had not attained the age of twenty-one or a female who had not attained the age of eighteen. Today, in most states, the **age of majority** (the age at which a person is no longer a minor) for contractual purposes has been changed by statute to eighteen years for both sexes.[1] In addition, some states provide for the termination of minority upon marriage. Subject to certain exceptions, the contracts entered into by a minor are voidable at the option of that minor. The minor may avoid legal obligations by exercising the option to *disaffirm* the contract. Note, however, that an adult who enters into a contract with a minor cannot avoid his or her contractual duties on the ground that the minor can do so. Unless the minor exercises the option to avoid the contract, the adult party is bound by it.

MINORS' RIGHTS TO DISAFFIRM   The general rule is that a minor can enter into any contract that an adult can enter into, provided that the contract is not one prohibited by law for minors (for example, the sale of alcoholic beverages). Although minors can enter into contracts, they also have the right to disaffirm their contracts. Exceptions to this rule exist and will be discussed later in this section.

Disaffirmance in General   In order for a minor to exercise the option to avoid a contract, he or she need only manifest an intention not to be bound by the contract. The minor avoids the contract by disaffirming it. The technical definition of **disaffirmance** is the legal avoidance, or setting aside, of a contractual obligation. Words or conduct may serve to express this intent. Suppose James Caldwell, a seventeen-year-old, enters into a contract to sell his car to Joseph Reed, an adult. Caldwell can avoid the contract and avoid his legal duty to deliver possession of the car to Reed either by telling Reed that he refuses to abide by the contract or by selling the car to a third person. In other words, Caldwell can disaffirm the contract

by expressing his intention in words or by acting inconsistently with his duties under the contract.

The contract can ordinarily be disaffirmed at any time during minority or for a reasonable time after the minor comes of age. In some states, however, a minor's disaffirmance of certain contracts is prohibited under a statute. For example, in the case of a contract for the sale of land by a minor, the rule in most states is that a minor can disaffirm only after attaining his or her majority. Other statutes include complete proscriptions of a minor's right to avoid contracts for student loans, medical care, and insurance policies and contracts that a minor makes pursuant to running a business. On grounds of public policy, other promises of a minor may be enforced, particularly when they entail something that the law would compel anyway—supporting an illegitimate child, for example.

If a minor fails to disaffirm a contract within a reasonable time after reaching the age of majority, the court must determine whether the conduct constitutes *ratification*, binding the minor in contract, or *disaffirmance*, allowing the minor's avoidance. Generally, if the contract is fully performed by both parties (executed), it is presumed to be ratified. If the contract is still executory (not yet fully performed by both parties), it is considered disaffirmed.

For example, assume that the age of majority in your state is eighteen. Your sister, age seventeen, contracts to purchase a bicycle from an adult for $125. Your sister then turns eighteen. If she has not taken possession of the bicycle or paid the $125 purchase price, an executory contract exists. If she fails to take possession of and pay for the bicycle within a reasonable time after her eighteenth birthday, most courts would hold her conduct to be an act of disaffirmance. On the other hand, if she has taken possession of the bicycle and paid the purchase price, an executed contract exists, and most courts would hold her failure to actively disaffirm within a reasonable time after her eighteenth birthday to be an act of ratification. A minor must disaffirm the entire contract in order to disaffirm it at all. For example, the minor cannot decide to keep part of the goods and return the remainder.

In the following case, a minor asserts the defense of incapacity to avoid liability for her indorsement of a check. The reasoning of the court illustrates the public policy underlying a minor's right to disaffirm contractual obligations.

---

1. Although the age of majority applicable in contracts has been changed to eighteen in many states, it may still be twenty-one for some purposes, including the purchase and consumption of alcohol. The word *infant* is usually used synonymously with the word *minor*.

BACKGROUND AND FACTS   *April Iverson's uncle, John Polachek, obtained a life insurance policy through his employer, Scholl, Inc. The policy, issued by Bankers Life and Casualty, named April as the sole beneficiary. April, the plaintiff, was eleven years old when her uncle died and when Bankers mailed the $10,000 death-benefit check to her. The check was made out in her name because Scholl had not informed Bankers that April was a minor. Subsequently, April's father misappropriated the funds by having April sign (indorse) the check. Later, April sued Bankers and Scholl for the $10,000. Bankers claimed that her indorsement discharged its obligation to her. She claimed that as a minor she did not have the capacity to discharge this contractual obligation. The trial court dismissed her complaint against Scholl and Bankers, and April appealed.*

 Case 10.1

IVERSON v. SCHOLL INC.
Appellate Court of Illinois, First District, 1985.
136 Ill.App.3d 962, 91 Ill.Dec. 407, 483 N.E.2d 893.

STAMOS, Presiding Judge.
*   *   *   *

The fundamental question posed *   *   * is whether there has been an effective and valid discharge of Bankers' obligation to pay the life insurance proceeds to plaintiff. Plaintiff, as the named beneficiary of the policy issued by Bankers to John Polachek, was a third party beneficiary of that contract [one for whose benefit a promise is made in a contract to which he or she is not a party]. Therefore, upon the death of the insured, plaintiff acquired a vested [accrued or settled] right to the proceeds of the policy. As a general matter, Bankers was contractually required to remit the proceeds of that policy to the named beneficiary. The law is settled that an insurer is discharged from liability on an insurance policy if it, while acting in good faith, pays the proceeds to the named beneficiary. The insurer's obligation of good faith requires a reasonable investigation by the insurer when it is aware of suspicious circumstances regarding a beneficiary. The obligation of good faith is not violated unless a reasonable investigation would have disclosed facts sufficient to defeat the named beneficiary claim.

The general principles cited above, however, must be read in conjunction with the law as it relates to minors, like plaintiff. The public policy of Illinois is to protect minors and their property from the consequences of dealing with others. As such, the courts of this state have consistently and assiduously guarded the rights of minors. The protection afforded to minors is especially prominent in the area of contracts. The general rule applicable to all contracts, other than for necessaries [e.g., food, clothing], is that the contract of a minor is voidable and may be repudiated by the minor during minority or within a reasonable time upon achieving majority absent a ratification. "The exercise of a minor's right to disaffirm his contract may operate injuriously and sometimes unjustly against the other party, but the right exists for the protection of the infant against his own improvidence and may be exercised entirely in his discretion." The ignorance of one party to the contract of the minority of the other party is, generally, of no consequence and does not operate as a bar to the right of the minor to disaffirm. The right to disaffirm applies whether the contract is wholly executory or fully executed and, if the consideration is lost or expended, the minor is not bound to make restitution.

The crucial question thus becomes, in light of the foregoing principles, whether plaintiff has discharged Bankers' obligation to pay the proceeds. This court holds that plaintiff, as a minor, was legally incapable of discharging Bankers' obligation and that Bankers must draw another check, in favor of plaintiff, and pay the proceeds to either plaintiff's legal representative or to another person able to legally discharge Bankers on plaintiff's behalf or for plaintiff's benefit.
*   *   *   *

*   *   * It is without consequence that Bankers had no knowledge that plaintiff was a minor or that it acted in good faith. Also, the filing of suit is sufficient evidence of plaintiff's desire to disaffirm any purported discharge given by her under the cajoling influence of her father. The fact that Bankers has paid once is of no consequence to this plaintiff's suit. The law recognizes that entities deal with a minor at their own peril, and the law protecting minors has been enforced even when it results in unfairness or injury to the other party. The cases are numerous where the courts have jealously guarded the rights of minors vis-a-vis the careless, unsuspecting, or unscrupulous others. This court therefore reverses the order dismissing Bankers and remands the action for a trial.

As to Scholl [the minor's uncle's employer] there is no set of facts plaintiff could allege in order to raise a viable claim against it. Scholl was not a party to the contract of insurance on which Bankers remains liable. Also, Scholl does not owe a duty, as the employer of the insured, to the named beneficiary. Scholl's sole obligation was to notify Bankers of the fact of the death of an insured and provide Bankers with the name of the beneficiary.

DECISION AND REMEDY   *The appellate court affirmed the dismissal of the claim against Scholl but reversed the trial court's decision with respect to Bankers Life and Casualty. Bankers was still obligated to pay April the proceeds from the insurance policy.*

Duty of Restoration   When a contract has been executed, minors cannot disaffirm without returning whatever goods they may have received, or paying for their reasonable value. This is called the minor's *duty of restoration*. Although many states recognize this duty, most place certain limitations on it. Under the majority view, the minor need only return the goods (or other consideration), provided such goods are in the minor's possession or control. Even if the goods have been used, damaged, or ruined, the minor's right to disaffirm the contract is not affected. Suppose Pat Boland, a seventeen-year-old, purchases a used Ford Taurus from Jane Crow, an adult. Boland is a bad driver and negligently runs the car into a telephone pole. The next day he returns the car to Crow and disaffirms the contract. Under the majority view, this return fulfills Boland's duty of restoration, even though the auto is now wrecked.

A few states, either by statute or by court decision, have placed an additional duty on the minor—the *duty of restitution*. This duty accords with the maxim that one's youth may be used as a shield, but not as a sword. The theory is that the adult should be returned to his or her position before the contract was made. The duty of restitution requires Boland to pay Crow for the damage done to the car in addition to returning it. Some states do not require full restitution. A minor must pay only a "reasonable" amount to compensate the adult.

When a minor disaffirms, all property that he or she has transferred to the adult as consideration may be recovered, even if it is then in the hands of a third party. If the property itself cannot be returned, the adult must pay the minor its equivalent value. Under UCC 2-403(1), which deals with the sale of or the contract to sell *goods*, a minor cannot recover the goods transferred to a third party who is a bona fide purchaser[2] ("a good faith purchaser for value"). For example, Mary, a minor, sells her stereo to Ann, an adult, for $100. Ann immediately sells the stereo to Grant for $110. Later, Mary wishes her stereo back and notifies Ann of her intent to disaffirm the contract. Even though Mary has a legal right to disaffirm the contract with Ann, Mary cannot require Grant, a bona fide purchaser, to return the stereo to her.

The Effect of a Minor's Misrepresentation of Age   Suppose a minor tells a seller that she is twenty-one years old when she is actually only seventeen. Ordinarily, the minor can disaffirm the contract even though she misrepresented her age. Moreover, in certain jurisdictions, a minor will not be held liable under the tort theory of deceit for misrepresenting his or her age, because, indirectly, the judgment might force the minor to perform the contract.

In many jurisdictions, however, legislatures or courts have declared certain circumstances under which a minor will be bound to a contract despite his or her misrepresentation of age. First, several states have enacted statutes for precisely this purpose. In these states, misrepresentation of age is enough to prohibit disaffirmance. Other statutes

---

2. Defined as "purchaser for a valuable consideration paid or parted with in the belief that the vender had a right to sell, and without any suspicious circumstances to put him on inquiry." [Merritt v. Railroad Co., 12 Barb. 605 (1852)].

prohibit a minor who has engaged in business as an adult from disaffirming contracts negotiated in carrying out this business.[3]

Second, some courts refuse to allow minors who misrepresented their age to disaffirm executed contracts unless they can return the consideration received. In these cases, the courts reason that the combination of misrepresentation and unjust enrichment estops (prevents) minors from asserting contractual incapacity.

_____

3. See, for example, statutes in Iowa, Kansas, Utah, and Washington.

Third, some courts allow a misrepresenting minor to disaffirm a contract but hold the minor liable for damages in tort, and the defrauded party may sue the minor for misrepresentation or fraud. A split in authority exists on this point, since some courts, as previously pointed out, have recognized that allowing a suit in tort is equivalent to indirectly enforcing the minor's contract.

In the following case, an Ohio appellate court had to deal with the problem of a minor's false representation of her age as the inducement to a contract. At the time this case was decided, the age of majority in Ohio was twenty-one.

BACKGROUND AND FACTS *The plaintiff is Haydocy Pontiac, a seller of automobiles. The defendant, Lee, was twenty years of age when she contracted to purchase the automobile, but she represented to the plaintiff-seller that she was twenty-one years old. The defendant purchased the car by making a trade-in and financing the rest of the purchase price. She executed a note for the unpaid purchase price, including financing charges and insurance charges. The total amount of the note was approximately $2,000.*

Immediately following delivery of the automobile, Lee turned the car over to a third person. She never at any time thereafter had possession of the automobile. Lee made no further attempt to make payment on the contract and attempted to disaffirm the contract. She did not return the automobile to the plaintiff-seller, nor did she offer to return it. She merely announced that she was a minor at the time of purchase, that she had not ratified the agreement to purchase the car, and that she was repudiating her contract and would not be bound by it. The trial court applied the general rule of law permitting a minor to avoid a transaction without being required to restore the consideration received. Haydocy Pontiac appealed.

 Case 10.2

HAYDOCY PONTIAC, INC. v. LEE

Court of Appeals of Ohio, Franklin County, 1969. 19 Ohio App.2d 217, 250 N.E.2d 898.

STRAUSBAUGH, Judge.

＊   ＊   ＊   ＊

The cases we have examined in this regard all relate to the question whether the infant can recover from the vendor the purchase price paid and the right of the vendor to counterclaim rather than the facts of this case where the vendor, in the original petition, seeks to recover the property or, in lieu thereof, the balance due on the purchase price. Many of the cases use language to the effect that when the property received by the infant is in his possession, or under his control, to permit him to rescind the contract without requiring him to return or offer to return it would be to permit him to use his privilege as a "sword rather than a shield."

＊   ＊   ＊   ＊

To allow infants to avoid a transaction without being required to restore the consideration received where the infant has used or otherwise disposed of it causes hardship on the other party. We hold that where the consideration received by the infant cannot be returned upon disaffirmance of the contract because it has been disposed of the infant must account for the value of it, not in excess of the purchase price, where the other party is free from any fraud or bad faith and where the contract has been induced by a false representation of the age of the infant. *Under this factual situation the infant is estopped* [prevented] *from pleading infancy as a defense where the contract has been induced by a false representation that the infant was of age.* [Emphasis added.]

The necessity of returning the consideration as a prerequisite to obtaining equitable relief is still clearer where the infant misrepresents age and perpetrated an actual fraud on the other party. The disaffirmance of an infant's contract is to be determined by equitable principles, whether sought in a proceeding in equity or a case at law.

The common law has bestowed upon the infant the privilege of disaffirming his contracts in conservation of his rights and interests. Where the infant, 20 years of age, through falsehood and deceit enters into a contract with another who enters therein in honesty and good faith and, thereafter, the infant seeks to disaffirm the contract without tendering back the consideration, no right or interest of the infant exists which needs protection. The privilege given the infant thereupon becomes a weapon of injustice.

DECISION
AND REMEDY
The judgment of the trial court was reversed. The Ohio appellate court allowed the seller, Haydocy Pontiac, Inc., to recover the fair market value of the automobile from the defendant, Lee. The only restriction imposed by the court was that the fair market value could not be in excess of the original purchase price of the automobile.

Liability for Necessaries   A minor who enters into a contract for *necessaries* (food, clothing, shelter, and other items, as will be discussed below) may disaffirm the contract but will still remain liable for the reasonable value of the goods. If the minor has a parent or guardian who is able to provide the minor with necessaries, but fails to do so, the parent or guardian will be liable for the reasonable value of any necessary goods, such as clothing, purchased by the minor. The legal duty to pay a reasonable value does not arise from the contract itself but is imposed by law under a theory of quasi-contract (implied-in-law contract). Parents' liability will be discussed later in this chapter.

The minor's right to disaffirm a contract has economic ramifications in that sellers are likely to refuse to deal with minors because of it. If minors can at least be held liable for the reasonable value of the goods, sellers' reluctance to enter into contracts with minors will be offset. This theory explains why the courts narrow the subject matter to necessaries. Without such a rule, minors might be denied the opportunity to purchase necessary goods.

Note, though, that the minor is liable only for the reasonable value (quasi-contract theory) of the goods (because with disaffirmance there is no contract and therefore no contract price to which the

court can refer). Suppose Hank Olsen, a minor, purchases a suit that is list priced at $150. After wearing the suit for several weeks, Olsen wants to disaffirm his contract with the clothier. He can do so, but he is liable for the reasonable value of the suit. If the court deems the value of the suit to be $115, then the clothier can recover only that amount, even if this deprives the clothier of some of the profit that he thought he would realize on the sale.

There is no firm, universally accepted definition of necessaries. At a minimum, necessaries include food, clothing, shelter, medicine, and hospital care. In some cases, however, courts have not limited necessaries to items required for physical existence but have extended the term to include whatever is believed to be necessary to maintain a person's financial and social status. Thus, what will be considered necessaries for one person may not be for another. Moreover, necessaries have been held to include education as well as services that are reasonably necessary to enable a minor to earn a living.

Generally, courts determine on a case-by-case basis what constitutes necessaries. Even housing, in the form of a leased apartment, may not constitute a necessary in certain circumstances—as the following case illustrates.

BACKGROUND AND FACTS *Webster Street was a partnership that owned apartments in Omaha, Nebraska. On September 18, 1982, Webster leased one second-floor apartment to Mathew Sheridan and his friend, Pat Wilwerding. Both made the rental deposit of $150 and signed the lease for a six-month term at $250 per month. Both Sheridan and Wilwerding were minors (below the age of majority in Nebraska, which is twenty-one) and had left home with the understanding that they could return at any time.*

Unable to continue paying the rent, both minors abandoned the apartment in November. In January of 1983, the attorney for Sheridan and Wilwerding notified Webster Street that his clients would not pay the rental amount that Webster Street claimed; indeed, the attorney demanded the return of the $150 rental deposit. Webster Street commenced suit against Sheridan and Wilwerding for the amount of the rent due at that time under the lease. The trial court found for the minors but awarded Webster Street money for cleanup and repairs and rent for the month during which Sheridan and Wilwerding had occupied the premises. Webster Street appealed.

 Case 10.3

WEBSTER STREET PARTNERSHIP, LTD. v. SHERIDAN

Supreme Court of Nebraska, 1985.
220 Neb. 9, 368 N.W.2d 439.

KRIVOSHA, Chief Justice.
❖　❖　❖　❖

As a general rule, an infant does not have the capacity to bind himself absolutely by contract. The right of the infant to avoid his contract is one conferred by law for his protection against his own improvidence and the designs of others. The policy of the law is to discourage adults from contracting with an infant; they cannot complain if, as a consequence of violating that rule, they are unable to enforce their contracts. As stated in *Curtice Co. v. Kent:* "The result seems hardly just to the [adult], but persons dealing with infants do so at their peril. The law is plain as to their disability to contract, and safety lies in refusing to transact business with them."

However, the privilege of infancy will not enable an infant to escape liability in all cases and under all circumstances. For example, it is well established that an infant is liable for the value of necessaries furnished him. An infant's liability for necessaries is based not upon his actual contract to pay for them but upon a contract implied by law, or, in other words, a quasi-contract.

Just what are necessaries, however, has no exact definition. The term is flexible and varies according to the facts of each individual case. In *Cobbey v. Buchanan*, we said: " 'The meaning of the term "necessaries" cannot be defined by a general rule applicable to all cases; the question is a mixed one of law and fact, to be determined in each case from the particular facts and circumstances in such case.' " A number of factors must be considered before a court can conclude whether a particular product or service is a necessary. As stated in *Schoenung v. Gallet*:

"The term 'necessaries,' as used in the law relating to the liability of infants therefor, is a relative term, somewhat flexible, except when applied to such things as are obviously requisite for the maintenance of existence, and depends on the social position and situation in life of the infant, as well as upon his own fortune and that of his parents. The particular infant must have an actual need for the articles furnished; not for mere ornament or pleasure. The articles must be useful and suitable, but they are not necessaries merely because useful or beneficial. Concerning the general character of the things furnished, to be necessaries the articles must supply the infant's personal needs, either those of his body or those of his mind. However, the term 'necessaries' is not confined to merely such things as are required for a bare subsistence. There is no positive rule by means of which it may be determined what are or what are not necessaries, for what may be considered necessary for one infant may not be necessaries for another infant whose state is different as to rank, social position, fortune, health, or other circumstances, the question being one to be determined from the particular facts and circumstances of each case."

This appears to be the law as it is generally followed throughout the country.

*   *   *   *

" 'To enable an infant to contract for articles as necessaries, he must have been in actual need of them, and obliged to procure them for himself. They are not necessaries as to him, however necessary they may be in their nature, if he was already supplied with sufficient articles of the kind, or if he had a parent or guardian who was able and willing to supply them. The burden of proof is on the plaintiff to show that the infant was destitute of the articles, and had no way of procuring them except by his own contract.' "

*   *   *   *

[Quoting from a legal treatise, the court stated:]

Thus, articles are not necessaries for an infant if he has a parent or guardian who is able and willing to supply them, and an infant residing with and being supported by his parent according to his station in life is not absolutely liable for things which under other circumstances would be considered necessaries.

The undisputed testimony is that both tenants were living away from home, apparently with the understanding that they could return home at any time. *   *   *

*   *   * It would therefore appear that in the present case neither Sheridan nor Wilwerding was in need of shelter but, rather, had chosen to voluntarily leave home, with the understanding that they could return whenever they desired. *   *   * We therefore find that both the municipal court and the district court erred in finding that the apartment, under the facts in this case, was a necessary.

*   *   *   *

Because the rental of the apartment was not a necessary, the minors had the right to avoid the contract, either during their minority or within a reasonable time after reaching their majority. Disaffirmance by an infant completely puts an end to the contract's existence, both as to him and as to the adult with whom he contracted. Because the parties then stand as if no contract had ever existed, the infant can recover payments made to the adult, and the adult is entitled to the return of whatever was received by the infant.

The record shows that Pat Wilwerding clearly disaffirmed the contract during his minority. Moreover, the record supports the view that when the agent for Webster Street ordered the minors out for failure to pay rent and they vacated the premises, Sheridan likewise disaffirmed the contract. The record indicates that Sheridan reached majority on November 5. To suggest that a lapse of 7 days was not disaffirmance within a reasonable time would be foolish. Once disaffirmed, the contract became void; therefore, no contract existed between the parties, and the minors were entitled to recover all of the moneys which they paid and to be relieved of any further obligation under the contract.

DECISION
AND REMEDY

The judgment of the district court was reversed. Sheridan and Wilwerding were entitled to all of the monies that they had paid over to Webster Street without exception.

Insurance and Loans Traditionally, insurance has not been viewed as a *necessary*, so minors can ordinarily disaffirm their contracts and recover all premiums paid. Some jurisdictions, however, prohibit the right to disaffirm—for example, when minors contract for life or medical insurance. Other jurisdictions allow a minor to disaffirm but limit recovery to the value of premiums paid, less the insurance company's actual cost of protecting the minor under the policy. Suppose Bob Berzak takes out an automobile insurance policy and pays $1,000 in premiums. Bob has an accident for which his insurance company, State Farm, pays a claim of $700. In states following the traditional rule, Bob's recovery upon disaffirmance will be $1,000, the full value of the premiums. In states limiting his recovery, Bob can recover only $300, the excess of the value of the premiums over State Farm's actual cost under the policy.

In and of itself, a loan is seldom viewed as a necessary, even if the minor spends the money on necessaries. If, however, the lender makes a loan for the express purpose of enabling the minor to purchase necessaries, and the lender personally makes sure the money is so spent, the minor is normally obligated to repay the loan.

RATIFICATION   In contract law, **ratification** is the act of accepting and giving legal force to an obligation that previously was not enforceable. In relation to minors' contracts, *ratification* may be defined as an act or expression in words by which a minor, upon or after reaching majority, indicates an *intention* to become bound by the contract. Ratification must occur, if at all, after the individual comes of age, since any attempt to become legally bound prior to majority is no more effective than the original contractual promise. This protects the minor and is consistent with the theory that the contracts of a minor are voidable at his or her option.

Express Ratification   Suppose John Lawrence enters into a contract to sell a stereo to Carol Ogden. At the time of the contract Carol is a minor. Naturally, Carol can avoid her legal duty to pay for the stereo by disaffirming the contract. Imagine, instead, that Carol reaches majority and writes a letter to John stating that she still agrees to buy the stereo. Carol thus ratifies the contract and is now legally bound. John can sue for breach of contract if Carol refuses to perform her part of the bargain. This is an example of *express* ratification.

Implied Ratification   The contract can also be ratified by *conduct*. Suppose, as a minor, Carol takes possession of the stereo and continues to use it after reaching the age of majority. This conduct evidences an intent to abide by the contract and is a form of *implied* ratification. Again, Carol is legally bound, and John can sue her for breach of contract if she fails to perform her duty to pay the purchase price. When an individual, after reaching majority, continues to use and make payments on property purchased as a minor, the continued use and payment are inconsistent with disaffirm-

ance and implicitly indicates an intention to be bound by the contract.

In general, any act or conduct showing an intention to affirm the contract will be deemed to be ratification. As previously discussed, however, silence after reaching the age of majority does not in and of itself constitute ratification of an executory contract in most situations. If Carol had said nothing to John and had not taken possession or made payment, she would not have ratified the contract, since she had expressed no intention to abide by it. On the other hand, the minor may have a duty to speak in some circumstances. Suppose that after coming of age, a former minor seller fails to disaffirm, knowing that the purchaser is making costly improvements on the property sold. In this case the minor cannot disaffirm the contract.

NON-VOIDABLE CONTRACTS AND TORTS

Minors   Many states have passed statutes restricting the ability of minors to avoid certain contracts. For example, as previously discussed, some states prohibit minors from disaffirming certain insurance contracts. Other states hold that loans for education or medical care received by minors create binding legal duties that they cannot avoid.[4]

In addition, certain statutes specifically require minors to perform legal duties. Suppose James Dornan, a minor, wants to legally seize the property of Davis Snowden for default of a loan. In some states, Dornan is required to file a bond before the legal seizure, or attachment, can occur. After filing the bond, Dornan cannot avoid the obligations of the bonding agreement, since the bond is a legal duty imposed by state statute. In such situations, a minor cannot rely on the common law rule that the bonding contract is voidable. Similar legal duties are imposed on minors with respect to bank accounts and transfers of stocks.

Some contracts cannot be avoided, simply as a matter of law, on the grounds of public policy. For example, marriage contracts and contracts to enlist in the armed services fall into this category.

Torts   In Chapters 4 and 5, we discussed the area of law called torts, defined as private wrongs committed upon a person or property independent of

---

4. New York Education Law, Sec. 281 (McKinney 1969); Cal. Civil Code Sec. 36 (West 1982).

contract. Generally, minors are liable for their torts. Courts do, however, weigh the factors of age, mental capacity, and maturity before determining a minor's liability. As has been pointed out, a breach of contract is normally not treated as a tort for which the minor is liable. When the tort is more than a simple misfeasance (that is, improper performance of some lawful act) in the performance of a contract, however, and when it is separate from and independent of the contract, the court may rule against the minor. The test of whether an action against the minor can be brought is whether a basis for establishing liability exists apart from the contract. For example, suppose a minor rents a boat. The rental agreement provides that the minor will use due care to prevent damage to the boat. Nonetheless, the minor's careless use of the boat damages it. Will a court uphold an action in tort for negligence? The answer to this question depends on whether the court interprets imposing tort liability on the minor as directly or indirectly enforcing the minor's promise, which, because of a lack of contractual capacity, is voidable. The minor may be held liable, however, to any third parties injured by the minor's negligence.

PARENTS' LIABILITY   As a general rule, parents are not liable for the contracts made by their minor children. This is why businesses ordinarily require parents to sign any contract made with a minor. The parents then become personally obligated under the contract to perform the conditions of the contract, even if their child avoids liability.

Parents who have neglected the care of their minor child can be held liable for the reasonable value of necessaries supplied to the child, even when they have not signed a contract. In other words, if a child purchases shoes because his or her parents refuse to provide any shoes, the parents can be held liable for the reasonable value of the shoes.

Under the common law, parents were not held liable for the torts of their minor children simply because of the parent-child relationship. In some states, the courts have adopted a rule that requires a separate determination of the parent's negligence. In those states, a parent may be liable if he or she fails to exercise proper parental control over the minor child and the parent knew, or should have known, from the minor's habits and tenden-

cies, that failure to exercise control posed an unreasonable risk of harm to others.

Other states have enacted statutes imposing on parents legal responsibility for the consequences of the tortious acts of their children. These statutes vary. For example, in some states, liability will be imposed on parents only for the "wilful, malicious or wanton" acts of their minor children.

Intoxicated Persons

A contract entered into by an intoxicated person can be <u>either voidable</u> or <u>valid</u>. If the person was intoxicated enough to lack mental capacity, then the transaction is voidable at the option of the intoxicated person even if the intoxication was purely voluntary. In order for the contract to be voidable, it must be proved that the intoxicated person's reason and judgment were impaired to the extent that he or she did not comprehend the legal consequences of entering into the contract. If, despite intoxication, the person understands these legal consequences, the contract will be enforceable. Simply because the terms of the contract are foolish or obviously favor the other party does not mean that the contract is voidable (unless the other party *fraudulently* induced the person to become intoxicated). Problems often arise in determining whether a party was intoxicated enough to avoid legal duties. Many courts prefer to look at objective indications to determine whether the contract is voidable because of intoxication rather than inquire into the intoxicated party's mental state.

The following case on page 197 shows an unusual business transaction in which boasts, brags, and dares "after a few drinks" resulted in a binding sale and purchase transaction. It should be noted that avoidance due to intoxication is very rare.

AVOIDANCE OR RATIFICATION   If a contract is held to be voidable because of a person's intoxication, that person has the option of disaffirming (avoiding) it—the same option available to a minor. The vast majority of courts, however, require the intoxicated person to make full restitution (fully return consideration received) as a condition of disaffirmance, except in cases involving necessaries, as discussed below. For example, suppose a person contracts to purchase a set of encyclopedias while intoxicated. If the books are delivered, the purchaser can disaffirm the executed contract (get-

BACKGROUND AND FACTS   *W. O. Lucy and J. C. Lucy, the plaintiffs, filed suit against A. H. Zehmer and Ida Zehmer, the defendants, to compel the Zehmers to convey title of their property, known as the Ferguson Farm, to the Lucys for $50,000, as allegedly the Zehmers had agreed to do. The transaction had come about in a most unusual manner. Lucy had known Zehmer for fifteen or twenty years and for the last eight years or so had been anxious to buy the Ferguson Farm from Zehmer. One night, Lucy stopped in to visit the Zehmers in the combination restaurant, filling station, and motor court they operated. While there, Lucy tried to buy the Ferguson Farm once again. This time he tried a new approach. According to the trial court transcript, Lucy said to Zehmer, "I bet you wouldn't take $50,000 for that place." Zehmer replied, "Yes, I would too; you wouldn't give fifty."*

Throughout the evening the conversation returned to the sale of the Ferguson Farm for $50,000. At the same time, the parties continued to drink whiskey and engage in light conversation. The conversation repeatedly returned to the subject of the Ferguson Farm. Eventually, Lucy enticed Zehmer to write up an agreement to the effect that Zehmer would agree to sell to Lucy the Ferguson Farm for $50,000 complete. Zehmer first wrote that out on the back of a restaurant check. He tore up the first copy because he had written "I do hereby agree" and thought it had better read "we" because Mrs. Zehmer would have to sign it too. Zehmer rewrote the agreement and asked Mrs. Zehmer to sign it. She agreed.

Lucy sued Zehmer to go through with the sale. Zehmer argued that he was drunk and that the offer was made in jest and hence was unenforceable. The trial court agreed with the Zehmers.

BUCHANAN, Justice.
*   *   *   *

The instrument sought to be enforced was written by A. H. Zehmer on December 20, 1952, in these words: "We hereby agree to sell to W. O. Lucy the Ferguson Farm complete for $50,000.00, title satisfactory to buyer," and signed by the defendants, A. H. Zehmer and Ida S. Zehmer.

A. H. Zehmer admitted that *   *   * W. O. Lucy offered him $50,000 cash for the farm, but that he, Zehmer, considered that the offer was made in jest; that so thinking, and both he and Lucy having had several drinks, he wrote out "the memorandum" quoted above and induced his wife to sign it; that he did not deliver the memorandum to Lucy, but that Lucy picked it up, read it, put it in his pocket, attempted to offer Zehmer $5 to bind the bargain, which Zehmer refused to accept, and realizing for the first time that Lucy was serious, Zehmer assured him that he had no intention of selling the farm and that the whole matter was a joke. Lucy left the premises insisting that he had purchased the farm.
*   *   *   *

The discussion leading to the signing of the agreement, said Lucy, lasted thirty or forty minutes, during which Zehmer seemed to doubt that Lucy could raise $50,000. Lucy suggested the provision for having the title examined and Zehmer made the suggestion that he would sell it "complete, everything there," and stated that all he had on the farm was three heifers.

Lucy took a partly filled bottle of whiskey into the restaurant with him for the purpose of giving Zehmer a drink if he wanted it. Zehmer did, and he and Lucy had one or two drinks together. Lucy said that while he felt the drinks he took he was not intoxicated, and from the way Zehmer handled the transaction he did not think he was either.

 Case 10.4

W. O. LUCY AND J. C. LUCY v. A. C. ZEHMER AND IDA S. ZEHMER

Supreme Court of Appeals of Virginia, 1954.
196 Va. 493, 84 S.E.2d 516.

*   *   *   *

The defendants insist that *   *   * the writing sought to be enforced was prepared as a bluff or dare to force Lucy to admit that he did not have $50,000; that the whole matter was a joke; that the writing was not delivered to Lucy and no binding contract was ever made between the parties.

It is an unusual, if not bizarre, defense. *   *   *

In his testimony, Zehmer claimed that he "was high as a Georgia pine," and that the transaction "was just a bunch of two doggoned drunks bluffing to see who could talk the biggest and say the most." That claim is inconsistent with his attempt to testify in great detail as to what was said and what was done. *   *   * The record is convincing that Zehmer was not intoxicated to the extent of being unable to comprehend the nature and consequences of the instrument he executed, and hence that instrument is not to be invalidated on that ground. *   *   *

*   *   *   *

The appearance of the contract, the fact that it was under discussion for forty minutes or more before it was signed; Lucy's objection to the first draft because it was written in the singular, and he wanted Mrs. Zehmer to sign it also; the rewriting to meet that objection and the signing by Mrs. Zehmer; the discussion of what was to be included in the sale, the provision for the examination of the title, the completeness of the instrument that was executed, the taking possession of it by Lucy with no request or suggestion by either of the defendants that he give it back, are facts which furnish persuasive evidence that the execution of the contract was a serious business transaction rather than a casual, jesting matter as defendants now contend.

*   *   *   *

Not only did Lucy actually believe, but the evidence shows he was warranted in believing, that the contract represented a serious business transaction and a good faith sale and purchase of the farm.

In the field of contracts, as generally elsewhere, "*We must look to the outward expression of a person as manifesting his intention rather than to his secret and unexpressed intention.* [Emphasis added.] 'The law imputes to a person an intention corresponding to the reasonable meaning of his words and acts.' "

*   *   *   *

Whether the writing signed by the defendants and now sought to be enforced by the complainants was the result of a serious offer by Lucy and a serious acceptance by the defendants, or was a serious offer by Lucy and an acceptance in secret jest by the defendants, in either event it constituted a binding contract of sale between the parties.

DECISION   *The Supreme Court of Virginia determined that the writing was an enforceable*
AND REMEDY   *contract and reversed the ruling of the lower court. The Zehmers were required*
by court order to carry through with the sale of the Ferguson Farm to the Lucys.

ting back the payment made) only by returning the encyclopedias.

An intoxicated person, after becoming sober, may ratify expressly or implicitly, just as a minor may upon reaching majority. Implied ratification occurs when a person enters into a contract while intoxicated and fails to disaffirm the contract within a *reasonable* time after becoming sober. Acts or conduct inconsistent with an intent to disaffirm— for example, continued use of property purchased

under a voidable contract—will also ratify the contract.

In addition, contracts for necessaries are voidable (as in the case of minors), but the intoxicated person is liable in quasi-contract for the reasonable value of the consideration received.

The lack of contractual capacity due to intoxication while the contract is being made must be distinguished from capacity (or the lack thereof) of an alcoholic. If a contract is made while an alcoholic is sober, there is no lack of capacity.[5] Exhibit 10-1 illustrates a classification of contracts made by intoxicated persons.

Mentally Incompetent Persons

Contracts made by mentally incompetent persons can be either void, voidable, or valid. If a person has been adjudged mentally incompetent by a court of law and a guardian has been appointed, any contract made by the mentally incompetent person is void—no contract exists. Only the guardian can enter into binding legal duties on the incompetent person's behalf.

Mentally incompetent persons not so adjudged by a court may enter into voidable contracts if they do not know they are entering into the contract or if they lack the mental capacity to comprehend its subject matter, nature, and consequences. In such situations the contracts are voidable at the option of the mentally incompetent person, although the other party does not have this option.[6]

Such contracts may be disaffirmed or ratified. Ratification must occur after the person has be-

come mentally competent or after a guardian has been appointed and ratifies the contract. Like minors and intoxicated persons, mentally incompetent persons are liable in quasi-contract for the reasonable value of necessaries they receive.

A contract entered into by a mentally incompetent person may also be valid. A person may be able to understand the nature and effect of entering into a certain contract, yet simultaneously lack capacity to engage in other activities. In such cases the contract will be valid, since the person is not legally mentally incompetent for contractual purposes.[7] Similarly, an otherwise mentally incompetent person may have a *lucid interval*—that is, a temporary restoration of sufficient intelligence, judgment, and will to enter into contracts without disqualification—during which he or she will be considered to have full legal capacity. Exhibit 10-2 illustrates contract classifications of mentally incompetent persons.

_____

5. Olsen v. Hawkins, 90 Idaho 28, 408 P.2d 462 (1965).
6. This asymmetry applies to all voidable contracts.

7. Modern courts no longer require a person to be completely irrational to disaffirm contracts on the basis of mental incompetency. A contract may be voidable if, by reason of a mental illness or defect, an individual was unable to act reasonably with respect to the transaction and the other party had reason to know of the condition. See Ortelere v. Teachers' Retirement Bd., 25 N.Y.2d 196, 303 N.Y.S.2d 362, 250 N.E.2d 460 (1969).

Exhibit 10-1 Contract Classification—Intoxicated Persons

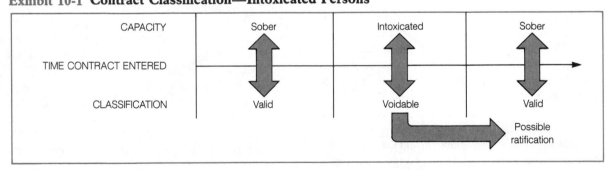

Exhibit 10-2 Contract Classification—Mentally Incompetent Persons

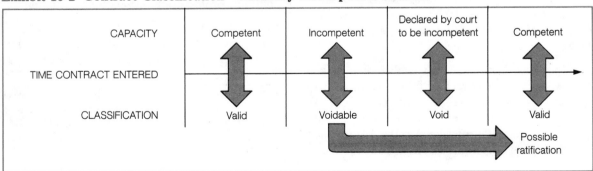

Aliens

An alien is a citizen of another country who resides in this country. Generally, aliens who are legally in this country have the same contractual rights as U.S. citizens. They may be sued and they may sue in the courts in order to enforce their contractual rights. Some states restrict the right of an alien to own real property. In virtually all cases, an *enemy alien* (that is, a citizen of a country with which we are at war) will not be able to enforce a contract, although the contract can be held in abeyance (temporarily set aside) until the war is over.

GENUINENESS OF ASSENT

It is possible for a contract to be voidable even though two parties with full legal capacity have entered into an agreement for a legal purpose and even though it is supported by consideration. This can occur when there is no *genuine assent* to the terms of the contract because of mistake, misrepresentation, undue influence, or duress.

Mistakes

It is important to distinguish between mistakes *in judgment as to value or quality* and mistakes *as to facts*. Only the latter have legal significance. Suppose Jane Simpson plans to buy ten acres of land in Montana. If she believes the land is worth $100,000, and it is worth only $40,000, her mistake is one of value or quality. If she believes, however, that the land is the ten acres owned by the Boyds, and it is actually the ten acres owned by the Deweys, her mistake is one of fact. Only a mistake as to fact allows a contract to be avoided.

Mistakes occur in two forms—*unilateral* and *mutual (bilateral)*. A unilateral mistake is made by only one of the contracting parties; a mutual, or bilateral, mistake is made by both.

UNILATERAL MISTAKES   A unilateral mistake occurs when one contracting party makes a mistake as to some *material fact*—that is, a fact important to the subject matter of the contract. In general, a unilateral mistake does not afford the mistaken party any right to relief from the con-

tract.[8] For example, John intends to sell his stereo for $550. He learns that Jane is interested in buying a used stereo. John writes a letter to Jane offering to sell his stereo, but he mistakenly types in the figure price of $500. Jane immediately writes back, accepting John's offer. Even though John intended to sell his stereo for $550, his unilateral mistake falls on him. He is bound in contract to sell the stereo to Jane for $500.

There are two exceptions to the general rule. First, the rule is not applied when the *other* party to the contract knows or should have known that a mistake was made. Second, some states will not enforce the contract against the mistaken party if the error was due to a mathematical mistake in addition, subtraction, division, or multiplication and if it was done inadvertently and without gross negligence (a mistake of this nature is sometimes referred to as a *scrivener's error*—meaning a writer's, or scribe's, error).

For an example of how these exceptions are applied, consider the following case. Odell Construction Co. made a bid to install the plumbing in a proposed apartment building. When Herbert Odell, the president, added up his costs, his secretary forgot to give him the figures for the pipe fittings. Because of the omission, Odell's bid was $6,500 below that of the other bidders. The prime contractor, Sunspan Inc., accepted Odell's bid. If Sunspan was not aware of Odell's mistake and could not reasonably have been aware of it, the contract will be enforceable, and Odell will be required to install the plumbing at the bid price. If it can be shown that Odell's secretary mentioned her error to Sunspan, however, or if Odell's bid was so far below the others that, as a contractor, Sunspan should reasonably have known the bid was a mistake, the contract can be rescinded. Sunspan would not be allowed to accept the offer knowing it was made by mistake.[9] The law of contracts protects only *reasonable* expectations.

MUTUAL MISTAKES OF MATERIAL FACT When both parties are mistaken as to the same material fact, the contract can be rescinded by

---

8. Restatement, Second, Contracts, Section 153, liberalizes this rule to take into account the modern trend of allowing avoidance although only one party has been mistaken.

9. Peerless Glass Co. v. Pacific Crockery Co., 121 Cal. 641, 54 P. 101 (1898).

either party.[10] Again, the mistake must be about a material fact—a fact important to the subject matter of the contract. In the following case, the court applied the mutual mistake doctrine to a situation in which an insurance contract was canceled on the basis of a mutual mistake of fact.

10. Restatement, Second, Contracts, Section 152.

 Case 10.5

BOYD v. AETNA LIFE INS. CO.

Appellate Court of Illinois, Fourth District, 1941.
310 Ill.App. 547, 35 N.E.2d 99.

BACKGROUND AND FACTS *The plaintiff, Christine Boyd, was named beneficiary in a policy insuring her husband's life. The policy, issued by Aetna Life (the defendant), contained a provision for payment of benefits in the event of the husband's permanent total disability. The couple separated, but Mrs. Boyd continued to pay the premiums, keeping the policy in force subject to valid claims. Later, since she did not know the whereabouts of her husband or his state of health, she contacted the insurance company and it was agreed that she should surrender the policy for the cash surrender value. After she surrendered the policy, Mrs. Boyd learned that her husband had become disabled. His disability had occurred before she surrendered the policy, and had she known about it, she would not have surrendered the policy. She asked the court to rescind her surrender agreement with Aetna Life and to order Aetna to pay her the disability benefits due under the policy on the ground of "mutual mistake of fact." Aetna argued "that notwithstanding her conscious want of ignorance of the condition of health of her husband she had elected to surrender the policy in question and take the cash surrender value thereof, in lieu of paying any further premiums on the policy, and by such action waived any rights she had under the policy of insurance."*

STONE, Presiding Justice.
*　*　*　*

The decisive and practically sole question for the consideration of this court is whether the facts alleged in the amended complaint set forth a sufficient mistake of fact, in the legal acceptation of the term, as to justify the intervention of a court of equity, and relieve against the consequences of that alleged mistake of fact, in the entering into the contract of rescision.

*　*　* *"Mistake of fact" has been defined to be a mistake, not caused by the neglect of a legal duty on the part of the person making the mistake, and consisting in an unconscious ignorance or forgetfulness of a fact past or present material to the contract, or belief in the present existence of a thing material to the contract which does not exist, or in the past existence of a thing which has not existed.* [Emphasis added.]

[A]t the time of cancellation plaintiff had a perfectly valid claim, but she and the company were both at that time *　*　* ignorant of the fact that there was a claim in existence, due to the total permanent disability of insured. The supposed element of doubt as to the health of Boyd never entered into the contemplation of either party, nor did it form any part of the consideration for the cancellation and surrender of the policy. It would be quite natural that they would assume, as they evidently did, that the insured was in good health. As matter of fact such is the express allegation of the amended complaint.

*　*　*　*

In the instant case, the insured's state of health was not merely incidental, nor was it a matter that would merely enhance the amount of damages. The subject matter of the mistake was intrinsic to the transaction. As set forth in plaintiff's amended complaint, "if she had known the true facts as to said Jimmie Boyd's total permanent disability *　*　* she would not have surrendered same (the policy) to the defendant." This policy was in full force and effect at the time of total permanent disability. Upon that contingency coming to pass the liability of defendant was fixed. The cancellation was not intended to reach back and absolve defendant from any liability which it had already incurred.

DECISION
AND REMEDY
Aetna was held liable to Mrs. Boyd as a beneficiary for payment of benefits under the policy, since she had been paying premiums on the policy up to and including the time when her ex-husband became disabled. At the time of his disability, Aetna became indebted to Mrs. Boyd as beneficiary for those payments. Therefore, there was indeed a mutual mistake of fact, since neither she nor Aetna knew of her ex-husband's disability, which entitled her to payment. The court permitted Mrs. Boyd to rescind her surrender agreement with Aetna and ordered Aetna to pay her the disability benefits.

Mutual Mistake in Identity of Subject Matter The classic case on mutual mistake of fact involved a ship named *Peerless* that was to sail from Bombay with certain cotton goods on board. More than one ship named *Peerless* sailed from Bombay that winter, however. The consequent mistake as to the identity of the subject matter of the contract was mutual, and it was about a material fact.

Case 10.6
RAFFLES v. WICHELHAUS AND ANOTHER
Court of Exchequer, England, 1864.
159 Eng.Rep. 375.

BACKGROUND AND FACTS *The defendant, Wichelhaus, purchased a shipment of Surat cotton from the plaintiff, Raffles, "to arrive ex 'Peerless' from Bombay." The defendant expected the goods to be shipped on the Peerless sailing from Bombay in October. The plaintiff expected to ship the goods on another Peerless, which sailed from Bombay in December. By the time the goods arrived and the plaintiff tried to deliver them, the defendant was no longer willing to accept them.*

Per Curiam. [An opinion by the whole court.]
* * * *

Declaration. For that it was agreed between the plaintiff and the defendants, to wit, at Liverpool, that the plaintiff should sell to the defendants, and the defendants buy of the plaintiff, certain goods, to wit, 125 bales of Surat cotton, guaranteed middling fair merchant's Dhollorah,[a] to arrive ex "Peerless" from Bombay; and that the cotton should be taken from the quay, and that the defendants would pay the plaintiff for the same at a certain rate, to wit, at the rate of 17¼d. per pound, within a certain time then agreed upon after the arrival of the said goods in England. Averments: that the said goods did arrive by the said ship from Bombay in England, to wit, at Liverpool, and the plaintiff was then and there ready, and willing and offered to deliver the said goods to the defendants, &c. Breach: that the defendants refused to accept the said goods or pay the plaintiff for them.

Plea. That the said ship mentioned in the said agreement was meant and intended by the defendants to be the ship called the "Peerless," which sailed from Bombay, to wit, in October; and that the plaintiff was not ready and willing and did not offer to deliver to the defendants any bales of cotton which arrived by the last mentioned ship, but instead thereof was only ready and willing and offered to deliver to the defendants 125 bales of Surat cotton which arrived by another and different ship, which was also

[a. "Guaranteed middling fair merchant's Dhollorah" means that the quality of the delivered Dhollorah cotton would be somewhere between middling and fair. It is common among merchants to establish a tolerance interval for the quality of bulk goods actually delivered.]

called the "Peerless," and which sailed from Bombay, to wit, in December.

*   *   *   *

There is nothing on the face of the contract to show that any particular ship called the "Peerless" was meant; but the moment it appears that two ships called the "Peerless" were about to sail from Bombay there is a latent ambiguity, and parol evidence[b] may be given for the purpose of shewing that the defendant meant one "Peerless," and the plaintiff another. That being so, there was no consensus ad idem, and therefore no binding contract.

The judgment was for the defendant, Wichelhaus.

**DECISION
AND REMEDY**

The court held that no mutual assent existed, because each party attached a materially different meaning to an essential term of the written contract. This being so, oral testimony would have been needed to determine whether the parties had actually meant the same ship. If both had meant the same ship, then the contract would have been enforceable.

COMMENTS

|b.   With respect to contracts, *parol evidence* is evidence that the document itself does not furnish but that other sources (such as, in this case, oral testimony) provide. See Chapter 12.|

MUTUAL MISTAKES IN VALUE   Value is variable. Depending on the time, place, and other circumstances, the same item may be worth considerably different amounts. When parties contract, their agreement establishes the value of the object of their transaction—for the moment. At the next moment, the value may change. Either party may be mistaken as to the shape that change will take, but a mistake as to value will almost never justify voiding a contract. Each party is considered to have assumed the risk that the value will change or prove to be different from what he or she thought. Without this rule, almost any party who did not receive what he or she considered a fair bargain could argue mistake.

Suppose Daniel Murray, after seeing Beverly Beale's violin, buys it for $250. Neither party knows that it is a Stradivarius built in 1717 and worth thousands of dollars. Although Beverly may claim a mutual mistake has been made, the mistake is not one that warrants contract rescission (cancellation). Both Murray and Beale mistook the value of that particular violin. Therefore, the contract cannot be rescinded.

As pointed out above, if the parties are mistaken as to some fact that is material to their transaction, the transaction may be avoided. This rule applies when the fact affects the value of the subject matter of the parties' deal. For example, an early Michigan case[11] involved two farmers who entered into a contract for the purchase of a cow. Both the owner and the purchaser thought the cow was barren (incapable of breeding and producing calves). Based on this belief, they negotiated a price several hundred dollars less than it would have been had the cow been capable of breeding. Just before delivery, the owner discovered the cow had conceived a calf, and he refused to deliver the much more valuable cow to the purchaser. In a split decision, the court held that "a barren cow is substantially a different creature than a breed[:] one."

Misrepresentation—Fraud

Although **fraud** is a tort, it also affects the genuineness of the innocent party's consent to the contract. Thus, the transaction is not voluntary in the sense of involving "mutual assent." When an innocent party is fraudulently induced to enter into a contract, the contract normally can be avoided, because that party has not *voluntarily* consented to its terms.[12] Normally, the innocent party can either rescind the contract and be restored to the original position or can enforce the contract and

---

11. Sherwood v. Walker, 66 Mich. 568, 33 N.W. 919 (1887).
12. Restatement, Second, Contracts, Sections 163 and 164.

seek damages for any injuries resulting from the fraud.

The word *fraudulent* is used in various senses in the law. Generally, fraudulent misrepresentation refers only to misrepresentation that is consciously false and is intended to mislead another. That is, the perpetrator of the fraudulent misrepresentation must know or believe that the assertion is not true, or must be lacking the confidence that he or she states or implies in the truth of the assertion, or must know that he or she does not have the basis stated or implied for the assertion.[13]

What is at issue is whether the defendant believes that the plaintiff is substantially certain to be misled as a result of the misrepresentation. For example, Jones makes a statement to ABC Credit Rating Company about his financial condition that he knows is untrue. Jones realizes that ABC will publish this information for its subscribers. Marchetti, a subscriber, receives the published information. Relying on that information, Marchetti is induced to make a contract to lend money to Jones. Jones's statement is a fraudulent misrepresentation. The contract is voidable by Marchetti.

Typically, fraud consists of the following elements:

1. A misrepresentation of a material fact has occurred.
2. There is an intent to deceive.
3. The innocent party has justifiably relied on the misrepresentation.
4. The innocent party has been injured.

We will examine each of these elements in turn.

MISREPRESENTATION HAS OCCURRED The first element of proving fraud is to show that misrepresentation of a material fact has occurred. This misrepresentation can be in words or actions. For example, the statement "This sculpture was created by Michelangelo" is an express misrepresentation of fact if the statue was sculpted by another artist. The misrepresentation as to the identity of the artist would certainly be a *material* fact in the formation of a contract.

Misrepresentation can also take place by the conduct of a party. One such form of conduct is concealment. Concealment is basically an act that keeps the other party from learning of a material fact.[14] Suppose Quid contracts to buy a new car from Ray, a dealer in new automobiles. The car was used as a demonstration model for prospective customers to test drive, but Ray turned back the odometer. Quid cannot tell from the odometer reading that the car has been driven nearly five hundred miles, and Ray does not tell Quid the distance the car has actually been driven. The concealment constitutes fraud because of Ray's conduct. Likewise, if a salesperson shows a sample from the top of a large box but does not show the samples at the bottom, a misrepresentation by conduct has occurred if there is a marked difference in quality between the top and bottom merchandise.

Representations of future facts (predictions) or statements of opinion are generally not subject to a claim of fraud. Every person is expected to exercise care and judgment when entering into contracts, and the law will not come to the aid of one who simply makes an unwise bargain. For example, statements like "This land will be worth twice as much next year" or "This car will last for years and years" are statements of opinion, not fact. Contracting parties should recognize them as such and not rely on them. An opinion is usually subject to contrary or conflicting views; a fact is objective and verifiable. A seller of goods, then, is allowed to use *puffery* to sell his or her wares without liability for fraud.

In certain cases, however, opinions may entitle the innocent party to rescission or reformation. These cases almost always involve an "expert" giving a naive purchaser an opinion, and they are decided on equitable grounds. The courts usually hold it to be unfair to allow an expert to take advantage of a novice, especially if the expert knows the novice is relying on the expert's opinion. Thus, an expert's statement of opinion to a layperson is treated as fact.

The following case illustrates how a dance instructor with superior knowledge made statements of opinion concerning plaintiff's dance potential that were treated as misrepresentations of a material fact.

---

13. Restatement, Second, Contracts, Section 162.

14. Restatement, Second, Contracts, Section 160.

BACKGROUND AND FACTS   *The defendant, Arthur Murray, Inc., operated dancing schools throughout the nation through local, franchised operators, one of whom was the defendant. The plaintiff, Audrey E. Vokes, a widow without family, wished to become "an accomplished dancer" and to find "a new interest in life." In 1961 she was invited to attend a "dance party" at J. P. Davenport's "School of Dancing." Vokes went to the school and received elaborate praise from her instructor for her grace, poise, and potential as "an excellent dancer." The instructor sold her eight half-hour dance lessons for $14.50 each, to be utilized within one calendar month.*

Subsequently, over a period of less than sixteen months, Vokes bought a total of fourteen dance courses, which amounted to 2,302 hours of dancing lessons for a total cash outlay of $31,090.45, all at Davenport's school. She filed suit against the school. When the trial court dismissed her complaint, she appealed.

 Case 10.7

VOKES v. ARTHUR MURRAY, INC.

District Court of Appeal of Florida, Second District, 1968.
212 So.2d 906.

PIERCE, Judge.
*   *   *   *

These dance lesson contracts and the monetary consideration therefor of over $31,000 were procured from her by means and methods of Davenport and his associates which went beyond the unsavory, yet legally permissible, perimeter of "sales puffing" and intruded well into the forbidden area of undue influence, the suggestion of falsehood, the suppression of truth, and the free exercise of rational judgment, if what plaintiff alleged in her complaint was true. From the time of her first contact with the dancing school in February, 1961, she was influenced unwittingly by a constant and continuous barrage of flattery, false praise, excessive compliments, and panegyric encomiums [elaborate praise], to such extent that it would be not only inequitable, but unconscionable, for a Court exercising inherent chancery power [powers of equity] to allow such contracts to stand.

She was incessantly subjected to overreaching blandishment and cajolery. She was assured she had "grace and poise"; that she was "rapidly improving and developing in her dancing skill"; that the additional lessons would "make her a beautiful dancer, capable of dancing with the most accomplished dancers"; that she was "rapidly progressing in the development of her dancing skill and gracefulness," etc., etc. She was given "dance aptitude tests" for the ostensible purpose of "determining" the number of remaining hours of instructions needed by her from time to time.

At one point she was sold 545 additional hours of dancing lessons to be entitled to the award of the "Bronze Medal" signifying that she had reached "the Bronze Standard," a supposed designation of dance achievement by students of Arthur Murray, Inc.

Later she was sold an additional 926 hours in order to gain the "Silver Medal," indicating she had reached "the Silver Standard," at a cost of $12,501.35.

At one point, while she still had to her credit about 900 unused hours of instructions, she was induced to purchase an additional 24 hours of lessons to participate in a trip to Miami at her own expense, where she would be "given the opportunity to dance with members of the Miami Studio."

She was induced at another point to purchase an additional 126 hours of lessons in order to be not only eligible for the Miami trip but also to become "a life member of the Arthur Murray Studio," carrying with it certain dubious emoluments [advantages], at a further cost of $1,752.30.

At another point, while she still had over 1,000 unused hours of instruction she was induced to buy 151 additional hours at a cost of $2,049.00 to be eligible for a "Student Trip to Trinidad," at her own expense as she later learned.

Also, when she still had 1100 unused hours to her credit, she was prevailed upon to purchase an additional 347 hours at a cost of $4,235.74, to qualify her to receive a "Gold Medal" for achievement, indicating that she had advanced to "the Gold Standard."

On another occasion, while she still had over 1200 unused hours, she was induced to buy an additional 175 hours of instruction at a cost of $2,472.75 to be eligible "to take a trip to Mexico."

Finally, sandwiched in between other lesser sales promotions, she was influenced to buy an additional 481 hours of instruction at a cost of $6,523.81 in order to "be classified as a Gold Bar Member, the ultimate achievement of the dancing studio."

All the foregoing sales promotions, illustrative of the entire fourteen separate contracts, were procured by defendant Davenport and Arthur Murray, Inc., by false representations to her that she was improving in her dancing ability, that she had excellent potential, that she was responding to instructions in dancing grace, and that they were developing her into a beautiful dancer, whereas in truth and in fact she did not develop in her dancing ability, she had no "dance aptitude," and in fact had difficulty in "hearing the musical beat." The complaint alleged that such representations to her "were in fact false and known by the defendant to be false and contrary to the plaintiff's true ability, the truth of plaintiff's ability being fully known to the defendants, but withheld from the plaintiff for the sole and specific intent to deceive and defraud the plaintiff and to induce her in the purchasing of additional hours of dance lessons." It was averred that the lessons were sold to her "in total disregard to the true physical, rhythm, and mental ability of the plaintiff." In other words, while she first exulted that she was entering the "spring of her life," she finally was awakened to the fact there was "spring" neither in her life nor in her feet.

*   *   *   *

It is true that "generally a misrepresentation, to be actionable, must be one of fact rather than of opinion." But this rule has significant qualifications, applicable here. It does not apply where there is a fiduciary relationship [one of trust] between the parties, or where there has been some artifice or trick employed by the representor, or where the parties do not in general deal at "arm's length" as we understand the phrase, or where the representee does not have equal opportunity to become apprised of the truth or falsity of the fact represented.

A statement of a party having *   *   * superior knowledge may be regarded as a statement of fact although it would be considered as opinion if the parties were dealing on equal terms.

It could be reasonably supposed here that defendants had "superior knowledge" as to whether plaintiff had "dance potential" and as to whether she was noticeably improving in the art of terpsichore. And it would be a reasonable inference from the undenied averments of the complaint that the flowery eulogiums heaped upon her by defendants as a prelude to her contracting for 1944 additional hours of instruction in order to attain the rank of the Bronze Standard, thence to the bracket of the Silver Standard, thence to the class of the Gold Bar Standard, and finally to the crowning plateau of a Life Member of the Studio, proceeded as much or more from the urge to "ring the cash register" as from any honest or realistic appraisal of her dancing prowess or a factual representation of her progress.

*   *   *   *

*   *   * "[W]hat is plainly injurious to good faith ought to be considered as a fraud sufficient to impeach a contract," and *   *   * an improvident agreement may be avoided "because of surprise, or mistake, *want of freedom, undue influence, the suggestion of falsehood, or the suppression of truth*." [Emphasis added.]

DECISION AND REMEDY   *Vokes's complaint, which had originally been dismissed from the trial court, was reinstated, and the case was returned to the trial court to allow Vokes to prove her case.*

Fraud is an ambiguous concept in law. It includes various degrees of misrepresentation, which can be separated into three tort categories: (1) intentional behavior, (2) negligent behavior, and (3) strict liability for certain behavior. In all cases involving the tort of misrepresentation and the contract defense of fraud, the defendant must misrepresent a fact or facts, and the plaintiff must reasonably believe the misrepresentation to be true and must rely on it with resulting damages.

COMMENTS

Misrepresentation of Law   Misrepresentation of law does not *ordinarily* entitle the party to relief from a contract. For example, Sarah has a parcel of property that she is trying to sell to Brad. Sarah knows that a local ordinance prohibits building anything on the property higher than three stories. Nonetheless, she tells Brad, "You can build a condominium fifty stories high if you want to." Brad buys the land and later discovers that Sarah's statement is false. Normally, Brad cannot avoid the contract because at common law people are assumed to know state and local law where they reside. Additionally, a layperson should not rely upon a statement made by a nonlawyer about a point of law.

Exceptions to this rule occur when the misrepresenting party is in a profession that is known

to require greater knowledge of the law than the average citizen possesses. The courts are recognizing an increasing number of such professions. For example, the courts recognize that real estate brokers are expected by their clients to know the law governing real estate sales, land use, and so on. If Sarah, in the preceding example, were a lawyer or a real estate broker, her misrepresentation of the area's zoning status would probably constitute fraud.[15]

The following case demonstrates an attempt by one party to bring an action based on deceit against a hotel owner for his misrepresentation of state law.

---

15. Restatement, Second, Contracts, Section 170.

BACKGROUND AND FACTS   *Two, Inc., contacted Gilmore regarding an opportunity to operate a discotheque in the Jerome Hotel, a hotel in Aspen, Colorado, owned by Gilmore. Gilmore told Two, Inc., that if it agreed to a "management agreement," it could by law share in his liquor license. Gilmore's opinion of the law on this matter had been previously questioned by others. A short time thereafter Gilmore discovered that the agreement was illegal, as it did not conform with state liquor codes. Gilmore contacted Two, Inc., to negotiate a new agreement, but an impasse occurred over the liquor license. Gilmore indicated he would notify the liquor distributors that Two, Inc., did not have a license to buy or sell liquor. Two, Inc., abandoned the premises and filed a lawsuit seeking damages on grounds of deceit based on fraud. The trial court entered a judgment for Gilmore, and Two, Inc., appealed.*

Case 10.8
TWO, INC. v. GILMORE
Colorado Court of Appeals, 1984.
679 P.2d 116.

PIERCE, Judge.
✷   ✷   ✷   ✷

The trial court concluded, as a matter of law, that Gilmore's representation to Two that a management agreement was tantamount to a lease and would allow for the sharing of liquor license privileges was a representation of law and, therefore, not actionable. We agree.

A representation of law is only an expression of opinion and is impotent to void a contract or support an action for damages. ✷   ✷   ✷ A representation of what the law will or will not permit to be done is one upon which the party to whom it is made has no right to rely. The truth or falsehood of such a representation can be tested by ordinary vigilance and attention. * * * Therefore the fact that Gilmore's opinion as to the state of the law had previously been questioned by others is no bar to his defense against this deceit claim. * * *

Here, Gilmore's representation to Two constitutes an individual's belief and opinion concerning statutes controlling the dispensation, purchase, and sale of liquor. Therefore, under the facts of this case, Two cannot obtain remedial relief. * * *

DECISION AND REMEDY   *The court affirmed the ruling of the trial court and denied Two, Inc., any damages.*

Silence   Ordinarily, neither party to a contract has a duty to come forward and disclose facts. Therefore, a contract cannot be set aside because certain pertinent information is not volunteered.

For example, suppose you have an accident that requires extensive body work on one side of your car. After the repair, the car's appearance and operation are the same as they were before the accident. One year later you decide to sell your car. Do you have a duty to volunteer the information about the accident to the seller? The answer is no. In this case, silence does not constitute misrepresentation. On the other hand, if the purchaser asks you if the car has had extensive body work and you lie, you have committed a fraudulent misrepresentation.

Some exceptions to this rule exist. If a *serious* defect or *serious* potential problem is known to the seller but cannot reasonably be suspected by the buyer, the seller may have a duty to speak. Expanding the example just given, suppose your car occasionally vibrates dangerously because of the earlier accident. In this case, you have a duty to speak. Similarly, if the foundation of a factory is cracked, creating a potential for serious water damage, the seller must reveal this fact. Likewise, when a city fails to disclose to bidders subsoil conditions that will cause great expense in constructing a sewer, the city is guilty of fraud.[16]

Failure to disclose important facts also constitutes fraud if the parties have a relationship of trust and confidence, called a **fiduciary relationship.** In such a relationship, if one party knows any facts that materially affect the other's interests, they must be disclosed. An attorney, for example, has a duty to disclose material facts to a client. Other such relationships include partners in a partnership, directors of corporations and shareholders, and guardians and wards.[17]

A seller's silence, coupled with active concealment, constitutes misrepresentation. In the Ray-Quid example discussed above, for example, Ray not only failed to disclose the true mileage to Quid but concealed the true mileage by turning back the odometer. Disclosing some, but not all, of the facts can be equally deceitful. Such would be the case if Ray had mentioned that the car actually had "a few more miles on it" than shown by the odometer—which registered three miles. In addition, if circumstances change so that what once was true is now false, the party knowing of the change has a duty to inform the other.

Statutes provide other exceptions to the general rule of nondisclosure. The Truth-in-Lending Act, for example, requires disclosure of certain facts (see Chapter 46). Statutes may even specify the type size to be used in the document providing the information.

KNOWLEDGE OF THE FALSE REPRESENTATION —INTENT TO DECEIVE   The second element of fraud is knowledge on the part of the misrepresenting party that facts have been falsely represented. This element, normally called **scienter,** or "guilty knowledge," signifies that there was an *intent to deceive.* Proof of intent is not necessary if the circumstances surrounding a transaction are such that one can *infer* the intent. The act of misrepresentation of fact combined with knowledge of the fact's falsity normally constitutes an intent to deceive. Statements made with reckless disregard for the truth may satisfy the intent requirement.

---

16. City of Salinas v. Souza & McCue Constr. Co., 66 Cal.2d 217, 424 P.2d 921, 57 Cal.Rptr. 337 (1967). Normally, the seller must disclose only "latent" defects—that is, ones that would not readily be discovered even by an expert. Thus, termites in a house would not be a latent defect, since an expert could readily discover their presence.

17. Restatement, Second, Contracts, Sections 161 and 173.

Suppose that Roper has owned a 1986 Oldsmobile for two years and suddenly, for no apparent reason, quits driving it. Roper then advertises the automobile for sale. Chipper asks Roper how the engine runs, and Roper says, "This Olds runs like a Swiss watch; there is nothing wrong with it." So Chipper buys the Olds, only to discover the next day that there is a crack in the engine block requiring replacement of the entire engine. Here a court can *infer* that Roper knew that the engine block was cracked (at least in the absence of another explanation from Roper), since he suddenly quit driving the two-year-old car and put it up for sale.

RELIANCE ON THE MISREPRESENTATION   The third element of fraud is *justifiable reliance* on the misrepresentation of fact. The deceived party must have justifiable reason for relying on the misrepresentation, and the misrepresentation must be an important factor in inducing the party to enter into the contract, though it need not be the sole factor.

Reliance is not justified if the innocent party knows the true facts or relies on obviously extravagant statements. Suppose a used-car dealer tells you, "This old Cadillac will get fifty miles to the gallon." You would not normally be justified in relying on the statement. Or suppose Phelps, a bank director, induces Scott, a co-director, to sign a guarantee that the bank's assets will satisfy its liabilities, stating, "We have plenty of assets to satisfy our creditors." If Scott knows the true facts, he will not be justified in relying on Phelps's statement. If, however, Scott does not know the true facts *and has no way of finding them out*, he will be justified in relying on the statement. The same rule applies to defects in property sold. If the defects are obvious, the buyer cannot justifiably rely on the seller's representations. If the defects are hidden or latent (that is, not apparent on the surface), the buyer is justified in relying on the seller's statements.

INJURY TO THE INNOCENT PARTY   The final element of fraud is injury to the innocent party. The courts are divided on this issue. Some do not require a showing of injury when the action is to *rescind or cancel* the contract. Since rescission returns the parties to the position they were in before they made the contract, showing injury to the innocent party has been held to be unnecessary.[18]

In an action to recover *damages* caused by the fraud, proof of an injury is universally required. The measure of damages is ordinarily equal to what the value of the property would have been if it had been delivered as represented, less what it is actually worth. In effect, this gives the innocent (non-breaching) party the *benefit of the bargain* rather than reestablishing the party's position prior to the contract. In actions based on fraud, courts often award **exemplary,** or **punitive, damages,** which are defined as damages awarded to a plaintiff over and above the proved, actual compensation for the loss. Punitive damages are based on the public policy consideration of *punishing* the defendant or setting an example for similar wrongdoers.

In the following case, Hazel Gales applied for auto insurance, stating falsely that she had not been in an auto accident in the past five years and had not received a ticket for a moving violation in the past three years. The defendant, Plains Insurance Co., claimed that such false representations made her policy void from the beginning (void *ab initio*). The company contended that it would not have sold the policy at the specified rate and perhaps would not have sold it at all if Gales had provided true information about her driving record. Thus, the insurance company contended that it had not engaged in a genuine assent (that is, there was no consent).

18. For example, Kaufman v. Jaffee, 244 App.Div. 344, 279 N.Y.S. 392 (1935).

BACKGROUND AND FACTS   *The plaintiff in this action, D. C. Miller, sued the insurance company of the owner and driver of the automobile in which his wife was killed. The owner and operator of the automobile, Hazel Gales, also perished in the crash. She was insured by Plains Insurance Company, the defendant. The policy provided, among other things, $500 medical expense coverage and up to $10,000 uninsured motorists coverage. This coverage provides*

 Case 10.9

MILLER v. PLAINS INS. CO.

Springfield Court of Appeals, Missouri 1966.
409 S.W.2d 770.

for payment to the insured in case the insured is involved in an accident in which someone else is at fault and does not have any insurance.

At the trial, Miller was awarded both $500 in medical expenses and $10,000 under the uninsured motorists provision. On appeal, the defendant argued that had it known certain representations were untrue, it would not have undertaken the risk in insuring Gales, who had a record of moving traffic violations and, in particular, of hazardous driving, for which she had been cited in another state. She did not disclose these facts when applying for the policy.

TITUS, Judge.
*   *   *   *

What is a material misrepresentation? A misrepresentation that would likely affect the conduct of a reasonable man in respect to his transaction with another is material. [Emphasis added.] Materiality, however, is not determined by the actual influence the representation exerts, but rather by the possibility of its so doing. A representation made to an insurer that is material to its determination as to what premium to fix or to whether it will accept the risk, relates to a fact actually material to the risk which the insurer is asked to assume. The word "risk" does not relate to an actual increase in danger but to a danger determined by the insurer's classification of the various circumstances affecting rates and insurability. That the fact misrepresented has no actual subsequent relation to the manner in which the event insured against occurred, does not make it any the less material to the risk. Thus, whether a misrepresentation is material in an application for an automobile insurance policy, is determined by whether the fact, if stated truthfully, might reasonably have influenced the insurance company to accept or reject the risk or to have charged a different premium, and not whether the insurer was actually influenced.
*   *   *   *

It is a well-known fact insurance companies rely on expense, loss, and other statistical data to measure differences among risks and thus ascertain rates to be charged for individual risks in accordance with standards for measuring variations in hazards. This is recognized and, to some extent, controlled by our statutes. Questions as to traffic violations of prospective insureds and as to previous accidents in which they have been involved are legitimate fields of research for insurance companies, for these are not only rate-determining facts but may also determine if the risk will even be insured. In consideration of the authorities previously cited, *   *   * we are of the opinion the misrepresentations involved in this case might reasonably be expected to have influenced the insurance company to have accepted or rejected Mrs. Gales as an insured or to have charged her a different premium for issuing her a policy. As the only evidence in this case is that if defendant had known the truth it would have declined the risk, we are drawn to the conclusion the misrepresentations were material and should permit defendant to avoid its liability under the policy.

DECISION AND REMEDY   *The trial court's ruling was reversed. The defendant, Plains Life Insurance Company, did not have to pay the $10,000 uninsured motorists claim or the $500 medical expense coverage because of the material misrepresentation of fact made by Hazel Gales when she filled out the application on which her insurance policy was issued. In essence, the court decided there was no true assent by the insurance company to insure Gales under that premium for that policy. No insurance contract ever came into existence.*

INNOCENT MISREPRESENTATION   If a person makes a statement that he or she believes to be true but that actually misrepresents material facts, the person is guilty only of an **innocent misrepresentation,** not of fraud. If an innocent misrepresentation occurs, the aggrieved party can rescind the contract but usually cannot seek damages. Basically, an innocent misrepresentation, in the contract sense, is viewed as a mistake rather than as a fraud.

NEGLIGENT MISREPRESENTATION Sometimes a party will make a misrepresentation through carelessness believing the statement is true. This misrepresentation is negligent, if he or she fails to exercise reasonable care in uncovering or disclosing the facts or does not use the skill and competence that his or her business or profession requires. For example: A real estate broker assures Sneed that a particular house is entirely insulated, even though the broker knows only that the attic is insulated. In virtually all states, such **negligent misrepresentation** is equal to *scienter*, or to knowingly making a misrepresentation. In other words, culpable ignorance of the truth supplies the intention to mislead, even if the defendant can claim, "I didn't know."

Undue Influence

Undue influence arises from special kinds of relationships in which one party can greatly influence another party, thus overcoming that party's free will. Minors and elderly people are often under the influence of guardians. If the guardian induces a young or elderly ward to enter into a contract that benefits the guardian, undue influence may have been exerted. Undue influence can arise from a number of fiduciary relationships: attorney-client, doctor-patient, guardian-ward, parent-child, husband-wife, or trustee-beneficiary. The essential feature of undue influence is that the party being taken advantage of does not, in reality, exercise free will in entering into a contract. A contract entered into under excessive or undue influence lacks genuine assent and is therefore voidable.[19]

To determine whether undue influence has been exerted, a court must ask: To what extent was the transaction induced by domination of the mind or emotions of the person in question? It follows, then, that the mental state of the person in question will often show to what extent the persuasion from the outside influence was "unfair."

When a contract enriches a party at the expense of another who is in a relationship of trust and confidence or one of dominance with the enriched party, the court will often *presume* that the contract was made under undue influence. For example, if a ward challenges a contract made by his or her guardian, the presumption will normally be that the guardian has taken advantage of the ward. To rebut this presumption successfully, the guardian has to show that *full disclosure* was made to the ward, that consideration was adequate, and that the ward received independent and competent advice before completing the transaction.

In cases where the relationship is one of trust and confidence, such as between an attorney and a client, the dominant party (the attorney) is held to extreme or utmost good faith in dealing with the subservient party. Suppose a long-time attorney for an elderly man induces him to sign a contract for the sale of some of his assets to a friend of the attorney at below-market prices. The contract is probably voidable. The attorney has not upheld good faith in dealing with the man (unless this presumption can be rebutted).

Duress

Undue influence involves conduct of a *persuasive* nature; **duress** involves conduct of a *coercive* nature. That is, assent to the terms of a contract is not genuine if one of the parties is *forced* into agreement. Recognizing this, the courts allow that party to rescind the contract. Forcing a party to enter into a contract under the fear of threats is legally defined as *duress*.[20] For example, if Piranha Loan Co. threatens to harm you or your family unless you sign a promissory note for the money that you owe, Piranha is guilty of duress. In addition, threatening blackmail or extortion to induce consent to a contract constitutes duress. Duress is both a defense to the enforcement of a contract and a ground for rescission or cancellation. Therefore, the party upon whom the duress is exerted can choose to carry out the contract or to avoid the entire transaction. (This is true in most cases in which assent is not real.)

Generally, the threatened act must be wrongful or illegal. Threatening to exercise a legal right is not ordinarily illegal and usually does not constitute duress. Suppose that Donovan injures Jaworski in an auto accident. The police are not

---

19. Restatement, Second, Contracts, Section 177.

20. Restatement, Second, Contracts, Sections 174 and 175.

called. Donovan has no automobile insurance, but she has substantial assets. Jaworski is willing to settle the potential claim out of court for $3,000. Donovan refuses. After much arguing, Jaworski loses her patience and says, "If you don't pay me $3,000 right now, I'm going to sue you for $35,000." Donovan is frightened and gives Jaworski a check for $3,000. Later in the day, she stops payment on the check. Jaworski comes back to sue her for the $3,000. Donovan argues that she was the victim of duress. The threat of a civil suit is normally not duress, however.

Being in need is generally not a circumstance that will lead to a finding of duress, even when one party exacts a very high price for whatever it is the other party needs. If the party exacting the price also creates the need, however, duress may be found. For example, the Internal Revenue Service assessed a large tax and penalty against Sam Thompson. Thompson retained Earl Eyman, an attorney, to resist the assessment. The last day before the deadline for filing a reply with the Internal Revenue Service, Eyman declined to represent Thompson unless he signed a very high contingency fee agreement for his services. The agreement was unenforceable.[21] Although Eyman had threatened only to withdraw his services, something that he was legally entitled to do, he was responsible for delaying the withdrawal until the last day. Since it would have been impossible at that late date to obtain adequate representation elsewhere, Thompson was forced into either signing the contract or losing his right to challenge the IRS assessment.

In the following case, the court examines whether the consent obtained in an agreement was the result of duress.

---

21. Thompson Crane & Trucking Co. v. Eyman, 123 Cal.App.2d 904, 267 P.2d 1043 (1954).

Case 10.10
GARSHMAN v. UNIVERSAL RESOURCES HOLDING, INC.
United States District Court for the District of New Jersey, 1986.
641 F.Supp. 1359.

BACKGROUND AND FACTS *In 1981, Columbia Gas Transmission (Transmission) entered into a five-year contract with Universal Resources Holdings under which Transmission leased to Universal a tract of land with existing natural gas reserves. The lease provided that Universal was obligated to deliver to Transmission all gas extracted from the land. Transmission was to take or pay for at least 75 percent of Universal's gas production from this land at a set price. There was also a provision that allowed Transmission to temporarily suspend its performance in any given year. Such "take or pay" contracts are common in the gas industry.*

In the early 1980s, the price of gas decreased dramatically, and paying the price set by the contract would create huge losses for Transmission. Transmission sought to renegotiate the contract with Universal in 1983 and threatened not to renew the lease and to exercise its right to suspend performance temporarily unless Universal agreed to renegotiate the lease at a lower price. Because of the economic impact Universal would suffer from a temporary suspension, it agreed to lower the price. In 1985, Daniel Garshman, who funded natural gas exploration, sued several gas producers and pipeline companies, including Universal Resources Holding and Columbia Gas Transmission, for unfair competition; but this suit was dismissed. Universal, however, cross-claimed to enforce the original contract with Transmission claiming that it had been forced to enter into a modified contract under duress. Transmission moved to dismiss the claim.

BROTMAN, District Judge.
*   *   *   *

Universal contends *   *   * that Transmission's actions, as enumerated in the crossclaim, constitute a breach of its contracts with Universal. Specifically, Universal alleges that Transmission's renegotiation efforts contravened its contractual obligation to pay the maximum lawful price for natural gas under the contracts and to take the volume of gas required by such contracts.

Universal's breach of contract claim is rooted in Transmission's alleged "coercion and duress." According to the crossclaim, Transmission breached its existing contracts by wielding its economic power arbitrarily and unfairly. In addition, Universal claims that the renegotiated contract it eventually signed was obtained by coercion and is therefore voidable and subject to recission.

* * * Under New York law, a claim of duress has four elements: (1) a threat; (2) unlawfully made; (3) that caused involuntary acceptance; (4) because the circumstances permitted no alternative. * * *

To establish that contract acceptance was involuntary because the circumstances permitted no alternative, a party must show that "a breach of contract action would have been impossible when the threat was made." * * *

Universal nowhere alleges that a breach of contract action would have been impossible or inadequate when Transmission "extorted" price concessions. Transmission first approached Universal about renegotiating their contracts in early 1983. Discussions continued until August 1984, when Universal agreed to renegotiate. Because Universal failed to pursue a legal remedy for alleged breach of contract then, its present claim for duress is inadequate as a matter of law.

A "threat" is a necessary element of duress, and an announced intention to exercise a legal right cannot constitute a threat. Transmission contends that by announcing that it would curtail its purchases and take other steps to reduce its "take" from Universal, it was merely exercising its contractual rights.

The original "take or pay" contract contained several provisions limiting Transmission's actual obligation to purchase and take gas during any given year. Section 6.1 provides that although Transmission promises to take all the gas the seller has available "insofar as it can consistently do so having regard for its other related interests . . ."

[I]t is further expressly understood and agreed that Buyer may restrict the flow or discontinue the taking of the gas temporarily, when and for such length of time as in its judgment it is deemed expedient so to do, Buyer's judgment being based upon consideration of market demand, its then existing pipeline facilities, the line pressure it deems necessary to maintain, and the competitive and other conditions in the various fields in which it is purchasing or producing gas.

In addition, Section 6.4 provides that "[i]t is recognized that Buyer may not be able to take and need not take gas from seller hereunder . . . during any definite period," and Section 6.5 provides that so long as the volume of gas specified in the take or pay clause is taken or paid for, "all gas delivered hereunder may be taken in whatever manner and at such times as will best suit the convenience of the Buyer."
* * * *

Even if Transmission did threaten to reduce the amount of gas it took from Universal, Transmission did not exceed its contractual authority. * * * The "threats" alleged by Universal do not support a claim of duress as a matter of law.

The district court dismissed Universal's claim of economic duress against Transmission.　　　　　**DECISION AND REMEDY**

Adhesion Contracts and Unconscionability

Modern courts are beginning to strike down terms dictated by a party with overwhelming bargaining power. **Adhesion contracts** arise in situations in which the signer must agree to certain dictated terms or go without the commodity or service in question. An adhesion contract is written *exclusively* by one party (the dominant party) and presented to the other party (the adhering party) with no opportunity to negotiate. Adhesion contracts usually contain copious amounts of fine print disclaiming the maker's liability for everything imaginable. Standard lease forms are often called adhesion contracts. Many automobile retailers have used contracts containing several pages of fine print when selling a car. In the past, nearly every company excluded liability for personal injuries suffered as a result of using the product. The average consumer buying a car was in no position to bargain for personal injury coverage. The consumer could either go without an automobile or buy the auto, risking personal injury for which he or she could not hold the auto manufacturer liable.

Standard form contracts are used by a variety of businesses and include life insurance policies, residential leases, loan agreements, and employment agency contracts. In order to avoid enforcement of the contract or of a particular clause, the aggrieved party must show substantially unequal bargaining positions and show that enforcement would be manifestly unfair or oppressive. If the required showing is made, the contract or particular term is deemed *unconscionable* and not enforced. Technically, unconscionability under the

UCC applies only to contracts for the sale of goods.[22] Many courts, however, have broadened the concept and applied it in other situations.

Although unconscionability will be discussed in the next chapter, it is important to note here that the great degree of discretion permitted a court to invalidate or strike down a contract or clause as being unconscionable has met with resistance. As a result, some states have not adopted Section 2-302 of the UCC. In those states, the legislature and the courts prefer to rely on traditional notions of fraud, undue influence, and duress. In one respect, this gives certainty to contractual relationships, since parties know they will be held to the exact terms of their contracts. But on the other hand, public policy does dictate that there be some limit on the power of individuals and businesses to dictate the terms of a contract.

---

22. See UCC 2-302.

CONCEPT SUMMARY: Genuineness of Assent

PROBLEMS OF ASSENT	RULES
Mistakes 1. Bilateral	If both parties' mistake relates to a material fact, such as identity, either party can avoid the contract. If the mistake goes to value or quality, either party can enforce the contract.
2. Unilateral	Generally, the mistaken party is bound by the contract, *unless* (1) the other party knows or should have known of the mistake or (2) in some states, the mistake is an inadvertent mathematical error—in addition, subtraction, etc.—committed without gross negligence.
Misrepresentation 1. Fraud	Four elements are necessary to establish fraud: 1. A misrepresentation of a material fact has occurred. 2. There is intent to deceive. 3. The innocent party has justifiably relied on the misrepresentation. 4. For damages, the innocent party has been injured. Usually, the innocent party can enforce or avoid the contract.
2. Other	Intent to deceive need not be shown. Usually, the innocent party can rescind the contract but cannot seek damages. A misrepresentation of law generally does not permit a person to avoid the contract.
Influence/Coercion 1. Undue influence	Arises from special relationships, such as fiduciary relationships, in which one party's free will has been overcome by the undue influence exerted by the other party. Usually, the contract is voidable.

CONCEPT SUMMARY: Genuineness of Assent (Continued)	
PROBLEMS OF ASSENT	**RULES**
2. Duress	Defined as forcing a party to enter into a contract under the fear of a threat, for example, the threat of violence or economic pressure. The party forced to enter the contract can rescind the contract.
Unconscionability	Concerned with one-sided bargains in which one party has substantially superior bargaining power and can dictate the terms. Typically occurs in: 1. Standardized contract form's fine print provision purporting to shift a risk normally borne by one party to the other (for example, a liability disclaimer). 2. "Take it or leave it" adhesion contracts by which the buyer cannot procure goods or services from a seller without agreeing to the seller's dictated terms (that is, the buyer has no choice).

QUESTIONS AND CASE PROBLEMS

1. Seling, a minor, sold her bicycle to Adam, an adult, for $100. Adam took possession and paid Seling. Two months later, Adam sold the bicycle to Bonnet, a bona fide purchaser, for value. Seling's parents became upset when they learned of her sale. Seling, who has not yet reached the age of majority, seeks to disaffirm the contract with Adam and recover the bicycle from Bonnet. Discuss whether Seling can recover the bicycle from Bonnet, and discuss Adam's liability to Seling.

2. Treat is a seventeen-year-old minor who has just graduated from high school. She is attending a university 200 miles from home and has contracted to rent an apartment near the university for one year at $250 per month. She is working at a convenience store to earn enough money to be self-supporting. She moves into the apartment and has paid four months' rent when a dispute arises between her and the landlord. Treat, still a minor, moves out and returns the key to the landlord. The landlord wants to hold Treat liable for the balance of the lease, $2,000. Discuss fully Treat's liability on the lease.

3. John is an elderly man who lives with his nephew, Samuel. John is totally dependent on Samuel's support. Samuel tells John that unless he transfers a tract of land he owns to Samuel for a price 15 percent below market value, Samuel will no longer support and take care of him. John enters into the contract. Discuss fully whether John can set aside this contract.

4. Martin owns a forty-room motel on Highway 100. Tanner is interested in purchasing the motel. During the course of negotiations, Martin tells Tanner that the motel netted $30,000 last year and that it will net at least $45,000 next year. The motel books, which Martin turns over to Tanner before the purchase, clearly show that Martin's motel netted only $15,000 last year. Also, Martin fails to tell Tanner that a bypass to Highway 100 is being planned that will redirect most traffic away from the front of the motel. Tanner purchases the motel. During the first year under Tanner's operation, the motel nets only $18,000. It is at this time that Tanner learns of the previous low profitability of the motel and the planned bypass. Tanner wants his money back from Martin. Discuss fully Tanner's probable success in getting his money back.

5. Discuss which of the following contracts are fully enforceable:

(a) Simmons finds a stone in his pasture that he believes to be quartz. Jenson, who also believes that the stone is quartz, contracts to purchase it for $10. Just before delivery, the stone is discovered to be a diamond worth $1,000.

(b) Jacoby's barn is burned to the ground. He accuses Goldman's son of arson and threatens to bring criminal action unless Goldman agrees to pay him $5,000. Goldman agrees to pay.

(c) Kober, a *new* salesperson, innocently tells Larry that a lawn mower he is selling has a five-year manufacturer's warranty. Larry contracts to purchase the lawn mower in reliance on that information. Larry and Kober are transacting business for the first time. At the time of delivery, it is discovered that the manufacturer only warrants the lawn mower for one year.

6. Michael LaFleur was injured when a forklift blade fell on his right foot while he was on the job at C. C. Pierce, Inc. The doctor for the company's insurance carrier told LaFleur that the injury was not serious and that x-rays showed no fracture or complication. In reliance on the doctor's statements, LaFleur settled his insurance claim

with C. C. Pierce, Inc., for $4,000 and signed a release that read, "This is a complete and final settlement of my claim and I will not be able to reopen my claim or seek further benefits because of this injury." The agreement covered "all injuries received by Michael LaFleur on or about January 21 and February 15, 1975." LaFleur later discovered that he suffered from Buerger's disease, a rare arterial occlusive disease. LaFleur had the disease before the accident, but the injury aggravated the condition and made it much worse. Under tort law, aggravating a preexisting condition is actionable for the full amount of the damages resulting. Discuss whether LaFleur can rescind his contract with C. C. Pierce because of a mutual mistake. [LaFleur v. C. C. Pierce Co., Inc., 398 Mass. 254, 496 N.E.2d 827 (1986)]

7. In 1982, William Schmalz was hired by the Hardy Salt Company under an employment contract that stated that he was entitled to six months' severance pay in the event that he was laid off. The company did not have to pay in the event of any voluntary separation or involuntary termination for other reasons, such as for poor performance or for cause. In mid-1983, Schmalz was asked to resign after having an affair with the chairman's executive secretary. Schmalz was told that if he did not resign he would be fired but that if he did resign the company would keep him on the payroll for another six weeks. Schmalz resigned and signed an agreement releasing Hardy Salt from any liability for breach of the employment contract. Schmalz claimed that he signed the release under duress and sued Hardy Salt for the six months' severance pay under his employment contract. Discuss whether Schmalz's claim for duress should succeed. [Schmalz v. Hardy Salt Company, 739 S.W.2d 765 (Mo.App.1987)]

8. Smith purchased a car on credit from Bobby Floars Toyota, Inc., a month before his eighteenth birthday. Smith made regular monthly payments for eleven months but then returned the car to the dealer and made no further payments on it. The dealer sold the car and sued Smith to recover the difference between the amount obtained from the sale of the car and the money Smith still owed to the dealer. Smith refused to pay on the ground that he had been a minor at the time of purchase and had disaffirmed the contract after he had reached the age of majority. Will the car dealer succeed in its claim that the ten monthly payments made after Smith turned eighteen constituted a ratification of the purchase contract? [Bobby Floars Toyota, Inc. v. Smith, 48 N.C.App. 580, 269 S.E.2d 320 (1980)]

9. Kevin Green, a sixteen-year-old minor, entered into a sales agreement to purchase a Camaro from Star Chevrolet for $4,642.50. The title for the car was drawn up in Kevin's name, and the money came from Kevin's personal bank account. The question of Kevin's age was not raised by him or the car dealership. He used the car daily to drive six miles to school and back and to drive about one mile to his place of part-time work. Kevin brought the car back several times for repairs, and he later discovered that the engine was not the size and power that it was supposed to be. Finally, when the main head gasket blew, Kevin's at-

torney informed Star Chevrolet that Kevin was disaffirming the contract. Kevin repaired the gasket and continued to use the car until an accident destroyed the car more than a year after the purchase. He then returned the Camaro. Discuss whether Kevin can recover the full amount of the car's sales price from Star Chevrolet. [Star Chevrolet Co. v. Green by Green, 473 So.2d 157 (Miss. 1985)]

10. William and Lilly Adams obtained a divorce in 1985 and began the process of dividing their property. They inventoried their worldly possessions and decided that certain property would go to Mrs. Adams and the remainder, including the debts on the community property, would remain with Mr. Adams. Mrs. Adams testified that Mr. Adams consistently told her that she must take the property as offered and agree not to seek alimony. She stated that Mr. Adams threatened to declare bankruptcy and force Mrs. Adams to accept the responsibility for her share of the community debts if she did not agree. Mrs. Adams also said that Mr. Adams frequently cursed her but did not in any way threaten physical harm. Mrs. Adams received a copy of the proposed community property settlement and stated that she basically understood it. She casually spoke to two different attorneys about the settlement contract, but both said that they would need time to investigate before giving advice. Mrs. Adams signed anyway. She later claimed that she had done so under duress and because of fraudulent misrepresentation. Discuss whether Mrs. Adams can rescind the settlement contract on these bases. [Adams v. Adams, 503 So.2d 1052 (La.App.2 Cir. 1987)]

11. Allen Apfelblat began suffering from mental illness in the summer of 1983. In November of that same year, he executed three notes to Michigan National Bank in order to purchase three automobiles. On January 6, 1984, Apfelblat was involuntarily committed to a psychiatric hospital, where he was successfully treated. Upon Apfelblat's release, the bank threatened to pursue legal recourse if Apfelblat did not pay on the notes. In response, Apfelblat agreed, at the insistence of the bank, to execute new notes to cover the accrued debts and to make several interest payments that were in arrears. Apfelblat later filed an action to discharge the notes due because of lack of capacity at the time the original notes were executed. Apfelblat also claimed that he did not intend to legally ratify the contract or to accept liability from a voidable contract when he did not have to. Discuss whether Apfelblat's contract is enforceable by Michigan National Bank. [Apfelblat v. National Bank of Wyandotte-Taylor, 158 Mich.App. 258, 404 N.W.2d 725 (1987)]

12. In 1973, James Halbman, Jr., a minor, entered into an agreement to buy a 1968 Oldsmobile from Michael Lemke for $1,250. He paid the $1,000 downpayment and took possession of the automobile immediately. After experiencing problems with the car, Halbman took it into a garage for repairs. When he failed to pay the garage bill of $637, the garage removed the vehicle's engine and transmission. Halbman subsequently disaffirmed the sale contract with Lemke and returned the title to the Oldsmobile. Halbman also successfully sued to obtain the return of the money that he had paid to Lemke. Can Lemke countersue for restitution on the automobile's decline in value because of the removed auto parts? [Halbman v. Lemke, 99 Wis.2d 241, 298 N.W.2d 562 (1980)]

13. Sheehan sold a 1965 Buick Riviera to Rose, a minor, for $5,176. While still a minor, Rose elected to disaffirm the purchase and notified Sheehan of his intention, offering to return the vehicle for a full refund. Sheehan refused, claiming that Rose appeared to be adult and acted and negotiated like an adult. In addition, Sheehan claimed that the vehicle was a necessary item for Rose because it was used to carry on his school, business, and social activities. Discuss whether Rose can disaffirm the sale and if so whether Sheehan is entitled to an offsetting amount for depreciation in the value. [Rose v. Sheehan Buick, Inc., 204 So.2d 903 (Fla.App. 1967)]

14. Carol Ann White, nineteen (a minor), went to Dr. Demetrios Cidis and asked him to furnish her with contact lenses. They agreed on a price of $225, and Carol gave Cidis her personal check for $100. The doctor examined Carol on Thursday evening, ordered the lenses on Friday, and the doctor received them on Saturday. The cost to the doctor for the lenses was $110. On Monday, at the insistence of her father, Carol called and cancelled the contract and stopped payment on the check. At the time, Carol lived at home, had a full-time job, and paid her parents a sum each month for room and board. The lenses could be used by no one but Carol and thus had no market value. Dr. Cidis brought suit, claiming that the lenses were a necessity. Carol claims her minority as a defense to any liability. Discuss whether contact lenses are necessaries. [Cidis v. White, 71 Misc.2d 481, 336 N.Y.S.2d 362 (1972)]

15. Lawrence Gerard and Firejet American contracted to be the exclusive distributorship in North, Central, and South America, plus Germany and Japan, for the sale of Firejet extinguishers. The extinguishers were invented by Almouli and manufactured by Alchem in Israel. The extinguishers were small-sized, portable aerosol extinguishers that were easy to use. The distributorship agreed to purchase a substantial quantity. Although the Firejet extinguisher did not have Underwriters Laboratories (UL) approval, it had passed all but one UL test. It was felt that UL approval, necessary for sales in the United States, would be given within six to seven months. It was known that UL approval usually requires a minimum of three years and can require up to fifteen years. When delivery was later tendered by Alchem, the distributorship refused delivery because of the lack of UL approval. Almouli and Alchem filed suit, claiming that the distributorship was in breach of its exclusive distributorship agreement for failure to make good faith efforts to sell the product and that the length of time for UL approval was a mutual mistake of fact. Discuss whether there was a mutual mistake

of fact as to the time period for UL approval. [Gerard v. Almouli, 746 F.2d 936 (2d Cir. 1984)]

16. Division West Chinchilla Ranch made numerous TV advertisements that induced listeners to go into the business of raising chinchillas. The advertisements stated that, for a payment of $2,150 or more, Division would send one male and six female chinchillas and—for an additional sum—cages, feed, and supplies. Division's representations were that "chinchilla ranching can be done in the basement, [and] spare rooms, . . . with minor modifications. . . ," and that chinchillas were "odorless and practically noiseless" and "a profitable pastime that can explode into a FIVE FIGURE INCOME. . . ." All statements would lead one to believe that no special skill was needed in the raising of chinchillas. Based on these representations, Adolph Fischer and others (the plaintiffs) purchased the chinchillas from Division. None of the plaintiffs was a sophisticated businessperson or highly educated. It soon became apparent that greater skill than that advertised was required to raise chinchillas and that certain statements made by Division's sales representatives as to the value of the pelts proved to be untrue. None of the plaintiffs had financial success with their growing (ranching) of chinchillas over a three-year period. The plaintiffs seek to rescind the contracts to get their money back, claiming fraud on the part of Division. Discuss whether Division's statements constitute fraud. [Fischer v. Division West Chinchilla Ranch, 310 F.Supp. 424 (D.Minn. 1970)]

17. In July 1965, Loral Corporation was awarded a $6 million contract to produce radar sets for the Navy. For this contract Loral needed to purchase 40 precision gear parts. Loral awarded to Austin Instrument a subcontract to supply 23 of the 40 gear parts. In May of 1966 Loral was awarded a second contract to produce more radar sets. Loral solicited bids for 40 more gear parts. Austin submitted a bid for all 40 but was told by Loral that the subcontract would be awarded only for items for which Austin was the lowest bidder. Austin's president told Loral that it would not accept an order for less than 40 gear parts and, one day later, told Loral that Austin would cease deliveries on the existing contract unless (1) Loral awarded Austin a contract for all 40 gear part units and (2) Loral consented to substantial increases for the price of all gear sets under the existing contract. Ten days later Austin ceased making deliveries. Loral tried to find other suppliers to furnish the gear sets, but none were available. Because of deadlines and liquidated damage clauses in the Navy contract, plus possible loss of reputation of Loral with the government, Loral agreed to Austin's terms. After Austin's last delivery, Loral filed suit to recover the increased prices Austin charged on the grounds that the agreement to pay these prices was based on duress. Discuss Loral's claim. [Austin Instrument, Inc. v. Loral Corp., 29 N.Y.2d 124, 272 N.E.2d 533, 324 N.Y.S.2d 22 (1971)]

Chapter 11

Legality

In order for a contract to be enforced in court, the contract must not call for the performance of an illegal act. A contract is illegal if either its formation or its performance is criminal, tortious, or otherwise opposed to public policy. The first part of this chapter will consider what makes a bargain illegal—being contrary to state or federal statutes or to public policy. The second part will consider the *effects* of an illegal bargain. Such contracts are normally void—that is, they really are not contracts.

CONTRACTS CONTRARY TO STATUTE

Statutes often prescribe the terms of contracts. In some instances, the laws are specific, even providing for the inclusion of certain clauses and their wording. Other statutes prohibit certain contracts on the basis of their subject matter, the time at which they are entered into, or the status of the contracting parties.

Usury

Every state has statutes that set the maximum rates of interest that can be charged for different types of transactions, including ordinary loans. A lender who makes a loan at an interest rate above the lawful maximum is guilty of **usury.** The maximum rate of interest varies from state to state.

The maximum rate of interest should not be confused with either the **legal rate of interest** or the **judgment rate of interest.** The legal rate of interest is a rate fixed by statute when the parties to a contract intend an interest rate to be paid but do not fix the rate in the contract. This rate is frequently the same as the maximum rate of interest permitted by statute. A judgment rate of interest is a rate fixed by statute that is applied to monetary judgments from the moment the judgment is awarded by a court until the judgment is paid. In some states, the legal rate is also the *pre-judgment rate.* That is, it is the rate of interest that accrues on the amount of a judgment from the time of the filing of the suit to the issuance of the judgment.

In order to determine how much interest is being charged on a loan and whether the loan is usurious, many states require that fees, service charges, credit insurance, "points,"[1] and the like imposed by the lender be included in the calculation. For example, suppose you are charged $100 per year to borrow $1,000. In addition, the lender charges you $25 in service charges and requires you to take out credit insurance that costs another $25. The true annual rate of interest is 15 percent (the total of $150 in charges divided by the principal amount of $1,000).

For some loans, the lender imposes a discount from the principal as interest. Suppose that the lender is willing to loan you $1,000, payable at the end of one year at a discount of $150. You will receive only $850, but at the end of the loan year you must pay the lender $1,000.

Not all charges are included in the calculation for interest. Many statutes provide that charges for additional services primarily of benefit to the borrower should not be included if they are reasonable. Examples of such charges are certain filing fees, attorneys' fees, and inspection or investigation charges.

EXCEPTIONS Although usury statutes place a ceiling on allowable rates of interest, exceptions have been made in order to facilitate business transactions. For example, many states exempt corporate loans from the usury laws. In addition, almost all states have adopted special statutes allowing much higher interest rates on small loans. In some cases, the interest (including other charges) can exceed 100 percent of the loan. Such high rates are allowed because many borrowers simply cannot get loans at interest rates below the normal lawful maximum and might otherwise be forced to turn to loan sharks.

EFFECTS OF USURY The effects of a usurious loan differ from state to state. A number of states allow the lender to recover the principal of a loan along with interest up to the legal maximum. In effect, the lender is denied recovery of the excess interest. In other states, the lender can recover the principal amount of the loan but not the interest. In a few states, a usurious loan is a void transaction, and the lender cannot recover either the principal or the interest.

Gambling

In general, wagers and games of chance are illegal. All states have statutes that regulate gambling—defined as any scheme for the distribution of property by chance among persons who have paid a valuable consideration for the opportunity to receive the property.[2] Gambling is the creation of risk for the purpose of assuming it. A few states do permit gambling, some only as long as the prizes or winnings do not exceed $100 to $500.[3] In addition, a number of states have recognized the substantial revenues that can be obtained from gambling and have legalized state-operated lotteries, horse racing, and lotteries arranged for charitable purposes (such as bingo).

Sometimes it is difficult to distinguish a gambling contract from the risk-sharing inherent in almost all contracts. For example, it might appear that a person selling or buying a futures contract (a contract for the future purchase or sale of a commodity, such as corn or wheat) is essentially gambling on the future price of the commodity. Since, however, the seller of the futures contract either already has a property interest in the commodity or can purchase the commodity elsewhere and deliver the commodity as required in the futures contract, courts have upheld the legality of such contracts.

The following case illustrates a court's analysis of the difference between a contest of chance and one of skill in forecasting the results of football games to be played.

---

1. Points are commonly required in the financing of real estate transactions. A point is defined as 1 percent of the amount of the loan, and the lender collects it only once—at the time the loan is made. It is a fee or charge imposed in addition to the constant, long-term, stated interest rate on the loan, but it may be tax-deductible as interest. See *Real Estate Sales Handbook* (Chicago: Realtors National Marketing Institute of the National Association of Realtors, 1979).

---

2. See *Wishing Well Club v. Akron*, 66 Ohio Law Abs. 406, 112 N.E.2d 41 (1951).

3. Iowa and Florida are two such states.

Case 11.1

**SEATTLE TIMES CO.
v. TIELSCH**

Supreme Court of Washington,
En Banc, 1972.
80 Wash.2d 502, 495 P.2d 1366.

BACKGROUND AND FACTS *The* Seattle Times *ran a football fore-casting contest that it named "Guest-Guesser." The Seattle chief of police claimed that the contest was illegal because it was a lottery. When the* Times *petitioned the court to determine the legality of the contest, the trial court found that the contest was an illegal lottery. The* Times *appealed.*

ROSELLINI, J.
*   *   *   *

The result of a football game may depend upon weather, the physical condition of the players and the psychological attitude of the players. It may also be affected by sociological problems between and among the members of a football team. The element of chance is an integral part of the game of football as well as the skill of the players.

The lure of the "Guest-Guesser" contest is partially the participant's love of football, partially the challenge of competition and partially the hope enticingly held out, which is often false or disappointing, that the participant will get something for nothing or a great deal for a very little outlay *   *   *.

The elements of a lottery are prize, consideration and chance *   *   *.

The appellant maintains that chance is not a dominant element in football fore-casting contests. *   *   * The trial court found to the contrary upon that evidence, and we think the finding is justified. The appellant's expert statistician who testified at the trial did not state that chance plays no part in the outcome of such a contest or even that it does not play a dominant role. He merely testified that such a contest is not one of "pure chance." Pure chance he defined as a 50-50 chance. He acknowledged that a contestant who consistently predicted the outcome of 14 out of 20 games correctly would be a "highly skilled" contestant. *   *   *

Where a contest is multiple or serial, and requires the solution of a number of problems to win the prize, the fact that skill alone will bring contestants to a correct solution of a greater part of the problems does not make the contest any the less a lottery if chance enters into the solution of another lesser part of the problems and thereby proximately influences the final result *   *   *.

Our research has revealed only one case involving a football forecasting game and the game there was a "pool," that is, a gambling game wherein wagers were placed. The Superior Court of Pennsylvania held that it was a lottery. What is most relevant in the case for our consideration here is the court's discussion of the element of chance in forecasting the result of football games. The court said: It is true that for an avid student of the sport of football the chance taken is not so great as for those who have little interest in the game. However, it is common knowledge that the predictions even among these so-called "experts" are far from infallible. Any attempt to forecast the result of a single athletic contest, be it football, baseball, or whatever, is fraught with chance. This hazard is multiplied directly by the number of predictions made. The operators of the scheme involved in this case were all cognizant of this fact for the odds against a correct number of selections were increased from 5 to 1 for three teams picked up to 900 to 1 for fifteen teams.

The trial court in the instant case recognized the same basic realities attendant upon the enterprise of football game-result forecasting. We are convinced that it correctly held that chance, rather than skill, is the dominant factor in the Times' "Guest-Guesser" contest. The very name of the contest conveys quite accurately the promoters' as well as the participants' true concept of the nature of the contest.

We conclude that the contest, however harmless it may be in the opinion of the participants and the promoters, is a lottery.

**DECISION
AND REMEDY**

The trial court's ruling was upheld. The "Guest-Guesser" game was indeed a lottery. The contest, even though harmless in the opinion of the participants and the promoters, was illegal.

Sabbath Laws

Statutes called Sabbath, or Sunday, laws prohibit the formation or performance of certain contracts on Sunday. At common law, in the absence of this statutory prohibition, such contracts are legal. Most states, however, have enacted some type of Sunday statute.

Some states have statutes making all contracts entered into on Sunday illegal. Statutes in other states prohibit only the sale of merchandise, particularly alcoholic beverages, on Sunday. (These are often called *blue laws*.) A number of states have laws that forbid the carrying on of "all secular labor and business on The Lord's Day." In such states, contracts made on Sunday are normally illegal and unenforceable *as long as they remain executory* (not performed).

Exceptions to Sunday laws permit contracts for necessities, such as food, and works of charity. In addition, a contract entered into on Sunday that has been fully performed (that is, an *executed* contract) cannot be rescinded, or cancelled. Active enforcement of Sunday laws varies from state to state and even among communities within a particular state. Many do not enforce the Sunday laws, and some of these laws have been held to be unconstitutional on grounds that they are contrary to the freedom of religion.

Licensing Statutes

All states require members of certain professions or callings to obtain licenses allowing them to practice. Doctors, lawyers, real estate brokers, construction contractors, electricians, and stockbrokers are but a few of the people who must be licensed. Obtaining some licenses requires extensive schooling and examinations, which indicates to the public that a special skill has been acquired. Obtaining others requires only good moral character.

When a person enters into a contract with an unlicensed individual, the contract may be enforceable despite the lack of a license. The nature of the statute itself often tells if such a contract is enforceable. Some statutes expressly provide that the lack of a license for people engaged in certain occupations will bar enforcement of any work-related contracts they enter into.

If the statute does not expressly state this, one must look to the underlying purpose of the licensing requirements for that occupation. If the underlying purpose of the licensing statute is to raise revenues, a contract entered into with an unlicensed practitioner will be enforceable. The sanction instead will usually be a fine on the unlicensed practitioner. If the underlying purpose is to protect the public from unauthorized practitioners, however, then the contract will be illegal and unenforceable. For example, if you enter into a contract involving the professional services of an unlicensed chiropractor, the chiropractor cannot enforce the contract. The licensing of chiropractors is designed to protect the public from persons who are not capable (or who have not shown their capability) of practicing their trade. The following case illustrates this principle.

BACKGROUND AND FACTS   *Paris is a real estate broker licensed under the laws of the state of Georgia. After learning that certain Gulf County, Florida, acreage owned by Hilton & Associates was on the market, Paris contacted Cooper, a Florida resident who was interested in purchasing the property. Paris visited the property in Florida, helped prepare Cooper's written offer of purchase, worked with Cooper's attorney on the sales contract, and attended the closing of the sale in Panama City, Florida. As a result of this sale, Paris received a $315,070 commission in the form of a $215,070 note secured by the real property and a check for $100,000 from Cooper. Paris then returned the $100,000 check to Cooper and, in return, was given a check for $25,000 and a demand note for $75,000.*

Cooper subsequently defaulted on his payments to both Hilton & Associates and Paris. When Hilton & Associates initiated foreclosure proceedings in circuit court, Paris filed suit against Cooper seeking recovery under the promissory

 Case 11.2

COOPER v. PARIS
District Court of Appeal of Florida, First District, 1982.
413 So.2d 772.

notes. Cooper, in turn, filed suit against Paris, seeking to have Paris's conduct declared to be that of an unlicensed real estate broker, which would invalidate the promissory notes held by Paris. Cooper also sought recovery of the sums he had already paid to Paris, $25,000 and $12,904. The $12,904 figure constituted payment on the $75,000 demand note.

The trial court held that Paris had acted in the capacity of a unlicensed real estate broker in the state of Florida, thereby invalidating the promissory notes held by Paris. The court also held, however, that the payments already made to Paris could not be recovered by Cooper. Cooper appealed from this decision.

McCORD, Judge
*   *   *   *

Both parties agree, and decisional law overwhelmingly supports the view, that this contract was void and illegal *ab initio* [from the beginning]:

> The broad basis for the doctrine that contracts of certain unlicensed persons are unenforceable is that the courts should not lend their aid to the enforcement of contracts where performance would tend to deprive the public of the benefits of regulatory measures.

*   *   * This general rule is subject to the exception that where the parties are not *in pari delicto* [equally at fault], the innocent party may recover. Here, Paris argued that Cooper is *in pari delicto* with him because both Cooper and his attorney knew that Paris was not licensed to transact real estate business in Florida. While the evidence is conflicting on whether Cooper himself knew that Paris was not licensed, Cooper's attorney admitted that he knew Paris was not licensed as a real estate agent in Florida. However, even if Cooper knew of Paris's status and nevertheless participated in making the illegal contract, this fact would not prevent him from maintaining an action for restitution:

> When the legislature enacts a statute forbidding certain conduct for the purpose of protecting one class of persons from the activities of another, a member of the protected class may maintain an action *notwithstanding the fact that he has shared in the illegal transaction*. The protective purpose of the legislation is realized by allowing the plaintiff to maintain his actions against the defendant within the class primarily to be deterred. In this situation it is said that the plaintiff is not *in pari delicto*. This rule is applied in favor of a person seeking to recover back money for services performed by a person lacking a required license to perform such services.

The manifest purpose of Chapter 475, Florida Statutes, is to prevent unscrupulous real estate practices and to promote the protection of the consumer/purchaser. The public interest is protected where personal service is to be rendered by the licensed real estate agent through a requirement that the license may be issued only upon satisfactory proof of honesty, truthfulness, good reputation, competency, and experience. To this end, the Act subjects the unlicensed real estate agent not only to forfeiture of his right to compensation but also to criminal liability. While we certainly do not condone the actions of Cooper or his attorney, the statute prescribes punishment against only one party to the agreement, Paris. Therefore, to refuse to return the monies paid would affront this Court's affirmative duty to see that the party violating public policy not benefit in any way as a result of his wrongdoing.

Otherwise, Paris stands to be rewarded for his illegal activities, a result to which this Court cannot subscribe. Moreover, by allowing Paris to keep these monies this Court would implicitly encourage unlicensed persons to seek up-front money, thereby eviscerating the salutary purpose of Chapter 475 by permitting those persons to keep any funds garnered prior to a judicial declaration that the contract is void. *   *   *

The appellate court held that Cooper was entitled to restitution for payments made, even if he knew that Paris was not licensed to transact business in Florida and participated in making an illegal contract for the sale of Florida land. The court wished to prevent unlicensed brokers from benefiting from illegal activities.

DECISION AND REMEDY

Contracts to Commit a Crime

Any contract to commit a crime is a contract in violation of a statute.[4] Thus, a contract to sell an illegal drug (the sale of which is prohibited by statute) is not enforceable. Should the object or performance of the contract be rendered illegal by statute after the contract has been entered into, the contract is said to be discharged by law. (See the discussion under "Impossibility of Performance" in Chapter 14).

CONTRACTS CONTRARY TO PUBLIC POLICY

Although contracts are entered into by private parties, some are not enforceable because of the neg-

_____
4. See, for example, McConnell v. Commonwealth Pictures Corp., 7 N.Y.2d 465, 166 N.E.2d 494, 199 N.Y.S.2d 483 (1960).

ative impact they would have on society. These contracts are said to be *contrary to public policy*. Numerous examples exist. Any contract to commit an immoral act falls in this category. Contracts that prohibit marriage have been held to be illegal on this basis. Suppose Dangerfield promises a young man $500 if he will refrain from marrying Dangerfield's daughter. If the young man accepts, the resulting contract is void. Thus, if he married Dangerfield's daughter, Dangerfield could not sue him for breach of contract.

In the following case, the defendant claimed that a contract was void because it contravened public policy.

BACKGROUND AND FACTS *A. M. Kashfi (plaintiff) is an Iranian citizen currently residing in California. Phibro-Salomon (defendant) is incorporated in Delaware and has its offices in New York. It is a trading and marketing organization that deals with commodities, including oil, metals, and minerals.*

A letter agreement between Phibro and Kashfi provided that Kashfi would be paid a commission of 1 percent of the value of any oil that was sold as part of an oil barter transaction that was being proposed. The services rendered by Kashfi consisted of arranging meetings between the defendant and key officials of the Iranian government in connection with the oil barter transaction. According to the plaintiff, Phibro proposed to facilitate the sale of Iranian oil on behalf of Iran, and the proceeds of the oil sales would be used by Iran to purchase military equipment from the United States.

The plaintiff alleged that between March and June of 1976 he set up a series of meetings between the defendant and various "key" Iranian officials and that he arranged to have Iranian officials forward Phibro's proposal to the Shah of Iran for his consideration and approval. The plaintiff contended that in June 1976, the Shah approved the oil barter transaction and that the agreement resulted in the sale of $2.4 billion worth of Iranian oil, the proceeds of which were used by the Iranian government to purchase American-made military aircraft.

Case 11.3
KASHFI v. PHIBRO-SALOMON, INC.
United States District Court for the Southern District of New York, 1986.
628 F.Supp. 727.

Based on the letter agreement, Kashfi alleged that Phibro owed him $24 million for the services he rendered during 1976. The defendant contended the agreement violated both Iranian and United States law and was thus void.

TENNEY, District Judge.
*   *   *   *

The letter agreement at issue here also contravenes the public policy of the United States. Exercising personal or political influence with government officials in order to obtain a government contract is expressly prohibited by 41 U.S.C. § 254(a) (the "Procurement Statute").

("[C]ourts will decline to enforce contingent fee contracts when an attempt to introduce personal solicitation and personal influence into dealings with government is actually intended or in fact results."); ("If part of the services bargained for consist in the exercise of personal or political influence on legislators or officials, made effective by personal solicitation, it is clear that the bargain is unlawful.").

The federal Procurement Statute prohibits paying a commissioned fee to an individual for arranging a contract between the United States government and a third party. *   *   *

Obviously the letter agreement in the instant case is not invalidated by the federal Procurement Statute, since the United States government was not involved. However, Kashfi is seeking compensation for the efforts he expended in attempting to secure a contract for the defendant with the government of Iran, which is exactly the kind of practice that Congress condemned when it enacted the Procurement Statute in this country.

The Iranian Influence law is similar to the federal Procurement Statute, and—based on the plain language of the Influence Law—it appears that the objectives of both laws are the same. The purpose of the Procurement Statute is threefold: (1) to prevent the use of improper influence in connection with securing government contracts; (2) to eliminate arrangements which encourage inequitable and exorbitant fees that bear no reasonable relationship to the services rendered; and (3) to prevent contracts being awarded on a basis other than merit.

("[Contingent fee] arrangements could easily result in higher prices for government goods and services as well as contracts which would not have been awarded had all the potential contractors been afforded equal consideration.") These objectives can also be ascribed to the Iranian Influence Law. In order to enforce the Letter Agreement in this case, the Court would essentially have to disregard these objectives. Thus, for the reasons set forth above, the Court concludes that the letter agreement is unenforceable.

DECISION AND REMEDY *The district court held that since the letter agreement contravened public policy, as expressed in the purposes of the U.S. procurement and Iranian influence statutes, it was unenforceable.*

Contracts in Restraint of Trade

An example of contracts that adversely affect the public are contracts in restraint of trade. For example, competitors who agree to set the levels or ranges of the prices they will charge for their products or services inhibit competition, and public policy favors competition in the economy. Such price-fixing arrangements may be horizontal (between competitors) or vertical (between manufac-turers and distributors concerning resale prices). Contracts in restraint of trade usually violate one or more **antitrust statutes** that have been enacted to encourage competition within the economy.[5] Some contracts in restraint of trade are considered

---

5. Some of these statutes are the Sherman Antitrust Act, the Clayton Act, and the Federal Trade Commission Act. States also have separate antitrust statutes. Antitrust and contracts in restraint of trade are discussed in Chapter 48.

to be illegal *per se*—that is, a court will hold them to be illegal as a matter of law without examining whether they restrain trade in fact. Prior to the adoption of antitrust statutes, however, the common law prohibited certain contracts that had the effect of restraining trade.

Although most contracts in restraint of trade are illegal, an exception is recognized for some restraints that are considered to be *reasonable* and interpreted as being integral to certain contracts. Many such exceptions involve a type of restraint that is called a covenant not to compete, or a restrictive covenant.

COVENANTS NOT TO COMPETE   *Covenants not to compete* are often contained in contracts for the sale of an ongoing business. The seller agrees not to open a new store within a certain geographical area surrounding the old store for a specified period of time. When covenants, or agreements, not to compete are accompanied by the sale of an ongoing business, the agreements are usually upheld as legal if they are "reasonable," usually in terms of time and area. The purpose of these covenants is to enable the seller to sell, and the purchaser to buy, the goodwill and reputation of an ongoing business. If these covenants were not valid, then the valuable business interest of goodwill and reputation could not be transferred. For example, suppose the seller has built up an established clientele because the business is known for its high-quality product and service. If the buyer desires to keep the opportunity to serve the established clientele, he or she will include a covenant that imposes reasonable restrictions on the seller—for example, that the seller shall not establish a similar business within a two-mile radius for a period of two years. The seller, in turn, receives consideration in return for giving up his or her legal right to compete under the conditions prescribed. In this way, the seller is prevented from opening a similar business down the block and drawing away the buyer's customers.

If the agreement not to compete is made without an accompanying sales agreement, it is void because it tends to restrain trade and is contrary to public policy. Even when ancillary to a primary agreement, an agreement not to compete can be contrary to public policy if it is unreasonably broad or restrictive as to time or geographic area. Sup-

pose Orian Capital, doing business in San Francisco sells its loan and finance business to Bankers Life Company. If Orian Capital agrees not to open another business in the state of California, the agreement not to compete is unreasonably broad. After all, the threat of losing customers to Orian is not very severe in San Diego. On the other hand, if the agreement covers only the San Francisco Bay area, it will probably be upheld.

Ancillary agreements not to compete can also be held contrary to public policy if they cover an unreasonably long period of time. In the preceding example, if Orian agrees not to compete for a hundred years, the contract will be contrary to public policy. On the other hand, a five-year agreement is reasonable and enforceable (and in some cases, depending on the situation, up to twenty years would be reasonable).

Agreements not to compete can be ancillary to employment contracts. It is increasingly common for many middle- and upper-level management personnel to agree not to work for competitors or not to start a new business for a specified period of time after terminating employment. If such an agreement is not ancillary to an employment contract, it is illegal. If the agreement is ancillary to an employment contract, it is legal as long as it is not excessive in scope or duration.

On occasion, when a covenant not to compete has been construed to be unreasonable in its essential terms, some courts have *reformed* the covenant, converting its terms into reasonable ones. Instead of declaring the covenant illegal and unenforceable, the courts have applied the rule of reasonableness and changed the contract so that its basic, original intent could be enforced. For example, in the Orian Capital case, if Orian is forbidden to open another business anywhere in California for a period of one hundred years, the court may either declare the entire covenant null and void or reform the covenant terms to cover only the San Francisco Bay area for a period of five years. (This presents a problem, however, in that the judge becomes a party to the contract. Consequently, contract reformation is usually carried out by a court only when necessary to prevent undue burdens or hardships.)

In the following case, the covenant not to compete was held to be unreasonable as to duration and therefore unenforceable.

Case 11.4

**NATIONWIDE
MUTUAL
INSURANCE
COMPANY v. HART**

Court of Special Appeals of
Maryland, 1988.
73 Md.App. 406, 534 A.2d 999.

BACKGROUND AND FACTS *On May 14, 1984, Robert Hart joined Nationwide Mutual Insurance Company as an employee-agent and began in-service training in Nationwide's new agent development program. When he was hired, Hart signed an agent's employment agreement that described the terms of his employment and contained the restrictive covenant that is at issue in this case. Paragraph 11 of the agreement provided as follows:*

> *Agent agrees that he/she will not compete, either directly or indirectly by and for himself or as agent for another or through others as agent, solicitor, representative or broker in any way connected with the sale, advertising or solicitation of fire, casualty, health or life insurance in the area described below for a period of one year from the date of the voluntary or involuntary termination of employment with the Companies or, should the Companies find it necessary by legal action to enjoin Agent from competing with Companies, one year after the date such injunction is obtained [emphasis added] in the following area: Within twenty-five miles of the principal place of business located at 6910 York Road, Baltimore, Maryland.*

Hart resigned from Nationwide on March 31, 1986, and on that day he began working for a competing insurance firm, Grau and Associates, Inc. After he resigned, Nationwide wrote to Hart, reminded him of his obligations under the non-competition clauses, and informed him that Nationwide would enforce the agreement if necessary. Soon after he began working for Grau, Hart sent a letter to some of his former Nationwide customers informing them of his new association with Grau. The letter read as follows:

> *I just want to notify you that I have found it best for my clients that I become an independent agent. For this reason, you will not be able to find me at Nationwide. However, I certainly would hope to hear from you if I can be of any service to you. I currently represent several companies in all lines of insurance, and have found that the competitive rates available put me in a better position to provide my clients with the coverage they need at more affordable prices.*

Nationwide filed suit, alleging that Hart had breached the restrictive covenant contained in Paragraph 11 of the agreement. Although one year had lapsed from the date of Hart's employment termination, Nationwide asked for an injunction to restrain Hart while the lawsuit was pending based on the extension of the covenant in Paragraph 11. The injunction was denied, and Nationwide appealed.

BISHOP, Judge.
*   *   *   *

During the hearing on the injunction, the attorney for Nationwide told the trial judge that Nationwide was not seeking to prevent Hart "from a license anywhere within the State of Maryland" but that Nationwide sought "that he only be prohibited from *selling* insurance within a twenty-five mile radius." *   *   * To prohibit the selling of insurance within a limited area is quite different from prohibiting licensure.

The former clearly falls within the category of the type of service which may be the subject of restrictive agreements under Maryland law.

While the determination of enforceability depends on the facts and circumstances present in each particular case, a comparative examination of the cases in this State which have considered this issue indicates a consistency in the holdings of this Court.

These decisions demonstrate that Maryland follows the general rule that restrictive covenants may be applied and enforced only against those employees who provide unique services, or to prevent the future misuse of trade secrets, routes or lists of clients, or solicitation of customers.

Having reached this conclusion, we would ordinarily reverse and remand with direction that the court [re]consider the matter; however, we have an additional problem.

Hart terminated his employment with Nationwide on March 31, 1986, and therefore the one-year restriction in Paragraph 11 would terminate on March 30, 1987. That period has elapsed. Nonetheless, there is an extension of time "should [Nationwide] find it necessary by legal action to enjoin [Hart] from competing" to "one year after the date of the obtaining of the injunction." It is with the extension of time that we have difficulty.

* * * [R]estrictive covenants in a contract of employment * * * will be sustained if the restraint is confined within limits which are *no wider as to area and duration* than are reasonably necessary for the protection of the business of the employer and do not impose undue hardship on the employee or disregard the interests of the public.

The restrictive covenant contained in Paragraph 11, although reasonable as to area, is unreasonable as to duration because, as written, it restricts Hart's activities as an insurance salesman for "one year after the date [the] injunction is obtained," regardless of the date he terminates his employment and regardless of the date of the issuance of the injunction. Although restrictive covenants of one year or more have been upheld, the covenants in those cases went into effect on the date the employment contract was terminated, not some indefinite date in the future as in the situation presented here.

The court affirmed the judgment of the lower court. The provision in Paragraph 11 of the agreement by which the duration of the restriction could be extended beyond one year from the date of the termination of employment was held to be unreasonable because it was potentially unlimited in duration.

DECISION AND REMEDY

Exculpatory Clauses

Ordinarily, a court does not look at the fairness or equity of a contract. That is, the courts generally do not inquire into the adequacy of consideration, as discussed in Chapter 9. Persons are assumed to be reasonably intelligent, and the courts will not come to their aid just because they have made an unwise or foolish bargain. In certain circumstances, however, bargains are so oppressive that the courts relieve innocent parties of part or all of their duties. Such bargains are called **unconscionable.**

Contracts attempting to absolve parties of negligence or other wrongs are often held to be unconscionable. For example, suppose Jones and Laughlin Steel Company hires a laborer and has him sign a contract stating:

Said employee hereby agrees with employer, in consideration of such employment, that he will take

upon himself all risks incident to his position and will in no case hold the company liable for any injury or damage he may sustain, in his person or otherwise, by accidents or injuries in the factory, or which may result from defective machinery or carelessness or misconduct of himself or any other employee in service of the employer.

This contract provision attempts to remove Jones and Laughlin's potential liability for injuries occurring to the employee, and it is usually contrary to public policy.[6]

Such clauses, which may also be found in rental and ordinary sales agreements, are called **exculpatory clauses.** For our purposes, they may be defined as clauses that purport to release a party from all liability for property damage or personal

---

6. For a case with similar facts, see Little Rock & Ft. Smith Ry. Company v. Eubanks, 48 Ark. 460, 3 S.W. 808 (1887). In such a case the clause may also be illegal on the basis of a violation of the state workers' compensation law.

injury arising within contexts related to the subject matter of the contract.

Exculpatory clauses are sometimes found in commercial and residential property leases. In the majority of cases involving leases for commercial property, these clauses are held to be contrary to public policy. Additionally, they are almost universally held to be illegal and unenforceable when they are included in residential property leases.

The following case illustrates the illegality of an exculpatory clause in an application form for membership in an athletic club.

Case 11.5
**BROWN v.
RACQUETBALL
CENTERS, INC.**
Superior Court of Pennsylvania,
1987.
369 Pa.Super. 13, 534 A.2d 842.

BACKGROUND AND FACTS   *When LeRoy F. Brown (plaintiff) became a member of Racquetball Centers, Inc. (defendant) on September 27, 1984, he was required to complete and sign a two-sided application form that included the following release:*

I, LeRoy F. Brown, voluntarily enter the Westend Racquet Club, . . . to participate in the athletic, physical and social activities therein. I have inspected the premises and know of the risks and dangers involved in such activities as are conducted therein and that unanticipated and unexpected dangers may arise during such activities. I hereby and do assume all risks of injury to my person and property that may be sustained in connection with the stated and associated activities in and about these premises. [Emphasis added.]

In consideration of the permission granted to me to enter the premises and participate in the stated activities, I hereby, for myself, my heirs, administrators and assigns, release, remise and discharge the owners, operators and sponsors of the premises and its activities and equipment and their respective servants, agents, officers, and all other participants in those activities of and from all claims, demands, actions and causes of action of any sort, for injury sustained to my person and/or property during my presence on the premises and my participation in those activities due to negligence or any other fault.

On May 19, 1985, as Brown was leaving the shower facilities at the club, he slipped on the wet tile floor and fell, hitting his head and suffering numerous injuries. Brown claimed that the accident was a direct and proximate result of the club's negligent maintenance of the shower room. The club contended that the application form signed by Brown operated to release the club from liability for Brown's injuries. The Court of Common Pleas found in favor of the club, and Brown appealed from the judgment.

DEL SOLE, Judge.
* * * *

Generally, an exculpatory clause is valid if:

(a) it does not contravene any policy of the law, that is, if it is not a matter of interest to the public or state; (b) the contract is between persons relating entirely to their own private affairs; (c) each party is a free bargaining agent and the clause is not in effect a mere contract of adhesion whereby one party simply adheres to a document which he is powerless to alter, having no alternative other than to reject the transaction entirely.

In [this case] there is no need to address whether the release contravened public policy or satisfied the other criteria, since we find that in no way does this release absolve the releasee of liability for its own acts of negligence.

The law requires that before an exculpatory clause will be interpreted and construed to relieve a person of liability for that party's own or its servants' or agents' acts of negligence it must:

> spell out the intention of the parties with the greatest of particularity * * * and show the intent to release from liability beyond doubt by express stipulation and no inference from words of general import can establish it.

The release in question does not spell out the intention of the parties with the necessary particularity. The language does not set forth in an unambiguous manner that the releasor, in signing the agreement, intends to absolve the releasee of liability for the releasee's own negligence. Instead, the language can more clearly be interpreted to relieve the Club of liability as the result of injuries sustained by a member while participating in certain activities of the Club.

Contracts providing for immunity from liability from one's own negligent acts are disfavored by the law and therefore require strict adherence to the above elaborated standards. The release signed by Appellant Brown does not satisfy these standards.

The Superior Court of Pennsylvania reversed the lower court's ruling and held that the exculpatory clause was unenforceable.

DECISION AND REMEDY

Adhesion Contracts and Unconscionability

Contracts entered into because of one party's vastly superior bargaining power may also be deemed unconscionable. For example, if every auto manufacturer were to insert an exculpatory clause (a clause freeing the manufacturer from liability for personal injury or monetary damage) in contracts for the sale of autos, consumers presumably would have no chance to bargain for the elimination of the clause from a given contract. (These contracts, which were discussed in the preceding chapter, are also called *adhesion contracts*.) Essentially, the consumer's choice would be to take a contract or leave it. In order to combat such clauses, courts have held them to be unconscionable.[7] The consumer has no choice, so the contract is contrary to public policy.

Another example of an unconscionable contract is a contract in which the terms of the agreement "shock the conscience" of the court. Suppose a welfare recipient with a fourth-grade education agrees to purchase a refrigerator for a price of $2,000, signing a two-year, non-usurious installment contract. The same type of refrigerator usually sells for $400 on the market. Some courts have held this type of contract unconscionable de-spite the general rule that the courts will not inquire into the adequacy of consideration.[8] Typically, the cases have involved consumer transactions in which the buyer was not aware of the actual price he or she was agreeing to pay.

Both the Uniform Commercial Code (UCC) and the Uniform Consumer Credit Code (UCCC) embody the unconscionability concept—the former with regard to the sale of goods[9] and the latter with regard to consumer loans and the waiver of rights.[10]

To illustrate, UCC 2-302, which deals with the sale of goods, basically provides that as a matter of law a court can declare an entire contract or any clause in a contract illegal because of unconscionability. Whether the court will so hold depends frequently upon the commercial setting and all the circumstances of the transaction, such as the education, income, and position of the buyer relative to the seller (as in the refrigerator example).

In the following case, a potato grower attempts to avoid contractual obligations by claiming that the contract is unconscionable. The court discusses factors typically considered in determining whether a contract or clause is unconscionable.

---

7. See Henningsen v. Bloomfield Motors, Inc., 32 N.J. 358, 161 A.2d 69 (1960).

8. Jones v. Star Credit Corp., 59 Misc.2d 189, 298 N.Y.S.2d 264 (1969).

9. See, for example, UCC Sections 2-302 and 2-719.

10. See, for example, UCCC Sections 5.108 and 1.107.

Case 11.6

DOUGHTY v. IDAHO FROZEN FOODS CORP.

Court of Appeals of Idaho, 1987.
112 Idaho 791, 736 P.2d 460.

BACKGROUND AND FACTS *In 1983, Doughty contracted to sell a portion of his anticipated potato crop to Idaho Frozen Foods (IFF) in order to secure financing for the growing of the crop. To express the terms of their agreement, the parties used a "form" contract that had been developed through negotiations between IFF and the Potato Growers of Idaho (PGI). Under the contract, Doughty was to receive a base price if the potato crop contained a certain percentage of potatoes weighing ten ounces or more. If the crop contained a higher percentage, the price would be increased. Conversely, if the crop contained a lower percentage, the price would be reduced. These provisions in the contract reflected IFF's desire to have potatoes a certain size in order to meet its processing needs. The contract also provided IFF with the option to refuse or accept delivery of the potatoes if less than 10 percent of them weighed ten ounces or more. Doughty had no such option. Doughty contracted to sell only a portion of his crop to IFF. The potatoes that Doughty did not sell to IFF, he sold to another processor on the "fresh pack" market for $4.69 per hundredweight. In the fresh pack market, potatoes are packaged in sacks and containers and sold for whole use, such as for baking potatoes. In the fresh pack market, no preharvest contract is used. The potatoes are sold after harvest. Unfortunately, because of poor weather conditions, only 8 percent of Doughty's potato crop consisted of ten-ounce potatoes. Because of the small percentage of ten-ounce potatoes, Doughty was entitled to only $2.57 per hundredweight for his potatoes under the terms of the IFF contract. After four days of delivery under the contract, Doughty refused to deliver any more potatoes to IFF. IFF brought suit for breach of contract. Doughty claimed that the contract was not enforceable because it was unconscionable and therefore void. The trial court held that the contract was enforceable, and Doughty appealed.*

WALTERS, Chief Judge.

* * * *

Doughty argues that the contract is unconscionable because the terms were disproportionately skewed in favor of IFF. Specifically, Doughty invites a comparison of the built-in step decreases in the contract price based on the percentage of smaller potatoes and the step increases in price for higher percentages of larger potatoes. Doughty contends the contract is unconscionable because the price decreases are steeper than the price increases. Doughty also contends that it was unconscionable for IFF to have the option not to accept the potatoes if they consisted of less than ten percent ten-ounce or larger size potatoes. [T]his Court recognized that a claim of unconscionability may have procedural and substantive aspects. We stated that procedural unconscionability may arise in the bargaining process leading to an agreement. Procedural unconscionability "is characterized by great disparity in the bargaining positions of the parties, by extreme need of one party to reach some agreement (however unfavorable), or by threats short of duress. These circumstances taint the bargaining process, producing a result that does not reflect free market forces." * * * Regarding substantive unconscionability, * * * "[o]nly in special circumstances may a court of equity set aside contracts fairly and freely negotiated." We further noted that such "special circumstances" turn on "whether at the time of making of the contract, and in light of the general commercial background and commercial needs of a particular case, [the contract is] so one-sided as to oppress or unfairly surprise one of the parties."

Doughty's allegations encompass aspects of both procedural and substantive unconscionability. Under either aspect, we do not find the contract to be unconscionable. Although Doughty was not a member of PGI, the group which negotiated the contract with IFF, PGI represented a significant number of growers. Doughty has not shown that he was in any way different from those potato growers who were members of PGI. Moreover, the record clearly establishes that PGI did have substantial bargaining power and negotiating expertise. The contract was generally negotiated over a period of time with both PGI and IFF, attempting to meet their needs. Testimony by IFF's buyer indicated that one year a PGI-approved contract was not used because the two sides could not agree on terms. That, at the least, indicates that PGI did have substantial negotiating strength.

Doughty entered into the contract freely and sought the benefits which the collective bargaining power of PGI had obtained. Apparently, Doughty was not dissatisfied with the contract *until* his crop produced small potatoes. There is no indication that Doughty tried or wanted to negotiate different terms under the contract. In fact, the contract would appear to be to the advantage of a farmer such as Doughty—one who through innovation, skill, and aggressiveness sought to produce a crop that would fulfill not only the IFF contract, but also his other processing contract, plus produce potatoes for the "fresh pack" market. Had Doughty's efforts produced the ten-ounce potatoes he sought, Doughty would have had a very beneficial contract. There was no indication that Doughty was forced by "extreme need" into the contract. Although Doughty's bank required a contract in order to provide the financing to grow the potatoes, that requirement does not indicate extreme need. For instance, Doughty might have avoided any use of the IFF contract by simply contracting with the other processor who bought portions of Doughty's crop on terms different from the IFF contract. Finally, there is no indication from the record of any threats to Doughty that caused him to enter into the IFF contract.

The contract also does not reflect any substantively unconscionable aspects. The prices were based on the size and quality of potatoes that IFF desired and that Doughty hoped he could produce. The pricing variations, as well as the option to refuse potatoes not meeting the contract requirements, do not appear to be unreasonable considering the product the contract was intended to produce—ten-ounce or larger potatoes. The contract was a preharvest contract. Therefore Doughty could attempt to manipulate and manage the crop to produce exactly the size potatoes that would be most financially rewarding. Doughty was thwarted by unexpected weather conditions. Doughty's assertions reflect an attempt to reap the benefits that the contract would have produced if he had grown the kind of potatoes he intended to, yet escape the negative aspects resulting from his inability to produce that type of potato. The contract simply does not appear to be "so one-sided as to oppress or unfairly surprise one of the parties."

Each party accepted certain risks by signing the preharvest contract. IFF took a chance that market prices might decline, while Doughty took a chance on growing a certain size potato. IFF did have an option to reject potatoes that did not meet IFF's size criteria. However, contracts do not necessarily give identical rights to all parties. That is part of the bargaining process. It does not necessarily make a contract unconscionable. We conclude that the contract was not unconscionable in this case.

The court of appeals held that the circumstances of the negotiation and execution of the contract did not render the contract unconscionable and affirmed the trial court's decision.

DECISION AND REMEDY

Discriminatory Contracts

Contracts in which a party promises to discriminate in terms of color, race, religion, national origin, or sex are contrary to statute and contrary to public policy.[11] For example, if a property owner promises in a contract not to sell the property to

---

11. Federal Civil Rights Act of 1964, 42 U.S.C.A., Section 2000e, *et seq.*

a member of a particular race, the contract is unenforceable. Public policy underlying these prohibitions is very strong, and the courts are quick to invalidate discriminatory contracts. Thus, the law attempts to ensure that people will be treated equally.

Contracts for the Commission of a Tort

Contracts that require a party to commit a civil wrong, or a tort, have been held to be contrary to public policy. Remember that a *tort* is an act that is wrongful to another individual in a private sense, even though it may not necessarily be criminal in nature (an act against society).

Contracts Injuring Public Service

Contracts that interfere with a public officer's duties are contrary to public policy. For example, contracts to pay legislators for favorable votes are obviously harmful to the public. Often, a fine line is drawn between lobbying efforts and agreements to influence voting. When a lobbying group provides certain factual information in order to influence the outcome of legislation, the group is not engaging in an illegal activity. But if the group enters into a contingency-fee agreement, whereby the legislator receives a certain amount of money if a certain bill is passed or a certain contract is awarded, the agreement is illegal because it is deemed contrary to public policy. In the United States, people are not entitled to buy and sell votes. Therefore, agreements to do so are illegal.

Agreements that involve a *conflict of interest* are often illegal. Public officers cannot enter into contracts that cause conflict between their official duties as representatives of the people and their private interests. Statutes require many public officers to liquidate their interests in private businesses before serving as elected representatives. Other statutes merely require that while they are in office they take no part in the operation of, or decisions concerning, any business in which they have an interest, so that private and public responsibilities remain separate.

Suppose Ladd is a county official in charge of selecting land for the building of a new courthouse. He makes a contract for the state to buy land that he happens to own. This is a conflict of interest. If the state discovers later that Ladd owned the land, it can normally use this information to show a conflict of interest and to void the contract.

Agreements Obstructing the Legal Process

Any agreement that is intended to delay, prevent, or obstruct the legal process is illegal. For example, an agreement to pay some specified amount if a criminal prosecution is terminated is illegal. Likewise, agreements to suppress evidence in a legal proceeding or to commit fraud upon a court are illegal. Tampering with a jury by offering jurors money in exchange for their votes is illegal.

In a trial, most witnesses (except expert witnesses) are paid a flat fee to compensate them for their expenses. Offering to pay one witness more than another is contrary to public policy, since the extra payment can provide an incentive for the witness to lie.

A promise to refrain from prosecuting a criminal offense in return for a reward is void because it is against public policy. A reward given under the threat of arrest or prosecution is also void.

EFFECT OF ILLEGALITY

In general, an illegal contract is void. That is, the contract is deemed never to have existed, and the courts will not aid either party. In most illegal contracts, both parties are considered to be equally at fault—**in pari delicto.** In such cases the contract is void. If it is executory (not yet fulfilled), neither party can enforce it. If it is executed, there can be neither contractual nor quasi-contractual recovery.

Suppose Sonatrach, Algeria's national oil company, contracts to sell oil to Tenneco without government approval. Algerian law prohibits the export of oil without government approval. Therefore, the contract is illegal and unenforceable. If Tenneco sues to enforce delivery of the oil, the suit will be dismissed, since the contract is void. Even if Tenneco has paid for some of the oil, the contract cannot be enforced. Tenneco cannot even get back the money it paid under the illegal contract. In general, the courts takes a hands-off attitude toward illegal contracts.

That one wrongdoer in an illegal contract is unjustly enriched at the expense of the other is of no concern to the law—except under certain special circumstances that will be discussed below. The major justification for this hands-off attitude is that it is improper to place the machinery of justice at the disposal of a plaintiff who has broken the law by entering into an illegal bargain. Another justification is the hoped-for deterrent effect of this general rule. A plaintiff who suffers loss because of it should presumably be deterred from entering into similar illegal bargains.

Exceptions to the General Rule

Some persons are excepted from the general rule that neither party to an illegal bargain can sue for breach and neither can recover for performance rendered:

1. Persons justifiably unaware or ignorant of facts that make the agreement illegal.
2. Persons protected by statutory law.
3. Persons who withdraw from an illegal agreement before the transaction is performed.
4. Persons induced to enter into an illegal contract through fraud, duress, or undue influence.

JUSTIFIABLE IGNORANCE OF THE FACTS When one of the parties is relatively innocent, that party can often obtain restitution or recovery of benefits conferred in a partially executed contract. In this case, the courts will not enforce the contract but will allow the parties to return to their original positions.

It is also possible for an innocent party who has fully performed under the contract to enforce the contract against the guilty party. For example, a truck carrier contracts with Gillespie to carry goods to a specific destination for a normal fee of $500. The truck carrier delivers the goods and later finds out that the contents of the shipped crates were illegal. Although the law specifies that the shipment, use, and sale of the goods were illegal, the carrier, being an innocent party, can still legally collect the $500 from Gillespie.

MEMBERS OF PROTECTED CLASSES When a statute is clearly designed to protect a certain class of people, a member of that class can enforce a contract in violation of the statute even though the other party cannot. A statute that prohibits employees from working more than a specified number of hours per month is designed to protect those employees. An employee who works more than the maximum can recover for those extra hours

of service. Flight attendants are subject to a federal statute that prohibits them from flying more than a certain number of hours every month. Even if an attendant exceeds the maximum, the airline must pay for those extra hours of service.

Another example of statutes designed to protect a particular class of people concerns **blue sky laws,** state legislation that regulates and supervises securities offerings and sales to protect members of the public from fraudulent investment schemes. Such laws are intended to stop the sale of stock in fly-by-night concerns such as visionary oil wells and distant gold mines. Investors are protected as a class and can sue to recover the purchase price of stock issued in violation of such laws.

Most states also have statutes regulating the sale of insurance. If the insurance company violates a statute when selling insurance, *the purchaser can nevertheless enforce the policy*. For example, assume Indemnity Insurance Company is not qualified to sell insurance in Montana but does so anyway. A purchaser who buys a policy to insure his auto has an accident and seeks to recover. The insurer cannot avoid payment under the policy, even though the contract is illegal. The statutes regulating insurance companies are designed to protect policyholders, so the buyer can recover from the insurer.

WITHDRAWAL FROM ILLEGAL AGREEMENT If the illegal agreement has been only partly performed and the illegal part of the bargain has not yet been performed, the party rendering performance can withdraw from the bargain. That party can recover the performance or its value. For example, Sam and Jim decide to wager (illegally) on the outcome of a boxing match. Each deposits money with a stakeholder, who agrees to pay the winner of the bet. At this point, each party has performed part of the agreement, but the illegal part of the agreement will not occur until the money is paid to the winner. Before such payment occurs, either party is entitled to withdraw from the agreement by giving notice of repudiation to the stakeholder.

ILLEGAL CONTRACT THROUGH FRAUD, DURESS, OR UNDUE INFLUENCE Often, illegal contracts involve two blameworthy parties, but one party is more at fault than the other. When a party has been induced to enter into an illegal bargain by fraud, duress, or undue influence of the other party to the agreement, that party will be allowed to recover for performance or its value.

Consider the following example: Mildred Pfeiffer has a number of creditors threatening to file suit for debts she owes. Pointing out that in a successful suit, the creditors might be able to "get their hands on" Mildred's expensive investment diamonds, her confidante Harry persuades her to "sell" the diamonds to him for a nominal price. Harry promises to "sell" the diamonds back to her at the same price after she has "gotten the creditors off her back." Believing Mildred to have insufficient assets to pay her debts in full, the creditors agree to accept less than they are owed and release her from further liability. When Mildred demands that Harry sell the diamonds back to her, he says that unless she pays him the diamonds' full market value, he will tell the creditors about the deal. At first she agrees, but on second thought, she decides to sue Harry. Although Mildred undertook the original "sale" to defraud her creditors, who could have had it set aside had they discovered it, a court would allow her to recover the diamonds from Harry. Harry used Mildred's confidence in him to unduly influence her to participate in the first transaction. His coercion in the "resale" constitutes duress.

Severable, or Divisible, Contracts

A *severable* contract consists of distinct parts that can be performed separately, with separate con-sideration provided for each part. If a contract is severable into legal and illegal portions, and the illegal portion does not go to the essence of the bargain, the legal portion can be enforced. This is consistent with the basic policy of courts to enforce the legal intentions of the parties wherever possible.

Suppose Norman Harrington contracts to buy ten pounds of bluegrass seed for $25 and five gallons of herbicide for $30. At the time, Harrington does not know that the Food and Drug Administration has banned sale of the herbicide and that the contract for its sale is therefore illegal. Here, the contract is severable because separate considerations were stated for the bluegrass seed ($25) and the herbicide ($30). Therefore, the portion of the contract for the sale of bluegrass seed is enforceable; the other portion is not.

In contrast, a contract would be indivisible if the parties intended that each party's complete performance was essential, even if the contract contained a number of seemingly separate provisions. For instance, a contract for the sale of a business might contain, as one of its clauses, a covenant not to compete—which would prevent the seller from opening a competing business nearby. Although this clause would seem to be a separate and divisible provision of the contract, in fact, it goes to the heart of the contract. Without such a clause, the buyer might not obtain the good-will attaching to the business and the seller's former customers.

 QUESTIONS AND CASE PROBLEMS

1. A famous New York City hotel, Hotel Lux, is noted for its food as well as its luxury accommodations. Hotel Lux contracts with a famous chef, Chef Perlee, to become its head chef at $6,000 per month. The contract states that should Perlee leave the employment of Hotel Lux for any reason, he will not work as a chef for any hotel or restaurant in the states of New York, New Jersey, or Pennsylvania for a period of one year. During the first six months of the contract, Hotel Lux substantially advertises Perlee as its head chef, and business at the hotel is excellent. Then a dispute arises between the hotel management and Perlee, and Perlee terminates his employment. One month later, he is hired by a famous New Jersey restaurant just across the New York state line. Hotel Lux learns of Perlee's employment through a large advertisement in a New York City newspaper. It seeks to enjoin Perlee from working in that restaurant as a chef for one year. Discuss how successful Hotel Lux will be in its action.

2. State X requires a person to be eighteen years old before being permitted to purchase alcoholic beverages. The state also has passed a law that persons who prepare and serve liquor in the form of drinks in commercial establishments must be licensed. The only requirement for obtaining a yearly license is that the person be at least eighteen years old. Michael, age thirty-five, is hired as a bartender for the Lone Star Restaurant. George, a staunch alumnus of a nearby university, brings twenty of his friends to the restaurant to celebrate a football victory that afternoon. George has ordered four rounds of drinks, and the

bar bill exceeds $150. George learns that Michael failed to renew his bartender's license, and George refuses to pay, claiming the contract is unenforceable. Discuss whether George is correct.

3. The Constitution provides for the separation of church and state. The government can in no way support or affiliate itself with any particular religion or group of religions. (Note that across-the-board legislation, such as tax exemptions for religious organizations, is not prohibited by this constitutional provision.) Illinois enacted a law requiring all retailers who do not sell food to remain closed on Sunday. A local retailer challenged the law as a violation of the constitutional provision calling for separation of church and state. Do you think such a "Sunday closing law" is unconstitutional? Discuss fully.

4. Walsh was shopping at W. T. Grant Co. when she was approached by a saleswoman, who asked her if she wanted to open a charge account. The saleswoman's "pitch" was that she needed points for a contest. Walsh agreed to open a charge account and was given a booklet of coupons with a stated value of $200. She was told by the saleswoman that she would be charged only for the coupons she used. In reality, the agreement Walsh signed was an installment sales contract, obligating her to pay a total of $246.01 over a twenty-month period at $10 per month. Walsh failed to make the first payment. W. T. Grant Co. filed suit. Is the agreement illegal? If so, for what reasons? [W. T. Grant Co. v. Walsh, 100 N.J.Super. 60, 241 A.2d 46 (1968)]

5. Womack was a well-known gambler in Saline County. Judge Maner, a friend of Womack, not only knew of Womack's gambling enterprises but approved of them. From time to time over a period of several years, Womack paid money to the judge to ensure that he would not be prosecuted. As a result of this long-standing agreement, Womack paid the judge a total of $1,675. Womack then claimed that the consideration for which he paid the judge was void and unlawful at the time the contract was entered into as well as at the present time. Therefore, Womack sued Judge Maner to rescind the contract and to get back the $1,675 he had paid. Should Womack recover? [Womack v. Maner, 277 Ark. 786, 301 S.W.3d 438 (1957)]

6. In 1970, Overbeck received a Sears credit card. In 1974 he charged several purchases on the card. If Overbeck had paid for each purchase within thirty days, no service charge would have been added to the outstanding balance. But he chose to let the account "revolve." Therefore, under the credit card agreement between Overbeck and Sears, a service charge of 1.5 percent (18 percent annually) was added each month. Overbeck claimed that the 18 percent annual interest was usurious and contrary to the laws of Indiana, which set the maximum legal rate at 6 percent. Was Overbeck correct? [Overbeck v. Sears, Roebuck and Company, 169 Ind.App. 501, 349 N.E.2d 286 (1976)]

7. Jo Anne Hall's husband induced her to consent to be divorced. She claimed that her former husband represented that the divorce was needed for business reasons. He promised that after the divorce they would continue living together as man and wife, and he would support her as he had in the past. The divorce was granted, and they lived together for three months. He then left her so he could marry another woman. Mrs. Hall filed suit, claiming, among other allegations, breach of contract. Discuss whether a contract to get a divorce and to cohabitate after the divorce is illegal. [Hall v. Hall, 455 So.2d 813 (Ala. 1984)]

8. Roeber and the Swift & Courtney & Beecher Company were both engaged in the business of manufacturing matches. Swift desired to purchase Roeber's business, which was quite lucrative. Pursuant to the sale agreement between Swift and Roeber, Roeber agreed not to engage in the match business in any state in the United States other than Nevada and Montana for ninety-nine years. Was the contract enforceable? [Diamond Match Company v. Roeber, 106 N.Y 473, 13 N.E. 419 (1887)]

9. On June 10, 1984, Bennett (plaintiff) entered an amateur bicycle race sanctioned and conducted by the United States Cycling Federation (defendant). Bennett signed a document provided by the Cycling Federation that stated in part: "In consideration of the acceptance of my application for entry in the above event, I hereby waive, release and discharge any and all claims for damage which I may have, or which may hereafter accrue to me, as a result of my participation in said event." The release also included a clause by which Bennett was to assume risks associated with bicycle racing. While participating in the scheduled racing event, Bennett collided with an automobile driven by James Ketchum and owned by John Gismond. Bennett alleged that, during the race, the vehicle was permitted onto the track by agents or servants of the defendants, who knew, or should have known, of the hazard it presented to the cyclists. The defendant claimed it had no liability, because of the release signed by Bennett. What is the outcome? [Bennett v. U.S. Cycling Federation, 193 Cal.App.3d 1485, 239 Cal.Rptr. 55 (1987)]

10. Margaret R. Shehab worked as a licensed real estate agent in the state of Michigan for Products, Inc., which subsequently became Xanadu, Inc. On the representation of S. L. McNiece, president of Products, Inc., that she did not need a Texas real estate license, she agreed to relocate to San Antonio, Texas, and to become sales manager of Lafayette Place, an apartment house that was being converted into condominiums. A letter agreement was ultimately given to her by Products, Inc., confirming that she was to act as sales manager and receive as her compensation 1 percent of the sales price of each unit she sold. She was provided with a rent-free apartment at Lafayette Place and was "on call" twenty-four hours a day to show units to prospective buyers. During the period from 1978 through 1981, she successfully sold and received commissions on more than 140 units. Sometime in the latter half of 1980, Shehab sold the remaining 54 units to Williston H. Clover. She was denied her commission on these remaining units on the ground that she was unlicensed in Texas to sell real estate. Shehab filed suit to recover her commission. Will she be able to get it? [Shehab v. Xanadu, Inc., 698 S.W.2d 491 (Tex.App. 13 Dist. 1985)]

11. Carolyn Murphy is a welfare recipient with four minor children. Brian McNamara is in the busi-

ness of renting and selling television and stereo sets. After seeing McNamara's advertisement for "rent to own" televisions, Murphy signed a lease agreement with McNamara for a twenty-five-inch Philco console color TV at $16 per week. The lease payments were to run for seventy-eight weeks, after which she would become the owner. At no time did McNamara tell Murphy that the total lease payments amounted to $1,268, including delivery charge. The retail sale price of the set was $499. Murphy had paid about $436 when she read a newspaper article criticizing the lease plan. When she learned that she was required to pay $1,268,

Murphy stopped making payments. McNamara's employees attempted to take possession and made threats through telephone and written communications. Murphy filed suit, alleging that the contract violated the Connecticut Unfair Trade Practices Act and state usury laws and that the contract terms were unconscionable under Section 2-302 of the Uniform Commercial Code. Discuss her allegations, particularly her claim that the contract is unconscionable under the UCC. [Murphy v. McNamara, 36 Conn.Supp. 183, 416 A.2d 170 (1979)]

Chapter 12

Writing and Form

Suppose I meet you on the street and orally offer to sell you my used personal computer for $800. You accept my offer. Later, upon your tender of the $800, I refuse to transfer my personal computer to you because I have had a better offer from another person. You threaten to sue me. After all, we did have an *oral* contract. The question is whether an oral contract is enforceable. In most cases, it is, but the party seeking to enforce it must establish the existence of the contract as well as its actual terms. Naturally, when the parties have no writing or memorandum about the contract, only oral testimony can be used in court to establish the existence of the terms of the contract. The problem with oral testimony is that parties are sometimes willing to perjure themselves in order to win lawsuits.

Therefore, at early common law, parties to a contract were not allowed to testify. This led to the practice of hiring third party witnesses. As early as the seventeenth century, the English recognized the many problems presented by this practice and enacted a statute to help deal with it. The statute, passed by the English Parliament in 1677, was known as "An Act for the Prevention of Frauds and Perjuries." The act required that certain types of contracts, in order to be enforceable, had to be evidenced by a writing and signed by the party against whom enforcement was sought. For example, our oral contract for the sale of my computer would fall under the act and could not be enforced by you in a court action. In the United States, the descendant of the British act is called the Statute of Frauds.

CONTRACTS THAT MUST BE IN WRITING

Today almost every state has a Statute of Frauds, modeled after the English act. The actual name of the Statute of Frauds is misleading, since it neither applies to fraud nor invalidates any type of contract. Rather, it denies enforceability to certain contracts that do not comply with its requirements. The primary purpose of the act is evidentiary—to provide reliable evidence of the existence and terms of certain classes of contracts deemed historically to be important or complex. Although the statutes vary slightly from state to state, all require the following types of contracts to be in writing or evidenced by written memorandum.[1]

---

1. Restatement, Second, Contracts, Section 110.

1. Contracts involving interests in land.
2. Contracts that cannot *by their terms* be performed within one year from the date of formation.
3. Collateral, or secondary, contracts, such as promises to answer for the debt or duty of another and promises by the administrator or executor of an estate to pay a debt of the estate personally—that is, out of his or her own pocket.
4. Promises made in consideration of marriage.
5. Contracts for the sale of goods priced at $500 or more.

CONTRACTS INVOLVING INTERESTS IN LAND

Under the Statute of Frauds, a contract involving an interest in land must be attested to by a writing.

Sale of Land

A contract calling for the sale of land is not enforceable unless it is in writing or evidenced by a written memorandum. Land is real property and includes all physical objects that are permanently attached to the soil, such as buildings, fences, trees, and the soil itself. The Statute of Frauds operates as a *defense* to the enforcement of an oral contract for the sale of land. Therefore, even if both parties acknowledge the existence of an oral contract for the sale of land, under most circumstances the contract will still not be enforced.[2] If Sam contracts orally to sell Blackacre to Betty but later decides not to sell, under most circumstances Betty cannot enforce the contract. Likewise, if Betty refuses to close the deal, Sam cannot force Betty to pay for the land.

Frequently it is necessary to distinguish between real property, which is property affixed to the land, and personal property. A contract for the sale of land ordinarily involves the entire interest in the real property, including buildings, growing crops, vegetation, minerals, timber, and anything else affixed to the land. Therefore, a fixture (personal property so affixed or so used as to become a part of the realty) is treated as real property. But anything else, such as a couch, is treated as personal property.

Other Interests

The Statute of Frauds requires written contracts for the transfer of other interests in land. Interests in land include life estates, real estate mortgages, and easements. Each of these interests, which will be described in detail in Chapter 52, is discussed briefly here.

LIFE ESTATES A **life estate** is an ownership interest in land that lasts for a person's lifetime. For example, if Sally Manne sells Edenfarm to Mary Johnson "for life, then after Johnson's death, to Nancy Smole," Johnson has a life estate in the farm. This means that Johnson can live on and farm the land during her lifetime, but when Johnson dies Smole will have a full estate in the farm—that is, she will own it entirely.[3]

MORTGAGES A real estate **mortgage** is a conveyance of an interest in land as a security for repayment of a loan. If Nancy Smole, now full owner of Edenfarm, wants to borrow money from First National Bank, First National will require *collateral* for the loan. By giving conditional title of Edenfarm to the bank, Smole can get the loan. When she pays off the debt, Edenfarm will be hers once again in total ownership.

EASEMENTS An **easement** is a legal right to use land without owning it. Easements are created expressly or impliedly. An express easement arises when the owner of land expressly agrees to allow another person to use the land. To be enforceable the agreement must be in writing. Implied easements can arise from the past conduct of the parties. For example, when a farmer has used a certain path to reach the back forty acres of his farm for twenty years, and the path goes across a neighbor's property, the farmer has an *implied* easement to cross the neighbor's property. Implied easements need not be in writing and rarely are, because of the way they are created.

LEASES A **lease** is a transfer without title of real property for a certain period of time. Because a lease represents a transfer of a property interest, leases originally fell under the Statute of Frauds. Most states, however, now have statutes expressly providing that short-term oral leases are enforceable. Thus, any lease lasting more than this period

---

2. The contract will be enforced, however, if the parties admit to the existence of the oral contract in court or admit to its existence pursuant to discovery before trial.

---

3. Full ownership like Nancy Smole's is called a *fee simple absolute*. See Chapter 52.

must be in writing. These statutory periods vary. For example, Indiana allows leases to be oral for up to three years. Leases are discussed in detail in Chapter 53.

THE ONE-YEAR RULE

A contract that cannot, *by its own terms*, be performed within one year from the date it was formed must be in writing to be enforceable.[4] Since disputes over such contracts are unlikely to occur until some time after the contracts have been made, resolution of these disputes is difficult unless the contract terms have been put in writing.

Possibility of Performance

In order for a particular contract to fall under the one-year rule of the Statute of Frauds, contract performance within a year from the date of contract formation must be objectively impossible. If the contract, by its terms, makes complete performance within the year *possible* (not probable), the contract is not covered by the Statute of Frauds and need not be in writing.

Suppose Bankers Life orally contracts to loan $40,000 to Janet Lawrence "as long as Lawrence and Associates operates its financial consulting firm in Omaha, Nebraska." The contract is not within the Statute of Frauds—no writing is required—because Lawrence and Associates could go out of business in one year or less. In this event, the contract would be fully performed within one year. Although this occurrence is unlikely, it is nevertheless possible, and that possibility removes the contract from the province of the Statute of Frauds.[5]

Suppose, on the other hand, that Bankers Life agrees to loan the money to Lawrence "for a period of two years with the provision that there will be no acceleration or prepayment for the period." Lawrence and Associates could go out of business in one year or less. Since the debtor is not allowed to accelerate payments on the loan or prepay the remainder at any time, he or she cannot perform the contract within one year without breaching the contract's terms. Therefore, this contract is

subject to the Statute of Frauds and must be evidenced by a writing to be enforceable. Compare the specified two years in this contract to the statement in the preceding example, where the words "as long as" were used.

Next, assume that the contract states that the loan will last for two years but may be "terminable at the end of six months, subject to review of Lawrence and Associates' financial condition." Here the contract is not subject to the Statute of Frauds because, by the terms of the contract, it can be fully performed within one year.

The one-year period begins to run *the day after the contract is made*.[6] Suppose you graduate from college on June 1. An employer orally contracts to hire you immediately (June 1) for one year at $2,000 per month. This contract is not subject to the Statute of Frauds (and thus need not be in writing in order to be enforceable) because the one-year period to measure performance begins on June 2. Since your performance of one year can begin immediately, it would take you exactly one year from the date of entering the contract to perform.

Suppose that on March 1 the dean of your college, in your presence, orally contracts to hire your professor for the next academic year (a nine-month period) at a salary of $35,000. The academic year begins on September 1. Does this contract have to be in writing to be enforceable? The answer is yes. The one-year period used to measure whether performance by contract terms is possible begins on March 2. Since the nine-month contract could not begin until September 1 and would end on May 31 of the next year, the contract performance period exceeds the one-year measurement period by three months. Thus, this contract is within the Statute of Frauds. But if this oral contract had been entered into at any time between June 1 and September 1, the contract, by its terms, would be performed within one year of the date of contract formation (acceptance of the offer), and the oral contract would be enforceable.

In summary, the test to determine whether an oral contract is enforceable under the one-year rule of the Statute of Frauds is not whether an agreement is *likely* to be performed within a year from the date of making the contract. Rather, the ques-

---

4. Restatement, Second, Contracts, Section 130.

5. See Warner v. Texas & Pac. Ry. Co., 164 U.S. 418, 17 S.Ct. 147, 41 L.Ed. 495 (1896).

6. 2 Corbin on Contracts, Section 444.

tion revolves around whether performance within a year is *possible*. Even if performance actually takes more than one year, an oral contract is binding so long as performance was possible in less than a year. Exhibit 12-1 illustrates graphically the application of the one-year rule.

COLLATERAL PROMISES

A collateral, or secondary, promise is one ancillary to a primary contractual relationship. This term is used to refer to any promise that is ancillary to a principal transaction. Two collateral promises are covered by the Statute of Frauds:

1. Promises by the administrator or executor of an estate to pay personally the debts of the estate.
2. Promises to answer for the debt or duty of another.[7]

Promises by the Administrator or Executor of an Estate to Pay Personally the Debts of the Estate

The administrator (or executor) of an estate has the duty of paying the debts of the deceased and distributing any remainder to the deceased's heirs. The administrator can contract orally on behalf of the estate. A writing is required only when the administrator promises to pay the debts of the estate personally. Suppose Edward Post (administrator) contracts with Martha Lynch for legal services. If Post contracts on behalf of the estate,

an oral contract is valid, and the estate is bound to pay Lynch for her legal services. But if Post agrees to pay Lynch's legal fees personally out of his own pocket, the contract must be in writing. Otherwise it is not enforceable, and Lynch cannot recover.

Promises to Answer for the Debt or Duty of Another

Promises made by one person to pay the debts or discharge the duties of another if the latter fails to perform are subject to the Statute of Frauds and must be in writing. Three elements must be present in this collateral promise situation in order to require that the agreement be in writing:

1. Three parties are involved.
2. Two promises are involved.
3. The secondary, or collateral, promise is to pay a debt or fulfill a duty only if the first promisor fails to do so.

This set of requirements is illustrated in Exhibit 12-2.

The Statute of Frauds applies only to promises made by a third party to fulfill the obligations of a principal party to a contract if that party does not perform.[8] Assume, for example, that David wants to borrow $10,000 from Bancroft. Owens, David's parent, forms a contract with Bancroft whereby Owens promises to pay the $10,000 if David fails to pay the debt when it becomes due.

---

7. Restatement, Second, Contracts, Section 112.

8. Such promises are referred to as *suretyship* or *guaranty* contracts. See Chapter 30 for definitions and a more detailed discussion of these terms.

Exhibit 12-1 Contracts Impossible to Perform within One Year

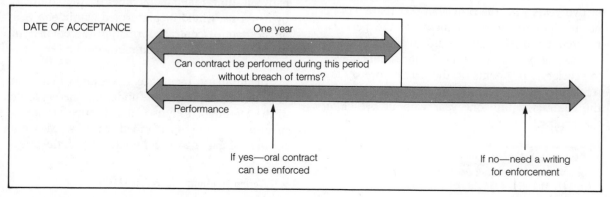

Exhibit 12-2 **Collateral Promises**

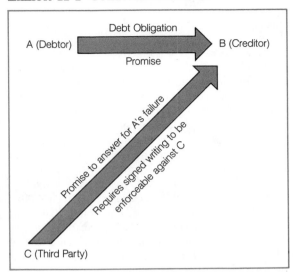

Owens's promise to Bancroft is secondary (collateral) to the David-Bancroft contract and must be in writing to be enforceable. The underlying purpose behind this provision of the Statute of Frauds is to ensure that a person will not be forced to pay the debt of another on the basis of oral testimony—which could be perjured.

The key point here is that the obligation of the guarantor (Owens, in the above example) is secondary, and the guarantor's liability for the obligation is thus secondary—Owens will not become liable *unless* David is unable or unwilling to pay the $10,000. David, in contrast, is primarily liable for the obligation, and the David-Bancroft contract does not have to be in writing to be enforceable. The Statute of Frauds only applies if the guarantor's obligation is contingent upon the principal debtor's refusal or inability to pay the creditor.

THE "MAIN PURPOSE RULE" EXCEPTION   The oral promise to answer for the debt of another is covered by the Statute of Frauds unless the guarantor is effectively a debtor because his or her main purpose in accepting secondary liability is to secure a pecuniary (monetary) benefit. This type of contract need not be in writing.[9] The assumption is that a court can infer from the circumstances of any given case whether the "leading objective" of the promisor was to secure a pecuniary advantage.

Consider an example. Oswald contracts with Machine Manufacturing Company to have some machines custom-made for Oswald's factory. She promises Machine Materials Supply Company, Machine Manufacturing's supplier, that if Machine Materials continues to deliver materials to Machine Manufacturing, Oswald will guarantee payment. This promise need not be in writing, even though the effect may be to pay the debt of another, since Oswald's main purpose is to serve her own pecuniary benefit.[10]

Another typical application of the so-called main purpose doctrine occurs when one creditor guarantees the debtor's debt to another creditor for the purpose of forestalling litigation so as to allow the debtor to remain in business long enough to generate enough profits to pay *both* creditors.

The following case illustrates an application of the main purpose doctrine. A creditor of a development complex guaranteed the general contractor's payments to a subcontractor to ensure that the development would be completed on time. Failure of the development project to be completed as contracted would have markedly decreased tenant revenue, placing the principal debtor in default on its loan to the bank.

---

9. Restatement, Second, Contracts, Section 116.

10. Kampman v. Pittsburgh Contracting and Engineering Co., 316 Pa. 502, 175 A. 396 (1934).

BACKGROUND AND FACTS *Wilson Floors contracted to provide flooring materials for a residential and commercial development known as "The Cliffs," which was owned by the defendant bank, Sciota Park, Ltd. When the general contractor for Sciota fell behind in payments to Wilson, Wilson stopped work on the project. The defendant assured Wilson that he would be paid if he returned to work. After Wilson's final bill was not paid, Wilson proceeded with this action against the defendant.*

 Case 12.1

WILSON FLOORS CO. v. SCIOTA PARK, LTD.

Supreme Court of Ohio, 1978.
54 Ohio St.2d 451, 377 N.E.2d 514.

SWEENEY, Justice.

The central issue in this cause is whether the bank's oral promise to Wilson that payments would be forthcoming upon a resumption of work at The Cliffs project constituted an enforceable oral contract.

[Under Ohio law:]

No action shall be brought whereby to charge the defendant, upon a special promise, to answer for the debt, default, or miscarriage of another person *   *   * unless the agreement upon which such action is brought, or some memorandum or note thereof, is in writing and signed by the party to be charged therewith or some other person thereunto by him or her lawfully authorized.

When the leading object of the promisor is not to answer for another, but to subserve some pecuniary or business purpose of his own, involving a benefit to himself, or damage to the other contracting party, his promise is not within the statute of frauds, although it may be in form a promise to pay the debt of another, and its performance may incidentally have the effect of extinguishing that liability.

In applying the leading object rule to the facts in this cause, the Court of Common Pleas, finding that the bank assumed a "direct undertaking" when it guaranteed Wilson payment for future services rendered, held that the bank's promise was enforceable by Wilson. No significance was given to the fact that [the general contractor] remained primarily liable for the debt owed Wilson, *i.e.*, that Wilson continued to send its progress billings to [the general contractor] for reimbursement.

The Court of Appeals, on the other hand, finding that the bank became only secondarily liable to Wilson when it guaranteed payment to the subcontractor, held that the bank's promise came within the provisions of the statute of frauds and therefore was unenforceable. The fact that the promise by the bank to guarantee payments was made to further the bank's own business interest was found not to be determinative of the cause.

*   *   *   *

In many cases the test whether a promise is or is not within the statute of frauds is to be found in the fact that the original debtor does or does not remain liable on his undertaking; if he is discharged by a new arrangement made on sufficient consideration, with a third party, this third party may be held on his promise though not in writing; but if the original debtor remains liable and the promise of the third party is only collateral to his, it will in strictness be nothing more than a promise to answer for the other's debt. But where the third party is himself to receive the benefit for which his promise is exchanged, it is not usually material whether the original debtor remains liable or not.

The above explanation of the leading object rule indicates that, in a determination of whether an oral promise is enforceable to pay the debt of another, the court may employ one of two tests. The court may inquire as to whether the promisor becomes primarily liable on the debt owed by another to a third party. If it is found that the promisor does not become primarily liable for payment of the debt, the court may inquire as to whether the promisor's leading object was to subserve his own business or pecuniary interest.

Because it is unquestioned that the bank in the instant cause did not become primarily liable when it guaranteed the subcontractors that they would be paid the court must apply the second test *   *   * to determine the enforceability of the verbal agreement.

Under the second test, it is of no consequence that when such promise is made, the original obligor remains primarily liable or that the third party continues to look to the original obligor for payment. So long as the promisor undertakes to pay the subcontractor whatever his services are worth irrespective of what he may owe the general contractor, and so long as the main purpose of the promisor is to further his own business or pecuniary interest, the promise is enforceable. Thus, under this test it is not required to show as a condition precedent for enforceability of the oral contract that the original debt is extinguished.

The facts in the instant cause [the case under review] reflect that the bank made its guarantee to Wilson to subserve its own business interest of reducing costs to complete the project. Clearly, the bank induced Wilson to remain on the job and rely on its credit for future payments. To apply the statute of frauds and hold that the bank had no contractual duty to Wilson despite its oral guarantees would not prevent the wrong which the statute's enactment was to prevent, but would in reality effectuate a wrong.

Judgment was entered in favor of Wilson. The bank's main purpose (leading object) was to derive a benefit for itself. Therefore, the promise to pay the general contractor's debts was not within the Statute of Frauds.

DECISION AND REMEDY

PROMISES MADE IN CONSIDERATION OF MARRIAGE

A unilateral promise to pay a sum of money or to give property in consideration of a promise to marry must be in writing. If Bill MacAdams promises $10,000 to Bruce Coby if Coby promises to marry his daughter, Sally MacAdams, MacAdams's promise must be in writing to be enforceable. The same rule applies to *prenuptial agreements* (agreements made before marriage), which define the ownership rights of each partner in the other partner's property. For example, a prospective husband may wish to limit the amount his prospective wife could obtain if the marriage should end in divorce. Another common situation involving prenuptial agreements occurs when a man and woman who wish to get married both have separate assets and children from prior marriages. A prenuptial arrangement may be highly desirable in this case. Prenuptial arrangements made in consideration of marriage must be in writing to be enforceable.

CONTRACTS FOR THE SALE OF GOODS

The UCC contains several Statute of Frauds provisions that require written evidence of a contract. Section 2-201 contains the major provision, which generally requires a writing or memorandum for the sale of goods priced at $500 or more. A writing that will satisfy the Code requirement need only state the quantity term, and that need not be stated "accurately," as long as it adequately reflects both parties' intentions. The contract will not be enforceable, however, for any quantity greater than that set forth in the writing. In addition, the writing must be signed by the person to be charged—that is, the person who refuses to perform or the one being sued. Beyond these two requirements, the writing need not designate the buyer or seller, the terms of payment, or the price.

Exceptions to the writing requirements, contained in UCC 2-201, are discussed in detail in Chapter 16. A few of the more important exceptions are discussed here as well.

Goods Made Specially to Order

Contracts for goods made specially for the buyer—that is, goods that cannot be resold by the seller in the ordinary course of the seller's business—are enforceable even when not in writing, provided that the seller has made a substantial beginning of manufacture or commitment for their procurement.[11] Suppose Kareem Abdul-Jabbar orally contracts with a furniture factory for $250,000 of furniture specially designed on a larger-than-normal scale to accommodate his larger-than-normal physique. Once the factory has committed itself to the manufacture of, or has made a substantial beginning in manufacturing, the furniture, the oral contract is enforceable.

Confirmation of an Oral Contract between Merchants

If one merchant sends to another a written confirmation of an oral contract, the merchant receiving the confirmation (with knowledge of its terms) must object in writing within ten days of its receipt, or the oral contract will be enforceable by either party.[12]

---

11. UCC 2-201(3)(a).
12. UCC 2-201(2).

Suppose Rodriguez in Los Angeles calls Cohen in New York City on June 1, and an oral contract is formed for Cohen's purchase of a new $10,000 machine. The next day Rodriguez sends Cohen a telegram that states, "This is to confirm our telephone contract of June 1 for your purchase of the Model 12 machine at $10,000. Thank you for your order." Cohen receives the telegram the same day. On June 15 Cohen discovers that a similar machine can be purchased for $9,000. Cohen claims the Statute of Frauds as a defense for his refusal of Rodriguez's tender of the machine. Cohen will lose against Rodriguez's suit for breach because he failed to object in writing within ten days of receiving Rodriguez's confirmation.

Admissions

If a party to an oral contract "admits" in "pleading, testimony or otherwise in court that a contract for sale was made," the contract will be enforceable, but only to the extent of the quantity admitted.[13] Thus, if the president of Windblown Sailboats admits under testimony that an oral agreement was made for fifty sails, the agreement will be enforceable to that extent.

PARTIAL PERFORMANCE

As stated above, the Statute of Frauds is a defense against the enforcement of an oral contract. Executed contracts—that is, contracts that have been fully performed—are not subject to the Statute of Frauds. Problems arise when an oral contract has been partially performed. For example, a buyer may have paid part of the purchase price and taken complete or partial possession of the seller's property.

Sale of Land

In cases involving contracts relating to the transfer of interests in land, if the purchaser has paid part of the price, taken possession, and made permanent improvements to the property and the parties cannot be returned to their pre-contract status quo, a court may grant *specific performance* (that is, performance of the contract according to the precise terms agreed on).

---

13. UCC 2-201(3)(b).

Whether the courts will enforce an oral contract for an interest in land when partial performance has taken place is usually determined by the degree of injury that would be suffered if the court chose not to enforce the oral contract.[14] The following examples illustrate this approach:

1.   The purchase price of the land has been paid, but the buyer has not taken possession. In this case, since the parties can be returned to their original positions without injury, the courts will usually not grant specific performance.
2.   The buyer has paid part of the purchase price and taken possession. Some states allow enforcement of the contract, since the parties cannot be returned to their pre-contract status quo.
3.   When part of the purchase price has been paid, possession has been taken by the buyer, and permanent improvements have been made on the land, most states allow enforcement of the contract. Once these three things have been done, the courts can be fairly sure that there was actually a contract in existence, even if it was an oral contract. The parties could not be returned to their pre-contract status quo without substantial injury.

Sale of Goods

Under the UCC, an oral contract is enforceable to the extent that a seller accepts payment or a buyer accepts delivery of the goods[15] contracted for. For example, Windblown Sailboats makes an oral contract with Sunset Sails to have Sunset make 750 sails for Windblown's new nineteen-foot Day Sailer. Windblown repudiates the agreement after the sails have been made and after two dozen have been delivered. The contract will be enforceable to the extent of the two dozen sails accepted by Windblown.

SUFFICIENCY OF THE WRITING

To be safe, all contracts should be fully set forth in a writing signed by all the parties. This assures that if any problems arise concerning performance of the contract, a written agreement can be introduced into court. The Statute of Frauds and the

---

14. In some states, mere *reliance* on an oral contract is enough to remove it from the Statute of Frauds.
15. UCC 2-201(3)(c).

UCC require either a written contract or a written memorandum signed by the party against whom enforcement is sought or a legally recognized exception, such as partial performance. For a memorandum, any confirmation, invoice, sales slip, check, or telegram can constitute a writing sufficient to satisfy the Statute of Frauds.[16] The signature need not be placed at the end of the document but can be anywhere in the writing. It can even be an initial rather than the full name.

A memorandum evidencing the oral contract need only contain the essential terms of the contract. Under the UCC, for the sale of goods, the writing need only name the quantity term and be signed by the party to be charged. Under most provisions of the Statute of Frauds, the writing must also name the parties, the subject matter, the consideration, and the essential terms with reasonable certainty. *Essential terms* in contracts for the sale of land, for example, include location and price. *With reasonable certainty* means with sufficient clarity to allow the terms to be determined from the memo itself, without reference to any outside sources.[17]

As indicated above, only the party to be held liable on the oral contract need sign the writing. In other words, the party against whom enforcement of the contract is sought must have signed it. Thus, a contract may be enforceable by one of its parties but not by the other. Suppose Ota and Warrington orally contract for the sale of Ota's lake house and lot for $55,000. Ota writes Warrington a letter confirming the sale by identifying the parties and the essential terms—price, method of payment, and legal address—and signs the letter. Ota has made a written memorandum of the oral land contract. Since she signed the letter, she can be held to the oral contract by Warrington. Since Warrington has not signed or entered into a written contract or memorandum, however, he can plead the Statute of Frauds as a defense, and Ota cannot enforce the contract against him.

The following case illustrates the writing criteria required in one state for a memorandum to satisfy the Statute of Frauds.

---

16. Even if the Statute of Frauds is satisfied, the existence and terms of the contract must be proved in court.

17. Rhodes v. Wilkins, 83 N.M. 782, 498 P.2d 311 (1972).

BACKGROUND AND FACTS   *Michael Elrod, as agent for Kenneth Katz, offered in writing to buy certain real estate owned by Joiner and his wife, the defendants. The written contract (offer) sent to Joiner provided an earnest money payment (deposit) by Katz of $1,000. Over the telephone, Joiner told Katz on October 13, 1985, that "everything was agreeable, that we had a deal, that [Joiner] was going to execute the contract and mail it back." Katz then pointed out to Joiner that the contract contained a provision by which the offer would be revoked unless the contract was executed (signed) and delivered by Joiner by October 14. Katz and Joiner agreed to disregard the provision. On October 20, Joiner mailed the executed contract, and Katz deposited the earnest money in a trust account with the title company. Joiner then sent a telegram that read, "I have signed and returned contract but have changed my mind. Do not wish to sell property." Elrod sued the Joiners for specific performance (to enforce the contract). The trial court found that a valid and enforceable contract existed, and the Joiners appealed.*

 Case 12.2

C. P. JOINER v. ELROD

Court of Appeals of Texas, Corpus Christi, 1986. 716 S.W.2d 606.

SEERDEN, Justice.
* * * *

Appellants contend * * * that the trial court erred as a matter of law in finding the existence of an enforceable contract for the sale of the property, based on "the oral modification of a written offer within the Statute of Frauds." Under this point, appellants argue that no contract was ever formed, and characterize the transaction as offer and counteroffer. They also urge that any contract is unenforceable because the oral modification was material.

The evidence establishes that a contract for the sale of land was formed during the telephone conversation of October 13, when there was a meeting of the minds about the terms of the transaction. *   *   *

Under Texas law, oral contracts to convey land are not void, but unenforceable if the party against whom enforcement is sought raises the Statute of Frauds as a defense. *   *   *

A memorandum is required not for the purpose of obtaining a written contract, but merely to furnish written evidence, signed by the party to be charged, of the obligation to be enforced against him. The written memorandum may be made after the agreement. The writing may consist of correspondence, receipts, telegrams, or a combination of documents. The writing does not need to contain all of the stipulations on which the parties have agreed. *   *   *   *

The question in this case is whether the execution was valid. Evidence shows that the execution was pursuant to an oral agreement to delete [the revocation provision]. That Joiner agreed to the contract and subsequent modification is evidenced by his behavior in delivering the contract on October 20 and by the contents of his telegram. The contract became enforceable when Joiner delivered the executed writing by placing it in the mail.

A party may waive strict performance of a contract which is required to be in writing, or extend its terms by oral agreement. An offerer may waive strict compliance with provisions specifying a time limit, even where time is the essence of the contract.

DECISION AND REMEDY *The appellate court affirmed the decision of the lower court and held that a valid and enforceable contract for the sale of land had been made.*

CONCEPT SUMMARY: Contracts Subject to the Statute of Frauds

TYPES OF CONTRACTS	APPLICATIONS AND EXCEPTIONS
Contracts involving an interest in realty	*Application* Applies to any contract for an interest in realty, such as sale, mortgage, easement grant, and life tenancy interest. *Exceptions* 1. Partial performance: principle in equity where parties cannot be restored to status quo. 2. Statute: most states provide for enforcement of short-term oral leases.
Contracts whose terms are impossible to perform within one year of contract formation	*Application* Applies only to contracts objectively impossible to perform fully within one year from the date of formation. *Exception* None.
Contracts to answer for the debt of another	*Application* Applies only to express contracts made between the guarantor and creditor whose terms make the guarantor secondarily liable. *Exception* Main purpose, or leading object, doctrine.
Promises in consideration of marriage	*Application* Applies to promises to pay money or give property in consideration of a promise to marry and to prenuptial agreements. *Exception* None.

CONCEPT SUMMARY: Contracts Subject to the Statute of Frauds (Continued)	
TYPES OF CONTRACTS	**APPLICATIONS AND EXCEPTIONS**
Sale of goods priced at $500 or more	*Application* Applies to: the sale of goods whose purchase price (excluding taxes) is $500 or more, UCC 2-201(1).
	Exceptions 1. When one party sends a written confirmation and the receiver does not object in writing within ten days, UCC 2-201(2), (between merchants). 2. Specially ordered goods, when the seller has made a substantial beginning of manufacture or commitment for procurement, UCC 2-201(3)(a). 3. Admission under oath of an oral contract, UCC 2-201(3)(b). 4. Partial performance, at least to the extent the buyer has paid for or possesses the goods, UCC 2-201(3)(c).
EXCEPTION TO CONTRACTS OTHERWISE UNENFORCEABLE UNDER STATUTE OF FRAUDS	
Memorandum Written evidence of an oral contract signed by the party against whom enforcement is sought. Generally, the writing must name the parties, identify the subject matter of the contract, and, in the sale of goods, the quantity; in the sale of land, it must name essential terms, such as property description and price.	

THE PAROL EVIDENCE RULE

The **parol evidence rule** prohibits the introduction at trial of evidence of the parties' prior negotiations or agreements or contemporaneous oral agreements that contradict or vary the terms of written contracts.[18] The written contract is ordinarily assumed to be the complete embodiment of the parties' agreement.

Because of the rigidity of the parol evidence rule, courts make several exceptions. These exceptions are listed and explained in Exhibit 12–3.

The major key in determining if the general rule excluding parol evidence is applied is basically whether the parties intended the writing to be a complete and final embodiment of the terms of their agreement. If so, the writing is referred to as an **integrated contract,** and parol evidence is excluded. If the written agreement is only partially integrated, evidence of consistent additional terms are admissible to supplement it.[19]

The following case deals with the admissibility of parol evidence that contradicts the terms of a written contract. In making its decision, the court considers (1) whether a fully integrated written contract existed and (2) whether the oral promise modifying the contract terms was made prior to or contemporaneous with the formation of the written contract or subsequent to it.

18. Restatement, Second, Contracts, Section 213.

19. Restatement, Second, Contracts, Section 216.

BACKGROUND AND FACTS   *Alan Bronfman owned 80 percent of the stock of Distributors, Inc., a corporation that distributed kitchen appliances to builders in the Kansas City area. He signed a personal guaranty to Centerre Bank of Kansas City, the plaintiff, to secure a line of credit[a] that Centerre extended to Distributors. Because of a slump in the economy, Bronfman wanted to sell his interest in Distributors. He agreed to sell his entire interest in the company to Dan Brown and members of Brown's family. Brown inquired at the bank whether this change of ownership would affect Centerre's lending to Distributors. William McDaniel, a loan officer at the bank who handled Dis-*

Case 12.3

CENTERRE BANK OF KANSAS CITY v. DISTRIBUTORS, INC.
Missouri Court of Appeals,
1985.
705 S.W.2d 42.

tributors' account, orally promised that if Bronfman continued to guaranty the loans and if the Brown family would agree to give personal guaranties for Distributors' borrowings, then Centerre would continue to lend to Distributors.

After Dan Brown had provided these additional guaranties, Centerre withdrew its financing and demanded that Distributors' demand notes be paid within sixty days. The bank cited Distributors' poor performance over the past few years and the low credit rating that bank examiners had given the firm. The bank sued the corporation and its guarantors to collect the unpaid balance on the notes. The defendants filed counterclaims against the bank for damages for breach of the oral commitment to continue to extend credit that accompanied the written guaranties. The trial jury awarded a multimillion-dollar judgment for the defendants. The bank appealed.

TURNAGE, Judge.
*   *   *   *

The Bank contends the trial court improperly admitted evidence that McDaniel said the Bank would continue to extend credit to Distributors if each of the Browns delivered their personal guaranty of the Distributors' note because such evidence violated the parol evidence rule. The Browns contend the evidence does not violate the parol evidence rule because the guaranty was not an integrated agreement. They further contend that although they were bound on their guaranty the evidence shows that the guaranty was executed and delivered pursuant to their obligation under the oral agreement.

The argument that the guaranty is not an integrated agreement is easily answered. An integrated agreement simply means that the writing in question is a complete statement of the bargain made between the parties. The reason for the rule, of course, is that the parol evidence rule only prohibits evidence of prior or contemporaneous agreements which vary or contradict the terms of an unambiguous and complete writing. Here, the guaranty stated that "there are no conditions or limitations to this guaranty except those written or printed herein, and no alteration, change, or modification shall be made except in writing" and signed by the parties. This demonstrates that the writing was fully integrated and contained the complete agreement of the parties.

The Browns further contend that the evidence of the separate oral agreement for the continuation of credit does not vary or contradict the terms of the guaranty. The guaranty provided that the Browns unconditionally guaranteed payment when due of all indebtedness of Distributors to the Bank. The oral agreement claimed by the Browns would certainly contradict this term. The agreement calls for the Bank to extend further credit to Distributors and to not call the note due and in effect means the Browns would not be obligated to pay the Distributors' note when it was called due. Thus, the Browns would escape liability because under their alleged oral agreement the note was agreed not to be called in favor of further credit being extended.
*   *   *   *

In this case, the intention of the parties to create a complete unambiguous guaranty appears on the face of the guaranty. The written agreement is flatly contradicted by the oral agreement which the Browns seek to find from the testimony that the Bank would continue to extend credit to Distributors if the personal guaranties were delivered. The parol evidence rule is a rule of substantive law and not a rule of evidence and evidence offered in violation of it must be ignored. Therefore, the evidence of the statement by McDaniel that the Bank would continue to extend credit to Distributors if the Browns delivered their personal guaranties violated the parol evidence rule and such evidence must be ignored. It necessarily follows that such evidence could not be considered for the purpose of establishing an oral agreement between the Browns and the Bank. The court erred in submitting a verdict [instruction] which authorized a verdict in favor of the Browns if the jury found an agreement to extend credit to Distributors on the delivery of the Browns' personal guaranties.

The court held that the judgment in favor of the defendants should be reversed and that the trial court erred in allowing the parol evidence. The case was remanded to the lower court.

DECISION AND REMEDY

Note that the oral promise by the bank was contemporaneous with the written guaranties. If that promise had been made later, the defendants might have been able to claim that the promise was an effective subsequent modification of the prior contract arrangement.

COMMENTS

a. In this case, a *line of credit* is the limit of credit the Centerre Bank extended to Distributors—in other words, the full extent of credit the company could use in its dealings with the bank. When a line of credit is nearly exhausted, a customer is expected to reduce the indebtedness before drawing on it further.

Exhibit 12–3 Circumstances under Which Parol Evidence Is Admissible

CIRCUMSTANCE	RATIONALE
Subsequent modification of contract	Since courts assume all prior and contemporaneous negotiations and agreements are merged in the written contract, there is no reason to forbid evidence of changes in the written contract as long as they occur *after* the writing—unless the modification brings the contract under the Statute of Frauds, in which case the modification must be in writing to be enforceable.
Void or voidable contract	If one of the parties was deceived into agreeing to the terms of a written contract through mistake, fraud, or misrepresentation, evidence attesting to the deception should not be excluded.
Ambiguous contract terms	When the terms of a written contract are ambiguous, evidence is admissible to show the meaning of the terms.
Incomplete contract	If a written contract is incomplete because it lacks one or more essential terms, courts will allow evidence to fill in the gaps existing in the written contract.
Prior course of dealing or usage of trade	When buyers and sellers deal with each other over extended periods of time, certain customary practices develop. They are often overlooked in the writing of the contract, so courts allow the introduction of evidence to show how the parties have acted in the past or what is customary within the trade.
Contract subject to an agreed-upon condition	Parol evidence is admissible if the existence of the entire agreement is subject to an orally agreed-upon condition. Proof of the condition does not *alter* or *modify* the written terms but involves the very *enforceability* of the written contract. For example, Carvelli agrees, in a written contract with Jackson, to purchase real property from Jackson for $100,000. Prior to signing the contract, the parties orally agree that the contract is binding *only on the condition* that Carvelli's attorney approves the deal. Evidence concerning this condition is admissible because what is at issue is whether the contract is enforceable.
Obvious mistake (typographical, clerical, etc.)	When an *obvious* or *gross* typographical or clerical error exists that would clearly not represent the agreement of the parties, evidence is admissible to correct the error.

INTERPRETATION OF CONTRACTS

When considering the rules that govern the courts' interpretation of contracts, the most important principle to keep in mind is that the law attempts not only to enforce a contract but to enforce *the contract the parties made*. The rules, which emerged and developed in the common law over hundreds of years, provide the courts with guidelines for determining the meaning of and giving effect to the contract the parties made.

The Plain Meaning Rule

In most cases in which the meaning of a contract or its terms is in doubt, the dispute concerns the writing. As indicated in the discussion of the parol evidence rule, if the words used in a contract appear to be plain and unambiguous (that is, not subject to conflicting meanings), their meaning must be determined from *the face of the instrument*—that is, the written document alone.

This is sometimes referred to as the *plain meaning rule*. Under this rule, in interpreting a contract's words, the meaning of which appears to be clear and unambiguous, a court cannot consider *extrinsic evidence* (that is, evidence not contained in the body of the document) of any kind.

This amounts to excluding more than just parol evidence. When a court decides that the language in question has a plain meaning, evidence of trade usage, prior dealing, and course of performance may be excluded. A *usage of trade* is a practice, method, or custom commonly observed in a particular trade. *Prior dealing* refers to previous conduct that may be regarded as establishing a common basis of understanding for interpreting the parties' expressions and subsequent conduct. *Course of performance* refers to what each party, with the other party's knowledge and acceptance, has been doing in fulfilling the contract.

For example, imagine a contract for the "July–August" delivery of "1,000" of a certain breed of turkey. The contract makes no mention of who will pay the freight charges. For purposes of this example, assume that within the turkey trade, "July–August" indicates that delivery is to be spread over two months rather than made all at once and that "1,000" actually signifies 1,200. Further, assume that in the course of dealing with other tur-

key buyers, the seller has always included crossbred animals with purebreds in fulfilling contracts. Finally, imagine that during July, the buyer pays the freight charges without objection. Whether or not a court admits evidence of the meaning given these terms according to trade usage and course of dealing and performance would significantly affect the result of any litigation between the parties under the contract.[20]

Other Rules of Interpretation[21]

When the writing is clear and unequivocal, a court will enforce it according to its plain terms, and there is no need for the court to interpret the language of the contract. When the writing is ambiguous, a court will interpret the language to give effect to the parties' intent *as expressed in their contract*. This is the primary purpose of the rules of interpretation—to determine the parties' intent from the language used in their agreement and give effect to that intent. A court will not make or remake a contract nor interpret the language according to what the parties claim their intent was when they made it.

As much as possible, a reasonable, lawful, and effective meaning will be given to all of a contract's terms. It is presumed that persons who make a contract intend it to be legal, reasonable, and effective rather than illegal, invalid, or unreasonable or ineffective in its provisions. A contract will be interpreted as a whole; individual, specific clauses will be considered subordinate to the contract's general intent. All writings that are part of the same transaction will be interpreted together. Nevertheless, terms that were the subject of separate negotiation will be given greater consideration than standardized terms and terms that were not negotiated separately.

A word will be given its ordinary, commonly accepted meaning, and a technical word or term

---

20. In Section 2-202, the UCC permits extrinsic evidence even if there is no ambiguity and provides that the words' meaning is subject to evidence of course of dealing and usage of trade. On the other hand, Sections 1-205(4) and 2-208(2) provide in effect that inconsistent customs may not change the meaning of the contracts' words. Thus, cases decided under the UCC have had conflicting outcomes.

21. This section includes in paraphrase parts of the text of the Restatement, Second, Contracts Sections 201, 202, 203, and 206. The UCC has adopted these same principles in whole or in part; see UCC 1-205, 2-202, and 2-208.

will be given its technical meaning, unless the parties clearly intended something else. Specific and exact wording will be given greater consideration than general language. Written or typewritten terms prevail over printed ones.[22]

Because a contract should be drafted in clear and unambiguous language, a party who uses ambiguous expressions is held to be responsible for the ambiguities. Thus, where the language used has more than one meaning, it will be interpreted against the party who drafted the contract.

---

22. See, for example, UCC 2-317 and 3-118.

Finally, where evidence of trade usage, prior dealing, and course of performance is admitted, what each of the parties does in pursuance of the contract will be interpreted as consistent with what the other does and with any relevant usage of trade and course of dealing and performance. In these circumstances, express terms are given the greatest weight, followed by course of performance, course of dealing, and usage of trade, in that order. When considering custom and usage, a court will look at the customs and usage of trade of the particular business and the locale where the contract was made or is to be performed.

QUESTIONS AND CASE PROBLEMS

1. On May 1, by telephone, Yu offers to hire Benson to perform personal services. On May 5, Benson returns Yu's call and accepts the offer. Discuss fully whether this contract falls under the Statute of Frauds under the following circumstances:

(a) The contract calls for Benson to be employed for one year, with the right to begin performance immediately.

(b) The contract calls for Benson to be employed for nine months, with performance of services to begin on September 1.

(c) The contract calls for Benson to submit a written research report, with a deadline of two years for submission.

2. In December 1988, Kaplin ordered 11,000 yards of madras at 75 cents a yard from Reich. The order was made over the telephone. On January 9, 1989, Reich sent Kaplin a bill that included a statement of the quantity that Reich had sent Kaplin. On February 18, 1989, Kaplin wrote to Reich, stating:

Replying to your letter of the 18th, please be advised that we examined a few pieces of merchandise that were billed to us against your invoice No. 10203, and found that it was not up to our standard. We are, therefore, unable to accept this shipment. * * * Very truly yours, (signed) Isador Kaplin.

Reich sued Kaplin for payment owed under the contract. Kaplin defended on the ground that the contract was entered into over the telephone and therefore failed to meet Statute of Frauds requirements. Is Kaplin's argument convincing?

3. William Rowe was admitted to General Hospital, suffering from the effects of a severe gastric hemorrhage. On the day Rowe was admitted, Rowe's son informed an agent for the hospital that his father had no financial means but that he would pay for his father's medical services. Subsequently, the son stated, "Well, we want you to do everything you can to save his life, and we don't want you to spare any expense. Whatever he needs, Doctor, you go ahead and get it, and I will pay you." After Rowe was discharged from the hospital, his son refused to pay the medical bills. Can the hospital enforce the son's oral promise?

4. Roger is interested in starting a restaurant on Lake Faithful. He locates an old, vacant mansion on the lake, which, with alterations, would be ideal for the restaurant. The mansion is owned by Striker. Roger calls Striker on the telephone and contracts to lease the mansion, to be used as a restaurant with agreed alterations, for ten years at a lease price of $12,000 per year, with Roger to pay six months' rent in advance. Roger is to have immediate right to possession. He sends Striker a check for $6,000, noting on the check, "six months advance payment on ten-year lease—Striker mansion." Striker cashes the check upon receipt. Roger does not take immediate possession, but he does contract with Smith & Associates to make alterations to the mansion. Work on the alterations had not yet begun when, one month later, Striker has an opportunity to sell the mansion to a buyer at a substantial price. Striker tenders back to Roger $6,000, claiming the ten-year lease is unenforceable under the Statute of Frauds. Is Striker correct? Discuss fully.

5. The following oral contracts deal with the sale of goods. Discuss fully which of them are enforceable and which are unenforceable under the Statute of Frauds:

(a) Carrigan contracts to purchase for $2,000 napkins and tablecloths with the name of his restaurant, "Harvest House," embroidered on each.

(b) Harper, a merchant, sends Proctor, another merchant, a confirmation of their oral contract. Proctor receives this confirmation on May 1 and does not respond until May 20, at which time he refutes the contract.

6. Butler Brothers was the main contractor for a highway construction project near Minneapolis. Butler hired another contractor, Ganley Brothers, to perform some of the highway construction work. At the time

the contract was formed, Butler made several false representations to Ganley. If Ganley had known Butler's statements were fraudulent, Ganley would never have entered into the contract. The written contract between Butler and Ganley included the following clause: "The contractor [Ganley] has examined the said contracts * * * and is not relying upon any statement made by the company in respect thereto." In light of this clause, can Ganley introduce evidence of Butler's fraudulent misstatements at trial? [Ganley Bros. Inc. v. Butler Bros. Bldg. Co., 170 Minn. 373, 212 N.W. 602 (1927)]

7. Rimshot, director of a local basketball camp, wished to increase his business by advertising his camp. He discussed the possibility of printing up flyers about the camp with Lyal, a local printer. Rimshot told Lyal that not only did he want Lyal to print the flyers, he wanted him to distribute them to local merchants. Lyal said that he usually distributed about 20 flyers to each merchant and charged a small publication fee. Subsequently, Lyal and Rimshot entered into a written agreement under which Lyal agreed to print 1,000 flyers for Rimshot and to distribute them locally. Lyal printed the flyers but distributed them to only four merchants, giving 250 to each. After the poorest turnout in his basketball camp's history, Rimshot sued Lyal for breach of contract. Can he introduce parol evidence concerning Lyal's statements about how he normally distributed flyers? [See similar fact pattern in Stoops v. Smith, 100 Mass. 63, 97 Am.Dec. 76 (1868)]

8. Fernandez orally promised Pando that if Pando helped her win the New York state lottery, she would share the proceeds equally with him. Pando agreed to purchase the tickets in Fernandez's name, select the lottery numbers, and pray for divine intervention from a saint to help them win. Fernandez won $2.8 million in the lottery, which was to be paid over a ten-year period. When Fernandez failed to share the winnings equally, Pando sued for breach of her contractual obligation. Fernandez countered that the contract was unenforceable under the Statute of Frauds, since the contract could not be performed within one year. Could the contract be performed within a year? Explain. [Pando by Pando v. Fernandez, 127 Misc.2d 224, 485 N.Y.S.2d 162 (1984)]

9. Lero McClam, a widow, was trying to pay off the mortgage that was due on her home. Because this payment would deplete her financially, she asked her daughters to sign over to her their interest in two tracts of land in which the daughters held ownership interests. For this, McClam would hold the land during her lifetime; and upon her death all of her land, including her home, would be divided equally among all the children. McClam's attorney sent a signed letter to the daughters outlining McClam's intentions and included in the letter a legal description of the lands. McClam later orally repeated the promise to the daughters when they signed over the deeds. McClam, however, failed to will the property to all her children but instead left the land to one son, Donald McClam. The daughters sued for their interest in the land. Would the attorney's letter satisfy the Statute of Frauds requirement even if no actual agreement was made until later? If the letter is sufficient, would parol evidence be permitted

if it included matters not in the letter? [Smith v. McClam, 289 S.C. 452, 346 S.E.2d 720 (1986)]

10. Nichols Vasels and John LoGuidice orally contracted for the sale of land owned by Vasels. Vasels and LoGuidice signed a document entitled "Escrow Instructions." It contained a description of approximately twenty-seven acres of land but clearly provided that the acreage was to be split into four parcels. The purchase provision of this document related only to "Parcel 1," although the buyer was given an option to buy the remainder of the land. The document did not include a specific description of Parcel 1; according to the document, the specific boundaries were to be determined in the following manner: "seller shall deliver into escrow the legal description covering 'Parcel 1' prior to the close of escrow on 'Parcel 1.' Said legal description is to be approved by all parties in the writing." LoGuidice, the buyer, made the initial $50,000 payment but failed to make the second payment. Vasels sued to enforce the agreement, but LoGuidice claimed that the memorandum was too vague to be enforced under the Statute of Frauds and sued for the return of his $50,000 payment. Discuss LoGuidice's defense and his chances of success. What if both parties had orally agreed that Parcel 1 would constitute a specific area of land? [Vasels v. LoGuidice, 740 P.2d 1375 (Utah App. 1987)]

11. Donald Laird and Joseph Martin, land developers, orally contracted with Chesapeake Financial Corporation to undertake a joint venture to develop some real estate in Maryland. According to the agreement, Chesapeake was to provide the financing for the venture. Chesapeake later refused to provide the necessary funding, and Laird and Martin sued for damages as a result of Chesapeake's alleged misrepresentation. Chesapeake asserted the Statute of Frauds as a defense, claiming that it had not anticipated completing the project within one year's time and thus that the oral contract was unenforceable. Under the Maryland Statute of Frauds, "any agreement that is not to be performed within the space of one year from the making thereof" is required to be in writing. Discuss whether this oral contract falls under the Statute of Frauds. [Chesapeake Financial Corporation v. Laird, 289 Md. 594, 425 A.2d 1348 (1981)]

12. Alice was attempting to bid on a contract to supply uniforms to the U.S. government. Alice asked Robett Manufacturing whether it could act as a subcontractor for the project and make an offer for supplying the shirts and trousers. Robett sent a letter that stated, "We are pleased to offer 3,500 shirts at $4.00 each and the trousers at $3.00 each with delivery approximately ninety days after receipt of order." The letter was not signed but contained Robett's name and letterhead. Alice claimed that it accepted this offer from Robett. One week later, the U.S. government asked Robett to bid on the same contract; Robett did so and received the contract from the government. Alice sued Robett Manufacturing, claiming that a contract existed because Alice had accepted Robett's offer and that the written letter from Robett constituted a complete memorandum and satisfied the Statute of Frauds. Discuss whether Alice can succeed against Robett's Statute of Frauds defense. [Alice v. Robett Manufacturing Co., 328 F.Supp. 1377 (N.D.Ga. 1970)]

13. In 1974, George Wackenhut decided to install a sophisticated closed-circuit television camera security system for his home, which is known as the "Castle." Impossible Electronic Security discussed the use of their products with Wackenhut, and Wackenhut allowed an Impossible dealer, Jackson & Church, to begin installing the $47,000 system in his home. Wackenhut was unhappy to learn after the installation began that one component part in each of six cameras had to be replaced every three months for $5,000 each. He cancelled the order with Jackson & Church (and the dealer cancelled the order with Impossible) and decided to buy a cheaper security system from Jackson & Church manufactured by a competitor of Impossible. Jackson & Church had executed a written purchase order to Impossible, and Wackenhut had executed a written purchase order to Jackson & Church, but nothing in writing to Impossible. Impossible claims an oral contract was made that was later denied by Wackenhut. When Impossible sued Wackenhut for breach of the oral contract, Impossible relied on the purchase orders to meet the UCC writing requirement for the Statute of Frauds. Both orders contained a description of the product and the quantity involved. Impossible's order from the dealer described only a wholesale price, while Wackenhut's order described the retail price he was to pay to Jackson & Church. Discuss whether these two orders can be used by Impossible to evidence a contract under the UCC. Could Impossible win by showing that the security system is a specially manu-

factured good, thus removing the requirement of written evidence of the oral contract? Discuss. [Impossible Electronic Techniques, Inc. v. Wackenhut Protective Systems, Inc., 669 F.2d 1026 (5th Cir. 1982)]

14. Illinois Bell Telephone (IBT) and the Reuben H. Donnelly Corporation (RHD) had by contract jointly produced telephone directories in Illinois for over sixty years. While in the process of oral negotiations to renew the contracts, IBT notified RHD by letter that the existing contracts were being cancelled pursuant to contract terms. These contract terms required RHD to turn over records, to assign advertising contracts, to refrain from using certain information in any future directories RHD may publish, and so on. The termination clause under which IBT cancelled stated that "either party may cancel this agreement by giving prior written notice to the other one year in advance of the effective date of cancellation." The requirements imposed on RHD were to take place upon "termination." In anticipation that RHD's and IBT's interpretation of the contract terms and the time when RHD's obligations would become effective would differ, IBT filed suit seeking specific performance of its demand for RHD to meet the termination requirements immediately. RHD moved to dismiss the suit, claiming that the words of the contract were clear and that such demands were not effective until one year after "the effective date of cancellation." Discuss who is correct. [Illinois Bell Tel. Co. v. Reuben H. Donnelley Corp., 595 F.Supp. 1192 (N.D.Ill. 1984)]

Chapter 13

Third Party Rights

Once it has been determined that a valid and legally enforceable contract exists, attention can be turned to the rights and duties of the parties to the contract. Since a contract is a private agreement between the parties who have entered into it, it is fitting that these parties alone should have rights and liabilities under the contract. This idea is referred to as **privity of contract,** and it establishes the basic concept that third parties have no rights in a contract to which they are not a party.

To illustrate, suppose I offer to sell you my watch for $100, and you accept. Later, I refuse to deliver the watch to you even though you tender the $100. You decide to overlook my breach, but your close friend, Ann, is unhappy with my action and files suit. Can she receive judgment? The answer is obviously no, as she was not a party to the contract. You, as a party, have rights under the contract and could file a successful suit, but Ann has *no standing in court* (no right to sue).

There are two exceptions to this rule. The first involves a **third party beneficiary contract.** Here the parties to a contract make it with the intent to benefit a third party, and the third party has rights in the contract and may sue the promisor and under some circumstances the promisee to have it enforced. The second exception involves an **assignment of rights** or a **delegation of duties.** Here one of the original parties *transfers* contractual rights or obligations to a third party, giving the third party the rights or obligations of the transferor.

THIRD PARTY BENEFICIARY CONTRACTS

When the promisee to a contract intends at the time of contracting that the contract performance benefit a third person, the third person becomes a beneficiary of the contract and as a beneficiary has legal rights in the contract.

This means that three parties, instead of the traditional two, have rights under third party beneficiary contracts: (1) the one making the promise (the promisor) that benefits the third party; (2) the one to whom the promise is made (the promisee); and (3) the third party on whom the promisee intends to confer a benefit under the contract (the third party beneficiary). If the promisor fails to keep the promise that benefits the third party, the third party can bring an action against the promisor to have the contract enforced.

For example, Abbott contracts with Baker to pave Baker's driveway upon Baker's promise to pay Carlson $375. Carlson is a third party beneficiary (since Abbott intends him to benefit from Baker's promise). The courts will uphold Carlson's right to enforce the contract against Baker. Exhibit 13–1 illustrates the relationships of the parties in a third party beneficiary contract.

Note that only **intended beneficiaries** have legal rights. Third parties who benefit from a contract only *incidentally* are **incidental beneficiaries** and have no legal rights under the contract; they cannot sue to have the contract enforced.

Intended Beneficiaries

In determining whether a third party beneficiary is an intended or incidental beneficiary, the best question to ask is: to whom is performance to be given according to the language of the contract? In other words, according to the language of the contract, was the promisee's purpose to obtain the benefit for himself or herself primarily or to confer a benefit on another directly? Traditionally, third party beneficiaries were divided into two types: creditor beneficiaries and donee beneficiaries. These two major categories will be discussed below, but bear in mind that any *intended* beneficiary to a contract may sue to enforce the promise.[1]

---

1. The Restatement, Second, Contracts dispenses with the terms *creditor beneficiary* and *donee beneficiary* and distinguishes only between intended and incidental beneficiaries. Because the traditional terms appear in court decisions and are still occasionally used by the courts, we retain their usage here.

CREDITOR BENEFICIARIES If a promisee's main purpose in making a contract is to discharge a duty or debt he or she already owes to a third party, then the third party is a **creditor beneficiary**.[2] The creditor beneficiary contract arises when another person (the promisor) promises the debtor (the promisee) to pay the debtor's debt to the creditor (the third party). Although not a party to the contract, the creditor is *intended* as the beneficiary and can thus enforce the promise against the promisor.

Allowing a creditor beneficiary to sue the promisor directly results in a reduction of the number of potential lawsuits before the courts. For example, assume Abbott owes Carlson $5,000 and the debt is due. Abbott has to sell her car to pay the debt and finds a buyer, Baker. Abbott transfers title to her car to Baker in return for Baker's promise to pay Abbott's debt to Carlson. Abbott and Baker have created a third party beneficiary contract in which Baker is the promisor (because he made the promise benefiting the third party), Abbott is the promisee (because Baker made the promise to Abbott), and Carlson is the creditor beneficiary. If Baker breaches his promise to Abbott and fails to pay Carlson, Carlson can, of course, bring an action against Abbott to collect the debt because, under their prior contract, Abbott owes Carlson the money. Abbott, in turn, could then sue Baker for breach of contract. Allowing the

---

2. Restatement, Second, Contracts, Section 302(1)(a).

Exhibit 13-1 Third Party Beneficiary Contract Relationships

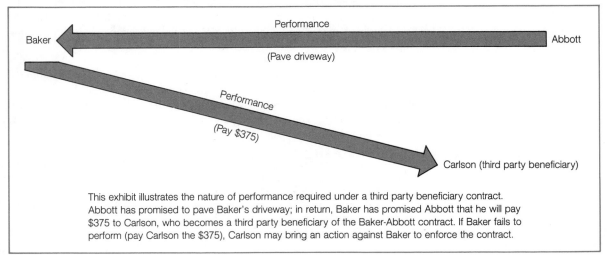

This exhibit illustrates the nature of performance required under a third party beneficiary contract. Abbott has promised to pave Baker's driveway; in return, Baker has promised Abbott that he will pay $375 to Carlson, who becomes a third party beneficiary of the Baker-Abbott contract. If Baker fails to perform (pay Carlson the $375), Carlson may bring an action against Baker to enforce the contract.

creditor beneficiary (Carlson) to sue the promisor (Baker) directly, however, renders the litigation more efficient: By circumventing the middle person (Abbott), the same result is achieved with one legal action instead of two.

In the following case, a creditor beneficiary to a contract sued the promisor directly for payment of the debt. This case, one of the earliest in a U.S. court in which an exception to the rule of privity was allowed, is a landmark in the law governing third party beneficiary contracts and is often cited by the courts.

Case 13.1

LAWRENCE v. FOX

Court of Appeals of New York,
1859.
20 N.Y. 268.

BACKGROUND AND FACTS   *Holly owed Lawrence (the plaintiff) $300. Fox (the defendant) suggested that Holly give him the money and promised to pay it to Lawrence to discharge Holly's debt. (Sufficient consideration was present in this transaction to create a contract between Holly and Fox.) Fox never paid Lawrence, so Lawrence sued the defendant, considering himself a third party beneficiary of the contract between Holly and Fox. The court decided that the plaintiff had a legal right to sue the defendant for failing to pay the $300 as promised, even though the plaintiff was never "in privity"; that is, he was not a direct party to the contract.*

GRAY, Justice.
*   *   *   *

In this case the promise was made to Holly and not expressly to the plaintiff;
*   *   * As early as 1806 it was announced by the Supreme Court of this State, upon what was then regarded as the settled law of England, "That where one person makes a promise to another for the benefit of a third person, that third person may maintain an action upon it." *Schermerhorn v. Vanderheyden* has often been re-asserted by our courts and never departed from.
*   *   *   *

In *Hall v. Marston* the court [said]: "It seems to have been well settled that if A promises B for a valuable consideration to pay C, the latter may maintain assumpsit [an action to enforce the agreement] for the money;" and in *Brewer v. Dyer*, the recovery was upheld, as the court said, "upon the principle of law *long recognized and clearly established*, that when one person, for a valuable consideration, engages with another, by a simple contract, to do some act for the benefit of a third, the latter, who would enjoy the benefit of the act, may maintain an action for the breach of such engagement; that it does not rest upon the ground of any actual or supposed relationship between the parties as some of the earlier cases would seem to indicate, but upon the broader and more satisfactory basis, that the law operating on the act of the parties creates the duty, establishes a privity, and implies the promise and obligation on which the action is founded."
*   *   *   *

In this case the defendant, upon ample consideration received from Holly, promised Holly to pay his debt to the plaintiff; the consideration received and the promise to Holly made it as plainly his duty to pay the plaintiff as if the money had been remitted to him for that purpose, and as well implied a promise to do so as if he had been made a trustee of property to be converted into cash with which to pay.
*   *   *   *

No one can doubt that he [Holly] owes the sum of money demanded of him, or that in accordance with his promise it was his duty to have paid it to the plaintiff; nor can it be doubted that whatever may be the diversity of opinion elsewhere, the adjudications in this State, from a very early period, approved by experience, have established the defendant's liability *   *   *."

The judgment should be affirmed.

Judgment was for the plaintiff, Lawrence. Fox was required to pay the plaintiff $300 to fulfill his original contract with Holly.

DECISION AND REMEDY

DONEE BENEFICIARIES If a promisee's main purpose in making a contract is to confer a gift upon a third party, then the third party is a **donee beneficiary.**[3] A donee beneficiary can enforce the promise of a promisor just as a creditor beneficiary can. To illustrate, suppose Abbott goes to her attorney, Baker, and enters into a contract in which Baker promises to draft a will naming Abbott's son, Carl, as an heir. Carl is a donee beneficiary, and if Baker does not prepare the will properly, Carl can sue Baker.[4] Or suppose Abbott offers to paint Baker's house if Baker pays $750 to Carl, Abbott's son. Abbott wants to give the money to Carl as a gift. Carl is a donee beneficiary and can enforce Baker's promise to pay $750.

The most common third party beneficiary contract involving a donee beneficiary is a life insurance contract. In a typical contract, Abbott, the promisee, pays premiums to Old Life, a life insurance company, and Old Life promises to pay a certain amount of money upon Abbott's death to anyone Abbott designates as beneficiary. The designated beneficiary, Carl, is a donee beneficiary under the life insurance policy and can enforce payment against the insurance company upon Abbott's death.

Incidental Beneficiaries

The benefit that an incidental beneficiary receives from a contract between two parties is unintentional. Therefore, an incidental beneficiary cannot enforce a contract to which he or she is not a party. Several factors must be examined to determine whether a party is an incidental beneficiary. The presence of one or more of the factors listed below strongly indicates an *intended* (rather than an incidental) benefit to the third party.

1. Performance rendered directly to the third party.

2. The rights of the third party to control the details of performance.
3. Express designation in the contract.

The following are examples of incidental beneficiaries. The third party has no rights in the contract and cannot enforce it against the promisor.

1. Jon contracts with Pat to build a factory on Pat's land. Jon's plans specify that Ad Pipe Company pipe fittings must be used in all plumbing. Ad Pipe Company is an incidental beneficiary and cannot enforce the contract against Jon by attempting to require Jon to purchase its pipe.
2. Ken contracts with Stu to build a recreational facility on Stu's land. Once the facility is constructed, it will greatly enhance the property values in the neighborhood. If Ken subsequently refuses to build the facility, Pete, a neighboring property owner, cannot enforce the contract against Ken by attempting to require Ken to build the facility.
3. Hank is an employee of Mary. Hank has been promised a promotion if his employer obtains a contract with Jones. Mary is unable to obtain the contract with Jones. Hank is an incidental beneficiary to that contract and has no right to sue Jones for being the cause of his failure to be promoted to a better-paying position. Indeed, Hank cannot sue Jones even if Hank loses his job as a result of the failure of Mary and Jones to reach an agreement.

Enforceable Rights—When The Rights of a Third Party Vest

Until the rights of a third party vest, the third party cannot enforce a contract against the original parties. When a right is *vested*, it is fixed or it takes effect. The rights of a third party vest when the original parties *cannot rescind or change the contract without the consent of the third party.*

The rights of an intended third party beneficiary vest (and the power of the original contracting parties to change, alter, or rescind the contract

---

3. Restatement, Second, Contracts, Section 302(1)(b).

4. Lucas v. Hamm, 56 Cal.2d 583, 364 P.2d 685, 15 Cal.Rptr. 821 (1961).

terminates) whenever one of the following three things happens:

1. The third party beneficiary learns of the contract and manifests assent to it at the request of the promisor and promisee.
2. The third party beneficiary brings suit upon the contract.
3. The third party materially alters his or her position in detrimental reliance on the contract.[5]

Suppose, for example, that Carlson learns of Baker's intention to give him $375 after the driveway has been paved. Before Carlson agrees to accept the payment, however, Baker decides to make payment elsewhere. Carlson's right to the payment will not have vested, since Carlson did not assent prior to the contract revision.

If the contract expressly reserves to the contracting parties the right to cancel, rescind, or modify the contract, the rights of the third party beneficiary are subject to any change that results. In such a case, the vesting of the third party's rights will not terminate the power of the original contracting parties to alter their legal relationship.[6] This is particularly true in most life insurance contracts, where the right to change the beneficiary is reserved.

ASSIGNMENT OF RIGHTS AND DELEGATION OF DUTIES

When third parties acquire rights or assume duties arising from a contract to which they were not parties, the *rights* are transferred to them by *assignment* and the *duties* are transferred by *delegation*. Assignment, or delegation, occurs *after* the original contract has been made, when one of the parties transfers an interest or duty in the contract to a third party.

Assignments are important because they are involved in many financing devices for businesses. Probably the most common contractual right that is assigned is the right to the payment of money, such as an account receivable. For instance, a retailer who sells to consumers on credit may need funds to finance the business. To obtain cash, the retailer may assign the right to the consumers' payments on their accounts to a third party, typically a financial institution, in exchange for an amount less than the amount due. The discount compensates the financial institution for the loss of the use of its money between the time it purchases the right and the time it collects from the consumers.

Assignments of accounts receivable, the proceeds from contracts not yet performed, and *general intangibles* (that is, property that is a right rather than a physical object—for example, stocks, bonds, and the goodwill of a business) *secure* (that is, act as assurances of payment for) millions of dollars of loans daily, providing working capital without which many businesses could not continue to operate. (Secured financing is subject to UCC Article 9, which is discussed in Chapter 29.)

Assignments also arise in a nonfinancing context and may not be subject to Article 9. For example, a claim that is not evidenced by a note or some other negotiable instrument can only be transferred by assignment. Collection agencies often purchase overdue accounts of businesses for, perhaps, fifty cents on the dollar and seek to compel the debtors to pay up. If the agency succeeds, it keeps whatever it collects.

A distinction must be made between assignment (or delegation), and novation (see Chapter 14). A *novation* is a written agreement entered into by *all* the parties whereby one party is substituted for another party; that is, one party is completely dismissed from the contract, and another is substituted. The dismissed party is no longer liable under the original contract. Such is not the case with assignment and delegation.

Assignments

In every bilateral contract, the two parties have corresponding rights and duties. One party has a *right* to require the other to perform some task, and the other has a *duty* to perform it. The transfer of *rights* to a third person is known as an *assignment*. When rights under a contract are assigned unconditionally, the rights of the assignor (the party making the assignment) are extinguished.[7] The third party (the assignee, or party receiving the assignment) has a right to demand perfor-

---

5. Restatement, Second, Contracts, Section 311.

6. Defenses raised against third party beneficiaries are given in Restatement, Second, Contracts, Section 309.

---

7. Restatement, Second, Contracts, Section 317.

Exhibit 13–2 **Assignment Relationships**

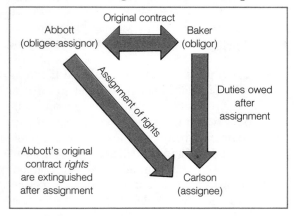

mance from the other original party to the contract (the obligor). This is illustrated in Exhibit 13–2.

For example, once Abbott has assigned her rights under the original contract with Baker to Carlson, Carlson can enforce the contract against Baker if Baker fails to perform. The assignee takes only those rights that the assignor originally had. For example, suppose Baker owes Abbott $50, and Abbott assigns to Carlson the right to receive the $50. Here, a valid assignment of a debt exists, and Baker must pay the $50 to Carlson (the assignee) or Carlson will be entitled to enforce payment in a court of law.

Furthermore, the assignee's rights are subject to the defenses that the obligor has against the assignor. To illustrate, suppose Baker contracts to sell her boat to Abbott for $40,000. The contract calls for delivery of the boat to Abbott or his assignee upon presentation of a receipt of payment signed by Baker. Abbott fraudulently gives Baker a worthless check, and Baker signs the receipt, noting thereon "payment by check." Abbott is in debt to Carlson and in satisfaction of the debt assigns to Carlson the contract rights for the delivery of the boat. Baker, upon discovery of the worthless check, has a legal right to avoid the contractual obligation to deliver the boat to Abbott. Since the assignee Carlson's rights are subject to this same defense, Carlson cannot require Baker to transfer the boat, even though she is an innocent party to these events.

STATUTE OF FRAUDS In general, an assignment can take any form, oral or written. Naturally, it is more difficult to prove the occurrence of an

oral assignment, so it is practical to put all assignments in writing.

Of course, assignments covered by the Statute of Frauds must be in writing to be enforceable. As noted in Chapter 12, assignments of an interest in land, contracts that cannot be performed within one year, promises to answer for the debts of another, promises in consideration of marriage, and promises of an administrator or an executor to personally pay the debts of an estate must also be in writing. In addition, most states require contracts for the assignment of wages to be in writing.[8]

CONSIDERATION An assignment need *not* be supported by legally sufficient consideration to be effective. A gratuitous assignment is just as effective as an assignment made for money. The absence of consideration becomes significant, however, when the assignor wants to revoke the assignment. If the assignment was made for consideration, the assignor cannot revoke it. If no consideration is involved, the assignor can revoke, thereby cancelling the right of the third party to demand performance or to sue for failure to render that performance.[9] Gratuitous assignments can be revoked by:

1. The subsequent assignment of the same right to another third party.
2. The death of the assignor.
3. The bankruptcy of the assignor.
4. A notice of revocation given to the assignee.

RIGHTS THAT CANNOT BE ASSIGNED As a general rule, all rights can be assigned, except in special circumstances. The following is a list of these special circumstances with examples:

1. If a statute expressly prohibits assignment, the right in question cannot be assigned. Suppose John is a new employee of Craft, Inc. Craft is an employer under workers' compensation statutes in this state, and thus John is a covered employee. John has a relatively high-risk job. In need of a loan, John borrows the money from Shady, assigning to Shady all workers' compensation benefits due him should he be injured on the job. This type of assignment of *future* workers' compensa-

---

8. See, for example, California Labor Code, Section 300. There are other assignments that must be in writing, as well.

9. Restatement, Second, Contracts, Section 332.

tion benefits is prohibited by state statute and thus cannot be assigned.

2. If a contract stipulates that the rights cannot be assigned, then, *ordinarily*, they cannot be assigned.[10] Suppose Baker agrees to build a house for Abbott. The contract between Abbott and Baker states: "The contract cannot be assigned by Abbott. Any assignment renders this contract void, and all rights hereunder will thereupon terminate." Abbott then attempts to assign her rights to Carlson. Carlson cannot enforce the contract against Baker by trying to get Baker to build the house because the contract expressly prohibits the assignment of rights. (But once the house is built, the rights to the monetary payment are assignable.)

3. When a contract is uniquely *personal* in nature, the rights under the contract cannot be assigned unless all that remains is a money payment. Suppose Baker signs a contract to be a tutor for

Abbott's children. Abbott then attempts to assign her right in Baker's services to Carlson. Carlson cannot enforce the contract against Baker because the contract called for the rendering of a unique personal service.[11]

4. Finally, a right cannot be assigned if assignment will materially increase or alter the risk of the obligor.[12] Assume Abbott takes out an insurance policy on her hotel with Preventive Casualty, an insurance company. The policy insures against fire, theft, floods, and vandalism. Abbott then attempts to assign the insurance policy to Carlson, who also owns a hotel. The assignment is ineffective because it substantially alters Preventive Casualty's risk. Insurance companies evaluate the particular risk associated with a certain party and tailor their policies to fit that exact risk. If the policy is assigned to a third party, the insurance risk will be materially altered. Therefore, the assignment will not operate to give Carlson any rights against Preventive Casualty.

In the following case, the central issue was whether a company that sold a spa to another company could assign to the buyer membership contracts that included exculpatory clauses limiting liability for personal injuries. The claim of nonassignability due to the personal nature of the contract is discussed.

---

10. Several exceptions to this rule exist. First, a contract cannot prevent assignment of the right to receive money. This exception exists to encourage the free flow of money and credit in modern business settings. Second, the assignment of rights in real estate normally cannot be prohibited, because this would be contrary to public policy. Such prohibitions are called *restraints against alienation* (to alienate, in this context, means to freely sell or transfer land interests). Third, the assignment of negotiable instruments cannot be prohibited. Fourth, in a sale-of-goods contract, the right to receive damages for breach of contract or for payment of an account owed may be assigned even though the sales contract prohibits assignment [UCC 2-210(2)].

11. Restatement, Second, Contracts, Sections 317 and 318.

12. See UCC 2-210(2).

Case 13.2

PETRY v. COSMOPOLITAN SPA INTERNATIONAL, INC.

Court of Appeals of Tennessee, Eastern Section, 1982. 641 S.W.2d 202.

BACKGROUND AND FACTS   *On August 8, 1978, the plaintiff, Shirley Petry, entered into a contract with the defendant, Cosmopolitan Spa International, Inc. (Cosmopolitan). The contract was for a spa membership that was to include "processing, program counseling, and facilities usage." The written contract contained an exculpatory clause. The pertinent part of the clause stated, "Member fully understands and agrees that in participating in one or more of the courses, or using the facilities maintained by Cosmopolitan, there is the possibility of accidental or other physical injury. Member further agrees to assume the risk of such injury and further agrees to indemnify Cosmopolitan from any and all liability to Cosmopolitan by either the Member or third party as the result of the use by the Member of the facilities and instructions as offered by Cosmopolitan."*

On or around January 1, 1980, Cosmopolitan sold the spa to Holiday Spa of Tennessee, Inc. (Holiday). On February 25, 1980, the plaintiff, Shirley Petry, injured her back when she sat on an exercise machine and it collapsed under her. She brought this suit against both Cosmopolitan and Holiday for damages for personal injuries resulting from the defendants' negligence in properly maintaining the exercise machine. The defendants claimed that the exculpatory clause negated their liability. Petry argued that Holiday could not use the exculpatory clause as a defense because it was part of a contract for personal services, and therefore the contract was not assignable. The trial court granted a summary judgment to the defendants, and Petry appealed.

PARROTT, Presiding Judge.

* * * *

The Supreme Court of Tennessee [has] held * * * that an exculpatory clause of almost the exact type and wording as the one in this case was valid and enforceable. That case is both factually and legally on point with this one. The trial judge below correctly recognized this in his summary judgment opinion. Like the court below, we are compelled by the doctrine of stare decisis to follow this holding. [The Supreme Court of Tennessee case referred to above] is a clear and unambiguous decision by the highest court of this state and has never been altered or overruled.

* * * *

Appellant also contends that if the exculpatory clause is valid, it does not protect appellee, Holiday, from liability because it could not be assigned. Again, we must disagree. The exculpatory clause in this contract was a right of appellee Cosmopolitan. Generally, contractual rights can be assigned [unless:]

(a) the substitution of a right of the assignee for the right of the assignor would materially change the duty of the obligor, or materially increase the burden or risk imposed on him by his contract, or materially impair his chance of obtaining return performance, or materially reduce its value to him, or

(b) the assignment is forbidden by statute or is otherwise inoperative on grounds of public policy, or

(c) assignment is validly precluded by contract.

None of the above exceptions to assignability can be successfully raised as to this exculpatory clause. Appellant contends that the assignment was invalid because the contract was of a personal nature and that she never consented to the assignment. We find this unpersuasive. This contract was primarily for the use of spa facilities and not of a personal nature.

The exculpatory clause in this case was clearly enforceable, and the contract containing it was assignable to Holiday. Petry's suit was barred as a matter of law and was properly dismissed by summary judgment.

DECISION AND REMEDY

ANTI-ASSIGNMENT CLAUSES Anti-assignment clauses in contracts are increasing in both number and importance. If the promisor makes it clear that a right is *not* to be assignable, generally no subsequent assignment will be effective. (As pointed out in footnote 10, however, there are some important exceptions.)

Anti-assignment clauses have appeared in leases for many years. Now they are being used more frequently in other types of contracts as well. Recently, they have appeared in mortgage contracts, where they represent attempts to restrict the assumption of mortgages by new owners of real property. The typical lease or mortgage today cannot be assigned without the landlord's or mortgagee's consent.

Typical clauses in mortgages are due-on-sale (DOS) provisions. Under such provisions, a purchaser of mortgaged realty cannot assume the mortgage without the mortgagee's consent. The due-on-sale provision accelerates the entire loan, making the mortgage fully payable. Therefore the loan would have to be fully paid (by the buyer) or the buyer would have to secure a new mortgage (at the current interest rate). The Supreme Court has upheld such clauses for federally insured financial institutions, and most states, either by statute or judicial decision, permit and enforce DOS clauses in mortgage contracts.

Certain contracts provide that if the promisee assigns his or her rights under the contract to a third party, the contract itself will become void. These contract provisions are frequently found in insurance policies. They stipulate that the policy rights will be forfeited if the policyholder assigns the policy. If the assignment is attempted before a loss is incurred, the company can declare that the policy is void. (On the other hand, if the assignment is made after the loss, the claim is reduced to a monetary right, and the assignee can recover.) Typically, when an anti-assignment clause restrains the alienation (transfer or sale) of property, the clause becomes subject to judicial review.

Restraints on the power to assign only operate against the parties themselves. They do not effectively prohibit an assignment by operation of law, such as an assignment pursuant to bankruptcy or death.

NOTICE OF THE ASSIGNMENT   Once a valid assignment of rights has been made to a third party, the third party should notify the obligor (Baker in Exhibit 13–2) of the assignment. This is not legally necessary, because an assignment is effective immediately, whether or not notice is given. Two major problems arise, however, when notice of the assignment is not given to the obligor:

1.   If the assignor assigns the same right to two different persons, the question arises as to which one has priority (right) to the performance by the obligor. Although the rule most often observed in the United States is that the first assignment in time is the first in right, some states follow the English rule, which basically gives priority to the first assignee who gives notice.[13]

_____

13. At common law, there were three different rules. The first rule was called the English rule. Assignees second in time to the first assignee prevailed in every case in which they had paid value, had taken the assignment without notice of the prior assignment, and had given the *obligor* notice of the assignment before the first assignee gave such notice. Another rule, called the New York rule, essentially stated that the first assignment in time is first in right. According to the third rule, the Massachusetts rule, the first assignee prevailed provided the first assignment was not revocable at the time the second assignment was made.

For example, suppose Baker owes Abbott $1,000 on a contractual obligation. On May 1, Abbott assigns this monetary claim to Carlson. No notice of assignment is given Baker. On June 1, for services Dullus has rendered to Abbott, Abbott assigns the same monetary claim from Baker to Dullus. Dullus immediately notifies Baker of the assignment. Although in the majority of states Carlson would have priority to receive payment, because Carlson's assignment was first in time, in some states Dullus would have priority because Dullus gave first notice.

2.   Until the obligor has notice of assignment, the obligor can discharge his or her obligation by performance to the assignor, and performance by the obligor to the assignor constitutes a discharge to the assignee. Once the obligor receives proper notice, only performance to the assignee can discharge the obligor's obligations.

To illustrate, suppose Baker owes Abbott $1,000 on a contract obligation. Abbott assigns this monetary claim to Carlson. No notice of assignment is given to Baker. Baker pays Abbott the $1,000. Although the assignment was valid, Baker's payment to Abbott was a discharge of the debt, and Carlson's failure to give notice to Baker of the assignment caused Carlson to lose the right to collect the money from Baker. If Carlson had given Baker notice of the assignment, Baker's payment to Abbott would not have discharged the debt, and Carlson would have had a legal right to require payment from Baker.

Delegation of Duties

Just as a party can transfer rights under a contract through an assignment, a party can also transfer duties. Duties are not assigned, however. They are *delegated*. Normally, a delegation of duties does not relieve the party making the delegation—the delegator—of the obligation to perform in the event that the party who has been delegated the duty—the delegatee—fails to perform.

FORM OF THE DELEGATION   No special form is required to create a valid delegation of duties. As long as the delegator expresses a present intention to make the delegation, it is effective. The delegator need not even use the word *delegate*.

DUTIES THAT CAN BE DELEGATED   As a general rule, any duty can be delegated. Exhibit

13–3 illustrates the relationships involved in a delegation. There are, however, some exceptions to this rule. Delegation is prohibited in the following situations:

1. When performance depends on the *personal* skill or talents of the obligor.
2. When special trust has been placed in the obligor.
3. When performance by a third party will vary materially from the performance expected by the obligee under the contract.
4. Usually, when a contract restricts either party's right to delegate duties.

Suppose Baker contracts with Abbott to tutor Abbott in the various aspects of financial underwriting and investment banking. Baker is an experienced businessperson who is well known for his expertise in finance. Further, assume that Baker wants to delegate his duties to teach Abbott to a third party, Carlson. This delegation would be ineffective, since Baker has contracted to render a service to Abbott that is founded upon Baker's *expertise*. It would represent a change from Abbott's expectancy under the contract. Therefore, Carlson cannot perform Baker's duties.

Suppose Baker, an attorney, contracts with Abbott, a banker, to advise Abbott on a proposed merger with a savings and loan association. Baker wishes to delegate this duty to advise the bank to Carlson, a law firm across town. Services of an attorney are *personal in nature*. Baker's delegation will be ineffective.

Exhibit 13-3 Delegation Relationships

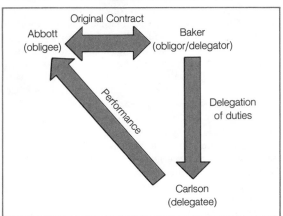

Finally, assume that Baker contracts with Abbott to pick up and deliver heavy construction machinery to Abbott's property. Baker then delegates this duty to Carlson, who is in the business of delivering heavy machinery. The delegation is effective. The performance required is of a *routine and nonpersonal nature* and does not change Abbott's expectancy under the contract.

EFFECT OF A DELEGATION OF DUTIES   If a delegation of duties is enforceable, the obligee (Abbott in the exhibit) must accept performance from the delegatee. The obligee can legally refuse performance from the delegatee only if the duty is one that may not be delegated. A valid delegation of duties *does not relieve* the delegator (Baker in the exhibit) of obligations under the contract.[14] If the delegatee (Carlson in the exhibit) fails to perform, the delegator is still liable to the obligee.

LIABILITY OF THE DELEGATEE TO THE OBLIGEE.   If the delegatee fails to perform, whether the obligee can hold the delegatee liable comes into issue. If the delegatee has made a promise of performance that will directly benefit the obligee, there is an assumption of duty. Breach of this duty makes the delegatee liable to the obligee.

Suppose Abbott contracts with Carlson to build Carlson a house according to Carlson's blueprint plans. Abbott becomes seriously ill and contracts to have Baker build the house for Carlson. Baker fails to build the house. Is Baker (the delegatee) liable to Carlson (the obligee)? The answer is yes. Carlson can sue Baker *or* Abbott (the delegator), or both, for damages (but can only collect from one of them). This is an area in which the law governing third party beneficiaries overlaps with delegation law. In effect, Carlson's position here is the same as that of a third party beneficiary to the Abbott-Baker contract.

When a contract provides for "assignment of all rights," this wording may also be treated as a delegation and an assumption of duties. The traditional view was that under this type of assignment, Carlson did not assume any duties. This view was based on the theory that the acceptance of the benefits of the contract was not sufficient

---

14. Crane Ice Cream Co. v. Terminal Freezing Co., 147 Md. 588, 128 A. 280 (1925).

to imply a promise to assume the duties of the contract.

Modern authorities, however, take the view that the probable intention in using such general words is to create an assignment of rights and a delegation and an assumption of duties.[15] There-

---

15. UCC 2-210(1) (where there is a general assignment of a contract for the sale of goods). Restatement, Second, Contracts, Section 328.

fore, when general words are used (for example, "I assign the contract" or "all my rights under the contract"), the contract is construed as implying an assignment of rights and a delegation and an assumption of duties.

Finally, note that the delegator has no further liability after a novation has occurred. We return to the concept of novation in the next chapter.

QUESTIONS AND CASE PROBLEMS

1. John has been accepted as a freshman to attend a college 200 miles from his home for the fall semester. John's roommate is his close friend, Daniel. John's father, Michael, makes a contract with auto dealer Jackson to purchase a new car for $10,000 to be delivered to John, with the title in John's name. Daniel is delighted to hear of Michael's purchase for John, since Daniel will not have a car of his own at college and will benefit if John has a car. Michael pays the full purchase price and takes off for a six-month vacation in Europe. Jackson never delivers the car, and John files an action against Jackson. Discuss fully whether John can recover for Jackson's breach of contract. Would your answer be any different if Daniel sued Jackson for breach of contract?

2. Five years ago, Jane purchased a house. At that time, being unable to pay the full purchase price, she borrowed money from Thrift Savings and Loan, which in turn took an 8 percent mortgage on the house. The mortgage contract did not prohibit the assignment of the mortgage. Now Jane has secured a new job in another city and has sold the house to Sylvia. The purchase price included payment to Jane of the value of her equity and the assumption of the mortgage held by Thrift. At the time of this contract, Thrift did not know of or consent to the sale. On the basis of these facts, if Sylvia defaults in making the house payments to Thrift, what are Thrift's rights?

3. Thomas is a student attending college. He signs a one-year lease agreement that runs from September 1 to August 31. The lease agreement specifies that the lease cannot be assigned without the landlord's consent. Thomas decides not to go to summer school and assigns the balance of the lease (three months) to a close friend, Fred. The landlord objects to the assignment and denies Fred access to the apartment. Thomas claims Fred is financially sound and should be allowed the full rights and privileges of an assignee. Discuss fully whether the landlord or Thomas is correct.

4. Ben Cartwright sells the mineral rights to 1,000 acres on the Ponderosa to Ajax Mining Company for royalty payments of $1,000 per month for the term of the agreement. One month later, Ben assigns the royalties to his son, Little Joe, as a gift. Later, Little Joe's actions around the Ponderosa cause him to fall out of favor with his father. Ben, in need of working capital, contracts with banker John for a loan of $50,000, with Ben assigning the royalty payments to John for the repayment of this loan. The next royalty payment arrives. Discuss who is entitled to the royalty payment, Little Joe or banker John.

5. Diane has a specific set of plans to build a sailboat. The plans are detailed in nature, and any boat builder can build the boat. Diane secures bids, and the low bid is made by the Whale of a Boat Corporation. Diane contracts with Whale to build the boat for $4,000. Whale then receives unexpected business from elsewhere. In order to meet the delivery date in the contract with Diane, Whale assigns (delegates) the contract, without Diane's consent, to Quick Brothers, a reputable boat builder. When the boat is ready for delivery, Diane learns of the assignment and refuses to accept delivery, even though the boat is built to specifications. Discuss fully whether Diane is obligated to accept and pay for the boat. Would your answer be any different if Diane did not have a specific set of plans but instead contracted with Whale to design and build a sailboat for $4,000? Explain.

6. Christopher wrote a letter to Donald claiming that Donald owed him $3,000 for the shipment of string bikinis he sent Donald three months ago. Donald wrote back, saying that the bikinis were defective and that he therefore refused to pay. Christopher wrote back that his lawyer had advised him that it was questionable whether Donald had informed him of the defect in time and that Christopher might have a valid claim for the purchase price of $3,000 despite any defects. About a month later, Donald wrote back to Christopher informing him that Jerry, who owed Donald $3,000 from a previous contract, had agreed with Donald to make the payment to Christopher. Thereafter, Jerry failed to make the payment to Christopher. Can Christopher sue Jerry?

7. Owens, a federal prisoner, was transferred from federal prison to the Nassau County Jail pursuant to a contract between the U.S. Bureau of Prisons and the county. The contract included a policy statement that required the receiving prison to provide for the safekeeping and protection of transferred federal prisoners. While in the Nassau County Jail, Owens was beaten severely by prison officials and suffered lacerations, bruises, and a lasting impairment that caused blackouts. Can Owens, as a third party beneficiary, sue the county for breach of its agreement with the U.S. Bureau of Prisons? [Owens v. Haas, 601 F.2d 1242 (2d Cir. 1979)]

8. Clement was seriously injured in a car accident with King. Clement sued King. King retained Prestwich as her attorney. Because of the alleged negligence of Prestwich, Clement was able to obtain a $21,000 judgment on her claim against King. Clement received from King a purported written assignment of King's malpractice claim against Prestwich as settlement for the judgment against her. Can King assign her cause of action against Prestwich to Clement? [Clement v. Prestwich, 114 Ill.App.3d 479, 448 N.E.2d 1039, 70 Ill.Dec. 161 (1983)]

9. Fox Brothers agreed to convey to Canfield Lot 23 together with a one-year option to purchase Lot 24 in a subdivision known as Fox Estates. The agreement did not contain any prohibitions, restrictions, or limitations against assignments. Canfield paid the price of $20,000 and took title to Lot 23. Thereafter, Canfield assigned his option rights in Lot 24 to the Scotts. When the Scotts tried to exercise their right to the option, Fox Brothers refused to convey the property to them. The Scotts then brought suit for specific performance. What was the result? [Scott v. Fox Brothers Enterprises, Inc., 667 P.2d 773 (Colo.App. 1983)]

10. Rensselaer Water Company was under contract to the city of Rensselaer, New York, to provide water to the city, including water at fire hydrants. A warehouse owned by H. R. Moch Company was totally destroyed by a fire which could not be extinguished because of inadequate water pressure at the fire hydrants. Moch brought suit against Rensselaer Water Company for damages, claiming that Moch was a third-party beneficiary to the city's contract with the water company. Will Moch be able to recover damages from the water company on the basis that the water company breached its contract with the city? Explain. [H. R. Moch Co. v. Rensselaer Water Co., 247 N.Y. 160, 159 N.E. 896 (1928)]

Chapter 14

Performance and Discharge

Just as rules are necessary to determine when a legally enforceable contract exists, so also are they necessary to determine when one of the parties can justifiably say, "I have fully performed, so I am now discharged from my obligations under this contract." The legal environment of business requires the identification of some point at which one or both parties can reasonably know their duties are at an end.

The **discharge** (termination) of a contract is ordinarily accomplished when both of the parties perform those acts promised in the contract. For example, a buyer and seller have a contract for the sale of a bicycle for $50. This contract will be discharged upon the buyer's payment of $50 to the seller and the seller's transfer of possession of the bicycle to the buyer.

Although a contract is ordinarily discharged by the parties' performance of their contractual duties, discharge can also occur in other ways. In this chapter, we will discuss some of the more important ways in which contracts can be discharged.[1] Broadly speaking, contracts can be discharged by the following:

1. The occurrence or failure of a *condition* upon which a contract is based.
2. *Performance* (or breach of contract, in which case the nonbreaching party is discharged from the duty of performance).
3. *Agreement of the parties* (through rescission, novation, or accord and satisfaction).
4. *Operation of law* (resulting from material alteration of the contract, the statute of limitations, bankruptcy, or impossibility or commercial impracticability of performance).

CONDITIONS

In most contracts, promises of performance are not *expressly* conditioned or qualified. Rather, they are *absolute promises*. They must be performed,

---

1. Looking at *all* of them would take an entire book.

or the party promising the act will be in breach of contract. For example, I promise to pay you $100 on September 1. The promise is unconditional. If I do not pay you the $100, I am in breach of contract.

In some cases, however, performance may be beneficial only if a certain event either does or does not occur. Therefore, *a condition* is inserted into the contract, either expressly by the parties or impliedly by courts. If this condition is not satisfied, the obligations of the parties are discharged.

Suppose I offer to purchase a tract of your land on the condition that your neighbor to the south agrees to sell me her land. You accept my offer. Our obligations (promises) are conditioned upon your neighbor's willingness to sell her land. Should this condition not be satisfied (for example, if your neighbor refuses to sell), our obligations to each other are discharged and cannot be enforced.

Thus, a **condition** is a possible future event, the occurrence or nonoccurrence of which will trigger the performance of a legal obligation or terminate an existing obligation under a contract.[2]

Although there is a fundamental distinction between the breach of an absolute promise and the failure or nonoccurrence of an express condition, both can occur in a single contract.

For example, if you say to Bob, "If you wash my car, I will pay you $10," your duty to pay is subject to the condition that Bob wash your car.

Bob made no promise to wash your car. If there is a failure of the condition—that is, if Bob does not wash your car—you are under no liability to him.

Imagine, however, that you say to Bob, "I will pay you $10 if you wash my car, provided you also promise to wash my car," and Bob says, "I promise to wash your car." Now, if Bob does not wash your car, your duty to pay is discharged, and Bob is liable for breach of contract for failure to perform his promise.

Three types of conditions can be present in contracts—conditions *precedent*, conditions *subsequent*, and conditions *concurrent*.

Conditions Precedent

A condition that must be fulfilled before a party's performance is due is called a **condition precedent.** The condition precedes the absolute duty to perform. For example, Fisher promises to contribute $1,000 to the Salvation Army if Calvin completes college. Fisher's promise is subject to the (express) condition precedent of Calvin's completing college. Until the condition is fulfilled or satisfied, Fisher's promise to donate to charity does not become absolute.

The following case concerns a condition precedent in a contract for the sale of a pharmacy.[3]

---

2. Restatement, Second, Contracts, Section 224, defines a condition as "an event, not certain to occur, which must occur, unless its nonoccurrence is excused, before performance under a contract becomes due."

3. As a practical matter, the difference between conditions precedent and conditions subsequent is relatively unimportant from a substantive point of view, but very important procedurally. Usually, as in the following case, the plaintiff must prove conditions precedent, since usually, it is he or she that claims there is a duty to be performed. Similarly, the defendant must usually prove conditions subsequent, since it is usually he or she that claims a duty no longer exists.

BACKGROUND AND FACTS *On June 8, 1983, the plaintiff, K & K Pharmacy, Inc., entered into a written contract with the defendant, James R. Barta, for the sale of a pharmacy to Barta. The pharmacy was situated in a shopping mall with other stores, and the pharmacy premises were leased from the owner of this mall, Larsen Enterprises. The contract between K & K and Barta contained a provision that stated: "This Agreement shall be contingent upon Buyer's ability to obtain a new lease from Larsen Enterprises, Inc., for the premises presently occupied by Seller. In the event Buyer is unable to obtain a new lease satisfactory to Buyer, this Agreement shall be null and void." Barta wanted to sell certain foodstuffs in the pharmacy, as he did in his other stores, but another lessee in the shopping mall had an exclusive right to sell groceries and refused to give the necessary concession. As a result, Barta refused to sign*

 Case 14.1

K & K PHARMACY, INC. v. BARTA

Supreme Court of Nebraska, 1986.
222 Neb. 215, 382 N.W.2d 363.

a lease with Larsen and notified K & K Pharmacy that he would not go through with the sale. K & K Pharmacy sued to recover damages for alleged breach of the contract. The district court gave summary judgment for Barta, and the plaintiff appealed.

BOSLAUGH, Justice.
*   *   *   *

The case turns on the meaning and effect of the "New Lease" provision in the contract. Generally, in negotiating a contract the parties may impose any condition precedent, a performance of which is essential before the parties become bound by the agreement. The provision entitled "13. *New Lease*" was clearly a condition precedent to the existence of binding contractual obligations between the parties. The contract was *contingent* upon the defendant's obtaining a new lease *satisfactory* to him. This court has held that "where a contract is executed but its effectiveness is dependent upon the fulfillment of an agreed condition before it can become a binding contract, such contract cannot be enforced unless the condition is performed."
*   *   *   *

The lease provision in the contract was not only a condition precedent but it was also a satisfaction clause. However, its terms were not ambiguous, and a reading of the plain language shows that the contract depended upon the buyers' satisfaction with a new lease. This court has stated that "[i]f the agreement leaves no doubt that honest satisfaction and no more is meant, the condition does not occur if the obligor is honestly, even though unreasonably, dissatisfied." While a mere statement of dissatisfaction is not conclusive, the evidence need only show honest dissatisfaction and no more.

This court has also stated that, ordinarily, such a question of honest satisfaction is one of fact. However, summary judgment is an appropriate remedy when there is no genuine issue as to any material fact.

In the present case summary judgment was correctly granted if the pleadings and depositions show that there was no genuine issue as to the defendant's satisfaction with a new lease. The plaintiffs do not allege any bad faith or dishonest dissatisfaction on the defendant's part, but merely allege a breach of contract which would require proof that the condition precedent occurred. There simply is no evidence to support that contention.

Assuming the truth of all of the evidence offered by the plaintiff, there is no evidence of performance of the condition precedent which was necessary before the contract could be enforced against the defendant. The evidence is undisputed that the defendant was not able to obtain a lease satisfactory to him. The defendant was not able to obtain a lease allowing him to employ his established marketing policy. Further, there is no evidence that defendant was anything but honestly dissatisfied with the lease. This was not a case where the party who had some obligation as to the condition precedent refused to make a good faith effort to perform the condition.

DECISION AND REMEDY
The appellate court held that the contract was not enforceable, because the condition precedent had not occurred. Thus, the decision of the lower court in favor of the defendant was affirmed.

Conditions Subsequent

When a condition operates to terminate a party's duty to perform, it is called a **condition subsequent.** The condition follows, or is subsequent to, the absolute duty to perform. If the condition occurs, the party need not perform any further. For example, if Hartman promises to work for the San Pedro Company for one year unless he is admitted to Stanford's Graduate School of Business, the absolute duty to work is conditioned upon his not being admitted. Hartman's promise to work for San Pedro continues to be absolute until he is admitted to Stanford. Once Hartman is officially admitted, the absolute duty to work for San Pedro ends, and Hartman is released from the contract.[4]

Concurrent Conditions

When each party's absolute duty to perform is conditioned on the other party's absolute duty to perform, there are **concurrent conditions.** Concurrent conditions occur only when the parties expressly or impliedly are to perform their respective duties *simultaneously.* For example, if a buyer promises to pay for goods when they are delivered by the seller, each party's absolute duty to perform is conditioned upon the other party's absolute duty to perform. The buyer's duty to pay for the goods does not become absolute until the seller either delivers or tenders the goods. Likewise, the seller's duty to deliver the goods does not become absolute until the buyer tenders or actually makes payment. Therefore, neither can recover from the other for breach unless he or she first tenders his or her own performance.

Express and Implied Conditions

Conditions can also be classified as: (1) express, (2) implied in fact, or (3) implied in law.

Express conditions are provided for by the parties' agreement. An express condition is usually prefaced by the word *if, provided, after,* or *when.* Conditions *implied in fact* are similar to express conditions because they are understood to be part of the agreement, but they are not expressly found in the language of the agreement. The court infers them from the promises.

Finally, *implied-in-law,* or *constructive,* conditions are imposed by the law in order to achieve justice and fairness. They are not contained in the language of the contract or even necessarily im-

plied.[5] For example, a contract in which a builder is supposed to build a house for a buyer can omit the date on which the buyer is supposed to pay the builder. Nonetheless, a court would consider it an implied condition that the buyer not be obliged to pay the builder until the house is fully or substantially completed, because the buyer should not be compelled to perform unless the builder has performed.

DISCHARGE BY PERFORMANCE

The great majority of contracts are discharged by performance. The contract comes to an end when both parties fulfill their respective duties by performing the acts they have promised. Performance can also be accomplished by tender. **Tender** is an unconditional offer to perform by one who is ready, willing, and able to do so. Therefore, a seller who places goods at the disposal of a buyer has tendered delivery and can demand payment. A buyer who offers to pay for goods has tendered payment and can demand delivery of the goods. Once performance has been tendered, the party making the tender has done everything possible to carry out the terms of the contract. If the other party then refuses to perform, the party making the tender can sue for breach of contract.

The Degree of Performance Required

It is important to distinguish among three types performance: (1) complete, (2) substantial, and (3) inferior. Failure of a required performance usually constitutes a material breach of the contract.

One typically uses a *reasonable expectations test* for determining which of these categories a performance fits. *Complete performance* occurs when performance is within the bounds of reasonable expectations. *Substantial performance* occurs when performance is slightly below reasonable expectations. A *material breach* occurs when performance is far below reasonable expectations.

Although in most contracts the parties fully discharge their obligations by complete performance, sometimes a party fulfills most, but not all, the duties or completes the duties in a manner contrary to the terms of the contract. The issue then arises as to whether this failure of complete

---

4. It is possible that a condition may be subsequent in form but precedent in fact. For example, if a promissory note is expressly conditioned to be void if the quantity of goods entering a certain port is greater during a stated period than it was during the same period in the preceding year, the language describes a condition subsequent. But obviously, the note would not be payable until after the stated period, when the quantity of imports could be determined, and thus, its payment would be subject to a condition precedent. Conditions subsequent in form but precedent by operation are common in insurance policies. Generally, conditions precedent are common; conditions subsequent are rare. The Restatement, Second, Contracts, deletes the terms *condition subsequent* and *condition precedent* as they are confusing.

5. Restatement, Second, Contracts, Section 226.

performance acts as a discharge of the performance required of the other party.

For example, a home building contract specifies installation of Fuller brand plasterboard for the walls. The builder cannot secure the Fuller brand and installs Honeyrock. All other aspects of construction conform to the contract. Does this deviation discharge the buyer from paying for the house upon completion? The answer depends on a single question: Does the term in dispute constitute either an express or an implied-in-fact condition? If so, then only complete performance can discharge the promise. If the term of the contract is interpreted as *constructive* (that is, a promise to install plasterboard of Fuller brand quality), then *substantial*, not complete, performance is required. In the event that the term is interpreted as constructive, it must be determined whether the performance is substantial. If it is not, the party is in material breach (a topic to be discussed later).

CONDITIONS AND COMPLETE PERFORMANCE
Normally, conditions expressly stated in the contract must fully occur in all aspects. Any deviation operates as a discharge. In the illustration above, if the terms in the specifications had stated that *only Fuller brand* plasterboard was to be used, a court could construe this term as an express condition. The builder's use of the Honeyrock brand, even though its quality is equal to that of Fuller, would not fulfill this express condition precedent to payment, and therefore the builder would not be entitled to payment.

A typical illustration of a condition precedent to payment is a life insurance policy in which one of the conditions for enforcement of the policy is the payment of the life insurance premium. The premium must be paid prior to the death of the insured, or the insurance company will not be obligated to pay benefits.

SUBSTANTIAL PERFORMANCE Human nature dictates that performance will not always fully sat-

isfy the parties. Therefore, for the sake of justice and fairness, the courts hold that a party must fulfill his or her obligation to perform as long as the other party has fulfilled the terms of the contract with *substantial performance*. In order to qualify as substantial, the performance must not vary greatly from the performance promised in the contract. If performance is substantial, the other party's duty to perform remains absolute, less damages, if any, for the minor deviations.

In the Fuller illustration, if the specification for Fuller plasterboard is construed as a constructive term, then the only issue is whether the substitution of Honeyrock plasterboard constitutes substantial performance. Obviously, if Honeyrock is of similar quality, substantial performance by the builder has taken place, and the buyer may be obligated to pay according to the contract.[6] This kind of deviation from the terms of a contract, however, must not be grossly negligent. The courts differ as to whether an intentional variation from a contract, even if made with good motives, prevents substantial performance.

Substantial performance does not operate to eliminate any breach of contract arising from less than full performance. Although substantial performance does not prevent discharge (as the breach is not material), a breach of contract—however slight—has occurred. If the plasterboard substituted for Fuller brand had been of a somewhat lower quality than Fuller, reducing the value of the house by $300, the builder would still be allowed to recover the contracted building price, less than $300. Remedies will be discussed in detail in the next chapter.

The following case, also involving a contract for the construction of a house, will help to clarify when there has been substantial performance by the contractor.

---

6. For an excellent analysis of substantial performance, see Judge Cardozo's opinion in Jacob & Youngs v. Kent, 230 N.Y. 239, 129 N.E. 889 (1921).

Case 14.2

PLANTE v. JACOBS
Supreme Court of Wisconsin,
1960.
10 Wis.2d 567, 103 N.W.2d
296.

BACKGROUND AND FACTS *The Jacobses entered into a written contract with the plaintiff, Plante, to furnish the materials and construct a house on their lot, in accordance with plans and specifications, for a sum of $26,765. During the course of construction, the plaintiff was paid $20,000. Disputes arose between the parties concerning the work being done. The Jacobses refused to continue paying. The plaintiff did not complete the house. The trial court* *found that the contract was substantially performed. The Jacobses were required to pay $4,152.90 plus interest and court costs. The defendants appealed.*

HALLOWS, Justice.

* * * *

The defendants argue the plaintiff cannot recover any amount because he has failed to substantially perform the contract. The plaintiff conceded he failed to furnish the kitchen cabinets, gutters and downspouts, sidewalk, closet clothes poles, and entrance seat amounting to $1,601.95. This amount was allowed to the defendants. The defendants claim some 20 other items of incomplete or faulty performance by the plaintiff and no substantial performance because the cost of completing the house in strict compliance with the plans and specifications would amount to 25 to 30 per cent of the contract price. The defendants especially stress the misplacing of the wall between the living room and the kitchen, which narrowed the living room in excess of one foot. The cost of tearing down this wall and rebuilding it would be approximately $4,000. The record is not clear why and when this wall was misplaced, but the wall is completely built and the house decorated and the defendants are living therein. Real estate experts testified that the smaller width of the living room would not affect the market price of the house.

* * * *

Substantial performance as applied to construction of a house does not mean that every detail must be in strict compliance with the specifications and the plans. Something less than perfection is the test of specific performance unless all details are made the essence of the contract. This was not done here. There may be situations in which features or details of construction of special or of great personal importance, if not performed, would prevent a finding of substantial performance of the contract. In this case the plan was a stock floor plan. No detailed construction of the house was shown on the plan. There were no blueprints. The specifications were standard printed forms with some modifications and additions written in by the parties. Many of the problems that arose during the construction had to be solved on the basis of practical experience. No mathematical rule relating to the percentage of the price, of cost of completion or of completeness can be laid down to determine substantial performance of a building contract. Although the defendants received a house with which they are dissatisfied in many respects, the trial court was not in error in finding the contract was substantially performed.

The Wisconsin Supreme Court upheld the trial court's judgment. Substantial performance was evident.

DECISION AND REMEDY

PERFORMANCE TO THE SATISFACTION OF ANOTHER   Contracts often state that completed work must personally satisfy one of the parties or a third person. The question then arises whether this satisfaction becomes a condition precedent, requiring actual personal satisfaction or approval for discharge, or whether the test of satisfaction is an absolute promise requiring such performance as would satisfy a "reasonable person" (substantial performance).

When the subject matter of the contract is personal, a contract to be performed to the satisfaction of one of the parties is conditioned, and perfor-mance must actually satisfy that party. For example, contracts for portraits, works of art, medical or dental work, and tailoring are considered personal. Therefore, only the personal satisfaction of the party will be sufficient to fulfill the condition. Suppose Williams agrees to paint a portrait of Hirshon's daughter for $500. The contract provides that Hirshon must be satisfied with the portrait. If Hirshon is not, she will not be required to pay for it. The only requirement imposed on Hirshon is that she act honestly and in good faith. If she expresses dissatisfaction only to avoid paying for the portrait, the condition of satisfaction is excused, and her duty to pay becomes absolute. (Of course, the jury, or the judge acting as a jury, will have to decide whether she is acting honestly.[7])

Contracts that involve mechanical fitness, utility, or marketability need only be performed to the satisfaction of a reasonable person. For example, construction contracts or manufacturing contracts are usually *not* considered to be personal, so the party's personal satisfaction is normally irrelevant. As long as the performance will satisfy a reasonable person, the contract is fulfilled. For example, assume Duplex Safety Boiler Company agrees to rebuild Garden's boiler "to Garden's satisfaction." After the company rebuilds the boiler, it operates properly, but Garden is dissatisfied and refuses to pay for the repair work. Most courts would not construe these terms as a condition; if a reasonable person would be satisfied with the boiler's operation, Duplex is entitled to be paid for the repair work.[8]

At times, contracts also require performance to the satisfaction of a third party (not a party to the contract). For example, assume you contract to pave several city streets. The contract provides that the work will be done "to the satisfaction of Phil Hopper, the supervising engineer." In this situation, the courts are divided. A minority of courts require the personal satisfaction of the third party, here Phil Hopper. If Hopper is not satisfied, you will not be paid, even if a reasonable person would be satisfied. Again, the personal judgment must be made honestly, or the condition will be excused. A majority of courts require the work to be satisfactory to a reasonable person. So even if Hopper were dissatisfied with the cement work, you would be paid, as long as a qualified supervising engineer would have been satisfied.

All of the above examples demonstrate the necessity for *clear, specific wording in contracts*. Also, one must never underestimate the importance of reading the small print in contracts.

Material Breach of Contract

A **breach of contract** is the nonperformance of a contractual duty. When the breach is *material*,[9] or performance is not substantial—in other words, when there has been a failure of consideration—the nonbreaching party is excused from the performance of contractual duties and has a cause of action to sue for damages caused by the breach. If the breach is *minor* (not material), the nonbreaching party's duty to perform can sometimes be suspended until the breach is remedied but is not entirely excused. Once the minor breach has been cured, the nonbreaching party must resume performance of the contractual obligations undertaken. Any breach entitles the nonbreaching party to sue for damages, but only a material breach discharges the nonbreaching party from the contract. The policy underlying these rules allows contracts to go forward when only minor problems occur but terminates them if major problems occur.[10]

Suppose Raytheon Corp. contracts with the United States government to build an all-weather tactical force system that uses Hawk missiles coated with paint that will deflect defensive weapons' heat-sensor guidance systems. The total contract price is $15.2 billion, of which $1,000,000 is the cost of obtaining and applying the paint. Raytheon builds the system on schedule and according to the contract, except that the Hawk missiles function effectively only under good weather conditions. The government will be entitled to treat the contract as breached, since the lack of the all-weather capability contracted for makes the system virtually useless. In addition, the government can sue Raytheon and recover damages caused by the system's ineffectiveness. On the other hand, if Raytheon builds the system on schedule and according to the contract, except for a failure to coat the Hawk missiles with the deflective paint, which is easily obtainable, the government will not be able to treat the contract as discharged, since the damage is easily curable and the breach is thus only minor. Of course, the government can sue Raytheon for damages that its failure to paint has caused.

---

7. For a classic case, see Gibson v. Cranage, 39 Mich. 49 (1878).

8. If, however, the contract specifically states that it is to be fulfilled to the "personal" satisfaction of one or more of the parties, and the parties so intended, the outcome will probably be different.

---

9. Restatement, Second, Contracts, Section 241.

10. See UCC 2-612 dealing with installment contracts for the sale of goods.

A nonbreaching party need not treat a material breach as a discharge of the contract but can treat the contract as being in effect and simply sue for damages. In the above example, if Raytheon delays four months on the first stage of the project, the government can treat the contract as still being in effect and sue for damages caused by the delay.

Anticipatory Breach

Duties of the nonbreaching party can be discharged by *anticipatory repudiation* of the contract by the other party. This type of repudiation constitutes a material breach.

Before either party to a contract has a duty to perform, one of the parties may refuse to perform his or her contractual obligations. This is called **anticipatory breach,** or **repudiation.**[11] For example, De La Tour made a contract with Hochster in March to employ Hochster as a courier for three months—June, July, and August. On May 11, De La Tour wrote to Hochster, "I am going abroad this summer and will not need a courier." This is an anticipatory breach of the employment contract. Since De La Tour repudiated the contract, Hochster *could* treat the act as a present, material breach. Furthermore, he could sue to recover damages *immediately*, without having to wait until June 1 to sue.[12]

There are two reasons for treating an anticipatory breach as a present, material breach:

1. The nonbreaching party should not be required to remain ready and willing to perform when the other party has already repudiated the contract.

2. The nonbreaching party should have the opportunity to seek a similar contract elsewhere.

Thus, Hochster should not be required to remain ready to serve as De La Tour's courier until June 1, since that would be a waste of time. In the meantime, Hochster could be working elsewhere.

It is important to note that until the nonbreaching party treats this early repudiation as a breach, the breaching party can retract his or her anticipatory repudiation by proper notice and restore the parties to their original obligations.[13]

Quite often an anticipatory breach occurs when a sharp fluctuation in market prices causes the contract, if performed, to be extremely unfavorable to one of the parties. For example, Martin Corporation contracts to manufacture and sell 100,000 personal computers to Com-age, a retailer of computer equipment that has 500 outlet stores. Delivery is to be made six months from the date of the contract. The contract price is based on the seller's present costs of acquiring inventory parts purchased from others. One month later, three inventory suppliers raise their prices to Martin. Based on these prices, if Martin manufactures and sells the personal computers to Com-age at the contract price, it stands to lose $500,000. Martin immediately writes Com-age that it cannot deliver the 100,000 computers at the contract price. Even though you may feel sorry for Martin, Martin's letter is an anticipatory repudiation of the contract that allows Com-age the option to treat the repudiation as a material breach and to proceed immediately to pursue remedies, even though the actual contract delivery date is still five months away.[14]

Time for Performance

If no time for performance is stated in the contract, a *reasonable time* is implied.[15] If a specific time is stated, the parties must usually perform by that time. However, unless time is expressly stated to be vital, a delay in performance will not destroy the performing party's right to payment. When time is expressly stated to be vital, or when it is construed to be "of the essence," the time for performance must usually be strictly complied with. The time element becomes a condition.

For example, a contract for the sale of soybeans must be performed within a reasonable time, even if it does not mention time. A contract for the sale

---

11. Restatement, Second, Contracts, Section 253, and UCC 2-610.

12. The doctrine of anticipatory breach first arose in this landmark case [Hochster v. De La Tour, 2 Ellis and Blackburn Reports 678 (1853)], when the English court recognized the delay and expense inherent in a rule requiring a nonbreaching party to wait until the time for performance to sue on an anticipatory breach.

13. See UCC 2-611.

14. See Reliance Cooperage Corp. v. Treat, 195 F.2d 977 (8th Cir. 1952), as a further illustration.

15. See UCC 1-204.

of soybeans "on or before April 1" may be performed by April 2 or 3. (But the party rendering late performance will have to pay for any damages caused by the delay.) A contract for the sale of soybeans "on or before April 1—necessary for immediate shipment abroad on April 2" must be performed by April 1. Time is of the essence because the buyer plans on immediate resale. Delivery after April 1 will prevent the buyer from exporting the soybeans and will constitute a material breach.

DISCHARGE BY AGREEMENT

Any contract can be discharged by agreement of the parties. The agreement can be contained in the original contract, or the parties can form a new contract for the express purpose of discharging the original contract.

Discharge by Rescission

Rescission is the process whereby the parties cancel the contract and are returned to the positions they occupied prior to forming it. In order for **mutual rescission** to take place, the parties must make another agreement, which must also satisfy the legal requirements for a contract. There must be an *offer*, an *acceptance*, and *consideration*. Ordinarily, if the parties agree to rescind the original contract, their promises not to perform those acts promised in the original contract will be legal consideration for the second contract. This occurs when the performance of each is executory (not yet completed).

The rescission agreement is generally enforceable even if made orally. This applies even if the original agreement was in writing except if the new agreement falls within the Statute of Frauds (discussed in Chapter 12). Another exception applies to agreements rescinding a contract for the sale of goods regardless of price under the UCC where the contract requires written rescission.[16]

When one party has fully performed, however, an agreement to call off the original contract will not normally be enforceable. Because the performing party has received no consideration for the

promise to call off the original bargain, additional consideration will be necessary.

To illustrate: Suppose Alberto's Food Company contracts to buy forty truckloads of oranges from Citrus Products, Inc. Later, representatives of Alberto's and Citrus get together and decide to call off the deal (rescind the original contract). This agreement is enforceable, since neither party has yet performed. The consideration that Citrus receives for calling off the deal is freedom from performing what it was legally bound to perform under the contract—that is, not having to deliver the forty truckloads of oranges. The consideration Alberto's receives for calling off the deal is not having to pay for the oranges, an obligation it would otherwise have had to honor.

On the other hand, if Citrus had already delivered the oranges, an agreement to call off the deal would not normally be enforceable. In this case, Citrus would receive no consideration for its promise to call off the deal.

In sum, contracts that are *executory* on *both* sides (contracts on which neither party has performed) can be rescinded solely by agreement.[17] But contracts that are *executed on one side* (contracts on which one party has performed) can be rescinded only if the party who has performed receives consideration for the promise to call off the deal.

Discharge by Novation or Substituted Agreement

The process of **novation** substitutes a new party for one of the original parties. Essentially, the parties to the original contract and one or more new parties get together and agree to substitute the new party for one of the original parties. The requirements of a novation are:

1. A previous valid obligation.
2. An agreement of all the parties to a new contract.
3. The extinguishment of the old obligation (discharge of the prior party).
4. A new contract that is valid.

---

16. UCC 2-209(2)(4).

17. Certain sales made to consumers at their homes can be rescinded by the consumer within three days for no reason at all. This three-day "cooling-off" period is designed to aid consumers who are susceptible to high-pressure door-to-door sales tactics. See Chapter 46 and 15 U.S.C. Section 1635(a).

Suppose Union Carbide Corporation contracts to sell its petrochemical business in Europe, Bakelite Xylonite, Ltd., to British Petroleum Company for $200 million. Before the transfer is completed, British Petroleum learns from its financial experts that this acquisition is not in its best interests. British Petroleum has known for some time that BP Chemicals has a strong interest in acquiring Bakelite to expand its European market. British Petroleum wants to substitute BP Chemicals as purchaser of Bakelite. In order to accomplish this, the parties agree to a novation. Union Carbide, British Petroleum, and BP Chemicals all get together and agree that BP Chemicals will buy the Bakelite Xylonite stock from Union Carbide. As long as the new contract is supported by consideration, the novation will discharge the original contract (between Union Carbide and British Petroleum) and replace it with the new contract (between Union Carbide and BP Chemicals).

Substitution of a new contract between the same parties expressly or impliedly revokes and discharges a prior contract.[18] The parties involved may simply want a new agreement with somewhat different terms, so they expressly state in a new contract that the old contract is now discharged. They can also make the new contract without expressly stating that the old contract is discharged. If the parties do not expressly discharge the old contract, it will be *impliedly* discharged because of the change or because of the new contract's different terms, which are inconsistent with the old contract's terms.

For example, suppose Triangle Pacific Corp. contracts to sell its lumber manufacturing facilities in Slocan, British Columbia, to a Canadian investor group for $7.9 million in cash and $800,000 in a five-year note. Before the sale is closed, however, Triangle Pacific Corp. decides that it wants $6.9 million in cash and $1.8 million in a five-year note. The Canadian investor group agrees, and the parties draw up a new contract with these terms of sale. If the second agreement states, "Our previous contract to accept payment of $7.9 million in cash, balance in a five-year note is hereby revoked," the original contract will be expressly

discharged by substitution. If the second agreement does not state this, the original contract will nevertheless be discharged by implication. Triangle Pacific Corp. cannot sell the same lumber manufacturing facilities under two different terms of payment. Since the terms are inconsistent, a court will enforce the terms that were decided upon most recently. In this case, the sale would be for $6.9 million in cash and $1.8 million in a five-year note.

A *compromise*, or settlement agreement, that arises out of a bona fide dispute over the obligations under an existing contract will be recognized at law. Such an agreement will be substituted as a new contract, and it will either expressly or impliedly revoke and discharge the obligations under any prior contract.

Discharge by Accord and Satisfaction

For a contract to be discharged by **accord and satisfaction,** the parties must agree to accept performance different from the performance originally promised. An **accord** is defined as an executory contract (that is, one that has not yet been performed) to perform some act to satisfy an existing contractual duty.[19] The duty is not yet discharged. A **satisfaction** is the performance of the accord agreement. An accord and its satisfaction (performance) discharge the original contractual obligation.

Once the accord has been made, the original obligation is merely suspended. (This differs from substitution of a new contract, which, as pointed out above, operates to discharge the original obligation.) The obligor can discharge the obligation by performance of the obligation agreed to in the accord. Likewise, if the obligor refuses to perform the accord, the obligee can bring action on the original obligation or seek a decree for specific performance on the accord.

To illustrate, Matthews obtains a judgment against Brown for $3,000. Later both parties agree that the judgment can be satisfied by Brown's transfer of her stamp collection to Matthews. This agreement to accept the stamps in lieu of $3,000 in cash is the accord. If Brown transfers her collection to Matthews, the accord agreement has

---

18. It is this immediate discharge of the prior contract that distinguishes a substituting contract from accord and satisfaction, discussed in the next section.

19. Restatement, Second, Contracts, Section 281.

been fully performed, and the $3,000 debt is discharged. If Brown refuses to transfer her stamps, the accord has been breached. Since the original obligation is merely suspended, Matthews can bring action to enforce the judgment for $3,000 in cash or, in most states, obtain a decree for specific performance for the transfer of the collection and the discharge of the debt.

As pointed out in Chapter 9, on consideration, acceptance by a creditor of a debtor's payment on a disputed, or unliquidated, debt operates as both accord and satisfaction of the debt claim of the creditor, resulting in a discharge.

DISCHARGE BY OPERATION OF LAW

Under certain circumstances, contractual duties may be discharged by operation of law. These circumstances include material alteration of the contract, the running of the statute of limitations, and the impossibility or impracticability of performance.

Alteration of the Contract

In order to discourage parties from altering written contracts, the law operates to allow an innocent party to be discharged when the other party has materially altered a written contract without consent. For example, contract terms such as quantity or price might be changed without the knowledge or consent of all parties. If so, the party who was unaware of the change can treat the contract as discharged or terminated.[20]

Statutes of Limitations

Statutes of limitations limit the period during which a party can sue on a particular cause of action. (A cause of action is the basis or reason for suing or bringing an action.) After the applicable limita-

---

20. The contract is voidable, and the innocent party can also treat the contract as in effect, either on the original terms or on the terms as altered. A buyer who discovers that a seller altered the quantity of goods in a sales contract from 100 to 1,000 by secretly inserting a zero can purchase either 100 or 1,000 of the items.

tions period has passed, a suit can no longer be brought in a court of law or equity.

For example, the limitations period for bringing suits for breach of oral contracts is usually two to three years; for written contracts, four to five years; for recovery of amounts awarded in judgment, ten to twenty years, depending on state law.

Section 2-725 of the UCC deals with the statute of limitations applicable to certain contracts for the sale of goods. For purposes of applying this section, the UCC does not distinguish between oral and written contracts. Section 2-725 provides that an action for the breach of any contract for sale must be commenced within four years after the cause of that action has accrued. The cause of action accrues when the breach occurs, regardless of the aggrieved party's lack of knowledge of the breach. By original agreement, the parties can reduce this four-year period to a one-year period. They cannot, however, extend it beyond the four-year limitation period.

Technically, the running of a statute of limitations bars access only to *judicial* remedies; it does not extinguish the debt or the underlying obligation. The statute precludes access to the courts for collection. But if the party who owes the debt or obligation agrees to perform (that is, makes a new promise to perform), the cause of action barred by the statute of limitations will be revived. For the old agreement to be revived by a new promise in this manner, many states require that the promise be in writing or that there be evidence of partial performance.

For example, suppose Burlington Northern Railroad contracts for sixty-three new miles of track to be laid between Dalhart and Amarillo, Texas. Martin Marietta Corp. supplies four tons of cast iron railway for the project and is paid $22,000 of the $30,000 purchase price. Texas's statute of limitations for collection of this debt is four years, but Martin Marietta Corp. fails to collect the debt or sue for collection during that four-year period after delivery of the iron. Therefore, Martin Marietta Corp. can no longer sue. It is barred by the statute of limitations. But if Burlington Northern Railroad agrees, in writing, to pay the remaining $8,000, or if it actually pays part of the $8,000, Marietta Corp. can again sue to collect the full debt. The statute of limitations is no longer a bar, and the cause of action for recovery of the full debt is revived.

Bankruptcy

A **discharge in bankruptcy** will ordinarily bar enforcement of most of a debtor's contracts by the creditors. (Bankruptcy is fully discussed in Chapter 31.) Bankruptcy can be entered into voluntarily or involuntarily.[21] A proceeding in bankruptcy attempts to allocate the assets the debtor owns at bankruptcy to the creditors in a fair and equitable fashion. Once the assets are allocated, the debtor receives a discharge in bankruptcy. Partial payment of a debt barred *after* discharge in bankruptcy will not revive the debt.

Discharge by Impossibility or Impracticability of Performance

After a contract has been made, performance may become impossible in an objective sense. This is known as **impossibility of performance** and may discharge a contract.[22] Occasionally, if circumstances arise after the contract is formed that make performance *extremely* difficult or costly, courts may allow the contract to be discharged under the **doctrine of commercial impracticability.** These two legal excuses from performance under a contract are discussed below.

OBJECTIVE IMPOSSIBILITY Certain basic types of situations generally qualify under the objective impossibility of performance rules that discharge contractual obligations:

1. One of the essential parties to a personal contract *dies or becomes incapacitated* prior to performance.[23]

To illustrate this type of impossibility, suppose Jane, a famous actress, contracts to play the lead-ing role in a movie. Before the picture starts, she becomes ill and dies. Her personal performance was essential to the completion of the contract. Thus her death discharges the contract and her estate's liability for her nonperformance.

2. The *specific* subject matter of the contract is destroyed.[24]

For example, Pappagoras contracts to sell 10,000 bushels of apples to be harvested "from his Green Valley apple orchard in the state of Washington." Volcanic ash from Mount St. Helens destroys his apples. Because the contracted apples were to come specifically from his Green Valley orchard, his performance has been rendered impossible by the eruption of Mount St. Helens. Thus, this contract is discharged.

Another example of the second type of impossibility is a contract to lease a building when the building is destroyed by fire, or a contract to sell oil from a particular well when the well goes dry.

3. A change in *law* renders performance illegal.[25]

Examples of the third type include a contract to loan money at 20 percent when the usury rate is changed to make loans in excess of 12 percent illegal and a contract to build an apartment building when the zoning laws are changed to prohibit the construction of residential rental property. Both changes render the contracts impossible to perform.

The following case illustrates objective impossibility where the plaintiff could not continue to take dance lessons under a contract due to a serious injury.

---

21. A Chapter 12 or 13 case can be initiated only by a debtor's filing of a voluntary petition.

22. Restatement, Second, Contracts, Section 261.

23. Restatement, Second, Contracts, Section 262.

24. Restatement, Second, Contracts, Section 263.

25. Restatement, Second, Contracts, Section 264.

BACKGROUND AND FACTS *In November 1959, the plaintiff, Parker, went to the Arthur Murray Dance Studio to redeem a certificate entitling him to three free dance lessons. At the time, Parker was a thirty-seven-year-old college-educated bachelor who lived alone in a one-room attic apartment. During the free lessons, the instructor told Parker that he had exceptional potential to become an accomplished dancer and generally encouraged him to take more lessons. Parker signed a contract for seventy-five hours of lessons at a cost of $1,000. At the bottom of the contract, "NON-CANCELLABLE NEGOTIABLE CONTRACT" was printed in boldface type.*

 Case 14.3

PARKER v. ARTHUR MURRAY, INC.

Appellate Court of Illinois, Second Division, First District, 1973.

10 Ill.App.3d 1000, 295 N.E.2d 487.

Parker attended lessons regularly. He was praised and encouraged by the instructors despite his lack of progress. Contract extensions and new contracts for additional instructional hours were executed. Each contract and each extension contained the same boldface words: "NON-CANCELLABLE CONTRACT." Some of the agreements contained the statement, "I UNDERSTAND THAT NO REFUNDS WILL BE MADE UNDER THE TERMS OF THIS CONTRACT," also in boldface.

On September 24, 1961, Parker was seriously injured in an automobile collision. The accident rendered him incapable of continuing his dance lessons. By that time, he had contracted for a total of 2,734 hours of lessons for which he had paid $24,812.80. Despite Parker's repeated written demands, the Arthur Murray Dance Studio refused to return any of Parker's money. The trial court allowed for rescission of the contract. Arthur Murray, Inc., and the Arthur Murray Dance Studio appealed.

STAMOS, Presiding Justice.

The sole issue raised by defendants is whether the terms of the contracts barred plaintiff from asserting the doctrine of impossibility of performance as the basis for seeking rescission.

*   *   *   *

Plaintiff was granted rescission [by the trial court] on the ground of impossibility of performance. The applicable legal doctrine is expressed in the Restatement of Contracts, § 459, as follows:

A duty that requires for its performance action that can be rendered only by the promisor or some other particular person is discharged by his death or by such illness as makes the necessary action by him impossible or seriously injurious to his health, unless the contract indicates a contrary intention or there is contributing fault on the part of the person subject to the duty.

*   *   *   *

In Illinois impossibility of performance was recognized as a ground for rescission in *Davies v. Arthur Murray, Inc.*, wherein the court nonetheless found for the defendant because of the plaintiff's failure adequately to prove the existence of an incapacitating disability.

Defendants do not deny that the doctrine of impossibility of performance is generally applicable to the case at bar. Rather they assert that certain contract provisions bring this case within the Restatement's limitation that the doctrine is inapplicable if "the contract indicates a contrary intention." It is contended that such bold type phrases as "NON-CANCELLABLE CONTRACT," "NON-CANCELLABLE NEGOTIABLE CONTRACT" and "I UNDERSTAND THAT NO REFUNDS WILL BE MADE UNDER THE TERMS OF THIS CONTRACT" manifested the parties' mutual intent to waive their respective rights to invoke the doctrine of impossibility. This is a construction which we find unacceptable. Courts engage in the construction and interpretation of contracts with the sole aim of determining the intention of the parties. We need rely on no construction aids to conclude that plaintiff never contemplated that by signing a contract with such terms as "NON-CANCELLABLE" and "NO REFUNDS" he was waiving a remedy expressly recognized by Illinois courts. Were we also to refer to established tenets of contractual construction, this conclusion would be equally compelled. An ambiguous contract will be construed most strongly against the party who drafted it. Exceptions or reservations in a contract will, in case of doubt or ambiguity, be construed least favorably to the party claiming the benefit of the exceptions or reservations. Although neither party to a contract should be relieved from performance on the ground that good business judgment was lacking, a court will not place upon language a ridiculous construction. We conclude that plaintiff did not waive his right to assert the doctrine of impossibility.

Defendants have also contended, albeit indirectly, that plaintiff failed to establish the existence of an incapacitating disability. In contrast to *Davies v. Arthur Murray, Inc., supra,* wherein the plaintiff relied solely upon his own uncorroborated testimony, plaintiff in the case at bar produced both lay witnesses and expert medical testimony corroborating the severity and permanency of his injuries. That testimony need not be recited; suffice it to say that overwhelming evidence supported plaintiff's contention that he was incapable of continuing his lessons.

The trial court's ruling that impossibility of performance was grounds for rescission was upheld. Parker was entitled to recover the prepaid sums of money representing unused lessons.

DECISION AND REMEDY

COMMERCIAL IMPRACTICABILITY Courts will at times excuse performance under a contract when the performance becomes much more difficult or expensive than originally contemplated at the time the contract was formed. For someone to invoke successfully the doctrine of commercial impracticability, however, the anticipated performance must become *extremely* difficult or costly.[26]

To illustrate, the California Supreme Court held that a contract was discharged because it would cost ten times more than the original estimate to excavate a certain amount of gravel.[27] In another case, commercial impracticability was not found when a carrier of goods was to deliver wheat from the West Coast of the United States to a safe port in Iran.[28] The Suez Canal, the usual route, was nationalized by Egypt and closed, forcing the carrier to travel around Africa and the Cape of Good Hope, through the Mediterranean and go to Iran. The added expense was approximately $42,000 above and beyond the contract price of $306,000, and the original journey of 10,000 miles was extended by 3,000 miles. Nevertheless, the court held that the contract was not commercially impracticable to perform, because the closing of the Suez Canal was foreseeable. Therefore, caution should be used in invoking commercial impracticability. The added burden of performing must

be *extreme* and, more importantly, must *not* have been within the cognizance of the parties when the contract was made.

A closely allied theory is the doctrine of **frustration of purpose.** In principle, a contract will be discharged if supervening circumstances make it impossible to attain the purpose both parties had in mind when making the contract. The origins of the doctrine lie in the old English "coronation cases." A coronation procession was planned for Edward VII when he became king of England following the death of his mother, Queen Victoria. Hotel rooms along the coronation route were rented at exorbitant prices for that day. When the king became ill and the procession was canceled, the purpose of the room contracts was "frustrated." A flurry of lawsuits resulted. Hotel and building owners sought to enforce the room rent bills against would-be parade observers, and would-be parade observers sought to be reimbursed for rental monies paid in advance on the rooms. Would-be parade observers were excused from their duty of payment. It was from this situation that the court developed its theory of recovery known as *frustration of purpose.*

TEMPORARY IMPOSSIBILITY An occurrence or event that makes it temporarily impossible to perform the act for which a party has contracted will operate to *suspend* performance until the impossibility ceases. Then, ordinarily, the parties must perform the contract as originally planned. However, if the lapse of time and the change in circumstances surrounding the contract make it substantially more burdensome to perform the promised acts, the parties will be discharged.

---

26. Restatement, Second, Contracts, Sections 265 and 266, and UCC 2-615.

27. Mineral Park Land Co. v. Howard, 172 Cal. 289, 156 P. 458 (1916).

28. Transatlantic Financing Corp. v. United States, 363 F.2d 312 (D.C. Cir. 1966).

The leading case on this subject, *Autry v. Republic Productions*,[29] involved an actor who was drafted into the army in 1942. Being drafted rendered his contract temporarily impossible to perform, and it was suspended until the end of the war. When the actor got out of the army, the value of the dollar had so changed that performance of the contract would have been substantially burdensome for him. Therefore, the contract was discharged.

29. 30 Cal.2d 144, 180 P.2d 888 (1947).

CONCEPT SUMMARY: Discharge of Contracts

METHOD	TYPES AND BASIC RULES
Discharge by occurrence or failure of a condition	1. *Failure of condition precedent to exist or occur* Duty to perform does not become absolute absent compliance with condition precedent. 2. *Occurrence of condition subsequent.*
Discharge by performance (or breach of contract)	1. *Performance* Complete (if terms are construed as express conditions) or substantial. 2. *Breach* Material nonperformance discharges the nonbreaching party's performance.
Discharge by agreement	1. *Mutual rescission* An enforceable agreement to restore parties to their precontract positions. 2. *Novation* By valid contract, a new party is substituted for an original party, thereby terminating the old contract. 3. *Accord and satisfaction* An agreement whereby the original contract can be discharged by a different performance.

Discharge by operation of law	1. *Alteration* An innocent party is discharged by material alteration without consent.
	2. *Statute of limitations* The plaintiff's delay in filing suit bars availability of judicial remedies, thus discharging the defendant's duty to perform.
	3. *Bankruptcy* The decree discharges most of the debtor's contractual obligations.
	4. *Impossibility or impracticability of performance*
	  a. A person whose performance is essential to completion of the contract dies or is incapacitated.
	  b. The specific subject matter of the contract is destroyed prior to transfer.
	  c. Performance is declared illegal.
	  d. Performance becomes commercially impracticable.
	  e. Temporary impossibility of performance: If performance is temporarily suspended because of events or occurrences (such as war), and subsequent circumstances make the contract substantially more difficult to perform, the parties may be discharged.

QUESTIONS AND CASE PROBLEMS

1. The Rosenbergs own a real estate lot, and they contract with Faithful Construction, Inc., to build a house thereon for $60,000. The specifications list "all plumbing bowls and fixtures . . . to be Crane brand." The Rosenbergs leave on vacation, and during their absence Faithful is unable to buy and install Crane plumbing fixtures. Instead, Faithful installs Kohler brand fixtures, an equivalent in the industry. Upon completion of the building contract, the Rosenbergs, on inspection, discover the substitute and refuse to accept the house, claiming Faithful had breached the conditions set forth in the specifications. Discuss fully the Rosenbergs' claim.

2. Junior owes creditor Carlton $1,000, which is due and payable on June 1. Junior has been in a car accident, missed a great deal of work, and consequently will not have the money on June 1. Junior's father, Fred, offers to pay Carlton $1,100 in four equal installments if Carlton will discharge Junior from any further liability on the debt. Carlton accepts. Discuss the following:

 (a) Is the transaction a novation, or is it accord and satisfaction? Explain.

 (b) Does the contract between Fred and Carlton have to be in writing to be enforceable? (Review the Statute of Frauds' discussion in Chapter 12.) Explain.

3. ABC Clothiers, Inc., has a contract with retailer Taylor & Sons to deliver 1,000 summer suits to Taylor's place of business on or before *May 1*. On *April 1*, Taylor senior receives a letter from ABC informing him that ABC will not be able to make the delivery as scheduled. Taylor is very upset, as he had planned a big ad sale campaign. He wants to file suit against ABC immediately (April 2). Taylor's son, Tom, tells his father that a suit is not proper until ABC actually fails to deliver the suits on May 1. Discuss fully who is correct, Taylor or his son Tom.

4. The following events take place after the formation of the contracts. Discuss which of these contracts are now discharged by virtue of the events rendering the contracts impossible of performance.

 (a) Jimenez, a famous singer, contracts to perform in your nightclub. He dies prior to performance.

 (b) Raglione contracts to sell you her land. Just before title is to be transferred, she dies.

 (c) Oppenheim contracts to sell you 1,000 bushels of apples from her orchard in the state of Washington. Because of a severe frost, she is unable to deliver the apples.

 (d) Maxwell contracts to lease a service station for ten years. His principal income is from the sale of gasoline. Due to an oil embargo by foreign oil-producing nations, gasoline is rationed, cutting sharply into Maxwell's gasoline sales. He cannot make his lease payments.

5. Murphy contracts to purchase from Lone Star Liquors six cases of French champagne for $1,200. The contract states that delivery is to be made at the Murphy residence "on or before June 1, to be used for daughter's wedding reception on June 2." The champagne is carried regularly in Lone Star's stock. On June 1, Lone Star's delivery van is involved in an accident, and the champagne is not delivered that day. On the morning of June 2, Murphy discovers the nondelivery. Unable to reach Lone Star because its line is busy, Murphy purchases the champagne from another dealer. That afternoon, just before the wedding reception, Lone Star tenders delivery of the champagne at Murphy's residence. Murphy refuses tender, and Lone Star sues for breach of contract. Discuss fully the result.

6. John Agosta and his brother Salvatore had formed a corporation, but disagreements between the two brothers caused John to petition for voluntary dissolution of the corporation. According to the dissolution agreement, the total assets of the corporation, which included a warehouse and inventory, would be split between the brothers by Salvatore's selling his stock to John for $500,000. This agreement was approved, but shortly before the payment was made, a fire totally destroyed the warehouse and inventory, which were the major assets of the corporation. John refused to pay Salvatore the $500,000, and Salvatore brought suit for breach of contract. Discuss whether the destruction of the major assets of the corporation affects John's required performance. [In the Matter of Fontana v. D'Oro Foods Inc., 122 Misc.2d 1091, 472 N.Y.S.2d 528 (1983)]

7. Zilg is author of *DuPont: Behind the Nylon Curtain*, a historical account of the DuPont family in America's social, political, and economic affairs. Prentice-Hall signed Zilg to a contract to publish the book exclusively. There was no provision to have Prentice-Hall use its best efforts to promote the book; rather, it was left up to the publisher to use its discretion as to the number of volumes printed and the level of promotion. Prentice-Hall printed 13,000 volumes, authorized an advertising budget of $5,500, distributed over 600 copies to reviewers, and purchased ads in major newspapers. Zilg claims that Prentice-Hall cut its first printing by 5,000 copies and its advertising budget by $9,500, and these cuts were evidence that Prentice-Hall had not made a "best effort" to fully promote the book. Prentice-Hall claimed that its reduction came after careful review and was based on sound and valid business decisions. Based on these facts only, discuss whether Prentice-Hall has fulfilled its contractual duty to Zilg. [Zilg v. Prentice-Hall, Inc., 717 F.2d 671 (2d Cir. 1983)]

8. Sun Maid Raisin signed a contract to buy 1,800 tons of raisins from Victor Packing Company in 1976. Victor planned to supply the raisins by purchasing them in the market during that year but to wait until very late to get a good price. It waited too long. Because of heavy, "disastrous" rains that year, 50 percent of the crop was destroyed, and the price of raisins skyrocketed from $860 per ton to $1,600 per ton. Victor Packing could not meet Sun Maid's contract demand without sustaining equally "disastrous" losses, and it notified Sun Maid that it was repudiating the contract. Sun Maid sued for damages for breach of contract, and Victor Packing claimed, among other things, that performance was impracticable. Discuss whether Victor Packing's defense should succeed. [Sun Maid Raisin Growers v. Victor Packing Co., 146 Cal.App.3d 787, 194 Cal.Rptr. 612 (5 Dist. 1983)]

9. Grane, a homeowner, contracted with Butkovich & Sons to enlarge Grane's basement and build a new room over the new basement area. Butkovich was also to lay a new garage floor and construct a patio area. The parties agreed to a price of $19,290 for the work. When the construction was completed, Grane refused to pay the contractor the $9,290 balance he still owed, claiming that Butkovich had failed to install water stops and reinforcing wire in one concrete floor in accordance with Grane's specifications and that the main floor of the addition was 8⅞ inches lower than the plans had called for. As a mortgage holder on the property, the State Bank of St. Charles was named co-defendant, as its interests would be affected by a judgment against Grane if the latter could not pay. But-kovich claimed that it had substantially performed the contract. Grane claimed that performance was of poor quality and that failure to follow contract specifications constituted a material breach. Discuss who should win. [Butkovich & Sons, Inc. v. State Bank of St. Charles, 62 Ill.App.3d 810, 379 N.E.2d 837, 20 Ill.Dec. 4 (1978)]

10. International Harvester, a manufacturer of farm equipment and trucks, entered into an agreement to sell selected assets and liabilities to Tenneco. Tenneco had franchises around the country that sold Case machinery and equipment. Many of these dealerships competed with the newly acquired International Harvester franchises. Because Tenneco would lose substantial amounts of money by operating competing franchises, many of the International Harvester dealerships were closed. One of the franchises acquired by Tenneco was run by Groseth; and in January of 1985, Groseth was informed that his franchise was terminated. Groseth was not informed why, nor was he given six months' notice of his termination and an opportunity to rectify any claim of breach, which was his right under the franchise agreement. When Groseth sued, Tenneco raised the defense of frustration of purpose. Will Tenneco succeed in this defense? [Groseth International, Inc. v. Tenneco, Inc., 410 N.W.2d 159 (S.D. 1987)]

Chapter 15

Breach of Contract and Remedies

Whenever a party fails to perform part or all of the duties under a contract, that party is in breach of contract. *Breach of contract* is the failure to perform what a party is under an absolute duty to perform.[1] Once a party has failed to perform or has performed inadequately, the other party—the nonbreaching party—can choose one or more of several remedies. A *remedy* is the relief provided for an innocent party when the other party has breached the contract. It is the means employed to enforce a right or to redress an injury. Strictly speaking, the remedy is not a part of a lawsuit, but the result thereof, the object for which the lawsuit is presented and the end to which all litigation is directed. The most common remedies available to a nonbreaching party include:

1. Damages.
2. Rescission and restitution.
3. Specific performance.
4. Reformation.[2]

DAMAGES

A breach of any contract entitles the nonbreaching party to sue for money (damages). *Damages* are designed to compensate the nonbreaching party for the loss of the bargain. When a party loses the benefit of the bargain or contract, the breaching party must make up this loss to the nonbreaching party. Often, courts say that innocent parties are to be placed in the position they would have occupied had the contract been fully performed.[3]

Types of Damages

Four broad categories of damages will be discussed in this chapter:

1. Compensatory.
2. Consequential.
3. Punitive.
4. Nominal.

---

1. Restatement, Second, Contracts, Section 235(2).
2. As discussed in Chapter 1, an award of damages is a remedy at law. Rescission and restitution, specific performance, and reformation are equitable remedies.
3. Restatement, Second, Contracts, Section 347, and UCC 1-106(1).

COMPENSATORY DAMAGES   Damages compensating the nonbreaching party for the *loss of the bargain* are known as **compensatory damages.** These damages compensate the injured party only for injuries actually sustained and proved to have arisen directly from the loss of the bargain caused by the breach of contract. They simply replace the loss caused by the wrong or injury. To illustrate: Wilcox contracts to perform certain services exclusively for Hernandez during the month of March for $2,000. Hernandez cancels the contract and is in breach. Wilcox is able to find another job during the month of March, but can only earn $500. He can sue Hernandez for breach and recover $1,500 as compensatory damages.

The measurement of compensatory damages varies by type of contract. Certain types of contracts deserve special mention. They are contracts for the sale of goods, land contracts, and construction contracts.

Sale of Goods   In a contract for the sale of goods, the usual measure of compensatory damages is an amount equal to the difference between the contract price and the market price.[4] Suppose Chrysler Corporation contracts to buy ten model UTS 400 computer terminals from Sperry Rand Corporation for $8,000 apiece. If Sperry Rand fails to deliver the ten terminals and the current market price of the terminals is $8,150, Chrysler's measure of damages in this case is $1,500 (ten times $150).

Sale of Land   Ordinarily, because each parcel of land is unique, the remedy for a seller's breach of a contract for a sale of real estate is *specific performance* (that is, the buyer is awarded the piece of property he or she bargained for). When this remedy, which is discussed more fully later in this chapter, is unavailable (for example, when the seller has sold the property to someone else), or when the breach is on the part of the buyer, the measure of damages is ordinarily the same as in contracts for the sale of goods—that is, the difference between the contract price and the market price of the land. The majority of states follow this rule. A minority of states, however, follow a different rule when the seller breaches the contract and the

breach is not deliberate.[5] In such a case, these states allow the prospective purchaser to recover any down payment plus any expenses incurred (such as fees for title searches, attorneys, and escrows). This minority rule effectively places purchasers in the position they occupied prior to the sale.

Construction Contracts   The measure of damages in a building or construction contract varies depending upon which party breaches and when the breach occurs. The owner can breach at three different stages of the construction:

1.   Before performance begins.
2.   During performance.
3.   After performance has been completed.

If the owner breaches *before performance begins*, the contractor can recover only the profits that would have been made on the contract (that is, the total contract price less the cost of materials and labor). If the owner breaches *during performance*, the contractor can recover the profits plus the costs incurred in partially constructing the building. If the owner breaches *after the construction has been completed*, the contractor can recover the entire contract price[6] plus interest.

When the *construction contractor breaches the contract* by stopping partway through the project, the measure of damages is the cost of completion, which includes reasonable compensation for any delay in performance. If the contractor substantially performs, the courts may use the cost-of-completion formula, but only if there is no substantial economic waste in requiring completion.[7] If the contractor finishes late, the measure of damages will be the loss of use.

---

4. At the time and place where the goods were to be delivered or tendered. See UCC 2-708 and UCC 2-713.

5. A deliberate breach includes the vendor's failure to convey the land because the market price has gone up. A nondeliberate breach includes the vendor's failure to convey the land because an unknown easement (right of use over another's property) rendered title unmarketable. See Chapter 52.

6. Actually, this is true for most contracts; the nonbreaching party is normally owed the contract profit plus the cost of performance.

7. Economic waste occurs when the cost of additional resources to finish the project exceeds any conceivable value placed on the additional work done. For example, if a contractor discovers that it will cost $10,000 to move a large coral rock eleven inches as specified in the contract, and the change in the rock's position will alter the appearance of the project only a trifle, full completion will involve economic waste.

Exhibit 15-1 **Measurement of Damages in Breached Construction Contracts**

PARTY IN BREACH	TIME OF BREACH	MEASUREMENT OF DAMAGES
Owner	Before construction begins	Profits (contract price less cost of materials and labor)
Owner	During construction	Profits plus costs incurred up to time of breach
Owner	After construction has been completed	Contract price
Contractor	During construction	Generally, all costs incurred by owner to complete construction

These rules concerning the measurement of damages in breached construction projects are summarized in Exhibit 15-1.

In the following case, the plaintiff substantially performed a construction project for the defendant, with whom the plaintiff had no express, written contract. The plaintiff sought recovery under the theory of *quantum meruit* (Latin for "as much as he deserved"—that is, recovery of the fair value of his services).

BACKGROUND AND FACTS *The plaintiff, Davies, a construction firm, agreed to construct four duplexes for Olson and Lund at "cost plus $6,000 builder's profit per duplex." The cost per duplex was undetermined because the specifications for each duplex had not been agreed upon. Davies prepared a breakdown of costs, but Olson, without Lund's participation, requested numerous changes and additions to the duplex specifications. There was never any "meeting of minds" regarding what changes in the plans would be made, however, and no express written contract was ever finally agreed upon or executed. Davies began work on the duplexes and substantially completed the work, but Olson's financing was insufficient to cover all of the construction costs that Davies incurred. When Olson failed to pay any more costs, Davies sued for* quantum meruit *and breach of contract. After an extensive trial, the trial court found that Davies should recover from Olson the reasonable cost of construction, $365,353, less the amount already received, $313,580, or $51,773. Both parties were unhappy with the decision, and both appealed the case.*

 Case 15.1

DAVIES v. OLSON
Court of Appeals of Utah, 1987.
746 P.2d 264.

BILLINGS, Judge.
* * * *

Because we remand for further proceedings, we attempt to provide some guidance to the trial court. *Quantum meruit* is an action initiated by a plaintiff to recover payment for labor performed in a variety of circumstances in which that plaintiff, for some reason, would not be able to sue on an express contract. Recovery under *quantum meruit* presupposes that no enforceable written or oral contract exists. Confusion surrounds the use and application of *quantum meruit*, because courts have used the terms *quantum meruit*, contract implied in fact, contract implied in law, quasi-contract, unjust enrichment, and/or restitution without analytical precision. * * *

Quantum meruit has two distinct branches. Both branches, however, are rooted in "justice," to prevent the defendant's enrichment at the plaintiff's expense.

Contract implied in law, also known as quasi-contract or unjust enrichment, is one branch of *quantum meruit*. A quasi-contract is not a contract at all, but rather is a legal action in restitution. The elements of a quasi-contract, or a contract implied in law, are: (1) the defendant received a benefit; (2) an appreciation or knowledge by the defendant of the benefit; (3) under circumstances that would make it unjust for the defendant to retain the benefit without paying for it. The measure of recovery under quasi-contract, or contract implied in law, is the value of the benefit conferred on the defendant (the defendant's gain) and not the detriment incurred by the plaintiff, or necessarily the reasonable value of the plaintiff's services.

A contract implied in fact is the second branch of *quantum meruit*. A contract implied in fact is a "contract" established by conduct. The elements of a contract implied in fact are: (1) the defendant requested the plaintiff to perform work; (2) the plaintiff expected the defendant to compensate him or her for those services; and (3) the defendant knew or should have known that the plaintiff expected compensation. * * * "Technically, recovery in contract implied in fact is the amount the parties intended as the contract price. If that amount is unexpressed, courts will infer that the parties intended the amount to be the reasonable market value of the plaintiff's services." * * *

In the case before us, the trial court, correctly found that there was no express contract, and thus that plaintiffs' recovery must be based on *quantum meruit*. The court further held that plaintiffs should recover their reasonable costs of constructing the duplexes. The court correctly found a contract implied in fact. It is undisputed that defendant Olson orally requested plaintiff Davies to construct the duplexes, that plaintiffs expected Olson to compensate them for those services, and that Olson knew that plaintiffs expected compensation. Thus, we remand as to defendant Olson for a determination of the reasonable value of plaintiffs' services in constructing the duplexes, and an entry of judgment against him for that amount.

We are unable to determine what the court found as to defendant Lund. Thus we remand as to defendant Lund for findings on whether he requested plaintiffs to perform work, and if so, to what extent, or whether he received any unjust benefits as a result of plaintiff's efforts.

DECISION AND REMEDY   *The appellate court remanded the case to the trial court to (1) determine the reasonable value of Davies's services under* quantum meruit *and (2) determine to what extent Lund was liable.*

CONSEQUENTIAL (SPECIAL) DAMAGES Foreseeable damages that result from a party's breach of contract are called *consequential damages*. They differ from compensatory damages in that they are caused by special circumstances beyond the contract itself. They flow from the consequences, or results, of a breach.

For example, if a seller fails to deliver goods with knowledge that a buyer is planning to resell these goods immediately, consequential damages will be awarded for the loss of profit from the planned resale. The buyer will also recover compensatory damages for the difference between the contract price and the market price of the goods.

In order to recover consequential damages, the breaching party must know (or have reason to know) that special circumstances will cause the nonbreaching party to suffer an additional loss. The rationale here is to give the nonbreaching party the whole benefit of the bargain, provided the breaching party knew of the special circumstances when the contract was made.

For example, Leed contracts to have a specific part shipped to her—one that she desperately needs to repair her printing press. In contracting with the shipper who is to return the part, Leed tells the shipper that she must receive it by Monday or she will not be able to print her paper and will lose $750. If the shipper is late, Leed can recover the consequential damages caused by the delay (that is, the $750 in lost profits).

Similarly, when a bank wrongfully dishonors a check, the drawer of the check (a customer of the bank) may recover consequential damages (such as those resulting from slander of credit or reputation) if he or she is arrested or prosecuted.[8]

A leading case on the necessity of giving notice of consequential circumstances is *Hadley v. Baxendale*, decided in England in 1854. The case involved a broken crankshaft used in a mill operation. In the mid-1800s, it was very common for large mills, such as the one the plaintiffs operated, to have more than one crankshaft in case the main one broke and had to be repaired, as it did in this case. Also, in those days it was common knowledge that flour mills had spares. It is against this background that the parties argued whether or not the damages resulting from profits lost while the crankshaft was out for repair were "too remote" to be recoverable.

---

8. Weaver v. Bank of America, 59 Cal.2d 428, 380 P.2d 644, 30 Cal.Rptr. 4 (1963). A checking account is a contractual arrangement. See UCC 4-402.

BACKGROUND AND FACTS *The Hadleys (plaintiffs) ran a flour mill in Gloucester. The crankshaft attached to the steam engine in the mill broke, causing the mill to shut down. The shaft had to be sent to a foundry located in Greenwich so that the new shaft could be made to fit the other parts of the engine. Baxendale, the defendant, was a common carrier who transported the shaft from Gloucester to Greenwich. The Hadleys claimed that they had informed Baxendale that the mill was stopped and that the shaft must be sent immediately. The freight charges were collected in advance, and Baxendale promised to deliver the shaft the following day. It was not delivered for several days, however. As a consequence, the mill was closed for several days. The Hadleys sued to recover the profits lost during that time. Baxendale contended that the loss of profits was "too remote." The court held for the plaintiffs, and the jury was allowed to take into consideration the lost profits. The defendant appealed.*

Case 15.2
HADLEY v. BAXENDALE
Court of Exchequer, 1854.
9 Exch. 341, 156 Eng.Rep. 145.

ALDERSON, B.
✻   ✻   ✻   ✻

Now we think the proper rule in such a case as the present is this:—Where two parties have made a contract which one of them has broken, the damages which the other party ought to receive in respect of such breach of contract should be such as may fairly and reasonably be considered either arising naturally, i.e., according to the usual course of things, from such breach of contract itself, or such as may reasonably be supposed to have been in the contemplation of both parties, at the time they made the contract, as the probable result of the breach of it. Now, if the special circumstances under which the contract was actually made were communicated by the plaintiffs to the defendants, and thus known to both parties, the damages resulting from the breach of such a contract, which they would reasonably contemplate, would be the amount of injury which would ordinarily follow from a breach of contract under these special circumstances so known and communicated. But, on the other hand, if these special circumstances were wholly unknown to the party breaking the contract, he, at the most, could only be supposed to have had in his contemplation the amount of injury which would arise generally, and in the great multitude of cases not affected by any special circumstances, from such a breach of contract. For, had the special circumstances been known, the parties might have specially provided for the breach of contract by special terms as to the damages in that case; and of this advantage it would be very unjust to deprive them. Now the above principles are those by which we think the jury ought to be guided in estimating the damages arising out of any breach of contract.
✻   ✻   ✻   ✻

Now, in the present case, if we are to apply the principles above laid down, we find that the only circumstances here communicated by the plaintiffs to the defendants at the time the contract was made, were, that the article to be carried was the broken shaft of a mill, and that the plaintiffs were the millers of that mill. But how do these circumstances show reasonably that the profits of the mill must be stopped by an unreasonable delay in the delivery of the broken shaft by the carrier to the third person? Suppose the plaintiffs had another shaft in their possession put up or putting up at the time, and that they only wished to send back the broken shaft to the engineer who made it; it is clear that this would be quite consistent with the above circumstances, and yet the unreasonable delay in the delivery would have no effect upon the intermediate profits of the mill. Or, again, suppose that, at the time of the delivery to the carrier, the machinery of the mill had been in other respects defective, then, also, the same results would follow. Here it is true that the shaft was actually sent back to serve as a model for a new one, and that the want of a new one was the only cause of the stoppage of the mill, and that the loss of profits really arose from not sending down the new shaft in proper time, and that this arose from the delay in delivering the broken one to serve as a model. But it is obvious that, in the great multitude of cases of millers sending off broken shafts to third persons by a carrier under ordinary circumstances, such consequences would not, in all probability, have occurred; and these special circumstances were here never communicated by the plaintiffs to the defendants. It follows, therefore, that the loss of profits here cannot reasonably be considered such a consequence of the breach of contract as could have been fairly and reasonably contemplated by both the parties when they made this contract.

DECISION AND REMEDY   *The Court of Exchequer ordered a new trial. According to the court, the special circumstances that caused the loss of profits had never been sufficiently communicated by the plaintiffs to the defendants. The plaintiffs would have to have given express notice of these circumstances in order to collect consequential damages.*

COMMENTS   *When damages are awarded, compensation is given only for those injuries that the defendant could reasonably have foreseen as a probable result of the usual course of events following a breach. If the injury complained of is outside the usual and foreseeable course of events, it must be shown specifically that the defendant had reason to know the facts and foresee the injury.*

PUNITIVE DAMAGES Punitive, or exemplary, damages are generally not awarded in a breach of contract action. Punitive damages are designed to punish a guilty party and to make an example of the party in order to deter similar conduct in the future. Such damages have no legitimate place in contract law, since they are, in essence, penalties, and a breach of contract is not unlawful in a criminal or societal sense. A contract is simply a civil relationship between the parties. The law may compensate one party for the loss of bargain, no more and no less.

In a few situations, a person's actions can cause both a breach of contract and a tort. For example, the parties can establish by contract a certain rea-

sonable standard or duty of care. Failure to live up to that standard is a breach of contract, and the act itself may constitute negligence.

A careful review of Chapters 4 and 5, which deal with torts, will indicate that some intentional torts could also be tied to a breach of the terms of a contract. In such cases it is possible for the nonbreaching party to recover punitive damages for the commission of the tort in addition to compensatory and consequential damages for breach of contract.

Also, some jurisdictions—California, for instance—recognize that a breach of the implied covenant of good faith and fair dealing is actionable as a tort and may warrant an award of punitive damages. In these states, for example, in breach of employment-contract situations, employees have used this form of action to recover damages for *wrongful termination*—that is, termination of employment in violation of an employment contract. (Employer-employee relationships are discussed in more detail in Chapters 33 and 49.)

NOMINAL DAMAGES   *Nominal damages* have been defined as those awarded when only a technical injury is involved and no actual damages have been suffered. In other words, when no financial loss results from a breach of contract, the court may award nominal damages to the innocent party. Nominal damage awards are often trifling, such as a dollar, but they do establish that the defendant acted wrongfully. For example, suppose that Jackson contracts to buy potatoes from Stanley at 50 cents a pound. Stanley breaches the contract and does not deliver the potatoes. In the meantime, the price of potatoes has fallen. Jackson is able to buy them in the open market at half the price he contracted for with Stanley. He is clearly better off because of Stanley's breach. Thus, in a breach of contract suit, Jackson may be awarded only nominal damages for the technical injury he sustained, because no monetary loss was involved. Most lawsuits for nominal damages are brought as a matter of principle under the theory that a breach has occurred and some damages must be imposed regardless of actual loss.

Mitigation of Damages

In most situations, when a breach of contract occurs, the innocent injured party is held to a duty to mitigate, or reduce, the damages that he or she suffers. Under this **mitigation of damages** doctrine, the duty owed depends on the nature of the contract. For example, some states require the lessor to use reasonable means to find a new tenant if the lessee abandons the premises and fails to pay rent. If an acceptable tenant becomes available, the landlord is required to lease the premises to this tenant to mitigate the damages recoverable from the former lessee. The former lessee is still liable for the difference between the amount of the rent under the original lease and the rent received from the new lessee. If the lessor has not taken the reasonable means necessary to find a new tenant, presumably a court can reduce the award made by the amount of rent he or she could have received had such reasonable means been taken.

In the majority of states, wrongfully terminated employees owe the duty to mitigate damages suffered by their employers' breach. The damages they receive are their salaries less the incomes they would have received in similar jobs that they could have obtained by reasonable means. It is the employer's burden to prove the existence of such a job and to prove that the employee could have been hired. (The employee is, of course, under no duty to take a job that is not of the same type and rank.)

Liquidated Damages versus Penalties

A **liquidated damages** provision in a contract specifies a certain amount to be paid in the event of a future default or breach of contract. For example, a provision requiring a construction contractor to pay $100 for every day he or she is late in completing the construction is a liquidated damages provision. Liquidated damages differ from penalties. **Penalties** specify a certain amount to be paid in the event of a default or breach of contract *and are designed to penalize* the breaching party. Liquidated damage provisions are enforceable; penalty provisions are not.

In order to determine if a particular provision is for liquidated damages or for a penalty, two questions must be answered. First, when the contract was entered into, was it apparent that damages would be difficult to estimate in the event of a breach? Second, was the amount set as damages a reasonable estimate and not excessive?[9] If both answers are yes, the provision will be enforced. If either answer is no, the provision will not be enforced. In a construction contract, for example, it is difficult to estimate the amount of damages caused by a delay in completing construction, so liquidated damage clauses are often used. The following case demonstrates the application of liquidated damages to a contractor who was responsible for delays in the completion of a project.

---

9. Restatement, Second, Contracts, Section 356(1), and see UCC 2-718(1), which applies both tests.

Case 15.3

VRGORA v. LOS ANGELES UNIFIED SCHOOL DISTRICT

Court of Appeal, Second
District, 1984.
152 Cal.App.3d 1178,
200 Cal.Rptr. 130.

BACKGROUND AND FACTS *Vrgora, a general contractor, entered into a contract with the Los Angeles Unified School District (LAUSD) to construct an "automotive service shed" and a specifically enclosed room outfitted with an electronic vehicle performance tester. The contract specified a price of $167,195.09, a completion time of 250 days from commencement, and a liquidated damages clause of $100 per day for late completion.*

Vrgora began construction on January 31, 1977, with an expected completion date of July 29, 1977. Delays in the project arose when the manufacturer of the tester did not receive approval for the tester until September 23, 1977 (a delay of over six months). The tester arrived on November 15, 1977, but because of a conflict over its payment, the manufacturer removed the tester. Upon payment, the manufacturer re-delivered the tester on December 23, 1977, and Vrgora completed the project on May 2, 1978. LAUSD assessed $20,700 as liquidated damages against Vrgora. In the suit that followed, the trial court determined that Vrgora was liable for the damages, and Vrgora appealed.

STEPHENS, Associate Justice.

* * * *

[Vrgora's] final argument rests with the fact that LAUSD actually used and occupied a portion of the facility prior to its completion. With this premise, appellant insists that LAUSD should not be allowed to claim full liquidated damages. Particularly, appellant maintains that "[i]f the specified daily rate is a reasonable approximation of the amount necessary to compensate [LAUSD] because [it] cannot occupy the entire building, then, presumably, it would not be a reasonable approximation as to only a portion of the building when another portion is actually occupied." Although at first blush the argument appears plausible, appellant's logic is flawed.

Under California law, liquidated damages are viable if it is established that at the formative stages of the contract [:(1) that] it was mutually recognized that damages from a breach would be impracticable or extremely difficult to determine with certainty; and (2) that the amount or formula stipulated by the parties represented a reasonable endeavor to ascertain what such damages might be. * * * In the context of a public construction contract, it has often been determined as a matter of law that contractor-induced damages, described as "inconvenience and loss of use by the public," are incalculable. * * * Further, this type of liquidated damages provision is legislatively presumed valid " * * * unless manifestly unreasonable under the circumstances existing at the time the contract was made." * * *

In the case at bench, it is most evident that at the formative stages of the contract damages in the event of a breach could not have been ascertained with any reasonable degree of certainty. Moreover, the per diem [per day] assessment does *not* appear manifestly unreasonable. * * *

* * * *

For our purposes, we find it significant that the appellate court's award was made *notwithstanding the fact that the school district occupied and used some of the school rooms.* * * *

* * * *

Because the judgment is supported by substantial evidence in the record, an implicit finding that appellant was sufficiently on notice that the vehicle performance tester's laboratory approval was his contractual responsibility negates his contentions to the contrary. Likewise, substantial evidence requires that we affirm an implicit finding that appellant was the sole source of any delays and thus was obligated under the terms of the contract for the agreed liquidated damages. Finally, the fact that actual injury is uncertain militates against any "setoff" due to possible unjust enrichment of LAUSD.

The court upheld the lower court's finding making Vrgora liable for liquidated damages of $20,700.

RESCISSION AND RESTITUTION

Rescission is essentially an action to undo, or cancel, a contract—to return the contracting parties to the positions they occupied prior to the transaction.[10] Where fraud, a mistake, duress, undue influence, misrepresentation, or lack of capacity to contract is present, unilateral rescission is available.[11] The failure of one party to perform entitles the other party to rescind the contract. The rescinding party must give prompt notice to the breaching party. Generally, to rescind a contract, both parties must make **restitution** to each other by returning goods, property, or money previously conveyed.[12] If the goods or property received can be restored *in specie*—that is, if the actual goods or property can be returned—they must be. If the goods or property have been consumed, restitution must be made in an equivalent amount of money.

Essentially, restitution refers to the plaintiff's recapture of a benefit conferred on the defendant through which the defendant has been unjustly enriched. For example, Ann conveys $10,000 to Bob in return for Bob's promise to design a house for her. The next day Bob calls Ann and tells her that he has taken a position with a large architectural firm in another state and cannot design the house. Ann decides to hire another architect that afternoon. Ann can obtain restitution of the $10,000.

---

10. The rescission discussed here is *unilateral* rescission, in which only one party wants to undo the contract. In mutual rescission, both parties agree to undo the contract. Mutual rescission discharges the contract; unilateral rescission is generally available as a remedy for breach of contract.

11. Many states have statutes allowing consumers to rescind unilaterally contracts made at home with door-to-door salespersons. Rescission is allowed within three days for any reason or for no reason at all. See, for example, California Civil Code, Section 1689.5.

12. Restatement, Second, Contracts, Section 370.

SPECIFIC PERFORMANCE

The equitable remedy of *specific performance* calls for the performance of the act promised in the contract. This remedy is quite attractive to the nonbreaching party, since it provides the exact bargain promised in the contract. It also avoids some of the problems inherent in a suit for money damages.

There are three basic reasons for the attractiveness of the remedy of specific performance. First, the nonbreaching party need not worry about collecting the judgment.[13] Second, the nonbreaching party need not look around for another contract. Third, the actual performance is more valuable than the money damages.

Although the equitable remedy of specific performance is often preferable to other remedies, specific performance will not be granted unless the party's legal remedy (money damages) is inadequate.[14] For example, contracts for the sale of goods rarely qualify for specific performance. The legal remedy, money damages, is ordinarily adequate in such situations because substantially identical goods can be bought or sold in the market. If the goods are unique, however, a court of equity will decree specific performance. For example, paintings, sculptures, or rare books or coins are so unique that money damages will not enable a buyer to obtain substantially identical substitutes in the market.

Sale of Land

Specific performance is granted to a buyer in a contract for the sale of land. The legal remedy for

---

13. Courts enter judgments as final dispositions of cases. The judgment, of course, must be collected, and collection may pose problems. For example, the judgment debtor may be broke or have only a very small net worth.

14. Restatement, Second, Contracts, Section 359.

breach of a land sales contract is inadequate because every piece of land is considered to be unique. Money damages will not compensate a buyer adequately because the same land in the same location obviously cannot be obtained elsewhere. Only when specific performance is unavailable (for example, when the seller has sold the property to someone else) will damages be awarded instead.

Contracts for Personal Services

Personal service contracts require one party to work personally for another party. Courts of equity normally refuse to grant specific performance of personal service contracts. If the contract is not deemed personal, the remedy at law may be adequate if substantially identical service (for example, lawn mowing) is available from other persons.

In individually tailored personal service contracts, courts will not order specific performance by the party who was to be employed, because public policy strongly discourages involuntary servitude.[15] Moreover, the courts do not want to have to monitor a continuing service contract if supervision would be difficult—as it would be if the contract required the exercise of personal judgment or talent. For example, if you contracted with a brain surgeon to perform brain surgery on you, and the surgeon refused to perform, the court would not compel (and you certainly would not want) the surgeon to perform under those circumstances. A court cannot assure meaningful performance in such a situation.[16]

REFORMATION

Reformation is an equitable remedy used when the parties have *imperfectly* expressed their agreement in writing. Reformation allows the contract

to be rewritten to reflect the parties' true intentions. It applies most often where fraud or mutual mistake (for example, a clerical error) are present. Reformation is almost always sought so that some other remedy may then be pursued.

For example, if Gilge contracts to buy a certain parcel of land from Cavendish, but their contract mistakenly refers to a parcel of land different from the one being sold, the contract does not reflect the parties' intentions. Accordingly, a court of equity can reform the contract so that it conforms to the parties' intentions and accurately refers to the parcel of land being sold. Gilge could then show that Cavendish breached the contract as reformed. She can then claim specific performance.

Two other examples deserve mention. The first involves two parties who have made a binding oral contract. They further agree to reduce the oral contract to writing, but in doing so, they make an error in stating the terms. Universally, the courts will allow into evidence the correct terms of the oral contract, thereby reforming the written contract.

The second example deals with written agreements (covenants) not to compete (see Chapter 11, Legality). If the covenant is for a valid and legitimate purpose (such as the sale of a business) but the area or time restraints of the covenant are unreasonable, some courts will reform the restraints by making them reasonable and will enforce the entire contract as reformed. Other courts, however, will throw out the entire restrictive covenant as illegal.

RECOVERY BASED ON QUASI-CONTRACT

As stated in Chapter 7, quasi-contract is an equitable theory through which an obligation is imposed in the absence of an agreement. The courts use this theory to prevent unjust enrichment. Hence quasi-contract provides an equitable basis for equitable relief. The legal obligation, or duty, arises because the law considers that a promise to pay for benefits received is implied by the party accepting the benefits. Generally, when one party has conferred a benefit on another party, justice requires the party receiving the benefit to pay the

---

15. The Thirteenth Amendment to the United States Constitution prohibits involuntary servitude, but *negative* injunctions (that is, injunctions prohibiting rather than ordering certain conduct) are possible. Thus, whereas you may not be able to compel a person to perform under a personal service contract, you may be able to restrain that person from engaging in similar contracts for a period of time.

16. Similarly, courts often refuse to order specific performance of construction contracts because courts are not set up to operate as construction supervisors or engineers.

reasonable value for it. The party receiving the benefit should not be unjustly enriched at the other party's expense.

Quasi-contractual recovery is useful where one party has partially performed under a contract that is unenforceable. It can be used as an alternative to a suit for damages and will allow the party to recover the reasonable value of the partial performance, measured in some cases according to the benefit received and in others according to the detriment suffered.

In order to recover on a quasi-contract, the party seeking recovery must show that:

1. He or she has conferred a benefit on the other party.
2. He or she conferred the benefit with the reasonable expectation of being paid.
3. He or she did not act as a volunteer in conferring the benefit.
4. The party receiving the benefit would be unjustly enriched by retaining the benefit without making payment.

For example, suppose Abrams contracts to build two oil derricks for the Texas Gulf Sulfur Co. For financial reasons, Texas Gulf stipulates that the derricks are to be built over a period of three years, but the parties do not make a written contract. Enforcement of the contract will therefore be barred by the Statute of Frauds.[17] If Abrams completes one derrick before Texas Gulf tells him that the contract is unenforceable, Abrams can sue in quasi-contract because: (1) a benefit has been conferred on Texas Gulf Sulfur, since one oil derrick has been built; (2) Abrams built the derrick (conferred the benefit) expecting to be paid; (3) Abrams did not volunteer to build the derrick but built it under an unenforceable oral contract; and (4) allowing Texas Gulf to retain the derrick without compensating Abrams would enrich the company unjustly. Therefore, Abrams should be able to recover the reasonable value of the oil derrick (under the theory of *quantum meruit*—"as much as he deserved") measured according to the benefit Texas Gulf received.

ELECTION OF REMEDIES

In many cases, a nonbreaching party has several remedies available, but they may be inconsistent with each other. Therefore, the party must choose which remedy to pursue.

The purpose of the *election of remedies* doctrine is to prevent double recovery. Suppose McCarthy agrees to sell his land to Tally. Then McCarthy changes his mind and repudiates the contract. Tally can sue for compensatory damages or for specific performance. If she receives damages, she should not be able to get specific performance of the sales contract, since failure to deliver title to the land was the cause of the injury for which she received damages. If Tally could seek compensatory damages in addition to specific performance, she would recover twice for the same breach of contract. The doctrine of election of remedies requires Tally to choose the remedy she wants, and it eliminates any possibility of double recovery. In other words, the election doctrine represents the legal embodiment of the adage "you can't have your cake and eat it, too."

Unfortunately, the doctrine has been applied in a rigid and technical manner, leading to some harsh results. For example, in a Wisconsin case,[18] Carpenter was fraudulently induced to buy a piece of land for $100. He spent $140 moving onto the land and then discovered the fraud. Instead of suing for damages, Carpenter sued to rescind the contract. The court denied recovery of the $140 because the seller, Mason, did not receive the $140 and was therefore not required to reimburse Carpenter for his moving expenses. So Carpenter suffered a net loss of $140 on the transaction. If Carpenter had sued for damages, he could have recovered the $100 and the $140. Because of such problems, the doctrine of election of remedies has been eliminated in contracts for the sale of goods. The UCC expressly rejects the doctrine. (See UCC 2-703 and UCC 2-711.) Remedies under the UCC are not exclusive but cumulative in nature and include all the available remedies for breach of contract. Thus, for example, under UCC 2-721, in a suit based on fraud, the defrauded party may obtain rescission of the contract, restitution of the

---

17. Contracts that by their terms cannot be performed within one year must be in writing to be enforceable. See Chapter 12.

18. Carpenter v. Mason, 181 Wis. 114, 193 N.W. 973 (1923).

benefits conferred, and any damages due to the fraud.

WAIVER OF BREACH

Under certain circumstances, a nonbreaching party may be willing to accept a defective performance of the contract. This knowing relinquishment of a legal right (that is, the right to require satisfactory and full performance) is called a **waiver.**[19] When a waiver of a breach of contract occurs, the party waiving the breach cannot take any later action on the theory that the contract was broken. In effect, the waiver erases the past breach; the contract continues as if the breach had never occurred. Of course, the waiver of breach of contract extends only to the matter waived and not to the whole contract. Businesspersons often waive breaches of contract by the other party in order to get whatever benefit possible out of the contract.

For example, a seller contracts with a buyer to deliver to the buyer 10,000 tons of coal on or before November 1. The contract calls for the buyer's payment to be made by November 10 for coal delivered. Because of a coal miners' strike, coal is scarce. The seller breaches the contract by not tendering delivery until November 5. The buyer may be well advised to waive the sellers' breach, accept delivery of the coal, and pay as contracted.

Ordinarily, the waiver by a contracting party will not operate to waive subsequent, additional, or future breaches of contract. This is always true when the subsequent breaches are unrelated to the first breach. For example, an owner who waives the right to sue for late completion of a stage of construction does not waive the right to sue for failure to comply with engineering specifications.

A waiver will be extended to subsequent defective performance if a reasonable person would conclude that similar defective performance in the future would be acceptable. Therefore, a *pattern of conduct* that waives a number of successive breaches will operate as a continued waiver. In order to change this result, the nonbreaching party

should give notice to the breaching party that full performance will be required in the future.

To illustrate: Suppose the construction contract mentioned above was to be completed in six stages two months apart, spanning a period of one year. The question is whether the waiver of the right to object to lateness of performance of stage 1 will operate as a waiver of the time requirements for stages 2 through 6. If only the first stage's time requirements have been waived, the waiver will not extend to the other five stages. However, if the first five stages have all been late (and the right to object to the lateness was always waived), the waivers will extend to the final stage unless the owner has given proper notice that future performance is to be on time.

The party who has rendered defective or less-than-full performance remains liable for the damages caused by the breach of contract. In effect, the waiver operates to keep the contract going. The waiver prevents the nonbreaching party from calling the contract to an end or rescinding the contract. The contract continues, but the nonbreaching party can recover damages caused by defective or less-than-full performance.

CONTRACT PROVISIONS LIMITING REMEDIES

A contract can include provisions stating that no damages can be recovered for certain types of breaches or that damages must be limited to a maximum amount. In addition, the contract can provide that the only remedy for breach is replacement, repair, or refund of the purchase price. Provisions stating that no damages can be recovered are called *exculpatory clauses*. (See Chapter 11). Provisions that affect the availability of certain remedies are called *limitation of liability clauses*.

Because of the importance of these clauses and their uses, some discussion and illustrative situations are offered here.

Mutual Assent to Limitation Required

Initially, a court must determine if the provision limiting remedies has been made a part of the contract by offer and acceptance. In order for a

---

19. Restatement, Second, Contracts, Sections 84, 246, and 247. The Restatement uses the term *promise* rather than *waiver*.

term or provision to become part of a contract, both parties must consent to it. Therefore, courts will analyze whether the provision was noticed by the parties—whether, for example, the provision was in fine print or on the back of a lengthy contract. If either party did not know about the provision, it will not be a part of the contract and will not be enforced.[20]

For example, when motorists park their cars in lots, they often receive small ticket stubs that exclude liability for damages to cars parked in the lot. If a reasonable person would have noticed such an exculpatory clause, it will be enforced. If the clause is not conspicuous and a reasonable person would not have noticed it, the clause will not normally be enforced, and the motorist can sue for damage caused to his or her car.[21]

Type of Breach Covered

Once it has been determined that the provision or clause is part of the contract, the analysis must focus on the type of breach that is exculpated. For example, a provision excluding liability for injuries that are inflicted intentionally or that occur as a result of fraud will not be enforced. Likewise, a clause excluding liability for illegal acts or violations of law will not be enforced. On the other hand, a clause excluding liability for negligence may be enforced in appropriate cases. When an exculpatory clause for negligence is contained in a contract made between parties with roughly equal bargaining positions, the clause usually will be enforced.

For example, assume Delta Airlines buys six DC-9s from Douglas Aircraft. In the contract for sale, a clause excludes liability for errors in design and construction of the aircraft. The clause will be upheld because both parties are large corporations with roughly equal bargaining positions. The equality of bargaining power assures that the exculpatory clause was not dictated by one of the parties and forced upon the other.

Limited Remedies—UCC

Under the UCC, in a contract for the sale of goods, remedies can be limited, but rules different from those just discussed apply. If only a certain remedy is desired, the contract must state that the remedy is exclusive. Suppose you buy an automobile and the sales contract limits your remedy to repair or replacement of defective parts. Under the UCC, the sales contract must state that the *sole* and *exclusive* remedy available to the buyer is repair and/or replacement of the defective parts.[22] If the contract states that the remedy is exclusive, then the specified remedy will be the only one ordinarily available to the *buyer* (provided the contract is not *unconscionable*).[23]

When circumstances cause an exclusive remedy to fail in its essential purpose, then it will not be exclusive. [See UCC 2-719(2).] Suppose the car you bought breaks down several times and the dealer is unable to fix or replace the defective parts. In that case, the exclusive remedy fails in its essential purpose, and all the other remedies under the UCC become available.

Under the UCC, a sales contract may also limit or exclude consequential damages, provided the limitation is not unconscionable. Where the buyer is purchasing consumer goods, the limitation of liability for personal injury is *prima facie* unconscionable and will not normally be enforced. Where the buyer is purchasing goods for commercial use, the limitation of liability for personal injury is not necessarily unconscionable.

Suppose that you have purchased a small printing press for your teenage son. It is a present to him for his birthday. He will be using it to print leaflets and pamphlets for his social club. The contract for purchase states that consequential damages arising from personal injury as a result of a defect in the small printing press are excluded. This exclusion or limitation of liability is *prima facie* unconscionable. It will not be enforced. On the other hand, if you buy a printing press for your business, the limitation will not necessarily be unconscionable and may be enforceable.

---

20. See, for example, the Magnuson-Moss Warranty Act discussion in Chapter 20.

21. See California State Auto v. Barrett Garages, Inc., 257 Cal.App.2d 71, 64 Cal.Rptr. 699 (1967).

---

22. UCC 2-719(1).

23. See Chapter 11 for a discussion of unconscionability and UCC 2-719(3).

QUESTIONS AND CASE PROBLEMS

1. Under which of the following breach of contract situations would specific performance be an appropriate remedy? Discuss fully.

(a) Thompson contracts to sell her house and lot to Cousteau. Then, upon finding another buyer willing to pay a higher purchase price, she refuses to deed the property to Cousteau.

(b) Amy contracts to sing and dance in Fred's nightclub for one month, beginning May 1. She then refuses to perform.

(c) Hoffman contracts to purchase a rare coin owned by Erikson, as Erikson is breaking up his coin collection. At the last minute Erikson decides to keep his coin collection intact and refuses to deliver the coin to Hoffman.

(d) There are three shareholders of the ABC Corporation: Panozzo, who owns 48 percent of the stock; Chang, who owns another 48 percent; and Ryan, who owns 4 percent. Ryan contracts to sell her 4 percent to Chang. Later, Ryan refuses to transfer the shares to Chang.

2. Cohen contracts to sell his house and lot to Windsor for $100,000. The terms of the contract call for Windsor to put up 10 percent of the purchase price as "earnest money," a down payment. The terms further stipulate that should the buyer breach the contract, the earnest money would be treated as liquidated damages. Windsor puts up the earnest money, but because her expected financing of the $90,000 balance falls through, she breaches the contract. Two weeks later Cohen sells the house and lot to Ballard for $105,000. Windsor demands her $10,000 back, but Cohen refuses, claiming that Windsor's breach and contract terms entitle him to keep the "earnest money" payment. Discuss who is correct.

3. Ken owns and operates a famous candy store. He makes most of the candy sold in the store, and business is particularly heavy during the Christmas season. Ken contracts with Sweet, Inc., to purchase 10,000 pounds of sugar to be delivered on or before November 15. Ken has informed Sweet that this particular order is to be used for the Christmas season business. Because of production problems the sugar is not tendered to Ken until December 10, at which time Ken refuses it as being too late. Ken has been unable to purchase the quantity of sugar needed to meet the Christmas orders and has had to turn down numerous regular customers, some of whom have indicated that they will purchase candy elsewhere in the future. What sugar Ken has been able to purchase has cost him 10 cents per pound above the price contracted for with Sweet. Ken sues Sweet for breach of contract, claiming as damages the higher price paid for sugar from others, lost profits from this year's lost Christmas sales, future lost profits from customers who

have indicated that they will discontinue doing business with him, and punitive damages for failure to meet the contracted delivery date. Sweet claims Ken is limited to compensatory damages only. Discuss who is correct.

4. Wallechinsky purchases an automobile from Anderson Motors, paying $1,000 down and agreeing to pay off the balance in thirty-six monthly payments of $200 each. The terms of the agreement call for Wallechinsky to make each payment on or before the first of each month. During the first six months, Anderson receives the $200 payments before the first of each month. During the next six months, Wallechinsky's payments are never made until the fifth of each month. Anderson has accepted and cashed the payment check each time. When Wallechinsky tenders the thirteenth payment on the fifth of the next month, Anderson refuses to accept the check, claiming that Wallechinsky is in breach of contract and demands the entire balance owed. Wallechinsky claims that Anderson cannot hold her in breach. Discuss the result fully.

5. Putnam contracts to buy a new Oldsmobile from Old Century Motors, paying $2,000 down and agreeing to make twenty-four monthly payments of $350 each. He takes the car home and, after making one payment, learns that his Oldsmobile has a Chevrolet engine in it rather than the famous Olds Super V-8 engine. Old Century never informed Putnam of this fact. Putnam immediately notifies Old Century of his dissatisfaction and tenders back the car to Old Century. Old Century accepts the car and returns to Putnam the $2,000 down payment plus the one $350 payment. Two weeks later Putnam, without a car and angry, files a suit against Old Century, seeking damages for breach of warranty and fraud. Discuss the effect of Putnam's actions.

6. Ballard was working for El Dorado Tire Company. He was discharged, and he sued for breach of the employment contract. The trial court awarded damages to Ballard, and El Dorado Tire appealed. In the appeal, El Dorado claimed that the trial court failed to reduce Ballard's damages by the amount that he might have earned in other employment during the remainder of the breached contract. El Dorado Tire introduced as evidence the fact that there was an extremely low rate of unemployment for professional technicians and managers in the area. The implication was that Ballard had not taken advantage of the opportunity for mitigating damages. Was El Dorado correct? [Ballard v. El Dorado Tire Co., 512 F.2d 901 (5th Cir. 1975)]

7. Kerr Steamship Company delivered to RCA a twenty-nine-word coded message to be sent to Kerr's agent in Manila. The message included instructions on loading cargo onto one of Kerr's vessels. Kerr's profits on the carriage of the cargo were to be about $6,600. RCA mislaid the coded message, and it was never sent. Kerr sued RCA for the $6,600 in profits that it lost because RCA never sent the message. Can Kerr recover? [Kerr Steamship Co. v. Radio Corp. of America, 245 N.Y. 284, 157 N.E. 140 (1927)]

8. Teachers Insurance and Annuity Association of America (T.I.A.A.) agreed to lend City Centre One Associates

$14.5 million for the construction of an office building in Salt Lake City. City Centre, however, refused to go through with the closing on the loan, and T.I.A.A. sued for specific performance of their contract. Courts have in the past granted specific performance of lending agreements when requested by the *borrower* if failure to go through with the loan would result in irreparable injury to the borrower, who may be unable to secure alternate financing. Should T.I.A.A., as a *lender*, succeed in its request for specific performance? [City Centre One Associates v. Teachers Insurance and Annuity Association, 656 F.Supp. 658 (D.Utah 1987)]

9. Sawyer Fruit, Vegetable & Cold Storage Co. purchased a machine for producing quick-frozen fruit from Lewis Refrigeration Company. Lewis warranted that the machine would process 6,000 pounds of fruit per hour. The sales contract provided that if the machine failed to perform as warranted, Lewis had the right to repair or replace promptly any parts required in order for the machine to function properly. If Lewis was unable to correct the problem through repair or replacement of parts, Sawyer's sole remedy under the contract was rescission; consequential damages were excluded. When the machine did not process the volume warranted, Sawyer had trouble meeting its contracts to supply its customers with frozen fruit. Sawyer did not want to rescind the contract and return the faulty machine, because this would cause the company to fall even further behind in filling its orders. When Sawyer failed to pay the amount still owing on the purchase price of the machine, Lewis sued Sawyer to recover the balance. Sawyer counterclaimed for consequential damages (lost profits). Discuss fully whether under the UCC Sawyer is entitled to consequential damages, notwithstanding the clause in the sales contract excluding consequential damages as a remedy. [Lewis Refrigeration Co. v. Sawyer Fruit, Vegetable & Cold Storage Co., 709 F.2d 427 (6th Cir. 1983)]

10. Southwestern Bell Telephone executed a license agreement that gave United Video authority to construct and operate a cable television system using poles and conduits owned by Bell. The agreement specified that United Video would make a down payment for rent and telephone wire service. By law, Bell was required to locate and mark underground facilities, upon request, before any excavation so that no disruption of the telephone lines would take place. Bell had provided this service free of charge for many years, and it performed the service for United Video before United Video installed its lines. After United Video had substantially completed its installation, Bell notified the company of its intention to charge for the locating and marking service. The charge was not a part of the oral or written contract, and United Video refused to pay. Bell sought to recover based on *quantum meruit*. Discuss whether Bell should succeed in its claim. [Southwestern Bell Telephone Company v. United Video Cablevision of St. Louis, Inc., 737 S.W.2d 474 (Mo.App. 1987)]

11. W. A. and Lola Dunn were payees of several installment promissory notes issued by General Equities of Iowa. Each note contained an acceleration clause that permitted the holder of the note to accelerate and demand full payment of the note should any installment not be paid when due. Over a period of time the Dunns accepted late installment payments from General Equities without invoking the acceleration clause. General Equities made a further late payment. The Dunns returned the General Equities check and demanded payment of the entire balance, with interest, in accordance with the acceleration clause. General Equities claimed that the acceptance of the previous late payments constituted a waiver of the Dunns' right to invoke the acceleration clause. Discuss whether the previous acceptance of late payments waived the Dunns' right to accelerate payment. [Dunn v. General Equities of Iowa, Ltd., 319 N.W.2d 515 (Iowa 1982)]

12. Paul Lewis has operated a sawmill in Cove, Arkansas, since 1956. Lewis decided to install hydraulic equipment in 1963 to better meet the demands of competition. Upon installing the equipment, Frank Rowe, a local Mobil Oil dealer, suggested that Ambrex 810 oil be used with the hydraulic machinery. From the record, it appears that this oil did not have the necessary chemical additives to allow it to function in hydraulic equipment. The system first broke down six months after it was installed. Lewis asked Rowe to make sure the correct type of oil was being used, and, after consultation with Mobil, Rowe continued to supply Ambrex 810. During the next two years of operation six new pumps had to be installed to operate the hydraulic equipment. Lewis changed the brand of pump used, but, with the use of the Ambrex 810 oil recommended by Mobil, this pump broke down almost immediately. Finally, when the next pump was installed, a new oil was used that contained the necessary chemical additives, and the pump has functioned satisfactorily for two and one-half years. Lewis filed suit against Mobil Oil Corporation for damages, including consequential damages, claiming that Mobil had breached its warranty of fitness for a particular purpose. The trial court awarded Lewis $89,250, which included lost profits as consequential damages. Discuss whether the seller should be held liable for lost profits as a result of the recommended oil's failure to perform as warranted. [Lewis v. Mobil Oil Corporation, 438 F.2d 500 (8th Cir. 1971)]

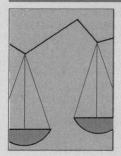

Focus on Ethics

Contract Law and the Application of Ethics

Numerous areas of contract law lend themselves to ethical analysis. Business people certainly face ethical questions when they deal with the application of black-letter law to contracts. (Black-letter law is an informal term for the principles of law that courts generally accept and/or that are embodied in statutes.) Courts, for example, generally will not inquire into the adequacy of the consideration given in a contract. In other words, a court will not reevaluate a contract to determine whether what each party gave is equivalent to what each party received. As long as each party gives some sort of consideration, the courts will conclude that the parties intended to make a binding agreement. The requirement that contracts be supported by consideration also makes parties aware that they can be bound by the contract. Thus, a businessperson could knowingly arrange an exchange in which consideration was far less than value received and successfully argue in court that the consideration was adequate to make the contract legally enforceable. Nonetheless, that person may still be violating the ethics of society.

CONTRACT LAW AND CHANGE

Much of contract law has changed to coincide with the changing ideas of fairness. Consider several examples, which are, of course, not exhaustive of ethical concerns in contract law.

Impossibility

The doctrine of impossibility of performance is based to some extent on the ethical question of whether one party should suffer economic loss when it is impossible to perform a contract. The rule that one is "bound by his or her contracts" is not followed when performance is made impossible. The doctrine of impossibility of performance is applied to relieve a contracting party of liability for failure to perform. This doctrine, however, is applied only when the parties themselves did not allocate the risk of the events that rendered performance impossible. Furthermore, this doctrine rests upon the assumption that the party claiming the defense of impossibility has acted ethically. In other words, a party cannot arrange events intentionally to make performance impossible.

A contract is discharged, for example, if the performance of the contract calls for the delivery of a particular car and through no fault of either party this car is stolen and completely demolished in an accident. Yet the doctrine of impossibility of performance is not available if the party agreeing to sell his or her car either crashed the car to avoid performance of the contract or caused the car's destruction by his or her negligence. The well-known English case of *Taylor v. Caldwell* is also illustrative of the doctrine of impossibility of performance [122 Eng.Rep. 309 (K.B. 1863)]. In *Taylor,* the plaintiff entered into a contract with the defendant to rent the defendant's music hall for a series of concerts. Before the first concert, but after the contract had been entered into, the music hall was destroyed by fire. The court held that the defendant was discharged from performing. Furthermore, because performance was impossible, his failure to perform was not a breach of contract.

Prior to the late nineteenth century, courts were reluctant to discharge a contract even when it appeared that performance was literally impossible. Just as society's ethics change with the passage of time, however, law also makes a transition to reflect society's new perceptions of ethical behavior. Today courts are much more willing to discharge a contract when its performance has become literally impossible. Holding a party in breach of contract, when performance has become literally impossible through no fault of the party claiming the defense of impossibility, no longer coincides with society's notions of fairness.

Frustration of Purpose

The doctrine of frustration of purpose is based upon the idea that when one party's purpose is completely or almost completely frustrated by supervening events, that party should not be required to perform the contract, even though performance of the contract is not rendered impossible. When such a "frustration of purpose" occurs, most courts will discharge a party from performing.

In determining whether to discharge a party from performing a contract, courts will frequently consider whether the alleged frustrating event was foreseeable. The more foreseeable the event, the less likely it is that a court will allow this defense. Hence, the doctrine of frustration of purpose embodies society's ethical notion that it is unfair to require a party to perform a contract in a situation in which the party's object in making the contract has been frustrated.

Mistake

The notion that mistake in contracts should release the contracting parties from their obligations has gained strength as the ethics of society have changed. If one were to study the cases of several hundred years ago, one would find much less acceptance of mistake as an excuse to avoid a contractual obligation than exists today.

Mistakes can arise in numerous contexts surrounding the making of a contract. A mistake may be unilateral in that it is made by only one party. In *Steinmeyer* v. *Schroeppel* [226 Ill. 9 (1907)], for example, a bidder on a construction project incorrectly calculated his costs and therefore submitted an offer that was substantially lower than it would have been if he had correctly calculated his costs. The Illinois court held that the bidder was not entitled to rescind the contract. The court further stated that rescission based upon a unilateral mistake may not be obtained when the mistake results from a failure to exercise reasonable care and diligence. More recent court decisions, however, appear to be less harsh. Some courts have concluded that rescission on account of computation errors is permissible when the only injury to the other party is the loss of the expectancy engendered by a favorably low bid. Thus, ideas of fairness to each of the contracting parties change over time.

Unconscionability

The doctrine of unconscionability represents a good example of the law's attempting to enforce ethical behavior. This doctrine suggests that some contracts may be so unfair to one party as to be unenforceable, even though that party originally agreed to the contract's terms.

Section 2-302 of the Uniform Commercial Code provides that a court will consider the fairness of contracts and may consider a contract or any clause of a contract to have been unconscionable at the time it was made. If so, the court may refuse to enforce the contract, or it may enforce the contract without the unconscionable clause, or it may limit the application of the clause so as to avoid an unconscionable result.

The UCC does not define the term *unconscionability.* The drafters of the UCC, however, have added explanatory comments to the relevant sections of the Code, and these comments serve as guidelines to the Code's application. Comment 1 to Section 2-302 suggests that the basic test for unconscionability is whether, under the circumstances existing at the time of the making of the contract, the clause in question was so one-sided as to be unconscionable. This test is to be applied against the general commercial background of the contract. Obviously, this test provides only general guidance.

Unconscionable action is comparable to unethical action and is incapable of precise definition. Information about the particular facts and specific circumstances surrounding the contract is necessary. For example, a contract with a marginally literate consumer might be seen as unfair and unenforceable, whereas the same contract with a major business firm would be upheld by the courts.

The doctrine of unconscionability could be used broadly to ensure that all contracts appeared perfectly ethical, but the courts have not used it in this way. Only contracts that are so extremely one-sided as to "shock the conscience" of the court have been found unconscionable. Judges have been reluctant to overturn contracts that present difficult ethical questions. Unconscionability is an area in which law and ethics overlap, but even here the law does not resolve all ethical matters.

Contractual Capacity

Chapter 10 pointed out that in order for a contract to be valid and enforceable, the individuals entering into it must have contractual capacity. Consequently, except under certain circumstances, minors can avoid contractual obligations. The question of whether or not a minor should be held responsible for his or her acts is clearly an ethical one. Our set of shared beliefs currently dictates that minors should not be held responsible for contracts except under special circumstances.

For example, in most states minors are allowed to avoid contracts for the sale of nonnecessaries. Merely by making a good-faith attempt to return the purchased goods, a minor can receive a full refund of any monies paid. An ethical issue arises, however, when the minor has diminished the value of the goods prior to returning them or is unable to return them. Because it does not seem "fair" to most people that the merchant should suffer because of the minor's actions, some states require that the merchant be compensated for any reduction in value of the goods.

The Equitable Remedy of Quasi-Contract

Quasi-contracts, often referred to as contracts implied in law, arise to establish justice and fairness. The term quasi-contract is misleading, however, in that a quasi-contract is not a contract at all. The parties have not made any agreement. Rather, a court imposes a

quasi-contract upon the parties when justice requires; these contracts are used to prevent unjust enrichment. The doctrine of unjust enrichment is based upon the theory that individuals should not be allowed to profit or enrich themselves inequitably at the expense of others. This belief is fundamental in our society. Thus, imposing contract liability on an unconsenting party in order to prevent a result perceived by society as unfair (unjust enrichment) is clearly an action inspired by ethical considerations.

A typical situation in which a court, as a matter of judicial policy, may impose a quasi-contract upon the parties arises when one person renders emergency services to another person without first entering into a contract. In these circumstances, courts generally allow the person who renders the emergency services to recover in quasi-contract the reasonable fee for his or her emergency services. This recovery is allowed irrespective of the fact that the parties never entered into a contract. Thus, ethical considerations suggest that it is sometimes necessary for courts to impose a quasi-contract in order to prevent unfairness or unjust enrichment.

CONTRACT LAW, THE INDIVIDUAL, AND BIG BUSINESS

According to one school of legal and economic thought, contract law as interpreted in this unit does not mesh with reality. This school asserts that the individual as a consumer no longer contracts in the traditional sense with huge companies such as Exxon and General Motors. Consequently, it is suggested that the traditional contract elements of offer, acceptance, consideration, and so on may

not be the most appropriate way to analyze consumer purchases.

Some critics argue that an individual consumer has no bargaining position and, hence, must buy on the merchant's terms or not at all. If this theory is correct, ethical considerations no longer play as important a part in an understanding of common law contract doctrine as they did a hundred years ago. In other words the relationship between the seller, the corporation, and the eventual buyer, the consumer, has become so attenuated that the traditional personal interaction between buyers and sellers is no longer present to inspire ethical considerations. A company produces a product and sells it to a wholesaler, who then sells it to a distributor-dealer, who in turn may sell it to the ultimate consumer. This school of thought de-emphasizes the effect of ethical considerations on the part of companies and concludes that big business in general has had a detrimental effect on society.

Another school of thought asserts that no matter how large a firm is, it must please the consumer in order to maximize profits. That is, the ultimate "director" of the firm is the consumer, who still has the choice of buying a smaller quantity or none at all of whatever products are offered in the marketplace. This school of thought perceives consumers to be relevant actors. Furthermore, in markets that include more than one firm, competition forces the firms to offer the consumer products at a price and quality that will maximize profits. Because most producers make the highest profits by inducing repeat sales, they have a profit incentive to treat their clients ethically—in a way that pleases them. Thus, to some extent, ethical issues are hidden by the effect of the producers' notion of profit maximization.

Since both schools of thought are convinced that they are right, the debate may continue indefinitely.

DISCUSSION QUESTIONS

1. Although minors have the power to avoid contracts, the adults with whom the minors contract do not. Because of this one-sided power, some observers have suggested that the law confers on minors a privilege, and that thus, it is inaccurate to speak of the "limited" capacity of minors. But there is another side to consider. Adults often refuse to contract with minors, because minors cannot provide legal assurance that they will not disaffirm. From this point of view, minors are under a legal and practical disability, and their power of avoidance may work against their own best interests. As is often the case, the protection of the law limits the liberty of the protected person. Is the price of this protection too high? Would the interests of minors be best served by granting them full freedom of contract? Or should a different balance be struck—perhaps by instituting a younger age of majority or permitting minors to avoid only those contracts that are not beneficial to them?

2. Suppose you contract to purchase steel at a fixed price per ton. There is a lengthy steelworkers' strike, causing the price of steel to triple from the contract price. If you demand that the supplier fulfill the contract, it will go out of business. Compare the ethical and business aspects of the situation.

3. When selling products, companies often include in the sales contracts exculpatory clauses, in which the consumer agrees not to sue the manufacturer for damages or in which damages are limited. Even if a consumer signs a contract containing an exculpatory clause, is it ethical for the company to insist upon such a clause? Might an exculpatory clause be unconscionable?

Unit Three

COMMERCIAL TRANSACTIONS AND THE UNIFORM COMMERCIAL CODE

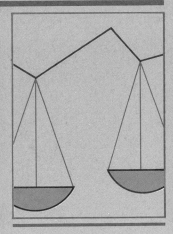

Chapter 16

Introduction to Sales Contracts and Their Formation

Almost every day of our lives we make purchases—the daily newspaper, groceries, clothes, textbooks, compact discs, a car, and so on. Usually we purchase goods rather than real property. For this reason studying the law relating to the sale of goods is relevant to our daily lives.

The people from whom we buy our goods are, to us, sellers. But our sellers are in turn buyers from their suppliers, who are in turn buyers from manufacturers. The law of sales is the study of the rights and responsibilities of those in the purchase-and-sale-of-goods chain, from the original maker of the item to the ultimate user. A **sale** is a contract that, by its terms, transfers title to goods from a seller to a buyer for a price.

HISTORICAL PERSPECTIVE

Today's law of sales originated centuries ago in the customs and traditions of merchants and traders. The *Lex Mercantoria* (Law Merchant) was a system of rules, customs, and usages self-imposed by early commercial traders and merchants to settle disputes and to enforce obligations among themselves. These rules were established at "fairs," where merchants met to exchange goods and settle differences through "fair courts" established and operated by the merchants themselves.

By the end of the seventeenth century, the principles of the Law Merchant were widely accepted and quite naturally became part of the common law. From that time on, judges, not merchants, refined the principles of mercantile law into the modern commercial law of sales.

Numerous attempts were made in the United States to produce a uniform body of laws relating to commercial transactions. Two major proposals, the Uniform Negotiable Instruments Law (1896) and the Uniform Sales Act (1906), were widely adopted by the states. Several other proposed "uniform acts" followed, although most were not widely adopted.

In the 1940s the need to integrate the half-dozen or so uniform acts covering commercial transactions into a single, comprehensive body of statutory law was recognized. Accordingly, the National Conference of Commissioners on Uniform State Laws developed the Uniform Commercial Code (UCC, or simply "the Code") to serve that purpose.

Shift from Common Law to Statutory Law

It is important to note that when we focus on sales contracts, the subject of this chapter, we move away from common law principles and into a body of statutory law. The UCC is the statutory framework we will use, since it has been adopted as law by all states (with the exception of Louisiana, which has adopted only part of it). Relevant sections of the UCC are noted in the following discussion of sales contracts. The reader should refer to Appendix C in the back of the book while examining these notations. Many similarities to the contract law studied in Chapters 7 through 15 will be apparent. Indeed, such similarities should be expected, since the UCC represents the codification of much of the existing common law of contracts.

The Uniform Commercial Code

The UCC is the single most comprehensive codification of the broad spectrum of laws involved in a total commercial transaction. The Code views the entire "commercial transaction for the sale of and payment for goods" as a single legal occurrence having numerous facets.

To illustrate: Review the titles of the ten articles of the UCC in Appendix C. Now consider a consumer who buys a refrigerator from an appliance store and agrees to pay for it on an installment plan. Several articles of the UCC can be applied to this single commercial transaction. Since there is a contract for sale of goods, Article 2 will apply. If a check is given as the down payment on the purchase price, it will be negotiated and ultimately passed through one or more banks for collection. This process is the subject matter of Article 3, Commercial Paper, and Article 4, Bank Deposits and Collections. If the appliance store extends credit to the consumer through the installment plan, and if it retains a right in the refrigerator (the collateral), then Article 9, Secured Transactions, will be applicable.

Suppose, in addition, the appliance company must first obtain the refrigerator from its manufacturer's warehouse, after which it is to be delivered by common carrier to the consumer. The storage and shipment of goods is the subject matter of Article 7, Documents of Title. If the appliance company arranges to pay the manufacturer, located in another state, for the refrigerator supplied, a letter of credit, which is the subject matter of Article 5, may be used.

Thus, the Code attempts to provide a consistent and integrated framework of rules to deal with all the phases *ordinarily arising* in a commercial sales transaction from start to finish.[1]

THE SCOPE OF ARTICLE 2: THE SALE OF GOODS

No body of law operates in a vacuum removed from other principles of jurisprudence. A sales contract is governed by the same common law principles applicable to all contracts—offer, acceptance, consideration, capacity, and legality—and these principles should be reexamined when sales are studied. The law of sales, found in Article 2 of the UCC, is a part of the law of contracts.

Two things should be kept in mind. First, Article 2 deals with the sale of *goods*, not real property (real estate), services, or intangible property such as stocks and bonds. Second, in some cases, the rules may vary quite a bit, depending upon whether the buyer or seller is a *merchant*. It is always a good idea to note the subject matter of a dispute and the kind of people involved. If the subject is goods, then the UCC will govern. If it is real estate or services, then the common law will apply.

What Is a Sale?

Section 2-102 of the Code states that Article 2 "applies to transactions in goods." This implies a

---

1. Two articles of the UCC seem not to apply to the "ordinary" commercial sales transaction. Article 6, Bulk Transfers, involves merchants who sell off the major part of their inventory (sometimes pocketing the money and disappearing, leaving creditors unpaid). Since such bulk sales do not ordinarily arise in a commercial transaction for the sale of goods, they are treated separately. Article 8, Investment Securities, deals with transactions involving certain negotiable securities (stocks and bonds), transactions that do not fall within the concept of sale of or payment for *goods*. However, the subject matter of Articles 6 and 8 was considered by the Code's drafters to be related *sufficiently* to commercial transactions to warrant inclusion in the UCC.

broad scope for this article, covering gifts, purchases of goods, and bailments. (A bailment involves delivery of personal property without title for a specific purpose, as when, for example, an individual drops off his or her clothes at the cleaner's. Bailments are discussed more fully in Chapter 51.) For the purposes of this chapter, we will treat Article 2 as applicable only to an actual sale. A sale is officially defined "as the passing of title from the seller to the buyer for a price" [UCC 2-106(1)]. The price may be payable in money or in other goods, services, or realty (real estate).

What Are Goods?

To be characterized as a *good*, an item must be *tangible*, and it must be *movable*.

A tangible item has physical existence—it can be touched or seen, as a horse, a car, or a chair. Thus, intangible property, such as corporate stocks and bonds, promissory notes, bank accounts, patents and copyrights, or ordinary contract rights, have only conceptual existence and do not come under Article 2.

A *movable* item can be carried from place to place. Hence, real estate is excluded from Article 2.

Two basic areas of dispute arise in determining whether the object of the contract is goods and thus whether Article 2 is applicable. One dispute concerns *goods associated with realty*, such as crops or timber, and the other concerns contracts involving a combination of *goods and services*.

GOODS VERSUS REALTY   Goods associated with real estate fall under Article 2. Section 2-107 provides the following rules:

1.   A contract for the sale of minerals or the like (including oil and gas) or of a structure (such as a building) is a contract for the sale of goods *if severance, or removal, is to be made by the seller*. If the buyer is to sever the subject of the contract from the land, the contract is considered a sale of real estate governed by the principles of real property law, not the UCC.

To illustrate: Sue agrees to sell Ben a quantity of oil that is located under Sue's property. If Ben is to drill the wells to remove the oil, their contract is a contract for the sale of real estate. If the agreement provides that Sue is to drill the wells to obtain the oil, the transaction is a sale of goods.

Similarly, if Sue agrees to sell Ben an old barn located on Sue's farm with Ben to remove the barn, the agreement is a contract for the sale of real estate. If Sue is to remove the barn, the transaction is characterized as a sale of goods under UCC Article 2.

2.   A sale of growing crops or timber to be cut is a sale of goods *regardless of who severs them*.

3.   Other "things attached" to realty but capable of severance without *material harm* to the land are considered goods regardless of who severs them.[2]

GOODS VERSUS SERVICES   When goods and services are combined, courts have disagreed over whether a particular transaction involves the sale of goods or the rendering of a service. For example, is the blood furnished to a patient during an operation a sale of goods or the performance of a medical service? Some courts say a good; some say a service. Whether the transaction in question involves the sale of goods or services is important because the majority of courts treat services as being excluded by the UCC. In discussing their decisions, the courts try to determine which factor is predominant—the good or the service.

The same kind of "mixed transaction" problem is encountered when a beautician applies hair dye to a customer in a beauty shop. The Code does not provide the answer, and court decisions are in conflict.

The Code does stipulate, however, that serving food or drink to be consumed either on or off restaurant premises involves a sale of goods, at least for the purpose of an implied warranty of merchantability [UCC 2-314(1)]. Also, a contract for specially manufactured goods is one for goods, not services [UCC 2-105(1)]. Several other special cases are explicitly characterized as goods by the Code, including the unborn young of animals, rare coins, and other forms of money as a commodity.

Who Is a Merchant?

Article 2 governs the sale of goods in general. It applies to sales transactions between all buyers and sellers. In a limited number of instances, however, the Code presumes that in certain phases of sales transactions involving professional merchants,

---

2. The Code avoids using the word *fixtures* here because of the numerous definitions of this term. (See Chapter 52.)

special business standards ought to be imposed because of the merchants' degree of commercial expertise.[3] Such standards do not apply to the casual or inexperienced seller or buyer. Section 2-104 defines three ways in which merchant status can occur:

1. A merchant is a person who deals in goods of the kind involved in the sales contract. Thus, a retailer, a wholesaler, or a manufacturer is a merchant of those goods sold in the business. A merchant for one type of goods is not necessarily a merchant for any other type. For example, a sporting equipment retailer is a merchant when buying tennis equipment but not when buying stereo equipment.

2. A merchant is a person who, by occupation, holds himself or herself out as having knowledge

and skill peculiar to the practices or goods involved in the transaction. This is a broad definition that can include banks or universities as merchants.

3. A person who employs a merchant as a broker, agent, or other intermediary has the status of merchant in that transaction. Hence, if a "gentleman farmer" who ordinarily does not run the farm hires a broker to purchase livestock, the farmer is considered a merchant in the livestock transaction.

In summary, a person is a merchant when that person, acting in a mercantile capacity, possesses or uses an expertise specifically related to the goods being sold. This basic distinction, however, is not always clear-cut. For example, disagreement has arisen over whether a farmer is a merchant. The answer depends upon the particular goods involved, the transaction, and whether, in the particular situation, the farmer has special knowledge concerning the goods involved in the transaction. The following case illustrates how the courts decide whether a person is a merchant and therefore subject to the UCC version of the Statute of Frauds.

---

3. The provisions that apply only to merchants deal principally with the Statute of Frauds, firm offers, confirmatory memoranda, warranties, and contract modification. These special rules reflect expedient business practice commonly known to merchants in the commercial setting. They will be discussed later in this chapter.

Case 16.1
**CHISOLM v.
CLEVELAND**

Court of Appeals of Texas, Fort
Worth, 1987.
741 S.W.2d 619.

BACKGROUND AND FACTS *Courts K. Cleveland, Jr., is a seller of various types of feed. R. J. "Buck" Chisolm is a dairy farmer who raises his own dairy feed. On those occasions when he anticipates not being able to raise enough feed, he purchases the remainder from a feed supplier. Chisolm agreed orally to buy, and Cleveland agreed orally to sell, one and one-half bags of green chop, which is a feed crop. Chisolm wanted to purchase by weight, but Cleveland wanted to sell by volume (per bag). When the feed was delivered, Chisolm understood the truck driver to say that Cleveland had agreed to Chisolm's terms of sale by weight. After the sale, Cleveland sent Chisolm a written confirmation of the contract, to which Chisolm did not respond in writing within ten days. When Chisolm balked at paying per volume, a lawsuit resulted. The trial court awarded Cleveland $9,885 for breach of an oral contract to purchase cattle feed. The court held that both parties were merchants and that Chisolm's failure to object to Cleveland's written confirmation removed the Statute of Frauds as a defense. Chisolm appealed.*

HILL, Justice.
*　*　*　*

If Courts K. Cleveland, Jr. can establish the existence of an oral contract, he can enforce that contract regardless of the Statute of Frauds, if he can show that the transaction fell within section 2.201(b) of the Texas Business and Commerce Code. Section 2.201(b) provides that the Statute of Frauds is satisfied if the contract is between merchants, and if a writing confirming the contract is sent within a reasonable time and the party receiving it has reason to know its contents and does not give written notice of objection within ten days of receipt. Whether the transaction falls within section 2.201(b) depends upon whether R. J. "Buck" Chisolm was a "merchant" within the meaning of the section.

"Merchant" was defined by the court as "a person who deals in goods of the kind or otherwise by his occupation holds himself out as having knowledge or skill peculiar to the practices or goods involved in the transaction. . . ." This definition is taken from the longer definition of merchant found in section 2.104(a) of the Texas Business and Commerce Code.

The purpose of this definition of "merchant" is to distinguish professionals in a given field from a casual or inexperienced seller or buyer. If Chisolm were a merchant, then section 2.201(b) of the Texas Business and Commerce Code would hold Chisolm to the oral contract with Cleveland according to the terms stated in Cleveland's letter of confirmation unless Chisolm disputed those terms in writing within ten days. The evidence was clear that Chisolm did not dispute Cleveland's terms or respond to the bill in any manner. The evidence here did not show that Chisolm had ever bought and sold green chop, and the evidence showed that he only occasionally bought other types of feed for his cattle, in years when he anticipated that the amount of feed that he had raised would not be sufficient. This evidence establishes that Chisolm is a casual or inexperienced buyer, not that he was a professional buyer or seller of green chop, or any other kind of cattle feed. Since he was only a casual or inexperienced buyer or seller, as opposed to a professional, he was not a merchant as defined by section 2.104(a).

Since Chisolm was not a merchant, as defined by section 2.104(a), his failure to respond to the written confirmation of the contract within ten days did not remove the contract from the application of the Statute of Frauds. Thus, Courts K. Cleveland, Jr. must establish a written contract with R. J. "Buck" Chisolm before he can enforce it.

DECISION AND REMEDY

The court of appeals reversed the judgment of the lower court. The oral contract was not enforceable under the Texas Statute of Frauds because Chisolm was not a merchant.

COMMENTS

In order for Cleveland to prevail, he had to show (1) that the contract was between merchants, and (2) that Chisolm had not objected in writing within ten days after receipt of the confirmation. Cleveland was not able to prove the first element, and thus it was immaterial whether or not Chisolm responded within the ten-day time frame.

FORMATION OF A SALES CONTRACT

The policy of the UCC is to recognize that the law of sales is part of the general law of contracts. The Code often restates general principles or is silent on certain subjects. In those situations, the common law of contracts and applicable state statutes govern. The following sections summarize the ways that UCC provisions *change* the effect of the general law of contracts.

Offer

In general contract law, the moment a definite offer is met by an unqualified acceptance, a bind-ing contract is formed. In commercial sales transactions, the verbal exchanges, the correspondence, and the actions of the parties may not reveal exactly when a binding contractual obligation arises. The Code states that an agreement sufficient to constitute a contract can exist even if the moment of its making is undetermined [UCC 2-204(2)].

OPEN TERMS According to contract law, an offer must be definite enough for the parties (and the courts) to ascertain its essential terms when it is accepted. The UCC states that a sales contract will not fail for indefiniteness even if one or more terms are left open, as long as: (1) the parties intended to make a contract and (2) there is a reasonably certain basis for the court to grant an appropriate remedy [UCC 2-204(3)].

The Code has lessened the requirements for definiteness of essentials in contracts for sale, but it has not removed the common law requirement that the contract be at least definite enough for the court to identify the agreement so as to enforce it or award appropriate damages on its breach. Two factors should be kept in mind. First, the more terms left open, the less likely the courts will find that the parties intended to form a contract. Second, as a general rule, if the *quantity* term is left open, the courts will have no basis for determining a remedy, and the sales contract will fail unless the contract is either an output or a requirements contract [UCC 2-306]. (An *output contract* is a buyer's agreement to purchase a seller's entire output for a stated period; a *requirements contract* is a seller's agreement to supply a buyer with all the buyer's requirements for certain goods used in his or her operations. Output and requirements contracts are discussed in detail in Chapter 9.)

Open Price Term   If the parties have not agreed on a price, the court will determine "a reasonable price *at the time for delivery*" [UCC 2-305(1)]. If either the buyer or the seller is to determine the price, the price is to be fixed in good faith [UCC 2-305(2)].

Sometimes the price fails to be fixed through the fault of one of the parties. In that case, the other party can treat the contract as cancelled or fix a reasonable price. For example, Axel and Beatty enter into a contract for the sale of goods and agree that Axel will fix the price. The agreement becomes economically burdensome to Axel, and Axel refuses to fix the price. Beatty can either treat the contract as cancelled or can set a reasonable price [UCC 2-305(3)].

Open Payment Term   When parties do not specify payment terms, payment is due at the time and place at which the buyer is to receive the goods [UCC 2-301(a)]. Generally, credit is not used. The buyer can tender payment in cash or a commercially acceptable substitute, such as a check or a credit card. If the seller demands payment in actual cash, the buyer must be given a reasonable time to obtain it [UCC 2-511(2)]. This is especially important when a definite and final time for performance is stated in the contract.

Open Delivery Term   When no delivery terms are specified, the buyer normally takes delivery at the seller's place of business [UCC 2-308(a)]. If the seller has no place of business, then the seller's residence is used. When goods are located in some other place and both parties know it, then delivery is made there. When the time for shipment or delivery has not been clearly specified in the sales contract, the court will infer a "reasonable" time under the circumstances for performance [UCC 2-309(1)].

The following case illustrates a court's determination of what constitutes a reasonable time for the delivery of produce to be sold at market.

Case 16.2

MENDELSON-ZELLER CO., INC. v. JOSEPH WEDNER & SON CO.
U.S. Department of Agriculture, 1970.
7 UCC Rep. Serv. 1045.

BACKGROUND AND FACTS   *On or about January 18, 1968, Mendelson-Zeller Co., Inc. (plaintiff), contracted orally to sell to Joseph Wedner & Son Co. (defendant) a mixed truckload of produce consisting of 400 cartons of lettuce and 500 cartons of lemons, which were to be handled on consignment. (In a consignment sale, title remains with the seller but the buyer has the right to sell the goods.) The plaintiff shipped the lettuce on January 18, 1968, at 9:40 P.M. from El Centro, California, and shipped the lemons on the same truck from Yuma, Arizona, on January 19, 1968, at 4:30 A.M. Wedner claimed that the goods were to arrive at Pittsburg, Pennsylvania, between 2:00 and 3:00 A.M. on Monday, January 22, 1968, so that they would be available for the market of that morning. The truckload of produce did not arrive at the defendant's place of business until 12:30 P.M. on January 22, 1968, however. Wedner's docking superintendent refused to unload the truck and instructed the driver to return the next morning at 2:00 A.M. to have the truck unloaded in time for Tuesday's market. The driver locked the truck and did not return until 6:30 A.M. on Tuesday. Although the produce was delivered on the scheduled delivery date (Monday, January 22), according to Wedner it arrived nine* *and one-half hours late (at 12:30 P.M. on that date). Wedner eventually sold the lettuce and remitted the net proceeds of $1,028.93 to Mendelson-Zeller. Mendelson-Zeller then sued for $871.07, the difference between the contract price of $1,900.00 and the sum paid, $1,028.93.*

FLAVIN, Judicial Officer. [A judicial officer functions as a judge or magistrate.]

*   *   *   *

There is evidence that the trucker was under some pressure to get the lettuce to respondent [Wedner & Son] for Monday morning's market.

*   *   *   *

It is evident * * * that [seller] * * * distinguishes between an estimated delivery time and a delivery time which is specified as a part of the contract terms. Neither party submitted a broker's memorandum covering the sale which would presumably show whether there was a specified contract delivery time. In addition the bill of lading does not disclose a specified arrival time though a blank space is provided in which such information can be entered. All of the statements relevant to arrival time other than [buyer] Wedner's statement can be interpreted to mean estimated or anticipated arrival time rather than a time specified as a contract condition.

Respondent [Wedner] as the party alleging that a specified arrival time was a part of the contract of sale had the burden of proving by a preponderance of the evidence that its allegation was true. In view of the foregoing discussion we conclude that respondent has not met its burden of proof.

Section 2-309(1) of the Uniform Commercial Code provides that the time for delivery in the absence of an agreed time shall be a reasonable time. Section 2-503(1) provides that tender of delivery must be at a reasonable hour. The evidence shows that the truck left Yuma at 4:30 A.M. January 19 and arrived at respondent's warehouse at 12:30 P.M. January 22. Although the trucker offered to pay overtime for unloading, respondent's docking superintendent refused to unload. Wedner testified that he thought the truck arrived well after business hours. However, he also testified that respondent's office hours are 9 A.M. to 5 P.M. and the hours at its warehouse and terminal on Mondays are 4 A.M. to anywhere from 11:30 to 12:30 P.M. There is no evidence as to the exact time the warehouse closed on January 22. It is unnecessary to resolve whether the tender on January 22 was within a reasonable hour or whether, as complainant contends, respondent accepted delivery by ordering the truckers to return the next morning. The load was tendered and accepted at 6:30 A.M. January 23, about 97 hours after the truck left Yuma. Although there was some testimony indicating that the normal transit time is 72 hours, the trucking company states that this is an impossibility in the winter time. The truck was actually in transit about 80 hours between Yuma and Pittsburgh. Under the circumstances, we are unable to say that delivery on January 23, was not within a reasonable time.

DECISION AND REMEDY

The seller, Mendelson-Zeller Co., prevailed. The delivery was made in reasonable time; hence, Wedner's failure to pay the full contract price of the lettuce was a breach of contract. The court awarded Mendelson-Zeller damages plus interest on the amount owing.

Duration of an Ongoing Contract   A single contract may specify successive performances but may not indicate how long the parties are required to deal with one another. Although either party may terminate the ongoing contractual relationship, principles of good faith and sound commercial practice call for reasonable notification before termination so as to give the other party reasonable time to seek a substitute arrangement [UCC 2-309(2)(3)].

Options and Cooperation Regarding Performance   When no specific shipping arrangements have been made but the contract contemplates shipment of the goods, the *seller* has the right to make these arrangements in good faith, using commercial reasonableness in the situation [UCC 2-311].

When terms relating to the assortment of goods are omitted from a sales contract, the *buyer* can specify the assortment. For example, Harley and Babcock contract for the sale of 1,000 pens. The pens come in a variety of colors, but the contract is silent on which colors are ordered. Babcock, the buyer, has the right to take whatever colors he wishes. Babcock, however, must make the selection in good faith and must use commercial reasonableness [UCC 2-311].

MERCHANT'S FIRM OFFER   The firm offer is in the special category of rules applicable only to merchants. Under regular contract principles, an offer can be revoked any time before acceptance. The major common law exception is an option contract, in which the offeree pays consideration for the offeror's irrevocable promise to keep the offer open for a stated period.

The UCC creates a second exception that applies only to *firm offers* for the sale of goods made *by a merchant* (regardless of whether or not the offeree is a merchant). If the merchant gives *assurances* in a *signed writing* that the offer will remain open, the merchant's firm offer is irrevocable without the necessity of consideration[4] for the stated period or, if no definite period is specified, a reasonable period (neither to exceed three months) [UCC 2-205].

To illustrate: Daniels, a used-car dealer, writes a letter to Peters on January 1 stating, "I have a 1984 Dodge Dart on the lot that I'll sell you for $4,200. This offer will remain open until the end of the month." By January 18, Daniels has heard nothing from Peters, so he sells the Dodge Dart to another person. On January 23, Peters tenders $4,200 to Daniels and asks for the car. When Daniels tells him the car has already been sold, Peters claims that Daniels has breached a good contract. Peters is right. Since Daniels is a merchant of used cars, he is obligated to keep his offer open until the end of January. Since he has not done so, he is liable for breach.

It is necessary, however, that the offer be both *written and signed* by the offeror.[5] Where a firm offer is contained in a form contract prepared by the offeree, a *separate* firm offer assurance must be signed as well. The purpose of the merchant's firm offer rule is to give effect to a merchant's deliberate intent to be bound to a firm offer. If the firm offer is buried in one of the pages of the offeree's form contract amid copious language, the offeror might inadvertently sign the contract without realizing it, thus defeating the purpose of the rule.

Acceptance

Generally, acceptance of an offer to buy or sell goods may be made in any reasonable manner and by any reasonable means. If the response indicates a definite acceptance of the offer, a contract is formed, even if the response includes additional or different terms—so long as acceptance is not made expressly conditional on the offeror's assent to the new terms. An offeree's additional terms are considered proposals, and the contract is formed on the offeror's terms, unless the parties are both merchants. These points are examined in the following sections.

METHODS OF ACCEPTANCE   The general common law rule is that an offeror can specify, or authorize, a particular means of acceptance, making that means the only one effective for the contract. The common law rule has been altered recently, however, so that even unauthorized means of communication are effective as long as the acceptance is received by the specified deadline. For example, suppose the offer states, "Answer by telegraph within five days." If the offeree sends a letter, and it is received by the offeror within five days, a valid contract is formed.

When the offeror does not specify a means of acceptance, the Code provides that acceptance can be made by any means of communication reasonable under the circumstances, even if the acceptance is not received within the designated time

---

4. If the offeree pays consideration, then an *option contract* and not a *merchant's firm offer* is formed.

5. "Signed" includes any symbol executed or adopted by a party with present intention to authenticate a writing [UCC 1-201(39)]. A complete signature is not required. Therefore, initials, a thumbprint, a trade name, or any mark used in lieu of a written signature will suffice, regardless of its location on the document.

[UCC 2-206(1)]. For example, Alpha Corporation writes Beta Corporation a letter offering to sell Beta $1,000 worth of goods. The offer states that Alpha will keep the offer open for only ten days from the date of the letter. Before the ten-day period has lapsed, Beta sends Alpha a telegram of acceptance. The telegram is misdirected by the telegraph company and does not reach Alpha until after the deadline. Is a valid contract formed? The answer is probably yes, since the telegraph appears to be a commercially reasonable medium of acceptance under the circumstances. Acceptance would be effective upon Alpha's delivery of the message to the telegraph office, which occurred before the offer lapsed.

The UCC permits acceptance of an offer to buy goods for current or prompt shipment by either a *promise* to ship or *prompt shipment* of the goods to the buyer [UCC 2-206(1)(b)]. This provision of the Code retains the common law acceptance of an offer (performance by delivery of conforming goods—that is, goods that are in accordance with the contract terms—to the carrier) and adds as acceptance the commercial practice of sellers who send promises to ship conforming goods. These promises are effective when sent, if they meet the test of being sent by a medium that is commercially reasonable under the circumstances.

The Code goes one step further and provides that if the seller does not promise to ship conforming goods but instead ships (in response to the order) *nonconforming goods,* this shipment constitutes both an *acceptance* and a *breach.* This rule does not apply if the seller seasonably (within the time agreed on or within a reasonable time) notifies the buyer that the nonconforming shipment is offered only as an *accommodation.* The notice of accommodation must clearly indicate to the buyer that the shipment does not constitute an acceptance and that, therefore, no contract has been formed.

For example, Barrymore orders 1,000 *blue* widgets from Stroh. Stroh ships 1,000 *black* widgets to Barrymore, notifying Barrymore that since Stroh has only black widgets in stock, these are sent as an accommodation. The shipment of black widgets is not an acceptance but a counteroffer, and a contract will be formed only if Barrymore accepts the black widgets.

If, however, Stroh ships 1,000 black widgets instead of blue without notifying Barrymore that the goods are being shipped *as an accommodation,* Stroh's shipment acts as both an acceptance of Barrymore's offer and a *breach* of the resulting contract. Barrymore may sue Stroh for any appropriate damages.

At common law, since a unilateral offer invites acceptance by a performance, the offeree need not notify the offeror of performance unless the offeror would not otherwise know about it. The UCC is more stringent than common law, stating that "Where the beginning of requested performance is a reasonable mode of acceptance an offeror who is not notified of acceptance within a reasonable time may treat the offer as having lapsed before acceptance" [UCC 2-206(2)].

To illustrate: Johnson writes the Scroll Bookstore on Monday, "Please send me a copy of *West's Business Law* for $45, COD," signed "Johnson." Scroll receives the request on Tuesday. Scroll immediately prepares the book for shipment but does not ship it for four weeks. Upon its arrival, Johnson rejects the shipment, claiming that the book has arrived too late to be of value.

In this case, since Johnson heard nothing from Scroll for a month, he was justified in assuming that the store did not intend to deliver *West's Business Law.* Johnson could consider that the offer had lapsed because of the length of time.

ADDITIONAL TERMS Under traditional common law, if Able makes an offer to Baker, and Baker in turn accepts but adds some slight qualification, there is no contract. The so-called mirror-image rule, which requires that the acceptance exactly mirror the offer, makes Baker's action a rejection of and a counteroffer to Able's offer.

The UCC generally takes the position that if the offeree's response indicates a *definite* acceptance of the offer, a contract is formed, even if the acceptance includes terms in addition to or different from the original offer [UCC 2-207(1)]. The Code, however, provides that the offeree's expression cannot be construed as an acceptance if the modifications are subject to (conditional upon) the offeror's assent.

For example, Trevor offers to sell Perry 500 pounds of chicken breasts at a specified price and on specified delivery terms. Perry responds, "I accept your offer for 500 pounds of chicken breasts, as evidenced by a city scale weight certificate, at the price and delivery terms stated in your offer."

Perry's response constitutes a contract even though the acceptance adds the words "as evidenced by a city scale weight certificate. If, however, Perry says, "I accept your offer for 500 pounds of chicken breasts on the condition that the weight be evidenced by a city scale weight certificate," there will be no contract unless Trevor so agrees.

If it is determined that a contract exists, the issue is to determine under whose terms performance will be measured: the offeror's or the offeree's (with modifications). The Code also addresses this issue in an attempt to solve the so-called "battle of the forms" between commercial buyers and sellers. (Battle of the forms is an informal term describing the effect of buyers' and sellers' use of many forms to accept and to confirm terms expressed in other forms. [See UCC 2-207(2).])

Exhibit 16–1 is an example of a purchase order. The front of the form is the actual order for particular goods. The back contains standard contract clauses and terms governing the sale. These clauses are sometimes modified to meet a particular purchase requirement. The clauses will have even more meaning as you read the following materials on sales.

Rules When Seller or Buyer Is a Non-merchant When either the seller or the buyer is a non-merchant, or when both are non-merchants, the additional terms are construed as mere proposals (suggestions), and the modified terms do not become a part of the contract. Thus, the contract is formed on the offeror's terms [UCC 2-207(2)].

For example, O'Hare offers to sell his *personal* car to Green for $1,000. Green replies, "I accept your offer to purchase your car for $1,000. I would like a new spare tire to be included as part of the purchase price." Green has given O'Hare a definite expression of acceptance, creating a contract, even though Green's acceptance also suggests an added term for the offer. Since O'Hare is not a merchant, the additional term is merely a proposal (suggestion), and O'Hare is not legally obligated to comply. On the other hand, if Green made the spare tire a *condition* of acceptance, then Green would be making a counteroffer and rejecting the original offer.

Rules between Merchants The Code rule for additional terms in the acceptance is a little different

when the transaction occurs between merchants (that is, when both buyer and seller are merchants). Between merchants, the additional proposed terms *automatically* become part of the contract unless:

1. They materially alter the original contract.
2. The offer expressly states that no terms other than those in the offer will be accepted.
3. The offeror objects to the modified terms in a timely fashion [UCC 2-207(2)].

Suppose Vinson and Brady are merchants. Vinson offers to sell Brady 1,000 pen-and-pencil sets at $10 per set *plus* freight. Brady responds, "I accept your offer. Price is $10.01 per set, *including* freight." There is a contract between Vinson and Brady because Brady made a definite expression of acceptance. Unless Vinson objects to the modification within a reasonable time after receiving notice of the change, Vinson is bound to the $10.01 price per set including freight.

Such is not the case, however, if the modification is one that materially alters the contract. What constitutes a material alteration is frequently a question of fact that only a court can decide. Generally, if the modification involves no unreasonable element of surprise or hardship for the offeror, the court will hold that it did not materially alter the contract. If, in the example just presented, the actual freight charge and the 1 cent per set were within a reasonable range of each other, the modification would *probably* not be considered material.

Now suppose that Vinson's offer states, "1,000 pen-and-pencil sets at a price of $10 per set plus freight. Your acceptance on these terms and these terms only." Brady's definite expression of acceptance with the modified freight terms still constitutes a contract, but because Vinson's offer specifically restricts his obligations to the terms of his offer, the contract is formed on Vinson's terms of "$10 per set plus freight."

In the following case, the court considers the question of whether a carpet manufacturer's written confirmation of a carpet dealer's oral orders for carpet was an "acceptance expressly conditioned on the buyer's consent to additional terms" (specifically, an arbitration provision), which would bring their situation within UCC 2-207(1), and whether the written confirmation between mer-

Exhibit 16–1 An Example of a Purchase Order (Front)

IBM

Purchase Order

NUMBER DATE

IBM DATA

SUPPLIER	MACH	U/M	OC	SUC	PP	REC	EXP	COMMODITY	MM	DEPT. ORDER	ALT	JOB NO.	DEPT. CHG.	APPROP.	CC	PR ORIG.	CHG. RN

REC. NO.	B.J. S.O. OR REF. NO.	ACCOUNT NO.	COMMITMENT

REMIT TO→

NOTIFY BUYER IMMEDIATELY IF REMIT TO ADDRESS IS DIFFERENT ON INVOICE.

SHIP TO: IBM 11400 BURNET ROAD AUSTIN, TEXAS 78758 BLDG.

OTHER THAN ABOVE

CODE

TAXES
DO NOT CHARGE TEXAS SALES USE TAX SINCE WE PAY DIRECT OUR DIRECT PAY AUTHORIZATION NUMBER IS:
3-000001-7281-4

SPECIFICATION CODE
1. Print Attached.
2. Specifications Attached.
3. Sample Attached.
4. Print in Your Possession.
5. Specification in Your Possession.
6. Sample in Your Possession.

SEE CODE BELOW | SHIP VIA | IBM DATA | F.O.B. SHIP POINT | DESTINATION | IBM DATA | YOUR TERMS OF PAYMENT

IMPORTANT
1. SHOW OUR COMPLETE ORDER NUMBER, ITEM NUMBER AND IBM PART NUMBER (IF ANY) ON ALL INVOICES, SHIPPING CONTAINERS, PACKING LISTS AND CORRESPONDENCE.
2. SECURELY ATTACH PACKING SLIP TO OUTSIDE OF CARTON.
3. PACKAGES WEIGHING OVER 75 LBS MUST BE PACKAGED FOR HANDLING WITH A MECHANICAL DEVICE.

TRANSPORTATION ROUTING GUIDELINES
(DO NOT INSURE OR DECLARE VALUE)

0-99 (45kg.) United Parcel Service, if available. If not,
0-40 (18kg.) Parcel Post *(Zones 1-8)* up to $1000 value.
All other Ship as indicated in "ship via" block.

ITEM	PART NUMBER		E/C LEVEL	SHIP TO ARRIVE	QUANTITY	U/M	UNIT PRICE	U/M

*TOTAL QUANTITY OF ITEM ORDERED

"SUBJECT TO THE TERMS AND CONDITIONS ON THE BACK HEREOF WHICH ARE INCORPORATED AND MADE A PART HEREOF"

ADDRESS ALL INVOICES TO:
INTERNATIONAL BUSINESS MACHINES CORP.
Attn: Accounts Payable
P. O. Box 9928
Austin, Texas 78766

AUTHORIZED SIGNATURE 512-838-3300 EXT.

942-0262-4

Source: Reprinted with the permission of the IBM Corporation. © 1985. Copyright: IBM.

Exhibit 16–1 (Continued) An Example of a Purchase Order (Back)

STANDARD TERMS AND CONDITIONS

IBM EXPRESSLY LIMITS ACCEPTANCE TO THE TERMS SET FORTH ON THE FACE AND REVERSE SIDE OF THIS PURCHASE ORDER AND ANY ATTACHMENTS HERETO:

PURCHASE ORDER CONSTITUTES COMPLETE AGREEMENT	This Purchase order, including the terms and conditions on the face and reverse side hereof and any attachments hereto, contains the complete and final agreement between International Business Machines Corporation (IBM) and Seller. Reference to Seller's bids or proposals, if noted on this order, shall not affect terms and conditions hereof, unless specifically provided to the contrary herein, and no other agreement or quotation in any way modifying any of said terms and conditions will be binding upon IBM unless made in writing and signed by IBM's authorized representative.
ADVERTISING	Seller shall not, without first obtaining the written consent of IBM, in any manner advertise, publish or otherwise disclose the fact that Seller has furnished, or contracted to furnish to IBM, the material and/or services ordered hereunder.
APPLICABLE LAW	The agreement arising pursuant to this order shall be governed by the laws of the State of New York. No rights, remedies and warranties available to IBM under this contract or by operation of law are waived or modified unless expressly waived or modified by IBM in writing.
CASH DISCOUNT OR NET PAYMENT PERIOD	Calculations will be from the date an acceptable invoice is received by IBM. Any other arrangements agreed upon must appear on this order and on the invoice.
CONFIDENTIAL INFORMATION	Seller shall not disclose to any person outside of its employ, or use for any purpose other than to fulfill its obligations under this order, any information received from IBM pursuant to this order, which has been disclosed to Seller by IBM in confidence, except such information which is otherwise publicly available or is publicly disclosed by Seller's receipt of such information or is rightfully received by Seller from a third party. Upon termination of this order, Seller shall return to IBM upon request all drawings, blueprints, descriptions or other material received from IBM and all materials containing said confidential information. Also, Seller shall not disclose to IBM any information which Seller deems to be confidential, and it is understood that any information received by IBM, including all manuals, drawings and documents will not be of a confidential nature or restrict, in any manner, the use of such information by IBM. Seller agrees that any legend or other notice on any information supplied by Seller, which is inconsistent with the provisions of this article, does not create any obligation on the part of IBM.
GIFTS	Seller shall not make or offer gifts or gratuities of any type to IBM employees or members of their families. Such gifts or offerings may be construed as Seller's attempt to improperly influence our relationship.
IBM PARTS	All parts and components bailed by IBM to Seller for incorporation in work being performed for IBM shall be used solely for such purposes.
OFF-SPECIFICATION	Seller shall obtain from IBM written approval of all off-specification work.
PACKAGES	Packages must bear IBM's order number and show gross, tare and net weights and/or quantity.
PATENTS	Seller will settle or defend, at Seller's expense (and pay any damages, costs or fines resulting from), all proceedings or claims against IBM, its subsidiaries and affiliates and their respective customers, for infringement, or alleged infringement, by the goods furnished under this order, or any part or use thereof of patents (including utility models and registered designs) now or hereafter granted in the United States or in any country where Seller, its subsidiaries or affiliates, heretofore has furnished similar goods. Seller will, at IBM's request, identify the countries in which Seller, its subsidiaries or affiliates, heretofore has furnished similar goods.
PRICE	If price is not stated on this order, Seller shall invoice at lowest prevailing market price.
QUALITY	Material is subject to IBM's inspection and approval within a reasonable time after delivery. If specifications are not met, material may be returned at Seller's expense and risk for all damages incidental to the rejection. Payment shall not constitute an acceptance of the material nor impair IBM's right to inspect or any of its remedies.
SHIPMENT	Shipment must be made within the time stated on this order, failing which IBM reserves the right to purchase elsewhere and charges Seller with any loss incurred, unless delay in making shipment is due to unforeseeable causes beyond the control and without the fault or negligence of Seller.
SUBCONTRACTS	Seller shall not subcontract or delegate its obligations under this order without the written consent of IBM. Purchases of parts and materials normally purchased by Seller or required by this order shall not be construed as subcontracts or delegations.
(NON-U.S. LOCATIONS ONLY)	Seller further agrees that during the process of bidding or production of goods and services hereunder, it will not re-export or divert to others any IBM specification, drawing or other data, or any product of such data.
TAXES	Unless otherwise directed, Seller shall pay all sales and use taxes imposed by law upon or on account of this order. Where appropriate, IBM will reimburse Seller for this expense.
TOOLS	IBM owned tools held by Seller are to be used only for making parts for IBM. Tools of any kind held by Seller for making IBM's parts must be repaired and renewed by Seller at Seller's expense.
TRANSPORTATION	Routing—As indicated in transportation routing guidelines on face of this order. F.O.B.—Unless otherwise specified, ship collect, F.O.B. origin. Prepaid Transportation (when specified)—Charges must be supported by a paid freight bill or equivalent. Cartage) No charge allowed Premium Transportation) unless authorized Insurance) by IBM. Consolidation—Unless otherwise instructed, consolidate all daily shipments to one destination on one bill of lading.
COMPLIANCE WITH LAWS AND REGULATIONS	Seller shall at all times comply with all applicable Federal, State and local laws, rules and regulations.
EQUAL EMPLOYMENT OPPORTUNITY	There are incorporated in this order the provisions of Executive Order 11246 (as amended) of the President of the United States on Equal Employment Opportunity and the rules and regulations issued pursuant thereto with which the Seller represents that he will comply, unless exempt.
EMPLOYMENT AND PROCUREMENT PROGRAMS	There are incorporated in this order the following provisions as they apply to performing work under Government procurement contracts: Utilization of Small Business Concerns (if in excess of $10,000) (Federal Procurement Regulation (FPR) 1-1.710-3(a)); Small Business Subcontracting Program (if in excess of $500,000) (FPR 1-1.710-3 (b)); Utilization of Labor Surplus Area Concerns (if in excess of $10,000) (FPR 1-1.805-3(a)); Labor Surplus Area Subcontracting Program (if in excess of $500,000) (FPR 1-1.805-3 (b)); Utilization of Minority Enterprises (if in excess of $10,000) (FPR 1-1.1310-2 (a)); Minority Business Enterprises Subcontracting Program (if in excess of $50,000) (FPR 1-1.1310-2(b)); Affirmative Action for Handicapped Workers (if $2,500 or more) (41 CFR 60-741.4); Affirmative Action for Disabled Veterans and Veterans of the Vietnam Era (if $10,000 or more) (41 CFR 60-250.4); Utilization of Small Business Concerns and Small Business Concerns Owned and Controlled by Socially and Economically Disadvantaged Individuals (if in excess of $10,000) (44 Fed. Reg. 23610 (April 20, 1979)); Small Business and Small Disadvantaged Business Subcontracting Plan (if in excess of $500,000) (44 Fed. Reg. 23610 (April 20, 1979)).
WAGES AND HOURS	Seller warrants that in the performance of this order Seller has complied with all of the provisions of the Fair Labor Standards Act of 1938 of the United States as amended.
WORKERS' COMPENSATION, EMPLOYERS' LIABILITY INSURANCE	If Seller does not have Workers' Compensation or Employer's Liability Insurance, Seller shall indemnify IBM against all damages sustained by IBM resulting from Seller's failure to have such insurance.

Source: Reprinted with the permission of the IBM Corporation. © 1985. Copyright: IBM.

chants automatically became part of the contract unless they "materially altered it," which would bring the action within the provisions of UCC 2-207(2).

 Case 16.3

DORTON v. COLLINS & AIKMAN CORP.
United States Court of Appeals, Sixth Circuit, 1972.
453 F.2d 1161.

BACKGROUND AND FACTS *The Carpet Mart, a carpet dealer, and Collins & Aikman Corp., a carpet manufacturer, typically did business orally. Their oral transactions were followed by acknowledgment forms that were generally recognized as confirmations of prior oral agreements. In this particular instance, Collins & Aikman attempted to introduce in their confirmation form an additional term concerning an arbitration provision. The court was not able to resolve who should prevail, because a final decision required additional findings of fact from the trial court. The court merely provided a framework within which the trial court could proceed after the additional information had been gathered.*

CELEBREZZE, Circuit Judge.

* * * *

* * * *Under the common law, an acceptance or a confirmation which contained terms additional to or different from those of the offer or oral agreement constituted a rejection of the offer or agreement and thus became a counter-offer.* [Emphasis added.] The terms of the counter-offer were said to have been accepted by the original offeror when he proceeded to perform under the contract without objecting to the counter-offer. Thus, a buyer was deemed to have accepted the seller's counter-offer if he took receipt of the goods and paid for them without objection.

Under Section 2-207 the result is different. This section of the Code recognizes that in current commercial transactions, the terms of the offer and those of the acceptance will seldom be identical. Rather, under the current "battle of the forms," each party typically has a printed form drafted by his attorney and containing as many terms as could be envisioned to favor that party in his sales transactions. Whereas under common law the disparity between the fine-print terms in the parties' forms would have prevented the consummation of a contract when these forms are exchanged, Section 2-207 recognizes that in many, but not all, cases the parties do not impart such significance to the terms on the printed forms. * * *

* * * *

[We assume], for purposes of analysis, that the arbitration provision was an addition to the terms of The Carpet Mart's oral offers * * *.

Because Collins & Aikman's acceptances were not expressly conditional on the buyer's assent to the additional terms within the proviso of Subsection 2-207(1) a contract is recognized under Subsection (1), and the additional terms are treated as "proposals" for addition to the contract under Subsection 2-207(2). Since both Collins & Aikman and The Carpet Mart are clearly "merchants" as that term is defined in Subsection 2-104(1), the arbitration provision will be deemed to have been accepted by The Carpet Mart under Subsection 2-207(2) unless it materially altered the terms of The Carpet Mart's oral offers.

If Collins & Aikman's acknowledgments are in fact acceptances and the arbitration provision is additional to the terms of Carpet Mart's oral orders, the contracts will be recognized under the provisions of UCC 2-207(1). The arbitration clause will then be viewed as a proposal under UCC 2-207(2), and it will be deemed to have been accepted by Carpet Mart, as both parties are merchants, unless it materially altered the oral agreement.

DECISION AND REMEDY

Consideration

The UCC radically changes the common law rule that contract modification must be supported by new consideration. Section 2-209(1) states that "an agreement modifying a contract needs no consideration to be binding." Of course, contract modification must be sought in good faith [UCC 1-203]. Modifications *extorted* from the other party are in bad faith and, therefore, unenforceable.

For example, Hal agrees to manufacture and sell certain goods to Betty for a stated price. Subsequently, a sudden shift in the market makes it difficult for Hal to sell the items to Betty at the given price without suffering a loss. Hal tells Betty of the situation, and Betty agrees to pay an additional sum for the goods. Later Betty reconsiders and refuses to pay more than the original price. Under Section 2-209(1) of the UCC, Betty's promise to modify the contract needs no consideration to be binding. Hence, Betty is bound by the modified contract.

In the example above, a shift in the market provides an example of a *good faith* reason for contract modification. In fact, Section 1-203 states: "Every contract or duty within this act imposes an obligation of good faith in its performance or enforcement." Good faith in the case of a merchant is defined to mean honesty in fact and the observance of reasonable commercial standards of fair dealing in the trade [UCC 2-103(1)(b)]. But what if there really was no shift in the market, and Hal knew that Betty needed the goods immediately but refused to deliver unless Betty agreed to pay an additional sum of money? This sort of extortion of a modification without a legitimate commercial reason would be ineffective because it would violate the duty of good faith. Hal would not be permitted to enforce the higher price.

WHEN MODIFICATION WITHOUT CONSIDERATION REQUIRES A WRITING   There are situations in which modification without consideration must be written in order to be enforceable. For example, the contract itself may prohibit its modification or rescission except by signed writing. Therefore, only those changes agreed to in the signed writing are enforceable [UCC 2-209(2)]. If a consumer (non-merchant buyer) is dealing with a merchant, and the merchant supplies the form that contains the prohibition against oral modifi-

cation, the consumer must sign a separate acknowledgment of the clause.

Also, any modification that brings the contract under the Statute of Frauds must usually be in writing to be enforceable. Thus, if an oral contract for the sale of goods priced at $400 is modified so that the contracted goods are priced at $600, the modification will have to be in writing to be enforceable since under that statute contracts for the sale of goods for the price of $500 or more must be in writing to be enforceable [UCC 2-209(3)]. If, however, the buyer accepts delivery of the goods after the modification, he or she is bound to the $600 price [UCC 2-201(3)(c)].

Statute of Frauds

Section 2-201(1) of the UCC contains a Statute of Frauds provision that applies to contracts for the sale of goods. The provision requires a writing for the contract to be enforceable if the price of the goods is $500 or more. The parties can have an initial oral agreement, however, and satisfy the Statute of Frauds by having a subsequent written memorandum of their oral agreement. In each case the writing must be signed by the party against whom enforcement is sought.

WRITTEN CONFIRMATION BETWEEN MERCHANTS   Once again the UCC provides a special rule for a contract for the sale of goods between merchants. Merchants can satisfy the requirements of a writing for the Statute of Frauds if, after the parties have agreed orally, one of the merchants sends a signed written confirmation to the other merchant. The communication must indicate the terms of the agreement, and the merchant receiving the confirmation must have reason to know of its contents. Unless the merchant who receives the confirmation gives written notice of objection to its contents within ten days after receipt, the writing will be sufficient against the receiving merchant even though he or she has not signed anything.

For example, Jonas is a Miami merchant buyer. He contracts over the telephone to purchase $5,000 worth of goods from Sarah, a New York City merchant seller. Two days later Sarah sends written confirmation detailing the terms of the oral contract, and later Jonas receives it. If Jonas wishes to use the Statute of Frauds as a defense against enforcement of the contract against him, he must give Sarah written notice of objection to the contents of the written confirmation within ten days of receipt.

RELAXED REQUIREMENTS   The UCC has greatly relaxed the requirements for the sufficiency of a writing to satisfy the Statute of Frauds. A written contract or a memorandum will be sufficient as long as a sales contract is indicated and, with the exception for contracts between merchants mentioned above, as long as it is signed by the party against whom enforcement is sought. Except in the case of output and requirements contracts, a contract is not enforceable beyond the quantity of goods shown in the writing. All other terms can be proved in court by oral testimony. Often, terms that are not agreed upon can be supplied by the open term provisions of Article 2 itself.

EXCEPTIONS   Section 2-201 defines three exceptions to the Statute of Frauds requirement [UCC 2-201(3)]. A contract, if proved to exist, will be enforceable despite the absence of a writing even if it involves a sale of goods for the price of $500 or more under the following circumstances:

1.   *The oral contract is for (a) specially manufactured goods for a particular buyer; (b) these goods are not suitable for resale to others in the ordinary course of the seller's business; and (c) the seller has substantially started to manufacture the goods or made commitments for the manufacture of the goods.* In this situation, once the seller has taken action, the buyer cannot repudiate the agreement claiming the Statute of Frauds as a defense.

To illustrate: Archer orders a uniquely styled cabinet from Collins, a cabinetmaker. The price of the cabinet is $1,000, and the contract is oral. Collins finishes the cabinet and offers to deliver it to Archer. Archer refuses to pay for it even though the job is completed on time. Archer claims that he is not liable because the contract is oral. If the unique style of the cabinet makes it improbable that Collins can find another buyer, then Archer is liable to Collins. Note that Collins must have made a substantial beginning in manufacturing the specialized item prior to Archer's repudiation. Of course, the court must be convinced that there was an oral contract.

2.   *The party against whom enforcement of a contract is sought can admit in pleadings (written answers), testimony, or other court proceedings that a contract for sale was made.* In this case the contract

will be enforceable even though it was oral, but enforceability is limited to the quantity of goods admitted.

To illustrate: Archer and Collins negotiate an agreement over the telephone. During the negotiations, Archer requests a delivery price for 500 gallons of gasoline and a separate price for 700 gallons of gasoline. Collins replies that the price would be the same, $1.10 per gallon. Archer verbally orders 500 gallons. Collins honestly believes that Archer has ordered 700 gallons and tenders that amount. Archer refuses the shipment of 700 gallons, and Collins sues for breach. Archer's answer and testimony admit an oral contract was made, but only for 500 gallons. Since Archer admits the existence of the oral contract, Archer cannot plead the Statute of Frauds as a defense. However, the contract is enforceable only to the extent of the quantity admitted, 500 gallons.

3.   *An oral agreement will be enforceable to the extent that payment has been made and accepted or to the extent that goods have been received and accepted.* This is the "partial performance" exception. The oral contract will be enforced at least according to the amount of performance that *actually* took place.

For example, Archer orally contracts to sell Collins ten chairs at $100 each. Before delivery, Collins sends Archer a check for $500, which Archer cashes. Later, when Archer attempts to deliver the chairs, Collins refuses delivery, claiming the Statute of Frauds as a defense, and demands the return of his $500. Under the UCC's partial performance rule, Archer can enforce the oral contract by tender of delivery of five chairs for the $500 accepted. Similarly, if Collins had made no payment but had accepted the delivery of five chairs from Archer, the oral contract would have been enforceable against Collins for $500, the price of the five chairs delivered.

Parol Evidence

If the parties to a contract set forth its terms in a confirmatory memorandum (a writing expressing offer and acceptance of the deal) or in a writing intended as their final expression, the terms of the contract cannot be contradicted by evidence of any prior or contemporaneous oral or written agreements. The terms of the contract can be explained or supplemented by consistent additional terms, however, or by course of dealing, usage of trade, or course of performance [UCC 2-202].

CONSISTENT ADDITIONAL TERMS If the court finds an ambiguity in a writing that is supposed to be a complete and exclusive statement of the agreement between the parties, it may accept evidence of consistent additional terms to clarify or remove the ambiguity. The court will not, however, accept evidence of contradictory terms. This is the rule under both the Code and the common law of contracts.

COURSE OF DEALING AND USAGE OF TRADE In construing a commercial agreement, the court will assume that the course of prior dealing between the parties and the usage of trade were taken into account when the agreement was phrased [UCC 2-202 and 1-201(3)]. The Code states, "A course of dealing between the parties and any usage of trade in the vocation or trade in which they are engaged or of which they are or should be aware give particular meaning to [the terms of an agreement] and supplement or qualify the terms of [the] agreement" [UCC 1-205(3)].

The Code has determined that the meaning of any agreement, evidenced by the language of the parties and by their action, must be interpreted in light of commercial practices and other surrounding circumstances.

A *course of dealing* is a sequence of previous conduct between the parties to a particular transaction that establishes a common basis for their understanding [UCC 1-205(1)]. Course of dealing is restricted, literally, to the sequence of conduct between the parties that has occurred prior to the agreement in question.

Usage of trade is defined as any practice or method of dealing having such regularity of observance in a place, vocation, or trade as to justify an expectation that it will be observed with respect to the transaction in question [UCC 1-205(2)]. Further, the expressed terms of an agreement and an applicable course of dealing or usage of trade will be construed to be consistent with each other whenever reasonable. When such construction is *unreasonable*, however, the expressed terms in the agreement will prevail [UCC 1-205(4)].

In the following case, the court permitted the introduction of evidence of usage and custom in the trade to explain the meaning of quantity figures that the parties took for granted when the contract was formed.

Case 16.4

HEGGBLADE-MARGULEAS-TENNECO, INC. v. SUNSHINE BISCUIT, INC.

Court of Appeals of California, 5th District, 1976. 59 Cal.App.3d 948, 131 Cal.Rptr. 183.

BACKGROUND AND FACTS *Heggblade-Marguleas-Tenneco (HMT) contracted with Sunshine Biscuit (Bell Brand) to supply potatoes to be used in the production of potato-snack foods. HMT had never marketed processing potatoes before. Heinie Hoffman, who had over twenty years' experience in the potato-processing industry, was hired by HMT on October 1, 1970, to obtain more marketing contracts for its potatoes and to assist in selling the potatoes HMT was planning to grow. Hoffman signed formal contracts with Sunshine Biscuit for HMT on October 5, 1970. The quantity mentioned in the contract negotiations was 100,000 sacks of potatoes. It was agreed that the amount of potatoes to be supplied would vary somewhat with Sunshine Biscuit's needs. Subsequently, a decline in demand for Sunshine Biscuit's products severely reduced its need for potatoes, and it prorated the reduced demand among its suppliers, including HMT, as fairly as possible. Sunshine Biscuit was able to take only 60,105 sacks out of the 100,000 previously estimated. In HMT's suit for breach of contract, Sunshine Biscuit attempted to introduce evidence that it is customary in the potato-processing industry for the number of potatoes specified in sales contracts to be reasonable estimates rather than exact numbers that a buyer intends to purchase. The trial court held for Sunshine Biscuit. HMT appealed.*

FRANSON, Acting Presiding Justice.
*   *   *   *

California Uniform Commercial Code section 2202 states the parol evidence rule applicable to the sale of personal property [and, in] subdivision (a), permits a trade usage to be put in evidence "as an instrument of interpretation." The Uniform Commercial Code comment to subdivision (a) of section 2202 states that evidence of trade usage is admissible "*   *   * in order that the true understanding of the parties as to the agreement may be reached. Such writings are to be read on the assumption that *   *   * the usages of trade were taken for granted when the document was phrased. Unless *carefully negated* they have become an element of the meaning of the words used. Similarly, the course of actual performance by the parties is considered the best indication of what they intended the writing to mean."

*   *   *   *

*   *   * Since the contracts in question are silent about the applicability of the usage and custom, evidence of such usage and custom was admissible to explain the meaning of the quantity figures.

*   *   *   *

Appellant's [HMT's] argument that the evidence of custom should not have been considered by the jury in interpreting the contracts because the officers of HMT were inexperienced in the marketing of processing potatoes and lacked knowledge of the custom is similarly without merit. Mr. Hoffman was knowledgeable in the processing potato business and was aware of the trade custom. Since appellant pleaded that the contracts had been entered into on October 15, 1970, and Hoffman had been employed by HMT on October 1, 1970, his knowledge was imputed to HMT.

Moreover, persons carrying on a particular trade are deemed to be aware of prominent trade customs applicable to their industry. The knowledge may be actual or constructive, and it is constructive if the custom is of such general and universal application that the party must be presumed to know it.

*   *   * Because potatoes are a perishable commodity and their demand is dependent upon a fluctuating market, and because the marketing contracts are signed eight or nine months in advance of the harvest season, common sense dictates that the quantity would be estimated by both the grower and processor. Thus, it cannot be said as a matter of law that HMT was ignorant of the trade custom.

We conclude that the trial court properly admitted the evidence of usage and custom to explain the meaning of the quantity figures in the contracts.

DECISION AND REMEDY   *The trial court's judgment was affirmed. Bell Brand did not have to pay HMT for the difference between the 100,000 sacks of potatoes it estimated it would need and the 60,105 sacks of potatoes it actually purchased.*

COMMENTS   *Parol evidence of usage and custom that is not inconsistent with the terms of the written agreement can be introduced in situations in which both parties knew or should have known of the existence of the particular custom or usage in that industry in that locality. Such evidence is supplemental and shows the meaning that the parties attach to the particular language. It does not alter the contract terms. Just as a previous course of dealing between parties can be regarded as establishing a common basis for interpreting their expressions and conduct [UCC 1-205(1)], so, too, can a usage of trade—a regularly observed practice or method of dealing that is normally accepted and followed in a place, vocation, or trade—establish a common basis for interpreting expressions or conduct [UCC 1-205(2)].*

COURSE OF PERFORMANCE   Course of performance is the conduct that occurs under the terms of a particular agreement. The course of performance actually undertaken is the best indication of what the parties to an agreement intended it to mean, since presumably the parties themselves know best what they meant by their words [UCC 2-208].

To illustrate: Akron Lumber Company contracts with Blauveldt to sell Blauveldt a specified number of "2-by-4s." Akron agrees to deliver the lumber in five separate deliveries. Blauveldt accepts the first three deliveries but rejects the fourth, claiming that Akron has breached the contract by delivering lumber measuring 1 ⅞ inches by 3 ¾ inches rather than 2 inches by 4 inches. Akron can argue that in the trade (usage of trade) 2-by-4s are commonly 1 ⅞ inches by 3 ¾ inches and that Blauveldt, by accepting the lumber without objection in the three previous deliveries under the agreement (course of performance), attested to his understanding that "2 by 4" actually means "1 ⅞ by 3 ¾."

The Code provides *rules of construction.* Express terms, course of performance, course of dealing, and usage of trade are to be construed together when they do not contradict one another. When such construction is unreasonable, however, the following order of priority controls: (1) express terms, (2) course of performance, (3) course of dealing, and (4) usage of trade [UCC 1-205(4) and 2-208(2)].

Unconscionability

An unconscionable contract is one that is so unfair and one-sided that enforcing it would be unreasonable. Section 2-302 allows the court to evaluate a contract or any clause in a contract. If the court deems it to be unconscionable *at the time it was made,* the court can (1) refuse to enforce the contract, or (2) enforce the remainder of the contract without the unconscionable clause, or (3) limit the application of any unconscionable clauses to avoid an unconscionable result.

The court, in determining whether a contract or clause is unconscionable, must decide whether, in light of general commercial practice and the commercial needs of the particular trade involved, the clauses are so one-sided as to be unconscionable under the circumstances at the time the contract was made. In this day of consumer law, more and more consumer sales contracts are being attacked as unconscionable. Typical cases involve high-pressure salespersons and uneducated consumers who contract away their basic rights. In general, the courts have concluded that unequal bargaining power, coupled with unscrupulous dealings by one party, will result in an unenforceable, unconscionable contract.

It is noteworthy that the doctrine of unconscionability expressed explicitly in Section 2-302 is a codification of a pre-UCC notion. The right of the courts to refuse to enforce all of the terms agreed to by the parties to a contract has been recognized for centuries. Equity courts have refused to grant performance of a contract deemed unfair (unconscionable). One of the leading cases involved Campbell Soup Company.[6] The form contract prepared by Campbell Soup contained a clause that excused the company from accepting goods under certain circumstances. Additionally, the clause prohibited the seller of the goods from selling them elsewhere without Campbell's written consent. The court refused to grant specific performance in this classic case on the basis that this clause was unconscionable.

The inclusion of Section 2-302 in the UCC reflects an increased sensitivity to certain realities of modern commercial activities. Classical contract theory holds that a contract is a bargain in which the terms have been worked out *freely* between parties that are equals. In many modern commercial transactions, this premise is invalid. Standard form contracts are often signed by consumer-buyers who understand few of the terms used and who often do not even read them. Virtually all of the terms are advantageous to the parties supplying the standard form contract. With Section 2-302, the courts have a powerful weapon for policing such transactions, as the next case illustrates.

---

6. Campbell Soup Co. v. Wentz, 172 F.2d 80 (3d Cir. 1948).

Case 16.5

JONES v. STAR CREDIT CORP.

Supreme Court of New York, Nassau County, 1969.
59 Misc.2d 189, 298 N.Y.S.2d 264.

BACKGROUND AND FACTS   *The Joneses (plaintiffs), welfare recipients, agreed to purchase a freezer for $900 as the result of a salesperson's visit to their home. Sales taxes and financing charges raised the total price to $1,439.69. At trial, the freezer was found to have a maximum retail value of approximately $300. The plaintiffs sued to have the purchase contract declared unconscionable under the UCC.*

WACHTLER, Justice.

*   *   *   *

*   *   * The question is whether this transaction and the resulting contract could be considered unconscionable within the meaning of Section 2-302 of the Uniform Commercial Code *   *   * .

There was a time when the shield of "caveat emptor" ["let the buyer beware"] would protect the most unscrupulous in the marketplace—a time when the law, in granting parties unbridled latitude to make their own contracts, allowed exploitive and callous practices which shocked the conscience of both legislative bodies and the courts.

The effort to eliminate these practices has continued to pose a difficult problem. On the one hand it is necessary to recognize the importance of preserving the integrity of agreements and the fundamental right of parties to deal, trade, bargain, and contract. On the other hand there is the concern for the uneducated and often illiterate individual who is the victim of gross inequality of bargaining power, usually the poorest members of the community.

*   *   *   *

Section 2-302 of the Uniform Commercial Code enacts the moral sense of the community into the law of commercial transactions. It authorizes the court to find, as a matter of law, that a contract or a clause of a contract was "unconscionable at the time it was made," and upon so finding the court may refuse to enforce the contract, excise the objectionable clause or limit the application of the clause to avoid an unconscionable result. "The principle," states the Official Comment to this section, "is one of the prevention of oppression and unfair surprise." It permits a court to accomplish directly what heretofore was often accomplished by construction of language, manipulations of fluid rules of contract law and determinations based upon a presumed public policy.

There is no reason to doubt, moreover, that this section is intended to encompass the price term of an agreement. In addition to the fact that it has already been so applied, the statutory language itself makes it clear that not only a clause of the contract, but the contract in toto, may be found unconscionable as a matter of law. Indeed, no other provision of an agreement more intimately touches upon the question of unconscionability than does the term regarding price.

Fraud, in the instant case, is not present; nor is it necessary under the statute. The question which presents itself is whether or not, under the circumstances of this case, the sale of a freezer unit having a retail value of $300 for $900 ($1,439.69 including credit charges and $18 sales tax) is unconscionable as a matter of law. The court believes it is.

Concededly, deciding the issue is substantially easier than explaining it. No doubt, the mathematical disparity between $300, which presumably includes a reasonable profit margin, and $900, which is exorbitant on its face, carries the greatest weight. Credit charges alone exceed by more than $100 the retail value of the freezer. These alone, may be sufficient to sustain the decision. Yet, a caveat is warranted lest we reduce the import of Section 2-302 solely to a mathematical ratio formula. It may, at times, be that; yet it may also be much more. The very limited financial resources of the purchaser, known to the sellers at the time of the sale, is entitled to weight in the balance. Indeed, the value disparity itself leads inevitably to the felt conclusion that knowing advantage was taken of the plaintiffs. In addition, the meaningfulness of choice essential to the making of a contract, can be negated by a gross inequality of bargaining power.

There is no question about the necessity and even the desirability of instalment sales and the extension of credit. Indeed, there are many, including welfare recipients, who would be deprived of even the most basic conveniences without the use of these devices. Similarly, the retail merchant selling on instalment or extending credit is expected to establish a pricing factor which will afford a degree of protection commensurate with the risk of selling to those who might be default prone. However, neither of these accepted premises can clothe the sale of this freezer with respectability.

    *   *   *   *

Having already [been] paid more than $600 toward the purchase of this $300 freezer unit, it is apparent that the defendant has already been amply compensated. In accordance with the statute, the application of the payment provision should be limited to amounts already paid by the plaintiffs and the contract be reformed and amended by changing the payments called for therein to equal the amount of payment actually so paid by the plaintiffs.

DECISION AND REMEDY   *Judgment was entered for the plaintiffs. The contract was reformed so that they were required to make no further payments.*

COMMENTS   *A court may be reluctant to find a contract unconscionable if the retail price and the total installment-payment purchase price differ only slightly or if credit charges are reasonable in light of current interest rates.*

CONCEPT SUMMARY: The Formation of Sales Contracts

Offer and Acceptance	1. The acceptance of unilateral offers can be made by a promise to ship or by shipment itself. UCC 2-206(1)(b)
	2. Not all terms have to be included for a contract to result. UCC 2-204
	3. Particulars of performance can be left open. UCC 2-204(3), 2-311(1)
	4. Firm written offers made by a *merchant*, the duration of which is three months or less, cannot be revoked. UCC 2-205
	5. Acceptance by performance requires notice within a reasonable time; otherwise, the offer can be treated as lapsed. UCC 2-206(2)
	6. The price does not have to be included to have a contract. UCC 2-305
	7. Variations in terms between the offer and the acceptance may not be a rejection but may be an acceptance. UCC 2-207(1)
	8. Acceptance may be made by any reasonable means of communication; it is effective when dispatched. UCC 2-206(1)(a)
Consideration	1. A modification of a contract for the sale of goods does not require consideration. UCC 2-209(1)
Requirements under the Statute of Frauds	1. All contracts for the sale of goods priced at $500 or more must be in writing. A writing is sufficient so long as it indicates a contract between the parties and it is signed by the party against whom enforcement is sought. A contract is not enforceable beyond the quantity shown in the writing.
	2. Exceptions to the requirement of a writing exist in the following situations:
	a. When written confirmation of an oral contract *between merchants* is not objected to in writing by the receiver within ten days. UCC 2-201(2)

CONCEPT SUMMARY: The Formation of Sales Contracts (Continued)	
Requirements under the Statute of Frauds (Continued)	b. When the oral contract is for specially manufactured goods not suitable for resale to others, and the seller has substantially started to manufacture the goods. UCC 2-201(3)(a) c. When the defendant admits in pleadings, testimony, or other court proceedings that an oral contract for the sale of goods was made. In this case the contract will be enforceable to the quantity of goods admitted. UCC 2-201(3)(b) d. When payment has been made and accepted under the terms of an oral contract. The oral agreement will be enforceable to the extent that such payment has been received and accepted or to the extent that goods have been received and accepted. UCC 2-201(3)(c)

Parol Evidence	1. The terms of a clearly and completely worded written contract cannot be contradicted by oral or other evidence.
	
	2. Parol evidence is admissible to clarify the terms of a writing:
	
	  a. If the contract terms are ambiguous.
	  b. If evidence of course of dealing, usage of trade, or course of performance is necessary to learn or to clarify the intentions of the parties to the contract.

Unconscionability	An unconscionable contract is one that is so unfair and one-sided that it would be unreasonable to enforce it. If the court deems a contract to be unconscionable at the time it was made, the court can (1) refuse to enforce the contract; (2) refuse to enforce the unconscionable clause of the contract; or (3) limit the application of any unconscionable clauses to avoid an unconscionable result. UCC 2-302.

LEASES

The UCC also now applies to leases of goods under a separate section, Article 2A. In short, Article 2A is a repetition of Article 2, except that it applies to leases, instead of sales, of goods.

Article 2A covers any transaction that creates a lease and includes subleases [UCC 2A-102, 2A-103(k)]. The article defines a **lease agreement** as the lessor and lessee's bargain, as found in their language and as implied from other circumstances, including course of dealing and usage of trade or course of performance [UCC 2A-103(k)]. A **lessor** is one who sells the right to possession and use of goods under a lease [UCC 2A-103(p)]. A **lessee** is one who acquires the right to possession and use of goods under a lease [UCC 2A-103(o)].

Article 2A is included in the full text of the UCC in Appendix B.

QUESTIONS AND CASE PROBLEMS

1. A. B. Zook, Inc., is a manufacturer of washing machines. Over the telephone, Zook offers to sell Radar Appliances 100 Model-Z washers at a price of $150 per unit. Zook agrees to keep this offer open for ninety days. Radar tells Zook that the offer appears to be a good one and that it will let Zook know of its acceptance within the next two to three weeks. One week later, Zook sends and Radar receives notice that Zook has withdrawn its offer. Radar immediately thereafter telephones Zook and accepts the $150-per-unit offer. Zook claims, first, that there never was a sales contract formed between it and Radar and, second, that if there was a contract, the contract is unenforceable. Discuss Zook's contentions.

2. Flint, a retail seller of television sets, orders 100 Model Color-X sets from manufacturer Martin. The order specifies the price and that the television sets are to be *shipped* by Humming Bird Express on or before October 30. The order is received by Martin on October 5. On October 8 Martin writes Flint a letter indicating that the order was received and that the sets will be shipped as directed, at the specified price. This letter is received by Flint on October 10. On October 28, Martin, in preparing the shipment, discovers it has only 90 Color-X sets in stock. Martin ships the 90 Color-X sets and 10 television sets of a different model, stating clearly on the invoice that the 10 are being shipped only as an accommodation. Flint claims Martin is in breach of contract. Martin claims the shipment was not an acceptance and therefore no contract was formed. Explain who is correct and why.

3. Shane has a requirements contract with Sky that obligates Sky to supply Shane with all the gasoline Shane needs for his delivery trucks for one year at $1 per gallon. A clause inserted in small print in the contract by Shane, and not noticed by Sky, states, "The buyer reserves the right to reject any shipment for any reason without liability." For six months Shane has ordered and Sky has delivered under the contract without any controversy. Because of price actions by OPEC, the price of gasoline to Sky has increased substantially. Sky contacts Shane and tells Shane he cannot possibly fulfill the requirements contract unless Shane agrees to pay $1.10 per gallon. Shane, in need of the gasoline, agrees in writing to modify the contract. Later that month, Shane learns he can buy gasoline at $1.05 per gallon from Collins. Shane refuses delivery of his most recent order to Sky, claiming, first, that the contract allows him to do so without liability, and, second, that he is required to pay only $1 per gallon if he accepts the delivery. Discuss fully Shane's contentions.

4. Hatter owns 360 acres of land in Bear County. Hatter makes three separate contracts, in writing, with Bean concerning the land. First, Hatter contracts to sell Bean 500 tons of gravel from a quarry located on the land for a stated price. The contract calls for Bean to remove the gravel. The second contract sells to Bean all the wheat presently growing on a forty-acre tract. Hatter is obligated under the contract to harvest and deliver the wheat to Bean. The third contract is for the sale of the northeast ninety acres with all corn standing. Discuss fully which of these contracts, if any, fall under the UCC.

5. Strike offers to sell Bailey 1,000 shirts for a stated price. The offer states that shipment will be made by the Dependable Truck Line. Bailey replies, "I accept your offer for 1,000 shirts at the price quoted. Delivery to be by Yellow Express Truck Line." Both Strike and Bailey are merchants. Three weeks later, Strike ships the shirts by the Dependable Truck Line, and Bailey refuses shipment. Strike sues for breach of contract. Bailey claims, first, that there never was a contract because the modification of carriers did not constitute an acceptance and, second, that even if there was a contract, Strike is in breach by shipping the shirts by Dependable contrary to the contract terms. Discuss fully Bailey's claims.

6. Fred and Zuma Palermo contacted Colorado Carpet for a price quotation on providing and installing new carpeting and tiling in their home. In response, Colorado Carpet submitted a written proposal to provide and install the carpet at a certain price per square foot of material, *including* labor. The total was in excess of $500. The proposal was never accepted in writing by the Palermos, and the parties disagreed over how much of the proposal had been agreed to orally. After the installation of the carpet and tiling had begun, Mrs. Palermo became dissatisfied and sought the services of another contractor. Colorado Carpet then sued the Palermos for breach of the oral contract. The trial court held that the contract was one for services and was thus enforceable (that is, it didn't fall under the Statute of Frauds [UCC 2-201], which requires contracts for the sale of *goods* for the price of $500 or more to be in writing in order to be enforceable). Discuss fully whether the contract between the Palermos and Colorado Carpet was primarily for the sale of goods or the sale of services. [*Colorado Carpet Installation, Inc. v. Palermo*, 668 P.2d 1384 (Colo. 1983)]

7. Loeb & Company entered into an oral agreement with Schreiner, a farmer, whereby Schreiner was to sell Loeb 150 bales of cotton, each weighing 480 pounds. Shortly thereafter, Loeb sent Schreiner a letter confirming the terms of the oral contract. Schreiner neither acknowledged receipt of the letter nor objected to its terms. When delivery came due, Schreiner ignored the oral agreement and sold his cotton on the open market because the price of cotton had more than doubled (from 37 cents to 80 cents per pound) since the oral agreement was made. In a lawsuit by Loeb & Company against Schreiner, can Loeb & Company recover? [*Loeb & Co. v. Schreiner*, 294 Ala. 722, 321 So.2d 199 (1975)]

8. McNabb agreed to sell soybeans to Ralston Purina Company. Severe weather damaged a significant portion of all soybean crops that year. When McNabb was unable to meet the November 30 delivery deadline, Ralston Purina modified the contract without additional consideration to allow delivery as late as February 28 of the following year. Between November and February, the price of soybeans rose substantially. If Ralston Purina's extensions of the delivery date were intended to *maximize* damages in the event of McNabb's breach, would the modifications to the contract be enforceable? [*Ralston Purina Co. v. McNabb*, 381 F.Supp. 181 (D.Tenn. 1974)]

9. Helvey received electricity from the Wabash County REMC, the county electrical utility. When a mistake in the electrical line resulted in damage to Helvey's household appliances, Helvey sued Wabash County for breach of express and implied contractual warranties. Households require only 110 volts, and Wabash delivered 135 volts or more. Wabash County claimed that under UCC 2-725 a four-year statute of limitations existed and that Helvey had no claim because more than four years had elapsed since the accident. Indiana has a shorter statute of limitations period for sales of goods than for service contracts, however. Helvey claimed that the UCC provision did not apply because electricity is a service and not a good.

Discuss whether the UCC should be applied in this case. [Helvey v. Wabash County REMC, 151 Ind.App. 176, 278 N.E.2d 608 (1972)]

10. In 1961, Clark and American Sand & Gravel discussed the possibility of a purchase by Clark of 25,000 tons of sand at 45 cents per ton. Although both parties found the terms of the possible sale agreeable, no sale was ever made. About eighteen months later, Clark requested his truck driver to obtain about 1,500 tons of sand from American Sand & Gravel. American Sand & Gravel supplied the sand, but no purchase price was ever mentioned. Subsequently, American charged Clark 55 cents per ton for the sand. Is there a contract between American and Clark? If so, what price can American charge for the sand? [American Sand & Gravel, Inc. v. Clark and Fray Constr. Co., 2 Conn.Cir. 284, 198 A.2d 68 (1963)]

11. R-P Packaging is a manufacturer of cellophane wrapping material. The plant manager for Flowers Baking Company decided to improve its packaging of cookies. The plant manager contacted R-P Packaging for the possible purchase of cellophane wrap imprinted with designed "artwork." R-P took measurements to determine the appropriate size of the wrap and submitted to Flowers a sample size with the artwork to be imprinted. After agreeing that the artwork was satisfactory, Flower gave a verbal order to R-P for the designed cellophane wrap at a price of $13,000. When the wrap was tendered, although it conformed to the measurements and design, Flowers complained that the wrap was too short and the design off-center. Flowers rejected the shipment. R-P sued. Flowers contended that the oral contract was unenforceable under the Statute of Frauds. Discuss this contention. [Flowers Baking Company v. R-P Packaging, Inc., 229 Va. 370, 329 S.E.2d 462 (1985)]

12. Peggy Holloway was a real estate broker who guaranteed payment for shipment of over $11,000 worth of mozzarella cheese sold by Cudahy Foods Company to Pizza Pride in Jamestown, North Carolina. The entire arrangement was made orally. Cudahy mailed to Holloway an invoice for the order, and Holloway did not object in writing to the invoice within ten days of receipt. Later, when Cudahy demanded payment from Holloway, Holloway denied ever guaranteeing payment for the cheese and raised the Statute of Frauds (UCC 2-201) as an affirmative defense. Cudahy claims that the Statute of Frauds cannot be used as a defense as both Cudahy and Holloway are merchants, and Holloway failed to object within ten days to Cudahy's invoice. Discuss Cudahy's argument. [Cudahy Foods Company v. Holloway, 286 S.E.2d 606 (N.C.App.Ct. 1982)]

13. Tie Manufacturing, Inc., contracted to purchase from General Instrument Corporation certain electrical components. Tie Manufacturing sent General Instrument its purchase order, which stated on the reverse side that the contract "shall be governed by and in accordance with the laws of the State of New York." The purchase order terms also provided that the buyer was not bound by terms in the seller's acknowledgment that varied the terms of the purchase order without the buyer's written consent. The seller's acknowledgment form contained a choice-of-law clause that restricted jurisdiction of disputes to the state in which the "chief executive offices of the seller are located," which was Connecticut. Tie did not object to this clause. A dispute arose, and the parties claimed that their respective choice-of-law clauses controlled the resolution of the dispute. Discuss whose contract terms governed the dispute. [General Instrument Corp. v. Tie Mfg., Inc., 517 F.Supp. 1231 (S.D.N.Y. 1981)]

14. Harry Starr orally contracted to purchase a new automobile from Freeport Dodge, Inc. Starr signed an order form describing the car and made a downpayment of $25. The dealer did not sign the form, and the form stated that "this order is not valid unless signed and accepted by the dealer." The dealer deposited the $25, and such was noted on the order form. On the day scheduled for delivery, a sales representative for the dealer told Starr that an error had been made in determining the price and that Starr would be required to pay an additional $175 above the price on the order form. Starr refused to pay the additional amount and sued for breach of contract. Dodge claims that the contract falls under the Statute of Frauds, and, since Dodge did not sign the contract, the oral contract is not enforceable. Discuss Freeport Dodge's contention. [Starr v. Freeport Dodge, Inc., 54 Misc.2d 271, 282 N.Y.S.2d 58 (N.Y.Dist.Ct. 1967)]

15. Auburn Plastics submitted price quotations to CBS for the manufacture of eight cavity molds to be used in making parts for CBS's toys. Each quotation price specified that the offer must be accepted within fifteen days or the offer would lapse at Auburn's option. The offer also specified that CBS would be subject to a 30-percent charge for engineering services if CBS ever required delivery of the molds. After a lapse of four months, CBS sent a purchase order to Auburn for the cavity molds. In CBS's purchase order, it was stated that CBS had the right to demand delivery of the molds from Auburn at any time without payment of an engineering charge and that acceptance of the order was to accord with the terms of the purchase order. Auburn's acknowledgment form, as an acceptance of CBS's purchase order, stated that the sale was subject to the conditions and terms of its price quotations. CBS paid Auburn for the molds, and Auburn began to manufacture the toy parts. When Auburn announced a price increase for the toy parts, CBS demanded delivery of the molds. Auburn refused to deliver the molds unless CBS paid the 30-percent engineering-service fee. CBS obtained an order directing the sheriff to seize the molds. Discuss whose sales contract terms govern the duties and rights of the parties. [CBS, Inc. v. Auburn Plastics, Inc., 67 A.D.2d 811, 413 N.Y.2d 50 (N.Y.App.Div. 1979)]

Chapter 17

SALES
Title, Risk, and Insurable Interest

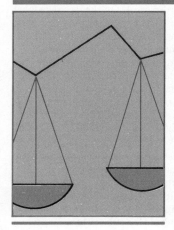

The sale of goods transfers ownership (title) from seller to buyer. Often a sales contract is signed before the actual goods are available. For example, a sales contract for oranges is signed in May, but the oranges are not ready for picking and shipment until October. Any number of things can happen between the time a sales contract is signed and the time the goods are actually transferred to the buyer's possession. Fire, flood, or frost can destroy the orange groves. The oranges may be lost or damaged in transit. The parties may want to obtain casualty insurance on the goods. The government may levy a tax on the oranges.

Before the creation of the UCC, *title*—right of ownership—was the central concept in sales law, controlling all issues of rights and remedies of the parties to a sales contract. Frequently, however, it was difficult to determine when title actually passed from seller to buyer. Therefore, the UCC divorced the question of title as completely as possible from the question of the rights and obligations of buyers, sellers, and third persons (such as subsequent purchasers, creditors, or the tax collector).

In some situations title is still relevant under the Code, and the UCC has special rules for locating title. These rules will be discussed in the materials that follow. In most situations, however, the Code replaces the concept of title with three other concepts: (1) identification, (2) risk of loss, and (3) insurable interest.

IDENTIFICATION

Before any interest in specific goods can pass from the seller to the buyer, two conditions must prevail: (1) The goods must be in existence, and (2) they must be identified to the contract. If either condition is lacking, only a contract to sell (not a sale) exists [UCC 2-105(2)]. Goods that are not both existing and identified to the contract are called *future goods*. For example, a contract to purchase next year's crop of hay would be a contract for future goods, a crop yet to be grown.

For passage of title, the goods must be identified in a way that will distinguish the particular goods to be delivered under the sales contract from all other similar goods.[1] **Identification** is a designation of goods as the subject matter of the sales contract.

In many cases identification is simply a matter of specific designation. For example, you contract to purchase a fleet of five cars by the serial numbers listed for the cars, or you agree to purchase all the wheat in a specific bin at a stated price per bushel. Problems usually occur only when a quantity of goods is purchased from a larger mass, such as 1,000 cases of peas from a 10,000-case lot.

There is a general rule that when a purchaser buys a quantity of goods to be taken from a larger mass, identification can be made only by separation of the contracted goods from the mass. Therefore, until the seller separates the 1,000 cases of peas from the 10,000-case lot, title and risk of loss remain with the seller.

There are a few exceptions to this general rule. For example, a seller owns approximately 5,000 chickens (hens and roosters). A buyer agrees to purchase all the hen chickens at a stated price. Most courts would hold that "all the hen chickens" is a sufficient identification, and title and risk can pass to the buyer without the goods identified in the contract being physically separated from the other goods (the hens from the roosters). The reasoning is that the contract identification serves as sufficient separation.

The most common exception deals with fungible goods [UCC 1-201(17)]. Fungible goods are goods that are alike by nature, agreement, or trade usage. Typical examples are wheat, oil, and wine. If these goods are held or intended to be held by owners in common (owners that have undifferentiated shares of the entire mass), an owner can pass title and risk of loss to a buyer without an actual separation. The buyer replaces the seller as an owner in common [UCC 2-105(4)].

For example, Abraham, Bush, and Carroll are farmers. They deposit, respectively, 5,000 bushels, 3,000 bushels, and 2,000 bushels of the same

grade of grain in a bin. The three become owners in common, with Abraham owning 50 percent of the 10,000 bushels, Bush 30 percent, and Carroll 20 percent. Abraham could contract to sell 5,000 bushels of grain to Tyson and, since the goods are fungible, pass title and risk of loss to Tyson without physically separating 5,000 bushels. Tyson now becomes an owner in common with Bush and Abraham.

Identification is significant because it gives the buyer the right to obtain insurance on (have an insurable interest in) the goods and the right to recover from third parties who damage the goods. In certain circumstances, identification allows the buyer to take the goods from the seller. In other words, the concept of identification is easier to understand if one looks at its consequences.

Parties can agree on whether identification will take place in their contract; but if they do not so specify, in addition to the preceding rules, the following rules apply [UCC 2-501(1)]:

1. Identification takes place at the time the contract is made *if the contract calls for the sale of specific and ascertained goods already existing.*

2. If the sale involves unborn young animals that will be born within twelve months from the time of the contract, identification will take place when the young are conceived. If it involves crops to be harvested within twelve months (or the next harvest season occurring after contracting, whichever is longer), identification will take place when the crops are planted or begin to grow.

3. In other cases, identification takes place when the goods are marked, shipped, or somehow designated by the seller as the particular goods to pass under the contract. The seller can delegate the right to identify goods to the buyer.

When Title Passes

Once goods exist and are identified, the provisions of UCC 2-401 apply to the passage of title.

BY AGREEMENT Parties can expressly agree to when and under what conditions title will pass to the buyer. In virtually all subsections of UCC 2-401, the words "unless otherwise explicitly agreed" appear, meaning that any explicit understanding between the buyer and the seller will determine when title passes.

IN ABSENCE OF AGREEMENT Unless an agreement is explicitly made, title passes to the buyer

---

1. According to UCC 2-401, each provision of Article 2 "with respect to the rights, obligations, and remedies of the seller, the buyer, purchasers or other third parties applies irrespective of title to the goods except where the provisions refer to such title." These provisions referring to title include: UCC 2-312, warranty of title by seller; UCC 2-326(3), consignment sales; UCC 2-327(1)(a), sale on approval and "risk of loss"; UCC 2-403(1), entrustment; UCC 2-501(2), insurable interest in goods; and UCC 2-722, who can sue third parties for injury to goods.

at the time when and the place where the seller performs the physical delivery of the goods [UCC 2-401(2)]. The delivery terms determine when this occurs.

Shipment Contracts   Under shipment contracts, the seller is required or authorized to ship goods by carrier. Here, the seller is required only to deliver the goods into the hands of a carrier (such as a trucking company), and title passes to the buyer at the time and place of shipment [UCC 2-401(2)(a)].

Destination Contracts   With destination contracts, the seller is required to deliver the goods to a particular destination, usually directly to the buyer but sometimes to the buyer's designate. Title passes to the buyer when the goods are tendered at that destination [UCC 2-401(2)(b)].

Contracts for Delivery without Seller's Moving the Goods   When the contract of sale does not call for the seller's shipment or delivery (when the buyer is to pick up the goods), the passage of title depends on whether the seller must deliver a document of title, such as a bill of lading or a warehouse receipt, to the buyer. A *bill of lading* is a receipt for goods that is signed by a carrier and that serves as a contract for the transportation of the goods. A *warehouse receipt* is a receipt issued by a warehouser for goods stored in his or her warehouse. See Exhibits 17–1 and 17–2. When a document of title is required, title passes to the buyer *when and where the document is delivered.* Thus, if the goods are stored in a warehouse, title passes to the buyer when the appropriate documents are delivered. The goods need not move. In fact, the buyer can choose to leave the goods at the same warehouse for a period of time, and the buyer's title to those goods will be unaffected.

When no documents of title are required, and delivery is made without the goods being moved, title passes at the time and place the sales contract was made, if the goods have already been identified. If the goods have not been identified, then title does not pass until identification occurs. Consider an example: Fein sells lumber to Ozo. It is agreed that Ozo will pick up the lumber at the yard. If the lumber has been identified (segregated, marked, or in any other way distinguished from all other lumber), title will pass to Ozo when the contract is signed. If the lumber is still in storage bins at the mill, however, title will not pass to Ozo until the particular pieces of lumber to be sold under this contract are identified [UCC 2-401(3)].

RISK OF LOSS

Under the UCC, several concepts replace the concept of title in determining the rights and remedies of parties to a sales contract. For example, risk of loss does not necessarily pass with title. The question of who suffers a financial risk if goods are damaged, destroyed, or lost is resolved primarily under Sections 2-509 and 2-319. Risk of loss depends on whether or not a sales contract has been breached at the time of loss [UCC 2-510].

Passage of Risk of Loss Absent a Breach of Contract

In the absence of agreement, risk of loss generally passes to the buyer upon some form of the seller's delivery, or tender of delivery, of the goods to the buyer. The following sections discuss the basic rules governing passage of risk of loss.

BY AGREEMENT   Risk of loss can be assigned through an agreement by the parties, preferably in writing. Therefore, the parties can generally control the exact moment risk of loss passes from the seller to the buyer. Of course, at the time so agreed, the goods must be in existence and identified to the contract for this contract provision to be enforceable.

DELIVERY WITHOUT PHYSICAL MOVEMENT OF THE GOODS   Frequently, the goods are to be picked up from the seller by the buyer. In absence of agreement, if the seller is a merchant, risk of loss passes to the buyer only upon the buyer's taking physical possession of the goods. If the seller is a nonmerchant, risk passes to the buyer upon the seller's tender of delivery [UCC 2-509(3)].

CARRIER CASES—SALES REQUIRING DELIVERY BY MOVEMENT OF GOODS   Assuming that there is no specification in the agreement, the following rules apply to so-called carrier cases.

Contract Terms   The following specific terms in the contract, even though used in connection with a stated price, assist one in determining when risk

Exhibit 17–1 A Sample Negotiable Bill of Lading

UNIFORM MOTOR CARRIER ORDER BILL OF LADING

1st Sheet

Original—Domestic

Shipper's No._____

Agent's No._____

CENTRAL FREIGHT LINES INC.

RECEIVED, subject to the classifications and tariffs in effect on the date of the issue of this Bill of Lading,

From		, Date	19

At	Street,	City,	County,	State

the property described below, in apparent good order, except as noted (contents and condition of contents of packages unknown) marked, consigned and destined as shown below, which said company (the word company being understood throughout this contract as meaning any person or corporation in possession of the property under the contract) agrees to carry to its usual place of delivery at said destination, if within the scope of its lawful operations, otherwise to deliver to another carrier on the route to said destination. It is mutually agreed, as to each carrier of all or any of said property over all or any portion of said route to destination, and as to each party at any time interested in all or any of said property, that every service to be performed hereunder shall be subject to all the conditions not prohibited by law, whether printed or written, herein contained, including the conditions on back hereof, which are hereby agreed to by the shipper and accepted for himself and his assigns.

The surrender of this Original ORDER Bill of Lading properly indorsed shall be required before the delivery of the property. Inspection of property covered by this bill of lading will not be permitted unless provided by law or unless permission is indorsed on this original Bill of lading or given in writing by the shipper.

Consigned to Order of

Destination	Street,	City,	County,	State

Notify

At	Street,	City,	County,	State

I. C. C. No.   **Vehicle No.**

Routing

No. Pack-ages	Description of Articles, Special Marks, and Exceptions	*Weight (Subject to Correction)	Class or Rate	Check Column	Subject to Section 7 of Conditions, if this shipment is to be delivered to the consignee without recourse on the consignor, the consignor shall sign the following statement:
					The carrier shall not make delivery of this shipment without payment of freight and all other lawful charges.
					(Signature of consignor.)
					If charges are to be prepaid write or stamp here, "To be Prepaid."
					Received $_____ to apply in prepayment of the charges on the property described hereon.
					Agent or Cashier.
					Per_____ (The signature here acknowledges only the amount prepaid.)

SAMPLE

*If the shipment moves between two ports by a carrier by water, the law requires that the bill of lading shall state whether it is "carrier's or shipper's weight."

Note—Where the rate is dependent on value, shippers are required to state specifically in writing the agreed or declared value of the property.

The agreed or declared value of the property is hereby specifically stated by the shipper to be not exceeding

_____ per _____

Charges advanced:

$_____

Shipper		Agent.
Per	Per	
Permanent address of Shipper	Street,	City,	State

Source: Reprinted with permission of Central Freight Lines Inc. © 1985 Central Freight Lines, Inc.
Note: This form is printed in yellow to warn holders that it is an order bill of lading. The back of the form permits negotiation by indorsement.

Exhibit 17–2 A Sample Nonnegotiable Warehouse Receipt

Warehouse Receipt – Not Negotiable

Agreement No. _____   Vault No. _____ _____ _____ _____ _____

Service Order _____

Receipt and
Lot Number _____   Date of Issue _____ 19 ____

Received for the account of and deliverable to * _____

whose latest known address is _____

SAMPLE

_____ the goods enumerated on the inside or attached schedule to be

stored in Company warehouse, located at _____
which goods are accepted only upon the following conditions set forth below:

READ CAREFULLY That the value of all goods stored, including the contents of any container, and all goods hereafter stored for Depositor's account to be not over $ _____ per pound † per article unless a higher value is noted in the schedule, for which an additional monthly storage charge of _____ ¢ on each $ _____ valuation in excess of $ _____ per pound † per article or fraction thereof will be made.

If there are any items enumerated in this receipt valued in excess of the above limitations per pound per article and not so noted in the schedule, return this receipt within 10 days with proper values so indicated in writing in order that the receipt may be re-issued and proper higher storage rates assessed.

OWNERSHIP. The Customer, Shipper, Depositor, or Agent represents and warrants that he is lawfully possessed of goods to be stored and/or has the authority to store or ship said goods. (If the goods are mortgaged, notify the Company the name and address of the mortgagee.)

PAYMENT OF CHARGES. Storage bills are payable monthly in advance for each month's storage or fraction thereof. Labor charges, cartage and other services rendered are payable upon completion of work. All charges shall be paid at the warehouse location shown hereon, and if delinquent, shall incur interest monthly at the rate of _____ per cent ( ) per year. The Depositor will pay reasonable attorney's fee incurred by The Company in collecting delinquent accounts.

LIABILITY OF COMPANY. The company shall be liable for any loss or injury to the goods caused by its failure to exercise such care as a reasonably careful man would exercise under like circumstances. The company will not be liable for loss or damage to fragile articles not packed, or articles packed or unpacked by other than employees of this company. Depositor specifically agrees that the warehouse will not be liable for contamination of or for insect damage to articles placed in drawers of furniture by the depositor. Periodic spraying of the warehouse premises shall constitute ordinary and proper care, unless the Depositor requests in writing and pays for anti-infestation treatment of articles in drawers and compartments of stored furniture.

CHANGE OF ADDRESS. Notice of change of address must be given the Company in writing, and acknowledged in writing by the Company.

TRANSFER OR WITHDRAWAL OF GOODS. The warehouse receipt is not negotiable and shall be produced and all charges must be paid before delivery to the Depositor, or transfer of goods to another person; however, a written direction to the Company to transfer the goods to another person or deliver the goods may be accepted by the Company at its option without requiring tender of the warehouse receipt.

ACCESS TO STORAGE, PARTIAL WITHDRAWAL. A signed order from the person in whose name the receipt is issued is required to enable others to remove or have access to goods. A charge is made for stacking and unstacking, and for access to stored goods.

BUILDING—FIRE—WATCHMAN. The Company does not represent or warrant that its building cannot be destroyed by fire or that the contents of said buildings including the said property cannot be destroyed by fire. The Company shall not be required to maintain a watchman or sprinkler system and its failure to do so shall not constitute negligence.

CLAIMS OR ERRORS. All claims for non-delivery of any article or articles and for damage, breakage, etc., must be made in writing within ninety (90) days from delivery of goods stored or they are waived. Failure to return the warehouse receipt for correction within ( ) days after receipt thereof by the depositor will be conclusive that it is correct and delivery will be made only in accordance therewith.

FUTURE SERVICE. This Contract shall extend and apply to future services rendered to the Depositor by the Company and to any additional goods deposited with the Company by the Depositor.

WAREHOUSEMAN'S LIEN. The Company reserves the right to sell the goods stored, in accordance with the provisions of the Uniform Commercial Code (Business and Commerce Code if stored in Texas), for all lawful charges in arrears.

TERMINATION OF STORAGE. The Company reserves the right to terminate the storage of the goods at any time by giving to the Depositor thirty (30) days' written notice of its intention so to do, and, unless the Depositor removes such goods within that period, the Company is hereby empowered to have the same removed at the cost and expense of the Depositor, or the Company may sell them at auction in accordance with state law.

DEPOSITOR WILL PAY REASONABLE LEGAL FEES INCURRED BY WAREHOUSE IN COLLECTING DELINQUENT CHARGES.

THIS DOCUMENT CONTAINS THE WHOLE CONTRACT BETWEEN THE PARTIES AND THERE ARE NO OTHER TERMS, WARRANTIES, REPRESENTATIONS, OR AGREEMENTS OF EITHER DEPOSITOR OR COMPANY NOT HEREIN CONTAINED.

Storage per month or fraction thereof	$ _____
Warehouse labor	$ _____
Cartage	$ _____
Packing at residence . . .	$ _____
Wrapping and preparing for storage	$ _____
Charges advanced	$ _____
	$ _____
	$ _____

By _____

*Insert "Mr. and/or Mrs." or, if military personnel, appropriate rank or grade.
† Delete the words "per pound" if the declared value is per article.
For goods stored for military personnel under PL 245, the contractor's liability for care of goods is as provided in Basic Agreement with U.S. Government.

THIS PROPERTY HAS NOT BEEN INSURED BY THIS COMPANY FOR FIRE OR ANY OTHER CASUALTY
SCHEDULE OF GOODS ON FOLLOWING PAGE OR ATTACHED

W-1 (1981) Approved by SW W T4 ©   Re-order from Hart Graphics, Austin, Texas

Source: Reprinted with permission of Hart Graphics, Inc. of Austin, Texas. © 1985 Hart Graphics, Inc.

of loss passes to the buyer. Four such terms should be noted:

1. **F.O.B.** (free on board) means that delivery is at the seller's expense to a specific location. The parties can agree that delivery be either at place of shipment (for example, seller's city or place of business) or at place of destination (for example, buyer's city or place of business). Absent a contrary agreement, when the term is F.O.B. the place of shipment, the risk of loss passes when the seller puts the goods into the carrier's possession. When the term is F.O.B. the place of destination, the risk of loss passes when the seller tenders delivery [UCC 2-319(1)].

2. **F.A.S.** (free alongside) requires the seller at his own expense and risk to deliver the goods alongside the ship before risk passes to the buyer [UCC 2-319(2)].

3. **C.I.F. or C.&F.** (cost, insurance, and freight, or just cost and freight) requires, among other things, that the seller "put the goods in possession of a carrier" before risk passes to the buyer [UCC 2-320(2)].

4. **Delivery ex-ship** (from the carrying vessel) means that risk of loss does not pass to the buyer until the goods leave the ship or are otherwise properly unloaded [UCC 2-322].

Shipment Contracts   In a shipment contract, if the seller is required or authorized to ship goods by carrier (not required to deliver them to a particular destination), risk of loss passes to the buyer when the goods are duly delivered to the carrier [UCC 2-509(1)(a)].

For example, a seller in New York sells 10,000 tons of sheet metal to a buyer in California, F.O.B. New York (free on board in New York—that is, buyer pays the transportation charges from New York). The contract authorizes a shipment by carrier; it does not require the seller to tender the metal in California. Risk passes to the buyer when the conforming goods are properly placed in the possession of the carrier. If the goods are damaged in transit, the loss falls on the buyer. (Actually, buyers may have recourse against carriers, subject to tariff rule limitations, and they usually insure the goods from the time they leave the seller.) Generally, all contracts are assumed to be shipment contracts if nothing to the contrary is stated in the contract.

Destination Contracts   In a destination contract, the seller is required to deliver the goods to a particular destination. The risk of loss passes to the buyer when the goods are tendered to the buyer at that destination. In the preceding example, if the contract had been F.O.B. California, risk of loss during transit to California would have fallen on the seller.

In the following case, the court reviewed UCC 2-509(1) as it relates to passage of the risk of loss. Under the Code, an F.O.B. term indicates whether the contract is a shipment contract or a destination contract and thus indicates when the risk of loss passes. The F.O.B. terminology controls. In this case, the contract contained neither delivery terms, such as F.O.B., nor specific terms for allocation of loss while goods were in transit.

BACKGROUND AND FACTS   *Defendant Karinol Corp. contracted "to ship" watches to the plaintiff in Chetumal, Mexico. The contract, formed in Florida and governed by Florida's codification of the UCC, contained a "ship to" address but did not otherwise indicate it should be considered a destination contract. The plaintiff-buyer made a deposit, and the watches were shipped, but they were lost in transit. The plaintiff sought a refund for the deposit, claiming risk of loss was on the seller. Defendant-seller Karinol claimed that the plaintiff suffered the risk of loss and owed the balance of the purchase price. The trial court held for the defendant. The plaintiff appealed.*

 Case 17.1

PESTANA v. KARINOL CORP.

District Court of Appeal of Florida, Third District, 1979. 367 So.2d 1096.

HUBBART, Judge.
*   *   *   *

Where the risk of loss falls on the seller at the time the goods sold are lost or destroyed, the seller is liable in damages to the buyer for non-delivery unless the seller tenders a performance in replacement for the lost or destroyed goods. On the other hand, where the risk of loss falls on the buyer at the time the goods sold are lost or destroyed, the buyer is liable to the seller for the purchase price of the goods sold.

In the instant case, we deal with the normal shipment contract involving the sale of goods. The defendant Karinol pursuant to this contract agreed to send the goods sold, a shipment of watches, to the plaintiff's decedent in Chetumal, Mexico. There was no specific provision in the contract between the parties which allocated the risk of loss on the goods sold while in transit. In addition, there were no delivery terms such as F.O.B. Chetumal contained in the contract.

All agree that there is sufficient evidence that the defendant Karinol performed its obligations as a seller under the Uniform Commercial Code if this contract is considered a shipment contract. Karinol put the goods sold in the possession of a carrier and made a contract for the goods safe transportation to the plaintiff's decedent; Karinol also promptly notified the plaintiff's decedent of the shipment and tendered to said party the necessary documents to obtain possession of the goods sold.

The plaintiff Pestana contends, however, that the contract herein is a destination contract in which the risk of loss on the goods sold did not pass until delivery on such goods had been tendered to him at Chetumal, Mexico—an event which never occurred. He relies for this position on the notation at the bottom of the contract between the parties which provides that the goods were to be sent to Chetumal, Mexico. We cannot agree. A "send to" or "ship to" term is a part of every contract involving the sale of goods where carriage is contemplated and has no significance in determining whether the contract is a shipment or destination contract for risk of loss purposes. As such, the "send to" term contained in this contract cannot, without more, convert this into a destination contract.

DECISION AND REMEDY	*The buyer was liable to the seller for the full contract price of the watches.*

BAILEE CASES—SALES REQUIRING DELIVERY WITHOUT MOVEMENT OF GOODS When a bailee[2] is holding goods for a person who has contracted to sell them and the goods are to be delivered without being moved, the risk of loss passes to the buyer when: (1) the buyer receives a negotiable (transferrable by indorsement or delivery)[3] document of title for the goods, or (2) the bailee acknowledges the buyer's right to possess the goods, or (3) the buyer receives a nonnegotiable document of title *and* has had a *reasonable time* to present the document to the bailee and demand the goods. Obviously, if the bailee refuses to honor the document, the risk of loss remains

with the seller [UCC 2-509(2) and 2-503(4)(b)]. (See Exhibit 17–1 for a sample negotiable bill of lading and Exhibit 17–2 for a sample nonnegotiable warehouse receipt.)

To illustrate: McKee stores goods in Hardy's warehouse and takes a negotiable warehouse receipt for them. On the following day, McKee indorses the receipt (in this instance, signs his name on the document) and sells it to Byne for cash. The day after that, Hardy's warehouse burns down, and the goods are completely destroyed. The risk of loss is on Byne because it accompanied the negotiable warehouse receipt that gave him title to the goods.

In the following case, goods stored in a warehouse were destroyed by fire just a few days after they had been sold. The court had little difficulty in determining that title to the goods had passed from seller to buyer at the time the transfer was entered on the warehouse books—before the fire occurred. Because the goods were uninsured at the time of the fire, the significant issue for the parties involved was whether risk of loss had also passed to the buyer prior to the fire.

---

2. Under the UCC, a bailee is a party who by bill of lading, warehouse receipt, or other document of title acknowledges possession of goods and contracts to deliver them. A warehousing company, for example, or a trucking company that normally issues documents of title for goods it receives is a bailee. Bailments are the subject of Chapter 51.

3. Chapter 23 discusses negotiable and nonnegotiable instruments generally. UCC 7-104 states what constitutes negotiable and nonnegotiable documents of title.

BACKGROUND AND FACTS *In December of 1982, Peter Eckrich & Sons contracted to buy from Jason's Foods 38,000 pounds of "St. Louis style" pork ribs. It was arranged that the ribs would be transferred from Jason's account in an independent warehouse to Eckrich's account in the same warehouse, without any actual movement of the ribs. In its confirmation of the agreement, Jason's notified Eckrich that the transfer would be effected between January 10 and January 14. On January 13, Jason's telephoned the warehouse and requested that the transfer be made. The transfer was entered on the warehouse books immediately, but no warehouse receipt was sent to Eckrich until January 17 or 18, and Eckrich did not receive the receipt—and thus did not know the transfer had occurred—until January 24. The warehouse burned down on January 17, and Jason's subsequently sued Eckrich to recover the contract price. The trial court held that Eckrich was not liable because risk of loss had not passed to Eckrich prior to the fire. The trial court judge granted summary judgment for Eckrich, and Jason's appealed.*

Case 17.2

JASON'S FOODS, INC. v. PETER ECKRICH & SONS, INC.

United States Court of Appeals, Seventh Circuit, 1985.

774 F.2d 214.

POSNER, Circuit Judge.

* * * *

Eckrich argues with great vigor that it cannot be made to bear the loss of goods that it does not know it owns. But that is not so *outré* a circumstance as it may sound. If you obtain property by inheritance, you are quite likely to own it before you know you own it. And Eckrich's position involves a comparable paradox: that Jason's continued to bear the risk of loss of goods that it knew it no longer owned. So the case cannot be decided by reference to what the parties knew or did not know; and neither can it be decided, despite Jason's' urgings, on the basis of which party could have insured against the loss. Both could have. Jason's had sufficient interest in the ribs until the risk of loss shifted to Eckrich to insure the ribs until then. You do not have to own goods to insure them; it is enough that you will suffer a loss if they are lost or damaged, as of course Jason's would if the risk of loss remained on it after it parted with title. Section 2-509(2) separates title from risk of loss. Title to the ribs passed to Eckrich when the warehouse made the transfer on its books from Jason's' account to Eckrich's, but the risk of loss did not pass until the transfer was "acknowledged."

A related section of the Uniform Commercial Code, section 2-503(4)(a), makes acknowledgment by the bailee (the warehouse here) a method of tendering goods that are sold without being physically moved; but, like section 2-509(2)(b), it does not indicate to whom acknowledgment must be made. The official comments on this section, however, indicate that it was not intended to change the corresponding section of the Uniform Sales Act, section 43(3). And section 43(3) had expressly required acknowledgment to the buyer. Rules on tender have, it is true, a different function from rules on risk of loss; they determine at what point the seller has completed the performance of his side of the bargain. He may have completed performance, but if the goods are still in transit the risk of loss does not shift until the buyer receives them, if the seller is a merchant. In the case of warehouse transfers, however, the draftsmen apparently wanted risk of loss to conform to the rules for tender. For comment 4 to section 2-509 states that "where the agreement provides for delivery of the goods as between the buyer and seller without removal from the physical possession of a bailee, the provisions on manner of tender of delivery apply on the point of transfer of risk." And those provisions as we have said apparently require (in the case where no document of title passes) acknowledgment to the buyer. The acknowledgment need not, by the way, be in writing, so far as we are aware. Jason's could have instructed the warehouse to call Eckrich when the transfer was complete on the warehouse's books. * * *

* * * *

* * * Does "acknowledgment" mean receipt, as in the surrounding subsections of 2-509(2), or mailing? Since the evidence was in conflict over whether the acknowledgment was mailed on January 17 (and at what hour), which was the day of the fire, or on January 18, this could be an important question—but in another case. Jason's waived it. The only theory it tendered to the district court, or briefed and argued in this court, was that the risk of loss passed either on January 13, when the transfer of title was made on the books of the warehouse, or at the latest on January 14, because Eckrich knew the ribs would be transferred at the warehouse sometime between January 10 and 14. We have discussed the immateriality of the passage of title on January 13; we add that the alternative argument, that Eckrich knew by January 14 that it owned the ribs, exaggerates what Eckrich knew. By the close of business on January 14 Eckrich had a well-founded expectation that the ribs had been transferred to its account; but considering the many slips that are possible between cup and lips, we do not think that this expectation should fix the point at which the risk shifts.   *   *   *

     *   *   *   *

DECISION AND REMEDY

The court of appeals, affirming the decision of the trial court, held that the risk of loss passes when there is "acknowledgment" to the buyer that the goods have been transferred to its account. Jason could have instructed the warehouse supervisor to call Eckrich and acknowledge the transfer when the transfer was completed on the books. Since Jason's chose not to give these instructions, "acknowledgment" took place when Eckrich received the receipt on January 24. Thus, when the warehouse burned down on January 17, the risk of loss had not yet been transferred to Eckrich.

CONCEPT SUMMARY: Passage of Title and Risk of Loss for Goods in Existence and Identified in Absence of Express Agreement	
SITUATION	**BASIC RULES**
Contract terms call for goods to be *shipped* (i.e., F.O.B. seller's business or city)	1. In absence of agreement, title and risk pass upon seller's delivery of conforming goods to the carrier. UCC 2-401(2)(a), UCC 2-509(1)(a)
Contract terms call for goods to be delivered at *destination* (i.e., F.O.B. buyer's warehouse)	1. In absence of agreement, title and risk pass upon seller's *tender* of delivery of conforming goods to the buyer at the point of destination. UCC 2-401(2)(b), UCC 2-509(1)(b)

Contract terms call for goods to be delivered *without physical movement* (i.e., the buyer must pick up the goods)	1. In absence of agreement, if the goods are not represented by a document of title—
	    a. Title passes upon the formation of the contract. UCC 2-401(3)(b)
	    b. Risk passes to the buyer, if seller is a merchant, upon buyer's *receipt* of the goods or, if seller is a nonmerchant, upon seller's *tender* of delivery of the goods. UCC 2-509(3)
	 2. In absence of agreement, if the goods are represented by a document of title—
	    a. If negotiable, and goods are held by a bailee, title and risk pass upon the buyer's *receipt* of the document. UCC 2-401(3)(a), UCC 2-509(2)(a)

CONCEPT SUMMARY: Passage of Title and Risk of Loss for Goods in Existence and Identified in Absence of Express Agreement, (Continued)	
SITUATION	**BASIC RULES**
	b. If nonnegotiable, and goods are held by a bailee, title passes upon the buyer's receipt of the document, but risk does *not* pass until the buyer, after receipt of the document, has had reasonable time to present the document to demand the goods. UCC 2-401(3)(a), UCC 2-509(2)(c), UCC 2-503(4)(b)
	3. In absence of agreement, if the goods are held by a bailee and no document of title is transferred, risk passes to the buyer when the bailee acknowledges the buyer's right to the possession of the goods. UCC 2-509(2)(b)

Sale on Approval and Sale or Return Contracts

A **sale on approval** is not a sale until the buyer accepts (approves) the offer. A **sale or return** is a sale that can be rescinded by the buyer without liability. In each case, passage of title and risk of loss depend upon the conditional event's happening or not happening, since these transactions are conditional by their very nature.

SALE ON APPROVAL   When a seller offers to sell goods to a buyer and permits the buyer to take the goods on a trial basis, a sale on approval is made. The term *sale* here is a misnomer, since only an *offer* to sell has been made, along with a bailment created by the buyer's possession.

Therefore, title and risk of loss (from causes beyond the buyer's control) remain with the seller until the buyer accepts (approves) the offer. Acceptance can be made expressly, by any act inconsistent with the *trial* purpose or seller's ownership, or by the buyer's election not to return the goods within the trial period. If the buyer does not wish to accept, the buyer may notify the seller of that fact within the trial period, and the return is at the seller's expense and risk [UCC 2-327(1)]. Goods held on approval are not subject to the claims of the buyer's creditors until acceptance.

SALE OR RETURN   The sale or return (sometimes called *sale and return*) is a species of contract by which the seller delivers a quantity of goods to the buyer, on the understanding that if the buyer wishes to retain any portion of those goods (for use or resale), the buyer will consider the portion retained as having been sold to him or her and will pay accordingly. The balance will be returned to the seller or will be held by the buyer as a bailee subject to the seller's order. When the buyer receives possession at the time of sale, the title and risk of loss pass to the buyer. Both remain with the buyer until the buyer returns the goods to the seller within the time period specified. If the buyer fails to return the goods within this time period, the sale is finalized. The return of the goods is at the buyer's risk and expense. The goods held on a sale or return contract are subject to the claims of the buyer's creditors while they are in the buyer's possession.

Under a contract for sale or return, the title vests immediately in the buyer, who has the privilege of rescinding the sale [UCC 2-326]. It is often difficult to determine from a particular transaction which exists—a sale on approval or a contract for sale or return. The Code states that (unless otherwise agreed) if the goods are for the buyer to use, the transaction is a sale on approval; if the goods are for the buyer to resell, the transaction is a sale or return [UCC 2-326(1)].

The Code treats a **consignment** as a sale or return. Under a consignment, the owner of goods (the *consignor*) delivers them to another (the *consignee*) for the consignee to sell. If the consignee sells the goods, he or she must pay the consignor for them. If the goods are not sold, they may simply be returned to the consignor. While the goods are in the possession of the consignee, the consignee holds title to them, and creditors of the consignee will prevail over the consignor in any action to repossess the goods. The Code does make an exception to this rule if the person making delivery (the consignor) does one of the following:

1. Complies with an applicable law providing for a consignor's interest or the like to be evidenced by a sign.
2. Establishes that the person conducting the business (the consignee) is generally known by his or her creditors to be substantially engaged in selling the goods of others.
3. Complies with the filing provisions of Article 9 (to be discussed in Chapters 29 and 30) [UCC 2-326(3)].

Risk of Loss in a Breached Sales Contract

There are many ways to breach a sales contract, and the transfer of risk operates differently depending on whether the seller or the buyer breaches. Generally, the party in breach bears the risk of loss.

SELLER'S BREACH If the goods are so nonconforming that the buyer has the right to reject them, the risk of loss will not pass to the buyer until the defects are cured or until the buyer accepts the goods in spite of their defects (thus waiving the

right to reject). For example, a buyer orders blue widgets from a seller, F.O.B. seller's plant. The seller ships black widgets, giving the buyer the right to reject. The widgets are damaged in transit. The risk of loss falls on the seller (although the risk would have been on the buyer if blue widgets had been shipped) [UCC 2-510].

If a buyer accepts a shipment of goods and later discovers a latent defect, acceptance can be revoked. Revocation allows the buyer to pass the risk of loss back to the seller, at least to the extent that the buyer's insurance does not cover the loss [UCC 2-510(2)].

BUYER'S BREACH The general rule is that when a buyer breaches a contract, the risk of loss *immediately* shifts to the buyer. There are three important limitations to this rule:

1. The seller must already have identified the goods under the contract. (Regardless of the delivery arrangements, the risk will shift.)
2. The buyer will bear the risk for only a *commercially reasonable time* after the seller learns of the breach.
3. The buyer will be liable only to the extent of any *deficiency* in the seller's insurance coverage [UCC 2-510(3)].

The following case is a good example of how a seller's failure to conform to the contract can result in the risk of loss remaining with the seller.

Case 17.3

MOSES v. NEWMAN

Court of Appeals of Tennessee, 1983.
658 S.W.2d 119.

BACKGROUND AND FACTS *Newman, the plaintiff, in response to an advertisement offering a "trailer, complete set-up," purchased a mobile home from Moses, the defendant, on February 7, 1981. On February 9, 1981, the defendant delivered the mobile home to the plaintiff's lot, blocked up and leveled (balanced) the home, removed the tires and axles, and connected sewer and water pipes. The defendant failed to anchor the mobile home. The plaintiff notified the defendant that the home had a broken window and water pipe and that there were no door keys. An installation crew was to return the following day; however, on February 10, 1981, a windstorm totally destroyed the mobile home. Newman claimed the loss of the mobile home fell on the seller.*

The evidence at the trial on the issue of whether the plaintiff had accepted the mobile home was sharply disputed. The trial judge concluded that the plaintiff had not accepted the mobile home at the time of the loss. On appeal, the appellate court also held that the plaintiff had not accepted tender of the mobile home and then addressed the issue of which party bore the risk of loss.

FRANKS, Judge.

*   *   *   *

The risk of loss provisions of the Uniform Commercial Code are contained in T.C.A., §§ 47-2-509, 47-2-510. In the instant case defendant argues T.C.A., § 47-2-509(3) applies and passes the risk of loss to the buyer on receipt of the goods where the seller is a merchant. Plaintiff argues T.C.A., § 47-2-510(1) applies, which provides: "Where a tender or delivery of goods so fails to conform to the contract as to give a right of rejection the risk of their loss remains on the seller until cure or acceptance."

Under the chancellor's factual determination the delivery of the trailer failed to conform to the contract giving rise to a right of rejection. The right of rejection under T.C.A., § 47-2-601 arises if the goods "fail in any respect to conform to the contract." *   *   * Whether the mobile home conformed to the contract is tested by the definition in T.C.A., § 47-2-106(2): "Goods or conduct including any part of a performance are 'conforming' or conform to the contract when they are in accordance with the obligations under the contract." In this case, plaintiff contracted for a habitable mobile home plus the installation. Accordingly, since the loss occurred before the installation was complete, the defendant had not delivered conforming goods which would shift the risk of loss to plaintiff.

For the risk to shift to the purchaser, the purchaser must receive the goods and the seller must fulfill his contractual obligations. "Under subsection (1) the seller by his individual action cannot shift the risk of loss to the buyer unless his action conforms with all the conditions resting on him under the contract." Comment 1 to T.C.A., § 47-2-510.

The appellate court upheld the trial court's determination that the risk of loss had not shifted from the defendant seller to the plaintiff. The seller had to bear the cost of the loss because of his failure to conform completely to the contract.	**DECISION AND REMEDY**

INSURABLE INTEREST

Buyers and sellers often obtain insurance coverage to protect against damage, loss, or destruction of goods. But any party purchasing insurance must have a "sufficient interest" in the insured item to obtain a valid policy. Insurance laws—not the Code—determine sufficiency. (See Chapter 54.) The Code is helpful, however, because it contains certain rules regarding a buyer's and a seller's insurable interest in goods on a sales contract.

Buyer's Insurable Interest

Buyers have an insurable interest in *identified* goods. The moment the goods are identified to the contract by the seller, the buyer has this special property interest, which allows the buyer to obtain necessary insurance coverage for the goods even before the risk of loss has passed [UCC 2-501(1)].

Consider an example: In March a farmer sells a cotton crop he hopes to harvest in October to a buyer. After the crop is planted, the buyer insures it against hail damage. In September a hailstorm ruins the crop. When the buyer files a claim under her insurance policy, the insurer refuses to pay the claim, asserting that the buyer has no insurable interest in the crop. The insurer is not correct. The buyer acquired an insurable interest in the crop when it was planted, since she had a contract to buy it. The rule in UCC 2-501(1)(c) states that a buyer obtains an insurable interest in the goods by identification, which occurs "when the crops are planted or otherwise become growing crops *   *   * if the contract is *   *   * for the sale of crops to be harvested within twelve months or the next normal harvest season after contracting, whichever is longer."

Seller's Insurable Interest

Sellers have an insurable interest in goods as long as they retain title to the goods. However, even after title passes to a buyer, a seller who has a "security interest" in the goods (a right to secure payment) still has an insurable interest and so can insure the goods [UCC 2-501(2)].

Hence, both a buyer and a seller can have an insurable interest in identical goods at the same time. In all cases, one must sustain an actual loss in order to have the right to recover from an insurance company.

BULK TRANSFERS

Special problems arise when a major portion of a business's assets are transferred. This is the subject of UCC Article 6, Bulk Transfers, which are defined as any transfer of a major part of the material, supplies, merchandise, or other inventory *not made in the ordinary course of the transferor's business* [UCC 6-102(1)]. Problems arise, for example, when a business owing numerous creditors sells a substantial part of its equipment and inventories to a buyer. If the merchant uses the proceeds to pay off debts, no problems arise. But what if the merchant spends the money on a trip around the world, leaving the creditors without payment? Can the creditors lay any claim to the goods that were transferred in bulk to the buyer? To prevent this problem from arising, Article 6 lays out certain requirements for bulk transfer.

Requirements of Article 6

A party's bulk transfer of assets is ineffective against any creditor of the transferor, and thus a creditor may disregard the transfer and levy on the goods as if they still belonged to the transferor, unless the following requirements are met:

1. The seller (transferor) must furnish to the buyer (transferee) a sworn list of the seller's existing creditors. This list must include those whose claims are disputed, stating names, business addresses, and amounts due [UCC 6-104(1)(a)].
2. The buyer and the seller must prepare a schedule of the property transferred [UCC 6-104(1)(b)].
3. The buyer must preserve the list of creditors and the schedule of property for six months. He or she must permit inspection thereof by any creditor of the seller or file the list and the schedule of property in a designated public office [UCC 6-104(1)(c)].

4. Notice of the proposed bulk transfer must be given by the buyer to each creditor of the seller at least ten days before the buyer takes possession of the goods or makes payments for them, whichever happens first [UCC 6-105]. (Some states also require the buyer to apply the proceeds from the sale to payment of the seller's creditors.)

If all of these steps are undertaken, then the bulk transfer complies with the statutory requirements. The buyer acquires title to the goods free of all claims of creditors of the seller.

Notice to Creditors

The specific requirements for the contents of the notice to creditors are as follows:

1. A statement that a bulk transfer is about to be made.
2. Names and business addresses of the seller in bulk and buyer in bulk.
3. Information about whether all debts of the seller in bulk are to be paid in full as a result of the bulk transfer and, if so, the addresses to which creditors should send their bills [UCC 6-107(1)].

Whenever the debts of the transferor in bulk are not to be paid in full as they fall due, the notice to creditors must also state such things as the location and general description of the property to be transferred, the address at which the schedule of property and list of creditors may be inspected, and whether the transfer is for new consideration or to pay existing debts [UCC 6-107(2)].

When Failure to Comply Occurs

When the requirements of Article 6 are not complied with, goods in possession of the transferee continue to be subject to the claims of the unpaid creditors of the seller for a period of six months [UCC 6-111]. Nonetheless, a bona fide purchaser of these goods from the transferee who pays value in good faith, not knowing that the goods are still subject to the claims of the transferor's creditors, acquires the goods free of any claim of those creditors.

If the creditor did not receive notice and such is due to the fault of the seller (such as not being on the seller's list), the seller is liable to the buyer for any loss incurred by the buyer. If the failure to receive notice is the buyer's fault and the seller's creditor satisfies his or her claim from the property transferred, the buyer can only recover from the seller the amount of the debt the seller owed to that creditor (quasi-contractual theory).

SALES BY NONOWNERS

Special problems arise when persons who acquire goods with imperfect titles attempt to resell them. UCC 2-402 and 2-403 deal with the rights of two parties who lay claim to the same goods, sold with imperfect titles.

Imperfect Title

Sometimes a seller of goods does not possess full ownership rights (good title) to the goods being sold. This can happen, for example, if the seller has stolen the goods or obtained them fraudulently. In such situations, does the buyer acquire title to the goods? The answer to this question, as discussed below, depends on the circumstances. Generally, a buyer acquires at least whatever title the seller has to the goods sold.

VOID TITLE   A buyer may unknowingly purchase goods from a seller who is not the owner of the goods. If the seller is a thief, the seller's title is *void*—legally, no title exists. Thus, the buyer acquires no title, and the real owner can reclaim the goods from the buyer.

For example, if Thomas steals goods owned by Carl, Thomas has *void title* (no legally recognized title) to those goods. If Thomas sells the goods to Benson, Carl can reclaim them from Benson even though Benson acted in good faith and honestly had no knowledge that the goods were stolen.

VOIDABLE TITLE   A seller has a *voidable title* if the goods that he or she is selling were obtained

by fraud; paid for with a check that is later dishonored; purchased on credit, when the seller was insolvent; or purchased from a minor. Purchasers of goods acquire all title that their transferors either had or had the power to transfer. A purchaser of a limited interest acquires rights only to the extent of the interest purchased. A seller with voidable title has power, nonetheless, to transfer a good title to a good faith purchaser for value.

A **good faith purchaser** is one who buys without knowledge of circumstances that would make a person of ordinary prudence inquire about the seller's title to the goods. In other words, such circumstances exist, but the purchaser is unaware of them. The real owner cannot recover goods from a good faith purchaser for value [UCC 2-403(1)]. If the buyer of the goods is not a good faith purchaser for value, then the actual owner of the goods can reclaim them from the buyer (or from the seller, if the goods are still in the seller's possession).

To illustrate: Martin sells his bicycle to Allen, who pays for the bicycle with a check that is later dishonored by the bank because of insufficient funds in Allen's account. Before Martin can retrieve the bicycle from Allen, Allen sells it to Peter. Peter, who has no knowledge that Allen has only voidable title to the bicycle, pays Allen with a check that is honored by the bank. Martin cannot recover his bicycle from Peter, because Peter is a good faith purchaser. Peter gets to keep the bicycle, and Martin's only recourse is to sue Allen for the price of the bike—if Allen is anywhere to be found.

The defendant in the following case had some warning that there was something suspicious about the transaction in which he was participating.

BACKGROUND AND FACTS   *Fred H. Lane (plaintiff) was the owner of Lane's Outboard, and he was engaged in the business of selling boats, motors, and trailers. He sold a new boat, motor, and trailer to a person who called himself John W. Willis. Willis took possession of the goods and paid for them with a check for $6,285. The check was later dishonored.*

About six months later, the defendant, Jimmy Honeycutt, bought the boat, motor, and trailer from a man identified as "Garrett," who was renting a summer

 Case 17.4

LANE v. HONEYCUTT

Court of Appeals of North Carolina, 1972.
14 N.C.App. 436, 188 S.E.2d 604.

beach house to the defendant that year. The defendant had known Garrett for several years.

The plaintiff sought to recover the boat, motor, and trailer from the defendant. The defendant's sole defense was that he was a good faith purchaser and therefore the plaintiff should not be able to recover from him. The trial court held for the plaintiff, and the defendant appealed.

VAUGHN, Judge.

*   *   *   *

Contrary to the contentions of plaintiff, we hold that the goods were delivered under a transaction of purchase and that the consequences of this purchase are governed by G.S. [General Statutes] § 25-2-403 [North Carolina's version of UCC 2-403].

The question which we consider to be determinative of this appeal is whether there is any evidence to support the following findings of fact by the court. "(2) The Defendant, Jimmy Honeycutt, did not purchase the boat, motor and trailer in good faith."

[Next, the court carefully reviewed the defendant's testimony concerning "Mr. Garrett," who had sold the defendant a boat, motor, and trailer worth over $6,000 for a mere $2,500.]

"Mr. Garrett first approached me about buying his house on the beach that I was staying in, and told me he wanted $50,000.00 for it, and I told him I couldn't afford anything like that. He said, 'Well, let me sell you a boat out there.' And I said, 'Well, I couldn't afford that either.' *   *   *

*   *   *   *

"*   *   * As to whether or not, in other words, this boat looked like it was fairly expensive, well, I thought it would be a little more than it was. He told me the price and I was very pleasantly surprised *   *   *. [H]e sells fishing tackle and stuff of that nature, and beer. He also sells gasoline for boats. Yes, sir, that is about all he sells down there. He rents small fishing boats and motors too. No, he doesn't sell them, he doesn't sell boats as far as I know *   *   *."

Garrett told defendant that he would let defendant have the boat for $2500. Defendant then paid Garrett a deposit of $100. Garrett had nothing to indicate that he was the owner of the boat, motor or trailer. Garrett told defendant he was selling the boat for someone else. "This guy comes down, you know, and does some fishing."

Two weeks later defendant returned to Garden City, South Carolina, with $2400, the balance due (on a boat, and trailer which had been sold new less than six months earlier for $6,285.00). On this occasion,

"Mr. Garrett had told me—well, he always called him, 'this guy' see, so I really didn't know of any name or anything, but he told me, 'this guy does a lot of fishing around here but I can't seem to get ahold of him.' He said, 'I've called him, but I can't get ahold of him, so since you have the money and you're here after the boat[,] *   *   * I don't believe he would object, so I'll just go ahead and sign this title for you so you can go on and get everything made out to you.' He then signed the purported owner's name on the documents and he signed the title over to me then."

The so-called "document" and "title," introduced as defendant's exhibit No. 8, was nothing more than the "certificate of number" required by G.S. § 75A-5 and issued by the North Carolina Wildlife Resources Commission. This "certificate of number" is not a "certificate of title" to be compared with that required by G.S. § 20-50 for vehicles intended to be operated on the highways of this State. Upon the change of ownership of a motor boat, G.S. § 75A-5(c) authorizes the issuance of a new "certificate of number" to the transferee upon proper application. The application for transfer of the number, among other things, requires the seller's *signature*. A signature is "the name of a person written with his own hand." Webster's Third New International Dictionary (1968). Defendant observed Garrett counterfeit the signature of the purported owner, John P. Patterson, on the exhibit. Following the falsified signature on defendant's exhibit No. 8, the "date sold" is set out as "June 12, 1970" and the buyer's "signature" is set out as "George (illegible) Williams." There was no testimony as to who affixed the "signature" of the purported buyer, George Williams, and there is no further reference to him in the record.

* * * *

We hold that the evidence was sufficient to support the court's finding that defendant was not a good faith purchaser.

The trial court's ruling was affirmed. The defendant was not a good faith purchaser. The plaintiff was determined to be the owner and to be entitled to immediate possession of the boat, motor, and trailer. The plaintiff was also awarded damages against the defendant for wrongful detention of the property.

DECISION AND REMEDY

ENTRUSTMENT According to Section 2-403(2), entrusting goods to a merchant *who deals in goods of that kind* gives the merchant the power to transfer all rights to a *buyer in the ordinary course of business. Entrusting* includes both delivering the goods to the merchant and leaving the purchased goods with the merchant for later delivery or pickup [UCC 2-403(3)]. A "buyer in the ordinary course" is a person who buys in good faith from a person who deals in goods of that kind. The buyer cannot have knowledge that the sale violates the ownership rights of a third person.

For example, Sue leaves her watch with a jeweler to be repaired. The jeweler sells both new and used watches. The jeweler sells Sue's watch to Ann, a customer, who does not know that the jeweler has no right to sell it. Ann gets *good title* against Sue's claim of ownership.

The good faith buyer, however, obtains only those rights held by the person who entrusted the goods. For example, Sue's watch is stolen by Thomas. Thomas leaves the watch with a jeweler for repairs. The jeweler sells the watch to Betty, who does not know that the jeweler has no right to sell it. Betty gets good title against Thomas, the entrustor, but not against Sue, who neither entrusted the watch to Thomas nor authorized Thomas to entrust it.

SELLER'S RETENTION OF SOLD GOODS Ordinarily, sellers do not retain goods in their possession or use after the goods have been sold. A seller who retained goods after they were sold could mislead creditors into believing that the seller's assets were more substantial than they really were.

Retention of the goods, and particularly their use by the seller, is basic evidence of an intent to defraud creditors. If a creditor can prove that the retention is in fact fraud, or if the state has a statute providing that such retention creates a presumption of fraud (and if the presumption is unrebutted), the creditor can set aside the sale to the buyer.

UCC 2-402(2), however, recognizes that it is not necessarily a fraud upon creditors if a *merchant* seller retains possession in good faith for a "commercially reasonable time" in order to accomplish some legitimate purpose (for example, repairs or adjustments).

A seller can defraud creditors by selling items at something substantially less than "fair consideration," thereby depleting the seller's assets. This is fraud on the seller's creditors if the seller is insolvent at the time of the sale, is made insolvent by the sale, or actually intended to defraud or delay actions by the creditors. Assets sold at less than fair consideration often are sold to a friend or relative of the seller. Such sales are considered sham transactions used to conceal assets.

For example, suppose that FL Boat Company is on the verge of bankruptcy. Many of the loans that FL's owner has taken out are personally secured by him, so his creditors can go after his personal assets to recover what he owes them. Knowing this, FL's owner sells several expensive cars to his father for only $3,000 apiece, and he sells his personal yacht to his brother-in-law for $10,000 (although it is worth $110,000). He has an implicit understanding with his father and his brother-in-law that he will retain control over these assets but that they will have title. If the creditors find out about the sham transactions, they can void the sales.

QUESTIONS AND CASE PROBLEMS

1. On May 1, Peale goes into Carson's retail clothing store to purchase a suit. Peale finds a suit he likes for $190 and buys it. The suit needs alteration. Peale is to pick up the altered suit at Carson's store on May 10. Consider the following separate sets of circumstances:

(a) One of Carson's major creditors obtains a judgment on the debt Carson owes and has the court issue a writ of execution to collect on that judgment all clothing in Carson's possession.

(b) On May 9, through no fault of Carson, his store burns down, and all contents are a total loss.

Discuss *Peale's* rights to the suit on which the major creditor has levied. Between Carson and Peale, who suffers the loss of the suit destroyed by fire? Explain.

2. Mackey orders from Pride 1,000 cases of Greenie brand peas from Lot A at list price to be shipped F.O.B. Pride's city via Fast Freight Lines. Pride receives the order and immediately sends Mackey an acceptance of the order with a promise to ship promptly. Pride later separates the 1,000 cases of Greenie peas and prints Mackey's name and address on each case. The peas are placed on Pride's dock, and Fast Freight is notified to pick up the shipment. The night before the pickup by Fast Freight, through no fault of Pride, a fire destroys the 1,000 cases of peas. Pride claims that title passed to Mackey at the time the contract was made and risk of loss passed to Mackey upon the marking of the goods with Mackey's name and address. Discuss Pride's contentions.

3. Zeke, who sells lawn mowers, tells Lewis, a regular customer, about a special promotional campaign. Upon receipt of a $50 down payment, Zeke will sell Lewis a new Universal lawn mower for $200, even though it normally sells for $350. Zeke further states to Lewis that if Lewis does not like the performance of the lawn mower, he can return it within thirty days and Zeke will refund the $50 down payment. Lewis pays the $50 and takes the mower. On the tenth day the lawn mower is stolen through no fault of Lewis. Lewis calls Zeke and demands the return of his $50. Zeke claims that Lewis should suffer the risk of loss and that he still owes Zeke the remainder of the purchase price, $150. Discuss whether Lewis or Zeke is correct.

4. In the following situations, two parties lay claim to the same goods sold. Discuss which of the parties would prevail in each situation.

(a) Thomas steals Dean's television set and sells the set to Bosky, an innocent purchaser, for value. Dean learns Bosky has the set and demands its return.

(b) Kerr takes her television set for repair to Martin, a merchant who sells new and used television sets. By accident, one of Martin's employees sells the set to Gale, an innocent purchaser-customer, who takes possession. Kerr wants her set back from Gale.

5. Benes contracts to purchase from Glover 100 cases of Knee High Corn to be shipped F.O.B. Glover's warehouse by Reliant Truck Lines. Glover, by mistake, delivers 100 cases of Green Valley Corn to the Reliant Truck Lines. While in transit, the Green Valley Corn is stolen. Between Benes and Glover, who suffers the loss?

6. The Ryans borrowed money from Evanston Building & Loan Company to buy a modular home manufactured by Fuqua Homes. They purchased the home from a partnership acting as an intermediary-dealer for Fuqua. After receiving the proceeds of the sale, the partners in the intermediary-dealership disappeared without making any payment to Fuqua Homes. Fuqua claimed that, since it had not been paid and still held the certificate of title to the modular home, it still had title to the home. Is Fuqua correct? [Fuqua Homes, Inc. v. Evanston Building & Loan Co., 52 Ohio App.2d 399, 370 N.E.2d 780 (1977)]

7. Harold Shook agreed with Graybar Electric Co. to purchase three reels of burial cable for use in Shook's construction work. When the reels were delivered, each carton was marked "burial cable," although two of the reels were in fact aerial cable. Shook accepted the conforming reel of cable and notified Graybar that he was rejecting the two reels of aerial cable. Because of a trucker's strike, Shook was unsuccessful in arranging for the return of the reels to Graybar. He stored the reels in a well-lighted space near a grocery store owner's dwelling, which was close to his work site. About four months later, he noticed that one of the reels had been stolen. On the following day he notified Graybar of the loss and, worried about the safety of the second reel, arranged to have it transported to a garage for storage. Before the second reel was transferred, however, it was also stolen, and Shook notified Graybar of the second theft. Graybar sued Shook for the purchase price, claiming that Shook had agreed to return to Graybar the noncomforming reels and had failed to do so. Shook contended that he had agreed only to contact a trucking company to return the reels and that, since he had contacted three trucking firms to no avail (owing to the strike), his obligation had been fulfilled. Discuss who bears the risk of loss for the stolen reels. [Graybar Electric Co. v. Shook, 283 N.C. 213, 195 S.E.2d 514 (1973)]

8. Hargo Woolen Mills had purchased bales of card waste, used in Hargo's manufacture of woolen cloth, from Shabry Trading Company for many years. On this occasion, however, Shabry shipped twenty-four bales to Hargo without an order. Rather than pay for reshipment, both parties decided that Hargo would retain possession of the bales and pay for what it used. Hargo kept the bales separate inside its warehouse and eventually used, and was billed for, eight bales. The remaining sixteen bales were still kept separate by Hargo. Hargo went bankrupt, and everything in its warehouse was taken by the receiver, Meinhard-Commercial Corp. Shabry claimed that it was the owner and title holder of the bales and requested their return, but Meinhard refused. Should Shabry be able to retake possession of the bales? [Meinhard-Commercial Corp. v. Hargo Woolen Mills, 112 N.H. 500, 300 A.2d 321 (1972)]

9. Crump, a television fanatic, purchased a television antenna and antenna tower from Lair Company. Crump purchased the antenna and tower under a ten-year conditional sales contract that obligated him to make monthly payments. The sales contract provided that Lair Company would retain title until Crump had completed all payments under the contract. The purchase contract stated, among other things, that Crump was not to move or tamper with the antenna during the ten-year payment period. About a year later, lightning struck and destroyed Crump's new antenna. At Crump's request, Lair Company performed extensive repairs on the antenna. Crump refused to pay, claiming that risk of loss or damage resulting from the lightning should be borne by Lair Company. Will Lair be successful in a suit for the cost of its repairs? [Lair Distributing Co. v. Crump, 48 Ala.App. 72, 261 So.2d 904 (1972)]

10. A new car owned by a New Jersey car rental agency was stolen in 1967. The agency collected the full price of the car from its insurance company, Home Indemnity Company, and assigned all its interest in the automobile to the insurer. Subsequently, a thief sold the car to an automobile wholesaler, who in turn sold it to a retail car dealer. Schrier purchased the automobile from the car dealer without knowledge of the theft. Home Indemnity Insurance Company sued Schrier to recover the car. Can Home Indemnity recover? [Schrier v. Home Indemnity Co., 273 A.2d 248 (D.C.App. 1971)]

11. Marcella Mattek, the plaintiff, was the owner of an automobile. She left the car with her son. She knew her son's intention was to sell the car, but she did not authorize him to do so. Her son took the car to Doug Frakes, a licensed used-car dealer, and authorized him to display the car but not to sell it. Frakes put his dealer's license plate on it and sold it to another licensed used-car dealer, the defendant, Malofsky. Frakes kept the money, and Mattek sued to recover her car. No certificate of title was ever delivered to Malofsky. Malofsky claimed to have good title, as he was a buyer in the ordinary course of business to a car entrusted by Mattek to a merchant, Frakes. Discuss fully whether Mattek is entitled to the return of her car. [Mattek v. Malofsky, 42 Wis.2d 16, 165 N.W.2d 406 (1969)]

12. A men's clothing manufacturer in Los Angeles sold $2,216 of men's clothing to a store in Westport, Connecticut. The contract stated that the shipment was to be "F.O.B. Los Angeles." The Los Angeles manufacturer arranged for shipping via common carrier to Connecticut. Upon arrival of the clothes, the purchaser's agent refused to unload them. The carrier's agent also refused to unload the goods, indicating that it was the purchaser's obligation to unload. The carrier left with the shipment, which subsequently disappeared. The Los Angeles manufacturer sued the purchaser for the contract price. Had the risk of loss passed to the Connecticut purchaser at the time of delivery of the clothes to the common carrier? [Ninth Street East, Ltd. v. Harrison, 5 Conn.Cir. 597, 259 A.2d 772 (1968)]

13. Ray Schock (buyer) negotiated to purchase a mobile home that was owned by Pablo and Colette Ronderos (sellers) and located on their property. On April 15, 1985, Schock appeared at the Ronderos's home and paid them the agreed-upon purchase price of $3,900. On that date, with the sellers' permission, Schock prepared the mobile home for removal. His preparations included the removal of the skirting around the mobile home's foundation, the removal of the "tie-downs," and the removal of the foundation blocks, which caused the mobile home to rest on the wheels of its chassis. Schock intended to remove the mobile home from the sellers' property on the following Monday, April 22, 1985, and the sellers had no objection to having the mobile home remain on their premises until that time. On Friday evening, April 19, 1985, the mobile home was destroyed by high winds as it sat on the sellers' property. Thereafter, Schock sued the sellers for the return of the $3,900 purchase money on the ground that when the mobile home was destroyed, the risk of loss was on the sellers. The sellers filed an answer alleging that they were entitled to keep the purchase price because the risk of loss had shifted to Schock on April 15, 1985, by tender of delivery. Which party will prevail? [Schock v. Ronderos, 394 N.W.2d 697 (N.D. 1986)]

14. Kumar Corporation agreed to sell 700 television sets to Nava, a Venezuelan wholesaler. Kumar and Nava expressly agreed that Nava would not pay for the television sets until it received and actually sold the merchandise in Venezuela. Kumar loaded the goods from its Miami warehouse into a trailer and delivered the trailer to the freight handler but failed to procure insurance. The shipping documents reflected that the goods were sold by Kumar to Nava for $144,417.00, C.I.F. Venezuela. Several days later, the trailer was discovered missing and was subsequently found abandoned and empty. Kumar sued the carrier. The carrier challenged Kumar's standing (right) to sue on the ground that the term C.I.F. (or its equivalent) required Kumar, the seller, to perform certain obligations with respect to the goods, including placing the goods in possession of the carrier, and that when these obligations were properly performed, the risk of loss or damage to the goods passed to Nava, the buyer. Since Nava suffered the loss, only Nava had standing to sue. Is this argument persuasive in light of all of the terms of the contract? [Kumar Corporation v. Nopal Lines, Ltd., 462 So.2d 1178 (Fla.App. 1985)]

15. Isis Foods, Inc., located in St. Louis, wished to purchase a shipment of food from Pocasset Food Sales, Inc. The sale of food was initiated by a purchase order from Isis stating that the shipment was to be made "F.O.B. St. Louis." Pocasset made the shipment by delivery of the goods to the carrier. Pocasset's invoices contain a provision stating: "Our liability ceases upon delivery of merchandise to carrier." The shipment of food was destroyed in transit before reaching St. Louis. Discuss which party has the risk of loss and why. [In re Isis Foods, Inc., 38 B.R. 48 (Bkrtcy. W.D.Mo. 1983]

16. Samuel Porter was the owner of a Maurice Utrillo painting entitled "Chateau de Lion-sur Mer." Harold Von Maker, who called himself Peter Wertz, bought a different painting from Porter, paying $50,000 cash and giving Porter ten promissory notes for $10,000 each. At the

same time, Wertz talked Porter into allowing Wertz to hang the Utrillo painting in Wertz's home while he decided whether to buy it. When the first promissory note was not paid, Porter learned that he was dealing with Von Maker, a man with a history of arrests and judgments against him. Von Maker told Porter that the Utrillo painting was on consignment and would be returned or Porter would receive $30,000. Actually, the painting had already been sold to Feigen Gallery, which had in turn sold it to Irwin Brenner, trading under the name Irwin Brenner Gallery. The painting is now in Venezuela. Porter filed suit against Wertz, the Feigen Gallery, and Irwin Brenner to recover either possession of the painting or its value. Feigen Gallery and Irwin Brenner claim that they had good title under UCC 2-403 and that Porter is estopped to repossess the painting or the value thereof. Discuss whether Porter is entitled to repossession or the value of the Utrillo painting. [Porter v. Wertz, 68 A.D.2d 141, 416 N.Y.S.2d 254 (1979)]

17. Donald Hayward agreed to buy a thirty-foot Revel Craft Playmate Yacht from Herbert F. Postma, a yacht dealer, on February 7, 1967. The boat was to be delivered to a slip on Lake Macatawa during April 1967. Hayward signed a security agreement on March 1, 1967, and gave a promissory note for $13,095.60 to Postma's dealership. The note was subsequently assigned to a bank. The security agreement provided clauses requiring the buyer to keep the boat in first-class order or repair and to keep the boat fully insured at all times. Prior to the delivery of the boat to Hayward, the boat was destroyed by fire. Neither Postma nor Hayward had insured the boat, and Hayward requested that Postma pay off the note or reimburse him for payments made. Postma refused, and Hayward sued. Discuss whether Hayward or Postma has the risk of loss as to the boat destroyed in the fire. [Hayward v. Postma, 31 Mich.App. 720, 188 N.W.2d 31 (1971)]

Chapter 18

SALES
Performance
and Obligation

To understand the performance that is required of a seller and of a buyer under a sales contract, it is necessary to know the duties and obligations each party has assumed under the terms of the contract. Keep in mind that "duties and obligations" under the terms of the contract here include those specified by the agreement, the custom, and the Code.

DUTY OF GOOD FAITH AND
COMMERCIAL REASONABLENESS

Sometimes the sales contract leaves open some particulars of performance and permits one of the parties to specify them. The obligations of "good faith" and "commercial reasonableness," however, underlie every sales contract within the UCC. They are objective obligations, and they can form the basis for a breach of contract suit later on. These standards are read into every contract, and they provide a framework in which the parties can specify particulars of performance. "Any such specification must be made in good faith and within limits set by commercial reasonableness" [UCC 2-311(1)].

The duty of cooperation between the parties required by Section 2-311 must be read along with the Code's "good faith" provision, which can never be disclaimed. "Every contract or duty within this Act imposes an obligation of good faith in its performance or enforcement" [UCC 1-203]. Good faith in the case of a merchant means honesty in fact *and* the observance of reasonable commercial standards of fair dealing in the trade [UCC 2-103(1)(b)].

Thus, when one party delays specifying particulars of performance for an unreasonable period of time or fails to cooperate with the other party, the innocent party is excused from any resulting delay in performance. In addition, the innocent party can proceed to perform in any reasonable manner. If the innocent party has performed as far as is reasonably possible under the circumstances, then the other party's failure to specify particulars or failure to cooperate can be treated as a breach of contract.

Good faith can mean that one party must not take advantage of another party by manipulating contract terms. Good faith applies to both parties, even the nonbreaching party. The principle of good faith applies through both the performance and the enforcement of all agreements or duties within a contract. Good faith is a question of fact for the jury. As previously mentioned, it means honesty in fact.

The following case deals with the issue of good faith in the termination of a franchise contract.

Case 18.1
ZAPATHA v. DAIRY MART, INC.
Massachusetts Supreme Judicial Court, 1980.
408 N.E.2d 1370.

BACKGROUND AND FACTS *In 1973, the Zapathas entered into a franchise agreement with the defendant, Dairy Mart, Inc. The agreement permitted either party to terminate the relationship without cause on ninety days' written notice. A second franchise agreement was executed in 1974, when the Zapathas moved their store to a new location. In 1977, the Zapathas refused to sign a new agreement submitted by the defendant. Dairy Mart then gave written notice to the Zapathas that their contract would be terminated in ninety days. The Zapathas brought an action seeking to enjoin the termination of the agreement, alleging that the contract provision allowing termination without cause was unconscionable and that Dairy Mart had not acted in good faith. The trial court held for the Zapathas, and Dairy Mart appealed.*

WILKINS, Judge.
*   *   *   *

[In determining whether the termination clause was unconscionable, the court concluded that the clause offered no potential for unfair surprise to the Zapathas.]

We further conclude that there was no oppression in the inclusion of a termination clause in the franchise agreement. We view the question of oppression as directed to the substantive fairness to the parties of permitting the termination provisions to operate as written. The Zapathas took over a going business on premises provided by Dairy Mart, using equipment furnished by Dairy Mart. As an investment, the Zapathas had only to purchase the inventory of goods to be sold but, as Dairy Mart concedes, on termination by it without cause Dairy Mart was obliged to repurchase all the Zapathas' saleable merchandise inventory, including items not purchased from Dairy Mart, at 80% of its retail value. There was no potential for forfeiture or loss of investment. There is no question here of a need for a reasonable time to recoup the franchisees' initial investment. The Zapathas were entitled to their net profits through the entire term of the agreement. They failed to sustain their burden of showing that the agreement allocated the risks and benefits connected with termination in an unreasonably disproportionate way and that the termination provision was not reasonably related to legitimate commercial needs of Dairy Mart. To find the termination clause oppressive merely because it did not require cause for termination would be to establish an unwarranted barrier to the use of termination at will clauses in contracts in this Commonwealth, where each party received the anticipated and bargained for consideration during the full term of the agreement.

We see no basis on the record for concluding that Dairy Mart did not act in good faith, as that term is defined in the sales article ("honesty in fact and the observance of reasonable commercial standards of fair dealing in the trade"). There was no evidence that Dairy Mart failed to observe reasonable commercial standards of fair dealing in the trade in terminating the agreement. If there were such standards, there was no evidence of what they were.

The question then is whether there was evidence warranting a finding that Dairy Mart was not honest "in fact." The judge concluded that the absence of any commercial purpose for the termination other than the Zapathas' refusal to sign a new franchise agreement violated Dairy Mart's obligation of good faith. Dairy Mart's right to terminate was clear, and it exercised that right for a reason it openly disclosed. The sole test of "honesty in fact" is whether the person was honest. We think that, whether or not termination according to the terms of the franchise agreement may have been arbitrary, it was not dishonest.

The lower court's judgment for the plaintiffs was reversed. Dairy Mart was allowed to terminate the agreement.

DECISION AND REMEDY

PERFORMANCE OF A SALES CONTRACT

A seller has the basic obligation to *transfer and deliver conforming goods*. The buyer has the basic obligation to *accept and pay for conforming goods* in accordance with the contract [UCC 2-301]. Overall performance of a sales contract is controlled by the agreement between the buyer and the seller. When the contract is unclear, or when terms are indefinite in certain respects and disputes arise, the Code provides built-in standards and rules for interpreting the agreement.

CONCURRENT CONDITIONS OF PERFORMANCE

The delivery of goods by the seller and the payment of the purchase price by the buyer are said to be *concurrent conditions*—conditions that are mutually dependent and are to be performed at the same time. The theoretical assumption is that delivery and payment can occur simultaneously. In reality this rarely happens.

Section 2-301 of the Code provides that "the obligation of the seller is to transfer and deliver and that of the buyer is to accept and pay *in accordance with the contract*" (emphasis added). If the contract expressly provides that the seller must first deliver the goods before receiving payment or that the buyer must pay before receiving the goods, then the terms of the contract control. When the agreement does not specifically provide otherwise, however, the Code charges both parties with the duty to proceed. In other words, in order for either party to maintain an action against the other for breach, the party bringing suit must put the other party in default by performing. This is accomplished in one of three ways—through (1) performance according to the contract,

(2) tender of performance according to the contract, or (3) excuse from tender of performance.[1]

For example, Laval agrees to deliver goods to Boyd on September 1, and Boyd agrees to pay on September 15. If Laval fails to deliver the goods, Boyd can sue Laval on or after September 2. Since Laval is in default, Boyd can proceed without first tendering the purchase price.

SELLER'S OBLIGATION— TENDER OF DELIVERY

Tender of delivery requires that the seller have and hold *conforming* goods at the buyer's disposal and give the buyer whatever notification is reasonably necessary to enable the buyer to take delivery [UCC 2-503(1)].

Tender must occur at a *reasonable hour* and in a *reasonable manner*. In other words, a seller cannot call the buyer at 2:00 A.M. and say, "The goods are ready. I'll give you twenty minutes to get them." Unless the parties have agreed otherwise, the goods must be tendered for delivery at a reasonable time and must be kept available for a reasonable period of time in order to enable the buyer to take possession of them [UCC 2-503(1)(a)].

All goods called for by a contract must be tendered in a single delivery unless the parties agree otherwise [UCC 2-612] or the circumstances are such that either party can rightfully request delivery in lots [UCC 2-307]. Hence, an order for 1,000 shirts cannot be delivered two shirts at a time. If seller and buyer contemplate, though, that the shirts will be delivered in four orders of 250 each as they are produced for summer, winter, fall, and spring stock and the price can be appor-

---

1. To *tender* is to offer or make available money or property in pursuance of a contract in such a way that nothing further remains to be done to fulfill the obligation of the party tendering.

tioned accordingly, it may be commercially reasonable to follow this course.

Place of Delivery

The UCC provides for the place of delivery pursuant to a contract, if the contract does not. Of course, the parties may agree on a particular destination, or their contract's terms or the circumstances may indicate the place.

NON-CARRIER CASES If the contract does not designate where the goods will be delivered, and the buyer is expected to pick them up, the place of delivery is the *seller's place of business* or, if the seller has none, the *seller's residence* [UCC 2-308]. If the contract involves the sale of *identified goods* (see Chapter 17 for a discussion of such goods) and the parties know when they enter into the contract that these goods are located somewhere other than at the seller's place of business (such as at a warehouse or in the possession of a bailee), then the *location of the goods* is the place for their delivery [UCC 2-308].

For example, Laval and Boyd live in San Francisco. In San Francisco, Laval contracts to sell to Boyd five used railroad dining cars, which both parties know are located in Atlanta. If nothing more is specified in the contract, the place of delivery for the railroad cars is Atlanta.

Assume further that the railroad cars are stored in a warehouse and that Boyd will need some type of document to show the warehouse (bailee) in Atlanta that Boyd is entitled to take possession of the five dining cars. The seller tenders delivery without moving the goods. The seller may deliver either by giving the buyer a *negotiable document of title* or by obtaining the *bailee's* (warehouse's) *acknowledgment* that the buyer is entitled to possession.[2]

CARRIER CASES In many instances, resulting either from attendant circumstances or from delivery terms contained in the contract, it is apparent that the parties intend that a carrier be used to move the goods. There are two ways a seller can complete performance of the obligation to deliver the goods—through a shipment contract or a destination contract.

Shipment Contracts A shipment contract requires or authorizes the seller to ship goods by a carrier. The contract does not require the seller to deliver the goods at a particular destination [UCC 2-509 and 2-319]. Unless otherwise agreed, the seller must [UCC 2-504]:

1. Put the goods into the hands of the carrier.
2. Make a contract for their transportation that is reasonable according to the nature of the goods and their value. (For example, certain types of goods need refrigeration in transit.)
3. Obtain and promptly deliver for tender to the buyer any documents necessary to enable the buyer to obtain possession of the goods from the carrier.
4. Promptly notify the buyer that shipment has been made.

If the seller fails to notify the buyer that shipment has been made or fails to make a proper contract for transportation, and a *material loss* of the goods or a *delay* results, the buyer can reject the shipment. Of course, the parties can agree that a lesser amount of loss or a delay will be grounds for rejection.

Destination Contracts Under destination contracts, the seller agrees to see that the goods will be duly tendered to the buyer at a particular destination. Once the goods arrive, the seller must tender the goods at a reasonable hour and hold conforming goods at the buyer's disposal for a reasonable length of time, giving appropriate notice. The seller must also provide the buyer with any documents of title necessary to enable the buyer to obtain delivery from the carrier. Although not a part of the seller's tender, unless otherwise agreed, the buyer must furnish facilities reasonably suited for the receipt of the goods [UCC 2-503].

CONTRACT TERMS As discussed in Chapter 17, specific terms in the sales contract, such as F.O.B., F.A.S., delivery ex-ship, and C.I.F. (or C. & F.) are also delivery terms. As a brief review:

F.O.B. Contracts In contracts specifying that the goods, price, or delivery are F.O.B. (free on board) to a particular point, the F.O.B. point is the delivery point [UCC 2-319(1)].

---

2. If the seller delivers a nonnegotiable document of title or merely writes instructions to the bailee to release the goods to the buyer without the bailee's *acknowledgment* of the buyer's rights, this will also be a sufficient tender, unless the buyer objects [UCC 2-503(4)]. But risk of loss will not pass until the buyer has had a reasonable time to present the document or the instructions.

F.A.S. Contracts   F.A.S. vessel (free alongside) contracts involve transportation by ship or other seagoing vessel. In contracts specifying that the goods, price, or delivery are F.A.S, the seller must deliver the goods alongside the vessel, usually on a dock designated by the buyer. The seller must obtain and tender a receipt, which is delivered to the buyer. Once delivered, the F.A.S. contract is complete [UCC 2-319(2)].

Ex-ship Contracts   If the contract calls for delivery of goods ex-ship (from the carrying vessel), the shipper must ship conforming goods and unload the goods at the port of destination.

C.I.F. Contracts   In C.I.F. (cost, insurance, and freight) or C. & F. (cost and freight) contracts, unless otherwise agreed, the seller is required to deliver and load the goods on board the carrier, obtain a bill of lading showing freight has been paid, obtain proper insurance coverage, prepare an invoice and other necessary documents, and forward all documents to the buyer [UCC 2-320 and 2-321].

EXCEPTIONS TO THE PERFECT TENDER RULE

As previously noted, the seller has an obligation to ship or tender *conforming goods,* and this entitles the seller to acceptance by and payment from the buyer according to the terms of the contract. At common law the seller was obligated to deliver goods in conformity with the terms of the contract in every detail. This was called the *perfect tender* doctrine. The UCC, in Section 2-601, preserves the perfect tender doctrine by providing that "if goods or tender of delivery fail *in any respect* to conform to the contract" (emphasis added), the buyer has the right to accept the goods, reject the entire shipment, or accept part and reject part.

For example, the buyer contracts to purchase 100 cases of Brand X peas to be delivered at the buyer's place of business on or before October 1. On September 28, the seller discovers that there are only 99 cases of Brand X in inventory but there will be another 500 cases within the next two weeks. So the seller tenders delivery of the 99 cases of Brand X on October 1, with the promise that the other case will be delivered within three weeks. Since the seller failed to make a per-fect tender of 100 cases of Brand X, the buyer has the right to reject the entire shipment and hold the seller in breach.

There are, however, many exceptions to the perfect tender rule.

Agreement of the Parties

If the parties have agreed, for example, that defective goods or parts will not be rejected if the seller is able to repair or replace them within a reasonable time, then the perfect tender rule does not apply.

Cure

The term **cure** is not specifically defined in the Code, but it refers to the seller's right to repair, adjust, or replace defective or nonconforming goods [UCC 2-508].

When any tender or delivery is rejected because of nonconforming goods and the time for performance has not yet expired, the seller can notify the buyer promptly of the intention to cure and can then do so *within the contract time for performance* [UCC 2-508(1)].

For example, Horn sells Gill a white refrigerator, to be delivered on or before September 15. Horn delivers a yellow refrigerator on September 10, and Gill rejects it. Horn can cure by notifying Gill that he intends to cure and by delivering a white refrigerator on or before September 15.

Once the time for performance under the contract has expired, the seller can still exercise the right to cure if the seller had *reasonable grounds to believe that the nonconforming tender would be acceptable to the buyer.*

Although frequently the seller tenders nonconforming goods with some type of price allowance, he or she may still have a reasonable belief that the goods will be accepted by the buyer for other reasons. For example, Demsetz has been supplying auto body paint to Hall Body, an auto body paint shop, for several years. Demsetz and Hall have a contract for R-Z type paint. In the past, when Demsetz could not obtain R-Z type paint, he substituted R-Y type paint, and Hall accepted without any objection. Hall signs a new contract for R-Z type paint to be delivered on April 30. Demsetz realizes that, with the paint supply on hand, only half the order can be filled with R-Z type paint, so he completes the other half of the order with R-Y type paint. The order is delivered on April 30. Hall rejects. Demsetz, knowing from their prior course of dealing that R-Y had always been an acceptable substitute, had "reasonable grounds to believe" that R-Y would be acceptable. Therefore, Demsetz can cure within a reasonable time, even though conforming delivery will occur after the actual time for performance under the contract.

As just pointed out, the seller may offer a price allowance with the tender of nonconforming goods. This frequently creates a presumption that a buyer will accept the fortuitous offer. Suppose a buyer contracts to purchase 100 Model Z hand calculators at a price of $20 each from a seller, to be delivered on or before October 1. The seller cannot deliver 100 Model Z calculators but tenders 100 new, more sophisticated, more expensive Model A-1 calculators at the same price as the 100 Model Z calculators contracted for on October 1. The buyer rejects the delivery. If the seller *notifies* the buyer of intent to cure, the seller has a *reasonable time* (after October 1) to substitute a conforming tender of Model Z calculators.

The seller's right to cure substantially restricts the buyer's right to reject. If the buyer refuses a tender of goods as nonconforming but does not disclose the nature of the defect to the seller, the buyer cannot later assert the defect as a defense if the defect is one that the seller could have cured. The buyer must act in good faith and state specific reasons for refusing to accept the goods [UCC 2-605].

Substitution of Carriers

Where an agreed manner of delivery (such as particular loading or unloading facilities) becomes impracticable or unavailable through no fault of either party but a commercially reasonable substitute is available, this substitute performance is sufficient tender to the buyer [UCC 2-614(1)].

For example, a sales contract calls for the delivery of a large piece of machinery to be shipped by ABC Truck Lines on or before June 1. The contract terms clearly state the importance of the delivery date. The employees of ABC Truck Lines go on strike. The seller will be entitled to make a reasonable substitute tender, perhaps by rail. Note that the seller here is responsible for any additional shipping costs, unless contrary arrangements have been made in the sales contract.

Installment Contracts

An **installment contract** is a single contract that requires or authorizes delivery in two or more separate lots to be accepted and paid for separately. In an installment contract, a buyer can reject an installment *only if the nonconformity substantially impairs the value of the installment* and cannot be cured [UCC 2-612(2), 2-307]. Notice how this is a substantial limitation on the perfect tender rule.

The entire installment contract is breached only when one or more nonconforming installments *substantially* impair the value of the *whole contract*. If the buyer subsequently accepts a nonconforming installment and fails to notify the seller of cancellation, then the contract is reinstated, however. Also, if the buyer brings an action with respect only to past installments or demands performance as to future installments, the aggrieved party has reinstated the contract [UCC 2-612(3)].

A major issue to be determined is what constitutes *substantial* impairment of the "value of the whole." For example, consider an installment contract for the sale of twenty carloads of plywood. The first carload does not conform to the contract because 9 percent of the plywood in the car deviates from the thickness specifications. The buyer cancels the contract, and immediately thereafter the second and third carloads of plywood arrive at the buyer's place of business. The court would have to grapple with the question of whether the 9 percent of nonconforming plywood substantially impaired the value of the whole.[3]

A more clear-cut example is an installment contract that involves parts of a machine. Suppose that the first part is delivered and is irreparably defective but is necessary for the operation of the machine. The failure of this first installment will be a breach of the whole contract. Even when the defect in the first shipment is such that it gives the buyer only a "reasonable apprehension" about the ability or willingness of the seller to properly complete the other installments, the breach on the

---

3. Continental Forest Products v. White Lumber Sales, Inc., 256 Or. 466, 474 P.2d 1 (1970). The court held that the deviation did not substantially impair the value of the whole contract. Additionally, the court stated that the nonconformity could be cured by an adjustment in the price.

first installment may be regarded as a breach of the whole.

The point to remember is that the UCC substantially alters the right of a buyer to reject the entire contract in installment sales contracts. Such contracts are broadly defined in the UCC, which strictly limits rejection to cases of substantial nonconformity.

Commercial Impracticability

Whenever occurrences unforeseen by either party when the contract was made make performance commercially impracticable, the rule of perfect tender no longer holds. According to UCC 2-615(a), delay in delivery or nondelivery in whole or in part is not a breach when performance has been made impracticable "by the occurrence of a contingency the nonoccurrence of which was a basic assumption on which the contract was made." The seller, however, must notify the buyer as soon as it is practicable to do so that there will be a delay or nondelivery.

The notion of commercial impracticability is closely allied with contract law theories of impossibility of performance and frustration of purpose.[4] Increased costs resulting from inflation do not in and of themselves excuse performance. This is the kind of risk ordinarily assumed by a seller conducting business. The unforeseen contingency must alter the essential nature of the performance, such as would occur with a sudden, severe shortage of raw materials.

---

4. See Chapter 14 under "Discharge by Impossibility or Impracticability of Performance."

For example, a major oil company that receives its supplies from the Middle East has a contract to supply a buyer with 100,000 gallons of oil. Because of an oil embargo by the Organization of Petroleum Exporting Countries (OPEC), the seller is prevented from securing oil supplies to meet the terms of this contract. Because of the same embargo, the seller cannot secure oil from any other source. This situation comes under the commercial impracticability exception to the perfect tender doctrine.

Sometimes the unforeseen event only *partially* affects the seller's capacity to perform. As a result, the seller is able to fulfill the contract partially but cannot tender total performance. In this event, the seller is required to allocate in a fair and reasonable manner any remaining production and deliveries among the contracted customers. The buyer must receive notice of the allocation, with the obvious right to accept or reject it.

For example, a grower of cranberries in the state of Washington, Cran Plan, has contracted to sell this season's production to a number of customers, including the G & G grocery chain. G & G has contracted to purchase 2,000 crates of cranberries. Cran Plan has sprayed some of its bogs of cranberries with a chemical called Green. The Department of Agriculture discovers that persons who eat products sprayed with Green may develop cancer. An order prohibiting the sale of these products is effected. Cran Plan has harvested all the bogs not sprayed with Green but cannot fully meet all contract deliveries. In this case, Cran Plan is required to allocate its production, notifying G & G of the amount it is able to deliver.

The following case illustrates an application of the doctrine of commercial impracticability.

BACKGROUND AND FACTS *In 1977, the Urbana and Champaign Sanitary District was planning two waste-water treatment facilities. CRS Group Engineers (Clark Dietz Division) set the specifications for the facilities, and all equipment had to meet with Dietz's approval. Belt filter presses were among the many types of equipment required. Dietz's specifications required certain performance capabilities, as well as exact conformity of the mechanical components. The mechanical specifications were set with reference to a machine manufactured by the Ralph B. Carter Co. The Waldinger Corporation, a subcontractor on the project, took bids from four belt filter press manufacturers. Ashbrook, the co-defendant, was selected by Waldinger to provide the belt filter presses. Ashbrook's machines could meet the performance specifications, but the*

Case 18.2
WALDINGER CORP. v. CRS GROUP ENGINEERS, INC.

United States Court of Appeals, Seventh Circuit, 1985.
775 F.2d 781.

mechanical components varied from those required by Dietz. Ashbrook's machine was thus not approved by Dietz, and Waldinger was forced to buy the belt filter presses from the Ralph B. Carter Co. at a higher price. Waldinger sued Ashbrook for breach of contract (and CRS Group Engineers for wrongful interference with Waldinger's contract with Ashbrook). Ashbrook claimed that Dietz intentionally or negligently drafted restrictive mechanical specifications and that Dietz's specifications made it commercially impracticable for Ashbrook to fulfill its contract. The Central District Court of Illinois found for Ashbrook, holding that Ashbrook was excused from performance because Dietz had made performance impracticable. Waldinger appealed.

WOOD, Circuit Judge.
*   *   *   *

Waldinger challenges the district court's conclusion that Ashbrook was excused from performing its contract with Waldinger on the ground of commercial impracticability. [UCC] § 2-615. Assuming the seller has not assumed the greater obligation under the agreement, three conditions must be satisfied before performance is excused: (1) a contingency has occurred; (2) the contingency has made performance impracticable; and (3) the nonoccurrence of that contingency was a basic assumption upon which the contract was made. The rationale for the defense of commercial impracticability is that the circumstance causing the breach has rendered performance "so vitally different from what was anticipated that the contract cannot be reasonably thought to govern." Because the purpose of a contract is to place the reasonable risk of performance upon the promisor, however, it is presumed to have agreed to bear any loss occasioned by an event that was foreseeable at the time of contracting.

The applicability of the defense of commercial impracticability, then, turns largely on foreseeability. The relevant inquiry is whether the risk of the occurrence of the contingency was so unusual or unforeseen and the consequences of the occurrence of the contingency so severe that to require performance is to grant the buyer an advantage he did not bargain for in the contract. If the risk of the occurrence of the contingency was unforeseeable, the seller cannot be said to have assumed that risk. *   *   * [I]f a contingency is foreseeable, the section 2-615 defense is unavailable because the party disadvantaged by the fruition of the contingency might have contractually protected itself.
*   *   *   *

The district court found that a basic assumption of the contract between Waldinger and Ashbrook was that Ashbrook equipment was competitive and would comply with the specifications drafted by Dietz. That assumption was based upon the belief that Dietz would interpret its specifications in a competitive and nonrestrictive manner. Because Dietz did not do so, performance by Ashbrook was rendered impracticable.
*   *   *   *

The district court found that it was not foreseeable at the time of contracting that Dietz would require strict compliance with all specifications. *   *   * True, Ashbrook knew that Dietz's approval was required and that at the time it signed the purchase orders Dietz had not expressly approved its 1-V machine. The refusal of an engineer to waive certain mechanical specifications is foreseeable, and a supplier normally assumes the risk of non-approval. But these general principles cannot be deemed to apply where an engineer's insistence on literal compliance with exclusionary specifications has no scientific or rational basis. Given industry practice on waiver of mechanical specifications and the EPA [Environmental Protection Agency] regulations [the plant was to be built according to EPA standards] prohibiting exclusionary specifications upon which Ashbrook could rightly rely, Ashbrook could not have foreseen the possibility that Dietz would require it to build a Carter machine even if its machine met the performance specifications. The section 2-615 defense is therefore available to Ashbrook if performance was rendered commercially impracticable by Dietz's insistence upon compliance with the exclusionary specifications.

* * * *

Under the contract documents, then, Ashbrook was required to guarantee performance. This, the evidence shows, it could not do if required to build its filter press according to Dietz's mechanical specifications. We conclude that Ashbrook's inability to supply a filter press that would both satisfy Dietz's mechanical specifications and perform as required is sufficient to establish that performance of its contract with Waldinger was commercially impracticable.

The court of appeals affirmed the district court's decision. Ashbrook, the co-defendant, did not have to pay any damages to Waldinger because performance of the contract would have been commercially impracticable. Therefore, Ashbrook was excused from fulfilling the terms of the contract.

DECISION AND REMEDY

Destruction of Identified Goods

The Code provides that when a casualty occurs that totally destroys *identified goods* under a sales contract through no fault of either party and *before risk passes to the buyer*, the seller and buyer are excused from performance [UCC 2-613(a)]. If the goods are only partially destroyed, however, the buyer can inspect them and either treat the contract as void or accept the damaged goods with an allowance off the contract price.

Consider an example. Antioch Appliances has on display six ABC dishwashers of a discontinued model. Five are white, and one is harvest gold. No others of that model are available. Chavez, who is not a merchant, clearly specifies that he needs the harvest gold dishwasher because it fits in his kitchen's color scheme. Chavez buys the harvest gold dishwasher. Unfortunately, before Antioch can deliver it, it is destroyed by a fire. In such a case, under Section 2-613, Antioch Appliance will not be liable to Chavez for failure to deliver the harvest gold dishwasher. The goods here suffered a casualty without fault of either party before the risk of loss passed to the buyer, and the loss was total, so the contract is avoided. Clearly, Antioch has no obligation to tender that dishwasher. Of course, Chavez has no obligation to pay for it, either.

Change the example somewhat. Chavez purchases a discontinued dishwasher model but does not specify the color. If the harvest gold dishwasher is destroyed by fire, Antioch is still obliged to tender one of the other discontinued models,

and Chavez is obligated to accept and to make payment. Only if Antioch's entire stock of the discontinued model were destroyed by the fire would it be excused from performance in this instance.

Assurance and Cooperation

Two other exceptions to the perfect tender doctrine apply equally to the seller and buyer.

The right of assurance stems from the concept that the essential purpose of a contract is performance by both parties, and thus when one party has reason to believe the other party will not perform, forcing the first party to perform creates an undue hardship.

The Code provides that should a seller (or buyer) have "reasonable grounds" to believe the buyer (or seller) will not perform as contracted, he or she may "in writing demand adequate assurance of due performance" from the other party; and until such assurance is received, he or she may "suspend" further performance without liability. The grounds for such belief and action must be reasonable. Between merchants, the grounds are determined by commercial standards [UCC 2-609]. The assurances requested also must be reasonable. If such assurances are not forthcoming within a reasonable time (not to exceed thirty days), the failure to respond may be treated as a *repudiation* of the contract.

For example, Hilary has contracted to ship Jenkins 100 dozen shirts on or before October 1, with Jenkins's payment due within thirty days of delivery. Hilary has made two previous shipments, neither of which has been paid for by Jenkins. On September 20, Hilary demands in writing certain assurances of payment (such as payment of the last two orders to bring the account up to date) before she will ship the 100 dozen shirts. If these assurances are reasonable, Hilary can suspend shipment of the shirts without liability pending Jenkins's compliance. If Jenkins does not provide the payments within a reasonable time (no longer than thirty days), Hilary can hold Jenkins in breach of contract without having made the contracted shipment.

Sometimes the performance of one party depends on the cooperation of the other. The Code provides that when such cooperation is not forthcoming, the other party can suspend his or her own performance without liability and hold the uncooperative party in breach [UCC 2-311(3)].

For example, Amati is required by contract to deliver 1,200 Model Z washing machines to locations in the state of California to be specified later by Farrell. Deliveries are to be made on or before October 1. Amati has repeatedly requested the delivery locations, and Farrell has not responded. The 1,200 Model Z machines are ready for shipment on October 1, but Farrell still refuses to give Amati delivery locations. Amati does not ship on October 1. Can Amati be held liable? The answer is no. Amati is excused for any resulting delay of performance because of Farrell's failure to cooperate.

BUYER'S OBLIGATIONS

Once the seller has adequately tendered delivery, the buyer is obligated to accept the goods and pay for them according to the terms of the contract. In the absence of any specific agreements, the buyer must:

1. Furnish facilities reasonably suited for receipt of the goods [UCC 2-503(1)(b)].
2. Make payment at the time and place the buyer *receives* the goods, even if the place of shipment is the place of delivery [UCC 2-310(a)].

Payment

When a sale is made on credit, the buyer is obliged to pay according to credit terms (for example, 60, 90, or 120 days), *not* when the goods are received. The credit period usually begins on the *date of shipment* [UCC 2-310(d)].

Payment can be made by any means agreed upon between the parties. Cash can be used, but the buyer can also use any other method generally acceptable in the commercial world. If the seller demands cash when the buyer offers a check, credit card, or the like, then the seller must permit the buyer reasonable time to obtain legal tender [UCC 2-511].

Right of Inspection

Unless otherwise agreed, or for C.O.D. (collect on delivery) goods, the buyer's right to inspect the goods is absolute. This right allows the buyer to verify, before making payment, that the goods tendered or delivered are what were contracted for or ordered. If the goods are not what the buyer ordered, there is no duty to pay. *An opportunity for inspection is therefore a condition precedent to the seller's right to enforce payment* [UCC 2-513(1)].

Unless otherwise agreed, inspection can take place at any reasonable place and time and in any reasonable manner. Generally, what is reasonable is determined by custom of the trade, past practices of the parties, and the like. The Code also provides for inspection after arrival when goods are to be shipped.

Costs of inspecting conforming goods are borne by the buyer unless agreed otherwise [UCC 2-513(2)].

C.O.D. SHIPMENTS If a seller ships goods to a buyer C.O.D. (or under similar terms), the buyer can rightfully *reject* them (unless the contract expressly provides for a C.O.D. shipment). This is because C.O.D. does not permit inspection before payment, and the effect is a denial of the buyer's right of inspection. But when the buyer has agreed to a C.O.D. shipment in the contract or has agreed to pay for the goods upon the presentation of a bill of lading, no right of inspection exists, because it was negated by the agreement[UCC 2-513(3)].

PAYMENT DUE—DOCUMENTS OF TITLE Under certain contracts, payment is due on the receipt of the required documents of title, even though the goods themselves may not have arrived at their destination. With C.I.F. and C. & F. contracts, payment is required upon receipt of the documents unless the parties have agreed otherwise.

Thus, payment is required prior to inspection, and it must be made unless the buyer knows that the goods are nonconforming [UCC 2-310(b), 2-513(3)].

Acceptance

The buyer can manifest assent to the delivered goods in different ways, each of which will constitute acceptance:

1. The buyer can expressly accept the shipment by words or conduct. For example, there is an acceptance if the buyer, after having had a reasonable opportunity to inspect, signifies agreement to the seller that either the goods are conforming or they are acceptable despite their nonconformity [UCC 2-606(1)(a)].
2. Acceptance will be presumed if the buyer has had a reasonable opportunity to inspect the goods and has failed to reject them within a reasonable period of time [UCC 2-606(1)(b), 2-602(1)].
3. The buyer can accept the goods by performing any act inconsistent with the seller's ownership. For example, any use or resale of the goods will generally constitute an acceptance. Limited use for the sole purpose of testing or inspecting the goods is not an acceptance, however [UCC 2-606(1)(c)].

Revocation of Acceptance

Acceptance of the goods by the buyer precludes the buyer from exercising the right of rejection. Acceptance does not in and of itself impair the right of the buyer to pursue remedies. (Remedies are discussed in Chapter 19.) But if the buyer accepts nonconforming goods and fails to notify the seller of the breach when it is discovered (or when it should have been discovered), then the buyer is barred from pursuing any remedy against the seller. What is at issue here is the necessity for the buyer to inform the seller of the breach within a reasonable time. The burden is on the buyer to establish the existence of a breach of contract once the goods have been accepted [UCC 2-607(3)].

After a buyer accepts a lot or a *commercial unit*,[5] acceptance can still be revoked if nonconformity *substantially* impairs the value of the unit or lot and if one of the following factors also is present:

1. Acceptance was predicated on the reasonable assumption that the nonconformity would be cured, and it has not been seasonably cured [UCC 2-608(1)(a)].
2. The buyer does not discover the nonconformity, and his or her acceptance was reasonably induced by the difficulty of discovery before acceptance or by the seller's assurances that the goods conform [UCC 2-608(1)(b)].

In the following case, the court stresses the elements that must be present before a buyer can revoke acceptance after having accepted the goods.

---

5. A commercial unit is a unit of goods that, by commercial usage, is viewed as a single whole for purposes of sale and that cannot be divided without materially impairing the character of the unit, its market value, or its use [UCC 2-105]. A commercial unit can be a single article (such as machine), a set of articles (such as a suite of furniture or an assortment of sizes), or a quantity (such as a bale, gross, or carload), or any other unit treated in the trade as a single whole.

BACKGROUND AND FACTS   *Susan Thomas, the defendant, was visiting in Arizona in February 1984 and heard about Raxx, a Russian Arabian stallion, during a horse show. The defendant visited the horse farm of George Alpert and Lee Wolfman, the plaintiffs and the owners of Raxx. She spoke to the plaintiffs' general manager, Mallory, about purchasing Raxx for breeding purposes; and a few days later, the price of $175,000 was set. Thomas told Mallory that she wished to have a collection of Raxx's sperm to test the stallion's breeding soundness, and Mallory assured the defendant that he would take care of it.*

Thomas agreed to purchase Raxx, made a payment of part of the price set for the stallion, and took him to Vermont. Despite breeding efforts, Raxx was unable to impregnate any of Thomas's Arabian mares. Thomas contacted Mal-

Case 18.3
ALPERT v. THOMAS
United States District Court,
District of Vermont, 1986.
643 F.Supp. 1406.

lory about these failures, and Mallory continued to assure her of Raxx's breeding soundness. After several failures, Dr. Woods of the New York College of Veterinary Medicine was called, and he determined that Raxx was an unsatisfactory prospective breeder. A stallion's value decreases significantly when it is not readily breedable, and Raxx's condition was not likely to improve, according to Dr. Woods.

The plaintiffs filed suit against Thomas to recover the remaining purchase price for the stallion. Thomas counterclaimed for rescission of sale, claiming she had revoked any acceptance (or, alternatively, for damages due to breach of express and implied warranties).

BILLINGS, District Judge.
*   *   *   *

As a result of Raxx's non-conformity to the express and implied warranties that he would be breeding sound, Thomas claims that she revoked her acceptance of Raxx. A buyer's revocation of acceptance of goods must satisfy the provisions of § 2-608. *   *   * There are four elements to proper revocation under § 2-608: (1) the goods' non-conformity with the contract substantially impairs the value to the buyer; (2) the buyer's acceptance was (a) forthcoming on the reasonable assumption that the non-conformity would be cured (discovery at time of acceptance) or (b) reasonably induced by the difficulty of the discovery or by the seller's assurances (no discovery at the time of acceptance); (3) revocation occurred within a reasonable time after the nonconformity was discovered or should have been discovered; and (4) revocation took place before a substantial change occurred in the condition of the goods not caused by their own defects.

As to the first element, Raxx's status as an unsatisfactory prospective breeder rendered him in non-conformity with the purchase and sale agreement's express and implied warranties that he would be merchantable as a breeder. Because Thomas was purchasing Raxx for breeding purposes, this non-conformity substantially impaired his value to her.

The second element of proper revocation under § 2-608 is also satisfied because Thomas was induced to accept Raxx without discovering his non-conformity as a result of Mallory's assurances that Georgian Hill Arabians would perform the breeding soundness evaluation and that Raxx was guaranteed to be breeding sound. *   *   *

*   *   * Thomas satisfied the third element of proper revocation in that she formally revoked within a reasonable time after Raxx's non-conformity was discovered or should have been discovered. Among the facts relevant to this finding are: plaintiffs' assurances that they would perform a breeding soundness test rendered the timing of Thomas's discovery of Raxx's infertility reasonable; Thomas promptly notified plaintiffs that Raxx's breedability had become suspect; Thomas *   *   * attempted several times to discuss the problem with plaintiffs and Mallory repeatedly replied that plaintiffs would "make it right"; and [a veterinarian contacted by the defendant] concurred with [the plaintiff's veterinarian's] recommendation made at the time of discovery, that Thomas should wait a few months and see if Raxx's problem would correct itself.

As to the final element of revocation under § 2-608, the Court found that there was no substantial damage in Raxx's condition not caused by his inability to breed.

In sum, the facts of this case indicate that all four elements of § 2-608 have been satisfied. Accordingly, Thomas properly revoked her acceptance of Raxx. Pursuant to § 2-608(3), she had the same rights and duties with regard to the horse as if she had rejected it. This includes the right to no longer be subject to the requirement, contained in § 2-607(4), that the buyer must prove any breach with respect to goods accepted. Once Thomas properly revoked her acceptance of Raxx, the burden falls upon plaintiffs, as sellers, to prove that Raxx conformed to the contract at the time of the sale.

The court rejected the plaintiffs' complaint and entered judgment for Thomas on her counterclaim. The court allowed Thomas to recover the $94,879.28 she had already paid for Raxx and $25,560.00 for transportation and care that she had reasonably incurred after the purchase.

DECISION AND REMEDY

NOTICE OF REVOCATION REQUIRED Revocation of acceptance will not be effective until notice is given to the seller, and that must occur within a reasonable time after the buyer either discovers or should have discovered the grounds for revocation. Also, revocation must occur before the goods have undergone any substantial change that was not caused by their own defects (such as spoilage) [UCC 2-608(2)].

PARTIAL ACCEPTANCE If some of the goods delivered do not conform to the contract and the seller has failed to cure, the buyer can make a *partial* acceptance [UCC 2-601(c)]. The same is true if the nonconformity was not reasonably discoverable before acceptance. A buyer cannot accept less than a single commercial unit, however.

Anticipatory Repudiation

The buyer and the seller have concurrent conditions of performance. But what if, before the time for either performance, one party clearly communicates to the other the intention not to perform? Such an action is a breach of the contract by *anticipatory repudiation*. When this occurs, the aggrieved party can, according to UCC 2-610:

1. For a commercially reasonable time await performance by the repudiating parties.
2. Resort to any remedy for breach even if the aggrieved party has notified the repudiating party that he or she awaits the latter's performance and has urged retraction.
3. In either case, *suspend performance* or proceed in accordance with the provisions of this article on the seller's right to identify goods notwithstanding breach or to salvage unfinished goods.

The key to anticipatory breach is that the repudiation takes place before the time that the party is required under contract to tender performance.

The nonbreaching party has a choice of two responses. He or she can treat the repudiation as a final breach by pursuing a remedy; or he or she can wait, hoping that the repudiating party will decide to honor the obligations required by the contract despite the avowed intention to renege.

Should the latter course be pursued, the Code permits the breaching party (subject to some limitations) to "retract" his or her repudiation. The retraction can be made by any method that clearly indicates an intent to perform. Once retraction has been made, the rights of the repudiating party under the contract are reinstated [UCC 2-611].

To illustrate: Wagner has contracted to deliver to Leonard 100,000 tons of coal on or before October 1. On September 15, Wagner tells Leonard that he will not make delivery until December 1. This statement of intent not to deliver until two months after the required delivery date is an anticipatory breach, and Leonard could pursue any of the remedies discussed in the next chapter.

But suppose Leonard responds that he expects Wagner to perform as obligated. Then, on September 28, Wagner informs Leonard that the 100,000 tons will be delivered as contracted, and a tender is made on October 1. Leonard has learned in the meantime that the same amount of coal can be purchased elsewhere (later in October) at a lower price. Therefore, Leonard refuses the tender, claiming Wagner breached the contract on September 15.

In this case Leonard, not Wagner, is in breach of contract. Wagner's notice was a retraction of the earlier repudiation. Since Leonard had not resorted to a remedy, or materially changed his position, or indicated that the repudiation was final, the retraction reinstated Wagner's rights under the contract. Therefore, Wagner's proper tender obligated Leonard to accept and pay for the coal tendered, and Leonard's refusal constitutes a breach.

QUESTIONS AND CASE PROBLEMS

1. Ames contracts to ship to Curley 100 Model Z television sets. The terms of delivery are F.O.B. Ames's city, by Green Truck Lines, with delivery on or before April 30. On April 15, Ames discovers that, because of an error in inventory control, all Model Z sets have been sold and the stock has not been replenished. Ames has Model X, a similar but slightly more expensive unit, in stock. On April 16, Ames ships 100 Model X sets, with notice that Curley will be charged the Model Z price. Curley (in a proper manner) rejects the Model X sets tendered on April 18. Ames does not wish to be held in breach of contract, even though he has tendered nonconforming goods. Discuss Ames's options.

· 2. Thal contracts to deliver to Hurwitz 1,000 bushels of corn at market price. Delivery and payment are to be made on October 1. On September 10, Hurwitz informs Thal that because of financial reverses she cannot pay on October 1. Thal immediately notifies Hurwitz that he is holding Hurwitz in breach of contract. On September 15, Thal files suit for breach of contract. On October 3, Hurwitz files an answer to Thal's lawsuit. Hurwitz claims that had Thal tendered delivery on October 1, she would have paid for the corn. Since no delivery was tendered, Hurwitz claims she cannot be held liable. Discuss whether Thal can hold Hurwitz liable for breach.

3. Kirk has contracted to deliver to Doolittle 1,000 cases of brand Wonder beans on or before October 1. Doolittle is to specify the means of transportation twenty days prior to date of shipment. Payment for the beans is to be made by Doolittle upon tender of delivery. On September 10, Kirk prepares the 1,000 cases for shipment. Kirk asks Doolittle how he would like the goods to be shipped, but Doolittle does not respond. On September 21, Kirk demands in writing assurance that Doolittle will be able to pay upon tender of the beans. Kirk's demand is that the money be placed in escrow prior to October 1 in a bank in Doolittle's city named by Kirk. Doolittle does not respond to any of the requests made by Kirk, but on October 5 he wants to file suit against Kirk for breach of contract for failure to deliver the beans as contracted. Discuss Kirk's liability for failure to tender delivery on October 1.

4. Gibson contracts to deliver 100 Model X color television sets to a new retail customer, Beaver, on May 1, with payment to be made upon delivery. Gibson tenders delivery in her own truck. Gibson notices that one or two cartons have scrape marks on them. Beaver inquires of Gibson whether the sets might have been damaged upon loading. Gibson assures Beaver that the sets are in perfect condition. Beaver tenders Gibson a check, but Gibson refuses the check, claiming that the first delivery to new customers is

always for cash. Beaver promises to have the cash within two days. Gibson leaves the sets with Beaver, who stores them in a warehouse pending an "opening sale" date. Two days later, Beaver opens some of the cartons and discovers that a number of the televisions are damaged beyond ordinary repair. Gibson claims Beaver has accepted the sets and is in breach by not paying on delivery. Discuss fully Gibson's claims.

5. Oberg purchased a car from Phillips. Soon after the purchase, Oberg discovered several defects in the automobile, including problems with the engine, the body paint, and the steering. Oberg returned the car to Phillips for repairs on numerous occasions. Phillips had the car at the shop for almost half of a three-month period. Oberg felt these repairs were unsatisfactory and gave Phillips a deadline in which to complete repairs. Phillips did not meet this deadline, and Oberg gave written notification of revocation of his acceptance. Oberg brought a suit against Phillips for breach of contract. Phillips insisted that the defects were only minor, that the car was under a one-year express warranty, and that these factors did not give Oberg a basis for his revocation. Did Oberg have a valid claim for revoking his acceptance of the car under this contract and suing for breach of contract? [Oberg v. Phillips, 615 P.2d 1022 (Okla.App. 1980)]

6. In August of 1979, A. B. Parker purchased a Ford-manufactured F-100 pickup truck from Bell Ford, Inc., for $6,155.40. Parker made several complaints to Bell Ford of excessive tire wear, and Bell Ford gave Parker a purchase order to have the vehicle aligned at an independent alignment shop. Though the problem was not cured, Parker never returned the vehicle to Bell Ford, nor did he make further complaint. A later inspection of the vehicle disclosed a defective wheel housing which had caused the tires to wear excessively. Parker sued Bell Ford and Ford Motor Company for breach of warranty. Bell Ford and Ford Motor Company claim Parker's continued acceptance of the vehicle under the circumstances precluded Parker's action. Discuss Bell Ford and Ford Motor Company's contention. [A. B. Parker v. Bell Ford, Inc., 425 So.2d 1101 (Ala. 1983)]

7. On February 6, 1978, Dreyfus Company, Inc., entered into a contract for the sale to Royster Company of 5,000 bushels of Arkansas Certified Bragg soybean seed at $13.50 per bushel. The contract of sale was conditioned on certification of the beans. Dreyfus informed Royster that the beans being sold would have to be purchased by Dreyfus from a company in Parkin, Arkansas. The parties did not communicate until May, when Dreyfus informed Royster that the beans had failed certification. Hours later, Dreyfus phoned and informed Royster that replacement certified beans had been located. Royster refused delivery, claiming the original beans suffered a casualty loss by failing certification under Section 2-613 of the UCC. Dreyfus sued for breach of contract. Discuss Royster's contention that UCC 2-613 relieved him from liability. [Dreyfus Company, Inc. v. Royster Company, 501 F.Supp. 1169 (E.D.Arkansas 1980)]

8. Leemar Steel Company manufactured counterweight inserts for CMI Corp., according to blueprints from CMI, and shipped them to CMI. CMI prepared an internal memo rejecting the shipment for nonconformance two days after it was received. CMI did not send the rejection notice to Leemar. Instead, a few weeks later, it notified Leemar by phone that there was a "problem with the inserts." CMI paid for the inserts and attempted, with Leemar's aid, to have the inserts ground to the correct tolerances during the next few months. Since this could not be accomplished, CMI filed suit to cancel the contract and to recover the money that it had paid Leemar pursuant to the contract. Discuss whether CMI has accepted the goods. Can it still revoke its acceptance and get its money back? [CMI Corp. v. Leemar Steel Co., Inc., 733 F.2d 1410 (10th Cir. 1984)]

9. T. W. Oil, Inc., the plaintiff, purchased fuel oil that was still at sea on a tanker. The oil company then contracted to sell to Consolidated Edison (C Ed), the defendant, this cargo of oil. When the plaintiff purchased the oil shipment, it received a certificate from the foreign refinery that stated the sulfur content of the oil was 0.52 percent. When the oil company then contracted with Con Ed to sell the oil to the latter, the oil company specified that the sulfur content was 0.5 percent, rounding off the 0.52 percent, as was the custom in the trade. During the negotiations with Con Ed, the oil company learned that Con Ed was authorized to buy and burn oil with a sulfur content of up to 1 percent and would mix oils containing more and less than that to maintain that figure.

When the oil shipment arrived, its sulfur content was found to be 0.92 percent. Con Ed rejected the shipment. The oil company offered a reduced price, which was also rejected by Con Ed. The next day, T. W. Oil offered to cure with a substitute shipment of conforming oil on a tanker due to arrive approximately one month after the original delivery date. Con Ed rejected the offer to cure. T. W. Oil sued for breach of contract, and the trial court held for the plaintiff, T. W. Oil, holding that the plaintiff's "reasonable and timely offer to cure" was improperly rejected. Discuss whether Con Ed was required to accept the substitute shipment. [T. W. Oil, Inc. v. Consolidated Edison Company, 57 N.Y.2d 574, 443 N.E.2d 932, 457 N.Y.S.2d 458 (1982)]

10. Bryant Lewis contracted to sell Ross Cattle Company four hundred head of cattle at $47.50 per hundredweight. Ross made an $8,000 down payment. Before delivery, Lewis heard a rumor that Ross was in poor financial condition, and Lewis demanded that he receive full payment before delivering the animals. Ross told Lewis the balance would be paid upon delivery, based on the weight of the cattle delivered. Lewis refused to deliver the cattle and sold them to a third party. Ross filed suit. Lewis claimed that the refusal of Ross to pay was an anticipatory repudiation of the contract. Discuss whether Lewis was correct and what action Lewis could have taken on the basis of the rumor. [Ross Cattle Co. v. Lewis, 415 So.2d 1029 (Miss. 1982)]

11. Wilson purchased a new television set from Scampoli in 1965. When the set was delivered, Wilson found that it did not work properly; the color was defective. Scampoli's repairperson could not correct the problem, and Wilson refused to allow the repairperson to dismantle and take the set back to the shop to determine the cause of difficulty. Instead, Wilson demanded that Scampoli deliver a new television set or return the purchase price. Scampoli refused to refund Wilson's money and insisted that he receive the opportunity to correct the malfunction of Wilson's set before replacing it or issuing a refund. Discuss whether Scampoli has the right to attempt to cure the product according to UCC 2-508. [Wilson v. Scampoli, 228 A.2d 848 (D.C. Cir. 1967)]

12. Rheinberg-Kellerei GMBH is a German wine producer and export seller who sold 1,245 cases of wine to Vineyard Wine Company, Inc. The contract did not specify delivery terms to any specific destination, and Rheinberg, through its agent, selected the port of Wilmington for the port of entry. Rheinberg delivered the wine to the boat carrier in early December 1978. On or about January 24, 1979, Vineyard learned that the wine had been lost in the North Atlantic sometime between December 12 and December 22, when the boat sank with all hands aboard. Vineyard refused to pay Rheinberg. Rheinberg filed an action for the purchase price, claiming that risk of loss had passed to the buyer, Vineyard, upon delivery of the wine to the carrier. Vineyard claimed that, because of Rheinberg's failure to give prompt notice of shipment (not until after the ship was lost at sea), risk of loss had not passed to the buyer. Discuss fully who is correct. [Rheinberg-Kellerei GMBH v. Vineyard Wine Co., 281 S.E.2d 425 (N.C.App. 1981)]

13. Can-Key Industries manufactured a newly developed product, a turkey hatching unit, which it sold to Industrial Leasing Corp. (ILC). ILC agreed to buy the unit only on the condition that it was accepted by a customer, Rose-A-Linda, who would lease the unit from ILC. When Rose-A-Linda did not lease the unit because it failed to meet its specifications, ILC refused to go through with the contract of sale with Can-Key. Rose-A-Linda had tried four times to have the unit changed to meet its specifications and kept the hatching unit for over fifteen months. Can-Key sued ILC for breach of contract, alleging that ILC and Rose-A-Linda had accepted the hatching unit by keeping it so long in use and by making several alterations in the goods that were inconsistent with the right of rejection. Discuss whether ILC and its lessee did accept the hatching unit or whether they still have the right to reject the goods offered by Can-Key. [Can-Key Industries, Inc. v. Industrial Leasing Corp., 286 Or. 173, 593 P.2d 1125 (1979)]

14. In June of 1973, Maple Farms, Inc. formed an agreement with the school district to supply the school district with milk for the 1973–1974 school year. The agreement was in the form of a requirements contract, whereby Maple Farms would sell to the school district all the milk the district required at a fixed price—which was the June market price of milk. By December of 1973, however, the price of raw milk had increased by 23 percent over the price specified in the contract. This meant that if

the terms of the contract were fulfilled, Maple Farms would lose $7,350. Because it had similar contracts with other school districts, Maple Farms stood to lose a great deal if it was held to the price stated in the contracts. When the school district would not agree to release Maple Farms from its contract, Maple Farms brought an action for a declaratory judgment. It contended that the price of raw milk was an event not contemplated by the parties when the contract was formed, and that, given the increased price, performance of the contract was commercially impracticable. Discuss whether Maple Farms should be released from the contract on the grounds of commercial impracticability. [Maple Farms, Inc. v. City School District of Elmira, 76 Misc.2d 1080, 352 N.Y.S.2d 784 (1974)]

15. On March 19, 1975, Moulton Cavity & Mold, Inc. agreed to sell twenty-six innersole molds (molds for the manufacture of shoes) to Lyn-Flex Industries for $600. Moulton understood that Lyn-Flex was in immediate need of the molds, and Moulton agreed to produce the molds within five weeks. The molds turned out to be quite complicated, and Moulton had to take some thirty tests to meet Lyn-Flex's specifications and also to fit the molds to Lyn-Flex's machines. After ten weeks, Lyn-Flex indicated that the model was approved as far as the fit was concerned but that other problems remained unsolved. Moulton went ahead and produced the twenty-six molds, and Lyn-Flex rejected them. When Moulton sued for damages for Lyn-Flex's alleged breach of contract, the trial court instructed the jury that substantial performance was sufficient to find for Moulton. Discuss whether this is true based upon the UCC. [Moulton Cavity & Mold, Inc. v. Lyn-Flex Ind., 396 A.2d 1024 (Me. 1979)]

Chapter 19

Remedies of Buyer and Seller for Breach

When a sales contract is breached, the aggrieved party may have a number of remedies from which to choose [UCC 2-703, 2-711]. These remedies range from retaining the goods to requiring the breaching party's performance under the contract. The general purpose of these remedies is to put the aggrieved party "in as good a position as if the other party had fully performed." It is important not only that the nonbreaching party know what remedies are available but that he or she know which remedy is most appropriate for a given situation [UCC 1-106(1)].

REMEDIES OF THE SELLER

The remedies available to a seller when the buyer is in breach under the UCC include:

1. The right to withhold delivery of the goods.
2. The right to stop a carrier or bailee from delivering goods to an insolvent or defaulting buyer.
3. A limited right to reclaim goods in the possession of an insolvent buyer.
4. The right to identify and/or resell goods identified to the contract.
5. The right to recover the purchase price plus incidental damages in certain cases.
6. The right to recover damages for the buyer's wrongful repudiation or nonacceptance of the contract.
7. The right to cancel the sales contract.

The Right to Withhold Delivery of the Goods

In general, sellers can withhold or discontinue performance of their obligations under a sales contract when buyers are in breach. If the breach is due to the buyer's insolvency, the seller can refuse to deliver the goods unless the buyer pays in cash [UCC 2-702(1)]. A person is **insolvent** under the UCC when that person ceases to pay "his debts in the ordinary course of business or cannot pay his debts as they become due or is insolvent within the meaning of the federal bankruptcy law" [UCC 1-201(23)].

Consider an example. On September 1, Simpson receives an order from Bentley for ten cases of ballpoint pens to be shipped on September 13. Bentley wants the goods put on his thirty-day open account. On September 6, Bentley files involuntary bankruptcy. On September 9, Simpson learns of Bentley's bankruptcy and therefore refuses to ship the goods on September 13. The court-appointed trustee of Bentley's assets now claims that Simpson has breached his contract with Bentley by not shipping the goods on September 13 as agreed. The trustee will not prevail, because Simpson was under no obligation to ship goods on credit to an insolvent buyer. The trustee, of course, could still obtain the goods for the benefit of Bentley's bankrupt estate by paying cash for them.

If a buyer has wrongfully rejected or revoked acceptance of the goods, failed to make proper and timely payment, or repudiated a part of the contract, the seller can withhold delivery of the goods in question. Furthermore, the seller can withhold the entire undelivered balance of the goods if the buyer's breach is material [UCC 2-703]. (Recall that a material breach is one that substantially impairs the value of the entire contract.)

The Right to Stop a Carrier or Bailee from Delivering Goods in Transit

If the seller has delivered the goods to a carrier or a bailee but the buyer has not yet received them, the goods are said to be *in transit*. If the seller learns of the buyer's insolvency while the goods are in transit, the seller can stop the carrier or bailee from delivering the goods to the buyer on the basis of the buyer's insolvency, regardless of the quantity shipped.

If the buyer is not insolvent but repudiates the contract or gives the seller some other right to withhold or reclaim the goods, the seller can stop the goods in transit only if the quantity shipped is at least a carload, a truckload, a planeload, or a larger shipment[1] [UCC 2-705(1)].

Consider an example. On January 1, Beel orders a carload of onions from Sneed. Sneed is to ship them on January 8, and Beel is to pay for

them on January 10. Sneed ships on time, but Beel does not pay on January 10. As soon as Sneed learns of this, she orders the carrier to stop the carload in transit. Since the carload is still on its way to Beel's city, the carrier is able to stop shipment. Beel cannot claim that Sneed and the carrier have performed a wrongful act by stopping the shipment, for a seller can always stop a carload of goods in transit when a buyer commits some breach of contract that gives the seller the right to withhold or reclaim the goods. Had the contract called for a shipment of ten bags of onions, rather than a carload, Sneed could not have stopped the goods in transit unless Beel was unable to pay for the goods (insolvent).

In order to stop delivery, the seller must *timely notify* the carrier or other bailee that the goods are to be returned or held for the seller. If the carrier has sufficient time to stop delivery, then the goods must be held and delivered according to the instructions of the seller, who is liable to the carrier for any additional costs incurred. If the carrier fails to act properly, it will be liable to the seller for any loss [UCC 2-705(3)].

The right of the seller to stop delivery is lost when:

1. The buyer obtains possession of the goods.
2. The carrier acknowledges the buyer's rights by reshipping or storing the goods for the buyer.
3. A bailee of the goods other than a carrier acknowledges that he or she is holding the goods for the buyer.
4. A negotiable document of title covering the goods has been negotiated to the buyer [UCC 2-705(2)].

Under general contract law, circumstances that make it unlikely that a party will be able to fulfill his or her contract may sometimes be treated as an anticipatory breach. As discussed in Chapter 18, under the UCC, circumstances that increase the risk of nonperformance but that do not clearly indicate that performance will not be forthcoming may not be treated as repudiation immediately. A seller may withhold performance, which includes stopping delivery, pending the buyer's assurances that performance will be forthcoming at the proper time. If adequate assurances are not given within a reasonable time (thirty days), the seller may treat the contract as repudiated. What is adequate, of course, depends on the circumstances [UCC 2-609].

---

1. This limitation of stoppage to larger shipments when the stoppage is due to reasons other than insolvency recognizes the burden that stoppage represents to carriers [UCC 2-705, Comment 1].

For example, imagine that in the Sneed-Beel onion deal described above, Sneed hears a rumor on January 9 that Beel is in financial trouble. Reasonably believing that the rumor may have a basis in fact, Sneed can order the delivery stopped in transit and demand assurance from Beel that payment will be made. A financial report from Beel's banker showing good financial condition would be adequate assurance, and on its receipt, Sneed must order the delivery resumed. On the other hand, if Beel provides no assurance, Sneed may consider the failure a repudiation.

The Right to Reclaim Goods in the Possession of an Insolvent Buyer

When a seller discovers that a buyer has received goods on credit while insolvent (as previously defined), the seller can demand return of the goods, if such demand is made within ten days of the buyer's receipt of the goods. The seller can demand and reclaim the goods at any time if the buyer misrepresented his or her solvency in writing within three months prior to the delivery of the goods [UCC 2-702(2)].

The seller's right to reclaim, however, is subject to the rights of a good faith purchaser or other buyer in the ordinary course of business who purchases the goods from the buyer before the seller reclaims.[2]

It is obvious that the seller who successfully reclaims goods under the UCC receives preferential treatment over the buyer's other creditors. Because of this, the Code provides that reclamation *bars* the seller from pursuing any other remedy as to these goods [UCC 2-702(3)].

This section of the UCC is extremely important should the buyer go through federal bankruptcy. The 1978 Bankruptcy Reform Act, as amended, provides in Section 546(c) that the rights and powers of the bankruptcy trustee are "subject to any statutory right or common law right of a seller . . . if the debtor has received such goods while insolvent." The seller need only make a demand for the return of the goods within ten days after receipt of the goods by the buyer.

---

2. A *buyer in the ordinary course of business* is a person who, in good faith and without knowledge that the sale violates the ownership rights or security interest of a third party, buys in ordinary course from a person (other than a pawnbroker) in the business of selling goods of that kind [UCC 1-201(9)].

The Right to Identify and/or Resell Goods Identified to the Contract after the Buyer Has Breached

Sometimes a buyer breaches or repudiates a sales contract while the seller is still in possession of finished or partially manufactured goods. In this event, the seller can identify to the contract the conforming goods that are still in his or her possession or control, even if they were not identified at the time of the breach. Then the seller can resell the goods and seek to recover damages from the breaching party [UCC 2-704].

When the goods contracted for are unfinished at the time of breach, the seller can treat the unfinished goods in two ways. First, the seller can cease manufacturing the goods and resell them for scrap or salvage value. Second, the seller can complete the manufacture, identify the goods to the contract, and resell them. In choosing between these two alternatives, the seller must exercise reasonable commercial judgment in order to mitigate the loss and obtain maximum realization of value from the unfinished goods [UCC 2-704(2)].

When a seller possesses or controls the goods at the time of the buyer's breach (because of the buyer's wrongful rejection or revocation of acceptance of the goods, failure to pay, or repudiation of the contract) or when the seller rightfully reacquires the goods by stopping them in transit, then the seller has the right to resell the goods. The resale must be made in good faith and in a commercially reasonable manner. The seller can recover any deficiency between the resale price and the contract price, along with **incidental damages,** defined as those costs to the seller resulting from stopping delivery of and transporting, caring for, and reselling the goods and other similar actions undertaken because of the breach [UCC 2-706(1), 2-710]. Obviously, it would be unfair for a buyer to profit from his or her own breach. Therefore, the Code encourages the seller's use of the remedy of resale by providing that the seller is *not liable* to the buyer for any profits made on the resale [UCC 2-706(6)].

The resale can be private or public, and the goods can be sold as a unit or in parcels. The seller must give the original buyer reasonable notice of the resale, unless the goods are perishable or will rapidly decline in value [UCC 2-706(2), 2-706(3)]. In the latter case, the seller has a duty to resell the goods as rapidly as possible in order to mitigate damages. A bona fide purchaser in a resale takes the goods free of any of the rights of the original buyer, even if the seller fails to comply with these requirements of the Code [UCC 2-706(5)].

Consider some examples. Cohen contracts on Monday to sell his car to Leuhrs for $5,000, with delivery of the car and payment for it due on the following Monday. When Cohen tenders delivery on Monday, Leuhrs refuses to accept or pay for the car. Cohen informs Leuhrs that he will resell the car at a private sale. Cohen sells the car to Devins for $2,000 on Tuesday. The following day, Cohen sues Leuhrs for $3,200—$3,000 being the difference between the resale price and the contract price and $200 being the value of incidental damages, the expense of arranging the sale. In this example, the seller would be unlikely to recover the $3,000 difference between the resale price and the contract price, because the resale was obviously not made in good faith or in a commercially reasonable manner. But if Cohen can prove incidental damages of $200, he will be likely to recover them.

Suppose that Cohen contracts to sell Leuhrs a prize bull for $10,000, with delivery and payment due on Monday. On Monday, Cohen tenders delivery of the prize bull, but Leuhrs refuses to accept or pay for it. Cohen tells Leuhrs that he is going to sell the bull at an area livestock auction the next day. At the auction, there are few bidders for the prize bull. Leuhrs decides to bid on the bull himself and obtains it for $9,000. Cohen then demands $1,100 in damages from Leuhrs—$1,000 for the difference between the contract price and the resale price plus $100 for incidental expenses in getting the prize bull to the auction. In this example, the total sum could probably be recovered by Cohen, assuming he can substantiate his incidental expenses. The livestock auction was a reasonable place for resale, and the resale was done in a commercially reasonable manner.

As a third example, Cohen contracts on Monday to sell 4,000 heads of romaine lettuce to Leuhrs for 30 cents per head, with delivery and payment due on Friday. On Wednesday, Cohen has 14,000 heads of romaine lettuce in his inventory, but he has not yet identified the 4,000 he intends to sell to Leuhrs. On that day, Leuhrs telephones Cohen to inform him that he will not accept or pay for the lettuce. Leuhrs claims that, since the 4,000 heads of romaine lettuce for his contract have not

yet been identified, Cohen cannot resell and recover damages from him. Leuhrs is incorrect here. Cohen has the right to identify the 4,000 heads of lettuce for Leuhrs's contract and the right to resell the lettuce. Cohen can recover the difference between the resale price received and the contract price of 30 cents per head, plus any incidental damages [UCC 2-704(1), 2-706(1), 2-710].

The Right to Recover the Purchase Price Plus Incidental Damages

Before the UCC was adopted, a seller could not sue for the purchase price of the goods unless title had passed to the buyer. Under the Code, an unpaid seller can bring an action to recover the purchase price and incidental damages, but only under one of the following circumstances:

1. When the buyer has accepted the goods and has not revoked acceptance, in which case title would have passed to the buyer.
2. When conforming goods have been lost or damaged after the risk of loss has passed to the buyer.
3. When the buyer has breached after the goods have been identified to the contract and the seller is unable to resell the goods [UCC 2-709(1)].

An action to recover the purchase price and incidental damages, available to the seller only under the circumstances just described, is distinct from an action to recover damages for breach of the sales contract.

If a seller sues for the contract price of goods that he or she has been unable to resell, the goods must be held for the buyer. The seller can resell at any time prior to the collection of the judgment from the buyer, but the net proceeds from the sale must be credited to the buyer. This is an example of the duty to mitigate damages.

To illustrate: Suppose Loomis has contracted to sell Zetting 200 tablecloths with the name of Zetting's restaurant inscribed on them. Loomis delivers the 200 tablecloths to Zetting, but Zetting refuses to pay. Or suppose Loomis tenders the 200 tablecloths to Zetting but Zetting refuses to accept them. In either case, Loomis has, as a proper remedy, an action for the purchase price.

In the first situation, Zetting accepted conforming goods, but he is in breach by failure to pay. In the second situation, the goods have been identified to the contract, and it is obvious that Loomis could not sell tablecloths inscribed with Zetting's restaurant's name to anyone else. Thus, both situations fall under UCC 2-709.

The Right to Recover Damages for Buyer's Wrongful Repudiation or Nonacceptance

If a buyer repudiates a contract or wrongfully refuses to accept the goods, a seller can maintain an action to recover damages. The seller may recover the difference between the contract price and the market price (at the time and place of tender of the goods) plus incidental damages [UCC 2-708(1)].

The time and place of tender are frequently given by such terms as F.O.B., F.A.S., C.I.F., and the like, which determine whether there is a shipment or destination contract.

If the difference between the contract price and the market price is too small to place the seller in the position that he or she would have been in if the buyer had fully performed, the proper measure of damages includes the seller's lost profits [UCC 2-708(2)].

The question of wrongful repudiation of a sales contract concerning specially manufactured roller wheels for skateboards is the subject of the next case.

BACKGROUND AND FACTS *Chicago Roller Skate Manufacturing Company entered into a sales contract with Sokol Manufacturing Company to provide the latter with truck and wheel assemblies with plates and hangers for use in the manufacture of skateboards. Chicago sent the requested goods to Sokol. At that time there was a balance due of $12,860. But since the skateboard fad had ended, Sokol decided to return, without Chicago's consent, a quantity of the goods purchased and demanded full credit on the contract price. These goods were not suitable for any other use; nor could they be resold. Chicago held them for seven months. Chicago offered Sokol a credit of 70 cents per unit, which Sokol neither accepted nor rejected. Finally, Chicago disassembled, cleaned, and rebuilt the units to make them suitable for use on normal roller skates. The rebuilt units had a reasonable value of between 67 cents and 69 cents. Thus, the salvage operation cost Chicago Roller Skate $3,540.76. Profits lost amounted to an additional $2,572. Chicago, disregarding its expense, credited Sokol with 70 cents per unit and brought suit for the balance due of $4,285. It recovered this sum in a judgment in the trial court. Sokol appealed.*

Case 19.1
CHICAGO ROLLER SKATE MANUFACTURING COMPANY v. SOKOL MANUFACTURING COMPANY
Supreme Court of Nebraska, 1970.
185 Neb. 515, 177 N.W.2d 25.

NEWTON, Justice.
* * * *

In accordance with section 2-709, U.C.C., plaintiff was entitled to hold the merchandise for defendant and recover the full contract price of $12,860. Plaintiff did not elect to enforce this right, but recognizing that there was no market for the goods or resale value and that they were consequently worthless for the purpose for which they were designed, it attempted to mitigate defendant's damages by converting the goods to other uses and credited defendant with the reasonable value of the goods as converted or rebuilt for use in roller skates. In so doing, plaintiff was evidencing good faith [UCC 1-203] and conforming to the general rule requiring one damaged by another's breach of contract to reduce or mitigate damages. * * *

The Uniform Commercial Code contemplates that it shall be supplemented by existing principles of law and equity [UCC 1-103]. It further contemplates that the remedies provided shall be liberally administered to the end that an aggrieved party shall be put in as good a position as it would have been in if the contract had been performed [UCC 1-106]. Here the buyer was demanding of the seller credit for the full contract price for goods that had become worthless. The seller was the aggrieved party and a return of worthless goods did not place it in as good a position as it would have been in had the contract been performed by the buyer paying the contract price. On the other hand, the crediting to defendant of the reasonable value of the rebuilt materials and recovery of the balance of the contract price did reasonably reimburse plaintiff. This procedure appears to be contemplated by section 2-718(4), U.C.C., which requires that a seller paid in goods credit the buyer with the reasonable value of the goods.

* * * [We] agree with defendant in its contention that the controlling measure of damages is that set out in section 2-708(2), U.C.C. This section provides that the measure of damages is the profit which the seller would have made from full performance by the buyer, together with any incidental damages resulting from the breach and costs reasonably incurred. Defendant overlooks the provision for allowance of incidental damages and costs incurred. The loss of profits, together with the additional costs or damage sustained by plaintiff amount to $6,112.76, a sum considerably in excess of that sought and recovered by plaintiff. Although the case was tried by plaintiff and determined on an erroneous theory of damages, the error is without prejudice to defendant. There being no cross-appeal, the judgment of the district court is affirmed.

DECISION AND REMEDY   *Sokol had to pay the $4,285 to Chicago Roller Skate Manufacturing Company.*

The Right to Cancel the Sales Contract

A seller can cancel a contract if the buyer wrongfully rejects or revokes acceptance of conforming goods, fails to make proper payment, or repudiates the contract in part or in whole. The contract can be canceled with respect to the goods directly involved, or the entire contract can be canceled if the breach is material [UCC 2-703].

The seller must *notify* the buyer of the cancellation, and at that point all remaining obligations of the seller are discharged. The buyer is not discharged from all remaining obligations but is in breach and can be sued under any of the subsections mentioned in UCC 2-703 and UCC 2-106(4).

If the seller's cancellation is not justified, then the seller is in breach of the contract, and the buyer can sue for appropriate damages.

Seller's Lien

Under certain circumstances, a seller's rights go beyond the remedies provided for under the UCC. One such right is a seller's common law lien in the goods being sold. A **lien** is an interest in property to secure payment of a debt or performance of an obligation. Technically, a lien is a right that is incident to the sale rather than a remedy for breach of contract. A seller's lien enables the seller to retain possession of the goods until the buyer pays for them.

The seller's lien can be waived or lost through: (1) express agreement, (2) acts inconsistent with the lien's existence, (3) payment or tender of payment by the buyer, or (4) voluntary and unconditional delivery of the goods to a carrier or other bailee or to the buyer or an authorized agent of the buyer.

If the sales agreement provides for an extension of credit to the buyer, the seller normally has no lien on the goods, since the act of extending credit is inconsistent with the existence of the lien. The seller will have a lien on the goods, however, if the buyer becomes insolvent or if the credit period expires while the goods are still in the seller's possession.

The tender of payment or the actual payment of the debt that the lien secures will ordinarily discharge the lien. This occurs when the buyer pays the full price for the goods and the seller gives up possession. When the buyer gives a promissory note, the lien ordinarily will *not* be discharged until the note is paid, even if the seller relinquishes possession of the goods.

Finally, sellers lose their liens when they voluntarily deliver possession of the goods to the buyer or to an authorized agent of the buyer. The lien is not lost, though, when delivery is qualified— that is, when the seller reserves his or her rights

CONCEPT SUMMARY: Seller's Remedies for Buyer's Breach	
SITUATIONS	**SELLER'S REMEDIES**
	The remedies available to a seller are basically determined by who has possession of the goods at the time of the buyer's breach.
Goods are in the seller's possession	1. Withhold delivery. UCC 2-703(a) 2. Resell. UCC 2-706 3. Sue for breach of contract. UCC 2-708 4. Cancel (and rescind). UCC 2-703 5. Identify goods to the contract. UCC 2-704

Goods are in transit	1. Stoppage in transit:
	   a. Any size shipment if reason is buyer's insolvency.
	   b. Carload, truckload, planeload, or larger shipment for reasons other than buyer's insolvency. UCC 2-705

Goods are in the buyer's possession	1. Sue for purchase price. UCC 2-709 2. Reclaim goods received by insolvent buyer (excludes all other remedies on reclamation). UCC 2-702

to the lien—or when the buyer obtains possession fraudulently.

Consider the following illustration. Williams, the plaintiff, sold his Chevrolet sedan to the Greers, the defendants. The defendants paid $4,280 by check and $400 in cash. After the Greers received possession of the Chevrolet, they stopped payment on the check. Williams went to court to regain possession of the auto by enforcing his seller's lien. The court upheld his complaint, allowing him to regain possession of the auto and to keep it until the Greers paid the $4,280. Essentially, the Greers had obtained possession fraudulently; therefore, they had a voidable title. Williams could validly enforce his lien because he had the right to void the title.

REMEDIES OF THE BUYER

Under the UCC, the remedies available to the buyer include:

1. The right to reject nonconforming or improperly delivered goods.
2. The right to recover identified goods upon the seller's insolvency.
3. The right to obtain specific performance.

4. The right to replevy the goods.
5. The right to retain the goods and enforce a security interest in them.
6. The right to cancel the contract.
7. The right of cover.
8. The right to recover damages for nondelivery or repudiation by the seller.
9. The right to recover damages for breach in regard to accepted goods.

The Right to Reject Nonconforming or Improperly Delivered Goods

If either the goods or the seller's tender of the goods fails to conform to the contract *in any respect,* the buyer can reject the goods. If some of the goods conform to the contract, the buyer can keep the conforming goods and reject the rest [UCC 2-601].

TIMELINESS AND REASON FOR REJECTION REQUIRED Goods must be rejected within a reasonable time and the seller must be seasonably notified [UCC 2-602]. Recall that notification is seasonable if it occurs before there is any substantial change in the goods not caused by their own defects—for example, before perishable goods perish. Furthermore, the buyer must designate particular defects that are ascertainable by reasonable inspection. Failure to do so precludes the buyer from using such defects to justify rejection or to establish breach when the seller could have cured the defects if they had been stated seasonably [UCC 2-605]. After rejecting the goods, the buyer cannot exercise any right of ownership over them. If the buyer acts inconsistently with the seller's ownership rights, the buyer will be deemed to have accepted the goods [UCC 2-606].

MERCHANT BUYER'S DUTIES WHEN GOODS ARE REJECTED

If a *merchant buyer* rightfully rejects goods, and the seller has no agent or business at the place of rejection, the buyer is required to follow any reasonable instructions received from the seller with respect to the goods controlled by the buyer. The buyer is entitled to reimbursement for the care and cost entailed in following the instructions [UCC 2-603]. The same requirement holds if the buyer rightfully revokes acceptance [UCC 2-608(3)].

If no instructions are forthcoming and the goods are perishable or threaten to decline in value quickly, the buyer can resell the goods in good faith, taking the appropriate reimbursement from the proceeds [UCC 2-603(1)]. If the goods are not perishable, the buyer may store them for the seller's account or reship them to the seller [UCC 2-604].

The Right to Recover Identified Goods from an Insolvent Seller

If a buyer has made a partial or a full payment for goods that remain in the possession of the seller, the buyer can recover the goods if the seller becomes insolvent within ten days after receiving the first payment and if the goods are identified to the contract. To exercise this right, the buyer must tender to the seller any unpaid balance of the purchase price [UCC 2-502].

The Right to Obtain Specific Performance

A buyer can obtain specific performance when the goods are unique or in other proper circumstances [UCC 2-716(1)]. Although it is not stated in this section of the Code, an award of specific performance is usually considered inappropriate unless the buyer's remedy at law is inadequate. Ordinarily, a suit for money damages will be sufficient to place a buyer in the position he or she would have occupied if the seller had fully performed. However, when the contract is for the purchase of a particular work of art, patent, copyright, or similarly unique item, money damages may not be sufficient. Under these circumstances, equity will require the seller to perform exactly (a remedy of specific performance) by delivering the unique goods.

To illustrate: Casey contracts to sell an antique car to Hammer for $30,000, with delivery and payment due on June 14. Hammer tenders payment on June 14, but Casey refuses to deliver. Can Hammer force delivery of the car? Probably, because the antique car is unique. Therefore, Hammer can obtain specific performance of the contract from Casey.

The Right to Replevy the Goods

Closely associated with a buyer's right to obtain specific performance is a buyer's right to replevy the goods. **Replevin** is an action to recover goods that are identifiable to the contract and that are in the hands of a breaching party who is unlawfully withholding them from the other party. The buyer can replevy the goods if the seller has repudiated or breached the contract. Additionally, buyers must usually show that they were *unable to cover*. As will be discussed below, *cover* is the right of a buyer, after the seller's breach, to purchase goods in substitution for those due under the contract; but the purchase must be made in good faith and without unreasonable delay [UCC 2-716(3)].

Consider the following example. On July 1, Salvador contracts to sell her tomato crop to Bryan, with delivery and payment due on August 10. By August 1, it is clear that the local tomato crop will be bad and that the price of tomatoes is going to rise. Salvador contracts to sell her tomato crop to Green for a higher price and then informs Bryan that she will not deliver on August 10 as agreed. Bryan indicates that cover is unavailable and that he is therefore going to bring a replevin action against Salvador to force her to deliver her tomatoes to him on August 10.

This replevin action will normally succeed. Although a tomato crop is not unique, a buyer of goods identifiable to the contract for which no cover is available has a right to a replevin. In a normal tomato year, cover would probably have been available, and Bryan would have been limited to an action for damages.

The Right to Retain and Enforce a Security Interest in the Goods

Buyers who rightfully reject goods or who justifiably revoke acceptance of goods that remain in their possession or control have a security interest in the goods (basically, a lien to recover expenses, costs, and the like). The security interest encompasses any payments the buyer has made for the goods as well as any expenses incurred with regard to inspection, receipt, transportation, care, and custody of the goods [UCC 2-711(3)]. A buyer with a security interest in the goods is a "person in the position of a seller." This gives the buyer the same rights as an unpaid seller. Thus, the buyer can resell, withhold delivery, or stop delivery of the goods. A buyer who chooses to resell must account to the seller for any amounts received in excess of the amount of the security interest [UCC 2-711(3), 2-706(6)].

The Right to Cancel the Contract

When a seller fails to make proper delivery or repudiates the contract, the buyer can cancel or rescind the contract. In addition, a buyer who has rightfully rejected or revoked acceptance of the goods can cancel or rescind. Under these circumstances, the buyer can cancel or rescind that portion of the contract directly involved in the breach. If the seller's breach is material and substantially impairs the value of the whole contract, the buyer can cancel or rescind the whole contract. Upon notice of cancellation, the buyer is relieved of any further obligations under the contract but still retains all remedy rights that can be assessed against the seller.

The Right of Cover

In certain situations, buyers can protect themselves by obtaining *cover* (by purchasing goods in substitution for those due under the contract). This option is available to a buyer who has rightfully rejected goods or revoked acceptance. It is also available when the seller repudiates the contract or fails to deliver the goods. In obtaining cover,

the buyer must act in good faith without unreasonable delay [UCC 2-712].

After purchasing substitute goods, the buyer can recover from the seller the difference between the cost of cover and the contract price, plus incidental and consequential damages less the expenses (such as delivery costs) that were saved as a result of the seller's breach [UCC 2-712, 2-715]. Consequential damages include any loss suffered by the buyer that the seller could have foreseen at the time of contract and any injury to the buyer's person or property proximately resulting from a breach of warranty[3] [UCC 2-715(2)].

Suppose Samms contracts to sell Byerly 10,000 pounds of sugar at 20 cents per pound. Delivery is to be on or before November 15. Samms knows that Byerly is going to use the sugar to make candy for Christmas sales. Byerly usually makes a $15,000 profit from these sales. Samms fails to deliver on November 15. Byerly attempts to purchase the sugar on the open market, but she must pay 30 cents per pound and take delivery on December 8. Because of this late delivery date, Byerly can prepare and sell only half as much Christmas candy as usual.

Byerly can recover from Samms the difference between the cover price and the contract price of sugar ($3,000 − $2,000 = $1,000) plus any incidental damages (costs incurred in effecting the cover). In addition, since Samms knew the reason for Byerly's purchase, Byerly is entitled to consequential damages. In this case, Byerly could probably include as part of her damages against Samms the lost profits from the Christmas candy sales ($7,500—half of the $15,000 profit usually made).

Buyers are not required to cover, and failure to cover will not bar them from using any other remedies that are available under the UCC [UCC 2-712(3)]. But a buyer who fails to cover when it is reasonably possible to do so may *not* be able to collect consequential damages that he or she could have avoided by purchasing substitute goods [UCC 2-715(2)(a)]. Thus, the UCC encourages buyers to cover in order to mitigate damages. For ex-

---

3. *Warranties*, which are discussed more fully in Chapter 20, may be defined generally as a seller's statements or representations referring to the character, quality, or title of his or her goods and constituting part of the contract of sale. Under the UCC, certain warranties are implied in a sale of goods.

ample, if a wholesaler is supposed to supply a grocer with eggs for resale and the wholesaler is unable to deliver them, the grocer has the option of covering. If the grocer covers, he or she can recover any lost profits resulting from the wholesaler's breach of the contract. If the grocer does not cover and has no eggs to sell, he or she cannot recover lost profits to the extent that cover could have reasonably prevented their loss.

The Right to Recover Damages for Nondelivery or Repudiation

If a seller repudiates the sales contract or fails to deliver the goods, the buyer can sue for damages. The measure of recovery is the difference between the contract price and the market price of the goods at the time that the buyer *learned* of the breach. The market price is determined at the place where the seller was supposed to deliver the goods. In some cases, the buyer can also recover incidental and consequential damages less the expenses that were saved as a result of the seller's breach [UCC 2-713]. Note that the damages here are based upon the time and place a buyer would normally obtain cover.

Consider an example. Billings orders 10,000 bushels of wheat from Sneed for $5 a bushel, with delivery due on June 14 and payment due on June 20. Sneed does not deliver on June 14. On June 14, the market price of wheat is $5.50 per bushel.

Billings chooses to do without the wheat. He sues Sneed for damages for nondelivery. Billings can recover $5,000 plus any expenses the breach may have caused him to incur. Here, the measure of damages is the market price less the contract price at the date that Billings was to have received delivery. (Any expenses Billings saved by the breach would have to be deducted from the damages.)

The Right to Recover Damages for Breach in Regard to Accepted Goods

A buyer who has accepted nonconforming goods must notify the seller of the breach within a reasonable time after the defect was or should have been discovered. Otherwise, the buyer cannot complain about defects in the goods [UCC 2-607(3)]. In addition, the parties to a sales contract can insert a provision requiring the buyer to give notice of any defects in the goods within a certain prescribed period. Such a requirement is ordinarily binding on the parties.

MEASURE OF DAMAGES IF A WARRANTY IS BREACHED   When the seller breaches a warranty, the measure of damages equals the difference between the value of the goods as accepted and their value if they had been as warranted. The measure of damages under UCC 2-714 when the seller breaches a warranty is illustrated by the following case.

Case 19.2

CHATLOS SYSTEMS, INC. v. NATIONAL CASH REGISTER CORP.

United States Court of Appeals, Third Circuit, 1982. 670 F.2d 1304.

BACKGROUND AND FACTS   *Chatlos Systems (plaintiff) purchased a computer from National Cash Register (defendant) for $46,020, a bargain price. The computer failed to operate as National Cash Register had warranted, and Chatlos sued for damages. Applying UCC 2-714(2), the trial judge found that the value of the system delivered was $6,000 and the fair market value of the system that would perform as National Cash Register had warranted was $207,826. A judgment was rendered for Chatlos for $201,826, plus prejudgment interest (that is, interest on the award of $201,826 calculated from the date that the system was delivered). National Cash Register appealed, contending that basing damages on the value of computers to the plaintiff rather than on the contract price was "substituting a Rolls Royce for a Ford."*

PER CURIAM [by the whole court].
*   *   *   *

Appellee did not order, nor was it promised, merely a specific NCR computer model, but an NCR computer system with specified capabilities. The correct measure of damages *   *   * is the difference between the fair market value of the goods accepted and the value they would have had if they had been as warranted. Award of that sum is not confined to instances where there has been an increase in value between date of ordering and date of delivery. It may also include the benefit of a contract price which, for whatever reason quoted, was particularly favorable for the customer. Evidence of the contract price may be relevant to the issue of fair market value, but it is not controlling. Appellant limited its fair market value analysis to the contract price of the computer model it actually delivered. Appellee developed evidence of the worth of a computer with the capabilities promised by NCR, and the trial court properly credited the evidence.

Appellee was aided, moreover, by the testimony of Frank Hicks, NCR's programmer, who said that he told his company's officials that the "current software was not sufficient in order to deliver the program that the customer [Chatlos] required. They would have to be rewritten or a different system would have to be given to the customer." Hicks recommended that Chatlos be given an NCR 8200 but was told, "that will not be done." Gerald Greenstein, another NCR witness, admitted that the 8200 series was two levels above the 399 in sophistication and price. This testimony supported Brandon's [Chatlos' expert witness] statement that the price of the hardware needed to perform Chatlos' requirements would be in the $100,000 to $150,000 range.

Essentially, then, the trial judge was confronted with the conflicting value estimates submitted by the parties. Chatlos' expert's estimates were corroborated to some extent by NCR's supporters. NCR, on the other hand, chose to rely on contract price. Credibility determinations had to be made by the district judge. * * *

Upon reviewing the evidence of record, therefore, we conclude that the computation of damages for breach of warranty was not clearly erroneous.

The judgment of the district court in favor of Chatlos was affirmed.

DECISION AND REMEDY

COMMENTS

The general purpose of the remedies in the UCC is to put the aggrieved party "in as good a position as if the other party had fully performed" [UCC 1-106(1)]. Chatlos was promised a system that was worth $207,826, but the system delivered was worth only $6,000. Thus, in order to put the company in as good a position as if National Cash Register had performed, Chatlos would have to be awarded $201,826 [UCC 2-714(2)].

SUIT BY A BUYER'S CUSTOMER RESULTING FROM THE SELLER'S BREACH OF WARRANTY When a buyer resells defective goods that were originally sold by a breaching seller, the buyer's customer can sue the buyer. Under these circumstances the buyer has two alternatives:

1. The buyer can notify the seller of the pending litigation. The notice should state that the seller can come into the action against the buyer and defend. The notice should also point out that if, after seasonable receipt of the notice, the seller does not come in, the seller may nevertheless be bound by determinations of fact in the customer's action against the buyer. If the buyer brings a subsequent action against the seller, the seller cannot relitigate factual issues that are common to both the buyer's action against the seller and the buyer's customer's action against the buyer and

that were determined in the customer's action [UCC 2-607(5)(a)].

2. The buyer can also defend against the customer's suit and later bring an action against the original seller. This situation arises most frequently when there is a manufacturer-dealer arrangement—for example, where a car dealer sells a defective automobile and the customer sues the dealer but not the manufacturer.

OTHER MEASURES OF DAMAGES The Code also allows for two additional methods or remedies for damages for accepted goods. Both can also be applied when there has been a breach of warranty.

The first applies when the buyer has accepted nonconforming goods. The buyer is entitled to recover for any loss "resulting in the ordinary course of events * * * as determined in any manner which is reasonable." Thus, this remedy

CONCEPT SUMMARY: Buyer's Remedies For Seller's Breach	
SITUATIONS	**BUYER'S REMEDIES** The remedies available to a buyer are basically determined by the facts of the situation.
Seller refuses to deliver, or seller tenders nonconforming goods and buyer rejects them	1. Cancel and, with notice, rescind. UCC 2-711 2. Cover. UCC 2-712 3. Sue for breach of contract. UCC 2-713
Seller tenders nonconforming goods and buyer accepts them	1. Sue for ordinary damages. UCC 2-714(1) 2. Sue for breach of warranty. UCC 2-714(2) 3. Deduct damages from the price of the goods. UCC 2-717
Seller refuses delivery and buyer wants the goods	1. Sue for specific performance. UCC 2-716(1) 2. Exercise right of replevin. UCC 2-716(3) 3. Recover goods from seller on seller's insolvency (when the buyer has paid part or all of the purchase price). UCC 2-502

is available for both a breach of warranty situation and any other failure of the seller to perform according to the contractual obligations [UCC 2-714(1)].

The second remedy is extremely important to a buyer, as the buyer not only has possession of the goods but also determines the amount of damages. The UCC permits the buyer, with proper notice to the seller, to deduct all or any part of the damages from the price still due and payable to the seller [UCC 2-717].

Suppose Reese is under contract to deliver 100 pairs of dress shoes at $50 each to Boone. The shoes are tendered, and upon inspection Boone discovers that 10 pairs are high-quality work shoes, not dress shoes. Boone accepts all 100 pairs and notifies Reese of the breach. At the time for contracted payment by Boone, Boone notifies Reese that she will not be able to sell the work shoes as quickly or for the same price or profit as the dress shoes and that she is tendering a check for $4,750 instead of the full $5,000 to reflect this loss. If Reese accepts and cashes Boone's check, Boone's measurement of damages is final.

When the buyer still has the goods, a court will have to consider whether to award damages in an amount calculated according to the basic formula in UCC 2-714(2), when the circumstances may indicate some other amount.

STATUTE OF LIMITATIONS FOR ACTIONS BROUGHT UNDER THE UNIFORM COMMERCIAL CODE

An action brought by a buyer or seller for breach of contract must be commenced under the Code *within four years after the cause of action accrues*. In addition to filing suit within the four-year period, an aggrieved party must ordinarily notify the breaching party of a defect within a reasonable time [UCC 2-607(3)(a)]. By agreement in the contract, the parties can reduce this period to not less than one year, but they cannot extend the period beyond the stated four years [UCC 2-725(1)].

A cause of action accrues for breach of warranty when the seller makes *tender* of delivery. This is the rule even if the aggrieved party is unaware that the cause of action has accrued [UCC 2-725(2)]. Remember, tender of delivery takes place in a shipment contract upon delivery of the goods to the carrier and in a destination contract upon tender of the goods at the specified destination delivery location. The one-year limitation in these cases may have a tremendous impact if the goods purchased are going to be stored primarily for future use. To avoid this impact, the Code provides that when a warranty explicitly extends to future performance, discovery of its breach must await the time of that performance [UCC 2-725(2)]. The statute of limitations also begins to run at that time.

For example, Hoover purchases a central air-conditioning unit for his restaurant. The unit is warranted to keep the temperature below a certain level. The unit is installed in the winter, but when summer comes, the restaurant does not stay cool. Therefore, discovery of the warranty's breach is made in the summer and not when the unit was delivered in the winter. The statute of limitations does not begin to run until the summer.

The following case illustrates how the expectation of the parties extends the time of warranty performance to a future date for statute of limitation purposes.

BACKGROUND AND FACTS *Puget Sound Plywood, Inc., manufactured certain lauan siding that Dennis and Lois Moore purchased during the construction of their house in 1970–71. By October 1977, the Moores had noticed some "problems" with the appearance of the siding. The problem, delamination, resulted because the particular species of lauan tree used in making the siding was not susceptible to being glued with the resin that Puget Sound used. The Moores began investigating a remedy for the situation in 1979, but they had difficulty determining who had manufactured the siding. An action was filed in April of 1981. The Moores alleged damages of $4,550, but two lower courts dismissed their case, holding that the period of limitations had lapsed. The Moores appealed.*

Case 19.3
MOORE v. PUGET SOUND PLYWOOD, INC.
Supreme Court of Nebraska, 1983.
214 Neb. 14, 332 N.W.2d 212.

CAPORALE, Justice.
* * * *

This analysis is required by reason of the operation of Neb. U.C.C. § 2-313(1)(b) as delineated in *England v. Leithoff*, decided after the municipal court trials herein. That opinion foreshadows the outcome of this case. We held therein that an oral representation concerning the origin of goods, made in the course of a sale, constitutes an express warranty under § 2-313(1)(b), which provides, among other things, that any description of goods which becomes a part of the basis of the bargain creates an express warranty that the goods shall conform to the description. According to the parties, the description of the goods as "siding" carried with it the representation that it would last the lifetime of the house. Therefore, the requisite elements of § 2-313(1)(b) are present; that is, the description of the goods became a part of the bargain and created in the minds of the parties the expectation that the siding would last the lifetime of the house. Section 2-725(2) provides in part: "A breach of warranty occurs when tender of delivery is made, except that where a warranty explicitly extends to future performance of the goods and discovery of the breach must await the time of such performance the cause of action accrues when the breach is or should have been discovered." The instant breach did not occur upon tender of delivery since, in light of the expectations of the parties, the warranty herein necessarily extended explicitly to future performance.

The case * * * relied upon by Puget Sound is not factually apposite here. Therein, discovery could, and in fact did, occur shortly after completion of the construction project; that is, the plaintiff knew about the defect prior to the tolling of the period of limitations but failed to act until after it had tolled. In this case, discovery could occur at any time between installation and the "life" of the house. The Moores acted within a reasonable period of time after they discovered the latent defect.

DECISION
AND REMEDY
The Supreme Court of Nebraska agreed with the Moores that the two lower courts were in error. The court remanded the case with instructions that a judgment be entered in favor of the Moores in the sum of $4,550.

Actions Not Falling within the Uniform Commercial Code

When a buyer or seller brings suit on a legal theory unrelated to the Code, the limitations periods specified above do not apply, even though the claim relates to goods.

For example, Nilsson buys tires for his automobile. The tires prove to have an inherently dangerous defect. Four years and one month after purchasing the tires, Nilsson loses control of the car and injures several passengers as well as himself. Nilsson can bring a suit against the tire manufacturer based on strict liability in tort. The suit will not be governed by the Code's statute of limitations but rather by the state's tort statute of limitations.

CONTRACTUAL PROVISIONS AFFECTING REMEDIES

The parties to a sales contract can vary their respective rights and obligations by contractual agreement. Certain restrictions are placed on the ability of parties to contract to limit their rights and remedies under the Code, but provisions that the parties frequently include are:

1. The liquidation or limitation of damages.
2. The limitation of remedies.
3. The waiver of defenses.

Liquidated Damages and Limitation of Damages

The parties can provide that a specified amount of damages will be paid in the event that either party breaches. These damages, called *liquidated damages,* must be reasonable in amount in view of the anticipated or actual loss caused by the breach, the difficulties of proof of loss, and the inconvenience or nonfeasibility of otherwise obtaining an adequate remedy. If the provision is valid, the aggrieved party is limited to recovering the amount of damages agreed on. If the amount of liquidated damages is unreasonably large, the provision is void as a penalty, and the court will determine the appropriate amount of damages [UCC 2-718].

Consider as an example the sale of an uncommon antique. Seuss contracts with Barnes to sell it for $3,000. The contract contains a liquidated damages clause that holds the breaching party liable for $1,000 in case of a breach by either party. Payment and delivery of the antique are due on January 1. Barnes tenders payment on that date, but Seuss refuses to deliver for no valid reason. Can Barnes demand $1,000 in damages? Because we are dealing with an uncommon antique, Barnes will probably be able to recover. Seuss's breach might cause Barnes a loss of $1,000 in that the object in question is probably not easily acquired on the open market for the price of $3,000. If, instead, the object in question were easily obtainable for the agreed price, then Barnes probably would not be able to recover the $1,000. The normal measure of damages would then be the market price of the object less the contract price. The $1,000 damage clause in the contract would, in essence, be imposing a penalty upon Seuss and therefore would be void under UCC 2-718(1). The court could determine that a smaller damage amount was appropriate, however.

A buyer often makes a down payment when a contract is executed. If the buyer defaults and the contract contains a liquidated damages provision, the seller retains the down payment as damages, and the buyer can recover only the part of the down payment that exceeded the amount specified as liquidated damages. The buyer is entitled to this sum as restitution. If the contract contains no provision for liquidated damages, the seller's damages are deemed to be 20 percent of the purchase price or $500, whichever is less [UCC 2-718(2)(b)]. The amount by which the buyer's down payment exceeds this sum must be returned to the buyer. If the seller can prove that his or her actual damages are higher, the buyer can recover only the excess over the seller's actual damages.

For example, Rieken pays $1,250 down on a $10,000 lathe. Rieken then breaches, and Shaneyfelt, the seller, offers no proof of the actual damages. In the absence of a liquidated damages clause, Rieken is entitled to restitution of $750 ($1,250 less $500). If Rieken had put $350 down on a $500 lathe, he would have been entitled to $250 ($350 less $100, which is 20 percent of the purchase price).

Limitation of Remedies

A seller and a buyer can expressly provide for remedies in addition to those provided in the Code. They can also provide for remedies in lieu of those provided in the Code, or they can change the measure of damages. The seller can provide that the buyer's only remedy upon breach of warranty will be repair or replacement of the item, or the seller can limit the buyer's remedy to return of the goods and refund of the purchase price. A remedy that is so provided is in addition to remedies provided in the Code unless the parties expressly agree that the remedy is exclusive of all others [UCC 2-719(1)].

If the parties state that a remedy is exclusive of all other remedies, then it is the sole remedy. But when circumstances cause an exclusive remedy to fail in its essential purpose, the remedy will no longer be exclusive [UCC 2-719(2)]. For example, a sales contract that limits the buyer's remedy to repair or replacement fails in its essential purpose if the item cannot be repaired and no replacements are available. Of course, any clause limiting remedies in an unconscionable manner is void.

Suppose Bing buys a motorcycle from merchant Simple. The sales contract is accompanied by an express warranty stating that the exclusive remedy is repair or replacement of defective parts. The contract explicitly provides that Simple will not be responsible for consequential loss. Bing discovers numerous defects in her motorcycle after only a few days' use. After discovering each defect, she returns the motorcycle for repairs. Some of the parts are out of stock and will take months to arrive at Simple's repair station. Bing sues Simple. A trier of fact in this situation may return a verdict for Bing in an amount far exceeding the cost of repairs. The reason is that the exclusive remedy of repair or replacement of defective parts would have failed in its essential purpose, since the motorcycle could not operate as it should have, free of defects.

In the following case, the court examines a limitation clause concerning *when* a claim can be brought for inferior-quality wool.

BACKGROUND AND FACTS *Wilson Trading Corp. entered into a contract with David Ferguson, Ltd., for the sale of yarn. A clause in the contract stated that "no claims relating to excessive moisture content, short weight, count variations, twist, quality or shade shall be allowed if made after weaving, knitting, or processing, or more than 10 days after receipt of shipment." In an apparent contradiction to this clause, defendant David Ferguson, Ltd., failed to make payment because, according to the defendant, after the yarn had been cut and knitted into sweaters and then washed, the color changed in a way that made the sweaters unmarketable. At trial, plaintiff Wilson Trading Corp. won summary judgment for the contract price of the yarn, on the ground that the notice of the alleged breach of warranty for defect in the coloration of the yarn was not given within the time expressly limited by the contract. The appellate division affirmed the trial court's decision without an opinion, and the buyer appealed.*

Case 19.4
WILSON TRADING CORP. v. DAVID FERGUSON, LTD.
Court of Appeals of New York 1968.
23 N.Y.2d 398, 244 N.E.2d 685, 297 N.Y.S.2d 108.

JASEN, Judge.
*   *   *   *

    *   *   * [S]ection 2-719 (subd. [2]) of the Uniform Commercial Code provides that the general remedy provisions of the code apply when "circumstances cause an

exclusive or limited remedy to fail of its essential purpose." As explained by the official comments to this section: "where an apparently fair and reasonable clause because of circumstances fails in its purpose or operates to deprive either party of the substantial value of the bargain, it must give way to the general remedy provisions of this article." (Uniform Commercial Code, § 2-719, official comment 1.) Here, paragraph 2 of the contract bars all claims for shade and other specified defects made after knitting and processing. Its effect is to eliminate any remedy for shade defects not reasonably discoverable within the time limitation period. It is true that parties may set by agreement any time not manifestly unreasonable whenever the code "requires any action to be taken within a reasonable time" (Uniform Commercial Code, § 1-204, subd. [1]), but here the time provision eliminates all remedy for defects not discoverable before knitting and processing and section 2-719 (subd. [2]) of the Uniform Commercial Code therefore applies.

Defendant's affidavits allege that sweaters manufactured from the yarn were rendered unmarketable because of latent shading defects not reasonably discoverable before knitting and processing of the yarn into sweaters. If these factual allegations are established at trial, the limited remedy established by paragraph 2 has failed its "essential purpose" and the buyer is, in effect, without remedy. The time limitation clause of the contract, therefore, insofar as it applies to defects not reasonably discoverable within the time limits established by the contract, must give way to the general code rule that a buyer has a reasonable time to notify the seller of breach of contract after he discovers or should have discovered the defect. (Uniform Commercial Code, § 2-607, subd. [3], par. [a].) * * *

In sum, there are factual issues for trial concerning whether the shading defects alleged were discoverable before knitting and processing, and, if not, whether notice of the defects was given within a reasonable time after the defects were or should have been discovered. If the shading defects were not reasonably discoverable before knitting and processing and notice was given within a reasonable time after the defects were or should have been discovered, a further factual issue of whether the sweaters were rendered unsaleable because of the defect is presented for trial.

DECISION AND REMEDY   *The judgment in favor of the seller was reversed. The case was remanded for a new trial.*

LIMITING CONSEQUENTIAL DAMAGES A contract can limit or exclude consequential damages provided the limitation is not unconscionable. When the buyer is a consumer, the limitation of consequential damages for personal injuries resulting from a breach of warranty is *prima facie* unconscionable. The limitation of consequential damages is not necessarily unconscionable when the loss is commercial in nature—for example, lost profits and property damage [UCC 2-719(3)].

Waiver of Defenses

A buyer can be precluded from objecting to a breach of warranty by a seller in certain situations. For example, when a buyer purchases on credit, the seller usually assigns the note or account to a financial institution in order to obtain ready cash. To facilitate the assignment of these notes or accounts, the seller will include a waiver of defense clause in the sales contract. By entering into the contract, the buyer agrees not to assert against the assignee defenses that may apply to the seller. In essence, the buyer must complain directly to the seller, and the buyer cannot withhold payment for breach of warranty. Thus, this waiver—if enforceable—would give the assignee rights similar to those of a **holder in due course** (a purchaser who took the note in good faith, for value, and without notice of any claims or defenses against it, as described in Chapter 25), and no personal defense could be asserted against the assignee [UCC 9-206].

In such cases, buyers are in the same position as if they had signed a waiver. Because of this, many states, including those that have adopted the Uniform Consumer Credit Code, have invalidated such clauses in sales contracts for consumer goods. In addition, Federal Trade Commission rules provide that in consumer purchases on credit, any personal defense of the debtor-buyer against the seller is equally applicable against *any* holder, including a holder in due course. Therefore, these clauses are invalid in consumer transactions.

LEMON LAWS

Some purchasers of automobiles found that the remedies provided by the UCC, after limitations had been imposed by the seller, were inadequate when they purchased an automobile that proved to be defective, or what is sometimes called a "lemon." In response to the frustrations of these buyers, many state legislatures during the early 1980s enacted *lemon laws*. The majority of the states have enacted such laws.

Basically, lemon laws provide that if an automobile under warranty possesses a defect that significantly affects the vehicle's value or use, and the defect has not been remedied by the seller within a specified number of opportunities (usually four), the buyer is entitled to a new car, replacement of defective parts, or return of all consideration paid.

Because disputes arise concerning these criteria, most state statutes require the aggrieved purchaser to state his or her case before an appeal jury. Appeal juries are arbitration panels designated or sponsored by automobile manufacturers. Their decisions are binding on the manufacturer (that is, cannot be appealed by the manufacturer to the courts) but not usually on the purchaser. To date, car manufacturers have set up a network of appeal juries to hear purchasers' complaints. For example, General Motors has contracted with numerous Better Business Bureaus throughout the United States to act as appeal juries.

 QUESTIONS AND CASE PROBLEMS

1. Scopes contracts to ship Keen via Quickway Truck Line 100 cases of Knee High brand corn, F.O.B. Keen's city, at $6.50 per case. Keen is to make a 10-percent down payment. The payment is to be received at Scopes's place of business before shipment occurs. Scopes ships the corn as contracted, although he has not yet received the down payment, and the goods arrive in Keen's city. There they remain in the delivery van. Since Keen has failed to make the down payment, Scopes orders Quickway not to make the delivery to Keen's warehouse. Keen claims that the transit has ended and that Scopes has no right to stop the delivery of the corn. Discuss the validity of Keen's claim and Scopes's action.

2. Bullard has contracted to sell Lorwin 500 washing machines of a certain model at list price. Bullard is to ship the goods on or before December 1. Bullard produces 1,000 washing machines of this model but has not yet prepared Lorwin's shipment. On November 1, Lorwin repudiates the contract. Discuss the remedies available to Bullard.

3. Roy has contracted with Schnee for the purchase and delivery of 100 Model Z dryers. At the time for that contracted tender, Schnee tenders 80 Model Z dryers and 20 Model X dryers. Schnee does not have 100 Model Z dryers in stock and does not expect to acquire any for at least three months. Roy wants 100 Model Z dryers or none at all. Discuss the remedies available to Roy under these circumstances.

4. McDonald has contracted to purchase 500 pairs of shoes from Vetter. Vetter manufactures the shoes and tenders delivery to McDonald. McDonald accepts the shipment. Later, upon inspection, McDonald discovers that 10 pairs of the shoes are poorly made and will have to be sold to customers as seconds. If McDonald decides to keep all 500 pairs of shoes, what remedies are available to her?

5. Lehor is an antique car collector. He contracts to purchase spare parts for a 1938 engine from Beem. These parts are not made any more and are scarce. To get the contract with Beem, Lehor has agreed to pay 50 percent of the purchase price in advance. On May 1, Lehor sends the payment, which is received on May 2. On May 3, Beem, having found another buyer willing to pay substantially more for the parts, informs Lehor that he will not deliver as contracted. That same day, Lehor learns that Beem is insolvent. Beem has the parts, and Lehor wants them. Discuss fully any possible remedies available to Lehor to get these parts.

6. In a contract between Associated Metals & Minerals Corp. and Kaiser Trading Company, Associated promised to deliver to Kaiser 4,000 tons of cryolite over the next sixteen months. After Associated had delivered about one-eighth of the cryolite to Kaiser, it repudiated the contract.

Kaiser sought to enforce the contract and requested the court to grant it specific performance against Associated. Kaiser presented convincing proof at trial that only a few hundred tons of cryolite were available on the open market and that Kaiser needed the 4,000 tons that Associated had promised to deliver in order for Kaiser to fulfill its contractual obligations to a number of other industrial companies. Should the court grant specific performance in this case? [Kaiser Trading Co. v. Associated Metals and Minerals Corp., 321 F.Supp. 923 (N.D.Cal. 1970)]

7. Kaiden placed a $5,000 deposit on a Rolls-Royce in August. The order form did not specify a delivery date, but correspondence between the parties indicated delivery was expected in November. On November 21, Kaiden notified the automobile dealer that she had purchased another Rolls-Royce elsewhere and requested a refund of her deposit. Under the liquidated damages clause of the written contract, the dealer was to retain the entire cash deposit in the event of a breach by the purchaser. The car was sold before Kaiden brought suit to recover her deposit. The dealer's actual damages amounted to $2,075. Should the court allow the dealer to retain the $5,000? [Lee Oldsmobile, Inc. v. Kaiden, 32 Md.App. 556, 363 A.2d 270 (1976)]

8. Rancher Baden purchased bull semen from Curtiss Breeding to use for artificial insemination. The semen was defective, so no calves were born. When Baden sued Curtiss, he contended that his consequential damages should include not only the value of the calf crop not born that year but also the value of the calf crop that would have been born the following year from the first calf crop. Should Baden be awarded these additional consequential damages? [Baden v. Curtiss Breeding Service, 380 F.Supp. 243 (D.Mont. 1974)]

9. Lupofresh, Inc., the plaintiff, contracted to sell a quantity of hops to the defendant Pabst Brewing Company. Lupofresh processed the hops and notified Pabst that the hops were ready for shipment. Pabst responded with a letter indicating acceptance of the hops but later refused to issue shipping orders, claiming that the price determination violated antitrust laws. Lupofresh sued for the full purchase price under UCC 2-709(1)(a). Pabst claimed that the goods had not been accepted but merely identified to the contract and that Lupofresh was required to attempt to resell the hops before it was entitled to recover the purchase price. Discuss fully who was correct. [Lupofresh, Inc. v. Pabst Brewing Co., 505 A.2d 37 (Super.Ct.Del. 1985)]

10. In July 1976, Engineering Measurements Company (EMCO) agreed to manufacture and deliver to International Technical Instruments (ITI) a specified number of optical communication links (an optical communication link is a device that allows wireless communication between two points). The links were to be delivered in stated installments. During a seven-month period, ITI continually complained that EMCO had failed to meet delivery schedules and had delivered some defective units. ITI did not refuse any shipment during this period. ITI filed suit, claiming EMCO had breached its contract by failing to meet its delivery schedules and by delivering defective units. EMCO argued that ITI had accepted the goods and that by failing to revoke its acceptance and give notice, ITI was precluded from any remedy under UCC 2-607(3)(a). Discuss fully whether ITI was able to recover under its suit for breach of contract. [International Technical Instruments, Inc. v. Engineering Measurements Co., 678 P.2d 558 (Colo.App. 1983)]

11. Servbest Foods had a contract with Emessee whereby Emessee was to purchase 200,000 pounds of beef trimmings from Servbest at 52.5 cents per pound. Servbest delivered to Emessee the warehouse receipts and invoices for the beef trimmings. The price of beef trimmings then fell significantly, and Emessee returned the documents to Servbest and canceled the contract. Servbest then sold the beef trimmings for 20.25 cents per pound and sued Emessee for damages (the difference between the contract price and the market price at which it had been forced to sell the trimmings) for breach of contract, plus incidental damages. Discuss whether Servbest Foods exercised a proper remedy and was entitled to the damages alleged in its lawsuit. [Servbest Foods, Inc. v. Emessee Industries, Inc., 82 Ill.App.3d 662, 403 N.E.2d 1, 37 Ill.Dec. 945 (1980)]

12. Bigelow-Sanford, Inc., entered into a contract to buy 100,000 yards of jute at $0.64 per yard from Gunny Corp. Gunny delivered 22,228 yards to Bigelow but informed the company that no more would be delivered. Several other suppliers to Bigelow defaulted, and Bigelow was forced to go into the market one month later to purchase a total of 164,503 yards of jute for $1.21 per yard. Bigelow sued Gunny for the difference between the market price and the contract price of the amount of jute that Gunny had not delivered. Discuss whether Bigelow could recover this amount from Gunny. [Bigelow-Sanford, Inc. v. Gunny Corp., 649 F.2d 1060 (5th Cir. 1981)]

13. Mrs. French rather imprudently bid on eight antique guns for sale at Sotheby's auction in London, England, on March 22, 1965. The guns finally sold for $24,886.27. Mrs. French never took possession of the guns. Mrs. French could not make payment for the goods, and Sotheby sued for the balance due on the sale. Mrs. French argued that this was not the correct amount for a court to award because Sotheby could resell the guns. She claimed that, given the circumstances, the correct amount was the difference between the market price of the guns and French's contract price. Discuss what remedies are available to Sotheby. [French v. Sotheby & Co., 470 P.2d 318 (Ok. 1970)]

Chapter 20

SALES
Introduction to
Sales Warranties

In the past, *caveat emptor*—let the buyer beware—was the prevailing philosophy in sales contract law. This may not have been an unrealistic approach when buyers and sellers were more or less equally capable of judging the quality (or lack of it) of the goods that were the subjects of their bargains. In twentieth-century America, however, it is unlikely that any buyer will comprehend the workings of any but a few of the goods he or she purchases, much less grasp all of the risks and be able to assume them intelligently and pay for any resulting injuries or damage. Thus, *caveat emptor* has given way to a consumer-oriented approach. This change, of course, has not been without cost to consumers, who generally pay higher prices imposed by sellers and their insurers to cover their increased costs.

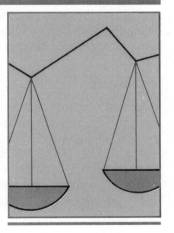

The concept of *warranty* is based upon the seller's assurance to the buyer that the goods will meet certain standards. The UCC designates five types of warranties that can arise in a sales contract:

1. Warranty of title [UCC 2-312].
2. Express warranty [UCC 2-313].
3. Implied warranty of merchantability [UCC 2-314].
4. Implied warranty of fitness for a particular purpose [UCC 2-315].
5. Implied warranty arising from the course of dealing or trade usage [UCC 2-314(3)].

In the law of sales, since a warranty imposes a duty upon the seller, a breach of warranty is a breach of the seller's promise. If the parties have not agreed to limit or modify the remedies available to the buyer on the seller's breach of warranty, the buyer can sue to recover damages against the seller. Under some circumstances, a breach can allow the buyer to rescind the agreement.[1]

WARRANTY OF TITLE

Title warranty arises automatically in most sales contracts. UCC 2-312 imposes three types of warranties of title.

---

1. Rescission can occur by rejection of goods before acceptance or by revocation by the buyer after acceptance.

Good Title

In most cases, sellers warrant that they have good and valid title to the goods sold and that transfer of the title is rightful [UCC 2-312(1)(a)]. For example, Alice steals goods from Ophelia and sells them to Betty, who does not know that they are stolen. If Ophelia discovers that Betty has the goods, then Ophelia has the right to reclaim them from Betty. Under this Code provision, however, Betty can then sue Alice for breach of warranty, because a thief has no title to stolen goods and thus cannot give good title in a subsequent sale. When Alice sold Betty the goods, Alice *automatically* warranted to Betty that the title conveyed was valid and that its transfer was rightful. Since this was not in fact the case, Alice breached the warranty of title imposed by UCC 2-312(1)(a) and became liable to the buyer for appropriate damages.

No Liens

A second warranty of title provided by the Code protects buyers who are *unaware* of any encumbrances (claims or liens) against goods at the time of the contract [UCC 2-312(1)(b)]. This warranty protects buyers who, for example, unknowingly purchase goods that are subject to a creditor's security interest. (See Chapter 29.) If a creditor legally repossesses the goods from a buyer who *had no actual knowledge of the security interest*, then the buyer can recover from the seller for a breach of warranty. (The buyer who has *actual knowledge* of a security interest has no recourse against a seller.)

To illustrate: Henderson buys a used color television set from Sneed for cash. A month later, Reynolds repossesses the set from Henderson, proving that she, Reynolds, has a valid security interest in the set. She proves that Sneed is in default, having missed five payments. Henderson demands his money back from Sneed. Under Section 2–312(2)(b), Henderson will be able to recover because the seller of goods warrants that the goods shall be delivered free from any security interest or other lien of which the buyer has no knowledge.

No Infringements

A third category of title warranty is the warranty against infringement. A merchant is deemed to warrant that the goods delivered are free from any

patent, trademark, or copyright claims of a third person[2] [UCC 2-312(3)]. If this warranty is breached and the buyer is sued by the claim holder, the buyer *must notify the seller* of litigation within a reasonable time to enable the seller to decide whether to defend the lawsuit. If the seller states in writing that he or she has decided to defend and agrees to bear all expenses, including that of an adverse judgment, then the buyer must let the seller undertake litigation; otherwise the buyer loses all rights against the seller if any infringement liability is established [UCC 2-607(3)(b), (5)(b)].

This infringement warranty does not apply to buyers who furnish specifications for goods to be made in a particular way. In fact, it is the buyer who must indemnify the seller against any third person's claims of infringement arising out of goods manufactured to the buyer's specifications [UCC 2-312(3)]. The same requirements of notice apply to a seller who is sued for breach of an infringement warranty for which the buyer is under an obligation in good faith to indemnify the seller for any loss suffered [UCC 2-607(6)].

To illustrate: Green orders a custom-made machine from Beryl, a manufacturer of such machines. It is built strictly to Green's specifications. While the machine is being built, Patton files a suit against Beryl for patent infringement. Beryl immediately informs Green in writing of this suit and demands that Green take over the expense of the litigation. Green refuses to do so. Beryl settles with Patton out of court by paying Patton modest damages. Beryl now wishes to be reimbursed by Green. Beryl will be able to collect because a buyer who orders custom-built goods from a seller and who furnishes the seller with the specifications warrants to the seller that the specifications do not infringe any patent.

Disclaimer of Title Warranty

In an ordinary sales transaction, the title warranty can be disclaimed or modified only by *specific language* in a contract. For example, sellers may assert that they are transferring only such rights, title, and interest as they have in the goods.

---

2. Recall from Chapter 16 that a *merchant* is defined in UCC 2-104(1) as a person who deals in goods of the kind involved in the sales contract or who, by occupation, presents himself or herself as having knowledge or skill peculiar to the goods involved in the transaction.

In certain cases, the circumstances of the sale are sufficient to indicate clearly to a buyer that no assurances as to title are being made. The classic example is a sheriff's sale, where buyers know that the goods have been seized to satisfy debts and it is apparent that the goods are not the property of the person selling them [UCC 2-312(2)].

EXPRESS WARRANTY

A seller can create an **express warranty** by making representations concerning the quality, condition, description, or performance potential of the goods. Under UCC 2-313, express warranties arise when a seller indicates that:

1. The goods will conform to any *affirmation or promise* of fact that the seller makes to the buyer about the goods. Such affirmations or promises are usually made during the bargaining process. Statements such as "These drill bits will *easily* penetrate stainless steel—and without dulling" constitute express warranties.

2. The goods will conform to any *description* of them—for example, in a label that states "crate contains one 150-horsepower diesel engine" or a contract that calls for delivery of a "camel's hair coat."

3. The goods will conform to any *sample* or *model*. For example, an express warranty arises when the sales representative of a textile firm says to a prospective customer, "The bolts of cloth we deliver will match this swatch."

Basis of the Bargain

The Code requires that for any express warranty to be created, the affirmation, promise, description, or sample must become part of the "basis of the bargain." Just what constitutes the basis of the bargain is hard to say. The Code does not define the concept, and each case presents a question of fact whether a representation came at such a time and in such a way that it induced the buyer to enter the contract.

Are certain vague telephone statements part of the basis of the bargain? That is the question addressed in the following case.

BACKGROUND AND FACTS   *Riegle sold a standard-bred race horse to Sessa for $25,000. Prior to the sale, Sessa sent a friend, Maloney, to examine the horse. Maloney reported that he "liked him." Additionally, during a telephone conversation, Riegle stated to Sessa that Sessa would like the horse and that he was a "good one" and "sound." After the sale had been consummated and after delivery, the horse almost immediately went lame in the hind legs. Experts were unable to identify the cause. They could not establish if the condition had been present before Riegle shipped the horse. Even though the horse—Tarport Conaway—was later able to race, Sessa sued for damages.*

Case 20.1
SESSA v. RIEGLE
United States District Court for the Eastern District of Pennsylvania, 1977.
427 F.Supp. 760, affirmed without opinion 568 F.2d 770 (3d Cir. 1978).

HANNUM, District Judge.
*   *   *   *

Sessa contends that certain statements made by Riegle during that conversation constitute express warranties on which Riegle is liable in this action. The most important of these is Riegle's alleged statement that, "The horse is sound," or words to that effect.

In deciding whether statements by a seller constitute express warranties, the court must look to UCC § 2-313 which presents three fundamental issues. First, the court must determine whether the seller's statement constitutes an "affirmation of fact or promise" or "description of the goods" under § 2-313(1)(a) or (b) or whether it is rather "merely the seller's opinion or commendation of the goods" under § 2-313(2). Second, assuming the court finds the language used susceptible to creation of a warranty, it must then be determined whether the statement was "part of the basis of the bargain." If it was, an express warranty exists and, as the third issue, the court must determine whether the warranty was breached.

With respect to the first issue, the court finds that in the circumstances of this case, words to the effect that "The horse is sound" spoken during the telephone conversation between Sessa and Riegle constitute an opinion or commendation rather than express warranty. This determination is a question for the trier of fact. There is nothing talismanic or thaumaturgic [magical or miraculous] about the use of the word "sound." Whether use of that language constitutes warranty, or mere opinion or commendation depends on the circumstances of the sale and the type of goods sold. While § 2-313 makes it clear that no specific words need be used and no specific intent need be present, not every statement by a seller is an express warranty.

*   *   *   *

Also mitigating against a finding of express warranty is the nature of the conversation between Sessa and Riegle. It seemed largely collateral to the sale rather than an essential part of it. Although Sessa testified that Riegle's "personal guarantee" given during the conversation was the quintessence of the sale, the credible evidence suggests otherwise. While on the telephone, Riegle made statements to the effect that "the horse is a good one" and "you will like him." These bland statements are obviously opinion or commendation, and the statement, "The horse is sound," falling within their penumbra takes on their character as such.

*   *   *   *

Even assuming that Riegle's statements could be express warranties, it is not at all clear that they were "part of the basis of the bargain," the second requisite of § 2-313. This is essentially a reliance requirement and is inextricably intertwined with the initial determination as to whether given language may constitute an express warranty since affirmations, promises, and descriptions tend to become part of the basis of the bargain. It was the intention of the drafters of the U.C.C. not to require a strong showing of reliance. In fact, they envisioned that all statements of the seller became part of the basis of the bargain unless clear affirmative proof is shown to the contrary. See Official Comments 3 and 8 to U.C.C. § 2-313, 12A P.S. § 2-313.

It is Sessa's contention that his conversation with Riegle was the principal factor inducing him to enter the bargain. He would have the court believe that Maloney was merely a messenger to deliver the check. The evidence shows, however, that Sessa was relying primarily on Maloney to advise him in connection with the sale. Maloney testified that he had talked to Sessa about the horse on several occasions and expressed the opinion that he was convinced "beyond the shadow of a doubt" that he was a good buy. With respect to his authority to buy the horse he testified

> "Well, Mr. Sessa said he had enough confidence and faith in me and my integrity and honesty that I, what I did say about the horse, I was representing the horse as he is or as he was, and that if the horse, in my estimation, was that type of a horse and at that given price, the fixed price of $25,000, he would buy the horse."

*   *   *   *

The court believes that Maloney's opinion was the principal, if not the only, factor which motivated Sessa to purchase the horse. The conversation with Riegle played a negligible role in his decision.

DECISION AND REMEDY   *The court decided that no express warranty had been made. The court further concluded that even if the defendant's statements gave rise to an express warranty, those statements were not relied on as part of the bargain.*

Statements of Opinion and Value— Use of Formal Words Not Required

According to Section 2-313(2), "It is not necessary to the creation of an express warranty that the seller use formal words such as 'warrant' or 'guar-antee' or that he has a specific intention to make a warranty *   *   *." It is necessary only that a reasonable buyer would regard the representation as part of the basis of the bargain.

On the other hand, if the seller merely makes a statement that relates to the value or worth of the goods or makes a statement of opinion or recommendation about the goods, the seller is not creating an express warranty [UCC 2-313(2)]. For example, a seller claims, "This is the best used car to come along in years; it has four new tires and a 200-horsepower engine just rebuilt this year." The seller has made several *affirmations of fact* that can create a warranty: The automobile has an engine; it is a 200-horsepower engine; it was rebuilt this year; there are four tires on the automobile; the tires are new. But the seller's *opinion* that it is "the best used car to come along in years" is known as *puffing* and creates no warranty. (Puffing is the expression of an opinion by a seller that is not made as a representation of fact.) A statement relating to the value of the goods, such as "it's worth a fortune" or "anywhere else you'd pay $10,000 for it," will not normally create a warranty.

The ordinary seller can give an opinion that is not a warranty. If the seller is an expert and gives an opinion as an expert, however, then a warranty can be created. For example, Saul is an art dealer and an expert in seventeenth-century paintings. If Saul states to Lauren, a purchaser, that in his opinion a particular painting is a Rembrandt, Saul has warranted the accuracy of his opinion.

What constitutes an express warranty and what constitutes puffing is not easy to resolve. Merely recognizing that some statements are not warranties does not tell us where one should draw the line between puffs and warranties. The reasonableness of the buyer's reliance appears to be the controlling criterion in many cases. For example, a salesperson's statements that a ladder "will never break" and will "last a lifetime" are so clearly improbable that no reasonable buyer should rely on them. Also, the context within which a statement is made might be relevant in determining the reasonableness of the buyer's reliance. For example, any statement made in a written advertisement is more likely to be relied upon by a reasonable person than a statement made orally by a salesperson. Another factor is the specificity of the statements made. For example, a car dealer's statement that a vehicle is in "excellent" or "mint" condition may be too nonspecific for a court to deem it an express warranty—as is illustrated by the following case.

BACKGROUND AND FACTS *The plaintiff, Web Press Services Corporation, purchased a used 1980 Ford Bronco from the defendant, New London Motors, Inc., in July 1984. During the course of the sales negotiation, the defendant told the plaintiff's agent that the truck was "excellent" and in "mint condition." The agent took the truck for a test drive and agreed to the purchase. Mechanical troubles developed almost immediately. Many problems were minor and were remedied by the defendant. The Bronco had a major structural defect in the rear axle however, and the defendant did not remedy this defect. In October 1984, the plaintiff tendered the Bronco back to the defendant and revoked its acceptance of the vehicle. The plaintiff then requested the return of the purchase price, and the defendant refused. The plaintiff brought an action for breach of express warranties, among other actions. The trial court found that the defendant did not breach any express warranties, and Web Press Services Corporation appealed.*

Case 20.2
WEB PRESS SERVICES CORPORATION v. NEW LONDON MOTORS, INC.
Supreme Court of Connecticut, 1987.
203 Conn. 342, 525 A.2d 57.

DANNEHY, Justice.
*   *   *   *

We next consider the plaintiff's claim that the court should have found a breach of an express warranty. According to the plaintiff, the defendant's repeated statements to the effect that the vehicle was an "excellent" and "unusual" one, and that it was in "mint" and "very good" condition, amounted to an express warranty under General Statutes § 42a-2-313(1)(a). *   *   * In concluding that the defendant's statements did not amount to an express warranty, the trial court relied on [a case in which] the court held that words such as "[t]his car is in A-1 condition" did not create an express warranty but were merely "seller's talk."
*   *   *   *

* * * Drawing the line between puffing and the creation of a warranty is often difficult, but several factors have been identified as helpful in making that determination. One such factor is the specificity of the statements made. A statement such as "this truck will give not less than 15.1 miles to the gallon when it is driven at a steady 60 miles per hour" is more likely to be found to create an express warranty than a statement such as "this is a top-notch car." Statements to the effect that a truck was in "good condition" and that a motor was in "perfect running order" have been held not to create express warranties. Another factor to be considered in determining whether a statement creates an express warranty is whether it was written or oral, the latter being more likely to be considered puffing.

The defendant['s] * * * statements certainly cannot be considered specific in nature. Moreover, the plaintiff was allowed to examine and test drive the vehicle prior to purchase. Under the facts of this case the trial court's failure to find an express warranty * * * cannot be considered clearly erroneous.

DECISION AND REMEDY   *The court held that the defendant's statements about the condition of the car did not create an express warranty. The court did remand the case back to the trial court, however, with directions to articulate the legal and factual basis upon which it had found that the defendant had not violated the Connecticut Unfair Trade Practices Act, which was one of the other legal theories upon which the plaintiff based its action.*

IMPLIED WARRANTIES

An **implied warranty** is one that *the law derives* by implication or inference from the nature of the transaction or the relative situation or circumstances of the parties.

For example: Kaplan buys an axe at Enrique's Hardware Store. No express warranties are made. The first time she chops wood with it, the axe handle breaks, and Kaplan is injured. She immediately notifies Enrique. Examination shows that the wood in the handle was rotten but that the rottenness could not have been noticed by either Enrique or Kaplan. Nonetheless, Kaplan notifies Enrique that she will hold him responsible for the medical bills. Enrique is responsible because a merchant seller of goods warrants that the goods he or she sells are fit for the ordinary purposes for which such goods are used. This axe was obviously not fit for those purposes.

Implied Warranty of Merchantability

An **implied warranty of merchantability** automatically arises in every sale of goods made *by a merchant* who deals in goods of the kind sold [UCC 2-314]. Thus, a retailer of ski equipment makes

an implied warranty of merchantability every time the retailer sells a pair of skis, but a neighbor selling skis at a garage sale does not.

Goods that are *merchantable* are "reasonably fit for the ordinary purposes for which such goods are used." They must be of at least average, fair, or medium-grade quality. The quality must be comparable to quality that will pass without objection in the trade or market for goods of the same description. In addition, the goods, to be merchantable, must be adequately packaged and labeled as provided by the agreement, and they must conform to the promises or affirmations of fact made on the container or label, if any.

Some examples of nonmerchantable goods include light bulbs that explode when switched on, pajamas that burst into flames upon slight contact with the heating elements of an electric room heater, high heels that break off shoes under normal use, or shotgun shells that explode prematurely.

A sale is also accompanied by an implied warranty of merchantability that imposes on the merchant liability for the safe performance of the product. It makes no difference whether the merchant knew of or could have discovered a defect that makes the product unsafe. (Of course, merchants are not absolute insurers against *all* accidents arising in connection with the goods. For example, a bar of soap is not unmerchantable merely because a user can slip and fall by stepping on it.) In an action based on breach of warranty, it is necessary to show:

1. That an implied warranty existed.
2. That the warranty was broken.
3. That the breach of warranty was the proximate cause of the damage sustained.

The serving of food or drink to be consumed on or off the premises is recognized as a sale of goods subject to the warranty of merchantability [UCC 2-314(1)]. Merchantable food means food that is fit to eat. Any object within the food that a buyer would ordinarily expect to accompany the food does not render the food nonmerchantable. Thus, a bone swallowed by a buyer eating fish would not subject the merchant seller to liability, but a nail would.

The following is a classic case of a court's interpretation of whether a fish bone in fish chowder is a foreign substance rendering the chowder unwholesome or not fit to be eaten.

BACKGROUND AND FACTS *Webster brought the following action against the Blue Ship Tea Room for personal injuries she sustained when consuming a bowl of its fish chowder. Her theory was breach of implied warranty of merchantability. A jury rendered a verdict for the plaintiff. The defendant appealed.*

 Case 20.3

WEBSTER v. BLUE SHIP TEA ROOM
Supreme Judicial Court of Massachusetts, 1964.
347 Mass. 421, 198 N.E.2d 309.

REARDON, Justice.

[The plaintiff] ordered a cup of fish chowder. Presently, there was set before her "a small bowl of fish chowder * * *. After 3 or 4 spoonfulls she was aware that something had lodged in her throat because she couldn't swallow and couldn't clear her throat by gulping and she could feel it." This misadventure led to two esophagoscopies at the Massachusetts General Hospital, in the second of which, on April 27, 1959, a fish bone was found and removed. The sequence of events produced injury to the plaintiff which was not insubstantial.

We must decide whether a fish bone lurking in a fish chowder, about the ingredients of which there is no other complaint, constitutes a breach of implied warranty under applicable provisions of the Uniform Commercial Code * * * . As the judge put it in his charge, "Was the fish chowder fit to be eaten and wholesome? * * * [N]obody is claiming that the fish itself wasn't wholesome. * * * But the bone of contention here—I don't mean that for a pun—but was this fish bone a foreign substance that made the fish chowder unwholesome or not fit to be eaten?"

* * * *

[We think that i]t is not too much to say that a person sitting down in New England to consume a good New England fish chowder embarks on a gustatory adventure which may entail the removal of some fish bones from his bowl as he proceeds. We are not inclined to tamper with age old recipes by any amendment reflecting the plaintiff's view of the effect of the Uniform Commercial Code upon them. We are aware of the heavy body of case law involving foreign substances in food, but we sense a strong distinction between them and those relative to unwholesomeness of the food itself, e.g., tainted mackerel (*Smith v. Gerrish*), and a fish bone in a fish chowder. Certain Massachusetts cooks might cavil at the ingredients contained in the chowder in this case in that it lacked the heartening lift of salt pork. In any event, we consider that the joys of life in New England include the ready availability of fresh fish chowder. We should be prepared to cope with the hazards of fish bones, the occasional presence of which in chowders is, it seems to us, to be anticipated, and which, in the light of a hallowed tradition, do not impair their fitness or merchantability. While we are bouyed up in this conclusion by *Shapiro v. Hotel Statler Corp.*, in which the bone which afflicted the plaintiff appeared in "Hot Barquette of Seafood Mornay," we know that the United States District Court of Southern California, situated as are we upon a coast, might be expected to share our views. We are most impressed, however, by

Allen v. Grafton, where in Ohio, the Midwest, in a case where the plaintiff was injured by a piece of oyster shell in an order of fried oysters, Mr. Justice Taft (now Chief Justice) in a majority opinion held that "the possible presence of a piece of oyster shell in or attached to an oyster is so well known to anyone who eats oysters that we can say as a matter of law that one who eats oysters can reasonably anticipate and guard against eating such a piece of shell *   *   *."

DECISION AND REMEDY   *The court "sympathized with a plaintiff who has suffered a peculiarly New England injury," but entered a judgment for the defendant, Blue Ship Tea Room.*

Implied Warranty of Fitness for a Particular Purpose

The implied warranty of fitness for a particular purpose arises when *any seller* (merchant or non-merchant) knows the particular purpose for which a buyer will use the goods *and* knows that the buyer is relying upon the seller's skill and judgment to select suitable goods [UCC 2-315].

A "particular purpose of the buyer" differs from the "ordinary purpose for which goods are used." Goods can be merchantable—suitable for the use to which such goods are ordinarily put—but still not fit for the buyer's particular purpose. For example, house paints suitable for painting ordinary walls are not suitable for painting stucco walls.

A contract can include both a warranty of merchantability and a warranty of fitness for a particular purpose, which relates to a specific use or to a special situation in which a buyer intends to use the goods. For example, a seller recommends a particular pair of shoes, *knowing* that a customer is looking for mountain climbing shoes. The buyer purchases the shoes *relying* on the seller's judgment. If the shoes are found to be not only improperly made but suitable only for walking, not for mountain climbing, the seller has breached

both the warranty of fitness for a particular purpose and the warranty of merchantability.

A seller does not need "actual knowledge" of the buyer's particular purpose. It is sufficient if a seller "has reason to know" the purpose. However, the buyer must have relied upon the seller's skill or judgment in selecting or furnishing suitable goods in order for an implied warranty of fitness to be created.

For example, Josephs buys a shortwave radio from Radio Shack, telling the salesperson that she wants a set strong enough to pick up Radio Luxembourg, which is 8,000 miles away. Radio Shack sells Josephs a Model XYZ set. The set works, but it will not pick up Radio Luxembourg. Josephs wants her money back. Here, since Radio Shack is guilty of a breach of implied warranty of fitness for the buyer's particular purpose, Josephs will be able to recover. The salesperson knew specifically that she wanted a set that would pick up Radio Luxembourg. Furthermore, Josephs relied upon the salesperson to furnish a radio that would fulfill this purpose. Since the salesperson did not do so, the warranty was breached.

In the next case, a seller helped a buyer solve a painting problem and became the defendant in a lawsuit for breach of an implied warranty of fitness.

Case 20.4

CATANIA v. BROWN

Circuit Court of Connecticut,
Appellate Division, 1967.
4 Conn.Cir. 344, 231 A.2d 668.

BACKGROUND AND FACTS   *The defendant, Brown, was engaged in the retail paint business. Catania, the plaintiff, asked Brown to recommend a paint to cover the exterior stucco walls of his house. Brown recommended and sold to Catania a certain brand of paint called "Pierce's Shingle and Shake" paint. Brown also advised Catania how to prepare the walls before applying the paint and how to mix the paint in proper proportion to the thinner. Catania followed Brown's instructions, but the paint blistered and peeled soon after it was applied.*

JACOBS, Judge.

*   *   *

Under the statute governing implied warranty of fitness for a particular purpose (§ 42a-2-315), two requirements must be met: (a) the buyer relies on the seller's skill or judgment to select or furnish suitable goods; and (b) the seller at the time of contracting has reason to know the buyer's purpose and that the buyer is relying on the seller's skill or judgment. "It is a question of fact in the ordinary case whether these conditions have been met and the warranty arises."

*   *   * "The raising of an implied warranty of fitness depends upon whether the buyer informed the seller of the circumstances and conditions which necessitated his purchase of a certain character of article or material and left it to the seller to select the particular kind and quality of article suitable for the buyer's use. *   *   * So when the buyer orders goods to be supplied and trusts to the judgment or skill of the seller to select goods or material for which they are ordered, there is an implied warranty that they shall be reasonably fit for that purpose." "Reliance can, of course, be more readily found where the *retailer* selects the product or recommends it."

*   *   * [T]he buyer, being ignorant of the fitness of the article offered by the seller, justifiably relied on the superior information, skill and judgment of the seller and not on his own knowledge or judgment, and under such circumstances an implied warranty of fitness could properly be claimed by the purchaser.

The plaintiff prevailed on the theory of implied warranty of fitness for a particular purpose. The defendant had created and breached a warranty of fitness by recommending the particular paint as suitable for stucco walls.

DECISION AND REMEDY

Implied Warranty Arising from Course of Dealing or Trade Usage

The Code recognizes in Section 2-314(3) that implied warranties can arise [or be excluded or modified under UCC 2-316(3)(c)] from course of dealing, course of performance, or usage of trade. In the absence of evidence to the contrary, when both parties to a sales contract have knowledge of a well-recognized trade custom, the courts will infer that they both intended that custom to apply to their contract. For example, in the sale of a new car, where the industry-wide custom includes lubricating the car before delivery, a seller who fails to do so can be held liable to a buyer for resulting damages for breach of implied warranty. This, of course, would also be negligence on the part of the dealer.

OVERLAPPING WARRANTIES

Sometimes two or more warranties are made in a single transaction. An implied warranty of merchantability or of fitness for a particular purpose, or both, can exist in addition to an express warranty. For example, where a sales contract for a new car states that "this car engine is warranted to be free from defects for 12,000 miles or twelve months, whichever comes first," there is an express warranty against all defects and an implied warranty that the car will be fit for normal use.

The rule of UCC 2-317 is that express and implied warranties are construed as cumulative if they are consistent with one another. If the warranties are inconsistent, the courts will usually hold that:

1.   Express warranties will displace inconsistent implied warranties except implied warranties of fitness for a particular purpose.

2.   Samples will take precedence over inconsistent general descriptions.

3.   Technical specifications will displace inconsistent samples or general descriptions.

Suppose that when Josephs buys a shortwave radio at Radio Shack, the contract expressly warrants that the radio will receive radio waves transmitted from as far as 4,000 miles away. She tries to pick up Radio Luxembourg—the stated purpose of her purchase—which is 8,000 miles away. The set cannot perform that well. Josephs claims that Radio Shack is guilty of breach of warranty of fitness. The express warranty takes precedence over any implied warranty of merchantability that a shortwave set should pick up any station anywhere in the world. Josephs does have a good claim for the breach of implied warranty of fitness for a specific purpose, however, because she had made it clear that she was buying the set to pick up Radio Luxembourg. In cases of inconsistency between an express warranty and a warranty of fitness for a buyer's particular purpose, the warranty of fitness for the buyer's particular purpose normally prevails [UCC 2-317(c)].

THIRD PARTY BENEFICIARIES OF WARRANTIES

One of the general principles of contract law is that a person who is not one of the parties to a contract has no rights under the contract. (Notable exceptions are assignments and third party beneficiary contracts. See Chapter 13.) The connection that exists between the contracting parties is called **privity of contract.** It was established at common law that privity must exist between a plaintiff and a defendant for any action based upon a contract to be maintained.

For example, I purchase a ham from retailer Ralph. I invite you to my house that evening. I prepare the ham properly. You are served first, since you are my guest, and you become severely ill because the ham is spoiled. Can you sue retailer Ralph for breach of the implied warranty of merchantability? Since warranty is based on a contract for the sale of goods, under the common law you would normally have warranty rights only if you were a party to the purchase of the ham. Therefore, the warranty would extend only to me, the purchaser.

In the past this hardship was sometimes resolved by court decisions removing privity as a requirement to hold manufacturers and sellers liable for certain defective products (notably food, drugs, and cosmetics) that were sold. The UCC, reflecting some of these decisions, has addressed the problem of privity, at least to the extent of giving the state the option to determine when privity is no longer required.

There is sharp disagreement over how far warranty liability should extend. In order to satisfy opposing views of the various states, the drafters of the UCC proposed three alternatives for liability under UCC 2-318. Accordingly, some states have adopted alternative A; others, alternative B; and still others, alternative C. All three alternatives are intended to eliminate the privity requirement with respect to certain enumerated types of injuries (personal versus property) for certain beneficiaries (for example, household members or bystanders).

ALTERNATIVE A   All sellers' warranties (express or implied) extend to any *natural person* (as opposed to a legally created entity, such as a corporation) in the buyer's family or household or to anyone who is a guest in the home, when it is reasonable to expect that such persons will use, consume, or be affected by the goods or be personally injured because of a breach of the warranty. Consider this example: Anderson buys an electric washing machine from E-Z Appliances. One month after the purchase, Anderson's mother-in-law, who has been living with his family for a year, receives a severe electric shock from a defective wire while using the machine. Anderson's mother-in-law claims damages from E-Z Appliances for breach of the warranty of merchantability. She can recover because the defective wire made the washing machine unfit for normal use. Since she was living with Anderson's family, she naturally would use the washing machine if she helped with housekeeping chores. Anderson's mother-in-law therefore qualifies as a third party beneficiary of the warranty.

ALTERNATIVE B   Alternative B extends the seller's warranty (express or implied) to any *natural person* who can reasonably be expected to use, consume, or be affected by the goods and who suffers personal injury because of the breach of warranty. This is a broader basis for liability than alternative A, since protection is not limited to family or household members.

Note the restrictions here, however. As with alternative A, the seller's warranty extends only to persons, not to corporations. It also limits the right of recovery of those not in privity to personal injury damages and therefore eliminates the possibility of suing for property damages. A seller may not exclude or limit the warranties given under alternatives A or B.

ALTERNATIVE C Alternative C offers the broadest coverage of all. It extends to any person (including a corporation) who is injured. It extends the rule to damages beyond injuries to the person. It does not allow the seller to exclude or limit its liability for personal injuries.

WARRANTY DISCLAIMERS

Courts view warranty disclaimers with disfavor, especially when consumers are involved. As discussed below, even when sellers have adhered exactly to the methods of disclaimer specified by the UCC, courts have often held that the disclaimers are unconscionable. Also, there are other federal and state statutes (for example, the Magnuson-Moss Warranty Act, which is considered below) that may make disclaimers of a particular warranty unenforceable. And a buyer prevented from claiming breach of warranty may be able to sue successfully on a theory of negligence or strict liability (each of which is discussed in more detail in Chapter 21).

Obviously, then, the seller's best protection from being held accountable for affirmations of fact or promises that relate to the goods is not to make them in the first place. Of course, a contract normally involves a sale of something describable and described. A clause purporting to disclaim all warranties cannot negate the seller's obligation with respect to this description and therefore cannot be given literal effect [UCC 2-313, Comment 4]. Thus, the manner in which a seller can disclaim or qualify any warranty varies with the way the warranty is created. For example, a seller's description of his or her merchandise as an "automobile" creates an express warranty that what will be delivered to a buyer is an automobile. Stating that goods are being sold "as is" cannot disclaim this warranty; and thus, a seller cannot deliver a car without wheels or a motor and avoid liability.

Express Warranties

Any affirmation of fact or promise, description of the goods, or use of samples or models by a seller creates an express warranty. Obviously, then, express warranties can be excluded if the seller has carefully refrained from making any promise or affirmation of fact relating to the goods, or describing the goods, or selling by means of a sample or model [UCC 2-313].

The parol evidence rule protects the seller from a buyer's false claims that an oral warranty was created. Under this rule, if the parties intended the written contract to be the complete expression of their agreement, the buyer cannot offer evidence of an oral warranty. Nevertheless, a court may conclude that the contract was not a complete expression of the parties' intentions and permit proof of oral terms.

The Code does permit express warranties to be negated or limited by specific and unambiguous language, provided this is done in a manner that protects the buyer from surprise. Therefore, a written disclaimer in language that is clear and conspicuous, and called to a buyer's attention, could negate all oral express warranties not included in the written sales contract [UCC 2-316(1)].

Implied Warranties

Generally speaking, and unless circumstances indicate otherwise, implied warranties (of merchantability and fitness) are disclaimed by the expressions "as is," "with all faults," or other similar expressions that in common understanding for *both* parties call the buyer's attention to the fact that there are no implied warranties [UCC 2-316(3)(a)].

The Code also permits a seller to specifically disclaim the implied warranty either of fitness or of merchantability [UCC 2-316(2)]. To disclaim the implied warranty of fitness, the disclaimer *must* be in writing and conspicuous. The word *fitness* does not have to be mentioned in the writing; it is sufficient, for example, for the disclaimer to state: "There are no warranties that extend beyond the description on the face hereof."

A merchantability disclaimer must be more specific; it must mention *merchantability*. It need not be written; but if it is, the writing must be conspicuous. According to UCC 1-201(10):

> A term or clause is conspicuous when it is so written that a reasonable person against whom it is to operate ought to have noticed it. A printed heading in capitals is conspicuous. Language in the body of a form is conspicuous if it is in large or other contrasting type or color.

To illustrate: Merchant Logan sells Breen a particular lawn mower selected by Logan with the characteristics clearly requested by Breen. At the time of the sale, Logan orally tells Breen that he does not warrant the merchantability of the mower, as it is last year's model. The mower proves to be defective and will not work. Breen wishes to hold Logan liable for breach of implied warranty of merchantability and of fitness for a particular purpose.

Breen can hold Logan liable for breach of the warranty of fitness but not of the warranty of merchantability. Logan's oral disclaimer mentioning the word *merchantability* is a proper disclaimer. For Logan to have disclaimed the implied warranty of fitness, a conspicuous writing would have been required. Since no written disclaimer was made, Logan can still be held liable.

Buyer's Refusal to Inspect

If a buyer actually examines the goods (or a sample or model) as fully as desired before entering a contract or if the buyer refuses to examine the goods, *there is no implied warranty with respect to defects that a reasonable examination will reveal.*

Suppose, in the earlier illustration concerning Kaplan's purchase of an axe from Enrique's Hardware Store, the defect in Kaplan's axe could easily have been spotted by normal inspection. Kaplan, even after Enrique asked, refused to inspect the axe before buying it. After being hurt by the defective axe, she will not be able to hold Enrique liable for breach of warranty of merchantability because she could have spotted the defect during an inspection [UCC 2-316(3)(b)].

Failure to examine the goods is not refusal to examine them; it is not enough that the goods were available for inspection and the buyer failed to examine them. A refusal occurs only when the seller *demands* that the buyer examine the goods. Of course, the seller always remains liable for latent (hidden) defects that ordinary inspection would not reveal. What the examination ought to reveal depends on a particular buyer's skill and method of examination. Therefore, an auto mechanic purchasing a car should be responsible for the discovery of some defects that a nonexpert would not be expected to find. The circumstances of each case determine what defects a so-called reasonable inspection should reveal.

UNCONSCIONABILITY AND WARRANTY DISCLAIMERS

The Code sections dealing with warranty disclaimers do not refer specifically to unconscionability as a factor. Eventually, however, the courts will test warranty disclaimers with reference to the unconscionability standards of Section 2-302. Such things as lack of bargaining position, "take it or leave it" choices, and failure of a buyer to understand or know of a warranty disclaimer provision will become relevant to the issue of unconscionability. Note in the following pre-UCC landmark decision the court's recognition of the consumer's "bargaining" position with respect to large auto manufacturers.

Case 20.5
HENNINGSEN v. BLOOMFIELD MOTORS, INC.
Supreme Court of New Jersey, 1960.
32 N.J. 358, 161 A.2d 69.

BACKGROUND AND FACTS   *This case involves the recovery of damages from an automobile manufacturer for injuries sustained by the owner and driver of a new car manufactured by Chrysler. The standard form purchase order used in the transaction contained an express warranty by which the manufacturer warranted the vehicle to be free from defects in material or workmanship. The manufacturer promised to correct any defects found without cost to the purchaser for a ninety-day period or four thousand miles, whichever came first. In addition, the purchase order contained a disclaimer, in fine print, of any and all other express or implied warranties. The disclaimer purported to absolve Chrysler and the dealer from all liability for the implied warranty of merchantability against injuries suffered. The standard form purchase order became part of the Chrysler contract when a consumer purchased an automobile. Hence, the express warranty that was offered instead of all other warranties, express or implied, was intended to set the limits of Chrysler's liability.*

FRANCIS, Justice.

* * * *

Plaintiff Claus H. Henningsen purchased a Plymouth automobile, manufactured by defendant Chrysler Corporation, from defendant Bloomfield Motors, Inc. His wife, plaintiff Helen Henningsen, was injured while driving it and instituted suit against both defendants to recover damages on account of her injuries. * * * The complaint was predicated upon breach of express and implied warranties and upon negligence. [The jury awarded damages to the Henningsens, and the manufacturer appealed.]

* * * *

I.
The Claim of Implied Warranty against the Manufacturer.

* * * *

Chrysler points out that an implied warranty of merchantability is an incident of a contract of sale. It concedes, of course, the making of the original sale to Bloomfield Motors, Inc., but maintains that this transaction marked the terminal point of its contractual connection with the car. Then Chrysler urges that since it was not a party to the sale by the dealer to Henningsen, there is no privity of contract between it and the plaintiffs, and the absence of this privity eliminates any such implied warranty.

* * * *

Under modern conditions the ordinary layman, on responding to the importuning of colorful advertising, has neither the opportunity nor the capacity to inspect or to determine the fitness of an automobile for use; he must rely on the manufacturer who has control of its construction, and to some degree on the dealer who, to the limited extent called for by the manufacturer's instructions, inspects and services it before delivery. In such a marketing milieu his remedies and those of persons who properly claim through him should not depend "upon the intricacies of the law of sales. The obligation of the manufacturer should not be based alone on privity of contract."

* * *

Accordingly, we hold that under modern marketing conditions, when a manufacturer puts a new automobile in the stream of trade and promotes its purchase by the public, an implied warranty that it is reasonably suitable for use as such accompanies it into the hands of the ultimate purchaser. [Emphasis added.] Absence of agency between the manufacturer and the dealer who makes the ultimate sale is immaterial.

II.
The Effect of the Disclaimer and Limitation of Liability Clauses on the Implied Warranty of Merchantability.

* * * In a society such as ours, where the automobile is a common and necessary adjunct of daily life, and where its use is so fraught with danger to the driver, passengers and the public, the manufacturer is under a special obligation in connection with the construction, promotion and sale of his cars. Consequently, the courts must examine purchase agreements closely to see if consumer and public interests are treated fairly.

What influence should these circumstances have on the restrictive effect of Chrysler's express warranty in the framework of the purchase contract? As we have said, *warranties originated in the law to safeguard the buyer and not to limit the liability of the seller or manufacturer.* [Emphasis added.] * * * But does the doctrine that a person is bound by his signed agreement, in the absence of fraud, stand in the way of any relief?

* * * *

The traditional contract is the result of free bargaining of parties who are brought together by the play of the market, and who meet each other on a footing of approximate economic equality. * * * But in present-day commercial life the standardized mass contract has appeared. It is used primarily by enterprises with strong bargaining power and position. * * *

* * * *

The warranty before us is a standardized form designed for mass use. It is imposed upon the automobile consumer. He takes it or leaves it, and he must take it to buy an automobile. No bargaining is engaged in with respect to it. In fact, the dealer through whom it comes to the buyer is without authority to alter it; his function is ministerial— simply to deliver it. The form warranty is not only standard with Chrysler but, as mentioned above, it is the uniform warranty of the Automobile Manufacturers Association.   *   *   *

The gross inequality of bargaining position occupied by the consumer in the automobile industry is thus apparent.   *   *   *
*   *   *   *

    *   *   * Courts keep in mind the principle that the best interests of society demand that persons should not be unnecessarily restricted in their freedom to contract. But they do not hesitate to declare void as against public policy contractual provisions which clearly tend to the injury of the public in some way.

    *   *   * *[W]e are of the opinion that Chrysler's attempted disclaimer of an implied warranty of merchantability and of the obligations arising therefrom is so inimical to the public good as to compel an adjudication of its invalidity.* [Emphasis added.]

III.
The Dealer's Implied Warranty.

The principles that have been expounded as to the obligation of the manufacturer apply with equal force to the separate express warranty of the dealer. This is so, irrespective of the absence of the relationship of principal and agent between these defendants, because the manufacturer and the Association establish the warranty policy for the industry. The bargaining position of the dealer is inextricably bound by practice to that of the maker and the purchaser must take or leave the automobile, accompanied and encumbered as it is by the uniform warranty.
*   *   *   *

For the reason set forth in Part I hereof, *we conclude that the disclaimer of an implied warranty of merchantability by the dealer, as well as the attempted elimination of all obligations other than replacement of defective parts, are violative of public policy and void.* [Emphasis added.]

DECISION AND REMEDY   *The court upheld the right of the plaintiffs, the Henningsens, to recover damages for injuries notwithstanding the attempted warranty disclaimer on the part of the defendants, Chrysler Corporation and Bloomfield Motors, Inc.*

CONCEPT SUMMARY: Warranties under the UCC

TYPE OF WARRANTY	HOW CREATED	POSSIBLE DEFENSES
Warranty of title UCC 2-312	Upon transfer of title, the seller warrants— 1. That he or she has the right to pass good and rightful title. 2. That the goods are free from unstated liens or encumbrances. 3. When the seller is a merchant, that the goods are free from infringement claims.	Specific language or circumstances excluded or modified warranty. UCC 2-312(2)

CONCEPT SUMMARY: Warranties under the UCC (Continued)

TYPE OF WARRANTY	HOW CREATED	POSSIBLE DEFENSES
Express warranty UCC 2-313	As part of a sale or bargain, a seller may create an express warranty by— 1. An affirmation of fact or promise. 2. A sale by description. 3. A sample shown as conforming to bulk.	1. Statement that is purported to create warranty was an opinion. 2. Specific language or conduct negated or limited warranty. UCC 2-316(1)
Implied warranty of merchantability UCC 2-314	This warranty arises when— 1. The seller is a merchant who deals in goods of the kind sold.	1. Warranty was specifically disclaimed (disclaimer can be oral or in writing, but must mention *merchantability* and, if in writing, must be conspicuous). UCC 2-316(2) 2. Sale was stated to be "as is" or "with all faults." UCC 2-316(3)(a) 3. The buyer examined the goods and is therefore bound by all defects that were found or should have been found. If the buyer refused or failed to examine, the buyer is bound by obvious defects. UCC 2-316(3)(b) 4. Course of dealing, performance, or usage of trade. UCC 2-316(3)(c)
Implied warranty of fitness for a particular purpose UCC 2-315	This warranty arises when— 1. The buyer's purpose or use is expressly or impliedly known by the seller, and 2. The buyer purchases in reliance on the seller's selection.	1. Specific disclaimer excluded or modified warranty (disclaimer must be in writing and be conspicuous. "There are no warranties which extend beyond the description on the face hereof."). UCC 2-316(2) 2. Same as items 2–4 under merchantability, above.
Implied warranty arising from course of dealing or trade usage UCC 2-314(3)	This warranty is created by prior dealings and/or custom of trade.	1. Warranty was excluded by specific language or as provided under UCC 2-316.

MAGNUSON-MOSS WARRANTY ACT

The Magnuson-Moss Warranty Act[3] (enacted in 1975) was designed to prevent deception in warranties by making them easier to understand. The act is mainly enforced by the Federal Trade Commission (FTC). Additionally, the Attorney General or a consumer who has been injured can enforce the act if informal procedures for settling disputes prove to be ineffective. The Magnuson-Moss Warranty Act modifies UCC warranty rules

3. 15 U.S.C. Sections 2301–12.

to some extent where *consumer* sales transactions are involved. However, the UCC remains the primary codification of warranty rules for industrial and commercial transactions.

No seller is *required* to give a written warranty for consumer goods sold under the Warranty Act. But if a seller chooses to make an express written warranty and the cost of the consumer goods is more than $10, the warranty must be labeled as either full or limited. In addition, if the cost of the goods is more than $15 (by FTC regulation), the warrantor is required to make certain disclosures fully and conspicuously in a single document in "readily understood language." This disclosure states the names and addresses of the warrantors, what specifically is warranted, procedures for enforcement of the warranty, any limitations on warranty relief, and that the buyer has legal rights.

Although a *full warranty* may not cover every aspect of the consumer product sold, what it covers ensures some type of buyer satisfaction in case the product is defective. Full warranty requires free repair or replacement of any defective part; if it cannot be repaired within a reasonable time, the consumer has the choice of either a refund or a replacement without charge. The full warranty frequently does not have a time limit. Any limitation on consequential damages must be *conspicuously* stated. Also, the warrantor need not perform warranty services if the problem with the product was caused by unreasonable use or damage by the consumer.

A *limited warranty* arises when the written warranty fails to meet one of the minimum requirements for a full warranty. The fact that a seller is giving only a limited warranty must be conspicuously designated. If only a time limitation would distinguish a limited warranty from a full warranty, then the Warranty Act allows the seller to designate the warranty as full by such language as "full twelve-month warranty."

Although, under the UCC, express warranties can be created by description or sample or model, only written promises or affirmations of fact are covered by the Magnuson-Moss Warranty Act. Thus, for purposes of the Warranty Act:

1. An express warranty is *any written promise* or *affirmation of fact* made by the seller to a consumer indicating the quality or performance of the product and affirming or promising that the product is either free of defects or will meet a specific level of performance over a period of time—for example, "this watch will not lose more than one second a year."

2. An express warranty is a written agreement to refund, repair, or replace the product if it fails to meet written specifications. This is typically a service contract.

Implied warranties do not arise under the Magnuson-Moss Warranty Act. They continue to be created according to the UCC provisions. Where an express warranty is made in a sales contract or a combined sales and service contract (where the service contract is undertaken within ninety days of the sale), the Magnuson-Moss Warranty Act prevents sellers from disclaiming or modifying the implied warranties of merchantability and fitness for a particular purpose. Sellers can impose a time limit on the duration of an implied warranty, but the time limit has to correspond to the duration of the express warranty.[4]

---

4. The time limit on an implied warranty occurring by virtue of the seller's express warranty must, of course, be reasonable, conscionable, and set forth in clear and conspicuous language on the face of the warranty.

QUESTIONS AND CASE PROBLEMS

1. Quid contracted to purchase a used car from Johnson's Quality Used Cars. During the oral negotiations for the sale, Johnson told Quid that this used car was in "A-1 condition" and would get sixteen miles to the gallon. Quid asked if the car used oil. Johnson replied that he had personally checked the car, and in his opinion the car did not use oil. Since delivery, Quid has used the car for one month (400 miles of driving) and is unhappy with it. The car needs numerous repairs, does not get sixteen miles to the gallon, and has used two quarts of oil. Quid claims Johnson is in breach of express warranties as to the condition of the car, gas mileage, and oil use. Johnson claims no express warranties were made. Discuss who is correct.

2. Jeremy is a farmer who needs to place a 2,000-pound piece of equipment in his barn. This will require lifting the equipment 30 feet up into a hayloft. Jeremy goes to Davidson Hardware and tells Davidson that he needs some heavy-duty rope to be used on his farm. Davidson recommends a one-inch-thick nylon rope, and Jeremy purchases 200 feet of the rope. Jeremy ties the rope around the piece of equipment, puts it through a pulley, and, with a tractor, lifts the equipment off the ground. Suddenly the rope breaks. In the crash to the ground the equipment is severely damaged. Jeremy files suit against Davidson for breach of implied warranty of fitness. Discuss how successful Jeremy will be in his suit.

3. Darrow purchases a new car from Slippery Motors. The retail installment contract states immediately above the buyer's signature in large, bold type: "There are no warranties that extend beyond the description on the face hereof" and "There are no express warranties that accompany this sale unless expressly written in this contract." Before purchasing the car, Darrow specifically informed Slippery's salesperson that he wanted a car that could be driven in a dusty area without needing mechanical repairs. Slippery's salesperson said to Darrow, "Nothing will go wrong with this car, but if it does, return it to us, and we will repair it without cost to you." Neither this statement nor any similar to it appears in the retail sales contract. Darrow drives the car into a dust storm. The air filter gets plugged up and the car engine overheats, causing motor damage. Slippery Motors refuses to repair the engine under any warranty. Darrow claims Slippery is liable for breach of the implied warranty of fitness, that such cannot be disclaimed because of the Magnuson-Moss Warranty Act, and that there is a breach of the salesperson's express warranty. Discuss Darrow's claims.

4. Terry has a used television set that she wishes to sell. Howard contracts to purchase the set. At the time of the making of the contract, Terry demands that Howard inspect the set to be sure it is exactly what he wants. Howard tells Terry that he does not have the time to do so. The set is delivered and paid for. Howard, upon using the set, discovers that the picture has a tendency to "jump" and that the vertical control does not always correct that tendency. The cost to repair the set is $50. Howard claims that the set is neither merchantable nor fit for its purpose. Terry claims she has no liability. Discuss who is correct.

5. John buys a one-karat diamond ring from Shady Sallor for $500. John is assured by Shady that the ring belonged to his deceased mother and that the only reason the price is so low is that he is behind in making payments on his car. John has no reason to believe differently. Bekins, a neighbor, admires the ring and offers to purchase it for $1,000. John agrees to sell the ring to Bekins, stating that he is transferring only such right and title as he has. Two months later, the police confiscate the ring as property stolen in a burglary of Owen's home. Bekins seeks to hold John liable. Discuss Bekins's action under warranty laws.

6. Robinson purchased a truck from Branch Moving and Storage Company "as is" without inspecting it. Branch diligently and repeatedly advised Robinson of the risk he was taking by purchasing the unit without inspection. When the truck required a number of repairs because of defects in it, Robinson sued Branch for breach of warranty. At trial, Robinson won. Branch appealed. What was the result? [Robinson v. Branch Moving and Storage Co., 28 N.C.App. 244, 221 S.E.2d 81 (1976)]

7. A disclaimer of the implied warranty of fitness must be in writing and must be conspicuous. If the implied warranty of merchantability is to be excluded by means of a writing, that writing must also be conspicuous. The following paragraph appeared in a sales contract. The page contained other type of larger and smaller sizes and boldface print, but no other words on the page were printed in italics.

The equipment covered hereby is sold subject only to the applicable manufacturer's standard printed warranty, if any, in effect at the date hereof, receipt of a copy of which is hereby acknowledged, and no other warranties, express or implied, including without limitation, the implied warranties of *merchantability and fitness for a particular purpose shall apply.*

Is this an effective disclaimer of the implied warranties according to UCC 2-316? [Dorman v. International Harvester Co., 46 Cal.App.3d 11, 120 Cal.Rptr. 516 (1975)]

8. Myrtle Carpenter purchased hair dye from a drugstore. The use of the dye caused an adverse skin reaction. She sued the local drugstore and the manufacturer of the dye, Alberto Culver Company. She claimed that a sales clerk indicated that several of Myrtle's friends had used the product and that their hair came out "very nice." The clerk purportedly also told Myrtle that she would get very fine results. On the package, there were cautionary instructions telling the user to make a preliminary skin test to determine if the user was susceptible in any unusual way to the product. Myrtle stated that she did not make the preliminary skin test. Did the seller make an express warranty about the hair dye? [Carpenter v. Alberto Culver Co., 28 Mich.App. 399, 184 N.W.2d 547 (1970)]

9. In 1984, the Lindemann farm's cotton crop fared poorly because of lack of weed control. That year, and every year since the early 1960s, the Lindemanns (plaintiffs) used Treflan, an herbicide manufactured by the defendants, Eli Lilly and Co. The label specifically stated that Treflan would control weeds when used according to label instructions. The Treflan label recommended that the herbicide be incorporated into the soil twice after it had been sprayed. The purpose of the double incorporation was to provide greater uniformity in the herbicide's distribution. The Lindemanns, in an effort to create still greater uniformity in the distribution of the Treflan, made an application by spraying half the amount of a normal application in one direction and half in the opposite direction. Each spraying was incorporated into the soil after it had been applied. If the directions did not contain a specific directive calling for a single application, could the Lindemanns recover for breach of express warranty of the herbicide to control weeds? [Lindemann v. Eli Lilly and Company, 816 F.2d 199 (5th Cir. 1987)]

10. On December 22, 1980, Jack M. Crothers purchased a used 1970 Dodge from Maurice Boyd, a sales agent employed by Norman Cohen, the owner of Norm's Auto Sales.

On December 23, 1980, Crothers was seriously injured when the Dodge he had just purchased went out of control and crashed into a tree. Crothers filed suit, asserting breach of an express warranty based on Boyd's representation to Crothers that the 1970 Dodge had a rebuilt carburetor and was a "good runner." Did Boyd's representations amount to an express warranty? [Crothers by Crothers v. Cohen, 384 N.W.2d 562 (Minn.App. 1986)]

11. On March 13, 1980, Judith Roth went to the hairdresser she had been using for the last seven years to have her hair bleached. The hair stylist used a new bleaching product, manufactured by Roux Laboratories, on Mrs. Roth's hair. Although other Roux products had been used previously with excellent results, the use of the new product resulted in damage to Mrs. Roth's hair that caused her embarrassment and anguish for the next several months as her hair grew back. The product's label had guaranteed it would not cause damage to a user's hair. Roth sued Ray-Stel's Hair Stylists and Roux Laboratories, Inc., alleging, among other claims, breach of express warranty resulting in personal injuries to her. Discuss whether there was a breach of express warranty. [Roth v. Ray-Stel's Hair Stylists, Inc., 18 Mass.App. 975, 470 N.E.2d 137 (1984)]

12. While passing by the American Kennels pet store, owned by defendant George Rosenthal, Ruby Dempsey, the plaintiff, decided to purchase a pedigreed white poodle. Dempsey told the salesperson that she wanted a dog suitable for breeding purposes. She purchased the poodle, whom she named Mr. Dunphy. Five days later, the dog was examined by a veterinarian and discovered to have a congenital defect. Dempsey returned to the store and demanded a refund of the purchase price. The store refused, and Dempsey filed suit. Dempsey claimed that the defendant was guilty of breach of the implied warranties of merchantability and fitness for a particular purpose. The defendant claimed that the poodle was still capable of breeding and thus no warranties had been breached. Discuss fully whether Dempsey was successful. [Dempsey v. Rosenthal, 121 Misc.2d 612, 468 N.Y.S.2d 441 (1983)]

Chapter 21

SALES
Product Liability

Often retailers serve simply as go-betweens, selling manufacturers' goods to consumers in prepackaged, sealed containers. Even so, retailers may be liable to purchasers on express or implied warranties despite the fact that they cannot always examine the goods prior to resale. In the past, courts frequently addressed the question of whether the injured party should recover from the manufacturer, the processor, or the retailer for damages caused by a defective product. Today, liability has been extended to manufacturers and processors through the application of new and old principles of the law.

Manufacturers and sellers of goods can be held liable to consumers, users, and bystanders for physical harm or property damage that is caused by the goods. This is called **products liability,** and it encompasses the contract theory of *warranty* and tort theories such as *negligence* and *strict liability*.

WARRANTY THEORY

Today, warranty law is an important part of the entire spectrum of laws relating to product liability. Consumers, purchasers, and even users of goods can recover *from any seller* for losses resulting from breach of implied and express warranties. A manufacturer is a *seller*. Therefore, a person who purchases goods from a retailer can recover from the retailer or manufacturer if the goods are not merchantable, because in most states *privity of contract* is no longer a prerequisite for breach-of-warranty recovery for personal injuries.

Since warranty laws were discussed in Chapter 20, the balance of this chapter will deal with the tort theories of recovery for damages and injuries caused by defective products.

LIABILITY BASED ON NEGLIGENCE

Chapter 4 defined *negligence* as failure to use that degree of care that a reasonable, prudent person would have used under the circumstances. The failure to exercise reasonable care under circumstances that cause an injury is the basis of liability for negligence. Thus, the manufacturer of a product must exercise "due care" to make that product safe to be used as intended. Due care must be exercised in designing the product, in selecting the materials, in using the appropriate production process, in assembling and testing the product, and in placing adequate warnings on the label informing the user of dangers of which an ordinary person might not be aware. The duty of care extends to the inspection and testing of purchased products used in the final product sold by the manufacturer. The failure to exercise due care is negligence.

Privity of Contract Not Required

An action based upon negligence does not require privity of contract between the injured plaintiff and the negligent defendant-manufacturer. Section 395 of the Restatement, Second, Torts states:

> A manufacturer who fails to exercise reasonable care in the manufacture of a chattel [movable good] which, unless carefully made, he should recognize as involving an unreasonable risk of causing substantial bodily harm to those who lawfully used it for a

purpose for which it was manufactured and to those whom the supplier should expect to be in the vicinity of its probable use, is subject to liability for bodily harm caused to them by its lawful use in a manner and for a purpose for which it is manufactured.

Simply stated, a manufacturer is liable for its failure to exercise due care to any person who sustains an injury proximately caused by a negligently made (defective) product. (The analysis of whether a product is so defective as to be *unreasonably dangerous* applies equally to actions based on strict tort liability and is discussed below.)

In the following landmark case, the New York court dealt with the liability of a manufacturer that failed to exercise reasonable care in manufacturing a finished product. The *MacPherson* case is the classic negligence case in which privity of contract was not required between the plaintiff and the defendant to establish liability. This is a forerunner to product liability, although it does not use product liability theory. Its subject matter, defectively manufactured wooden wheels for automobiles, is dated, but the principles involved are not.

Case 21.1

MacPHERSON v. BUICK MOTOR CO.

Court of Appeals of New York, 1916.
217 N.Y. 382, 111 N.E. 1050.

BACKGROUND AND FACTS   *The defendant, Buick Motor Company, was sued by Donald C. MacPherson, the plaintiff, who suffered injuries while riding in a Buick automobile that suddenly collapsed because one of the wheels was made of defective wood. The spokes crumbled into fragments, throwing MacPherson out of the vehicle and injuring him.*

The wheel itself had not been made by Buick Motor Company; it had been bought from another manufacturer. There was evidence, however, that the defects could have been discovered by reasonable inspection and that no such inspection had taken place. Although there was no charge that Buick knew of the defect and willfully concealed it, MacPherson charged Buick with negligence for putting a human life in imminent danger.

Keep in mind that MacPherson sued the manufacturer directly, despite the fact that the automobile was purchased from a retail Buick dealer. The trial court held for MacPherson, and Buick Motor Company appealed.

CARDOZO, Justice.
*   *   *   *

The question to be determined is whether the defendant owed a duty of care and vigilance to any one but the immediate purchaser.

The foundations of this branch of the law, at least in this state, were laid in *Thomas v. Winchester.* A poison was falsely labeled. The sale was made to a druggist, who in turn sold to a customer. The customer recovered damages from the seller who affixed the label. "The defendant's negligence," it was said, "put human life in imminent danger." A poison, falsely labeled, is likely to injure any one who gets it. *Because the*

danger is to be foreseen, there is a duty to avoid the injury. [Emphasis added.] *   *   *
Thomas v. Winchester became quickly a landmark of the law. In the application of its
principle there may, at times, have been uncertainty or even error. There has never
in this state been doubt or disavowal of the principle itself. *   *   *

These early cases suggest a narrow construction of the rule. Later cases, however,
evince a more liberal spirit. First in importance is *Devlin v. Smith.* The defendant, a
contractor, built a scaffold for a painter. The painter's servants were injured. The
contractor was held liable. He knew that the scaffold, if improperly constructed, was
a most dangerous trap. He knew that it was to be used by the workmen. He was building
it for that very purpose. Building it for their use, he owed them a duty, irrespective of
his contract with their master, to build it with care.

From *Devlin v. Smith* we *   *   * turn to the latest case in this court in which
Thomas v. Winchester was followed. That case is *Statler v. Ray Mfg. Co.* The defendant
manufactured a large coffee urn. It was installed in a restaurant. When heated, the
urn exploded and injured the plaintiff. We held that the manufacturer was liable. We
said that the urn "was of such a character inherently that, when applied to the purposes
for which it was designed, it was liable to become a source of great danger to many
people if not carefully and properly constructed."

It may be that *Devlin v. Smith* and *Statler v. Ray Mfg. Co.* have extended the
rule of *Thomas v. Winchester.* If so, this court is committed to the extension. The
defendant argues that things imminently dangerous to life are poisons, explosives, deadly
weapons—things whose normal function it is to injure or destroy. But whatever the
rule in *Thomas v. Winchester* may once have been, it has no longer that restricted
meaning. A scaffold *(Devlin v. Smith)* is not inherently a destructive instrument. It
becomes destructive only if imperfectly constructed. A large coffee urn *(Statler v. Ray
Mfg. Co.)* may have within itself, if negligently made, the potency of danger, yet no
one thinks of it as an implement whose normal function is destruction. *   *   *
*   *   *   *

We hold, then, that the principle of *Thomas v. Winchester* is not limited to poisons,
explosives, and things of like nature, to things which in their normal operation are
implements of destruction. If the nature of a thing is such that it is reasonably certain
to place life and limb in peril when negligently made, it is then a thing of danger. Its
nature gives warning of the consequences to be expected. If to the element of danger
there is added knowledge that the thing will be used by persons other than the purchaser,
and used without new tests, then, irrespective of contract, the manufacturer of this
thing of danger is under a duty to make it carefully. *   *   * It is possible to use almost
anything in a way that will make it dangerous if defective. That is not enough to charge
the manufacturer with a duty independent of his contract. *   *   * There must also
be knowledge that in the usual course of events the danger will be shared by others
than the buyer. Such knowledge may often be inferred from the nature of the transaction. But it is possible that even knowledge of the danger and of the use will not
always be enough. The proximity of remoteness of the relation is a factor to be considered. We are dealing now with the liability of the manufacturer of the finished
product, who puts it on the market to be used without inspection by his customers. If
he is negligent, where danger is to be foreseen, a liability will follow.

We are not required, at this time, to say that it is legitimate to go back of the
manufacturer of the finished product and hold the manufacturers of the component
parts. To make their negligence a cause of imminent danger, an independent cause
must often intervene; the manufacturer of the finished product must also fail in his
duty of inspection. It may be that in those circumstances the negligence of the earlier
members of the series is too remote to constitute, as to the ultimate user, an actionable
wrong. *   *   * There is here no break in the chain of cause and effect. In such
circumstances, the presence of a known danger, attendant upon a known use, makes
vigilance a duty. *   *   *

From this survey of the decisions, there thus emerges a definition of a duty of a
manufacturer which enables us to measure this defendant's liability. Beyond all ques-

tion, the nature of an automobile gives warning of probable danger if its construction is defective. This automobile was designed to go 50 miles an hour. Unless its wheels were sound and strong, injury was almost certain. It was as much a thing of danger as a defective engine for a railroad. The defendant knew the danger. It knew also that the car would be used by persons other than the buyer. This was apparent from its size; there were seats for three persons. It was apparent also from the fact that the buyer was a dealer in cars, who bought to resell. The maker of this car supplied it for the use of purchasers from the dealer just as plainly as the contractor in *Devlin v. Smith* supplied the scaffold for use by the servants of the owner. * * *
* * * *

It is true that * * * "an automobile is not an inherently dangerous vehicle." * * * The meaning is that danger is not to be expected when the vehicle is well constructed. The court left it to the jury to say whether the defendant ought to have foreseen that the car, if negligently constructed, would become "imminently dangerous." Subtle distinctions are drawn by the defendants between things inherently dangerous and things imminently dangerous, but the case does not turn upon these verbal niceties. If danger was to be expected as reasonably certain, there was a duty of vigilance, and this whether you call the danger inherent or imminent. * * *

We think the defendant was not absolved from a duty of inspection because it bought the wheels from a reputable manufacturer. It was not merely a dealer in automobiles. It was a manufacturer of automobiles. It was responsible for the finished product. It was not at liberty to put the finished product on the market without subjecting the component parts to ordinary and simple tests. * * * The obligation to inspect must vary with the nature of thing to be inspected. The more probable the danger the greater the need of caution.

DECISION AND REMEDY   *The New York Court of Appeals, the highest court in the New York state system, affirmed the judgment of the original trial court and the intermediate review court that the defendant, Buick Motor Company, was liable to Donald C. MacPherson for the injuries he sustained when he was thrown from the vehicle.*

COMMENTS   *This case has been interpreted to cover all articles that imperil life when negligently made. Prior to* MacPherson, *manufacturers escaped liability to consumers when their contractual dealings were with distributors or retailers. Since* MacPherson, *that is no longer the case.*

Defenses to Negligence

Any manufacturer, seller, or processor who can prove that due care was used in the manufacture of its product has an appropriate defense against a negligence suit, since failure to exercise due care is one of the major elements of negligence.

But there are other defenses, and their use and application vary from state to state. One area of variation is the tying of the breach (failure to exercise reasonable care) to the injury, referred to as causation (see Chapter 4). Numerous events, involving different people, take place between the time a product is manufactured and the time of its use. If any of these events can be shown to have caused or contributed to the injury, the manufacturer will claim, on the basis of this intervening cause, no liability.

Two other defenses are contributory negligence and, where recognized, assumption of risk (both also discussed in Chapter 4). For example, assume that the manufacturer of an industrial grinder states in its instruction manual that the grinder's operator should wear safety goggles. The owner of a machine tool repair shop purchases a grinder, has her employees read the manufacturer's instructions, and reminds them to wear safety goggles when they use the machine. Employee Joe

Kidd chooses to ignore the warnings. As Kidd begins using the grinder to sharpen a sawblade's cutting edge, a tiny spark of hot metal flies into and causes the loss of his right eye. Kidd files suit, claiming the manufacturer was negligent in failing to warn that the grinder might throw off hot metal sparks. The manufacturer-defendant would claim that Kidd's own knowledge of the risk and voluntary use of the product with such knowledge was an unreasonable assumption of risk and was the proximate cause of the injury.

Likewise, any time a plaintiff misuses a product or fails to make a reasonable effort at preserving his or her own welfare, the manufacturer or seller will claim that the plaintiff contributed to causing the injuries. The claim is that the plaintiff's negligence offsets the negligence of the manufacturer or seller. In some states, the contributory negligence of the plaintiff is an absolute defense for the defendant-manufacturer or seller. In many others, the negligence of both these parties is compared (comparative negligence), and damages are based on the proportion of negligence attributed to the defendant.

Violation of Statutory Duty as Basis of Liability

Numerous federal and state laws impose duties upon manufacturers of cosmetics, drugs, foods, toxic substances, and flammable materials. These duties involve appropriate description of contents, labeling, branding, advertising, and selling. For example, federal statutes include the Flammable Fabrics Act; the Food, Drug, and Cosmetic Act; and the Hazardous Substances Labeling Act. In a tort action for damages, a violation of statutory duty is often held to constitute *negligence per se*.

Consider an example: Jason Manufacturing Company produces pipe fittings *specifically* for use in the construction of homes in Monroe County. The fittings do not comply with county building codes. One of the pipe fittings bursts in a home, allowing hot water to spray on the homeowner. The homeowner can bring a negligence action for personal damages on the ground that failure to comply with the building codes is in and of itself an automatic breach of the manufacturer's duty of reasonable care. Of course, the homeowner has to show proximate cause—that is, he or she must relate the injury to the careless act.

FRAUDULENT AND NONFRAUDULENT MISREPRESENTATION

When a fraudulent misrepresentation has been made to a user or consumer and that misrepresentation ultimately results in an injury, the basis of liability may be the tort of fraud. Examples are the intentional mislabeling of packaged cosmetics and the intentional concealment of a product's defects.

A more interesting basis of liability is nonfraudulent misrepresentation, when a merchant *innocently* misrepresents the character or quality of goods. A famous example involved a drug manufacturer and a victim of addiction to a prescription medicine called Talwin. The manufacturer, Winthrop Laboratories, a division of Sterling Drug, Inc., innocently indicated to the medical profession that the drug was not physically addictive. Using this information, a physician prescribed the drug for his patient, who developed an addiction that turned out to be fatal. Even though the addiction was a highly unusual reaction resulting from the victim's highly unusual susceptibility to this product, the drug company was still held liable.[1]

THE DOCTRINE OF STRICT LIABILITY

A fairly recent development of tort law is the revival of the old doctrine of strict liability. Under this doctrine, people may be held liable for the results of their acts regardless of their intentions or their exercise of reasonable care. For example, a company that uses dynamite in constructing a road is strictly liable for any damages that it causes, even if it takes reasonable and prudent precautions to prevent such damages. In essence, the blasting company becomes liable for any personal injuries it causes and thus is an absolute insurer—that is, the company is liable for damages regardless of fault.

The English courts accepted the doctrine of strict liability for many years. Often, persons whose conduct resulted in the injury of another were held

1. Crocker v. Winthrop Laboratories, Div. of Sterling Drug, Inc., 514 S.W.2d 429 (Tex. 1974).

liable for damages, even if they had not intended to injure anyone and had exercised reasonable care. This approach was abandoned around 1800 in favor of the *fault* approach, in which an action was considered tortious only if it was wrongful or blameworthy in some respect.

Strict liability was reapplied in several landmark cases involving manufactured goods in the 1960s and has since become a common method of holding manufacturers liable. Section 402A of the Restatement, Second, Torts, promulgated in 1965 and now adopted by most of the states, clearly espouses the doctrine of strict liability in tort.

The Restatement of Torts

The Restatement, Second, Torts designates how the doctrine of strict product liability should be applied. It is a precise and widely accepted statement of the liabilities of sellers of goods (including manufacturers) and deserves close attention. Section 402A of Restatement, Second, Torts states:

(1) One who sells any product in a defective condition unreasonably dangerous to the user or consumer or to his property is subject to liability for physical harm thereby caused to the ultimate user or consumer or to his property, if
   (a) the seller is engaged in the business of selling such a product, and
   (b) it is expected to and does reach the user or consumer without substantial change in the condition in which it is sold.
(2) The rule stated in Subsection (1) applies although

(a) the seller has exercised all possible care in the preparation and sale of his product, and
(b) the user or consumer has not bought the product from or entered into any contractual relation with the seller.

Under this doctrine, liability does not depend on privity of contract. The injured party does not have to be the buyer or a third party beneficiary, as required under contract warranty theory [UCC 2-318]. Indeed, this type of liability in law is not governed by the provisions of the UCC. Under this doctrine, liability does not depend on proof of negligence. If the requirements discussed in the following section are met, the manufacturer's liability to an injured party may be virtually unlimited.

Strict liability is imposed by law as a matter of public policy. This public policy rests on the threefold assumption that (1) consumers should be protected against unsafe products; (2) manufacturers and distributors should not escape liability for faulty products simply because they are not in privity of contract with the ultimate users of those products; and (3) manufacturers and sellers of products are in a better position to bear the costs associated with injuries caused by their products—costs that they can ultimately pass on to all consumers in the form of higher prices.

California was the first state to impose strict liability in tort on manufacturers. In the landmark decision that follows, the California Supreme Court sets out the reasons for applying tort law rather than contract law to cases in which consumers are injured by defective products.

Case 21.2

GREENMAN v. YUBA POWER PRODUCTS, INC.

Supreme Court of California, 1962.
59 Cal.2d 57, 377 P.2d 897, 27 Cal.Rptr. 697.

BACKGROUND AND FACTS   *The plaintiff, Greenman, wanted a Shopsmith, a combination power tool that could be used as a saw, drill, and wood lathe, after having seen the tool demonstrated by a retailer and having studied a brochure prepared by the manufacturer. The plaintiff's wife bought him one for Christmas. More than a year later, a piece of wood flew out the lathe attachment of the Shopsmith while the plaintiff was using it, inflicting serious injuries on him. About ten and a half months later, the plaintiff sued both the retailer and the manufacturer for breach of warranties and negligence. The jury found for the plaintiff, and the defendants appealed.*

TRAYNOR, Justice.
*   *   *   *

Plaintiff introduced substantial evidence that his injuries were caused by defective design and construction of the Shopsmith. His expert witnesses testified that inadequate set screws were used to hold parts of the machine together so that normal vibration caused the tailstock of the lathe to move away from the piece of wood being turned permitting it to fly out of the lathe. They also testified that there were other more positive ways of fastening the parts of the machine together, the use of which would have prevented the accident. The jury could therefore reasonably have concluded that the manufacturer negligently constructed the Shopsmith. The jury could also reasonably have concluded that statements in the manufacturer's brochure were untrue, that they constituted express warranties, and that plaintiff's injuries were caused by their breach.

   *   *   *   *

[But] to impose strict liability on the manufacturer under the circumstances of this case, it was not necessary for plaintiff to establish an express warranty * * *. A manufacturer is strictly liable in tort when an article he places on the market, knowing that it is to be used without inspection for defects, proves to have a defect that causes injury to a human being. Recognized first in the case of unwholesome food products, such liability has now been extended to a variety of other products that create as great or greater hazards if defective.

   *   *   * [The] theory of an express or implied warranty running from the manufacturer to the plaintiff, the abandonment of the requirement of a contract between them, the recognition that the liability is not assumed by agreement but imposed by law, and the refusal to permit the manufacturer to define the scope of its own responsibility for defective products make clear that the liability is not one governed by the law of contract warranties but by the law of strict liability in tort. Accordingly, rules defining and governing warranties that were developed to meet the needs of commercial transactions cannot properly be invoked to govern the manufacturer's liability to those injured by their defective products unless those rules also serve the purposes for which such liability is imposed.

   *   *   * The purpose of such liability is to insure that the costs of injuries resulting from defective products are borne by the manufacturers that put such products on the market rather than by the injured persons who are powerless to protect themselves. Sales warranties serve this purpose fitfully at best. In the present case, for example, plaintiff was able to plead and prove an express warranty only because he read and relied on the representations of the Shopsmith's ruggedness contained in the manufacturer's brochure. Implicit in the machine's presence on the market, however, was a representation that it would safely do the jobs for which it was built. Under these circumstances, it should not be controlling whether plaintiff selected the machine because of the statements in the brochure, or because of the machine's own appearance of excellence that belied the defect lurking beneath the surface, or because he merely assumed that it would safely do the jobs it was built to do. It should not be controlling whether the details of the sales from manufacturer to retailer and from retailer to plaintiff's wife were such that one or more of the implied warranties of the sales act arose. "The remedies of injured consumers ought not to be made to depend upon the intricacies of the law of sales." To establish the manufacturer's liability it was sufficient that plaintiff proved that he was injured while using the Shopsmith in a way it was intended to be used as a result of a defect in design and manufacture of which plaintiff was not aware that made the Shopsmith unsafe for its intended use.

The jury verdict for the plaintiff was upheld.

DECISION AND REMEDY

Requirements of Strict Products Liability

Just because a person is injured by a product does not mean he or she will have a cause of action against the manufacturer of the product. A cause of action will exist only if the following six basic requirements of strict product liability are met:

1. The product must be in a defective condition when the defendant sells it.

2.   The defendant must normally be engaged in the business of selling that product.

3.   The product must be unreasonably dangerous to the user or consumer because of its defective condition.[2]

4.   The plaintiff must incur physical harm to self or property by use or consumption of the product.

5.   The defective condition must be the proximate cause of the injury or damage.

6.   The goods must not have been substantially changed from the time the product was sold to the time the injury was sustained.

Thus, in any action against a manufacturer or seller, the plaintiff does not have to show why or in what manner the product became defective. The plaintiff does, however, have to show that at the time the injury was sustained, the condition of the product was essentially the same as it was when it left the hands of the defendant manufacturer or seller.

The plaintiff must also show that the product was so defective as to be *unreasonably dangerous*. A court may consider a product so defective as to be unreasonably dangerous if either (1) the product was dangerous beyond the expectation of the ordinary consumer or (2) a less dangerous alternative was economically feasible for the manufacturer, but the manufacturer failed to produce it.

Under the feasible-alternative approach, courts will consider: a product's utility and desirability; the availability of other, safer products; the dangers that have been identified prior to an injured user's suit; the dangers' obviousness; the normal expectation of danger, particularly for established products; the probability of injury and its likely seriousness; the avoidability of injury by care in the product's use, including the contribution of instructions and warnings; and the viability of eliminating the danger without appreciably impairing the product's function or making the product too expensive. For example, people often cut themselves on knives, but a court would consider that knives are very useful. Reasoning that there is no way to avoid injuries without making the product useless and that the danger is obvious to users, a court would not find a knife to be unreasonably dangerous and would not hold a supplier of knives liable.

On the other hand, a court may consider a snowblower without a safety guard over the opening through which the snow is blown to be in a condition that is unreasonably dangerous, even if it carries warnings to stay clear of the opening. The danger may be within the user's expectations, but the court will also consider the likelihood of injury and its probable seriousness, as well as the cost of putting a guard over the opening and the guard's effect on the blower's operation.

Some products are safe when used as their manufacturers and distributors intend but not safe when used in other ways. Suppliers are generally required to expect reasonably foreseeable misuses and to design products that are either safe when misused or marketed with, for example, child-proof caps.

In the following case, the plaintiffs sought to recover from Honda Motor Company for injuries sustained while using Honda's mini–trail bike, even though the bike was not being used as directed by the manufacturer when the injuries occurred. An important factor considered by the court was whether Honda had adequately warned consumers of the potential dangers of using the bike in ways not intended by the manufacturer.

---

2. This element is no longer required in some states—for example, California.

Case 21.3
BAUGHN v. HONDA MOTOR COMPANY, LTD.
Supreme Court of Washington, 1986.
107 Wash.2d 127, 727 P.2d 655.

BACKGROUND AND FACTS   *On August 14, 1972, Douglas Bratz and Bradley Baughn were injured while riding a Honda Z50AK3 mini–trail bike. Both boys were just two months shy of their ninth birthdays. Bratz, who was driving the bike while Baughn rode as a passenger behind him, ran three stop signs without stopping before colliding with a truck. Bratz did not see the truck because, at the time of the accident, he was looking behind him at a girl chasing them on another mini–trail bike. Bratz wore a helmet, but it flew off on impact because it was unfastened. Baughn was not wearing a helmet. The mini–trail* *bike had a prominent warning label on it, immediately in front of the operator, stating:*

READ OWNER'S MANUAL CAREFULLY. THIS VEHICLE WAS MANUFACTURED FOR OFF-THE-ROAD USE ONLY. DO NOT OPERATE ON PUBLIC STREETS, ROADS OR HIGHWAYS.

The owner's manual contained similar explicit instructions against driving on public streets and roads and urged users to "Always Wear a Helmet."

The parents of the injured boys filed suit against Honda, alleging that the mini–trail bike was unreasonably dangerous. Honda claimed it had sufficiently warned consumers of potential dangers if the bike was not used as directed. The trial court granted Honda's motion for summary judgment, and the plaintiffs appealed.

ANDERSEN, Justice.

*   *   *   *

There is a considerable degree of overlap in the issues presented in the 415 pages of briefs filed in this case, out of which emerges one ultimate issue. *   *   * Is a manufacturer liable when children are injured while riding one of its mini–trail bikes on a public road in violation of manufacturer and parental warnings? *   *   * Where there are no design or manufacturing defects in the product, and where the warnings concerning its use are adequate, a manufacturer is not liable for an accident and resulting injuries. *   *   * On appeal, Baughn argues that Honda is liable under [various] theories, [including] strict liability. *   *   * Bratz discusses the same theories *   *   *.

Though the plaintiffs raise many issues under the heading of strict liability, the principal issue is Baughn's challenge to the standard set forth in [*Seattle-First Nat'l Bank v. Tabert*] for determining when a product may be considered defective, as is required in order to establish strict liability. In *Tabert*, this court held that a manufacturer may be held strictly liable for manufacturing a defective product if that product is not reasonably safe. "This means that it must be unsafe to an extent beyond that which would be reasonably contemplated by the ordinary consumer."

The *Tabert* "consumer expectations" test has been consistently applied by Washington courts in determining whether a manufacturer is strictly liable for manufacturing an unreasonably dangerous and therefore defective product. *Tabert* is widely recognized as a leading case in setting forth standards for imposing strict liability for a defective product.

*   *   *   *

In *Tabert*, we made clear the view of this court that "[t]he doctrine of strict liability does not impose legal responsibility simply because a product causes harm. Such a result would embody absolute liability which is not the import of strict liability."

*   *   *   *

A comment to § 402A of the Restatement (Second) of Torts is dispositive of the plaintiffs' *   *   * contention that Honda should be held strictly liable for manufacturing an unreasonably unsafe or dangerous product. Comment j states that to prevent a product from being unreasonably dangerous, a seller may be required to give directions or warnings as to its use. The comment adds:

Where warning is given, the seller may reasonably assume that it will be read and heeded; and a product bearing such a warning, which is safe for use if it is followed, is not in defective condition, nor is it unreasonably dangerous.

*   *   *   *

Baughn and Bratz argue that *   *   * [Honda's] warnings were inadequate because they did not describe what might happen if a child did ride a mini–trail bike on a public street. They also criticize Honda for failing to advise parents how to determine if their child was ready to ride a mini–trail bike.

*   *   *   *

Honda did not warn of every conceivable danger that could be encountered if children rode its mini–trail bikes on public streets and roadways. It did, however, specifically instruct that they were intended for off-the-road use only and that riders should wear helmets. There was no contention that Douglas or Bradley could not read the sticker prominently displayed on the mini–trail bike. There is no evidence that they read the owner's manual; Vernon Bratz said he only checked it to see how to adjust the mini–trail bike.

Honda did not inform parents how to determine if their child was ready to ride a mini–trail bike. In this case, however, both fathers owned motorcycles and had previously bought mini–trail bikes for their children which their children could ride. We cannot perceive that they did not think their children were ready to ride them.

While Honda did not warn Bradley and Douglas of the precise danger they eventually encountered, their parents did and did so repeatedly. The two boys were almost 9 years old. They were apparently normal children and undoubtedly knew that riding their mini–trail bikes on public roads and ignoring stop signs could cause them injury. Despite Honda's warnings and their parents' warnings, they rode into the street through several stop signs, did not watch where they were going and were injured when they collided with a truck they had not seen. The trial court did not err when it ruled that Honda satisfied its duty to warn under the law of negligence and strict liability.

DECISION AND REMEDY   *The Supreme Court of Washington affirmed the lower court's decision to grant summary judgment to Honda.*

Liability Sharing

As in cases involving product liability under other theories, a plaintiff must prove under a theory of strict liability in tort that the defective product that caused his or her injury was the product of a specific defendant. Recently, in cases in which plaintiffs could not prove which of many distributors of a harmful product supplied the particular product that caused the plaintiffs' injuries, courts have dropped this requirement. This has occurred in several cases involving DES (diethylstilbestrol), a drug administered in the past to prevent miscarriages. DES's harmful character was not realized until, a generation later, daughters of the women who took DES developed health prob-

lems, including vaginal carcinoma, that were linked to the drug. Partly due to the passage of time, a plaintiff-daughter could not prove which pharmaceutical company—of as many as 300—marketed the DES her mother ingested. In these cases, some courts applied *industrywide liability*, holding that all firms that manufactured and distributed DES during the period in question were liable for the plaintiffs' injuries in proportion to the firms' respective shares of the market.

The following case is illustrative of the market-share approach to liability and the application of the rule of apportionment used by the courts in determining each firm's respective liability to the plaintiff.

Case 21.4
MARTIN v. ABBOTT LABORATORIES
Supreme Court of Washington, 1984.
102 Wash.2d 581, 689 P.2d 368.

BACKGROUND AND FACTS   *Rita Rene Martin (the plaintiff) was born on October 4, 1962. Her mother, Shirley Ann Martin, had obtained a prescription for diethylstilbestrol (DES), which she took from May 1962 until the date Rita Martin was born. On January 4, 1980, Rita was diagnosed as suffering from carcinoma of the vagina. On February 21, 1980, as a result of the cancer, Rita underwent a radical hysterectomy and a partial vaginectomy.*

Shirley Martin could not remember which drug company manufactured the DES she ingested. Moreover, because of the passage of time and because DES was marketed generically, neither Shirley's physician nor her pharmacist could remember which company manufactured or marketed the drug Shirley ingested. The only thing Shirley Martin could substantiate was that she took the drug in 100-milligram doses.

Shirley and Rita Martin sued numerous drug companies (the defendants)— on the theories of negligence, strict liability, and breach of warranty—for personal injuries, pain, suffering, and destruction of the parent-child relationship. The Martins alleged that all of the pharmaceutical companies were liable for their injuries because of the companies' concerted, or joint, action to gain FDA approval and to market DES. The drug companies contended that none of them had been identified as the actual manufacturer or distributor of the DES ingested by Shirley Martin and that the plaintiffs had thus failed to state a cause of action for which relief could be granted. The trial court ruled that the plaintiffs had stated a valid cause of action, and from this ruling the defendants appealed.

DORE, Justice.

*   *   *   *

*   *   * [T]he crux of the problem facing this DES plaintiff is that she cannot identify the drug company that she alleges caused her injury. Numerous commentators and courts have identified several reasons for this plight. First, DES was, for the most part, produced in a "generic" form which did not contain any clearly identifiable shape, color, or markings. DES was a fungible drug produced with a chemically identical formula, and often pharmacists would fill DES prescriptions from whatever stock they had on hand, whether or not a particular brand was specified in the prescription. Second, it has been estimated that possibly as many as 300 drug companies produced or marketed DES during the 24 years DES was on the market, with companies entering and leaving the market throughout this period. Third, it appears that many drug companies may not have kept, or may not be able to locate, pertinent records as to when, where, and what type of DES they produced or marketed. These problems result from the passage of many years between the plaintiff's in utero exposure and the manifestation of cancer. During the intervening years, memories may have faded, medical and pharmaceutical records may have been lost or destroyed, and witnesses may have died.

We are presented with a conflict between the familiar principle that a tortfeasor [one who commits a tort] may be held liable only for damage that it has caused, and the sense of justice which urges that the victims of this tragedy should not be denied compensation because of the impossibility of identifying the individual manufacturer of these generic tablets if their manufacture and distribution were otherwise culpable.

*   *   *   *

Because certain manufacturers and distributors produced or marketed an allegedly defective drug for accidents of pregnancy, those manufacturers and distributors all contributed to the risk of injury, even though they may not have contributed to the actual injury of a given plaintiff. Although the defendants in this case have not acted in concert, *   *   * all participated in either gaining approval of DES for use in pregnancy or in producing or marketing DES in subsequent years. Each defendant contributed to the *risk* of injury to the public and, consequently, the risk of injury to individual plaintiffs. Thus, each defendant shares in some measure, a degree of culpability in producing or marketing DES. Moreover, *as between the injured plaintiff and the possibly responsible drug company, the drug company is in a better position to absorb the cost of the injury. The drug company can either insure itself against liability, absorb the damage award, or pass the cost along to the consuming public as a cost of doing business.* [Emphasis added.] We conclude that it is better to have drug companies or consumers share the cost of the injury than to place the burden solely on the innocent plaintiff.

We hold that plaintiff need commence suit against only one defendant and allege the following elements: that the plaintiff's mother took DES; that DES caused the plaintiff's subsequent injuries; that the defendant produced or marketed the type of DES taken by the plaintiff's mother; and that the defendant's conduct in producing or marketing the DES constituted a breach of a legally recognized duty to the plaintiff. At the trial, the plaintiff will have to prove each of these elements to the satisfaction of the trier of fact. We emphasize, however, that the plaintiff need not prove that a defendant produced or marketed the precise DES taken by the plaintiff's mother. Rather, the plaintiff need only establish by a preponderance of the evidence that a defendant produced or marketed the *type* (e.g., dosage, color, shape, markings, size, or other identifiable characteristics) of DES taken by the plaintiff's mother; the plaintiff need not allege or prove any facts related to the time or geographic distribution of the subject DES. While the type of DES ingested by the mother should be within the domain of her knowledge, facts relating to time and distribution should be particularly within the domain of knowledge of the DES manufacturers and distributors.

The defendants that are unable to exculpate [clear or excuse] themselves from potential liability are designated members of the plaintiffs' DES market; defined by the specificity of the evidence as to geographic market area, time of ingestion, and type of DES. These defendants are initially presumed to have equal shares of the market and are liable for only the percentage of plaintiff's judgment that represents their presumptive share of the market. These defendants are entitled to rebut this presumption and thereby reduce their potential liability by establishing their respective market share of DES in the plaintiff's particular geographic market. Upon proof of a market share by a preponderance of the evidence, that particular defendant is only liable for its share of the market as it relates to the total judgment. To the extent that other defendants fail to establish their actual market share, their presumed market share is adjusted so that 100 percent of the market is accounted for.

Application of this rule of apportionment is illustrated by the following hypotheticals. Assume that plaintiff's damages are $100,000 and defendants X and Y remain subject to liability after exculpation by other named defendants. If neither establishes its market share then they are presumed to have equal shares of the market and are liable respectively for 50 percent of the total judgment, X, $50,000 and Y, $50,000.

Assume defendant X establishes that it occupies 20 percent of the relevant market, and defendant Y fails to prove its market share. Defendant X is then liable for 20 percent of the damages, or $20,000, and defendant Y is subject to the remaining 80 percent, or $80,000.

Assume that defendant X establishes a market share of 20 percent and defendant Y a 60 percent market share. Then defendant X is subject to 20 percent of the judgment, $20,000, and defendant Y to 60 percent of the judgment, $60,000. The plaintiff does not recover her entire judgment because the remaining 20 percent of the market share is the responsibility of unnamed defendants.

DECISION AND REMEDY   *The Supreme Court of Washington determined that the plaintiffs had stated a valid cause of action, and the case was remanded to the trial court so that it could proceed in accordance with the appellate court's opinion.*

Limitations on Recovery

Some courts have limited the application of the strict liability doctrine to cases in which personal injuries have occurred. Thus, when a defective product causes only *property damage*, the seller may not be liable under a theory of strict liability, depending on the law of the particular jurisdiction. In addition, until recently, recovery for *eco-*

nomic loss was not available in an action based on strict liability (and even today it is rarely available). Note, however, that recovery for *breach of warranty* may be available, depending upon the type of injury and which alternative section of UCC 2-318 is in effect.

Finally, **statutes of repose** enacted by a number of states limit the time within which a plaintiff can file a product liability suit. Typically, a statute of repose begins to run at an earlier date and runs for a longer time than a statute of limitation. For example, a statute of repose may proscribe any claims not brought within twelve years from the date of *sale* or *manufacture* of the defective product. Therefore, it is immaterial that the product is defective or causes the injury if the injury occurs after the statutory period has lapsed. In addition, some of these legislative enactments have limited the application of the doctrine of strict liability to new goods. Some states, such as Massachusetts, have refused to recognize strict product liability. In these states, recovery is gained mainly via breach of warranty or negligence.

Defenses

Frequently, negligent misconduct or misuse of the product by the harmed person or a third party, coupled with the product's defect, causes damage or injury. If the misconduct or misuse can be charged to a claimant, it may be a defense to reduce the claimant's recovery or bar it altogether.

In some states, assumption of risk is a defense in an action based on strict liability in tort. In order for such a defense to be established, the defendant must show the following basic elements:

1. That the plaintiff voluntarily engaged in the risk while realizing the potential danger.
2. That the plaintiff knew and appreciated the risk created by the defect.
3. That the plaintiff's decision to undertake the known risk was unreasonable.

MISUSE OF THE PRODUCT Similar to the defense of voluntary assumption of risk is that of misuse of the product. Here the injured party did not know that the product was dangerous for a particular use, but that use was not the one for which the product was designed. (Contrast this with assumption of risk.) This defense has been severely limited by the courts, however. If the misuse is reasonably foreseeable, the seller must take measures to guard against it.

In the following case, the court examines the question of whether the injured party's misuse of the product was foreseeable by the manufacturer.

BACKGROUND AND FACTS *The plaintiff, Beverly Landrine, sued on behalf of her deceased infant daughter. The infant died after she swallowed a balloon while playing with a doll known as "Bubble Yum Baby." The doll could simulate the blowing of a bubble-gum bubble when a balloon was inserted into its mouth and inflated by pumping of its arm. The balloon was manufactured by Perfect Products Co. Mego Corporation, the distributor of the product, and Bell Arbor Novelty, the owner of the doll's trademark, were also defendants in the lawsuit. The plaintiff claimed that the balloon was defectively made or inherently unsafe when used by children and that the defendants had failed to warn of dangers associated with the balloon's usage. The defendants moved for summary judgment, which the trial court denied. Perfect Products Co. appealed.*

 Case 21.5

LANDRINE v. MEGO CORPORATION

Supreme Court, Appellate Division, 1983.
464 N.Y.S.2d 516.

MEMORANDUM DECISION.

*　*　*　*

*　*　* On this record neither plaintiff nor the crossclaimants have established that the balloons were unreasonably dangerous or defectively made. Absent a finding that all balloons are inherently dangerous, and that consequently a warning of the possible dangers must be given, Perfect cannot be held liable. Balloons in and of themselves are not dangerous. Their characteristics, features, and propensities are well-known, to children and adults alike. No duty to warn exists where the intended or foreseeable use of the product is not hazardous. Furthermore, "there is no necessity to warn a customer already aware—through common knowledge or learning—of a specific hazard." *　*　* Digestion of a balloon is not an intended use, and to the extent it is a foreseeable one, it is a misuse of the product for which the guardian of children must be wary. Were it otherwise, anything capable of being swallowed would have to be kept from a child. Even if a warning were required in this case it would have had to be directed to the guardian since the "legal responsibility, if any, for injury caused by [a product] which has possible dangers incident to its use should be shouldered by the one in the best position to have eliminated those dangers." * * * We see no need for such a warning. The ingestion of a balloon—which is not its intended use— is an act fraught with peril. Like a caution to drive carefully when operating heavy equipment * * * a self-evident warning is unnecessary.

DECISION AND REMEDY   *The appellate court reversed the trial court's ruling and granted summary judgment to Perfect, thereby freeing it of any liability for the infant's death.*

COMMENTS   *This case illustrates that a manufacturer is not absolutely liable for harm resulting from the use of its products. The basic elements of strict liability must still be met; that is, the product must be defective and unreasonably dangerous (and a foreseeable cause of an injury or damage) when sold by a merchant. In this case, the defense of misuse of product was successful. Balloons in and of themselves are not dangerous. Their characteristics and features are well known to both parents and children. The ingestion of a balloon is not an intended use; therefore, it is a misuse of the product for which the guardians of children must be responsible.*

COMPARATIVE FAULT As pointed out in Chapter 4, at common law, in any action based on negligence, contributory negligence of the injured party either completely barred recovery or reduced the amount of recovery under the rule of comparative negligence. In principle, contributory negligence is immaterial in any action based on the theory of strict liability in tort and in fact has been abolished as a defense by most courts.

Recent developments in the area of comparative negligence are affecting the doctrine of strict liability. Whereas previously the plaintiff's conduct was not a defense to strict liability, today a growing number of jurisdictions consider the negligent or intentional actions of the plaintiff in the apportionment of liability and damages. This "comparing" of the plaintiff's conduct to the defendant's strict liability results in an application of the doctrine of comparative negligence. States that have adopted this doctrine, either legislatively or through court decisions, include Minnesota, Alabama, Alaska, Kansas, New Jersey, Texas, California, Oregon, Florida, and Hawaii.[3] Al-

though comparative negligence in strict liability is presently the minority view, its recent growth may have a pervasive effect on this area of tort law.

Strict Liability to Bystanders

All courts extend the strict liability of manufacturers and other sellers to injured bystanders, although the drafters of Restatement, Second, Torts, Section 402A did not take a position on bystanders. For example, the manufacturer of an automobile was held liable for injuries caused by the explosion of the car's motor while the car was in traffic. A cloud of steam that resulted from the explosion caused multiple collisions because it kept other drivers from seeing well.[4]

In the following case, the court extends the protections of Section 402A to bystanders whose injuries from defective products are reasonably foreseeable. Thus, someone injured by an exploding bottle in a supermarket was able to seek damages from the manufacturer for an injury caused by the defective product.

---

3. W. Page Keeton et al., *Prosser and Keeton on Torts*, 5th ed. (St. Paul: West Publishing Co., 1984), pp. 478, 712.

4. Giberson v. Ford Motor Co., 504 S.W.2d 8 (Mo. 1974).

BACKGROUND AND FACTS *The plaintiff, Embs, was buying some groceries at Stamper's Cash Market. Unnoticed by her, a carton of 7-Up was sitting on the floor at the edge of the produce counter about one foot from where she was standing. Several of the 7-Up bottles exploded. Embs's leg was injured severely enough that Embs had to be taken to the hospital by a managing agent of the store. The trial court dismissed her claim. The appellate court now takes up the case.*

LUKOWSKY, Judge.

* * * *

Our expressed public policy will be furthered if we minimize the risk of personal injury and property damage by charging the costs of injuries against the manufacturer who can procure liability insurance and distribute its expense among the public as a cost of doing business; and since the risk of harm from defective products exists for mere bystanders and passersby as well as for the purchaser or user, there is no substantial reason for protecting one class of persons and not the other. The same policy requires us to maximize protection for the injured third party and promote the public interest in discouraging the marketing of products having defects that are a menace to the public by imposing strict liability upon retailers and wholesalers in the distributive chain responsible for marketing the defective product which injures the bystander. *The imposition of strict liability places no unreasonable burden upon sellers because they can adjust the cost of insurance protection among themselves in the course of their continuing business relationship.* [Emphasis added.]

We must not shirk from extending the rule to the manufacturer for fear that the retailer or middleman will be impaled on the sword of liability without regard to fault. Their liability was already established under Section 402A of the Restatement of Torts 2d. As a matter of public policy the retailer or middleman as well as the manufacturer should be liable since the loss for injuries resulting from defective products should be placed on those members of the marketing chain best able to pay the loss, who can then distribute such risk among themselves by means of insurance and indemnity agreements.

* * * *

The result which we reach does not give the bystander a "free ride." When products and consumers are considered in the aggregate, bystanders, as a class, purchase most of the same products to which they are exposed as bystanders. Thus, as a class, they indirectly subsidize the liability of the manufacturer, middleman and retailer and in this sense do pay for the insurance policy tied to the product.

Public policy is adequately served if parameters are placed upon the extension of the rule so that it is limited to bystanders whose injury from the defect is reasonably foreseeable.

For the sake of clarity we restate the extension of the rule. The protections of Section 402A of the Restatement, Second, Torts extend to bystanders whose injury from the defective product is reasonably foreseeable.

The appellate court reversed the trial court's directed verdict that dismissed Embs's claim. The case was remanded to the lower court for a new trial.

Case 21.6

EMBS v. PEPSI-COLA BOTTLING CO. OF LEXINGTON, KENTUCKY, INC.
Court of Appeals of Kentucky, 1975.
528 S.W.2d 703.

DECISION AND REMEDY

Crashworthiness Doctrine

Certain courts have adopted the doctrine of crashworthiness, which imposes liability for defects in the design or construction of motor vehicles that increase the extent of injuries to passengers if an accident occurs. The doctrine holds even when the defects do not actually cause the accident.[5] By

5. Turner v. General Motors Corp., 514 S.W.2d 497 (Texas Civ.App. 1974).

accepting the crashworthiness doctrine, the courts reject the argument of automobile manufacturers that involving a car in a collision does not constitute "ordinary use" of the car. There are, however, strong differences of opinion among the courts on this issue.

Strict Liability of Suppliers of Component Parts and Lessors of Movable Goods

Under the rule of strict liability in tort, the basis of liability has been expanded to include suppliers of component parts and lessors of movable goods. Thus, if General Motors buys brake pads from a subcontractor and puts them in Chevrolets without changing their composition, and if those pads are defective, both the supplier of the brake pads and General Motors will be held strictly liable for the damages caused by the defects.

Liability for personal injuries caused by defective goods extends to those who lease such goods.

Section 408 of the Restatement, Second, Torts states that:

One who leases a chattel as safe for immediate use is subject to liability to those whom he should expect to use the chattel, or to be endangered by its probable use, for physical harm caused by its use in a manner for which and by a person for whose use it is leased, if the lessor fails to exercise reasonable care to make it safe for such use or to disclose its actual condition to those who may be expected to use it.

Some courts have held that a leasing agreement gives rise to a contractual *implied warranty* that the leased goods will be fit for the duration of the lease. Under this view, if Hertz Rent-a-Car leases a Chevrolet that has been improperly maintained and a passenger in the Chevrolet is injured in an accident, the passenger can sue Hertz. (Liability is based on the contract theory of warranty, not tort.)

CONCEPT SUMMARY: Comparison of Negligence and Strict Liability in the Area of Product Liability		
	NEGLIGENCE	**STRICT LIABILITY**
Applicability	All products.	Products dangerously defective in design or manufacture.
Basic test	Considering all of the circumstances, was reasonable care exercised?	Is there a defect making the product unreasonably dangerous?[a]
Elements	1. Duty of care. 2. Breach of the duty. 3. Breach causes injury or damage.	1. Unreasonably dangerous defect. 2. Defect causes[b] injury or damage.[c]

Defenses	1. Exercise of reasonable care.
	 2. Intervening or superseding event caused injury or damage.
	 3. Claimant unreasonably assumed risk.
	 4. Claimant was also negligent:
	   a. Contributory-negligence jurisdiction—absolute defense.
	   b. Comparative-negligence jurisdiction—damages apportioned.
		1. Defect did not exist when product was in defendant's hands.
		 2. Claimant misused product in an unforeseeable way.
		 3. Claimant unreasonably assumed risk.
		 4. Claimant was also negligent:[d]
		   a. Contributory-negligence jurisdiction—absolute defense.
		   b. Comparative-negligence jurisdiction—damages apportioned.

a. As mentioned, some jurisdictions do not require that a defect render a product unreasonably dangerous.
b. In a few jurisdictions, under the crashworthiness doctrine, the defect need not have caused the accident that resulted in an injury. It need only have increased the extent of the injury.
c. Some jurisdictions limit awards to cases involving personal injuries. A few jurisdictions permit recovery of economic losses.
d. This defense is available in only a few states.

QUESTIONS AND CASE PROBLEMS

1. Susan buys a television set manufactured by Quality TV Appliance, Inc. She is going on vacation, so she takes the set to her mother's house for her mother to use. Because the set is defective, it explodes, causing considerable damage to her mother's house. Susan's mother sues Quality for the damages to her house. Discuss the theories under which Susan's mother can recover from Quality.

2. Perfect Drug Company manufactures and has placed on the market a drug for airsickness. Jacob purchases the drug from Green's Drug Store. Jacob is going on a trip and takes two of the tablets as directed. Jacob loses consciousness because of the side effects of the drug, and he falls down a flight of stairs at the airport, breaking an arm and a leg. Perfect knew of the possible side effects but did not place any warning on the label. Also, it is learned that Perfect failed to meet minimum federal drug standards in the manufacture of the drug—standards that would have reduced the side effects. Jacob wants to file an action based on Perfect's negligence.
   (a) Discuss Jacob's burden of proof.
   (b) Discuss how the situation would change if a warning had been placed on the package and minimum standards had been met.

3. Colt manufactures a new pistol. Firing of the pistol is dependent on an enclosed high-pressure device. The pistol has been thoroughly tested in two laboratories in the Midwest, and it has been designed and manufactured according to current technology. Wayne purchases one of the new pistols from Hardy's Gun and Rifle Emporium. When he uses the pistol in the high altitude of the Rockies, the difference in pressure causes the pistol to misfire, resulting in serious injury to Wayne. Colt can prove that all due care was used in the manufacturing process, and it refuses to pay for Wayne's injuries. Discuss Colt's liability in tort.

4. Baxter manufactures electric hair dryers. Julie purchases a Baxter dryer from her local Ace Drug Store. Green, a friend and guest in Julie's home, has taken a shower and wants to dry her hair. Julie tells Green to use the new Baxter hair dryer that she has just purchased. As Green plugs in the dryer, sparks fly out from the motor and continue to do so as she operates it. Despite this, Green begins drying her hair. Suddenly, the entire dryer ignites into flames, severely burning Green's scalp. Green sues Baxter on the basis of the torts of negligence and strict liability. Baxter admits the dryer was defective but denies liability, particularly since Green did not purchase the dryer. Discuss the validity of any defense claimed by Baxter.

5. Gina is standing on a street corner waiting for a ride to work. Barney has just purchased a new car manufactured by Optimal Motors. Barney is driving down the street when suddenly the steering mechanism breaks, causing him to run over Gina. Gina suffers permanent injuries. Barney's total income per year has never exceeded $15,000. Gina files suit against Optimal under the theory of strict liability in tort. Optimal pleads no liability because (1) due care was used in the manufacture of the car, (2) Optimal is not the manufacturer of the steering mechanism (Smith is), and (3) the Restatement governing strict liability applies only to users or consumers, and Gina is neither. Discuss the validity of the defenses claimed by Optimal.

6. Ryder Truck Rental leased one of its trucks to Gagliardi Brothers, Inc. While the truck was being operated by one of Gagliardi's employees in the scope of his employment, the brakes failed. The truck struck one car, which then collided with a car driven by Martin. Martin's car was damaged and she received injuries. If Martin wishes to sue Ryder, can she bring her suit under the theory of strict liability? [Martin v. Ryder Truck Rental, Inc., 353 A.2d 581 (Del. 1976)]

7. Ford Motor Company manufactured and distributed the Ford Cortina, which had only a cardboard shield separating the fuel tank from the passenger compartment. Nanda suffered severe disabling burns when the gas tank in his car exploded upon being struck in the rear by another car. In a strict liability action by Nanda against Ford Motor Company, Nanda argued that the absence of a fire wall or metal shield between the fuel tank and passenger compartment constituted an unreasonably dangerous defect in the product and that his injuries were caused by this defect. What was the result? [Nanda v. Ford Motor Co., 509 F.2d 213 (7th Cir. 1974)]

8. A two-year-old child lost his leg when he became entangled in a grain auger on his grandfather's farm. The auger had a safety guard that prevented any item larger than 4⅝ inches from coming into contact with the machine's moving parts. The child's foot was smaller than the openings in the safety guard. Was such an injury reasonably foreseeable? [Richelman v. Kewanee Machinery & Conveyor Co., 59 Ill.App.3d 578, 375 N.E.2d 885, 16 Ill.Dec. 778 (1978)]

9. During the 1960s, Aluminum Company of America (Alcoa) designed, patented, manufactured, and marketed a closure system for applying aluminum caps to carbonated soft-drink bottles. In 1969, Alcoa sold a capping machine to Houston 7-Up Bottling Company. On June 3, 1976, James Alm suffered a severe eye injury when an aluminum bottle cap exploded off a thirty-two-ounce bottle of 7-Up that had come from the Houston 7-Up Bottling Company. Alm sued Alcoa, alleging that, as the manufacturer, Alcoa had a duty to warn consumers of the dangers of a possible bottle-cap explosion. Alcoa argued that it had not had a duty to warn Alm because it had not manufactured or sold any component part or the final product that injured Alm. Alcoa had mentioned possible cap explosions in the machine users' manual, wall charts, and technical information that it had provided to the Houston 7-Up Bottling Company. Which allegation is correct? [Alm v. Aluminum Company of America, 717 S.W.2d 588 (Tex. 1986)]

10. Odell Kennedy was employed by the Georgetown Ice Company to operate ice-making machinery. Ice was carried up a conveyer from the machine

to a freezer for storage, and when the ice became stuck, employees had to climb onto a catwalk over the conveyer to dislodge it. In July 1976, Odell's arm was pulled off when he was accidentally pulled into the conveyer. The accident would not have occurred if protective shields had been incorporated over the top of the machine. The machinery involved in the accident was designed and installed by Custom Ice Equipment, and the catwalk was made by Odell's employer, Georgetown. Odell sued Custom for negligently designing the machine in a way that failed to take into account foreseeable dangers and on the basis of strict liability in tort. Discuss whether Odell should succeed against Custom on the theory that Custom should have foreseen that users of the machines would add catwalks or similar devices. [Kennedy v. Custom Ice Equipment Co., Inc., 271 S.C. 171, 246 S.E.2d 176 (1978)]

11. Frances Ontai entered the Straub Clinic and Hospital to have an x-ray examination of the colon. Ontai was placed in a vertical position on a table manufactured by General Electric. The footrest on the table broke, and Ontai fell to the floor of the examination room, suffering injuries. Ontai filed suit against Straub and General Electric. Ontai's suit against General Electric was based on strict liability in tort, negligence, and implied warranties. Discuss briefly each of these theories of liability. [Ontai v. Straub Clinic and Hospital, Inc., 66 Hawaii 237, 659 P.2d 734 (1983)]

Chapter 22

Basic Concepts of Commercial Paper

To some extent, commercial law is a reflection of customs and usages of trade in the business world. The development of the law concerning commercial paper—promissory notes, checks, and the like—grew from commercial necessity. As early as the thirteenth century, merchants dealing in foreign trade were using commercial paper in order to finance and conduct their affairs. Problems in transportation and in the safekeeping of gold or coins had prompted this practice. Since the king's common law courts of those times did not recognize the validity of commercial paper, the merchants had to develop their own rules governing its use, and these rules were enforced by "fair" or "borough" courts. For this reason, the early law governing commercial paper was part of the Law Merchant. (See Chapter 16.)

Later, the Law Merchant was codified in England in the Bills of Exchange Act of 1882. In 1896, the National Conference of Commissioners on Uniform Laws drafted the Uniform Negotiable Instruments Law. This law was reviewed by the states, and by 1920 all the states had adopted it. The Uniform Negotiable Instruments Law was the forerunner of Article 3 of the Uniform Commercial Code.

Commercial paper can be defined as any written promise or order to pay a sum of money. Drafts, checks, and promissory notes are typical examples. Commercial paper is transferred more readily than ordinary contract rights, and persons who acquire it are normally subject to less risk than the ordinary assignee of a contract right.

FUNCTIONS AND PURPOSES OF COMMERCIAL PAPER

Commercial paper has two functions. It serves as a substitute for money and as a credit device.

Debtors sometimes use currency, but for convenience and safety they often use commercial paper instead. For example, commercial paper is being used when a debt is paid by check. The substitute-for-money function of commercial paper developed in the Middle Ages. As mentioned previously, merchants deposited their precious metals with bankers in order to avoid the dangers of loss or theft. When they needed funds to pay for the goods

417

that they were buying, they gave the seller a written order addressed to the bank. This authorized the bank to deliver part of the precious metals to the seller. These orders, called *bills of exchange*, were sometimes used as a substitute for money. Today people use checks the same way. They also use drafts, promissory notes, and certificates of deposit that are payable either on demand or on some specified date in the future.

Commercial paper may represent an extension of credit. When a buyer gives a seller a promissory note, the terms of which provide that it is payable within sixty days, the seller has essentially extended sixty days of credit to the buyer. The credit aspect of commercial paper was developed in the Middle Ages soon after bills of exchange began to be used as substitutes for money. Merchants were able to give sellers bills of exchange that were not payable until a future date. Since the seller would wait until the maturity date to collect, this was a form of extending credit to the buyer. The holder of a promissory note payable in sixty or ninety days who wishes to sell this instrument to a third party may do so for immediate cash. Typically, banks buy these instruments and wait until their maturity date to receive payment. In order to induce a bank to buy a promissory note, the holder of the instrument accepts a discount of, say, 5, 10, or 15 percent of the face amount. In effect,

the bank pays less than the amount it will eventually collect as a way of charging interest.

For commercial paper to operate practically as a substitute for money or as a credit device, it is essential that the paper be easily transferable without danger of being uncollectible. This is the function that characterizes *negotiable* commercial paper. Each rule studied in this chapter can be examined in light of this function.

TYPES OF COMMERCIAL PAPER

UCC 3-104 specifies four types of instruments—drafts, checks, notes, and certificates of deposit.

Drafts

A **draft** (bill of exchange) is an unconditional written order. The party creating it (the **drawer**) orders another party (the **drawee**) to pay money, usually to a third party (the **payee**). Exhibit 22–1 shows a typical draft. The drawee must be obligated to the drawer either by agreement or through a debtor-creditor relationship in order for the drawee to be obligated to the drawer to honor the order.

TIME AND SIGHT DRAFTS   A *time draft* is a draft that is payable at a definite future time. A *sight*

Exhibit 22–1 Typical Time Draft: A Bill of Exchange

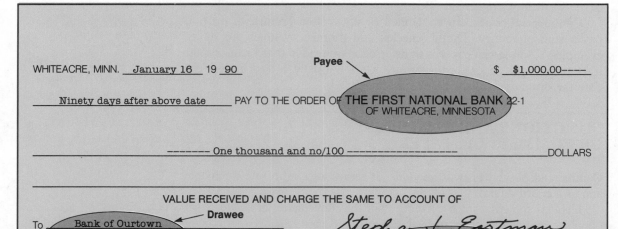

(or demand) *draft* is payable on sight—that is, when the holder presents it for payment—or at a stated time after sight.[1]

TRADE ACCEPTANCES   The **trade acceptance** is a draft that is frequently used in the sale of goods. The seller is both the drawer and the payee on this draft. Essentially, the draft orders the buyer to pay a specified sum of money to the seller, usually at a stated time in the future.

To illustrate: Good Yard Company sells $50,000 of fabric to Lane Dresses, Incorporated, each fall on terms requiring payment to be made in ninety days. One year Good Yard needs cash, so it draws a *trade acceptance* that orders Lane to pay $50,000 to the order of Good Yard Company ninety days hence. Good Yard presents the paper to Lane. Lane *accepts* by signing the face of the paper and returns it to Good Yard. Lane's acceptance creates an enforceable promise to pay the instrument when it comes due in ninety days. Good Yard can sell the trade acceptance in the commercial money market more easily than it can assign the $50,000 account receivable (for the reasons covered in Chapter 13, on assignments, and in subsequent chapters in this area). Thus, trade acceptances are

the standard credit instruments in sales transactions. Exhibit 22–2 shows a trade acceptance.

Checks

A **check** is a distinct type of draft, *drawn* on a *bank* and payable on *demand*. Checks are discussed more fully in Chapter 27. Note here, however, that with certain types of checks the bank is both the drawer and the drawee. For example, *cashier's checks* drawn by the bank on itself are payable on demand when issued. In addition, a check can be drawn by a bank on another bank. This instrument is known as a **bank draft.**

When *traveler's checks* are drawn on a bank, they are checks, but they require the purchaser's authorized signature before becoming payable. (Technically, most traveler's checks are not checks but drafts, because the drawee—for example, American Express—is ordinarily not a bank.)

Promissory Notes

The **promissory note** is a written promise between two parties. One party is the maker of the promise to pay, and the other is the payee, or the one to whom the promise is made. A promissory note, commonly referred to as a **note,** can be made payable at a definite time or on demand. It can name a specific payee or merely be payable to bearer. A sample promissory note is shown in Exhibit 22–3.

---

1. Or a sight draft may be payable on **acceptance,** the drawee's written promise (engagement) to pay the draft when it comes due. The usual manner of accepting is by writing the word *accepted* across the face of the instrument, followed by the date of acceptance and the signature of the drawee.

Exhibit 22–2 **Typical Time Draft: A Trade Acceptance**

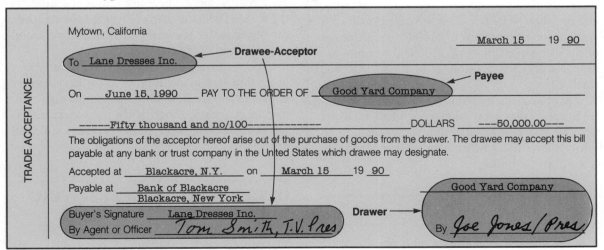

Exhibit 22–3 Typical Promissory Note

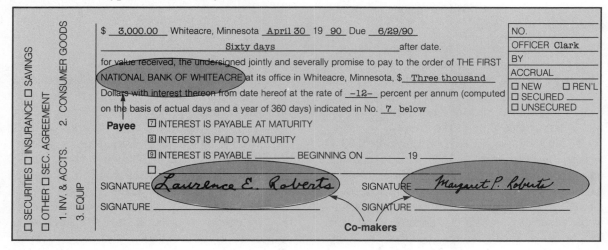

Notes are used in a variety of credit transactions and often carry the name of the transaction involved. For example, in real estate transactions, a promissory note for the unpaid balance on a house, secured by a mortgage on the property, is called a *mortgage note*. A note that is secured by personal property is called a *collateral note*. And a note payable in installments, such as for payment of a color television set over a twelve-month period, is called an *installment note*.

Certificates of Deposit

A **certificate of deposit (CD)** is an acknowledgment by a bank of the receipt of money with an engagement to repay it [UCC 3-104(2)(c)]. Certificates of deposit in small denominations are often sold by savings and loan associations, savings banks, and commercial banks. They are called small CDs and are for amounts up to $100,000. Certificates of deposit for amounts of $100,000 or more are called large CDs. Exhibit 22–4 shows a typical small CD.

Large and small certificates of deposit pay interest, and most large and some small CDs are negotiable. Their negotiability allows them to be sold, to be used to pay debts, or to serve as security (collateral) for a loan.

LETTERS OF CREDIT

A **letter of credit** is neither a draft nor a note. It is an agreement that the issuer will pay drafts

drawn by the creditor. Letters of credit are made by a bank or other person at the request of a customer and can be revocable or irrevocable commitments. Letters of credit are frequently used by buyers in the purchase of goods in commerce.

For example, a corporate buyer in California wishes to purchase manufacturing equipment from a West German seller. The buyer goes to its bank and through a loan agreement gets the bank to issue and to send a letter of credit to the seller in West Germany. The letter of credit provides that upon the seller's presentation of certain documents (bill of lading, invoice, customs receipts, and the like) to the bank, the bank will pay any drafts drawn by the seller on the buyer up to a stated amount. As the drafts are presented to the bank for payment, the bank remits the funds to the seller. The bank then collects the amount from the buyer under the terms of the loan agreement. (See Exhibit 22–5.)

Today, letters of credit are used for a variety of lending arrangements (such as the development of real estate) for both domestic and foreign commercial purposes. Much of the law governing letters of credit is found in Article 5 (Letters of Credit) in the UCC.

OTHER WAYS OF CLASSIFYING COMMERCIAL PAPER

The preceding classifications of commercial paper follow the language of the UCC. There are nu-

Exhibit 22–4 Typical Small CD

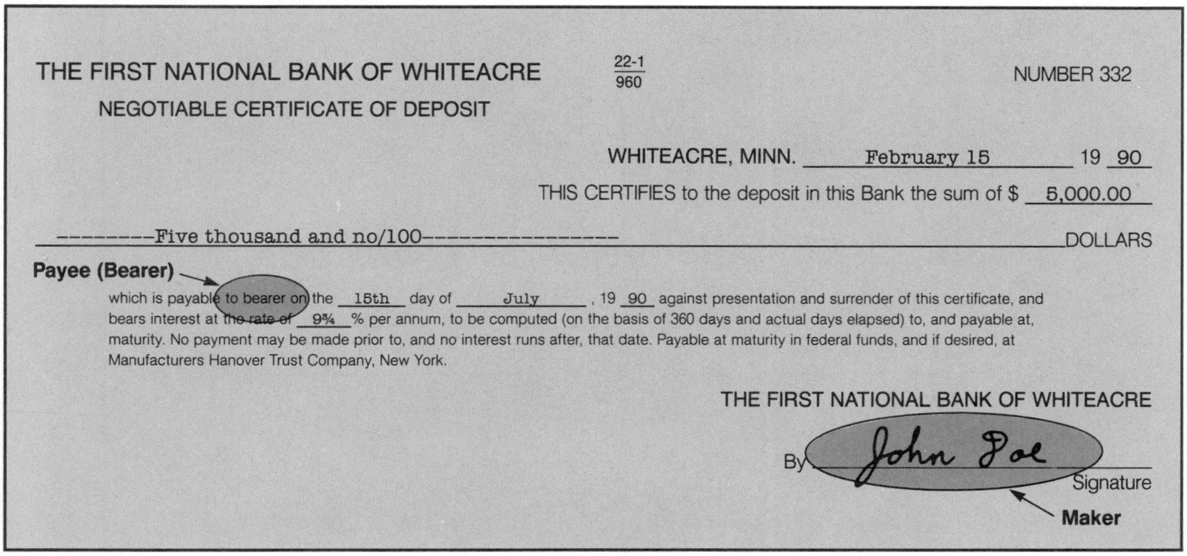

THE FIRST NATIONAL BANK OF WHITEACRE $\frac{22\text{-}1}{960}$ NUMBER 332

NEGOTIABLE CERTIFICATE OF DEPOSIT

WHITEACRE, MINN.   February 15   19 90

THIS CERTIFIES to the deposit in this Bank the sum of $ 5,000.00

————————Five thousand and no/100————————————DOLLARS

Payee (Bearer)

which is payable to bearer on the 15th day of July , 19 90 against presentation and surrender of this certificate, and bears interest at the rate of 9¾ % per annum, to be computed (on the basis of 360 days and actual days elapsed) to, and payable at, maturity. No payment may be made prior to, and no interest runs after, that date. Payable at maturity in federal funds, and if desired, at Manufacturers Hanover Trust Company, New York.

THE FIRST NATIONAL BANK OF WHITEACRE

By *John Doe*
Signature
Maker

merous other ways to classify commercial paper, some of which are treated here.

Demand Instruments and Time Instruments

Commercial paper can be classified as demand instruments or as time instruments. A demand instrument is payable on demand, that is, whenever the holder—a possessor *to whom the instrument runs*—chooses to present it to the maker in the case of a note or to the drawee in the case of a draft. (Instruments payable on demand include those payable on sight or on presentation and in which no time for payment is stated [UCC 3-108].) All checks are demand instruments because, by definition, they must be payable on demand; therefore, checking accounts are called **demand deposits.** Time instruments are payable at a future date.

Orders to Pay and Promises to Pay

Commercial paper involving the payment of money must contain either a *promise* to pay or an *order* to pay. Thus, commercial paper can be classified as either promises to pay or orders to pay. Accordingly, a check and a draft are orders to pay. On the other hand, a certificate of deposit and a promissory note are promises to pay.

Negotiable and Nonnegotiable Instruments

All commercial paper is either *negotiable* or *nonnegotiable*. For business to run smoothly, commercial paper must be negotiable—that is, generally, as acceptable as money. To encourage acceptability, paper must freely transfer the right to payment. When transferability is limited, the paper may be said to be nonnegotiable.

Both its form and its content determine whether commercial paper is negotiable. All the elements listed in UCC 3-104 must be present for negotiability. This topic is of sufficient importance that all of Chapter 23 is devoted to it. Note that when an instrument is negotiable, its transfer from one person to another is governed by Article 3 of the UCC. Indeed, UCC 3-102(e) defines *instrument* as a "negotiable instrument." For that reason, wherever the term *instrument* is used in this book, it refers to a negotiable instrument. Transfers of nonnegotiable instruments are governed by rules of assignment of contract rights. (See Chapter 13.)

PARTIES TO COMMERCIAL PAPER

To review, a note or a certificate of deposit has two original parties—the maker and the payee. A

Exhibit 22–5 Letter of Credit Transaction

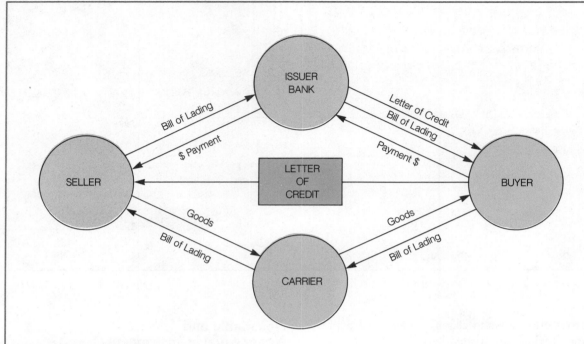

CHRONOLOGY OF EVENTS

1. Buyer contracts with issuer bank to issue a letter of credit; this sets forth the bank's obligation to pay on the letter of credit and buyer's obligation to pay the bank.

2. Letter of credit is sent to seller, informing seller that upon compliance with the terms of the letter of credit (such as presentment of necessary documents—for example, a bill of lading), the bank will issue a payment for the goods.

3. Seller delivers goods to carrier and receives a bill of lading.

4. Seller delivers the bill of lading to issuer bank and, if the document is proper, receives payment.

5. Issuer bank delivers the bill of lading to buyer.

6. Buyer delivers the bill of lading to carrier.

7. Carrier delivers the goods to buyer.

8. Buyer settles with issuer bank.

---

draft or a check has three original parties—the drawer, the drawee, and the payee. Sometimes two of the parties to a draft can be the same person (drawer-drawee or drawer-payee). Once an instrument is issued, additional parties can become involved. **Issue** is defined as the "first delivery of an instrument to a holder" [UCC 3-102(1)(a)]. The liability of these parties is discussed in Chapter 26.

Maker

A **maker** is the person who issues a promissory note or a CD promising to pay a certain sum of money to a payee or bearer. The maker's signature must appear on the face of the promissory note or CD for the maker to be liable on the note.

Drawer, Drawee, and Payee

When a check or other draft is issued, the person who issues it, known as the *drawer*, orders the *drawee* (who is a bank in the case of a check) to pay a certain sum of money to a *payee* (or to the bearer of the instrument).

To illustrate: Smith has a checking account with West Wind Bank. At the end of the month,

Smith receives his utility bill of $52 from the Tower Power and Light Corporation. Smith writes a check payable to the order of the utility, signing it in the lower right-hand corner. Smith is the *drawer* of the check. The West Wind Bank, which has been ordered to pay the check, is the *drawee*. Tower Power and Light, to which Smith has issued the check, is the *payee*.

Indorser

The payee of a note or draft may transfer it by signing (indorsing) it and delivering it to another person. By doing this, the payee becomes an **indorser.** For example, Carol receives a graduation check for $25. She can transfer the check to her mother (or anyone) by signing it on the back. Carol is an indorser.

Indorsee

The person who receives the indorsed instrument is the **indorsee.** In the example above, Carol's mother is the indorsee. She is entitled to the $25 payment by virtue of Carol's indorsement. Carol's mother can indorse the check to someone else and thus become an indorser as well.

Bearer

A **bearer** is any person who has physical possession of an instrument that either is payable to anyone without specific designation or is indorsed in blank. Bearer paper is payable to whoever possesses it. If a note is expressly made "payable to bearer" or if a check that already has imprinted "pay to the order of" is made to read "pay to the order of bearer," the person who possesses that note or check is the bearer. One of the most common methods of creating bearer paper is to make a check read "pay to the order of cash." A check payable to the order of a named person and indorsed by that named person in blank on the back makes its possessor a bearer also.

Holder

The term **holder** includes any person in possession of an instrument drawn, issued, or indorsed to him or her or to his or her order or to bearer or in blank.[2] To illustrate: If John Doe has in his possession a check made payable to the order of John Doe, John Doe is a holder of the check. A promissory note written by Sarah Smith promises to pay a sum of money to the order of Tom Jones. While the note is in Jones's possession, Jones is a holder. If Jones signs (indorses) the back of the note—which, since it is indorsed in blank, becomes bearer paper—and transfers (negotiates) it to Adam White, White becomes the holder.

The holder and the owner of negotiable paper can be, but are not necessarily, the same person. For example, a thief who steals a bearer instrument is a *holder* under commercial law principles (but obviously the thief is not the owner). Nonetheless, the thief can legally transfer (negotiate) the bearer instrument to another person, who then becomes a *holder*.

HOLDER IN DUE COURSE Under UCC 3-302, a holder in due course (HDC) is a person who acquires an instrument for value in good faith and without notice that it is defective or overdue or that any person has a claim to or defense against it.

HDCs are discussed fully in Chapter 25. At this point, the most important concept to remember, and one of the reasons a holder would want to become an HDC, is that it is easier for an HDC to collect payment on an instrument because the HDC is protected from all but a few defenses.

HOLDER THROUGH A HOLDER IN DUE COURSE An ordinary holder whose manner of acquisition fails to meet the requirements of a holder in due course can still be afforded HDC protection by proving that any prior holder qualified as a holder in due course [UCC 3-201(1)].

Acceptor

An **acceptor** is a drawee of a draft or check who has, by signing the instrument, manifestly agreed to pay the draft when due. For example, when the buyer "agrees" to pay the trade acceptance of the seller, drawn on the buyer (drawee), the buyer

---

2. UCC 1-201(20) defines *holder* as "a person who is in possession of a document of title or an instrument or an investment security drawn, issued, or indorsed to him or to his order or to bearer or in blank."

becomes an acceptor of the draft. (See Exhibit 22–2.) The same result takes place when a drawee bank certifies a check drawn on that bank.

Accommodation Party

An **accommodation party** is one who signs an instrument in any capacity to lend "his name to another party to it" [UCC 3-415(1)]. The accommodation party actually lends his or her credit to the party to whom the accommodation is made and is classified according to the accommodated party's status (that is, if the accommodated party is, for example, the drawer, the accommodation party is liable on the instrument as if he or she was the drawer).

For example, Barrow seeks a loan from the West Wind Bank. The bank will make the loan only if Barrow will get a third party with a good credit rating to co-sign the note. Able qualifies and agrees to accommodate Barrow by signing the note below Barrow's signature. Barrow is the *maker*, and Able is the *accommodation maker*. If, prior to the instrument's due date, Smith acquires it through the negotiation process, Able is still liable in the capacity in which she signed, even though Smith knows of the accommodation [UCC 3-415(2)].

In any case, Able, as the accommodation party, is not liable to Barrow. Able is liable to Smith, who took the note for value. But if Able pays the instrument, she has the right of recourse on the instrument against Barrow [UCC 3-415(5)].

QUESTIONS AND CASE PROBLEMS

1. Adam Smith, a college student, wished to purchase a new component stereo system from John Locke Stereo, Inc. Since Smith did not have the cash to pay for the entire stereo system, he offered to sign a note promising to pay $150 per month for the next six months. Locke Stereo, anxious to sell the system to Smith, agreed to accept the promissory note as long as Smith had one his professors sign it. Smith did this and tendered a note to John Locke Stereo that stated, "I, Adam Smith, promise to pay John Locke Stereo or its order the sum of $150 per month for the next six months." The note was signed by Adam Smith and his business law professor. About a week later, John Locke Stereo, which was badly in need of cash, signed the back of the note and sold it to Fidelity Bank. Give the specific designation of each of the four parties on this note.

2. A partnership called Larson and Adkins is a law firm. Larson had just won a case for her client, Brown, against Bill Bucks. When Larson went to collect the judgment from Bucks, Bucks wrote out a check that read: "Pay to the order of Larson and Adkins $60,000 [Signed] Bill Bucks." On the top of the check were the words "Hanover Trust." When Larson went to deposit the check in the trust account that she had set up for her client, she signed the back of the check "L. Larson." How are each of these parties designated in commercial paper law?

3. Negotiable instruments play an important part in commercial transactions. Different needs can be fulfilled by use of different types of instruments in certain ways. For instance, many insurance companies use a form of draft instead of a check to remit insurance benefits. The insurance company is both the drawer and the drawee; the beneficiary (the person receiving the money) is the payee; and the draft is made payable through a named bank in which the insurance company maintains a large account. What are the advantages of using such a draft?

4. Often, when two parties to a sale are strangers to each other and the sale is for a substantial amount of money, the selling party will insist that the purchaser make payment with a cashier's check. A cashier's check is a check for which the bank is both the drawer and the drawee. To purchase a cashier's check, a person goes to a bank teller, tenders the amount of money for which the check is to be payable, and supplies the teller with the name of the person who is to be the payee of the check. Once the payee's name is inscribed on the check, only the payee (or a person to whom the payee negotiates the check) will be able to receive money for the check. What problem might arise if a seller asked a prospective buyer of goods to make payment with a cashier's check, and the buyer purchased the check, naming the seller as the payee? How might this problem be avoided?

5. Identify the following types of commercial paper or parties involved in the use of commercial paper.

   (a) A draft drawn on a bank payable to a payee on demand.

   (b) A written acknowledgment by a bank of a receipt of money with an obligation to repay it.

   (c) A written promise to pay another (or holder) a certain sum of money.

   (d) An instrument drawn by a bank on itself payable on demand.

   (e) Any person who acquires the instrument as a payee, by indorsement, or by delivery.

   (f) A person who issues a promissory note payable to a named payee.

(g) A payee who transfers an order instrument by signing the instrument.

6. A California statute makes possession of a check with intent to defraud a crime. Norwood had in his possession an instrument that had the following title in the upper right-hand corner: "AUDITOR CONTROLLER'S GENERAL WARRANT COUNTY OF LOS ANGELES." Below this the instrument stated, "The treasurer of the County of Los Angeles will pay to the order of John Norwood $5,000." At trial the district attorney proved that Norwood had intended to defraud the County of Los Angeles of $5,000 while in possession of the above instrument. You are Norwood's attorney, and you are now appealing the case. What argument would appear to be the strongest to overturn Norwood's conviction? [People v. Norwood, 26 Cal.App.3d 148, 103 Cal.Rptr. 7 (1972)]

Chapter 23

COMMERCIAL PAPER
The Negotiable Instrument

For business and commerce to operate smoothly, commercial paper must be generally accepted as money. For it to be readily accepted, it must be freely transferable. The law creating and governing the negotiable instrument is primarily designed, therefore, to urge its use as a substitute for money.

It is important to know whether an instrument is negotiable because, if it is, any dispute concerning the instrument is resolved under Article 3 of the UCC. If the instrument is nonnegotiable, disputes must be resolved under ordinary contract law. We open this chapter with a brief discussion of the significance of this distinction for the parties involved. We then examine the factors that make an instrument negotiable and the requirements of what must appear *on the face of* negotiable instruments. Indorsements, which usually appear *on the back of* the instrument, are covered in the following chapter.

CONTRACT LAW VERSUS ARTICLE 3

The basic principles of contract law govern when simple contract rights are assigned to a third party, when a nonnegotiable instrument is transferred to a third party, and when a negotiable instrument is improperly negotiated to a third party (transferee). The contract rights of assignees or transferees are burdened with every legal defense that existed between prior parties regardless of the extent of their knowledge of them. Persons who transfer or assign contractual or nonnegotiable rights pass on only the rights that they had.

For example, Martin contracts in writing to purchase a used word processor from Francis for $600. Martin needs the word processor in his business. He pays $200 down and agrees to pay the balance, plus 10 percent interest, in six equal installments. Francis, as part of the sale, makes certain assertions as to the amount of prior use and the condition of the word processor. Shortly after the sale and transfer, Francis sells and assigns the contract and the balance due to Arlene. Martin learns that Francis has lied about the prior use and the condition of the processor. He refuses to make any further payments on the contract, claiming fraud and breach of warranty. Arlene insists that she has no knowledge of the deceit, is an innocent party, and wants to enforce the contractually obligated payments against Martin. Because Arlene as assignee is subject to any defense Martin has against the assignor, Francis, Arlene is subject to Martin's claims and defenses. Of course, if Martin's claim proves unsuccessful, the debt is still collectible.

Now assume that, instead of creating an installment contract, Martin pays Francis with a $600 check. Francis, who owes Arlene $600, indorses the check to Arlene in payment of the debt. Before Arlene cashes the check, however, Martin requests his bank to stop payment on the check because he has learned of Francis's fraud and breach of warranty. In this situation, because she is the holder of a *negotiable* instrument (the check), Arlene may be entitled to payment notwithstanding Martin's stop-payment order. Under the holder-in-due-course (HDC) doctrine in Article 3 of the UCC, if Arlene can show that she is an HDC, she will not be subject to Martin's defense against payment. To qualify as an HDC, Arlene would have to demonstrate that she took the check in good faith, for value, and without notice that it was overdue or dishonored or of any claim or defense against it. Of course, Arlene might have known that Francis lied to Martin about the word processor, in which case she would not qualify as an HDC and would not be entitled to payment.

The HDC doctrine is very important in the law governing commercial paper and will be discussed at length in Chapters 25 and 26. These examples serve to show, however, that the distinction between negotiable and nonnegotiable instruments can be very important for the parties involved in terms of legal consequences.

THE REQUIREMENTS FOR A NEGOTIABLE INSTRUMENT

UCC 3-104(1) specifies that in order for an instrument to be negotiable, it must:

1. Be in writing.
2. Be signed by the maker or the drawer.
3. Be an unconditional promise or order to pay.
4. State a specific sum of money.
5. Be payable on demand or at a definite time.
6. Be payable to order or to bearer.

A Writing

Negotiable instruments must be in *written form*. Clearly, an oral promise can create the danger of fraud or make it difficult to determine liability. Negotiable instruments must possess the quality of certainty that only formal written expression can give.

There are certain practical limitations concerning the writing and the substance on which it is placed.

1. The writing must be on material that lends itself to *permanence*. A carved block of ice or a writing in the sand, for example, would be too impermanent to qualify as a negotiable instrument. Thus, if Mary writes in the sand, "I promise to pay $100 to the order of Tom," this is not a writing, because it lacks permanence. Using the shirt off your back as the medium on which you make out a check to the IRS to pay your taxes would probably be acceptable, however.

2. The writing must have *portability*. This is not a legal requirement, but if an instrument is not movable, it cannot meet the requirement that it be freely transferable. A promise to pay written on the side of a cow, for example, is technically correct, but a cow cannot easily be transferred in the ordinary course of business.

Signed by the Maker or the Drawer

For an instrument to be negotiable, it must be signed by the maker if it is a note or a certificate of deposit or by the drawer if it is a draft or a check [UCC 3-104(1)(a)].

Extreme latitude is granted in determining what constitutes a **signature.** UCC 1-201(39) defines the word *signed* as "[including] any symbol executed or adopted by a party with present intention to authenticate a writing." UCC 3-401(2) expands upon this: "A signature is made by use of any name, including any trade or assumed name, upon an instrument, or by any word or mark used in lieu of a written signature." Thus, initials, an X, or a thumbprint will suffice. A trade name or an assumed name is sufficient even if it is false. A rubber stamp bearing a person's signature is permitted and frequently used in the business world.

If necessary, parol evidence (see Chapter 12) is admissible in identifying the signer. When the signer is identified, the signature becomes effective.

PLACEMENT OF THE SIGNATURE The location of the signature on the document is unimportant. The usual place is the lower right-hand corner, but this is not required. A *handwritten* statement on the body of the instrument, such as "I, Mary Jones, promise to pay John Doe," is sufficient to act as Mary's signature.

There are virtually no limitations on the manner in which a signature can be made, but it is necessary to be careful when receiving an instrument that has been signed in an unusual way. Furthermore, an unusual signature clearly decreases the marketability of an instrument because it creates uncertainty.

If the signature's genuineness is denied, the signature is nevertheless presumed valid. The party against whom it operates must provide some evidence of the signature's invalidity. The party asserting the signature's validity must then provide proof of the signature's genuineness.

SIGNATURE BY AUTHORIZED REPRESENTATIVE If a person with the *authority* to do so signs an instrument as the agent for the maker or drawer, the maker or drawer has effectively signed the instrument. No particular form of appointment as an agent is necessary to show such authority; all that is needed is proof that the agent has such authority [UCC 3-403].

If the agent has authority, the maker or drawer is liable on the instrument, just as if he or she had actually signed it. If the agent has authority and clearly has signed the instrument in a representative capacity, he or she will not be personally liable. If the agent has no such authority, or if the agent did not clearly sign in a representative capacity, the agent is personally liable. The importance of the liability of the parties in these situations will be discussed in detail in Chapter 26.

Unconditional Promise or Order To Pay

The terms of a promise or order must be included in the writing on the face of a negotiable instrument. These terms must not be conditioned upon the occurrence or nonoccurrence of some other event or agreement. Nor can the promise state that it is to be paid only out of a particular fund or source [UCC 3-105(2)].

PROMISE OR ORDER In order for an instrument to be negotiable, it must contain an express order or promise to pay. A mere acknowledgment of the debt, which might logically *imply* a promise, is not sufficient under the UCC because the promise must be an *affirmative* undertaking [UCC 3-102(1)(c)].

For example, the traditional I.O.U. is only an acknowledgment of indebtedness, not a negotiable instrument. But if such words as *to be paid on demand* or *due on demand* are added, the need for an affirmative promise is satisfied. For example, if a buyer executes a promissory note using the words, "I promise to pay $1,000 to the order of the seller for the purchase of goods X, Y, Z," then the requirement for a negotiable instrument is satisfied.

A certificate of deposit is different. Here, the requisite promise is satisfied because the bank's acknowledgment of the deposit and the other terms of the instrument clearly indicate a promise.

An *order* is associated with three-party instruments, such as trade acceptances, checks, and drafts. An order directs a third party to pay the instrument as drawn. In the typical check, the word *pay* (to the order of a payee) is a command to the drawee bank to pay the check when presented, and thus it is an order. The order is mandatory even if it is written in a courteous form with words like *please pay* or *kindly pay*. Precise language must be used, however. An order stating, "I wish you would pay," does not fulfill the requirement of precision.

In addition to being precise, an effective order must specifically identify the drawee (the person who must pay) [UCC 3-102(1)(b)]. A bank's name printed on the face of a check, for example, sufficiently designates the bank as drawee.

UNCONDITIONAL A negotiable instrument's utility as a substitute for money or as a credit device would be dramatically reduced if the promises attached to it were conditional. Investigating such conditional promises would be expensive and time-consuming, and therefore, the free transferability of the negotiable instrument would be greatly reduced. Substantial administrative costs would be associated with processing conditional promises. Furthermore, the payee would risk the possibility that the condition would not occur.

If Martin promises to pay Paula $10,000 only if a certain ship reaches port safely, anyone interested in purchasing the promissory note would have to investigate whether the ship arrived. The facts that the investigation disclosed might be incorrect. To avoid such problems, the UCC provides that only unconditional promises or orders can be negotiable [UCC 3-104(1)(b)].

The Code expands the definition of *unconditional*, however, in order to make sure that certain conditions commonly used in business transactions do *not* render an otherwise negotiable instrument nonnegotiable. These are resolved by UCC 3-105(1):

> A promise or order otherwise unconditional is not made conditional by the fact that the instrument
> (a) is subject to implied or constructive conditions; or
> (b) states its consideration * * * or the transaction which gave rise to the instrument * * *; or
> (c) refers to or states that it arises out of a separate agreement * * *; or
> (d) states that it is drawn under a letter of credit; or
> (e) states that it is secured, whether by mortgage, reservation of title or otherwise; or
> (f) indicates a particular account to be debited or any other fund or source from which reimbursement is expected; or
> (g) is limited to payment out of a particular fund or the proceeds of a particular source, if the instrument is issued by a government or governmental agency unit; or
> (h) is limited to payment out of the entire assets of a partnership, unincorporated association, trust or estate * * *.

Some of these conditions are very common and will be briefly discussed here.

Implied or Constructive Conditions   If the rule did not allow implied or constructive conditions, no instrument could be negotiable. Implied conditions, such as good faith and commercial reasonableness, appear in virtually every example of a negotiable instrument. For instance, every check implies that in the bank on which the check is drawn, there is an account containing sufficient funds to pay the check.

Statements of Consideration   Many instruments state the terms of the underlying agreement as a matter of standard business practice. Somewhere on its face, the instrument refers to the transaction or agreement for which it is being used in payment. The policy of the UCC is to integrate standard trade usages into its provisions.

For example, the words *as per contract* or *this debt arises from the sale of goods X and Y* do not render an instrument nonnegotiable.

If James Quinta writes, "On July 14, 1990, I promise to pay to the order of Louis Sneed $100 in full payment for the television set that Louis Sneed delivered to me on July 2, 1990, [signed] James Quinta," this promissory note is a negotiable instrument. The statement concerning the television set is not a condition. It describes the consideration for which the note was given. On the other hand, if the following words were added, the instrument would become nonnegotiable: "If this television set fails to suit my tastes and preferences in any way whatsoever on July 13, then the maker's obligation hereunder shall be null and void."

Reference to Other Agreements   The UCC provides that mere reference to another agreement does not affect negotiability. If, on the other hand, the instrument is made subject to the other agreement, it will be nonnegotiable [UCC 3-105(2)(a)]. A reference to another agreement is normally inserted for the purpose of keeping a record or giving information to anyone who may be interested. Notes frequently refer to separate agreements that give special rights to a creditor for an acceleration of payment or to a debtor for prepayment. References to these rights do not destroy the negotiability of the instrument.

For example, an instrument states, "On January 23, 1990, I promise to pay to the order of Patricia Senior $1,000, this note being secured under a security agreement and lien upon my 1987 Chevy Caprice, noted upon the title certificate thereof, [signed] Henry Winn." This instrument is negotiable. A statement that an instrument's payment is secured by collateral will not render an otherwise negotiable instrument nonnegotiable [UCC 3-112(1)(b)]. In fact, this statement adds to the salability and marketability of the instrument.

In the following case, a promissory note that incorporated another agreement was rendered nonnegotiable.

Case 23.1
MITCHELL v. RIVERSIDE NATIONAL BANK
Court of Civil Appeals of Texas—Houston (14th District), 1981.
613 S.W.2d 802.

BACKGROUND AND FACTS   *In order to make certain improvements to his property, Mitchell signed a builder's and mechanic's lien contract (which permits a claim against the property itself if the note for the improvements is not paid) and a note in the amount of $4,435 payable to the contractor who was to perform the work. The note specifically provided that it was secured by a lien and "subject to and governed by said contract, which is hereby expressly referred to, incorporated herein and made a part hereof." The lien contract provided that in the event the improvements were not completed, the owner and holder of the note would have a lien against the property for the contract price less the cost to complete the improvements according to the contract. Before the note matured, the contractor assigned it to Riverside National Bank for a discounted price of $3,548. The contractor began the improvements but never finished them. Mitchell then was forced to hire another contractor to complete the job at a cost of $3,400. When the note became due, Mitchell refused to pay it. Riverside filed suit for the face amount of the note and for a lien against the property to force payment of that amount. Mitchell claimed that the note was nonnegotiable and that the bank's remedy was limited to the lien contract. The trial court awarded the bank the amount it had paid for the note ($3,548) and gave it a lien on Mitchell's property. Mitchell appealed.*

JUNELL, Justice.
*   *   *   *

Mitchell contends that [the language in the note referring] to the contract burdens the note with the conditions of the contract, thereby making the note non-negotiable and subjecting recovery on the note to any defenses available under the contract. We agree. Use of the terms "subject to and governed by" in referring to an extrinsic contract in an otherwise negotiable instrument destroys the negotiability of the instrument and renders the instrument burdened by the terms within the extrinsic contract. *   *   *

The face amount of the note being $4,435.00 and the cost of completion being stipulated by the parties to be $3,400.00, we hold that Riverside has a lien against Mitchell's property for $1,035.00, plus interest at the rate of ten percent per annum
*   *   *.

DECISION AND REMEDY   *Because it incorporated the terms "subject to and governed by said contract," the note was nonnegotiable, and recovery was governed by the terms of the lien contract. The defendant was only liable to the bank for the amount of the improvements actually completed by the original contractor. The appellate court reformed the judgment of the trial court to this lower amount.*

Secured by a Mortgage   A simple statement in an otherwise negotiable note indicating that the note is secured by a mortgage does not destroy its negotiability. Actually, such a statement might make the note even more acceptable in commerce. Note that the statement that a note is secured by a mortgage must not stipulate that the maker's promise to pay is *subject* to the terms and conditions of the mortgage.

Indication of Particular Funds or Accounts   In many instruments, it is indicated expressly or impliedly that payment should come from a particular fund or that a particular account is to be debited. For example, a check is drawn impliedly on funds in a particular checking account.

Generally, mere reference to the account to be debited or to the fund from which payment is preferred will not affect the negotiability of the instrument. However, if payment is expressly limited to payment *only* from a particular fund, the instrument is rendered nonnegotiable [UCC 3-105(2)(b)]. The condition obviously restricts the acceptability of the instrument as a substitute for money, as a holder's payment depends on whether such a fund exists and whether it is sufficient to pay the instrument.

For example, a note dated March 3, 1990, reads, "Gilbert Corporation promises to pay to the order of the Miami Herald $150 on demand, charged to advertising expense, [signed] Harold Henry, Treasurer, Gilbert Corporation." This note is negotiable. The phrase "charged to advertising expense" is merely a posting instruction to the corporation's accounting department. If a note states that "Jones plans to liquidate real estate to pay this obligation," the note is still considered negotiable.[1] On the other hand, if a note reads "payment to be made within the next thirty days from jobs now under construction," the note will be held nonnegotiable, because it does not contain an unconditional promise.

Consider another example. A note states that "payment of said obligation is restricted to payment from accounts receivable." In this case, payment is conditioned from one particular source—accounts receivable—and this renders the instrument nonnegotiable. It does not make the note uncollectible, however. The contract may still be assigned under contract rules of assignment.

The two exceptions to this rule are instruments issued by government agencies that are payable out of particular revenue funds and instruments limited to partnership, unincorporated association, estate, or trust assets [UCC 3-105(1)(g), (h)].

Sum Certain in Money

Negotiable instruments must state the amount to be paid in a *sum certain in money*. This requirement promotes clarity and certainty in determining the value of the instrument [UCC 3-104(1)(b)]. Any promise to pay in the future is risky because the value of money (purchasing power) fluctuates. Nonetheless, the present value of such an instrument can still be estimated with a reasonable degree of accuracy by financial experts. If the in-

strument's value were stated in terms of goods or services, it would be too difficult to ascertain the market value of those goods and services at the time the instrument was to be discounted.

The UCC mandates that negotiable commercial paper be paid wholly in money. For example, a promissory note that provides for payment in diamonds or in 1,000 hours of services is not payable in money. Thus, the note is nonnegotiable.

SUM CERTAIN The term *sum certain* means an amount that is ascertainable from the instrument itself without reference to an outside source. A demand note payable with 12 percent interest meets the requirement of sum certain because its amount can be determined at the time it is payable. UCC 3-106(1) states that the sum is not rendered uncertain by the fact that it is to be paid:

(a) with stated interest or by stated installments; or
(b) with stated different rates of interest before and after default or a specified date; or
(c) with a stated discount or addition if paid before or after the date fixed for payment * * *.

The basic test is whether any holder who receives the instrument can determine by calculation the amount required to be paid when the instrument is due. Thus, instruments that provide simply for payment of interest at prevailing bank rates are generally nonnegotiable, because bank rates fluctuate. A mortgage note tied to a variable rate of interest that fluctuates as a result of market conditions is not negotiable. Similarly, a note is nonnegotiable if it indexes the amount to be paid to the consumer price index in an attempt to avoid the effects of inflation. When an instrument is payable at the legal rate or at a judgment rate or as fixed by state law, however, the instrument can be negotiable.

In international trade, notes that are to be paid in another currency satisfy the sum certain requirement. If X promises in a note to pay 1,000 French francs, this note meets the certainty requirement even though the parties must refer to exchange rates that are not embodied in the instrument. The Code, therefore, makes an exception to its own general rule because of the realities of international trade [UCC 3-107(2)].

Often, instruments have provisions authorizing collection costs and attorneys' fees upon de-

---

1. Southern Baptist Hospital v. Williams, 89 So.2d 769 (La.App. 1956).

fault. UCC 3-106(1)(e) indicates that an instrument with such provisions still meets the sum certain requirement and therefore is still negotiable. Providing for collection costs and attorneys' fees lessens some of the costs and risks that a bank (or other institution) dealing in commercial paper would otherwise incur. Note, though, that a few states have invalidated such provisions either by statute or by judicial decision. In states where such provisions are legal, the fees must be reasonable, or the clause will be voided as being against public policy.

The elements that determine negotiability must be present on the face of the instrument. In the following case, a note was nonnegotiable because it did not specify a sum certain in money.

Case 23.2
HINCKLEY v. EGGERS
Court of Civil Appeals of Texas—Dallas, 1979.
587 S.W.2d 448.

BACKGROUND AND FACTS   *Hinckley, plaintiff and appellant, held a deed of trust (a security lien on realty) and a note signed by the trustee of a joint venture (a group of investors including Eggers and others). Hinckley sued to enforce both the deed of trust and the note against the trustee and against the members of the joint venture. A clause in the note stated that if there was a default in payments under the deed of trust, the "sole remedy of the legal holder hereof or payee * * * shall be the foreclosure of the property covered by the deed of trust * * * and the maker's personal liability and responsibility to pay to payee or the subsequent holder hereof on demand that dollar amount equal to all taxes * * * due and payable on the property for the current year plus all interest * * * accrued." The trial court separated the case against the trustee from the case against the joint venture and entered judgment against the trustee. The trial court granted a summary judgment in favor of the joint venture, however, holding that the note was negotiable but that, since none of the investors had signed the note or the deed of trust, they had no liability. Hinckley appealed, alleging that the note was nonnegotiable because it did not contain a sum certain in money. Hinckley argued that therefore, under basic contract law, he could introduce parol evidence, which he wanted to do to show that the trustee signed the note as an agent for the joint venture and, that as principals, the members of the joint venture were liable.*

HUMPHREYS, Associate Justice.
*   *   *   *

The test of negotiability is prescribed by Tex.Bus. & Comm.Code Ann. § 3.104(a)(2) which provides that the instrument must "contain an unconditional promise or order to pay a sum certain in money." Appellant argues that the note in question is not negotiable because it is not an unconditional promise in that it is to be paid only out of a particular fund. In this connection, appellant cites section 3.105(b)(2), which provides that a promise is not unconditional if it "states that it is to be paid out of a particular fund or source," with certain exceptions not applicable here.

We agree that the note does not contain an unconditional promise to pay the principal sum. *   *   *

[Its] provisions have the effect of making the note payable out of a particular fund or source, namely, the proceeds of a sale of the property covered by the deed of trust. That is the only fund to which the holder may look for payment, although, of course, the maker may pay with any funds available. It would be contradictory to characterize as unconditional a promise that can be completely enforced only if a sale of the collateral produces sufficient funds. Under the clear provisions of the Code, such a note is not negotiable.

We recognize that the note provides personal liability for an amount equal to the taxes due on the property and the interest accrued on the note at the time of acceleration or foreclosure, and that the present suit is brought to enforce the personal liability.

This provision does not establish negotiability. In the first place, this amount is not a "sum certain" within section 3.104(a)(2) because the amount of the taxes can be determined only from sources outside the instrument. Second, even if we disregard the taxes, we find no authority supporting the view that a note may be negotiable with respect to the interest when it is not negotiable with respect to the principal. We interpret the phrase "a sum certain in money" in section 3.104(a)(2) to mean the principal sum, which, of course, may be payable "with stated interest," under section 3.106(a)(1). Consequently, we hold that a note is not negotiable if it provides that the maker has no personal liability for the principal sum and that the holder's only remedy on default is foreclosure on the collateral, even though the note also contains an unconditional promise to pay a determinable amount of interest.

The court held that the note was nonnegotiable because it was conditioned to be paid out of a particular fund (proceeds from the sale of the realty) and it did not contain a sum certain to be paid (lack of the principal sum). The obligations under the note were thus determined by basic contract law, and parol evidence could be admitted to prove that the members of the joint venture were liable as principals on the note. The appellate court reversed the summary judgment in favor of the joint venture rendered by the trial court and remanded the case for trial.

DECISION AND REMEDY

MONEY AND NO OTHER PROMISE UCC 3-104(1)(b) provides that a sum certain is to be payable in "money and no other promise." The Code defines money as "a medium of exchange authorized or adopted by a domestic or foreign government as a part of its currency" [UCC 1-201(24)].

Suppose that the maker of a note promises "to pay on demand $1,000 in U.S. gold." Since gold is not a medium of exchange adopted by the U.S. government, the note is not payable in money. The same result would occur if the maker promised "to pay $1,000 *and* fifty liters of 1964 Chateau Lafite-Rothschild wine," as the instrument is not payable *entirely* in money.

An instrument "payable in $1,000 U.S. currency or an equivalent value in gold" would be nonnegotiable, if the *maker* reserved the option of paying in money or gold. If the option were left to the *payee*, some legal scholars argue that the instrument would be negotiable.

Under UCC 3-107(2), any instrument payable in the United States with a face amount stated in a foreign currency can be paid in the equivalent in U.S. dollars at the due date, unless the paper expressly requires payment in the foreign currency.

To summarize, only instruments payable in money are negotiable. An instrument payable in U.S. government bonds or in shares of IBM stock is not negotiable, because neither bonds nor stocks are a medium of exchange recognized by the U.S. government.

Payable on Demand or at a Definite Time

UCC 3-104(1)(c) requires that a negotiable instrument "be payable on demand or at a definite time." Clearly, in order to ascertain the value of a negotiable instrument, it is necessary to know when the maker, drawee, or acceptor is required to pay. It is also necessary to know when the obligations of secondary parties—drawers, indorsers, and accommodation parties—will arise. Futhermore, it is necessary to know when an instrument is due in order to calculate when the statute of limitations may apply. And finally, with an interest-bearing instrument, it is necessary to know the exact interval during which the interest will accrue in order to determine the present value of the instrument.

PAYABLE ON DEMAND Instruments that are payable on demand include those that contain the words *payable at sight* or *payable upon presentment* and those that say nothing about when payment is due. The very nature of the instrument may indicate that it is payable on demand. For example, a check, by definition, is payable on demand [UCC 3-104(2)(b)]. If no time for payment is specified and the person responsible for payment must pay upon the instrument's presentment, the instrument is payable on demand [UCC 3-108].

PAYABLE AT A DEFINITE TIME To be negotiable, time instruments must be payable at a definite time that is specified on the face of the instrument. The maker or drawee is under no obligation to pay until the specified time has elapsed.

Often, instruments contain additional terms that seem to conflict with the definite time requirement. UCC 3-109 attempts to clear up some of these potential problems:

(1) An instrument is payable at a definite time if by its terms it is payable:

(a) on or before a stated date or at a fixed period after a stated date; or

(b) at a fixed period after sight; or

(c) at a definite time subject to any acceleration; or

(d) at a definite time subject to extension at the option of the holder, or to extension to a further definite time at the option of the maker or acceptor or automatically upon or after a specified act or event.

(2) An instrument which by its terms is otherwise payable only upon an act or event uncertain as to time of occurrence is not payable at a definite time even though the act or event has occurred.

To illustrate: An instrument dated June 1, 1990, states, "One year after the death of my grandfather, James Taylor, I promise to pay to the order of Henry Winkler $500. [Signed] Mary Taylor." This instrument is nonnegotiable. Because the date of the grandfather's death is uncertain, the maturity date is uncertain, even though the event is bound to occur or has occurred. Even if the grandfather has already died, the note does not specify the time for payment.

When an instrument is payable on or before a stated date, it is clearly payable at a definite time, although the maker has the option of paying before the stated maturity date. This uncertainty does not violate the definite time requirement. Suppose Lee gives Zenon an instrument dated May 1, 1990, that indicates on its face that it is payable on or before May 1, 1991. This instrument satisfies the requirement. On the other hand, an instrument

that is undated and made payable "one month after date" is clearly nonnegotiable. There is no way to determine the maturity date from the face of the instrument.

Drafts stating that they are payable at a fixed period after sight are considered payable at a definite time [UCC 3-109(1)(b)]. The term *sight* means the moment that the draft is presented for payment or for acceptance by the drawee. The Code further requires that such instruments be presented for acceptance to the drawee in order to determine the maturity date [UCC 3-501(1)(a)]. Presenting an instrument for acceptance to the drawee establishes the sight and the time period, which runs from the date the instrument is presented.

ACCELERATION CLAUSES An **acceleration clause** allows a payee or other holder of a time instrument to demand payment of the entire amount due, with interest, if a certain event occurs, such as a default in payment of an installment when due. There must be, of course, a good faith belief that payment will not be made before an acceleration clause is invoked.

For example, Carl lends $1,000 to Debra. Debra makes a negotiable note promising to pay $100 per month for eleven months. The note may contain a provision that permits Carl or any holder to accelerate all the payments plus interest if Debra fails to pay an installment in any given month. If, for example, Debra fails to make the third payment, the note will be due and payable in full. If Carl accelerates the unpaid balance, Debra will owe Carl the remaining principal plus interest.

Under UCC 3-109(1)(c), instruments that include acceleration clauses are negotiable because the exact value of the instrument can be ascertained, and the instrument will be payable on a fixed date if the event allowing acceleration does not occur. Thus, the fixed date is the outside limit used to determine the value of the instrument.

Furthermore, the payee or holder cannot accelerate the instrument even if it contains an acceleration clause unless it is done in good faith. Section 1-208 indicates that the acceleration clause "shall be construed to mean that [the holder of the instrument] shall have the power [to accelerate] only if he in good faith believes that the prospect of payment or performance is impaired." But the burden of proving a lack of good faith is on the borrower—the maker of the note.

EXTENSION CLAUSES The reverse of an acceleration clause is an **extension clause,** which allows the date of maturity to be extended into the future. To keep the instrument negotiable, the interval of the extension must be specified if the right to extend is given to the maker of the instrument. If, on the other hand, the holder of the instrument can extend it, the maturity date does not have to be specified.

Suppose a note reads, "The maker [obligor] has the right to postpone the time of payment of this note beyond its definite maturity date of January 1, 1990. However, this extension shall be for no more than a reasonable time." A note with this language is not negotiable because it does not satisfy the definite time requirement. The right to extend is the maker's, and the maker has not indicated when the note will become due after the extension.

A note that reads "The holder of this note at the date of maturity, January 1, 1991, can extend the time of payment until the following June 1 or later, if the holder so wishes" is a negotiable instrument. The length of the extension does not have to be specified because the option to extend is solely that of the holder. After January 1, 1991, the note is, in effect, a demand instrument.

Payable to Order or to Bearer

Since one of the functions of a negotiable instrument is to substitute for money, freedom to transfer is an essential requirement. To ensure that a proper transfer can be made, one of the requirements of a negotiable instrument is that it be "payable to order or to bearer" [UCC 3-104(1)(d)]. These required words indicate that at the time issuance it is expected that unknown persons—not just the immediate party—will eventually be the owners.

ORDER INSTRUMENTS UCC 3-110(1) defines an instrument as an order to pay "when by its terms it is payable to the order * * * of any person therein specified with reasonable certainty * * *." This section goes on to state that an order instrument can be payable to the order of:

(a) the maker or drawer; or
(b) the drawee; or
(c) a payee who is not maker, drawer, or drawee; or

(d) two or more payees together or in the alternative; or
(e) the representative of an estate, trust, or fund or his successor; or
(f) an office or officer by title [such as a tax assessor]; or
(g) a partnership or unincorporated association.

The purpose of order paper is to allow the maker or drawer to transfer the instrument to a specific person. In turn that person may transfer the instrument to whomever he or she wishes. Thus, the maker or drawer agrees to pay the person specified or to pay whomever that person designates. In this way, the instrument retains its transferability.

Suppose an instrument states, "payable to the order of Sam Smith" or "pay to Sam Smith or order." The maker or drawer has indicated that a payment will be made to Smith or to whomever Smith designates. The instrument is negotiable.

If the instrument states, "payable to Sam Smith" or "pay to Sam Smith only," however, the instrument loses its negotiability. The maker or drawer has indicated only that Smith will be paid.

In addition, except for bearer paper, the person specified must be named with *certainty*, because the transfer of an order instrument requires an indorsement. (See Chapter 24.) If an instrument is "payable to the order of my kissing cousin," the instrument is nonnegotiable, as a holder could not be sure which cousin was intended to indorse and properly transfer the instrument.

BEARER INSTRUMENT UCC 3-111 defines a bearer instrument as one that does not designate a specific payee. The term *bearer* means the person in possession of an instrument that is payable to bearer or indorsed in blank [UCC 1-201(5)]. Here, the maker or drawer agrees to pay anyone who presents the instrument for payment, and complete transferability is implied.

Any instrument containing the following terms is a bearer instrument: "Payable to the order of bearer," "Payable to Sam Sneed or bearer," "Payable to bearer," "Pay cash," or "Pay to the order of cash." In addition, an instrument that contains "any other indication which does not purport to designate a specific payee" is bearer paper [UCC 3-111(c)]. The use of such designations can cause problems and should be avoided. A check made payable to the order of "Uncle Sam" would probably be considered to designate a payee, the United States government, and would thus be an order instrument. An instrument "payable to the order of one case of beer" would not designate a specific payee and would be a bearer instrument.

When an instrument is made payable to order *and* to bearer, the instrument is a bearer instrument if the bearer words are handwritten or typewritten but an order instrument if the bearer words are in a printed form [UCC 3-110(3)]. The next case distinguishes bearer paper from order paper.

Case 23.3 **BROADWAY MANAGEMENT CORP. v. BRIGGS** Appellate Court of Illinois, Fourth District, 1975. 30 Ill.App.3d 403, 332 N.E.2d 131.	**BACKGROUND AND FACTS** *Broadway Management Corp., the plaintiff, brought suit on a note signed by Briggs, the defendant, which read in part: "Ninety days after date, I, we, or either of us, promise to pay to the order of Three Thousand Four Hundred Ninety Eight and 45/100---Dollars." The underlined words and symbols had been typed on the note; the remainder was printed material. There were no blanks on the face of the note; all unused space was filled in with hyphens. No payee was named. The lawsuit was instituted against Briggs when the note was not paid at maturity. The trial court ruled in favor of Broadway Management, and Briggs appealed. The central issues on appeal were whether the note was order or bearer paper and how that affected its negotiability.*

CRAVEN, Justice.

*   *   *   *

*   *   *   The official comments to [UCC § 3-111] note that an instrument made payable "to the order of _____" is not bearer paper, but an incomplete order instrument unenforceable until completed in accordance with authority. U.C.C., § 3-115.

The instrument here is not bearer paper. We cannot say that it "does not purport to designate a specific payee." Rather, we believe the wording of the instrument is clear in its implication that the payee's name is to be inserted between the promise and the amount, so that the literal absence of blanks is legally insignificant.

DECISION AND REMEDY   *With the payee's name omitted from the blank reserved for such purpose, the name of the payee could not be determined from the face of the note. The instrument was thus incomplete order paper, and its negotiability was destroyed until a name was inserted. The decision of the trial court was reversed, and the case was remanded.*

OMISSIONS THAT DO NOT AFFECT NEGOTIABILITY

UCC 3-112 lists the following terms and omissions that do not affect negotiability:

1.   The omission of a statement of any consideration.

2.   The omission of the name of the place where the instrument is drawn or payable.

3.   The promise or power to maintain or protect collateral or to give additional collateral.

4.   The term in a draft indicating that the payee, by indorsing or cashing the draft, acknowledges full satisfaction of the obligation of the drawer.

OTHER FACTORS THAT DO NOT AFFECT NEGOTIABILITY

There are other factors that do not affect the negotiability of an instrument, and the UCC provides rules for clearing up ambiguous terms. Some of these factors and rules are as follows:

1.   Unless the date of an instrument is necessary to determine a definite time for payment, the fact that an instrument is undated does not affect its negotiability. A typical example is an undated check [UCC 3-114(1)].

2.   Postdating or antedating an instrument does not affect negotiability [UCC 3-114(1)].

3.   Handwritten terms outweigh typewritten and printed terms, and typewritten terms control those that are printed [UCC 3-118(b)]. For example, if your check is printed "Pay to the order of," and in handwriting you insert in the blank "John Smith or bearer," the check is a bearer instrument. An instrument reading "Pay to the order of John Smith or bearer" is payable to order *unless* the bearer words are handwritten or typewritten [UCC 3-110(3)].

4.   Words outweigh figures unless the words are ambiguous [UCC 3-118(c)]. This is important when the numerical amount and written amount on a check differ.

5.   Unless otherwise specified, when interest is provided for, the rate is the *judgment rate* (that is, the rate provided by law for a judgment) at the place of payment and runs from the date of the instrument or, if undated, from the date of its issue [UCC 3-118(d)].

CONCEPT SUMMARY: Eight Requirements for Negotiable Instruments

REQUIREMENTS	BASIC RULES
Must be in writing UCC 3-104(1)	1. A writing can be on anything that is readily transferable and that has a degree of permanence. [See also UCC 1-201(46).]
Must be signed by the maker or drawer UCC 3-104(1)(a) UCC 3-401(2) UCC 1-201(39)	1. The signature can be anyplace on the instrument. 2. It can be in any form (such as a word, mark, or rubber stamp) that purports to be a signature and authenticates the writing. 3. It can be signed in a representative capacity.
Must be a definite promise or order UCC 3-104(1)(b)	1. A promise must be more than a mere acknowledgement of a debt. 2. The words "I/We promise" or "Pay" meet this criterion.
Must be unconditional UCC 3-104(1)(b) UCC 3-105	1. Payment cannot be expressly conditional upon the occurrence of an event. 2. Payment cannot be made subject to or governed by another agreement. 3. Payment cannot be paid only out of a particular fund (except for a government-issued instrument).
Must be an order or promise to pay a sum certain UCC 3-104(1)(b) UCC 3-106	1. An instrument may state a sum certain even if payable in installments, with interest, at a stated discount, or at an exchange rate. 2. Inclusion of costs of collection and attorneys' fees does not disqualify the statement of a sum certain.
Must be payable in money UCC 3-104(1)(b) UCC 3-107	1. Any medium of exchange recognized as the currency of a government is money. 2. The maker or drawer cannot retain the option to pay the instrument in money or something else.

(Continued on the next page)

CONCEPT SUMMARY: Eight Requirements for Negotiable Instruments (Continued)

REQUIREMENTS	BASIC RULES
Must be payable on demand or at a definite time UCC 3-104(1)(c) UCC 3-108 UCC 3-109	1. Any instrument payable on sight, presentation, or issue is a demand instrument. 2. An instrument is still payable at a definite time even though it is payable on or before a stated date or within a fixed period after sight or the drawer or maker has an option to extend time for a definite period. 3. Acceleration clauses, even if unenforceable, do not affect the negotiability of the instrument.
Must be payable to order or bearer UCC 3-104(1)(d) UCC 3-110 UCC 3-111	1. An order instrument must name the payee with reasonable certainty. 2. An instrument whose terms intend payment to no particular person is payable to bearer.

QUESTIONS AND CASE PROBLEMS

1. The following note is written by Mary Ellen on the back of an envelope: "I, Mary Ellen, promise to pay to Kathy Martin or bearer $100 on demand." Discuss fully whether this constitutes a negotiable instrument.

2. A promissory note is signed by Peter Paul. The note is dated May 1, 1990. Assuming that all other terms in the note meet the requirements for negotiability, discuss fully whether the following clause would render the note non-negotiable: "This note is payable 100 years from date, but payment of principal plus interest is due and payable immediately upon the death of the maker."

3. The following instrument was written on a sheet of paper by Moss Martin: "I, the undersigned, do hereby acknowledge that I owe Sam Smith one thousand dollars, with interest, payable out of the proceeds of the sale of my horse, Thundercloud, next month. Payment is to be made on or before six months from date." Discuss specifically why this instrument is nonnegotiable.

4. You have signed a year's lease for an apartment near campus. The October rent is due and payable. You write a check for the rent due. On the check you write the following, "Payment for October rent as per lease agreement."
(a) Does this statement render the instrument non-negotiable? Explain.
(b) Would your answer be any different if the written clause read, "Payment subject to the terms of a signed lease dated September 1, 1990"?

5. Martin Moss is in need of a loan. He borrows $500 from his friend, Paula Peters, signing a promissory note. Two clauses in the note are as follows:
(a) "On or before July 1, 1990, I promise to pay to Paula Peters or bearer $550 in cash or title to my 1982 car, at the holder's option."
(b) "The maker hereof reserves the right to extend the time of payment of said note for six months; however, the holder reserves the right to extend the time of payment indefinitely."
Explain whether either clause or both clauses render Martin's note nonnegotiable.

6. In October 1970, Hall issued a draft that included the following: "Pay to L. Westmoreland and B. Bridges or order $1,000 on demand." Before he handed it to Bridges, Hall scratched out the words *or order* with his pen. Does the fact that the draft is payable to two payees destroy its negotiability? Does the scratching out of the words *or order* destroy the draft's negotiability? [First Federal Sav. and Loan Ass'n v. Branch Banking and Trust Co., 282 N.C. 44, 191 S.E.2d 683 (N.C. 1972)]

7. The Williamsons held a note secured by a second mortgage on a farm they had sold to the Wanlasses. The Wanlasses sometimes made payments later than the first of the month, but they never missed a payment. The Williamsons brought suit to enforce the acceleration clause in the note. Could the Williamsons prove that they believed in good faith that payment or performance might be impaired? [Williamson v. Wanlass, 545 P.2d 1145 (1976)]

8. McDonald, the personal representative of the Marion Cahill estate, made out a check to himself on the estate checking account. The payee and the amount of the check read: "Pay to the order of Emmett E. McDonald $10,075.00 Ten hundred seventy-five . . . Dollars." The bank paid to

McDonald and charged the estate account for $10,075—the numerical rather than the written amount. McDonald then absconded with the money. Yates, who succeeded McDonald as the personal representative of the estate, sued the bank to recover the $9,000 difference between $1,075 and $10,075, alleging that the bank should have paid only the smaller amount, which had been written on the check in words. The trial court dismissed the claim, and Yates appealed. Should Yates prevail on appeal? [Yates v. Commercial Bank & Trust Company, 432 So.2d 725 (Fla.App. 1983)]

9. Appliances, Inc., performed electrical heating and plumbing work for Yost Construction totaling approximately $7,000 during a three-year period. Appliances, Inc., was never paid by Yost Construction for any of these jobs. Yost, in both his capacity as president of the construction company and in his individual capacity, signed an undated ninety-day promissory note in favor of Appliances in order to reduce Yost Construction's debt and to have Appliances perform services for Yost as an individual. Neither Yost in his individual capacity nor Yost Construction paid the note, and Appliances filed suit. The trial court held that the undated note was totally unenforceable. Should Appliances prevail on appeal by arguing that the note was negotiable? [Appliances, Inc. v. Yost, 181 Conn. 207, 435 A.2d 1 (Conn. 1980)]

10. Higgins, a used-car dealer, sold a 1977 Corvette to Holsonback, the defendant. Holsonback paid for the car with a draft drawn on First State Bank of Albertville, the plaintiff. On the draft were the following words: "ENCLOSED—TITLE ON 77 CHEV. VETT. FREE OF ALL LIENS AND ENCUMBRANCE." The bank paid Higgins. First State presented the draft to Holsonback for payment, but Holsonback refused to pay, claiming that Higgins was in breach of contract. First State Bank filed suit against Holsonback on his draft. Holsonback claimed that the draft was nonnegotiable because the draft's reference to the title rendered the draft conditional. Discuss Holsonback's contention. [Holsonback v. First State Bank of Albertville, 394 So.2d 381 (Ala.Civ.App. 1980)]

Chapter 24

COMMERCIAL PAPER
Transferability and Negotiation

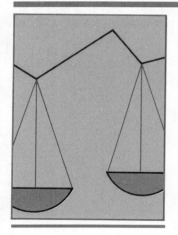

Commercial paper must be freely transferable. Once a negotiable instrument circulates beyond the original parties, the commercial law principles of negotiation come into play. The method of transfer that is used to pass a negotiable instrument from person to person determines the rights and duties that are passed with it.

Strictly speaking, negotiation occurs at the first delivery of a negotiable instrument to a holder, when the maker or drawer *issues* the instrument [UCC 3-102(1)(a)]. Typically, however, in commercial practice, the term *negotiation* is used to identify transfers occurring in a particular way after the instrument has been issued.

As already pointed out, the method of transfer determines the rights and duties that are passed with the negotiable instrument. Furthermore, whether the instrument is an order or bearer instrument (as discussed in Chapter 23) determines how one *initially* negotiates it.

ASSIGNMENT AND NEGOTIATION

Once issued, a negotiable instrument can be transferred by assignment or by negotiation.

Assignment

Assignment is a transfer of rights under a contract. Recall from Chapter 13 that under general contract principles, a transfer by assignment to an assignee gives the assignee only those rights that the assignor possessed. Any defenses that can be raised against an assignor can be raised against the assignee (unless there is an enforceable waiver of defense clause). Article 3 applies only to negotiable instruments; there can be no negotiation of a nonnegotiable instrument. When a transfer fails to qualify as a negotiation, it becomes an assignment, and the transferee does not become a holder.

Negotiation

Negotiation is the transfer of an instrument in such form that the transferee becomes a holder [UCC 3-202(1)]. Under UCC principles, a transfer by negotiation creates a holder who, at the very least, receives the rights of the previous possessor [UCC 3-201(1)]. Unlike an assignment, a transfer by negotiation can make it possible for a holder to receive *more* rights in the instrument than the prior possessor [UCC 3-305]. (A holder who receives greater rights is known as a *holder in due course.* See Chapter 25.) There are two methods of negotiating an instrument so that the receiver becomes a holder.

NEGOTIATING ORDER PAPER *Order paper* contains the name of a payee capable of indorsing, as in "pay to the order of Jane Smith." Order paper is also paper that has as its last or only indorsement a *special* indorsement, as in "Pay to Smith. [Signed] Jones." If the instrument is order paper, it is negotiated by delivery with any necessary indorsements. For example, the Transco Company issues a payroll check "to the order of Jane Smith." Smith takes the check to the supermarket, signs her name on the back (an indorsement), gives it to the cashier (a delivery), and receives cash. Smith has negotiated the check to the supermarket [UCC 3-202(1)].

NEGOTIATING BEARER PAPER If an instrument is payable to bearer, it is negotiated by delivery— that is, by transfer into another person's possession. Indorsement is not necessary [UCC 3-202(1)]. The use of *bearer paper* involves more risk through loss or theft than the use of order paper.

Assume Bob Robles writes a check "payable to cash" and hands it to Debbie Myers (a delivery). Robles has negotiated the check (a bearer instrument) to Myers. Myers places the check in her wallet, which is subsequently stolen. The thief has possession of the check. At this point, negotiation has not occurred, because delivery must be voluntary on the part of the transferor. If the thief "delivers" the check to an innocent third person, however, negotiation will be complete. All rights to the check will be passed *absolutely* to that third person, and Myers will lose all right to recover the proceeds of the check from the third person [UCC 3-305]. Of course, she can recover her money from the thief if the thief can be found.

CONVERTING ORDER TO BEARER PAPER AND VICE VERSA The method used for negotiation depends upon the character of the instrument at the time the negotiation takes place. For example,

a check originally payable to "Cash" but subsequently indorsed "Pay to Salk" must be negotiated as order paper (by indorsement and delivery), even though it was previously bearer paper [UCC 3-204(1)].

An instrument payable to the order of a named payee and indorsed in blank (see Exhibit 24-1) becomes a bearer instrument [UCC 3-204(2)]. To illustrate: A check is made payable to the order of Axel Amundsen. The check is issued to Amundsen, and Amundsen indorses it by signing his name on the back. The instrument can now be negotiated by delivery only. Amundsen can negotiate the check to whomever he wishes by delivery, and that person in turn can negotiate by delivery without indorsement. If Amundsen, after such indorsement, loses the check, then a finder can negotiate it further.

Exhibit 24–1 Blank Indorsement

INDORSEMENTS

Indorsements are required whenever the instrument being negotiated is classified as an order instrument. (Many transferees of bearer paper require indorsement for identification purposes, even though the UCC does not require it.) An **indorsement** is a signature with or without additional words or statements. It is most often written on the back of the instrument itself. If there is no room on the instrument, indorsements can be written on a separate piece of paper called an **allonge.** The allonge must be "so firmly affixed" to the instrument "as to become a part thereof" [UCC 3-202(2)]. Attachment by pins or paper clips will not suffice. Some courts hold that staples are sufficient.

One purpose of an indorsement is to effect the negotiation of order paper. Sometimes the transferee of bearer paper will request the holder-transferor to indorse. This is done to impose liability on the indorser. The liability of indorsers will be discussed later, in Chapter 26.

Once an instrument qualifies as a negotiable instrument, the form of indorsement will have no effect on the character of the underlying instrument. Indorsement relates to the right of the holder to negotiate the paper and the manner in which negotiation must be done.

Types of Indorsements

We will examine four categories of indorsements:

1. Blank.
2. Special.
3. Qualified.
4. Restrictive.

BLANK INDORSEMENTS   A **blank indorsement** specifies no particular indorsee and can consist of a mere signature [UCC 3-204(2)]. Hence, a check payable "to the order of Rosemary White" can be indorsed in blank simply by having her signature written on the back of the check. Exhibit 24–1 shows a blank indorsement.

As mentioned, an instrument payable to order and indorsed in blank becomes payable to bearer and can be negotiated by delivery alone [UCC 3-204(2)]. In other words, a blank indorsement converts an order instrument to a bearer instrument, which anybody can cash. If De Wert indorses in blank a check payable to her order and then loses it on the street, Ketchum can find it and sell it to Lucas for value without indorsing it. This constitutes a negotiation, because Ketchum makes delivery of a bearer instrument (which was an order instrument until it was indorsed).

SPECIAL INDORSEMENTS   A **special indorsement** indicates the specific person to whom the indorser intends to make the instrument payable; that is, it names the indorsee [UCC 3-204(1)]. No special words of negotiation are needed. Words such as "pay to the order of Wilson" or "pay to Wilson" followed by the signature of the indorser are sufficient. When an instrument is indorsed in this way, it is order paper.

To avoid the risk of loss from theft, one may convert a blank indorsement to a special indorsement. This reconverts the bearer paper to order paper. UCC 3-204(3) allows a holder to "convert a blank indorsement into a special indorsement by writing over the signature of the indorser in blank any contract consistent with the character of the indorsement."

For example, a check is made payable to Arthur Engles. He indorses his name by blank indorsement on the back of the check and negotiates the check to Sam Wilson. Sam, not wishing to cash the check immediately, wants to avoid any risk should he lose the check. He therefore writes "pay to Sam Wilson" above Arthur's blank indorsement. In this manner Sam has converted Arthur's blank indorsement into a special indorsement. Further negotiation now requires Sam Wilson's indorsement plus delivery. (See Exhibit 24–2.)

Exhibit 24–2 Special Indorsement

In the following case, the indorser of a check, instead of writing the indorsee's name on the back of the check, attached a removable sticker containing the indorsee's name. Does this constitute a special indorsement? That is the question before the court.

Case 24.1
WALCOTT v. MANUFACTURERS HANOVER TRUST

Civil Court of the City of New York, Kings County, Trial Part 31, 1986.
133 Misc.2d 725, 507 N.Y.S.2d 961.

BACKGROUND AND FACTS *Kenneth Walcott, the plaintiff, alleged that he mailed his paycheck together with a money order to Midatlantic Mortgage Company in payment of his mortgage. He claimed he signed (indorsed) his name in blank to the back of the check and placed his mortgage number and the Midatlantic mailing sticker on the back of the check. Shortly thereafter, Midatlantic notified Walcott that his mortgage payment was late. Walcott investigated and discovered that his paycheck had been cashed at Bilko Check Cashing Corp. by a third party. Bilko had deposited the check into its account at defendant Manufacturers Hanover Trust. The payroll check had cleared and* *been charged to Walcott's employer's account. A copy of the back of the check showed Walcott's indorsement and his mortgage number; but it showed no sign of the sticker. Walcott filed suit against Bilko and against Manufacturers Hanover Trust, claiming his indorsement was either special or restrictive. Both Bilko and the bank claimed that the indorsement was in blank and thus the check had been properly cashed by Bilko.*

HARKAVY, Judge.

* * * *

The store manager of Bilko had testified previously in a prior trial of this case before this Court which ended in a mistrial. Her testimony from the prior trial was incorporated on consent of all parties into the retrial. She testified that in order for a * * * check to be cashed, two pieces of identification are required, usually an employee identification card containing an individual's social security number, and a drivers license. She further testified that the person presenting the check in question must have had such identification since the notations as to the calculation of the check cashing fees on the front of the check indicate that identification was shown.

* * * *

Examination of the back of the check, a photocopy of which, as previously stated, was introduced into evidence, reveals that Mr. Walcott did not specify any particular indorsee. * * * The back of the check shows no sticker attached at all. Even if it had originally been affixed thereto, as plaintiff claims, it obviously became detached easily, thus failing to meet the indorsement requirements under the UCC to constitute a special indorsement.

As to the numbers written underneath plaintiff's signature, they did not have the effect of restricting plaintiff's indorsement. "An indorsement is restrictive which either

(a) is conditional; or

(b) purports to prohibit further transfer of the instrument; or

(c) includes the words 'for collection,' 'for deposit,' 'pay any bank,' or like terms signifying a purpose of deposit or collection; or

(d) otherwise states that it is for the benefit or use of the indorser or of another person." UCC § 3-205.

This section of the Uniform Commercial Code is very specific. The series of numbers representing plaintiff's mortgage account was insufficient to restrict negotiation of plaintiff's check.

Plaintiff's indorsement had the effect of converting the check into a bearer instrument. * * * Consequently, since plaintiff failed to limit his blank indorsement, the check was properly negotiated by delivery to third party defendant Bilko and properly cashed by them.

The court held for the defendants, Manufacturers Hanover Trust and Bilko Check Cashing Corp., and dismissed the complaint.

DECISION AND REMEDY

QUALIFIED INDORSEMENTS Generally, an indorser, *merely by indorsing*, impliedly promises to pay the holder or any subsequent indorser the amount of the instrument in the event that the drawer or maker defaults on the payment [UCC 3-414(1)]. A **qualified indorsement** is used by an indorser to disclaim or limit this liability on the instrument. In this form of indorsement, the no-

tation *without recourse* is commonly used. A sample is shown in Exhibit 24–3.

A qualified indorsement is often used by persons acting in a representative capacity. For instance, insurance agents sometimes receive checks payable to them that are really intended as payment to the insurance company. The agent is merely indorsing the payment through to the principal

Exhibit 24–3 Qualified Indorsement

> *Without recourse*
> *Arthur Engle*

and should not be required to make good on the check if it is later dishonored. The "without recourse" indorsement absolves the agent. If the instrument is dishonored, the holder cannot obtain recovery from the agent who indorsed "without recourse" unless the indorser has breached one of the warranties listed in UCC 3-417(2), (3).

Usually, blank and special indorsements are *unqualified* indorsements. That is, the blank or special indorser is guaranteeing payment of the instrument *in addition to* transferring title to it. The qualified indorser is not guaranteeing such payment. Nonetheless, the qualified indorsement ("without recourse") still transfers title to the indorsee; an instrument bearing a qualified indorsement can be further negotiated.

Qualified indorsements are accompanied by either a special or a blank indorsement that determines further negotiation. Therefore, a special qualified indorsement makes the instrument an order instrument, and it requires an indorsement plus delivery for negotiation. A blank qualified indorsement makes the instrument a bearer instrument, and only delivery is required for negotiation.

To illustrate: A check is made payable to the order of Maggie Mede. Maggie wants to negotiate the check specifically to Harold Hollis with a qualified indorsement. Maggie would indorse the check, "Pay to Harold Hollis, without recourse. [Signed] Maggie Mede." For Harold to further negotiate the check to George Green, he would have to indorse and deliver the check to George.

RESTRICTIVE INDORSEMENTS Prior to the existence of the UCC, a **restrictive indorsement** was thought to prohibit the further negotiation of an instrument. Although some who indorse in this manner still believe the restrictive indorsement prevents any further transfer, the Code holds to the contrary. UCC 3-206(1) states that "no restrictive indorsement prevents further transfer or negotiation of the instrument." The restrictive indorsement requires indorsees to comply with cer-

tain instructions regarding the funds involved. Restrictive indorsements come in many forms. UCC 3-205 categorizes four separate types.

Conditional Indorsements When payment is dependent on the occurrence of some specified event, the instrument has a conditional indorsement [UCC 3-205(a)]. Exhibit 24–4 illustrates a conditional indorsement.

Exhibit 24–4 Conditional Indorsement

> *Pay to Bob Block, provided he completes renovations on building number 23 by September 1, 1990*
> *Ted Smith*

Except against an intermediary bank (defined in Chapter 27), or a payor bank that is not the depository bank, the indorsement is enforceable, and neither Bob Block nor any subsequent holder has the right to enforce payment against Smith on the note before the condition is met [UCC 3-206(2)(3)].

It is important to note that a conditional indorsement does not prevent further negotiation of the instrument. If the conditional language had appeared on the face of the instrument, however, the instrument would not have been negotiable because it would not have met the requirement that it contain an unconditional promise to pay.

Indorsements Prohibiting Further Indorsement An indorsement such as "Pay to Bill Jones only. [Signed] Sue Wong," does not prevent further negotiation. Jones can negotiate the paper to a holder just as if it read "Pay to Bill Jones. [Signed] Sue Wong" [UCC 3-206(1)]. This type of restrictive indorsement has the same legal effect as a special indorsement. It is rarely used [UCC 3-205(b)].

Indorsement for Deposit or Collection A common type of restrictive indorsement is one that makes the indorsee (almost always a bank) a collecting *agent* of the indorser. (See Exhibit 24–5 for an illustration of such an indorsement of a check payable and issued to Mary Smith.)

Exhibit 24–5 For Deposit—For Collection Indorsement

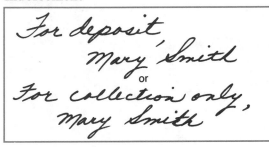

For deposit,
     Mary Smith
or
For collection only,
   Mary Smith

Exhibit 24–6 Trust Indorsements

Pay to Ann North
in trust for
Johnny North
    R. P. North
or
Pay to Ann North
as agent for
R. P. North
    R. P. North

In particular, an indorsement of "Pay any bank or banker" or "For deposit only" has the effect of locking the instrument into the bank collection process. Only a bank can acquire rights of a holder following this indorsement until the item has been specially indorsed by a bank to a person who is not a bank [UCC 4-201(2)]. A bank's liability for payment of an instrument with a restrictive indorsement is discussed in Chapter 27.

Trust, or Agency, Indorsements Indorsements that state that they are for the benefit of the indorser or a third person are trust, or agency, indorsements. Samples are shown in Exhibit 24–6.

The indorsement results in legal title vesting in the original indorsee. To the extent that the original indorsee pays or applies the proceeds consistently with the indorsement (for example, "in trust for Johnny North * * *"), the indorsee is a holder and can become a holder in due course, described in Chapter 25 [UCC 3-205(d), 3-206(4)].

The fiduciary restrictions on the instrument do not reach beyond the original indorsee.[1] Any subsequent purchaser can qualify as a holder in due course unless he or she has actual notice that the instrument was negotiated in breach of the fiduciary duty.[2]

---

1. Compare this to the rule governing conditional indorsements. A conditional indorsement binds all subsequent indorsers (except certain banks) and primary parties to see that the money is applied consistently with the condition. Agency, or trust, indorsements limit this responsibility to the original indorsee. Subsequent parties are not encumbered with this restriction.

2. See Quantum Dev. v. Joy, 397 F.Supp. 329 (D.C.Virgin Is. 1975).

CONCEPT SUMMARY: Types of Indorsements and Their Consequences		
WORDS COMPRISING THE INDORSEMENT	**TYPE OF INDORSEMENT**	**INDORSER'S SIGNATURE LIABILITY[a]**
"Rosemary White"	Blank	Unqualified signature liability upon proper presentment and notice of dishonor.[b]
"Pay to Sam Wilson, Rosemary White"	Special	Unqualified signature liability upon proper presentment and notice of dishonor.
"Without recourse, Rosemary White"	Qualified (blank for further negotiation)	No signature liability. Transfer warranty liability if breach.[c]
"Pay to Sam Wilson, without recourse, Rosemary White"	Qualified (special for further negotiation)	No signature liability. Transfer warranty liability if breach.

(Continued on the next page)

CONCEPT SUMMARY: Types of Indorsements and Their Consequences, (Continued)		
WORDS COMPRISING THE INDORSEMENT	**TYPE OF INDORSEMENT**	**INDORSER'S SIGNATURE LIABILITY[a]**
"Pay to Sam Wilson on condition he completes painting my house at 23 Elm Street by 9/1/90, Rosemary White"	Restrictive—conditional (special for further negotiation)	Signature liability only if condition is met. If condition is met, signature liability upon proper presentment and notice of dishonor.
"Pay to Sam Wilson only, Rosemary White"	Restrictive—prohibitive (special for further negotiation)	Signature liability only on Sam Wilson receiving payment. If Wilson receives payment, signature liability upon proper presentment and notice of dishonor.
"For Deposit, Rosemary White"	Restrictive—for deposit (blank for further negotiation)	Signature liability only on White having amount deposited in her account. If deposit is made, signature liability upon proper presentment and notice of dishonor.
"Pay to Ann South in trust for John North, Rosemary White"	Restrictive—trust (special for further negotiation)	Signature liability only on payment to Ann South for John North's benefit. If restriction is met, signature liability upon proper presentment and notice of dishonor.

a. *Signature liability* refers to the liability of a party who signs an instrument. The basic questions include whether there is any liability and, if so, whether it is unqualified or restricted. Signature liability is discussed in more detail in Chapter 26.

b. When an instrument is dishonored—that is, when, for example, a drawer's bank refuses to cash the drawer's check upon proper presentment—an indorser of the check may be liable on it if he or she is given proper *notice of dishonor*. Dishonor and notice of dishonor are discussed in Chapter 26.

c. The transferor of an instrument makes certain warranties to the transferee and subsequent holders, and thus, even if the transferor's signature does not render him or her liable on the instrument, he or she may be liable for breach of a transfer warranty. Transfer warranties are discussed in Chapter 26. See also UCC 3-417(2) and (3).

Unauthorized Signatures

People are not normally liable to pay on negotiable instruments unless their signatures appear on the instruments. Hence, an unauthorized signature is wholly inoperative and will not bind the person whose name is forged.[3] There are exceptions to this rule, found in UCC 3-404(1). If the person whose unauthorized signature was used ratifies that signature or is in some way precluded from denying it, then the unauthorized signature is operative. Additionally, an unauthorized signature will operate as "the signature of the unauthorized signer in favor of any person who in good faith pays the instrument or takes it for value" [UCC 3-404(1)].

_____

3. On the other hand, a drawee is charged with knowledge of the *drawer's* signature. The drawee cannot recover money it pays out to a holder in due course on a negotiable instrument bearing a forged drawer's signature. (See UCC 3-418.)

Generally, when there is a forged or unauthorized *indorsement*, the burden of loss falls on the first party to take the forged indorsement. In other words, a forged indorsement does not transfer title; and thus, whoever takes an instrument with a forged indorsement cannot become a holder. In effect, for purposes of negotiation and transferring title, a forged indorsement is no indorsement. For example, if Doc's Check Cashing Service cashes Carol's alimony check for Ed, who has forged Carol's signature on the check, Doc's is not legally entitled to payment from Carol's ex-husband's bank account. (This rule is considered more fully in Chapters 26 and 27.) In two situations involving forged indorsements, however, the resulting loss falls on the drawer or maker. These situations are as follows:

1. When an imposter induces the maker or drawer of an instrument to issue it to the imposter.

2. When a person signs as or on behalf of a maker or drawer, intending that the payee will have no interest in the instrument, or when an agent or employee of the maker or drawer has supplied him or her with the name of the payee, also intending the payee to have no such interest [UCC 3-405(1)]. These situations often involve an employee who wishes to swindle an employer by padding bills or payrolls. This is frequently referred to as the *fictitious payee rule*.

Imposter Rule

An **imposter** is one who, by use of the mails, telephone, or personal appearance, induces a maker or drawer to issue an instrument in the name of an impersonated payee. The maker or drawer honestly believes that the imposter is actually the named payee and issues the instrument to the imposter. Since the maker or drawer did issue and intend the imposter to receive the instrument, the indorsement by the imposter is not treated as unauthorized when the instrument is transferred to an innocent party.

In such situations, the unauthorized indorsement of a payee's name can be as effective as if the real payee had signed. The *imposter rule* of UCC 3-405 provides that an imposter's indorsement will be effective—that is, not a forgery—insofar as the drawer goes.

For example, a man walks into John Green's clothing store and purports to be Jerry Lewis soliciting contributions for his annual fund raising for muscular dystrophy. John Green has heard of the Lewis Telethon but has never met or seen Jerry Lewis. Wishing to support a worthy cause, Green writes out a check for $500 payable to Jerry Lewis and hands it to the imposter. The imposter forges the signature of Jerry Lewis and negotiates the check to a Stop and Shop convenience store. Green discovers the fraud and stops payment on the check, claiming the payee's signature is forged. Since the imposter rule is in effect, Green cannot claim a forgery against Stop and Shop, and he must seek redress from the imposter. If Green had sent the check to the real Jerry Lewis but the check had been stolen and negotiated to the store by a forged indorsement, the imposter rule would not apply, and Stop and Shop would have to seek redress against the forger. In either instance, the party who assumes the risk of loss is the party in the best position to guard against an instrument's transfer to an imposter or forger.

Fictitious Payee Rule

The so-called **fictitious payee rule** deals with an instrument issued in the name of a payee with the intention that the payee have no interest in the instrument. The payee need not be fictitious (that is, the payee may be a real person). The determining factor is that the maker or drawer, or another party who has supplied the payee's name to the maker or drawer, intends that the payee not be the party to receive the proceeds when payment is made on the instrument. This most often takes place when (1) a dishonest employee deceives the employer, the maker or drawer, into signing an instrument payable to a party with no right to receive the instrument, or (2) the dishonest employee or agent has the authority to so issue the instrument on behalf of the maker or drawer. In these situations, the payee's indorsement is not treated as a forgery, and the maker or drawer is held liable on the instrument by an innocent holder.

Assume that the Revco Company gives its bookkeeper, Sam Snyde, general authority to issue checks in the company name drawn on Second Federal Bank so that Snyde can pay employees and pay other corporate bills. Snyde decides to cheat Revco out of $10,000 by issuing a check payable to Fanny Freid, an old acquaintance of his. Snyde does not intend Freid to receive any of the money, and Freid is not an employee or creditor of the company.

Snyde indorses the check in Freid's name, naming himself as indorsee. Snyde cashes the check with a local bank, which collects payment from the drawee bank, Second Federal. Second Federal then charges Revco's account $10,000.

Revco discovers the fraud and demands that its account be recredited. Who bears the loss? Neither the local bank that first accepted the check nor Second Federal is liable. The rule of UCC 3-405 provides the answer. Since Snyde's indorsement in the name of a payee with no interest in the instrument is effective, there is no forgery. Hence, the collecting bank is protected in paying on the check, and the drawee bank is protected in charging Revco's account. It is the employer-drawer, Revco, that bears the loss.[4] Of course,

---

4. May Dept. Stores Co. v. Pittsburgh Nat. Bank, 374 F.2d 109 (3rd Cir. 1967).

Revco has recourse against Snyde, who, however, has most likely spent the money or absconded with it.

Whether a dishonest employee actually signs the check or merely supplies his or her employer with names of fictitious creditors (or with true names of creditors having fictitious debts), the Code makes no distinction in result. For example, Ned Norris draws up the payroll list from which em-ployee checks are written. Norris fraudulently adds the name Sue Swift (a fictitious person) to the payroll, thus causing checks to be issued to her. Again, it is the employer-drawer who bears the loss, because the employer is in the best position to prevent such fraud.

In the following case, the court must determine whether a bank should bear the loss for checks paid to and indorsed by a fictitious payee.

Case 24.2
CITY OF PHOENIX v. GREAT WESTERN BANK & TRUST

Court of Appeals of Arizona, Division 1, Department A, 1985.
148 Ariz. 53, 712 P.2d 966.

BACKGROUND AND FACTS *Jay Maisel was employed by the city of Phoenix under a program to assist ex-convicts. After five months in a nonsensitive position, Maisel was promoted to a position in which he was responsible for preparing documentation for issuance of warrants (orders authorizing payment from the municipal treasury) to vendors. Six months later, Maisel prepared duplicate claims for which the city issued warrants, each in the amount of $514,320.40, to the order of Duncan Industries. One warrant was sent to the vendor in Chicago, and the other was sent to Maisel's partner, Gary Hann, in Tucson. In the meantime, Hann had set up a checking account at Great Western Bank & Trust in the name of Duncan Industries, telling the bank that the company was a sole proprietorship involved in investments. Hann provided a taxpayer identification number for the business, his social security number, a local telephone number, a local business address, a post office box number, his driver's license number, and his hospital patient card. Four days after the account had been opened, Hann deposited the fraudulent warrant, which was accepted with a four-day hold to prevent withdrawals prior to payment by the drawee bank. Four days after the warrant had been deposited, Hann began making withdrawals from the account. Within ten days, he had withdrawn over $441,000 from the account. The city of Phoenix sued Great Western Bank & Trust to recover for payment of the check, claiming that the bank had been negligent and had acted in bad faith in accepting such a large amount and allowing such a large withdrawal within ten days. The bank claimed it was protected by the fictitious payee rule. The trial court granted a summary judgment in favor of the bank, and the city of Phoenix appealed.*

CORCORAN, Judge.

* * * *

[Arizona Revised Statutes] Section 47-3405(A)(3), often referred to as the "ficitious payee rule," provides in pertinent part:

A. An indorsement by any person in the name of a named payee is *effective* if:

. . .

3. An agent or employee of the maker or drawer has supplied him with the name of the payee intending the latter to have no such interest.
(Emphasis added.)

The exception places the loss from the activities of a faithless employee upon the employer rather than upon the drawee bank. The loss is shifted by making the endorsement "effective" although it is unauthorized. Since the endorsement is "effective" the "instrument passes as though there had been no forgery and as between a collecting bank and the drawer of the check, the loss must fall on the drawer employer." The rule, as applied, also eliminates any liability of a collecting bank for breach of warranty of the genuineness of the signatures, §§ 47-3417 and 47-4207, because a signature that is "effective" is to be regarded as "genuine" for the purpose of warranty liability. Thus, in this case, the City, as assignee of drawee Valley National Bank, has no recourse against the Great Western Bank based on the warranties contained in §§ 47-3417 and 47-4207 owed by the Bank to the drawee Valley National Bank.

The basis of the fictitious payee rule is explained in UCC § 3-405, Official Comment 4:

> The principle followed is that the loss should fall upon the employer as a risk of his business enterprise rather than upon the subsequent holder or drawee. The reasons are that the employer is normally in a better position to prevent such forgeries by reasonable care in the selection or supervision of his employees, or, if he is not, is at least in a better position to cover the loss by fidelity insurance; and that the cost of such insurance is properly an expense of his business rather than of the business of the holder or drawee.

The factual circumstances for application of § 47-3405(A)(3) are met in this case. Maisel, an "employee" of the drawer, the City of Phoenix, supplied the City, as to the duplicate warrant, with the name of a "payee," Duncan Industries, with the intent of creating no interest in Duncan Industries.

The Bank claims that it is shielded from liability by the terms of § 47-3405. The City responds that the Bank's failure to exercise reasonable care in opening the Hann account, accepting the warrant for deposit and allowing Hann to withdraw almost the entire amount of the check in ten days estops the Bank from asserting the fictitious payee rule as a defense.

*   *   *   *

The lack of an explicit standard of care in § 47-3405 has created confusion as to the standard for liability for a fictitious payee loss. In our view the fictitious payee rule is not intended to provide an *absolute* defense. [Emphasis added.] Although there is no good faith requirement specifically set forth in § 47-3405, banks are obligated to act in "good faith" in all contracts and duties. Thus, to successfully assert the effectiveness of an endorsement under § 47-3405 a bank must have acted in good faith.

*   *   *   *

The City claims that the Bank should have realized that the circumstances of the deposit of the warrant were suspicious and therefore it should have carefully investigated the warrant before accepting it. But, the City concedes that there is no evidence that any Bank employee acted as a confederate with either Maisel or Hann. The facts the City points to are: the youth of the depositer, the amount of the warrant (approximately 2.5 percent of the branch's average daily deposit), and the proximity in time of the deposit to the opening of the account by a depositor previously unknown to the Bank.

*   *   *

The facts pointed to by the City do not indicate a lack of good faith on the part of the Bank. The warrant was made payable to the order of the named depositor. It was appropriately indorsed by him and deposited in his account at the Bank. There were no alterations on the face of the warrant nor were there any other suggestions sufficient to invoke a duty to inquire in connection with the deposit. Mere negligence or knowledge of suspicious circumstances is not sufficient to show bad faith. From these facts the trial court correctly decided as a matter of law that the Bank acted in good faith—with "honesty in fact in the conduct or transaction concerned."

*   *   *   *

The City also claims that but for the Bank's negligence in opening the account, the fraudulent warrant check would not have been passed. This assertion has no merit. The Bank's lack of good faith, notice or negligence cannot be judged by looking at unrelated and dissimilar transactions as though they were one incident. Rather, lack of good faith must be established by reference to the conduct or transaction concerned. In the opening of the account, the Bank acted in good faith with honesty in fact.

The City argues that the Bank acted in bad faith in allowing Hann to withdraw almost the full amount of his deposit within ten days after the deposit of the warrant.

*   *   *

*   *   *   *

In the instant case there were three distinct transactions: the opening of the bank account, the deposit of the warrant, and withdrawals from the bank account. The only transaction relevant to our inquiry of good faith is the deposit of the warrant. The trial court correctly decided that the warrant was deposited in good faith. We further note that the opening of the account and the withdrawals were conducted in good faith, so that even if "conduct or transactions concerned" was interpreted as the interrelation of the three events, the trial court was justified in concluding that the Bank acted in good faith.

The facts relating to the opening of the account do not provide foresight to anticipate the deposit of a fraudulent warrant; nor, do the circumstances of the withdrawals provide hindsight that a fraudulent warrant had been passed. Clearly, good faith neither requires 20/20 foresight nor 20/20 hindsight as to preceding and subsequent unrelated and dissimilar events and transactions.

DECISION AND REMEDY *The court of appeals affirmed the trial court's summary judgment in favor of the bank. The fictitious payee rule precluded recovery against the bank for breach of warranty of genuineness of signatures. The signatures were regarded as genuine for purposes of warranty liability.*

Miscellaneous Indorsement Problems

Of course, a variety of other problems may arise where indorsements are concerned. Some of these problems are discussed below.

NO STANDARD CATEGORY Sometimes an indorsement does not seem to fit into any of the standard categories. For example, the indorsement can read: "I hereby assign all my right and title and interest in this note. [Signed] Beverly Hatch." The signature is an effective indorsement despite the additional language of transfer. Use of the word *assign* does not change the negotiation into a mere assignment. Clearly, Beverly Hatch did not intend to limit the rights of the person to whom she was transferring the instrument [UCC 3-202(4)].

CORRECTION OF NAME An indorsement should be identical to the name that appears on the instrument. The payee or indorsee whose name is misspelled can indorse with the misspelled name, or the correct name, or both [UCC 3-203].

For example, Susan Lock receives a check payable to the order of "Susan Locke." She can indorse the check either "Susan Locke" or "Susan Lock." The usual practice is to indorse the name as it appears on the instrument and follow it by the correct name.[5]

BANK INDORSEMENTS When a customer deposits a check with a bank and fails to indorse it, the bank has the right to supply any necessary indorsement for its customer unless the instrument *specifically prohibits it* [UCC 4-205(1)].

For example, Morty Adams deposits his government check with First National Bank and forgets to indorse it. Since government checks typically state "Payee's indorsement required," the bank will not supply the indorsement. The check will be returned to Adams for his signature.

Ordinarily, checks do not specifically require the payee's indorsement. The bank merely stamps or marks the check, indicating that it was deposited by the customer or credited to the customer's account [UCC 4-205].

Commercial paper must move rapidly through banking channels. In the process of clearing through collection, a check can be transferred between banks by use of any agreed-upon method of indorsement that identifies the transferor bank [UCC 4-206]. For example, a bank can indorse using its Federal Reserve number instead of its name.

MULTIPLE PAYEES An instrument payable to two or more persons *in the alternative* (for example, "Pay to the order of Capron or Baker") requires the indorsement of only one of the payees [UCC 3-116(a)]. If an instrument is payable to two or more persons *jointly* (for example, "Pay to the order of Carl and Doris" or "Pay to the order of

---

5. Watertown Federal Sav. and Loan v. Spanks, 346 Mass. 398, 193 N.E.2d 333 (1963).

Glenda, Harold"), then all the payees' indorsements are necessary for negotiation [UCC 3-116(b)].

UNINDORSED ORDER PAPER If order paper is transferred without indorsement, it is a transfer by assignment, not by negotiation. The receiver is merely a transferee, not a holder, and does not qualify as a holder in due course. If, however, the transfer is made for value given, the unqualified indorsement of the transferor can be compelled by law by the transferee unless the parties have agreed otherwise. The effect is the negotiation of the instrument. The transferee becomes a holder and can negotiate the instrument further [UCC 3-201(3)]. Compare this rule with that governing the bank's right upon deposit of an unindorsed check, as previously discussed.

AGENTS OR OFFICERS A negotiable instrument can be drawn payable to a legal entity such as an estate, a partnership, or an organization. For example, if a check reads "Pay to the order of the Red Cross," an authorized representative of the Red Cross can negotiate it.

Similarly, negotiable paper can be payable to a public officer. For example, checks reading "Pay to the order of the County Tax Collector," or "Pay to the order of Larry White, Receiver of Taxes," can be negotiated by whoever holds the office [UCC 3-110(1)(b)].

QUESTIONS AND CASE PROBLEMS

1. A check drawn by Daniel for $200 is made payable to the order of Paula. The check is issued to Paula. Paula owes her landlord $200 in rent and transfers the check to her landlord with the following indorsement: "For rent paid. [Signed] Paula." Paula's landlord has contracted to have Peter Plumber repair a number of apartment leaks. The plumber insists on immediate payment. The landlord transfers the check to Peter without indorsement. Later, in order to pay for plumbing supplies at Facet's Store, Peter transfers the check with the following indorsement: "Pay to Facet's Store, without recourse. [Signed] Peter Plumber." Facet sends the check to its bank indorsed "For deposit only. [Signed] Facet's Store."

   (a) Classify each of these indorsements.

   (b) Was the transfer from Paula's landlord to Peter Plumber, without indorsement, an assignment or a negotiation? Explain.

2. Dan David drafts a check for $500 payable to the order of Jane Petrie. Petrie wants to purchase Fred Flint's 1972 Chevy for $500 and contracts to do so, with payment to be immediate and delivery of the car to be seven days thereafter. Petrie indorses David's check to Flint by writing "Pay to Flint, upon condition of delivery of his 1972 Chevy. [Signed] Jane Petrie." Flint takes the check and indorses it, "For deposit. [Signed] Fred Flint." Assume that Dan David has a legal right to stop payment on the check, and assume that Flint has not delivered the car.

   (a) How is each of the indorsements above classified?

   (b) What is the legal effect of Petrie's indorsement under the circumstances?

3. Lonny Ledger has been Ann Green's employee accountant for five years. During that time, Green has relied more and more on Ledger to prepare payment checks for suppliers, payroll checks, and the like. Unknown to Green, Ledger is a compulsive gambler and is deeply in debt. Ledger, believing that his life is at stake, prepares two checks payable to nonexistent suppliers. Green signs both checks without knowledge of these events. Ledger indorses both suppliers' names and adds "Pay to Lonny Ledger" above both names. Ledger takes the checks and deposits them at his bank without indorsement. Later, he withdraws the funds from his bank. His bank sends the checks through the collection process. The checks are paid by Green's bank, the drawee. Green discovers Ledger's action after Ledger has left town. Green claims that Ledger's indorsement of the suppliers' names constituted a forgery, that Ledger's bank did not have Ledger's indorsement, and that the bank must therefore recredit her account. Discuss Green's contentions.

4. John and Martha Whelan ordered a clock from a catalog seller. John sent the seller a check for $50 with the order. The seller cashed the check. When the seller found she could not deliver the clock, she drew and sent a refund check to the Whelans. When the Whelans received the check, they noticed that it was made payable to Jonathan and Martha Whelan. Martha Whelan is now away visiting her mother, and John needs to negotiate the check to pay an overdue bill.

   (a) Can John properly negotiate the check without Martha's indorsement? Explain.

   (b) John is concerned that the check is made payable to Jonathan, not John. Would this prohibit John from negotiating the check under any circumstances? Explain.

5. Jay Jones is an Elevated Party candidate for the city council in a large city. It is common knowledge that Jones is personally soliciting funds throughout the neighborhood. Frank Francis has been a member of the Elevated Party for years. He receives a phone call from Sam Shady, who pretends to be Jay Jones and asks for financial help. Over the phone Francis agrees to write a check for $200 payable to Jay Jones. Shady gives Francis a post office box address.

Francis writes the check and sends it to the box as directed. Shady has nothing to do with the campaign of Jones, and the box is his own. Shady immediately takes the check and indorses the name of Jones and then his own name. Shady now negotiates the check to a friend, Judy Green, who has no knowledge of Shady's activities. Shady leaves the country. Later, Francis learns of the fraud. Francis claims that since the signature of Jones was forged by Shady, Francis is not liable to Green on the check. Discuss the contention of Francis.

6. Dynamics Corp. and Marine Midland Bank had a long-standing agreement under which Marine Midland received checks payable to Dynamics and indorsed and deposited them in Dynamics' account. Dynamics never saw the checks. They were made out to the order of Dynamics and delivered directly to Marine Midland. Marine Midland stamped the backs of the checks with Dynamics' name and insignia and transferred them. Within the meaning of the UCC, is the act of sending checks to Marine Midland Bank a negotiation? If Marine Midland transfers the checks to other parties, is this a negotiation? [Marine Midland Bank–New York v. Graybar Electric Co., 41 N.Y.2d 703, 363 N.E.2d 1139, 395 N.Y.S.2d 403 (1977)]

7. A life insurance policy was taken out on the life of Robert Agaliotis by Louis Agaliotis, his father. A provision in the policy allowed Louis to request that $1,852 be paid to him as the owner of the policy. Through a clerical error, the insurance company made the check payable to Robert, but it was correctly delivered to Louis. If Louis indorsed Robert's name and cashed the check, was he liable for wrongfully indorsing the check? [Agaliotis v. Agaliotis, 38 N.C.App. 42, 247 S.E.2d 28 (1978)]

8. F. Mitchell, assistant treasurer of Travco Corporation, caused two checks payable to a fictitious company, L. and B. Distributors, to be drawn on the corporation's account. Mitchell took both checks to his personal bank, indorsed them "F. Mitchell," and gave them to the teller. The teller cashed them. When Travco learned of the embezzlement, it demanded reimbursement from the bank. The bank contended that under the rule concerning fictitious payees and imposters, Mitchell's indorsement was valid and that therefore the bank should be allowed to collect. Is the bank's contention true? [Travco Corp. v. Citizens Federal Sav. & Loan Ass'n, 42 Mich.App. 291, 201 N.W.2d 675 (1972)]

9. On or about November 15, 1979, Warnock purchased a cashier's check for $53,541.93, payable to her order and drawn on the Pueblo Bank and Trust Company. Between November 15, 1979, and November 30, 1979, Warnock indorsed "Katherine Warnock" on the reverse side of the check, and Warnock's attorney, Jerry Quick, wrote the words "deposit only" under Warnock's indorsement. On November 30, 1979, Quick deposited the check into the Marquez Trust account, which was an account maintained by Quick at La Junta State Bank. Warnock did not at any time maintain an account with the bank. Warnock died on November 10, 1981. Robert Travis, a personal representative of the estate of Warnock, filed an action against La Junta State Bank seeking recovery of the amount of the cashier's check. Travis alleged that the words "deposit only" constituted a restrictive indorsement placed on the check by Quick for the benefit of Warnock and that, consequently, the bank had a duty to either deposit the item into an account for Warnock or to undertake further investigation of the indorsement before crediting the sum to any account other than to an account for Warnock. Is Travis correct? [La Junta State Bank v. Travis, 727 P.2d 48 (Colo. 1986)]

10. In January of 1973, Keith and Joyce Alves loaned Joyce Alves's parents, Beatrice and William Baldaia, $15,000. In return, the Baldaias executed a promissory note payable to Joyce Alves. In February of 1978, Keith and Joyce Alves divorced. The separation agreement contained the following provision: "Wife agrees to assign to Husband any and all right, title, and interest she may have in a certain note, executed by her parents, dated January 3, 1973 on or before date of final hearing." Joyce Alves later wrote on the promissory note, "Pay to the order of Keith R. Alves. [Signed] Joyce Ann Alves." Some time later, Keith Alves tried to collect payment on the note from the Baldaias, who refused to pay it. Alves then sought payment from his former wife, who had since remarried and taken the name of Schaller. Schaller claimed that her transfer of the promissory note to Alves, pursuant to the separation agreement, constituted an "assignment" of her rights and interests in the note and not a formal "negotiation" of the note. Was the transfer of the promissory note an assignment or a negotiation? [Alves v. Baldaia, 14 Ohio App.3d 187, 470 N.E.2d 459 (1984)]

Chapter 25

COMMERCIAL PAPER
Holder in Due Course

Commercial paper is not money; rather, it is an instrument that is payable in money. The body of rules contained in Article 3 of the UCC govern a party's right to payment of a check, draft, note, or certificate of deposit.[1] The third party is characterized as either an ordinary *holder* or a *holder in due course*.[2] (The party can also be a transferee according to UCC 3-201.)

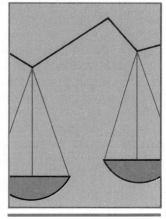

Litigation concerning commercial paper occurs when there is a dispute about who should be paid. Issues of litigation usually turn on which party can obtain payment on an instrument when it is due or on whether some defense can be asserted to discharge or to cancel liability on an instrument. For these reasons, it becomes important for a person seeking payment to have the rights of a holder in due course. A holder in due course takes a negotiable instrument free of all claims and most defenses of other parties. That means that the holder in due course has the right to collect payment on that instrument, and this right will take priority over the claims of other parties.[3]

Our discussion of holders in due course will be concerned primarily with *negotiable* instruments that have been *negotiated*.

HOLDER VERSUS HOLDER IN DUE COURSE

As pointed out in Chapter 22, a holder is a person who possesses a negotiable instrument "drawn, issued, or indorsed to him or his order or to bearer or

---

1. The rights and liabilities on checks, drafts, notes, and certificates of deposit are determined under Article 3 of the UCC. Other kinds of commercial paper, such as stock certificates or bills of lading and other documents of title, meet the requirements of negotiable instruments, but the rights and liabilities of the parties on these documents are covered by Articles 7 and 8 of the Code. See Chapter 51 on bailments for information on Article 7.

2. *Holder*, as the term is used in Article 3 of the UCC, applies here only in the context of negotiable instruments.

3. UCC 3-305(2) specifically sets forth the very limited number of real *defenses* that defeat payments to a holder in due course. A holder in due course takes commercial paper free from personal (as opposed to real) defenses. These are discussed more thoroughly in Chapter 26.

in blank" [UCC 1-201(20)]. To be a holder, a person must have possession and good title (free of forgeries of those names necessary to the chain of title). The holder is the person who, by the terms of the instrument, is legally entitled to payment. The holder of an instrument need not be its owner in order to transfer it, negotiate it, discharge it, or enforce payment of it in his or her own name [UCC 3-301].

A holder has the status of an assignee of a contract right. A transferee of a negotiable instrument who is characterized merely as a holder (as opposed to a holder in due course) obtains only those rights that the predecessor-transferor had in the instrument. In the event that there is a conflicting, superior claim or defense to the instrument, an ordinary holder will not be able to collect payment.

A **holder in due course** (HDC) is a special-status transferee of a negotiable instrument who, by meeting certain acquisition requirements, takes the instrument *free* of most defenses or adverse claims to it. Stated another way, an HDC can normally acquire a higher level of immunity to defenses against payment on the instrument or claims of ownership to the instrument by other parties.

REQUIREMENTS FOR HOLDER-IN-DUE-COURSE STATUS

The basic requirements for attaining HDC status are set forth in UCC 3-302. First, the instrument must be negotiable, and whoever seeks HDC status must be a holder. The holder must take the instrument (1) for value, (2) in good faith, and (3) without notice that it is overdue, or that it has been dishonored, or that any person has a defense against it or a claim to it.

The underlying requirement for HDC status is that a person must first be a holder of that instrument. Regardless of other circumstances surrounding acquisition, only a holder has a chance to become an HDC.

Taking for Value

An HDC must have given *value* for the instrument [UCC 3-303]. A person who receives an instru-

ment as a gift or who inherits it has not met this requirement. In these situations, the person becomes an ordinary holder and does not possess the rights of an HDC.[4]

The Code provides for a holder to take the instrument for value in one of three ways. Basically, a holder gives value:

1. To the extent that the agreed-upon consideration has been paid or a security interest or lien acquired.

2. By payment of or as security for an *antecedent*, or prior, *claim*.

3. By giving a negotiable instrument or irrevocable commitment as payment.

AGREED-UPON CONSIDERATION PERFORMED
The concept of value in the law of negotiable instruments is not the same as the concept of consideration in the law of contracts. An executory promise (a promise to give value in the future) is a clearly valid consideration to support a contract [UCC 1-201(44)]. It does not, however, normally constitute value sufficient to make one an HDC. UCC 3-303 provides that a holder takes the instrument for value only to the extent that the agreed-upon consideration has been performed. Therefore, if the holder plans to pay for the instrument later or plans to perform the required services at some future date, the holder has not yet given value. In that case, the holder is not yet a holder in due course.

Suppose Ted Green draws a $500 note payable to Roger Evans in payment for goods. Evans negotiates the note to Irene Franks, who promises to pay him for it in thirty days. During the next month, Franks learns that Evans breached the contract by delivering defective goods and that Green will not honor the $500 note. Evans has left town. Whether Franks can hold Green liable on the note will depend on Franks's status as a holder in due course. Since Franks has given no value at the time she learns of Green's defense, she is a mere holder, not a holder in due course. Thus, Green's defense is valid not only against Evans but also against Franks. If Franks had paid Evans for the note on the transfer (which would mean

---

4. There is one way an ordinary holder who fails to meet the value requirement can qualify as a holder in due course. The "shelter provision" of the Code allows an ordinary holder to succeed to HDC status if any prior holder was an HDC. This exception is discussed later in the chapter [UCC 3-201(1)].

the agreed-upon consideration had been performed), she would be a holder in due course and could hold Green liable on the note even though Green had a valid breach of contract or warranty defense against Evans.

UCC 3-303(a) provides that a holder takes an instrument for value only to the extent that the agreed-upon consideration has been performed. For example, Arnolds negotiates a $1,000 note to Raymonds for a total (discounted) price of $950, with $700 payable now and $250 due in thirty days. Raymonds is immediately an HDC to the extent of $700, and when she completes payment of $250, she will become an HDC for the full $1,000 face amount of the note.

Do not be confused when the value of the agreed-upon consideration differs from the face amount of the instrument. When a time instrument is sold, it is usually discounted to allow for transfer costs, collection costs, and interest charges. Thus, a $1,000 note due in ninety days may be sold for $950 cash to a financial institution. The requirement of agreed-upon consideration is satisfied by the $950 payment. And when the instrument comes due, the holder will collect the full $1,000. If the discrepancy between the purchase amount and face value is great, however, this discrepancy can be considered along with other factors to indicate either that the purchaser lacks good faith or that only a partial payment is being made, reducing the HDC status to this amount. The good faith element will be discussed later in this chapter.

A holder takes an instrument for value to the extent that the holder acquires a security interest in or lien on the instrument. It is not unusual for an instrument to be given as security for a loan or other obligation.

If, for example, Norris issues a $1,000 note payable to Lomond, Lomond can use the note to secure a $700 loan from Hilton. (Lomond gets $700 cash; Hilton holds the note as security.) Hilton's $700 loan qualifies her as a holder for value. If Lomond does not repay the $700, Hilton can collect the note. But what if Norris has a personal defense (such as breach of contract or fraud in the inducement) against Lomond? Hilton, as an HDC, is free and clear of the defense, but *only to the extent of $700*. Hence, the rule is: "a purchaser of a limited interest can be a holder in due course only to the extent of the interest purchased" [UCC 3-302(4)].

A holder can also take for value by acquiring a lien on the instrument through an agreement rather than through operation of law. For example, a payee of a note pledges it to a bank as security for a loan. The terms of the pledge agreement give the bank a lien on the instrument. The bank is a holder for value to the extent of its lien.

ANTECEDENT CLAIM When an instrument is given in payment of (or as security for) an **antecedent claim,** the value requirement is met [UCC 3-303(b)]. Here again, commercial law and contract law produce different results. An antecedent claim is not valid consideration under general contract law, but it does constitute value sufficient to satisfy the requirement for HDC status in commercial law.

Assume Cary owes Dwyer $2,000 on a past due account. If Cary negotiates a $2,000 note to Dwyer and Dwyer accepts it to discharge the overdue account balance, Dwyer has given value for the instrument.

NEGOTIABLE INSTRUMENT AS VALUE UCC 3-303(c) provides that a holder takes the instrument for value "when he gives a negotiable instrument for it, or makes an irrevocable commitment to a third person."

To illustrate: Martin has issued a $500 negotiable promissory note to Paula. The note is due six months from the date issued. Paula's financial circumstances are such that she does not want to wait for the maturity date to collect. Therefore, she negotiates the note to her friend Susan, who pays her $200 in cash and writes her a negotiable check for the balance of $300. Susan has given full value for the note by paying $200 in cash and issuing Paula the check for $300.

A negotiable instrument has value when issued, not when the underlying obligation is finally paid. In the preceding example, assume that before Paula cashes Susan's check, Susan learns that the maker of the note has a personal defense against Paula. In this event, Susan has the protection of HDC status. Commercial practicality requires this rule because a negotiable instrument, by its nature, carries the possibility that it might be negotiated to a holder in due course. If it is, the party that issued it generally cannot refuse to pay [UCC 3-303].

CHECK DEPOSITS AND WITHDRAWALS Occasionally, a commercial bank can become an HDC when honoring other banks' checks for its own customers. In this situation, the bank becomes an "involuntary" holder in due course, in that at the time of giving value the bank has no intention of becoming an HDC.

Assume that on Monday morning at the end of the month Pat Stevens has $400 in her checking account at the First National Bank. That morning Stevens deposits her payroll check for $300 drawn by her employer on the Second National Bank. During her lunch hour she issues a check to her landlord for $425. The landlord cashes the check at the First National Bank. Later, the Second National Bank returns the payroll check marked "insufficient funds." In most cases, First National would charge this check against Stevens's account. If that cannot be done, however, is the First National Bank an HDC of the employer's check? The answer is yes. According to what is referred to as the first-money-in, first-money-out rule, First National Bank has paid to the landlord $25 of its own funds [UCC 4-208(2)]. Therefore, First National is an HDC to the extent it has given value—$25.

SPECIAL CASES   In a few exceptional circumstances, a holder can take an instrument even for value but still not be accorded HDC status. UCC 3-302(3) specifies the following situations:

1. Purchase at a judicial sale (for example, a bankruptcy sale) or taking under legal process.
2. Acquisition when taking over an estate (as administrator).

3. Purchase as part of a bulk transfer (as when a corporation buys the assets of another corporation).

In these situations, the UCC limits the rights of the holder to those of an ordinary holder.

Taking in Good Faith

The second requirement for HDC status is that the holder take the instrument in good faith [UCC 3-302(1)(b)]. This means that the purchaser-holder must have acted honestly in the process of acquiring the instrument. **Good faith** is defined in UCC 1-201(19) as "honesty in fact in the conduct or transaction concerned."

Because of the good faith requirement, one must ask whether the purchaser, when acquiring the instrument, honestly believed the instrument was not defective. If a person purchases a $10,000 note for $100 from a stranger on a street corner, the issue of good faith can be raised on the grounds of the suspicious circumstances *and* the grossly inadequate consideration. The Code does not provide clear guidelines to determine good faith. Thus, each situation will be examined separately.

In the following case, the court focused on the issue of the admissibility of evidence regarding the adequacy of consideration for the sale of a negotiable instrument when considering whether the purchase was made in good faith.

Case 25.1
FUNDING CONSULTANTS, INC. v. AETNA CASUALTY AND SURETY COMPANY

Supreme Court of Connecticut, 1982.
187 Conn. 637, 447 A.2d 1163.

BACKGROUND AND FACTS   *Benjamin Priesner and Aetna Casualty and Surety Co., the defendants, were co-makers of a promissory note (the Priesner note) that was given to Paul King in connection with the sale of King's insurance company to Priesner. The Priesner note was a non-interest-bearing negotiable instrument in the amount of $68,000 payable in four equal annual installments. King sold the Priesner note to the plaintiff, Funding Consultants, Inc., shortly thereafter. In return for the Priesner note, King received $5,000 cash and a promissory note for $35,000 (the Funding note). The Funding note was a non-interest-bearing negotiable instrument payable in four equal installments, one every two months. Priesner, after formal demand, refused to make any payments on the Priesner note, alleging he had been induced to make the note by fraudulent misrepresentations about the financial condition of King's insurance company. Funding Consultants declared the whole amount due and payable and filed suit to collect, claiming it was a holder in due course (HDC) and that the fraud defense could thus not be used against payment. To establish its HDC status, the plaintiff relied on the testimony of its president, Richard*

Splain, that he had little knowledge of or experience in the purchase of negotiable instruments. The defendants sought to counter this testimony by offering testimony by an expert witness that the plaintiff had given inadequate consideration ($40,000 for a $68,000 note) for the Priesner note and that this amounted to taking the note in bad faith. The trial court disallowed the expert's testimony, and the jury found the plaintiff to be a holder in due course. The defendants appealed.

PETERS, Justice.
*   *   *   *

   *   *   * In order to decide whether a holder of an instrument acted in good faith, the trier of fact must determine the intent or state of mind of the party concerned. As in other determinations concerning intent, the trier is entitled to consider not only the testimony of the interested party but also evidence of surrounding circumstances that inferentially illuminate his honesty in fact in view of his actual knowledge. *   *   * [I]f a party pays for an instrument an amount far less than its face value, such evidence is a factor that a trier may reasonably consider in weighing whether a purchase was made in good faith. The sale of an instrument at a substantial discount may in fact have alerted a prospective purchaser to a possible defense to which he may not wilfully close his eyes. We therefore hold that the defendant was entitled to introduce evidence in this case to show that there was such inadequacy of consideration that this factor, among others, should have been weighed by the jury in its determination of the plaintiff's good faith.

   *   *   * The expert testimony was offered by the defendant to show what a commercial bank would have paid for the Priesner note and what the effective rate of return on the plaintiff's investment would have been. It is not an answer to this offer of proof that the plaintiff's president had testified about his inexperience with the purchase of negotiable paper and his ignorance of the practices and procedures of commercial banks. The jury might have chosen to disregard some or all of this testimony. The expert's evidence would have provided the jury with some basis for assessing the present value of both the Priesner note and the Funding note. It is not unreasonable to offer a lay jury expert assistance in the proper calculation of values that are not obvious on the face of the instruments to be compared. The proffered evidence was relevant because it would have enabled the jury to make a more accurate assessment of whether the plaintiff took the Priesner note in good faith.

The Supreme Court of Connecticut held that the trial court had improperly excluded the expert testimony and that the defendants were entitled to a new trial to determine the holder-in-due-course status of Funding Consultants. The judgment of the trial court was set aside, and the case was remanded for new trial.

DECISION AND REMEDY

Taking without Notice

The third requirement for HDC status involves notice [UCC 3-304]. A person will not be afforded HDC protection if he or she knew or should have known at the time the instrument was acquired that it was defective in any one of the following ways [UCC 3-302(1)(c)]:

1. It was overdue.
2. It had been dishonored.

3. There was a defense against it.
4. There was another claim to it.

The main provisions of UCC 3-304 spell out the common circumstances that, as a matter of law, constitute notice of a claim or defense and notice of an overdue instrument. *Notice of a fact* involves [UCC 1-201(25)]: (1) actual knowledge of the fact, (2) receipt of notice of the fact, or (3) reason to know that the fact exists, given all the facts and circumstances known at the time in question.

UCC 3-304(4) contains a list of specific facts that do not in themselves constitute notice of a defense or claim. The list can be reviewed in the full text of the Code contained in Appendix B. In short, the Code's position is that certain kinds of information about the instrument or about parties to it can raise some suspicion regarding the ultimate enforceability of the paper, but the information falls short of indicating a defense or claim. Also, knowledge from a public notice—for example, through newspapers or official records—is not automatically imputed to a purchaser; it must be shown that the information was read [UCC 3-304(5)]. Recall that the basic test of good faith is honesty in fact. The key concern is whether this particular purchaser honestly knew something was wrong with a particular instrument at the time it was acquired.

OVERDUE INSTRUMENTS All negotiable paper is either payable at a definite time (time instrument) or payable on demand (demand instrument). What will constitute notice that an instrument is overdue or has been dishonored will vary depending upon whether it is demand or time paper.

Time Instruments A holder of a time instrument who takes the paper the day after its expressed due date is "on notice" that it is overdue. Nonpayment by the due date should indicate to any purchaser who is obligated to pay that the primary party has a defense to payment. Thus, a promissory note due on May 15 must be acquired before midnight on May 15. If it is purchased on May 16, the purchaser will be an ordinary holder, not an HDC.

Sometimes instruments read, "Payable in thirty days." A note dated December 1 that is payable in thirty days is due by midnight on December 31. But what if a note is dated December 2 and is payable in thirty days? When is it due? If the payment date falls on a Sunday or holiday, the instrument is payable on the next business day, so the note is due on January 2.

A large debt is often broken down into successive payments. The debt can be evidenced by a single, large-denomination note payable in installments; or a series of notes in smaller denominations can be issued, each identified as part of the same indebtedness. In the case of an installment note, notice that the maker has defaulted on any installment of principal (but not interest payments) will prevent a purchaser from becoming an HDC [UCC 3-304(3)(a)]. Most installment notes provide specifically that any payment made on the note shall be applied first to interest, with the balance to principal. Thus, any payment that is less than the amount due on that installment will put a holder on notice that some of the principal is overdue.

The same result occurs when a series of notes with successive maturity dates is issued at the same time for a single indebtedness. Default in payment of any one note of the series will constitute overdue notice for the entire series. Prospective purchasers then know that they cannot qualify as HDCs.

Suppose a note reads, "Payable May 15, but may be accelerated if the holder feels insecure." A purchaser, unaware that a prior holder has elected to accelerate the due date on the instrument, buys the instrument prior to May 15. UCC 3-304(3)(b) provides that such a purchaser can be a holder in due course unless he or she has reason to know that the acceleration has occurred.

Demand Instruments A purchaser has notice that a demand instrument is overdue if he or she takes the instrument knowing that demand has been made or takes it an unreasonable length of time after its issue. "A reasonable time for a check drawn and payable within the states and territories of the United States and the District of Columbia is *presumed* to be 30 days" [UCC 3-304(3)(c)]. [Emphasis added.]

Obviously, what constitutes a reasonable time period depends on the circumstances. Except for a domestic check, in which a reasonable time is presumed to be thirty days, there are no exact measurements for determining a reasonable time. Past cases indicate, however, that a reasonable time for payment of an interest-bearing demand instrument is longer than for one payable without interest.

In the following case, the court held that a one-year-old check was an overdue instrument. This fact precluded the holder from attaining HDC status, even though the holder had checked with the drawer of the check before depositing it.

BACKGROUND AND FACTS *On October 25, 1983, in payment for cattle sold at auction, Fort Pierre Livestock Auction, Inc., issued check number 19074 for $31,730.23 to its customer, Gene Hunt. Later, Fort Pierre discovered it had miscounted the cattle, and on October 31, 1983, it issued check number 19331 for $36,343.95 to Hunt. This check was meant to replace check 19074, but no notation to that effect was written on it. Fort Pierre did not ask Hunt to return check 19074 but attempted to stop payment on it. Its bank had no record of such an attempt. Approximately one year later, on October 26, 1984, a representative of the Northwest South Dakota Production Credit Association (PCA) met with Hunt to arrange repayment of a delinquent loan. Hunt agreed to give PCA checks 19074 and 19331 in exchange for the forgiveness of his remaining debt. PCA did not know that one check had replaced the other or that Fort Pierre had attempted to stop payment on check 19074. PCA called Fort Pierre's manager and told him that a couple of old "Hunt" checks would be deposited. Fort Pierre's manager called its bank (American State Bank of Pierre) and warned it not to accept the checks without full indorsements. Upon discovering in January 1985 that both checks had cleared, Fort Pierre informed PCA that one check was meant to replace the other and demanded repayment for check 19074. PCA refused, asserting holder-in-due-course status. Fort Pierre sued to recover. The trial court found that PCA was a holder in due course and denied Fort Pierre's recovery. Fort Pierre appealed.*

KONENKAMP, Circuit Judge.

*   *   *   *

The holder of an instrument has the burden of proving that he is an HDC when defenses or claims are shown. PCA took check 19074 for value and in good faith, but knew it was a year old; therefore, the only issue is whether PCA had notice check 19074 was overdue.

*   *   *   *

*   *   * [W]e can envision instances where a delay of more than thirty days may be legitimate in the ordinary course of commerce, but PCA offered no justification for a year's delay. *   *   *

PCA concedes that it knew the check was a year old, but argues its telephone call to Fort Pierre warning of its imminent deposit of old Hunt checks along with Fort Pierre's apparent acquiescence overcomes the presumed notice that check 19074 was overdue. *   *   *

When a holder has no notice of a defect in an instrument at the time it comes into his hands, later events will not alter his HDC status. If knowledge acquired after the taking of an instrument is immaterial, then logically, a holder with notice that an instrument is overdue at the time it is taken should not be able to undo that notice except in the most extraordinary circumstances. When PCA's agent called Fort Pierre he made no mention of the check numbers, their amounts or dates, and Fort Pierre's manager made no comment which would lead the agent to believe the checks were not overdue, but only acknowledged the agent's intention to deposit them.

PCA's warning to Fort Pierre that it was about to deposit Hunt's "old checks" was insufficient to negate what was plainly visible on the check's face: a year-old date. Since it had notice that check 19074 was overdue PCA was not a holder in due course.

The Supreme Court of South Dakota reversed the lower court's judgment, holding that PCA was not a holder in due course since it had sufficient notice that the checks were overdue.

Case 25.2
AMERICAN STATE BANK OF PIERRE v. NORTHWEST SOUTH DAKOTA PRODUCTION CREDIT ASSOCIATION
Supreme Court of South Dakota, 1987.
404 N.W.2d 517.

DECISION AND REMEDY

DISHONORED INSTRUMENTS Actual knowledge that an instrument has been dishonored or knowledge of facts that would lead a holder to suspect that such has happened puts a holder on notice. Thus, a person who takes a check clearly stamped "insufficient funds" is put on notice. No notice exists without this knowledge. For example, Burton holds a demand note dated March 1 on Kayto, Inc., a local business firm. On March 19, she demands payment, and Kayto refuses (that is, dishonors the instrument). On March 20, Burton negotiates the note to Reynolds, a purchaser who lives in another state. Reynolds does not know and has no reason to know that the note has been dishonored, so Reynolds is not put on notice and can therefore become an HDC.

DEFENSES AGAINST OR CLAIMS TO AN INSTRUMENT Knowledge of claims or defenses can be imputed to the purchaser in certain situations because (1) they are apparent from an examination of the face of the instrument or (2) they are extraneous to the instrument but apparent from the facts surrounding the transaction.

The Code provides that a purchaser of a negotiable instrument has "notice of a claim or defense if * * * the instrument is so incomplete, bears such visible evidence of forgery or alteration, or is otherwise so irregular as to call into question its validity, terms of ownership * * * or * * * that the obligation of any party is voidable in whole or in part, or that all parties have been discharged" [UCC 3-304(1)(a)(b)].

Incomplete Instruments A purchaser cannot expect to become an HDC of an instrument so incomplete on its face that an element of negotiability is lacking (for example, the name of the payee on order paper is missing or the amount is not filled in). Minor omissions are permissible because these do not call into question the validity of the instrument. For example, omission of connective words, such as the "on" in "Pay to Johnson on order," does not affect negotiability, and neither does omission of the date from a check that has the month and year [UCC 3-304(1)(a), 3-114(1)].

When a person accepts an instrument without knowing that it is incomplete, then that person can take it as an HDC and enforce it as completed. To illustrate: Stuart Morgan asks Joan Nelson to buy a textbook for him when she goes to the campus bookstore. Morgan writes a check payable to the campus store, leaves the amount blank, and tells her to fill in the price of the textbook. Assume the textbook costs $15.50 in each of the following situations.

1. If Nelson gives the store the check with the amount entirely blank, the check is so incomplete that it is nonnegotiable (it has no certain amount) and the bookstore cannot qualify as an HDC.

2. If the cashier sees that the check is blank, watches Nelson complete the amount as $65.50, and then gives her $50 in change, the store will probably still be an HDC if the cashier is without notice that the filling in of the amount is improper [UCC 3-304(4)(d)].

3. If Nelson fills in the check for $65.50 before she gets to the bookstore, the store sees only a properly completed instrument. Therefore, it will take the check as an HDC and can enforce it for the full $65.50. The unauthorized completion is not a sufficient defense against the store in this situation [UCC 3-407, 3-115].

Irregular Instruments Any noticeable irregularity on the face of an instrument that should indicate to a purchaser that something is wrong with the paper will bar HDC status. For example, a note bearing a payee's signature that has been lined through with bold strokes and has had a second name penciled above it is highly irregular and will disqualify a taker from HDC status [UCC 3-304(1)(a)].

On the other hand, a note that is otherwise negotiable, containing the notation "payable at Newark," will not be the subject of inquiry, because such notation does not raise questions essential to the terms, ownership, or validity of the note, nor does it create an ambiguity as to who is the party required to pay [UCC 3-3041(1)(a)].

A difference between the handwriting used in the body of a check and that used in the signature will not in and of itself make an instrument irregular. Postdating or antedating a check or stating the amount in digits but failing to write out the numbers will not make a check irregular [UCC 3-114(2)].

Visible evidence of forgery of a maker's or drawer's signature or alterations to material elements of negotiable paper will disqualify a purchaser from HDC status. Conversely, a careful forgery of a maker's or drawer's signature or alteration can go undetected by reasonable examination; and therefore, the purchaser can qualify as an HDC [UCC 3-304(1)(a)]. Losses that result from careful forgeries, however, usually fall on the party to whom the forger transferred the instrument (assuming, of course, that the forger cannot be found). Also, as pointed out in Chapter 24, a forged indorsement does not transfer title, and thus a person obtaining an instrument that has a forged indorsement of a name necessary to title cannot normally become a holder or an HDC.

Voidable Obligations It stands to reason that a purchaser who knows that a party to an instrument has a defense that entitles that party to avoid the obligation in any way cannot be a holder in due course. At the very least, good faith requires *honesty in fact* of the purchaser in a transaction. For example, a potential purchaser who knows that the maker of a note has breached the underlying contract with the payee cannot thereafter purchase the note as an HDC [UCC 3-304(1)(b)].

For example, knowledge of one defense precludes a holder from becoming an HDC to all other defenses. Litchfield, knowing that the note he has taken has a forged indorsement, presented it to the maker for payment. The maker refuses to pay on the grounds of breach of the underlying contract by the payee, Juarez. The maker can assert this defense against Litchfield even though Litchfield had no knowledge of the breach because his knowledge of the forgery alone prevents him from being an HDC in *all* circumstances.

Knowledge that a fiduciary has wrongfully negotiated an instrument is sufficient notice of a claim against the instrument to preclude HDC status. Suppose Jordan, a trustee of a university, improperly writes a check on the university trust account to pay a personal debt. Farley knows that the check has been improperly drawn on university funds, but she accepts it anyway. Farley cannot claim to be an HDC. When a purchaser knows that a fiduciary is acting in breach of trust, HDC status is denied [UCC 3-304(2)].

Payee as HDC

Under certain circumstances, a payee may qualify as an HDC [UCC 3-302(2)]. In order to be an HDC, a payee must exercise good faith, give value, and take the instrument without notice of a defense against it or claim to it.

To illustrate, Marshall Reed is an attorney for Dana Smith. Marshall recently had minor office surgery performed by Dr. Peters and owes Dr. Peters $600. Marshall has agreed to draft a land sales contract for Dana next week, on condition that Dana issue a check payable to Dr. Peters for $600. Dana sends the check to Dr. Peters with a note, "in payment of medical services rendered to Marshall Reed." Marshall leaves town and never performs the services for Dana. Dana stops payment on the check. Can Dr. Peters enforce payment as an HDC? The answer is yes. Although Dr. Peters is the payee, she gave value (medical services), took the check in good faith, and took without notice of dishonor, defense, claim, or that the check was overdue.

Logic dictates that in the majority of instances, if there are defenses to the instrument, the payee will know or have reason to know about them. To illustrate: Baker Painters contracts with Amex Company to paint the exterior of its new office building for $4,000. Amex issues a negotiable promissory note to Baker Painters for $4,000, due thirty days later. When the note comes due, Baker tries to collect the $4,000 from Amex. Amex refuses to pay the note, claiming that the paint was defective; it washed off during a rainstorm. Since Baker Painters obviously knows about the defective paint, Baker Painters is not an HDC. Amex can disavow liability on the note based on the breach of the underlying contract.

HOLDER THROUGH A HOLDER IN DUE COURSE

A person who does not qualify as a holder in due course but who derives his or her title *through a holder in due course* can acquire the rights and privileges of a holder in due course. According to UCC 3-201(1):

> Transfer of an instrument vests in the transferee such rights as the transferor has therein, except that a transferee who has himself been a party to any fraud or illegality affecting the instrument or who as a prior holder had notice of a defense or claim against it cannot improve his position by taking from a later holder in due course.

This is sometimes called the **shelter principle.** This rule seems to detract from the basic holder-in-due-course philosophy. It is, however, in line with the concept of marketability and free transferability of commercial paper, as well as with contract law, which provides that assignees acquire the rights of assignors. The transfer rule extends the holder-in-due-course benefits, and it is designed to aid the HDC in disposing of the instrument readily.

Anyone, no matter how far removed from an HDC, who can trace his or her title ultimately back to an HDC comes within the shelter principle. Normally, a person who acquires an instrument from an HDC or from someone with HDC rights gets HDC rights on the principle that the transferee of an instrument gets at least the rights that the transferor had.

Limitations on the Shelter Principle

UCC 3-201(1) explicitly indicates, however, that certain persons who formerly held instruments cannot improve their positions by later reacquiring them from HDCs. Thus, if a holder was a party to fraud or illegality affecting the instrument or if, as a prior holder, he or she had notice of a claim or defense against an instrument, that holder is not allowed to improve his or her status by repurchasing from a later HDC. In other words, a person is not allowed to "launder" the paper by passing it into the hands of an HDC and then buying it back.

To illustrate: Bailey and Zopa collaborate to defraud Manor. Manor is induced to give Zopa a negotiable note payable to Zopa's order. Zopa then specially indorses the note for value to Adams, an HDC. Bailey and Zopa split the proceeds. Adams negotiates the note to Stanley, another HDC. Stanley then negotiates the note for value to Bailey. Bailey, even though he got the note through an HDC, cannot acquire HDC rights, for he participated in the original fraud.

The following case demonstrates the importance of establishing a prior transferor as an HDC to gain the rights of an HDC under the shelter principle.

Case 25.3
ROZEN v. NORTH CAROLINA NAT. BANK
United States Court of Appeals, Fourth Circuit, 1978.
588 F.2d 83.

BACKGROUND AND FACTS   *The defendant, North Carolina National Bank (NCNB), had made a long-term loan to Sharpe Hosiery Mill. In October of 1974, NCNB issued a $20,000 certificate of deposit (CD) to Sharpe. A few days later Allen Stein bought Sharpe. As a result of the sale, NCNB was able to call for payment of the long-term loan and set off the CD, as well as Sharpe's checking account balance, against the unpaid balance. Stein refused to return the CD and instead used it as partial collateral for a personal loan from Manufacturers Hanover Bank and Trust, which did not know of the NCNB claim. When the CD matured, Manufacturers sent the CD to NCNB for collection. NCNB dishonored and retained the CD. Thereafter Stein had the plaintiff, Rozen, his brother-in-law, purchase all rights in the CD from Manufacturers. Rozen claimed the rights of an HDC as to the CD. When the plaintiff sued NCNB for the value of the CD, however, the trial court held that the plaintiff was not protected by the shelter principle.*

HAYNSWORTH, Chief Judge.
*   *   *   *

Rozen argues that Manufacturers enjoyed holder-in-due-course status and that, under § 3-201, Manufacturers transferred this protection to him along with its assignment of rights in the paper. Therefore, Rozen argues, the trial judge should have directed a verdict in his favor, since a holder in due course takes an instrument free from "all claims to it on the part of any person . . . and . . . all defenses of any party to the instrument with whom the holder has not dealt." U.C.C. § 3-305.

The difficulty with this contention, however, is that the jury was thoroughly justified in finding that Rozen's assignor was Allen Stein, not Manufacturers.* * * *

Even if we should consider Manufacturers as being Rozen's assignor, however, it does not assist Rozen. The pledgee of a negotiable instrument may qualify as a holder in due course, U.C.C. § 3-302, Comment 4, but the pledgee's rights are limited by his secured creditor's status. * * * A secured creditor's interest in collateral ceases when the debt is paid in full, see U.C.C. § 1-201(37), so whatever rights Manufacturers had as a holder in due course of the NCNB certificate were terminated when Allen Stein paid Manufacturers the money he owed. Thus at the time that Manufacturers executed the purported assignment to Rozen, the only rights it had in the NCNB certificate of deposit were those of a secured creditor which had been paid in full, and those rights are nothing.

Because Stein was not a holder in due course, Rozen could not have become a holder in due course derivatively. See U.C.C. § 3-201. Not surprisingly, Rozen makes no claim of having independently acquired the status of a holder in due course. See U.C.C. § 3-302. Since he never had possession of the certificate of deposit, he never became a holder of any kind. See U.C.C. § 1-201(20).

The shelter principle seeks to ensure that a holder in due course always enjoys a ready market for the paper he owns. This principle applies with greatest vigor to holders of time instruments yet to come due, for in such cases the holder cannot collect from the maker. If the holder needs immediate funds, he must turn to the market. If, however, notice of claims and defenses are widespread, free transfer will be inhibited. Thus, § 3-201 protects the transferee so as to create a market for the transferor.

In this case, however, Manufacturers never sought the benefits of § 3-201 for itself.

* * *

Moreover, the policy underlying the exception to the shelter principle counsels affirmance. The exclusion from the shelter principle of one who, having had notice of prior claims, takes back an instrument from a holder in due course rests upon sound principle and simple logic. Operation of the shelter principle in favor of such a person would defeat the purpose of subjecting him to defenses of the maker. Without the exception to the shelter principle, one not a holder in due course, by a transfer and an agreement to repurchase, could readily avoid the limitations under which he held the instrument in the first place.

Because Manufacturers held the CD as collateral on Stein's loan, Stein was the true assignor of the CD. Stein was not an HDC, so Rozen could not become an HDC under the shelter principle. **DECISION AND REMEDY**

CONCEPT SUMMARY: Rules and Requirements for Status of a Holder in Due Course

BASIC REQUIREMENTS	RULES
1. Must be a *holder*	*Holder* is defined as a person who is in possession of an instrument "drawn, issued or indorsed to him or his order or to bearer or in blank" [UCC 1-201(20)].
2. Must take for *value*	Holder gives value: a. To the extent agreed-upon consideration has been paid or a security interest or lien acquired. b. By payment of or as security for an antecedent claim. c. By giving a negotiable instrument or irrevocable commitment as payment [UCC 3-303].
3. Must take in *good faith*	*Good faith* is defined as "honesty in fact in the conduct or transaction concerned" [UCC 1-291(19)].

(Continued on the next page)

CONCEPT SUMMARY: Rules and Requirements for Status of a Holder in Due Course (Continued)

BASIC REQUIREMENTS	RULES
4. Must take without *notice.* a. Instrument is *overdue*	1. Time instruments are overdue the moment after due date for payment. 2. Demand instruments are overdue after a reasonable time has lapsed from issue. 3. Domestic checks are *presumed* overdue after thirty days from issue. 4. A note is overdue if any part of the *principal* is not paid when due. 5. If any acceleration of a time instrument has taken place, the instrument is overdue [UCC 3-304(3)].
b. Instrument has been *dishonored*	1. Actual knowledge or knowledge of facts that would lead a person to suspect an instrument has been dishonored is notice of dishonor [UCC 3-302(1)(c)].
c. Knowledge of a *claim* or *defense*	1. Notice exists if a person has actual knowledge of a claim or defense against an instrument. 2. Notice exists if an instrument is so incomplete, bears such visible evidence of forgery or alteration, or is so irregular that a reasonable person would be put on notice from examination or from facts surrounding the transaction [UCC 3-304(1)].

SPECIAL SITUATIONS	RULES
1. Shelter principle—holder through a holder in due course	A holder who cannot qualify as a holder in due course has the *rights* of a holder in due course if he or she derives title through a holder in due course [UCC 3-201].
2. Payee	A payee who meets the requirements can be a holder in due course [UCC 3-302(2)].
3. Purchasers not holders in due course	The following acquisitions cannot result in the holder's having HDC status: a. Purchase at a judicial sale. b. Purchase of a bulk transfer. c. Acquisition as part of an estate [UCC 3-302(3)].

QUESTIONS AND CASE PROBLEMS

1. Janice Kurtz issues a ninety-day negotiable promissory note payable to the order of Dennis Nolan. The amount of the note is left blank, pending a determination of the amount of money Nolan will need to purchase a bull for Kurtz. Kurtz authorizes any amount not to exceed $2,000. Nolan, without authority, fills in the note in the amount of $5,000 and thirty days later sells the note to the First National Bank of Texas for $4,500. Nolan not only does not buy the bull but leaves the state. The First National Bank has no knowledge that the instrument was incomplete when issued or that Nolan had no authority to complete the instrument in the amount of $5,000.

(a) Does the bank qualify as a holder in due course, and, if so, for what amount? Explain.

(b) If Nolan had sold the note to a stranger in a bar for $500, would the stranger qualify as a holder in due course? Explain.

2. Dana draws and issues a $100 check payable to the order of Peter. The check is dated and issued on May 1. On May 25, Peter indorses the check by special indorsement to his son, Sam, as a gift. On June 5, Sam negotiates the check for value by blank indorsement to Helen. Meanwhile, Dana has stopped payment on the check, claiming that Peter is in breach of contract. Helen claims that she has the rights of a holder in due course. Discuss Helen's contention.

3. Daniel is a well-known industrialist in the community. He has agreed to purchase a rare coin from Helen's Coin Shop. The purchase price is to be determined by independent appraisal. Payment is to be by Daniel's check. Daniel is going out of town and informs Helen that his agent will bring her a check during his absence. Daniel draws up a check payable to Helen, leaves the amount blank, and gives the check to his agent, Max. Max, without authority, fills in the amount for $10,000 and presents it to Helen, who now has the appraisal. The appraisal price is $7,000. Max tells Helen that Daniel wanted to be sure the check would cover the appraisal and that he (Max) is authorized to receive the coin plus the balance in cash. Helen gives Max the coin plus $3,000. When Daniel discovers Max's fraud, Daniel stops payment on the check and offers Helen $7,000 for the coin. Helen claims she is a holder in due course and is entitled to the face value of the check, $10,000. Discuss whether Helen is an HDC and can therefore successfully pursue her claim.

4. Martha has just opened a small copy reproduction store. She has numerous clients, and she bills them at the end of the month. Her operation was begun with limited financial resources. Her bank balance with the First National Bank is $200. She receives in the morning mail two checks. One is from the Buckhorn Corporation for $500, and the other is from Shady Acres Magazine Sales for $300. Martha deposits both checks at the First National Bank. Later, a paper supply saleswoman presents Martha with an overdue bill of $800. Martha writes a check in that amount, and the check is paid by the First National Bank. Later, one of the checks deposited by Martha is returned to the First National Bank. It is from Shady Acres and is marked "insufficient funds." Can the First National Bank be a holder in due course of the check written by Shady Acres? Explain.

5. Erwin has taken from dishonest payees through negotiation two checks under the following conditions:

(a) The drawer issued a check to the payee for $7. The payee cleverly altered the numeral on the check from $7 to $70 and the written word from *seven* to *seventy*.
(b) The drawer issued a check to the payee without filling in the amount. The drawer authorized the payee to fill in the amount for no more than $70. The payee filled in the amount of $700.

Discuss whether under these circumstances Erwin, by giving value to the payees, can qualify as a holder in due course.

6. The Sahara-Nevada Hotel billed Affinity Pictures for hotel charges in the amount of $3,046. Affinity's president, Saka, refused to pay the full amount, claiming that only $800 was owed. Saka signed a blank check and gave it to his agent. He instructed the agent to make the check out for $800, cash it, and give the cash to the Sahara-Nevada Hotel. Instead, the agent made the check payable for $3,046, the amount claimed by the hotel, and delivered it to the hotel's manager without mentioning the instructions. Is the Sahara-Nevada Hotel, the payee, a holder in due course? [Saka v. Sahara-Nevada Corp., 92 Nev. 703, 558 P.2d 535 (1976)]

7. By making several fraudulent misrepresentations, a builder induced several homeowners in Washington, D.C., to sign contracts authorizing home improvements. The homeowners obtained financing to pay the builder's fees from Jefferson Federal Savings and Loan Association, a local lending institution. In exchange for the financing, the homeowners issued promissory notes to Jefferson. The builder's fees were exorbitant, and the promissory notes were issued by the homeowners in the exact amounts of the fees charged. In addition, it was the builder's agent who introduced the homeowners to the loan manager of Jefferson Savings and Loan. The loan manager was aware of the fact that this person was the builder's agent. About a month later, after the homeowners had realized that the prices for the home improvements were exorbitant, they refused payment on the notes held by Jefferson. If Jefferson qualifies as a holder in due course, it will have every right to payment. Does Jefferson qualify? [Slaughter v. Jefferson Federal Sav. and Loan Ass'n, 538 F.2d 397 (D.C.Cir. 1976)]

8. Paul Tibbs, trading as Paul's Auto Sales, had a course of dealing over a twenty-two year period with the Virginia Capital Bank and with James K. Mathews, president of Mathews General Insurance Corporation. Aetna Casualty and Surety was the insurer of Virginia Capital Bank. Tibbs would purchase business insurance through Mathews and borrow money from the bank to finance the premium. Tibbs would sign a promissory note, leaving the amount blank. Mathews would ascertain the amount of the premium, fill in the blank on the note, and deliver the note to the bank. The bank would pay Mathews. On one note, Mathews filled in the amount for $9,600 rather than for $960—the premium owed. Mathews added the indorsement of his corporation, presented the note to the bank, and was paid. Tibbs learned of the unauthorized incompletion and refused to pay the note. The bank filed suit, claiming it was a holder in due course and entitled to the face amount of the note. Discuss the bank's contention. [Virginia Capital Bank v. Aetna Casualty & Surety Company, 231 Va. 283, 343 S.E.2d 81 (1986)]

9. On September 9, 1976, Rob-Glen Enterprises, Inc., executed and delivered promissory notes payable to the Dolly Cam Corp. in return for a loan of $46,000. In addition, to secure the loan a number of individuals of Rob-Glen Enterprises executed identical guarantees of payment for the notes. Shortly thereafter, prior to the notes' maturity, Dolly Cam indorsed the notes in blank and delivered them to the First National Bank of Long Island pursuant to an existing general loan and security agreement for past and future debts. Rob-Glen, at the date of maturity, refused to pay the notes held by First National Bank. First National Bank claimed it was entitled to payment as a holder in due course. Rob-Glen claimed the bank was not a holder in

due course because it had given no value. Discuss whether First National Bank was a holder in due course. [First National Bank of Long Island v. Rob-Glen Enterprises, Inc., 101 A.D.2d 848, 476 N.Y.S.2d 161 (1984)]

10. Dennis Bowling was a friend and neighbor of David Dabney. Bowling had no indication that Dabney was financially troubled. Indeed, by all evidence, Dabney was quite well off: He owned four grocery stores; he drove a Cadillac; his wife owned a new sports car; he had race horses, lived in an expensive home, and also (Bowling had been led to believe) owned real estate in other areas. In the fall of 1983, Dabney admitted to Bowling that he had "cash flow" problems and borrowed $40,000 from Bowling. At the same time, Dabney proposed they become partners in his grocery business, and discussions concerning this prospect ensued over the following weeks. At one point, Dabney asked Bowling for a signed blank check that would be deposited with a new grocery supplier as "security" and would never be used without Bowling's consent. If it was, Dabney promised, he would reimburse Bowling's account appropriately. Shortly thereafter, Dabney dated and filled out Bowling's blank check for $10,606.79 and gave the check to his major supplier and creditor, Bierhaus & Sons. Dabney owed Bierhaus more than $400,000 for past deliveries; and, after having received ten to twenty bad checks from Dabney, Bierhaus required cash or cashier's checks from Dabney for any deliveries. Dabney had told Bierhaus about the supposedly imminent partnership with Bowling, and under those circumstances, Bierhaus's agent accepted the $10,606.79 check from Bowling in payment for a delivery of groceries. Bowling's check was returned to Bierhaus, as there were insufficient funds in Bowling's account to cover it. Dabney had filed for bankruptcy protection. Bierhaus sought to collect the amount of the check from Bowling. Is Bierhaus a holder in due course? [E. Bierhaus & Sons v. Bowling, 486 N.E.2d 598 (Ind.App. 1 Dist. 1985)]

11. In the fall of 1980, the Williams Brothers Asphalt Paving Company contracted with two local communities in Michigan to resurface some of their streets. During the course of the jobs, Williams incurred debts to its supplier, Rieth-Riley Construction Company, in the amount of $45,960. When the work was completed, Williams received a total of $188,433 from the two communities and deposited the funds into its checking account at First Security Bank. Although the amount owed to Rieth-Riley ($45,960) was to have been set aside by the communities in a special trust (the Michigan Builders' Trust Fund), it was not. Williams owed a secured debt to First Security Bank and so immediately paid to the bank the entire amount it had received. The payment was in the form of checks drawn on Williams's checking account at the bank and made payable to the bank's order. Williams later filed for bankruptcy, and Rieth-Riley sought to get its money from the bank, contending that Williams Brothers had no right to the $45,960 still owed to Rieth-Riley and thus could not negotiate it (via the checks Williams Brothers had made payable to the bank) to the bank. Is the bank a holder in due course in this instance? [In re Williams Brothers Asphalt Paving Company, 59 B.R. 71 (Bkrtcy.W.D.Mich. 1986)]

Chapter 26

COMMERCIAL PAPER
Defenses, Liability, and Discharge

When the holder of a negotiable instrument seeks payment from its drawer or maker, there are certain defenses that will be effective to bar collection. As a matter of public policy, certain defenses are assertable against all parties, including a holder in due course (HDC). Others, which constitute most of the traditional defenses to contract actions generally, cannot be used against an HDC unless the individual asserting the defense dealt personally with the HDC.

In this chapter, we will consider the defenses available to prevent liability and then discuss the two kinds of liability associated with negotiable instruments. Finally, we will review the various ways a person can be discharged from an obligation on a negotiable instrument.

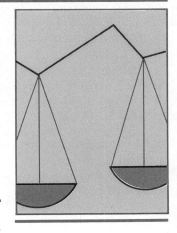

DEFENSES

Defenses fall into two general categories—real (or universal) defenses and personal defenses. Real defenses are used to avoid payment to all holders of a negotiable instrument, including an HDC or a holder through an HDC (under the shelter principle) [UCC 3-305(2)]. Personal defenses are used to avoid payment to an ordinary holder of a negotiable instrument [UCC 3-306].

Real Defenses

Real (universal) defenses, as noted, are valid against *all* holders, including HDCs or holders through HDCs.

FORGERY Forgery of a maker's or a drawer's signature cannot bind the person whose name is used (unless that person ratifies the signature or is precluded from denying it) [UCC 3-401 and 3-401(1)]. Thus, when a person forges an instrument, the person whose name is used has no liability to pay any holder or any HDC the value of the forged instrument. In addition, a principal can assert the defense of unauthorized signature against any holder or HDC when an agent has exceeded his or her authority to sign negotiable paper on behalf of the principal [UCC 3-403]. (Forgery is discussed briefly in Chapter 24, and unauthorized signatures will be discussed later in this chapter, in the section on liability.)

FRAUD IN THE EXECUTION If a person is deceived into signing a negotiable instrument, believing that he or she is signing something other than a negotiable instrument (such as a receipt), fraud in the execution (*in factum*) or inception is committed against the signer. For example, suppose a consumer unfamiliar with the English language signs a paper that is presented by a salesperson as a request for an estimate but that is in fact a promissory note. Even if the note is negotiated to an HDC, the consumer has a valid defense against payment. This defense cannot be raised, however, when a reasonable inquiry would have revealed the nature and terms of the instrument.[1] Thus, the signer's age, experience, and intelligence are relevant, since they frequently determine whether the signer should have known the nature of the transaction before he or she signed.

MATERIAL ALTERATION An alteration is material if it changes the contract terms between any two parties in any way. Examples of material alterations are [UCC 3-407(1)]:

1. A change in the number or relations of the parties.
2. The completion of an instrument in an unauthorized manner.
3. An addition to the writing as signed or the removal of any part of it.

Thus, cutting off part of the paper of a negotiable instrument, adding clauses, or any change in the amount, the date, or the rate of interest—even if the change is only one penny, one day, or 1 percent—is material. But it is not a material alteration to correct the maker's address, to have a red line drawn across the instrument to indicate that an auditor has checked it, or to correct the total final payment due when a mathematical error is discovered in the original computation. If the alteration is not material, any holder is entitled to enforce the instrument according to its original terms.

Material alteration is a *complete* defense against an ordinary holder but is at best only a *partial* defense against an HDC. An ordinary holder can

recover nothing on an instrument if it has been materially altered [UCC 3-407(2)].

If an original term, such as the monetary amount payable, has been altered, an HDC can enforce the instrument against the maker or drawer according to the original terms. If the instrument was incomplete and later completed in an unauthorized manner, alteration no longer can be claimed as a defense against an HDC, and the HDC can enforce the instrument as completed [UCC 3-407(2)(3)]. If the alteration is readily apparent, then obviously the holder has notice of some defect or defense, and such a holder cannot be an HDC [UCC 3-302(1)(c), 3-304(1)(a)].

DISCHARGE IN BANKRUPTCY Discharge in bankruptcy is an absolute defense on any instrument regardless of the status of the holder because the purpose of bankruptcy is to settle finally all of the insolvent party's debts [UCC 3-305(2)(d)].

MINORITY Minority, or infancy, is a real defense only to the extent that state law recognizes it as such [UCC 3-305(2)(a)]. (See Chapter 10.) Thus, this defense renders the instrument voidable rather than void, as discussed in the next three sections ("Illegality," "Mental Incapacity," and "Extreme Duress"). Since state laws on minority vary, so do determinations of whether minority is a real defense as against an HDC.

For example, in some states, when a minor misrepresents his or her age, the minor is prohibited from exercising the right of disaffirmance. In those states, minority is not allowed as a real defense if a minor who signs a negotiable instrument misrepresents his or her age. In other states, a minor is allowed to disaffirm (and is liable only for a tort of deceit) despite the misrepresentation of age, and therefore minority is a real defense.

ILLEGALITY When the law declares that an instrument is *void* because it has been executed in connection with illegal conduct, then the defense is absolute against both an ordinary holder and an HDC. If the law merely makes it *voidable*, as in the personal defense of illegality, to be discussed below, then it is still a defense against a holder but not against an HDC. The courts are sometimes prone to treat the word *void* in a statute as meaning

---

1. Burchett v. Allied Concord Financial Corp., 74 N.M. 575, 396 P.2d 186 (1964).

"voidable" in order to protect a holder in due course[2] [UCC 3-305(2)(b)].

MENTAL INCAPACITY   If a person is adjudicated mentally incompetent by state proceedings, any instrument issued by that person thereafter is void. If a negotiable instrument, that an incompetent issued, would be *void ab initio* (from the beginning), it is unenforceable by any holder or any HDC [UCC 3-305(2)(b)].

EXTREME DURESS   When a person signs and issues a negotiable instrument under such extreme duress as an immediate threat of force or violence (for example, at gunpoint), the instrument is *void* and unenforceable by any holder or HDC [UCC 3-305(2)(b)]. (Ordinary duress, to be discussed shortly, is only a personal defense.)

Personal Defenses

As mentioned above, personal defenses are used to avoid payment to an ordinary holder of a negotiable instrument. Personal defenses include every defense available in ordinary contract actions.

BREACH OF CONTRACT   When there is a breach of the underlying contract for which the negotiable instrument was issued, the maker of a note can refuse to pay it or the drawer of a check can stop payment. Breach of the contract can be claimed as a defense to liability on the instrument. For example, Peter purchases several cases of imported wine from Walter. The wine is to be delivered in four weeks. Peter gives Walter a promissory note for $1,000, which is the price of the wine. The wine arrives, but many of the bottles are broken, and several bottles that are tested have turned to vinegar. Peter refuses to pay the note on the basis of breach of contract and breach of warranty. (Under sales law, a seller impliedly promises that the goods are at least merchantable; see Chapter 20.) If the note is no longer in the hands of the payee seller but is presented for pay-

ment by an HDC, the maker buyer will not be able to plead breach of contract as a defense against liability on the note.

LACK OR FAILURE OF CONSIDERATION   The absence of consideration may be a successful defense in instances involving commercial paper [UCC 3-306(c), 3-408]. For example, if, without more, Tony says to Cleo, "I will sign a note promising to pay you $100,000," and Cleo says, "Okay," there is no consideration for Tony's promise to sign the note, and a court will not enforce the promise.

Similarly, if delivery of goods becomes impossible, a party who has agreed to issue or has issued a draft or note under the contract has a defense for not issuing the note or for not paying the note if it has been issued. Thus, in the hypothetical wine transaction just described, if delivery of the wine became impossible due to its loss in an accident, Walter could not subsequently sue successfully to enforce Peter's promise to pay the $1,000 promissory note.

FRAUD IN THE INDUCEMENT   A person who issues a negotiable instrument based on false statements by the other party will be able to avoid payment on that instrument. To illustrate: Peter agrees to purchase Sam's used tractor for $24,500. Sam, knowing his statements to be false, tells Peter that the tractor is in good working order and that it has been used for only one harvest. In addition, he tells Peter that he owns the tractor free and clear of all claims. Peter pays Sam $4,500 in cash and issues a negotiable promissory note for the balance. As it turns out, Sam still owes the original seller $10,000 on the purchase of the tractor, and the tractor is subject to a filed security interest (discussed in detail in Chapter 29). In addition, the tractor is three years old and has been used in three harvests. Peter can refuse to pay the note if it is held by an ordinary holder; but if Sam has negotiated the note to an HDC, Peter must pay the HDC. Of course, Peter can then sue Sam.

The following case illustrates not only that it is important to read a contract before signing but also that fraud in some circumstances is only a personal defense and cannot be used against a holder in due course.

---

2. W. Hawkland, *Commercial Paper and Bank Deposits and Collections* (Brooklyn: Foundation Press, 1979), p. 249.

Case 26.1
BURCHETT v. ALLIED CONCORD FINANCIAL CORP.

Supreme Court of New Mexico,
1964.
74 N.M. 575, 396 P.2d 186.

BACKGROUND AND FACTS *Mr. and Mrs. Burchett and Mr. and Mrs. Beevers, the plaintiff appellees, signed contracts with Kelly, a representative of Consolidated Products, to install aluminum siding on their homes. The original offer (made orally and accompanied by a written statement) indicated that each house would serve as a show house for advertising purposes and that the owners would receive $100 credit on each contract sold in a specific area of their town. Neither the Burchetts nor the Beeverses read their contract. In a few days, the first installment of the contract that they had actually signed—a mortgage contract that had been recorded against their property— came due. The mortgage note had been purchased from Consolidated Products by the appellant in this case, Allied Concord Financial Corporation. When Allied Concord notified the appellees that payment was due, the appellees realized the nature of the contracts they had signed and brought this action against the finance company to have the notes and mortgages canceled and declared void. The trial court determined that since the notes and mortgages were obtained fraudulently, Allied Concord Financial Corporation could not recover. Allied Concord appealed.*

CARMODY, Justice.
*　*　*　*

Following the explanation by Kelly, both families agreed to the offer and were given a form of a printed contract to read. While they were reading the contract, Kelly was filling out blanks in other forms. After the appellees had read the form of the contract submitted to them, they signed, *without reading*, the form or forms filled out by Kelly, assuming them to be the same as that which they had read and further assuming that what they signed provided for the credits which Kelly assured them they would receive. Needless to say, what appellees signed were notes and mortgages on the properties to cover the cost of the aluminum siding, and contracts containing no mention of credits for advertising or other sales.
*　*　*　*

[The] trial court found that the notes and mortgages, although signed by the appellees, were fraudulently procured. The court also found that the appellant paid a valuable consideration for the notes and mortgages, although at a discount, and concluded as a matter of law that the appellant was a holder in due course. *　*　*
*　*　*　*

*　*　* The only real question in the case is whether, under these facts, appellees, by substantial evidence, satisfied the provisions of the statute relating to their claimed defense as against a holder in due course.

In 1961, by enactment of ch. 96 of the session laws, our legislature adopted, with some variations, the Uniform Commercial Code. The provision of the code applicable to this case is as follows:

"To the extent that a holder is a holder in due course he takes the instrument free from
　"*　*　*

"(2) all defenses of any party to the instrument with whom the holder has not dealt except
　"*　*　*

"(c) such misrepresentation as has induced the party to sign the instrument with neither knowledge nor reasonable opportunity to obtain knowledge of its character or its essential terms; *　*　* "

We believe that the official comments following § 3-305(2)(c), Comment No. 7, provide an excellent guideline for the disposition of the case before us.
*　*　*　*

The test of the defense here stated is that of excusable ignorance of the contents of the writing signed. The party must not only have been in ignorance, but also have had no reasonable opportunity to obtain knowledge. In determining what is a reasonable opportunity all relevant factors are to be taken into account, including the age and sex of the party, his intelligence, education and business experience; his ability to read or to understand English, the representations made to him and his reason to rely on them or to have confidence in the person making them; the presence or absence of any third person who might read or explain the instrument to him, or any other possibility of obtaining independent information; and the apparent necessity, or lack of it, for acting without delay.

"Unless the misrepresentation meets this test, the defense is cut off by a holder in due course."

* * * *

Applying the elements of the test to the case before us, Mrs. Burchett was 47 years old and had a ninth grade education, and Mr. Burchett was approximately the same age, but his education does not appear. Mr. Burchett was foreman of the sanitation department of the city of Clovis and testified that he was familiar with some legal documents. Both the Burchetts understood English and there was no showing that they lacked ability to read. Both were able to understand the original form of contract which was submitted to them. * * * (T)he Burchetts had never had any prior association with Kelly and the papers were signed upon the very day that they first met him. There was no showing of any reason why they should rely upon Kelly or have confidence in him. The occurrences took place in the homes of appellees, but other than what appears to be Kelly's "chicanery," no reason was given which would warrant a reasonable person in acting as hurriedly as was done in this case. None of the appellees attempted to obtain any independent information either with respect to Kelly or Consolidated Products, nor did they seek out any other person to read or explain the instruments to them. As a matter of fact, they apparently didn't believe this was necessary because, like most people, they wanted to take advantage of "getting something for nothing." There is no dispute but that the appellees did not have actual knowledge of the nature of the instruments which they signed, at the time they signed them. Appellant urges that appellees had a reasonable opportunity to obtain such knowledge but failed to do so, were therefore negligent, and that their defense was precluded.

We recognize that the reasonable opportunity to obtain knowledge may be excused if the maker places reasonable reliance on the representations. The difficulty in the instant case is that the reliance upon the representations of a complete stranger (Kelly) was not reasonable, and all of the parties were of sufficient age, intelligence, education, and business experience to know better. In this connection, it is noted that the contracts clearly stated, on the same page which bore the signatures of the various appellees, the following:

"No one is authorized on behalf of this company to represent this job to be 'A SAMPLE HOME OR A FREE JOB.' ' * * *

Although we have sympathy with the appellees, we cannot allow it to influence our decision. They were certainly victimized, but because of their failure to exercise ordinary care for their own protection, an innocent party cannot be made to suffer.

DECISION AND REMEDY

The finance company, Allied Concord Financial Corporation, as a holder in due course, took the instrument free from the defenses claimed. Thus, the Burchetts and the Beeverses were liable for the amount of the notes.

COMMENTS

Consumer protection legislation might alter the outcome of similar cases in some states. Also, had this action been brought after the FTC holder-in-due-course rule (to be discussed shortly) was put into effect in 1976, then the outcome might have been different. The FTC rule requires that the subsequent holder of a promissory note resulting from a consumer credit contract be informed that he or she takes the note simply as a contract assignee and that the consumer credit contract is subject to all claims and demands that the debtor could assert against the promisee or payee named therein.

ILLEGALITY   Certain types of illegality constitute personal defenses. Other types constitute real defenses. Some transactions are prohibited under state statutes or ordinances, and some of these statutes fail to provide that the prohibited transactions are void. If a statute provides that an illegal transaction is voidable, the defense is personal. If a statute makes an illegal transaction void, the defense is a real defense and can successfully be asserted against an HDC. For example, a state may make gambling contracts illegal and void but be silent on payments of gambling debts. Thus, the payment of a gambling debt becomes voidable.

MENTAL INCAPACITY   There are various types and degrees of incapacity. Incapacity is ordinarily only a personal defense. If a maker or drawer is so extremely incapacitated that the transaction becomes a nullity, then the instrument is void. In that case, the defense becomes real, and it is good against an HDC as well [UCC 3-305(2)(b)].

If the maker drafts a negotiable instrument while mentally incompetent but before a formal court hearing declares (adjudicates) him or her to be mentally incompetent, many courts declare the obligation thereon to be voidable. If, however, the maker has been declared mentally incompetent by a court, a guardian has been appointed, and then the note is written, many courts hold the obligation null and void.

ORDINARY DURESS OR UNDUE INFLUENCE
Duress involves threats of harm or force. Ordinary duress—for example, the threat of a boycott—is a personal defense. As stated before, when the threat of force or harm becomes so violent and overwhelming that a person is deprived of his or her free will (comprising extreme duress), it becomes a real defense, good against all holders, including HDCs [UCC 3-305]. Thus, for example, an instrument signed at the point of a gun is void, even in the hands of an HDC, but one signed under a threat to prosecute the son or daughter of

the maker for theft may be merely voidable, so that the defense is not good against an HDC.

DISCHARGE BY PAYMENT OR CANCELLATION   If commercial paper is paid before its maturity date, the maker will ordinarily demand the return of the instrument itself or will note on the face of the instrument that payment has been made. Otherwise, it is possible for the instrument to continue circulating. If it comes into the hands of an HDC who demands payment at maturity, the defense of discharge by payment, which is merely a personal defense, will not allow the maker to avoid paying a second time on the same note [UCC 3-601(1)(a), 3-602]. (But in a quasi-contract action, the maker should be able to pass the additional liability on to the party who received the payment yet continued the instrument's circulation. Quasi-contracts are discussed in Chapters 7 and 15.)

UNAUTHORIZED COMPLETION OF AN INCOMPLETE INSTRUMENT   It is unwise for a maker or drawer to sign any negotiable instrument that is not complete. For example, Daniel signs a check, leaves the amount blank, and gives it to Dorman, an employee, instructing Dorman to make certain purchases and to complete the check "for not more than $500." Dorman fills in the amount as $5,000 *contrary to instructions.* If Daniel can stop payment in time, Daniel *may* be able to assert the defense of unauthorized completion and avoid liability to an ordinary holder. If the check is negotiated to an HDC, however, the instrument is payable as completed [UCC 3-115, 3-407, 3-304(4)(d), 4-401(2)(b)].

NONDELIVERY   If a bearer instrument is lost or stolen, the maker or drawer of the instrument has the defense of nondelivery against an ordinary holder. Recall that delivery means "voluntary transfer of possession" [UCC 1-201(14)]. This defense, however, is not good against an HDC [UCC 3-305, 3-306(c)].

CONCEPT SUMMARY: Valid Defenses against Holders of a Negotiable Instrument	
DEFENSES	**TYPES**
Real defenses UCC 3-305 Valid against all holders, including holders in due course and holders with the rights of holders in due course (through the shelter rule)	1. Forgery. 2. Fraud in the execution. 3. Material alteration. 4. Discharge in bankruptcy. 5. Minority, if the contract is voidable. 6. Illegality, incapacity, or duress, if the contract is void under state law.
Personal defenses UCC 3-306 Valid against ordinary holders but not against holders in due course or holders with the rights of holders in due course	1. Breach of contract (including breach of contract warranties). 2. Lack or failure of consideration. 3. Fraud in the inducement. 4. Illegality, incapacity (other than minority), or duress, if the contract is voidable. 5. Previous payment of the instrument. 6. Unauthorized completion of an incomplete instrument. 7. Nondelivery of the instrument.

FEDERAL LIMITATIONS ON HOLDER-IN-DUE-COURSE RIGHTS

The holder-in-due-course doctrine has been abused in consumer transactions. For example, a merchant would sell shoddy goods on credit, sell the promissory notes to a finance company, and cease doing business. When the goods proved to be defective, consumers would discover the empty storefront and stop paying on the notes. Consequently, the finance company would sue. Because the finance company was a holder in due course, consumers could not successfully assert personal defenses, such as breach of warranty, and would be held liable on the notes.

To protect consumers, the Federal Trade Commission (FTC) promulgated a rule[3] that effectively abolished the holder-in-due-course doctrine in consumer transactions. This FTC rule limits the rights of an HDC over an instrument that evidences a debt arising out of a *consumer credit* transaction. (Payment by check is not a credit transaction.) The rule, entitled "Preservation of Consumers' Claims and Defenses," attempts to prevent a situation in which a consumer is required to make payment for a defective product to a third party who is a holder in due course of a promissory note that formed part of the contract with the dealer who sold the defective good.

The FTC rule requires that any seller or lessor of goods or services who takes or receives a consumer credit contract or who accepts as full or partial payment for such sale or lease the proceeds of any purchase-money loan made in connection with any consumer credit contract include in the contract the following provision:

NOTICE
ANY HOLDER OF THIS CONSUMER CREDIT CONTRACT IS SUBJECT TO ALL CLAIMS AND DEFENSES WHICH THE DEBTOR COULD ASSERT AGAINST THE SELLER OF GOODS OR SERVICES OBTAINED PURSUANT HERETO OR WITH THE PROCEEDS HEREOF. RECOVERY HEREUNDER BY THE DEBTOR SHALL NOT

---

3. Volume 16 of the Code of Federal Regulations, Section 433.2. The rule was enacted pursuant to the FTC's authority under the Federal Trade Commission Act, Title 15, U.S.C. Section 41 *et seq.*

EXCEED AMOUNTS PAID BY THE DEBTOR HEREUNDER.

Obviously, the purpose of this notice is to inform any holder that, upon acquisition of a negotiable commercial paper, he or she is subject to all claims and demands that the debtor could assert against the promisee or payee named in the paper. In essence, the FTC rule places a holder in due course of the paper or of the negotiable instrument in the position of a contract assignee. The FTC rule clearly reduces the degree of transferability of commercial paper resulting from consumer credit contracts.

LIABILITY

Two kinds of liability are associated with negotiable instruments: liability based on contract and warranty liability. *Liability based on contract* is likely to arise not from a specific contract but from UCC rules relating to the signature on the instrument. Those who sign commercial paper are potentially liable for payment of the amount stated on the instrument. *Warranty liability,* on the other hand, extends to both signers and nonsigners. A breach of warranty can occur when the instrument is transferred or presented for payment.

The following sections cover the liability of the parties who sign the instrument—for example, drawers of drafts and checks, makers of notes and certificates of deposit, and indorsers. They also cover the liability of accommodation parties and the warranty liability of those who *transfer* with or without a signature.

Note that the focus is on liability *on the instrument itself or on warranties connected with transfer or presentment of the instrument* as opposed to liability for the underlying contract.

LIABILITY BASED ON SIGNATURES

The key to liability on a negotiable instrument is a **signature,** which is defined in UCC 3-401(2) as "any name, including any trade or assumed name, upon an instrument, or * * * any word or mark used in lieu of a written signature." A signature can be handwritten, typed, or printed; or it can

be made by mark, by thumbprint, or in virtually any manner. According to UCC 1-201(39), "signed" refers to any symbol executed or adopted by a party with the "present intention to authenticate a writing."

The requirement of a signature has its origin in the Law Merchant and is based simply on the need to know whose obligation the instrument represents. The critical element with any signature is a "present intention to authenticate a writing." Parol evidence can be used to identify the signer, and, once identified, the signature is effective against the signer no matter how it is made. UCC 3-401(1) states the general rule: "No person is liable on an instrument unless his [or her] signature appears thereon."

The few exceptions to the general rule are contained in UCC 3-404, which covers unauthorized signatures:

1. Any unauthorized signature is wholly inoperative unless the person whose name is signed ratifies it or is precluded from denying it [UCC 3-404(1)]. For example, a signature made by an agent exceeding the scope of actual, implied, or apparent authority can be ratified by the principal. A Pennsylvania court held that a wife's acceptance and retention of benefits from a promissory note constituted ratification of an otherwise unauthorized signature made by her husband.[4] Moreover, a person who writes and signs a check, leaving blank the amount and the name of the payee, and who then leaves the check in a place available to the public can be estopped (prevented), on the basis of negligence, from denying liability for its payment [UCC 3-115, 3-406, 4-401(2)(b)].

2. An unauthorized signature operates as the signature of the unauthorized signer in favor of an HDC. For example, if Frank forges Nick's name as the maker of a check, Katz, a subsequent holder in due course, can hold Frank personally liable on the check [UCC 3-404; see also 3-401(2)].

Agents' Signatures

The general law of agency covered in Chapters 32 and 33 applies to negotiable instruments. Agents can sign negotiable instruments and thereby bind their principals [UCC 3-403(1)]. Without such a

---

4. Rehrig v. Fortunak, 39 Pa. D. & C.2d 20 (1966).

rule, all corporate commercial business would stop. As Chapter 41 will show, every corporation can and must act through its agents. Because of the critical function the signature plays in determining liability on a negotiable instrument, however, we will go into some detail here concerning the potential problems of agents' signatures.

Generally, an authorized agent must indicate that he or she is signing an instrument on behalf of a *clearly named* principal in order to bind the principal on the instrument. The agent must write out the principal's name (by signature, mark, or some symbol) and his or her own name, or the agent can supply only the principal's signature.[5] To illustrate: The following signatures by Yokum as agent for Peter would bind Peter on the instrument:

1. Peter, by Yokum, agent.
2. Peter.
3. Peter, Yokum (by parol evidence).

If an authorized agent signs just his or her own name, the principal will not be bound on the instrument. Under UCC 3-403(2)(a), when an agent carelessly signs only his or her own name, the agent is *personally* liable on the instrument even though the parties know of the agency relationship. In addition, parol evidence (see Chapter 12) is not admissible to establish that the signature

was made for a principal. In such situations, form prevails over intent.

Under UCC 3-403(2)(b), two other situations in which an agent is held personally liable on a negotiable instrument can arise. If the instrument is signed in both the agent's name and the principal's name—"Peter, Yokum"—but nothing on the instrument indicates the agency relationship, the agent cannot be distinguished from the principal. In such a case, the form of the signature binds the agent (and it can also bind the principal). Since inclusion of both the agent's and the principal's names without indication of their relationship is ambiguous, parol evidence is admissible in controversies arising *between the immediate parties* to prove the agency relationship.

Another situation envisioned under UCC 3-403(2)(b) occurs when an agent signs a negotiable instrument and indicates agency status but fails to name the principal—for example, "Barry Scott, agent." Against any subsequent holder the agent is *personally* liable, but the unnamed principal cannot be held liable on the instrument. Since the indication of agency status without naming of the principal is ambiguous, parol evidence is admissible in controversies arising *between the immediate parties* to prove the agency relationship and to establish the liability of the unnamed principal [UCC 3-403(2)(b)].

In the following case, an agent who signed a check without disclosing that he was signing in a representative capacity was held personally liable.

---

5. If the agent signs the principal's name, the Code presumes that the signature is authorized and genuine [UCC 3-307(1)(b)].

BACKGROUND AND FACTS   *The plaintiff, O. B. Ellinger, doing business as Ellinger Paint and Dry Wall, sued Percy Griffin, the defendant, on three checks drawn on the account of Greenway Building Company and signed by Griffin, the company president. The checks, totaling $3,950, were issued to Ellinger in payment for labor and materials furnished to Greenway for a construction project. Greenway was the prime contractor for the project, and Griffin was authorized to sign checks as president of the company. The bank refused to honor the checks because of insufficient funds in the Greenway account.*

The major question before the court was whether Griffin's signature on a corporate check, without any indication of his representative capacity, obligated him personally and individually for the amount of the check.

Case 26.2
GRIFFIN v. ELLINGER
Supreme Court of Texas, 1976.
538 S.W.2d 97.

DOUGHTY, Justice.
*   *   *   *

*   *   * [Defendant] contends that the drafts show conclusively on their face that he was signing in a representative capacity only. Second, petitioner contends that extrinsic evidence establishes as a matter of law that the parties understood his signature to be in a representative capacity.

*   *   *   *

Each of the three drafts signed by Griffin were in essentially the same form. A copy of one of the drafts is reproduced below.

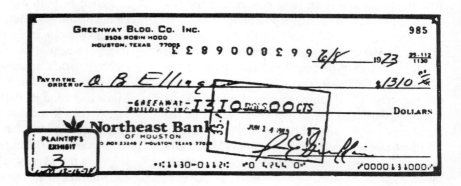

The first question is whether the draft shows on its face that Griffin signed in a representative capacity only. Although the draft clearly names the person represented, it does not show that Griffin signed only in his capacity as president of Greenway. Griffin contends, however, that considering the instrument as a whole, and taking into account the normal business usage of personalized checks, it should be apparent from the instrument itself that Griffin signed only as an authorized agent of Greenway. We disagree. We recognize that it is unusual to demand the individual obligation of a corporate officer on checks drawn on the corporate account, and that the more usual way of obtaining the personal obligation of an officer on such a check would be by endorsement. Business practice and usage are proper factors to be considered in construing the particular instrument under consideration. We also recognize that an instrument may disclose on its face that a signature was executed only in a representative capacity even though the particular office or position of the signer is not disclosed thereon.

*   *   * [W]e can find nothing on the face of the checks in the present case to show that Griffin intended to sign only in a representative capacity. [Defendant] points out that each check is stamped by a "check protector," which imprinted not only the amount of the draft but also the company's name. Although the stamp clearly reveals the name of the principal, it does not aid [defendant] because it gives no information as to the capacity in which *he* signed the instrument.

The fact that the name of the corporation appears on the check indicates that the account drawn upon is that of the corporation and that the funds in the account are the corporation's. While the drawer of a check is ordinarily the owner of the funds in the account drawn upon, the Code does not require that this be so. Under Section 3.413, *any person* who signs a draft engages that, upon dishonor, he will pay the amount thereof to the holder. Indeed, under Section 3.404, the signer of a draft who has no authority to draw upon the account is nevertheless liable upon his contract as drawer to any person who takes the instrument in good faith for value. [Defendant] points out that, since a corporation can only act through its agents, a personal signature is always required to authorize withdrawal of funds from a corporate account. Under Section 3.403, however, one signing an instrument is personally liable thereon even though he is authorized to and does in fact bind his principal, if he does not disclose that he is signing only in a representative capacity. In short, the burden is on the signer to relieve himself of personal liability by disclosing his agency. The fact that the instrument is an authorized draft drawn on a corporate account is not enough to disclose the representative character of the signature thereon. Section 3.403(c) expressly provides that the signer of an instrument may avoid personal liability by disclosing both the name of the organization of which he is an agent and the office he holds with the organization. Absent such a disclosure or its equivalent, the signer is personally liable on the instrument according to its terms, unless "otherwise established between the immediate parties" under subsection (b)(2). We hold that the checks in question do not show on their face that Griffin signed only in a representative capacity. * * *

The plaintiff, Ellinger, was able to collect the $3,950 from Griffin personally because Griffin had failed to disclose the representative character of his signature.

DECISION AND REMEDY

Although this case represents the majority rule, there are differences among states on the issue of personal liability. When the question of personal liability arises, and the instrument either names the principal or shows the fact of representation, the signer can offer evidence to prove that he or she acted in a representative capacity and may thus overcome the presumption that he or she is personally obligated.

COMMENTS

When a negotiable instrument is signed in the name of an organization (any legal or commercial entity [UCC 1-201(28)]) and the organization's name is preceded or followed by the name and office of an authorized individual, the organization will be bound; the individual who has signed the instrument in the representative capacity will not be bound [UCC 3-403(3)].

If the agent had no authority, either apparent or implied, to sign the principal's name, the "unauthorized signature is wholly inoperative as that of the person whose name is signed * * *" [UCC 3-404(1)]. Assume that Mary Night is the principal and Arthur King is her agent. King, without authority, signs a promissory note as follows: "Mary Night, by Arthur King, agent." Since Mary Night's "signature" is unauthorized, she cannot be held liable on the note, but King will be liable. This would be true even if King had merely signed the note "Mary Night," without indicating any agency. In either case, the unauthorized signer, King, is liable on the instrument.

Signature Liability

PRIMARY AND SECONDARY LIABILITY Every party, except a *qualified indorser*,[6] who signs a ne-

gotiable instrument is either primarily or secondarily liable for payment of that instrument when it comes due.

If a person is primarily liable on a negotiable instrument, then that person is absolutely required to pay the instrument, subject to certain real defenses [UCC 3-305]. Unless a real defense exists, a party who is primarily liable on an instrument will remain subject to that obligation until the applicable statute of limitations runs out. Only *makers* and *acceptors* are primarily liable [UCC 3-413(1)].

The liability of a party who is secondarily liable on a negotiable instrument is similar to that of a guarantor in a simple contract. Drawers and indorsers have secondary liability. Secondary liability is "contingent liability." In the case of notes, an indorser's secondary liability does not arise until the maker, who is primarily liable, has defaulted on the instrument [UCC 3-413(1), 3-414].

With regard to drafts and checks, a drawer's secondary liability does not arise until the drawee fails to pay or to accept the instrument, whichever is required. Note, however, that the drawee is not primarily liable. Makers of notes promise to pay, but drawees are ordered to pay. Therefore, drawees are not primarily liable unless they promise to pay—for example, by certifying a check. Nor are drawees even secondarily liable on an instrument. As stated in UCC 3-409, "a check or draft does not of itself operate as an assignment of any funds

---

6. A qualified indorser—one who indorses without recourse— undertakes no obligation to pay. A qualified indorser merely assumes warranty liability, which is discussed later in this chapter.

in the hands of the drawee available for its payment * * *." Thus, unless a drawee *accepts*,[7] the drawee's only obligation is to honor the drawer's orders.

The parties to a negotiable instrument are bound by all of the terms implied by their signatures by operation of law. Once it is established that a party signed this instrument (or that it was signed by that party's authorized agent), the Code defines the party's liability. The liability is contractual in the sense that each party voluntarily incurs it and thus can modify it.

PRIMARY LIABILITY OF THE MAKER OR ACCEPTOR   The maker of a note promises to pay the note. The words "I promise to pay" embody the maker's obligation to pay the instrument according to the terms as written at the time of the signing. If the instrument is incomplete when the maker signs it, then the maker's obligation is to pay it as completed, assuming that the instrument is properly completed [UCC 3-413(1), 3-115].

A maker guarantees that certain facts are true by signing a promissory note. In particular, Section 3-413(3) specifies that a maker admits to all subsequent parties that the payee in fact exists and that the payee has current capacity to indorse the note (for example, that the payee is not a minor at the time the note is signed). Primary liability is unconditional. The primary party's liability is immediate when the note becomes due. No action by the holder of the instrument is required.

The drawee-acceptor is in virtually the same position as the maker of a note [UCC 3-413(1), (3)]. A drawee who does not accept owes a contractual duty to the drawer to pay in accordance with the drawer's orders, but a drawee owes no duty to either the payee or any holder.

For example, Pope buys from Whitney goods costing $2,000. The goods will be shipped to arrive on September 1. Instead of giving Whitney cash, Pope draws a draft on Fairweather Finance Company for $2,000 payable to Whitney on September 1. At this point, Fairweather is not liable on the draft, and it will not become liable on the draft unless and until it accepts the draft.

A holder must present the instrument to a drawee for acceptance in three situations:

1.   When the instrument requires such presentation (see, for example, trade acceptances, discussed in Chapter 22).
2.   When the draft is to be payable at an address different from that of the drawee.
3.   When the draft's payment date is dependent on such presentment—for example, when the draft is payable thirty days after acceptance or sight.

Presentment in these situations is required to charge the drawer and indorsers with secondary liability [UCC 3-501(1)(a)].

If the drawee accepts the instrument as presented, the drawee becomes an acceptor and is primarily liable to all subsequent holders. A drawee who refuses to accept such a draft has dishonored the instrument. In refusing to accept, the drawee retains his or her original status and owes no duty to the payee or any holder.

A check is a special type of draft that is drawn on a bank and is payable on demand. Acceptance of a check is called *certification*. Certification is not necessary on checks, and a bank is under no obligation to certify. (See Chapter 27 for details.) However, upon certification, the drawee bank occupies the position of an acceptor and is primarily liable on the check to holders [UCC 3-411].

SECONDARY LIABILITY   Dishonoring an instrument triggers the liability of secondarily liable parties on the instrument—that is, the drawer, unqualified indorsers, and accommodation indorsers. Parties who are secondarily liable on a negotiable instrument promise to pay on that instrument only if:

1.   The instrument is properly and timely presented.
2.   The instrument is dishonored.
3.   Notice of dishonor is timely given to the secondarily liable party.[8]

These requirements are necessary for a secondarily liable party to have signature liability on a

---

7. To accept a draft, the drawee must place his or her signature on it [UCC 3-410].

8. An instrument can be drafted to provide a waiver of the presentment, dishonor, and notice of dishonor requirements. Presume for simplicity's sake that no such waivers have been incorporated into the instruments described in this chapter.

negotiable instrument, but they are not necessary for a secondarily liable party to have warranty liability (to be discussed later in this chapter) [UCC 3-414, 3-501, 3-502].

UCC 3-413(2) provides that "upon dishonor of the draft and any necessary notice of dishonor * * * [the drawer] will pay the amount of the draft to the holder or to any indorser who takes it up." For example, Nancy Oliver writes a check on her account at Third National Bank payable to the order of Joel Andrews. If Third National does not pay the check when Andrews presents it for payment, then Oliver is liable to Andrews on the basis of her secondary liability. Drawers are secondarily liable on drafts unless they disclaim their liability by drawing the instruments without recourse [UCC 3-413(2)].

Since drawers are secondarily liable, their liability does not arise until presentment and notice of dishonor have been made *properly* and in a *timely* way. If a draft (or check) is payable at a bank, improper presentment or notice relieves the drawer from secondary liability only when the drawee bank is insolvent and the drawer is thereby deprived of funds that would have covered the draft [UCC 3-502].

An *unqualified indorser* promises that in the event of presentment, dishonor, and notice of dishonor he or she will pay the instrument. Thus, the liability of an indorser is much like that of a drawer, with one major exception: Indorsers are *relieved* of their contractual liability to the holder of the instrument by (1) improper (late) presentment or (2) late notice or failure to notify the indorser of dishonor [UCC 3-414, 3-501, 3-502].

When an indorser has actively caused an instrument to be dishonored, the requirements of presentment and notice of dishonor are excused [UCC 3-511(2)(b)].

PROPER PRESENTMENT The Code spells out what constitutes a proper presentment. Basically, presentment by a holder must be made to the proper person, must be made in a proper manner, and must be timely [UCC 3-503, 3-504].

A note or CD must be presented to the maker for payment. A draft is presented by the holder to the drawee for acceptance or payment, or both, whichever is required. A check is presented to the drawee for payment [UCC 3-504].

Presentment can be properly made in any one of the following three manners, depending on the type of instrument [UCC 3-504(2)]:

1. By mail (but presentment is not effective until receipt of the mail).
2. Through a clearinghouse procedure, as for deposited checks.
3. At the place specified in the instrument for acceptance or payment—or, if the instrument is silent as to place, at the place of business or the residence of the person required to accept or pay.

One of the most crucial criteria for proper presentment is timeliness [UCC 3-503]. Failure to present on time is the most prevalent reason for improper presentment and consequent discharge of unqualified indorsers from secondary liability. See Exhibit 26–1, bearing in mind that its contents are somewhat oversimplified.

PROPER NOTICE Once the instrument has been dishonored, proper notice must be given in order for secondary parties to be held liable. The rules of proper notice are basically as follows [UCC 3-508]:

1. Notice operates for the benefit of all parties who have rights on an instrument against the party notified [UCC 3-508(8)]. For example, assume there are four indorsers on a note that its maker dishonors, and the holder gives timely notice to indorsers one and four. If the holder collects payment from indorser four, indorser four does not have to give notice to indorser one again to collect from indorser one.

It is important to remember that if more than one indorsement appears on an instrument, each indorser is liable for the full amount to any later indorser or to any holder. For example, imagine a note (Ernest's) indorsed by four indorsers (Hadley, Pauline, Martha, and Mary) before coming into the possession of a holder (Jack). If Ernest, the maker, dishonors the note at maturity, Jack, the holder, may demand and recover payment from Mary, indorser number four, who may then recover the full amount from any prior indorser. If Mary collects from Pauline (indorser number two), Pauline gets the note and may seek payment from Hadley. But Pauline cannot sue Martha, who is a later indorser, because liability moves only *up* the indorsement chain.

Exhibit 26-1 Time for Proper Presentment [UCC 3-503]

TYPE OF INSTRUMENT	FOR ACCEPTANCE	FOR PAYMENT
Time	On or before due date	On due date
Demand	Within a reasonable time (after date or issue or after secondary party becomes liable thereon)	
Check (domestic)	Not applicable	Presumed to be:[a] Within thirty days (of date on the instrument or the issue date, whichever is later) to hold drawer secondarily liable Within seven days (of indorsement) to hold indorser secondarily liable

a. In the case of a domestic, uncertified check, these are the time periods within which to present for payment *or* to initiate the bank collection process.

2. Except for dishonor of foreign drafts, notice may be given in any reasonable manner. This includes oral or written notice and notice written or stamped on the instrument itself [UCC 3-508(3)]. To give notice of dishonor of a foreign draft (a draft drawn in one country and payable in another country), a formal notice called a *protest* is required [UCC 3-509].

3. Any necessary notice must be given by a bank before its midnight deadline (midnight of the next banking day after receipt) [UCC 4-104(1)(h)] and by all others before midnight of the third *business* day after either dishonor or receipt of notice of dishonor [UCC 3-508(2)]. Written notice is effective when sent, not when received [UCC 3-508(4)].

4. Notice to a partner is notice to a partnership [UCC 3-508(5)]. Similarly, when a party is deceased, incompetent, or bankrupt, notice may be given to his or her representative [UCC 3-508(6), (7)].

ACCOMMODATION PARTIES An **accommodation party** is one who signs an instrument for the purpose of lending his or her name to another party in credit to the instrument [UCC 3-415(1)]. Accommodation parties are one form of security against nonpayment on a negotiable instrument.

For example, a bank about to lend money, a seller taking a large order for goods, or a creditor about to extend credit to a prospective debtor all want some reasonable assurance that the debts will be paid. A party's uncertain financial condition or the fact that the parties to a transaction are complete strangers can make a creditor reluctant to rely solely on the prospective debtor's ability to pay. To reduce the risk of nonpayment, the creditor can require the joining of a third person as an accommodation party on the instrument.

If the accommodation party signs on behalf of a maker, he or she will be an *accommodation maker* and will be primarily liable on the instrument. If the accommodation party signs on behalf of a payee or other holder (usually to make the instrument more marketable), he or she will be an *accommodation indorser* and will be secondarily liable. Any indorsement not in the ordinary chain of title gives notice of its accommodation character [UCC 3-415(2), (4)]. For example, a signature that appears on an instrument above that of the payee, who would normally be the first indorser, would be outside the chain of title. An accommodation party is never, however, liable to the party accommodated, and if the accommodation party pays the instrument, he or she has a right of recourse against the party accommodated [UCC 3-415(5)].

WARRANTY LIABILITY

In addition to the signature liability discussed in the preceding sections, transferors make certain implied warranties regarding the instruments that they are negotiating. Liability under these warranties is not subject to the conditions of proper presentment, dishonor, and notice of dishonor. These warranties arise even when a transferor does not indorse the instrument (as in delivery of bearer paper) [UCC 3-417]. Warranties fall into two categories, those that arise upon the *transfer* of a negotiable instrument and those that arise upon *presentment*.

Transfer Warranties

Five *transfer warranties* are described in UCC 3-417(2). They provide that any person who *indorses* an instrument and *receives consideration* warrants to *all* subsequent transferees and holders who take the instrument in good faith that:

1. The transferor has good title to the instrument or is otherwise authorized to obtain payment or acceptance on behalf of one who does have good title.
2. All signatures are genuine or authorized.
3. The instrument has not been materially altered.
4. No defense of any party is good against the transferor.
5. The transferor has no knowledge of any insolvency proceedings against the maker, the acceptor, or the drawer of an unaccepted instrument.

A qualified indorser who indorses an instrument without recourse limits the fourth warranty to a warranty that he or she has no knowledge of such a defense rather than that there is no defense [UCC 3-417(3)].

The manner of transfer and the negotiation that is used determine how far and to whom a transfer warranty will run. Transfer by indorsement and delivery of order paper extends warranty liability to any subsequent holder who takes the instrument in good faith. The warranties of a person who transfers without indorsement (by delivery of bearer paper), however, extend only to the immediate transferee [UCC 3-417(2)].

For example, Asher forges Martin's name as maker of a promissory note. The note is made payable to Asher. Asher indorses the note in blank, negotiates it to Paula, and leaves the country. Paula, without indorsement, delivers the note to Bill. Bill, in turn without indorsement, delivers the note to Helen. Upon Helen's presentment of the note to Martin, the forgery is discovered. Helen can hold Bill (the immediate transferor) liable for breach of warranty that all signatures are genuine. Helen cannot hold Paula liable, because Paula is not Helen's immediate transferor but is a prior non-indorsing transferor. This example shows the importance of the distinction between transfer by indorsement and delivery of order paper and transfer by delivery of bearer paper without indorsement.

A *Concept Summary* of the law on transfer warranty liability appears at the end of this discussion.

Presentment Warranties

Any person who seeks payment or acceptance of a negotiable instrument impliedly warrants to any other person who in good faith pays or accepts the instrument that:

1. The party presenting has good title to the instrument or is authorized to obtain payment or acceptance on behalf of a person who has good title.
2. The party presenting has no knowledge that the signature of the maker or the drawer is unauthorized.
3. The instrument has not been materially altered.

These warranties exist under UCC 3-417(1) and are often referred to as **presentment warranties** because they protect the person to whom the instrument is presented.

The second and third warranties do not apply in certain cases (to certain persons) in which the presenter is a holder in due course. It is assumed, for example, that a drawer or maker will recognize his or her own signature or that a maker or acceptor will recognize whether an instrument has been materially altered.

Both transfer and presentment warranties attempt to shift liability back to a wrongdoer or to the person who dealt face to face with a wrongdoer and thus was in the best position to prevent the wrongdoing.

The following case illustrates an accommodation indorser's possible signature and warranty liability.

Case 26.3
OAK PARK CURRENCY EXCHANGE, INC. v. MAROPOULOS

Appellate Court of Illinois, 1977.
48 Ill.App.3d 437, 363 N.E.2d
54, 6 Ill.Dec. 525.

BACKGROUND AND FACTS   *Bugay came into the possession of a check drawn on the American National Bank to the order of Henry Sherman, Inc. He fraudulently indorsed "Henry Sherman" on the back of the check. Then Bugay asked the defendant, Maropoulos, to help him cash it. Maropoulos took Bugay to the Oak Park Currency Exchange, Inc., the plaintiff, because Maropoulos was known by the personnel of that company. While on the company premises, Maropoulos identified himself and induced the company to cash the check. Oak Park Currency Exchange agreed to cash the check only if Maropoulos would indorse it. He did so, received the money, and immediately gave it to Bugay. When Oak Park subsequently indorsed the check and deposited it in the Belmont National Bank, the "Henry Sherman" indorsement was found to be a forgery. The bank recovered full payment from plaintiff Oak Park. Plaintiff in turn attempted to receive reimbursement from defendant Maropoulos on his indorsement and for breach of warranty. At trial, the court directed a verdict in favor of Maropoulos. Oak Park appealed.*

GOLDBERG, Presiding Justice.
*   *   *   *

In this court, plaintiff urges that defendant breached his warranty of good title when he obtained payment of a check on which the payee's indorsement was forged and that there was sufficient evidence to support a directed verdict in favor of plaintiff. Plaintiff's contentions are based exclusively on Section 3-417(1) of the Code. Defendant contends that an accommodation indorser does not make warranties under Section 3-417(1) and that the trial court properly directed a verdict for the defendant.

A party who signs an instrument "for the purpose of lending his name to another party to *   *   *" that instrument is an accommodation party. Section 3-415(1). Such a party "is liable in the capacity in which he has signed *   *   *." Section 3-415(2). Therefore defendant is an accommodation indorser and would be liable to plaintiff under his indorser's contract, provided that he had received timely notice that the check had been presented to the drawee bank and dishonored. Section 3-414. Because these conditions precedent to the contractual liability of an indorser have not been met, defendant is not liable on his contract as an accommodation indorser.

Furthermore, the drawee bank, American National, did not dishonor the check but paid it. This operated to discharge the liability of defendant as an accommodation indorser.
*   *   *   *

An additional theory requires affirmance of the judgment appealed from. Subsection 3-417(2) of the Code provides that one "who transfers an instrument and receives consideration warrants to his transferee *   *   *" that he has good title. *   *   * The evidence presented in the case at bar establishes that defendant received no consideration for his indorsement. Though [plaintiff's employee] testified that she saw Bugay hand defendant some money as the two left the currency exchange, she also testified that defendant stated that he was doing a favor for his friend; that she was not paying close attention to the two men and that she did not watch them as they walked away from her. Thus her testimony was considerably weakened by her own qualifying statements and it was strongly and directly contradicted by the positive and unshaken testimony of defendant that he received nothing in return for his assistance. The simple fact standing alone that this witness saw Bugay hand some money to defendant, even if proved, would have no legal significance without additional proof of some type showing that the payment was consideration for defendant's indorsement.

DECISION AND REMEDY   *The appellate court affirmed the trial court's directed verdict in favor of Maropoulos. He was not required to repay Oak Park Currency Exchange, Inc.*

CONCEPT SUMMARY: Transfer Warranty Liability for Transferors Who Receive Consideration	
TYPES	**TO WHOM WARRANTIES EXTEND**
General indorsers	The five transfer warranties listed below extend to *all* subsequent holders: 1. Transferor has good title or is otherwise authorized to obtain payment or acceptance on behalf of one who does have good title. 2. All signatures are genuine or authorized. 3. Instrument has not been materially altered. 4. No defense of any party is good against transferor. 5. Transferor has no knowledge of insolvency proceedings against the maker, acceptor or drawer of an accepted instrument.
Non-indorsers	Same as for the general indorser, but warranties extend *only* to the *immediate transferee.*
Qualified indorsers	Same as for the general indorser, except that a qualified indorsement (without recourse) limits the fourth warranty to a warranty that indorser has no knowledge of such a defense rather than that there is no defense. The warranties extend to *all* subsequent holders.

DISCHARGE

Discharge from liability on an instrument can come from payment, cancellation, or, as previously discussed, material alteration. Discharge can also occur if a party reacquires an instrument, if a holder impairs another party's right of recourse, or if a holder surrenders collateral without consent [UCC 3-601].

Discharge by Payment

According to UCC 3-601(1)(a) and 3-603, all parties to a negotiable instrument will be discharged when the party primarily liable on it pays to a holder the amount due in full.[9] The same is true if the drawee of an unaccepted draft or check makes payment in good faith to the holder. In these situations, all parties on the instruments are usually discharged. By contrast, such payment made by any other party (for example, an indorser) will discharge only the indorser and subsequent parties on the instrument. The party making such a payment still has the right to recover on the instrument from any prior parties.

A party will not be discharged when paying in bad faith to a holder who acquired the instrument by theft or who obtained the instrument from someone else who acquired it by theft (unless, of course, the person has the rights of a holder in due course) [UCC 3-603(1)(a)]. Finally, a party who pays on a restrictively indorsed instrument cannot claim discharge if the payment is made in a manner inconsistent with the terms of the restrictive indorsement [UCC 3-603(1)(b)].

Once payment or other satisfaction has been made to the holder in return for the surrender of the instrument, the liability of the maker or drawer is discharged, and the transaction comes to an end. There are numerous ways in which makers or drawers can effect payment or satisfaction.

Discharge by Cancellation

The holder of a negotiable instrument can discharge any party to the instrument by cancellation. UCC 3-605(1)(a) explains how cancellation can oc-

---

9. This is true even if the payment is made "with knowledge of a claim of another person to the instrument unless prior to such payment or satisfaction the person making the claim either supplies indemnity deemed adequate by the party seeking the discharge or enjoins payment or satisfaction by order of a court of competent jurisdiction in an action in which the adverse claimant and the holder are parties" [UCC 3-603(1)].

cur: "The holder of an instrument may even without consideration discharge any party in a manner apparent on the face of the instrument or the indorsement, as by intentionally cancelling the instrument or the party's signature by destruction or mutilation, or by striking out the party's signature." For example, writing the word "Paid" across the face of an instrument constitutes cancellation. Tearing up a negotiable instrument cancels the instrument. Crossing out a party's indorsement cancels that party's liability and the liability of subsequent indorsers who have already indorsed the instrument, but not the liability of any prior parties.

Destruction or mutilation of a negotiable instrument is considered cancellation only if it is done with the intention of eliminating obligation on the instrument [UCC 3-605(1)(a)]. Thus, if destruction or mutilation occurs by accident, the in-

strument is not discharged, and the original terms can be established by parol evidence [UCC 3-804].

Discharge by Reacquisition

A person who reacquires an instrument that he or she held previously discharges all intervening indorsers against subsequent holders who do not qualify as holders in due course [UCC 3-208, 3-601(3)(a)].

Discharge by Impairment of Recourse or of Collateral

Sometimes a party to an instrument will post or give collateral to secure that his or her performance will occur. When a holder surrenders that collateral without consent of the parties who would benefit from the collateral in the event of nonpayment, those parties to the instrument are discharged [UCC 3-606(1)(b)].

 QUESTIONS AND CASE PROBLEMS

---

1. On December 1, Daniel drew a check payable to Peter for $100 for services to be rendered on or before January 1. Peter indorsed the check in blank to Smith on December 15 as payment of a debt. Smith was unable to cash the check during the Christmas holidays. Finally, on January 5 he negotiated the check to Harold, without indorsement, as payment for a cord of wood delivered. Peter never performed the services, and Daniel had stopped payment on the check by the time Harold attempted to cash it. Harold contended that he could hold Daniel liable on the check. Daniel claimed that his defense was good against Harold. Discuss the contentions of Daniel and Harold.

2. Martin makes out a negotiable promissory note payable to Peter. Peter indorses the note "without recourse, Peter" and transfers it for value to Susan. Susan, in need of cash, negotiates the note to Helen by indorsing it "Pay to Helen, Susan." On the due date, Helen presents the note to Martin for payment, only to learn that Martin has filed for bankruptcy and will have all debts (including the note) discharged in bankruptcy. With these facts, discuss fully whether Helen can hold Martin, Peter, and Susan liable on the note.

3. Martin makes out a $500 negotiable promissory note payable to Peter. By special indorsement, Peter transfers the note for value to Susan. By blank indorsement, Susan transfers the note for value to Martha. By special indorse-

ment, Martha transfers the note for value to Harold. In need of cash, Harold transfers the instrument for value by blank indorsement *back* to Susan. When told that Peter has left the country, Susan strikes out Peter's indorsement. Later she learns that Peter is a wealthy restaurant owner in Miami and that Martin is financially unable to pay the note. Susan contends she can hold either Peter, Martha, or Harold liable on the note as an HDC. Discuss fully Susan's contentions.

4. Jerry Foster is a recent college graduate. A stranger comes to his door with a package. The stranger tells Jerry that the package is a gift from an anonymous friend and asks Jerry to sign a delivery receipt. Jerry, without reading what he is signing, signs at the place designated by the stranger and marked with an X. Jerry opens the package, and inside are two recently published novels. Jerry does not give the incident a second thought until six months later, when a holder in due course demands $1,000 from Jerry. Jerry now learns that he signed a six-month, negotiable promissory note instead of a delivery receipt. He is the victim of fraud. Discuss fully whether Jerry is obligated to pay the holder in due course $1,000.

5. Julie Willsted is a purchasing agent for Greenville, Inc., a manufacturer of video tape recorders. Julie has authority to sign checks in payment of purchases made by Greenville. Julie makes out three checks to suppliers and signs each one differently, as follows:

    (a) Greenville, Inc., by Julie Willsted, purchasing agent.

    (b) Julie Willsted, purchasing agent.

    (c) Julie Willsted.

Discuss briefly whether Julie is personally liable on each signature and whether parol evidence is admissible to hold Greenville, Inc., liable.

6. Fidelity Mortgage Investors established a line of credit with Sterling National Bank and Trust Company in the amount of $2 million. In exchange for the credit, Fidelity issued a promissory note to Sterling for this same amount. Interest on the note was 9¼ percent. A notation "9¼" was penciled on the face of the note by Sterling. This accorded with standard bank practices in that locality. Fidelity later claimed that this notation constituted a fraudulent and material alteration of the instrument in that it represented an attempt by Sterling to set the post-maturity interest at the same rate as the pre-maturity interest. In the absence of agreement, the post-maturity rate would be 6 percent (by statute). What effect did the notation "9¼" have on each of the parties to the promissory note? [Sterling Nat'l Bank and Trust Co. v. Fidelity Mortgage Investors, 510 F.2d 870 (2d Cir. 1975)]

7. James Balkus died without leaving a will. A few days later, Ann Vesely, his sister, discovered in his personal effects two promissory notes made payable to her in the amount of $6,000. She presented the notes to the Security First National Bank of Sheboygan Trust Department, the personal representative for the estate of Balkus, for payment. The personal representative refused, claiming that Vesely was not a holder in due course and that nondelivery of the notes to her was a proper defense. The trial court upheld the personal representative's claim, and Vesely appealed. Discuss whether nondelivery is a proper defense against Vesely. [Vesely v. Security First National Bank of Sheboygan Trust Department, 128 Wis.2d 246, 381 N.W.2d 593 (App. 1985)]

8. Gary Culver, a Missouri farmer, made a business arrangement in 1984 with Nasib Ed Kalliel. Kalliel was to manage the business end of the farming enterprise, while Culver did the actual farming. Culver was to receive a salary and a percentage of the profits. In the summer of 1984, Culver notified Kalliel that he urgently needed money to prevent foreclosure. One week later, Culver received $30,000 from the Rexford State Bank of Rexford, Kansas. Culver thought that the money had come from Kalliel and that Kalliel was responsible for repayment. About a week later, a representative from the Rexford Bank, Jerry Gilbert, approached Culver and requested Culver's signature on a blank promissory note form, stating that "Rexford State Bank wanted to know where the $30,000.00 went, * * * for their records." Apparently, Gilbert led Culver to believe that the document was merely a receipt for the $30,000. The maturity date, interest rate, and amount of the promissory note were later filled in, only the amount read $50,000 instead of $30,000. It was later verified that $50,000 had been deposited in Kalliel's Rexford Bank account, from which the $30,000 sent to Culver had been drawn. Subsequent to these events, the Rexford Bank became insolvent, and the Federal Deposit Insurance Corporation (FDIC) purchased the bank's outstanding notes, including the one signed by Culver. The FDIC sought recovery on the note, since the note had matured and no money had ever been paid on it, and moved for summary judgment against Culver. Culver claimed that he should not be liable on the note because Gilbert's misrepresentations of the nature of the note constituted fraud in the execution. Can Culver successfully raise the real defense of fraud in the execution to avoid liability on the note? [Federal Deposit Insurance Corp. v. Culver, 640 F.Supp. 725 (D.Kan. 1986)]

9. On May 25, 1964, Kroyden Industries, Inc., a New Jersey corporation, was prohibited by court order from making certain representations to its customers in connection with the sale of carpeting. In August of 1964, in violation of this order, one of Kroyden's employees offered to give Anna Berenyi and her husband carpeting free of charge if they referred prospective buyers to Kroyden Industries. Mr. and Mrs. Berenyi agreed to this condition and, relying upon the employee's offer, Anna Berenyi signed a promissory note for $1,521, from which "finder's fees" would be deducted when prospective buyers were referred to Kroyden Industries. Kroyden subsequently negotiated the note to the plaintiff in this case, New Jersey Mortgage & Investment Corporation. When Berenyi refused to pay the note, the plaintiff brought this legal action against her to recover the debt. Berenyi claimed that she was not liable on the note because the contract with Kroyden was illegal, having been prohibited by court order. Can Berenyi avoid her obligations on the note on the basis of illegality? [New Jersey Mortgage & Investment Company v. Berenyi, 140 N.J.Super. 406, 356 A.2d 421 (App.Div. 1976)]

Chapter 27

COMMERCIAL PAPER
Checks and the Banking System

Checks are the most common kind of commercial paper regulated by the Uniform Commercial Code. Checks, credit cards, and charge accounts are rapidly replacing currency as a means of payment in almost all transactions for goods and services. It is estimated that 60 billion personal and commercial checks are written each year in the United States. Checks are more than a daily convenience; checkbook money is an integral part of the economic system.

This chapter will identify the legal characteristics of checks and the legal duties and liabilities that arise when a check is issued. Then it will consider the check deposit-and-collection process—that is, the actual procedure by which checkbook money moves through banking channels, causing the underlying cash dollars to be shifted from bank account to bank account.

CHECKS

Recall from Chapter 22 that a **check** is a special type of draft that is drawn on a *bank*, ordering it to pay a sum of money on *demand* [UCC 3-104(2)(b)]. The person who writes the check is called the *drawer* and is usually a depositor in the bank on which the check is drawn. The person to whom the check is payable is the *payee*. The bank or financial institution on which the check is drawn is the *drawee*. If Anne Gordon writes a check from her checking account to pay her school tuition, she is the drawer, her bank is the drawee, and her school is the payee.

The payee can indorse the check to another person, thereby making that receiver a holder. Recall that a holder is a person who is in rightful possession of an instrument that is drawn to that person's order (or drawn to bearer) or that is indorsed to that person (or in blank) [UCC 1-201(20)]. The *payee as a holder* of a check has the right to transfer or negotiate it or to demand its payment in his or her own name, *as does any subsequent holder*.

A check does not, in and of itself, operate as an assignment of funds [UCC 3-409(1)]. The drawee bank is not liable to a payee or holder who presents the check for payment, even though the drawer has sufficient funds to pay the check. The payee's, or holder's, only recourse is against the drawer. (The drawer, however, may subsequently hold the bank liable for its wrongful refusal to pay.)

Cashier's Checks

Checks are usually three-party instruments, but on certain types of checks, the bank can serve as both the drawer and the drawee. For example, when a bank draws a check upon itself, the check is called a **cashier's check** and is a negotiable instrument upon issue. (See Exhibit 27–1.) In effect, with a cashier's check, the bank lends its credit to the purchaser of the check, thus making it available for immediate use in banking circles. A cashier's check is therefore an acknowledgment of a debt drawn by the bank upon itself.

Traveler's Checks

A **traveler's check** has the characteristics of a cashier's check. It is an instrument on which a financial institution is both the drawer and the drawee. The institution is directly obligated to accept and pay its traveler's check according to the instrument's terms. The purchaser must provide his or her authorized signature on the traveler's check at the time it is bought and when it is used. (See Exhibit 27–2.)

Certified Checks

When a person writes a check, it is assumed that he or she has money on deposit to cover that check when it is presented for payment. To ensure against dishonor for insufficient funds, a check may be certified by the drawee bank. A **certified check** is recognized and accepted by a bank officer as a valid appropriation of the specified amount that is drawn against the funds held by the bank. (See Exhibit 27–3.) The usual method of certification is for the cashier or teller to write across the face of the check, over the signature, a statement that it is good when properly indorsed.

The certification should contain the date, the amount being certified, and the name and title of the person certifying. Certification prevents the bank from denying liability. It is a promise that sufficient funds are on deposit and *have been set aside* to cover the check. Certified checks are used in many business dealings, especially when the buyer and seller are strangers. Sometimes, certified checks (or cashier's checks) are the required form of payment under state law—for example, in purchases at a sheriff's sale.

A drawee bank is not obligated to certify a check, and failure to do so is not a dishonor of the check [UCC 3-411(2)]. When a bank agrees to certification, it immediately charges the drawer's account with the amount of the check and

Exhibit 27–1 Cashier's Check

Exhibit 27–2 Traveler's Check

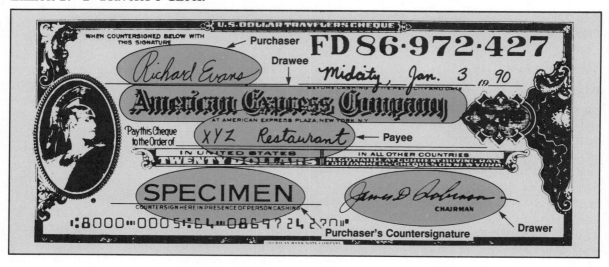

Exhibit 27–3 Certified Check

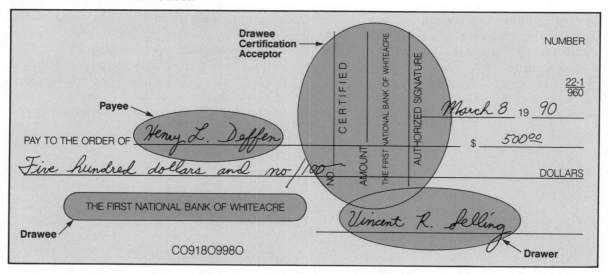

transfers those funds to its own certified check account. In effect, the bank is agreeing in advance to accept that check when it is presented for payment and to make payment from those funds reserved in the certified check account [UCC 3-411(1)].

DRAWER'S REQUEST FOR CERTIFICATION The legal liability of the drawer varies on the basis of whether the certification is requested by the drawer or the holder. The drawer who obtains certification remains *secondarily liable* on the instrument if for some reason the certifying bank cannot or does not honor the check when it is presented for payment.

For example, Epstein buys Stiple's car for $5,000. Epstein writes out a check for that amount and takes it to the bank, where it is certified. In the unlikely event that the bank fails to honor the check when it is presented for payment, Stiple can hold Epstein liable for payment of the $5,000.

HOLDER'S REQUEST FOR CERTIFICATION   If the check is certified at the request of the holder, then the drawer and any indorsers prior to certification are completely discharged. A holder's request for certification is viewed as choice of the bank's promise to pay over the drawer's and any indorser's promises. In this situation, the holder can look only to the bank for payment. Suppose in the example above Epstein had written a $5,000 check to Stiple, but Stiple had taken the check to the drawee bank for certification. Upon certification, Epstein would have been released from all liability, and Stiple would have been able to look only to the bank for his $5,000 [UCC 3-411(1)].

REVOCATION OF CERTIFICATION   The bank's ability to revoke certification is extremely limited. If a good faith holder has changed position in reliance on that certification, the bank cannot revoke. Furthermore, since certification constitutes *acceptance* of an instrument under the Uniform Commercial Code, a bank can never revoke certification against an HDC regardless of whether the HDC has changed position in reliance on the certification [UCC 3-418].

ALTERATION OF A CERTIFIED CHECK   A bank will be liable for payment of an altered check only if the check was altered prior to certification. Upon certification, the drawee bank becomes an acceptor and becomes liable for the instrument according to its tenor (the very words and figures on the instrument) at the time of certification. Alterations after certification are not binding on the bank.

The following case involves a certified check that was altered. Because of the alteration, it was dishonored when presented to the bank. The court held the bank liable for only the original amount of the check.

BACKGROUND AND FACTS   *The Franklin National Bank (defendant) certified a check payable to Sam Goody, Inc., in the amount of $16. The certification stamp of the defendant bank did not show the amount for which the check was certified. The check had been presented to the defendant bank for certification by either the depositor or an accomplice. After the certification was procured, the amount of the check was altered from $16 to $1,600. The check was later presented to the plaintiff, Sam Goody, Inc., in payment for merchandise. The customer who presented the check represented that it was a bonus check. The customer had ordered the merchandise on the previous day and had stated that he would secure from his employer a certified check drawn directly to the plaintiff, Sam Goody, to pay the balance owing. Subsequently, the bank refused to honor the check because of the alteration. The plaintiff sued the bank for the full $1,600. The bank asserted that it was responsible only for the amount it had certified originally—that is, $16.*

Case 27.1
SAM GOODY, INC. v. FRANKLIN NAT'L BANK OF LONG ISLAND
Supreme Court of New York, 1968.
57 Misc.2d 193, 291 N.Y.S.2d 429.

FARLEY, Justice.
*   *   *   *

The fraudulent scheme perpetrated in this case was obviously made possible by the knowledge that the certification stamp of the defendant Bank would not disclose the amount for which the check was certified. The plaintiff claims the negligence of the Bank in this respect caused the loss and that the Bank is estopped [prevented] from asserting the defense of alteration under Section 3-406 of the Uniform Commercial Code.
*   *   *   *

A bank, when certifying a check, does no more than to affirm the genuineness of the signature of the maker, that he has funds on deposit to meet the item, and that the funds will not be withdrawn to the prejudice of the holder. The certification constitutes an acceptance of the check to this extent (U.C.C., § 3-411), but the bank by its certification does not guaranty the body thereof *   *   * and engages only to pay the item according to its tenor at the time certification is procured (U.C.C., § 3-413). Furthermore, a holder of a check, by having it certified, is deemed to have warranted to the bank that the instrument has not been materially altered. The Code makes one exception to this rule by providing that the same warranty is not given by a holder in due course whether the alteration is made before or after certification (U.C.C., §§ 3-417(1), 3-413). Consequently, under the Code, where a check is certified *after the amount has been altered*, the bank runs the risk of sustaining the loss if the instrument passes into the hands of a holder in due course. [Emphasis added.] * * *

The rule, however, is otherwise where the certification of the check is procured by the maker. In such case, the bank does not incur the risk of an alteration prior to its acceptance, and only agrees to pay the instrument according to its tenor at the time of certification even as to a holder in due course (U.C.C., § 3-413[1]).

The evidence in this case does not disclose whether the maker or his accomplice procured certification of the check, but the controlling fact that alteration occurred after certification of the instrument is not disputed. The bank, in checking its records, discovered the alteration and refused payment. Under these circumstances, the negligence of the bank, if any, is not a substantial or proximate cause of the loss, and in accordance with the rules mentioned above, it is not liable to the plaintiff except for the amount for which the check was originally drawn.

DECISION AND REMEDY   *The defendant, Franklin National Bank, was liable for only $16, the original amount of the certified check.*

COMMENTS   *Notice that the court did not discuss UCC 3-406 at length. Rather, the court made it clear that it did not believe that the bank was negligent.*

THE BANK-CUSTOMER RELATIONSHIP

The bank-customer relationship begins when the customer opens a checking account and deposits money that will be used to pay for checks written. The rights and duties of the bank and the customer are contractual and depend upon the nature of the transaction.

Article 4 of the UCC is a statement of the principles and rules of modern bank deposit-and-collection procedures. It governs the relationship of banks with one another as they process checks for payment, and it establishes a framework for deposit and checking agreements between a bank and its customers.

Article 3 of the UCC, which deals with the use of commercial paper, sets forth the requirements for negotiable instruments. The extent to which any party is either charged with or discharged from liability on a check is established according to the provisions of Article 3. Note that a check can fall within the scope of Article 3 as a negotiable

instrument and yet be subject to the provisions of Article 4 while it is in the course of collection. In the case of a conflict between Articles 3 and 4, Article 4 controls [UCC 4-102(1)].

A creditor-debtor relationship is created between a customer and a bank when, for example, the customer makes cash deposits into a checking account or when final payment is received for checks drawn on other banks. (Creditor-debtor relationships generally are discussed in Chapters 29, 30, and 31.)

A principal-agent relationship underlies the check collection process. A check does not operate as an immediate legal assignment of funds between the drawer and the payee [UCC 3-409]. The money in the bank represented by that check does not move from the drawer's account to the payee's account; nor is any underlying debt discharged until the drawee bank honors the check and makes final payment. To transfer checkbook dollars among different banks, each bank acts as the agent of collection for its customer [UCC 4-201(1)]. (Agency relationships generally are discussed in Chapters 32 and 33.)

DUTIES OF THE BANK

A commercial bank serves its customers primarily in two ways:

1. By honoring checks for the withdrawal of funds on deposit in its customers' accounts.
2. By accepting deposits in U.S. currency and collecting checks written to or indorsed to its customers that are drawn on other banks.

HONORING CHECKS

When a commercial bank provides checking services, it agrees to honor the checks written by its customers with the usual stipulation that there be sufficient funds available in the account to pay each check. When a drawee bank *wrongfully* fails to honor a check, it is liable to its customer for damages resulting from its refusal to pay. The Code does not attempt to specify the theory under which the customer may recover for wrongful dishonor; it merely states that the drawee is liable. Thus, the drawer customer does not have to prove that the drawee bank breached its contractual commitment, or slandered the customer's credit, or was negligent [UCC 4-402]. When the bank properly dishonors a check for insufficient funds, it has no liability to the customer.

On the other hand, a bank may charge against a customer's account an *overdraft*—that is, a check that is paid from that account even though the account contains insufficient funds to cover the check [UCC 4-401(1)]. Once a bank makes special arrangements with its customer to accept overdrafts on an account, the payor bank can become liable to its customer for damages proximately caused by its wrongful dishonor of overdrafts. The charging of overdrafts will be discussed later in this chapter.

The customer's agreement with the bank includes a general obligation to keep sufficient money on deposit to cover all checks written. The customer is liable to the payee or to the holder of a check in a civil suit if a check is not honored. If intent to defraud can be proved, the customer can also be subject to criminal prosecution for writing a bad check.

The following case illustrates that when a bank agrees with a customer to pay overdrafts, the bank's refusal to honor checks on an overdrawn account is a wrongful dishonor.

BACKGROUND AND FACTS *Lawrence and Linda Kendall were officers and the principal shareholders of Kendall Yacht Corporation, a corporation formed to build yachts on special order from customers. The corporation had never issued stock and was in need of more operating funds.*

The corporation had a payroll checking account and a general business checking account with United California Bank. When the corporation ran into financial problems, Mr. Kendall spoke with Ron Lamperts, a loan officer at the bank, in an effort to obtain financing for the corporation.

The bank agreed to honor overdrafts on the corporate account until such time as the corporation was financially more stable. The Kendalls continued to write checks for supplies, payroll, and other operating expenses of the corporation from about mid-October through December. The corporate bank account was badly overdrawn, and a number of the checks had been dishonored by the bank.

The Kendalls brought this lawsuit against United California Bank, charging that its wrongful dishonor of checks that it had initially agreed to accept as overdrafts caused damage to the Kendalls' personal and credit reputation. The trial court held for Kendall, and the bank appealed.

McDANIEL, Associate Justice.
*   *   *   *

During October, November, and December, the Bank honored overdrafts of the Corporation totaling in excess of $15,000. There were also a number of overdrafts

Case 27.2
KENDALL YACHT CORP. v. UNITED CALIFORNIA BANK
Court of Appeals of California, 1975.
50 Cal.3d 949, 123 Cal.Rptr. 848.

written during these months which were not honored by the Bank. Some of these were to suppliers and others were payroll checks to employees. In addition, the Bank failed to honor a check written to Insurance Company of North America to cover a premium for workmen's compensation insurance. The Kendalls were not aware that this check had been "bounced" until after one of their employees had been injured and they had been notified by Insurance Company of North America that their insurance had been terminated for nonpayment of premium.

After the collapse of the business, the Kendalls understandably had a number of enemies in the community. They were accused of having breached the trust of their former suppliers and employees and of having milked the Corporation of its funds and placed them in a Swiss bank account. They were repeatedly threatened with legal action and physical harm; they suffered acts of vandalism such as eggs and oil being thrown at their cars. Mr. Kendall's subsequent employer was contacted and threatened by creditors of the Corporation. Criminal charges were brought against Mrs. Kendall for writing checks against insufficient funds; the charges were dismissed shortly before she was brought to trial on them. The Kendalls were required to appear and answer charges in administrative proceedings involving dishonored payroll checks and the Corporation's failure to carry workmen's compensation insurance. Each testified to experiencing severe emotional distress and humiliation as a result of these matters. They also testified to marital problems which were allegedly caused by the stress brought on by the failure of the business.

* * * *

The Bank contends first that under Commercial Code section 4402 the wrongful dishonor of a check of a *corporation* does not give a cause of action for damages to individual officers and shareholders of the corporation. Commercial Code section 4402, which represents section 4-402 of the Uniform Commercial Code, reads as follows: "A payor bank is liable to its customer for damages proximately caused by the wrongful dishonor of an item. When the dishonor occurs through mistake liability is limited to actual damages proved."

[It] was entirely foreseeable that the dishonoring of the Corporation's checks would reflect directly on the personal credit and reputation of the Kendalls and that they would suffer the adverse personal consequences which resulted when the Bank reneged on its commitments.

* * * *

[It] has been held in this state that a cause of action for wrongful dishonor of a check sounds in tort as well as in contract, and "if the conduct is tortious, damages for emotional distress may be recovered despite the fact that the conduct also involves a breach of contract."

DECISION AND REMEDY *The court awarded the Kendalls $26,000 each as compensatory damages for the bank's wrongful dishonor of the checks.*

Stale Checks

The bank's responsibility to honor its customers' checks is not absolute. A bank is not obliged to pay an uncertified check presented more than six months from its date [UCC 4-404]. Commercial banking practice regards a check outstanding for longer than six months as a **stale check.** UCC 4-404 gives a bank the option of paying or not paying on a stale check. The usual banking practice is to consult the customer, but if a bank pays in good faith without consulting the customer, it has the right to charge the customer's account for the amount of the check.

In the following case, a bank's payment of a stale check is at issue. The court's discussion of this issue is illustrative.

BACKGROUND AND FACTS   *Granite Equipment Leasing Corporation issued a check to Overseas Equipment Company. After five days, Overseas indicated that the check had not been received. Granite ordered payment on the check stopped and wired the funds to Overseas. Approximately one year later, the check cleared, and Granite's account was charged. Granite sued the bank for return of the funds to its account, maintaining that the bank had a duty to inquire into the circumstances of the stale check. The bank based its defense on the premise that the stop-payment order had expired and that it had acted in good faith.*

Case 27.3
GRANITE EQUIPMENT LEASING CORP. v. HEMPSTEAD BANK
Supreme Court of New York, 1971.
68 Misc.2d 350, 326 N.Y.S.2d 881.

HARNETT, Justice.

*   *   *   *

Under the Uniform Commercial Code, does a bank have a duty of inquiry before paying a stale check? Does it matter that the stale check had been previously stopped under a stop payment order which expired for lack of renewal? So this case goes.

*   *   *   *

There is no doubt the check is stale. There is no doubt the stop payment order was properly given at the outset, and that it was never renewed. Granite essentially maintains the Bank had a duty to inquire into the circumstances of that stale check, and should not have paid in face of a known lapsed stop order without consulting its depositor.

The Uniform Commercial Code, which became effective in New York on September 27, 1964, provides that:

"(1) A customer may by order to his bank stop payment of any item payable for his account *   *   * (2) *   *   * A written [stop] order is effective for only six months unless renewed in writing." UCC § 4-403.

*   *   *   *

Granite cannot be permitted to predicate liability on the part of the Bank on its failure to inquire about and find a stop payment order which had become terminated in default of renewal.

*   *   *   *

Neither may Granite predicate a claim of liability upon the Bank's payment of a stale check. *   *   *

*   *   *   *

There is no obligation under the statute of the Bank to search its records to discover old lapsed stop payment orders. The Bank does not have to pay a stale check, but it may pay one in "good faith." Significantly, UCC § 1-201(19) defines "good faith" as "honesty in fact in the conduct or transaction concerned." In the absence of any facts which could justify a finding of dishonesty, bad faith, recklessness, or lack of ordinary care, in the face of circumstances actually known, or which should have been known, the Bank is not liable to Granite for its payment of the check drawn to Overseas.

Granite's complete remedy lies in its pending Florida action against Overseas to recover the extra payment.

The court dismissed the complaint and entered judgment in favor of the bank, which was not required to pay Granite Equipment the amount of the check. The court ruled that Hempstead Bank had acted in good faith.

DECISION AND REMEDY

Missing Indorsements

Depository institutions[1] are allowed to supply any necessary indorsements of a customer. (This rule does not apply if the item expressly requires the payee's indorsement.) The depository bank places a statement on the item to the effect that it was deposited by a customer or credited to that customer's account [UCC 4-205(1)].

Death or Incompetence of a Customer

UCC 4-405 provides that if, at the time a check is issued or its collection has been undertaken, a bank does *not know* of an adjudication of incompetence, a check can be paid and the bank will not incur liability. Neither death nor incompetency revokes the bank's authority to pay an item until the bank knows of the situation and has had reasonable time to act. Even when a bank *knows* of the death of its customer, for ten days after the date of death, it can pay or certify checks drawn

on or prior to the date of death—unless a person claiming an interest in that account, such as an heir or an executor of the estate, orders the bank to stop all payment. Without this provision, banks would constantly be required to verify the continued life and competency of their drawers.

Stop-Payment Orders

Only a customer can order his or her bank to pay a check, and only a customer can order payment to be stopped. This right does not extend to holders—that is, payees or indorsees—because the drawee bank's contract is only with its drawers. A customer has no right to stop payment on a check that has been certified or that has been accepted by a bank. A stop-payment order must be received within a reasonable time and in a reasonable manner to permit the bank to act on it [UCC 4-403(1)].

A stop-payment order can be given orally, usually by phone.[2] An oral order is binding on the bank for only fourteen calendar days unless confirmed in writing. (See Exhibit 27–4.) A written stop-payment order or an oral order confirmed in

---

1. A *depository institution* is the party or institution—such as a bank or a trust company—that receives and takes responsibility for a deposit, which, as used in this chapter, refers generally to negotiable instruments and specifically to checks. *Depositary* should not be confused with *depository*, a term that describes the *physical* place in which the deposit is placed.

2. Some states do not recognize oral stop-payment orders; they must be in writing.

Exhibit 27–4 Stop-Payment Order

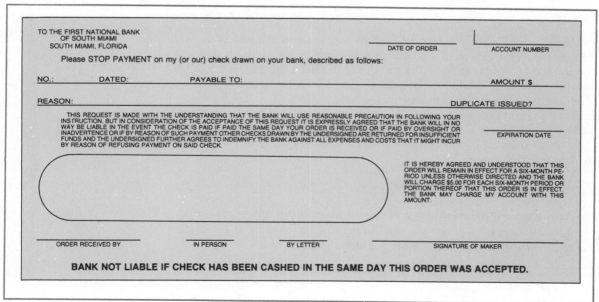

writing is effective for six months only, unless renewed in writing [UCC 4-403(2)].

Should the drawee bank pay the check over the customer's properly instituted stop-payment order, the bank will be obligated to recredit the account of the drawer customer. The bank, however, is liable for no more than the actual loss suffered by the drawer because of the wrongful payment.

For example, suppose Pat Davis orders one hundred used typewriters at $50 each from Jane Greer. Davis pays in advance for the goods with her check for $5,000. Later that day, Greer tells Davis that she is not going to deliver any typewriters. Davis immediately calls her bank and stops payment on the check. Two days later, in spite of this stop-payment order, the bank inadvertently honors Davis's $5,000 check to Greer for the undelivered typewriters. The bank will be liable to Davis for the full $5,000.

The result would be different if Greer had delivered ninety-nine typewriters. Since Davis would have owed Greer $4,950 for the goods delivered,

she would have been able to establish actual losses of only $50 resulting from the bank's payment over her stop-payment order. The bank would be liable to Davis for only $50.

A stop-payment order has its risks for a customer. The drawer must have a *valid legal ground* for issuing such an order; otherwise the holder can sue the drawer for payment. (Of course, the holder cannot sue the drawee bank for honoring a stop-payment order for which the drawer had no valid legal ground.) Moreover, defenses sufficient to prevent payment against a payee may not be valid grounds to prevent payment against a subsequent holder in due course [UCC 3-305].

A person who wrongfully stops payment on a check will not only be liable to the payee for the amount of the check but may also be liable for *special* damages resulting from the wrongful order. Special damages, however, must be separately pleaded and proved at trial. The following case illustrates the problem of proving special damages when payment of a check is wrongfully stopped.

BACKGROUND AND FACTS *Sanford was fired from his job in a restaurant owned by Vickrey. Vickrey gave Sanford a number of checks for wages due to him, plus a stock refund check for $720 that Sanford had invested in Vickrey's other businesses. Sanford told Vickrey that he needed the money to pay his bills and to get to Las Vegas where he could get another job. Vickrey gave him a check for $720 on which he wrote, "Refund for stock deposit." After depositing the checks in his bank, Sanford returned to the restaurant where he cursed and threatened Vickrey and then set out for Las Vegas. Vickrey stopped payment on the $720 check. Sanford's bank got in touch with Sanford a few days later and asked him to sign a note for the $720. Sanford made two trips back to Texas to straighten out the matter. He sought recovery from Vickrey for the amount of the check and, as special damages, the expenses he had incurred in making the two trips to Texas. The trial court awarded Sanford $1,750 in damages, and Vickrey appealed.*

Case 27.4
VICKREY v. SANFORD
Court of Appeals of Texas, 1974.
506 S.W.2d 270.

BREWSTER, Justice.
*   *   *

On the occasion when Vickrey had given the $720.00 check to Sanford, Sanford had advised Vickrey that he needed the money to pay up bills and to get to Las Vegas, Nevada, at which place he could get a job.

After Sanford had done the cursing at the "Sirloin Stockade," he, on the same day, left for Las Vegas, Nevada, and was there hired at the Golden Nugget as a dealer and to work at the roulette wheel.

A few days later Sanford called home and was told by his wife that payment had been stopped on the $720.00 check and that Mr. Allen, a vice-president of Denton

County National Bank, where he had cashed it, wanted to get in touch with him. He called Allen and Allen wanted him to sign a note for the $720.00.

*   *   *   *

Sanford sought in this case to recover the amount of the check ($720.00) plus interest thereon, plus the expenses that he incurred in making the two trips back to Denton, plus exemplary [punitive] damages.

[The court had no trouble deciding that Vickrey was responsible for paying the $720 plus interest. It was Sanford's most unusual request for the cost of traveling between Nevada and Texas to straighten out the mess that gave the court cause for concern.]

If plaintiff, Sanford, is legally entitled to recover for expenses incurred in making the two trips from Nevada back to Texas plus the loss of salary due to losing his job, it would only be on the theory that they were special damages that were within the contemplation of the parties at the time the contract was executed. This is a necessary element if the expenses sought to be recovered are in the category of special damages.

*   *   *   *

There was no evidence tending to show that the entire transaction with reference to Sanford signing the note to the Bank could not have been handled by mail, thus rendering both of Sanford's trips to Texas unnecessary. There was no evidence offered to the effect that it was necessary that this note be signed in Denton.

DECISION AND REMEDY   *The court permitted Sanford to recover only the amount of the $720 check in damages. The court held that there was insufficient evidence to uphold Sanford's claim for special damages.*

Overdrafts

When the bank receives an item properly payable from its customer's checking account but there are insufficient funds in the account to cover the amount of the check, the bank can either dishonor the item or pay the item and charge the customer's account, creating an overdraft [UCC 4-401(1)]. The bank can subtract the difference from the customer's next deposit because the check carries with it an enforceable implied promise to reimburse the bank.

When a check "bounces," a holder can resubmit the check, hoping that at a later date sufficient funds will be available to pay it. The holder must notify any indorsers on the check of the first dishonor; otherwise they will be discharged from their signature liability.

Payment on a Forged Signature of the Drawer

A forged signature on a check has no legal effect as the signature of a drawer [UCC 3-404(1)]. Banks require signature cards from each customer who opens a checking account. The bank is responsible for determining whether the signature on a customer's check is genuine. The general rule is that the bank must recredit the customer's account when it pays on a forged signature.

The bank has no right to recover from a holder who, without knowledge, cashes a check bearing a forged drawer's signature. The holder merely guarantees that he or she has no knowledge that the signature of the drawer is unauthorized. Unless the bank can prove that the holder has such knowledge, its only recourse is against the forger [UCC 3-418, 4-207(1)(b)].

CUSTOMER NEGLIGENCE   When the customer's negligence substantially contributes to the forgery, the bank will not normally be obliged to recredit the customer's account for the amount of the check. Suppose Axelrod Corporation uses a mechanical check-writing machine to write its payroll and business checks. Axelrod discovers that one of its employees used the machine to write himself a check for $10,000 and that the bank subsequently honored it. Axelrod requests the bank to recredit $10,000 to its account for incorrectly paying on a forged check. If the bank can show that Axelrod failed to take reasonable care in controlling access to the check-writing equipment, Axelrod cannot require the bank to recredit its account for the amount of the forged check [UCC 3-406].

TIMELY EXAMINATION REQUIRED A customer has an *affirmative duty* to examine monthly statements and canceled checks promptly and with reasonable care and to report any forged signatures promptly [UCC 4-406(1)]. This includes forged signatures of indorsers, to be discussed later [UCC 4-406].

Failure to so examine and report, or any carelessness by the customer that results in a loss to the bank, makes the customer liable for the loss [UCC 4-406(2)(a)]. Even if the customer can prove that reasonable care was taken against forgeries, the Code provides that unless discovery of such forgeries and notice to the bank takes place within specific time frames the customer cannot require the bank to recredit his or her account.

When a series of forgeries by the same wrongdoer takes place, the Code provides that the customer, in order to recover for all the forged items, must discover and report the forgery to the bank within fourteen calendar days of the receipt of the bank statement and canceled checks that contain the first forged item [UCC 4-406(2)(b)]. Failure to notify within this period of time discharges the bank's liability for all similar forged checks prior to notification, unless the customer can establish that the bank failed to exercise ordinary care in paying the checks.

For example, Middletown Bank sends out monthly statements and canceled checks on the last day of each month. Bradley, owner of a small store, unknowingly has had a number of his blank checks stolen by employee Harry. On April 20, Harry forges Bradley's signature and cashes check number 1. On April 22, Harry forges Bradley's signature and cashes check number 2. The checks canceled in April (including the forged ones) and the April statement from the Middletown Bank are received on May 1. Bradley sets aside the statement and does not reconcile his checking account.

On May 20 Harry forges Bradley's signature and cashes check number 3. The checks canceled in May and the May statement are received by Bradley on June 1. Upon immediate examination of both statements, Bradley discovers the forgeries and demands that the bank recredit his account for all forged checks.

Must the bank do so? The answer is no, assuming the bank was not negligent in paying the forged checks [UCC 4-406(3)]. The two forged checks in April were made available to Bradley for inspection on May 1. Liability for any forged check in this series fell on Bradley after May 15 (fourteen days after receipt of the April statement). In addition, if Bradley's negligence in failing to examine his April statement promptly resulted in a loss to the Middletown Bank, the bank's liability to recredit Bradley's account for any forged item would be reduced by the amount of this loss.

Had Bradley examined his April statement immediately upon receipt and reported the two April forgeries, the bank would have been obligated to fully recredit Bradley's account. If the bank could have proved that Bradley's carelessness in permitting the blank checks to be stolen substantially contributed to the forgery, however, Bradley—not the bank—would have been liable [UCC 3-406, 4-406].

Regardless of the degree of care exercised by the customer or the bank, the Code places an absolute time limit on the liability of a bank for forged customer signatures. UCC 4-406(4) provides that a customer who has not reported his or her forged signature one year from the date that the statement and canceled checks were made available for inspection loses the legal right to have the bank recredit his or her account.

In the following case, the customer's duty to discover and report an unauthorized signature was at issue.

BACKGROUND AND FACTS *Ossip-Harris Insurance Company, Inc., the plaintiff, maintained a checking account with Barnett Bank of South Florida, N.A., the defendant, during 1980 and 1981. From May 1980 through June 1981, Ossip's bookkeeper, Edgerly, used a facsimile signature stamp to forge the name of Ossip's president, Harris, to ninety-nine checks totaling $19,711.90. When the canceled checks came back to Ossip, Edgerly would replace the payee name (her own name or the name of one of her creditors) with one of a legitimate Ossip business expense. Throughout this period, Harris periodically reviewed the monthly statements and canceled checks but did not*

Case 27.5
OSSIP-HARRIS INSURANCE, INC. v. BARNETT BANK OF SOUTH FLORIDA, N.A.

District Court of Appeal of Florida, 1983.
428 So.2d 363.

detect the forgeries until June of 1981. At that time, Harris notified Barnett, and no further forged instruments were paid by Barnett. Ossip alleged that Barnett wrongfully paid the ninety-nine checks drawn on Ossip's account, but the trial court entered a summary judgment in favor of Barnett. Ossip appealed the summary judgment.

HENDRY, Judge.

*   *   *   *

Resolution of this dispute turns on the provisions of subsections (1) through (3) of Section 674.406, Florida Statutes (1981), which [use the same language as UCC 4-406(1) through (3) regarding a customer's duty] to "exercise reasonable care and promptness" in examining bank statements and items to discover any unauthorized signatures or alterations. If this duty is not complied with, paragraph (b) of subsection (2) of the statute precludes recovery from the bank on any checks containing an un-authorized signature which were paid by the bank at least fourteen days after the first item and statement were made available to the customer. *   *   * Subsection (3) of the statute provides, however, that subsection (2) is inapplicable where the "customer establishes lack of ordinary care on the part of the bank in paying the item(s)."

We find that Barnett met its burden, as movant [one making a motion before the court] for summary judgment, of conclusively showing that Ossip failed to meet its initial burden under subsection (1) of the statute in that it did not "exercise reasonable care and promptness to examine the statement and items to discover" the unauthorized signatures. The undisputed evidence demonstrates that Ossip received bank statements from Barnett each month from May 1980 to June 1981 and that the statements contained the cancelled checks alleged to be forgeries. In response to a question posed by Ossip's own attorney, Edward Harris admitted that he did not actually review the signature on all of the company's cancelled checks and even admitted that he didn't pay attention to the signatures on the checks but was more concerned with the amounts and whether it was "the kind of check [Ossip-Harris] would normally pay." The checks were thus not scrutinized for unauthorized signatures as required by statute, nor was reasonable notice given to Barnett of any wrongdoing after the first statement and checks were made available to Ossip within the meaning of Section 674.406 (2)(b). Consequently, the evidence supports the conclusion, as a matter of law, that Ossip failed to exercise the degree of care required by statute *   *   * [and] is therefore precluded from re-covering against Barnett unless it can establish lack of ordinary care by Barnett in paying the forgeries.

Under Section 674.406(3), the burden of proving Barnett's lack of ordinary care falls squarely on Ossip-Harris. *   *   * Deposition testimony by Estella Brown, an employee of Barnett that handled the Ossip-Harris account, established that she had received six months of on-the-job training and that she examined each check against the signature card on file with the bank to determine the validity of the signature. When any problems arose with regard to signatures, she would bring the checks to the attention of her supervisor. Ossip presented no evidence of either the accepted standard of ordinary care in the banking world, or that Barnett's method of detecting forgeries did not meet this standard. Ossip's only argument in this regard, that the bank was negligent in not detecting the forgery, is particularly unavailing [futile] in light of the fact that Edward Harris failed to detect the forgery of his own signature. To require Barnett's employees to be handwriting experts as Ossip seems to imply, would establish a higher standard than that required by the statute, which is simply ordinary care.

DECISION AND REMEDY   *The appellate court sustained the summary judgment entered by the trial court. Plaintiff Ossip could not recover the $19,711.90 paid out of its account by the defendant, Barnett Bank.*

This case illustrates the importance of reconciling your bank statement promptly **COMMENTS**
upon receipt and notifying your bank of any alteration or unauthorized signature.

Payment on a Forged Indorsement

A bank that pays a customer's check bearing a forged indorsement must recredit the customer's account or be liable to the drawer-customer for breach of contract.

For example, Baker issues a $50 check "to the order of Thelma." Larry steals the check, forges Thelma's indorsement, and cashes the check. When the check reaches Baker's bank, the bank pays it and debits Baker's account. Under UCC 4-401, the bank must recredit Baker's account $50 because it failed to carry out Baker's order to pay "to the order of Thelma." Baker's bank will in turn recover—under breach of warranty principles—from the bank that cashed the check [UCC 4-207(1)(a)].

The customer, in any case, has a duty to examine the returned checks and statements received by the bank and to report forged indorsements upon discovery or notice. Failure to report forged indorsements within a three-year period after the items containing the forgeries have been made available to the customer relieves the bank of liability [UCC 4-406(4)].

Payment on an Altered Check

The customer's instruction to the bank is to pay the exact amount on the face of the check to the holder. The bank must examine each check before making final payment. If it fails to detect an alteration, it is liable to its customer for the loss because it did not pay as the drawer-customer ordered. The loss is the difference between the original amount of the check and the amount actually paid. Suppose a check written for $11 is altered to read $111 and the drawee bank fails to detect the alteration and pays the $111. The bank may charge the customer's account for only $11 (the amount the customer ordered it to pay) [UCC 4-401(2)(a)].

The bank may recover the remaining $100 from the party who presented the check for payment[3] on the ground of breach of the presentment warranty that the instrument had not been altered. If the bank were the drawer, however, it could not recover the $100 on this ground from the presenting party, if the party was an HDC who was acting in good faith [UCC 3-417(1)(c), 4-207(1)(c)]. The reason is that an instrument's drawer is in a better position than an HDC to know whether the instrument has been altered.

Similarly, an HDC, acting in good faith in presenting a certified check for payment, does not warrant to the check's certifier that the check was not altered before it was certified (and the HDC acquired it after the certification) or that it was not altered after its certification [UCC 3-417(1)(c), 4-207(1)(c)]. For example, Selling, the drawer, draws a check for $500 payable to Deffen, the payee. Deffen alters the amount to $5,000. The First National Bank of Whiteacre, the drawee, certifies the check for $5,000. Deffen negotiates the check to Evans, an HDC. The drawee-bank pays Evans $5,000. On discovering the mistake, the bank cannot recover from Evans the $4,500 paid by mistake, even though the bank was not in a superior position to detect the alteration. This is in accord with the purpose of certification, which is to obtain the definite obligation of a bank to honor a definite instrument.

A customer's negligence can shift the risk of loss. A common example occurs when a person carelessly writes a check, leaving large gaps around the numbers and words so that additional numbers and words can be inserted. (See, for example, Exhibit 27–5.)

Similarly, a person who signs a check and leaves the dollar amount for someone else to fill in is barred from protesting when the bank unknowingly and in good faith pays whatever amount is shown [UCC 4-401(2)(b)]. Finally, if the bank can trace its loss on successive altered checks to the customer's failure to discover the initial alteration,

---

3. Usually, the party presenting an instrument for payment is a bank's customer or a collecting bank. A bank's customers include its account holders, which may include other banks [UCC 4-104(1)(e)]. A collecting bank is any bank handling an item for collection except the payor bank [UCC 4-105(d)].

Exhibit 27–5 A Poorly Filled Out Check

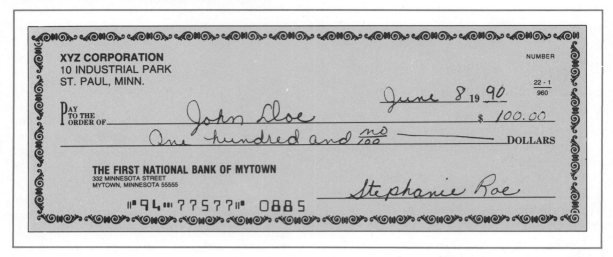

then the bank can alleviate its liability for reimbursing the customer's account[4] [UCC 4-406]. The law governing the customer's duty to examine monthly statements and canceled checks and to discover and report alterations to the drawee bank is the same as that applied to forged customer signatures.

In every situation involving a forged drawer's signature or an alteration, a bank must observe reasonable commercial standards of care in paying on a customer's checks [UCC 4-406(3)]. The customer's contributory negligence can be asserted only if the bank has exercised ordinary care.

ACCEPTING DEPOSITS

A second fundamental service a commercial bank provides for its checking account customers is that of accepting deposits of cash and checks. Cash deposits made in U.S. currency are received into the customer's account without being subject to further collection procedures. This section will focus on what happens to checks after they have been deposited. In most situations, deposited checks

are from parties who do business at different banks, but sometimes checks are written between customers of the same bank. Either situation brings into play the bank collection process as it operates within the statutory framework of Article 4 of the UCC.

Definitions

The first bank to receive a check for payment is the **depositary bank**.[5] When a person deposits his or her IRS tax refund check into a personal checking account at the local bank, that bank acts as a depositary bank. The bank on which a check is drawn (the drawee bank) is called the **payor bank.** Any bank except the payor bank that handles a check during some phase of the collection process is a **collecting bank.** Any bank except the payor bank or depositary bank to which an item is transferred in the course of this collection process is called an **intermediary bank.**

The Collection Process

During the collection process, any bank can take on one or more of the above roles. For example, a buyer in New York writes a check on her New York bank and sends it to a seller in San Francisco. The seller deposits the check in her San Francisco

---

4. The bank's defense is the same whether successive payments were made on a forged drawer's signature or an altered check. The bank must prove that prompt notice would have prevented its loss. For example, notification might have alerted the bank not to pay further items or enabled it to catch the forger.

---

5. All definitions in this section are found in UCC 4-105.

CONCEPT SUMMARY: Bank-Customer Relationships

SITUATION	BASIC RULES
Bank's charge against customer's account UCC 4-401	The bank has the right to charge a customer's account for any item properly payable even if the charge results in an overdraft.
Wrongful dishonor UCC 4-402	The bank is liable to its customer for wrongful dishonor due to mistake for actual damages proved. Damages can include those proximately caused by consequent arrest or prosecution, as well as other consequential damages.
Stop-payment order UCC 4-403	The customer must make a stop-payment order in time for the bank to have a reasonable opportunity to act. Oral orders are binding for only fourteen days unless they are confirmed in writing. Written orders are effective for only six months, unless renewed in writing. The bank is liable for wrongful payment over a timely stop-payment order.
Stale check UCC 4-404	The bank is not obligated to pay an uncertified check presented more than six months after its date, but it may do so in good faith without liability.
Death or incompetence of customer UCC 4-405	As long as the bank does not know of the death or incompetence of a customer, the bank can pay an item without liability. Even with knowledge of a customer's death, a bank can honor or certify checks (in the absence of a stop-payment order) for ten days after the date of the customer's death.
Unauthorized signature or alteration UCC 4-406	The customer has a duty to examine account statements with reasonable care upon receipt and to notify the bank promptly of any unauthorized signatures or alterations. On a series of unauthorized signatures or alterations by the same wrongdoer, examination and report must be given within fourteen calendar days of receipt of the statement. Failure to comply releases the bank from any liability unless the bank failed to exercise reasonable care. Regardless of care or lack of care, the customer is estopped from holding the bank liable after one year for unauthorized customer signatures or alterations and after three years for unauthorized indorsements.

bank account. The seller's bank is both a *depositary bank* and a *collecting bank*. The buyer's bank in New York is the *payor bank*. As the check travels from San Francisco to New York, any collecting bank (other than the depositary bank) holding the item in the collection process is an *intermediary bank*.

BANK'S LIABILITY FOR RESTRICTIVE INDORSEMENTS
A bank is not bound by any restrictive indorsements of any person except the immediate holder who transfers or presents the instrument

for payment [UCC 3-206(2)]. This means that *only the first bank to which the item is presented for collection must pay in a manner consistent with any restrictive indorsement* [UCC 3-206(3)]. This bank is called the depositary bank [UCC 4-105(a)].

To illustrate: Elliott writes a check on his New York bank account and sends it to Barton. Barton indorses the check with a restrictive indorsement that reads, "For deposit into account #4921 only." A Miami bank is the first bank to which this check is presented for payment (the depositary bank), and it must act consistently with the terms of the restrictive indorsement. Therefore, it must credit account #4921 with the money or be liable to Barton for conversion. Elliot's check leaves the Miami bank indorsed "for collection." As the check moves through the collection network of intermediary banks to Elliot's New York bank for payment, each intermediary bank is only bound by the preceding bank's indorsement to collect.

The division of responsibility between types of banks is necessary. Collecting banks process huge numbers of commercial instruments, and there is no practical way for them to examine and comply with the effect of each restrictive indorsement. Therefore, the only reasonable alternative is to charge the depositary bank with the responsibility of examining and complying with any restrictive indorsements.

CHECK COLLECTION BETWEEN CUSTOMERS OF THE SAME BANK An item payable by the depositary bank that receives it is called an "on-us item." If the bank does not dishonor the check by the opening of the second banking day following its receipt, it is considered paid [UCC 4-213(4)(b)]. For example, Harriman and Goldsmith each have a checking account at First National Bank. On Monday morning, Goldsmith deposits into his own checking account a $300 check from Harriman. That same day, First National issues Goldsmith a "provisional credit" for $300. When the bank opens on Wednesday, Harriman's check is considered honored and Goldsmith's provisional credit becomes a final payment.

CHECK COLLECTION BETWEEN CUSTOMERS OF DIFFERENT BANKS Once a depositary bank receives a check, it must arrange to present it either directly or through intermediary banks to the appropriate payor bank. Each bank in the collection chain must pass the check on before midnight of the next banking day following its receipt [UCC 4-202(2)]. Thus, for example, a collecting bank that receives a check on Monday must forward it to the next collection bank before midnight on Tuesday. Unless the payor bank dishonors the check or returns it by midnight on the next banking day following receipt, the payor bank is accountable for the face amount of the check [UCC 4-302].

To facilitate an even flow of the many items handled by banks daily, the Code permits what is called deferred posting, or delayed return. *Deferred posting* permits posting of checks received after a certain time (say 2:00 P.M.) to be deferred until the next day. Thus, a check received by a payor bank at 3:00 P.M. on Monday would be deferred for posting until Tuesday. In this case, the payor bank's deadline would be midnight Wednesday [UCC 4-301(1)].

THE FEDERAL RESERVE SYSTEM CLEARS CHECKS The Federal Reserve System has greatly simplified the clearing of checks—that is, the method by which checks deposited in one bank are transferred to the banks on which they were written. Suppose Samuel Evans of Chicago writes a check to John Lucky of San Francisco. When Lucky receives the check in the mail, he deposits it in his bank. His bank then deposits the check in the Federal Reserve Bank of San Francisco, which sends the check to the Federal Reserve Bank of Chicago. That Federal Reserve Bank then sends the check to Evans's bank, where the amount of the check is deducted from Evans's account. Exhibit 27–6 illustrates this process.

EXPEDITED FUNDS AVAILABILITY ACT In 1987, Congress passed an act to improve the check-processing system and to shorten the period between the time a customer deposits funds and the time the funds are made available to the customer. The major problem Congress addressed in this legislation was the practice by which depository institutions (depositary banks) placed a "hold" on deposited checks—that is, did not allow the depositor to draw on these funds (either as cash or by means of a check) until the check had been honored (paid) by the payor bank. Many hold periods were lengthy, and many institutions placed holds lasting a week or longer even on deposited government checks.

The act, known as the Expedited Funds Availability Act (12 U.S.C. Section 4001 *et seq.*), required that a temporary "availability" schedule be effected by September 1, 1988, and that a permanent schedule be implemented by the Federal Reserve on or before September 1, 1990. Basically, under the temporary availability schedule, any local check deposited must be available for withdrawal by check or as cash within two business days from the date of deposit. The Federal Reserve Board has designated check processing regions, and if the depositary and payor banks are located in the same region, the check is classified as a local check. For nonlocal checks, the avail-

Exhibit 27–6 How a Check Is Cleared

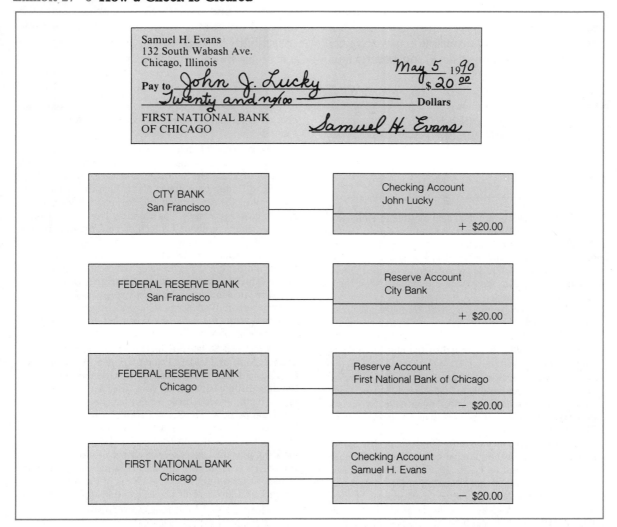

ability period for withdrawal is not more than six business days. By September 1, 1990, these time periods are to be reduced to one business day (for local checks) and four business days (for nonlocal checks).

In addition, the act requires the following:

1. That funds be available on the *next business day* for cash deposits and wire transfers, government checks, the first $100 of a day's check deposits, cashier's checks, certified checks, and checks for which the depositary and payor banks are branches of the same institution.

2. That, for cash withdrawals, the first $100 of any deposit be available on the opening of the next

business day after deposit. If a local check was deposited, the next $400 will be available for withdrawal by no later than 5:00 P.M. the next business day. The remainder will be available as provided in the schedule. If, for example, you deposit a local check for $500 on Monday, you can withdraw $100 in cash at the opening of the business day on Tuesday, and an additional $400 must be available for withdrawal by no later than 5:00 P.M. on Wednesday.

There is a different availability schedule for deposits made at *nonproprietary* automated teller machines (ATMs)—ATM machines that are not owned or operated by the depository institution.

Basically, a six-day hold is permitted on all deposits, including cash deposits, made at nonproprietary ATMs. Also, a depository institution has eight days to make funds available in new accounts (those open less than thirty days) and an extra four days on deposits over $5,000 (except deposits of government and cashier's checks), on accounts with repeated overdrafts, or on checks of questionable collectibility (if the institution tells the depositor it suspects fraud or insolvency).

QUESTIONS AND CASE PROBLEMS

1. Daniel drafts a check for $1,000 payable to Paula and drawn on the West Bank. After issue of the check, Paula, by blank indorsement, negotiates the check to Fred. Fred finds an ideal real estate lot for sale, but to close the deal he needs to make a $1,000 down payment by certified check. Fred takes the check to West Bank and requests West Bank to certify Daniel's check.

(a) If West Bank refuses to certify Daniel's check, can either Daniel or Fred hold the bank liable? Explain.

(b) If West Bank certifies the check, explain fully the liability of Daniel as drawer to Fred and to Paula as indorser.

2. On January 5, Daniel drafts a check for $3,000 drawn on the East Bank and payable to his secretary, Sylvia. Daniel puts last year's date on the check by mistake. Sylvia has not yet cashed the check at the East Bank when, on January 7, Daniel is killed in an automobile accident. The East Bank is aware of Daniel's death. On January 10, Sylvia presents the check to the East Bank, and the bank honors the check by payment to Sylvia. Daniel's widow, Martha, claims that the East Bank has wrongfully paid Sylvia, since it knew of Daniel's death and since the check was by date over one year old. Martha, as executrix of Daniel's estate and sole heir by his will, demands that East Bank recredit Daniel's estate for the check paid Sylvia. Discuss fully East Bank's liability in light of Martha's demand.

3. Daniel goes grocery shopping and carelessly leaves his checkbook in his shopping cart. His checkbook, with two blank checks remaining, is stolen by Thomas. On May 5, Thomas forges Daniel's name on a check for $100 and cashes the check at Daniel's bank, the First Bank of Jonestown. Daniel has not reported the theft to his bank. On June 1, Daniel receives his monthly bank statement and canceled checks from Jonestown Bank, including the forged check by Thomas. Daniel does not reconcile his checking account. On June 20, Thomas forges Daniel's last check. This check is for $1,000 and is cashed at the West Bank, a bank with which Thomas has previously done business. The West Bank sends the check through the collection process, and the Jonestown Bank honors it. On July 1, upon receipt of Jonestown Bank's statement and canceled checks, Daniel discovers both forgeries and immediately notifies Jonestown Bank. Thomas cannot be found. Daniel claims that Jonestown must recredit his account for both checks, as his signature was forged. Discuss fully Daniel's claim.

4. Diana takes her television set to Honest John's TV Service Store for repairs. The set is supposedly repaired, at a cost of $125. On Saturday, Diana writes out a check payable to Honest John drawn on the First Greenville Bank. Diana takes the set home and discovers that virtually no repairs have been made. On Monday, Diana calls Honest John to complain about his lack of performance. Honest John insists the repairs were made and refuses even to look at the television set. Diana immediately calls the First Greenville Bank and issues a stop-payment order over the phone. Three weeks later, Honest John cashes Diana's check at a drive-in window of the First Greenville Bank. Diana is furious upon discovery of the bank's payment to Honest John and wants the bank to recredit her account. Discuss fully the First Greenville Bank's liability in this matter.

5. Daniel has $5,000 in his checking account with the Second Bank of Fielder. Daniel writes a check for $500 payable to Peter. This check is in settlement of a long-standing dispute between the two. Peter deposits the check in his bank. Peter's bank sends the check through the collection process. The Second Bank, by mistake, returns the check to Peter's bank marked "insufficient funds." Peter's bank returns the check to Peter, charging his account for $500, plus the bank's service charge of $10 for returned checks. Peter is furious and files criminal charges against Daniel. Discuss fully the Second Bank of Fielder's liability for wrongful dishonor of Daniel's check.

6. In September 1976, Edward and Christine McSweeney opened a joint checking account with the United States Trust Company of New York. Between April and July of 1978, 195 checks totaling $99,063 were written. In July 1978, activity in the account ceased. Ninety-five of the 195 checks, totaling $16,811, were written by Christine, and the balance were written by Edward. After crediting of deposits during the period, the checks amounted to a cumulative overdraft of $75,983. Can a bank knowingly honor a check when payment creates an overdraft, or must the bank dishonor the check? If the bank pays a check creating an overdraft, can the bank collect the amount of overdraft from its customer? [U.S. Trust Company of New York v. McSweeney, 91 A.D.2d 7, 457 N.Y.S.2d 276 (1982)]

7. Rees Plumbing Company, Inc., and Weldon Douglas both maintained checking accounts at the Citizens Bank of Jonesboro. On August 19, 1966, Rees drew a check payable to Douglas in the amount of $1,000 and delivered it to Douglas. On that same day, Douglas presented the check to Citizens Bank for deposit in his own checking account. Deposit slips were prepared, and a teller of the bank stamped the back of the check with the August 19 date and the statement "pay to any bank—prior indorsement guaranteed, Citizens Bank of Jonesboro, Jonesboro, Arkansas." On August 20, 1966, the bank dishonored the check because of insufficient funds and debited the amount of the check from Douglas's account. Did the bank, by stamping the indorsement on the check deposited by Douglas and by delivering a deposit slip to Douglas, "accept" the check? Assume that instead of giving Douglas a provisional credit to his account, the Citizens Bank had cashed the check. Could it then have debited Douglas's account upon dishonor of the check? [Douglas v. Citizens Bank of Jonesboro, 244 Ark. 168, 424 S.W.2d 532 (1968)]

8. Reinhard purchased a cashier's check made payable to The Patchworks Co. from Marine Midland Bank. The check was delivered to The Patchworks in exchange for goods purchased by Reinhard. Because he was dissatisfied with the goods, Reinhard told the bank that he had lost the check and asked that payment be stopped. Can Reinhard stop payment? [Moon Over the Mountain, Ltd. v. Marine Midland Bank, 87 Misc.2d 918, 386 N.Y.S.2d 974 (1976)]

9. Northwest Shopping Center owned and operated a shopping center in Texas. Kaiser was one of its tenants. Pursuant to the rental agreement, Kaiser paid a monthly rent of $500 with a check that it mailed to Northwest. Northwest retained one of these rent checks for over nine months. If Northwest then presented it to Kaiser's bank for payment, was the bank obligated to pay? If the bank refused to pay, was Kaiser still liable? [Kaiser v. Northwest Shopping Center, 544 S.W.2d 785 (Tex. Civ. App. 1976)]

10. Ralston pledged stock certificates as collateral for a loan. The proceeds of the loan, $38,000, were used to open a new checking account at the lending bank. Ralston immediately had the bank certify a $21,000 check payable to a second bank. Later that day the lending bank learned that the stock certificates were stolen and notified the payee bank that certification of the check was rescinded. The payee bank had accepted the check for deposit to Ralston's account but had given no value for it (no checks had been honored against the deposit). As a holder of the certified check, could the payee bank prevent the lending bank's revocation of certification? [Rockland Trust Co. v. South Shore National Bank, 366 Mass. 74, 314 N.E.2d 438 (1974)].

11. [image] Susan Wolf forged her employer's name on more than ninety checks drawn on the employer's bank account. The bank cashed the checks, debiting the employer's account, and Wolf wrongfully received a total of more than $22,500. When the forgeries were discovered, the employer brought a criminal action against Wolf but later dropped the charges and settled out of court. The employer also demanded that the bank credit its account for the amount of the forged checks. The bank refused. Assuming there was no evidence that the employer's negligence had substantially contributed to the forgery, was the employer entitled to have the bank credit its account? [SCCI, Inc. v. United States National Bank of Oregon, 78 Or.App. 176, 714 P.2d 1113 (1986)]

12. On September 14 Parr sent a check to Champlin Oil Company in payment of a bill she owed them. On September 15 she called the bank and requested that payment on the check be stopped. She gave the bank her account number and the check number, the date the check was written, the payee on the check, and the amount. All information was correctly given to the bank except for the amount, which was substantially different than what she had actually written on the check. On September 16 she went to the bank and executed a written stop-payment order. The written order also contained the erroneous amount. On September 17, the bank paid the check. Parr sued the bank for wrongfully paying the check over her stop-payment order. The bank claimed that Parr's error on the stop-payment request concerning the amount of the check relieved it of liability. Will the bank succeed in this defense? Explain. [Parr v. Security National Bank, 680 P.2d 648 (Okl.App. 1984)]

13. In July of 1979 Read & Read, Inc., a corporation owned by Thomas and Emerson Read, hired Judy Bode as a sales secretary. She was promoted to executive secretary shortly thereafter and worked primarily for Emerson Read. Judy Bode eventually assumed responsibility for overseeing nearly all of Read's checking accounts, including his personal account. She also reviewed the bank statements for each account and reconciled them to the corresponding checkbooks. As a result of a hunting accident, Mr. Read lost his hand and, to facilitate check signing, had a rubber signature stamp made. Ms. Bode had easy access to the stamp. From September 1980 until January 1981, Ms. Bode used the rubber stamp to forge a total of fourteen checks for her own purposes on Read's accounts, including one check for over $8,000. Read, who did not review any bank statements during this entire period of time, was unaware of the forgeries. When the forgeries were discovered in January of 1981, Read sued his bank, the South Carolina National Bank, to recover the amount of the forged checks that he alleged had been wrongfully honored by the bank. The trial court held for the bank, and Read appealed. Can Read recover from the bank the funds lost as a result of Judy Bode's forgeries? [Read v. South Carolina National Bank, 286 S.C. 534, 335 S.E.2d 359 (1985)]

Chapter 28

Electronic Fund Transfers

The application of computer technology to banking, in the form of **electronic fund transfer systems (EFTS),** promises to relieve banking institutions of the burden of having to move mountains of paperwork in order to process fund transfers. An **electronic fund transfer** is a transfer of money made with the use of an electronic terminal, a telephone, a computer, or magnetic tape. Automatic payments, direct deposits, and other fund transfers are now made electronically; no physical transfers of cash, checks, or other negotiable instruments are involved. Through the use of EFTS, transactions that would otherwise take days can now be completed in minutes. For example, Hannah in New York could pay a debt to Barbara in Miami by entering into a computer a bank order to pay it. Chase Manhattan, the drawee bank, could instantly debit Hannah's account and transfer the credit to the First National Bank of Miami, Barbara's bank, which could immediately credit her account. EFT transactions eliminate the **float time** that the drawer of a check currently enjoys by retaining the use of funds during the period between the check's issuance and final payment.

Electronic fund transfers are governed by contract law. Consumer transactions utilizing EFTS, however, are subject to the Electronic Fund Transfer Act,[1] which was passed in 1978 and went into full effect in 1980. Currently, a committee of the Permanent Editorial Board of the Uniform Commercial Code is cooperating with the American Law Institute in drafting a Uniform New Payments Code (UNPC) covering EFTS, as well as all other payment systems except those involving cash.

TYPES OF ELECTRONIC TRANSFERS

There are principally four types of EFTS in use: (1) automated teller machines, (2) point-of-sale systems, (3) systems handling direct deposits and withdrawals of funds, and (4) pay-by-telephone systems. To initiate a transaction on one of the machines involved, a consumer often uses a card that provides access to the computer system. Each card has an accompanying

---

1. 15 U.S.C. Section 1693 *et seq.*

personal identification number (PIN) that is given only to the account holder—a number that is meant to be kept secret so as to inhibit others' use of the card. A sample access card is shown in Exhibit 28–1.

Automated Teller Machines

A major EFTS development has involved the **automated teller machine (ATM),** also called a customer-bank communication terminal or remote service unit. ATMs are located either on a bank's premises or at convenient locations such as supermarkets, drugstores, and shopping centers. Once the access card activates an ATM, the ATM can receive deposits, dispense funds from checking or savings accounts, transfer funds between accounts, make credit card advances, and receive payments on loan accounts. ATMs are usually connected on-line to the bank's computers.

Point-of-Sale Systems

Point-of-sale systems allow consumers to transfer funds to merchants to pay for purchases. On-line terminals are located at checkout counters in, for example, grocery stores. Instead of receiving cash or a check from the customer, the checkout person inserts the customer's card into a terminal, which reads the data encoded on the card. The computer at the customer's bank verifies that the card and identification code are valid and that there are enough funds in the customer's account to cover the purchase. After the payment is made, the customer's account is debited for the amount of the purchase.

For the grocer, direct payment from customers by means of point-of-sale systems involves, under current law, less risk of nonpayment or "bounced" checks. For the customer, the electronic transfer makes bills and check writing unnecessary.

Direct Deposits and Withdrawals

Automated clearinghouses are similar to the ordinary clearinghouses in which checks are cleared between banks. The main difference is that entries are made in the form of electronic signals; no checks are used. Thus, these systems do not further automate the handling of checks; they replace checks. This type of EFTS allows a bank to complete a transaction for less than the cost of clearing a check.

A direct deposit may be made to a customer's account through an electronic terminal when the customer has authorized the deposit in advance. The federal government often uses this EFTS to deposit Social Security payments directly into beneficiaries' accounts. Similarly, an employer may agree to make payroll and pension payments directly into an employee's account at specified intervals.

A customer may also authorize the bank (or other financial institution at which the customer's

Exhibit 28–1 A Sample Access Card

a. Front Side

b. Back Side

©1988 by Home Federal. Reprinted with permission.

funds are on deposit) to make automatic payments at regular, recurrent intervals to a third party. For example, insurance premiums, utility bills, and home mortgage and automobile installment loan payments may sometimes be made automatically.

Pay-by-Telephone Systems

When it is undesirable to arrange in advance for an automatic payment—as, for example, when the amount of a regular payment varies—some financial institutions permit their customers to pay bills through a pay-by-telephone system. This allows the customer to access the institution's computer system by telephone and direct a transfer of funds. Utility bills frequently are paid directly by customers using pay-by-telephone systems. Customers may also be permitted to transfer funds between accounts—for example, to withdraw funds from a savings account and make a deposit in a checking account—in this way.

CONSUMER TRANSFERS: THE ELECTRONIC FUND TRANSFER ACT

Congress stated in 1978 that the use of electronic systems to transfer funds promised to provide substantial benefits for consumers. But Congress also concluded that, given the unique characteristics of EFTS, existing consumer protection legislation governing the rights and obligations of consumers, financial institutions, and intermediaries was inadequate with respect to the types of fund transfers occurring by means of EFTS. Thus, in 1978, Congress passed the Electronic Fund Transfer Act (EFTA) "to provide a basic framework establishing the rights, liabilities, and responsibilities of participants in electronic fund transfers." The EFTA is essentially a disclosure law benefiting consumers; it requires financial institutions to inform consumers of their rights with respect to EFTS. The EFTA is not concerned with commercial electronic fund transfers—transfers between businesses or between businesses and financial institutions.

Under the EFTA, the Federal Reserve System's board of governors is authorized to administer the act and to promulgate regulations to carry out the purposes of the act. The board of gover-

nors has issued a set of rules, called **Regulation E,** to protect users of EFTS; this regulation should be consulted for a complete understanding of the EFTA. Also, the board has drafted model clauses for financial institutions that utilize electronic systems to use in disclosing information.

Institutions and Transactions Covered

The EFTA governs financial institutions that offer electronic fund transfers involving a customer's account. The EFTA defines **financial institutions** to include banks, savings and loan institutions, credit unions, and any other business entities that directly or indirectly hold accounts belonging to consumers. Thus, securities brokerage houses that permit consumers to make electronic transfers to and from money market fund accounts are included.

The types of accounts covered include demand accounts, savings accounts, and other asset accounts established for personal, family, or household purposes. All electronic fund transfers involving such accounts are covered by the EFTA. Note that, although telephone transfers are included in the definition of an electronic fund transfer, they are only covered by the EFTA if they are made *pursuant to a prearranged plan under which periodic or recurring transfers are contemplated*. This holds even if an imposter, posing as an account holder, calls a bank official and requests a fund transfer. If the bank complies with the request, the owner of the account cannot hold the bank liable, under the EFTA, for the erroneously transferred funds. This does not mean that the owner has no legal recourse to recover the funds; it simply means that his or her cause of action will not lie under the EFTA.[2]

Disclosure of Terms and Conditions

The EFTA requires that the terms and conditions of electronic fund transfers involving a customer's account must be disclosed in readily understandable language at the time the customer contracts for the services. Included among the required disclosures are:

1. The customer's liability for unauthorized transfers resulting from the loss or theft of the card, code, or other access device.

2. Kashanchi v. Texas Commerce Medical Bank, N.A., 703 F.2d 936 (5th Cir. 1983).

2. Whom and what phone number to call to report a theft or loss.

3. The charges for using the EFTS.

4. What systems are available and the limits on frequency and dollar amounts.

5. The customer's right to see evidence of transactions in writing.

6. How errors can be corrected.

7. The customer's right to stop payments.

8. The financial institution's liability to the customer.

9. Rules concerning disclosure of account information to third parties.

Exhibit 28–2 shows a disclosure form containing the requisite information.

Documentation Regarding Transactions

The EFTA considerably reduces the amount of paper used in transferring funds. Financial institutions are required to provide the customer with written documentation—a receipt—of each transfer made from an electronic terminal at the time of the transfer. (Receipts are not required for telephone transfers, even when a telephone transfer is otherwise subject to the EFTA.) The receipt must clearly state the date, the type of transfer, the amount, the identity of the customer's account, the identity of any third party involved (such as a merchant accepting the customer's card as a means of paying for purchased goods), and the location of the terminal involved. Exhibit 28–3 shows an automatic teller machine (ATM) transaction receipt.

In addition, financial institutions must give customers periodic statements describing types, amounts, dates, transferees, and locations of transfers for each account through which an EFTS provides access. The type of account and the frequency with which the customer uses it determine the timing of the statements. Monthly statements are required for every month in which there is an electronic transfer of funds. Otherwise, statements must be provided quarterly.

The statement must show the amount and date of the transfer, the fees charged, the location or identification of the terminal, and the name of the retailer or third party, if any, involved. Also, the statement must provide an address and phone number for inquiries and error notices.

Financial institutions must also notify customers if an automatic deposit is not made as scheduled. This helps customers to avoid overdrawing their accounts.

Preauthorized Transfers

A **preauthorized transfer** is a transaction authorized in advance to recur at substantially regular intervals. For example, an employee may be able to arrange with an employer and a bank for the direct deposit of payroll checks into his or her checking account. Similarly, an individual might authorize a monthly transfer from his or her account to pay insurance premiums or installments on a home mortgage or automobile loan.

A credit to a customer's account from the same payor at least once in each successive sixty-day period requires the financial institution to notify the customer, if the payor does not, when the credit is made, or, as noted in the preceding section, if it is not made as scheduled. When the service is contracted for, the parties can agree on the manner of notice. In other words, if an employee has arranged with his or her employer for the direct deposit of weekly payroll checks, the bank handling the receipt of the checks must notify the employee weekly, if the employer does not, whether a check has been deposited as arranged.

As its name implies, a preauthorized transfer must be authorized by the customer in advance. The authorization must be in writing, and a copy of it must be provided to the customer when it is made. To stop payment of a preauthorized EFT, a customer may notify the financial institution orally or in writing at any time up to three business days before the scheduled date of the transfer. The institution may require the customer to provide written confirmation within fourteen days of an oral notification. For example, suppose Temple has arranged with his bank, Manufacturers Hanover Trust, to have the bank make automatic payments on his automobile installment loan. If Temple wishes to make a given payment on the loan personally, he must order the bank more than three days before the automatic payment is scheduled to be made not to make the payment.

Stop Payment and Reversibility

Under the EFTA, then, a customer may cancel a *preauthorized* transfer before the transfer is made,

Exhibit 28–2 A Sample Form Disclosing Terms and Conditions as Required under the EFTA

This disclosure contains the terms and conditions for all Home Federal electronic banking services, in addition to specific information about pre-authorized electronic payments and deposits.

As someone who uses these services, you should read this information, as it pertains to your rights and responsibilities, as well as the terms and conditions of their use.

Electronic transactions may be payments or deposits, authorized by you, to or from your checking or savings account(s) or loan(s), or to or from a third party. They include:
- Anytimeteller℠ transactions
- STAR SYSTEM® network transactions
- EXPLORE℠ point-of-sale network (participating gas stations, grocery stores, and other merchants) transactions
- Pre-authorized debits and credits (includes Automatic Payroll Deposit)
- Direct Deposit service
- Telephone Transfer service
- SurePay (automatic loan payments and electronic deposit or payment transactions to or from your checking or savings account)
- Electronic payment or deposit transactions to or from your checking or savings account through an Automated Clearing House (ACH)

Business Days

Our business days are Monday through Friday, except holidays. When allowing processing time, it is important to only count business days. Weekends and holidays are not considered business days.

Privacy

Home Federal may disclose account information to third parties under any of the following conditions:
1. Where it is necessary for completing transfers;
2. To verify the existence and condition of your account for a third party, such as a credit bureau or merchant;
3. To comply with a legitimate request from a government agency, or a court order;
4. With your written permission.

Home Federal Liability/Change of Terms

If Home Federal does not complete a transfer to or from your account at the specified time, or in the specified amount, according to our Agreement with you, we will be liable for any losses or damages to you, with these exceptions:

Home Federal will not be liable if:
1. There are insufficient funds in your account to make a transfer or payment, for reasons beyond the control of this Association;
2. A transfer would exceed the credit limit on your line of credit;
3. The electronic banking system or terminal was not working properly at the time you initiated a transfer, and you were aware of this malfunction.

Home Federal may cease to offer any electronic banking service at any time. Service users will be given prior notice of any such change in policy.

Home Federal may change any term of the Agreement, including changes which will affect your cost or liability, by giving you at least 21 days written notice.

NOTE: There may be additional exceptions which apply, as stated in our Agreement with you.

Errors and Questions

In case of errors or questions about your electronic transactions, please contact your branch of account. Home Federal must hear from you within 60 days from the date of the first statement on which the problem or error appears. Failure to do so may result in your being held fully liable for the amount of the error.

Notification by phone or in person requires a written follow-up within 10 working days.

To Resolve an Error

When notifying Home Federal in writing of a suspected error:
1. Include your name, address, and account number.
2. Describe in detail the transaction in question and explain as clearly as you can why you believe it is an error or why you need more information.
3. Indicate the dollar amount of the suspected error.

Home Federal will investigate the error and report to you, usually within 10 business days.

Point-of-sale transactions, however, may take up to 20 business days to investigate.

We may take up to 45 days to investigate a reported error. If so, Home Federal will provisionally recredit your account within 10 business days (or 20 days for point-of-sale transactions) for the amount in question, so that you may have use of the money during the investigation period. This recrediting to your account may not occur if we have not received your notification in writing within the 10 business days.

If it is determined that no error occurred, we will notify you in writing within 3 business days following the investigation. Any amounts recredited to your account during the course of the investigation will be debited from your account. Copies of documents used in our investigation will be available to you upon request.

Anytimecard℠ Safety

For your protection, please:
1. Be sure to keep your Anytimecard in a safe place, and don't allow anyone to use it.
2. Keep your Personal Identification Number (PIN) a secret. Do not write it on your Anytimecard or otherwise make it available to anyone.
3. Notify Home Federal immediately of any loss, theft, or unauthorized use of your Anytimecard or PIN. Lost or stolen Anytimecards can be reported 24 hours a day, 7 days a week.

Anytimecard Consumer Liability

1. It is your responsibility to notify Home Federal immediately if your Anytimecard and/or Personal Identification Number (PIN) has been lost or stolen. Provided you notify Home Federal within 2 business days after you discover the possible loss or theft, your loss will be limited to a maximum of $50 if your Anytimecard and PIN are used without your permission.
2. If you fail to notify Home Federal within 2 business days of the possible loss or theft of your Anytimecard or PIN, and it can be proven that such notification could have prevented the unauthorized use of your Anytimecard or PIN, your loss could be as much as $500.
3. If you fail to notify Home Federal within 60 days, and it can be proven that such notification could have prevented the unauthorized use of your Anytimecard or PIN, you may not be able to recover

©1988 Home Federal. Reprinted with permission.

Exhibit 28–3 An ATM Receipt

ments provided by the financial institution handling his or her account or accounts. Within sixty days after the institution has sent a statement, the customer must notify the institution of any errors that appear on it. Whether oral or written, the notice must contain the following information:

1. The customer's name and account number.
2. A sentence stating that an error has been made and its alleged amount.
3. The reasons the customer believes an error has been made.

The institution is required to investigate and report the results within ten business days. If the institution needs more than ten days, it may take up to forty-five, but it must recredit the customer's account for the amount alleged to be in error until the problem is resolved. If it determines that an error did occur, it has one business day to adjust the customer's account. Even if no mistake has been made, the institution has to give the customer a full, written report with conclusions. Failure to investigate in good faith makes the institution liable to the customer for **treble damages**—three times the amount of provable damages.

Banks are held to strict compliance with the terms of the EFTA, and if they fail to adhere to the letter of the law of the EFTA they will be held liable for violation, as is illustrated in the following case.

just as a drawer—the person who signs a check—may stop payment on a check before it is paid. For other EFT transactions, however, the EFTA does not provide for the reversal of an electronic transfer of funds, once it has occurred. This is because the uniquely instantaneous nature of an electronic transfer of funds provides no float time during which an effective reversal of an order to pay can be made.

Mistakes and Corrections

Under the EFTA, a customer has a duty to examine the periodic—monthly or quarterly—state-

---

BACKGROUND AND FACTS *Ms. Bisbey (the plaintiff) opened a checking account with the District of Columbia National Bank (the defendant) in January of 1981. Subsequently, she authorized the bank to debit her checking account for fund transfer directives that were submitted monthly by the New York Life Insurance Company (NYLIC) for payment of her insurance premiums. In September 1981, Ms. Bisbey's account lacked sufficient funds to cover the insurance directive, and no transfer was made. NYLIC resubmitted the September directive in October, with the October monthly directive. Bisbey's funds were insufficient to satisfy either submission, but the bank covered the premiums. As a result, two overdraft notices were sent to Bisbey, each in the amount of her monthly insurance premium. Bisbey, having forgotten her nonpayment in September, believed that the bank had erroneously made two payments in October. At this point, Bisbey informed a customer representative of the bank that she believed that an error had occurred with regard to the preauthorized transfers. Approximately ten days later, an official of the bank telephoned Bisbey*

Case 28.1
**BISBEY v. D.C.
NATIONAL BANK**
United States Court of Appeals,
District of Columbia Circuit,
1986.
793 F.2d 315.

and orally explained that there had been no improper duplication of her insurance premiums. Bisbey, however, still considered the matter unresolved, and she filed suit under the EFTA, alleging that the bank had unlawfully failed to properly advise her about the result of its investigation into the alleged duplication error in the transfers from her checking account. Under the EFTA, a bank's notification to a customer that no error has been made must be in writing. The trial court ruled in favor of the bank, and Bisbey appealed.

EDWARDS, Circuit Judge.

* * * *

* * * Section 908(d) of the [Electronic Fund Transfer] Act imposed a duty upon the Bank to "deliver or mail" the results of its investigation to Ms. Bisbey and to advise her of her right to request reproductions of all documents which it relied upon to conclude that no error occurred. The oral notice given to appellant was insufficient with respect to the [statute's] required "explanation," and it did not even purport to give "notice of the right to request reproductions" as required by the statute.

The Bank's foregoing failures to comply with the statute give rise to civil liability under section 915 of the Act. That section provides that "any person who fails to comply with any provision of [the Act] with respect to any consumer, except for an error resolved in accordance with section 908, is liable to such consumer" for actual damages or for a symbolic award. Thus, under the plain terms of the Act, civil liability attaches to *all* failures of compliance with respect to *any* provision of the Act, including Section 908.

* * * *

It may seem odd that the Bank is held liable for a transaction that benefited the plaintiff. Ms. Bisbey's account contained insufficient funds to cover either of the premium requests submitted by NYLIC. Though she had no overdraft agreement, the Bank did not charge an overdraft fee. Thus, the effect of the Bank's payments was to provide her, at no cost, with insurance coverage she would not have had otherwise. Upon Bisbey's inquiry, the Bank gave her a correct report but neglected to send it in writing, as the statute requires. Ms. Bisbey conceded below that she had suffered no damage and the District Court's surmise that she may have been benefited seems correct. Despite this, the litigation has continued for nearly three years, and the statute compels a finding that the Bank is liable. * * *

The "fail[ure]s to comply" with the EFTA in the instant case are plain; moreover, they are failures to which civil liability attaches for they have not been resolved in accordance with section 908. * * *

DECISION AND REMEDY   *The court of appeals reversed the trial court's decision and remanded the case to the lower court for determination of the amount of an award of damages and attorneys' fees.*

COMMENTS   *Although there was no evidence of bad faith on the part of the bank and the plaintiff did not suffer a loss, it is nonetheless clear that the bank officials failed to comply with the provisions of the EFTA. Thus, the bank was held liable for violating the provisions of the act.*

Customer Liability for Unauthorized Transfers

Before a customer can be held liable for any unauthorized transfer, under the EFTA, it must be established that the transfer resulted from the use of an accepted means of access and that the customer had been provided with a means of identifying himself or herself to that means of access. For example, a bank's customer will not be held liable for unauthorized withdrawals from the customer's checking account unless the bank has provided the customer with a card (such as the one illustrated in Exhibit 28–1) and a secret number for access to the bank's EFTS.

In the event that the access card or other device is lost, stolen, or misplaced, the EFTA limits the customer's liability for any unauthorized transfers of funds to $50 if the customer notifies the financial institution within two business days of learning of the loss or theft. If the customer does not inform the institution until after the second day, his or her liability climbs to $500. The customer's liability may be unlimited if notification does not occur within sixty days of the customer's receipt of a periodic statement that reflects an unauthorized transfer.

To recover, the institution must prove first that the customer and the institution had an agreement under which the customer agreed to this liability and second that the customer knew that the access device had been lost, stolen, or misplaced. In the case of an unauthorized transfer appearing on the statement, the institution must show that any loss of funds due to the unauthorized transfer would not have occurred but for the customer's failure to report the unauthorized transfer's appearance on the statement within sixty days of the statement's transmittal.

To illustrate: On May 1, Wistful goes to an automatic teller machine belonging to Citicorp, his bank, to make a withdrawal from his checking account. He discovers that his access card is missing but fails to tell Citicorp until May 15. On May 12, Warp, a thief, made a $100 withdrawal from the account using Wistful's card and number. Wistful, as the account's owner, is liable for the full $100 because Wistful did not notify Citicorp that the card had been stolen or lost prior to Warp's illegal withdrawal. If Wistful had failed to tell Citicorp at all that the card was missing and Warp had continued to use it to withdraw funds, Wistful could have been held liable for the entire amount withdrawn.

The following case involves a bank customer who, trying to do a good deed, allowed another person (an alleged bank representative) to use his access card. The alleged bank representative, who had earlier surreptitiously observed the customer enter his PIN into the ATM, withdrew funds from the customer's account. The issue before the court is whether these actions resulted in an authorized or an unauthorized transfer of funds.

BACKGROUND AND FACTS   *Frederick P. Ognibene (the plaintiff) sought to recover from Citibank (the defendant) $400 that had been withdrawn from his account at the defendant bank by an unauthorized person using an automated teller machine. Ognibene claimed that he was the victim of a scam that the defendant had been aware of for some time. On August 16, 1981, Ognibene went to the ATM area at one of the defendant's branches and activated one of the machines with his Citibank card. He pressed in his personal identification code and withdrew $20. While he did this, a person who was using the telephone between Ognibene's machine and the adjoining machine said into the telephone, "I'll see if his card works in my machine." Thereupon the stranger, purporting to be a bank representative, asked Ognibene if he could use Ognibene's card to check whether the other machine was working. Ognibene handed the card to him and saw him insert it into the adjoining machine at least two times while stating into the telephone, "Yes, it seems to be working." The bank's computer records in evidence showed that two withdrawals of $200 each from Ognibene's account were made on August 16, 1981, on the machine adjoining the one Ognibene used for his $20 withdrawal. The two $200 withdrawals were made at 5:42 P.M. and 5:43 P.M.; Ognibene's $20 withdrawal was made at 5:41 P.M. At the time, Ognibene was unaware that any withdrawals from his account were being made on the adjoining machine. After later learning that $400 had been withdrawn from his checking account, Ognibene filed suit against the bank under the Electronic Fund Transfer Act, alleging that, since the withdrawal was not authorized by him, the bank should bear the loss.*

Case 28.2
OGNIBENE v. CITIBANK, N.A.
Civil Court of the City of New York, 1981.
112 Misc.2d 219, 446 N.Y.S.2d 845.

THORPE, Judge.

*   *   *   *

The EFT Act places various limits on a consumer's liability for electronic fund transfers from his account if they are "unauthorized." Insofar as is relevant here, a transfer is "unauthorized" if (1) it is initiated by a person other than the consumer and without actual authority to initiate such transfer, (2) the consumer receives no benefit from it, and (3) the consumer did not furnish such person "with the card, code, or other means of access" to his account. *   *   *

*   *   *   *

The EFT Act requires that the consumer have furnished to a person initiating the transfer the "card, code, or other means of access" to his account to be ineligible for the limitations on liability afforded by the act when transfers are "unauthorized." The evidence establishes that in order to obtain access to an account via an automated teller machine, both the card and the personal identification code must be used. Thus, by merely giving his card to the person initiating the transfer, a consumer does not furnish the "means of access" to his account. To do so, he would have to furnish the personal identification code as well. *   *   *

The court finds that plaintiff did not furnish his personal identification code to the person initiating the $400 transfer within the meaning of the EFT Act. There is no evidence that he deliberately or even negligently did so. On the contrary, the unauthorized person was able to obtain the code because of defendant's own negligence. Since the bank had knowledge of the scam and its operational details (including the central role of the customer service telephone), it was negligent in failing to provide plaintiff customer with information sufficient to alert him to the danger when he found himself in the position of a potential victim. Although in June, 1981, after the scam came to the defendant's attention, it posted signs in its ATM areas containing a red circle approximately 2½ inches in diameter in which is written "Do Not Let Your Citicard Be Used For Any Transaction But Your Own," the court finds that this printed admonition is not a sufficient security measure since it fails to state the reason why one should not do so. Since a customer of defendant's electronic fund transfer service must employ both the card and the personal identification code in order to withdraw money from his account, the danger of loaning his card briefly for the purpose of checking the functioning of an adjoining automated teller machine would not be immediately apparent to one who has not divulged his personal identification number and who is unaware that it has been revealed merely by virtue of his own transaction with the machine.

Since the bank established the electronic fund transfer service and has the ability to tighten its security characteristics, the responsibility for the fact that plaintiff's code, one of the two necessary components of the "access device" or "means of access" to his account, was observed and utilized as it was must rest with the bank.

For the foregoing reasons and in view of the fact that the primary purpose of the EFT Act and the regulation promulgated thereunder is the protection of individual consumers, the court concludes that plaintiff did not furnish his code to anyone within the meaning of the act. Accordingly, since the person who obtained it did not have actual authority to initiate the transfer, the transfer qualifies as an "unauthorized" one and the bank cannot hold plaintiff fully liable for the $400 withdrawal.

To avail itself of the limited liability imposed by the act upon a consumer in the event of an "unauthorized" transfer, the bank must demonstrate (1) that the means of access utilized for the transfer was "accepted" and (2) that the bank has provided a way [in] which the user of the means of access can be identified as the person authorized to use it. One definition of "accepted" under the act is that the consumer has used the means of access. Both of the foregoing conditions of liability have been met here since plaintiff used the means of access to his account to withdraw the $20 and had been given a personal identification code.

Additionally, the bank must prove that it disclosed to the consumer his liability for unauthorized electronic fund transfers and certain information pertaining to notification of the bank in the event the consumer believes that an unauthorized transfer has been or may be effected.

Defendant did not establish that it made such disclosures to the plaintiff. Accordingly, it is not entitled to avail itself of the benefit of the limited liability for unauthorized transfers imposed upon consumers by the act.

The court deemed that the transfer was unauthorized under the criteria established by the EFTA and that the bank, because of its own negligence in failing to post effective warnings to customers concerning the scam, should be liable for the unauthorized transfer. The court awarded a judgment in favor of Ognibene for $400.

DECISION AND REMEDY

Liability of the Financial Institution

A financial institution is liable to a customer for all damages *proximately caused* by its failure to make an electronic fund transfer according to the terms and conditions of an account, in the correct amount, or in a timely manner when the customer properly instructs it to do so.

There are exceptions. The institution will not be liable if:

1. The customer's account has insufficient funds through no fault of the institution.
2. The funds are subject to legal process, such as attachment (see Chapter 30).
3. The transfer would exceed an established credit limit.
4. An electronic terminal has insufficient cash.
5. Circumstances beyond the institution's control prevent the transfer.

The institution is also liable for failure to stop payment of a preauthorized transfer from a customer's account when instructed to do so under the account's terms and conditions.

For an institution's violation of EFTA, a consumer may recover actual damages and punitive damages of not more than $1,000 or less than $100. (Unlike actual damages, punitive damages are assessed to punish a defendant or to set an example for similar wrongdoers.) In a class action suit, the punitive damage limit is the lesser of $500,000 or 1 percent of the institution's net worth.

It is a federal misdemeanor to violate the EFTA. Criminal sanctions include a $5,000 fine and up to one year's imprisonment. It is a federal felony for people to use EFTS access devices fraudulently. In those cases, sanctions include a $10,000 fine and ten years' imprisonment.

CONCEPT SUMMARY: Electronic Fund Transfer Act of 1978

AREA OF COVERAGE	ESSENTIAL PROVISIONS
Disclosure	Terms and conditions must be disclosed in readily understandable language.
Documentation	1. The customer must be provided with a written receipt for each transfer made from an electronic terminal at the time of the transfer. 2. Financial institutions must provide customers with periodic statements of each account to which an electronic fund transfer system provides access.
Preauthorized transfers	*Deposits*—Banks must notify the customer when the account is credited if the payor does not notify the customer or if the credit is not made as scheduled. *Transfers*—Authorization must be in writing; three days' notice is required to stop a preauthorized transfer.

(Continued on the next page)

CONCEPT SUMMARY: Electronic Fund Transfer Act of 1978 (Continued)

AREA OF COVERAGE	ESSENTIAL PROVISIONS
Mistakes and corrections	1. The customer must notify the institution of a mistake within sixty days after the statement has been mailed. 2. The institution is required to investigate and report the results within ten business days; it can have up to forty-five days but must recredit the customer's account until the problem has been resolved. 3. The institution must give the customer a full written report, even if no mistake occurred.
Customer liability for unauthorized transfers	1. Liability is limited to $50 if the customer notifies the financial institution within two business days of learning of loss or theft of access card or device. 2. Liability limit is $500 if the customer fails to notify the institution within two business days but notifies within sixty days. 3. Liability may be unlimited if the customer fails to notify the bank within sixty days of receipt of the bank statement reflecting an unauthorized transfer.
Liability of financial institution	1. The institution is liable for all damages proximately caused by its failure to make electronic fund transfers according to the terms and conditions of an account. Punitive damages may be assessed against the insitution. 2. The institution is liable for failure to stop payment of a preauthorized transfer when instructed to do so under the terms and conditions of the EFTA. 3. Violation of the EFTA constitutes a federal misdemeanor.

COMMERCIAL ELECTRONIC FUND TRANSFERS

Nearly all commercial electronic fund transfers are excluded from coverage under the Uniform Commercial Code and federal and state electronic fund transfer statutes. Currently, contract and tort common law and, indirectly, federal and state laws that regulate the financial institutions involved govern these transfers. Eventually, they may be subject to the Uniform New Payments Code, which, as noted, concerns EFTS and is being drafted by a committee of the Permanent Editorial Board of the Uniform Commercial Code.

Generally, the contracts or customary courses of dealing on which commercial electronic fund transfer systems are based allocate the risk of error, fraud, and loss among the systems' users. When parties utilizing commercial electronic fund transfers systems are unable to resolve disputes on their own and choose to litigate, the courts apply common law contract or tort principles. Thus, when a transfer is not effected as ordered, a transfer is made to the wrong party, or it is uncertain whether a transfer has been received or completed, a court may take into consideration the facts of the particular case.

For example, a court may consider an award of damages in a situation involving an institution's negligent failure to effect an ordered transfer. The court may consider whether the injured party acted prudently—that is, mitigated the damages—and whether the institution could have expected the consequences of its negligence. By comparison, the Uniform Commercial Code protects collecting banks, when they lose checks, from consequential damages. That is, under the UCC, damages for failure to exercise ordinary care in handling a check are limited to the amount of the item [UCC 4-103(5)].

FUTURE DEVELOPMENTS

The Permanent Editorial Board of the Uniform Commercial Code and the American Law Institute began cooperating in 1974 on a project to draft a uniform set of rules governing all payment systems except cash. The proposed Uniform New Payments Code (UNPC) will cover credit cards, checks, and EFTS. The basis of the UNPC is that the parties' rights and liabilities should not depend on the form of payment system used.

It has been argued that consumer interests are better served if the rules vary with the payment system, since the relationships among the parties involved often vary among systems. For example, the holder or presenter of a check may not be known to the bank on which the check is drawn; and thus, reversibility might not be possible. On the other hand, a retailer who accepts a credit card in payment for goods may have an ongoing relationship with the financial institution that issued the card. In that situation, permitting reversibility could protect consumers against flawed merchandise, if it could be charged back against the merchant.

Others argue that it is premature to establish a uniform set of rules, since the technology is still developing. Among the newer developments are systems that use personal computers and television monitors to allow customers to pay bills, buy merchandise, and conduct banking transactions from home.

There is little doubt that the expense of processing checks and credit card paperwork has caused financial institutions to turn increasingly to the use of EFTS. We can expect that in the future, as computerized banking systems continue to develop and expand, serious attention will also have to be given to defining the rights, obligations, and liabilities of parties utilizing these systems.

QUESTIONS AND CASE PROBLEMS

---

1. Just before going home for Christmas vacation, Jim noticed that his November bank statement was $200 short of funds. Upon closer inspection, he noted that on November 28 there had been a $200 cash withdrawal from an automatic teller machine. Jim had not used his ATM card in over two months. He immediately notified the bank by telephone of the error and advised the bank that he was going to be out of town until January 18, but he gave the bank the address and telephone number at which he could be reached. Jim wrote a letter to the bank confirming his telephone conversation and once again gave the bank this address and telephone number. On January 18, when Jim arrived back in town, he still had not heard from the bank. When he called the bank, the bank officer said that he was sorry that nothing had been done to try to resolve the problem. The reason for the delay, the bank officer stated, was that many bank employees had been on Christmas vacation, causing the bank to be understaffed for about a month. The bank officer told Jim that the bank would try to get back in touch with him within two weeks concerning the matter. Jim, unhappy with this answer, decided to file suit against the bank for violation of the Electronic Fund Transfer Act. Will Jim succeed in his suit? If so, how much money will he be able to recover?

2. Kim has a checking account at First National Bank. She has had this bank account for over five years and has never had a check returned for insufficient funds. Kim works at Monmouth Medical Center and has arranged with her employer for direct deposit of her monthly paycheck into her checking account at First National. For an unexplained reason, Kim's July 1 paycheck was not deposited in her checking account. On July 15, Kim received four notices from the bank stating that four of her checks had not been honored because her account was overdrawn. She incurred late charges from her creditors and charges from the bank for the overdrawn checks. Kim files suit against her bank. Can she recover any money from the bank? If so, under what theory and how much?

3. Sandy has a checking account at Texas Bank. She frequently uses her access card to obtain money from the automatic teller machines. She always withdraws $50 when she makes a withdrawal, but she never withdraws more than $50 in any one day. When she received the April statement on her account, she noticed that on April 13 two withdrawals for $50 each had been made from the account. Believing this to be a mistake, she went to her bank on May 10 to inform the bank of the error. A bank officer told her that the bank would investigate and inform her of the result. On May 26, the bank officer called her and said that bank personnel were having trouble locating the error but would continue to try to find it. On June 20, the bank sent her a full written report advising her that no error had been made. Sandy, unhappy with the bank's explanation, filed suit against the bank, alleging that it had violated the Electronic Fund Transfer Act. What was the outcome of the suit? Would it matter if the bank could show that on the day in question it had deducted $50 from Sandy's account to cover a check that Sandy had written to a local department store and that had cleared the bank on that day?

4. Tom was a member of Health Club International, a national racquetball and fitness club. He had been a member of this club for five years and had paid his $50 monthly membership fee on the first day of every month by a preauthorized transfer of funds. Tom grew increasingly dissatisfied with the overcrowding in the health club and threatened to terminate his membership. Finally, on August 29, he instructed his bank by phone to make no more $50 payments to the health club. The bank notified him that it would discontinue paying but that it needed a letter from him confirming his desire to stop the preauthorized transfer. Tom forgot to send the letter, and the bank subsequently paid $50 to the health club on September 1 and October 1. On October 10, Tom filed a lawsuit against his bank to recover the $100, alleging that the bank had violated the Electronic Fund Transfer Act. Discuss whether Tom was able to recover his money.

5. On August 23, 1983, Robert Porter tried to withdraw $100 from his checking account at an automatic teller machine. When no money was dispensed from the machine after the necessary buttons had been pushed, he reported the incident to a bank official. A few weeks later, on September 5, Robert tried to withdraw $200. When no money appeared after two tries, he again reported the problem to a bank official. As a result of these two incidents, Robert's next bank statement showed one withdrawal of $100 and two of $200 each (for a total of $500). Robert filed suit against the bank to recover the $500 debit on his checking account for money he never received. Discuss whether Robert was able to recover the $500. [Porter v. Citibank, N.A., 123 Misc.2d 28, 472 N.Y.S.2d 582 (1984)]

6. Parviz Haghighi Abyaneh and Iran Haghighi were co-owners of a savings account at First State Bank. On May 23, 1984, a person identifying himself as Abyaneh entered the Raleigh, North Carolina, office of Citizens Savings and Loan Association of Rocky Mount (Citizens) and opened a savings account. He then called the First State Bank and asked a bank employee to transfer funds from Abyaneh's First State account into the newly created account. As a result, $53,825.66 was transferred to the new account, and subsequently, the funds were withdrawn. When the true owners of the First State Bank account learned of the transfer, they filed suit against Merchants Bank, North, successor by merger to First State Bank, for violating the Electronic Fund Transfer Act. Discuss whether Abyaneh will be able to recover the $53,825.66. [Abyaneh v. Merchants Bank, North, 670 F.Supp. 1298 (M.D.Pa. 1987)]

7. Dorothy Judd and her husband had a joint checking account at a Citibank branch in New York. They also had Citicards that gave them access to the computer via the bank's automatic teller machines. Each card, before it could access the computer, had to be validated by the bank. Although Mrs. Judd had gone to the bank to receive her personal identification number and have her card validated, her husband had not yet done so. Thus, only Mrs. Judd's card could be used to obtain cash or make any other transaction via the ATM, and then only if the user knew her PIN—which she said she had given to no one and which she had not even written down but had memorized. The Judds were thus stunned to learn that $800 had been charged to their checking account as a result of two transactions, one made on February 26 and the other on March 28. The bank maintained that there was no way the funds could have been withdrawn without the use of Mrs. Judd's card and PIN. Mrs. Judd said she had been at work at the times of both withdrawals, and a letter from her employer confirmed her statement. Mrs. Judd sued for the return of the $800, which she claimed had been erroneously charged to her account by Citibank. On the basis of these facts, discuss whether the bank should have been held liable. [Judd v. Citibank, 107 Misc.2d 526, 435 N.Y.S.2d 210 (1980)]

Focus on Ethics

Commercial Transactions and the Uniform Commercial Code

Transactions involving the sale of goods constitute a major portion of business activity in the commercial and manufacturing sectors of this economy. Since the 1960s, the sale of goods has been governed by the Uniform Commercial Code in virtually every state. Many of the Code provisions express our ethical standards. Much of the conduct of businesspersons in the business world has an ethical basis.

INDEFINITENESS IN THE SALES CONTRACT

It would seem that the requirements for the formation of the sales contract would be detailed and explicit. In fact, there is no contract if the terms are unduly indefinite. The UCC [2–204(3)], however, states that a sales contract will not fail for indefiniteness even if one or more terms are left open, so long as the parties intend to make the contract and there is a reasonably certain basis for the court to grant an appropriate remedy. For example, there can be open price terms, open delivery terms, and open payment terms, and a valid contract will still exist.

Yet the tolerance for indefiniteness in contracts was not always so great. Older common law cases required a much higher degree of specificity with respect to the terms of a contract. In the often-cited case of *Sun Printing and Publishing Assn.* v. *Remington Paper & Power Co., Inc.* [235 N.Y. 338 (1923)], Judge Cardozo, writing for the New York Court of Appeals, held that the contract that stated that the price of the newsprint was to be agreed upon by the parties, but in no event was the price to be higher than the contract price charged by the Canadian Export Paper Company, failed for indefiniteness. Cardozo concluded that since the contract did not specify how the fluctuations in the Canadian price were to affect the contract price, it must fail. But, over time, society's perceptions of the contracting environment, as well as its ideas on fairness, have changed. Thus, a lesser degree of specificity is presently tolerated with respect to the terms of a contract.

As long as the court determines that the parties have intended to make a contract and that there is any reasonably certain basis for granting a remedy, it may attempt to supply the missing term. The Code attempts to maximize the probability that two willing parties will engage in a mutually beneficial economic transaction. Underlying this effort is the notion that commercial transactions form the basis of our country's economic well-being. Rather than make such transactions difficult, the UCC attempts to facilitate commercial transactions.

Businesspersons at times try to take advantage of the flexibility of the UCC's requirements for a valid sales contract. Occasionally, one reads of a business scandal in which an unscrupulous seller, for example, requires buyers of a product to sign a written sales contract with a number of blanks. The blanks are filled in later in a manner not agreed upon by the two parties prior to signature. Our shared beliefs reject the notion that businesspersons should be able to take advantage of customers in such a way. And, in fact, both the competitive nature of the marketplace and the UCC's imposition of an obligation of good faith and commercial reasonableness in the performance of every contract minimize the success of unscrupulous businesspersons who desire to operate in an unethical fashion.

THE EFFECT OF A COMPETITIVE MARKETPLACE

Ideally, the competitive marketplace limits unethical behavior by businesspersons. Many successful businesses, particularly those dealing in goods, require repeat customers to thrive and profit. Unethical dealings with customers may become known, and hence such repeat customers dwindle and deter others from purchasing products from the unethical business. In this situation, the unethical businessperson will ultimately fail.

Unfortunately, the market does not always work so perfectly. Consumers may lack the information about businesses necessary to penalize unethical business-persons. Even if the system works, the first-time buyers must suffer the results of unethical behavior. Plus, some businesses—such as resorts catering largely to one-time tourists—may not require repeat business. And, of course, inevitably there are some "fly-by-night" companies that simply deceive one set of buyers and then pick up and move their operations to a different locale and deceive another set of buyers, and so on.

GOOD FAITH AND COMMERCIAL REASONABLENESS

"Good faith" and "commercial reasonableness" are two key concepts that permeate the Uniform Commercial Code and help to prevent the success of unethical behavior by business-persons. These standards are objective, even though the terms are subjective.

The concepts of good faith and commercial reasonableness are read into every contract and impose certain duties on all parties. Section 2–311(1) indicates that when parties leave the particulars of performance to be specified by one of the parties, "[a]ny such specification must be made in good faith and within limits set by commercial reasonableness." The requirement of commercial reasonableness means that the term subsequently supplied should not come as a surprise to one party. Thus, commercial reasonableness indicates that there is a permissible variation that is determined according to commercial standards. Courts frequently look to course of dealing, usage of trade, and the surrounding circumstances in determining commercial reasonableness.

Even though all commercial actions, including performance and enforcement of contract terms, must exhibit commercial reasonableness, the UCC makes it clear that innocent parties can be excused from certain types of nonperformance. Nonperformance of a contract may be excused when the nonperformance is the result of a commercially reasonable intervening phenomenon. Indeed, the doctrine of commercial impracticability relies on a theory of reasonability. The fact that the word "reasonable" appears about ninety times in Article 2 of the UCC demonstrates the UCC's opposition to imposing undue hardship upon merchants and upon those with whom they deal. A merchant is expected to act in a reasonable manner according to reasonable commercial customs. Also, throughout the UCC merchants are held to a higher standard than are nonmerchants. Under UCC 2–314(1), for example, a warranty that goods shall be merchantable is only implied in a contract for their sale if the seller is "a merchant with respect to goods of that kind." This higher standard clearly represents an ideal that the drafters of the UCC were seeking.

With respect to good faith, under previous law the only time this concept was discussed in any detail was normally in an equitable proceeding where the "ethics" of a situation has always been emphasized more strongly (for example, "He who seeks equity must do equity"). By making good faith a clear obligation in every contract for the sale of goods, and then defining good faith as *honesty in fact,* the drafters of the UCC are stating a very broad policy principle—one that maintains a high standard.

The concept of good faith, which is read into every contract, implies that one party will not take advantage of another party by manipulating contract terms. Furthermore, it is implicitly understood that good faith applies to both *actions* and *intent.* The obligation of good faith is particularly important in "requirements" and "output" contracts. Requirements contracts provide that the buyer purchase all of his or her needs for a specific good from the seller. An output contract provides that the buyer will purchase the seller's entire output. Without the obligation of good faith, it is clear that the potential for abuse would be tremendous. If, for example, the cost of producing the good that is the subject of a requirements contract suddenly increases and the market price of the good unexpectedly quadruples, the buyer could claim that his or her needs are now equivalent to the entire output of the seller. Then, after buying all the seller's output at a price that is substantially below the market price, the buyer could turn around and resell the goods the buyer does not need for his or her own use at the new, higher market price.

Under the UCC, however, this type of unethical behavior is prohibited. Even though contracts that call for the buyer to purchase all of his or her needs from the seller are explicitly authorized under the Code, such contracts are construed to involve actual requirements that may occur in good faith. Under UCC 2–306(1), no quantity "unreasonably disproportionate to any stated estimate or in the absence of a stated estimate to any normal or otherwise comparable prior output or requirements may be tendered or demanded." Thus, the requirements of "good faith" and of not demanding a quantity "unreasonably disproportionate" make it clear that *no speculation* is allowed under requirements contracts. The UCC reflects ethical considerations in prohibiting such abuses of contracts.

WARRANTIES

The higher standard to which merchants must conform carries over to warranties. The term "warranty" is used in the UCC to reflect a promise or a guarantee made by a seller of goods that these goods will have certain characteristics. In expressing ideas of fairness in particular situations, the UCC makes it difficult for merchants to disclaim warranties and requires that any such disclaimers be conspicuous. In other words, disclaimers must not be hidden.

Both express and implied warranties are recognized by the Code. Under UCC 2–314(2) goods sold by a merchant must be fit for the ordinary purposes for which such goods are used, be of proper quality, and be properly labeled and packaged. A description of goods is an express warranty, and, hence, a seller of goods may be found in breach of contract if the goods fail to conform to the previously made description. Recognizing descriptions as express warranties is an effort by the Code to inject greater fairness into contractual situations. The UCC acknowledges the fact that a buyer may often reasonably believe that a seller is warranting his or her product, even though the seller may not use formal words such as "warrant" or "guarantee." Thus, the law imposes an ethical obligation upon merchants in statutory form.

It is generally believed that the implied warranties of merchantability and fitness for a particular purpose are necessary to help the consumer in a world of complex problems (although some scholars have argued that, in fact, the UCC sections addressing disclaimer, waiver, and modification, when properly used, have *reduced* the effectiveness of such warranty protection for the consumer). The creation of the Consumer Product Safety Commission (CPSC) occurred after numerous congressional studies showed a need for greater consumer protection. The CPSC presumably was created because the marketplace somehow failed to provide products that were sufficiently safe. The federal government concluded that the warranty provisions of the UCC had failed to provide adequate protection for consumers.

The businessperson has not only a legal obligation to provide safe products, but also an ethical one. When faced with the possibility of providing additional safety at no extra cost, every ethical business-person will indeed opt for a safer product. At issue, however, is the policy relating to what a producer should do when a safer product requires higher costs and therefore higher consumer prices. The marketplace presumably will determine the optimal level of safety; however, that level has been deemed too low by many, and for this reason the Consumer Product Safety Commission was created. Arguably, unsafe products lead to social costs because injured individuals must sometimes receive medical care, and often at public expense. Furthermore, dependents of injured individuals may find themselves in financial difficulties and require "welfare" payments from the state.

ETHICS VERSUS EFFICIENCY

Contracts can be analyzed in terms of economic efficiency. Economic efficiency exists when no change in the current use of resources will increase the material welfare of society. It can be argued that the law of contracts leads to economic efficiency because it establishes a set of rules that businesspersons can rely on when they engage in commercial transactions. When such persons know what the outcome of court cases will be, they have an incentive to avoid behavior that is not in conformance with the law of contracts. In other words, businesspersons attempt to minimize the amount of their resources spent on litigation, since litigation expenses increase costs and lower profits.

Much contractual litigation results in reduction in the wealth of one party and an increase in the wealth of the other. Consider the following example: An individual enters into a contract with a merchant. For a specified sum of money, the merchant is to provide a certain tool. The tool is to be used for a specified activity. The purchaser of the tool uses it for another activity and in so doing permanently injures himself. He sues the merchant, which is an extremely large company. If the trier of fact (which in some cases will be a judge and in others a jury) finds in favor of the merchant, the wealth of the injured plaintiff will be decreased and the company will be better off than it would have been had it been forced to compensate the plaintiff for the injuries resulting from the use of its tool. If, on the other hand, the trier of facts rules in favor of the plaintiff, the plaintiff's wealth will be increased, and the company's wealth will be correspondingly decreased.

From an ethical point of view, is it fair to require the company to compensate the plaintiff when the plaintiff's injuries resulted from a disregard for the company's explicit instructions? Some people argue that, since the company can better "afford" to lose wealth (via payment to the injured plaintiff for injuries), the trier of fact should rule in favor of the plaintiff. Others, however, question the fairness of determining the outcome of a particular case on the basis of who can best absorb the cost.

From the point of view of economic efficiency, placing liability on the merchant will lead to undesirable results. After all, the contract between the two parties specified that the tool was to be used in a particular activity. The plaintiff used the tool in a different activity. If,

because of injury from improper use of the tool, the plaintiff is awarded damages, a signal will be sent to other individuals that they too will be awarded compensation for any injuries sustained by careless or negligent use of such tools. Arguably, this rule will lead to greater carelessness by consumers, since they will no longer need to be concerned with suffering the consequences of their carelessness. The company, on the other hand, may be the subject of many more suits by consumers attempting to recover damages for injuries sustained as a result of their careless use of the merchant's tool. Paying out compensation to injured, careless plaintiffs will increase the company's costs. If other companies that produce substantially the same tool are also sued and the courts similarly award damages to the careless plaintiffs, the price of this tool will eventually go up to reflect the costs of compensating careless plaintiffs. Consumers in general will have to pay more for this tool because of the carelessness of relatively few individuals. Economic efficiency clearly will suffer.

The results of recent court cases involving personal injuries indicate that there is a greater concern in our society for proper compensation of injuries than for economic efficiency. The ethical concern that victims who are injured using products deserve to be compensated appears to predominate in court decisions, however careless the plaintiffs may have been. Thus, particularly in the area of product liability, the increasing number of actions brought by plaintiffs has frequently resulted

in defendant companies' settling questionable claims in order to save the expense of litigation.

CHECKS AND THE BANKING SYSTEM

Numerous moral and ethical questions face members of the banking community. Banks and other financial institutions offer a variety of services to their customers. Some financial institutions would certainly like to prevent customers from using stop-payment orders. Stop payment occurs when a financial institution permits its customers to stop payment on a check for whatever reason. The marketplace, as well as custom and law, nonetheless provides for the customer's use of such stop payments. How much should a bank or other financial institution be allowed to charge a customer for the use of a stop payment? If the bank or other financial institution charges too much for this service, is it in fact effectively removing that service by over-pricing it? The same issue applies to returned checks (usually for insufficient funds). What is the appropriate bank charge?

DISCUSSION QUESTIONS

1. To what extent does competition in the marketplace obviate the need for ethical business standards?
2. Should the question of product safety be decided according to economic analysis only? Or is product safety simply an ethical consideration? How far removed is economic analysis from ethical considerations here? For example, is it ethical to produce a product, such as asbestos, that may contribute to human lung cancer?

3. U.S. automobile manufacturers have re-emphasized quality in their cars—perhaps, in part, in response to foreign competition. Increasing quality, however, often means increasing costs to consumers. To what extent do companies have an ethical responsibility to produce high-quality products? How does a company decide whether to spend the money to improve the quality of its products?

4. Can a human life be subjected to cost-benefit analysis? For example, consider the following situation: A rule is proposed that will require all commercial airlines to use jets that have two additional emergency exit doors. Given the average number of airline crashes per year and the average number of individuals injured or killed in such crashes, it is estimated that the new safety standard will save an additional ten lives per year. Should the standard therefore be instituted? What if it costs $10 million? $50 million? $3 billion? To what extent, if any, is cost relevant where human life is concerned?

5. Does a person have an ethical duty to perform obligations under a sales contract, even if he or she no longer has a legal duty to do so? Is not a contract a form of promise? What are the ethical responsibilities of making such a promise?

Unit Four

CREDITORS' RIGHTS AND BANKRUPTCY

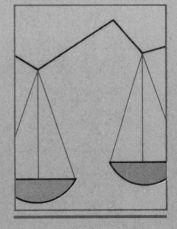

Chapter 29

Secured Transactions

The concept of a secured transaction is as basic to modern business practice as the concept of credit. Few purchasers (manufacturers, wholesalers, retailers, consumers) have the resources to pay cash for all the goods they purchase. Lenders are reluctant to lend money to a debtor solely upon the debtor's promise to repay the debt. The simple fact is that sellers and lenders want to minimize the risk of loss due to nonpayment and will not sell goods or lend money unless the promise of payment is somehow guaranteed.

To minimize the risk of loss, the creditor often requires the debtor to provide some type of security beyond the mere promise that the debt will be paid. When this security takes the form of personal property owned by the debtor or in which the debtor has a legal interest, the transaction becomes known as a **secured transaction.**

The importance of being a secured creditor cannot be overemphasized. Business, as we know it, could not exist without the presence of secured transaction law. Secured creditors are generally not hampered by certain state laws favorable to debtors, and secured creditors have a favored position should the debtor become bankrupt.

A key to understanding this area of the law is to consider a transaction from a creditor's point of view. From this perspective, the basic questions are:

1. Does the creditor have an enforceable security interest in the debtor's property?
2. If the creditor has an enforceable security interest and the debtor defaults on the underlying obligation, will the creditor's interest take *priority* over other creditors' claims?

The answers to these two questions form the basis for the law of secured transactions and involve two important concepts: **attachment** and **perfection.** A security interest is not enforceable unless the creditor's rights have attached to the **collateral** (the property the debtor offered as security). What has to be done for a security interest to attach will be considered in this chapter, following a brief introduction to Article 9 of the Code and the key terminology of secured transactions. The chapter will then discuss the process of perfection and its importance in establishing priority over other creditors' claims. Basically, perfection is what the creditor must do in the way of giving legal notice to make his or her security interest effective against the debtor's other creditors.

ARTICLE 9 OF THE UCC

Prior to adoption of the UCC, creditors used a great number of security devices, such as chattel mortgages, conditional sales contracts, assignment of accounts, and trust receipts. Each had its own rules and terminology. Article 9 of the UCC has eliminated the distinctions among the various forms of financing, simplified the terminology, and provided a framework for the law of secured transactions.

Article 9 applies to any transaction that is intended to create a security interest in personal property, the sale of accounts, chattel paper,[1] and fixtures.[2] Transactions excluded from Article 9 include real estate mortgages, landlords' liens, mechanics' liens, claims arising from judicial proceedings, and so on [UCC 9-104]. In general, these transactions do not deal with personal property and are excluded because they are extensively treated in other areas of the law.

As will become evident, the law of secured transactions tends to favor the rights of creditors; but, to a lesser extent, it offers debtors some protection, too.

DEFINITIONS

The terminology used under the Code is now uniformly adopted in all documents drawn in secured transaction situations:

1. Security interest. Every interest "in *personal property or fixtures* [emphasis added] which secures payment or performance of an obligation" is a security interest [UCC 1-201(37)].

---

1. A *chattel* is an article of personal property. (Generally, personal property is all property that is not real estate.) *Chattel paper* is the document or documents evidencing both a financial obligation and a security interest in or a lease of specific goods [UCC 9-105(1)(b)].

2. A *fixture* is an article of what was originally personal property that has been permanently affixed to real estate and thus has become so related to the real estate that an interest in it arises under real estate law [UCC 9-313(1)(a)]. For example, a building's heating or air conditioning system is a fixture. By comparison, a *trade fixture* is an article that a commercial tenant affixes to his or her business premises to conduct the business and that can be removed without injury to the property. Display shelving and removable display counters are trade fixtures.

2. Secured party. A lender, seller, or any person in whose favor there is a security interest, including a person to whom accounts or chattel paper have been sold, is a secured party [UCC 9-105(1)(m)].

3. Debtor. The party who owes payment or performance of the secured obligation, whether or not that party actually owns or has rights in the collateral, is a debtor. The term *debtor* includes sellers of accounts or chattel paper. When the debtor and owner of the collateral are not the same person, the term *debtor* refers to the actual owner of the collateral or describes the obligor on an obligation, or both, depending upon the context in which the term is used [UCC 9-105(1)(d)].

4. Security agreement. The agreement that creates or provides for a security interest between the debtor and a secured party is called a security agreement [UCC 9-105(1)(l)].

5. Collateral. The property subject to a security interest, including accounts and chattel paper that have been sold, is collateral [UCC 9-105(1)(c)]. See Exhibit 29-4 on pages 539-540 for definitions.

These basic definitions form the concept under which a debtor-creditor relationship becomes a secured transaction relationship. (See Exhibit 29-1.)

ATTACHMENT—CREATING AN ENFORCEABLE SECURITY INTEREST

Before a creditor can become a secured party, the creditor must have a security interest in the collateral of the debtor. Three requirements must be met in order for a creditor to have an enforceable security interest.

1. Unless the creditor has possession of the collateral, there must be an agreement in writing.
2. The creditor must give value to the debtor.
3. The debtor must have rights in the collateral.

Once these requirements have been met, the creditor's rights are said to "attach" to the collateral. This means that the creditor has an *enforceable* security interest against the debtor. Attachment ensures that the security interest between the debtor and the secured party is effective [UCC 9-203].

Exhibit 29–1 **Secured Transactions—Concepts and Terminology**

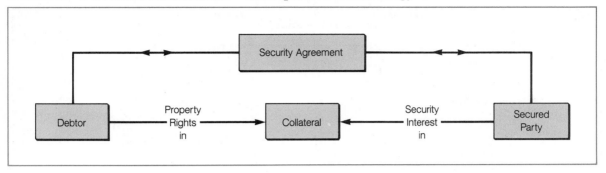

Written Agreement

Unless the collateral is in the possession of the secured party (the creditor), there must be a *written security agreement* describing the collateral and signed by the debtor. (It is not necessary for the creditor to sign.) See Exhibit 29–2 for a detailed sample agreement. The security agreement creates or provides for a security interest. For example, it might read "Debtor hereby grants to secured party a security interest in the following goods."

The description must reasonably identify the collateral [UCC 9-203(1), 9-110]. For example, the description "my truck" is sufficient if the debtor has only one truck.

Value Given to Debtor

The secured party must give *value*. According to UCC 1-201(44), value is any consideration that supports a simple contract. In addition, value can be security given for a preexisting (antecedent) obligation or any binding commitment to extend credit. Normally, the value given by a secured party involves a direct loan or a commitment to sell goods on credit.

Debtor Has Rights in Collateral

The debtor must have *rights* in the collateral; that is, the debtor must have some ownership interest or right to obtain possession of that collateral. The debtor's rights can represent either a current or a future legal interest in the collateral. For example, a retailer-debtor can give a secured party a security interest not only in existing inventory owned by the retailer but also in future inventory to be acquired by the retailer.

PURCHASE-MONEY SECURITY INTEREST

Often, sellers of consumer durable goods, such as stereos and television sets, agree to extend credit for part of the purchase price of those goods.[3] Also, lenders not necessarily in the business of selling such goods often agree to lend much of the purchase price for the goods. There is a special name for the security interest that the seller or the lender obtains when such a transaction occurs. It is called a **purchase-money security interest.** Formally, such an interest obtains when:

1. A seller retains or takes a security interest in collateral to secure part or all of the collateral's purchase price.
2. Some other party takes a security interest in collateral to secure the party's advances or other obligation that enables the debtor to acquire rights in or to use the collateral—for example, a financing agency takes a purchase-money security interest when it makes advances to a buyer to enable him or her to buy goods from a seller, and the buyer uses the money for that purpose [UCC 9-107].

In either case, a lender or seller has essentially provided a buyer with the purchase money to buy goods. To illustrate, suppose Barbara wants to purchase a stereo from Sanko. The purchase price is $900. Not being able to pay cash, Barbara signs a security agreement to pay $100 down and $50 per month until the balance plus interest is fully

3. Under the Federal Trade Commission's unfair credit practices rules, it is a violation of Section 5 of the FTC Act for a lender or retail seller to take or receive a *nonpossessory, non-purchase*-money security interest in household goods.

Exhibit 29–2 A Sample Security Agreement

SECURITY AGREEMENT

DEBTOR _____

DEBTOR'S RESIDENCE _____
       OR
PLACE OF BUSINESS _____

SECURED PARTY _____

SECURED PARTY'S ADDRESS _____

_____

SECURITY INTEREST In order to secure the payment of the Debt described below and the obligations of this Security Agreement, Debtor gives Secured Party a security interest in the following Collateral under Article 9 of the Uniform Commercial Code (UCC):

COLLATERAL _____

_____

_____

_____

_____

AFTER-ACQUIRED PROPERTY AND PROCEEDS The Collateral includes: all proceeds, increases, substitutions, replacements, additions, improvements and accessions to the Collateral, all proceeds from insurance on the Collateral, and all refunds of unearned premiums for insurance; but does not include any consumer goods (other than accessions) acquired by Debtor more than 10 days after the loan proceeds are advanced. This provision shall not be construed to mean that Debtor is authorized to sell, lease, or dispose of the Collateral without the consent of Secured Party.

DEBT $_____ Note dated _____, 19____ payable to Secured Party.

FUTURE ADVANCES AND OTHER DEBTS The debt includes: any renewals or extensions of the Note; any amounts advanced by Secured Party to protect its security interest in the Collateral; any future amounts advanced by Secured Party at its option to Debtor; any and all other liabilities of Debtor to Secured Party, now existing or later incurred, matured or unmatured, direct or contingent; any costs or expenses that may be lawfully assessed against Debtor for the collection of the Debt, including attorney's fees;

LOCATION OF COLLATERAL Debtor agrees to keep the Collateral
[ ] at the Debtor's address stated above;
[ ] at the following location: _____

_____

REAL ESTATE If marked here [ ], the Collateral is either [ ] a fixture that is, or will be, attached to the following described real estate; or [ ] crops growing or to be grown upon the following described real estate: _____

_____
whose record owner is: _____ .

FARM PRODUCTS If marked here [ ], the Collateral is farm products and includes the offspring and increase of any livestock or crops given as such Collateral and all feed, seed, fertilizer and other supplies now owned or later acquired in connection with such farming operations, all of which is located upon the above described real estate.

LOCATION OF RECORDS If marked here [ ], the Collateral consists of accounts, instruments, chattel paper, documents or other general intangibles and the records concerning such Collateral are kept at _____

_____

POSSESSION BY SECURED PARTY If marked here [ ], the Collateral will be retained in the possession of Secured Party, and the following provisions in this section shall be applicable. Secured Party's duty with reference to the Collateral shall be solely to use reasonable care in the custody and preservation of the Collateral in its possession and to receive collections, earnings, dividends, remittances and payments on such Collateral as and when made. Secured Party shall have the option of applying the amounts so received, after deduction for any collection costs that may be lawfully charged, as payment of any debt secured by this Security Agreement, or holding such amounts for the benefit of Debtor. Secured Party shall not be responsible in any way for any depreciation in value of the Collateral, nor shall Secured Party have any duty or responsibility to take any steps to preserve rights against other parties or to enforce collection of the Collateral.

USE OF COLLATERAL The Collateral will be used primarily for the purposes checked below:
[ ] Personal, family, or household purposes
[ ] Business operations (other than farming)
[ ] Farming operations

OWNERSHIP OF COLLATERAL Debtor is the owner of the Collateral, or if marked here [ ], Debtor is purchasing the Collateral with the proceeds of the Note described above. Except for the security interest created by this Security Agreement, the Collateral is free from any lien, security interest, encumbrance, or claim. With respect to any instruments, chattel paper, documents or other general intangibles given as Collateral, Debtor warrants and represents that: they are genuine, free from adverse claims, default, prepayment or defenses; all persons appearing to be obligated thereon have authority and capacity to contract and are bound thereon; and they comply with applicable laws concerning form, content, and manner of preparation and execution. Debtor will, at Debtor's cost and expense, defend any action which may affect Secured Party's security interest in, or Debtor's title to, the Collateral.

FINANCING STATEMENT No Financing Statement covering the Collateral or any part thereof or any proceeds thereof is on file in any public office and, at Secured Party's request, Debtor will join in executing all necessary Financing Statements in forms satisfactory to Secured Party and will pay the cost of filing and will further execute all other necessary instruments deemed necessary by Secured Party and pay the cost of filing.

SALE OR ENCUMBRANCE OF COLLATERAL Debtor will not, without the written consent of Secured Party, sell, contract to sell, lease, encumber, or dispose of the Collateral or any interest therein until this Security Agreement and all debts secured thereby have been fully satisfied.

Exhibit 29-2 (Continued)

INSURANCE If the Collateral is tangible property and is insurable, Debtor will insure the Collateral with companies acceptable to Secured Party against such casualties and in such amounts as Secured Party shall reasonably require with a loss payable clause in favor of Debtor and Secured Party as their interest may appear, and Secured Party is hereby authorized to collect sums which may become due under any of said policies and apply the same to the obligations hereby secured.

PROTECTION OF COLLATERAL If the Collateral is tangible property, Debtor will keep the Collateral in good order and repair and will not waste or destroy the Collateral or any part thereof. Debtor will not use the Collateral in violation of any statute or ordinance and Secured Party will have the right to examine and inspect the Collateral at any reasonable time.

TAXES Debtor will pay promptly when due all taxes and assessments on the Collateral or for its use and operation.

DECREASE IN VALUE OF COLLATERAL If in Secured Party's judgment the Collateral has materially decreased in value or if Secured Party shall at any time deem that Secured Party is insecure, Debtor shall either provide enough additional Collateral to satisfy Secured Party, or shall reduce the total indebtedness by an amount sufficient to satisfy Secured Party.

REIMBURSEMENT OF EXPENSES At the option of Secured Party, Secured Party may discharge taxes, liens, interest, or perform or cause to be performed for and on behalf of Debtor any actions and conditions, obligations, or covenants which Debtor has failed or refused to perform, and may pay for the repair, maintenance, and preservation of the Collateral, including, to the extent but only to the extent such amounts may be lawfully collected, attorney's fees, court costs, agent's fees, or commissions, or any other costs or expenses. All sums so expended shall bear interest from the date of payment at the rate of interest stated in the Note described above, if such rate of interest can be lawfully collected and if not then at the maximum legal rate, and shall be payable on demand at the place designated in the Note and shall be secured by this Security Agreement.

CHANGE OF RESIDENCE OR PLACE OF BUSINESS Debtor will promptly notify Secured Party of any change of the Debtor's residence, place of business, or place where records are kept.

TIME OF PERFORMANCE AND WAIVER In performing any act under this Security Agreement and the Note secured thereby, time shall be of the essence. Secured Party's acceptance of partial or delinquent payments, or the failure of Secured Party to exercise any right or remedy shall not be a waiver of any obligation of Debtor or right of Secured Party or constitute a waiver of any other similar default subsequently occurring.

DEFAULT Debtor shall be in default under this Security Agreement on the happening of any of the following events or conditions:
(1) Default in the payment or performance of any obligation, covenant, or liability contained or referred to in the Note or in this Security Agreement;
(2) Any warranty, representation, or statement made or furnished to Secured Party by or on behalf of Debtor proves to have been false in any material respect when made or furnished;
(3) Loss, theft, substantial damage, destruction, sale, or encumbrance to or of any of the Collateral, or the making of any levy, seizure, or attachment thereof or thereon;
(4) Any time Secured Party believes that the prospect of payment of any indebtedness secured hereby or the performance of this Security Agreement is impaired;
(5) Death, dissolution, termination of existence, insolvency, business failure, appointment of a receiver for any part of the Collateral, assignment for the benefit of creditors or the commencement of any proceeding under any bankruptcy or insolvency law by or against Debtor or any guarantor or surety for Debtor.

REMEDIES Upon the occurrence of any such event of default, and at any time thereafter, Secured Party may declare all obligations secured immediately due and payable and may proceed to enforce payment of the same and exercise any and all of the rights and remedies provided by the Uniform Commercial Code as well as other rights and remedies either at law or in equity possessed by Secured Party.

Secured Party shall have the right to remove the Collateral from the premises of Debtor and, for purposes of removal and possession, Secured Party or its representatives may enter any premises of the Debtor without legal process and the Debtor hereby waives and releases Secured Party of and from any and all claims in connection therewith or arising therefrom.

Secured Party may require Debtor to assemble the Collateral and make it available to Secured Party at any place to be designated by the Secured Party which is reasonably convenient to both parties. Unless the Collateral is perishable or threatens to decline speedily in value or is of a type customarily sold on a recognized market, Secured Party will give the Debtor reasonable notice of the time and place of any public sale thereof or of the time after which any private sale or any other intended disposition thereof is to be made. The requirements of reasonable notice shall be met if such notice is mailed, postage prepaid, to the address of Debtor shown at the beginning of this Security Agreement at least five days before the time of the sale or disposition. Expenses of retaking, holding, preparing for sale, selling, or the like shall include Secured Party's reasonable attorney's fees and legal expenses, to the extent but only to the extent such amounts may be lawfully collected.

TEXAS LAW TO APPLY This Agreement shall be construed under and in accordance with the Uniform Commercial Code and other applicable laws of the State of Texas and all obligations of the parties created hereunder are performable in the County of the Secured Party's address stated above.

PARTIES BOUND This Agreement shall be binding on and inure to the benefit of the parties hereto and their respective heirs, executors, administrators, legal representatives, successors, and assigns. If there is more than one Debtor, their obligations shall be joint and several.

LEGAL CONSTRUCTION In case any one or more of the provisions contained in this Agreement shall for any reason be held to be invalid, illegal, or unenforceable in any respect, such invalidity, illegality, or unenforceability shall not affect any other provision thereof and this Agreement shall be construed as if such invalid, illegal, or unenforceable provision had never been contained herein. Notwithstanding anything else herein to the contrary, if the Debt secured by this Security Agreement is a loan made under any chapter of the Texas Credit Code that limits charges and expenses that may be collected by Secured Party, the provisions of such Code shall govern in the event of any conflict between the provisions of this Security Agreement and the provisions of such Code.

Executed _____ ,19_____ .

Secured Party: Debtor:

_____   _____

paid. Sanko is to retain a security interest in the purchased stereo until full payment has been made.

The same result would occur if Barbara went to the West Bank and borrowed the $900 to buy the stereo from Sanko. After Barbara signs a security agreement with West Bank, with the to-be-purchased stereo as collateral, West Bank has a purchase-money security interest the moment the stereo is purchased from Sanko. To protect its investment of the purchase money and thereby its security interest, West Bank might arrange to pay the $900 directly to Sanko.

The importance of a purchase-money security interest is basically twofold:

1. It allows for the automatic perfection of a security interest in consumer goods without the secured party's possession or filing (to be discussed later in this chapter).
2. It ordinarily gives a secured party priority over a party with a non-purchase-money security interest in the same collateral (to be discussed later in this chapter).

THE SCOPE OF A SECURITY INTEREST

A security agreement can cover various types of property in addition to collateral already in the debtor's possession—the proceeds of sale, after-acquired property, inventory, and future advances.

Proceeds

A secured party has an interest in the **proceeds** of (that is, whatever is received from) the sale, exchange, or other disposal of the collateral [UCC 9-203(3), 9-306(2)]. To illustrate, suppose a bank has a perfected security interest in the inventory of a retail seller of TV sets. The retailer sells a TV set out of this inventory to you, a buyer in the ordinary course of business. Since you cannot pay cash, you sign a retail security agreement by which you will make twenty-four monthly payments. If the retailer should default on the loan from the bank, the bank is entitled to the remaining payments you owe to the retailer as proceeds.

After-acquired Property

After-acquired property of the debtor is property acquired after the execution of the security agreement. In other words, after-acquired property is property that a debtor does not own or have the rights to at the time the debtor enters into a security agreement but that he or she will acquire at some time in the future.

The security agreement itself may provide for coverage of after-acquired property [UCC 9-204(1)]. This is particularly useful for inventory financing arrangements, because a secured party whose security interest is in existing inventory knows that the debtor will sell that inventory, thereby reducing the collateral subject to the security interest. Generally, the debtor will purchase new inventory to replace the inventory sold. The secured party wants this newly acquired inventory to be subject to the *original* security interest. Thus, the after-acquired property clause extends the secured party's claim to any inventory acquired thereafter. (This is not to say that such an original security interest will be superior to the rights of all other creditors with regard to this after-acquired inventory, as will be discussed later.)

Consider a typical example. Anderson buys factory equipment from Blonsky on credit, giving as security an interest in all of her equipment—both what she is buying and what she already owns. The security interest contains an after-acquired property clause. Six months later, Anderson pays cash to another seller for more equipment. Six months after that, Anderson goes out of business before she has paid off her debt to Blonsky. Blonsky has a security interest in *all* of Anderson's equipment, even the equipment bought from the other seller.

An after-acquired property clause normally does not allow for attachment of a security interest in consumer goods "unless the debtor acquired rights in them within 10 days after the secured party gives value" [UCC 9-204(2)]. Presumably, this protects consumers from encumbering all their present and future property.

Future Advances

Often a debtor has a continuing *line of credit* under which the debtor can borrow intermittently. As evidence of this arrangement, the debtor may be issued a *letter of credit* in which the issuer of the letter states that it has agreed to pay drafts drawn on the debtor's line of credit by the debtor's creditors (as explained in Chapter 22). A letter of credit, typically issued by a bank, has three parties: the issuer, the customer, and a beneficiary who will draw the drafts under it. Letters of credit typically specify not only a maximum amount but a specified time duration. Advances against lines of credit can be subject to a properly perfected security interest in certain collateral.

The security agreement may provide that any future advances made against the line of credit are also subject to the security interest in the same collateral. For example, Tobrun is the owner of a small manufacturing plant with equipment valued at $1,000,000. Tobrun is in immediate need of $50,000 of working capital. Tobrun secures a loan from West Bank, signing a security agreement putting up all his equipment as security. In the security agreement Tobrun can borrow up to $500,000 in the future, using the same equipment as collateral (future advances). In such cases, it is not necessary to execute a new security agreement and perfect a security interest in the collateral each time an advance is made to the debtor [UCC 9-204(3)].

The Floating Lien Concept

When collateral is sold, exchanged, or otherwise disposed of, a security interest shifts automatically to the proceeds. Under most circumstances, a creditor may also take a security interest in a debtor's after-acquired property; and the obligations a security agreement covers may include future advances. Because Article 9 provides for these possibilities, it is often referred to as a **floating lien** statute. Floating liens commonly arise in the financing of inventories, for example. A creditor is not interested in specific pieces of inventory, because they are constantly changing.

Suppose that Ptarmigan Products, a cross-country ski dealer, has a line of credit with Seattle First National Bank to finance its inventory. Ptarmigan and Seattle First enter into a security agreement that provides for coverage of proceeds, after-acquired property, inventory, and future advances. Seattle First perfects its security interest in Ptarmigan's inventory according to the appropriate method (as described later).

One day, Ptarimigan sells a new pair of the latest cross-country skis, for which it receives a used pair in trade. That same day, it purchases two new pairs of skis from a local manufacturer with an additional amount of money obtained from Seattle First. Seattle First gets a perfected security interest in the used pair of cross-country skis under the proceeds clause, has a perfected security interest in the two new pairs of skis purchased from the local manufacturer under the after-acquired property clause, and has the new amount of money advanced to Ptarimigan secured by the futrure-advance clause. All of this is done under the original perfected security agreement. The various items in the inventory have changed, but Seattle First still has a perfected security interest in Ptarimigan's inventory, and hence it has a floating lien on the inventory.

Similarly, the concept of a floating lien can apply to a stock of goods as it is processed and sold. Under Section 9-205, the lien can start with raw materials and follow them as they become finished goods and inventories and as they are sold, turning into accounts receivable, chattel paper, or cash.

PERFECTING A SECURITY INTEREST

As mentioned in this chapter's introduction, a creditor has two main concerns if the debtor defaults—satisfaction of the debt out of certain predesignated property and priority over other creditors. The concept of *attachment,* which establishes the criteria for creating an enforceable security interest, deals with the former concern; the concept of *perfection* deals with the latter.

Even though a security interest has attached, the secured party must take steps in order to protect his or her claim to the collateral over claims that third parties may have, such as other secured creditors, general creditors, trustees in bankruptcy, and purchasers of the collateral that is the subject matter of the security agreement. Perfection represents the legal process by which a secured party is protected against the claims of third parties who may wish to have their debts satisfied out of the same collateral.

Methods of Perfection

There are three basic methods of perfection:

1. **By transfer of collateral.** The debtor can transfer possession of the collateral itself to the secured party. This occurs, for example, in a pawnshop transaction, in which a party trades possession of a necklace or some other item for a sum of money. For most collateral, possession by the secured party is impractical, as it denies the debtor the right to use, sell, or derive income from the property to pay off the debt. With respect to certain instruments (negotiable according to UCC 3-104) or to certificated securities (as defined in UCC 8-102), except in a few cases in which temporary perfections may be obtained, the *only* way for proper perfection is by possession by the secured party. This type of transfer is called a **pledge** [UCC 9-302(1)(a), 9-304(1), 9-305].

Consider an example. Ulster borrows $2,000 from Levine, giving Levine possession of three antique guns as collateral for the loan. Several months later, before Ulster has repaid the loan, a creditor obtains a judgment against Ulster. The creditor seeks to have the sheriff take the valuable antique guns away from Levine. Even though no financing statement has been filed, the creditor cannot touch the antique guns because Levine perfected his security interest in them when he took possession of them.

2. **Automatic perfection.** In certain circumstances, the security interest can be perfected automatically at the time of a credit sale—that is, at the time that the security interest is created under a written security agreement. Note that this *automatic perfection rule*—or *perfection by attachment*—applies only when there is a purchase-money security interest and the goods are *consumer goods* (defined as goods bought or used by the debtor primarily for personal, family, or household purposes). The seller in this situation need do nothing more to protect his or her interest. There are exceptions to this rule, however, that cover security interests in fixtures and in motor vehicles [UCC 9-302(1)(d)]. For those states that have not adopted the 1972 UCC amendments,[4] a purchase-money security interest in farm equipment under a certain statutory value is also automatically perfected by attachment.

Another instance of automatic perfection occurs when a person assigns a small portion of his or her accounts receivable, usually to a collecting agent known as a *factor*. Perfection is automatic as long as the assignment does not by itself or in conjunction with other assignments to the same assignee constitute a transfer of a significant part of the outstanding accounts of the debtor. Other situations in which perfection is automatic (but which are somewhat less important) are listed in UCC 9-302(1).

3. **By filing.** The third and most common method of perfection is by filing a *financing statement*. The UCC requires a financing statement to have: (a) the signature of the debtor, (b) the addresses of both the debtor and the creditor, and (c) a description of the collateral by type or item[5] [UCC 9-402(1)]. Filing is generally the means of perfection to use—unless, of course, the collateral is the kind that a secured party can or must take possession of in order to perfect (such as a money pledge) or unless the creditor has a purchase-money security interest in consumer goods. See Exhibit 29–3 for a sample financing statement.

The financing statement must contain a description of the collateral in which the secured party has a security interest. The purpose of including a description of collateral in a financing statement is to put persons who might later wish to lend to the debtor on notice that certain goods in the debtor's possession are already subject to a perfected security interest. Sometimes the description given in the security agreement varies from that given in the financing statement, with the description in the security agreement being more precise and the description in the financing statement more general. For example, a security agreement drafted as part of a loan to a manufacturer may list all the manufacturer's equipment subject to the loan by serial number, whereas the financing statement may simply describe it as "all equipment owned or hereafter acquired."

---

4. The following states have *not* adopted the 1972 amendments in whole or in part: Louisiana, Missouri, South Carolina, and Vermont.

5. For certain types of collateral—crops, timber to be cut, minerals, accounts, and goods that are to become fixtures—the financing statement must include more than a description of the collateral itself. For example, a description of the real estate concerned is also required in some of these cases [UCC 9-402(1)(5), 9-103(5), 9-313].

Exhibit 29–3 **A Sample Financing Statement**

This FINANCING STATEMENT is presented for filing pursuant to the California Uniform Commercial Code.

1. DEBTOR (LAST NAME FIRST—IF AN INDIVIDUAL)	1A. SOCIAL SECURITY OR FEDERAL TAX NO.	
1B. MAILING ADDRESS	1C. CITY, STATE	1D. ZIP CODE
2. ADDITIONAL DEBTOR (IF ANY) (LAST NAME FIRST—IF AN INDIVIDUAL)	2A. SOCIAL SECURITY OR FEDERAL TAX NO.	
2B. MAILING ADDRESS	2C. CITY, STATE	2D. ZIP CODE
3. DEBTOR'S TRADE NAMES OR STYLES (IF ANY)	3A. FEDERAL TAX NUMBER	

4. SECURED PARTY

NAME

MAILING ADDRESS

CITY   STATE   ZIP CODE

4A. SOCIAL SECURITY NO., FEDERAL TAX NO. OR BANK TRANSIT AND A.B.A. NO.

5. ASSIGNEE OF SECURED PARTY (IF ANY)

NAME

MAILING ADDRESS

CITY   STATE   ZIP CODE

5A. SOCIAL SECURITY NO., FEDERAL TAX NO. OR BANK TRANSIT AND A.B.A. NO.

6. This FINANCING STATEMENT covers the following types or items of property **(include description of real property on which located and owner of record when required by instruction 4).**

As security for and in consideration of all present and any future advances or other obligations debtor hereby grants United California Bank a security interest in all of the following types or items of property ("Collateral" herein) in which the debtor now has or hereafter acquires any right, title, or interest, or rights present and future, wheresoever located and whether in the possession of the debtor, a warehouseman, bailee, trustee or any other person, and all increases, therein and replacements, products, and proceeds thereof. Proceeds include but are not limited to inventory, returned merchandise, accounts, chattel paper, general intangibles, insurance proceeds, documents, money, goods, equipment, instruments, and any other tangible or intangible property arising under the sale, lease or other disposition of collateral:

7. CHECK IF APPLICABLE [X]   7A. ☐ PRODUCTS OF COLLATERAL ARE ALSO COVERED

7B. DEBTOR(S) SIGNATURE NOT REQUIRED IN ACCORDANCE WITH INSTRUCTION 5(c) ITEM:
☐ (1)   ☐ (2)   ☐ (3)   ☐ (4)

8. CHECK IF APPLICABLE [X]   ☐ DEBTOR IS A "TRANSMITTING UTILITY" IN ACCORDANCE WITH UCC § 9105 (1) (n)

9.   DATE:

►

SIGNATURE(S) of DEBTOR(S)

TYPE OR PRINT NAME(S) OF DEBTOR(S)

►

SIGNATURE(S) OF SECURED PARTY(IES)

TYPE OR PRINT NAME(S) OF SECURED PARTY(IES)

11. *Return copy to:*

NAME

ADDRESS

CITY

STATE

ZIP CODE

(1) FILING OFFICER COPY

CODE
1
2
3
4
5
6
7
8
9
0

10. THIS SPACE FOR USE OF FILING OFFICER (DATE, TIME, FILE NUMBER AND FILING OFFICER)

FORM UCC-1—FILING FEE $3.00
Approved by the Secretary of State

MS-336 10-78

To avoid problems that might be caused by different descriptions, a secured party may repeat exactly the security agreement's description in the financing statement; file the security agreement as a financing statement, assuming it meets the previously discussed criteria; or, where permitted, file a combination security agreement–financing statement form.

The following case illustrates the importance of the description of collateral in a security agreement—a security interest is granted in the collateral only to the extent of the collateral's description in the security agreement. If the description in the financing statement is different, the security agreement's description prevails.

Case 29.1
ALLIS-CHALMERS CORP. v. STAGGS
Appellate Court of Illinois, Fifth District, 1983.
117 Ill.App.3d 428, 453 N.E.2d 145, 72 Ill.Dec. 840.

BACKGROUND AND FACTS   On July 19, 1979, debtor Staggs Farm Equipment, Inc. (the defendant), an Allis-Chalmers dealer, granted Allis-Chalmers (the plaintiff) a security interest pursuant to the terms of a security agreement. The property named as collateral in the agreement with Allis-Chalmers Corp. was described as follows:

> The Debtor's inventory of new machinery manufactured or sold by Secured Party, attachments, accessories and replacement parts therefor now owned or hereafter acquired by the Debtor from the Secured Party plus all proceeds derived therefrom. The collateral is more specifically described in Debtor's purchase orders, invoices, and periodic inventories signed by both parties. For the purpose of identification, such purchase orders, invoices and inventories, as and when executed, are by reference made a part hereof.

On July 25, 1979, the plaintiff filed the financing statement with the Illinois Secretary of State. The financing statement described the property as follows:

> The debtor's inventory of new and used Farm Equipment, new and used Lawn and Garden Equipment, together with implements, attachments and accessories thereto and replacement parts therefor manufactured by or offered for sale by Allis-Chalmers Corporation now owned or hereafter acquired, on which the debtor has given or hereafter grants Allis-Chalmers Corporation a security interest. Proceeds of Collateral are also covered.

On February 20, 1980, Staggs purchased a farm implement business from Bailey, pursuant to the terms of a contract for sale executed on that date. To secure part of the purchase price, Bailey took a security interest in parts in stock as inventoried on February 1, 1980, and valued at $100,000. Bailey filed a financing statement with the Illinois Secretary of State on February 29, 1980, in which the collateral was described as follows:

> All stock in trade, inventory, parts and replacement parts now owned or hereinafter acquired and all accounts receivable and chattel paper now owned or hereinafter acquired.

Staggs discontinued business operations in August 1981, and on September 28, 1981, Allis-Chalmers brought an action in order to recover from Bailey (also a defendant) the inventory of Staggs in which Allis-Chalmers had a security interest.

The trial court granted summary judgment for the plaintiff. The court reasoned that Allis-Chalmers's security interest had priority, since Allis-Chalmers had filed its financing statement covering the debtor's inventory before

Bailey filed his financing statement covering the same inventory. Under UCC 9-312(5)(a) conflicting security interests are ranked according to priority in time of filing.

On appeal, Bailey contended that the plaintiff's security interest was limited to the terms of its security agreement and that the inventory acquired from Bailey under the contract of February 20, 1980, would not have come within the description of property covered by the plaintiff's security interest.

JONES, Justice.

* * * *

Inconsistency between the financing statement and the security agreement may * * * arise where the financing statement states a greater or lesser quantity than the security agreement. The description in the financing statement can neither reduce nor enlarge the security interest actually created by the parties. Consequently, when the financing statement describes a greater quantity of property or additional property beyond that described in the security agreement, the "surplus" description has no effect; *the security interest is only as extensive as the property described in the security agreement* and the financing statement is not effective to do more than perfect the interest in that property. [Emphasis added.]

Applying this rule to the instant case, we find that the trial court erred in determining the parties' rights in the disputed property by reference to the description of collateral contained in the plaintiffs' financing statements. The plaintiffs' security interest was limited, therefore, to that portion of Staggs' inventory that was owned by Staggs on July 19, 1979, or acquired thereafter by Staggs from Allis-Chalmers, and it could not be extended by the broader description contained in the plaintiffs' financing statements. We note parenthetically that the trial court overlooked the final clause of the financing statement description that referred to inventory "on which the debtor has given or hereafter grants Allis-Chalmers Corporation a security interest" in making its ruling. Since the plaintiffs had no interest in Allis-Chalmers inventory acquired after July 19, 1979, from a third party, Bailey is entitled to this inventory by virtue of his purchase money security interest in property sold under the contract of February 20, 1980.

* * * *

In holding that a broader description of collateral in a financing statement is ineffective to extend a security interest beyond that stated in the security agreement, courts have noted that it is the security agreement itself that "creates or provides for a security interest." The function of the financing statement is merely to put third parties on notice that the secured party who filed it may have a perfected security interest in the collateral described. The Code further provides that a security agreement "is effective according to *its* terms." [A] security interest is not effective against third parties unless the debtor has signed a security agreement which contains a description of the collateral. These provisions indicate that a security interest cannot exist in the absence of a security agreement, and it follows that a security interest is limited to property described in the security agreement.

This view has been expressed by the authors of the Illinois Code Comment in referring to section 9-110 of the Code, which states the requirement for sufficiency of a description under Article 9. They observe:

It is important to bear in mind * * * that a general description adequate in a financing statement (§ 9-402) may not be sufficient in the underlying security agreement (§ 9-203(1)(a)). The former is solely to give notice: the latter creates substantive rights in collateral. * * * The security agreement and the financing statement are double screens through which the secured party's rights to collateral are viewed, and his rights are measured by the narrower of the two.

The court of appeals reversed the judgment of the trial court. Bailey was entitled to the inventory covered by the February 20, 1980, contract.

DECISION AND REMEDY

CLASSIFICATION OF COLLATERAL DETERMINES WHERE TO FILE In order for the place of filing to be determined, goods must be classified as consumer goods, equipment, farm products, or inventory. Collateral also may be classified by legal scholars as indispensable paper, consisting of chattel paper, documents of title, and instruments, or as other intangible collateral, such as accounts and general intangibles. The classes of goods are mutually exclusive; *the same property cannot at the same time and to the same person be both equipment and inventory,* for example. Is a physician's car equipment or a consumer good? Is a farmer's jeep equipment or a consumer good? The principal *use* to which the property is put by the debtor determines its classification. If the physician puts the car primarily to personal use, then it is a consumer good; if it is used primarily for his or her medical practice, then it is equipment. If a farmer's jeep is necessary for farming operations and is used primarily for that, then the jeep is classified as farm equipment. But the car and jeep can never be categorized as both equipment and consumer goods [UCC 9-109].

Goods can fall into different classes at different times. For example, a CB radio is inventory when it is in the hands of a dealer [UCC 9-109(4)]. But when it is purchased by a consumer for use in a private car, it becomes a consumer good [UCC 9-109(1)]. When it is bought and installed in a police patrol car, it is equipment [UCC 9-109(2)]. Under the Code, the majority rule is that the classification and filing are based on the *primary use* being made of the collateral at the time of filing.

Depending upon the classification of collateral, filing is either centrally with the secretary of state or locally with a county official, or both, according to state law. According to UCC 9-401, a state may choose one of three proposed alternative systems.[6] In general, financing statements for consumer goods or for any collateral used or arising from a farmer's business should be filed with the county clerk. Other kinds of collateral require filing with the secretary of state [UCC 9-401].

It is important to note that if a secured party fails to perfect properly, the perfection is void and a later, properly perfected, security interest has

priority. For example, suppose a state has adopted the second alternative of UCC 9-401. This alternative provides for central filing (usually with the secretary of state) if the collateral is inventory. West Bank loans retail seller Alger $5,000, and Alger puts up all existing inventory and any after-acquired inventory as collateral. Alger signs a security agreement and a financing statement. By error, West files the financing statement locally (with the county clerk). Later, Alger, in need of working capital, secures a loan from Friendly Savings and Loan. Alger puts up as collateral some newly acquired inventory she paid for previously with cash. Alger signs a security agreement and a financing statement. Friendly Savings perfects its security interest by filing centrally. If Alger goes into default on both loans, Friendly's proper perfection gives it priority to the after-acquired inventory because West Bank's perfection, although prior in time, was improperly filed and therefore void.

There is an exception. A financing statement filed in an improper place is effective against any party who has actual knowledge of the contents of the improperly filed statement [UCC 9-401(2)]. Thus, in the example just given, if, in a search of financing statements filed locally, Friendly had discovered West Bank's statement, Friendly's subsequent properly filed statement covering the same property would not have priority over West Bank's defectively filed statement.

According to UCC 9-401, once the security agreement is properly filed, any change in the use of the collateral will not endanger the security interest of the secured party. State laws other than the UCC control when filing is done for each category of collateral. Exhibit 29–4 summarizes the various classifications of collateral and the methods of perfecting a security interest.

Perfection of a Security Interest in Proceeds

Perfection of a security interest in proceeds is available automatically upon perfection of the secured party's security interest and remains perfected for ten days after receipt of the proceeds by the debtor. One way to extend the ten-day automatic period is to provide for such extended coverage in the original security agreement. This is typically done when the collateral is of the type that is likely to be sold.

---

6. Approximately half the states have adopted the second alternative. See UCC 9-401 in Appendix B. Filing fees range from as low as $3 to as high as $25.

Exhibit 29–4 Types of Collateral and Methods of Perfection

TYPE OF COLLATERAL	DEFINITIONS	PERFECTION METHOD	UCC SECTIONS
Tangible	All things that are *movable* at the time the security interest attaches or that are *fixtures* [UCC 9-105(1)(h)]. This includes timber to be cut, growing crops, and unborn animals.		
1. Consumer goods	Goods used or bought primarily for personal, family, or household purposes—for example, household furniture [UCC 9-109(1)].	For purchase-money security interest, attachment is sufficient; for boats, motor vehicles, and trailers, filing or compliance with a certificate of title statute is required; for other consumer goods, general rules of filing or possession apply.	9-302(1)(d), 9-302(3), 9-302(4), 9-305
2. Equipment	Goods bought for or used primarily in business—for example, a delivery truck [UCC 9-109(2)].	Filing or possession by secured party.	9-302(1), 9-305
3. Farm products	Crops, livestock, and supplies used or produced in a farming operation in the possession of a farmer-debtor. This includes products of crops or livestock—for example, milk, eggs, maple syrup, and ginned cotton [UCC 9-109(3)].	Filing or possession by secured party.	9-302(1), 9-305
4. Inventory	Goods held for sale or lease and materials used or consumed in the course of business—for example, raw materials or the floor stock of a retailer [UCC 9-109(4)].	Filing or possession by secured party.	9-302(1), 9-305
5. Fixtures	Goods that become so affixed to realty that an interest in them arises under real estate law—for example, a central air conditioning unit [UCC 9-313(1)(a)].	Filing only.	9-313(1)
Intangible	Nonphysical property that exists only in connection with something else.		
1. Chattel paper	Any writing that evidences both a *monetary obligation* and a *security interest*—for example, a thirty-six-month-payment retail security agreement and note signed by a buyer to purchase a car [UCC 9-105(1)(b)].	Filing or possession by secured party.	9-304(1), 9-305
2. Documents of title	Paper that entitles the person in possession to hold, receive, or dispose of the paper or goods the document covers—for example, bills of lading, warehouse receipts, and dock warrants [UCC 9-105(1)(f), 1-201(15), 7-201].	Filing or possession by secured party.	9-304(1)(3); 9-305
3. Instruments	Any writing that evidences a right to payment of money and that is not a security agreement or lease, and any negotiable instrument or certificated security that in the ordinary course of business is transferred by delivery with any necessary indorsement or assignment—for example, stock certificates, promissory notes, and certificates of deposit [UCC 9-105(1)(i), 3-104, 8-102(1)(a)].	Unless temporary perfected status, possession only.	9-304(1), (4), (5); 9-305

(Continued on the next page)

Exhibit 29-4 Types of Collateral and Methods of Perfection (Continued)

TYPE OF COLLATERAL	DEFINITIONS	PERFECTION METHOD	UCC SECTIONS
4. Accounts	Any right to payment for goods sold or leased or services rendered that is not evidenced by an instrument or chattel paper—for example, accounts receivable and contract right payments [UCC 9-106].	Filing (with exceptions).	9-302(1)(e), (g)
5. General intangibles	Any personal property other than that defined above—for example, a patent, a copyright, goodwill, or a trademark [UCC 9-106].	Filing only.	9-302(1)

The UCC provides three methods by which the security interest in proceeds may remain perfected for longer than ten days after the receipt of the proceeds by the debtor. They are as follows:

1. When a filed financing statement covers the original collateral and the proceeds are collateral in which a security interest may be perfected by filing in the office or offices where the financing statement has been filed. Furthermore, a secured creditor's interest automatically perfects in property that the debtor acquires with cash proceeds, if the original filing would have been effective as to that property and the financing statement indicates the types of property constituting those proceeds [UCC 9-306(3)(a)]. (See Exhibit 29-3 for an example of the appropriate phrasing.)

2. When there is a filed financing statement that covers the original collateral and the proceeds are identifiable cash proceeds [UCC 9-306(3)(b)].

3. When the security interest in the proceeds is perfected before the expiration of the ten-day period [UCC 9-306(3)(c)].

Collateral Moved to Another Jurisdiction

Obviously, collateral may be moved by the debtor from one jurisdiction (state) to another. When this occurs, a problem arises in that only parties who check the records in the county (local filing) or state (central filing) in which perfection properly took place are actually aware of the secured party's filing, even though the law imputes constructive notice to all. Frequently, the secured party is not even aware that the collateral has been moved out of the jurisdiction. A subsequent lender who per-

fects his or her security interest in the same collateral could wrongly believe that he or she has first priority on the debtor's default.

The Code addresses these problems and at the same time furthers the concept of the floating lien. In general, a properly perfected security interest in collateral moved into a new jurisdiction continues to be perfected in the new jurisdiction for a period of up to four months from the date it was moved or for the period of time remaining under the perfection in the original jurisdiction, whichever expires first [UCC 9-103(1)(d), 9-103(3)(e)]. Collateral moved from county to county *within* a state where local filing is required, however, may not have a four-month limitation, and the original filing may have continuous priority. [See UCC 9-403(3).]

To illustrate: Suppose that on January 1 Calvin secures a loan from a Kansas bank by putting up all his wheat–threshing equipment as security. The Kansas bank files the security interest centrally with the secretary of state. In June, Calvin has an opportunity to harvest wheat crops in South Dakota and moves his equipment into that state on June 15. Under the UCC, the Kansas bank's perfection remains effective in South Dakota for a period of four months from June 15. If the equipment remains in South Dakota, and the Kansas bank wishes to retain its perfection priority longer than four months, it must perfect properly in South Dakota during this four-month period. Should it fail to do so, its perfection will be lost after four months, and subsequent perfected security interests in the same collateral in South Dakota will prevail.

Among mobile goods, automobiles pose one of the biggest problems. If either the new or the original jurisdiction requires a certificate of title as part of its perfection process for an automobile, perfection does not automatically end after four months. Instead, perfection ends as soon as the automobile is registered again (after the end of the four-month period) and a "clean" certificate of title is obtained [UCC 9-103(2)].

The Effective Time of Perfection

The Code furthers the floating lien concept with provisions affecting the time period during which a properly perfected security interest has priority. A filing statement is effective for five years from the date of filing [UCC 9-403(2)]. If a continuation statement is filed *within six months* prior to the expiration date, the effectiveness of the original statement is continued for another five years, starting with the expiration date of the first five-year period [UCC 9-403(3)]. The effectiveness of the statement can be continued in the same manner indefinitely.

PRIORITIES

The consequences of perfection and nonperfection are important in determining priorities among parties having conflicting interests in the same collateral.

Perfection is important because the Code makes it clear that an *unperfected* security interest is of little value when challenged by a third party. According to UCC 9-301, certain categories of persons prevail over the unperfected security interest:

1. A person who has a perfected security interest in the same collateral.
2. A lien creditor—that is, a creditor who acquires a lien on property by attachment or **levy** (judicial process), including a trustee in bankruptcy [UCC 9-301(3)].
3. A person who is a transferee in bulk (see UCC Article 6 and Chapter 17) or other buyer not in the ordinary course of business (under the Food Security Act of 1985, discussed below, buyers of farm products are buyers in the ordinary course of business), to the extent that that person gives value and receives delivery of the collateral without knowledge of the security interest and before it is perfected.

4. A person who is a transferee of accounts or general intangibles, to the extent that the transferee gives value without knowledge of the security interest and before it is perfected.

Assuming a party has an enforceable security interest, his or her priority will depend upon the time at which the security interest attached (became enforceable) or the time at which it became perfected, or both, according to the following rules:

1. *Conflicting perfected security interests.* When two or more secured parties have perfected security interests in the same collateral, generally the *first to perfect* (file or take possession of collateral) wins [UCC 9-312(5)(a)].
2. *Conflicting unperfected security interests.* When two conflicting security interests are unperfected, the *first in time* to attach has priority [UCC 9-312(5)(b)].
3. *Conflicting perfected security interests in commingled or processed goods.* When goods with two or more perfected security interests are so manufactured or commingled that they lose their separate identities into a product or mass, the perfected security interests attach to the new product or mass "according to the ratio that the cost of goods to which each interest originally attached bears to the cost of the total product or mass" [UCC 9-315(2)].

EXCEPTIONS TO PERFECTION PRIORITY RULES

Under certain circumstances, the perfection of a security interest will not protect a secured party against certain other third parties having claims to the collateral. The following discussion covers these exceptions to perfection priority rules.

Non-purchase-Money versus Purchase-Money Perfected Security Interests

The general rule, as previously stated, is that the first in time to perfect is first in priority rights to the collateral. This rule is always applicable when the first in time to perfect is a purchase-money security interest. The Code provides, however, that under certain conditions a purchase-money security interest, properly perfected, will prevail over a non-purchase-money security interest in after-acquired collateral, even though the non-purchase-money security interest was perfected first in time.

If the collateral is *inventory*, a perfected purchase-money security interest will prevail over a previously perfected non-purchase-money security interest, provided (generally) that the purchase-money secured party perfects *and* gives the non-purchase-money secured party written notice of his or her interest *before* the debtor takes possession of the newly acquired inventory [UCC 9-312(3)].

If the collateral is other than inventory, a purchase-money security interest will have priority over a previously perfected non-purchase-money security interest provided that the purchase-money security interest is perfected either before or within ten days *after* the debtor takes possession. No notice is required [UCC 9-312(4)].

To illustrate: Retailer Mary needs a loan of money to be used as working capital. On May 1, she secures a one-year installment loan from West Bank, signing a security agreement and putting up her present inventory plus any after-acquired inventory as collateral. That same date, West Bank perfects by filing a financing statement centrally. On August 1, Mary learns that she can purchase directly from Martin, a manufacturer, $10,000 worth of new inventory, which is a bargain. Since she cannot pay this amount in cash, she signs a security agreement with Martin, giving Martin a security interest in the newly purchased inventory. Delivery of the new inventory is to be on September 1. The new inventory is delivered on September 1 as ordered. On September 7, a fire destroys most of Mary's store and warehouse. There remains only a part of the new inventory, and its value is insufficient to cover both debts. Who has priority with regard to the remaining inventory, West Bank or Martin?

If Martin perfected by filing and gave West Bank notice of its security interest prior to September 1, the date Mary received possession, Martin prevails. If Martin did not meet these conditions, West Bank prevails.

Suppose the collateral is equipment, rather than inventory, and Martin perfected on September 8, after the fire. Since Martin properly perfected its

purchase-money security interest within ten days after Mary received delivery, Martin prevails over West Bank for the remaining after-acquired equipment.

Buyers in the Ordinary Course of Business

Since buyers should not be required to find out if there is an outstanding security interest on a merchant's inventory, the Code provides that a person who buys "in the ordinary course of business" will take the goods free from any security interest in the merchant's inventory, even if the security interest is perfected and even if the buyer knows of its existence [UCC 9-307(1)]. A *buyer in the ordinary course of business* is defined as any person who in good faith, and without knowledge that the sale is *in violation* of the ownership rights or security interest of a third party in the goods, buys in ordinary course from a person in the business of selling goods of that kind [UCC 1-201(9)].

Suppose retail seller Carl secures a loan from West Bank and puts up his existing appliance inventory and any appliance inventory thereafter acquired as collateral. Carl signs a security agreement and a financing statement, which West Bank properly perfects. Later Carl sells an appliance from inventory covered by the security agreement to Lee, with Lee paying cash. If Carl goes into default on the loan, West Bank's prior perfected security has no effect upon Lee. Lee took the appliance completely free of West Bank's security interest, even though perfected, and West Bank loses this item of collateral for satisfaction of the default. (Of course, West Bank has rights in any identifiable cash proceeds.)

In the case on the following page, the court must determine at what point a buyer becomes a buyer in the ordinary course of business.

Buyers of Farm Products

Under the UCC, a buyer of farm products from a farmer takes the products subject to a security interest, even if the buyer knows nothing about the existence of a security agreement [UCC 9-307(1)]. Under the Food Security Act of 1985 (7 U.S.C. Section 1631), however, buyers in the ordinary course of business include buyers of farm products from a farmer. Under the Food Security

BACKGROUND AND FACTS   *The Big Knob Volunteer Fire Department (the plaintiff) agreed to buy a fire truck from Hamerly Custom Productions, Inc., which was in the business of assembling component parts into fire trucks. The plaintiff paid Hamerly $48,000 toward the $51,836 purchase price. Under their contract, Hamerly agreed to deliver the truck within twenty to seventy days of receiving the chassis from a third-party supplier. The contract also provided that title to the truck would not pass to the plaintiff until the price had been paid in full. Hamerly ordered the chassis from Lowe & Moyer Garage, Inc. (the defendant), and on receiving the chassis began transforming it into a fire truck, painting "Big Knob Volunteer Fire Department" on the cab. The chassis was subject to a security interest. However, Hamerly neither paid the defendant for the chassis nor completed the truck and delivered it to the plaintiff. Consequently, both plaintiff and defendant sued Hamerly. Hamerly surrendered the truck to the defendant, which dropped its suit. The plaintiff obtained a default judgment against Hamerly for specific performance and then sued Hamerly and the defendant to replevy (repossess) the truck. The trial court found in favor of the defendant for the chassis or its value, reasoning that since title had not passed, the plaintiff was not a buyer in the ordinary course of business. The plaintiff appealed.*

Case 29.2
BIG KNOB VOLUNTEER FIRE COMPANY v. LOWE & MOYER GARAGE, INC.
Superior Court of Pennsylvania, 1985.
338 Pa.Super. 257, 487 A.2d 953.

SPAETH, President Judge.

*   *   *   *

*   *   * The trial court held that the Volunteer Fire Department was not a buyer in ordinary course because there was no sale to it. Relying on the definition of "sale" as "the passing of title from the seller to the buyer for a price," § 2-106(a), the trial court held that "[n]either title to the truck passed, nor was delivery made to plaintiff."

The point at which a person becomes a buyer in ordinary course is subject to considerable controversy because the Code does not specify the moment at which the status is conferred. The controversy arises in the context of both § 9-307(a) and § 2-403(b) of the Code.

*   *   *   *

The cases are divided. Cases denying recovery to a party on the ground that the party was not a buyer in ordinary course reason that a sale is required, § 1-201; a sale requires transfer of title, § 2-106(a); and a transfer of title occurs either when agreed upon by the parties or upon physical delivery, § 2-401(2). Absent satisfaction of these criteria, the buyer will not prevail even though some or all of the purchase price has been paid. *   *   * This reasoning places the buyer who has paid in advance for goods not yet delivered in an extremely vulnerable position.

Emphasis upon a title-passing test means that *until* title passes, either according to the contract or through seller's delivery of the goods, the "executory buyer's" status is in jeopardy. He is subject to the superior rights of an inventory secured party and runs the risk of being advised that the sale to him is in violation of the security agreement, so that he may never become a buyer in ordinary course of business.

The modern trend in contests between a buyer without possession and a secured creditor, typically the inventory financer, is to ignore or deemphasize the concept of "sale." Instead of focusing on passage of title (delivery), courts and commentators increasingly favor identification as the critical moment that determines when a buyer becomes a buyer in ordinary course.

*   *   *   *

*   *   * [C]ourts have with increasing frequency held that passing of title (when agreed to or occurring upon delivery, § 2-401(2)) is not essential to a person becoming a buyer in ordinary course of business. We agree with these courts, and hold that identification rather than delivery is the point at which a person becomes a buyer in ordinary course of business. Since here the fire truck was identified to the contract, the Volunteer Fire Company did become a buyer in ordinary course of business. Upon entrusting the goods to Hamerly, which dealt in goods of that kind, Lowe & Moyer gave Hamerly the power to transfer its rights to a buyer in ordinary course of business, and Hamerly exercised that power when it painted the Volunteer Fire Department's name on the cab of the fire truck, identifying the goods to the contract and making the Volunteer Fire Department a buyer in ordinary course of business. *   *   *

DECISION AND REMEDY   *The Big Knob Volunteer Fire Company was held to be a buyer in the ordinary course of business, even though title would not pass until the purchase price was fully paid. Therefore, the Volunteer Fire Company was entitled to possession of the truck free of the security interest.*

Act, a secured party is not protected against a buyer of farm products from a farmer unless one of the following occurs:

1.   The buyer has received notice of the security interest within one year before the purchase.
2.   The buyer fails to register with the secretary of state before the purchase, and the secured party has properly perfected his or her interest centrally.
3.   The buyer received notice from the secretary of state that the farm products being sold are subject to an *effective financing statement* (EFS). An EFS is a form that a secured party must file in addition to an Article 9 financing statement to protect his or her interest in a farmer's products in those states with EFS filing systems.

Secondhand Goods: Goods Sold by a Consumer to a Consumer

Carla, a consumer, purchases a refrigerator on credit because she cannot pay the full purchase price. A written security agreement exists in which the seller takes a purchase-money security interest in the consumer goods under this type of credit plan. Further, the seller need not file a financing statement because, when a purchase-money security interest is taken in consumer goods, *perfection occurs automatically* [UCC 9-302(1)(d)]. Later, Carla sells the refrigerator to her next door neighbor, Nan, who purchases it for home use without any knowledge of the credit arrangements between Carla and the original seller. Subsequently, Carla defaults on the credit payments to the seller. What are the seller's rights? The seller had a perfected purchase-money security interest in the refriger-

ator when it was held by Carla. Under UCC 9-307(2), however, the perfection is not good against the next door neighbor.

UCC 9-307(2) requires that a person in the position of this next door neighbor must purchase (give value for) the goods for personal, family, or household use, without knowledge of the original seller's security interest, and that the purchase must take place *before* the secured party has filed a financing statement. In this case, recall that the seller took a purchase-money security interest, which is perfected automatically. No filing was required. Hence, the next door neighbor purchased the refrigerator free and clear before the seller had filed a financing statement. The seller could have avoided this possibility simply by *filing* a financing statement, even though a purchase-money security interest had been perfected.

Buyers of Chattel Paper and Instruments

Another purchaser who may not be subject to a secured party's interest despite perfection is the purchaser of chattel paper and instruments. This protection is provided by Section 9-308. As previously defined, *chattel paper* is a writing or writings that evidence both a monetary obligation and a security interest in specific goods. *Instrument* means a negotiable instrument as defined in UCC 3-104, or a certificated security as defined in UCC 8-102, or basically any other writing that evidences a right to the payment of money and is not itself a security agreement or lease transferred in the ordinary course of business [UCC 9-105(1)(i)].

Chattel paper is a very important class of collateral used in financing arrangements, especially in automobile financing. When it is sold by a creditor, the creditor can deliver it over to the assignee, who is then responsible for collecting the debt directly from the debtor. This arrangement is known as *notification* or *direct collection*. As an alternative, a creditor can sell chattel paper to an assignee with the understanding that the creditor will retain the chattel paper, make collections from the debtor, and then remit the money to the assignee. This kind of transaction is *nonnotification* or *indirect collection*. The widespread use of both methods of dealing with chattel paper is recognized by the Code, and hence the Code permits perfection of a chattel paper security interest either by filing or by taking possession of the chattel paper.

Problems arise when perfection is made by filing only. If the chattel paper is thereafter sold to another purchaser who gives *new value* and takes *possession* of the paper in the *ordinary course of business*, *without knowledge* that it is subject to a security interest, the new purchaser will have priority over the secured creditor. (Of course, the creditor has rights in the proceeds.)

The *Concept Summary* on page 546 deals with the priority of claims to a debtor's collateral.

THE RIGHTS AND DUTIES OF DEBTORS AND CREDITORS UNDER THE UCC

The security agreement itself determines most of the rights and duties of the debtor and the creditor. The UCC, however, imposes some rights and duties that are applicable in the absence of a security agreement to the contrary.

Information Request by Creditors

Under UCC 9-407(1), a creditor has the option, when making the filing, of asking the filing officer to make a note of the file number, the date, and the hour of the original filing on a copy of the financing statement. The filing officer must send this copy to the person making the request. Under UCC 9-407(2), a filing officer must also give information to a person who is contemplating obtaining a security interest from a prospective debtor. The filing officer must give a certificate that provides information on possible perfected financing statements with respect to the named debtor. The filing officer will charge a fee for copies provided.

Assignment, Amendment, and Release

At any time, a secured party of record can release part or all of the collateral described in a filed financing statement. This ends his or her security interest in the collateral [UCC 9-406]. A secured party can assign part or all of the security interest to another, called the assignee. That assignee becomes the secured party of record if, for example, he or she either makes a notation of the assignment somewhere on the financing statement or files a written statement of assignment [UCC 9-405(2)].

It is also possible to amend a financing statement that has already been filed. The amendment must be signed by *both* parties. The debtor has to sign the security agreement, the original financing statement, and the amendments [UCC 9-402(4)]. All other secured transaction documents, such as releases, assignments, continuations of perfection, perfections of collateral moved into another jurisdiction, and termination statements, need only be signed by the secured party.

Reasonable Care of Collateral

If a secured party is in possession of the collateral, he or she must use reasonable care in preserving it. Otherwise, the secured party is liable to the debtor [UCC 9-207(1),(3)]. If the collateral increases in value, the secured party can hold this increased value or profit as additional security unless it is in the form of money, which must be remitted to the debtor or applied toward reducing the secured debt [UCC 9-207(2)(c)]. Additionally, the collateral must be kept in identifiable condition unless it is fungible [UCC 9-207(2)(d)]. Finally, the debtor must pay for all reasonable charges incurred by the secured party in preserving, operating, and taking care of the collateral in possession [UCC 9-207(2)(a)].

The Status of the Debt

During the time in which the secured debt is outstanding, the debtor may wish to know the status of the debt. If so, the debtor need only sign a

CONCEPT SUMMARY: The Priority of Claims to a Debtor's Collateral

PARTIES	PRIORITY
Unperfected secured party	Prevails over unsecured creditors and creditors who have obtained judgments against the debtor but who have not begun the legal process to collect on those judgments (UCC 9-301).
Purchaser of debtor's collateral	1. Goods purchased in the ordinary course of business: Purchaser prevails over a perfected secured party even if the purchaser knows of the security interest [UCC 9-307(1)].
	2. Farm products purchased in the ordinary course of business: Purchaser prevails unless purchaser: a. Received notice of the security interest within one year before the purchase. b. Fails to register with the secretary of state before the purchase, and the secured party has properly perfected his or her interest centrally. c. Received notice from the secretary of state that the farm products being sold are subject to an effective financing statement.
	3. Consumer goods purchased out of the ordinary course of business: Purchaser prevails over a perfected secured party, providing the purchaser purchased: a. For value. b. Without actual knowledge of the security interest. c. For use as a consumer good. d. Prior to secured party's perfection by *filing* [UCC 9-307(2)].
	4. The chattel paper purchaser prevails over a perfected secured party, providing the purchaser: a. Gave new value. b. Took possession. c. Took in the ordinary course of business. d. Took without *actual* knowledge of secured party's perfection (UCC 9-308).
	5. The purchaser of negotiable instruments, documents, and securities prevails over a perfected secured party, particularly if the purchaser is a holder in due course, a holder to whom the document has been duly negotiated, or a bona fide purchaser of a security (UCC 9-308, 9-309).

Perfected secured parties to same collateral	Between two perfected secured parties to the same collateral, the general rule is that first in time of perfection is first in right to the collateral [UCC 9-312(5)]. Exceptions are:
	 a. *Crops*—New value to produce crops given within three months of planting has priority over prior six-month perfected interest [UCC 9-312(2)].
	 b. *Purchase-money security interest*—Even if second in time of perfection (when first in time of perfection is a non-purchase-money security interest), it has priority providing:
	   i. In the case of inventory, that the purchase-money security interest is perfected and proper notice is given to non-purchase-money perfected security interest holder *on* or *before* time that debtor takes possession [UCC 9-312(3)].
	   ii. In the case of other collateral, that the purchase-money security interest has priority, providing such is perfected within ten days after debtor receives possession [UCC 9-312(4)].

statement that indicates the aggregate amount of the unpaid debt at a specific date (and perhaps a list of the collateral covered by the security agreement). The secured party must then approve or correct this statement in writing. The creditor must comply with the request within two weeks of receipt; otherwise, the creditor is liable for any loss caused to the debtor by the failure to do so [UCC 9-208(2)]. One such request is allowed without charge every six months. For each additional request, the secured party can require a fee not exceeding $10 per request [UCC 9-208(3)].

DEFAULT

Article 9 defines the rights, duties, and remedies of a secured party and of the debtor upon a debtor's default. Should the secured party fail to comply with its duties, the debtor is afforded particular rights and remedies.

The topic of default is one of great concern to secured lenders and to the lawyers who draft security agreements. What constitutes default is not always clear. In fact, Article 9 does not define the term. Thus, parties are encouraged in practice and by the Code to include in their security agreements certain standards to be applied in the event that default actually comes about. Consequently, parties can stipulate the conditions that will constitute a default [UCC 9-501(1)].

Typically, because of the disparity in bargaining position between a debtor and a creditor, these critical terms are shaped with exceeding breadth by the creditor in order to give some sense of security. The ultimate terms, however, are not allowed to go beyond the limitations imposed by the good faith requirement of UCC 1-208 and the unconscionability doctrine.

Although any breach of the terms of the security agreement can constitute default, default occurs most commonly when the debtor fails to meet the scheduled payments that the parties have agreed upon or when the debtor becomes bankrupt. If the security agreement covers equipment, however, the debtor may have warranted that he or she is the owner of the equipment or that no liens or other security interests are pending on that equipment. Breach of any of these representations can result in default.

Basic Remedies

According to UCC 9-501, upon default, a secured creditor can reduce a claim to judgment, foreclose, or enforce a security interest by any available judicial process. Where the collateral consists of documents of title, a secured party can proceed against either the documents or the underlying goods.

A secured party's remedies can be divided into two basic categories:

1. A secured party can relinquish a security interest and proceed to judgment on the underlying debt, followed by execution and levy.[7] This is rarely done unless the value of the secured collateral has been greatly reduced below the amount of the debt and the debtor has other nonexempt assets available to satisfy the debt [UCC 9-501(1)].

2. A secured party can take possession of the collateral covered by the security agreement [UCC 9-503]. Upon taking possession, the secured party can retain the collateral covered by the security agreement for satisfaction of the debt [UCC 9-502(2)] or can resell the goods and apply the proceeds toward the debt [UCC 9-504].

Under UCC 9-501(1), a creditor's rights and remedies are *cumulative;* therefore, if a creditor is unsuccessful in enforcing rights by one method, another method can be pursued. The UCC does not require election of remedies between an action on the underlying obligation and repossession of the collateral.[8]

When a security agreement covers both real and personal property, the secured party can proceed against the personal property in accordance with the remedies of Article 9. On the other hand, the secured party can proceed against the entire collateral under procedures set down by local real estate law, in which case the Code does not apply [UCC 9-501(4)].

For example, this situation occurs when the security interest on a corporate loan applies to the

---

7. *Execution and levy* refers to the legal process through which any creditor may obtain satisfaction on a debt. Basically, it entails the creditor's obtaining a favorable judgment, the court's issuing a writ of execution directing an officer (the sheriff, for example) to seize the defendant-debtor's nonexempt property and sell it, and the officer's doing as directed (that is, seizing and selling the property).

8. See J. White and R. Summers, *Uniform Commercial Code,* 2nd ed. (St. Paul: West Publishing Co., 1980), pp. 1093–1094.

manufacturing plant (real property) and also to the inventory (personal property). Determining whether particular collateral is personal or real property can prove to be difficult, especially with regard to fixtures—things affixed to real property. Under certain circumstances, the Code allows the removal of fixtures upon default; however, such removal is subject to the provisions of Article 9 [UCC 9-313].

The Secured Party's Right to Take Possession

The secured party has the right to take possession of the collateral upon default unless the security agreement states otherwise. As long as there is no breach of the peace, the secured party can simply repossess the collateral. Otherwise the secured party must resort to the judicial process [UCC 9-503].

What constitutes a breach of the peace is of prime importance to both parties, for such an act can open the secured party to tort liability. The Code does not define *breach of the peace*. Therefore, parties must resort to state law to determine it.

Generally, neither the creditor nor the creditor's agent can enter a debtor's home, garage, or place of business without permission. Consider a situation in which an automobile is collateral. A repossessing party who walks onto the debtor's premises, proceeds up the driveway, enters the vehicle without entering the garage, and drives off will probably not be considered to have breached the peace. In some states, however, satisfying the elements of an action for wrongful trespass could provide the grounds necessary to initiate an action for breach of the peace. (Most car repossessions occur when the car is parked on a street or in a parking lot.)

In the following case, the court determines whether a breach of the peace occurred when a secured party repossessed the collateral—cattle.

Case 29.3 **HILLIMAN v. COBADO** Supreme Court, Cattaraugus County, 1986. 131 Misc. 2d 206, 499 N.Y.S.2d 610.	**BACKGROUND AND FACTS** *Kent Cobado (defendant) sold John Szata (plaintiff) a herd of cattle subject to an agreement giving the defendant a security interest in the herd—"68 cows and 1 bull"—and the plaintiff's farm, which was owned by Szata's in-laws, the Hillimans. After the cattle's delivery, the plaintiff culled some of the poorer stock from the herd. This annoyed the defendant, who nevertheless replaced thirty-seven cows. Over time, as he made payments on the contract, the plaintiff continued to cull poor stock from the herd. This increasingly annoyed the defendant, until one day, without warning, he drove out to the plaintiff's farm with two deputy sheriffs to repossess the cattle. The plaintiff told them that he was not in default under the security agreement and tried to persuade the defendant to leave. The defendant turned and ran to the barn, saying, "To hell with this. We're taking the cows." As the defendant was in the barn releasing the cattle, one of the deputies told the plaintiff, who was a cripple and could move about only with the aid of a cane, that he—the plaintiff—would be arrested if he got out of line. Unable to reach his attorney over the phone, the plaintiff again urged the defendant to stop. The defendant simply laughed at him, beating the cattle to herd them through a small opening in the barn door. Before the cattle had been loaded onto the defendant's assembled trucks, Lt. Ernie Travis of the Sheriff's Department arrived on the scene and advised the defendant that if he left with the cattle he would be arrested. The defendant ignored the warning, and when he left with the cattle he was arrested for possession of stolen property. Before the court's decision in this case, no disposition had been made of the criminal charge. The court considered the defendant's right to use self-help in repossessing the cattle.*

HOREY, Acting Justice.
*   *   *   *

The right to self help by way of repossession is an assignment of the exclusive power of the sovereignty of a state. This is true because it represents a delegation of the exclusively governmental function of resolving disputes. The delegation of the right of repossession to a secured party [in UCC 9-503] is not a carte blanche one. Rather it is specifically limited and exerciseable only without a breach of the peace. Its exercise should be strictly confined to those situations, rare as they may be, when the repossession can be accomplished peaceably. Physical confrontation or the threat thereof is not necessary to effect a breach of the peace.

Certain it is that in ignoring the order of the purchasers to desist and remove himself from the premises; in ignoring the admonition of Lt. Travis of the Sheriff's Department to desist; in demonstrating his contempt for all restraint by his statement "to hell with this we're taking the cows"; by proceeding to release the cows, beating and herding them to the trucks, without heed of the warning that his continuance would result in his arrest, the defendant Cobado not only engaged in conduct which was likely to produce violence and consternation but did in fact produce violence, consternation and disorder.

This court finds as a matter of fact and law that the retaking of the plaintiff's cattle was a "breach of the peace."

The court found that the taking of the cattle involved a breach of the peace and therefore was not authorized by the UCC and was unlawful. The court held in favor of the plaintiff and ordered that the cattle be returned to him.   **DECISION AND REMEDY**

REASONABLE CARE OF THE COLLATERAL REQUIRED   Once the secured party comes into possession of the collateral by repossession after breach, the rights, remedies, and duties provided by Section 9-207, as previously discussed, come into play. The main requirement of that section calls for the secured party to exercise "reasonable care" in the custody and preservation of any collateral in his or her possession.

This duty cannot be disclaimed, and any exculpatory (excusing) clause will be unenforceable [UCC 1-102(3)]. Reasonable limitations as to what will be required, however, can be agreed upon by the parties. Where the collateral consists of instruments or chattel paper, reasonable care extends to taking necessary steps to preserve rights against parties with prior rights unless otherwise agreed. Should the secured party fail to meet his or her obligations as prescribed in UCC 9-207, that party will be liable for any damages occasioned by such failure. The secured party does not, however, lose the security interest for failure to exercise reasonable care.

ASSEMBLING THE COLLATERAL   UCC 9-503 provides authorization for security agreements to require that, upon default, the debtor assemble the collateral and make it available to the secured party at a location designated by that party. The

location must be reasonably convenient to both parties. This provision is important to a creditor when the collateral is located in several places or when the debtor is in a better position to assemble it.

The Code also recognizes the inherent practical problems involved in removal and disposition of collateral when it is heavy equipment. Removal and storage costs could quickly reach an impractical level. The Code therefore authorizes the secured party to render such equipment "unusable" to the debtor (by locking it, for example) and to dispose of the collateral on the debtor's premises [UCC 9-503]. This authorization does not permit unreasonable action by the secured party, because every aspect of the repossession and disposition must comply with the standards of commercial reasonableness of Section 9-504.

Disposition of Collateral

Once default has occurred, and the secured party has obtained possession of the collateral, the secured party is faced with several alternatives to satisfy the debt. The party can retain the collateral [UCC 9-505(2)] or sell, lease, or otherwise dispose of the collateral in any commercially reasonable manner [UCC 9-504(1)]. Any sale is always subject to procedures established by state law.

RETENTION OF COLLATERAL BY SECURED PARTY AFTER DEFAULT The Code recognizes that parties are sometimes better off if they do not sell the collateral. Therefore, a secured party can retain collateral, but this general right is subject to several conditions. The secured party must send written notice of the proposal to the debtor if the debtor has not signed a statement renouncing or modifying his or her rights after default. With consumer goods, no other notice has to be given. In all other cases, notice must be sent to any other secured party from whom the secured party has received written notice of a claim of interest in the collateral in question. If within twenty-one days after the notice has been sent the secured party receives an objection in writing from a person entitled to receive notification, then the secured party must dispose of the collateral under UCC 9-504. If no such written objection is forthcoming, the secured party can retain the collateral in full satisfaction of the debtor's obligation [UCC 9-505(2)].

CONSUMER GOODS When the collateral is *consumer goods* with a *purchase-money security interest,* and the debtor has paid *60 percent* of the *cash price* or *loan,* then the secured party must dispose of the collateral under UCC 9-504 within ninety days. Failure to comply opens the secured party to an action for conversion or other liability under UCC 9-507(1) unless the consumer-debtor signed a written statement *after default* renouncing or modifying the right to demand the sale of the goods [UCC 9-505(1)].

DISPOSITION PROCEDURES A secured party who does not choose to retain the collateral must resort to the disposition procedures prescribed under UCC 9-504. The Code allows a great deal of flexibility with regard to disposition. The only real limitation is that it must be accomplished in a commercially reasonable manner. UCC 9-507(2) supplies some examples of what does or does not meet the standard of commercial reasonableness:

> The fact that a better price could have been obtained by a sale at a different time or in a different method from that selected by the secured party is not of itself sufficient to establish that the sale was not made in a commercially reasonable manner. If the secured party either sells the collateral in the usual manner in any recognized market therefor or if he sells at the price currently in such a market at the time of sale or if he has otherwise sold in conformity with reasonable commercial practices among dealers in the type of property sold, he has sold in a commercially reasonable manner.

A secured party is not compelled to resort to public sale to dispose of the collateral. The party is given the latitude under the Code to seek out the best terms possible in a private sale. Generally, no specific time requirements must be met; however, the time must ultimately meet the standard of commercial reasonableness.

Generally, in order for a sale to be classified as a sale conducted in a commercially reasonable manner, notice of the place, time, and manner of sale is required. Notice must be sent by the secured party to the debtor if the debtor has not signed a statement renouncing or modifying the right to notification of sale after default. For consumer goods, no other notification need be sent. In all other cases, notification must be sent to any other secured party from whom the secured party has received written notice of claim of an interest in the collateral [UCC 9-504(3)]. No such notice is necessary, however, when the collateral is perishable or threatens to decline speedily in value or when it is of a type customarily sold on a recognized market.

PROCEEDS FROM DISPOSITION Proceeds from the disposition must be applied in the following order:

1. Reasonable expenses stemming from the retaking, holding, or preparing for sale are covered first. When authorized by law and if provided for in the agreement, these can include reasonable attorneys' fees and legal expenses.
2. Satisfaction of the balance of the debt owed to the secured party must then be made.
3. Subordinate security interests whose written demands have been received prior to the completion of distribution of the proceeds are covered third [UCC 9-504(1)].
4. Any surplus generally goes to the debtor.

DEFICIENCY JUDGMENT Often, after proper disposition of the collateral, the secured party has not collected all that was owed by the debtor. Unless otherwise agreed, the debtor is liable for any deficiency. On the other hand, if the underlying transaction was a sale of accounts or of chattel paper, the secured party can collect a deficiency judgment only if the security agreement so provides [UCC 9-504(2)].

REDEMPTION RIGHTS At any time before the secured party disposes of the collateral or enters into a contract for its disposition or before the debtor's obligation has been discharged through the secured party's retention of the collateral, the debtor or any other secured party can exercise the right of *redemption* of the collateral. The debtor or other secured party can do this by tendering performance of *all* obligations secured by the collateral, by paying the expenses reasonably incurred by the secured party, and by retaking the collateral and maintaining its care and custody [UCC 9-506].

TERMINATION

When a debt is paid, the secured party generally must send to the debtor or file with the filing officer to whom the original financing statement was given a termination statement. If the financing statement covers consumer goods, the termination statement must be filed by the secured party within one month after the debt has been paid or within ten days of the debtor's requesting a filing in writing after the debt has been paid, whichever is earlier [UCC 9-404(1)]. In all other cases, the termination statement must be filed or furnished to the debtor within ten days after a written request has been made by the debtor. If the affected secured party fails to file such a termination statement, as required by UCC 9-404(1), or fails to send the termination statement within ten days after proper demand, the secured party will be liable to the debtor for $100. Additionally, the secured party will be liable for any loss caused to the debtor.

QUESTIONS AND CASE PROBLEMS

1. Discuss how each secured party would properly perfect his or her security interest in the following cases.

(a) Martin is a manufacturer of refrigerators. Ray, a retailer, buys a number of these refrigerators. Ray signs a security agreement giving Martin a security interest in the refrigerators.

(b) Mary sells a refrigerator to Carla, to be used in Carla's home. Carla signs a security agreement giving Mary a security interest in the refrigerator.

(c) Ray sells a refrigerator to Dr. Dodd, to be used in his office to store medicines. Dr. Dodd signs a security agreement giving Ray a security interest in the refrigerator.

(d) Mary sells a refrigerator to farmer Ames, who needs it to store eggs not sold at market. Ames signs a security agreement giving Mary a security interest in the refrigerator.

2. Marion has a prize horse named Thunderbolt. Marion is in need of working capital. To secure it, she borrows $5,000 from Rodriguez, with Rodriguez taking possession of Thunderbolt as security for the loan. No written agreement is signed. Discuss whether, in absence of written agreement, Rodriguez has a security interest in Thunderbolt *and* whether Rodriguez can be a perfected secured party without filing a financing statement.

3. Ray is a seller of electric generators. He purchases a large quantity of generators from manufacturer Martin Corporation by making a down payment and signing a security agreement to make the balance of payments over a period of time. The agreement gives Martin Corporation a security interest in the generators and the proceeds. Martin Corporation files a financing statement on its security interest centrally. Ray receives the generators and immediately sells one of them to Green on an installment contract, with payment to be made in twelve equal installments. At the time of sale, Green knows of Martin's security interest. Two months later Ray goes into default on his payments to Martin. Discuss Martin's rights against purchaser Green in this situation.

4. Martin is a manufacturer of washing machines. On September 1, in need of working capital, Martin contacts Smith, a loan officer for the First Bank. Martin asks to borrow $200,000, putting up all its equipment as security. Smith agrees to make the loan. In the security agreement signed by Martin's president is a clause stating that this loan is secured not only by the existing equipment presently located at Martin's plant but by any equipment acquired in the future by Martin. The First Bank files a financing statement centrally on *September 5*. On *November 1*, Martin has an opportunity to purchase from Daniel Equipment Corporation some newly manufactured Daniel equipment at a bargain price of $50,000. On that same date, Martin contracts by a security agreement to purchase the equipment from Daniel, paying $20,000 down and the balance in monthly payments over a three-year period, with Daniel having a security interest in the purchased equipment. The new equipment is delivered on *December 1*. On *December 7*, Daniel perfects its security interest in the newly delivered equipment by filing a financing statement centrally. Later Martin goes into default to both parties. Discuss who has priority over the new equipment, the First Bank or Daniel.

5. Ray is a retail seller of television sets. Ray sells a color television set to Clara for her apartment for $600. Clara cannot pay cash and signs a security agreement, paying $100 down and agreeing to pay the balance in twelve equal installments of $50 each. The security agreement gives Ray a security interest in the television set sold. Clara makes six payments on time; then she goes into default because of unexpected financial problems. Ray repossesses the set and wants to keep it in full satisfaction of the debt. Discuss Ray's rights and duties in this matter.

6. Denise owns and operates a successful restaurant. One year ago she borrowed money from West Bank to make two purchases, an expensive television set for her home and a piece of restaurant equipment. Denise signed security agreements for both purchases with West Bank, giving West Bank a security interest in all of the collateral. West Bank filed a financing statement locally for perfection of its security interest in the television set and centrally for the restaurant equipment. Denise has now made the last payments on both. Discuss West Bank's duties and liabilities to Denise for its failure to file termination statements on the security interests.

7. Ms. Calcote obtained an automobile loan from Citizens & Southern National Bank, with the Bank maintaining a security interest in the car. On March 28, 1984, after Ms. Calcote had defaulted on the loan, the bank repossessed the vehicle. On the following day, the bank sent a certified letter, return receipt requested, to Ms. Calcote informing her of the repossession, of the bank's plans to sell the auto at a private sale in May of 1984, and of her right to demand a public sale of the vehicle. Although the letter was sent to the address on the bank's records and at which the bank had repossessed the car, Ms. Calcote never received the letter. On April 19, 1984, it was returned to the bank stamped "unclaimed." On May 11, 1984, the car was sold at a private sale to which over 150 dealers had been invited. When Ms. Calcote learned that the car had been sold, she brought an action against the bank, claiming she had not been properly notified of the repossession and sale and that the private sale was not a commercially reasonable method of disposition. Discuss fully her claims. [Calcote v. Citizens & Southern National Bank, 179 Ga.App. 132, 345 S.E.2d 616 (1986)]

8. On June 12, 1985, Edward Dye purchased a 1985 Buick Riviera from his close friend of over thirty years, Gordon McGrath, d/b/a (doing business as) McGrath Auto Sales. Under the terms of the sale, Dye purchased the vehicle for the price that the dealer had paid for it. Dye used a set of dealer's license plates, and no certificate of title was assigned to him. McGrath on several occasions asked to use the vehicle to show other clients. The Bank of Illinois provided "floor plan" (inventory) financing to McGrath's automobile dealership and had a perfected security interest in all McGrath's new automobiles. When McGrath defaulted on his loan to the bank, the bank sought to gain possession of the automobile from Dye. Did the bank have a claim to the automobile? Discuss. [Bank of Illinois v. Dye, 163 Ill.App.3d 1018, 517 N.E.2d 38, 115 Ill.Dec. 73 (1987)]

9. McGovern Auto Specialty, Inc., the debtor, granted Kay Automotive Warehouse, Inc., a security interest in various personal property that it owned. Both the security agreement and the financing statement listed the name of the debtor as McGovern Auto and Truck Parts, Inc. Later, the debtor filed a petition to reorganize its capital structure under Chapter 11 of the Bankruptcy Code. Under the Bankruptcy Code, the debtor in possession is given the powers and rights of a trustee in bankruptcy. A trustee can void any unperfected security interest. The debtor claimed that the erroneous listing of the debtor's name in the filing caused the security interest to be unperfected. Kay claimed that the error was minor and that it held a perfected security interest in the personalty with rights superior to those of unsecured creditors and the debtor. Discuss whether Kay was a properly perfected secured party. [In re McGovern Auto Specialty, Inc., 51 B.R. 511 (Bkrtcy.E.D.Pa. 1985)]

10. The First National Bank of North Dakota (plaintiff) loaned Freddie Mutschler, a prominent farmer in Jamestown, North Dakota, $3 million. Mutschler gave the bank a lien on his crops as partial security for the loan. The loan agreement provided that when Mutschler sold his grain, he would be obligated to turn over the proceeds to cover the indebtedness. Mutschler was also the owner, but not the manager, of the Jamestown Farmers Elevator, which bought and sold various farmers' grain. In the fall of 1982, Mutschler sold his crop to the Jamestown Farmers Elevator but did not apply the proceeds to the debt at the bank. The elevator in turn sold some of the grain to the Pillsbury Company, which knew of the bank's security interest but did not know the terms of the security agreement. The bank did not discover these events until Mutschler and the Jamestown Farmers Elevator filed for bankruptcy in early 1983. The bank sued Pillsbury for conversion of the collateral. Which party prevailed? [First Bank of North Dakota v. Pillsbury Company, 801 F.2d 1036 (8th Cir. 1986)]

11. In July of 1978, Dr. Jose B. Namer executed to Citizens and Southern National Bank a note in the amount of $35,000 with an accompanying security agreement in the following property: "All equipment of the debtor of every description used or useful in the conduct of the debtor's business, now or hereafter existing or acquired. . . . The listed assets held for collateral are presently located at 4385 Hugh Howell Rd., Tucker, Ga." In July of 1980, Dr. Namer moved some of his equipment to a new office owned by Hudson Properties, Inc., in Fairburn, Georgia. In order to finance this move, Dr. Namer procured a loan from a Fairburn bank, and Hudson co-signed the note. The Fairburn bank prepared a security agreement covering the same equipment as the 1978 security agreement. In September of 1980, Dr. Namer defaulted on the first note and absconded with the equipment in the Fairburn office. Hudson received an insurance payment as cash proceeds for the missing equipment. Citizens and Southern National Bank claimed priority rights to the missing equipment or proceeds, even though the equipment had been moved to Fairburn. Could Citizens and Southern National Bank recover this insurance money from Hudson? [Hudson Properties, Inc. v. Citizens & Southern National Bank, 168 Ga.App. 331, 308 S.E.2d 708 (1983)]

Chapter 30

Rights of Debtors and Creditors

The law of debtor-creditor relations has undergone various changes over the years. Historically, debtors and their families have been subjected to punishment for their inability to pay debts, including involuntary servitude, imprisonment, and dismemberment. The modern legal system has moved away from a punishment philosophy in dealing with debtors. In fact, many observers say that it has moved too far in the other direction, to the detriment of creditors. Today, consumer protection is emphasized, and the legal system is designed to aid and protect the debtor and the debtor's family.

This chapter deals with various rights and remedies available through statutory laws, common law, and contract law to assist the debtor and creditor in resolving their disputes without the debtor's having to resort to bankruptcy. The next chapter discusses bankruptcy as a last resort to resolve debtor-creditor problems.

LAWS ASSISTING CREDITORS

As pointed out in Chapter 29, if a debtor defaults, a secured creditor's priority can determine whether the creditor recoups complete, partial, or no payment of amounts he or she is owed. Creditors with no priority are paid last, of course—if at all.

A perfected security interest, in the case of personal property, or a mortgage, in the case of real estate, may be referred to as a *consensual lien*. A **lien** is a claim or charge on a debtor's property that must be satisfied before the property (or its proceeds) is available to satisfy the claims of other creditors. Referring to the lien as *consensual* indicates that its basis is the parties' agreement. Consensual liens on personal property are the subject of Article 9 of the UCC and were discussed in Chapter 29. Enforcing payment under a consensual lien on real estate is discussed later in this chapter.

A lien may also arise under a statute or the common law or through a judicial proceeding. Statutory liens include mechanic's liens. Liens created at common law include artisan's liens and innkeeper's liens. Judicial liens include those that represent a creditor's efforts to collect on a debt before a judgment (for example, through prejudgment attachment) or after it (for example, through a writ of execution). These terms are defined in the discussion of remedies that follows.

It is important to remember that a lien creditor has priority only to the extent of the value of his or her collateral. To illustrate, imagine that McInerney owns property worth $100,000, including a cache of furs worth $40,000. McInerney owes Bret $40,000, Easton $50,000, and Ellis $60,000. Bret has a lien on the furs. On McInerney's default, Bret has the first right to the furs or the proceeds from their sale. If the furs turned out to be worth only $20,000, Bret's claim for the other $20,000 would have no greater priority than the claims of Easton and Ellis.

To further reduce the risks involved in extending credit, a creditor may use a surety or a guaranty. Basically, these terms (the difference between them is explained below) refer to a third person who promises to pay a debt or perform an obligation if the principal debtor does not pay or perform. A surety or a guaranty may be used in addition to or instead of security in collateral or realty, when, for example, security is unavailable or too costly.

Mechanic's Lien on Real Property

When a person contracts for labor, services, or material to be furnished for the purpose of making improvements on real property but does not immediately pay for the improvements, a creditor can place a **mechanic's lien** (also known as a *materialman's lien*) on the property. This creates a special type of debtor-creditor relationship wherein the real estate itself becomes security for the lien (debt).

For example, a roofer repairs a leaky roof at the request of a homeowner. The homeowner owes the roofer the agreed-upon price for the materials, labor, and services performed. If the homeowner cannot pay or pays only a portion of the charges, a mechanic's lien against the property can be created. The roofer is the lienholder, and the real property is encumbered with a mechanic's lien for the amount owed. If the homeowner does not pay the lien, the property can be sold to satisfy the debt.

The procedures by which a mechanic's lien is created are controlled by state law. Generally, the lienholder must file a written notice of lien against the particular property involved. The notice of lien must be filed within a specific time period, measured from the last date on which materials or labor were provided (usually within 60 to 120 days). Failure to pay the debt entitles the lienholder to foreclose on the real estate on which the improvements were made and to sell it in order to satisfy the amount of the debt. Of course, the lienholder is required by statute to give notice to the owner of the property prior to foreclosure and sale. The sale proceeds are used to pay the debt and the costs of the legal proceedings; and the surplus, if any, is paid to the former owner.

Artisan's and Innkeeper's Liens on Personal Property

An **artisan's lien** and an **innkeeper's lien** are security devices created at common law. They are similar to a mechanic's lien but are liens on personal property to secure the payment of a debt for labor done, for value added, or for care of the personal property.

For example, Ann leaves her watch at the jeweler's to be repaired and to have her initials engraved on the back. In absence of agreement, the jeweler can keep the watch until Ann pays for the repairs and services that the jeweler provides. Should Ann fail to pay, the jeweler has an artisan's lien on Ann's watch for the amount of the bill and can sell the watch in satisfaction of the lien.

An artisan's lien is a *possessory lien*. The lienholder ordinarily must have retained possession of the property and have expressly or impliedly agreed to provide the services on a *cash, not a credit, basis*. Usually, the lienholder retains possession of the property. In this case, the lien remains in existence as long as the lienholder maintains possession and is terminated once possession is voluntarily surrendered—unless the surrender is only temporary. When the surrender is temporary, there must be an agreement that the property will be returned to the lienholder. Even with such an agreement, if a third party obtains rights in that property while it is out of the lienholder's possession, the lien is lost. The only way a lienholder can protect a lien and surrender possession at the same time is to record notice of the lien in accordance with state lien and recording statutes.

Modern statutes permit the holder of an artisan's lien to foreclose and sell the property subject to the lien in order to satisfy payment of the debt. As with the mechanic's lien, the lienholder is required to give notice to the owner of the property prior to foreclosure and selling. The sale proceeds are used to pay the debt and the costs of the legal proceedings, and the surplus, if any, is paid to the former owner.

An innkeeper's lien is given on the baggage of guests for the agreed-upon charges that remain unpaid. If no express agreement was made on those charges, then the lien will be the reasonable value of the accommodations furnished. The innkeeper's lien is terminated either by the guest's payment of the hotel's charges or by surrender of the baggage to the guests, unless such surrender is temporary. Also, the lien is terminated by *conversion* (that is, simply the assumption of ownership) of the guest's baggage by the innkeeper. Although state statutes permit conversion by means of a public sale, there is a trend toward requiring that the guest first be given an impartial judicial hearing.[1]

Writ of Execution

A debt must be past due in order for a creditor to commence legal action against a debtor. If the creditor is successful, the court awards the creditor a judgment against the debtor (usually for the amount of the debt plus any interest and legal costs incurred in obtaining the judgment). Attorneys' fees are not included in this amount unless provided for by statute or contract.

Frequently, it is easy to secure a judgment, but this is only half the battle. If the debtor does not or cannot pay the judgment, the creditor is entitled to go back to the court and obtain a **writ of execution.** This writ is an order, usually issued by the clerk of the court, directing the sheriff or other officer to seize (levy) and sell any of the debtor's nonexempt real or personal property that is within the court's geographic jurisdiction (usually the county in which the courthouse is located). The proceeds of the sale are used to pay the judgment and the costs of the sale. Any excess is paid to the debtor. The debtor can pay the judgment and redeem the nonexempt property at any time before the sale takes place. Because of exemption and bankruptcy laws, many judgments are virtually uncollectible.

Attachment

Attachment is a court-ordered seizure and taking into custody of property that is in controversy because of a debt.[2] Attachment rights are created by state statutes. Attachment is normally a *prejudgment* remedy. It occurs either at the time of or immediately after the commencement of a lawsuit but before the entry of a final judgment. By statute, the restrictions and requirements for a creditor to attach before judgment are very specific and limited. The due process clause of the Fourteenth Amendment to the Constitution limits a court's power to authorize seizure of a debtor's property without notice to the debtor or a hearing on the facts. In recent years, a number of state attachment laws have been held to be unconstitutional.

In order to use attachment as a remedy, the creditor must have an enforceable right to payment of the debt under law, and the creditor must follow certain procedures. Otherwise, the creditor can be liable for damages for wrongful attachment. He or she must file with the court an affidavit stating that the debtor is in default and stating the statutory grounds under which attachment is sought. A bond must be posted by the creditor to cover court costs, the value of the loss of use of the good suffered by the debtor, and the value of the property attached. When the court is satisfied that all the requirements have been met, it issues a **writ of attachment.** This writ is similar to a writ of execution in that it directs the sheriff or other officer to seize nonexempt property. If the creditor prevails at trial, the seized property can be sold to satisfy the judgment.

The following case illustrates that strict compliance with every specific procedure established by the state's attachment statute is required in order for the property to be subject to an enforce-

1. Klim v. Jones, 315 F.Supp. 109 (D.C.N.D.Cal. 1970).

2. *Attachment* under the UCC's Article 9, as discussed in Chapter 29, refers to the process through which a security interest becomes enforceable against a debtor with respect to the debt's collateral [UCC 9-203]. In the present context, *attachment* refers to the process through which a debtor's property is seized to secure the debt or a creditor's claim prior to a judgment. In many cases, the creditor will want to assure that there will be some assets of the debtor against which to execute the judgment.

able writ of attachment, because a writ of attachment operates against a debtor's property simply on the strength of the creditor's sworn statement that a debt is owed.

Case 30.1

TOPJIAN PLUMBING AND HEATING, INC. v. BRUCE TOPJIAN, INC.

Supreme Court of New Hampshire, 1987.
129 N.H. 481, 529 A.2d 391.

BACKGROUND AND FACTS *Topjian Plumbing and Heating, Inc., the plaintiff, sought prejudgment writs of attachment to satisfy an anticipated judgment in a contract action against Bruce Topjian, Inc., the defendant. Topjian Plumbing did not petition the court for permission to effect the attachments but merely completed the forms, served them on the defendant and on the Fencers—the owners of a parcel of land that had previously belonged to the defendant—and recorded them at the registry of deeds. The Fencers objected to the attachment of their property, and in the course of the hearing on their objection, the superior court invalidated all of the attachments, holding that they were not in compliance with the New Hampshire prejudgment attachment statute RSA 511–A:8. This statute requires application to the court for an order to attach property. Topjian Plumbing appealed.*

THAYER, Justice.
* * * *

The superior court invalidated the plaintiff's attachments because of the plaintiff's failure to petition the court for permission to attach the property prior to serving the attachments on the defendants and recording them at the registry of deeds. RSA 511-A:8 clearly requires that application must be made to the court for an order authorizing an *ex parte* [for the benefit of one party] pre-judgment attachment, "[t]he purpose of [which] is to obtain security for the payment of a plaintiff's judgment should [plaintiff] prevail."
* * * *

In 1984, this court, interpreting RSA chapter 511-A, determined that the standard requirements of due process, such as notice and hearing, must be adhered to before property interests can be encumbered by a pre-judgment attachment.
* * * The proper procedure for obtaining an *ex parte* attachment is for the plaintiff to petition the court for permission to obtain an *ex parte* attachment order before serving the attachment on the defendant and recording it at the registry of deeds.

Furthermore, the Superior Court Rules pertaining to *ex parte* pre-judgment attachments require plaintiffs to petition the court for permission to attach the property prior to service or entry of any writ of summons or other pleading.

DECISION AND REMEDY *The Supreme Court of New Hampshire affirmed the decision of the lower court, holding that the attachments were invalid because the plaintiff had failed to comply with the attachment statute.*

Garnishment

Garnishment is similar to attachment except that it is a collection remedy directed not at the debtor but at the debtor's property or rights held by a third person. The third person, the garnishee, owes a debt to the debtor or has property that belongs to the debtor, such as wages or a bank account. Typically, a garnishment judgment is served on a person's employer so that part of the person's usual paycheck will be paid to the creditor.

Both federal laws and state laws limit the amount of money that can be garnished from a debtor's weekly take-home pay.[3] Federal law provides a minimal framework to protect debtors from losing

---

3. A few states (for example, Texas) do not permit garnishment of wages, except under a child-support order.

all their income to the payment of judgment debts.[4] State laws also provide dollar exemptions, and these amounts are often larger than those provided by federal law. State and federal statutes can be applied together to help create a pool of funds sufficient to enable a debtor to continue to provide for family needs while also reducing the amount of the judgment debt in a reasonable way.

Under federal law, garnishment of an employee's wages for any one indebtedness cannot be grounds for dismissal of an employee.

The legal proceeding for a garnishment action is governed by state law. As a result of a garnish-

---

4. For example, the federal Consumer Credit Protection Act, 15 U.S.C. Section 1601 *et seq.*, provides that a debtor can retain either 75 percent of the disposable earnings per week or the sum equivalent to thirty hours of work paid at federal minimum wage rates, whichever is greater.

ment proceeding, the debtor's employer is ordered by the court to turn over a portion of the debtor's wages to pay the debt. Garnishment operates differently from state to state, however. According to the laws in some states, the judgment creditor need obtain only one order of garnishment, which will then continuously apply to the judgment debtor's weekly wages until the entire debt has been paid. In other states, the judgment creditor must go back to court for a separate order of garnishment for each pay period.

The following case illustrates that the public policy behind a state's statutory restrictions on the use of prejudgment attachment and garnishment of wages inhibits even that state, as an employer, from setting off debts owed it by an employee against wages due that employee.

BACKGROUND AND FACTS An *audit report of the California Medical Facility at Vacaville reported that in 731 instances, employees had been overpaid. The total amount of the overpayments was $463,113. The state of California began notifying affected employees of the overpayments and of its repayment plan to deduct up to $400 from each affected employee's net salary warrant and 40 percent of net overtime pay. (A warrant is an order authorizing someone to pay a particular amount.) The state contended that Section 17051 of the California Government Code authorizes this method of repayment. Section 17051 provides that when a warrant is drawn in favor of a payee with a claim against the state and facts that affect the validity or amount of the claim are discovered prior to payment, the warrant may be held for payment of the state's claim first. The California State Employees' Association contended that this general provision must give way to the more specific wage garnishment law and that the state's repayment plan constituted an unlawful garnishment of wages. The court refused to compel the state to make full salary payments to employees without deductions to recoup prior alleged overpayments. The California State Employees' Association appealed.*

Case 30.2
CALIFORNIA STATE EMPLOYEES' ASSOCIATION v. STATE OF CALIFORNIA
Court of Appeal, First District, Fifth Division, 1988.
198 Cal.App.3d 374, 243 Cal.Rptr. 602.

HANING, Associate Judge.
* * * *

Insofar as the attachment law and wage garnishment law reflect or establish public policy, it is obvious that they provide substantial protection for wages against both pretrial attachments and enforcement of judgments. "The policy underlying the state's wage exemption statutes is to insure that regardless of the debtor's improvidence, the debtor and his or her family will retain enough money to maintain a basic standard of living, so that the debtor may have a fair chance to remain a productive member of the community. Moreover, fundamental due process considerations underlie the prejudgment attachment exemption. Permitting appellant to reach respondent's wages by setoff would let it accomplish what neither it nor any other creditor could do by attachment and would defeat the legislative policy underlying that exemption. We conclude that an employer is not entitled to a setoff of debts owing it by an employee against any wages due that employee."
* * * *

*   *   * Government Code section 17051 deals generally with "claim[s] against the State," and refers merely to "facts or circumstances . . . which would *affect the validity or alter the amount of the claim.*" It also requires the agency in question to "pay the portion of the claim *then due* and payable." Presumably, wages actually earned during the current pay period are due, and the fact that the employee owed a debt to the state, even for a prior overpayment, does not "affect the validity or alter the amount of the [current] claim" for wages earned. We conclude that this general language is superseded by the specific provisions of the attachment and wage garnishment laws protecting earnings from such extra-judicial seizures.

DECISION AND REMEDY   *The court of appeal reversed the lower court's ruling and remanded the case to the lower court with instructions to issue a writ commanding the state to make normal salary payments without deductions to the affected employees.*

Creditors' Composition Agreements

As discussed in Chapter 9, creditors may contract with a debtor for discharge of the debtor's liquidated debts upon payment of a sum less than that owed. (The contract discharges only those debts of creditors who agree to be bound.) These agreements are called compositions or creditors' composition agreements and are usually held to be enforceable. Note, however, that they may be superseded by the debtor's bankruptcy.

Secured Transactions—Article 9

Chapter 29 discussed in detail a secured party's rights upon a debtor's default. One such right is the repossession of the collateral upon breach of the security agreement. Upon repossession, the secured party has the right to keep the collateral in full satisfaction of the debt (unless there is a purchase-money security interest in consumer goods with 60 percent or more of the price or loan paid or unless proper objection is received). Alternatively, the secured party can sell the collateral and use the proceeds to discharge the debt. If the proceeds are insufficient to cover the balance owed, the secured party is entitled to a deficiency judgment and can proceed with a writ of execution, as previously discussed. Therefore, either way, a debt resolution can be accomplished.

Mortgage Foreclosure on Real Property

A real estate mortgage agreement provides that when the **mortgagor** (debtor/borrower) *defaults* in making payment in accordance with the terms of the agreement, the **mortgagee** (creditor/lender) can declare that the entire mortgage debt is due immediately. The mortgagee/creditor can enforce payment in full by a legal action called **foreclosure.**

Four statutory methods of foreclosure are permitted in the United States:

1. Strict foreclosure is permitted in only a few states. Upon default and after a specified period, the mortgagee acquires absolute title to the property.

2. Entry, or writ of entry, is permitted in only a few states. Upon default, the mortgagee obtains a writ entitling him or her to possession; after a specified statutory period, the mortgagee receives absolute title.

3. Power of sale is permitted in most states. Instead of following statutory guidelines for the judicial sale of the property, the sale provisions are stated in the mortgage agreement.

4. Foreclosure sale (to be discussed) is the usual method. Statutory procedures must be followed to protect the rights of the mortgagor.

A **deed of trust** in some states is basically equivalent to a mortgage. The major difference between a mortgage and a deed of trust is that the legal title to the real property is placed with a trustee to secure payment of the loan for the realty. In most states, upon the debtor's default, the terms of the deed of trust and the statutory treatment thereof result in a foreclosure similar to that for a mortgage.

FORECLOSURE SALES   A foreclosure sale is a judicial sale at which the real estate covered by the mortgage is sold.[5] If the proceeds of the sale are sufficient to cover both the costs of the foreclosure and the mortgaged debt, any surplus is received by the debtor. If, on the other hand, the sale proceeds are insufficient to cover the foreclosure costs and the mortgaged debt, the mortgagee can seek to recover the difference from the mortgagor by obtaining a *deficiency judgment*. This type of judgment represents the "deficiency amount"—that is, the difference between the mortgaged debt and the amount actually received from the proceeds of the foreclosure sale. A deficiency judgment is obtained in a separate legal action that is pursued subsequent to the foreclosure action. It entitles the creditor to recover the deficiency from the sale of other nonexempt property owned by the debtor. A number of states do not allow for a deficiency judgment for certain types of real estate interests.

From the time of default until the time of the foreclosure sale, a mortgagor can redeem the property by paying the full amount of the debt, plus any interest and other costs that have accrued. This mortgagor's right is known as the **equity of redemption.** In some states, the mortgagor may even redeem within a statutory period after the judicial sale. This period is called a **statutory period of redemption,** and the deed to the property is usually not delivered to the purchaser until the expiration of this period.

Assignment for Benefit of Creditors

Both common law and statutes may provide for a debtor's assignment of assets to a trustee or assignee for the benefit of the debtor's creditors. In these situations, the debtor voluntarily transfers title to assets owned to a trustee or assignee, who in turn sells or liquidates these assets, tendering payment to the debtor's creditors on a *pro rata* (proportionate) basis. Each creditor may accept the tender (and discharge the debt owed to him or her) or reject it (and attempt to collect the debt in another way).

The flexibility and informality of an assignment for the benefit of creditors may save creditors time and expense and result in better prices when a debtor's property is liquidated. Nevertheless, creditors may decide that this option does not adequately protect their rights. Under the bankruptcy laws, creditors of a certain number with a certain amount of claims may have administration of the debtor's property transferred to the bankruptcy court—in other words, force the debtor into involuntary bankruptcy. (See Chapter 31.) Thus, like a creditors' composition agreement, a debtor's bankruptcy may supersede an assignment for the benefit of creditors—even if the bankruptcy is initiated by creditors.

Bulk Sales—Article 6 of the UCC

As discussed in Chapter 17, a creditor may have certain rights when a seller-debtor sells a substantial portion of the assets of his or her business to a purchaser. Such a sale is referred to as a bulk sale or transfer—that is, one not normally made in the seller's ordinary course of business. Because a creditor's recovery against the debtor could be substantially diminished by the bulk sale or transfer of assets to an innocent purchaser, the Code treats such transfer as a potential fraud on creditors.

To avoid any possibility of fraud and to protect the rights of the creditors and of the purchaser of the bulk goods, the UCC sets forth certain procedures for bulk transfers. Basically, the bulk seller is required to give the purchaser a sworn list of creditors, and the purchaser is obligated to give the seller's creditors notice of the pending sale at least ten days prior to payment or to the purchaser's taking possession. Creditors who receive notice must act within that ten-day period or their claims will be cut off by the sale. Any creditor not receiving notice of the sale, however, can take action against the debtor-seller and can levy against the goods so transferred to the purchaser for a period of up to six months. In this way, creditors' interests are protected in the bulk transfer of a debtor's business assets.

Fraudulent Conveyances

As discussed in Chapter 17, any conveyance by a debtor through sale (or gift) to a third person that is expressly or impliedly *fraudulent* allows the

---

5. This is true even if the property is the debtor's homestead. A mortgage is one debt that is *not* subject to the homestead statutory exemption, which exempts the homestead from execution of any general debts of a householder or head of a family. The homestead exemption is discussed later in this chapter.

creditor to set aside the transfer and proceed against the property (even if the property is in the possession of a third person, except a good faith purchaser for value).

There are two types of fraud: fraud in fact and fraud implied in law. Fraud in fact is the transfer of the property with the *intent* to defraud the creditor. Fraud implied in law occurs when the transfer is made in such a manner that a non-merchant transferor retains *possession* (and usually use) of the property. In the latter case, fraud is presumed, but it can be rebutted.

SURETYSHIP AND GUARANTY

When a third person promises to pay a debt or perform an obligation owed by another in the event that the debtor does not pay or perform, a suretyship or guaranty relationship is created. Exhibit 30–1 illustrates these relationships. The third person's credit becomes the security for the debt owed.

Suretyship

A contract of suretyship is a promise to a creditor made by a third person (the surety) to be responsible for the debtor's obligation. The surety is *primarily* liable. In other words, the creditor can hold the surety responsible for payment of the debt the moment the debt is due, without first exhausting all legal remedies against the debtor. A surety agreement does not have to be in writing to be enforceable—as, for example, when the surety makes the promise directly to the obligee—but it usually is.

For example, David Brown wants to borrow money from the bank to buy a used car. Because David is still in college, the bank will not lend him the money unless his father will co-sign the note. When his father co-signs the note, his father becomes primarily liable to the bank. On the note's due date, the bank can, without first making an effort to collect from David, seek payment from his father or, without attempting to collect from his father, seek payment from David, or seek payment from both.

Guaranty

A guaranty contract is similar to one of suretyship—it also includes a promise to answer for the

Exhibit 30–1 Suretyship Parties

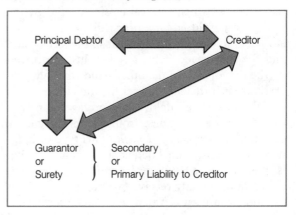

principal's obligation. Unlike a surety, who is primarily liable, however, a guarantor (the person making the guaranty) is *secondarily* liable. When the contract involves a debt, for instance, the guarantor can be required to answer for the obligation only after the principal has defaulted. Usually, the creditor must also have attempted to collect from the principal, since usually a debtor would not otherwise be declared to be in default.

For example, AB Corporation approaches Norwest Bank to borrow money to meet its payroll. Doubting AB's creditworthiness, Norwest asks Merrimack, the company's president and owner of 70 percent of its stock, to sign an agreement making him personally liable if AB does not pay off the loan. If Merrimack signs, he becomes the loan's guarantor, but Norwest cannot hold him liable until AB is in default.

The contract between the guarantor and the creditor must be in writing to be enforceable unless the "main purpose" exception applies. That is, if the guaranty agreement's main purpose is to benefit the guarantor, the contract will be enforceable even if it is not in writing. (See Chapter 12 for a more detailed discussion.)

The guaranty contract's terms determine the extent and length of time of the guarantor's liability. For example, a guaranty can cover only a single transaction or be *continuing* (that is, cover a series of transactions). Similarly, a guaranty can be *limited* or *unlimited* as to time or amount.

The rights and defenses of the surety and the guarantor are basically the same. Therefore, the following discussion applies to both.

Defenses of the Surety

A creditor must try to prevent certain actions that will release the surety from the obligation. Any material change in the terms of the original contract between the principal debtor and the creditor without the prior consent of the surety may discharge the surety completely. Even a material change that does not affect the surety's risk could effect a discharge. Such changes include extensions of time for making payment, providing the extension agreement is binding on the creditor, and (for a compensated surety) the surety suffers a loss.

A release of the principal debtor without the surety's consent releases the surety unless the creditor expressly reserves his or her rights against the surety. A release with a reservation is treated as a covenant not to sue (discussed in Chapter 9) rather than a release.

Naturally, if the principal obligation is paid by the debtor or by another person on behalf of the debtor, the surety is discharged from obligation. Similarly, if valid tender of payment is made and the creditor for some reason rejects it with knowledge of the surety's existence, then the surety is released from any obligation on the debt.

Generally, any defenses available to a principal debtor can be used by the surety to avoid liability on the obligation to the creditor, except that the surety cannot use defenses personal to the debtor, such as the debtor's incapacity or bankruptcy. The ability of the surety to assert any defenses the debtor may have against the creditor is the most important concept in suretyship, since most defenses available to the surety are those of the debtor.

Obviously, a surety may have his or her own defenses—for example, incapacity or bankruptcy. Another defense is available when the creditor has fraudulently induced the surety to guaranty the debt of the debtor. In most states, prior to formation of the suretyship contract, the creditor has a legal duty to inform the surety of material facts known by the creditor that would materially increase the surety's risk. Failure to so inform is fraud and makes the suretyship obligation voidable.

In addition, if a creditor surrenders or impairs the value of the debtor's collateral while knowing of the surety and without the surety's consent, the surety is released to the extent that the surety would suffer a loss from the creditor's actions—as the following case illustrates. The primary reason for this principle of suretyship law is to protect the surety who agreed to become obligated only because the debtor's collateral was in the possession of the creditor.

BACKGROUND AND FACTS   *Hallmark Cards, Inc., sued Edward Peevy, who had guaranteed an obligation owed to Hallmark by Garry Peevy. At the time of Edward Peevy's guaranty, Hallmark had in its possession property pledged as security by Garry Peevy. Before suit was filed, Hallmark sold the pledged property without notice to Edward Peevy. Since the property sold did not cover the loan balance, Hallmark sued for the balance, seeking a deficiency judgment. Edward Peevy contended that because Hallmark had sold the property pledged by Garry Peevy as security for the obligation without notifying him, Hallmark was not entitled to a deficiency judgment against him. Hallmark contended that Edward Peevy was not entitled to notice of the sale of the collateral and was not required to give consent. The court granted Edward Peevy's motion for a summary judgment, holding that notice to a guarantor of the sale of collateral was a necessary prerequisite to seeking a deficiency judgment against the guarantor. Hallmark appealed.*

Case 30.3
HALLMARK CARDS, INC. v. PEEVY
Supreme Court of Arkansas, 1987.
293 Ark. 594, 739 S.W.2d 691.

NEWBERN, Justice.
*   *   *   *

The notice requirement with which we are concerned here is stated in the relevant part of Ark. Stat. Ann. § 85-9-504(3) as follows: ". . . reasonable notification of the time after which any private sale or other intended disposition is to be made shall be sent by the secured party to the debtor. . . ." Hallmark argues Edward H. Peevy was not a "debtor" and thus was not entitled to notice. "Debtor" is defined by Ark. Stat. Ann. § 85-9-105(1)(d) as:

> . . . the person who owes payment or other performance of the obligation secured, whether or not he owns or has rights in the collateral, and includes the seller of accounts or chattel paper. Where the debtor and the owner of the collateral are not the same person, the term "debtor" means the owner of the collateral in any provision of the Article [chapter] dealing with the collateral, the obligor in any provision dealing with the obligation, and may include both where the context so requires.
>
> *   *   *   *
>
> Other jurisdictions have held, virtually unanimously, that a guarantor is a debtor for purposes of the notice requirement.
>
> *   *   * Simple fairness requires that the term "debtor" to whom notice is required include one who is responsible for payment upon default of the principal obligor.
>
> *   *   *   *
>
> *   *   * Our holding here is that a secured party who has failed to comply with the requirement that a debtor be notified of the sale of collateral may not recover the deficiency established between the sale price and the obligation owed to the creditor by the debtor.

DECISION AND REMEDY   *The Supreme Court of Arkansas affirmed the lower court's holding that Hallmark's failure to notify the guarantor of the sale of property securing an obligation precluded Hallmark's recovery of the remainder of the debt from the guarantor.*

Rights of the Surety

When the surety pays the debt owed to the creditor, the surety is entitled to certain rights. First, the surety has a legal **right of subrogation.** Simply stated, this means that any right the creditor had against the debtor now becomes the right of the surety. Included are creditor rights in bankruptcy, rights to collateral possessed by the creditor, and rights to judgments secured by the creditor. In short, the surety now stands in the shoes of the creditor.

Second, the surety has a **right of reimbursement** from the debtor. This right stems from either the suretyship contract or equity. Basically, the surety is entitled to receive from the debtor all outlays the surety has made on behalf of the suretyship arrangement. These can include expenses incurred as well as the actual amount of the debt paid the creditor.

Third, if there are *co-sureties* (two or more sureties on the same obligation owed by the debtor), a surety who pays more than his or her proportionate share upon a debtor's default is entitled to recover from the co-sureties the amount paid above the surety's obligation. This is referred to as the surety's **right of contribution.** Generally, a co-

surety's liability either is determined by agreement or, in absence of agreement, is set at the maximum liability under the suretyship contract.

For example, suppose two co-sureties are obligated under a suretyship contract to guarantee the debt of a debtor. One surety's maximum liability is $15,000, and the other's is $10,000. The debtor owes $10,000 and is in default. The surety with the $15,000 maximum liability pays the creditor the entire $10,000. In the absence of other agreement, this surety can recover $4,000 from the other surety ($10,000/$25,000 × $10,000 = $4,000, this co-surety's obligation).

PROTECTION OF THE DEBTOR—EXEMPTIONS

In most states, certain types of real and personal property are exempt from levy of execution or attachment. Probably the most familiar of these exemptions is the **homestead exemption.** Each state permits the debtor to retain the family home, either in its entirety or up to a specified dollar amount, free from the claims of unsecured creditors or trustees in bankruptcy. The purpose is to

CONCEPT SUMMARY: Remedies Available to Creditors

REMEDY	DEFINITION
Mechanic's lien	A nonpossessory, filed lien on an owner's real estate for labor, services, or materials furnished to or made on the realty.
Artisan's or innkeeper's lien	A possessory lien on an owner's personal property for labor performed, value added, or care of said personal property for which no payment was received.
Writ of execution	In cases of unsatisfied judgments, a court order directing the sheriff or other officer to seize and sell sufficient nonexempt property of the judgment debtor to satisfy the judgment.
Attachment	A court-ordered seizure of property (generally prior to full resolution of the creditor's rights resulting in judgment). Attachment is only available upon posting of bond and in strict compliance with the applicable state statutes.
Garnishment	A collection remedy that allows the creditor to attach a debtor's money (such as wages owed or bank accounts) or other property that is held by a third person.
Secured transaction (UCC Article 9)	Upon the debtor's default, a secured party's right to repossess collateral subject to the secured party's security interest and either keep or sell the collateral to satisfy the debt.
Mortgage foreclosure	The creditor's selling or taking title to realty to satisfy the mortgage debt upon the debtor's default on the mortgage payments.
Creditors' composition agreements	A contract between the debtor and creditors whereby the debtor's debts are discharged by payment of a sum less than that owed in the original debt.
Assignment for benefit of creditors	The debtor's assignment of certain assets to a trustee or assignee, who sells or liquidates these assets and tenders payments to creditors on a *pro rata* basis. Acceptance of this payment by a creditor is discharge of the debt.
Other Legal Protection for Creditors' Investments	
Suretyship or guaranty	A contract in which a third person agrees to be primarily or secondarily liable for the debt owed by the principal debtor. A creditor can turn to this third person for satisfaction of the debt.
Fraudulent conveyance (express or implied)	The creditor's right to set aside a transfer to a third party, if the conveyance is fraudulent, and proceed against the property conveyed.

ensure that the debtor will retain some form of shelter.

For example, Daniels owes Carey $40,000. The debt is the subject of a lawsuit, and the court awards Carey a judgment of $40,000 against Daniels. The homestead of Daniels is valued at $50,000. There are no outstanding mortgages or other liens on his homestead. To satisfy the judgment debt, Daniels's family home is sold at public auction for $45,000. Assume the homestead exemption is $25,000. The proceeds of the sale are distributed as follows:

1. Daniels is paid $25,000 as his homestead exemption.
2. Carey is paid $20,000 toward the judgment debt, leaving a $20,000 deficiency judgment (that is, "leftover debt") that can be satisfied (paid)

from any other nonexempt property (personal or real) that Daniels may have, if allowed by state law.

In some states, statutes permit the homestead exemption only if the judgment debtor has a family. The policy behind this type of statute is to protect the family. If a judgment debtor does not have a family, a creditor may be entitled to collect the full amount realized from the sale of the debtor's home.

State exemption statutes usually include both real and personal property. Personal property that is most often exempt from satisfaction of judgment debts includes:

1. Household furniture up to a specified dollar amount.
2. Clothing and certain personal possessions, such as family pictures or a bible.
3. A vehicle (or vehicles) for transportation (at least up to a specified dollar amount).
4. Certain classified animals, usually livestock but including pets.
5. Equipment the debtor uses in a business or trade, such as tools or professional instruments, up to a specified dollar amount.

SPECIAL PROTECTION FOR THE CONSUMER-DEBTOR

Numerous *consumer* protection statutes and rules apply to the debtor-creditor relationship. Although most of these are discussed in detail in Chapter 46, a brief listing and discussion here will illustrate the breadth and importance of these consumer-oriented protection laws.

Consumer Credit Protection Act (CCPA)

The Consumer Credit Protection Act (CCPA), a federal statute, is commonly known as the Truth-in-Lending Act. It is basically a disclosure law, administered by the Board of Governors of the Federal Reserve System, that requires sellers and lenders to disclose credit terms on loans so that a consumer-debtor can shop around for the best financing arrangements. Generally, the creditor must clearly indicate to consumer-debtors what charges they are incurring for the privilege of paying the debt over a period of time, including what the total annual percentage rate and finance charges are.

Uniform Consumer Credit Code (UCCC)

In an attempt to make consumer credit laws at the state level uniform, the National Conference of Commissioners on Uniform State Laws proposed legislation called the Uniform Consumer Credit Code (UCCC). The essential results are as follows:

1. To place statutory ceilings on interest rates and other finance charges.
2. To require disclosure similar to that required by the federal Truth-in-Lending Act.
3. To limit garnishment actions against take-home wages to a certain amount and to prohibit discharge of an employee solely because of garnishment proceedings.
4. To allow cancellation of a contract solicited by a seller in the consumer-debtor's home within three business days of the solicitation.
5. To limit the application of the holder-in-due-course (HDC) concept to sellers who accept checks, rather than other types of negotiable instruments, from consumer-debtors.
6. To prohibit referral sales—sales in which sellers offer rebates or discounts to buyers for furnishing the names of other prospective purchasers.
7. To provide criminal as well as civil penalties for violations.

Only a handful of states have adopted the UCCC even though it has undergone numerous drafts. Other states have passed laws similar to some of the provisions of the UCCC, such as laws concerning home-solicitation sales.

Federal Trade Commission Rule—Holder in Due Course (HDC)

As part of the consumer protection movement, the Federal Trade Commission (FTC) promulgated a rule that limited the rights of an HDC with regard to a negotiable promissory note executed by a debtor-buyer as a part of a consumer transaction. As stated in Chapter 26, the rule provides that the seller must disclose clearly in the sales agreement that any personal defenses the buyer could assert against the seller can also be asserted against an HDC.

This rule basically eliminates the use of buyer's waiver of defense clauses in consumer transactions. These clauses in security agreements, otherwise permitted under UCC 9-206, waive any claim or defense the debtor might have against a good faith assignee for value of a security interest.

QUESTIONS AND CASE PROBLEMS

1. Sylvia takes her car to Crank's Auto Repair Shop. A sign in the window states that all repairs must be paid for in cash unless credit is approved in advance. Sylvia and Crank agree that Crank will repair Sylvia's car engine and put in a new transmission. No mention is made of credit. Because Crank is not sure how much engine repair will be necessary, he refuses to give Sylvia an estimate. He repairs the engine and puts in a new transmission. When Sylvia comes to pick up her car, she learns that the bill is $795. Sylvia is furious, refuses to pay Crank that amount, and demands possession of her car. Crank demands payment. Discuss the rights of the parties in this matter.

2. James is employed by the Cross-Bar Packing Corporation and earns take-home pay of $400 per week. He is $2,000 in debt to the Holiday Department Store for goods purchased on credit over the past eight months. Most of this property is nonexempt and is presently located in James's apartment. James is in default on his payments to Holiday. Holiday learns that James has a girlfriend in another state and that he plans on giving her most of this property for Christmas. Discuss what actions are available and should be taken by Holiday to resolve the debt owed by James.

3. Ann is a student at Slippery Stone University. In need of funds to pay for tuition and books, she attempts to secure a short-term loan from West Bank. The bank agrees to make a loan if Ann will have someone financially responsible guarantee the loan payments. Sheila, a well-known businesswoman and a friend of Ann's family, calls the bank and agrees to pay the loan if Ann cannot. Because of Sheila's reputation, the loan is made. Ann is making the payments, but because of illness she is not able to work for one month. She requests that West Bank extend the loan for three months. West Bank agrees, raising the interest rate for the extended period. Sheila has not been notified of the extension (and therefore has not consented to it). One month later Ann drops out of school. All attempts to collect from Ann have failed. West Bank wants to hold Sheila liable. Discuss West Bank's claim against Sheila.

4. Higgins is the owner of a relatively old home valued at $45,000. He notices that the bathtubs and fixtures in both bathrooms are leaking and need to be replaced. He contracts with Plumber to replace the bathtubs and fixtures. Plumber replaces them, and on June 1 she submits her bill of $4,000 to Higgins. Because of financial difficulties, Higgins does not pay the bill. Higgins's only asset is his home, which, under state law, is exempt up to $40,000 as a homestead. Discuss fully Plumber's remedies in this situation.

5. Kloster-Madsen, Inc., a general contractor, entered into a contract with the owner of a building to do certain remodeling work. About a month later, pursuant to the contract, an electrical subcontractor removed several light fixtures from one of the ceilings, cutting four holes in the ceiling and placing the removed light fixtures in the holes. Immediately after this work was begun, a new owner, Tafi's, Inc., purchased the building. Several thousand dollars' worth of material and labor was expended before Tafi's informed the general contractor that it did not wish to have the building remodeled. Can Kloster-Madsen impose a mechanic's lien on the building even though it entered into the building contract with a different owner? [Kloster-Madsen, Inc. v. Tafi's, Inc., 303 Minn. 59, 226 N.W.2d 603 (1975)]

6. A. J. Kellos Construction Co. was the general contractor for the construction of a building in Georgia. Kellos entered into a subcontract with Roofing Specialists, Inc., for the construction of the roof of this project. A bond was executed by Balboa Insurance Co. in favor of Kellos underwriting Roofing Specialists' performance of its contract. When the roofing was condemned by the state architect, Kellos sued Balboa on the bond for damages resulting from Roofing Specialists' default on the contract. Was the bond executed by Balboa in favor of Kellos a contract of insurance or of suretyship? [A. J. Kellos Const. Co., Inc. v. Balboa Ins. Co., 495 F.Supp. 408 (S.D. Ga. 1980)]

7. John Shumate parked his car in a vacant lot where he had left it several times previously. When he returned, he was informed that the car had been towed at the property owner's request. Thomas Younger had a collision with another car. His car was towed from the scene of the accident at the request of the police while Younger was discussing his accident with the police. The towing companies informed both car owners that they must pay towing and storage charges before their autos would be returned. The car owners sued to challenge this claim of a possessory lien asserted by the towing companies. Could the owners be prevented from removing their cars until payment was made? [Younger v. Plunkett, 395 F.Supp. 702 (E.D.Pa. 1975)]

8. Greg Weeman was a regular patron of the Linebacker Tavern, owned by Arthur Church. After spending the evening at the tavern, Greg left in his car and, several hours later, had an automobile accident and died. Greg was highly intoxicated at the time of his death. Greg's estate filed suit against the tavern, claiming that its owners had been grossly negligent in serving alcohol to Greg when he was obviously intoxicated and because they knew or should have known he would be driving a motor vehicle when he left. The plaintiff's only witness testified that he had arrived at the tavern after Greg arrived, had one beer with Greg, and then left the premises with him. The plaintiff applied for a writ of attachment (a prejudgment action) against the tavern, pending judgment on the gross negligence suit, and the

court granted the application. The defendant appealed, claiming that the plaintiff should not have been allowed to attach its property because the evidence was not sufficient to establish probable cause that its employees had served Greg alcohol when he was intoxicated or that the alcohol he consumed at the tavern had caused his death. Discuss the merits of the defendant's claim. [Weeman v. Church, 11 Conn.App. 420, 527 A.2d 1226 (1987)]

9. Harmony Unlimited obtained a judgment against John Chivetta and his company, JMC Enterprises. At the time of the judgment, John lacked sufficient funds to pay. Just before Harmony obtained the judgment, John transferred $126,000 to his mother, Nettie, who signed a promissory note. Harmony served a garnishment summons on Nettie, claiming that she was a party to a fraudulent scheme by her son to conceal his assets and was holding funds that belonged to her son. The note for $126,000 was payable on demand, carried no interest, and contained a provision that barred John from obtaining a money judgment against his mother. Nettie paid some of John's bills after the transfer of money from her son to her. Nettie argued that Har-mony's rights against her could not be any greater than John's rights against her and that since John could not obtain a judgment against her for the money, Harmony could not do so either. Discuss Harmony's right of garnishment against Nettie. [Harmony Unlimited, Inc. v. Chivetta, 743 S.W.2d 884 (Mo.App. 1987)]

10. In February of 1973, Gladys Schmidt borrowed $4,120 from the National Bank of Joliet to finance the purchase of a Cadillac. The bank held a security interest in the automobile and had perfected this interest by filing in the office of the secretary of state. In August of 1973, Schmidt took the car to Bergeron Cadillac for repairs, which cost approximately $2,000. When Schmidt failed to pay for the repairs, Bergeron Cadillac retained possession of the car and placed an artisan's lien upon it. In September, Schmidt defaulted on her payments to the bank, and the bank later filed an action to gain possession of the Cadillac from Bergeron. Discuss which party had a right to possession of the vehicle—Bergeron Cadillac or the National Bank. [National Bank of Joliet v. Bergeron Cadillac, Inc., 66 Ill.2d 140, 361 N.E.2d 1116, 5 Ill.Dec. 588 (1977)]

Chapter 31

Bankruptcy and Reorganization

The U.S. Constitution, Article I, Section 8, provides that "The Congress shall have the power * * * to establish * * * uniform laws on the subject of bankruptcies throughout the United States." Bankruptcy proceedings are rooted in federal laws; bankruptcy courts are special federal courts; and bankruptcy judges are federally appointed.

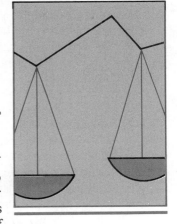

FEDERAL BANKRUPTCY LAW—HISTORICAL BACKGROUND

Bankruptcy law is designed to accomplish two main goals. The first is to provide relief and protection to debtors who have "gotten in over their heads." The second is to provide a fair means of distributing a debtor's assets among all creditors. Thus, the law attempts to protect the rights of both the debtor and the creditor.

The original Bankruptcy Act was enacted in 1898 and was amended by the 1938 Chandler Act. A major overhaul of the federal bankruptcy law occurred in 1978 with the passage of the Bankruptcy Reform Act of 1978. The 1978 act was amended in 1984, basically to correct what many felt to be deficiencies brought about by the 1978 major overhaul, and again in 1986 to increase the number of bankruptcy judgeships,[1] provide for U.S. trustees, and create a new Chapter 12 in bankruptcy to aid the family farmer.

Bankruptcy proceedings are held in bankruptcy courts. The bankruptcy courts' primary function is to hold *core proceedings*[2] dealing with the procedures required to administer the estate of the debtor in bankruptcy. Bankruptcy courts are under the authority of U.S. district courts, and rulings from bankruptcy courts can be appealed to the district courts.

---

1. For example, twelve judgeships were assigned to the Central District of California, while states such as Alaska, Delaware, Hawaii, Idaho, Montana, Nebraska, New Hampshire, North Dakota, Rhode Island, South Carolina, South Dakota, Vermont, and Wyoming were each assigned one.
2. Core proceedings are procedural functions, such as allowance of claims, decisions on preferences, automatic stay proceedings, confirmation of bankruptcy plans, discharge of debts, and so on.

Fundamentally, a bankruptcy court fulfills the role of an administrative court for the district court concerning matters in bankruptcy. Decisions on personal injury, wrongful death, and other civil proceedings affecting the debtor are now resolved in federal or state courts.

Although the Bankruptcy Act is a federal law, state laws on secured transactions, liens, judgments, and exemptions also play a role in a federal bankruptcy proceeding.

THE BANKRUPTCY REFORM ACT OF 1978 AS AMENDED

The Bankruptcy Reform Act of 1978, as amended—hereinafter called the Code—is contained in Title 11 of the United States Code and has eight chapters. Chapters 1, 3, and 5 include general definitional provisions and provisions governing case administration, creditors, the debtor,[3] and the estate. These three chapters apply generally to all kinds of bankruptcies. The next five chapters set forth the different types of relief that debtors may seek. Chapter 7 provides for liquidation (the selling of all remaining nonexempt assets for cash). Chapter 9 governs the adjustment of debts of a municipality. Chapter 11 governs reorganizations. Chapter 12 (family farmers) and Chapter 13 (individuals) provide for adjustment of debts by parties with regular incomes.

The following sections deal with Chapter 7 liquidations, Chapter 11 reorganizations, and Chapter 12 and 13 plans. The latter three chapters have been referred to as "rehabilitation" chapters.

The 1984 Bankruptcy Amendments require the clerk of the court to give all *consumer-debtors*[4] written notice of each chapter under which they may proceed prior to the commencement of a filing. The purpose of this amendment is to fully inform a consumer-debtor of the various types of relief available.

---

3. It is noteworthy that the term *bankrupt* no longer exists under the Code. Those who were *bankrupts* under the old Bankruptcy Act are now merely *debtors* under the Code.

4. Defined here as individuals whose debts are primarily consumer debts.

CHAPTER 7 LIQUIDATIONS

Chapter 7 liquidation is the most familiar type of bankruptcy proceeding and is often referred to as an ordinary or "straight" bankruptcy. Put simply, a debtor in a straight bankruptcy states his or her debts and turns his or her assets over to a trustee. The trustee sells the nonexempt assets and distributes the proceeds to creditors. With certain exceptions, the balance of the debts is then discharged (extinguished), and the debtor is relieved of his or her obligation to pay the debts. Any "person"—defined as including individuals, partnerships, and corporations[5]—may be a debtor under Chapter 7. Railroads, insurance companies, banks, savings and loan associations, and credit unions cannot be Chapter 7 debtors, however. Other chapters of the Code, or federal or state statutes, apply to them.

Filing the Petition

A straight bankruptcy may be commenced by the filing of either a voluntary or an involuntary petition.

VOLUNTARY BANKRUPTCY A voluntary petition in bankruptcy is brought by the debtor, who files official forms designated for that purpose in the bankruptcy court. The 1984 amendments require a consumer-debtor who has selected Chapter 7 to state in the petition, at the time of filing, that he or she understands the relief available under other chapters of the Code and has chosen to proceed under Chapter 7. If the consumer-debtor is represented by an attorney, the attorney must file an affidavit stating that he or she has informed the debtor of the relief available under each chapter. A debtor does not have to be insolvent to file or petition in bankruptcy. Anyone liable to a creditor can declare bankruptcy.[6]

---

5. The definition of *corporation* includes unincorporated companies and associations. It also covers labor unions.

6. The inability to pay debts as they become due is known as *equitable* insolvency. A *balance sheet* insolvency, which exists when a debtor's liabilities exceed assets, is not the test. Thus, it is possible for debtors to be thrown into involuntary bankruptcy even though their assets far exceed their liabilities. This may occur when a debtor's cash flow problems become severe.

The voluntary petition contains the following schedules:

1. A list of both secured and unsecured creditors, their addresses, and the amount of debt owed to each.

2. A statement of the financial affairs of the debtor.

3. A list of all property owned by the debtor, including property claimed by the debtor to be exempt.

4. A listing of current income and expenses. (This schedule was added by the 1984 amendments to provide creditors and the court with relevant information on the debtor's ability to pay creditors a reasonable amount from future income. This information *could* permit a court, on its own motion, to dismiss a consumer-debtor's Chapter 7 petition after a hearing,[7] and to encourage the filing of a Chapter 13 petition, where that would result in a substantial improvement of a creditor's receipt of payment.)

The official forms must be completed accurately, sworn to under oath, and signed by the debtor. To conceal assets or knowingly supply false information on these schedules is a crime under the bankruptcy laws. If the voluntary petition for bankruptcy is found to be proper, the filing of the petition will itself constitute an *order for relief*. Once a consumer-debtor's voluntary petition has been filed, the clerk of the court (or person directed) must give the trustee and creditors mailed notice of the order of relief not more than twenty days after entry of the order. A new feature allows a husband and wife to file jointly for bankruptcy under a single petition.

INVOLUNTARY BANKRUPTCY An involuntary bankruptcy occurs when the debtor's creditors force the debtor into bankruptcy proceedings. An involuntary case cannot be commenced against a farmer[8] or charitable institution. For an involuntary case to be filed against other debtors, the following requirements must be met. If the debtor has twelve or more creditors, three or more of these creditors having unsecured claims totaling at least $5,000 must join in the petition. If a debtor has fewer than twelve creditors, one or more creditors having a claim of $5,000 may file.

If the debtor challenges the involuntary petition, a hearing will be held and the bankruptcy court will enter an *order for relief* if it finds either of the following:

1. The debtor is generally not paying debts as they become due.

2. A general receiver, assignee, or custodian took possession of or was appointed to take charge of substantially all of the debtor's property within 120 days before the filing of the petition.

If the court grants an order for relief, the debtor will be required to supply the same information in the bankruptcy schedules as in a voluntary bankruptcy.

An involuntary petition should not be used as an everyday debt-collection device, and the Code provides penalties for the filing of frivolous petitions against debtors. Judgment may be granted against the petitioning creditors for the costs and attorneys' fees incurred by the debtor in defending against an involuntary petition that is dismissed by the court. If the petition is filed in bad faith, damages can be awarded for injury to the debtor's reputation. Punitive damages may also be awarded.

Automatic Stay

The moment a petition, either voluntary or involuntary, is filed, there exists an **automatic stay,** or suspension, of virtually all litigation and other action by creditors against the debtor or the debtor's property. In other words, once a petition has been filed, creditors cannot commence or continue most legal actions, such as foreclosure of liens, execution on judgments, trials, or any action to repossess property in the hands of the debtor. A

---

7. For example, Marcy has recently graduated from a school of law and earns an annual salary of $50,000. She has few assets. While attending school, she acquired numerous debts. To silence her creditors, she files for Chapter 7 bankruptcy. Her creditors would be better off if the court would deny her petition for Chapter 7 bankruptcy. Note, however, that the law does give the debtor a presumption in favor of granting an order of relief under whatever chapter in the Code is requested by the debtor.

8. The definition of *farmer* includes persons who receive more than 80 percent of their gross income from farming operations, such as tilling the soil, dairy farming, ranching, or the production or raising of crops, poultry, or livestock. Corporations and partnerships may qualify under certain conditions.

secured creditor, however, may petition the bankruptcy court for relief from the automatic stay in certain circumstances.

Underlying the Code's automatic stay provision for a secured creditor is a concept known as *adequate protection*. The adequate protection doctrine, among other things, protects secured creditors from losing their security as a result of the automatic stay. The bankruptcy court can provide adequate protection by requiring the debtor or trustee to make periodic cash payments or a one-time cash payment (or to provide additional collateral or replacement liens) to the extent that the stay may actually cause the value of the property to decrease. Or the court may grant other relief that is the "indubitable equivalent" of the secured party's interest in the property, such as a guaranty by a solvent third party to cover losses suffered by the secured party as a result of the stay.

For example, suppose Speedy Express, a delivery service, owns three delivery trucks in which First Bank has a security interest. Speedy Express has failed to make its monthly payments for two months. Speedy Express files a petition in bankruptcy, and the automatic stay prevents First Bank from repossessing the trucks. Meanwhile, the trucks (whose collective value is already less than the balance due) are depreciating at a rate of several hundred dollars a month. First Bank's inability to repossess and immediately resell the trucks is harming the bank to the extent of several hundred dollars per month. The bankruptcy court may protect First Bank from being harmed by requiring Speedy Express to make a one-time cash payment or periodic cash payments (or to provide additional collateral or replacement liens) to the extent that the delivery trucks are depreciating in value. If the debtor is unable to provide adequate protection, the court may vacate the stay as applied to First Bank and allow it to repossess the trucks.

A creditor's failure to abide by an automatic stay can be costly. The 1984 amendments provide that if a creditor *knowingly* violates the automatic stay (a willful violation), any party injured, including the debtor, is entitled to recover actual damages, costs, and attorneys' fees and may be entitled to recover punitive damages.

The Trustee

Promptly after the order for relief in a Chapter 7 proceeding has been entered, an interim or provisional trustee is appointed by the **United States Trustee** to preside over the debtor's property until the first meeting of creditors. At this first meeting, either a permanent trustee is elected or the interim trustee becomes the permanent trustee. The trustee's principal duty is to collect and reduce to money the "property of the estate" and to close up the estate as expeditiously as is compatible with the best interests of the parties.

Creditors' Meeting

Within a reasonable time after the order of relief has been granted (not less than ten days nor more than thirty days) the bankruptcy court must call a meeting of creditors listed in the schedules filed by the debtor. The bankruptcy judge does not attend this meeting.

The debtor is required to attend the meeting (unless excused by the court) and to submit to examination under oath by the creditors and the trustee. Failing to appear when required or making false statements under oath may result in the debtor's being denied a discharge of bankruptcy.

Proof of claims by creditors must normally be filed within ninety days of the meeting.[9]

Property of the Estate

Upon the commencement of a Chapter 7 proceeding, an *estate in property* is created. The estate consists of all the debtor's legal and equitable interests in property presently held, wherever located, together with community property, property transferred in a transaction voidable by the trustee, proceeds and profits from the property of the estate, and certain after-acquired property. Interests in certain property—such as gifts, inheritances, property settlements (divorce), or life insurance death proceeds—to which the debtor becomes entitled *within 180 days after filing* may also become part of the estate. Thus, the filing of a bankruptcy petition generally fixes a dividing line: Property acquired prior to the filing of the petition becomes property of the estate, and property acquired after the filing of the petition, except as just noted, remains the debtor's.

---

9. This same ninety-day rule applies in Chapter 12 and Chapter 13 bankruptcies as well. In Chapter 11 bankruptcies, the court fixes the time within which proof of claims may be filed.

Exemptions

The trustee takes control over the debtor's property, but an individual debtor is entitled to exempt certain property from the bankruptcy. Prior to the enactment of the Code, state law exclusively governed the extent of the exemptions. (See Chapter 30.) The Code establishes a federal exemption scheme, however. An individual debtor (or a husband and wife who file jointly) now may choose between the exemptions provided under the applicable state law or the federal exemptions.[10] The Bankruptcy Code exempts the following property:

1. Up to $7,500 in equity in the debtor's residence and burial plot.

2. Interest in a motor vehicle up to $1,200.

3. Interest, up to $200 for a particular item, in household goods and furnishings, wearing apparel, appliances, books, animals, crops, or musical instruments (the 1984 amendments, however, limit the aggregate total of all items to $4,000).

4. Interest in jewelry up to $500.

5. Interest in any other property worth up to $400, plus any unused part of the $7,500 homestead exemption up to $3,750.[11]

6. Interest in, up to $750, any tools of the debtor's trade.

7. Any unmatured life insurance contract owned by the debtor.

8. Certain interests in accrued dividends or interest under life insurance contracts owned by the debtor.

9. Professionally prescribed health aids.

10. The right to receive Social Security and certain welfare benefits, alimony and support, and certain pension benefits.

11. The right to receive certain personal injury and other awards.

---

10. Individual states have the power to pass legislation precluding the use of the federal exemptions by debtors residing within their borders. As of January 1, 1987, the following states had such legislation: Alabama, Alaska, Arizona, Arkansas, California, Colorado, Delaware, Florida, Georgia, Idaho, Illinois, Indiana, Iowa, Kansas, Kentucky, Louisiana, Maine, Maryland, Missouri, Montana, Nebraska, Nevada, New Hampshire, New York, North Carolina, North Dakota, Ohio, Oklahoma, Oregon, South Carolina, South Dakota, Tennessee, Utah, Virginia, West Virginia, and Wyoming.

11. The 1984 amendments placed a cap of $3,750 on the unused part of the homestead exemption to prevent some debtors from receiving a windfall.

Trustee's Powers

The basic duty of the trustee is to collect the debtor's available estate and reduce it to money for distribution, preserving the interests of both the debtor and unsecured creditors. This requires that the trustee be accountable for administering the debtor's estate. To enable the trustee to accomplish this duty, the Code gives the trustee certain powers, stated in both general and specific terms.

General powers are described by the statement that the trustee occupies a position *equivalent* in rights to that of other parties. For example, the trustee has the same rights as a *lien creditor* on a simple contract who could have obtained a judicial lien on the debtor's property or who could have levied execution on the debtor's property. This means that a trustee has priority over an unperfected secured party to the debtor's property. A trustee also has power equivalent to that of a *bona fide purchaser* of real property from the debtor.

Nevertheless, a creditor with a purchase-money security interest may prevail against a trustee, if the creditor files within ten days of the debtor's receipt of the collateral, even if the bankruptcy petition is filed before the creditor perfects. For example, Jill loaned Jack $20,000 on January 1, taking a security interest in the machinery Jack purchased with the $20,000. On January 27, before Jill perfected her security interest, Jack filed for bankruptcy. The trustee can invalidate Jill's security interest, because it was unperfected when Jack filed the bankruptcy petition. Jill could assert a claim as an unsecured creditor. But if Jack had filed for bankruptcy on January 7, and Jill had perfected her security interest on January 8, she would prevail, because she perfected her purchase-money security interest within ten days of Jack's receipt of the machinery.

The trustee has specific *powers of avoidance*—that is, the trustee can set aside a sale or other transfer of the debtor's property, taking it back as a part of the debtor's estate. These powers include any voidable rights available to the debtor, preferences, certain statutory liens, and fraudulent transfers by the debtor. Each will be discussed in more detail below.

The debtor shares most of the trustee's avoiding powers. Thus, if the trustee does not take action to enforce one of his or her rights (for example, to recover a preference), the debtor in a

Chapter 7 bankruptcy can nevertheless enforce that right.[12]

Under these powers, persons holding the debtor's property at the time the petition is filed are required to deliver the property to the trustee.

VOIDABLE RIGHTS   A trustee steps into the shoes of the debtor. Thus, any reason that a debtor can use to obtain return of his or her property can be used by the trustee as well. These grounds include fraud, duress, incapacity, and mutual mistake.

For example, Ben sells his boat to Frank. Frank gives Ben a check, knowing that there are insufficient funds in his bank account to cover the check. Frank has committed fraud. Ben has the right to avoid that transfer and recover the boat from Frank. Once an order for relief under Chapter 7 of the Code has been entered for Ben, the trustee can exercise the same right to recover the boat from Frank, and it becomes a part of the debtor's estate.

PREFERENCES   A debtor is not permitted to transfer property or to make a payment that favors one creditor over others. The trustee is allowed to recover payments made both voluntarily and involuntarily to one creditor in preference over another.

To have made a preferential payment that can be recovered, an *insolvent* debtor *generally* must have transferred property, for a *preexisting* debt, within *ninety days* of the filing of the petition in bankruptcy. The transfer must give the creditor more than the creditor would have received upon liquidation and distribution under the chapter proceedings. The trustee does not have to prove insolvency, as the Code provides that the debtor is presumed to be insolvent during this ninety-day period.

For example, suppose Connally borrows $10,000 from the First National Bank of Texas on January 1, and repays the loan on June 1 as promised, and files a bankruptcy petition on July 1. The bankruptcy trustee can recover the $10,000 payment because Connally made it within ninety days of filing. If Connally had not filed until September 1, however, the trustee could not have recovered the $10,000. If a friend of Connally's

had paid off the loan, the payment could not have been recovered, regardless of whether it was made within ninety days, because it was not made with Connally's money or other property. If, on February 1, at the bank's insistence that the loan be secured, Connally had provided a mortgage on the Connally ranch and then had not repaid the loan before declaring bankruptcy, the trustee could have avoided the mortgage if it would have given the bank more than the bank would have received in the Chapter 7 proceeding (that is, if Connally's property was insufficient to pay all unsecured creditors in full).

Sometimes the creditor receiving the preference is an *insider*—an individual, partner, partnership, officer, or director of a corporation (or a relative of one of these) who has a close relationship with the debtor. If such is the case, the avoidance power of the trustee is extended to transfers made within *one year* before filing; however, the *presumption* of insolvency is confined to the ninety-day period. Therefore, the trustee must prove that the debtor was insolvent at the time of earlier transfer.

Not all transfers are preferences. To be a preference, the transfer must be made for something other than current consideration. Therefore, it is generally assumed by most courts that payment for services rendered within ten to fifteen days prior to the payment of the current consideration is not a preference. If a creditor receives payment in the ordinary course of business, such as payment of last month's telephone bill, the payment cannot be recovered by the trustee in bankruptcy. To be recoverable, a preference must be a transfer for an antecedent debt, such as a year-old printing bill. In addition, the 1984 amendments permit a consumer-debtor to transfer any property to a creditor up to a total value of $600, without the transfer's constituting a preference.

If a preferred creditor has sold the property to an innocent third party, the trustee cannot recover the property from the innocent party, but the creditor generally can be held accountable for the value of the property.

LIENS ON DEBTOR'S PROPERTY   The trustee is permitted to avoid the fixing of certain statutory liens, such as a landlord's lien, on property of the debtor. Liens that first become effective on the bankruptcy or insolvency of the debtor are voidable by the trustee. Liens that are not per-

---

12. Under Chapter 11 (to be discussed later), for which no trustee generally exists, the debtor has the same avoiding powers as a trustee under Chapter 7. Under Chapters 12 and 13 (also to be discussed later) a trustee must be appointed.

fected or enforceable on the date of the petition against a bona fide purchaser are voidable.

FRAUDULENT TRANSFERS The trustees may avoid fraudulent transfers or obligations if they are made within one year of the filing of the petition or if they are made with actual intent to hinder, delay, or defraud a creditor. Transfers made for less than a reasonably equivalent consideration are also vulnerable if by making them the debtor became insolvent, was left engaged in

business with an unreasonably small amount of capital, or intended to incur debts that he or she could not pay.

The following case illustrates fraudulent transfers made by a debtor to his daughters. The transfers involved no consideration, and after the transfer the debtor retained control and derived benefits from the property. The trustee in bankruptcy sought to set aside the transfers, and the creditors and wife of the debtor filed actions to deny the debtor a discharge in bankruptcy.

BACKGROUND AND FACTS *Ralph I. Lazar (the debtor) was sued for wrongful interference with a contractual relationship in another case. Lazar had submitted to one disposition by an attorney for the plaintiffs in that suit. Three weeks later, Lazar made the first of several transfers of his assets to his daughters, Arlene and Betty Lazar. One such transfer was his entire interest in a note and mortgage ($180,000), which was paid to his daughters. His daughters deposited the funds in certificates of deposit for approximately four months. The funds were then withdrawn. With these funds and with a transfer by Ralph Lazar of personal funds, plus $104,000 transferred from his solely owned pension trust fund, Arlene purchased a yacht. Title to the yacht was held by Arbet Enterprises, Inc., a closely held corporation in which the daughters were the sole shareholders. Arbet Enterprises was formed solely to take title to the yacht. The yacht was then sold, a sixty-foot Chris Craft yacht was purchased (with title held by Arbet Enterprises) with half the proceeds, and the remaining funds were deposited to be used by the debtor and his daughters for their support. The debtor used the Chris Craft as his place of residence and for his personal benefit and enjoyment. Ralph Lazar lost the lawsuit for wrongful interference with a contractual relationship, resulting in a judgment against him for $2 million. When the judgment creditors attempted to execute the judgment, Lazar filed a Chapter 7 bankruptcy petition, having stripped himself of his assets by the transfers to his daughters. The trustee filed a claim against Lazar for fraudulent transfer and sought to have the money held by Arbet Enterprises (as Lazar's alter ego—second self) and the Chris Craft yacht turned over to the trustee as part of the debtor's estate. The creditors and wife of Lazar filed independent actions seeking to deny him a discharge in bankruptcy due to his fraudulent actions.*

Case 31.1
IN RE LAZAR[a]
United States Bankruptcy Court,
Southern District of Florida,
1988.
81 B.R. 148.

WEAVER, Bankruptcy Judge.

*   *   *   *

*   *   * The transfers of the Note and Mortgage and the Pension Trust funds described above are marked by several of the "badges of fraud" which the Florida courts have identified as factors tending to indicate the presence of a fraudulent transfer. Specifically, the subject transfers were made to family members for no consideration, and after the transfers the debtor retained full control over, and derived the primary benefit from, the use of the funds and the assets subsequently purchased therewith.

---

a.   *In re* means concerning or regarding. It is a method of entitling a judicial proceeding in which there are no adversary parties but only some thing as to which some action is taken—in this case, a debtor's estate in bankruptcy.

The Court finds that the debtor's intent in making the aforesaid transfers, and the legal effect of said transfers, was to hinder, delay and defraud the creditors. Under these circumstances, the trustee has sufficiently proven his claim.

* * * *

As a separate and independent basis for awarding the turnover of the yacht * * * to the trustee, this Court finds that the corporation known as Arbet Enterprises, Inc. is the alter ego of the debtor. Arbet Enterprises, Inc. was at all times the mere instrumentality of the debtor [that is, completely under the debtor's control], created to aid the debtor in defrauding the creditors and concealing his ownership of [the yachts].

In addition to the trustee's claim, both the creditors and the debtor's spouse filed independent actions seeking to block the discharge of the debtor. These claims were consolidated for trial with the trustee's claim. The objections to the discharge are mainly premised upon the provisions of 11 U.S.C. § 727(a). In connection with the claimed objections to the debtor's discharge, the Court finds that the debtor, with the intent to hinder, delay and defraud the creditors, did engage in the continuous concealment of his assets during the one year period prior to the filing of the bankruptcy petition, which satisfies the requirements of § 727(a)(2) of the Bankruptcy Code.

DECISION AND REMEDY *The court held that the transfers Ralph Lazar made to his daughters were fraudulent and that the trustee could set aside those transfers, which included the yacht and remaining funds. In addition, Lazar was denied the right to receive a discharge in bankruptcy.*

Claims of Creditors

Generally, any legal obligation of the debtor is a claim. In the case of a disputed or unliquidated claim, the bankruptcy court will set the value of the claim. Any creditor holding a debtor's obligation can file a claim against the debtor's estate. These claims are automatically allowed unless contested by the trustee, debtor, or another creditor.

The Code, however, does not allow claims for breach of employment contracts or real estate leases for terms longer than one year. Such claims are limited to one year's rent or wages, despite the remaining length of either contract in breach.

Distribution of Property

Creditors are either secured or unsecured. The rights of secured creditors were discussed in Chapter 29. A *secured* creditor has a security interest in collateral that secures the debt. Before passage of the 1984 amendments, secured parties were frequently forced to wait for months concerning the disposition of the secured collateral held by the debtor, because of the automatic stay provisions. Today, the law provides that a consumer-debtor, within thirty days of filing a Chapter 7 petition or before the date of the first meeting of the creditors (whichever is first), must file with the clerk a statement of intention with respect to the secured collateral. The statement must indicate whether the debtor will retain or surrender the collateral to the secured party.[13] The trustee is obligated to enforce the debtor's statement within forty-five days after it is filed.

If the collateral is surrendered to the secured party, the secured creditor can enforce the security interest either by accepting the property in full satisfaction of the debt or by foreclosing on the collateral and using the proceeds to pay off the debt. Thus, the secured party has priority over unsecured parties as to the proceeds from the disposition of the collateral. Indeed, the Code provides that if the value of the collateral exceeds the secured party's claim, the secured party also has priority as to the proceeds in an amount that will cover reasonable fees and costs incurred because of the debtor's default. Any excess over this amount is used by the trustee to satisfy the claims of unsecured creditors. Should the collateral be insufficient to cover the secured debt owed, the secured creditor becomes an unsecured creditor for the difference.

---

13. Also, if applicable, the debtor must specify whether the collateral will be claimed as exempt property and whether the debtor intends to redeem the property or reaffirm the debt secured by the collateral.

Bankruptcy law establishes an order of priority for classes of debts owed to *unsecured* creditors, and they are paid in the order of their priority. Each class must be fully paid before the next class is entitled to any of the remaining proceeds. If there are insufficient proceeds to pay fully all the creditors in a class, the proceeds are distributed *proportionately* to the creditors in the class, and classes lower in priority receive nothing. The order of priority among classes of unsecured creditors is as follows:

1. Administrative expenses—including court costs, trustee fees, and attorneys' fees.
2. In an involuntary bankruptcy, expenses incurred by the debtor in the ordinary course of business from the date of the filing of the petition up to the appointment of the trustee or the issuance by the court of an order of relief.
3. Unpaid wages, salaries, and commissions earned within ninety days of the filing of the petition, limited to $2,000 per claimant. Any claim in excess of $2,000 is treated as a claim of a general creditor (listed as number 8 below).
4. Unsecured claims for contributions to be made to employee benefit plans, limited to services performed during 180 days prior to the filing of the bankruptcy petition and $2,000 per employee.
5. Claims by farmers and fishermen, up to $2,000, against debtor operators of grain storage or fish storage or processing facilities.
6. Consumer deposits of up to $900 given to the debtor before the petition was filed in connection with the purchase, lease, or rental of property that was not received or provided. Any claim in excess of $900 is treated as a claim of a general creditor (listed as number 8 below).
7. Certain taxes and penalties due to government units, such as income and property taxes.
8. Claims of general creditors.

If any amount remains after the priority classes of creditors have been satisfied, it is turned over to the debtor.

In a bankruptcy case in which the debtor has no assets, creditors are notified of the debtor's petition for bankruptcy but are instructed not to file a claim. In such a case, the unsecured creditors will receive no payment and most, if not all, of these debts will be discharged.

Discharge

From the debtor's point of view, the primary purpose of a Chapter 7 liquidation is to obtain a fresh start through the discharge of debts.[14] Certain debts, however, are not dischargeable in bankruptcy. Also, certain debtors may not qualify to have all debts discharged in bankruptcy. These situations are discussed below.

EXCEPTIONS TO DISCHARGE Discharge of a debt may be denied because of the nature of the claim or the conduct of the debtor. Claims that are not dischargeable under Chapter 7 include the following:

1. Claims for back taxes accruing within three years prior to bankruptcy.
2. Claims against property or money obtained by the debtor under false pretenses or by false representations.
3. Claims by creditors who were not notified of the bankruptcy; these claims did not appear on the "schedules" the debtor was required to file.
4. Claims based on fraud or misuse of funds by the debtor while he or she was acting in a fiduciary capacity or claims involving the debtor's embezzlement or larceny.
5. Alimony and child support.
6. Claims based on willful or malicious conduct by the debtor toward another or the property of another.
7. Certain fines and penalties payable to governmental units.
8. Certain student loans, unless payment of the loans imposes an undue hardship on the debtor and the debtor's dependents.
9. Consumer debts of more than $500 for luxury goods or services owed to a single creditor incurred within forty days of the order of relief. This denial of discharge is a rebuttable presumption, and any debts reasonably incurred to support the debtor or dependents are not classified as luxury goods or services.
10. Cash advances totaling more than $1,000 as extensions of open-end consumer credit obtained

---

14. Discharges are granted only to *individuals* who are debtors under Chapter 7, not to corporations or partnerships. The latter may use Chapter 11, or they may terminate under state law.

by the debtor within twenty days of the order of relief. This is also a rebuttable presumption.

11. Judgments or consent decrees awarded against a debtor as a result of the debtor's operation of a motor vehicle while legally intoxicated.

In the following case, the question of the discharge of a student loan is at issue.

Case 31.2
BAKER v. UNIVERSITY OF TENNESSEE AT CHATTANOOGA (IN RE BAKER)
United States Bankruptcy Court, Eastern District of Tennessee, 1981.
10 B.R. 870.

BACKGROUND AND FACTS   *Mary Lou Baker attended three different institutions of higher learning, the University of Tennessee at Chattanooga, Cleveland State Community College, and the Baroness Erlanger School of Nursing. At these three schools, she received educational loans totaling $6,635. After graduation, she was employed; but her monthly take home pay was less than $650. Monthly expenses for herself and her three children were approximately $925. Her husband had left town and provided no child or other financial support. She received no public aid and had no other income. In January of 1981, just prior to this action, Mary Lou Baker's church paid her gas bill so that she and her children could have heat in their home. One child had reading difficulty, and another required expensive shoes. She had not been well and had been unable to pay her medical bills. Baker filed for bankruptcy. In her petition, she sought a discharge of her educational loans based on the hardship provision, which is the issue before the court.*

KELLEY, Bankruptcy Judge.

This cause came on to be heard on May 5, 1981, on debtor's complaint to determine dischargeability of certain educational loans. The complaint alleges that debtor is entitled to relief under 11 U.S.C. 523 (a)(8) which reads as follows:

Exceptions to discharge.

(a) A discharge under section 727, 1141, or 1328(b) of this title does not discharge an individual debtor from any debt—

*   *   *   *

(8) to a governmental unit, or a nonprofit institution of higher education, for an educational loan, unless—

(B) excepting such debt from discharge under this paragraph will impose an undue hardship on the debtor and the debtor's dependents;

*   *   *   *

In 1976 the Congress passed the Educational Amendments which restricted a discharge in bankruptcy. The restriction was designed to remedy an abuse by students who, immediately upon graduation, would file bankruptcy to secure a discharge of educational loans. These students often had no other indebtedness and could easily pay their debts from future wages.

*   *   *   *

As noted in 3 *Collier on Bankruptcy*, 15th edition, at paragraph 523.18:

Paragraph (B) of subdivision (a)(8) is the "hardship" provision that permits the court to discharge a student loan otherwise nondischargeable, if excepting the debt from discharge will impose an undue hardship on the debtor or the debtor's dependents. This exemption from the exception to discharge is discretionary with the bankruptcy judge who will have to determine whether payment of the debt will cause undue hardship on the debtor and his dependents thus defeating the "fresh start" concept of the bankruptcy laws. There may well be circumstances that justify failure to repay a student loan such as illness, incapacity or other extenuating circumstances. Where the court finds that such circumstances exist, it may order the debt discharged.

The court concludes that under the circumstances of this case, requiring the debtor to repay the debts owed to the *three* defendants in the amount of $6,635.00 plus interest would impose upon her and her dependents an undue hardship. In passing the Educational Amendments of 1976 and including these amendments in the Bankruptcy Reform Act of 1978, Congress intended to correct an abuse. It did not intend to deprive those who have truly fallen on hard times of the "fresh start" policy of the new Bankruptcy Code.

The debtor's student loans were discharged.

DECISION AND REMEDY

OBJECTIONS TO DISCHARGE In addition to the exceptions to discharge previously listed, other circumstances will cause a bankruptcy court to deny the discharge of a debt or debts. When the court denies the discharge of the debtor (as opposed to the debt), the assets of the debtor are still distributed to the creditors, but the debtor remains liable for the unpaid portion of all claims. Some grounds for the denial of discharge of the debtor include:

1. The debtor's concealment or destruction of property with the intent to hinder, delay, or defraud a creditor.
2. The debtor's fraudulent concealment or destruction of financial records.
3. The debtor's refusal to obey a lawful order of a bankruptcy court.
4. The debtor's failure to satisfactorily explain the loss of assets.
5. The granting of a discharge to the debtor within six years of the filing of the petition.
6. The debtor's written waiver of discharge approved by the court.

Prior to the 1984 amendments, creditors were reluctant to challenge and object to the granting of a discharge to a debtor. If the challenge was denied, the creditor was liable in judgment to the debtor for all costs and reasonable attorneys' fees. To encourage legitimate objections, the amendments provide that even if the creditor loses on the challenge, the creditor is liable for costs and attorneys' fees only if the challenge was not *substantially justified*.

EFFECT OF DISCHARGE The primary effect of a discharge is to void any judgment on a discharged debt and enjoin any action to collect a discharged debt. A discharge does not affect the liability of a co-debtor.

REVOCATION OF DISCHARGE The Code provides that a debtor may lose his or her bankruptcy discharge by revocation upon petition by the trustee or a creditor. The bankruptcy court may within one year revoke the discharge decree if it is discovered that the debtor acted fraudulently or dishonestly during the bankruptcy proceedings. The revocation renders the discharge null and void, allowing creditors not satisfied by the distribution of the debtor's estate to proceed with their claims against the debtor.

REAFFIRMATION OF DEBT A debtor may voluntarily wish to pay off a dischargeable debt. This is called a *reaffirmation of the debt*. The 1984 amendments completely revised the rules concerning reaffirmation agreements. To be enforceable, reaffirmation agreements must be made before the debtor is granted a discharge. The agreement must be filed with the court. If the debtor is represented by an attorney, court approval is not required if the attorney files a declaration or affidavit stating that the debtor has been fully informed of the consequences of the agreement, the agreement is voluntarily made, and the agreement does not impose a hardship on the debtor or dependents. If the debtor is not represented by an attorney, court approval will be required, and the agreement will be approved only if the court finds that it will cause no undue hardship and will be in the best interest of the debtor.

In addition, the debtor can rescind the agreement at any time prior to discharge or within sixty days of the filing of the agreement, whichever is later. This rescission period must be stated *clearly* and *conspicuously* in the reaffirmation agreement.

CHAPTER 11 REORGANIZATIONS

The type of bankruptcy proceeding used most commonly by a corporate debtor is the Chapter 11 reorganization. In a reorganization, the creditors and the debtor formulate a plan under which the debtor pays a portion of his or her debts and is discharged of the remainder. The debtor is allowed to continue in business. Although this type of bankruptcy is commonly a corporate reorganization, any debtor (except a stockbroker or a commodities broker) who is eligible for Chapter 7 relief is eligible for Chapter 11 relief. In addition, railroads are eligible for Chapter 11 relief.

The same principles that govern the filing of a Chapter 7 petition apply to Chapter 11 proceedings. The case may be brought either voluntarily or involuntarily. The same principles govern the entry of the order for relief. The automatic stay and adequate protection provisions are applicable in reorganizations. The automatic stay provisions and the use of a plan to discharge unsecured debts have been used to prevent injured parties from securing judgments in lawsuits and debtors from breaking collective bargaining agreements. This has resulted in much controversy. The courts and the 1984 amendments have attempted to clarify some of these issues, particularly collective bargaining agreements, which will be discussed later in this chapter.

In some instances, creditors may prefer private, negotiated adjustments of creditor-debtor relations, also known as **workouts,** to bankruptcy proceedings. Often these out-of-court workouts are much more flexible and thus more conducive to a speedy settlement. Speed is critical, since delay is one of the most costly elements in any bankruptcy proceeding.

Another advantage of workouts is that they avoid the various administrative costs of bankruptcy proceedings. Thus, under Section 305(a) of the Bankruptcy Code, a court, after notice and a hearing, may dismiss or suspend all proceedings in a case at any time if dismissal or suspension would better serve the interests of the creditors. Section 1112 also allows a court, after notice and a hearing, to dismiss a case under Chapter 11 "for cause." Cause includes the absence of a reasonable likelihood of rehabilitation, the inability to effectuate a plan, and an unreasonable delay by the debtor that is prejudicial to creditors.[15]

In the following case, creditors of Johns-Manville Corporation seek to dismiss, under Section 1112, a voluntary petition filed by Manville.

---

15. See 11 U.S.C. Section 1112(b).

Case 31.3

IN RE JOHNS-MANVILLE CORP.

United States Bankruptcy Court,
Southern District of New York,
1984.
36 B.R. 727.

BACKGROUND AND FACTS *On August 26, 1982, Johns-Manville Corporation, a highly successful industrial enterprise and major producer of asbestos, filed for protection under Chapter 11 of the Bankruptcy Code. This filing came as quite a surprise to some of Manville's creditors, as well as to some of the other corporations that were being sued, along with Manville, for injuries caused by asbestos exposure. Manville asserted that the approximately 16,000 lawsuits pending as of the filing date and the potential lawsuits of people who had been exposed but who would not manifest asbestos-related diseases until sometime in the future necessitated its filing. The creditors of Manville, including people harmed by asbestos exposure who had won lawsuits or settlements, contended that Johns-Manville had not filed in good faith and that the voluntary Chapter 11 petition should thus be dismissed under Section 1112 of the Bankruptcy Code.*

LIFLAND, Bankruptcy Judge.
* * * *

In determining whether to dismiss under Code Section 1112(b), a court is not necessarily required to consider whether the debtor has filed in "good faith" because that is not a specified predicate under the Code for filing. Rather, according to Code Section 1129(a)(3), good faith emerges as a requirement for the confirmation of a plan.

* * * It is thus logical that the good faith of the debtor be deemed a predicate primarily for emergence out of a Chapter 11 case. It is after confirmation of a concrete and immutable reorganization plan that creditors are foreclosed from advancing their distinct and parochial interests in the debtor's estate.

A "principal goal" of the Bankruptcy Code is to provide "open access" to the "bankruptcy process." * * *

Accordingly, the drafters of the Code envisioned that a financially beleaguered debtor with real debt and real creditors should not be required to wait until the economic situation is beyond repair in order to file a reorganization petition. The "Congressional purpose" in enacting the Code was to encourage resort to the bankruptcy process. This philosophy not only comports with the elimination of an insolvency requirement, but also is a corollary of the key aim of Chapter 11 of the Code, that of avoidance of liquidation. * * *

In the instant case, not only would liquidation be wasteful and inefficient in destroying the utility of valuable assets of the companies as well as jobs, but, more importantly, liquidation would preclude just compensation of some present asbestos victims and all future asbestos claimants. This unassailable reality represents all the more reason for this Court to adhere to this basic potential liquidation avoidance aim of Chapter 11 and deny the motions to dismiss. Manville must not be required to wait until its economic picture has deteriorated beyond salvation to file for reorganization. * * * *

In sum, Manville is a financially beseiged enterprise in desperate need of reorganization of its crushing real debt, both present and future. The reorganization provisions of the Code were drafted with the aim of liquidation avoidance by great access to Chapter 11. Accordingly, Manville's filing does not abuse the jurisdictional integrity of this Court.

The motions to dismiss the Manville petition were denied. The court concluded that a bankruptcy proceeding was appropriate in this situation.

DECISION AND REMEDY

Debtor in Possession

Upon entry of the order for relief, the debtor generally continues to operate his or her business as a *debtor in possession*. The court, however, may appoint a trustee to operate the debtor's business if gross mismanagement of the business is shown or if for some other reason appointing a trustee is in the best interests of the estate. As soon as practicable after entry of the order for relief, a creditors' committee of unsecured creditors is appointed. The committee may consult with the debtor in possession (or the trustee) concerning the administration of the case or the formulation of the plan.

Creditors' Committees

Additional creditors' committees may be appointed to represent special-interest creditors. Orders affecting the estate generally will not be entered without either the consent of the committee or a hearing in which the judge hears the position of the committee.

The Plan

A Chapter 11 plan of rehabilitation is a plan to conserve and administer the debtor's assets in the hope of an eventual return to successful operation and solvency. The plan must be fair and equitable and must:

1. Designate classes of claims and interests.
2. Specify the treatment to be afforded the classes. (The plan must provide the same treatment for each claim in a particular class.)
3. Provide an adequate means for execution.

FILING THE PLAN Only the debtor may file a plan within the first 120 days after the date of the order for relief. If the debtor does not meet the 120-day deadline, however, or if the debtor fails to obtain the required creditor consent within 180 days, any party may propose a plan.

Once the plan has been developed, it is submitted to each class of creditors for acceptance. Each class must accept the plan unless the class is not adversely affected [11 U.S.C. Section 1129(8)]. A class has accepted the plan when a majority of the creditors, representing two-thirds of the amount of the total claim, vote to approve it.

CONFIRMATION OF THE PLAN Each plan submitted is almost a case history in itself, and each plan varies from others. Each plan, however, must be "in the best interests of the creditors." Even when all classes of creditors accept the plan, the court may refuse to confirm it if it fails to meet this requirement. Conversely, even if only one class accepts the plan, the court may still confirm it under the Code's so-called *cram down* provision.

The plan is binding upon confirmation. Upon confirmation, the debtor is given a Chapter 11 discharge from all claims not protected under the plan. This discharge, however, does not apply to any claims denied discharge under Chapter 7 (as previously discussed).

Collective Bargaining Agreements

Under the 1978 Reform Act, questions arose as to whether a Chapter 11 debtor could reject a recently negotiated collectively bargained labor contract. In *National Labor Relations Board v. Bildisco and Bildisco,* the Supreme Court held that a collective bargaining agreement subject to the National Labor Relations Act is an "executory contract" and thus subject to *rejection* by a debtor in possession.[16] The Court emphasized that such a rejection should not be permitted unless there is a finding that the policy of Chapter 11 (successful rehabilitation of debtors) would be served by the action. Hence, when the bankruptcy court determines that a rejection of a collective bargaining agreement should be permitted, it must make a reasoned finding *on the record* as to *why* it has determined that a rejection should be permitted.

The 1984 amendments are an attempt to reconcile federal policies favoring collective bargaining with the need to allow a debtor company to reject executory labor contracts while trying to reorganize under Chapter 11 of the Code. A new section has been added to the Bankruptcy Code that sets forth standards and procedures under

which collective bargaining contracts can be assumed or rejected under a Chapter 11 filing.

In general, a collective bargaining contract can be rejected if the debtor has first proposed necessary contractual modifications to the union and the union has failed to adopt them without good cause. The company is required to provide the union with the relevant information needed to evaluate this proposal and to confer in good faith in attempting to reach a mutually satisfactory agreement on the modifications.

CHAPTER 13 PLANS

Chapter 13 of the Bankruptcy Code provides for "Adjustment of Debts of an Individual with Regular Income." Individuals (not partnerships or corporations) with *regular income* who owe fixed unsecured debts of less than $100,000 or fixed secured debts of less than $350,000 may take advantage of Chapter 13. This includes individual proprietors and individuals who live on welfare, Social Security, fixed pensions, or investment income.[17] Many small business debtors have a choice of filing a plan under Chapter 11 or Chapter 13. There are several advantages in filing a Chapter 13 plan. One advantage is that it is less expensive and less complicated than a Chapter 11 proceeding or even a Chapter 7 liquidation.

Filing the Petition

A Chapter 13 case can be initiated only by the filing of a voluntary petition by the debtor. Certain Chapter 7 and Chapter 11 cases may be converted to Chapter 13 cases with the consent of the debtor.[18] A trustee, who will make payments under the plan, must be appointed.

Automatic Stay

Upon the filing of a Chapter 13 petition, the automatic stay previously discussed takes effect. It

---

16. 465 U.S. 513, 104 S.Ct. 1188, 79 L.Ed.2d 482 (1984).

17. Prior to passage of the new Bankruptcy Act, self-employed persons could not file under Chapter 13.

18. A Chapter 13 case may be converted to a Chapter 7 case at the request of either the debtor or, under certain circumstances denominated "for cause," a creditor. A Chapter 13 case may be converted to Chapter 11 after a hearing. In either instance, farmers are protected from creditor-requested conversions.

enjoins creditors from taking action against co-obligors of the debtor. Although the stay applies to all or part of a consumer debt, it does not apply to any business debt incurred by the debtor. A creditor has the right to seek relief from the automatic stay. A 1984 amendment was enacted to save the creditor time and money in seeking court approval to vacate (remove) the stay and recover from the co-debtor. The new law provides that upon the creditor's request to vacate the stay against the co-debtor, unless written objection is filed, twenty days later the stay against the co-debtor is automatically terminated without a hearing.

The Plan

A Chapter 13 plan of rehabilitation must:

1. Provide for the turnover to the trustee of such future earnings or income of the debtor as is necessary for execution of the plan.
2. Provide for full payment in deferred cash payments of all claims entitled to priority.
3. Provide for the same treatment of each claim within a particular class. (The 1984 amendments permit the debtor to list co-debtors, such as guarantors or sureties, as a separate class.)

FILING THE PLAN   Only the debtor may file a plan under Chapter 13. This plan may provide either for payment of all obligations in full or for payment of a lesser amount. The time for payment under the plan may not exceed three years unless the court approves an extension. The term, with extension, may not exceed five years.

The 1984 amendments require the debtor to make "timely" payments, and the trustee is required to ensure that the debtor commence these payments. The law now provides that the debtor must commence making payments under the proposed plan within thirty days after the plan has been *filed*. If the plan has not been confirmed, the trustee is instructed to retain the payments until the plan is confirmed and then distribute them accordingly. If the plan is denied, the trustee will return the payments to the debtor less any costs. Failure of the debtor to make timely payments or to commence payments within the thirty-day period will allow the court to convert the case to a Chapter 7 bankruptcy or to dismiss the petition.

CONFIRMATION OF THE PLAN   After the plan is filed, the court holds a confirmation hearing at which interested parties may object to the plan. The court will confirm a plan with respect to each claim of a secured creditor under any of the following circumstances:

1. If the secured creditors have àccepted the plan.
2. If the plan provides that creditors retain their liens and if the value of the property to be distributed to them under the plan is not less than the secured portion of their claims.
3. If the debtor surrenders the property securing the claim to the creditors.

OBJECTION TO THE PLAN   Unsecured creditors do not have a vote to confirm a Chapter 13 plan, but they can object to it. The court can approve a plan over the objection of the trustee or any unsecured creditor only in one of the following situations:

1. When the value of the property to be distributed under the plan is at least equal to the amount of the claims.
2. When all the debtor's projected disposable income to be received during the three-year plan period will be applied to making payments. Disposable income is all income received *less* amounts needed to support the debtor and dependents and/or amounts needed to meet ordinary expenses to continue the operation of a business.

MODIFICATION OF THE PLAN   Prior to completion of payments, the plan may be modified upon request of either the debtor, the trustee, or an unsecured creditor. If there is an objection by any interested party to the modification, the court must hold a hearing to determine approval or disapproval of the modified plan.

Discharge

After completion of all payments under a Chapter 13 plan, the court grants a discharge of all debts provided for by the plan. The exemptions to discharge are for certain long-term debts. Except for claims constituting priority debts and except for alimony and child support, all other debts are dischargeable. Priority debts must be paid because the priority claims are a minimum requirement of what must be included in a plan. A Chapter 13 discharge is sometimes referred to as a "super-discharge." One of the reasons for this is that the law

CONCEPT SUMMARY: Bankruptcy—A Comparison of Chapters 7, 11, 12, and 13

ISSUE	CHAPTER 7	CHAPTER 11	CHAPTERS 12 AND 13
Purpose	Liquidation.	Reorganization.	Adjustment.
Who can petition	Debtor (voluntary) or creditors (involuntary).	Debtor (voluntary) or creditors (involuntary).	Debtor (voluntary) only.
Who can be a debtor	Any "person" (including partnerships and corporations) except railroads, insurance companies, banks, savings and loan institutions, and credit unions. Farmers and charitable institutions cannot be involuntarily petitioned.	Any debtor eligible for Chapter 7 relief; railroads are also eligible.	*Chapter 12*—Any family farmer whose gross income is at least 50 percent farm-dependent and whose debts are at least 80 percent farm-related or any partnership or closely held corporation at least 50 percent owned by a farm family, where total debt does not exceed $1,500,000. *Chapter 13*—Any individual (not partnerships or corporations) with regular income who owes fixed unsecured debt of less than $100,000 or secured debt of less than $350,000.
Procedure leading to discharge	Nonexempt property is sold with proceeds to be distributed (in order) to priority groups. Dischargeable debts are terminated.	Plan is submitted; and if it is approved and followed, debts are discharged.	Plan is submitted (must be approved if debtor turns over disposable income for three-year period); and if it is approved and followed, debts are discharged.
Advantages	Upon liquidation and distribution, most debts are discharged, and debtor has opportunity for fresh start.	Debtor continues in business. Creditors can accept plan, or it can be "crammed down" on them. Plan allows for reorganization and liquidation of debts over plan period.	Debtor continues in business or possession of assets. If plan is approved, most debts are discharged after a three-year period.

allows a Chapter 13 discharge to include fraudulently incurred debt and claims resulting from malicious or willful injury. Therefore, a Chapter 13 discharge is much more beneficial to some debtors than a Chapter 7 discharge.

Even if the debtor does not complete the plan, a hardship discharge may be granted if failure to complete the plan was due to circumstances beyond the debtor's control and if the value of the property distributed under the plan was greater than would have been paid in a Chapter 7 liquidation. A discharge can be revoked within one year if it was obtained by fraud.

CHAPTER 12 PLANS

On November 27, 1986, the Family Farmer Bankruptcy Act became law. In order to help relieve economic pressure on small farmers, Congress created a new chapter (Chapter 12) in the Bankruptcy Code. The new law defines a *family farmer* as one whose gross income is at least 50 percent farm-dependent and whose debts are at least 80 percent farm-related. The total debt must not exceed $1,500,000. A partnership or closely held corporation (at least 50 percent owned by the farm family) can also take advantage of this new law.

A Chapter 12 filing is very similar in procedure to a Chapter 13 filing. The farmer-debtor must file a plan not later than ninety days after the order of relief. The filing of the petition acts as an automatic stay against creditors' and co-obligors' actions against the estate.

A secured creditor can petition to lift the automatic stay for adequate protection of his or her interest if the value of the collateral is less than the amount of the secured debt owed the creditor. Before the enactment of Chapter 12, some courts held that "adequate protection" required the farmer-debtor, as is required of other debtors under other chapters of the Code, to compensate the secured creditor for so-called "lost opportunity costs." Lost opportunity costs represent a sum equal to the interest that the undercollateralized secured creditor might earn on an amount of money equal to the value of the collateral securing the debt. The rationale behind requiring these payments as part of adequate protection is that the Code's automatic stay provisions preclude the creditor from foreclosing its interest and reinvesting the proceeds.

Because farmland values have dropped substantially, family farmers are usually unable to pay lost opportunity costs. Thus, family farm reorganizations were often throttled on a creditor's motion to lift the automatic stay. Chapter 12 adds a different means for providing adequate protection—payment of reasonable market rental payments—to protect the value of the property and thereby the operation of a farm as a going concern. Generally, the amount of reasonable market rental has been based on the gross rental value of the farmland and its income potential, considering crop requirements, government payments, and so on.

The content of a Chapter 12 plan is basically the same as that of a Chapter 13 filing. The plan can be modified by the farmer-debtor but, except for cause, must be confirmed or denied within forty-five days of the filing of the plan.

Court confirmation of the plan is the same as for a Chapter 13 plan. In summary, the plan must provide for payment of secured debts at the value of the collateral. If the secured debt exceeds the value of the collateral, the remaining debt is unsecured. For unsecured debtors, the plan must be confirmed if either the value of the property to be distributed under the plan equals the amount of the claim or the plan provides that all of the farmer-debtor's disposable income to be received in a three-year period (longer by court approval) will be applied to making payments.

Disposable income is all income received less amounts needed to support the farmer-debtor and family and to continue the farming operation. Completion of payments under the plan is a discharge of all debts provided for by the plan.

The new law also allows a farmer who has already filed under Chapter 11 or 13 to convert to Chapter 12. Chapter 12, like Chapters 11 and 13, allows for the farmer-debtor to convert to liquidation under Chapter 7.

QUESTIONS AND CASE PROBLEMS

1. Carlton has been a rancher all his life, raising cattle and crops. His ranch is valued at $500,000, almost all of which is exempt under state law. Carlton has eight creditors and a total indebtedness of $70,000. Two of his largest creditors are Samson ($30,000 owed) and Greed ($25,000 owed). The other six creditors have claims of less than $5,000 each. A drought has ruined all of Carlton's crops and forced him to sell many of his cattle at a loss. He cannot pay off his creditors.

(a) Under the Code, can Carlton, with a $500,000 ranch, voluntarily petition himself into bankruptcy? Explain.

(b) Could either Samson or Greed force Carlton into involuntary bankruptcy? Explain.

2. Sam is a retail seller of television sets. He sells Martha a $900 set on a retail installment security agreement in which she pays $100 down and agrees to pay the balance in equal installments. Sam retains a security interest in the set, and he perfects that interest by filing a financing statement locally. Two months later, Martha is in default on her payments to Sam and is involuntarily petitioned into bankruptcy by her creditors. Sam wants to repossess the television set as provided for in the security agreement, and he wants to have priority over the trustee in bankruptcy as to any proceeds from the disposal of the set. Discuss fully Sam's right to repossess and whether he has priority over the trustee in bankruptcy as to any proceeds from disposal of the set.

3. Green is not known for his business sense. He started a greenhouse and nursery business two years ago and because of his lack of experience, he soon was in debt to a number of creditors. On February 1, Green borrowed $5,000 from his father to pay some of these creditors. On May 1, Green paid back the $5,000, depleting his entire working capital. One creditor, the Cool Springs Nursery Supply Corporation, extended credit to Green on numerous purchases. Cool Springs pressured Green for payment, and on July 1, Green paid Cool Springs half the money owed. On September 1, Green voluntarily petitioned himself into bankruptcy. The trustee in bankruptcy claimed that both Green's father and Cool Springs must turn over to the debtor's estate the amounts Green paid to them. Discuss fully the trustee's claims.

4. Gordon petitioned himself into voluntary bankruptcy. There were three major claims against his estate. One was made by Carlton, a friend who held Gordon's negotiable promissory note for $2,500; one was made by Elmer, an employee who was owed three months' back wages of $4,500; and one was made by the United Bank of the Rockies on an unsecured loan of $5,000. In addition, Dietrich, an accountant retained by the trustee, was owed $500, and property taxes of $1,000 were owed to Rock County. Gordon's nonexempt property was liquidated, with proceeds of $5,000. Discuss fully what amount each party will receive and why.

5. The East Bank was a secured party on a $5,000 loan it made to Sally. Sally experienced financial difficulty, and creditors other than the East Bank petitioned her into involuntary bankruptcy. The value of the secured collateral had substantially decreased in value. Upon its sale, the debt to East Bank was reduced to $2,500. Sally's estate consisted of $100,000 in exempt assets and $2,000 in nonexempt assets. After the bankruptcy costs and back wages to Sally's employees had been paid, nothing was left for unsecured creditors. Sally received a discharge in bankruptcy. Later she decided to go back into business. By selling a few exempt assets and getting a small loan, she would be able to buy a small but profitable restaurant. She went to East Bank for the loan. East Bank claimed that the balance of its secured debt had not been discharged in bankruptcy. Sally signed an agreement to pay East Bank the $2,500, as the bank had not been a party to petitioning her into bank-

ruptcy. Because of this, East Bank made the new unsecured loan to Sally.

(a) Discuss East Bank's claim that the balance of its secured debt had not been discharged in bankruptcy.
(b) Discuss the legal effect of Sally's agreement to pay East Bank $2,500 after the discharge in bankruptcy.
(c) If one year after buying the restaurant Sally went into voluntary bankruptcy, what effect would the bankruptcy proceedings have on the new unsecured loan?

6. Tracey Service Co., Inc., filed a petition for a Chapter 11 reorganization. Acar Supply Co., one of Tracey's creditors, filed a motion to convert the case to a Chapter 7 liquidation. The court found that the debtor corporation had no place of business, no inventory, no equipment, no employees, and no business phone. Should Tracey Service be permitted to reorganize under Chapter 11? [In re Tracey Service Co., Inc., 17 B.R. 405 (Bkrtcy.E.D.Pa.1982)]

7. Donald Lewis filed a voluntary petition for bankruptcy. One of the debts on which he sought discharge was $1,500 judgment that had been entered against him for assault on Betty Dunson. Lewis testified in the bankruptcy court that he put both hands around Dunson's neck and told her to leave his wife alone or he would break her neck. Will the court grant a discharge of the judgment claim? [In re Lewis, 17 B.R. 341 (Bkrtcy.S.D.Ohio 1982)]

8. Prior to filing for bankruptcy, Bray was making loan payments to his company's credit union through payroll deductions. Bray's employer continued to deduct the loan payments from Bray's paychecks after being notified of the bankruptcy petition. Is this a violation of the Bankruptcy Code? [In re Bray, 17 B.R. 152 (Bkrtcy.N.D.Ga. 1982)]

9. In 1983, Beech Acceptance Corporation financed the sale of three airplanes to Gull Air, Inc. Approximately three years later, Gull Air defaulted on its obligations to Beech Acceptance, and Beech filed suit. Before the trial, Gull Air and Beech negotiated a workout agreement that provided for large monthly payments over a certain period. Despite the workout agreement, Gull Air filed a Chapter 11 petition in bankruptcy. Gull Air claimed that payments made under the workout agreement during the ninety days prior to the filing of the Chapter 11 petition amounted to a preference and must be returned to the debtor in possession (Gull Air). There was no question that Beech had received more than it would have under a Chapter 7 liquidation. Beech claimed that the payments had been made in the ordinary course of business. Discuss who is correct. [In re Gull Air, Inc., 82 B.R. 1 (Bkrtcy.D.Mass. 1988)]

10. In 1985, the United States, under the Comprehensive Environmental Response, Compensation and Liability Act, filed suit for costs in connection with the cleaning up of asbestos released from a facility owned and operated by Nicolet, Inc. Before the lawsuit was completed, Nicolet filed a petition for Chapter 11 bankruptcy. Nicolet argued that the petition in bankruptcy operated as an automatic stay of the government's right to continue civil proceedings against it to recover the cleanup costs. The Bankruptcy Code provides an exception to the automatic stay order when the debtor has filed the petition. This exception provides that the stay is not available against a governmental

unit exercising its police and regulatory powers. Discuss whether the civil action by the United States to recover cleanup costs falls under the automatic stay order or under the exception of a governmental unit exercising its police and regulatory powers. [United States v. Nicolet, Inc., 81 B.R. 310 (E.D.Pa. 1988)]

11. John Patrick Goulding filed for Chapter 7 bankruptcy relief in 1987. In his schedules, he listed assets of $62,000 and debts of over $670,000. The majority of these debts were unsecured and were not consumer debts. The Federal Deposit Insurance Corporation (FDIC), as successor to two banks, was the largest unsecured creditor ($379,000). The FDIC and the trustee learned that Goulding was the beneficiary of three irrevocable spendthrift trusts (the assets of which cannot be reached by creditors) that provided him with $12,000 per month, and that he would receive from the corpus (principal) of one trust $200,000 on January 30, 1988. The trustee and the FDIC filed a joint motion requesting the court to dismiss Goulding's Chapter 7 petition. Discuss whether the court should have dismissed Goulding's petition and whether any payments made from the trusts were part of the debtor's estate. [In re Goulding, 79 B.R. 874 (Bkrtcy.W.D.Mo. 1987)]

Focus on Ethics

Creditors' Rights and Bankruptcy

We are certainly many years away from that period in our history when debtors' prisons existed. Some say, however, that we have proceeded too far in the opposite direction, making it too easy for debtors to avoid paying what they legally owe.

THE GENERAL QUESTION OF CREDITORS' RIGHTS

When a debtor fails to meet his or her financial obligations, the creditor has numerous remedies, such as a mechanic's lien on real property, an artisan's lien on personal property, foreclosure, attachment, and garnishment. When such rights and remedies are invoked, the creditor is often considered by the general public to employ "unfair" tactics. There is clearly a distinction in people's minds between the nonrepayment of a loan and the theft of personal property. But from a purely economic point of view, the result is the same—the wealth of the creditor-seller is reduced.

An ethical question arises as to whether the creditor or the debtor should be favored when the debtor has not performed. For many, this ethical question revolves around the way in which the debtor has reduced the net worth of the creditor.

Also, the public at large often judges the debtor's action on the basis of the purpose for which the debt was incurred. If the debt was incurred for a "needed" item, such as a refrigerator, then common opinion seems to be that such a debtor should be dealt with in a lenient manner. On the other hand, if the debt was incurred for a trip to the Bahamas, the ethical issue appears to be significantly different.

THE EFFECT OF NONPAYMENT OF LOANS

Whatever the ethical issue may be when a debtor fails to perform, the economic consequence is clear: The cost of nonperformance is imposed on all of those debtors who do perform. This cost takes the form of higher average interest rates. That is, the greater the percentage of loan agreements not consummated according to the agreement, the larger the "risk factor" added to normal interest rates. Creditors deal in a highly competitive market. They expect to earn a normal rate of return for investment in such an industry. If costs increase because of nonperformance by debtors, those costs will have to be recouped somewhere. In

general, the only way to recoup them is to charge all debtors a higher interest rate.

ETHICS AND ECONOMICS: AN EXAMPLE

Although there is a tendency to sympathize with a person who becomes unable to pay his or her debts, the ethical issue is not quite that simple. If creditors are unable to enforce repayment rights against delinquent debtors, the result will be higher interest charges to other borrowers of money. Consider an example of a court decision and the ethical and economic issues involved.

To purchase furniture and consumer durable goods, people who live and make their purchases in low-income areas must sometimes sign an agreement stating that failure to make timely payment can result in the repossession not only of the goods purchased under the present contract but also of any goods purchased earlier under similar contracts from the same vendor. This provision is often called a cross-collateralization or add-on clause.

Suppose that Mrs. Jenks, a poor, divorced mother of three children, makes three separate purchases at a store. First she buys a television, then a stereo, and then a couch. Each of these items is purchased on credit. Every time she purchases an item, she signs a contract containing the add-on clause described above. She duly makes all payments on the first two items but fails to make payments for the last item. The vendor, invoking its rights under the add-on clause, repossesses not only the couch but also the stereo and the television. Mrs. Jenks sues.

How should the court decide? For many, the add-on clause offends their sense of justice. Why should Mrs. Jenks relinquish those items that she has paid for? When cases such as this one have reached the courts, judgments have tended to favor plaintiffs, striking down the add-on clause on such grounds as unconscionability.

But consider the long-run implications of such a court decision. Add-on clauses allowing for repossession (replevin) of previously purchased items, in addition to the one under contract, give vendors in low-income areas additional security to reduce the costs of nonperformance. Such clauses may not be found in higher-income areas because such security is less necessary. Without the additional security in a low-income area, vendors might reduce the amount of credit offered. They might screen applicants more carefully, eliminating those who previously might have obtained credit. The long-term result might be a reduction in the amount of credit available in low-income areas. Thus, a ruling in Mrs. Jenks's favor might actually harm poor people in the long run. This complicates the ethical issue considerably.

But the analysis cannot stop here. The economic considerations just discussed assume that the market in which Mrs. Jenks buys goods is freely functioning and competitive. Some creditors, however, may possess considerable market power in low-income areas, and Mrs. Jenks may have no other source of credit. These creditors may use the add-on clauses only to extract unusually high profits and may make no additional credit available to the community. Customers in these areas may also be poorly educated and may be unaware of the implications of the add-on clauses that they sign. Is it fair to hold Mrs. Jenks to a deal that she could not comprehend? Moreover, without adequate information, how can the ideal free market in credit function properly? Perhaps courts that have favored the plaintiffs in cases like Mrs. Jenks's have reached the proper decision. This example, though, shows how ethical concerns are affected by economics and may be more complex than they initially appear.

GARNISHMENT OF WAGES

Ethical considerations are invariably involved in the issue of garnishment of wages. There will always be a conflict between creditors' rights and the needs of the debtor. The employer must be considered, as well. Certainly, many an employer would like to terminate an individual's employment because of garnishment proceedings. Certainly, a creditor would like to use garnishment to allow for repayment of a debt at the earliest possible date. But the employee must continue working. Also, there must be enough income left over after garnishment for the employee to survive and indeed to have an incentive to continue working.

Most states have statutes that allow for garnishment of wages to enforce compliance with child-support orders. Is this an acceptable form of government intrusion? Texas, one of two states that did not (until recently) allow garnishment of wages for any purpose, has a long history of protecting the rights of individuals against excessive governmental intrusion. It is difficult to balance the rights of an individual against the legal duty of parents to support their minor children. Yet a balance must be reached; and since the garnishment of wages has proved to be the most effective method for enforcing child-support payments, society has generally concluded that the garnishment of wages in situations in which child support is not being paid is the most equitable solution. After all, noncompliance with child-support orders may transfer the burden of child support onto the public—a situation that many regard as unfair. Therefore, in 1984, Texas changed its law and now permits garnishment of wages to enforce child-support orders.

BANKRUPTCY

The first goal of bankruptcy law is to provide relief and protection to debtors who have "gotten in over their heads." But consider the concept of bankruptcy from the point of view of the creditor. The creditor has extended a transfer of purchasing power from himself or herself to the debtor. That transfer of purchasing power represents a transfer of an asset for an asset. The debtor obtains the asset of money, goods, or services; and the creditor obtains the asset called a *secured* or *unsecured* legal obligation to pay. Once the debtor is in bankruptcy, voluntarily or involuntarily, the asset that the creditor owns most often has a diminished value. Indeed, in many circumstances, that asset has no value. Bankruptcy law attempts to provide a "fair" means of distributing to creditors the assets remaining in the debtor's possession.

Society has generally concluded that everyone should be given the chance to start over again. Thus, bankruptcy law is a balancing act between providing such a chance and ensuring that creditors are given "a fair shake." But the question of "moral hazard" arises with bankruptcy law just as it does with product liability law. The easier it becomes for debtors to hide behind bankruptcy laws, the greater will be the incentive for debtors to use such laws to avoid payment of legally owed sums of money. That also means that the more easily a debtor can hide behind bankruptcy laws, the more a creditor will charge, because of the increased degree of risk. The fact is that the total number of bankruptcies has increased since the enactment of the Bankruptcy Reform Act of 1978. What this phenomenon means is that creditors incur higher risks in making loans. In order to compensate for these higher risks, creditors will do one or more of the following: increase the interest rates charged to everyone, require more security (collateral), or be more selective in the granting of credit. Thus, a trade-off situation exists: The more lenient bankruptcy laws are, the better off will be those debtors who find themselves in bankruptcy; but those debtors who will never be in bankruptcy will be worse off. Ethical concerns here must be matched with the economic concerns of

other groups of individuals affected by the law.

CHAPTER 11 FILING

Particularly controversial are questions concerning at what point and in what circumstances companies should be entitled to file a Chapter 11 petition for reorganization under the Bankruptcy Reform Act of 1978. Filing a Chapter 11 petition automatically stays the commencement, continuation, or enforcement of proceedings against the debtor. As previously stated, the bankruptcy law attempts to provide a refuge to the honest debtor who is unable to pay his or her debts. The "rehabilitation" of the debtor, rather than the liquidation of the debtor's estate (Chapter 7), is the primary purpose of Chapter 11.

Manville Corporation's Chapter 11 filing raises many ethical issues. Many critics argue that the Manville filing was an abuse of the federal bankruptcy law, since the company was still earning profits. The Manville Corporation filed for Chapter 11 reorganization on August 26, 1982, and at that time the corporation's reported assets were valued at $2.2 billion. The fact that Manville Corporation was solvent when it filed for Chapter 11 reorganization led many people to question the "fairness" behind Chapter 11. Should a bankruptcy court be used by a solvent company facing potential tort liability? Do companies such as Manville deserve the "fresh start" available under Chapter 11— which allows debtors to escape the pressures that drove them into bankruptcy?

Manville officials contended that the petition for reorganization was the only way to save the corporation from the

pending 16,500 lawsuits for asbestos-related diseases. A research firm commissioned by Manville in 1982 estimated that the company would have incurred liability as high as $4.8 billion by the year 2009. Furthermore, the Bankruptcy Code is drafted so as to allow the filing for Chapter 11 reorganization by a "solvent" debtor. The theory behind allowing solvent debtors to file is that creditors will be better protected if debtors file for reorganization while their assets are still available to pay creditors' claims. As long as a debtor is "honest," bankruptcy courts have been willing to discharge the debtor from pre-petition debts and some post-petition debts.

Yet even though the filing by Manville was consistent with the letter of the Bankruptcy Code, questions still arise as to whether Manville filed in good faith and deserved a "fresh start." There is no doubt that Manville knew that exposure to asbestos resulted in asbestos-related diseases such as asbestosis, lung cancer, and cancer of the stomach, colon, and rectum. Court cases also resulted in findings that Manville withheld this knowledge from its employees. Given this evidence, is Manville truly deserving of a fresh start?

COMPETITION AND CHAPTER 11

Competition often induces manufacturers to take risks that may subsequently harm society, thus precipitating the manufacturer's own economic downfall. Some critics argue, however, that the imposition of punitive damages in product liability cases may in effect be "overkill." In other words, punitive damages administered to punish the offender and to deter this type of conduct in the future may make the difference between a company's filing or not filing a petition for Chapter 11 reorganization. Thus, the economic consequences of our punishment and deterrence objectives appear much more complex than upon first glance. How can we punish and deter unethical conduct by a company that has done much good in the past and has the potential to do much good in the future without inviting it to file for Chapter 11? Remember, the filing of a petition in bankruptcy automatically stays the commencement of proceedings against the debtor. What happens to potential plaintiffs then?

Another aspect of Chapter 11 also raises ethical considerations (and is controversial as well). In recent years competition in many industries has increased dramatically. After the deregulation of the airline industry, for example, some airlines overexpanded and eventually became insolvent. Furthermore, as the industry grew from 36 to 156 airlines, fare wars began to characterize the industry. Thus, some companies—such as Braniff and Air Florida—were unsuccessful under deregulation and ultimately declared bankruptcy. Others—such as Eastern and Pan Am—have high debts and little cash. In this type of situation, it may be tempting for a company not to deal in good faith because it knows that resort to Chapter 11 is always available. Chapter 11 may become a bargaining chip for management to use against labor during wage negotiations, as noted earlier. The threat of Chapter 11 can leave employees in a very vulnerable position as they try to predict whether a company is actually considering Chapter 11 as a viable alternative or is merely bluffing.

DISCUSSION QUESTIONS

1. Is bankruptcy ethical? Doesn't a person have a moral responsibility to pay his or her debts? After his haberdashery went bankrupt in the 1930s, President Harry S Truman went on to pay all his creditors over the next decade, even though he had no legal obligation to do so. Should all bankrupt individuals acknowledge their responsibilities as President Truman did?

2. What should be the balance between creditors' and debtors' rights?

3. How moral and ethical is it for a business to refuse to deal with a customer simply because that person once went into bankruptcy, even though that person is now a good credit risk in every other way?

Unit Five

AGENCY AND EMPLOYMENT

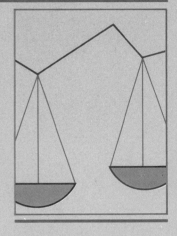

Chapter 32

Agency Relationships

One of the most common, important, and pervasive legal relationships is that of agency. In an **agency** relationship between two parties, one of the parties, called the **agent,** agrees to represent or act for the other, called the **principal.** The principal has the right to control the agent's conduct in matters entrusted to the agent. More formally, the Restatement, Second, Agency,[1] defines *agency* as "the fiduciary relation[2] which results from the manifestation of consent by one person to another that the other shall act in his behalf and subject to his control, and consent by the other so to act." In general, the law of agency is based on the maxim that "one acting by another is acting for himself."

THE NATURE OF AGENCY

An agent acts for his or her principal. By using agents a principal can conduct multiple business operations simultaneously in various locations. Thus, for example, contracts that bind the principal can be made at different places with different persons at the same time. A familiar example of an agent is a corporate officer who serves in a representative capacity for the owners of the corporation. In this capacity, the officer has the authority to bind the principals to a contract. Indeed, agency law is essential to the existence and operation of a corporate entity, because only through its agents can a corporation function and enter into contracts.

KINDS OF AGENCY RELATIONSHIPS

The first step in analyzing an agency relationship is to determine whether such a relationship exists. Traditional analysis in the law of agency distinguishes three categories of relationships:

---

1. Restatement, Second, Agency, Section 1(1). The Restatement, Second, Agency, is an authoritative summary of the law of agency, which is often referred to by jurists in decisions and opinions.
2. A fiduciary relationship involves a high degree of trust and a duty to act for someone else's benefit.

1. Principal and agent.
2. Employer and employee.
3. Principal and independent contractor.

It is important to note that the principal-agent relationship can also be found within an employer-employee or a principal–independent contractor relationship.

Principal-Agent

In a principal-agent relationship, the parties have agreed that the agent will act *on behalf of and instead of* the principal in negotiating and transacting business with third persons. The agent has *derivative authority* in carrying out the principal's business. This relationship will affect the principal's rights and duties. Thus, an agent is empowered to perform legal acts that are binding on the principal.

For example, Earl is hired as a booking agent for a rock group—Harry and the Rockets. As the group's agent, Earl can negotiate and sign contracts for the rock group to appear at concerts. The contracts will be binding and thus legally enforceable against the group.

Employer-Employee

Prior to the industrial revolution, the terms *employer* and *employee* had no significance in common law rules of agency. The original term used to denote an employer-employee relationship was *master-servant relationship*. The terms *master* and *servant* are now archaic and outdated; but because they have been traditionally used in the law governing agency relationships, they are still encountered occasionally.

Today's law defines a *servant* as an employee and a *master* as an employer. An **employee** is defined as one whose physical conduct is *controlled*, or subject to control, by the employer. An employee can be an agent if the employee has an appointment or contract for hire with authority to represent the employer.

For example, Dana owns a dress shop. She employs Sandy, Sheila, and Sue as salespeople and Sara as a janitor. Dana is the employer (master); the other women are the employees (servants). The key feature of the employer-employee rela-

tionship is that the employer has the right to control the employee in the performance of the tasks involved in the employment. The employees do not have *independent* business discretion. Dana can thus tell her salespeople not only to sell the dresses but also how to sell them. In selling the dresses, however, they are agents as well as employees. They have been given the authority by Dana to contract for and represent Dana in creating sales with customers. Sara, however, because she is not a salesperson, has no authority with respect to selling dresses and thus is not an agent in that respect. In fact, she may have no authority to represent Dana in any dealings with others, including receiving deliveries of janitorial supplies.

All employment laws (state and federal) apply only to the employer-employee relationship. Statutes governing Social Security, withholding taxes, workers' compensation, unemployment compensation, workplace safety laws, and the like are applicable only where there is employer-employee status. *These laws do not apply to the independent contractor.*

Principal–Independent Contractor

Independent contractors are not employees, because their principals have no control over the details of their physical performance. Restatement, Second, Agency, Section 2, defines an independent contractor as:

> a person who contracts with another to do something for him but who is not controlled by the other nor subject to the other's right to control with respect to his physical conduct in the performance of the undertaking. He may or may not be an agent.

The following factors are relevant in determining whether a person is an independent contractor or an employee:

1. How much control can the principal exercise over the details of the work?
2. Is the employed person engaged in an occupation or business distinct from that of the principal?
3. Is the work usually done under the principal's direction, or is it done by a specialist without supervision?
4. Does the principal supply the tools at the place of work?
5. For how long is the person hired or retained?

6. What is the method of payment—by time period or at the completion of the job?

7. What is the degree of skill required to do whatever it is the person was hired or retained to do?

Building contractors and subcontractors are independent contractors; a property owner does not control the acts of either of these professionals. Truck drivers who own their equipment and hire out on an *ad hoc* basis are independent contractors; however, truck drivers who drive company trucks on a regular basis are usually employees. A collection agency is another example of an independent contractor.

The relationship between a principal and an independent contractor also may or may not involve an agency relationship. To illustrate: An owner of real estate who hires a real estate broker to negotiate a sale of his or her property has not only contracted with an independent contractor (the real estate broker) but has also established an agency relationship for the specific purpose of assisting in the sale of the property.

The following case demonstrates the criteria by which courts decide whether an employer-employee or principal–independent contractor relationship exists.

BACKGROUND AND FACTS   *Dr. George Hall, the defendant, normally worked from 8:00 A.M. to 6:00 P.M. on weekdays and frequently on weekends. He had neither the time nor the capacity for household maintenance, so he hired Ivan Davey, who was the partner of the plaintiff, Tom Amear, to do landscaping and other work around the house. Hall would tell Davey what needed to be done, and then Davey, Amear, or other employees would accomplish the work. Davey and Amear controlled their own hours and methods of accomplishing the work. In February of 1977, Hall asked Davey to install fiberglass over four spaces formed by exposed beams connecting the carport and the house. The beams were purely decorative with no structural purpose, and Hall did not instruct Davey how to install the fiberglass. It was Amear's idea to climb out on the beams to install it. Once he was on the beams, the nails in each end of the beam supporting him pulled through the beam, and he fell and severely injured himself. Amear claimed that he was an employee and that Hall had failed to provide and maintain safe working conditions. Hall claimed that Amear was an independent contractor. The trial court entered judgment in favor of Hall, and Amear appealed.*

Case 32.1
AMEAR v. HALL
Court of Appeals of Georgia, 1982.
164 Ga.App. 163,
296 S.E.2d 611.

QUILLIAN, Chief Justice.
*   *   *   *

The test historically applied by this Court [in determining] whether a person employed is a servant or an independent contractor is whether the employer, under the contract, whether oral or written, has the right to direct the time, the manner, the methods, and the means of the execution of the work, as contradistinguished from the right to insist upon the contractor producing results according to the contract, or whether the contractor in the performance of the work contracted for is free from any control by the employer of the time, manner, and method in the performance of the work.
*   *   * Under either test, the evidence demanded a finding that plaintiff was an independent contractor.
*   *   *   *

An individual contractor is expected to determine for himself whether his place of employment is safe or unsafe, and ordinarily may not recover against the owner for injuries sustained in the performance of the contract. *   *   * Unless the owner and an injured employee have a relationship of master-servant, the employer is generally not responsible for injuries occasioned by the method by which work is done by the employee. *   *   * "It is also the general rule that the employer is under no duty to take affirmative steps to guard or protect the [individual] contractor's employees against the consequences of the contractor's negligence or to provide for their safety."

DECISION   *The court of appeals found Davey and Amear to be independent contractors.*
AND REMEDY   *Therefore, Hall was not liable for the injury to Amear, and the judgment of the trial court was affirmed.*

FORMATION OF THE AGENCY RELATIONSHIP

The following discussion will emphasize the usual form that an agency relationship takes. An agency relationship is a *consensual* relationship; that is, it comes about by voluntary consent and agreement between the parties. It is a consensual relationship because it must be based on some affirmative indication that the agent agrees to act for the principal and the principal agrees to have the agent so act.

The Agency Agreement

Generally, no formalities are required to create an agency. An agency relationship can be created by oral agreement, by written contract, or by acts or conduct of the parties that imply an agency relationship.

There are two main exceptions to oral agency agreements. A **power of attorney** (to be discussed in the following chapter) grants an agent either full or restricted authority to act in the principal's behalf and must be executed in a notarized writing.

In many states, the Statute of Frauds (discussed in Chapter 12) requires that whenever agency authority empowers the agent to enter into a contract that the Statute of Frauds requires to be in writing, the agent's authority from the principal must also be in writing. This is known as the **equal dignity rule.** It applies most frequently to contracts for the sale of an interest in land or contracts that cannot be performed within one year. An exception to the equal dignity rule exists in modern business practice. An executive of a corporation, when acting for the corporation in an ordinary business situation, is not required to obtain written authority from the corporation.

An agency agreement, as noted, can be implied from conduct. For example, a hotel expressly allows Jack Andrews to park cars, but Andrews has no employment contract there. The hotel's conduct amounts to a manifestation of its willingness that Jack park its customers' cars, and Jack can infer from the hotel's conduct that he has authority to act as a valet. It can be implied that for that purpose he is an agent for the hotel.

Legal Capacity and Purpose

A principal must have legal capacity to enter into contracts. The logic is simple. A person who can-

CONCEPT SUMMARY: Agency—Legal Relationships	
TYPE OF LEGAL RELATIONSHIP	**DESCRIPTION**
Principal-agent	An agent has the authority to act on behalf of and instead of the principal, using a certain degree of his or her own *discretion*.
Employer-employee	The employer has the right to *control* the physical conduct of the employee.
Principal–independent contractor	The contractor is not an employee, and the principal has *no control* over the details of physical performance. Except for real estate and collection agencies, the contractor is not usually an agent.

not legally enter into contracts directly should not be allowed to do it indirectly through an agent. An agent derives the authority to enter into contracts from the principal, and a contract made by an agent is legally viewed as a contract of the principal. It is immaterial whether the agent personally has the legal capacity to make that contract. Thus, a minor can be an agent but cannot be a principal appointing an agent (in some states).[3] In states that permit a minor to be a principal, any resulting contracts will be voidable by the minor principal but not by the adult third party. Thus, any person can be an agent, regardless of whether he or she has the capacity to contract. Even a person who is legally incompetent can be appointed an agent.

An agency relationship can be created for any *legal* purpose. One created for an illegal purpose or contrary to public policy is unenforceable. If Jones (as principal) contracts with Smith (as agent) to sell narcotics illegally, the agency relationship is unenforceable, because selling narcotics illegally is a felony and therefore against public policy. It is also illegal for medical doctors and other licensed professionals to employ unlicensed agents to perform professional acts.

Agency by Ratification or Estoppel

On occasion, a person who is in fact not an agent, or who is an agent acting outside the scope of his or her authority, may make a contract on behalf of another (a principal). If the principal approves or affirms that contract by word or by action, an agency relationship is created by **ratification.** Ratification is a matter of intent, and intent can be expressed by either words or conduct.

An agency relationship can also be created by **estoppel.** When a *principal* causes a third person to believe that another person is his or her agent, and the third person deals with the supposed agent, the principal is "estopped to deny" the agency relationship.

Ratification and estoppel, since they pertain to relationships between principals and agents and third parties, will be discussed in detail in the following chapter.

---

3. Exceptions have been granted by some courts to allow a minor to appoint an agent for the limited purpose of contracting for the minor's necessities of life. [Casey v. Kastel, 237 N.Y. 305, 142 N.E. 671 (1924)]

Agency by Operation of Law

In some cases, the courts have found it desirable to find an agency relationship in the absence of a formal agreement. This may occur when family relationships are involved. For example, suppose one spouse purchases certain basic necessaries and charges them to the other spouse's charge account. The courts will often rule that the latter is liable for payment for such necessaries. Such rulings may be based on a social policy of promoting the general welfare of the spouse who made the purchases or on the assumption that the other spouse has a legal duty to supply necessaries to family members.

Sometimes agency by operation of law is created to give an agent emergency power to act under unusual circumstances that are not covered by the agreement when failure to act would cause a principal substantial loss. If the agent is unable to contact the principal, the courts will often grant this emergency power. (See the *Concept Summary* on the following page for a comparison of the ways in which agency relationships are formed.)

DUTIES OF AGENTS AND PRINCIPALS

Once the principal-agent relationship has been created, both parties have duties that govern their conduct. The principal-agent relationship is *fiduciary*—one of trust. In it, each party owes the other the duty to act with the utmost good faith. Neither party may keep from the other information that has any bearing on their agency relationship.

Agent's Duties to Principal

The duties that an agent owes to a principal are set forth in the agency agreement or arise by operation of law. They are implied from the agency relationship *whether or not the identity of the principal is disclosed to a third party.* Generally, the agent owes the principal the following five duties:

1. Performance.
2. Notification.
3. Loyalty.
4. Obedience.
5. Accounting.

CONCEPT SUMMARY: Formation of Principal-Agent Relationship

METHOD OF FORMATION	DESCRIPTION
By agreement	Formed through express consent (oral or written) or implied from conduct.
By ratification	Principal either by act or agreement ratifies conduct by a person who is not in fact an agent or who acted outside his or her scope of authority.
By estoppel	Principal causes a third person to believe that another person is his or her agent, and the third person acts to his or her detriment in reasonable reliance on that belief.
By operation of law	Based on a social duty (such as the need to support family members) or formed in emergency situations when the agent is unable to contact the principal.

DUTY OF PERFORMANCE An implied condition in every agency contract is the agent's agreement to use reasonable diligence and skill in performing the work. When an agent fails to perform his or her duties entirely, he or she will generally be liable for breach of contract.

The degree of skill or care required of an agent is usually that expected of a reasonable person under similar circumstances. Although in most cases this is interpreted to mean ordinary care, an agent may have presented himself or herself as possessing special skills (such as those that an accountant or attorney possesses). In these situations, the agent is expected to exercise the skill or skills claimed. Failure to do so constitutes a breach of the agent's duty.

For example, an insurance agent who fails to obtain the insurance coverage requested by a principal is guilty of breach of contract. When an agent performs carelessly or negligently, the agent can be liable in tort as well.

In many situations, an agent who does not act for money (a gratuitous, or free, agent) can be subject to the same standards of care and duty to perform as other agents. A gratuitous agent cannot be liable for breach of contract, because there is no contract. A gratuitous agent is subject only to tort liability. Once the agent has begun to act in an agency capacity, however, he or she has the duty to continue to perform in this capacity in an acceptable manner.

For example, Alex Paul's friend, Amy Foster, is a real estate broker. She (the agent) gratuitously

offers to sell Paul's (the principal's) farm, Black Acre. If she never attempts to sell Black Acre, Paul has no legal cause of action to force her to do so. But assume that Foster finds a buyer. She keeps promising the buyer a sales contract but fails to provide one within a reasonable period of time. The buyer becomes disgruntled and seeks another property, and the sale ultimately falls through. Paul has a cause of action in tort for negligence— because Foster failed to use the degree of care reasonably expected of real estate brokers.

DUTY OF NOTIFICATION There is a maxim in agency law that "all the agent knows, the principal knows." This maxim means that a principal will be presumed to know of any statement made by an agent to a third party—because the principal may be bound by it or be liable for any damages resulting from it. Thus, it is only logical that the agent is required to notify the principal of all significant or material matters that come to his or her attention concerning the subject matter of the agency. This is the duty of notification.

For example, Able is Paul's agent for the purchase of a certain property from Tom. In the course of dealing, Able discovers that many years ago Green obtained subsurface mineral rights in this property. Thinking that this is unimportant, Able neglects to tell Paula. The purchase of the land takes place subject to Green's right to mine and remove the minerals. Paula does not have recourse against Tom; that is, Paula cannot rescind the sale or use the existence of Green's right to remove minerals as a defense to avoid going through with the sale. Able had the duty to notify Paula. The fact that he failed to do so and breached his fiduciary duty cannot be allowed to prejudice the rights of the innocent third party, Tom. Paula, however, does have recourse against Able for damages.

DUTY OF LOYALTY Loyalty is one of the most fundamental duties in a fiduciary relationship. Basically stated, the agent has the duty to act solely for the benefit of his or her principal and not in the interest of the agent or a third party.

Numerous principles result from this duty. For example, an agent cannot represent two principals in the same transaction unless both know of the dual capacity and consent to it. Thus, a real estate agent cannot represent both the seller and the buyer in collecting commissions, unless the seller and the buyer so agree. A salesperson representing Avon cannot sell products of a competing line at the same time unless Avon consents. In addition, an agent who owns property cannot sell the property to the principal without indicating that ownership prior to the sale. Furthermore, an agent cannot make "secret" profits—that is, an agent employed by a principal to buy cannot buy from himself or herself, and an agent employed to sell cannot become the purchaser without the principal's consent. In short, the agent's loyalty must be undivided. The agent's actions must be strictly for the benefit of the principal and must not result in any secret profit for the agent.

The duty of loyalty means that any information or knowledge acquired through the agency relationship is considered confidential. It would be a breach of loyalty to disclose such information either during the agency relationship or after its termination. Typical examples of confidential information are trade secrets and customer lists compiled by the principal. Note, however, that an agent has the right to use skills and basic knowledge acquired during the course of agency employment in his or her own behalf (such as sales techniques learned during the agency relationship), as long as such actions do not violate confidentiality.

DUTY OF OBEDIENCE When an agent is acting on behalf of the principal, a duty is imposed on the agent to follow all lawful and clearly stated instructions of the principal. The agent violates this duty whenever he or she deviates from such instructions. For example an automobile salesperson may be liable to the dealer (the salesperson's principal) if, in an effort to close a sale, he or she makes a more extensive warranty than the dealer has indicated it is willing to make and if the buyer subsequently takes advantage of that warranty.

During emergency situations, however, when the principal cannot be consulted, the agent may deviate from such instructions without violating this duty if the circumstances so warrant. When instructions are not clearly stated, the agent can fulfill the duty of obedience by acting in good faith and in a manner reasonable under the circumstances.

DUTY OF ACCOUNTING Unless an agent and a principal agree otherwise, the agent has the duty to keep and make available to the principal an account of all property and money received and paid out on behalf of the principal. This includes gifts from third persons in connection with the agency. For example, a gift from a customer to a salesperson for prompt deliveries made by the salesperson's firm belongs to the firm. The agent has a duty to maintain separate accounts for the principal's funds and for personal funds, and no *commingling* (mixing) of these accounts is allowed. When a licensed professional violates this duty to account, he or she may be subject to disciplinary proceedings by the appropriate regulatory institution. In addition, the agent is liable to the principal for failure to account.

Duties Owed by Subagents

A **subagent** is any person employed or appointed by an agent to assist the agent in transacting the affairs of the principal. If the agent has authority to appoint a subagent, the subagent has authority to bind the principal. Consequently, there exists a fiduciary relationship between the subagent and the principal as well as between the subagent and the agent. Generally, the principal's authorization is needed for the hiring of subagents except in emergencies. On the other hand, if the agent is normally expected in his or her line of work to hire subagents, they may be hired without the *explicit* authorization of the principal. For example, agents typically may hire subagents to perform mechanical or minor functions that do not involve any significant decision making without the explicit authorization of the principal. Subagents owe the same duties to agents and to principals as agents owe to principals.

If an agent hires a subagent without the principal's authority, then the subagent has no legal relationship to the principal—expressed, implied, or apparent. Since the subagent and the principal have no agency relationship to one another, no duties arise between them. A principal will not be liable to third parties for the subagent's acts. The agent who hires the subagent without authority, however, will be liable to the principal or third parties if the subagent acts wrongfully, and the agent will bear the loss.

Principal's Duties to Agent

The principal also has certain duties to the agent. Generally these duties include the following:

1. Compensation.
2. Reimbursement and indemnification.
3. Cooperation.
4. Safe working conditions.

The principal's duties to an agent may be expressed, or they may be implied by law.

DUTY OF COMPENSATION   Except in a gratuitous agency relationship, the principal must pay the agreed-upon value (or reasonable value) for an agent's services. When the amount of compensation is agreed upon by the parties, the principal owes the duty to pay it upon completion of the agent's specified activities. If no amount is expressly agreed upon, then the principal owes the agent the customary compensation for such services. If no amount is established either by custom or by law, the principal owes the agent the reasonable value of his or her services.

In general, when a principal requests certain services from an agent, the agent reasonably expects payment. A duty is therefore implied for the principal to pay the agent for services rendered. For example, when an accountant or an attorney is asked to act as an agent, compensation is implied. The principal has the duty to pay that compensation in a timely manner.

DUTY OF REIMBURSEMENT AND INDEMNIFICATION   Whenever an agent disburses sums of money at the request of the principal, and whenever the agent disburses sums of money to pay for necessary expenses in the course of a reasonable performance of his or her agency duties, the principal has the duty to reimburse. Agents cannot recover for expenses they incur through their own misconduct or negligence, however.

The principal has the duty to reimburse an agent for authorized payments and to *indemnify* (compensate) an agent for liabilities incurred because of authorized and lawful acts and transactions and also for losses suffered because of the principal's failure to perform any duties.

The amount of indemnification is usually specified in the agency contract. If it is not, the courts will look to the nature of the business and the type of loss in order to determine the amount.

Authorized subagents can recover from either the principal or the agent who hires them, since the subagent is in a fiduciary relationship to both. If the authorized subagent obtains indemnification from the agent who does the hiring, the agent can then seek indemnification from the principal.

DUTY OF COOPERATION   A principal has a duty both to cooperate with and to assist an agent in performing his or her duties. The principal must do nothing to prevent such performance. For example, when a principal grants an agent an exclusive territory, the principal cannot compete with the agent or appoint or allow another agent to so compete in violation of the *exclusive agency*. Such competition would expose the principal to liability for the agent's lost sales or profits.

DUTY TO PROVIDE SAFE WORKING CONDITIONS   The common law requires the principal to provide safe premises, equipment, and conditions for all agents and employees. The principal has a duty to inspect working conditions and to warn agents and employees about any unsafe areas. If the relationship is one of employment, the employer's liability is frequently covered by worker's compensation insurance, which is the primary remedy for an employee's injury on the job.

REMEDIES AND RIGHTS OF AGENTS AND PRINCIPALS

It is said that every wrong has its remedy. In business situations, disputes between agents and principals may arise out of either contract or tort laws and carry corresponding remedies. These remedies include monetary damages, termination of the agency relationship, injunction, and required accountings.

Agent's Rights and Remedies against Principal

For every duty of the principal, the agent has a corresponding right. Therefore, the agent has the right to be compensated, reimbursed, and indemnified and to work in a safe environment. An agent also has the right to perform agency duties without interference by the principal.

Remedies of the agent for breach of duty by the principal follow normal contract and tort remedies. For example, under appropriate circumstances, an agent can lawfully withhold further performance and demand that the principal give an accounting.

When the principal-agent relationship is not contractual, an agent has no right to specific performance. An agent can recover for past services and future damages but cannot force the principal to allow him or her to continue acting as an agent.

Principal's Rights and Remedies against Agent

In general, a principal has contract remedies for an agent's breach of fiduciary duties. The principal also has tort remedies for fraud, misrepresentation, negligence, deceit, libel, slander, and trespass committed by the agent. In addition, any breach of a fiduciary duty by an agent may justify the principal's termination of the agency.

The main actions available to the principal are constructive trust, avoidance, and indemnification.

CONSTRUCTIVE TRUST   Anything an agent obtains by virtue of the employment or agency relationship belongs to the principal. It is a breach of an agent's fiduciary duty to retain secretly benefits or profits that, by right, belong to the principal. Courts in this case will imply a **constructive trust.** The agent actually holds the money on behalf of the principal, and the principal can recover it in a lawsuit. For example, Andrews, a purchasing agent, gets cash rebates from a customer. If Andrews keeps the rebates, he violates his fiduciary duty to his principal, Metcalf. Upon finding out about the cash rebates, Metcalf can sue Andrews and recover them.

An agent is also prohibited from taking advantage of the agency relationship to obtain goods or property that the principal wants to purchase. For example, Peterson (the principal) wants to purchase property in the suburbs. Cox, Peterson's agent, learns that a valuable tract of land has just become available. Cox cannot buy the land for herself. Peterson gets the right of first refusal. If Cox purchases the land for her benefit, the courts will impose a constructive trust on the land; that is, the land will be held for and on behalf of the principal despite the fact that the agent attempted to buy it in her own name.

AVOIDANCE   When an agent breaches the agency agreement or agency duties under a contract, the principal has a right to avoid any contract entered into with the agent. This right of avoidance is at the election of the principal.

In the following case, a real estate agent was supposedly acting on behalf of a landowner for the sale of a piece of property. The trial court decided that the agent had no cause of action.

BACKGROUND AND FACTS   *Ramsey, the plaintiff, was a licensed real estate broker and was also in the business of buying and holding land for resale. Gordon, the defendant, was the owner of approximately 181 acres of land and engaged Ramsey's services as a broker to find a buyer for the property. Ramsey, when he heard that the land was rapidly appreciating in value, told Gordon that he would buy the land himself. Gordon then agreed to sell Ramsey the tract of land for $800 per acre. A contract of sale to convey the property was drawn up; but before the contract was executed, Gordon conveyed the property to a third party for the same price ($800 per acre).*

Meanwhile, Ramsey, acting for himself, began negotiating for the resale of that property to another customer for a price of $1,250 per acre. Naturally, when Ramsey learned that Gordon had conveyed the property to another buyer,

Case 32.2
RAMSEY v. GORDON
Court of Civil Appeals of Texas, Waco, 1978.
567 S.W.2d 868.

he blamed Gordon for his lost profits. Ramsey claimed that he lost over $90,000 in profits on the resale of the property and brought an action against Gordon to recover this amount. Gordon maintained that Ramsey had breached his fiduciary duties as Gordon's agent by not finding a purchaser for the best price available. The trial court held for Gordon and Ramsey appealed.

HALL, Justice.
* * * *

Ramsey does not challenge the finding that the property was increasing in value when the contract was being negotiated and made with Gordon, nor the findings that he knew the value was increasing and failed to disclose that fact to Gordon. Indeed, he may not do so because they are amply supported by the evidence and its inferences. His response to the conclusion that he breached his duties as Gordon's agent is to argue that he was only a purchaser and to cite Gordon's testimony that Gordon believed $800.00 per acre was a fair price when he made the contract. The over-all import of the record is that when it served Ramsey's purposes he would claim that under the contract he was Gordon's agent, but that in fact he used the contract to speculate with the property to his personal advantage without disclosure to Gordon. As we have said, the [trial] court found that Ramsey was Gordon's agent. Ramsey's testimony supports that finding.

Whenever an agent breaches his duty to his principal by becoming personally interested in an agency agreement, the contract is voidable at the election of the principal without full knowledge of all the facts surrounding the agent's interest. [Emphasis added.]
* * * [It is a] "settled rule" that "an agent in dealing with a principal on his own account owes it to the principal not only to make no misstatements concerning the subject matter of the transaction, but also to disclose to him fully and completely all material facts known to the agent which might affect the principal; and that unless this duty on the party of the agent has been met, the principal cannot be held to have ratified the transaction."

DECISION AND REMEDY   *The judgment of the trial court was affirmed. Ramsey was denied recovery because an agency relationship existed between Ramsey and Gordon, and Ramsey had breached his duties under this relationship.*

INDEMNIFICATION   A principal can be sued by a third party for an agent's negligent conduct, and in certain situations the principal can sue the agent for an equal amount of damages. This is called **indemnification.** The same holds true if the agent violates the principal's instructions. For example, Lewis (the principal) tells his agent, Moore, who is a used car salesman, to make no warranties for the used cars. Moore is eager to make a sale to Walters, the third party, and makes a warranty for the car's engine. Lewis is not absolved from liability to Walters for engine failure, but if Walters sues Lewis, Lewis can then sue Moore for indemnification for violating his instructions.

Sometimes it is difficult to distinguish between instructions of the principal that limit an agent's authority and those that are merely advice. For example, Willis (the principal) owns an office supply company; Jones (the agent) is the manager. Willis tells Jones, "Don't order any more supplies this month." Willis goes on vacation. A large order comes in from a local business, and the present inventory is insufficient to meet it. What is Jones to do? In this situation, Jones probably has the inherent power to order more supplies despite Willis's statement. It is unlikely that Jones would be required to indemnify Willis in the event that the local business subsequently canceled the order.

TERMINATION OF AN AGENCY

Agency law is similar to contract law in that both an agency and a contract terminate by an act of the parties or by operation of law. Once the relationship between the principal and the agent has ended, the agent no longer has actual authority to bind the principal—that is, he or she lacks the principal's consent to act in the principal's behalf. Under some circumstances, third persons may also need to be notified when the agency has been terminated.

Termination by Act of the Parties

The parties may terminate the authority by including in their agreement some express or implied condition or limitation, the occurrence of which will terminate the agency. This may consist of a certain date or some particular event. Furthermore, at any time, the parties may simply agree to end their relationship.

LAPSE OF TIME An agency agreement may specify the time period during which the agency relationship will exist. If so, the agency ends when that time expires. For example, Able signs an agreement of agency with Paula "beginning January 1, 1987, and ending December 31, 1992." The agency is automatically terminated on December 31, 1992. Of course, the parties can agree to continue the relationship, in which case the same terms will apply.

If no definite time is stated, then the agency continues for a reasonable time and can be terminated at will by either party. What constitutes a reasonable time depends upon the circumstances and the nature of the agency relationship. For example, Paula asks Able to sell her car. If after two years Able has not sold Paula's car and there has been no communication between Paula and Able, it is safe to assume that the agency relationship has terminated. Able no longer has the authority to sell Paula's car.

PURPOSE ACHIEVED An agent can be employed to accomplish a particular objective, such as the purchase of stock for a cattle rancher. In that case, the agency automatically ends after the cattle have been purchased.

If more than one agent is employed to accomplish the same purpose, such as the sale of real estate, the first agent to complete the sale automatically terminates the agency relationship for all the others.

OCCURRENCE OF A SPECIFIC EVENT An agency can be created to terminate upon the happening of a certain event. For example, Paula appoints Able to handle her business affairs while she is away. When Paula returns, the agency automatically terminates.

Sometimes one aspect of the agent's authority terminates on the occurrence of a particular event, but the agency relationship itself does not terminate. For example, Paula, a banker, permits Able, the credit manager, to grant a credit line of $1,000 to certain depositors who maintain a balance of $1,000 in a savings account. If any customer's savings account balance falls below $1,000, Able can no longer make the credit line available to that customer. But Able's right to extend credit to the other customers maintaining the minimum balance will continue.

MUTUAL AGREEMENT Recall from basic contract law that parties can cancel (rescind) a contract by mutually agreeing to terminate the contractual relationship. The same holds true in agency law regardless of whether the agency contract is in writing or whether it is for a specific duration. For example, Paula no longer wishes Able to be her agent, and Able does not want to work for Paula any more. Either party can communicate to the other the intent to terminate the relationship. Agreement to terminate effectively relieves each of the rights, duties, and powers inherent in the relationship.

TERMINATION BY ONE PARTY As a *general* rule, either party can terminate the agency relationship. The agent's act is said to be a renunciation of authority. The principal's act is a revocation of authority. Although both parties may have the *power* to terminate—because agency is a consensual relationship, and thus neither party can be compelled to continue in the relationship—they may not possess the *right* to terminate and may therefore be liable for breach of contract. Wrongful termination can subject the canceling party to a suit for damages.

For example, Able has a one-year employment contract with Paula to act as her agent for $18,000. Paula can discharge Able before the contract period expires (Paula has the *power* to breach the contract); however, Paula will be liable to Able for money damages because Paula has no *right* to breach the contract.

Even in an agency at will (that is, an agency that either party may terminate at any time), the principal who wishes to terminate must give the agent a reasonable notice—that is, at least sufficient notice to allow the agent to recoup his or her expenses and, in some cases, to make a normal profit.

The next case involves the wrongful termination of an agency relationship.

Case 32.3
DOWD MORE CO. REALTORS v. McDONALD
Court of Civil Appeals of Texas, Houston (1st Dist.), 1973. 494 S.W.2d 282.

BACKGROUND AND FACTS   *The appellant, Dowd More Co. Realtors (a real estate broker), entered into a contract to sell the home of the appellees, the McDonalds. The contract was to be in force for an agreed-upon and stated period of time. Under the contract, the agent had an exclusive right to sell the property. Dowd More advertised the property and showed it to prospective purchasers. While the agency contract was still in force, the McDonalds sold their property to a purchaser. Dowd More claimed it was entitled to a commission, and the McDonalds refused to pay it. Dowd More filed suit for its commission. The trial court held for the McDonalds on the theory that the sale by the McDonalds revoked the agency contract and that no commission was earned by Dowd More since the property was sold by the owners. Dowd More appealed.*

EVANS, Justice.
*   *   *   *

In this case the appellants Dowd More established the essential facts which entitle them to a recovery for breach of contract. While the appellants were admittedly not the procuring cause of the sale, it is undisputed that appellants had initiated performance under the contract and had advertised the property for sale, had placed their "For Sale" sign in the yard, had listed the property with Multiple Listing Service and had shown the property to prospective customers. The contract was *   *   * a bilateral agreement which appellees could not unilaterally revoke by a sale to a third party.

This principle is, we believe, clearly set forth in *McDonald v. Davis*, wherein this court speaking through Chief Justice Bell said:
*   *   *   *

"The principal may of course revoke an agent's authority where not coupled with an interest, but there is a distinction between his power to revoke and his right to revoke. He at any time before full performance can revoke the authority of an agent so the agent will lose his authority to bring the principal into legal relations with a third party. However, if he has no right to revoke it, he will be liable for damages suffered by the agent by reason of the wrongful revocation. Where, as here, there is a bilateral contract, the principal has no right to revoke to the prejudice of the agent.

Where a principal breaches the contract, he becomes liable in damages. Where, as here, suit is for breach of a contract granting the agent the exclusive right for a definite period of time to sell property, the damages are for breach of contract and not for the commission promised if the agent sold. He is entitled to recover the reasonable profit he would have made. Prima facie that profit is the amount represented by the stipulated commission."

As stated above, appellants' compensation under the exclusive real estate listing contract was stipulated to be 6% of the listed price of $18,500.00, or $1100.00. In the absence of satisfactory evidence that appellants' reasonable profits were in a lesser sum than the stipulated commission the sum specified in the contract is prima facie evidence of their damages. Accordingly, the judgment of the trial court is reversed and judgment is rendered for the appellants in the amount of $1100.00 with interest at 6% per annum from and after September 3, 1971.

The trial court's judgment for the McDonalds was reversed. The court held that the McDonalds had wrongfully terminated the agency and were liable for damages equivalent to the amount of what would have been Dowd More's commission.

DECISION AND REMEDY

AGENCY COUPLED WITH AN INTEREST An agency *coupled with an interest* (also referred to as a *power coupled with an interest* or a *power given as a security*) is a relationship created for the benefit of the agent. The agent actually acquires a beneficial interest in the subject matter of the agency. Under these circumstances, it is not equitable to permit a principal to terminate at will. Hence, this type of agency is "irrevocable."

Since, in an agency coupled with an interest, the interest is not created for the benefit of the principal, it is not really an agency in the usual sense. Therefore, any attempt by the principal to revoke an agency coupled with an interest normally has no legal force or effect and is not terminated by the death of either the principal or the agent.

For example, Sarah Roberts needs $10,000. John Hartwell agrees to lend her the money, but not without security. Consequently, Roberts delivers some of her jewelry to Hartwell and signs a letter giving him the power, in case she fails to repay the loan, to sell the jewelry as her agent for the best price that can be obtained and to pay out of the proceeds the unpaid amount of the loan, giving any surplus to her. Having obtained the money, Roberts tells Hartwell that she revokes the power to sell. Under the law of agency, the power is not revoked. Subsequently, Roberts dies. The power is still not affected.

An agency coupled with an interest should not be confused with a situation in which the agent merely derives proceeds or profits from the sale of the subject matter. For example, an agent who merely receives a commission from the sale of real property does not have a beneficial interest in the property itself. Likewise, an attorney whose fee is a percentage of the recovery (a contingency fee) merely has an interest in the proceeds. These agency relationships are revocable by the principal, subject to any express contractual arrangements between the principal and the agent.

Termination by Operation of Law

Certain events will terminate agency authority automatically, since their occurrence makes it impossible for the agent to perform or improbable that the principal would continue to want performance. These events include death or insanity, loss of the agency's subject matter, changed circumstances, bankruptcy, and war.

DEATH OR INSANITY The general rule is that death or insanity of either the principal or the agent automatically and immediately terminates the ordinary agency relationship. Knowledge of the death is not required. For example, Paula sends Able to the Far East to purchase a rare book. Before Able makes the purchase, Paula dies. Able's agent status is terminated at the moment of death, even though Able does not know that Paula has died. (Some states, however, have changed this common law by statute.)

An agent's transactions that occur after the death of the principal are not binding on the principal's estate. Assume Able is hired by Paula to collect a debt from Tom (a third party). Paula dies, but Able still collects the money from Tom, not knowing of Paula's death. Tom's payment to Able is no longer legally sufficient to discharge Tom's debt to Paula, because Able no longer has Paula's authority to collect the money. If Able absconds with the money, Tom must pay the debt again, to Paula's estate.

IMPOSSIBILITY When the specific subject matter of an agency is destroyed or lost, the agency terminates. For example, Paula employs Able to sell Paula's house. Prior to any sale, the premises are destroyed by fire. Able's agency and authority to sell Paula's house terminate. Similarly, when it is impossible for the agent to perform the agency lawfully, because of war or because of a change in the law, the agency terminates.

CHANGED CIRCUMSTANCES When an event occurs that has such an unusual effect on the subject matter of the agency that the agent can reasonably infer that the principal will not want the agency to continue, the agency terminates. Paula hires Able to sell a tract of land for $10,000. Subsequently, Able learns that there is oil under the land and that the land is therefore worth $1 million. The agency and Able's authority to sell the land for $10,000 are terminated.

BANKRUPTCY Bankruptcy of the principal or the agent *usually* terminates the agency relationship.[4] Some situations, such as those involving a serious financial loss, might indicate to parties with whom the agent might otherwise contract on behalf of the principal that no future contracts should be made.

WAR When the principal's country and the agent's country are at war with each other, the agency is terminated.

Notice Required for Termination

When an agency terminates by operation of law because of death, insanity, or some other unforeseen circumstance, there is no duty to notify third persons, unless the agent's authority is coupled with an interest.[5] If, however, the parties themselves have terminated the agency, it is the principal's duty to inform any third parties who know of the existence of the agency that it has been terminated.

An agent's *actual authority* continues until the agent receives some notice of termination. Notice to third parties, however, follows the general rule that an agent's *apparent authority* continues until the third person is notified (from any source of information) that such authority has been terminated.[6]

The principal is expected to notify *directly* any third person the principal knows has dealt with the agent. For third persons who have heard about the agency but have not dealt with the agent, *constructive* notice is sufficient.[7]

No particular form of notice is required. The principal can actually notify the agent, or the agent can learn of the termination through some other means. For example, Marshall bids on a shipment of steel, and Smith is hired as an agent to arrange transportation of the shipment. When Smith learns that Marshall has lost the bid, Smith's authority to make the transportation arrangement terminates.

If the agent's authority is written, it must be revoked in writing, and the writing must be shown to all people who saw the original writing that established the agency relationship. Otherwise, the principal may still be bound by the agent's apparent authority. Sometimes a written authorization (like that granting power of attorney) contains an expiration date. The passage of the expiration date is sufficient notice of termination for third parties.

---

4. Insolvency, as distinguished from bankruptcy, does not necessarily terminate the relationship.

5. There is an exception to this rule in banking. UCC 4-405 provides that the bank as the agent can continue to exercise specific types of authority even after the customer's death or insanity unless it has knowledge of the death or insanity. When it has knowledge of the customer's death, it has authority for ten days after the death to pay checks (but not notes or drafts) drawn by the customer unless it receives a stop-payment order from someone who has an interest in the account, such as an heir. (This rule does not apply to insanity.)

---

6. Generally, *apparent authority* exists when the principal causes a third party to believe that an agent has authority, even though the agent has none, and the third party acts in reliance on the principal's representations. See Chapter 33.

7. *Constructive notice* is information or knowledge of a fact imputed by law to a person if he or she could have discovered the fact by proper diligence. Contructive notice is often accomplished pursuant to a statute by newspaper publication.

CONCEPT SUMMARY: Termination of an Agency

TYPE OF TERMINATION OF AGENCY	RULES	TERMINATION OF AGENT'S AUTHORITY
ACT OF THE PARTIES		NOTICE TO THIRD PERSONS REQUIRED
1. Lapse of time	Automatic at end of stated time.	1. Direct to those who have dealt with agency
2. Purpose achieved	Automatic upon completion of purpose.	2. Constructive to all others
3. Mutual rescission	Need mutual consent or acceptance of consideration.	

4. Termination by one party
  a. Revocation by principal
  b. Renunciation by agent
	At will agencies—generally no breach. Cannot revoke an agency coupled with an interest. Specified time agencies—breach unless legal cause.	

OPERATION OF LAW		
1. Death or insanity	Automatic upon death or insanity of either principal or agent (except when agency is coupled with an interest).	
2. Impossibility— destruction of the specific subject matter	Applies any time agency cannot be performed because of event beyond parties' control.	NO NOTICE REQUIRED— AUTOMATIC UPON THE HAPPENING OF THE EVENT
3. Changed circumstances	Events so unusual, it would be inequitable to allow agency to continue to exist.	
4. Bankruptcy	Bankruptcy decree terminates—not mere insolvency.	
5. War between principal's and agent's countries	Automatically suspends or terminates—no way to enforce legal rights.	

QUESTIONS AND CASE PROBLEMS

1. Paul Gett is a well-known, wealthy financier living in the city of Torris. Adam Wade, a friend of Gett, tells Timothy Brown that he is Gett's agent for the purchase of rare coins. Wade even shows Brown a local newspaper clipping mentioning Gett's interest in coin collecting. Brown, knowing of Wade's friendship with Gett, contracts with Wade to sell a rare coin valued at $25,000 to Gett. Wade takes the coin and disappears with it. On the date of contract payment Brown seeks to collect from Gett, claiming Wade's agency made Gett liable. Gett does not deny that Wade was a friend, but he claims that Wade was never his agent. Discuss fully whether an agency was in existence at the time the contract for the rare coin was made.

2. Adam is hired by Peter as an agent to sell a piece of property owned by Peter. The price to be obtained is not to be less than $30,000. Adam discovers that because a shopping mall is planned for the area of Peter's property, the fair market value of the property will be at least $45,000 and could be higher. Adam forms a real estate partnership with his cousin Carl, and Adam prepares for Peter's signature a contract for $32,000 for sale of the property to Carl. Peter signs the contract. Just before closing and passage of title, Peter learns about the shopping mall and the increased fair market value of his property. Peter refuses to deed the property to Carl. Carl claims that Adam, as

agent, solicited a price above that agreed upon in the creation of the agency and that the contract is therefore binding and enforceable. Discuss fully whether Peter is bound to this contract.

3. John Paul Corporation made the following contracts:
    (a) A contract with Able Construction to build an addition to the corporate office building.
    (b) A contract with a CPA, a recent college graduate, to head the cost accounting section.
    (c) A contract with a salesperson to travel a designated area to solicit orders (contracts) for the corporation.
Able contracts with Apex for materials for the addition; the CPA hires an experienced accountant to advise her on certain accounting procedures; and the salesperson contracts to sell a large order to Green, agreeing to deliver the goods in person within twenty days. Able refuses to pick up the materials, the CPA is in default in paying the hired consultant, and the salesperson does not deliver on time. Apex, the accountant, and Green claim John Paul Corporation is liable under agency law. Discuss fully whether an agency relationship was created by John Paul with Able, the CPA, or the salesperson.

4. Able is hired by Peters as a traveling salesperson. Able not only solicits orders but delivers the goods and collects payments from his customers. Able places all payments in his private checking account and at the end of each month draws sufficient cash from his bank to cover the payments made. Peters is totally unaware of this procedure. Because of a slowdown in the economy, Peter tells all his salespeople to offer 20 percent discounts on orders. Able solicits orders, but he offers only 15 percent discounts, pocketing the extra 5 percent paid by customers. Able has not lost any orders by this practice, and he is rated one of Peter's top salespersons. Peters learns of Able's actions. Discuss fully Peters's rights in this matter.

5. When the Mileses applied for a mortgage loan, the bank president told them a termite inspection was always required and arranged for by the bank. The bank president was advised that termites had been found on the property and that extermination would be necessary, but he did not advise the Mileses. Do the Mileses have a cause of action against the bank? [Miles v. Perpetual Sav. & Loan Co., 58 Ohio St.2d 93, 388 N.E.2d 1364 (1979)]

6. During the course of the administration of the estate of Baldwin M. Baldwin, it became necessary to sell a vast apartment complex owned by the estate, known as Baldwin Hills Village. Lemby, a real estate broker, doing business as Skyline Realty, was commissioned to make the sale. A number of prospective purchasers were contacted, and they were present at the private sale of Baldwin Hills Village. On a number of prior occasions, Lemby had indicated to the executors of Baldwin's estate that he was interested in purchasing the property. At the private sale, Lemby outbid all others and bought Baldwin Hills Village. Lemby then sought his commission on the sale from the Baldwin estate. Will anything in agency law prevent Lemby from recovering? [In re Estate of Baldwin, 34 Cal.App.3d 596, 110 Cal.Rptr. 189 (1973)]

7. On October 11, 1973, John Gray, owner of a 50 percent interest in a government oil and gas lease, assigned 20 percent of the operating rights and working interest to John Tylle in consideration of Tylle's payment of $10,000. The assignment was in writing and stated: "Until further notice assignee hereby appoints and designates assignor as agent and operator of the said lease for the purpose of development and management." A few weeks later, John Gray died unexpectedly. Tylle filed a claim against Gray's estate, seeking to recover the $10,000 he paid Gray. In order for Tylle to be successful, he must show that the agency relationship between him and Gray had been terminated. Will Tylle be successful? [In re Estate of Gray, 37 Colo.App. 47, 541 P.2d 336 (1975)]

8. Evan Smith experienced a heart attack in the emergency room of Baptist Memorial Hospital after being given a dose of penicillin for a sore throat. Smith sued the attending physician as well as the hospital. The hospital called itself a full-service hospital with emergency room facilities. Baptist Memorial considered the doctors as independent contractors, not agents. For example, for tax and accounting purposes the doctors were not treated as employees of the hospital. Based on this information, discuss whether the doctors who treated patients in the emergency room were independent contractors or agents. [Smith v. Baptist Memorial Hospital System, 720 S.W.2d 618 (Tex. App.– San Antonio 1986)]

9. Howard Bankerd left his wife and gave a power of attorney to Arthur King, instructing King to sell Bankerd's property "on such terms as to him seem best." Howard left town and could not be located for several years. In the meantime, Mrs. Bankerd convinced King to transfer the property by deed to her without consideration (as a gift). Bankerd later sued his former attorney for breach of the duty of loyalty and trust. Discuss whether King had the right, based on Bankerd's instructions, to deed the property by gift. [King v. Bankerd, 303 Md. 98, 492 A.2d 608 (1985)]

10. Broyles signed a sales representative's agreement with NCH Corp. that included covenants not to compete and not to solicit NCH customers after termination of the agreement. NCH maintained detailed and costly records of its routes and customers. It considered this information to be valuable and sensitive, although all the data was readily ascertainable from other sources. Broyles transcribed the names and information with intent to use this material after he left NCH's employ. He later voluntarily terminated his employment with NCH and went to work for a competing firm. Based on the information he had transcribed while an employee of NCH, he solicited business from some of his former customers. NCH sued Broyles, claiming that the use of his list was a breach of his employment contract and a breach of his fiduciary duty to NCH. Discuss whether NCH was successful in its claim that Broyles had breached his fiduciary duty. [NCH Corp. v. Broyles, 749 F.2d 247 (5th Cir. 1985)]

Chapter 33

Liability to Third Parties and Employer-Employee Relationships

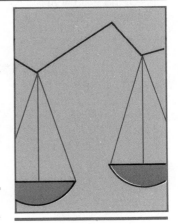

Once the principal-agent relationship has been created, attention often focuses on the rights of third persons who deal with the agent. The first part of this chapter is concerned with the rights of these third parties when they *contract* with agents. Such contracts will make an agent's principal liable to the third party only if the agent had authority to make the contract or if the principal ratified, or was estopped from denying, the agent's acts.

The second part of the chapter will deal with an agent's liability to third parties in contract and tort and the principal's liability to third parties because of an agent's torts. The chapter concludes with a basic discussion of employer-employee relationships.

SCOPE OF AGENT'S AUTHORITY

A principal's liability in a contract with a third party arises from the authority given the agent to enter legally binding contracts on the principal's behalf. An agent's authority to act stems from three types of sources:

1. Express (or specific). ⎫
2. Implied. ⎬ Actual authority
3. Apparent (or by estoppel). ⎭

If an agent contracts outside the scope of his or her authority, the principal may still become liable by ratifying the contract.

Express Authority

Express authority is embodied in that which the principal has engaged the agent to do. It can be given orally or in writing. For example, giving an agent a power of attorney confers express authority.[1] Like all agency relationships, a power of attorney can be special—permitting the agent to do specified acts only—or it can be general—permitting the agent to transact all business dealings for the principal. Of course, if the appointment comes

---

1. An agent who holds the power of attorney is called an attorney in fact for the principal. The holder does not have to be an attorney at law.

within the statute of frauds (discussed in Chapter 12), it must be in writing to be enforceable. See Exhibit 33–1.

As discussed in Chapter 32, the *equal dignity* rule in most states requires that if the contract being executed is or must be in writing, then the agent's authority must also be in writing. A principal may, however, ratify in writing an act done originally without written authority. For example, Palmer (the principal) orally asks Larkins (the agent) to sell a ranch that Palmer owns. Larkins finds a buyer and signs a sales contract (a contract for an interest in realty must be in writing) on behalf of Palmer to sell the ranch. The buyer cannot enforce the contract unless Palmer subsequently ratifies Larkins's agency status *in writing*. Once the contract has been ratified, either party can enforce rights under the contract.

The following case illustrates the formalities required for a power of attorney to give the holder the right to convey real estate.

Case 33.1 **BLOOM v. WEISER** District Court of Appeal of Florida, Third District, 1977. 348 So.2d 651.	**BACKGROUND AND FACTS** *Joseph Weinberg and Rachela Weiser purchased a condominium unit as joint tenants with right of survivorship.[a] Thereafter Weinberg executed a general power of attorney making his son, Arthur Winters, his agent. Winters conveyed Weinberg's one-half interest in the condominium to Weinberg's daughter, Miriam Bloom. After Weinberg's death, Bloom wanted to sell the condominium, but Weiser claimed complete ownership by right of survivorship on the ground that the agent had no authority to transfer the real estate to Bloom.*

HAVERFIELD, Judge.

*   *   *   *

The established rule is that a power of attorney must be strictly construed and the instrument will be held to grant only those powers which are specified. We are of the view that for a power of attorney to authorize a conveyance of real estate, the authority of the agent to do so must be plainly stated. Reviewing the power of attorney granted Winters, we find the instrument contains no specific grant of power authorizing him to convey real estate. Therefore, the July 18 deed executed by Winters and purporting to convey Weinberg's one-half interest in the subject condominium unit to Miriam Bloom is void.

DECISION AND REMEDY   *The deed executed by Winters was void. Title to the condominium belonged to Weiser.*

a. As will be discussed in Chapter 50, in a *joint tenancy* each tenant owns an undivided interest in the property; on the death of a tenant, his or her interest becomes the property of the surviving tenant.

Implied Authority

Implied authority is conferred by custom, can be inferred from the position the agent occupies, or is implied by virtue of being reasonably necessary to carry out express authority.

For example, Adams is employed by Packard Grocery to manage one of its stores. Packard has not specified (expressly stated) Adams's authority to contract with third persons. In this situation, authority to manage a business implies authority to do what is reasonably required (as is customary or can be inferred from a manager's position) to operate the business. This includes making contracts for obtaining employee help, for buying merchandise and equipment, and even for advertising the products sold in the store.

Because implied authority is conferred on the basis of custom, it is important for third persons to be familiar with the custom of the trade. The list of rules that have developed to determine what authority is implied based on custom or on the agent's position is extensive. Generally, implied authority is authority customarily associated with

Exhibit 33–1 Sample Power of Attorney

POWER OF ATTORNEY

GENERAL

Know All Men by These Presents: That I, _____

_____

the undersigned (jointly and severally, if more than one) hereby make, constitute and appoint _____

as true and lawful Attorney for me and in my name, place and stead and for my use and benefit:

    (a) To ask, demand, sue for, recover, collect and receive each and every sum of money, debt, account, legacy, bequest, interest, dividend, annuity and demand (which now is or hereafter shall become due, owing or payable) belonging to or claimed by me, and to use and take any lawful means for the recovery thereof by legal process or otherwise, and to execute and deliver a satisfaction or release therefor, together with the right and power to compromise or compound any claim or demand;

    (b) To exercise any or all of the following powers as to real property, any interest therein and/or any building thereon: To contract for, purchase, receive and take possession thereof and of evidence of title thereto; to lease the same for any term or purpose, including leases for business, residence, and oil and/or mineral development; to sell, exchange, grant or convey the same with or without warranty; and to mortgage, transfer in trust, or otherwise encumber or hypothecate the same to secure payment of a negotiable or non-negotiable note or performance of any obligation or agreement;

    (c) To exercise any or all of the following powers as to all kinds of personal property and goods, wares and merchandise, choses in action and other property in possession or in action: To contract for, buy, sell, exchange, transfer and in any legal manner deal in and with the same; and to mortgage, transfer in trust, or otherwise encumber or hypothecate the same to secure payment of a negotiable or non-negotiable note or performance of any obligation or agreement;

    (d) To borrow money and to execute and deliver negotiable or non-negotiable notes therefor with or without security; and to loan money and receive negotiable or non-negotiable notes therefor with such security as he shall deem proper;

    (e) To create, amend, supplement and terminate any trust and to instruct and advise the trustee of any trust wherein I am or may be trustor or beneficiary; to represent and vote stock, exercise stock rights, accept and deal with any dividend, distribution or bonus, join in any corporate financing, reorganization, merger, liquidation, consolidation or other action and the extension, compromise, conversion, adjustment, enforcement or foreclosure, singly or in conjunction with others of any corporate stock, bond, note, debenture or other security; to compound, compromise, adjust, settle and satisfy any obligation, secured or unsecured, owing by or to me and to give or accept any property and/or money whether or not equal to or less in value than the amount owing in payment, settlement or satisfaction thereof;

    (f) To transact business of any kind or class and as my act and deed to sign, execute, acknowledge and deliver any deed, lease, assignment of lease, covenant, indenture, indemnity, agreement, mortgage, deed of trust, assignment of mortgage or of the beneficial interest under deed of trust, extension or renewal of any obligation, subordination or waiver of priority, hypothecation, bottomry, charter-party, bill of lading, bill of sale, bill, bond, note, whether negotiable or non-negotiable, receipt, evidence of debt, full or partial release or satisfaction of mortgage, judgment and other debt, request for partial or full reconveyance of deed of trust and such other instruments in writing of any kind or class as may be necessary or proper in the premises.

Giving and Granting unto my said Attorney full power and authority to do and perform all and every act and thing whatsoever requisite, necessary or appropriate to be done in and about the premises as fully to all intents and purposes as I might or could do if personally present, hereby ratifying all that my said Attorney shall lawfully do or cause to be done by virtue of these presents. The powers and authority hereby conferred upon my said Attorney shall be applicable to all real and personal property or interests therein now owned or hereafter acquired by me and wherever situate.

    My said Attorney is empowered hereby to determine in his sole discretion the time when, purpose for and manner in which any power herein conferred upon him shall be exercised, and the conditions, provisions and covenants of any instrument or document which may be executed by him pursuant hereto; and in the acquisition or disposition of real or personal property, my said Attorney shall have exclusive power to fix the terms thereof for cash, credit and/or property, and if on credit with or without security.

    The undersigned, if a married woman, hereby further authorizes and empowers my said Attorney, as my duly authorized agent, to join in my behalf, in the execution of any instrument by which any community real property or any interest therein, now owned or hereafter acquired by my spouse and myself, or either of us, is sold, leased, encumbered, or conveyed.

    When the contest so requires, the masculine gender includes the feminine and/or neuter, and the singular number includes the plural.

WITNESS my hand this _____ day of _____ , 19_____

_____   _____

State of California,   } SS.
    County of _____

On _____ , before me, the undersigned, a Notary Public in and for said State, personally appeared _____

known to me to be the person _____ whose name _____ subscribed to the within instrument and acknowledged that _____ executed the same.

Witness my hand and official seal.   (Seal) _____

                                                  Notary Public in and for said State.

the position occupied by the agent or authority that can be inferred from the express authority given to the agent to fully perform his or her duties. The test is whether it was reasonable for the agent to believe that he or she had the authority to enter the contract in question.

Apparent Authority and Estoppel

Actual authority arises from what the principal manifests *to the agent*. Apparent authority exists when the principal, by either word or action, causes a *third party* reasonably to believe that an agent has authority to act, even though the agent has no express or implied authority. If the third party changes his or her position in reliance on the principal's representations, the principal may be *estopped* from denying that the agent had authority.

For example, a traveling salesperson has no express authority to collect for orders solicited from customers. Since the agent neither possesses the goods ordered nor delivers them, the agent also has no implied authority to collect. Assume that a customer, Carla, pays an agent, Adam, for a solicited order. Adam then takes the payment to the principal's accounting department. An accountant accepts payment and sends Carla a receipt. This procedure is thereafter followed for other orders solicited and paid for by Carla. Later Adam solicits an order, and Carla pays Adam as before. This time, however, Adam absconds with the money. Can Carla claim that the payment to Adam was authorized and thus, in effect, a payment to the principal? The answer is yes, because the principal's *repeated* acts of accepting Carla's payment led Carla reasonably to believe that Adam had authority to receive payments for goods solicited. Although Adam did not have express or implied authority, the principal's conduct gave Adam apparent authority to collect. The principal would be estopped from claiming that the agent had no authority to collect in this particular case.

Sometimes a principal will go beyond mere statements or actions that convince a third party that a certain person is the principal's agent. If, for example, the principal has "clothed the agent" with both possession and apparent ownership of the principal's property, the agent has very broad powers and can deal with the property as if he or she were the true owner.

For example, to deceive certain creditors, Baker (the principal) and Hunter (the agent) agree verbally that Hunter will hold certain stock certificates for Baker. Since the certificates are bearer paper (that is, they do not require indorsement to be transferred), Hunter's possession and apparent ownership of the stock certificates are such strong indications of ownership that a reasonable person would conclude that Hunter was the actual owner. If Hunter negotiates the stock certificates to a third person, Baker will be estopped from denying Hunter's authority to transfer the stock.

Where land is involved, courts have held that possession alone is not a sufficient indication of ownership. (See Chapter 52 for details.) If, on the other hand, the agent also possesses the deed to the property and sells the property against the principal's wishes to an unsuspecting buyer, the principal cannot cancel the sale or assert a claim to title.

Emergency Powers

When an unforeseen emergency demands action by the agent to protect or preserve the property and rights of the principal, but the agent is unable to communicate with the principal, the agent has emergency power.

For example, Fisher (the agent) is an engineer for Pacific Railroad (the principal). While Fisher is acting within the scope of his employment, he falls under the train many miles from home and is severely injured. Davis, the conductor (also an agent), directs Thompson, a doctor, to give medical aid to Fisher and to charge Pacific for the medical services. Davis has no express authority to bind Pacific Railroad for the services of Thompson. Yet, because of the emergency situation, the law recognizes him as having authority to act appropriately under the circumstances.

Ratification

Ratification is the affirmation of a previously unauthorized contract or act. Ratification can be either express or implied. Generally, only a principal can ratify. The principal must be aware of all material facts; otherwise, the ratification is not effective. Ratification binds the principal to the agent's acts and treats the acts or contracts as if they had been authorized by the principal *from the outset*. If the principal does not ratify, there is no contract binding the principal, and the third party's agreement with the agent is viewed merely as an unaccepted offer. Because the third party's agreement is treated as an unaccepted offer, the third party can revoke the offer (rescind the agreement) at any time before the principal ratifies, without liability. The agent, however, may well be liable to the third party for misrepresenting his or her authority.

The principal's acceptance (that is, the ratification) is binding only if the principal *knows* all the terms of the contract. If not, the principal can thereafter rescind ratification unless, of course, the third party has proceeded to change position in reliance on the contract.

Suppose an agent, without authority, contracts with a third person on behalf of a principal for repair work to the principal's office building. The principal learns of the contract from the agent and agrees to "some repair work," thinking that it will involve only patching and painting the exterior of the building. In fact, the contract includes resurfacing the parking lot, which the principal does not want done. Upon learning of the additional provision, the principal rescinds the contract. If the third party has made no preparations to do the work (such as purchasing materials, hiring additional workers, or renting equipment), then the principal can still rescind. But if the third party has, to his or her detriment, relied on the principal's ratification by making preparations, the principal must reimburse the third party for the cost of the preparations.

Two important points must be stressed. First, it is immaterial whether the principal's lack of knowledge results from the agent's fraud or is simply a mistake on the principal's part. If the third party has not changed position in reliance on the principal, the principal can repudiate the ratification. The unauthorized contract remains an offer, and the principal's acceptance is not valid, because contract law provides that one cannot accept terms one does not know about. Second, the whole transaction must be ratified; a principal cannot affirm the desirable parts of a contract and reject the undesirable parts.

Death or incapacity of the third party *before* ratification will void an unauthorized contract. Most courts will also recognize an intervening and extraordinary change of circumstances as a basis for setting aside a principal's ratification to permit a third party to revoke.

Assume that Able, without authority, enters into a contract with a third party who wants to purchase Paula's shopping center. The following night the shopping center is destroyed by fire. Paula's subsequent ratification will not be effective to bind the third party. The courts will reason that it is unjust to hold a third party liable in such a case and will permit the transaction to be avoided despite ratification.

EXPRESS RATIFICATION If a principal's statements or conduct express an intent to be bound, the prior unauthorized act will be ratified, and the principal will become a party to the contract.

For example, Smith (the agent) negotiates the sale of a shipment of oranges to World Markets without the authorization of Samuelson (the principal). Samuelson sees the completed paperwork and tells Smith to go ahead with it. Samuelson thus expressly ratifies the sale and is now bound to the terms of the sales contract.

IMPLIED RATIFICATION Implied ratification occurs most commonly when a principal decides to accept the benefits of a previously unauthorized transaction. In the preceding example, if Samuelson had known of the unauthorized acts and failed to repudiate or object to them within a reasonable time, the contract would have been ratified. In addition, if World Markets had paid for the oranges and if Samuelson, upon learning that World Markets had paid, did not object or repudiate, Samuelson would have impliedly ratified the contract.

REQUIREMENTS FOR RATIFICATION SUMMARIZED The previous discussion can be put in the form of a list of requirements for ratification, as follows:

1. The presumptive agent must have purportedly acted on behalf of a principal who subsequently ratifies.
2. The principal must know of all material facts involved in the transaction.
3. The agent's act must be affirmed in its entirety by the principal.
4. The principal must have the legal capacity to authorize the transaction at the time the agent engages in the act and at the time the principal ratifies.
5. The principal's affirmance must occur prior to the withdrawal of the third party from the transaction or prior to a change in circumstances that would make holding the third party to the transaction unjust.

6. The principal must observe the same formalities when he or she approves the act purportedly done by the agent on his or her behalf as would have been required to authorize it initially.

7. Ratification is irrevocable.

The following case illustrates the need of the principal promptly to repudiate unauthorized acts of an agent, once he or she knows about them, to avoid ratification.

Case 33.2
THEIS v. duPONT,
GLORE FORGAN INC.
Supreme Court of Kansas, 1973.
212 Kan. 301, 510 P.2d 1212.

BACKGROUND AND FACTS *Charles Theis, the plaintiff, maintained an investment account with the brokerage firm of duPont, Glore Forgan Inc., the defendant. Theis discovered that Benjamin, a duPont account executive, was making unauthorized transactions in his account and reprimanded him. Theis finally closed the account when Benjamin directly contravened Theis's order not to buy on May 24, 1968. Theis filed suit against duPont for all the unauthorized trading by Benjamin from the inception of the Theis account. The trial court allowed recovery on only the May 24 transaction. Theis appealed.*

FROMME, Justice.
* * * *

* * * On acquiring knowledge of the unauthorized act of an agent, the principal should promptly repudiate the act, otherwise it will be presumed he has ratified and affirmed the act.
* * * *

The record is clear the trial court correctly applied [the principles governing ratification. T]here were 36 transactions in the Theis account. The court determined that by Theis's failure to promptly repudiate unauthorized transactions he had either authorized or ratified the first 35 transactions. However, the court found that Theis promptly repudiated the final transaction of May 24 when he learned it had been made contrary to his express orders. This was evidenced not only by registering a protest with Benjamin but also by closing his commodities account with the broker.

It is pointed out the requirement of prompt repudiation is to prevent an investor from withholding his disapproval until the market has taken a turn for the worse, and then deciding to assert the alleged wrongdoing. In such case if prompt repudiation were not required he might sit back and quietly accept profits resulting from an unauthorized trade when it turned out to be to his advantage.

In the present case Theis had previously absorbed the losses, as well as the gains, resulting from Benjamin's unauthorized transactions. However, on May 24 Theis did not hesitate in closing his account as soon as he learned that Benjamin had bought in his short position contrary to express instructions. The record shows he did so without waiting to see whether the market price would ultimately rise or fall. His actions indicate he was unconcerned with the wisdom of the May 24 purchase. He was irate over the unauthorized purchase by Benjamin. The action of Theis in closing his account with duPont was found by the trial court to be an express repudiation of the May 24 transaction and this finding is supported by substantial evidence. Whether there has been a repudiation within a reasonable time in a question of fact and the ratification of a former unauthorized act is not the ratification of another entirely distinct act.

DECISION
AND REMEDY
Although the court found Theis had ratified Benjamin's earlier actions, duPont, Glore Forgan Inc. was liable for the unauthorized act of its employee on May 24.

PRINCIPAL'S AND AGENT'S LIABILITY FOR CONTRACTS

Principals are classified as disclosed, partially disclosed, or undisclosed.[2] **disclosed principal** is a principal whose identity is known by the third party at the time the contract is made by the agent. A **partially disclosed principal** is a principal whose identity is not known by the third party, but the third party knows that the agent is or may be acting for a principal at the time the contract is made. An **undisclosed principal** is a principal whose identity is totally unknown by the third party, and the third party has no knowledge that the agent is acting in an agency capacity at the time the contract is made.

Disclosed and Partially Disclosed Principals

If an agent acts within the scope of his or her authority, a disclosed or partially disclosed principal is liable to a third party for a contract made by the agent. Ordinarily, if the principal is disclosed, an agent has no contractual liability for the nonperformance of the principal or of the third party.

If the agent has no authority but nevertheless contracts purportedly on behalf of a disclosed principal, the principal cannot be held liable in contract by a third party, but the agent is liable in contract.

In most states, if the principal is partially disclosed, the principal and agent are both treated as parties to the contract, and the third party can hold either liable for contractual nonperformance.[3]

Undisclosed Principals

When neither the fact of agency nor the identity of the principal is disclosed, a third party is deemed to be dealing with the agent personally, and the agent is liable as a party on the contract.

For example, in a contract for the sale of a horse, a third party knows only that Scammon (the agent) wants to purchase the horse. The third party does not know that Scammon is actually negotiating for Johnson (the principal). Scammon signs a written contract in her own name, not indicating any agency relationship. She delivers the horse to Johnson, who is in fact the principal, but Johnson refuses to pay her. Scammon tries to return the horse to the third party, who refuses to take it. The third party is entitled to hold Scammon liable for payment. The agent's subjective intent is not relevant. The third party contracted with the agent on the basis of the *agent's* credit and reputation, not the undisclosed principal's. Therefore, the agent is liable.

If the agent has acted within the scope of authority, the undisclosed principal is fully bound to perform just as if the principal had been fully disclosed at the time the contract is made unless:

1. The undisclosed principal was expressly excluded as a party in the contract. For example, an agent contracts for a lease of a building with a landlord. The landlord does not know of the agency and the lease specially lists the agent as tenant, with no right of assignment without the landlord's consent. The undisclosed principal cannot enforce the lease.

2. The contract is a negotiable instrument. Here, the UCC provides that only the agent is liable if the instrument neither names the principal nor shows that the agent signed in a representative capacity.[4]

3. The performance of the agent is personal to the contract, allowing the third party to refuse the principal's performance. Typical examples involve extensions of credit and highly personal service contracts.

If the agent is forced to pay the third party, and if the agent has contracted within the scope of authority granted, the agent is entitled to indemnification by the principal. It was the principal's duty to perform even though his or her identity was undisclosed,[5] and failure to do so will make the principal ultimately liable. Once the undisclosed principal's identity is revealed, the third

---

2. Restatement, Second, Agency, Section 4.

3. Restatement, Second, Agency, Section 321.

4. UCC 3-401(1) and 3-403(2)(a). Extrinsic evidence to show an agency relationship is not normally admissible.

5. If Abel is a gratuitous agent, and the principal accepts the benefits of Abel's contract with a third party, then the principal will be liable to Abel on the theory of quasi-contract.

party has the right to *elect* to hold either the principal or the agent liable on contract. (In some states no election is necessary.)

In the following case, the undisclosed principal creates a liability problem for the travel agent.

Case 33.3
ROSEN v. DEPORTER-BUTTERWORTH TOURS, INC.
Appellate Court of Illinois, 1978.
62 Ill.App.3d 762, 379 N.E.2d
407, 19 Ill.Dec. 743.

BACKGROUND AND FACTS   *The plaintiff, Rosen, purchased a package tour for an African safari from the defendant, Deporter-Butterworth Tours, Inc. The travel bureau failed to disclose that it was in fact a special agent for the tour's sponsor, World Trek. Prior to the purchase of the package, the plaintiff had direct contact with the travel bureau but never with the tour sponsor. Hence, the tour sponsor, World Trek, was an undisclosed principal.*

The plaintiff planned to travel through Europe and then to join the tour in Egypt. Before leaving the United States, the plaintiff told the travel bureau where he could be reached in Europe and in Egypt prior to the start of the tour. The tour itinerary had to be changed. The travel bureau failed to contact the plaintiff overseas, leaving the plaintiff stranded in Egypt for a week. The plaintiff sued the travel bureau for damages sustained. The travel bureau claimed that it was not liable because it was merely an agent for World Trek and that World Trek was the proper party to the lawsuit. The trial court held for Rosen, and the travel bureau appealed.

BARRY, Presiding Justice.
*   *   *   *

The final issue presented for review is whether the trial court erred in finding defendant [the travel bureau] liable to the plaintiff for the price of the tour. Inherent in a decision of this issue is a determination of the relationship between the plaintiff and defendant and defendant and the tour sponsor, World Trek. *   *   * [I]n the normal situation between a travel bureau and its traveler client a special agency relationship arises for the limited object of the one business transaction between the two parties. It is clear in the present case that the plaintiff employed the defendant travel bureau as his special agent for the limited purpose of arranging the African Safari Tour sponsored by World Trek.

Although the sponsor of the tour, World Trek, as advertised in the brochure, was not a party to this lawsuit, their relationship to the defendant is an important factor in deciding liability. The record contains a letter from defendant to World Trek as plaintiff's exhibit No. 4, which admits to defendant's selling of World Trek's tour to the plaintiff and hints of a principal-agency relationship between World Trek and the defendant. The evidence also disclosed that the defendant received a 10% commission from World Trek for selling its tour. *The legal principle that an agent is liable as a principal [to] a third party in the case of an undisclosed agency relationship* is well established and needs no citation for authority. [Emphasis added.] In the instant case the plaintiff was aware that World Trek was sponsoring the tour but was without knowledge as to whether the defendant was truly representing him as his special agent for arranging the tour or whether defendant was acting as an agent for World Trek in selling its tour to plaintiff.

The traditional relationship between a travel bureau, such as defendant, and the tour sponsors of the various tours sold has been categorized as one of agent and principal particularly in the field of tort liability of the travel bureau for injuries that occur to the traveler. No sound reason exists for not finding the same principal-agent relationship between a tour sponsor and a travel bureau in the case of alleged liability for breach of an agreement involving the ultimate sale of the tour to an ordinary member of the traveling public, such as the plaintiff.

*   *   * [I]f an agent does not disclose the existence of an agency relationship and the identity of his principal, he binds himself to the third party with whom he acts as *if he, himself, were the principal.* [Emphasis added.] * * * The fact that the plaintiff knew that World Trek and not defendant was the tour sponsor does not satisfy the necessary disclosure to prevent defendant from becoming liable as principal. * * *

The appellate court held that the travel bureau was liable to the plaintiff because the travel bureau had not revealed that it was acting as an agent for World Trek, an undisclosed principal.

DECISION AND REMEDY

Warranties of Agent

When the agent lacks authority or exceeds the scope of authority, the agent's liability to a third party is based on the theory of breach of implied warranty of authority, not on breach of the contract itself.[6]

The agent's implied warranty of authority can be breached intentionally or by a good-faith mistake.[7] The agent's liability remains, as long as the third party has relied on the agency status. Conversely, when the third party knows at a time of the contract that the agent is mistaken, or when

the agent indicates to the third party *uncertainty* about the extent of authority, the agent is not personally liable for breach of warranty.

LIABILITY FOR AGENT'S TORTS

Obviously, an agent is liable for his or her own torts. A principal may also be liable for an agent's torts if they result from:

1. The principal's own tortious conduct.
2. The principal's authorization of a tortious act.
3. The agent's unauthorized but tortious misrepresentation.

If the agent is an employee, whose conduct the principal-employer controls, the principal-employer

---

6. The agent is not liable on the contract because the agent was never personally intended to be a party to the contract.

7. If the agent intentionally misrepresents his or her authority, then the agent can also be liable in tort for fraud.

CONCEPT SUMMARY: Authority of Agent to Bind Principal and Third Party

AUTHORITY OF AGENT	DEFINITION	EFFECT ON PRINCIPAL AND THIRD PARTY
Express authority	Authority expressly given by the principal to the agent.	Principal and third party are bound in contract.
Implied authority	Authority implied by custom, from the position in which the principal has placed the agent, or because it is necessary to carry out expressly authorized duties and responsibilities.	
Apparent authority	Authority created when the conduct of the principal leads a third party to believe the principal's agent has authority.	
Unauthorized acts	Acts committed by an agent that are outside the scope of his or her express, implied, or apparent authority.	Principal and third party are not bound in contract—*unless* the principal ratifies prior to the third party's withdrawal.

may be liable for an unauthorized tort committed by the employee in the course of employment. If the agent is an independent contractor, whose conduct is not subject to the principal's control, the principal is not liable for harm resulting from the agent's negligent conduct if the principal did not intend or authorize the method of performance or the result.

Principal's Tortious Conduct

A principal conducting an activity through an agent may be liable for harm resulting from the principal's own negligence or recklessness, which may include giving improper instructions, authorizing the use of improper materials or tools or the like, establishing improper rules, or failing to prevent others' tortious conduct while they are on the principal's property or using the principal's equipment, materials, or tools.

For instance, if Jack knows that Jill cannot drive but nevertheless authorizes her to take the company truck to pick up water pails for his business inventory, he will be liable for his own negligence to anyone injured by her negligent driving.

Principal's Authorization of Tortious Conduct

Similarly, a principal who authorizes an agent to commit a tortious act may be liable to persons or property injured thereby, because the act is considered to be the principal's. For example, if John directs Warren, an agent he retained to oversee the harvest of crops he bought, to cut the corn on specific acreage, which neither of them has the right to, the harvest is a trespass, and John is liable to whoever owns the corn.

In the same light, if Victoria instructs Albert, her real estate agent, to tell prospective purchasers that there is oil beneath her property, when she knows there is not, she will be liable to anyone who buys the property in reliance on the statements.

Misrepresentation

A principal is exposed to tort liability whenever a third person sustains loss due to the agent's misrepresentation. The keys to a principal's liability are whether the agent was actually or apparently authorized to make representations and whether such representations were made within the scope of the agency.

Assume Lewis is a demonstrator for Moore's products. Moore sends Lewis to a home show to demonstrate products and to answer questions from consumers. Moore has given Lewis authority to make statements about the products. If Lewis makes only true representations, all is fine; but if he makes false claims, Moore will be liable for any injuries or damages sustained by third parties in reliance on Lewis's false representations.

An interesting series of cases has arisen on the theory that when a principal has placed an agent in a position to defraud a third party, the principal is liable for the agent's fraudulent acts.

For example, Pratt is a loan officer at First Security Bank. In the ordinary course of the job, Pratt approves and services loans and has access to the credit records of all customers. Pratt falsely represents to a borrower, McMillan, that the bank feels insecure about McMillan's loan and intends to call it in unless McMillan provides additional collateral, such as stocks and bonds. McMillan gives Pratt numerous stock certificates, which Pratt keeps in her own possession and later uses to make personal investments. The bank is liable to McMillan for losses sustained on the stocks even though the bank had no direct role or knowledge of the fraudulent scheme.

The legal theory used here is that the agent's position conveys to third persons the impression that the agent has the authority to make statements and perform acts consistent with the ordinary duties that are within the scope of the position. When an agent appears to be acting within the scope of the authority that the position of agency confers but is actually taking advantage of a third party, the principal who placed the agent in that position is liable. In the example above, if a bank teller or a security guard had told McMillan that the bank required additional security for a loan, McMillan would not have been justified in relying on either person's authority to make that representation. However, McMillan could reasonably expect that the loan officer was telling the truth.

INNOCENT MISREPRESENTATION Tort liability based on fraud requires proof that a material misstatement was made knowingly and with the intent to deceive. An agent's innocent mistakes occurring in a contract transaction or involving a warranty contained in the contract can provide grounds for the third party's rescission of the contract and the award of damages. Moreover, justice dictates that when a principal knows that an agent is not accurately advised of facts but does not correct either the agent's or the third party's impressions, the principal is directly responsible to the third party for resulting damages. The point is that the principal is always directly responsible for an agent's misrepresentation made within the scope of authority.

Doctrine of *Respondeat Superior*

The principal-employer is liable for harm caused by an agent-employee in the scope of employment. The theory of liability involves the doctrine of **respondeat superior**.[8] This doctrine imposes vicarious liability on the employer—that is, liability without regard to the personal fault of the employer for torts committed by an employee in the course or scope of employment.[9]

SCOPE OF EMPLOYMENT   The Restatement, Second, Agency, Section 229, indicates the general factors that courts will consider in determining whether or not a particular act occurred within the course and scope of employment. They are:

1.   Whether the act was authorized by the employer.
2.   The time, place, and purpose of the act.
3.   Whether the act was one commonly performed by employees on behalf of their employers.
4.   The extent to which the employer's interest was advanced by the act.
5.   The extent to which the private interests of the employee were involved.
6.   Whether the employer furnished the means or instrumentality (for example, a truck or a machine) by which the injury was inflicted.
7.   Whether the employer had reason to know that the employee would do the act in question and whether the employee had done it before.

8.   Whether the act involved the commission of a serious crime.

LIABILITY FOR INDEPENDENT CONTRACTOR'S ACTS

The general rule concerning liability for the acts of independent contractors is that the principal is not liable for physical harm caused to a third person by the negligent act of an independent contractor in the performance of the contract. A principal who has no legal power to control the details of the physical performance of a contract cannot be held liable. Here again the test is the *right to control*. Since a principal bargains with an independent contractor only for results and retains no control over the manner in which those results are achieved, the principal is generally not expected to bear the responsibility for torts committed by an independent contractor. A collection agency is a typical example of an independent contractor. The creditor is generally not liable for the acts of the collection agency because collection is a distinct business occupation.

Generally, an exception to this doctrine prevails when exceptionally hazardous activities are involved. Typical examples of such activities include blasting operations, the transportation of highly volatile chemicals, and the use of poisonous gases. In these cases, a principal cannot be shielded from liability merely by using an independent contractor. Strict liability is imposed upon the principal as a matter of law. Also, in some states, strict liability is imposed by statute.

LIABILITY FOR AGENT'S CRIMES

Obviously, an agent is liable to third persons for his or her own crimes. A principal or employer is not liable for an agent's or employee's crime simply because the agent or employee committed the crime while otherwise acting within the scope of authority or employment, unless the principal or employer participated by conspiracy or other action.

In some jurisdictions, under specific statutes, a principal may be liable for an agent's violating,

---

8. The doctrine of *respondeat superior* applies not only to employer-employee relationships but also to principal-agent relationships as long as the principal has the right of control over the agent.

9. The theory of *respondeat superior* is similar to the theory of strict liability covered in Chapters 4 and 21. This doctrine may not apply if the employer has sovereign or charitable organization immunity. The practice of granting such immunity is diminishing in most states.

in the course and scope of employment, such regulations as those governing sanitation, prices, weights, and the sale of liquor.

LIABILITY FOR SUBAGENT'S ACTS

There are three instances in which an agent can hire a subagent:

1. To perform mechanical or minor duties.
2. When it is the business custom.
3. For unforeseen emergencies.

If an agent is authorized to hire subagents for the principal under any one of these circumstances, then the principal is liable for the acts of the subagents. There is a slight difference in result if the agent hires for an *undisclosed principal*. In that case, the agent is responsible for the subagent in contract law for such things as wages. The undisclosed principal, however, is generally held to be liable for tort injuries. The doctrine of *respondeat superior* imposes liability on the true "master." An agent's unauthorized hiring of a subagent generally does not create any legal relationship between the principal and the subagent.

EMPLOYER-EMPLOYEE RELATIONSHIPS

Employer-employee relationships are generally created by an express or an implied contract. The contract gives the employer the right basically to control the employee's conduct, workplace, and work habits and the benefits enjoyed within the scope of the employee's employment.

If the employee is also an agent of the employer, the employee has the authority to act on behalf of the employer. The rights, duties, and liabilities afforded this relationship have already been discussed.

Statutory regulations that deal with employment discrimination, the health of the employee, the safety of the workplace, wrongful discharge, labor-management agreements, and the like apply only to the employer-employee relationship. These laws are discussed in Chapter 49.

Employment Contracts

An employment contract is generally a mutual agreement formed by an employer and an employee. Basic contract rules apply. The parties can include any contract terms they desire, as long as these terms are not in violation of statute or against public policy. For example, a contract for wages so low as to be in violation of the Fair Labor Standards Act would be illegal. Frequently, employment contracts are governed by collective bargaining agreements made with the employer on behalf of the employees by a union.

COVENANTS NOT TO COMPETE   In some employment contracts, an employee agrees that should he or she ever leave his or her employment, for whatever reason, he or she will not accept another employment position with an employer who is presently a competitor. These are called covenant-not-to-compete clauses. When these clauses are only a subordinate part of the total employment contract and the scope of the prohibition is reasonable in geographic area and duration, the covenants are generally enforceable by injunction.

COMPENSATION   The duties of the employee are set forth generally in the contract, and for fulfillment of these duties the employee is entitled to compensation. Where permitted, a creditor, through a legal procedure, can garnish the wages of an employee in satisfaction of a debt.

SHOP RIGHT   An interesting question arises when an employee invents a product and the employer (or principal as an employer) claims a right to the invention or to the patent. The **shop right doctrine,** or rule, is involved here. This doctrine says that if the employee's duties do not include conducting research and making inventions, the employer is not entitled to the invention but merely has a shop right interest in it. This interest allows the employer a nonexclusive right to use the invention without paying any royalties to the employee. The employee retains ownership and, subject to the shop right interest, full rights to the invention, which he or she may sell to others or license others to use. The employer's right is irrevocable even after the employment relationship ends. The rights of an employer under the shop right doctrine are illustrated in the following case.

BACKGROUND AND FACTS *Leroy Rowland was hired by Aetna as a general staff engineer. He was not hired as a design engineer, but during his employment at Aetna he designed a machine table (the IHI table) useful to Aetna's assembly line. He designed the table with the help of his supervisor, Remner, using Aetna's tools and on work time. Rowland and Remner received a patent from the government. Rowland was subsequently laid off by Aetna. Aetna insisted that Rowland assign the patent for the machine table to Aetna, because Rowland had built the machine on company time. When Rowland refused to assign his interest to Aetna, the firm sued Rowland. The lower court held in Rowland's favor, and Aetna appealed.*

Case 33.4
AETNA-STANDARD ENGINEERING CO. v. ROWLAND
Superior Court of Pennsylvania, 1985.
343 Pa. Super. 64, 493 A.2d 1375.

CIRILLO, Judge.

* * * *

* * * [T]he absence from the employment contract of an express agreement to assign will not preclude the employer as a matter of law from asserting a claim to the employee's invention. Instead, a court must closely scrutinize the employment contract, so that, absent an express contrary agreement, an employee must assign his invention to his employer if he was hired for the purpose of using his inventive ability to solve a specific problem or to design a certain procedure or device for the employer; in such a case, the invention is the precise subject of the employment contract. Given the personal, intellectual nature of the inventive process, the courts must otherwise hesitate to imply agreements to assign.

Although an employer might not be entitled to an assignment of the employee's invention—that is, of his patent—the employer will likely have a license or "shop right" to use the invention without paying the employee any additional compensation as royalties; the shop-right rule thus creates an exception from the employee's patent right to exclude others from making or using his invention. As in the law on assignment of inventions, the employment relationship, standing alone, does not give the employer a shop right; the employer might have to show an express agreement for the right. A shop right will arise, however, where the employee devises the invention on the employer's time and at the latter's expense, using his materials and facilities, and allows him to use the invention without special compensation.

The Pennsylvania courts, and the federal courts sitting in Pennsylvania, have long applied the Supreme Court's rules on employers' and employees' rights to inventions virtually verbatim. In the early case of *Slemmer's Appeal*, the plaintiffs claimed to be joint inventors with the defendant employee of a patented invention. Our Supreme Court could not agree with the plaintiffs, as such a holding would invalidate the patent, an action beyond the Court's jurisdiction. Instead, the Court applied a license theory, and stated:

[I]f a person employed in the manufactory of another, while receiving wages, makes experiments at the expense of his employer, constructs the article invented and permits his employer to use it, no compensation for the use being paid or demanded, and then obtains a patent, these facts will justify the presumption of a license to use the invention.

* * * *

On these facts, appellant is not entitled to an assignment of appellee's invention of the table. Appellee was hired as a general staff engineer; he was not recruited specifically to design the IHI table. * * * He received no special compensation for his work on the IHI contract; rather, that work was simply within the normal scope of his duties as an Aetna engineer. More importantly, he had no express agreement with appellant, written or oral, to assign to it any inventions he created during his employment. Finally, appellant asked appellee to sign the disclosure document and, most significantly, the patent application, as a joint inventor with Remner: appellant made no claim to the patent until after it had discharged appellee. On these facts, we cannot imply an agreement in appellee's employment contract to assign his invention to appellant.

However, we find that, under the case-law discussed above, appellant has a shop right to use the patented table. Appellee testified that he assumed appellant would own any inventions he designed. The table was designed at appellant's place of business and with its resources for appellant's IHI contract. While appellant has no right to appellee's patent interest, it is entitled to the royalty-free, non-exclusive use of the table in its IHI project.

DECISION AND REMEDY   *The superior court affirmed the lower court's decision that Aetna was not entitled to an assignment of Rowland's interest but only to a royalty-free, nonexclusive use of the invention.*

TERMINATION Contracts of employment are either at will (involving no specific time period) or for a specific term. Contracts at will can generally be terminated by proper notice at any time without liability.

Employment at Will A common employment relationship, familiar to most students, is employment at will. Employment at will involves an employment contract for an unspecified term; thus, both the employer and the employee have the option of terminating the employment contract at any time. Traditionally, an employer could discharge an at-will employee for any (or no) reason without liability. In recent decades, some grounds that employers could formerly use with impunity to discharge at-will employees have emerged as violative of statutes or public policy—for example, termination in violation of civil rights laws, which is discussed in detail in Chapter 49.

Recent legislative acts and, in some jurisdictions, court decisions have carved out other exceptions to the employment-at-will doctrine. For example, an employee may have a cause of action for damages on grounds of wrongful discharge if the employee is terminated for "whistle-blowing" —that is, reporting, testifying against, or aiding in an investigation of an employer who is breaking the law.

Similarly, an at-will employee may have a civil cause for damages when he or she is terminated for refusing to break the law or for exercising his or her legal rights—filing a workers' compensation claim, for example, or participating in union activities. Also, courts have construed requirements of good faith and fair dealing in at-will employment relationships to hold that discharges are wrongful when they are undertaken with the intent of undercutting employee's benefits in an employer's favor—for example, to avoid paying sales commissions or pensions.

In some instances, courts have interpreted employee manuals or other statements by a company's management or personnel department as part of an employment contract. Thus, for example, if an employee manual describes a procedure that it purports will be followed before an employee is discharged—including, perhaps, written notice and a hearing before disinterested company personnel—an employee cannot be discharged without the notice and hearing, or the employer may be liable for damages. Even a statement that "no employee will be discharged without good cause" may prompt a court to require that an employer establish that the reason for an employee's discharge constituted a "good cause."

The following case involves a former at-will employee who brought suit against his former employer for wrongful discharge. The case is illustrative of the three major exceptions to the employment-at-will doctrine that are allowed in some states and jurisdictions.

Case 33.5
WAGNER v. CITY OF GLOBE
Supreme Court of Arizona, 1986.
150 Ariz. 82, 722 P.2d 250.

BACKGROUND AND FACTS *Edward Wagner was hired by the city of Globe as a police officer. The local magistrate and Wagner's police chief became upset with Wagner when he pointed out that a prisoner had been arrested illegally and held far beyond the required jail term. Wagner was fired by the department soon thereafter for no specific reason. Wagner sued the city for wrongful discharge and discrimination (Wagner was a Mexican-American).*

The lower court held for the city without submitting the evidence to a trial, and Wagner appealed the charge of wrongful discharge.

GORDON, Vice Chief Justice.

*   *   *   *

The doctrine of employment-at-will found fertile ground in the laissez-faire climate of nineteenth century America and thrived until very recently. Increasingly, however, the doctrine is under attack. Today three-fifths of the states have recognized some form of a cause of action for "wrongful discharge." The trend has been to modify the at-will doctrine by creating exceptions to its operation. Three major exceptions have been developed: the "implied contract" exception, which relies upon proof of an implied promise of continued employment absent just cause for termination to protect the legitimate expectations of workers, and which may be established by oral representations, a course of dealing, personnel manuals or memoranda; the "public policy" exception, which permits recovery upon a finding that the employer's conduct undermined some important public policy; and the implied covenant of "good faith and fair dealing," which protects employees from termination for bad cause.

*   *   *   *

Employees should not have to choose between their jobs and the demands of important public policy interests; thus courts have developed the public policy exception to the at-will doctrine. Actions for wrongful discharge in breach of public policy are essentially breaches of duties imposed by law, and are best characterized as actions in tort rather than contract. The tort of wrongful discharge in violation of public policy has been variously labeled: discharge for bad cause, retaliatory discharge, improper discharge, etc. Whatever the nomenclature, our concern remains the same: employees should not be discharged because they performed an act that public policy would encourage, or refused to do that which public policy condemns.

*   *   *   *

The employee who chooses to report illegal or unsafe conduct by his employer differs significantly from the employee forced to choose between his job and actual participation in illegal behavior. The latter is the paradigmatic case of a public policy violation; in contrast the whistleblower faces the arguably less onerous choice of either ignoring the known or suspected illegality or becoming an instrument of law enforcement. Nonetheless, whistleblowing employees have gained a measure of judicial protection.

*   *   *   *

*   *   * [We] believe that the petitioner's behavior is best characterized as whistleblowing behavior. Wagner took affirmative steps to investigate and rectify the illegal detention and called it to the attention of the police chief and city magistrate. Wagner was not forced to a Hobson's choice between his job and illegal activity; he chose to take affirmative remedial action. *   *   *

We believe that whistleblowing activity which serves a public purpose should be protected. So long as employees' actions are not merely private or proprietary, but instead seek to further the public good, the decision to expose illegal or unsafe practices should be encouraged. We recognize that there is a tension between the obvious societal benefits in having employees with access to information expose activities which may be illegal or which may jeopardize health and safety, and accepted concepts of employee loyalty; nevertheless we conclude that on balance actions which enhance the enforcement of our laws or expose unsafe conditions, or otherwise serve some singularly public purpose, will inure to the benefit of the public. Indeed, our legislature has recognized that whistleblowing activity is worthy of protection. In 1985 the legislature enacted A.R.S. § 38-532, which protects state and county employees from retaliation for their whistleblowing activity. While A.R.S. § 38-532 is not applicable to this case, it evinces a legislative expression of public policy fully consonant with our decision.

*   *   *   *

If the petitioner's allegations are true, as we must assume they are for purposes of this appeal, then he has stated a valid cause of action for wrongful discharge in violation of public policy. No exhaustive canvass of constitutional or statutory authority is necessary to support the proposition that there is no public policy more important or fundamental than the one favoring the effective protection of the lives, liberty, and property of our people. No one will disagree with the proposition that public policy is furthered when the civil rights of our citizens are protected from abuse; for when the rights of even one citizen may be so cavalierly dispatched none may rest easy. The petitioner's successful attempt to free Hicks [the illegally arrested prisoner] from illegal confinement was a refreshing and laudable exercise which should be protected, not punished. The police, who are charged with the responsibility of enforcing our laws, should be encouraged to zealously guard the civil rights of our people and not be deterred from rectifying or reporting the abuse of those rights for fear of discharge.

DECISION AND REMEDY   *The Supreme Court of Arizona reversed the decision and remanded the case for a trial on the merits.*[a]

a. A *trial on the merits* is a trial of the substantive issues in a case, as opposed to a hearing on a motion or other matter. In this case, as noted above, the lower court made its decision without submitting the evidence to a trial.

Contracts for a Specified Duration   Contracts for a specified duration can usually be terminated, without employer liability, only for good and sufficient cause or by the employee's acceptance of some form of severance consideration. A termination without cause is a breach of contract and can make the employer liable for the balance of the compensation due under the term contract and/or damages. On occasion, the employer may be required to reinstate the employee.

What is good and sufficient cause for termination is sometimes at the heart of an employee's lawsuit. Generally, an employee's serious nonperformance of duties, insubordination, disloyalty, incompetency or disability that seriously affects work performance, and wrongful conduct are grounds for a good-cause termination.

An employee can be held liable by an employer for wrongful termination under a contract for a specific duration. The employer cannot force (through specific performance) the employee to continue to work for the employer, as that would constitute a form of involuntary servitude, which is a constitutional violation. The employer can, however, seek damages, making termination by the employee less attractive.

Employment Torts

Considerable legal attention is given to an employer's tort liability for injuries suffered by the employee and to suits by third persons who are harmed by the torts of the employee. This section briefly discusses the employer's liability in these situations.

EMPLOYER'S NEGLIGENCE   Under common law principles, the employer is required to provide the employee a safe working environment with safe tools and equipment and competent co-workers. An employee can refuse to work in an unsafe environment and such refusal cannot be a basis for termination of employment.[10] In the event the employee is injured within the scope of employment, if the employer's negligence caused the injury, the employee may be entitled to actual damages.

Of course, as in any situation involving negligence (see Chapter 4), the employer can assert such defenses as the employee's contributory negligence. The employer might also claim that the risk of the injury was a risk the employee assumed on taking the job. When an employee negligently injures a co-worker, the employer may avoid liability for the injury under the *fellow servant doctrine*, unless the injury was caused by an irresponsible worker hired by the employer (which constitutes negligence on the part of the employer) or was caused by a superior or supervisor.

WORKERS' COMPENSATION STATUTES   In all states, workers' compensation statutes cover at least

---

10. For example, under the Occupational Safety and Health Act of 1970, employees are protected from discharge or discrimination for refusal to work because of a reasonable apprehension of death or serious injury. See Whirlpool Corp. v. Marshall, 445 U.S. 1, 100 S.Ct. 883, 63 L.Ed.2d 154 (1980).

some employment-related injuries. Typically, these statutes provide that certain employees are entitled to fixed amounts of compensation for injuries that occur in accidents arising in the course of employment. Either the employer or the employer's insurer pays the compensation, which may include amounts for wages lost because of the injury and for medical and death benefits.

Under these statutes, an injured employee need not prove negligence but may be compensated no matter who was at fault. To avoid a claim, an employer might argue that the injury was not related to the employment, that it was not as serious as the employee claimed, or that the employee purposely inflicted the injury or was intoxicated at the time the injury occurred. Liability cannot be avoided on grounds of the employee's contributory negligence or assumption of risk, or under the fellow servant doctrine.

EMPLOYER'S LIABILITY FOR EMPLOYEE'S NEGLIGENCE Third persons injured through the negligence of an employee can sue either the employee who was negligent or the employer, if the employee's negligent conduct occurred while the employee was acting within the scope of employment. Liability of the employer, when the employer is not personally at fault, is based on the doctrine of *respondeat superior,* discussed earlier in this chapter.

At early common law, a servant (employee) was viewed as the master's (employer's) property. The master was deemed to have absolute control over the servant's acts and was held strictly liable for them no matter how carefully the master supervised the servant. The rationale for the doctrine of *respondeat superior* is based on the principle of social duty that requires every person to manage his or her affairs, whether accomplished by the person or through agents or servants, so as not to injure another. Liability is imposed on employers because they are deemed to be in a better financial position to bear the loss. The superior financial position carries with it the duty to be responsible for damages.

Today the doctrine continues, but employers carry liability insurance and spread the cost of risk over the entire business enterprise. Public policy requires that an injured person be afforded effective relief, and recovery from a business enterprise provides far more effective relief than recovery

from an individual employee. Liability rights exist under law because of public policy protections of third parties. Thus, a master (employer) cannot contract with a servant (employee) to disclaim responsibilities for injuries resulting from the servant's acts, because such disclaimers are against public policy.

For the employer to be liable, the act causing injury must have occurred within the scope of the employee's employment. For example, Sutton (the employee) is a delivery driver for Schwartz (the employer). Schwartz provides Sutton with a vehicle and instructs him to use it for making company deliveries. Nevertheless, one day Sutton drives his own car instead of the company vehicle and negligently injures Walker. Even though Sutton's act (driving the car) was unauthorized, the negligence occurred as part of Sutton's regular duties of employment (making deliveries). Hence, Schwartz is still liable to Walker for the injuries caused by Sutton, even though Sutton used his own car contrary to Schwartz's instructions. Only if Sutton's acts had exceeded the scope of employment duties in a way that the employer could not reasonably have expected would Schwartz have been relieved of liability.

An employee going to and from work or to and from meals is usually considered outside the scope of employment. All travel time of a traveling salesperson, however, is normally considered within the scope of employment for the duration of the business trip, including the return trip home.

When an employee goes off on his or her own—that is, departs from the employer's business to take care of personal affairs—is the employer liable? It depends. If the employee's activity is a substantial departure akin to an utter abandonment of the employer's business, then the employer is not liable.

For example, a traveling salesperson is driving the employer's vehicle to call on a customer for a possible sales order. On the way to the customer's place of business, the employee deviates one block to mail a letter at the post office. As the employee approaches the post office, she negligently runs into a parked vehicle owned by Ann. The departure of the employee from the employer's business to take care of a personal affair is not substantial. The employee is still within the scope of employment, and the employer is liable to Ann. If the employee had decided to pick up a few friends for cocktails in another city, and in the process had negligently run her vehicle into Ann, Ann could not have held the employer liable, only the employee.

The following case is a classic in master-servant law. Although it is over 150 years old, the legal principle for which it stands is still viable in employment law today.

Case 33.6
JOEL v. MORISON
Court of Exchequer, England, 1834.
6 Carrington & Payne Reports 501.

BACKGROUND AND FACTS *The plaintiff was walking across Bishopsgatestreet when he was knocked down by a cart driven negligently by a servant of the defendant. The plaintiff suffered a fractured leg and multiple injuries. The plaintiff took the position that the defendant was liable for his injuries because the defendant's servant was driving the cart that caused the injuries. The defendant argued that his cart was never driven in the neighborhood in which the plaintiff was injured. Moreover, it was suggested that the defendant's servant had gone out of his way for his own purposes and might have taken the cart at a time when it was not wanted for business purposes to pay a visit to some friends.*

PARKE, Judge.
*   *   *   *

His Lordship afterwards, in summing up, said—This is an action to recover damages for an injury sustained by the plaintiff, in consequence of the negligence of the defendant's servant. There is no doubt that the plaintiff has suffered the injury, and there is no doubt that the driver of the cart was guilty of negligence, and there is no doubt also that the master, if that person was driving the cart on his master's business, is responsible. If the servants, being on their master's business, took a detour to call upon a friend, the master will be responsible. If you think the servants lent the cart to a person who was driving without the defendant's knowledge, he will not be responsible. Or, if you think that the young man who was driving took the cart surreptitiously, and was not at the time employed on his master's business, the defendant will not be liable. The master is only liable where the servant is acting in the course of his employment. If he was going out of his way, against his master's implied commands, when driving on his master's business, he will make his master liable; but if he was going on a frolic of his own, without being at all on his master's business, the master will not be liable. As to the damages, the master *   *   * [although not himself] guilty of any offence, *   *   * is only responsible in law, therefore the amount should be reasonable.

DECISION AND REMEDY *The verdict was for the plaintiff, and he was awarded damages of £30. In this case, the master was held liable for the acts of his servant.*

BORROWED SERVANTS Employers can lend the services of their employees to other employers. Suppose that an employer leases ground-moving equipment to another employer and sends along an employee to operate the machinery. Who is liable for injuries caused by the employee's negligent actions on the job site? Liability turns on *which employer had the primary right to control* the employee at the time the injuries occurred. Generally, the employer who rents out the equipment is presumed to retain control over his or her employee. If the rental is for a relatively long period of time, however, control may be deemed to pass to the employer who is renting the equipment and presumably controlling and directing the employee.

NOTICE OF DANGEROUS CONDITIONS The employer is charged with knowledge of any dangerous conditions discovered by an employee and pertinent to the employment situation. To illustrate, a maintenance employee in Martin's apartment building notices a lead pipe protruding from the ground in the building's courtyard. The employee neglects either to fix it or to inform the employer of the danger. Sam falls on the pipe and is injured. The employer is charged with knowledge of the dangerous condition regardless of whether or not the employee actually informed the employer. That knowledge is imputed to the employer by virtue of the employment relationship.

EMPLOYER'S LIABILITY FOR EMPLOYEE'S INTENTIONAL TORTS

Most intentional torts that employees commit have no relation to their employment; and thus, their employers will not be held liable. Under *respondeat superior*, however, the employer is liable for intentional torts of the employee committed within the scope of employment, just as the employer is liable for negligence. For example, an employer is liable when an employee commits assault and battery or false imprisonment while acting within the scope of employment. Of course, questions concerning whether the employee's act was within the scope of employment or constituted a "frolic" still apply in this context.

An employee acting at the employer's direction can be liable as a **tortfeasor** (one who commits a wrong, or tort), along with the employer, for committing the tortious act even if the employee was unaware of the wrongfulness of the act. For example, an employer directs an employee to burn out a field of crops. The employee does so, assuming that the field belongs to the employer, which it does not. Both can be found liable to the owner of the field for damages.

An employer who knows or should know that an employee has a propensity for committing tortious acts is liable for the employee's acts even if they would not ordinarily be considered within the scope of employment. For example, the Blue Moon employs Joe Green as a bouncer, knowing that he has a history of arrests for assault and battery. While he is working one night within the scope of his employment, he viciously attacks a patron who "looks at him funny." The Blue Moon will bear the responsibility for Green's acts because it knew that he had a propensity for committing tortious acts.

Also, an employer is liable for permitting an employee to engage in reckless acts that can injure others. For example, an employer observes an employee smoking while filling containerized trucks with highly flammable liquids. Failure to stop the employee will cause the employer to be liable for any injuries that result.

QUESTIONS AND CASE PROBLEMS

1. Adam is a traveling salesperson for Peter Petri Plumbing Supply Corporation. Adam has express authority to solicit orders from customers and to offer a 5 percent discount if payment is made within thirty days of delivery. Petri has said nothing to Adam about extending credit. Adam calls on a new prospective customer, John's Plumbing Firm. John tells Adam that he will place a large order for Petri products if Adam will give him a 10 percent discount with payment due in equal installments thirty, sixty, and ninety days from delivery. Adam says he has authority to make such a contract. John calls Petri and asks if Adam is authorized to make contracts giving a discount. No mention is made of payment terms. Petri replies that Adam has authority to make discounts on purchase orders. On the basis of this information, John orders $10,000 worth of plumbing supplies and fixtures. The goods are delivered and are being sold. One week later John receives a bill for $9,500, due in thirty days. John insists he owes only $9,000 and can pay it in three equal installments, at thirty, sixty, and ninety days from delivery. Discuss the liability of Petri and John only.

2. Alice Adams is a purchasing agent–employee for the A & B Coal Supply partnership. Adams has authority to purchase the coal needed by A & B to satisfy the needs of its customers. While Adams is leaving a coal mine from which she has just purchased a large quantity of coal, her car breaks down. She walks into a small roadside grocery store for help. While there, she runs into Will Wilson. Wilson owns 360 acres back in the mountains with all mineral rights. Wilson, in need of money, offers to sell Adams the property at $1,500 per acre. Upon inspection of the property, Adams forms the opinion that the subsurface contains valuable coal deposits. Adams contracts to purchase the property for A & B Coal Company, signing the contract "A & B Coal Supply, Alice Adams, agent." The closing date is August 1. Adams takes the contract to the partnership. The managing partner is furious, as A & B is not in the property business. Later, just before closing, both Wilson and the partnership learn that the value of the land is at least $15,000 per acre. Discuss the rights of A & B and Wilson concerning the land contract.

3. Paula Development Enterprises hires Able to act as its agent to purchase a 1,000-acre tract of land from Thompson for $1,000 per acre. Paula Enterprises does not wish Thompson to know that it is the principal or that Able is

its agent. Paula wants the land for a new country housing development, and Thompson may not sell the land for that purpose or may demand a premium price. Able makes the contract for the purchase, signing only Able's name as purchaser and not disclosing to Thompson the agency relationship. The closing and transfer of deed are to take place on September 1.

(a) If Thompson learns of Paula's identity on August 1, can Thompson legally refuse to deed the property on September 1? Explain.

(b) Paula gives Able the money for the closing, but Able absconds with the money, causing a breach of Able's contract at the date of closing. Thompson then learns of Paula's identity and wants to enforce the contract. Discuss fully Thompson's rights under these circumstances.

4. Able is hired as a traveling salesperson for the ABC Tire Corporation. Able has a designated geographic area and time schedule within which to solicit orders and service customers. Able is given a company car to use in covering the territory. One day, Able decides to take his personal car to cover part of his territory. It is 11:00 A.M., and Able has just finished calling on all customers in the city of Tarrytown. Able's next appointment is in the city of Austex, twenty miles down the road, at 2:00 P.M. Able starts out for Austex, but halfway there he decides to visit a former college roommate who runs a farm ten miles off the main highway. Able is enjoying his visit with his former roommate when he realizes that it is 1:45 P.M. and that he will be late for the appointment in Austex. Driving at a high speed down the country road to reach the main highway, Able crashes his car into Thomas's tractor, severely injuring Thomas, a farmer. Thomas claims he can hold the ABC Tire Corporation liable for his injuries. Discuss fully ABC's liability in this situation.

5. Adam is an agent for Fish Galore, Inc. Adam has express authority to solicit orders and receive payments in advance of shipment. He is well known as an agent in the region. One of his customers, Seafood Quality, has been a regular customer for five years, has usually made large orders, and has always paid Adam in advance to get the discount offered by Fish Galore. Fish Galore learns that Adam has incurred large gambling debts and has recently used some of the customers' payments to pay off these debts. When Adam cannot reimburse Fish Galore, he is fired. Fish Galore hires a new agent and publishes in regional newspapers the fact that the new agent will be covering the territory. Desperately in need of cash, Adam solicits a large order from Seafood Quality and receives payment. Then he calls on a new customer, Catfish Heaven, who also gives Adam an order and payment. Adam absconds with the money. Fish Galore refuses to honor either order. Seafood Quality and Catfish Heaven claim Fish Galore is in breach of contract. Discuss fully their claims.

6. Under the Fair Housing Act, racial discrimination in housing practices (including the renting of apartments) is prohibited. Leach owned two apartment complexes in Columbus, Mississippi, and employed Jenkins as office manager of the apartments. For the entire time that she managed the apartments, Jenkins did not rent to any blacks, even though blacks made up about 37 percent of the local population. The United States Attorney General brought suit against Leach for violations of the Fair Housing Act. Leach contended that Jenkins did all the renting and made all the decisions as to whom she rented the apartments to. Did the government win its case against Leach? [United States v. Real Estate Development Corp., 347 F.Supp. 776 (N.D.Miss. 1972)]

7. Richard Lanno worked for the Thermal Equipment Co. as a project engineer. Lanno was allowed to keep a company van and tools at his home because he routinely drove to work sites directly from his home and because he was often needed for unanticipated trips during his off hours. The arrangement had been made for the convenience of Thermal Equipment, even though Lanno's managers permitted him to make personal use of the van. Lanno was involved in a collision with Lazar while driving the van home from work. At the time of the accident, Lanno had taken a detour in order to stop at a store—he had intended to purchase a few items and then go home. Lazar sued Thermal Equipment, claiming that Lanno had acted while within the scope of his employment. Discuss whether Lazar was able to recover and why. Can employees act on behalf of their employers and themselves at the same time? [Lazar v. Thermal Equipment Corp., 148 Cal.App.3d 458, 195 Cal.Rptr. 890 (1983)]

8. Fred Hash worked for Van Stavern Construction Company as a field supervisor in charge of constructing a new plant facility. Hash entered into a contract with Sutton's Steel & Supply to supply steel to the construction site in several installments. Hash gave the name of B. D. Van Stavern, the president and owner of the construction firm, instead of the firm name as the party for whom he was acting. The contract and the subsequent invoices all had B. D. Van Stavern's name on them. Several loads were delivered by Sutton. All of the invoices were signed by Van Stavern employees, and corporate checks were made out to Sutton. When Sutton Steel later sued Van Stavern personally for unpaid debts totaling $40,437, it claimed that Van Stavern had ratified the acts of his employee, Hash, by allowing payment on previous invoices. Although Van Stavern had had no knowledge of the unauthorized arrangement, had he legally ratified the agreement by his silence? Explain. [Sutton's Steel & Supply, Inc. v. Van Stavern, 496 So.2d 1360 (La.App. 1986)]

9. Garcia was an employee of Van Groningen & Sons, which operated an orchard, and one of Garcia's duties was to drive a tractor through the orchard pulling machinery behind. On one particular occasion, Garcia invited his nephew Perez to accompany him on the job as he drove the tractor through the orchard. Perez had to sit on the tool box because there was only one seat on the tractor. Perez was knocked off by a tree branch and was severely injured when the tractor machinery ran over his leg. Perez sued Van Groningen & Sons under the theory of *respondeat superior*. Van Groningen testified that the company forbade anyone but the driver to ride on the tractor because of the danger and that Garcia had personally been advised of this rule. Discuss what chance Perez has of recovering under the doctrine of *respondeat superior*. [Perez v. Van Groningen & Sons, Inc., 41 Cal.3d 962, 719 P.2d 676, 227 Cal.Rptr. 106 (1986)]

Focus on Ethics

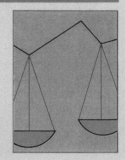

Agency and Employment

Agency law is concerned with duties, rights, and liabilities of principals and agents. Foremost in the area of agency is the nature of duty.

THE DUTY OF THE AGENT TO THE PRINCIPAL

What is the nature of the duty that an agent owes to a principal in an employment situation? Does the agent have the duty to disclose all favorable information that could be used by the principal to increase the principal's profits? Or does the agent have the right to use some of the information gleaned during the course of normal employment for his or her own benefit? In order to understand the answers to these questions, we must understand the kind of relationship that exists between a principal and an agent.

The very nature of the principal-agent relationship is one of trust, which we call a fiduciary relationship. Because of this, it is expected that an agent owes certain duties to the principal. These duties include being loyal and obedient, informing the principal of important facts concerning the agency, accounting to the principal for property or money

received, and performing with reasonable diligence and skill.

Thus, ethical conduct would prevent an agent from representing two principals in the same transaction, or making a secret profit from the agency, or failing to disclose the interest of the agent in property the principal was purchasing. The expected ethical conduct of the agent has evolved into rules that, if breached, cause the agent to be held liable.

What about looking beyond the duty to the principal and considering one's duty to society? Those employees of Firestone who knew of the company's defective tires in the early 1980s presumably could have divulged that information to the public (at the risk of losing their jobs, of course). Furthermore, employees aware of deliberate and fraudulent cost overruns on government contracts could make this information public, once again at the risk of losing their jobs. Some scholars have argued that many of the greatest "evils" in the past twenty-five years have been accomplished in the name of "duty" to the principal. Duty in this context means placing the well-being of the principal above that of the public.

AGENCY BY ESTOPPEL

Sometimes a third person may be led to believe, by either the agent or the principal, that an individual is acting in the capacity of an agent. For the most part, agency law seems to follow ethical considerations in such situations; the notion of agency by estoppel is one in which the potential harm caused by the apparent agency relationship to the innocent third party is either prevented altogether or minimized.

THE DUTY OF THE PRINCIPAL TO THE AGENT

Assuming that agents owe certain fiduciary duties to their principals, do principals have corresponding ethical duties to agents? In the law, principals have certain defined duties, such as compensation and reimbursement of certain expenses.

Principals also owe their agents a duty of cooperation. One might expect most principals to cooperate with their agents out of self-interest, but this is not universally the case. Suppose a principal hires an agent on commission to sell a building, and the agent puts considerable time and expense into the process. If the principal changes his or her mind and decides to retain the building, he or she might want to prevent the agent from completing a sale. Is such action ethical, or does it violate a principal's duty of cooperation? What alternatives would such a principal have?

Another duty of principals is to provide safe working conditions. The principal therefore should not expose agents to unreasonable hazards as they go about their work. The definition of *safe* remains a difficult one, however, as every job probably entails some degree of unavoidable risk. Suppose an employer hires a delivery person and supplies a truck. Must the truck contain seat belts to ensure safe working conditions? What about airbags or special safety glass?

Significantly, most of the duties described above are negotiable at law. In forming a contract, the principal and the agent can extend or abridge many of the ordinary duties owed in such a relationship. Legal rules generally come into play when the contract is silent or ambiguous on a point. Allowing the parties to negotiate their relative duties seems ethically fair, so long as the parties are able to understand their rights and make informed decisions.

RESPONDEAT SUPERIOR

Additional ethical issues arise concerning the doctrine of *respondeat superior,* under which the employer may be liable for the torts of employees. Why should an innocent employer be required to pay for the actions of others? Consider the following examples from the world of sports.

Traditionally, the doctrine of assumption of risk has prevented plaintiffs from recovering damages for sports injuries on the assumption that the players have "consented" to participate in the sports. Thus, in *Moe v. Steenberg* [275 Minn. 448, 147 N.W.2d 587 (1966)], a plaintiff ice skater was denied recovery for injuries sustained when another skater, the defendant, was skating backwards and collided with the plaintiff. The general notion prevailed that the participant in a sport assumes the risks that are inherent in it. The question arises, however, as to what type of recovery should be allowed with respect to intentional actions committed by members of a professional sports team. More specifically, should potential plaintiffs be allowed to bring an action against team owners under the doctrine of *respondeat superior* and to recover damages for intentional torts committed by the teams' players? Does our collection of shared beliefs require that this doctrine be extended in such a way? Several cases have indicated a new trend toward recovery by a professional athlete from an opposing team's owner.

In 1973, in a game between the Denver Broncos and the Cincinnati Bengals, Dale Hackbart was playing safety for the Broncos and Charles Clark was playing fullback for the Bengals. When Hackbart attempted to block Clark to make room for a teammate to run with an intercepted pass, Clark hit Hackbart in the back of the head with his right forearm. This blow resulted in a severe neck injury, which forced Hackbart to end his career. A trial court dismissed Hackbart's

actions on the grounds that he had assumed the risk of such an injury and that the judiciary was not "well suited" to determine which civil restraints should be applied to professional football. The Tenth Circuit, in *Hackbart v. Cincinnati Bengals, Inc.* [601 F.2d 516 (10th Cir. 1979)], however, reversed the trial court's decision and held that the owner of the team (as well as Clark) could be liable under the doctrine of *respondeat superior.*

Do you agree with the Tenth Circuit's recognition of a cause of action based on *respondeat superior* and its conclusion that an owner of a professional sports team may be held liable for intentional torts committed by team members? Even though it doesn't seem "fair" to treat professional sports differently from employer-employee relationships, it is still interesting to explore the policy rationales behind the doctrine of *respondeat superior* as applied in this context.

The prevailing rationale for retaining *respondeat superior* in our laws is based upon the employer's assumed ability to pay. Our collection of shared beliefs suggests that an injured party should be afforded the most effective relief possible. Thus, even though an employer may be absolutely innocent, the employer has a "deeper pocket" and will be more likely to have the funds necessary to make the injured party whole. Yet this rationale begins to weaken in the area of professional sports. Professional athletes are presently among the highest-paid employees in our society. In this context, does it seem ethical to apply the doctrine of *respondeat superior* and impose liability upon owners without fault? Unlike many other employment relationships, professional athletes frequently have the ability to pay a substantial damage claim.

Another rationale for the doctrine of *respondeat superior* is based upon the theory of deterrence. This rationale proposes that employers will take greater precautions to deter wrongful acts by their employees if they know that they may be liable for their employees' wrongful conduct. Yet wouldn't holding a player liable for his or her own wrongful conduct be more effective in deterring this type of undesirable behavior? Isn't it reasonable to assume that deterrence might be better served if a player knew that he or she, not the team owner, would be held solely liable for such conduct?

DISCUSSION QUESTIONS

1. How much obedience and loyalty does an employee owe an employer? How should this duty be balanced against the public interest?

2. If an agent injures a third party during the course of employment, to what extent should the employer be held liable for the agent's actions? Does the amount of negligence on the part of an agent have any bearing on your answer? Is there any situation in which the agent should be held personally liable for his or her actions that harm third parties?

3. The question above relates to the doctrine of *respondeat superior.* What ethical considerations generated this doctrine?

4. Agency by estoppel occurs when the principal's actions create the appearance of authority in a presumed agent. Do you think that agency by estoppel should be allowed under all circumstances? Or, rather, do you believe that the third person should be required to prove that he or she reasonably believed that the agent had authority?

5. The termination of an agency agreement can occur by operation of law. In particular, when unforeseen circumstances (such as impossibility of performance or bankruptcy) occur, termination by operation of law may take place. What ethical considerations are involved here?

BUSINESS ORGANIZATIONS

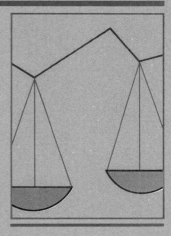

Chapter 34

Forms of Business Organization

There are basically three types of business organizations—sole proprietorships, partnerships, and corporations. Other types of business organizations also exist—among them joint ventures, syndicates or investment groups, joint stock companies, business trusts, and cooperatives—but these are essentially hybrid forms of partnerships or of corporations.

This chapter will first describe these various forms of business organization and will then compare a partnership with a corporation in more detail.

SOLE PROPRIETORSHIP

The simplest form of business is a sole proprietorship. The owner is the business. This form is used by anyone who does business without creating a business entity. One usually associates a sole proprietorship with small enterprises, although this is not necessarily the case. The sole proprietor's personal estate is liable for his or her business debts. The advantages and disadvantages of a sole proprietorship are discussed later in this chapter.

PARTNERSHIP

A partnership arises from an agreement, express or implied, between two or more persons to carry on a business for profit. Partners are co-owners of a business and have joint control over its operation and the right to share in its profits. Partners are also agents of one another and may individually bind the entire partnership in agreements. Both partnerships and sole proprietorships are creatures of common law rather than of statute. No particular form of partnership agreement is necessary for the creation of a partnership, although it is desirable that the agreement be in writing. The Uniform Partnership Act (UPA), adopted in forty-nine states,[1] governs the

---

1. Only the state of Louisiana has not adopted the UPA. Guam, the District of Columbia, and the Virgin Islands have also adopted the UPA. See Appendix C for the complete text of the UPA.

operation of partnerships *in the absence* of express agreements. Basically, the partners may agree to almost any terms when establishing the partnership so long as they are not illegal or contrary to public policy. The UPA comes into play only if the partners have neglected to include a necessary term. In a sense, then, the UPA is a gap-filler. It is not a code that must be followed in order for a partnership to be created.

A partnership is a legal entity for limited purposes, such as the partnership name and title of ownership and property. Otherwise, it is not a legal entity. Rather, the personal net worth of the partners is subject to partnership obligations. The partnership itself is not subject to levy for federal income taxes; only an information return must be filed. A partner's profit from the partnership (whether or not the partner actually receives the income during that tax year) is taxed as individual income to the partner.

Chapter 35 will detail the creation and termination of general partnerships. Chapter 36 will deal with the duties, rights, and liabilities of partners to each other and to third persons.

Limited Partnerships

A special—and popular—form of partnership is the limited partnership, which consists of at least one general partner and one or more limited partners. One of the major benefits of becoming a limited partner is limited liability, with respect to both lawsuits brought against the partnership and money at risk. The maximum money at risk for the limited partners is defined by the limited partnership agreement, which specifically states how much each limited partner must contribute to the partnership.

The limited partnership is created by an agreement; but unlike a general partnership, the limited partnership does not come into existence until a certificate of partnership is filed appropriately in a state. Furthermore, unlike a general partnership, a limited partnership is completely a creature of statute. If the statute is not followed almost to the letter, the courts will hold that a general partnership exists instead. Then those who thought their liability was limited by their investment in a limited partnership will be held generally liable to the full extent of their personal net worth.

Once a limited partnership has been created, the law treats the general partner exactly the same as any partner in ordinary partnership. The limited partner is treated basically as an investor; that is, the limited partner contributes capital but does not participate in the management or control of the partnership. As long as the limited partner's activities are confined to the investor role, the limited partner's liability is limited to his or her capital contribution, and personal assets are not subject to partnership obligations. Limited partnerships are discussed in more detail in Chapter 37.

All states permit limited partnerships. Thirteen states have adopted the Uniform Limited Partnership Act (ULPA) and thirty-six its revision, the Revised Uniform Limited Partnership Act (RULPA). These acts govern the organization and operation of limited partnerships. The ULPA and RULPA have been included as Appendices D and E in this text.

BUSINESS CORPORATIONS

The most important form of business organization is the corporation. A corporation comes into existence by an act of the state and therefore is a legal entity. It typically has perpetual existence. One of the key features of a corporation is that the liability of its owners is limited to their investments. Their personal estates are usually not liable for the obligations of the corporation.

Corporations consist of shareholders, who are the owners of the business. A board of directors, elected by the shareholders, manages the business. The board of directors normally employs officers to oversee day-to-day operations.

The law governing the formation, management and operation, liability, and termination of corporations will be discussed in detail in Chapters 38 to 43.

OTHER FORMS OF BUSINESS ORGANIZATION

There are a number of other, less common forms of business organization. They include joint ventures; syndicates, or investment groups; joint stock companies; business trusts; and cooperatives.

Joint Ventures

When two or more persons or entities combine their interests in a particular business enterprise and agree to share in losses or profits jointly or in proportion to their contributions, they are engaged in a joint venture. The joint venture is treated in much the same way as a partnership, but it differs in that it is created in contemplation of a limited activity or a single transaction.

For example, Able and Cain pool their resources to buy an old boat, remodel it, and sell it, dividing the profits. This does not create a partnership but a joint venture. The same is true if Able, owning a piece of land, and Cain, owning an adjoining piece of land, agree to sell both parcels together as one unit to the highest bidder and then divide the proceeds proportionately to the value of each parcel.

Members of a joint venture usually have limited powers to bind their co-venturers. A joint venture is normally not a legal entity and therefore cannot be sued as such, but its members can be sued individually. Usually, joint ventures are taxed as partnerships are. They range in size from very small activities to huge, multimillion-dollar joint actions engaged in by some of the world's largest corporations.

Syndicates, or Investment Groups

A group of individuals getting together to finance a particular project, such as the building of a shopping center or the purchase of a professional basketball franchise, is called a syndicate or an investment group. The form of such groups varies considerably. They may exist as corporations or as general or limited partnerships. In some cases, the members merely own property jointly and have no legally recognized business arrangement.

Joint Stock Companies

A joint stock company or association is a true hybrid of a partnership and a corporation. It has many characteristics of a corporation but is usually treated as a partnership. For example, the joint stock company resembles a corporation in that its ownership is represented by transferable shares of stock, it is usually managed by directors and officers of the company or association, and it can have a perpetual existence.

Most of its other features, however, are more characteristic of a partnership. For example, the joint stock company is formed by agreement (not statute); property is usually held in the names of the members; shareholders have personal liability; and generally the company is not treated as a legal entity for purposes of a lawsuit. Shareholders are not treated as agents of each other, however, as would be the case if the company were a true partnership.

The joint stock company is not widely used, but a modern example is the American Express Company, which was a joint stock association until 1965.

Business Trusts

A business trust is created by a written trust agreement that sets forth the interests of the beneficiaries and the obligations and powers of the trustees. With a business trust, legal ownership and management of the property of the business stays with one or more of the trustees, and the profits are distributed to the beneficiaries.

The business trust was started in Massachusetts and represented an attempt on the part of its founders to obtain the limited liability advantage of corporate status while avoiding certain restrictions on a corporation's ownership and development of real property. The business trust was more popular at the turn of the century than it is today. Its decline is a result of antitrust laws (discussed in detail in Chapter 48).

The business trust resembles a corporation in many aspects. Death or bankruptcy of a beneficiary does not terminate the trust, and beneficiaries are not personally responsible for the debts or obligations of the business trust. In fact, in a number of states business trusts must pay corporate taxes. In a few states only, the beneficiaries are treated as partners, and they are personally liable to business creditors; thus the limited-liability advantage is eliminated.

Cooperatives

A cooperative is an association, either incorporated or not, that is organized to provide an economic service without profit to its members (or shareholders). An incorporated cooperative is subject to state laws governing nonprofit corporations.

It will make distributions of dividends, or profits, to its owners on the basis of their transactions with the cooperative rather than on the basis of the amount of capital they contributed. Cooperatives that are unincorporated are often treated as partnerships. The members have joint liability for the cooperatives' acts. Cooperatives are generally formed by groups of individuals who wish to pool their resources in order to gain some advantage in the marketplace. Consumer purchasing co-ops are formed to obtain lower prices through quantity discounts. Seller marketing co-ops are formed to control the market and thereby obtain higher prices from consumers. Often, cooperatives are exempt from certain federal laws—for example, antitrust statutes—because of their special status.

THE ADVANTAGES AND DISADVANTAGES OF A SOLE PROPRIETORSHIP

A major advantage of a sole proprietorship is that the proprietor receives all the profits, because he or she takes all the risk. In addition, it is often easier and less costly to start a sole proprietorship than to start any other kind of business. Few legal forms must be completed; and since the proprietor makes all the decisions, the problem of reaching agreement among a number of people is avoided. The sole proprietor is also free from corporate income taxes, paying only personal income taxes on profits. These taxes are not necessarily lower than those for a corporation; however, "double taxes" are avoided. (That is, a corporation may have to pay taxes on its profits, which are then distributed to shareholders, who are also taxed on their earnings.) Furthermore, the operation may receive credit not only to the extent that the business's balance sheet warrants but to the full extent that the sole proprietor's resources justify.

A major disadvantage of the sole proprietorship is that, as sole owner, the proprietor alone bears the risk of losses. In addition, the proprietor's opportunity to raise capital is limited to personal funds and the funds of those who are willing to make loans. Additionally, and perhaps more importantly for many potential entrepreneurs, the sole proprietor has unlimited liability, or legal re-

sponsibility, for all obligations incurred in doing business.

COMPARING A PARTNERSHIP WITH A CORPORATION

Exhibit 34–1 offers an abbreviated comparison of a partnership and a corporation, giving the essential advantages and disadvantages of each. Other points of comparison concern the liability of owners, tax considerations, and the need for capital.

Liability of Owners

The form of the organization does not always absolutely determine the liability of the owners. Generally, sole proprietorships and general partners have personal liability, and limited partners and shareholders of corporations have liability limited to their investment. Because of this, creditors frequently look to personal liability in extending credit. For example, a bank may be unwilling to lend money to a corporation that is relatively small and has only a few shareholders. The corporate form of the business does not guarantee that it is a better risk for the bank. Typically, in such situations, the relatively few shareholders must personally sign for any loans made to the corporation. That is, the shareholders agree to become personally liable for the loan. In essence, they must be guarantors for the corporation's debt. Hence, the corporate form of business does not prevent them from having personal liability in such a case, because they have assumed the liability voluntarily.

Tax Considerations

Various tax considerations must be taken into account in a comparison of a partnership with a corporation. These considerations are listed in Exhibit 34–2.

Need for Capital

One of the most common reasons for changing from a sole proprietorship to a partnership or a corporation is the need for additional capital to finance expansion. A sole proprietor can seek partners who will bring capital with them. The part-

Exhibit 34–1 Comparing a Partnership with a Corporation

CHARACTERSTIC	PARTNERSHIP	CORPORATION
1. Method of creation	Created by agreement of the parties.	Charter issued by state—created by statutory authorization.
2. Legal position	Not a separate legal entity in many states.	Always a legal entity separate and distinct from its owners—a legal fiction that allows it to own property and be a party to litigation.
3. Liability	Unlimited liability (except for limited partners in a limited partnership).	Limited liability of shareholders—shareholders are not personally liable for the debts of the corporation.
4. Duration	Terminated by agreement of the partners, by the death of one or more of the partners, by withdrawal of a partner, by bankruptcy, etc.	Can have perpetual existence.
5. Transferability of interest	Although partnership interest can be assigned, assignee does not have full rights of a partner.	Shares of stock can be transferred.
6. Management	Each general partner has a direct and equal voice in management unless expressly agreed otherwise in the partnership agreement. (A limited partner has no rights in management in a limited partnership.)	Shareholders elect directors, who set policy and appoint officers.
7. Taxation	Each partner pays *pro rata* share of income taxes on net profits, whether or not they are distributed.	Double taxation—corporation pays income tax on net profits, with no deduction for dividends, and shareholders pay income tax on disbursed dividends they receive.
8. Organizational fees, annual license fees, and annual reports	None.	All required.
9. Transaction of business in other states	Generally no limitation.[a]	Normally must qualify to do business and obtain certificate of authority.

[a] A few states have enacted statutes requiring that foreign partnerships qualify to do business there—for example, 3 N.H.Rev.Stat.Ann. Chapter 305-A in New Hampshire.

nership might be able to secure more funds from potential lenders than could the sole proprietor. But when a firm wants to expand greatly, simply increasing the number of partners can lead to too many partners and make it difficult for the firm to operate effectively. Therefore, incorporation may be the best choice for an expanding business or-ganization. There are many possibilities for obtaining more capital by issuing shares of stock. The original owners will find that although their proportion of ownership has been reduced, they are able to expand much more rapidly by selling shares in the company.

Exhibit 34–2 Partnership versus Corporation—Tax Considerations

TAX ASPECT	PARTNERSHIP	CORPORATION
1. Federal income tax	Partner is taxed on proportionate share of partnership income, even if not distributed; the partnership files information returns only.	Income of the corporation is taxed; stockholders are also taxed on distributed dividends. Corporation must file corporate income tax forms.
2. Accumulation	Partners are taxed on accumulated as well as distributed earnings.	Corporate stockholders are not taxed on accumulated earnings. In some instances, however, the corporation must pay a penalty tax for accumulations of income.
3. Capital gains	All partners are taxed on their proportionate share of capital gains, which are taxed at ordinary income rate.	Corporation is taxed on capital gains and losses.
4. Exempt interest (Exempt interest can come, for example, from municipal bonds.)	Partners are not taxed on exempt interest received from the firm.	Any exempt interest distributed by a corporation is fully taxable income to the stockholders.
5. Pension plan	Partners can adopt a Keogh Plan, an IRA, or a 401-K Plan.	Employees and officers who are also stockholders can be beneficiaries of a pension trust. The corporation can deduct its payments to the trust.
6. Social security	Partners must pay a self-employment tax (13.3 percent by 1990).	All compensation to officers and employee stockholders is subject to social security taxation up to the maximum.
7. Death benefits (excluding those provided by insurance)	There is no exemption for payments to partners' beneficiaries.	Benefits up to $5,000 can be received tax-free by stockholders' and employees' beneficiaries.
8. State taxes	The partnership is not subject to taxes. State income taxes are paid by each partner.	The corporation is subject to state income taxes (although these taxes can be deducted on federal returns).

QUESTIONS AND CASE PROBLEMS

1. Suppose Ann, Betty, and Carla are college graduates, and Ann has come up with an idea for a new product that she believes could make the three of them very rich. Her idea is to manufacture beer dispensers for home use, and her goal is to market them to consumers throughout the Midwest. Ann's personal experience qualifies her to be both first-line supervisor and general manager of the new firm. Betty is a born salesperson. Carla has little interest in sales or management but would like to invest a large sum of money that she has inherited from her aunt. What should

Ann, Betty, and Carla consider in deciding which form of business organization to adopt?

2. In the situation described in Question 1, assume that Carla is willing to put her inherited money in the business but does not want any further liability should the beer dispenser manufacturing business fail. Alternatively, the bank is willing to lend some capital at a 14 percent interest rate, but it will do so only if certain restrictions are placed on management decisions. The bank's plan is not satisfactory to Ann or Betty, and the two decide to bring Carla into the business. Under these circumstances, discuss which types of business organizations are best suited to meet the needs of Carla.

3. The limited-liability aspect of the corporation is one of the most important reasons that firms choose to organize as corporations rather than as partnerships or sole proprietorships. Limited liability means that if a corporation is not able to meet its obligations with corporate assets, creditors will not be allowed to look to the owners (stockholders) of the corporation to satisfy their claims. Assume that Ann and Betty (from Question 1) do not have a wealthy friend like Carla who wishes to go into business with them and that therefore they must borrow money to start their business. Ann and Betty decide to incorporate. What do you think a lender will ask them when they seek a loan? What effect does this have on the "advantage" of limited liability under incorporation?

4. Assume that Bateson Corporation is considering entering into two contracts, one with a joint stock company that distributes home products east of the Mississippi River, and the other with a business trust formed by a number of sole proprietors who are sellers of home products on the West Coast. Both contracts involve large capital outlays for the Bateson Corporation to supply each business with beer dispensers. In both business organizations, at least two shareholders or beneficiaries are personally wealthy, but each business organization has limited financial resources. The owner-managers of Bateson Corporation are not familiar with either form of business organization. Since each form resembles a corporation, they are concerned with the possibility of liability in the event that either business organization breaches the contract by failing to make the deferred payments. Discuss fully Bateson's concern.

5. Gustave Peterson contacted his family doctor, Leland C. Reichelt, complaining of abdominal pain. The doctor recommended gallbladder surgery. Dr. George Fortier performed the surgery, and Dr. Reichelt assisted. It was Dr. Reichelt's normal practice to refer patients to Dr. Fortier for surgery, and each charged the patient separately for his services. During the operation, a metal clip was inadvertently left inside Peterson's abdominal cavity. It eventually formed a stone, which later caused Peterson chest and gastric pain. Peterson repeatedly complained to Dr. Reichelt, who diagnosed the problem as related to either a hernia or stress. Peterson finally sought the advice of another physician, Dr. S. J. Spellman, who upon performing surgery discovered the metal clip. Peterson filed suit against both Dr. Reichelt and Dr. Fortier for malpractice under the theory that Fortier and Reichelt were engaged in a joint enterprise (joint venture). Discuss whether the two doctors were joint venturers. [Peterson v. Fortier, 406 N.W.2d 563 (Minn.App. 1987)]

6. Rusty Holler, the defendant, was looking for someone to pasture cattle on his land in 1971. He entered into a contract with the partnership of L. W. Maxfield and Bill Poage. The contract called for Holler to furnish grass for slightly over a thousand head of cattle. The partnership was to furnish the cattle and pay for trucking costs and labor. After these costs were deducted, Holler and the partnership would split the profits fifty-fifty. There was no agreement as to sharing of losses. For three years the parties made a profit, but in the fourth year they suffered a loss. The partnership wanted to hold Holler liable as either a partner or a joint venturer. Discuss the partnership's claims. [P & M Cattle Co. v. Holler, 559 P.2d 1019 (Wyo. 1977)]

Chapter 35

PARTNERSHIPS
Creation and Termination

To a great extent, partnership law derives from agency law. (See Chapters 32 and 33.) Each partner is considered an agent of the partnership. Thus, to a certain extent, agency concepts apply.

In one important way, however, partnership law is distinct from agency law. A partnership is based on a voluntary contract between two or more competent persons, who agree to place some or all of their money, effects, labor, and skill in a business with the understanding that profits and losses will be proportionately shared. On the other hand, in an agency relationship, one person (the agent) can be compensated from business profits but does not agree to share the ordinary business losses and has no ownership interest in the business.

Partnership law in the United States is codified in the Uniform Partnership Act (UPA). The UPA, which has been adopted in forty-nine states, replaces the body of common law principles dealing with partnerships.[1] As pointed out in the preceding chapter, a partnership agreement can include virtually any terms that the partners wish, unless they are illegal or contrary to public policy. Only when certain essential terms are left out does the UPA come into play.

In the past, attempts to formulate a concrete definition of the term *partnership* caused endless controversy among judges, lawyers, and members of the business community. A **partnership** is defined by the UPA as "an association of two or more persons to carry on as co-owners a business for profit."[2] Therefore, three essential elements of a partnership are (1) a common ownership interest in an ongoing business, (2) the sharing of the profits and losses of the business, and (3) the right to manage the operations of the partnership.

NATURE OF PARTNERSHIPS

A partnership is sometimes called a *firm* or a company, terms that connote an entity separate and apart from its aggregate members. Sometimes the

1. The UPA was first passed in 1915 by Pennsylvania.
2. UPA Section 6(1).

law of partnership recognizes the independent entity, but for certain other purposes, the law treats the partnership as an aggregate of individual partners. At common law, a partnership was never treated as a separate legal entity. Thus, a common law suit could never be brought by or against the firm in its own name; each individual partner had to sue or be sued.

Partnership as an Entity

Many states today provide specifically that the partnership can be treated as an entity for certain purposes. This usually includes the capacity to sue or be sued, to collect judgments, and to have all accounting procedures in the name of the partnership. In addition, the UPA recognizes that partnership property may be held in the name of the partnership rather than in the names of the individual partners. Finally, federal procedural laws frequently permit the partnership to be treated as an entity in such matters as suits in federal courts, bankruptcy proceedings, and filing of informational federal tax returns. These will be discussed here in some detail.

LEGAL CAPACITY States vary on how a partnership is viewed as a party in a legal suit. Some permit a partnership to sue and be sued in the firm name; others allow a partnership to be sued as an entity but not to sue others in its firm name (that is, the partnership must use the names of the individual partners). Federal courts recognize the partnership as an entity that can sue or be sued when a federal question is involved. Otherwise, federal courts follow the practice adopted by the state in which the federal court is located.

JUDGMENTS Partnership liability is first paid out of partnership assets when a judgment is rendered *against the firm name*. In a general partnership, the personal assets of the individual members are subject to liability if the partnership's assets are inadequate. Even in limited partnerships, at least one of the partners—the general partner—subjects his or her personal assets to liability for the partnership's obligations. Good legal practice dictates that where state law permits a firm to be sued, the partners should be joined as parties to the suit. This ensures that a wide range of assets will be available for paying the judgment.

The general rule is that a judgment creditor of a partnership (a creditor in whose favor a money

judgment has been entered) can execute the judgment against the partners either jointly or severally. In some states, the judgment creditor must, however, exhaust the remedies against partnership property before proceeding to execute against the individual property of the partners. This is referred to as the doctrine of **marshalling assets.** Marshalling assets is a common law equitable doctrine; it is not statutory.

MARSHALLING ASSETS The arrangement or ranking of assets in a certain order toward the payment of debts outstanding is involved in marshalling assets. In particular, when there are two classes of assets and some creditors can enforce their claims against both whereas others can enforce their claims against only one, then the creditors of the former class are compelled to exhaust the assets against which they alone have a claim before they can have recourse to the other assets. This provides for the settlement of as many claims as possible.

As applied to a partnership, the doctrine of marshalling assets requires that the partnership's creditors have first priority to the partnership's assets and that personal creditors of the individual partners have first priority to the individual assets of each partner. When the partnership's assets are insufficient to satisfy a partnership creditor, that creditor does not have access to the assets of any individual partner until the personal creditors of that partner have been satisfied from such assets. This doctrine does not apply to partnerships that are in Chapter 7 proceedings in bankruptcy. (See Chapter 31.)

Consider an example. X, Y, and Z are equal partners. On dissolution of the partnership, the partnership has assets of $100,000 and liabilities of $70,000. The partners therefore have a net equity of $10,000 each. X, Y, and Z have no personal assets but owe $10,000 each in personal debts. Under the rule of marshalling of assets, the personal creditors of X, Y, and Z cannot reach the partnership assets until the $70,000 of partnership liabilities have been paid off. After that, each partner's personal creditors may resort to each partner's $10,000 equity to satisfy their personal claims.

Now assume that the partnership liabilities are $130,000 rather than $70,000 and that partners X and Y are insolvent. Z, on the other hand, has personal assets of $25,000 and personal liabilities of $25,000. The partnership's creditors cannot resort to Z's personal assets, because Z's personal creditors come first and will, in this hypothetical example, exhaust them.

BANKRUPTCY In federal court, an adjudication of bankruptcy *in the firm name* applies only to the partnership entity. It does not constitute personal bankruptcy for the partners. Similarly, the personal bankruptcy of an individual partner does not bring the partnership entity or its assets into bankruptcy.

The doctrine of marshalling assets is modified when a partnership is granted an order of relief in bankruptcy. In such situations, if partnership assets are insufficient to cover debts owed to partnership creditors, each general partner becomes personally liable to the bankruptcy trustee for the amount of the deficiency.

CONVEYANCE OF PROPERTY The title to real or personal property can be held in the firm name. This means that the partnership as an entity can own property apart from that owned by its individual members.[3] Thus, the property can be conveyed (transferred) without each individual partner's joining in the transaction.

At common law, title to real estate could not be held in a partnership's firm name. Each partner was regarded as a co-owner (known in legal terminology as a *tenant in partnership*).[4] Each partner had to join in all conveyances. Although the modern rule of partnership property ownership disregards the need for aggregate action to convey property, there are some practical difficulties to consider.

Most states do not require public records to keep lists of members of a partnership. Hence, in determining the validity of a conveyance in a partnership's name, it may be impossible to tell whether the person executing the deed is actually a partner and has authority to convey. Some states, however, have passed laws requiring firms to file a statement of partnership. This list names members of the firm authorized to execute conveyances on behalf of the firm.

---

3. UPA Section 8(3).

4. The UPA retained this concept. UPA Section 25(1). That is, although property may be held in the name of the partnership, partners are still regarded as co-owners.

Aggregate Theory of Partnership

When the partnership is not regarded as a separate legal entity, it is treated as an *aggregate* of the individual partners. For example, for federal income tax purposes, a partnership is not a taxpaying entity. The income or losses incurred by it are "passed through" the partnership framework and attributed to the partners on their individual tax returns. The partnership as an entity has no tax liability. It is an entity only for the filing of an informational return with the IRS, indicating the profit and loss that each partner will report on his or her individual tax return.

FORMATION OF A PARTNERSHIP

A partnership is ordinarily formed by an agreement among the parties. The law does recognize another form of partnership—*partnership by estoppel*. This form arises when persons who are not partners represent or hold themselves out as partners when dealing with third parties. The liability of partners by estoppel is covered later in this chapter.

A partnership is a voluntary association of individuals. As such, a *true partnership* is generally based on an agreement among the parties that reflects their intention to create a partnership, contribute capital, share profits and losses, and participate in management. The partnership relationship involves a high degree of trust and reliance. Each partner is an agent for the other partners.

Formalities

As a general rule, agreements to form a partnership can be *oral, written,* or *implied by conduct*. Some partnership agreements, however, must be in writing to be legally enforceable within the Statute of Frauds. (See Chapter 12 for details.) For example, a partnership agreement that, by its terms, is to continue for more than one year or one that authorizes the partners to deal in real property transfers must be evidenced by a sufficient writing. A sample partnership agreement is shown in Exhibit 35-1.

Practically speaking, it is better if the provisions of any partnership agreement are in writing.

Exhibit 35–1 Sample Partnership Agreement

PARTNERSHIP AGREEMENT

This agreement, made and entered into as of the _____, by and among _____ _____ (hereinafter collectively sometimes referred to as "Partners").

WITNESSETH:

Whereas, the Parties hereto desire to form a General Partnership (hereinafter referred to as the "Partnership"), for the term and upon the conditions hereinafter set forth;

Now, therefore, in consideration of the mutual covenants hereinafter contained, it is agreed by and among the Parties hereto as follows:

Article I
BASIC STRUCTURE

Form. The Parties hereby form a General Partnership pursuant to the Laws of _____ _____.

Name. The business of the Partnership shall be conducted under the name of _____ _____.

Place of Business. The principal office and place of business of the Partnership shall be located at _____, or such other place as the Partners may from time to time designate.

Term. The Partnership shall commence on _____, and shall continue for _____ years, unless earlier terminated in the following manner: (a) By the completion of the purpose intended, or (b) Pursuant to this Agreement, or (c) By applicable _____ law, or (d) By death, insanity, bankruptcy, retirement, withdrawal, resignation, expulsion, or disability of all of the then Partners.

Purpose—General. The purpose for which the Partnership is organized is _____

Article II
FINANCIAL ARRANGEMENTS

Each Partner has contributed to the initial capital of the Partnership property in the amount and form indicated on Schedule A attached hereto and made a part hereof. Capital contributions to the Partnership shall not earn interest. An individual capital account shall be maintained for each Partner. If at any time during the existence of the Partnership it shall become necessary to increase the capital with which the said Partnership is doing business, then (upon the vote of the Managing Partner(s)): each party to this Agreement shall contribute to the capital of this Partnership within _ days notice of such need in an amount according to his then Percentage Share of Capital as called for by the Managing Partner(s).

The Percentage Share of Profits and Capital of each Partner shall be (unless otherwise modified by the terms of this Agreement) as follows:

Names	Initial Percentage Share of Profits and Capital

No interest shall be paid on any contribution to the capital of the Partnership. No Partner shall have the right to demand the return of his capital contributions except as herein provided. Except as herein provided, the individual Partners shall have no right to any priority over each other as to the return of capital contributions except as herein provided.

Distributions to the Partners of net operating profits of the Partnership, as hereinafter defined, shall be made at _____. Such distributions shall be made to the Partners simultaneously.

For the purpose of this Agreement, net operating profit for any accounting period shall mean the gross receipts of the Partnership for such period, less the sum of all cash expenses of operation of the Partnership, and such sums as may be necessary to establish a reserve for operating expenses. In determining net operating profit, deductions for depreciation, amortization, or other similar charges not requiring actual current expenditures of cash shall *not* be taken into account in accordance with generally accepted accounting principles.

(Continued on the next page)

Exhibit 35–1 (Continued)

No Partner shall be entitled to receive any compensation from the Partnership, nor shall any Partner receive any drawing account from the Partnership.

Article III
MANAGEMENT

The Managing Partner(s) shall be _____.

The Managing Partner(s) shall have the right to vote as to the management and conduct of the business of the Partnership as follows:

Names   **Vote**

Article IV
DISSOLUTION

In the event that the Partnership shall hereafter be dissolved for any reason whatsoever, a full and general account of its assets, liabilities and transactions shall at once be taken. Such assets may be sold and turned into cash as soon as possible and all debts and other amounts due the Partnership collected. The proceeds thereof shall thereupon be applied as follows:

(a) To discharge the debts and liabilities of the Partnership and the expenses of liquidation.

(b) To pay each Partner or his legal representative any unpaid salary, drawing account, interest or profits to which he shall then be entitled and in addition, to repay to any Partner his capital contributions in excess of his original capital contribution.

(c) To divide the surplus, if any, among the Partners or their representatives as follows: (1) First (to the extent of each Partner's then capital account) in proportion to their then capital accounts. (2) Then according to each Partner's then Percentage Share of [*Capital//Income*].

No Partner shall have the right to demand and receive property in kind for his distribution.

Article V
MISCELLANEOUS

The Partnership's fiscal year shall commence on January 1st of each year and shall end on December 31st of each year. Full and accurate books of account shall be kept at such place as the Managing Partner(s) may from time to time designate, showing the condition of the business and finances of the Partnership; and each Partner shall have access to such books of account and shall be entitled to examine them at any time during ordinary business hours. At the end of each year, the Managing Partner(s) shall cause the Partnership's accountant to prepare a balance sheet setting forth the financial position of the Partnership as of the end of that year and a statement of operations (income and expenses) for that year. A copy of the balance sheet and statement of operations shall be delivered to each Partner as soon as it is available.

Each Partner shall be deemed to have waived all objections to any transaction or other facts about the operation of the Partnership disclosed in such balance sheet and/or statement of operations unless he shall have notified the Managing Partner(s) in writing of his objectives within thirty (30) days of the date on which such statement is mailed.

The Partnership shall maintain a bank account or bank accounts in the Partnership's name in a national or state bank in the State of _____. Checks and drafts shall be drawn on the Partnership's bank account for Partnership purposes only and shall be signed by the Managing Partner(s) or their designated agent.

Any controversy or claim arising out of or relating to this Agreement shall only be settled by arbitration in accordance with the rules of the American Arbitration Association, one Arbitrator, and shall be enforceable in any court having competent jurisdiction.

Witnesses   **Partners**

_____   _____

_____   _____

Dated: _____

The terms of an oral agreement are difficult to prove, because a court must evaluate oral testimony given by persons with an interest in the eventual decision. In addition, in the course of drafting a written agreement, the partners may see potential problems that they would not have seen otherwise.

For instance, Tomkins and Fredericks plan to enter into a partnership agreement to sell tires. Among the provisions to be included is that Tomkins is to provide two-thirds of the capital to start up the business and is to receive two-thirds of the profits in return. The agreement is made orally. Tomkins now sues because Fredericks claims that one-half of the profits should be his. Without a writing, Tomkins may have a hard time overcoming the presumption that he is entitled to only one-half of the profits of a two-person partnership.[5] A partnership agreement, called *articles of partnership*, usually specifies each partner's share of the profits and is binding regardless of how uneven the distribution appears to be.

Duration of Partnership

The partnership agreement can specify the duration of the partnership in terms of a date or the completion of a particular project. This is called a *partnership for a term*. A dissolution without the consent of all the partners prior to the expiration of the partnership term constitutes a breach of the agreement, and the responsible partner can be liable for any losses resulting from it.

If no fixed duration is specified, the partnership is a *partnership at will*. Any partner can dissolve this type of partnership at any time without violating the agreement and without incurring liability for losses to other partners that result from the termination.

Capacity

Any person having the capacity to enter a contract can become a partner. A partnership contract entered into with a minor as a partner is voidable and can be disaffirmed by the minor. (See Chapter 10 for details.)

Lack of legal capacity due to insanity at the time of the agreement likewise allows the purported partner either to avoid the agreement or to enforce it. If a partner is adjudicated mentally incompetent during the course of the partnership, the partnership is not automatically dissolved, but dissolution can be decreed by a court upon petition.

The Corporation as Partner

Disagreement exists on whether a corporation can become a partner. After all, general partners are personally liable for the debts incurred by the partnership. But if one of the general partners is a corporation, then what does personal liability mean?

One view is that a corporation cannot be a partner unless the corporation's articles of incorporation specifically empower it to enter into a partnership as a partner. The opposite view, which prevails today, is contained in the Model Business Corporation Act (see Appendix F), which allows corporations generally to make contracts and incur liabilities. Basically, then, the capacity of corporations to contract is a question of corporation law. The UPA, on the other hand, specifically permits a corporation to be a partner. By definition, "a partnership is an association of two or more persons," and the UPA defines a person as including corporations.[6]

Many states restrict the ability of corporations to become partners, though such restrictions have become less common over the years. Many decisions in jurisdictions that do not permit corporate partners nevertheless validate the arrangements by characterizing them as joint ventures rather than as partnerships.

Mutual Consent

A partnership is a voluntary association of co-owners. It cannot be forced upon anyone. The *intent* to associate is a key element of a partnership, and one cannot join a partnership unless all other partners consent.[7]

---

5. The law assumes that members of a partnership share profits and losses equally unless a partnership agreement provides otherwise [UPA Section 18(a)].

6. UPA Section 2.

7. UPA Section 18(g).

Factors Indicating Partnership Status

Parties commonly find themselves in conflict over whether their business enterprise is a legal partnership, especially in the absence of a formal written contract. To answer this question, the UPA and the courts have developed broad guidelines for interpreting partnership status.

In determining whether a partnership exists, the court usually looks for the three essential elements of partnership mentioned earlier in this chapter:

1. A sharing of profits or losses.
2. A joint ownership of the business.
3. An equal right of management of the business.

A problem arises when evidence is insufficient to establish all three factors. The UPA provides a set of guidelines to be used in this event. For example, the sharing of profits and losses from a business is considered *prima facie* evidence that a partnership has been created. No such inference is made, however, if the profits were received as payment of:

1. A debt by installments or interest on a loan.
2. Wages of an employee.
3. Rent to a landlord.
4. An annuity to a widow or representative of a deceased partner.
5. A sale of goodwill of a business or property.[8]

To illustrate: A debtor businessperson owes a creditor $5,000 on an unsecured debt. To repay the debt, the debtor agrees to pay (and the creditor to accept) 10 percent of the debtor's monthly profits until the loan with interest has been paid. Although the creditor is sharing profits from the business, the debtor and creditor are not presumed to be partners.

Consider another example in which a young college graduate wants to start a retail dress shop. The graduate leases a building from the landlord. Both the landlord and the graduate know that it will take time to establish a clientele, and standard equal rental payments could severely restrict the graduate's ability to purchase inventory. Thus, the lease calls for a minimum low rental payment plus a percentage of the monthly profits for the term of the lease. This sort of arrangement does not make the landlord and tenant partners, even though there is a sharing of profits.

Joint ownership of property, obviously, does not in and of itself create a partnership. Therefore, the fact that MacPherson and Bunker own real property as joint tenants or as tenants in common (a form of joint ownership) does not establish a partnership. In fact, the sharing of gross returns and even profits from such ownership is usually not enough to create a partnership.[9] Thus, if MacPherson and Bunker jointly owned a piece of rural property and leased the land to a farmer, the sharing of the profits from the farming operation by the farmer in lieu of set rental payments would ordinarily not make MacPherson, Bunker, and the farmer partners.

In the following case, a widow attempted to persuade the court that she and her late husband were business partners.

---

8. UPA Section 7(4).

9. UPA Section 7(2),(3).

Case 35.1
MILLER v. CITY BANK & TRUST CO., N.A.
Court of Appeals of Michigan, 1978.
82 Mich.App. 120, 266 N.W.2d 687.

BACKGROUND AND FACTS   *The plaintiff, Miller, was a widow who for tax reasons attempted to establish that a partnership had existed between herself and her late husband. At the trial, she testified that her husband had asked her to marry him and move with him to another city to help run his nursery business. They married, and the plaintiff gave up her well-paying job to move south with her new husband.*

The year after the plaintiff married her husband, a business registration certificate was filed for the nursery, indicating that the business was a partnership. Checking accounts, vehicles, and other equipment were bought and held under the business name. On the other hand, annual tax forms and schedules and a Michigan business activities form indicated that the business was a sole proprietorship. There was never any formal, written partnership agreement.

The plaintiff stated at trial that her husband had described the relationship when he asked her to marry him and at all times since as one of partnership. She was under the impression that they were business partners. Furthermore, the plaintiff testified that her husband told her that she was "the best partner he ever had." The trial court held that no partnership existed, and Miller appealed.

DANHOF, Chief Judge.

*   *   *   *

*   *   * The elements of a partnership are generally considered to include a voluntary association of two or more people with legal capacity in order to carry on, via co-ownership, a business for profit. Co-ownership of the business requires more than merely joint ownership of the property and is usually evidenced by joint control and the sharing of profits and losses. With the intentions of the party to form a partnership as our polestar [guide] we will review the trial court's finding.

It is not disputed that the parties were involved in a business venture for profit and had the legal capacity to form a partnership. However, the evidence relating to co-ownership does not indicate that a legal partnership was contemplated. Prior to the marriage, Mr. Miller [the plaintiff's husband] operated the business and owned all the property. Mrs. Miller [the plaintiff] made no capital contributions except her services. Even though plaintiff worked long and hard hours, this does not establish that the parties had an agreement to form a partnership. This evidence could also be viewed as consistent with an employee-employer relationship or that of a helpful wife who assisted her husband without them intending a legal partnership.

Co-ownership is also indicated by profit sharing. In fact, profit sharing is prima facie evidence of a partnership. However, the [trial] court did not find an agreement to share profits and we cannot say that this was clearly erroneous. [When an appellate court reviews a trial court's findings of fact, it will not disturb the resulting judgment unless there is absolutely no factual evidence to support the trial court's conclusion. In this case, the appellate court showed that there were many possible interpretations to be made from the fact that Mr. and Mrs. Miller each received monthly payments from the business.] That Mr. and Mrs. Miller each received monthly payments from the nursery checking account does not necessarily establish profit sharing. The payments could also be reasonably viewed as salary or wages. Another possible interpretation would be that Mr. Miller was withdrawing money from his sole proprietorship and was dividing it equally because he felt an obligation to share equally with his wife, as a wife rather than a business partner.

Another indicia of co-ownership is mutual agency and control. That Mrs. Miller kept the books, wrote checks, and hired and fired does not necessarily establish any control other than that which might be given to a trusted employee. However, it is not necessary that this control be exercised as long as it exists. In view of the absence of the exercise of control or mutual agency, evidence of an agreement in respect to the division of control is about the only way to prove mutual agency and control. However, no evidence of an agreement with respect to mutual control was presented.

*   *   *   *

The evidence introduced *   *   * indicated that the deceased did not intend to form a legal partnership with his wife. First, there is no written agreement and there is only plaintiff's testimony in support of an oral one. The income tax returns and schedules listed the business as a sole proprietorship, listed Mr. Miller's income as wages and Mrs. Miller's occupation as a housewife. In 1964, Mr. Miller applied for a self-employee retirement deduction plan as a sole proprietorship. Mr. Miller's social security forms listed the business as a sole proprietorship. All the capital contributions came from Mr. Miller and the property remained in his name (or his and his wife's name), and none was transferred to the partnership. Shortly before his death, Mr. Miller deeded his homestead to his wife and himself as tenants by the entirety and this would seem needless if they already owned it as partners. Although none of these facts are conclusive, they are all factors to be weighed in the decision.

DECISION AND REMEDY   *After reviewing the entire trial court record, the appellate court agreed that the presumption of partnership established by the filing of business registration papers was rebutted by other competent evidence, which tended to show that Mr. Miller had intended the business to be run as a sole proprietorship. The trial court's judgment that no partnership existed was affirmed.*

Partnership by Estoppel

Parties who are not partners can hold themselves out as partners and make representations that third persons rely on in dealing with the alleged partners. The law of partnership imposes liability on the alleged partner or partners, but it does not confer any partnership rights on these persons.

There are two aspects of liability. The person representing himself or herself to be a partner in an actual or alleged partnership is liable to any third person who extends credit in good faith reliance on such representations. Similarly, a person who expressly or impliedly *consents* to such misrepresentation of an alleged partnership relationship is also liable to third persons who extend credit in good faith reliance.[10]

For example, Moore owns a small shop. Knowing that the Midland Bank will not make a loan on his credit alone, Moore represents that Lewis, a financially secure businesswoman, is a partner in Moore's business. Lewis knows of Moore's misrepresentation but fails to correct the bank's information. Midland Bank, relying on the strength of Lewis's reputation and credit, extends a loan to Moore. Moore will be liable to the bank for the loan repayment. In many states, Lewis would also be held liable to the bank in such a loan transaction. Lewis has impliedly consented to the misrepresentation and will normally be estopped from denying that she is a partner of Moore. She will be regarded as if she were in fact a partner in Moore's business to the extent that this loan is concerned.

When a real partnership exists and a partner represents that a non-partner is a member of the firm, the non-partner is regarded as an agent whose acts are binding on the partner.

For example, Middle Earth Movers has three partners—Johnson, Mathews, and Huntington. Mathews represents to the business community that Thompson is also a partner. If Thompson negotiates a contract in Middle Earth Movers' name, the contract will be binding on Mathews but normally not on Johnson and Huntington (unless, of course, Johnson and Huntington knew and consented to Mathews's representation).

Again, partnership by estoppel requires that a third person reasonably and detrimentally rely on the representation that a person was part of the partnership.

PARTNERSHIP TERMINATION

Any change in the relations of the partners that demonstrates unwillingness or inability to carry on partnership business dissolves the partnership, resulting in termination.[11] If any of the partners wish to continue the business, they are free to reorganize into a *new* partnership.

The termination of a partnership has two stages—dissolution and winding up. Both must take place before termination is complete.

Dissolution occurs when any partner ceases to be associated with the carrying on of partnership business. *Winding up* is the actual process of collecting and distributing the partnership's assets.

Dissolution is the principal remedy of a partner against co-partners. Events causing the dis-

---

10. UPA Section 16.

11. UPA Section 29.

solution can be grouped into three basic categories:

1. Acts of partners.[12]
2. Operation of law.[13]
3. Judical decree.[14]

---

12. UPA Section 31(1),(2).
13. UPA Section 31(3),(4),(5).
14. UPA Sections 31(6) and 32.

Dissolution terminates the right of a partnership to exist as a going concern, but the partnership continues to exist long enough to wind up its affairs. When winding up is complete, the partnership's *legal* existence is terminated. The concepts of dissolution, winding up, and termination are discussed by the Supreme Court of Minnesota in the next case.

BACKGROUND AND FACTS *The plaintiff, Mary Stilinovich, and the defendant, Nick Maras, were a sister and brother who had formed a partnership by oral agreement with assets left to them by their deceased father. There were accusations of misappropriation on both sides, and a referee was appointed. The referee ordered the dissolution of the partnership because of irreconcilable differences between the partners. It was the referee's task to liquidate the assets of the partnership. Maras tendered a written offer to buy out his sister for $65,000. No such offer was submitted by the plaintiff. A hearing was held, and the referee ordered an accounting (a partner's right to have his or her interest determined by a third party). After the accounting, he ordered the business to be sold to Maras for $65,000. The plaintiff brought this action, contending that the referee had erred in his order. The trial court affirmed the referee's judgment, and Stilinovich appealed.*

Case 35.2
MARAS v. STILINOVICH
Supreme Court of Minnesota, 1978.
268 N.W.2d 541.

YETKA, Justice.
* * * *

[This] was essentially a partnership dissolution in which the undivided two-thirds interest in the land and building was treated as a partnership asset. * * * [W]hether a sale could be ordered to one partner over the objection of the other [is contested.] The parties stipulated that the assets were partnership assets and not subject to mere partition. We find the stipulation is broad enough to allow sale to one partner where the other fails to tender a timely bid.
* * * *

After dissolution, a partnership continues until liquidated or wound up. Although dissolution of a partnership is usually followed by liquidation, a withdrawing partner may be paid his partnership contribution and share of accumulated profits and no liquidation need occur. Minn. [law] provides, in effect, that the partnership affairs must be wound up after dissolution unless otherwise agreed. Crane and Bromberg, Law of Partnership, § 86, suggests that the most logical buyers of a dissolved partnership are the remaining partners, and in the stipulation the parties agreed to one of the partners carrying on the business. Agreements for continuation of partnership business after dissolution are generally valid and enforceable. Oral agreements are generally sufficient to establish a partnership relationship, and we hold that the oral agreement in this case was sufficient to establish the framework for dissolution of a partnership. The referee was clearly acting within the scope of his powers by ordering the sale to Nick Maras.

The court examined the proceedings and concluded that the dissolution was fair. The trial court's judgment was therefore affirmed.

DECISION AND REMEDY

Dissolution of a partnership may come about through the following acts of the partners: by agreement, by the withdrawal of a partner, by the addition of a partner, or by the transfer of a partner's interest.

BY AGREEMENT A partnership can be dissolved when certain events stipulated in the partnership agreement occur. For example, when a partnership agreement expresses a fixed term or a particular business objective to be accomplished, the passing of the date or the accomplishment of the project dissolves the partnership. Partners do not have to abide by the stipulations in the agreement, however. They can mutually agree to dissolve the partnership early or to extend it. If they agree to continue in the partnership, they become *partners at will*, with all the rights and duties remaining as originally agreed.

PARTNER'S POWER TO WITHDRAW A partnership is a personal legal relationship among co-owners. No person can be compelled either to become a partner or to remain one. Implicit in a partnership is each partner's *power* to disassociate from the partnership at any time. For example, Jake and Carla form a partnership with no definite term and no particular undertaking specified— that is, a partnership at will. Both Jake and Carla have the power and the right to withdraw from the partnership. The partnership continues for three years, until one day Carla announces that she no longer wishes to continue in the partnership. Even assuming that Carla's sudden withdrawal will not do irreparable damage to the firm, her act may be sufficient to begin the process of dissolution.

ADMISSION OF NEW PARTNERS A change in the composition of the partnership, whether by the withdrawal of a partner or by the *admission of a new partner* (without the consent of all the partners), results in dissolution. If the remaining or new partners agree to continue in the firm's business, a new partnership arises. The new partnership carries the debts of the dissolved partnership. Creditors of the prior partnership become creditors of the one that is continuing the business.[15]

TRANSFER OF A PARTNER'S INTEREST The UPA provides that neither a voluntary transfer of a part-

ner's interest[16] nor an involuntary sale of a partner's interest for the benefit of creditors[17] by itself dissolves the partnership. (A transferee acquires the right to the transferring partner's profits but does not become a partner; thus, a transferee has no say in the management or administration of the partnership affairs nor a right to inspect the partnership books.) Either occurrence, however, can ultimately lead to judicial dissolution of the partnership, as will be discussed.

Dissolution by Operation of Law

A partnership is dissolved by operation of law in the event of death, bankruptcy, or illegality.

DEATH A partnership is dissolved upon the death of any partner, even if the partnership agreement provides for carrying on the business with the executor of the decedent's estate. Any change in the composition among partners results in a new partnership. (But there is always the possibility of a reformation of the partnership upon the death of a partner.)

BANKRUPTCY The bankruptcy of a partner will dissolve a partnership. Insolvency alone will not result in dissolution. Naturally, bankruptcy of the firm itself will result in dissolution.

ILLEGALITY Any event that makes it unlawful for the partnership to continue its business or for any partner to carry on in the partnership will result in dissolution. Even if the illegality of the partnership business is a cause for dissolution, however, the partners can decide to change the nature of their business and continue in the partnership.

For example, Moran and Becker enter a partnership agreement to run a tuna fishing business. Subsequently, a maritime law prohibiting tuna fishing by private concerns is passed. Moran and Becker must dissolve their partnership if their sole business is to fish for tuna. They can choose to remain partners, however, and fish for something that is not prohibited.

When the illegality applies to an individual partner, the dissolution *must* occur. For example,

---

15. UPA Section 41.

16. A single partner cannot make another person a partner in a firm merely by transferring his or her interest to that person [UPA Section 27].

17. UPA Section 28.

suppose the state legislature passes a law making it illegal for magistrates to engage in the practice of law. If an attorney in a law firm is appointed a magistrate, the partnership must be dissolved. The next case deals with dissolution of a partnership due to illegality.

BACKGROUND AND FACTS　*The plaintiff, Williams, sued the defendant, Burrus, for an accounting and dissolution of their partnership. To form the partnership Williams had provided property to serve as collateral so that Burrus could obtain a bank loan to assist in the purchasing of a restaurant. The partnership agreement, in addition to providing that Williams would supply the collateral, stated that the business would be in Burrus's name and that Burrus alone would apply for a liquor license without mentioning Williams. At the time Williams was an unacceptable licensee according to the Washington State Liquor Control Board. To receive a license issued to a partnership, all members of the partnership have to be qualified to obtain a license. The trial court found the partnership agreement illegal and unenforceable and dismissed Williams's complaint. Williams appealed.*

ANDERSEN, Judge.

* 　* 　* 　*

No state retail liquor license of any kind can be issued to a partnership unless all of the members thereof are qualified to obtain a license, and no licenseholder can allow any other person to use such a license.

Furthermore, a partnership is dissolved by any event which makes it unlawful for the business of the partnership to be carried on or for the members to carry it on in partnership.

The issue of illegality may be raised at any time.

Under the general rule that the courts will not aid either party to an illegal agreement where a partnership is formed to carry out an illegal business or to conduct a lawful business is an illegal manner, the courts will refuse to aid any of the parties thereto in an action against the other. 　* 　* 　*

The appellate court affirmed the trial court's dismissal of Williams's case. Since the partnership was illegal, neither party had any rights that a court would enforce.

The partnership agreement between the partners was not enforceable because it was illegally formed. Both partners were at fault in the making of the contract. When both parties are equally at fault (in pari delicto) the court leaves the parties as it found them. Therefore, the court refused to aid either party in an action against the other.

Case 35.3
WILLIAMS v. BURRUS
Court of Appeals of Washington, Division 1, 1978.
20 Wash.App. 494, 581 P.2d 164.

DECISION AND REMEDY

COMMENTS

Dissolution by Judicial Decree

Dissolution of a partnership can result from judicial decree. For dissolution to occur, an application or petition must be made in an appropriate court. The court then either denies the petition or grants a decree of dissolution. Noting that a court may decree a dissolution under whatever circumstances render it equitable, UPA Section 32 also cites the following situations in which a court can dissolve a partnership: insanity, incapacity, business impracticality, and improper conduct.

INSANITY　A partnership can obtain a judicial declaration of dissolution when a partner is adjudicated insane or is shown to be of unsound mind. This action often involves a series of complex tests and standards.

INCAPACITY   When it appears that a partner has become incapable of performing his or her duties under the partnership agreement, a decree of dissolution may be required. It must appear that the incapacity is permanent and will substantially affect the partner's ability to discharge his or her duties to the firm.

BUSINESS IMPRACTICALITY   When it becomes obvious that the firm's business can be operated only at a loss, judicial dissolution may be ordered.

IMPROPER CONDUCT   A partner's impropriety involving partnership business (for example, fraud perpetrated upon the other partners) or improper behavior reflecting unfavorably upon the firm (for example, habitual drunkenness resulting in gross neglect of the partnership's business) will provide grounds for a judicial decree of dissolution.

Dissolution may also be granted when personal dissension between partners becomes so persistent and harmful as to undermine the confidence and cooperation necessary to carry on the firm's business. (In general, courts are reluctant to allow partners to sue each other except for dissolution.)

If a partner seeks judicial dissolution of the partnership, is this action the same as a withdrawal from the partnership? This question became important in the following case, in which a partnership agreement provided for damages upon a partner's withdrawal from the partnership.

Case 35.4
**IMPERIAL LITHO/
GRAPHICS v. M. J.
ENTERPRISES**
Court of Appeals of Arizona,
Division 1, 1986.
152 Ariz. 68, 730 P.2d 245.

BACKGROUND AND FACTS   *Morris Lerner and Jerry Wisotsky were sole and equal shareholders in Imperial Litho/Graphics (Imperial) and were sole and equal partners in M. J. Enterprises, a real estate partnership formed in 1963 to lease property to Imperial and provide tax benefits to the individual partners. The partnership agreement provided for damages and for a specific division of assets if a partner withdrew. As a result of deterioration in their personal relationship, in 1982 Wisotsky purchased all of the stock in Imperial. In the purchase agreement, Lerner agreed by covenant to not compete or malign the good name of Wisotsky or Imperial. Except for this covenant, the partnership was not affected by the agreement. Wisotsky (Imperial) filed an action in 1983 claiming that the partnership and Lerner had breached the covenant. Lerner (the partnership), in his counterclaim, sued for judicial dissolution of the partnership. Wisotsky answered the counterclaim by opposing dissolution of the partnership and claiming that Lerner had withdrawn from the partnership by filing for dissolution. If Lerner had withdrawn, he would have to pay damages according to the partnership agreement. The trial court found Lerner to be a withdrawing partner and to be bound by the provisions of the partnership agreement relating to withdrawing partners. The agreement allowed each partner to receive half of the partnership's capital account. Because the capital account had a balance of $279,612, Wisotsky alleged that Lerner owed the partnership half of this amount. The trial court denied Lerner's petition for judicial dissolution of the partnership. Lerner and the partnership appealed.*

JACOBSON, Presiding Judge.
The major issue in this appeal is whether a partnership agreement that provides methods by which the partnership can be terminated precludes dissolution of the partnership under the Uniform Partnership Act.
*   *   *   *
Lerner first contends that under the provisions of the Uniform Partnership Act, he was entitled to a dissolution of the partnership and the trial court erred in failing to grant such dissolution. Corollary to this argument is the contention that the trial court erred in considering Lerner a "withdrawing" partner under the partnership agreement.

Lerner's basic contention is that under the provisions of the Uniform [Partnership] Act he has an absolute right to seek dissolution of the partnership. We agree. A.R.S. [Arizona Revised Statutes] § 29-231 provides two methods by which a partnership may be dissolved, either without breach of the partnership agreement (in the words of the Uniform Act, "without violation of the agreement") or in breach of the partnership agreement (again in the words of the Uniform Act, "in contravention of the agreement"). Thus, whether Lerner breaches the partnership agreement by seeking dissolution only goes to the amount that he may recover upon dissolution and not the absolute right granted under the act to have dissolution occur.

* * *

Wisotsky does not seriously argue that Lerner cannot at anytime seek a dissolution of the partnership, but argues that by seeking such a dissolution he becomes a "withdrawing" partner under the partnership agreement and is entitled to be reimbursed only for his partnership interest as a "withdrawing" partner and cannot, under any circumstances, seek a judicial dissolution of the partnership. * * *

* * * *

We agree with the reasoning of *Cooper v. Isaacs:*

We do not believe it can be said at this time . . . that the partnership agreement involved here was clearly meant to exclude the possibility of dissolution of the partnership by decree of court under [§ 32 of the Uniform Partnership Act—A.R.S. § 29-232]. True, the partnership agreement does discuss certain ways by which the partnership can be terminated and states that their partnership 'shall continue until terminated as herein provided.' [Citation omitted.] However, it may well be that the parties did not consider the possibility that serious disagreements would arise at the time they made the agreement; the language limiting the methods of terminating the partnership may have been intended only to prevent a partner from dissolving the partnership voluntarily and without good cause.

Like in *Cooper*, the partnership agreement here is silent as to dissolution for cause and distribution of partnership assets in such a situation. The agreement only speaks to voluntary dissolution upon agreement of all partners. Moreover, the agreement is silent as to what constitutes a "withdrawal" by a partner. Under these circumstances, we hold that Lerner was entitled to seek judicial dissolution of the partnership for cause. We further hold that the mere filing of such a complaint does not constitute an intention to withdraw within the meaning of the partnership agreement. * * *

DECISION AND REMEDY

The court reversed the judgment of the trial court, holding that dissolution and distribution by law is allowable even though the partnership agreement did not provide for it. The appellate court remanded the question of whether there was ground for dissolution to the trial court.

COMMENTS

If the appellate court had upheld the trial court's ruling and found that Lerner had withdrawn from the partnership, Lerner could have been liable for damages resulting from a breach of the partnership agreement. Upon a holding by the trial court on remand that dissolution occurred, the partnership assets would be divided equally between the two partners.

Notice of Dissolution

Dissolution ends the partnership as a business enterprise. Thereafter, it remains viable only for the purpose of winding up its affairs. In some circumstances, however, a partnership or a withdrawing partner can become bound to a contract made after dissolution has begun but before winding up is complete.

NOTICE TO PARTNERS The intent to dissolve or to withdraw from a firm must be communicated to each partner. This notice of intent can come from the words of a partner (actual notice) or from the actions of a partner (constructive notice). All partners will share liability for the acts of any partner who continues conducting business for the firm without knowing that the partnership has been dissolved. For example, Ann, Doreen, and Carlo have a partnership, Ann tells Doreen of her intent to withdraw. Before Carlo learns of Ann's intentions, he enters into a contract with a third party. The contract is equally binding on Ann, Doreen, and Carlo. Unless the other partners have notice, the withdrawing partner will continue to be bound as a partner to all contracts created for the firm.

NOTICE TO THIRD PARTIES   To avoid liability for obligations a partner incurs after dissolution of a partnership, notice must be given to all affected third persons. The manner of giving notice depends upon the third person's relationship to the firm. Any third person who has extended credit to the partnership must receive *actual notice*. For all others, a newspaper announcement or similar public notice is sufficient.

Winding Up

Once dissolution has occurred and partners have been notified, they cannot create new obligations on behalf of the partnership. Their only authority is to complete transactions begun but not finished at the time of dissolution and to wind up the business of the partnership. Winding up includes collecting and preserving partnership assets, discharging liabilities (paying debts), and accounting to each partner for the value of his or her interest in the partnership.

When dissolution is caused by a partner's act that violates the partnership agreement, the innocent partners may have rights to damages resulting from the dissolution. Also, the innocent partners have the right to buy out the offending partner and to continue the business instead of winding up the partnership.

Dissolution resulting from the death of a partner vests all partnership assets in the surviving partners. The surviving partners act as fiduciaries in settling partnership affairs in a quick, practicable manner and in accounting to the estate of the deceased partner for the value of the decedent's interest in the partnership. The surviving partners are entitled to payment for their services in winding up the partnership as well as to reimbursement for any costs incurred in the process.[18]

The following case deals with a partner's failure to manage partnership assets properly after the partnership was dissolved.

18. UPA Section 18(f).

Case 35.5
HOOPER v. YODER
Supreme Court of Colorado,
1987.
737 P.2d 852.

BACKGROUND AND FACTS   *In the fall of 1976, Steven Hooper and David Yoder formed a partnership to market frozen yogurt bars. No formal partnership agreement was drawn. They agreed to share equally in the management, risks, and profits of the business. In 1977, they decided to incorporate the business in the name of Beautiful Daydreams, Inc. Hooper was president, and Yoder was vice-president and secretary; they were also the only members of the board of directors. During the following year, each loaned the corporation $10,000. Although the corporation retired the debt to Yoder by periodic payments, Hooper was never repaid. To secure further financing, they received a loan from Market West (a food-brokerage firm). When it appeared that they could not repay the loan, Market West agreed to accept stock in Beautiful Daydreams, Inc., in partial payment and to add Brian Bradley (a Market West officer) as a member of the board of directors. Disputes between Yoder and Hooper arose.*

In November 1978, without Yoder's knowledge, the other two directors adopted a resolution issuing ninety-five shares of stock to Hooper to cancel $9,500 of the corporate debt to him and five shares to Market West to cancel $500 of the corporate debt to Market West. On January 15, 1979, by a written "Action of Shareholders without a Meeting," Hooper and Market West, acting through

Bradley, removed the entire board of directors of Beautiful Daydreams and elected Hooper and Bradley the only directors. The two directors met and elected Hooper president and treasurer and Bradley vice-president and secretary. Yoder received no notice of this meeting. On February 1, 1979, Hooper told Yoder that he was laid off permanently. Yoder then filed an action against Hooper, alleging breach of fiduciary duty in the winding up of the partnership. The trial court, sitting without a jury, held that: (1) a partnership was formed in 1977, (2) the parties agreed to continue their partnership enterprise in corporate form, and (3) Hooper, in the winding up of the partnership, breached his fiduciary duty to his partner, Yoder, by excluding Yoder from participating equally in the issuance of corporate stock and by withdrawing a salary from the business without the assent or knowledge of Yoder. (Hooper, as president, had received a total salary of $141,500 prior to the filing of the suit.) The court awarded Yoder $70,750 (half of Hooper's salary) and 47½ shares of corporate stock (half of the 95 shares issued to Hooper). Hooper appealed.

LOHR, Justice.

*   *   *   *

As a general rule, when partners organize a corporation to operate the business of the partnership and transfer the assets to the corporation, the partnership is dissolved. This is so because such action usually reflects the express will of the parties that the partnership be dissolved.

*   *   * We find no support in the record for a finding that the parties intended that the partnership would continue after the corporation was organized. As the trial court found, the partners agreed to incorporate, and the essential term of that agreement was that stock ownership would be equal. Based on this record, we conclude that the partnership between Hooper and Yoder was dissolved upon the incorporation of Beautiful Daydreams.

The dissolution of a partnership, however, does not automatically terminate the existence of the partnership. The Uniform Partnership Law provides that "[o]n dissolution the partnership is not terminated but continues until the winding up of partnership affairs is completed. *   *   * The winding up includes the entire process of settling the partnership affairs after dissolution."

When partners organize a corporation to continue the business of the firm, the winding up of the partnership includes the transfer of the partnership assets to the corporation in exchange for corporate stock. Here, the winding up of the partnership remained incomplete pending issuance of corporate stock to Hooper and Yoder in equal amounts pursuant to the agreement they made as partners prior to incorporation. Because there were no shares of stock issued upon incorporation of Beautiful Daydreams, it cannot be said that the property of the partnership was exchanged for stock in the corporation and that the stock was then distributed to the partners, thereby winding up the partnership affairs. The circumstances of this case bring us to the conclusion that the winding up of the partnership was not accomplished upon incorporation and, therefore, the partnership continued to exist.

Because the partnership continued to exist, so did the fiduciary duties that one partner owes to another. Partners in a business enterprise owe to one another the highest duty of loyalty; they stand in a relationship of trust and confidence to each other and are bound by standards of good conduct and square dealing. Each partner has the right to demand and expect from the other a full, fair, open and honest disclosure of everything affecting the relationship. During the winding up of partnership affairs, the partners continue to owe to each other the same duty of loyalty and fair dealing.

*   *   *   *

*   *   * Hooper's actions in causing the issuance of 95 shares of stock to himself and none to Yoder and in drawing a salary from the business without the assent or knowledge of Yoder are the very antithesis of the type of fair dealing required between partners in winding up a partnership. The trial court's conclusion that "Mr. Hooper breached his fiduciary duty by not issuing fifty percent of the shares of stock to Mr. Yoder in November of 1978 and by freezing him out of the corporation after January 15, 1979 and by drawing a salary for himself" is factually supported by the record and is legally correct.

*   *   *   *

Under ordinary circumstances, and in absence of agreement, a partner is not entitled to salary or other compensation for services in conducting the partnership business. This is true even if the services rendered by one partner are disproportionately valuable to any services performed by the others. However, the Uniform Partnership Law does recognize a surviving partner's right to "reasonable compensation" for those services necessary to the winding up of partnership affairs after its dissolution. Any such entitlement to compensation during the winding up period is tempered by equitable considerations. Courts have denied compensation to a partner for services in winding up a partnership where the partner acted wrongfully.

In the initial partnership agreement in this case, Hooper and Yoder agreed to equal salaries. Yoder was subsequently prevented from participating in the corporate decision-making process when Hooper breached his fiduciary duty by excluding Yoder from stock ownership. Hooper proceeded to take a salary from the business without Yoder's consent or knowledge. Under these circumstances, the trial court's decision to deny compensation to Hooper for his services was a proper exercise of its equitable powers.

*   *   *   *

In summary, Hooper and Yoder agreed to incorporate their business enterprise, which previously had been conducted as a partnership. The essential term of the agreement was that stock ownership would be equal. Upon incorporation the partnership was dissolved. All that remained to be done to terminate the partnership was the distribution of corporate stock in accordance with the parties' agreement. This simple process of winding up the partnership affairs never occurred. Therefore, the fiduciary duties of the parties as partners continued in effect at all times pertinent to this lawsuit. Hooper breached those duties by issuing stock to himself without providing an equal amount to Yoder and by paying salary to himself without Yoder's knowledge or approval. The trial court provided appropriate remedies for these breaches by *   *   * requiring Hooper to share the stock and salary equally with Yoder in accordance with the partnership agreement between them.

DECISION AND REMEDY   *The Supreme Court of Colorado affirmed the decision of the lower court.*

Distribution of Assets

Both creditors of the partnership and creditors of the individual partners can make claims on the partnership's assets. Creditors of the partnership have priority over creditors of individual partners in the distribution of partnership assets; the converse priority is followed in the distribution of individual partner assets, except under the new Bankruptcy Act. This act provides that a partner's individual assets may be utilized to pay claims against a partnership involved in certain bankruptcy proceedings.[19] (Bankruptcy law in general is discussed in Chapter 31.)

The distribution of a partnership's assets is made *after* third-party debts have been paid. The priorities, after third-party debts, are as follows:[20]

1. Refund of advances (loans) made to or for the firm by a partner.
2. Return of capital contribution to a partner.
3. Distribution of the balance, if any, to partners in accordance with the relative proportions of their respective shares in the profits.

If the partnership's liabilities are greater than its assets, the partners bear the losses—in the absence of a contrary agreement—in the same proportion in which they shared the profits (rather

---

19. 11 U.S.C. Section 723.

20. UPA Section 40(b).

than, for example, in proportion to their contributions to the partnership's capital). If the partnership is insolvent, the partners must still contribute their respective shares. If one of the partners does not contribute, the other or others must provide the additional amounts necessary to pay the liabilities; but he, she, or they have a right of contribution against whoever has not paid his or her share.[21]

The distribution of partnership assets begins with the subtraction of the partnership's total liabilities from its total assets (or vice versa, in the case of an insolvent partnership). Liabilities include amounts owed to creditors, to partners for their capital contributions, and to partners for other than capital and profit. Amounts that remain after payment of the liabilities are distributed to the partners according to the profit-sharing ratio. If, on the other hand, the partnership has suffered

an aggregate loss, the total loss is shared as agreed or in the same ratio as the partners share profits.

PARTNERSHIP BUY-AND-SELL AGREEMENTS

Usually, when people enter into partnerships, they are getting along with each other. To prepare for the possibility that the situation may change and they may become unable to work together amicably, the partners should make express arrangements during the formation of the partnership to provide for its smooth dissolution. A provision may be made for one or more partners to buy out the other or others should the situation warrant. To agree beforehand on who buys what, under what circumstances, and, if possible, at what price, may eliminate costly negotiations or litigation later. Alternatively, it may be agreed that one or more partners will determine the value of the interest being sold and the other or others can decide whether to buy or sell.

---

21. If an individual partner is insolvent and for that reason cannot pay his or her share of the loss, however, the solvent partner or partners will be unable to recover their additional contributions from the insolvent partner.

QUESTIONS AND CASE PROBLEMS

1. Daniel is the owner of a chain of shoe stores. He hires Martin as the manager of a new store, which is to open in Grand Rapids, Michigan. Daniel, by written contract, agrees to pay Martin a monthly salary. In addition, Daniel and Martin have agreed to an 80-20 percent split in profits. Without Daniel's knowledge, Martin represents himself to Carlton as Daniel's partner, showing Carlton the agreement to share profits. Carlton extends credit to Martin. Martin defaults. Discuss whether Carlton can hold Daniel liable as a partner.

2. Adam wishes to purchase some real property owned by Tropical Gardens. He learns that Tropical Gardens is a partnership owned by Waldheim, Berry, and Lamont. He also learns that the partnership needs capital and that the need for capital is one of the major reasons the partners are selling their real property. Since Tropical Gardens is a partnership, Adam has the following concerns:

    (a) Can the partnership convey the land in the name of Tropical Gardens?

    (b) If there is a breach of contract, against whom must Adam file a lawsuit?

    (c) If he obtains a judgment against Tropical Gardens, against whom can he execute it?

Discuss Adam's concerns.

3. Two individuals, Smother and Ono, orally agree to form a partnership to run a television sales and repair business. No specific term of partnership duration is stated. Smother is an adult, and Ono is a minor. The oral partnership agreement provides that each partner will contribute capital of $5,000, with Ono's contribution due at the end of the first year's operation. Two months prior to the end of the first year's operation, Smother and Ono orally agree to take in Super TV Supply Corporation as a third partner. Two weeks later, both Super TV Supply Corporation and Ono assert that neither of them had the capacity to become a partner and that, in any event, there was no written agreement to form a partnership. Discuss whether Ono and Super TV Supply Corporation can disclaim partnership responsibility to Smother.

4. Alister, Bentley, and McCoy have formed a twenty-year partnership to purchase land, develop it, manage it, and then sell the property. The partnership agreement calls for the partners to devote their full time to the business. Discuss fully which of the following acts will constitute a dissolution of the partnership and whether there is any ensuing liability of Alister.

    (a) After two years, Bentley and McCoy agree that the working hours of the partnership will be from 8:00 A.M. to 6:00 P.M. rather than the previously established schedule of 9:00 A.M. to 5:00 P.M. Alister refuses to come to work before 9:00 A.M. and quits promptly at 5:00 P.M.

    (b) After two years, Alister quits the partnership and walks out.

(c) After two years, Alister becomes insolvent.

(d) After two years, Alister dies.

5. Susan and Dominic formed a partnership. At the time of formation, Susan's capital contribution was $10,000, and Dominic's was $15,000. Later, Susan made a $10,000 loan to the partnership when it needed working capital. The partnership agreement provided that profits were to be shared, with 40 percent for Susan and 60 percent for Dominic. The partnership was dissolved by Dominic's death. At the end of the dissolution and the winding up of the partnership, the partnership's assets were $50,000, and the partnership's debts were $8,000. Discuss fully how the assets should be distributed.

6. Karen, Doug, and Charlie were partners in a partnership at will. Karen and Doug excluded Charlie from partnership management affairs and then sought a dissolution of the partnership. A trial court dissolved the partnership and ordered a sale of the partnership asset, a shopping center. Karen and Doug were the highest bidders at the court-ordered sale and were therefore able to retain the shopping center. Will the courts protect Charlie from this type of freeze-out?

7. Lynne, Ernest, and Stanley Timmermann established a partnership in 1965 for the purpose of engaging in farming activities. In January 1969, Lynne stated to the other two partners that he no longer wished to be involved in the partnership. It was not until August 31, 1970, however, that Lynne ceased to participate in the farming activities of the partnership. In January 1972, Lynne attempted to bring about a forced liquidation of the partnership through a lawsuit. In January 1969, the value of the partnership was approximately $50,000. On August 31, 1970, the value of the partnership was slightly less than $10,000; and in January 1972, the value of the partnership was more than $300,000. Assuming Lynne had a one-third interest in the partnership, approximately how much should he have received when he withdrew? Explain your answer. [Timmermann v. Timmermann, 272 Or. 613, 538 P.2d 1254 (1975)]

8. On September 28, 1958, Reid and three others entered into a written partnership agreement for the purpose of leasing for profit certain real property located in Montgomery County, Pennsylvania. Reid was to manage the property, and the others were to perform the physical labor necessary to maintain the premises in good condition. One year later, Reid notified the others that she was dissolving the partnership and requested that the partnership assets be liquidated as soon as possible. Had dissolution occurred? Assuming dissolution had occurred, could the other partners recover damages for breach of partnership agreement on the ground that the partnership was a partnership for a particular undertaking and hence not terminable at will? [Girard Bank v. Haley, 460 Pa. 237, 332 A.2d 443 (1975)]

9. Carola and Grogan were partners in a law firm. The partnership began business in 1974 and was created by an oral agreement. On September 6, 1976, Carola withdrew from the partnership some of its files, furniture, books, and various other items of office equipment. The next day, Carola informed Grogan he had withdrawn from the partnership. Were Carola's actions on September 6, 1976 effective notice of dissolution to Grogan? [Carola v. Grogan, 102 A.D.2d 934, 477 N.Y.S.2d 525 (1984)]

10. In 1964, Alex Gershunoff and Lawrence Silk formed a partnership to syndicate and manage apartment houses. Jacob Oliker served the partnership as legal counsel. In 1969, Oliker joined the partnership, known as the Alex Company, as an equal partner. Oliker paid $5,000 to the partnership and gave up his legal practice as consideration for entering the partnership, but there was never a written partnership agreement. The partnership functioned smoothly from 1969 until 1974. The partnership bought apartment houses and called itself a "development company." At one point, the partnership organized two limited partnerships: an "ownership company" to buy the property from the development company and a "leasing company" to lease the property to another leasing company, which operated the apartment complexes under a management contract with a corporation, PIC, in which Gershunoff, Silk, and Oliker were the sole shareholders. In March 1974, Oliker withdrew from the partnership. After Oliker's withdrawal, the value of land owned by the partnership greatly appreciated. For two and a half years, the parties failed to agree on the amount of Oliker's interest. In November of 1976, Gershunoff and Silk sent Oliker a "final accounting," which Oliker rejected. Oliker filed suit, requesting a formal accounting and a court-supervised winding up of affairs, with his interest to be determined as of its value at the time of the court-ordered accounting. Discuss whether Oliker was entitled to an equal share in the increased value of partnership assets. [Oliker v. Gershunoff, 195 Cal.App.3d 1288, 241 Cal.Rptr. 415 (2d Dist. 1987)]

11. During June and July of 1981, Taylor Rental Center rented pumps and sandblasting equipment for use on the *M/V Courtney D*, a seagoing vessel. Apparently, the vessel was owned by Paramount Petroleum Corporation. When the request for rental was submitted, Taylor checked the authorization to rent by telephoning the number given. The phone was answered by a business calling itself "Paramount," and Taylor was instructed by phone to send invoices for the rental charges to the Houston post office box of the company. The identification of the employees picking up the equipment was also checked by Taylor. A second request to rent equipment was made by a captain claiming to represent Paramount Steamship Company, Ltd. Since the equipment was to be used on the *Courtney D*, and since the invoices were to be sent to the same address as the earlier rental, Taylor assumed the two Paramount firms were a single enterprise or a partnership. The invoices went unpaid, and Taylor learned that Paramount had apparently gone out of business. Taylor then sought payment from Paramount Petroleum, claiming that it was liable for the bill and that, if it was not the same corporation as Paramount Steamship, it was at least its partner. When the trial court held for Taylor, Paramount Petroleum appealed. Discuss whether the sharing of telephone and post office facilities by the two companies constitutes a partnership by estoppel. [Paramount Petroleum Corporation v. Taylor Rental Center, 712 S.W.2d 534 (Tex.Civ.App.–Houston (14th Dist.) 1986)]

Chapter 36

PARTNERSHIPS
Operation and Duties

The rights and duties of partners are governed largely by the specific terms of their partnership agreement. In the absence of provisions to the contrary in the partnership agreement, the law imposes the rights and duties discussed in this chapter. The character and nature of the partnership business generally influence the application of these rights and duties.

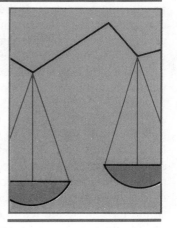

RIGHTS AMONG PARTNERS

The rights held by partners in a partnership relate to the following areas: management, interest in the partnership, compensation, inspection of books, accounting, and property rights.

Management

"All partners have equal rights in the management and conduct of partnership business." [1] Management rights belong to all partners in an ordinary partnership. [2] Unless the partners agree otherwise, each has one vote in management matters *regardless of the proportional size of his or her interest in the firm*. Often, in a large partnership, partners will agree to delegate daily management responsibilities to a management committee made up of one or more of the partners.

The majority rule controls decisions in ordinary matters connected with partnership business, unless otherwise specified in the agreement. Unanimous consent of the partners is required to bind the firm in any of the following actions, however:

1. To alter the essential nature of the firm's business as expressed in the partnership agreement or to alter the capital structure of the partnership.
2. To admit new partners or to enter a wholly new business. [3]
3. To assign partnership property into a trust for the benefit of creditors.
4. To dispose of the partnership's goodwill.
5. To confess judgment against the partnership or submit partnership claims to arbitration. (A *confession of judgment* is the act of a debtor in

1. UPA Section 18(e).
2. In limited partnerships, limited partners may not generally participate in management without affecting their limited-liability status. See Chapter 37.
3. UPA Section 18(g),(h).

permitting a judgment to be entered against him or her by a creditor, for an agreed sum, without the institution of legal proceedings.)

6. To undertake any act that would make further conduct of partnership business impossible.[4]

7. To amend the articles of the partnership agreement.

Each of these matters significantly affects the nature of the partnership.

Interest in the Partnership

Each partner is entitled to the proportion of business profits and losses that is designated in the partnership agreement. If the agreement does not apportion profits or losses, the UPA provides that profits are to be shared equally and losses are to be shared in the same ratio as profits.[5]

For example, Dawson and Maubrey form a partnership. The partnership agreement provides for capital contributions of $6,000 from Dawson and $4,000 from Maubrey, but it is silent as to how Dawson and Maubrey will share profits or losses. In this case, Dawson and Maubrey will share both profits and losses equally. Had the partnership agreement provided for profits to be shared in the same ratio as capital contributions, Dawson would have been entitled to 60 percent of profits and Maubrey to 40 percent; and had it been silent as to losses, losses would have been shared in the same ratio.

Compensation

Devoting time, skill, and energy to partnership business is a partner's duty and generally not a compensable service. Partners can, of course, agree otherwise. For example, the managing partner of a law firm often receives a salary in addition to his or her share of profits for performing special administrative duties in office and personnel management. UPA Section 18(f) provides that a surviving partner is entitled to compensation for services in winding up partnership affairs (and reimbursement for expenses incurred in the process) above and apart from his or her share in the partnership profits.

Each partner impliedly promises to subordinate his or her own economic interests to those of

the partnership. Assume that Hunter, Brooks, and Palmer enter into a partnership as consultants to outside firms. Palmer undertakes independent consulting for an outside firm without the consent of Hunter and Brooks. Palmer's compensation from the outside firm is considered partnership income.[6] A partner cannot engage in any independent competitive activities without the other partners' consent. Even with a noncompetitive activity, Palmer can breach his fiduciary duty if the partnership suffers a loss from his efforts. Of course, the partnership agreement or the unanimous consent of the partners can permit a partner to engage in any activity.

Inspection of Books

Partnership books and records must be kept accessible to all partners. Each partner has the right to receive (and the corresponding duty to produce) full and complete information concerning the conduct of all aspects of partnership business.[7] Each firm retains books in which to record and secure such information. Partners contribute the information, and a bookkeeper typically has the duty to preserve it. The books must be kept at the firm's principal business office unless the partners agree otherwise.[8] Every partner, whether active or inactive, is entitled to inspect all books and records upon demand and can make copies of the materials. The personal representative of a deceased partner's estate has the same right of access to partnership books and records that the decedent would have had.

Accounting

An accounting of partnership assets or profits is done to determine the value of each partner's proportionate share in the partnership. An accounting can be called for voluntarily, or it can be compelled by the order of a court in equity.[9] Formal

---

4. UPA Section 9(3), various subsections.

5. UPA Section 18(a).

6. UPA Section 21.

7. UPA Section 20.

8. UPA Section 19.

9. The principal remedy of a partner against co-partners is an equity suit for dissolution, an accounting, or both. With minor exceptions, a partner cannot maintain an action against other firm members for damages until partnership affairs are settled and an accounting is done. This rule is necessary because legal disputes among partners invariably involve conflicting claims to shares in the partnership. Logically, the value of each partner's share must first be determined by an accounting.

accounting occurs by right in connection with dissolution proceedings, but, under UPA Section 22, a partner also has the right to a formal accounting in the following situations:

1. When the partnership agreement provides for a formal accounting.
2. When a partner is wrongfully excluded from the business, from access to the books, or both.
3. When any partner is withholding profits or benefits belonging to the partnership in breach of the fiduciary duty.
4. When circumstances "render it just and reasonable."

Property Rights

A partner has three basic property rights. They are:

1. An interest in the partnership.
2. A right in specific partnership property.
3. A right to participate in the management of the partnership, as previously discussed.[10]

There is an important legal distinction between a partner's rights in specific property belonging to the firm to be used for business purposes and a partner's right to share in the firm's earned profits to the extent of his or her interest in the firm. No individual partner has an absolute right to specific property of the firm. A partner is co-owner with his or her partners of specific partnership property, holding as a tenant in partnership. A specific asset may constitute partnership property even when title to it is in an individual partner's name. Among factors courts may consider in determining whether a specific asset is partnership property is how closely the asset is connected to the partnership's operation.

Chapter 35 discussed the rights of creditors in regard to partnerships. A judgment creditor of an individual partner has no right to execute or attach specific partnership property, but he or she can obtain the partner's share of profits. A creditor of the firm can levy directly upon partnership property.

PARTNER'S INTEREST IN THE FIRM   A partner's interest in the firm is a personal asset consisting of a proportionate share of the profits earned[11]

and a return of capital after dissolution and winding up.

A partner's interest is susceptible to assignment or to a judgment creditor's lien. Judgment creditors can attach a partner's interest by petitioning the court that entered the judgment to grant the creditors a *charging order*. This order entitles the creditors to profits of the partner and to any assets available to the partner upon dissolution.[12] Neither an assignment nor a court's charging order entitling a creditor to receive a share of the partner's money will cause dissolution of the firm.[13]

PARTNERSHIP PROPERTY   UPA Section 8(1) provides that "all property originally brought into the partnership's stock or subsequently acquired, by purchase or otherwise, *on account of the partnership,* is partnership property." (Emphasis added.) For example, in the formation of a partnership, a partner may bring into the partnership property he or she owns as a part of his or her capital contribution. This property becomes partnership property even though title is still in the name of the contributing partner.

Indications that the assets were acquired with the intention that it be a partnership asset is the heart of the phrase *on account of the partnership.* Thus, the more closely an asset is associated with the business operations of the partnership, the more likely it is to be a partnership asset. Moreover, when such an asset is purchased with partnership funds, it will belong to the partnership unless a contrary intention is shown. If, for example, a piece of property is purchased with partnership funds, it is presumed to be partnership property even if title is taken in the name of one of the partners.

Partners are *tenants in partnership* of all firm property.[14] Tenancy in partnership has several important effects. If a partner dies, the surviving partners, not the heirs of the deceased partner, have the right of survivorship to the specific property. Although surviving partners are entitled to possession, they have a duty to account to the decedent's estate for the *value* of the deceased partner's interest in said property.[15]

---

10. UPA Section 24.
11. UPA Section 26.

12. UPA Section 28.
13. UPA Section 27.
14. UPA Section 25(1).
15. UPA Section 25(2)(d),(e).

A partner has no right to sell, assign, or in any way deal with a particular item of partnership property other than for partnership purposes.[16] Nor is a partner's personal credit related to partnership property; creditors cannot use partnership property to satisfy the personal debts of a partner. Partnership property is available only to satisfy partnership debts, to enhance the firm's credit, or to achieve other business purposes.

Every partner is a co-owner with all other partners of specific partnership property, such as office equipment, paper supplies, and vehicles. Each partner has equal rights to possess partnership property for business purposes or in satisfaction of firm debts, but not for any other purpose without the consent of all the other partners.

The following case deals with an attempt by a deceased partner's widow to claim, as her husband's heir, an interest in partnership property.

---

16. UPA Section 25(2)(a),(b).

Case 36.1
CATES v. INTERNATIONAL TELEPHONE AND TELEGRAPH CORP.
United States Court of Appeals, Fifth Circuit, 1985.
756 F.2d 1161.

BACKGROUND AND FACTS *James Cates and three other persons formed two partnerships, SanJac International (SJI) and SanJac Association (SJA). The partnerships provided group life, health, and accident insurance to small employers who could not obtain the lower rates charged to larger employers. To facilitate their program, the partnerships contracted with insurance providers, including the defendant firms, ITT Life Insurance Company and Lloyds of London. When the partnerships were later dissolved, and while Cates was still in the process of winding up the affairs of the partnerships, Cates died. At the time of his death, Cates was involved in a lawsuit against ITT Life and Lloyds of London for—among other things—failure to pay claims promptly and entering into contracts with the fraudulent intent not to perform them. Upon Cates's death, his wife intervened in the suit, claiming, as Cates's heir, an interest in partnership property (that is, the damages to be awarded in the lawsuit). The district court held for the defendants, and Mrs. Cates appealed.*

GARWOOD, Circuit Judge.
*   *   *   *

*   *   * [T]he widow, heirs, legatees, or personal representatives of a deceased partner have neither any interest in or right to possess specific partnership property nor any right to the management or administration of partnership affairs, all such interests and rights vesting in the remaining partner or partners. Accordingly, even if any or all of the *   *   * contentions of Cates are well taken, a point we do not decide, nevertheless, his widow *   *   *, Mrs. Cates, would not, merely by reason of any or all such matters, be able to maintain suit on the partnership causes of action.

Mrs. Cates, however, urges that the situation is otherwise because, although neither partnership had terminated, "the partnerships were not only in dissolution, but . . . Cates took charge of the winding-up process and thus had the right to institute suits or take other steps to complete the winding-up process." *   *   * She contends that where a partnership is in dissolution and the partner conducting the winding-up process dies, that the right to complete the winding up passes to the deceased partner's personal representative. That is true, however, *only* with respect to the death of the *last* surviving partner. At his death, Cates was not the last surviving partner in either SJA or SJI. [Under the Texas Uniform Partnership Act (TUPA)] section 25(2)(d) the rights of a deceased partner to specific partnership property vest "in the surviving partner" and *not* in the deceased partner's personal representative, except only "where the deceased was the last surviving partner." And, section 37 provides that "the legal representative of the last surviving partner, not bankrupt, has the right to wind up the partnership affairs." In the commentary to section 37 of the TUPA, Professor Alan R. Bromberg states:

In giving the surviving partners authority to wind up, § 37 is buttressed by § 25(2)(d) which gives them all the rights of a deceased partner in specific partnership property. Thus, partnership assets are not subject to administration in the estate of a deceased partner (unless he was the last).

Mrs. Cates may not bring an action on behalf of the partnership solely because she is the heir of one of the partners. Partnership property rights pass to the partnership and not to the heirs of a deceased partner.

DECISION AND REMEDY

DUTIES AND POWERS OF PARTNERS

The duties and powers of partners consist of a fiduciary duty of each partner to the other and general agency powers.

Fiduciary Duty

Partners stand in a fiduciary relationship to one another just as principals and agents do. (See Chapter 32.) It is a relationship of extraordinary trust and loyalty. The fiduciary duty imposes a responsibility upon each partner to act in utmost good faith for the benefit of the partnership. It requires that each partner subordinate his or her personal interests to the mutual welfare of the partners.

This fiduciary duty underlies the entire body of law pertaining to partnership and to agency. From it, certain other duties are commonly implied. Thus, a partner must account to the partnership for any personal profits or benefits derived without the consent of all of the partners in any partnership transaction.[17] These include transactions among partners or with third parties connected with the formation, conduct, or liquidation of the partnership or with any use of partnership property.[18]

Upon the death of a partner, the surviving partner is under a fiduciary duty to liquidate partnership assets without delay and to credit the estate of the deceased partner for the value of the decedent's interest in the partnership. The fiduciary duty of good faith owed the deceased partner extends by implication to the personal representative of the deceased partner's estate as well. The principles of fiduciary duty and property rights are illustrated in the next case.

---

17. In this sense, to account to the partnership means not only to divulge the information but also to determine the value of any benefits or profits derived and to hold that money or property in trust on behalf of the partnership.

18. UPA Section 21.

BACKGROUND AND FACTS *About forty-five doctors, including Dr. Witlin, owned and operated a health center as partners. When Witlin died, the other doctors, in accordance with their partnership agreement, purchased his share of the center, paying his widow $65,228. The partnership agreement provided that on Witlin's death a management committee of the partnership was required to make a good faith determination of the fair market value of Witlin's share. The partnership had the option to offer this amount to Witlin's widow. The $65,228 offer, however, was based only on the book value of the partnership's assets. (Book value is the value at which assets are carried on the books—that is, cost less depreciation. It does not include the good will or the going business value of a successful business, factors which are likely to be considered in determining fair market value.) In addition, although the partnership was in the process of bargaining to sell the health center at a price that would have doubled Mrs. Witlin's proportionate share, the partnership did not inform her of that fact. Later, Mrs. Witlin sought a greater amount for her husband's share, even though she had accepted the partnership's offer. The trial court held for Witlin's widow, and the doctors appealed.*

Case 36.2
ESTATE OF WITLIN
California Court of Appeal, 1978.
83 Cal.App.3d 167, 147 Cal.Rptr. 723.

COBEY, Associate Justice.

*   *   *   *

Appellants [the forty-five doctors] owed [a fiduciary] * * * duty to plaintiff as the widow and executrix [personal representative] of their deceased partner in purchasing from her their deceased partner's interest in the partnership. Throughout the transaction they were bound to act toward her "in the highest good faith" and they were forbidden to obtain any advantage over her in the matter by, among other things, the slightest concealment. Yet the management committee never revealed to plaintiff or her representative, King, that the basic value in their formula for determining the fair market value of the partnership was book value alone. Likewise, as already noted, the management committee did not mention to King the possibility that the hospital might be shortly sold.

This possibility of sale was quite real. It appears from plaintiff's improperly rejected offers of proof that the management committee reached in 1969 a tentative agreement with General Health Services to sell the partnership's assets to it for approximately $60,000 a percentage point, that between April and September 28, 1971, the management committee and the American Cyanamid Corporation were discussing a sale of the partnership to it for at least $93,000 a percentage point, and, as already noted from the evidence itself, that the partnership's assets were finally sold in June 1972 to Hospital Corporation of America for about $84,000 a percentage point.

The management committee knew all of this, but they apparently never breathed a word of it to either plaintiff or her attorney. It seems that in discussing the fair market value of the partnership they talked out of both sides of their mouths. They talked to plaintiff and her attorney in terms of $16,000 and $24,600 per percentage point while they were more or less simultaneously talking to conglomerates interested in purchasing the hospital and the other assets of the partnership in terms of selling prices ranging from $60,000 to $93,500 per percentage point. Given this situation, how could their offer of $24,600 per percentage point to plaintiff have been a good faith determination on their part of the fair market value of the partnership? Obviously the jury's verdict was correct and solidly supported in this respect.

DECISION AND REMEDY *The trial court's judgment was affirmed on appeal. The partners were held to have breached their fiduciary duty to their deceased partner by failing to make a full and fair disclosure.*

General Agency Powers

Each partner is an *agent* of every other partner and acts as both a principal and an agent in any business transaction within the scope of the partnership agreement. Each partner is a general agent of the partnership in carrying out the usual business of the firm. Thus, every act of a partner concerning partnership business and every contract signed in the partnership name bind the firm.[19]

The UPA affirms general principles of agency law that pertain to the authority of a partner to bind a partnership in contract. Under the same principles, a partner may subject a partnership to liability in tort. When a partner is apparently car-

rying on partnership business with third persons in the usual way, both the partner and the firm share liability. It is only when third persons *know* that the partner has no such authority that the partnership is not liable.

For example, Peter, a partner in Firm X, applies for a loan on behalf of the partnership without authorization from the other partners. The bank manager knows Peter has no authority. If the bank manager grants the loan, Peter will be personally bound, but the firm will not be liable.

JOINT LIABILITY In most states, partners are subject to joint liability on partnership debts and contracts.[20] *Joint liability* means that if a third party

---

19. UPA Section 9(1).

20. UPA Section 15(b).

sues a partner on, for example, a partnership debt, the partner has the right to insist that the other partners be sued with him or her. In fact, if the third party does not sue all of the partners, those partners sued cannot be required to pay a judgment, and the assets of the partnership cannot be used to satisfy the judgment. (Similarly, the third party's release of one partner releases all.) In other words, to bring a successful claim against the partnership on a debt or contract, a plaintiff must name all the partners as defendants.

To simplify this rule, some states[21] have enacted statutes providing that a partnership may be sued in its own name and a judgment will bind the partnership's and the individual partners' property even though not all the partners are named in the complaint.

If the third party is successful, he or she may collect on the judgment against the assets of one or more of the partners. In other words, each partner is liable and may be required to pay the entire amount of the judgment. When one partner pays the entire amount, the partnership is required to indemnify that partner.[22] If the partnership cannot do so, the obligation falls on the other partners.

JOINT AND SEVERAL LIABILITY In some states,[23] partners are jointly and severally liable for partnership debts and contracts. In all states, partners are jointly and severally liable for torts and breaches of trust.[24]

Joint and several liability means a third party may sue any one or more of the partners without suing all of them or the partnership itself. (That is, a third party may sue one or more of the partners separately or all of them together, at his or her option.) This is true even if the partner did not participate in, ratify, or know about whatever it was that gave rise to the cause of action.

A judgment against one partner on his several liability does not extinguish the others' liability. (Similarly, a release of one partner discharges the partners' joint but not several liability.) Thus, those not sued in the first action may be sued subsequently. However, the first action may have been

conclusive on the question of liability. If, for example, in an action against one partner, the court held that the partnership was in no way liable, the third party cannot bring an action against another partner and succeed on the issue of the partnership's liability.

If the third party is successful, he or she may collect on the judgment only against the assets of those partners named as defendants. However, the partner who committed the tort is required to indemnify the partnership for any damages it pays.

LIABILITY OF INCOMING PARTNER A newly admitted partner to an existing partnership has limited liability for whatever debts and obligations the partnership incurred prior to the new partner's admission. UPA Section 17 provides that the new partner's liability can be satisfied only from partnership assets. This means that the new partner has no personal liability for these debts and obligations but any capital contribution made by him or her is subject to them.

TRADING VERSUS NON-TRADING PARTNERSHIPS—A DIGRESSION At common law, prior to the UPA, a distinction was drawn between trading and non-trading partnerships. Essentially, any partnership business that had goods in inventory and made profits buying and selling those goods was considered a trading partnership. All other partnerships were non-trading. The distinction between these two types of partnerships is important in discussing the apparent authority of the partnership and of its individual members. The UPA does not expressly adopt the distinction between these two types of partnerships, but many cases decided under the UPA nonetheless followed the distinction.

AUTHORITY OF PARTNERS Agency concepts relating to apparent authority, actual authority, and ratification are also applicable to partnerships. The extent of *implied authority* is generally broader for partners than for ordinary agents. The character and scope of the partnership business and the customary nature of the particular business operation determine the scope of implied powers. For example, the usual course of business in a trading partnership involves buying and selling commodities. Consequently, each partner in a trading partnership has a wide range of implied powers to borrow money in the firm name and to extend the

---

21. California, for example.

22. UPA Section 18(b).

23. Alabama, Arizona, Colorado, Missouri, North Carolina, Tennessee, and Texas.

24. UPA Section 15(a).

firm's credit in issuing or indorsing negotiable instruments.

In an ordinary partnership, firm members can exercise all implied powers reasonably necessary and customary to carry on that particular business. Some customarily implied powers include the authority to make warranties on goods in the sales business, the power to convey real property in the firm name where such conveyances are part of the ordinary course of partnership business, the power to enter contracts consistent with the firm's regular course of business, and the power to make admissions and representations concerning partnership affairs.[25]

If a partner acts within the scope of authority, the partnership is bound to third parties. For example, a partner's authority to sell partnership products carries with it the implied authority to transfer title and to make usual warranties. Hence,

---

25. UPA Section 11.

in a partnership that operates a retail tire store, any partner negotiating a contract with a customer for the sale of a set of tires can warrant that "each tire will be warranted for normal wear for 40,000 miles."

This same partner, however, does not have the authority to sell office equipment, fixtures, or the partnership office building without the consent of all the other partners. In addition, since partnerships are formed for profit, a partner does not generally have the authority to make charitable contributions without the consent of the other parties. No such action is binding on the partnership unless it is ratified by all of the other partners.

Like the law of agency, the law of partnership imputes one partner's knowledge of all matters pertaining to partnership affairs to all other partners, because members of a partnership stand in a fiduciary relationship to one another. In other words, it is presumed that each partner discloses to every other partner all relevant information pertaining to the business of the partnership.

QUESTIONS AND CASE PROBLEMS

1. Meyer, Knapp, and Cavanna form a partnership to operate a window washing service. Meyer contributes $10,000 to the partnership, and Knapp and Cavanna contribute $1,000 each. The partnership agreement is silent on how profits and losses will be shared. One month after the partnership has begun operation, Knapp and Cavanna vote, over Meyer's objection, to purchase another truck for the firm's operation. Meyer believes that since he contributed $10,000, no major commitment to purchase by the partnership can be made over his objection. In addition, Meyer claims that, in absence of agreement, profits must be divided in the same ratio as capital contributions. Discuss Meyer's contentions.

2. Lisa, Betty, and Carla form a partnership to operate a hairstyling salon. After one year's operation, the salon has become very busy and profitable. Most customers have a preference as to which partner's services they use. Lisa becomes ill, and Betty and Carla start working sixty-hour weeks. It appears that Lisa will not return to work for at least two months. Betty and Carla want to bring in Dana as a new partner. Lisa objects to Dana and refuses to consent to Dana's admission into the partnership. Betty and Carla insist that they be paid extra compensation for having to work additional hours because of Lisa's illness. Discuss

whether Betty and Carla are entitled to the compensation claimed and whether Dana can be admitted as a new partner by majority vote.

3. Gershwin and Spring are partners in a law firm. Gershwin has substantial personal assets. Gershwin, driving his own car, is on his way to take a deposition from a witness when he negligently runs into Thomas. The damages and injuries to Thomas amount to $5,000. Unknown to Gershwin, Spring at the same time contracts to purchase $9,000 worth of word processing equipment from Copycat, Inc. Both partners have express partnership authority to purchase office equipment. Gershwin is angry about the purchase and wrongfully cancels the contract with Copycat. Both Copycat and Thomas want to sue. Discuss the nature of the partners' liability in both cases.

4. Arnold and Mueller operate as partners a car dealership. The partnership has existing debts of $300,000 with General Motors. Arnold and Mueller take in a new partner, Bullard. Bullard contributes to the partnership land valued at $100,000 to be used by the partnership as a used car lot. Bullard is new to the car dealership business and, in making his first sale, warrants to a customer that the partnership will repair the car at no cost for a period of two years regardless of mileage. General Motors sues the partners jointly on the debt and obtains a judgment. Arnold and Mueller insist that Bullard's warranty to the customer is not binding on the partnership.

    (a) Discuss Bullard's liability to General Motors.

    (b) Discuss Arnold's and Mueller's claim that Bullard's warranty is not binding on the partnership.

5. Nanterre, Francis, and Litsi form a television repair partnership. Profits are to be shared equally. Each partner

draws a monthly salary of $1,000. Without Nanterre's and Francis's knowledge, Litsi, who has principal authority to purchase supplies and equipment, is receiving a rebate from large orders made with a supplier. Also, Litsi keeps the books and records at his home and continually denies Nanterre and Francis access to the books. Nanterre and Francis want an accounting. Discuss fully whether they are entitled to it.

6. Oddo and Ries entered into a partnership agreement in March 1978 to create and publish a book describing how to restore F-100 pickup trucks. Oddo was to write the book and Ries was to provide the capital. Oddo supplied Ries with the manuscript, but Ries was dissatisfied and hired someone else to revise the manuscript. The book Ries finally published contained substantial amounts of Oddo's work. Can Oddo require Ries to formally account for the profits on the book? [Oddo v. Ries, 743 F.2d 630 (9th Cir. 1984)]

7. Plaintiff Hodge brought an action against a partnership that owned a movie theater for specific performance of a contract for the sale of land. Volar, the managing partner of the partnership, had signed a contract for the sale to Hodge of real estate adjacent to the theater and belonging to the partnership. The agreement reserved an easement for use as a driveway into the premises. At trial, Volar claimed that prior to signing he had told Hodge that Hodge would have to present him with a plan of the property and that Volar's other partners would have to approve before the sale of the property would be final. At trial, Hodge denied this. The partners argued that, in any event, Volar did not have authority to sell the property. Did he? [Hodge v. Garrett, 101 Idaho 397, 614 P.2d 420 (1980)]

8. Birch and DeLong formed Birch-DeLong Construction Company in 1972 as a partnership. They agreed that all proceeds from the sale of houses would be deposited in a bank and that funds would be disbursed only by mutual agreement or authorization. Initially, both men signed all the checks, but in 1974 DeLong agreed that Birch would take over the accounting and disburse funds for the business. In 1980 the business was suffering and DeLong realized Birch had been paying some personal expenses out of partnership funds. Would DeLong have had a valid claim to an accounting of the funds Birch used to cover his personal expenses? [State of Washington v. Birch, 36 Wash.App. 405, 675 P.2d 246 (1984)]

9. Pat McGowan, Val Somers, and Brent Roberson were general partners in Vermont Place, a limited partnership formed to construct duplexes on a tract of land in Fort Smith, Arkansas. In 1984 the partnership mortgaged the property so that it could build there. McGowan owned a separate company, Advance Development Corp., that was hired by the partnership to develop the project. On September 3, 1984, Somers and Roberson discovered that McGowan had not been paying the suppliers to the project, including National Lumber Company, nor making the mortgage payments. The suppliers and the bank sued the partnership and the general partners individually. Discuss whether Somers and Roberson could be held individually liable for the debts incurred by McGowan. [National Lumber Co. v. Advance Development Corp., 293 Ark. 1, 732 S.W.2d 840 (1987)]

10. B. Darryl Clubb and Jeffere F. Van Liew formed a partnership to develop North Coast Park in northern San Diego County, California. The two were to share equally in the ownership and profits, and Clubb was to receive a 6-percent development fee. Later, Clubb claimed, he was forced to accept R. W. Wortham, III, as a partner, thereby reducing his interest to one-third. Subsequently, Wortham and Van Liew formed a new partnership called North Coast Park II in which Clubb had no interest. Without Clubb's consent, Van Liew and Wortham transferred by sale improved North Coast property to the new partnership. Clubb sued Wortham and Van Liew, claiming—among other things—that the sale (transfer) of the North Coast property was in breach of the partnership agreement. To prove this and other information concerning the two partnerships, Clubb, during the discovery phase of the trial, moved for a court order requiring Lawrence T. Dougherty, an attorney for both partnerships, to disclose certain information. Dougherty refused, claiming attorney-client privilege. Clubb claimed that information known by one partner must be made available to all partners. Discuss whether Dougherty could be compelled to give Clubb the information. [Wortham & Van Liew v. Superior Court (Clubb), 188 Cal.App.3d 927, 233 Cal.Rptr. 725 (1987)]

11. Three brothers, James, John, and Claude, purchased several parcels of land, taking title to the land either in their names or in their partnership name, Strother Brothers. The brothers never executed a written partnership agreement. After James died, John and Claude, along with their mother Minnie, brought suit to have Minnie declared owner of a one-fourth interest in the lands. This would leave James's heirs with only a one-fourth interest in the partnership instead of a one-third interest. Before trial Minnie died, leaving all her property to John and Claude. Discuss whether John and Claude succeeded in their attempt to increase their share of the partnership's property at the expense of their deceased brother's estate. [Strother v. Strother, 436 So.2d 847 (Ala. 1983)]

Chapter 37

PARTNERSHIPS
Limited Partnerships

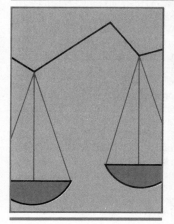

This chapter will look in detail at the formation, management, and termination of limited partnerships.

DEFINITION OF LIMITED PARTNERSHIP

Limited partnerships are formed by compliance with statutory requirements. They consist of at least one general partner and one or more limited partners.[1] The general partner (or partners) assumes management responsibility of the partnership and, as such, has full personal liability for all debts of the partnership. The limited partner (or partners) contributes cash (or other property) and owns an interest in the firm but does not undertake any management responsibilities and is not personally liable for partnership debts beyond the amount of his or her investment. A limited partner can forfeit limited liability by taking part in managing the business. In many respects, limited partnerships are like general partnerships, discussed in Chapters 35 and 36. They are sometimes referred to as special partnerships, in contrast to general partnerships.

The Uniform Limited Partnership Act

The Uniform Limited Partnership Act (ULPA) was promulgated in 1916. At one time, all states but Louisiana had adopted the 1916 version of the ULPA. Today thirty-six states have replaced their versions of ULPA with the revised ULPA discussed below.[2] The great virtue of both acts is that they expressly provide protection to limited partnerships against technical defects in their formation if there has been substantial compliance with statutory requirements.[3] Under either act, a limited partnership can conduct any business that can be carried on by a general partnership unless there is an exception in the state statutes.[4] The predominant exceptions involve the banking and insurance industries.

---

1. ULPA Section 1, RULPA Section 101(7).
2. Several states—including California and Delaware—made considerable changes in the revised ULPA before adopting it.
3. ULPA Section 2(2), RULPA Section 201(b).
4. ULPA Section 3, RULPA Section 106.

The Revised Uniform Limited Partnership Act

On August 5, 1976, the National Conference of Commissioners on Uniform State Laws approved the Revised Uniform Limited Partnership Act (RULPA). It contains eleven articles and sixty-four sections and was made available to state legislatures in 1977. In August, 1985, the commissioners approved a superseding version of RULPA. It is, however, very similar to the 1976 RULPA.[5]

For a comparison of the basic characteristics of general partnerships, limited partnerships, and those limited partnerships formed under the Revised Uniform Limited Partnership Act, see Exhibit 37–1.

FORMATION

The creation of a limited partnership is a public and formal proceeding that must follow statutory requirements. Contrast this with the informal, private, and voluntary agreement that usually suffices for a general partnership, as described in Chapter 35. For a limited partnership, there must be two or more partners, and they must sign a certificate that sets forth, at minimum, the following information:[6]

1. Firm name.
2. Character of the business.
3. Location of the principal place of business.
4. Name and place of residence of each member and whether each is a general or a limited partner.
5. Duration of the partnership.
6. Amount of cash and description and agreed-upon valuation of any other property contributed by each limited partner.

7. Additional contributions (if any) to be made by each limited partner and the times at which they are to be made.
8. Rights related to changes in partnership personnel (if any) and subsequent continuance of the business.
9. Share of profits or other compensation that each limited partner is entitled to receive.

In essence, the content of the certificate and the method of filing resemble those for the corporate charter (to be discussed in Chapter 39). Often, there are private, informal agreements covering matters that do not have to be stated in the certificate, such as the profit shares of the general partners. See Exhibit 37–2 for a sample certificate of limited partnership.

Where to File Certificates

The certificate must be filed with the designated state official. It is usually open to public inspection. The official is normally in the county where the principal business of the firm will be carried on. Some states require multiple filings for a business that will be carried on in numerous counties. Others require only one filing, usually at the state capital. The RULPA requires the filing of the certificate in the office of the secretary of state. Constructive notice (by reason of law) does not usually exist for a certificate filed in another state. Thus, if a limited partnership chooses to do business where no certificate is filed, a court can rule that its failure to file locally makes it a general partnership. This is similar to the qualification rules for foreign corporation (a corporation doing business in one state although chartered or incorporated in another). Some states require newspaper publication of certificates, or at least summaries of them, in addition to filings.

Number of Limited Partners

Originally, limited partnerships were conceived to accommodate only a few limited partners. There seems, however, to be no statutory limit to the number of partners; and in some cases, very large groups have been assembled.

---

5. This chapter will discuss ULPA and the 1976 RULPA and note the significant differences in the 1985 RULPA.

6. ULPA Section 2(1), RULPA Section 201. The 1985 RULPA Section 201 requires only the name of the limited partnership, the name and address of an agent for service of process, the name and address of each general partner, and the latest date on which the limited partnership is to dissolve. Since, under these amendments, limited partners are not required to sign the certificate, they would not be potentially liable for false statements in it.

Exhibit 37–1 **Basic Comparison of Partnerships**

CHARACTERISTIC	GENERAL PARTNERSHIP (UPA)	LIMITED PARTNERSHIP (ULPA)	LIMITED PARTNERSHIP (RULPA)
Creation	By agreement of two or more persons to carry on a business as co-owners for profit.	By agreement of two or more persons, one or more general partners and one or more limited partners, to carry on a business as co-owners for profit. Filing of certificate in appropriate state office is required.	Same as limited partnership, except filing of certificate with the state's secretary of state is required.
Sharing of profits and losses	By agreement, or in absence thereof, profits are shared equally by partners and losses are shared in same ratio as profits.	Profits are shared as required in certificate agreement, and losses are shared likewise, except limited partners share losses only up to their capital contribution.	Same as limited partnership, except in absence of provision in certificate agreement, profits and losses are shared on basis of percentages of capital contributions.
Liability	Unlimited personal liability of all partners.	Unlimited personal liability of all general partners; limited partners only to extent of capital contributions.	Same as limited partnership.
Capital contribution	No minimal or mandatory amount; set by agreement.	Set by agreement; may be cash, property, or any obligation except services.	Same as limited partnership, except contribution of services is allowed.
Management	By agreement, or in absence thereof, all partners have an equal voice.	General partners by agreement, or else each has an equal voice. Limited partners have no voice or else are subject to liability as general partners.	Same as limited partnership, except limited partner involved in partnership management is liable as a general partner *only* if third party has knowledge of such involvement. Limited partner may act as agent or employee of partnership and may vote on amending certificate and on sale or dissolution of partnership.
Duration	By agreement, or can be dissolved by action of partner (including withdrawal), operation of law (including death or bankruptcy), or court decree.	By agreement in certificate, by court decree, or by withdrawal, death, or insanity of general partner in absence of right of other general partners to continue the partnership. Death of a limited partner, unless he or she is the only remaining limited partner, does not terminate the partnership.	Same as limited partnership, except it enlarges class of activities by general partner that result in termination.
Assignment	Interest can be assigned, although assignee does not have rights of partner without consent of other partners.	Same as general partnership. If partners consent to assignee's becoming a partner, certificate must be amended.	Same as limited partnership. Upon assignment of all interest, partner ceases to be a partner.

Exhibit 37–1 **Basic Comparison of Partnerships (Continued)**

CHARACTERISTIC	GENERAL PARTNERSHIP (UPA)	LIMITED PARTNERSHIP (ULPA)	LIMITED PARTNERSHIP (RULPA)
Priorities (order) upon liquidation	1. Outside creditors. 2. Partner creditors. 3. Capital contribution of partners. 4. Profits of partners.	1. Outside creditors and limited partner creditors. 2. Profits to limited partners. 3. Limited partner capital contributions. 4. General partner creditors. 5. Profits to general partners. 6. Capital contributions of general partners.	1. Outside creditors and partner creditors. 2. Amounts to which partners are entitled before withdrawal under the partnership agreement. 3. Capital contributions—limited and general partners. 4. Profits—limited and general partners.

RIGHTS AND LIABILITIES OF LIMITED PARTNERS

General partners, unlike limited partners, are personally liable to the partnership's creditors; thus, a limited partnership must include at least one general partner so that someone has personal liability. This policy can be circumvented in states that allow a corporation to be the general partner in a partnership. Since a corporation's liability is limited to the extent of its assets, no one in such a limited partnership actually has personal liability.

Limited Partners Cannot Participate in Management

The exemptions from personal liability of the limited partners rest on their not participating in management.[7] First, the contribution of a limited partner cannot be in his or her services as manager—it has to be in cash or other property.[8] Second, the surname of a limited partner cannot be included in the partnership name.[9] A violation of either of these provisions renders the limited partner just as liable as a general partner to any creditor who does not know that he or she is a limited partner.[10]

Note that no law expressly bars the participation of limited partners in the management of the partnership. Rather, the threat of personal liability deters their participation.

Under the RULPA, only if the third party had knowledge of the limited partner's management activities is the limited partner liable as a general partner.[11] How much actual review and advisement a limited partner can engage in before being exposed to liability is an unsettled question.[12]

The issue of the degree of control of the limited partner comes up in the following case.

---

7. ULPA Section 7, RULPA Section 303.

8. ULPA Section 4. See, however, RULPA Section 101(2), in which *contribution* is defined to include "services rendered."

9. ULPA Section 5, RULPA Section 102.

10. ULPA Sections 5, 7; RULPA Section 303.

11. RULPA Section 303(a).

12. Compare ULPA Section 7 with RULPA Section 303(b), (c).

Exhibit 37–2 **Sample Certificate of Limited Partnership**[a]

CERTIFICATE OF LIMITED PARTNERSHIP

The undersigned, desiring to form a Limited Partnership under the Uniform Limited Partnership Act of the State of _____ , make this certificate for that purpose.

§ 1.   Name.   The name of the Partnership shall be "_____ _____ ".

§ 2.   Purpose.   The purpose of the Partnership shall be to [*describe*].

§ 3.   Location.   The location of the Partnership's principal place of business is _____County, _____ .

§ 4.   Members and Designation.   The names and places of residence of the members, and their designation as General or Limited Partners are:

_____	[*Address*]	General Partner
_____	[*Address*]	General Partner
_____	[*Address*]	Limited Partner
_____	[*Address*]	Limited Partner

§ 5.   Term.   The term for which the Partnership is to exist is indefinite.

§ 6.   Initial Contributions of Limited Partners.   The amount of cash and a description of the agreed value of the other property contributed by each Limited Partner are:

[*Name*]	[*Describe*]
[*Name*]	[*Describe*]

§ 7.   Subsequent Contributions of Limited Partners.   Each Limited Partner may (but shall not be obliged to) make such additional contributions to the capital of the Partnership as may from time to time be agreed upon by the General Partners.

§ 8.   Profit Shares of Limited Partners.   The share of the profits which each Limited Partner shall receive by reason of his contribution is:

[*Name*]	_____ %
[*Name*]	_____ %

Signed _____ , 19_____

_____
_____
_____
_____

Signed and sworn before me, the undersigned authority, this _____ _____ , 19_____ .

Notary Public
_____County, _____

---

a. This certificate illustrates the information required under ULPA Section 2. Under RULPA Section 201, as it was originally drafted, all of the information above was required, as well as the name and address of an agent for service of process and a listing of the contributions and profit shares of the general partners. Under RULPA's 1985 amendments, no information pertaining to limited partners or to any partner's contributions or shares is required, nor do the limited partners need to sign the certificate; but the latest date on which the limited partnership is to dissolve must be included.

BACKGROUND AND FACTS   *Richard Gast, an engineer, was employed by LNG Services, a limited partnership. When he left LNG he submitted a claim for back pay and reimbursement of expenses. LNG did not pay, and Gast sued the company, the general partner, Petsinger, and the limited partners. Gast claimed that although they called themselves limited partners, they were, by virtue of their participation in the business, general partners and should therefore be held personally liable for the money LNG owed him. The trial court granted a summary judgment (without a jury) for the limited partners, and Gast appealed.*

Case 37.1
GAST v. PETSINGER
Superior Court of Pennsylvania, 1974.
228 Pa.Super. 394, 323 A.2d 371.

HOFFMAN, Judge.
*   *   *   *

The organization of LNG Services is in conformance with the Uniform Limited Partnership Act. The certificate is in good order, and the Agreement delineates the powers, rights and liabilities of the General and Limited Partners in express terms. None of the powers mentioned therein exceed the degree of "control" which converts the status of a limited partner to that of general partner. In two sections of the U.L.P.A., the statute clearly limits the liability of the limited partner: "A limited partner shall not become liable as a general partner unless, in addition to the exercise of his rights and powers as a limited partner, *he takes part in the control of the business.*"
*   *   *   *

Only Dr. Garwin and Jerome Apt, Jr., appear to have acted in capacities which require some discussion and evaluation. In addition to receiving reports and attending meetings wherein status reports and additional capital investments were discussed, Dr. Garwin was employed by the Partnership as an independent engineering consultant with respect to certain projects undertaken by LNG Services for which service he was retained by the General Partner and in which, he and the General Partner assert, he remained subject to the supervision and control of Petsinger, the General Partner. Apt was also engaged from time to time as an independent consultant on certain projects. These individuals were described as "Project Managers" on several booklets which were attached to appellant's deposition as exhibits.
*   *   *   *

The key issue before the lower court was whether the appellant had presented an arguable case demonstrating that some or all of the appellees had "take[n] part in the control of the business." *   *   *
*   *   *   *

An analysis of [other court] cases reveals that they were decided on their own facts and are of little use in forming rules or standards. In each case, it was not the position of the limited partner that was stated as permissible, but the actual role and degree of participation that each had in relation to the general partner. A reading of those cases reinforces the belief of this Court that the determination must be made on an *ad hoc* basis, and while employment may not be conflicting with the status of a limited partner, the "control" that partner has in the day-to-day functions and operations of the business is the key question. Does the limited partner have decision-making authority that may not be checked or nullified by the general partner? *   *   *

Here, the appellant testified that partners Apt and Garwin acted in the partnership as "Project Managers." He stated in his deposition that the appearance of their names on brochures and reports, the obvious weight their "advice" carried in their recommendations and report on key projects, and their managerial responsibilities, all contributed to a belief that they exercised "control." The defendant Petsinger, the General Partner, confirms the fact that these two individuals acted as independent "consultants" on various "projects." He denies their authority or right to control the business decisions.
*   *   *

It may be true that once all of the facts are in the appellees, Apt and Garwin, will have been found not to have exercised the degree of "control" necessary to impose general liability upon them. We agree that the nature of the business of LNG Services, described as having as its purposes "the management of the development, engineering, and technical advice relating to the development or uses for liquefied natural gas, etc., . . ." required the utilization of expert opinion of technical minds. It is not apparent from the face of the record that the technical skills and training of Apt and Garwin did not by virtue of their retention as "Project Managers" place them in a position where their "advice" did influence and perhaps, control the decisions of the General Partner, whose particular expertise is unknown.

DECISION AND REMEDY

The judge remanded the case so that the trial court could examine the degree of control exercised by two limited partners whose expertise and roles in the company, as consultants to the general partner, may have been so dominant that they actually did participate in the day-to-day management of LNG. If they participated in management, they should be held liable as general partners.

COMMENTS

The courts acknowledge that the determination of whether a limited partner actively engages in the management of the limited partnership must be made on a case-by-case basis. Because a limited partner invests money in the business, he or she does have an interest in seeing that the business is managed well. Sometimes a limited partner is as knowledgeable as the general partner(s) in the type of business the limited partnership is formed to pursue. This frequently makes it difficult for the limited partner not to actively try to influence the decisions of the general partners; and when such activity becomes active management, the limited partner loses the limitation of liability to his or her investment.

The case above was tried under the Uniform Limited Partnership Act. Under the Revised Uniform Limited Partnership Act, a limited partner "does not participate in the control of the business * * * solely by * * * being a contractor for or an agent or employee of the limited partnership or of a general partner, [or] consulting with and advising a general partner with respect to the business of the limited partnership." In addition, the limited partner is only liable to persons who transact business with the limited partnership with "actual knowledge of his participation in control." Had the RULPA been in effect, it is highly unlikely that Apt and Garwin would have been considered active participants in the management of the limited partnership.

Liability of Limited Partners

A limited partner may be liable to creditors to the extent of any contribution that he or she promised to the firm or any part of a contribution that he or she withdrew from the firm.[13] If the firm is defectively organized and the limited partner fails to renunciate (withdraw from the partnership) on discovery of the defect, the partner can be held personally liable to the firm's creditors. Note, though, that the ULPA and the RULPA allow individuals to remain limited partners regardless of whether they comply with statutory technicalities. Decisions on liability for false statements in a partnership certificate run in favor of persons who have relied on the false statements and against members who sign the certificate knowing of the

---

13. See ULPA Section 7 and RULPA Section 502.

falsity.[14] A limited partnership is formed by good faith compliance with the requirements for signing and filing the certificate, even if the certificate is incomplete or defective. When a limited partner discovers a defect in the formation of the limited partnership, he or she can obtain shelter from future liability by renouncing an interest in the profits of the partnership, thereby avoiding any future reliance by third parties.[15]

The liability of a limited partner is limited to the capital that he or she contributes or agrees to contribute to the partnership. By contrast, the liability of a general partner for partnership indebtedness is virtually unlimited. In a recent case, the general partner of a limited partnership remained personally liable for partnership debts after the limited partnership went through a Chapter 7 bankruptcy.[16]

The following case deals with an attempt by a bank creditor to hold limited partners liable on notes that represented their capital contributions.

---

14. See ULPA Section 6 and RULPA Section 207. The 1985 RULPA Section 204 does not require that limited partners sign the certificate or its amendments.

15. ULPA Section 11. Compare RULPA Section 304, under which the limited partner can also avoid liability if, on discovering the mistake, he or she causes an appropriate certificate or amendment to be filed.

16. Rohdie v. Washington, 641 S.W.2d 317 (Tex.Ct.App. 1982).

BACKGROUND AND FACTS   *Chemical Bank of Rochester filed suit against the limited partners of a partnership to recover funds advanced on a note. Stanndco Developers was the sole general partner in Meadowbrook Farm Apartments. In exchange for Stanndco's promise to transfer apartment units to the Meadowbrook limited partnership, eighteen limited partners executed promissory notes payable to Meadowbrook for their "shares" in the limited partnership. The notes totaled $101,000. Stanndco later sought a $101,000 bank loan for purposes unrelated to Meadowbrook and used the notes given by the Meadowbrook limited partners as collateral. Stanndco indorsed the notes to itself without the consent or ratification of the limited partners. The bank sought to collect on the notes from the limited partners.*

Case 37.2
CHEMICAL BANK OF ROCHESTER v. ASHENBURG
Supreme Court of Monroe County, 1978.
94 Misc.2d 64, 405 N.Y.S.2d 175.

SCHNEPP, Justice.
*   *   *   *

Plaintiff [bank] had knowledge that Stanndco was negotiating the instruments in a transaction for its own benefit, without authority, and in breach of its duty as a fiduciary. Plaintiff knew from the outset of the transaction, when Stanndco first approached it for a corporate loan, that the notes were not being used by Stanndco for a partnership purpose. *   *   * In the face of these facts, plaintiff acted in bad faith. Chemical Bank had actual knowledge or knowledge of facts sufficient to impute notice on the infirmities, defects and defenses to the instrument. In short, plaintiff, having taken the notes with notice and in bad faith, is not entitled to the rights of a holder in due course.
*   *   *   *

It is held that plaintiff takes subject to the defendants' claim that the notes were negotiated for the individual purpose of a general partner in breach of its fiduciary duty. Plaintiff, a non–holder in due course, may not recover on the notes against the defendant makers *   *   *.

*   *   * The defendants, as both makers of the notes and limited partners, had a legitimate expectation that the provisions of the Partnership Law would be followed. They had no cause to anticipate that a general partner would exceed his authority by assigning their rights in specific partnership property without their written consent or ratification and thus effectively terminate their right to have their contribution returned. It was the written consent or ratification of each defendant limited partner that was required for the proper negotiation of the notes—and this is what Stanndco failed to secure. Clearly, each defendant maker is offended and damaged by Stanndco's breach of duty, because each is a limited partner.

* * * Plaintiff's conduct permitted the diversion of the partnership assets and it should not profit from its own wrongdoing. Under these circumstances it would be unconscionable not to permit the defendants to assert their claim as a defense against plaintiff. * * *

DECISION AND REMEDY   *The court dismissed Chemical Bank's lawsuit against the limited partners. Since Chemical Bank knew that Stanndco was transferring the notes for other than legitimate partnership purposes, it was not permitted to recover any money from the limited partners.*

Rights of the Limited Partner

Subject to the limitations described above, limited partners have essentially the same rights as general partners: the right of access to partnership books, the right to an accounting of partnership business, and the right to participate in the dissolution and the winding up of the partnership. They are entitled to a return of their contributions in accordance with the partnership certificate.[17] They can also assign their interests subject to specific clauses in the certificate.[18]

LIMITED PARTNER'S RIGHT TO SUE   In jurisdictions that have considered the matter, courts seem to recognize fully the limited partner's right to sue, either individually or on behalf of the firm, for economic injury to the firm by general partners or outsiders. The RULPA provides a limited partner with the right to sue on behalf of the firm if the general partners with authority to do so have refused to file suit.[19] In addition, investor protection legislation, such as security laws (discussed in Chapter 43), may give some protection to limited partners.

THE USE OF A LIMITED PARTNERSHIP

The limited partnership is a less effective liability shield than the corporation. In many respects, the corporation is more flexible, and its charter does not require frequent amendments as a limited partnership certificate does.[20] One might conclude

that limited partnerships have little utility, except for special reasons.

Before World War II, limited partnerships were used sparingly, but during and after the war their number increased, largely because of high federal income tax rates, particularly on corporations. A limited partnership allows the limited partners to deduct expenses or losses against other income directly and to be protected from personal liability.

There are three primary uses for limited partnerships today:

1.   To buy, build, and lease commercial property, hold it for a period of five or more years, and then resell it.
2.   To purchase and lease heavy equipment.
3.   To loan money and take back first mortgages.

Also, limited partnerships have been used extensively to finance oil and gas ventures, film productions, and research and development.

Nevertheless, it is most likely that only more sophisticated investors will structure a business as a limited partnership, and then only under circumstances that make other investments less desirable. Limited partnerships have proved to have some popularity with people who are starting new Individual Retirement Accounts (IRAs). A limited partnership funded with capital from IRAs might include a small number of investors, each with a large amount of capital, or a large number of investors, each with a small amount of capital.

DISSOLUTION

A limited partnership is dissolved in much the same way as an ordinary partnership. The retirement, death, or insanity of a general partner can dissolve the partnership, but not if the business can be continued by one or more of the other

---

17. ULPA Section 10, RULPA Section 201(a)(10).

18. ULPA Section 19, RULPA Sections 702, 704.

19. RULPA Section 1001.

20. ULPA Section 24(2). Amendment is required considerably less frequently under the RULPA's Section 202(b).

general partners in accordance with their certificate or by consent of all members.[21] The death or assignment of interest of a limited partner does not dissolve the limited partnership.[22] With respect to dissolution, limited partnerships resemble corporations more closely than they do general partnerships. Public filings, passive (non-managing) investors, and limited liability are all features of both corporations and limited partnerships.

Causes of Dissolution

A limited partnership is dissolved by the expiration of its term or the completion of its undertaking. When there is no definite term or undertaking, the express will of any general partner will usually dissolve the partnership. Under the ULPA, limited partners do not have the power to dissolve the partnership unless they have rightfully, but unsuccessfully, demanded the return of their contribution.[23] Under the RULPA, limited partners have neither the right nor the power to dissolve the firm, except by court decree.[24] If, however, the general partners dissolve the partnership without the consent of the limited partners before the end of the term fixed by the certificate, this dissolution is considered a breach.

Illegality, expulsion, and bankruptcy of the general partners may lead to the dissolution of a limited partnership. Bankruptcy of a limited partner will not, however, unless it causes the bankruptcy of the firm.

The retirement of a general partner causes a dissolution unless the members consent to a continuation by the remaining general partners or unless this contingency is provided for in the certificate.

Consequences of Dissolution

The consequences of the dissolution of general partnerships apply to limited partnerships (see Chapter 35). Therefore, the firm continues in operation while winding up. The general partners of a limited partnership have the authority to wind up, as in an ordinary partnership. The representatives of general partners, not the limited partners, succeed the general partners. Limited partners have the right to obtain dissolution and winding up by court decree.[25]

Assuming that the general partners continue the business, the limited partners generally have the right to be paid the value of their interests at dissolution, plus profits or interest on that value from dissolution until payment.

Priorities in Distribution of Assets

Upon dissolution, under the ULPA, creditors' rights to assets precede partners' rights, and limited partners' rights precede general partners' rights. Limited partners take their share of profits and of contributed capital before general partners receive anything.[26] Under the RULPA, creditors' rights, including those of partners who are creditors, come first; then partners and former partners receive unpaid distributions of partnership assets and, except as otherwise agreed, amounts representing a return of their contributions and amounts proportionate to their share of the distributions.[27]

---

21. ULPA Section 20, RULPA Section 801.
22. ULPA Section 21, RULPA Section 705.
23. ULPA Section 16.
24. RULPA Section 802.

---

25. ULPA Section 10(c), RULPA Sections 802, 803.
26. ULPA Section 23, and see Exhibit 37–1.
27. RULPA Section 804, and see Exhibit 37–1.

QUESTIONS AND CASE PROBLEMS

1. Asner and Burton form a limited partnership with Asner as the general partner and Burton as the limited partner.

Burton puts up $15,000, and Asner contributes some office equipment that he owns. A certificate of limited partnership is properly filed, and business is begun. One month later, Asner becomes ill. Instead of hiring someone to manage the business, Burton takes over complete management himself. While Burton is in control, he makes a contract with Thomas involving a large sum of money. Asner returns to work. Because of other commitments, the Thomas contract is breached. Thomas contends that he can hold Asner and

Burton personally liable if his judgment cannot be satisfied out of the assets of the limited partnership. Discuss this contention.

2. Alfred, Barton, and Carrie want to form a limited partnership. Alfred and Barton are recent college graduates with no business experience. They are to be the general partners. Carrie, an experienced businesswoman, is to be the limited partner. Carrie is to put up $10,000 and to manage the business for the first six months, until Alfred and Barton gain experience. For this, the partnership will list her capital contribution as $15,000. Profits are to be divided equally. The limited partnership name has not been determined. For the present, the partners plan on simply using their surnames. Discuss what advice an attorney might give Alfred, Barton, and Carrie on forming a limited partnership.

3. Elsie, Liz, and Elena form a limited partnership. Elsie is a general partner, and Liz and Elena are limited partners. Consider each of the separate events below and discuss fully which constitute a dissolution of the limited partnership.
   (a) Liz assigns her partnership interest to Diana.
   (b) Elena is petitioned into involuntary bankruptcy.
   (c) Elsie dies.

4. Otto and Klaus form a limited partnership to operate a retail jewelry business. Otto is the general partner and Klaus the limited partner. The certificate of partnership does not specify a definite term for the partnership's existence. Otto and Klaus disagree over Otto's management of the business. Klaus demands, in writing, the return of his contribution. Discuss fully the following:
   (a) Can a limited partner dissolve the partnership?
   (b) If the limited partnership is dissolved, who has authority to wind up the affairs of the partnership?

5. Cochran and Wolf form a limited partnership, with Cochran as the general partner. During the existence of the partnership, Cochran's contribution of capital is $2,000, and Wolf's is $50,000. The limited partnership is dissolved, and the sale of partnership assets in the winding up of the partnership affairs results in proceeds of $100,000. Partnership creditors have claims totaling $45,000, and the profit accounts of Cochran and Wolf are $5,000 each. Discuss the priorities to the $100,000.

6. In a limited partnership having one general partner, the general partner loaned over $1 million to the partnership and executed notes payable to herself. The limited partner knew that these notes were carried as outstanding debts on the partnership books for seven years. When the general partner died, the limited partner maintained that the partnership agreement did not authorize the general partner to borrow money and that the amount constituted a contribution to capital rather than loans. How did the court treat the money? [Park Cities Corp. v. Byrd, 522 S.W.2d 572 (Tex.Civ.App. 1975)]

7. The Sports Factory, Inc., executed a lease with Ridley Park Associates, a limited partnership, to operate a health and racquetball club. William Chanoff was the general partner of Ridley Park Associates. Over several months, Ridley Park failed to meet the original agreement with Sports Factory, Inc., in several respects, including altering architectural plans for the racquetball courts and failing to acquire the zoning changes needed for operation of a health spa.

If Sports Factory brought a cause of action for breach of its agreement with Ridley Park, who would be found liable? [Sports Factory, Inc. v. Chanoff, 586 F.Supp. 342 (E.D.Pa. 1984)]

8. Columbia-Heather was a limited partnership engaged in the construction of an apartment complex in Toledo, Ohio. Partnership Equities, Inc., the plaintiff, was one of the general partners, and Amin Khoury and James Marten, the defendants, were two of the limited partners. In becoming limited partners, the defendants had agreed to make contributions over a four-year period. The defendants refused to make contributions for the last two years. They claimed that the general partners had breached the partnership agreement and therefore the limited partners were not obligated to make continued contributions to the limited partnership. The general partners sued for the unpaid contributions under Section 17 of the Uniform Limited Partnership Act (Section 502 of the Revised Uniform Limited Partnership Act). Discuss who will prevail. [Partnership Equities, Inc. v. Marten, 15 Mass.App. 42, 443 N.E.2d 134 (1982)]

9. Combat Associates was formed as a limited partnership to promote an exhibition boxing match between Lyle Alzado (a professional football player) and Muhammed Ali. Alzado and others had formed Combat Promotions; and this organization was to be the general partner, and Blinder, Robinson & Co., Inc., the limited partner, in Combat Associates. The general partner's contribution consisted of assigning all contracts pertaining to the match, and the limited partner's contribution was a $250,000 letter of credit to ensure Ali's compensation. Alzado personally guaranteed to repay Blinder, Robinson for any amount of loss if the proceeds of the match were less than $250,000. In preparation for the match, at Alzado's request, Blinder, Robinson's president participated in interviews and a promotional rally and the company sponsored parties and allowed its local office to be used as a ticket sales outlet. The proceeds of the match were insufficient, and Blinder, Robinson sued Alzado on his guaranty. Alzado counterclaimed by asserting that Blinder, Robinson took an active role in the control and management of Combat Associates and should be held liable as a general partner. How did the court rule on Alzado's counterclaim? [Blinder, Robinson & Co., Inc. v. Alzado, 713 P.2d 1314 (Colo.App. 1985)]

10. Mt. Hood Meadows, Oregon, Ltd., was a limited partnership established to carry on the business of constructing and operating a winter sports development in the Hood River area of Oregon. Elizabeth Brooke and two of the other limited partners were dissatisfied because, for all the years in which profits were earned after 1974, the general partner distributed only 50 percent of the limited partners' taxable profits. The remaining profits were retained and reinvested in the business. Each of the limited partners was taxed on his or her distributable share of the profits, however, regardless of whether the cash was actually distributed. Brooke and the others brought this action to compel the general partner to distribute all of the limited partnership's profits. Discuss whether the limited partners could compel the general partner to distribute all of the profits. [Brooke v. Mt. Hood Meadows Oregon, Ltd., 81 Or.App. 387, 725 P.2d 925 (1986)]

Chapter 38

CORPORATIONS
Nature & Classifications

The corporation can be owned by a single person, or it can have hundreds, thousands, or even millions of shareholders. The shareholder form of business organization developed in Europe at the end of the seventeenth century. The firms were called *joint stock companies,* and they frequently collapsed because their organizers absconded with the funds or proved to be incompetent.

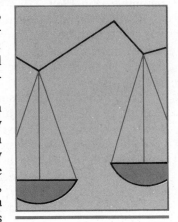

The most famous collapse involved the South Sea Company, which assumed England's national debt in 1711 and obtained in return a monopoly over British trade with the South Sea Islands in South America plus an annual interest payment. The shares of the company were driven up by speculation, fraud was exposed, and a collapse followed. The event came to be known as the South Sea Bubble, and it led to the Bubble Act of 1720, a law that curtailed the use of joint stock companies in England for over a hundred years. Because of this history of fraud and collapse, organizations resembling corporations were regarded with suspicion in the United States during its early years.

In the eighteenth century, a typical U.S. corporation was a municipality. Although several business corporations were formed after the Revolutionary War, it was not until the nineteenth century that the corporation came into common use for private business. In 1811, New York passed a general incorporation law allowing businesses to incorporate. Incorporation was permissible by five or more persons for the manufacture of textiles, glass, metals, and paint. The corporation could have capital of $100,000 (about $750,000 in today's dollars) and a life of twenty years.

The significance of the New York law was that it allowed voluntary incorporation through standard bureaucratic procedures rather than special acts of the legislature, which were usually available only to businesspersons with political influence. By the mid-nineteenth century, railroads predominated among corporations. After the Civil War, manufacturing corporations became numerous.

THE CORPORATION AS A CREATURE OF STATUTE

The corporation is a creature of statute. Its existence depends generally upon state law, although some corporations, especially public organizations, can be created under federal law. Each state has its own body of corporate law, and these laws are not entirely uniform. The Model Business Corporation Act (often called the Model Act) is a codification of modern corporation law. It enunciates principles of corporate law that have been adopted to some degree by every state.

The Model Business Corporation Act (MBCA) was originally patterned after the Illinois Business Corporation Act of 1933. It was first published in its complete form in 1933 by the Committee on Corporate Laws of the Section of Corporation, Banking, and Business Law of the American Bar Association. Since 1933, the act has undergone several changes and was subsequently revised and renumbered in 1969.

The 1969 act underwent revisions over the years, and the Committee on Corporate Laws decided that all provisions of the act should be revised so that its language would be internally consistent and uniform.

The Revised Model Business Corporation Act (RMBCA), as approved in June 1984, was drafted as a convenient guide for revision of state business corporation acts. It was designed for use by both publicly held and closely held corporations and includes provisions for the rights and duties of shareholders, management, and directors. Already, a number of states have amended their corporation laws, to a limited degree, based on the RMBCA.

Neither the 1969 act nor the 1984 act has been totally adopted by any state in its current form. The 1969 act, however, has been influential in codification of corporation statutes in thirty-seven states[1] and the District of Columbia. It should be kept in mind, however, that there is considerable variation among the statutes of the states that have used the Model Act as a basis for their statutes. Because of this, individual state corporation laws should be relied upon rather than the MBCA.

The MBCA and selections from the RMBCA have been included in this text as Appendix F and Appendix G, respectively.

THE NATURE OF A CORPORATION

A **corporation** is a legal entity created and recognized by state law. It can consist of one or more persons identified under a common name.

The Corporation as a Legal "Person"

A corporation is recognized under state and federal law as a "person," and it enjoys many of the same rights and privileges that U.S. citizens enjoy.

The Bill of Rights guarantees a "person," as a citizen, certain protections, and corporations are considered persons in most instances. For example, a corporation has the same right as a natural person to equal protection of the laws under the Fourteenth Amendment. It has the right of access to the courts as an entity that can sue or be sued. It also has the right of due process before denial of life, liberty, or property, as well as freedom from unreasonable search and seizures and from double jeopardy.

Under the First Amendment, corporations are entitled to freedom of speech;[2] however, only the corporation's individual officers and employees possess the Fifth Amendment right against self-incrimination.[3] In addition, the privilege and immunities clause of the federal Constitution (Article 4, Section 2) does not protect corporations, nor does it protect unincorporated associations.[4] This means that a state may restrict a *foreign corporation's* activities within that state. (In this instance, a corporation incorporated in one state is a foreign corporation as to other states.)

An unsettled area of corporation law has to do with the criminal acts of a corporation. It is obvious that a corporation cannot be sent to prison even though, under law, it is a person. Most courts hold a corporation that has violated the criminal statutes liable for fines. When criminal conduct can be attributed to corporate officers or agents,

---

1. Alaska, Alabama, Arizona, Arkansas, Colorado, Connecticut, Florida, Georgia, Idaho, Iowa, Kentucky, Louisiana, Maine, Maryland, Massachusetts, Michigan, Mississippi, Montana, Nebraska, New Jersey, New Mexico, New York, North Carolina, North Dakota, Oregon, Rhode Island, South Carolina, South Dakota, Tennessee, Texas, Utah, Vermont, Virginia, Washington, West Virginia, Wisconsin, Wyoming.

2. Pacific Gas & Elec. Co. v. P.U.C. of California, 475 U.S. 1, 106 S.Ct. 903, 89 L.Ed.2d 1 (1986).

3. In re Grand Jury No. 86-3 (Will Roberts Corp.), 816 F.2d 569 (11th Cir. 1987).

4. W.C.M. Window Co., Inc. v. Bernardi, 730 F.2d 486 (7th Cir. 1984).

those individuals, as natural persons, are held liable and can be imprisoned for their acts.

Characteristics of the Corporate Entity

A corporation is an artificial person, with its own corporate name, owned by individual shareholders. It is a legal entity with rights and responsibilities. The corporation substitutes itself for its shareholders in conducting corporate business and in incurring liability. Its authority to act and the liability for its actions are separate and apart from the individuals who own it, although in certain limited situations the "corporate veil" can be pierced (that is, liability for the corporation's obligations can be extended to shareholders). In some instances, shareholders can voluntarily make themselves personally liable for some or all of the debts of the corporation. This is particularly true with smaller corporations that attempt to obtain financing.

Responsibility for overall management of the corporation is entrusted to a board of directors, which is elected by shareholders.[5] Corporate officers and other employees are hired by the board of directors to run the daily business operations of the corporation.

The following sections briefly discuss the relationships and responsibilities of the shareholders, the board of directors, the officers, and the employees in the management of the corporation. More detail will be found in Chapter 41.

SHAREHOLDERS　The acquisition of a share of stock makes a person an owner or shareholder in a corporation. Unlike the members in a partnership, the body of shareholders can change constantly without affecting the continued existence of the corporation. Thus, a corporation is not affected by the death of a shareholder, whereas the death of a partner dissolves a partnership.

Generally, shareholders are owners without direct control over the management of the corporation's business. Only through the election of the board of directors can they exercise influence over corporate policy. They are neither managers nor agents of the corporation.

As a general rule, a shareholder is not personally liable for the corporation's business debts; nor is the corporation responsible for a shareholder's personal debts. Each shareholder's liability is limited to the amount of the investment (that is, the money actually paid when the stock was acquired).[6]

Thus, if Paul Ginsberg purchases one hundred shares of Ace Manufacturing stock at $1 per share and Ace Manufacturing goes bankrupt owing creditors millions of dollars, Ginsberg's loss is limited to the $100 purchase price that he originally paid for the shares. The converse is also true. If Ginsberg declares bankruptcy and owes creditors thousands of dollars, Ace Manufacturing Company is not liable, and the creditors can claim only the one hundred shares of stock.

Each shareholder has an ownership interest in a corporation, proportionate to his or her ownership of shares in the corporation. Shareholders have certain rights during a corporation's existence and are entitled to proportional parts of corporate assets on the winding up of corporate business (subject, of course, to corporate liabilities and obligations).

A shareholder can sue the corporation, and the corporation can sue a shareholder. Also, under certain circumstances, a shareholder can sue on behalf of a corporation. A shareholder's action to enforce a corporate cause of action, called a **derivative suit,** is based upon a primary right of a corporation but is asserted on its behalf by the stockholder because of the corporation's failure, deliberate or otherwise, to act upon the primary right. The shareholder's derivative suit and the special responsibility of majority shareholders of the corporation will be discussed in the next two chapters. Majority shareholders are those who hold a majority of the shares of the corporation's stock and, thus, may control the corporation's management or elect the directors.

BOARD OF DIRECTORS　A general rule in corporate law says, "Directors must direct the corporate business affairs." The board of directors is elected by shareholders and is periodically accountable to them for reelection.

The board is responsible for making decisions about overall policy. Directors declare dividends, authorize major corporate contracts, appoint or remove officers and set their salaries, issue au-

---

5. MBCA Sections 35, 36; RMBCA Sections 8.01, 8.03

6. MBCA Section 25, and RMBCA Section 6.22.

thorized shares of stock, and recommend changes in the corporate charter. They delegate the day-to-day operation of corporate affairs to the officers and other employees of the corporation. The board can organize itself into executive committees and delegate to these committees particular responsibilities to act on behalf of the entire board or to report back to it. Then, it acts as a unit.

OFFICERS AND OTHER EMPLOYEES   Officers are agents of the corporation. They answer to the board of directors rather than to the shareholders directly, and they can be removed at any time by the board.

TAX CONSIDERATIONS   Since a corporation is a separate legal entity, corporate profits are taxed by the state and federal governments. Corporations can do one of two things with corporate profits—retain them or pass them on to shareholders in the form of dividends. The corporation receives no tax deduction for dividends distributed to shareholders.

When dividends are money payments, they are again taxable (except when they represent distributions of capital) as ordinary income to the shareholder receiving them. This double taxation feature of the corporate organization is one of its major disadvantages. On the other hand, retained earnings, if invested properly, will yield higher corporate profits in the future and thus cause the price of the company's stock to rise. Individual shareholders can then reap the benefits of these retained earnings in the gains they receive when they sell their shares, but they still do not avoid taxation.

DOMESTIC, FOREIGN, AND ALIEN CORPORATIONS

The corporation is referred to as a **domestic corporation** by its home state (the state in which it incorporated). As mentioned, a corporation formed in one state but doing business in another is referred to in that other state as a **foreign corporation**. A corporation formed in another country, say Mexico, doing business within the United States is referred to in the United States as an **alien corporation.**

A foreign corporation does not have an automatic right to do business in a state other than its state of incorporation. It must obtain a *certificate of authority* in the states where it plans to do business. Usually, the process of obtaining a certificate is a mere formality, but often the foreign corporation must comply with standards of financial responsibility before the certificate will be issued.

Should a foreign corporation do business without obtaining a certificate, the state can fine it, deny it the privilege of using state courts, and even hold its officers, directors, or agents personally liable for corporate obligations incurred in that state.[7]

Once the certificate has been issued, the powers conferred upon a corporation by its home state generally can be exercised in the other state. Numerous states have specific laws designed to regulate foreign corporations. One such law is the requirement that foreign corporations maintain a registered office or agent (address) in the state. One of the purposes of such a statute is to provide a place to serve process in the event of a suit against the corporation. Frequently, state laws governing corporations apply equally to domestic and foreign corporations. When these statutes relate to internal corporate affairs, however, they normally do not apply to foreign corporations.

Some jurisdictions require a foreign corporation to post a bond before it is permitted to do business. This bond is intended to ensure the performance of the foreign corporation's contracts within the state.

Frequently, the biggest issue in dealing with foreign corporations is whether such corporations are actually doing business within the state. A single transaction or the mere presence of the corporation's product in the state or contacts with the state may not be enough to constitute doing business there.

Before a state court can hear a dispute in which a foreign corporation is the defendant, the state court must have *jurisdiction* over the defendant. A state court only has jurisdiction over foreign corporations that have sufficient *contacts* with the state. A foreign corporation that has its home office within the state or has manufacturing plants in the state meets this "minimum contacts" requirement. A foreign corporation whose only contact with the state is the fact that one of its directors resides

---

7. Robertson v. Levy, 197 A.2d 443 (D.C. Ct. App. 1964).

there does not have sufficient contact with the state for the state court to exercise jurisdiction over it.[8]

The following case illustrates a court's application of the "minimum contacts" test in determining jurisdiction.

_____

8. The "minimum contacts" requirement was established in the landmark case International Shoe Co. v. Washington, 326 U.S. 310, 66 S.Ct. 154, 90 L.Ed. 95 (1945).

BACKGROUND AND FACTS *The plaintiff, Pesaplastic, is a Venezuelan corporation that manufactures and distributes large plastic products in South America. The defendant, Milacron, is an Ohio corporation engaged in the manufacture and sale of large injection molding machines. Milacron's principal place of business is in Cincinnati, but it also maintains a Latin American sales and service office in North Miami Beach, Florida. The plaintiff sued Tedruth, a New Jersey corporation that sold molds, and its agent, Milacron, for breach of contract and breach of warranty made in a sales contract under which Pesaplastic had purchased a Tedruth mold. The district court found that it had jurisdiction over Tedruth under Florida law. The basis of this decision was the jury's finding that Milacron was an agent of Tedruth. Tedruth argued that the complaint against it should have been dismissed for lack of jurisdiction.*

Case 38.1
PESAPLASTIC, C.A. v. CINCINNATI MILACRON CO.
United States Court of Appeals, Eleventh Circuit, 1985.
750 F.2d 1516.

FAY, Circuit Judge.
*   *   *   *

This court generally evaluates a jurisdictional problem by looking first at the applicable state statute and then at federal due process requirements. In diversity cases such as this one, "the federal court is bound by state law concerning the amenability [answerability] of a person or a corporation to suit, so long as state law does not exceed the limitations imposed by the Due Process Clause of the Fourteenth Amendment."
*   *   *

Jurisdiction over Tedruth must therefore be determined by looking first at the law of the state of Florida. The applicable Florida statute *   *   * provides that any person, whether or not a citizen or resident of Florida, who personally or *through an agent* operates, conducts, engages in, or carries on a business or business venture in Florida, or who maintains an office or agency in that state, thereby submits himself to the jurisdiction of the Florida courts.
*   *   *   *

*   *   * In the instant case, the jury specifically found that Milacron acted as Tedruth's agent with respect to the transaction with Pesaplastic. There is ample evidence in the record to support this conclusion. When a trier of fact specifically finds that an agency relationship exists between two corporations, and the agent corporation is authorized and does conduct business in Florida for the benefit of the principal corporation, we are of the opinion that the Florida jurisdictional statute clearly brings the principal corporation, in this case Tedruth, within the jurisdiction of the Florida courts.

Having upheld the district court's finding of jurisdiction under the Florida statute, we next turn to the constitutional considerations regarding jurisdiction. The due process clause of the Fourteenth Amendment requires that Tedruth have such minimum contacts with Florida so that "maintenance of the suit does not offend 'traditional notions of fair play and substantial justice.' " *   *   *

Applying the mode of analysis developed in *International Shoe*, we must first define the extent of Tedruth's activities in Florida. *   *   * Tedruth has never officially sought authority to transact business in Florida nor does it have any offices or agents in that state. Clearly Tedruth does not engage in continuous and systematic activities in Florida. Where such is the case, "jurisdiction depends on the relationship between the cause of action on the one hand and the nature and quality of defendant's activities on the other hand." *   *   * Moreover, the burden is on Pesaplastic to make a prima facie showing of the facts on which jurisdiction is predicated. *   *   *

In the instant case, we find from the record that Pesaplastic has shown numerous Miami-based activities which led directly to the sale of the Tedruth mold. The link between Tedruth and these activities is *   *   * Helfenstein, Milacron's Miami-based sales representative. The record is uncontroverted that Helfenstein advised Pesaplastic of the availability of the Tedruth mold, furnished price quotations, made several sales pitches concerning the mold, and in fact traveled to Venezuela for the purpose of discussing, among other things, the metric mold. The record also indicates that Pedro Hoffman, President and Director of Pesaplastic, and Mario Fernandez, former Managing Director of Pesaplastic, met with Helfenstein in Miami to further discuss this matter.

Throughout the course of these negotiations, numerous telexes concerning the mold were sent from Helfenstein's Miami office to both Pesaplastic and Tedruth. The contents of these telexes leaves little doubt that Tedruth and Milacron were acting in concert to persuade Pesaplastic to buy the Tedruth mold. When Pesaplastic wanted samples of the pallets, it was Helfenstein who worked out the air freight and customs clearance arrangements. All of the contacts with Pesaplastic made prior to Pesaplastic's representative's trip to the Tedruth plant were made by Helfenstein from his Miami office. In addition, the details for that visit were also made by Helfenstein in Miami, and he accompanied Pesaplastic's representatives to New Jersey. Tedruth was well aware of Helfenstein's efforts and at some point agreed to pay him $3,000 as a commission on the sale of the mold.

These activities are clearly an integral part of Pesaplastic's cause of action and as such, they constitute the sufficient minimum contacts necessary to support jurisdiction. Accordingly, we find no error in the district court's refusal to dismiss the complaint on these grounds.

DECISION AND REMEDY   *The court held that the district court did have jurisdiction over Tedruth, the New Jersey corporation, under Florida law. The jurisdiction is based on the Florida activities of Milacron, Tedruth's agent. The district court's judgment was affirmed, and Tedruth, along with Milacron, had to pay compensatory damages for the breach of contract. Tedruth also paid punitive damages.*

PUBLIC AND PRIVATE CORPORATIONS

A public corporation is one formed by the government to meet some political or governmental purpose. Cities and towns that incorporate are common examples. In addition, many federal government organizations, such as the U.S. Postal Service, the Tennessee Valley Authority, and Amtrak, are public corporations.

Public corporations should not be confused with *publicly traded* or *held* corporations. The latter are corporations whose shares are traded to and among the general public, as opposed to *privately held* or *traded* corporations (also known as close corporations and discussed below), whose shares

are not. Both publicly and privately held or traded corporations are private corporations.

Private corporations are created either wholly or in part for private benefit. Most corporations are private. Private corporations can serve a public purpose, as a public utility does, but they are nonetheless owned by private persons rather than the government.

NONPROFIT CORPORATIONS

Some corporations are formed without a profit-making purpose. These are called nonprofit, not-for-profit, or eleemosynary (charitable) corporations. They are usually (although not necessarily) private corporations. They can be used in conjunction with an ordinary corporation to facilitate making contracts with the government. Private hospitals, educational institutions, charities, religious organizations, and the like are frequently organized as nonprofit corporations.

Although shares of stock can be issued by such corporations, dividends are not paid to the members. Formation of nonprofit corporations often follows state statutes based on the Model Nonprofit Corporation Act. Under corporation statutes, the organization of nonprofit corporations is similar to the organization of other types of corporations. The nonprofit corporation is a convenient form of organization that allows various groups to own property and to form contracts without the individual members' being personally exposed to liability.

CLOSE CORPORATIONS

Close corporations—often referred to as closely held corporations, family corporations, or privately held corporations—are corporations whose shares are held by members of a family or by relatively few persons. Usually, the members of the small group involved in a close corporation are personally known to each other. Because the number of shareholders is so small, there is no trading market for the shares. In practice, a close corporation is often operated as a partnership is. A few states recognize this in the special statutory provisions that cover close corporations.

Close Corporation Statutes

In order to be eligible for close corporation status in states with close corporation statutes, a corporation must have a limited number of shareholders, the transfer of corporation stock must be subject to certain restrictions, and the corporation must not make any public offering of its securities.[9] Close corporation statutes provide greater flexibility by expressly permitting close corporations to vary significantly from traditional corporations.[10]

A Statutory Close Corporation Supplement has recently been promulgated by the Committee on Corporate Laws of the Section of Corporation, Banking, and Business Law of the American Bar Association. Where adopted, it applies only to eligible corporations that elect close corporation status. To be eligible, a corporation must have less than fifty shareholders. As under some states' statutes, the supplement relaxes most of the nonessential formalities to the operation of a closely held corporation.

Management

The close corporation has a single shareholder or a closely knit group of shareholders, and these individuals usually hold the positions of directors and officers. The management of a close corporation resembles that of a sole proprietorship or a partnership. In the eyes of the law, however, it is still a corporation and must meet the same legal requirements as other corporations, unless it is subject to the special statutes just mentioned.

In states that do not have special statutes governing close corporations, the small corporation may find it difficult to meet the requirements of state corporation law. Often, however, these difficulties are not insurmountable. Consider an example in which a state law requires that a corporation have two directors, and a close corporation has only one shareholder. In the articles of incorporation, the number of directors can be set at two, but the corporation can operate with a permanent vacancy on the board of directors. Alternatively, a disinterested person, usually a friend, can be convinced to put his or her name down as director.

Transfer of Shares

Since, by definition, a close corporation has a small number of shareholders, the transfer of shares of one shareholder to someone else can cause serious management problems. In other words, the other shareholders may find themselves required to share control with someone they do not know or like. To avoid this problem, it is usually advisable for the close corporation with several shareholders to specify restrictions on the transferability of stock in its articles of incorporation.

Consider an example. Deke, Allen, and Henry Wallingford are forming a corporation, Walling-

---

9. See, for example, Del. Code Annotated, Title 8, Section 342. This section limits the number of shareholders in a close corporation to no more than thirty.

10. For example, in some states (such as Maryland), the close corporation need not have a board of directors.

ford Boat Company, in which they will be the only shareholders. Deke and Allen do not want Henry to sell his shares to an unknown third person. The articles of corporation might therefore restrict the transferability of shares to outside persons. For example, the articles might stipulate a right of first refusal—that is, a provision that the shareholders will offer their shares to the corporation or other shareholders before seeking an outside purchaser.

Another way in which control of a close corporation can be stabilized is through the use of a

shareholder agreement. Agreements among shareholders to vote their stock in a particular way are generally upheld. Shareholder agreements can also provide that when one of the original shareholder dies, his or her shares of stock in the corporation will be divided in such a way that the proportionate holdings of the survivors, and thus their proportionate control, will be maintained.

The following case deals with the enforcement of a provision of a shareholder agreement.

Case 38.2

GALLER v. GALLER

Supreme Court of Illinois, 1964.
32 Ill.2d 16, 203 N.E.2d 577.

BACKGROUND AND FACTS   *Benjamin and Isadore Galler were brothers and 50 percent shareholders in a wholesale drug business that was incorporated under Illinois law as the Galler Drug Company.*

The corporation prospered, and in July 1955 Benjamin and Isadore and their wives entered into a carefully drafted agreement among themselves and the corporation. The written agreement purported to provide that, in the event of the death of either brother, the corporation would provide income for the support and maintenance of his immediate family. In addition, the family of the deceased brother would have equal control over the corporation.

Benjamin died in 1957. Shortly thereafter, his widow, Emma, requested that Isadore, the surviving brother, comply with the terms of the 1955 agreement. Isadore refused to cooperate. Emma sued, seeking specific performance of the 1955 agreement. The trial court agreed with Emma, holding that the shareholder agreement was valid. The intermediate appellate court subsequently held that the 1955 agreement was void on the ground of public policy. The Illinois Supreme Court reviewed the case.

UNDERWOOD, Justice.
*   *   *   *

The power to invalidate the agreements on the grounds of public policy is so far reaching and so easily abused that it should be called into action to set aside or annul the solemn engagement of parties dealing on equal terms only in cases where the corrupt or dangerous tendency clearly and unequivocally appears upon the face of the agreement itself or is the necessary inference from the matters which are expressed, and the only apparent exception to this general rule is to be found in those cases where the agreement, though fair and unobjectionable on its face, is a part of a corrupt scheme and is made to disguise the real nature of the transaction.
*   *   *   *

At this juncture it should be emphasized that we deal here with a so-called close corporation. Various attempts at definition of the close corporation have been made. For our purposes, a close corporation is one in which the stock is held in a few hands, or in a few families, and wherein it is not at all, or only rarely, dealt in by buying or selling. Moreover, it should be recognized that shareholder agreements similar to that in question here are often, as a practical consideration, quite necessary for the protection of those financially interested in the close corporation. While the shareholder of a public-issue corporation may readily sell his shares on the open market should management fail to use, in his opinion, sound business judgment, his counterpart of the close corporation often has a large total of his entire capital invested in the business and has no ready market for his shares should he desire to sell. He feels, understandably, that he is more than a mere investor and that his voice should be heard concerning all corporate activity. Without a shareholder agreement, specifically enforceable by the courts, insuring him a modicum of control, a large minority shareholder might find himself at the mercy of an oppressive or unknowledgeable majority. Moreover, as in the case at bar, the shareholders of a close corporation are often also the directors and officers thereof. With substantial shareholding interests abiding in each member of the board of directors, it is often quite impossible to secure, as in the large public-issue corporation, independent board judgment free from personal motivations concerning corporate policy. For these and other reasons too voluminous to enumerate here, often the only sound basis for protection is afforded by a lengthy, detailed shareholder agreement securing the rights and obligations of all concerned.

* * * *

The Appellate Court correctly found many of the contractual provisions free from serious objection, and we need not prolong this opinion with a discussion of them here. That court did, however, find difficulties in the stated purpose of the agreement as it relates to its duration [and] the election of certain persons to specific offices for a number of years * * *. [The court also considered the effect of the stated purpose of the agreement upon its validity.]

* * * While limiting voting trusts in 1947 to a maximum duration of 10 years, the [Illinois State] legislature has indicated no similar policy regarding straight voting agreements although these have been common since prior to 1870. In view of the history of decisions of this court generally upholding, in the absence of fraud or prejudice to minority interests or public policy, the right of stockholders to agree among themselves as to the manner in which their stock will be voted, we do not regard the period of time within which this agreement may remain effective as rendering the agreement unenforceable.

The clause that provides for the election of certain persons to specified offices for a period of years likewise does not require invalidation.

We turn next to a consideration of the effect of the stated purpose of the agreement upon its validity. The pertinent provision is: "The said Benjamin A. Galler and Isadore A. Galler desire to provide income for the support and maintenance of their immediate families." Obviously, there is no evil inherent in a contract entered into for the reason that the persons originating the terms desired to so arrange their property as to provide post-death support for those dependent upon them. Nor does the fact that the subject property is corporate stock alter the situation so long as there exists no detriment to minority stock interests, creditors or other public injury.

The Illinois Supreme Court held that the shareholder agreement was enforceable.   **DECISION AND REMEDY**

S CORPORATIONS

Certain corporations can choose to qualify under Subchapter S of the Internal Revenue Code to avoid the imposition of income taxes at the corporate level while retaining all the advantages of a corporation, particularly limited legal liability. In 1982, Congress enacted the Subchapter S Revision Act, the purpose of which was "to minimize the effect of Federal income taxes on choices of the form of business organizations and to permit the incorporation and operation of certain small businesses without the incidence of income taxation at both the corporated and shareholder level." [11]

Additionally, Congress decreed that all corporations are divided into two groups: **S corporations** (formerly Subchapter S corporations), which have elected Subchapter S treatment, and C corporations, which are all other corporations.

Although the S corporation has the advantages of the corporate form without the double taxation of income (since corporate income is not taxed

---

11. Senate Committee Report No. 97-640.

separately), it does have some disadvantages. One of the most important tax disadvantages is that an S corporation's fringe-benefit payments to employee-shareholders who own more than 2 percent of the stock are not tax deductible.

Requirements for S Corporation Qualification

A corporation must meet numerous requirements to qualify as an S corporation. The following are some of the more important:

1. The corporation must be a domestic corporation.
2. The corporation must not be a member of an affiliated group of corporations.
3. The shareholders of the corporation must be individuals, estates, or certain trusts. Corporations, partnerships, and nonqualifying trusts cannot be shareholders.
4. The corporation must have thirty-five or fewer shareholders.
5. The corporation can have only one class of stock. Not all shareholders need have the same voting rights.
6. No shareholder of the corporation can be a non-resident alien.

Benefits of S Corporation Status

At times it is beneficial for a regular corporation to elect S corporation status. The following is a checklist of the reasons such status can be beneficial.

1. When the corporation has losses, S status allows the shareholders to use the losses to offset other income.
2. When the stockholders are in a lower tax bracket than the corporation, S status causes their entire income to be taxed in the shareholders'

bracket, whether or not it is distributed. This is particularly attractive when the corporation wants to accumulate earnings for some future business purpose.
3. Only a single tax on corporate income is imposed at individual income tax rates at the shareholder level (taxable to shareholders whether or not the income is actually distributed).

PROFESSIONAL CORPORATIONS

Professional corporations are relatively new in corporate law. In the past, professional persons, such as physicians, lawyers, dentists, and accountants, could not incorporate. Today they can, and their corporations are typically called professional service associations or professional corporations. They can be identified by the letters S.C. (service corporation), P.C. (professional corporation), Inc. (incorporated), or P.A. (professional association). In general, a professional corporation is formed in the same way as an ordinary business corporation.

Originally, the professional corporation lightened the tax burden on professionals. By 1981, however, this form of enterprise had come to be widely viewed as permitting unacceptable tax avoidance through many tax-deductible investments, including certain kinds of pension plans. Since 1981, stringent limitations exacted by Congress have helped stop the growth of professional corporations and eliminate the tax loopholes available to those who formed this type of corporation.

State statutes regarding the operations of corporations have been applied to professional corporations. (The MBCA has a Model Professional Corporation Supplement.) The following case illustrates the application of New York corporate law to a professional corporation.

Case 38.3
WE'RE ASSOCIATES COMPANY v. COHEN, STRACHER & BLOOM, P.C.

Supreme Court, Appellate Division, Second Department, 1984.
103 A.D.2d 130, 478 N.Y.S.2d 670.

BACKGROUND AND FACTS *On October 7, 1980, the defendant, Cohen, Stracher & Bloom, P.C., a legal firm organized as a professional corporation under New York law, entered into an agreement with the plaintiff, We're Associates Company, for the lease of office space located in Lake Success, New York. The lease was signed for the landlord by one of the partners of the plaintiff company and for the defendant professional corporation by Paul J. Bloom, as vice-president. Bloom and the two other defendants, Cohen and Stracher, were the sole officers, directors, and stockholders of the professional corporation. The professional corporation became delinquent in paying its rent, and the plaintiff brought an action in May 1983 to recover rents and other charges of approxi-*

mately $9,000 alleged to be due and owing under the lease. The complaint was filed against the professional corporation and each individual shareholder of the corporation. The individual shareholders moved to dismiss the action against them individually. The trial court granted their motion, holding they could not be held individually liable for past-due rent. The landlord appealed.

BROWN, Justice.
*   *   *   *

It is well established that in the absence of some constitutional, statutory or charter provision, the shareholders of a corporation are not liable for its contractual obligations and that parties having business dealings with a corporation must look to the corporation itself and not the shareholders for payment of their claims. Indeed, this insulation from individual liability for corporate obligations is one of the fundamental purposes of operating through the corporate form. Where the Legislature has intended to depart from this general rule of limited liability and impose the obligations of the corporation upon the individual shareholder, it has made explicit provisions for such obligations.

A review of the [applicable New York law and its legislative history discloses t]he clear intent of the Legislature [to be] that, except for the specific statutory provisions regarding liability arising from the rendition of professional services, the members of professional corporations are to enjoy the same benefits of limited liability afforded to shareholders of any other form of corporation. We find that those benefits, which include insulation from ordinary corporate business debts, were intended to be available to the members of any professional corporation, regardless of the nature of the profession involved. There is, therefore, no basis for concluding that attorneys who practice in a professional corporation have some exceptional legal obligation over and above that of other professionals simply by virtue of their particular profession. Any analysis of the possible ethical considerations or moral obligations of attorneys in this situation is a separate matter and does not bear upon the substantive legal issue of the scope of liability under the statute.

Accordingly, we hold that the individual members of the professional corporation at bar may not be held liable for the rents and charges alleged to be due under the lease and that [the lower court] correctly struck their names from the complaint.

The reviewing court held that the individual members of the professional corporation could not be held liable for the rents and charges alleged to be due under the lease. In a professional corporation, liability for contractual obligations is strictly limited to the assets of the professional corporation.

DECISION AND REMEDY

Tort Liability of Members

Subject to certain exceptions, the shareholders of a professional corporation have limited liability. There are two basic areas of liability that deserve brief attention:

1. Malpractice of a member.
2. Torts unrelated to professional activities.

MALPRACTICE OF A MEMBER Of course, each member of a professional corporation is *personally* liable for his or her own torts. The liability of a member for the malpractice of another member is not clear. For example, in a partnership, dentists Dryden, Fox, and Kraus are each unlimitedly liable for whatever malpractice liability is incurred by the others within the scope of the partnership. If the three formed a professional corporation, however, the orthodox corporate law rule would usually apply, and none of the dentists would be liable for the malpractice of the others. Unlike statutes limiting personal liability in the ordinary business corporation, however, many professional corporation statutes retain a provision holding professional persons personally liable for their acts and for professional acts performed under their supervision.

The MBCA's Model Professional Corporation Supplement Section 11 provides three alternatives. A state may limit liability as in a business corporation, impose liability as in a partnership, or limit personal liability in an amount conditioned on the corporation's demonstrating financial responsibility by obtaining insurance or a surety bond. (In this context, a *surety bond* represents a third party's obligation to pay for injuries caused by the professional's malpractice if the professional does not.)

TORTS UNRELATED TO PROFESSIONAL ACTIVITIES Torts that are not related to malpractice are often treated differently from malpractice. A shareholder in a professional corporation is protected from the liability imposed because of torts committed by other members. If a secretary has been sent from the office to pick up tax forms from the IRS and, in the process, runs into another car, both the corporation (under the doctrine of *respondeat superior*) and the secretary will be held liable. Ordinarily, the shareholder in a professional corporation will not be held personally liable.

QUESTIONS AND CASE PROBLEMS

1. Jonathan, Gary, and Rob are active members of a partnership called Swim City. The partnership manufactures, sells, and installs outdoor swimming pools in the states of Texas and Arkansas. The partners want to continue to be active in management and to expand the business into other states as well. They are concerned about rather large recent judgments entered against swimming pool companies throughout the United States. Based on these facts only, discuss whether the partnership should incorporate.

2. The Swim City partnership decides to incorporate in the state of Texas under the name of Swim City, Inc. The partners also decide that they want to continue to do business in the state of Arkansas. Later, a man from Oklahoma comes into the corporate office in Texas and purchases an outdoor swimming pool. The swimming pool is shipped to Oklahoma and installed personally by the new owner. The owner is injured while swimming in the pool and claims his injury is due entirely to the defective manufacture of the pool. Discuss fully how the corporation can continue to do business in Arkansas. Also discuss the corporation's liability with respect to a suit filed by the injured man in an Oklahoma state court.

3. When Jonathan, Gary, and Rob decide to form the Texas corporation, Swim City, Inc., it is their desire that the only shareholders be the former partners. Discuss what they can and should do to limit the management, ownership, and control to the three of them and still incorporate.

4. Jonathan, Gary, and Rob, as partners in Swim City, decide that they need to incorporate in order to have limited personal liability. They wish to avoid double taxation, however. Discuss whether, upon incorporation, there is any way the partners can avoid paying corporate income taxes without incurring criminal liability.

5. Young, Cassidy, and Chi are doctors who have formed a partnership. Recently they have become concerned about their individual personal liability in the event that one of them is sued for malpractice or even in the event that one of them is guilty of ordinary negligence in the course of driving his or her personal car to make a house call. Discuss how the doctors can avoid personal liability should any of these kinds of torts be committed by one of the doctors in the partnership.

6. Leslie R. Barth was president of five corporations. During the course of an investigation for failure to file corporate and personal income tax returns, the IRS served an administrative summons for Barth to turn over prescribed corporate records. Barth only partially complied, and the IRS took Barth to district court. The court ordered the corporations to furnish the requested information and to designate an agent to testify for the corporations "without revoking their personal privileges against self-incrimination." Barth appealed the order, claiming that such an order violated the "agent's" (his) constitutional right against self-incrimination and that this Fifth Amendment protection extended to the corporations. Discuss whether corporations possess Fifth Amendment privileges against self-incrimination and whether Barth's individual privilege against self-incrimination was denied by the district court's order. [United States v. Barth, 745 F.2d 184 (2nd Cir. 1984)]

7. Pacific Development, Inc., was incorporated in the District of Columbia for the purpose of international brokerage consulting. Pacific's founder, president, and sole shareholder was Tongsun Park, a South Korean who was on close terms with South Korea's president, Park Chung Hee. The government alleged that Park's main purpose was to influence Congress to give economic and military aid to South Korea. The IRS assessed $4.5 million in back taxes against Park in 1977. It then seized the assets of Pacific Development, Inc., claiming that the company was a mere alter ego of Park. Valley Finance, Inc., was another corporation wholly owned by Park. It had loaned money to Pacific Development, and it held a second deed of trust on the real property that the IRS had seized. Both Pacific

Development and Valley Finance attempted to obtain the return of Pacific Development's assets that the IRS had seized. The plaintiffs claimed that the IRS had improperly pierced the corporate veil of Pacific. Do you agree? [Valley Finance, Inc. v. United States, 629 F.2d 162 (D.C. Cir. 1980)]

8. Michigan-Wisconsin Pipeline Company was a Delaware corporation. It operated a natural gas pipeline that extended through more than a dozen states, including Kentucky. In that state, it had a warehouse as well as a compressor station. Twenty-one individuals were employed by Michigan-Wisconsin to carry on its business in Kentucky. No gas was either acquired or marketed in Kentucky. It simply flowed through a pipeline. The pipeline company claimed that it was exempt from Kentucky regulations because it was not doing business there. Do you agree? [Michigan-Wisconsin Pipeline Co. v. Kentucky, 474 S.W.2d 873 (Ky. 1971)]

9. In February of 1955, Robert Leihser, Albert Rench, and Claude Mullen purchased Lloyd Trucking Corporation. The three held the business as a close corporation, dividing the shares equally among themselves. In 1955, they each signed an agreement stating that, should any of them die or wish to sell his shares, the remaining shareholder(s) would purchase the shares according to a specific procedure. In 1961, Mullen wanted to sell his shares; and although the specific procedure was not followed, Leihser and Rench each purchased half of Mullen's shares. Each assigned one share of stock to his spouse, which was in violation of the 1955 agreement. In 1981, Rench died, and Leihser tendered payment to Rench's widow for Rench's shares. Mrs. Rench was willing to sell, but they could not agree on a price. Leihser sued to compel the sale according to the 1955 transfer agreement. Discuss whether the 1955 agreement was binding on Mrs. Rench. [Rench v. Leihser, 139 Ill.App.3d 889, 487 N.E.2d 1201, 94 Ill.Dec. 324 (1986)]

10. Zagoria and Stoner were the only shareholders of a professional corporation. They were both attorneys. While closing a real estate deal, Zagoria issued checks to clients in connection with the real estate and other loan closings. These checks were dishonored because of withdrawals from the professional corporate checking account. Does Stoner share personal liability for these dishonored checks? [First Bank & Trust Co. v. Zagoria, 250 Ga. 844, 302 S.E.2d 674 (1983)]

Chapter 39

CORPORATIONS
Formation and
Corporate Financing

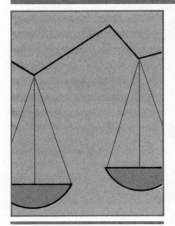

Incorporation refers to the procedural mechanics of forming a corporation. The corporation is entirely a creature of statute. Therefore, it must meet the requirements of the state's statutes. Although state statutes differ, their basic requirements for incorporation are similar. This chapter will not only deal with these basic requirements but will discuss pre-incorporation arrangements and activities.

In addition, since the formation and continued existence of corporations require financing, this chapter will briefly discuss the securities used to finance corporations.

PROMOTERS' ACTIVITIES

Before a corporation becomes a reality, people invest in the proposed corporation as subscribers, and contracts are frequently made by promoters on behalf of the future corporation. **Promoters** are those who, for themselves or others, take the preliminary steps in organizing a corporation. They issue the prospectus[1] for the proposed organization and secure a charter.

It is not unusual for a promoter to purchase or lease property with a view to selling it to the corporation to be organized. In addition, the promoter enters into contracts with attorneys, accountants, architects, and other professionals whose services will be needed in planning for the proposed corporation. Finally, a promoter induces people to purchase stock in the corporation.

Some interesting legal questions arise in regard to the promoter's activities. The most important problem centers on whether the promoter is personally liable for contracts made on behalf of a corporation that does not yet legally exist. In addition, once the corporation is formed, does it assume liability on these contracts, or is the promoter still personally liable?

As a general rule, a promoter is held personally liable on pre-incorporation contracts. Courts simply hold that promoters are not agents when a corporation has yet to come into existence. If, however, the promoter secures

---

1. A prospectus is a document, required by federal or state securities laws and regulations, that contains material facts concerning the financial operations of the corporation, allowing an investor to make an informed decision.

the contracting party's agreement to hold only the corporation (not the promoter) liable on the contract, the promoter will not be liable in the event of any breach of contract.

Basically, the promoter remains personally liable on the contract even after incorporation, unless the third party *releases* the promoter. In most states, this rule is applied whether or not the promoter made the agreement in the name of, or with reference to, the proposed corporation.

Once the corporation is formed (the charter issued), the promoter remains personally liable until the corporation assumes the pre-incorporation contract by *novation*. (See Chapter 14.) Novation releases the promoter and makes the corporation personally liable for performing the

contractual obligations. In some cases, the corporation *adopts* the promoter's contract by undertaking to perform it. Most courts hold that adoption in and of itself does not discharge the promoter from contractual liability. Obviously, a corporation cannot normally *ratify* a pre-incorporation contract, as there was no principal in existence at the time the contract was made.

Incorporation does not make the corporation automatically liable for pre-incorporation contracts. Until the newly formed corporation consents, the third party cannot enforce the promoter's contract against the corporation.

The following case deals with the personal liability of the promoter for pre-incorporation contracts.

BACKGROUND AND FACTS *Skandinavia, Inc., the plaintiff, was a manufacturer of Polypro underwear and was short of capital. As a result, Skandinavia's president entered into a series of contracts with Odilon Cormier, the defendant, an experienced textile manufacturer. Cormier was to act as a marketing agent to sell certain inventory of Skandinavia and to manufacture and sell new inventory under trade names Skandinavia transferred by sale to Cormier. For this, Cormier was to pay commissions to Skandinavia and to act as a promoter in forming a new corporation, Polypro, Inc., with Cormier to assign all rights and obligations to the newly formed corporation. In keeping with its obligation under the contract, Skandinavia transferred the inventory to Cormier. One month later, Cormier did form the new corporation called Polypro, Inc. Eight months later, Skandinavia claimed Cormier had breached the purchase-and-sale agreement by failing to make commission payments. Skandinavia sued Cormier individually; and under a pre-trial motion, the Polypro corporation was added as a defendant. The trial court dismissed all claims against Polypro, finding that Polypro was not Cormier's assignee under the purchase-and-sale agreement and had not adopted or participated in a novation of the agreement with Skandinavia. The court held that Cormier alone was liable to Skandinavia for damages. Cormier appealed, alleging that the lower court had erred in finding him, as a promoter, liable under the agreement instead of the newly formed corporation, Polypro.*

Case 39.1
SKANDINAVIA, INC. v. CORMIER
Supreme Court of New Hampshire, 1986.
128 N.H. 215, 514 A.2d 1250.

BATCHELDER, Justice.

We first address whether the [lower court] correctly found Cormier and not Polypro, Inc. liable under the agreement. Cormier raises several arguments in an effort to avoid personal liability. First, he argues that Polypro, Inc., rather than himself, is liable under the agreement because he acted only as a promoter for the corporation. In support of his contention, he refers to paragraph three of the agreement: "It is understood by the parties that in order to complete this transaction, Cormier shall have a new corporation, 'Polypro, Inc.' formed and shall assign all of his right and obligation under this agreement to said Corporation."

We agree with the [lower court] that Cormier's attempt to avoid contractual liability by claiming the status of a promoter is unavailing. The contractual language quoted above does not discharge Cormier.

As a general rule promoters are personally liable on contracts which they have entered into personally, even though they have contracted for the benefit of a projected corporation; the promoter is not discharged from liability by the subsequent adoption of the contract by the corporation when formed, unless there is a novation.

Cormier further contends that Polypro, Inc. was incorporated and acted in reliance on the agreement, thereby vesting rights in the corporation and making the corporation liable under the agreement. This argument is unpersuasive because the corporation took no action to adopt or ratify the agreement. Although the defendant contends that the corporation assumed the rights and obligations of the agreement, we find that Polypro, Inc. did not adhere to the statutory formalities required for the conduct of business affairs. No contracts were authorized by the corporation's board of directors, and no authority was granted by the corporation to any of its officers to purchase the inventory from Cormier. Accordingly, we agree with the [lower court's] finding that Polypro, Inc. did not become liable under the agreement.

We also reject Cormier's argument that he was released from liability by assignment. The record discloses no assignment of interest or obligation by Cormier. An express statement in a contract that a party *shall* assign its liability in the future only sets the stage for an assignment; it does not operate as one. In order to assign thousands of dollars worth of goods, formal contractual requirements imposed by statute must be met. In attempting to assign his rights and obligations to Polypro, Inc., Cormier did not comply with these statutory requirements or with the terms of the agreement, which requires any amendment to be in writing.

Likewise, we are not persuaded that a novation occurred. "A novation is a substituted contract that includes as a party one who was neither the obligor nor the obligee of the original duty." A novation requires "(1) a previous, valid obligation; (2) the agreement of all parties to a new contract; (3) the extinguishment of the old contract; and (4) validity of the new one."

A promoter may be discharged from liability . . . on a pre-incorporation contract by a novation if the corporation assumes the contract and the other contracting party assents to the substitution of the corporation for the promoter. . . . [But t]he doctrine of novation is highly technical, and a true novation seldom occurs in promotion cases.

Cormier could not unilaterally discharge himself from the contract he signed with the plaintiff; some affirmative action by the plaintiff was needed to release Cormier individually. The evidence indicates that the plaintiff relied on Cormier's personal wealth in entering into this unsecured agreement. We find no express intent on the plaintiff's part to release Cormier from liability. Accordingly, no express novation occurred. * * * The [lower court] ruled that this was not one of the exceptional instances in which a novation occurred after a corporate promotion contract because there was no evidence of assent to such a substitution on the plaintiff's part. [It] found that the evidence "demonstrated that no assignment, release, accord and satisfaction, equitable assignment, or express or implied novation occurred."

DECISION AND REMEDY   *The court affirmed the lower court's decision that Cormier, and not Polypro, was liable under the contract and affirmed the award of damages against Cormier.*

Subscribers and Subscriptions

Prior to the actual formation of the corporation, the promoter can contact potential individual investors, and they can agree to purchase capital stock in the future corporation. This agreement is often called a subscription agreement, and the potential investor is called a subscriber. Depending on state law, subscribers become shareholders as soon as the corporation is formed or as soon as the corporation accepts the agreement. Thus, if the corporation becomes insolvent, the trustee in bankruptcy can collect the consideration for any unpaid stock from a pre-incorporation subscriber.

Most courts view pre-incorporation subscriptions as continuing offers to purchase corporate stock. On or after its formation, the corporation can choose to accept the offer to purchase. Most courts also treat a subscription as a contract between the subscribers. A subscription is therefore irrevocable except with the consent of *all* of the subscribers. Under Section 17 of the Model Business Corporation Act, a subscription is irrevocable for a period of six months unless other provisions are made in the subscription agreement or unless all the subscribers agree to the revocation of the subscription.[2]

A minority of courts do not follow the Model Act, and in those jurisdictions the pre-incorporation subscriber can revoke the offer to purchase before acceptance without liability.

A promoter can avoid the problem of revocation in various ways. One way is to set up a trust with the promoter as trustee and the corporation as beneficiary (under the law of trusts, a beneficiary need not exist at the creation of the trust). Then the promoter-trustee enters into a contract with the subscriber. By the terms of the contract, the subscriber promises to buy the stock. If the subscriber fails to subscribe or fails to pay, he or she is liable to the promoter-trustee for breach of contract. Additionally, many statutes permit a forfeiture of partial payments on subscriptions, if later installments are not paid.

A typical problem in pre-incorporation subscription agreement cases arises when the corporation actually formed differs from the corporation in which the subscriber originally agreed to invest. The rule of thumb is that if the departure is minimal (for example, merely a change in name), the agreement is likely to be upheld. But if the change is material (such as entry into a different business entirely), the agreement will not be enforced against an unwilling investor. More important problems arise, however, when the corporation is not formed or when it fails after formation.

---

2. See RMBCA Section 6.20 for the same irrevocable period.

INCORPORATION PROCEDURES AND REQUIREMENTS

Exact procedures for incorporation differ among states, but the basic requirements are relatively similar.

State Chartering

Since state incorporation laws differ, individuals have found some advantage in looking for the states that offer the most advantageous tax or incorporation provisions. Delaware has historically had the least restrictive laws. Consequently, a significant number of corporations, including a number of the largest, have incorporated there. Delaware's statutes permit firms to incorporate in Delaware and carry out business and locate operating headquarters elsewhere. (Most other states now permit this.) On the other hand, close corporations, particularly those of a professional nature, generally incorporate in the state where their principal stockholders live and work.

Articles of Incorporation

The primary document needed to begin the incorporation process is called the articles of incorporation (see Exhibit 39–1). The articles include basic information about the corporation and serve as a primary source of authority for its future organizational and business functions. The person or persons who execute the articles are called incorporators.

Generally, the following should be included in the articles of incorporation:

1. Corporate name.
2. Purpose.
3. Duration.
4. Capital structure.
5. Internal organization.
6. Registered office and agent.
7. Incorporators.

CORPORATE NAME   The choice of a corporate name is subject to state approval to ensure against duplication or deception. Fictitious-name statutes usually require that the secretary of state run a check on the proposed name in the state of incorporation. Once cleared, a name can be reserved

Exhibit 39–1 Articles of Incorporation (Minimum Requirements) for the Hypothetical State of New Pacum

---

ARTICLE ONE

The name of the corporation is _____.

ARTICLE TWO

The period of its duration is perpetual (may be a number of years or until a certain date).

ARTICLE THREE

The purpose(s) for which the corporation is organized is (are) _____

_____.

ARTICLE FOUR

The aggregate number of shares that the corporation shall have authority to issue is _____ of the par value of _____ dollar(s) each (or without par value).

ARTICLE FIVE

The corporation will not commence business until it has received for the issuance of its shares consideration of the value of $1,000 (can be any sum not less than $1,000).

ARTICLE SIX

The address of the corporation's registered office is _____,
New Pacum and the name of its registered agent at such address is _____
_____.

(Use the street or building or rural route address of the registered office, not a post office box number.)

ARTICLE SEVEN

The number of initial directors is _____, and the names and addresses of the directors are _____
_____
_____.

ARTICLE EIGHT

The name and address of the incorporator is _____
_____.

(signed) _____

                                        Incorporator

Sworn to on _____ by the above-named incorporator.
              (date)

_____

Notary Public _____ County, New Pacum

(Notary Seal)

---

for a short time, for a fee, pending the completion of the articles of incorporation. Most states require the corporation name to include the word *corporation, incorporated, limited,* or an abbreviation of one of these terms.

Some states require that the name of the corporation be expressed in English letters or characters. States usually require that a corporate name

not be the same as, or deceptively similar to, the name of an existing corporation doing business within the state.

For example, if an existing corporation is named General Dynamics, Inc., the state will not allow another corporation to be called General Dynamic, Inc. Not only would that name be deceptive to third parties, but it would impliedly transfer a part of the goodwill established by the first corporate user to the second corporation.

PURPOSE   The intended business activities of the corporation must be specified in the articles, and, naturally, they must be lawful. A general statement of corporate purpose is usually sufficient to give rise to all of the powers necessary or convenient to the purpose of the organization. The corporate charter can state, for example, that the corporation is organized "to engage in the production and sale of agricultural products." There is a trend toward allowing corporate charters to state that the corporation is organized for any legal business with no mention of specifics.

Some states have prohibitions against the incorporation of certain professionals, such as doctors or lawyers, except pursuant to a professional incorporation statute. In some states, certain industries, such as banks, insurance companies, or public utilities, cannot be operated in the general corporate form and are governed by special incorporation statutes.

DURATION   A corporation can have perpetual existence under most state corporate statutes. A few states, however, prescribe a maximum duration after which the corporation must formally renew its existence.

CAPITAL STRUCTURE   The capital structure of the corporation is generally set forth in the articles. A few state statutes require a minimum capital investment (for example, $1,000) for ordinary business corporations, while corporations engaged in the insurance or banking industry can be required to have a greater capital investment. The number of shares of stock authorized for issuance, their par value, the various types or classes of stock authorized for issuance, and other relevant information concerning equity, capital, and credit must be outlined in the articles. The range of possibilities is discussed later in this chapter.

INTERNAL ORGANIZATION   Whatever the internal management structure of the corporation, it may be described in the articles, although it can be included in bylaws adopted after the corporation has been formed. The articles of incorporation commence the corporation; the bylaws are formed after commencement by the board of directors.

Bylaws are subject to and cannot conflict with the incorporation statute or the corporation's charter. Section 27 of the Model Act, for example, provides that "the power to alter, amend, or repeal the bylaws or adopt new bylaws shall be vested in the board of directors unless reserved to the shareholders by the articles of incorporation." That section further indicates that the bylaws must be consistent with the articles of incorporation. Typical bylaw provisions describe the quorum and voting requirements for shareholders, the election of the board of directors, the methods of replacing directors, and the manner and time of fixing shareholder and board meetings.

REGISTERED OFFICE AND AGENT   The corporation must indicate the location and address of its registered office within the state. Usually, the registered office is also the principal office of the corporation. The corporation must give the name and address of a specific person who has been designated an *agent* and who can receive legal documents on behalf of the corporation. These legal documents include service of process.

INCORPORATORS   Each incorporator must be listed by name and address. An incorporator is a person—including another corporation—who applies to the state on behalf of the corporation to obtain its corporate charter. The incorporator need not be a subscriber and need not have any interest at all in the corporation. Many states do not impose residency or age requirements for incorporators. States vary on the required number of incorporators; it can be as few as one or as many as three. Incorporators *must* sign the articles of incorporation when they are submitted to the state; often this is their only duty. In some states, they participate at the first organizational meeting of the corporation.

Certificate of Incorporation

Once the articles of incorporation have been prepared, signed, and authenticated by the incorporators, they are sent to the appropriate state official, usually the secretary of state, along with the appropriate filing fee. In many states, the secretary of state then issues a *certificate of incorporation* representing the state's authorization for the corporation to conduct business. The certificate and a copy of the articles are returned to the incorporators, who then hold the initial organizational meeting that completes the details of incorporation.

First Organizational Meeting

The first organizational meeting is provided for in the articles of incorporation but is held after the charter has actually been granted. At this meeting, the incorporators elect the first board of directors and complete the routine business of incorporation (pass bylaws, issue stock, and so forth). Sometimes, the meeting is held after the election of the board of directors, and the business to be transacted depends upon the requirements of the state's incorporation statute, the nature of the business, the provisions made in the articles, and the desires of the promoters.

Adoption of bylaws is probably the most important function of the first organizational meeting. The bylaws are the internal rules of management for the corporation. The shareholders, directors, and officers must abide by them in conducting corporate business. Unless they have knowledge of the bylaws, corporation employees and third persons dealing with the corporation are not bound by them.

CORPORATE STATUS

The procedures for incorporation are very specific. If they are not followed precisely, errors can be made that allow others to challenge the existence of the corporation.

Proper incorporation procedures can become important when, for example, a third person attempts to enforce a contract or bring suit for a tort injury and fortuitously learns of the defect in the incorporation procedure. The plaintiff could then seek to make the shareholders personally liable.

Also, when the corporation seeks to enforce a contract against a defaulting party and the defaulting party learns of the defective incorporation, he or she may seek to avoid liability on that ground. Courts have developed three theories to prevent the windfall that would occur if a contracting party were given the benefit of the stockholders' personal liability. The theories are *de jure* corporation, *de facto* corporation, and corporation by estoppel.

De Jure Corporation

If there is at least substantial compliance with all conditions precedent to incorporation, the cor-

poration is said to have *de jure* existence in law. In most states the certificate of incorporation is viewed as evidence that all mandatory statutory provisions have been met. This means that the corporation is properly formed, and neither the state nor a third party can attack its existence.

To illustrate, Bick Motor Company, Inc., a domestic corporation, is being sued by a customer, Fred Muris, for an injury sustained at Bick's headquarters. Muris wants to challenge Bick's corporate status because he knows that the personal assets of the owners, Gary and Edward Bick, far exceed the company's assets. Muris discovers that the address of one of the incorporators is incorrectly listed in the articles and argues that this error means that the corporation was improperly formed. Hence it is not a duly authorized corporation, and Gary and Edward Bick are personally liable. The law, however, does not regard such inconsequential procedural defects as bars to substantial compliance, and courts will uphold the *de jure* status of Bick Motor Company. Fred Muris can sue only Bick Motor Company as a corporate entity.

De Facto Corporations

In some situations, there is a defect in compliance with statutory mandates—for example, inadvertently failing to pay the required fee when filing the articles of incorporation. Under these circumstances, the corporation is not *de jure*. Nevertheless, it may have *de facto* status and be recognized as a corporation for most purposes, and its existence cannot be challenged by third persons (except for the state). The following elements are required for *de facto* status:

1. There must be a state statute under which the corporation can be incorporated validly.
2. The parties must have made a *good faith* attempt to comply with the statute.
3. The enterprise must already have undertaken to do business as a corporation.

Practically speaking, the concept of *de facto* status has limited utility in modern corporate law. The Model Business Corporation Act (Section 56) and most state statutes agree that the issuance of a certificate of incorporation (charter) by the secretary of state is *prima facie* evidence of corporate status (that is, *de jure* corporation). The right of the state to command a corporation to correct irregularities in corporate formation can be enforced under the *de facto* doctrine, however.

Corporation by Estoppel

Sometimes a corporation has neither *de jure* nor *de facto* status. When justice requires, the courts treat an alleged corporation as if it were an actual corporation for the purpose of determining the rights and liabilities involved in a particular situation. Corporation by estoppel is thus determined by the situation. It does not extend recognition of corporate status beyond the resolution of the problem at hand.

For example, suppose a buyer in good faith believes erroneously that the articles of his or her corporation have been filed. Based on this belief, the buyer enters into a contract with a seller to purchase typewriters. The seller is relying solely on the credit of the corporation. The corporation is not formed, and the buyer breaches the contract. The seller wants to hold the buyer personally liable. Based on these facts, the seller is "estopped" from denying the existence of the corporation and can look only to the corporation for liability.[3]

If an association that is neither an actual corporation nor a *de facto* or *de jure* corporation holds itself out as being a corporation, it will be estopped from denying corporate status in a lawsuit by a third party. This usually occurs when a third party contracts with an association that claims to be a corporation but does not hold a certificate of incorporation. When the third party brings suit

---

3. Cranson v. International Business Machines (IBM), Inc., 234 Md. 477, 200 A.2d 33 (1964).

naming the "corporation" as the defendant, the association may not escape liability on the ground that no corporation exists.

The same statutory provisions that effectively eliminate the *de facto* doctrine also eliminate the estoppel doctrine. This is especially true in jurisdictions with statutes imposing personal liability on anyone who acts as a corporation without authority to do so (see, for example, MBCA Section 146 and RMBCA Section 2.04).

DISREGARDING THE CORPORATE ENTITY

In some unusual situations, a corporate entity is used by its owners to perpetrate a fraud, circumvent the law, or in some other way accomplish an illegitimate objective. In these cases, the court will ignore the corporate structure by *piercing the corporate veil*, exposing the shareholders to personal liability.

Inadequate Capitalization

A corporation may have insufficient capital at the time it is formed to meet its prospective debts or potential liabilities. Under-capitalization is exacerbated when a corporation fails to obtain the amount of insurance that any reasonable business can be expected to have in the interest of public responsibility. In such situations, victims who are injured may be able to reach the personal assets of stockholders to satisfy their claims. This is illustrated by the following case.

BACKGROUND AND FACTS *Minton, the plaintiff, sued Seminole Hot Springs Corporation for negligence after his daughter drowned in a public swimming pool operated by that corporation. A trial court awarded Minton a judgment against the corporation. When Minton could not have that judgment satisfied from the assets of the corporation, he instituted a suit against Cavaney, the defendant, who had been a director and the secretary-treasurer of Seminole. Cavaney argued that he could not be held personally liable for the judgment against the corporation. He stated that Seminole had never had any assets and had never functioned as a corporation. No stock had ever been issued by Seminole. The trial court entered a judgment against Cavaney, and Cavaney appealed.*

Case 39.2
MINTON v. CAVANEY
Supreme Court of California, 1961.
56 Cal.2d 576, 364 P.2d 473, 15 Cal.Rptr. 641.

TRAYNOR, Justice.

* * * *

The figurative terminology "alter ego" and "disregard of the corporate entity" is generally used to refer to the various situations that are an abuse of the corporate privilege. The equitable owners of a corporation, for example, are personally liable when they treat the assets of the corporation as their own and add or withdraw capital from the corporation at will; when they hold themselves out as being personally liable for the debts of the corporation; or when they provide inadequate capitalization and actively participate in the conduct of corporate affairs.

In the instant case the evidence is undisputed that there was no attempt to provide adequate capitalization. Seminole never had any substantial assets. It leased the pool that it operated, and the lease was forfeited for failure to pay the rent. Its capital was " 'trifling compared with the business to be done and the risks of loss * * *.' " The evidence is also undisputed that Cavaney was not only the secretary and treasurer of the corporation but was also a director. The evidence that Cavaney was to receive one-third of the shares to be issued supports an inference that he was an equitable owner, and the evidence that for a time the records of the corporation were kept in Cavaney's office supports an inference that he actively participated in the conduct of the business.

DECISION AND REMEDY

The Supreme Court of California held that Cavaney could be liable as an individual for the debts and liabilities of the corporation. The court noted, however, that it did not have the power to render a judgment against Cavaney because to do so would violate Cavaney's due process rights. Cavaney had not been a party to the original lawsuit, in which the Seminole Corporation was found negligent in operating the swimming pool, and thus was not able to make any arguments disputing such negligence. The court noted that plaintiff Minton could file a new lawsuit, pleading the negligence cause of action, and could "pierce the corporate veil" to hold Cavaney personally liable.

Commingling of Personal and Corporate Interests

Often, corporations are formed according to law by a single person or by a few family members. The corporate entity and the sole stockholder (or family member stockholders) must carefully preserve the separate status of the corporation and its owners. Certain practices invite trouble for the one-person or family-owned corporation—the commingling of corporate and personal funds, the failure to hold and record minutes of board of directors' meetings, or the shareholders' continuous personal use of corporate property (for example, vehicles). When the corporate privilege is abused for personal benefit and the corporate business is treated in such a careless manner that the corporation and the shareholder in control are no longer separate entities, the court will require an owner to assume personal liability to creditors for the corporation's debts.

In short, where the facts show that great injustice would result from use of a corporation to avoid individual responsibility, a court of equity will look behind the corporate structure to the individual stockholder.

General corporation law has no specific prohibition against a stockholder lawfully lending money to his or her corporation. When an officer or director lends money and takes back security in the form of corporate assets, however, the courts will scrutinize the transaction closely. Any such transaction must be made in good faith and for fair value.

In the following case, two shareholders made a lawful loan of money to a corporation (which later became insolvent) and in return took a security interest in certain pieces of corporate property. When the corporation became insolvent, some creditors charged that the shareholders' loan transaction had not been made in good faith and that their security interest should therefore be set aside.

BACKGROUND AND FACTS   *The plaintiffs (InterTherm, Inc.) were creditors of Olympic Homes Systems, Inc. (Olympic). Two of Olympic's shareholders, Langley and Clayton, the defendants, had made a sizable loan to the corporation. In return, they took a security interest in certain corporate property.*

When the corporation became insolvent, the general creditors attempted to set aside the priority of the defendants' security interest. The defendants argued that the general creditors had failed to show either that there was any fraud involved in the making of the loan or that the loan was not a legitimate transaction. Moreover, according to the defendants, the general creditors had not established that the defendants' relationship to the corporation was fiduciary or that they showed a lack of good faith in the loan transaction. The trial court entered judgment for the general creditors, and the shareholders appealed.

Case 39.3
INTERTHERM, INC. v. OLYMPIC HOMES SYSTEMS, INC.
Court of Appeals of Tennessee, 1978.
569 S.W.2d 467.

DROWOTA, Judge.

* * * *

* * * As a fiduciary, the officer or director has a strong influence on how the corporation conducts its affairs, and a correspondingly strong duty not to conduct those affairs to the unfair detriment of others, such as minority shareholders or creditors, who also have legitimate interests in the corporation but lack the power of the fiduciary.

It is also generally held that courts will closely scrutinize the transactions of a majority, dominant, or controlling shareholder with his corporation, and will place the burden of proof upon the shareholder when the good faith and fairness of such a transaction is challenged. * * * It is obvious, however, that the reason for applying the rule to a shareholder is the same as the reason for applying it to an officer or director, that is, that he occupies a fiduciary position with regard to the corporation and those interested in it. Unless it is shown that a shareholder owns a majority of the stock or that he otherwise controls or dominates a corporation, however, a shareholder cannot be said to be a fiduciary and the reason for closely scrutinizing his transactions with the corporation disappears. Further, in reviewing the cases in which the courts have closely scrutinized transactions between a corporation and a shareholder and have put the burden of justifying them on the latter, we find that they almost invariably involve a majority, dominant, or controlling shareholder. Accordingly, it is clear that courts should apply the rule of close scrutiny and place the burden on the shareholder to justify a transaction with his corporation only when the shareholder owns a majority of stock, or is shown to dominate or control the corporation to a significant degree in some other way.

In the instant case, defendants contend that their secured loan to Olympic should be upheld under the general rule that shareholders may lawfully contract with their corporation. Plaintiffs, on the other hand, argue that this Court should scrutinize this transaction closely and put the burden of justifying it on defendants who, plaintiffs further argue, have failed to carry that burden. We hold that the instant transaction should not be subjected to close scrutiny, and that the burden of proof should not be on defendant shareholders, because plaintiffs have offered no evidence from which we could conclude that defendants owned a majority of Olympic's stock or otherwise dominated it in such a way as to justify imposing fiduciary responsibilities on them.

There is no evidence in this record that either defendant Langley or defendant Clayton was ever an officer or director of Olympic. The evidence is that each owned 15% of the capital stock of Olympic. It is clear that both were involved in setting up the corporation, but there is nothing to show that they participated in the business afterward. There is evidence that they did not intend to participate in the corporation's everyday affairs. * * * In short, there is no evidence of any degree of power or control by defendants over the corporation at any time. * * *

Plaintiffs, then, by failing to show that defendants Langley and Clayton had any fiduciary capacity with Olympic, have failed to shift from themselves the burden of proving fraud or absence of good faith in the loan transaction.

DECISION AND REMEDY   *The Supreme Court of Tennessee reversed the lower court's decision and held that the defendants, Langley and Clayton, held a valid security interest in the property of Olympic and were entitled to priority over the general creditors.*

CORPORATE FINANCING

In order to obtain financing, corporations issue **securities**—evidence of the obligation to pay money or of the right to participate in earnings and the distribution of corporate trusts and other property. The principal method of long-term and initial corporate financing is the issuance of stocks—equity—and bonds—debt—both of which are sold to investors. **Stocks,** or equity securities, represent the purchase of ownership in the business firm. **Bonds,** or debt securities, represent the borrowing of money by firms (and governments). Of course, not all debt is in the form of debt securities. Some is in the form of accounts payable, some in the form of notes payable, and still more in the form of leaseholds. Accounts and notes payable are typically short-term debts. Bonds are simply a way for the corporation to split up its long-term debt so that it can market it more easily.

Bonds

Bonds are issued by business firms and by governments at all levels as evidence of the funds they are borrowing from investors. Bonds almost always have a designated maturity date—the date when the principal, or face amount, of the bond (or loan) is returned to the investor. Bonds are sometimes referred to as *fixed-income securities* because their owners receive fixed dollar interest payments during the period of time prior to maturity.

Bonds can be sold below their face value at a *discount* or above their face value at a *premium*. Bonds sold at premiums have yields that are less than their coupon, or stated, rates; those sold at a discount have yields that are greater than the face rate.

CORPORATE BONDS   The characteristics of corporate bonds vary widely, in part because cor-

porations differ in their ability to generate the earnings and cash flow necessary to make interest payments and to repay the principal amount of the bonds at maturity. Furthermore, corporate bonds are only a part of the total debt and the overall financial structure of corporate business.

Because debt financing represents a legal obligation on the part of the corporation, various features and terms of a particular bond issue are specified in a lending agreement called a **bond indenture.** A corporate trustee, often a commercial bank trust department, represents the collective well-being of all bondholders in ensuring that the terms of the bond issue are met by the corporation.

The bond indenture specifies the maturity date of the bond and the pattern of interest payments until maturity. Most corporate bonds pay semiannually a coupon rate of interest on the face amount of the bond.

For example, the owner of a 6 percent corporate bond with a face value of $1,000 would receive $30 interest every six months. The indenture indicates whether any portion of the bond is to be retired each year in a series of *sinking fund payments*, and it specifies any collateral for the bond issue, such as buildings or equipment. Additionally, the indenture indicates how the bondholder (and other creditors of the business firm) will fare if the firm gets into serious financial difficulty and is unable to meet all its legal obligations.

There are a number of different types of corporate bonds, designated below.

Debenture Bonds   No specific assets of the corporation are pledged as backing for debenture bonds. Rather, they are backed by the general credit rating of the corporation, plus any assets that can be seized if the corporation allows the debenture bonds to go into default.

Mortgage Bonds Mortgage bonds pledge specific property. If the corporation defaults on the bonds, the bondholders can take the mortgage property.

Equipment Trust Bonds The collateral for the equipment trust bond, or chattel mortgage bond (loan), is a specific piece of equipment. Title to the equipment is vested in a trustee, who holds it for the benefit of the bond owners.

Collateral Trust Bonds Collateral trust bonds are secured by intangibles such as shares of stock in another corporation or accounts receivable.

Convertible Bonds Convertible bonds can be exchanged for a specified number of shares of common stock when and if the bondholder so desires. The rate of conversion is determined when the convertible bond is issued.

Callable Bonds Callable bonds, which may be debentures or any other kind of bonds, may be called in and the principal repaid at specified times or under specified conditions. The callable provision is included in the bond when it issued.

Stocks

Issuing stocks is another way corporations obtain financing. Stocks represent ownership in a business firm; bonds represent borrowing by the firm.

The most important characteristics of stocks are as follows:

1. The purchase price need not be paid back by the corporation.
2. The stockholder receives dividends only when so voted by the directors.
3. Stockholders are the last investors to be paid off upon dissolution.
4. Stockholders vote for management and on major issues.

The two major types of stock are preferred stock and common stock.

COMMON STOCK **Common stock** represents the true ownership of a corporation. Ownership of this stock represents a threefold proportionate interest in the corporation with regard to:

1. Control.
2. Earning capacity.
3. Net assets.

A shareholder's interest is generally in proportion to the number of shares he or she owns out of the total number of shares issued.

Voting rights in a corporation apply to election of the firm's board of directors and to any proposed changes in the ownership structure of the firm.[4] For example, a holder of common stock generally has the right to vote in a decision on a proposed merger, since mergers can change the proportion of ownership. Many small investors in giant corporations probably feel that their small number of votes has little impact on the business firm—particularly when incumbent management owns or obtains the right to vote shares by proxy and thus has a significant and often controlling proportion of the total votes. Still, voting rights are an important characteristic of common stock and one that some investors take seriously.

There is no obligation to return a principal amount per share to each holder of common stock. No firm can ensure that the market price per share of its common stock will not go down over time. Neither does the issuing firm guarantee a dividend; indeed, some business firms never pay dividends. Considering these negative aspects, why would an individual even consider investing in common stock? The answer, of course, is that a stockholder is at least one, if not the only, owner of a corporation, and all owners are entitled to their proportional share of the corporation's after-tax earnings. If Janet Gray owns 100 shares (0.01 percent of 1 million shares outstanding) of a firm that earns $3 million after taxes, she has a property right to a proportional share of those earnings, or $300. Earnings are the key to the benefits that an investor receives from common stock.

Either the earnings of a corporation are paid out in the form of cash dividends to shareholders, or they are retained in the business for the express purpose of enhancing future earnings. If the board of directors of Janet Gray's firm (and it is *her* firm, because she owns common stock) declares a dividend of $1.20 per share, then she receives $120 of her $300 earnings now as a tangible benefit, and the other $180 is retained by the corporation. Her other tangible benefit is the market price per share that she will receive if and when she ultimately sells part or all of her 100 common shares.

---

4. State corporation law specifies the types of issues on which shareholder approval must be obtained.

Market price depends, among other things, on the recent earnings (and dividends) of the firm and, more importantly, on the expectations for future earnings and dividends, as well as on the overall economic well-being of the country.

Holders of common stock, then, are a group of investors who assume a *residual* position in the overall financial structure of a business. In terms of receiving payment for their investment, they are last in line. The earnings to which they are entitled also depend on the corporation's paying all the other groups—suppliers, employees, managers, bankers, governments, bondholders, and holders of preferred stock—what is due them first. Once those groups have been paid, however, the owners of common stock may be entitled to *all* the remaining earnings. (But the board of directors is not normally under any duty to declare the remaining earnings as dividends.) This is the central feature of ownership in any business, be it a corner grocery, a retail store, an architectural firm, or a giant international oil corporation. In each instance, the owners of common stock occupy the riskiest position, but they can expect a correspondingly greater return on their investment. Again, it can be seen why the return and risk pattern holds. As one moves from savings accounts and U.S. government bonds to corporate bonds with different ratings to preferred stock and, finally, to common stock, expected returns increase to compensate for the higher risks that are undertaken. Exhibit 39–2 offers a comparison of stocks and bonds.

Authorized, Issued, and Outstanding Shares   A share of stock is the basic unit of ownership of the corporation. **Authorized shares** are those that the corporation is allowed to issue by its articles of incorporation. Under modern law, there generally is no limit on the number of authorized shares. **Issued shares** are those that are actually issued to shareholders. There is no specific percentage of authorized shares that must be issued. The number of issued shares does not always equal the number of outstanding shares because corporations sometimes repurchase some of their shares. **Outstanding shares** are those still held by the shareholders. Repurchased shares are known as **treasury shares;** these shares are authorized and issued but not outstanding.

Par Value and No Par Shares   The specific monetary value assigned to shares in the articles of incorporation is called *par value.* It is the face value of a share. Although of historical interest, par value is no longer of primary importance. Its one lingering effect is that the price per common share initially sold must be greater than or equal to par value. This creates no problem when nominal amounts are used for par value.

The issuance of *no par shares* is permitted in most jurisdictions. As their name implies, these shares are assigned no dollar value. Some statutes provide that the board of directors has the right to fix the price for no par shares issued, but the articles of incorporation may expressly reserve this right for the shareholders.

Exhibit 39–2 How Do Stocks and Bonds Differ?

STOCKS	BONDS
1. Stocks represent ownership.	1. Bonds represent owed debt.
2. Stocks (common) do not have a fixed dividend rate.	2. Interest on bonds must always be paid, whether or not any profit is earned.
3. Stockholders can elect a board of directors, which controls the corporation.	3. Bondholders usually have no voice in or control over management of the corporation.
4. Stocks do not have a maturity date; the corporation does not usually repay the stockholder.	4. Bonds have a maturity date on which the bondholder is to be repaid the face value of the bond.
5. Most corporations issue or offer to sell stocks. This is the usual definition of a business corporation.	5. Corporations do not necessarily issue bonds.
6. Stockholders have a claim against the property and income of a corporation after all creditors' claims have been met.	6. Bondholders have a claim against the property and income of a corporation that must be met before the claims of stockholders.

PREFERRED STOCK   **Preferred stock** is a stock with *preferences*. Usually this means that holders of preferred stock have priority over holders of common stock to dividends and to payment upon dissolution of the corporation. Preferred shareholders may or may not have the right to vote.

From an investment standpoint, preferred stock is more similar to bonds than to common stock, but it is not included among the liabilities of a business, because it represents equity. Like all equity securities, preferred shares have no fixed maturity date on which they must be retired by the firm. Occasionally, firms do retire preferred stock, but they are not legally obligated to do so.

Preferred shareholders receive periodic dividend payments, usually established as a fixed percentage of the face amount of each preferred share. A 7 percent preferred stock with a face amount of $100 per share would pay its owner a $7 dividend each year. Payment of dividends is not a legal obligation on the part of the firm, whereas the interest payments due to bondholders are legal obligations.

There are a number of different types of preferred stock, which are designated as follows:

Cumulative Preferred Stock   Any dividend payment on cumulative preferred stock not made in a given year must be paid in a subsequent year before any dividends can be paid to owners of common stock. If, for example, a corporation fails to pay dividends for three years on a stock with a $100 par value and a $5 annual dividend preference, then the company must pay the cumulative preferred stock owners $15 per share at the end of the three years before any dividends can be paid to owners of common stock. Sometimes there are limits on the extent to which dividend arrears may accumulate—for example, there may be three- or five-year cumulative limits.

Participating Preferred Stock   The owner of participating preferred stock can share to some extent in additional dividends that are paid by the firm. Usually, the preferred stockholders are paid their agreed-upon rate of, say, $8 per share (the dividend preference), and then common stockholders are paid an equal percentage rate, after which any additional dividends declared by the board of directors are distributed equally among preferred and common stockholders.

Convertible Preferred Stock   The owner of shares of convertible preferred stock has an option of converting each share into a specified number of common shares. Sometimes convertible preferred stock can be exchanged for common stock in another company. In any event, the exchange ratio is determined when the convertible preferred shares are issued. Hence, if there is an increase in the market value of the corporation's common stock, the market value of the convertible preferred stock also rises. See Exhibit 39–3 for a cumulative convertible preferred stock certificate.

Redeemable, or Callable, Preferred Stock   Redeemable, or callable, preferred stock is issued by a corporation under the express condition that the corporation has the right to buy back the shares of stock from the preferred stockholders at some future time. The terms of such a buy-back arrangement are specified when the preferred stock is issued. Corporations issue callable preferred stock so that they can call in the higher-cost preferred stock and reissue lower-cost shares if interest rates fall in the future.

THE CAUTIOUS POSITION OF THE PREFERRED STOCKHOLDER   Holders of preferred stock are investors who have assumed a rather cautious position in their relationship to the corporation. They have a stronger position than common shareholders with respect to dividends and claims on assets, but as a result, they will not share in the full prosperity of the firm if it grows successfully over time.

A preferred stockholder receives fixed dividends periodically, and there may be changes in the market price of the shares. The return and the risk associated with a share of preferred stock lie somewhere between those associated with bonds and common stock. As a result, preferred stock is often categorized with corporate bonds as a fixed-income security, even though the legal status is not the same. As mentioned above, preferred stock is more similar to bonds than to common stock, even though preferred stock appears in the ownership section of the firm's balance sheet.

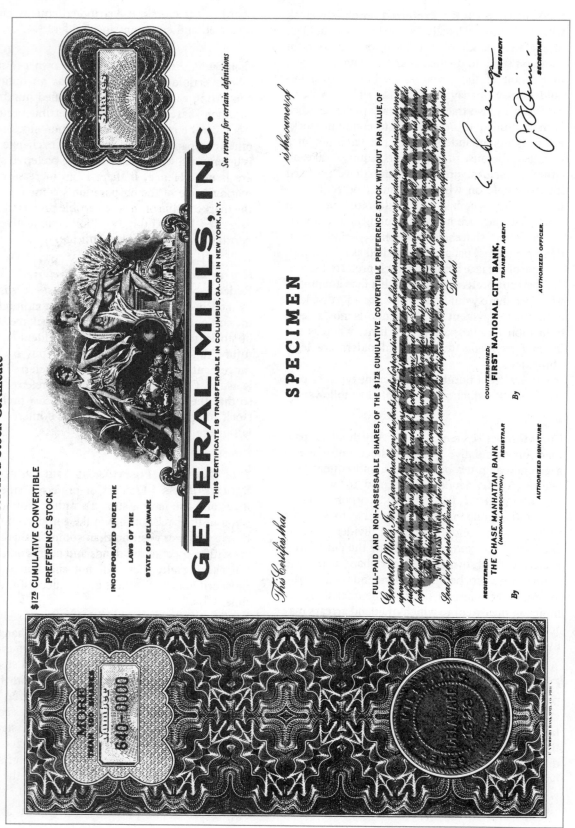

Exhibit 39–3 A Sample Cumulative Convertible Preferred Stock Certificate

CONCEPT SUMMARY: Stocks

TYPE	DEFINITION
Common stock	Voting shares that represent ownership interests in a corporation. Common stock has lowest priority with respect to payment of dividends and distribution of assets upon the corporation's dissolution.
Preferred stock	Shares that have priority over common shares as to payment of dividends and distribution of assets upon corporate dissolution. Dividend payments are usually a fixed percentage of the face value of the share.
Cumulative preferred stock	Preferred shares for which required dividends not paid in a given year must be paid in a subsequent year before any common stock dividends are paid.
Participating preferred stock	Preferred shares entitling owner to receive dividends from funds available after preferred shareholders receive required dividends and common shareholders receive prescribed dividends.
Convertible preferred stock	Preferred shares giving holders the option to convert the shares into a specified number of common shares in the issuing corporation or, sometimes, in another corporation.
Redeemable or callable preferred stock	Preferred shares issued with the express condition that the issuing corporation has the right to repurchase the shares as specified.
Authorized shares	Shares allowed to be issued by the articles of incorporation.
Issued shares	Shares that have actually been transferred to shareholders.
Outstanding shares	Authorized and issued shares still held by shareholders.
Treasury shares	Shares authorized and issued but not outstanding (reacquired by the corporation).
No par value shares	Shares issued with no stated value. The price is usually fixed by the board of directors or shareholders.
Par value shares	Shares issued and priced at a stated value per share.

QUESTIONS AND CASE PROBLEMS

1. Cummings, Marvin, and Taft are recent college graduates who want to form a corporation to manufacture and sell personal computers. Peterson tells them he will set in motion the formation of their corporation. First, Peterson makes a contract for the purchase of a piece of land for $20,000 with Owens. Owens does not know of the prospective corporate formation at the time of the signing of the contract. Second, Peterson makes a contract with Babcock to build a small plant on the property being purchased. Babcock's contract is conditional on the corporation's for-mation. Peterson secures all necessary subscription agreements and capitalization, and he files the articles of incorporation. A charter is issued.

   (a) Discuss whether the newly formed corporation or Peterson or both are liable on the contracts with Owens and Babcock.

   (b) Discuss whether the corporation is automatically liable to Babcock upon being formed.

2. As a promoter forming a new corporation, Peterson enters into three pre-incorporation subscription agreements with Mary, Anne, and Harry. The three subscribers each agree to purchase a thousand shares of stock of the future corporation for $2,000. Two months later, just prior to the issuance of the corporate charter, Mary tells Peterson she is withdrawing from the agreement. The charter is issued the next week. Just before the first organizational meeting of the corporation, Harry also withdraws from the agree-

ment. Discuss fully whether Mary or Harry or both can withdraw from their subscription agreements without liability.

3. Cartwright, Gomez, and Bush form a corporation. The state laws governing incorporation require that the articles of incorporation be signed by three incorporators. A charter is issued, and the corporation begins to do business. Thomas extends credit to the corporation. Because of a national recession, the corporation becomes insolvent. At this time, Thomas learns that Cartwright failed to sign the articles of incorporation. Thomas claims that the corporation's formation was improper and that Cartwright, Gomez, and Bush are personally liable. Discuss Thomas's claim.

4. Jim, Allen, and Ed are brothers who form a corporation to build swimming pools. They are the sole shareholders, members of the board of directors, and officers of the corporation. No meetings are held, and corporate trucks are put to personal use on weekends. In addition, the brothers lend the corporation money, taking a security interest in the corporate property when they cannot get unsecured credit from others because of previous unsecured indebtedness. The corporation becomes insolvent, and the brothers claim they have priority over unsecured creditors on the basis of their security interest. The unsecured creditors claim not only that the security interest can be set aside but that the brothers are personally liable. Discuss these claims.

5. A new corporation is formed. By its articles of incorporation, it has 100,000 shares of authorized common stock at a par value of $2 per share. The corporation has limited property assets, since its major function is that of a service corporation. The corporation issues 50,000 shares. Soon it needs additional financing. Profits for the first year are relatively low, but the future of the corporation is bright. The corporation needs $90,000 of additional financing, but it wants to plow back next year's profits into the corporation.

(a) Would you recommend funding by issuance of corporate bonds? Discuss.

(b) Would you recommend the issuance of preferred or common stock? Discuss.

6. Pointer formed a corporation with $1,000 capital and later loaned over $400,000 to the corporation. Six days after he was notified that Tigrett had filed suit against his corporation, Pointer transferred corporate assets amounting to $400,000 to himself as repayment of the loans. Pointer then transferred these assets to another corporation, of which he was the sole shareholder. The second corporation took over all the business and duties of the original corporation. By the time Tigrett was awarded a judgment against the original corporation, it had no assets. Is there any way for Tigrett to collect the amount of her judgment? [Tigrett v. Pointer, 580 S.W.2d 375 (Tex.Civ.App. 1978)]

7. Harvey's is a group of New York corporations. Five of these entered into an agreement with Flynt Distributing Company for Flynt to distribute their magazines. Following this agreement Harvey failed to pay Flynt or to ship the magazines to Flynt, causing Flynt injury. Two of Harvey's shareholders converted the assets of the five corporations

to their own use, which left the corporations undercapitalized. Discuss whether this conduct amounts to an abuse of corporate business, which would allow Flynt to pierce the corporate veil. [Flynt Distributing Co., Inc. v. Harvey, 734 F.2d 1389 (9th Cir. 1984)]

8. On January 27, 1982, Joseph E. Walker, acting as president on behalf of Music City Sawmill Company, purchased a wheel-loaded machine from Thompson & Green Machinery Company (T & G). Walker was also president of Music City Lumber Company. To effect the sale, Walker signed, on behalf of Music City Sawmill, a promissory note. At the time of the purchase, unknown to Walker, Music City Sawmill was not incorporated, but it became so the next day. When Music City Sawmill was unable to make payments on the note, T & G sued Music City Sawmill, Music City Lumber Company, and Walker individually. Walker claimed that even though Music City Sawmill was not incorporated at the time he signed the note as the purported president, a corporation by estoppel existed and he could not be held personally liable. Discuss whether Walker was correct. [Thompson & Green Machinery Co., Inc. v. Music City Lumber Co., Inc., 683 S.W.2d 340 (Tenn.App. 1984)]

9. Richard Bice, the promoter and incorporator of Hog Heaven Corporation, signed a farm management contract with Midland Farm Management Company prior to filing Hog Heaven's articles of incorporation. Once these articles had been filed, Hog Heaven adopted the contract by accepting its benefits and burdens (that is, the benefits of having the farm managed by Midland and the burden of paying for such management). Eventually, Midland breached the contract, and Hog Heaven brought suit to enforce the contract terms. Midland claimed that since Hog Heaven was not in existence at the time the contract was entered into, Hog Heaven lacked capacity to enforce the contract. Could Hog Heaven bring an action for breach of contract even though it was not yet in existence when the contract was made? [Hog Heaven Corp. v. Midland Farm Management Co., 380 N.W.2d 756 (Iowa App. 1985)]

10. Morque and the other members of a real estate partnership secured a mortgage loan from First Federal Savings and Loan to renovate a building in order to open a bar. Later, the partners executed another agreement with First Federal. The second agreement provided that if First Federal foreclosed on the mortgage, the partners would transfer their liquor license for the property to any party designated by First Federal. Two months after signing these agreements, Morque and his partners formed a corporation called Himax and had the liquor license for the bar transferred to Himax. Himax operated the bar and leased the first floor of the building from the real estate partnership. The stock in Himax changed hands several times, and new officers and directors took charge. When the bar failed to generate sufficient revenues to make the required mortgage payments, First Federal started foreclosure proceedings against Morque and sought a court injunction barring transfer of the liquor license by Himax to any party other than one approved by First Federal. Himax claimed that it was not bound by any pre-incorporation agreement made by the partners. The present officers and directors claimed that they had not signed and had no knowledge of the transfer restriction agreement and thus had not adopted or created a novation of the agreement. Should Himax be bound by the pre-incorporation agreement barring transfer of the liquor license to a party other than one approved by First Federal under these circumstances? [Federal Savings and Loan Insurance Corp. v. Morque, 372 N.W.2d 872 (N.D. 1985)]

11.   Charles Wolfe was the sole shareholder and president of Wolfe & Company, a firm that leased tractor-trailers. The corporation had no separate bank account. Banking transactions were conducted through Wolfe's personal accounts, and employees were paid from them. Wolfe never consulted with any other corporate directors. During the tax years 1974–1976, the corporation incurred $114,472.91 in federal tax liabilities for employment, fuel, and highway-use taxes and for penalties, fees, and interest. The government held Wolfe personally liable. Wolfe paid the tax bill and then brought an action against the government for disregarding his corporate entity. Discuss whether the government can disregard the corporate entity in Wolfe's case and hold Wolfe personally liable for corporate taxes. [Wolfe v. United States, 798 F.2d 1241 (9th Cir. 1986)]

Chapter 40

CORPORATIONS
Corporate Powers and Management

The power of a corporation is derived from several sources. We first examine them and then look at powers of shareholders and directors.

CORPORATE POWERS

Corporations have both express and implied powers. These are distinguished and defined below.

Express Powers

The express powers of a corporation are found in its articles of incorporation, in the law of the state of incorporation, and in the state and federal constitutions. The order of priority used when conflicts arise among documents involving corporations is as follows:

1. The U.S. Constitution.
2. State constitutions.
3. State statutes.
4. The certificate of incorporation (charter).
5. Bylaws.
6. Resolutions of the board of directors.

It is important to keep in mind that the corporation is a "legal person." Under modern law, except as limited by charters, statutes, or constitutions, *a corporation can engage in all acts and enter into any contract available to a natural person in order to accomplish the purposes for which it was created.*

Implied Powers

Certain inherent powers attach when a corporation is created. Barring express constitutional, statutory, or charter prohibitions, the corporation has the implied power to do all acts reasonably appropriate and necessary to accomplish its corporate purposes. For this reason, a corporation has the implied power to borrow money within certain limits, to lend money or to extend credit to those with whom it has a legal or contractual relationship, and to make charitable contributions.[1]

To borrow money, the organization acts through its board of directors to authorize the execution

of negotiable paper. Most often, the president or chief executive officer of the corporation executes the necessary papers on behalf of the corporation. In so doing, corporate officers have the implied power to bind the corporation in matters directly connected with the *ordinary* business affairs of the enterprise.

The issue in the following case is whether the corporation's power to issue stock is an implied power or a power expressly granted by the state.

---

1. Corporations are prohibited from making political contributions in federal elections by the Federal Elections Campaign Act [18 U.S.C. Section 321]. Early law held that a corporation had no implied authority to make charitable contributions, because making charitable contributions was contrary to the primary purpose of the corporation to make a profit. Modern law, by statutes and court decisions, now holds that a corporation can make charitable contributions.

BACKGROUND AND FACTS *Several members of the Malvern Country Club, including Dewey Allen, sued the club to enforce their rights as purported stockholders. Allen and several others had filed the articles of incorporation of the club with a provision that stock could and would be sold. The club, a nonprofit corporation, claimed that the issuance of stock was contradictory to its nature and the incorporation laws of Arkansas (as a matter of law, a nonprofit organization could not give individuals an equitable claim in the assets or retained earnings of the corporation). Allen claimed that the right to issue stock was an implied power of all corporations and expressly provided for in the articles of incorporation. The original laws of incorporation in Arkansas did not prohibit the issuance of stock for such corporations, but neither did they provide for issuance. Prior to this lawsuit, however, Arkansas amended the law expressly to prohibit the issuance of stock by nonprofit corporations, but this did not affect any corporations that had already been incorporated properly. Allen made a motion to dismiss the club's defense that nonprofit corporations could not have stockholders, but the lower court declined. Allen appealed that decision.*

Case 40.1
ALLEN v. MALVERN COUNTRY CLUB
Supreme Court of Arkansas, 1988.
295 Ark. 65, 746 S.W.2d 546.

HOLT, Judge.
*   *   *   *

In 1956, a petition for incorporation was filed with the Hot Spring County Circuit Court requesting that the court enter an order incorporating the Malvern Country Club as a nonprofit corporation—the object and purpose of the Club being to promote the pleasure, recreation, and bodily health of its members by means of a private country club. The petition, which was approved by the circuit court, included a proposed constitution which contained articles of incorporation. In relevant part, article five provided:

> STOCK CERTIFICATE HOLDING MEMBERS: 200 members may be elected to membership in this class upon payment of a stockholder's fee of $350.00. This class will constitute the sole voting membership of the Club. A certificate of stock shall be issued, entitling the holder thereof to all the privileges of the Club upon such terms and conditions as may be prescribed by the By-Laws, and further entitling such members to share in the property or assets of the organization.

The articles of incorporation also provided for additional classes of members not authorized to own stock. *   *   *

*   *   * Nonprofit corporations such as the Club are now governed by the 1963 Arkansas Nonprofit Corporation Act *   *   *.

Sometime in 1969, the Club filed its articles of incorporation with the Secretary of State pursuant to the new Act. In May 1987, allegedly without notice to several stockholders, certain amendments to the articles of incorporation were proposed and adopted by the Club's members, some of whom did not hold shares of stock. In June 1987, appellants filed the underlying action seeking a declaration of their rights as stockholders and for other relief.

A review of superseded sections reveals absolutely no authority for the issuance of stock by nonprofit corporations such as the Club. *   *   *

Appellants argue that the Act would not affect corporations chartered under preexisting statutes. Subsection (a), however, explicitly requires that such corporations originally be chartered in accordance with the laws of this state prior to the effective date of the new Act. It is clear that the Club was not chartered in accordance with the statutes in effect at the time of incorporation as those statutes did not give entities such as the Club the power to issue stock. We reach the inescapable conclusion that there is not now, nor has there ever been, statutory authority for the issuance of stock by the appellee Club.

Corporations organized under the laws of this state are but creatures of the legislature, and the legislative power to create corporations cannot be delegated to the courts. Hence, we find no support for appellants' argument that court approval in 1956 of provisions for the issuance of stock in the Club's articles of incorporation, absent statutory authority therefor, in any way validated the stock.

The laws of a particular state which grant or restrict the powers of a corporation become part of the articles of incorporation or charter of that corporation. Anyone seeking to obtain the benefit of provisions within such articles of incorporation or charter takes that benefit with the burdens prescribed by the relevant statutes, and if there is a conflict between the charter and the statutes under which the charter was issued, the charter must yield to the laws of the state.

Much like the power to create the corporate status, the power to create corporate stock is a legislative function which must be exercised for such stock to have legal existence; the power to issue stock must be specifically granted by the statutes under which a corporation is formed, which results in the rule that the power to issue stock is not held to be among the incidental or implied powers of a corporation. As such, we reject appellants' contention that the issuance of stock was incidental to the purpose of the Club or that it was an implied power of the Club.

The inevitable consequence of the absence of specific statutory authorization for the issuance of stock is that, by law, such stock is void, confers no rights on the person to whom issued, and creates no liabilities; the rule of voidness applies to disputes between shareholders or between shareholders and the corporation. In light of the foregoing, application of the 1963 Act can work no deprivation of property since the stock at issue was void from the outset.

DECISION AND REMEDY   *The Supreme Court of Arkansas affirmed the decision of the lower court and held that not-for-profit corporations do not have an implied power to issue stock. Such power must be expressly granted by a state statute. Because the Arkansas statute did not grant such power, Allen and the other members were not legal stockholders in the club and could not exert stockholders' rights.*

Ultra Vires Doctrine

The term *ultra vires* means "beyond the powers." In corporate law, acts of a corporation that are beyond the authority given to it under its charter or under the statutes by which it was incorporated are ***ultra vires* acts.**

Ultra vires acts can be understood only within the context of the particular stated purpose for which the corporation was organized. Acts in furtherance of the corporation's expressed purposes are within the corporate power; acts beyond the scope of corporate business as described in the charter are *ultra vires*. Of course, an illegal act is inherently *ultra vires*.

The stated purposes in the articles of the corporation set the limits of the activities the corporation can legally pursue. Any time the corporation takes on activities outside the stated purposes, the corporation can be charged with committing an *ultra vires* act. Because of this, corporations are increasingly aware of the benefit of adopting a very broad statement of purpose in their articles of incorporation to include virtually all conceivable activities. Corporate statues in many states permit the expression "any lawful purpose" to be a legally sufficient stated purpose in the articles of incorporation.

In certain cases, the law recognizes the right of a shareholder to sue the board of directors for its alleged wrongful action of pursuing *ultra vires* acts. A stockholder can bring what is called a *derivative suit* against the corporation after first demanding that the directors correct the wrong. If the directors fail to act, the stockholder can ask the court to enforce the corporate right.

Judicial Treatment of *Ultra Vires* Contracts

The current trend in dealing with *ultra vires* contracts is embodied in statutory enactments similar to Section 7 of the Model Act, which upholds the validity and enforceability of an *ultra vires* contract as between the parties involved. Note, however, that the right of shareholders on behalf of the corporation, the right of the corporation itself to recover damages from the officers and directors who caused the transaction, and the right of the attorney general of the state to institute an injunction against the transaction or to institute dissolution proceedings against the corporation for *ultra vires* acts have been upheld.

The following case deals with an action that was held by the court to be *ultra vires*.

BACKGROUND AND FACTS   *The Seabrook Island Property Owners Association was created to preserve the value and amenities of every apartment owner within the Seabrook Island development. The bylaws of the association provided that it could assess an annual maintenance fee as fixed by the board of directors of the association in order to maintain the street, open spaces, and other common facilities for the owner-members. Each homeowner was required to pay these annual charges because of a binding covenant included in the purchase contract. The bylaws of the association did not empower the board of directors to levy any assessments other than this annual maintenance charge. Nevertheless, the board adopted a resolution to assess a special charge to finance a beach restoration project and bridge construction. Such an assessment could not in any way be considered a maintenance charge. Lovering and other lot owners in the development sued to prevent the association from making such an assessment. The Court of Common Pleas granted summary judgment for the association, and Lovering appealed.*

Case 40.2
LOVERING v. SEABROOK ISLAND PROPERTY OWNERS ASSOCIATION
Court of Appeals of South Carolina, 1986.
344 S.E.2d 862.

BELL, Judge.
*   *   *   *

The main question presented by this appeal is whether the Association had authority to levy the emergency budget assessment. We hold that the levying of an emergency budget assessment was an *ultra vires* action by the Association.

A corporation may exercise only those powers which are granted to it by law, by its charter or articles of incorporation, and any by-laws made pursuant thereto. Acts beyond the scope of a corporation's powers as defined by law or its charter are *ultra vires*. In determining a corporation's powers, its charter is to be construed strictly; any ambiguity in the terms of a corporate charter must operate against the corporation. The specification of certain powers operates as a limitation on such objects as are embodied therein and is an implied prohibition of the exercise of other and distinct powers.

A similar rule of strict construction applies to the enforcement of covenants against real property. Covenants purporting to impose affirmative obligations on the grantee are to be strictly construed and not enforced unless the obligation is imposed in clear and unambiguous language which is sufficiently definite to guide the courts in its application.

The Association contends it may impose special assessments for any corporate purpose pursuant to the general statement of purposes in its by-laws. The Association specifically directs our attention to a provision in the by-laws stating that the purpose of the Association is, among other things, "to engage in such other activities as may be to the mutual benefit of the owners of property on Seabrook Island." This provision, it contends, authorizes it to impose special assessments for corporate purposes.

The general statement of corporate purposes relied on is not sufficient, standing alone, to authorize the levying of special assessments on property owners. In order to constitute an enforceable power of assessment in the Association, an assessment provision must: (1) express a sufficiently definite standard by which to measure liability for the assessment; (2) describe with particularity the property to be maintained; and (3) provide an ascertainable standard by which the purpose for which the assessment is levied can be objectively determined. A standard such as "any other thing necessary or desirable in the opinion of the Board of Directors" is too vague to be enforceable.

As a matter of general law, a nonprofit corporation has the power to enforce the collection of dues and charges in accordance with the provisions of its by-laws. In this case, however, neither the protective covenants nor the by-laws give the Association power to levy special assessments. The protective covenants and the by-laws authorize the Association to impose only an annual maintenance charge. The annual maintenance charge must be based on the assessed value of the property for tax purposes. It may be adjusted from year to year, but still must be based on assessed value for taxation. The moneys collected are to be used only for the purposes enumerated in the by-laws.

Under the rules of construction outlined above, the specification of the power to levy an annual maintenance charge limits the power of the Association to impose other assessments on property owners within the Seabrook Island subdivision. It operates as an implied prohibition against the levying of special assessments. Therefore, the Association was without power to impose a special assessment, even if its object was to carry out a legitimate corporate purpose. A permissible purpose cannot be accomplished by a prohibited means.

DECISION AND REMEDY   *The court of appeals reversed the decision of the lower court and held for Lovering. The association had acted* ultra vires *in levying the special assessment.*

COMMENTS   *The* ultra vires *doctrine is of declining importance in corporate law because courts have held that any legal action that a corporation undertakes to profit its shareholders is allowable and proper. The doctrine is still of some importance, however, and was applied in this case because property owners are subject to greater risk of abuse by their property associations than are most stockholders by their corporations.*

Torts and Criminal Acts

A corporation is liable for the torts committed by its agents or officers within the course and scope of their employment. A corporation can act only through its agents and servants. This principle applies to a corporation exactly as it applies to the ordinary agency relationships discussed in

Chapter 33. It follows the doctrine of *respondeat superior*.

At common law, a corporation could not be held liable for a crime, particularly one that required intent. Under modern criminal law, however, a corporation can sometimes be held liable for the criminal acts of its agents and employees, provided the punishment can be applied to the corporation.[2]

The Model Penal Code (discussed in Chapter 6) provides that a corporation may be convicted of a crime in the following situations:

1. The criminal act by the corporation's agent or employee is within the scope of his or her employment and the purpose of the statute defining the act as a crime is to impose liability on corporations.
2. The crime consists of a failure to perform a specific affirmative duty imposed on corporations by law.
3. The crime was authorized, requested, commanded, committed, or recklessly tolerated by one of the corporation's high managerial agents.

When a law requires intent as an element of a crime, the agent's or employee's intent may be imputed to the corporation. An important factor is how high in the corporate hierarchy the individual stands. Is he or she high enough in the management structure that his or her conduct can be interpreted without proof of authorization as the corporation's acts? This is known as the "high managerial agent" rule.

Crimes for which corporations have been indicted or convicted include manslaughter, homicide, arson, and grand theft.

CORPORATE MANAGEMENT— SHAREHOLDERS

As a general rule, shareholders have no responsibility for the daily management of the corporation (except when identical ownership and management is desired, as is the case in many closely held corporations). Shareholders are ultimately re-

sponsible for choosing the board of directors, which does have such control. Ordinarily, corporate officers and other employees owe no direct duty to individual stockholders. Their duty is to the corporation as a whole. A director is in a fiduciary relationship to the corporation and therefore serves the interests of the shareholders as a group.

In some cases, a majority shareholder, or a few acting together, may be regarded as having a fiduciary duty to the corporation and the minority shareholders. This might occur, for example, if he, she, or they owned enough shares to exercise *de facto* control over the corporation.

Under these circumstances, the majority shareholder may also have a fiduciary duty to the corporation's creditors. Generally, however, there is no legal relationship between shareholders and creditors of the corporation. Shareholders can, in fact, be creditors of the corporation and have the same rights of recovery against the corporation as any other creditor. The rights and liabilities of shareholders are discussed in Chapter 41.

Shareholder Powers

Shareholders must approve fundamental changes affecting the corporation before the changes can be effected. Hence, shareholders are empowered to amend the articles of incorporation (charter) and bylaws, approve merger or dissolution of the corporation, and approve the sale of all or substantially all of the corporation's assets. Some of these powers are subject to prior board approval.

Election and removal of the board of directors are accomplished by a vote of the shareholders. The first board of directors is either named in the articles of incorporation or chosen by the incorporators to serve until the first shareholders' meeting. From that time on, selection and retention of directors are exclusively a shareholder function.

Directors usually serve their full term. If they are unsatisfactory, they are simply not reelected. Shareholders have the inherent power to remove a director from office *for cause* (breach of duty or misconduct) by a majority vote.[3] Some state statutes permit removal of directors without cause by the vote of a majority of the holders of outstanding

---

2. Obviously, a corporation cannot be imprisoned; however, it can be fined and possibly dissolved.

3. A director can often demand court review of removal for cause.

shares entitled to vote.[4] Some corporate charters expressly provide that shareholders by majority

vote can remove a director at any time *without cause*.

In the following case, the plaintiff sued to be reinstated on a corporate board of directors after having been removed from office by a majority vote of the shareholders.

---

4. Most states allow cumulative voting for directors (discussed later in this chapter). In these states, a director cannot be removed without cause over the negative vote that would be sufficient to elect that director in the first place. See, for example, California Corporate Code Section 303A. Also see Section 39 of the Model Act.

Case 40.3
KAMIN v. KOREN
United States District Court for
the Southern District of New
York, 1985.
621 F.Supp. 444.

BACKGROUND AND FACTS *The plaintiffs, Bernard Kamin and his associated corporation, Mosport Park, Ltd., agreed to purchase 1,295 shares of stock from the New York Grand Prix Corporation for $500,000. As part of this agreement, Grand Prix allowed Mosport Park to name Kamin to Grand Prix's board of directors. But when Mosport Park failed to pay all of the installments of the $500,000 purchase price, Grand Prix terminated Kamin's directorship. Grand Prix's bylaws specified that directors could be removed "with or without cause." Mosport Park and Kamin sued Grand Prix to have Kamin reinstated. Grand Prix replied (1) that it was not obligated to keep Kamin on its board of directors after Mosport Park's default and (2) that even if Mosport Park had not defaulted, Grand Prix was entitled to remove any director without cause according to its bylaws. The plaintiffs also tried to have Grand Prix's major shareholder and director, Daniel Koren, removed from Grand Prix's board of directors by a show of cause after Koren made a substantial withdrawal of corporate funds without the countersignature required under Grand Prix's bylaws.*

WEINFELD, District Judge.
*   *   *   *

In the light of the default upon the failure to pay the $100,000 due on December 1, 1984 and January 1, 1985, plaintiffs nonetheless contend that this did not affect Mosport's claim under the consulting agreement nor Kamin's right to remain as Mosport's designee on the Board of Directors under the shareholders agreement. *   *   * [T]hey assert that the default was waived orally and a new agreement entered into which substantially modified the written agreements of November 12, 1984. The Court finds otherwise. Under the shareholders agreement, Mosport agreed to purchase 1,295 shares of New York Grand Prix for a total purchase price of $500,000 "subject to the terms and conditions of a Subscription Agreement of even date which is attached hereto as Exhibit C." That subscription agreement provided that "no shares . . . shall be issued to the undersigned until the full purchase price has been paid." Thus, Mosport never became an unconditional shareholder of New York Grand Prix. While the interested parties discussed the plaintiff's default, it was never waived and no new agreement was entered into. Moreover, the shareholders agreement itself provides that "no modification, amendment, or waiver of any provision of this Agreement shall be effective unless in writing and signed by the parties against whom enforcement thereof is sought." Under New York law, such provisions are binding on the parties absent a showing that an oral agreement was entered into and that there was partial performance or substantial reliance. Plaintiffs have made no such showing.
*   *   *   *

Plaintiffs contend that the removal of Kamin from the Board of Directors by the shareholders violated the shareholders agreement and was unlawful. New York Grand Prix's by-laws provide for the removal of directors at any time "with or without cause."

The evidence at trial supports a finding that Kamin's removal was justified whether with or without cause. Moreover, Mosport's right under the shareholders agreement to designate a member of the Board of Directors was dependent upon its being a shareholder of New York Grand Prix. As noted above, upon Mosport's default after making the first payment of $50,000, it was not entitled to receive shares of stock, none were issued to it, and the $50,000 was converted into a subordinated loan. Kamin is not entitled to reinstatement on the Board of Directors.

Finally, plaintiffs allege Koren issued two New York Grand Prix checks, one in the sum of $3,500 and the other in the sum of $20,000, upon his sole signature and contrary to a requirement of the shareholders agreement that checks in excess of $2,000 be countersigned by one other officer and checks in excess of $5,000 be countersigned by two other officers. Accordingly, plaintiffs urge that these actions warrant the removal of Koren as an officer and director. While the physical signature of another officer does not appear on the checks at issue, Rosart, whose testimony the Court finds credible on this and other matters, testified that because he was in Toronto at the time, he telephoned an executive at the Bank where New York Grand Prix funds were on deposit and authorized the payment of the checks, the payees of which had rendered services to New York Grand Prix and to whom the amounts of the checks were due. It is undisputed that both checks were issued in payment of obligations due to the payees from New York Grand Prix. While the check for $20,0000 signed by Koren and approved by Rosart did not contain a third signature as required under the shareholders agreement and therefore breached that agreement, the Court finds the issuance of that check in payment of a corporate debt did not result in any damage to plaintiffs or New York Grand Prix. In the absence of injury to Mosport, assuming it was a shareholder at the time of the issuance of the check, or to New York Grand Prix, that single incident furnishes no ground for plaintiffs' contention that Koren should be removed from his position as an officer and director of the corporation. This was no instance of diversion of corporate funds.

The district court held in favor of the defendants. The court found (1) that Mosport Park was in default of its agreement and therefore Grand Prix was not obligated to retain Kamin on its board; (2) that even if there had been no default by Mosport Park, Grand Prix could remove directors without a showing of cause; and (3) that without a shareholder vote to remove a director, a show of cause must be made by Mosport Park to remove Koren from the board of directors, and Mosport Park did not show such cause.

DECISION AND REMEDY

Shareholders' Forum

Shareholders' meetings must occur at least annually, but special meetings can be called to take care of urgent matters. Since it is usually not practical for owners of only a few shares of stock of publicly traded corporations to attend the shareholders' meetings, they normally give third persons a written authorization to vote their shares at the meetings. This authorization, called a *proxy*, will be discussed later.

NOTICE OF MEETINGS   Notice of meetings, including the day and the hour, is announced in writing to each shareholder at a reasonable length of time prior to the date of the shareholders' meeting.[5] Special meeting notices must include a statement of the purpose of the meeting; business transacted at a special meeting is limited to that purpose.

---

5. The shareholder can waive the requirement of written notice by signing a waiver form. A shareholder who did not receive written notice, but who learned of the meeting and attended without protesting the lack of notice, is said to have waived notice by such conduct. State statutes and corporate bylaws typically set forth the time within which notice must be sent, what methods can be used, and what the notice must contain.

SHAREHOLDER VOTING   In order for shareholders to act, a minimum number of them (in terms of number of shares held) must be present at a meeting. This minimum number, called a *quorum,* is generally more than 50 percent. Corporate business matters are presented in the form of *resolutions,* which shareholders vote to approve or disapprove. Some states provide that the unanimous written consent of shareholders is a permissible alternative to holding a shareholders' meeting.

Once a quorum is present, a majority vote of the shares represented at the meeting is usually required to pass resolutions. Assume that Midwestern Supply, Inc., has 10,000 outstanding shares of voting stock. Its articles set the quorum at 50 percent of outstanding shares and provide that a majority vote of shares present is necessary to pass on ordinary matters. At the shareholders' meeting, a *quorum* of stockholders representing 5,000 outstanding shares must be present to conduct business, and a *vote* of at least 2,501 of those shares is needed to pass ordinary resolutions. If more than 5,000 are present, of course, a larger vote is needed.

At times, a statute or the corporation charter requires that the vote be carried by a number greater than a simple majority of shares represented at the meeting. Extraordinary corporate matters, such as merger, consolidation, or dissolution of the corporation (to be discussed in Chapter 42), will require passage by a higher percentage of the representatives of *all* corporate shares entitled to vote, not just a majority of those present at that particular meeting.

VOTING LISTS   Voting lists are prepared by the corporation prior to each shareholders' meeting. Persons whose names appear on the corporation's stockholder records as the record owners of the shares are the persons ordinarily entitled to vote.[6] The voting list contains the name and address of each shareholder as shown on the corporate records on a given cutoff date (record date). It also includes the number of voting shares held by each owner. The list is usually kept at the corporate headquarters and is available for inspection by shareholders.

VOTING TECHNIQUES   Most states permit or require shareholders to elect directors by *cumulative voting,* a method of voting designed to allow minority shareholders representation on the board of directors.[7] Cumulative voting operates as follows: The number of members of the board to be elected is multiplied by the total number of voting shares held. The result equals the number of votes a shareholder has, and this total can be cast for one or more nominees for director. All nominees stand for election at the same time. Where cumulative voting is not required either by statute or under the articles, the entire board can be elected by a majority of shares at a shareholders' meeting.

To illustrate: A corporation has 10,000 shares issued and outstanding. The minority shareholders hold only 3,000 shares, and the majority shareholders hold the other 7,000 shares. Three members of the board are to be elected. The majority shareholders' nominees are Mott, Gregory, and Dunsworth. The minority shareholders' nominee is Diamond. Can Diamond be elected by the minority shareholders?

If cumulative voting is allowed, the answer is yes. The minority shareholders have 9,000 votes among them (the number of directors to be elected times the number of shares equals 3 times 3,000, which equals 9,000 votes). All of these votes can be cast to elect Diamond. The majority shareholders have 21,000 votes (3 times 7,000 equals 21,000 votes), but these votes have to be distributed among their three nominees. The principle of cumulative voting is that no matter how the majority shareholders cast their 21,000 votes, they will not be able to elect all three directors if the minority shareholders cast all of their 9,000 votes for Diamond, as illustrated in Exhibit 40–1.

SHAREHOLDER AGREEMENTS   A group of shareholders can agree in writing prior to the meeting to vote their shares together in a specified manner. Voting agreements are usually held to be valid and enforceable.

PROXY VOTING   A shareholder can appoint a voting agent. A proxy, as mentioned, is a written authorization to cast the shareholder's vote, and a person can solicit proxies from a number of

---

6. When the legal owner is deceased, bankrupt, incompetent, or in some other way under a legal disability, his or her vote can be cast by a person designated by law to control and manage the owner's property.

7. See, for example, the California Corporate Code Section 708.

Exhibit 40–1 Cumulative Voting—Sample Balloting Results

BALLOT	MAJORITY SHAREHOLDER VOTES			MINORITY SHAREHOLDER VOTES	DIRECTORS ELECTED
	Mott	*Gregory*	*Dunsworth*	*Diamond*	
1	10,000	10,000	1,000	9,000	Mott, Gregory, Diamond
2	9,001	9,000	2,999	9,000	Mott, Gregory, Diamond
3	6,000	7,000	8,000	9,000	Gregory, Dunsworth, Diamond

shareholders in an attempt to concentrate voting power.

VOTING TRUSTS   Shareholders can enter into an agreement (a trust contract) whereby legal title (record ownership on the corporate books) is transferred to a trustee, who is then responsible for voting the shares. The agreement can specify how the trustee is to vote, or it can allow the trustee to use his or her discretion. The trustee takes physical possession of the actual stock certificate and in return gives the shareholder a *voting trust certificate*. The shareholder retains all of the rights of ownership (for example, the right to receive dividend payments) except for the power to vote.

A voting trust is not the same thing as a proxy, for the latter can be revoked more easily. The holder of a proxy has neither legal title to the stock nor possession of the certificates, whereas voting trustees have both.[8]

CORPORATE MANAGEMENT—DIRECTORS

Every corporation is governed by directors. Subject to statutory limitations, the number of directors is set forth in the corporation's articles or bylaws. Historically, the minimum number of directors has been three, but today many states permit fewer.

Directors' Election and Term of Office

Normally, the first board of directors is appointed by the incorporators upon the creation of the corporation, or directors are named by the corporation itself in the articles. The first board serves until the first annual shareholders' meeting. Subsequent directors are elected by majority vote of the shareholders.

The term of office for a director is usually one year—from annual meeting to annual meeting. Longer and staggered terms are permissible under most state statutes. A common practice is to elect one-third of the board members each year for a three-year term. In this way, there is greater management continuity.

A director can be removed *for cause*, either as specified in the articles or bylaws or by shareholder action. Even the board of directors itself may be given power to remove a director for cause, subject to shareholder review. In most states, unless the shareholders have reserved the right at the time of election, a director cannot be removed without cause.

When death or resignation creates a vacancy on the board of directors or when a new position is created through amendment of the articles or bylaws, either the shareholders or the board itself can fill the position, depending on state law or the provisions of the bylaws.

Directors' Qualifications and Compensation

Few qualifications are legally required of directors. Only a handful of states retain minimum age and residency requirements. A director is sometimes a shareholder, but this is not a necessary qualification unless, of course, statutory provisions, corporate articles, or bylaws require ownership.

Compensation for directors is ordinarily specified in the corporate articles or bylaws. Because directors have a *fiduciary* relationship to the share-

---

8. Under Section 34 of the Model Act, the term of a voting trust cannot exceed ten years. Most states limit the duration of a proxy to eleven months (see MBCA Section 33).

holders and to the corporation, an express agreement or provision for compensation is necessary for them to receive money from the funds they control or for which they have responsibility.

Management Responsibilities

Directors have responsibility for all policy-making decisions necessary to the management of all corporate affairs. Just as shareholders cannot act individually to bind the corporation, the directors must act as a body in carrying out routine corporate business. In other words, management powers belong to the board as a whole, not to the directors individually. One director has one vote, and generally the majority rules.

The general areas of responsibility of the board of directors include:

1. Declaration and payment of corporate dividends to shareholders.[9]
2. Authorization for major corporate policy decisions—for example, the initiation of proceedings for the sale or lease of corporate assets outside of the regular course of business, the determination of new product lines, and the overseeing of major contract negotiations and major management-labor negotiations.
3. Appointment, supervision, and removal of corporate officers and other managerial employees and the determination of their compensation.
4. Financial decisions involving such things as the issuance of authorized shares or bonds.

The Board of Directors' Forum

The board of directors conducts business by holding formal meetings with recorded minutes.[10] The date upon which regular meetings are held is usually established in the articles and bylaws or by board resolution, and no further notice is customarily required. Special meetings can be called with notice sent to all directors.

Quorum requirements can vary among jurisdictions. Many states leave the decision to the corporate articles or bylaws. In the absence thereof, most states provide that a quorum is a majority of the number of directors authorized in the articles or bylaws. Voting is done *in person* (unlike voting at shareholders' meetings, which can be done by proxy).[11] The rule is one vote per director. Ordinary matters generally require a simple majority vote of those present, if there is a quorum; certain extraordinary issues may require a higher number.

Delegation of Board of Directors' Powers

The board of directors can delegate some of its functions to an executive committee or to corporate officers. In doing so, the board does not avoid its responsibility for directing the affairs of the corporation. Rather, the daily responsibilities of corporate management are given over to corporate officers and managerial personnel, who are empowered to make decisions relating to ordinary corporate affairs within well-defined guidelines.

EXECUTIVE COMMITTEE   Most states permit the board of directors to elect an executive committee from among its members to handle management decisions that arise between board meetings, as provided in the bylaws. The *executive committee* is limited to making management decisions about ordinary business matters.

CORPORATE OFFICERS   The officers and other executive employees are hired by the board of directors or, in rare instances, by the shareholders. In addition to being responsible for the duties articulated in the bylaws, corporate and managerial officers are agents of the corporation, and the ordinary rules of agency apply or have been applied to their employment (unlike the board of directors, whose powers are conferred by the state).

Qualifications are determined at the discretion of the corporation and are included in the articles or bylaws. In most states, a person can hold more than one office and can be both an officer and a director of the corporation. Corporate officers can be removed by the board of directors at any time with or without cause and regardless of the terms of the employment contract, although the corporation can still be liable for breach-of-contract damages.

---

9. See Dodge v. Ford Motor Co., 204 Mich. 459, 170 N.W. 668 (1919).

10. Some states, such as Michigan and Texas (and the Model Act, Sections 43 and 44), now have a corporate statute authorizing conference telephone calls for board meetings.

---

11. Except in Louisiana, where a director can vote by proxy under certain circumstances.

QUESTIONS AND CASE PROBLEMS

1. The board of directors of Chromics, Inc., has to decide whether or not to make the following three transactions, none of which is expressly covered in the articles or bylaws of the corporation: a charitable gift of $100,000 to a private university noted for the education of minority students; a secured loan of corporate surplus funds at a high interest rate; and an extension of credit to another corporation in which Chromics owns shares. Discuss whether Chromics, Inc., through action by its board, has the authority and the power to make these transactions.

2. Saxon Wells, Inc., was formed for the purpose of drilling and servicing water wells. This purpose is specifically stated in its articles of incorporation. One year after the formation of the corporation, the board of directors entered into a contract with an independent oil driller, Thomas, to purchase and market all the oil Thomas produced from his wells during a five-year period. The contract has been performed for two years, and Saxon Wells has expended corporate funds to set up storage and marketing facilities. Thomas now refuses to sell any more oil to Saxon Wells, claiming the corporation contracted outside its powers. Discuss this claim.

3. Ann owns 10 shares of Monmouth Corporation. Monmouth Corporation has 100,000 outstanding issued common shares. Ann believes that many decisions of the board of directors do not consider the preservation of the environment. Two pending proposals approved by the board deal with the purchase of timberland for conversion into condominiums. Both proposals require an amendment to the corporate charter and need a two-thirds shareholder vote. Ann knows other shareholders who she believes would oppose these proposals. Unfortunately, most shareholders live a considerable distance from the site of the shareholders' meeting and will be unable to attend. Discuss any techniques Ann can use to oppose these proposals.

4. Carter Corporation has issued and has outstanding 100,000 shares of common stock. Four stockholders own 60,000 of these shares, and for the past six years their entire slate of nominees for membership on the board has been elected. John and twenty other shareholders, who own 20,000 shares, are dissatisfied with corporate management and want a representative on the board who shares their views. Explain the circumstances under which John and the minority shareholders can elect their representative to the board.

5. Kathy is elected to the board of directors of a corporation. The board consists of nine members. The articles and bylaws are silent as to what constitutes a quorum. The bylaws do permit the board itself, by majority vote, to elect board members to fill vacancies created by death or resignation. The bylaws also require majority votes for ordinary corporate decisions made at regular corporate board meetings. Just prior to a regular meeting, a board member dies. At the scheduled regular meeting, a proposal is to be made that Kathy opposes. She cannot attend the meeting and sends her proxy. The meeting takes place with five members in attendance. By a vote of three to two, John is elected to fill the board vacancy, and the proposal is passed. Kathy's proxy is declared invalid by the chairman of the board. Kathy challenges both votes. Discuss whether her challenges will be successful.

6. Mohawk Rubber Company was a corporation organized under the law of the state of Ohio. Fawcett and Ernst were the principal executives of Mohawk. The board of directors of Mohawk included Fawcett and Ernst and five outside directors. The board directed Ernst to consider a new stock option plan, as Mohawk was earning good profits and would likely be the target of a takeover bid. On January 4, 1983, sixteen days before the regularly scheduled board of directors meeting at which Ernst was to present his stock option plan, Ernst telephoned each of the directors individually to obtain their approval for the plan. No prior written notice was given to the directors, and the plan was not before them in written form prior to the telephone calls. Each director orally approved the plan as it was described to him. "Minutes of the Board of Directors Meeting" were prepared that outlined the events of January 4, 1983, as if it had been a formal meeting. Later, a proxy statement was issued urging the shareholders to give prompt attention to the plan and indicating that the board of directors had unanimously recommended a vote for the plan. Fradkin, a Mohawk shareholder, filed a derivative suit to stop the plan. To cure the omission of the formal meeting, Ernst and Fawcett presented a document entitled "Approval of Directors of the Mohawk Rubber Company to Action without a Meeting" at a subsequent board meeting. All of the directors signed the document. Discuss whether Fradkin was successful in his derivative suit. [Fradkin v. Ernst, 571 F.Supp. 829 (N.D.Ohio, 1983)]

7. Harris Lumber Company was a corporation organized under the law of the state of Arkansas. Harris was the president of the corporation; Nelson was its secretary and treasurer; and Jones was its remaining director and shareholder. Several years after its incorporation, Harris Lumber owed Merchants and Farmers Bank $4,500. A promissory note was executed for the amount of the debt, and a mortgage was executed on certain personal property owned by Harris Lumber to secure payment. Nelson, who at the time was general manager of Harris Lumber, signed both the note and the mortgage. Payments amounting to $2,150 were made over the next two and one-half years on the promissory note. At that point, payment ceased, and Merchants Bank brought suit to recover the balance of the sum owed. Harris Lumber Company never objected to the execution of the mortgage or the note or to any of the payments under the note until Merchants Bank filed the suit. At that point, however, Harris Lumber claimed that Nelson did not have the authority to sign promissory notes or to execute mortgages on behalf of Harris Lumber. In fact, neither the corporate charter nor any of the board of directors' resolutions vested the general manager with any authority to bind the corporation. Was Merchants Bank successful in

its suit against Harris Lumber Company? [Merchants and Farmers Bank v. Harris Lumber Co., 103 Ark. 283, 146 S.W. 508 (1912)]

8. John Field's employment as president of Continental Trans-Company was terminated by the board of directors of that company in December of 1976. The board agreed to pay Field the sum of $25,000 and to execute a note for the same amount in return for Field's stock holdings and debentures in the company. At the time of this transaction, Continental was insolvent and prohibited by the laws of Oregon from repurchasing any of its own stock. Field sued when the notes were in default. He conceded that the undertaking of the debt obligation by the corporation was *ultra vires* but claimed that this was not a defense to his cause of action in Oregon. Assuming that Field was correct and *ultra vires* was not a defense, should he have succeeded in his suit? [Field v. Haupert, 58 Or.App. 117, 647 P.2d 952 (1982)]

9. William T. Cloney was the president of the Boston Athletic Association (BAA), a nonprofit corporation whose principal purpose is to present the annual Boston Marathon. At a 1981 BAA board of directors' meeting, Cloney was "authorized and directed to negotiate and to execute in the name of and in behalf of [the BAA] such agreements as he deems in the best interest of the Association for the perpetuation, sponsorship, or underwriting of the Boston A. A. Marathon." For past marathons, Cloney himself had undertaken to secure contracts with individual sponsors, and the BAA had full control over the presentation of the Marathon. This time, however, Cloney contracted with International Marathons, Inc. (IMI) for IMI to be the exclusive promoter of the race. Under the terms of the contract, (1) BAA transferred all rights to use the Boston Marathon name and logos to IMI, (2) the agreement was to be automatically renewable from year to year, and (3) IMI was entitled to keep any profits beyond the first $400,000, which would be paid to BAA. In short, the contract with IMI prevented the BAA from having any significant control over the sponsorship or presentation of the race, which was essentially the reason for its corporate existence. When the board of directors learned of Cloney's agreement with IMI, it brought an action to have the agreement set aside on the ground that Cloney had exceeded the authorization vested in him by the board. IMI claimed that Cloney had been given the authority to make the contract and it should therefore be enforced. Discuss who is correct. [Boston Athletic Association v. International Marathons, Inc., 392 Mass. 356, 467 N.E.2d 58 (1984)]

Chapter 41

CORPORATIONS
Rights and Duties of Directors, Managers, and Shareholders

A corporation joins the efforts and resources of a large number of individuals for the purpose of producing greater returns than those individuals could have obtained individually. Sometimes actions that benefit the corporation as a whole do not coincide with the separate interests of these individuals. This chapter focuses on the rights and duties of directors, managers, and shareholders and the ways in which conflicts among them are resolved.

THE ROLE OF OFFICERS AND DIRECTORS

A director occupies a position of responsibility unlike that of other corporate personnel. Directors are sometimes inappropriately characterized as *agents* because they act for and on behalf of the corporation. No *individual* director, however, can act as an agent to bind the corporation; and as a group, directors collectively control the corporation in a way that no agent can control a principal. Directors are often incorrectly characterized as *trustees* because they occupy positions of trust and control over the corporation. Unlike trustees, however, they do not own or hold title to property for the use and benefit of others.

The Business Judgment Rule

Directors are expected to use their best judgment in guiding corporate management, but they are not insurers of business success. Honest mistakes of judgment and poor business decisions on their part do not make them liable to the corporation for resulting damages. This is the *business judgment rule*. The rule immunizes directors—and officers—from liability when a decision is within managerial authority, as long as the decision complies with management's fiduciary duties (discussed below) and as long as acting on the decision is within the powers of the corporation. Consequently, if there is a reasonable basis for a business decision, it is unlikely that a court will interfere with that decision, even if the corporation suffers thereby.

To benefit from the rule, directors and officers must act in good faith, in what they consider to be the best interests of the corporation, and with the care that an ordinarily prudent person in a like position would exercise in similar circumstances.[1] This requires an informed decision, with a rational basis, and with no conflict between the decision maker's personal interest and the interest of the corporation.

To be informed, the director or officer must do what is necessary to become informed: attend presentations, ask for information from those who have it, read reports, review other written materials such as contracts—in other words, carefully study a situation and its alternatives. To be free of conflicts of interest, the director must not engage in self-dealing. For instance, a director should not oppose a *tender offer* (an offer to purchase shares in the company made by another company directly to the shareholders) in the corporation's best interest because its acceptance may cost the director his or her position. For a decision to have an apparently rational basis, the decision itself must appear to have been made reasonably. For example, a director should not accept a tender offer with only a moment's consideration based solely on the market price of the corporation's shares.

Fiduciary Duties

Directors manage the corporation through the officers who are selected by the board; these officers are agents of the corporation. Directors and officers are deemed *fiduciaries* of the corporation. Their relationship with the corporation and its shareholders is one of trust and confidence. The fiduciary duties of the directors and officers include the duty of care and the duty of loyalty.

THE DUTY OF CARE   As pointed out above, directors are obligated to be honest and to use prudent business judgment in the conduct of corporate affairs. Directors must exercise the same degree of care that reasonably prudent people use in the conduct of their own personal business affairs.

Breach of the Duty of Care   Directors can be held answerable to the corporation and to the shareholders for breach of their duty of care. When directors delegate work to corporate officers and employees, they are expected to use a reasonable amount of supervision. Otherwise, they will be held liable for *negligence* or *mismanagement* of corporate personnel.

For example, a corporate bank director failed to attend any board of directors' meetings in five and a half years and never inspected any of the corporate books or records. Meanwhile, the bank president made various improper loans and permitted large overdrafts. The corporate director was held liable to the corporation for losses of nearly $20,000 resulting from the unsupervised actions of the bank president and the loan committee.

Directors and officers are expected to act in accordance with their own knowledge and training. Directors may, however, make decisions in reliance on information furnished by competent officers or employees, professionals such as attorneys and accountants, or even an executive committee of the board without being accused of acting in bad faith or failing to exercise due care if such information turns out to be faulty.

Directors are expected to attend board of directors' meetings, and their votes should be entered into the minutes of corporate meetings. Unless a dissent is entered, the director is presumed to have assented. Directors who dissent rarely are held individually liable for mismanagement of the corporation with regard to the matter voted upon. It is for this reason that a director who is absent from a given meeting sometimes registers with the secretary of the board a dissent to actions taken at the missed meeting with which he or she disagrees.

As indicated previously, directors are expected to be informed on corporate matters and to familiarize themselves with legal and other professional advice rendered to the board. For example, a court may consider directors negligent for failing to scrutinize financial reports that, if studied, would have revealed improper or illegal use of corporate funds by subordinates. A director who is unable to carry out these responsibilities should resign.

Even when the required duty of care has not been exercised, directors and officers are liable only for the damages caused to the corporation by their negligence (according to the causation rules of negligence law discussed in Chapter 4).

THE DUTY OF LOYALTY   Perhaps the best way to describe the concept of loyalty is by a definition given by Justice Cardozo:

Many forms of conduct permissible in a workaday world for those acting at arm's length, are forbidden

---

1. Section 35 of the MBCA. See also RMBCA Section 8.30.

to those bound by fiduciary ties. Not honesty alone, but the punctilio [observance in minute detail] of an honor the most sensitive, is then the standard of behavior. As to this there has developed a tradition that is unbending and inveterate.[2]

The essence of the duty requires subordination of self-interest to the interest of the entity to which the duty is owed. The duty of loyalty prohibits directors from using corporate funds or confidential corporate information for their personal advantage. It requires officers and directors to disclose fully any corporate opportunity or any possible conflict of interest that might occur in a transaction involving the directors and the corporation.

---

2. Meinhard v. Salmon, 249 N.Y. 458, 464, 164 N.E. 545, 546 (1928).

Cases dealing with violations of fiduciary duty typically involve one or more of the following:

1. Competing with the corporation.
2. Usurping a corporate opportunity.
3. Having an interest that conflicts with the interest of the corporation.
4. Engaging in insider trading (See Chapter 43.)
5. Authorizing some corporate transaction that is detrimental to minority shareholders.
6. Selling control over the corporation.

In the following case, the Alabama supreme court reviewed a situation in which officers, directors, and shareholders attempted to secure advantages for themselves at the expense of the corporation.

BACKGROUND AND FACTS *The defendants, Morad and Thomson, were officers, directors, and shareholders of Bio-Lab, Inc. Bio-Lab had one additional shareholder, the plaintiff, Coupounas. While serving as officers and directors of Bio-Lab, the defendants incorporated and operated a competing business, Med-Lab, Inc. The plaintiff brought a derivative suit on behalf of Bio-Lab against the defendants and Med-Lab, alleging that, in opening the competing business, they had usurped a corporate opportunity of Bio-Lab. The trial court held for the plaintiff, and the defendants appealed.*

 Case 41.1

MORAD v. COUPOUNAS
Supreme Court of Alabama, 1978.
361 So.2d 6.

FAULKNER, Justice.
* * * *

"[I]f there is presented to a corporate officer or director a business opportunity which the corporation is financially able to undertake, [and which] is, from its nature, in the line of the corporation's business and is of practical advantage to it, [and] one in which the corporation has an interest or a reasonable expectancy, and, by embracing the opportunity, the self-interest of the officer or director will be brought into conflict with that of his corporation, the law will not permit him to seize the opportunity for himself."
* * *

"[N]umerous factors are to be weighed, including the manner in which the offer was communicated to the officer; the good faith of the officer; the use of corporate assets to acquire the opportunity; the financial ability of the corporation to acquire the opportunity; the degree of disclosure made to the corporation; the action taken by the corporation with reference thereto; and the need or interest of the corporation in the opportunity. These, as well as numerous other factors, are weighed in a given case. The presence or absence of any single factor is not determinative of the issue of corporate opportunity." * * *

Here the trial court specifically found that one of the corporate purposes of Bio-Lab was to expand into specific new areas, including Tuscaloosa. Ample evidence in the record supports this conclusion. Bio-Lab's certificate of incorporation declared that one of the purposes of the business was "to have one or more offices." * * *
* * * *

* * * [T]estimony revealed that $44,000 had been required to establish Med-Lab. At the end of 1974 Bio-Lab had only $24,300 available for this purpose. But, Raburn [a certified public accountant, familiar with the books of both Med-Lab and

Bio-Lab] also testified that in 1974 Bio-Lab had paid a "rather high" dividend of $20,000. His testimony indicated that the payment of dividends is often restricted when a corporation wishes to expand. Thus, if the dividend had not been paid, Bio-Lab clearly should have had the financial ability to expand to Tuscaloosa, with or without a loan. In light of this testimony the trial court's finding that defendants improperly formed Med-Lab to the detriment of Bio-Lab is clearly supportable and will not be disturbed by this Court on appeal.

DECISION AND REMEDY *The Alabama supreme court determined that the appropriate remedy for the defendants' breach of duty of loyalty was for the court to impose a "constructive trust," which would require all profits of Med-Lab to be paid to Bio-Lab.*

CONFLICTS OF INTEREST Corporate directors often have many business affiliations, and they can even sit on the board of more than one corporation. Of course, they are precluded from entering into or supporting any business that operates in direct competition with the corporation. The fiduciary duty requires them to make a full disclosure of any potential *conflicts of interest* that might arise in any corporate transaction.

Sometimes the corporation will enter into a contract or engage in a transaction in which an officer or director has a material interest. The director or officer must make a *full disclosure* of that interest and should abstain from voting on the proposed transaction.

For example, Pacific Business Corporation needs office space. Louis Allen, one of its five directors, owns the building adjoining the corporation's offices. He negotiates a lease with Pacific Business for the space, making a full disclosure to Pacific Business and the other four board directors. The lease arrangement is fair and reasonable, and it is unanimously approved by the corporation's board of directors. In such a case, the contract is valid. The rule is one of reason; otherwise, directors would be prevented from ever giving financial assistance to the corporations they serve.

The various state statutes contain different standards, but a contract will generally not be voidable if:

1. It was fair and reasonable to the corporation at the time it was made.
2. There is a full disclosure of the interest of the officers or directors in the transaction.
3. The contract is approved by a majority of the disinterested directors or shareholders.

(See Section 41 of the Model Business Corporation Act and Section 8.31 of the Revised Model Business Corporation Act.)

Often, contracts are negotiated between corporations whose boards have a member or members in common. Such transactions require great care, as they are closely scrutinized by courts.

RIGHTS OF DIRECTORS

A director of a corporation has a number of rights. These include the right of participation, the right of inspection, the right of indemnification, and the right of compensation.

Right of Participation

A corporate director must have certain rights in order to function properly in that position. The main right is to be notified of board of directors' meetings, so as to participate in them. As pointed out in Chapter 40, regular board meetings are usually established by the bylaws or board resolution, and no notice of these meetings is required. If special meetings are called, however, notice is required unless waived by the director.

Right of Inspection

A director must have access to all corporate books and records in order to make decisions and to exercise the necessary supervision. This right is virtually absolute and cannot be restricted.

Right of Indemnification

It is not unusual for corporate directors to become involved in lawsuits by virtue of their position and their actions as directors. Most states (and MBCA

Section 5) permit a corporation to indemnify a director for legal costs, fees, and judgments involved in defending corporation-related suits.

At common law, a director had no right to be indemnified; however, there was little objection to indemnification if the director was absolved of liability. Today, statutes and court decisions allow indemnification even if the director is not absolved of liability, as long as his or her actions were made in good faith, based on a reasonable belief that such actions were in the best interests of the corporation.

Criminal convictions usually require bad faith, but bad faith is not presumed merely because the director settles the litigation, pleads *nolo contendere* (no contest), or even is found liable civilly. Many states specifically permit a corporation to purchase liability insurance for the directors and officers (D & O insurance) to cover indemnification. When the statutes are silent on this matter, the power to purchase such insurance is usually considered to be part of the corporation's implied power.

Right of Compensation

Historically, directors have had no inherent right to compensation for their services as directors. Officers receive compensation, and nominal sums are often paid as honoraria to directors. In many cases, directors are also chief corporate officers and receive compensation in their managerial positions. Most directors, however, gain through indirect benefits, such as business contacts, prestige, and other rewards.

There is a growing trend toward providing more than nominal compensation for directors, especially in large corporations where directorships can be enormous burdens in terms of time, work, effort, and risk. Many states permit the corporate articles or bylaws to authorize compensation for directors; and in some cases, the board can set its own compensation unless the articles or bylaws provide otherwise.

RIGHTS AND DUTIES OF CORPORATE OFFICERS AND MANAGERS

Corporate officers and other high-level managers are employees of the company, and their rights are defined by employment contracts.

The duties of corporate officers are the same as the duties of directors, because their respective corporate positions involve both of them in decision making and place them in similar positions of control. Hence, they are viewed as having the same fiduciary duty of care and loyalty in their conduct of corporate affairs. Officers are subject to the same obligations concerning corporate opportunities and conflicts of interest as are directors.

SHAREHOLDER RIGHTS

Shareholders own the corporation. Their rights are established in the articles of incorporation and under the state's general incorporation law.

The Right to a Stock Certificate

A stock certificate evidences ownership. In jurisdictions that require the issuance of stock certificates, shareholders have the right to demand that the corporation issue a certificate and record their names and addresses in the corporate stock record books. In an increasing number of jurisdictions (and under MBCA Section 23), boards of directors may provide that shares of stock be uncertificated (that is, that actual, physical stock certificates need not be issued). In that circumstance, it may be required that the corporation send the holders of uncertificated shares letters or some other form of notice containing the same information required to be included on the face of stock certificates.

Stock is *intangible* personal property—the ownership right exists independently of the certificate itself. A stock certificate may be lost or destroyed, but ownership is not destroyed with it.

A new certificate can be issued to replace one that has been lost or destroyed.[3] Notice of shareholder meetings, dividends, and operational and financial reports are all distributed according to the recorded ownership listed in the corporation's books, not on the basis of possession of the certificate.

---

3. To have a lost or destroyed certificate reissued, a shareholder is normally required to furnish an indemnity bond to protect the corporation against potential loss should the original certificate reappear at some future time in the hands of a bona fide purchaser [UCC 8-302, 8-405(2)].

Assume that Betty Anderson's certificate showing ownership of corporate stock in Chrysler Corporation is destroyed in a fire on September 1. The corporation declares a dividend on September 5. According to corporate records, Betty Anderson is the "record owner" and receives the dividend even though she no longer physically has the certificate.

Of course, to sell or otherwise transfer the shares, indorsement and delivery of the actual certificate to the transferee are required.

Preemptive Rights

A **preemptive right** is a common law concept in which a preference is given to a shareholder over all other purchasers to subscribe to or purchase a prorated share of a new issue of stock. This allows the shareholder to maintain his or her portion of control, voting power, and financial interest in the corporation. Most statutes either grant preemptive rights (but allow them to be negated in the corporation's articles) or deny preemptive rights (except to the extent that they are granted in the articles). The result is that the articles of incorporation determine the existence and scope of preemptive rights. Generally, preemptive rights apply only to additional stock sold for cash. They do not apply to treasury shares reissued or to authorized but unissued shares. Generally, such rights must be exercised within a specified time period (usually thirty days).

For example, Paula Gudmundson purchases one hundred shares of National Clothing stock. National Clothing had authorized and issued one thousand shares, of which Paula now owns 10 percent. Subsequently, National Clothing, by vote of its shareholders, authorizes the issuance of another one thousand shares (amending the articles of incorporation). This increases its capital stock to a total of two thousand shares.

If preemptive rights have been provided, Paula can purchase one additional share of the new stock being issued for each share she currently owns—or one hundred additional shares. Thus, she can own two hundred of the two thousand shares outstanding, and her relative position as a shareholder will be maintained. If preemptive rights are not reserved, her proportionate control and voting power will be diluted from that of a 10 percent shareholder to that of a 5 percent shareholder be-

cause of the issuance of the additional one thousand shares.

Preemptive rights are far more significant in a close corporation because of the relatively small number of shares and the substantial interest each shareholder controls.

Stock Warrant Rights

When preemptive rights exist and a corporation is issuing additional shares, each shareholder is usually given stock warrants. A **stock warrant** is a transferable option to acquire a given number of shares from the corporation at a stated price (usually below the current market price). Warrants are often publicly traded on securities exchanges. When the warrant option will expire after a short period of time, the stock warrants are usually referred to as *rights*.

Dividend Rights

A dividend is a distribution of corporate profits or income *ordered by the directors* and paid to the shareholders in proportion to their shares in the corporation. Dividends can be paid in cash, property, stock of the corporation that is paying the dividends, or stock of other corporations.[4]

State laws vary, but every state determines the general circumstances and legal requirements under which dividends are paid. State laws also control the sources of revenue to be used; only certain funds are legally available for paying dividends. Once declared, a cash dividend becomes a corporate debt enforceable at law like any other debt.[5]

Under statutes that limit the sources of funds from which dividends may be paid, prescribed sources include the following:

1. *Retained earnings.* All states allow dividends to be paid from the undistributed net profits earned by the corporation, including capital gains from the sale of fixed assets. The undistributed net profits are called earned surplus or retained earnings.
2. *Net profits.* A few state statutes allow dividends to be issued from current net profits without regard to deficits in prior years.

---

4. Technically, dividends paid in stock are not dividends. They maintain each shareholder's proportional interest in the corporation. On one occasion, a distillery declared and paid a "dividend" in bonded whiskey.

5. An insolvent corporation cannot declare a dividend.

3. *Surplus*. A number of state statutes allow dividends to be paid out of any kind of surplus.

When directors fail to declare a dividend, shareholders can ask a court of equity for a mandatory injunction to compel the directors to meet and to declare a dividend. It must be shown that the directors have acted so unreasonably in withholding the dividend that their conduct is an abuse of discretion.

Often, large money reserves are accumulated for a bona fide purpose such as expansion, research, or other legitimate corporate goals. The mere fact that sufficient corporate earnings or surplus are available to pay a dividend is not enough to compel directors to distribute funds that, in the board's opinion, should not be paid.

As is illustrated in the following case, the courts are circumspect about interfering with corporate operations and will not compel directors to declare dividends unless abuse of discretion is clearly shown. Thus, directors are not ordinarily *required* to declare dividends to shareholders.

BACKGROUND AND FACTS   In April 1980, Grand Metropolitan (Grand Met) made a tender offer (an offer to purchase directly from shareholders) for all of Liggett Group Inc.'s 8.4 million common shares at the price of $50 per share. During the first quarter of 1980, the shares had traded at between $34 and $42 on the New York Stock Exchange. The Liggett board of directors rejected this tender offer and advised the shareholders to reject it. On May 12, Standard Brands Inc. made a rival tender offer for 4 million shares at a price of $65 per share. The Liggett board endorsed the Standard Brands offer. Grand Met increased its offer to $69 per share on May 14, and on the same date Standard Brands withdrew its offer. The Liggett board approved the amended offer and recommended to the shareholders that they accept the price as fair. Grand Met acquired 87.4 percent of Liggett's outstanding common stock as a result of the tender offer. In its tender offer, Grand Met informed the shareholders of Liggett that a merger of Liggett with Grand Met would occur as soon as possible and that shares not tendered would be purchased for $69. Gabelli surrendered its shares in August 1980 for the $69 cash-out price. Historically, Liggett had paid quarterly dividends of $0.625 per share in March, June, September, and December. Liggett had paid its June dividend prior to the merger, but no third-quarter dividend was declared or paid. Gabelli alleged that Grand Met breached its fiduciary duty to Liggett's minority shareholders when it did not declare a third-quarter dividend so that it could obtain the dividend money for itself once the merger had been completed. The trial court dismissed Gabelli's claim on a motion for summary judgment. Gabelli appealed.

Case 41.2
GABELLI & CO. v. LIGGETT GROUP INC.
Supreme Court of Delaware, 1984.
479 A.2d 276.

HERRMANN, Chief Justice.
*   *   *   *

In our view, this case commenced as, and continues to be, no more nor less than an action to compel the declaration and payment of a dividend by the Board of Directors of Liggett for the benefit of about 13% of its stockholders who were then in the final stages of being cashed-out in a merger transaction for a price conceded to be fair for the acquisition of all of the assets of Liggett.

As so simplified, it is abundantly clear upon the undisputed facts that summary judgment for the defendants was correctly granted.

There is no showing by the plaintiff anywhere in this case that, given the extraordinary circumstances existing in Liggett's affairs in late July 1980, the Board of Liggett abused its discretion in the exercise of its business judgment by not declaring a third-quarter dividend in accord with the corporation's dividend history of prior years. In the absence of such showing, the plaintiff may not prevail in this action to compel the dividend.

It is settled law in this State that the declaration and payment of a dividend rests in the discretion of the corporation's board of directors in the exercise of its business judgment; that, before the courts will interfere with the judgment of the board of directors in such matter, fraud or gross abuse of discretion must be shown. *   *   *

Gabelli has not alleged fraud; and it has made no showing that the failure of Liggett's Board to declare a third-quarter dividend, under the undisputed facts and circumstances of this case, is explicable only on the theory of a gross or oppressive abuse of discretion. *   *   *

On the record before us, the non-payment of a final dividend by the Liggett Board in the final stages of the cash-out merger, is reasonably "explicable" *   *   * for at least 2 reasons: (1) It would have been unfair to the holders of 87% of the stock, who accepted the tender offer upon the recommendation of the Board, to reward by a "farewell" or "bonus" dividend the holders of the remaining 13% who, for some unannounced reason, declined to accept the tender-offer and held out for the merger cash-out with the risk-free assurance of receiving the same price per share; and (2) It would have been unreasonable to supplement the $69 per share, which had been approved by the Board as a fair price for Liggett and all of its assets, by a last minute dividend declared in the final stages of the merger cash-out process.
*   *   *   *

The plaintiff has placed nothing on this record to raise a genuine issue of material fact as to whether (1) Grand Met actually "prevented" the Liggett Board from declaring the dividend; or (2) the Liggett Board actually would have "otherwise" declared the dividend. The undisputed facts before us, and the reasonable inferences to be drawn therefrom, are to the contrary.

DECISION AND REMEDY   *The Supreme Court of Delaware affirmed the trial court's grant of summary judgment to Liggett. It held that the board of directors did not abuse its discretion in electing not to declare a dividend.*

ILLEGAL DIVIDENDS   A dividend paid while the corporation is *insolvent* is automatically an illegal dividend, and shareholders can be liable for returning the payment to the corporation or its creditors.

As noted, dividends are generally required by statute to be distributed only from certain authorized corporate accounts representing profits. Sometimes dividends are improperly paid from an unauthorized account, or their payment causes the corporation to become insolvent. Generally, in this case, shareholders must return illegal dividends only if they knew that the dividends were illegal when they received them.

In all cases of illegal and improper dividends, the board of directors can be held personally liable for the amount of the payment. When directors can show that a shareholder *knew* a dividend was illegal when it was received, however, the directors are entitled to reimbursement from the shareholder.

The Right to Vote

Shareholders exercise ownership control through the power of their votes. In the early development of corporate law, each shareholder was entitled to one vote per share. This rule still holds today, but the voting techniques discussed in Chapter 40 (shareholder agreements, voting trusts, cumulative voting methods, and so on) all enhance the power of the shareholder's vote.

The articles can exclude or limit voting rights, particularly to certain classes of shares. For example, owners of preferred shares are usually denied the right to vote. Treasury shares, held by the corporation, cannot be voted until they have been reissued by the corporation.

Inspection Rights

Shareholders in a corporation enjoy both common law and statutory inspection rights. At common law, shareholders enjoy qualified rights to inspect and copy corporate books and records, such as the bylaws and minutes of the board of directors' meetings and the shareholders' meetings, as well as documents such as contracts, correspondence, and tax returns. They even have the right to inspect the corporate headquarters. At common law, the shareholder's right of inspection is limited, however, to inspection and copying of corporate books and records for a *proper purpose*, provided they make the request in advance. The shareholder must prove the purpose is proper.

The statutory right to inspect requires a statement of purpose, and under the MBCA, the corporation must prove the purpose is improper. Either the shareholder can inspect in person, or an attorney, agent, accountant, or other assistant can do so.

The power of inspection is fraught with potential abuses, and the corporation is allowed to protect itself from them. For example, a shareholder can properly be denied access to corporate records to prevent harassment or to protect trade secrets or other confidential corporate information. MBCA Section 52 requires that the shareholder must have held his or her shares for at least six months immediately preceding the demand to inspect *or* must hold five percent of all outstanding shares.

A corporation's improper refusal to allow access to its records can result in severe and costly liability to the corporation, however. Under the MBCA, the penalty is 10 percent of the value of the shares owned by the shareholder who has been denied access to the books.

The following case illustrates a court's dilemma in determining whether a stockholder-competitor could inspect the corporate books for limited purposes.

BACKGROUND AND FACTS   *The plaintiff, Uldrich, was a shareholder and former director, officer, and employee of Datasport, Inc., the defendant, a Minnesota corporation. Datasport terminated Uldrich's employment, directorship, and office. Uldrich maintained his status as a stockholder, and he also became a competitor of Datasport. While Uldrich was still a director and an officer of Datasport, he was prohibited from marketing his competing product for one year, by a court order granted upon Datasport's request. After his dismissal, Uldrich was denied access to Datasport's books and records. He sought a writ of mandamus from the court commanding Datasport to permit inspection. The trial court ordered the writ, and Datasport appealed.*

Case 41.3
ULDRICH v. DATASPORT, INC.
Court of Appeals of Minnesota, 1984.
349 N.W.2d 286.

PARKER, Judge.

*   *   *   *

The trial court found that Uldrich has good faith reasons for seeking access to the corporate books and records of Datasport, i.e., to place a monetary value on his stock interests and to evaluate the conduct and affairs of the other shareholders, officers and directors. [In a previous case] the Supreme Court held such reasons sufficient to compel inspection of corporate books and records by mandamus.

Respondent is concerned that the corporate records reflect that virtually all of Datasport's sales revenues are "eaten up" by operating expenses. He is concerned about the other shareholders (who are officers and directors) using Datasport assets to benefit their other business interests. The other shareholders of Datasport own a partnership called Studio Time; Studio Time leases office space to Datasport. These shareholders also own a corporation called Multi-Data, which promotes a product relating health and weather; Multi-Data offices are also located in the same space as Datasport offices. The officers of Multi-Data are also the officers of Datasport. Datasport sold computer time to Multi-Data and Multi-Data's services were used by Datasport at one time. All of the remaining shareholders, officers and directors of Datasport own a company called Reel Time, a television production company which was operated out of the Datasport offices. In three and one-half years, with over $1.5 million in sales, [Uldrich] has received less than $1,000 in return on his investment.

Datasport contends that the documents requested are "confidential business information" and that the order directs Datasport to make available "significant portions of its corporate records which cannot be included within any reasonable definition of books of account * * * " [, which, under the applicable Minnesota statute, every shareholder has a right to examine.]

Neither the statute nor case law defines "books of account." [Datasport] argues that the trial court's order includes information in these various records that are the supporting documentation for the books of account, "but do not themselves form a part of the books of account."

Under the circumstances here, when the shareholders, officers and directors of Datasport have multiple business interests operated on the same premises as, and doing business with, Datasport, and when [Uldrich's] return on his investment appears trivial in view of a substantial sales record, the trial court properly recognized that equity required a broad scope be given to the concept of shareholder access.

The trial court recognized that misuse might be made of some of the information sought and enjoined use of it for any competitive purpose.

DECISION AND REMEDY *The court of appeals affirmed the writ of mandamus compelling Datasport to allow Uldrich to exercise his shareholder's right of inspection.*

COMMENTS *The court's order in this case balanced the interests of the shareholder's access to corporate records and the sensitivities of a corporation to its competitors. Apparently because of this, the court did not impose a 10 percent penalty.*

The Right to Transfer Shares

Corporate stock represents an ownership right in intangible personal property. The law generally recognizes the right of an owner to transfer property to another person unless there are valid restrictions on its transferability. Although stock certificates are negotiable and freely transferable by indorsement and delivery, transfer of stock in closely held corporations is generally restricted by contract, the bylaws, or a restriction stamped on the stock certificate. The existence of any restrictions on transferability should always be noted on the face of the stock certificate, and these restrictions must be reasonable.

THE RIGHT OF FIRST REFUSAL Sometimes corporations or their shareholders restrict transferability by reserving the option to purchase any shares offered for resale by a shareholder. The option remains with the corporation or the shareholders for only a specified or reasonable time. Variations on the purchase option are possible. For example, a shareholder might be required to offer the shares to other shareholders or to the corporation first.

CORPORATE RECORDS When shares are transferred, a new entry is made in the corporate stock book to indicate the new owner. Until the corporation is notified and the entry is complete, voting rights, notice of shareholders' meetings, dividend distribution, and so forth are all held by or made to the current record owner.

Rights upon Dissolution

When a corporation is dissolved and its outstanding debts and the claims of its creditors have been satisfied, the remaining assets are distributed on a pro rata basis among the shareholders. Certain classes of preferred stock can be given priority to the extent of their contractual preference. If no preference as to distribution of assets upon liquidation are given to any class of stock, then the stockholders share the remaining assets.

COMPELLING RECEIVERSHIP Suppose a minority shareholder knows that the board of directors is mishandling corporate assets or is permitting a deadlock to threaten or irreparably injure the corporation's finances. The minority shareholder is not powerless to intervene. He or she can petition a court to appoint a receiver and to liquidate the business assets of the corporation.

MBCA Section 97 and RMBCA Section 14.30 permit any shareholder to institute such an action when it appears that:

1. The directors are deadlocked in the management of corporate affairs, shareholders are unable to break that deadlock, and irreparable injury to the corporation is being suffered or threatened.
2. The acts of the directors or those in control of the corporation are illegal, oppressive, or fraudulent.
3. Corporate assets are being misapplied or wasted.
4. The shareholders are deadlocked in voting power and have failed, for a specified period (usually two annual meetings), to elect successors to directors whose terms have expired or would have expired with the election of successors.

SHAREHOLDER LIABILITIES

One of the hallmarks of the corporate organization is that shareholders are not personally liable for the debts of the corporation. If the corporation fails, shareholders can lose their investment, but that is generally the limit of their liability. In certain instances of fraud, undercapitalization, or careless observance of corporate formalities, a court will pierce the corporate veil (disregard the corporate entity) and hold the shareholders individually liable. But these situations are the exception, not the rule.

Although rare, there are three additional situations in which a shareholder can be held personally liable. These situations relate to:

1. Stock subscriptions.
2. Watered stock issued.
3. Illegal dividends (previously discussed).

Stock Subscriptions

As discussed in Chapter 39, a preincorporation stock subscription agreement is treated as a continuing offer, and it is usually irrevocable (for up to six months under the MBCA). Once the corporation has been formed, it can sell shares to shareholder-investors. In either case, once the subscription agreement or stock offer is accepted,

a binding contract is formed. Any refusal to pay constitutes a breach resulting in the personal liability of the shareholder.

Watered Shares

Shares of stock can be paid for by property or by services rendered, instead of cash. Shares cannot be purchased with promissory notes. The general rule is that for par value shares sold, the corporation must receive a value at least equal to the par value amount. For no par shares, the corporation must receive the value of the shares as determined by the board or by shareholders. When shares are issued by the corporation for less than these stated values, the shares are referred to as **watered stock.** In most cases, the shareholder who receives watered stock must pay the difference to the corporation (the shareholder is personally liable). In some states, the shareholder who receives watered stock may be liable to creditors of the corporation for unpaid corporate debts.

To illustrate the concept of watered stock, suppose that during the formation of a corporation, Garcia, as one of the incorporators, transferred his property, Greenacre, to the corporation for 10,000 shares of stock at a par value of $100 per share for a total price of $1 million. The property is transferred and the shares are issued. Greenacre is carried on the corporate books at a value of $1 million. Upon appraisal, it is discovered that the market value of the property at the time of transfer was only $500,000. The shares issued to Garcia are therefore watered stock, and he is liable to the corporation for the difference.

DUTIES AND LIABILITIES OF MAJOR SHAREHOLDERS

As mentioned in Chapter 40, in some cases, a majority shareholder is regarded as having a fiduciary duty to the corporation and to the minority shareholders. This occurs when a single shareholder (or a few acting in concert) owns a sufficient number of shares to exercise *de facto* control over the corporation. In these situations, majority shareholders owe a fiduciary duty to the minority shareholders and creditors when they sell their shares, because such a sale is, in fact, a transfer of control of the corporation.

QUESTIONS AND CASE PROBLEMS

1. Otts Corporation negotiates with the Wick Construction Company for the renovation of the Otts corporate headquarters. Wick, owner of the Wick Construction Company, is also one of the five members of the board of directors of Otts. The contract terms are standard for this type of contract. Wick has previously informed two of the other directors of his interest in the construction company. The contract is approved by Otts's board on a three-to-two vote, with Wick voting with the majority. Discuss whether this contract is binding on the corporation.

2. Rheingold, Inc., has a board of directors consisting of three members (Evans, Goodrich, and Mortimer) and approximately five hundred shareholders. At a regular meeting of the board, the board selects Green as president of the corporation by a two-to-one vote, with Evans dissenting. The minutes of the meeting do not register Evans's dissenting vote. Later, upon an audit, it is discovered that Green is a former convict and has openly embezzled $500,000 from Rheingold, Inc. This loss is not covered by insurance. The corporation wants to hold directors Evans, Goodrich, and Mortimer liable. Evans claims no liability. Discuss the personal liability of the directors to the corporation.

3. Ann owns 10,000 shares (10 percent) of Superal Corporation. Superal authorized 100,000 shares and issued all of them during its first six months in operation. Later, Superal reacquired 10,000 of these shares. With shareholder approval, Superal amended its articles so as to authorize and issue another 100,000 shares and also, by a resolution of the board of directors, to reissue the 10,000 shares of treasury stock. There is no provision in the corporate articles dealing with shareholders' preemptive rights. Because of her previous ownership of 10 percent of Superal, Ann claims that she has the preemptive right to purchase 10,000 shares of the new issue and 1,000 shares of the stock being reissued. Discuss her claims.

4. Lucy has acquired one share of common stock of a multimillion-dollar corporation with over 500,000 shareholders. Lucy's ownership is so small that she is questioning what her rights are as a shareholder. For example, she wants to know whether this one share entitles her to:

    (a) Attend and vote at shareholder meetings.

    (b) Inspect the corporate books.

    (c) Receive yearly dividends.

Discuss Lucy's rights in these three matters.

5. Riddle has made a pre-incorporation subscription agreement to purchase 500 shares of a newly formed corporation. The shares have a par value of $100 per share. The corporation is formed, and Riddle's subscription is accepted by the corporation. Riddle transfers a piece of land he owns to the corporation, and the corporation issues 250 shares for it. One year later, with the corporation in serious financial difficulty, the board declares and pays a $5 per share dividend. It is now learned that the land transferred by Riddle had a market value of $18,000. Discuss any liability shareholder Riddle has to the corporation or to creditors of the corporation.

6. Klinicki and Lundgren formed Berlinair, a closely held Oregon corporation, to provide air transportation out of West Germany. Klinicki, who owned 33 percent of the company stock, was the vice-president and a director. Lundgren, who also owned 33 percent of the stock, was the president and a director. Lelco, Inc., a corporation owned by Lundgren and his family, owned 33 percent of Berlinair, and Berlinair's attorney owned the last 1 percent of stock. One of the goals of Berlinair was to obtain the contract with BFR, a West German consortium of travel agents, to provide BFR with air charter service.

Later, Lundgren learned that the BFR contract might become available. Lundgren then incorporated Air Berlin Charter Company, of which he was the sole owner, and bid for the BFR contract. Lundgren won the BFR contract for Air Berlin while using Berlinair working time, staff, money, and facilities without the knowledge of Klinicki. When Klinicki learned of the BFR contract he filed a derivative suit, as a minority stockholder, against Air Berlin for usurping a corporate opportunity. Should Klinicki recover against Air Berlin? If so, what should Klinicki be awarded as damages? [Klinicki v. Lundgren, 67 Or.App. 160, 678 P.2d 1250 (1984)]

7. Engdahl was a 10 percent stockholder, a director, and the treasurer of Aero Drapery, Inc. In May of 1967, several Aero employees expressed to Engdahl their dissatisfaction with their employment with Aero. Later that month, at Engdahl's suggestion, Engdahl met with the employees and suggested that they join together and form a new enterprise. In early June, they decided to go into the custom-drapery business in direct competition with Aero. Later that month, the new business associates decided upon a location for the new business, contacted suppliers, and secured an advertisement in the Yellow Pages. In July 1967, Engdahl tendered his resignation as director and treasurer of Aero Drapery, Inc.? Has Engdahl breached any duty to Aero Drapery, Inc.? Would your answer be different if Engdahl had resigned early in May of 1967? (What additional fact do you need to know to answer the latter question?) [Aero Drapery of Kentucky, Inc. v. Engdahl, 507 S.W.2d 166 (Ky.App. 1974)]

8. Hartung, Odle, and Burke were architects. In 1971 they organized as a corporation. Their association, however, was riddled with dissent from the start. As it became apparent that the corporate turmoil would eventually result in reorganization of the corporation, Hartung began conferring with several clients of the firm, informing them that he was willing to continue as their architect after his withdrawal from the corporation. The corporation was later dissolved, and several of its clients continued to do business with Hartung. Do Odle and Burke have any recourse against Hartung for his activities? [Hartung v. Architects Hartung/Odle/Burke, Inc., 157 Ind.App. 546, 301 N.E.2d 240 (1973)]

9. Atlantic Properties, Inc., had only four shareholders, each of whom owned 25 percent of the capital stock. The bylaws required an 80 percent affirmative vote of the shareholders on all actions taken by the corporation. This provision had the effect of giving any of the four original shareholders a veto in corporate decisions. One shareholder refused for seven years to vote for any dividends, although he was warned that his actions might expose the corporation to Internal Revenue Service penalties for unreasonable accumulation of corporate earnings and profits. The Internal Revenue Service did impose such penalties on the corporation. Can the dissenting shareholder be held personally liable for these penalties? [Smith v. Atlantic Properties, Inc., 12 Mass.App. 201, 422 N.E.2d 798 (1981)]

10. Frederick Valerino and his family owned 50 percent of the stock in EMA (Electrical-Mechanical of America, Inc.), and the remaining 50 percent was owned by Charles Little. Both Valerino and Little participated actively in operating the corporation until 1979, when a dispute arose, resulting in a stalemate. For two years no shareholders' meeting was held and no board of directors could be elected. Little held a shareholders' meeting in 1981 and sent a telegram to Valerino stating that the purpose of the meeting was "[f]or the sale and purchase of the Capital Stock of EMA." Valerino did not attend and sent a reply letter indicating that he did not wish to sell any of his stock. Actually, Little held the meeting with the intention of issuing more stock to himself and his family, thus reducing Valerino's ownership to 25 percent. Valerino sued to enforce his preemptive rights in the corporation and to set aside the new stock issuance because of fraud. Discuss whether Valerino should succeed in his claim. [Valerino v. Little, 62 Md.App. 588, 490 A.2d 756 (1985)]

Chapter 42

CORPORATIONS
Merger, Consolidation, and Termination

Corporations increase their holdings for a number of reasons. They may wish to enlarge their physical plants, increase their property or investment holdings, or acquire the assets, know-how, or goodwill of another corporation. Sometimes acquisition is motivated by a desire to eliminate a competitor, to accomplish diversification, or to ensure adequate resources and markets for the acquiring corporation's product. Whatever the reason, the corporation typically extends its operations by combining with another corporation through:

1. Merger.
2. Consolidation.
3. Purchase of assets.
4. Purchase of a controlling interest of the other corporation.

This chapter will examine the various ways in which merger or consolidation alters the fundamental structure of the corporation. Dissolution and liquidation are the combined processes by which a corporation terminates its existence. The last part of this chapter will discuss the typical reasons for and methods used in terminating a corporation.

MERGER AND CONSOLIDATION

The terms *merger* and *consolidation* are often used interchangeably, but they refer to two legally distinct proceedings. Whether a combination is in fact a merger or a consolidation, however, the rights and liabilities of shareholders, the corporation, and its creditors are the same.

Merger

A **merger** involves the legal combination of two or more corporations. After a merger, only one of the corporations continues to exist. For example, Corporation A and Corporation B decide to merge. It is agreed that A will absorb B; so upon merger, B ceases to exist as a separate entity, and A continues as the *surviving corporation*.

After the merger, A is recognized as a single corporation, possessing all the rights, privileges, and powers of itself and B. A automatically acquires all of B's property and assets without the necessity of formal transfer. A becomes liable for all B's debts and obligations. Finally, A's articles of incorporation are deemed *amended* to include any changes that are stated in the *articles of merger*.

In a merger, the surviving corporation is vested with the disappearing corporation's preexisting legal rights and obligations. For example, if the disappearing corporation had a right of action against a third party, the surviving corporation could bring suit after the merger to recover the disappearing corporation's damages.

Consolidation

In the case of a **consolidation,** two or more corporations combine so that each corporation ceases to exist and a new one emerges. Corporation A and Corporation B consolidate to form an entirely new organization, Corporation C. In the process, A and B both terminate. C comes into existence as an entirely new entity.

The results of consolidation are essentially the same as the results of merger. C is recognized as a new corporation and a single entity; A and B cease to exist. C accedes to all the rights, privileges, and powers previously held by A and B. Title to any property and assets owned by A and B passes to C without formal transfer. C assumes liability for all debts and obligations owed by A and B. The articles of consolidation *take the place of* A's and B's original corporate articles and are thereafter regarded as C's corporate articles.

When a merger or a consolidation takes place, the surviving corporation or newly formed corporation will issue shares or pay some fair consideration to the shareholders of the corporation that ceases to exist.

The Procedure

All states have statutes authorizing mergers and consolidations for *domestic* corporations, and most states allow the combination of domestic (in-state) and foreign (out-of-state) corporations. Although the procedures vary somewhat among jurisdictions, in each case the basic requirements are as outlined below:

1. The board of directors of *each* corporation involved must approve a merger or consolidation plan.

2. The shareholders of *each* corporation must vote approval of the plan at a shareholders' meeting. Most state statutes require the approval of two-thirds of the outstanding shares of voting stock, although some states require only a simple majority and others require a four-fifths vote. Frequently, statutes require that each class of stock approve the merger; thus, the holders of non-voting stock must also approve. A corporation's bylaws can dictate a stricter requirement.

3. Once approved by *all* the directors and the shareholders, the plan (articles of merger or consolidation) is filed, usually with the secretary of state.

4. When state formalities are satisfied, the state issues a certificate of merger to the surviving corporation or a certificate of consolidation to the newly consolidated corporation.

Short-Form (Parent-Subsidiary) Mergers

The MBCA provides a simplified procedure for the merger of a substantially owned subsidiary corporation into its parent corporation. Under these provisions, a **short-form merger** can be accomplished *without approval of the shareholders* of either corporation.

The short-form merger can be utilized only when the parent corporation owns at least 90 percent of the outstanding shares of each class of stock of the subsidiary corporation. The simplified procedure requires that a plan for the merger be approved by the board of directors of the parent corporation before it is filed with the state. A copy of the merger plan must be sent to each shareholder of record of the subsidiary corporation.

Appraisal Rights

What if a shareholder disapproves of the merger or consolidation but is outvoted by the other shareholders? The law recognizes that a dissenting shareholder should not be forced to become an unwilling shareholder in a corporation that is new or different from the one in which the shareholder originally invested. The shareholder has the right to dissent and may be entitled to be paid *fair value* for the number of shares held on the date of the merger or consolidation.

This right is referred to as the shareholder's **appraisal right.** An appraisal right is given by state statute and is available only when the statute specifically provides for it. It is normally extended to regular mergers, consolidations, short-form mergers, sales of substantially all the corporate assets not in the ordinary course of business, and, in certain states, adverse amendments to the articles of incorporation.

The appraisal right may be lost if the elaborate statutory procedures are not precisely followed. Whenever the right is lost, the dissenting shareholder must go along with the objectionable transaction.

One of the basic procedures usually followed requires that a written notice of dissent be filed by the dissenting shareholder or shareholders prior to the vote of the shareholders on the proposed transaction. This notice of dissent is also basically a notice to all shareholders of costs that may be imposed by dissenting shareholders should the merger or consolidation be approved. In addition, after approval the dissenting shareholders must make a written demand for payment and for fair value.

Valuation of shares is often a point of contention between the dissenting shareholder and the corporation. The MBCA Section 81 provides that the "fair value of shares" is the value on the day prior to the date on which the vote was taken.[1] The corporation must make a *written* offer to purchase a dissenting shareholder's stock, accompanying the offer with a current balance sheet and income statement for the corporation. If the shareholder and the corporation do not agree on the fair value, a court will determine it.

Once a dissenting shareholder elects appraisal rights under statute, in some jurisdictions, the shareholder loses his or her shareholder status. Without that status, a shareholder cannot vote, receive dividends, or sue to enjoin whatever action prompted his or her dissent. In some of those jurisdictions, statutes provide or courts have held that shareholder status may be reinstated during the appraisal process (for example, if the shareholder decides to withdraw from the process and the corporation approves). In other jurisdictions, the status may not be reinstated until the appraisal has concluded. Even if the status is lost, courts may allow an individual to sue on grounds of fraud or other illegal conduct associated with the merger.

The following case illustrates the frequently encountered problem of determining the fair value of shares under appraisal rights.

---

1. Any appreciation or depreciation of the stock in anticipation of the approval is excluded.

Case 42.1
ROSENBLATT v. GETTY OIL CO.
Supreme Court of Delaware,
1985.
493 A.2d 929.

BACKGROUND AND FACTS *In 1976, the defendant, Getty Oil, began negotiating for the merger of that corporation with Skelly Oil. Both acknowledged the desirability of a merger and agreed that an exchange of common stock would be the method of achieving that result. An engineering firm, D & M, and several investment banking and accounting firms were hired to assist in estimating asset values. Getty Oil and Skelly Oil immediately took an adversarial approach as each tried to value its own assets as high as possible. Eventually, Skelly agreed to an exchange ratio of 0.5875 shares of Getty stock for 1 share of Skelly stock. The boards of directors of both companies agreed to the merger and submitted the question to their respective shareholders; and with shareholder approval, the companies were merged in 1977.*

Rosenblatt, a minority shareholder in Skelly Oil, brought a class action suit on behalf of himself and other Skelly Oil shareholders who disapproved of the merger. The plaintiffs challenged the fairness of the price and asset valuations and sought a review by the courts. Part of their claim was based on the fact that the valuation of Skelly assets was substantially below the liquidation price that the plaintiffs' appraisers had determined. Thus, Rosenblatt claimed that liquidation would be the only fair course for Skelly given the lower price offered by Getty Oil. The court of chancery, however, held that the exchange ratio was fair to all shareholders, and the plaintiffs appealed.

MOORE, Justice.

* * * *

The plaintiffs challenge the fairness of the transaction, including the exchange ratio and the propriety of delegating the final subsurface asset valuation to D & M.

* * *

As to the fairness of the merger price, plaintiffs claim that exclusive use of the Delaware Block method [a method of assigning weights to asset value, market value, and earnings potential] yielded a value of $110 per share, considerably less than Skelly's appraised asset value of $195 per share. * * *

* * * *

* * * [W]e note initially that "in a non-fraudulent transaction . . . price may be the preponderant consideration outweighing other features of the merger." Fair price involves all relevant economic factors of the proposed merger, such as asset value, market value, earnings, future prospects, and any other elements that affect the inherent or intrinsic value of a company's stock. Thus, in [the] *Weinberger* [case] we authorized proof of value in appraisal and other stock valuation cases by any techniques or methods generally considered acceptable in the financial community and otherwise admissible in court. In addition, we ruled that the Delaware Block formula was no longer the *exclusive* mechanism of value precluding other generally accepted techniques. We stated further that only speculative elements of value due to the accomplishment of the merger are excluded * * * . However, elements of future value known or susceptible of proof at the date of the merger do not fall within this narrow exclusion and may be considered[.] * * *

While the plaintiffs challenge the defendant's use of the Delaware Block method, that was the only valuation technique permitted at that time. * * * We find no legal error or abuse of discretion by the Chancellor's action in accepting its use here.

* * * *

After careful scrutiny of the methods employed by the parties, the process of information gathering, the negotiations, and all relevant economic and financial factors, we conclude that the Chancellor's findings regarding fairness of the price paid the Skelly minority shareholders were entirely correct.

As noted earlier, Getty and Skelly were given a legal opinion on mergers under Delaware law at the July 15, 1976 meeting. Thus, from the outset, both sides were aware of the exclusive valuation method then approved by the courts of this State, the so-called Delaware Block formula. Both parties sought to follow this method in reaching the ultimate stock exchange ratio. They were entirely correct in doing so. * * *

The record indicates that with the block formula in mind, Getty and Skelly embarked on a lengthy and detailed review of their asset values, which both companies justifiably believed were of primary importance. This approach was based on legal opinions and on the recognition, shared by both corporations, that the real worth of an oil company is centered in its reserves. The record shows that this belief in the importance of asset value was still shared as of the final rounds of bargaining on November 1 and 7, 1976. Getty and Skelly diverted substantial resources to their respective asset reviews, each using hundreds of employees and retaining reputable investment bankers. Getty and Skelly also employed D & M, a petroleum consulting engineering firm with a worldwide reputation and more importantly, with nearly 37 years of experience in estimating Getty's and Skelly's respective oil and natural gas reserves.

* * * *

After an exhaustive review of the facts and evidence relating to the issue of fairness, we conclude that Getty dealt fairly with Skelly's minority shareholders from the genesis of the merger through approval by the respective boards of the two companies. We also conclude that the price received by the Skelly shareholders was fair.

DECISION   *The Supreme Court of Delaware affirmed the decision of the lower court and*
AND REMEDY   *held that the exchange ratio was fair to all shareholders.*

Shareholder Approval

Shareholders invest in a corporate enterprise with the expectation that the board of directors will manage the enterprise and will approve ordinary business matters. Actions taken on extraordinary matters must be authorized by the board of directors and the shareholders. Often, modern statutes require that certain types of extraordinary matters be approved by a vote of the shareholders. Typically, matters requiring shareholder approval include the sale, lease, or exchange of all or substantially all corporate assets outside of the corporation's regular course of business. Other examples include amendments to the articles of incorporation, transactions concerning merger or consolidation, and dissolution.

Hence, when any extraordinary matter arises, the corporation must proceed as authorized by law to obtain shareholder and board of director approval. Sometimes a transaction can be characterized as not to seem to require shareholder approval, but a court will use its equity powers to require such approval. In order to determine the nature of the transaction, the courts will look not only to the details of the transaction but also to its consequences.

The following case involves a sale of corporate assets that was negotiated without the shareholders' approval. The shareholders opposing the sale sought injunctive relief from the court.

Case 42.2
**SCHWADEL v.
UCHITEL**
District Court of Appeal of
Florida, Third District, 1984.
455 So.2d 401.

BACKGROUND AND FACTS   *Mike and Peter Schwadel, the plaintiffs, were major shareholders in HJU Sales & Investments, Inc. Over several years the assets of the corporation had been sold off until only one asset remained— a restaurant called "The Place for Steak." The plaintiffs sued the president and third major shareholder of the corporation, Hy Uchitel, when he entered into a contract to sell this remaining asset. Florida state law prohibits the sale of all or substantially all of a corporation's assets without shareholder approval. The Schwadels sought an injunction to prevent the sale of the restaurant, but the lower court denied the request. The plaintiffs appealed.*

BASKIN, Judge.
*   *   *   *

The prerequisites of section 607.241 [of Florida statutes] must be satisfied when a contemplated sale of major assets of a corporation will substantially limit the corporate business. The Place for Steak was the sole asset of Southern Caterers of North Bay Village, Inc., the wholly owned subsidiary of HJU, and the last of several restaurants owned by parent corporation HJU. It is undisputed that the fundamental purpose in forming the parent corporation and in operating the corporate enterprise through various subsidiaries was, and continues to be, to engage in the restaurant business. Thus, the sale of The Place for Steak constitutes a sale of "substantially all" the corporate assets and is subject to the statutory rights and protections extended to stockholders under Florida's shareholder "consent" provisions governing such transactions.

The purpose of a shareholder "consent" provision is "to protect the shareholders from fundamental change, or more specifically to protect the shareholders from the destruction of the means to accomplish the purposes or objects for which the corporation was incorporated and actually performs." When Hy Uchitel entered into a contract for the sale of the last major corporate asset, he violated shareholders' statutory rights to receive prior notice to consider the transaction and effectively barred their participation in a decision which fundamentally changes the nature of the corporation. This court must therefore decide whether injunctive relief is appropriate under these circumstances.

The general rule is that a court of equity is empowered to issue injunctive relief to prevent officers or directors of a corporation from wrongfully dealing with corporate assets and to prevent such wrongful actions from infringing upon shareholders' voting rights. The proposed sale of the remaining corporate asset constituted a breach of Uchitel's fiduciary duties to the corporation and to its stockholders, and deprived shareholders of their statutory rights to notice and to vote prior to the transfer of the last corporate asset. Injunctive relief is appropriate because appellants have a clear legal right to prior notice and a vote, and legal remedies are inadequate to prevent the irreparable harm that would result from Uchitel's unilateral decision to change the fundamental nature of the corporate enterprise. An award of damages would not compensate the shareholders for the destruction of the corporation caused by the transfer of the last major corporate asset. The pending sale is therefore enjoined.

The court of appeals reversed the lower court's decision and granted an injunction to the plaintiffs. **DECISION AND REMEDY**

PURCHASE OF ASSETS

When a corporation acquires all or substantially all of the assets of another corporation by direct purchase, the purchasing or *acquiring* corporation simply extends its ownership and control over more physical assets. Since no change in the legal entity occurs, the *acquiring corporation* is not required to obtain shareholder approval for the purchase.[2]

Although the acquiring corporation may not be required to obtain shareholder approval for such an acquisition, the U.S. Department of Justice has issued guidelines that significantly constrain and often prohibit mergers that could result from a purchase of assets, including takeover bids. These guidelines are part of the federal antitrust laws to enforce Section 7 of the Clayton Act (discussed in Chapter 48).

Note that the corporation that is *selling* all its assets is substantially changing its business position and perhaps its ability to carry out its corporate purposes. For that reason, the corporation whose assets are *acquired* must obtain both board of director and shareholder approval. In most states and under the MBCA, a dissenting shareholder of the selling corporation can demand appraisal rights.

Generally, a corporation that purchases the assets of another corporation is not responsible for the liabilities of the selling corporation. Exceptions to this rule are made in the following circumstances:

1. When the purchasing corporation impliedly or expressly assumes the seller's liabilities.
2. When the sale amounts to what in fact is a merger or a consolidation.
3. When the purchaser continues the seller's business and retains the same personnel (same shareholders, directors, and officers).
4. When the sale is fraudulently executed to escape liability.

In any of these situations, the acquiring corporation will be held to have assumed both the assets and the liabilities of the selling corporation.

In the following case, the court evaluates a creditor's claim that the debtor corporation fraudulently sold its assets to avoid liability for its debts and that the sale of assets was a *de facto* merger. Under the *de facto* merger doctrine, if a sale of assets constitutes—for all practical purposes—a merger, the acquiring corporation will be responsible for the liabilities of the selling corporation.

---

2. If the acquiring corporation plans to pay for the assets with its own corporate stock and not enough authorized unissued shares are available, the shareholders must vote to approve issuance of additional shares by amendment of the corporate articles. Also, acquiring corporations whose stock is traded in a national stock exchange can be required to obtain their own shareholders' approval if they plan to issue a significant number of shares, such as a number equal to 20 percent or more of the outstanding shares.

Case 42.3
**LUMBARD v.
MAGLIA, INC.**
United States District Court for
the Southern District of New
York, 1985.
621 F.Supp. 1529.

BACKGROUND AND FACTS *From 1975 until mid-1984, Carla Leather manufactured, distributed, and sold women's leather apparel. Meritum Corporation loaned Carla Leather several million dollars for operations and held a continuing security interest in Carla Leather's present and after-acquired inventory, products, and proceeds. In early 1982, after Carla Leather had sustained substantial operating losses, the founder, Carla Maglia, allegedly arranged for the creation of another corporate entity to carry on her business free from debt. As part of Carla Leather's liquidation, most of the tangible and intangible assets were sold to this new corporation for little or no consideration. The new corporation was called Maglia, Inc., and began business in 1982 with Carla Leather's personnel, products, customers, suppliers, and business equipment. Maglia, Inc., was financed by a credit agency called Brancorp, which had earlier refused to extend credit to Carla Leather because Meritum held the position of senior creditor. Eliot Lumbard, as trustee for the estate of Meritum Corporation, filed suit on behalf of Meritum against Maglia, Inc., to recover the assets previously owned by Carla Leather. Lumbard also sued Brancorp for participating in the allegedly fraudulent avoidance of debt. Maglia, Inc., moved to dismiss the claim.*

GOETTEL, District Judge.
*   *   *   *

For a *de facto* merger to occur, there must be continuity of the successor and predecessor corporation as evidenced by (1) continuity of ownership; (2) a cessation of ordinary business and dissolution of the predecessor as soon as practically and legally possible; (3) assumption by the successor of the liabilities ordinarily necessary for the uninterrupted continuation of the business of the predecessor; and (4) a continuity of management, personnel, physical location, assets, and general business operation. "Not all of these factors are needed to demonstrate a merger; rather, these factors are only indicators that tend to show a *de facto* merger."

Brancorp's assertion that identity of ownership is a prerequisite to successor liability finds no support in the case law. Not only is identity of ownership one of several factors, but the cases uniformly hold that continuity, not uniformity, is the significant variable. One court stated,

> We think that the dissolution of [predecessor] and the organization of [successor] had but one purpose, and that was to avoid the contractual liability of [predecessor]. . . . It is true that preferred stock in [successor] was issued to a number of persons who were not stockholders in [predecessor]; but the fact remains that the plant and business of the older corporation were taken over by the later one, the same organization was continued, and the names of the two corporations differ only by reason of the addition of the abbreviation "Inc."

*   *   *   *

[W]e deem the later organization merely a continuation of the former.

The defendants' contention that the plaintiffs cannot state any claim for successor liability because Carla had no viable business to transfer at the time of the alleged merger is also meritless. In fact, Carla's insolvency argues for the application of the various theories of successor liability. Where a transferor, like Carla, receives little if anything in exchange for its assets, it cannot respond to actions by creditors. Creditors must then pursue the transferee, here Maglia.

[The plaintiff's complaint] clearly describes the wholesale transformation of one company, Carla, into another, Maglia. [It] alleges that Maglia continued the enterprise of Carla with the same employees, assets, and management. It further states that these transactions reduced Carla to a "shell." Viewed in a light most favorable to the plaintiffs, these allegations are sufficient to state a *de facto* merger claim against Maglia.

The district court refused to dismiss the claim against Maglia, Inc., and Brancorp. **DECISION AND REMEDY**

PURCHASE OF STOCK

An alternative to the purchase of another corporation's assets is the purchase of a substantial number of the voting shares of its stock. This enables the acquiring corporation to control the acquired, or *target,* corporation. The acquiring corporation deals directly with the shareholders in seeking to purchase the shares they hold.

Tender Offers

When the acquiring corporation makes a public offer to all shareholders of the target corporation, it is called a *tender offer* (an offer that is publicly advertised and addressed to all shareholders of the target company). The price of the stock in the tender offer is generally higher than the market price of the target stock prior to the announcement of the tender offer. The higher price induces shareholders to tender their shares to the acquiring firm.

The tender offer can be conditional upon the receipt of a specified number of outstanding shares by a specified date. The offering corporation can make an *exchange* tender offer in which it offers target stockholders its own securities in exchange for their target stock. In a cash tender offer, the offering corporation offers the target stockholders cash in exchange for their target stock.

Federal securities laws strictly control the terms, duration, and circumstances under which most tender offers are made. In addition, a majority of states have passed takeover statutes that impose additional regulations on tender offers when in-state companies are involved.

The use of the tender offer as a method of gaining corporate control began in the mid-1960s. Highly contested legal battles and enormous expenses involved in complying with federal and state regulations have worked in some cases to discourage the use of tender offers as a vehicle for obtaining control of a corporation through stock purchase.

Recently, many tender offers have received national attention. In some cases, tenders have resulted in the purchaser's making millions of dollars under a buy-out agreement with the target corporation.

Target Responses

As discussed in Chapter 41, the directors of a corporation owe a fiduciary duty to the shareholders. In the context of a tender offer, this requires that, after full consideration, the directors make a good faith decision as to whether the shareholders' acceptance or rejection of the offer would be most beneficial. In making any recommendation, the directors must fully disclose all **material facts.** A fact is material if there is a substantial likelihood that a reasonable shareholder would consider it important in deciding how to vote. For example, information indicating a good price for the stock would be considered material.

Sometimes, a target firm's board of directors will see a tender offer as favorable and recommend to the shareholders that they accept it. Alternatively, to resist a takeover, a target company may make a *self tender,* which is an offer to acquire stock from its own shareholders and thereby retain corporate control.

To resist a takeover, a target company may solicit a merger with a third party, which then, of course, makes a better (often simply a higher) tender offer to the target's shareholders. This third party has been called a *white knight.* A white knight that interferes once the acquiring and target companies have agreed to merge may be held to have wrongfully interfered with a contractual relationship. This was the determination in the recent case involving Pennzoil's suit against Texaco, whose acquisition of Getty Oil after Getty had agreed to merge with Pennzoil prompted a trial court to award $10.5 billion to Pennzoil.[3]

Alternatively, the target company may attempt its own takeover of the acquiring corporation. This has been called the *Pac-man defense.* Because the self tender, the white knight defense, and the Pac-

---

3. On appeal, the trial court's judgment was affirmed, but the award was reduced. This case is presented in Chapter 5 on pages 92–94.

man defense use tender offers, they are subject to the same federal and state laws as the tender offers that prompted their use as defensive takeover tactics.

Other oppositional strategies include the target company's making itself less financially attractive to the acquiring corporation. The target may implement *scorched earth* tactics, by which it sells off assets or divisions or takes out loans that it agrees to repay in the event of a takeover. To make a takeover more difficult, a target company may change its articles of incorporation or bylaws. For example, the bylaws may be amended to require that a larger number of shareholders approve the firm's combination. This tactic has been described as *shark repellant,* as it casts an acquiring corporation in the role of a shark.

Another tactic, called a *poison pill,* involves the target's issuing to its stockholders shares that can be turned in for cash if a takeover is successful. This makes the takeover undesirably or even prohibitively expensive for the acquiring corporation. In response, parties intent on taking over a particular target have sometimes grouped together to enhance their financial position and made group bids.

A target may also seek an injunction against an acquiring corporation on grounds that the attempted takeover violates antitrust laws (the subject of Chapter 48), which are intended to prevent the illegal restraint of competition. This defense may succeed if the takeover would, in the eyes of a court, result in a substantial increase in the acquiring corporation's market power.

An acquiring corporation may challenge its target's defensive tactics as violations of the target management's fiduciary duties to maximize the interests of the target's shareholders.

When a takeover is successful, top management is usually changed. With this in mind, many top executives have secured *golden parachutes,* which guarantee them certain attractive payments if they are discharged or demoted because of a takeover.

Even if a takeover attempt does not succeed, it may still be lucrative to the acquiring corporation. To regain control, the target company may pay an exceptional price to repurchase the stock the acquiring corporation bought. Indeed, when a takeover is attempted through a gradual accumulation of target stock rather than a tender offer, the intent may be to get the target company to buy back the accumulated shares. This has been called *greenmail.*

Insider Trading

An *insider* is an individual with material information about a publicly traded corporation that is not available to the public. **Insider trading**—that is, the buying or selling of corporate securities by a person in possession of material, nonpublic information—is covered under Sections 10(b) and 16(b) of the Securities Exchange Act of 1934 and Rule 10b-5 of the Securities and Exchange Commission and is considered more fully in Chapter 43. At this point, it may be said that one who possesses inside information has a duty to disclose it to whoever is on the other side of the transaction.[4]

Perhaps the most famous instances of insider trading involved Ivan Boesky, Dennis Levine, and others in trades that made use of inside information concerning many of the largest takeover attempts in the 1980s. Curiously, among those involved were young lawyers and investment bankers with salaries in the hundreds of thousands of dollars and more. Once the scheme was exposed, none of these individuals retained their high-salaried positions. On conviction, all of them paid large fines, and some went to prison.

TERMINATION

Termination of a corporate life, like termination of a partnership, has two phases—dissolution and liquidation. **Dissolution** is the legal death of the artificial "person" of the corporation. **Liquidation** is the process by which corporate assets are converted into cash and distributed among creditors and shareholders according to specific rules of preference.[5]

Dissolution

Dissolution can be brought about in any of the following ways:

---

4. Under the Insider Trading Sanctions Act of 1984, insiders may be fined as much as triple the amount of any profit made or loss avoided on each illegal transaction, up to $50,000.

5. Upon dissolution, the liquidated assets are first used to pay creditors. Any remaining assets are distributed to shareholders according to their respective stock rights; preferred stock has priority over common stock, generally by charter.

1. An act of a legislature in the state of incorporation.
2. The expiration of the time provided in the certificate of incorporation.
3. The voluntary approval of the shareholders and the board of directors.
4. Unanimous action by all shareholders.
5. Court decree brought about by the attorney general of the state of incorporation for any of the following reasons: (a) failure to comply with administrative requirements (for example, failure to pay annual franchise taxes or to submit an annual report or to have a designated registered agent), (b) the procurement of a corporate charter through fraud or misrepresentation upon the state, (c) the abuse of corporate powers (*ultra vires* acts), (d) the violation of the state criminal code after the demand to discontinue has been made by the secretary of state, (e) the failure to commence business operations, or (f) the abandonment of operations before starting up.[6]

Sometimes an involuntary dissolution of a corporation is necessary—for example, when a board of directors is deadlocked. Courts hesitate to order involuntary dissolution in such circumstances unless there is specific statutory authorization to do so, but if the deadlock cannot be resolved by the shareholders and if it will irreparably injure the corporation, the court will proceed with an involuntary dissolution. Courts can also dissolve a corporation for mismanagement.[7]

In the following case, a minority shareholder—one of the two shareholders in a close corporation—sued to have the corporation dissolved because he had been "frozen out" of the business by the allegedly oppressive tactics of the majority shareholder. Note the court's reluctance to grant the extreme remedy of dissolution, even though it deemed that a "freeze-out" had occurred.

---

6. See MBCA Section 94 and RMBCA Section 14.20.

7. See MBCA Section 97 and RMBCA Section 14.30.

BACKGROUND AND FACTS *In 1984, the plaintiff, Elmer Balvik, and the defendant, Thomas Sylvester, decided to turn their partnership into a corporation because of the tax benefits that would result. The new Weldon Corporation carried on the partnership's old business of electrical contracting. Sylvester received 70 percent of the stock of the new corporation and Balvik the remaining 30 percent, in proportion to the capital that each contributed. Both took positions as directors and officers of the corporation, and each was entitled to one vote per share of stock. Balvik was at all times a minority voice in the company. Although Sylvester and Balvik had had no problems during their years as partners, difficulties emerged soon after incorporation. Sylvester believed that excess profits should be reinvested in the corporation, while Balvik wanted them withdrawn and paid out as bonuses or dividends. Balvik was fired from his job, allegedly because of poor performance, and he began working for another company. Balvik was unable to take any of his capital contribution in the corporation with him and no longer received a salary from the corporation. Balvik sued to have the corporation dissolved under North Dakota law, which allows dissolution for illegal, oppressive, or fraudulent acts by corporate directors or those in control of the corporation toward minority shareholders. The district court ordered dissolution and appointed a receiver, and the defendant appealed.*

Case 42.4
BALVIK v. SYLVESTER
Supreme Court of North Dakota, 1987.
411 N.W.2d 383.

VANDE WALLE, Justice.
*   *   *   *

"The word 'oppressive,' as used in the statute does not carry an essential inference of imminent disaster; it can contemplate a continuing course of conduct. The word does not necessarily savor of fraud, and the absence of 'mismanagement, or misapplication of assets,' does not prevent a finding that the conduct of the dominant directors or officers has been oppressive. It is not synonymous with 'illegal' and 'fraudulent.' "

The statutory concept of oppressive conduct, and the broad and imprecise definitions of the term given by the courts, is best understood by examining the nature and characteristics of close corporations. The typical attributes of a close corporation are that: (1) the shareholders are few in number, often only two or three; (2) the shareholders usually live in the same geographical area, know each other, and are well acquainted with each other's business skills; (3) all or most of the shareholders are active in the business, usually serving as directors or officers or as key participants in some managerial capacity; and (4) there is no established market for the corporate stock. Thus it is generally understood that, in addition to supplying capital and labor to a contemplated enterprise and expecting a fair return, parties comprising the ownership of a close corporation expect to be actively involved in its management and operation.
* * * *

The limited market for stock in a close corporation and the natural reluctance of potential investors to purchase a noncontrolling interest in a close corporation that has been marked by dissension can result in a minority shareholder's interest being held "hostage" by the controlling interest, and can lead to situations where the majority "freeze out" minority shareholders by the use of oppressive tactics.

Freeze-outs are actions taken by the controlling shareholders to deprive a minority shareholder of her interest in the business or a fair return on her investment. A variety of freeze-out techniques exist, with the withholding of dividends being by far the most commonly applied technique. This technique is often combined with the discharge of the minority shareholder from employment and removal of the minority shareholder from the board of directors. If the minority shareholder is employed by the corporation full time, as is typical, and if she relies on her salary as her primary means of obtaining a return on her investment, as is typical, she is suddenly left with little or no income and little or no return on her investment. The controlling shareholders may effectively deprive the minority shareholder of every economic benefit that she derives from the corporation. Meanwhile, the controlling shareholders may continue to receive a substantial return based on their continuing employment with the corporation. The minority shareholder's investment serves only to ensure the success of the corporation for the benefit of the controlling shareholders.

Because of the predicament in which minority shareholders in a close corporation are placed by a "freeze out" situation, courts have analyzed alleged "oppressive" conduct by those in control in terms of "fiduciary duties" owed by the majority shareholders to the minority and the "reasonable expectations" held by the minority shareholders in committing their capital and labor to the particular enterprise.
* * * *

* * * [C]onsidering Sylvester's inclination to reinvest profits in the corporation, the possibility of a declaration of dividends in the near future appears remote. We find little relevance in whether Sylvester discharged Balvik from employment for cause, or in the fact that Balvik's removal as a director and officer of the corporation occurred only after Balvik brought the instant suit. The ultimate effect of these actions is that Balvik clearly has been "frozen out" of a business in which he reasonably expected to participate. As a result, Balvik is entitled to relief.
* * * *

We have recognized that forced dissolution of a corporation is a drastic remedy which should be invoked with extreme caution and only when justice requires it. In a sense, a forced dissolution allows minority shareholders to exercise retaliatory "oppression" against the majority. * * *

Under the circumstances, we believe the trial court abused its discretion in ordering the extreme remedy of dissolution. Weldon is apparently an on-going business and, under the facts presented, ordering its dissolution and liquidation is unduly harsh. Balvik, in his complaint, sought as an alternative remedy that "the Defendant pay to the Plaintiff the true value of his stock in the Corporation. . . ." * * * [W]e believe [this] is the appropriate remedy here. Consequently, we remand this case for the entry of an order requiring either Weldon or Sylvester to purchase Balvik's stock at a price determined by the court to be the fair value thereof. The court may conduct any further proceedings it deems necessary for resolution of the issue. The parties are, of course, free to agree to other alternative methods of resolving this dispute.

The Supreme Court of North Dakota affirmed the decision of the lower court that Balvik had been "frozen out" of the corporation. The court refused to dissolve the corporation, however, but remanded the case so that another remedy could be sought.

DECISION AND REMEDY

Liquidation

When dissolution takes place by voluntary action, the members of the board of directors act as trustees of the corporate assets. As trustees, they are responsible for winding up the affairs of the corporation for the benefit of corporate creditors and shareholders. This makes the board members personally liable for any breach of their fiduciary trustee duties.

Liquidation can be accomplished without court supervision unless the members of the board do not wish to act in this capacity or unless shareholders or creditors can show cause to the court why the board should not be permitted to assume the trustee function. In either case, the court will appoint a receiver to wind up the corporate affairs and liquidate corporate assets. A receiver is always appointed by the court if the dissolution is involuntary.

QUESTIONS AND CASE PROBLEMS

1. Gretz is chairman of the board of directors of Faraday, Inc., and Williams is chairman of the board of directors of Firebrand, Inc. Faraday is a manufacturing corporation, and Firebrand is a transportation corporation. Gretz and Williams meet to consider the possibility of combining their corporations and activities into a single corporate entity. They consider two alternative courses of action: acquisition by Faraday of all the stock and assets of Firebrand or combination of the two corporations to form a new corporation, Farabrand, Inc. Both chairmen are concerned about the necessity of formal transfer of property, liability for existing debts, and the problem of amending articles of incorporation. Discuss what the two proposed combinations are called and what legal effect each has on the transfer of property, the liabilities of the combined corporations, and the need to amend the articles of incorporation.

2. Ann owns 10,000 shares of Ajax Corporation. Her shares represent a 10 percent ownership in Ajax. Zeta Corporation is interested in acquiring Ajax in a merger, and the board of directors of each corporation has approved the merger. The shareholders of Zeta have already approved the acquisition, and Ajax has called for a shareholders' meeting to approve the merger. Ann disapproves of the merger and does not want to accept Zeta shares for the Ajax shares she holds. The market price of Ajax shares is $20 per share the day before the shareholder vote and drops to $16 on the day the shareholders of Ajax approve the merger. Discuss Ann's rights in this matter, beginning with notice of the proposed merger.

3. Green Corporation wants to acquire all the assets of Red Dot Corporation. Green plans to pay for the assets by issuing its own corporate stock. Green's board of directors has already approved the merger. Discuss whether shareholder approval is required for this merger.

4. Alitech Corporation is a small midwestern business that owns a valuable patent. Alitech has approximately 1,000 shareholders with 100,000 authorized and outstanding shares. Block Corporation would like to have use of the patent, but Alitech refuses to give Block a license. Block has tried to acquire Alitech by purchasing Alitech's assets, but Alitech's board of directors has refused to approve the acquisition. Alitech's shares are presently selling for $5 per share. Discuss how Block Corporation might proceed in order to gain the control and use of Alitech's patent.

5. Saunders Corporation has been losing money for several years but still has valuable fixed assets. The shareholders see little hope that the corporation will ever make a profit. Another corporation, Topway Corporation, has failed to pay state taxes for several years or to file annual reports required by statute. In addition, Topway is accused of being guilty of gross and persistent *ultra vires* acts. Dis-

cuss whether these corporations will be terminated and how the assets of each would be handled upon dissolution.

6. Galdi was a shareholder of BankEast Corporation. BankEast proposed a merger with another bank, and Galdi voted against the merger and exercised her right to statutory appraisal. BankEast and Galdi could not agree on the value of the stock, so each appointed an appraiser, who appointed a third appraiser. All three appraisers agreed on the value of the stock. Galdi, still not pleased with the price, withdrew from the appraisal process. BankEast went to court to compel Galdi to accept the appraisal and transfer the stock. What was the result? [BankEast Corp. v. Galdi, 125 N.H. 280, 480 A.2d 136 (1984)]

7. Burack, Inc., was a family-operated close corporation that sold plumbing supplies in New York. The founder, Israel Burack, transferred his shares in the corporation to other family members; and when Israel died in 1974, the position of president passed to his son, Robert Burack. Robert held a one-third interest in the company, and the remainder was divided among Israel's other children and grandchildren. All shareholders participated in the corporation as employees or officers and thus relied on salaries and bonuses, rather than dividends, for distribution of the corporation's earnings. In 1976, several of the family-member employees requested a salary increase from Robert, who claimed that company earnings were not sufficient to warrant any employee salary increases. Shortly thereafter, a shareholders' meeting was held (the first in the company's fifty-year history), and Robert was removed from his position as president and denied the right to participate in any way in the corporation. Robert sued to have the company dissolved because he had been "frozen out." Discuss whether Robert should succeed in his suit or whether the court would choose another alternative. [Burack v. I. Burack, Inc., 137 A.D.2d 523, 524 N.Y.S.2d 457 (1988)]

8. CMCREC was a real estate holding corporation with 2,179,892 shares of common stock outstanding in 1986. Another corporation, CMC, owned 96 percent of the stock. CMC decided to merge CMCREC into the parent corporation for various financial, legal, and tax reasons and held a shareholder meeting to vote on this specific matter. The decision to merge was passed overwhelmingly. David Rosenstein and several others, who owned 5 shares of CMCREC among them, opposed the merger. They claimed that the merger was unfair because it prevented them from continuing participation in CMCREC. Rosenstein also claimed that the reimbursement amount was grossly inadequate. Rosenstein sued CMC to have the merger set aside. Discuss whether Rosenstein should succeed in his suit or whether another remedy was available. [Rosenstein v. CMC Real Estate Corp., 168 Ill.App.3d 92, 522 N.E.2d 221, 118 Ill.Dec. 766 (1988)]

9. Albert Martin owned 50 percent of the stock in Martin's News Service, Inc., and the remaining 50 percent was owned by his brother, Raymond Martin. Albert and Raymond had difficulty working together and communicated only through their accountant. For ten years, there were no corporate meetings, elections to the board of directors, or other corporate formalities. During that time, Raymond operated the business much as a sole proprietorship, failing to consult Albert on any matter and making all of the decisions himself. The corporation, however, was a viable concern that had grown successfully through the years. Albert sued to have the corporation dissolved. Should he succeed? [Martin v. Martin's News Service, Inc., 9 Conn.App. 304, 518 A.2d 951 (1986)]

10. On March 6, 1981, Carolyn Hamaker lost three fingers from her left hand while operating a notcher machine (a lathe) at her place of employment in South Dakota, Pallets and Wood Products. The notching machine had been manufactured by Kenwel Machine Company. On December 31, 1975, Kenwel sold its assets to John and Rosemary Jackson, who created a new company called Kenwel-Jackson Machine Company. Kenwel Machine Company terminated its existence in August of 1977. Kenwel-Jackson Machine Company continued to manufacture notchers, but it made several design changes and was in fact producing a different machine from the one that injured Carolyn Hamaker. As a result of her injuries, Hamaker brought a suit for damages against Kenwel-Jackson, since Kenwel Machine Company no longer existed. Discuss whether Kenwel-Jackson is liable for injuries caused by a machine manufactured by a company purchased by Kenwel-Jackson. [Hamaker v. Kenwel-Jackson Machine Co., Inc., 387 N.W.2d 515 (S.D. 1986)]

Chapter 43

CORPORATIONS
Financial Regulation
and Investor Protection

After the great stock market crash of 1929, various studies showed a need for regulation of securities markets. Basically, securities regulation legislation was enacted to provide investors with more information in order to help them to make more informed buying and selling decisions. Furthermore, regulation was designed to prohibit deceptive, unfair, and manipulative practices. Today, the sale and transfer of securities are heavily regulated by federal and state statutes and by government agencies. This is a complex area of the law. This chapter will outline the nature of federal securities regulations and their effect on the business world.

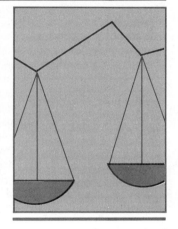

The most important federal securities regulations are the Securities Act of 1933 and the Securities Exchange Act of 1934. These acts and others are administered by the Securities and Exchange Commission.

THE SECURITIES AND EXCHANGE COMMISSION

Congress has delegated to the Securities and Exchange Commission (SEC) the responsibility of administering all federal securities law. The SEC is an independent regulatory agency established by the Securities Exchange Act of 1934. The SEC's major responsibilities are as follows:

1. Requiring disclosure of facts concerning offerings of securities listed on national securities exchanges and of certain securities traded over the counter (OTC).
2. Regulating the trade in securities on the thirteen national and regional securities exchanges and in the over-the-counter markets.
3. Investigating securities fraud.
4. Regulating the activities of securities brokers, dealers, and investment advisers and requiring their registration.
5. Supervising the activities of mutual funds.
6. Recommending administrative sanctions, injunctive remedies, and criminal prosecution against those who violate securities laws.

THE SECURITIES ACT OF 1933

The Securities Act of 1933[1] was designed to prohibit various forms of fraud and to stabilize the
securities industry by requiring that all essential
information concerning the issuance of securities,
except those exempted under the act, be made
available to the investing public. The 1933 act
basically requires disclosure.

Definition of Security

Generally, a **security** is any document evidencing
a debt or a property interest. Under Section 2(1)
of the Securities Act, securities include:

> any note, stock, treasury stock, bond, debenture,
> evidence of indebtedness, certificate of interest or
> participation in any profit-sharing agreement, col-
> lateral-trust certificate, preorganization certificate or
> subscription, transferable share, investment con-
> tract, voting-trust certificate, certificate of deposit
> for a security, fractional undivided interest in oil,
> gas, or other mineral rights, or, in general, any
> interest or instrument commonly known as a "se-
> curity," or any certificate of interest or participation
> in, temporary or interim certificate for, receipt for,
> guarantee of, or warrant or right to subscribe to or
> purchase, any of the foregoing.[2]

---

1. 15 U.S.C. Sections 77a–77aa.
2. 15 U.S.C. Section 77b(1). The 1982 amendments added
stock options.

Basically, the courts have interpreted this definition to mean that a security exists in any transaction in which a person (1) invests (2) in a common enterprise (3) reasonably expecting profits
(4) derived *primarily* or *substantially* from others'
managerial or entrepreneurial efforts.

For our purposes, it is probably most convenient to think of securities in their most common
form—stocks and bonds issued by corporations.
Bear in mind, however, that securities can take
many forms and have been held to include whiskey, cosmetics, worms, beavers, boats, vacuum
cleaners, muskrats, and cemetery lots, as well as
investment contracts in condominiums, franchises, limited partnerships, oil or gas or other
mineral rights, and farm animals accompanied by
care agreements.

In determining what constitutes a security under the 1933 act, courts have often cited *SEC v.
W. J. Howey*, presented below. In this classic case,
in which citrus groves qualified as securities, the
Supreme Court held that for a security to exist an
investor's profits must be derived *solely* from other's efforts. Later court decisions, however, have
required only that the profits be derived *primarily*
or *substantially* from the efforts of others.[3]

---

3. See, for example, SEC v. Glenn W. Turner Enterprises,
Inc., 474 F.2d 476 (9th Cir. 1973), cert. denied 414 U.S. 821,
94 S.Ct. 117, 38 L.Ed.2d 53 (1973), in which pyramid sales
arrangements were held to involve investment contracts and
securities because the profits realized were due *primarily* or
substantially to others' efforts.

Case 43.1
**SECURITIES AND
EXCHANGE
COMMISSION v. W. J.
HOWEY CO.**

Supreme Court of the United
States, 1946.
328 U.S. 293, 66 S.Ct. 1100, 90
L.Ed. 1244.

BACKGROUND AND FACTS   *The Howey Company (Howey) owned
large tracts of citrus acreage in Lake County, Florida. For several years, it
planted about five hundred acres annually, keeping half of the groves itself and
offering the other half to the public to help finance additional development.
Howey-in-the-Hills Service, Inc., was a service company engaged in cultivating
and developing these groves, including the harvesting and marketing of the
crops. Each prospective customer was offered both a land sales contract and a
service contract, after being told that it was not feasible to invest in a grove
unless service arrangements were made. Of the acreage sold by Howey, 85 percent
was sold with a service contract with Howey-in-the-Hills Service, Inc. Howey
did not register with the SEC or meet the other administrative requirements
that issuers of securities must fulfill. The SEC sued to enjoin Howey from
continuing to offer the land sales and service contracts. Howey responded that
no SEC violation existed because no securities were issued. The district court
and the circuit court of appeals refused to issue the injunction. The SEC, as*

the petitioner, appealed to the United States Supreme Court against Howey, the respondent.

MURPHY, Judge.

*   *   *   *

*   *   * The legal issue in this case turns upon a determination of whether, under the circumstances, the land sales contract, the warranty deed and the service contract together constitute an "investment contract" within the meaning of § 2 (1) [of the Securities Act.] An affirmative answer brings into operation the registration requirements of § 5 (a), unless the security is granted an exemption under § 3 (b). The lower courts, in reaching a negative answer to this problem, treated the contracts and deeds as separate transactions involving no more than an ordinary real estate sale and an agreement by the seller to manage the property for the buyer.

The term "investment contract" is undefined by the Securities Act or by relevant legislative reports. But the term was common in many state "blue sky" laws [laws requiring registration with the appropriate state commission] in existence prior to the adoption of the federal statute and, although the term was also undefined by the state laws, it has been broadly construed by state courts so as to afford the investing public a full measure of protection. Form was disregarded for substance and emphasis was placed upon economic reality. An investment contract thus came to mean a contract or scheme for "the placing of capital or laying out of money in a way intended to secure income or profit from its employment." This definition was uniformly applied by state courts to a variety of situations where individuals were led to invest money in a common enterprise with the expectation that they would earn a profit solely through the efforts of the promoter or of some one other than themselves.

By including an investment contract within the scope of § 2 (1) of the Securities Act, Congress was using a term the meaning of which had been crystallized by this prior judicial interpretation. It is therefore reasonable to attach that meaning to the term as used by Congress, especially since such a definition is consistent with the statutory aims. In other words, an investment contract for purposes of the Securities Act means a contract, transaction or scheme whereby a person invests his money in a common enterprise and is led to expect profits solely from the efforts of the promoter or a third party, it being immaterial whether the shares in the enterprise are evidenced by formal certificates or by nominal interests in the physical assets employed in the enterprise. Such a definition necessarily underlies this Court's decision in *S. E. C. v. Joiner Corp.*, and has been enunciated and applied many times by lower federal courts. It permits the fulfillment of the statutory purpose of compelling full and fair disclosure relative to the issuance of "the many types of instruments that in our commercial world fall within the ordinary concept of a security." It embodies a flexible rather than a static principle, one that is capable of adaptation to meet the countless and variable schemes devised by those who seek the use of the money of others on the promise of profits.

The transactions in this case clearly involve investment contracts as so defined. The respondent companies are offering something more than fee simple interests in land, something different from a farm or orchard coupled with management services. They are offering an opportunity to contribute money and to share in the profits of a large citrus fruit enterprise managed and partly owned by respondents. They are offering this opportunity to persons who reside in distant localities and who lack the equipment and experience requisite to the cultivation, harvesting and marketing of the citrus products. Such persons have no desire to occupy the land or to develop it themselves; they are attracted solely by the prospects of a return on their investment. Indeed, individual development of the plots of land that are offered and sold would seldom be economically feasible due to their small size. Such tracts gain utility as citrus groves only when cultivated and developed as component parts of a larger area. A common enterprise managed by respondents or third parties with adequate personnel and equipment is therefore essential if the investors are to achieve their paramount aim of a return on their investments. Their respective shares in this enterprise are evidenced by land sales contracts and warranty deeds, which serve as a convenient method of determining the investors' allocable shares of the profits. The resulting transfer of rights in land is purely incidental.

* * * *

This conclusion is unaffected by the fact that some purchasers choose not to accept the full offer of an investment contract by declining to enter into a service contract with the respondents. The Securities Act prohibits the offer as well as the sale of unregistered, non-exempt securities. Hence it is enough that the respondents merely offer the essential ingredients of an investment contract.

We reject the suggestion of the Circuit Court of Appeals, that an investment contract is necessarily missing where the enterprise is not speculative or promotional in character and where the tangible interest which is sold has intrinsic value independent of the success of the enterprise as a whole. *The test is whether the scheme involves an investment of money in a common enterprise with profits to come solely from the efforts of others.* [Emphasis added.] If that test be satisfied, it is immaterial whether the enterprise is speculative or non-speculative or whether there is a sale of property with or without intrinsic value. The statutory policy of affording broad protection to investors is not to be thwarted by unrealistic and irrelevant formulae.

DECISION AND REMEDY *The Supreme Court reversed the decision of the circuit court of appeals and found that the investment contract was, in fact, a security. Howey was required to file a registration statement.*

Requirements of the Registration Statement

Section 5 of the act broadly provides that if a security does not qualify for an exemption, that security must be *registered* before it is offered to the public through the use of either the mails or any facility of interstate commerce, including securities exchanges. Issuing corporations must file a *registration statement* with the SEC. Investors must be provided with a *prospectus* that describes the security being sold, the issuing corporation, and the investment or risk attaching to the security. In principle, the registration statement and the prospectus supply sufficient information to enable unsophisticated investors to evaluate the financial risk involved.

CONTENTS OF THE REGISTRATION STATEMENT The registration statement must contain detailed information about the securities offering and the offeror, including the following:

1. A description of the significant provisions of the security offered for sale, including the relationship between that security and the other capital securities of the registrant. Also, the corpo-

ration must disclose how it intends to use the proceeds of the sale.

2. A description of the registrant's properties and business.

3. A description of the management of the registrant and its security holdings, remuneration, and other benefits, including pensions and stock options. Any interests of directors or officers in any material transactions with the corporation must be disclosed.

4. A financial statement certified by an independent public accounting firm.

5. A description of material pending lawsuits.

WHAT THE REGISTERING CORPORATION CAN DO BEFORE, DURING, AND AFTER REGISTRATION Before filing the registration statement and the prospectus with the SEC, the corporation is allowed to obtain an *underwriter* who will monitor the distribution of the new issue. There is a twenty-day waiting period after registration before the sale can take place. During this period, oral offers between interested investors and the issuing corporation concerning the purchase and sale of the proposed securities may take place; very limited written advertising is allowed. At this time, the so-called *red herring* prospectus may be distributed. It gets its name from the red legend printed across it stating that the registration has been filed but has not become effective.

After the waiting period, the registered securities can be legally bought and sold. Written advertising is allowed in the form of a so-called *tombstone ad,* so named because the format resembles a tombstone. Such ads simply tell the investor where and how to obtain a prospectus. Normally, any other type of advertising is prohibited.

Exemptions

A corporation can avoid the high cost and complicated procedures associated with registration by taking advantage of certain exemptions. SEC regulations provide that the following offerings are exempt:

1.   Private, noninvestment company offerings up to $500,000 in any one year are exempt if no general solicitation or advertising is used, the SEC is notified of the sales, and precaution is taken against nonexempt, unregistered resales.[4] The limits on advertising and unregistered resales do not apply if the offering is made solely in states that provide for registration and disclosure and the securities are sold in compliance with those provisions.[5]

2.   Noninvestment company offerings up to $5 million in any twelve-month period are exempt, regardless of the number of **accredited investors** (banks, insurance companies, investment companies, the issuer's executive officers and directors, and persons whose income or net worth exceeds certain limits), so long as there are no more than thirty-five unaccredited investors, no general solicitation or advertising is used, the SEC is notified of the sales, and precaution is taken against nonexempt, unregistered resales. If the sale involves *any* unaccredited investors, *all* investors must be given material information about the offering

company, its business, and the securities before the sale. The issuer is not required to believe that each unaccredited investor "has such knowledge and experience in financial and business matters that he is capable of evaluating the merits and the risks of the prospective investment." [6]

3.   Private offerings in unlimited amounts that are not generally solicited or advertised are exempt if the SEC is notified of the sales, precaution is taken against nonexempt, unregistered resales, and the issuer believes that each unaccredited investor has sufficient knowledge or experience in financial matters to be capable of evaluating the investment's merits and risks. There may be no more than thirty-five unaccredited investors, although there may be an unlimited number of accredited investors. If there are *any* unaccredited investors, the issuer must provide to *all* purchasers material information about itself, its business, and the securities before the sale.[7]

This last exemption is perhaps most important to those that want to raise funds through the sale of securities without registering them. It is often referred to as the *private placement* exemption, because it exempts "transactions not involving any public offering." [8] This provision applies to private offerings to a limited number of persons who are sufficiently sophisticated and in a sufficiently strong bargaining position so as to be able to assume the risk of the investment (and who thus have no need for federal registration protection) and to private offerings to similarly situated institutional investors.

Also exempt are intrastate transactions involving purely local offerings.[9] This exemption applies to offerings restricted to residents of the state in which the issuing company is organized and doing business. The exemption requires that 80 percent of the issuer's assets be located in the state of issue, 80 percent of the issuer's gross revenue be from business conducted within the state, and 80 percent of the net income from the sale of the issue be used in the state. Also, for nine months after the last sale, no resale may be made to a nonres-

---

4. Precautions to be taken against nonexempt, unregistered resales include: asking the investor whether he or she is buying the securities for others; before the sale, disclosing to each purchaser in writing that the securities are unregistered and thus cannot be resold, except in an exempt transaction, without first being registered; and indicating on the certificate that the securities are unregistered and restricted.

5. SEC Regulation D, 17 C.F.R. Section 230.504.

---

6. SEC Regulation D, 17 C.F.R. Section 230.505.

7. SEC Regulation D, 17 C.F.R. Section 230.506.

8. 15 U.S.C. Section 77d(2).

9. 15 U.S.C. Section 77c(a)(11).

ident, and precautions must be taken against this possibility. (Precautions include obtaining a statement of residence in writing from each investor, as well as indicating on the securities certificates that they are unregistered and subject to resale only to state residents.) These offerings remain subject to applicable laws in the state of issue.

Among securities exempt from the registration requirement in consideration of the "small amount involved," [10] other than those mentioned above, is an issuer's offer of up to $1.5 million in securities in any twelve-month period. Under the SEC's Regulation A,[11] the issuer must file with the SEC notice of the issue and an offering circular, which must also be provided to investors before the sale;

but this is a much simpler and less expensive process than the procedures associated with registration.

Also, an offer made *solely* to accredited investors is exempt if its amount is not more than $5 million. Any number of accredited investors may participate, but no unaccredited investors may do so. No general solicitation or advertising may be used, the SEC must be notified of all sales, and precaution must be taken against nonexempt, unregistered resales (because these are restricted securities and may be resold only by registration or in an exempt transaction).[12]

These exemptions under the Securities Act of 1933 and SEC regulations are summarized in the following *Concept Summary*.

---

10. 15 U.S.C. Section 77c(b).

11. 17 C.F.R. Sections 230.251–230.264.

12. 15 U.S.C. Section 77d(6).

CONCEPT SUMMARY: Exemptions Under the 1933 Act for Securities Offerings by Businesses

TYPE OF OFFERING	REQUIRED CONDITIONS
Private, noninvestment company offerings up to $500,000 in any 12-month period	1. No general solicitation or advertising (unless state provides for registration and disclosure). 2. SEC is notified of sales. 3. Precaution is taken against nonexempt, unregistered resales.
Noninvestment company offerings up to $5 million in any 12-month period	1. Unlimited number of accredited investors. 2. No more than 35 unaccredited investors. 3. If *any* unaccredited investors, material information about offering firm must be disclosed. 4. No general solicitation or advertising. 5. SEC is notified of sales. 6. Precaution is taken against nonexempt, unregistered resales.
Private placement (private offerings in unlimited amounts that are generally not solicited or advertised)	1. Unlimited number of accredited investors. 2. No more than 35 unaccredited investors. 3. If *any* unaccredited investors, (a) material information about offering firm must be disclosed, and (b) issuer must reasonably believe that each unaccredited investor is experienced in financial matters and capable of evaluating risks involved in investment. 4. SEC is notified of sales. 5. Precaution is taken against nonexempt, unregistered resales.
Intrastate transactions (offerings restricted to residents of the state in which issuing company is organized and doing business)	1. 80 percent of issuer's assets are located in the state of issue. 2. 80 percent of issuer's gross revenue is from business conducted within the state. 3. 80 percent of net income from the sale of the issue is used in the state. 4. No resale is made to a nonresident for 9 months after last sale, and precautions are taken to prevent such resale.

CONCEPT SUMMARY: Exemptions Under the 1933 Act for Securities Offerings by Businesses (Continued)	
TYPE OF OFFERING	**REQUIRED CONDITIONS**
Offerings up to $1.5 million in any 12-month period (under SEC Regulation A)	1. Notice of the issue and an offering circular are filed with SEC and provided to investors.
Offerings up to $5 million in any 12-month period	1. Unlimited number of accredited investors. 2. No unaccredited investors. 3. No general solicitation or advertising. 4. SEC is notified of sales. 5. Precaution is taken against nonexempt, unregistered resales.

Additional Exempt Securities

Other exempt securities are:[13]

1. All bank securities sold prior to July 27, 1933.

2. Commercial paper if the maturity date does not exceed nine months.

3. Securities of charitable organizations.

4. Securities resulting from a corporate reorganization issued for exchange with the issuer's existing security holders and certificates issued by trustees, receivers, or debtors in possession under the Bankruptcy Act (bankruptcy is discussed in Chapter 31).

5. Securities issued exclusively for exchange with the issuer's existing security holders, provided no commission is paid (for example, stock dividends and stock splits).

6. Securities issued to finance the acquisition of railroad equipment.

7. Any insurance, endowment, or annuity contract issued by state-regulated insurance company.

8. Government-issued securities.

9. Securities issued by banks, savings and loan associations, farmers' cooperatives, and similar institutions subject to supervision by governmental authorities.

Registration violations of the 1933 act are not treated lightly. In the following case, the BarChris Construction Corporation was sued by the purchasers of the corporation's debentures under Section 11 of the Securities Act of 1933. Section 11 imposes liability when a registration statement or a prospectus contains material false statements or material omissions.

---

13. 15 U.S.C. Section 77c.

BACKGROUND AND FACTS *This lawsuit was brought by purchasers of BarChris debenture bonds under Section 11 of the Securities Act of 1933. The plaintiffs alleged that the registration statement filed with the Securities and Exchange Commission, which became effective on May 16, 1961, contained material false statements and material omissions.*

The defendants fell into three categories: (1) the persons who signed the registration statement, (2) the underwriters (consisting of eight investment banking firms), and (3) BarChris's auditors—Peat, Marwick, Mitchell & Co. Included in the group of defendants who signed the registration statement were: (1) BarChris's nine directors, (2) BarChris's controller, (3) one of BarChris's attorneys, (4) two investment bankers who were later named as directors of the BarChris Corporation, and (5) numerous other persons participating in the preparation of the registration statement.

Case 43.2
ESCOTT v. BARCHRIS CONSTR. CORP.

United States District Court for the Southern District of New York, 1968.
283 F.Supp. 643.

BarChris grew out of a business that was started in 1946 to build bowling alleys. The introduction of automatic pin-setting machines in 1952 sparked rapid growth in the bowling industry. BarChris benefited from this increased interest in bowling, and its construction operations expanded rapidly. It was estimated that in 1960 BarChris installed approximately 3 percent of all bowling lanes built in the United States. BarChris's sales increased dramatically between 1956 and 1960, and the company was recognized as a significant factor in the bowling construction industry.

BarChris was in constant need of cash to finance its operations, a need that grew more and more pressing as operations expanded. In 1959, BarChris sold over a half-million shares of its common stock to the public. By early 1961, it needed additional working capital, and this time it decided to sell debentures.

BarChris filed a registration statement of the debentures with the SEC and received the proceeds of the financing. Nevertheless, it experienced increasing financial difficulties, which in time became insurmountable. By early 1962, it was painfully apparent that BarChris was beginning to fail. In October of that year, BarChris filed a petition for an arrangement under the Bankruptcy Act, and it defaulted on the interest due in November on the debentures.

The plaintiffs challenged the accuracy of the registration statement and charged that the text of the prospectus—including many of the figures—was false and that material information had been omitted.

The federal district court reviewed all of the figures and statements included in the prospectus.

McLEAN, District Judge.

*   *   *   *

The action is brought under Section 11 of the Securities Act of 1933. *   *   *

*   *   *   *

On the main issue of liability, the questions to be decided are (1) did the registration statement contain false statements of fact, or did it omit to state facts which should have been stated in order to prevent it from being misleading; (2) if so, were the facts which were falsely stated or omitted "material" within the meaning of the Act.

*   *   *   *

It is a prerequisite to liability under Section 11 of the Act that the fact which is falsely stated in a registration statement, or the fact that it is omitted when it should have been stated to avoid misleading, be "material." The regulations of the Securities and Exchange Commission pertaining to the registration of securities define the word as follows:

"The term 'material', when used to qualify a requirement for the furnishing of information as to any subject, limits the information required to those matters as to which an average prudent investor ought reasonably to be informed before purchasing the security registered."

What are "matters as to which an average prudent investor ought reasonably to be informed"? It seems obvious that they are matters which such an investor needs to know before he can make an intelligent, informed decision whether or not to buy the security.

Early in the history of the Act, a definition of materiality was given in *Matter of Charles A. Howard*, which is still valid today. A material fact was there defined as: "a fact which if it had been correctly stated or disclosed would have deterred or tended to deter the average prudent investor from purchasing the securities in question."

The average prudent investor is not concerned with minor inaccuracies or with errors as to matters which are of no interest to him. The facts which tend to deter him from purchasing a security are facts which have an important bearing upon the nature or condition of the issuing corporation or its business.

Judged by this test, there is no doubt that many of the misstatements and omissions in this prospectus were material. This is true of all of them which relate to the state of affairs in 1961, i.e., the overstatement of sales and gross profit for the first quarter, the understatement of contingent liabilities as of April 30, the overstatement of orders on hand and the failure to disclose the true facts with respect to officers' loans, customers' delinquencies, application of proceeds and the prospective operation of several alleys.

BarChris Corporation itself and all the signers of the registration statement for the debentures, the underwriters, and the corporation's auditors were held liable.

DECISION AND REMEDY

THE SECURITIES EXCHANGE ACT OF 1934

The Securities Exchange Act of 1934 provides for the regulation and registration of securities exchanges, brokers, dealers, and national securities associations (such as the National Association of Securities Dealers, NASD). It regulates the markets in which securities are traded by maintaining a continuous disclosure system for all corporations with securities on the securities exchanges and for those companies that have assets in excess of $5 million and five hundred or more shareholders. These corporations are referred to as Section 12 companies, since they are required to register their securities under Section 12 of the 1934 act. The act regulates proxy solicitation for voting, and it allows the SEC to engage in market surveillance to regulate undesirable market practices such as fraud, market manipulation, misrepresentation, and stabilization (*Stabilization* is a market-manipulating technique whereby securities underwriters bid for securities to stabilize their price during their issuance.)

Insider Trading— Section 10(b) and SEC Rule 10b-5

One of the most important parts of the 1934 act relates to so-called *insider trading*. Because of their positions, corporate directors and officers often obtain advance inside information that can affect the future market value of the corporate stock. Obviously, their positions can give them a trading advantage over the general public and shareholders. The 1934 Securities Exchange Act extends liability to officers and directors in their personal transactions for taking advantage of such information when they know it is unavailable to the person with whom they are dealing.

Section 10(b) of the 1934 act and SEC Rule 10b-5 cover not only corporate officers, directors, and majority shareholders but also certain "outside" persons having access to receiving information of a nonpublic nature on which trading is based. Those persons to whom the material information is transmitted are known as *tippees*. A tipee is liable only if he or she knowingly received inside information from a person who knowingly violated a fiduciary duty by disclosure of the information.

Some of the most famous (or infamous) instances of insider trading occurred in the 1980s, when Ivan Boesky, Dennis Levine, and other lawyers and investment bankers traded securities on the basis of inside information concerning some of the decade's largest takeover bids.

Disclosure under SEC Rule 10b-5

Any material omission or misrepresentation of material facts in connection with the purchase or sale of a security may violate Section 10(b) and Rule 10b-5. The key to liability (which can be civil or criminal) under this rule is whether the insider's information is "material."

Following are some examples of material facts calling for a disclosure under the rule:

1. A new ore discovery.
2. Fraudulent trading in the company stock by a broker-dealer.
3. A dividend change (whether up or down).
4. A contract for the sale of corporate assets.
5. A new discovery (process or product).
6. A significant change in the firm's financial condition.

WHEN MUST DISCLOSURE UNDER RULE 10b-5 BE MADE? Courts have struggled with the problem of when information becomes public knowledge. Clearly, when inside information becomes public knowledge, all insiders should be allowed to trade without disclosure. The courts have suggested that insiders should refrain from trading for a "reasonable waiting period" when the news is not readily translatable into investment action. Presumably, this gives the news time to filter down and to be evaluated by the investing public. What constitutes a reasonable waiting period is not at all clear, however.

The following is one of the landmark cases interpreting Rule 10b-5. The SEC sued Texas Gulf Sulphur for issuing a misleading press release. The release underestimated the magnitude and the value of a mineral discovery. The SEC also sued several of Texas Gulf Sulphur's directors, officers, and employees under Rule 10b-5 after these persons had purchased large amounts of the corporate stock prior to the announcement of the corporation's rich ore discovery.

Case 43.3
SECURITIES AND EXCHANGE COMM. v. TEXAS GULF SULPHUR CO.
United States Court of Appeals, Second Circuit, 1968.
401 F.2d 833.

BACKGROUND AND FACTS *Texas Gulf Sulphur Co. (TGS) drilled a hole on November 12, 1963, near Timmins, Ontario, that appeared to yield a core with exceedingly high mineral content. Since TGS did not own the mineral rights in the surrounding regions, it maintained secrecy about the results of the core samples. Evasive tactics were undertaken to camouflage the drill site, and a second hole was drilled. TGS completed an extensive land acquisition program and then began drilling this lucrative site. Rumors began to spread, and by early April 1964, a "tremendous staking rush [was] going on."*

On April 11, 1964, an unauthorized report of the extraordinary mineral find hit the papers. On April 12, TGS issued a press release that played down the discovery and stated that it was too early to tell whether the ore finding would be significant. Later, TGS announced to the press a strike of at least 25 million tons of ore. Charles Fogarty, executive vice-president of TGS, had already purchased 1,700 shares of stock during the month of November 1963 and an additional 300 shares in December. In March 1964, he bought 400 shares, and in April he bought 300 shares. Other TGS officials also purchased stock. They accepted stock options[a] on February 20, 1964.

The Securities and Exchange Commission filed suit against TGS and several of its officers, directors, and employees to enjoin (prevent) TGS's continued violation of the Securities Exchange Act of 1934 and to compel the individual defendants to rescind the securities transactions they had made. The complaint alleged that, on the basis of material inside information concerning the results of TGS's drilling, the defendants either personally or through agents purchased TGS stock, while the information concerning the drill site remained undisclosed to the investing public. The SEC further charged that certain of the defendants (tippers) had divulged information to certain others (tippees) for their use in purchasing TGS stock before the information was disclosed to the public or to other sellers. In addition, certain defendants had accepted options to purchase TGS stock without disclosing material information about the progress of the drilling to either the stock option committee or the TGS board of directors. Finally, the complaint charged that TGS issued a deceptive press release on April 12, 1964. (The deceptive press release should be the focus in a reading of the following case.)

The trial court judge held that the issuance of the press release was lawful because it was not issued for the purpose of benefiting the corporation, and there was no evidence that any insider had used the information in the press release to personal advantage. Thus it was not "misleading or deceptive on the basis of the facts then known." The trial court went on to find that most of the defendants had not violated Rule 10b-5, and the SEC appealed.

WATERMAN, Circuit Judge.
*   *   *   *

I. THE INDIVIDUAL DEFENDANTS
*   *   *   *

In each case, *   *   * whether facts are material within Rule 10b-5 when the facts relate to a particular event and are undisclosed by those persons who are knowledgeable thereof will depend at any given time upon a balancing of both the indicated probability that the event will occur and the anticipated magnitude of the event in light of the totality of the company activity. Here, *   *   * knowledge of the possibility, which surely was more than marginal, of the existence of a mine of the vast magnitude indicated by the remarkably rich drill core located rather close to the surface (suggesting mineability by the less expensive openpit method) within the confines of a large anomaly (suggesting an extensive region of mineralization) might well have affected the price of TGS stock and would certainly have been an important fact to a reasonable, if speculative, investor in deciding whether he should buy, sell, or hold. After all, this first drill core was "unusually good and *   *   * excited the interest and speculation of those who knew about it."
*   *   *   *

Finally, a major factor in determining whether the *   *   * discovery was a material fact is the importance attached to the drilling results by those who knew about it. In view of other unrelated recent developments favorably affecting TGS, participation by an informed person in a regular stock-purchase program, or even sporadic trading by an informed person, might lend only nominal support to the inference of the materiality of the *   *   * discovery; nevertheless, the timing by those who knew of it of their stock purchases and their purchases of *short-term* calls[b]—purchases in some cases by individuals who had never before purchased calls or even TGS stock—virtually compels the inference that the insiders were influenced by the drilling results.
*   *   *   *

We hold, therefore, that all transactions in TGS stock or calls by individuals apprised of the drilling results *   *   * were made in violation of Rule 10b-5. Inasmuch as the visual evaluation of that drill core (a generally reliable estimate though less accurate then a chemical assay) constituted material information, those advised of the results of the visual evaluation as well as those informed of the chemical assay traded in violation of law.

II. THE CORPORATE DEFENDANT

*   *   *   *

At 3:00 P.M. on April 12, 1964, evidently believing it desirable to comment upon the rumors concerning the Timmins project, TGS issued the press release. *   *   * It read in pertinent part as follows:
*   *   *   *

> Recent drilling on one property near Timmins has led to preliminary indications that more drilling would be required for proper evaluation of this prospect. The drilling done to date has not been conclusive, but the statements made by many outside quarters are unreliable and include information and figures that are not available to TGS.
>
> The work done to date has not been sufficient to reach definite conclusions and any statement as to size and grade of ore would be premature and possibly misleading. When we have progressed to the point where reasonable and logical conclusions can be made, TGS will issue a definite statement to its stockholders and to the public in order to clarify the Timmins project.

*   *   *   *

It does not appear to be unfair to impose upon corporate management a duty to ascertain the truth of any statements the corporation releases to its shareholders or to the investing public at large. Accordingly, we hold that Rule 10b-5 is violated whenever assertions are made, as here, in a manner reasonably calculated to influence the investing public, e.g., by means of the financial media, if such assertions are false or misleading or are so incomplete as to mislead irrespective of whether the issuance of the release was motivated by corporate officials for ulterior purposes. It seems clear, however, that if corporate management demonstrates that it was diligent in ascertaining that the information it published was the whole truth and that such diligently obtained information was disseminated in good faith, Rule 10b-5 would not have been violated.

*   *   *   *

We conclude, then, that, having established that the release was issued in a manner reasonably calculated to affect the market price of TGS stock and to influence the investing public, we must remand to the district court to decide whether the release was misleading to the reasonable investor and if found to be misleading, whether the court in its discretion should issue the injunction the SEC seeks.

DECISION AND REMEDY   *The appellate court's judgment was favorable to the SEC. The information contained in the press release was material, and the transaction in stock by the insiders who knew of it had violated Rule 10b-5. Thus, the options of the individual defendants were rescinded. The questions of whether the press release was misleading and what remedies should be imposed, however, were remanded to the trial court for decision. A trial court is bound to apply the law as enunciated by the court of appeals in making this type of decision.*

COMMENTS   *Texas Gulf Sulphur Company was not only sued by the SEC. Additionally, numerous civil actions for damages were brought against it by plaintiff-investors who had sold their TGS stock as a result of the deceptively gloomy press release regarding the corporation's mineral exploration. All these suits were settled in 1972.[c] In a federal lawsuit filed against TGS some two years after the initial case, a court of appeals held that investors who had sold stock in reliance upon the representations in the press release could recover damages from the corporation and the officers who drafted the release. The court went on to state that the proper measure of damages was the difference between the selling price and the price at which the investors could have reinvested within a reasonable period of time after they became aware of TGS's curative press release announcing the 25-million-ton strike.*

The court held that a diligent and reasonable investor would have become informed of the curative press release within four days of its issue, and investors who sold their stock more than four days after the second press release was issued could not recover under the Securities Exchange Act on the basis of reliance on the earlier, deceptive release.

a. A *stock option* is a contract that gives the holder the right to purchase a set number of shares of stock at a fixed price upon demand. Stock options are often used by corporations as bonuses to employees.
[b. A *call* is an option to buy a certain amount of stock at a fixed price within a certain time.]
c. Cannon v. Texas Gulf Sulphur, 55 F.R.D. 308 (S.D.N.Y. 1972).

WHEN DOES RULE 10b-5 APPLY?   Rule 10b-5 applies in virtually all cases concerning the trading of securities, whether on organized exchanges, in over-the-counter markets, or in private transactions. The rule covers notes, bonds, certificates of interest and participation in any profit-sharing agreement, agreements to form a corporation, and

joint venture agreements; in short, it covers just about any form of security. It is immaterial whether a firm has securities registered under the 1933 act for the 1934 act to apply.

Rule 10b-5 is applicable only when the requisites of federal jurisdiction, such as the use of the mails, of stock exchange facilities, or of any instrumentality of interstate commerce, are present. Rarely can a commercial transaction be completed without such contact. In addition, the states have corporate securities laws, many of which include provisions similar to Rule 10b-5.

In *Chiarella* v. *United States*,[14] the Supreme Court considered the role Rule 10b-5 plays when there is no use of interstate commerce, the mails, or any of the facilities of any national securities exchange. Chiarella was a printer who worked at a New York composing room and handled announcements of corporate takeover bids. Even though the documents that were delivered to the printer concealed the identity of the target corporations by blank spaces and false names, Chiarella was able to deduce the names of the target companies. Without disclosing his knowledge, he purchased stock in the target companies and sold the shares immediately after the takeover attempts were made public. He realized a gain of slightly more than $30,000 in the course of fourteen months.

In 1978, Chiarella was indicted on seventeen counts of violating Section 10(b) of the Securities Exchange Act of 1934 and SEC Rule 10b-5. The trial court convicted him on all counts, and the court of appeals affirmed that conviction. The Supreme Court, however, reversed. The Court held that Chiarella could not be convicted for his failure to disclose his knowledge to stockholders or to target companies since he was under no duty to disclose his knowledge. Chiarella was under no duty to disclose because he had no prior dealing with the stockholders and was not their agent, nor was he a person in whom sellers had placed their trust and confidence. Thus, an "outsider" such as Chiarella who comes into possession of nonpublic market information does not violate Rule 10b-5 if he or she fails to disclose this information. A duty to disclose does not arise from mere possession of nonpublic market information.

In the following case, the Supreme Court examined the liability of a person who had received material nonpublic information from "insiders" of a corporation with which he had no connection.

---

14. 445 U.S. 222, 100 S.Ct. 1108, 63 L.Ed.2d 348 (1980).

BACKGROUND AND FACTS   *Dirks was an officer of a New York broker-dealer firm who specialized in providing investment analysis of insurance company securities to institutional investors. On March 6, 1973, Dirks received information from Ronald Secrist, a former officer of Equity Funding of America. Secrist alleged that the assets of Equity Funding were vastly overstated as a result of fraudulent corporate practices, and he urged Dirks to verify the fraud and disclose it publicly. Dirks decided to investigate the allegations, and through his investigation he openly discussed the information he had obtained with a number of clients and investors. The Securities and Exchange Commission (SEC) subsequently filed a complaint against Equity Funding and also found that Dirks had aided and abetted violations of Section 17(a) of the Securities Act of 1933, Section 10(b) of the Securities Exchange Act of 1934, and SEC Rule 10b-5 by repeating the allegations of fraud to members of the investment community, who later sold their Equity Funding stock. Dirks sought review in the court of appeals, which entered a judgment against him. The United States Supreme Court granted certiorari.*

Case 43.4
DIRKS v. SECURITIES AND EXCHANGE COMMISSION
Supreme Court of the United States, 1983.
463 U.S. 646, 103 S.Ct. 3255, 77 L.Ed.2d 911 (1983).

POWELL, Justice.
*   *   *   *

In the seminal [influential] case of *In re Cady, Roberts & Co.*   *   *   * the SEC recognized that the common law in some jurisdictions imposes on "corporate 'insiders,' particularly officers, directors, or controlling stockholders" an "affirmative duty to disclosure . . . when dealing in securities."   *   *   * The SEC found that not only did breach of this common-law duty also establish the elements of a Rule 10b-5 violation, but that individuals other than corporate insiders could be obligated either to disclose material nonpublic information before trading or to abstain from trading altogether.
*   *   *

*   *   *   *

We were explicit in *Chiarella* in saying that there can be no duty to disclose where the person who has traded on inside information "was not [the corporation's] agent, . . . was not a fiduciary, [or] was not a person in whom the sellers [of the securities] had placed their trust and confidence." *   *   *

The SEC's position, as stated in its opinion in this case, is that a tippee "inherits" the *Cady, Roberts* obligation to shareholders whenever he receives inside information from an insider. *   *   *
*   *   *   *

In effect, the SEC's theory of tippee liability in both cases appears rooted in the idea that the antifraud provisions require equal information among all traders. This conflicts with the principle set forth in *Chiarella* that only some persons, under some circumstances, will be barred from trading while in possession of material nonpublic information. *   *   *

Imposing a duty to disclose or abstain solely because a person knowingly receives material nonpublic information from an insider and trades on it could have an inhibiting influence on the role of market analysts, which the SEC itself recognizes is necessary to the preservation of a healthy market. *   *   * It is in the nature of this type of information, and indeed of the markets themselves, that such information cannot be made simultaneously available to all of the corporation's stockholders or the public generally.

The conclusion that recipients of inside information do not invariably acquire a duty to disclose or abstain does not mean that such tippees always are free to trade on the information. The need for a ban on some tippee trading is clear. Not only are insiders forbidden by their fiduciary relationship from personally using undisclosed corporate information to their advantage, but they may not give such information to an outsider for the same improper purpose of exploiting the information for their personal gain. *   *   *
*   *   *   *

In determining whether a tippee is under an obligation to disclose or abstain, it thus is necessary to determine whether the insider's "tip" constituted a breach of the insider's fiduciary duty. All disclosures of confidential corporate information are not inconsistent with the duty insiders owe to shareholders. *   *   * Thus, the test is whether the insider personally will benefit, directly or indirectly, from his disclosure. Absent some personal gain, there has been no breach of duty to stockholders. And absent a breach by the insider, there is no derivative breach. *   *   *
*   *   *   *

Under the inside-trading and tipping rules set forth above, we find that there was no actionable violation by Dirks. It is undisputed that Dirks himself was a stranger to Equity Funding, with no pre-existing fiduciary duty to its shareholders. He took no action, directly or indirectly, that induced the shareholders or officers of Equity Funding to repose trust or confidence in him. There was no expectation by Dirks' sources that he would keep their information in confidence. Nor did Dirks misappropriate or illegally obtain the information about Equity Funding. Unless the insiders breached their *Cady, Roberts* duty to shareholders in disclosing the nonpublic information to Dirks, he breached no duty when he passed it on to investors as well as to the *Wall Street Journal*.

DECISION AND REMEDY   *The judgment of the court of appeals was reversed. Dirks, under the circumstances of this case, had no duty to refrain from use of the inside information that he had acquired.*

COMMENTS   *There was no breach of duty to the stockholders of Equity Funding, since neither Secrist nor the other employees of Equity Funding benefited directly or indirectly by their disclosure, under the test established by the Supreme Court in this case. Thus, in the absence of a breach of duty to the shareholders by the insiders, there could be no derivative breach by Dirks.*

Insider Reporting and Trading—Section 16(b)

Officers, directors, and certain large stockholders[15] of Section 12 corporations are required to file reports with the SEC concerning their ownership and trading of the corporation's securities.[16] In order to discourage such insiders from using nonpublic information about their company to their personal benefit in the stock market, Section 16(b) of the 1934 act provides for the recapture by the corporation of all profits realized by the insider on any purchase and sale or sale and purchase of the corporation's stock within any six-month period.[17] It is irrelevant whether the insider actually used inside information; all such "short-swing" profits must be returned to the corporation.

Section 16(b) applies not only to stock but to warrants, options, and securities convertible into stock. In addition, the courts have fashioned complex rules for determining profits. Corporate insiders are wise to seek competent counsel prior to trading in the corporation's stock. Exhibit 43–1 compares the effects of Rule 10b-5 and Section 16(b).

The Insider Trading Sanctions Act of 1984

The Insider Trading Sanctions Act of 1984[18] permits the SEC to bring suit in a federal district court against anyone violating or aiding in a violation of the 1934 act or SEC rules by purchasing or selling a security while in the possession of material nonpublic information. The violation must occur on or through the facilities of a national securities exchange or from or through a broker

---

15. Those stockholders owning 10 percent of the class of equity securities registered under Section 12 of the 1934 act (15 U.S.C. Section 78*l*).

16. 15 U.S.C. Section 78*l*.

17. 15 U.S.C. Section 78p(b). In a declining stock market, one can realize profits by selling at a high price and repurchasing later at a lower price.

18. 15 U.S.C. Section 78u(d)(2)(A).

Exhibit 43–1 Comparison of Coverage, Application, and Liabilities under Rule 10b-5 and Section 16(b)

	RULE 10b-5	SECTION 16(b)
1. What is subject matter of transaction?	Any security (does not have to be registered).	Any security (does not have to be registered).
2. What transactions are covered?	Purchase or sale.	Short-swing purchase and sale or short-swing sale and purchase.
3. Who is subject to liability?	Virtually anyone with inside information—including officers, directors, controlling stockholders, and tippees.	Officers, directors, and certain 10 percent stockholders.
4. Is omission, scheme, or misrepresentation necessary for liability?	Yes.	No.
5. Are any transactions exempt?	No.	Yes, there are a variety of exemptions.
6. Is direct dealing with the party necessary?	No.	No.
7. Who can bring an action?	A person transacting with an insider, or the SEC, or a purchaser or a seller damaged by a wrongful act.	Corporation and shareholder by derivative action.

or dealer. Transactions pursuant to a public offering by an issuer of securities are excepted.

The court may assess as a penalty as much as triple the profits gained or the loss avoided by the guilty party. For purposes of the act, profit or loss is defined as "the difference between the purchase or sale price of the security and the value of that security as measured by the trading price of the security at a reasonable period of time after public dissemination of the nonpublic information." [19]

The act also increased the criminal penalty from $10,000 to $100,000.[20] This act does not, however, have any effect on other actions the SEC may take nor on actions private investors may bring.

Proxy Statements

Section 14(a) of the Securities Exchange Act of 1934 regulates the solicitation of proxies from shareholders of Section 12 companies.[21] The SEC regulates the content of proxy statements sent to shareholders by corporate managers who are requesting authority to vote on behalf of the shareholders in a particular election on specified issues. Whoever solicits a proxy must fully and accurately disclose all facts that are pertinent to the matter to be voted on. SEC Rule 14a-9 is similar to the antifraud provisions of Rule 10b-5. Remedies for violation are extensive, ranging from injunctions to preventing a vote from being taken, to monetary damages.

REGULATION OF INVESTMENT COMPANIES

Investment companies, and mutual funds in particular, grew rapidly in World War II. Such companies were at that time regulated by the Investment Company Act of 1940.[22] This act provides for SEC regulation of investment company activities. It was expanded by the Investment Company Act Amendments of 1970. Further minor changes were made in the Securities Act Amendments of 1975.

19. 15 U.S.C. Section 78u(d)(2)(C).
20. 15 U.S.C. Section 78ff(a).
21. 15 U.S.C. Section 78n(a).
22. 15 U.S.C. Sections 80a-1 to 80a-64.

The 1940 Act Coverage

The 1940 act requires that every investment company register with the SEC and imposes restrictions on the activities of such companies and persons connected with them. For the purposes of the act, an investment company is defined as an entity that (a) "is * * * engaged primarily * * * in the business of investing, reinvesting, or trading in securities" or (b) is engaged in such business and has more than 40 percent of its assets in investment securities. Excluded from coverage are banks, insurance companies, savings and loan associations, finance companies, oil and gas drilling firms, charitable foundations, tax-exempt pension funds, and other special types of institutions, such as closely held corporations.

Regulation of Mutual Fund Activities

All investment companies must register with the SEC by filing a notification of registration. Each year, registered companies must file reports with the SEC.

In order to safeguard company assets, all securities must be held in the custody of a bank or stock exchange member, and that bank or stock exchange member must follow strict procedures established by the SEC.

No dividends may be paid from any source other than accumulated, undistributed net income. Furthermore, there are restrictions on investment activities. For example, investment companies are not allowed to purchase securities on the margin (pay for only part of the total price, borrowing the rest), sell short (sell shares not yet owned), or participate in joint trading accounts.

The Foreign Corrupt Practices Act

In 1977, the Foreign Corrupt Practices Act (FCPA) was passed as an amendment to the Securities Exchange Act of 1934. Congress had discovered that several hundred American corporations had been giving bribes or other questionable payments, in their transactions abroad, to foreign government officials and others in order to obtain favorable business conditions or contracts. Those companies that made the payments argued that such payments were customary and necessary in many foreign countries. Nevertheless, since 1977 it has been a crime under the FCPA for any American firm to offer, promise, or make payments or gifts of anything of value to foreign officials in exchange for favored treatment. The FCPA also prohibits offers of payments to foreign political parties and to foreign candidates for political office.

Facilitating payments, often known as "grease payments," are currently made throughout the world to numerous lower-level government officials. The FCPA does not prohibit these payments as long as the recipient has no discretion in carrying on a government function. For example, if a payment is made by a firm to a foreign government official simply to speed up an import licensing process, the FCPA has not been violated.

The FCPA provides for companies to be fined up to $1 million for violations of the act. Additionally, directors, officers, employees, or agents who participate in violations can be fined up to $10,000 and be given prison terms of up to five years.

STATE SECURITIES LAWS

Today, all states have their own corporate securities laws that regulate the offer and sale of securities within individual state borders.[23] Often

---

23. These laws are cataloged and annotated in *Blue Sky Law Reporter* (Commerce Clearing House), a loose-leaf service.

referred to as **blue sky laws,** they are designed to prevent "speculative schemes which have no more basis than so many feet of blue sky." Since the adoption of the 1933 and 1934 federal securities acts, the state and federal governments have regulated securities concurrently. Indeed, both federal acts specifically preserve state securities laws.

Certain features are common to all state blue sky laws. They have antifraud provisions, many of which are patterned after Rule 10b-5. Also, most state corporate securities laws regulate securities brokers and dealers. Typically, these laws also provide for the registration or qualification of securities offered or issued for sale within the state. Unless an applicable exemption from registration is found, issuers must register or qualify their stock with the appropriate state official, often called a corporations commissioner.

There is a difference in philosophy among state statutes. Many are like the Securities Act of 1933 and mandate certain disclosures before registration is effective and a permit to sell the securities is issued. Others have fairness standards that a corporation must meet in order to offer or sell stock in the state. The Uniform Securities Act, which has been adopted in part by several states, was drafted to be acceptable to states with differing regulatory philosophies.

 ## QUESTIONS AND CASE PROBLEMS

1. Maresh, an experienced geologist, owned certain oil and gas leases covering land in Nebraska. To raise money for the drilling of a test well, he undertook to sell fractional interests in the leases. He approached Garfield, a man with whom he had done business in the past. Garfield had mentioned that he would be interested in investing in some of Maresh's future oil ventures. Garfield had wide business experience in the stock market and in oil stocks. He felt that the investment in Maresh's gas leases could be lucrative. Based on Garfield's promise to wire the money promptly, Maresh began drilling. Soon after, when Maresh realized that the land was dry, Garfield refused to pay his

share of the investment. Garfield claimed that he could rescind the agreement to invest, since the investment offered by Maresh was a security within the meaning of the Securities Act of 1933 and it had not been registered. Did Maresh offer a security within the meaning of the 1933 act? [Garfield v. Strain, 320 F.2d 116 (10th Cir. 1963)]

2. Zabriskie purchased certain notes from Lewis in connection with a real estate venture that Lewis was trying to establish. The notes bore a maturity date of eight months after the date of purchase. The Securities Act of 1933 excludes from its definition of securities any note that has a maturity date not exceeding nine months at the time of issue. Knowing that the Securities Act is an attempt to control the sales of *investment* securities, can a better test be devised than this strict nine-month rule? [Zabriskie v. Lewis, 507 F.2d 546 (10th Cir. 1974)]

3. Emerson Electric Company owned 13.2 percent of Dodge Manufacturing Company's stock. Within six months of the purchase of this stock, Emerson sold enough shares

to a broker to reduce its holding to 9.96 percent of its former Dodge holdings. One week later (but still less than six months after Emerson's initial purchase), Emerson sold its remaining shares of Dodge stock. The sole purpose of Emerson's initial sale of just over 3 percent of its Dodge stock was to avoid liability under Section 16 of the Securities Exchange Act of 1934, which prohibits short-swing trading. Assuming Emerson made no profit on the initial sale of stock but made substantial profits when it sold the remaining 9.96 percent of Dodge stock, must it disgorge the profits it made on the sale? [Reliance Electric Co. v. Emerson Electric Co., 404 U.S. 418, 92 S.Ct. 596, 30 L.Ed.2d 575 (1972)]

4. Leston Nay owned 90 percent of the stock of First Securities Company. Between the years 1942 and 1966, Hochfelder sent large sums of money to Nay to be invested in escrow accounts of First Securities. The whole investment scheme was a fraud, and Nay converted the money sent by Hochfelder to his own use. Hochfelder sued Ernst & Ernst, First Securities' auditor, for failing to use proper auditing procedures and thus negligently failing to discover the fraudulent scheme. Was Ernst & Ernst found guilty of violating Section 10(b) of the 1934 Securities Exchange Act and Rule 10b-5? [Ernst & Ernst v. Hochfelder, 425 U.S. 185, 96 S.Ct. 1375, 47 L.Ed.2d 668 (1976)]

5. Lakeside Plastics and Engraving Company was a close corporation incorporated in Minnesota. The company suffered losses from the time it was incorporated in 1946. Of its four shareholders, only one was involved in management of the firm. Notwithstanding its earlier difficulties, by 1954 the firm was apparently about to become profitable. Without informing the other shareholders of this fact, the shareholder-manager bought out the remaining shareholders. He accomplished this by making numerous misrepresentations to them. Assuming the shareholder-manager used none of the instrumentalities of interstate commerce, including the mails or the telephone, in making these misrepresentations, could the remaining shareholders bring an action under Section 10(b) of the Securities Exchange Act of 1934? If not, did the remaining shareholders have any legal recourse? [Myzel v. Fields, 386 F.2d 718 (8th Cir. 1967)]

6. American Breeding Herds (ABH) offered a cattle breeding plan under which Ronnett contracted to buy thirty-six Charolais cows at $3,000 per head and a one-quarter interest in a Charolais bull at $5,000, totalling $113,000. The ABH agreement described itself as a "tax shelter program * * * unlike the purchase of securities such as stock and bonds." Ronnett entered into the agreement after receiving investment advice from Shannon, an investment counselor. The cows were tagged and sent to an ABH-approved breeding ranch. Ronnett signed a maintenance agreement and paid a monthly maintenance fee. Was the ABH plan a security, and should it have been registered under the Securities Act of 1933? [Ronnett v. American Breeding Herds, Inc., 124 Ill.App.3d 842, 464 N.E.2d 1201, 80 Ill.Dec. 218 (1984)]

7. Ronald Rodeo's investment group purchased limited partnership interests in certain Illinois apartment buildings and separately, by contract, acquired an option to buy out the remaining interests of the general partners. According to the arrangement, the general partners would operate the apartments, and the limited partners would provide essential capital while retaining their limited liability. Rodeo could not actively intervene in the business without losing his limited liability. He therefore had to rely solely upon the general partners for the enterprise's profitability. Two years later, Rodeo became disenchanted with the operation of the apartment enterprise and sued R. Dean Gillman and the other general partners under the Illinois blue sky act. In his claim, Rodeo stated that material misrepresentations and omissions had been made during the negotiation of the limited partnership contracts in violation of the state securities act. The general partners responded that no securities were involved and that, because of the buy-out option, the limited partners actually had ultimate control over the management of the apartments. Discuss the definition of *security* and whether the limited partnership contracts meet this definition. [Rodeo v. Gillman, 787 F.2d 1175 (7th Cir. 1986)]

8. U.S. News and World Report, Inc., set up a profit-sharing plan in 1962 that allotted to certain employees specially issued stock known as bonus or anniversary stock. The stock was given to the employees for past services and could not be traded or sold to anyone other than the corporate issuer, U.S. News. This special stock was issued only to employees and for no other purpose but as bonuses. Since there was no market for the stock, U.S. News hired an independent appraiser to estimate the fair value of the stock so that the employees could redeem the shares. Charles Foltz and several other employees held stock through this plan and sought to redeem the shares with U.S. News, but Foltz disputed the value set by the appraisers. Foltz sued U.S. News for violation of securities regulations. What defense would allow U.S. News to successfully resist Foltz's claim? [Foltz v. U.S. News & World Report, Inc., 627 F.Supp. 1143 (D.D.C. 1986)]

9. In early 1985, FMC made plans to buy some of its own stock as part of a restructuring of its balance statement. Unknown to FMC management, the brokerage firm FMC employed—Goldman, Sachs & Co.—disclosed information on the stock purchase that found its way to Ivan Boesky. FMC was one of the seven major corporations in whose stock Ivan Boesky allegedly traded using inside information. Boesky made purchases of FMC's stock between February 18 and February 21 and between March 12 and April 4. Boesky's purchases amounted to a substantial portion of the total volume of FMC stock traded during these periods. The price of FMC stock increased from $71.25 on February 20, 1986, to $97.00 on April 25, 1986. As a result, FMC paid substantially more for the repurchase of its own stock than anticipated. Upon the discovery of Boesky's knowledge of FMC's recapitalization plan, FMC sued Boesky for the excess price it had paid—approximately $220 million. Discuss whether FMC should recover under Section 10(b) of the Securities Exchange Act and SEC Rule 10b-5. [FMC Corp. v. Boesky, 673 F.Supp. 242 (N.D.Ill. 1987)]

10. Management Assistance, Inc., (MAI) bought and leased computers for which IBM provided maintenance services. The chairman of the board (Oreamuno) and president (Gonzalez) of MAI learned that IBM was going to increase its maintenance prices dramatically. The increases would cut MAI's profits by 75 percent per month. Just before the IBM maintenance price increases were announced, Oreamuno and Gonzalez sold their MAI stock for $28 per share. After IBM publicly announced its price increase, the price of MAI stock fell to $11 per share. Diamond, a shareholder of MAI, brought a derivative action on behalf of MAI to recover the difference in profits. When corporate fiduciaries have breached their duty to the corporation by using nonpublic information, may a derivative action be brought by a shareholder for any profit resulting from the breach of duty? Discuss. [Diamond v. Oreamuno, 24 N.Y.2d 494, 248 N.E.2d 910, 301 N.Y.S.2d 78 (1969)]

Chapter 44

Private Franchises

The Federal Trade Commission has defined a **franchise** as "an arrangement in which the owner of a trademark, a trade name, or a copyright licenses others, under specified conditions or limitations, to use the trademark, trade name, or copyright in purveying goods or services." The franchise system has also been described as an organization composed of distributive units established and administered by a supplier as a medium for expanding and controlling the market of its products. Each franchise dealer is a legally independent but economically dependent unit of the integrated business system. The individual **franchisee** (the holder of the franchise) can operate as an independent business; yet it can obtain the advantages of a regional or national organizational affiliation with the **franchisor** (the licensor of the franchise) to supply products, advertising, and other services.

The use of franchises has expanded rapidly in recent years. It began in the early part of the century. Between 1910 and 1940, franchising was used in the automobile industry, sports, and the soft drink bottling industry. Now franchises account for about 25 percent of all retail sales and more than 14 percent of the gross national product in the United States. The franchise pattern of business development is a particularly appealing form of capitalistic enterprise. It has the advantage of enabling groups of individuals with small amounts of capital to become entrepreneurs.

THE LAW OF FRANCHISING

The growth in franchise operations has outdistanced the law of franchising. There has yet to be developed a solid body of appellate decisions under federal or state laws relating to franchises. In the absence of case law precisely addressed to franchising, the courts tend to apply general common law principles and appropriate federal or state statutory definitions and rules. The franchise relationship has characteristics associated with agency law, employment law, and independent contracting; yet it does not truly fit into any of these traditional classifications.

Some statutory requirements specifically relating to franchising have been enacted at the federal level. Automobile dealership franchisees are protected from automobile manufacturers' bad faith termination of their franchises by the Automobile Dealers' Franchise Act (enacted in 1956), also known as the Automobile Dealers' Day in Court Act.[1] If a manufacturer-franchisor terminates a franchise for a dealer-franchisee's failure to comply with unreasonable demands (for example, failure to attain an unrealistically high sales quota), the manufacturer is liable for damages.

Other federal statutes include the Petroleum Marketing Practices Act (PMPA),[2] which was adopted in 1979 to protect gasoline station franchisees' reasonable expectations in the continuation of their franchises. Before the PMPA's passage, gasoline franchisors were notorious for imposing high minimum rents and gallonage requirements, and the situation only worsened during the energy crisis in the early 1970s. The PMPA prescribes the grounds and conditions under which a franchisor may terminate or decline to renew a franchise. Federal antitrust laws (discussed in Chapter 48) may also apply if there is an illegal price-fixing agreement affecting the relationship between a franchisor and franchisee.

In 1979, the Federal Trade Commission (FTC) issued regulations that require franchisors to disclose material facts necessary to a prospective franchisee's making an informed decision concerning the purchase of a franchise. These regulations are discussed more fully later in this chapter.

Many states currently have statutes dealing with franchise law. State legislation tends to be similar to federal statutes and the FTC regulations. That is, state laws are generally designed to protect prospective franchisees from dishonest franchisors and to prohibit franchisors from terminating franchises without good cause. For example, a law might require the disclosure of information that is material to making an informed decision regarding the purchase of a franchise. This could include such information as the actual costs of operation, recurring expenses, and profits earned and facts substantiating these figures.

When a franchise exists primarily for the sale of products manufactured by the franchisor, the law governing sales as expressed in Article 2 of the Uniform Commercial Code (discussed in Unit Three) applies.

---

1. 15 U.S.C. Section 1222.
2. 15 U.S.C. Section 2801.

TYPES OF FRANCHISES

There are three types of franchises: distributorships, chain-style businesses, and manufacturing or processing plants.

1.   A *distributorship* relationship is established when a manufacturing concern (franchisor) licenses a dealer (franchisee) to sell its product. Often, a distributorship covers an exclusive territory. An example of this type of franchise is an automobile dealership.

2.   A *chain-style business* operation exists when a franchisee operates under a franchisor's trade name and is identified as a member of a select group of dealers that engages in the franchisor's business. The franchisee is generally required to follow standardized or prescribed methods of operation. Often, the franchisor requires that minimum prices and standards of operation be maintained. In addition, sometimes the franchisee is obligated to deal exclusively with the franchisor to obtain materials and supplies. Examples of this type of franchise include McDonald's and most other fast food chains.

3.   A *manufacturing or processing plant* arrangement is one in which the franchisor transmits to the franchisee the essential ingredients or formula to make a particular product. The franchisee then markets the product either at wholesale or at retail in accordance with the franchisor's standards. Examples of this type of franchise are Coca-Cola and other soft drink corporations.

THE FRANCHISE AGREEMENT

The franchise relationship is defined by a contract between the franchisor and the franchisee. Each franchise relationship and each industry has its own characteristics, so it is difficult to describe the broad range of details a franchising contract may include. The following sections, however, define the essential characteristics of the franchise relationship.

Entering the Franchise Relationship

Prospective franchisees must initially decide on the type of business they wish to undertake. Then they must obtain information about the business from the franchisor. Usually, franchisors make numerous statistics and market studies available for prospective franchisees to examine. The inexperienced franchisee must rely heavily on the franchisor in evaluating and setting up the initial business organization.

Payment for Franchise

The franchisee ordinarily pays an initial fee or lump-sum price for the franchise license (the privilege of being granted a franchise). This fee is separate from the various products that the franchisee purchases from or through the franchisor. In some industries, the franchisor relies heavily on the initial sale of the franchise for realizing a profit. In other industries, the continued dealing between the parties brings profit to both.

In most situations, the franchisor receives a stated percentage of the annual sales or annual volume of business done by the franchisee. The franchise agreement may also require the franchisee to pay a percentage of advertising costs and certain administrative expenses incurred throughout the duration of the franchise arrangement.

Location and Business Organization

Typically, the franchisor determines the territory to be served. The franchise agreement can specify whether the premises for the business must be leased or purchased outright. In some cases, construction of a building is necessary to meet the terms of the franchise agreement.

In addition, the agreement specifies whether the franchisor supplies equipment and furnishings for the premises or whether this is the responsibility of the franchisee. When the franchise is a service operation, such as a motel, the contract often provides that the franchisor will establish certain standards for the facility and will make inspections to ensure that the standards are being maintained in order to protect the franchise name and reputation.

The business organization of the franchisee is of great concern to the franchisor. Depending on the terms of the franchise agreement, the franchisor may specify particular requirements for the form and capital structure of the business. The franchise agreement may provide that standards of operation, such as sales quotas, quality standards, or record keeping, be conducted by the franchisor. Furthermore, a franchisor may wish to retain stringent control over the training of personnel involved in the operation and over administrative aspects of the business. Although the day-to-day operation of the franchise business is normally left up to the franchisee, the franchise agreement may provide for whatever amount of supervision and control the parties agree upon.

One area of franchises that causes a great deal of conflict is the territorial exclusivity of the franchise. Many franchise agreements, while they do define the territory alloted to a particular franchise, specifically state that the franchise is nonexclusive. The ramifications of non-exclusivity can be severe, because it allows the franchisor to establish additional franchises in the same territory as the existing franchisee. This problem is illustrated by the following case.

Case 44.1

IMPERIAL MOTORS, INC. v. CHRYSLER CORPORATION

United States District Court for the District of Massachusetts, 1983.
559 F.Supp. 1312.

BACKGROUND AND FACTS *In 1976, plaintiff Imperial Motors, Inc., entered into direct dealer agreements for Chrysler and Plymouth dealerships with the defendant, Chrysler Corporation. The direct dealer agreements explicitly provided that Imperial would not have the exclusive right to purchase for resale defendant's cars in a four-town area of South Carolina. The Chrysler district manager, however, told Imperial that Imperial's Chrysler-Plymouth dealership would be the only one in these four towns.*

In August of 1976, Chrysler allowed another Chrysler-Plymouth dealer, Carroll Motors, to move to a new showroom seven miles from Imperial's location. Imperial claimed that Chrysler had violated the Automobile Dealers' Day in Court Act by approving the relocation of Carroll Motors. Chrysler moved for summary judgment.

ZOBEL, District Judge.
*   *   *   *

Defendant's motion for summary judgment is proper as to that part of plaintiff's claim which alleges that defendant's approval of Carroll's relocation was a violation of the Act. The Act covers only those actions of a franchisor which amount to a "failure . . . to act in good faith in performing or complying with any of the terms or provisions of the franchise, or in terminating, cancelling, or not renewing the franchise with a dealer." 15 U.S.C. § 1222. Good faith is narrowly defined as "the duty of each party . . . to act in a fair and equitable manner toward each other so as to guaranty the one party freedom from coercion, intimidation or threats of coercion or intimidation by the other party. 15 U.S.C. § 1221. The failure to abide by the terms of a franchise agreement cannot by itself constitute a violation of the act. *   *   * Moreover, the Act explicitly defines a franchise as a "written agreement"; accordingly, oral promises are not part of a franchise agreement and cannot form the basis of a claim of bad faith.

Chrysler's motion for summary judgment was granted, and it was held that allowing a franchise to Carroll in the same area was not a violation of the franchise agreement or of the Automobile Dealers' Day in Court Act.

DECISION AND REMEDY

The franchisee in this case was left unprotected by his franchise agreement as far as territorial exclusivity was concerned. The same denial of relief resulted from a suit filed under the Unfair Trade Practices Act by a Ford automobile dealer (with a non-exclusive franchise agreement) after Ford Motor Company granted another Ford dealership near his. [See McLaughlin Ford, Inc. v. Ford Motor Company, 192 Conn. 558, 473 A.2d 1185 (1984).] Franchisees must obtain exclusivity rights in their contracts to be protected.

COMMENTS

Price and Quality Controls

Franchises provide the franchisor with an outlet for the firm's goods and services. Depending upon the nature of the business, the franchisor may require the franchisee to purchase products from the franchisor at an established price. Of course, a franchisor cannot set the prices at which the franchisee will resell the goods, as this is a violation of state or federal antitrust laws, or both. A franchisor can suggest retail prices but cannot insist on them. Also, although a franchisor can require franchisees to purchase supplies from it, requiring a franchisee to purchase *exclusively* from the franchisor may violate federal antitrust laws.

As a general rule, there is no question of the validity of a provision permitting the franchisor to enforce certain quality standards. Since the franchisor has a legitimate interest in maintaining the quality of the product or service in order to protect its name and reputation, it can exercise greater control in this area than would otherwise be tolerated.

Termination of the Franchise Agreement

The duration of the franchise is a matter to be determined between the parties. Generally, a franchise will initially be formed for a short term, such as a year, so that the franchisee and the franchisor can determine whether they want to stay in business with one another. Usually the franchise agreement will specify that termination must be "for cause," such as death or disability of the franchisee, insolvency of the franchisee, breach of the franchise agreement, or failure to meet specified sales quotas. Most franchise contracts provide that notice of termination must be given. If no notice requirements are specified in the franchise agreement, then a reasonable notice will be implied. A franchisee must be given reasonable time to wind up the business—that is, to do the accounting and return the copyright or trademark or any other property of the franchisor.

Much franchise litigation has arisen over termination provisions. Since the franchise agreement is normally a form contract drawn and prepared by the franchisor, and since the bargaining power of the franchisee is rarely equal to that of the franchisor, the termination provisions of contracts are generally more favorable to the franchisor. The franchisee normally invests a substantial amount of time and money in the franchise operation to make it successful. Despite this fact, the franchisee may receive little or nothing for the business upon termination. The franchisor owns the trademark and hence the business. It is in this area that Congress, regulatory agencies, and state legislatures have attempted to provide franchisees with protection. Before these measures existed, the courts often struggled to offer a terminated franchisee some kind of relief, as is illustrated in the next case.

Case 44.2
ATLANTIC RICHFIELD CO. v. RAZUMIC

Supreme Court of Pennsylvania, 1978.
480 Pa. 366, 390 A.2d 736.

BACKGROUND AND FACTS *The plaintiff, Atlantic Richfield Company (Arco), entered into a "dealer lease" with the defendant, Razumic, in 1953. The defendant expended $5,000 in inventory, equipment, and capital. Arco financed the initial supply of gasoline to get the service station on its feet, and the defendant opened for business. Over the years, the parties signed numerous agreements resembling the first dealer lease, as well as various forms concerning the use of Arco's promotional campaign materials, the purchase of fuel, and credit card sale arrangements.*

In 1970, Razumic moved into a new service station built by Arco and signed a three-year dealer lease. On June 29, 1973, Arco notified Razumic that the lease would not be renewed and directed Razumic to vacate the premises in thirty days. Razumic refused to leave, and Arco filed suit to force termination of the lease agreement. The trial court found for Arco, holding that the dealership agreement could be terminated at will for any reason.

ROBERTS, Justice.
* * * *

In his pleadings, at trial, and on appeal to this Court, Razumic has urged that he and Arco were parties to a franchise agreement Arco could not terminate at will. Arco, on the other hand, has contended throughout that the dealership agreement could be terminated for any reason. We agree with Razumic.
* * * *

* * * We believe that the 1970 writing and its riders embody a franchise agreement. * * * Given the comprehensive terms of the writing obligating Razumic to operate the Arco service station in a manner Arco determined would reflect favorably upon the public image of the Arco trademark, report and share gross receipts with Arco pursuant to a "FRANCHISE RENT SCHEDULE," and allow Arco to inspect the station to assure Razumic's continued compliance with the many provisions of the form writing, it is clear that Razumic was not pursuing solely his own business interests. Rather, Razumic conducted his business and sold his products in accordance with methods prescribed by Arco.
* * * *

The writing provides Arco the right to terminate the "lease" should Razumic abandon the premises or close them "for a period of seventy-two hours." Razumic's negligence or willful misconduct causing damages to a substantial portion of the premises gives Arco "the right to terminate this lease without liability." Razumic's failure to make timely payment of rent, his death or insolvency, or governmental taking also permit Arco to terminate the "lease." Further, Razumic's "fail[ure] to comply with any of his other obligations" set forth in the writing permits Arco to terminate the agreement if Razumic fails to remedy the situation after fifteen days' notice of non-compliance.

The writing does not, however, contain any provision granting Arco the right to terminate the franchise agreement at will. In view of the provisions authorizing Arco to terminate the parties' franchise agreement for limited, business reasons and an additional provision authorizing Razumic, upon giving "at least sixty days advance written notice," to terminate the agreement without reason upon the anniversary of a term where the stated term exceeds one year, the absence of a similar term authorizing Arco to terminate the agreement without reason is striking.

* * * *

An Arco dealer has his own expectations. He knows that his good service will in many instances produce regular customers. He also realizes, however, that much of his trade will be attracted because his station offers the products, services, and promotions of the well-established and well-displayed name "Arco." Unlike a tenant pursuing his own interests while occupying a landlord's property, a franchisee such as Razumic builds the goodwill of both his own business and Arco.

In exchange, an Arco dealer such as Razumic can justifiably expect that his time, effort, and other investments promoting the goodwill of Arco will not be destroyed as a result of Arco's arbitrary decision to terminate their franchise relationship. Consistent with these reasonable expectations, and Arco's obligation to deal with its franchisees in good faith and in a commercially reasonable manner, Arco cannot arbitrarily sever its franchise relationship with Razumic. A contrary conclusion would allow Arco to reap the benefits of its franchisees' efforts in promoting the goodwill of its name without regard for the franchisees' interests.

* * * *

For the above reasons, the writing's leasehold terminology stating a three year term of occupancy does not govern the duration of the comprehensive contractual business relationship between Razumic and Arco. Rather, the language establishes a right of occupancy which the franchisee Razumic can reasonably expect will not be abruptly halted. Consistent with Razumic's reasonable expectations, principles of good faith and commercial reasonableness, Arco may not arbitrarily recover possession of the service station and thereby summarily terminate the franchise relationship.

DECISION AND REMEDY

The Supreme Court of Pennsylvania reversed the trial court's decision. Arco was prohibited from terminating the franchise agreement without good cause.

COMMENTS

The UCC requirements of good faith in contract dealings are often applied to ongoing franchise relationships when the franchise involves the sale of goods. The UCC provisions have ordinarily not been applied to franchise agreements that extend to the leasing of premises, however.

DETERMINATION OF RELIEF In the absence of specific legislation, the courts and legal commentators have applied many theories to protect a franchisee's rights upon termination. Some courts have held that every contract contains an implied covenant of good faith and fair dealing. Others have held that if a franchise investment is substantial and the relationship has been established for an indefinite duration, it cannot be terminated until after a reasonable period of time has elapsed. What constitutes a reasonable time depends upon the circumstances in each case. Some of the circumstances that the courts consider are:

1. The amount of preliminary and promotional expenditures made.
2. The length of time the franchise has been in operation before notice of termination was given.
3. The prospects for forfeiture of profits.
4. Whether or not the franchise has proved to be profitable during its actual operation.

If contract provisions allow for termination, even though the provisions may be unfair to the franchisee, it is possible that no cause of action will be found. The Uniform Commercial Code, Section 2-302, has been used by some courts to find that termination provisions dispensing with notification are invalid if their effect is unconscionable. The courts have generally refused to find that franchises terminable by notice at any time or at the end of a specific time are unconscionable *per se.*

MEASURE OF DAMAGES   The courts have also struggled to determine how best to measure damages to prevent injustice or unfairness when misconduct occurs in a franchise relationship. Since franchising is a rather peculiar form of capitalist enterprise, serious franchising problems warrant legislative attention. In situations covered by a state or federal franchise statute, a franchisee need not rely on common law principles to obtain protection in the courts from franchisor abuses. Which law to apply is dealt with in the following case.

Case 44.3
HUGHES v. SINCLAIR MARKETING, INC.
Supreme Court of Minnesota,
1986.
389 N.W.2d 194.

BACKGROUND AND FACTS   *In early 1972, Donald Hughes and Clair Anderson contacted a representative of Sinclair Oil concerning a service station franchise in Crystal, Minnesota. The representative told Hughes and Anderson that Sinclair wanted a dealer on a long-term basis. The representative did not, at the time, inform Hughes and Anderson that Sinclair leased the station property from Minnesota-Ohio Oil Company and that the lease would terminate in December 1976. Hughes and Anderson signed a dealer agreement and station lease in April 1972 and regularly renewed the lease until 1976. During this period, Sinclair began to convert its franchises into company-owned stations with salaried managers. At the end of 1976, in light of the imminent expiration of Sinclair's lease, Hughes and Anderson voluntarily vacated the property under an agreement by which Sinclair was to negotiate in good faith to purchase the property from Minnesota-Ohio in order to renew their franchise. Over the next several months, it became clear to Hughes and Anderson that Sinclair planned neither to purchase the station nor offer them an alternative franchise. Hughes and Anderson filed a suit for damages, alleging that Sinclair had violated the Minnesota franchise statute by (1) improper nonrenewal and (2) misrepresentation. The franchise statute permits a recovery of "actual damages sustained by the plaintiff." In addition, the plaintiffs claimed common law misrepresentation, which limits damages to out-of-pocket losses. The trial court awarded Hughes and Anderson $144,164, basing liability solely on improper nonrenewal (wrongful termination). Sinclair filed motions for a judgment notwithstanding the verdict (j.n.o.v.) and a new trial. Sinclair denied the plaintiffs' allegations and claimed that for improper nonrenewal, injunction was the exclusive remedy. The trial court denied these motions, and Sinclair appealed. The court of appeals sustained the award of damages, but on the basis of misrepresentation under the franchise act rather than improper termination. The appellate court deemed that, under the act, damages included future profits lost because of the franchise termination. Sinclair appealed to the Supreme Court of Minnesota. After concluding that the jury verdict could be sustained on all three bases of liability—misrepresentation under the act, common law fraud, and improper nonrenewal of a franchise—the supreme court considered Sinclair's contentions regarding the relief awarded to Hughes and Anderson.*

YETKA, Justice.
*   *   *   *

Appellant [Sinclair] *   *   * argues that the court of appeals erred by allowing lost future profits as actual damages for misrepresentation under the franchise act and that the district court was limited to injunctive relief for improper non-renewal. If the court allows lost future profits on either basis, appellant also disputes the amount awarded.

Respondents [Hughes and Anderson] maintain that "actual damages" awarded for misrepresentation under the act include lost future profits. They also claim that the actual damages provision applies to improper non-renewal. * * *

The traditional recovery for common law misrepresentation in Minnesota is limited to out-of-pocket loss. The district court instructed the jury that, on either theory of misrepresentation, damages would not include benefit of the bargain [future profits]. The court of appeals, however, found that the language of the franchise act indicates that damages for misrepresentation under the act are not to be limited to out-of-pocket losses. [The statute provides:]

> A person who violates any provision of sections 80C.01 to 80C.13 and 80C.15 to 80C.22 or any rule or order thereunder shall be liable to the franchisee or subfranchisor who may sue for damages caused thereby, for rescission, or other relief as the court may deem appropriate.
>
> * * * *
>
> Any suit authorized under this section may be brought to recover the actual damages sustained by the plaintiff together with costs and disbursements plus reasonable attorney's fees.

The court of appeals reasoned that the term "actual damages" expanded the available remedies beyond out-of-pocket losses to include any damages caused by the violation. Since the damages included the loss of a business, the court found that future profits were properly awarded.

The meaning of the term "actual damages" as used in [the act] has not been resolved by this court. The purpose behind limiting damages for common law misrepresentation to out-of-pocket loss is to avoid speculative damages and assure that the award is measured by the natural and proximate loss sustained by the defrauded party. The court has recognized an exception to the general rule when out-of-pocket damages fail to return a party to the status quo. This court has also ruled that the proper measure of damages for interruption of an established business includes lost future profits. In the present case, Sinclair's misrepresentations induced the respondents to forego their renewal rights under the franchise act and thereby lose their business. Since the district court found that the record did not sustain a finding of out-of-pocket loss, application of the common law rule would fail to return Hughes and Anderson to their condition before Sinclair's misrepresentations. We hold that, under the circumstances of this case, lost future profits may be recovered by the respondents as "actual damages" for misrepresentation under the act.

DECISION AND REMEDY *The decision of the court of appeals was affirmed, and the court held that lost future profits could be included in the measure of actual damages.*

CONSUMER AND FRANCHISEE PROTECTION The consumer protection movement and pressures from franchise investors have prompted the passage of numerous statutes to protect franchisees from bad faith termination of their franchise contracts. For example, as noted above, the federal Automobile Dealers' Day in Court Act allows an auto dealer who contends that the franchisor did not act in good faith in terminating the franchise to take the matter to court for a judicial determination. Moreover, various states have passed laws in recent years that spell out certain conditions and circumstances under which a franchise can be terminated. These laws, however, are subject to serious constitutional challenges under the impairment of contracts clause, the due process clause, and the interstate commerce clause of the U.S. Constitution.

The realities of the franchise industry demonstrate a need for uniform regulation. Common law theories and existing statutory remedies have little application to franchising problems. The franchise system is a complex and unique business enterprise. It is growing so fast that it seems almost impossible to design a regulatory scheme that is both comprehensive and flexible enough to meet the needs of this system of business enterprise.

REGULATION OF THE FRANCHISING INDUSTRY

Any industry that expands rapidly without a uniform regulatory scheme is likely to engage in certain abusive and destructive practices. The franchising industry is no exception. The Federal Trade Commission has investigated whether illegal methods have been used to compel restaurant franchises to purchase goods and services at artificially inflated prices. Other abusive practices have been discovered in the form of hidden markups on the capital assets and equipment that must be purchased by a franchisee either from the franchisor or from approved vendors. Cases of misrepresentation occur in the initial sale of many franchises. More than a few unsuspecting franchisees have learned, after entering into the franchise contract, that in order to operate the business and to meet the established sales quotas, they must work an inordinate number of hours a week.

The franchise relationship grows out of a contract. But because of the nature of the franchise system, the common law remedies that have been applied to contract and sales contract situations do not provide adequate relief. Furthermore, not all states have enacted statutes to govern franchise relationships. Thus, what is permissible in one state may not be permissible in another. Such lack of uniformity creates serious problems for franchise arrangements, especially when they are operated on a national scale.

The Franchise Contract: Disclosure Protection

A franchise purchaser can suffer substantial losses if the franchisor has not provided full and complete information regarding the franchisor-franchisee relationship, as well as the details of the

contract under which the business will be operated. When misrepresentation permeates the initial sale of a franchise operation, the common law remedy of fraud in the inducement provides inadequate relief. In most cases, the franchisee has already paid the franchise purchase price and may also have incurred substantial losses in the initial operating phases of the business. Furthermore, alleging that the franchisor intentionally misstated or misrepresented a material fact upon which the franchisee relied places a great burden of proof on the franchisee.

Before 1979, fewer than twenty states had included disclosure provisions in legislation concerning franchising. California was the first state to enact a franchise disclosure law, and it has served as a model for other disclosure statutes. The California Franchise Investment Law[3] (enacted in 1970 and effective on January 1, 1971) sets out twenty-two items that must be disclosed in a registration filed with the state. Some of the items of disclosure include:

1. The name and business address of the franchisor.
2. The business experience of any persons affiliated with the franchisor.
3. Whether any person associated with the franchisor has been convicted of a felony.
4. A recent financial statement.
5. A typical franchise agreement.
6. A statement of all fees that the franchisee is required to pay.
7. Other information that the commissioner of corporations may reasonably require.

Some courts have attempted to apply the Securities Act of 1933 and various state blue sky laws to franchise agreements. The franchise agree-

---

3. The California Franchise Investment Law provides: "California franchisees have suffered substantial losses where the franchisor or his representative has not provided full and complete information regarding the franchisor-franchisee relationship, the details of the contract between the franchisor and the franchisee, and the prior business experience of the franchisor. It is the intent of this law to provide each prospective franchisee with the information necessary to make an intelligent decision regarding the franchise being offered." Cal. Corp. Code Section 31001.

ment could possibly be considered an "investment contract" within the meaning of blue sky laws and the 1933 Securities Act. Thus, it would be subject to the registration and disclosure requirements of the securities laws.

This theory, however, has not met with much success on the federal level. The United States Supreme Court has defined an investment contract as "a contract, transaction or scheme whereby a person invests his (or her) money in a common enterprise and is led to expect profits solely from the efforts of the promoter or third party."[4] The typical franchise agreement fails this test for determining "investment contracts" because a franchisee must make an effort to make money. Thus, franchise agreements are usually not considered securities under the Securities Act.

Federal law prohibits mail fraud. According to 18 U.S.C. Section 1341, the U.S. mails cannot be used to further a scheme to defraud. The mail fraud provision penalizes misrepresentations made by use of the mails. This is not a very effective means for preventing fraud or misrepresentation in a franchisor's negotiations with a potential franchisee, however, because it affords only an after-the-fact remedy.

Similarly, the Federal Trade Commission, under Section 5 of the FTC Act, has the power to stop unfair or deceptive practices in commerce and to prohibit deceptive advertising. Both the FTC provisions and the mail fraud provisions lack the affirmative protection that disclosure laws would afford a potential purchaser of a franchise.

The FTC Franchise Rule

The FTC franchise rule was promulgated in response to widespread evidence of deception and unfair practices in connection with the resale of franchises and business opportunity ventures. This rule requires that, within a specified time, franchisors and franchise brokers furnish the information that prospective franchisees need in order to make an informed decision about entering into a franchise relationship. The rule sets forth the circumstances under which a franchisor or broker can make claims about the projected sales income or profits of existing or potential outlets. The rule also imposes requirements that concern the establishment and termination of the franchise relationship.

INDICATIONS OF AGENCY IN THE FRANCHISE RELATIONSHIP

The mere licensing of a trade name does not create an agency relationship. The courts, however, have determined that certain factors in the franchisor-franchisee relationship indicate the existence of an agency relationship:

1. The terms of the agreement create an agency relationship.
2. The franchisor exercises a high degree of control over the franchisee's activities.
3. A third person looking at the relationship between the franchisor and the franchisee would reasonably believe that there is an agency relationship.
4. The franchisor derives an especially great benefit from the franchisee's activities. (The greater the benefit, the more likely an agency relationship will be found.)

If these factors show a very close relationship between the franchisor and the franchisee, then their relationship will be deemed to be that of an employer and employee or a principal and agent. If the factors show a high degree of independence between the franchisee and franchisor, then the franchisee will be deemed an independent contractor without agency authority.

The characterization of the relationship has tax implications and implications for the regulatory treatment of the business organization. In addition, if an agency relationship is found, the franchisor is liable for the franchisee's improper actions or injuries to third parties both in tort and in contract, according to the principles of agency law discussed in Chapters 32 and 33.

---

4. SEC v. W. J. Howey Co., 328 U.S. 293, 66 S.Ct. 1100, 90 L.Ed. 1244 (1946). This case was presented in the text of the preceding chapter.

QUESTIONS AND CASE PROBLEMS

1. John Jefferson had a franchise beer distributorship. He built up this distributorship over ten years into a very profitable business. Last year, Jefferson decided to sell a soft drink and distribute it to the outlet retailers and businesses that purchased beer from him. The beer company franchisor was unhappy with the arrangement. There was nothing in the franchise agreement to prohibit Jefferson from distributing a noncompeting product, but there was a provision that required Jefferson to give his full attention to the franchise. The beer company demanded that Jefferson cease distributing the soft drink, and Jefferson refused. The franchisor beer company immediately terminated the franchise agreement. Discuss the franchisee's rights in this matter.

2. Ann has been interested in securing a particular high-quality ice cream franchise. The franchisor is willing to give Ann a franchise. A franchise agreement is made that calls for Ann to sell the ice cream only at a specific location, to buy all the ice cream from the franchisor, to order and sell all the flavors produced by the franchisor, and to refrain from selling any ice cream stored for more than two weeks after delivery by the franchisor, as this ice cream decreases in quality after that period. After two months of operation, Ann believes that she can increase her profits by moving the store to another part of the city. She also refuses to order even a limited quantity of the "fruit delight" flavor because of its higher cost, and she has sold ice cream that has been stored longer than two weeks without customer complaint. Ann claims that the franchisor has no right to restrict her in these practices. Discuss her claims.

3. Solomon is approached by Apex Company, a franchisor, to sell Apex products under a franchise agreement. The franchise contract calls for Solomon to pay Apex $20,000 and for Apex to supply Solomon with all Apex products on low-interest credit terms. The contract also provides that Apex will advertise its products in the area and furnish Solomon, who has had no previous business experience, with bookkeeping and other management services. Solomon borrows the money and pays Apex $20,000. Apex is a sole proprietorship on shaky financial ground. Not only does Apex fail to provide the promised management services to Solomon, but it also fails to advertise its products in Solomon's area. In addition, Apex is often late in filling Solomon's orders. Solomon wants to hold Apex liable for substantial losses. Discuss the theories under which Solomon will claim relief.

4. Blake is interested in becoming a service station dealer. He contacts Esco Oil Corporation and obtains a franchise contract in which Esco agrees to furnish Blake all gasoline, oil, and related products necessary to run the service station. In addition, Esco provides Blake with Esco signs and promotional materials. A sign reading "Blake's Esco Service" is provided for the front of the station. In return for supplying all the products Blake requires, promotional materials and signs, and other services, Esco is to receive a percentage on all products sold. Esco advertises that it stands behind its dealers. The relationship between Blake and Esco is challenged. Discuss whether the relationship is strictly franchisor-franchisee or whether it is a principal-agent (employer-employee) relationship.

5. A fifteen-year-old employee was injured while using a slicing machine at a fast food franchise, the Yankee Doodle Dandy restaurant. Federal law prohibits the operation of meat-slicing machines by persons under eighteen years of age. Under the franchise agreement, the franchisor had the power to terminate the agreement if the franchisee failed to comply with local, state, and federal laws. The franchisor knew that the franchisee was not conforming to the law. Could the franchisor be held liable for the negligent supervision of the franchisee? [Coty v. U.S. Slicing Machine Co., Inc., 58 Ill.App.3d 237, 373 N.E.2d 1371, 15 Ill.Dec. 687 (1978)]

6. Ger-Ro-Mar, Inc., was a manufacturer and distributor of lingerie and swimwear. Through its multilevel marketing program, Ger-Ro-Mar enlisted the services of men and women throughout the country to sell its products at wholesale and retail. Under the selling arrangement, franchisees were required to buy an inventory before they could participate in the program. A prospective franchisee could enter at any of three levels—key distributor, senior key, or supervisor. Entry at a particular level was based on the amount of inventory initially purchased by the franchisee. To induce individuals to become franchisees, Ger-Ro-Mar distributed various promotional materials that described the marketing system and illustrated how an individual could earn large sums of money by building a large personal group of salespeople through recruitment. The illustration in Ger-Ro-Mar's brochures promised that district managers could earn up to $56,000 and regional managers up to $90,000 yearly. Concerning the regional manager position, Ger-Ro-Mar's promotional brochure promised, "ANYONE CAN ACHIEVE THIS LEVEL." An investigation by the FTC revealed that the success promised in the brochure was dependent upon the franchisee's recruitment of salespersons, who in turn would recruit salespersons to work under them. Is there anything wrong with Ger-Ro-Mar's franchising scheme? Why might the FTC wish to order Ger-Ro-Mar to cease and desist distribution of its promotional brochure? [Ger-Ro-Mar, Inc. v. FTC, 518 F.2d 33 (2d Cir. 1975)]

7. A franchise agreement entered into between Shakey's Inc., as franchisor, and Charles Martin, as franchisee, included the following provision: "Upon termination of this agreement, for a period of one year thereafter, the franchisee shall not engage in the production or sale of pizza products in a location within a radius of thirty miles from the franchised premises." After operating a Shakey's pizza franchise for several years, Martin ceased doing business as Shakey's, removed all indications of Shakey's trade name from the premises, and proceeded to do business as "Martin's Pizza Parlor." Has Martin violated his agreement not to compete? What business interest does Shakey's have, if any? Is the agreement not to compete a reasonable one? [Shakey's Inc. v. Martin, 91 Idaho 758, 430 P.2d 504 (1967)]

8. E. T. Runyan and Pacific Air Industries, Inc., entered into a written franchise agreement whereby, in consideration of Runyan's payment of $25,000, he was awarded an exclusive photogrammetric franchise for four southern California counties. Under the agreement, Pacific was obligated to train Runyan in the rudiments of photogrammetry (measurement by use of aerial photography), including twenty-five hours of sales and technical assistance for an initial period. In the meantime, Runyan resigned his position with Tidewater Oil Company. Since Runyan was entering a technical field in which he had no experience, he relied on Pacific's promise. Pacific's training program proved to be entirely inadequate. Runyan nevertheless attempted to operate his franchise, but when he realized that he was unable to do so, he attempted to rescind. Could Runyan rescind the franchise agreement? [Runyan v. Pacific Air Indust., Inc., 2 Cal.3d 304, 466 P.2d 682, 85 Cal.Rptr. 138 (1970)]

9. Ernst and Barbara Larese (the plaintiffs) entered into a ten-year franchise agreement with Creamland Dairies, Inc. (the defendant) in 1974. The franchise agreement provided that the franchisee "shall not assign, transfer or sublet this franchise, or any of [the] rights under this agreement, without the prior written consent of Area Franchisor [Creamland] and Baskin Robbins, any such unauthorized assignment, transfer or subletting being null and without effect." The plaintiffs attempted to sell their franchise rights in February and August 1979, but Creamland refused to consent to the sales. The plaintiffs brought suit, alleging that Creamland had interfered with their contractual relations with the prospective buyers by unreasonably withholding its consent; they held that the defendant had a duty to act in good faith and in a commercially reasonable manner when a franchisee sought to transfer its rights under the franchise agreement. The defendant contended that the contract gave it an unqualified right to refuse to consent to proposed sales of the franchise rights. Which party prevailed? [Larese v. Creamland Dairies, Inc., 767 F.2d 716 (10th Cir. 1985)]

10. In 1981, the Huangs entered into a franchise agreement with Holiday Inns, Inc., whereby the Huangs agreed to adhere to the quality standards established by Holiday Inns and to comply in every respect with the Holiday Inns Standards Manual. In November of 1983, the district director of Holiday Inns made a courtesy inspection which revealed cracked windows, damaged and discolored walls, inoperative smoke detectors, broken light fixtures, poultry being stored at room temperature, and numerous other indications that the Huangs were not maintaining quality standards in accordance with the franchise agreement. A formal inspection in February of 1984 revealed no significant improvement in quality standards, and the hotel was given an official rating of "unacceptable." The Huangs, who had been given detailed reports concerning the findings of both inspections, were advised that if the noted deficiencies were not remedied within sixty days, Holiday Inns would have grounds to terminate the franchise. When an inspection in April of 1984 revealed that the deficiencies had not been cured, Holiday Inns notified the Huangs that the franchise would be terminated on July 30 unless the deficiencies were remedied by June 28. The Huangs, who in May had begun renovations on the hotel costing $55,000, requested a ninety-day extension to the June 28 deadline, which Holiday Inns refused to grant. The Huangs then petitioned the court for a preliminary injunction against Holiday Inns' termination of the franchise, claiming that Holiday Inns had acted "capriciously and arbitrarily" by (1) not stating precisely the nature of the deficiencies and what was required to make repairs and improvements and (2) not giving the Huangs a reasonable time in which to remedy the deficiencies. Discuss fully whether Holiday Inns should be enjoined from terminating the franchise, given these circumstances. [Huang v. Holiday Inns, Inc., 594 F.Supp. 352 (C.D.Cal.1984)]

Focus on Ethics

Business Organizations

Whenever a discussion of business organizations occurs, the central issue is usually the large American business corporation. To be sure, numerous ethical issues are involved in partnership law and in the nature of other specialized forms of business organizations. For example, what should be the treatment of joint ventures—should the individuals involved be treated simply as partners? What about the use of hybrid forms of business organization that are devised to gain either a limitation of liability (e.g., limited partnerships) or tax advantages (e.g., S corporations)? Even though the ethical questions about these other forms of business organizations are important, the issue of big business dominates ethical concerns both in economics and in law in this country. One of the most important ethical considerations is the nature of the control of the large corporation.

WHO CONTROLS THE CORPORATION?
Consider a corporation with literally millions of shareholders. Does any one shareholder affect the way in which the modern corporation governs itself? The answer has to be no.

Indeed, the separation of ownership and management is basic. Management of a corporation apparently can do whatever it wants within the scope of the charter of the corporation. The directors and officers have a duty to perform, but perform for whom? If a director's action cannot be controlled by the individual owners of the corporation, then by what means is such an action controlled?

There is an ethical question at the heart of all actions of directors and officers. What is the nature of their duty to the entity called the corporation? What is the nature of their duty to society? What is the nature of their duty to the corporation's employees? All of these ethical responsibilities can be considered elements of the question of corporate social responsibility.

CORPORATE SOCIAL RESPONSIBILITY
For a number of years now, numerous speakers have debated the social responsibility of the corporation as an institution. What should be the primary corporate goal? Should the growth of the firm or long-term profit maximization be the primary corporate goal, or should social responsibility be

given considerable weight in assessing corporate goals? The way in which corporate goals and social responsibility are perceived ultimately involves ethical considerations.

At one end of the spectrum is the notion that the corporation's sole responsibility is to maximize profits within the limits set by the law. Commentators at this end of the spectrum assert that the social duty of a business enterprise is actually long-term profit maximization. From this perspective, professional managers are regarded as trustees and the corporation is simply viewed as an extension of its shareholders. Non-profit-making activities will diminish the shareholders' wealth and are therefore not considered appropriate management conduct. Residual profits belong to the stockholders and are not to be devoted to the public interest.

At the other end of the spectrum is the notion that the directors and officers of a corporation have a duty higher than that of mere profit maximization or growth of the firm. According to this view, corporate management should engage only in those activities that benefit society as a whole. Therefore, if the corporation produces a type of baby food that babies like and that mothers buy but that is not "good" for babies because of a high MSG or sugar content, the corporation should not market the baby food.

Defining Corporate Responsibility

One of the major problems in discussing corporate social responsibility is our inability to define it objectively. We might have some notion of the nature of socially responsible actions when publicly appointed or elected officials are under study, but we have much less clear-cut notions about socially responsible actions when the directors or officers of a private corporation are concerned. In addition, critics of the entire concept of corporate social responsibility argue that they do not want private citizens, in their roles as directors and officers of private corporations, engaging in activities that those individuals have judged to be socially responsible. Besides, are business executives equipped to fashion appropriate corporate responses to social demands? What exactly is in society's best interest? This query has been a subject of dispute for decades, and many critics contend that the political process is the appropriate forum for decisions concerning social responsibility, not the corporate boardroom.

The December 1984 Union Carbide tragedy in Bhopal, India, raised numerous ethical considerations. Was this company exhibiting corporate responsibility in its Bhopal operations? When twenty-five tons of the agricultural pesticide methyl isocyanate leaked from the U.S.-owned company's Bhopal plant, 2,000 deaths and 100,000 injuries resulted in the city of Bhopal. Union Carbide insisted that the Bhopal factory

was built according to the same safety standards as its U.S. factories. There was, however, no computerized safety system installed in the Bhopal plant, even though one was installed in a sister plant in West Virginia.

Many experts contend that U.S. companies frequently locate factories in developing countries in order to escape the many U.S. environmental and safety regulations. Is it ethical for a company to take advantage of lax regulations in Third World countries? Such companies are not violating any *laws.*

It is further alleged that companies such as Union Carbide are lacking in social responsibility when they locate factories with lethal materials in areas of high population density. Many of the survivors of the Bhopal tragedy alleged that they were completely unaware of the fact that lethal materials were manufactured so near to them. Do companies have a responsibility to inform residents near their factories as to the nature of their products? If so, how far should this responsibility extend?

CORPORATE SOCIAL RESPONSIVENESS

At early common law, a corporation was absolutely prohibited from giving to charity because all profits belonged to shareholders. But the law has changed to allow private corporations to give to charity. Corporate nonprofit activity is justified by public policy reasons. The argument is that the wealth of the nation is no longer primarily in the hands of private individuals. Much of the nation's wealth is in corporate hands. Additionally, since the size of government has increased dramatically since the 1930s, taxation has increased

accordingly. Thus, the philanthropic abilities of private individuals have been diminished.

Although corporations as a group are often criticized as lacking social responsiveness, most major corporations do engage in philanthropic activities. Corporations routinely donate to hospitals, the arts, universities, and the like. Most major corporations employ one or more individuals to screen charitable requests and to determine which organizations should be the recipients of charitable contributions. B. Dalton Bookseller, for example, put up $3 million to launch a massive drive against functional illiteracy. The Bank of America has created a $10 million revolving-loan program in which funds are loaned to community development groups at a 3 percent interest rate.

A considerable number of corporations have also acknowledged moral and political considerations in their social responsiveness. Coca-Cola has established the National Hispanic Business Agenda—a major program to expand ties with the Hispanic community. This corporation has agreed to patronize more Hispanic firms, employ more Hispanic people, and support Hispanic educational and job-training programs.

SOCIAL INVESTING

Social investing, the buying and selling of securities on the basis of moral or social criteria, has become a popular subject of debate. The question frequently arises: How do you determine whether a company is socially responsible? Socially conscious investors have begun using social-responsibility criteria— such as pollution control, charitable donations, safety conditions, and equal employment opportunities—in identifying socially responsible companies. Some investment advisors rely upon the nature of the products or services that a company provides in order to determine whether a company is socially responsible. Others, however, look to the internal operations of a company in evaluating social responsibility.

Yet, irrespective of the widespread attention recently given to the subject of social investing, the goal of most investors is still simply to make a profit. Even though people claim to be, and probably are, concerned with social responsibility, most still don't really want to commit their funds on any basis other than expected profits. Moral and social scrutiny is appealing, but it does have its problems. How exactly do you determine which company is socially responsible and which is not? How far do you have to look to determine whether a company is socially responsible? Furthermore, does social investing make good financial sense at all? Many individuals allege that when social investing is done properly, the corporation and the public do see a benefit.

THE CORPORATION'S DUTY TO THE CONSUMER

What is the nature of the corporation's duty to the consumer? This issue often dominates discussions of product quality, pricing, and advertising. The layperson's notion is that he or she has absolutely no effect on the pricing, quality, and nature of the products and services offered by the modern-day giant corporation. Therefore, some consumers believe that corporations should be severely

regulated by the government and the courts in order to maintain the consumer's rights.

But what, really, is at issue here? Can the corporation willfully ignore the well-being of the consumer? As previously discussed, the critics of modern-day corporations assert that profit maximization is basically the only duty of a corporation. The supporters of modern-day corporations, however, claim that it is impossible for the well-being of the consumer to be ignored. In fact, they take one further step and assert that the ultimate control of the corporation actually lies in the hands of the consumer. After all, they argue, the consumer freely chooses to buy or not to buy a corporation's product. Even in the absence of effective competition, the consumer can purchase a smaller quantity of the product being offered. Thus, it is in the corporation's best long-term interest to attempt to satisfy the consumer.

Irrespective of the alleged power of the consumer to control the corporation, an ethical question remains. The process of competition takes time. Information is costly to obtain and never perfect. If corporate leaders know or suspect that certain of their products may have deleterious long-run effects on the consumer, shouldn't such corporate leaders have an ethical responsibility to inform the consumer? Eli Lilly, for example, failed to recognize an ethical responsibility that resulted in the death of an 81-year-old woman who had taken Lilly's arthritis drug, Oraflex, and a $6 million punitive verdict was rendered against Lilly. Lilly had Oraflex approved for sale in the United States without informing the Food and Drug Administration of thirty-two

overseas deaths associated with the use of this drug.

Furthermore, what about an ethical responsibility to citizens in other countries? If the Food and Drug Administration has prohibited the sale of a particular substance in the United States because it might have long-run carcinogenic effects, should the producer attempt to sell it in those countries where it is still legal?

THE CORPORATION'S DUTY TO ITS EMPLOYEES

What are the corporation's duties to its employees? The answer to this ethical question is not an easy one because of the necessary trade-offs involved. To the extent that the corporation provides higher-than-competitive wages, better-than-"reasonable" working conditions, and the like, its costs per unit of production will be higher. That means that the price of the product will be higher. Who has a greater "right," the employee or the consumer? Also, there is a conflict between the shareholder and the employee. The more employees obtain, presumably, the less shareholders will obtain. No easy solution to such conflict is available.

THE CORPORATION'S DUTY TO ITS SHAREHOLDERS

In many ethical controversies, management's duty to shareholders seems to conflict with duties to society as a whole. Consequently, the duty to shareholders may be minimized in importance. In other cases, though, management's duty to shareholders may conflict with the self-interest of management itself. May management protect itself, or must management concern itself exclusively with shareholder interests?

The possible ethical conflict usually arises in connection with a *hostile takeover*. When an outside corporation intends to take over a target company and oust management, must management meekly stand by and accept its fate? All agree that management may fight for the rights of the target company's shareholders and try to obtain the best price for their shares. But what if management seeks out a *white knight*—a company that will complete the takeover but leave management officers in their jobs? For example, when Mobil Corporation made a tender offer for Marathon Oil, Marathon's management sought out U.S. Steel, which topped Mobil's offer and agreed to retain most of Marathon's management officers. Does this process place the self-interest of management over the welfare of the shareholders?

Anticipating the possibility of a hostile takeover, some high-level management officials have obtained *golden parachute* provisions in their contracts. Golden parachutes provide that if the management officer is fired, that person becomes entitled to possibly enormous benefits and severance pay. For example, when Bendix Corporation released William Agee after a failed takeover

attempt, Agee received a $4 million payment. While such a provision protects management, it may also deter outside companies from even attempting a takeover, thereby depriving the shareholders of a better price for their shares. Some, however, contend that golden parachutes are essential for companies to attract high-quality officers.

Shareholders may attempt to protect their own interests through a shareholders' derivative suit. In a shareholders' derivative suit, a minority of shareholders may object to the actions of their company's management. The derivative suit may be an attempt to compel management action in their interest. Through the application of the business judgment rule, courts have begun to limit the availability of this action. The business judgment rule may allow the board of directors to have the derivative suit dismissed if it believes that the suit is not in the corporation's best interests. The directors, however, must be disinterested in the sense that they must not have participated in the challenged transactions or have a personal interest in the outcome of the suit. Therefore, ethically, interested directors cannot dismiss a suit brought against them. Yet how exactly does one go about determining a personal interest? How strong

or how weak can this personal interest be? How does one know whether the directors have exercised good faith in their business decisions?

DISCUSSION QUESTIONS

1. If shareholders as individuals own too small a percentage of a corporation to have an effect on its actions, how do they exert control over the corporation? Some argue that their control is through the sale of shares in companies with whose actions they are dissatisfied. How would such a sale of shares have any effect on the company's future activities?

2. Should a company act ethically toward its competitors? Toward its suppliers? If so, in what way?

3. Should conservation of natural resources and other environmental considerations be concerns to which businesses address themselves?

4. Management officers have a legal and ethical responsibility to shareholders, whose money they manage. Does this responsibility extend to sacrificing their own jobs to a hostile takeover?

5. What ethical responsibilities do shareholders have to management or to other workers in their corporation?

GOVERNMENT REGULATION

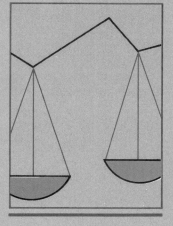

Chapter 45

Introduction and Administrative Law

Every year, federal agencies issue tens of thousands of pages filled with words in fine print containing rules that regulate business activities. A company that violates these rules may end up paying millions of dollars in liability damages. In some cases, the company's officers may be subject to criminal penalties. Federal rules cover virtually all aspects of a business operation—from its creation and financing to its hiring and firing of employees, from the way it manufactures its products to the manner in which it markets those products, and so on. These detailed federal regulations are supplemented by thousands of administrative regulations at the state and local level. As state and local rules vary widely by jurisdiction, this chapter will focus on federal administrative law.

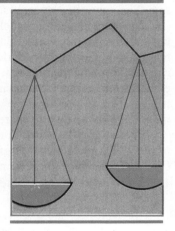

Most business regulations are directly established by **administrative agencies,** sometimes called the bureaucracy, rather than by the Congress. These agencies do not possess their own constitutional authority but have only the power that Congress has granted them by enabling statutes. In some cases, though, Congress has passed broad enabling statutes, delegating to the agencies great authority to regulate business.

For example, the Federal Trade Commission (FTC) may force a company to cease an advertising campaign whenever the commission considers those advertisements to be "unfair or deceptive" to consumers. The Federal Communications Commission (FCC) has the power to grant or deny multimillion-dollar television licenses to broadcasters, guided only by the law's requirement that its actions be in the "public interest."

The breadth of power possessed by these agencies has led some to call them the headless fourth branch of government. Those subject to agency rules may find themselves frustrated by an apparent lack of accountability on the part of federal administrators. Most agencies are considered part of the executive branch and are thus subject to the authority of the president. Some **independent regulatory agencies** have somewhat greater protection from presidential influence, however, and their officials cannot be removed from office without cause. Virtually all agencies have a broad range of authority that seems legislative and judicial, as well as executive, in nature.

HISTORICAL BACKGROUND

Administrative law was largely unknown in the early years of our nation. At that time, the United States had a relatively simple, non-industrial economy that required little regulation. As business grew, however, demands for regulation developed. The first true regulatory agency was the Interstate Commerce Commission (ICC), which was created in 1887 to regulate the railroads. Early regulation focused primarily on setting prices and deciding disputes between regulated companies. The extent of regulation increased dramatically during the Great Depression of the 1930s as President Franklin D. Roosevelt strove to increase employment and escape the depression. In 1934, such agencies as the Securities and Exchange Commission (SEC) and the National Labor Relations Board (NLRB) were created. Most of this regulation was known as economic regulation, because it was intended to make the free market work better. Securities laws and regulations, for example, were established to ensure that purchasers of stock would have sufficient information to make informed judgments about buying shares of a company.

An even greater growth in regulation took place in the 1960s and 1970s. Congress empowered the Consumer Product Safety Commission (CPSC) in 1972, the Environmental Protection Agency (EPA) in 1970, and the Occupational Safety and Health Administration (OSHA) in 1970. More than one-third of all current federal agencies were created between 1970 and 1979. This new regulation is usually called social regulation, because it attempts to protect the public from potentially harmful consequences of the free market. For example, certain industries may produce air pollution, which endangers the public health. EPA regulations are designed to prevent or control such pollution. During the 1970s, the number of administrative rules increased markedly, and agencies played a greater role in shaping federal policies. Indeed, the total number of pages of regulations and pronouncements issued by federal agencies increased from 20,036 pages in 1970 to 85,650 in 1980.

Recently, in the 1980s, there has been something of a backlash against the bureaucracy and especially against economic regulation. Agency rules seemed to create unreasonable and unnecessarily high costs of compliance for businesspersons. Although some **deregulation** has taken place in response to this pressure, a considerable amount of regulation is unquestionably here to stay. Some deregulation efforts have been overturned by the courts. The following case illustrates the controversy surrounding administrative regulation today.

Case 45.1
PUBLIC CITIZEN v.
STEED
United States Court of Appeals,
District of Columbia Circuit,
1984.
733 F.2d 93.

BACKGROUND AND FACTS *Congress passed legislation in 1966 that required the National Highway Traffic Safety Administration (NHTSA) to adopt automobile safety standards. Among the standards required by Section 203 of the act are rules for grading the quality of automobile tires. In 1975, the NHTSA adopted treadwear regulations based on certain road testing procedures. In 1983, as part of the Reagan administration's program of deregulation, the NHTSA indefinitely suspended the tire-quality regulations. The NHTSA contended that the standards were too costly for the economically troubled U.S. automobile industry and that the test procedures were not sufficiently reliable. Public Citizen, a public-interest group, sued the NHTSA, claiming that the suspension of the tire-quality standards was arbitrary and capricious.*

MIKVA, Circuit Judge.
*   *   *   *

NHTSA justified the instant suspension on the ground that the treadwear grading system was affirmatively misleading consumers about actual treadwear of tires, thereby frustrating the purpose of section 203. NHTSA claimed that the unreliability of treadwear information was caused by two factors: variability in test results caused by the test procedures themselves and variability in grade assignment practices by the tire manufacturers. Rather than attempt to correct these deficiencies in the treadwear grading program, NHTSA decided to suspend the program altogether while it further studied the pervasiveness of the variability problem and identified specific sources of variability.

We find that decision to be arbitrary and capricious for two reasons. First, the record does not support NHTSA's finding that the magnitude of the variability problem justified suspending the treadwear grading requirements, rather than retaining them while improvements in the test procedures and in the manufacturers' grade assignment practices could be developed. Second, NHTSA failed to explain why alternatives, which the rulemaking record indicates were available to the agency, could not correct many of the variability problems that NHTSA had identified.

* * * *

It is hard to imagine a more sorry performance of a congressional mandate than that carried out by NHTSA and its predecessors under section 203 of the Act. Between inaction, foot-dragging, and field reversal, the track record of agency performance is very muddy indeed.

In light of the express statutory command that a tire grading program be established by 1968, NHTSA's "indefinite suspension" of the most meaningful component of that program was arbitrary and capricious. The agency did not "cogently explain" why suspension was necessary when the old system could have been retained while improvements were developed.

DECISION AND REMEDY

The court granted Public Citizen's petition. The suspension of the tire-quality standards was judged unlawful. Consequently, the suspension was lifted, and the 1975 standards were reinstated.

PURPOSES AND METHODS OF REGULATION

The growth of regulation by administrative agencies is due largely to two factors: (1) the recognition that an absolutely free and totally unregulated market may not best serve the nation's welfare and (2) the inability of Congress to specify detailed rules for regulating the market. The far-reaching responsibilities and competing demands of Congress prevent that body from focusing on the details of regulation. For example, Congress has neither the knowledge nor the time to establish detailed safety requirements for nuclear power plants. Agencies, by contrast, are limited to smaller, more narrowly defined areas and can develop considerable expertise in their respective jurisdictions. Thus, the Nuclear Regulatory Commission (NRC), with its many staff members, was established in 1974 (replacing the Atomic Energy Commission) to become expert in nuclear safety and create specific regulations to prevent the chance of a nuclear accident. When creating an agency, Congress generally passes an enabling statute that sets forth a broad outline for regulation and gives the agency

the power to adopt more specific rules to further Congress's general purpose.

Purposes of Regulation

In various laws, Congress has made clear the reasons for and objectives of regulation. These reasons and objectives have evolved over time and reflect the expanding role of government in our economy.

CONTROLLING MONOPOLY POWER An early objective of economic regulation was to control **monopoly power,** through which a single company controls an entire market and charges more than a competitive price for its product. In the nineteenth century, railroads were something of a natural, or unavoidable, monopoly, and the Interstate Commerce Commission was created to prevent the railroads from abusing their monopoly power at the expense of shippers and consumers. Since then, other laws have been passed to prevent what was perceived to be "excessive competition." Airline regulation, for example, was a response to the fear that competition would become destructive of the industry, compromising safety and other concerns of consumers.

RATIONING SCARCE RESOURCES Another important objective of economic regulation is to ration scarce resources. Past regulation of oil and natural gas was largely a response to the fear of a growing scarcity of these resources. The Federal Communications Commission, which was created in 1934, regulates the radio and television industries because the spectrum for transmission of their signals is limited. The FCC limits radio stations to a specific frequency and requires that frequencies be separated to ensure that a clear signal can be received. The FCC may also require stations to broadcast a certain amount of news or other public-service programming.

CORRECTING UNEQUAL BARGAINING POWER Some economic regulation seeks to correct unequal bargaining power in the free market. The National Labor Relations Board establishes rules governing unions and labor relations to create fairness in labor-management relations and bargaining. The Securities and Exchange Commission seeks to promote fairness in securities transactions.

SOCIAL REGULATION Most social regulation is intended to correct for harms resulting from the free-market system. Even a freely and fairly functioning market may cause harm to society as a whole. The market for automobiles, for example, fails to account for the social harm caused by the air pollution automobiles produce. Therefore, regulation may be required to discourage polluting activities. In 1906, Congress, having concluded that individuals lacked the information necessary for a free market in consumer drugs, established the Food and Drug Administration (FDA). Today, the FDA requires that drugs be both safe and effective before they can be marketed. Other major regulated activities are summarized in Exhibit 45–1.

Methods of Regulation

Given the many different industries to be regulated and the varying purposes of regulation, it is not surprising that agencies currently employ many different methods of regulation.

RATE SETTING Traditional regulation consisted primarily of **rate setting,** in which federal agencies actually set the prices at which certain companies could sell their goods and services. Agencies historically have used rate setting to control monopoly pricing by utilities, railroads, and other natural and legal monopolies. Agencies examine the cost of providing services and set prices for regulated businesses. The set prices allow for a "fair" profit.

LICENSING Another common regulatory approach is **licensing.** The Federal Communications Commission licenses broadcasters and grants them exclusive rights to a portion of the available broadcast spectrum. The Food and Drug Administration licenses products such as drugs as a precondition to their being marketed. Government protection of exclusive rights through patents and

Exhibit 45–1 **Regulated Activities**

Transportation	Government historically has regulated transportation activities, including railroads, trucking, and air travel. Although significant deregulation has occurred in the transportation area, the Interstate Commerce Commission still regulates many activities, and the Federal Aviation Administration regulates air safety.
Utilities	Electric, water, and gas services tend to be local monopolies, regulated by state and local governments.
Communications	The Federal Communications Commission allocates available airwaves. It has also established rules to prevent obscenity on the airwaves and to maintain "fairness" in the treatment of political candidates.
Banking	Banks are subject to extensive reporting and other Federal Reserve Board regulations to ensure good management and solvency.
Consumer Products	The government sets safety standards for numerous consumer products and may conduct recalls when necessary.
General Industry	Many rules are not industry-specific but apply across the board to many companies. These include antipollution regulations, labor and worker-safety rules, and many others.

trademarks is also a kind of licensing regulation. Other agencies place information requirements on regulated enterprises. Some rules require the disclosure of certain information to consumers, and some attempt to prevent false and misleading advertising claims. Adhering to such rules is a condition of obtaining a license.

STANDARD SETTING   Probably the most common type of regulation is **standard setting.** In this process, an agency sets specific standards that companies must meet. Thus, the Environmental Protection Agency may require that given industrial plants install certain specific types of pollution control devices, and the Occupational Safety and Health Administration may demand the installation of defined health and safety protections for workers.

REQUIREMENTS OF ADMINISTRATIVE LAW

It should be obvious from the preceding discussion that agencies possess considerable authority over many businesses. Indeed, as mentioned, it is often said that the federal administrative agencies have legislative, judicial, and executive powers. Although agencies are considered part of the executive branch of government, their ability to adopt binding regulations is very much like Congress's power to pass laws. The agencies' authority to judge individual cases of alleged rule violations is closely analogous to the courts' power of adjudication. Individuals appearing before a regulatory agency may feel that the agency unfairly acts as their prosecutor, judge, and jury. These agency powers are not unchecked, however, because Congress has created rules for the agencies themselves and has provided the opportunity for judicial review of agency actions.

Agency Rulemaking— the "Legislative Power"

The best-known and most common actions of agencies involve **rulemaking,** which occurs when new regulations are promulgated (formally adopted) or old regulations are amended. Such rules typically set prospective requirements for future activities of regulated enterprises. Thus, the Federal

Trade Commission created a new rule governing the advertising and sale of used cars. This rule required that dealers disclose whether they offered any warranty on the car and, if so, what the nature of the warranty was. Used-car dealers were also required to disclose all known major repairs to the car. Virtually all agencies possess rulemaking powers, which are akin to legislative powers. Moreover, the extent and importance of this rulemaking authority has grown considerably over the years.

Agency rulemaking powers are governed primarily by the Administrative Procedure Act (APA), which created both procedural and substantive requirements for regulatory actions.[1] The APA arose out of the first great regulatory controversy in the 1930s, when business complained that the newly created agencies were acting irresponsibly. Agencies such as the Securities and Exchange Commission and the National Labor Relations Board were making regulatory decisions that seemed arbitrary and lacking in uniform procedures. Congress passed the APA in 1946 to regularize agency procedures and promote fairness in the decision making.

PROCEDURAL REQUIREMENTS FOR RULEMAKING   Slightly different APA requirements apply to different types of rulemaking activity. Most rules regulating business activity, however, must follow the procedures described below. A *rule*, subject to these APA procedures, is defined as "the whole or part of an agency statement of general or particular applicability and future effect designed to implement, interpret, or prescribe law or policy."[2] Failure to follow the required procedures will invalidate the resulting regulation.

A new rulemaking is typically triggered by a factor such as an agency investigation of the regulated industry, congressional pressure, or public petitions. An agency may not simply establish a new binding rule, however, but must follow specific procedures defined by the APA and described below. To illustrate the general description, we include a discussion of a controversial automobile

---

1. The text of the APA can be found at 5 U.S.C. Sections 551–706.

2. 5 U.S.C. Section 551(4).

safety regulation and the specific rulemaking procedures involved.[3]

The Notice of Proposed Rulemaking Even informal "notice-and-comment" rulemakings generally must begin with a Notice of Proposed Rulemaking (NPRM), which describes the intended purpose and nature of the planned rule and usually includes a draft of the current proposal.[4] The NPRM also must disclose any specific information on which the agency intends to rely. This notice must be published in the *Federal Register*, which is the official record for all federal agency actions. The *Federal Register* takes the form of a lengthy daily journal of rules and administrative statements. At present, the *Federal Register* consists of nearly a hundred thousand pages per year. A sample page from the *Federal Register* is reproduced in Exhibit 45–2.

When the Department of Transportation was implementing the National Traffic and Motor Vehicle Safety Act of 1966, it proposed a rule requiring all new cars to have air bags and published an NPRM in the *Federal Register*. This controversial rule was first proposed in 1967 and reproposed in 1976. The department projected that the rule would save 12,000 lives every year.

Public Comments The purpose of publishing the NPRM is to allow interested private groups to comment on the agency's plan for regulation. Typically, the public is given sixty or more days in which to submit written comments to the agency. Most regulations involve "informal rulemaking," and in this situation there may be no opportunity for oral comment. When statutes require formal rulemaking, however, the agency must also provide for a public hearing at which individuals may present their views orally to the administrators.[5] All the comments received in response to the NPRM become part of the "rulemaking record."

The proposed air-bag rule prompted written comments from many parties. Auto safety organizations and insurance companies wrote in to encourage the rule's adoption. General Motors, Ford, Chrysler, and other automobile companies argued

that the air-bag requirement was too expensive and was unnecessary. They contended that the Department of Transportation should encourage greater seat-belt usage instead, possibly through the use of automatic, "self-buckling" seat belts. These comments were placed in the record for the department to study.

The Final Rule After the public has been given an opportunity to comment on the proposed rule, the agency reviews this information and may publish a final rule in the *Federal Register*. This rule will have binding legal effect unless overturned by subsequent judicial review. In many instances, an agency may adopt only those rules that find support in the rulemaking record, which also forms the basis of any court review of the agency decision.

In the air-bag controversy, the Department of Transportation eventually adopted a final rule in 1977 that required "passive restraints" in new cars—either air bags or automatic seat belts, to be phased in over several years. In 1981, this passive-restraint rule was repealed, reflecting the Reagan administration's emphasis on deregulation. The 1981 *Federal Register* notice summarizing the background of the passive restraint rule and repealing its requirements appears in Exhibit 45–2.

***Ex Parte* Contacts** A particular regulatory problem is presented by ***ex parte* contacts.** These are informal communications to the agency not contained within the rulemaking record. Sometimes, other agencies or private parties communicate their rulemaking advice to agencies privately and off the record. For example, an executive might choose to call an agency official informally to express his or her displeasure with a proposed rule. Although such comments are not necessarily illegal in informal rulemaking, they have become controversial and have been the subject of some criticism. The APA does not prohibit the agency from listening to such comments, but a rule adopted by the agency must find adequate support in the public record and cannot rely exclusively on ex parte contacts.[6] The following case illustrates the state of the law regarding ex parte contacts.

---

3. This chapter's summary of the air-bag regulation is highly condensed. The actual regulation involved extensive rulemaking over a period of decades.

4. 5 U.S.C. Section 553.

5. 5 U.S.C. Section 556.

---

6. Administrative Conference of the United States, *A Guide to Federal Agency Rulemaking* (1983), p. 155.

Exhibit 45–2 A Page from the *Federal Register*

Federal Register / Vol. 46, No. 209 / Thursday, October 29, 1981 / Rules and Regulations   53419

National Highway Traffic Safety Administration

49 CFR Part 571

[Docket No. 74–14; Notice 25]

Federal Motor Vehicle Safety Standards; Occupant Crash Protection

AGENCY: National Highway Traffic Safety Administration, Department of Transportation.

ACTION: Final rule.

SUMMARY: The purpose of this notice is to amend Federal Motor Vehicle Safety Standard No. 208, Occupant Crash Protection, to rescind the requirements for installation of automatic restraints in the front seating positions of passenger cars. Those requirements were scheduled to become effective for large and mid-size cars on September 1, 1982, and for small cars on September 1, 1983.

The automatic restraint requirements are being rescinded because of uncertainty about the public acceptability and probable usage rate of the type of automatic restraint which the car manufacturers planned to make available to most new car buyers. This uncertainty and the relatively substantial cost of automatic restraints preclude the agency from determining that the standard is at this time reasonable and practicable. The reasonableness of the automatic restraint requirements is further called into question by the fact that all new car buyers would be required to pay for automatic belt systems that may induce only a few additional people to take advantage of the benefits of occupant restraints.

The agency is also seriously concerned about the possibility that adverse public reaction to the cost and presence of automatic restraints could have a significant adverse effect on present and future public acceptance of highway safety efforts.

Under the amended standard, car manufacturers will continue to have the current option of providing either automatic or manual occupant restraints.

DATES: The rescission of the automatic restraint requirements of Standard No. 208 is effective December 8, 1981. Any petitions for reconsideration must be received by the agency not later than December 3, 1981.

ADDRESS: Any petitions for reconsideration should refer to the docket number and notice number of this notice and be submitted to: Administrator, National Highway Traffic Safety Administration, 400 Seventh Street, S.W., Washington, D.C. 20590.

FOR FURTHER INFORMATION CONTACT: Mr. Michael Finkelstein, Associate Administrator for Rulemaking, National Highway Traffic Safety Administration, Washington, D.C. 20590 (202–426–1810).

SUPPLEMENTARY INFORMATION: On April 9, 1981, the Department of Transportation published a notice of proposed rulemaking (NPRM) setting forth alternative amendments to the automatic restraint requirements of Standard No. 208 (46 FR 21205). The purpose of proposing the alternatives was to ensure that Standard No. 208 reflects the changes in circumstances since the automatic restraint requirements were issued (42 FR 34289; July 5, 1977) and to ensure that the standard meets the requirements of the National Traffic and Motor Vehicle Safety Act of 1966 and Executive Order 12291, "Federal Regulations" (February 17, 1981).

Background and NPRM

The automatic restraint requirements were adopted in 1977 in response to the high number of passenger car occupants killed annually in crashes and to the persistent low usage rate of manual belts. The manual belt is the type of belt which is found in most cars today and which the occupant must place around himself or herself and buckle in order to gain its protection. Then, as now, there were two types of automatic restraints, i.e., restraints that require no action by vehicle occupants, such as buckling a belt, in order to be effective. One type is the air cushion restraint (air bag) and the other is the automatic belt (a belt which automatically envelopes an occupant when the occupant enters a vehicle and closes the door).

In view of the greater experience with air bags in large cars and to spread out capital investments, the Department established a large-to-small car compliance schedule. Under that schedule, large cars were required to begin compliance on September 1, 1981, mid-size cars on September 1, 1982, and small cars on September 1, 1983.

On April 6, 1981, after providing notice and opportunity for comment, the Department delayed the compliance date for large cars from September 1, 1981, to September 1, 1982. As explained in the April 6, final rule, that delay was adopted

. . . because of the effects of implementation in model year 1982 on large car manufacturers, because of the added significance which those effects assume due to the change in economic circumstances since the schedule was adopted in 1977, and because of the undermining by subsequent events of the rationale underlying the original phase-in schedule.

Simultaneous with publishing the one-year delay in the effective date for large cars, the Department also issued a proposal for making further changes in the automatic restraint requirements. This action was taken in response to a variety of factors that raised questions whether the automatic restraint requirements represented the most reasonable and effective approach to the problem of the low usage of safety belts. Among these factors were the uncertainty about public acceptability of automatic restraints in view of the absence of any significant choice between automatic belts and air bags and the nature of the automatic belt designs planned by the car manufacturers, the consequent uncertainties about the rate of usage of automatic restraints, and the substantial costs of air bags even if produced in large volumes.

The three principal proposals were reversal of phase-in sequence, simultaneous compliance, and rescission. The reversal proposal would have changed the large-to-small car order of compliance to a requirement that small cars commence compliance on September 1, 1982, mid-size cars on September 1, 1983, and large cars on September 1, 1984. The proposal for simultaneous compliance would have required all size classes to begin compliance on the same date, March 1, 1983. The rescission proposal would have retained the manufacturers' current option of equipping their cars with either manual or automatic restraints.

In addition, the Department proposed that, under both the first and second alternatives, the automatic restraint requirements be amended so that such restraints would not be required in the front center seating position.

Following the close of the period for written comments on the April NPRM, NHTSA decided, in its discretion, to hold a public meeting on the alternatives. The purpose of the meeting was to permit interested parties to present their views and arguments orally before the Administrator and ensure that all available data were submitted to the agency. The notice announcing the meeting indicated that participants at the hearing would be permitted to supplement their previous comments. The notice also urged participants to consider the issues raised in former Secretary Coleman's June 14, 1976 proposal regarding occupant restraints and in former

Case 45.2

**SIERRA CLUB v.
COSTLE**

United States Court of Appeals,
District of Columbia Circuit,
1981.
657 F.2d 298.

BACKGROUND AND FACTS   *In 1976, the Environmental Protection
Agency proposed a rule establishing new pollution-control standards for coal-
fired steam generators. The agency gave notice and received comments in the
manner prescribed by the Administrative Procedure Act. After the public comments had been received, the EPA received informal suggestions from members
of Congress and other federal officials. In 1979, the EPA published its final
standards. Several environmental groups protested these standards, arguing that
they were too lax. As part of this protest, the groups complained that political
influence from Congress and other federal officials had encouraged the EPA to
relax the proposed standards. The groups went on to argue that these ex* parte
*comments were themselves illegal or, at least, that such comments should have
been summarized in the record.*

ROBB, Circuit Judge.
*   *   *   *

   The statute does not explicitly treat the issue of post-comment period meetings
with individuals outside EPA. Oral face-to-face discussions are not prohibited anywhere,
anytime, in the Act. The absence of such prohibition may have arisen from the nature
of the informal rulemaking procedures Congress had in mind. Where agency action
resembles judicial action, where it involves formal rulemaking, adjudication, or quasi-
adjudication among "conflicting private claims to a valuable privilege," the insulation
of the decisionmaker from ex parte contacts is justified by basic notions of due process
to the parties involved. But where agency action involves informal rulemaking of a
policymaking sort, the concept of ex parte contacts is of more questionable utility.

   Under our system of government, the very legitimacy of general policymaking
performed by unelected administrators depends in no small part upon the openness,
accessibility, and amenability of these officials to the needs and ideas of the public
from whom their ultimate authority derives, and upon whom their commands must
fall. As judges we are insulated from these pressures because of the nature of the judicial
process in which we participate; but we must refrain from the easy temptation to look
askance at all face-to-face lobbying efforts, regardless of the forum in which they occur,
merely because we see them as inappropriate in the judicial context. Furthermore, the
importance to effective regulation of continuing contact with a regulated industry, other
affected groups, and the public cannot be underestimated.
*   *   *   *

   It still can be argued, however, that if oral communications are to be freely permitted
after the close of the comment period, then at least some adequate summary of them
must be made in order to preserve the integrity of the rulemaking docket, which under
the statute must be the sole repository of material upon which EPA intends to rely.
The statute does not require the docketing of all post-comment period conversations
and meetings, but we believe that a fair inference can be drawn that in some instances
such docketing may be needed. *   *   *

**DECISION
AND REMEDY**   *The court affirmed the EPA standards. The court found only "small procedural
errors" that did not justify overturning the standards.*

**SUBSTANTIVE REQUIREMENTS FOR RULEMAK-
ING**   Although most restrictions on agency rules
are procedural, the APA also permits some judicial
review of the substance of final regulations. Those
adversely affected by a regulation possess *standing*

to challenge a newly promulgated rule[7]—that is,
they have a sufficiently direct interest in the rule
to be proper plaintiffs. An affected person may

_____

7. 5 U.S.C. Section 702.

contend that a rule misinterprets the applicable law or goes beyond the agency's statutory authority. It is difficult, however, to support a claim that a regulation should be overturned simply because the agency made a mistake in judgment.

Under the APA, a person questioning an agency judgment on this basis must demonstrate that it is "arbitrary and capricious."[8] Courts have not formulated a clear definition of arbitrary and capricious, but the standard is a relatively easy one for the agency to meet—it is similar to the rational-basis test under the equal protection clause of the Constitution. To meet the standard, the person challenging the rule must show a serious flaw in

---

8. 5 U.S.C. Section 706(2)(a).

the agency's judgment, such as internal inconsistency or refusal to consider reasonable alternatives to its rule. Moreover, the reviewing court is largely limited to the findings of fact made by the agency and the rulemaking record it compiled.

Substantive review was ultimately sought in the dispute over the air-bag regulation. Before the passive-restraint requirement was put into effect, the newly elected Reagan administration's Department of Transportation conducted another rulemaking and repealed the regulation in 1981, as part of a program of deregulation. The insurance companies objected and sued, claiming that the repeal of the rule was arbitrary and capricious. The case ultimately reached the Supreme Court, which issued the following decision.

BACKGROUND AND FACTS   *In 1977, the Department of Transportation adopted a passive-restraint standard (known as Standard 208) that required new cars to have either air bags or automatic seat belts. By 1981, it became clear that all the major auto manufacturers would install automatic seat belts to comply with this rule. The Department of Transportation determined that most purchasers of cars would detach their automatic seat belts, thus making them ineffective. Consequently, the department repealed the regulation.*

State Farm Mutual and other insurance companies sued in the District of Columbia Circuit Court of Appeals for a review of the Department of Transportation's repeal of the regulation. That court held that the repeal was arbitrary and capricious because the Department of Transportation had reversed its rule without sufficient support. The motor vehicle manufacturers then appealed this decision to the United States Supreme Court.

 Case 45.3

MOTOR VEHICLE MANUFACTURERS ASSOC. v. STATE FARM MUTUAL AUTOMOBILE INS. CO.

Supreme Court of the United States, 1983.
463 U.S. 29, 103 S.Ct. 2856, 77 L.Ed.2d 443.

WHITE, Justice.
*   *   *   *

The Department of Transportation accepts the applicability of the "arbitrary and capricious" standard. It argues that under this standard, a reviewing court may not set aside an agency rule that is rational, based on consideration of the relevant factors, and within the scope of the authority delegated to the agency by the statute. We do not disagree with this formulation. The scope of review under the "arbitrary and capricious" standard is narrow and a court is not to substitute its judgment for that of the agency. Nevertheless, the agency must examine the relevant data and articulate a satisfactory explanation for its action including a "rational connection between the facts found and the choice made." In reviewing that explanation, we must "consider whether the decision was based on a consideration of the relevant factors and whether there has been a clear error of judgment." *   *   * Normally, an agency rule would be arbitrary and capricious if the agency has relied on factors which Congress has not intended it to consider, entirely failed to consider an important aspect of the problem, offered an explanation for its decision that runs counter to the evidence before the agency, or is so implausible that it could not be ascribed to a difference in view or the product of agency expertise. *   *   *
*   *   *   *

The first and most obvious reason for finding the rescission arbitrary and capricious is that NHTSA apparently gave no consideration whatever to modifying the Standard to require that airbag technology be utilized. Standard 208 sought to achieve automatic crash protection by requiring automobile manufacturers to install either of two passive restraint devices: airbags or automatic seatbelts. There was no suggestion in the long rulemaking process that led to Standard 208 that if only one of these options were feasible, no passive restraint standard should be promulgated. *   *   *

*   *   *

*   *   * Given the effectiveness ascribed to airbag technology by the agency, the mandate of the Act to achieve traffic safety would suggest that the logical response to the faults of detachable seatbelts would be to require the installation of airbags. At the very least this alternative way of achieving the objectives of the Act should have been addressed and adequate reasons given for its abandonment. But the agency not only did not require compliance through airbags, it also did not even consider the possibility in its 1981 rulemaking. Not one sentence of its rulemaking statement discusses the airbags-only option. *   *   *

*   *   *   *

*   *   * It is true that rulemaking "cannot be found wanting simply because the agency failed to include every alternative device and thought conceivable by the mind of man . . . regardless of how uncommon or unknown that alternative may have been. . . ." But the airbag is more than a policy alternative to the passive restraint Standard; it is a technological alternative within the ambit of the existing Standard. We hold only that given the judgment made in 1977 that airbags are an effective and cost-beneficial life-saving technology, the mandatory passive restraint rule may not be abandoned without any consideration whatsoever of an airbags-only requirement.

DECISION AND REMEDY   *The Supreme Court held that the rescission of the standard was arbitrary and capricious. The Court remanded the case to the court of appeals, with directions to remand to the Department of Transportation for further consideration of the air-bag rule.*

On some occasions, an agency may be held to a standard that is slightly stricter than the arbitrary and capricious test. The statute authorizing a particular agency may require that rules be based on "substantial evidence." This standard is usually used in cases of formal rulemaking, which include oral hearings and cross-examination of witnesses, as in court.[9] Under this standard, an agency's finding must be supported by substantial evidence in the record. Although stricter than the arbitrary and capricious test, the substantial-evidence standard still accords considerable deference to agency conclusions.

Agency Adjudication— the "Judicial Power"

In addition to the authority to make rules, most agencies possess the power to judge some types of individual disputes.[10] Sometimes the agency may use adjudication to make policy, by deciding whether a particular action violates the statute that the agency is charged with administering. More frequently, an agency adjudicates a factual dispute concerning whether a person has violated a rule.

ADMINISTRATIVE LAW JUDGES Most agency adjudications are initially resolved by a special kind of officer known as an **administrative law**

---

9. 5 U.S.C. Section 706(2)(f) applies this substantial-evidence test to formal rulemakings conducted under Sections 556 and 557. Other laws may also require the use of this standard.

10. Requirements for adjudication are found at 5 U.S.C. Section 544.

judge (ALJ). Administrative law judges are not judges in the conventional sense but are employees of the agency conducting the adjudication. The office of ALJ has evolved into an independent one, however.

The APA provides a set of protections for the independence of ALJs. ALJs cannot be fired by an agency but only by the Civil Service Commission after a full hearing. Their pay is set independently to protect them from agency reprisals for unpopular decisions. The Civil Service Commission also establishes requirements for hiring ALJs, sets "grades," or promotion levels, for all current ALJs, and controls their case assignments. Prior to 1972, these judges were called "trial examiners," but their title was changed to enhance their prestige. Administrative law judges lack the full independence of the federal judiciary, but they are generally well regarded and paid nearly as much as federal district judges.

PROCEDURES   Agency adjudication is much like a court hearing, complete with penalties, and therefore individuals involved in adjudication have more procedural protections than those involved in rulemaking. Among other rights, these persons have a right to be represented by counsel and a right to cross-examine witnesses. Most adjudications begin with a complaint filed by the agency against a business charged with violating a rule or statute. This is followed by a hearing before the administrative law judge, who conducts the hearing and rules on all motions raised by the parties. At the hearing, the agency is represented by counsel, who presents evidence in support of the complaint. There is no jury in agency adjudications. Unlike the courts, which restrict the admissibility of evidence, administrative hearings have liberal rules that permit almost any relevant evidence to be introduced.[11]

AN EXAMPLE OF AGENCY ADJUDICATION Consider the following example of agency adjudication. In 1970, the Federal Trade Commission embarked upon a policy requiring that advertising claims be "substantiated" by testing. This policy left open many questions regarding what types of claims must be substantiated and what degree of substantiation is necessary. Questions of the latter type were settled through adjudication. For example, the FTC believed that advertisements for a certain sunburn ointment were misleading and insufficiently substantiated; and in 1971 the commission filed a complaint against Pfizer, Inc., the drug company responsible for the advertising.

At the Pfizer hearing, the FTC presented evidence that the advertising claim was invalid and unsupported by careful scientific studies. Pfizer then presented its case, in which it argued that detailed scientific substantiation should not be required. As in other courtroom trials, witnesses were cross-examined and procedural objections were raised. Both parties submitted legal briefs and proposed findings to the administrative law judge. The ALJ then rendered an **initial order** in favor of Pfizer. The APA defines an initial order as "the whole or a part of a final disposition, whether affirmative, negative, injunctive, or declaratory in form, of an agency in a matter other than a rulemaking."[12]

An ALJ's initial decision becomes the order of the agency unless it is appealed. In contrast, a **recommended order** is one in which the presiding employee (not always an ALJ) recommends the order to the agency.[13] The recommended order is generally adopted if neither the agency counsel nor the respondent objects. The final order may take the form of civil monetary penalties or a **cease-and-desist order,** which is much like a court's injunction.

Although an ALJ's initial decision is likely to carry considerable weight with the agency, the APA specifically states that "on appeal from review of the initial decision, the agency has all the powers which it would have in making the initial decision, except as it may limit the issues on notice or by rule." Review by an agency differs from most instances of judicial review in that the agency is not required to defer to the administrative law judge's findings of fact. The FTC enforcement staff appealed the Pfizer case to the full commission, asking that the ALJ's decision be overturned. The following decision of the commission affirmed the basic advertising substantiation rule but also upheld the ALJ's verdict.

---

11. Federal Administrative Law Judge Hearings, *Statistical Report*, p. 33.

12. 5 U.S.C. Section 551(6).
13. 5 U.S.C. Section 557(b).

Case 45.4

IN RE PFIZER, INC.

Federal Trade Commission,
1972.
81 F.T.C. 23.

BACKGROUND AND FACTS *The Federal Trade Commission staff's advertising substantiation rule held that advertisements must be substantiated by well-controlled scientific studies, or such claims would be considered deceptive. The staff then brought an action against Pfizer over advertisements for a sunburn treatment, which were allegedly unsupported by direct studies on humans. Pfizer argued that it had other forms of evidence sufficient to support its advertising claims.*

The ALJ who heard this adjudication dismissed the complaint against Pfizer, holding that no controlled scientific studies should be required. The staff appealed this dismissal to the commission itself.

KIRKPATRICK, Commissioner.

The Commission's staff counsel, who have the burden of proving the allegations of the complaint, challenge certain advertising by Pfizer for the product "UN-BURN," a nonprescription product recommended for use on minor burns and sunburn. The complaint cited the following radio and television advertising for Un-Burn as typical and representative:

New Un-Burn actually anesthetizes *nerves* in sensitive sunburned skin.

Un-Burn relieves pain *fast*. Actually *anesthetizes nerves* in sensitive sunburned skin.

Sensitive skin * * * Sunburned skin is sensitive skin * * * Sensitive sunburned skin needs * * * UN-BURN. New UN-BURN contains the same local anesthetic doctors often use. * * * Actually anesthetizes nerves in sensitive sunburned skin. I'll tell you what I like about UN-BURN. It's the best friend a blonde ever had! * * * I'm a blonde * * * and I know what it means to have sensitive skin. Why I'm half afraid of moon burn! That's why I'm mad about UN-BURN. It stops sunburn pain in * * * less time than it takes me to slip out of my bikini. That's awfully nice to know when you're the sensitive type.
* * *

The complaint alleges that the foregoing advertising claims were not substantiated by Pfizer by "adequate and well-controlled scientific studies or tests prior to the making of such statements."
* * * *

Given the imbalance of knowledge and resources between a business enterprise and each of its customers, economically it is more rational, and imposes far less cost on society, to require a manufacturer to confirm his affirmative product claims rather than impose a burden upon each individual consumer to test, investigate, or experiment for himself. The manufacturer has the ability, the knowhow, the equipment, the time and the resources to undertake such information by testing or otherwise—the consumer usually does not.

Turning to that part of the complaint which challenges respondent's marketing practices as unfair, the Commission is of the view that it is an unfair practice in violation of the Federal Trade Commission Act to make an affirmative product claim without a reasonable basis for making the claim. Fairness to the consumer, as well as fairness to competitors, dictates this conclusion. Absent a reasonable basis for a vendor's affirmative product claims, a consumer's ability to make an economically rational product choice, and a competitor's ability to compete on the basis of price, quality, service or convenience, are materially impaired and impeded.
* * * *

Pfizer's director of Marketing testified that he took three measures to satisfy himself as to the efficacy of the product Un-Burn. First, he received "complete assurance" from Pfizer's medical people that the claims he planned to use for Un-Burn could be supported by the two active ingredients in the quantities in which they were to be used in the product. He was assured that the way a topical anesthetic works is to anesthetize nerves and thereby stop pain. He was also assured by the "medical people" that the product was patterned very closely after the market leader, Solarcaine. Secondly, he was assured that all available literature or information on these two active ingredients had been thoroughly reviewed and favorable conclusions derived from this review as to the efficacy of the ingredients as topical anesthetics. Finally, he personally reviewed all competitive advertising to satisfy himself that Pfizer would not be claiming anything more than other products with the same active ingredients. The director of marketing testified that Pfizer did not conduct tests on humans to determine whether the efficacy claims could be supported, but consciously "accepted another method of satisfying" themselves by going over the history of the ingredients. No specific tests were conducted on human beings to prove that Un-Burn anesthetizes nerve ends.

*   *   *   *

While the Commission finds that respondent failed in its attempt to demonstrate affirmatively the existence of a reasonable basis for its Un-Burn advertising, the evidence is not sufficient to prove that respondent in fact *lacked* a reasonable basis for its advertising claims. The record evidence is simply inconclusive with regard to the adequacy of the medical literature and clinical experience relied upon by respondent, and with regard to the reasonableness of such reliance.

The commission affirmed the ALJ's decision and dismissed the complaint against Pfizer. In so doing, the commission upheld the concept that advertising must be substantiated, but it went on to hold that the staff had not met its burden of proof in demonstrating that Pfizer's advertising was insufficiently substantiated.	**DECISION AND REMEDY**

If the agency rules *against* the private party following an adjudication, further appeal is still possible. In adjudications, courts review whether the agency has afforded a party all the procedures guaranteed by statute and the due process clause of the Constitution. If the agency's fact-finding procedures are inadequate, the court may conduct a full *de novo* **review**.[14] In a *de novo* review, the court does not defer to the agency, as it ordinarily would on a question of fact. Rather, the reviewing court reconsiders the case and all the evidence as if it had not been heard before the agency. When such a review occurs, a court is much more likely to substitute its judgment on the facts and overturn the agency decision. In addition, the court will consider whether the result is consistent with the statute authorizing agency action.

Agency Enforcement and Administration—the "Executive Power"

Administrative agencies perform executive functions, such as investigating legal violations and prosecuting them in court. Agencies have the powers necessary to carry out their designated func-

tions. These include investigatory, enforcement, and administrative powers.

INVESTIGATORY POWERS In order for agencies to regulate businesses effectively, they must be able to obtain information. When an agency has been delegated the power to issue rules prescribing standards of conduct, it is essential that the agency have access to complete and accurate information. Some companies, however, may consider it to be in their best interests to resist disclosure in an effort to avoid or impede further regulation. Consequently, Congress has delegated to agencies various degrees of investigatory powers. These powers include the authority to issue subpoenas for documents or testimony, inspect records, and request information. For example, the Federal Trade Commission may subpoena records and require reports as part of its program to ensure accuracy in advertising. Companies may thus be compelled to provide their substantiation to the agency even before an actual adjudication takes place.

Investigatory powers of agencies are constrained by constitutional limitations, however. Both procedural and substantive due process protect businesses against arbitrary, capricious, and unreasonable agency demands. In addition, the

---

14. 5 U.S.C. Section 706(2)(f).

Fourth Amendment requires an agency to obtain a warrant before searching the premises of a business.[15] If the Occupational Safety and Health Administration (OSHA) wants to conduct a routine inspection to see if a company has unsafe working conditions, the agency must obtain a warrant before it may require an inspection of the workplace. As a practical matter, however, OSHA has little difficulty obtaining these warrants. Although the Fifth Amendment protection against self-incrimination does not apply to corporations, individuals may refuse to provide information on the grounds that it may tend to incriminate them.

ENFORCEMENT POWERS   Most agencies also possess enforcement powers, including the power to issue orders to parties found to be in violation of rules or statutes. All final orders carry the weight of statutory law and have prescribed penalties for violations. These penalties are binding unless a reviewing court reverses the agency decision. Failure to comply with the prescribed penalties is treated like any other violation of the law. In most cases, violations are considered to be civil matters, and thus a violator is held liable for money damages or is required to take some specific action, such as the installation of new pollution-control equipment. In 1986, for example, Gulf States Oil and Refining Company of Houston was fined over $2.5 million for violating rules on the maximum amount of lead permitted in fuel. Currently, there is a trend toward issuing criminal as well as civil penalties. Violators, including corporate officers, may be subject to jail sentences. For example, violators of the insider trading prohibitions of the securities acts may be jailed for up to five years and fined up to $100,000 per offense. The Securities and Exchange Commission has the power to pursue these penalties through criminal prosecution in court. In 1987, an office manager, a reporter, and the well-known investor Ivan Boesky were sentenced to jail terms ranging from eighteen months to three and one-half years for violation of federal securities laws.

ADMINISTRATIVE POWERS   Many agencies possess other significant executive powers as well.

They have whatever internal management powers are necessary to accomplish their objectives. Thus, agencies have the necessary authority to hire employees, hire subcontractors, and make rules for office management. Agencies may also have the authority to disburse money through grants or loans to public and private entities. The Environmental Protection Agency, for example, makes grants to develop or test innovative approaches to pollution control.

PUBLIC ACCOUNTABILITY

It should be clear from the preceding discussion that federal agencies possess far-reaching powers. In recent years there has been some reaction against the perceived abuse of this administrative authority. During the Reagan administration, new limits were placed on agency decision making, and some areas were deregulated. The Civil Aeronautics Board, which regulated airline schedules and fares, was abolished altogether. Many regulations, especially those of OSHA and the EPA, were suspended by the Reagan administration, and other rules were subjected to intensive White House review. Even prior to the Reagan administration, however, genuine public concern existed over the powers exercised by administrative agencies. As a result of this concern, several laws were passed to make agencies more accountable to the public. The most significant of these laws are the Freedom of Information Act, the Government-in-the-Sunshine Act, and the Regulatory Flexibility Act.

Freedom of Information Act

The Freedom of Information Act (FOIA), which was passed by Congress in 1966, requires the federal government to disclose certain "records" to "any person" upon request.[16] The person requesting information need not disclose the reason for the request. Although the request must comply with FOIA procedures, it need only contain a reasonable description of the information sought. If the agency denies the request or simply fails to respond, the person making the request can go to a federal district court to obtain an order compelling disclosure. Many state governments have

---

15. Marshall v. Barlow's, Inc., 436 U.S. 307, 98 S.Ct. 1816, 56 L.Ed.2d 305 (1978). But note that warrants are not *always* required—for example, they are not required for searches in highly regulated industries and seizures of contaminated food.

16. 5 U.S.C. Section 552.

their own versions of the Freedom of Information Act that are applicable to state agencies.

An agency must disclose requested information unless it falls within specific, statutorily defined exemptions from the FOIA. These exemptions include the following:

1. Classified information related to national defense or foreign affairs.
2. Information related solely to the internal personnel rules and practices of an agency.
3. Information specifically exempted by other statutes.
4. Trade secrets and privileged commercial information obtained by the government from private persons.
5. Certain private intra-agency or inter-agency memoranda.

6. Personnel and medical files.
7. Information related to the supervision of financial institutions.
8. Privileged geological data.
9. Investigatory records that may be related to future prosecutions.

The last exemption is to prevent statutory violators from "previewing" the government's investigations of or cases against the violators. When an agency claims that information is exempt from disclosure, courts tend to review this claim critically and with a presumption that information should be disclosed to the interested members of the public. The following case illustrates a court's review of FOIA exemption claims.

BACKGROUND AND FACTS *In 1971, Sears, Roebuck & Co. requested that the National Labor Relations Board disclose all advice and appeals memoranda on a certain issue of labor law. These documents reflect the board's internal disposition of certain labor disputes. For example, if the board decides not to issue a complaint on a labor law violation, an appeals memorandum is prepared and effectively terminates the case. Sears sought these documents under the FOIA to determine when the NLRB was likely to allege a labor law violation. The NLRB claimed that these documents were exempt from disclosure as intra-agency memoranda under an exemption of FOIA. The district court and court of appeals ruled for Sears, and the NLRB appealed to the Supreme Court of the United States.*

 Case 45.5

NATIONAL LABOR RELATIONS BOARD v. SEARS, ROEBUCK & CO.
Supreme Court of the United States, 1975.
421 U.S. 132, 95 S.Ct. 1504, 44 L.Ed.2d 29.

WHITE, Justice.
*   *   *   *

*   *   * It is sufficient to note for present purposes that the Act seeks "to establish a general philosophy of full agency disclosure unless information is exempted under clearly delineated statutory language." As the Act is structured, virtually every document generated by an agency is available to the public in one form or another, unless it falls within one of the Act's nine exemptions.
*   *   *   *

Sears claims, and the courts below ruled, that the memoranda sought are expressions of legal and policy decisions already adopted by the agency and constitute "final opinions" and "instructions to staff that affect a member of the public," both categories being expressly disclosable under § 552(a)(2) of the Act, pursuant to its purposes to prevent the creation of "secret law."
*   *   *   *

[The court then considered the NLRB's claim that disclosure was exempted as intra-agency memoranda.]

*   *   * Manifestly, the ultimate purpose of this long-recognized privilege is to prevent injury to the quality of agency decisions. The quality of a particular agency decision will clearly be affected by the communications received by the decisionmaker on the subject of the decision prior to the time the decision is made. However, it is difficult to see how the quality of a decision will be affected by communications with respect to the decision occurring after the decision is finally reached; and therefore equally difficult to see how the quality of the decision will be affected by forced disclosure of such communications, as long as prior communications and the ingredients of the decisionmaking process are not disclosed.

DECISION AND REMEDY   *The Supreme Court affirmed the decision of the lower courts with respect to appeals memoranda that represented the final disposition of a case. The Court noted that other documents, which involved the NLRB's preparation of a case, could be exempted as intra-agency memoranda.*

Government-in-the-Sunshine Act

The Sunshine Act, or "open meeting law," was passed by Congress in 1976 and requires that "every portion of every meeting of an agency" that is "headed by a collegial body" must be open to "public observation." [17] When a group of agency officials meets to deliberate or to take action on agency business, the Sunshine Act applies. This act also requires procedures to ensure that the public is provided with adequate advance notice of the planned meeting and its agenda. The Sunshine Act also contains statutorily specified exceptions to this rule, which are similar to the FOIA disclosure exemptions. Additional exceptions permit the closing of meetings at which matters will be discussed (1) that involve accusing any person of a crime, (2) that would frustrate the implementation of a future agency action, or (3) that involve agency participation in future rulemaking or litigation. The courts have interpreted the Sunshine Act strictly to require openness whenever possible.

Regulatory Flexibility Act

Congress has been particularly concerned over the effect of regulation on small business. To mitigate this regulatory burden, Congress passed the Reg-

ulatory Flexibility Act in 1980.[18] Under this act, whenever a new rule will have a "significant impact upon a substantial number of small entities," the agency must conduct a regulatory flexibility analysis. This analysis must measure the costs of regulation on small business and consider alternatives that might be less burdensome. In addition, the Regulatory Flexibility Act contains provisions to help alert small business entities about forthcoming regulations. Due in part to the Regulatory Flexibility Act, small business has been relieved of some record-keeping requirements relating to hazardous-waste management and other rules.

The Trend toward Control over Administrative Agencies

Public accountability requirements, such as the Regulatory Flexibility Act, represent a continuing trend toward controlling perceived excesses of agency power. The greatest restrictions, however, remain in the detailed procedural requirements of the APA and in the political influence of Congress and the president. Notwithstanding these checks, agencies possess considerable power and will continue to establish scores of regulations affecting business in the United States.

---

17. 5 U.S.C. Section 552(b).

18. 5 U.S.C. Sections 601–612.

QUESTIONS AND CASE PROBLEMS

1. Assume that the Securities and Exchange Commission has a policy not to enforce rules prohibiting insider trading

except when the insiders make monetary profits for themselves. Then the SEC modifies this policy by a determination that the agency has the statutory authority to bring an enforcement action against an individual even if he or she does not personally profit from the insider trading. In modifying the policy, the SEC does not conduct a rulemaking but simply announces its new decision. A securities organization objects and says that the policy was unlawfully developed without opportunity for public comment. In a lawsuit challenging the new policy, should the policy be overruled under the Administrative Procedure Act?

2. Assume that the Food and Drug Administration, using proper procedures, adopts a rule describing its future investigations. This new rule covers all future cases in which the FDA wants to regulate food additives. Under the new rule, the FDA says that it will not regulate food additives without giving food companies an opportunity to cross-examine witnesses. Some time later, the FDA wants to regulate methylisocyanate, a food additive. In doing so, the FDA conducts a normal notice-and-comment rulemaking, without cross-examination, and regulates methylisocyanate. Producers protest, saying that the FDA promised cross-examination. The FDA responds that the Administrative Procedure Act does not require such cross-examination and that its promise could simply be withdrawn. How should the court rule?

3. For decades, the Federal Trade Commission resolved fair trade and advertising disputes through individual adjudications. In the 1960s, the FTC began promulgating rules that defined fair and unfair trade practices. In cases involving violations of these rules, the due process rights of participants were more limited and did not include cross-examination. This was because, although anyone found violating a rule would receive a full adjudication, the legitimacy of the rule itself could not be challenged in the adjudication. If a party had violated a rule, it was almost certain to lose the adjudication. Affected parties complained, arguing that their rights before the FTC were unduly limited by the new rules. Were the rules illegal?

4. The Department of Commerce issued a flammability standard that required all mattresses, including crib mattresses, to pass a test that involved contact with a burning cigarette. The manufacturers of crib mattresses petitioned the court to exempt their product from the test procedure, but the department refused to do so. The crib manufacturers sued the department and argued that applying such a rule to crib mattresses was arbitrary and capricious because infants do not smoke. Should this rule be overturned? [Bunny Bear, Inc. v. Peterson, 473 F.2d 1002 (1st Cir. 1973)]

5. The Atomic Energy Commission was engaged in rulemaking proceedings for nuclear reactor safety. An environmental group sued the commission, arguing that its proceedings were inadequate. The commission had carefully complied with all requirements of the Administrative Procedure Act. The environmentalists argued, however, that the very hazardous and technical nature of the reactor safety issue required more elaborate procedures above and beyond those of the APA. A federal circuit court of appeals agreed and overturned the Atomic Energy Commission rules. The commission appealed the case to the Supreme Court of the United States. How should the Court rule? [Vermont Yankee Nuclear Power Corp. v. Natural Resources Defense Council, Inc., 435 U.S. 519, 98 S.Ct. 1197, 55 L.Ed.2d 460 (1978)]

6. The Interstate Commerce Commission proposed a rule to regulate airline practices related to sponsored tours. After receiving public comments, the ICC decided that in order for the rule to be effective it should apply to travel agents as well. Consequently, the ICC's final rule applied to both airlines and travel agents. An association of travel-agent tour brokers protested the final rule, arguing that its members had had no notice that the rule might apply to travel agents and no effective opportunity to comment on the rule as applied to agents. Should the court uphold the rule? [National Tour Brokers Ass'n v. United States, 591 F.2d 896 (D.C. Cir. 1978)]

7. The Truth-in-Lending Act requires merchants who regularly extend credit to consumers to disclose the amount of the finance charge. The act also gives the Federal Reserve Board (FRB) the authority to adopt regulations under the act. The board issued a regulation requiring disclosure whenever a finance charge was imposed or when goods were sold and "payable in more than four installments." A magazine seller offered a subscription for installment payments but failed to comply with the regulation. The magazine seller argued that the regulation went beyond the FRB's authority and was illegal. The court of appeals agreed and overturned the rule. The FRB appealed to the Supreme Court. How should the Court rule? [Mourning v. Family Publications Service, Inc., 411 U.S. 356, 93 S.Ct. 1652, 36 L.Ed.2d 318 (1973)]

8. The Interstate Commerce Act required certain companies to obtain ICC approval for the expansion of trucking services. The approval was known as a certificate of convenience and necessity. At about the same time, two separate trucking concerns applied for such certificates to serve the mid-Atlantic region. The two applications covered the same route origins, similar commodities, and similar destinations. The ICC approved one application and denied the other, but it gave no explanation or justification for its decision. The company whose application was denied sued the ICC. Should the court uphold the ICC's determination? [Contractors Transport Corp. v. United States, 537 F.2d 1160 (4th Cir. 1976)]

9. Historically, unions have organized new company hiring practices in "hiring halls." A hiring hall is an agency or office run by the union, or by the union and the employer jointly. Hiring halls tend to favor union members. The National Labor Relations Board held this practice to be legal. Then the NLRB reconsidered its decision and held that the use of hiring halls was illegal. A case arose involving an employee who had been hired through a hiring hall before the NLRB changed its rule. The NLRB applied its new rule retroactively and held that the employee was hired illegally through an unfair labor practice. The company sued, claiming that penalizing it for a practice that was legal at the time was unfair. How should the court rule? [NLRB v. E&B Brewing Co., 276 F.2d 594 (6th Cir. 1960)]

10. The Food and Drug Administration has authority to protect the public health from misbranded or dangerous food products. After the FDA found that a company was marketing a product, "Nutrilite Food Supplement," that was mislabeled, the FDA seized all inventory from the company's warehouse. The FDA did so without granting the company a hearing. The company sued, arguing that this action was destroying its business. Should the court uphold the FDA's decision? [Ewing v. Mytinger & Casselberry, Inc., 339 U.S. 594, 70 S.Ct. 870, 94 L.Ed. 1088 (1950)]

11. A state statute required vehicle dismantlers—that is, persons whose business includes dismantling automobiles and selling the parts—to be licensed and keep records regarding the vehicles and parts in their possession. The statute also authorized warrantless administrative inspections—that is, without first obtaining a warrant, agents of the state department of motor vehicles or police officers could inspect a vehicle dismantler's license, records, and vehicles on the premises. Pursuant to this statute, police officers entered an automobile junkyard and asked to see the owner's license and records. The owner replied that he did not have the documents. The officers inspected the premises and discovered stolen vehicles and parts. Charged with possession of stolen property and unregistered operation as a vehicle dismantler, the junkyard owner argued that the warrantless inspection statute was unconstitutional under the Fourth Amendment. The trial court disagreed, reasoning that the junkyard business was a highly regulated industry. On appeal, the highest state court concluded that the statute had no truly administrative purpose and impermissibly authorized searches only to discover stolen property. The state appealed to the Supreme Court of the United States. Should the Court uphold the statute? [New York v. Burger, __ U.S. __, 107 S.Ct. 2636, 96 L.Ed.2d 601 (1987)]

Chapter 46

Consumer Protection

For most of America's history, the government assumed that business and free enterprise would satisfy the needs and wants of consumers. The legal watchword that accompanied this assumption was *caveat emptor,* or "let the buyer beware." Consumers were free to contract as they chose, and if they struck a bad bargain or purchased a faulty product, the government would not interfere. Over the last several decades, however, this attitude has changed considerably. A spate of federal and state legislation now protects consumers against unfair trade practices, faulty or unsafe products, discriminatory practices on the part of creditors, and so on. Now it is the seller who must be wary lest he or she violates one of the many consumer protection statutes. *Caveat emptor* has been replaced by *caveat venditor*—"let the seller beware."

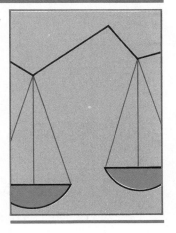

There are several important and distinct sources of government consumer protection. The federal government has passed many laws specifically to protect consumers. (See Exhibit 46–1 for examples.) In addition, under the authority of those laws, federal agencies have developed numerous regulations and guidelines to ensure the welfare of consumers. Further consumer protection exists at the state level. Most states have passed specific consumer protection laws, and all states have adopted parts of the Uniform Commercial Code, which contains important consumer protection provisions. Although in this chapter we focus primarily on federal legislation— because of its broader applicability—state laws nonetheless provide a significant amount of protection for consumers.

ADVERTISING

The earliest federal consumer protection law, and still one of the most important, is the Federal Trade Commission Act. This 1914 law created the Federal Trade Commission (FTC) as an independent regulatory agency with five members. To ensure a bipartisan commission, the law requires that no more than three members belong to the same political party. The act, as amended in 1938, authorizes the FTC to prohibit "unfair or deceptive

Exhibit 46-1 Federal Consumer Protection Statutes

POPULAR NAME	PURPOSE	STATUTE REFERENCE
ADVERTISING		
Federal Trade Commission Act (1914/1938)	Prohibits deceptive and unfair trade practices	15 U.S.C. Sections 45 *et seq.*
LABELING AND PACKAGING		
Wool Products Labeling Act (1939)	Requires accurate labeling of wool products	15 U.S.C. Section 68
Fur Products Labeling Act (1951)	Prohibits misbranding of fur products	15 U.S.C. Section 69
Cigarette Labeling and Advertising Act (1965)	Requires labels warning of possible health hazards	15 U.S.C. Sections 1331 *et seq.*
Child Protection and Toy Safety Act (1966)	Requires child-proof devices and special labeling	15 U.S.C. Sections 1261 *et seq.*
Fair Packaging and Labeling Act (1966)	Requires accurate names, quantities, weights	15 U.S.C. Sections 1451 *et seq.*
Smokeless Tobacco Act (1986)	Requires labels disclosing possible health hazards of smokeless tobacco; prohibits advertising via electronic media of smokeless tobacco products	15 U.S.C. Sections 4401 *et seq.*
SALES AND WARRANTIES		
Interstate Land Sales Act (1968)	Requires disclosure in interstate land sales	15 U.S.C. Section 1701
Real Estate Settlement Procedures Act (1974)	Requires disclosure of home-buying costs	12 U.S.C. Sections 2601 *et seq.*
Magnuson-Moss Warranty Act (1975)	Provides rules that govern content of warranties	15 U.S.C. Sections 2301 *et seq.*
CREDIT		
Consumer Credit Protection Act (Truth-in-Lending Act) (1968)	Offers comprehensive protection covering all phases of credit transactions	15 U.S.C. Sections 1601 *et seq.*
Fair Credit Reporting Act (1970)	Protects consumers' credit reputations	15 U.S.C. Section 1681
Equal Credit Opportunity Act (1974)	Prohibits discrimination in the extending of credit	15 U.S.C. Section 1691
Fair Credit Billing Act (1974)	Protects consumers in credit-card billing errors and other disputes	15 U.S.C. Sections 1666 *et seq.*
Fair Debt Collection Practices Act (1977)	Prohibits debt collectors' abuses	15 U.S.C. Section 1692
HEALTH AND SAFETY		
Federal Food, Drug, and Cosmetic Act (1938)	Protects consumers from unsafe food products and from unsafe and/or ineffective drugs	21 U.S.C. Sections 301 *et seq.*
Flammable Fabrics Act (1953)	Prohibits the sale of highly flammable clothing	15 U.S.C. Sections 1191 *et seq.*
Consumer Product Safety Act (1972)	Established the Consumer Product Safety Commission to regulate all potentially hazardous consumer products	15 U.S.C. Sections 2051 *et seq.*

acts or practices."[1] Under this authority, one of the important functions of the FTC is to ensure that consumers are not misled by deceptive advertising.

1. 15 U.S.C. Section 45.

FTC Procedures

The FTC learns of a possibly deceptive advertisement through its own investigations or through a complaint by a consumer or competitor. The commission then investigates the situation and may subpoena documentary evidence (legally compel a party to give over the documents). Then, if the FTC believes the advertisement is unfair or deceptive and the company disagrees, an agency adjudication is held before an administrative law judge, as described in the preceding chapter.

After a hearing that is much like a trial, the administrative law judge rules. If the company loses, it may appeal the decision to the FTC commissioners. If the company loses again, it may then appeal to a U.S. court of appeals. The court will tend to defer to the FTC's judgment, however, and will normally overturn the commission's decision only when the commission's finding is not supported by substantial evidence.

Cease-and-Desist Orders

When the FTC succeeds in proving that an advertisement is unfair or deceptive, it usually issues a **cease-and-desist order** requiring that the challenged advertising be stopped. A company that fails to obey such an order may be fined $10,000 for each consequent illegal advertisement. In addition, the FTC may initiate a "consumer redress" action that rescinds or reforms contracts made under the earlier misleading advertisement.

Counter-advertising

A recent and controversial type of sanction imposed by the FTC is known as **counter-advertising.** When a firm has been found liable for deceptive advertising, a counter-advertising order by the FTC would require the company to utilize new advertisements in print, on radio, or on television to correct the earlier misinformation. For example, Listerine advertised that its mouthwash could prevent or cure colds and sore throats. This claim

was found to be unsupported, and the FTC required Listerine to state in future advertisements that its product did not prevent colds or sore throats.[2] Although this power is seldom used, it remains a part of the FTC's enforcement arsenal.

"Unfair or Deceptive Acts"

The terms *unfair* and *deceptive* are very broad, and the FTC has a difficult task defining exactly what types of advertising are illegal. Advertising may be deemed deceptive if it is scientifically untrue. For example, in an early case, a claim that a cosmetic cream would "rejuvenate" skin was held to be misleading.[3] Advertisements by Wonder Bread were held to mislead the consuming public into believing that the bread was more nutritious than other breads.[4] Certain scientific claims made in advertising must be substantiated. As discussed in Chapter 45, this requirement demands that a company have supporting documentation for advertising claims.

The FTC has also attacked deceptive price advertising. For example, a paint retailer advertised that it would sell two cans for the price of one but then established a very high price for a single can of paint. The courts agreed that this practice was deceptive.[5]

In the following case, an advertising practice involving pain relievers was found to be misleading.

---

2. Warner-Lambert Co. v. FTC, 562 F.2d 749 (D.C. Cir. 1977).

3. Charles of the Ritz Distributors Corp. v. FTC, 143 F.2d 676 (2d Cir. 1944).

4. I.T.T. Continental Baking Co., CCH Trade Reg. Rep., Paragraph 20,182 (1972).

5. FTC v. Mary Carter Paint Co., 382 U.S. 46, 86 S.Ct. 219, 15 L.Ed.2d 128 (1965).

BACKGROUND AND FACTS   *The Federal Trade Commission issued a complaint against American Home Products Corp. (AHP) for that company's advertisements regarding Anacin and Arthritis Pain Formula (APF). The complaint alleged that the advertisements were unsubstantiated and misleading. After extensive hearings, an administrative law judge ruled against AHP, holding that the advertisements were misleading. On appeal, the full FTC affirmed the findings of the administrative law judge. The commission ordered that AHP cease and desist in certain advertising claims. AHP appealed this ruling to a federal court of appeals.*

Case 46.1
AMERICAN HOME PRODUCTS CORP. v. FEDERAL TRADE COMMISSION
United States Court of Appeals, Third Circuit, 1982.
695 F.2d 681.

ADAMS, Circuit Judge.

* * * *

The complaint charged, among other things, that AHP's advertisements had falsely claimed that Anacin has a unique pain-killing formula that has been conclusively proven to be superior in effectiveness to all other non-prescription analgesics, and that Anacin is a tension reliever. Another of the complaint's accusations was that the petitioner misrepresented that APF is superior to competing products in that it causes less frequent side effects. AHP's answer, filed May 29, 1973, denied any violation of the Federal Trade Commission Act. The petitioner's position was that it did not make the advertising claims which the complaint accused it of making, and that any claims it did make were truthful.

* * * *

AHP's advertising that Anacin and APF possessed more of an active ingredient than did their competitors' products was, similarly, an attempt at false product differentiation. One series of television advertisements announced that the consumer shown on camera "found medically proved Anacin overpowers headache pain. For most headaches, all three leading pain relievers reach an effective level in your bloodstream in minutes. But in the final analysis the highest level is reached by Anacin. This higher level is the extra pain reliever Anacin provides for your headache." * * * Yet other products on the market possess as much aspirin as Anacin and four widely available products— APF, Arthritis Strength Bufferin, Cope, and Midol—contain *greater* amounts. Even more misleading are those advertisements that convey the impression that Anacin has *twice as much* pain reliever as all other non-prescription products. For example, one advertisement had it that

> 2 Anacin Tablets have more of the one pain reliever doctors recommend most than 4 of the other leading extra strength tablets. . . . 2 Anacin contain more of this specific pain reliever than 4 of the others.

Another advertisement proclaims:

> Anacin's fortified formula has more of this specific pain reliever than any other leading headache tablet. In fact, Anacin is formulated twice as strong in the amount of this specific pain reliever as the other leading extra-strength tablet.

The ALJ quoted these two advertisements, along with several others.

[The court then confirmed that these statements were literally false.]

DECISION   *The court affirmed the commission's findings that the advertisements were*
AND REMEDY *misleading. The court also affirmed the commission's cease-and-desist order after slightly modifying it for clarification.*

The FTC also regulates advertising that contains an endorsement by a celebrity. Such ads may be deemed deceptive if the celebrity actually makes no use of the endorsed product. For example, a company owned by Pat Boone (the well-known pop singer of the 1950s and 1960s) advertised an anti-acne product with the claim that his daughters had used the product successfully. In truth, his daughters had never used the product, and the FTC compelled an end to the false advertising and restitution to consumers who had purchased the product during the illegal advertising campaign.[6]

Advertising will be deemed deceptive only if a reasonable consumer would be misled. If an advertising claim is expressed in vague generalities or is obviously exaggerated, the ad will be legal. This practice is known as **puffing,** and the government assumes that it will not likely fool consumers. Thus, the claim that "when you're out of Schlitz, you're out of beer" is legal, even though it is literally false. Generalized claims that a product is "the best" will also usually be legal unless accompanied by other deceptive comments.

Bait-and-Switch Advertising

In some cases, the FTC has promulgated more specific rules to govern advertising. One of its

---

6. 92 F.T.C. 310 (1978).

more important rules, called "Guides on Bait Advertising,"[7] is designed to prohibit advertisements that specify a remarkably low price for a particular item, which may not even be in stock. The low price is the "bait" to lure the consumer into the store, whereupon a salesperson tries to "switch" the consumer to some other, more expensive item. According to FTC guidelines, **bait advertising** oc-

curs when the seller refuses to show the advertised item, fails to have adequate quantities of it available, fails to promise or deliver the advertised item within a reasonable time, or discourages employees from selling the item.

Numerous techniques fall into the bait-and-switch category. In the following case, sales personnel not only were directed to engage in a bait-and-switch sales ploy but were rewarded for doing so.

7. 16 C.F.R. Section 238.

 Case 46.2

ALL-STATE INDUSTRIES OF NORTH CAROLINA, INC. v. FEDERAL TRADE COMMISSION

United States Court of Appeals, Fourth Circuit, 1970.
423 F.2d 423.

BACKGROUND AND FACTS *All-State Industries, a producer of residential aluminum siding, storm windows, and other products, used a bait-and-switch sales technique in selling its products. The "ADV" lower-cost grade of aluminum was featured in the company's ads, but salespersons, following the training manual, attempted to sell the "PRO" grade after contacting the customers. The Federal Trade Commission found this practice to be an "unfair and deceptive" practice under the FTC Act and issued a cease-and-desist order. All-State Industries appealed.*

BRYAN, Circuit Judge.

*   *   *   *

Respondents' sales technique, or "pitch" is devised to create, first, a demand for the "ADV" product. Through inflated promotion it is presented as a "special offer" with "limited time" prices. But the Examiner found the "ADV" is actually priced uniformly and without time limit. He held as untrue All-State's claim that they deal directly from their factory with the output "100% guaranteed."

Inquiries or "leads" are answered by a supposed "sales manager." He attempts to pressure the prospect into signing a contract, a note and a deed, committing him to the purchase of "ADV" articles but leaving blank the monetary obligation. As soon as the contract is executed, the salesperson brings out a sample of the "ADV" and points out deficiencies in it, "whether real or imaginary." The "PRO" is then shown in contrast, to the detriment of the "ADV." Whenever possible the "PRO" is then sold "at the highest price obtainable from the individual customer." The salesmen have incentives to substitute the "PRO"—they receive no commission on "ADV" but only on "PRO" sales.

This "bait and switch" artifice, the Examiner discovered, was fully set forth in the sales force's training manual and was employed generally. He also reported that All-State's agents utilized "gimmicks whereby the original prices quoted for respondents' products can be reduced." For example, the representative would promise a potential buyer a special discount, even below the quoted sale price, if the latter would allow the use of his home for demonstration or display purposes. Rarely, however, would a patron's home be so utilized. It was found as a bare inducement to overcome "sales resistance at a higher price" and provide "some apparently reasonable basis for the reduction in price."

The cease-and-desist order was enforced against All-State Industries as well as against each of All-State's sales agents. Such a bait-and-switch scheme is clearly in violation of the Federal Trade Commission's "Guides on Bait Advertising."

DECISION AND REMEDY

LABELING AND PACKAGING LAWS

In addition to the general restrictions on advertising, the federal government has passed laws dealing with specific products. For example, cigarette packages and advertising must contain one of several warnings about the dangers of smoking.[8] The 1966 Fair Packaging Act requires that consumer goods have labels that identify the product, the manufacturer, the packer or distributor and its place of business, the net quantity of the contents, and the quantity of each serving if the number of servings is stated.[9] Still other laws regulate the labeling and packaging of individual products, such as drugs and cosmetics, food products, and fabrics.

SALES

Through its regulatory power, the Federal Trade Commission has the authority to go beyond deceptive advertising and control other unfair sales practices as well.

Door-to-Door Sales

An important early FTC rule applied to door-to-door sales. These sales were often unfair to consumers, who sometimes purchased unnecessary products just to get the salespersons to leave their homes. Furthermore, because repeat purchases are an insignificant part of the door-to-door business, sellers were less concerned with building goodwill among customers and more willing to use unfair bargaining practices.

The commission, by regulation, now protects consumers against certain door-to-door sales practices. Among other protections, the FTC rule requires door-to-door salespersons to give consumers three days in which to cancel any sale. This "cooling off period" allows a customer who purchased an item from a door-to-door sales agent to change his or her mind and avoid the purchase within three days. The FTC rule protects consumers in other ways as well. In one case, agents of a door-to-door encyclopedia sales firm would

mislead individuals to gain access to their homes. An FTC cease-and-desist order required each of the company's salespersons, before entering a home, to give the resident a card disclosing that the agent was selling encyclopedias.[10]

Industry-Specific Regulation

More recently, the FTC has regulated specific industries that were considered to be abusive in dealing with consumers. The commission's 1981 "used-car rule" requires dealers to affix a "Buyer's Guide" window disclosure label to all cars for sale. This label must (1) disclose whether the car has a warranty or is being sold "as is"; (2) give information on any service contract or promises; and (3) suggest that the consumer obtain an inspection of the car and get all promises in writing.

The FTC also has regulated funeral homes. As of 1984, funeral homes must provide customers with itemized prices of all aspects of a funeral. Moreover, funeral homes are not allowed to require specific embalming procedures or specific types of caskets for bodies that are going to be cremated. The commission rule also safeguards against funeral-home misrepresentations about local legal requirements and charges. Thus, funeral homes can no longer imply that local laws require particular caskets or fees for burial when this is not the case.

The used-car and funeral-home rules are just two examples of the many ways in which the FTC prohibits unfair sales procedures within specific industries.

Real Estate

In 1968, Congress passed the Interstate Land Sales Full Disclosure Act. There are many examples of misled purchasers who, while living in a state such as New York, invested their life savings to purchase land in Florida for a retirement home only to discover that the property was located in an uninhabitable swamp. Now, interstate sellers of land must file a "statement of record" with the Department of Housing and Urban Development (HUD). This permits HUD to ensure that potential purchasers have all the necessary facts to make an informed judgment about purchasing the land. If this law is violated, purchasers may legally rescind the land sale (avoid the contract and recover

---

8. 15 U.S.C. Sections 1331 *et seq.*
9. 15 U.S.C. Sections 1451 *et seq.*

10. Grolier, Inc. v. FTC, 699 F.2d 983 (9th Cir. 1983).

their purchase money), and sellers are subject to criminal penalties.

In 1974, Congress enacted the Real Estate Settlement Procedures Act (RESPA) to ensure that buyers of residential property are given all necessary information about the settlement process, including closing costs. Purchasing a house is not only an enormous investment, it may also be legally complex. Settlement may require title insurance, attorneys' fees, appraisal fees, taxes, insurance, and broker's fees. RESPA prohibits kickbacks (secret payments for business referrals) and requires that buyers be informed of settlement procedures, protections, and costs. RESPA also requires that a lender inform the buyer of the effective mortgage rate on a housing loan.

CREDIT PROTECTION

In the past, some lenders and bill collectors were extremely abusive to consumers. In response, the federal government has passed a series of laws that regulate the extension of credit and the recovery of debts.

Truth-in-Lending Act

In 1968, Congress passed the Consumer Credit Protection Act, which has become better known as the Truth-in-Lending Act (TILA). TILA does not regulate interest rates but simply requires creditors to disclose certain loan terms, so that the prospective debtor understands the contract and can shop around for the best financing arrangements.

TRANSACTIONS COVERED BY TILA Not all creditors and transactions are subject to TILA. The act applies to persons who, in the ordinary course of their business, (1) lend money, (2) sell on credit, or (3) arrange for the extension of credit. Thus, sales or loans between two consumers are not covered by TILA. Nor are corporations pro-

tected—the act applies only to natural persons taking out loans. Significantly, the act only applies to loans of $25,000 or less. Larger loans are not covered. Transactions covered by TILA typically include retail and installment loans, car loans, home improvement loans, and certain small real estate loans.

DISCLOSURE REQUIREMENTS If a transaction does fall within TILA, certain specific disclosure requirements apply. These disclosure rules are found in **Regulation Z,** which was promulgated by the Federal Reserve Board. This regulation includes a model form that must be used to disclose to consumers detailed information concerning the amount to be financed and the annual percentage rate of interest (APR).

Suppose you purchase a $10,000 car on credit from a dealer. The dealer also offering credit must disclose the finance charge and the annualized percentage rate on the loan. This means that the dealer must inform you of the total interest charges to be paid over the life of the loan as well as the percent of interest applicable to the loan. The dealer must also tell you the number of loan payments, the dollar amount of each payment, and when each payment is due. Finally, the dealer must disclose any terms applying to prepayment—such as whether an interest penalty attaches if you prepay the loan.

Various penalties apply to creditors that violate the terms of TILA. Federal agencies, including the FTC and the Justice Department, may sue the violator. Criminal penalties include one year in jail and a $5,000 fine for each violation. In addition, consumers have their own *private right of action* under TILA if they sue within one year from the date of the violation. If successful, the consumer may recover actual damages, two times the finance charge, and attorneys' fees. In no event may damages exceed $1,000, however.

The following case illustrates the need for creditors to comply with all of the requirements of TILA.

BACKGROUND AND FACTS *Mary Smith, the plaintiff, purchased a car from Don Chapman Motor Sales, the defendant. Smith brought an action alleging that the sales contract violated the Truth-in-Lending Act and the Texas Consumer Credit Code (TCCC). Chapman argued that, although he had not specifically complied with the terms of the two consumer protection statutes, he*

 Case 46.3

SMITH v. CHAPMAN
United States Court of Appeals,
Fifth Circuit, 1980.
614 F.2d 968.

was in substantial compliance and, further, that since Smith understood all the terms of the contract, Chapman had achieved the purposes of the statutes and should not be penalized. The trial court held for Smith, and Chapman appealed.

BROWN, Circuit Judge.

* * * *

First, the purpose of TILA is to promote the "informed use of credit * * * [and] an awareness of the cost thereof by consumers" by assuring "a meaningful disclosure of credit terms so that the consumer will be able to compare more readily the various credit terms available to him. * * *"

It is now well-settled that an objective standard is used in determining violations of TILA. It is not necessary that the plaintiff-consumer actually have been deceived in order for there to be a violation. TILA is primarily enforced through lawsuits filed by consumers acting as "private attorneys general." In fact, consumers who are aware of the true terms of a contract are more able to see that these terms are not clearly and conspicuously disclosed on the installment sales contract form. Thus, the purpose of the Act is more readily served by allowing lawsuits by these consumers who are less easily deceived.

Second, the applicable standard is strict compliance with the technical requirements of the Act. Only adherence to a strict compliance standard will promote the standardization of terms which will permit consumers readily to make meaningful comparisons of available credit alternatives.

* * * *

The "Motor Vehicle Contract" that Smith entered into with Chapman Motors was a one-page document with terms printed on both sides of the page. The front of this document did not mention the security interest that the seller retained in the car; this was set forth as Condition No. 1 on the back of the page. Delinquency charges were stated on the front and as Condition No. 6 on the back of the document as follows:

The Seller, at its option, shall collect a delinquency charge on each installment in default for a period of more than ten days in an amount not to exceed 5% of each installment or $5.00 whichever is less, or, in lieu thereof, interest after maturity on each such installment, not to exceed the highest lawful contract rate.

The specific interest rate after maturity, imposed by Condition No. 10 on the back of the contract, was ten percent (10%) per annum. At the bottom of both sides of the page was printed: "NOTICE, SEE REVERSE SIDE FOR IMPORTANT INFORMATION, ALL TERMS OF WHICH ARE INCORPORATED BY REFERENCE."

Smith alleged in her complaint that the failure to state these provisions on the front side of the page was a violation of Regulation Z, 12 CFR § 226.8(a)(1) * * *.

The general rule for disclosures is that they "be made clearly, conspicuously, in meaningful sequence, in accordance with the further requirements of [§ 226], and at the time and in the terminology prescribed in applicable sections."

Chapman first contends that he has complied with the requirements of § 226.8(a)(1) by including the notice of incorporation by reference of terms on both sides of the page. Under a strict compliance standard, incorporating by reference terms on the backside of a page when it is explicitly required that these terms appear on the front side, would be a violation of TILA.

* * * *

Chapman next takes issue with the District Court's holding that the listing of the sales tax on the automobile contract form as an "official fee," and not in the blank labelled "Cash Price (Including Sales Tax)," violated Regulation Z and the TCCC.

* * * *

The District Court inferred from § 226.4(b)(3) that taxes must be included either in the cash price or be listed as a finance charge. We are mindful of the confusion potentially created when taxes, which are imposed regardless of whether or not credit is extended, are listed as finance charges and how, as Chapman urges, this goes against the policy of TILA to make installment sales contracts more easily understood by consumers. Yet, this is what the regulation implies, and this how we have interpreted it in the past. Any changes in the regulation are not for us, but for the Federal Reserve Board to make. We agree with the District Court's interpretation of § 226.4(b)(3).

* * * *

We reiterate that the purpose of TILA is to "assure a meaningful disclosure of credit terms," and that Regulation Z, § 226(a), requires that disclosures be made clearly, conspicuously and in meaningful sequence. To place the tax figure in the wrong space when another space is specifically provided is not a clear disclosure in the meaningful sequence. And when the form states the sales tax is included in the figure stated, but in fact it is not, it is, furthermore, misleading. A misleading disclosure is as much a violation of TILA as a failure to disclose at all.

Because this disclosure is misleading, and because it contradicts the definition of "official fees," which under Texas law do not include sales taxes, it is also in violation of TCCC.

The judgment of the district court was affirmed. Statutory penalties of twice the amount of the finance charges connected with the transaction, plus attorneys' fees, were imposed for violation of the federal law and for violation of the state regulations. The entire penalty totaled four times the finance charge.	**DECISION AND REMEDY**

Credit Cards

Credit cards now represent a major source of consumer debt. TILA also applies to certain credit-card transactions. In 1974, Congress amended TILA with the Fair Credit Billing Act. The key provision of this amendment permits a credit-card purchaser to withhold payment until a dispute over a faulty product is resolved. The credit-card issuer must intervene and try to obtain a settlement between the credit-card user and the seller of the objectionable product. A purchaser does not have an *unlimited* right to stop payment, however. He or she must first make a good faith effort to obtain satisfaction from the seller. The buyer then may stop payment. Although the purchaser is not legally required personally to notify the credit company, that action is probably advisable.

Other provisions of this act relate to billing disputes. If the debtor believes that there is an error in a bill, the credit-card company must investigate, and the debtor may suspend payments in the interim. The cardholder simply writes to the company within sixty days of receipt of the bill and explains why he or she believes that an error exists. The credit company must acknowledge the letter within thirty days and resolve the dispute within ninety days. During that period,

the debtor has no liability for the amount in dispute. If no error is found, the debtor may owe the amount plus any finance charges for the period in which payments were not made during the investigation. If the bill is in error, the debtor need not pay the mistaken amount.

TILA contains other protections for credit-card users as well. One provision limits the liability of a cardholder to $50 per card for unauthorized charges made prior to the time the creditor is notified. Suppose, for example, that Jones loses his American Express card in the street. Prentice finds it and buys $200 worth of goods with the card. The next day, Jones discovers the card is missing and notifies the issuer. American Express later bills Jones for the $200 of goods bought by Prentice. Jones is only liable for $50. Had Jones notified the issuer *before* Prentice's purchase, Jones would owe nothing on Prentice's purchases.

Another TILA provision prohibits a credit-card company from billing a consumer for unauthorized charges if the credit card was improperly issued by the company. Suppose that American Express mails a credit card to Farmer, who has neither applied for such a card nor held one in the past. The envelope is stolen out of Farmer's mailbox, and the thief buys $200 worth of goods with the card. American Express bills Farmer for this $200, but Farmer legally owes nothing because American Express performed a prohibited act by sending an unsolicited card.

Other Federal Laws

Other federal legislation offers further credit protection to consumers. In 1970, for example, Congress enacted the Fair Credit Reporting Act as part of the Truth-in-Lending Act. This law protects consumers from inaccurate or unfair credit reports. Consumers are entitled, upon request, to be informed of the nature and scope of a credit

investigation, the kind of information that is being compiled, and the names of the persons who will be receiving the credit report. Inaccurate or misleading material must be removed from the file. If there is an unresolvable dispute about the accuracy of certain parts of the report, the consumer has the right to add a one-hundred-word statement to the file defending his or her position with regard to the disputed matter.

The following case illustrates the liability exposure of companies that maintain credit reports and ratings.

Case 46.4

THOMPSON v. SAN ANTONIO RETAIL MERCHANTS ASSOC.
United States Court of Appeals, Fifth Circuit, 1982.
682 F.2d 509.

BACKGROUND AND FACTS *The San Antonio Retail Merchants Association (SARMA) maintained credit reports on consumers. In 1974, William Daniel Thompson allowed his account at a jewelry store to become delinquent. SARMA placed a derogatory credit rating into Thompson's file but failed to include his Social Security number. In 1978, William Douglas Thompson applied for credit with Gulf Oil Corporation and Montgomery Ward in San Antonio. SARMA erroneously reported to both firms the bad-debt record of William Daniel Thompson. As a result, both Gulf and Montgomery Ward denied credit to William Douglas Thompson. Initially, William Douglas Thompson believed he had been denied credit because of his 1976 burglary conviction. In 1979, however, he learned the true reason. After discovering the error, William Douglas Thompson attempted to get SARMA to correct the error. SARMA, however, repeatedly sent him letters addressed to William Daniel Thompson and failed to correct the erroneous credit report. William Douglas Thompson sued SARMA, and the district court ruled for him. The court further awarded Thompson $10,000 in damages for mental distress, plus attorneys' fees of $4,485. SARMA appealed this decision.*

PER CURIAM.
*   *   *   *

Under 15 U.S.C. § 1681o of the Fair Credit Reporting Act (Act), a "consumer reporting agency" is liable to "any consumer" for negligent failure to comply with "any requirement imposed" by the Act. In the instant case, the district court determined that SARMA was liable under section 1681o for negligent failure to comply with section 1681e(b) of the Act, which provides:

When a consumer reporting agency *prepares* a consumer report, it shall follow *reasonable procedures* to assure *maximum possible accuracy* of information concerning the individual about whom the report relates.

Section 1681e(b) does not impose strict liability for any inaccurate credit report, but only a duty of reasonable care in preparation of the report. That duty extends to updating procedures, because "preparation" of a consumer report should be viewed as a continuing process and the obligation to insure accuracy arises with every addition of information. The standard of conduct by which the trier of fact must judge the adequacy of agency procedures is what a reasonably prudent person would do under the circumstances.

Applying the reasonable-person standard, the district court found two acts of negligence in SARMA's updating procedures. First, SARMA failed to exercise reasonable care in programming its computer to automatically capture information into a file without requiring any minimum number of "points of correspondence" between the consumer and the file or having an adequate auditing procedure to foster accuracy. Second, SARMA failed to employ reasonable procedures designed to learn the disparity in social security numbers for the two Thompsons * * *

* * * *

SARMA asserts that Thompson failed to prove any actual damages, or at best proved only minimal damages for humiliation and mental distress. There was evidence, however, that Thompson suffered humiliation and embarrassment from being denied credit on three occasions. Thompson testified that the denial of credit hurt him deeply because of his mistaken belief that it resulted from his felony conviction:

I was trying to build myself back up, trying to set myself up, get back on my feet again. I was working sixty hours a week and sometimes seventy. I went back to school. I was going to school at night three nights a week, four nights a week, three hours a night, and [denial of credit] really hurt. It made me disgusted with myself.

DECISION AND REMEDY

The appellate court upheld the district court's finding for Thompson and its estimate of $10,000 in damages for mental distress. Because the Fair Credit Reporting Act specifically authorizes the payment of attorneys' fees, this finding was also affirmed.

In 1974, Congress enacted the Equal Credit Opportunity Act as part of TILA. This law prohibits discrimination in credit based on race, religion, national origin, color, sex, marital status, age, or receipt of certain types of income, such as public assistance. Under this law, creditors may not request information that is to be used for unlawful discrimination.

DEBT COLLECTION

In the past, debt collectors have employed a variety of harassing acts in their efforts to collect overdue payments. Some of these practices—such as threatening violence, making late-night phone calls, and informing neighbors and co-workers of the debt—were held by Congress to be unduly abusive. Consequently, the legislature adopted the Fair Debt Collection Practices Act in a 1977 amendment to TILA.

Illegal Debt Collection Practices

The Fair Debt Collection Practices Act does not apply to the creditors themselves but only to specialized debt-collection agencies that regularly collect debts owed to someone else (usually for a percentage of the amount owed). The act outlaws

several specific collection practices, including the following:

1. Contacting the consumer at his or her place of employment, if the employer objects.
2. Contacting the consumer at inconvenient or unusual times (such as 3:00 A.M.) or contacting the consumer at any time, if he or she is represented by an attorney.
3. Contacting third parties other than parents, spouses, or financial advisers about the payment of a debt, unless specifically authorized to do so by a court.
4. Using harassment or intimidation (such as abusive language) or using false and misleading approaches (such as posing as a police officer).
5. Communicating with the consumer after receipt of notice that the consumer is refusing to pay the debt, except to advise the consumer of further action to be taken by the collection agency.

Garnishment

When a debt has gone uncollected for a prolonged period of time, the creditor may seek to garnish the debtor's wages. **Garnishment** is a legal procedure by which the creditor may directly seize a portion of the debtor's wages in order to pay off the debt. State law has always regulated this procedure, which may only be obtained after a court hearing and the entry of a judgment for the creditor, but TILA added federal protections. In brief, wages cannot be garnished beyond 25 percent of an individual's after-tax earnings and must leave individuals with a certain minimum income.

HEALTH AND SAFETY

Federal legislation also regulates the safety of consumer products. The first consumer safety law, which regulated food and drugs, was passed in 1906. This law was amended in 1938 and now exists as the Federal Food, Drug, and Cosmetic Act. This act and subsequent laws extend federal protection to food products, which are regulated to prevent adulteration or misbranding. Separate laws regulate cosmetics, children's toys, and fabric flammability to ensure that safety standards are met. Federal auto safety laws also exist, as discussed in Chapter 45.

Consumer Product Safety Act

The most far-reaching federal regulatory authority related to product safety is found in the Consumer Product Safety Act, which was passed in 1972. This law created the Consumer Product Safety Commission (CPSC) and empowered it to regulate potentially hazardous consumer products. The commission has authority over "any article, or component part thereof produced or distributed for sale to a consumer for use in or around a permanent or temporary household or residence, a school, in recreation or otherwise, or for the personal use, consumption or enjoyment of a consumer." Some products, such as tobacco, guns, and automobiles, are exempted from the CPSC's control.

The commission conducts research on product safety and maintains a clearinghouse of information on the risks associated with various consumer products. After investigation, the CPSC may set safety standards for consumer products. For example, one 1982 rule established requirements for power lawn mowers—such as safety guards around the blades—in order to reduce the 60,000 injuries this product had been causing annually.

The commission may even ban products that are found to present an "unreasonable risk" to the user. For example, in the late 1970s the commission banned various types of fireworks, unsafe baby cribs, and many products containing asbestos or vinyl chloride (substances that can cause cancer). The commission has also banned more than four hundred toys that were considered to be hazardous because they contained sharp points or small, removable components. In each case, the CPSC concluded that the risks inherent in marketing the product outweighed its benefits.

For a time, the CPSC was fairly vigorous in regulating product safety, particularly during the 1970s. It has become generally less active in the late 1980s, however.

STATE LAWS

In addition to the extensive federal legislation described above, important state laws also provide protection for consumers. In some cases, the state protection significantly exceeds that provided by federal law.

Uniform Commercial Code

Portions of the UCC, which was covered in detail in Unit Three, form a part of the law of all the states. Perhaps the most significant consumer protection provision of the UCC is the doctrine of unconscionability, found in UCC Section 2-302. This doctrine, as defined by the courts, prohibits the enforcement of transactions that are so patently unfair that they "shock the conscience" of the court. It should be noted that not all states have adopted the unconscionability provisions of the UCC. The UCC also governs consumer warranties and places restrictions on the ability of sellers to limit their liability for personal injuries caused by defective consumer products.

Uniform Consumer Credit Code

In 1968, the National Conference of Commissioners on Uniform State Laws promulgated the Uniform Consumer Credit Code (UCCC). The UCCC is an attempt to create a comprehensive, uniform body of rules governing the most important aspects of consumer credit and covers most types of sales, including real estate. This uniform code has only been adopted in substantial part by eleven states. Many other states have statutes containing closely related provisions, however.

The UCCC has its own truth-in-lending provisions and restrictions on garnishment. It sets maximum credit service rates for various amounts of debt and contains unconscionability provisions related to debtors. Other UCCC provisions protect consumers from abusive home-solicitation sales practices, limit creditor repossession rights, and limit interest rates. Some of these provisions have been resisted as unduly disruptive of free-market operations.

State Consumer Protection Laws

In addition to adopting portions of the uniform codes, most states have established their own consumer protection statutes. Some of these laws are quite strict, considerably exceeding federal protections. These laws vary from state to state and are difficult to summarize. Thus, a wise businessperson will acquaint himself or herself with the coverage and prohibitions of local laws.

State consumer protection laws do have some common aspects. They are typically directed at deceptive trade practices, such as a seller's providing consumers with misleading information. For example, the 1973 Texas Deceptive Trade Practices Act actually prohibits sellers from inducing consumers to purchase items that they do not need or cannot afford. The California Civil Code permits consumers to keep unsolicited goods without payment.[11] Some state laws even permit consumers to recover treble damages and attorneys' fees in the event of violation. The following Texas case demonstrates that state laws are sometimes stricter than common law or even federal statutory consumer protection laws.

---

11. Under federal law, if unsolicited goods are sent by mail, the recipient is entitled to treat the goods as a gift with the "right to retain, use, discard, or dispose of [them] in any manner he [or she] sees fit without any obligations whatsoever to the sender." Merchandise mailed by a charitable organization soliciting contributions is excepted. Postal Reorganization Act of 1970, 39 U.S.C. Section 3009.

BACKGROUND AND FACTS   *In May 1975, J. W. Singleton, who was not a merchant, sold his used boat, motor, and trailer to Charles Pennington. Singleton orally stated that he had just spent $500 to repair the boat, and that the boat was in "excellent" or "perfect" condition and "just like new." In fact, the gear housing of the motor was cracked and had been repaired inadequately. Singleton had not experienced any problems with the boat and was unaware of this problem. Pennington, after buying the boat, discovered the cracked gear housing and spent $481.68 to have it repaired. Pennington then sued Singleton for fraud and for violation of the Texas Deceptive Trade Practices Act (DTPA). The district court held for Singleton on the fraud count but for Pennington on the DTPA count. Pennington received treble damages under the DTPA. Singleton appealed this decision, and the court of appeals reversed in his favor. Pennington then appealed to the Texas Supreme Court.*

Case 46.5
PENNINGTON v. SINGLETON
Supreme Court of Texas, 1980.
606 S.W.2d 682.

McGEE, Justice.
*   *   *   *

Pennington contends that subdivisions (5) and (7) of § 17.46(b) [of the DPTA] are applicable to the misrepresentations made about the boat.

Subdivision (5) prohibits representing that a good has characteristics, uses, or benefits that it does not have. The boat sold to Pennington was represented to have the characteristics of a "new" boat or a boat in "excellent" or "perfect" condition. The boat did not have these characteristics because of the cracked gear housing. The boat was also represented to produce the uses and benefits of a "new" boat or a boat in "excellent" or "perfect" condition. Because of the cracked gear housing, the boat could not produce those benefits. A good may lack its claimed characteristics or fail to bring about its claimed uses or benefits because it is not in good mechanical condition, or for other reasons such as its design or manufacture. In *United Postage Corp.* v. *Kam-*

meyer, a vending machine was represented to have a certain selling capacity. Because it lacked that capacity, it was held to lack its claimed characteristics, uses, or benefits. We do not agree with Singleton's argument that false statements about the boat's mechanical condition did not relate to its characteristics, uses, or benefits. Regardless of the reason, when a good does not have the characteristics it is represented to have, or perform as represented, the injury to the consumer is the same. There is no justification for excluding some misrepresentations and including others on the basis of the reason for their falsity.

Subdivision (7) prohibits representing that a good is of a particular standard, quality, grade, style, or model if it is of another. Quality is a measure of degree; as to particular goods quality may be calibrated by standard or grade, as with eggs or meat, or specified by style or model, as with machinery. Even when specific categories are not devised, the good may still be described with more general words of quality. Words like "excellent" and "perfect" are words indicating a high degree of quality. Because the boat was in poor mechanical condition, its condition was of poor quality and the representations were false.

DECISION AND REMEDY *The Texas Supreme Court reversed the appellate court and restored the district court's finding in favor of Pennington under the DTPA. Singleton's false statement of quality was held to violate the act. The court also approved the granting of treble damages to Pennington.*

Increasingly, state officials have enforced both state and federal consumer protection laws. In recent years, such officials have successfully prosecuted a major fraud case involving disconnected odometers on Chrysler cars, a case involving misleading health claims by the makers of Campbell soup, and many other actions.

Government regulation on behalf of consumers has increased over the past decades. Nevertheless, most consumer disputes are still settled by contract law. Only in cases of particularly unfair or misleading business practices does regulation play a major role.

QUESTIONS AND CASE PROBLEMS

1. Andrew, a California resident, received a flyer in the U.S. mail announcing a new line of regional cookbooks distributed by the Every-Kind Cookbook Company. Andrew was not interested and threw the flyer away. Two days later, Andrew received in the mail an introductory cookbook entitled "Lower Mongolian Regional Cookbook," as announced in the flyer, on a "trial basis" from Every-Kind. Andrew was not interested but did not go to the trouble to return the cookbook. Every-Kind demanded payment of $20.95 for the Lower Mongolian Regional Cookbook. Should Andrew be required to pay?

2. Green receives two new credit cards on May 1. One was solicited from the King Department Store, and the other was unsolicited from the Flyways Airline. During the month of May, Green makes several credit-card purchases from King, but she does not use the Flyways Airline card. On May 31, a burglar breaks into Green's home and steals both credit cards, among other items. Green notifies the King Department Store of the theft of the King credit card on June 2, but she fails to notify Flyways Airline. Using the King credit card, the burglar makes a $500 purchase on June 1 and a $200 purchase on June 3. The burglar then charges $1,000 on the Flyways Airline card on June 5. Green receives the bills for these charges and refuses to pay. For which, if any, of these charges is Green liable?

3. Roseman was employed as a debit agent for the John Hancock Insurance Company. He resigned following accusations that he had been dishonest with his company expense account. Before his resignation, he reimbursed the account. Part of the information concerning Roseman's resignation was contained in a credit report held by the Retail Credit Company. Subsequently, Roseman was denied a position with another insurance company based on this credit report. Roseman claimed that Retail Credit had behaved illegally in failing to notify him of this information

so that he could place a statement in the files explaining the situation. Was Roseman correct? [Roseman v. Retail Credit Co., Inc., 428 F.Supp. 643 (E.D.Pa. 1977)]

4. Roger Gonzalez purchased a Ford from Schmerler Ford on credit. The installment credit agreement that Gonzalez signed named Ford Motor Credit Corporation as the payee of the loan. Nowhere on the loan form or the disclosure documents did the name Schmerler Ford appear. Schmerler Ford, however, helped Gonzalez fill out the loan forms and then forwarded them to Ford Motor Credit Corporation. Schmerler lacked the authority to negotiate the interest rate charged on the loan and lacked the ability to approve Gonzalez's loan. Gonzalez's loan was made solely by the Ford Motor Credit Corporation. Later, it was discovered that the loan forms failed to disclose all of the relevant information required under the Truth-in-Lending Act. Who could be held liable—Schmerler Ford, Ford Motor Credit Corporation, or both? [Gonzalez v. Schmerler Ford, 397 F.Supp. 323 (N.D.Ill. 1975)]

5. In the summer of 1972, Robert Martin applied for and was issued an American Express credit card. Approximately three years later, in April 1975, Martin gave his card to E. L. McBride, a business associate, and orally authorized McBride to charge up to $500 on the credit card. He also wrote to American Express, requesting that charges on his account be limited to $1,000. In June 1975, however, Martin received a statement from American Express indicating that the amount owed on his credit card was approximately $5,300. Under the Truth-in-Lending Act, what is the extent of Martin's liability to American Express? [Martin v. American Express, Inc., 361 So.2d 597 (Ala.Civ.App. 1978)]

6. On July 16, Polly Ann Barber entered into a retail installment contract with Kimbrell's, Inc., for the purchase of various items of household furniture for a total price of $592. Barber later sued Kimbrell's for violating the Truth-in-Lending Act because Kimbrell's used the term *total time balance* in its disclosure document, rather than *total of payments* as the act required. At the same time, Barber sued Furniture Distributors, Inc., claiming that it too was liable as a creditor under the act. Furniture Distributors, Inc, participated in the development and preparation of the standard contract form and distributed it for use in all the retail stores in the Kimbrell's chain. It was also the parent company of Kimbrell's and had extensive knowledge of the credit terms for all the consumer credit sales that Kimbrell's made. Each time one of the Kimbrell's stores made a consumer credit sale, the installment contract was sent to Furniture Distributors for review. If Kimbrell's is in violation of the Truth-in-Lending Act, can Barber also hold Furniture Distributors liable? [Barber v. Kimbrell's, Inc., 577 F.2d 216 (4th Cir. 1978)]

7. Milhollin purchased an automobile and financed it with a standard retail installment contract with Ford Motor Credit Company. The front page of the contract disclosed certain features of the agreement as required by the Truth-in-Lending Act and Regulation Z. On a later page, in the body of the agreement, the contract contained an acceleration clause, which enabled the creditor to accelerate the entire debt upon the buyer's default. The presence of this acceleration clause was not disclosed on the front page. Milhollin sued and alleged that the failure to disclose this acceleration clause violated the Truth-in-Lending Act. Should Milhollin win? [Ford Motor Credit Co. v. Milhollin, 444 U.S. 555, 100 S.Ct. 790, 63 L.Ed.2d 22 (1980)]

8. Thompson Medical Company marketed a new cream called Aspercreme that was supposed to help arthritis victims and others suffering from minor aches. Aspercreme contained no aspirin. Thompson's television advertisements stated that the product provided "the strong relief of aspirin right where you hurt" and showed the announcer holding up aspirin tablets as well as a tube of Aspercreme. The Federal Trade Commission held that the advertisements were misleading, because they led consumers to believe that Aspercreme contained aspirin. Thompson Medical Company appealed this decision and argued that the advertisements never actually stated that its product contained aspirin. How should the court rule? [Thompson Medical Co., Inc. v. Federal Trade Commission, 791 F.2d 189 (D.C. Cir. 1986)]

9. Sears adopted a new advertising program to boost sales of its Lady Kenmore dishwashers. The new ads claimed that these dishwashers "completely eliminated" the need for rinsing dishes before placing them in the dishwasher. The owner's manuals accompanying the machines, however, recommended pre-rinsing. Interviews with consumers indicated that pre-rinsing was still required for truly clean dishes. In an action against Sears, the FTC held that the advertising was misleading. The FTC's remedial order required that Sears keep records to support all future advertising claims for all "major home appliances" and submit them to the FTC. Sears conceded that its dishwasher advertising was misleading but argued that the remedial order, which covered other appliances, was overly broad and unfair. Is the FTC's broad order legal? [Sears, Roebuck & Co. v. Federal Trade Commission, 676 F.2d 385 (9th Cir. 1982)]

10. Between 1960 and 1971, Norman R. Saindon owned and operated a chain of health clubs in the St. Louis area. He offered lifetime memberships to the public for $360, payable in twenty-four monthly installments of $15 each. Purchasers were required to pass a credit check before being approved for such memberships. The health club then sold the rights to the future installment payments to several finance companies. In addition, the health club sold a few memberships for full cash payment at discounts of 10 to 15 percent off the total installment price. Purchasers under the installment plan sued Saindon and the finance companies, arguing that the discount reflected a hidden credit charge, which was not disclosed as required by the Truth-in-Lending Act. Were these purchasers correct? [Joseph v. Norman's Health Club, Inc., 532 F.2d 86 (8th Cir. 1976)]

Chapter 47

Environmental Protection

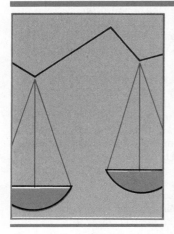

Historically, neither business nor government was much concerned with what we now call pollution. Waste products were simply burned into the air, poured into the water, or dumped on the ground with little or no thought for the consequences. We eventually discovered, however, that this process was poisoning our environment as well as ourselves. Many pollutants, such as carbon monoxide and certain airborne particulates, are known to cause disease and death. Consequently, environmental protection laws were passed to control pollution.

Environmental laws, which are only a little more than two decades old, have already led to some noticeable improvement in air and water quality. For example, the outdoor levels of sulfur dioxide, an air pollutant that can cause lung damage, decreased 36 percent between 1975 and 1985.[1] The Cuyahoga River in Cleveland, which once was so polluted that it actually caught fire, is much cleaner today, as are some of our other waterways. Many environmental problems remain, however, and pollution levels in many cities and rivers are still unacceptable. The Cuyahoga is still dirty, and major American cities (including Los Angeles, Houston, Denver, and many others) still have air-pollution levels in excess of federal standards. Thus, many citizens are working to expand and strengthen environmental protection requirements.

Compliance with environmental laws has become a significant and expensive part of a company's operation. The modern business firm must now worry about two different sets of environmental obligations: (1) compliance with federal and state regulations and (2) liability in damages.[2] This chapter will discuss the major laws affecting business in the context of these two obligations.

COMPLIANCE WITH REGULATIONS

The leading, and the most costly, environmental regulations are those created by the federal government. These laws, for the most part, are classified

1. *Environmental Management Report*, Summer 1986, p. VII-2.
2. For a good summary of important environmental legislation, see Arbuckle, Brown, Bryson, Frick, Hall, Miller, Miller, Sullivan, Vanderver, and Wegman, *Environmental Law Handbook* (1986).

according to the type of pollution addressed by the legislation (air pollution, water pollution, hazardous waste, and so on). The major federal environmental statutes discussed in this chapter are listed and summarized in Exhibit 47–1.

Air Pollution

In 1963, Congress passed the Clean Air Act, the first major piece of modern environmental legislation. The Environmental Protection Agency (EPA) was established in 1970 to coordinate federal regulation of environmental pollution. Various Clean Air Act amendments, particularly in 1970 and 1977, strengthened the government's authority to regulate air pollution. The Clean Air Act, as amended, empowers the EPA to promulgate rules to control emissions of various types of pollutants. Some of these air pollutants are responsible for the ugly "smog" that affects the inhabitants of major cities. Other air pollutants are unseen but may cause cancer when breathed.

AUTOMOBILE POLLUTION Air pollution from motor vehicles may represent the single most difficult pollution problem facing the nation. Congress in 1970 took the unusual step of legislatively mandating a 90 percent reduction in the emission of most automobile pollutants. This standard was later relaxed somewhat, but the car companies largely achieved the original goal, primarily through pollution-control devices known as catalytic converters.

Automobile production is regulated to ensure continued compliance with EPA regulations. If General Motors, for example, wants to introduce a new car, a prototype must be certified for compliance with EPA standards. Certification is required to demonstrate that emission controls are effective up to at least 50,000 miles of driving. The EPA may go into GM's manufacturing facilities and conduct assembly-line tests to ensure that production models also meet the standards. The Clean Air Act also imposes a statutory warranty that vehicles will meet air-quality standards for their entire useful lives, which means in the case of light-duty passenger vehicles a period of five years or 50,000 miles, whichever occurs first. Suppose that our hypothetical new car fails this standard in actual driving. The EPA may then require the cars already sold to be recalled and modified at the manufacturer's expense. To date, the EPA has required several manufacturers to recall thousands of automobiles for repair or replacement of pollution control equipment.

Exhibit 47–1 Federal Environmental Statutes

POPULAR NAME	PURPOSE	STATUTE REFERENCE
Federal Insecticide, Fungicide and Rodenticide Act (1947)	Controlling exposure to dangerous pesticides	7 U.S.C. Sections 135 *et seq.*
Federal Water Pollution Control Act (FWPCA) (1948)	Controlling water pollution from major sources	33 U.S.C. Sections 1251 *et seq.*
Clean Air Act (1963)	Controlling air pollution from cars and stationary sources	42 U.S.C. Sections 7401 *et seq.*
National Environmental Policy Act (NEPA) (1969)	Limiting environmental harm from federal government activities	42 U.S.C. Sections 4321 *et seq.*
Endangered Species Act (1973)	Protecting animals that are threatened with extinction	16 U.S.C. Sections 1531 *et seq.*
Safe Drinking Water Act (1974)	Regulating contaminants in drinking water	42 U.S.C. Sections 300f *et seq.*
Resource Conservation and Recovery Act (RCRA) (1976)	Establishing standards for new waste disposal sites	42 U.S.C. Sections 6901 *et seq.*
Toxic Substances Control Act (1976)	Regulating new and existing toxic substances	15 U.S.C. Sections 2601 *et seq.*
Comprehensive Environmental Response, Compensation and Liability Act (CERCLA) (Superfund) (1980)	Establishing liability and providing money to clean up existing waste disposal sites	42 U.S.C. Sections 9601 *et seq.*

The Clean Air Act also authorizes the EPA to control the makeup of automobile fuel and fuel additives. The most significant of these rules regulates the lead content of gasoline. The following case reviews a challenge to the EPA's restrictions on lead.

Case 47.1

ETHYL CORP. v. ENVIRONMENTAL PROTECTION AGENCY

United States Court of Appeals, District of Columbia Circuit, 1976.
541 F.2d 1.

BACKGROUND AND FACTS *Ethyl Corporation, a leading producer of antiknock compounds for increasing gasoline octane ratings, filed for judicial review of the Environmental Protection Agency (EPA) order that required annual reductions in the lead content of gasoline. The Clean Air Act authorized the agency to regulate gasoline additives that endanger public health and welfare. Review of agency actions under the Clean Air Act is available only in the U.S. Court of Appeals for the District of Columbia Circuit.*

WRIGHT, Circuit Judge.
*   *   *   *

On October 28, 1973, as a result of a motion filed in *Natural Resources Defense Council, Inc. v. EPA*, this court ordered EPA to reach within 30 days a final decision on whether lead additives should be regulated for health reasons. * * * [The EPA Document] candidly discusses the various scientific studies, both pro and con, underlying this information, and ultimately concludes that lead from automobile emissions will endanger the public health. * * * Under the final regulations, lead in all gasoline would be reduced over a five-year period to an average of 0.5 grams per gallon.

* * * Our scope * * * requires us to strike "agency action, findings, and conclusions" [only if] we find [them] to be "arbitrary, capricious, an abuse of discretion, or otherwise not in accordance with law." This standard of review is a highly deferential one. It presumes agency action to be valid. Moreover, it forbids the court's substituting its judgment for that of the agency * * *.

This is not to say, however, that we must rubber-stamp the agency decision as correct. To do so would render the appellate process a superfluous (although time-consuming) ritual. Rather, the reviewing court must assure itself that the agency decision was "based on a consideration of the relevant factors * * *."

Petitioners [Ethyl Corp.] vigorously attack both the sufficiency and the validity of the many scientific studies relied upon by the Administrator, while advancing for consideration various studies allegedly supportive of their position. The record in this case is massive—over 10,000 pages. Not surprisingly, evidence may be isolated that supports virtually any inference one might care to draw. * * *

Because of the importance of the issues raised, we have accorded this case the most careful and exhaustive consideration. We find that in this rule-making proceeding the EPA has complied with all the statutory procedural requirements and that its reasons as stated in its opinion provide a rational basis for its action. Since we reject all of petitioners' claims of error the Agency may enforce its low-lead regulations.

DECISION AND REMEDY   *The Environmental Protection Agency regulations were affirmed by the court of appeals. The court accorded substantial deference to the EPA's conclusion, and thus the EPA was permitted to enforce its low-lead regulations.*

STATIONARY SOURCES   The Clean Air Act also controls stationary sources of air pollution, such as utilities and manufacturing plants. Section 108 of the act sets ambient standards for several common pollutants.[3] An **ambient standard** sets the maximum level allowed in the air. The act leaves

---

3. 42 U.S.C. Section 7408.

it to the states to establish emission controls on particular sources to reduce air-pollution levels. Several major cities still have air-pollution levels that exceed the ambient standards. Thus, these locales must attempt to reduce pollution further. It is sometimes very difficult for a business to open a new facility in a city that has not attained the ambient standards.

Section 111 of the act provides for New Source Performance Standards (NSPSs) for new, large, stationary sources.[4] These standards require that newly built sources of air pollution use the *best available technology* to reduce air-pollution emissions. In the oil industry, for example, NSPSs apply to new refineries, storage facilities, and bulk-gasoline terminals.

Section 112 applies to certain particularly hazardous pollutants, such as those that may cause cancer.[5] Under this authority, the EPA has regulated air emissions of asbestos, vinyl chloride, arsenic, radiation, and other cancer-causing substances. For these pollutants, the EPA adopts National Emission Standards for Hazardous Air Pollutants (NESHAPs). These standards may be strict, for they must be set at levels that protect the public health with "an ample margin of safety." The following case involves a controversy over what the NESHAP for vinyl chloride should be and whether the EPA can consider the costs of emission controls in setting standards.

_____

4. 42 U.S.C. Section 7411.

5. 42 U.S.C. Section 7412.

BACKGROUND AND FACTS   *In 1976, the EPA established air-emission standards for vinyl chloride, a cancer-causing chemical used in the manufacture of plastic. The vinyl chloride emission standard was set under the authority of Section 112 of the Clean Air Act, which directs that standards be set "at a level which * * * provides an ample margin of safety to protect the public health." The standard was set at the emission-reduction level obtainable through use of the best available pollution-control technology. The resulting standard reduced vinyl chloride emissions by 95 percent but left a small risk that some (1 out of every 100,000) exposed individuals would get cancer. Environmental groups protested the standard, arguing that it was not strict enough to protect fully the public health. In 1977, the EPA responded to criticisms of the standard by starting another rulemaking investigation. No action was taken until 1985, when the EPA decided not to modify the earlier standard. In so doing, the EPA determined that a further reduction in the emission limits was not feasible and would be unreasonably costly. The Natural Resources Defense Council, an environmental group, sued the EPA, arguing that the standard was not strict enough and that it violated the requirements of Section 112.*

 Case 47.2

NATURAL RESOURCES DEFENSE COUNCIL, INC. v. U.S. ENVIRONMENTAL PROTECTION AGENCY

United States Court of Appeals, District of Columbia Circuit, 1987.
824 F.2d 1146.

BORK, Judge.
*   *   *   *

Since we cannot discern clear congressional intent to preclude consideration of cost and technological feasibility in setting emission standards under section 112, we necessarily find that the [EPA] Administrator may consider these factors. We must next determine whether the Administrator's use of these factors in this case is "based on a permissible construction of the statute."
*   *   *   *

Thus, in setting emission standards for carcinogenic pollutants, the Administrator has decided to determine first the level of emissions attainable by best available control technology. He will then determine the costs of setting the standard below that level and balance those costs against the risk to health below the level of feasibility. If the costs are greater than the reduction in risk, then he will set the standard at the level of feasibility. This exercise, in the Administrator's view, will always produce an "ample margin of safety."

*   *   *   *

We find that the congressional mandate to provide "an ample margin of safety" "to protect the public health" requires the Administrator to make an initial determination of what is "safe." This determination must be based exclusively upon the Administrator's determination of the risk to health at a particular emission level. *   *   *

*   *   *   *

We wish to reiterate the limited nature of our holding in this case because it is not the court's intention to bind the Administrator to any specific method of determining what is "safe" or what constitutes an "ample margin." We hold only that the Administrator cannot consider cost and technological feasibility in determining what is "safe." This determination must be based soley upon the risk to health. *   *   *

DECISION AND REMEDY   *The D.C. Circuit Court of Appeals held that the EPA had failed to use the proper standards under Section 112. The case was remanded to the EPA for reconsideration of the vinyl chloride emission limits under the legal rules set forth in the opinion.*

The EPA's air-pollution regulations are likely to increase in the future as the agency addresses new problems, such as acid rain and the destruction of the ozone layer.

Water Pollution

In 1948, Congress passed the Federal Water Pollution Control Act. This law, which was significantly amended in 1965, 1972, and 1977, is commonly known as the Clean Water Act.

The Clean Water Act approaches water-pollution control in several ways. One of the most important is the National Pollutant Discharge Elimination System (NPDES). This system requires any person discharging pollution into the water to report the volume and nature of the discharges. The discharger must obtain a permit from the EPA, and the EPA is empowered to set pollution-control restrictions on any such permits. Other specific water-pollution standards apply to particularly toxic discharges, to oil spills, and to companies that discharge into publicly owned waste treatment facilities.

Hazardous Waste

Currently, the most controversial environmental issue may be that of hazardous waste disposal. Leaking wastes at Love Canal in New York created a major public health risk that required evacuation of the entire local community. In 1976, Congress passed the Resource Conservation and Recovery Act (RCRA), which regulates all new disposal of hazardous wastes. The RCRA should be of great concern to all businesses. Even the supposedly clean "high-tech" industries, such as semiconductor manufacturing, must dispose of some very hazardous wastes or byproducts.

Suppose a new company is starting up. The company first must determine whether it will generate any hazardous wastes. The EPA maintains a list of regulated substances; this list includes hundreds of chemicals. If the company will have to dispose of some hazardous substance, either as a single chemical or in a mixture, the company must follow detailed EPA requirements.

First, the company must notify the EPA and obtain an identification number, so that the waste can be traced. Second, the company must prepare the Uniform Hazardous Waste Manifest, which identifies the waste by number and accompanies the waste at all times from its point of generation to its point of disposal. Third, when the waste is to be transported off-site, the company must ensure that it is properly packaged and labeled. Fourth, the company should ensure that the disposal facility for the waste meets all the detailed EPA safety requirements. The company also must file regular reports to EPA on the transport and disposal of its wastes. Some particularly hazardous wastes may not be disposed of on land at all. For example, wastes containing dioxin (a chemical highly likely to cause cancer) are banned from land disposal.

Other Laws

Several other environmental laws are important. The 1976 Toxic Substances Control Act requires that new chemicals be tested before they can be marketed. This law also permits the EPA to ban certain uses of substances that present an unreasonable risk to health. The 1974 Safe Drinking Water Act empowers the EPA to set public health standards for maximum levels of contaminants in drinking water. The Endangered Species Act of 1973 protects wildlife species in danger of extinction. The National Environmental Policy Act (NEPA), passed in 1969, requires the federal government to produce environmental impact statements for any major federal actions that significantly affect the environment. Private companies contracting for major federal actions may also need to prepare such statements.

LIABILITY FOR DAMAGES

Until recently, most environmental law simply involved compliance with federal and state regulations. Now, more and more frequently, individuals and the government are suing companies for damages resulting from environmental pollution.

Common Law Liability

Some common law causes of action for injuries caused by pollution have been recognized for centuries. These claims were rarely used, however, until recently. More aggressive plaintiffs are now suing businesses, seeking damages for health injuries caused by pollution.

NEGLIGENCE AND STRICT LIABILITY   Some common law pollution cases may be brought under negligence and strict liability theories, which are discussed in Chapter 4. A company may be negligent by polluting, especially if it is violating state or federal standards. When a pest-exterminating company contaminated a household water supply with a toxic chemical, a jury found the company to be negligent in its use of chemicals and in its failure to warn the residents of the potential risk.[6] Alternatively, companies may be subject to strict liability if their pollution is held to constitute an ultrahazardous activity. As discussed in Chapter 4, strict liability means that a plaintiff need not even show that the defendant was negligent in order to recover damages.

Plaintiffs in these cases have always had trouble proving causation. It is very difficult to link a specific disease or diseases to the air or water pollution emitted by a particular industry or firm. Some medical experts, however, may testify to the probability that a given source of pollution caused a particular disease. When such testimony is given and a jury finds for the plaintiffs, a company may be liable for millions of dollars in damages for health injuries. Punitive damages may also run into the millions. The following case involves a defendant held liable for extensive damages for harms caused by its polluting activities.

---

6. Laxton v. Orkin Exterminating Co., Inc., 639 S.W.2d 431 (Tenn. 1982).

BACKGROUND AND FACTS   *Velsicol maintained a large site for the disposal of chemical waste in Tennessee from 1964 to 1973, when the site was determined to be hazardous and closed. A group of five local residents sued Velsicol, claiming that the water in their home wells had become contaminated by hazardous chemicals that had leaked from Velsicol's disposal site. As a result of their exposure, the plaintiffs claimed to have suffered various health harms, including vision difficulty, risk of future cancer, and mental anguish. These plaintiffs sued under both strict liability and negligence theories.*

 Case 47.3

STERLING v. VELSICOL CHEMICAL CORP.

United States District Court for the Western District of Tennessee, 1986.
647 F.Supp. 303.

HORTON, Judge.

Strict Liability
*   *   *   *

    *   *   * [T]he Court concludes that Velsicol's activity on the farm was not only ultrahazardous activity, but also abnormally dangerous activity and therefore the de-

fendant is strictly liable for any damages that have occurred. This conclusion is made for * * * the following reasons:

1. There was a high degree of risk of some harm to the person, land or chattels of others * * *;
2. There was a likelihood that the harm that results would be great, such as the increased risk of many diseases including cancer, and the destruction of plaintiffs' quality of life;
3. The inability to eliminate the risk by the exercise of reasonable care;
4. The extent to which the activity at the dump was not a matter of common usage and as a means of disposal and violated the state of the art;
5. The inappropriateness of the location of the dump where it was carried out; and
6. The extent to which its value to the community (none) was outweighed by its dangerous attributes (great).

* * * *

Common Law Negligence

The Court concludes the doctrine of common law negligence applies to this case and Velsicol is clearly guilty of negligence in this case for the following reasons:

1. The Court concludes that there was a duty, a standard of conduct, imposed by law on Velsicol to protect others from unreasonable harm arising from the dumping of the chemicals on its farm; and
2. The Court further concludes that defendant breached that duty by its failure to do the following:

   a. Defendant failed to investigate the geological makeup or strata under the dumpsite prior to its purchase or operation;

   b. Defendant failed to investigate the hydrological, or water bearing zones under the dumpsite prior to its purchase or operation;

   c. Defendant failed to hire knowledgeable persons to investigate the geological and hydrogeological area under the dumpsite prior to its purchase or operation;

   d. Defendant failed to install proper monitoring procedures in and around the dumpsite prior to commencing dumping operations at the dumpsite;

   e. Defendant failed to investigate the geological and hydrogeological situation at the dumpsite after being warned by the [U.S. Geological Survey] in 1967 that their chemicals were escaping from their burial trenches and were in fact contaminating the local water table aquifer[.]

DECISION AND REMEDY   *After finding that the plaintiffs' harms had been proximately caused by the defendant's chemicals, the court awarded the plaintiffs over $5.2 million in actual damages. In addition, the court awarded the plaintiffs $7.5 million in punitive damages.*

NUISANCE   Polluters may also be held liable under the doctrine of nuisance. In general, a person has the right to use his or her land in any manner he or she chooses. A nuisance arises when one uses his or her own property in a manner that unreasonably interferes with another's use or enjoyment of real property or endangers the public welfare. For example, one defendant's manufacturing plant spewed out black smoke that settled as dust on a neighbor's residential property. The court found this to be a nuisance, particularly in view of the fact that an alternative fuel and modern emission-control systems were available to prevent the air pollution.[7] When deciding nuisance cases, courts usually "balance the equities" between the harm caused by the pollution and the costs of stopping the pollution.

Superfund

In 1980, Congress passed the Comprehensive Environmental Response, Compensation and Lia-

---

7. McCarty v. Natural Carbonic Gas Co., 189 N.Y. 40, 81 N.E. 549 (1907).

bility Act (CERCLA), which is more commonly known as Superfund. This law's approach to pollution control differed from the approach of earlier acts. Rather than establishing rules for controlling pollution, Superfund established a $1.6 billion federal fund—which has since been expanded to $5 billion—that can be used to clean up dangerous old hazardous waste disposal sites. In addition, Superfund authorized the government to sue individual companies for the cost of cleaning up these sites.

When a release or threatened release from a hazardous waste site occurs, the EPA may clean up the site to correct the problem. The government may then recover its cleanup costs from (1) the person who generated the wastes disposed at the site; (2) the person who transported wastes to the site; (3) the person who owned or operated the site at the time of the waste disposal; or (4) the current owner and operator of the site.[8] Many companies may thus be liable for their past actions in waste disposal.

Moreover, Superfund mandates a harsh standard of liability. Strict liability applies by statute. In addition, liability among multiple defendants may be held to be joint and several. *Joint and several liability* means that a company that is responsible for only a fraction of the waste may nonetheless be liable for all of the cleanup costs. Available defenses under Superfund are few. Moreover, as illustrated by the following case, the government may not be required to show that the defendant's waste actually caused the problem at the disposal site.

_____

8. 42 U.S.C. Section 9607.

BACKGROUND AND FACTS *During the 1970s, South Carolina Recycling and Disposal, Inc. (SCRDI), maintained a disposal facility for wastes. Many chemical companies ("generators") used the site for waste disposal. The site eventually accumulated 7,200 fifty-five gallon drums of hazardous substances, which were stored somewhat haphazardly. Some of the wastes were leaking into the ground, and several fires occurred. The EPA began cleanup operations on the site under Superfund and sued several generators for the cleanup costs. Five of these generators argued that they should not be liable. According to the generators, the EPA had no evidence that their specific wastes had leaked or otherwise contributed to the hazard. Thus, the generators argued, the EPA had failed to show causation. The EPA contended that it need only show that the generators sent wastes to the site at some time in the past. Both sides filed for summary judgment.*

 Case 47.4

UNITED STATES v. SOUTH CAROLINA RECYCLING AND DISPOSAL, INC.
United States District Court for the District of South Carolina, 1986.
653 F.Supp. 984.

SIMONS, Judge.
* * * *

Generator defendants would * * * have this court require plaintiff to prove that hazardous substances traceable to each generator were released at the Bluff Road site or that their specific substances were more than a *de minimis* factor in a release or threatened release. Significantly, similar "causation" arguments were recently expressly rejected by the Eastern District of Pennsylvania in *United States v. Wade*, a case on all fours factually with this one.

In *Wade*, the court held that to require specific proof of causation would not only be at odds with the express language of the statute, but also would effectively "eviscerate the statute" because of the technological infeasibility of "fingerprinting" a given generator's substances at a site. * * * This court agrees with the conclusions reached in *Wade* and therefore rejects defendants' causation arguments. Plaintiff's burden of proof is defined by and limited to the express terms of the statute. Applying those terms to the undisputed facts, it is clear that each of the generator defendants made arrangements with SCRDI or its predecessors for disposal or treatment of wastes containing hazardous substances and that, as evidenced by the identification of each generator's drums at the Bluff Road site, such wastes were shipped to the site. It is further undisputed that hazardous substances like those of each of the generator defendants were present at the site at the time of cleanup, as shown by samples taken at the site; that there were releases and threatened releases of hazardous substances at the site; and that the government incurred costs in responding to those releases and threatened releases. Thus, based on the undisputed facts, each of these generator defendants is subject to liability under Section 107 of [Superfund].

DECISION AND REMEDY   *The district court ruled in favor of the government, holding that the generators were liable even in the absence of evidence that their particular wastes had created any hazard. In addition, the court held that the generators were each jointly and severally liable for the entirety of the cleanup costs.*

THE COSTS OF POLLUTION CONTROL

Businesspersons are beginning to chafe under the high costs and rigorous technical requirements of environmental regulation. Consider, for example, an oil company, even a small one. Air-pollution regulations under the Clean Air Act affect most of the company's operations. Refineries have to be equipped with special equipment to comply with one set of regulations for emissions of particulates, carbon monoxide, and sulfur dioxide. Even storage tanks must be equipped with new emission-control equipment for volatile organic compounds (chemical vapors that have been linked to cancer and other diseases). Other standards regulate emissions during the distribution of gasoline to stations. An entirely different set of standards under a different section of the Clean Air Act requires special equipment to control leaks of benzene, a hazardous byproduct of gasoline production. Other rules affect the company's product, such as regulations limiting the lead content in the company's gasoline. Proposed new rules would require all service stations in America to replace existing gas pumps with new technologies.

Full compliance with water-pollution regulations may also be both complex and expensive. For example, a California refinery operated by Union Oil obtained a permit providing for maximum discharge levels of various water pollutants. To comply with the terms of the permit, Union Oil established an expensive pollution-control program that first segregated the waste into two different streams. The first stream alone required one pretreatment operation to separate wastes, then two different types of treatment to remove wastes, and then another highly advanced treatment to clarify the water. Notwithstanding this elaborate process, unusually heavy rains caused the system to become overloaded, and Union Oil was held to have violated the terms of its permit.[9]

Each of the environmental protection requirements discussed in this chapter involve compliance costs—sometimes heavy ones—for businesspersons. In addition to these costs, business firms may also be required to pay extensive liability damages to private citizens or the government for harms caused by pollution-generating activities. These costs seem likely to increase in the future. Total cleanup costs under Superfund alone are estimated at $44 billion, and the cost of defending Superfund lawsuits may reach $8 billion.[10] The modern businessperson obviously must be aware of the many environmental regulations that pertain to his or her business activities, as well as the types of liability to which he or she might be exposed for harms resulting from pollution.

---

9. Sierra Club v. Union Oil Co. of California, 25 Environment Reporter (BNA) 1801 (9th Cir. 1987).

10. *Oversight Hearings on Superfund Reauthorization: Judicial and Legal Issues, Before the Subcomm. on Administrative Law and Governmental Relations of the House Judiciary Comm.*, 99th Cong., 1st Sess. 305 (1985) (statement of Timothy Harker of the EPA).

QUESTIONS AND CASE PROBLEMS

1. The EPA has set ambient standards for several pollutants, including sulfur dioxide, specifying the maximum concentration allowable in the outdoor air. One way to meet these standards is to reduce emissions. Companies discovered, however, that they could also meet the standards at less cost by building very high smokestacks. When emitted from such high stacks, pollutants were more widely dispersed and remained below the concentration level specified by the ambient standards. Environmental groups claimed that the Clean Air Act was designed to reduce pollution, not disperse it, and argued that industry should not be allowed to rely on tall stacks. Are the environmental groups correct, or should industry be allowed to use the less expensive dispersal method?

2. Current scientific knowledge indicates that there is no safe level of exposure to a cancer-causing agent. In theory, even one molecule of such a substance has the potential for causing cancer. Section 112 of the Clean Air Act requires that all cancer-causing substances be regulated to ensure a margin of safety. Some environmental groups have argued that all emissions of such substances must be eliminated in order for such a margin of safety to be reached. Such a total elimination would likely shut down many major U.S. industries. Should the EPA totally eliminate all emissions of cancer-causing chemicals?

3. Moonbay is a development home building corporation that primarily develops retirement communities. Farmtex owns a number of feedlots in Sunny Valley. Moonbay purchased 20,000 acres of farmland in the same area and began building and selling homes on this acreage. In the meantime Farmtex continued to expand its feedlot business, and eventually only 500 feet separated the two operations. Because of the odor and flies from the feedlots, Moonbay found it difficult to sell the homes in its development. Moonbay wants to enjoin Farmtex from operating its feedlots in the vicinity of its retirement home development. Discuss under what theory Moonbay would file this action. Discuss whether Farmtex has violated any federal environmental laws.

4. Union Electric operates three coal-fired generators in the St. Louis area. The company was in violation of the EPA's Section 108 air-pollution standards for sulfur dioxide. After proving that its generators could not meet the standards, Union Electric was granted a one-year variance, temporarily exempting it from the standards. After the year was up, Union Electric sued the EPA, arguing that the sulfur dioxide emission limits were economically and technologically infeasible. Should Union Electric be exempted from compliance with the standards? [Union Electric Co. v. EPA, 427 U.S. 246, 96 S.Ct. 2518, 49 L.Ed.2d 474 (1976)]

5. The EPA promulgated water-pollution discharge limits for several mining industries. These standards authorized variances exempting mining operations from their coverage if the operations could show that they used special processes or facilities that made the standards inapplicable. Cost was not a consideration in granting the variances. An industry trade association sued, claiming that the EPA should consider costs in granting variances, and the Fourth Circuit Court of Appeals agreed. Should the Supreme Court overturn this decision or affirm it and let costs be considered in the granting of variances under the Clean Water Act? [EPA v. National Crushed Stone Association, 449 U.S. 64, 101 S.Ct. 295, 66 L.Ed.2d 268 (1980)]

6. The Resource Conservation and Recovery Act gives the EPA authority to require a company to clean up a hazardous-waste site that presents an "imminent and substantial endangerment" to public health or to the environment. A company disposed of dioxin by discharging it into a pond located on its property. The EPA ordered that the company stop the disposal and clean up the site. The company argued that the EPA had no evidence of any actual harm to the health of nearby residents. Should the company be compelled to clean up the dioxin even in the absence of evidence of actual harm? [United States v. Vertac Chemical Corp., 489 F.Supp. 870 (E.D.Ark. 1980)]

7. The United States Navy conducted practice bombing runs in Puerto Rico. Sometimes, pilots missed their targets, and the bombs were dropped into water. Although there were no established effluent standards for the bombs, the activity violated the terms of the Clean Water Act, because the Navy had no NPDES permit for polluting the water. Puerto Rico sought an injunction, requesting that the bombing runs be stopped because they violated the Clean Water Act. The Navy contended that it should be allowed to continue, regardless of the violation. How should the court rule? [Weinberger v. Romero-Barcelo, 456 U.S. 305, 102 S.Ct. 1798, 72 L.Ed.2d 91 (1982)]

8. Cities Service Company operated a phosphate rock mine that included large settling ponds for the extraction of phosphate. A dam outside of one of these ponds broke, sending a billion gallons of phosphate slimes into the nearby Peace River, killing fish and causing other damage. The state of Florida sued Cities Service under strict liability for damages. Given these facts, should Cities Service be liable? [Cities Service Co. v. State, 312 So.2d 799 (Fla.App. 1975)]

9. Portland General Electric Company maintained a turbine facility. Nearby residents complained that the facility emitted low-frequency sound waves that caused them to suffer loss of sleep, emotional distress, and mental strain. Consequently, these residents sued the company, claiming that it was creating a nuisance. The defendant contended that the plaintiffs had suffered no special harm. The district court dismissed the plaintiffs' complaint, and the plaintiffs appealed the decision. Should the appellate court affirm the dismissal? [Frady v. Portland General Electric Co., 55 Or.App. 344, 637 P.2d 1345 (1981)]

Chapter 48

Antitrust

Today's **antitrust laws** are intended to discourage **monopolies** and control the exercise of monopoly power—that is, the power to fix prices and exclude competition in a particular market. They are the descendants of long-standing principles found in old English common law. As early as the fifteenth century, certain restraints on free trade were held to be illegal. Attempts to corner the market by "engrossing" (buying crops while still in the fields) and "regrating" (buying crops and hoarding them) were prohibited under common law.

Although common law rules favoring competition continued to evolve, they failed to keep pace with the rapid industrialization that occurred in the nineteenth century. In America, with the growth of national markets after the Civil War, a number of small companies combined to form large companies and began to obtain monopoly control over certain product markets. These organizations were typically known as **trusts,** after an arrangement used by John D. Rockefeller and Standard Oil, in which owners could combine together and receive a share of the pooled earnings of several jointly managed companies.

People felt that the trusts abused their power by driving small competitors out of business and then raising prices to earn excessive monopoly profits. Entire industries became dominated by a single company. Congress responded in 1890 by passing the Sherman Act. This law created the first statutory controls on monopolies, and numerous companies are still sued under the Sherman Act today. In 1914, Congress supplemented the requirements of the Sherman Act with a new law, the Clayton Act, which addressed more specific antitrust problems. This chapter will consider the important requirements of these two leading antitrust laws.

THE SHERMAN ACT

The Sherman Act does not tell businesses how they must act. Rather, by proscribing particular acts, it tells them how they may *not* act.

The important provisions of the Sherman Act are found in the first two sections, which constitute very different prohibitions. These sections read as follows:

Section 1: Every contract, combination in the form of trust or otherwise, or conspiracy, in restraint of trade or commerce among the several States, or with foreign nations, is hereby declared to be illegal [and is a felony punishable by fine or imprisonment].

* * *

Section 2: Every person who shall monopolize, or attempt to monopolize, or combine or conspire with any other person or persons, to monopolize any part of the trade or commerce among the several States, or with foreign nations, shall be deemed guilty of a felony [and is similarly punishable].* * *

Note that Section 1 prohibits *agreements* that restrain trade and thus requires two or more participants. This section is aimed primarily at competitors who agree to restrict competition. Section 2 applies to any individual or company seeking to retain or obtain monopoly power over a market. This section requires no specific agreement but only the presence of unlawful monopoly power or attempts to obtain such power. We will discuss these sections in greater detail after we review some other aspects of the Sherman Act and its applicability.

Other Aspects of the Sherman Act

The Sherman Act does not apply to all businesses, nor may a party bring an action under the act unless the party has standing to sue. The following subsections briefly summarize the jurisdictional and other aspects of the Sherman Act.

JURISDICTION   Although the Sherman Act has broad jurisdiction, it is not universal. The act applies only to firms or individuals engaged in interstate commerce. The courts have construed the meaning of interstate commerce more and more broadly, however, bringing even such local activities as dentistry within the Sherman Act if such activities have a significant anticompetitive effect on interstate commerce.[1] Significantly, the Sherman Act also extends to U.S. nationals abroad who are engaged in activities that affect U.S. commerce. This concept is discussed further in Chapter 58, on international law.

---

1. Federal Trade Commission v. Indiana Federation of Dentists, 476 U.S. 447, 106. S.Ct. 2009, 90 L.Ed.2d 445 (1986). See Case 48.1 on page 835.

EXEMPTIONS   Certain activities are exempt from the antitrust laws. Exempted activities include those carried out by the following:

1. Labor unions.
2. Public utilities, such as some electric, gas, and telephone companies.
3. Other highly regulated industries, such as banking and the insurance business (but not boycotts, coercion, or intimidation on the part of insurance companies).
4. Cooperatives formed by farm and livestock producers and by fisheries.
5. Professional baseball organizations.
6. Government bodies, so long as these activities are pursuant to a legitimate state interest.
7. American exporters with regard to certain cooperative activities.
8. Certain cooperative research ventures.

Professionals such as doctors and lawyers are *not* exempt and have increasingly been subjected to antitrust laws.

STANDING TO SUE   The Department of Justice may sue to enforce the Sherman Act on behalf of the federal government's interest. State governments may also be active in enforcing antitrust laws. In addition, private parties injured by antitrust violations may sue for damages. Indeed, most antitrust lawsuits are private actions. For a private party to have standing to sue, the party must show (1) that the antitrust violation either directly caused or was a substantial factor in causing the injury and (2) that the antitrust violation injured the business activities of the plaintiff. Suppose, for example, that a new company, Service Airlines, is formed to provide air transportation over some profitable local routes. The major air carriers agree to lower prices below costs on these routes in order to drive Service Airlines out of business. Once this has occurred, Service Airlines can sue the major carriers in a private action for violating the antitrust laws. A private plaintiff who wins an antitrust case will receive *treble damages*—three times the actual damages—and attorneys' fees.

REMEDIES AND SANCTIONS   The treble-damages award in private actions serves as a major deterrent to antitrust violations. In addition, any person found guilty of violating the Sherman Act is subject to criminal prosecution for a felony.

Upon conviction, a person can be fined up to $100,000 and imprisoned for three years. A corporation can be fined $1 million. In the late 1950s, several leading electrical equipment manufacturers, including General Electric and Westinghouse, conspired together to set prices for government bids. Seven executives in these companies were convicted of crimes.[2] The sentences were relatively short (thirty days), but the public embarrassment was considerable and civil penalties were substantial.

In addition to civil damages and criminal penalties, the government may obtain a court order requiring the defendant to divest itself of property. Called a **divestiture,** this is the means through which a monopoly is broken up into separate companies. AT&T, for example, had long controlled virtually all telephone services in America, as well as the manufacture of telephone equipment. The government brought an antitrust action against AT&T, and a 1982 court decision required local telephone services to be operated by smaller, regional companies that are independent of AT&T.[3] The telephone equipment market was also opened to competition.

Per Se Violations versus the Rule of Reason

Some anticompetitive agreements are considered to be so objectionable that the courts hold them to be *per se* **violations** of Section 1 of the Sherman Act. Price-fixing agreements, for example, are illegal *per se* under Section 1. This means that price fixing is automatically and invariably illegal and that the courts will not even consider a defendant's attempted justification of the price-fixing arrangement.

Other anticompetitive agreements may be legitimate, however, and are analyzed under the **rule of reason.** When the rule of reason applies, a court will balance the important, legitimate reasons for the agreement against the potential anticompetitive effect of the agreement. If legitimate competitive benefits, such as economic efficiency, outweigh anticompetitive effects, the agreement will be held lawful.

Justice Brandeis formulated a classic expression of the rule of reason when he wrote:

> [T]he legality of an agreement or regulation cannot be determined by so simple a test, as whether it restrains competition. Every agreement concerning trade, every regulation of trade, restrains. To bind, to restrain, is of their very essence. The true test of legality is whether the restraint imposed is such as merely regulates and perhaps thereby promotes competition or whether it is such as may suppress or even destroy competition. To determine that question the court must ordinarily consider the facts peculiar to the business to which the restraint is applied; its condition before and after the restraint was imposed; the nature of the restraint and its effect, actual or probable. The history of the restraint, the evil believed to exist, the reason for adopting the particular remedy, the purpose or end sought to be attained, are all relevant facts.[4]

Section 1 and Horizontal Agreements

Section 1 of the Sherman Act is most directly concerned with controlling **horizontal agreements** among businesspersons. Horizontal agreements are those between direct competitors. If General Motors and Ford conspired together, that action would represent behavior that might violate Section 1.

PRICE FIXING   Perhaps the most blatant violation of Section 1 is horizontal price fixing. If GM and Ford agreed to set minimum prices for new cars, they would be involved in horizontal price fixing. As mentioned earlier, price fixing is deemed to be illegal *per se* under Section 1 of the Sherman Act.

GROUP BOYCOTTS   **Group boycotts** among competitors are also illegal *per se* under the antitrust laws. An individual firm generally has the right to deal with whoever it wishes, but the Sherman Act prohibits a group of competitors from agreeing to boycott a particular person or firm. In one case, a department store chain was facing serious competition from a smaller appliance store. The chain used its leverage to induce many appliance manufacturers to stop selling to the smaller store. This type of group boycott was held to be illegal under Section 1.[5]

2. United States v. Westinghouse Electric Corp., *et al.*, 1960 Trade Cas. (CCH) 69,699 (E.D.Pa 1960).

3. United States v. AT&T, 552 F.Supp. 131, (D.D.C. 1982).

4. Chicago Board of Trade v. United States, 246 U.S. 231, 38 S.Ct. 242, 62 L.Ed. 683 (1918).

5. Klor's, Inc. v. Broadway-Hale Stores, Inc., 359 U.S. 207, 79 S.Ct. 705, 3 L.Ed.2d 741 (1959).

Another illegal agreement between horizontal competitors is discussed in the following Supreme Court decision. Because this case was not a complete boycott, the Court used a rule-of-reason analysis.

BACKGROUND AND FACTS *In an attempt to control costs, dental health insurers adopted a policy that required dentists to submit diagnostic dental X rays to the insurance company for review before the company would approve payment for treatment. The Indiana Federation of Dentists objected to this policy and adopted a resolution not to submit X rays as requested by the insurers. Most dentists complied with this resolution and refused to submit X rays. In 1978, the Federal Trade Commission issued a complaint against the federation and found that the joint refusal to submit X rays was a violation of antitrust laws. According to the commission, the policy of not submitting X rays had the effect of encouraging unnecessary dental procedures and raising costs. The federation appealed this finding, and the Seventh Circuit Court of Appeals overturned the FTC's ruling. The appellate court contended that the commission had not shown that the federation's policy had an anticompetitive effect. The FTC then appealed to the United States Supreme Court.*

Case 48.1
FEDERAL TRADE COMMISSION v. INDIANA FEDERATION OF DENTISTS
Supreme Court of the United States, 1986.
476 U.S. 447, 106 S.Ct. 2009, 90 L.Ed.2d 445.

WHITE, Justice.
* * * *

The question remains whether these [facts] are legally sufficient to establish a violation of § 1 of the Sherman Act—that is, whether the Federation's collective refusal to cooperate with insurers' requests for x rays constitutes an "unreasonable" restraint of trade. * * *
* * * *

Application of the Rule of Reason to these facts is not a matter of any great difficulty. The Federation's policy takes the form of a horizontal agreement among the participating dentists to withhold from their customers a particular service that they desire—the forwarding of x rays to insurance companies along with claim forms. "While this is not price fixing as such, no elaborate industry analysis is required to demonstrate the anticompetitive character of such an agreement." A refusal to compete with respect to the package of services offered to customers, no less than a refusal to compete with respect to the price term of an agreement, impairs the ability of the market to advance social welfare by ensuring the provision of desired goods and services to consumers at a price approximating the marginal cost of providing them. Absent some countervailing procompetitive virtue—such as, for example, the creation of efficiencies in the operation of a market or the provision of goods and services—such an agreement limiting consumer choice by impeding the "ordinary give and take of the market place" cannot be sustained under the Rule of Reason. No credible argument has been advanced for the proposition that making it more costly for the insurers and patients who are the dentists' customers to obtain information needed for evaluating the dentists' diagnoses has any such procompetitive effect.

The Supreme Court reversed the lower court's decision and approved the FTC order. The Court held that the commission's findings were supported by substantial evidence and that the Indiana Federation of Dentists had violated Section 1 of the Sherman Act. The Court reinstated the FTC's order requiring the federation to cease its practice of jointly refusing to provide dental X rays to insurers.

DECISION AND REMEDY

HORIZONTAL MARKET DIVISION   Another *per se* violation of Section 1 occurs when competing firms agree to divide the market between themselves. For example, if two interstate cement companies normally sell throughout the entire state of California, they cannot enter into an agreement by which one of them sells only in southern California and the other sells only in northern California. In one leading case, a British firm and a French firm agreed to divide up geographic markets, including the United States, for certain antifriction bearings, which are widely used in many types of manufacturing. The Supreme Court held that this agreement violated Section 1 of the Sherman Act.[6]

TRADE ASSOCIATIONS   The rule of reason would apply to many activities of trade associations. Almost every industry has a trade association in which

competitors join together to promote certain common interests. For example, the major oil producers belong to the American Petroleum Institute (API), which was formed in 1919 and has its headquarters in Washington, D.C. Trade associations undertake such activities as exchanging important business information, representing the entire industry before the government, and setting safety standards for their member companies.

A small company might argue that trade association safety standards violate Section 1. These standards might be expensive to meet and might therefore hurt small firms and reduce competition. Under the rule of reason, however, a court would also consider the public benefits to be derived from the standards. In this case, the safety standards would probably be held to be lawful, unless their primary purpose was to restrict competition.

The following decision illustrates a representative rule-of-reason analysis of trade association rules.

---

6. Timken Roller Bearing Co. v. United States, 341 U.S. 593, 71 S.Ct. 971, 95 L.Ed. 1199 (1951).

Case 48.2

NATIONAL SOCIETY OF PROFESSIONAL ENGINEERS v. UNITED STATES

Supreme Court of the United States, 1978.
435 U.S. 679, 98 S.Ct. 1355, 55 L.Ed.2d 637.

BACKGROUND AND FACTS   *The National Society of Professional Engineers is a trade association that includes most of the professional engineers in the United States. The society adopted an ethical principle that its members should not engage in competitive bidding for engineering services. Thus, clients were forced to select engineers on the basis of reputation rather than price. In 1972, the U.S. attorney general sued the society, arguing that this principle was a violation of Section 1 of the Sherman Act. Both the district court and the circuit court of appeals held for the United States and found the practice to be illegal. The society appealed to the United States Supreme Court.*

STEVENS, Justice.
*   *   *   *

A.   *The Rule of Reason.*
*   *   *   *

  *   *   * The Rule of Reason, with its origins in common-law precedents long antedating the Sherman Act, *   *   * has been used to give the Act both flexibility and definition, and its central principle of antitrust analysis has remained constant. Contrary to its name, the Rule does not open the field of antitrust inquiry to any argument in favor of a challenged restraint that may fall within the realm of reason. Instead, it focuses directly on the challenged restraint's impact on competitive conditions.
*   *   *   *

B.   *The Ban on Competitive Bidding.*

  Price is the "central nervous system of the economy," and an agreement that "interfere[s] with the setting of price by free market forces" is illegal on its face. In this case we are presented with an agreement among competitors to refuse to discuss prices with potential customers until after negotiations have resulted in the initial selection of an engineer. While this is not price fixing as such, no elaborate industry analysis is required to demonstrate the anticompetitive character of such an agreement. It operates as an absolute ban on competitive bidding, applying with equal force to both complicated and simple projects and to both inexperienced and sophisticated customers. As the District Court found, the ban "impedes the ordinary give and take of the market place," and substantially deprives the customer of "the ability to utilize and compare prices in selecting engineering services." On its face, this agreement restrains trade within the meaning of § 1 of the Sherman Act.

The Society's affirmative defense confirms rather than refutes the anticompetitive purpose and effect of its agreement. The Society argues that the restraint is justified because bidding on engineering services is inherently imprecise, would lead to deceptively low bids, and would thereby tempt individual engineers to do inferior work with consequent risk to public safety and health. The logic of this argument rests on the assumption that the agreement will tend to maintain the price level; if it had no such effect, it would not serve its intended purpose. The Society nonetheless invokes the Rule of Reason, arguing that its restraint on price competition ultimately inures to the public benefit by preventing the production of inferior work and by insuring ethical behavior. As the preceding discussion of the Rule of Reason reveals, this Court has never accepted such an argument.

The Supreme Court affirmed the holding and the remedy of the lower federal court. The court entered a judicial order prohibiting the society from adopting any official opinion, policy statement, or guideline stating or implying that competitive bidding is unethical.	**DECISION AND REMEDY**

JOINT VENTURES   The rule of reason also applies to **joint ventures** between competitors. A joint venture is similar to a business partnership for a specific purpose. Thus, two computer companies might pool their resources in research and development in order to create new products. Even though such cooperation might reduce competition in violation of the antitrust laws, the combination would probably be legal under those laws if the companies could show strong, legitimate reasons for the joint venture (such as innovation). Indeed, in 1984 Congress passed specific legislation authorizing this particular type of research joint venture.[7] In another significant recent case, the FTC permitted an auto manufacturing joint venture between General Motors and Toyota to go forward.[8]

Section 1 and Vertical Agreements

Restrictions on **vertical agreements** under the antitrust laws are more controversial than those on horizontal agreements. Vertical agreements are made not between direct competitors but between firms at different levels in the chain of product distribution. For example, Westinghouse appliances (the producer) and an appliance store (the retailer) are in a vertical relationship.

RESALE PRICE MAINTENANCE   **Resale price maintenance** occurs when a manufacturer specifies what the retail price of its products must be. For most of this century, resale price maintenance was legally authorized by **fair trade laws** in forty-six states and permitted by Congress under the Miller-Tydings Amendment of 1937 and the McGuire Act of 1952. Then, in the 1975 Consumer Goods Pricing Act, Congress withdrew authorization for the fair trade laws. The practice of resale price maintenance is now illegal *per se* under Section 1 of the Sherman Act. Thus, if Westinghouse required that independent retailers, such as Sears, sell its refrigerators at a specific price, the action would be illegal. Westinghouse may, however, specify prices at its own stores, such as Westinghouse outlet stores. Westinghouse may also *suggest* retail prices for other independent stores, but it may not enforce these prices.

VERTICAL MARKET DIVISION   Sometimes, manufacturers may place territorial or customer restrictions upon their retailers. For example, a manufacturer may choose to grant a retailer an exclusive territory, so that there are no other re-

---

7. National Cooperative Research Act, 15 U.S.C. Section 4301.
8. General Motors Corp., 103 F.T.C. 374 (1984).

tailers of the same product within the retailer's area. Thus, a television manufacturer may sell through only one retailer in a certain locale. In this way, manufacturers may obtain greater advertising or service benefits for their products. These territorial or customer restrictions are judged under the rule of reason and may be legal, as illustrated in the following case.

Case 48.3

CONTINENTAL T.V., INC. v. GTE SYLVANIA, INC.

Supreme Court of the United
States, 1977.
433 U.S. 36, 97 S.Ct. 2549, 53
L.Ed.2d 568.

BACKGROUND AND FACTS *Prior to 1962, like most other television manufacturers, Sylvania sold its televisions to independent or company-owned distributors, who in turn resold to a large and diverse group of retailers. In 1962, Sylvania phased out its wholesale distributors and began to sell its televisions directly to franchised retailers. Sylvania limited the number of franchises granted for any given area and required each franchisee to sell the Sylvania products from only the locations of the franchise. A franchise did not constitute an exclusive territory, and Sylvania retained sole discretion to increase the number of retailers in an area, depending on the success or failure of existing retailers in developing their market. Continental T.V., a Sylvania franchisee, withheld all payments due for Sylvania products after a dispute over additional locations sought by Continental. John P. Maguire & Co., the finance company that handled the credit arrangements between Sylvania and its franchisees, sued Continental for payment and for the return of secured merchandise. Continental claimed that Sylvania had violated Section 1 of the Sherman Act by entering into and enforcing franchise agreements that permitted the sale of Sylvania products only in specified locations. The trial court held for Continental, and Sylvania appealed.*

POWELL, Justice.
*   *   *   *

In the present case it is undisputed that title to the televisions passed from Sylvania to Continental. Thus, the *Schwinn per se* rule applies unless Sylvania's restriction on locations falls outside Schwinn's prohibition against a manufacturer's attempting to restrict a "retailer's freedom as to where and to whom it will resell the products." As the Court of Appeals conceded, the language of *Schwinn* is clearly broad enough to apply to the present case. Unlike the Court of Appeals, however, we are unable to find a principled basis for distinguishing *Schwinn* from the case now before us.

Both Schwinn and Sylvania sought to reduce but not to eliminate competition among their respective retailers through the adoption of a franchise system. Although it was not one of the issues addressed by the District Court or presented on appeal by the Government, the Schwinn franchise plan included a location restriction similar to the one challenged here. These restrictions allowed Schwinn and Sylvania to regulate the amount of competition among their retailers by preventing a franchisee from selling franchised products from outlets other than the one covered by the franchise agreement. To exactly the same end, the Schwinn franchise plan included a companion restriction, apparently not found in the Sylvania plan, that prohibited franchised retailers from selling Schwinn products to nonfranchised retailers. In *Schwinn* the Court expressly held that this restriction was impermissible under the broad principle stated there. In intent and competitive impact, the retail-customer restriction in *Schwinn* is indistinguishable from the location restriction in the present case. In both cases the restrictions limited the freedom of the retailer to dispose of the purchased products as he desired. The fact that one restriction was addressed to territory and the other to customers is irrelevant to functional antitrust analysis and, indeed, to the language and broad thrust of the opinion in *Schwinn*. As Mr. Chief Justice Hughes stated: "Realities must dominate the judgment. *   *   * The Anti-Trust Act aims at substance."
*   *   *   *

Vertical restrictions reduce intrabrand competition by limiting the number of sellers of a particular product competing for the business of a given group of buyers. Location restrictions have this effect because of practical constraints on the effective marketing area of retail outlets. Although intrabrand competition may be reduced, the ability of retailers to exploit the resulting market may be limited both by the ability of consumers to travel to other franchised locations and, perhaps more importantly, to purchase the competing products of other manufacturers. None of these key variables, however, is affected by the form of the transaction by which a manufacturer conveys his products to the retailers.

Vertical restrictions promote interbrand competition by allowing the manufacturer to achieve certain efficiencies in the distribution of his products. These "redeeming virtues" are implicit in every decision sustaining vertical restrictions under the rule of reason. Economists have identified a number of ways in which manufacturers can use such restrictions to compete more effectively against other manufacturers. For example, new manufacturers and manufacturers entering new markets can use the restrictions in order to induce competent and aggressive retailers to make the kind of investment of capital and labor that is often required in the distribution of products unknown to the consumer. Established manufacturers can use them to induce retailers to engage in promotional activities or to provide service and repair facilities necessary to the efficient marketing of their products. Service and repair are vital for many products, such as automobiles and major household appliances. The availability and quality of such services affect a manufacturer's goodwill and the competitiveness of his product. Because of market imperfections * * *, these services might not be provided by retailers in a purely competitive situation, despite the fact that each retailer's benefit would be greater if all provided the services than if none did.

The Supreme Court reversed the trial court's holding that Sylvania had violated Section 1 of the Sherman Act.	**DECISION AND REMEDY**
In this case, the Supreme Court focused directly on the applications of a strict per se rule. Its rejection of a rigid rule in favor of a rule-of-reason approach has been extended to other important areas of antitrust law. Thus, the courts and antitrust enforcers will look at the challenged restraint's impact on competition. In this case, the Court found no overall harm to competition.	**COMMENTS**

The practices outlined above are but a few of the acts prohibited by Section 1 of the Sherman Act. Theoretically, any agreement may violate Section 1 if it unduly restrains competition. Some other specific types of agreements are directly controlled by the Clayton Act, which is discussed later in the chapter. First, however, we will consider Section 2 of the Sherman Act.

Section 2 and Monopolization

Section 1 of the Sherman Act prohibits agreements and conspiracies between separate entities. In contrast, a single company may violate the Section 2 prohibition of unlawful monopolization of a market. It should be noted that the Sherman Act does not define *monopoly*. Strictly speaking, a monopoly exists where only one firm controls the entire market for a product. In practice, courts have defined a *monopoly* as a firm that controls such a high percentage of the market that it is able to control prices or exclude competition. Section 2 also prohibits *attempts* to monopolize a market, even if they are unsuccessful.

To establish a Section 2 monopolization violation, two things must be proved. First, the federal government or other plaintiff must show that the defendant's market share is large enough to provide the defendant with monopoly power in a particular product market. Second, the plaintiff must show that the defendant has willfully acquired or maintained that monopoly power.

MONOPOLY POWER The primary measure of monopoly power is the **market-share test.** Before a court can determine a company's market share, however, it must first define the market itself. Defining a market is a more difficult undertaking than one might think. For example, do hot breakfast cereals and cold breakfast cereals make up one market or two different markets?

In one well-known case, du Pont was sued for monopolizing the cellophane market, in which the company controlled about 75 percent of all production. Du Pont contended, however, that other packaging materials competed with cellophane and that the company had a rather small share of the market for all flexible packaging materials. The United States Supreme Court found that there was a great deal of interchangeability between these materials. For example, 32 percent of the snack industry used cellophane, but even more of the industry used other materials. Consequently, the Court held that the relevant product market included all flexible packaging materials, and that du Pont was not a monopolist in this broader market.[9]

In defining a product market, then, the key question is the degree of interchangeability between somewhat different products. If one such product is a good substitute for another, the two products are considered part of the same market. If not, they are in different markets. In one interesting case, the market for gospel music was held to be different from the general music market.[10]

Courts also must consider the geographic boundaries of a market. A company with a small share of the national market may nevertheless possess monopoly power in one region of the country. In one case, the beer companies of Pabst and Blatz sought to merge. At the time, these were the tenth and eighteenth largest beer companies in the United States, and the merger did not threaten national competition. In Wisconsin, however, Blatz and Pabst were the first and fourth largest beer sellers, and the merger was prohibited as leading to undue concentration in a local geographic market.[11]

Once the market has been defined, courts must also determine what share of the market a company must control in order for the control to be objectionable. No specific level is always unlawful, but the Justice Department has set guidelines. See Exhibit 48–1.

THE INTENT REQUIREMENT Simple possession of monopoly power through a large market share is not itself illegal. If that share was acquired through a superior product or mere historical accident, the resultant market power is legal. If, however, the monopolist has undertaken some purposeful act to acquire or preserve monopoly power, Section 2 has been violated.

Many actions of a company may satisfy the intent requirement. When Alcoa had a very large market share for aluminum, that company simply kept increasing its production capacity to supply all future demand for aluminum. The United States Supreme Court held that this pattern of increasing capacity to fill demand served to prevent competitors from entering the market and qualified as a purposeful act under Section 2.[12] Thus, even a relatively innocuous act may become illegal when performed by a company that possesses monopoly market power.

In the following case, a skiing company's refusal to participate in a joint marketing venture was held to violate Section 2.

---

9. United States v. E. I. du Pont De Nemours & Co., 351 U.S. 377, 76 S.Ct. 994, 100 L.Ed. 1264 (1956).

10. Affiliated Music Enterprises, Inc. v. Sesac, Inc., 268 F.2d 13 (2d Cir. 1959).

11. United States v. Pabst Brewing Co., 384 U.S. 546, 86 S.Ct. 1665, 16 L.Ed.2d 765 (1966).

12. United States v. Aluminum Company of America, 148 F.2d 416 (2d Cir. 1945).

Case 48.4

ASPEN SKIING CO. v. ASPEN HIGHLANDS SKIING CORP.

Supreme Court of the United States, 1985.
472 U.S. 585, 105 S.Ct. 2847, 86 L.Ed.2d 467.

BACKGROUND AND FACTS *Aspen, Colorado, is a leading ski resort, and private investors developed four major facilities there for downhill skiing: Ajax, Aspen Highlands, Buttermilk, and Snowmass. The facilities were owned by independent investors, and they jointly offered an "all-Aspen ticket," which could be used for skiing at any of the facilities. Receipts from the ticket were paid to the various facilities in a manner proportionate to their use, as based on surveys of skiers. By 1977, Aspen Skiing Co. (Ski Co.) had acquired ownership of Ajax, Buttermilk, and Snowmass, and Aspen Highlands was owned by the*

Aspen Highlands Skiing Corp. At this time, the two companies were engaged in a dispute over the proper distribution of receipts from the all-Aspen ticket. Ski Co. discontinued the all-Aspen ticket and replaced it with a three-area ticket that covered only its own facilities. Aspen Highlands' share of the local downhill skiing market declined from over 20 percent in 1976–1977 to 11 percent in 1980–1981. Aspen Highlands filed an antitrust complaint against Ski Co., alleging that Ski Co. had monopolized the market for downhill skiing services at Aspen, in violation of Section 2 of the Sherman Act. Aspen Highlands argued that the discontinuation of the all-Aspen ticket was a purposeful act with intent to monopolize the market. The district court issued a judgment in favor of Aspen Highlands, and the Tenth Circuit Court of Appeals affirmed in all respects. Ski Co. appealed to the Supreme Court.

STEVENS, Justice.
*   *   *   *

In this Court, Ski Co. contends that even a firm with monopoly power has no duty to engage in joint marketing with a competitor, that a violation of § 2 cannot be established without evidence of substantial exclusionary conduct, and that none of its activities can be characterized as exclusionary. *   *   *
*   *   *   *

*   *   * In the actual case that we must decide, the monopolist did not merely reject a novel offer to participate in a cooperative venture that had been proposed by a competitor. Rather, the monopolist elected to make an important change in a pattern of distribution that had originated in a competitive market and had persisted for several years. The all-Aspen, 6-day ticket with revenues allocated on the basis of usage was first developed when three independent companies operated three different ski mountains in the Aspen area. It continued to provide a desirable option for skiers when the market was enlarged to include four mountains, and when the character of the market was changed by Ski Co.'s acquisition of monopoly power. Moreover, since the record discloses that interchangeable tickets are used in other multimountain areas which apparently are competitive, it seems appropriate to infer that such tickets satisfy consumer demand in free competitive markets.
*   *   *   *

Perhaps most significant, however, is the evidence relating to Ski Co. itself, for Ski Co. did not persuade the jury that its conduct was justified by any normal business purpose. Ski Co. was apparently willing to forgo daily ticket sales both to skiers who sought to exchange the coupons contained in Highlands' Adventure Pack, and to those who would have purchased Ski Co. daily lift tickets from Highlands if Highlands had been permitted to purchase them in bulk. The jury may well have concluded that Ski Co. elected to forgo these short-run benefits because it was more interested in reducing competition in the Aspen market over the long run by harming its smaller competitor.

The Supreme Court affirmed the decision of the lower federal courts. The original jury had found that Aspen Highlands had suffered $2.5 million in actual damages, which were trebled under the Sherman Act to an award of $7.5 million. This award was affirmed by the Supreme Court.

DECISION AND REMEDY

ATTEMPTED MONOPOLIZATION Section 2, as mentioned, also prohibits attempted monopolization of a market. Maintaining an attempted-monopolization action involves two different tests.

First, there must be a specific intent to exclude competitors and gain monopoly power in a given market. Second, this attempt must have a dangerous probability of success. Proof of actual mo-

Exhibit 48–1 A New Way of Judging Industrial Concentration

The traditional way to measure concentration has been to add the market shares of the four largest companies, A, B, C, and D. Their combined 50 percent market share would make this a fairly concentrated industry. If D and F wanted to merge, creating the industry's largest producer with 17 percent of the market, the merger would be suspect.

Under the new guidelines, the Justice Department assures that any merger that does not raise the Herfindahl Index above 1000 is legal. Antitrusters would look at the makeup of the industry after the merger. Combining D's 10 percent and F's 7 percent, and squaring them, raises the index to 997, virtually assuring legality.

COMPANIES	OLD METHOD (MARKET SHARE)	HERFINDAHL INDEX (SHARE SQUARED)
A	16%	256
B	13	169
C	11	121
D	10	100
E	8	64
F	7	49
G	6	36
H	5	25
I	4	16
Others (24)	20	(Est.) 21
Total	100%	857

INDUSTRIAL SECTORS WITH THE HIGHEST HERFINDAHL INDEXES		
Military tanks		5823
Telephone and telegraph equipment		5026
Sewing machines		4047
Cellulosic synthetic fibers		3189
Turbines		2443

. . . AND THE LOWEST		
Specialty dies & tools		11
Concrete blocks		27
Metal plating & polishing		31
Commercial lithography		32
Ready-mix concrete		32

Source: John E. Kwoka, using 1972 data from Economic Informations Systems, Inc. Reprinted by permission of McGraw-Hill from *Business Week*, May 17, 1982, p. 20.

nopolization is not required, but attempted monopolization is illegal only if the defendant presents a real threat.

THE CLAYTON ACT

Whereas the Sherman Act is expressed in rather general terms, the Clayton Act tends to prohibit more specific types of anticompetitive behavior. The Clayton Act also makes it easier to challenge these behaviors based on probable future anticom-

petitive effects, without proof of current harms. In addition to the Antitrust Division of the Department of Justice, the Federal Trade Commission has authority to enforce the Clayton Act. As under the Sherman Act, private parties may sue and recover treble damages and attorneys' fees under the Clayton Act. When the FTC brings an action against an alleged violation, it is often settled with a consent decree, in which the defendant accepts certain penalties but admits no guilt. This procedure makes defendants less vulnerable to subsequent private lawsuits. The exemptions discussed above under the Sherman Act also apply to the Clayton Act.

Section 2 and Price Discrimination

In 1936, Congress amended Section 2 of the Clayton Act through the Robinson-Patman Act. This law prohibits certain types of **price discrimination.** Price discrimination occurs when a seller charges different prices to different buyers for the same product. For example, suppose Coca-Cola sold its syrup to both McDonald's and Wendy's at the same time but charged McDonald's more. This could constitute illegal price discrimination under Section 2 of the Clayton Act.

Under Section 2 of the Clayton Act, as amended, it is illegal for any person (1) engaged in interstate commerce (2) to price discriminate between different purchasers (3) for goods of like grade and quality, when (4) the effect may be substantially to lessen competition. The act applies only to goods (not services) and only to sales that occur roughly at the same time. Furthermore, the seller must be "engaged" in interstate commerce, and price discrimination is illegal only if it has a substantial anticompetitive effect. Suppose, for example, that a large national producer of frozen desserts typically sells its product for $4.00. Then a relatively small local company in Utah starts selling a similar product for $3.00. This new company begins to take away a large portion of the Salt Lake City market. The large national producer then cuts prices for its frozen desserts in Utah to $2.50, while keeping prices at $4.00 in other states. As a consequence, the local Utah company goes out of business. Here, the price discrimination obviously has a substantial anticompetitive effect and is thus in violation of Section 2 of the Clayton Act.[13]

Several defenses are available in a price-discrimination case. First, a defendant may justify price differentiation between customers by showing cost differences in serving those buyers. A New York seller may charge California customers more than local customers because of higher freight expenses or other costs of doing business out of state. A defendant may also justify price discrimination when changing conditions make price changes necessary. For example, strawberries initially sold to restaurants at $2 per pint may be reduced in price to $1 per pint when they must be sold quickly to avoid spoilage. Price discrimination is also lawful when the lower price was offered in good faith to meet a competitor's equally low price.

The application of Section 2 of the Clayton Act is illustrated in the following decision.

---

13. This hypothetical case is a slightly simplified and exaggerated version of an actual case—Utah Pie Co. v. Continental Baking Co., 386 U.S. 685, 87 S.Ct. 1326, 18 L.Ed.2d 406 (1967).

BACKGROUND AND FACTS *Morton Salt Company (the respondent) sold table salt to wholesalers and retail grocery chains. The company sold its leading brand, called "Blue Label," on a quantity discount basis. Purchasers of over 50,000 cases were charged $1.35 per case, purchasers of 5,000 cases were charged $1.40, and purchasers of less than a carload paid $1.60 per case. Only five companies purchased sufficient quantities of salt to obtain the lowest price. The Federal Trade Commission issued a complaint that the quantity price differentials were not cost-justified and represented illegal price discrimination under the Robinson-Patman Act. The commission therefore ordered Morton Salt to cease offering its quantity discounts. On appeal, a circuit court of appeals found no violation and overturned the FTC ruling. The commission then appealed to the United States Supreme Court.*

 Case 48.5

FEDERAL TRADE COMMISSION v. MORTON SALT CO.

Supreme Court of the United States, 1948.
334 U.S. 37, 68 S.Ct. 822, 92 L.Ed. 1196.

BLACK, Justice.

Respondent's basic contention, which it argues this case hinges upon, is that its "standard quantity discounts, available to all on equal terms, as contrasted, for example, to hidden or special rebates, allowances, prices or discounts, are not discriminatory within the meaning of the Robinson-Patman Act." Theoretically, these discounts are equally available to all, but functionally they are not. For as the record indicates (if reference to it on this point were necessary) no single independent retail grocery store, and probably no single wholesaler, bought as many as 50,000 cases or as much as $50,000 worth of table salt in one year. Furthermore, the record shows that, while certain purchasers were enjoying one or more of respondent's standard quantity discounts, some of their competitors made purchases in such small quantities that they could not qualify for any of respondent's discounts, even those based on carload shipments. The legislative history of the Robinson-Patman Act makes it abundantly clear that Congress considered it to be an evil that a large buyer could secure a competitive advantage over a small buyer solely because of the large buyer's quantity purchasing ability. The Robinson-Patman Act was passed to deprive a large buyer of such advantages except to the extent that a lower price could be justified by reason of a seller's diminished costs due to quantity manufacture, delivery or sale, or by reason of the seller's good faith effort to meet a competitor's equally low price.

*   *   *   *

It is argued that the findings fail to show that respondent's discriminatory discounts had in fact caused injury to competition. There are specific findings that such injuries had resulted from respondent's discounts, although the statute does not require the Commission to find that injury has actually resulted. The statute requires no more than that the effect of the prohibited price discriminations "may be substantially to lessen competition . . . or to injure, destroy, or prevent competition." After a careful consideration of this provision of the Robinson-Patman Act, we have said that "the statute does not require that the discriminations must in fact have harmed competition, but only that there is a reasonable possibility that they 'may' have such an effect." Here the Commission found what would appear to be obvious, that the competitive opportunities of certain merchants were injured when they had to pay respondent substantially more for their goods than their competitors had to pay. The findings are adequate.

DECISION AND REMEDY   *The Supreme Court overturned the appellate court's decision and reinstated the FTC's cease-and-desist order prohibiting Morton Salt's quantity-discount pricing system. Any future quantity discounts would have to be justified by cost differentials.*

The prohibition on price discrimination remains a controversial one. Many economists question whether this law is necessary to control undue market power. Section 2 of the Clayton Act has not been actively used by the government. Nevertheless, some price-discrimination prosecutions continue to occur.

Section 3 and Exclusionary Practices

Section 3 of the Clayton Act prohibits certain types of exclusionary practices. Most such practices involve the attempts of one company to prevent another from purchasing the products of competing firms. The major types of illegal exclusionary practices include tying arrangements, exclusive dealing contracts, and requirements contracts.

TYING ARRANGEMENTS   Section 3 of the Clayton Act prohibits certain restrictive agreements, including **tying arrangements.** A tying arrangement occurs when a seller refuses to sell one product unless the buyer also agrees to buy another product. The sale of the first product is thus *tied* to the purchase of the second. For example, a hypothetical leading producer of beer, ABC Company, might attempt to diversify into other alcoholic products. To do so, ABC Company might agree to sell its beer (the "tying" product) only to customers who also agree to buy its new line of Newport Beach Wine Coolers (the "tied" product). This action would represent a tying arrangement. For a tying arrangement to be illegal, the following three requirements must be met:

1.   **Two different products.** First, there must be two different products involved—the tying product and the tied product. Sometimes this standard raises difficulties. For example, are shoes and

shoelaces together one product or two? Courts have suggested that they should be considered a single product.

2. Substantial market power. Second, the seller must have sufficient market power in the tying product to coerce the purchase of the tied product.

3. Substantial amount of commerce. Finally, the tying arrangement must affect a substantial amount of commerce involving the products in question.

If these three requirements are met, the tying arrangement will generally be illegal under Section 3 of the Clayton Act. Tying arrangements may also be illegal under the rule of reason under Section 1 of the Sherman Act. Under the Sherman Act, tying goods with services may be illegal, whereas the Clayton Act only prohibits the tying of goods with other goods.

In 1936, the Supreme Court held that IBM's practice of requiring the purchase of tabulating cards (the tied product) as a condition of leasing its tabulation machines (the tying product) was unlawful.[14] The Court, however, has not applied a strict rule against tying arrangements. In another case, the Court ruled in favor of U.S. Steel despite the existence of a tie-in between the purchase of prefabricated homes (the tying product) and available credit (the tied product).[15] Since there was no evidence that U.S. Steel had significant market power in either the prefabricated-home market or the credit market, the arrangement was found to be lawful.

EXCLUSIVE DEALING CONTRACTS   Section 3 of the Clayton Act also prohibits **exclusive-dealing contracts** when the effect of these contracts would be "to substantially lessen competition or tend to create a monopoly."

Exclusive-dealing contracts arise when a seller or manufacturer requires that a buyer not purchase the products of the seller's competitors. Despite its similarity to a tying contract, an exclusive-dealing arrangement is subject to a different judicial standard: The courts generally apply a *modified rule of reason* and focus on the effects of the exclusive-dealing contract on competition.

The leading exclusive-dealing decision was reached in *Standard Oil Co. of California v. United States.*[16] In this case, the largest gasoline seller in the nation made exclusive-dealing contracts with independent stations in seven western states. The contracts involved 16 percent of all retail outlets, whose sales comprised approximately 7 percent of all retail sales in the market. The United States Supreme Court found that these contracts violated Section 3 of the Clayton Act.

Courts in recent years have become less likely to hold exclusive-dealing contracts illegal. This is because such contracts may offer real economic benefits. For example, the assurance of exclusive dealing may help producers plan future production needs and enable them to offer lower prices than they otherwise could.

REQUIREMENTS CONTRACTS   One particular type of exclusive-dealing arrangement is a requirements contract. As discussed in Chapter 9, a requirements contract requires that the buyer of a particular commodity purchase all of the commodity he or she will need over a particular period from a particular seller. The legality of these requirements contracts depends on whether they substantially lessen competition in a market. In *Tampa Elec. Co. v. Nashville Coal Co.,*[17] the United States Supreme Court upheld a contract under which Nashville Coal Company was to supply all the coal required by Tampa Electric Company for electricity generation. In its decision, the Court emphasized that the coal company had a very small market share in the relevant geographic region.

Section 7 and Mergers

Section 7 of the Clayton Act prohibits certain mergers between or among persons—which include individuals, sole proprietorships, partnerships, corporations, and so on. The merger of two companies into a larger concern obviously may raise the risk of undue concentration of market power. Different kinds of mergers are judged by different standards. Under the Reagan administration, the federal government has relaxed the standards for challenging mergers somewhat, but some mergers remain illegal under the antitrust laws.

14. International Business Machines Corp. v. United States, 298 U.S. 131, 56 S.Ct. 701, 80 L.Ed. 1085 (1936).

15. United States Steel Corp. v. Fortner Enterprises, Inc., 429 U.S. 610, 97 S.Ct. 861, 51 L.Ed.2d 80 (1977).

16. 337 U.S. 293, 69 S.Ct. 1051, 93 L.Ed. 1371 (1949).

17. 365 U.S. 320, 81 S.Ct. 623, 5 L.Ed.2d 580 (1961).

HORIZONTAL MERGERS The most objectionable kind of merger, in theory, is a **horizontal merger** between competitors. Whether the merger will be legal depends in large part on the market share of each of the two merging firms before they combine and the market share of the resulting firm. If the two firms control only a few percentage points of the relevant market, the merger is likely to be legal. If the firms have a larger share, however, the government is likely to challenge the merger. The Justice Department now uses a formula known as the Herfindahl Index to determine the acceptability of horizontal mergers in terms of market share. Exhibit 48–1 illustrates the application of the Herfindahl Index.

This market-share test is not the only standard by which mergers are judged. Courts will also look at other likely effects of the merger. If the combination of two companies eliminates a particularly vigorous competitor or makes collusion more likely, even a merger of relatively small firms may be illegal. Conversely, when a horizontal merger will increase efficiency without unduly harming competition, the merger is likely to be legal. Although these factors are important, the Herfindahl Index remains the best test of the effects of mergers on free competition. The index is applied in the following case.

Case 48.6

FEDERAL TRADE COMMISSION v. PPG INDUSTRIES, INC.

United States Court of Appeals, District of Columbia Circuit, 1986.
798 F.2d 1500.

BACKGROUND AND FACTS *PPG Industries is the world's largest producer of high-technology aircraft transparencies (windows and the like). PPG sought to merge with Swedlow, Inc., another large producer of these transparencies. The Federal Trade Commission objected to the merger and brought an action to obtain a preliminary injunction blocking the merger. The district court ruled against the FTC but adopted a "hold separate" order, which allowed the acquisition to proceed but required that the companies be operated separately until a final antitrust ruling could be obtained. The FTC appealed this decision, seeking a complete preliminary injunction.*

BORK, Judge.
* * * *

PPG Industries is a publicly-held manufacturer of glass products, automotive and industrial coatings, and chemicals. It is the world's largest producer of glass aircraft transparencies—windows, windshields, and canopies used in civilian and military fixed-wing aircraft and helicopters. It is also a substantial supplier of acrylic and composite (mixed glass/acrylic) transparencies. Swedlow is a closely-held corporation and the world's largest manufacturer of acrylic aircraft transparencies. Swedlow does not produce glass transparencies. While PPG and Swedlow produce transparencies from different materials, the district court found the corporations to be "frequent competitors for contracts to supply transparencies to major U.S. airframe manufacturers." * * *
* * * *

* * * The relevant geographic market was found to be the United States market for such aircraft transparencies. Because it had no accurate figures for the emerging high technology market, the court used the closest relevant market, that for all transparencies, and noted that this market is already highly concentrated with the top four firms accounting for over 80% of all sales in 1984, a statistic which yields a 1943 on the Herfindahl-Hirschmann Index ("HHI"). The merger of PPG, the largest manufacturer with a 30% market share, and Swedlow, the second largest manufacturer with a 23% market share, would create an entity with a combined market share two-and-one-half times larger than that of the nearest competitor and raise the HHI to 3295.
* * * *

* * * The *Department of Justice Merger Guidelines* define as "unconcentrated" a market with an HHI below 1000, as "moderately concentrated" a market with an HHI between 1000 and 1800, and as "highly concentrated" a market with an HHI over 1800. The pre-acquisition HHI calculated by the district court shows that the relevant market, as the court defined it, is already "highly concentrated" and the effect of the acquisition would be a dramatic increase in concentration.

The circuit court held for the Federal Trade Commission and granted the preliminary injunction, which prevented the merger from proceeding.

DECISION AND REMEDY

VERTICAL MERGERS **Vertical mergers** occur when a company at one stage of production or distribution acquires a company at a higher or lower stage of production or distribution. The acquisition of a tire plant by an automobile manufacturer would constitute *backward* vertical integration, whereas the acquisition by the same auto manufacturer of a car-rental agency would constitute *forward* vertical integration. The legality of vertical mergers depends on a number of factors, including the definition of the relevant product market in geographic areas as well as the merger's predictable effect on competition in that market. If a vertical merger forecloses a major market from competitors, for example, the merger may be illegal.

In one leading case, *Brown Shoe*, the country's fourth largest shoe manufacturer sought to acquire the G. R. Kinney Company, a leading shoe retailer. Because of a trend toward vertical mergers in the shoe industry and the fear that retail markets would be foreclosed to other manufacturers, the United States Supreme Court held this merger to be illegal.[18]

---

18. Brown Shoe Co. v. United States, 370 U.S. 294, 82 S.Ct. 1502, 8 L.Ed.2d 510 (1962).

CONGLOMERATE MERGERS A *conglomerate* is a company composed of seemingly unrelated subsidiaries. A **conglomerate merger** occurs when a company in one industry combines with a company in another industry. The merger of a car company with a food company, for example, would constitute a conglomerate merger. The Gulf & Western Corporation provides a graphic real-world example. In 1960, Gulf & Western was a relatively small car-bumper manufacturer, but during the following decade the company acquired numerous other firms, including a producer of zinc, Paramount Pictures, major sugar producers, Consolidated Cigar Company, an air-conditioning concern, Brown Paper, the New York Knicks, and thirty-three wholesalers of automotive parts, among dozens of other companies.

Conglomerate mergers by definition combine unrelated, noncompeting companies, and such mergers usually do not seriously injure competition. Courts will look at the overall effect of such mergers, however, and even conglomerate mergers may be found illegal when they actually threaten competition. The following case, which concerns a product-extension conglomerate merger, demonstrates how such mergers may in fact violate the antitrust laws.

BACKGROUND AND FACTS   *The Federal Trade Commission argued that Procter & Gamble's acquisition of Clorox Chemical Company violated the Clayton Act and substantially lessened competition in the household liquid bleach market. At the time of the merger, Clorox was the leading manufacturer of household bleach in a highly concentrated market. Purex, the major competitor, did not sell its product in some markets, primarily in the northeast and mid-Atlantic states. Procter & Gamble was a large, diversified producer of high-turnover household products. Its large advertising budget, along with other factors, allowed it to enjoy economic advantages in advertising its products. The commission found that extensive advertising expenditures could increase Clorox's market share. The commission argued that Procter & Gamble's acquisition of Clorox would discourage entry and competition in this market.*

 Case 48.7

FEDERAL TRADE COMMISSION v. PROCTER & GAMBLE CO.

Supreme Court of the United States, 1967.
386 U.S. 568, 87 S.Ct. 1224, 18 L.Ed.2d 303.

DOUGLAS, Justice.

* * * *

At the time of the acquisition, Clorox was the leading manufacturer of household liquid bleach, with 48.8% of national sales * * * . The industry is highly concentrated; in 1957, Clorox and Purex accounted for almost 65% of the Nation's household liquid bleach sales, and, together with four other firms, for almost 80%. * * *

Since all liquid bleach is chemically identical, advertising and sales promotion are vital. In 1957 Clorox spent almost $3,700,000 on advertising, imprinting the value of its bleach in the mind of the consumer. * * * The Commission found that these heavy expenditures went far to explain why Clorox maintained so high a market share despite the fact that its brand, though chemically indistinguishable from rival brands, retailed for a price equal to or, in many instances, higher than its competitors.

Procter is a large, diversified manufacturer of low-price, high-turnover household products sold through grocery, drug, and department stores. Prior to its acquisition of Clorox, it did not produce household liquid bleach. * * * Its primary activity is in the general area of soaps, detergents, and cleansers; in 1957, of total domestic sales, more than one-half * * * were in this field. Procter was the dominant factor in this area.

* * * *

The decision to acquire Clorox was the result of a study conducted by Procter's promotion department designed to determine the advisability of entering the liquid bleach industry. * * *

The final report confirmed the conclusions of the initial report and emphasized that Procter would make more effective use of Clorox's advertising budget and that the merger would facilitate advertising economies. A few months later, Procter acquired the assets of Clorox in the name of a wholly owned subsidiary, the Clorox Company, in exchange for Procter stock.

The Commission * * * found that the substitution of Procter with its huge assets and advertising advantages for the already dominant Clorox would dissuade new entrants and discourage active competition from the firms already in the industry due to fear of retaliation by Procter. * * *

The anticompetitive effects with which this product-extension merger is fraught can easily be seen: (1) the substitution of the powerful acquiring firm for the smaller, but already dominant, firm may substantially reduce the competitive structure of the industry by raising entry barriers and dissuading the smaller firms from aggressively competing; (2) the acquisition eliminates the potential competition of the acquiring firm.

The liquid bleach industry was already oligopolistic [dominated by only a few firms] before the acquisition, and price competition was certainly not as vigorous as it would have been if the industry were competitive. * * *

DECISION AND REMEDY   *The FTC order that Procter & Gamble divest itself of the Clorox Company was upheld by the Supreme Court of the United States.*

STATE-ACTION DEFENSE

As suggested earlier in this chapter, actions taken by states have historically been exempt from the antitrust laws. Now, however, the use of the state-action defense is somewhat more complex. Government entities are not automatically exempted from antitrust law simply because of their status.

In *California Liquor Dealers v. Midcal Aluminum, Inc.*,[19] the Supreme Court formally recognized two requirements for obtaining antitrust immunity under the **state-action doctrine.** First, the challenged restraint must be "one clearly articulated and affirmatively expressed as state policy," and

---

19. 445 U.S. 97, 100 S.Ct. 937, 63 L.Ed.2d 233 (1980).

second, the policy must be "actively supervised" by the state itself. A recent decision held that even a combination of private companies engaged in price setting would be legal if the action were both authorized and actively supervised by a state government.[20]

Another recent United States Supreme Court decision held that the state-action defense applied

to local municipalities as well.[21] The U.S. Congress has also exempted local governments and their officials from monetary damages under the antitrust laws by passing the Local Government Antitrust Act of 1984.[22]

---

20. Southern Motor Carriers Rate Conference, Inc. v. United States, 471 U.S. 48, 105 S.Ct. 1721, 85 L.Ed.2d 36 (1985).

21. Town of Hallie v. City of Eau Claire, 471 U.S. 34, 105 S.Ct. 1713, 85 L.Ed.2d 24 (1985).

22. 15 U.S.C. Sections 34–36.

QUESTIONS AND CASE PROBLEMS

1. Discuss *fully* whether each of the following situations violates the Sherman Act.

(a) Trujillo Foods, Inc., is the leading seller of frozen Mexican foods in three southwestern states. The various retail outlets that sell Trujillo products are in close competition, and customers are very price conscious. Trujillo has conditioned its sales to retailers with the agreement that the retailers will not sell below a minimum price nor above a maximum price. The retailers are allowed to set any price within these limits.

(b) Franklin, Inc., Green, Inc., and Fill-It, Inc., are competitors in the manufacture and sale of microwave ovens sold primarily east of the Mississippi River. As a patriotic gesture and to assist the unemployed, the three competitors agree to lower their prices on all microwave models by 20 percent for a three-month period that includes the Fourth of July and Labor Day.

(c) Foam Beer, Inc., sells its beer to distributors all over the United States. Foam sends each of its distributors a recommended price list, explaining that past records indicate that selling beer at those prices should ensure the distributor a reasonable rate of return. The price list clearly states that the sale of beer by Foam to the distributor is not conditioned upon the distributor's reselling the beer at the recommended price and that the distributor is free to set the price.

2. Mickey's Appliance Store was a new retail seller of appliances in Sunwest City. Mickey's innovative sales techniques and financing caused a substantial loss of sales from the appliance department of Luckluster Department Store. Luckluster was a large department store and part of a large chain with substantial buying power. Luckluster told a number of appliance manufacturers that if they continued to sell to Mickey's, Luckluster would stop purchasing from them. The manufacturers immediately stopped selling appliances to Mickey's. Mickey's filed suit against Luckluster

and the manufacturers, claiming their actions constituted an antitrust violation. Luckluster and the manufacturers could prove that Mickey's was a small retailer with a small portion of the market. Since the relevant market was not substantially affected, they claimed they were not guilty of restraint of trade. Discuss *fully* whether there was an antitrust violation.

3. Quick Photo, Inc., is a manufacturer of photographic film. At present, Quick Photo has approximately 50 percent of the market. Quick Photo launches a campaign whereby the purchase price of Quick Photo film includes photo processing by Quick Photo, Inc. Quick Photo claims that its film processing is specially designed to improve the quality of the finished photos when Quick Photo's film is used. Discuss *fully* whether Quick Photo's combination of film purchase and film processing is an antitrust violation.

4. Bock Brewery, Inc., is a regional producer and seller of Suds Beer. In its five-state area, Bock has 15 percent of the beer market. Barrel Tap, Inc., is a corporation that has exclusive beer sales concessions in taverns in all major airports in a twenty-state area. Barrel Tap purchases beer from Bock, Miller, and Anheuser-Busch, Inc. Bock acquires the stock and assets of Barrel Tap, Inc. What type of merger is this? Discuss *fully* whether this merger is in violation of the Clayton Act, Section 7.

5. Spray-Rite was an authorized distributor of Monsanto herbicides from 1957 to 1968 and typically sold these herbicides at discount prices. Monsanto manufactures a variety of chemical products in addition to these herbicides. In October 1968, Monsanto declined to renew Spray-Rite's distributorship after receiving complaints from other distributors. Spray-Rite sued Monsanto under Section 1 of the Sherman Act. In its complaint, Spray-Rite alleged that Monsanto and some of its distributors had conspired to fix the resale price of Monsanto herbicides. Monsanto contended that Spray-Rite's distributorship had been terminated because of its failure to hire trained sales personnel and promote sales to dealers adequately. The court of appeals concluded that proof that Spray-Rite's termination had occurred subsequent to competitor complaints was sufficient to support an inference of concerted action in violation of the Sherman Act. Should illegal price fixing be inferred from the fact that a manufacturer terminated a price-cutting distributorship after complaints from other distributors? [Monsanto Co. v. Spray-Rite Service Corp., 465 U.S. 752, 104 S.Ct. 1464, 79 L.Ed.2d 775, rehearing denied, 466 U.S. 994, 104 S.Ct. 2378, 80 L.Ed.2d 850 (1984)]

6. Edwin G. Hyde, a certified anesthesiologist, applied for a position on the medical staff of East Jefferson Parish Hospital. The hospital had entered into a contract under which all anesthesiological services required by the hospital's patients were to be performed by a certain professional medical corporation. Consequently, the hospital denied Hyde's application. Hyde brought suit under Section 1 of the Sherman Act, alleging that the contract was an illegal tying arrangement. Should Hyde prevail? [Jefferson Parish Hospital District No. 2 v. Hyde, 466 U.S. 2, 104 S.Ct. 1551, 80 L.Ed.2d 2 (1984)]

7. Febco, Inc., manufactured lawn and turf equipment. The Colorado Pump and Supply Company was a wholesale distributor of such equipment in Colorado. An important item that Colorado Pump distributed was a control device for sprinkling systems. Although Febco manufactured one of the better sprinkler controls, a number of other manufacturers competed in the field with competitive and satisfactory substitutes for the Febco controllers. Under an agreement between Febco and Colorado Pump giving Colorado Pump the right to distribute Febco products, Colorado Pump was required to stock an entire line of Febco products. It could also stock other brands. Industry data proved that it was important for distributors to protect the goodwill of manufacturers by carrying a complete line of a manufacturer's goods or none at all. Is the agreement between Febco and Colorado an illegal tying arrangement? [Colorado Pump & Supply Co. v. Febco, Inc., 472 F.2d 637 (10th Cir. 1973)]

8. Meister Brau, Inc., was engaged in the business of brewing beers, malts, and ales. It acquired the Berger Meister Beer Company through purchase of the latter's common stock. Berger Meister sold the beer it brewed through distributors who operated as individual businesses separate from Berger Meister. Soon after Meister Brau acquired Berger Meister, it terminated some of Berger Meister's distributorships. The distributors handled the products of a number of other breweries, but they complained that the reduced sales volume that would result from termination by Meister Brau would drive them out of business. The distributors therefore sued Meister Brau, arguing that its agreement with its new subsidiary, Berger Meister, to terminate the distributorships constituted a conspiracy to restrain trade in violation of Section 1 of the Sherman Act. The distributors alleged that the terminations would reduce competition in a market that was already tending toward concentration. Discuss whether Meister Brau violated Section 1. [Ricchetti v. Meister Brau, Inc., 431 F.2d 1211 (9th Cir. 1970)]

9. American Oil Company was a producer and distributor of oil, gas, and related products. Olson was engaged in bulk distribution and retail sales of oil products. Early in 1967, American decided to acquire control of Olson's bulk-distribution operation, and it purchased substantially all of Olson's assets. Thereafter, American hired Lawrence McMullin to assume control of the Olson operation for American. Under the agreement, McMullin was to take charge of the Olson plant and was to be paid on a commission basis in lieu of salary for the bulk petroleum sales that he procured. In addition, the contract between American and McMullin imposed certain territorial limitations and price restrictions on sales by the operation that McMullin was to control. Could the agreement between McMullin and American Oil imposing price restrictions and territorial controls constitute a violation of Section 1 of the Sherman Antitrust Act? [American Oil Co. v. McMullin, 508 F.2d 1345 (10th Cir. 1975)]

10. The National Collegiate Athletic Association (NCAA) plays an important role in regulating amateur collegiate sports. As a result of various surveys and reports, the NCAA concluded that television adversely affects college football game attendance and that the telecasting of such games could seriously threaten the collegiate athletic system. The NCAA subsequently imposed regulations that restrained the ability of member colleges to negotiate and contract for the telecasting of college football games. Some member colleges began to assert that colleges with major football programs deserved to have greater input in the formulation of policies on televising college games. When some member colleges entered into a television agreement with NBC on their own, the NCAA announced that it would take disciplinary action against any member college that complied with the contract. Did the NCAA violate the Sherman Act? Should this case be considered under the rule of reason or according to the assumptions related to *per se* violation? [National Collegiate Athletic Association v. University of Oklahoma et al., 468 U.S. 85, 104 S.Ct. 2948, 82 L.Ed.2d 70 (1984)]

11. Certain medical foundations in Arizona organized to promote fee-for-service medical care and compete with health maintenance organizations. These foundations established a specific schedule of *maximum* fees for health services that could be charged to policyholders of specified insurance plans. The state sued the foundations, arguing that the fee schedule was a violation of Section 1 of the Sherman Act. Was the state correct? [Arizona v. Maricopa County Medical Society, 457 U.S. 332, 102 S.Ct. 2466, 73 L.Ed.2d 48 (1982)]

12. The National Football League (NFL) is an association of professional football teams. For a time, the NFL was the only national professional football league in major markets. Another business group formed the United States Football League (USFL) to compete with the NFL. After several years of operation, the USFL encountered severe financial problems and sued the NFL, arguing that the NFL monopolized the market unlawfully under Section 2. The USFL alleged, for example, that the NFL had television contracts with all three major television networks (ABC, CBS, and NBC), which tended to deprive the USFL of television revenue. The NFL argued that the USFL simply provided an inferior product. Who should prevail? [United States Football League v. National Football League, 644 F.Supp. 1040 (S.D.N.Y. 1986)]

13. Waste Management, Inc., was the largest waste collection and disposal company operating in the United States. Waste Management attempted to purchase EMW Ventures, Inc., another large waste disposal company. The resultant merger would have left Waste Management with nearly 49 percent of the total waste disposal market and would have increased the Herfindahl Index of concentration in the market to more than 2700. Entry of new companies into this market was very easy, however, as people could operate waste disposal operations out of their homes with only one truck. The United States sued to prevent the merger, arguing that the resulting concentration would injure competition. Should the merger be blocked under the Clayton Act? [United States v. Waste Management, Inc., 743 F.2d 976 (2d Cir. 1984)]

Chapter 49

Employment and Labor Relations Law

Traditionally, employment relationships were governed by contract law, and little government regulation of these relationships existed. Most employer-employee contracts were considered to be "at will." In an **at-will contract,** historically, either party may terminate the contractual relationship at any time and for any reason. In practice, this meant that employers could fire workers without good cause and even for such unjustified reasons as racial discrimination.

In recent decades, however, the government has stepped in to regulate certain aspects of the employment relationship. At-will employment contracts still exist, but the employer no longer has the flexibility to fire employees for any reason whatsoever. Discharges based on certain prohibited reasons are now illegal and may subject employers to liability for damages under federal statutes, state statutes, contract law, or tort law.

The federal government responded to public pressure in the 1930s to protect employees' rights to unionize. In the 1960s and 1970s, Congress passed additional legislation to protect workers from certain types of discrimination, to protect the safety of workers, and to ensure the security of employee pension-plan investments. State governments have introduced other employee protection laws, and the common law has also evolved to limit some employer rights. This chapter will discuss the major government actions affecting employment relationships.

UNIONS AND COLLECTIVE BARGAINING

Early regulation of the employment relationships focused on protecting workers' rights to unionize and collectively bargain with their employers. These early laws ensured that workers could form unions and that the unions could negotiate with employers over wages and other terms of employment. In this way, workers were better able to defend their own interests against employers. In 1932, Congress passed the Norris-LaGuardia Act, which protected peaceful strikes and picketing by workers. In 1935, Congress passed the National Labor Relations Act (popularly known as the Wagner Act), which conclusively established the rights of employees to form unions and negotiate with an employer. Consequently, workers can group together in their own organization and present a united front in bargaining.

The Wagner Act also created the National Labor Relations Board (NLRB) to oversee and enforce that law's requirements. The NLRB is a five-member federal agency that supervises and enforces the labor laws. These laws apply to all employers affecting interstate commerce. The law applies only to labor employees, however, and not to independent contractors or management workers.

Since their passage, these labor laws have been significantly amended by further acts of Congress. In 1947, the Taft-Hartley Act was passed. This law was hotly disputed because it introduced provisions that protected employers from certain union practices. In 1959, Congress passed the Landrum-Griffin Act to control some internal business procedures of unions. Now, union elections are regulated to prevent corruption or fraud. Exhibit 49–1 illustrates the evolution of federal labor law. The following discussion provides a more detailed explanation of the major provisions of contemporary labor law.

The Right to Organize

The centerpiece of federal labor law protects the right of employees to form and join unions. When employees want to form a union, they first must seek support from a majority of workers in their job category at their worksite. They do so by getting other workers to sign authorization cards supporting a union election. Once 30 percent of the employees in a job category have signed such cards, a union election will be initiated voluntarily by the employer or required by the NLRB.

In such elections, the union organizers will campaign for unionization, and the employer often will campaign against the union, but the employer cannot interfere with the organization or election procedure. Each side will present information to convince a majority of workers to vote for or against the union. The NLRB oversees election procedures to ensure that they are fair.

Unfair Labor Practices

The NLRB protects fairness by proscribing certain **unfair labor practices.** For example, an employer campaigning against a union cannot threaten to fire the workers or close the plant if they vote for the union. Nor can the employer discriminate against union organizers or members of a union. Another rule makes it an unfair labor practice for any employer to dominate or interfere in its workers' formation of a union. Exhibit 49–2 lists the principal unfair labor practices of both employers and unions.

Arguments over alleged unfair labor practices are first decided by the NLRB and may then be appealed to federal court. The following case, which involved a representative dispute over allegedly unfair labor practices, illustrates this process.

BACKGROUND AND FACTS *Some garment workers at Luxuray's production facility in Fort Plain, New York, attempted to form a union. The management of the plant began holding meetings of employees during working hours to discourage the formation of a union. At one such meeting, the management showed a film entitled "And Women Must Weep." This fictional film dramatically depicts certain alleged risks of unionization. Union supporters filed a complaint with the National Labor Relations Board, which held that showing the film constituted an unfair labor practice. The NLRB issued an order prohibiting the company from showing the film to the remainder of its employees. The employer appealed this decision, contending that showing the film was a protected exercise of its freedom of speech.*

 Case 49.1

LUXURAY OF NEW YORK v. NATIONAL LABOR RELATIONS BOARD

United States Court of Appeals, Second Circuit, 1971.
447 F.2d 112.

KAUFMAN, Judge.
* * * *

The only issue before us is whether Luxuray violated Section 8(a)(1) of the [Wagner] Act by showing to employees at one of the anti-union meetings from which pro-union

employees were excluded, a film, which might appropriately be characterized as prop-
aganda, entitled "And Women Must Weep." Prior to showing the film, Sidney Foreman, Director of Manufacturing of the Consumer Product Division of Beaunit Corporation read to the employees a prepared written statement to the effect that the events
depicted were true although the film was a dramatization by professional actors. Foreman also observed that the setting of the strike portrayed in the film was a small town
like Fort Plain and warned that similar events "could happen to us people, our community, our friends."

The film itself has apparently become something of a standard tool in anti-union
campaigns. The Fifth Circuit has accurately described its contents:

> It is in color. It tells the story of a strike in Princeton, Indiana. The actors and
> actresses are professionals. The film is narrated by one of the actresses who plays
> the part of the wife of a minister whose parishioners are involuntarily involved in
> the strike as members of the union. They are among the union members who are
> dictatorially mistreated by the majority of the union members. The majority pro-
> voked the strike to serve the wrongful ends of one union officer. The minority of
> the members who oppose the strike are deprived of their rights by the majority.
> The strike was called without consulting the International.

Among other baneful events, the film shows picket line violence, the minister being
jeered, smashed windshields, slashed tires, and upturned automobiles, all caused by
the majority members of the union. The minister's wife is threatened by an anonymous
caller who announces that her home will be the next to be bombed. The minister is
shown with a rifle, sitting through the night, in an effort to protect his family. The
climax of the fray is reached when the strikers fire into the trailer home of a dissenting
union member and a bullet strikes his baby in the head. The film closes with the end
of the strike and with the announcement that the baby will live. The closing words of
the narrator are: "All you have to do is ask yourself, could my town be next? And if
you think that the answer of what happened to us couldn't happen to you, remember
that is what we thought in the beginning. Must you wait to come face to face with
tyranny as we did[?]"

*   *   *   *

The showing of "And Women Must Weep" undoubtedly illustrated the management's anti-union attitude more graphically than did its speeches and pamphlets. But
a mere expression of anti-union sentiment by an employer is an exercise of free speech
protected by at least Section 8(c) and most likely by the First Amendment. The film,
in the context of its showing, cannot even be said to have implied a "prediction." A
fairer characterization would be that by showing the film, the employer expressed an
opinion that in the past local union officials have abused their power and called wildcat strikes to the detriment of the union membership, and that similar abuses might
accompany unionization in the future, particularly at Fort Plain. The Board does not
assert that local unions have in fact never been corrupted and their power never abused
to advance the selfish ends of their leaders. Thus, the film is a one-sided brief against
unionism, devoid of significant rational content perhaps, but nonetheless not reasonably
to be construed as threatening retaliation or force. Nowhere in the film does the
employer or his representative appear or make any representation. The film, in short,
may be characterized as a exposé of what happens to union members when dominated
by ruthless and unthinking union officials.

**DECISION
AND REMEDY**

*Having found that the NLRB order violated the rights of the employer, the
court denied enforcement of that portion of the NLRB order prohibiting the
showing of the film. Employers' anti-union advocacy can only be prohibited if
it uses threats of reprisal for unionization or promises of future benefit for non-
unionization.*

Exhibit 49–1 The Evolution of Federal Labor Law

YEAR	POPULAR NAME	PRIMARY PROVISIONS
1932	Norris-LaGuardia Act	Established the right to strike and picket peacefully; prohibited federal judicial injunctions against lawful strikes.
1935	Wagner Act	Established the National Labor Relations Board; defined certain employer unfair labor practices; instituted NLRB oversight over union elections and other provisions of the act.
1947	Taft-Hartley Act	Established certain labor practices by unions as unfair; created a cooling-off period preventing work stoppage for eighty days when a strike threatens to create a national emergency.
1959	Landrum-Griffin Act	Created "bill of rights" for union members to ensure union democracy and prevent corruption by union officials.

Exhibit 49–2 Unfair Labor Practices

UNFAIR LABOR PRACTICES OF EMPLOYERS
Discriminating against union members or organizers. Interfering with free election through threats of reprisal. Dominating labor organization of workers. Interfering with workers' attempts to unionize. Refusing to bargain in good faith with NLRB-certified union. Discriminating against workers for filing charges with NLRB.

UNFAIR LABOR PRACTICES OF UNIONS
Engaging in secondary boycotts through strikes or picketing. Causing employer to discriminate against non-union workers. Refusing to bargain in good faith with employer. Forcing employer to pay for non-working employees ("featherbedding"). Coercing workers or employer to prevent them from exercising their legal rights.

Collective Bargaining

Once a legal union is formed, it becomes the exclusive bargaining representative for its members. This means that the employer must bargain over terms of employment with that legally recognized union. **Collective bargaining** is the term used to denote negotiations between a union and an employer. When working out a new contract, these parties typically bargain over wage rates, fringe benefits, employment conditions, and other terms. Both sides are required to bargain in good faith, which means that they must sincerely try to work out a voluntary contract agreement.

Strikes

If the collective bargaining process breaks down despite the best efforts of the parties, the union may call a strike. By refusing to work and picketing the job site, employees hope to pressure the employer into making bargaining concessions. Employers have a right to try to replace the workers and go on with business if possible. In the 1987 professional football players' strike, for example, the team owners continued playing games by using replacement players (sometimes disparagingly called "scabs"). A few regular players crossed the strike picket lines and returned to their teams to play in the replacement games. After three weeks of replacement games, the strike was called off. Once a strike has ended, an employer cannot discriminate against employees who participated in the strike but must give them a fair chance to be rehired. Thus, the regular football players returned to work after the strike. A few replacement players were able to stay on with their teams, however.

Illegal Strikes

The NLRB declares certain strikes to be illegal. Foremost among these is the **secondary boycott.** Workers may only strike against their own employer, known as the primary employer. Strikes or picketing directed against other companies that do business with the primary employer—in order to pressure the primary employer into concessions—are illegal secondary boycotts under Section 8(b) of the National Labor Relations Act. "Hot cargo" agreements, in which employers agree with unions not to deal with non-union companies, are also illegal secondary boycotts. The following case analyzes the current Supreme Court opinion on secondary boycotts and the difficulty of determining whether a picket line actually constitutes such an illegal strike.

Case 49.2
NATIONAL LABOR RELATIONS BOARD v. RETAIL STORE EMPLOYEES UNION, LOCAL 1001, RETAIL CLERKS INTERNATIONAL ASSN., AFL-CIO

Supreme Court of the United States, 1980.
447 U.S. 607, 100 S.Ct. 2372, 65 L.Ed.2d 377.

BACKGROUND AND FACTS *Safeco Title Insurance Company underwrites real estate title insurance in the state of Washington. The company maintains close ties with five local title companies. Local 1001 is the union representing the workers of Safeco. After collective bargaining failed, the union went on strike and picketed the offices of Safeco. The union also picketed each of the five local title companies, asking consumers to support the union by canceling their Safeco policies. Safeco and a title company protested to the NLRB, arguing that the picketing of the individual title companies was an illegal secondary boycott. The NLRB agreed and ordered the union to cease such picketing. The union appealed, and the court of appeals overturned the NLRB order. The companies then appealed to the United States Supreme Court.*

POWELL, Justice.
*   *   *   *

Section 8(b)(4)(ii)(B) of the National Labor Relations Act makes it "an unfair labor practice for a labor organization . . . to threaten, coerce, or restrain" a person not party to a labor dispute "where . . . an object thereof is . . . forcing or requiring [him] to cease using, selling, handling, transporting, or otherwise dealing in the products of any other producer . . . or to cease doing business with any other person. . . ."

In *Tree Fruits*, the Court held that § 8(b)(4)(ii)(B) does not prohibit all peaceful picketing at secondary sites. There, a union striking certain Washington fruit packers picketed large supermarkets in order to persuade consumers not to buy Washington apples. Concerned that a broad ban against such picketing might run afoul of the First Amendment, the Court found the statute directed to an " 'isolated evil.' " The evil was use of secondary picketing "to persuade the customers of the secondary employer to cease trading with him in order to force him to cease dealing with, or to put pressure upon, the primary employer." Congress intended to protect secondary parties from pressures that might embroil them in the labor disputes of others, but not to shield them from business losses caused by a campaign that successfully persuades consumers "to boycott the primary employer's goods." Thus, the Court drew a distinction between picketing "to shut off all trade with the secondary employer unless he aids the union in its dispute with the primary employer" and picketing that "only persuades his customers not to buy the struck product." The picketing in that case, which "merely follow[ed] the struck product," did not " 'threaten, coerce, or restrain' " the secondary party within the meaning of § 8(b)(4)(ii)(B).
*   *   *   *

As long as secondary picketing only discourages consumption of a struck product, incidental injury to the neutral is a natural consequence of an effective primary boycott. But the Union's secondary appeal against the central product sold by the title companies in this case is "reasonably calculated to induce customers not to patronize the neutral parties at all." The resulting injury to their businesses is distinctly different from the injury that the Court considered in *Tree Fruits*. Product picketing that reasonably can be expected to threaten neutral parties with ruin or substantial loss simply does not square with the language or the purpose of § 8(b)(4)(ii)(B). Since successful secondary picketing would put the title companies to a choice between their survival and the severance of their ties with Safeco, the picketing plainly violates the statutory ban on the coercion of neutrals with the object of "forcing or requiring [them] to cease . . . dealing in the [primary] produc[t] . . . or to cease doing business with" the primary employer.

The Supreme Court reversed the decision of the court of appeals and remanded the case with directions to enforce the NLRB's order prohibiting secondary picketing of the five local title companies.

DECISION AND REMEDY

As an example of illegal secondary action, suppose that grocery store workers at Consolidated Foods are engaged in a strike. To put additional pressure on Consolidated Foods, these workers might want to picket the offices of TransAmerica Trucking, a transportation company that delivers products to the Consolidated Foods store. The workers might even be able to get their union allies who work for TransAmerica to refuse to deliver products to the Consolidated Foods store. This secondary boycott, however, would be illegal under the labor laws.

Some other types of strikes may also be illegal. Only strikes adopted by a majority of union members are lawful. "Wildcat" strikes by a minority of the employees are not legal. Violent strikes are also unlawful, as are "sitdown" strikes, in which the employees refuse to leave the plant but simply sit down on the job. If a strike in a critical industry would create a national emergency, the president of the United States may obtain an eighty-day injunction stopping the strike. This injunction creates an eighty-day "cooling-off" period during which the parties can reconsider their disagreements and, ideally, work out a compromise. President Eisenhower obtained such an injunction against striking steel workers in 1959; President Nixon, against striking dockworkers in 1971; and President Carter, against striking coal miners in 1978.

EMPLOYMENT DISCRIMINATION

At the present time, employment discrimination law may be the leading employment law issue for private employers. Title VII of the Civil Rights Act of 1964 prohibits certain types of discrimination by such employers. Title VII is the short name for the several sections of the act that require equal employment opportunity. This legislation has had a significant effect on the workplace.

General Requirements of Title VII

Compliance with the Civil Rights Act is monitored by the Equal Employment Opportunity Commission (EEOC). This commission has five members, appointed by the president to five-year terms, and thousands of staff members. The EEOC has power to issue guidelines for interpreting the law and to bring lawsuits against organizations that violate the law.

COVERAGE Title VII covers employers in interstate commerce who have fifteen or more employees. Because interstate commerce is defined very broadly, the vast majority of employers are covered, as are employment agencies and labor organizations. This title only applies to employer-employee discrimination, however, and does not prohibit other forms of discrimination, such as discrimination against other companies or clients.

PROTECTED CLASSES The concept of a **protected class** is an important one under Title VII, which does not protect workers against every conceivable form of employment discrimination. Discrimination against homosexuals, for example, is not prohibited under Title VII. The protected classes include those defined by race, sex, color, religion, and national origin. Employment discrimination based on any of these criteria is strictly prohibited.

PROCEDURES AND REMEDIES A victim who has suffered discrimination may not simply file a lawsuit under Title VII. First, the person must file a claim with the EEOC, which investigates the facts and seeks to achieve a voluntary **conciliation** through which the employer and employee settle the dispute. If conciliation is not forthcoming, the EEOC may sue the employer under Title VII. If the EEOC chooses not to sue, then the victim may bring his or her own Title VII suit. Suppose Katherine Jones believes that she was unjustly fired because of discrimination. The EEOC may disbelieve her case and refuse to sue her employer. Nevertheless, Katherine may bring her own lawsuit against the employer.

If the plaintiff successfully proves that unlawful discrimination occurred, he or she may receive damages for back pay or retroactive promotions. Thus, Katherine Jones might receive back wages from the time of her firing to the time of the decision in her case and might also be granted any promotions that she was denied because of illegal discrimination. Employer liability under Title VII may be considerable. In 1983, the last year for which such statistics are available, the EEOC obtained over $40 million in damages for employees under Title VII. The court may also grant an injunction prohibiting future violations and correcting for past discrimination.

Disparate-Treatment Discrimination

When one thinks of employment discrimination, one is likely to imagine a job supervisor who is overtly racist. In one early case, only black workers were forced to do custodial work, because blacks "clean better." [1] Or an employer might simply refuse to hire minorities for white-collar jobs. This

blatant, intentional discrimination is known as **disparate treatment.**

Because intent may sometimes be difficult to prove, courts have established certain procedures for resolving disparate-treatment cases. Suppose a woman applies for employment with a construction firm and is rejected. If she sues on grounds of disparate-treatment discrimination, she must meet a four-part test. In a hiring discrimination case, these requirements are:

1.   That the plaintiff is a member of a protected class.
2.   That the plaintiff applied and was qualified for the job in question.
3.   That the plaintiff was rejected by the employer.
4.   That the employer continued to seek applicants for the position or filled the position with a person not in a protected class.

If the plaintiff can meet these relatively easy tests, she makes out a *prima facie* **case** of illegal discrimination. Making out a *prima facie* case of discrimination means that the plaintiff has met her initial burden of proof and will win in the absence of an employer response. The burden then shifts to the employer-defendant to articulate a legal reason for not hiring the plaintiff. For example, the employer might say that the plaintiff was not hired because she lacked sufficient experience or training. The plaintiff must then show that the employer's reason is a pretext (not the true reason) and that discriminatory intent actually motivated the employer's decision. Evidence of sexist statements by the employer might be used to show such a pretext. The resolution of a disparate-treatment action is shown in the following decision.

---

1. Slack v. Havens, 522 F.2d 1091 (9th Cir. 1975).

Case 49.3

TEXAS DEPT. OF COMMUNITY AFFAIRS v. BURDINE

Supreme Court of the United States, 1981.
450 U.S. 248, 101 S.Ct. 1089, 67 L.Ed.2d 207.

BACKGROUND AND FACTS   *In 1972, Burdine was an accounting clerk working for the Texas Department of Community Affairs. She was promoted to Field Services Coordinator in 1972 and soon applied for another promotion, to Project Director. She was refused the promotion, and the job remained vacant for six months; then a male was hired. When in 1973 the department had to make cutbacks, Burdine was terminated from her position. She sued, alleging discrimination based upon her sex. Burdine made out a* prima facie *case, but the district court accepted the defendant's explanation that it had denied her the promotion for nondiscriminatory reasons. Consequently, the district court ruled for the defendant, the Department of Community Affairs. The Fifth Circuit Court of Appeals reversed the lower court's ruling. The appellate court* *held that the department had failed to demonstrate that the male hired as Project Director was "more qualified" than Burdine. The Texas Department of Community Affairs appealed this decision to the United States Supreme Court.*

POWELL, Justice.

* * * *

The burden of establishing a prima facie case of disparate treatment is not onerous. The plaintiff must prove by a preponderance of the evidence that she applied for an available position for which she was qualified, but was rejected under circumstances which give rise to an inference of unlawful discrimination. The prima facie case serves an important function in the litigation: it eliminates the most common nondiscriminatory reasons for the plaintiff's rejection. As the Court explained in *Furnco Construction Corp.* v. *Waters*, the prima facie case "raises an inference of discrimination only because we presume these acts, if otherwise unexplained, are more likely than not based on the consideration of impermissible factors." Establishment of the prima facie case in effect creates a presumption that the employer unlawfully discriminated against the employee. If the trier of fact believes the plaintiff's evidence, and if the employer is silent in the face of the presumption, the court must enter judgment for the plaintiff because no issue of fact remains in the case.

The burden that shifts to the defendant, therefore, is to rebut the presumption of discrimination by producing evidence that the plaintiff was rejected, or someone else was preferred, for a legitimate, nondiscriminatory reason. The defendant need not persuade the court that it was actually motivated by the proffered reasons. It is sufficient if the defendant's evidence raises a genuine issue of fact as to whether it discriminated against the plaintiff. To accomplish this, the defendant must clearly set forth, through the introduction of admissible evidence, the reasons for the plaintiff's rejection. The explanation provided must be legally sufficient to justify a judgment for the defendant. If the defendant carries this burden of production, the presumption raised by the prima facie case is rebutted, and the factual inquiry proceeds to a new level of specificity. Placing this burden of production on the defendant thus serves simultaneously to meet the plaintiff's prima facie case by presenting a legitimate reason for the action and to frame the factual issue with sufficient clarity so that the plaintiff will have a full and fair opportunity to demonstrate pretext. The sufficiency of the defendant's evidence should be evaluated by the extent to which it fulfills these functions.

The plaintiff retains the burden of persuasion. She now must have the opportunity to demonstrate that the proffered reason was not the true reason for the employment decision. * * *

* * * *

In summary, the Court of Appeals erred by requiring the defendant to prove by a preponderance of the evidence the existence of nondiscriminatory reasons for terminating the respondent and that the person retained in her stead had superior objective qualifications for the position. When the plaintiff has proved a prima facie case of discrimination, the defendant bears only the burden of explaining clearly the nondiscriminatory reasons for its actions.

The Supreme Court reversed the Fifth Circuit Court's decision and remanded the case to district court for further proceedings consistent with the procedures set forth in the opinion.

DECISION AND REMEDY

Disparate-Impact Discrimination

As Title VII law developed, courts discovered that many instances of discrimination appeared to be unintentional. Some apparently neutral and fair employment practices might have a discriminatory *effect*. For example, consider an employer who requires that all workers have a high school diploma. In some circumstances, this requirement might have the effect of discriminating against minority groups.

To make out a **disparate-impact discrimination** case, the plaintiff must meet two requirements. In a race discrimination case, for example, the plaintiff must first show that the employer's percentage of minority employees is much smaller than would be expected, considering the number of minority applicants or the percentage of the minority in the local population. Then, the plaintiff must show that the low percentage on the job is due to some employer practice, such as requiring high school diplomas, that has the effect of

excluding large numbers of minority applicants. This makes out a *prima facie* case, and no evidence of discriminatory intent need be shown.

The EEOC's nonbinding guidelines elaborate on the disparate-impact test with an "80 percent rule." If the selection rate for one protected class (such as black applicants) is less than 80 percent of the selection rate for another class (such as white applicants), the EEOC presumes that the selection procedures have an unlawful disparate impact. Statistical analysis can be complex, however, and the following case illustrates the difficulty of statistically proving an unlawful disparate impact.

Case 49.4

NEW YORK CITY TRANSIT AUTHORITY v. BEAZER

Supreme Court of the United States, 1979.
440 U.S. 568, 99 S.Ct. 1355, 59 L.Ed.2d 587.

BACKGROUND AND FACTS *The New York City Transit Authority maintains a policy against hiring individuals who use narcotic drugs, including methadone. Methadone is a drug legally given by public agencies as a treatment for heroin addiction. Several individuals undergoing methadone treatment were denied employment with the Transit Authority (TA). These individuals sued TA under Title VII and the equal protection clause of the Constitution, claiming that the policy was discriminatory in effect. Approximately 80 percent of narcotics users were either black or Hispanic, and the policy therefore excluded a disproportionately large number of minorities. The district court held for the plaintiffs. This court held that TA could exclude methadone users from "safety-sensitive" jobs, such as subway car drivers, but not from other custodial jobs. The court of appeals affirmed the district court's decision. TA then appealed to the United States Supreme Court.*

STEVENS, Justice.
*   *   *   *

A prima facie violation of the Act may be established by statistical evidence showing that an employment practice has the effect of denying the members of one race equal access to employment opportunities. Even assuming that respondents have crossed this threshold, when the entire record is examined it is clear that the two statistics on which they and the District Court relied do not prove a violation of Title VII. *   *   *

First, the District Court noted that 81% of the employees referred to TA's medical director for suspected violation of its narcotics rule were either black or Hispanic. But respondents have only challenged the rule to the extent that it is construed to apply to methadone users, and that statistic tells us nothing about the racial composition of the employees suspected of using methadone. Nor does the record give us any information about the number of black, Hispanic, or white persons who were dismissed for using methadone.
*   *   *   *

Second, the District Court noted that about 63% of the persons in New York City receiving methadone maintenance in public programs—i.e., 63% of the 65% of all New York City methadone users who are in such programs—are black or Hispanic. We do not know, however, how many of these persons ever worked or sought to work for TA. This statistic therefore reveals little if anything about the racial composition of the class of TA job applicants and employees receiving methadone treatment. More particularly, it tells us nothing about the class of otherwise-qualified applicants and employees who have participated in methadone maintenance programs for over a year—

the only class improperly excluded by TA's policy under the District Court's analysis. The record demonstrates, in fact, that the figure is virtually irrelevant because a substantial portion of the persons included in it are either unqualified for other reasons—such as the illicit use of drugs and alcohol—or have received successful assistance in finding jobs with employers other than TA. * * *

* * * *

At best, respondents' statistical showing is weak; even if it is capable of establishing a prima facie case of discrimination, it is assuredly rebutted by TA's demonstration that its narcotics rule (and the rule's application to methadone users) is "job related."

The Supreme Court reversed the decision of the lower courts and ruled in favor of TA. The statistical evidence did not prove that TA had violated Title VII.	**DECISION AND REMEDY**

Defenses

Once an employee has made out a *prima facie* case of discrimination, the employer-defendant has an opportunity to respond. The employer may attempt to disprove the plaintiff's case. In addition, the employer may use certain defenses to justify its employment practices.

BUSINESS NECESSITY DEFENSE   Defendants may use a **business necessity defense** in disparate-impact cases. To do so, the employer must show a strong business reason for the practice that has a discriminatory effect. An employer might show, for example, that a high school education is required for workers to do a good job. Courts have held that educational requirements are a business necessity for some jobs, but they have rejected educational requirements for less complicated positions that primarily require manual labor. In one case, a company that converted wood into paper products was hiring for various positions, some skilled and some unskilled. Historically, the company had hired blacks for the unskilled jobs. After passage of the Civil Rights Act, the company adopted certain standardized psychological tests as a prerequisite for employment in skilled jobs. Use of these tests had a discriminatory effect, because blacks consistently scored lower than whites. When the company argued a business necessity defense, the court held that the tests were not closely job-related and thus did not qualify as a business necessity.[2]

BFOQ DEFENSE   In addition to the business necessity defense in disparate-impact cases, Title VII offers other defenses to employers charged with discrimination. One such defense is that of **bona fide occupational qualification** (BFOQ). This defense applies when apparent and even intentional discrimination against a particular protected class is essential to the job itself. An employer, therefore, may restrict hiring to one sex or religion under some circumstances. For example, a men's fashion magazine could hire only male models because of the BFOQ defense. Under Title VII, however, the *race* of the worker may never be a BFOQ. The defense applies only to other protected classes.

Many controversies have arisen over this defense, particularly in sex-discrimination cases. Some companies have argued that being a male is a BFOQ for jobs requiring heavy lifting,[3] while others have contended that being a female is a BFOQ for flight attendants.[4] Courts have rejected both these defenses and have generally restricted the BFOQ defense to instances when the employee's gender is of the "essence" of the job.

SENIORITY SYSTEM DEFENSE   Another statutory defense protects "bona fide seniority systems." In some cases, a company may have had a past history of discrimination. Even if the company now seeks to be unbiased, it may have no minorities in upper-level positions simply because of the past discrimination. The company may face

2. Albemarle Paper Co. v. Moody, 422 U.S. 405, 95 S.Ct. 2362, 45 L.Ed.2d 280 (1975).

3. Rosenfeld v. Southern Pacific Co., 444 F.2d 1219 (9th Cir. 1971).

4. Diaz v. Pan American World Airways, Inc., 442 F.2d 385 (5th Cir. 1971).

a lawsuit seeking an order for minorities to be promoted ahead of schedule to compensate for past discrimination. If a present intent to discriminate is not proven, and promotions or other job benefits are governed by a fair, or bona fide, seniority system, the employer has a good defense against the lawsuit.

Affirmative Action

One of the first attempts by the federal government to regulate discrimination among private employers was an executive order issued by President Roosevelt in 1941, encouraging full participation by all citizens in the national defense effort. Subsequent executive orders prohibited race discrimination on the part of employers who contracted with the government and permitted cancellation and exclusion from future contracts for violators. Executive orders issued in the 1960s— particularly Executive Order 11246, issued by President Johnson in 1965—expanded the obligation not to discriminate on the basis of race, national origin, religion, and sex to *any work* the contractor performed during the period the employer was performing a government contract. Pursuant to these orders, the Department of Labor issued regulations and guidelines requiring government contractors to undertake affirmative recruiting efforts and ensure nondiscriminatory treatment of employees and applicants.

The use of racial classifications to benefit rather than burden racial or ethnic minorities has been much debated.[5] Among the practices on which the debate has focused is giving qualified members of minorities preferential treatment in hiring and promotions to atone for past discriminatory actions. The objections have been directed principally at the use of racial preferences and quotas.[6]

Under Title VII, a white worker challenged an affirmative action plan that his employer had adopted pursuant to a union agreement. The plan reserved 50 percent of the openings in an in-plant training program for blacks until the proportion of black workers at the plant approximated the proportion of blacks in the surrounding area's labor force. The seniority of a number of whites— including the plaintiff—who had applied for the program and had been turned down was greater than the seniority of some of the blacks selected for training. In *United Steelworkers of America v. Weber*[7] the United States Supreme Court held that Title VII did not prohibit an employer or a union from adopting a voluntary affirmative action plan in an attempt to remedy racial imbalances in traditionally segregated job categories. The Court pointed out that the program was temporary and left a fair number of training slots open for whites.

The United States Supreme Court has also ruled that Title VII does not prohibit an employer from considering sex as a factor when evaluating qualified applicants for jobs in which women have been significantly underrepresented.[8] When a female employee who scored slightly lower on promotion selection criteria than a male employee was promoted ahead of the male employee, he sued the employer under Title VII. The Court pointed out that, like the *Weber* case discussed above, this case involved traditionally segregated job categories. The Court concluded that the promoted woman was amply qualified, that the male employees' rights had not been trammeled, and that no absolute bar to their advancement had been constructed.

Affirmative action may be illegal, however, when it requires workers to be fired from their existing jobs. When a school board laid off white teachers with more seniority than some teachers it retained in order to maintain a black-white balance among teachers, the United States Supreme Court held that the action was illegal.[9] Although the law is somewhat unclear, it seems that some forms of affirmative action are probably legal in

---

5. One of the first major affirmative-action cases involved not employment but student admissions and arose under Title VI of the Civil Rights Act of 1964. Title VI prohibits racial discrimination by recipients of federal funds. In that case, the United States Supreme Court invalidated a plan that gave clear preferences to minorities. Five justices indicated, however, that they would uphold a program that considered race as a factor without using strict preferences. Regents of the University of California v. Bakke, 438 U.S. 265, 98 S.Ct. 2733, 57 L.Ed.2d 750 (1978).

6. There are two basic forms of affirmative action. A quota may be set reserving a specific number of places for minority members and a specific number for nonminority members. Alternatively, separate standards may be set giving preferential treatment to minority members without the use of a quota.

---

7. 443 U.S. 193, 99 S.Ct. 2721, 61 L.Ed.2d 480 (1979).

8. Johnson v. Transportation Agency, ___ U.S. ___, 107 S.Ct. 1442, 94 L.Ed.2d 615 (1987).

9. Wygant v. Jackson, 476 U.S. 267, 106 S.Ct. 1842, 90 L.Ed.2d 260 (1986). This case involved a public employer and was decided under the Fourteenth Amendment. A similar result is likely under Title VII also.

hiring decisions but that affirmative action may be illegal in determining which employees are to be fired.

Sexual Harassment

Title VII is increasingly used to attack sexual harassment in the workplace. If a supervisor forces sexual advances upon a subordinate worker, the supervisor is presumably discriminating because of the worker's gender, in violation of Title VII.

Two types of sexual harassment are recognized by the courts. The first type is *quid pro quo* harassment, whereby sexual favors are demanded in return for hiring, promoting, or granting other employment benefits to a person. The second type is known as harassing-environment discrimina-

tion. Here, the sexual advances may create a very uncomfortable working environment, which is also illegal. Repeated sexual comments, jokes, and touching may constitute such a harassing environment.

In sexual-harassment cases the employer may be liable, even though an employee actually did the harassing. If the culpable employee is in a supervising position, the company will usually be held automatically liable for the behavior. If a lower-level employee is responsible for the harassment, the company will be held liable only if it knew or should have known about the harassment and failed to take corrective action.

The following case is a leading example of the law as applied to sexual harassment and employer liability.

BACKGROUND AND FACTS *Mechelle Vinson began work in 1974 as a teller at Meritor Savings Bank. She claimed that a supervisory employee, Jack Taylor, began making sexual advances toward her, to which she ultimately acquiesced. She further testified that Taylor fondled her in front of other employees and even forcibly raped her. Taylor denied these charges. Vinson sued, claiming sex discrimination. The district court noted that Vinson had received a series of promotions during the time she worked at the bank and held that the sexual relationship had no relationship to her continued employment at the bank. Finding no* quid pro quo *discrimination, the court ruled in favor of the bank. Vinson appealed, and the appellate court ruled in her favor, finding that she had made out a case of harassing-environment discrimination. The bank appealed to the United States Supreme Court.*

 Case 49.5

MERITOR SAVINGS BANK, FSB v. VINSON
Supreme Court of the United States, 1986.
447 U.S. 57, 106 S.Ct. 2399, 91 L.Ed.2d 49.

REHNQUIST, Justice.
*   *   *   *

Respondent argues, and the Court of Appeals held, that unwelcome sexual advances that create an offensive or hostile working environment violate Title VII. Without question, when a supervisor sexually harasses a subordinate because of the subordinate's sex, that supervisor "discriminate[s]" on the basis of sex. Petitioner apparently does not challenge this proposition. It contends instead that in prohibiting discrimination with respect to "compensation, terms, conditions, or privileges" of employment, Congress was concerned with what petitioner describes as "tangible loss" of "an economic character," not "purely psychological aspects of the workplace environment." *   *   *
*   *   *   *

Since the guidelines were issued, courts have uniformly held, and we agree, that a plaintiff may establish a violation of Title VII by proving that discrimination based on sex has created a hostile or abusive work environment. As the Court of Appeals for the Eleventh Circuit wrote in *Henson v. Dundee*:

> Sexual harassment which creates a hostile or offensive environment for members of one sex is every bit the arbitrary barrier to sexual equality at the workplace that racial harassment is to racial equality. Surely, a requirement that a man or woman run a gauntlet of sexual abuse in return for the privilege of being allowed to work and make a living can be as demeaning and disconcerting as the harshest of racial epithets.

DECISION
AND REMEDY

The Supreme Court affirmed the appellate court's decision in favor of Vinson and remanded the case to district court for further proceedings. The Court held that the bank's liability for the actions of its supervisory employees should be determined by common law principles of agency.

Religious Discrimination

Title VII also prohibits discrimination based on religion, but this provision creates special legal problems. Under the First Amendment, some employers may have a constitutional right to discriminate based on religion. A church, for example, cannot be compelled to hire a minister of a different religion. In this case, religion would be a BFOQ.

Title VII does not define religion, and disputes have arisen over just when a set of beliefs constitutes a religion. Courts generally have defined religion broadly, requiring simply that the plaintiff have a genuine commitment to principles that occupy a central place in his or her approach to life. Title VII also prohibits discrimination against atheists or other persons who profess no religious beliefs.

Secular employers may not discriminate on the basis of religion and must make "reasonable accommodation" to the religious requirements of their employees. The leading religious discrimination case is *Trans World Airlines, Inc. v. Hardison*.[10] In this case, Hardison, a TWA machinist, adhered to religious beliefs that precluded working on Saturdays. TWA arranged a schedule that permitted Hardison to take Saturdays off. The problem arose when TWA needed Hardison to take over for an absent worker on a Saturday. To get an alternative worker, TWA would have been required to violate its seniority system or pay a much higher wage rate. Hardison refused to work on Saturday and was fired. When Hardison sued, the United States Supreme Court ruled in favor of TWA, holding that the company was not required to make further accommodation for Hardison's religion.

In another common circumstance, an employee's religion may oppose membership in a union.

Companies and unions have argued that this claim is simply an attempt to avoid paying union dues. In such a case, a court has held that an employee cannot be required to join the union but that the worker must pay an amount equivalent to union dues to a mutually acceptable charity.[11]

Age Discrimination

Age discrimination does not fall under Title VII but is governed by a special statute, the Age Discrimination in Employment Act of 1967 (ADEA). This law prohibits discrimination based on age. The law protects only those forty years of age and older, however. Thus, a thirty-five-year-old victim of age discrimination has no recourse.

The ADEA works much like Title VII. Intentional age discrimination is illegal under disparate-treatment analysis, in which the procedures are similar to those previously discussed. Disparate-impact analysis may also be applied to age discrimination. In one case, an employer declined to hire certain individuals with a great deal of experience and, therefore, a higher wage requirement. A court held this to have the effect of discriminating based on age in violation of the ADEA.[12] Under recent amendments, the ADEA prohibits mandatory retirement for non-managerial workers.

Defenses under the ADEA are also similar to those under Title VII. A business-necessity defense applies to disparate-impact cases, and a BFOQ defense is also available when applicable. Coverage of ADEA is limited to firms that have twenty or more employees and that affect interstate commerce.

---

10. 432 U.S. 63, 97 S.Ct. 2264, 53 L.Ed.2d 113 (1977).

11. Tooley v. Martin-Marietta Corp., 648 F.2d 1239 (9th Cir. 1981).

12. Geller v. Markham, 635 F.2d 1027 (2d Cir. 1980).

WRONGFUL DISCHARGE

Traditionally, employers could fire workers at will. Federal laws, such as the Wagner Act and Title VII, have modified this rule somewhat. Courts have also eroded the at-will employment doctrine through a series of relatively recent common law rulings that restrict the right of employers to fire workers. Because this is a common law issue, the rules vary from state to state. There is a definite trend toward recognizing exceptions to the at-will doctrine, however, and some courts have even awarded punitive damages against employers in wrongful-discharge litigation. Wise employers will discharge employees only for good cause and will obtain documentation to support their position. Wise employees will be familiar with and follow company policies.

Public Policy Theory

The most widespread common law exception to the at-will employment doctrine is the public policy exception. Under this rule, an employer may not fire a worker for reasons that violate fundamental public policies of the jurisdiction. For example, courts may prevent an employer from firing a worker who serves on a jury and therefore cannot work scheduled hours. Sometimes, an employer will direct an employee to do something that violates the law. If the employee refuses to perform the illegal act, the employer might decide to fire the worker. Most states have held that firing the worker under these circumstances violates public policy. The public policy theory generally protects employees from being required to violate the law but does not always protect employees when no legal violation is involved.

Whistle-blowing

Some states have extended the public policy exception to cover **whistle-blowing.** Whistle-blowing occurs when an employee tells the government or the press that his or her employer is engaged in some unsafe or illegal activity. For example, an employee might tell the Environmental Protection Agency (EPA) that the employer has been violating pollution laws. In a state that protects whistle-blowing, the employer could not discharge the employee for informing the EPA. Other states, though, have not gone this far in protecting whistle-blowers. Federal law may also protect employees who "blow the whistle." For example, if an employee of a defense contractor reveals overcharges on weapons, the employee is protected. In one case, when trucking-company employees were fired for reporting safety violations, the Department of Labor ordered that the employees be reinstated.[13]

Contract Theory

Some courts have used contract theory to protect employees from arbitrary discharges. Many of these courts have held that an *implied* employment contract exists between the employer and the employee. If the employee is fired outside the terms of the implied contract, he or she may succeed in a breach-of-contract action.

For example, a company's handbook or personnel bulletins may state that, as a matter of policy, the company will only dismiss workers for good and sufficient cause. If the employee is aware of this policy and continues to work for the company, a court may find that there is an implied contract, based on the terms of the company policy. If an employer makes promises to employees regarding discharge policy, those promises may also be considered part of an implied contract. If the company fires the worker in a manner contrary to the manner promised, a court may hold that the company has violated the implied contract and is liable for damages. Most state courts will consider this claim and judge it by traditional contract standards.

A few states have gone even further and held that all employment contracts contain an **implied covenant of good faith.** This means that both sides promise to abide by the contract in good faith. If the employer fires an employee for an arbitrary or unjustified reason, the employee can claim that the covenant of good faith was breached and the contract violated.

In the following case, a discharged employee claimed that the employer's personnel policy manual constituted an implied employment contract, which had been breached by his employer.

---

13. *See* Brock v. Roadway Express, Inc., ___ U.S. ___, 107 S.Ct. 1740, 95 L.Ed.2d 239 (1987).

Case 49.6

WOOLLEY v. HOFFMANN-La ROCHE, INC.

Supreme Court of New Jersey, 1985.
99 N.J. 284, 491 A.2d 1257.

BACKGROUND AND FACTS *Richard Woolley was hired in 1969 to work in the engineering department of Hoffmann-La Roche. The parties had no written employment contract. Woolley did receive the company's personnel policy manual, which stated that employees would be fired only for good cause. Woolley received several promotions until 1978, when he wrote a memorandum about piping problems within one of the company's buildings. Within a month, the company requested his resignation. When Woolley refused to resign, the company fired him. Woolley sued, claiming that the personnel manual created an implied contract and that he had been fired without good cause. Hoffmann-La Roche argued that no such implied contract existed and moved for summary judgment. The trial court ruled for Hoffmann-La Roche, and the appellate court affirmed this judgment. Woolley then appealed to the state supreme court.*

WILENTZ, Chief Justice.
*   *   *   *

Hoffmann-La Roche contends that the formation of the type of contract claimed by plaintiff to exist—Hoffmann-La Roche calls it a permanent employment contract for life—is subject to special contractual requirements: the intent of the parties to create such an undertaking must be clear and definite; in addition to an explicit provision setting forth its duration, the agreement must specifically cover the essential terms of employment—the duties, responsibilities, and compensation of the employee, and the proof of these terms must be clear and convincing; the undertaking must be supported by consideration in addition to the employee's continued work. Woolley claims that the requirements for the formation of such a contract have been met here and that they do not extend as far as Hoffmann-La Roche claims. Further, Woolley argues that this is not a "permanent contract for life," but rather an employment contract of indefinite duration that may be terminated only for good cause and in accordance with the procedure set forth in the personnel policy manual. Both parties agree that the employment contract is one of indefinite duration; Hoffmann-La Roche contends that in New Jersey, when an employment contract is of indefinite duration, the inescapable legal conclusion is that it is an employment at will; Woolley claims that even such a contract—of indefinite duration—may contain provisions requiring that termination be only for cause.
*   *   *   *

In recognizing a cause of action to provide a remedy for employees who are wrongfully discharged, we must balance the interests of the employee, the employer, and the public. Employees have an interest in knowing they will not be discharged for exercising their legal rights. Employers have an interest in knowing that they can run their businesses as they see fit as long as their conduct is consistent with public policy. The public has an interest in employment stability and in discouraging frivolous lawsuits by dissatisfied employees.
*   *   *   *

Whatever their worth in dealing with individual long-term employment contracts, these requirements, over and above those ordinarily found in contract law, have no relevancy when a policy manual is involved. In that case, there is no individual lifetime employment contract involved, but rather, if there is a contract, it is one for a group of employees—sometimes all of them—for an indefinite term, and here, fairly read, one that may not be terminated by the employer without good cause.

DECISION AND REMEDY *The New Jersey supreme court reversed the lower courts' summary judgment against Woolley. The case was remanded for trial, at which Woolley would have an opportunity to prove his claims.*

Tort Theory

In extreme cases, the discharge of an employee may give rise to a tort cause of action. Abusive discharge procedures may represent intentional infliction of emotional distress or defamation (false statements injurious to the employee's reputation).

One Massachusetts case involved a restaurant called the Ground Round. The restaurant had suffered some thefts of supplies, and the manager announced that he would start firing waitresses alphabetically until the thief was identified. Debra Agis, the first waitress fired, said that she suffered great emotional distress as a result. The state supreme court upheld her claim as stating a valid cause of action.[14]

WORKER SAFETY AND WELFARE

The United States Congress and the states have passed a series of laws that are intended to protect workers' safety and welfare. Unions frequently bargain for the safety and financial well-being of their member workers, but the following laws provide protection over and above that afforded by union contracts.

State Workers' Compensation

Tragically, many thousands of workers are injured or killed on the job. Historically, such workers relied upon the tort system to recover damages, usually under negligence law. The resultant suits overburdened the courts, however, and too many workers went uncompensated for their injuries because of their contributory negligence or a finding that a fellow worker was at fault.

Between 1900 and 1920, most states passed workers' compensation laws. Now, all states have such laws. Workers' compensation laws establish an administrative procedure for compensating injured workers. Rather than going to court, an injured worker files a claim with the state. The less formal administrative process provides swifter and more certain compensation to such workers.

In exchange for this simpler and more efficient compensation system, employees must accept workers' compensation as their exclusive remedy for injuries. Thus, workers give up their right to sue in court for on-the-job injuries. Today, many of these workers could receive larger awards in a court suit—if they won. (Average recoveries under workers' compensation are less than half those in comparable tort suits.)

The administrative process differs in other ways from court adjudication. Under workers' compensation laws, strict liability applies, so the employee need no longer show negligence on the part of the employer. An injured worker may receive medical costs, rehabilitation costs, and lost future income. For most injuries, such as the loss of a limb, states maintain a fixed schedule of specific damages. For example, in Georgia a worker who loses his or her hand will receive $21,600. In Iowa, however, the loss of a hand is compensated at over $100,000.

Before a worker can recover for an injury, he or she must prove two things. First, the worker must prove that he or she is an employee and not an independent contractor. Second, the worker must prove that the injury arose out of or in the course of employment. For typical on-the-job injuries, these standards are obviously met.

Some disputes arise over the course-of-employment test, however. What if an employee is injured at a company picnic? If the picnic is considered to be for the benefit of the employer, most states will permit the worker to recover. What if an employee is injured going to or from work? Commuting to and from work is not covered by most workers' compensation laws, unless this travel is part of the employee's job (as it is, for example, if the employee is a traveling salesperson).

Occupational Safety and Health Act

Congress passed the Occupational Safety and Health Act in 1970 to reduce the rate of injury and disease among workers. This law created the Occupational Safety and Health Administration (OSHA), a federal agency that implements the act. Virtually every U.S. employer is subject to OSHA requirements.

SETTING SAFETY STANDARDS   OSHA's most important power may be setting safety standards. The agency establishes regulations requiring em-

14. Agis v. Howard Johnson Co., 371 Mass. 140, 355 N.E.2d 315 (1976).

ployers to increase workplace safety. Agency regulations attempt to prevent both accidental injuries and disease. These regulations are established through the rulemaking procedures described in Chapter 45. OSHA may also adopt emergency temporary standards without following so many procedures. The law requires that all OSHA standards be "feasible" for employers to meet. In addition, OSHA health standards may only control "significant" risks and cannot regulate very low level risks to employees.

OSHA has developed thousands of standards. Many of them govern workplace equipment, as OSHA establishes requirements for ladders, scaffolding, cranes, assembly-line machinery, and numerous other kinds of equipment. OSHA health standards set maximum exposure levels for such hazardous chemicals as benzene and arsenic. OSHA standards also specify that workers have a right to know the chemicals to which they may be exposed and the possible risks of this exposure.

COMPLIANCE AND ENFORCEMENT   OSHA has broad powers to enforce its standards. The agency may conduct surprise inspections of companies. If a violation is discovered, OSHA will issue the employer a citation. The citation typically will direct the company to correct or abate the situation, and OSHA may assess civil penalties against the company. If OSHA deems that the violation is not serious, there may be no civil penalty, but penalties may amount to as much as $1,000 per serious violation or $10,000 for willful or repeated violations.

To enforce a civil penalty for serious violations, OSHA must show (1) that a standard applies, (2) that the employer violated the standard, (3) that workers were in danger of being exposed to the hazardous situation,[15] and (4) that the company was aware of the workplace conditions that violated the standard. As defenses, the company may prove that compliance with the standard was not feasible or that the violation was due to unpreventable employee misconduct. For example, if a worker removed safety devices from a machine unbeknownst to the employer, the employer may not be responsible for a resultant accident.

GENERAL-DUTY CLAUSE   In addition to specific standards, the Occupational Safety and Health Act also imposes a general duty on all employers to keep their workplaces free from recognized hazards. This duty applies even if there is no federal standard applicable to the situation. To show a violation of this clause, the government must prove (1) that a hazard was present, (2) that it was recognized as a hazard, (3) that the hazard was likely to cause death or serious physical harm; and (4) that feasible steps were available to remedy the hazard.

ERISA

In 1974, Congress passed the Employee Retirement Income Security Act (ERISA). This law was intended to ensure the availability of worker pensions and other negotiated benefit plans. In some cases, employers had promised pensions to workers but had failed to maintain an adequate fund to pay out pensions at the promised levels. In other cases, pension managers had embezzled pension funds or invested poorly. ERISA was intended to correct such abuses.

ERISA does not require an employer to establish a pension plan or other worker benefit plan. A company may legally choose not to provide pension-plan benefits. Where such a plan exists, however, ERISA establishes standards for its management.

Vesting

A key provision of ERISA concerns **vesting** standards. Vesting gives the employee a legal right to receive pension benefits at some future date when he or she ceases to work. Before ERISA, some workers who had been employed by companies for twenty or even thirty years ultimately received no pension benefits because those benefits had not vested.

ERISA establishes complex vesting rules. In summary, all employee contributions to pension plans vest immediately. If these plans are funded in part through wage deductions, the worker has an immediate vested right to all such employee contributions. Employer contributions may be handled in several ways. Under any procedure, though, the employee's pension rights are fully vested after ten years of service.

---

15. With regard to this standard, employers have the burden of proving that workers were not exposed.

Investment Guarantees

In order to prevent the mismanagement of pension funds, ERISA has established rules on how they must be invested. Pension managers must invest as would a "prudent" person. This requires managers to be relatively cautious in their investments and to refrain from investing more than 10 percent of the fund in securities of the employer. ERISA also contains highly detailed record-keeping and reporting requirements.

OTHER EMPLOYMENT LAWS

This chapter has discussed the most controversial aspects of employment law. Many other laws af-

fect business employment decisions. For example, federal legislation restricts discrimination against the handicapped, in the Rehabilitation Act of 1973; [16] provides for disability and old age insurance, in the Social Security Act of 1935; [17] and establishes a minimum wage, in the Fair Labor Standards Act of 1938.[18] Employers thus must be familiar with a myriad of legal requirements that influence their employment decisions.

---

16. 29 U.S.C. Sections 701–796.

17. 42 U.S.C. Section 301.

18. 29 U.S.C. Section 201.

QUESTIONS AND CASE PROBLEMS

1. Suppose that Consolidated Stores is undergoing a unionization campaign. Prior to the election, management says that the union is unnecessary to protect workers. Management also provides bonuses and wage increases to the workers during this period. The employees reject the union. Union organizers protest that the wage increases during the election campaign unfairly prejudiced the vote. Should these wage increases be regarded as an unfair labor practice?

2. A hospital had a policy that prohibited employees from distributing literature except in certain locker rooms and restrooms. Workers who wanted to establish a union distributed literature in the cafeteria, in violation of the hospital policy. Union organizers and the NLRB argued that the hospital's policy was unduly restrictive and an unfair labor practice. The hospital argued that its restrictions were essential to preventing doctors and patients from being disturbed, though the hospital had allowed some charities to solicit funds in the cafeteria. Who should prevail? [Beth Israel Hospital v. NLRB, 437 U.S. 483, 98 S.Ct. 2463, 57 L.Ed.2d 370 (1978)]

3. The employees of Berger Transfer & Storage Company were engaged in a campaign to unionize the company. Management officers questioned workers about whether they had signed authorization cards and why they supported the union. The employer also announced to workers that if the unionization succeeded, some employees would probably be laid off. The NLRB contended that these practices represented unfair labor practices. Should the court uphold the NLRB? [NLRB v. Berger Transfer & Storage Co., 678 F.2d 679 (7th Cir. 1982)]

4. Frouge was a general contractor working on a housing project in Philadelphia. Frouge had originally ordered pre-machined doors produced by non-union employees. Frouge's union refused to hang the pre-machined doors under a "will not handle" clause in the employment contract. Frouge substituted doors cut by union employees on the jobsite. The producers of the pre-machined doors complained that the "will not handle" clause represented an illegal secondary boycott. Should the court strike down this provision? [National Woodwork Manufacturers Association v. NLRB, 386 U.S. 612, 87 S.Ct. 1250, 18 L.Ed.2d 357 (1967)]

5. Donnell was a black General Motors employee who applied for admission into a skilled-trade apprenticeship position. Donnell was rejected because he failed to meet the requirement that all applicants must have completed high school. Donnell sued under Title VII, claiming that the requirement had a discriminatory impact and was unjustified by business necessity. Should Donnell prevail? [Donnell v. General Motors Corp., 576 F.2d 1292 (8th Cir. 1978)]

6. In 1966, Corning Glass Works decided to open up jobs on the night shift to women and consolidated its male and female seniority lists. This enabled women to exercise their seniority to obtain certain higher-paying night jobs as vacancies occurred. Then, in 1969, a new collective bargaining agreement abolished the higher wages for night-shift jobs. The agreement did allow for a higher "red circle" rate for night-shift workers employed prior to 1969, however. This "red circle" rate effectively locked in the higher wages for male workers but prevented new workers from receiving these wages. Was this practice a violation of Title VII? [Corning Glass Works v. Brennan, 417 U.S. 188, 94 S.Ct. 2223, 41 L.Ed.2d 1 (1974)]

7. Dianne Rawlinson applied for employment as an Alabama prison guard and was rejected for two reasons. First, she failed to meet a requirement that guards be at least five feet two inches tall and weigh at least 120 pounds. Raw-

linson argued, however, that this requirement had a disparate impact against women and was illegal under Title VII. Second, the Alabama prisons had a policy against employing women in "contact positions" in maximum-security prisons, which included most of the system's jobs. Rawlinson argued that this provision was also illegal under Title VII. Should the court strike down these Alabama requirements? [Dothard v. Rawlinson, 433 U.S. 321, 97 S.Ct. 2720, 53 L.Ed.2d 786 (1977)]

8. At an REA Express shipping terminal, a conveyor belt was inoperative because an electrical circuit had shorted out. The manager called a licensed electrical contractor. When the contractor arrived, REA's maintenance supervisor was in the circuit breaker room. The floor was wet, and the maintenance supervisor was using sawdust to try to soak up the water. While the licensed electrical contractor was attempting to fix the short circuit, standing on the wet floor, he was electrocuted. Simultaneously, REA's maintenance supervisor, who was standing on a wooden platform, was burned and knocked unconscious. OSHA sought to fine REA Express $1,000 for failure to furnish a place of employment free from recognized hazards. Should OSHA be upheld? [REA Express, Inc. v. Brennan, 495 F.2d 822 (2d Cir. 1974)]

9. Ray Palmateer worked in a managerial position for International Harvester for sixteen years. Palmateer reported another employee to local law enforcement authorities for certain disputed minor thefts. International Harvester decided that Palmateer had recklessly resorted to the criminal justice system for minor personnel problems and fired him. Palmateer sued, claiming that his discharge vi-

olated public policy. How should the court rule? [Palmateer v. International Harvester Co., 85 Ill.2d 124, 421 N.E.2d 876, 52 Ill.Dec. 13 (1981)]

10. Wayne Pugh had been employed by See's Candies for thirty-two years, during which time he had worked his way up from dishwasher to vice-president in charge of production. Then, the company abruptly terminated Pugh without giving any reason. Pugh theorized that he had been fired because of pressure from the company's union. Pugh had been told orally that it was the company's practice not to terminate administrative personnel except for good cause. He argued that these representations had created an implied contract and that he had been unlawfully fired without good cause. For whom should the court rule? [Pugh v. See's Candies, Inc., 116 Cal.App.3d 311, 171 Cal.Rptr. 917 (1981)]

11. Wise, a female employee of Mead Corporation, became involved in a dispute in the lunchroom of her place of employment with another employee, Pruitt. A fight ensued, and Wise kicked and scratched Pruitt and used "abusive and uncivil" language. Because of this behavior, Wise's employment at Mead was terminated by her employer. Wise brought suit, alleging sex discrimination on the part of Mead Corporation in violation of Title VII of the Civil Rights Act of 1964, on the grounds that at least four other fights at Mead had occurred under similar circumstances and none of the participants had been fired. None of the other fights had involved a female. Did Wise's employment termination constitute sex discrimination by Mead Corporation? Discuss. [Wise. v. Mead Corp., 614 F.Supp. 1131 (M.D.Ga. 1985)]

Focus on Ethics

Government Regulation

Government regulation is pervasive in our economic and legal system. It includes consumer protection, environmental protection, antitrust law, employment and labor relations law, and other issues. In all areas of government regulation, one can ask the question, "Why does government regulation exist?" Pure capitalist ideology has as its basis a belief that government intervention in the economic system should be minimal. Yet today virtually every area of economic activity is regulated by government. Is this increased government regulation due to a change in the capitalist ideology or to a change in the ethical concerns of society?

EMPLOYMENT DISCRIMINATION

Society has definitely changed its thinking with respect to employment. In the past, employers were not required to hire, retain, and promote employees with equality. Equal opportunity regulations were therefore designed to reduce or eliminate discriminatory practices. Attempts at "making up" for past patterns of discrimination have resulted in affirmative action programs.

Many of these affirmative action programs have resulted in what has been termed "reverse discrimination" against majority groups. Such reverse discrimination raises the ethical issue of how far society should go in trying to remedy the effects of past discrimination against minorities.

In the well-known case of *Regents of the University of California v. Bakke* [438 U.S. 265, 98 S.Ct. 2733, 57 L.Ed.2d 750 (1978)], for example, Alan Bakke, a Vietnam veteran and engineer who had been turned down for medical school at the Davis campus of the University of California, discovered that his academic record was better than those of some of the minority applicants who had been admitted to the program. He sued the University of California regents, alleging reverse discrimination. The Supreme Court held that a public university may give favorable weight to minority applicants as part of a plan to increase minority enrollment. The Court, however, stated that the use of a quota system, in which a certain number of seats is explicitly reserved for minority applicants, is unconstitutional. In other words, public universities may consider race or ethnic

background as a factor in attempting to obtain the benefits that flow from an ethnically diverse student body, but they may not utilize a quota system for the benefit of minorities.

Burlington Northern settled a ten-year-old discrimination case by agreeing not only to pay $10 million in back wages to current and former black employees but also to give priority consideration to black applicants who had been previously rejected for jobs. Burlington Northern is not using a quota system to reserve a certain number of jobs for black applicants. Rather, Burlington Northern is merely giving priority preference to the black applicants previously rejected.

Reverse discrimination was also addressed in the case of *Firefighters Local Union No. 1784 v. Stotts* [467 U.S. 561, 104 S.Ct. 2576, 81 L.Ed.2d 482 (1984)]. In this case, Stotts, a black member of the Memphis, Tennessee, fire department, filed a class action alleging that the department and certain city officials were violating Title VII of the Civil Rights Act of 1964 by engaging in a pattern or practice of hiring and promoting on the basis of race.

A consent decree was subsequently entered into for

the purpose of remedying the department's hiring and promotion practices with respect to blacks. The goal of the decree was to increase minority representation in each fire department job classification to approximately the proportion of blacks in the local labor force. To this end, 50 percent of the department's annual job vacancies were to be filled by qualified black applicants. Also, 20 percent of the promotions within each job classification were to be given to qualified blacks. Nothing was said about the existing seniority system, layoffs, or reductions in rank.

After the consent decree had been entered into, the city of Memphis announced that projected budget deficits necessitated a reduction of city employees, including firefighters. Layoffs were to be based on seniority—that is, the last hired would be the first to be laid off. In effect, layoffs on the basis of seniority would counter the goal of the consent decree, as the blacks recently hired would be the first to go. The district court proceeded to enjoin the department from adhering to its seniority system in determining who would be laid off. The court concluded that the proposed layoffs would have a racially discriminatory effect and that the seniority system was not a bona fide one. The court of appeals affirmed, and the United States Supreme Court granted the petitions for certiorari.

The Supreme Court held that the consent decree did not include the displacement of white employees with seniority over blacks and hence that the district court's injunction did not merely enforce the agreement of the parties as embodied in the consent decree. The Court

concluded that, since Title VII protects bona fide seniority systems, it is inappropriate to deny an innocent employee the benefits of his or her seniority in order to provide a remedy unless intentional discrimination is proven.

How much should the current generation of white employees and other members of majority groups have to pay for past discriminatory practices of employers? To what extent, and in what ways, should the government regulate employment conditions to ensure equal opportunity? These are the questions facing society—and the courts—today.

ENVIRONMENTAL CONCERNS

To what extent is business required to concern itself with the conservation of natural resources? Does a company have to wait until it is besieged by protesters before it acts, as in the case of Weyerhauser in the Northwest? This forest products company found itself under attack by protesters who accused it of raping the forest. It ultimately set up an extensive program of replanting trees and became more selective in its cutting, thereafter cutting in a manner to conserve natural resources.

For business enterprises generally, the emphasis has been on maximizing short-term profits and, thus, observing the minimal environmental protections required by law. But the effect of large corporations' activities on the environment has now become a subject of public concern. Throughout this nation's history, Americans have tended to view large corporations with a somewhat critical eye. Whereas in the past corporations have been criticized for failing to create

enough jobs or for failing to produce a sufficient quantity or quality of goods and services, these same corporations are now being criticized for failing to consider as their ethical responsibility the protection of the environment. Yet the fact is that companies typically cannot protect the environment without incurring higher production costs. This result is generally not happily received by stockholders—even those having environmentalist leanings. Pollution control clearly involves costs that must be absorbed somewhere—by shareholders, in the form of smaller dividends; by consumers, in the form of higher prices; or by employees, in the form of lower wages.

In a competitive economic system, companies cannot be socially responsible alone. If an individual firm tries to accept this responsibility and other firms don't, lower profits for the socially responsible firm and its eventual demise may result. Consequently, we can argue that it is because of our competitive system that we require government regulation and that this need is particularly great in the environmental protection area.

But does this mean that it is only through government regulation of all competitors that we will achieve a reduction in the amount of environmental destruction caused by production processes? Is it possible to combine profit-making activities *and* environmental protection programs? Dow Chemical thought so. That firm devised and implemented a massive program of pollution control directed toward waste reduction and the conservation of raw materials. Manufacturing processes were closely scrutinized to increase operating efficiency, to recycle raw materials formerly vented into the air or lost to the sewer, and to use waste products. Although in its press releases Dow emphasized its good citizenship, it nonetheless profited by these programs. Pollution control meant savings that could be transformed directly into higher company profits.

ANTITRUST

In the last quarter-century, antitrust sanctions have been applied to individual corporate officers and directors who have knowingly violated antitrust laws. Jail sentences were given to officers and directors of a corporation as a result of antitrust violations for the first time in the 1960s. One must ask whether a director or officer of a corporation should knowingly allow the corporation to engage in activities that are clearly in violation of antitrust laws. Again we are faced with the problem of where the duty of loyalty lies for a director or officer of a corporation. If the only duty is to the shareholders, then we would not have a difficult time arguing that directors and officers of a corporation should ignore antitrust laws "as long as they can get away with it." On the other hand, if the ethical responsibility of directors and officers of a corporation is to the public at large, then deliberate acts in violation of antitrust laws should never be performed.

But what about antitrust laws that, in fact, seem unreasonable? In particular, the Robinson-Patman Act has been lambasted by lawyers, businesspersons, and economists alike for many years. In principle, this statute was passed to protect the small businessperson from the buying power of chain stores by limiting price concessions granted to powerful buyers. Thus, the statute prohibited price discrimination unless such discrimination was supported by cost savings or was otherwise necessary to meet a competitor's price. In practice, however, it has been used on numerous occasions by small stores to extort tribute from large firms. In other words, every time a large operation was able to undercut the price of a smaller operation in the same line of business, the smaller concern entered into antitrust litigation citing violation of the Robinson-Patman Act. This use of the Robinson-Patman Act has been severely criticized as being anticompetitive and contrary to the guiding principles of the antitrust laws.

Numerous economic studies have shown that the Robinson-Patman Act has probably resulted in economic inefficiency. But does that mean it should be repealed? Not necessarily, because we may have an ethical responsibility to maintain a large number of small businesses in the United States. After all, the larger the business, presumably, the greater the amount of political and economic power. Thus, an objective of antitrust policy may be to limit the social and political power of big business and to increase that of small business. This objective is quite logical, considering the fact that the antitrust laws were enacted during a period of distrust of concentrations of size and power. Therefore, we should not be surprised when the free play of market forces is interrupted in favor of ethical responsibilities such as preserving and encouraging small business. If we wish to maintain diffused political power in our society, perhaps we should foster legislation such as the Robinson-Patman Act, which prevents small firms from being forced out of business by larger firms—even if the latter are more efficient.

THE ECONOMICS OF REGULATION

Most regulation is motivated by government's concern for the social welfare. Corporations may be criticized for using technicalities or loopholes to escape the letter of the law while violating its spirit. Yet regulation is not always an unmitigated blessing, even for its intended beneficiaries.

Consider the example of rent control. Local governments have placed regulations on landlords to prevent them from raising rents and thereby driving out low-income tenants. Most people are sympathetic to this concern, but the long-run implications of rent control must still be considered. Rent control restricts the profitability of residential housing and discourages the construction of new rental units, which may be needed by the community. Some have suggested that rent control shares some responsibility for the now-major problem of homelessness. Thus, though rent control may have benefits, its full consequences should be explored.

DISCUSSION QUESTIONS

1. Some government regulation, such as antitrust law, may be enforced by private corporations. Are these private suits always ethical and proper, or should we consider the motive of the plaintiff company? For example, when MCI won a

large antitrust award from AT&T, some suggested that federal courts were being used as part of market competition. Might not companies be using antitrust laws to enhance their own market share and to restrict competition?

2.   In view of the many consumer protection laws that exist, should corporations have any ethical obligations to consumers beyond the letter of the law? Don't consumers have the responsibility to bargain for any additional protections?

3.   Both environmental and occupational safety laws strive to protect the public health from hazardous substances. Should standards in these two contexts be the same? Or should employees be allowed to voluntarily accept some greater risk in return for a higher wage scale?

4.   An employer's affirmative-action policy may conflict with the interests of its current employees and their union. How should such a company balance its duties under labor law with those under discrimination law?

PROPERTY AND ITS PROTECTION

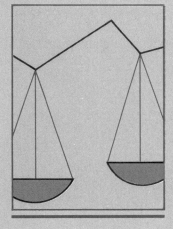

Chapter 50

Personal Property

Property consists of the legally protected rights and interests a person has in anything with an ascertainable value that is subject to ownership. Property would have little value if the law did not define the right to use it, to sell or dispose of it, and to prevent trespassing upon it. In the United States, the ownership of property receives special protection under the law. The Bill of Rights states that "no person shall ⋆ ⋆ ⋆ be deprived of life, liberty, or property, without due process of law; nor shall private property be taken for public use, without just compensation." The Fourteenth Amendment provides that "no State shall ⋆ ⋆ ⋆ deprive any person of life, liberty, or property, without due process of law."

THE NATURE OF PERSONAL PROPERTY

Property may be divided into real property and personal property. **Real property** (sometimes called *realty* or *real estate*) means the land and everything permanently attached to the land. When structures are permanently attached to the land, then everything attached permanently to the structures is also realty. (Real property is discussed in detail in Chapters 52 and 53.) Everything else is **personal property** (or *personalty*). Attorneys sometimes refer to all personal property as **chattel,** a more comprehensive term than *goods* because it includes living as well as inanimate property. Often, instead of saying personal property, the law will refer to goods as chattel.

Since personal property and real property differ significantly, the law has developed different sets of rules to deal with their acquisition and disposition. For example, a lease of real property conveys a *property interest* from the landlord (lessor) to the tenant (lessee). A lease of personal property merely transfers a *possessory interest*, creating a bailment (to be discussed in the next chapter).

Personal property can be tangible or intangible. *Tangible personal property* such as a television set, heavy construction equipment, or a car, has physical substance. *Intangible personal property* represents some set of rights and duties, but it has no real physical existence. Stocks and bonds are intangible personal property. So, too, are patents, trademarks, and copyrights, already discussed in Chapter 5.

877

The Expanding Nature of Personal Property

In a dynamic society, the concept of personal property must expand to take account of new types of ownership rights. For example, gas, water, and telephone services are now considered personal property for the purpose of criminal prosecution when they are stolen or used without payment. Federal and state statutes protect against the copying of musical compositions. It is a crime now to engage in the "bootlegging"—illegal copying for resale—of records and tapes. The theft of computer programs and services is usually considered a theft of personal property. (See Chapter 55, "Computers and the Law.")

PROPERTY RIGHTS AND OWNERSHIP TITLE[1]

Property can be viewed as a bundle of rights. These rights include the right to possession of the property and the right to dispose of the property—by sale, gift, rental, lease, and so on.

Fee Simple

A person who holds the entire bundle of rights is said to be the owner in **fee simple.** The owner in fee simple is entitled to use, possess, and dispose of the property as he or she chooses during his or her lifetime; and upon death, the owner's interest in the property descends to his or her heirs.

Concurrent Ownership

Persons who share ownership rights simultaneously in a particular piece of property are said to be *concurrent* owners. There are two principal types of **concurrent ownership:** tenancy in common and joint tenancy.

Tenancy in common is co-ownership in which each of two or more persons owns an undivided fractional interest in the property. Upon one tenant's death, that interest passes to his or her heirs. For example, suppose Reband and Charnock own a rare stamp collection as tenants in common. If Reband died before Charnock, one-half of the stamp collection would become the property of Reband's

---

1. The principles discussed in this section apply equally to real property ownership, discussed in Chapter 52.

heirs. If Reband had sold her interest to French before she died, French and Charnock would have become co-owners as tenants in common. If French died, his interest in the personal property would pass to his heirs, and they in turn would own the property with Charnock as tenants in common.

Joint Tenancy

In a **joint tenancy,** each of two or more persons owns an undivided interest in the whole (personal property), and a deceased joint tenant's interest passes to the surviving joint tenant or tenants. Joint tenancy can be terminated at any time before the joint tenant's death by gift or by sale. If no termination occurs, then upon the death of a joint tenant, his or her interest transfers to the remaining joint tenants, not to the heirs of the deceased joint tenant. If Reband and Charnock from the preceding example were joint tenants and if Reband died before Charnock, the entire collection would become the property of Charnock. Reband's heirs would receive absolutely no interest in the collection. If, prior to Reband's death, she had sold her interest to French, French and Charnock would have become co-owners. Reband's sale, however, would have terminated the joint tenancy, and French and Charnock would have become owners as tenants in common.

A joint tenancy can also be transferred by *partition;* that is, the tenants can physically divide the property into equal parts. Since a joint tenant's interest is capable of being conveyed without the consent of the other joint tenants, it can be levied against by the tenant's creditors. This characteristic is also true of the tenancy in common.

At common law, unless a clear intention to create a tenancy in common was shown, there was a presumption that any co-tenancy was a joint tenancy. Modern statutes, however, reverse this presumption. Most statutes now presume that a co-tenancy is a tenancy in common unless there is a clear intention to establish a joint tenancy. Thus, the language "to Jerrold and Eva as joint tenants with right of survivorship, and not as tenants in common" would create a joint tenancy.

Less Common Ways of Holding Property

There are two less common types of concurrent ownership. One is tenancy by the entirety, and the other is community property ownership.

TENANCY BY THE ENTIRETY Tenancy by the entirety is less common today than it once was. Typically, it is created by a conveyance (transfer) to a husband and wife. It is distinguished from joint tenancy by the inability of either spouse to transfer separately his or her interest during his or her life. Since neither can voluntarily convey his or her interest, the creditors of one spouse cannot levy on the property. In some states where statutes give the wife the right to convey her property, this form of concurrent ownership has been effectively abolished. A divorce, either spouse's death, or mutual agreement will terminate a tenancy by the entirety.

COMMUNITY PROPERTY Community property ownership applies only in Arizona, California, Idaho, Louisiana, Nevada, New Mexico, Texas, Washington, Wisconsin, and Puerto Rico. Each spouse technically owns an *undivided* one-half interest in property. This type of ownership applies to most personal property acquired by the husband and/or wife during the course of marriage. It generally does not apply to property acquired prior to the marriage or to property acquired by gift or inheritance during the marriage. After a divorce, community property is divided equally.

ACQUIRING OWNERSHIP OF PERSONAL PROPERTY

The ownership of personal property can be acquired by possession, purchase, production, gift, will or inheritance, and accession. Each of these is discussed below.

Possession

One example of acquiring ownership by possession is the capture of wild animals. Wild animals belong to no one in their natural state, and the first person to take possession of a wild animal normally owns it. The killing of a wild animal amounts to assuming ownership of it. Merely being in hot pursuit does not give title, however. There are two exceptions to this basic rule. First, any wild animals captured by a trespasser are the property of the landowner, not the trespasser. For instance, the fish in a pond on a farmer's land are the farmer's property, not the property of a tres-

passer who fishes for and catches them. Second, if wild animals are captured or killed in violation of wild game statutes, the capturer does not obtain title to the animals; rather, the state does. Other illustrations of acquiring ownership by possession are presented later in this chapter.

Purchase

Purchase is one of the most common means of acquiring and transferring ownership of personal property. The purchase and sale of personal property (called goods) are covered in depth in Chapters 16 to 19.

Production

Production—the fruits of labor—is another means of acquiring ownership of personal property. For example, writers, inventors, and manufacturers all produce personal property and thereby acquire title to it. (In some situations—for example, situations in which researchers are hired for that purpose—the producer does not own what is produced.)

Gift

A **gift** is another fairly common means of acquiring or transferring ownership of property. A gift is essentially a *voluntary* transfer of property ownership. It is not supported by legally sufficient consideration, since the very essence of a gift is giving without consideration. A gift must be transferred or delivered in the present rather than in the future. For example, suppose that your aunt tells you that she is going to give you a new Mercedes-Benz for your next birthday. This is simply a *promise* to make a gift. It is not considered a gift until the Mercedes-Benz is delivered.

There are three requirements for an effective gift—delivery, donative intent, and acceptance by the donee (the one receiving the gift).

DELIVERY Delivery is obvious in most cases, but some objects cannot be relinquished physically. Then the question of delivery depends upon the surrounding circumstances. When the physical object cannot be delivered, a symbolic delivery, or **constructive delivery,** will be sufficient. Constructive delivery does not confer actual possession of the object in question. It is a general term for all those acts that the law holds to be equivalent to acts of real delivery. Suppose that you want to make a gift of various old rare coins that you have stored in a safety deposit box. You certainly cannot deliver the box itself to the donee, and you do not want to take the coins out of the bank. Instead, you can simply deliver the key to the box to your donee. This constitutes symbolic, or constructive, delivery of the contents of the box.

Delivery of intangible personal property *must* be accomplished by symbolic or constructive delivery. For example, ownership interests in firms are often represented by stock certificates, and delivery of the certificate entitles the holder to dividends. Other examples of intangible personal property that must be constructively delivered include insurance policies, contracts, promissory notes, and chattel mortgages.

An effective delivery also requires giving up *complete dominion and control* (ownership rights) over the subject matter of the gift. The outcome of disputes often turns on the retaining or relinquishing of control over the subject matter of the gift. The Internal Revenue Service scrutinizes transactions between relatives when one relative has given away income-producing property. A relative who does not relinquish complete control over a piece of property will have to pay taxes on the income from that property. Under the tax laws, it may be illegal to assign or to give away income while retaining control over the property that produces the income (unless a special trust is set up).

Delivery can be accomplished by means of a third person. The third person may be the agent of the donor (the one making the gift) or the donee. If the person is the agent of the donor, the gift is effective when the agent delivers to the donee. If, on the other hand, the third person is the agent of the donee, the gift is effective when the donor delivers the property to the donee's agent.[2] When there is doubt as to whose agent the third party is, he or she is generally presumed to be the agent of the donor. Naturally, no delivery is necessary if the gift is already in the hands of the donee. All that is necessary to complete the gift in such a case is the required intent and acceptance by the donee.

DONATIVE INTENT　Donative intent is determined from the language of the donor and the surrounding circumstances. For example, when a gift is challenged in court, the court may look at the relationship between the parties and the size of the gift in relation to the donor's other assets. A gift to an archenemy will be viewed with suspicion. Likewise, when a person has given away a large portion of his or her assets, the court will scrutinize the transactions to determine what the mental capacity of the donor was and whether fraud or duress was used.

In the following case, the court looks at the intent of the donor and the question of delivery.

---

2. Bickford v. Mattocks, 95 Me. 547, 50 A.894 (1901).

Case 50.1
ESTATE OF PIPER
Missouri Court of Appeals,
1984.
676 S.W.2d 897.

BACKGROUND AND FACTS　*Gladys Piper died intestate (without a will) in 1982. At the time of her death, she owned personal property consisting of household goods, two old automobiles, farm machinery, and "miscellaneous" items totaling $5,150. This did not include jewelry or cash. When Gladys died, she had $206.75 in cash and her two diamond rings, known as the "Andy Piper" rings, in her purse. The contents of Gladys's purse were taken by her niece Wanda Brown upon Gladys's death, allegedly to preserve them for the estate. Clara Kauffmann, a friend of Gladys Piper, filed a claim against the estate for $4,800. From October 1974 until Gladys's death in 1982, Clara had taken Gladys to the doctor, beauty shop, and grocery store, written her checks to pay her bills, and helped her care for her home. Clara maintained that Gladys had promised to pay her for these services and that the diamond rings were a gift to her. The trial court denied Clara's request for payment of $4,800 on the basis that the services had been voluntary. Clara then filed a petition for delivery of personal property, the rings, which was granted by the trial court. The defendants—Gladys's heirs and her estate by the administrator—appealed.*

GREENE, Judge.

* * * *

We direct our attention to that portion of the judgment declaring that the rings were the property of Clara Kauffman. Clara's petition claimed the rings belonged to her by reason of "a consummated gift long prior to the death of Gladys Piper." The only evidence of the gift issue came from two witnesses. James Naylor, who had known Gladys for over 20 years, testified that when he saw Gladys "[b]etween the time of her last admission to the hospital and the date of her death," Gladys told him, after Naylor had complimented her on her rings, that "these are Clara's, but I am wearing them until I am finished with them, or until I am dead or whatever she may have said * * *." Beverly Marcus testified that Gladys told her "when she was through with those rings, they were to be Clara's."

There was no evidence of any actual delivery to Clara, at any time, of the rings. A person claiming an inter vivos gift [a gift made during the life of the donor] of personal property has the burden of proving it by clear and convincing evidence. * * * The essentials of such a gift are 1) a present intention to make a gift on the part of the donor, 2) a delivery of the property by donor to donee, and 3) an acceptance by donee, whose ownership takes effect immediately and absolutely. * * *

While no particular form is necessary to effect a delivery, and while the delivery may be actual, constructive, or symbolical, there must be some evidence to support a delivery theory. What we have here, at best, through the testimony of James Naylor and Beverly Marcus, was an intention on the part of Gladys, at some future time, to make a gift of the rings to Clara. Such an intention, no matter how clearly expressed, which has not been carried into effect, confers no ownership rights in the property in the intended donee. * * * Language written or spoken, expressing an intention to give, does not constitute a gift, unless the intention is executed by a complete and unconditional delivery of the subject matter, or delivery of a proper written instrument evidencing the gift. * * * There is no evidence in this case to prove delivery, and, for such reason, the trial court's judgment is erroneous.

The judgment of the trial court was reversed. No effective gift of the rings had been made because Gladys had never delivered the rings to Clara.

DECISION AND REMEDY

ACCEPTANCE The final requirement of a valid gift is acceptance by the donee. This rarely presents any problems, since most donees readily accept their gifts. The courts generally assume acceptance unless shown otherwise.

GIFTS *INTER VIVOS* AND GIFTS *CAUSA MORTIS*
Gifts **inter vivos** are made during the donor's lifetime. Gifts **causa mortis** and made in contemplation of imminent death. Gifts *causa mortis* do not become absolute until the donor dies from the contemplated illness or disease. The donee must survive to take the gift, and the donor must not have revoked the gift prior to death. A gift *causa mortis* is revocable at any time up to the death of the donor and is automatically revoked if the donor recovers.

Suppose Stevens is to be operated on for a cancerous tumor. Before the operation, he delivers an envelope to a close business associate. The envelope contains a letter saying, "I realize my days are numbered and I want to give you this check for $1,000,000 in the event of my death from this operation." The business associate cashes the check. The surgeon performs the operation and removes the tumor. Stevens recovers fully. Several months later, Stevens dies from a heart attack that is totally unrelated to the operation. If Stevens's personal representative (the party charged with administering Stevens's estate) tries to recover the

$1,000,000, she will succeed. The gift *causa mortis* is automatically revoked if the donor recovers. The *specific event* that was contemplated in making the gift was death from a particular operation. Since Stevens's death was not the result of this event, the gift is revoked, and the $1,000,000 passes to Stevens's estate.[3]

Will or Inheritance

Ownership of property may be transferred by will or by inheritance under state statutes. These transfers, called bequests, devises, or inheritances, are dealt with in Chapter 56.

Accession

Accession means "something added." It occurs when someone adds value to a piece of personal property by use of either labor or materials. Generally, there is no dispute about who owns the property after accession has occurred, especially when the accession is accomplished with the owner's consent.

For example, a Corvette customizing specialist comes to Sam's house. Sam has all the materials necessary. The customizing specialist uses them to add a unique bumper to Sam's Corvette. Sam simply pays the customizer for the value of the labor, obviously retaining title to the property.

Two situations in which ownership can be in issue after the occurrence of an accession are:

1. A situation in which a party has wrongfully caused the accession.
2. A situation in which the materials added or labor expended greatly increase the value of the property or change the identity of the property.

Some general rules can be applied when these situations occur.

If the accession was caused wrongfully (without the owner's consent) and in bad faith, the courts will generally favor the owner over the improver, even if the value of the property was increased substantially. In addition, many courts will deny the improver (wrongdoer) any compensation for the value added; for example, a car thief who put new tires on the stolen car would ob-

viously not be compensated for the value of the new tires.

If the accession is performed in good faith, however, even without the owner's consent, ownership of the improved item most often depends on the actual increase in the value of the property or change of identity of the property. The greater the increase, the more likely that ownership will pass to the improver. Obviously, when this occurs, the improver must compensate the original owner for the value the property had prior to the accession. If the increase in value is not sufficient for ownership to be passed to the improver, most courts require the owner to compensate the improver for the value added.

To illustrate: Suppose Angelo is walking in a large country field and discovers a huge stone that is shaped approximately like the Lone Ranger's horse, Silver. Angelo comes back for twenty-seven weeks and transforms the stone into an exact replica of Silver. Angelo's artist friends are very impressed and convince him to move the stone horse to a gallery, where it is valued at $50,000. The owner of the field in which Angelo found the stone now wants to claim title to it. Normally, the courts will give Angelo title to the stone because the changes he made caused it to greatly increase in value and the accession was performed in good faith. But Angelo will have to pay the owner of the field for the reasonable value of the stone before it was altered.

Confusion

Confusion is defined as the commingling of goods so that one person's personal property cannot be distinguished from another's. It frequently involves goods that are fungible.[4] *Fungible goods* are goods of which each particle is identical with every other particle, such as grain and oil. For example, if two farmers put their number 2 grade winter wheat into the same silo, confusion will occur. If the confusion of goods is caused by a person who wrongfully and willfully mixes his or her goods with those of another in order to render them indistinguishable, the innocent party acquires title to the total.

This rule does not apply when confusion occurs by agreement, honest mistake, or the act of

3. Brind v. International Trust Co., 66 Colo. 60, 179 P. 148 (1919).

4. See UCC 1-201(17).

some third party. When any of these three events occurs, the owners all share ownership as tenants in common. Suppose that you enter into a cooperative arrangement with five other farmers in your local community of Midway, Iowa. Each fall everyone harvests the same amount of number 2 yellow corn. The corn is stored in silos that are held by the cooperative. Each of you owns one-sixth of the total corn in the silos. If anything happens to the corn, each of you will bear the loss in equal proportions of one-sixth.

But suppose you share ownership in some other proportion. Often, owners do not have equal interests. In such a case, the owners must keep careful records of their respective proportions. If a dispute over ownership or loss arises, the courts will presume that everyone has an equal interest in the goods. So you must be prepared to prove that you own more or less than an equal part.

Suppose you own two-thirds of the corn in the Midway co-op silos. Further assume that the silos are damaged by a tornado and thunderstorm. How much have you lost if one-half of the corn is blown away by the storm? You have lost one-half of your two-thirds, or one-third of the total. When corn is stored by several owners, each owning a different proportion of the total, loss is shared proportionally.

Confusion that results from negligent conduct creates a different problem. When there is a loss by fire, theft, or destruction, the person responsible for the commingling must bear the entire loss. If the wrongdoer can show that no injury occurred, however, and can prove what portion he or she contributed to the whole, then the wrongdoer can recover that portion.

Suppose you are the vice-president in charge of purchasing for a salad oil company. You buy 10,000 gallons of high-grade salad oil and have it delivered to a field warehouse company. The warehouse company stores many grades of oil, and your oil is negligently mixed with oil of a much lower grade. The oil was worth $.64 per gallon before it was confused, but now it is worth only $.32 per gallon. Here you should be entitled to claim your 10,000 gallons of oil and sue the warehouse for $3,200 in damages caused by the negligent confusion. On the other hand, suppose the grades of oil were exactly the same but you had contracted to have your oil stored in a separate bin. There may have been a technical breach of

contract, but you will not normally recover any damages, because there has been no injury.[5]

MISLAID, LOST, OR ABANDONED PROPERTY

As already noted, one of the methods of acquiring ownership of property is to possess it. Simply finding something and holding onto it, however, does not necessarily entitle the finder to it. If the property has been *mislaid*, the finder does not have first claim to it. Its true owner does, and if the owner does not assert this claim, the owner of the premises on which it was discovered may claim it. If it has been *lost*, the finder has first claim to it—after its true owner. If it has been intentionally *abandoned*, the finder's possession entitles him or her to its title.

Mislaid Property

Property that has been voluntarily placed somewhere by the owner and then inadvertently forgotten is **mislaid property.** Suppose you go to the theater and leave your gloves on the concession stand. The gloves are mislaid property, and the theater owner is entrusted with the duty of reasonable care for the goods. When mislaid property is found, the finder does not obtain title to or possession of the goods.[6] Instead, the owner of the place where the property was mislaid becomes the caretaker of the property because it is highly likely that the true owner will return.[7]

Lost Property

Property that is *involuntarily* left is **lost property.** A finder of lost property can claim title to the property against the whole world, *except the true owner*. If the true owner demands that the lost

---

5. As a matter of commercial reality, very few, if any, warehouses contract for storage in separate facilities. If they did, many people would want separate facilities for fear of confusion. But this would negate the savings in warehouse storage. Here we are really dealing with *fungible* goods.

6. The finder is an involuntary bailee. See Chapter 51.

7. He or she is a bailee with right of possession against all except the true owner.

property be returned, the finder must return it. If a third party attempts to take possession of lost property from a finder, the third party cannot assert a better title than the finder.

When a finder knows who the true owners of property are and fails to return it to them, that finder is guilty of a tort known as *conversion* (see Chapter 4). Finally, many states require the finder to make a reasonably diligent search to locate the true owner of lost property.

Suppose Arnolds works in a large library at night. In the courtyard on her way home, she finds a piece of gold jewelry that contains several apparently precious stones. Arnolds decides to take it to a jeweler to have it appraised. While pretending to weigh the jewelry, an employee of the jeweler removes several of the stones. If Arnolds brings an action to recover the stones from the jeweler, she will win, because she found lost property and holds valid title against everyone *except the true owner*. Since the property was *lost* and not *mislaid,* the owner of the library is not the caretaker of the jewelry. Instead, Arnolds acquires title good against the whole world (except the true owner).[8]

---

8. See Armory v. Delamirie, 1 Strange 505 (K.B. 1722). If Arnolds has found the jewelry during the course of her em-

Many states have **estray statutes** to encourage and facilitate the return of property to its true owner and then to reward the finder for honesty if the property remains unclaimed. Such statutes provide an incentive for finders to report their discoveries by making it possible for them, after passage of a specified period of time, to acquire legal title to the property they have found. Such statutes usually require the county clerk to advertise the property in an attempt to enhance the opportunity of the owner to recover what has been lost.

There are always some preliminary questions to be resolved before the estray statute can be employed. The item must be *lost property*, not mislaid or abandoned property. When the situation indicates that the property was probably lost and not mislaid or abandoned, as a matter of public policy, loss is presumed, and the estray statute applies. Such a situation occurred in the following case.

---

ployment, however, her employer would be the involuntary bailee. (See Chapter 51, on bailments.) Further, many courts now say that lost property recovered in a private place allows the owner of the place, *not* the finder, to become the bailee (even if the finder is not a trespasser).

Case 50.2 **PASET v. OLD ORCHARD BANK & TRUST CO.** Appellate Court of Illinois, First District, Third Division, 1978. 62 Ill.App.3d 534, 378 N.E.2d 1264, 19 Ill.Dec. 389	**BACKGROUND AND FACTS** *Paset, a safety deposit box subscriber, brought an action against the Old Orchard Bank and Trust Co., the defendant, seeking a declaratory judgment that the state estray statute applied to her finding $6,325 on a chair in the examination booth in the bank's safety deposit vault area. The bank wrote to everyone who had been in the safety deposit vault area either on the day of, or on the day preceding, the discovery. The money was not claimed within the statutory period of one year. Hence, the plaintiff petitioned the court to grant her ownership of the money. The trial court entered an order refusing to determine ultimate ownership of the money. Paset appealed.*

SIMON, Justice.

* * * *

The bank's position is that the estray statute is not applicable because the money was not lost in the sense the word "lost" is used in that statute. The bank contends that, under the common law, the money was mislaid by its owner rather than lost, and that the estray statute does not apply to mislaid property. In the alternative, the bank argues that the money was discovered not in a public place, but in a private area with access restricted to safety deposit box subscribers. The bank claims, therefore, that the money always was in its constructive possession or custody, either as owner of the premises or as bailee for an unknown and unidentified safety deposit box subscriber, and that property in someone's constructive possession or custody cannot be lost. As against the plaintiff, the bank claims to have the superior right to hold the money indefinitely, and in fact is required to do so until the true owner puts in his appearance.

* * * *

[W]e do not accept the bank's initial argument that the money was mislaid rather than lost. It is complete speculation to infer, as the bank urges, that the money was deliberately placed by its owner on the chair located partially under a table in the examining booth, and then forgotten. If the money was intentionally placed on the chair by someone who forgot where he left it, the bank's notice to safety deposit box subscribers should have alerted the owner. The failure of an owner to appear to claim the money in the interval since its discovery is affirmative evidence that the property was not mislaid.

Because the evidence, though ambiguous, tends to indicate that the money probably was not mislaid, and because neither party contends that the money was abandoned, we conclude that the ambiguity should, as a matter of public policy, be resolved in favor of the presumption that the money was lost. * * * Accordingly, we reject the bank's first contention that the money was mislaid and the estray statute irrelevant, and conclude that the money was "lost," and so encompassed by the Illinois estray statute.

We also reject the bank's alternative argument that the money, having been found in a place from which the general public was excluded, was always in the bank's constructive custody or possession, and therefore could not have been "lost," as that word is used in the estray statute.

* * * *

* * * The bank's record of its safety deposit box subscribers who visited the vault on the day of or the day preceding the plaintiff's discovery gave the bank the opportunity to search for the owner among this limited group. The bank also had sufficient time to contact any subscriber who had not been in his box since the date the plaintiff discovered the money. Consequently, in view of the opportunities the bank had to search out the owner of the money among this limited group, of the notice the bank gave to that group and of the plaintiff's undisputed compliance with the estray statute, vesting the ownership of the money in the finder is a more pragmatic and sensible solution than having the bank continue to hold the money indefinitely.

The appellate court decided that the estray statute should be applied and that the ownership of the money should be vested in the finder, Paset.	**DECISION AND REMEDY**

Abandoned Property

Property that has been *discarded* by the true owner, who has *no intention* of claiming title to it, is **abandoned property.** Someone who finds abandoned property acquires title to it, and such title is good against the whole world, *including the original owner.* The owner of lost property who eventually gives up any further attempt to find the lost property is frequently held to have abandoned the property.

For example, assume that Starr is driving with the windows down in her car. Somewhere along her route, a valuable scarf blows out the window. She retraces her route but cannot find the scarf. She finally decides that further search is useless and proceeds to her destination 500 miles away. Starr makes no further attempt to find the scarf. Six months later, Frye, a hitchhiker, finds the scarf. Frye has acquired title, which is good even against Starr. (Of course, the same result would occur if Starr had deliberately discarded the scarf along the highway.)

A trespasser who finds an item of abandoned personal property does not acquire title to it, however. The owner of the real property on which it was found does. The same rule applies if the property was lost. Similarly, if, for example, a landowner employs a crew to install an underground septic tank and the crew digs up a cache of pioneer relics, the landowner has first claim to the relics, since they were buried in his ground.

On the other hand, if the crew had unearthed money, gold, silver, plate, or bullion (instead of pewter dishes, tin cups, brass buttons, and old muskets), the find could be classified as **treasure trove,** and the crew might be able to keep it. In the United States, in the absence of a statute, a finder has title to treasure trove against all but the true owner. (In Great Britain, the Crown gets it.)

Generally, to constitute treasure trove, property need not have been buried—it could have been hidden in some other private place, such as behind loose bricks in an old chimney—but its owner must be unknown, and its finders must not have been trespassing.[9]

___

9. Danielson v. Roberts, 44 Or. 1008, 74 P. 913 (1904).

QUESTIONS AND CASE PROBLEMS

1. John has a severe heart attack and is taken to the hospital. He is not expected to live, and he knows it. Since he is a bachelor without close relatives nearby, John gives his car keys to his close friend, Fred, telling Fred that he is expected to die and that the car is Fred's. John survives the heart attack, but two months later he dies from pneumonia. Uncle Sam, the executor of John's estate, wants Fred to return the car. Fred refuses, claiming the car was given to him by John as a gift. Discuss whether Fred will be required to return the car to John's estate.

2. Sally goes into Meyer's Department Store to do some Christmas shopping. She becomes engrossed in looking over a number of silk blouses but suddenly realizes she has a dinner engagement. She hastily departs from the store, inadvertently leaving her purse on a sales counter. Julie, a sales clerk at the store, notices the purse on the counter but leaves it there, expecting Sally to return for it. Later, when Sally returns, the purse is gone. Sally files an action against Meyer's Department Store for the loss of her purse. Discuss the probable success of her suit.

3. Bill Heise is a janitor for the First Mercantile Department Store. While walking to work, Bill discovers an expensive watch lying on the curb. Later that day, while Bill is cleaning the aisles of the store, he discovers a wallet containing $500 but no identification. Bill turns over the wallet to his supervisor, Joe Frances, and gives the watch to his son, Gordon. Two weeks later, Martin Avery, the owner of the watch, discovers that Bill found the watch and demands it back from Gordon. Bill decides now to claim the wallet with its $500, but Joe refuses to turn it over, saying that Bill is not the true owner and that the money is really the property of the store. Discuss who is entitled to the watch and who is entitled to the wallet containing $500.

4. Fred McDuff has a son named Don. Fred wants to give his son a new car that he has recently purchased. Fred and his son have been on bad terms during the past few years, and Fred feels part of this is his fault. He goes to his son's house, wanting to make amends by giving the car to Don. When Fred arrives at Don's house, his daughter-in-law (Don's wife) tells Fred that Don is out of town and will return the next day. Fred gives the keys to the new car to his daughter-in-law, tells her to hold the keys for his son, and says that he will return the next day. Two hours later, Fred has second thoughts about giving Don the car. He retrieves the keys from his daughter-in-law before she can turn them over to Don. Don returns from his trip, learns of the events, and demands possession of the car, claiming a gift was made. Is Don entitled to the car?

5. James DeCante owns a 1967 Chevy. The car has had continual mechanical problems, and James's repair expenses have been considerable. One day, in disgust, James parks the car on a city-owned vacant lot two blocks from his house. The car sits there for four months. During this period Sam Green observes the car, which has been unattended by James. Sam takes the car and makes improvements and repairs valued at $500. Later, James learns that Sam has the car, has it running smoothly, and is treating it as if it were his. James demands the car, claiming title. Sam refuses to surrender the car, claiming that he has title. Discuss who is correct and what rights, if any, each person has against the other.

6. Welton, an experienced businessperson, transferred to Gallagher bearer bonds, stating that the bonds were hers (Gallagher's) with "no strings attached" and that she should place the bonds in her safe deposit box for safekeeping. Later, Welton wanted Gallagher to return the bonds to him, claiming that he was still the owner. Gallagher refused, claiming that Welton's transfer was a gift of the bonds to her. Discuss fully whether Welton's transfer of the bearer bonds was a gift. [Welton v. Gallagher, 2 Hawaii App. 242, 630 P.2d 1077 (1981)]

7. Troop and Rust were partners in an oil and gas operation. Troop owned a three-fourths interest in the operation, and Rust owned a one-fourth interest. After eight years of operation, a dispute arose as to whether Rust had contributed his share of the expenses. As a result of the dispute, the partnership was dissolved. In attempting to divide up the oil, Rust learned that Troop had commingled the partnership's oil with oil from another lease that Troop owned. At trial, Troop was unable to show how much of the commingled oil had come from his other operation. How much of the oil should each of the parties receive? [Troop v. St. Louis Union Trust Co., 25 Ill.App.2d 143, 166 N.E.2d 116 (1960)]

8. Richard Coddington, a single man, opened a joint savings account with his mother. They signed a signature card that stated that the account was owned by them as joint tenants with the right of survivorship. New York banking

law provides that joint tenancy has been created when a bank account is opened in the names of two persons and is "payable to either or the survivor." However, no statement was made on the passbook as to survivorship. Later, Richard married Margaret. Richard died. Margaret claimed a share of the savings account on the ground that it was not a joint tenancy because the passbook did not contain words of survivorship. She also claimed that the statutory presumption of a joint tenancy was negated by Richard's past behavior—his withdrawal of substantial sums from the account throughout his life. At trial, the court awarded the entire account to Richard's mother. Margaret appealed. What was the result? [In re Estate of Richard N. Coddington, 56 App.Div.2d 697, 391 N.Y.S.2d 760 (1977)]

9. In June of 1983, the First National Bank of Chicago (First Chicago) sold some of its used office furniture to Walter Zibton, a dealer in new and secondhand office supplies and furniture. Included among the items of furniture were some file cabinets that were locked and presumed to be empty. Keys for the file cabinets were unavailable. Zibton sold one of the file cabinets to Charles Strayve and included three other file cabinets free of charge. Strayve later gave one of the cabinets to his friend Richard Michael, the plaintiff in this case. About six weeks after Michael had received the cabinet, it fell over in his garage, burst open, and exposed the contents—$6,687,948.85 worth of certificates of deposit. Michael took the certificates to the FBI for safekeeping and brought action to determine ownership of the certificates, claiming that they were abandoned property and that he, as the finder, was thus the rightful owner. First Chicago claimed that the certificates were lost property. Discuss who was correct. [Michael v. First Chicago Corp., 139 Ill.App.3d 374, 487 N.E.2d 403, 93 Ill.Dec. 736 (1985)]

10. Leonard Charrier, an amateur archeologist in Louisiana, uncovered artifacts from a several-hundred-year-old Indian burial ground. The artifacts had been made by the ancestors of the present-day Tunica Indian tribe of Louisiana. The Tunica tribe asked the court to award it custody of the property, which included burial pots, ornaments, and pottery. Charrier claimed that the property had been abandoned and that he had the right to title because he had taken possession of the property. Discuss whether the Tunica tribe, as heirs to the former owners of the property, should succeed in their claim to the artifacts or whether the property was abandoned. [Charrier v. Bell, 496 So.2d 601 (La.App. 1 Cir. 1986)]

11. Danny Smith and his brother discovered a sixteen-foot boat lying beside a roadway in Alabama. Danny Smith informed the police, who immediately impounded the boat and stored it in a city warehouse. Although Smith acquiesced to the police action, he told the police that if the true owner did not claim the boat he wanted it. When the true owner did not come forward, the police refused to relinquish the boat to Smith and instead told Smith he planned to auction it to the highest bidder on behalf of the city. Smith sued for custody of the boat. Since Smith never physically held the boat but rather allowed the police to take possession, should Smith succeed in his claim to title as finder? Could Smith defeat a claim if the true owner sought to retake the boat? [Smith v. Purvis, 474 So.2d 1131 (Ala.Civ.App. 1985)]

Chapter 51

Bailments

Virtually every individual and business is affected by the law of bailments at one time or another (and sometimes even on a daily basis). For example, doing any of the following creates a bailment relationship: shipping goods via public or private means, storing goods in a warehouse, renting a car, leaving a car in a public garage, or leaving a watch or typewriter to be repaired. When individuals deal with bailments, whether they realize it or not, they are subject to the obligations and duties that arise from the bailment relationship. A **bailment** is formed by the delivery of personal property, without transfer of title, by one person, called a **bailor,** to another, called a **bailee,** usually under an agreement for a particular purpose (for example, loan, storage, repair, or transportation). Upon completion of the purpose, the bailee is obligated to return the bailed property in the same or better condition to the bailor or to a third person or to dispose of it as directed. Most bailments are created by agreement, but not necessarily by contract law, because in many bailments not all of the elements of a contract (such as mutual assent or consideration) are present. For example, if you loan your business law text to a friend so that your friend can read tomorrow's assignment, a bailment is created, but not by contract, because there is no consideration. On the other hand, many commercial bailments, such as the delivery of your suit or dress to the cleaners for dry cleaning, are based on contract.

A bailment is distinguished from a sale or a gift in that possession is transferred without passage of title or intent to transfer title. In a sale or a gift, title is transferred from the seller or donor to the buyer or donee.

The number, scope, and importance of bailments created daily in the business community and in everyday life make it desirable for any person to understand the elements necessary for the creation of a bailment and to know what rights, duties, and liabilities flow from bailments.

ELEMENTS OF A BAILMENT

Not all transactions involving the delivery of property from one person to another create a bailment. The basic elements of bailment creation are as follows:

1. Personal property.
2. Delivery of possession (without title).
3. Agreement that the property be returned to the bailor or otherwise disposed of according to its owner's directions.

Personal Property Requirement

Bailment involves only personal property. A bailment of persons is not possible. Although a bailment of your luggage is created when it is transported by an airline, as a passenger you are not the subject of a bailment. Also, you cannot bail realty; thus, leasing your house to a tenant is not bailment.

Bailments involving *tangible* items, such as jewelry, cattle, and automobiles, are more frequent than bailments of *intangible* personal property, such as promissory notes and shares of corporate stock.

Delivery of Possession

Delivery of possession means transfer of possession of property to the bailee in such a way that:

1. The bailee is given exclusive possession and control over the property.
2. The bailee *knowingly* accepts the personal

property.[1] In other words, the bailee *intends* to exercise control over it.

If either delivery of possession or knowing acceptance is lacking, there is no bailment relationship. For example, suppose that Stevenson is in a hurry to catch his plane. He has a package he wants to check at the airport. He arrives at the airport check-in station, but the person in charge has gone on a coffee break. Stevenson decides to leave the package on the counter. Even though there has clearly been physical transfer of the package, the person in charge of the check-in station has not knowingly accepted the personal property. Therefore, there has been no effective delivery. The same result would occur in the following example: Delacroix checks her coat at a restaurant. In the coat pocket is a $20,000 diamond necklace. By accepting the coat, the bailee does not *knowingly* accept the necklace.

The following case distinguishes between a lease of space and a bailment.

---

1. We are dealing here with *voluntary* bailments. Under some circumstances, regardless of whether a person *intentionally* accepts possession of someone else's personal property, the law imposes on him or her the obligation to redeliver it. For example, if property is *accidentally* left in another's possession without negligence on the part of its owner, the person in whose possession it has been left may be responsible for its return. This is referred to as *involuntary* bailment.

BACKGROUND AND FACTS *Plaintiff Nelson parked his airplane at a facility owned and operated by the defendant, Shroeder Aerosports, Inc. The parking spaces contained tie-down facilities to secure the aircraft. Nelson tied his plane down when he left it at the facility. The defendant later moved Nelson's plane to another space and tied it down. A later attempt was made by the defendant to move the aircraft, but the tie-down knots were so secure that the aircraft was not disturbed. At all times Nelson retained the keys to the plane. After the weather bureau issued a storm warning, the defendant checked all aircraft in tie-down spaces and found that the tie-downs for Nelson's plane were securely tied. During the storm, Nelson's plane was turned over by high winds, and Nelson sought recovery from the defendant for the damage. The trial court held for the defendant, and the plaintiff appealed.*

Case 51.1
NELSON v. SHROEDER AEROSPORTS, INC.
Supreme Court of South Dakota, 1979.
280 N.W.2d 107.

DUNN, Justice.

Plaintiff argues that a bailor-bailee relationship arose between the parties in that a prima facie case was presented for the existence of a bailment. Plaintiff correctly states the elements for a showing of such a prima facie case, to wit: (1) the delivery of the property to defendant, (2) its value, (3) defendant's failure to return the property in good condition upon demand, and (4) the damages resulting from the failure to deliver.

Plaintiff fails, however, to recognize that the delivery contemplated above for the existence of a bailment turns on whether possession and control of the property is retained by the owner or is delivered to defendant. To constitute sufficient delivery, the generally recognized test is whether there is a full transfer of the property so as to amount to relinquishment of exclusive possession, control and dominion over the property for the duration of the relationship so that the person to whom delivery is made can exclude the possession of the owner and all other persons within the limits of the agreement between the parties.

* * * *

The evidence shows that plaintiff kept the keys to the aircraft and gave a third party permission to fly the aircraft. This exhibits plaintiff's retained control over the aircraft.

* * *

We must conclude that plaintiff did not relinquish exclusive possession, control and dominion over the aircraft. We hold that under the circumstances present in this case, where plaintiff's aircraft was placed in the airport parking or tie-down space and defendant was not given and did not assert exclusive control over the aircraft, there was no delivery giving rise to a bailor-bailee relationship and only a lease relating to the space occupied by the aircraft was created as opposed to a bailment of the aircraft into the hands of defendant.

DECISION AND REMEDY   *The trial court's judgment for the defendant was upheld. Because the defendant was not given exclusive control over the aircraft, no bailment was created.*

COMMENT   *Note, however, that in some cases dealing with* paid-for *parking privileges, the court has held that a bailment is created even though the car owner locks up the car and retains the keys.*

ACTUAL DELIVERY   A distinction is made between a restaurant patron who checks a coat with an attendant and a patron who hangs the coat on a coat rack. Giving the coat to the attendant constitutes an actual, physical delivery and thereby creates a bailment. The attendant (hence the restaurant) has exclusive possession and control over the retention and removal of the coat. By contrast, the self-hung coat can be removed at any time by the patron or anyone else so inclined. The restaurant does not have substantial control over the property and is not considered a bailee.

CONSTRUCTIVE DELIVERY   Constructive delivery is an implied or symbolic delivery. What is physically delivered to the bailee is not the actual property bailed but something so related to the property that the requirement of delivery is satisfied. For example, Lyssenko owns a boat that she wishes to loan to Brady for the weekend. It is moored at a municipal marina. Lyssenko gives Brady the boat registration papers so that the harbor master will allow Brady to board the boat.

Lyssenko has made constructive delivery of the boat to Brady.

In certain unique situations, a bailment is found despite the apparent lack of the requisite elements of control and knowledge. In particular, safe deposit box rental is usually held to constitute a bailor-bailee relationship between the bank and its customer, despite the bank's lack of knowledge of the contents and its inability to have exclusive control of the property. The bank may contractually avoid a bailment, however, by merely leasing the safe deposit box.[2]

Another example of such a situation occurs when the bailee acquires the property accidentally or by mistake—as when someone finds lost or mislaid property. A bailment is created even though the bailor did not voluntarily deliver the property to the bailee. Such bailments are called *involuntary* bailments.

---

2. By statute or by express contract, a safe deposit box may be a lease of space or license, depending on the jurisdiction or the facts or both.

The Bailment Agreement

A bailment agreement can be *express* or *implied*. Although no written agreement is required for bailments of less than one year (that is, the Statute of Frauds does not apply), it is a good idea to have one, especially when valuable property is involved.

The bailment agreement expressly or impliedly provides for the return of the bailed property to the bailor or to a third person or provides for disposal by the bailee. The agreement presupposes that the bailee will return the identical goods originally given by the bailor. In a bailment of *fungible goods*[3]—uniform identical goods—or a bailment with the *option to purchase*, however, only equivalent property must be returned.

For example, Sanchez, Basen, and Kerlly each store 1,000 pounds of grain of the same type and grade in Hansen's Warehouse every year, and each receives receipts. When Sanchez returns to reclaim "his grain," Hansen's Warehouse is obligated to give him 1,000 pounds of wheat grain—but not necessarily the particular kernels he originally deposited. Sanchez cannot claim that Hansen's Warehouse is guilty of conversion (see Chapter 4) in not returning to him the exact wheat that he put into storage. As long as it returns goods of the same *type*, *grade*, and *quantity*, Hansen's Warehouse—the bailee—has performed its obligation.

A bailment with an option or offer to purchase allows the prospective buyer the right to hold or use the property while deciding whether to purchase. At the end of an agreed-upon period, the bailee must either return the property to the bailor-seller or agree to purchase the property (such as by paying cash to the seller). If he or she agrees to purchase the property, the bailee-buyer returns to the bailor-seller "equivalent" property (promise or payment of money), terminating the bailment and creating a sale.

A typical example is a *sale on approval*. Suppose Rand is interested in buying a lawn mower. The seller gives him possession of a new model, telling him to take it home and try it out. The sales price is $280. If Rand does not like the lawn mower, he can bring it back within two weeks. If he does not bring it back within this period or if he approves the offer, the seller will bill him. Thus, a bailment is created, and Rand has the duty to either return the lawn mower or approve the offer and return the equivalent in the form of the purchase price.

ORDINARY BAILMENTS

There are three types of ordinary bailments. The distinguishing feature among them is *which party receives a benefit from the bailment*. Ultimately, the courts will use this factor to determine the standard of care required by the bailee while in possession of the personal property, and this factor will dictate the rights and liabilities of the parties. (See Exhibit 51–1.)

The three types of ordinary bailments are:

1. *Bailment for the sole benefit of the bailor.* This is a type of gratuitous bailment (one that involves no consideration) for the convenience and benefit of the bailor. The bailee is liable only for gross negligence. (Negligence is discussed in Chapter 4.)

2. *Bailment for the sole benefit of the bailee.* This is typically a loan of an article to a person (the bailee) solely for that person's convenience and benefit. The bailee is liable for even slight negligence.

3. *Bailment for the mutual benefit of the bailee and the bailor.* This is the most common kind of bailment and involves some form of compensation for storing items or holding property. It is a contractual bailment. The bailee is liable for ordinary negligence, or the failure to observe ordinary care, which is the care that a reasonably prudent person would use under the circumstances.

Although the standard of care required by the bailee often depends on the type of bailment, recently most courts have tended to use *reasonable standards of care* regardless of the type of bailment arrangement in effect.

RIGHTS AND DUTIES OF A BAILEE

In a bailment situation, both the bailee and the bailor have rights and duties. These rights and

---

3. Fungible goods are defined in UCC 1-201(17) and discussed in Chapter 17 ("Sales—Title, Risk, and Insurable Interest"). UCC 7-207(1) states clearly, "Fungible goods may be commingled."

Exhibit 51–1 **Standard of Care Required of a Bailee**

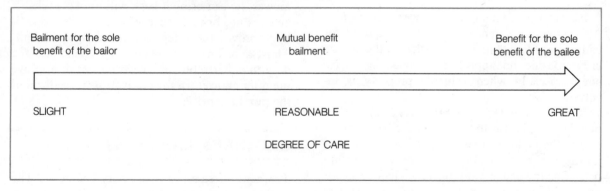

duties of the bailee are discussed below. A bailor's rights and duties will be discussed in the following section.

Rights of the Bailee

The bailee takes possession of personal property for a specified purpose, after which that property is returned (in the same or a *pre*specified altered form). Thus, implicit in the bailment agreement is the right of the bailee to take possession, to utilize the property in accomplishing the purpose of the bailment, and to receive some form of compensation (unless the bailment is intended to be gratuitous). Depending upon the nature of the bailment and the terms of the bailment agreement, these bailee rights are present (with some limitations) in varying degrees in all bailment transactions.

RIGHT OF POSSESSION   Temporary control and possession of property that ultimately is to be returned to the owner is the hallmark of a bailment. The meaning of "temporary" depends upon the terms of the bailment agreement. If a specified period is expressed in the bailment agreement, then the bailment is continuous for that time period. Earlier termination by the bailor is a breach of contract (if the bailment involves consideration), and the bailee can recover damages from the bailor. If no duration is specified, the bailment ends when either the bailor or the bailee so demands.

A bailee's right of possession, even though temporary, permits the bailee to recover damages from any third persons for damage or loss to the property. For example, No Spot Dry Cleaners sends all suede leather garments to Cleanall Com-

pany for special processing. If Cleanall loses or damages any leather goods, No Spot has the right to recover against Cleanall.

If the personal property is stolen from the bailee during the bailment, the bailee has a legal right to regain possession of (recapture) the goods or to obtain damages from any third person who has wrongfully interfered with the bailee's possessory rights.

RIGHT TO USE BAILED PROPERTY   Naturally, the extent to which bailees can use the personal property entrusted to them depends upon the terms of the bailment contract. Where no provision is made, the extent of use depends upon how necessary it is for the goods to be at the bailee's disposal in order for the ordinary purpose of the bailment to be carried out. For example, when leasing drilling machinery, the bailee is expected to use the equipment to drill. On the other hand, when providing long-term storage for a car, the bailee is not expected to use the car, because the ordinary purpose of a storage bailment does not include use of the property (unless an emergency dictates such use to protect the car).

RIGHT OF COMPENSATION   A bailee has a right to be compensated as provided for in the bailment agreement or reimbursed for costs and services rendered in the keeping of the bailed property, or both. In mutual-benefit bailments, the amount of compensation is often expressed in the bailment contract. For example, in a rental (bailment) of a car, the contract provides for charges on the basis of time, mileage, or a combination of the two, plus other possible charges. In nonrental bailments, when a car is left at a service station for an oil change, the bailee makes a service charge.

Even in a gratuitous bailment, a bailee has a right to be reimbursed or compensated for costs incurred in the keeping of the bailed property. For example, Ann loses her pet dog, which is found by Jesse. Jesse takes Ann's dog to his home and feeds it. Even though he takes good care of the dog, it becomes ill, and a veterinarian is called. The bill for the veterinarian's services and the medicine is paid by Jesse. Jesse is normally entitled to be reimbursed by Ann for all reasonable costs incurred in the keeping of her dog.

To enforce the right of compensation, the bailee has a right to place a *possessory* lien (claim) on the specific bailed property until he or she has been fully compensated. This lien on specific bailed property is sometimes referred to as an **artisan's lien.** The lien is effective only as long as the bailee has not agreed to extend credit to the bailor and the bailee retains possession over the bailed property.

If the bailor refuses to pay or cannot pay the charges (compensation), the bailee is entitled in most states to foreclose on the lien. This means that the bailee can sell the property and be paid out of the proceeds for the amount owed from the bailment, returning any excess to the bailee.

For example, Peter takes his car to the garage and enters into an agreement for repairs. The repairs are to be paid for in cash. Upon completion of the repairs, the garage tenders Peter his car, but because of unexpected bills he cannot pay the garage. The garage has a right to retain possession of Peter's car, exercising a *bailee's lien.* Unless Peter can make arrangements for payment, the garage will normally be entitled to sell the car in order to be compensated for the repairs.

RIGHT TO LIMIT LIABILITY "Ordinary" bailees have the right to limit their bailment liability by type of risk or by monetary amount, or both, as long as:

1. The limitations are called to the attention of the bailor.
2. The limitations are not against public policy.

Any enforceable limitation imposed by the ordinary bailee must be brought to the bailor's attention. Although the bailee is not required to read orally or interpret the limitation for the bailor, it is essential that the bailor in some way know of the limitation. Thus, a sign in Joe's garage stating that Joe will not be responsible "for loss due to theft, fire, or vandalism" may or may not be held to be notice to the bailor. Whether the notice will be effective will depend on the size of the sign, its location, and any other circumstances affecting the likelihood of its being noticed by Joe's patrons. The same holds true with limitations placed on the back of identification receipts (stubs) for parked cars, checked coats, or stored bailed goods. Most courts require additional notice, since the bailor rarely reads the receipt and usually treats it merely as an identification number to be used when reclaiming the bailed goods.

Even if the bailor has received notice, certain types of disclaimers of liability are considered to be against public policy and therefore illegal. Clauses, called *exculpatory clauses,* that limit a person's liability for his or her own wrongful acts are carefully scrutinized by the courts, and in bailments they are quite often held to be illegal. The classic illustration of an exculpatory clause is found on parking receipts: "We assume no risk for damage to or loss of automobile or its contents regardless of cause. It is agreed that the vehicle owner assumes all such risks." Even though the language may vary, if the bailee attempts to exclude liability for the bailee's own negligence, the result is the same—the clause is unenforceable as being against public policy. This is especially true in the case of bailees providing quasi-public services.

Duties of the Bailee

The bailee has two basic responsibilities: (1) to take proper care of the property and (2) to surrender or dispose of the property at the end of the bailment. The bailee's duties are based on a mixture of tort law and contract law. The duty of care involves the standards and principles of tort law discussed previously and in Chapter 4. A bailee's failure to exercise appropriate care in handling the bailor's property results in tort liability. The duty to relinquish the property in a mutual-benefit bailment at the end of the bailment is grounded in contract law principles. Failure to return the property is a breach of contract, and, with one exception, the bailee is liable for damages. The exception exists when the obligation is excused because the goods or chattel have been destroyed, lost, or stolen through no fault of the bailee (or claimed by a third party with a superior claim).

DUTY OF CARE   As previously discussed, bailees must exercise proper care over the property in their possession to prevent its loss or damage. The three types of bailments demand different degrees of care (although the trend is toward enforcement of reasonable standards of care). When a bailment exists for the sole benefit of the bailee, great care, or the highest level of care, is required. When the bailment exists for the mutual benefit of the bailor and the bailee, reasonable care is the standard. When the bailment exists for the sole benefit of the bailor, slight care, or something less than ordinary or reasonable care, is expected.

DUTY TO RETURN BAILED PROPERTY   At the end of the bailment, the bailee normally must relinquish the identical undamaged property (unless it is fungible) to either the bailor or someone the bailor designates or must otherwise dispose of it

as directed. This is usually a *contractual* duty arising from the bailment agreement (contract). Failure to give up possession at the time the bailment ends is breach of a contract term and could constitute the tort of conversion.

DELIVERY OF GOODS TO THE WRONG PERSON   A bailee may be liable if the goods being held or delivered are given to the wrong person. Hence, a bailee must be satisfied that the person to whom the goods are being delivered is the actual owner or has authority from the owner to take possession of the goods. Should the bailee deliver in error, particularly when the bailee knows that the goods are stolen or that there is another claim of ownership against the goods, then the bailee may be liable for conversion or mis-delivery.

The following case presents an example of this principle.

Case 51.2
**CAPEZZARO v.
WINFREY**

Superior Court of New Jersey,
1977.
153 N.J.Super. 267, 379 A.2d
493.

BACKGROUND AND FACTS   *The plaintiff was a robbery victim who sued the city and its police officers after the police had arrested a person who the plaintiff claimed had stolen money. During their apprehension of the suspect, the police removed the money from the suspect's clothing, and the police department kept it. When the suspect was released from custody, she went to the police station and demanded return of the money. The police officers gave it to her. The robbery victim claimed to be the rightful owner of the money and sued the city for negligence because police officers in the city's employ had released the money. The jury found for the robbery victim, and the police officers and the city appealed this judgment.*

PER CURIAM.
*   *   *   *

It has been said that a constructive bailment or a bailment by operation of law may be created when a person comes into possession of personal property of another, receives nothing from the owner of the property, and has no right to recover from the owner for what he does in caring for the property. Such person is ordinarily considered to be a gratuitous bailee, liable only to the bailor for bad faith or gross negligence.

Where possession has been acquired accidentally, fortuitously, through mistake or by an agreement for some other purposes since terminated, the possessor, "upon principles of justice," should keep it safely and restore or deliver it to its owner. Under such circumstances, the courts have considered the possessions *quasi-contracts* [implied contracts created by law] of bailment or constructive and involuntary bailments.
*   *   *   *

Ordinarily, a person who has possession of property may be presumed by another to be the rightful owner thereof in the absence of any knowledge to the contrary. However, here the police were fully aware of plaintiff's adverse claim, but notwithstanding such knowledge and without notice to plaintiff turned the money over to Winfrey.
*   *   *   *

Defendants *   *   * contend that when the indictment was dismissed any claim by plaintiff lost its validity and they were obligated to return the monies in question to Winfrey as bailor. We disagree. A bailee with knowledge of an adverse claim makes delivery to the bailor at his peril, and only if he is ignorant of such a claim will he be protected against a subsequent claim by the rightful owner. The position of a bailee in such situation and his possible courses of action are set forth in 9 *Williston on Contracts* (3 ed. 1967), § 1036 at 897–898:

* * * If a bailee knows goods are stolen, or that the bailor is acting adversely to a clearly valid right, even though the true owner has as yet made no demand for them, the bailee will be liable to him for conversion if delivery is made to the bailor. In case, therefore, that the bailee knows or has been notified of an adverse claim, he will deliver to the bailor at his peril. The bailee must, for his own protection, choose one of two courses:

First, he may satisfy himself of the validity of one of the two claims and obtain authority from the owner of the claim to refuse delivery to all other claimants. In such a case he may plead at law to an action by any but the rightful owner the title of the latter, or the right of one having a superior right to immediate possession. If this title or right can be proved, a perfect defense is established. Second, if no actual adverse claim has been made, but the bailee knows of the existence of adverse right, or if the bailee cannot determine which of two claimants has the better title, and neither claimant will give a bond indemnifying the bailee from all damage caused by delivery to him, the only course open to the bailee is to file a bill of interpleader against the several possible owners, praying a temporary injunction against actions against himself until the true ownership of the goods is determined. And it should be added that a bailee who redelivers the goods to the bailor, or upon his order, in ignorance of his lack of title, is fully protected against subsequent claims of the rightful owner.

The police returned the money to Winfrey after being informed by the warden of the county jail that the indictments had been dismissed. They did not contact plaintiff before doing so, even though they were on notice of his adverse claim. The dismissal of the indictment for the reasons here present did not vitiate [weaken] plaintiff's adverse claim to the money. Inherent in the jury's verdict is a finding that defendants were negligent in releasing the money without a determination of the validity of the adverse claim. Such finding and the verdict are amply supported by the evidence.

The judgment of the trial court was affirmed. The police officers and the city were liable to the robbery victim.

DECISION AND REMEDY

PRESUMPTION OF NEGLIGENCE Sometimes the duty to return and the duty of care are combined to determine bailee liability. At the end of the bailment, a bailee has the duty to return the bailor's property in the condition in which it was received (allowing for ordinary wear and aging). In some cases, the bailor can sue the bailee in tort for damage to or loss of goods on the theory of *negligence* or *conversion*. But often it is not possible for the bailor to discover and prove what specific acts of negligence or conversion committed by the bailee caused damage or loss to the property.[4] Thus,

the law of bailments recognizes a rule whereby a bailor's proof that damage or loss to the property has occurred will, in and of itself, raise a *presumption* that the bailee is guilty of negligence or conversion. Once this is shown, the bailee must prove that he or she was not at fault. A bailee who is able to *rebut* (contradict) the presumption is not liable to the bailor. When damage to goods is of the type that normally results only from someone's negligence, and when the bailee had full control of the goods, it is more likely than not that the damage was caused by the bailee's negligence. Therefore, the bailee's negligence is presumed.

Determining whether a bailee exercised an appropriate degree of care is usually a question of fact. This means that the trier of fact (a judge or

---

4. The basic formula for finding negligence requires proof that (1) a duty exists, (2) a breach of that duty occurred, and (3) the breach is the proximate cause of damage or loss.

a jury) weights the facts of a particular situation and concludes that the bailee did or did not exercise the requisite degree of care at the time the loss or damage occurred. The failure to exercise appropriate care is negligence, and the bailee is liable for the loss or damage in tort.

The following case illustrates that once a bailment is created, failure of the bailee to return the bailed property to the bailor upon demand results in a presumption of conversion (or negligence).

Case 51.3
MUELLER v. SOFFER
Appellate Court of Illinois, Fifth District, 1987.
160 Ill.App.3d 699, 112 Ill.Dec. 589, 513 N.E.2d 1198.

BACKGROUND AND FACTS *Marvin Mueller, the president of Vin-Mar Supply, Inc., purchased approximately 1,150 railroad luggage carts from the Missouri Pacific Railroad. Mueller made an oral contract with Larry Soffer to store the luggage carts in Soffer's warehouse. Subsequently, a fire destroyed the warehouse, and the carts were either destroyed or severely damaged. Without Mueller's consent, the damaged carts were removed in the clean-up operation as scrap metal. Mueller demanded that Soffer return all carts "in a salvage condition." When no carts were returned, Mueller filed suit, alleging that Soffer and the warehouse (the defendants) were negligent in the care they exercised over the bailed property. The trial court held that Mueller and Vin-Mar Supply (the plaintiffs) had established a prima facie case of bailment and that failure to return the bailed property upon demand raised a presumption of negligence. The court also concluded that the defendants had failed to rebut the presumption of negligence and held for the plaintiffs. The defendants appealed.*

KASSERMAN, Justice.
* * * *

On appeal defendants contend that plaintiffs failed to meet their burden of proving that defendants were negligent in failing to return the carts. Defendants assert that plaintiffs do not claim defendants' negligence caused the fire, that plaintiffs cannot therefore claim recovery for loss of the carts at their pre-fire value, and that the only issue is their alleged negligence in failing to return the carts in their post-fire condition. We disagree.

In order properly to plead the existence of and the right to recovery under a bailment theory, the following elements must be alleged: an agreement, express or implied, to create a bailment; delivery of the property in good condition; acceptance of the items bailed by the bailee; and nonreturn or redelivery of the property in a damaged condition. We conclude that the complaint herein, although inartfully drafted, satisfies these requirements. Defendants have admitted in their answer their duty as bailee to exercise ordinary care in regard to the storage and safekeeping of the carts, as alleged in the complaint. Furthermore, since proof of delivery and nonreturn of bailed goods gives rise to a presumption of negligence on the part of the bailees, we conclude that the complaint raises both the issue of defendants' negligence in allowing the fire to damage plaintiffs' carts and the issue of defendants' negligence in allowing the damaged carts to be removed from the premises without plaintiffs' authority.
* * * *

At trial, plaintiffs established an agreement between plaintiffs and defendants, the delivery of the carts to defendants' warehouse, and the nonreturn of the carts. Therefore, plaintiffs established a prima facie case and raised a presumption of defendants' negligence.
* * * *

We conclude that [the] evidence does not rebut the presumption of negligence. Defendants, as bailees, were under a duty to exercise reasonable care under the circumstances. In the case at bar, Edward Soffer testified that no effort was made to determine whether plaintiffs' property was salvageable, yet he authorized [the removal of] all the debris without seeking plaintiffs' authority or permission and without accounting to plaintiffs for the scrap value of the carts. We note that Powell received cash for some of the scrap from the site on September 20, and 21, 1984, *i.e.*, after Soffer received Mueller's demand letter. A bailee is not excused from failing to exercise ordinary care because the bailee would have been equally careless with his own property. Furthermore, in the face of the evidence presented by plaintiffs, defendants failed to present any evidence to rebut the presumption that the fire which resulted in a destruction of plaintiffs' property was a result of defendants' negligence.

The appellate court affirmed the trial court's findings that a bailment had been created, that the bailee had had a duty to exercise reasonable care over the bailed carts, and that failure to return the bailed property on demand had raised a presumption of negligence (that reasonable care had not been exercised). Since the defendants had failed to rebut this presumption, the defendants were liable for damages.

DECISION AND REMEDY

RIGHTS AND DUTIES OF A BAILOR

As explained below, a bailee's duties and a bailor's rights are complementary. A bailor's basic duty is to provide a bailee with property free from latent defects that could injure the bailee.

Rights of a Bailor

The bailor's rights are essentially a complement to the bailee's duties. A bailor has the right to expect the following:

1. The property will be protected with reasonable care while in the possession of the bailee.
2. The bailee will utilize the property as agreed in the bailment agreement (or not at all).
3. The property will be relinquished at the conclusion of the bailment according to directions given by the bailor.
4. The bailee will not convert (alter) the goods except as agreed.
5. The bailor will not be bound by any limitations on the bailee's liability unless such are known and are enforceable by law.
6. Repairs or service on the property will be completed without defective workmanship.

Duties of a Bailor

A bailor has a single, all-encompassing duty to provide the bailee with goods or chattels that are free from hidden defects that could cause injury to the bailee. This duty translates into two rules:

1. In a *mutual-benefit bailment*, the bailor must notify the bailee of all known defects and any hidden defects that the bailor knew of or could have discovered with reasonable diligence and proper inspection.
2. In a *bailment for the sole benefit of the bailee*, the bailor must notify the bailee of any known defects.

The bailor's duty to reveal defects is based on a negligence theory of tort law. A bailor who fails to give the appropriate notice is liable to the bailee and to any other person who might reasonably be expected to come into contact with the defective article.

To illustrate: Rentco (the bailor) leases four tractors to Hopkinson. Unknown to Rentco (but discoverable by reasonable inspection), the brake mechanism on one of the tractors is defective at the time the bailment is made. Hopkinson uses the defective tractor without knowledge of the brake problem and is injured along with two other field workers when the tractor rolls out of control. Rentco is liable on a negligence theory for injuries sustained by Hopkinson and the two others.

This is the analysis: Rentco has a mutual-benefit bailment and a *duty* to notify Hopkinson of the discoverable brake defect. Rentco's failure to notify is the *proximate cause* of injuries to farm workers who might be expected to use or have contact with the tractor. Therefore, Rentco is *liable* for the resulting injuries.

A bailor can also incur *warranty liability* based on contract law for injuries resulting from bailment of defective articles. Property leased by a bailor must be *fit for the intended purpose of the bailment.* The bailor's knowledge or ability to discover any defects is immaterial. Warranties of fitness arise by law in sales contracts and have been applied by judicial interpretation in the case of bailments "for hire." Article 2A of the UCC extends implied warranties of merchantability and fitness for a particular purpose to bailments [UCC 2A-212, 2A-213].

TERMINATION OF BAILMENT

Bailments for a specific term end when the stated period lapses. When no duration is specified, the bailment can be terminated at any time by the following events:

1. The mutual agreement of both parties.
2. A demand by either party.
3. The completion of the purpose of the bailment.
4. An act by the bailee that is inconsistent with the terms of the bailment.
5. The operation of law.

SPECIAL FEATURES OF SPECIFIC BAILMENTS

Most of this chapter has concerned itself with ordinary bailments, in which bailees have a duty, as regards property entrusted to them, to use ordinary care. Some bailment transactions warrant special consideration. These include bailments in which the bailee's duty of care is extraordinary— that is, his or her liability for loss or damage to the property is absolute—as is generally true in cases involving common carriers and innkeepers. Warehouse companies have the same duty of care as ordinary bailees; but like carriers, they are subject to extensive coverage of federal and state laws, including the UCC's Article 7.

Documents of Title and Article 7

Any commercial transaction may involve a shipment or storage of goods covered by a bill of lading, a warehouse receipt, or a delivery order. These documents of title are subject to Article 7 of the UCC.[5] To be a **document of title,** a document "must purport to be issued by or addressed to a bailee and purport to cover goods in the bailee's possession which are either identified or are fungible portions of an identified mass" [UCC 1-201(15), 7-102(1)(e); see also UCC 7-401].

A **bill of lading** is a document verifying the receipt of goods for shipment issued by a person engaged in the business of transporting or forwarding goods [UCC 1-201(6)]. A **warehouse receipt** is a receipt issued by a person engaged in the business of storing goods for hire [UCC 1-201(45); see also UCC 7-201, 7-202].[6] A **delivery order** is a written order to deliver goods directed to a warehouseman, carrier, or other person who in the ordinary course of business issues warehouse receipts or bills of lading [UCC 7-102(1)(d)].

Simply, a document of title is a receipt for goods in the charge of a bailee-carrier or a bailee-warehouseman and a contract for the shipment or storage of identified goods.

NEGOTIABILITY OF DOCUMENTS OF TITLE Negotiability is a concept that applies to documents of title when—as in situations involving commercial paper[7]—they contain the words "bearer" or "to the order of" [UCC 7-104(1)]. If a document of title is negotiable—that is, if it specifies that the goods are to be delivered to bearer or to the order of a named person—the following are also possible:

1. The possessor of the document of title is entitled to receive, hold, and dispose of the document and the goods it covers.
2. A good faith purchaser of the document may acquire greater rights to the document and the goods it covers than the transferor had or had the authority to convey (that is, a good faith purchaser

---

5. Of course, where applicable, federal law is paramount (see UCC 7-103). For example, the Federal Bills of Lading Act (49 U.S.C. Sections 81–124), enacted in 1916, applies to bills of lading issued by a common carrier for goods shipped in interstate or foreign commerce, and the United States Warehouse Act (7 U.S.C. Sections 241–243), enacted in 1916, applies to receipts covering agricultural products stored for interstate or foreign commerce.

6. UCC 7-102(h) defines the person engaged in the storing of goods for hire as a *warehouseman.*

7. Commercial paper is the subject of UCC Article 3, which is discussed in detail in Chapters 22 through 27.

may take free of the claims and defenses of prior parties).

If a document of title is nonnegotiable—that is, if it is not made payable to the order of any named person or to bearer—it may be transferred by assignment but not negotiation [UCC 7-104(2)].

In other words, documents of title constitute a class of commercial paper representing commodities in storage or transportation. Thus, for example, just as—under Article 3—the holder in due course of a negotiable promissory note cuts off prior ownership claims, so—under Article 7—the holder of a negotiable warehouse receipt who takes by *due negotiation* does the same.[8]

DUE NEGOTIATION   The concepts of Articles 3 and 7 are similar.[9] There are important distinctions between them, however. Article 7 relates to paper that purports to cover specific goods, but Article 3 paper does not cover or represent any particular money. Also, Article 7 refers to the negotiability process as **due negotiation.** Due negotiation requires not only that the purchaser of a document of title take it in good faith without notice of a defense against or claim to it and pay value, but also that he or she do so in the regular course of business or financing and not in the settlement or payment of a money obligation [UCC 7-501(4)]. In other words, even if all other requirements are met, transfer of a negotiable document of title to a nonbusinessperson is not due negotiation. In that case, the transferee acquires only those rights the transferor had or had the authority to convey [UCC 7-504].[10]

On due negotiation, however, a transferee can acquire greater rights in a document of title than the transferor had. The transferee obtains title to the document and to the goods, including rights to goods delivered to the bailee after the document

was issued, and takes free of all prior claims and defenses of which he or she had no notice. The document's issuer remains obligated to store or deliver the goods according to the document's terms [UCC 7-502]. Under this provision, business people can extend credit on documents of title without concern for adverse claims of third parties.

To prevent a thief or a finder of goods from defeating the rights of the true owner (by, for example, taking them to a warehouse and subsequently negotiating the warehouse receipt to a third party who would otherwise take free of the claims of others), the goods must be delivered to the issuer of the document of title by their owner or the owner's agent [UCC 7-503(1)]. Otherwise, the document does not represent title to the goods. Even if the document does not represent title, however, the bailee will not be liable if he or she acts in good faith and observes reasonable commercial standards in receiving and delivering the goods [UCC 7-404].

In other words, a carrier or warehouseman who receives goods from a thief or finder and delivers them according to that individual's instructions is not liable to the goods' true owner. The reason for this rule is that carriers and warehousemen are not links in the chain of title and do not represent the owner in transactions affecting title but simply furnish a service necessary to trade and commerce.

Common Carriers

Common carriers are publicly licensed to provide transportation services to the general public. They are distinguished from private carriers, which operate transportation facilities for a select clientele. A private carrier is not bound to provide service to every person or company making a request. The common carrier, however, must arrange carriage for all who apply, within certain limitations.[11]

The common-carrier contract of transportation creates a *mutual-benefit bailment*. But, unlike the

---

8. Compare UCC 3-305 and 7-502.

9. For example, a delivery order under Article 7 is analogous to a draft under Article 3. A draft is an order by a drawer to a drawee to pay money to a payee. A delivery order is an order by a bailor to a bailee to deliver goods to a deliveree.

10. And until the bailee is notified of the transfer, the transferee's rights may be defeated by certain creditors of the transferor; by a buyer from the transferor in the ordinary course of business, if the bailee has delivered the goods to the buyer; or by the bailee who has dealt with the transferor in good faith [UCC 7-504(2)].

11. A common carrier is not required to take any and all property anywhere in all instances. Public regulatory agencies, such as the Interstate Commerce Commission, govern commercial carriers, and carriers may be restricted to geographical areas. They may also be limited to carrying certain kinds of goods or to providing only special types of transportation equipment.

bailee in ordinary mutual-benefit bailments, the common carrier is held to a standard of care based on *strict liability*, rather than reasonable care, in protecting the bailed personal property. This means that the common carrier is absolutely liable, regardless of negligence, for all loss or damage to goods except loss or damage caused by one of the five common law exceptions:

1. An act of God.
2. An act of a public enemy.
3. An order of a public authority.
4. An act of the shipper.
5. The inherent nature of the goods.

UCC 7-309(1) provides that the UCC "does not repeal or change any law or rule of law which imposes liability on a common carrier for damages not caused by its negligence."

Common carriers are treated as if they were absolute insurers for the safe delivery of goods to the destination, but actually they are not. They cannot contract away this liability for damaged goods; but subject to government regulations, they are permitted to limit their dollar liability to an amount stated on the shipment contract.[12]

Except for the five exceptions given, the common carrier is liable for any damage to goods in shipment, even that caused by the willful acts of third persons or by sheer accident. Thus, a common-carrier trucking company moving cargo is liable for acts of vandalism, mechanical defects in refrigeration units, or a dam bursting, if any of these acts results in damage to the cargo. But damage caused by acts of God—an earthquake or lightning, for example—is the shipper's loss.

There are many interesting cases concerning what constitutes an "act of God." The following extract is from a case in which a common carrier learned that a flood was *not* necessarily enough of an "act of God" to excuse liability:

> The only acts of God that excuse common carriers from liability for loss or injury to goods in transit are those operations of the forces of nature that could not have been anticipated and provided against and that by their super human force unexpectedly injure or destroy goods in the custody or control of the carrier. Extreme weather conditions which operate to foil human obligations of duty are regarded as acts of God. However, every strong wind, snow-storm, or rainstorm cannot be termed an act of God merely because it is of unusual or more than average intensity. Ordinary, expectable, and gradual weather conditions are not regarded as acts of God even though they may have produced a disaster, because man had the opportunity to control their effects.[13]

SHIPPER'S LOSS The shipper bears any loss occurring through its own faulty or improper crating or packaging procedures. For example, if a bird dies because its crate was poorly ventilated, the shipper bears the loss, not the carrier.

In the following case, the United States Supreme Court deals with the question of whether a common carrier that has exercised reasonable care and has complied with the instructions of the shipper is nonetheless liable to the shipper for spoilage in transit of an interstate shipment of perishable commodities.

---

12. UCC 7-309(2). Federal laws and Interstate Commerce Commission regulations require common carriers to offer shippers the opportunity to obtain higher dollar limits for loss by paying a higher fee for the transport. For interstate rail transportation, the matter is settled by the Carmack Amendment to the Interstate Commerce Act [49 U.S.C. Section 20(11)], which is discussed in the case that follows.

---

13. Southern Pac. Co. v. Loden, 19 Ariz.App. 460, 508 P.2d 347 (1973).

Case 51.4
MISSOURI PACIFIC RAILWAY CO. v. ELMORE & STAHL
Supreme Court of the United States, 1964.
377 U.S. 134, 84 S.Ct. 1142, 12 L.Ed.2d 194.

BACKGROUND AND FACTS *Elmore & Stahl, a fruit shipper, contracted with the Missouri Pacific Railway Co. to ship melons from Rio Grande City, Texas, to Chicago. At trial, the jury was convinced that Missouri Pacific and its connecting carriers performed all the required transportation services without negligence. The jury also found that the evidence showed that the condition of the melons on arrival in Chicago was defective and that the condition was not due solely to an inherent defect in the melons. The trial judge ruled against the carrier, and the court of appeals affirmed, as did the Texas Supreme Court. The ground for affirmation was, basically, that Missouri Pacific* *did not show that the spoilage or decay was due entirely to the inherent nature of the goods—in other words, that the damage was caused solely by natural deterioration. The United States Supreme Court reviewed the case.*

STEWART, Justice

*   *   *   *

The Carmack Amendment of 1906, § 20(11) of the Interstate Commerce Act, makes carriers liable "for the full actual loss, damage, or injury *   *   * caused by" them to property they transport, and declares unlawful and void any contract, regulation, tariff, or other attempted means of limiting this liability. It is settled that this statute has two undisputed effects crucial to the issue in this case: First, the statute codifies the common-law rule that a carrier, though not an absolute insurer, is liable for damage to goods transported by it unless it can show that the damage was caused by "(a) the act of God; (b) the public enemy; (c) the act of the shipper himself; (d) public authority; (e) or the inherent vice or nature of the goods." *   *   * Second, the statute declares unlawful or void any "rule, regulation, or other limitation of any character whatsoever" purporting to limit this liability. *   *   * Accordingly, under federal law, in an action to recover from a carrier for damage to a shipment, the shipper establishes his prima facie case when he shows delivery in good condition, arrival in damaged condition, and the amount of damages. Thereupon, the burden of proof is upon the carrier to show both that it was free from negligence and that the damage to the cargo was due to one of the expected causes relieving the carrier of liability *   *   *.

The disposition of this case in the Texas courts was in accordance with these established principles. It is apparent that the jury were unable to determine the cause of the damage to the melons. "[T]he decay of the perishable cargo is not a cause; it is an effect. It may be the result of a number of causes, for some of which, such as the inherent defects of the cargo *   *   * the carrier is not liable." But the jury refused to find that the carrier had borne its burden of establishing that the damaged condition of the melons was due solely to "inherent vice," as defined in the instruction of the trial judge—including "the inherent nature of the commodity which will cause it to deteriorate with a lapse of time." The petitioner [Missouri Pac. Ry. Co.] does not challenge the accuracy of the trial judge's instruction or the jury's finding. Its position is simply that if goods are perishable, and the nature of the damage is spoilage, and the jury affirmatively find that the carrier was free from negligence and performed the transportation services as required by the shipper, then the law presumes that the cause of the spoilage was the natural tendency of perishables to deteriorate even though the damage might, in fact, have resulted from other causes, such as the acts of third parties, for which no exception from carrier liability is provided. Consequently, it is argued, the question of "inherent vice" should not have been submitted to the jury, since the carrier in such a case does not bear the affirmative burden of establishing that the damage was caused by the inherent vice exception of the common law.

*   *   *   *

Finally, all else failing, it is argued that as a matter of public policy, the burden ought not to be placed upon the carrier to explain the cause of spoilage, because where perishables are involved, the shipper is peculiarly knowledgeable about the commodity's condition at and prior to the time of shipment, and is therefore in the best position to explain the cause of the damage. Since this argument amounts to a suggestion that we now carve out an exception to an unquestioned rule of long standing upon which both shippers and carriers rely, and which is reflected in the freight rates set by the carrier, the petitioner must sustain a heavy burden of persuasion. The general rule of carrier liability is based upon the sound premise that the carrier has peculiarly within its knowledge "[a]ll the facts and circumstances upon which [it] may rely to relieve [it] of [its] duty. *   *   * In consequence, the law casts upon [it] the burden of the loss which [it] cannot explain or, explaining, bring within the exceptional case in which [it] is relieved from liability." We are not persuaded that the carrier lacks adequate means to inform itself of the condition of goods at the time it receives them from the shipper, and it cannot be doubted that while the carrier has possession, it is the only one in a position to acquire the knowledge of what actually damaged a shipment entrusted to its care.

DECISION AND REMEDY

The Court upheld the judgment of the Texas Supreme Court. Even if a common carrier exercises reasonable care, it is liable for spoilage in transit unless it can prove that the cause of the spoilage was the natural tendency of the commodities to deteriorate.

CONNECTING CARRIERS A bill of lading that specifies one or more connecting carriers is called a *through bill of lading*. When connecting carriers are involved in transporting goods under a through bill of lading, the shipper can recover from the original carrier or any connecting carrier [UCC 7-302]. Normally, the *last* carrier is presumed to have received the goods in good condition.

Warehouse Companies

Warehousing is the business of providing storage of property for compensation. Like ordinary bailees, warehouse companies are liable for loss or damage to property and possession resulting from *negligence*. UCC 7-204(1) provides that a warehouseman must "exercise such care * * * as a reasonably careful [person] would exercise under like circumstances but unless otherwise agreed he [or she] is not liable for damages which could not have been avoided by the exercise of such care." Under UCC 7-204(2), a warehouse company can limit the dollar amount of liability, but the bailor must be given the option of paying an increased storage rate for an increase in the liability limit.

Innkeepers

At common law, innkeepers, hotel owners, and similar operators were held to the same strict liability as common carriers with respect to property brought into the rooms by guests. Today, only those who provide lodging to the public for compensation as a *regular* business are covered under this rule of strict liability. Moreover, the rule applies only to those who are *guests*, as opposed to *lodgers*. A lodger is a permanent resident of the hotel or inn, whereas a guest is a traveler.

STATUTORY CHANGES In most states, innkeepers can avoid strict liability for loss of guests' valuables and money by providing a safe in which to keep them. Each guest must be clearly notified of the availability of such a safe. For articles that are not kept in the safe or articles of such a nature that they are not normally kept in a safe, statutes will often limit innkeepers' liability.

Consider an example. Jackson stays for a night at Hideaway Hotel. When he returns from eating breakfast in the hotel restaurant, he discovers that the people in the room next door have forced the lock on the door between the two rooms and stolen his suitcase—which, of course, he could not put in the hotel safe. Jackson claims that the hotel is liable for his loss. The hotel denies liability because of the lack of negligence on its part. At common law, innkeepers are actually insurers of the property of their guests, and so the hotel will be liable.

Today, however, state statutes limit the strict liability imposed by the common law. These statutes vary from state to state. In many states, the monetary damages for which the innkeeper is liable are limited in amount. Indeed, these statutes may even provide that the innkeeper has no liability in the absence of negligence. Many statutes require these limitations to be posted or the guest to be notified. The posting (notice) is frequently found on the door of each room in the motel or hotel.

Normally, the innkeeper assumes no responsibility for the safety of a guest's automobile, because the guest usually retains possession and control. If, on the other hand, the innkeeper provides parking facilities and the guest's car is entrusted to the innkeeper or to an employee, the innkeeper will be liable under the rules that pertain to parking lot bailees (ordinary bailments).

CONCEPT SUMMARY: Rights and Duties of a Bailee

BAILEE	BASIC RULES
Rights	1. A bailee has the right to be compensated or reimbursed for keeping bailed property. This right is based in contract or quasi-contract.
	2. Unpaid compensation or reimbursement entitles the bailee to a lien (usually possessory) on the bailed property and the right of foreclosure.
	3. A bailee has the right to limit his or her liability. An ordinary bailee can limit type of risk or monetary amount or both, provided proper notice is given and the limitation is not against public policy. In special bailments, limitations on types of risk are usually not allowed, but limitations on the monetary amount at risk are permitted by regulation.
	4. The right of possession allows actions against third persons who damage or convert the bailed property and allows actions against the bailor for wrongful breach of the bailment.
	5. The right to an insurable interest in the bailed property allows the bailee to insure and recover under the insurance policy for loss or damage to the property.
Duties	1. A bailee must exercise reasonable care over property entrusted to him or her. A common carrier (special bailee) is held to a standard of care based on *strict liability* unless the bailed property is lost or destroyed due to: (a) an act of God, (b) an act of a public enemy, (c) an act of a governmental authority, (d) an act of a shipper, or (e) the inherent nature of the goods.
	2. Bailed goods in a bailee's possession must be returned to the bailor or disposed of according to bailor's directions. Failure of return gives rise to a presumption of negligence.
	3. A bailee cannot use or profit from bailed goods except by agreement or in situations in which the use is implied to further the bailment purpose.

QUESTIONS AND CASE PROBLEMS

1. Curtis is an executive on a business trip to the West Coast. He has driven his car on this trip and checks into the Hotel Ritz. The hotel has a guarded underground parking lot. Curtis gives his car keys to the parking lot attendant but fails to notify the attendant that his wife's $10,000 fur coat is in a box in the trunk. The next day, upon checking out, he discovers that his car has been stolen. Curtis wants to hold the hotel liable for both the car and the coat. Discuss the probable success of his claim.

2. Discuss the standard of care required from the bailee for the bailed property in the following situations, and determine whether the bailee breached that duty:

(a) Adam borrows Tom's lawn mower because his own lawn mower needs repair. Adam mows his front yard. In order to mow the back yard, he needs to move some hoses and lawn furniture. He leaves the mower in front of his house while doing so. When he returns to the front, he discovers the mower has been stolen.

b) Mary owns a valuable speedboat. She is going on vacation and asks her neighbor, Regina, to store the boat in one stall of Regina's double garage. Regina consents, and the boat is moved into the garage. Regina, in need of some grocery items for dinner, drives to the store. In doing so, she leaves the garage door open, as is her custom. While she is at the store, the speedboat is stolen.

3. Lee owns and operates a service station. Walter's car needs some minor repairs. Walter takes his car to Lee's station. Lee tells Walter that he will be unable to do the work until the next day and that Walter can either bring the car back at that time or leave it overnight. Walter leaves the car with Lee. The next afternoon Walter comes to pick up his car. Lee presents Walter with a bill for $220 and refuses to return the car until he is paid. Upon inspecting the car, Walter discovers that the mileage indicator shows 150 more miles on the car than when he brought it in. Lee claims he was legally allowed to let one of his employees road-test the car by taking it to his home on the preceding evening and driving it. Discuss Walter's and Lee's legal rights under these circumstances.

4. Paul borrows from his neighbor, Max, a gasoline-driven lawn edger. Max has not used the lawn edger for two years. Paul is not familiar with using a lawn edger, since he has never owned one. Max previously used this edger often, and if he had made a reasonable inspection, he would have discovered that the blade was loose. Paul is injured when the blade becomes detached while he is edging his yard.

    (a) Can Paul hold Max liable for his injuries?

    (b) Would your answer be any different if Paul had rented the edger from Max and paid a fee? Explain.

5. Franklin Washer, Inc., delivered to the Western Central Railroad one hundred crated washing machines to be shipped to Rocky High Appliance Store in Denver, Colorado. Western Central received the goods on Thursday and stored them in its warehouse pending loading into boxcars the next day. On the Western Central shipping invoice was a clause printed in big, bold type that excluded the carrier from liability resulting from loss of goods under control of the carrier because of acts of vandalism, fire, or theft. The clause also limited liability to $500 per shipment unless a higher evaluation was declared and a fee paid. That evening a riot broke out. Some of the one hundred crated washing machines were stolen, some were damaged by the rioters, and some were destroyed by fire. Franklin wants to hold the carrier liable for the entire value of the one hundred machines. Western claims, first, that it has no liability by virtue of the contractual limitation against liability for loss by fire, theft, or vandalism; and second, that if it were liable, its damage cost responsibility would be only $500. Discuss the validity of Western's claims.

6. Procter & Gamble was a distributor of soybean oils. Its buyer, Allied Crude Vegetable Oil Refining Corp., persuaded Procter & Gamble to engage in a practice known as field warehousing. Under this arrangement, Procter & Gamble shipped oil to Field Warehousing Corp., which stored the oil in its tanks. In exchange for the oil, Field Warehousing gave Procter & Gamble warehousing receipts. This allowed Procter & Gamble to sell the oil to Allied by merely selling the receipts (which were evidence of title to the oil). Thus, Procter & Gamble did not have to ship any of the oil in order to make a sale. About six months after it began storing oil at Field Warehousing, Procter & Gamble sold a large number of its warehouse receipts to Allied, and it was discovered that the oil was missing. Who was liable for the missing oil? [Procter & Gamble Distributing Co. v. Lawrence American Field Warehousing Corp., 16 N.Y.2d 344, 213 N.E.2d 873, 266 N.Y.S.2d 785 (1965)]

7. Buchanan entered into an agreement with Byrd and Barksdale by which Buchanan would pay $40 a month for Byrd and Barksdale to feed and keep Buchanan's horse on their five-acre tract in Irving, Texas. One night, the horses were in one of the pastures rather than in their stalls. All of them escaped around midnight, apparently through an open gate. Buchanan's horse was killed by a train a mile away. Buchanan sued for damages. What was the result? [Buchanan v. Byrd, 519 S.W.2d 841 (Texas 1975)]

8. Rena, in her will, bequeathed her jewelry to her daughter Linda. Upon Rena's death, Edward, Rena's husband and Linda's stepfather, gave Linda one ring, a gift to Rena from a prior husband, but put the other jewelry in his home in a dresser drawer. While Edward was in the hospital with a heart ailment, the jewelry was stolen from the dresser drawer. Edward never told Linda, nor did he file an insurance claim or a police report. When Linda found out, she sued her stepfather for negligence for failure to exercise reasonable care over her bailed property. What was the result? [Estate of Murrell, 454 So.2d 437 (Miss. 1984)]

9. The plaintiff (Augustine) attended a dental seminar held at a Marriott Hotel. The sponsor of the seminar had rented the banquet room in which the seminar was held and had requested the hotel to place a movable coat rack outside the room, in the public lobby. Augustine placed his cashmere coat on the rack before entering the seminar. When he tried to find the coat at the noon recess, however, he noted that the rack had been moved a distance down the lobby and around a corner, near an exit. To his dismay, his coat was missing. Claiming the hotel was liable for the loss, Augustine brought this action. Discuss whether the hotel is a bailee of the coat and thus liable to its owner for the loss. [Augustine v. Marriott Hotel, 132 Misc.2d 180, 503 N.Y.S.2d 498 (Town Ct. N.Y. 1986)]

10.   Robert Freeman owned a broken Bulova watch. Its band was encrusted with gold nuggets and contained two jade stones. He took the watch to John Garcia's jewelry store for repairs. Garcia did not have the necessary equipment to make all the repairs, so he sent the watch to Douglas Viers Base Watch Repair Lab. While it was at Viers's shop, the watch, along with several others, was stolen. Viers did not have insurance, nor did he have any burglar alarm or other safeguards on the premises. Freeman, claiming the watch had been worth $25,000, sued both Garcia and Viers for the value of the watch. Discuss whether Garcia or Viers or both are liable for the loss of the watch. [Freeman v. Garcia, 495 So.2d 351 (La.App. 1986)]

11. Obadiah and Rose Simmons, the plaintiffs, purchased a bedroom suite on layaway from Max's Discount Furniture, a store owned by Max Yelverton, the defendant. As part of the bargain, Max's salesperson agreed that after the purchase price had been paid, Max would continue to hold the furniture in storage until the Simmonses wanted to claim it or until Max needed the warehouse space. Two years after the final payment had been made, the Simmonses attempted to pick up the furniture, only to discover that Max had gone out of business and that the furniture was nowhere to be found. Discuss Yelverton's liability, assuming that there is no evidence that the loss of the furniture was due to lack of care on the part of Max's

Discount Furniture. [Simmons v. Yelverton, 513 So.2d 504 (La.App. 1987)]

12. K-2 Petroleum, Inc. (K-2), and El Dorado Oil and Gas, Inc. (El Dorado), were engaged in a joint-venture drilling project. They operated under an agreement whereby El Dorado provided a working electric generator for K-2's working interest in the well. The generator became non-functional, and K-2 sought to have El Dorado replace or repair it. El Dorado refused. K-2 subsequently contracted with Stewart and Stevenson Services, Inc. (S & S), for the repair of the generator. Shortly after receiving the generator for repair, S & S was notified by El Dorado that it was the true owner of the generator. El Dorado identified it by model and serial number and demanded its return upon completion of repairs. Since S & S knew of the common practice among oil field companies of switching, loaning, and borrowing equipment among themselves, it allowed El Dorado to take possession of the generator after El Dorado had paid for the repair. Before K-2 received any notice of S & S's delivery to El Dorado, K-2 and El Dorado terminated their joint venture and agreed that all salvageable equipment and supplies from the project were the property of K-2. K-2 later filed suit against S & S, claiming that S & S's failure to return the generator to K-2 and its delivery of the generator to El Dorado constituted the tort of conversion. Discuss K-2's claim. [Stewart & Stevenson Services, Inc. v. Kratochvil, 737 S.W.2d 65 (Tex.App.–San Antonio 1987)]

Chapter 52

Nature and Ownership of Real Property

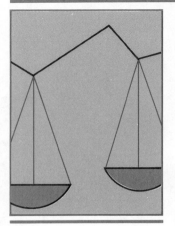

From earliest times, property has provided a means for survival. Primitive peoples lived off the fruits of the land, eating the vegetation and wildlife. Later, as the wildlife was domesticated and the vegetation cultivated, property provided pasturage and farmland. In the twelfth and thirteenth centuries, the power of feudal lords was exemplified by the amount of land that they held; the more land they held, the more powerful they were. After the age of feudalism passed, property continued to be an indicator of family wealth and social position.

NATURE OF REAL PROPERTY

Real property consists of land and the buildings, plants, and trees that it contains. Whereas personal property is movable, real property—also called real estate or realty—is immovable. Real property usually means land, but it also includes subsurface and air rights, plant life and vegetation, and fixtures.

Land

Land includes the soil on the surface of the earth and the natural products or artificial structures that are attached to it. It further includes all the waters contained on or under its surface and the air space above it (subject, of course, to the use of aviators). In other words, absent a contrary statute or case law, a landowner has the right to everything existing permanently below the surface of his or her property to the center of the earth and above it to infinity.

Subsurface and Air Rights

The owner of real property has relatively exclusive rights to the air space above the land as well as the soil and minerals underneath it. Until fifty years ago, the right to use air space was not too significant, but today, commercial airlines and high-rise office buildings and apartments use the air space regularly. Early cases involving air rights dealt with matters such as whether a telephone wire could be run across a person's property when the wire did not touch any of the property[1] and whether a bullet shot over the person's land constituted trespass.[2]

Today, cases involving air rights present questions such as the right of commercial and private planes to fly over property and the right of individuals and governments to seed clouds and produce artificial rain. Flights over private land do not normally violate the property owners' rights unless the flights are low and frequent, causing a direct interference with the enjoyment and use of the land.[3]

Significant limitations on either air rights or subsurface rights normally have to be indicated on the deed transferring title at the time of purchase. When no such encumbrances are noted, a purchaser can expect to have an unfettered right to possession of the property. If any preexisting covenant unknown to the purchaser interferes with these rights, the purchaser can sue the seller for breach of warranty of title. However, most state statutes limit the time period in which the purchaser can sue. An alternative lawsuit is for breach of the covenant of quiet enjoyment. There is also a limit on the time for bringing such a suit, but it does not begin to run until after the discovery of the breach.

SEPARATION OF SURFACE AND SUBSURFACE RIGHTS   Ownership of the surface of land can be separated from ownership of its subsurface. Subsurface rights can be extremely valuable when beneath the surface are, for instance, minerals, oil, or natural gas. But a subsurface owner's rights would be of little value if he or she could not use the surface to exercise those rights. Hence, a subsurface owner will have an easement to, for example, find and remove minerals. (An **easement**

is a right of use over the property of another. Easements are discussed later in this chapter.)

Of course, conflicts may arise between surface and subsurface owners when attempts are made to excavate below the surface. At common law, a landowner has the right to have the land supported in its natural condition by the owners of the interests under the surface. If the owners of the subsurface rights excavate, they are absolutely liable if their excavation causes the surface to subside, even if the excavation is done without negligence.

If the excavation causes the collapse of or damage to structures on the land, the excavators are not liable at common law unless the landowner shows that the excavation would have caused the land in its natural state to have collapsed. If the land would not have collapsed in its natural state, the excavator is liable for the damage if the excavation was done negligently.

Today, many states have statutes that extend excavators' liability to include damage to structures on the property. Typically, these statutes provide exact guidelines as to the support requirements for excavations of various depths.

Plant Life and Vegetation

Plant life, both natural and cultivated, is also considered to be real property. In many instances, the natural vegetation, such as trees, adds greatly to the value of the realty. When a parcel of land is sold and the land has growing crops on it, the sale includes the crops, unless otherwise specified in the sales contract. When crops are sold by themselves, however, they are considered to be personal property or goods. Consequently, the sale of crops is a sale of goods, and it is governed by the Uniform Commercial Code rather than by real property law ([UCC 2-107(2)].

Fixtures

Certain personal property can become so closely associated with the real property to which it is attached that the law views it as real property. Such property is known as a **fixture**—a thing affixed to realty. A thing is *affixed* to realty when it is attached to it by roots, embedded in it, or permanently attached by means of cement, plaster, bolts, nails, or screws. The fixture can be physi-

---

1. Butler v. Frontier Telephone Co., 186 N.Y. 486, 79 N.E. 716 (1906). Stringing a wire across someone's property violates the air rights of that person. Leaning walls, buildings, projecting eave spouts and roofs also violate the air rights of the property owner.

2. Herrin v. Sutherland, 74 Mont. 587, 241 P. 328 (1925). Shooting over a person's land constitutes trespass.

3. United States v. Causby, 328 U.S. 256, 66 S.Ct. 1062, 90 L.Ed. 1206 (1946).

cally attached to real property, be attached to another fixture, or even be without any actual physical attachment to the land, as long as the owner *intends* the property to be a fixture.

Fixtures are included in the sale of land if the sales contract does not provide otherwise. The sale of a house includes the land and the house and garage on it, as well as the cabinets, plumbing, and windows. Since these are permanently affixed to the property, they are considered to be a part of it. Unless otherwise agreed, however, the curtains and throw rugs are not included. Items such as drapes and window-unit air conditioners are difficult to classify. Thus, a contract for the sale of a house or commercial realty should indicate which items of this sort are included in the sale.

In order to determine whether or not a certain item is a fixture, the *intention* of the party who placed the property must be examined. If the facts indicate that the person intended the item to be a fixture, then it will be a fixture.

When the intent of the party who placed the fixture on the realty is in dispute, the courts usu-

ally determine the intent based on either or both of the following factors:

1. If the property attached cannot be removed without causing substantial damage to the remaining realty, it is usually deemed a fixture.
2. If the property attached is so adapted to the rest of the realty as to become a part thereof, it is usually deemed a fixture.

Certain items can only be attached to property permanently; such items are fixtures. It is assumed that the owner intended them to be fixtures, since they had to be permanently attached to the property. A tile floor, cabinets, and carpeting are examples. Also, when an item of property is custom-made for installation on real property, such as storm windows, the property is usually classified as a fixture. Again, it is assumed that the owner intended the item of property to become part of the real property.

The following case illustrates a court's interpretation of whether certain items are considered fixtures.

Case 52.1
PAUL v. FIRST NATIONAL BANK OF CINCINNATI
Common Pleas Court of Ohio, Hamilton County, 1976.
52 Ohio Misc. 77, 369 N.E.2d 488.

BACKGROUND AND FACTS *The plaintiff, Paul, purchased an elegant residence known as Long Acres from the defendant bank, First National Bank of Cincinnati, the executor of the estate of Augustine Long. When possession was delivered to the plaintiff, he found items missing from the property. Long's will left to his children "all household furnishings, appliances, decoration, and equipment." The plaintiff claimed that the children had wrongfully removed and converted certain fixtures that should have remained with the property. The trial court held for the plaintiff, and the defendant appealed.*

BLACK, Judge.
*   *   *   *

The converted items must be considered in two groups, as follows:
(1) 4 Handmade lighting fixtures around swimming pool
    Lighting fixture in living quarters of apartment over stable
    2 Lighting fixtures removed from chapel
    3 Metal cranes
    4 Garden statues.
(2) Ornamental housing over well
    Mercury statue
    Walnut organ bench.

In the court's judgment, group (1) are legally classified as "fixtures," and group (2) are "appurtenances" [articles adapted for use to the property to which they are connected], under the intent and meaning of the purchase contract. This conclusion is based on three considerations: the law of fixtures, the intent and meaning of the purchase contract, and the intent and meaning of the testamentary gift to the children.
*   *   *   *

In *Masheter v. Boehm* the Supreme Court designated, in paragraph two of the syllabus, six "facts" to be considered in determining whether an item is a fixture:

(1) The nature of the property;

(2) The manner in which the property is annexed to the realty;

(3) The purpose for which the annexation is made;

(4) The intention of the annexing party to make the property a part of the realty;

(5) The degree of difficulty and extent of any loss involved in removing the property from the realty; and

(6) The damage to the severed property which such removal would cause.

* * * *

Using the Supreme Court's considerations, the light "fixtures" (there is no other available word) from the swimming pool, the stable apartment and the chapel are clearly fixtures in contemplation of law. They are of a type universally recognized as fixtures. This is true even though the pool "fixtures" were hung on brackets and could be unplugged and simply lifted off the brackets. But they were designed and produced solely and only for the swimming pool, from the same design as was used for the light fixture in the porte cochere (which was not removed). Further, the poles from which they were taken are barren and incomplete without them.

The three metal cranes and the four garden statues also meet five of the six criteria, in the judgment of the court. The "nature" of these items is that they were a part of the total elegance of Long Acres. They are not the type of fixture which would be commonly found on other lawns or in other gardens in Hamilton County, but they are an integral part of this sumptuous country estate. The cranes were "annexed" by being bolted or screwed into concrete foundations in a manner similar to the annexation of the marble table in the Great Hall, an item clearly admitted by all defendants to be a fixture passing with the real estate. The 4 garden statues (busts?) were not simply placed on top of their columns, but were held in place by 6-inch pipe protruding from the columns into the bases of the statues. The purpose of fixing these into position was to ensure their presence and preservation as part and parcel of the landscape and approach to Long Acres. These cranes and statues were not items moved about at the whim of the owner or according to the seasons: they were permanent implacements, intended to be part of the continuing visual effect of the estate. * * *

Group (2), being the ornamental well housing, the Mercury statue and the organ bench, were not attached in a permanent way. However, interpreting the contract from its four corners, in the light of all the facts and circumstances in evidence, the Court concludes that these items were "appurtenances" to the real estate, both in contemplation of law and in interpretation of this word as used in the purchase contract.

The word "appurtenance" means more than rights of way or other incorporeal rights: it includes an article adapted to the use of the property to which it is connected and which is intended to be a permanent accession to the freehold.

All three items in group (2) form a part of the character of Long Acres and enhance the style of its elegance. They are appurtenant to Long Acres in the sense that they are necessarily connected with the use and enjoyment of this country estate. They are incidental to the total value of this estate. The source of that value is not only the grand design but also all of the details whereby that design is executed: the location of the house on the property, the sweep of the driveway as it approaches the porte cochere, the spread-out location of the barns and other outbuildings, the majesty of the formal gardens, the spaciousness of the lawns on every side, and all the details of the exterior and interior of the mansion itself.

* * * *

The Mercury statue is pictured in two photographs included in the appraisal of Long Acres which was considered by plaintiff before purchase. It may have been moved from the pedestal from time to time by the Long family, and it was not a "sun dial," despite this label in the appraisal. But interpreting the contract in the light of all facts and circumstances in evidence, the Court concludes that these items were appurtenances passing with the real estate.

* * * *

However, the Long children plainly had no right to cut down and remove light fixtures, or to remove and refuse to return the other items comprising group (1). The status of these items is not and was not in doubt, in the judgment of this Court, and the taking was accomplished with knowledge (both actual and constructive) of the legal status of the items, with purpose to deprive the purchaser of them permanently, without a reasonable or lawful excuse, and to the purchaser's injury.

* * * *

The conclusion of the court is that with respect to the conversion of property (Count 1), damages shall be the fair market value of replacement articles (determined as of the day of taking); the principle is to restore plaintiff fairly and reasonably to his position before the wrongful taking of these articles.

DECISION AND REMEDY *The trial court's judgment for the plaintiff was affirmed. The plaintiff recovered the fair market value of the fixtures and appurtenances improperly taken from the estate.*

OWNERSHIP INTERESTS IN REAL PROPERTY—ESTATES IN LAND

Ownership of property is an abstract concept that cannot exist independently of the legal system. No one can actually possess or *hold* a piece of land, the air above, the earth below, and all the water contained on it. The legal system therefore recognizes certain rights and duties that constitute the ownership interest in real property.[4]

Freehold Estates

Rights of ownership in real property, called **estates,** are classified according to their nature, interest, and extent. Two major categories of estates are freehold estates, which are held indefinitely, and less-than-freehold estates, which are held for a predetermined time. There are two kinds of freehold estates—estates in fee and life estates.

ESTATES IN FEE   There are two kinds of estates in fee: the fee simple absolute and the fee simple defeasible.

The Fee Simple Absolute   In a **fee simple absolute,** or fee simple, the owner has the greatest aggregation of rights, privileges, and power pos-

sible. The fee simple is limited absolutely to a person and his or her heirs and is assigned forever without limitation or condition. The rights that accompany a fee simple include the right to use the land for whatever purpose the owner sees fit, subject to laws that prevent the owner from unreasonably interfering with another person's land and subject to applicable zoning laws.

A fee simple is potentially infinite in duration and can be disposed of by deed or by will (by selling or giving away). When the owner of a fee simple dies without a will, the fee simple passes to the owner's legal heirs. The owner of a fee simple absolute also has the rights of *exclusive* possession and use.

At early common law, a fee simple absolute could be conveyed to A only by the statement that the conveyance was "to A and his heirs." The words "and his heirs" denoted the fee simple as infinite in duration and distinguished it from other estates such as the *fee simple defeasible* (which is defined below). In the United States today, these so-called words of limitation have been eliminated and a conveyance "to A" as well as "to A and his heirs" will convey a fee simple.

The Fee Simple Defeasible   The term **fee simple defeasible** encompasses a number of estates that *almost* constitute absolute ownership. The word *defeasible* refers to an owner's ability to lose ownership of property, whether the loss is voluntary or involuntary. For our purposes, these estates include the fee simple determinable (also referred to as the *fee simple subject to special limitation*), the fee simple subject to a condition subsequent,

---

4. The principles considered in these sections apply to instances of sole ownership and to instances of *concurrent ownership*—that is, situations in which persons share ownership of these rights simultaneously in a particular piece of property. Concurrent ownership is discussed in detail in Chapter 50.

and the fee simple subject to an executory interest. Generally, it may said these are fee simple estates that terminate or may terminate upon the occurrence of a specified condition or event.

A conveyance, for example, "to A and his heirs as long as the land is used for charitable purposes" creates a fee simple defeasible. In this type of conveyance, the original owner retains a *partial* ownership interest. As long as the specified condition occurs, A has full ownership rights, but if the specified condition does not occur and the land ceases to be used for charitable purposes, then the land reverts, or returns, to the original owner. If the original owner is not living at the time, the land passes to his or her heirs. In other words, once the condition fails, A is divested of rights regardless of whether the original owner to (or through) whom the land reverts is alive.

In this example, the interest that the original owner retains is called a *future interest,* since if it arises it will arise in the future. (But a so-called future interest is still a form of present property ownership that has a current market value.) The future interest that the owner holds is known as a *possibility of reverter.* In the conveyance "to A, but if the premises are ever used for the sale of alcoholic beverages then to B," the original owner has conveyed the entire interest. The owner has conveyed a fee simple defeasible to A and a future interest to B.

Consider another example. Simon deeds some land to XYZ Church "for as long as this land is used for church purposes and no longer." For two years, the land is used by the church for a playground for the children going to Sunday School. The church then sells the land to Smith, who intends to build an apartment building on it. As soon as Simon learns of the sale to Smith, he begins a court action to have himself declared the owner of the land. Since Simon deeded a fee simple determinable to XYZ Church, he will succeed in his court action. The instant the condition was broken, legal ownership automatically vested in Simon.

XYZ Church can even sell the land (or otherwise dispose of it) to Smith, and it would not revert to Simon if Smith will also use it for church purposes.

THE LIFE ESTATE A **life estate** is an estate that lasts for the life of some specified individual. A conveyance "to A for his life" creates a life estate. A less common type of life estate is created by the conveyance "to A for the life of B." This is known as an estate *pur autre vie,* or an estate for the life of another.

In a life estate, the life tenant has fewer rights of ownership than the holder of a fee simple defeasible. The life tenant has the right to use the land provided no waste (injury to the land) is committed. In other words, the life tenant cannot injure the land in a manner that would adversely affect the owner of the future interest in it. The life tenant can use the land to harvest crops, or, if mines and oil wells are already on the land, can extract minerals and oil from it. But the life tenant cannot exploit the land by creating new wells or mines.

Consider an example. Michaelson deeds land to Hitchcock for life. Oil is found under that land. Agents of Mobil Oil Company negotiate an oil and gas lease with Hitchcock, but Mobil never contacts Michaelson. Mobil simply starts drilling an oil well. When Michaelson learns of this, he demands that Mobil stop drilling or negotiate a lease with him. Michaelson can enforce his demand because a life tenant alone cannot make a binding oil and gas lease upon the property if no drilling was taking place at the time the life estate was created. By the same token, Hitchcock cannot sell any of the timber that is on the land without Michaelson's approval, because the removal of standing timber will reduce the value of the land.

But Hitchcock has the right to possess the land and, if it is farmland, to cultivate it and grow cash crops, retaining the proceeds, or to raise animals for market. Neither activity will reduce the value of the land, and such use is what was intended when the life estate was created.

The life tenant has the right to mortgage the life estate and create liens, easements, and leases; but none can extend beyond the life of the tenant. In addition, the owner of a life estate has the right to exclusive possession during his or her life. Exclusive possession, however, is subject to the rights of the future interest holder to come onto the land and protect the future interest.

Along with these rights, the life tenant also has some *duties*—to keep the property in repair and to pay property taxes. In short, the owner of the life estate has the same rights as a fee simple owner except that the value of the property must be kept intact for the future interest holder, less the decrease in value resulting from normal use of the property allowed by the life tenancy.

Nonfreehold Estates

The **less-than-freehold estates** are possessory real estate interests treated for some purposes as personal rather than real property. They are covered in this chapter for the sake of convenience because they relate to ownership of an interest in land. These estates include:

1. A tenancy for years.
2. A periodic tenancy.
3. A tenancy at will.
4. A tenancy at sufferance.

All, except a tenancy at sufferance, involve the transfer of the right to possession for *a specified period of time*.

The owner or lessor (landlord) conveys the property to the lessee (tenant) for a certain period of time. In every nonfreehold estate, the tenant has a *qualified* right to exclusive possession (qualified by the right of the landlord to enter upon the premises to assure that no waste is being committed). This is called a **leasehold estate.** The tenant can use the land—for example, by harvesting crops—but cannot injure the land by such activities as cutting down timber for sale or extracting oil.

TENANCY FOR YEARS   A **tenancy for years** is created by an express contract (which can sometimes be oral) by which property is leased for a specified period of time, such as a month, a year, or a period of years. For example, signing a one-year lease to occupy an apartment creates a tenancy for years. At the end of the period specified in the lease, the lease ends (without notice) and possession of the apartment returns to the lessor. If the tenant dies during the period of the lease, the lease passes to the tenant's heirs as personal property. Often, leases include renewal or extension provisions.

PERIODIC TENANCY   A **periodic tenancy** is created by a lease that does not specify how long it is to last but does specify that rent is to be paid at certain intervals. This type of tenancy is automatically renewed for another rental period unless properly terminated. For example, a periodic tenancy is created by a lease that states, "Rent is due

on the tenth day of every month." This provision creates a tenancy from month to month. This type of tenancy can also be from week to week or from year to year. A periodic tenancy sometimes arises when a landlord allows a tenant under a tenancy for years to hold over and continue paying monthly or weekly rent.

At common law, in order to terminate a periodic tenancy, the landlord or tenant must give one period's notice to the other party. If the tenancy is month to month, one month's notice must be given. If the tenancy is week to week, one week's notice must be given. State statutes often require a different period for notice of termination in a periodic tenancy, however.

TENANCY AT WILL   Suppose a landlord rents an apartment to a tenant "for as long as both agree." In such a case, the tenant receives a leasehold estate known as a **tenancy at will.** At common law, either party can terminate the tenancy without notice (that is, "at will"). This type of estate usually arises when a tenant who has been under a tenancy for years retains possession after the termination date of that tenancy with the landlord's consent. Before the tenancy has been converted into a periodic tenancy (by the periodic payment of rent), it is a tenancy at will, terminable by either party without notice. Once the tenancy is treated as a periodic tenancy, a termination notice must conform to the one already discussed. The death of either party or the voluntary commission of waste by the tenant will terminate a tenancy at will.

TENANCY AT SUFFERANCE   A **tenancy at sufferance** is not a true tenancy. It is the mere possession of land without right. A tenancy at sufferance is not an estate, since it is created by a tenant *wrongfully* retaining possession of property. Whenever a life estate, tenancy for years, periodic tenancy, or tenancy at will ends and the tenant continues to retain possession of the premises without the owner's permission, a tenancy at sufferance is created.

TERMINATION   As long as a tenancy exists, a landlord can collect rent in full, regardless of whether the premises are actually occupied by the tenant. Thus, when a tenant wrongfully abandons the premises and refuses to pay rent, the landlord can permit the premises to remain vacant, refuse to recognize the attempted surrender by the ten-

---

CONCEPT SUMMARY: The Basic Forms of Ownership of Real Property

FORMS OF OWNERSHIP	TYPES AND DEFINITIONS

Freehold Estate (held indefinitely)	1. Estate in fee—
	  a. Fee simple absolute—Most complete form of ownership.
	  b. Fee simple defeasible—Fee simple that can end if specified condition or event occurs.
	2. Life estate—Lasts for the life of a specified individual; rights subject to the rights of the future interest holder.

Nonfreehold estate (possessory interests held for a specified period of time)	1. Tenancy for years—Lasts for periods of time stated by express contract. 2. Periodic tenancy—Period determined by frequency of rent payments; automatically renewed unless proper notice is given. 3. Tenancy at will—For as long as both parties agree; no notice of termination required. 4. Tenancy at sufferance—Possession of land without legal right.

---

ant, and bring a lawsuit to collect the rent as it comes due. A tenant who wrongfully abandons the premises and refuses to pay rent cannot require that the landlord find another tenant to pay the rent. In many circumstances, however, the landlord has a duty created by statute or judicial decisions to mitigate his or her damages. As a result, if other tenants are available, the landlord may be unable to collect damages for the tenant's breach of the lease.

TRANSFER OF OWNERSHIP

Ownership of real property can pass from one person to another in a number of ways. They include inheritance, eminent domain, adverse possession, and deed. Conveyance by deed includes transfer by sale and by gift.

Transfer by Inheritance

Property that is transferred on an owner's death is passed by *inheritance*. If the owner of land dies with a will, that land passes according to the terms of the will. If the owner dies without a will, state statutes prescribe how and to whom the property will pass.

Eminent Domain

Even if ownership in real property is in fee simple absolute, there is still a superior ownership that limits the fee simple absolute. It is called **eminent domain**, and it is sometimes referred to as the condemnation power of the government to take land for public use. It gives a right to the government to acquire possession of real property in the manner directed by the Constitution and the laws of the state whenever the public interest requires it. Property may not be taken for private benefit but only for public use.

For example, when a new public highway is to be built, the government must decide where to build it and how much land to condemn. The power of eminent domain is generally invoked through condemnation proceedings. After the government determines that a particular parcel of land is necessary for public use, it brings a judicial proceeding to obtain title to the land. Then, in another proceeding, the court determines the *fair value* of the land, which is usually approximately equal to its market value. Under the Fifth Amendment, private property may not be taken for public use without "just compensation."

Adverse Possession

Adverse possession is a means of obtaining title to land without delivery of a deed. Essentially, when one person possesses the property of another for a certain statutory period of time (three to thirty years, with ten years being most common), that person, called the adverse possessor, acquires title to the land and cannot be removed from the land by the original owner. The adverse possessor is vested with a perfect title just as if there had been a conveyance by deed.

In order for property to be held adversely, four elements must be satisfied:

1. Possession must be actual and exclusive; that is, the possessor must take sole physical occupancy of the property.
2. The possession must be open, visible, and notorious, not secret or clandestine. The possessor must occupy the land for all the world to see.
3. Possession must be continuous and peaceable for the required period of time. This requirement means that the possessor must not be interrupted in the occupancy by the true owner or by the courts.
4. Possession must be hostile and adverse. In other words, the possessor must claim the property as against the whole world. He or she cannot live on the property with the permission of the owner.

Sale of Real Estate

Transfers of ownership interests in real property are frequently accomplished by means of a sale. The sale of real estate is similar to the sale of goods, since it involves a transfer of ownership, often with certain warranties. In the sale of real estate, however, certain formalities are observed that are not required in the sale of goods. To meet the requirements of law, a deed must be signed and delivered.[5]

Conveyance by Deed

Possession and title to land are also passed from person to person by means of a **deed**—the instrument of conveyance of real property. A deed is a writing signed by an owner of property by which title to it is transferred to another. Deeds must meet certain requirements.

Unlike a contract, a deed does not have to be supported by legally sufficient consideration. Gifts of real property are common, and they require

deeds even though there is no consideration for the gift. The necessary components of a valid deed are:

1. The names of the buyer (grantee) and seller (grantor).
2. Words evidencing an intent to convey (for example, "I hereby bargain, sell, grant, or give").
3. A legally sufficient description of the land.
4. The grantor's (and usually the spouse's) signature.
5. Delivery of the deed.

Types of Deeds

Deeds may be classified according to the interests they convey and the consequent degree of protection they offer against defects of title. Four types of deeds are discussed below.

WARRANTY DEED The **warranty deed** warrants the greatest number of things and thus provides the most extensive protection against defects of title. (See Exhibit 52–1.) In most states, special language is required to make a warranty deed. Thus, if a contract calls for "a warranty deed" without specifying the covenants to be included in the deed or if a deed states that the seller is providing the "usual covenants," most courts will infer from this language all of the following covenants (warranties) of title:

1. A **covenant of seisin** and a **covenant of the right to convey** warrant that the seller has title and the power to convey the estate that the deed describes. The *covenant of seisin* specifically assures the buyer that the grantor has the property in the quantity and quality that the grantor purports to convey. For example, if Lawson, the owner of a life estate in Whiteacre, attempts to convey a fee simple to Capron, Lawson has breached the covenant of seisin. If Capron is damaged by Lawson's breach, then Capron is entitled to recover from Lawson.
2. A **covenant against encumbrances** guarantees that the property being sold or conveyed is not subject to any outstanding rights or interests that will diminish the value of the land, except as stated. Examples of common encumbrances include mortgages, liens, profits, easements, and private deed restrictions on the use of land. Unless the deed expressly states that the conveyance is subject to a particular encumbrance, a covenant

---

5. The phrase *signed, sealed, and delivered* once referred to the requirements for transferring title to real property by deed. The seal has fallen from use, but signature and delivery are still required.

Exhibit 52–1 A Sample Warranty Deed

Date:　May 31, 1990

Grantor:　GAYLORD A. JENTZ AND WIFE, JOANN H. JENTZ

Grantor's Mailing Address (including county):
　　　4106 North Loop Drive
　　　Austin, Travis County, Texas

Grantee:　DAVID F. FRIEND AND WIFE, JOAN E. FRIEND AS JOINT TENANTS
　　　WITH RIGHT OF SURVIVORSHIP
Grantee's Mailing Address (including county):
　　　5929 Fuller Drive
　　　Austin, Travis County, Texas

Consideration:
For and in consideration of the sum of Ten and No/100 Dollars ($10.00) and other
valuable consideration to the undersigned paid by the grantees herein named, the
receipt of which is hereby acknowledged, and for which no lien is retained, either
express or implied.

Property (including any improvements):
Lot 23, Block "A", Northwest Hills, Green Acres Addition, Phase 4, Travis County,
Texas, according to the map or plat of record in volume 22, pages 331-336 of the
Plat Records of Travis County, Texas.

Reservations from and Exceptions to Conveyance and Warranty:

This conveyance with its warranty is expressly made subject to the following:

Easements and restrictions of record in Volume 7863, Page 53, Volume 8430,
Page 35, Volume 8133, Page 152 of the Real Property Records of Travis County,
Texas, Volume 22, Pages 335-339, of the Plat Records of Travis County, Texas;
and to any other restrictions and easements affecting said property which are
of record in Travis County, Texas.

　　Grantor, for the consideration and subject to the reservations from and exceptions to conveyance and warranty, grants, sells,
and conveys to Grantee the property, together with all and singular the rights and appurtenances thereto in any wise belonging, to
have and hold it to Grantee, Grantee's heirs, executors, administrators, successors, or assigns forever. Grantor binds Grantor
and Grantor's heirs, executors, administrators, and successors to warrant and forever defend all and singular the property to
Grantee and Grantee's heirs, executors, administrators, successors, and assigns against every person whomsoever lawfully
claiming or to claim the same or any part thereof, except as to the reservations from and exceptions to conveyance and warranty.

　　When the context requires, singular nouns and pronouns include the plural.

　　　　　　　　BY: _____
　　　　　　　　　　　Gaylord A. Jentz

　　　　　　　　BY: _____
　　　　　　　　　　　JoAnn H. Jentz

　　　　　　　　(Acknowledgment)

STATE OF TEXAS
COUNTY OF

　　This instrument was acknowledged before me on the　　31st day of　May　　, 1990
by　Gaylord A. and JoAnn H. Jentz

　　　　　　_____
　　　　　　Notary Public, State of Texas
　　　　　　Notary's name (printed): Rosemary Potter

　　　　Notary Seal　　　　Notary's commission expires: 1/31/1993

against encumbrances will be breached if the buyer discovers an undisclosed encumbrance. Again, as in the case of a covenant of seisin, the buyer is entitled to recover for any damage caused by the breach of this covenant.

3. A **covenant for quiet enjoyment** guarantees that the grantee or buyer will not be disturbed in his or her possession of the land by the grantor or any third persons. For example, suppose Janet Parker sells a two-acre lot and office building by warranty deed. Subsequently, a third person shows better title than Janet had and proceeds to evict the buyer. Here, the covenant for quiet enjoyment has been breached, and the buyer can recover the purchase price of the land plus any other damages incurred in being evicted.

The following case illustrates these covenants.

Case 52.2
BROWN v. LOBER
Supreme Court of Illinois, 1979.
75 Ill.2d 547, 389 N.E.2d 1188,
27 Ill.Dec. 780.

BACKGROUND AND FACTS *The plaintiff, Brown, purchased real property in 1957 and received a warranty deed. The deed contained no list of encumbrances. In 1974, the plaintiff granted a call option[a] to Consolidated Coal Company, giving the company rights to subsurface coal. Consolidated agreed to pay the plaintiff $6,000 for these rights. In 1976, it was discovered that the plaintiff did not own the subsurface mineral rights free and clear as indicated by the warranty deed of 1957. Instead, the plaintiff owned only one-third of the rights. The rights to the remaining two-thirds had been deeded away in 1947 by a prior grantor.*

The plaintiff had already been paid $2,000 by the coal company for its one-third interest. The coal company would not pay the remaining $4,000. The plaintiff then filed this lawsuit, seeking the $4,000 in damages against the prior grantor, Lober, the defendant.

Lober asserted that the ten-year statute of limitations for covenant of seisin barred the lawsuit. Brown asserted that a right of action was permitted for breach of the covenant of quiet enjoyment.

The trial court found for Lober, deciding that the ten-year statute of limitations had run from the time the deed was issued in 1957. Brown appealed.

UNDERWOOD, Justice.

* * * *

The deed which plaintiffs received * * * was a general statutory form warranty deed meeting the requirements of section 9 of "An Act concerning conveyances."

* * *

The effect of this provision is that certain covenants of title are implied in every statutory form warranty deed. Subsection 1 contains the covenant of seisin and the covenant of good right to convey. These covenants, which are considered synonymous, assure the grantee that the grantor is, at the time of the conveyance, lawfully seized and has the power to convey an estate of the quality and quantity which he professes to convey.

* * * *

Subsection 3 sets forth the covenant of quiet enjoyment, which is synonymous with the covenant of warranty in Illinois. By this covenant, "the grantor warrants to the grantee, his heirs and assigns, the possession of the premises and that he will defend the title granted by the terms of the deed against persons who may lawfully claim the same, and that such covenant shall be obligatory upon the grantor, his heirs, personal representatives, and assigns."

* * * *

Since the deed was delivered to the plaintiffs on December 21, 1957, any cause of action for breach of the covenant of seisin would have accrued on that date. The trial court held that this cause of action was barred by the statute of limitations. No question is raised as to the applicability of the 10-year statute of limitations. We conclude, therefore, that the cause of action for breach of the covenant of seisin was properly determined by the trial court to be barred by the statute of limitations since plaintiffs did not file their complaint until May 25, 1976, nearly 20 years after their alleged cause of action accrued.

* * * *

This court has stated on numerous occasions that, in contrast to the covenant of seisin, the covenant of warranty or quiet enjoyment is prospective in nature and is breached only when there is an actual or constructive eviction of the covenantee by the paramount titleholder.

The cases are also replete with statements to the effect that the mere existence of paramount title in one other than the covenantee is not sufficient to constitute a breach of the covenant of warranty or quiet enjoyment: "[T]here must be a union of acts of disturbance and lawful title, to constitute a breach of the covenant for quiet enjoyment, or warranty * * *."

* * * *

Since no one has, as yet, undertaken to remove the coal or otherwise manifested a clear intent to exclusively "possess" the mineral estate, it must be concluded that the subsurface estate is "vacant." As in [a previous case,] plaintiffs "could at any time have taken peaceable possession of it. [They have] in no way been prevented or hindered from the enjoyment of the possession by any one having a better right." Accordingly, until such time as one holding paramount title interferes with plaintiffs' right of possession (*e.g.*, by beginning to mine the coal), there can be no constructive eviction and, therefore, no breach of the covenant of quiet enjoyment.

DECISION AND REMEDY

The judgment of the trial court was affirmed. The statute of limitations barred an action for breach of the covenant of seisin. Further, the Browns could not recover for breach of the covenant of quiet enjoyment, because no one had interfered with their right of possession.

a. A call option permits its holder, who has paid a fee for the option, to demand delivery of certain amounts of commodities or stock at a stated price.

SPECIAL WARRANTY DEED In contrast to the warranty deed, the **special warranty deed** (also known as *deed with covenant against grantor's acts*) warrants only that the grantor or seller has not previously done anything to lessen the value of the real estate. If the special warranty deed discloses all liens or other encumbrances, the seller will not be liable to the buyer if a third person subsequently interferes with the buyer's ownership. If the third person's claim arises out of or is related to some act of the seller, however, the seller will be liable to the buyer for damages.

Both the special warranty deed and the warranty deed warrant that the seller has "marketable" title. Common defects that may render a title unmarketable include variations in the names of grantors and grantees, breaks in the chain of title, outstanding liens, and defectively executed deeds in the chain of title.

QUITCLAIM DEED A quitclaim deed warrants less than any other deed. Essentially, it simply conveys to the grantee whatever interest the grantor had. In other words, if the grantor had nothing, then the grantee receives nothing. Naturally, if the grantor had a defective title, or no title at all, a conveyance by warranty deed or special warranty deed would not cure the defects. Such deeds, however, will give the buyer a cause of action to sue the seller. A quitclaim deed gives no cause of action unless the seller had one.

A quitclaim deed can and often does serve as a release of the grantor's interest in a particular parcel of property. For instance, suppose Trump owns a strip of waterfront property on which he wants to build condominiums. Koch has an interest in a section of the property, which he might assert either to prevent the development or to insist on a share of its earnings. Trump can negotiate with Koch for a release of the claim. Koch's signing of a quitclaim deed would constitute such a release.

With a grant deed, the grantor simply states, "I grant the property to you" or "I convey, or bargain and sell, the property to you." By state statute, grant deeds may carry with them an implied warranty that the grantor owns the property being transferred and has not previously encumbered it or conveyed it to someone else.

Recording Statutes

Recording statutes are in force in every jurisdiction. The purpose of these statutes is to provide prospective buyers with a way to check whether there has been an earlier transaction. Hence, recording a deed gives constructive notice to the world that a certain person is now the owner of a particular parcel of real estate.[6] Placing everyone on notice as to the true owner is intended to prevent the previous owners from fraudulently conveying the land to a subsequent purchaser.

Properly notarized deeds are generally recorded in the county where the property is recorded. Many state statutes require that the grantor sign the deed in the presence of two attesting witnesses before it can be recorded. There are three basic types of recording statutes:

1. A *race statute* provides that the first purchaser to record a deed has superior rights to the property, regardless of whether he or she knew that someone else had already bought it but had failed to record the deed.[7] Under these statutes, recording is a "race," and whoever files first "wins."

2. A *pure notice statute* provides that, regardless of who files first, a person who knows that someone else has already bought the property cannot claim priority. On the other hand, a subsequent bona fide purchaser who, at the time he or she acquires a deed, has no notice of a previous deed—because, for example, it has not been recorded—may successfully assert a superior claim to the property. (A **bona fide purchaser** is one who purchases for value, in good faith, and without notice.)

3. A *notice-race statute* protects a purchaser who does not know that someone else has already bought the property and who records his or her deed first.

Irrespective of the particular type of recording statute adopted by a state, recording a deed involves a fee. The grantee typically pays this fee, since he or she is the one who will be protected by recording the deed.

Warranty of Habitability

The common law rule of *caveat emptor* ("let the buyer beware") held that the seller of a home made no warranties with respect to the soundness or fitness of the home unless such a warranty was specifically included in the deed or contract of sale. Although *caveat emptor* is still the rule of law in a minority of states, there is currently a strong trend against it and in favor of an **implied warranty of habitability.** Under this new approach, the courts hold that the seller of a new house warrants that it will be fit for human habitation regardless of whether any such warranty is included in the deed or contract of sale. This warranty is similar to the UCC's implied warranty of merchantability for sales of personal property. In recent years, some states, such as Virginia, have passed legislation creating such warranties for newly constructed residences.

Essentially, under an implied warranty of habitability, the seller warrants that the house is in reasonable working order and is of reasonably sound construction. The purchaser is only required to prove that the home he or she purchased was somehow defective and to prove the damages caused by the defect in order to recover. Thus, under the warranty of habitability theory, the seller of a new home is in effect a guarantor of the home's fitness.

---

6. In this situation, constructive notice operates to impute to a person knowledge of the ownership, regardless of whether the individual *actually* knows about it. This is because he or she is in a position that involves a duty to inquire; and proper diligence—for example, searching the public records—would reveal the fact of the ownership.

7. Only two states use a race statute. Usage in the rest of the states is split about evenly between the pure notice statute and the notice-race statute.

FUTURE INTERESTS

The common law recognizes a number of estates that are nonpossessory. **Future estates** consist of estates that *may* or *will* become possessory in the future. These estates are in direct contrast to estates that are *possessory*.

A person can convey an estate that is limited by a specified period of time; by the life of the grantor, grantee, or other person; or by an occurrence. The person to whom such an estate is conveyed has a *present possessory interest*. Life estates, terms for years, and fee simple determinable estates are examples of of estates that carry present possessory interests. These estates, however, unlike other possessory estates, are accompanied by a residuary interest that may or may not have been disposed of by the grantor. This residuary interest is a *future interest*, and it can take several forms.

Reversionary Interests and Powers of Termination

When a grantor owns a fee simple estate in land and conveys an estate to another with a duration that is less than the duration of the estate that the grantor owns, an undisposed residue remains in the grantor. That undisposed residue is called a **reversion.**

Suppose, for example, that Owen owns a fee simple estate and conveys a life estate in Blackacre to Ann. Owen has not disposed of the interest in the land remaining after Ann's life. Thus, Owen has automatically retained a reversion that will become possessory, upon Ann's death, in Owen or his heirs. Ann's life estate is an estate in possession, whereas Owen has a *vested* future interest—that is, an absolute right to possession of Blackacre at some point in the future. Furthermore, even though Owen holds a future interest, this interest exists in the present in the sense that Owen can convey his future interest.

Suppose, however, that Owen conveys Blackacre "to Ann and her heirs." It is clear that Owen now holds no future interest in Blackacre, since he has conveyed his entire estate to Ann as a fee simple absolute. If, on the other hand, Owen conveys a fee simple determinable (such as "to Ann and her heirs as long as the property is used for educational purposes"), Owen has retained a **possibility of reverter** or a **power of termination.** A possibility of reverter is a future interest in favor of the grantor that is contingent on the happening of the event named in the conveyance. The conveyance of a fee simple determinable that gives rise to a possibility of reverter usually includes the words "so long as," "until," "while," or "during."

Remainders and Executory Interests

When an owner of real property conveys an estate that is less than a fee simple absolute and does not retain the residuary interest, then that interest will take the form of either a **remainder** or an **executory interest.**

A remainder differs from an executory interest in that a remainder occurs *immediately* upon the *natural termination* of a preceding estate—such as a life estate. As mentioned previously, a remainder can be either *vested* or *contingent*. Both are future interests, but the holder of a vested remainder has an absolute right to possession at the end of the prior estate, whereas the owner of a contingent remainder has only a *conditional* right to possession when the prior estate ends (that is, the vesting of the right depends on an event that may or may not occur). Yet both are estates in land in favor of persons other than the grantor, and both can be transferred to other persons.

Executory interests, like remainders, are future possessory interests in real property that are conveyed to persons other than the grantor at the time of a conveyance. Executory interests, however, take effect either *before* or *after*, rather than immediately on, the natural termination of a preceding estate. For example, Papinian, an owner in fee simple, sells certain real property "to Paul for life and one year after Paul's death to Johnson." In this example, Paul is given a life estate, the property reverts to Papinian for one year, and then Johnson takes possession, divesting Papinian's reversion.

An executory interest that divests the grantor's estate is a *springing interest* (also called a springing use). Because the interest springs out of the reversion in the grantor Papinian, in the previous example, Johnson has a springing executory interest.

An executory interest that divests a grantee's estate is a *shifting interest* (also called a shifting use). To illustrate: Owen conveys Blackacre "to Ann for twenty years, but *if* Ann should divorce, *then* Blackacre is to pass immediately to Carla." Carla has a future interest in Blackacre that will become a present possessory interest if Ann becomes divorced. Carla's future interest is a shifting executory interest, since the possessory interest would shift from Ann to Carla if Ann should divorce.

NONPOSSESSORY INTERESTS

Some interests in land do not include any rights of possession. These interests, known as nonpossessory interests, include easements, profits, and licenses. Because easements and profits are similar and the same rules apply to both, they will be discussed together.

Easements and Profits

An **easement** is the right of a person to make limited use of another person's property without taking anything from the property. An easement, for example, can be the right to walk across another's property. In contrast, a **profit** is the right to go onto land in possession of another and take away some part of the land itself or some product of the land. For example, Owen, the owner of Sandy View, gives Ann the right to go there and remove all the sand and gravel that she needs for her cement business. Ann has a profit. The difference between an easement and a profit is that an easement merely allows a person to use land without taking anything from it, whereas a profit allows a person to take something from the land. Easements and profits can be classified as either *appurtenant* or *in gross*.

EASEMENT (OR PROFIT) APPURTENANT
easement or profit appurtenant arises when the owner of one piece of land has a right to go onto (or remove things from) an adjacent piece of land owned by another. Suppose Owen, the owner of Whiteacre, has a right to drive his car across Green's land, Greenacre, which is adjacent to Whiteacre. This right-of-way over Greenacre is an easement appurtenant to Whiteacre and can be used only by the owner of Whiteacre. Owen can convey the easement when he conveys Whiteacre. Now imagine that the highway is on the other side of Black's property, Blackacre, which is on the other side of Greenacre. To reach the highway, White has an easement across both properties. Whiteacre and Blackacre are not adjacent, but White has an easement appurtenant nonetheless.

EASEMENT (OR PROFIT) IN GROSS An easement or profit in gross exists when the right to use or take things from another's land is not dependent upon the owner of the easement or profit owning an adjacent tract of land. Suppose Owen

owns a parcel of land with a marble quarry. Owen conveys to XYZ Corporation, which owns no land, the right to come onto his land and remove up to five hundred pounds of marble per day. XYZ Corporation owns a profit in gross. When a utility company is granted an easement to run its power lines across another's property, it obtains an easement in gross. An easement or profit in gross requires the existence of only one parcel of land, which must be owned by someone other than the owner of the easement or profit in gross.

EFFECT OF SALE OF PROPERTY When a parcel of land that is *benefited* by an easement or profit appurtenant is sold, the property carries the easement or profit along with it. Thus, if Owen sells Whiteacre to Thomas and includes the appurtenant right-of-way across Greenacre in the deed to Thomas, Thomas will own both the property and the easement that benefits it.

When a parcel of land that has the *burden* of an easement or profit appurtenant is sold, the new owner must recognize its existence only if he or she knew or should have known of it or if it was recorded in the appropriate office of the county. Thus, if Owen records his easement across Greenacre in the appropriate county office before Green conveys the land, the new owner of Greenacre will have to allow Owen, or any subsequent owner of Whiteacre, to continue to use the path across Greenacre.

CREATION OF AN EASEMENT (OR PROFIT)
Profits and easements can be created by *deed* or *will* or by *implication, necessity,* or *prescription*. Creation by *deed* or *will* simply involves the delivery of a deed or a disposition in a will by the owner of an easement stating that the grantee (the person receiving the profit or easement) is granted the rights in the easement or profit that the grantor had. An easement or profit, however, may be created by *implication* when the circumstances surrounding the division of a parcel of property imply its creation. If Barrow divides a parcel of land that has only one well for drinking water and conveys the half without a well to Dan, a profit by implication arises, since Dan needs drinking water. An easement may also be created by necessity. An easement by *necessity* does not require division of property for its existence. A person who rents an apartment, for example, has an easement by necessity in the private road leading up to it.

Easements and profits by *prescription* are created in much the same way as title to property is obtained by adverse possession (discussed previously). An easement arises by prescription when one person exercises an easement, such as a right-of-way, on another person's land without the landowner's consent and the use is apparent and continues for a period of time equal to the applicable statute of limitations (usually the same as for acquiring title by adverse possession).

TERMINATION OF AN EASEMENT (OR PROFIT) An easement or profit can be terminated or extinguished in several ways. The simplest way is to deed it back to the owner of the land that is burdened by it. Another way is to abandon it and create evidence of intent to relinquish the right to use it. Mere nonuse will not extinguish an easement or profit *unless it is accompanied by an intent to abandon*. Finally, when the owner of an easement or profit becomes the owner of the property burdened by it, then it is merged into the property.

Licenses

A license is the revocable right of a person to come onto another person's land. It is a personal privilege that arises from the consent of the owner of the land and that can be revoked by the owner. A ticket to attend a movie at a theater is an example of a license. If a theater owner issues a ticket entitling the holder to enter the property of the owner and Ann subsequently acquires the ticket and is refused entry into the theater, she has no right to force her way into the theater. The ticket is only a revocable license, not a conveyance of an interest in property.

LAND-USE CONTROL

Land-use control deals with *limitations* on property owners that either arise by agreement (covenants running with the land, equitable servitudes) or are imposed by the government (zoning).

Covenants Running with the Land

A **covenant running with the land** goes with the land and cannot be separated from it. A covenant runs with the land when the original parties *and* their successors, as opposed to the original parties alone, will be entitled to its benefit or burdened with its obligation. In other words, its benefit or obligation passes with the land's ownership.

Consider an example. Owen is the owner of Grasslands, a twenty-acre estate whose northern half contains a small reservoir. Owen wishes to convey the northern half to Arid City, but before he does, he digs an irrigation ditch connecting the reservoir with the lower ten acres, which he uses as farmland. When Owen conveys the northern ten acres to Arid City, he enters into an agreement with the city. The agreement, which is contained in the deed, states, "Arid City, its heirs and assigns, promises not to remove more than five thousand gallons of water per day from the Grasslands reservoir." Owen has created a *covenant running with the land* under which Arid City and all future owners of the northern ten acres of Grasslands are limited as to the amount of water they can draw from its reservoir.

Four requirements must be met for a covenant running with the land to be enforceable. If they are not met, a simple contract is created between the two original parties only.

1. The covenant running with the land must be created in a written agreement (covenant). It is usually contained in the document that conveys the land.

2. The parties must intend that the covenant *run with the land*. In other words, the instrument that contains the covenant must state not only that the promisor is bound by the terms of the covenant but that all the promisor's "successors, heirs, or assigns" will be bound.

3. The covenant must *touch and concern* the land. The limitations on the activities of the owner of the burdened land must have some connection with the land. For example, a purchaser of land cannot be bound by a covenant requiring him or her to drive only Ford pickups, since such a restriction has no relation to the land purchased.

4. The original parties to the covenant must be in *privity of estate* at the time the covenant is created. This requirement means that the relationship between them must be that of landlord and tenant, vendor and purchaser, testator and devisee, or the like.

Equitable Servitudes

Because of the confusion over the meaning and application of the privity of estate requirement, covenants running with the land have not been a very effective device for guiding the development of residential and commercial land. Therefore, courts of equity have utilized an alternative means of private land-use control known as **equitable servitudes.** The most significant difference between covenants running with the land and equitable servitudes is that privity of estate is not required for enforcement of an equitable servitude.

An equitable servitude is created by an instrument that complies with the Statute of Frauds, an intention that the use of land be restricted, and *notice* of the restriction to the person acquiring the burdened land. The notice may be constructive.

For example, in the course of developing a fifty-lot suburban subdivision, Levitt records a declaration of restrictions that effectively limits construction on each lot to one single-family house. In each lot's deed is a reference to the declaration with a provision that the purchaser and his or her successors are bound to those restrictions. Thus, each purchaser assumes ownership with notice of the restrictions. If an owner attempts to build a duplex (or any structure that does not comply with the restrictions) on a lot, the other owners may obtain a court order enjoining the construction.

In fact, Levitt might simply have included the restrictions on the subdivision's map, filed the map in the appropriate public office, and included a reference to the map in each deed. In this way, each owner would also have been held to have constructive notice of the restrictions.

Equitable servitudes are usually upheld; however, equitable servitudes and covenants running with the land have sometimes been used to perpetuate neighborhood segregation, and in these cases they have been invalidated by the courts. In the Supreme Court case of *Shelley v. Kraemer*,[8] restrictive covenants proscribing resale to minority groups were declared unconstitutional and could no longer be enforced in courts of law. In addition, the Civil Rights Act of 1968 (also known as the Fair Housing Act) prohibits all discrimination based on race, color, religion, or national origin in the sale and leasing of housing.

Zoning

The government is by far the most potent force in guiding the development and use of land. State and local governments have far greater resources and enforcement powers than do private individuals to control land use. Moreover, since ideally the government represents majority interests, it is in the best position to determine what land uses reflect the needs of society as a whole.

The state's power to control the use of land through legislation is derived from two sources: eminent domain and police power. Through eminent domain, the government can take land for public use, but it must pay just compensation. Consequently, eminent domain is an expensive method of land-use control. Under its police power, however, the state can pass laws aimed at protecting public health, safety, morals, and general welfare. These laws can affect owners' rights and uses of land, without the state's having to compensate the landowner. If a state law restricts a landowner's property rights too much, the state's regulation will be deemed a *confiscation,* or a *taking,* and may be subject to the eminent domain requirement that just compensation be paid.

Suppose Perez owns a large tract of land, which she purchased with the intent to subdivide and develop into residential properties. At the time of the purchase, there were no zoning regulations restricting use of the land. If the government attempts to zone Perez's entire tract of land as "public parkland only" and thus prohibit her from developing any part of it, the action will be deemed confiscatory, since the government will be denying her the ability to use her property for any reasonable income-producing or private purpose for which it is suited and because she had reasonable, investment-backed expectations in her develoment plans. The regulation will be held unconstitutional and void, or the government will have to compensate Perez, since it has effectively confiscated her land. Suppose, however, that the government zones Perez's parcel of land as "three-fourths residential, one-fourth park area" after her purchase. This zoning regulation is not confiscatory, since she will be able to use most of the property for building residences.

---

8. 334 U.S. 1, 68 S.Ct. 836, 92 L.Ed. 1161 (1948).

The state's power to regulate the use of land is limited in two other ways, both of which arise from the Fourteenth Amendment. First, the state cannot regulate the use of land arbitrarily or unreasonably, since this would be taking property without due process. There must be a *rational basis* for the classifications that the state imposes on property. Any act that is reasonably related to the health or general welfare of the public is deemed to have a rational basis.

Second, a state's regulation of land use control cannot be discriminatory. A zoning ordinance is considered discriminatory if it affects one parcel of land in a way in which it does not affect surrounding parcels and if there is no rational basis for the difference. Placing a single parcel or a limited number of parcels in a classification that does not accord with a general zoning scheme or comprehensive plan (referred to as *spot zoning*, discussed below) is often held invalid on grounds of unreasonable discrimination.

Also, a zoning ordinance cannot be racially discriminatory. For example, a small community near a large metropolitan area may not zone so as to exclude all low-income housing if the effect is racial discrimination. If the community could prove that other tracts within its limits were suitable for integrated housing, the ordinance might be allowed to stand, however. Similarly, a zoning ordinance cannot prohibit churches or otherwise burden the exercise of religion, but a community can reasonably regulate the churches' location sites.

FLOATING ZONES Generally, the state agency charged with the responsibility of land-use planning can take one of two approaches. The first is to designate, all at one time, use restrictions on each parcel of land located within the entire area to be zoned (usually a city or town). Alternatively, the agency can use "floating zones," deciding initially how much land should be designated for each of a variety of particular uses (commercial, residential, park, farming) and later assigning such designations at the request of landowners. The floating zone concept allows for flexibility in zoning and reduces arbitrariness.

SPOT ZONING One method that the agency charged with zoning an area may not use is **spot zoning.** Zoning ordinances are to apply to all property within the zone. Spot zoning occurs when an agency grants a parcel of land a classification different from the one it grants to surrounding property, if the difference between the classifications neither falls within the comprehensive zoning plan nor can be justified on the basis of health, safety, morals, or the community's general welfare. For example, spot zoning might involve granting an owner the right to construct a smelter in a residential neighborhood or limiting an owner to erecting a structure no higher than two stories when its neighbors are fifty-story skyscrapers.

VARIANCE A landowner whose land has been limited by a zoning ordinance to a particular use cannot make an alternative use of the land unless he or she first obtains a zoning variance. A landowner must meet three criteria to be entitled to a variance:

1. The landowner must find it impossible to realize a reasonable return on the land as zoned.

2. The adverse effect of the zoning ordinance must be particular to the person seeking the variance and not one that has a similar effect on the other landowners within the same zone.

3. A granting of the variance must not substantially alter the essential character of the zoned area.

By far the most important criterion used in granting a variance is whether it will substantially alter the character of the neighborhood. Courts tend to be rather lenient about the first two requirements. As the following case illustrates, courts also tend to defer to the discretion of zoning boards unless the board has abused its authority.

BACKGROUND AND FACTS *The city of Moline planned to build a new firehouse on land that was appropriately zoned for construction of a firehouse. The proposed firehouse, however, was slightly larger than the zoning ordinances permitted. Thus, in April 1963, Moline filed with the Board of Zoning Adjustment of St. Louis County for variances from the set-back and building line provisions in the ordinance. Essentially, the city's plans called for*

Case 52.3
CONNER v. HERD
Court of Appeals of Missouri, 1970.
452 S.W.2d 272.

construction of a building that would be set back about four feet farther than the zoning allowed. Alfred and Marie Conner, who owned property adjacent to the site of the new construction, objected to the variance. The variance was granted, and the Conners appealed the board's ruling to the courts.

SMITH, Commissioner.

*   *   *   *

*   *   * [A]ppellants contend the findings of the Board were arbitrary and capricious and not based upon competent and substantial evidence. We take these in order.

*   *   *   *

"JURISDICTION AND POWERS.—The Board of Zoning Adjustment is hereby authorized to: (5) Permit a variation in the yard requirements of any Zoning District or the building and set back lines for Major Highways as provided by law where there are practical difficulties or unnecessary hardships in the carrying out of these provisions due to an irregular shape of the lot, topographical or other conditions, provided such variation will not seriously affect any adjoining property or the general welfare."

This provision, under which the Board acted here, empowers the Board to give variances under specified circumstances where strict enforcement of the regulations would be unjust. It imposes standards for the Board's action and is not a grant of legislative power.

This brings us to the heart of this appeal, appellants' contention that the action of the Board was not based on competent and substantial evidence and was arbitrary and capricious. Neither this court nor the trial court can substitute its judgment on the evidence for that of the Board. We may only determine whether the Board could reach the conclusion it did upon the evidence before it. We hold it could.

*   *   *   *

The most efficient and satisfactory type of fire station for Moline's purposes is one where returning trucks can enter the back of the station from Clairmont Drive, remove the hoses and other equipment for cleaning, put clean equipment on the truck and move the truck into position for exit through the front onto Chambers Road for the next call. The lot in question is 165 feet in depth (after the widening of Chambers to 80 feet) and 80 feet in width. If the set-back line on Chambers Road, 80 feet, is adhered to there would not be enough room at the rear of the station (39 feet) for the large fire trucks to negotiate the turn from Clairmont Drive into the rear of the station. The entrance from Clairmont would also obviate the need for the trucks to back into the station from Chambers Road. There was also testimony that having the station located nearer the road than the old station would allow greater traffic safety in leaving the station in that both the dispatcher and the driver would have greater visibility along Chambers. *   *   *

The width of the lot is such that a 2 foot variance on the building line of Clairmont Drive would be necessary to get the proposed fire station on the property if the regulation of a 6 foot side yard on the west (next to appellants) is met. The granted variance is less than the previously existing encroachment.

*   *   *   *

The Board could find here that in the absence of a variance Moline would be confronted with substantial additional expense, interruption of fire protection service during the period of construction, and unnecessary inconvenience if not outright danger to the residents of the district. The Board is not required to ignore the source of the funds available to the district (taxpayers) in determining that additional expense constitutes an unnecessary hardship. Under *Rosedale-Skinker*, there exist sufficient "practical difficulties" and "unnecessary hardships" to the district to permit a variance and these arise from the inadequate size of the lot to contain a fire station. This was the essence of the Board's finding "that because of the requirements, the proposed new building and facilities cannot be erected as the eighty foot set back line on Chambers Road and the thirty foot building line on Clairmont Drive are intended."

*   *   *   *

The effect on general welfare finding is supported by the evidence of the need for the new building to render adequate fire protection to the district and by the testimony on the beneficial effect of the proposed construction upon traffic safety on Chambers Road, including the installation of a traffic light on Chambers Road to be controlled by the dispatcher when trucks leave the station.

The court held that the zoning board had enough evidence to grant the variance in accordance with the requirements of the zoning ordinance. The judgment of the circuit court, which had affirmed the action taken by the zoning board, was affirmed by the appellate court.   **DECISION AND REMEDY**

QUESTIONS AND CASE PROBLEMS

1. Elkins owned a tract of land, but he was not sure that he had full title to the property. When Maves expressed an interest in buying the property, Elkins sold Maves the land and executed a quitclaim deed. Maves properly recorded the deed immediately. Several months later, Elkins learned that he had had full title to the tract of land. He then sold the land to Jones by general warranty deed. Jones knew of the earlier purchase by Maves but took the deed anyway and later sued to have Maves evicted from the land. Jones claimed that since he had a general warranty deed, his title to the land was better than that of Maves's quitclaim deed. Will Jones succeed in claiming title to the land? Discuss.

2. Robert and Maria are neighbors. Robert's lot is extremely large, and his present and future use of it will not involve the entire area. Maria wants to build a single-car garage and driveway along the present lot boundary. Because of ordinances requiring buildings to be set back fifteen feet from an adjoining property line, and because of the placement of her existing structures, she cannot build the garage. Maria contracts to purchase ten feet of Robert's property along their boundary line for $3,000. Robert is willing to sell but will give Maria only a quitclaim deed, whereas Maria wants a general warranty deed. Discuss the differences between these deeds as they would affect the rights of the parties if the title to this ten feet of land later proved to be defective.

3. Harold was a wanderer twenty-two years ago. It was at that time that he decided to settle down on a vacant three-acre piece of land, which he did not own. People in the area indicated to him that they had no idea who owned it. Harold built a house on the land, got married, and raised three children while living there. He fenced in the land, placed a gate with a sign, "Harold's Homestead," above it, and had trespassers removed. Harold is now confronted by Joe Moonfeld, who has a deed in his name as owner of the property. Moonfeld orders Harold and family off the property, claiming his title ownership. Discuss who has best "title" to the property.

4. Anthony is the owner of a lakeside house and lot. He deeds the house and lot to "my wife, Sylvia, for life, with remainder to my son, David, providing he graduates from college with a B or better average during Sylvia's lifetime." Answer the following questions:

    (a) Does Anthony have any interest in the deeded lakeside house? Explain.

    (b) What is Sylvia's interest called? Explain.

    (c) What is David's interest called? Explain.

5. Murray owns 640 acres of rural land. A new highway is being built nearby by Ajax Corporation, Inc. Ajax purchases from Murray the rights to build and use a road across Murray's land. Construction vehicles will pass over the road and will remove sand and gravel required to build the highway. A deed is prepared and filed in the county by Ajax. Later, a dispute arises between Murray and Ajax, and Murray refuses Ajax the right to use the road or to remove sand and gravel. Ajax claims its property rights cannot be revoked by Murray. Discuss fully what property rights Ajax has in this matter.

6. The owners of the Seven Palms Motor Inn decided that their motel was in need of renovation. Accordingly, they ordered a large quantity of bedspreads, curtain rods, and drapes from Sears, Roebuck and Company. Thereafter, Seven Palms Motor Inn failed to pay its bill, which amounted to approximately $8,000, including installation. Under Missouri law, a supplier of fixtures can establish a lien on the land and the building to which the fixtures have become attached. Sears sought to establish such a lien to make it easier to recover the debt that Seven Palms owed it. Which, if any, of the above-named items will Sears be able to successfully argue are fixtures? [Sears, Roebuck & Co. v. Seven Palms Motor Inn, 530 S.W.2d 695 (Mo. 1975)]

7. Dixie Gardens, Inc., was a developer in Pasco County, Florida. Henry Sloane purchased a lot and residence in a Dixie Gardens development. The deed read in part as follows: "If the developer or the Crestridge Utilities Corporation causes garbage collection service bi-weekly to be made available, the owner of each lot shall pay the developer or its assigns, the sum of $1.75 per month therefor." Sloane wished to employ another contractor for garbage collection, but Dixie Gardens argued that Sloane was bound by the provision quoted above, which amounted to a covenant running with the land. Is Dixie Gardens correct? [Sloane v. Dixie Gardens, Inc., 278 So.2d 309 (Fla.App. 1973)]

8. In 1961, Mary Schaefers divided her real property and conveyed it to her children, William, Elfreda, Julienne, and Rosemary. The deed from Mary Schaefers to her daughter Rosemary contained the following language: "It is further mutually agreed by and between the grantor and the grantee that as part of the consideration set out above, the grantee agrees to provide a permanent home for my daughter, Elfreda, should she desire or request one, and for my son, William Schaefers, should he desire or request one. Failure to perform the above will be considered a material breach of the consideration set out herein." In 1974, Rosemary conveyed her portion of her mother's property to Edward and Arthur Apel. Subsequently, William Schaefers attempted to prevent the sale to the Apels from taking place by telling them that the house was encumbered by a covenant running with the land and that if they purchased the house, they would be bound to provide a home for William and Elfreda Schaefers. Is Rosemary's promise to provide a home for William and Elfreda (should they demand one) a covenant running with the land? [Schaefers v. Apel, 295 Ala. 277, 328 So.2d 274 (1976)]

9. Lawrence Reeves was a landowning farmer whose land was being foreclosed upon by his mortgage holder, Metropolitan Life Insurance Company. Prior to the foreclosure, Reeves had contracted with Production Sale Company to erect a grain-storage facility on the farm. Its total cost was $171,185.30. Prior to the foreclosure, Reeves had paid only $16,137.77. When Metropolitan brought the foreclosure proceedings, the question arose as to whether the grain-storage facility was a fixture to the realty or personal property. If it was considered to be a fixture, Metropolitan would receive the proceeds from the sale; if it was considered to be personal property, the proceeds would go to Production Sale Company. Discuss whether the facility was a fixture to the real property or personal property. [Metropolitan Life Insurance Co. v. Reeves, 223 Neb. 299, 389 N.W.2d 295 (1986)]

10. In 1882, Moses Webster owned a parcel of land that extended down to the Atlantic Ocean. He conveyed the strip of the property fronting the ocean to another party. The deed included the following statement: "Reserve being had for said Moses Webster the right of way by land or water." The strip of property is now owned by Margaret Williams, and the portion retained by Webster now belongs to Thomas O'Neill. Williams is denying O'Neill access to the ocean. O'Neill has brought an action to establish his title to an easement over Williams's property. Who will win, and why? [O'Neill v. Williams, 527 A.2d 322 (Me. 1987)]

11. Paul was the owner of real estate located in Putnam County, Florida. In 1982, while Paul was living with Lucille, he executed a deed conveying the property to himself and Lucille as joint tenants with right of survivorship. In 1985, Paul and Lucille stopped living together, and three months later Lucille conveyed her interest in the property to her daughter, Sandra. Review concurrent ownership discussed in Chapter 50. What type of interest does Sandra possess in the property, and why? [Foucart v. Paul, 516 So.2d 1035 (Fla.App. 1987)]

Landlord-Tenant Relationships

In the past century—and particularly in the past two decades—landlord-tenant relationships have become much more complex than they were before, as has the law governing them. Generally, the law has come to apply such contract doctrines as implied warranties, unconscionability, and so on to the landlord-tenant relationship. Increasingly, in recent years, landlord-tenant relationships have become subject to specific state and local statutes and ordinances as well. In 1972, in an effort to create more uniformity in the law governing landlord-tenant relationships, the National Conference of Commissioners on Uniform State Laws proposed the Uniform Residential Landlord and Tenant Act (URLTA).

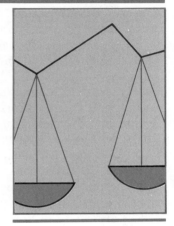

CREATION OF THE LANDLORD-TENANT RELATIONSHIP: THE LEASE

When a landowner transfers temporary, exclusive possession of his or her property to another party in exchange for the payment of rent, a **landlord-tenant relationship** is created. The owner is the landlord, or **lessor;** the party assuming temporary possession is the tenant, or **lessee;** and their rental agreement is the **lease.** (For an explanation of the types of tenancies the parties may create, see Chapter 52.)

The *temporary* nature of possession, under a lease, is what distinguishes a tenant from a purchaser, who acquires title to the property. The *exclusivity* of possession distinguishes a tenant from a licensee, who acquires the temporary right to a *nonexclusive* use, such as sitting in a theatre seat.

Leases may be oral or written. At common law, an oral lease is valid. As is the case with most oral agreements, however, a party who seeks to enforce an oral lease may have difficulty proving its existence. In most states, statutes mandate that leases be in writing for some tenancies (such as those exceeding one year).

The Lease Form

To create a landlord-tenant relationship, a document must:

1. Express an intent to establish the relationship.
2. Provide for transfer of the property's possession to the tenant at the beginning of the term.

3. Provide for the landlord's **reversionary interest,** which entitles the property owner to re-take possession at the end of the term.

4. Describe the property—for example, give its street address.

5. Indicate the length of the term, the amount of the rent, and how and when it is to be paid.

In the drafting of commercial leases, sound business practice dictates that the leases be written carefully and that the parties' rights and obligations be clearly defined in the lease agreements.

Illegality

A property owner cannot legally discriminate against prospective tenants on the basis of race, color, religion, national origin, or sex. Similarly, a tenant cannot legally promise to do something counter to laws prohibiting discrimination. A tenant, for example, cannot legally promise to do business only with members of a particular race. The public policy underlying these prohibitions is to treat all people equally.

State or local law often dictates permissible lease terms. URLTA, for example, prohibits the inclusion in a lease agreement of a clause under which the tenant agrees to pay the landlord's attorneys' fees in a suit to enforce the lease. Also, a statute or ordinance might prohibit leasing a structure that is in a certain physical condition or is not in compliance with local building codes.

Similarly, a statute may prohibit the leasing of property for a particular purpose. For example, a state law might prohibit gambling houses. Thus, if a landlord and tenant intend that the leased premises be used only to house an illegal betting operation, their lease is unenforceable. If a tenant's intended use of leased property is illegal under some circumstances but legal under others, the lease is unenforceable if the landlord intends that the property be put only to the illegal use. If the landlord does not so intend, he or she may enforce the lease.

Zoning ordinances present a special situation. Some courts have not invalidated leases made for purposes that violate zoning laws, when these ordinances provide for exceptions under certain circumstances. Sometimes, the courts reason that the parties drafted their lease with the understanding that the property would qualify for an exception to the zoning laws. When property is subject to zoning laws that may inhibit a tenant's intended use, the tenant should reserve an option to terminate the lease agreement if the intended use cannot be accomplished. Otherwise, of course, the tenant will be responsible for the performance of his or her obligation under the lease regardless of whether the intended use can be accomplished.

Unconscionability

The **unconscionability** concept is one of the most important of the contract doctrines applied to leases. Basically, as applied to leases in some jurisdictions (and under URLTA, Section 1.303), the concept follows the provision of UCC 2-302. Under this provision, a court may declare an entire contract or any of its clauses unconscionable and thus illegal, depending on the circumstances surrounding the transaction and the parties' relative bargaining positions.

For example, in a residential lease, a clause claiming to absolve a landlord from responsibility for interruptions in such essential services as central heating or air conditioning will not shield a landlord from liability if the systems break down when they are needed the most.

PARTIES' RIGHTS AND DUTIES

At common law, the parties to a lease had relative freedom to include whatever terms they chose. Currently, the trend is to base the rights and duties of the parties on the principles of real estate law and contract law. These rights and duties generally pertain to the four broad areas of concern for landlords and tenants—the possession, use, and maintenance of lease property and, of course, rent.

Possession

Possession involves the obligation of the landlord to deliver possession to the tenant at the beginning of the lease term and the right of the tenant to obtain possession and retain it until the lease expires.

LANDLORD'S DUTY TO DELIVER POSSESSION
A landlord is obligated to give a tenant possession of the property that the tenant has agreed to lease. The "English" rule, followed in many states, requires the landlord to provide actual *physical pos-*

session to the tenant. If, for example, a previous tenant is still living on the premises on the date the new tenant is entitled to possession, the landlord must remove the previous tenant or breach the obligation to the new tenant.

The "American" rule, followed in other states, requires the landlord to transfer only the *legal right to possession*. Under this rule, the new tenant in the preceding example would have been responsible for removing the previous tenant, who no longer had the legal right to possession.

URLTA follows the English rule and requires the landlord to provide the tenant with actual physical possession of the leased property, unless the parties agree otherwise.

TENANT'S RIGHT TO RETAIN POSSESSION
After obtaining possession, the tenant retains it exclusively until the lease expires, unless the lease provides otherwise or the tenant defaults under the terms of the lease. Most leases expressly give the landlord the right to come onto the property for the purpose of inspecting the property, making necessary repairs, or showing the property to prospective purchasers or (toward the end of an expiring term) to possible future tenants.

COVENANT OF QUIET ENJOYMENT   Under the **covenant of quiet enjoyment,** the landlord promises that during the lease term neither the landlord nor anyone having a superior title to the property will disturb the tenant's use and enjoyment of the property. This covenant forms the essence of the landlord-tenant relationship, and if it is breached, the tenant can terminate the lease and sue for damages.

DEPRIVING THE TENANT OF POSSESSION OR ENJOYMENT: EVICTION   If the landlord deprives the tenant of the tenant's possession of the leased property or interferes with his or her use or enjoyment of it, an **eviction** occurs. This is the case, for example, when the landlord changes the lock and refuses to give the tenant a new key. A **partial eviction** occurs if the landlord deprives the tenant of the use of a part—one room, for example—of the leased premises. Assuming the tenant has a legal right to possession of the property, he or she may either sue for damages or possession or consider the eviction a breach of condition and cease paying rent or terminate the lease.

Constructive Eviction   A **constructive eviction** occurs when the landlord wrongfully performs or fails to perform any of the undertakings the lease requires, thereby making the tenant's further use and enjoyment of the property exceedingly difficult or impossible. In order to claim that a constructive eviction has occurred, the tenant must first notify the landlord of the interference. If the landlord fails to remedy the situation within a reasonable period of time, the tenant must then abandon the premises. On vacating the premises, the tenant's obligation to pay further rent ceases. As in cases of wrongful eviction generally, the tenant may sue to move back onto the property or terminate the lease and seek damages. Examples of constructive eviction include a landlord's failure to provide heat in the winter, light, or other essential utilities.

Retaliatory Eviction   **Retaliatory eviction** occurs when a landlord evicts a tenant for complaining to a government agency about the condition of leased premises. Under some statutes, a retaliatory motive will be presumed if eviction proceedings are begun within a certain time after a tenant has complained. If a tenant can prove that a landlord's primary purpose in evicting or attempting to evict the tenant is retaliation for reporting violations—of a housing or sanitation code, for example—regardless of the time elapsed, the tenant may be entitled to stop the eviction proceedings or collect damages.

Using the Premises

If the parties do not limit the uses to which the property may be put, the tenant may make any use of it, so long as the use is legal and reasonably relates to the purpose for which the property is adapted or ordinarily used and does not injure the landlord's interest.

Also, the tenant is not entitled to create a **nuisance** by substantially interfering with others' quiet enjoyment of their property rights. To constitute a nuisance, conduct must be more than simply aggravating. For example, arguing with the neighbors may be annoying behavior, but it would probably not qualify as a nuisance, unless it took the form of harassment. Consistently playing drums in the middle of the night in an apartment complex, however, probably would constitute a nuisance.

TENANT'S DUTY NOT TO COMMIT WASTE

The tenant has no right to remove or otherwise damage leased property without the landlord's consent. The duty of a tenant not to damage the premises is a duty not to commit **waste,** which is the abuse or destructive use of property by one in rightful possession. For example, a tenant cannot knock out an inside wall in a leased house to enlarge a living room or remove a fence or a grove of trees to accommodate grazing livestock unless he or she first obtains the landlord's permission to do so.

The tenant is responsible for all damage he or she causes, intentionally or negligently, and the tenant may be held liable for the cost of returning the property to the physical condition it was in at the lease's inception. Unless the parties have agreed otherwise, the tenant is not responsible for ordinary wear and tear and the property's consequent depreciation in value.

If, at some time during the lease term, the tenant decides to stop using the property but to continue paying the rent, the lease may require the tenant to give the landlord notice of the nonuse. There is a greater chance of vandalism, fire, or some other cause of damage to property when it is not being used, and the nonuse may affect insurance coverage.

ALTERING THE PREMISES In most states, the tenant may make no alterations to the leased premises without the landlord's consent. In other jurisdictions, the tenant may make alterations, without being liable for the expense of their removal, if they were necessary for the tenant's use of the property and did not reduce its value. **Alterations** include improvements or changes that materially affect the condition of the property. Thus, for example, erecting additional structures probably would (and painting interior walls would not) be considered making alterations. Unless the parties have agreed otherwise, neither the landlord nor the tenant is required to make specific alterations or otherwise improve the property.

Once a residential tenant affixes an item of personal property—such as a storage cabinet—to real property, it becomes a **fixture** (see Chapter 52). In some jurisdictions, fixtures become the landlord's property and may not be removed at the end of the lease term. In other jurisdictions, fixtures can be removed at the end of the lease period,
if they can be taken without damage to the landlord's property.

Maintaining the Premises

At common law the landlord was under no duty to repair the leased premises or to warrant that they were habitable or suitable for the tenant's purposes. The tenant took the property "as is." Today, this common law rule has generally been replaced with statutes mandating a landowner's compliance with certain safety, health, and fire-protection standards. Also, in most states, statutes or judicial decisions impose a duty on a landlord who leases residential property to furnish premises that are *habitable*—that is, in a condition fit for human occupancy—and to make repairs not caused by the tenant's actions. Nevertheless, under a long-term commercial lease, a tenant may still assume the responsibility of making all necessary repairs, including, for example, rebuilding a structure after its destruction in a fire.

STATUTORY REQUIREMENTS Usually, the landlord must comply with state statutes and city ordinances that delineate specific standards for the construction and maintenance of buildings. Typically, these codes contain structural requirements common to the construction, wiring, and plumbing of residential and commercial buildings. In some jurisdictions, landlords of residential property are required by statute to maintain the premises in good repair.

The landlord is also responsible for maintaining **common areas**—halls, stairways, elevators, and so on. This duty relates not only to defects of which the landlord has actual knowledge but to those that the landlord should reasonably know about. A landlord, for example, cannot avoid responsibility for repairing a dilapidated but little-used back stairway by asserting that he or she never used it and did not know it needed to be fixed.

OBLIGATIONS UNDER THE LEASE In a long-term lease for the use of commercial property, the parties may choose to designate in the lease which of them has the responsibility to maintain the leased premises and to what extent. Generally, an express promise to repair is legally binding.

Under most circumstances, a residential tenant is not required to make such major repairs as replacing an old roof or laying a new foundation.

And without a lease provision under which the tenant assumes a duty to maintain the leased property, the tenant is under no obligation to do so. Ordinarily, however, the tenant is liable for repairs required as a result of his or her intentional or negligent actions.

IMPLIED WARRANTY OF HABITABILITY The **implied warranty of habitability** requires that a landlord who leases residential property furnish premises in a habitable condition—that is, in a condition that is safe and suitable for people to live in—at the beginning of a lease term and to maintain them in that condition for the lease's duration. Some state legislatures have enacted this warranty into law. In other jurisdictions, courts have based this warranty on the existence of a landlord's statutory duty to repair or simply applied it as a matter of public policy.

Generally, this warranty applies to major—or *substantial*—physical defects that the landlord knows or should know about and has had a reasonable time to repair—for example, a big hole in the roof. In deciding whether a defect is sufficiently substantial to be in violation of the warranty, courts may consider the following factors:

1. Whether the tenant caused the defect or is otherwise responsible for it.
2. How long the defect has existed.
3. The age of the building, since a newer dwelling would be expected to have fewer problems.
4. The defect's impact—potential and real—on the tenant's health, safety, and activities such as sleeping and eating.
5. Whether the defect contravenes applicable housing, building, or sanitation statutes.

An unattractive or annoying feature, such as a crack in the wall, may be unpleasant, but unless the crack is a structural defect or affects the residence's heating capabilities, it is probably not sufficiently substantial to make the place uninhabitable.

In the following case, the Supreme Court of Missouri departs from its former rulings based on the common law doctrine of *caveat emptor* ("let the buyer beware") in regard to leased property. The court's reasons concerning why and when the implied warranty of habitability should apply are illustrative of the public policy considerations behind the warranty.

Case 53.1

DETLING v. EDELBROCK

Supreme Court of Missouri, 1984.
671 S.W.2d 265.

BACKGROUND AND FACTS *Several tenants, including Dorothy Detling, sued their landlord, C. E. Edelbrock, for damages as a result of "enormous annoyance, discomfort, frustration, mental anxiety and mental distress." The tenants gave evidence that the property they leased exhibited "material and substantial" violations of the local municipal housing code, including rodent infestation, water leakage, and unstable steps. The lower court dismissed the suit because in Missouri no warranty of habitability existed; instead, Missouri courts applied the common law doctrine of "caveat emptor" against the tenants. The tenants appealed the dismissal to the Supreme Court of Missouri.*

WELLIVER, Judge.
* * * *

At common law a tenant leased property subject to the rule of caveat emptor and the landlord, with certain exceptions, had no duty to maintain and repair rental property or fixtures thereon. Our decision in *Turner v. Ragan* exemplifies this traditional learning:

> The landlord does not, by making the lease, impliedly warrant that the premises are safe or fit for the use to which the lessee may intend to put them. A rule similar to that of caveat emptor applies. It is the duty of the lessee to examine as to the existence of defects in the premises and to provide against their ill effects.

The common law rules as applied to leases for residential premises have come under heavy criticism in recent years as being outmoded for contemporary leasing arrangements. As a consequence, courts in many jurisdictions have abrogated the common law rules in favor of an implied warranty of habitability. Several rationales have been

advanced for replacing the common law with such a warranty, including: (1) doctrine changes in the law, including recognition of the contractual nature of modern lease agreements and the trend against caveat emptor in favor of a warranty of fitness in consumer transactions; (2) the widespread enactment of state and local housing regulations establishing minimum community standards of habitability; (3) the tenant's reasonable expectation that property leased for the purpose of human habitation for a designated period of time will be fit for that use for the duration of the lease; and (4) the belief that tenants lack the means or abilities either to fully inspect modern dwelling units or to maintain the premises during the term of the lease.
* * * *

We do not lightly depart from the teachings of the common law, but we are persuaded by the reasoning * * * that the time has come to abandon caveat emptor and the "no-repair" rule with respect to leases for residential property. We hold, therefore, that a landlord impliedly warrants the habitability of leased residential property. Specifically, we hold that a landlord warrants that the dwelling is habitable and fit for living at the inception of the [lease] and that it will remain so during the entire term. [The landlord warrants] that he will provide facilities and service vital to the life, health and safety of the tenant and to the use of the premises for residential purposes.
* * * *

Habitability is to be measured by community standards, reflected in most cases in local housing and property maintenance codes. To constitute a breach of the warranty, a tenant must allege and prove conditions of such a nature as to render the premises unsafe or unsanitary. * * *
* * * [W]e believe a tenant seeking to state a cause of action for breach of the warranty of habitability must allege facts satisfying the following elements: (1) entry into a lease for residential property; (2) the subsequent development of dangerous or unsanitary conditions on the premises materially affecting the life, health and safety of the tenant; (3) reasonable notice of the defects to the landlord; and (4) subsequent failure to restore the premises to habitability.

We believe that appellants have adequately pleaded these elements. Appellants plead that each of them entered into leases for residential apartments owned by respondent; that numerous "material and substantial" violations of the municipal codes affecting their individual apartments, common areas, and central building systems, including roach and rodent infestation, missing screens, exposed wiring, boiler malfunctions, water leakage, rubbish strewn in passageways, and unstable steps, render the leased premises "unsafe, unsanitary, and unfit for human habitation"; that respondent was given reasonable notice of [these conditions; and that the respondent failed to restore the premises to habitability].

DECISION AND REMEDY   *The Supreme Court of Missouri deemed that Edelbrock had breached an implied warranty of habitability. The court thus reversed the lower court's dismissal of the tenants' petition and remanded the case for a trial on the merits.*

REMEDIES FOR LANDLORD'S FAILURE TO MAINTAIN LEASED PROPERTY   The tenant's remedies for the landlord's failure to maintain the leased premises vary with the circumstances and with state laws.

Withholding Rent   Rent withholding is a remedy that is generally associated with the landlord's breach of the warranty of habitability. Where rent withholding is authorized under a statute (sometimes referred to as a "rent strike" statute), the tenant must usually put the amount withheld into an **escrow account.** This account is held in the name of the depositor (in this case, the tenant) and an **escrow agent** (in this case, usually the court or a government agency), and the funds are returnable to the depositor if the third person (in this case, the landlord) fails to fulfil the escrow condition.

Generally, the tenant may withhold an amount equal to the amount by which the defect rendering the premises unlivable reduces the property's rental value. How much that is may be determined in different ways, and the tenant who withholds more than is legally permissible is liable to the landlord for the excessive amount withheld.

Repairing and Deducting Under **repair and deduct** statutes or judicial recognition of a right to repair and deduct, the tenant pays for the repairs and deducts their cost from the rent. As in the case of rent withholding, this remedy is usually associated with the landlord's breach of the warranty of habitability.

Before a tenant can use this remedy, the problem—which in some states must concern a basic service, such as heat or water—must be the landlord's responsibility, and the landlord must be notified and fail to do anything about the problem within a reasonable time. Under some statutes, the deductible amount is restricted to a month's rent or some other fixed amount.

Canceling the Lease Terminating the lease is a remedy available to the tenant only when the landlord's failure to repair amounts to either constructive eviction or a breach of the warranty of habitability.

Suing for Damages Although a lawsuit for damages is always a possible course of action, it is not always economical. The amount a tenant can negotiate or be awarded may be based on the cost of a defect's repair or on the difference between the defective property's and the repaired property's rental values.

Rent

Rent is the tenant's payment to the landlord for the tenant's occupancy or use of the landlord's real property. Generally, the tenant must pay the rent even if the tenant refuses to occupy the property or moves out, as long as the refusal or the move is unjustifiable and the lease is in force. Rent is payable according to an applicable statute, custom, or what the parties decide. The amount may be subject to a legislated ceiling—as in Berkeley, California, and New York City—or it may be as much or as little as the market will bear. Usually, rent is payable in advance or periodically throughout the lease term, but rent payable in crops may not be due until the end of a term.

Some states provide that the landlord must wait for as many as ten days after the rent's due date before initiating proceedings to terminate the lease for failure on the part of the tenant to pay rent. Notice may be required before a suit can be filed. Also, the landlord may impliedly waive the right to prompt payment if in the past he or she has accepted late payments.

SECURITY DEPOSITS At the lease's inception, the landlord may require a deposit to secure the tenant's obligation to fulfill the lease. If the tenant fails to pay the rent or damages the property, the landlord may retain the deposit.

Under URLTA (for residential leases only), the amount of the deposit is limited to one month's rent and must be returned—less any amounts owed for damages or unpaid rent—at the end of the lease term within fourteen days of the tenant's request for the return of the deposit. Some states permit larger deposits and longer periods before their return. Under URLTA and some state laws, if the landlord withholds any amount from the deposit to cover damages, the tenant must be given an itemized list of the damages. In some states, the landlord must also pay interest on the deposit, less an appropriate sum as compensation for the effort involved in meeting this obligation. If the landlord fails to meet these requirements, the tenant may recover at least the amount due. In some states, the tenant may recover triple the amount due and attorneys' fees.

LATE CHARGES Legally, late charges can be imposed if a tenant does not pay rent when it is due. In general, the amount of a late charge may not be excessive, and it must bear some logical relation to the amount of the rent or to how long the payment has been overdue.

RENT ESCALATION Unless there is a clause in the lease providing otherwise, the amount of the rent cannot be increased during the lease term. If there is a clause allowing **rent escalation,** the amount may be linked to the landlord's operating costs, indexed to increases in the cost of living, or subject to a real or anticipated increase in a commercial tenant's business activity.

PROPERTY TAXES   In most jurisdictions, the tenant is not obligated to pay assessments and taxes on leased property. The responsibility of paying those charges may be transferred from the landlord to the tenant in the lease, however, or the lease may provide that the rent will be raised if the taxes increase. The tenant may be liable for the amount of the increase if the increase is due to improvements (such as the installation of trade fixtures) made by the tenant.

LANDLORD'S REMEDIES FOR TENANT'S FAILURE TO PAY RENT   Under the common law and in many states, when a tenant vacates leased property unjustifiably (not a result of constructive eviction or the landlord's breach of the warranty of habitability), the tenant remains obligated to pay the rent for the remainder of the lease term—however long that might be. The landlord may refuse to lease the premises to an acceptable, new tenant and let the property stand vacant.

In a growing number of jurisdictions, however, the landlord is required to *mitigate* his or her damages—that is, the landlord is required to make a reasonable attempt to lease the property to another party. In those jurisdictions, the tenant's liability for unpaid rent is restricted to the period of time that it would reasonably take for the landlord to lease the property to another tenant. Damages may also be allowed for the landlord's costs in reletting the property.

What is considered a reasonable period of time with respect to reletting the property varies with the type of lease and the location of the leased premises. Under a long-term residential lease, for example, this period might be three months. In some jurisdictions, if reasonable—but unsuccessful—attempts are made to relet, the tenant remains liable for the rent for the remainder of the lease.

Depending on the jurisdiction, if a tenant fails to pay rent or refuses to give up wrongful possession of leased property, the landlord can resort to one of three actions: a landlord's lien, a lawsuit, or recovery of possession.

Landlord's Lien   Under the common law, when a tenant did not pay the rent, the landlord could simply take and keep or sell whatever of the defaulting tenant's personal property was on the leased premises. Today, the landlord does not have this alternative unless the parties have contracted for it or it is permitted under a statute.

Among states that by statute preserve this remedy, known as a **landlord's lien,** some states grant the landlord a lien on all of the tenant's personal property but require the landlord to initiate court proceedings to exercise the lien. Typically, the court will authorize a sheriff to seize the tenant's property. Other states allow the landlord to seize specific items of the tenant's property and hold them as *security* for unpaid rent (that is, as protection or assurance that the landlord will recoup something on the tenant's obligation), but the landlord must obtain a court order to sell the property.

Lawsuit   Just as the landlord may sue the responsible tenant for damaging leased property, the landlord may also sue the defaulting tenant to collect unpaid rent.

Recovery of Possession   Under the common law, on the tenant's breach of the lease, the landlord could—with force, if necessary—evict the tenant and recover possession of the leased property without legal proceedings. Today, the landlord must use legal process, even if the parties have stipulated in the lease that the landlord has, and may exercise without legal proceedings, a **right of entry** (a right to retake possession peaceably).

There are two procedures to which the landlord may resort to evict the tenant. One is the common law remedy of **ejectment,** which requires the landlord to appear in court and show that the defaulting tenant is in wrongful possession. An action in ejectment does not take priority over other proceedings and, consequently, may be delayed for a long time. During the delay, the tenant can remain in possession. Thus, this action is used infrequently.

The remedy of ejectment has been modified under statutes that provide for a summary procedure often referred to as **unlawful detainer.** The landlord must show that the tenant is in breach of the lease or that the lease has expired and the tenant has not moved out. The court makes a decision quickly and, if the landlord prevails, orders a sheriff to remove the tenant.

LIABILITY FOR INJURIES ON THE PREMISES

Under the common law, whether a party in possession of property was liable to an individual who was injured on the property depended in part on that individual's classification as an invitee, a licensee, or a trespasser. An **invitee** is one whom the party in possession invites onto the premises for the possessing party's benefit, such as a customer. A **licensee** is one whom the party in possession invites or allows onto the premises for the licensee's benefit, such as a salesperson. A **trespasser** is one whom the party in possession does not invite and who has no other right to be on the premises. Each classification might require a different standard of care on the part of the person in possession of the property. Also, under certain circumstances, if the injured trespasser was a very young child who might be expected to be attracted onto the property, the **attractive nuisance doctrine** could apply to require yet a different standard of care.

These distinctions have not been entirely done away with, but today liability is more likely to depend on who controls the area where the injury occurred, and the governing standard is one of **reasonable care** under all circumstances. Applying the standard of reasonable care requires taking into consideration the predictability of a particular event (that is, applying the principle of **foreseeable risk**). The person who has responsibility for a particular part of the premises must take the same precautions regarding the area's safety as would a person of ordinary prudence in the same circumstances. Essentially, this is the same standard of care that is applied in cases of negligence.

Landlord's Liability

Traditionally, when the landlord surrendered possession of his or her property to the tenant, the landlord also relinquished responsibility for injuries occurring on the property. This was true regardless of whether the injury was caused by a condition that existed at the time the property was leased or a condition that developed later. Today, however, in recognition of the policies underlying the warranty of habitability, the landlord bears greater responsibility for the conditions of the premises and for injuries resulting from those conditions.

Currently, the landlord is generally liable for injuries occurring on the part of the property within the landlord's control—that is, common areas such as basements, hallways, and elevators. Also, when the landlord assumes an obligation to repair, the landlord's liability may extend to injuries attributable to failure to make repairs or to negligently made repairs. Thus, the landlord may be responsible for injuries that occur on the part of the premises subject to the tenant's control—that is, the apartment, the house, or the store that the tenant leased from the landlord—when that responsibility is based on the landlord's duty to repair.

INJURIES CAUSED BY DEFECTS ON THE PREMISES   The landlord's liability extends to injuries resulting from a dangerous condition that the landlord knew or should have known about, when the landlord fails to tell the tenant about it or actually conceals it. The landlord need not believe that the condition is unsafe; the situation need only be one that would lead a reasonable person to conclude that there is an unreasonable risk of harm. For example, the landlord may be liable if he or she knows that the caulking is very loose in a brick wall and a brick subsequently falls and injures a tenant.

In most states, the landlord is not under a duty to inspect residential premises before leasing them, unless there is reason to suspect that a potentially harmful defect exists. Also, the landlord is under no obligation to tell the tenant about conditions that the tenant knows about when he or she signs the lease or that are obvious, such as a lumpy carpet in the hall.

COMMERCIAL PROPERTY   When property is leased for public purposes, including commercial activities, the landlord does have an obligation to inspect the property and make repairs before the tenant takes possession to prevent unreasonable risks to members of the public. This does not include obvious conditions, which people can be expected to avoid. The landlord's liability covers only that part of the leased premises that is open to the public. If, for example, a customer disregards a sign reading "Employees Only," goes through the door, and is somehow injured on the other side, the landlord may not be liable. Similarly, the landlord is normally not liable for the tenant's negligence in maintaining the premises, assuming they were in good condition when the tenant moved in.

The liability of a landlord of leased commercial property is at issue in the following case. Note the importance of the distinction between obvious and latent conditions in the court's determination of whether the landlord should be held liable.

Case 53.2
ALABAMA POWER COMPANY v. DUNAWAY
Supreme Court of Alabama, 1987.
502 So.2d 726.

BACKGROUND AND FACTS *Alabama Power Company (APCO) leased property to David Garner, who operated Real Island Marina. The land was located on the waterfront of Lake Martin in Alabama, and under the lease APCO had no duty to repair or maintain the land. Garner operated the marina and charged the public for recreational use of the facilities. An employee picnic held at the marina was attended by David Dunaway and his family. Dunaway's son, Daniel, drowned in the lake after the family had camped for the night on the marina premises. No direct evidence existed as to how the accident occurred. Mrs. Dunaway sued APCO, Real Island Marina, and the company that sponsored the picnic for the wrongful death of her son, claiming that the property was unsafe and that lifeguards and guardrails on the seawall by the lake should have been provided. The circuit court found in favor of Dunaway, and APCO appealed.*

HOUSTON, Justice.
*   *   *   *

[A]s to the tenant, his servant, guest or others entering under his title, in the absence of a covenant to repair, . . . the landlord is only liable for injuries resulting from *latent defects, known to him at the time of the leasing, and which he concealed from the tenants.*

This Alabama law on landlord liability was reaffirmed by this Court in *Collier v. Duprel,* where the plaintiff broke his leg by tripping over an orange electrical cord supplying electricity to display signs at a lounge, operated by a lessee. We affirmed summary judgment in favor of the landlord, observing that the contention that the landlord knew of the existence of the electrical cord was irrelevant, because the alleged "defect" was not a "latent" one, which was defined as "a hidden or concealed defect, one which could not be discovered by reasonable and customary inspection."

Under these principles there is simply no factual basis for liability for APCO as landlord under either of the plaintiff's theories of negligence. The picnic pavilion and seawall were built by the lessee (Garner) and if there were a "defect" arising from the pavilion's proximity to the water, it was obvious to any observer. This was no "latent" defect. The testimony showed that the plaintiff, as well as Daniel's father, had been to Real Island Marina with Daniel and both knew of the location of the pavilion with respect to the water and of the absence of guardrails on the seawall. There were no lifeguards at the marina, and Garner had erected a sign reading "Danger, swim at your own risk." The lack of lifeguards is a condition which could have been discovered by Garner's invitees by their reasonable and customary inspection. Therefore, this was not a "latent defect."

The mere fact that APCO as landlord knew of the location of the pavilion in relation to the seawall and knew of the absence of guardrails on the seawall is irrelevant, because this "defect" was not a latent one. The same rule would apply as to the absence of lifeguards.

DECISION AND REMEDY *The Supreme Court of Alabama reversed the lower court's decision. APCO was under no duty to warn the public of obvious hazards and was not liable for the wrongful death of Daniel Dunaway.*

COMMON AREAS The landlord is responsible for—and liable for any injuries resulting from—the condition of common areas, as long as the areas are under his or her control. This responsibility includes a duty to inspect and repair such conditions as peeling lead-based paint, rotting stair railings, burned out or dim lighting, and defective water heaters and to otherwise correct such conditions as wet steps or a loose mat placed over the slippery surface of a polished floor.

When the landlord retains control over part of the premises leased to the tenant—for example, an apartment's walls—the landlord may be liable for injuries caused by that part's disrepair. The landlord is not, however, liable for injuries occurring on parts of his or her residential property where people could not be reasonably expected to go—for example, a roof or a closed basement.

REPAIRS In many jurisdictions, under building, housing, or sanitation codes or the warranty of habitability, the landlord is required to put or keep premises for lease in good repair. The breach of this duty may constitute negligence and establish the landlord's liability for any injuries caused thereby.

The landlord's express agreement to repair may be a basis for the landlord's liability if an injury is caused by the landlord's failure to fulfill the agreement. Ordinarily, the landlord has a reasonable time, after discovering or being told that a condition requires repair, within which to do the repair work or see that it is done.

Regardless of whether the landlord has agreed to make repairs, once the landlord undertakes them, he or she is liable for injuries attributable to negligence in the repair work. Once begun, a repair need not be completed, but reasonable care—which may consist of as little as a warning sign—is necessary.

INJURIES CAUSED BY CRIMES OF THIRD PERSONS The landlord is not normally required to set up an elaborate security system to protect tenants from criminals. But when crimes are reasonably foreseeable and the landlord takes no steps to prevent them, he or she may be liable if an injury results.

Courts consider several factors in determining whether a crime is foreseeable and preventable. It is logical to assume that some prior criminal activity in the geographical area in which the property is located is required to make future crimes reasonably predictable. Similarly, it is reasonable to base an expectation of future crime on how recently the previous crime occurred. Court decisions have varied as to what constitutes "recently" (possibly less than six months) and "area" (perhaps several blocks or perhaps no more than the leased property's parking lot or the building in which the leased premises are located).

Also, the type of crime may be considered. For example, a series of thefts from automobiles in an apartment complex's parking garage may make subsequent apartment break-ins foreseeable, and a few assaults on tenants could indicate that steps should be taken before an assault escalates into rape. The automobile break-ins, however, would not necessarily make murder a foreseeable risk.

In the following case, the heir to a victim of a crime that occurred on leased premises brought suit against the lessors, the tenants, and the subtenants for the wrongful death of the victim, claiming that the defendants had failed to provide sufficient security in a common area. Whether the crime was a significant, foreseeable possibility is the major factor in the court's determination.

BACKGROUND AND FACTS *Victor Iannelli entered a commercial office building in downtown Manhattan to keep a business appointment on March 17, 1976. The appointment was with the New York Typographical Union #6. The labor union leased several floors of the building from the owner and sublet part of the leased premises to the Graphic Arts Federal Credit Union, whose president was Bertram Powers. On that morning, an employee of the credit union entered the building and was held up by several masked robbers. Iannelli was shot and killed when he chanced to encounter the robbers on their way out. Iannelli's heir (the plaintiff) sued the building's owners, the labor union, and the credit union (the defendants) for the wrongful death of Iannelli, alleging that the defendants had been negligent in not providing better security, such as guards, alarms, and surveillance cameras. The heir claimed that the robbery was a foreseeable risk because the building was very near a "bad neighborhood"*

Case 53.3
IANNELLI v. POWERS
New York Supreme Court, Appellate Division, 1986.
114 A.D.2d 157, 498 N.Y.S.2d 377.

and the credit union—a banking institution—was thus a likely target of crime. The trial court held that the defendants were liable, and they appealed.

BRACKEN, Justice.

* * * *

* * * A person who possesses realty as either an owner or a tenant is under a duty to exercise reasonable care under the circumstances to maintain the property in a safe condition. That duty includes an obligation to take minimal precautions to protect members of the public from the reasonably foreseeable criminal acts of third persons.

However, the possessor of realty is not an insurer of the safety of those who enter upon such realty, and, in order to establish the existence of a duty on his part to take minimal protective measures, it must be shown "that he either knows or has reason to know from past experience 'that there is a likelihood of conduct on the part of third persons * * * which is likely to endanger the safety of the visitor.' " This is so "even when there is an extensive history of criminal conduct on the premises." For example [in *Nallan v. Helmsley Spear, Inc.*, in which] the plaintiff was shot by an unknown assailant as he was signing a guest register in the unattended lobby of the defendants' Manhattan office building, the plaintiff adduced evidence at trial that there had been 107 reported crimes in the building in the 21-month period immediately preceding the shooting, including at least 10 crimes against persons. The court concluded that although there was no proof that any of the prior crimes had occurred in the lobby:

> [A] rational jury could have found from the history of criminal activity in the other parts of the building that a criminal incident in the lobby was a significant, foreseeable possibility. If the jury found that defendants knew or had reason to know of the prior crimes in the building and further found that defendants should have anticipated a risk of harm from criminal activity in the lobby, it properly could have gone on to conclude that defendants failed in their obligation to take reasonable precautionary measures to minimize the risk and make the premises safe for the visiting public.

* * * *

In sharp contrast, the record in the case at bar contains little evidence of criminal activity prior to the date of the shooting. The employee of the twelfth floor tenant, who had apparently permitted the robbers to enter the building, testified only that the neighborhood surrounding the building was "a little scary," and that she had smelled marijuana in a nearby park. A retired New York City homicide detective, who had been involved in the investigation of Victor Iannelli's death, testified only that the neighborhood was located between several "bad" areas. In the building itself, just two relatively minor incidents had been reported: a camera had been taken from the union president's desk, and one of the owners had received a complaint from a tenant regarding a missing typewriter.

Under these circumstances, the evidence failed to establish that the appellants-respondents could have reasonably foreseen the robbery and ensuing homicide, so as to give rise to a corresponding duty on their part to adopt security measures. It simply cannot be said that the appellants-respondents had reason to know or should have known of a probability of criminal conduct on the part of third persons which was likely to pose a risk of harm to persons lawfully on the premises. The robbery and shooting by third persons in this case were superseding, intervening criminal acts which were not reasonably foreseeable and which severed any possible causal link between the appellants-respondents' conduct and the death of the plaintiff's decedent.

DECISION AND REMEDY   *This court reversed the decision of the lower court and held that there was no liability on the part of the defendants for the wrongful death of Iannelli.*

EXCULPATORY CLAUSES   A lease may contain a clause that claims to relieve the landlord from any liability for injuries or other damages, including those caused by the landlord's own negligence. Known as **exculpatory clauses,** these provisions are unenforceable if injury or damage results from the landlord's failure to fulfill a statutory duty, such as compliance with a state's building code. When included in a lease for residential property, an exculpatory clause releasing a landlord from liability for his or her negligence is unenforceable, in part because of the essential nature of housing.

Tenant's Liability

A tenant has a duty to maintain in a reasonably safe condition those areas under his or her control. When commercial property is involved, this duty extends to all parts of the premises onto which a customer or other member of the public might be expected to go—such as the aisles in a grocery store. The grocer's duty includes using care in displaying his or her wares so that they present no threat to customers' safety. For example, the goods should not be stacked so as to block an aisle or to fall onto a customer taking an item for purchase. Similarly, the grocer may be liable if a customer slips on the spilled contents of a broken jar and is injured.

In some situations—particularly when property is leased for commercial purposes—the tenant's duty may coincide with the landlord's duty, and thus both the landlord and the tenant may be liable for a third party's injuries. In the following case, for example, the plaintiff was injured in the parking lot of a shopping center when her shopping cart overturned. She had purchased the groceries in the cart from a grocer who had leased the premises from the owner of the shopping center. Although the landlord had agreed in the lease contract to maintain the parking lot, this provision did not relieve the tenant from liability for a customer's injury resulting from inadequate maintenance of the parking lot.

BACKGROUND AND FACTS   *National Tea Company operated a grocery store inside a shopping center in Ocean Springs, Mississippi. National Tea leased the building from Chrisler Properties, the owner of the center and parking lot. The lease provided in part that, "The premises under this lease include the free use of properly paved, lighted * * * parking lot * * * for the parking by lessee, its customers, agents, and employees. Said parking lot to be used in conjunction with other customers of lessees in this development, if any, and lessor agrees to maintain, light, and remove snow from all parking area." James Allday was the manager of National Tea's grocery store. The plaintiff, Romain Wilson, had purchased some groceries at the store and carried them in a cart through the parking lot. The cart wheel hit a pothole in the pavement, and the cart overturned, pulling Wilson to the ground. Wilson severely injured her back in the fall and sued Allday and the grocery store for damages. The trial court jury found for the plaintiff, but the judge granted a judgment notwithstanding the verdict for Allday and National Tea. Wilson appealed.*

Case 53.4
WILSON v. ALLDAY
Supreme Court of Mississippi,
1986.
487 So.2d 793.

ANDERSON, Justice.
*   *   *   *

The established law in this state is that the owner, occupant or person *in charge of premises* owes to an invitee or business visitor a duty of exercising reasonable or ordinary care to keep the premises in reasonably safe and suitable condition or of warning invitee of dangerous conditions not readily apparent which owner knows or should know of in the exercise of reasonable care. However, the owner, occupant or person in charge of property is not an insurer of the safety of an invitee—where the invitee knows or should know of an apparent danger, no warning is required.

*   *   *   *

[The court quotes as follows from various sources of landlord-tenant law:]

Where only part of a building or related premises is occupied by a tenant, but he has full control and possession of such part, he is, as to the public, under the duty of keeping his portion of the premises in repair, and he will be liable for injuries resulting from its unsafe condition to a person lawfully thereon. Thus he will be held so liable for injuries to one such as a cotenant or those under him. The duty of care applies even though the landlord may also have some control over the particular facility and is also liable for the injury. The duty of the tenant includes the duty to warn his invitees of any latent dangerous condition or defects on the premises.

Thus, it has been held that a tenant may be responsible for the condition of approaches and stairways or a *parking area*. His duty or responsibility also applies to parts of the premises used in common with other tenants which they are all obliged to maintain.

If the lessee's use of the premises was tantamount to possession and control, then the lessee owed a duty of ordinary and reasonable care to its invitees upon the premises. Whether there was a breach (notice, dangerous conditions, etc.) becomes a question of fact. Conversely, if lessee's use of the lot did not constitute control, there would be no duty owed and therefore no cause of action.

Whether or not there was a known obvious danger was a question to be resolved by the jury. Appellant argues that appellee did, in fact, have possession and exercised control of the parking lot in that appellee had erected a cart corral there and its employees went onto the lot at least twelve times each day to gather its carts. Further, it invited customers to park in the lot in front of the store and instructed its employees to park in other designated areas on the lot. Appellant contends that appellees' presence and activities on the lot put it in the position to know of dangers and thereby gave rise to a duty to at least warn its invitees of those dangers.

*   *   *   *

It would appear that a tenant/lessee/occupier of premises owes a duty of reasonable care to its invitees for the demised property and such necessary incidental areas substantially under its control (as the parking lot) and which he invites the public to use, notwithstanding a maintenance agreement with the landlord. While such agreement may serve as the basis for recovery against the lessor, it does not absolve the lessee of his duty to his invitees under the circumstances.

*   *   *   *

If the lessees occupied and controlled the premises in question, then there was a duty concurrent with both the lessee and lessor to repair the dangerous condition or to warn invitees coming onto the premises.

DECISION AND REMEDY   *The state supreme court held that the lower court was correct in submitting the issue to the jury for determination but that the lower court erred in overturning the jury's decision. The judgment of the lower court was thus reversed. Wilson could collect damages from Allday and National Tea for her injury.*

TRANSFERRING RIGHTS TO LEASED PROPERTY

Either the landlord or the tenant may wish to transfer his or her rights to the leased property during the term of the lease.

Transferring the Landlord's Interest

Just as any other real property owner can sell, give away, or otherwise transfer his or her property (see Chapter 52), so can a landlord—who is, of course, the leased property's owner. Furthermore, the landlord may make a deal involving only the lease, only the landlord's reversionary interest in the property after the lease has been terminated, only the rent accruable under the lease, or any of these property rights in combination.

If complete title—that is, the landlord's reversionary interest—to the leased property is transferred, the tenant becomes the tenant of the new owner. The new owner may collect subsequent rent but must then abide by the terms of the existing lease agreement.

Transferring the Tenant's Interest

The tenant's transfer of his or her entire interest in the leased property to a third person is an **assignment** of the lease. The tenant's transfer of all or part of the premises for a period shorter than the lease term is a **sublease.** Under neither an assignment nor a sublease can the assignee's or sublessee's rights against the landlord be *more* than those of the original tenant.

ASSIGNMENTS   A controlling statute or a clause in the lease may require the landlord's consent to the tenant's assignment of his or her interest in the lease. If the statute or lease does not also require that consent not be unreasonably withheld, some courts will impose that condition. Typically, clauses that require the landlord's consent to assignment are written as forfeiture restraints—that is, they provide that the landlord may terminate the tenancy if the tenant attempts to assign the lease without consent. This restriction is meant to protect the landlord from an assignee-tenant who might damage the property, fail to pay the rent, or otherwise be irresponsible. The landlord's knowing acceptance of rent from an assignee, however, may constitute a waiver of the consent requirement.

When an assignment is valid, the assignee acquires all of the tenant's rights under the lease. But an assignment does not release the assigning tenant from the obligation to pay rent should the assignee default. Also, if the assignee exercises an option under the original lease to extend the term, the assigning tenant remains liable for the rent during the extension, unless the landlord agrees otherwise.

SUBLEASES   The restrictions that apply to an assignment of the tenant's interest in the leased premises apply to a sublease. For example, if the landlord's consent is required, a sublease without such permission is ineffective. Also, a sublease does not release the tenant from his or her obligations under the lease any more than an assignment does.

To illustrate: A student, Ann, leases an apartment for a two-year period. Ann has been planning to attend summer school, but she is offered a job in Europe for the summer months and accepts. To avoid paying three months' rent for an unoccupied apartment, she can sublease the apartment to another student, unless the lease requires the landlord's permission, in which case the landlord's consent will have to be obtained. The sublessee will take the apartment under the same lease terms as Ann. The landlord can hold Ann liable should the sublessee violate those terms.

TERMINATION OR RENEWAL OF THE LEASE

Usually a lease terminates when its term ends. The tenant surrenders the property to the landlord, who retakes possession. If the lease does not contain an option for renewal and the parties have not agreed that the tenant may stay on, the tenant has no right to remain. If the lease is renewable and the tenant decides to exercise the option, the tenant must comply with any conditions requiring notice to the landlord of the tenant's decision.

Termination

In addition to the expiration of the lease term, a lease can be terminated in several other ways.

TERMINATION BY NOTICE   If the lease states the time it will end, the landlord is not required to give the tenant notice—that is, to remind the tenant the lease is going to expire—even as the time approaches. The lease terminates automatically. The lease may require that notice be given, however, or notice may be required under a statute. The procedures and time periods vary, but usually one or two months' notice is enough to end a tenancy for a year, and a week will suffice to end a tenancy for a shorter period.

On the other hand, a *periodic tenancy* will renew automatically unless one of the parties gives timely notice of termination. A periodic tenancy is a tenancy from week to week, month to month, or year to year. (Periodic tenancies are discussed in Chapter 52.)

RELEASE AND MERGER   A lease may give the tenant the opportunity to purchase the leased property during the term or at its end. Regardless of whether the lease provides this option, the landlord can convey his or her interest in the property to the tenant. This transfer is a **release,** and the tenant's interest in the property **merges** into the title to the property that he or she now holds. Of course, a release effectively relieves the tenant of his or her obligations under the lease while bestowing on him or her title to the property, as well as all of the former landlord's responsibilities regarding the property. Because a release is a transfer of real property, it is subject to the Statute of Frauds (discussed in Chapter 12) and thus must be in writing.

SURRENDER BY AGREEMENT   The parties may agree to end a tenancy before it would otherwise terminate. If the lease was subject to the Statute of Frauds, surrender of the property by agreement must be in writing, since, technically, the tenant is conveying his or her interest in the property to the landlord. Surrender of the property by operation of law, however, does not require a writing. A surrender by operation of law is sometimes held to occur when the tenant abandons the property.

ABANDONMENT   A landlord may treat a tenant's **abandonment** of the property—that is, the tenant's moving off the premises completely with no intention of returning—before the end of term as an offer of surrender, and the landlord's retaking of possession of the property will relieve the tenant of the obligation to pay rent. Sometimes, actions that the landlord takes to mitigate his or her damages—for example, refinishing an abandoned apartment's floors when preparing to lease it to another party—may be interpreted as accepting the tenant's offer of surrender, thereby absolving the tenant of responsibility for future rent payment.

FORFEITURE   **Forfeiture** is the termination of a lease, according to its terms or the terms of a statute, when one of the parties fails to fulfill a condition under the lease and thereby breaches it. For instance, if the lease provides that the tenant will forfeit his or her interest in the leased property on failing to pay rent when it is due, the tenant's late payment of rent could prompt the lease's forfeiture. Generally, the courts do not favor forfeiture, and when neither the lease nor a statute provides for it, the landlord may only claim damages.

DESTRUCTION OF THE PROPERTY   Under statutes in most states, destruction of the leased property brought about by a fire, flood, or other cause beyond the landlord's control can terminate a residential lease. Usually, the landlord is under no obligation to restore the premises.

Similarly, the destruction of an entire building leased for business purposes may release the commercial tenant from any responsibility for continued payment of rent. (Terms vary among leases. If there is, for example, a fire, a commercial tenant's rent may only be reduced proportionally, according to how much property has been destroyed, and the responsibility for restoring the property may rest on the tenant.)

Renewal

The lease may provide for renewal, or the landlord and the tenant may simply agree to renew it. When the lease provides for an option to renew, there is typically a requirement that the tenant notify the landlord within a specific period of time—usually days or months—before the lease expires as to whether the tenant will exercise the option. The tenant must comply with any particulars regarding the notice's form (for example, that it be in writing) or the renewal will be invalid, even if the tenant stays on the property. The tenant's attempt to alter other terms to which the renewal is subject can be interpreted as a choice not to exercise the option.

If a tenant neither renews a lease in accordance with its terms nor moves off the leased premises, but stays on without the landlord's consent, he or she can be treated as a trespasser. The tenant may be held liable to the landlord for damages.

QUESTIONS AND CASE PROBLEMS

1. Goodman contracts to lease an apartment near the campus from landlord Lopez for one year, with the monthly rent due and payable on the first of each month. At the end of the year, Goodman does not vacate the apartment, and Lopez does not object. Goodman continues to pay the rent on the first day of the month, and it is accepted by Lopez. Six months later, Lopez informs Goodman that the apartment has been leased to Green and that Goodman must vacate the premises by the end of the week. Goodman refuses to leave, and Lopez threatens eviction proceedings. Discuss the rights of the parties under these circumstances. (Review both Chapters 52 and 53).

2. Turner owns an apartment building. She contracts with Alvarez for one year to place coin-operated washing machines and dryers in laundry rooms in the building complex. The contract requires Alvarez to service the washers and dryers within twenty-four hours after notice is given that service is necessary. Some of the apartment leaseholders complain to Turner that Alvarez's service is poor and that Alvarez does not promptly refund money lost in the machines. After an argument, Turner orders Alvarez to remove all the machines within one week and not to come on the property again. Alvarez claims that he has a lease of the laundry rooms for one year. Turner claims that Alvarez has a revocable license (see Chapter 52). Discuss fully the property rights of the parties in this matter.

3. James owns a three-story building. James leases the ground floor to Juan's Mexican restaurant. The lease is to run for a five-year period and contains an express covenant of quiet enjoyment. One year later, James leases the top two stories to the Upbeat Club, a discotheque. The club's hours run from 5:00 P.M. to 11:00 P.M. The noise from the Upbeat Club is so loud that it is driving away customers from Juan's Mexican restaurant. Juan has notified the landlord of the interference and has called the police on a number of occasions. The landlord refuses to talk to the owners of the Upbeat Club or to do anything to remedy the situation. Juan abandons the premises. James files suit for breach of the lease agreement and for the rental payments still due under the lease. Juan claims that he was constructively evicted and has filed a countersuit for damages. Discuss who will be held liable.

4. Thomas has been a tenant of the Crestview Apartments for more than ten years. His tenancy is a month-to-month tenancy. During the ten years of his tenancy, the building's condition has steadily deteriorated. Indeed, the deterioration has reached the point at which the premises are in violation of city health and housing ordinances. Thomas has repeatedly complained to the landlord, but no repairs have been made. Thomas helps to organize a tenants' council, and the council reports numerous housing, building,

and health violations to the authorities. The authorities bring actions against the landlord.

(a) Assume that immediately after the authorities bring their actions, Thomas is given notice of termination of his lease. Thomas wants to prevent his eviction. Discuss how successful he will be.

(b) Assume Thomas and the other tenants want to withhold rent payments until the premises are repaired. Discuss whether the tenants may withhold the rent payments and, if so, to what extent and on what grounds.

5. Sarah has rented a house from Franks. The house is only two years old. Sarah's roof leaks every time it rains. The water that has accumulated in the attic has caused plaster to fall off ceilings in the upstairs bedrooms, and one ceiling has started to sag. Sarah has complained to Franks and asked Franks to have the roof repaired. Franks says he caulked the roof, but the roof still leaks. Franks claims that since Sarah has sole control of the leased premises, she has the duty to repair the roof. Sarah insists that the repair of the roof is Franks's responsibility. Discuss fully who is responsible for repairing the roof and, if the responsibility belongs to Franks, what remedies are available to Sarah.

6. You are a student in college and plan to attend classes for nine months. You sign a twelve-month lease for an apartment and pay a security deposit of $150. Discuss fully each of the following situations:

(a) You have a summer job in your home town and wish to assign the balance of your lease (three months) to a fellow student who will be attending summer school. Can you do so?

(b) You are graduating in May. The lease will have three months remaining. Can you terminate the lease without liability by giving a thirty-day notice to the landlord?

(c) The lease period has expired. Are you entitled to the return of your $150 security deposit?

7. Spirn, a shopping-mall tenant, sustained injuries when he fell while on the property of Joseph, the mall's owner. At the time of the injury, Spirn was on his way to a furnace room in the mall to check the furnace, which seemed to be malfunctioning. The furnace room was only accessible by an outside door, approximately twelve feet from the street. There was no paved walkway leading to the door, but a "trodden path" had been created in the snow by persons who had been called earlier by Joseph to repair the furnace. The repairpersons' footprints had made depressions in the snow, which had subsequently been iced over. Spirn slipped and injured himself. Spirn filed suit against Joseph, alleging that the path was an unnatural (or aggravated natural) condition of the premises created by agents of Joseph and that Joseph had a duty to maintain safe premises. Joseph had therefore been negligent in failing to warn Spirn of the condition of the path. Discuss whether Spirn was successful. [Spirn v Joseph, 144 Ill.App.3d 127, 493 N.E.2d 1197, 98 Ill.Dec. 176 (1986)]

8. A landlord of residential premises leased a building he owned nearby for use as a cocktail lounge. The residential tenants complained to the landlord about the late-evening and early-morning music and disturbances coming from the lounge. Although the lease for the lounge provided that entertainment had to be conducted so that it could not be heard outside the building and would not disturb residents of the apartments, the landlord was unsuccessful in remedying the problem. The tenants vacated their apartments. Was the landlord successful in a suit to collect rent from the tenants who vacated? [Blackett v. Olanoff, 371 Mass. 714, 358 N.E.2d 817 (1977)]

9. Jeanne Koferl, a single woman with an eight-year-old son, was a tenant of Highview Associates under a written lease that was to expire on May 26, 1983. Her apartment complex had become the target of burglars and thieves, and break-ins and thefts had become frequent. Prior to January 1983, she had suffered the traumatic experience of having a Peeping Tom peak through her window. This event was reported to the management. At the end of January 1983, two men attempted to burglarize her apartment at 3:00 A.M. She fled with her child to her mother's home and never returned to the apartment. The landlord was able to rent the apartment to another tenant before May of 1983. The landlord sued Koferl for unpaid rent for the months of February and March and for re-renting expenses. Was the tenant liable for the costs of re-renting her apartment prior to the end of the lease term? [Highview Associates v. Koferl, 124 Misc.2d 797, 477 N.Y.S.2d 585 (Dist.Ct. 1984)]

10. Denna Kostecki was an eleven-year-old minor who lived next door to an apartment building and frequently played with tenants' children. One day, Denna and some other children were playing a game of chase in the apartment building. Denna, while being chased, ran toward a door with fifteen small glass panes in it. The door opened into a common hallway. She was passing through the door as it was slowly closing. Suddenly, the door closed rapidly, causing her hand to shatter one of the glass panes. This, in turn, caused cuts on her hand resulting in partial disability, scarring, and disfigurement. The door had never closed in such a rapid fashion in the past, and there had been no complaints concerning the door. Denna filed suit (through her father) against the building's owners, Chris and Jay Pavlis, claiming that the closure mechanism was defective and the door was thus unreasonably dangerous. Discuss whether the owners were liable for Denna's injuries. [Kostecki by Kostecki v. Pavlis, 140 Ill.App.3d 176, 488 N.E.2d 644, 94 Ill.Dec. 645 (1986)]

11. Tachtronic Instruments leased office and warehouse space in a building owned by Provident Mutual Life Insurance Company. The three-year lease ran until October 31, 1985, and specified monthly payments to Provident in the amount of $2,463. Within the first year of the lease term, Tachtronic defaulted on its payments. When Provident brought an action to evict Tachtronic, the small firm paid a portion of the rent due, and the action was dismissed. By February of 1984, Tachtronic had largely vacated the premises. On March 1, 1984, Tachtronic met with representatives of Provident at the "leased" premises. The premises were inspected by Provident, and Tachtronic removed its remaining possessions, broom-swept the floor, and turned over the keys to Provident. Immediately thereafter, Provident sought a new tenant for the premises. A new tenant was found, and a more lucrative lease beginning November 1, 1984, was created between Provident and the new tenant. In June of 1984, Provident commenced an action to recover the rent due from Tachtronic prior to its departure from the leased premises and also the rent due and payable for the remainder of the lease. Discuss whether Provident could collect. [Provident Mutual Life Insurance Co. v. Tachtronic Instruments, Inc., 394 N.W.2d 161 (Minn.App. 1986)]

Chapter 54

Insurance

THE NATURE OF INSURANCE

Insurance is a contract whereby, for a stipulated consideration, one party agrees to compensate the other for any future loss on a specified subject by a specified peril. Insurance is a means to transfer and allocate risk. In many cases, **risk** can be described as a prediction concerning potential loss based on known and unknown factors. Insurance, however, involves much more than a game of chance.

There are many precautions that may be taken to protect against the hazards of life. For example, an individual may wear a seat belt to protect himself or herself against injury in an automobile accident. Likewise, a person may install smoke detectors to guard against the risk of fire. Of course, no one can predict whether an accident or a fire will ever occur, but individuals and businesses must establish plans to protect their personal and financial interests should some event threaten to undermine their security. This concept is known as **risk management.** Transferring certain risks from the individual to the insurance company is the most common method of risk management.

The Concept of Risk Pooling

All types of insurance use the principle of pooling of risk; that is, they spread the risk among a large number of people—the pool—to make the premiums small compared with the coverage offered. Consider life insurance. Only a small proportion of the individuals in any particular age group will die in any one year. If a large percentage of this age group pays premiums to a life insurance company in exchange for a benefit payment in case of premature death, there will be a sufficient amount of money to pay the beneficiaries of the policyholders who do die. Given a long enough time for correlation of data about the group and the particular disaster—in this case, premature death—insurance companies can predict the total number of disasters in any one year with great accuracy. Thus, they can estimate the total amount they will have to pay if they insure the group, and they can predict the rates they will have to charge each member of the group in order to make the necessary payments and make a profit for the company.

Terminology

An insurance contract is called a **policy;** the consideration paid to the insurer is called a **premium;** and the insurance company is sometimes called an **underwriter.**

The *parties* to an insurance policy are the *insurer* (the insurance company) and the *insured* (the person covered by its provisions). Insurance contracts are usually obtained through an *agent,* who ordinarily works for the insurance company, or a *broker,* who is ordinarily an independent contractor. When a broker deals with an applicant for insurance, the broker is, in effect, the applicant's agent. By contrast, an insurance agent is an agent of the insurance company.

In most situations, state law determines the status of all parties writing or obtaining insurance. State laws govern the incorporation, licensing, supervision, and liquidation of insurers and the licensing and supervision of insurance agents and brokers.

Classification of Insurance

Insurance is classified according to the nature of the risk involved. For example, fire insurance, casualty insurance, life insurance, and title insurance apply to different types of risk. Furthermore, policies of these types differ in the persons and interests they protect. This is reasonable, because the types of losses that are expected and the types that are foreseeable or unforeseeable vary with the nature of the activity. See Exhibit 54–1 for a list of various insurance classifications.

INSURABLE INTEREST

A person can insure anything in which he or she has an *insurable interest.* Without this insurable interest, there is no enforceable contract, and a transaction to insure would have to be treated as a wager.

Life

In the case of life insurance, one must have a reasonable expectation of benefit from the continued life of another in order to have an insurable interest in that person's life. The benefit may be pecuniary (related to money) or it may be founded upon the relationship between the parties (by blood or affinity).

Close family relationships give a person an insurable interest in the life of another. Generally, blood or marital relationships fit this category. A husband can take out an insurance policy on his wife and vice versa, parents can take out life insurance policies on their children, brothers and sisters on each other, and grandparents on grandchildren, as all these are close family relationships.

To illustrate the concept of insurable interest, assume that James Jones insures his life for $100,000 with Continental Insurance Company, naming Henry Mason as beneficiary of the policy. When Jones dies, Continental Insurance cannot refuse to pay Mason merely because he had no insurable interest in the life of Jones. The *beneficiary* of a life insurance policy need not have an insurable interest in the insured. Jones was actually insuring his own life for the benefit of Mason and is the owner of the policy. Obviously, Jones has an insurable interest in his own life. On the other hand, if Jones bought a policy with Continental Insurance to insure the life of his next-door neighbor, Robert Samuel, Continental Insurance could refuse to pay the face value of the policy upon Samuel's death because Jones had no insurable interest in Samuel's life.

The insurable interest in life insurance must exist *at the time the policy is obtained.* Because of this rule, in most states a divorce will not affect a policy. Similarly, under a key-person life insurance policy, it will not matter if the key person is no longer in the business's employ at the time of the loss—that is, the key person's death.

KEY-PERSON INSURANCE Key-person insurance (sometimes referred to as business insurance) involves an organization's insuring the life of a person who is important to that organization. Because the organization expects to receive some pecuniary gain from the continuation of the key person's life or some financial loss from the key person's death, the organization has an insurable interest.

Exhibit 54–1 **Insurance Classifications**

TYPE OF INSURANCE	COVERAGE
Accident	Covers expenses, losses, and suffering incurred by the insured because of accidents causing physical injury and consequent disability; sometimes includes a specified payment to heirs of the insured if death results from an accident.
All-risk	Covers all losses that insured may incur except those resulting from fraud on the part of the insured.
Automobile	May cover damage to automobiles resulting from specified hazards or occurrences (such as fire, vandalism, theft, or collision); normally provides protection against liability for personal injuries and property damage resulting from the operation of the vehicle.
Business	Protects a business in the event of the death or disability of a key employee; often referred to as key-person insurance.
Casualty	Protects against losses that may be incurred by the insured as a result of being held liable for personal injuries or property damage sustained by others.
Credit	Pays to a creditor the balance of a debt upon the disability, death, insolvency, or bankruptcy of the debtor; often offered by lending institutions.
Decreasing-term	Provides life insurance; requires uniform payments over the life (term) of the policy, but with a decreasing face value.
Employer's liability	Insures employers against liability for injuries or losses sustained by employees during the course of their employment; covers claims not covered under workers' compensation insurance.
Fidelity or guaranty	Provides indemnity against losses in trade or losses caused by the dishonesty of employees, the insolvency of debtors, or breaches of contract.
Fire	Covers losses caused to the insured as a result of fire.
Floater	Covers movable property, so long as the property is within the territorial boundaries specified in the contract.
Group	Provides individual life, medical, or disability insurance coverage but is obtainable through a group of persons, usually employees; the policy premium is paid either entirely by the employer or partially by the employer and partially by the employee.
Health	Covers expenses incurred by the insured resulting from physical injury or illness and other expenses relating to health and life maintenance.
Homeowners	Protects homeowners against some or all of the risks of loss to their residences and their contents or liability related to such property.
Liability	Protects against liability imposed on the insured resulting from injuries to the person or property of another.
Life	Covers the death of the policyholder. Upon the death of the insured, an amount specified in the policy is paid by the insurer to the insured's beneficiary.
Major medical	Protects the insured against major hospital, medical, or surgical expenses.
Malpractice	Protects professionals (doctors, lawyers, and others) against malpractice claims brought against them by their patients or clients; a form of liability insurance.
Marine	Covers movable property (ships, freight, or cargo) against certain perils or navigation risks during a specific voyage or time period.
Mortgage	Covers a mortgage loan; the insurer pays the balance of the mortgage to the creditor upon the death or disability of the debtor.
No-fault auto	Covers personal injury and (sometimes) property damage resulting from automobile accidents. The insured submits his or her claims to his or her own insurance company, regardless of who was at fault. A person may sue the party at fault or that party's insurer only in cases involving serious medical injury and consequent high medical costs. Governed by state "no-fault" statutes.

(Continued on the next page)

Exhibit 54–1 Insurance Classifications (Continued)

TYPE OF INSURANCE	COVERAGE
Term	Provides life insurance for a specified period of time (term) with no cash surrender value; usually renewable.
Title	Protects against any defects in title to real property and any losses incurred as a result of existing claims against or liens on the property at the time of purchase.

Typically, a partnership will insure the life of each partner, because the death of any one partner will legally dissolve the firm and cause some degree of loss to the partnership. Similarly, a corporation has an insurable interest in the life expectancy of a key executive whose death would result in financial loss to the company.

Property

In the case of real and personal property, an insurable interest exists when the insured derives a pecuniary benefit from the preservation and continued existence of the property. That is, one has an insurable interest in property when one would sustain a pecuniary loss from its destruction. For example, a mortgagor and a mortgagee both have an insurable interest in the mortgaged property. So do a landlord and a tenant in leased property, a secured party in the property in which he or she has an interest, a partner in partnership property, and a stockholder in corporate property. But John or Jane Doe cannot obtain fire insurance on the White House or auto insurance on A. J. Foyt's racing cars.

The existence of an insurable interest is a primary concern in determining liability under an insurance policy. The insurable interest in property must exist *when the loss occurs*.

In the following case, the insurance company claimed that the insured possessed no insurable interest in her former husband's house, since she had deeded her interest to him one year before his death.

Case 54.1
MOTORISTS MUTUAL INSURANCE COMPANY v. RICHMOND

Court of Appeals of Kentucky, 1984.
676 S.W.2d 478.

BACKGROUND AND FACTS *Linda Richmond and Eddie Durham were married, the parents of two children, and homeowners in Kentucky. When Richmond and Durham divorced, Richmond, the plaintiff, deeded her legal interest in the title to their home to Durham and moved out with their children. Shortly thereafter Durham died, leaving the two children as his only legal heirs. Richmond returned to the home with the children. She had been living there, making the mortgage payments, for more than one year when the home was totally destroyed by fire. Ten months prior to the fire, Richmond had secured fire insurance with the defendant, Motorists Mutual Insurance Company. She sought payment from Motorists for the destruction of the house, but Motorists refused to pay, claiming that she had no insurable interest in the house. The trial court awarded Richmond, her children, and the mortgage company $29,000. Motorists appealed.*

CLAYTON, Judge.
*   *   *   *

Seeking to avoid payment under the contract, Motorists would now cast Richmond as nothing more than a trespassing squatter who "surreptitiously" returned to the residence and thereafter fraudulently represented her true lack of ownership interest. * * * We cannot accept [this] base characterization. [It is] not supposed by the record or the law.

Linda Richmond, both before and after the death of her late former husband, made substantial monetary contribution to the maintenance and improvement of the destroyed residence. As natural guardian for her minor children, and later as administratrix of the Durham estate, she was obligated to provide for the care and custody of their offspring, including the duty to protect their home, of which the children became sole owners in fee simple by statute of descent upon the death of their father. Thus, when Richmond returned to the property following Durham's death she was not a surreptitious trespasser. Her offspring and she as their guardian were fully entitled to use and dominion over the premises. While not possessed of title, Richmond certainly possessed an insurable interest in the residence: first, by her status as natural guardian for the protection of her minor children's interest; and second, by her extensive pecuniary investment in the residence. * * *

Nor does the present record contain any suggestion of fraud or unwitting assumption of risk by Motorists. Richmond made no claim of ownership to the residence. Her only direct action with regard to the so-called "receipt" was to place her signature upon it. Motorists' own agent, Mosely, was responsible for completing the remainder of the document including the portion indicating Richmond's ownership. Had he so chosen, he could have easily verified his assumptions concerning Richmond's ownership simply by calling Farmers State Bank. It is a well settled principle of law in this state that an insurer as

principal is bound by the acts of his agent within the scope of his apparent authority, though his authority may in fact be limited, if the person dealing with him is ignorant of the limitation upon his authority. Few persons [understand] insurance who have not made it a special study. The agent who comes to get the insurance is the only person they deal with or know in the transaction. The rule that he represents the company and not the insured in taking the application is just and is generally recognized.

* * * Thus, the burden of any error in the nature of Richmond's insurable interest, rather than its existence, falls upon Motorists via the actions of its agent.

Motorists is further obligated to make payment by the definition provisions of its policy. Under that policy "insured" is defined as

You and the following representatives of your household:

a. your relatives

b. *any other person under the age of 21 who is in the care of any person named above.* [Emphasis added by the court.]

At the time of issuance of the policy, Linda's children, Melody and James, were each, by statute of descent, fee simple owners of an indivisible one-half interest in the residence. As minors under the age of 15, neither child was legally capable of contracting for insurance in his or her own behalf. Therefore, absent Linda's efforts in securing insurance, neither Melody nor James could have directly protected his or her ownership interest in the home. By defining the terms of its policy so as to include the ownership interest of the children, Motorists undertook exactly the risk it bargained for and should not now be able to successfully deny payment. In this respect no liberal construction of the policy of insurance is necessary to protect the insured.

The court held that Linda Richmond had an insurable interest in the home, for which Motorists was required to pay.

DECISION AND REMEDY

THE INSURANCE CONTRACT

An insurance contract is governed by the general principles of contract law. Policies generally are in standard form; and in some states, standardization of forms is required.

Application for Insurance

The application for insurance is usually attached to the policy and made a part of the insurance contract. An insurance applicant is bound by any false statements that appear in the application (subject to certain exceptions). Because the insurance company evaluates the risk factors based on the information included in the insurance application, misstatements or misrepresentations can void a policy, especially if the insurance company can show that it would not have extended insurance if it had known the facts.

When the Contract Becomes Effective

The effective date of an insurance contract is important. In some instances, the insurance applicant is not protected until a formal written policy is issued. In other situations, the applicant is protected between the time the application is received and the time the insurance company either accepts or rejects it.

A person who seeks insurance from an insurance company's agent will usually be protected from the moment the application is made, provided some form of premium has been paid. Between the time the application is received and either rejected or accepted, the applicant is covered (possibly subject to certain conditions, such as successfully passing a medical examination). Usually the agent will write a memorandum, or **binder,** indicating that a policy is pending and stating its essential terms.

According to general principles of agency law, if a broker (as opposed to an agent of an insurance company) fails to obtain policy coverage and the applicant is damaged as a result, then the broker is liable to the damaged applicant-principal for the loss.

If the parties agree that the policy will be issued and delivered at a later time, the contract is not effective until the policy is issued and delivered or sent to the applicant, depending upon the agreement. Thus, loss sustained between the time of application and the delivery of the policy is not covered.

Parties can agree that a life insurance policy will be binding at the time the insured pays the first premium. The policy, however, can be *expressly contingent* upon the applicant's passing a physical examination. If the applicant pays the premium and passes the examination, then the policy coverage is continuously in effect. If the applicant pays the premium but dies before having the physical examination, then the applicant's estate must show that the applicant would have passed the examination had he or she not died.

Coverage on an insurance policy, then, can begin when a binder is written, when the policy is issued, or, depending upon the terms of the contract, after a certain period of time has elapsed. The following case illustrates the kinds of problems that can arise concerning the effective date of coverage of an insurance policy.

Case 54.2
DAVIS AND LANDRY, INC. v. GUARANTY INCOME LIFE INSURANCE COMPANY

Court of Appeal of Louisiana, First Circuit, 1983. 442 So.2d 621.

BACKGROUND AND FACTS *On October 22, 1981, the partnership of Davis and Landry, Inc., the plaintiff, mailed two applications to Guaranty Income Life Insurance Co., the defendant, for $500,000 life insurance policies and a check for two years' advance premiums to insure the lives of the two principals, Davis and Landry. Davis and Landry believed that pending delivery of the policy they would receive $100,000 coverage under specific terms stated in a premium receipt. On October 27, 1981, the remainder of Davis's application package, a form entitled "Answers Made to the Medical Examiner," executed by a doctor, was received by Guaranty Income. Based on the answers given in this form, Guaranty Income decided it needed to obtain an "attending physician's statement" (APS) from the doctor. The request for this further statement was mailed to the doctor on November 2, 1981, and had not been returned by November 10, 1981, when Davis died. The partnership sued Guaranty Income to recover benefits under the insurance policy for Davis's death. The trial court granted a summary judgment for the insurance company, from which the plaintiff appealed.*

SHORTESS, Judge.

*   *   *   *

An insurance company is under a duty to act upon an application for insurance within a reasonable time, and a violation of that duty with resultant damages will subject the company to liability for negligence. What is a reasonable period must depend upon the facts in each case, and the burden is on plaintiff to show that a policy would have issued but for the delay caused by the neglect of the insurer. *   *   *

*   *   *

*   *   * [W]e find that the insurer did not breach any duty when it did not inform plaintiff that the physician had not returned Davis' APS. The APS had only been in the physician's possession on the date of the applicant's death for, at most, seven working days. This is simply not an unreasonable amount of time for the insurer to allow the physician to complete and return the APS. Moreover, even if it can be said that defendant breached a duty to this plaintiff, it is clear from the deposition of Fowler, the underwriter, that the policy would not necessarily have issued even upon prompt return of the APS. The APS, as returned on November 17, showed that Davis had suffered tingling and numbness in his hands and "a vague, interior chest wall discomfort" and that Dr. Walker had referred him to neurosurgeon, Dr. John Clifford, regarding this symptom. Fowler testified that, based upon this information, additional statements would have been required from Dr. Clifford. *   *   * Even assuming that the APS had been returned to defendant immediately upon receipt by the physician, there is no way for plaintiff to establish that the report which *would* have been requested by defendant from Dr. Clifford would have reached defendant before Davis' death. In other words, given that a report from Dr. Clifford would have been required by defendant, the amount of time it would have taken Dr. Clifford to return his report is a totally unknown and unknowable element which plaintiff would have to prove in order to show that "but for" defendant's negligence the application would have been approved.

*   *   *   *

There is no genuine issue as to the fact that the policy of insurance had not been issued on the life of Robert Davis before or on the date of his death. *   *   *

Plaintiff claims that it is entitled to a $100,000.00 coverage under the terms of the premium receipt. The receipt provides for a limited amount of coverage after the fulfillment of certain conditions, but before the delivery of the policy. The conditions are:

*   *   *

(3) Each person to be insured must be acceptable to the company (after investigation and medical examination, if required) under its underwriting rules, limits and standards for the plan and amount applied for, without modification, at the Company's standard rates.

*   *   *

If the above conditions have been fulfilled and the Company actually approves this application, until the policy applied for is actually delivered, the amount of insurance, including accidental death benefits, which may become effective under this receipt, shall not exceed the amount of insurance applied for or $100,000 whichever is smaller.

*   *   * Condition (3) was not fulfilled at any point before Davis' death. Plaintiff contends that the information eventually received from Dr. Clifford established that Davis had merely a minor nerve problem which caused his tingling and numbness and chest discomfort. According to plaintiff, this establishes that Davis was at the time of his death "acceptable" to the company. However, plaintiff neglects to read the entire text of the condition. It requires that the person be acceptable after an investigation and medical examination, if required under its underwriting rules.

*   *   * [Davis] could not have been acceptable *after* investigation because an investigation was taking place when he died. Furthermore, [the receipt requires] that the company "actually approves" the application in order for the receipt coverage to become effective. The fact that the company was still conducting an investigation of Davis' health negates any possibility that it had actually approved his application. * * * We therefore find that no policy had been issued and that the receipt coverage was not in effect due to nonfulfillment of all the conditions contained in the receipt.

Based on the foregoing, we find that there is no genuine issue of material fact and that defendant is entitled to a judgment as a matter of law. * * *

DECISION AND REMEDY   *The appellate court affirmed the lower court's grant of summary judgment for the defendant insurance company.*

COMMENTS   *This case illustrates the predicament of the "hopefully insured" waiting for the insurance application to be approved. The courts have granted insurance companies a "reasonable time" to act upon an application. What is a "reasonable time" depends upon the facts of each case. The premium receipt proved to be inadequate in protecting the plaintiff, so the plaintiff was left without any coverage.*

Important Provisions

PROVISIONS MANDATED BY STATUTE   If a statute mandates that a certain provision be included in insurance contracts, a court will deem that an insurance policy contains the provision regardless of whether the parties actually included it in the language of their contract. If a statute requires that any limitations regarding coverage be stated in the contract, a court will not allow an insurer to avoid liability for a claim through reliance on an unexpressed restriction.

INCONTESTABILITY CLAUSES   Statutes commonly require that a life or health insurance policy provide that after the policy has been in force for a specified length of time—often two or three years—the insurer cannot contest statements made in the application. This is known as an **incontestability clause.** Once a policy becomes incontestable, the insurer cannot later avoid a claim on the basis of, for example, the insured's fraud, unless the clause provides an exception for that circumstance. The clause does not prohibit an insurer's refusal or reduction of payment for a claim due to nonpayment of premiums, failure to file proof of death within a certain period, or lack of an insurable interest.

COINSURANCE CLAUSES   Often, when taking out fire insurance policies, property owners insure their property for less than its full value. Part of the reason for this is that most fires do not result in a total loss. To encourage owners to insure their property for an amount as close to full value as possible, a standard provision of fire insurance policies is a **coinsurance clause.** Typically, a coinsurance clause provides that if the owner insures the property up to a specified percentage—usually 80 percent—of its value, he or she will recover any loss up to the face amount of the policy. If the insurance is for less than the fixed percentage, the owner is responsible for a proportionate share of the loss. Coinsurance applies only in instances of partial loss. For example, if the owner of property valued at $100,000 took out a policy in the amount of $40,000 and suffered a loss of $30,000, the recovery would be $15,000. The formula for calculating the recovery amount is as follows:

$$\frac{\text{Amount of insurance } (\$40,000)}{\text{Coinsurance percent } (80\%) \times \text{property value } (\$100,000)} = \frac{\text{recovery percent } (50\%)}{}$$

Recovery percent (50%) × amount of loss ($30,000) = recovery amount ($15,000)

If the owner had taken out a policy in the amount of $80,000, then, according to the same formula, the full loss would have been recovered.

APPRAISAL AND ARBITRATION CLAUSES   Most fire insurance policies provide that if the parties cannot agree on the amount of a loss covered under the policy or the value of the property lost, an **appraisal** can be demanded. An appraisal is an estimate of the property's value determined by suitably qualified individuals who have no interest in the property. Typically, two appraisers are used—one being appointed by each party. A third party, or **umpire,** may be called on to resolve differences.

Other types of insurance policies also contain provisions for appraisal and arbitration when the insured and insurer disagree as to the value of a loss.

MULTIPLE INSURANCE COVERAGE If an insured has **multiple insurance coverage**—that is, policies with several companies covering the same insurable interest—and the amount of coverage exceeds the loss, the insured can collect from each insurer only the company's proportionate share of the liability to the total amount of insurance. Many fire insurance policies include a pro rata clause, which requires any loss to be shared proportionately by all carriers. For example, if Grumbling insured $50,000 worth of property with two companies, each of whose policies had a liability limit of $40,000, on the property's total destruction Grumbling could collect only $25,000 from each insurer.

ANTILAPSE CLAUSES A life insurance policy may provide, or a statute may require a policy to provide, that it will not automatically lapse if no payment is made on the date due. Ordinarily, under an **antilapse provision,** the insured has a **grace period** of thirty or thirty-one days within which to pay an overdue premium. If the insured fails to pay a premium altogether, there are alternatives to cancellation. The insurance company may:

1. Be required to extend the insurance for a period of time.
2. Issue a policy with less coverage to reflect the amount of the payments made.
3. Pay to the insured the policy's **cash surrender value**—the amount the insurer has agreed to pay on the policy's cancellation before the insured's death. (In determining this value, the following factors are considered: the period that the policy has already run, the amount of the premium, the insured's age and life expectancy, and amounts to be repaid on any outstanding loans taken out against the policy.)

When the insurance contract states that the insurer cannot cancel the policy, these alternatives are important.

CANCELLATION When an insurance company can cancel its insurance contract, the policy or a state statute usually requires that the insurer give advance written notice of the cancellation. Any premium paid in advance and not yet earned may be refundable. The insured may also be entitled to the policy's cash surrender value.

Cancellation can occur for various reasons depending on the type of insurance. For example, automobile insurance can be canceled for nonpayment of premiums or suspension of the insured's driver's license. Property insurance can also be canceled for nonpayment of premiums, as well as because of physical changes in the property that result in its becoming uninsurable, the insured's fraud or misrepresentation, conviction for a crime that increases the hazard insured against, or gross negligence that increases the hazard insured against. Life and health policies can be canceled (before the effective date of an incontestability clause) due to false statements made by the insured in the application.

An insurer cannot cancel a policy—or refuse to write a renewal policy—because of the national origin or race of an applicant. Moreover, an insurance company cannot cancel a policy to penalize an insured who has appeared as a witness in a case against the company.

Interpreting Provisions of an Insurance Contract

The courts are increasingly cognizant of the fact that most people do not have the special training necessary to understand the intricate terminology used in insurance policies. The words used in an insurance contract have their ordinary meaning and are interpreted by courts in light of the nature of the coverage involved. When there is an ambiguity in the policy, the provision is interpreted against the insurance company. When it is unclear whether an insurance contract actually exists because the written policy has not been delivered, the uncertainty will be determined against the insurance company. The court will presume that the policy is in effect unless the company can show otherwise.

The following case illustrates the problem of interpretation.

Case 54.3
**STANLEY v. SAFECO
INSURANCE
COMPANY OF
AMERICA**

Supreme Court of Washington,
1988.
109 Wash.2d 738, 747 P.2d
1091.

BACKGROUND AND FACTS   *Stanley, the plaintiff, was covered by an accidental death and dismemberment policy with Safeco Insurance Company of America, the defendant. The policy provided payment for "loss of . . . a foot if the loss was by actual severance at or above . . . the ankle joint." The plaintiff was struck by an automobile while jogging. He suffered an immediate loss of motor power and sensation in both legs and up to the abdominal area. An undisputed medical report revealed a dislocation of the twelfth thoracic vertebra. The report concluded that the plaintiff had a functional severance of the spinal cord with resulting permanent paralysis, including paralysis of the feet. The insurance company denied coverage, claiming that the injury did not come under this policy. The lower court granted a summary judgment in favor of Safeco, and Stanley appealed. The court of appeals reversed the lower court's decision, and Safeco appealed.*

BRACHTENBACH, Justice.

The issue is whether the loss of function of a foot caused by an accidental severance of the spinal cord comes within the coverage of an insurance policy which provides payment for "loss of . . . a foot if the loss was by actual severance at or above . . . the ankle joint"? We hold that benefits are payable.

*   *   *   *

SAFECO issued a group policy which provided *   *   * "Accidental Death and Dismemberment Insurance".

*   *   *   *

*   *   * [In the policy, t]here is no definition of "actual severance" or "loss of a foot."

*   *   *   *

The essence of SAFECO's argument is that the policy is a dismemberment policy which requires amputation of the foot as a condition of coverage. *   *   *

[A]n insurance policy should be given a practical and reasonable rather than a literal interpretation; that is, a fair and sensible construction, consonant with the apparent object and intent of the parties; a construction such as would be given by the average person purchasing insurance. If the policy is ambiguous, a meaning and construction most favorable to the insured must be applied. A policy provision is ambiguous when it is fairly susceptible to two different interpretations, both of which are reasonable. *   *   * [A] "loss" may occur as a result of loss of use or function.

*   *   * [T]he doctor, absent surgery, could not be certain of actual severance of the spinal cord, but the substantial subluxation [incomplete dislocation of a bone in a joint] together with all loss of use and function led him to conclude that plaintiff was completely and permanently paralyzed.

*   *   *   *

SAFECO would have us deny coverage here on the basis of the language in the caption at the top of the coverage page entitled "Accidental Death and Dismemberment Insurance." Thus, SAFECO focuses on the heading or caption of the coverage page as limiting the operative words in the body of the policy.

*   *   * [T]he language in the body of the policy provides *what* must occur (loss of foot) and *how* or *where* the loss is sustained (actual severance at or above the ankle joint). SAFECO's interpretation would modify the language of the body of the policy by taking from the caption the word "dismemberment" and inserting it in the coverage language. If carried to its logical extreme the caption would provide coverage only for "accidental death *and* dismemberment."

We conclude that *   *   * the language in the body of the policy is not ambiguous; it covers the plaintiff's loss. Even if the caption is a controlling part of the coverage language, the provision becomes ambiguous and is construed against SAFECO. It has long been our rule that the caption " 'should never of itself be taken to override the intention of the parties to an insurance policy as shown by the provisions and clauses inserted thereunder.' "

The Supreme Court of Washington affirmed the decision of the court of appeals. Stanley's loss was covered by the insurance policy.

DECISION AND REMEDY

Basic Duties and Rights

Essentially, the parties to an insurance contract are responsible for the obligations the contract imposes. These include the basic contractual duties discussed in Unit Two.

When applying for insurance, for example, the obligation to act in good faith means that a party must reveal everything necessary for the insurer to evaluate the risk. In other words, the applicant must disclose all **material facts.** Where insurance is concerned, these include all facts that would influence an insurer in determining whether to charge a higher premium or to refuse to issue a policy altogether.

Once the insurer has accepted the risk, and on the occurrence of an event giving rise to a claim, the insurer has a duty to investigate to determine the facts. When a policy provides insurance against third party claims, the insurer is obligated to make reasonable efforts to settle such a claim. If a settlement cannot be reached, then, regardless of the claim's merit, the insurer must defend any suit against the insured. Usually, a policy provides that in this situation the insured must cooperate. A policy provision may expressly require the insured to attend hearings and trials and to assist in obtaining evidence and witnesses and in reaching a settlement.

Defenses against Payment to the Insured

An insurance company can raise any of the defenses that would be valid in any ordinary action on a contract and some defenses that do not apply in ordinary contract actions. If the insurance company can show that the policy was procured by fraud, misrepresentation, or violation of warranties, it may have a valid defense for not paying a claim. The insurance company may also have the right to disaffirm or rescind an insurance contract. Improper actions, such as those that are against public policy or that are otherwise illegal, can give the insurance company a defense against the payment of a claim or allow it to rescind the contract.

The following case involves the issue of liability for fire damage resulting from the actions of one of the insured persons under a contract of insurance. Because the insured individuals were married, the company claimed that the wrongful act of one spouse was attributable to the other. This would prevent either from recovering fire insurance proceeds.

BACKGROUND AND FACTS *The plaintiffs, Herbert and Arlene Steigler, sued on an insurance policy issued by the defendant, the Insurance Company of North America (INA), for fire damage to their home. The lower court denied the plaintiffs' recovery. The plaintiffs were a husband and wife who owned the property as tenants in the entirety and who were insured under an INA policy. It was undisputed that the husband deliberately set fire to the house, that his actions constituted fraud under the terms of the policy, and that the policy was void and he could not recover under it. It was equally undisputed that the wife was not involved in any way in the act. The wife claimed that she was not barred from recovering under the policy, since she was an innocent co-tenant, and that she was entitled to her pro rata share of the fire insurance proceeds.*

Case 54.4
STEIGLER v. INS. CO. OF NORTH AMERICA
Supreme Court of Delaware, 1978.
384 A.2d 398.

DUFFY, Justice.

* * * *

As we have noted, the policy contained a standard fraud provision rendering the policy void "in case of any fraud * * * by the *insured* relating thereto" (emphasis added); and the policy insured two persons: "Herbert F. Steigler and Arlene R. Steigler."

The [first] critical question, of course, relates to the meaning of the word "insured" in the fraud provision. Does it mean one or both of the Steiglers? The answer is by no means clear because the word "insured" is singular while two persons are named as the "insured," i.e., Herbert F. Steigler and Arlene R. Steigler. Thus, construction of the term is required.

In resolving the ambiguity in the Steigler-INA contract we refer to two rules of construction. First, where ambiguous, the language of an insurance contract is always construed most strongly against the insurance company which has drafted it.

Second, "an insurance contract should be read to accord with the reasonable expectations of the purchaser so far as the language will permit."

Applying these principles, we hold that an "ordinary person owning an undivided interest in property, not vested in the nice distinctions of insurance law, would naturally suppose that his individual interest in the property was covered by a policy which named him without qualification as one of the persons insured."

In our judgment * * * Mrs. Steigler had an interest in the property, the policy named her without qualification as one of the persons insured and she should not be barred from recovering under the policy by the fraud of the other co-tenant.

INA contends that because the Steiglers are married the arson of the husband bars recovery by his wife. The theory is that the contract terms govern any claim, the contract is voided by fraud, and that husband and wife are one person, i.e., together and inseparably they hold the entire estate.

We are not persuaded that the "oneness" theory, which is, to say the least, somewhat "quaint" in this day and age, should override the other principles at stake here. When two persons own property as tenants in common, it is generally recognized, as INA concedes, that the interests may be separable and, therefore, an innocent tenant in common can recover a *pro rata* share of fire insurance proceeds. Thus, for example, had the Steiglers owned the property and the policy as "co-habitants" rather than as spouses, the general rule would have permitted rather than have barred her recovery. Without pausing to explore the equal protection problems which such a result might raise, we conclude that barring a wife from recovering because she is a wife would be contrary to the public policy clearly mandated by the Married Women's Act.

DECISION AND REMEDY *The lower court's ruling was reversed. The wife was entitled to half the insurance policy proceeds for the fire damage. The case was remanded to the trial court's jurisdiction under instruction to enter a ruling in the wife's favor and award her half the insurance proceeds.*

Rebuttal of the Defenses of the Insurance Company

There are certain ways in which the insurance company can be prevented from asserting some defenses that are normally available. State statutes and case law provide for such estoppel.

For example, if a company tells an insured that information requested on a form is optional and the insured provides it anyway, the company cannot use the information to avoid its contractual obligation under the insurance contract. Similarly, incorrect statements as to the age of the insured normally do not provide the insurance company with a way to escape payment upon the death of the insured.

In the following case, the court evaluates whether a false statement made on an application for a life insurance policy and the backdating of the application and policy should allow the insurer to avoid payment on the policy.

Case 54.5
ROBERTS v. NATIONAL LIBERTY GROUP OF COMPANIES
Appellate Court of Illinois, 1987.
159 Ill.App.3d 706, 512 N.E.2d
792, 111 Ill.Dec. 403.

BACKGROUND AND FACTS   *In the spring of 1982, Paul Roberts, then fifty-nine years of age, applied to the National Liberty Group of Companies for a $30,000 life insurance policy available only to individuals under sixty years of age. This first application was lost or misplaced by the insurance company, and Roberts submitted a second application in November of 1982. Because Roberts had by then had his sixtieth birthday, the second application was backdated to April 11, 1982 (a date prior to his birthday), as was the ensuing policy.*

Although Roberts had suffered slight hypertension in 1979 and had been seen and treated by a physician for this condition for a short time thereafter, he marked "no" to the question on the application concerning treatment for high blood pressure. In October of 1982, Roberts was diagnosed as having cancer, and he died from this disease in June of 1983. Roberts, although he knew of the cancer diagnosis when he submitted the second application, did not indicate this on the application form because the diagnosis had not been made at the time of his original application. Upon Roberts's death, his wife submitted a claim to the insurance company for $30,000. The insurance company denied the claim on the ground that the false statement concerning hypertension and the failure to mention the cancer diagnosis constituted misrepresentation. Mrs. Roberts sued the insurance company for the proceeds plus interest. The trial court found for the plaintiff, and the insurance company (the defendant) appealed.

WOMBACHER, Justice.

*   *   *   *

Under Illinois law, a false statement in an application for insurance is not in itself a ground for avoiding the insurance policy. The insurer must prove that the statements were made with intent to deceive or involved matters materially affecting the acceptance of the risk. *   *   *

*   *   *   *

Incomplete answers, or failure to disclose material information in response to a question in an application may constitute a material misrepresentation. Whether an applicant's statements are material is determined by the question of whether reasonably careful men would have regarded the facts stated as substantially increasing the chances of the events insured against, so as to cause a rejection of the application or different conditions. In the instant case, there was testimony at trial that high blood pressure such as indicated here did not usually result in the defendant refusing insurance. The defendant's representative testified that the rate of the premium would most likely be involved. The large volume of applications made to the company indicates that an affirmative response to the blood pressure question would result in only a telephone check to the applicant *   *   *.

Lastly, the defendant contends that the failure to disclose the cancer prior to the issuance of the policy in November of 1982 voided the policy. The cancer was diagnosed one month prior to the receipt of the application by the defendant. However, the policy which was issued predates by six months the date that the cancer was diagnosed. The trial court held that the backdating of the policy estopped the defendant from asserting the defense of nondisclosure.

*   *   * The test of estoppel is whether, considering all the circumstances of the case, conscience and honest dealing require that the defendant be estopped. Estoppel generally is based upon an insurance carrier's conduct and/or representations which mislead an insured to his detriment. We agree with the trial court. The defendant may not now adopt an inconsistent position or course of conduct to the loss of the plaintiff. Indeed, had the policy not been backdated then no policy would exist because Mr.

Roberts' sixtieth birthday occurred in April 1982. The insurance coverage in question was only available to individuals under 60 years of age. Equity requires that due to the defendants' action of backdating the application and policy, they now be barred from asserting the nondisclosure defense.

DECISION AND REMEDY — *The judgment of the trial court was affirmed; the insurance company could not avoid payment on the policy. In the interests of equity and fairness, the insurance company, because of its own conduct in backdating the application and policy, was not allowed to raise the defense of nondisclosure.*

TYPES OF INSURANCE

Four general types of insurance coverage held by individuals will be covered here:

1. Life insurance.
2. Fire and homeowners insurance.
3. Automobile insurance.
4. Business liability insurance.

First, each of these types of insurance will be discussed in terms of the kinds of coverage available. Then special features and provisions will be pointed out, with special emphasis on life and fire insurance policies as they relate to the law.

Life Insurance

There are four basic types of life insurance:

1. **Whole life,** sometimes referred to as straight life, ordinary life, or cash-value insurance. This type of insurance provides protection with a cumulated cash surrender value that can be used as collateral for a loan. Premiums are paid by the insured during the insured's entire lifetime, with a fixed payment to the beneficiary upon death.

2. **Limited-payment life,** such as a twenty-payment life policy. Premiums are paid for a stated number of years, after which the policy is paid up and fully effective during the insured's life. Naturally, premiums are higher than for whole life. This insurance does have a cash surrender value.

3. **Term** insurance. Fixed premiums are paid for a specified term. Payment on the policy is due only if death occurs within the term period. Premiums are less expensive than for whole life or limited-payment life, and there is usually no cash surrender value. Frequently, this type of insurance can be converted to another type of life insurance.

4. **Endowment** insurance. Fixed premium payments are made for a definite term. At the end of the term, a fixed amount is to be paid to the insured or, upon the death of the insured during the specified period, to a beneficiary. Thus, this type of insurance represents both term insurance and a form of **annuity** (the right to receive fixed, periodic payments for life or—as in this case—for a term of years). It has a rapidly increasing cash surrender value, but premiums are high, as payment is required at the end of the term even if the insured is still living.

5. **Universal life,** a new type of insurance that combines some aspects of term insurance and some aspects of whole life insurance. Every payment, usually called a "contribution," involves two deductions made by the issuing life insurance company. The first one is a charge for term insurance protection; the second is for company expenses and profit. The money that remains after these deductions earns interest for the policyholder at a rate determined by the company. The interest-earning money in the policy is called the policy's cash value, but that term does not mean the same thing as it does for a traditional whole life insurance policy. With a universal life policy, the cash value grows at a variable interest rate rather than at a predetermined rate.

The rights and liabilities of the parties in life insurance are basically dependent upon the insurance contract. A few features deserve special attention.

LIABILITY The insurance contract determines not only the extent of the insurer's liability but, generally, whether the insurer is liable upon the death of the insured. Most life insurance contracts exclude liability for death caused by suicide, military action during war, execution by a state or federal government, or even something that occurs while the insured is a passenger in a commercial vehicle. In the absence of exclusion, most courts today construe any cause of death to be one of the insurer's risks.

ADJUSTMENT DUE TO MISSTATEMENT OF AGE The insurance policy constitutes the agreement between the parties. The application for insurance is part of the policy and is usually attached to the policy. When the insured misstates his or her age in the application, an error takes place particularly as to the amount of premiums paid. Misstatement of age is not a material error sufficient to allow the insurer to void the policy. Instead, upon discovery of the error, the insurer will adjust the premium payments and/or benefits accordingly.

ASSIGNMENT Most life insurance policies permit the insured to change beneficiaries. When this is the case, in the absence of any prohibition or notice requirement, the insured has a right to assign the rights to the policy (for example, as security for a loan) without the consent of the insurer or the beneficiary. If the beneficiary right is vested—that is, has become absolute, entitling the beneficiary to payment of the proceeds—the policy cannot be assigned without the consent of the beneficiary. The vast majority of life insurance contracts permit assignment and only require notice to the insurer to be effective.

CREDITORS' RIGHTS Unless it is exempt under state law, the insured's interest in life insurance as an asset is subject to the rights of judgment creditors. These creditors generally can reach insurance proceeds payable to the insured's estate, proceeds payable to anyone if the payment of premiums constituted a fraud on creditors, and proceeds payable to a named beneficiary if the insured has reserved the right to change beneficiaries. Creditors, however, cannot compel the insured to make available the cash surrender value of the policy or to change the named beneficiary to that of the creditor. Almost all states exempt at least a part of the proceeds of life insurance from creditors' claims.

TERMINATION Although the insured can cancel and terminate the policy, the insurer generally cannot do so. Therefore, termination usually takes place only upon the occurrence of the following:

1. Default in premium payments that causes the policy to lapse.

2. Death and payment of benefits.
3. Expiration of term of policy.
4. Cancellation by the insured.

Fire and Homeowners Insurance

There are basically two types of insurance policies for a home—standard fire insurance policies and homeowners policies.

STANDARD FIRE INSURANCE POLICIES The standard fire insurance policy protects the homeowner against fire and lightning as well as damage from smoke and water caused by the fire or the fire department. Paying slightly more will extend the coverage to damage caused by hail, windstorms, explosions, and so on. Personal theft insurance and a comprehensive liability policy can also be added.

Most fire insurance policies are classified according to the type of property covered and the extent (amount) of the issuer's liability. Exhibit 54–2 lists typical fire insurance policies.

As with life insurance, certain features and provisions of fire insurance deserve special mention. In reading the following, it is important to note some basic differences in the treatment of life and fire policies.

Liability As with all forms of insurance, the insurer's liability is determined from the terms of the policy. Most policies, however, limit recovery to losses resulting from *hostile* fires—basically, those that break out or begin in places where no fire was intended to burn. A *friendly* fire—one burning in a place where it was intended to burn—is not covered. Therefore, smoke from a fireplace is not covered, but smoke from a fire caused by a defective electrical outlet is. Sometimes, owners add "extended coverage" to the fire policy to cover losses from friendly fires.

If the policy is a valued policy (described in Exhibit 54–2) and the subject matter is completely destroyed, the insurer is liable for the amount specified in the policy. If it is an open policy, then the extent of actual loss must be determined, and the insurer is liable only for the amount of the loss or for the maximum amount specified in the policy, whichever is less. For partial losses, actual loss must always be determined, and the insurer's liability is limited to that amount. Most insurance policies permit the insurer either to restore or replace the property destroyed or to pay for the loss.

Exhibit 54–2 Typical Fire Insurance Policies

TYPE OF POLICY	COVERAGE
Blanket policy	This policy covers a class of property rather than specific property, since the property is expected to shift or vary in nature. A policy covering the inventory of a business is an example.
Specific policy	This policy covers a specific item of property at a specific location. An example is a particular painting located in a residence or a piece of machinery located in a factory or business.
Floater policy	This policy usually supplements a specific policy. It is intended to cover property that may change in either location or quantity. To illustrate, if the painting mentioned under "Specific policy" were to be exhibited during the year at numerous locations throughout the state, a floater policy would be desirable.
Valued policy	This policy is one in which, by agreement, a specific value is placed on the subject to be insured to cover the eventuality of its total loss.
Open policy	This policy is one in which the value of the property insured is not agreed upon. The policy usually provides for a maximum liability of the insurer, but payment for loss is restricted to the fair market value of the property at the time of loss or to the insurer's limit, whichever is less.

Proof of Loss   Fire insurance policies require the insured to file with the insurer within a specified period or immediately (within a reasonable time) a proof of loss as a condition for recovery. Failure to comply *could* allow the insurance carrier to avoid liability. Courts vary somewhat on the enforcement of such clauses. So that this does not become a legal issue, the insured should always report a loss immediately to the insurer and file the proper statements covering the loss.

Occupancy Clause   Most standard policies require that the premises be occupied at the time of loss. The relevant clause states that if the premises become vacant or unoccupied for a given period, unless consent by the insurer is given, the coverage is suspended until the premises are reoccupied. Persons going on extended vacations should check their policies on this matter.

Assignment   Before a loss has occurred, a fire insurance policy is not assignable without the consent of the insurer. The theory is that the fire insurance policy is a personal contract between the insured and the insurer. The nonassignability of the policy is extremely important in the purchase of a house. The purchaser must procure his or her own insurance. If the purchaser wishes to assume the remaining insurance coverage period of the seller, consent of the insurer is essential.

To illustrate, Ann is selling her home and lot to Sam. Ann has a one-year fire policy with Ajax Insurance Company, with six months of coverage remaining at the date on which the sale is to close. Ann agrees to assign the balance of her policy, but Ajax has not given its consent. One day after passage of the deed, a fire totally destroys the house. Can Sam recover from Ajax?

The answer is no, as the policy is actually voided upon the closing of the transaction and the deeding of the property. The reason the policy is voided is that Ann no longer has an insurable interest at the time of loss; and Sam has no rights in a nonassignable policy.

HOMEOWNERS POLICIES   A homeowners policy provides protection against a number of risks under a single policy, allowing the policyholder to save over the cost of buying each protection separately. There are two basic types of homeowners policy coverage:

1.   *Property coverage* includes garage, house, and other private buildings on the policyholder's lot. It also includes the personal possessions and property of the policyholder at home, in travel, or at work. It pays additional living expenses for living away from home because of a fire or some other covered peril.

2.   *Liability coverage* is for personal liability in case someone is injured on the insured's property,

the insured damages someone else's property, or the insured injures someone else who is not in an automobile. It generally does not cover liability for professional malpractice.

Similar to liability coverage is coverage for the medical payments of others who are injured on the policyholder's property and coverage for property of others that is damaged by a member of the policyholder's family.

Forms of Homeowners Policies   There are five forms of homeowners and condominium owners policies. The essential difference among the five forms is the number of perils insured against. For example, one form (called the basic form) covers eleven perils, or risks; another (the broad form) covers eighteen; and another (the comprehensive form) covers those eighteen and all others.

Renters, too, take out insurance policies to cover losses to personal property. Renters insurance, called "residence contents broad form," covers personal possessions against the eighteen perils and includes additional living expenses and liability coverage.

Adding a Personal Articles or Effects Floater Policy   An insured may wish to pay a slightly higher premium to insure specific personal articles—for example, cameras, musical instruments, works of art, jewelry, and other valuables. This is accomplished by addition of a *personal articles floater* to a homeowners policy. The insured submits a list of the things to be covered and some affidavits giving their current market value. Insuring under a floater provides all-risk insurance, and the covered property can therefore be omitted from fire and theft policies.

A *personal effects floater* policy covers personal items that accompany the insured when he or she is traveling. In most cases, this coverage is not necessary, because a regular homeowners policy provides sufficient coverage. The personal effects floater covers articles only when they are taken off the insured's property. It does not cover theft from an unattended automobile unless there is evidence of forced entry, and even then, the company's liability is generally limited to 10 percent of the amount of insurance and no more than a specified amount, such as $250 or $500, for all property in

any one loss. This restriction can be removed by payment of an additional premium, however.

Automobile Insurance

There are two basic kinds of automobile insurance: liability insurance and collision and comprehensive insurance.

LIABILITY INSURANCE   Automobile liability insurance covers bodily injury and property damage liability. Liability limits are usually described by a series of three numbers, such as 100/300/50. This means that the policy will pay a maximum of $100,000 for bodily injury to one person and $300,000 to more than one person and a maximum of $50,000 for property damage in one accident. Many insurance companies offer liability up to $500,000 and sometimes higher.

Individuals who are dissatisfied with the maximum liability limits offered by regular automobile insurance coverage can purchase separate coverage under an *umbrella* policy. Umbrella limits sometimes go as high as $5 million. They also cover personal liability in excess of a homeowners policy's liability limits.

COLLISION AND COMPREHENSIVE INSURANCE   Collision insurance covers damage to the insured's car in any type of collision. Usually, it is not advisable to purchase full collision coverage (otherwise known as zero deductible). The price per year is quite high, because it is likely that small but costly repair jobs will be required each year. Most people prefer to take out $100, $250, or $500 deductible coverage, which costs substantially less than zero deductible coverage.

Comprehensive insurance covers loss, damage, and destruction by fire, hurricane, hail, vandalism, and theft. It can be obtained separately from collision insurance.

OTHER AUTOMOBILE INSURANCE   Other types of automobile insurance coverage include the following:

1. *Uninsured motorist coverage.* Uninsured motorist coverage insures the driver and passengers against injury caused by any driver without insurance or by a hit-and-run driver. Certain states

require that it be included in all insurance policies sold to drivers.

2. *Accidental death benefits.* Sometimes called *double indemnity,* accidental death benefits provide a lump sum to named beneficiaries if the policyholder dies in an automobile accident. This coverage generally costs very little, but it may not be necessary if the insured has a sufficient amount of life insurance.

3. *Medical payment coverage.* Medical payment coverage provided by an auto insurance policy pays hospital and other medical bills and sometimes funeral expenses. This type of insurance protects all the passengers in the insured's car when the insured is driving.

4. *Other-driver coverage.* An **omnibus,** or **other-driver, clause** protects the vehicle owner who has taken out the insurance and anyone who drives the vehicle with the owner's permission. This coverage may be held to extend to a third party who drives the vehicle with the permission of the person to whom the owner gave permission.

5. *No-fault insurance.* Under no-fault statutes, claims arising from an accident are made against the claimant's own insurer, regardless of whose fault the accident was. In some cases—for example, when injuries involve expensive medical treatment—an injured party may seek recovery from another party or insurer. In those instances, the injured party may collect the maximum amount of no-fault insurance and still sue for total damages from the party at fault, although usually, on winning an award, the injured party must reimburse the insurer for its no-fault payments.

Business Liability Insurance

A business may be vulnerable to all sorts of risks. A key employee may die or become disabled, a customer may be injured when using a manufacturer's product, the patron of an establishment selling liquor may leave the premises and injure a third party in an automobile accident, or a professional may overlook some important detail, causing liability for malpractice. Should the first situation arise (for instance, if the company president dies), the business may have some protection under a key-person insurance policy, discussed previously. In the other circumstances, other types of insurance may apply.

GENERAL LIABILITY Comprehensive general liability insurance can cover virtually as many risks as the insurer agrees to cover. For example, among the types of coverage that a business might wish to acquire is protection from liability for injuries arising from on-premises events not otherwise insured against, such as company social functions.

Some specialized establishments may be subject to liability in individualized circumstances, and policies can be drafted to meet their needs. For example, in many jurisdictions statutes impose liability on a seller of intoxicating liquor when a buyer of the liquor, intoxicated as a result of the sale, injures a third party. Legal protection may extend not only to immediately consequent injuries, such as quadriplegia in an automobile accident, but also to the loss of support suffered by a family because of the injuries. Insurance can provide coverage for these injuries and losses.

PRODUCT LIABILITY Manufacturers may be subject to liability for injuries that their products cause, and product liability insurance can be written to match specific products' risks. Coverage can be procured under a comprehensive general liability policy or under a separate policy. The coverage may include expenses involved in recalling and replacing a product that has proved to be defective. (For a comprehensive discussion of product liability, see Chapter 21.)

PROFESSIONAL MALPRACTICE In recent years, professionals—attorneys, physicians, architects, and engineers, for example—have increasingly become the targets of negligence suits. Professionals may purchase malpractice insurance to protect themselves against such claims. The large judgments in some malpractice suits have received considerable publicity and are sometimes cited in what has been termed "the insurance crisis," since they have contributed to a considerable increase in malpractice insurance premiums in recent years.

WORKERS' COMPENSATION Workers' compensation insurance covers payments to employees who are injured in accidents arising out of and in the course of employment (that is, on the job). Workers' compensation, which was discussed in detail in Chapter 49, is governed by state statutes.

QUESTIONS AND CASE PROBLEMS

1. Ann owns a house and has an elderly third cousin living with her. Ann decides she needs fire insurance on the house and a life insurance policy on her third cousin to cover funeral and other expenses that will result from her cousin's death. Ann takes out a fire insurance policy from Ajax Insurance Company and a $10,000 life insurance policy from Beta Insurance Company on her third cousin. Six months later, Ann sells the house to John and transfers title to him. Ann and her cousin move into an apartment. With two months remaining on the Ajax policy, a fire totally destroys the house; at the same time, Ann's third cousin dies. Both insurance companies tender back premiums but claim they have no liability under the insurance contracts, as Ann did not have an insurable interest. Discuss their claims.

2. John contracts with an Ajax Insurance Company agent for a $50,000 ordinary life insurance policy. The application form is filled in to show John's age as thirty-two. In addition, the application form asks whether John has ever had any heart ailments or problems. John answers no, forgetting that as a young child he was diagnosed as having a slight heart murmur. A policy is issued. Three years later John becomes seriously ill. A review of the policy discloses that John was actually thirty-three at the time of application and issuance of the policy and that he erred in answering the question about a history of heart ailments. Discuss whether Ajax can void the policy and escape liability upon John's death.

3. Ann has an ordinary life insurance policy on her life and a fire insurance policy on her house. Both policies have been in force for a number of years. Ann's life insurance names her son, Rory, as beneficiary. Ann has specifically removed her right to change beneficiaries, and the life policy is silent on right of assignment. Ann is going on a one-year European vacation and borrows money from Leonard to finance the trip. Leonard takes an assignment of the life insurance policy as security for the loan, as the policy has accumulated a substantial cash surrender value. Ann also rents out her house to Leonard and assigns to him her fire insurance policy. Discuss fully whether Ann's assignment of these policies is valid.

4. Frank has an open fire insurance policy on his home for a maximum liability of $60,000. The policy has a number of standard clauses, including the right of the insurer to restore or rebuild the property in lieu of a monetary payment, and it has a standard coinsurance clause. A fire in Frank's house virtually destroys a utility room and part of the kitchen. The fire was caused by an electric water heater overheating. The total damage to the property is $10,000. The property at the time of loss is valued at $100,000. Frank files a proof of loss claim for $10,000. Discuss the insurer's liability in this situation.

5. Lori has a large house. She secures two open fire insurance policies on the house. Her policy with the Ajax Insurance Company is for a maximum of $100,000, and her policy with Beta Insurance Company is for a maximum of $50,000. Lori's house burns to the ground. The value of the house at the time of the loss is $120,000. Discuss the liability of Ajax and Beta to Lori.

6. James and Hazel Gray signed a joint application for health insurance coverage with Great American Reserve Insurance Company. The application was taken by John L. Sides, who at the time was not an agent for Great American but an independent insurance broker. Upon signing the application, the Grays gave Sides $188.50, the first month's premium, and later alleged that Sides had told them the policy would become effective when the first payment was made. Sides then sent the application to Great American, along with his own application to become a salesperson for Great American. Sides subsequently was allowed to sell Great American insurance policies. After several initial problems, Great American received the Grays' policy application two and a half months after they had signed it, and only then did the company begin to process the application. Two days before Great American received the policy application, Mr. Gray was thrown from a horse and injured. Mrs. Gray notified Sides of the injury, but Sides learned from Great American that the Grays were not covered as of the date of the injury. James Gray then brought suit against Great American and Sides for breach of an insurance contract. Did the Grays have a valid insurance policy with Great American on the date of Mr. Gray's injury? Explain. [Gray v. Great American Reserve Insurance Co., 495 So.2d 602 (1986)]

7. Martin A. Gurrentz applied for life insurance from Federal Kemper Life Assurance Company through an insurance agent named Alfrey. In September 1982, Gurrentz filled out an application but paid no premiums. Between the submission of the application and the delivery of the first two policies, Gurrentz sought medical advice from a physician relative to an ear problem. A biopsy was done and he was advised that he had a throat malignancy, for which he subsequently received radiation treatments. Upon delivery of the policies, Gurrentz signed a statement stating that there had been no changes in his health status and he had not seen a doctor since filing the application for insurance. In April 1983, Federal learned of Gurrentz's throat problem when he filed a claim under a separate medical health policy. After an investigation, Federal notified Gurrentz in February 1984 that they were canceling the life insurance policies and refunding all premiums paid. Was Federal able to successfully rescind Gurrentz's life insurance policies? [Gurrentz v. Federal Kemper Life Assurance Co., 513 So.2d 241 (Fla.Dist.App. 1987)]

8. On April 16, 1982, Frances and Michael Berthiaume made a written application for mortgage life insurance with the Minnesota Mutual Life Insurance

Company. The policy sought was to provide $44,308.37 in insurance coverage to cover the amount of the Berthiaumes' loan balance on the mortgage for their house, for a monthly premium of $12.42. Mr. Berthiaume did not take a physical examination for the policy, but in filling out the application he answered "no" to a question asking whether he had ever been treated for or had ever been advised that he had high blood pressure. The answer Mr. Berthiaume gave was incorrect; in fact, he had been diagnosed as having hypertension four months before the application was made. In October of 1982, Mr. Berthiaume became ill, and he died two months later. When his widow submitted a claim for the mortgage insurance, the insurance company denied payment, citing Mr. Berthiaume's inaccurate answer on the application. Minnesota Mutual sought summary judgment, which was granted by the trial court. Mrs. Berthiaume appealed. Discuss whether Mr. Berthiaume's inaccurate answer on the insurance policy application voided Minnesota Mutual's obligation to pay on the policy. [Berthiaume v. Minnesota Mutual Life Ins. Co., 388 N.W.2d 15 (Minn.App. 1986)]

9. Claude and Mildred owned their home in Lexington and had a fire insurance policy on the home. Claude and Mildred contracted with Benjamin to build a new home for them in exchange for cash and transfer of their present home. After conveying the home to Benjamin, Claude and Mildred continued living there and paid both rent and the insurance premium. The fire insurance policy was never assigned to Benjamin. While Claude and Mildred were still living in their old home, a fire damaged it. The insurance company would not pay, claiming that Claude and Mildred had no insurable interest in the property at the time of the loss. Discuss *fully* how a court will rule. [O'Donnell v. MFA Insurance Company, 671 S.W.2d 302 (Mo.App. 1984)]

10. The insured brought an action to recover losses in excess of $100,000 sustained because of employee theft. The thefts occurred during the terms of two different policies but were not discovered until the second policy had replaced the first. Each policy limited recovery to $50,000 for employee dishonesty and provided that for a loss "which occurs partly during the Effective Period of this endorsement and partly during the period of other policies, the total liability of the Company shall not exceed in the aggregate the amount of this endorsement." The insured maintained that he was entitled to recover $50,000 on each policy. What did the court decide? [Davenport Peters Co. v. Royal Globe Ins. Co., 490 F.Supp. 286 (Mass. 1980)]

Focus on Ethics

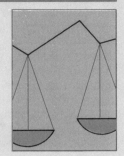

Property and Its Protection

The legal structures that support our ideas about property are crucial to the continuation of our economic system. Indeed, private property is at the heart of pure capitalist ideology. Nonetheless, alternative views about private property abound; for example, Marxists have often equated possession of private property with theft. Consider some questions relating to property that raise ethical issues.

PROBLEMS WITH NEW FORMS OF PERSONAL PROPERTY

Most of our laws were written to deal with traditional, tangible forms of property, such as a car or a book. In the modern economy, however, intangible personal property is increasingly important. Protection of rights in intangible property raises new difficulties.

For example, a company may expend tremendous amounts of time and money in developing a new and improved software program. But a consumer, after buying one copy of the program, can duplicate the software innumerable times on new diskettes at very little expense.

The company gets relatively little economic benefit from developing the software. As a consequence, the incentives for innovation in software development are diminished.

The consumer who copies software without permission is in a sense stealing the intangible personal property of the company. Yet many individuals do not even consider the ethics of copying intangible personal property. Even if this copying is deemed a civil or criminal wrong, the legal system can do little about it. Such small-scale and frequent theft could not be practicably prevented. We must depend largely upon the ethics of individuals in protecting property rights in many new forms of intangible property.

THE BETAMAX CONTROVERSY

As a result of recent technological advances in the area of home entertainment, significant ethical issues have arisen. The development of videocassette recorders (VCRs) certainly makes it possible, and indeed quite tempting, for us to tape TV programs for our viewing convenience. But how far can we go in taping other people's materials? What are

the limits? Is it fair to videotape a ball game, play it on a large screen, and invite customers to see it—all without paying anything?

This type of recording of copyrighted movies and TV programs has attracted widespread attention. Owners of copyrighted audio-visual works are clearly adversely affected by the home taping of movies and special programs, since the copyright owners are not compensated for the copies being made. Remember that the purpose of the copyright laws is to encourage and reward creativity by securing for copyright owners, for a limited time, the exclusive right to reproduce copyrighted works. This limited right clearly provides an economic incentive for people to be creative—and creativity is one of the primary ways by which society progresses.

The United States Supreme Court case of *Sony Corporation of America v. Universal City Studios* (464 U.S. 417, 104 S.Ct. 774, 78 L.Ed.2d 574 [1984]), frequently referred to as the Betamax case, focused on ethical considerations of the in-home taping of TV movies and programs. The Court specifically addressed the issue of whether the sale of videotape recorders, most certainly to be used for home video recording of free television programs, violates the exclusive right of copyright owners to reproduce copyrighted works. Universal City Studios, owners of copyrights on some TV programs that are broadcast on public airwaves, brought an action against the Sony Corporation, which manufactures and sells home VCRs. The plaintiffs contended that the defendants were liable for copyright infringement as either direct or contributory infringers because the home recording of their copyrighted programs by Betamax owners constituted a copyright infringement. No relief was sought against any Betamax consumer.

In a five-to-four decision, the Court held that the sale of the VCRs to the public does not constitute contributory infringement of the plaintiffs' copyrights. The Court concluded that, since many copyright holders who license their works for broadcast on free television would not object to home taping for noncommercial use, the equipment that makes such copying feasible should not be stifled simply because some copyright holders happen to object to this home taping. Furthermore, the Court stated that the plaintiffs had failed to show that noncommercial use of a copyrighted work is harmful or that, if this use should ever become widespread, it would adversely affect the potential market for the plaintiffs' copyrighted works. The fear of copyright owners that they had lost control over their property was disregarded. The district court's theory that it is not implausible that benefits from time-shifting for viewers' convenience could also accrue to the plaintiffs was also restated.

The effect of the Supreme Court's decision is to allow VCR manufacturers to benefit from this new market. The Supreme Court accepted the district court's findings that the time-shifting is a noncommercial, nonprofit activity falling within the "fair use" exemption of the copyright laws. But what if the Betamax were used to make copies for a commercial or profit-making purpose? In *Sony,* the Court stated that in such a case the use would presumptively be unfair and thus would not fall within the "fair use" doctrine. In order for a fair use privilege to be found, the value to the public must override the copyright holder's interest.

The closeness of the *Sony* decision emphasizes the difficulty in dealing with some of the legal ramifications of technological developments. Many people are unhappy with the Supreme Court's decision in this case and are looking to Congress for legislative action. Various proposed items of legislation seek to change the result reached in the Betamax case. Do you believe, for example, that a royalty fee should be paid by VCR manufacturers to copyright owners in return for a license? Solutions such as these are embodied in pending legislation.

THE QUESTION OF LAND-USE CONTROL

Legislation and regulation to control land use are prevalent throughout the United States. Often, such land-use control is undertaken in the name of "the public." But one must realize the consequences of such actions.

Consider the effect of legislation altering property owners' rights in coastal sections of the United States. Let's suppose that prior to passage of the legislation, owners of land in coastal areas could use that land in any way they wanted. They could build condominiums, golf courses, or do nothing. After the legislation goes into effect, a committee is formed that passes judgment on each requested change in the current use of the land. Suppose that a large amount of unaltered land is desired for coastal areas, even though that land is private property. If the committee routinely does not allow condominiums and housing developments to be built on the land, its market value will fall. Now we are entering into a taking issue, which is covered by the Fifth Amendment to the United States Constitution. Under this amendment, private property cannot be taken for public use without "just compensation." Government agencies maintain that land-use control does not involve a taking because the physical possession of the land remains in the hands of the private owner. From an economic point of view, however, a taking of potential income has occurred, because the net worth of the property owner subsequently falls when the land-use controls restrict the way in which the land can be used.

Who has a greater ethical concern in this issue—the private owner of the land and the potential occupants of condominiums and housing developments on the land or the nonowner who would like to see the land remain undeveloped and use the beaches and surrounding lands? No easy answer is available. Whatever decision is made concerning the use of the land, someone will benefit and someone will lose. Whenever there is a trade-off in terms of who benefits and who loses in the use of an economic resource, we can only make value judgments—we cannot provide a clear-cut answer as to what is appropriate.

INSURANCE

In the area of insurance, one of the major ethical concerns involves moral hazard. In the insurance industry, moral hazard occurs when individuals or companies have an incentive to act negligently or to engage in activities that will result in payment by an insurance company. For example, the businessperson who takes out a large insurance policy on a building has less incentive to take care that the building is protected from fire than an individual without an insurance policy. What is the ethical responsibility of the owner of the building when insurance is in effect? Is he or she exempt from taking precautions against a fire?

The same issue arises for insurance policies that cover losses due to theft. The smaller the deductible in such policies,

the less incentive the property owner has to prevent loss due to theft. For example, with insurance in effect, the property owner may have less incentive to install alarm systems, to pay for private patrol service, and so on. Of course, the more claims made on such insurance policies, the higher the average insurance rate per dollar amount insured. Thus, those individuals who are careless about protecting their own property impose costs on all individuals who buy property insurance.

Moral hazard exists with medical insurance as well. The smaller the deductible, the greater the incentive for the individual to neglect the practice of preventive medicine. What is the ethical responsibility of the individual citizen in terms of providing for his or her own well-being? Does the fact that health insurance is available for most individuals in the United States mean that these individuals should not be concerned about smoking, being overweight, and so on? Indeed, it is argued that in the United States, too many resources are devoted to the care of those who are already sick and too few resources to preventive medicine.

DISCUSSION QUESTIONS

1. How should society decide what objects should receive the protection granted by property rights? If we grant property rights in intangible objects, such as software, should we grant rights in even more intangible concepts, such as ideas?

2. Should an individual have some recognized property right in his or her job? How would such a right be protected at law?

3. Whose interests should come first in the question of land-use control?

4. Suppose an applicant for insurance makes a false statement concerning a material fact on the application form. Should an insurer have any responsibility to pay out on the subsequently issued insurance?

5. What limits can be placed on a person's use of private property? Consider an owner of oceanfront property who wants to develop a resort. What if such development would threaten the habitat for an endangered species? Should the individual defer to species protection? Should government intervene to compel species protection?

Unit Nine

SPECIAL TOPICS

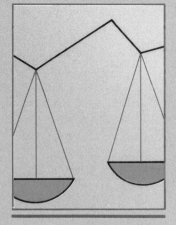

Chapter 55

Computers and the Law

We are living in a computer society. Virtually all of the financial transactions of the government and of most large businesses are handled by computers. Also, an increasing percentage of other forms of business activity is carried on through computers. In dollar volume, more funds are now transferred electronically—merely by changes in digital information within computer memories—than by the physical exchange of money. Rapidly advancing computer technology in the past decade has so reduced the size, expense, and operational complexity of computers that computers are no longer accessible only to large-scale institutions and business enterprises. Indeed, computers are quickly becoming nearly as commonplace as telephones in the business world, and computer equipment and software represent an increasing percentage of consumer expenditures as well.

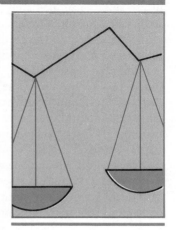

The many and diverse advantages brought about by the computer revolution are not risk-free, however. Computers have also created opportunities to harm individuals and to commit crimes—new forms of crime that are often difficult to detect and that are not always covered by existing criminal law statutes. As discussed in Chapter 1, in an era of rapid changes in the practices and customs of society, there is often a lag between the evolution of those new practices and the development of laws to govern them. In the area of computer uses and abuses, the law clearly is still in its formative stages. In some cases, existing laws have been extended—either by amendment or through judicial interpretation—to include computers. In other cases, new legislation has been enacted that specifically addresses situations unique to the computer age.

In this chapter, we discuss the emerging legal problems of the computer society and the ways in which courts and lawmakers are dealing with these problems. In addition to computer crime, these problems include the need for legal protection for software and the issue of privacy. We conclude the chapter with a brief discussion of how computers have aided lawyers.

COMPUTER CRIME

The American Bar Association defines **computer crime** as any act that is directed against computers and computer parts, that uses computers as instruments of crime, or that involves computers and constitutes abuse. Generally, computer crimes are classified as white-collar crimes, since ordinarily they do not involve physical violence. A recent study indicates that most computer crimes are committed by persons who are not well acquainted with computer technology, and most of the offenses tend to be no more sophisticated than entering false numbers into a computer system. In many cases, those who commit computer crimes are employees of the business organizations or government agencies against which they commit their offenses.

Computer crime is often difficult to detect; and if the crime is cleverly executed and no accounting discrepancy is immediately apparent, it may go undetected for some time. In some cases, victimized companies, and even the government, have discovered multimillion-dollar thefts only after a considerable lapse of time. Even when it is apparent that a computer crime has occurred, tracing the crime to the individual who committed it can be very difficult, because the individual's identity is "hidden" by the anonymous nature of the computer system. It is also frequently true that, in the case of an employee, no one with enough expertise to discover a crime is overseeing the perpetrator's activities. Even when computer crimes are detected and reported, the complexities of the computer systems involved have often frustrated the attempts of attorneys, police officers, jurors, and others to comprehend the offenses and prosecute the offenders successfully.

It may be that the full extent of computer crime in the United States is unrevealed. Companies adversely affected by computer crime do not want publicity, because they are afraid customers will doubt the security of their computer systems and the accuracy of their computer-generated material. For this reason and those mentioned above, cases involving computer crimes are often plea bargained rather than taken to trial. (In a **plea bargain,** the defendant agrees to plead guilty to a lesser offense in return for a lighter sentence than he or she might otherwise have received.)

Types of Computer Crime

Crimes committed with or against computers generally fall into five broad categories: financial crimes, property theft, the theft of data or services, *software piracy* (the unauthorized copying of another's

computer program), and vandalism and destructive programming.

FINANCIAL CRIMES In addition to using computers for information storage and retrieval, businesses increasingly use computers to conduct financial transactions. This is equally true of the government, which handles virtually all of its transactions via computer. These circumstances provide opportunities for employees and others to commit crimes that can involve serious economic losses. For example, employees of accounting and computer departments can, with little effort and without the risk involved in transactions evidenced by paperwork, transfer monies among accounts. The potential for crime in the area of financial transactions is great, and it is in this category of computer crime that most monetary losses are suffered.

Once a computer system has been accessed, information contained in the computer's records can be altered. An individual could, for example, remove a bad credit history and obtain loans that otherwise might not be obtainable. Alternatively, an individual could create a bad credit history to prevent or delay another party's receipt of borrowed funds.

PROPERTY THEFT The theft of computer equipment (hardware) has become easier and more commonplace as computer components have become smaller in size and thus more readily transportable. Computer-related theft may involve goods that are controlled and accounted for by means of a computer applications program. For example, an employee in a company's accounting department could manipulate inventory records to funnel orders for goods through a phony account and ship the merchandise elsewhere. Payments could also be made on the basis of dummy orders for goods that the company never received. Thefts of computer equipment and thefts of goods with computers are subject to the same criminal and tort laws as thefts of other property (see Chapters 4, 5, and 6).

THEFT OF DATA OR SERVICES Most people would agree that when an individual uses another's computer or computer information system without authorization, the individual is stealing. For example, an employee who uses a computer system or data stored in a computer system for private gain and without the employer's authorization would likely be considered a thief, as would a politician who uses a government computer to send out campaign brochures.

Nevertheless, stealing computer data and services does not fit within the common law definition of larceny (popularly known as theft) or its traditional statutory counterparts. At common law and under most criminal codes, larceny requires a physical taking and carrying away of property from another's possession. Under the common law, criminal statutes are to be strictly construed (that is, a criminal statute cannot be held to include offenses other than those that the statute clearly describes and provides for). Thus, since stealing computer data or services need not involve physically taking and carrying away property from another's possession, it could not be held to constitute larceny.

In a number of states, however, legislation has been passed to abolish or at least limit the application of the common law rule of strict construction of criminal statutes. For example, the Model Penal Code provides for construction "according to the fair import of [a statute's] terms" [Model Penal Code 1.02(3)]. Thus, under an increasing number of revised criminal codes or broad judicial interpretations of existing statutes, the unauthorized use of computer data or services is considered larceny.

Particularly vulnerable to the theft of data or services are systems to which more than one party has access. Even systems accessible only through *passwords* (codes designed to prohibit access to all but authorized users) are often used illegally, especially when the codes are not changed for long periods of time. Breaking a computer's security code or device and perusing the information in the system's records is commonly known as *hacking*. Some instances of hacking have been widely publicized and have generated considerable alarm. Such was the case, for example, in 1983 when a group of Wisconsin high school students discovered the passwords for the computer system at the defense research center in Los Alamos, New Mexico, and thereby gained access to it.

In the following case, two employees used their employer's computer facilities, without the employer's authorization, to develop an outside business interest. As you read the case, note how an existing criminal statute (governing mail fraud) is interpreted very broadly by the court so as to cover computer-assisted crime.

BACKGROUND AND FACTS *David Kelly and Mathew Palmer, Jr., were employed at Sperry Univac's applications development center, which develops and maintains programs to be used by Univac's customers. While employed at Univac, Kelly and Palmer developed a system—which they called the allegro system—for computerizing the generation of sheet music. In developing the program, they used substantial amounts of computer time and storage capacity within the central processing unit of the applications development center. They also contracted with Broomall Industries to help them develop and promote the allegro system. After this agreement was formed, Kelly, Palmer, Broomall's president, and another associate caused promotional materials to be mailed to music publishers, inviting them to send representatives to an allegro demonstration. At no time did anyone from Univac give Kelly or Palmer authority to use the company's computers to develop the allegro system.*

Kelly and Palmer's activities were finally discovered by the company, and they were indicted on five counts of mail fraud and one count of conspiracy to commit mail fraud. The indictment alleged that in using Sperry Univac's computer time and storage facilities without authorization, Kelly and Palmer had defrauded Univac of their services as employees and used the U.S. mails to further a fraudulent scheme. After a trial by jury, Kelly and Palmer were found guilty on all counts. They filed post-trial motions contending that their acts did not constitute a scheme or an attempt to defraud within the meaning of the mail fraud statute and that the mails had not been used to execute the scheme.

Case 55.1

UNITED STATES v. KELLY

United States District Court for the Eastern District of Pennsylvania, 1981. 507 F.Supp. 495.

DITTER, Judge.

*   *   *   *

*   *   * [I]t is necessary to consider the general purpose and scope of the mail fraud statute. *   *   * In pertinent part, 18 U.S.C. § [Section] 1341 provides:

> Whoever, having devised or intending to devise any scheme or artifice to defraud . . . for the purpose of executing such scheme or artifice or attempting to do so, places in any post office or authorized depository for mail matter, any matter or thing whatever to be sent or delivered by the Post Office . . . or knowingly causes to be delivered by mail according to the direction thereon . . . shall be fined not more than $1000.00 or imprisoned not more than five years or both.

The essential elements of mail fraud are (1) a scheme or artifice to defraud and (2) the use of the United States mails in execution of the scheme. The broad, amorphous statutory language, coupled with the lack of legislative history explaining its intended meaning, has generally permitted the courts considerable latitude in determining what types of schemes come within the purview of the statute. *   *   * [T]he Supreme Court held that the perimeters of the term "scheme or artifice to defraud" are not limited to common law concepts of fraud or false pretenses and that the existence of such a scheme is not contingent upon a violation of state law.

*   *   *   *

It is clear from this brief discussion that the propriety of defendants' mail fraud convictions cannot be evaluated in a technical or mechanistic fashion. Rather, they must be considered in light of the broad language of the statute itself, the expansive interpretation which it has been accorded by the courts, and its general utility in meeting the multifarious types of schemes, complex or simple, which may be devised.

*   *   *   *

*   *   * It is well established that a scheme which is directed at depriving an employer of the honest and faithful services of its employees or of its right to have its business conducted honestly may constitute a "scheme to defraud" within the meaning of the mail fraud statute.

*   *   *   *

[I]t is abundantly clear [from the] record that Kelly and Palmer were aware of Univac's policy against the use of its facilities for personal business ventures. They nevertheless made extensive use of the company's computer facilities in furtherance of their own pecuniary interests, took steps to conceal their activities and willfully failed to seek authorization for them. The evidence was more than sufficient to sustain the jury's determination that the defendants acted with intent to defraud.

*   *   *   *

*   *   * The defendants contend that the mailing of the promotional materials was related only to their goal of ultimately making money from the completed allegro system. It did not, they assert, further the unauthorized use of Univac's computer facilities and therefore was unrelated to the execution of the fraudulent scheme. In so arguing, defendants posit an unduly restrictive interpretation of the perimeters of their scheme to defraud. Under the terms of the indictment, Kelly and Palmer were charged with defrauding Univac by *using its resources for their own personal gain*. The evidence at trial clearly established that while the defendants were utilizing Univac's facilities to develop the technological viability of the system, they were actively engaged in attempting to develop a market for the completed allegro program.

*   *   *   *

Thus, the utilization of Univac's computer facilities cannot be viewed in isolation. As the evidence makes abundantly clear, the primary, if not exclusive, motivating factor in defendants' unauthorized use of their employer's computer storage facility was their desire to market the completed allegro system at a substantial pecuniary gain for themselves. Hence, Kelly and Palmer's attempts to develop the technological capabilities of the system cannot be viewed as distinct from their attempts to sell it. Both activities were directed at the achievement of a single goal—to derive financial gain from the marketing of the completed allegro system. Indeed without this goal, the computer use was merely an academic exercise * * *.

The obvious purpose of the promotional material was to solicit potential sales for the completed allegro system. Viewed in this context, the mailings were directly related to the achievement of the fruits of defendants' scheme. I therefore conclude that the mailing in question was "for the purpose of executing" the scheme to defraud.

The defendants' post-trial motions were denied and the convictions upheld. **DECISION AND REMEDY**

The defendants might have escaped liability for their unauthorized use of Univac's computer if they had not used the mails to further their scheme. **COMMENTS**

SOFTWARE PIRACY For the average consumer, software is expensive. It can also be expensive to produce. Often, considerable sums are invested in the research and development necessary to create new, innovative software programs. And, once marketed, new software requires that user support be provided during its life on the market. It is not surprising that, given the expense of software and the zealous competition in today's software market, many individuals and business firms have been tempted to steal software by decoding and making unauthorized copies of software programs. This is known as *software piracy*. It has been estimated that the annual loss to developers from this practice is more than $250 million.

At one time, manufacturers incorporated protective codes into their software to inhibit its duplication. Breaking through these security codes became little more than a game to some individuals, who then made illegal copies of the software. Consequently, some manufacturers ceased attempting to protect their software by this method, since little benefit was gained in comparison with the increased cost and software complexity required by the security measures. Many companies now take protective steps against software piracy by stressing the benefits—such as written instructions and user support—associated with using authorized copies. Others are suing the users of unauthorized copies in tort for copyright or patent infringement.

Software piracy is illegal, but the applicability of traditional criminal or tort law is made difficult by the unique nature of computer programs. For example, as with the theft of data or services, statutes designed to prohibit larceny—the taking of property without the owner's consent—may be difficult to apply. These statutes were originally enacted to prohibit the theft of *tangible* property. Computer programs, however, are *intangible*, or intellectual, property. As mentioned in Chapter 6, some states have dealt with the issue of program piracy by expanding their definitions of property to bring the theft of computer programs under their larceny statutes. At the federal level, existing laws protecting intellectual property (such as patent and copyright laws) have been amended in recent years to extend coverage to computer programs—as will be discussed later in this chapter.

VANDALISM AND DESTRUCTIVE PROGRAMMING On occasion, political activists, terrorists, and disgruntled employees have physically damaged computer hardware or ruined computer software. These acts have included such conduct as smashing computer equipment with a crowbar, shooting it with a pistol, and—in an attempt to make a political point—pouring blood over a computer. In one instance, to erase a company's records, an individual merely walked past computer storage banks with an electromagnet.

Other destructive acts have required greater technical awareness and facility. For example, a computer program can be designed to rearrange, replace, or even destroy data. Further, the program can be time-delayed and set—much like a time-bomb—to "explode" in the future. Similarly, lines can be inserted into an existing program to damage a system or, for example, to have funds transferred into a phony account. Thus, a knowledgeable individual can do a considerable amount of damage.

Preventing and Controlling Computer Crime

Protective measures against illegitimate access to computer information systems have been undertaken by business firms to prevent—or at least reduce—computer crime. In addition, at both the federal and state levels, legislation has been enacted in an attempt to define and control computer crime.

PRIVATE PROTECTIVE MEASURES—LIMITING ACCESS TO DATA An increasingly common practice among business firms and government institutions is restricting access to and use of information in a computer system through the use of various security measures.

In some cases, the data's availability can be limited to those with special security clearances. Establishing a system of security clearances may involve organizing data in specific categories. The category to which an individual is given access is related to the information the individual needs to perform his or her job. For example, the names of account holders can be kept separate from the accounts' balances. In this way, a party who needs to work with the balances can be prevented from learning the holders' identities.

Passwords may be attached to a system or to a portion of the data within a system to preclude unauthorized access. Considering the relative ease with which unauthorized individuals have discovered passwords in the past, however, it is advisable to change the passwords frequently.

Another means of limiting access to computer information is to encode the data contained within the system—that is, to translate the data into a secret code. Data can be encoded before it is stored or communicated to another party. The data is decoded when it is taken from storage or when the other party receives it.

As a further protective measure, a copy of the data can be stored outside the facilities in which a company's computer system is located. Then, if some of the information kept in the system is destroyed or lost, it can be reproduced.

FEDERAL COMPUTER CRIME CONTROL LEGISLATION Successful prosecution of computer crimes has often depended on a broad interpretation of existing statutes. In some cases, this is because an act, such as hacking, is not specifically forbidden under the applicable criminal code. In other cases, computer-assisted abuse may actually fall outside the traditional definition of a crime (as already noted, for example, the commonly used definition of larceny does not encompass intangible property such as the data stored in a computer).

Under existing federal statutes, computer-assisted crimes have been prosecuted with some success. Successful prosecutions include convictions under laws concerning theft and property offenses, transportation of stolen property, wire fraud, and mail fraud. The following case is representative of the types of problems encountered by courts in trying to apply traditional laws to situations involving computers. In this case, the issue was raised as to whether alterations of accounts payable documents that resulted in computer-issued checks to an improper payee constituted forgery.

Case 55.2
UNITED STATES OF AMERICA v. JONES
United States Court of Appeals,
Fourth Circuit, 1977.
553 F.2d 351.

BACKGROUND AND FACTS *Criminal indictments were returned against Amy Everston Jones, charging her with transporting in interstate and foreign commerce certain checks (securities) that she knew had been "stolen, converted or taken by fraud" in violation of federal law. The federal law excludes forgeries as violations. The purported crime was against a Canadian company, Inglis, Ltd., a subsidiary of Whirlpool, a U.S. corporation. Michael Everston, an alleged accomplice of Jones, was supervisor of Inglis's accounting department. Everston directed an accounting clerk to set up an account payable to A. L. E. Jones and, by changing vendor numbers and other computerized data, was able to convert documents properly payable to Whirlpool into the account of A. L. E. Jones. The computer ultimately issued checks to Jones, which she deposited in her account in Maryland. Jones admitted that the checks were forgeries, but since forgeries are excluded as violations under the federal statutes, she moved* *to dismiss the indictments. The district court agreed and dismissed the indictments against Jones. The United States appealed.*

FIELD, Judge.

* * * *

The sole issue is whether the alteration of accounts payable documents fed into a computer which resulted in the issuance of checks payable to an improper payee constituted a "falsely made, forged, altered, counterfeited or spurious" security within the meaning of the exclusionary clauses of [the federal law].

In considering the phrase "falsely made, forged, altered, or counterfeited" in the statutory sections the district court correctly noted that the terms "are substantially synonymous and refer to the crime of forgery." [*Greathouse v. United States*] We also agree with the district court's conclusion that the term "forgery" should be viewed in the light of its common law meaning:

> A forged writing was defined in *Greathouse* as one "which falsely purports to be the writing of another person than the actual maker." It seems apparent from the sources relied upon that this was intended to express the meaning of forgery as it was known at common law. Furthermore, the Supreme Court defined what it termed "the concept of 'federal' forgery" as being no broader than its common law counterpart, in the absence of some contrary indication in the statute or legislative history. * * * The area of consideration in this case is thus circumscribed by what would have been a forgery at common law.

However, we disagree with the district court's conclusion that the acts committed by Everston constituted common law forgery. The Supreme Court has noted that "[f]orgery * * * may * * * be defined (at common law) to be, 'the fraudulent making or alteration of a writing to the prejudice of another man's right.' * * *'" Significantly, then, "[a]n essential element of the crime of forgery is making the false writing" * * *.

* * * In the present case, the district court was of the opinion that Everston, in fact, made a false writing because "the individual who drafted the instrument in a practical sense was Everston, although he employed the computer as the instrumentality by which the checks were physically drawn." We think, however, that the acts of Everston did not constitute the making of a false writing, but rather amounted to the creation of a writing which was genuine in execution but false as to the statements of fact contained in such writing. The distinction is critical to the sufficiency of the indictment.

> In criminal cases the great weight of authority holds false statements in or fraudulent execution of otherwise valid instruments not to be forgery within the common law or unexpanded meaning.

The district court was of the opinion that the facts did not warrant the conclusion that false statements appeared on the face of the checks issued by Inglis to "A. L. E. Jones." We cannot agree. The checks state that the designated amount is payable "to the order of A. L. E. Jones," and implicit in such an unconditional order was the existence of an obligation running from Inglis, Limited, to the payee. There was, of course, no such obligation, but as the result of Everston's misconduct the accounting department of Inglis was defrauded into believing that the company owed a bona fide obligation to "A. L. E. Jones" and, accordingly, issued a genuine instrument containing a false statement of fact as to the true creditor.

We recognize that, at common law, one need not have physically counterfeited an instrument to be convicted of forgery. However, we note that in those circumstances the issuance of the instrument purporting to have legal efficacy "was neither intended nor issued as such by the purported maker." In the present case, the purported maker, Inglis, issued the check and "the instrument [was] of such nature that if not voidable for the defendant's fraud it could have some legal or prejudicial effect upon the signer."

* * * *

Since we conclude that the checks did not fall within the exclusion of the statutes as forgeries, the order of the district court dismissing the indictment must be reversed.

DECISION AND REMEDY   *The decision of the district court dismissing the indictments was reversed. The defendant sought review by the United States Supreme Court, but the writ of certiorari was denied.*

COMMENTS   *The common law definition of forgery requires that a writing falsely purport to be the writing of one other than the actual maker. In other words, the crime requires a lie about the genuineness of a document. Thus, the employee who pads a timecard does not commit forgery, because the lie does not relate to the timecard's genuineness but to the truth of the information on it. Similarly, in this case, the court reasoned that since the company actually issued the checks, the checks were genuine; it was the statements on them that were false.*

Counterfeit Access Device and Computer Fraud and Abuse Act   Congress has enacted legislation directed at specific computer abuses. The Counterfeit Access Device and Computer Fraud and Abuse Act (enacted in 1984) applies to those who infiltrate a computer system that they are not authorized to use and to those who are authorized to use a system but who use their access to commit an offense proscribed by the act. Under the act, it is a crime to access a computer knowingly for any of the following reasons:

1. To obtain restricted government information—which includes information protected for reasons of national defense or foreign relations and information restricted under the Atomic Energy Act—with the intent that the information be used to the injury of the United States or the advantage of a foreign nation.
2. To obtain information contained in a financial institution's financial records or in a consumer reporting agency's files on consumers.
3. To use, modify, destroy, or prevent the authorized use of a computer operated for or on behalf of the federal government or to disclose the information that it contains.

Electronic Fund Transfer Act   The Electronic Fund Transfer Act (EFTA), which is discussed in more detail in Chapter 28, concerns electronic fund transfers, such as direct payroll and social security deposits and transactions conducted at automatic teller machines (ATMs). These transfers provide opportunities for theft through such means as the interception and alteration of data involved in the transfers, the counterfeiting of ATM cards, and the use of stolen code numbers to gain access to financial information and accounts.

Under the EFTA, it is a crime to use, sell, furnish, or transport in interstate commerce any counterfeit, fictitious, altered, forged, lost, stolen, or fraudulently obtained device (such as an ATM card or code number) used to conduct an electronic fund transfer to obtain money, goods, services, or anything else of value. Penalties for violations include up to ten years' imprisonment and a fine of up to $10,000.

STATE COMPUTER CRIME CONTROL LEGISLATION   As previously pointed out, success in prosecuting computer crimes under state laws has often depended on broad interpretations of statutes directed at more traditional crimes. In recent years, several states have dealt with the problem of computer crime by passing laws that are more specific than federal crime control legislation. In Idaho, for example, accessing computer information without authorization is a misdemeanor, and illegally changing information is a felony. South Dakota has made it illegal to disclose passwords. All unauthorized computer use is a felony in Hawaii. Other states are also in the process of revising their laws to include the sort of specific computer offenses discussed in this chapter.

INTELLECTUAL PROPERTY PROTECTION FOR SOFTWARE

Even when special security programming is added to software in an attempt to prevent the software from being copied, a skilled computer enthusiast can make copies with little difficulty. Once the software has been decoded, a competitor can improve on the pirated material and market the improved product to the detriment of the original software's distributor. Thus, legal protection for their products is a primary concern for companies involved in researching, developing, and marketing new computer software.

As discussed in Chapter 5, statutory protection exists for **intellectual property** (that is, property resulting from intellectual, creative processes—the products of an individual's mind). An inventor may obtain a **patent** from the government and thereby secure an exclusive right to make, use, and sell an invention. Certain works of authors and artists are automatically given **copyright** protection against the unauthorized reproduction of those works. The law also provides protection for **trademarks**—that is, marks, words, symbols, or pictures used to distinguish goods in or on the market from competitive merchandise. Further, a business's **trade secrets** (that is, information or a process that gives a company an advantage over its competitors, who do not know the information or use the process) are protected against a competitor's appropriation.

Under current judicial decisions, it is possible for a software developer and manufacturer to have its product come under all of these protections simultaneously.

Patent Protection

A patent lasts seventeen years for an invention and a lesser period of time for a design. To be granted a patent, an applicant must show that—in the case of software, for example—a process is genuine, novel, useful, and not obvious. IBM obtained patents for some critical elements of its new personal computer, the PS/2. Patent protection may be difficult for developers and manufacturers of software to obtain, since many of these products simply automate procedures that can be performed manually. Also, the basis for software is often a mathematical equation or formula, which is not patentable.

Another obstacle to obtaining patent protection for software is in the procedure of obtaining patents. The process can be expensive and slow. The time element is a particularly important consideration for someone wishing to obtain a patent on software: In light of the rapid changes and improvements in computer technology, the delay could undercut the product's success in the market.

If a patent is infringed (see Chapter 5 for a discussion of what constitutes patent infringement), the patent holder may sue for an injunction, damages, the destruction of all infringing copies, and attorneys' fees and court costs. In the computer industry, patent protection is increasingly used as a bargaining tool in cooperative licensing arrangements.

Copyright Protection

A copyright protects a work from the moment of its creation until fifty years after its creator's death or, in the case of a corporation, for seventy-five years from creation. Under the Computer Software Copyright Act of 1980, amending the 1976 Copyright Reform Act, computer programs are included in the list of creative works protected by federal copyright law.

SOURCE AND OBJECT CODE PROTECTION   The 1980 statute defines a computer program as a "set of statements or instructions to be used directly or indirectly in a computer in order to bring about a certain result." This broad definition has posed some difficult problems for the courts. Unlike literary works, computer programs interact with machines and are "readable" by machines. But can a computer program's object code (the version of the program that is readable by the computer) be considered a "set of statements or instructions to be used directly or indirectly in a computer" and thus fall under the 1980 act? Or should copyright protection be limited to a computer program's source code (the version of the program that can be read by humans)? In the following landmark case, the court addressed these questions and extended copyright protection to both of these elements of computer programs.

Case 55.3
APPLE COMPUTER, INC. v. FRANKLIN COMPUTER CORPORATION

United States Court of Appeals, Third Circuit, 1983. 714 F.2d 1240.

BACKGROUND AND FACTS *Apple Computer, Inc., is a leading manufacturer of personal computers, related equipment, and computer programs. Franklin Computer Corporation is a small manufacturer of computers. It manufactures and sells the ACE 100 personal computer, which was designed to be "Apple compatible"—meaning that any software and peripheral equipment developed for use with the Apple II could be used with the ACE 100. Franklin used fourteen Apple operating programs stored on ROMs in manufacturing the ACE 100. A ROM (read only memory) is an internal permanent memory device consisting of a semiconductor chip that is incorporated into the circuitry of the computer. Apple sued Franklin, claiming infringement of its copyrights on the fourteen programs. The district court denied Apple's motion for a preliminary injunction because it doubted the copyrightability of Apple's programs. Apple appealed.*

SLOVITER, Judge.

*   *   *   *

Franklin's principal defense at the preliminary injunction hearing and before us is primarily a legal one, directed to its contention that the Apple operating system programs are not capable of copyright protection.

*   *   *   *

In 1976, after considerable study, Congress enacted a new copyright law to replace that which had governed since 1909. Under the law, two primary requirements must be satisfied in order for a work to constitute copyrightable subject matter—it must be an "original work of authorship" and must be "fixed in [a] tangible medium of expression." *   *   *

*   *   *   *

The 1980 amendments added a definition of a computer program:

A "computer program" is a set of statements or instructions to be used directly or indirectly in a computer in order to bring about a certain result. *   *   *

*   *   *   *

The district court here questioned whether copyright was to be limited to works "designed to be 'read' by a human reader (as distinguished from) read by an expert with a microscope and patience." The suggestion that copyrightability depends on a communicative function to individuals stems from the early decision of *White-Smith Music Publishing Co. v. Apollo Co.*, which held a piano roll was not a copy of the musical composition because it was not in a form others, except perhaps for a very expert few, could perceive. However, it is clear from the language of the 1976 Act and its legislative history that it was intended to obliterate distinctions engendered by *White-Smith*.

Under the statute, copyright extends to works in any tangible means of expression *"from which they can be perceived,* reproduced, or otherwise communicated, either directly or *with the aid of a machine or device."* Further, the definition of "computer program" adopted by Congress in the 1980 amendments is "sets of statements or instructions to be used *directly or indirectly* in a computer in order to bring about a certain result." As source code instructions must be translated into object code before the computer can act upon them, only instructions expressed in object code can be used "directly" by the computer. *   *   *

*   *   *   *

The district court also expressed uncertainty as to whether a computer program in object code could be classified as a "literary work." However, the category of "literary works," one of the seven copyrightable categories, is not confined to literature in the nature of Hemingway's *For Whom the Bell Tolls*. The definition of "literary works" includes expression not only in words but also "numbers, or other . . . numerical symbols or indicia," thereby expanding the common usage of "literary works." *   *   *

Thus a computer program, whether in object code or source code, is a "literary work" and is protected from unauthorized copying, whether from its object or source code version.

Just as the district court's suggestion of a distinction between source code and object code was rejected by our opinion in *Williams* issued three days after the district court opinion, so also was its suggestion that embodiment of a computer program on a ROM, as distinguished from in a traditional writing, detracts from its copyrightability. In *Williams* we rejected the argument that "a computer program is not infringed when the program is loaded into electronic memory devices (ROMs) and used to control the activity of machines." * * *

* * * *

* * * Therefore we reaffirm that a computer program in object code embedded in a ROM chip is an appropriate subject of copyright.

* * * *

Franklin's attack on operating system programs as "methods" or "processes" seems inconsistent with its concession that application programs are an appropriate subject of copyright. Both types of programs instruct the computer to do something. Therefore, it should make no difference * * * whether these instructions tell the computer to help prepare an income tax return (the task of an application program) or to translate a high level language program from source code into its binary language object code form (the task of an operating system program such as "Applesoft"). Since it is only the instructions which are protected, a "process" is no more involved because the instructions in an operating system program may be used to activate the operation of the computer than it would be if instructions were written in ordinary English in a manual which described the necessary steps to activate an intricate complicated machine. There is, therefore, no reason to afford any less copyright protection to the instructions in an operating system program than to the instructions in an application program.

* * * We believe that the 1980 amendments reflect Congress' receptivity to new technology and its desire to encourage, through the copyright laws, continued imagination and creativity in computer programming. Since we believe that the district court's decision on the preliminary injunction was, to a large part, influenced by an erroneous view of the availability of copyright for operating system programs and unnecessary concerns about object code and ROMs, we must reverse the denial of the preliminary injunction and remand for reconsideration.

The district court's denial of Apple's request for a preliminary injunction against Franklin was reversed and the case remanded to the district court for further proceedings. Franklin appealed to the Supreme Court of the United States, but its writ was denied. Before the district court proceedings commenced, the parties resolved the suit by settlement agreement.

DECISION AND REMEDY

PROGRAM STRUCTURE PROTECTION Copyright protection is not the same as patent protection. A patent protects the *application* of an idea; a copyright protects only its *expression*. Thus, an individual might develop a program to implement the idea underlying a competitor's software but might structure the program differently. As long as the source and object codes were substantially different, such implementation would not constitute an infringement of the competitor's copyright. In recent years, court decisions have expanded copyright protection to cover the total concept of a program, including its overall structure, sequence, and organization. Under these decisions, these program characteristics must also differ substantially from those of a competitor-plaintiff.[1]

---

1. See, for example, Whelan Associates, Inc. v. Jaslow Dental Laboratory, Inc., 797 F.2d 1222 (3d Cir. 1986).

Remedies against copyright infringement (discussed in detail in Chapter 5) are similar to those for patent infringement. Prior to initiating any lawsuit, the copyright owner must have registered or have sought to register the copyright with the U.S. Copyright Office.

Trademark Protection

Computer hardware and software trademarks are protected under federal law. Trademark registration provides protection for twenty years and is renewable. Once a trademark has been registered with the U.S. Patent and Trademark Office, its owner has the right to its exclusive and continued use, providing it does not become generic (the word *aspirin*, for example, was once a trademark).

Trademark infringement occurs when an unauthorized party copies the trademark to a substantial degree or uses it in its entirety, intentionally or unintentionally.

Protection of Trade Secrets

Protection of trade secrets extends both to ideas and to their expression. For this reason, and because it involves no registration or other time-consuming procedure, trade secret protection may be well suited for software. A secret is protected if it is not commonly known in the trade and if it gives its owner a competitive advantage. Of course, the secret—which can be a formula, a method, or any information used in a business—must be disclosed to some persons, most likely employees. To protect a secret, a business must take reasonable precautions, such as having all employees who use or know the process or information agree in their contracts never to reveal it.

Semiconductor Chip Protection Act

The Semiconductor Chip Protection Act of 1984 provides protection for **mask works,** which are defined as a series of images related to the pattern that the many layers of a semiconductor-chip product form.[2] A mask work must be fixed in the product to qualify for the protection, and within two years of initially taking commercial advantage

---

2. Prior to passage of the Semiconductor Chip Protection Act, a government study revealed that research and development costs for a single chip could exceed $4 million, while the costs of copying it could be less than $100,000.

of the mask work, the owner must register it with the U.S. Copyright Office. On registration, the owner of the protected mask work obtains the exclusive right, for ten years, to reproduce, import, or distribute the work or a semiconductor-chip product that contains it.

THE PRIVACY ISSUE

Computers have made information easier to obtain, retain, and retrieve than when it was subject to manual collection, storage, and dispersal. In virtually all interactions between individuals and institutions—banks, schools, insurance companies, the government, and others—data concerning the transactions are entered into computer files. Using computer retrieval systems provides for more rapid and efficient performance when information is needed. But it also allows individuals less control over the nature of that information, its accuracy and completeness, and its distribution. Thus, a balance must be struck between the need for information collection, storage, and retrieval and the rights of individuals to maintain their privacy.

Constitutional Right to Privacy

The U.S. Constitution does not explicitly mention a general right to privacy. In some contexts, however, the United States Supreme Court has recognized that such a right is implied under various constitutional provisions and has held that an individual's privacy should be protected against government intrusion. The Court has not yet held that the right to privacy limits governmental collection of data concerning private individuals, but it has indicated that the government can assemble and use data in which it has a legitimate interest and for which it provides adequate safeguards against misuse.

Common Law Doctrine

Individuals and businesses have been compelled to pay damages in actions based on invasion of privacy. This is a tort cause of action discussed generally in Chapter 4. In situations involving computers, relief may be accorded for unauthorized physical intrusions into, for example, an individual's private records. Courts have allowed suits for the unauthorized examination of a bank account.

Alternatively, an individual may be awarded compensation for the public disclosure of a private fact about him or her, when the nature of the disclosure is such that it would be highly objectionable to a reasonable person. This is true even when the party making the disclosure had a right to know the information in the first place.

Both of these causes of action present difficulties, particularly when computers are concerned. Demonstrating that private records were invaded when there has been no physical intrusion into, for instance, one's home is an example of the type of difficulty that can arise. Showing that a disclosure was "public" when only a few people were made privy to the revealed information—however disruptive that limited disclosure may have proved to be—is another.

Privacy Legislation

Congress has enacted numerous laws (see Exhibit 55–1) to control the collection and dispersal of

Exhibit 55–1 Federal Legislation Relating to Privacy

TITLE	PROVISIONS CONCERNING PRIVACY
Freedom of Information Act (1966)	Provides that individuals have a right to obtain access to information about them collected in government files.
Fair Credit Reporting Act (1970)	Provides that consumers have the right to be informed of the nature and scope of a credit investigation, the kind of information that is being compiled, and the names of the firms or individuals who will be receiving the report.
Crime Control Act (1973)	Safeguards the confidentiality of information amassed for certain state criminal systems.
Family Educational Rights and Privacy Act (1974)	Limits access to computer-stored records of education-related evaluations and grades in private and public colleges and universities.
Privacy Act (1974)	Protects the privacy of individuals about whom the federal government has information. Specifically, the act provides that: 1. Agencies originating, using, disclosing, or otherwise manipulating personal information must ensure the reliability of the information and provide safeguards against its misuse. 2. Information compiled for one purpose cannot be used for another without the concerned individual's permission. 3. Individuals must be able to find out what data concerning them is being compiled and how it will be used. 4. Individuals must be given a means through which to correct inaccurate data.
Tax Reform Act (1976)	Preserves the privacy of personal financial information.
Right to Financial Privacy Act (1978)	Prohibits financial institutions from providing the federal government with access to a customer's records unless the customer authorizes the disclosure.
Electronic Fund Transfer Act (1980)	Requires financial institutions to notify an individual if a third party gains access to the individual's account.
Counterfeit Access Device and Computer Fraud and Abuse Act (1984)	Prohibits use of a computer without authorization to retrieve data in a financial institution's or consumer reporting agency's files.
Cable Communications Policy Act (1984)	Regulates access to information collected by cable service operators on subscribers to cable services.
Electronic Communications Privacy Act (1986)	Prohibits the interception of information communicated by electronic means.

personal information as well as to provide ways to challenge the accuracy of information and to obtain relief for the use of inaccurate information.

Generally, the laws that states have enacted to address computer crime, which were discussed earlier in this chapter, are also necessarily concerned to some extent with the issue of privacy. The Privacy Act of 1974 has served as a model for many of the state laws regulating government records and recording practices.

COMPUTERIZED LEGAL RESEARCH

The days of the hunched-over, bespectacled law clerk searching through dusty tomes filled with ancient cases may not be completely over, but computers have greatly simplified the task of legal research. There are a number of law-related *data bases* that can be accessed through several high-speed data-delivery systems. The two most commonly used systems are WESTLAW and LEXIS. WESTLAW is West Publishing Company's computer-assisted legal research service. Mead Data Control, Inc., provides LEXIS. Each system has software that makes it possible for a researcher to interact with the delivery system.

WESTLAW, LEXIS, and similar computerized data-search systems allow for access to virtually all cases, statutes, federal regulations, and other law-related materials with a minimum of delay and physical effort. Often, the most recent court opinions are available through computer-assisted legal research systems long before they are available in bound volumes in a law library.

QUESTIONS AND CASE PROBLEMS

1. As a college student, you are required to write a term paper. You are currently employed part-time by ABC, Inc. Without ABC's permission, you secure access to ABC's computer and use the computer to generate certain data formulations for your paper. Discuss whether you could and should be liable to ABC for theft.

2. Upon graduation from college with a business degree in information systems, you are hired by the Greenville Corporation. Greenville is a government contractor and has a great deal of sensitive information stored in its computer system. Many of Greenville's employees need and use certain portions of this information. Because of the widespread access to the computer system, you are worried that some of Greenville's sensitive information may end up in the hands of a competitor. Discuss some measures you could take to protect against misuse of the stored data.

3. Adams, who owns and operates a restaurant, has had an account with Uptown Bank for over twenty years. All of Uptown's banking records are computerized. Greed, a competitor of Adams, pays a sum of money to a disgruntled Uptown employee to access Uptown's computer system and provide Greed with information on the financial position and activities of Adams. In addition to giving Greed this information, the employee gives one of Adams's creditors the access code of Uptown's computer system. The creditor, using its own computer, then gathers financial information on Adams. Uptown Bank learns of these activities and discharges the employee. Discuss whether any of the federal laws mentioned in this chapter are specifically applicable to these facts.

4. Franks is an employee of Beto, Inc., and frequently takes work home. Because he needs a computer to do some of the work, he takes one of Beto's older-model computers, Model 100Y, home without Beto's permission. Later, Franks learns that Beto is considering declaring the Model 100Y computers obsolete. Franks immediately takes the Model 100Y computer and trades it in for a new personal computer, which he gives to his daughter. Discuss whether Franks has committed theft. Could Franks be held liable in tort by Beto? (See Chapter 5.)

5. McGraw was employed by the city of Indianapolis as a computer operator. The city leased computer services on a fixed-charge, or flat-rate, basis; hence, its expense for computer services was constant, regardless of how much computer time was used. McGraw was provided with a terminal at his desk and assigned a portion of the computer's information storage capacity, or private library. McGraw became involved in a private sales venture and began using a small portion of his assigned library to maintain records associated with the venture. At the time he was hired, he received a handbook disclosing the general prohibition against the unauthorized use of city property, and he was reprimanded several times for selling his products in the office and on "office time." The relevant criminal theft statute reads: "A person who knowingly or intentionally exerts unauthorized control over property of another person with intent to deprive the other of any part of its value or use commits theft." Discuss whether McGraw should be convicted of theft because of his unauthorized use of city facilities. [State v. McGraw, 480 N.E.2d 552 (Ind. 1985)]

6. Atari owned the exclusive rights to the copyrighted PAC-MAN home video game. North American Philips Consumer Electronics Corporation later developed a game, called K. C. Munchkin, that Atari believed was similar to PAC-MAN. Atari brought suit, charging copyright infringement, and sought an injunction. Discuss how a court might go about determining whether home video games are similar for copyright purposes. [Atari, Inc. v. North American Philips Consumer Electronics Corp., 672 F.2d 607 (7th Cir. 1982)]

7. A computer programmer employed by the Board of Education of New York City was charged with theft of services for using his employer's computer for his own personal projects without permission. The statute outlawing theft of services defined the crime as the intentional use of "business, commercial, or industrial equipment or facilities of another person," when one knows he or she is not entitled to their use, with the "intent to derive a commercial or other substantial benefit." Discuss whether the board's computer is "business, commercial, or industrial equipment" as required by the statute. [People v. Weg, 113 Misc.2d 1017, 450 N.Y.S.2d 957 (1982)]

8. Data Cash Systems, Inc. (DCS) retained an independent consultant to design and develop a program for a computerized chess game. The program was then translated into machine language and used to create an object program in the form of a read-only-memory (ROM) silicon chip, which was installed as part of the computer's circuitry. All copies of the source program contained copyright notices, but neither the marketed game nor the ROM program contained any copyright notice. After DCS had filed a copy of the source program with the Register of Copyrights, it was issued a certificate of copyright registration. A year after DCS began marketing the chess game, JS&A Group, a competitor, began marketing a similar game that used a ROM identical to that of DCS. Investigation revealed that the new ROM was being manufactured by a Hong Kong firm for JS&A. DCS sued JS&A for copyright infringement and unfair competition. Should the copyright of the source program be extended to the ROM? [Data Cash Systems, Inc. v. JS&A Group, Inc., 628 F.2d 1038 (7th Cir. 1980)]

9. An insurance company hired a service that investigated injury claims to obtain medical information reports on two claimants who were patients of a Denver hospital. Through the use of the telephone, an agent obtained a verbatim reading of the medical reports, which he later transcribed and sent to the insurance company. The actual medical records themselves never left the hospital file room; only the medical information contained in the records was acquired. The relevant criminal theft statute reads: "A person commits theft when he knowingly obtains or exercises control over anything of value of another without authorization, by threat or deception, and: (a) intends to deprive the other person permanently of the use or benefit of the thing of value." Is medical information surreptitiously procured a "thing of value" and therefore governed by the theft statute? Would the answer be the same if this information had been secured by unauthorized entry into the Denver hospital's computer system? [People v. Home Insurance Co., 197 Colo. 260, 591 P.2d 1036 (1979)]

Chapter 56

Wills, Trusts, and Estates

The laws of succession of property are a necessary corollary to the concept of private ownership of property. The law requires that, upon death, title to the decedent's property must vest (full possession must be delivered) somewhere. The decedent can direct the passage of property after death by *will*, subject to certain limitations imposed by the state. If no valid will has been executed, the decedent is said to have died **intestate,** and state law prescribes the distribution of the property among heirs or next of kin. If no heirs or kin can be found, the property escheats (title is transferred to the state).

In addition, a person can transfer property through a *trust*.[1] The owner (settlor) of the property transfers legal title to a *trustee*, who has a duty imposed by law to hold the property for the use or benefit of another (the beneficiary).

PURPOSES OF INHERITANCE LAWS

State regulation of inheritance has developed in response to certain social and political goals. Three principles underlie U.S. inheritance and succession laws.

1.   *The concept of private property.* Any system of laws to regulate the passage of a decedent's estate must do so in the context of a firmly rooted tradition of private ownership of property.

2.   *Effectuation of the individual's testamentary intent.* The right to direct the distribution of one's own property to whomever one chooses (subject to the rights of the surviving spouse and children) is often taken as a basic tenet of U.S. jurisprudence. Many formalities surround the court's duty to ensure that when a will is offered for authentication, it is in fact the genuine and final expression of the decedent's wishes.

---

1. A trust can be set up by the property owner *during his or her life* (by a deed accompanied by a trust document) or *at his or her death* (by a will containing or accompanied by a trust document). This chapter discusses both types of trusts.

3. *The policy favoring family.* The protection of the family has been a cornerstone of inheritance laws throughout history. As noted earlier, intestate succession is inheritance by the heirs of the deceased. In contemporary law, this goal is reinforced by state statutes guaranteeing that an absolute portion of the decedent's estate will be allotted to the surviving spouse and children.

WILLS

A **will** is the final declaration of the disposition that a person desires to have made of his or her property after death. A will is referred to as a *testamentary disposition* of property. It is a formal instrument that must follow exactly the requirements of the appropriate state's statutes to be effective. The reasoning behind such a strict requirement is obvious. A will becomes effective only after death. No attempts to modify it after the death of the maker are allowed because the court cannot ask the maker to confirm the attempted modifications. (But sometimes the wording must be "interpreted" by the courts.)

A will can serve other purposes besides the distribution of property. It can appoint a guardian for minor children or incapacitated adults. It can also appoint a personal representative to settle the affairs of the deceased.

Vocabulary of Wills

Every area of law has its own special vocabulary, and the area of wills is no exception. A man who makes out a will is known as a **testator** (from the Latin *testari*—"to make a will"), and a woman who makes out a will is called a **testatrix.** The court responsible for administering any legal problems surrounding a will is called a **probate court.** When a person dies, a *personal representative* settles the affairs of the deceased. An **executor** or **executrix** is the personal representative named in the will; an **administrator** or **administratrix** is the personal representative appointed by the court for a decedent who dies without a will, who fails to name an executor in the will, who names an executor lacking the capacity to serve, or who writes a will that the court refuses to admit to probate. A gift of real estate by will is generally called a **devise,** and a gift of personal property under a will is called a **bequest** or **legacy.**

Types of Gifts

Gifts by will can be specific, general, or residuary. A *specific* devise or bequest (legacy) describes particular property that can be distinguished from all the rest of the testator's property. For example, Johnson's will provides, "I give my nephew, Tom, my gold pocket watch with the initials MTJ on it." Should the gold watch not be part of Johnson's property at the time of Johnson's death (if, for example, it has been sold, destroyed, or given away), the legacy is extinguished, or cancelled. This is known as *ademption by extinction*. If, before Johnson's death, Johnson gave the watch to Tom, the gift adeems *by satisfaction.*

A *general* devise or bequest (legacy) does not single out any particular item of property to be transferred by will. For example, "I give to my daughter, Dana, $10,000" is a general bequest. Usually, general legacies specify a sum of money.

On occasion, assets are insufficient to pay in full all of the bequests provided for in a will, as well as the taxes, debts, and expenses of administering the estate. When this happens, an *abatement,* by which the legatees receive reduced benefits, takes place. For example, Johnson's will leaves "$15,000 each to my children, Mary and Sam." Upon Johnson's death, only $10,000 is available to honor these bequests. By abatement, each child will receive $5,000. If bequests are more complicated, abatement may be more complicated. The testator's or testatrix's intent, as expressed in the will, controls. If the will is silent, there is a particular order in which the property and gifts abate. Usually, *intestate property* (property not disposed of in the will) and *residuary gifts* (bequests of that portion of the testator's or testatrix's estate that the will does not otherwise dispose of—for example, a bequest of "all the rest of my property to Melvin") abate before general bequests, then demonstrative bequests (discussed below) abate, and lastly specific bequests and devises abate.

A testator or testatrix may wish that a legatee receive a gift of a certain sum of money, stock, or other property from an identifiable source, such as a savings account in a particular bank or a portfolio managed by a certain brokerage firm, but intend that if the source is unavailable at the time of death, the bequest is to be satisfied from other estate assets. This is accomplished by means of a *demonstrative* bequest. In the will, the testator or testatrix designates a particular source from which the gift is to be made, additionally instructing that if that source is insufficient or no longer exists, the bequest be paid out of the general assets.

If the legatee dies prior to the death of the testator or testatrix or before the legacy is payable, a *lapsed legacy* occurs. At common law, the legacy failed. Today, under an anti-lapse statute, a legacy may not lapse if the legatee is in a certain blood relationship to the testator or testatrix—such as a child, grandchild, brother, or sister—and if the legatee also left a child or other surviving heir.

Sometimes, as noted, a will provides that any assets remaining after specific gifts are made and

debts are paid are to be distributed through a *residuary* clause. A residuary provision is used because the exact amount to be distributed cannot be determined until all other gifts and payouts are made. A residuary estate can pose problems, however, when the will does not specifically name the beneficiaries to receive the residue. In such a case, if the court cannot determine the testator's intent, the remainder of the residuary passes according to state laws of intestacy.

In the following case, the court had to decide how to distribute the residual assets of an estate.

Case 56.1
ESTATE OF CANCIK
Appellate Court of Illinois, First
District, Fifth Division, 1984.
121 Ill.App.3d 113, 459 N.E.2d
296, 76 Ill.Dec. 659.

BACKGROUND AND FACTS *Edward Cancik, the testator, died with a net estate valued at more than $200,000. Edward had intentionally omitted all his relatives from his will except his cousin Charles Cancik. Edward specifically willed to Charles all his personal and household goods and placed the residue in a testamentary trust for the maintenance of the Cancik family mausoleum. After Edward's death, Charles filed a complaint alleging that the value of the trust corpus (that is, the capital or principal, as distinguished from the interest) vastly exceeded the amount necessary to accomplish its purpose (to maintain the mausoleum) and asked that the residuum be distributed to him as the testator's only heir-at-law. Thomas, another relative of Edward, acting for any unknown heirs as guardian ad litem (a person appointed to protect the interests of parties unable to represent themselves) filed a petition to have the residuum distributed to all the testator's heirs by intestacy, twelve of whom were later found to be living in Czechoslovakia. The trial court held that the residue passed to all the heirs by the laws of intestacy. Charles appealed.*

SULLIVAN, Justice.
* * * *

[Edward Cancik (testator)] executed a will in which he bequeathed, in clause IV, all of his personal and household effects to Charles; and then, in clause V, placed the residue of his estate into a testamentary trust, the income of which was to be used for the perpetual maintenance of the mausoleum. * * * In the final clause of the will (clause VII), testator stated:

I have intentionally omitted the names of my relatives from this my Last Will and Testament for reasons I deem good and sufficient with the exception of my aforesaid cousin, CHARLES E. CANCIK.
* * * *

The object of testamentary construction is to ascertain the intention of the testator and, in so doing, the intention which must be given effect is that expressed in the language of the will, not one which the testator may have had in his mind but failed to express. * * * Although there is a presumption against intestacy, it is only a presumption and may not be used to overcome the language of the will or to supply language which has been omitted. Thus, where the testator has overlooked a contingency for which he probably would have provided had it occurred to him, the court may not speculate as to what that provision might have been; * * * rather, any property not specifically devised or bequeathed will pass under the residuary clause, but where there is no residuary provision or that clause itself has failed for some reason, the undisposed portion of the estate becomes intestate property and vests in the heirs of the testator according to their proportionate statutory shares. *   *   *

Here, Charles concedes that the will contained no specific dispository provision for the unused trust funds; nevertheless, he maintains that clause VII effectively disinherits all other heirs and thus creates, by implication, an alternate residuary bequest to him as the only heir who was not excluded from participating in the distribution of the estate. We find this argument unpersuasive. First, it is well-settled that heirs cannot be disinherited merely by a declaration that they are excluded from the will or that they take only a certain amount. *   *   * The only means by which a testator can disinherit an heir is to give the property to someone else; *   *   * thus, no matter how strong the intention to disinherit may be expressed in a will, the testator is presumed to know the law that where a testamentary gift fails, for whatever reason, and no alternate dispositional intention is expressed, the property passes by intestacy to the heirs at law. *   *   *

In our view, a reading of the will in its entirety, and of the language of clause VII in particular, does not give rise to an implication so strong as to leave no reasonable doubt that the testator intended Charles to inherit the entire excess residuum of his estate. It appears that his major concern was for the care and maintenance of the family mausoleum, and it was to this purpose that he directed, through clause V, the overwhelming bulk of his assets; and although he referred to Charles with a certain degree of affection, as his "beloved cousin," the bequest to Charles in clause IV of the will consisted of only personal property of minimal value when compared to the total estate. In the light of this vastly disproportionate division of property between the trust and Charles, we cannot conclude, as Charles suggests, that he (Charles) was so favored by the overall scheme of the will as to raise an inference that clause VII evidenced testator's intention to disinherit all other heirs; or, more importantly, that it created an alternate residuary bequest to him upon the termination or failure of the trust. As noted earlier, where a will is silent or where its provisions lend themselves to more than one interpretation, the courts may not supply gifts not found therein, and the property left undisposed then passes by intestacy to the heirs of the testator notwithstanding any attempts in the will to disinherit them.

The court held that the residuum of Edward's estate must go to his heirs rather than to Charles, who was merely the beneficiary of Edward's personal belongings.	**DECISION AND REMEDY**

The Uniform Probate Code

Probate laws vary from state to state. In 1969, the American Bar Association and the National Conference of Commissioners on Uniform State Laws approved the Uniform Probate Code (UPC). The UPC codifies general principles and procedures for the resolution of conflicts in settling estates and relaxes some of the requirements for a valid will contained in earlier state laws. Fifteen states have adopted some form of the UPC. References to UPC provisions will be included in the remainder of this chapter whenever general practice in most states is consistent. Since succession and inheritance laws vary widely among states, however, one should always check the laws of the state involved.[2]

Testamentary Capacity

Not everyone who owns property necessarily qualifies to make a valid disposition of that property by will. *Testamentary capacity* requires the testator to be of legal age and sound mind *at the time the will is made.* The legal age for executing a will varies, but in most states and under the UPC the minimum age is eighteen years [UPC 2-501]. Thus,

---

2. For example, California law differs *substantially* from the UPC.

a will of a twenty-one-year-old decedent written when the person was sixteen is invalid.

The concept of *sound mind* refers to the testator's ability to formulate and to comprehend a personal plan for the disposition of property. Further, a testator must intend the document to be his or her will. Courts have grappled with the requirement of sound mind for a long time, and their decisions have been inconsistent. Mental incapacity is a highly subjective matter and thus is not easily measured. The general test for testamentary capacity has the following provisions:

1. The testator must comprehend and remember the "natural objects of his or her bounty" (usually family members and persons for whom the testator has affection).

2. The testator must comprehend the kind and character of the property being distributed.

3. The testator must understand and formulate a plan for disposing of the property.

Less mental ability is required to make a will than to manage one's own business affairs or to enter into a contract. Thus, a testator may be feeble, aged, eccentric, or offensive in behavior and still possess testamentary capacity. Moreover, a person can be adjudged mentally incompetent or have delusions about certain subjects and yet, during lucid moments, still be of sound mind and make a valid will.

The problem of determining testamentary mental capacity is illustrated by the following case dealing with a testatrix in a nursing home.

Case 56.2
IN RE ESTATE OF UNGER
Court of Appeals of Oregon, 1980.
47 Or.App. 951, 615 P.2d 1115.

BACKGROUND AND FACTS *The issue in this will-contest case was whether the testatrix, Lena L. Unger, had sufficient testamentary capacity to execute a last will and testament on February 25, 1976. Unger was confined to a nursing home, and the staff testified that she was in a state of mental confusion at the time the will was executed. The probate court found that testatrix had sufficient testamentary capacity.*

ROBERTS, Judge.
*   *   *   *

The attorney was one of the subscribing witnesses [to the will]. He testified that he felt testatrix was competent to make the will as he had no data to indicate otherwise. The other subscribing witness, the attorney's secretary, also testified that, in her opinion, testatrix was competent, as she, too, had no reason to believe otherwise. The secretary was present when respondent read aloud the provisions of the will to testatrix in the reception area, but was unable to hear anything said by testatrix although testatrix appeared to the secretary to be asking questions. After respondent's explanation to testatrix and prior to testatrix's execution of the will, testatrix approached the secretary, asking something to the effect of "What is this, what am I doing, what do you want me to do?" The secretary did not recall that an explanation was given to testatrix by anyone. The secretary testified that the attorney then appeared and asked some cursory questions about testatrix's satisfaction with the document. The secretary did not hear testatrix say anything, but she did appear to nod her head. Testatrix then signed the document at the place indicated to her.

The testimony of the subscribing witnesses, aided by the presumption of competency which accompanies a will that has been duly executed, carries great weight in the determination of decedent's testamentary capacity. The reason for this is that the determination of testamentary capacity must focus on the moment the will is executed and subscribing witnesses are in a position to observe the decedent at the time of the execution. Nevertheless, this heavy reliance on the subscribing witnesses' testimony is not always appropriate.
*   *   *   *

Other witnesses who testified were nursing home personnel who had observed testatrix for a period of eight days prior to the signing of the will, and the physician who examined testatrix three days prior to the date the will was executed. These witnesses were disinterested and unanimous in their opinion that at the time the will was executed, testatrix was without testamentary capacity. Those on the nursing staff who were familiar with testatrix until her death, two and one-half years later, also indicated that at no time was she competent.

* * * *

Those individuals who testified that they observed testatrix frequently both prior to and subsequent to the execution of the will were a registered nurse, a licensed practical nurse, the nursing home's activities director, and the home's administrator. They all indicated that testatrix lacked testamentary capacity. Testatrix was described as being very confused; as wandering aimlessly about the nursing home; as being unable to distinguish her room or her possessions from [those of] other patients; as being unable to recognize the staff; as being unable to carry on a conversation; and as being able to communicate only on the most basic level and only if a short answer was required. Testimony indicated that her mental confusion left her unable to dress herself appropriately and caused her to have difficulty feeding herself and maintaining personal hygiene.

* * * *

We conclude the evidence of testatrix's mental acuity is not as persuasive as the testimony from the examining physician and the nursing home personnel, who were disinterested and who were dealing with testatrix on a more constant basis than the other witnesses during the period of time surrounding the date of the will's execution.

DECISION AND REMEDY

The probate court's judgment was reversed. The testatrix was determined to have lacked testamentary capacity, and the will executed on February 25, 1976, was therefore invalid.

COMMENTS

Unger died intestate. The property passed as though there had never been any will. It is important to stress that incapacity is difficult to prove.

Formal Requirements of a Will

A will must comply with statutory formalities designed to ensure that the testator or testatrix understood his or her actions at the time the will was made. These formalities are intended to help prevent fraud. Unless they are followed, the will is declared void, and the decedent's property is distributed according to the laws of intestacy of the state. The requirements are not uniform among jurisdictions. Most states, however, uphold the following basic requirements for executing a will.

1. *A will must be in writing.* A written document is generally required, although in some cases oral wills, called nuncupative wills (to be discussed later), are found valid [UPC 2-502]. The writing itself can be informal as long as it substantially complies with the statutory requirements. In some states, a will can be handwritten in crayon or ink. It can be written on a sheet or scrap of paper, on a paper bag, or on a piece of cloth. A will that is

completely in the handwriting of the testator is called a **holographic** (or olographic) **will.**

A will also can refer to a written memorandum that itself is not a will but that contains information necessary to carry out the will. For example, Thelma's will provides that a certain sum of money be divided among a group of charities named in a written memorandum that Thelma gave to the trustee *the same day the will was signed.* The written list of charities will be "incorporated by reference" into the will only if it was in existence when the will was executed (signed) and if it is sufficiently described so that it can be identified.

2. *A formal (nonholographic) will must be signed by the testator.* It is a fundamental requirement in almost all jurisdictions that the testator's or testatrix's signature be made with the requisite intent to validate the will; but so long as it is in the body of the will, it need not be at the end of the will. Each jurisdiction dictates by statute and court decision what constitutes a signature. Initials, an

"X" or other mark, and words like "Mom" have all been upheld as valid when it was shown that the testators intended them to be signatures.

3. *A formal (nonholographic) will must be witnessed.* A will must be attested by two and sometimes three witnesses. The number of witnesses, their qualifications, and the manner in which the witnessing must be done are generally set out in a state's statute.

A witness can be required to be disinterested—that is, not a beneficiary under the will. By contrast, the UPC provides that a will is valid even if it is attested by an interested witness [UPC 2-505]. There are no age requirements for witnesses, but they must be mentally competent.

Witnesses function to verify that the testator actually executed (signed) the will and had the requisite intent and capacity at the time. A witness does not have to read the contents of the will. Usually, the testator and witnesses must all sign in the sight or the presence of one another, but the UPC deems it sufficient if the testator acknowledges his or her signature to the witnesses [UPC 2-502]. The UPC does not require all parties to sign in the presence of one another.

4. *A will may be required to be "published."* Publication is an oral declaration by the maker to the witnesses that the document they are about to sign is his or her "last will and testament." Publication is becoming an unnecessary formality in most states, and it is not required under the UPC.

In general, strict compliance with the preceding formalities (except the one relating to witnesses and the one relating to publication) is required before a formal document is accepted as the decedent's will. Holographic wills constitute another exception in some jurisdictions. A holographic will must be signed by the decedent, however, and its material provisions must be in the testator's handwriting in order for them to be probated (validated) [UPC 2-503].

NUNCUPATIVE WILLS   A nuncupative will is an oral will made before witnesses. It is not permitted in most states. Where authorized by statute, such wills are valid only if made during the last illness or in expectation of the imminent death of the testator or testatrix, and usually before at least three witnesses. They are sometimes referred to as death-bed wills. Only personal property (not real property) can be transferred by a nuncupative

will. Statutes frequently permit soldiers and sailors to make nuncupative wills when on active duty.

Undue Influence

A valid will is one that represents the maker's intention to transfer and distribute his or her property. When it can be shown that the decedent's plan of distribution was the result of improper pressure brought by another person overriding the maker's intent, the will is declared invalid.

Undue influence may be inferred by the court if the testator or testatrix ignores blood relatives and names as beneficiary a nonrelative who is in constant close contact and in a position to influence the making of the will. For example, if a nurse or friend caring for the deceased at the time of death is named as beneficiary to the exclusion of all family members, the validity of the will might well be challenged on the basis of undue influence.

Revocation of Wills

An executed will is revocable by the maker at any time during the maker's lifetime. Wills can also be revoked by operation of law. Revocation can be partial or complete, and it must follow certain strict formalities.

ACT OF THE MAKER   Revocation of an executed will by the maker can be effected in either of two ways—by physical act or in writing.

Revocation by Physical Act   The testator or testatrix may revoke a will by intentionally burning, tearing, canceling, obliterating, or destroying it or by having someone else do so in the presence of the maker and at the maker's direction.[3] In some states, partial revocation by physical act of the maker is recognized. Thus, those portions of a will lined out or torn away are dropped, and the remaining parts of the will are valid. In no case, however, can a provision be crossed out and an additional or substitute provision written in. Such altered portions require reexecution (resigning) and reattestation (rewitnessing).

To revoke a will by physical act, it is necessary to follow the mandates of a state statute exactly.

---

3. The destruction cannot be inadvertent. The maker's intent to revoke must be shown. When a will has been burned or torn accidentally, it is normally recommended that the maker have a new document created so that it will not falsely appear that the maker intended to revoke the will.

When a state statute prescribes the exact methods for revoking a will by physical act, those are the only methods that will revoke the will.

Revocation in Another Writing A **codicil** is a written instrument separate from the will that amends or revokes provisions in the will. It eliminates the necessity of redrafting an entire will merely to add to it or amend it. A codicil can also be used to revoke an entire will. The codicil must be executed with the same formalities required for a will. It must refer expressly to the will. In effect, it updates a will, because the will is "incorporated by reference" into the codicil.

A *second will* can be executed that may or may not revoke the first or a prior will, depending upon the language used. The second will must use specific language like, "This will hereby revokes all prior wills." If the second will is otherwise valid and properly executed, it will revoke all prior wills. If the express *declaration of revocation* is missing, then both wills are read together. If any of the dispositions made in the second will are inconsistent with the prior will, the second will controls.

When a state statute details the requirements for revoking a will with another writing, those requirements must be strictly complied with, as illustrated by the following case.

BACKGROUND AND FACTS *Frances Maude Thompson, the decedent, executed a will on September 2, 1964, in Nebraska. Upon her death, Victor E. Thompson, her husband, filed a petition for the probate of her will. John E. Finley, son of the decedent through a prior marriage, filed a petition seeking a formal adjudication of his deceased mother's estate by intestacy. Finley's petition claimed that his mother executed a subsequent will that revoked the 1964 document offered for probate by the husband. Finley could not find the subsequent will, however. Finley's petition was dismissed, and the will was admitted to probate. Finley appealed.*

Case 56.3
ESTATE OF THOMPSON
Supreme Court of Nebraska, 1983.
214 Neb. 899, 336 N.W.2d 590.

CAPORALE, Justice.
*   *   *   *

*   *   * The only evidence concerning the issue is the testimony of the contestant son and his wife. It is to the effect that in July of 1965 they examined and read a one- or two-page typewritten document which the decedent, a Nebraska resident, showed them while she was visiting at their home in Colorado, and which she said was her will. The document began with the words, "Last Will and Testament of Frances Maude Thompson." It contained two signatures in addition to that of his mother, but they could not recall whose they were. According to the son, there was also "some kind of a mark on it for a notary." It bore a 1965 date, but he could not recall the month. The son believed, but could not "swear," that the document contained a clause revoking former wills. His wife recalled such a clause. The son testified further that "The Will specified that if [sic] the property was first to go to Vic Thompson and then to me without restriction, in other words, he wouldn't be deprived of this property during his lifetime. . . . It had nothing in there that said, specific words, for life." His wife generally corroborated the son in this regard. They could recall no other specific portions of the document.

It is the son's contention that although the above-cited testimony is insufficient to establish the distributive provisions of the 1965 will so as to entitle it to probate, the evidence is sufficient to establish that a will was duly made and executed after the 1964 will such as to destroy the earlier will. The effect of that circumstance would be that his mother would have died intestate and her property would therefore be subject to distribution under the laws of descent rather than under the 1964 document. *   *   * [Neb.Rev.Stat.] Section 30-2332 provides: "A will or any part thereof is revoked (1) by a subsequent will which, as is evident either from its terms or from competent evidence of its terms, revokes the prior will or part expressly or by inconsistency; or (2) by being burned, torn, canceled, obliterated, or destroyed, with the intent and for the purpose of revoking it by the testator or by another person in the presence of and by the direction of the testator." * * *

In the posture of this case the threshold question becomes whether the contestant's evidence meets the "clear, unequivocal, and convincing" standard required to establish that a subsequent will was duly executed. We find that it does not.

One need look no further than the first two sentences of the Comment to § 30-2332 to reach that conclusion. Those sentences read: "Revocation of a will may be by either a subsequent will or an act done to the document. If revocation is by a subsequent will, it must be *properly executed*." (Emphasis supplied.) The evidence does not tell us where the will was executed, what formalities, if any, the witnesses observed in affixing their signatures to the document, or what role a notary, if any, played in the execution process.

* * * *

In 1965, Neb.Rev.Stat. § 30-204 (Reissue 1964) provided that, except for nun-cupative wills, and wills properly executed in other jurisdictions, wills must be signed by the testator, or some person in his presence, and by his express direction, and attested and subscribed in the presence of the testator by two or more competent witnesses. No showing exists that these formalities were followed. Faced with the same language as to method of execution presently contained in Neb.Rev.Stat. § 30-2327 (Reissue 1979) that, except for holographic wills, certain written statements, and wills properly executed in other jurisdictions, every will is required "to be signed by at least two individuals each of whom witnessed either the signing or the testator's acknowledgement of the signature or of the will," the court in *Matter of Estate of Weidner*, held that where it could not be established that there was a second individual who had witnessed either the signing or the testator's acknowledgment of her signature, there was insufficient evidence to support a finding that the will was fully executed and thus it could not revoke a prior will. * * *

There was no evidence before the trial court herein as to the manner in which the 1965 document was executed. We conclude, therefore, that as a matter of law the evidence does not clearly, unequivocally, and convincingly establish that the 1965 document was properly executed as the last will and testament of the contestant's mother.

DECISION AND REMEDY   *The testatrix did not revoke her validly executed will by writing a second will because she did not strictly adhere to the state formalities of a properly executed will.*

REVOCATION BY OPERATION OF LAW Revocation by operation of law occurs when marriage, divorce or annulment, or the birth of children takes place after a will has been executed.

Marriage In the vast majority of states, when a testator marries *after* executing a will that does not include the new spouse, the spouse upon the testator's death can receive the amount he or she would have taken had the testator died intestate. In effect, this revokes the will to the extent of providing the spouse with an intestate share. The rest of the estate is passed under the will [UPC 2-301, 2-302]. If, however, the omission of a future spouse is intentional in the existing will or the spouse is otherwise provided for in the will (or by transfer of property outside of the will), the omitted spouse will not be given an intestate share.

Divorce or Annulment At common law and under the UPC, divorce does not necessarily revoke the entire will. A divorce or an annulment occurring after a will has been executed will revoke those dispositions of property made under the will to the former spouse [UPC 2-508].

Children Born after a Will Has Been Executed If a child is born after a will has been executed and if it appears that the testator would have made a provision for the child, then the child is entitled to receive whatever portion of the estate he or she is allowed under state intestate laws. Most state

CONCEPT SUMMARY: Wills

TYPE OF WILL	DEFINITION
Holographic	A will completely in the handwriting of the testator; valid where permitted by state statute.
Attested	A written will, signed by the testator, properly witnessed, and, where required, published; one that meets formal statutory requirements for a valid will.
Nuncupative	An oral will made before witnesses during the deathbed illness of the testator; it is only valid to transfer personal property, not real property.

METHOD OF REVOCATION OR MODIFICATION	DEFINITION
By act of the maker:	
Physical act	Tearing up, canceling, obliterating, or deliberately destroying part or all of a will.
Codicil	A formal separate document to amend or revoke an existing will.
New will	A new, properly executed will that expressly revokes the existing will.
By operation of the law:	
Marriage	Generally revokes a will written before the marriage. (Under the UPC, marriage does not revoke a previously executed will. The spouse takes as under intestacy laws.)
Divorce or annulment	Revokes dispositions made under a will to a former spouse.
Subsequently born children	It is *implied* that the child is entitled to receive the portion of the estate granted under intestate distribution laws.

TYPE OF GIFT	DEFINITION
Specific	A devise or bequest of a particular piece of property in the testator's estate.
General	A devise or bequest that does not single out a particular item in the testator's estate; usually a sum of money.
Residuary	A devise or bequest of any properties left in the estate after all specific and general gifts have been made.

laws allow a child to receive some portion of the estate if no provision is made in a will, unless it appears from the terms of the will that the testator intended to disinherit the child. Under the UPC, the rule is the same. The effect is to partially revoke the parent's will [UPC 2-302].

Rights under a Will

The law imposes certain limitations on the way a person can dispose of property in a will. For example, a married person who makes a will cannot avoid leaving a certain portion of the estate to the surviving spouse. In most states this is called a "forced share," "widow's share," or "elective share," and it is often one-third.

Beneficiaries under a will have rights as well. A beneficiary can renounce (disclaim) his or her share of the property given under a will. Further, a surviving spouse can renounce the amount given under a will and elect to take the "forced share" if the forced share is larger than the amount of the gift. State statutes provide the methods by which a surviving spouse accomplishes renunciation. The purpose of these statutes is to allow the spouse to obtain whichever distribution would be most advantageous. The UPC gives the surviving spouse an elective right to take one-third of the total estate [UPC 2-201].

STATUTES OF DESCENT AND DISTRIBUTION (INTESTACY LAWS)

The rules of descent are statutory. Each state regulates how property will be distributed when a person dies without a will. State laws attempt to carry out the likely intent and wishes of the decedent. These statutes are called **intestacy laws.**

The rules of descent vary widely from state to state. There is usually a special statutory provision for the rights of the surviving spouse and children, however. In addition, the law provides that first the debts of the decedent must be satisfied out of his or her estate and then the remaining assets can pass to the surviving spouse and to the children.

A surviving spouse usually receives a share of the estate—one-half if there is also a surviving child and one-third if there are two or more children. Only where no children or grandchildren survive the decedent will a surviving spouse succeed to the *entire estate.*

Assume that Foley dies intestate and is survived by his wife, Barbara, and his children, Carl and Diane. Foley's property passes according to intestacy laws. After Foley's outstanding debts have been paid, Barbara will receive the homestead (either in fee simple or as a life estate) and ordinarily a one-third to one-half interest in all other property. The remaining real and personal property will pass to Carl and Diane in equal portions.

Distribution

State statutes of descent and distribution specify the order in which heirs of an intestate share in the estate. When there is no surviving spouse or child, then grandchildren, brothers and sisters, and, in some states, parents of the decedents are the next in line to share. These relatives are usually called *lineal descendants.*

Generally, on the testator's or testatrix's death, title will descend before it will ascend. For example, property will pass to the deceased's chil-

dren before it will pass to his or her parents. (In either case, title by inheritance is called title by descent.) But because state statutes differ so widely, few other generalizations can be made about the laws of descent and distribution. It is extremely important to refer to the exact terms of the applicable state statutes when addressing any problem of intestacy distribution.

The UPC provides that a surviving spouse, in addition to taking an elective share of one-third of the decedent's estate, is entitled to the following:

1. A homestead allowance of $5,000.
2. A household and personal effects exemption, to a value not to exceed $3,500.
3. A family allowance for a period of up to one year after the death occurs to provide for daily expenses before the estate is settled, up to the amount of $6,000 [UPC 2-401, 2-402, 2-403, 2-404].

If there are no lineal descendants, then *collateral heirs* are the next group to share. Collateral heirs include nieces, nephews, aunts, and uncles of the decedent. If there are no survivors in any of those groups of people related to the decedent, most statutes provide that the property is to be distributed among the next of kin of any of the collateral heirs. Stepchildren and other relatives by marriage are not considered kin. However, legally adopted children are recognized as lawful heirs of their adoptive parents.

Whether an illegitimate child inherits depends on state statute. In all states, intestate succession between the mother and the child exists. In some states, intestate succession between the father and the child can occur only where the child is "legitimized" by ceremony or the child has been "acknowledged" by the father.

In the following case, the constitutionality of an illegitimacy statute was affirmed by the Ohio supreme court. The U.S. Supreme Court has allowed state illegitimacy statutes to stand on concluding that legitimate state purposes were served by the statutes.[4]

---

4. Labine v. Vincent, 401 U.S. 532, 91 S.Ct. 1017, 28 L.Ed.2d 288 (1971). In Trimble v. Gordon, 430 U.S. 762, 97 S.Ct. 1459, 52 L.Ed.2d 31 (1977), the Court ruled that an Illinois illegitimacy statute was unconstitutional because it did not bear a rational relationship to a legitimate state purpose.

BACKGROUND AND FACTS *Clarence Jackson died on January 17, 1975. His will left everything to his wife in the event she survived him. Since she had died earlier, the court appointed an administrator for his estate. The administrator, White, brought an action in probate court for a determination of the decedent's heirs-at-law. Randolph and Alice Marie Jackson, who claimed to be the decedent's illegitimate daughter, were among the defendants in this action. The probate court denied her status to inherit as an heir-at-law, and she appealed.*

Case 56.4
WHITE v. RANDOLPH
Supreme Court of Ohio, 1979.
59 Ohio St.2d 6, 391 N.E.2d
333.

PER CURIAM [by the whole court].
* * * *

The unanimous opinion of the Court of Appeals in the cause at bar was written by Judge Robert E. Holmes, now a Justice of this court. In our view, the position taken by Justice Holmes represents the correct one under the instant facts and, therefore, is incorporated at length:
* * * *

* * * Following a hearing on the matter [in Probate Court,] Judge Metcalf held, as a matter of law, that appellant was not entitled to inherit from the estate of Clarence Jackson because she introduced no evidence tending to show:

" '* * * that the decedent, alleged father, legitimized his illegitimate daughter, or formally acknowledged his daughter in Probate Court, or adopted such daughter, or provided for her in his will, or designated her as his heir at law * * *.'

"[Under Ohio statutes,] a child born out of wedlock is capable of inheriting from and through his mother, but may inherit from his father only under certain circumstances. The father may legitimatize an illegitimate child by afterwards marrying the mother of the illegitimate child and acknowledging the child as his. Further, the natural father of an illegitimate child may confer upon such child a right of inheritance from such father by several means: (1) by formal acknowledgement in Probate Court that the child is his with consent of the mother; (2) by designating the illegitimate child as his heir-at-law; (3) by adopting the illegitimate child; and (4) by making a provision for the child in his will.

"Appellant concededly cannot meet any of the above criteria. However, appellant contends that the [Fourteenth Amendment of the United States Constitution] requires that she be permitted to inherit from decedent if she can establish with sufficient competent evidence that decedent is, in fact, her father. In the cases considering this general issue before us, it has been rather uniformly pointed out that the rationality of the classification must be examined in light of the legitimate state purposes to which it is related.

"It has long been recognized in Ohio that proof of paternity, especially after the death of the alleged father, is difficult, and peculiarly subject to abuse. One of the resultants of such abuse would be the instability of land titles of real estate left by intestate fathers of illegitimate children.
* * * *

"[W]e believe that the Ohio statutory provisions present a reasonable middle ground for the recognition of certain categories of illegitimate children of intestate men. Through these laws inheritance rights may be reasonably recognized without jeopardizing the orderly settlement of estates or the dependability of titles to property passing under intestate laws.

"Clearly, the Ohio classification scheme is rationally related to the legitimate state purpose of assuring efficient disposition of property at death while avoiding spurious claims. Moreover, the Ohio provisions do not discriminate between legitimate and illegitimate children *per se*. All children may inherit from their mothers. Some illegitimate children and all legitimate children may inherit from their fathers. The group 'discriminated against' is that class of illegitimate children whose fathers did not formally acknowledge them or designate them as heirs-at-law."

* * * *

Subsequent to the decision of the Court of Appeals in the instant cause, the United States Supreme Court, in the case of *Lalli v. Lalli*, upheld the constitutionality of a New York statute which allowed illegitimate children to inherit from their father only if a court of competent jurisdiction, during the father's lifetime, entered an order declaring the child's paternity.

Recognizing the difficulty of proving paternity and the possibility of fraudulent assertions of paternity upon the estate of the decedent, the court found that the statutory differences afforded legitimate and illegitimate heirs under intestate succession were justified in furtherance of New York's substantial interest in the just and orderly disposition of property at death. In that regard, we conclude that the Ohio statutes in question in the cause at bar are substantially related to the important state interests discussed by the court in *Lalli*.

DECISION AND REMEDY   *The judgments of the probate court and the appellate court were affirmed. The Ohio statute was not unconstitutional. Ohio has a sufficient interest in the disposition of property at death to justify the differences in its laws regarding intestate succession for legitimate and illegitimate children.*

COMMENTS   *Most states have amended their intestacy statutes dealing with illegitimate children to provide a more liberal test for establishing inheritance rights. These states allow paternity to be established by evidence that the parents married after the child's birth, or by an adjudication before the death of the father, or by clear and convincing proof after the father's death [UPC 2-109].*

THE PATTERN OF INTESTACY DISTRIBUTION FOR GRANDCHILDREN When an intestate is survived by descendants of deceased children, a question arises as to what share the descendants (that is, grandchildren of the intestate) will receive. *Per stirpes* is a method of dividing an intestate share by which a class or group of distributees takes the share that the deceased ancestor of the group *would have been* entitled to inherit had that person lived. An example shows how this method might be applied to grandchildren. Assume that John, a widower, has three children, Tony, Barbara, and Clara. Tony has two children (Mark and Sally), Barbara has one child (Greg), and Clara has one child (Peter). At the time of John's death, Tony and Barbara have already died. If John's estate is distributed *per stirpes*, the following distribution will take place:

1. Mark and Sally: one-sixth each, taking Tony's one-third.

2. Greg: one-third, taking Barbara's share.

3. Clara: one-third, as the surviving child (Peter does not inherit).

Exhibit 56–1 illustrates the *per stirpes* method of distribution.

Another type of distribution of an estate is the *per capita* method. Under this method, each person takes an equal share of the estate. Assume that John, a widower, has two children, Tony and Barbara. Tony has two children (Mark and Sally), and Barbara has one child (Greg). At the time of John's death, Tony and Barbara have already died. If John's estate is distributed *per capita*. Mark, Sally, and Greg will each receive a one-third share. Exhibit 56–2 illustrates the *per capita* method of distribution.

In most states and under the Uniform Probate Code, in-laws do not share in an estate. If a child dies before his or her parents, the child's surviving spouse will not receive an inheritance on the death of the deceased's parents. For example, assume that John, a widower, has two married children,

Exhibit 56–1 *Per Stirpes* Distribution

Under this method of distribution, an heir takes the share that his or her deceased parent would have been entitled to inherit, had the parent lived. This may mean that a class of distributees—the grandchildren in this example—will not inherit in equal portions. (Note that Mark and Sally only receive one-sixth of John's estate, while Greg inherits one-third.)

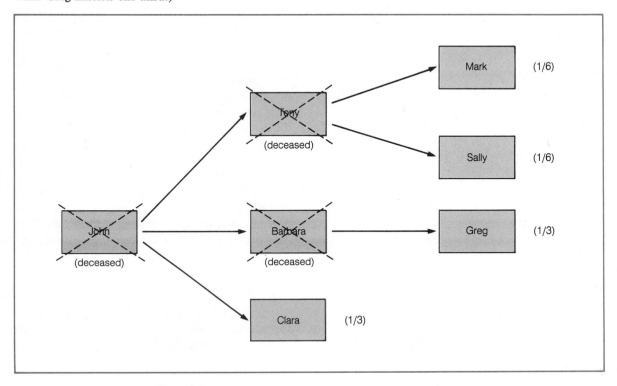

Exhibit 56–2 *Per Capita* Distribution

Under this method of distribution, all heirs in a certain class—in this case, the grandchildren—inherit equally. Note that Mark and Sally in this situation each inherit not one-sixth of John's estate (as they do under the *per stirpes* method of distribution), but one-third.

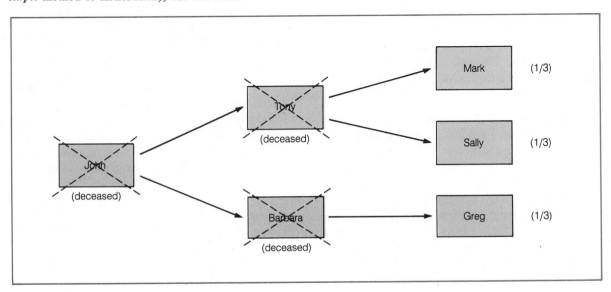

Tony and Barbara, and no grandchildren. If Tony predeceases his father, John's entire estate will go to Barbara. Tony's surviving wife will not inherit.

TRUSTS

A trust involves any arrangement whereby legal title to property is transferred from one person to be administered by a trustee for a third party's benefit. It can also be defined as a right or property, real or personal, held by one party for the benefit of another. A trust can be created for any purpose that is not illegal or against public policy. The essential elements of a trust are:

1. A designated beneficiary.
2. A designated trustee.
3. A fund sufficiently identified to enable title to pass to the trustee.
4. Actual delivery to the trustee with the intention of passing title.

If Sanford conveys his farm to South Miami First National Bank to be held for the benefit of his daughters, Sanford has created a trust. Sanford is the settlor (the one creating the trust, or grantor), South Miami First National Bank is the trustee, and Sanford's daughters are the beneficiaries.

Express Trusts

An express trust is one created or declared in expressed terms, usually in writing. It differs from one that is inferred by the law from the conduct or dealings of the parties (an implied trust, to be discussed later). The two types of express trusts that will be discussed here are *inter vivos* trusts and testamentary trusts.

INTER VIVOS TRUSTS An ***inter vivos* trust** is a trust executed by a grantor during his or her lifetime. The grantor executes a "trust deed," and legal title to the trust property passes to the named trustee. The trustee has a duty to administer the property as directed by the grantor for the benefit and in the interest of the beneficiaries. The trustee must preserve the trust property, make it productive, and, if required by the terms of the trust agreement, pay income to the beneficiaries, all in accordance with the terms of the trust. Once the *inter vivos* trust is created, the grantor has, in effect, given over the property for the benefit of beneficiaries.

TESTAMENTARY TRUSTS A **testamentary trust** is a trust created by will to come into existence upon the settlor's death. Although a testamentary trust has a trustee who maintains legal title to the trust property, actions of the trustee are subject to judicial approval. The trustee of a testamentary trust can be named in the will or be appointed by the court; thus, a testamentary trust will not fail because no trustee has been named in the will. The legal responsibilities of the trustees are the same in both an *inter vivos* and a testamentary trust. If the will setting up a testamentary trust is invalid, then the trust will also be invalid. The property that was supposed to be in the trust will then pass according to intestacy laws, not according to the terms of the trust.

Implied Trusts

Sometimes a trust is imposed by law, even in the absence of an express trust. Customarily, these implied trusts are divided into constructive and resulting trusts.

CONSTRUCTIVE TRUST A **constructive trust** differs from an express trust in that it arises by operation of law as an equitable remedy that enables plaintiffs to recover property (and sometimes damages) from defendants who would otherwise be unjustly enriched. In other words, when a transaction takes place in which the person who takes the legal estate in property cannot also enjoy the beneficial interest without violating some established principle of equity, the court will create a constructive trust. The legal owner is declared to be a trustee for the parties who, in equity, are actually entitled to the beneficial enjoyment that flows from the trust. One source of a constructive trust is a wrongful action, such as violation of a fiduciary relationship.

To illustrate: Jules and Spring are partners in buying, developing, and selling real estate. Jules learns through the staff of the partnership that a piece of land will soon come on the market that the staff will recommend that the partnership purchase. Jules purchases the property secretly in his own name, violating his fiduciary relationship. When these facts are discovered, a court will determine that Jules must hold the property in trust for the partnership.

RESULTING TRUST A **resulting trust** arises from the conduct of the parties. Here the trust results or is created when circumstances raise an inference that the party holding legal title to the property does so for the benefit of another, unless the inference is rebutted or the beneficial interest otherwise disposed of.

To illustrate: Thor purchases one acre of land from Lassen. Thor is going out of the country for two years and will be unable to attend the closing. She asks Lassen to deed the property, at the closing, to Thor's good friend, Crenshaw. Lassen does indeed convey the property to Crenshaw. If it is proved that Thor did not intend to make a gift of the land to Crenshaw, the property may be considered to be held in trust (a resulting trust), with Crenshaw as the trustee, for the benefit of Thor.

Other Kinds of Trusts

Certain trusts are created for special purposes. Three such trusts are charitable, spendthrift, and totten trusts.

CHARITABLE TRUSTS A trust designed for the benefit of a segment of the public or of the public in general is a **charitable trust.** It differs from a private trust in that the identities of the beneficiaries are uncertain. Usually, to be deemed a charitable trust, a trust must be created for charitable, educational, religious, or scientific purposes.

SPENDTHRIFT TRUST A trust that contains a provision for the maintenance of a beneficiary by prevention of his or her improvidence with the bestowed funds is a **spendthrift trust.** Essentially, the beneficiary is not permitted to transfer his or her right to future payments of income or capital. The majority of states allow spendthrift trust provisions that prohibit creditors from subjecting the beneficiary's interest in future distributions from the trust to the payment of debts.

TOTTEN TRUST A special type of trust created when one person deposits money in his or her own name as a trustee for another is a **totten trust.**

This trust is tentative in that it is revocable at will until the depositor dies or completes the gift in his or her lifetime by some unequivocal act or declaration (for example, delivery of the funds to the intended beneficiary). If the depositor should die before the beneficiary dies and if the depositor has not revoked the trust expressly or impliedly, a presumption arises that an absolute trust has been created for the benefit of the beneficiary. At the death of the depositor, the beneficiary obtains property rights to the balance on hand.

The Trustee

The trustee is the person holding the trust property. Anyone legally capable of holding title to and dealing in property can be a trustee. If the settlor of a trust fails to name a trustee, or if a named trustee cannot or will not serve, the trust does not fail—an appropriate court can appoint a trustee.

TRUSTEE'S DUTIES As obvious as it may sound, a trustee's basic duty is one of trust. Specifically, a trustee must act with honesty, good faith, and prudence in administering the trust and exercise a high degree of loyalty toward the trust beneficiary. The standard of care is the degree of care a prudent person would exercise in his or her personal affairs.[5] The duty of loyalty requires that the trustee act in the *exclusive* interest of the beneficiary.

Among specific duties, a trustee must keep clear and accurate accounts of the trust's administration and furnish complete and accurate information to the beneficiary. A trustee must keep trust assets separate from his or her own assets. A trustee has a duty to pay to an income beneficiary the net income of the trust assets at reasonable intervals. A trustee has a duty to distribute the risk of loss from investments by reasonable diversification and a duty to dispose of assets that do not represent prudent investments. Investments in federal, state, or municipal bonds, corporate bonds, and shares of preferred or common stock may be prudent investments under particular circumstances.

5. Revised Uniform Principal and Income Act Section 2(a)(3); Restatement (Second) of Trusts Section 227 (1959). Currently, this rule is in force in about thirty-five states by statute and five under the common law.

TRUSTEE'S POWERS When a settlor creates a trust, he or she may prescribe the trustee's powers and performance. Generally, state law[6] applies only to the extent that it does not conflict with the terms of the trust.[7] When state law does apply, it is most likely to restrict the trustee's investment of trust funds. Typically, statutes confine trustees to investments in conservative debt securities such as government, utility, and railroad bonds and first-mortgage loans on realty. However, it is common for a settlor to grant a trustee discretionary investment power. In that circumstance, any statute may be considered only advisory, with the trustee's decisions subject in most states to the prudent person rule.

A difficult question concerns the extent of a trustee's discretion to "invade" the principal and distribute it to an income beneficiary, if the income is found to be insufficient to provide for the beneficiary in an appropriate manner. A similar question concerns the extent of a trustee's discretion to retain trust income and add it to the principal, if the income is found to be more than sufficient to provide for the beneficiary in an appropriate manner. Generally, the answer to both questions is that the income beneficiary should be provided with a somewhat predictable annual income, but with a view to the safety of the principal. Thus, a trustee may make individualized adjustments in annual distributions.

Of course, a trustee is responsible for carrying out the purposes of the trust. If the trustee fails to comply with the terms of the trust or the controlling statute, he or she is personally liable for any loss.

ALLOCATIONS BETWEEN PRINCIPAL AND INCOME Frequently, a settlor will provide one beneficiary with a life estate and another beneficiary with the remainder interest in a trust. For example, a farmer may create a testamentary trust providing that the farm's income be paid to his or her surviving spouse and that on the surviving spouse's death, the farm be given to their children. Among the income and principal beneficiaries, questions may arise concerning the apportionment of receipts and expenses for the farm's management and the trust's administration between income and principal. Even when income and principal beneficiaries are the same, these questions may occur.

To the extent that a trust instrument does not provide instructions, a trustee must refer to applicable state law. The general rule is that ordinary receipts and expenses are chargeable to the income beneficiary, while extraordinary receipts and expenses are allocated to the principal beneficiaries.[8] For example, the receipt of rent from trust realty would be ordinary, as would the expense of paying the property's taxes, but the cost of long-term improvements and proceeds from the property's sale would be extraordinary.

Trust Termination

The terms of a trust should expressly state the event on which the settlor wishes it to terminate—for example, the beneficiary's or the trustee's death. If the trust instrument does not provide for termination on the beneficiary's death, the beneficiary's death will not end it. Similarly, without an express provision, a trust will not terminate on the trustee's death.

Typically, a trust instrument specifies a termination date. For example, a trust created to educate the settlor's child may provide that the trust ends when the beneficiary reaches the age of twenty-five. If the trust's purpose is fulfilled before that date, a court may order the trust's termination. If no date is specified, a trust will terminate when its purpose has been fulfilled. Of course, if a trust's purposes become impossible or illegal, the trust will terminate.

---

6. In ten states, the law consists, in part, of the Uniform Principal and Income Act, published in 1931. The Revised Uniform Principal and Income Act, issued in 1962, has been adopted in twenty-nine states. There are other uniform acts that may apply—for instance, about a third of the states have enacted the Uniform Trustees' Powers Act, promulgated in 1964. In addition, most states have their own statutes covering particular procedures and practices. In other words, as in other areas of estate planning, the laws concerning trusts differ among the states. Common law principles have been collected in the Restatement (Second) of Trusts (1959).

7. Revised Uniform Principal and Income Act Section 2(a)(1); Restatement (Second) of Trusts Section 164 (1959).

8. Revised Uniform Principal and Income Act Sections 3, 6, 8, 13; Restatement (Second) of Trusts Section 233 (1959).

ESTATE ADMINISTRATION

The orderly procedure used to collect assets, settle debts, and distribute the remaining assets when a person dies is the subject matter of estate administration. The rules and procedures for managing the estate of a deceased are controlled by statute. Thus, they vary from state to state. In every state, there is a special court, often called a probate court, that oversees the management of estates of decedents.

The first step after a person dies is usually to determine whether or not the decedent left a will. In most cases, the decedent's attorney will have that information. If there is uncertainty as to whether a valid will exists, the personal papers of the deceased must be reviewed. If a will exists, it probably names a personal representative (executor) to administer the estate. If there is no will, or if the will fails to name a personal representative, then the court must appoint an administrator. Under the UPC, the term *personal representative* refers to either an executor (person named in the will) or an administrator (person appointed by the court) [UPC 1-201(30)].

Principal Duties of the Personal Representative

The first duty of the personal representative is to inventory and collect the assets of the decedent. If necessary, the assets are appraised to determine their value. Both the rights of creditors and the rights of beneficiaries must be protected during the estate administration proceedings. In addition, the personal representative is responsible for managing the assets of the estate during the administration period and for not allowing them to be wasted or unnecessarily depleted.

The personal representative receives and pays valid claims of creditors and arranges for the estate to pay federal and state income taxes and estate taxes (or inheritance taxes, depending on the state). A personal representative is required to post a bond to ensure honest and faithful performance. Usually, the bond exceeds the estimated value of the personal estate of the decedent. Under most state statutes, the will can specify that the personal representative need not post a bond.

When the ultimate distribution of assets to the beneficiaries is determined, the personal repre-

sentative is responsible for distributing the estate pursuant to the court order. Once the assets have been distributed, an accounting is rendered to the court, the estate is closed, and the personal representative is relieved of any further responsibility or liability for the estate. Exhibit 56–3 lists the duties of the personal representative.

Probate versus Nonprobate

To probate a will means to establish its validity and to carry the administration of the estate through a court process. The process of probate can be time-consuming and costly, and the probate court may be involved in every step of the proceedings. Attorneys, accountants, and personal representatives will be involved in the probate process.

Many states have statutes that allow for the distribution of assets without probate proceedings. Faster and less expensive methods are used. For example, property can be transferred by affidavit (a written statement taken before a person who has authority to affirm it),[9] and problems or questions can be handled during an administrative hearing. In addition, some state statutes provide that title to cars, savings and checking accounts, and certain other property can be passed merely by the filling out of forms. This is particularly true when most of the property is held in joint tenancy with right of survivorship or when there is only one heir.

FAMILY SETTLEMENT AGREEMENTS A majority of states provide for *family settlement agreements*, which are private agreements among the beneficiaries. Once a will is admitted to probate, the family members can agree to settle among themselves the distribution of the decedent's assets. Although a family settlement agreement speeds the settlement process, a court order is still needed

---

9. For example, under the Virginia Small Estates Act (Va. Code Ann. Sections 64.1–132.4 [Cum. Supp. 1981]), modeled after UPC 3-1201 and 3-1202, a decedent's successor may collect the decedent's personal property by presenting an affidavit stating that (1) the value of the decedent's total personal property does not exceed $5,000, (2) sixty or more days have passed since the death, (3) no one has applied to be personal representative, (4) any will has been probated and a list of the heirs filed, and (5) the successor is entitled to payment or delivery of the property for the reason stated in the affidavit. The affidavit discharges a party paying, delivering, or transferring property in reliance on the affidavit, just as if the party had dealt with a personal representative.

Exhibit 56–3 The Duties of the Personal Representative

It would be impossible to indicate all the duties the executor must perform, but here are some

1. Managing the estate until it is settled, including:
   a. Collecting debts due the estate.
   b. Managing real estate and arranging for maintenance and repairs.
   c. Registering securities in the name of the estate.
   d. Collecting insurance proceeds.
   e. Running the family business, if necessary.
   f. Arranging for the family's support during probate.
   g. Properly insuring assets.

2. Collecting all assets and necessary records, including:
   a. Locating the will, insurance policies, real estate papers, car registrations, and birth certificates.
   b. Filing claims for pension, social security, profit sharing, and veteran's benefits.
   c. Taking possession of bank accounts, real estate, personal effects, and safe deposit boxes.
   d. Obtaining names, addresses, and social security numbers of all heirs.
   e. Making an inventory of all assets.
   f. Setting up records and books.

3. Determining the estate's obligations, including:
   a. Determining which claims are legally due.
   b. Obtaining receipts for all claims paid.
   c. Checking on mortgages and other loans.

4. Computing and then paying all death taxes due, which requires:
   a. Selecting the most beneficial tax alternatives.
   b. Deciding which assets to sell to provide necessary funds.
   c. Paying taxes on time to avoid penalties.
   d. Opposing any unfair valuations of estate property established by governmental taxing authorities.

5. Computing beneficiaries' shares and then distributing the estate, which includes:
   a. Determining who gets particular items and settling family disputes.
   b. Transferring title to real estate and other property.
   c. Selling off assets to pay cash legacies.
   d. Paying final estate costs.
   e. Preparing accountings for the court's approval.

to protect the estate from future creditors and to clear title to the assets involved.

SUMMARY PROCEDURES The use of summary procedures—which are shorter and simpler than regular proceedings—can save time and money in estate administration. The expense of a personal representative's commission, attorneys' fees, appraisers' fees, and so forth can be eliminated or at least minimized if the parties utilize summary administration procedures. But in some situations—for example, when a guardian must be appointed for minor children or for an incompetent person and a trust has been created to protect the minor or the incompetent person—probate procedures cannot be avoided. In the ordinary situation, a person can employ various will substitutes to avoid the cost of probate—for example, *inter vivos* trusts, life insurance policies with named beneficiaries, or joint tenancy arrangements. Not all methods are suitable for every estate, but there

are alternatives to a complete probate administration.

ESTATE TAXES

The death of an individual may result in tax liabilities at both the federal and state levels.

Federal Estate Tax

At the federal level, a tax is levied upon the total value of the estate after debts and expenses for administration have been deducted and after various exemptions have been allowed. The tax is on the estate itself rather than on the beneficiaries. Therefore, it does not depend on the character of any bequests or on the relationship of the beneficiary to the decedent, unless a gift to charity that is recognized by the IRS as deductible from the total estate for tax purposes is involved. Estate planning for larger estates also considers other deductions available under federal law. And an entire estate can pass free of estate tax if the estate is left to the surviving spouse.

State Inheritance Taxes

The majority of states assess a death tax in the form of an inheritance tax imposed on the recipient of a bequest rather than on the estate. Some states also have a state estate tax similar to the federal estate tax. In general, inheritance tax rates are graduated according to the type of relationship between the beneficiary and decedent. The lowest rates and largest exemptions are applied to a surviving spouse and the children of the decedent.

QUESTIONS AND CASE PROBLEMS

1. John is a widower who has two married children, Frank and Amy. Amy has two children, Phil and Paula. Frank has no children. John dies, leaving a typewritten will that gives all his property equally to his children, Frank and Amy, and provides that should a child predecease him, leaving grandchildren, the grandchildren are to take *per stirpes*. The will was witnessed by Amy and John's lawyer and signed by John in their presence. Amy has predeceased John. Frank claims the will is invalid.

   (a) Discuss whether the will is valid.

   (b) Discuss the distribution of John's estate if the will is invalid.

   (c) Discuss the distribution of John's estate if the will is valid.

2. James was a bachelor. While single, he made out a will naming his mother, Carol, as sole beneficiary. Later, James married Lisa.

   (a) If James died while married to Lisa without changing his will, would the estate go to his mother, Carol? Explain.

   (b) Assume James made out a new will upon his marriage to Lisa, leaving his entire estate to Lisa. Later he divorced Lisa and married Sue, but he did not change his will. Discuss the rights of Lisa and Sue to his estate after his death.

   (c) Assume James divorced Lisa, married Sue, and changed his will leaving his estate to Sue. Later, a daughter, Lori, was born. James died without having included Lori in his will. Discuss fully whether Lori had any rights in the estate.

3. Ann has drafted and properly executed a will. Assume the following clauses in her will and the following events:

   (a) Her will provides, "I leave my two-carat diamond ring to my sister, Sylvia." At the time of Ann's death, Sylvia has already died, leaving one child, Lindsay.

   (b) Her will provides, "I leave $5,000 to each of my nieces, Fern and Dorothy." At the time of Ann's death, only $4,000 remains in her estate.

   (c) Her will provides, "I leave to my nephew, Donald, my $10,000 Cadillac or equivalent value." Just prior to Ann's death she sold the Cadillac.

Discuss fully each situation, giving its name and describing its effect on the legatees.

4. Sam, an eighty-three-year-old invalid, employs a nurse, Sarah, to care for him. Prior to Sarah's employment, Sam executed a will leaving his entire estate to his only living relative—his great-grandson, Fred. Sarah convinces Sam that Fred is dead and gets Sam to change his will, naming Sarah as his sole beneficiary. After Sam's death, Fred appears and contests the will. Discuss the probable success of Fred's action.

5. The following transfers and events take place:

   (a) John lives in Europe. He transfers $20,000 to his good friend, Kate, and orally instructs her to invest and distribute the $20,000 and whatever it accrues so as to finance the MBA education of his daughter, JoAnn.

   (b) Fred is on the board of directors of the ABC Corporation and is the chairman of its research policy committee. Through his chairmanship he learns that ABC has come up with a cure for cancer. Fred purchases on the open market 20,000 shares of ABC stock at $10 per share. When the announcement of the cure is made, the market value of ABC's stock increases to $200 per share.

   (c) Sue is a successful businesswoman. She is engaged to marry John, a man of modest means who has ambitions to be an inventor. Sue creates a $20,000 joint savings account in the name of "Sue, in trust for John." Sue tells John that the purpose of the account is to encourage him to move forward in his business ventures.

Discuss fully whether a valid trust has been created in each situation, what each trust is called, and, where applicable, what its effect is.

6. Jesse Butterfield Morris died on February 11, 1967. On April 6, 1967, the Security First National Bank offered a document for probate as Morris's holographic will. The document was entirely in Morris's handwriting, but it contained no signatures of witnesses. The document was dated (November 1, 1965), was addressed to the Security First National Bank, and contained the initials J. B. M. at the end. Should Morris's will be probated? [In re Estate of Morris, 268 Cal.App.2d 638, 74 Cal.Rptr. 32 (1969)]

7. Harris executed a written instrument in which he named Bishop as trustee of $17,000 in bonds, notes, mortgages, and money. The instrument declared that Harris was transferring these assets to Bishop in trust for the benefit of the public library in Alexandria, Ohio, but Harris never delivered the instrument. Thereafter, Harris received interest

on some of the notes and still had access to the money and instruments that were the subject of the trust. Had Harris created a valid trust? Consider the requirements of making a valid gift. [Whitehead v. Bishop, 23 Ohio App. 315, 155 N.E. 565 (1925)]

8. In 1925, Campbell died, leaving a will in which the ninth clause read as follows: "My good friends Clark and Smith I appoint as my trustees. Each of my trustees is competent by reason of familiarity with the property, my wishes and friendships, to wisely distribute some portion at least of said property. I therefore give and bequeath to my trustees all my property in trust to make disposal by the way of a memento from myself, of such articles to such of my friends as they, my trustees, shall select. All of said property, not so disposed of by them, my trustees are directed to sell and the proceeds of such sale or sales to become and be disposed of as a part of the residue of my estate." Was this a valid trust? [Clark v. Campbell, 82 N.H. 281, 133 A. 166 (1926)]

9. H. W. Wolfe died at the age of sixty-seven, leaving personal property worth about $4,000 and more than five hundred acres of land. On July 31, 1911, not long before he died, he properly executed a will that contained the following provision: "I, H. W. Wolfe, will and bequeath to Miss Mary Lilly Luffman, a tract of land near Roaring Gap Post Office, on State Road and South Fork, adjoining the lands of J. M. Royal and others, the land bought by me from H. D. Woodruff. Witness my hand and seal, this thirty-first day of July, 1911." On August 14, 1911, Wolfe wrote another will that provided in part: "I, H. W. Wolfe, do make and declare this to be my last will and testament. I will and bequeath all my effects to my brothers and sisters, to be divided equally among them. Witness my hand and seal, this the fourteenth day of August, 1911." Both wills were properly signed and attested. Who was entitled to what under these wills? [In re Wolfe's Will, 185 N.C. 563, 117 S.E. 804 (1923)]

10. An elderly, childless widow had nine nieces and nephews. She devised her entire estate to be divided equally among two nieces and the husband of one of the nieces, who was also the attorney who drafted the will and the executor named in the will. The testatrix was definitely of sound mind when the will was executed. If you were one of the nieces or nephews omitted from the will, could you think of any way to have the will invalidated? [Estate of Eckert, 93 Misc.2d 677, 403 N.Y.S.2d 633 (1978)]

11. Robert and Everett Kling, two brothers, purchased rental property in Fenton, Missouri. Robert contributed $5,544 and Everett $5,624 toward the purchase price of $19,005. Title to the property was taken in the name of Everett's wife, Nancy. The brothers maintained an account in which they made deposits and from which they paid expenses related to the rental property. Although each brother had agreed to contribute $20 per month toward the remaining purchase price, Robert never did do so, and Everett consequently increased his contribution to $40 per month. When Robert died, Everett and Nancy claimed 100 percent ownership of the Fenton property. Robert's children, John and Janet, filed suit, claiming that Everett and Nancy held the property as a resulting trust and that they (John and Janet) were entitled to half of the property. Discuss whether a resulting trust had been created and, if so, what the distribution should be. [Estate of Kling, 736 S.W.2d 65 (Mo.App. 1987)]

12. Louie Villwok died on November 12, 1984, leaving an executed will that left everything to his present wife, Rose, if she survived him. If Rose predeceased him, his three daughters from a previous marriage would receive a general bequest of money and a portion of the residue. Rose survived Villwok, and when his will was offered for probate, the decedent's daughters contested the will. They claimed, among other things, that the will was a result of undue influence on the part of Rose. At the hearing, the daughters presented evidence to show that after Rose married the decedent, the relationship between her and the decedent's children deteriorated; that the decedent drank heavily on a daily basis and was intoxicated most of the time; and that Rose made concerted efforts to come between the decedent and his daughters. Each daughter also testified that her father had made statements to her expressly indicating that he did not want Rose or her children to have his property and that he wanted his daughters to receive all of his property. Discuss whether their contest should be successful based on this evidence. [In re Estate of Villwok, 226 Neb. 693, 413 N.W.2d 921 (1987)]

13. Myrtle Courziel executed a valid will that provided for the establishment of a scholarship fund designed to encourage the study of corrosion as it affects metallurgical engineering. The recipients were to be students in the upper half of their class at the University of Alabama. Subsequently, Myrtle died. John Calhoun, the eventual administrator of her estate, obtained access to Myrtle's safe deposit box to search for her will. He found the will intact, except that the last page of the will, which had contained Myrtle's signature and the signatures of the witnesses, had been removed from the document and was not in the safe deposit box or anywhere else to be found. Since Myrtle had had sole control over the will, should it have been presumed that her removal of the last page (or her having allowed it to be removed) effectively revoked the will? [Board of Trustees of University of Alabama v. Calhoun, 514 So.2d 895 (Ala. 1987)]

Chapter 57

Liability of Accountants

Accountants play a major role in a business's financial system. Accountants have the necessary expertise and experience in establishing and maintaining accurate financial records to design, control, and audit record-keeping systems, to prepare reliable statements that reflect an individual's or a business's financial status, and to give tax advice and prepare tax returns.

Accountants are subject to standards of conduct established by codes of professional ethics, by state statutes, and by judicial decisions. They are also governed by the contracts they enter into with their clients. When accountants enter into a contract, they must perform all the services for which they were hired, in addition to following standard accounting procedures. Accountants must comply with **generally accepted accounting principles (GAAP)** and **generally accepted auditing standards (GAAS).**

Under both common law and statutory provisions, accountants face potential legal liability in their work. Common law imposes liability for breach of contract, negligence, and fraud. An accountant may also be subject to federal statutory liability under the Securities Act of 1933 and under the Securities Exchange Act of 1934. These two acts impose civil and criminal liabilities for violations. Considering the many potential sources of legal liability that may be imposed upon accountants, an accountant should be well aware of his or her legal obligations.

POTENTIAL COMMON LAW LIABILITY TO CLIENTS

Under common law, accountants are liable to clients for breach of contract, negligence, or fraud.

Liability for Breach of Contract

Under common law, accountants face liability for any breach of contract. An accountant owes a duty to his or her client to honor the terms of the contract and to perform the contract within the stated time period. If the accountant fails to perform as agreed in the contract, then he or she has breached the contract and the client has the right to recover damages from the accountant. An accountant may be held liable for expenses incurred by his or her client in securing another accountant, for penalties imposed upon the client for failure to meet time deadlines, and also for any other reasonable and foreseeable monetary losses that arise from the accountant's breach.

Liability for Negligence

Accountants occupy a position similar to that of other professionals who render professional services for compensation. When a person holds himself or herself out as an accountant, he or she is held to the standard of care, knowledge, and judgment generally exercised by accountants in the community acting under the same or similar circumstances. An accountant is measured against a hypothetical reasonably prudent and skillful accountant.

As long as an accountant conforms to generally accepted accounting principles and acts in good faith, he or she will not be held liable to the client for incorrect judgment. As a general rule, an accountant is not required to discover every impropriety, defalcation (embezzlement), or fraud in his or her client's books. If, however, the impropriety, defalcation, or fraud has gone undiscovered because of an accountant's negligence or failure to perform an express or implied duty, the accountant will be liable for any resulting losses suffered by his or her client. Therefore, an accountant who uncovers suspicious financial transactions and fails to fully investigate the matter or to inform his or her client can be held liable to the client for the resulting loss. Typically, the amount of the loss resulting from an accountant's failure to exercise reasonable care according to generally accepted standards is substantially higher than the fee the client was to pay the accountant.

A violation of generally accepted accounting principles and generally accepted auditing standards will be considered *prima facie* evidence of negligence on the part of the accountant. Compliance with generally accepted accounting principles and generally accepted auditing standards, however, does not necessarily relieve an accountant from potential legal liability. An accountant may be held to a higher standard of conduct established by state statute and by judicial decisions.

If an accountant is deemed guilty of negligence, the client may collect damages for losses that arose from the accountant's negligence. An accountant, however, is not without possible defenses to a cause of action for damages based on negligence. Possible defenses include allegations that:

1. The accountant was not negligent.
2. If the accountant was negligent, this negligence was not the proximate cause of the client's losses.
3. The client was contributorily negligent.

Sometimes accountants are hired to prepare unaudited financial statements. Although a lesser standard of care is typically required for a "write up," accountants may still be held liable in this situation. Accountants may be subject to liability for failing, in accordance with standard accounting procedures, to delineate a balance sheet as "unaudited." An accountant will also be held liable for failure to disclose to a client facts or circumstances that give reason to believe that misstatements have been made or that a fraud has been committed.

Liability for Fraud

Actual fraud and constructive fraud present two different circumstances under which an accountant may be found liable. An accountant may be held liable for *actual fraud* when he or she intentionally misstates a material fact to mislead his or her client and the client justifiably relies on the misstated fact to his or her injury. A material fact is one that a reasonable person would consider important in deciding whether to act. On the other hand, an accountant may be held liable for *constructive fraud* whether or not he or she acted with fraudulent intent. For example, constructive fraud may be found when an accountant is grossly negligent in the performance of his or her duties. The intentional failure to perform a duty in reckless disregard of the consequences of such a failure would constitute gross negligence on the part of an accountant. Both actual and constructive fraud are potential sources of legal liability under which a client may bring an action against an accountant.

When a client is dissatisfied with the performance of an accounting firm, he or she will often sue on all three common law theories in the alternative. The Federal Rules of Civil Procedure permit a pleader, in a claim or defense, to make two or more statements that are not necessarily consistent with each other. Thus, a plaintiff may sue on several theories. In the following case, the court had to sift through claims for negligence, constructive fraud, and breach of contract. Notice how the court disposes of the latter two counts by its treatment of the negligence claim.

BACKGROUND AND FACTS   *The American Pacific Group (APG), planning a merger with one of its subsidiaries, The Hawaii Corporation (THC), engaged the accounting firm of Peat, Marwick, Mitchell & Co. (PMM) to prepare financial statements for both companies and also to express opinions as to the most advantageous means of combining them. When the merger resulted in an arguably unnecessary loss of $22,000,000, the trustee in reorganization sued PMM on grounds of, among others, accountant malpractice, based on the unusual method PMM had used in restructuring the companies. The plaintiff contended that, had PMM used the accounting method generally applied in such transactions, its financial statements would have reflected a more negative picture, and the merger would never have occurred.*

Case 57.1
IN RE THE HAWAII CORP.
United States District Court for the District of Hawaii, 1983. 567 F.Supp. 609.

PANNER, Judge.
*   *   *   *

Plaintiff's principal complaint is that the reorganization occurred. Plaintiff argues that, if the proper method of accounting had been applied to the transaction and if the financial facts had been made available, either the THC Board or one or more of the minority shareholders of THC would have prevented the reorganization.
*   *   *   *

I conclude that the plaintiff has failed to prove by a preponderance of the evidence that the defendant was negligent in the method of accounting for the transaction. It is not necessary to endorse such a procedure for application to all situations. Here it was appropriate. Even if *   *   * purchase accounting should have been used throughout the transaction, the results would have not been significantly different. *   *   * The income statement on the pro forma statements would not have changed and the figure reported as retained earnings on the balance sheet would have been somewhat higher. Under these circumstances, plaintiff has failed to prove that the merger would not have occurred, either by reason of director action or minority stockholder action.

Analysis of the testimony and the exhibits reflects thoughtful accounting decisions based on judgment in difficult matters.
*   *   *   *

Plaintiff alleges that PMM is liable for fraud because the comfort letter,[a] the financial statements, and pro forma balance sheets that PMM prepared contained material misrepresentations upon which THC relied in embarking on the THC-APG reorganization and related transactions. There is no contention of intentional fraud. Plaintiff asserts the misrepresentations were made with reckless disregard for their truth or falsity.
*   *   *   *

My findings with respect to the negligence claim are dispositive of plaintiff's fraud claim. Plaintiff has failed to prove that the comfort letter, financial statements, or pro forma balance sheets prepared by the defendant contained material misrepresentations.

PMM entered into written and oral contracts to perform auditing and accounting services for THC. Plaintiff's breach of contract claim is based upon the allegation that PMM negligently failed to perform its contractual undertakings with due care.

[a. A letter from PMM stating that the informal procedures used did not reveal any material changes in the financial statements since the last audit and that only an audit with certain established procedures could reliably supply that information.]

Plaintiff contends that PMM breached its express and implied duties and obligations under the contracts by negligently and recklessly acting as previously set forth, and seeks contract damages including all compensation paid by plaintiff to PMM for the services it rendered.

The requirement that an accountant or auditor exercise that degree of skill and competence reasonably expected of persons in those professions is implied in a contract for professional services. * * * Liability follows for breach of contract if there is negligence. * * *

In concluding that plaintiff failed to prove by a preponderance of the evidence that defendant was negligent in performing auditing and accounting services for plaintiff, I have also necessarily concluded that plaintiff cannot recover for breach of contract.

DECISION AND REMEDY   *The court found that the accounting method employed by PMM, while admittedly "creative," did not violate the negligence standard, since it produced a result essentially similar to that of the standard method. Furthermore, the court concluded that, even though the accounting was not done according to the usual method, it was arrived at by careful reasoning. Since that standard had been upheld, the court reasoned, there had been no breach of contract, fraud, or negligence. Judgment was for the defendant, PMM.*

POTENTIAL COMMON LAW LIABILITY TO THIRD PERSONS

Traditionally, an accountant did not owe any duty to a third person with whom he or she had no direct contractual relationship. An accountant's duty was only to his or her client. Violations of the federal securities laws, fraud, and other intentional or reckless acts of wrongdoing were the only exceptions to this general rule. Chief Judge Benjamin Cardozo's 1931 decision in *Ultramares Corp. v. Touche*[1] was the leading authority for this traditional view. In *Ultramares*, a lender alleged that its reliance on the accountants' negligently prepared statements had caused it to lose money on loans made to the client. The court, however, refused to impose liability upon the accountants and concluded that the accountants owed a duty of nonnegligence only to those persons for whose "primary benefit" the statements were intended. In this case, the client was the only person for whose "primary benefit" the statements were intended.

Over the past few years, however, the *Ultramares* rule has been severely criticized. Accountants perform much of their work for use by persons who are not parties to the contract; and thus,

it is asserted that they owe a duty to these third parties. Consequently, there has been an erosion of the *Ultramares* rule, and accountants have been exposed to potential liability to third parties.

Understanding an accountant's common law liability to third parties is critical, because often, when a business fails, its independent auditor (accountant) may be one of the few potentially solvent defendants. In order to hold an accountant liable for negligence, a third party must demonstrate not only that the accountant committed a tort but also that the third party was an "intended beneficiary" of the accountant's work. A person other than the client qualifies as an "intended beneficiary" when the accountant knows or should have known that the work was being done for the benefit of a third party who intended to rely on the accountant's work. Jurisdictions vary as to whether the accountant must be aware that his or her work product is intended for a *particular* third party. A third party may also hold an accountant liable for actual or constructive fraud.

In the following case, the accountant was held liable to a third party creditor for making incorrect financial statements prepared by use of nonstandard accounting procedures. The court found the accountant could be held liable, even though the accountant had labeled the statements as "unaudited" and included an express disclaimer as to their accuracy.

1. 255 N.Y. 170, 174 N.E. 441 (1931).

BACKGROUND AND FACTS *The defendant, Safranek, prepared regular financial statements for Agri-Products, Inc., a Nebraska company. Based on these documents, Seedkem, Inc., the plaintiff, advanced more than $700,000 in credit to Agri-Products. Later, Seedkem learned that the financial statements were incorrect and had been prepared by use of nonstandard procedures. The defendant argued that, since he had not certified the statements and had expressly disclaimed any opinion as to their validity, he could not be held liable for their inaccuracy. This action involved a motion to dismiss for failure to state a claim upon which relief could be granted. The federal court applied Nebraska law, since the claim was a state common law claim.*

Case 57.2
SEEDKEM, INC. v. SAFRANEK
United States District Court for the District of Nebraska, 1979. 466 F.Supp. 340.

DENNEY, Judge.
*   *   *   *

The Court notes that the Restatement (Second) of Torts § 552 takes the position that accountants may be liable to a third party, with whom they are not in privity, for negligence in the preparation of a financial statement under certain circumstances. *   *   * Significantly, both jurisdictions, Indiana and Nebraska, have followed the position taken by the Restatement in the area of strict liability in tort, *   *   * and have abandoned the requirement of privity in that area. Seemingly, these jurisdictions, when faced with the issue in question, could be expected to follow the position taken by the Restatement in this area as well and abandon the requirement of privity.

However, the defendant argues that this case represents an extreme situation distinguishable from those cases which have rejected the privity requirement and found an accountant liable to a third party. Defendant points out that the cases cited by the plaintiff in support of its position all involved either certified or audited financial statements or express representations by the accountant to the third party as to the accuracy of the statements. Defendant contends that this case, on the other hand, involves unaudited statements containing an express disclaimer of opinion without any contrary representation and is therefore thoroughly distinguishable.
*   *   *   *

The fact that the financial statements were expressly marked "unaudited" and contained an express disclaimer of opinion is not necessarily dispositive at this time. The observations and statements by the Iowa Supreme Court in *Ryan v. Kanne* are particularly persuasive:

*   *   * Although in this profession a distinction is made between certified audits where greater time and effort are expended to verify book items, and uncertified audits where greater reliance is placed on book items, it is clear to us that accountants, or any other professional persons, must perform those acts that they have agreed to do under the contract and which they claim have been done in order to make the determination set forth and presented in their report. Their liability must be dependent upon their undertaking, not their rejection of dependability. They cannot escape liability for negligence by a general statement that they disclaim its reliability.

He [the accountant-defendant] must perform as agreed whether the work is certified or not. This being so, we have here fact questions as to the substance of the agreement between the parties, as to the care exercised in its performance, and as to the representation made, rather than whether the report was certified or uncertified.

The court denied the motion to dismiss for failure to state a claim upon which relief could be granted. The court held that an accountant can be liable to a third party, who is not in privity, for negligence in preparing financial statements regardless of whether those statements have been certified.

DECISION AND REMEDY

POTENTIAL STATUTORY LIABILITY

Potential civil and criminal liabilities against accountants may be imposed by the Securities Act of 1933 and the Securities Exchange Act of 1934.

Liability under Section 11 of the Securities Act of 1933

Registration statements are required to be filed with the Securities and Exchange Commission (SEC) prior to an offering of securities (see Chapter 43). Accountants frequently prepare and certify the issuer's financial statements that are included in the registration statement. Section 11 of the federal Securities Act of 1933 imposes liability upon accountants for misstatements and omissions of material facts in registration statements. Therefore, an accountant may be found liable if he or she prepared any financial statements included in the registration statement that "contained an untrue statement of a material fact or omitted to state a material fact required to be stated therein or necessary to make the statements therein not misleading." [2]

Under Section 11 of the 1933 act, an accountant may be held liable for his or her misstatement or omission of a material fact in a registration statement by anyone who acquires a security covered by the registration statement. A purchaser of a security need only demonstrate that he or she has suffered a loss on the security. Proof of reliance upon the materially false statement or misleading omission is not usually required. Nor is there a requirement of privity between the accountant and the security purchasers.

Section 11 imposes a duty upon accountants to use "due diligence" in the preparation of financial statements included in the filed registration statements. After the purchaser has proved the loss on the security, the accountant bears the burden of showing that he or she exercised "due diligence" in the preparation of the financial statements. To avoid liability, the accountant must show that he or she had, "after reasonable investigation, reasonable grounds to believe and did believe, at the time such part of the registration statement

became effective, that the statements therein were true and that there was no omission of a material fact required to be stated therein or necessary to make the statements therein not misleading." [3] Further, the failure to follow generally accepted accounting principles and generally accepted auditing standards is also proof of a lack of due diligence.

In particular, the due diligence standard places a burden upon accountants to verify information furnished by a corporation's officers and directors. The burden of proving due diligence requires an accountant to demonstrate that he or she is free from negligence or fraud. For example, the accountants in *Escott v. BarChris Construction Corp.* [4] were held liable for a failure to detect danger signals in materials that, under generally accepted accounting standards, required further investigation under the circumstances. Merely asking questions is not always sufficient to satisfy the requirement of due diligence.

Besides proving that he or she has acted with due diligence, an accountant may defend by claiming that:

1. There were no misstatements or omissions.
2. The misstatements or omissions were not of material facts.
3. The misstatements or omissions had no causal connection to the plaintiff's loss.
4. The plaintiff purchaser invested in the securities knowing of the misstatements or omissions.

A purchaser bringing a suit under Section 11 of the Securities Act of 1933 may recover the difference between the amount paid for the security and one of the following:

1. The value of the security at the time the suit was brought.
2. The price at which the security was disposed of in the market before the suit.
3. The price at which the security was disposed of after the suit but before judgment, if such damages are less than the damages representing the difference between the amount paid for the security and its the value at the time the suit was brought. [5]

---

2. Securities Act of 1933, Section 11(a).

3. Securities Act of 1933, Section 11(b)(3).
4. 283 F.Supp. 643 (S.D.N.Y. 1968).
5. Securities Act of 1933, Section 11(e).

Liability under the Securities Exchange Act of 1934

Under Sections 18 or 10(b) of the Securities Exchange Act of 1934 or SEC Rule 10b-5, an accountant may be found liable for fraud. A plaintiff has a substantially heavier burden of proof under the 1934 act than under the 1933 act. Unlike the 1933 act, the 1934 act provides that an accountant need not prove due diligence in order to escape liability. Section 18 of the 1934 act imposes civil liability on an accountant who makes or causes to be made in any application, report, or document a statement that at the time and in light of the circumstances was false or misleading with respect to any material fact.[6]

Section 18 liability is narrow in that it applies only to applications, reports, documents, and registration statements filed with the SEC. This remedy is further limited in that it applies only to sellers and purchasers. Under Section 18, a seller or purchaser must prove one of the following:

1. That the false or misleading statement affected the price of the security.
2. That the purchaser or seller relied upon the false or misleading statement in making the purchase or sale and was not aware of the inaccuracy of the statement.

Even if a purchaser or seller proves these two elements, an accountant can be exonerated of liability upon proof of "good faith" in the preparation of the financial statement. To demonstrate good faith, an accountant must show that he or she had no knowledge that the financial statement was false and misleading. Acting in good faith requires the total absence of an intention on the part of the accountant to seek an unfair advantage or to defraud another party. Proving a lack of intent to deceive, manipulate, or defraud is frequently referred to as proving a lack of *scienter*. Absence of good faith can also be demonstrated by the accountant's reckless conduct and gross negligence. (Note that "mere" negligence in the preparation of a financial statement does not constitute liability under the 1934 act. This differs from provisions of the 1933 act, under which an accountant is liable for all negligent acts.) In addition to the good faith defense, accountants have

available as a defense the buyer's or seller's knowledge that the financial statement was false and misleading.

A court, under Section 18 of the 1934 act, also has the discretion to assess reasonable costs, including attorneys' fees, against accountants.[7] Sellers and purchasers may maintain a cause of action "within one year after the discovery of the facts constituting the cause of action and within three years after such cause of action accrued."[8]

The Securities Exchange Act of 1934 further subjects accountants to potential legal liability in its antifraud provisions. Section 10(b) of the 1934 act and SEC Rule 10b-5 contain the antifraud provisions. As stated in *Herman & MacLean v. Huddleston,* "a private right of action under Section 10(b) of the 1934 act and Rule 10b-5 has been consistently recognized for more than 35 years."[9]

Section 10(b) makes it unlawful for any person, including accountants, to use, in connection with the purchase or sale of any security, any manipulative or deceptive device or contrivance in contravention of SEC rules and regulations.[10] Rule 10b-5 further makes it unlawful for any person, by use of any means or instrumentality of interstate commerce:

1. To employ any device, scheme, or artifice to defraud.
2. To make any untrue statement of a material fact or to omit to state a material fact necessary to make the statements made, in light of the circumstances, not misleading.
3. To engage in any act, practice, or course of business that operates or would operate as a fraud or deceit upon any person, in connection with the purchase or sale of any security.[11]

Accountants may be held liable only to sellers or purchasers under Section 10(b) and Rule 10b-5.[12] The scope of these antifraud provisions is extremely wide. Privity is not necessary for a recovery. Under these provisions, an accountant

---

6. Securities Exchange Act of 1934, Section 18(a).

7. Securities Exchange Act of 1934, Section 18(a).

8. Securities Exchange Act of 1934, Section 18(c).

9. 459 U.S. 375, 103 S.Ct. 683, 74 L.Ed.2d 548 (1983).

10. Securities Exchange Act of 1934, Section 10(b).

11. 17 C.F.R. Section 240.10b-5.

12. See Blue Chip Stamps v. Manor Drug Stores, 421 U.S. 723, 95 S.Ct. 1917, 44 L.Ed.2d 539 (1975).

may be found liable not only for fraudulent misstatements of material facts in written material filed with the SEC but also for any fraudulent oral statements or omissions made in connection with the purchase or sale of any security.

In order for a plaintiff to recover from an accountant under the antifraud provisions of the 1934 act, he or she must, in addition to establishing status as a purchaser or seller, prove *scienter*,[13] a

---

13. See Ernst & Ernst v. Hochfelder, 425 U.S. 185, 96 S.Ct. 1375, 47 L.Ed.2d 668 (1976).

fraudulent action or deception, reliance, materiality, and causation. A plaintiff who fails to establish these elements cannot recover damages from an accountant under Section 10(b) or Rule 10b-5.

In the following case, the court wrestles with the reliance requirement on finding an accounting firm liable under Rule 10b-5. Ask yourself as you read the case if any evidence exists that actually shows reliance by the plaintiffs.

Case 57.3
SHARP v. COOPERS & LYBRAND

United States Court of Appeals,
Third Circuit, 1981.
649 F.2d 175.

BACKGROUND AND FACTS *Westland Minerals Corporation (WMC) was the promoter of a venture in which multiple limited partnerships were formed for the purpose of drilling for oil and gas. WMC requested from the accounting firm of Coopers & Lybrand (C&L) an opinion letter on behalf of one of its investors, a Mr. Muhammed Ali, who desired reassurance concerning the benefits offered by this classic tax shelter. WMC subsequently showed copies of the letter to other potential investors. Thereafter, C&L concluded that, for the purposes of encouraging potential investors, a more complete letter should be drafted. Hence, WMC was presented with a revised document for use in encouraging potential investors. When the Internal Revenue Service eventually denied deductions taken by the investors, some 210 of them sued C&L, partially on the basis of this revised document. The trial court held for the investors, and C&L appealed.*

ALDISERT, Judge.
*   *   *   *

The factual setting of this case combines Caribbean intrigue, creative accounting, and high finance against the backdrop of investors attempting to limit their tax obligations.
*   *   *   *

Here, two opinion letters were issued by C&L. The first went out on July 21, 1971, to WMC and was signed in the firm name by a partner. The letter was in response to a request by WMC in behalf of *one* of its investors. The second letter went out in October, 1971, after a partner, Wright, had learned that WMC was showing copies of the letter to investors generally as part of WMC's sales program. With full knowledge of the letter's intended use—a tool to be used by a securities seller as part of a sales program—the partnership, through a partner, made the calculated decision to send out a more complete letter. Moreover, it was also decided that the letter be signed, not in the name of a partner, but in the partnership name. These facts are central to the important inquiry, whether this activity propelled C&L into a position in which the investing public would place their trust and confidence in it. We determine that it did ascend to that position, and the ultimate issue turns on this determination.
*   *   *   *

Reliance is an element of a plaintiff's action for damages under rule 10b-5. The obvious reason for this requirement is that a plaintiff in a rule 10b-5 action should not be allowed to recover damages when the defendant's wrongful action had no relationship to the plaintiff's loss. Reliance is therefore one aspect of the ubiquitous requirement that losses be causally related to the defendant's wrongful acts. This precept is manifest in the Securities Exchange Act of 1934 in § 28(a), 15 U.S.C. § 78bb(a), which states in part that "no person permitted to maintain a suit for damages under the provisions of this chapter shall recover, through satisfaction of judgment in one or more actions, a total amount in excess of his actual damages on account of the act complained of." Normally, a plaintiff suing under rule 10b-5 bears the burden of proving all the elements of his case. Nevertheless, the necessity of an element to a valid claim does not determine the allocation of the burdens of going forward and persuasion with respect to that element.

The Supreme Court authoritatively addressed the requirement of proving reliance in rule 10b-5 actions in *Affiliated Ute Citizens of Utah v. United States*, stating:

> Under the circumstances of this case, involving primarily a failure to disclose, positive proof of reliance is not a prerequisite to recovery. All that is necessary is that the facts withheld be material in the sense that a reasonable investor might have considered them important in the making of this decision. This obligation to disclose and this withholding of a material fact establish the requisite element of causation in fact.

The Court has subsequently defined a material omission in the context of proxy statements under rule 14a-9 as "a substantial likelihood that a reasonable [investor] would consider it important. * * * [T]here must be a substantial likelihood that the disclosure of the omitted fact would have been viewed by the reasonable investor as having significantly altered the 'total mix' of information made available." We have held this standard of materiality applicable to the rule 10b-5 actions as well. *Affiliated Ute* makes clear that in at least some situations a presumption of reliance in favor of the rule 10b-5 plaintiff is proper. Our present task is to determine whether that presumption was properly applied in this case.

Both parties in this case cite decisions indicating that the presumption of reliance is proper in cases of alleged omissions, whereas no presumption arises in cases of alleged misrepresentations. This distinction has led C&L to argue that its wrongful conduct in this case arose from misrepresentations in the opinion letter, whereas the class representatives argue that the violation resulted from the appellant's failure to disclose certain material facts.

We have concluded that both misrepresentations and omissions are present in this case. The jury heard evidence that C&L had misrepresented certain crucial facts in the letter, such as its disclaimer of verification of the facts on which the opinion letter was based and its assertion that cash supplemental to the limited partner's contributions would be borrowed "from suitable banks or other lending agencies * * *." The jury also heard evidence that C&L had failed to disclose certain material facts, such as the affiliation between the putative lender, the Bahamian bank, and WMC. A strict application of the omissions-misrepresentation dichotomy would require the trial judge to instruct the jury to presume reliance with regard to the omitted facts, and not to presume reliance with regard to the misrepresented facts. Although this resolution would have great appeal to graduate logicians in a classroom, we are not persuaded to adopt it for use in a courtroom.

* * * *

We agree with the district court that the burden in this case should fall on C&L. The opinion letter issued by C&L was intended to influence the investment decisions of persons interested in WMC partnerships. The appellant undoubtedly foresaw that it would have that effect. As in *Affiliated Ute*, C&L by its action facilitated the transactions at issue but failed to disclose certain facts. Its misrepresentation of other facts should not alleviate its burden of proving nonreliance. Considering the likelihood that investors would rely on the opinion letter, we conclude that the trial judge properly placed the burden of refuting a presumption of reliance on the appellant.

The court held that the accounting firm had violated Rule 10b-5. Essential to the finding of the liability under Rule 10b-5 was the reliance of investors on **DECISION AND REMEDY** *the letter in their purchase of partnership interests. Note, however, that the court allowed reliance to be presumed under these facts; since the defendant had known the letter was going to potential investors, it could assume they would rely on it. At trial, the defendant had the burden of refuting that presumption.*

CONCEPT SUMMARY: Civil Liability of Accountants

TYPE OF LIABILITY	WHEN LIABLE
Common Law 1. Liability to client: a. Breach of contract	An accountant who fails to perform according to his or her contractual obligations can be held liable for breach of contract and resulting damages.
b. Negligence	An accountant in performance of his or her duties must use the care, knowledge, and judgment generally used by accountants under the same or similar circumstances. Failure to do so is negligence. Violating generally accepted accounting principles and standards is *prima facie* evidence of negligence.
c. Fraud	Actual intent to misrepresent a material fact to a client, when the client relies on the misrepresentation, is fraud. Gross negligence in performance of duties is constructive fraud.
2. Liability to third parties: a. Negligence	An accountant's duty of care to the client flows to any third person the accountant knows or should have known will benefit from the accountant's work.
b. Fraud	An accountant is liable for actual or constructive fraud perpetrated on a third person, the same as for a client.
Statutory Law 1. Securities Act of 1933, Section 11	An accountant who makes a false statement or omits a material fact in audited financial statements required for registration of securities under the law may be liable to anyone who acquires securities covered by the registration statement. The accountant's defense is basically the use of due diligence and the reasonable belief that the work was complete and correct. The burden of proof is on the accountant.
2. Securities Exchange Act of 1934, Sections 10(b) and 18	Accountants are held liable for false and misleading applications, reports, and documents required under the act. The burden is on the plaintiff, and the accountant has numerous defenses, including good faith and lack of knowledge that what was submitted was false.
3. Other acts	An accountant can be held liable under other acts, such as the Internal Revenue Code 1976 and 1978 acts, the Tax Act of 1982, and the Deficit Reduction Act of 1984. These acts impose penalties for failure to furnish a taxpayer a copy of a completed return, failure to sign as preparer or furnish an identification number, or understatement of a taxpayer's liability, among others.

CRIMINAL LIABILITY

An accountant may be found criminally liable under the Securities Act of 1933, the Securities Exchange Act of 1934, the Internal Revenue Code, and both state and federal criminal codes. Under both the 1933 act and the 1934 act, accountants may be subject to criminal penalties for *willful conduct*—imprisonment of up to five years and/or a fine of up to $10,000 under the 1933 act and $100,000 under the 1934 act.

WORKING PAPERS AND ACCOUNTANT-CLIENT COMMUNICATIONS

Performing an audit for a client involves an accumulation of *working papers*—the various documents used and developed during the audit. These include work plans, the testing of accounts and the results of this testing, and other records of pertinent data. Under the common law, which in this instance has been codified in a number of states, working papers remain the accountant's property. But because they reflect the client's financial situation, the client has a right of access to them. The client must give permission before they can be transferred to another accountant. Without the client's permission or a valid court order, their contents are not to be disclosed.

Disclosure would constitute a breach of the accountant's fiduciary duty to the client. On grounds of unauthorized disclosure, the client could initiate a malpractice suit. The accountant's best defense would be that the client gave permission for the papers' release.

As stated above, under a valid court order, the contents of working papers must be disclosed. In the context of accountant-client communications, the circumstances under which a court order is valid vary, however. In some states, statutes provide the client with a privilege, so that the material may not be revealed even in court or in court-sanctioned proceedings without the client's permission. This statutory privilege extends to all confidential communications between accountant and client and, thus, is also available as a valid ground for refusing to testify as to such communications.

In cases involving federal law, federal courts do not recognize a client's state-provided right to confidentiality. Thus, in those cases, in response to a court order, an accountant must provide the information sought.

 ## QUESTIONS AND CASE PROBLEMS

1. Larkin, Inc., retains Howard Perkins to manage its books and to prepare its financial statements. Perkins, a certified public accountant, is authorized to practice in Indiana and practices there. After twenty years, Perkins has become a bit bored with the format of generally accepted accounting principles and has become creative in his accounting methods. Now, though, Perkins has a problem, since he is being sued by Molly Tucker, one of Larkin's creditors. Tucker alleges that Perkins either knew or should have known that Larkin's financial statements would be distributed to various individuals. Furthermore, she asserts that these financial statements were negligently prepared and seriously inaccurate. What are the consequences of Larkin's failure to adopt generally accepted accounting standards? Under the traditional *Ultramares* rule, can Tucker recover damages from Perkins?

2. The accounting firm of Goldman, Walters, Johnson & Co. prepared financial statements for Lucy's Fashions, Inc. After reviewing the various financial statements, Happydays State Bank agreed to loan Lucy's Fashions $35,000 for expansion. When Lucy's Fashions declared bankruptcy under Chapter 11 six months later, Happydays State Bank promptly filed an action against Goldman, Walters, Johnson & Co., alleging negligent preparation of financial statements. Assuming that the court has abandoned the *Ultramares* approach, what is the result? What are the policy reasons for holding accountants liable to third parties with whom they are not in privity?

3. In early 1989, Bennett, Inc., offered a substantial number of new common shares to the public. Harvey Helms had a long-standing interest in Bennett, Inc., since his grandfather had once been president of the company. Upon receiving a prospectus prepared and distributed by Bennett, Inc., Helms was dismayed by the pessimism it embodied. After much debate, Helms decided to delay purchasing stock in the company. A few months later, Helms asserted that the prospectus prepared by the accountants was overly pessimistic. Moreover, Helms alleged that the prospectus contained materially misleading statements. How successful would Helms be in bringing a cause of action under Rule 10b-5 against the accountants of Bennett, Inc.?

4. The plaintiffs, Harry and Barry Rosenblum, brought an action against Touche Ross & Co., a prominent accounting firm. The plaintiffs alleged that they had relied upon the correctness of audits in acquiring Giant common stock in conjunction with the sale of their business to Giant. The financial statements of Giant were found to be fraudulent, and the stock that the Rosenblums had acquired proved to be worthless. The plaintiffs alleged that Touche's negligence in conducting the audits was the proximate cause of their loss. Does an auditor owe a duty to third persons known and intended by the auditor to be recipients of the audit? Furthermore, does an independent auditor owe a duty to anyone when the opinion he or she furnishes states no limitation in the certificate as to those to whom the company may disseminate the information contained in the financial statements? [H. Rosenblum, Inc. v. Adler, 93 N.J. 324, 461 A.2d 138 (1983)]

5. An accounting firm was engaged by two car rental companies to determine the net worth of those businesses by preparing an audited statement. At the request of their clients, the accountants did not audit the accounts receivable, made appropriate exceptions to the accounts receivable in the balance sheet, and qualified their accountants' opinion with a similar caveat. After the audit had been performed and on the basis of the figures reflected in the balance sheet, Stephens Industries, Inc., purchased two-thirds of the car rental companies' stock. The car rental businesses thereafter failed, and Stephens Industries, Inc., brought an action against the accounting firm for allegedly having misrepresented the status of the accounts receivable in the audit. What was the result? [Stephen Industries, Inc. v. Haskins & Sells, 438 F.2d 357 (10th Cir. 1971)]

6. The plaintiffs were the purchasers of all the stock in companies owned by the defendant sellers. Alleging fraud under the federal securities law and under the New York common law of fraud, the plaintiffs sued the defendant sellers and their accounting firm. What should be the result with respect to the accounting firm, assuming that the treatment of shipping costs and expenses and factoring charges was not in accordance with generally accepted accounting principles and hence created an inaccurate financial picture in the financial statement? [Berkowitz v. Baron, 428 F.Supp. 1190 (S.D.N.Y. 1977)]

7. Credit Alliance Corporation is a major financial service company engaged primarily in financing the purchase of capital equipment through installment sales and leasing agreements. As a condition of extending additional major financing to L. B. Smith, Credit Alliance required an audited financial statement. Smith provided Credit Alliance with an audited financial statement prepared by the accounting firm of Arthur Andersen & Co. Later, upon Smith's petitioning for bankruptcy, it was discovered that Smith, at the time of the audit, was in a precarious financial position. Credit Alliance filed suit against Arthur Andersen, claiming that Andersen had failed to conduct investigations in accordance with proper auditing standards and that Andersen's recklessness had resulted in misleading statements that caused Credit Alliance to incur damages. In addition, it was claimed that Andersen knew or should have known that Credit Alliance would rely on these statements in issuing credit to Smith. Discuss whether Credit Alliance, as a third party, could hold Arthur Andersen liable in a negligence action. [Credit Alliance Corp. v. Arthur Andersen & Co., 65 N.Y.2d 536, 483 N.E.2d 110, 493 N.Y.S.2d 435 (1985)]

8. Toro Co. was a major supplier of equipment and credit to Summit Power Equipment Distributors. Toro Co. required audited reports from Summit in order to evaluate the distributor's financial condition. Summit supplied Toro with reports prepared by Krouse, Kern & Co., an accounting firm. The reports allegedly contained mistakes and omissions regarding Summit's financial condition. Toro alleged that it had extended and renewed large amounts of credit to Summit in reliance on the audited reports. Summit was unable to repay these amounts, and Toro brought a negligence action against the accounting firm and the individual accountants. Evidence produced at the trial showed that Krouse knew that the reports it furnished to Summit were to be used by Summit to induce Toro to extend credit, but no evidence was produced to show either a contractual relationship between Krouse and Toro or a link between these companies evidencing Krouse's understanding of Toro's actual reliance on the reports. Indiana follows the *Ultramares* rule. What was the result? [Toro Co. v. Krouse, Kern & Co., 827 F.2d 155 (7th Cir. 1987)]

9. The accounting firm of Arthur Young & Co. was employed by DMI Furniture, Inc., to conduct a review of an audit prepared by Brown, Kraft & Co., certified public accountants, for Gillespie Furniture Co. DMI planned to purchase Gillespie and wished to determine its net worth. Arthur Young, by letter, advised DMI that Brown, Kraft had performed a high-quality audit and that Gillespie's inventory on the audit dates was fairly stated on the general ledger. Allegedly as a result of these representations, DMI went forward with its purchase of Gillespie. Subsequently, DMI charged Brown, Kraft & Co., Arthur Young, and Gillespie's former owners with violations of Section 10(b) of the Securities Exchange Act and SEC Rule 10b-5. DMI complained that Arthur Young's review had proved to be materially inaccurate and misleading, primarily because the inventory reflected in the balance sheet was grossly overstated. Arthur Young was charged "with acting recklessly in failing to detect, and thus failing to disclose, material omissions and reckless conduct on the part of Brown, Kraft, and in making affirmative misstatements in its letter" to DMI. DMI sought $8 million in compensatory damages and $8 million in punitive damages from the accounting firms. Did DMI have a valid cause of action under either Section 10(b) or Rule 10b-5? Discuss. [DMI Furniture, Inc. v. Brown, Kraft & Co., 644 F.Supp. 1517 (C.D.Cal. 1986)]

Chapter 58

The Effect of International Law in a Global Economy

International trade is increasingly important in business. United States exports—shipments of goods to other countries—exceed $200 billion, and imports are tens of billions of dollars greater. Many more billions of dollars change hands annually in international investments.

International business is conducted in a variety of ways. A U.S. company may export its product to foreign countries or may franchise retail outlets overseas. McDonald's, for example, has franchises throughout the world. Other companies are involved in importing products into the United States. Toyota, Nissan, Honda, and other Asian automobile companies are among the largest importers. Businesses may invest in land or corporations in certain foreign countries and may license information or technology in other nations. Increasingly, U.S. firms are entering into joint ventures with foreign companies. In 1986, for example, British Telecom and Du Pont formed an important joint venture to make laser and other advanced communications equipment for the world market.

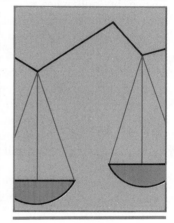

Businesspersons engaged in international trade must depend on international law. International law is less well developed than domestic law, however, and considerable uncertainty remains in many transactions. Even straightforward questions, such as what country's law should apply to a contract, may have complex or unclear answers. This chapter discusses some overriding issues in the developing international law governing commercial transactions.

THE CONTEXT OF INTERNATIONAL LAW

International law is considerably different from the United States domestic law studied so far. Domestic law applies universally throughout a jurisdiction, and judgments can be enforced effectively by the government. Usually, a considerable body of statutes or precedents offers clear guidance in resolving disputes. International law is somewhat less certain and may be less binding. Neither the United Nations nor the International Court of Justice has the power to enforce international law fully. For example, if a government undertakes an illegal military invasion, international law may provide no effective response. Nevertheless, international law may play a major role in business transactions.

Sources of International Law

International law stems from numerous sources. The most important of these are international organizations and conferences, trade agreements among nations, and international customs.

INTERNATIONAL ORGANIZATIONS AND CONFERENCES   International organizations and conferences, such as the United Nations, are the source of some international law. These organizations adopt resolutions, declarations, and other types of standards that often require particular behavior of nations. Many violations of these rules are without sanction, however. Disputes may be brought before the United Nations International Court of Justice, but only when nations voluntarily submit to its jurisdiction, and the court is often powerless to enforce its decisions even then.

REGIONAL MULTILATERAL AGREEMENTS   More important to international business law are regional multilateral agreements among nations. For example, the European Economic Community (EEC), or Common Market, establishes and enforces rules of international trade among European member states. Similarly, the Association of Southeast Asian Nations (ASEAN) establishes trade rules, including **tariffs** (taxes on imports), for Malaysia, the Philippines, Singapore, and Thailand. Anyone attempting to do business in these countries must be familiar with the rules of the regional association.

BILATERAL TRADE AGREEMENTS   Other important legal requirements may be established by bilateral trade agreements between two nations. For the United States, many of these bilateral agreements are created by formal treaties. A *treaty* is an agreement or contract between two or more nations that must be authorized and ratified by the responsible officials of each nation. Under Article II, Section 2, of the United States Constitution, the president can make treaties with foreign governments, subject to ratification by at least two-thirds of the Senate.

INTERNATIONAL CUSTOMS   Another important source of international law consists of international trade customs that have evolved over time among nations. Under Article 38(1) of the Statute of the International Court of Justice, an international custom is referred to as "evidence of a general practice accepted as law." Past practice may therefore actually become the unwritten, implied law. This may create considerable uncertainty, however, regarding when a customary voluntary practice evolves into a legal obligation.

Act of State Doctrine

The international legal rights of private businesses are limited by the sovereign power of nations in international law. Under the **act of state doctrine,** the judges of one country may not question the validity of official acts committed by a foreign government within its own country. The United States Supreme Court declared in *Underhill v. Hernandez* that "the courts of one country will not sit in judgment on * * * the acts of the government of another done within its own territory." [1] Consequently, if a foreign government nationalizes the overseas manufacturing operations of a United States company, that company may receive little or no compensation for its assets that were seized. In the early 1970s, Chile took over Kennecott Copper Company's holdings in a Chilean mine and declared that Kennecott's past "excess profits" from the mine eliminated the need for compensation for the nationalization. When companies do business overseas, they have very little international legal protection against the actions of the governments of the countries in which they operate.

Sovereign Immunity

Closely related to the act of state doctrine is the **doctrine of sovereign immunity,** the presence of which is usually established by treaty. Under certain conditions, this doctrine immunizes foreign nations from the jurisdiction of United States courts. In 1976, Congress codified this rule in the Foreign Sovereign Immunities Act (FSIA). [2] This law modified past practice somewhat by expanding the rights of plaintiff-creditors against foreign nations. Under Section 1610 of the act, plaintiffs may now sometimes attach the property of a foreign state "used for a commercial activity in the United States."

The FSIA exclusively governs the circumstances in which an action may be brought against a foreign nation in the United States, including attempts to attach a country's property. One of

---

1. 168 U.S. 250, 252, 18 S.Ct. 83, 84, 42 L.Ed. 456 (1897).
2. 28 U.S.C. Sections 1602–1611.

the primary purposes of this act was to have federal courts, rather than the State Department, determine claims of foreign sovereign immunity. This was expected to add a greater degree of certainty to such determinations and reduce the role of politics in this judicial sphere.

Sovereign immunity law can be important in international business transactions. Suppose that an American company, U.S. Consolidated Foods, enters into a contract for goods with the government of Venezuela or one of its subsidiary businesses. If the Venezuelan government breaks the contract or refuses to perform, U.S. Consolidated Foods may have no remedy against the foreign sovereign, unless the contract falls within the commercial-activity exception of the FSIA or is otherwise excepted from the act's coverage.

Passage of the FSIA has not resolved all legal questions. Disputes persist over which entities are protected as foreign states. Under Section 1603 of the FSIA, a *foreign state* is defined to include both a political subdivision of a foreign state and an instrumentality of such a state. The question of what is an exempt commercial activity has also been disputed. *Commercial activities* are broadly defined by this section to mean business activities by the foreign state carried on in the United States or causing a direct effect in the United States. But the particulars of what constitutes a commercial activity are not defined in the act. Rather, it is left up to the courts to decide whether a particular activity is governmental or commercial in nature—as is illustrated by the following case.

BACKGROUND AND FACTS *The plaintiffs, Texas Trading and three other trading companies, brought an action for breach of contract against the defendants, the Federal Republic of Nigeria and its central bank. The defendants had overbought quantities of cement from the plaintiffs. Unable to accept delivery of the cement, they repudiated the contract, alleging that they were entitled to immunity under the FSIA.*

Case 58.1
TEXAS TRADING & MILLING CORP. v. FEDERAL REPUBLIC OF NIGERIA
United States Court of Appeals, Second Circuit, 1981.
647 F.2d 300.

KAUFMAN, Judge.
* * * *

These four appeals grow out of one of the most enormous commercial disputes in history, and present questions which strike to the very heart of the modern international economic order. An African nation, developing at breakneck speed by virtue of huge exports of high-grade oil, contracted to buy huge quantities of Portland cement, a commodity crucial to the construction of its infrastructure. It overbought, and the country's docks and harbors became clogged with ships waiting to unload. * * * Unable to accept delivery of the cement it had bought, the nation repudiated its contracts. * * * For the ruling principles here, we must look * * * to a new and vaguely-worded statute, the Foreign Sovereign Immunities Act of 1976 * * * a law described by its draftsmen as providing only "very modest guidance" on issues of preeminent importance. For answers to those most difficult questions, the authors of the law "decided to put [their] faith in the U.S. courts." Guided by reason, precedent, and equity, we have attempted to give form and substance to the legislative intent.
* * *

* * * *

The determination of whether particular behavior is "commercial" is perhaps the most important decision a court faces in an FSIA suit. This problem is significant because the primary purpose of the Act is to "restrict" the immunity of a foreign state to suits involving a foreign state's public acts. * * * If the activity is not "commercial," it satisfies none of the three clauses of § 1605(a)(2), and the foreign state is (at least under that subsection) immune from suit. Unfortunately, the definition of "commercial" is the one issue on which the Act provides almost no guidance at all. * * * No provision of the Act * * * defines "commercial." Congress deliberately left the meaning open and, as noted above, "put [its] faith in the U.S. courts to work out progressively, on a case-by-case basis . . . the distinction between commercial and governmental." * * *

* * * *

Under [the FSIA] Nigeria's cement contracts and letters of credit qualify as "commercial activity." Lord Denning, writing in *Trendtex Trading Corp. v. Central Bank of Nigeria,* * * * with his usual erudition and clarity, stated: "If a government department goes into the market places of the world and buys boots or cement—as a commercial transaction—that government department should be subject to all the rules of the marketplace." Nigeria's activity here is in the nature of a private contract for the purchase of goods. Its purpose—to build roads, army barracks, whatever—is irrelevant.

DECISION AND REMEDY *The court of appeals held that under the Foreign Sovereign Immunities Act, the Federal Republic of Nigeria and its central bank were not immune from acts arising out of a breach of contract to purchase cement. This conclusion was based on the court's determination that the contract to purchase the cement was a commercial activity and, hence, the doctrine of sovereign immunity did not apply.*

An important exception to sovereign immunity exists when a foreign state has "waived its immunity either explicitly or by implication." [3] Sometimes treaties between nations will waive the governments' sovereign immunity. Explicit waivers of sovereign immunity may also be contained in private contracts between U.S. companies and foreign governments. Thus, if U.S. Consolidated Foods contracts to sell grain to Egypt, that contract might contain a provision in which Egypt agrees not to argue the defense of sovereign immunity in future contract disputes.

TRANSACTING BUSINESS ABROAD

Transacting business abroad has always been attended by many difficulties. International business transactions may be complex, difficult to enforce, and hedged by various legal restrictions. It is thus recommended that prospective international businesspersons acquaint themselves with the unique rules and practices governing these transactions.

Certain specific practices are necessary. Like all other commercial contracts, the transnational business contract should be in writing. In addition, this contract should contain a clause that

designates the official language to be used in interpreting the contractual terms. The basic contract of sale should include a legal definition of terms, the price and manner of payment, and a provision specifying acceptable currencies for payment. A *force majeure* clause, which protects the parties from international forces beyond their control, is also advisable.

Letters of Credit

Selling goods overseas involves particular risks because the buyer and the seller often are separated by thousands of miles. Sellers fear delivering goods for which they might not be paid. Buyers are reluctant to pay until there is evidence that the goods have been shipped. These risks are especially acute for small businesses. Thus, **letters of credit** are increasingly used to facilitate international business transactions.

In a typical letter-of-credit transaction, the *issuer* (a bank) agrees to issue a letter of credit and to ascertain the occurrence of certain acts (such as the shipment of goods) by the *beneficiary* (the seller). Issuers usually are banks with branches in both the importing and exporting countries. The issuer is bound to pay the beneficiary when the beneficiary has complied with the terms and conditions of the letter of credit. Typically, the letter of credit will require that the beneficiary deliver a bill of lading to prove that shipment has been made. In return, the *account party* (the buyer) promises to reimburse the issuer for the amount paid to the

---

3. 28 U.S.C. Section 1605(a)(1).

beneficiary. This letter-of-credit procedure offers important benefits to the parties in sales transactions. For example, the risk of the importer's creditworthiness is assumed by the issuer bank and not by the exporting company. The "life cycle" of a letter of credit is summarized in Exhibit 58–1.

After a letter of credit has been issued, courts may be required to determine compliance with its terms. In a transaction involving a letter of credit, there generally are at least three separate and distinct contracts. First, there is the contract for goods between the account party (the buyer) and the beneficiary (the seller). Second, there is the contract between the issuer (the bank) and the account party (the buyer). Third, there is the letter of credit itself, which involves the issuer and the beneficiary. Given the fact that these contracts are separate and distinct, the issuer's obligations are defined by the letter of credit and not by the underlying contract between the buyer and the seller. When disagreements arise, their resolution will depend on the degree to which the various parties have complied with the various contracts involved.

If the documents presented by the beneficiary comply with the terms of the letter of credit, the issuer must honor the letter of credit. The issuer must then pay the beneficiary whether or not the account party pays the issuer. (The account party might refuse to pay the issuer if, for example, on delivery, the goods proved to be defective.)

In other words, the issuer's only responsibility is to verify that the bill of lading covers the goods identified in the letter of credit and that any other documents called for in the letter comply with its requirements. The courts are presently divided as to whether strict compliance or substantial compliance with the terms of the letter of credit is required. Traditionally, courts required strict compliance with these terms.

Technology Transfer

An especially controversial international trade issue involves the transfer of information and technological advances across national boundaries. The United States is concerned that such technology transfer from our country will cost us a rare remaining competitive advantage over foreign nations. U.S. law currently restricts the export of certain technologies, especially those that are important to national security. Moreover, once technological information is transferred, international law must still be called upon to protect proprietary rights in that information.

Exhibit 58–1 The Life Cycle of a Letter of Credit

Although the letter of credit appears quite complex at first, it is not difficult to understand. It merely involves the exchange of documents (and money) through intermediaries. The following steps depict the letter-of-credit procurement cycle.

Step 1: The buyer and seller agree upon the terms of sale. The sales contract dictates that a letter of credit is to be used to finance the transaction.

Step 2: The buyer completes an application for a letter of credit and forwards it to his or her bank, which will issue the letter of credit.

Step 3: The issuing buyer's bank then forwards the letter of credit to a correspondent bank in the seller's country.

Step 4: The correspondent bank relays the letter of credit to the seller.

Step 5: Having received assurance of payment, the seller makes the necessary shipping arrangements.

Step 6: The seller prepares the documents required under the letter of credit and delivers them to the correspondent bank.

Step 7: The correspondent bank negotiates the documents. If it finds them in order, it sends them to the issuing bank and pays the seller in accordance with the terms of the letter of credit.

Step 8: The issuing bank, having received the documents, examines them. If they are in order, the issuing bank will charge the buyer's account and send the documents on to the buyer or his or her customs broker. The issuing bank also will reimburse the correspondent bank.

Step 9: The buyer or broker receives the documents and picks up the merchandise from the shipper (carrier).

Source: National Association of Purchasing Management.

In the United States, inventions are protected by patent law, which prevents others from copying the invention. U.S. patent laws provide no direct protection overseas, however. Consequently, to be protected overseas, an inventor must patent his or her invention under the varying patent laws of the world's nations. International treaties address international protection for inventors under the "Paris Convention." [4] This convention does not provide independent international patent protection, but it does guarantee nondiscriminatory treatment under the varying patent laws of independent nations. There is also some international protection of copyrights and trademarks. Under the "Berne Convention," member nations are prohibited from

discriminating against copyrighted works of other member nations, and copyright protection takes effect in other countries automatically without the necessity of government formalities. The United States may prohibit the importation of products that infringe upon patents registered in our country. And in *Wells Fargo & Co. v. Wells Fargo Express Co.*,[5] a United States court extended our trademark laws to cover violations by a foreign licensee of an American company.

The following case addresses the issue of whether an American firm, barred from marketing its product within the United States because of a competitor's superior patent claim, could nonetheless legally market the product abroad.

_____

4. See International Convention for Protection of Industrial Property, March 20, 1883, 21 U.S.T. 1583, T.I.A.S. No. 6923.

_____

5. 556 F.2d 406 (9th Cir. 1977).

Case 58.2
DEEPSOUTH PACKING CO. v. LAITRAM CORP.

Supreme Court of the United States, 1972.
406 U.S. 518, 92 S.Ct. 1700, 32 L.Ed.2d 273.

BACKGROUND AND FACTS *Laitram Corporation has valid United States patents for machinery used in the process of deveining shrimp. Under the U.S. patent code, no other company may "make" or "sell" the patented item in the United States. Deepsouth Packing Company began shipping components of deveining machinery similar to Laitram's to foreign customers. These components were shipped in three different boxes, but the entire machine could be assembled in less than an hour. Laitram argued that this practice violated its exclusive rights under the U.S. patent. The district court held for Deepsouth, but the Fifth Circuit Court of Appeals reversed and ruled that Deepsouth's foreign sales violated Laitram's patent. Deepsouth appealed to the United States Supreme Court.*

WHITE, Justice.
* * * *

* * * Petitioner and respondent both hold patents on machines that devein shrimp more cheaply and efficiently than competing machinery or hand labor can do the job. Extensive litigation below has established that respondent, the Laitram Corp., has the superior claim and that the distribution and use of petitioner Deepsouth's machinery in this country should be enjoined to prevent infringement of Laitram's patents. We granted certiorari to consider a related question: Is Deepsouth, barred from the American market by Laitram's patents, also foreclosed by the patent laws from exporting its deveiners, in less than fully assembled form, for use abroad?
* * * *

* * * [The] judgment of Laitram's patent superiority forecloses Deepsouth and its customers from any future use (other than a use approved by Laitram or occurring after the Laitram patent has expired) of its deveiners "throughout the United States." The patent provisions taken in conjunction with the judgment below also entitle Laitram to the injunction it has received prohibiting Deepsouth from continuing to "make" or, once made, to "sell" deveiners "throughout the United States." Further, Laitram may recover damages for any past unauthorized use, sale, or making "throughout the United States." This much is not disputed.

But Deepsouth argues that it is not liable for every type of past sale and that a portion of its future business is salvageable. Section 154 [of the patent code] and related provisions obviously are intended to grant a patentee a monopoly only over the United States market; they are not intended to grant a patentee the bonus of a favored position as a flagship company free of American competition in international commerce. Deepsouth, itself barred from using its deveining machines, or from inducing others to use them "throughout the United States," barred also from making and selling the machines in the United States, seeks to make the parts of deveining machines, to sell them to foreign buyers, and to have the buyers assemble the parts and use the machines abroad.

*　*　*

*　*　*　*

In conclusion, we note that what is at stake here is the right of American companies to compete with an American patent holder in foreign markets. Our patent system makes no claim to extraterritorial effect; "these acts of Congress do not, and were not intended to, operate beyond the limits of the United States," and we correspondingly reject the claims of others to such control over our markets. To the degree that the inventor needs protection in markets other than those of this country, the wording of 35 U.S.C. §§ 154 and 271 reveals a congressional intent to have him seek it abroad through patents secured in countries where his goods are being used.

The Supreme Court reversed the Fifth Circuit Court's holding. The Court held that Deepsouth's practice did not violate the United States patent laws.	**DECISION AND REMEDY**

DISPUTE RESOLUTION

Whatever precautions are taken in international transactions, there is always the possibility of disagreement, just as in a domestic contract dispute. Resolving the international business dispute, however, is somewhat more complicated.

Judicial Resolution

Unless otherwise specified, international legal disputes will be settled in court. But a businessperson who wants to sue over an international transaction faces a number of difficult questions: What nation's courts have jurisdiction over the dispute? What nation's law will be applied in resolving the dispute? Will crucial documents and witnesses be available at the trial? What enforceable remedies are available? Ideally, the contract in question will specify answers to these questions. If it does not, the parties enter a thicket of difficult and complex international precedents. The following case is illustrative.

BACKGROUND AND FACTS *In November 1967, Zapata, a Houston-based American corporation, contracted with Unterweser, a German corporation, to tow Zapata's drilling rig from Louisiana to Italy. A clause in the contract contained the following provision: "Any dispute arising must be treated before the London Court of Justice." Unterweser's ship, the Bremen, began the towing operation, but on January 9, 1968, a severe storm arose in the Gulf of Mexico. During this storm, the drilling rig was severely damaged, and the rig was towed to the nearest port, which was Tampa, Florida. On January 12, Zapata, ignoring the contract provision, sued in federal district court in Tampa, seeking damages for allegedly negligent towage. Unterweser argued that the U.S. courts lacked jurisdiction because of the contract provision. The district court rejected Unterweser's motion to dismiss the case, and Unterweser appealed. On appeal, a sharply divided Fifth Circuit Court of appeals affirmed the district court by an eight-to-six vote. Unterweser then appealed to the United States Supreme Court.*

Case 58.3
M/S BREMEN v. ZAPATA OFF-SHORE CO.
Supreme Court of the United States, 1972.
407 U.S. 1, 92 S.Ct. 1907, 32 L.Ed.2d 513.

BURGER, Justice.

* * * *

* * * For at least two decades we have witnessed an expansion of overseas commercial activities by business enterprises based in the United States. The barrier of distance that once tended to confine a business concern to a modest territory no longer does so. Here we see an American company with special expertise contracting with a foreign company to tow a complex machine thousands of miles across seas and oceans. The expansion of American business and industry will hardly be encouraged if, notwithstanding solemn contracts, we insist on a parochial concept that all disputes must be resolved under our laws and in our courts. * * *

Forum-selection clauses have historically not been favored by American courts. Many courts, federal and state, have declined to enforce such clauses on the ground that they were "contrary to public policy," or that their effect was to "oust the jurisdiction" of the court. Although this view apparently still has considerable acceptance, other courts are tending to adopt a more hospitable attitude toward forum-selection clauses. This view, advanced in the well-reasoned dissenting opinion in the instant case, is that such clauses are prima facie valid and should be enforced unless enforcement is shown by the resisting party to be "unreasonable" under the circumstances.

* * *

* * * *

* * * This approach is substantially that followed in other common-law countries including England. It is the view advanced by noted scholars and that adopted by the Restatement of the Conflict of Laws. It accords with ancient concepts of freedom of contract and reflects an appreciation of the expanding horizons of American contractors who seek business in all parts of the world. Not surprisingly, foreign businessmen prefer, as do we, to have disputes resolved in their own courts, but if that choice is not available, then in a neutral forum with expertise in the subject matter. Plainly, the courts of England meet the standards of neutrality and long experience in admiralty litigation. The choice of that forum was made in an arm's-length negotiation by experienced and sophisticated businessmen, and absent some compelling and countervailing reason it should be honored by the parties and enforced by the courts.

DECISION   *The Supreme Court held that the contract provision was controlling and that*
AND REMEDY   *U.S. courts lacked jurisdiction. Consequently, the Court vacated the decision*
                            on appeal and remanded the case for further proceedings consistent with its
                            opinion.

Even after a plaintiff company has won a case in a foreign court, its remedy is not ensured. That judgment must still be enforced in the nation where the defendant has assets to pay the judgment. Fortunately, if a company has won in a foreign court, that judgment will be presumed valid and enforced almost automatically in the United States and in many other nations. This is known as the **policy of comity.**

Arbitration

To help avoid many of the thorny questions that arise in judicial resolution of disputes, interna-

tional business contracts increasingly call for disputes to be settled by arbitration. Arbitration offers greater speed, less expense, greater privacy, and the promise of better future relations between the parties to a dispute. Consequently, *arbitration clauses* are now included in many private international agreements. Arbitration is discussed in detail in Chapter 2.

International arbitration clauses should specify the law to be applied and a means for selecting an arbitrator. Many arbitrators are certified for the job, and most are senior businesspersons or lawyers who have experience in resolving business disputes. The arbitration process itself is somewhat like a trial but much less formal. Both sides present their cases, largely unconstrained by rules of evidence, and the arbitrator attempts to reach a fair conclusion. In the original contract, the parties usually have agreed to be bound by the arbitrator's decision.

An arbitrator cannot enforce his or her decision, so the winner may have to go to court for enforcement, and the loser may challenge the arbitrator's decision. Courts are extremely reluctant to overturn an arbitrator's ruling, however, if both parties have voluntarily agreed to abide by the arbitrator's decision. Internationally, court enforcement of arbitration is governed by the United Nations Convention on the Recognition and Enforcement of Foreign Arbitral Awards,[6] which was originally drafted in 1958 and has since been adopted by most of the world's commercially significant nations. The United States adopted the terms of the Convention in 1970.[7] Under this Convention, court enforcement of arbitrators' decisions is automatic, except when arbitral procedures are manifestly unfair or when the arbitrator's award is contrary to the law or public policy of the nation where enforcement is sought.

A DEVELOPING INTERNATIONAL UCC?

As international business transactions become more extensive, there is increased recognition of the need for a settled body of law for resolving disputes. In response, the United Nations has developed a new Convention on Contracts for the International Sale of Goods.[8] This 1980 Convention is much like an international Uniform Commercial Code (UCC), because it provides rules for settling contract disputes. The current Convention's rules are generally similar to those of the UCC, but they differ in a few important respects, such as the following:

1. The Convention has no Statute of Frauds pro-

vision requiring sales of goods contracts to be in writing (in contrast to UCC 2-201).

2. Under the Convention, acceptances must mirror the language of the offer, or they will be considered counteroffers (in contrast to UCC 2-207).

3. A contract under the Convention is formed upon receipt of the acceptance, not upon its dispatch through a reasonable medium (in contrast to UCC 2-206).

Unfortunately, this United Nations Convention is not universally applicable. The Convention applies only to contracts between parties in two different countries when the governments of both countries have ratified the Convention. At this point, the Convention has only been ratified by a handful of nations, but these countries include the United States, France, Italy, and the People's Republic of China. On January 1, 1989, the Convention also took effect in Austria, Finland, Mexico, and Switzerland. Companies that want to avoid application of the Convention may do so by specifying in their contract that the terms of the Convention will not apply.

EXTRATERRITORIAL APPLICATION OF U.S. ANTITRUST LAWS

So far, this chapter has focused on international legal rules. Participants in international business dealings must be aware that some *national* laws may apply even to overseas transactions. For the United States, the most significant of these laws of extraterritorial application are the antitrust laws.

As you may recall from Chapter 48, United States antitrust laws prohibit certain agreements in restraint of trade and the monopolization of markets. Under recent legislation, extraterritorial application may exist when international conduct that would violate our antitrust laws "has a direct, substantial, and reasonably foreseeable effect" on business in the United States.[9] As is illustrated by the following case, U.S.-based multinational companies may not be able to insulate their activities abroad from the application of U.S. antitrust laws.

---

6. 3 U.S.T. 2517, T.I.A.S. No. 6997.

7. 9 U.S.C. Sections 201–208.

8. Final Act (April 10, 1980), U.N. Doc. A/Conf. 9 7/18, reprinted in 19 International Legal Materials 668 (1980).

9. 15 U.S.C. Section 6a.

Case 58.4
TIMBERLANE LUMBER CO. v. BANK OF AMERICA, N.T. & S.A.
United States Court of Appeals, Ninth Circuit, 1976.
549 F.2d 597.

BACKGROUND AND FACTS *Timberlane Lumber Company brought an antitrust action, arguing that officials of the Bank of America and others located in both the United States and Honduras conspired to prevent Timberlane from milling lumber in Honduras and exporting it to the United States, thereby maintaining control of the Honduran lumber export business in the hands of a few select individuals financed and controlled by the bank. This conspiracy, Timberlane argued, violated the U.S. antitrust laws and directly affected lumber prices in the U.S. market. The defendant bank argued that the injuries to Timberlane resulted from acts of the Honduran government, which should be beyond the jurisdiction of U.S. courts. The district court held for the defendant bank and dismissed the complaint. Timberlane appealed.*

CHOY, Judge.
* * * *

That American law covers some conduct beyond this nation's borders does not mean that it embraces all * * *. Extraterritorial application is understandably a matter of concern for the other countries involved. Those nations have sometimes resented and protested, as excessive intrusions into their own spheres, broad assertions of authority by American courts. * * *
* * * *

Even among American courts and commentators, however, there is no consensus on how far the jurisdiction should extend. The district court here concluded that a "direct and substantial effect" on United States foreign commerce was a prerequisite, without stating whether other factors were relevant or considered. * * *
* * * *

The effects test by itself is incomplete because it fails to consider other nations' interests. Nor does it expressly take into account the full nature of the relationship between the actors and this country. Whether the alleged offender is an American citizen, for instance, may make a big difference; applying American laws to American citizens raises fewer problems than application to foreigners. * * *
* * * *

A tripartite analysis seems to be indicated. As acknowledged above, the antitrust laws require in the first instance that there be *some* effect—actual or intended—on American foreign commerce before the federal courts may legitimately exercise subject matter jurisdiction under those statutes. Second, a greater showing of burden or restraint may be necessary to demonstrate that the effect is sufficiently large to present a cognizable injury to the plaintiffs and, therefore, a civil *violation* of the antitrust laws. Third, there is the additional question which is unique to the international setting of whether the interests of, and links to, the United States—including the magnitude of the effect on American foreign commerce—are sufficiently strong, vis-á-vis those of other nations, to justify an assertion of extraterritorial authority.
* * * *

The elements to be weighed include the degree of conflict with foreign law or policy, the nationality or allegiance of the parties and the locations or principal places of business of corporations, the extent to which enforcement by either state can be expected to achieve compliance, the relative significance of effects on the United States as compared with those elsewhere, the extent to which there is explicit purpose to harm or affect American commerce, the foreseeability of such effect, and the relative importance to the violations charged of conduct within the United States as compared with conduct abroad.

DECISION AND REMEDY *The court of appeals set aside the dismissal of Timberlane's claim because the district court had failed to consider all relevant factors. The case was remanded to the district court for further proceedings consistent with the opinion.*

Remember that the act of state or sovereign immunity doctrines may provide a defense to the extraterritorial application of antitrust laws to the actions of foreign governments. International organizations that control the price of raw materials, such as the Organization of Petroleum Exporting Countries (OPEC), may violate U.S. antitrust laws yet still be exempt from enforcement action. Private companies subject to foreign sovereign compulsion in pricing are likewise exempt.

IMPORT RESTRICTIONS

Virtually all countries, including the United States, place some restrictions on the importation of products and services. Nations may place a quota, or numerical limit, on imports. In recent years, Japan has abided by a "voluntary" quota on the number of Japanese cars imported into the United States. Nations also may place a tariff, or tax, on imported goods. Most of the world's leading trading nations abide by the General Agreement on Tariffs and Trade (GATT), which is designed to minimize trade barriers among nations. GATT was originally drafted in 1947 and has been renegotiated since. Major renegotiations in 1964–1967 created across-the-board tariff reductions among member countries, and others, in 1973–1979, instituted controls over nontariff barriers to trade.

Notwithstanding GATT, the United States has some specific laws aimed at what we consider unfair international trade practices. Some products may be "dumped" in the U.S. market. **Dumping** occurs when a foreign producer sells goods in our country at a price below the price of those goods in the exporting country. This practice is designed to underprice U.S. companies and thus seize a greater share of the large U.S. market.

The U.S. government has attempted to control this practice ever since the Antidumping Act of 1921.[10] Under current law, a U.S. company that is materially injured may complain of dumping to a federal agency known as the International Trade Commission (ITC). The ITC was established in 1974 and consists of six persons appointed by the president with the advice and consent of the Senate. If the ITC finds that unlawful dumping of foreign products has occurred, the Secretary of the Treasury may establish an extra tariff—known as an antidumping duty—on the imported goods in question. The duty is to equal the difference between the price charged in the United States and the price at which the goods are sold to consumers in the exporting country. Assessment of this duty may be retroactive to cover past dumping as well. Retroactive antidumping duties were imposed in the following case.

---

10. 19 U.S.C. Section 160 *et seq.*

BACKGROUND AND FACTS *ICC Industries was an importer of potassium permanganate from the People's Republic of China (PRC). The International Trade Administration (ITA) of the Department of Commerce conducted an antidumping investigation and concluded that this potassium permanganate was being imported at less than fair value (LTFV), in violation of U.S. law. Fair value is an estimate of the value of the product in the home market—in this case, the People's Republic of China. As a consequence of its investigation of ICC, the ITA imposed retroactive antidumping duties on its imports of potassium permanganate for the period 1981–1983. Imposition of these duties required a finding that ICC had known or should have known that the product was being imported at less than fair value. ICC argued that it was unaware of this fact. ICC emphasized that, since the People's Republic of China had a non-market economy, the company was unable to ascertain a home market value for potassium permanganate. ICC therefore appealed the ITA's order.*

Case 58.5
ICC INDUSTRIES, INC. v. UNITED STATES
United States Court of Appeals, Federal Circuit, 1987.
812 F.2d 694.

BISSELL, Judge.
* * * *

We address first whether the importers knew or should have known of the dumping. The antidumping statutes impose a duty when a foreign producer prices the exported merchandise at LTFV and sales of that merchandise cause or threaten to cause material injury to a domestic industry. Fair value is intended to be an estimate of foreign market value. Fair value can be based on several different factors. "[D]umping is generally defined to exist when the foreign market value is higher than the purchase price in the United States." We find unpersuasive the importers' argument that because the merchandise was imported from a non-market economy (NME) country they could never know that the merchandise is being imported below fair value. *   *   *
* * * *

*   *   * [In] NME countries, there is no home market price to which the United States price can be compared. Home market prices and costs are meaningless as a source of "fair value" in NME countries in view of the level of intervention by the government in setting relative prices. *   *   * Consequently, the statute requires the ITA to identify "surrogate" producers in market economy countries and to compare the prices of the NME country's imports to the prices charged by the surrogate.
* * * *

The importers assert that they did not know the price of potassium permanganate in the PRC. Notwithstanding, these importers averred to the "competitive" nature of the prices at which they purchased potassium permanganate and, in fact, knew the prices of this merchandise in Europe and the United States. The importers knew that:
(1) Spain and the PRC were the primary sources other than [one of ICC Industries' competitors] of this product in the United States.
(2) Spain is not a state controlled economy country.
(3) [D]uring the period of March–July, 1983, the unit price of potassium permanganate was 22% less than that imported from Spain and nearly 40% less than the price of the domestic product.
* * * *

This level of underselling, in this commercial environment, while under this administrative scrutiny, is sufficient to support the ITA's conclusion that these importers should have known that they were importing potassium permanganate at LTFV. Since importers have failed to point to any legal error in ITA's estimate of foreign market value, we hold that the conclusion reached by the ITA and affirmed by the trial court is supported by substantial evidence.

**DECISION
AND REMEDY**   *The court of appeals affirmed the International Trade Administration's order imposing antidumping duties.*

FOREIGN CORRUPT PRACTICES ACT

In 1977, Congress enacted the Foreign Corrupt Practices Act (FCPA). This law was passed as a result of public concern over the fact that U.S. corporations and businesspersons were bribing overseas government officials to obtain contracts and favors from their governments.

The FCPA prohibits American businesses from making payments to any official of a foreign government, if the purpose of the payments is to get that official to act in his or her official capacity to provide business opportunities. The FCPA also contains detailed bookkeeping requirements to ensure that any such payments will be uncovered. Companies in violation of the act may be fined up to $1 million, and business officers who willfully violate the act may be fined up to $10,000 and imprisoned for up to five years.

QUESTIONS AND CASE PROBLEMS

1. Suppose that Arnold Roth enters into an agreement to purchase sixty crates of widgets from Manufacturers, Inc. Roth secures an irrevocable letter of credit from Sunnydays Bank. When Manufacturers, Inc., places the sixty crates of widgets on board a steamship, it receives in return the invoices required under the letter of credit. Roth subsequently learns that Manufacturers, Inc., has filled the sixty crates with rubbish—not widgets. Given the fact that an issuer's obligation under a letter of credit is independent of the underlying contract between the buyer and seller, will the issuer be required to pay the draft? See UCC 5-114(2)(a).

2. Verlinden B.V., a Dutch corporation, entered into a contract for the purchase of 240,000 metric tons of cement by the Federal Republic of Nigeria. Verlinden B.V. subsequently sued the Central Bank of Nigeria in a U.S. federal court, alleging that the bank's actions constituted an anticipatory breach. Did Congress exceed the scope of Article III of the U.S. Constitution by granting federal district courts jurisdiction over actions brought by foreign corporations against foreign sovereigns? [Verlinden B.V. v. Central Bank of Nigeria, 461 U.S. 480, 103 S.Ct. 1962, 76 L.Ed.2d 81 (1983)]

3. Issues frequently arise as to whether a particular instrument is a letter of credit or an ordinary guaranty contract. A letter of credit creates a primary liability, whereas a guaranty contract imposes a secondary liability on the preexisting obligation of another. State statutes prohibit banks from guarantying the debt of another. Consider an instrument that is labeled a letter of credit. Further assume that the instrument requires the bank (issuer) physically to verify that certain business transactions have occurred. Is such an instrument a letter of credit or an ordinary guaranty contract? [Wichita Eagle & Beacon Publishing Co. v. Pacific National Bank of San Francisco, 493 F.2d 1285 (9th Cir. 1974)]

4. Section 1610(d)(1) of the Foreign Sovereign Immunities Act (FSIA) provides that the property of a foreign state that is used for commercial activity in the United States is not immune from attachment prior to the entry of a judgment if the foreign state has "explicitly waived its immunity from attachment prior to judgment." Banco Nacional, an instrumentality of the government of Costa Rica, entered into a written agreement with Libra Bank, LTD, the plaintiffs. In the agreement, Banco Nacional stated that it did not have "any right of immunity from suit from respect to the Borrower's obligations" under this particular agreement. Did Banco Nacional, the defendant, "explicitly" waive its immunity from prejudgment attachment as required by the FSIA? [Libra Bank, Ltd. v. Banco Nacional de Costa Rica, S.A., 676 F.2d 47 (2d Cir. 1982)]

5. The Swiss Credit Bank issued a letter of credit in favor of Antex Industries to cover the sale of 92,000 electronic integrated circuits manufactured by Electronic Arrays. The letter of credit specified that the chips would be transported to Tokyo by ship. Antex shipped the circuits by air. Payment on the letter of credit was dishonored because the shipment by air did not fulfill the precise terms of the letter of credit. Should a court compel payment? [Board of Trade of San Francisco v. Swiss Credit Bank, 728 F.2d 1241 (9th Cir. 1984)]

6. Both Mannington Mills and Congoleum Corporation are American producers of carpets and other floor coverings. Mannington alleged that Congoleum had fraudulently obtained foreign patents through false statements and misrepresentation of data. Mannington sued Congoleum, arguing that these actions violated U.S. antitrust laws. Congoleum argued that the U.S. courts had no jurisdiction. Congoleum contended that issuance of foreign patents came under the act of state doctrine or, at least, required deference to foreign nations. Should the U.S. exercise jurisdiction over this dispute? [Mannington Mills, Inc. v. Congoleum Corp., 595 F.2d 1287 (3d Cir. 1979)]

7. Alberto-Culver Company is an American company that manufactures and sells hair products. The company purchased three overseas businesses from Fritz Scherk, a German citizen. The contract provided that disputes were to be arbitrated before the International Chamber of Commerce in Paris. A year later, Alberto-Culver discovered that trademark rights purchased under the contract were much more limited than it had been led to understand. Alberto-Culver sued Scherk for securities fraud in federal district court in Illinois. Scherk moved for dismissal, contending that the case should be arbitrated. Alberto-Culver noted that parties could not waive their rights to judicial enforcement of the securities laws. Should the court grant Scherk's motion for dismissal? [Scherk v. Alberto-Culver Co., 417 U.S. 506, 94 S.Ct. 2449, 41 L.Ed.2d 270 (1974)]

8. American manufacturers of television sets brought suit against Japanese manufacturers, alleging that the Japanese manufacturers had illegally conspired to drive the American manufacturers from the American market by engaging in a predatory pricing scheme. Allegedly, the Japanese manufacturers conspired to fix and maintain artificially high prices for television sets they sold in Japan and, at the same time, to fix and maintain low prices for the sets they exported to and sold in the United States. Should the U.S. courts find the Japanese manufacturers in violation of U.S. antitrust laws? [Matsushita Electric Industrial Co. v. Zenith Radio Corp., 475 U.S. 574, 106 S.Ct. 1348, 89 L.Ed.2d 538 (1986)]

9. DBM Drilling Corporation contracted to purchase a drilling rig from GATX Leasing Corporation. DBM arranged with Frost National Bank to issue an irrevocable letter of credit to GATX to pay for the rig. GATX complied with all the provisions of the letter of credit. DBM argued, however, that the oil rig itself did not comply with the terms of the underlying contract between DBM and GATX. DBM therefore sued to enjoin the bank from paying GATX under the letter of credit. Should the court issue such an injunction? [GATX Leasing Corp. v. DBM Drilling Corp., 657 S.W.2d 178 (Tex.App. 1983)]

10. ☐ The Bank of Jamaica, which is wholly owned by the government of Jamaica, contracted with Chisholm & Company in January of 1981 for Chisholm to arrange for lines of credit from various U.S. banks and obtain $50 million in credit insurance from the Export-Import Bank of the United States. This Chisholm successfully did, but subsequently the deals arranged for by Chisholm were refused by the Bank of Jamaica. The bank had decided to do its own negotiating while having Chisholm work as well. When the bank refused to pay Chisholm for its services, Chisholm brought an action to obtain relief for the bank's breach of the implied contract. The Bank of Jamaica brought a motion to dismiss, claiming sovereign immunity and state action (act of state doctrine) as defenses. Discuss whether the Bank of Jamaica is immune from Chisholm's action for breach of contract in a U.S. federal court. [Chisholm & Co. v. Bank of Jamaica, 643 F.Supp. 1393 (S.D.Fla. 1986)]

Focus on Ethics

Special Topics and the Application of Ethics

Unique situations present special ethical problems. In this final *Focus on Ethics,* we consider a few special legal and ethical situations.

COMPUTER PIRACY

Tremendous growth in the microcomputer industry in recent years has raised numerous ethical considerations. Many people claim that copyright law has failed to keep up with the unethical behavior that is now possible in our legal system. Some types of computer programs are protected under the copyright laws; yet computer software can exist in several forms. In the past, manufacturers of computer software marketed their programs in an unreadable form stored in a silicon chip. But now technology has advanced to the point at which programs stored in these silicon chips can be "pirated."

Manufacturers have sought to "copy protect" their software. This means programming, or "locking," the disk, so that it cannot be copied. Copy protection has largely failed, however, and has created a new market in programs that "crack" the copy-protection codes. Do you think it is ethical for a company to make money

by selling computer programs that defeat copy-protection systems?

THE "LIVING WILL"

In recent years, ethical and legal issues surrounding the "right to die" have received considerable attention. In a recent California episode, a father had terminal cancer of the esophagus and lacked the capacity to act. His son, acting on previously expressed wishes of the father, forced a nurse at gunpoint to disconnect the mechanical ventilator that was keeping his comatose father alive. The son was subsequently charged with murder. This is an extreme example of a recurring problem, and the law has developed the "living will" to try to deal with this problem.

Wills generally deal solely with the distribution of property and take effect *only* upon a client's death. The living will, however, takes effect during the client's lifetime and concerns the *person,* rather than the *estate,* of the client.

The living will permits the client's physician to withhold or to terminate medical care when such care does not appear to be in the patient's interest and, moreover, is simply prolonging life. To put it mildly, this type of

will is very controversial. Many people feel that it is morally wrong to allow a person to consent to the withholding or termination of medical care and treatment. Thus, the question arises: Should we allow members of our society to obtain living wills? Quite often we do protect people from themselves, as is illustrated by the fact that people are required to wear motorcycle helmets and seat belts in many states and by the fact that many drugs are legally prohibited.

Furthermore, even if we conclude that the option of procuring a living will is acceptable in our society, the questions arise as to how and to what extent we want to recognize the use of living wills. On October 1, 1984, the Wisconsin Natural Death Act became effective. This act sets forth a procedure for obtaining and signing a living will. In addition, the act includes a specific form that may be used by attorneys, clients, and health care providers. Yet whenever a statute expresses a specific form for dealing with a particular situation, many people are reluctant to seek out variations on the statutory forms.

The question of restrictions upon living wills must be

considered. At what point should we allow termination of life-sustaining procedures? The Wisconsin act, for example, allows life-sustaining procedures to be terminated only if two physicians agree that death will occur within thirty days. The act also permits some kinds of life-support systems to be terminated, but not others. Yet why should we draw the lines here? Some people have suggested that we should ask whether the brain is functioning and whether there is any expectation that the patient will continue to enjoy what is truly life in determining who among us should live or die. Drawing these types of lines is extremely difficult.

It is not unheard of for a young, healthy individual to be injured in a severe automobile accident or to become a victim of a terminal disease. Thus, any individual should be aware of the position of his or her state with respect to living wills. If individuals are dissatisfied with the requirements and guidelines of a particular state's living-will statute or with the fact that a state does not have one, the possibility of amendment or enactment of a statute is always present. As stated throughout these sections on ethics, the law gradually evolves in order to embody society's changing perceptions of what is ethical.

THE BREADTH OF ACCOUNTANTS' ETHICAL RESPONSIBILITIES

Traditionally, accountants have been considered to be professionals—much like doctors or lawyers. Members of these professions have always considered their clients' welfare to be their foremost responsibility. Thus, a lawyer will zealously defend even a client whom he or she believes

to be guilty. A doctor will exert his or her greatest efforts on behalf of any human being without considering the external social consequences of treatment. Similarly, accountants have acted at the behest of their clients.

This client-centered ethic has spawned conflicts in the accounting profession. Third parties frequently rely on accounting statements to help them make essential investment decisions. The accountant who prepares misleading statements, at the request of a client, is participating in the fraud perpetrated on these individuals. Moreover, such an extreme devotion to clients threatens the credibility of the entire accounting profession. The law has recognized to some extent an accountant's liability to third parties.

Placing limits on accountants' representation of clients is not inconsistent with professionalism. Even lawyers face limits in their defense of their clients. For example, a lawyer cannot steal or destroy evidence to advance a client's interest. Similarly, in some circumstances, ethical duties to third parties may supersede an accountant's responsibility to his or her client.

Recognition of an accountant's responsibility to third parties is an important step but an incomplete one. Accountants remain confidential advisors and advocates for their clients. Fairness to third parties may demand the disclosure of negative facts or future prospects about the client. Although accountants may not participate in fraud, deciding what facts must be disclosed on statements can be difficult. Frequently, the significance or materiality of financial facts or future prospects is debatable.

Must the accountant undertake a complete and independent evaluation of all such facts before deciding whether disclosure is necessary?

THE FOREIGN CORRUPT PRACTICES ACT

Congress has attempted to legislate international ethics in the Foreign Corrupt Practices Act (FCPA). Broadly speaking, this act prohibits U.S. companies from bribing foreign governments for contracts or other favors. Prior to passage of the act, such payments were relatively commonplace and an accepted cost of doing business.

American firms have voiced frustration with the act. Foreign officials in some countries have traditionally expected payments for consideration in doing business. Such payments are not always considered unethical behavior in some countries but rather a supplemental tax for the use of official services. Higher-level officials may be fully aware of such payments and implicitly authorize them.

The FCPA only prohibits U.S. firms from making such payments—it cannot prevent foreign officials from expecting or demanding them. Thus, the act may not prevent overseas bribery but may merely shift such actions from U.S. to foreign corporations, thus placing American corporations at a competitive disadvantage in international trade. This disadvantage is especially undesirable in view of America's ongoing balance-of-payments deficit.

Business officials have experienced an additional ethical dilemma. An employee of an American corporation has a fiduciary duty to the corporation's shareholders. Yet the FCPA may prevent the employee from making sure the company competes effectively. The problem is further complicated when the U.S. firm can provide the best products or services to the foreign country. In this instance, the FCPA may injure the American company, its workers, and the foreign purchaser as well. Congress recently has amended the FCPA to reduce record-keeping requirements, but the fundamental proscription on bribery remains. Is bribery always unethical or can it be justified by the benefits that may result?

ETHICS IN INTERNATIONAL TRADE

The American government has become increasingly active in protecting consumers and the environment from hazardous products and industrial processes. Many foreign governments, however, lack the capability or the will to provide similar protections. As a consequence, U.S. firms may sell seemingly hazardous products overseas with little or no regulation.

Suppose that the U.S. government discovers that a pesticide causes cancer and prohibits the use of the chemical in this nation. The pesticide producer may have large stocks of the chemical in inventory. Moreover, sales of the chemical may be quite profitable for the company. Suppose that the producer elects to sell its inventory overseas or even to continue producing the pesticide

for foreign sales. Is this action ethical? Should not the company at least warn the foreign buyers of the cancer risk? Or should the company simply leave the matter in the hands of the foreign government?

Some persons have suggested that the United States should prohibit exports of any products banned for domestic use. Bear in mind, however, that foreign circumstances may differ from those in the United States. For example, the United States banned the pesticide DDT, primarily because of its adverse effects on wildlife. In Asia, however, DDT was a critical component of the mosquito control necessary to combat malaria. Perhaps foreign citizens would conclude that the benefits of a hazardous product outweigh the risks that it presents.

DISCUSSION QUESTIONS

1. An accounting firm is hired to prepare statements for a major company. A group of employees has recently sued the company, claiming sex discrimination and asking for millions of dollars in damages. The company and its lawyers assure the accountants that the lawsuit is frivolous and need not be disclosed as a future potential liability. Should the accountants seek an outside, independent assessment of the litigation to determine whether the potential liability should be disclosed?

2. What are the broader ethical implications of living wills? Is there a risk that withdrawing medical care will lead to less respect for human life? If so, might this precedent endanger other relatively powerless groups, such as the mentally disabled?

3. Suppose a foreign government official demands that a U.S. company make a payment to him before it can be granted a contract to provide water-supply facilities for the foreign nation. This payment would violate the Foreign Corrupt Practices Act. Company officials know that their company's bid is the lowest and believe that their company can do the best job of constructing the facilities. These officials further believe that the payment can be made secretly. Failure to make the payment will mean that the job will be given to a higher bidder from a European nation. Should the officials make the payment if they are unlikely to be caught?

4. Cigarette consumption in the United States has declined in the face of fears about the effects of smoking on health. Cigarette companies may, however, increase sales in foreign countries, where the health risks of smoking are less well known. Should cigarette companies include health warnings on all packs of cigarettes sold overseas, even though that country's law does not require this action? Is the warning alone enough to fulfill the companies' ethical obligations?

THE CONSTITUTION OF THE UNITED STATES

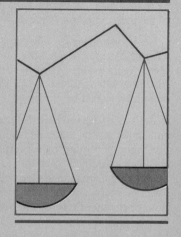

PREAMBLE

We the People of the United States, in Order to form a more perfect Union, establish Justice, insure domestic Tranquility, provide for the common defence, promote the general Welfare, and secure the Blessings of Liberty to ourselves and our Posterity, do ordain and establish this Constitution for the United States of America.

ARTICLE I

Section 1. All legislative Powers herein granted shall be vested in a Congress of the United States, which shall consist of a Senate and House of Representatives.

Section 2. The House of Representatives shall be composed of Members chosen every second Year by the People of the several States, and the Electors in each State shall have the Qualifications requisite for Electors of the most numerous Branch of the State Legislature.

No Person shall be a Representative who shall not have attained to the Age of twenty five Years, and been seven Years a Citizen of the United States, and who shall not, when elected, be an Inhabitant of that State in which he shall be chosen.

Representatives and direct Taxes shall be apportioned among the several States which may be included within this Union, according to their respective Numbers, which shall be determined by adding to the whole Number of free Persons, including those bound to Service for a Term of Years, and excluding Indians not taxed, three fifths of all other Persons. The actual Enumeration shall be made within three Years after the first Meeting of the Congress of the United States, and within every subsequent Term of ten Years, in such Manner as they shall by Law direct. The Number of Representatives shall not exceed one for every thirty Thousand, but each State shall have at Least one Representative; and until such enumeration shall be made, the State of New Hampshire shall be entitled to chuse three, Massachusetts eight, Rhode Island and Providence Plantations one, Connecticut five, New York six, New Jersey four, Pennsylvania eight, Delaware one, Maryland six, Virginia ten, North Carolina five, South Carolina five, and Georgia three.

When vacancies happen in the Representation from any State, the Executive Authority thereof shall issue Writs of Election to fill such Vacancies.

The House of Representatives shall chuse their Speaker and other Officers; and shall have the sole Power of Impeachment.

Section 3. The Senate of the United States shall be composed of two Senators from each State, chosen by the Legislature thereof, for six Years; and each Senator shall have one Vote.

Immediately after they shall be assembled in Consequence of the first Election, they shall be divided as equally as may be into three Classes. The Seats of the Senators of the first Class shall be vacated at the Expiration of the second Year, of the second Class at the Expiration of the fourth Year, and of the third Class at the Expiration of the sixth Year, so that one third may be chosen every second Year; and if Vacancies happen by Resignation, or otherwise, during the Recess of the Legislature of any State, the Executive thereof may make temporary Appointments until the next Meeting of the Legislature, which shall then fill such Vacancies.

No Person shall be a Senator who shall not have attained to the Age of thirty Years, and been nine Years a Citizen of the United States, and who shall not, when elected, be an Inhabitant of that State for which he shall be chosen.

The Vice President of the United States shall be President of the Senate, but shall have no Vote, unless they be equally divided.

The Senate shall chuse their other Officers, and also a President pro tempore, in the Absence of the Vice President, or when he shall exercise the Office of President of the United States.

The Senate shall have the sole Power to try all Impeachments. When sitting for that Purpose, they shall be on Oath or Affirmation. When the President of the United States is tried, the Chief Justice shall preside: And no Person shall be convicted without the Concurrence of two thirds of the Members present.

Judgment in Cases of Impeachment shall not extend further than to removal from Office, and disqualification to hold and enjoy any Office of honor, Trust, or Profit under the United States: but the Party convicted shall nevertheless be liable and subject to Indictment, Trial, Judgment, and Punishment, according to Law.

Section 4. The Times, Places and Manner of holding Elections for Senators and Representatives, shall be prescribed in each State by the Legislature thereof; but the Congress may at any time by Law make or alter such Regulations, except as to the Places of chusing Senators.

The Congress shall assemble at least once in every Year, and such Meeting shall be on the first Monday in December, unless they shall by Law appoint a different Day.

Section 5. Each House shall be the Judge of the Elections, Returns, and Qualifications of its own Members, and a Majority of each shall constitute a Quorum to do Business; but a smaller Number may adjourn from day to day, and may be authorized to compel the Attendance of absent Members, in such Manner, and under such Penalties as each House may provide.

Each House may determine the Rules of its Proceedings, punish its Members for disorderly Behavior, and, with the Concurrence of two thirds, expel a Member.

Each House shall keep a Journal of its Proceedings, and from time to time publish the same, excepting such Parts as may in their Judgment require Secrecy; and the Yeas and Nays of the Members of either House on any question shall, at the Desire of one fifth of those Present, be entered on the Journal.

Neither House, during the Session of Congress, shall, without the Consent of the other, adjourn for more than three days, nor to any other Place than that in which the two Houses shall be sitting.

Section 6. The Senators and Representatives shall receive a Compensation for their Services, to be ascertained by Law, and paid out of the Treasury of the United States. They shall in all Cases, except Treason, Felony and Breach of the Peace, be privileged from Arrest during their Attendance at the Session of their respective Houses, and in going to and returning from the same; and for any Speech or Debate in either House, they shall not be questioned in any other Place.

No Senator or Representative shall, during the Time for which he was elected, be appointed to any civil Office under the Authority of the United States, which shall have been created, or the Emoluments whereof shall have been increased during such time; and no Person holding any Office under the United States, shall be a Member of either House during his Continuance in Office.

Section 7. All Bills for raising Revenue shall originate in the House of Representatives; but the Senate may propose or concur with Amendments as on other Bills.

Every Bill which shall have passed the House of Representatives and the Senate, shall, before it become a Law, be presented to the President of the United States; If he approve he shall sign it, but if not he shall return it, with his Objections to the House in which it shall have originated, who shall enter the Objections at large on their Journal, and proceed to reconsider it. If after such Reconsideration two thirds of that House shall agree to pass the Bill, it shall be sent together with the Objections, to the other House, by which it shall likewise be reconsidered, and if approved by two thirds of that House, it shall become a Law. But in all such Cases the Votes of both Houses shall be determined by Yeas and Nays, and the Names of the Persons voting for and against the Bill shall be entered on the Journal of each House respectively. If any Bill shall not be returned by the President within ten Days (Sundays excepted) after it shall have been presented to him, the Same shall be a Law, in like Manner as if he had signed it, unless the Congress by their Adjournment prevent its Return in which Case it shall not be a Law.

Every Order, Resolution, or Vote, to which the Concurrence of the Senate and House of Representatives may be necessary (except on a question of Adjournment) shall be presented to the President of the United States; and before the Same shall take Effect, shall be approved by him, or being disapproved by him, shall be repassed by two thirds of the Senate and House of Representatives, according to the Rules and Limitations prescribed in the Case of a Bill.

Section 8. The Congress shall have Power To lay and collect Taxes, Duties, Imposts and Excises, to pay the Debts and provide for the common Defence and general Welfare of the United States; but all Duties, Imposts and Excises shall be uniform throughout the United States;

To borrow Money on the credit of the United States;

To regulate Commerce with foreign Nations, and among the several States, and with the Indian Tribes;

To establish an uniform Rule of Naturalization, and uniform Laws on the subject of Bankruptcies throughout the United States;

To coin Money, regulate the Value thereof, and of foreign Coin, and fix the Standard of Weights and Measures;

To provide for the Punishment of counterfeiting the Securities and current Coin of the United States;

To establish Post Offices and post Roads;

To promote the Progress of Science and useful Arts, by securing for limited Times to Authors and Inventors the exclusive Right to their respective Writings and Discoveries;

To constitute Tribunals inferior to the supreme Court;

To define and punish Piracies and Felonies committed on the high Seas, and Offenses against the Law of Nations;

To declare War, grant Letters of Marque and Reprisal, and make Rules concerning Captures on Land and Water;

To raise and support Armies, but no Appropriation of Money to that Use shall be for a longer Term than two Years;

To provide and maintain a Navy;

To make Rules for the Government and Regulation of the land and naval Forces;

To provide for calling forth the Militia to execute the Laws of the Union, suppress Insurrections and repel Invasions;

To provide for organizing, arming, and disciplining, the Militia, and for governing such Part of them as may be employed in the Service of the United States, reserving to the States respectively, the Appointment of the Officers, and the Authority of training the Militia according to the discipline prescribed by Congress;

To exercise exclusive Legislation in all Cases whatsoever, over such District (not exceeding ten Miles square) as may, by Cession of particular States, and the Acceptance of Congress, become the Seat of the Government of the United States, and to exercise like Authority over all Places purchased by the Consent of the Legislature of the State in which the Same shall be, for the Erection of Forts, Magazines, Arsenals, dock-Yards, and other needful Buildings;—And

To make all Laws which shall be necessary and proper for carrying into Execution the foregoing Powers, and all other Powers vested by this Constitution in the Government of the United States, or in any Department or Officer thereof.

Section 9. The Migration or Importation of such Persons as any of the States now existing shall think proper to admit, shall not be prohibited by the Congress prior to the Year one thousand eight hundred and eight, but a Tax or duty may be imposed on such Importation, not exceeding ten dollars for each Person.

The privilege of the Writ of Habeas Corpus shall not be suspended, unless when in Cases of Rebellion or Invasion the public Safety may require it.

No Bill of Attainder or ex post facto Law shall be passed.

No Capitation, or other direct, Tax shall be laid, unless in Proportion to the Census or Enumeration herein before directed to be taken.

No Tax or Duty shall be laid on Articles exported from any State.

No Preference shall be given by any Regulation of Commerce or Revenue to the Ports of one State over those of another: nor shall Vessels bound to, or from, one State be obliged to enter, clear, or pay Duties in another.

No Money shall be drawn from the Treasury, but in Consequence of Appropriations made by Law; and a regular Statement and Account of the Receipts and Expenditures of all public Money shall be published from time to time.

No Title of Nobility shall be granted by the United States: And no Person holding any Office of Profit or Trust under them, shall, without the Consent of the Congress, accept of any present, Emolument, Office, or Title, of any kind whatever, from any King, Prince, or foreign State.

Section 10. No State shall enter into any Treaty, Alliance, or Confederation; grant Letters of Marque and Reprisal; coin Money; emit Bills of Credit; make any Thing but gold and silver Coin a Tender in Payment of Debts; pass any Bill of Attainder, ex post facto Law, or Law impairing the Obligation of Contracts, or grant any Title of Nobility.

No State shall, without the Consent of the Congress, lay any Imposts or Duties on Imports or Exports, except what may be absolutely necessary for executing it's inspection Laws: and the net Produce of all Duties and Imposts, laid by any State on Imports or Exports, shall be for the Use of the Treasury of the United States; and all such Laws shall be subject to the Revision and Controul of the Congress.

No State shall, without the Consent of Congress, lay any Duty of Tonnage, keep Troops, or Ships of War in time of Peace, enter into any Agreement or Compact with another State, or with a foreign Power, or engage in War, unless actually invaded, or in such imminent Danger as will not admit of delay.

ARTICLE II

Section 1. The executive Power shall be vested in a President of the United States of America. He shall hold his Office during the Term of four Years, and, together with the Vice President, chosen for the same Term, be elected, as follows:

Each State shall appoint, in such Manner as the Legislature thereof may direct, a Number of Electors, equal to the whole Number of Senators and Representatives to which the State may be entitled in the Congress; but no Senator or Representative, or Person holding an Office of Trust or Profit under the United States, shall be appointed an Elector.

The Electors shall meet in their respective States, and vote by Ballot for two Persons, of whom one at least shall not be an Inhabitant of the same State with themselves. And they shall make a List of all the Persons voted for, and of the Number of Votes for each; which List they shall sign and certify, and transmit sealed to the Seat of the Government of the United States, directed to the President of the Senate. The President of the Senate shall, in the Presence of the Senate and House of Representatives, open all the Certificates, and the Votes shall then be counted. The Person having the greatest Number of Votes shall be the President, if such Number be a Majority of the whole Number of Electors appointed; and if there be more than one who have such Majority, and have an equal Number of Votes, then the House of Representatives shall immediately chuse by Ballot one of them for President; and if no Person have a Majority, then from the five highest on the List the said House shall in like Manner chuse the President.

But in chusing the President, the Votes shall be taken by States, the Representation from each State having one Vote; A quorum for this Purpose shall consist of a Member or Members from two thirds of the States, and a Majority of all the States shall be necessary to a Choice. In every Case, after the Choice of the President, the Person having the greater Number of Votes of the Electors shall be the Vice President. But if there should remain two or more who have equal Votes, the Senate shall chuse from them by Ballot the Vice President.

The Congress may determine the Time of chusing the Electors, and the Day on which they shall give their Votes; which Day shall be the same throughout the United States.

No person except a natural born Citizen, or a Citizen of the United States, at the time of the Adoption of this Constitution, shall be eligible to the Office of President; neither shall any Person be eligible to that Office who shall not have attained to the Age of thirty five Years, and been fourteen Years a Resident within the United States.

In Case of the Removal of the President from Office, or of his Death, Resignation or Inability to discharge the Powers and Duties of the said Office, the same shall devolve on the Vice President, and the Congress may by Law provide for the Case of Removal, Death, Resignation or Inability, both of the President and Vice President, declaring what Officer shall then act as President, and such Officer shall act accordingly, until the Disability be removed, or a President shall be elected.

The President shall, at stated Times, receive for his Services, a Compensation, which shall neither be increased nor diminished during the Period for which he shall have been elected, and he shall not receive within that Period any other Emolument from the United States, or any of them.

Before he enter on the Execution of his Office, he shall take the following Oath or Affirmation: "I do solemnly swear (or affirm) that I will faithfully execute the Office of President of the United States, and will to the best of my Ability, preserve, protect and defend the Constitution of the United States."

Section 2.   The President shall be Commander in Chief of the Army and Navy of the United States, and of the Militia of the several States, when called into the actual Service of the United States; he may require the Opinion, in writing, of the principal Officer in each of the executive Departments, upon any Subject relating to the Duties of their respective Offices, and he shall have Power to grant Reprieves and Pardons for Offenses against the United States, except in Cases of Impeachment.

He shall have Power, by and with the Advice and Consent of the Senate to make Treaties, provided two thirds of the Senators present concur; and he shall nominate, and by and with the Advice and Consent of the Senate, shall appoint Ambassadors, other public Ministers and Consuls, Judges of the supreme Court, and all other Officers of the United States, whose Appointments are not herein otherwise provided for, and which shall be established by Law; but the Congress may by Law vest the Appointment of such inferior Officers, as they think proper, in the President alone, in the Courts of Law, or in the Heads of Departments.

The President shall have Power to fill up all Vacancies that may happen during the Recess of the Senate, by granting Commissions which shall expire at the End of their next Session.

Section 3.   He shall from time to time give to the Congress Information of the State of the Union, and recommend to their Consideration such Measures as he shall judge necessary and expedient; he may, on extraordinary Occasions, convene both Houses, or either of them, and in Case of Disagreement between them, with Respect to the Time of Adjournment, he may adjourn them to such Time as he shall think proper; he shall receive Ambassadors and other public Ministers; he shall take Care that the Laws be faithfully executed, and shall Commission all the Officers of the United States.

Section 4.   The President, Vice President and all civil Officers of the United States, shall be removed from Office on Impeachment for, and Conviction of, Treason, Bribery, or other high Crimes and Misdemeanors.

ARTICLE III

Section 1.   The judicial Power of the United States, shall be vested in one supreme Court, and in such inferior Courts as the Congress may from time to time ordain and establish. The Judges, both of the supreme and inferior Courts, shall hold their Offices during good Behaviour, and shall, at stated Times, receive for their Services a Compensation, which shall not be diminished during their Continuance in Office.

Section 2.   The judicial Power shall extend to all Cases, in Law and Equity, arising under this Constitution, the Laws of the United States, and Treaties made, or which shall be made, under their Authority;—to all Cases affecting Ambassadors, other public Ministers and Consuls;—to all Cases of admiralty and maritime Jurisdiction;—to Controversies to which the United States shall be a Party;—to Controversies between two or more States;—between a State and Citizens of another State;—between Citizens of different States;—between Citizens of the same State claiming Lands under Grants of different States, and between a State, or the Citizens thereof, and foreign States, Citizens or Subjects.

In all Cases affecting Ambassadors, other public Ministers and Consuls, and those in which a State shall be a Party, the supreme Court shall have original Jurisdiction. In all the other Cases before mentioned, the supreme Court shall have appellate Jurisdiction, both as to Law and Fact, with such Exceptions, and under such Regulations as the Congress shall make.

The Trial of all Crimes, except in Cases of Impeachment, shall be by Jury; and such Trial shall be held in the State where the said Crimes shall have been committed; but when not committed within any State, the Trial shall be at such Place or Places as the Congress may by Law have directed.

Section 3.   Treason against the United States, shall consist only in levying War against them, or, in adhering to their Enemies, giving them Aid and Comfort. No Person shall be convicted of Treason unless on the Testimony of two Witnesses to the same overt Act, or on Confession in open Court.

The Congress shall have Power to declare the Punishment of Treason, but no Attainder of Treason shall work Corruption of Blood, or Forfeiture except during the Life of the Person attainted.

ARTICLE IV

Section 1.   Full Faith and Credit shall be given in each State to the public Acts, Records, and judicial Proceedings of every other State. And the Congress may by general Laws prescribe the Manner in which such Acts, Records and Proceedings shall be proved, and the Effect thereof.

Section 2.   The Citizens of each State shall be entitled to all Privileges and Immunities of Citizens in the several States.

A Person charged in any State with Treason, Felony, or other Crime, who shall flee from Justice, and be found in another State, shall on Demand of the executive Authority of the State from which he fled, be delivered up, to be removed to the State having Jurisdiction of the Crime.

No Person held to Service or Labour in one State, under the Laws thereof, escaping into another, shall, in Consequence of any Law or Regulation therein, be discharged from such Service or Labour, but shall be delivered up on Claim of the Party to whom such Service or Labour may be due.

Section 3.   New States may be admitted by the Congress into this Union; but no new State shall be formed or erected within the Jurisdiction of any other State; nor any State be formed by the Junction of two or more States, or Parts of States, without the Consent of the Legislatures of the States concerned as well as of the Congress.

The Congress shall have Power to dispose of and make all needful Rules and Regulations respecting the Territory or other Property belonging to the United States; and nothing in this Constitution shall be so construed as to Prejudice any Claims of the United States, or of any particular State.

Section 4.   The United States shall guarantee to every State in this Union a Republican Form of Government, and shall protect each of them against Invasion; and on Application of the Legislature, or of the Executive (when the Legislature cannot be convened) against domestic Violence.

ARTICLE V

The Congress, whenever two thirds of both Houses shall deem it necessary, shall propose Amendments to this Constitution, or, on the Application of the Legislatures of two thirds of the several States, shall call a Convention for proposing Amendments, which, in either Case, shall be valid to all Intents and Purposes, as part of this Constitution, when ratified by the Legislatures of three fourths of the several States, or by Conventions in three fourths thereof, as the one or the other Mode of Ratification may be proposed by the Congress; Provided that no Amendment which may be made prior to the Year One thousand eight hundred and eight shall in any Manner affect the first and fourth Clauses in the Ninth Section of the first Article; and that no State, without its Consent, shall be deprived of its equal Suffrage in the Senate.

ARTICLE VI

All Debts contracted and Engagements entered into, before the Adoption of this Constitution shall be as valid against the United States under this Constitution, as under the Confederation.

This Constitution, and the Laws of the United States which shall be made in Pursuance thereof; and all Treaties made, or which shall be made, under the Authority of the United States, shall be the supreme Law of the Land; and the Judges in every State shall be bound thereby, any Thing in the Constitution or Laws of any State to the Contrary notwithstanding.

The Senators and Representatives before mentioned, and the Members of the several State Legislatures, and all executive and judicial Officers, both of the United States and of the several States, shall be bound by Oath or Affirmation, to support this Constitution; but no religious Test shall ever be required as a Qualification to any Office or public Trust under the United States.

ARTICLE VII

The Ratification of the Conventions of nine States shall be sufficient for the Establishment of this Constitution between the States so ratifying the Same.

AMENDMENT I [1791]

Congress shall make no law respecting an establishment of religion, or prohibiting the free exercise thereof; or abridging the freedom of speech, or of the press; or the right of the people peaceably to assembly, and to petition the Government for a redress of grievances.

AMENDMENT II [1791]

A well regulated Militia, being necessary to the security of a free State, the right of the people to keep and bear Arms, shall not be infringed.

AMENDMENT III [1791]

No Soldier shall, in time of peace be quartered in any house, without the consent of the Owner, nor in time of war, but in a manner to be prescribed by law.

Amendment IV [1791]

The right of the people to be secure in their persons, houses, papers, and effects, against unreasonable searches and seizures, shall not be violated, and no Warrants shall issue, but upon probable cause, supported by Oath or affirmation, and particularly describing the place to be searched, and the persons or things to be seized.

AMENDMENT V [1791]

No person shall be held to answer for a capital, or otherwise infamous crime, unless on a presentment or indictment of a Grand Jury, except in cases arising in the land or naval forces, or in the Militia, when in actual service in time of War or public danger; nor shall any person be subject for the same offence to be twice put in jeopardy of life or limb; nor shall be compelled in any criminal case to be a witness against himself, nor be deprived of life, liberty, or property, without due process of law; nor shall private property be taken for public use, without just compensation.

AMENDMENT VI [1791]

In all criminal prosecutions, the accused shall enjoy the right to a speedy and public trial, by an impartial jury of the State and district wherein the crime shall have been committed, which district shall have been previously ascertained by law, and to be informed of the nature and cause of the accusation; to be confronted with the witnesses against him; to have compulsory process for obtaining witnesses in his favor, and to have the Assistance of Counsel for his defence.

AMENDMENT VII [1791]

In Suits at common law, where the value in controversy shall exceed twenty dollars, the right of trial by jury shall be preserved, and no fact tried by jury, shall be otherwise re-examined in any Court of the United States, than according to the rules of the common law.

AMENDMENT VIII [1791]

Excessive bail shall not be required, nor excessive fines imposed, nor cruel and unusual punishments inflicted.

AMENDMENT IX [1791]

The enumeration in the Constitution, of certain rights, shall not be construed to deny or disparage others retained by the people.

AMENDMENT X [1791]

The powers not delegated to the United States by the Constitution, nor prohibited by it to the States, are reserved to the States respectively, or to the people.

AMENDMENT XI [1798]

The Judicial power of the United States shall not be construed to extend to any suit in law or equity, commenced or prosecuted against one of the United States by Citizens of another State, or by Citizens or Subjects of any Foreign State.

AMENDMENT XII [1804]

The Electors shall meet in their respective states, and vote by ballot for President and Vice-President, one of whom, at least, shall not be an inhabitant of the same state with themselves; they shall name in their ballots the person voted for as President, and in distinct ballots the person voted for as Vice-President, and they shall make distinct lists of all persons voted for as President, and of all persons voted for as Vice-President, and of the number of votes for each, which lists they shall sign and certify, and transmit sealed to the seat of the government of the United States, directed to the President of the Senate;—The President of the Senate shall, in the presence of the Senate and House of Representatives, open all the certificates and the votes shall then be counted;—The person having the greatest number of votes for President, shall be the President, if such number be a majority of the whole number of Electors appointed; and if no person have such majority, then from the persons having the highest numbers not exceeding three on the list of those voted for as President, the House of Representatives shall choose immediately, by ballot, the President. But in choosing the President, the votes shall be taken by states, the representation from each state having one vote; a quorum for this purpose shall consist of a member or members from two-thirds of the states, and a majority of all states shall be necessary to a choice. And if the House of Representatives shall not choose a President whenever the right of choice shall devolve upon them, before the fourth day of March next following, then the Vice-President shall act as President, as in the case of the death or other constitutional disability of the President.—The person having the greatest number of votes as Vice-President, shall be the Vice-President, if such number be a majority of the whole number of Electors appointed, and if no person have a majority, then from the two highest numbers on the list, the Senate shall choose the Vice-President; a quorum for the purpose shall consist of two-thirds of the whole number of Senators, and a majority of the whole number shall be necessary to a choice. But no person constitutionally ineligible to the office of President shall be eligible to that of Vice-President of the United States.

AMENDMENT XIII [1865]

Section 1. Neither slavery nor involuntary servitude, except as a punishment for crime whereof the party shall have been duly convicted, shall exist within the United States, or any place subject to their jurisdiction.

Section 2. Congress shall have power to enforce this article by appropriate legislation.

AMENDMENT XIV [1868]

Section 1. All persons born or naturalized in the United States, and subject to the jurisdiction thereof, are citizens of the United States and of the State wherein they reside. No State shall make or enforce any law which shall abridge the privileges or immunities of citizens of the United States; nor shall any State deprive any person of life, liberty, or property, without due process of law; nor deny to any person within its jurisdiction the equal protection of the laws.

Section 2. Representatives shall be apportioned among the several States according to their respective numbers, counting the whole number of persons in each State, excluding Indians not taxed. But when the right to vote at any election for the choice of electors for President and Vice President of the United States, Representatives in Congress, the Executive and Judicial officers of a State, or the members of the Legislature thereof, is denied to any of the male inhabitants of such State, being twenty-one years of age, and citizens of the United States, or in any way abridged, except for participation in rebellion, or other crime, the basis of representation therein shall be reduced in the proportion which the number of such male citizens shall bear to the whole number of male citizens twenty-one years of age in such State.

Section 3. No person shall be a Senator or Representative in Congress, or elector of President and Vice President, or hold any office, civil or military, under the United States, or under any State, who having previously taken an oath, as a member of Congress, or as an officer of the United States, or as a member of any State legislature, or as an executive or judicial officer of any State, to support the Constitution of the United States, shall have engaged in insurrection or rebellion against the same, or given aid or comfort to the enemies thereof. But Congress may by a vote of two-thirds of each House, remove such disability.

Section 4. The validity of the public debt of the United States, authorized by law, including debts incurred for payment of pensions and bounties for services in suppressing insurrection or rebellion, shall not be questioned. But neither the United States nor any State shall assume or pay any debt or obligation incurred in aid of insurrection or rebellion against the United States, or any claim for the loss or emancipation of any slave; but all such debts, obligations and claims shall be held illegal and void.

Section 5. The Congress shall have power to enforce, by appropriate legislation, the provisions of this article.

AMENDMENT XV [1870]

Section 1. The right of citizens of the United States to vote shall not be denied or abridged by the United States or by any State on account of race, color, or previous condition of servitude.

Section 2. The Congress shall have power to enforce this article by appropriate legislation.

AMENDMENT XVI [1913]

The Congress shall have power to lay and collect taxes on incomes, from whatever source derived, without apportionment among the several States, and without regard to any census or enumeration.

AMENDMENT XVII [1913]

[1] The Senate of the United States shall be composed of two Senators from each State, elected by the people thereof, for six years; and each Senator shall have one vote. The electors in each State shall have the qualifications requisite for electors of the most numerous branch of the State legislatures.

[2] When vacancies happen in the representation of any State in the Senate, the executive authority of such State shall issue writs of election to fill such vacancies: *Provided*, That the legislature of any State may empower the executive thereof to make temporary appointments until the people fill the vacancies by election as the legislature may direct.

[3] This amendment shall not be so construed as to affect the election or term of any Senator chosen before it becomes valid as part of the Constitution.

AMENDMENT XVIII [1919]

Section 1. After one year from the ratification of this article the manufacture, sale, or transportation of intoxicating liquors within, the importation thereof into, or the exportation thereof from the United States and all territory subject to the jurisdiction thereof for beverage purposes is hereby prohibited.

Section 2. The Congress and the several States shall have concurrent power to enforce this article by appropriate legislation.

Section 3. This article shall be inoperative unless it shall have been ratified as an amendment to the Constitution by the legislatures of the several States, as provided in the Constitution, within seven years from the date of the submission hereof to the States by the Congress.

AMENDMENT XIX [1920]

[1] The right of citizens of the United States to vote shall not be denied or abridged by the United States or by any State on account of sex.

[2] Congress shall have power to enforce this article by appropriate legislation.

AMENDMENT XX [1933]

Section 1. The terms of the President and Vice President shall end at noon on the 20th day of January, and the terms of Senators and Representatives at noon on the 3d day of January, of the years in which such terms would have ended if this article had not been ratified; and the terms of their successors shall then begin.

Section 2. The Congress shall assemble at least once in every year, and such meeting shall begin at noon on the 3d day of January, unless they shall by law appoint a different day.

Section 3. If, at the time fixed for the beginning of the term of the President, the President elect shall have died, the Vice President elect shall become President. If the President shall not have been chosen before the time fixed for the beginning of his term, or if the President elect shall have failed to qualify, then the Vice President elect shall act as President until a President shall have qualified; and the Congress may by law provide for the case wherein neither a President elect nor a Vice President elect shall have qualified, declaring who shall then act as President, or the manner in which one who is to act shall be selected, and such person shall act accordingly until a President or Vice President shall have qualified.

Section 4. The Congress may by law provide for the case of the death of any of the persons from whom the House of Representatives may choose a President whenever the right of choice shall have devolved upon them, and for the case of the death of any of the persons from whom the Senate may choose a Vice President whenever the right of choice shall have devolved upon them.

Section 5. Sections 1 and 2 shall take effect on the 15th day of October following the ratification of this article.

Section 6. This article shall be inoperative unless it shall have been ratified as an amendment to the Constitution by the legislatures of three-fourths of the several States within seven years from the date of its submission.

AMENDMENT XXI [1933]

Section 1. The eighteenth article of amendment to the Constitution of the United States is hereby repealed.

Section 2. The transportation or importation into any State, Territory, or possession of the United States for delivery or use therein of intoxicating liquors, in violation of the laws thereof, is hereby prohibited.

Section 3. This article shall be inoperative unless it shall have been ratified as an amendment to the Constitution by conventions in the several States, as provided in the Constitution, within seven years from the date of the submission hereof to the States by the Congress.

AMENDMENT XXII [1951]

Section 1. No person shall be elected to the office of the President more than twice, and no person who has held the office of President, or acted as President, for more than two years of a term to which some other person was elected President shall be elected to the office of President more than once. But this Article shall not apply to any person holding the office of President when this Article was proposed by the Congress, and shall not prevent any person who may be holding the office of President, or acting as President, during the term within which this Article becomes operative from holding the office of President or acting as President during the remainder of such term.

Section 2. This article shall be inoperative unless it shall have been ratified as an amendment to the Constitution by the legislatures of three-fourths of the several States within seven years from the date of its submission to the States by the Congress.

AMENDMENT XXIII [1961]

Section 1. The District constituting the seat of Government of the United States shall appoint in such manner as the Congress may direct:

A number of electors of President and Vice President equal to the whole number of Senators and Representatives in Congress to which the District would be entitled if it were a State, but in no event more than the least populous state; they shall be in addition to those appointed by the states, but they shall be considered, for the purposes of the election of President and Vice

President, to be electors appointed by a state; and they shall meet in the District and perform such duties as provided by the twelfth article of amendment.

Section 2. The Congress shall have power to enforce this article by appropriate legislation.

AMENDMENT XXIV [1964]

Section 1. The right of citizens of the United States to vote in any primary or other election for President or Vice President, for electors for President or Vice President, or for Senator or Representative in Congress, shall not be denied or abridged by the United States, or any State by reason of failure to pay any poll tax or other tax.

Section 2. The Congress shall have power to enforce this article by appropriate legislation.

AMENDMENT XXV [1967]

Section 1. In case of the removal of the President from office or of his death or resignation, the Vice President shall become President.

Section 2. Whenever there is a vacancy in the office of the Vice President, the President shall nominate a Vice President who shall take office upon confirmation by a majority vote of both Houses of Congress.

Section 3. Whenever the President transmits to the President pro tempore of the Senate and the Speaker of the House of Representatives his written declaration that he is unable to discharge the powers and duties of his office, and until he transmits to them a written declaration to the contrary, such powers and duties shall be discharged by the Vice President as Acting President.

Section 4. Whenever the Vice President and a majority of either the principal officers of the executive departments or of such other body as Congress may by law provide, transmit to the President pro tempore of the Senate and the Speaker of the House of Representatives their written declaration that the President is unable to discharge the powers and duties of his office, the Vice President shall immediately assume the powers and duties of the office as Acting President.

Thereafter, when the President transmits to the President pro tempore of the Senate and the Speaker of the House of Representatives his written declaration that no inability exists, he shall resume the powers and duties of his office unless the Vice President and a majority of either the principal officers of the executive department or of such other body as Congress may by law provide, transmit within four days to the President pro tempore of the Senate and the Speaker of the House of Representatives their written declaration and the President is unable to discharge the powers and duties of his office. Thereupon Congress shall decide the issue, assembling within forty-eight hours for that purpose if not in session. If the Congress, within twenty-one days after receipt of the latter written declaration, or, if Congress is not in session, within twenty-one days after Congress is required to assemble, determines by two-thirds vote of both Houses that the President is unable to discharge the powers and duties of his office, the Vice President shall continue to discharge the same as Acting President; otherwise, the President shall resume the powers and duties of his office.

AMENDMENT XXVI [1971]

Section 1. The right of citizens of the United States, who are eighteen years of age or older, to vote shall not be denied or abridged by the United States or by any State on account of age.

Section 2. The Congress shall have power to enforce this article by appropriate legislation.

THE UNIFORM COMMERCIAL CODE

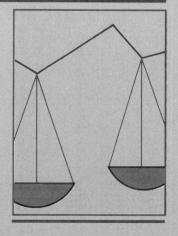

(Adopted in 52 jurisdictions; all 50 States, although Louisiana has adopted only Articles 1, 3, 4, and 5; the District of Columbia, and the Virgin Islands.)

The Code consists of 10 Articles as follows:

Art.

1. GENERAL PROVISIONS

2. Sales
    2A. Leases

3. Commercial Paper

4. Bank Deposits and Collections

5. Letters of Credit

6. Bulk Transfers

7. Warehouse Receipts, Bills of Lading and Other Documents of Title

8. Investment Securities

9. Secured Transactions: Sales of Accounts and Chattel Paper

10. Effective Date and Repealer

Article 1
GENERAL PROVISIONS

Part 1 Short Title, Construction, Application and Subject Matter of the Act

§ 1—101. Short Title.

This Act shall be known and may be cited as Uniform Commercial Code.

§ 1—102. Purposes; Rules of Construction; Variation by Agreement.

(1) This Act shall be liberally construed and applied to promote its underlying purposes and policies.

(2) Underlying purposes and policies of this Act are

(a) to simplify, clarify and modernize the law governing commercial transactions;

(b) to permit the continued expansion of commercial practices through custom, usage and agreement of the parties;

(c) to make uniform the law among the various jurisdictions.

(3) The effect of provisions of this Act may be varied by agreement, except as otherwise provided in this Act and except that the obligations of good faith, diligence, reasonableness and care prescribed by this Act may not be disclaimed by agreement but the parties may by agreement determine the standards by which the per-

formance of such obligations is to be measured if such standards are not manifestly unreasonable.

(4) The presence in certain provisions of this Act of the words "unless otherwise agreed" or words of similar import does not imply that the effect of other provisions may not be varied by agreement under subsection (3).

(5) In this Act unless the context otherwise requires

(a) words in the singular number include the plural, and in the plural include the singular;

(b) words of the masculine gender include the feminine and the neuter, and when the sense so indicates words of the neuter gender may refer to any gender.

§ 1—103. Supplementary General Principles of Law Applicable.

Unless displaced by the particular provisions of this Act, the principles of law and equity, including the law merchant and the law relative to capacity to contract, principal and agent, estoppel, fraud, misrepresentation, duress, coercion, mistake, bankruptcy, or other validating or invalidating cause shall supplement its provisions.

§ 1—104. Construction Against Implicit Repeal.

This Act being a general act intended as a unified coverage of its subject matter, no part of it shall be deemed to be impliedly repealed by subsequent legislation if such construction can reasonably be avoided.

§ 1—105. Territorial Application of the Act; Parties' Power to Choose Applicable Law.

(1) Except as provided hereafter in this section, when a transaction bears a reasonable relation to this state and also to another state or nation the parties may agree that the law either of this state or of such other state or nation shall govern their rights and duties. Failing such agreement this Act applies to transactions bearing an appropriate relation to this state.

(2) Where one of the following provisions of this Act specifies the applicable law, that provision governs and a contrary agreement is effective only to the extent permitted by the law (including the conflict of laws rules) so specified:

Rights of creditors against sold goods. Section 2—402.

Applicability of the Article on Leases. Sections 2A—105 and 2A—106.

Applicability of the Article on Bank Deposits and Collections. Section 4—102.

Bulk transfers subject to the Article on Bulk Transfers. Section 6—102.

Applicability of the Article on Investment Securities. Section 8—106.

Perfection provisions of the Article on Secured Transactions. Section 9—103.

§ 1—106. Remedies to Be Liberally Administered.

(1) The remedies provided by this Act shall be liberally administered to the end that the aggrieved party may be put in as good a position as if the other party had fully performed but neither consequential or special nor penal damages may be had except as specifically provided in this Act or by other rule of law.

(2) Any right or obligation declared by this Act is enforceable by action unless the provision declaring it specifies a different and limited effect.

§ 1—107. Waiver or Renunciation of Claim or Right After Breach.

Any claim or right arising out of an alleged breach can be discharged in whole or in part without consideration by a written waiver or renunciation signed and delivered by the aggrieved party.

§ 1—108. Severability.

If any provision or clause of this Act or application thereof to any person or circumstances is held invalid, such invalidity shall not affect other provisions or applications of the Act which can be given effect without the invalid provision or application, and to this end the provisions of this Act are declared to be severable.

§ 1—109. Section Captions.

Section captions are parts of this Act.

Part 2 General Definitions and Principles of Interpretation

§ 1—201. General Definitions.

Subject to additional definitions contained in the subsequent Articles of this Act which are applicable to specific Articles or Parts thereof, and unless the context otherwise requires, in this Act:

(1) "Action" in the sense of a judicial proceeding includes recoupment, counterclaim, set-off, suit in equity and any other proceedings in which rights are determined.

(2) "Aggrieved party" means a party entitled to resort to a remedy.

(3) "Agreement" means the bargain of the parties in fact as found in their language or by implication from other circumstances including course of dealing or usage of trade or course of performance as provided in this Act (Sections 1—205 and 2—208). Whether an agreement has legal consequences is determined by the provisions of this Act, if applicable; otherwise by the law of contracts (Section 1—103). (Compare "Contract".)

(4) "Bank" means any person engaged in the business of banking.

(5) "Bearer" means the person in possession of an instrument, document of title, or certificated security payable to bearer or indorsed in blank.

(6) "Bill of lading" means a document evidencing the receipt of goods for shipment issued by a person engaged in the business of transporting or forwarding goods, and includes an airbill. "Airbill" means a document serving for air transportation as a bill of lading does for marine or rail transportation, and includes an air consignment note or air waybill.

(7) "Branch" includes a separately incorporated foreign branch of a bank.

(8) "Burden of establishing" a fact means the burden of persuading the triers of fact that the existence of the fact is more probable than its non-existence.

(9) "Buyer in ordinary course of business" means a person who in good faith and without knowledge that the sale to him is in violation of the ownership rights or security interest of a third party in the goods buys in ordinary course from a person in the business of selling goods of that kind but does not include a pawnbroker. All persons who sell minerals or the like (including oil and gas) at wellhead or minehead shall be deemed to be persons in the business of selling goods of that kind. "Buying" may be for cash or by exchange of other property or on secured or unsecured credit and includes receiving goods or documents of title under a pre-existing contract for sale but does not include a transfer in bulk or as security for or in total or partial satisfaction of a money debt.

(10) "Conspicuous": A term or clause is conspicuous when it is so written that a reasonable person against whom it is to operate ought to have noticed it. A printed heading in capitals (as: NON-NEGOTIABLE BILL OF LADING) is conspicuous. Language in the body of a form is "conspicuous" if it is in larger or other contrasting type or color. But in a telegram any stated term is "conspicuous". Whether a term or clause is "conspicuous" or not is for decision by the court.

(11) "Contract" means the total legal obligation which results from the parties' agreement as affected by this Act and any other applicable rules of law. (Compare "Agreement".)

(12) "Creditor" includes a general creditor, a secured creditor, a lien creditor and any representative of creditors, including an assignee for the benefit of creditors, a trustee in bankruptcy, a receiver in equity and an executor or administrator of an insolvent debtor's or assignor's estate.

(13) "Defendant" includes a person in the position of defendant in a cross-action or counterclaim.

(14) "Delivery" with respect to instruments, documents of title, chattel paper, or certificated securities means voluntary transfer of possession.

(15) "Document of title" includes bill of lading, dock warrant, dock receipt, warehouse receipt or order for the delivery of goods, and also any other document which in the regular course of business or financing is treated as adequately evidencing that the person in possession of it is entitled to receive, hold and dispose of the document and the goods it covers. To be a document of title a document must purport to be issued by or addressed to a bailee and purport to cover goods in the bailee's possession which are either identified or are fungible portions of an identified mass.

(16) "Fault" means wrongful act, omission or breach.

(17) "Fungible" with respect to goods or securities means goods or securities of which any unit is, by nature or usage of trade, the equivalent of any other like unit. Goods which are not fungible shall be deemed fungible for the purposes of this Act to the extent that under a particular agreement or document unlike units are treated as equivalents.

(18) "Genuine" means free of forgery or counterfeiting.

(19) "Good faith" means honesty in fact in the conduct or transaction concerned.

(20) "Holder" means a person who is in possession of a document of title or an instrument or a certificated investment security drawn, issued, or indorsed to him or his order or to bearer or in blank.

(21) To "honor" is to pay or to accept and pay, or where a credit so engages to purchase or discount a draft complying with the terms of the credit.

(22) "Insolvency proceedings" includes any assignment for the benefit of creditors or other proceedings intended to liquidate or rehabilitate the estate of the person involved.

(23) A person is "insolvent" who either has ceased to pay his debts in the ordinary course of business or cannot pay his debts as they become due or is insolvent within the meaning of the federal bankruptcy law.

(24) "Money" means a medium of exchange authorized or adopted by a domestic or foreign government as a part of its currency.

(25) A person has "notice" of a fact when

(a) he has actual knowledge of it; or

(b) he has received a notice or notification of it; or

(c) from all the facts and circumstances known to him at the time in question he has reason to know that it exists.

A person "knows" or has "knowledge" of a fact when he has actual knowledge of it. "Discover" or "learn" or a word or phrase of similar import refers to knowledge rather than to reason to know. The time and circumstances under which a notice or notification may cease to be effective are not determined by this Act.

(26) A person "notifies" or "gives" a notice or notification to another by taking such steps as may be reasonably required to inform the other in ordinary course whether or not such other actually comes to know of it. A person "receives" a notice or notification when

(a) it comes to his attention; or

(b) it is duly delivered at the place of business through which the contract was made or at any other place held out by him as the place for receipt of such communications.

(27) Notice, knowledge or a notice or notification received by an organization is effective for a particular transaction from the time when it is brought to the attention of the individual conducting that transaction, and in any event from the time when it would have been brought to his attention if the organization had exercised due diligence. An organization exercises due diligence if it maintains reasonable routines for communicating significant information to the person conducting the transaction and there is reasonable compliance with the routines. Due diligence does not require an individual acting for the organization to communicate information unless such communication is part of his regular duties or unless he has reason to know of the transaction and that the transaction would be materially affected by the information.

(28) "Organization" includes a corporation, government or governmental subdivision or agency, business trust, estate, trust, partnership or association, two or more persons having a joint or common interest, or any other legal or commercial entity.

(29) "Party", as distinct from "third party", means a person who has engaged in a transaction or made an agreement within this Act.

(30) "Person" includes an individual or an organization (See Section 1—102).

(31) "Presumption" or "presumed" means that the trier of fact must find the existence of the fact presumed unless and until evidence is introduced which would support a finding of its non-existence.

(32) "Purchase" includes taking by sale, discount, negotiation, mortgage, pledge, lien, issue or re-issue, gift or any other voluntary transaction creating an interest in property.

(33) "Purchaser" means a person who takes by purchase.

(34) "Remedy" means any remedial right to which an aggrieved party is entitled with or without resort to a tribunal.

(35) "Representative" includes an agent, an officer of a corporation or association, and a trustee, executor or administrator of an estate, or any other person empowered to act for another.

(36) "Rights" includes remedies.

(37) "Security interest" means an interest in personal property or fixtures which secures payment or performance of an obligation. The retention or reservation of title by a seller of goods notwithstanding shipment or delivery to the buyer (Section 2—401) is limited in effect to a reservation of a "security interest". The term also includes any interest of a buyer of accounts or chattel paper which is subject to Article 9. The special property interest of a buyer of goods on identification of those goods to a contract for sale under Section 2—401 is not a "security interest", but a buyer may also acquire a "security interest" by complying with Article 9. Unless a consignment is intended as security, reservation of title thereunder is not a "security interest," but a consignment is in any event subject to the provisions on consignment sales (Section 2—326).

Whether a transaction creates a lease or security interest is determined by the facts of each case; however, a transaction creates a security interest if the consideration the lessee is to pay the lessor for the right to possession and use of the goods is an obligation for the term of the lease not subject to termination by the lessee, and

(a) the original term of the lease is equal to or greater than the remaining economic life of the goods,

(b) the lessee is bound to renew the lease for the remaining economic life of the goods or is bound to become the owner of the goods,

(c) the lessee has an option to renew the lease for the remaining economic life of the goods for no additional consideration or nominal additional consideration upon compliance with the lease agreement, or

(d) the lessee has an option to become the owner of the goods for no additional consideration or nominal additional consideration upon compliance with the lease agreement.

A transaction does not create a security interest merely because it provides that

(a) the present value of the consideration the lessee is obligated to pay the lessor for the right to possession and use of the goods is substantially equal to or is greater than the fair market value of the goods at the time the lease is entered into,

(b) the lessee assumes risk of loss of the goods, or agrees to pay taxes, insurance, filing, recording, or registration fees, or service or maintenance costs with respect to the goods,

(c) the lessee has an option to renew the lease or to become the owner of the goods,

(d) the lessee has an option to renew the lease for a fixed rent that is equal to or greater than the reasonably predictable fair market rent for the use of the goods for the term of the renewal at the time the option is to be performed, or

(e) the lessee has an option to become the owner of the goods for a fixed price that is equal to or greater than the reasonably predictable fair market value of the goods at the time the option is to be performed.

For purposes of this subsection (37):

(x) Additional consideration is not nominal if (i) when the option to renew the lease is granted to the lessee the rent is stated to be the fair market rent for the use of the goods for the term of the renewal determined at the time the option is to be performed, or (ii) when the option to become the owner of the goods is granted to the lessee the price is stated to be the fair market value of the goods determined at the time the option is to be performed. Additional consideration is nominal if it is less than the lessee's reasonably predictable cost of performing under the lease agreement if the option is not exercised;

(y) "Reasonably predictable" and "remaining economic life of the goods" are to be determined with reference to the facts and circumstances at the time the transaction is entered into; and

(z) "Present value" means the amount as of a date certain of one or more sums payable in the future, discounted to the date certain. The discount is determined by the interest rate specified by the parties if the rate is not manifestly unreasonable at the time the transaction is entered into; otherwise, the discount is determined by a commercially reasonable rate that takes into account the facts and circumstances of each case at the time the transaction was entered into.

(38) "Send" in connection with any writing or notice means to deposit in the mail or deliver for transmission by any other usual means of communication with postage or cost of transmission provided for and properly addressed and in the case of an instrument to an address specified thereon or otherwise agreed, or if there be none to any address reasonable under the circumstances. The receipt of any writing or notice within the time at which it would have arrived if properly sent has the effect of a proper sending.

(39) "Signed" includes any symbol executed or adopted by a party with present intention to authenticate a writing.

(40) "Surety" includes guarantor.

(41) "Telegram" includes a message transmitted by radio, teletype, cable, any mechanical method of transmission, or the like.

(42) "Term" means that portion of an agreement which relates to a particular matter.

(43) "Unauthorized" signature or indorsement means one made without actual, implied or apparent authority and includes a forgery.

(44) "Value". Except as otherwise provided with respect to negotiable instruments and bank collections (Sections 3—303, 4—208 and 4—209) a person gives "value" for rights if he acquires them

(a) in return for a binding commitment to extend credit or for the extension of immediately available credit whether or not drawn upon and whether or not a chargeback is provided for in the event of difficulties in collection; or

(b) as security for or in total or partial satisfaction of a pre-existing claim; or

(c) by accepting delivery pursuant to a preexisting .contract for purchase; or

(d) generally, in return for any consideration sufficient to support a simple contract.

(45) "Warehouse receipt" means a receipt issued by a person engaged in the business of storing goods for hire.

(46) "Written" or "writing" includes printing, typewriting or any other intentional reduction to tangible form.

Amended in 1962, 1972, 1977, and 1987.

§ 1—202. Prima Facie Evidence by Third Party Documents.

A document in due form purporting to be a bill of lading, policy or certificate of insurance, official weigher's or inspector's certificate, consular invoice, or any other document authorized or required by the contract to be issued by a third party shall be prima facie evidence of its own authenticity and genuineness and of the facts stated in the document by the third party.

§ 1—203. Obligation of Good Faith.

Every contract or duty within this Act imposes an obligation of good faith in its performance or enforcement.

§ 1—204. Time; Reasonable Time; "Seasonably".

(1) Whenever this Act requires any action to be taken within a reasonable time, any time which is not manifestly unreasonable may be fixed by agreement.

(2) What is a reasonable time for taking any action depends on the nature, purpose and circumstances of such action.

(3) An action is taken "seasonably" when it is taken at or within the time agreed or if no time is agreed at or within a reasonable time.

§ 1—205. Course of Dealing and Usage of Trade.

(1) A course of dealing is a sequence of previous conduct between the parties to a particular transaction which is fairly to be regarded as establishing a common basis of understanding for interpreting their expressions and other conduct.

(2) A usage of trade is any practice or method of dealing having such regularity of observance in a place, vocation or trade as to justify an expectation that it will be observed with respect to the transaction in question. The existence and scope of such a usage are to be proved as facts. If it is established that such a usage is embodied in a written trade code or similar writing the interpretation of the writing is for the court.

(3) A course of dealing between parties and any usage of trade in the vocation or trade in which they are engaged or of which they are or should be aware give particular meaning to and supplement or qualify terms of an agreement.

(4) The express terms of an agreement and an applicable course of dealing or usage of trade shall be construed wherever reasonable as consistent with each other; but when such construction is unreasonable express terms control both course of dealing and usage of trade and course of dealing controls usage trade.

(5) An applicable usage of trade in the place where any part of performance is to occur shall be used in interpreting the agreement as to that part of the performance.

(6) Evidence of a relevant usage of trade offered by one party is not admissible unless and until he has given the other party such notice as the court finds sufficient to prevent unfair surprise to the latter.

§ 1—206. Statute of Frauds for Kinds of Personal Property Not Otherwise Covered.

(1) Except in the cases described in subsection (2) of this section a contract for the sale of personal property is not enforceable by way of action or defense beyond five thousand dollars in amount or value of remedy unless there is some writing which indicates that a contract for sale has been made between the parties at a defined or stated price, reasonably identifies the subject matter, and is signed by the party against whom enforcement is sought or by his authorized agent.

(2) Subsection (1) of this section does not apply to contracts for the sale of goods (Section 2—201) nor of securities (Section 8—319) nor to security agreements (Section 9—203).

§ 1—207. **Performance or Acceptance Under Reservation of Rights.**

A party who with explicit reservation of rights performs or promises performance or assents to performance in a manner demanded or offered by the other party does not thereby prejudice the rights reserved. Such words as "without prejudice", "under protest" or the like are sufficient.

§ 1—208. **Option to Accelerate at Will.**

A term providing that one party or his successor in interest may accelerate payment or performance or require collateral or additional collateral "at will" or "when he deems himself insecure" or in words of similar import shall be construed to mean that he shall have power to do so only if he in good faith believes that the prospect of payment or performance is impaired. The burden of establishing lack of good faith is on the party against whom the power has been exercised.

§ 1—209. **Subordinated Obligations**

An obligation may be issued as subordinated to payment of another obligation of the person obligated, or a creditor may subordinate his right to payment of an obligation by agreement with either the person obligated or another creditor of the person obligated. Such a subordination does not create a security interest as against either the common debtor or a subordinated creditor. This section shall be construed as declaring the law as it existed prior to the enactment of this section and not as modifying it. Added 1966.

Note: *This new section is proposed as an optional provision to make it clear that a subordination agreement does not create a security interest unless so intended.*

Article 2
SALES

Part 1
Short Title, General Construction and Subject Matter

§ 2—101. **Short Title.**

This Article shall be known and may be cited as Uniform Commercial Code—Sales.

§ 2—102. **Scope; Certain Security and Other Transactions Excluded From This Article.**

Unless the context otherwise requires, this Article applies to transactions in goods; it does not apply to any transaction which although in the form of an unconditional contract to sell or present sale is intended to operate only as a security transaction nor does this Article impair or repeal any statute regulating sales to consumers, farmers or other specified classes of buyers.

§ 2—103. **Definitions and Index of Definitions.**

(1) In this Article unless the context otherwise requires

(a) "Buyer" means a person who buys or contracts to buy goods.

(b) "Good faith" in the case of a merchant means honesty in fact and the observance of reasonable commercial standards of fair dealing in the trade.

(c) "Receipt" of goods means taking physical possession of them.

(d) "Seller" means a person who sells or contracts to sell goods.

(2) Other definitions applying to this Article or to specified Parts thereof, and the sections in which they appear are:
"Acceptance". Section 2—606.
"Banker's credit". Section 2—325.
"Between merchants". Section 2—104.
"Cancellation". Section 2—106(4).
"Commercial unit". Section 2—105.
"Confirmed credit". Section 2—325.
"Conforming to contract". Section 2—106.
"Contract for sale". Section 2—106.
"Cover". Section 2—712.
"Entrusting". Section 2—403.
"Financing agency". Section 2—104.
"Future goods". Section 2—105.
"Goods". Section 2—105.
"Identification". Section 2—501.
"Installment contract". Section 2—612.
"Letter of Credit". Section 2—325.
"Lot". Section 2—105.
"Merchant". Section 2—104.
"Overseas". Section 2—323.
"Person in position of seller". Section 2—707.
"Present sale". Section 2—106.
"Sale". Section 2—106.
"Sale on approval". Section 2—326.
"Sale or return". Section 2—326.
"Termination". Section 2—106.

(3) The following definitions in other Articles apply to this Article:
"Check". Section 3—104.
"Consignee". Section 7—102.
"Consignor". Section 7—102.
"Consumer goods". Section 9—109.
"Dishonor". Section 3—507.
"Draft". Section 3—104.

(4) In addition Article 1 contains general definitions and principles of construction and interpretation applicable throughout this Article.

§ 2—104. Definitions: "Merchant"; "Between Merchants"; "Financing Agency".

(1) "Merchant" means a person who deals in goods of the kind or otherwise by his occupation holds himself out as having knowledge or skill peculiar to the practices or goods involved in the transaction or to whom such knowledge or skill may be attributed by his employment of an agent or broker or other intermediary who by his occupation holds himself out as having such knowledge or skill.

(2) "Financing agency" means a bank, finance company or other person who in the ordinary course of business makes advances against goods or documents of title or who by arrangement with either the seller or the buyer intervenes in ordinary course to make or collect payment due or claimed under the contract for sale, as by purchasing or paying the seller's draft or making advances against it or by merely taking it for collection whether or not documents of title accompany the draft. "Financing agency" includes also a bank or other person who similarly intervenes between persons who are in the position of seller and buyer in respect to the goods (Section 2—707).

(3) "Between merchants" means in any transaction with respect to which both parties are chargeable with the knowledge or skill of merchants.

§ 2—105. Definitions: Transferability; "Goods"; "Future" Goods; "Lot"; "Commercial Unit".

(1) "Goods" means all things (including specially manufactured goods) which are movable at the time of identification to the contract for sale other than the money in which the price is to be paid, investment securities (Article 8) and things in action. "Goods" also includes the unborn young of animals and growing crops and other identified things attached to realty as described in the section on goods to be severed from realty (Section 2—107).

(2) Goods must be both existing and identified before any interest in them can pass. Goods which are not both existing and identified are "future" goods. A purported present sale of future goods or of any interest therein operates as a contract to sell.

(3) There may be a sale of a part interest in existing identified goods.

(4) An undivided share in an identified bulk of fungible goods is sufficiently identified to be sold although the quantity of the bulk is not determined. Any agreed proportion of such a bulk or any quantity thereof agreed upon by number, weight or other measure may to the extent of the seller's interest in the bulk be sold to the buyer who then becomes an owner in common.

(5) "Lot" means a parcel or a single article which is the subject matter of a separate sale or delivery, whether or not it is sufficient to perform the contract.

(6) "Commercial unit" means such a unit of goods as by commercial usage is a single whole for purposes of sale and division of which materially impairs its character or value on the market or in use. A commercial unit may be a single article (as a machine) or a set of articles (as a suite of furniture or an assortment of sizes) or a quantity (as a bale, gross, or carload) or any other unit treated in use or in the relevant market as a single whole.

§ 2—106. Definitions: "Contract"; "Agreement"; "Contract for Sale"; "Sale"; "Present Sale"; "Conforming" to Contract; "Termination"; "Cancellation".

(1) In this Article unless the context otherwise requires "contract" and "agreement" are limited to those relating to the present or future sale of goods. "Contract for sale" includes both a present sale of goods and a contract to sell goods at a future time. A "sale" consists in the passing of title from the seller to the buyer for a price (Section 2—401). A "present sale" means a sale which is accomplished by the making of the contract.

(2) Goods or conduct including any part of a performance are "conforming" or conform to the contract when they are in accordance with the obligations under the contract.

(3) "Termination" occurs when either party pursuant to a power created by agreement or law puts an end to the contract otherwise than for its breach. On "termination" all obligations which are still executory on both sides are discharged but any right based on prior breach or performance survives.

(4) "Cancellation" occurs when either party puts an end to the contract for breach by the other and its effect is the same as that of "termination" except that the cancelling party also retains any remedy for breach of the whole contract or any unperformed balance.

§ 2—107. Goods to Be Severed From Realty: Recording.

(1) A contract for the sale of minerals or the like (including oil and gas) or a structure or its materials to be removed from realty is a contract for the sale of goods within this Article if they are to be severed by the seller but until severance a purported present sale thereof which is not effective as a transfer of an interest in land is effective only as a contract to sell.

(2) A contract for the sale apart from the land of growing crops or other things attached to realty and capable of severance without material harm thereto but not de-

scribed in subsection (1) or of timber to be cut is a contract for the sale of goods within this Article whether the subject matter is to be severed by the buyer or by the seller even though it forms part of the realty at the time of contracting, and the parties can by identification effect a present sale before severance.

(3) The provisions of this section are subject to any third party rights provided by the law relating to realty records, and the contract for sale may be executed and recorded as a document transferring an interest in land and shall then constitute notice to third parties of the buyer's rights under the contract for sale.

Part 2 Form, Formation and Readjustment of Contract

§ 2—201. **Formal Requirements; Statute of Frauds.**

(1) Except as otherwise provided in this section a contract for the sale of goods for the price of $500 or more is not enforceable by way of action or defense unless there is some writing sufficient to indicate that a contract for sale has been made between the parties and signed by the party against whom enforcement is sought or by his authorized agent or broker. A writing is not insufficient because it omits or incorrectly states a term agreed upon but the contract is not enforceable under this paragraph beyond the quantity of goods shown in such writing.

(2) Between merchants if within a reasonable time a writing in confirmation of the contract and sufficient against the sender is received and the party receiving it has reason to know its contents, its satisfies the requirements of subsection (1) against such party unless written notice of objection to its contents is given within ten days after it is received.

(3) A contract which does not satisfy the requirements of subsection (1) but which is valid in other respects is enforceable

(a) if the goods are to be specially manufactured for the buyer and are not suitable for sale to others in the ordinary course of the seller's business and the seller, before notice of repudiation is received and under circumstances which reasonably indicate that the goods are for the buyer, has made either a substantial beginning of their manufacture or commitments for their procurement; or

(b) if the party against whom enforcement is sought admits in his pleading, testimony or otherwise in court that a contract for sale was made, but the contract is not enforceable under this provision beyond the quantity of goods admitted; or

(c) with respect to goods for which payment has been made and accepted or which have been re-

ceived and accepted (Sec. 2—606).

§ 2—202. **Final Written Expression: Parol or Extrinsic Evidence.**

Terms with respect to which the confirmatory memoranda of the parties agree or which are otherwise set forth in a writing intended by the parties as a final expression of their agreement with respect to such terms as are included therein may not be contradicted by evidence of any prior agreement or of a contemporaneous oral agreement but may be explained or supplemented

(a) by course of dealing or usage of trade (Section 1—205) or by course of performance (Section 2—208); and

(b) by evidence of consistent additional terms unless the court finds the writing to have been intended also as a complete and exclusive statement of the terms of the agreement.

§ 2—203. **Seals Inoperative.**

The affixing of a seal to a writing evidencing a contract for sale or an offer to buy or sell goods does not constitute the writing a sealed instrument and the law with respect to sealed instruments does not apply to such a contract or offer.

§ 2—204. **Formation in General.**

(1) A contract for sale of goods may be made in any manner sufficent to show agreement, including conduct by both parties which recognizes the existence of such a contract.

(2) An agreement sufficient to constitute a contract for sale may be found even though the moment of its making is undetermined.

(3) Even though one or more terms are left open a contract for sale does not fail for indefiniteness if the parties have intended to make a contract and there is a reasonably certain basis for giving an appropriate remedy.

§ 2—205. **Firm Offers.**

An offer by a merchant to buy or sell goods in a signed writing which by its terms gives assurance that it will be held open is not revocable, for lack of consideration, during the time stated or if no time is stated for a reasonable time, but in no event may such period of irrevocability exceed three months; but any such term of assurance on a form supplied by the offeree must be separately signed by the offeror.

§ 2—206. **Offer and Acceptance in Formation of Contract.**

(1) Unless other unambiguously indicated by the language or circumstances

(a) an offer to make a contract shall be construed as inviting acceptance in any manner and by any medium reasonable in the circumstances;

(b) an order or other offer to buy goods for prompt or current shipment shall be construed as inviting acceptance either by a prompt promise to ship or by the prompt or current shipment of conforming or nonconforming goods, but such a shipment of non-conforming goods does not constitute an acceptance if the seller seasonably notifies the buyer that the shipment is offered only as an accommodation to the buyer.

(2) Where the beginning of a requested performance is a reasonable mode of acceptance an offeror who is not notified of acceptance within a reasonable time may treat the offer as having lapsed before acceptance.

§ 2—207. **Additional Terms in Acceptance or Confirmation.**

(1) A definite and seasonable expression of acceptance or a written confirmation which is sent within a reasonable time operates as an acceptance even though it states terms additional to or different from those offered or agreed upon, unless acceptance is expressly made conditional on assent to the additional or different terms.

(2) The additional terms are to be construed as proposals for addition to the contract. Between merchants such terms become part of the contract unless:

(a) the offer expressly limits acceptance to the terms of the offer;

(b) they materially alter it; or

(c) notification of objection to them has already been given or is given within a reasonable time after notice of them is received.

(3) Conduct by both parties which recognizes the existence of a contract is sufficient to establish a contract for sale although the writings of the parties do not otherwise establish a contract. In such case the terms of the particular contract consist of those terms on which the writings of the parties agree, together with any supplementary terms incorporated under any other provisions of this Act.

§ 2—208. **Course of Performance or Practical Construction.**

(1) Where the contract for sale involves repeated occasions for performance by either party with knowledge of the nature of the performance and opportunity for objection to it by the other, any course of performance accepted or acquiesced in without objection shall be relevant to determine the meaning of the agreement.

(2) The express terms of the agreement and any such course of performance, as well as any course of dealing and usage of trade, shall be construed whenever reasonable as consistent with each other; but when such construction is unreasonable, express terms shall control course of performance and course of performance shall control both course of dealing and usage of trade (Section 1—205).

(3) Subject to the provisions of the next section on modification and waiver, such course of performance shall be relevant to show a waiver or modification of any term inconsistent with such course of performance.

§ 2—209. **Modification, Rescission and Waiver.**

(1) An agreement modifying a contract within this Article needs no consideration to be binding.

(2) A signed agreement which excludes modification or rescission except by a signed writing cannot be otherwise modified or rescinded, but except as between merchants such a requirement on a form supplied by the merchant must be separately signed by the other party.

(3) The requirements of the statute of frauds section of this Article (Section 2—201) must be satisfied if the contract as modified is within its provisions.

(4) Although an attempt at modification or rescission does not satisfy the requirements of subsection (2) or (3) it can operate as a waiver.

(5) A party who has made a waiver affecting an executory portion of the contract may retract the waiver by reasonable notification received by the other party that strict performance will be required of any term waived, unless the retraction would be unjust in view of a material change of position in reliance on the waiver.

§ 2—210. **Delegation of Performance; Assignment of Rights.**

(1) A party may perform his duty through a delegate unless otherwise agreed or unless the other party has a substantial interest in having his original promisor perform or control the acts required by the contract. No delegation of performance relieves the party delegating of any duty to perform or any liability for breach.

(2) Unless otherwise agreed all rights of either seller or buyer can be assigned except where the assignment would materially change the duty of the other party, or increase materially the burden or risk imposed on him by his contract, or impair materially his chance of obtaining return performance. A right to damages for breach of the whole contract or a right arising out of the assignor's due performance of his entire obligation can be assigned despite agreement otherwise.

(3) Unless the circumstances indicate the contrary a prohibition of assignment of "the contract" is to be construed as barring only the delegation to the assignee of the assignor's performance.

(4) An assignment of "the contract" or of "all my rights under the contract" or an assignment in similar general terms is an assignment of rights and unless the language or the circumstances (as in an assignment for security) indicate the contrary, it is a delegation of performance of the duties of the assignor and its acceptance by the assignee constitutes a promise by him to perform those duties. This promise is enforceable by either the assignor or the other party to the original contract.

(5) The other party may treat any assignment which delegates performance as creating reasonable grounds for insecurity and may without prejudice to his rights against the assignor demand assurances from the assignee (Section 2—609).

Part 3 General Obligation and Construction of Contract

§ 2—301. **General Obligations of Parties.**

The obligation of the seller is to transfer and deliver and that of the buyer is to accept and pay in accordance with the contract.

§ 2—302. **Unconscionable Contract or Clause.**

(1) If the court as a matter of law finds the contract or any clause of the contract to have been unconscionable at the time it was made the court may refuse to enforce the contract, or it may enforce the remainder of the contract without the unconscionable clause, or it may so limit the application of any unconscionable clause as to avoid any unconscionable result.

(2) When it is claimed or appears to the court that the contract or any clause thereof may be unconscionable the parties shall be afforded a reasonable opportunity to present evidence as to its commercial setting, purpose and effect to aid the court in making the determination.

§ 2—303. **Allocations or Division of Risks.**

Where this Article allocates a risk or a burden as between the parties "unless otherwise agreed", the agreement may not only shift the allocation but may also divide the risk or burden.

§ 2—304. **Price Payable in Money, Goods, Realty, or Otherwise.**

(1) The price can be made payable in money or otherwise. If it is payable in whole or in part in goods each party is a seller of the goods which he is to transfer.

(2) Even though all or part of the price is payable in an interest in realty the transfer of the goods and the seller's obligations with reference to them are subject to this Article, but not the transfer of the interest in realty or the transferor's obligations in connection therewith.

§ 2—305. **Open Price Term.**

(1) The parties if they so intend can conclude a contract for sale even though the price is not settled. In such a case the price is a reasonable price at the time for delivery if

(a) nothing is said as to price; or

(b) the price is left to be agreed by the parties and they fail to agree; or

(c) the price is to be fixed in terms of some agreed market or other standard as set or recorded by a third person or agency and it is not so set or recorded.

(2) A price to be fixed by the seller or by the buyer means a price for him to fix in good faith.

(3) When a price left to be fixed otherwise than by agreement of the parties fails to be fixed through fault of one party the other may at his option treat the contract as cancelled or himself fix a reasonable price.

(4) Where, however, the parties intend not to be bound unless the price be fixed or agreed and it is not fixed or agreed there is no contract. In such a case the buyer must return any goods already received or if unable so to do must pay their reasonable value at the time of delivery and the seller must return any portion of the price paid on account.

§ 2—306. **Output, Requirements and Exclusive Dealings.**

(1) A term which measures the quantity by the output of the seller or the requirements of the buyer means such actual output or requirements as may occur in good faith, except that no quantity unreasonably disproportionate to any stated estimate or in the absence of a stated estimate to any normal or otherwise comparable prior output or requirements may be tendered or demanded.

(2) A lawful agreement by either the seller or the buyer for exclusive dealing in the kind of goods concerned imposes unless otherwise agreed an obligation by the seller to use best efforts to supply the goods and by the buyer to use best efforts to promote their sale.

§ 2—307. **Delivery in Single Lot or Several Lots.**

Unless otherwise agreed all goods called for by a contract for sale must be tendered in a single delivery and payment is due only on such tender but where the circumstances give either party the right to make or demand delivery in lots the price if it can be apportioned may be demanded for each lot.

§ 2—308. **Absence of Specified Place for Delivery.**

Unless otherwise agreed

(a) the place for delivery of goods is the seller's place of business or if he has none his residence; but

(b) in a contract for sale of identified goods which to the knowledge of the parties at the time of contracting are in some other place, that place is the place for their delivery; and

(c) documents of title may be delivered through customary banking channels.

§ 2—309. **Absence of Specific Time Provisions; Notice of Termination.**

(1) The time for shipment or delivery or any other action under a contract if not provided in this Article or agreed upon shall be a reasonable time.

(2) Where the contract provides for successive performances but is indefinite in duration it is valid for a reasonable time but unless otherwise agreed may be terminated at any time by either party.

(3) Termination of a contract by one party except on the happening of an agreed event requires that reasonable notification be received by the other party and an agreement dispensing with notification is invalid if its operation would be unconscionable.

§ 2—310. **Open Time for Payment or Running of Credit; Authority to Ship Under Reservation.**

Unless otherwise agreed

(a) payment is due at the time and place at which the buyer is to receive the goods even though the place of shipment is the place of delivery; and

(b) if the seller is authorized to send the goods he may ship them under reservation, and may tender the documents of title, but the buyer may inspect the goods after their arrival before payment is due unless such inspection is inconsistent with the terms of the contract (Section 2—513); and

(c) if delivery is authorized and made by way of documents of title otherwise than by subsection (b) then payment is due at the time and place at which the buyer is to receive the documents regardless of where the goods are to be received; and

(d) where the seller is required or authorized to ship the goods on credit the credit period runs from the time of shipment but post-dating the invoice or delaying its dispatch will correspondingly delay the starting of the credit period.

§ 2—311. **Options and Cooperation Respecting Performance.**

(1) An agreement for sale which is otherwise sufficiently definite (subsection (3) of Section 2—204) to be a contract is not made invalid by the fact that it leaves particulars of performance to be specified by one of the parties. Any such specification must be made in good faith and within limits set by commercial reasonableness.

(2) Unless otherwise agreed specifications relating to assortment of the goods are at the buyer's option and except as otherwise provided in subsections (1)(c) and (3) of Section 2—319 specifications or arrangements relating to shipment are at the seller's option.

(3) Where such specification would materially affect the other party's performance but is not seasonably made or where one party's cooperation is necessary to the agreed performance of the other but is not seasonably forthcoming, the other party in addition to all other remedies

(a) is excused for any resulting delay in his own performance; and

(b) may also either proceed to perform in any reasonable manner or after the time for a material part of his own performance treat the failure to specify or to cooperate as a breach by failure to deliver or accept the goods.

§ 2—312. **Warranty of Title and Against Infringement; Buyer's Obligation Against Infringement.**

(1) Subject to subsection (2) there is in a contract for sale a warranty by the seller that

(a) the title conveyed shall be good, and its transfer rightful; and

(b) the goods shall be delivered free from any security interest or other lien or encumbrance of which the buyer at the time of contracting has no knowledge.

(2) A warranty under subsection (1) will be excluded or modified only by specific language or by circumstances which give the buyer reason to know that the person selling does not claim title in himself or that he is purporting to sell only such right or title as he or a third person may have.

(3) Unless otherwise agreed a seller who is a merchant regularly dealing in goods of the kind warrants that the goods shall be delivered free of the rightful claim of any third person by way of infringement or the like but a buyer who furnishes specifications to the seller must hold the seller harmless against any such claim which arises out of compliance with the specifications.

§ 2—313. **Express Warranties by Affirmation, Promise, Description, Sample.**

(1) Express warranties by the seller are created as follows:

(a) Any affirmation of fact or promise made by the seller to the buyer which relates to the goods and becomes part of the basis of the bargain creates an express warranty that the goods shall conform to the affirmation or promise.

(b) Any description of the goods which is made part of the basis of the bargain creates an express warranty that the goods shall conform to the description.

(c) Any sample or model which is made part of the basis of the bargain creates an express warranty that the whole of the goods shall conform to the sample or model.

(2) It is not necessary to the creation of an express warranty that the seller use formal words such as "warrant" or "guarantee" or that he have a specific intention to make a warranty, but an affirmation merely of the value of the goods or a statement purporting to be merely the seller's opinion or commendation of the goods does not create a warranty.

§ 2—314. Implied Warranty: Merchantability; Usage of Trade.

(1) Unless excluded or modified (Section 2—316), a warranty that the goods shall be merchantable is implied in a contract for their sale if the seller is a merchant with respect to goods of that kind. Under this section the serving for value of food or drink to be consumed either on the premises or elsewhere is a sale.

(2) Goods to be merchantable must be at least such as

(a) pass without objection in the trade under the contract description; and

(b) in the case of fungible goods, are of fair average quality within the description; and

(c) are fit for the ordinary purposes for which such goods are used; and

(d) run, within the variations permitted by the agreement, of even kind, quality and quantity within each unit and among all units involved; and

(e) are adequately contained, packaged, and labeled as the agreement may require; and

(f) conform to the promises or affirmations of fact made on the container or label if any.

(3) Unless excluded or modified (Section 2—316) other implied warranties may arise from course of dealing or usage of trade.

§ 2—315. Implied Warranty: Fitness for Particular Purpose.

Where the seller at the time of contracting has reason to know any particular purpose for which the goods are required and that the buyer is relying on the seller's skill or judgment to select or furnish suitable goods, there is unless excluded or modified under the next section an implied warranty that the goods shall be fit for such purpose.

§ 2—316. Exclusion or Modification of Warranties.

(1) Words or conduct relevant to the creation of an express warranty and words or conduct tending to ne-

gate or limit warranty shall be construed wherever reasonable as consistent with each other; but subject to the provisions of this Article on parol or extrinsic evidence (Section 2—202) negation or limitation is inoperative to the extent that such construction is unreasonable.

(2) Subject to subsection (3), to exclude or modify the implied warranty of merchantability or any part of it the language must mention merchantability and in case of a writing must be conspicuous, and to exclude or modify any implied warranty of fitness the exclusion must be by a writing and conspicuous. Language to exclude all implied warranties of fitness is sufficient if it states, for example, that "There are no warranties which extend beyond the description on the face hereof."

(3) Notwithstanding subsection (2)

(a) unless the circumstances indicate otherwise, all implied warranties are excluded by expressions like "as is", "with all faults" or other language which in common understanding calls the buyer's attention to the exclusion of warranties and makes plain that there is no implied warranty; and

(b) when the buyer before entering into the contract has examined the goods or the sample or model as fully as he desired or has refused to examine the goods there is no implied warranty with regard to defects which an examination ought in the circumstances to have revealed to him; and

(c) an implied warranty can also be excluded or modified by course of dealing or course of performance or usage of trade.

(4) Remedies for breach of warranty can be limited in accordance with the provisions of this Article on liquidation or limitation of damages and on contractual modification of remedy (Sections 2—718 and 2—719).

§ 2—317. Cumulation and Conflict of Warranties Express or Implied.

Warranties whether express or implied shall be construed as consistent with each other and as cumulative, but if such construction is unreasonable the intention of the parties shall determine which warranty is dominant. In ascertaining that intention the following rules apply:

(a) Exact or technical specifications displace an inconsistent sample or model or general language of description.

(b) A sample from an existing bulk displaces inconsistent general language of description.

(c) Express warranties displace inconsistent implied warranties other than an implied warranty of fitness for a particular purpose.

§ 2—318. **Third Party Beneficiaries of Warranties Express or Implied.**

Note: If this Act is introduced in the Congress of the United States this section should be omitted. (States to select one alternative.)

Alternative A

A seller's warranty whether express or implied extends to any natural person who is in the family or household of his buyer or who is a guest in his home if it is reasonable to expect that such person may use, consume or be affected by the goods and who is injured in person by breach of the warranty. A seller may not exclude or limit the operation of this section.

Alternative B

A seller's warranty whether express or implied extends to any natural person who may reasonably be expected to use, consume or be affected by the goods and who is injured in person by breach of the warranty. A seller may not exclude or limit the operation of this section.

Alternative C

A seller's warranty whether express or implied extends to any person who may reasonably be expected to use, consume or be affected by the goods and who is injured by breach of the warranty. A seller may not exclude or limit the operation of this section with respect to injury to the person of an individual to whom the warranty extends. As amended 1966.

§ 2—319. **F.O.B. and F.A.S. Terms.**

(1) Unless otherwise agreed the term F.O.B. (which means "free on board") at a named place, even though used only in connection with the stated price, is a delivery term under which

  (a) when the term is F.O.B. the place of shipment, the seller must at that place ship the goods in the manner provided in this Article (Section 2—504) and bear the expense and risk of putting them into the possession of the carrier; or

  (b) when the term is F.O.B. the place of destination, the seller must at his own expense and risk transport the goods to that place and there tender delivery of them in the manner provided in this Article (Section 2—503);

  (c) when under either (a) or (b) the term is also F.O.B. vessel, car or other vehicle, the seller must in addition at his own expense and risk load the goods on board. If the term is F.O.B. vessel the buyer must name the vessel and in an appropriate case the seller must comply with the provisions of this Article on the form of bill of lading (Section 2—323).

(2) Unless otherwise agreed the term F.A.S. vessel (which means "free alongside") at a named port, even though used only in connection with the stated price, is a delivery term under which the seller must

  (a) at his own expense and risk deliver the goods alongside the vessel in the manner usual in that port or on a dock designated and provided by the buyer; and

  (b) obtain and tender a receipt for the goods in exchange for which the carrier is under a duty to issue a bill of lading.

(3) Unless otherwise agreed in any case falling within subsection (1)(a) or (c) or subsection (2) the buyer must seasonably give any needed instructions for making delivery, including when the term is F.A.S. or F.O.B. the loading berth of the vessel and in an appropriate case its name and sailing date. The seller may treat the failure of needed instructions as a failure of cooperation under this Article (Section 2—311). He may also at his option move the goods in any reasonable manner preparatory to delivery or shipment.

(4) Under the term F.O.B. vessel or F.A.S. unless otherwise agreed the buyer must make payment against tender of the required documents and the seller may not tender nor the buyer demand delivery of the goods in substitution for the documents.

§ 2—320. **C.I.F. and C. & F. Terms.**

(1) The term C.I.F. means that the price includes in a lump sum the cost of the goods and the insurance and freight to the named destination. The term C. & F. or C.F. means that the price so includes cost and freight to the named destination.

(2) Unless otherwise agreed and even though used only in connection with the stated price and destination, the term C.I.F. destination or its equivalent requires the seller at his own expense and risk to

  (a) put the goods into the possession of a carrier at the port for shipment and obtain a negotiable bill or bills of lading covering the entire transportation to the named destination; and

  (b) load the goods and obtain a receipt from the carrier (which may be contained in the bill of lading) showing that the freight has been paid or provided for; and

  (c) obtain a policy or certificate of insurance, including any war risk insurance, of a kind and on terms then current at the port of shipment in the usual amount, in the currency of the contract, shown to cover the same goods covered by the bill of lading and providing for payment of loss to the order of the buyer or for the account of whom it may concern; but the seller may add to the price the amount of the premium for any such war risk insurance; and

(d) prepare an invoice of the goods and procure any other documents required to effect shipment or to comply with the contract; and

(e) forward and tender with commercial promptness all the documents in due form and with any indorsement necessary to perfect the buyer's rights.

(3) Unless otherwise agreed the term C. & F. or its equivalent has the same effect and imposes upon the seller the same obligations and risks as a C.I.F. term except the obligation as to insurance.

(4) Under the term C.I.F. or C. & F. unless otherwise agreed the buyer must make payment against tender of the required documents and the seller may not tender nor the buyer demand delivery of the goods in substitution for the documents.

§ 2—321. C.I.F. or C. & F.: "Net Landed Weights"; "Payment on Arrival"; Warranty of Condition on Arrival.

Under a contract containing a term C.I.F. or C. & F.

(1) Where the price is based on or is to be adjusted according to "net landed weights", "delivered weights", "out turn" quantity or quality or the like, unless otherwise agreed the seller must reasonably estimate the price. The payment due on tender of the documents called for by the contract is the amount so estimated, but after final adjustment of the price a settlement must be made with commercial promptness.

(2) An agreement described in subsection (1) or any warranty of quality or condition of the goods on arrival places upon the seller the risk of ordinary deterioration, shrinkage and the like in transportation but has no effect on the place or time of identification to the contract for sale or delivery or on the passing of the risk of loss.

(3) Unless otherwise agreed where the contract provides for payment on or after arrival of the goods the seller must before payment allow such preliminary inspection as is feasible; but if the goods are lost delivery of the documents and payment are due when the goods should have arrived.

§ 2—322. Delivery "Ex-Ship".

(1) Unless otherwise agreed a term for delivery of goods "ex-ship" (which means from the carrying vessel) or in equivalent language is not restricted to a particular ship and requires delivery from a ship which has reached a place at the named port of destination where goods of the kind are usually discharged.

(2) Under such a term unless otherwise agreed

(a) the seller must discharge all liens arising out of the carriage and furnish the buyer with a direction which puts the carrier under a duty to deliver the goods; and

(b) the risk of loss does not pass to the buyer until the goods leave the ship's tackle or are otherwise properly unloaded.

§ 2—323. Form of Bill of Lading Required in Overseas Shipment; "Overseas".

(1) Where the contract contemplates overseas shipment and contains a term C.I.F. or C. & F. or F.O.B. vessel, the seller unless otherwise agreed must obtain a negotiable bill of lading stating that the goods have been loaded on board or, in the case of a term C.I.F. or C. & F., received for shipment.

(2) Where in a case within subsection (1) a bill of lading has been issued in a set of parts, unless otherwise agreed if the documents are not to be sent from abroad the buyer may demand tender of the full set; otherwise only one part of the bill of lading need be tendered. Even if the agreement expressly requires a full set

(a) due tender of a single part is acceptable within the provisions of this Article on cure of improper delivery (subsection (1) of Section 2—508); and

(b) even though the full set is demanded, if the documents are sent from abroad the person tendering an incomplete set may nevertheless require payment upon furnishing an indemnity which the buyer in good faith deems adequate.

(3) A shipment by water or by air or a contract contemplating such shipment is "overseas" insofar as by usage of trade or agreement it is subject to the commercial, financing or shipping practices characteristic of international deep water commerce.

§ 2—324. "No Arrival, No Sale" Term.

Under a term "no arrival, no sale" or terms of like meaning, unless otherwise agreed,

(a) the seller must properly ship conforming goods and if they arrive by any means he must tender them on arrival but he assumes no obligation that the goods will arrive unless he has caused the non-arrival; and

(b) where without fault of the seller the goods are in part lost or have so deteriorated as no longer to conform to the contract or arrive after the contract time, the buyer may proceed as if there had been casualty to identified goods (Section 2—613).

§ 2—325. "Letter of Credit" Term; "Confirmed Credit".

(1) Failure of the buyer seasonably to furnish an agreed letter of credit is a breach of the contract for sale.

(2) The delivery to seller of a proper letter of credit suspends the buyer's obligation to pay. If the letter of credit is dishonored, the seller may on seasonable notification to the buyer require payment directly from him.

(3) Unless otherwise agreed the term "letter of credit" or "banker's credit" in a contract for sale means an irrevocable credit issued by a financing agency of good repute and, where the shipment is overseas, of good international repute. The term "confirmed credit" means that the credit must also carry the direct obligation of such an agency which does business in the seller's financial market.

§ 2—326. **Sale on Approval and Sale or Return; Consignment Sales and Rights of Creditors.**

(1) Unless otherwise agreed, if delivered goods may be returned by the buyer even though they conform to the contract, the transaction is

(a) a "sale on approval" if the goods are delivered primarily for use, and

(b) a "sale or return" if the goods are delivered primarily for resale.

(2) Except as provided in subsection (3), goods held on approval are not subject to the claims of the buyer's creditors until acceptance; goods held on sale or return are subject to such claims while in the buyer's possession.

(3) Where goods are delivered to a person for sale and such person maintains a place of business at which he deals in goods of the kind involved, under a name other than the name of the person making delivery, then with respect to claims of creditors of the person conducting the business the goods are deemed to be on sale or return. The provisions of this subsection are applicable even though an agreement purports to reserve title to the person making delivery until payment or resale or uses such words as "on consignment" or "on memorandum". However, this subsection is not applicable if the person making delivery

(a) complies with an applicable law providing for a consignor's interest or the like to be evidenced by a sign, or

(b) establishes that the person conducting the business is generally known by his creditors to be substantially engaged in selling the goods of others, or

(c) complies with the filing provisions of the Article on Secured Transactions (Article 9).

(4) Any "or return" term of a contract for sale is to be treated as a separate contract for sale within the statute of frauds section of this Article (Section 2—201) and as contradicting the sale aspect of the contract within the provisions of this Article on parol or extrinsic evidence (Section 2—202).

§ 2—327. **Special Incidents of Sale on Approval and Sale or Return.**

(1) Under a sale on approval unless otherwise agreed

(a) although the goods are identified to the contract the risk of loss and the title do not pass to the buyer until acceptance; and

(b) use of the goods consistent with the purpose of trial is not acceptance but failure seasonably to notify the seller of election to return the goods is acceptance, and if the goods conform to the contract acceptance of any part is acceptance of the whole; and

(c) after due notification of election to return, the return is at the seller's risk and expense but a merchant buyer must follow any reasonable instructions.

(2) Under a sale or return unless otherwise agreed

(a) the option to return extends to the whole or any commercial unit of the goods while in substantially their original condition, but must be exercised seasonably; and

(b) the return is at the buyer's risk and expense.

§ 2—328. **Sale by Auction.**

(1) In a sale by auction if goods are put up in lots each lot is the subject of a separate sale.

(2) A sale by auction is complete when the auctioneer so announces by the fall of the hammer or in other customary manner. Where a bid is made while the hammer is falling in acceptance of a prior bid the auctioneer may in his discretion reopen the bidding or declare the goods sold under the bid on which the hammer was falling.

(3) Such a sale is with reserve unless the goods are in explicit terms put up without reserve. In an auction with reserve the auctioneer may withdraw the goods at any time until he announces completion of the sale. In an auction without reserve, after the auctioneer calls for bids on an article or lot, that article or lot cannot be withdrawn unless no bid is made within a reasonable time. In either case a bidder may retract his bid until the auctioneer's announcement of completion of the sale, but a bidder's retraction does not revive any previous bid.

(4) If the auctioneer knowingly receives a bid on the seller's behalf or the seller makes or procures such as bid, and notice has not been given that liberty for such bidding is reserved, the buyer may at his option avoid the sale or take the goods at the price of the last good faith bid prior to the completion of the sale. This subsection shall not apply to any bid at a forced sale.

Part 4 Title, Creditors and Good Faith Purchasers

§ 2—401. Passing of Title; Reservation for Security; Limited Application of This Section.

Each provision of this Article with regard to the rights, obligations and remedies of the seller, the buyer, purchasers or other third parties applies irrespective of title to the goods except where the provision refers to such title. Insofar as situations are not covered by the other provisions of this Article and matters concerning title became material the following rules apply:

(1) Title to goods cannot pass under a contract for sale prior to their identification to the contract (Section 2—501), and unless otherwise explicitly agreed the buyer acquires by their identification a special property as limited by this Act. Any retention or reservation by the seller of the title (property) in goods shipped or delivered to the buyer is limited in effect to a reservation of a security interest. Subject to these provisions and to the provisions of the Article on Secured Transactions (Article 9), title to goods passes from the seller to the buyer in any manner and on any conditions explicitly agreed on by the parties.

(2) Unless otherwise explicitly agreed title passes to the buyer at the time and place at which the seller completes his performance with reference to the physical delivery of the goods, despite any reservation of a security interest and even though a document of title is to be delivered at a different time or place; and in particular and despite any reservation of a security interest by the bill of lading

(a) if the contract requires or authorizes the seller to send the goods to the buyer but does not require him to deliver them at destination, title passes to the buyer at the time and place of shipment; but

(b) if the contract requires delivery at destination, title passes on tender there.

(3) Unless otherwise explicitly agreed where delivery is to be made without moving the goods,

(a) if the seller is to deliver a document of title, title passes at the time when and the place where he delivers such documents; or

(b) if the goods are at the time of contracting already identified and no documents are to be delivered, title passes at the time and place of contracting.

(4) A rejection or other refusal by the buyer to receive or retain the goods, whether or not justified, or a justified revocation of acceptance revests title to the goods in the seller. Such revesting occurs by operation of law and is not a "sale".

§ 2—402. Rights of Seller's Creditors Against Sold Goods.

(1) Except as provided in subsections (2) and (3), rights of unsecured creditors of the seller with respect to goods which have been identified to a contract for sale are subject to the buyer's rights to recover the goods under this Article (Sections 2—502 and 2—716).

(2) A creditor of the seller may treat a sale or an identification of goods to a contract for sale as void if as against him a retention of possession by the seller is fraudulent under any rule of law of the state where the goods are situated, except that retention of possession in good faith and current course of trade by a merchant-seller for a commercially reasonable time after a sale or identification is not fraudulent.

(3) Nothing in this Article shall be deemed to impair the rights of creditors of the seller

(a) under the provisions of the Article on Secured Transactions (Article 9); or

(b) where identification to the contract or delivery is made not in current course of trade but in satisfaction of or as security for a pre-existing claim for money, security or the like and is made under circumstances which under any rule of law of the state where the goods are situated would apart from this Article constitute the transaction a fraudulent transfer or voidable preference.

§ 2—403. Power to Transfer; Good Faith Purchase of Goods; "Entrusting".

(1) A purchaser of goods acquires all title which his transferor had or had power to transfer except that a purchaser of a limited interest acquires rights only to the extent of the interest purchased. A person with voidable title has power to transfer a good title to a good faith purchaser for value. When goods have been delivered under a transaction of purchase the purchaser has such power even though

(a) the transferor was deceived as to the identity of the purchaser, or

(b) the delivery was in exchange for a check which is later dishonored, or

(c) it was agreed that the transaction was to be a "cash sale", or

(d) the delivery was procured through fraud punishable as larcenous under the criminal law.

(2) Any entrusting of possession of goods to a merchant who deals in goods of that kind gives him power to transfer all rights of the entruster to a buyer in ordinary course of business.

(3) "Entrusting" includes any delivery and any acquiescence in retention of possession regardless of any con-

dition expressed between the parties to the delivery or acquiescence and regardless of whether the procurement of the entrusting or the possessor's disposition of the goods have been such as to be larcenous under the criminal law.

(4) The rights of other purchasers of goods and of lien creditors are governed by the Articles on Secured Transactions (Article 9), Bulk Transfers (Article 6) and Documents of Title (Article 7).

Part 5 Performance

§ 2—501. Insurable Interest in Goods; Manner of Identification of Goods.

(1) The buyer obtains a special property and an insurable interest in goods by identification of existing goods as goods to which the contract refers even though the goods so identified are non-conforming and he has an option to return or reject them. Such identification can be made at any time and in any manner explicitly agreed to by the parties. In the absence of explicit agreement identification occurs

(a) when the contract is made if it is for the sale of goods already existing and identified;

(b) if the contract is for the sale of future goods other than those described in paragraph (c), when goods are shipped, marked or otherwise designated by the seller as goods to which the contract refers;

(c) when the crops are planted or otherwise become growing crops or the young are conceived if the contract is for the sale of unborn young to be born within twelve months after contracting or for the sale of crops to be harvested within twelve months or the next normal harvest season after contracting whichever is longer.

(2) The seller retains an insurable interest in goods so long as title to or any security interest in the goods remains in him and where the identification is by the seller alone he may until default or insolvency or notification to the buyer that the identification is final substitute other goods for those identified.

(3) Nothing in this section impairs any insurable interest recognized under any other statute or rule of law.

§ 2—502. Buyer's Right to Goods on Seller's Insolvency.

(1) Subject to subsection (2) and even though the goods have not been shipped a buyer who has paid a part or all of the price of goods in which he has a special property under the provisions of the immediately preceding section may on making and keeping good a tender of any unpaid portion of their price recover them from the seller if the seller becomes insolvent within ten days after receipt of the first installment on their price.

(2) If the identification creating his special property has been made by the buyer he acquires the right to recover the goods only if they conform to the contract for sale.

§ 2—503. Manner of Seller's Tender of Delivery.

(1) Tender of delivery requires that the seller put and hold conforming goods at the buyer's disposition and give the buyer any notification reasonably necessary to enable him to take delivery. The manner, time and place for tender are determined by the agreement and this Article, and in particular

(a) tender must be at a reasonable hour, and if it is of goods they must be kept available for the period reasonably necessary to enable the buyer to take possession; but

(b) unless otherwise agreed the buyer must furnish facilities reasonably suited to the receipt of the goods.

(2) Where the case is within the next section respecting shipment tender requires that the seller comply with its provisions.

(3) Where the seller is required to deliver at a particular destination tender requires that he comply with subsection (1) and also in any appropriate case tender documents as described in subsections (4) and (5) of this section.

(4) Where goods are in the possession of a bailee and are to be delivered without being moved

(a) tender requires that the seller either tender a negotiable document of title covering such goods or procure acknowledgment by the bailee of the buyer's right to possession of the goods; but

(b) tender to the buyer of a non-negotiable document of title or of a written direction to the bailee to deliver is sufficient tender unless the buyer seasonably objects, and receipt by the bailee of notification of the buyer's rights fixes those rights as against the bailee and all third persons; but risk of loss of the goods and of any failure by the bailee to honor the non-negotiable document of title or to obey the direction remains on the seller until the buyer has had a reasonable time to present the document or direction, and a refusal by the bailee to honor the document or to obey the direction defeats the tender.

(5) Where the contract requires the seller to deliver documents

(a) he must tender all such documents in correct form, except as provided in this Article with respect to bills of lading in a set (subsection (2) of Section 2—323); and

(b) tender through customary banking channels is sufficient and dishonor of a draft accompanying the documents constitutes non-acceptance or rejection.

§ 2—504. **Shipment by Seller.**

Where the seller is required or authorized to send the goods to the buyer and the contract does not require him to deliver them at a particular destination, then unless otherwise agreed he must

(a) put the goods in the possession of such a carrier and make such a contract for their transportation as may be reasonable having regard to the nature of the goods and other circumstances of the case; and

(b) obtain and promptly deliver or tender in due form any document necessary to enable the buyer to obtain possession of the goods or otherwise required by the agreement or by usage of trade; and

(c) promptly notify the buyer of the shipment.

Failure to notify the buyer under paragraph (c) or to make a proper contract under paragraph (a) is a ground for rejection only if material delay or loss ensues.

§ 2—505. **Seller's Shipment Under Reservation.**

(1) Where the seller has identified goods to the contract by or before shipment:

(a) his procurement of a negotiable bill of lading to his own order or otherwise reserves in him a security interest in the goods. His procurement of the bill to the order of a financing agency or of the buyer indicates in addition only the seller's expectation of transferring that interest to the person named.

(b) a non-negotiable bill of lading to himself or his nominee reserves possession of the goods as security but except in a case of conditional delivery (subsection (2) of Section 2—507) a non-negotiable bill of lading naming the buyer as consignee reserves no security interest even though the seller retains possession of the bill of lading.

(2) When shipment by the seller with reservation of a security interest is in violation of the contract for sale it constitutes an improper contract for transportation within the preceding section but impairs neither the rights given to the buyer by shipment and identification of the goods to the contract nor the seller's powers as a holder of a negotiable document.

§ 2—506. **Rights of Financing Agency.**

(1) A financing agency by paying or purchasing for value a draft which relates to a shipment of goods acquires to the extent of the payment or purchase and in addition to its own rights under the draft and any document of title securing it any rights of the shipper in the goods including the right to stop delivery and the shipper's right to have the draft honored by the buyer.

(2) The right to reimbursement of a financing agency which has in good faith honored or purchased the draft under commitment to or authority from the buyer is not impaired by subsequent discovery of defects with reference to any relevant document which was apparently regular on its face.

§ 2—507. **Effect of Seller's Tender; Delivery on Condition.**

(1) Tender of delivery is a condition to the buyer's duty to accept the goods and, unless otherwise agreed, to his duty to pay for them. Tender entitles the seller to acceptance of the goods and to payment according to the contract.

(2) Where payment is due and demanded on the delivery to the buyer of goods or documents of title, his right as against the seller to retain or dispose of them is conditional upon his making the payment due.

§ 2—508. **Cure by Seller of Improper Tender or Delivery; Replacement.**

(1) Where any tender or delivery by the seller is rejected because non-conforming and the time for performance has not yet expired, the seller may seasonably notify the buyer of his intention to cure and may then within the contract time make a conforming delivery.

(2) Where the buyer rejects a non-conforming tender which the seller had reasonable grounds to believe would be acceptable with or without money allowance the seller may if he seasonably notifies the buyer have a further reasonable time to substitute a conforming tender.

§ 2—509. **Risk of Loss in the Absence of Breach.**

(1) Where the contract requires or authorizes the seller to ship the goods by carrier

(a) if it does not require him to deliver them at a particular destination, the risk of loss passes to the buyer when the goods are duly delivered to the carrier even though the shipment is under reservation (Section 2—505); but

(b) if it does require him to deliver them at a particular destination and the goods are there duly tendered while in the possession of the carrier, the risk of loss passes to the buyer when the goods are there duly so tendered as to enable the buyer to take delivery.

(2) Where the goods are held by a bailee to be delivered without being moved, the risk of loss passes to the buyer

(a) on his receipt of a negotiable document of title covering the goods; or

(b) on acknowledgment by the bailee of the buyer's right to possession of the goods; or

(c) after his receipt of a non-negotiable document of title or other written direction to deliver, as provided in subsection (4)(b) of Section 2—503.

(3) In any case not within subsection (1) or (2), the risk of loss passes to the buyer on his receipt of the goods if the seller is a merchant; otherwise the risk passes to the buyer on tender of delivery.

(4) The provisions of this section are subject to contrary agreement of the parties and to the provisions of this Article on sale on approval (Section 2—327) and on effect of breach on risk of loss (Section 2—510).

§ 2—510. Effect of Breach on Risk of Loss.

(1) Where a tender or delivery of goods so fails to conform to the contract as to give a right of rejection the risk of their loss remains on the seller until cure or acceptance.

(2) Where the buyer rightfully revokes acceptance he may to the extent of any deficiency in his effective insurance coverage treat the risk of loss as having rested on the seller from the beginning.

(3) Where the buyer as to conforming goods already identified to the contract for sale repudiates or is otherwise in breach before risk of their loss has passed to him, the seller may to the extent of any deficiency in his effective insurance coverage treat the risk of loss as resting on the buyer for a commercially reasonable time.

§ 2—511. Tender of Payment by Buyer; Payment by Check.

(1) Unless otherwise agreed tender of payment is a condition to the seller's duty to tender and complete any delivery.

(2) Tender of payment is sufficient when made by any means or in any manner current in the ordinary course of business unless the seller demands payment in legal tender and gives any extension of time reasonably necessary to procure it.

(3) Subject to the provisions of this Act on the effect of an instrument on an obligation (Section 3—802), payment by check is conditional and is defeated as between the parties by dishonor of the check on due presentment.

§ 2—512. Payment by Buyer Before Inspection.

(1) Where the contract requires payment before inspection non-conformity of the goods does not excuse the buyer from so making payment unless

(a) the non-conformity appears without inspection; or

(b) despite tender of the required documents the circumstances would justify injunction against honor under the provisions of this Act (Section 5—114).

(2) Payment pursuant to subsection (1) does not constitute an acceptance of goods or impair the buyer's right to inspect or any of his remedies.

§ 2—513. Buyer's Right to Inspection of Goods.

(1) Unless otherwise agreed and subject to subsection (3), where goods are tendered or delivered or identified to the contract for sale, the buyer has a right before payment or acceptance to inspect them at any reasonable place and time and in any reasonable manner. When the seller is required or authorized to send the goods to the buyer, the inspection may be after their arrival.

(2) Expenses of inspection must be borne by the buyer but may be recovered from the seller if the goods do not conform and are rejected.

(3) Unless otherwise agreed and subject to the provisions of this Article on C.I.F. contracts (subsection (3) of Section 2—321), the buyer is not entitled to inspect the goods before payment of the price when the contract provides

(a) for delivery "C.O.D." or on other like terms; or

(b) for payment against documents of title, except where such payment is due only after the goods are to become available for inspection.

(4) A place or method of inspection fixed by the parties is presumed to be exclusive but unless otherwise expressly agreed it does not postpone identification or shift the place for delivery or for passing the risk of loss. If compliance becomes impossible, inspection shall be as provided in this section unless the place or method fixed was clearly intended as an indispensable condition failure of which avoids the contract.

§ 2—514. When Documents Deliverable on Acceptance; When on Payment.

Unless otherwise agreed documents against which a draft is drawn are to be delivered to the drawee on acceptance of the draft if it is payable more than three days after presentment; otherwise, only on payment.

§ 2—515. Preserving Evidence of Goods in Dispute.

In furtherance of the adjustment of any claim or dispute

(a) either party on reasonable notification to the other and for the purpose of ascertaining the facts and preserving evidence has the right to inspect, test and sample the goods including such of them as may be in the possession or control of the other; and

(b) the parties may agree to a third party inspection or survey to determine the conformity or condition of the goods and may agree that the findings shall be binding upon them in any subsequent litigation or adjustment.

Part 6 Breach, Repudiation and Excuse

§ 2—601. **Buyer's Rights on Improper Delivery.**

Subject to the provisions of this Article on breach in installment contracts (Section 2—612) and unless otherwise agreed under the sections on contractual limitations of remedy (Sections 2—718 and 2—719), if the goods or the tender of delivery fail in any respect to conform to the contract, the buyer may

(a) reject the whole; or

(b) accept the whole; or

(c) accept any commercial unit or units and reject the rest.

§ 2—602. **Manner and Effect of Rightful Rejection.**

(1) Rejection of goods must be within a reasonable time after their delivery or tender. It is ineffective unless the buyer seasonably notifies the seller.

(2) Subject to the provisions of the two following sections on rejected goods (Sections 2—603 and 2—604),

(a) after rejection any exercise of ownership by the buyer with respect to any commercial unit is wrongful as against the seller; and

(b) if the buyer has before rejection taken physical possession of goods in which he does not have a security interest under the provisions of this Article (subsection (3) of Section 2—711), he is under a duty after rejection to hold them with reasonable care at the seller's disposition for a time sufficient to permit the seller to remove them; but

(c) the buyer has no further obligations with regard to goods rightfully rejected.

(3) The seller's rights with respect to goods wrongfully rejected are governed by the provisions of this Article on Seller's remedies in general (Section 2—703).

§ 2—603. **Merchant Buyer's Duties as to Rightfully Rejected Goods.**

(1) Subject to any security interest in the buyer (subsection (3) of Section 2—711), when the seller has no agent or place of business at the market of rejection a merchant buyer is under a duty after rejection of goods in his possession or control to follow any reasonable instructions received from the seller with respect to the goods and in the absence of such instructions to make reasonable efforts to sell them for the seller's account if they are perishable or threaten to decline in value speedily. Instructions are not reasonable if on demand indemnity for expenses is not forthcoming.

(2) When the buyer sells goods under subsection (1), he is entitled to reimbursement from the seller or out of the proceeds for reasonable expenses of caring for and selling them, and if the expenses include no selling commission then to such commission as is usual in the trade or if there is none to a reasonable sum not exceeding ten per cent on the gross proceeds.

(3) In complying with this section the buyer is held only to good faith and good faith conduct hereunder is neither acceptance nor conversion nor the basis of an action for damages.

§ 2—604. **Buyer's Options as to Salvage of Rightfully Rejected Goods.**

Subject to the provisions of the immediately preceding section on perishables if the seller gives no instructions within a reasonable time after notification of rejection the buyer may store the rejected goods for the seller's account or reship them to him or resell them for the seller's account with reimbursement as provided in the preceding section. Such action is not acceptance or conversion.

§ 2—605. **Waiver of Buyer's Objections by Failure to Particularize.**

(1) The buyer's failure to state in connection with rejection a particular defect which is ascertainable by reasonable inspection precludes him from relying on the unstated defect to justify rejection or to establish breach

(a) where the seller could have cured it if stated seasonably; or

(b) between merchants when the seller has after rejection made a request in writing for a full and final written statement of all defects on which the buyer proposes to rely.

(2) Payment against documents made without reservation of rights precludes recovery of the payment for defects apparent on the face of the documents.

§ 2—606. **What Constitutes Acceptance of Goods.**

(1) Acceptance of goods occurs when the buyer

(a) after a reasonable opportunity to inspect the goods signifies to the seller that the goods are conforming or that he will take or retain them in spite of their nonconformity; or

(b) fails to make an effective rejection (subsection (1) of Section 2—602), but such acceptance does not occur until the buyer has had a reasonable opportunity to inspect them; or

(c) does any act inconsistent with the seller's ownership; but if such act is wrongful as against the seller it is an acceptance only if ratified by him.

(2) Acceptance of a part of any commercial unit is acceptance of that entire unit.

§ 2—607. **Effect of Acceptance; Notice of Breach; Burden of Establishing Breach After Acceptance; Notice of Claim or Litigation to Person Answerable Over.**

(1) The buyer must pay at the contract rate for any goods accepted.

(2) Acceptance of goods by the buyer precludes rejection of the goods accepted and if made with knowledge of a non-conformity cannot be revoked because of it unless the acceptance was on the reasonable assumption that the non-conformity would be seasonably cured but acceptance does not of itself impair any other remedy provided by this Article for non-conformity.

(3) Where a tender has been accepted

(a) the buyer must within a reasonable time after he discovers or should have discovered any breach notify the seller of breach or be barred from any remedy; and

(b) if the claim is one for infringement or the like (subsection (3) of Section 2—312) and the buyer is sued as a result of such a breach he must so notify the seller within a reasonable time after he receives notice of the litigation or be barred from any remedy over for liability established by the litigation.

(4) The burden is on the buyer to establish any breach with respect to the goods accepted.

(5) Where the buyer is sued for breach of a warranty or other obligation for which his seller is answerable over

(a) he may give his seller written notice of the litigation. If the notice states that the seller may come in and defend and that if the seller does not do so he will be bound in any action against him by his buyer by any determination of fact common to the two litigations, then unless the seller after seasonable receipt of the notice does come in and defend he is so bound.

(b) if the claim is one for infringement or the like (subsection (3) of Section 2—312) the original seller may demand in writing that his buyer turn over to him control of the litigation including settlement or else be barred from any remedy over and if he also agrees to bear all expense and to satisfy any adverse judgment, then unless the buyer after seasonable receipt of the demand does turn over control the buyer is so barred.

(6) The provisions of subsections (3), (4) and (5) apply to any obligation of a buyer to hold the seller harmless against infringement or the like (subsection (3) of Section 2—312).

§ 2—608. **Revocation of Acceptance in Whole or in Part.**

(1) The buyer may revoke his acceptance of a lot or commercial unit whose non-conformity substantially impairs its value to him if he has accepted it

(a) on the reasonable assumption that its non-conformity would be cured and it has not been seasonably cured; or

(b) without discovery of such non-conformity if his acceptance was reasonably induced either by the difficulty of discovery before acceptance or by the seller's assurances.

(2) Revocation of acceptance must occur within a reasonable time after the buyer discovers or should have discovered the ground for it and before any substantial change in condition of the goods which is not caused by their own defects. It is not effective until the buyer notifies the seller of it.

(3) A buyer who so revokes has the same rights and duties with regard to the goods involved as if he had rejected them.

§ 2—609. **Right to Adequate Assurance of Performance.**

(1) A contract for sale imposes an obligation on each party that the other's expectation of receiving due performance will not be impaired. When reasonable grounds for insecurity arise with respect to the performance of either party the other may in writing demand adequate assurance of due performance and until he receives such assurance may if commercially reasonable suspend any performance for which he has not already received the agreed return.

(2) Between merchants the reasonableness of grounds for insecurity and the adequacy of any assurance offered shall be determined according to commercial standards.

(3) Acceptance of any improper delivery or payment does not prejudice the aggrieved party's right to demand adequate assurance of future performance.

(4) After receipt of a justified demand failure to provide within a reasonable time not exceeding thirty days such assurance of due performance as is adequate under the circumstances of the particular case is a repudiation of the contract.

§ 2—610. **Anticipatory Repudiation.**

When either party repudiates the contract with respect to a performance not yet due the loss of which will substantially impair the value of the contract to the other, the aggrieved party may

(a) for a commercially reasonable time await performance by the repudiating party; or

(b) resort to any remedy for breach (Section 2—703 or Section 2—711), even though he has notified the repudiating party that he would await the latter's performance and has urged retraction; and

(c) in either case suspend his own performance or proceed in accordance with the provisions of this Article on the seller's right to identify goods to the contract notwithstanding breach or to salvage unfinished goods (Section 2—704).

§ 2—611. **Retraction of Anticipatory Repudiation.**

(1) Until the repudiating party's next performance is due he can retract his repudiation unless the aggrieved party has since the repudiation cancelled or materially changed his position or otherwise indicated that he considers the repudiation final.

(2) Retraction may be by any method which clearly indicates to the aggrieved party that the repudiating party intends to perform, but must include any assurance justifiably demanded under the provisions of this Article (Section 2—609).

(3) Retraction reinstates the repudiating party's rights under the contract with due excuse and allowance to the aggrieved party for any delay occasioned by the repudiation.

§ 2—612. **"Installment Contract"; Breach.**

(1) An "installment contract" is one which requires or authorizes the delivery of goods in separate lots to be separately accepted, even though the contract contains a clause "each delivery is a separate contract" or its equivalent.

(2) The buyer may reject any installment which is nonconforming if the non-conformity substantially impairs the value of that installment and cannot be cured or if the non-conformity is a defect in the required documents; but if the non-conformity does not fall within subsection (3) and the seller gives adequate assurance of its cure the buyer must accept that installment.

(3) Whenever non-conformity or default with respect to one or more installments substantially impairs the value of the whole contract there is a breach of the whole. But the aggrieved party reinstates the contract if he accepts a non-conforming installment without seasonably notifying of cancellation or if he brings an action with respect only to past installments or demands performance as to future installments.

§ 2—613. **Casualty to Identified Goods.**

Where the contract requires for its performance goods identified when the contract is made, and the goods suffer casualty without fault of either party before the risk of loss passes to the buyer, or in a proper case

under a "no arrival, no sale" term (Section 2—324) then

(a) if the loss is total the contract is avoided; and

(b) if the loss is partial or the goods have so deteriorated as no longer to conform to the contract the buyer may nevertheless demand inspection and at his option either treat the contract as voided or accept the goods with due allowance from the contract price for the deterioration or the deficiency in quantity but without further right against the seller.

§ 2—614. **Substituted Performance.**

(1) Where without fault of either party the agreed berthing, loading, or unloading facilities fail or an agreed type of carrier becomes unavailable or the agreed manner of delivery otherwise becomes commercially impracticable but a commercially reasonable substitute is available, such substitute performance must be tendered and accepted.

(2) If the agreed means or manner of payment fails because of domestic or foreign governmental regulation, the seller may withhold or stop delivery unless the buyer provides a means or manner of payment which is commercially a substantial equivalent. If delivery has already been taken, payment by the means or in the manner provided by the regulation discharges the buyer's obligation unless the regulation is discriminatory, oppressive or predatory.

§ 2—615. **Excuse by Failure of Presupposed Conditions.**

Except so far as a seller may have assumed a greater obligation and subject to the preceding section on substituted performance:

(a) Delay in delivery or non-delivery in whole or in part by a seller who complies with paragraphs (b) and (c) is not a breach of his duty under a contract for sale if performance as agreed has been made impracticable by the occurrence of a contingency the nonoccurrence of which was a basic assumption on which the contract was made or by compliance in good faith with any applicable foreign or domestic governmental regulation or order whether or not it later proves to be invalid.

(b) Where the causes mentioned in paragraph (a) affect only a part of the seller's capacity to perform, he must allocate production and deliveries among his customers but may at his option include regular customers not then under contract as well as his own requirements for further manufacture. He may so allocate in any manner which is fair and reasonable.

(c) The seller must notify the buyer seasonably that there will be delay or non-delivery and, when allocation is required under paragraph (b), of the estimated quota thus made available for the buyer.

§ 2—616. **Procedure on Notice Claiming Excuse.**

(1) Where the buyer receives notification of a material or indefinite delay or an allocation justified under the preceding section he may by written notification to the seller as to any delivery concerned, and where the prospective deficiency substantially impairs the value of the whole contract under the provisions of this Article relating to breach of installment contracts (Section 2—612), then also as to the whole,

    (a) terminate and thereby discharge any unexecuted portion of the contract; or

    (b) modify the contract by agreeing to take his available quota in substitution.

(2) If after receipt of such notification from the seller the buyer fails so to modify the contract within a reasonable time not exceeding thirty days the contract lapses with respect to any deliveries affected.

(3) The provisions of this section may not be negated by agreement except in so far as the seller has assumed a greater obligation under the preceding section.

Part 7 Remedies

§ 2—701. **Remedies for Breach of Collateral Contracts Not Impaired.**

Remedies for breach of any obligation or promise collateral or ancillary to a contract for sale are not impaired by the provisions of this Article.

§ 2—702. **Seller's Remedies on Discovery of Buyer's Insolvency.**

(1) Where the seller discovers the buyer to be insolvent he may refuse delivery except for cash including payment for all goods theretofore delivered under the contract, and stop delivery under this Article (Section 2—705).

(2) Where the seller discovers that the buyer has received goods on credit while insolvent he may reclaim the goods upon demand made within ten days after the receipt, but if misrepresentation of solvency has been made to the particular seller in writing within three months before delivery the ten day limitation does not apply. Except as provided in this subsection the seller may not base a right to reclaim goods on the buyer's fraudulent or innocent misrepresentation of solvency or of intent to pay.

(3) The seller's right to reclaim under subsection (2) is subject to the rights of a buyer in ordinary course or other good faith purchaser under this Article (Section 2—403). Successful reclamation of goods excludes all other remedies with respect to them.

§ 2—703. **Seller's Remedies in General.**

Where the buyer wrongfully rejects or revokes acceptance of goods or fails to make a payment due on or before delivery or repudiates with respect to a part or the whole, then with respect to any goods directly affected and, if the breach is of the whole contract (Section 2—612), then also with respect to the whole undelivered balance, the aggrieved seller may

(a) withhold delivery of such goods;

(b) stop delivery by any bailee as hereafter provided (Section 2—705);

(c) proceed under the next section respecting goods still unidentified to the contract;

(d) resell and recover damages as hereafter provided (Section 2—706);

(e) recover damages for non-acceptance (Section 2—708) or in a proper case the price (Section 2—709);

(f) cancel.

§ 2—704. **Seller's Right to Identify Goods to the Contract Notwithstanding Breach or to Salvage Unfinished Goods.**

(1) An aggrieved seller under the preceding section may

    (a) identify to the contract conforming goods not already identified if at the time he learned of the breach they are in his possession or control;

    (b) treat as the subject of resale goods which have demonstrably been intended for the particular contract even though those goods are unfinished.

(2) Where the goods are unfinished an aggrieved seller may in the exercise of reasonable commercial judgment for the purposes of avoiding loss and of effective realization either complete the manufacture and wholly identify the goods to the contract or cease manufacture and resell for scrap or salvage value or proceed in any other reasonable manner.

§ 2—705. **Seller's Stoppage of Delivery in Transit or Otherwise.**

(1) The seller may stop delivery of goods in the possession of a carrier or other bailee when he discovers the buyer to be insolvent (Section 2—702) and may stop delivery of carload, truckload, planeload or larger shipments of express or freight when the buyer repudiates or fails to make a payment due before delivery or if for any other reason the seller has a right to withhold or reclaim the goods.

(2) As against such buyer the seller may stop delivery until

    (a) receipt of the goods by the buyer; or

(b) acknowledgment to the buyer by any bailee of the goods except a carrier that the bailee holds the goods for the buyer; or

(c) such acknowledgment to the buyer by a carrier by reshipment or as warehouseman; or

(d) negotiation to the buyer of any negotiable document of title covering the goods.

(3) (a) To stop delivery the seller must so notify as to enable the bailee by reasonable diligence to prevent delivery of the goods.

(b) After such notification the bailee must hold and deliver the goods according to the directions of the seller but the seller is liable to the bailee for any ensuing charges or damages.

(c) If a negotiable document of title has been issued for goods the bailee is not obliged to obey a notification to stop until surrender of the document.

(d) A carrier who has issued a non-negotiable bill of lading is not obliged to obey a notification to stop received from a person other than the consignor.

§ 2—706. Seller's Resale Including Contract for Resale.

(1) Under the conditions stated in Section 2—703 on seller's remedies, the seller may resell the goods concerned or the undelivered balance thereof. Where the resale is made in good faith and in a commercially reasonable manner the seller may recover the difference between the resale price and the contract price together with any incidental damages allowed under the provisions of this Article (Section 2—710), but less expenses saved in consequence of the buyer's breach.

(2) Except as otherwise provided in subsection (3) or unless otherwise agreed resale may be at public or private sale including sale by way of one or more contracts to sell or of identification to an existing contract of the seller. Sale may be as a unit or in parcels and at any time and place and on any terms but every aspect of the sale including the method, manner, time, place and terms must be commercially reasonable. The resale must be reasonably identified as referring to the broken contract, but it is not necessary that the goods be in existence or that any or all of them have been identified to the contract before the breach.

(3) Where the resale is at private sale the seller must give the buyer reasonable notification of his intention to resell.

(4) Where the resale is at public sale

(a) only identified goods can be sold except where there is a recognized market for a public sale of futures in goods of the kind; and

(b) it must be made at a usual place or market for public sale if one is reasonably available and except

in the case of goods which are perishable or threaten to decline in value speedily the seller must give the buyer reasonable notice of the time and place of the resale; and

(c) if the goods are not to be within the view of those attending the sale the notification of sale must state the place where the goods are located and provide for their reasonable inspection by prospective bidders; and

(d) the seller may buy.

(5) A purchaser who buys in good faith at a resale takes the goods free of any rights of the original buyer even though the seller fails to comply with one or more of the requirements of this section.

(6) The seller is not accountable to the buyer for any profit made on any resale. A person in the position of a seller (Section 2—707) or a buyer who has rightfully rejected or justifiably revoked acceptance must account for any excess over the amount of his security interest, as hereinafter defined (subsection (3) of Section 2—711).

§ 2—707. "Person in the Position of a Seller".

(1) A "person in the position of a seller" includes as against a principal an agent who has paid or become responsible for the price of goods on behalf of his principal or anyone who otherwise holds a security interest or other right in goods similar to that of a seller.

(2) A person in the position of a seller may as provided in this Article withhold or stop delivery (Section 2—705) and resell (Section 2—706) and recover incidental damages (Section 2—710).

§ 2—708. Seller's Damages for Non-Acceptance or Repudiation.

(1) Subject to subsection (2) and to the provisions of this Article with respect to proof of market price (Section 2—723), the measure of damages for non-acceptance or repudiation by the buyer is the difference between the market price at the time and place for tender and the unpaid contract price together with any incidental damages provided in this Article (Section 2—710), but less expenses saved in consequence of the buyer's breach.

(2) If the measure of damages provided in subsection (1) is inadequate to put the seller in as good a position as performance would have done then the measure of damages is the profit (including reasonable overhead) which the seller would have made from full performance by the buyer, together with any incidental damages provided in this Article (Section 2—710), due allowance for costs reasonably incurred and due credit for payments or proceeds of resale.

§ 2—709. **Action for the Price.**

(1) When the buyer fails to pay the price as it becomes due the seller may recover, together with any incidental damages under the next section, the price

(a) of goods accepted or of conforming goods lost or damaged within a commercially reasonable time after risk of their loss has passed to the buyer; and

(b) of goods identified to the contract if the seller is unable after reasonable effort to resell them at a reasonable price or the circumstances reasonably indicate that such effort will be unavailing.

(2) Where the seller sues for the price he must hold for the buyer any goods which have been identified to the contract and are still in his control except that if resale becomes possible he may resell them at any time prior to the collection of the judgment. The net proceeds of any such resale must be credited to the buyer and payment of the judgment entitles him to any goods not resold.

(3) After the buyer has wrongfully rejected or revoked acceptance of the goods or has failed to make a payment due or has repudiated (Section 2—610), a seller who is held not entitled to the price under this section shall nevertheless be awarded damages for non-acceptance under the preceding section.

§ 2—710. **Seller's Incidental Damages.**

Incidental damages to an aggrieved seller include any commercially reasonable charges, expenses or commissions incurred in stopping delivery, in the transportation, care and custody of goods after the buyer's breach, in connection with return or resale of the goods or otherwise resulting from the breach.

§ 2—711. **Buyer's Remedies in General; Buyer's Security Interest in Rejected Goods.**

(1) Where the seller fails to make delivery or repudiates or the buyer rightfully rejects or justifiably revokes acceptance then with respect to any goods involved, and with respect to the whole if the breach goes to the whole contract (Section 2—612), the buyer may cancel and whether or not he has done so may in addition to recovering so much of the price as has been paid

(a) "cover" and have damages under the next section as to all the goods affected whether or not they have been identified to the contract; or

(b) recover damages for non-delivery as provided in this Article (Section 2—713).

(2) Where the seller fails to deliver or repudiates the buyer may also

(a) if the goods have been identified recover them as provided in this Article (Section 2—502); or

(b) in a proper case obtain specific performance or replevy the goods as provided in this Article (Section 2—716).

(3) On rightful rejection or justifiable revocation of acceptance a buyer has a security interest in goods in his possession or control for any payments made on their price and any expenses reasonably incurred in their inspection, receipt, transportation, care and custody and may hold such goods and resell them in like manner as an aggrieved seller (Section 2—706).

§ 2—712. **"Cover"; Buyer's Procurement of Substitute Goods.**

(1) After a breach within the preceding section the buyer may "cover" by making in good faith and without unreasonable delay any reasonable purchase of or contract to purchase goods in substitution for those due from the seller.

(2) The buyer may recover from the seller as damages the difference between the cost of cover and the contract price together with any incidental or consequential damages as hereinafter defined (Section 2—715), but less expenses saved in consequence of the seller's breach.

(3) Failure of the buyer to effect cover within this section does not bar him from any other remedy.

§ 2—713. **Buyer's Damages for Non-Delivery or Repudiation.**

(1) Subject to the provisions of this Article with respect to proof of market price (Section 2—723), the measure of damages for non-delivery or repudiation by the seller is the difference between the market price at the time when the buyer learned of the breach and the contract price together with any incidental and consequential damages provided in this Article (Section 2—715), but less expenses saved in consequence of the seller's breach.

(2) Market price is to be determined as of the place for tender or, in cases of rejection after arrival or revocation of acceptance, as of the place of arrival.

§ 2—714. **Buyer's Damages for Breach in Regard to Accepted Goods.**

(1) Where the buyer has accepted goods and given notification (subsection (3) of Section 2—607) he may recover as damages for any non-conformity of tender the loss resulting in the ordinary course of events from the seller's breach as determined in any manner which is reasonable.

(2) The measure of damages for breach of warranty is the difference at the time and place of acceptance between the value of the goods accepted and the value they would have had if they had been as warranted, unless special circumstances show proximate damages of a different amount.

(3) In a proper case any incidental and consequential damages under the next section may also be recovered.

§ 2—715. Buyer's Incidental and Consequential Damages.

(1) Incidental damages resulting from the seller's breach include expenses reasonably incurred in inspection, receipt, transportation and care and custody of goods rightfully rejected, any commercially reasonable charges, expenses or commissions in connection with effecting cover and any other reasonable expense incident to the delay or other breach.

(2) Consequential damages resulting from the seller's breach include

(a) any loss resulting from general or particular requirements and needs of which the seller at the time of contracting had reason to know and which could not reasonably be prevented by cover or otherwise; and

(b) injury to person or property proximately resulting from any breach of warranty.

§ 2—716. Buyer's Right to Specific Performance or Replevin.

(1) Specific performance may be decreed where the goods are unique or in other proper circumstances.

(2) The decree for specific performance may include such terms and conditions as to payment of the price, damages, or other relief as the court may deem just.

(3) The buyer has a right of replevin for goods identified to the contract if after reasonable effort he is unable to effect cover for such goods or the circumstances reasonably indicate that such effort will be unavailing or if the goods have been shipped under reservation and satisfaction of the security interest in them has been made or tendered.

§ 2—717. Deduction of Damages From the Price.

The buyer on notifying the seller of his intention to do so may deduct all or any part of the damages resulting from any breach of the contract from any part of the price still due under the same contract.

§ 2—718. Liquidation or Limitation of Damages; Deposits.

(1) Damages for breach by either party may be liquidated in the agreement but only at an amount which is reasonable in the light of the anticipated or actual harm caused by the breach, the difficulties of proof of loss, and the inconvenience or nonfeasibility of otherwise obtaining an adequate remedy. A term fixing unreasonably large liquidated damages is void as a penalty.

(2) Where the seller justifiably withholds delivery of goods because of the buyer's breach, the buyer is entitled to restitution of any amount by which the sum of his payments exceeds

(a) the amount to which the seller is entitled by virtue of terms liquidating the seller's damages in accordance with subsection (1), or

(b) in the absence of such terms, twenty per cent of the value of the total performance for which the buyer is obligated under the contract or $500, whichever is smaller.

(3) The buyer's right to restitution under subsection (2) is subject to offset to the extent that the seller establishes

(a) a right to recover damages under the provisions of this Article other than subsection (1), and

(b) the amount or value of any benefits received by the buyer directly or indirectly by reason of the contract.

(4) Where a seller has received payment in goods their reasonable value or the proceeds of their resale shall be treated as payments for the purposes of subsection (2); but if the seller has notice of the buyer's breach before reselling goods received in part performance, his resale is subject to the conditions laid down in this Article on resale by an aggrieved seller (Section 2—706).

§ 2—719. Contractual Modification or Limitation of Remedy.

(1) Subject to the provisions of subsections (2) and (3) of this section and of the preceding section on liquidation and limitation of damages,

(a) the agreement may provide for remedies in addition to or in substitution for those provided in this Article and may limit or alter the measure of damages recoverable under this Article, as by limiting the buyer's remedies to return of the goods and repayment of the price or to repair and replacement of non-conforming goods or parts; and

(b) resort to a remedy as provided is optional unless the remedy is expressly agreed to be exclusive, in which case it is the sole remedy.

(2) Where circumstances cause an exclusive or limited remedy to fail of its essential purpose, remedy may be had as provided in this Act.

(3) Consequential damages may be limited or excluded unless the limitation or exclusion is unconscionable. Limitation of consequential damages for injury to the person in the case of consumer goods is prima facie unconscionable but limitation of damages where the loss is commercial is not.

§ 2—720. Effect of "Cancellation" or "Rescission" on Claims for Antecedent Breach.

Unless the contrary intention clearly appears, expressions of "cancellation" or "rescission" of the contract or the like shall not be construed as a renunciation or discharge of any claim in damages for an antecedent breach.

§ 2—721. Remedies for Fraud.

Remedies for material misrepresentation or fraud include all remedies available under this Article for non-fraudulent breach. Neither rescission or a claim for rescission of the contract for sale nor rejection or return of the goods shall bar or be deemed inconsistent with a claim for damages or other remedy.

§ 2—722. Who Can Sue Third Parties for Injury to Goods.

Where a third party so deals with goods which have been identified to a contract for sale as to cause actionable injury to a party to that contract

(a) a right of action against the third party is in either party to the contract for sale who has title to or a security interest or a special property or an insurable interest in the goods; and if the goods have been destroyed or converted a right of action is also in the party who either bore the risk of loss under the contract for sale or has since the injury assumed that risk as against the other;

(b) if at the time of the injury the party plaintiff did not bear the risk of loss as against the other party to the contract for sale and there is no arrangement between them for disposition of the recovery, his suit or settlement is, subject to his own interest, as a fiduciary for the other party to the contract;

(c) either party may with the consent of the other sue for the benefit of whom it may concern.

§ 2—723. Proof of Market Price: Time and Place.

(1) If an action based on anticipatory repudiation comes to trial before the time for performance with respect to some or all of the goods, any damages based on market price (Section 2—708 or Section 2—713) shall be determined according to the price of such goods prevailing at the time when the aggrieved party learned of the repudiation.

(2) If evidence of a price prevailing at the times or places described in this Article is not readily available the price prevailing within any reasonable time before or after the time described or at any other place which in commercial judgment or under usage of trade would serve as a reasonable substitute for the one described may be used, making any proper allowance for the cost of transporting the goods to or from such other place.

(3) Evidence of a relevant price prevailing at a time or place other than the one described in this Article offered by one party is not admissible unless and until he has given the other party such notice as the court finds sufficient to prevent unfair surprise.

§ 2—724. Admissibility of Market Quotations.

Whenever the prevailing price or value of any goods regularly bought and sold in any established commodity market is in issue, reports in official publications or trade journals or in newspapers or periodicals of general circulation published as the reports of such market shall be admissible in evidence. The circumstances of the preparation of such a report may be shown to affect its weight but not its admissibility.

§ 2—725. Statute of Limitations in Contracts for Sale.

(1) An action for breach of any contract for sale must be commenced within four years after the cause of action has accrued. By the original agreement the parties may reduce the period of limitation to not less than one year but may not extend it.

(2) A cause of action accrues when the breach occurs, regardless of the aggrieved party's lack of knowledge of the breach. A breach of warranty occurs when tender of delivery is made, except that where a warranty explicitly extends to future performance of the goods and discovery of the breach must await the time of such performance the cause of action accrues when the breach is or should have been discovered.

(3) Where an action commenced within the time limited by subsection (1) is so terminated as to leave available a remedy by another action for the same breach such other action may be commenced after the expiration of the time limited and within six months after the termination of the first action unless the termination resulted from voluntary discontinuance or from dismissal for failure or neglect to prosecute.

(4) This section does not alter the law on tolling of the statute of limitations nor does it apply to causes of action which have accrued before this Act becomes effective.

Article 2A
LEASES

Part 1 General Provisions

§ 2A—101. Short Title.

This Article shall be known and may be cited as the Uniform Commercial Code—Leases.

§ 2A—102. Scope.

This Article applies to any transaction, regardless of form, that creates a lease.

§ 2A—103. Definitions and Index of Definitions.

(1) In this Article unless the context otherwise requires:

(a) "Buyer in ordinary course of business" means a person who in good faith and without knowledge that the sale to him [or her] is in violation of the ownership rights or security interest or leasehold interest of a third party in the goods buys in ordinary course from a person in the business of selling goods of that kind but does not include a pawnbroker. "Buying" may be for cash or by exchange of other property or on secured or unsecured credit and includes receiving goods or documents of title under a pre-existing contract for sale but does not include a transfer in bulk or as security for or in total or partial satisfaction of a money debt.

(b) "Cancellation" occurs when either party puts an end to the lease contract for default by the other party.

(c) "Commercial unit" means such a unit of goods as by commercial usage is a single whole for purposes of lease and division of which materially impairs its character or value on the market or in use. A commercial unit may be a single article, as a machine, or a set of articles, as a suite of furniture or a line of machinery, or a quantity, as a gross or carload, or any other unit treated in use or in the relevant market as a single whole.

(d) "Conforming" goods or performance under a lease contract means goods or performance that are in accordance with the obligations under the lease contract.

(e) "Consumer lease" means a lease that a lessor regularly engaged in the business of leasing or selling makes to a lessee, except an organization, who takes under the lease primarily for a personal, family, or household purpose, if the total payments to be made under the lease contract, excluding payments for options to renew or buy, do not exceed $25,000.

(f) "Fault" means wrongful act, omission, breach, or default.

(g) "Finance lease" means a lease in which (i) the lessor does not select, manufacture or supply the goods, (ii) the lessor acquires the goods or the right to possession and use of the goods in connection with the lease, and (iii) either the lessee receives a copy of the contract evidencing the lessor's purchase of the goods on or before signing the lease contract, or the lessee's approval of the contract evidencing the lessor's purchase of the goods is a condition to effectiveness of the lease contract.

(h) "Goods" means all things that are movable at the time of identification to the lease contract, or are fixtures (Section 2A—309), but the term does not include money, documents, instruments, accounts, chattel paper, general intangibles, or minerals or the like, including oil and gas, before extraction. The term also includes the unborn young of animals.

(i) "Installment lease contract" means a lease contract that authorizes or requires the delivery of goods in separate lots to be separately accepted, even though the lease contract contains a clause "each delivery is a separate lease" or its equivalent.

(j) "Lease" means a transfer of the right to possession and use of goods for a term in return for consideration, but a sale, including a sale on approval or a sale or return, or retention or creation of a security interest is not a lease. Unless the context clearly indicates otherwise, the term includes a sublease.

(k) "Lease agreement" means the bargain, with respect to the lease, of the lessor and the lessee in fact as found in their language or by implication from other circumstances including course of dealing or usage of trade or course of performance as provided in this Article. Unless the context clearly indicates otherwise, the term includes a sublease agreement.

(l) "Lease contract" means the total legal obligation that results from the lease agreement as affected by this Article and any other applicable rules of law. Unless the context clearly indicates otherwise, the term includes a sublease contract.

(m) "Leasehold interest" means the interest of the lessor or the lessee under a lease contract.

(n) "Lessee" means a person who acquires the right to possession and use of goods under a lease. Unless the context clearly indicates otherwise, the term includes a sublessee.

(o) "Lessee in ordinary course of business" means a person who in good faith and without knowledge that the lease to him [or her] is in violation of the ownership rights or security interest or leasehold interest of a third party in the goods, leases in ordinary course from a person in the business of selling or leasing goods of that kind but does not include a pawnbroker. "Leasing" may be for cash or by exchange of other property or on secured or unsecured credit and includes receiving goods or documents of title under a pre-existing lease contract but does not include a transfer in bulk or as security for or in total or partial satisfaction of a money debt.

(p) "Lessor" means a person who transfers the right to possession and use of goods under a lease. Unless the context clearly indicates otherwise, the term includes a sublessor.

(q) "Lessor's residual interest" means the lessor's interest in the goods after expiration, termination, or cancellation of the lease contract.

(r) "Lien" means a charge against or interest in goods to secure payment of a debt or performance of an obligation, but the term does not include a security interest.

(s) "Lot" means a parcel or a single article that is the subject matter of a separate lease or delivery, whether or not it is sufficient to perform the lease contract.

(t) "Merchant lessee" means a lessee that is a merchant with respect to goods of the kind subject to the lease.

(u) "Present value" means the amount as of a date certain of one or more sums payable in the future, discounted to the date certain. The discount is determined by the interest rate specified by the parties if the rate was not manifestly unreasonable at the time the transaction was entered into; otherwise, the discount is determined by a commercially reasonable rate that takes into account the facts and circumstances of each case at the time the transaction was entered into.

(v) "Purchase" includes taking by sale, lease, mortgage, security interest, pledge, gift, or any other voluntary transaction creating an interest in goods.

(w) "Sublease" means a lease of goods the right to possession and use of which was acquired by the lessor as a lessee under an existing lease.

(x) "Supplier" means a person from whom a lessor buys or leases goods to be leased under a finance lease.

(y) "Supply contract" means a contract under which a lessor buys or leases goods to be leased.

(z) "Termination" occurs when either party pursuant to a power created by agreement or law puts an end to the lease contract otherwise than for default.

(2) Other definitions applying to this Article and the sections in which they appear are:

"Accessions". Section 2A—310(1).
"Construction mortgage". Section 2A—309(1)(d).
"Encumbrance". Section 2A—309(1)(e).
"Fixtures". Section 2A—309(1)(a).
"Fixture filing". Section 2A—309(1)(b).
"Purchase money lease". Section 2A—309(1)(c).

(3) The following definitions in other Articles apply to this Article:

"Accounts". Section 9—106.
"Between merchants". Section 2—104(3).
"Buyer". Section 2—103(1)(a).
"Chattel paper". Section 9—105(1)(b).
"Consumer goods". Section 9—109(1).
"Documents". Section 9—105(1)(f).
"Entrusting". Section 2—403(3).
"General intangibles". Section 9—106.
"Good faith". Section 2—103(1)(b).
"Instruments". Section 9—105(1)(i).
"Merchant". Section 2—104(1).
"Mortgage". Section 9—105(1)(j).
"Pursuant to commitment". Section 9—105(1)(k).
"Receipt". Section 2—103(1)(c).
"Sale". Section 2—106(1).
"Sale on Approval". Section 2—326.
"Sale or Return". Section 2—326.
"Seller". Section 2—103(1)(d).

(4) In addition Article 1 contains general definitions and principles of construction and interpretation applicable throughout this Article.

§ 2A—104. **Leases Subject to Other Statutes.**

(1) A lease, although subject to this Article, is also subject to any applicable:

(a) statute of the United States;

(b) certificate of title statute of this State: (list any certificate of title statutes covering automobiles, trailers, mobile homes, boats, farm tractors, and the like);

(c) certificate of title statute of another jurisdiction (Section 2A—105); or

(d) consumer protection statute of this State.

(2) In case of conflict between the provisions of this Article, other than Sections 2A—105, 2A—304(3) and 2A—305(3), and any statute referred to in subsection (1), the provisions of that statute control.

(3) Failure to comply with any applicable statute has only the effect specified therein.

§ 2A—105. **Territorial Application of Article to Goods Covered by Certificate of Title.**

Subject to the provisions of Sections 2A—304(3) and 2A—305(3), with respect to goods covered by a certificate of title issued under a statute of this State or of another jurisdiction, compliance and the effect of compliance or noncompliance with a certificate of title statute are governed by the law (including the conflict of laws rules) of the jurisdiction issuing the certificate until the earlier of (a) surrender of the certificate, or (b) four months after the goods are removed from that jurisdiction and thereafter until a new certificate of title is issued by another jurisdiction.

§ 2A—106. Limitation on Power of Parties to Consumer Lease to Choose Applicable Law and Judicial Forum.

(1) If the law chosen by the parties to a consumer lease is that of a jurisdiction other than a jurisdiction in which the lessee resides at the time the lease agreement becomes enforceable or within 30 days thereafter or in which the goods are to be used, the choice is not enforceable.

(2) If the judicial forum chosen by the parties to a consumer lease is a forum that would not otherwise have jurisdiction over the lessee, the choice is not enforceable.

§ 2A—107. Waiver or Renunciation of Claim or Right After Default.

Any claim or right arising out of an alleged default or breach of warranty may be discharged in whole or in part without consideration by a written waiver or renunciation signed and delivered by the aggrieved party.

§ 2A—108. Unconscionability.

(1) If the court as a matter of law finds a lease contract or any clause of a lease contract to have been unconscionable at the time it was made the court may refuse to enforce the lease contract, or it may enforce the remainder of the lease contract without the unconscionable clause, or it may so limit the application of any unconscionable clause as to avoid any unconscionable result.

(2) With respect to a consumer lease, if the court as a matter of law finds that a lease contract or any clause of a lease contract has been induced by unconscionable conduct or that unconscionable conduct has occurred in the collection of a claim arising from a lease contract, the court may grant appropriate relief.

(3) Before making a finding of unconscionability under subsection (1) or (2), the court, on its own motion or that of a party, shall afford the parties a reasonable opportunity to present evidence as to the setting, purpose, and effect of the lease contract or clause thereof, or of the conduct.

(4) In an action in which the lessee claims unconscionability with respect to a consumer lease:

(a) If the court finds unconscionability under subsection (1) or (2), the court shall award reasonable attorney's fees to the lessee.

(b) If the court does not find unconscionability and the lessee claiming unconscionability has brought or maintained an action he [or she] knew to be ground-

less, the court shall award reasonable attorney's fees to the party against whom the claim is made.

(c) In determining attorney's fees, the amount of the recovery on behalf of the claimant under subsections (1) and (2) is not controlling.

§ 2A—109. Option to Accelerate at Will.

(1) A term providing that one party or his [or her] successor in interest may accelerate payment or performance or require collateral or additional collateral "at will" or "when he [or she] deems himself [or herself] insecure" or in words of similar import must be construed to mean that he [or she] has power to do so only if he [or she] in good faith believes that the prospect of payment or performance is impaired.

(2) With respect to a consumer lease, the burden of establishing good faith under subsection (1) is on the party who exercised the power; otherwise the burden of establishing lack of good faith is on the party against whom the power has been exercised.

Part 2 Formation and Construction of Lease Contract

§ 2A—201. Statute of Frauds.

(1) A lease contract is not enforceable by way of action or defense unless:

(a) the total payments to be made under the lease contract, excluding payments for options to renew or buy, are less than $1,000; or

(b) there is a writing, signed by the party against whom enforcement is sought or by that party's authorized agent, sufficient to indicate that a lease contract has been made between the parties and to describe the goods leased and the lease term.

(2) Any description of leased goods or of the lease term is sufficient and satisfies subsection (1)(b), whether or not it is specific, if it reasonably identifies what is described.

(3) A writing is not insufficient because it omits or incorrectly states a term agreed upon, but the lease contract is not enforceable under subsection (1)(b) beyond the lease term and the quantity of goods shown in this writing.

(4) A lease contract that does not satisfy the requirements of subsection (1), but which is valid in other respects, is enforceable:

(a) if the goods are to be specially manufactured or obtained for the lessee and are not suitable for lease or sale to others in the ordinary course of the lessor's business, and the lessor, before notice of repudiation is received and under circumstances that reasonably indicate that the goods are for the lessee, has made either a substantial beginning of their manufacture or commitments for their procurement;

(b) if the party against whom enforcement is sought admits in that party's pleading, testimony or otherwise in court that a lease contract was made, but the lease contract is not enforceable under this provision beyond the quantity of goods admitted; or

(c) with respect to goods that have been received and accepted by the lessee.

(5) The lease term under a lease contract referred to in subsection (4) is:

(a) if there is a writing signed by the party against whom enforcement is sought or by that party's authorized agent specifying the lease term, the term so specified;

(b) if the party against whom enforcement is sought admits in that party's pleading, testimony, or otherwise in court a lease term, the term so admitted; or

(c) a reasonable lease term.

§ 2A—202. Final Written Expression: Parol or Extrinsic Evidence.

Terms with respect to which the confirmatory memoranda of the parties agree or which are otherwise set forth in a writing intended by the parties as a final expression of their agreement with respect to such terms as are included therein may not be contradicted by evidence of any prior agreement or of a contemporaneous oral agreement but may be explained or supplemented:

(a) by course of dealing or usage of trade or by course of performance; and

(b) by evidence of consistent additional terms unless the court finds the writing to have been intended also as a complete and exclusive statement of the terms of the agreement.

§ 2A—203. Seals Inoperative.

The affixing of a seal to a writing evidencing a lease contract or an offer to enter into a lease contract does not render the writing a sealed instrument and the law with respect to sealed instruments does not apply to the lease contract or offer.

§ 2A—204. Formation in General.

(1) A lease contract may be made in any manner sufficient to show agreement, including conduct by both parties which recognizes the existence of a lease contract.

(2) An agreement sufficient to constitute a lease contract may be found although the moment of its making is undetermined.

(3) Although one or more terms are left open, a lease contract does not fail for indefiniteness if the parties have intended to make a lease contract and there is a reasonably certain basis for giving an appropriate remedy.

§ 2A—205. Firm Offers.

An offer by a merchant to lease goods to or from another person in a signed writing that by its terms gives assurance it will be held open is not revocable, for lack of consideration, during the time stated or, if no time is stated, for a reasonable time, but in no event may the period of irrevocability exceed 3 months. Any such term of assurance on a form supplied by the offeree must be separately signed by the offeror.

§ 2A—206. Offer and Acceptance in Formation of Lease Contract.

(1) Unless otherwise unambiguously indicated by the language or circumstances, an offer to make a lease contract must be construed as inviting acceptance in any manner and by any medium reasonable in the circumstances.

(2) If the beginning of a requested performance is a reasonable mode of acceptance, an offeror who is not notified of acceptance within a reasonable time may treat the offer as having lapsed before acceptance.

§ 2A—207. Course of Performance or Practical Construction.

(1) If a lease contract involves repeated occasions for performance by either party with knowledge of the nature of the performance and opportunity for objection to it by the other, any course of performance accepted or acquiesced in without objection is relevant to determine the meaning of the lease agreement.

(2) The express terms of a lease agreement and any course of performance, as well as any course of dealing and usage of trade, must be construed whenever reasonable as consistent with each other; but if that construction is unreasonable, express terms control course of performance, course of performance controls both course of dealing and usage of trade, and course of dealing controls usage of trade.

(3) Subject to the provisions of Section 2A—208 on modification and waiver, course of performance is relevant to show a waiver or modification of any term inconsistent with the course of performance.

§ 2A—208. Modification, Rescission and Waiver.

(1) An agreement modifying a lease contract needs no consideration to be binding.

(2) A signed lease agreement that excludes modification or rescission except by a signed writing may not be

otherwise modified or rescinded, but, except as between merchants, such a requirement on a form supplied by a merchant must be separately signed by the other party.

(3) Although an attempt at modification or rescission does not satisfy the requirements of subsection (2), it may operate as a waiver.

(4) A party who has made a waiver affecting an executory portion of a lease contract may retract the waiver by reasonable notification received by the other party that strict performance will be required of any term waived, unless the retraction would be unjust in view of a material change of position in reliance on the waiver.

§ 2A—209. Lessee under Finance Lease as Beneficiary of Supply Contract.

(1) The benefit of the supplier's promises to the lessor under the supply contract and of all warranties, whether express or implied, under the supply contract, extends to the lessee to the extent of the lessee's leasehold interest under a finance lease related to the supply contract, but subject to the terms of the supply contract and all of the supplier's defenses or claims arising therefrom.

(2) The extension of the benefit of the supplier's promises to the lessee does not: (a) modify the rights and obligations of the parties to the supply contract, whether arising therefrom or otherwise, or (b) impose any duty or liability under the supply contract on the lessee.

(3) Any modification or rescission of the supply contract by the supplier and the lessor is effective against the lessee unless, prior to the modification or rescission, the supplier has received notice that the lessee has entered into a finance lease related to the supply contract. If the supply contract is modified or rescinded after the lessee enters the finance lease, the lessee has a cause of action against the lessor, and against the supplier if the supplier has notice of the lessee's entering the finance lease when the supply contract is modified or rescinded. The lessee's recovery from such action shall put the lessee in as good a position as if the modification or rescission had not occurred.

§ 2A—210. Express Warranties.

(1) Express warranties by the lessor are created as follows:

(a) Any affirmation of fact or promise made by the lessor to the lessee which relates to the goods and becomes part of the basis of the bargain creates an express warranty that the goods will conform to the affirmation or promise.

(b) Any description of the goods which is made part of the basis of the bargain creates an express warranty that the goods will conform to the description.

(c) Any sample or model that is made part of the basis of the bargain creates an express warranty that the whole of the goods will conform to the sample or model.

(2) It is not necessary to the creation of an express warranty that the lessor use formal words, such as "warrant" or "guarantee," or that the lessor have a specific intention to make a warranty, but an affirmation merely of the value of the goods or a statement purporting to be merely the lessor's opinion or commendation of the goods does not create a warranty.

§ 2A—211. Warranties Against Interference and Against Infringement; Lessee's Obligation Against Infringement.

(1) There is in a lease contract a warranty that for the lease term no person holds a claim to or interest in the goods that arose from an act or omission of the lessor, other than a claim by way of infringement or the like, which will interfere with the lessee's enjoyment of its leasehold interest.

(2) Except in a finance lease there is in a lease contract by a lessor who is a merchant regularly dealing in goods of the kind a warranty that the goods are delivered free of the rightful claim of any person by way of infringement or the like.

(3) A lessee who furnishes specifications to a lessor or a supplier shall hold the lessor and the supplier harmless against any claim by way of infringement or the like that arises out of compliance with the specifications.

§ 2A—212. Implied Warranty of Merchantability.

(1) Except in a finance lease, a warranty that the goods will be merchantable is implied in a lease contract if the lessor is a merchant with respect to goods of that kind.

(2) Goods to be merchantable must be at least such as

(a) pass without objection in the trade under the description in the lease agreement;

(b) in the case of fungible goods, are of fair average quality within the description;

(c) are fit for the ordinary purposes for which goods of that type are used;

(d) run, within the variation permitted by the lease agreement, of even kind, quality, and quantity within each unit and among all units involved;

(e) are adequately contained, packaged, and labeled as the lease agreement may require; and

(f) conform to any promises or affirmations of fact made on the container or label.

(3) Other implied warranties may arise from course of dealing or usage of trade.

§ 2A—213. Implied Warranty of Fitness for Particular Purpose.

Except in a finance of lease, if the lessor at the time the lease contract is made has reason to know of any particular purpose for which the goods are required and that the lessee is relying on the lessor's skill or judgment to select or furnish suitable goods, there is in the lease contract an implied warranty that the goods will be fit for that purpose.

§ 2A—214. Exclusion or Modification of Warranties.

(1) Words or conduct relevant to the creation of an express warranty and words or conduct tending to negate or limit a warranty must be construed wherever reasonable as consistent with each other; but, subject to the provisions of Section 2A—202 on parol or extrinsic evidence, negation or limitation is inoperative to the extent that the construction is unreasonable.

(2) Subject to subsection (3), to exclude or modify the implied warranty of merchantability or any part of it the language must mention "merchantability", be by a writing, and be conspicuous. Subject to subsection (3), to exclude or modify any implied warranty of fitness the exclusion must be by a writing and be conspicuous. Language to exclude all implied warranties of fitness is sufficient if it is conspicuous and states, for example, "There is no warranty that the goods will be fit for a particular purpose".

(3) Notwithstanding subsection (2), but subject to subsection (4),

    (a) unless the circumstances indicate otherwise, all implied warranties are excluded by expressions like "as is" or "with all faults" or by other language that in common understanding calls the lessee's attention to the exclusion of warranties and makes plain that there is no implied warranty, and is conspicuous;

    (b) if the lessee before entering into the lease contract has examined the goods or the sample or model as fully as desired or has refused to examine the goods, there is no implied warranty with regard to defects that an examination ought in the circumstances to have revealed; and

    (c) an implied warranty may also be excluded or modified by course of dealing, course of performance, or usage of trade.

(4) To exclude or modify a warranty against interference or against infringement (Section 2A—211) or any part of it, the language must be specific, be by a writing, and be conspicuous, unless the circumstances, including course of performance, course of dealing, or usage of trade, give the lessee reason to know that the goods are being leased subject to a claim or interest of any person.

§ 2A—215. Cumulation and Conflict of Warranties Express or Implied.

Warranties, whether express or implied, must be construed as consistent with each other and as cumulative,

but if that construction is unreasonable, the intention of the parties determines which warranty is dominant. In ascertaining that intention the following rules apply:

    (a) Exact or technical specifications displace an inconsistent sample or model or general language of description.

    (b) A sample from an existing bulk displaces inconsistent general language of description.

    (c) Express warranties displace inconsistent implied warranties other than an implied warranty of fitness for a particular purpose.

§ 2A—216. Third-Party Beneficiaries of Express and Implied Warranties.

Alternative A

A warranty to or for the benefit of a lessee under this Article, whether express or implied, extends to any natural person who is in the family or household of the lessee or who is a guest in the lessee's home if it is reasonable to expect that such person may use, consume, or be affected by the goods and who is injured in person by breach of the warranty. This section does not displace principles of law and equity that extend a warranty to or for the benefit of a lessee to other persons. The operation of this section may not be excluded, modified, or limited, but an exclusion, modification, or limitation of the warranty, including any with respect to rights and remedies, effective against the lessee is also effective against any beneficiary designated under this section.

Alternative B

A warranty to or for the benefit of a lessee under this Article, whether express or implied, extends to any natural person who may reasonably be expected to use, consume, or be affected by the goods and who is injured in person by breach of the warranty. This section does not displace principles of law and equity that extend a warranty to or for the benefit of a lessee to other persons. The operation of this section may not be excluded, modified, or limited, but an exclusion, modification, or limitation of the warranty, including any with respect to rights and remedies, effective against the lessee is also effective against the beneficiary designated under this section.

Alternative C

A warranty to or for the benefit of a lessee under this Article, whether express or implied, extends to any person who may reasonably be expected to use, consume, or be affected by the goods and who is injured by breach of the warranty. The operation of this section may not be excluded, modified, or limited with respect to injury to the person of an individual to whom the warranty extends, but an exclusion, modification, or limitation of the warranty, including any with respect to rights and remedies, effective against the lessee is also effective against the beneficiary designated under this section.

§ 2A—217. Identification.

Identification of goods as goods to which a lease contract refers may be made at any time and in any manner explicitly agreed to by the parties. In the absence of explicit agreement, identification occurs:

(a) when the lease contract is made if the lease contract is for a lease of goods that are existing and identified;

(b) when the goods are shipped, marked, or otherwise designated by the lessor as goods to which the lease contract refers, if the lease contract is for a lease of goods that are not existing and identified; or

(c) when the young are conceived, if the lease contract is for a lease of unborn young of animals.

§ 2A—218. Insurance and Proceeds.

(1) A lessee obtains an insurable interest when existing goods are identified to the lease contract even though the goods identified are nonconforming and the lessee has an option to reject them.

(2) If a lessee has an insurable interest only by reason of the lessor's identification of the goods, the lessor, until default or insolvency or notification to the lessee that identification is final, may substitute other goods for those identified.

(3) Notwithstanding a lessee's insurable interest under subsections (1) and (2), the lessor retains an insurable interest until an option to buy has been exercised by the lessee and risk of loss has passed to the lessee.

(4) Nothing in this section impairs any insurable interest recognized under any other statute or rule of law.

(5) The parties by agreement may determine that one or more parties have an obligation to obtain and pay for insurance covering the goods and by agreement may determine the beneficiary of the proceeds of the insurance.

§ 2A—219. Risk of Loss.

(1) Except in the case of a finance lease, risk of loss is retained by the lessor and does not pass to the lessee. In the case of a finance lease, risk of loss passes to the lessee.

(2) Subject to the provisions of this Article on the effect of default on risk of loss (Section 2A—220), if risk of loss is to pass to the lessee and the time of passage is not stated, the following rules apply:

(a) If the lease contract requires or authorizes the goods to be shipped by carrier.

(i) and it does not require delivery at a particular destination, the risk of loss passes to the lessee when the goods are duly delivered to the carrier; but

(ii) if it does require delivery at a particular destination and the goods are there duly tendered while in the possession of the carrier, the risk of loss passes to the lessee when the goods are there duly so tendered as to enable the lessee to take delivery.

(b) If the goods are held by a bailee to be delivered without being moved, the risk of loss passes to the lessee on acknowledgment by the bailee of the lessee's right to possession of the goods.

(c) In any case not within subsection (a) or (b), the risk of loss passes to the lessee on the lessee's receipt of the goods if the lessor, or, in the case of a finance lease, the supplier, is a merchant; otherwise the risk passes to the lessee on tender of delivery.

§ 2A—220. Effect of Default on Risk of Loss.

(1) Where risk of loss is to pass to the lessee and the time of passage is not stated:

(a) If a tender or delivery of goods so fails to conform to the lease contract as to give a right of rejection, the risk of their loss remains with the lessor, or, in the case of a finance lease, the supplier, until cure or acceptance.

(b) If the lessee rightfully revokes acceptance, he [or she], to the extent of any deficiency in his [or her] effective insurance coverage, may treat the risk of loss as having remained with the lessor from the beginning.

(2) Whether or not risk of loss is to pass to the lessee, if the lessee as to conforming goods already identified to a lease contract repudiates or is otherwise in default under the lease contract, the lessor, or, in the case of a finance lease, the supplier, to the extent of any deficiency in his [or her] effective insurance coverage may treat the risk of loss as resting on the lessee for a commercially reasonable time.

§ 2A—221. Casualty to Identified Goods.

If a lease contract requires goods identified when the lease contract is made, and the goods suffer casualty without fault of the lessee, the lessor or the supplier before delivery, or the goods suffer casualty before risk of loss passes to the lessee pursuant to the lease agreement or Section 2A—219, then:

(a) if the loss is total, the lease contract is avoided; and

(b) if the loss is partial or the goods have so deteriorated as to no longer conform to the lease contract, the lessee may nevertheless demand inspection and at his [or her] option either treat the lease contract as avoided or, except in a finance lease that is not a consumer lease, accept the goods with due allowance from the rent payable for the balance of the lease term for the deterioration or the deficiency in quantity but without further right against the lessor.

Part 3 Effect Of Lease Contract

§ 2A—301. Enforceability of Lease Contract.

Except as otherwise provided in this Article, a lease contract is effective and enforceable according to its terms between the parties, against purchasers of the goods and against creditors of the parties.

§ 2A—302. Title to and Possession of Goods.

Except as otherwise provided in this Article, each provision of this Article applies whether the lessor or a third party has title to the goods, and whether the lessor, the lessee, or a third party has possession of the goods, notwithstanding any statute or rule of law that possession or the absence of possession is fraudulent.

§ 2A—303. Alienability of Party's Interest Under Lease Contract or of Lessor's Residual Interest in Goods; Delegation of Performance; Assignment of Rights.

(1) Any interest of a party under a lease contract and the lessor's residual interest in the goods may be transferred unless

(a) the transfer is voluntary and the lease contract prohibits the transfer; or

(b) the transfer materially changes the duty of or materially increases the burden or risk imposed on the other party to the lease contract, and within a reasonable time after notice of the transfer the other party demands that the transferee comply with subsection (2) and the transferee fails to comply.

(2) Within a reasonable time after demand pursuant to subsection (1)(b), the transferee shall:

(a) cure or provide adequate assurance that he [or she] will promptly cure any default other than one arising from the transfer;

(b) compensate or provide adequate assurance that he [or she] will promptly compensate the other party to the lease contract and any other person holding an interest in the lease contract, except the party whose interest is being transferred, for any loss to that party resulting from the transfer;

(c) provide adequate assurance of future due performance under the lease contract; and

(d) assume the lease contract.

(3) Demand pursuant to subsection (1)(b) is without prejudice to the other party's rights against the transferee and the party whose interest is transferred.

(4) An assignment of "the lease" or of "all my rights under the lease" or an assignment in similar general terms is a transfer of rights, and unless the language or the circumstances, as in an assignment for security, indicate the contrary, the assignment is a delegation of duties by the assignor to the assignee and acceptance by the assignee constitutes a promise by him [or her] to perform those duties. This promise is enforceable by either the assignor or the other party to the lease contract.

(5) Unless otherwise agreed by the lessor and the lessee, no delegation of performance relieves the assignor as against the other party of any duty to perform or any liability for default.

(6) A right to damages for default with respect to the whole lease contract or a right arising out of the assignor's due performance of his [or her] entire obligation can be assigned despite agreement otherwise.

(7) To prohibit the transfer of an interest of a party under a lease contract, the language of prohibition must be specific, by a writing, and conspicuous.

§ 2A—304. Subsequent Lease of Goods by Lessor.

(1) Subject to the provisions of Section 2A—303, a subsequent lessee from a lessor of goods under an existing lease contract obtains, to the extent of the leasehold interest transferred, the leasehold interest in the goods that the lessor had or had power to transfer, and except as provided in subsection (2) and Section 2A—527(4), takes subject to the existing lease contract. A lessor with voidable title has power to transfer a good leasehold interest to a good faith subsequent lessee for value, but only to the extent set forth in the preceding sentence. When goods have been delivered under a transaction of purchase the lessor has that power even though:

(a) the lessor's transferor was deceived as to the identity of the lessor;

(b) the delivery was in exchange for a check which is later dishonored;

(c) it was agreed that the transaction was to be a "cash sale"; or

(d) the delivery was procured through fraud punishable as larcenous under the criminal law.

(2) A subsequent lessee in the ordinary course of business from a lessor who is a merchant dealing in goods of that kind to whom the goods were entrusted by the existing lessee before the interest of the subsequent lessee became enforceable against the lessor obtains, to the

extent of the leasehold interest transferred, all of the lessor's and the existing lessee's rights to the goods, and takes free of the existing lease contract.

(3) A subsequent lessee from the lessor of goods that are subject to an existing lease contract and are covered by a certificate of title issued under a statute of this State or of another jurisdiction takes no greater rights than those provided both by this section and by the certificate of title statute.

§ 2A—305. Sale or Sublease of Goods by Lessee.

(1) Subject to the provisions of Section 2A—303, a buyer or sublessee from the lessee of goods under an existing lease contract obtains, to the extent of the interest transferred, the leasehold interest in the goods that the lessee had or had power to transfer, and except as provided in subsection (2) and Section 2A—511(4), takes subject to the existing lease contract. A lessee with a voidable leasehold interest has power to transfer a good leasehold interest to a good faith buyer for value or a good faith sublessee for value, but only to the extent set forth in the preceding sentence. When goods have been delivered under a transaction of lease the lessee has that power even though:

(a) the lessor was deceived as to the identity of the lessee;

(b) the delivery was in exchange for a check which is later dishonored; or

(c) the delivery was procured through fraud punishable as larcenous under the criminal law.

(2) A buyer in the ordinary course of business or a sublessee in the ordinary course of business from a lessee who is a merchant dealing in goods of that kind to whom the goods were entrusted by the lessor obtains, to the extent of the interest transferred, all of the lessor's and lessee's rights to the goods, and takes free of the existing lease contract.

(3) A buyer or sublessee from the lessee of goods that are subject to an existing lease contract and are covered by a certificate of title issued under a statute of this State or of another jurisdiction takes no greater rights than those provided both by this section and by the certificate of title statute.

§ 2A—306. Priority of Certain Liens Arising by Operation of Law.

If a person in the ordinary course of his [or her] business furnishes services or materials with respect to goods subject to a lease contract, a lien upon those goods in the possession of that person given by statute or rule of law for those materials or services takes priority over any interest of the lessor or lessee under the lease contract or this Article unless the lien is created by statute and the statute provides otherwise or unless the lien is

created by rule of law and the rule of law provides otherwise.

§ 2A—307. Priority of Liens Arising by Attachment or Levy on, Security Interests in, and Other Claims to Goods.

(1) Except as otherwise provided in Section 2A—306, a creditor of a lessee takes subject to the lease contract.

(2) Except as otherwise provided in subsections (3) and (4) of this section and in Sections 2A—306 and 2A—308, a creditor of a lessor takes subject to the lease contract:

(a) unless the creditor holds a lien that attached to the goods before the lease contract became enforceable, or

(b) unless the creditor holds a security interest in the goods that under the Article on Secured Transactions (Article 9) would have priority over any other security interest in the goods perfected by a filing covering the goods and made at the time the lease contract became enforceable, whether or not any other security interest existed.

(3) A lessee in the ordinary course of business takes the leasehold interest free of a security interest in the goods created by the lessor even though the security interest is perfected and the lessee knows of its existence.

(4) A lessee other than a lessee in the ordinary course of business takes the leasehold interest free of a security interest to the extent that it secures future advances made after the secured party acquires knowledge of the lease or more than 45 days after the lease contract becomes enforceable, whichever first occurs, unless the future advances are made pursuant to a commitment entered into without knowledge of the lease and before the expiration of the 45-day period.

§ 2A—308. Special Rights of Creditors.

(1) A creditor of a lessor in possession of goods subject to a lease contract may treat the lease contract as void if as against the creditor retention of possession by the lessor is fraudulent under any statute or rule of law, but retention of possession in good faith and current course of trade by the lessor for a commercially reasonable time after the lease contract becomes enforceable is not fraudulent.

(2) Nothing in this Article impairs the rights of creditors of a lessor if the lease contract (a) becomes enforceable, not in current course of trade but in satisfaction of or as security for a pre-existing claim for money, security, or the like, and (b) is made under circumstances which under any statute or rule of law apart from this Article would constitute the transaction a fraudulent transfer or voidable preference.

(3) A creditor of a seller may treat a sale or an identification of goods to a contract for sale as void if as against the creditor retention of possession by the seller is fraudulent under any statute or rule of law, but retention of possession of the goods pursuant to a lease contract entered into by the seller as lessee and the buyer as lessor in connection with the sale or identification of the goods is not fraudulent if the buyer bought for value and in good faith.

§ 2A—309. Lessor's and Lessee's Rights When Goods Become Fixtures.

(1) In this section:

(a) goods are "fixtures" when they become so related to particular real estate that an interest in them arises under real estate law;

(b) a "fixture filing" is the filing, in the office where a mortgage on the real estate would be recorded or registered, of a financing statement concerning goods that are or are to become fixtures and conforming to the requirements of subsection (5) of Section 9—402;

(c) a lease is a "purchase money lease" unless the lessee has possession or use of the goods or the right to possession or use of the goods before the lease agreement is enforceable;

(d) a mortgage is a "construction mortgage" to the extent it secures an obligation incurred for the construction of an improvement on land including the acquisition cost of the land, if the recorded writing so indicates; and

(e) "encumbrance" includes real estate mortgages and other liens on real estate and all other rights in real estate that are not ownership interests.

(2) Under this Article a lease may be of goods that are fixtures or may continue in goods that become fixtures, but no lease exists under this Article of ordinary building materials incorporated into an improvement on land.

(3) This Article does not prevent creation of a lease of fixtures pursuant to real estate law.

(4) The perfected interest of a lessor of fixtures has priority over a conflicting interest of an encumbrancer or owner of the real estate if:

(a) the lease is a purchase money lease, the conflicting interest of the encumbrancer or owner arises before the goods become fixtures, the interest of the lessor is perfected by a fixture filing before the goods become fixtures or within ten days thereafter, and the lessee has an interest of record in the real estate or is in possession of the real estate; or

(b) the interest of the lessor is perfected by a fixture filing before the interest of the encumbrancer or owner is of record, the lessor's interest has priority over any conflicting interest of a predecessor in title of the encumbrancer or owner, and the lessee has an interest of record in the real estate or is in possession of the real estate.

(5) The interest of a lessor of fixtures, whether or not perfected, has priority over the conflicting interest of an encumbrancer or owner of the real estate if:

(a) the fixtures are readily removable factory or office machines, readily removable equipment that is not primarily used or leased for use in the operation of the real estate, or readily removable replacements of domestic appliances that are goods subject to a consumer lease, and before the goods become fixtures the lease contract is enforceable; or

(b) the conflicting interest is a lien on the real estate obtained by legal or equitable proceedings after the lease contract is enforceable; or

(c) the encumbrancer or owner has consented in writing to the lease or has disclaimed an interest in the goods as fixtures; or

(d) the lessee has a right to remove the goods as against the encumbrancer or owner. If the lessee's right to remove terminates, the priority of the interest of the lessor continues for a reasonable time.

(6) Notwithstanding paragraph (a) of subsection (4) but otherwise subject to subsections (4) and (5), the interest of a lessor of fixtures is subordinate to the conflicting interest of an encumbrancer of the real estate under a construction mortgage recorded before the goods become fixtures if the goods become fixtures before the completion of the construction. To the extent given to refinance a construction mortgage, the conflicting interest of an encumbrancer of the real estate under a mortgage has this priority to the same extent as the encumbrancer of the real estate under the construction mortgage.

(7) In cases not within the preceding subsections, priority between the interest of a lessor of fixtures and the conflicting interest of an encumbrancer or owner of the real estate who is not the lessee is determined by the priority rules governing conflicting interests in real estate.

(8) If the interest of a lessor has priority over all conflicting interests of all owners and encumbrancers of the real estate, the lessor or the lessee may (a) on default, expiration, termination, or cancellation of the lease agreement by the other party but subject to the provisions of the lease agreement and this Article, or (b) if necessary to enforce his [or her] other rights and remedies under this Article, remove the goods from the real estate, free and clear of all conflicting interests of all owners and encumbrancers of the real estate, but he [or

she] must reimburse any encumbrancer or owner of the real estate who is not the lessee and who has not otherwise agreed for the cost of repair of any physical injury, but not for any diminution in value of the real estate caused by the absence of the goods removed or by any necessity of replacing them. A person entitled to reimbursement may refuse permission to remove until the party seeking removal gives adequate security for the performance of this obligation.

(9) Even though the lease agreement does not create a security interest, the interest of a lessor of fixtures is perfected by filing a financing statement as a fixture filing for leased goods that are or are to become fixtures in accordance with the relevant provisions of the Article on Secured Transactions (Article 9).

§ 2A—310. Lessor's and Lessee's Rights When Goods Become Accessions.

(1) Goods are "accessions" when they are installed in or affixed to other goods.

(2) The interest of a lessor or a lessee under a lease contract entered into before the goods became accessions is superior to all interests in the whole except as stated in subsection (4).

(3) The interest of a lessor or a lessee under a lease contract entered into at the time or after the goods became accessions is superior to all subsequently acquired interests in the whole except as stated in subsection (4) but is subordinate to interests in the whole existing at the time the lease contract was made unless the holders of such interests in the whole have in writing consented to the lease or disclaimed an interest in the goods as part of the whole.

(4) The interest of a lessor or a lessee under a lease contract described in subsection (2) or (3) is subordinate to the interest of

    (a) a buyer in the ordinary course of business or a lessee in the ordinary course of business of any interest in the whole acquired after the goods became accessions; or

    (b) a creditor with a security interest in the whole perfected before the lease contract was made to the extent that the creditor makes subsequent advances without knowledge of the lease contract.

(5) When under subsections (2) or (3) and (4) a lessor or a lessee of accessions holds an interest that is superior to all interests in the whole, the lessor or the lessee may (a) on default, expiration, termination, or cancellation of the lease contract by the other party but subject to the provisions of the lease contract and this Article, or (b) if necessary to enforce his [or her] other rights and remedies under this Article, remove the goods from the whole, free and clear of all interests in the whole, but

he [or she] must reimburse any holder of an interest in the whole who is not the lessee and who has not otherwise agreed for the cost of repair of any physical injury but not for any diminution in value of the whole caused by the absence of the goods removed or by any necessity for replacing them. A person entitled to reimbursement may refuse permission to remove until the party seeking removal gives adequate security for the performance of this obligation.

Part 4 Performance Of Lease Contract: Repudiated, Substituted And Excused

§ 2A—401. Insecurity: Adequate Assurance of Performance.

(1) A lease contract imposes an obligation on each party that the other's expectation of receiving due performance will not be impaired.

(2) If reasonable grounds for insecurity arise with respect to the performance of either party, the insecure party may demand in writing adequate assurance of due performance. Until the insecure party receives that assurance, if commercially reasonable the insecure party may suspend any performance for which he [or she] has not already received the agreed return.

(3) A repudiation of the lease contract occurs if assurance of due performance adequate under the circumstances of the particular case is not provided to the insecure party within a reasonable time, not to exceed 30 days after receipt of a demand by the other party.

(4) Between merchants, the reasonableness of grounds for insecurity and the adequacy of any assurance offered must be determined according to commercial standards.

(5) Acceptance of any nonconforming delivery or payment does not prejudice the aggrieved party's right to demand adequate assurance of future performance.

§ 2A—402. Anticipatory Repudiation.

If either party repudiates a lease contract with respect to a performance not yet due under the lease contract, the loss of which performance will substantially impair the value of the lease contract to the other, the aggrieved party may:

    (a) for a commercially reasonable time, await retraction of repudiation and performance by the repudiating party;

    (b) make demand pursuant to Section 2A—401 and await assurance of future performance adequate under the circumstances of the particular case; or

    (c) resort to any right or remedy upon default under the lease contract or this Article, even though the aggrieved party has notified the repudiating party that the aggrieved party would await the repudiating party's performance and assurance and has urged retraction. In addition, whether or not the aggrieved party is pursuing one of the foregoing remedies, the aggrieved party may suspend performance or, if the aggrieved party is the lessor, proceed in accordance with the provisions of this Article on the lessor's right to identify goods to the lease contract notwithstanding default or to salvage unfinished goods (Section 2A—524).

§ 2A—403. **Retraction of Anticipatory Repudiation.**

(1) Until the repudiating party's next performance is due, the repudiating party can retract the repudiation unless, since the repudiation, the aggrieved party has cancelled the lease contract or materially changed the aggrieved party's position or otherwise indicated that the aggrieved party considers the repudiation final.

(2) Retraction may be by any method that clearly indicates to the aggrieved party that the repudiating party intends to perform under the lease contract and includes any assurance demanded under Section 2A—401.

(3) Retraction reinstates a repudiating party's rights under a lease contract with due excuse and allowance to the aggrieved party for any delay occasioned by the repudiation.

§ 2A—404. **Substituted Performance.**

(1) If without fault of the lessee, the lessor and the supplier, the agreed berthing, loading, or unloading facilities fail or the agreed type of carrier becomes unavailable or the agreed manner of delivery otherwise becomes commercially impracticable, but a commercially reasonable substitute is available, the substitute performance must be tendered and accepted.

(2) If the agreed means or manner of payment fails because of domestic or foreign governmental regulation:

(a) the lessor may withhold or stop delivery or cause the supplier to withhold or stop delivery unless the lessee provides a means or manner of payment that is commercially a substantial equivalent; and

(b) if delivery has already been taken, payment by the means or in the manner provided by the regulation discharges the lessee's obligation unless the regulation is discriminatory, oppressive, or predatory.

§ 2A—405. **Excused Performance.**

Subject to Section 2A—404 on substituted performance, the following rules apply:

(a) Delay in delivery or nondelivery in whole or in part by a lessor or a supplier who complies with paragraphs (b) and (c) is not a default under the lease contract if performance as agreed has been made impracticable by the occurrence of a contingency the nonoccurrence of which was a basic assumption on which the lease contract was made or by compliance in good faith with any applicable foreign or domestic governmental regulation or order, whether or not the regulation or order later proves to be invalid.

(b) If the causes mentioned in paragraph (a) affect only part of the lessor's or the supplier's capacity to perform, he [or she] shall allocate production and deliveries among his [or her] customers but at his [or her] option may include regular customers not then under contract for sale or lease as well as his [or her] own requirements for further manufacture. He [or she] may so allocate in any manner that is fair and reasonable.

(c) The lessor seasonably shall notify the lessee and in the case of a finance lease the supplier seasonably shall notify the lessor and the lessee, if known, that there will be delay or nondelivery and, if allocation is required under paragraph (b), of the estimated quota thus made available for the lessee.

§ 2A—406. **Procedure on Excused Performance.**

(1) If the lessee receives notification of a material or indefinite delay or an allocation justified under Section 2A—405, the lessee may by written notification to the lessor as to any goods involved, and with respect to all of the goods if under an installment lease contract the value of the whole lease contract is substantially impaired (Section 2A—510):

(a) terminate the lease contract (Section 2A—505(2)); or

(b) except in a finance lease that is not a consumer lease, modify the lease contract by accepting the available quota in substitution, with due allowance from the rent payable for the balance of the lease term for the deficiency but without further right against the lessor.

(2) If, after receipt of a notification from the lessor under Section 2A—405, the lessee fails so to modify the lease agreement within a reasonable time not exceeding 30 days, the lease contract lapses with respect to any deliveries affected.

§ 2A—407. **Irrevocable Promises: Finance Leases.**

(1) In the case of a finance lease that is not a consumer lease the lessee's promises under the lease contract become irrevocable and independent upon the lessee's acceptance of the goods.

(2) A promise that has become irrevocable and independent under subsection (1):

(a) is effective and enforceable between the parties or against third parties including assignees of the parties, and

(b) is not subject to cancellation, termination, modification, repudiation, excuse, or substitution without the consent of the party to whom the promise runs.

Part 5 Default
A. In General

§ 2A—501. **Default: Procedure.**

(1) Whether the lessor or the lessee is in default under a lease contract is determined by the lease agreement and this Article.

(2) If the lessor or the lessee is in default under the lease contract, the party seeking enforcement has rights and remedies as provided in this Article and, except as limited by this Article, as provided in the lease agreement.

(3) If the lessor or the lessee is in default under the lease contract, the party seeking enforcement may reduce the party's claim to judgment, or otherwise enforce the lease contract by self-help or any available judicial procedure or nonjudicial procedure, including administrative proceeding, arbitration, or the like, in accordance with this Article.

(4) Except as otherwise provided in this Article or the lease agreement, the rights and remedies referred to in subsections (2) and (3) are cumulative.

(5) If the lease agreement covers both real property and goods, the party seeking enforcement may proceed under this Part as to the goods, or under other applicable law as to both the real property and the goods in accordance with his [or her] rights and remedies in respect of the real property, in which case this Part does not apply.

§ 2A—502. **Notice After Default.**

Except as otherwise provided in this Article or the lease agreement, the lessor or lessee in default under the lease contract is not entitled to notice of default or notice of enforcement from the other party to the lease agreement.

§ 2A—503. **Modification or Impairment of Rights and Remedies.**

(1) Except as otherwise provided in this Article, the lease agreement may include rights and remedies for default in addition to or in substitution for those provided in this Article and may limit or alter the measure of damages recoverable under this Article.

(2) Resort to a remedy provided under this Article or in the lease agreement is optional unless the remedy is expressly agreed to be exclusive. If circumstances cause an exclusive or limited remedy to fail of its essential purpose, or provision for an exclusive remedy is unconscionable, remedy may be had as provided in this Article.

(3) Consequential damages may be liquidated under Section 2A—504, or may otherwise be limited, altered, or excluded unless the limitation, alteration, or exclusion is unconscionable. Limitation of consequential damages for injury to the person in the case of consumer goods is prima facie unconscionable but limitation of damages where the loss is commercial is not.

(4) Rights and remedies on default by the lessor or the lessee with respect to any obligation or promise collateral or ancillary to the lease contract are not impaired by this Article.

§ 2A—504. **Liquidation of Damages.**

(1) Damages payable by either party for default, or any other act or omission, including indemnity for loss or diminution of anticipated tax benefits or loss or damage to lessor's residual interest, may be liquidated in the lease agreement but only at an amount or by a formula that is reasonable in light of the then anticipated harm caused by the default or other act or omission.

(2) If the lease agreement provides for liquidation of damages, and such provision does not comply with subsection (1), or such provision is an exclusive or limited remedy that circumstances cause to fail of its essential purpose, remedy may be had as provided in this Article.

(3) If the lessor justifiably withholds or stops delivery of goods because of the lessee's default or insolvency (Section 2A—525 or 2A—526), the lessee is entitled to restitution of any amount by which the sum of his [or her] payments exceeds:

(a) the amount to which the lessor is entitled by virtue of terms liquidating the lessor's damages in accordance with subsection (1); or

(b) in the absence of those terms, 20 percent of the then present value of the total rent the lessee was obligated to pay for the balance of the lease term, or, in the case of a consumer lease, the lesser of such amount or $500.

(4) A lessee's right to restitution under subsection (3) is subject to offset to the extent the lessor establishes:

(a) a right to recover damages under the provisions of this Article other than subsection (1); and

(b) the amount or value of any benefits received by the lessee directly or indirectly by reason of the lease contract.

§ 2A—505. **Cancellation and Termination and Effect of Cancellation, Termination, Rescission, or Fraud on Rights and Remedies.**

(1) On cancellation of the lease contract, all obligations that are still executory on both sides are discharged, but any right based on prior default or performance survives, and the cancelling party also retains any remedy for default of the whole lease contract or any unperformed balance.

(2) On termination of the lease contract, all obligations that are still executory on both sides are discharged but any right based on prior default or performance survives.

(3) Unless the contrary intention clearly appears, expressions of "cancellation," "rescission," or the like of the lease contract may not be construed as a renunciation or discharge of any claim in damages for an antecedent default.

(4) Rights and remedies for material misrepresentation or fraud include all rights and remedies available under this Article for default.

(5) Neither rescission nor a claim for rescission of the lease contract nor rejection or return of the goods may bar or be deemed inconsistent with a claim for damages or other right or remedy.

§ 2A—506. **Statute of Limitations.**

(1) An action for default under a lease contract, including breach of warranty or indemnity, must be commenced within 4 years after the cause of action accrued. By the original lease contract the parties may reduce the period of limitation to not less than one year.

(2) A cause of action for default accrues when the act or omission on which the default or breach of warranty is based is or should have been discovered by the aggrieved party, or when the default occurs, whichever is later. A cause of action for indemnity accrues when the act or omission on which the claim for indemnity is based is or should have been discovered by the indemnified party, whichever is later.

(3) If an action commenced within the time limited by subsection (1) is so terminated as to leave available a remedy by another action for the same default or breach of warranty or indemnity, the other action may be commenced after the expiration of the time limited and within 6 months after the termination of the first action unless the termination resulted from voluntary discontinuance or from dismissal for failure or neglect to prosecute.

(4) This section does not alter the law on tolling of the statute of limitations nor does it apply to causes of action that have accrued before this Article becomes effective.

§ 2A—507. **Proof of Market Rent: Time and Place.**

(1) Damages based on market rent (Section 2A—519 or 2A—528) are determined according to the rent for the use of the goods concerned for a lease term identical to the remaining lease term of the original lease agreement and prevailing at the time of the default.

(2) If evidence of rent for the use of the goods concerned for a lease term identical to the remaining lease term of the original lease agreement and prevailing at the times or places described in this Article is not readily available, the rent prevailing within any reasonable time before or after the time described or at any other place or for a different lease term which in commercial judgment or under usage of trade would serve as a reasonable substitute for the one described may be used, making any proper allowance for the difference, including the cost of transporting the goods to or from the other place.

(3) Evidence of a relevant rent prevailing at a time or place or for a lease term other than the one described in this Article offered by one party is not admissible unless and until he [or she] has given the other party notice the court finds sufficient to prevent unfair surprise.

(4) If the prevailing rent or value of any goods regularly leased in any established market is in issue, reports in official publications or trade journals or in newspapers or periodicals of general circulation published as the reports of that market are admissible in evidence. The circumstances of the preparation of the report may be shown to affect its weight but not its admissibility.

B. Default by Lessor

§ 2A—508. **Lessee's Remedies.**

(1) If a lessor fails to deliver the goods in conformity to the lease contract (Section 2A—509) or repudiates the lease contract (Section 2A—402), or a lessee rightfully rejects the goods (Section 2A—509) or justifiably revokes acceptance of the goods (Section 2A—517), then with respect to any goods involved, and with respect to all of the goods if under an installment lease contract the value of the whole lease contract is substantially impaired (Section 2A—510), the lessor is in default under the lease contract and the lessee may:

(a) cancel the lease contract (Section 2A—505(1));

(b) recover so much of the rent and security as has been paid, but in the case of an installment lease contract the recovery is that which is just under the circumstances;

(c) cover and recover damages as to all goods affected whether or not they have been identified to the lease contract (Sections 2A—518 and 2A—520), or recover damages for nondelivery (Sections 2A—519 and 2A—520).

(2) If a lessor fails to deliver the goods in conformity to the lease contract or repudiates the lease contract, the lessee may also:

> (a) if the goods have been identified, recover them (Section 2A—522); or

> (b) in a proper case, obtain specific performance or replevy the goods (Section 2A—521).

(3) If a lessor is otherwise in default under a lease contract, the lessee may exercise the rights and remedies provided in the lease contract and this Article.

(4) If a lessor has breached a warranty, whether express or implied, the lessee may recover damages (Section 2A—519(4)).

(5) On rightful rejection or justifiable revocation of acceptance, a lessee has a security interest in goods in the lessee's possession or control for any rent and security that has been paid and any expenses reasonably incurred in their inspection, receipt, transportation, and care and custody and may hold those goods and dispose of them in good faith and in a commercially reasonable manner, subject to the provisions of Section 2A—527(5).

(6) Subject to the provisions of Section 2A—407, a lessee, on notifying the lessor of the lessee's intention to do so, may deduct all or any part of the damages resulting from any default under the lease contract from any part of the rent still due under the same lease contract.

§ 2A—509. Lessee's Rights on Improper Delivery; Rightful Rejection.

(1) Subject to the provisions of Section 2A—510 on default in installment lease contracts, if the goods or the tender or delivery fail in any respect to conform to the lease contract, the lessee may reject or accept the goods or accept any commercial unit or units and reject the rest of the goods.

(2) Rejection of goods is ineffective unless it is within a reasonable time after tender or delivery of the goods and the lessee seasonably notifies the lessor.

§ 2A—510. Installment Lease Contracts: Rejection and Default.

(1) Under an installment lease contract a lessee may reject any delivery that is nonconforming if the nonconformity substantially impairs the value of that delivery and cannot be cured or the nonconformity is a defect in the required documents; but if the nonconformity does not fall within subsection (2) and the lessor or the supplier gives adequate assurance of its cure, the lessee must accept that delivery.

(2) Whenever nonconformity or default with respect to one or more deliveries substantially impairs the value of the installment lease contract as a whole there is a default with respect to the whole. But, the aggrieved party reinstates the installment lease contract as a whole if the aggrieved party accepts a nonconforming delivery without seasonably notifying of cancellation or brings an action with respect only to past deliveries or demands performance as to future deliveries.

§ 2A—511. Merchant Lessee's Duties as to Rightfully Rejected Goods.

(1) Subject to any security interest of a lessee (Section 2A—508(5)), if a lessor or a supplier has no agent or place of business at the market of rejection, a merchant lessee, after rejection of goods in his [or her] possession or control, shall follow any reasonable instructions received from the lessor or the supplier with respect to the goods. In the absence of those instructions, a merchant lessee shall make reasonable efforts to sell, lease, or otherwise dispose of the goods for the lessor's account if they threaten to decline in value speedily. Instructions are not reasonable if on demand indemnity for expenses is not forthcoming.

(2) If a merchant lessee (subsection (1)) or any other lessee (Section 2A—512) disposes of goods, he [or she] is entitled to reimbursement either from the lessor or the supplier or out of the proceeds for reasonable expenses of caring for and disposing of the goods and, if the expenses include no disposition commission, to such commission as is usual in the trade, or if there is none, to a reasonable sum not exceeding 10 percent of the gross proceeds.

(3) In complying with this section or Section 2A—512, the lessee is held only to good faith. Good faith conduct hereunder is neither acceptance or conversion nor the basis of an action for damages.

(4) A purchaser who purchases in good faith from a lessee pursuant to this section or Section 2A—512 takes the goods free of any rights of the lessor and the supplier even though the lessee fails to comply with one or more of the requirements of this Article.

§ 2A—512. Lessee's Duties as to Rightfully Rejected Goods.

(1) Except as otherwise provided with respect to goods that threaten to decline in value speedily (Section 2A—511) and subject to any security interest of a lessee (Section 2A—508(5)):

> (a) the lessee, after rejection of goods in the lessee's possession, shall hold them with reasonable care at the lessor's or the supplier's disposition for a rea-

sonable time after the lessee's seasonable notification of rejection;

(b) if the lessor or the supplier gives no instructions within a reasonable time after notification of rejection, the lessee may store the rejected goods for the lessor's or the supplier's account or ship them to the lessor or the supplier or dispose of them for the lessor's or the supplier's account with reimbursement in the manner provided in Section 2A—511; but

(c) the lessee has no further obligations with regard to goods rightfully rejected.

(2) Action by the lessee pursuant to subsection (1) is not acceptance or conversion.

§ 2A—513. Cure by Lessor of Improper Tender or Delivery; Replacement.

(1) If any tender or delivery by the lessor or the supplier is rejected because nonconforming and the time for performance has not yet expired, the lessor or the supplier may seasonably notify the lessee of the lessor's or the supplier's intention to cure and may then make a conforming delivery within the time provided in the lease contract.

(2) If the lessee rejects a nonconforming tender that the lessor or the supplier had reasonable grounds to believe would be acceptable with or without money allowance, the lessor or the supplier may have a further reasonable time to substitute a conforming tender if he [or she] seasonably notifies the lessee.

§ 2A—514. Waiver of Lessee's Objections.

(1) In rejecting goods, a lessee's failure to state a particular defect that is ascertainable by reasonable inspection precludes the lessee from relying on the defect to justify rejection or to establish default:

(a) if, stated seasonably, the lessor or the supplier could have cured it (Section 2A—513); or

(b) between merchants if the lessor or the supplier after rejection has made a request in writing for a full and final written statement of all defects on which the lessee proposes to rely.

(2) A lessee's failure to reserve rights when paying rent or other consideration against documents precludes recovery of the payment for defects apparent on the face of the documents.

§ 2A—515. Acceptance of Goods.

(1) Acceptance of goods occurs after the lessee has had a reasonable opportunity to inspect the goods and

(a) the lessee signifies or acts with respect to the goods in a manner that signifies to the lessor or the

supplier that the goods are conforming or that the lessee will take or retain them in spite of their nonconformity; or

(b) the lessee fails to make an effective rejection of the goods (Section 2A—509(2)).

(2) Acceptance of a part of any commercial unit is acceptance of that entire unit.

§ 2A—516. Effect of Acceptance of Goods; Notice of Default; Burden of Establishing Default after Acceptance; Notice of Claim or Litigation to Person Answerable Over.

(1) A lessee must pay rent for any goods accepted in accordance with the lease contract, with due allowance for goods rightfully rejected or not delivered.

(2) A lessee's acceptance of goods precludes rejection of the goods accepted. In the case of a finance lease, if made with knowledge of a nonconformity, acceptance cannot be revoked because of it. In any other case, if made with knowledge of a nonconformity, acceptance cannot be revoked because of it unless the acceptance was on the reasonable assumption that the nonconformity would be seasonably cured. Acceptance does not of itself impair any other remedy provided by this Article or the lease agreement for nonconformity.

(3) If a tender has been accepted:

(a) within a reasonable time after the lessee discovers or should have discovered any default, the lessee shall notify the lessor and the supplier, or be barred from any remedy.

(b) except in the case of a consumer lease, within a reasonable time after the lessee receives notice of litigation for infringement or the like (Section 2A—211) the lessee shall notify the lessor or be barred from any remedy over for liability established by the litigation; and

(c) the burden is on the lessee to establish any default.

(4) If a lessee is sued for breach of a warranty or other obligation for which a lessor or a supplier is answerable over:

(a) The lessee may give the lessor or the supplier written notice of the litigation. If the notice states that the lessor or the supplier may come in and defend and that if the lessor or the supplier does not do so he [or she] will be bound in any action against him [or her] by the lessee by any determination of fact common to the two litigations, then unless the lessor or the supplier after seasonable receipt of the notice does come in and defend he [or she] is so bound.

(b) The lessor or the supplier may demand in writing that the lessee turn over control of the litigation including settlement if the claim is one for infringement or the like (Section 2A—211) or else be barred from any remedy over. If the demand states that the lessor or the supplier agrees to bear all expense and to satisfy any adverse judgment, then unless the lessee after seasonable receipt of the demand does turn over control the lessee is so barred.

(5) The provisions of subsections (3) and (4) apply to any obligation of a lessee to hold the lessor or the supplier harmless against infringement or the like (Section 2A—211).

§ 2A—517. **Revocation of Acceptance of Goods.**

(1) A lessee may revoke acceptance of a lot or commercial unit whose nonconformity substantially impairs its value to the lessee if he [or she] has accepted it:

(a) except in the case of a finance lease, on the reasonable assumption that its nonconformity would be cured and it has not been seasonably cured; or

(b) without discovery of the nonconformity if the lessee's acceptance was reasonably induced either by the lessor's assurances or, except in the case of a finance lease, by the difficulty or discovery before acceptance.

(2) Revocation of acceptance must occur within a reasonable time after the lessee discovers or should have discovered the ground for it and before any substantial change in condition of the goods which is not caused by the nonconformity. Revocation is not effective until the lessee notifies the lessor.

(3) A lessee who so revokes has the same rights and duties with regard to the goods involved as if the lessee had rejected them.

§ 2A—518. **Cover; Substitute Goods.**

(1) After default by a lessor under the lease contract (Section 2A—508(1)), the lessee may cover by making in good faith and without unreasonable delay any purchase or lease of or contract to purchase or lease goods in substitution for those due from the lessor.

(2) Except as otherwise provided with respect to damages liquidated in the lease agreement (Section 2A—504) or determined by agreement of the parties (Section 1—102(3)), if a lessee's cover is by lease agreement substantially similar to the original lease agreement and the lease agreement is made in good faith and in a commercially reasonable manner, the lessee may recover from the lessor as damages (a) the present value, as of the date of default, of the difference between the total rent for the lease term of the new lease agreement and the total rent for the remaining lease term of the original lease agreement and (b) any incidental or consequential damages less expenses saved in consequence of the lessor's default.

(3) If a lessee's cover does not qualify for treatment under subsection (2), the lessee may recover from the lessor as if the lessee had elected not to cover and Section 2A—519 governs.

§ 2A—519. **Lessee's Damages for Non-Delivery, Repudiation, Default and Breach of Warranty in Regard to Accepted Goods.**

(1) If a lessee elects not to cover or a lessee elects to cover and the cover does not qualify for treatment under Section 2A—518(2), the measure of damages for non-delivery or repudiation by the lessor or for rejection or revocation of acceptance by the lessee is the present value as of the date of the default of the difference between the then market rent and the original rent, computed for the remaining lease term of the original lease agreement together with incidental and consequential damages, less expenses saved in consequence of the lessor's default.

(2) Market rent is to be determined as of the place for tender or, in cases of rejection after arrival or revocation of acceptance, as of the place of arrival.

(3) If the lessee has accepted goods and given notification (Section 2A—516(3)), the measure of damages for non-conforming tender or delivery by a lessor is the loss resulting in the ordinary course of events from the lessor's default as determined in any manner that is reasonable together with incidental and consequential damages, less expenses saved in consequence of the lessor's default.

(4) The measure of damages for breach of warranty is the present value at the time and place of acceptance of the difference between the value of the use of the goods accepted and the value if they had been as warranted for the lease term, unless special circumstances show proximate damages of a different amount, together with incidental and consequential damages, less expenses saved in consequence of the lessor's default or breach of warranty.

§ 2A—520. **Lessee's Incidental and Consequential Damages.**

(1) Incidental damages resulting from a lessor's default include expenses reasonably incurred in inspection, receipt, transportation, and care and custody of goods rightfully rejected or goods the acceptance of which is justifiably revoked, any commercially reasonable charges, expenses or commissions in connection with effecting cover, and any other reasonable expense incident to the default.

(2) Consequential damages resulting from a lessor's default include:

(a) any loss resulting from general or particular requirements and needs of which the lessor at the time of contracting had reason to know and which could not reasonably be prevented by cover or otherwise; and

(b) injury to person or property proximately resulting from any breach of warranty.

§ 2A—521. Lessee's Right to Specific Performance or Replevin.

(1) Specific performance may be decreed if the goods are unique or in other proper circumstances.

(2) A decree for specific performance may include any terms and conditions as to payment of the rent, damages, or other relief that the court deems just.

(3) A lessee has a right of replevin, detinue, sequestration, claim and delivery, or the like for goods identified to the lease contract if after reasonable effort the lessee is unable to effect cover for those goods or the circumstances reasonably indicate that the effort will be unavailing.

§ 2A—522. Lessee's Right to Goods on Lessor's Insolvency.

(1) Subject to subsection (2) and even though the goods have not been shipped, a lessee who has paid a part or all of the rent and security for goods identified to a lease contract (Section 2A—217) on making and keeping good a tender of any unpaid portion of the rent and security due under the lease contract may recover the goods identified from the lessor if the lessor becomes insolvent within 10 days after receipt of the first installment of rent and security.

(2) A lessee acquires the right to recover goods identified to a lease contract only if they conform to the lease contract.

C. Default by Lessee

§ 2A—523. Lessor's Remedies.

(1) If a lessee wrongfully rejects or revokes acceptance of goods or fails to make a payment when due or repudiates with respect to a part or the whole, then, with respect to any goods involved, and with respect to all of the goods if under an installment lease contract the value of the whole lease contract is substantially impaired (Section 2A—510), the lessee is in default under the lease contract and the lessor may:

(a) cancel the lease contract (Section 2A—505(1));

(b) proceed respecting goods not identified to the lease contract (Section 2A—524);

(c) withhold delivery of the goods and take possession of goods previously delivered (Section 2A—525);

(d) stop delivery of the goods by any bailee (Section 2A—526);

(e) dispose of the goods and recover damages (Section 2A—527), or retain the goods and recover damages (Section 2A—528), or in a proper case recover rent (Section 2A—529).

(2) If a lessee is otherwise in default under a lease contract, the lessor may exercise the rights and remedies provided in the lease contract and this Article.

§ 2A—524. Lessor's Right to Identify Goods to Lease Contract.

(1) A lessor aggrieved under Section 2A—523(1) may:

(a) identify to the lease contract conforming goods not already identified if at the time the lessor learned of the default they were in the lessor's or the supplier's possession or control; and

(b) dispose of goods (Section 2A—527(1)) that demonstrably have been intended for the particular lease contract even though those goods are unfinished.

(2) If the goods are unfinished, in the exercise of reasonable commercial judgment for the purposes of avoiding loss and of effective realization, an aggrieved lessor or the supplier may either complete manufacture and wholly identify the goods to the lease contract or cease manufacture and lease, sell, or otherwise dispose of the goods for scrap or salvage value or proceed in any other reasonable manner.

§ 2A—525. Lessor's Right to Possession of Goods.

(1) If a lessor discovers the lessee to be insolvent, the lessor may refuse to deliver the goods.

(2) The lessor has on default by the lessee under the lease contract the right to take possession of the goods. If the lease contract so provides, the lessor may require the lessee to assemble the goods and make them available to the lessor at a place to be designated by the lessor which is reasonably convenient to both parties. Without removal, the lessor may render unusable any goods employed in trade or business, and may dispose of goods on the lessee's premises (Section 2A—527).

(3) The lessor may proceed under subsection (2) without judicial process if that can be done without breach of the peace or the lessor may proceed by action.

§ 2A—526. Lessor's Stoppage of Delivery in Transit or Otherwise.

(1) A lessor may stop delivery of goods in the possession of a carrier or other bailee if the lessor discovers the lessee to be insolvent and may stop delivery of carload, truckload, planeload, or larger shipments of express or freight if the lessee repudiates or fails to make a payment

due before delivery, whether for rent, security or otherwise under the lease contract, or for any other reason the lessor has a right to withhold or take possession of the goods.

(2) In pursuing its remedies under subsection (1) the lessor may stop delivery until

(a) receipt of the goods by the lessee;

(b) acknowledgment to the lessee by any bailee of the goods, except a carrier, that the bailee holds the goods for the lessee; or

(c) such an acknowledgment to the lessee by a carrier via reshipment or as warehouseman.

(3) (a) To stop delivery, a lessor shall so notify as to enable the bailee by reasonable diligence to prevent delivery of the goods.

(b) After notification, the bailee shall hold and deliver the goods according to the directions of the lessor, but the lessor is liable to the bailee for any ensuing charges or damages.

(c) A carrier who has issued a nonnegotiable bill of lading is not obliged to obey a notification to stop received from a person other than the consignor.

§ 2A—527. **Lessor's Rights to Dispose of Goods.**

(1) After a default by a lessee under the lease contract (Section 2A—523(1)) or after the lessor refuses to deliver or take possession of goods (Section 2A—525 or 2A—526), the lessor may dispose of the goods concerned or the undelivered balance thereof in good faith and without unreasonable delay by lease, sale or otherwise.

(2) If the disposition is by lease contract substantially similar to the original lease contract and the lease contract is made in good faith and in a commercially reasonable manner, the lessor may recover from the lessee as damages (a) accrued and unpaid rent as of the date of default, (b) the present value as of the date of default of the difference between the total rent for the remaining lease term of the original lease contract and the total rent for the lease term of the new lease contract, and (c) any incidental damages allowed under Section 2A—530, less expenses saved in consequence of the lessee's default.

(3) If the lessor's disposition is by lease contract that for any reason does not qualify for treatment under subsection (2), or is by sale or otherwise, the lessor may recover from the lessee as if the lessor had elected not to dispose of the goods and Section 2A—528 governs.

(4) A subsequent buyer or lessee who buys or leases from the lessor in good faith for value as a result of a disposition under this section takes the goods free of the original lease contract and any rights of the original

lessee even though the lessor fails to comply with one or more of the requirements of this Article.

(5) The lessor is not accountable to the lessee for any profit made on any disposition. A lessee who has rightfully rejected or justifiably revoked acceptance shall account to the lessor for any excess over the amount of the lessee's security interest (Section 2A—508(5)).

§ 2A—528. **Lessor's Damages for Non-Acceptance or Repudiation.**

(1) Except as otherwise provided with respect to damages liquidated in the lease agreement (Section 2A—504) or determined by agreement of the parties (Section 1—102(3)), if a lessor elects to retain the goods or a lessor elects to dispose of the goods and disposition is by lease agreement that for any reason does not qualify for treatment under Section 2A—527(2), or is by sale or otherwise, the lessor may recover from the lessee as damages for non-acceptance or repudiation by the lessee (a) accrued and unpaid rent as of the date of default, (b) the present value as of the date of default of the difference between the total rent for the remaining lease term of the original lease agreement and the market rent at the time and place for tender computed for the same lease term, and (c) any incidental damages allowed under Section 2A—530, less expenses saved in consequence of the lessee's default.

(2) If the measure of damages provided in subsection (1) is inadequate to put a lessor in as good a position as performance would have, the measure of damages is the profit, including reasonable overhead, the lessor would have made from full performance by the lessee, together with any incidental damages allowed under Section 2A—530, due allowance for costs reasonably incurred and due credit for payments or proceeds of disposition.

§ 2A—529. **Lessor's Action for the Rent.**

(1) After default by the lessee under the lease contract (Section 2A—523(1)), if the lessor complies with subsection (2), the lessor may recover from the lessee as damages:

(a) for goods accepted by the lessee and for conforming goods lost or damaged within a commercially reasonable time after risk of loss passes to the lessee (Section 2A—219), (i) accrued and unpaid rent as of the date of default, (ii) the present value as of the date of default of the rent for the remaining lease term of the lease agreement, and (iii) any incidental damages allowed under Section 2A—530, less expenses saved in consequence of the lessee's default; and

(b) for goods identified to the lease contract if the lessor is unable after reasonable effort to dispose of them at a reasonable price or the circumstances reasonably indicate that effort will be unavailing, (i) accrued and unpaid rent as of the date of default, (ii) the present value as of the date of default of the rent for the remaining lease term of the lease agreement, and (iii) any incidental damages allowed under Section 2A—530, less expenses saved in consequence of the lessee's default.

(2) Except as provided in subsection (3), the lessor shall hold for the lessee for the remaining lease term of the lease agreement any goods that have been identified to the lease contract and are in the lessor's control.

(3) The lessor may dispose of the goods at any time before collection of the judgment for damages obtained pursuant to subsection (1) and the lessor may proceed against the lessee for damages pursuant to Section 2A—527 or Section 2A—528.

(4) Payment of the judgment for damages obtained pursuant to subsection (1) entitles the lessee to use and possession of the goods not then disposed of for the remaining lease term of the lease agreement.

(5) After a lessee has wrongfully rejected or revoked acceptance of goods, has failed to pay rent then due, or has repudiated (Section 2A—402), a lessor who is held not entitled to rent under this section must nevertheless be awarded damages for non-acceptance under Sections 2A—527 and 2A—528.

§ 2A—530. **Lessor's Incidental Damages.**

Incidental damages to an aggrieved lessor include any commercially reasonable charges, expenses, or commissions incurred in stopping delivery, in the transportation, care and custody of goods after the lessee's default, in connection with return or disposition of the goods, or otherwise resulting from the default.

§ 2A—531. **Standing to Sue Third Parties for Injury to Goods.**

(1) If a third party so deals with goods that have been identified to a lease contract as to cause actionable injury to a party to the lease contract (a) the lessor has a right of action against the third party, and (b) the lessee also has a right of action against the third party if the lessee:

    (i)   has a security interest in the goods;

    (ii) has an insurable interest in the goods; or

    (iii) bears the risk of loss under the lease contract or has since the injury assumed that risk as against the lessor and the goods have been converted or destroyed.

(2) If at the time of the injury the party plaintiff did not bear the risk of loss as against the other party to the lease contract and there is no arrangement between them for disposition of the recovery, his [or her] suit or set-

tlement, subject to his [or her] own interest, is as a fiduciary for the other party to the lease contract.

(3) Either party with the consent of the other may sue for the benefit of whom it may concern.

Article 3
COMMERCIAL PAPER

Part 1 Short Title, Form and Interpretation

§ 3—101. **Short Title.**

This Article shall be known and may be cited as Uniform Commercial Code—Commercial Paper.

§ 3—102. **Definitions and Index of Definitions.**

(1) In this Article unless the context otherwise requires

    (a) "Issue" means the first delivery of an instrument to a holder or a remitter.

    (b) An "order" is a direction to pay and must be more than an authorization or request. It must identify the person to pay with reasonable certainty. It may be addressed to one or more such persons jointly or in the alternative but not in succession.

    (c) A "promise" is an undertaking to pay and must be more than an acknowledgment of an obligation.

    (d) "Secondary party" means a drawer or indorser.

    (e) "Instrument" means a negotiable instrument.

(2) Other definitions applying to this Article and the sections in which they appear are:
"Acceptance". Section 3—410.
"Accommodation party". Section 3—415.
"Alteration". Section 3—407.
"Certificate of deposit". Section 3—104.
"Certification". Section 3—411.
"Check". Section 3—104.
"Definite time". Section 3—109.
"Dishonor". Section 3—507.
"Draft". Section 3—104.
"Holder in due course". Section 3—302.
"Negotiation". Section 3—202.
"Note". Section 3—104.
"Notice of dishonor". Section 3—508.
"On demand". Section 3—108.
"Presentment". Section 3—504.
"Protest". Section 3—509.
"Restrictive Indorsement". Section 3—205.
"Signature". Section 3—401.

(3) The following definitions in other Articles apply to this Article:
"Account". Section 4—104.

"Banking Day". Section 4—104.
"Clearing House". Section 4—104.
"Collecting Bank". Section 4—105.
"Customer". Section 4—104.
"Depositary Bank". Section 4—105.
"Documentary Draft". Section 4—104.
"Intermediary Bank". Section 4—105.
"Item". Section 4—104.
"Midnight deadline". Section 4—104.
"Payor Bank". Section 4—105.

(4) In addition Article 1 contains general definitions and principles of construction and interpretation applicable throughout this Article.

§ 3—103. Limitations on Scope of Article.

(1) This Article does not apply to money, documents of title or investment securities.

(2) The provisions of this Article are subject to the provisions of the Article on Bank Deposits and Collections (Article 4) and Secured Transactions (Article 9).

§ 3—104. Form of Negotiable Instruments; "Draft"; "Check"; "Certificate of Deposit"; "Note".

(1) Any writing to be a negotiable instrument within this Article must

(a) be signed by the maker or drawer; and

(b) contain an unconditional promise or order to pay a sum certain in money and no other promise, order, obligation or power given by the maker or drawer except as authorized by this Article; and

(c) be payable on demand or at a definite time; and

(d) be payable to order or to bearer.

(2) A writing which complies with the requirements of this section is

(a) a "draft" ("bill of exchange") if it is an order;

(b) a "check" if it is a draft drawn on a bank and payable on demand;

(c) a "certificate of deposit" if it is an acknowledgment by a bank receipt of money with an engagement to repay it;

(d) a "note" if it is a promise other than a certificate of deposit.

(3) As used in other Articles of this Act, and as the context may require, the terms "draft", "check", "certificate of deposit" and "note" may refer to instruments which are not negotiable within this Article as well as to instruments which are so negotiable.

§ 3—105. When Promise or Order Unconditional.

(1) A promise or order otherwise unconditional is not made conditional by the fact that the instrument

(a) is subject to implied or constructive conditions; or

(b) states its consideration, whether performed or promised, or the transaction which gave rise to the instrument, or that the promise or order is made or the instrument matures in accordance with or "as per" such transaction; or

(c) refers to or states that it arises out of a separate agreement or refers to a separate agreement for rights as to prepayment or acceleration; or

(d) states that it is drawn under a letter of credit; or

(e) states that it is secured, whether by mortgage, reservation of title or otherwise; or

(f) indicates a particular account to be debited or any other fund or source from which reimbursement is expected; or

(g) is limited to payment out of a particular fund or the proceeds of a particular source, if the instrument is issued by a government or governmental agency or unit; or

(h) is limited to payment out of the entire assets of a partnership, unincorporated association, trust or estate by or on behalf of which the instrument is issued.

(2) A promise or order is not unconditional if the instrument

(a) states that it is subject to or governed by any other agreement; or

(b) states that it is to be paid only out of a particular fund or source except as provided in this section.

§ 3—106. Sum Certain.

(1) The sum payable is a sum certain even though it is to be paid

(a) with stated interest or by stated installments; or

(b) with stated different rates of interest before and after default or a specified date; or

(c) with a stated discount or addition if paid before or after the date fixed for payment; or

(d) with exchange or less exchange, whether at a fixed rate or at the current rate; or

(e) with costs of collection or an attorney's fee or both upon default.

(2) Nothing in this section shall validate any term which is otherwise illegal.

§ 3—107. Money.

(1) An instrument is payable in money if the medium of exchange in which it is payable is money at the time

the instrument is made. An instrument payable in "currency" or "current funds" is payable in money.

(2) A promise or order to pay a sum stated in a foreign currency is for a sum certain in money and, unless a different medium of payment is specified in the instrument, may be satisfied by payment of that number of dollars which the stated foreign currency will purchase at the buying sight rate for that currency on the day on which the instrument is payable or, if payable on demand, on the day of demand. If such an instrument specifies a foreign currency as the medium of payment the instrument is payable in that currency.

§ 3—108. **Payable on Demand.**

Instruments payable on demand include those payable at sight or on presentation and those in which no time for payment is stated.

§ 3—109. **Definite Time.**

(1) An instrument is payable at a definite time if by its terms it is payable

   (a) on or before a stated date or at a fixed period after a stated date; or

   (b) at a fixed period after sight; or

   (c) at a definite time subject to any acceleration; or

   (d) at a definite time subject to extension at the option of the holder, or to extension to a further definite time at the option of the maker or acceptor or automatically upon or after a specified act or event.

(2) An instrument which by its terms is otherwise payable only upon an act or event uncertain as to time of occurrence is not payable at a definite time even though the act or event has occurred.

§ 3—110. **Payable to Order.**

(1) An instrument is payable to order when by its terms it is payable to the order or assigns of any person therein specified with reasonable certainty, or to him or his order, or when it is conspicuously designated on its face as "exchange" or the like and names a payee. It may be payable to the order of

   (a) the maker or drawer; or

   (b) the drawee; or

   (c) a payee who is not maker, drawer or drawee; or

   (d) two or more payees together or in the alternative; or

   (e) an estate, trust or fund, in which case it is payable to the order of the representative of such estate, trust or fund or his successors; or

   (f) an office, or an officer by his title as such in which case it is payable to the principal but the

incumbent of the office or his successors may act as if he or they were the holder; or

   (g) a partnership or unincorporated association, in which case it is payable to the partnership or association and may be indorsed or transferred by any person thereto authorized.

(2) An instrument not payable to order is not made so payable by such words as "payable upon return of this instrument properly indorsed."

(3) An instrument made payable both to order and to bearer is payable to order unless the bearer words are handwritten or typewritten.

§ 3—111. **Payable to Bearer.**

An instrument is payable to bearer when by its terms it is payable to

(a) bearer or the order of bearer; or

(b) a specified person or bearer; or

(c) "cash" or the order of "cash", or any other indication which does not purport to designate a specific payee.

§ 3—112. **Terms and Omissions Not Affecting Negotiability.**

(1) The negotiability of an instrument is not affected by

   (a) the omission of a statement of any consideration or of the place where the instrument is drawn or payable; or

   (b) a statement that collateral has been given to secure obligations either on the instrument or otherwise of an obligor on the instrument or that in case of default on those obligations the holder may realize on or dispose of the collateral; or

   (c) a promise or power to maintain or protect collateral or to give additional collateral; or

   (d) a term authorizing a confession of judgment on the instrument if it is not paid when due; or

   (e) a term purporting to waive the benefit of any law intended for the advantage or protection of any obligor; or

   (f) a term in a draft providing that the payee by indorsing or cashing it acknowledges full satisfaction of an obligation of the drawer; or

   (g) a statement in a draft drawn in a set of parts (Section 3—801) to the effect that the order is effective only if no other part has been honored.

(2) Nothing in this section shall validate any term which is otherwise illegal.

§ 3—113. **Seal.**

An instrument otherwise negotiable is within this Article even though it is under a seal.

§ 3—114. **Date, Antedating, Postdating.**

(1) The negotiability of an instrument is not affected by the fact that it is undated, antedated or postdated.

(2) Where an instrument is antedated or postdated the time when it is payable is determined by the stated date if the instrument is payable on demand or at a fixed period after date.

(3) Where the instrument or any signature thereon is dated, the date is presumed to be correct.

§ 3—115. **Incomplete Instruments.**

(1) When a paper whose contents at the time of signing show that it is intended to become an instrument is signed while still incomplete in any necessary respect it cannot be enforced until completed, but when it is completed in accordance with authority given it is effective as completed.

(2) If the completion is unauthorized the rules as to material alteration apply (Section 3—407), even though the paper was not delivered by the maker or drawer; but the burden of establishing that any completion is unauthorized is on the party so asserting.

§ 3—116. **Instruments Payable to Two or More Persons.**

An instrument payable to the order of two or more persons

(a) if in the alternative is payable to any one of them and may be negotiated, discharged or enforced by any of them who has possession of it;

(b) if not in the alternative is payable to all of them and may be negotiated, discharged or enforced only by all of them.

§ 3—117. **Instruments Payable With Words of Description.**

An instrument made payable to a named person with the addition of words describing him

(a) as agent or officer of a specified person is payable to his principal but the agent or officer may act as if he were the holder;

(b) as any other fiduciary for a specified person or purpose is payable to the payee and may be negotiated, discharged or enforced by him;

(c) in any other manner is payable to the payee unconditionally and the additional words are without effect on subsequent parties.

§ 3—118. **Ambiguous Terms and Rules of Construction.**

The following rules apply to every instrument:

(a) Where there is doubt whether the instrument is a draft or a note the holder may treat it as either. A draft drawn on the drawer is effective as a note.

(b) Handwritten terms control typewritten and printed terms, and typewritten control printed.

(c) Words control figures except that if the words are ambiguous figures control.

(d) Unless otherwise specified a provision for interest means interest at the judgment rate at the place of payment from the date of the instrument, or if it is undated from the date of issue.

(e) Unless the instrument otherwise specifies two or more persons who sign as maker, acceptor or drawer or indorser and as a part of the same transaction are jointly and severally liable even though the instrument contains such words as "I promise to pay."

(f) Unless otherwise specified consent to extension authorizes a single extension for not longer than the original period. A consent to extension, expressed in the instrument, is binding on secondary parties and accommodation makers. A holder may not exercise his option to extend an instrument over the objection of a maker or acceptor or other party who in accordance with Section 3—604 tenders full payment when the instrument is due.

§ 3—119. **Other Writings Affecting Instrument.**

(1) As between the obligor and his immediate obligee or any transferee the terms of an instrument may be modified or affected by any other written agreement executed as a part of the same transaction, except that a holder in due course is not affected by any limitation of his rights arising out of the separate written agreement if he had no notice of the limitation when he took the instrument.

(2) A separate agreement does not affect the negotiability of an instrument.

§ 3—120. **Instruments "Payable Through" Bank.**

An instrument which states that it is "payable through" a bank or the like designates that bank as a collecting bank to make presentment but does not of itself authorize the bank to pay the instrument.

§ 3—121. **Instruments Payable at Bank.**

Note: If this Act is introduced in the Congress of the United States this section should be omitted.
(States to select either alternative)

Alternative A—

A note or acceptance which states that it is payable at a bank is the equivalent of a draft drawn on the bank payable when it falls due out of any funds of the maker or acceptor in current account or otherwise available for such payment.

Alternative B—

A note or acceptance which states that it is payable at a bank is not of itself an order or authorization to the bank to pay it.

§ 3—122. Accrual of Cause of Action.

(1) A cause of action against a maker or an acceptor accrues

(a) in the case of a time instrument on the day after maturity;

(b) in the case of a demand instrument upon its date or, if no date is stated, on the date of issue.

(2) A cause of action against the obligor of a demand or time certificate of deposit accrues upon demand, but demand on a time certificate may not be made until on or after the date of maturity.

(3) A cause of action against a drawer of a draft or an indorser of any instrument accrues upon demand following dishonor of the instrument. Notice of dishonor is a demand.

(4) Unless an instrument provides otherwise, interest runs at the rate provided by law for a judgment

(a) in the case of a maker, acceptor or other primary obligor of a demand instrument, from the date of demand;

(b) in all other cases from the date of accrual of the cause of action.

Part 2 Transfer and Negotiation

§ 3—201. Transfer: Right to Indorsement.

(1) Transfer of an instrument vests in the transferee such rights as the transferor has therein, except that a transferee who has himself been a party to any fraud or illegality affecting the instrument or who as a prior holder had notice of a defense or claim against it cannot improve his position by taking from a later holder in due course.

(2) A transfer of a security interest in an instrument vests the foregoing rights in the transferee to the extent of the interest transferred.

(3) Unless otherwise agreed any transfer for value of an instrument not then payable to bearer gives the transferee the specifically enforceable right to have the unqualified indorsement of the transferor. Negotiation takes effect only when the indorsement is made and until that time there is no presumption that the transferee is the owner.

§ 3—202. Negotiation.

(1) Negotiation is the transfer of an instrument in such form that the transferee becomes a holder. If the instrument is payable to order it is negotiated by delivery with any necessary indorsement; if payable to bearer it is negotiated by delivery.

(2) An indorsement must be written by or on behalf of the holder and on the instrument or on a paper so firmly affixed thereto as to become a part thereof.

(3) An indorsement is effective for negotiation only when it conveys the entire instrument or any unpaid residue. If it purports to be of less it operates only as a partial assignment.

(4) Words of assignment, condition, waiver, guaranty, limitation or disclaimer of liability and the like accompanying an indorsement do not affect its character as an indorsement.

§ 3—203. Wrong or Misspelled Name.

Where an instrument is made payable to a person under a misspelled name or one other than his own he may indorse in that name or his own or both; but signature in both names may be required by a person paying or giving value for the instrument.

§ 3—204. Special Indorsement; Blank Indorsement.

(1) A special indorsement specifies the person to whom or to whose order it makes the instrument payable. Any instrument specially indorsed becomes payable to the order of the special indorsee and may be further negotiated only by his indorsement.

(2) An indorsement in blank specifies no particular indorsee and may consist of a mere signature. An instrument payable to order and indorsed in blank becomes payable to bearer and may be negotiated by delivery alone until specially indorsed.

(3) The holder may convert a blank indorsement into a special indorsement by writing over the signature of the indorser in blank any contract consistent with the character of the indorsement.

§ 3—205. Restrictive Indorsements.

An indorsement is restrictive which either

(a) is conditional; or

(b) purports to prohibit further transfer of the instrument; or

(c) includes the words "for collection", "for deposit", "pay any bank", or like terms signifying a purpose of deposit or collection; or

(d) otherwise states that it is for the benefit or use of the indorser or of another person.

§ 3—206. **Effect of Restrictive Indorsement.**

(1) No restrictive indorsement prevents further transfer or negotiation of the instrument.

(2) An intermediary bank, or a payor bank which is not the depositary bank, is neither given notice nor otherwise affected by a restrictive indorsement of any person except the bank's immediate transferor or the person presenting for payment.

(3) Except for an intermediary bank, any transferee under an indorsement which is conditional or includes the words "for collection", "for deposit", "pay any bank", or like terms (subparagraphs (a) and (c) of Section 3—205) must pay or apply any value given by him for or on the security of the instrument consistently with the indorsement and to the extent that he does so he becomes a holder for value. In addition such transferee is a holder in due course if he otherwise complies with the requirements of Section 3—302 on what constitutes a holder in due course.

(4) The first taker under an indorsement for the benefit of the indorser or another person (subparagraph (d) of Section 3—205) must pay or apply any value given by him for or on the security of the instrument consistently with the indorsement and to the extent that he does so he becomes a holder for value. In addition such taker is a holder in due course if he otherwise complies with the requirements of Section 3—302 on what constitutes a holder in due course. A later holder for value is neither given notice nor otherwise affected by such restrictive indorsement unless he has knowledge that a fiduciary or other person has negotiated the instrument in any transaction for his own benefit or otherwise in breach of duty (subsection (2) of Section 3—304).

§ 3—207. **Negotiation Effective Although It May Be Rescinded.**

(1) Negotiation is effective to transfer the instrument although the negotiation is

    (a) made by an infant, a corporation exceeding its powers, or any other person without capacity; or

    (b) obtained by fraud, duress or mistake of any kind; or

    (c) part of an illegal transaction; or

    (d) made in breach of duty.

(2) Except as against a subsequent holder in due course such negotiation is in an appropriate case subject to rescission, the declaration of a constructive trust or any other remedy permitted by law.

§ 3—208. **Reacquisition.**

Where an instrument is returned to or reacquired by a prior party he may cancel any indorsement which is not necessary to his title and reissue or further negotiate the instrument, but any intervening party is discharged as against the reacquiring party and subsequent holders not in due course and if his indorsement has been cancelled is discharged as against subsequent holders in due course as well.

Part 3 Rights of a Holder

§ 3—301. **Rights of a Holder.**

The holder of an instrument whether or not he is the owner may transfer or negotiate it and, except as otherwise provided in Section 3—603 on payment or satisfaction, discharge it or enforce payment in his own name.

§ 3—302. **Holder in Due Course**

(1) A holder in due course is a holder who takes the instrument

    (a) for value; and

    (b) in good faith; and

    (c) without notice that it is overdue or has been dishonored or of any defense against or claim to it on the part of any person.

(2) A payee may be a holder in due course.

(3) A holder does not become a holder in due course of an instrument:

    (a) by purchase of it at judicial sale or by taking it under legal process; or

    (b) by acquiring it in taking over an estate; or

    (c) by purchasing it as part of a bulk transaction not in regular course of business of the transferor.

(4) A purchaser of a limited interest can be a holder in due course only to the extent of the interest purchased.

§ 3—303. **Taking for Value.**

A holder takes the instrument for value

(a) to the extent that the agreed consideration has been performed or that he acquires a security interest in or a lien on the instrument otherwise than by legal process; or

(b) when he takes the instrument in payment of or as security for an antecedent claim against any person whether or not the claim is due; or

(c) when he gives a negotiable instrument for it or makes an irrevocable commitment to a third person.

§ 3—304. **Notice to Purchaser.**

(1) The purchaser has notice of a claim or defense if

    (a) the instrument is so incomplete, bears such visible evidence of forgery or alteration, or is otherwise so irregular as to call into question its validity, terms or ownership or to create an ambiguity as to the party to pay; or

(b) the purchaser has notice that the obligation of any party is voidable in whole or in part, or that all parties have been discharged.

(2) The purchaser has notice of a claim against the instrument when he has knowledge that a fiduciary has negotiated the instrument in payment of or as security for his own debt or in any transaction for his own benefit or otherwise in breach of duty.

(3) The purchaser has notice that an instrument is overdue if he has reason to know

(a) that any part of the principal amount is overdue or that there is an uncured default in payment of another instrument of the same series; or

(b) that acceleration of the instrument has been made; or

(c) that he is taking a demand instrument after demand has been made or more than a reasonable length of time after its issue. A reasonable time for a check drawn and payable within the states and territories of the United States and the District of Columbia is presumed to be thirty days.

(4) Knowledge of the following facts does not of itself give the purchaser notice of a defense or claim

(a) that the instrument is antedated or postdated;

(b) that it was issued or negotiated in return for an executory promise or accompanied by a separate agreement, unless the purchaser has notice that a defense or claim has arisen from the terms thereof;

(c) that any party has signed for accommodation;

(d) that an incomplete instrument has been completed, unless the purchaser has notice of any improper completion;

(e) that any person negotiating the instrument is or was a fiduciary;

(f) that there has been default in payment of interest on the instrument or in payment of any other instrument, except one of the same series.

(5) The filing or recording of a document does not of itself constitute notice within the provisions of this Article to a person who would otherwise be a holder in due course.

(6) To be effective notice must be received at such time and in such manner as to give a reasonable opportunity to act on it.

§ 3—305. **Rights of a Holder in Due Course.**

To the extent that a holder is a holder in due course he takes the instrument free from

(1) all claims to it on the part of any person; and

(2) all defenses of any party to the instrument with whom the holder has not dealt except

(a) infancy, to the extent that it is a defense to a simple contract; and

(b) such other incapacity, or duress, or illegality of the transaction, as renders the obligation of the party a nullity; and

(c) such misrepresentation as has induced the party to sign the instrument with neither knowledge nor reasonable opportunity to obtain knowledge of its character or its essential terms; and

(d) discharge in insolvency proceedings; and

(e) any other discharge of which the holder has notice when he takes the instrument.

§ 3—306. **Rights of One Not Holder in Due Course.**

Unless he has the rights of a holder in due course any person takes the instrument subject to

(a) all valid claims to it on the part of any person; and

(b) all defenses of any party which would be available in an action on a simple contract; and

(c) the defenses of want or failure of consideration, nonperformance of any condition precedent, non-delivery, or delivery for a special purpose (Section 3—408); and

(d) the defense that he or a person through whom he holds the instrument acquired it by theft, or that payment or satisfaction to such holder would be inconsistent with the terms of a restrictive indorsement. The claim of any third person to the instrument is not otherwise available as a defense to any party liable thereon unless the third person himself defends the action for such party.

§ 3—307. **Burden of Establishing Signatures, Defenses and Due Course.**

(1) Unless specifically denied in the pleadings each signature on an instrument is admitted. When the effectiveness of a signature is put in issue

(a) the burden of establishing it is on the party claiming under the signature; but

(b) the signature is presumed to be genuine or authorized except where the action is to enforce the obligation of a purported signer who has died or become incompetent before proof is required.

(2) When signatures are admitted or established, production of the instrument entitles a holder to recover on it unless the defendant establishes a defense.

(3) After it is shown that a defense exists a person claiming the rights of a holder in due course has the burden of establishing that he or some person under whom he claims is in all respects a holder in due course.

Part 4 Liability of Parties

§ 3—401. **Signature.**

(1) No person is liable on an instrument unless his signature appears thereon.

(2) A signature is made by use of any name, including any trade or assumed name, upon an instrument, or by any word or mark used in lieu of a written signature.

§ 3—402. **Signature in Ambiguous Capacity.**

Unless the instrument clearly indicates that a signature is made in some other capacity it is an indorsement.

§ 3—403. **Signature by Authorized Representative.**

(1) A signature may be made by an agent or other representative, and his authority to make it may be established as in other cases of representation. No particular form of appointment is necessary to establish such authority.

(2) An authorized representative who signs his own name to an instrument

    (a) is personally obligated if the instrument neither names the person represented nor shows that the representative signed in a representative capacity;

    (b) except as otherwise established between the immediate parties, is personally obligated if the instrument names the person represented but does not show that the representative signed in a representative capacity, or if the instrument does not name the person represented but does show that the representative signed in a representative capacity.

(3) Except as otherwise established the name of an organization preceded or followed by the name and office of an authorized individual is a signature made in a representative capacity.

§ 3—404. **Unauthorized Signatures.**

(1) Any unauthorized signature is wholly inoperative as that of the person whose name is signed unless he ratifies it or is precluded from denying it; but it operates as the signature of the unauthorized signer in favor of any person who in good faith pays the instrument or takes it for value.

(2) Any unauthorized signature may be ratified for all purposes of this Article. Such ratification does not of itself affect any rights of the person ratifying against the actual signer.

§ 3—405. **Impostors; Signature in Name of Payee.**

(1) An indorsement by any person in the name of a named payee is effective if

    (a) an impostor by use of the mails or otherwise has induced the maker or drawer to issue the instrument to him or his confederate in the name of the payee; or

    (b) a person signing as or on behalf of a maker or drawer intends the payee to have no interest in the instrument; or

    (c) an agent or employee of the maker or drawer has supplied him with the name of the payee intending the latter to have no such interest.

(2) Nothing in this section shall affect the criminal or civil liability of the person so indorsing.

§ 3—406. **Negligence Contributing to Alteration or Unauthorized Signature.**

Any person who by his negligence substantially contributes to a material alteration of the instrument or to the making of an unauthorized signature is precluded from asserting the alteration or lack of authority against a holder in due course or against a drawee or other payor who pays the instrument in good faith and in accordance with the reasonable commercial standards of the drawee's or payor's business.

§ 3—407. **Alteration.**

(1) Any alteration of an instrument is material which changes the contract of any party thereto in any respect, including any such change in

    (a) the number or relations of the parties; or

    (b) an incomplete instrument, by completing it otherwise than as authorized; or

    (c) the writing as signed, by adding to it or by removing any part of it.

(2) As against any person other than a subsequent holder in due course

    (a) alteration by the holder which is both fraudulent and material discharges any party whose contract is thereby changed unless that party assents or is precluded from asserting the defense;

    (b) no other alteration discharges any party and the instrument may be enforced according to its original tenor, or as to incomplete instruments according to the authority given.

(3) A subsequent holder in due course may in all cases enforce the instrument according to its original tenor, and when an incomplete instrument has been completed, he may enforce it as completed.

§ 3—408. **Consideration.**

Want or failure of consideration is a defense as against any person not having the rights of a holder in due course (Section 3—305), except that no consideration is necessary for an instrument or obligation thereon given in payment of or as security for an antecedent obligation of any kind. Nothing in this section shall be taken to displace any statute outside this Act under which a promise is enforceable notwithstanding lack or failure of consideration. Partial failure of consideration is a defense pro tanto whether or not the failure is in an ascertained or liquidated amount.

§ 3—409. **Draft Not an Assignment.**

(1) A check or other draft does not of itself operate as an assignment of any funds in the hands of the drawee available for its payment, and the drawee is not liable on the instrument until he accepts it.

(2) Nothing in this section shall affect any liability in contract, tort or otherwise arising from any letter of credit or other obligation or representation which is not an acceptance.

§ 3—410. **Definition and Operation of Acceptance.**

(1) Acceptance is the drawee's signed engagement to honor the draft as presented. It must be written on the draft, and may consist of his signature alone. It becomes operative when completed by delivery or notification.

(2) A draft may be accepted although it has not been signed by the drawer or is otherwise incomplete or is overdue or has been dishonored.

(3) Where the draft is payable at a fixed period after sight and the acceptor fails to date his acceptance the holder may complete it by supplying a date in good faith.

§ 3—411. **Certification of a Check.**

(1) Certification of a check is acceptance. Where a holder procures certification the drawer and all prior indorsers are discharged.

(2) Unless otherwise agreed a bank has no obligation to certify a check.

(3) A bank may certify a check before returning it for lack of proper indorsement. If it does so the drawer is discharged.

§ 3—412. **Acceptance Varying Draft.**

(1) Where the drawee's proffered acceptance in any manner varies the draft as presented the holder may refuse the acceptance and treat the draft as dishonored in which case the drawee is entitled to have his acceptance cancelled.

(2) The terms of the draft are not varied by an acceptance to pay at any particular bank or place in the United States, unless the acceptance states that the draft is to be paid only at such bank or place.

(3) Where the holder assents to an acceptance varying the terms of the draft each drawer and indorser who does not affirmatively assent is discharged.

§ 3—413. **Contract of Maker, Drawer and Acceptor.**

(1) The maker or acceptor engages that he will pay the instrument according to its tenor at the time of his engagement or as completed pursuant to Section 3—115 on incomplete instruments.

(2) The drawer engages that upon dishonor of the draft and any necessary notice of dishonor or protest he will pay the amount of the draft to the holder or to any indorser who takes it up. The drawer may disclaim this liability by drawing without recourse.

(3) By making, drawing or accepting the party admits as against all subsequent parties including the drawee the existence of the payee and his then capacity to indorse.

§ 3—414. **Contract of Indorser; Order of Liability.**

(1) Unless the indorsement otherwise specifies (as by such words as "without recourse") every indorser engages that upon dishonor and any necessary notice of dishonor and protest he will pay the instrument according to its tenor at the time of his indorsement to the holder or to any subsequent indorser who takes it up, even though the indorser who takes it up was not obligated to do so.

(2) Unless they otherwise agree indorsers are liable to one another in the order in which they indorse, which is presumed to be the order in which their signatures appear on the instrument.

§ 3—415. **Contract of Accommodation Party.**

(1) An accommodation party is one who signs the instrument in any capacity for the purpose of lending his name to another party to it.

(2) When the instrument has been taken for value before it is due the accommodation party is liable in the capacity in which he has signed even though the taker knows of the accommodation.

(3) As against a holder in due course and without notice of the accommodation oral proof of the accommodation is not admissible to give the accommodation party the benefit of discharges dependent on his character as such. In other cases the accommodation character may be shown by oral proof.

(4) An indorsement which shows that it is not in the chain of title is notice of its accommodation character.

(5) An accommodation party is not liable to the party accommodated, and if he pays the instrument has a right of recourse on the instrument against such party.

§ 3—416. Contract of Guarantor.

(1) "Payment guaranteed" or equivalent words added to a signature mean that the signer engages that if the instrument is not paid when due he will pay it according to its tenor without resort by the holder to any other party.

(2) "Collection guaranteed" or equivalent words added to a signature mean that the signer engages that if the instrument is not paid when due he will pay it according to its tenor, but only after the holder has reduced his claim against the maker or acceptor to judgment and execution has been returned unsatisfied, or after the maker or acceptor has become insolvent or it is otherwise apparent that it is useless to proceed against him.

(3) Words of guaranty which do not otherwise specify guarantee payment.

(4) No words of guaranty added to the signature of a sole maker or acceptor affect his liability on the instrument. Such words added to the signature of one of two or more makers or acceptors create a presumption that the signature is for the accommodation of the others.

(5) When words of guaranty are used presentment, notice of dishonor and protest are not necessary to charge the user.

(6) Any guaranty written on the instrument is enforcible notwithstanding any statute of frauds.

§ 3—417. Warranties on Presentment and Transfer.

(1) Any person who obtains payment or acceptance and any prior transferor warrants to a person who in good faith pays or accepts that

    (a) he has a good title to the instrument or is authorized to obtain payment or acceptance on behalf of one who has a good title; and

    (b) he has no knowledge that the signature of the maker or drawer is unauthorized, except that this warranty is not given by a holder in due course acting in good faith

        (i) to a maker with respect to the maker's own signature; or

        (ii) to a drawer with respect to the drawer's own signature, whether or not the drawer is also the drawee; or

        (iii) to an acceptor of a draft if the holder in due course took the draft after the acceptance or obtained the acceptance without knowledge that the drawer's signature was unauthorized; and

    (c) the instrument has not been materially altered, except that this warranty is not given by a holder in due course acting in good faith

        (i) to the maker of a note; or

        (ii) to the drawer of a draft whether or not the drawer is also the drawee; or

        (iii) to the acceptor of a draft with respect to an alteration made prior to the acceptance if the holder in due course took the draft after the acceptance, even though the acceptance provided "payable as originally drawn" or equivalent terms; or

        (iv) to the acceptor of a draft with respect to an alteration made after the acceptance.

(2) Any person who transfers an instrument and receives consideration warrants to his transferee and if the transfer is by indorsement to any subsequent holder who takes the instrument in good faith that

    (a) he has a good title to the instrument or is authorized to obtain payment or acceptance on behalf of one who has a good title and the transfer is otherwise rightful; and

    (b) all signatures are genuine or authorized; and

    (c) the instrument has not been materially altered; and

    (d) no defense of any party is good against him; and

    (e) he has no knowledge of any insolvency proceeding instituted with respect to the maker or acceptor or the drawer of an unaccepted instrument.

(3) By transferring "without recourse" the transferor limits the obligation stated in subsection (2) (d) to a warranty that he has no knowledge of such a defense.

(4) A selling agent or broker who does not disclose the fact that he is acting only as such gives the warranties provided in this section, but if he makes such disclosure warrants only his good faith and authority.

§ 3—418. Finality of Payment or Acceptance.

Except for recovery of bank payments as provided in the Article on Bank Deposits and Collections (Article 4) and except for liability for breach of warranty on presentment under the preceding section, payment or acceptance of any instrument is final in favor of a holder in due course, or a person who has in good faith changed his position in reliance on the payment.

§ 3—419. Conversion of Instrument; Innocent Representative.

(1) An instrument is converted when

    (a) a drawee to whom it is delivered for acceptance refuses to return it on demand; or

(b) any person to whom it is delivered for payment refuses on demand either to pay or to return it; or

(c) it is paid on a forged indorsement.

(2) In an action against a drawee under subsection (1) the measure of the drawee's liability is the face amount of the instrument. In any other action under subsection (1) the measure of liability is presumed to be the face amount of the instrument.

(3) Subject to the provisions of this Act concerning restrictive indorsements a representative, including a depositary or collecting bank, who has in good faith and in accordance with the reasonable commercial standards applicable to the business of such representative dealt with an instrument or its proceeds on behalf of one who was not the true owner is not liable in conversion or otherwise to the true owner beyond the amount of any proceeds remaining in his hands.

(4) An intermediary bank or payor bank which is not a depositary bank is not liable in conversion solely by reason of the fact that proceeds of an item indorsed restrictively (Sections 3—205 and 3—206) are not paid or applied consistently with the restrictive indorsement of an indorser other than its immediate transferor.

Part 5 Presentment, Notice of Dishonor and Protest

§ 3—501. When Presentment, Notice of Dishonor, and Protest Necessary or Permissible.

(1) Unless excused (Section 3—511) presentment is necessary to charge secondary parties as follows:

(a) presentment for acceptance is necessary to charge the drawer and indorsers of a draft where the draft so provides, or is payable elsewhere than at the residence or place of business of the drawee, or its date of payment depends upon such presentment. The holder may at his option present for acceptance any other draft payable at a stated date;

(b) presentment for payment is necessary to charge any indorser;

(c) in the case of any drawer, the acceptor of a draft payable at a bank or the maker of a note payable at a bank, presentment for payment is necessary, but failure to make presentment discharges such drawer, acceptor or maker only as stated in Section 3—502(1)(b).

(2) Unless excused (Section 3—511)

(a) notice of any dishonor is necessary to charge any indorser;

(b) in the case of any drawer, the acceptor of a draft payable at a bank or the maker of a note payable at a bank, notice of any dishonor is necessary, but

failure to give such notice discharges such drawer, acceptor or maker only as stated in Section 3—502(1)(b).

(3) Unless excused (Section 3—511) protest of any dishonor is necessary to charge the drawer and indorsers of any draft which on its face appears to be drawn or payable outside of the states, territories, dependencies, and possessions of the United States, the District of Columbia and the Commonwealth of Puerto Rico. The holder may at his option make protest of any dishonor of any other instrument and in the case of a foreign draft may on insolvency of the acceptor before maturity make protest for better security.

(4) Notwithstanding any provision of this section, neither presentment nor notice of dishonor nor protest is necessary to charge an indorser who has indorsed an instrument after maturity.

§ 3—502. Unexcused Delay; Discharge.

(1) Where without excuse any necessary presentment or notice of dishonor is delayed beyond the time when it is due

(a) any indorser is discharged; and

(b) any drawer or the acceptor of a draft payable at a bank or the maker of a note payable at a bank who because the drawee or payor bank becomes insolvent during the delay is deprived of funds maintained with the drawee or payor bank to cover the instrument may discharge his liability by written assignment to the holder of his rights against the drawee or payor bank in respect of such funds, but such drawer, acceptor or maker is not otherwise discharged.

(2) Where without excuse a necessary protest is delayed beyond the time when it is due any drawer or indorser is discharged.

§ 3—503. Time of Presentment.

(1) Unless a different time is expressed in the instrument the time for any presentment is determined as follows:

(a) where an instrument is payable at or a fixed period after a stated date any presentment for acceptance must be made on or before the date it is payable;

(b) where an instrument is payable after sight it must either be presented for acceptance or negotiated within a reasonable time after date or issue whichever is later;

(c) where an instrument shows the date on which it is payable presentment for payment is due on that date;

(d) where an instrument is accelerated presentment for payment is due within a reasonable time after the acceleration;

(e) with respect to the liability of any secondary party presentment for acceptance or payment of any other instrument is due within a reasonable time after such party becomes liable thereon.

(2) A reasonable time for presentment is determined by the nature of the instrument, any usage of banking or trade and the facts of the particular case. In the case of an uncertified check which is drawn and payable within the United States and which is not a draft drawn by a bank the following are presumed to be reasonable periods within which to present for payment or to initiate bank collection:

(a) with respect to the liability of the drawer, thirty days after date or issue whichever is later; and

(b) with respect to the liability of an indorser, seven days after his indorsement.

(3) Where any presentment is due on a day which is not a full business day for either the person making presentment or the party to pay or accept, presentment is due on the next following day which is a full business day for both parties.

(4) Presentment to be sufficient must be made at a reasonable hour, and if at a bank during its banking day.

§ 3—504. How Presentment Made.

(1) Presentment is a demand for acceptance or payment made upon the maker, acceptor, drawee or other payor by or on behalf of the holder.

(2) Presentment may be made

(a) by mail, in which event the time of presentment is determined by the time of receipt of the mail; or

(b) through a clearing house; or

(c) at the place of acceptance or payment specified in the instrument or if there be none at the place of business or residence of the party to accept or pay. If neither the party to accept or pay nor anyone authorized to act for him is present or accessible at such place presentment is excused.

(3) It may be made

(a) to any one of two or more makers, acceptors, drawees or other payors; or

(b) to any person who has authority to make or refuse the acceptance or payment.

(4) A draft accepted or a note made payable at a bank in the United States must be presented at such bank.

(5) In the cases described in Section 4—210 presentment may be made in the manner and with the result stated in that section.

§ 3—505. Rights of Party to Whom Presentment Is Made.

(1) The party to whom presentment is made may without dishonor require

(a) exhibition of the instrument; and

(b) reasonable identification of the person making presentment and evidence of his authority to make it if made for another; and

(c) that the instrument be produced for acceptance or payment at a place specified in it, or if there be none at any place reasonable in the circumstances; and

(d) a signed receipt on the instrument for any partial or full payment and its surrender upon full payment.

(2) Failure to comply with any such requirement invalidates the presentment but the person presenting has a reasonable time in which to comply and the time for acceptance or payment runs from the time of compliance.

§ 3—506. Time Allowed for Acceptance or Payment.

(1) Acceptance may be deferred without dishonor until the close of the next business day following presentment. The holder may also in a good faith effort to obtain acceptance and without either dishonor of the instrument or discharge of secondary parties allow postponement of acceptance for an additional business day.

(2) Except as a longer time is allowed in the case of documentary drafts drawn under a letter of credit, and unless an earlier time is agreed to by the party to pay, payment of an instrument may be deferred without dishonor pending reasonable examination to determine whether it is properly payable, but payment must be made in any event before the close of business on the day of presentment.

§ 3—507. Dishonor; Holder's Right of Recourse; Term Allowing Re-Presentment.

(1) An instrument is dishonored when

(a) a necessary or optional presentment is duly made and due acceptance or payment is refused or cannot be obtained within the prescribed time or in case of bank collections the instrument is seasonably returned by the midnight deadline (Section 4—301); or

(b) presentment is excused and the instrument is not duly accepted or paid.

(2) Subject to any necessary notice of dishonor and protest, the holder has upon dishonor an immediate right of recourse against the drawers and indorsers.

(3) Return of an instrument for lack of proper indorsement is not dishonor.

(4) A term in a draft or an indorsement thereof allowing a stated time for re-presentment in the event of any dishonor of the draft by nonacceptance if a time draft or by nonpayment if a sight draft gives the holder as against any secondary party bound by the term an option to waive the dishonor without affecting the liability of the secondary party and he may present again up to the end of the stated time.

§ 3—508. **Notice of Dishonor.**

(1) Notice of dishonor may be given to any person who may be liable on the instrument by or on behalf of the holder or any party who has himself received notice, or any other party who can be compelled to pay the instrument. In addition an agent or bank in whose hands the instrument is dishonored may give notice to his principal or customer or to another agent or bank from which the instrument was received.

(2) Any necessary notice must be given by a bank before its midnight deadline and by any other person before midnight of the third business day after dishonor or receipt of notice of dishonor.

(3) Notice may be given in any reasonable manner. It may be oral or written and in any terms which identify the instrument and state that it has been dishonored. A misdescription which does not mislead the party notified does not vitiate the notice. Sending the instrument bearing a stamp, ticket or writing stating that acceptance or payment has been refused or sending a notice of debit with respect to the instrument is sufficient.

(4) Written notice is given when sent although it is not received.

(5) Notice to one partner is notice to each although the firm has been dissolved.

(6) When any party is in insolvency proceedings instituted after the issue of the instrument notice may be given either to the party or to the representative of his estate.

(7) When any party is dead or incompetent notice may be sent to his last known address or given to his personal representative.

(8) Notice operates for the benefit of all parties who have rights on the instrument against the party notified.

§ 3—509. **Protest; Noting for Protest.**

(1) A protest is a certificate of dishonor made under the hand and seal of a United States consul or vice consul or a notary public or other person authorized to certify dishonor by the law of the place where dishonor occurs. It may be made upon information satisfactory to such person.

(2) The protest must identify the instrument and certify either that due presentment has been made or the reason why it is excused and that the instrument has been dishonored by nonacceptance or nonpayment.

(3) The protest may also certify that notice of dishonor has been given to all parties or to specified parties.

(4) Subject to subsection (5) any necessary protest is due by the time that notice of dishonor is due.

(5) If, before protest is due, an instrument has been noted for protest by the officer to make protest, the protest may be made at any time thereafter as of the date of the noting.

§ 3—510. **Evidence of Dishonor and Notice of Dishonor.**

The following are admissible as evidence and create a presumption of dishonor and of any notice of dishonor therein shown:

(a) a document regular in form as provided in the preceding section which purports to be a protest;

(b) the purported stamp or writing of the drawee, payor bank or presenting bank on the instrument or accompanying it stating that acceptance or payment has been refused for reasons consistent with dishonor;

(c) any book or record of the drawee, payor bank, or any collecting bank kept in the usual course of business which shows dishonor, even though there is no evidence of who made the entry.

§ 3—511. **Waived or Excused Presentment, Protest or Notice of Dishonor or Delay Therein.**

(1) Delay in presentment, protest or notice of dishonor is excused when the party is without notice that it is due or when the delay is caused by circumstances beyond his control and he exercises reasonable diligence after the cause of the delay ceases to operate.

(2) Presentment or notice or protest as the case may be is entirely excused when

   (a) the party to be charged has waived it expressly or by implication either before or after it is due; or

   (b) such party has himself dishonored the instrument or has countermanded payment or otherwise has no reason to expect or right to require that the instrument be accepted or paid; or

   (c) by reasonable diligence the presentment or protest cannot be made or the notice given.

(3) Presentment is also entirely excused when

   (a) the maker, acceptor or drawee of any instrument except a documentary draft is dead or in insolvency proceedings instituted after the issue of the instrument; or

(b) acceptance or payment is refused but not for want of proper presentment.

(4) Where a draft has been dishonored by nonacceptance a later presentment for payment and any notice of dishonor and protest for nonpayment are excused unless in the meantime the instrument has been accepted.

(5) A waiver of protest is also a waiver of presentment and of notice of dishonor even though protest is not required.

(6) Where a waiver of presentment or notice or protest is embodied in the instrument itself it is binding upon all parties; but where it is written above the signature of an indorser it binds him only.

Part 6 Discharge

§ 3—601. **Discharge of Parties.**

(1) The extent of the discharge of any party from liability on an instrument is governed by the sections on

(a) payment or satisfaction (Section 3—603); or

(b) tender of payment (Section 3—604); or

(c) cancellation or renunciation (Section 3—605); or

(d) impairment of right of recourse or of collateral (Section 3—606); or

(e) reacquisition of the instrument by a prior party (Section 3—208); or

(f) fraudulent and material alteration (Section 3—407); or

(g) certification of a check (Section 3—411); or

(h) acceptance varying a draft (Section 3—412); or

(i) unexcused delay in presentment or notice of dishonor or protest (Section 3—502).

(2) Any party is also discharged from his liability on an instrument to another party by any other act or agreement with such party which would discharge his simple contract for the payment of money.

(3) The liability of all parties is discharged when any party who has himself no right of action or recourse on the instrument

(a) reacquires the instrument in his own right; or

(b) is discharged under any provision of this Article, except as otherwise provided with respect to discharge for impairment of recourse or of collateral (Section 3—606).

§ 3—602. **Effect of Discharge Against Holder in Due Course.**

No discharge of any party provided by this Article is effective against a subsequent holder in due course unless he has notice thereof when he takes the instrument.

§ 3—603. **Payment or Satisfaction.**

(1) The liability of any party is discharged to the extent of his payment or satisfaction to the holder even though it is made with knowledge of a claim of another person to the instrument unless prior to such payment or satisfaction the person making the claim either supplies indemnity deemed adequate by the party seeking the discharge or enjoins payment or satisfaction by order of a court of competent jurisdiction in an action in which the adverse claimant and the holder are parties. This subsection does not, however, result in the discharge of the liability

(a) of a party who in bad faith pays or satisfies a holder who acquired the instrument by theft or who (unless having the rights of a holder in due course) holds through one who so acquired it; or

(b) of a party (other than an intermediary bank or a payor bank which is not a depositary bank) who pays or satisfies the holder of an instrument which has been restrictively indorsed in a manner not consistent with the terms of such restrictive indorsement.

(2) Payment or satisfaction may be made with the consent of the holder by any person including a stranger to the instrument. Surrender of the instrument to such a person gives him the rights of a transferee (Section 3—201).

§ 3—604. **Tender of Payment.**

(1) Any party making tender of full payment to a holder when or after it is due is discharged to the extent of all subsequent liability for interest, costs and attorney's fees.

(2) The holder's refusal of such tender wholly discharges any party who has a right of recourse against the party making the tender.

(3) Where the maker or acceptor of an instrument payable otherwise than on demand is able and ready to pay at every place of payment specified in the instrument when it is due, it is equivalent to tender.

§ 3—605. **Cancellation and Renunciation.**

(1) The holder of an instrument may even without consideration discharge any party

(a) in any manner apparent on the face of the instrument or the indorsement, as by intentionally cancelling the instrument or the party's signature by destruction or mutilation, or by striking out the party's signature; or

(b) by renouncing his rights by a writing signed and delivered or by surrender of the instrument to the party to be discharged.

(2) Neither cancellation nor renunciation without surrender of the instrument affects the title thereto.

§ 3—606. Impairment of Recourse or of Collateral.

(1) The holder discharges any party to the instrument to the extent that without such party's consent the holder

(a) without express reservation of rights releases or agrees not to sue any person against whom the party has to the knowledge of the holder a right of recourse or agrees to suspend the right to enforce against such person the instrument or collateral or otherwise discharges such person, except that failure or delay in effecting any required presentment, protest or notice of dishonor with respect to any such person does not discharge any party as to whom presentment, protest or notice of dishonor is effective or unnecessary; or

(b) unjustifiably impairs any collateral for the instrument given by or on behalf of the party or any person against whom he has a right of recourse.

(2) By express reservation of rights against a party with a right of recourse the holder preserves

(a) all his rights against such party as of the time when the instrument was originally due; and

(b) the right of the party to pay the instrument as of that time; and

(c) all rights of such party to recourse against others.

Part 7 Advice of International Sight Draft

§ 3—701. Letter of Advice of International Sight Draft.

(1) A "letter of advice" is a drawer's communication to the drawee that a described draft has been drawn.

(2) Unless otherwise agreed when a bank receives from another bank a letter of advice of an international sight draft the drawee bank may immediately debit the drawer's account and stop the running of interest pro tanto. Such a debit and any resulting credit to any account covering outstanding drafts leaves in the drawer full power to stop payment or otherwise dispose of the amount and creates no trust or interest in favor of the holder.

(3) Unless otherwise agreed and except where a draft is drawn under a credit issued by the drawee, the drawee of an international sight draft owes the drawer no duty to pay an unadvised draft but if it does so and the draft is genuine, may appropriately debit the drawer's account.

Part 8 Miscellaneous

§ 3—801. Drafts in a Set.

(1) Where a draft is drawn in a set of parts, each of which is numbered and expressed to be an order only if no other part has been honored, the whole of the parts constitutes one draft but a taker of any part may become a holder in due course of the draft.

(2) Any person who negotiates, indorses or accepts a single part of a draft drawn in a set thereby becomes liable to any holder in due course of that part as if it were the whole set, but as between different holders in due course to whom different parts have been negotiated the holder whose title first accrues has all rights to the draft and its proceeds.

(3) As against the drawee the first presented part of a draft drawn in a set is the part entitled to payment, or if a time draft to acceptance and payment. Acceptance of any subsequently presented part renders the drawee liable thereon under subsection (2). With respect both to a holder and to the drawer payment of a subsequently presented part of a draft payable at sight has the same effect as payment of a check notwithstanding an effective stop order (Section 4—407).

(4) Except as otherwise provided in this section, where any part of a draft in a set is discharged by payment or otherwise the whole draft is discharged.

§ 3—802. Effect of Instrument on Obligation for Which It Is Given.

(1) Unless otherwise agreed where an instrument is taken for an underlying obligation

(a) the obligation is pro tanto discharged if a bank is drawer, maker or acceptor of the instrument and there is no recourse on the instrument against the underlying obligor; and

(b) in any other case the obligation is suspended pro tanto until the instrument is due or if it is payable on demand until its presentment. If the instrument is dishonored action may be maintained on either the instrument or the obligation; discharge of the underlying obligor on the instrument also discharges him on the obligation.

(2) The taking in good faith of a check which is not postdated does not of itself so extend the time on the original obligation as to discharge a surety.

§ 3—803. Notice to Third Party.

Where a defendant is sued for breach of an obligation for which a third person is answerable over under this Article he may give the third person written notice of the litigation, and the person notified may then give similar notice to any other person who is answerable over to him under this Article. If the notice states that the person notified may come in and defend and that if the person notified does not do so he will in any action against him by the person giving the notice be bound by any determination of fact common to the two litigations, then unless after seasonable receipt of the notice the person notified does come in and defend he is so bound.

§ 3—804. Lost, Destroyed or Stolen Instruments.

The owner of an instrument which is lost, whether by destruction, theft or otherwise, may maintain an action in his own name and recover from any party liable thereon upon due proof of his ownership, the facts which prevent his production of the instrument and its terms. The court may require security indemnifying the defendant against loss by reason of further claims on the instrument.

§ 3—805. Instruments Not Payable to Order or to Bearer.

This Article applies to any instrument whose terms do not preclude transfer and which is otherwise negotiable within this Article but which is not payable to order or to bearer, except that there can be no holder in due course of such an instrument.

Article 4
BANK DEPOSITS AND COLLECTIONS

Part 1 General Provisions and Definitions

§ 4—101. Short Title.

This Article shall be known and may be cited as Uniform Commercial Code—Bank Deposits and Collections.

§ 4—102. Applicability.

(1) To the extent that items within this Article are also within the scope of Articles 3 and 8, they are subject to the provisions of those Articles. In the event of conflict the provisions of this Article govern those of Article 3 but the provisions of Article 8 govern those of this Article.

(2) The liability of a bank for action or non-action with respect to any item handled by it for purposes of presentment, payment or collection is governed by the law of the place where the bank is located. In the case of action or non-action by or at a branch or separate office of a bank, its liability is governed by the law of the place where the branch or separate office is located.

§ 4—103. Variation by Agreement; Measure of Damages; Certain Action Constituting Ordinary Care.

(1) The effect of the provisions of this Article may be varied by agreement except that no agreement can disclaim a bank's responsibility for its own lack of good faith or failure to exercise ordinary care or can limit the measure of damages for such lack or failure; but the parties may by agreement determine the standards by which such responsibility is to be measured if such standards are not manifestly unreasonable.

(2) Federal Reserve regulations and operating letters, clearing house rules, and the like, have the effect of agreements under subsection (1), whether or not specifically assented to by all parties interested in items handled.

(3) Action or nonaction approved by this Article or pursuant to Federal Reserve regulations or operating letters constitutes the exercise of ordinary care and, in the absence of special instructions, action or nonaction consistent with clearing house rules and the like or with a general banking usage not disapproved by this Article, prima facie constitutes the exercise of ordinary care.

(4) The specification or approval of certain procedures by this Article does not constitute disapproval of other procedures which may be reasonable under the circumstances.

(5) The measure of damages for failure to exercise ordinary care in handling an item is the amount of the item reduced by an amount which could not have been realized by the use of ordinary care, and where there is bad faith it includes other damages, if any, suffered by the party as a proximate consequence.

§ 4—104. Definitions and Index of Definitions.

(1) In this Article unless the context otherwise requires

(a) "Account" means any account with a bank and includes a checking, time, interest or savings account;

(b) "Afternoon" means the period of a day between noon and midnight;

(c) "Banking day" means that part of any day on which a bank is open to the public for carrying on substantially all of its banking functions;

(d) "Clearing house" means any association of banks or other payors regularly clearing items;

(e) "Customer" means any person having an account with a bank or for whom a bank has agreed to collect items and includes a bank carrying an account with another bank;

(f) "Documentary draft" means any negotiable or nonnegotiable draft with accompanying documents, securities or other papers to be delivered against honor of the draft;

(g) "Item" means any instrument for the payment of money even though it is not negotiable but does not include money;

(h) "Midnight deadline" with respect to a bank is midnight on its next banking day following the banking day on which it receives the relevant item or notice or from which the time for taking action commences to run, whichever is later;

(i) "Properly payable" includes the availability of funds for payment at the time of decision to pay or dishonor;

(j) "Settle" means to pay in cash, by clearing house settlement, in a charge or credit or by remittance, or otherwise as instructed. A settlement may be either provisional or final;

(k) "Suspends payments" with respect to a bank means that it has been closed by order of the supervisory authorities, that a public officer has been appointed to take it over or that it ceases or refuses to make payments in the ordinary course of business.

(2) Other definitions applying to this Article and the sections in which they appear are:
"Collecting bank" Section 4—105.
"Depositary bank" Section 4—105.
"Intermediary bank" Section 4—105.
"Payor bank" Section 4—105.
"Presenting bank" Section 4—105.
"Remitting bank" Section 4—105.

(3) The following definitions in other Articles apply to this Article:
"Acceptance" Section 3—410.
"Certificate of deposit" Section 3—104.
"Certification" Section 3—411.
"Check" Section 3—104.
"Draft" Section 3—104.
"Holder in due course" Section 3—302.
"Notice of dishonor" Section 3—508.
"Presentment" Section 3—504.
"Protest" Section 3—509.
"Secondary party" Section 3—102.

(4) In addition Article 1 contains general definitions and principles of construction and interpretation applicable throughout this Article.

§ 4—105. **"Depositary Bank"; "Intermediary Bank"; "Collecting Bank"; "Payor Bank"; "Presenting Bank"; "Remitting Bank".**

In this Article unless the context otherwise requires:

(a) "Depositary bank" means the first bank to which an item is transferred for collection even though it is also the payor bank;

(b) "Payor bank" means a bank by which an item is payable as drawn or accepted;

(c) "Intermediary bank" means any bank to which an item is transferred in course of collection except the depositary or payor bank;

(d) "Collecting bank" means any bank handling the item for collection except the payor bank;

(e) "Presenting bank" means any bank presenting an item except a payor bank;

(f) "Remitting bank" means any payor or intermediary bank remitting for an item.

§ 4—106. **Separate Office of a Bank.**

A branch or separate office of a bank [maintaining its own deposit ledgers] is a separate bank for the purpose of computing the time within which and determining the place at or to which action may be taken or notices or orders shall be given under this Article and under Article 3.

Note: *The brackets are to make it optional with the several states whether to require a branch to maintain its own deposit ledgers in order to be considered to be a separate bank for certain purposes under Article 4. In some states "maintaining its own deposit ledgers" is a satisfactory test. In others branch banking practices are such that this test would not be suitable.*

§ 4—107. **Time of Receipt of Items.**

(1) For the purpose of allowing time to process items, prove balances and make the necessary entries on its books to determine its position for the day, a bank may fix an afternoon hour of 2 P.M. or later as a cut-off hour for the handling of money and items and the making of entries on its books.

(2) Any item or deposit of money received on any day after a cut-off hour so fixed or after the close of the banking day may be treated as being received at the opening of the next banking day.

§ 4—108. **Delays.**

(1) Unless otherwise instructed, a collecting bank in a good faith effort to secure payment may, in the case of specific items and with or without the approval of any person involved, waive, modify or extend time limits imposed or permitted by this Act for a period not in excess of an additional banking day without discharge of secondary parties and without liability to its transferor or any prior party.

(2) Delay by a collecting bank or payor bank beyond time limits prescribed or permitted by this Act or by instructions is excused if caused by interruption of communication facilities, suspension of payments by another bank, war, emergency conditions or other circumstances beyond the control of the bank provided it exercises such diligence as the circumstances require.

§ 4—109. **Process of Posting.**

The "process of posting" means the usual procedure followed by a payor bank in determining to pay an item and in recording the payment including one or more of the following or other steps as determined by the bank:

(a) verification of any signature;

(b) ascertaining that sufficient funds are available;

(c) affixing a "paid" or other stamp;

(d) entering a charge or entry to a customer's account;

(e) correcting or reversing an entry or erroneous action with respect to the item.

Part 2 Collection of Items: Depositary and Collecting Banks

§ 4—201. **Presumption and Duration of Agency Status of Collecting Banks and Provisional Status of Credits; Applicability of Article; Item Indorsed "Pay Any Bank".**

(1) Unless a contrary intent clearly appears and prior to the time that a settlement given by a collecting bank for an item is or becomes final (subsection (3) of Section 4—211 and Sections 4—212 and 4—213) the bank is an agent or sub-agent of the owner of the item and any settlement given for the item is provisional. This provision applies regardless of the form of indorsement or lack of indorsement and even though credit given for the item is subject to immediate withdrawal as of right or is in fact withdrawn; but the continuance of ownership of an item by its owner and any rights of the owner to proceeds of the item are subject to rights of a collecting bank such as those resulting from outstanding advances on the item and valid rights of setoff. When an item is handled by banks for purposes of presentment, payment and collection, the relevant provisions of this Article apply even though action of parties clearly establishes that a particular bank has purchased the item and is the owner of it.

(2) After an item has been indorsed with the words "pay any bank" or the like, only a bank may acquire the rights of a holder

(a) until the item has been returned to the customer initiating collection; or

(b) until the item has been specially indorsed by a bank to a person who is not a bank.

§ 4—202. **Responsibility for Collection; When Action Seasonable.**

(1) A collecting bank must use ordinary care in

(a) presenting an item or sending it for presentment; and

(b) sending notice of dishonor or non-payment or returning an item other than a documentary draft to the bank's transferor [or directly to the depositary bank under subsection (2) of Section 4—212] *(see note to Section 4—212)* after learning that the item has not been paid or accepted as the case may be; and

(c) settling for an item when the bank receives final settlement; and

(d) making or providing for any necessary protest; and

(e) notifying its transferor of any loss or delay in transit within a reasonable time after discovery thereof.

(2) A collecting bank taking proper action before its midnight deadline following receipt of an item, notice or payment acts seasonably; taking proper action within a reasonably longer time may be seasonable but the bank has the burden of so establishing.

(3) Subject to subsection (1)(a), a bank is not liable for the insolvency, neglect, misconduct, mistake or default of another bank or person or for loss or destruction of an item in transit or in the possession of others.

§ 4—203. **Effect of Instructions.**

Subject to the provisions of Article 3 concerning conversion of instruments (Section 3—419) and the provisions of both Article 3 and this Article concerning restrictive indorsements only a collecting bank's transferor can give instructions which affect the bank or constitute notice to it and a collecting bank is not liable to prior parties for any action taken pursuant to such instructions or in accordance with any agreement with its transferor.

§ 4—204. **Methods of Sending and Presenting; Sending Direct to Payor Bank.**

(1) A collecting bank must send items by reasonably prompt method taking into consideration any relevant instructions, the nature of the item, the number of such items on hand, and the cost of collection involved and the method generally used by it or others to present such items.

(2) A collecting bank may send

(a) any item direct to the payor bank;

(b) any item to any non-bank payor if authorized by its transferor; and

(c) any item other than documentary drafts to any non-bank payor, if authorized by Federal Reserve regulation or operating letter, clearing house rule or the like.

(3) Presentment may be made by a presenting bank at a place where the payor bank has requested that presentment be made.

§ 4—205. Supplying Missing Indorsement; No Notice from Prior Indorsement.

(1) A depositary bank which has taken an item for collection may supply any indorsement of the customer which is necessary to title unless the item contains the words "payee's indorsement required" or the like. In the absence of such a requirement a statement placed on the item by the depositary bank to the effect that the item was deposited by a customer or credited to his account is effective as the customer's indorsement.

(2) An intermediary bank, or payor bank which is not a depositary bank, is neither given notice nor otherwise affected by a restrictive indorsement of any person except the bank's immediate transferor.

§ 4—206. Transfer Between Banks.

Any agreed method which identifies the transferor bank is sufficient for the item's further transfer to another bank.

§ 4—207. Warranties of Customer and Collecting Bank on Transfer or Presentment of Items; Time for Claims.

(1) Each customer or collecting bank who obtains payment or acceptance of an item and each prior customer and collecting bank warrants to the payor bank or other payor who in good faith pays or accepts the item that

(a) he has a good title to the item or is authorized to obtain payment or acceptance on behalf of one who has a good title; and

(b) he has no knowledge that the signature of the maker or drawer is unauthorized, except that this warranty is not given by any customer or collecting bank that is a holder in due course and acts in good faith

(i) to a maker with respect to the maker's own signature; or

(ii) to a drawer with respect to the drawer's own signature, whether or not the drawer is also the drawee; or

(iii) to an acceptor of an item if the holder in due course took the item after the acceptance or obtained the acceptance without knowledge that the drawer's signature was unauthorized; and

(c) the item has not been materially altered, except that this warranty is not given by any customer or collecting bank that is a holder in due course and acts in good faith

(i) to the maker of a note; or

(ii) to the drawer of a draft whether or not the drawer is also the drawee; or

(iii) to the acceptor of an item with respect to an alteration made prior to the acceptance if the holder in due course took the item after the acceptance, even though the acceptance provided "payable as originally drawn" or equivalent terms; or

(iv) to the acceptor of an item with respect to an alteration made after the acceptance.

(2) Each customer and collecting bank who transfers an item and receives a settlement or other consideration for it warrants to his transferee and to any subsequent collecting bank who takes the item in good faith that

(a) he has a good title to the item or is authorized to obtain payment or acceptance on behalf of one who has a good title and the transfer is otherwise rightful; and

(b) all signatures are genuine or authorized; and

(c) the item has not been materially altered; and

(d) no defense of any party is good against him; and

(e) he has no knowledge of any insolvency proceeding instituted with respect to the maker or acceptor or the drawer of an unaccepted item.

In addition each customer and collecting bank so transferring an item and receiving a settlement or other consideration engages that upon dishonor and any necessary notice of dishonor and protest he will take up the item.

(3) The warranties and the engagement to honor set forth in the two preceding subsections arise notwithstanding the absence of indorsement or words of guaranty or warranty in the transfer or presentment and a collecting bank remains liable for their breach despite remittance to its transferor. Damages for breach of such warranties or engagement to honor shall not exceed the consideration received by the customer or collecting bank responsible plus finance charges and expenses related to the item, if any.

(4) Unless a claim for breach of warranty under this section is made within a reasonable time after the person claiming learns of the breach, the person liable is discharged to the extent of any loss caused by the delay in making claim.

§ 4—208. Security Interest of Collecting Bank in Items, Accompanying Documents and Proceeds.

(1) A bank has a security interest in an item and any accompanying documents or the proceeds of either

(a) in case of an item deposited in an account to the extent to which credit given for the item has been withdrawn or applied;

(b) in case of an item for which it has given credit available for withdrawal as of right, to the extent of the credit given whether or not the credit is drawn upon and whether or not there is a right of charge-back; or

(c) if it makes an advance on or against the item.

(2) When credit which has been given for several items received at one time or pursuant to a single agreement is withdrawn or applied in part the security interest remains upon all the items, any accompanying documents or the proceeds of either. For the purpose of this section, credits first given are first withdrawn.

(3) Receipt by a collecting bank of a final settlement for an item is a realization on its security interest in the item, accompanying documents and proceeds. To the extent and so long as the bank does not receive final settlement for the item or give up possession of the item or accompanying documents for purposes other than collection, the security interest continues and is subject to the provisions of Article 9 except that

(a) no security agreement is necessary to make the security interest enforceable (subsection (1)(a) of Section 9—203); and

(b) no filing is required to perfect the security interest; and

(c) the security interest has priority over conflicting perfected security interests in the item, accompanying documents or proceeds.

§ 4—209. When Bank Gives Value for Purposes of Holder in Due Course.

For purposes of determining its status as a holder in due course, the bank has given value to the extent that it has a security interest in an item provided that the bank otherwise complies with the requirements of Section 3—302 on what constitutes a holder in due course.

§ 4—210. Presentment by Notice of Item Not Payable by, Through or at a Bank; Liability of Secondary Parties.

(1) Unless otherwise instructed, a collecting bank may present an item not payable by, through or at a bank by sending to the party to accept or pay a written notice that the bank holds the item for acceptance or payment. The notice must be sent in time to be received on or before the day when presentment is due and the bank must meet any requirement of the party to accept or pay under Section 3—505 by the close of the bank's next banking day after it knows of the requirement.

(2) Where presentment is made by notice and neither honor nor request for compliance with a requirement under Section 3—505 is received by the close of business on the day after maturity or in the case of demand items by the close of business on the third banking day after notice was sent, the presenting bank may treat the item as dishonored and charge any secondary party by sending him notice of the facts.

§ 4—211. Media of Remittance; Provisional and Final Settlement in Remittance Cases.

(1) A collecting bank may take in settlement of an item

(a) a check of the remitting bank or of another bank on any bank except the remitting bank; or

(b) a cashier's check or similar primary obligation of a remitting bank which is a member of or clears through a member of the same clearing house or group as the collecting bank; or

(c) appropriate authority to charge an account of the remitting bank or of another bank with the collecting bank; or

(d) if the item is drawn upon or payable by a person other than a bank, a cashier's check, certified check or other bank check or obligation.

(2) If before its midnight deadline the collecting bank properly dishonors a remittance check or authorization to charge on itself or presents or forwards for collection a remittance instrument of or on another bank which is of a kind approved by subsection (1) or has not been authorized by it, the collecting bank is not liable to prior parties in the event of the dishonor of such check, instrument or authorization.

(3) A settlement for an item by means of a remittance instrument or authorization to charge is or becomes a final settlement as to both the person making and the person receiving the settlement

(a) if the remittance instrument or authorization to charge is of a kind approved by subsection (1) or has not been authorized by the person receiving the settlement and in either case the person receiving the settlement acts seasonably before its midnight deadline in presenting, forwarding for collection or paying the instrument or authorization,—at the time the remittance instrument or authorization is finally paid by the payor by which it is payable;

(b) if the person receiving the settlement has authorized remittance by a non-bank check or obligation or by a cashier's check or similar primary obligation of or a check upon the payor or other remitting bank which is not of a kind approved by subsection (1)(b),—at the time of the receipt of such remittance check or obligation; or

(c) if in a case not covered by sub-paragraphs (a) or (b) the person receiving the settlement fails to seasonably present, forward for collection, pay or return a remittance instrument or authorization to it to charge before its midnight deadline,—at such midnight deadline.

§ 4—212. **Right of Charge-Back or Refund.**

(1) If a collecting bank has made provisional settlement with its customer for an item and itself fails by reason of dishonor, suspension of payments by a bank or otherwise to receive a settlement for the item which is or becomes final, the bank may revoke the settlement given by it, charge back the amount of any credit given for the item to its customer's account or obtain refund from its customer whether or not it is able to return the items if by its midnight deadline or within a longer reasonable time after it learns the facts it returns the item or sends notification of the facts. These rights to revoke, charge-back and obtain refund terminate if and when a settlement for the item received by the bank is or becomes final (subsection (3) of Section 4—211 and subsections (2) and (3) of Section 4—213).

[(2) Within the time and manner prescribed by this section and Section 4—301, an intermediary or payor bank, as the case may be, may return an unpaid item directly to the depositary bank and may send for collection a draft on the depositary bank and obtain reimbursement. In such case, if the depositary bank has received provisional settlement for the item, it must reimburse the bank drawing the draft and any provisional credits for the item between banks shall become and remain final.]

Note: *Direct returns is recognized as an innovation that is not yet established bank practice, and therefore, Paragraph 2 has been bracketed. Some lawyers have doubts whether it should be included in legislation or left to development by agreement.*

(3) A depositary bank which is also the payor may chargeback the amount of an item to its customer's account or obtain refund in accordance with the section governing return of an item received by a payor bank for credit on its books (Section 4—301).

(4) The right to charge-back is not affected by

(a) prior use of the credit given for the item; or

(b) failure by any bank to exercise ordinary care with respect to the item but any bank so failing remains liable.

(5) A failure to charge-back or claim refund does not affect other rights of the bank against the customer or any other party.

(6) If credit is given in dollars as the equivalent of the value of an item payable in a foreign currency the dollar amount of any charge-back or refund shall be calculated on the basis of the buying sight rate for the foreign currency prevailing on the day when the person entitled to the charge-back or refund learns that it will not receive payment in ordinary course.

§ 4—213. **Final Payment of Item by Payor Bank; When Provisional Debits and Credits Become Final; When Certain Credits Become Available for Withdrawal.**

(1) An item is finally paid by a payor bank when the bank has done any of the following, whichever happens first:

(a) paid the item in cash; or

(b) settled for the item without reserving a right to revoke the settlement and without having such right under statute, clearing house rule or agreement; or

(c) completed the process of posting the item to the indicated account of the drawer, maker or other person to be charged therewith; or

(d) made a provisional settlement for the item and failed to revoke the settlement in the time and manner permitted by statute, clearing house rule or agreement.

Upon a final payment under subparagraphs (b), (c) or (d) the payor bank shall be accountable for the amount of the item.

(2) If provisional settlement for an item between the presenting and payor banks is made through a clearing house or by debits or credits in an account between them, then to the extent that provisional debits or credits for the item are entered in accounts between the presenting and payor banks or between the presenting and successive prior collecting banks seriatim, they become final upon final payment of the item by the payor bank.

(3) If a collecting bank receives a settlement for an item which is or becomes final (subsection (3) of Section 4—211, subsection (2) of Section 4—213) the bank is accountable to its customer for the amount of the item and any provisional credit given for the item in an account with its customer becomes final.

(4) Subject to any right of the bank to apply the credit to an obligation of the customer, credit given by a bank for an item in an account with its customer becomes available for withdrawal as of right

(a) in any case where the bank has received a provisional settlement for the item,—when such settlement becomes final and the bank has had a reasonable time to learn that the settlement is final;

(b) in any case where the bank is both a depositary bank and a payor bank and the item is finally paid,—

at the opening of the bank's second banking day following receipt of the item.

(5) A deposit of money in a bank is final when made but, subject to any right of the bank to apply the deposit to an obligation of the customer, the deposit becomes available for withdrawal as of right at the opening of the bank's next banking day following receipt of the deposit.

§ 4—214. **Insolvency and Preference.**

(1) Any item in or coming into the possession of a payor or collecting bank which suspends payment and which item is not finally paid shall be returned by the receiver, trustee or agent in charge of the closed bank to the presenting bank or the closed bank's customer.

(2) If a payor bank finally pays an item and suspends payments without making a settlement for the item with its customer or the presenting bank which settlement is or becomes final, the owner of the item has a preferred claim against the payor bank.

(3) If a payor bank gives or a collecting bank gives or receives a provisional settlement for an item and thereafter suspends payments, the suspension does not prevent or interfere with the settlement becoming final if such finality occurs automatically upon the lapse of certain time or the happening of certain events (subsection (3) of Section 4—211, subsections (1)(d), (2) and (3) of Section 4—213).

(4) If a collecting bank receives from subsequent parties settlement for an item which settlement is or becomes final and suspends payments without making a settlement for the item with its customer which is or becomes final, the owner of the item has a preferred claim against such collecting bank.

Part 3 Collection of Items: Payor Banks

§ 4—301. **Deferred Posting; Recovery of Payment by Return of Items; Time of Dishonor.**

(1) Where an authorized settlement for a demand item (other than a documentary draft) received by a payor bank otherwise than for immediate payment over the counter has been made before midnight of the banking day of receipt the payor bank may revoke the settlement and recover any payment if before it has made final payment (subsection (1) of Section 4—213) and before its midnight deadline it

    (a) returns the item; or

    (b) sends written notice of dishonor or nonpayment if the item is held for protest or is otherwise unavailable for return.

(2) If a demand item is received by a payor bank for credit on its books it may return such item or send notice of dishonor and may revoke any credit given or recover the amount thereof withdrawn by its customer, if it acts within the time limit and in the manner specified in the preceding subsection.

(3) Unless previous notice of dishonor has been sent an item is dishonored at the time when for purposes of dishonor it is returned or notice sent in accordance with this section.

(4) An item is returned:

    (a) as to an item received through a clearing house, when it is delivered to the presenting or last collecting bank or to the clearing house or is sent or delivered in accordance with its rules; or

    (b) in all other cases, when it is sent or delivered to the bank's customer or transferor or pursuant to his instructions.

§ 4—302. **Payor Bank's Responsibility for Late Return of Item.**

In the absence of a valid defense such as breach of a presentment warranty (subsection (1) of Section 4—207), settlement effected or the like, if an item is presented on and received by a payor bank the bank is accountable for the amount of

    (a) a demand item other than a documentary draft whether properly payable or not if the bank, in any case where it is not also the depositary bank, retains the item beyond midnight of the banking day of receipt without settling for it or, regardless of whether it is also the depositary bank, does not pay or return the item or send notice of dishonor until after its midnight deadline; or

    (b) any other properly payable item unless within the time allowed for acceptance or payment of that item the bank either accepts or pays the item or returns it and accompanying documents.

§ 4—303. **When Items Subject to Notice, Stop-Order, Legal Process or Setoff; Order in Which Items May Be Charged or Certified.**

(1) Any knowledge, notice or stop-order received by, legal process served upon or setoff exercised by a payor bank, whether or not effective under other rules of law to terminate, suspend or modify the bank's right or duty to pay an item or to charge its customer's account for the item, comes too late to so terminate, suspend or modify such right or duty if the knowledge, notice, stop-order or legal process is received or served and a reasonable time for the bank to act thereon expires or the setoff is exercised after the bank has done any of the following:

    (a) accepted or certified the item;

    (b) paid the item in cash;

(c) settled for the item without reserving a right to revoke the settlement and without having such right under statute, clearing house rule or agreement;

(d) completed the process of posting the item to the indicated account of the drawer, maker or other person to be charged therewith or otherwise has evidenced by examination of such indicated account and by action its decision to pay the item; or

(e) become accountable for the amount of the item under subsection (1)(d) of Section 4—213 and Section 4—302 dealing with the payor bank's responsibility for late return of items.

(2) Subject to the provisions of subsection (1) items may be accepted, paid, certified or charged to the indicated account of its customer in any order convenient to the bank.

Part 4 Relationship Between Payor Bank and Its Customer

§ 4—401. When Bank May Charge Customer's Account.

(1) As against its customer, a bank may charge against his account any item which is otherwise properly payable from that account even though the charge creates an overdraft.

(2) A bank which in good faith makes payment to a holder may charge the indicated account of its customer according to

(a) the original tenor of his altered item; or

(b) the tenor of his completed item, even though the bank knows the item has been completed unless the bank has notice that the completion was improper.

§ 4—402. Bank's Liability to Customer for Wrongful Dishonor.

A payor bank is liable to its customer for damages proximately caused by the wrongful dishonor of an item. When the dishonor occurs through mistake liability is limited to actual damages proved. If so proximately caused and proved damages may include damages for an arrest or prosecution of the customer or other consequential damages. Whether any consequential damages are proximately caused by the wrongful dishonor is a question of fact to be determined in each case.

§ 4—403. Customer's Right to Stop Payment; Burden of Proof of Loss.

(1) A customer may by order to his bank stop payment of any item payable for his account but the order must be received at such time and in such manner as to afford the bank a reasonable opportunity to act on it prior to any action by the bank with respect to the item described in Section 4—303.

(2) An oral order is binding upon the bank only for fourteen calendar days unless confirmed in writing within that period. A written order is effective for only six months unless renewed in writing.

(3) The burden of establishing the fact and amount of loss resulting from the payment of an item contrary to a binding stop payment order is on the customer.

§ 4—404. Bank Not Obligated to Pay Check More Than Six Months Old.

A bank is under no obligation to a customer having a checking account to pay a check, other than a certified check, which is presented more than six months after its date, but it may charge its customer's account for a payment made thereafter in good faith.

§ 4—405. Death or Incompetence of Customer.

(1) A payor or collecting bank's authority to accept, pay or collect an item or to account for proceeds of its collection if otherwise effective is not rendered ineffective by incompetence of a customer of either bank existing at the time the item is issued or its collection is undertaken if the bank does not know of an adjudication of incompetence. Neither death nor incompetence of a customer revokes such authority to accept, pay, collect or account until the bank knows of the fact of death or of an adjudication of incompetence and has reasonable opportunity to act on it.

(2) Even with knowledge a bank may for 10 days after the date of death pay or certify checks drawn on or prior to that date unless ordered to stop payment by a person claiming an interest in the account.

§ 4—406. Customer's Duty to Discover and Report Unauthorized Signature or Alteration.

(1) When a bank sends to its customer a statement of account accompanied by items paid in good faith in support of the debit entries or holds the statement and items pursuant to a request or instructions of its customer or otherwise in a reasonable manner makes the statement and items available to the customer, the customer must exercise reasonable care and promptness to examine the statement and items to discover his unauthorized signature or any alteration on an item and must notify the bank promptly after discovery thereof.

(2) If the bank establishes that the customer failed with respect to an item to comply with the duties imposed on the customer by subsection (1) the customer is precluded from asserting against the bank

(a) his unauthorized signature or any alteration on the item if the bank also establishes that it suffered a loss by reason of such failure; and

(b) an unauthorized signature or alteration by the same wrongdoer on any other item paid in good faith by the bank after the first item and statement was available to the customer for a reasonable period not exceeding fourteen calendar days and before the bank receives notification from the customer of any such unauthorized signature or alteration.

(3) The preclusion under subsection (2) does not apply if the customer establishes lack of ordinary care on the part of the bank in paying the item(s).

(4) Without regard to care or lack of care of either the customer or the bank a customer who does not within one year from the time the statement and items are made available to the customer (subsection (1)) discover and report his unauthorized signature or any alteration on the face or back of the item or does not within three years from that time discover and report any unauthorized indorsement is precluded from asserting against the bank such unauthorized signature or indorsement or such alteration.

(5) If under this section a payor bank has a valid defense against a claim of a customer upon or resulting from payment of an item and waives or fails upon request to assert the defense the bank may not assert against any collecting bank or other prior party presenting or transferring the item a claim based upon the unauthorized signature or alteration giving rise to the customer's claim.

§ 4—407. Payor Bank's Right to Subrogation on Improper Payment.

If a payor bank has paid an item over the stop payment order of the drawer or maker or otherwise under circumstances giving a basis for objection by the drawer or maker, to prevent unjust enrichment and only to the extent necessary to prevent loss to the bank by reason of its payment of the item, the payor bank shall be subrogated to the rights

(a) of any holder in due course on the item against the drawer or maker; and

(b) of the payee or any other holder of the item against the drawer or maker either on the item or under the transaction out of which the item arose; and

(c) of the drawer or maker against the payee or any other holder of the item with respect to the transaction out of which the item arose.

Part 5 Collection of Documentary Drafts

§ 4—501. Handling of Documentary Drafts; Duty to Send for Presentment and to Notify Customer of Dishonor.

A bank which takes a documentary draft for collection must present or send the draft and accompanying documents for presentment and upon learning that the draft has not been paid or accepted in due course must seasonably notify its customer of such fact even though it may have discounted or bought the draft or extended credit available for withdrawal as of right.

§ 4—502. Presentment of "On Arrival" Drafts.

When a draft or the relevant instructions require presentment "on arrival", "when goods arrive" or the like, the collecting bank need not present until in its judgment a reasonable time for arrival of the goods has expired. Refusal to pay or accept because the goods have not arrived is not dishonor; the bank must notify its transferor of such refusal but need not present the draft again until it is instructed to do so or learns of the arrival of the goods.

§ 4—503. Responsibility of Presenting Bank for Documents and Goods; Report of Reasons for Dishonor; Referee in Case of Need.

Unless otherwise instructed and except as provided in Article 5 a bank presenting a documentary draft

(a) must deliver the documents to the drawee on acceptance of the draft if it is payable more than three days after presentment; otherwise, only on payment; and

(b) upon dishonor, either in the case of presentment for acceptance or presentment for payment, may seek and follow instructions from any referee in case of need designated in the draft or if the presenting bank does not choose to utilize his services it must use diligence and good faith to ascertain the reason for dishonor, must notify its transferor of the dishonor and of the results of its effort to ascertain the reasons therefor and must request instructions.

But the presenting bank is under no obligation with respect to goods represented by the documents except to follow any reasonable instructions seasonably received; it has a right to reimbursement for any expense incurred in following instructions and to prepayment of or indemnity for such expenses.

§ 4—504. Privilege of Presenting Bank to Deal With Goods; Security Interest for Expenses.

(1) A presenting bank which, following the dishonor of a documentary draft, has seasonably requested instructions but does not receive them within a reasonable time may store, sell, or otherwise deal with the goods in any reasonable manner.

(2) For its reasonable expenses incurred by action under subsection (1) the presenting bank has a lien upon the goods or their proceeds, which may be foreclosed in the same manner as an unpaid seller's lien.

Article 5
LETTERS OF CREDIT

§ 5—101. Short Title.

This Article shall be known and may be cited as Uniform Commercial Code—Letters of Credit.

§ 5—102. Scope.

(1) This Article applies

(a) to a credit issued by a bank if the credit requires a documentary draft or a documentary demand for payment; and

(b) to a credit issued by a person other than a bank if the credit requires that the draft or demand for payment be accompanied by a document of title; and

(c) to a credit issued by a bank or other person if the credit is not within subparagraphs (a) or (b) but conspicuously states that it is a letter of credit or is conspicuously so entitled.

(2) Unless the engagement meets the requirements of subsection (1), this Article does not apply to engagements to make advances or to honor drafts or demands for payment, to authorities to pay or purchase, to guarantees or to general agreements.

(3) This Article deals with some but not all of the rules and concepts of letters of credit as such rules or concepts have developed prior to this act or may hereafter develop. The fact that this Article states a rule does not by itself require, imply or negate application of the same or a converse rule to a situation not provided for or to a person not specified by this Article.

§ 5—103. Definitions.

(1) In this Article unless the context otherwise requires

(a) "Credit" or "letter of credit" means an engagement by a bank or other person made at the request of a customer and of a kind within the scope of this Article (Section 5—102) that the issuer will honor drafts or other demands for payment upon compliance with the conditions specified in the credit. A credit may be either revocable or irrevocable. The engagement may be either an agreement to honor or a statement that the bank or other person is authorized to honor.

(b) A "documentary draft" or a "documentary demand for payment" is one honor of which is conditioned upon the presentation of a document or documents. "Document" means any paper including document of title, security, invoice, certificate, notice of default and the like.

(c) An "issuer" is a bank or other person issuing a credit.

(d) A "beneficiary" of a credit is a person who is entitled under its terms to draw or demand payment.

(e) An "advising bank" is a bank which gives notification of the issuance of a credit by another bank.

(f) A "confirming bank" is a bank which engages either that it will itself honor a credit already issued by another bank or that such a credit will be honored by the issuer or a third bank.

(g) A "customer" is a buyer or other person who causes an issuer to issue a credit. The term also includes a bank which procures issuance or confirmation on behalf of that bank's customer.

(2) Other definitions applying to this Article and the sections in which they appear are:

"Notation of Credit". Section 5—108.
"Presenter". Section 5—112(3).

(3) Definitions in other Articles applying to this Article and the sections in which they appear are:

"Accept" or "Acceptance". Section 3—410.
"Contract for sale". Section 2—106.
"Draft". Section 3—104.
"Holder in due course". Section 3—302.
"Midnight deadline". Section 4—104.
"Security". Section 8—102.

(4) In addition, Article 1 contains general definitions and principles of construction and interpretation applicable throughout this Article.

§ 5—104. Formal Requirements; Signing.

(1) Except as otherwise required in subsection (1)(c) of Section 5—102 on scope, no particular form of phrasing is required for a credit. A credit must be in writing and signed by the issuer and a confirmation must be in writing and signed by the confirming bank. A modification of the terms of a credit or confirmation must be signed by the issuer or confirming bank.

(2) A telegram may be a sufficient signed writing if it identifies its sender by an authorized authentication. The authentication may be in code and the authorized naming of the issuer in an advice of credit is a sufficient signing.

§ 5—105. Consideration.

No consideration is necessary to establish a credit or to enlarge or otherwise modify its terms.

§ 5—106. Time and Effect of Establishment of Credit.

(1) Unless otherwise agreed a credit is established

(a) as regards the customer as soon as a letter of credit is sent to him or the letter of credit or an authorized written advice of its issuance is sent to the beneficiary; and

(b) as regards the beneficiary when he receives a letter of credit or an authorized written advice of its issuance.

(2) Unless otherwise agreed once an irrevocable credit is established as regards the customer it can be modified or revoked only with the consent of the customer and once it is established as regards the beneficiary it can be modified or revoked only with his consent.

(3) Unless otherwise agreed after a revocable credit is established it may be modified or revoked by the issuer without notice to or consent from the customer or beneficiary.

(4) Notwithstanding any modification or revocation of a revocable credit any person authorized to honor or negotiate under the terms of the original credit is entitled to reimbursement for or honor of any draft or demand for payment duly honored or negotiated before receipt of notice of the modification or revocation and the issuer in turn is entitled to reimbursement from its customer.

§ 5—107. Advice of Credit; Confirmation; Error in Statement of Terms.

(1) Unless otherwise specified an advising bank by advising a credit issued by another bank does not assume any obligation to honor drafts drawn or demands for payment made under the credit but it does assume obligation for the accuracy of its own statement.

(2) A confirming bank by confirming a credit becomes directly obligated on the credit to the extent of its confirmation as though it were its issuer and acquires the rights of an issuer.

(3) Even though an advising bank incorrectly advises the terms of a credit it has been authorized to advise the credit is established as against the issuer to the extent of its original terms.

(4) Unless otherwise specified the customer bears as against the issuer all risks of transmission and reasonable translation or interpretation of any message relating to a credit.

§ 5—108. "Notation Credit"; Exhaustion of Credit.

(1) A credit which specifies that any person purchasing or paying drafts drawn or demands for payment made under it must note the amount of the draft or demand on the letter or advice of credit is a "notation credit".

(2) Under a notation credit

(a) a person paying the beneficiary or purchasing a draft or demand for payment from him acquires a right to honor only if the appropriate notation is made and by transferring or forwarding for honor the documents under the credit such a person warrants to the issuer that the notation has been made; and

(b) unless the credit or a signed statement that an appropriate notation has been made accompanies the draft or demand for payment the issuer may delay honor until evidence of notation has been procured which is satisfactory to it but its obligation and that of its customer continue for a reasonable time not exceeding thirty days to obtain such evidence.

(3) If the credit is not a notation credit

(a) the issuer may honor complying drafts or demands for payment presented to it in the order in which they are presented and is discharged pro tanto by honor of any such draft or demand;

(b) as between competing good faith purchasers of complying drafts or demands the person first purchasing his priority over a subsequent purchaser even though the later purchased draft or demand has been first honored.

§ 5—109. Issuer's Obligation to Its Customer.

(1) An issuer's obligation to its customer includes good faith and observance of any general banking usage but unless otherwise agreed does not include liability or responsibility

(a) for performance of the underlying contract for sale or other transaction between the customer and the beneficiary; or

(b) for any act or omission of any person other than itself or its own branch or for loss or destruction of a draft, demand or document in transit or in the possession of others; or

(c) based on knowledge or lack of knowledge of any usage of any particular trade.

(2) An issuer must examine documents with care so as to ascertain that on their face they appear to comply with the terms of the credit but unless otherwise agreed assumes no liability or responsibility for the genuineness, falsification or effect of any document which appears on such examination to be regular on its face.

(3) A non-bank issuer is not bound by any banking usage of which it has no knowledge.

§ 5—110. Availability of Credit in Portions; Presenter's Reservation of Lien or Claim.

(1) Unless otherwise specified a credit may be used in portions in the discretion of the beneficiary.

(2) Unless otherwise specified a person by presenting a documentary draft or demand for payment under a credit relinquishes upon its honor all claims to the documents and a person by transferring such draft or demand or causing such presentment authorizes such re-

linquishment. An explicit reservation of claim makes the draft or demand noncomplying.

§ 5—111. **Warranties on Transfer and Presentment.**

(1) Unless otherwise agreed the beneficiary by transferring or presenting a documentary draft or demand for payment warrants to all interested parties that the necessary conditions of the credit have been complied with. This is in addition to any warranties arising under Articles 3, 4, 7 and 8.

(2) Unless otherwise agreed a negotiating, advising, confirming, collecting or issuing bank presenting or transferring a draft or demand for payment under a credit warrants only the matters warranted by a collecting bank under Article 4 and any such bank transferring a document warrants only the matters warranted by an intermediary under Articles 7 and 8.

§ 5—112. **Time Allowed for Honor or Rejection; Withholding Honor or Rejection by Consent; "Presenter".**

(1) A bank to which a documentary draft or demand for payment is presented under a credit may without dishonor of the draft, demand or credit

> (a) defer honor until the close of the third banking day following receipt of the documents; and

> (b) further defer honor if the presenter has expressly or impliedly consented thereto.

Failure to honor within the time here specified constitutes dishonor of the draft or demand and of the credit [except as otherwise provided in subsection (4) of Section 5—114 on conditional payment].

Note: *The bracketed language in the last sentence of subsection (1) should be included only if the optional provisions of Section 5—114(4) and (5) are included.*

(2) Upon dishonor the bank may unless otherwise instructed fulfill its duty to return the draft or demand and the documents by holding them at the disposal of the presenter and sending him an advice to that effect.

(3) "Presenter" means any person presenting a draft or demand for payment for honor under a credit even though that person is a confirming bank or other correspondent which is acting under an issuer's authorization.

§ 5—113. **Indemnities.**

(1) A bank seeking to obtain (whether for itself or another) honor, negotiation or reimbursement under a credit may give an indemnity to induce such honor, negotiation or reimbursement.

(2) An indemnity agreement inducing honor, negotiation or reimbursement

> (a) unless otherwise explicitly agreed applies to defects in the documents but not in the goods; and

> (b) unless a longer time is explicitly agreed expires at the end of ten business days following receipt of the documents by the ultimate customer unless notice of objection is sent before such expiration date. The ultimate customer may send notice of objection to the person from whom he received the documents and any bank receiving such notice is under a duty to send notice to its transferor before its midnight deadline.

§ 5—114. **Issuer's Duty and Privilege to Honor; Right to Reimbursement.**

(1) An issuer must honor a draft or demand for payment which complies with the terms of the relevant credit regardless of whether the goods or documents conform to the underlying contract for sale or other contract between the customer and the beneficiary. The issuer is not excused from honor of such a draft or demand by reason of an additional general term that all documents must be satisfactory to the issuer, but an issuer may require that specified documents must be satisfactory to it.

(2) Unless otherwise agreed when documents appear on their face to comply with the terms of a credit but a required document does not in fact conform to the warranties made on negotiation or transfer of a document of title (Section 7—507) or of a certificated security (Section 8—306) or is forged or fraudulent or there is fraud in the transaction:

> (a) the issuer must honor the draft or demand for payment if honor is demanded by a negotiating bank or other holder of the draft or demand which has taken the draft or demand under the credit and under circumstances which would make it a holder in due course (Section 3—302) and in an appropriate case would make it a person to whom a document of title has been duly negotiated (Section 7—502) or a bona fide purchaser of a certificated security (Section 8—302); and

> (b) in all other cases as against its customer, an issuer acting in good faith may honor the draft or demand for payment despite notification from the customer of fraud, forgery or other defect not apparent on the face of the documents but a court of appropriate jurisdiction may enjoin such honor.

(3) Unless otherwise agreed an issuer which has duly honored a draft or demand for payment is entitled to immediate reimbursement of any payment made under the credit and to be put in effectively available funds not later than the day before maturity of any acceptance made under the credit.

[(4) When a credit provides for payment by the issuer on receipt of notice that the required documents are in the possession of a correspondent or other agent of the issuer

(a) any payment made on receipt of such notice is conditional; and

(b) the issuer may reject documents which do not comply with the credit if it does so within three banking days following its receipt of the documents; and

(c) in the event of such rejection, the issuer is entitled by charge back or otherwise to return of the payment made.]

[(5) In the case covered by subsection (4) failure to reject documents within the time specified in sub-paragraph (b) constitutes acceptance of the documents and makes the payment final in favor of the beneficiary.]

Note: *Subsections (4) and (5) are bracketed as optional. If they are included the bracketed language in the last sentence of Section 5—112(1) should also be included.*

§ 5—115. **Remedy for Improper Dishonor or Anticipatory Repudiation.**

(1) When an issuer wrongfully dishonors a draft or demand for payment presented under a credit the person entitled to honor has with respect to any documents the rights of a person in the position of a seller (Section 2—707) and may recover from the issuer the face amount of the draft or demand together with incidental damages under Section 2—710 on seller's incidental damages and interest but less any amount realized by resale or other use or disposition of the subject matter of the transaction. In the event no resale or other utilization is made the documents, goods or other subject matter involved in the transaction must be turned over to the issuer on payment of judgment.

(2) When an issuer wrongfully cancels or otherwise repudiates a credit before presentment of a draft or demand for payment drawn under it the beneficiary has the rights of a seller after anticipatory repudiation by the buyer under Section 2—610 if he learns of the repudiation in time reasonably to avoid procurement of the required documents. Otherwise the beneficiary has an immediate right of action for wrongful dishonor.

§ 5—116. **Transfer and Assignment.**

(1) The right to draw under a credit can be transferred or assigned only when the credit is expressly designated as transferable or assignable.

(2) Even through the credit specifically states that it is nontransferable or nonassignable the beneficiary may before performance of the conditions of the credit assign his right to proceeds. Such an assignment is an assign-

ment of an account under Article 9 on Secured Transactions and is governed by that Article except that

(a) the assignment is ineffective until the letter of credit or advice of credit is delivered to the assignee which delivery constitutes perfection of the security interest under Article 9; and

(b) the issuer may honor drafts or demands for payment drawn under the credit until it receives a notification of the assignment signed by the beneficiary which reasonably identifies the credit involved in the assignment and contains a request to pay the assignee; and

(c) after what reasonably appears to be such a notification has been received the issuer may without dishonor refuse to accept or pay even to a person otherwise entitled to honor until the letter of credit or advice of credit is exhibited to the issuer.

(3) Except where the beneficiary has effectively assigned his right to draw or his right to proceeds, nothing in this section limits his right to transfer or negotiate drafts or demands drawn under the credit.

§ 5—117. **Insolvency of Bank Holding Funds for Documentary Credit.**

(1) Where an issuer or an advising or confirming bank or a bank which has for a customer procured issuance of a credit by another bank becomes insolvent before final payment under the credit and the credit is one to which this Article is made applicable by paragraphs (a) or (b) of Section 5—102(1) on scope, the receipt or allocation of funds or collateral to secure or meet obligations under the credit shall have the following results:

(a) to the extent of any funds or collateral turned over after or before the insolvency as indemnity against or specifically for the purpose of payment of drafts or demands for payment drawn under the designated credit, the drafts or demands are entitled to payment in preference over depositors or other general creditors of the issuer or bank; and

(b) on expiration of the credit or surrender of the beneficiary's rights under it unused any person who has given such funds or collateral is similarly entitled to return thereof; and

(c) a charge to a general or current account with a bank if specifically consented to for the purpose of indemnity against or payment of drafts or demands for payment drawn under the designated credit falls under the same rules as if the funds had been drawn out in cash and then turned over with specific instructions.

(2) After honor or reimbursement under this section the customer or other person for whose account the

insolvent bank has acted is entitled to receive the documents involved.

Article 6
BULK TRANSFERS

§ 6—101. **Short Title.**

This Article shall be known and may be cited as Uniform Commercial Code—Bulk Transfers.

§ 6—102. **"Bulk Transfers"; Transfers of Equipment; Enterprises Subject to This Article; Bulk Transfers Subject to This Article.**

(1) A "bulk transfer" is any transfer in bulk and not in the ordinary course of the transferor's business of a major part of the materials, supplies, merchandise or other inventory (Section 9—109) of an enterprise subject to this Article.

(2) A transfer of a substantial part of the equipment (Section 9—109) of such an enterprise is a bulk transfer if it is made in connection with a bulk transfer of inventory, but not otherwise.

(3) The enterprises subject to this Article are all those whose principal business is the sale of merchandise from stock, including those who manufacture what they sell.

(4) Except as limited by the following section all bulk transfers of goods located within this state are subject to this Article.

§ 6—103. **Transfers Excepted From This Article.**

The following transfers are not subject to this Article:

(1) Those made to give security for the performance of an obligation;

(2) General assignments for the benefit of all the creditors of the transferor, and subsequent transfers by the assignee thereunder;

(3) Transfers in settlement or realization of a lien or other security interests;

(4) Sales by executors, administrators, receivers, trustees in bankruptcy, or any public officer under judicial process;

(5) Sales made in the course of judicial or administrative proceedings for the dissolution or reorganization of a corporation and of which notice is sent to the creditors of the corporation pursuant to order of the court or administrative agency;

(6) Transfers to a person maintaining a known place of business in this State who becomes bound to pay the debts of the transferor in full and gives public notice of that fact, and who is solvent after becoming so bound;

(7) A transfer to a new business enterprise organized to take over and continue the business, if public notice of the transaction is given and the new enterprise assumes the debts of the transferor and he receives nothing from the transaction except an interest in the new enterprise junior to the claims of creditors;

(8) Transfers of property which is exempt from execution.

Public notice under subsection (6) or subsection (7) may be given by publishing once a week for two consecutive weeks in a newspaper of general circulation where the transferor had its principal place of business in this state an advertisement including the names and addresses of the transferor and transferee and the effective date of the transfer.

§ 6—104. **Schedule of Property, List of Creditors.**

(1) Except as provided with respect to auction sales (Section 6—108), a bulk transfer subject to this Article is ineffective against any creditor of the transferor unless:

(a) The transferee requires the transferor to furnish a list of his existing creditors prepared as stated in this section; and

(b) The parties prepare a schedule of the property transferred sufficient to identify it; and

(c) The transferee preserves the list and schedule for six months next following the transfer and permits inspection of either or both and copying therefrom at all reasonable hours by any creditor of the transferor, or files the list and schedule in (a public office to be here identified).

(2) The list of creditors must be signed and sworn to or affirmed by the transferor or his agent. It must contain the names and business addresses of all creditors of the transferor, with the amounts when known, and also the names of all persons who are known to the transferor to assert claims against him even though such claims are disputed. If the transferor is the obligor of an outstanding issue of bonds, debentures or the like as to which there is an indenture trustee, the list of creditors need include only the name and address of the indenture trustee and the aggregate outstanding principal amount of the issue.

(3) Responsibility for the completeness and accuracy of the list of creditors rests on the transferor, and the transfer is not rendered ineffective by errors or omissions therein unless the transferee is shown to have had knowledge.

§ 6—105. **Notice to Creditors.**

In addition to the requirements of the preceding section, any bulk transfer subject to this Article except one made by auction sale (Section 6—108) is ineffective against any creditor of the transferor unless at least ten days before he takes possession of the goods or pays for them, whichever happens first, the transferee gives notice of the transfer in the manner and to the persons hereafter provided (Section 6—107).

[§ 6—106. **Application of the Proceeds.**

In addition to the requirements of the two preceding sections:

(1) Upon every bulk transfer subject to this Article for which new consideration becomes payable except those made by sale at auction it is the duty of the transferee to assure that such consideration is applied so far as necessary to pay those debts of the transferor which are either shown on the list furnished by the transferor (Section 6—104) or filed in writing in the place stated in the notice (Section 6—107) within thirty days after the mailing of such notice. This duty of the transferee runs to all the holders of such debts, and may be enforced by any of them for the benefit of all.

(2) If any of said debts are in dispute the necessary sum may be withheld from distribution until the dispute is settled or adjudicated.

(3) If the consideration payable is not enough to pay all of the said debts in full distribution shall be made pro rata.]

Note: *This section is bracketed to indicate division of opinion as to whether or not it is a wise provision, and to suggest that this is a point on which State enactments may differ without serious damage to the principle of uniformity. In any State where this section is omitted, the following parts of sections, also bracketed in the text, should also be omitted, namely:*

Section 6—107(2)(e).

6—108(3)(c).

6—109(2).

In any State where this section is enacted, these other provisions should be also.

Optional Subsection (4)

[(4) The transferee may within ten days after he takes possession of the goods pay the consideration into the (specify court) in the county where the transferor had its principal place of business in this state and thereafter may discharge his duty under this section by giving notice by registered or certified mail to all the persons to whom the duty runs that the consideration has been paid into that court and that they should file their claims there. On motion of any interested party, the court may order the distribution of the consideration to the persons entitled to it.]

Note: *Optional subsection (4) is recommended for those states which do not have a general statute providing for payment of money into court.*

§ 6—107. **The Notice.**

(1) The notice to creditors (Section 6—105) shall state:

(a) that a bulk transfer is about to be made; and

(b) the names and business addresses of the transferor and transferee, and all other business names and addresses used by the transferor within three years last past so far as known to the transferee; and

(c) whether or not all the debts of the transferor are to be paid in full as they fall due as a result of the transaction, and if so, the address to which creditors should send their bills.

(2) If the debts of the transferor are not to be paid in full as they fall due or if the transferee is in doubt on that point then the notice shall state further:

(a) the location and general description of the property to be transferred and the estimated total of the transferor's debts;

(b) the address where the schedule of property and list of creditors (Section 6—104) may be inspected;

(c) whether the transfer is to pay existing debts and if so the amount of such debts and to whom owing;

(d) whether the transfer is for new consideration and if so the amount of such consideration and the time and place of payment; [and]

[(e) if for new consideration the time and place where creditors of the transferor are to file their claims.]

(3) The notice in any case shall be delivered personally or sent by registered or certified mail to all the persons shown on the list of creditors furnished by the transferor (Section 6—104) and to all other persons who are known to the transferee to hold or assert claims against the transferor.

§ 6—108. **Auction Sales; "Auctioneer".**

(1) A bulk transfer is subject to this Article even though it is by sale at auction, but only in the manner and with the results stated in this section.

(2) The transferor shall furnish a list of his creditors and assist in the preparation of a schedule of the property to be sold, both prepared as before stated (Section 6—104).

(3) The person or persons other than the transferor who direct, control or are responsible for the auction are collectively called the "auctioneer". The auctioneer shall:

(a) receive and retain the list of creditors and prepare and retain the schedule of property for the period stated in this Article (Section 6—104);

(b) give notice of the auction personally or by registered or certified mail at least ten days before it occurs to all persons shown on the list of creditors and to all other persons who are known to him to hold or assert claims against the transferor; [and]

[(c) assure that the net proceeds of the auction are applied as provided in this Article (Section 6—106).]

(4) Failure of the auctioneer to perform any of these duties does not affect the validity of the sale or the title of the purchasers, but if the auctioneer knows that the auction constitutes a bulk transfer such failure renders the auctioneer liable to the creditors of the transferor as a class for the sums owing to them from the transferor up to but not exceeding the net proceeds of the auction. If the auctioneer consists of several persons their liability is joint and several.

§ 6—109. **What Creditors Protected; [Credit for Payment to Particular Creditors].**

(1) The creditors of the transferor mentioned in this Article are those holding claims based on transactions or events occurring before the bulk transfer, but creditors who become such after notice to creditors is given (Sections 6—105 and 6—107) are not entitled to notice.

[(2) Against the aggregate obligation imposed by the provisions of this Article concerning the application of the proceeds (Section 6—106 and subsection (3)(c) of 6—108) the transferee or auctioneer is entitled to credit for sums paid to particular creditors of the transferor, not exceeding the sums believed in good faith at the time of the payment to be properly payable to such creditors.]

§ 6—110. **Subsequent Transfers.**

When the title of a transferee to property is subject to a defect by reason of his noncompliance with the requirements of this Article, then:

(1) a purchaser of any of such property from such transferee who pays no value or who takes with notice of such noncompliance takes subject to such defect, but

(2) a purchaser for value in good faith and without such notice takes free of such defect.

§ 6—111. **Limitation of Actions and Levies.**

No action under this Article shall be brought nor levy made more than six months after the date on which the transferee took possession of the goods unless the transfer has been concealed. If the transfer has been concealed, actions may be brought or levies made within six months after its discovery.

Note to Article 6: *Section 6—106 is bracketed to indicate division of opinion as to whether or not it is a wise provision, and to suggest that this is a point on which State enactments may differ without serious damage to the principle of uniformity.*

In any State where Section 6—106 is not enacted, the following parts of sections, also bracketed in the text, should also be omitted, namely:

Sec. 6—107(2)(e).
  6—108(3)(c).
  6—109(2).
In any State where Section 6—106 is enacted, these other provisions should be also.

Article 7
Warehouse Receipts, Bills of Lading and Other Documents of Title

Part 1 General

§ 7—101. **Short Title.**

This Article shall be known and may be cited as Uniform Commercial Code—Documents of Title.

§ 7—102. **Definitions and Index of Definitions.**

(1) In this Article, unless the context otherwise requires:

(a) "Bailee" means the person who by a warehouse receipt, bill of lading or other document of title acknowledges possession of goods and contracts to deliver them.

(b) "Consignee" means the person named in a bill to whom or to whose order the bill promises delivery.

(c) "Consignor" means the person named in a bill as the person from whom the goods have been received for shipment.

(d) "Delivery order" means a written order to deliver goods directed to a warehouseman, carrier or other person who in the ordinary course of business issues warehouse receipts or bills of lading.

(e) "Document" means document of title as defined in the general definitions in Article 1 (Section 1—201).

(f) "Goods" means all things which are treated as movable for the purposes of a contract of storage or transportation.

(g) "Issuer" means a bailee who issues a document except that in relation to an unaccepted delivery order it means the person who orders the possessor of goods to deliver. Issuer includes any person for whom an agent or employee purports to act in issuing a document if the agent or employee has real or apparent authority to issue documents, notwithstanding that the issuer received no goods or that the goods were misdescribed or that in any other respect the agent or employee violated his instructions.

(h) "Warehouseman" is a person engaged in the business of storing goods for hire.

(2) Other definitions applying to this Article or to specified Parts thereof, and the sections in which they appear are:

"Duly negotiate". Section 7—501.

"Person entitled under the document". Section 7—403(4).

(3) Definitions in other Articles applying to this Article and the sections in which they appear are:

"Contract for sale". Section 2—106.

"Overseas". Section 2—323.

"Receipt" of goods. Section 2—103.

(4) In addition Article 1 contains general definitions and principles of construction and interpretation applicable throughout this Article.

§ 7—103. **Relation of Article to Treaty, Statute, Tariff, Classification or Regulation.**

To the extent that any treaty or statute of the United States, regulatory statute of this State or tariff, classification or regulation filed or issued pursuant thereto is applicable, the provisions of this Article are subject thereto.

§ 7—104. **Negotiable and Nonnegotiable Warehouse Receipt, Bill of Lading or Other Document of Title.**

(1) A warehouse receipt, bill of lading or other document of title is negotiable

    (a) if by its terms the goods are to be delivered to bearer or to the order of a named person; or

    (b) where recognized in overseas trade, if it runs to a named person or assigns.

(2) Any other document is nonnegotiable. A bill of lading in which it is stated that the goods are consigned to a named person is not made negotiable by a provision that the goods are to be delivered only against a written order signed by the same or another named person.

§ 7—105. **Construction Against Negative Implication.**

The omission from either Part 2 or Part 3 of this Article of a provision corresponding to a provision made in the other Part does not imply that a corresponding rule of law is not applicable.

Part 2 Warehouse Receipts: Special Provisions

§ 7—201. **Who May Issue a Warehouse Receipt; Storage Under Government Bond.**

(1) A warehouse receipt may be issued by any warehouseman.

(2) Where goods including distilled spirits and agricultural commodities are stored under a statute requiring a bond against withdrawal or a license for the issuance of receipts in the nature of warehouse receipts, a receipt issued for the goods has like effect as a warehouse receipt even though issued by a person who is the owner of the goods and is not a warehouseman.

§ 7—202. **Form of Warehouse Receipt; Essential Terms; Optional Terms.**

(1) A warehouse receipt need not be in any particular form.

(2) Unless a warehouse receipt embodies within its written or printed terms each of the following, the warehouseman is liable for damages caused by the omission to a person injured thereby:

    (a) the location of the warehouse where the goods are stored;

    (b) the date of issue of the receipt;

    (c) the consecutive number of the receipt;

    (d) a statement whether the goods received will be delivered to the bearer, to a specified person, or to a specified person or his order;

    (e) the rate of storage and handling charges, except that where goods are stored under a field warehousing arrangement a statement of that fact is sufficient on a nonnegotiable receipt;

    (f) a description of the goods or of the packages containing them;

    (g) the signature of the warehouseman, which may be made by his authorized agent;

    (h) if the receipt is issued for goods of which the warehouseman is owner, either solely or jointly or in common with others, the fact of such ownership; and

    (i) a statement of the amount of advances made and of liabilities incurred for which the warehouseman claims a lien or security interest (Section 7—209). If the precise amount of such advances made or of such liabilities incurred is, at the time of the issue of the receipt, unknown to the warehouseman or to his agent who issues it, a statement of the fact that advances have been made or liabilities incurred and the purpose thereof is sufficient.

(3) A warehouseman may insert in his receipt any other terms which are not contrary to the provisions of this Act and do not impair his obligation of delivery (Section 7—403) or his duty of care (Section 7—204). Any contrary provisions shall be ineffective.

§ 7—203. **Liability for Nonreceipt or Misdescription.**

A party to or purchaser for value in good faith of a document of title other than a bill of lading relying in either case upon the description therein of the goods may recover from the issuer damages caused by the nonreceipt or misdescription of the goods, except to the extent that the document conspicuously indicates that the issuer does not know whether any part or all of the goods in fact were received or conform to the description, as where the description is in terms of marks or labels or kind, quantity or condition, or the receipt or description is qualified by "contents, condition and quality unknown", "said to contain" or the like, if such indication be true, or the party or purchaser otherwise has notice.

§ 7—204. Duty of Care; Contractual Limitation of Warehouseman's Liability.

(1) A warehouseman is liable for damages for loss of or injury to the goods caused by his failure to exercise such care in regard to them as a reasonably careful man would exercise under like circumstances but unless otherwise agreed he is not liable for damages which could not have been avoided by the exercise of such care.

(2) Damages may be limited by a term in the warehouse receipt or storage agreement limiting the amount of liability in case of loss or damage, and setting forth a specific liability per article or item, or value per unit of weight, beyond which the warehouseman shall not be liable; provided, however, that such liability may on written request of the bailor at the time of signing such storage agreement or within a reasonable time after receipt of the warehouse receipt be increased on part or all of the goods thereunder, in which event increased rates may be charged based on such increased valuation, but that no such increase shall be permitted contrary to a lawful limitation of liability contained in the warehouseman's tariff, if any. No such limitation is effective with respect to the warehouseman's liability for conversion to his own use.

(3) Reasonable provisions as to the time and manner of presenting claims and instituting actions based on the bailment may be included in the warehouse receipt or tariff.

(4) This section does not impair or repeal . . .

Note: *Insert in subsection (4) a reference to any statute which imposes a higher responsibility upon the warehouseman or invalidates contractual limitations which would be permissible under this Article.*

§ 7—205. Title Under Warehouse Receipt Defeated in Certain Cases.

A buyer in the ordinary course of business of fungible goods sold and delivered by a warehouseman who is also in the business of buying and selling such goods takes free of any claim under a warehouse receipt even though it has been duly negotiated.

§ 7—206. Termination of Storage at Warehouseman's Option.

(1) A warehouseman may on notifying the person on whose account the goods are held and any other person known to claim an interest in the goods require payment of any charges and removal of the goods from the warehouse at the termination of the period of storage fixed by the document, or, if no period is fixed, within a stated period not less than thirty days after the notification. If the goods are not removed before the date specified in the notification, the warehouseman may sell them in accordance with the provisions of the section on enforcement of a warehouseman's lien (Section 7—210).

(2) If a warehouseman in good faith believes that the goods are about to deteriorate or decline in value to less than the amount of his lien within the time prescribed in subsection (1) for notification, advertisement and sale, the warehouseman may specify in the notification any reasonable shorter time for removal of the goods and in case the goods are not removed, may sell them at public sale held not less than one week after a single advertisement or posting.

(3) If as a result of a quality or condition of the goods of which the warehouseman had no notice at the time of deposit the goods are a hazard to other property or to the warehouse or to persons, the warehouseman may sell the goods at public or private sale without advertisement on reasonable notification to all persons known to claim an interest in the goods. If the warehouseman after a reasonable effort is unable to sell the goods he may dispose of them in any lawful manner and shall incur no liability by reason of such disposition.

(4) The warehouseman must deliver the goods to any person entitled to them under this Article upon due demand made at any time prior to sale or other disposition under this section.

(5) The warehouseman may satisfy his lien from the proceeds of any sale or disposition under this section but must hold the balance for delivery on the demand of any person to whom he would have been bound to deliver the goods.

§ 7—207. Goods Must Be Kept Separate; Fungible Goods.

(1) Unless the warehouse receipt otherwise provides, a warehouseman must keep separate the goods covered by each receipt so as to permit at all times identification and delivery of those goods except that different lots of fungible goods may be commingled.

(2) Fungible goods so commingled are owned in common by the persons entitled thereto and the warehouseman is severally liable to each owner for that owner's share. Where because of overissue a mass of fungible

goods is insufficient to meet all the receipts which the warehouseman has issued against it, the persons entitled include all holders to whom overissued receipts have been duly negotiated.

§ 7—208. **Altered Warehouse Receipts.**

Where a blank in a negotiable warehouse receipt has been filled in without authority, a purchaser for value and without notice of the want of authority may treat the insertion as authorized. Any other unauthorized alteration leaves any receipt enforceable against the issuer according to its original tenor.

§ 7—209. **Lien of Warehouseman.**

(1) A warehouseman has a lien against the bailor on the goods covered by a warehouse receipt or on the proceeds thereof in his possession for charges for storage or transportation (including demurrage and terminal charges), insurance, labor, or charges present or future in relation to the goods, and for expenses necessary for preservation of the goods or reasonably incurred in their sale pursuant to law. If the person on whose account the goods are held is liable for like charges or expenses in relation to other goods whenever deposited and it is stated in the receipt that a lien is claimed for charges and expenses in relation to other goods, the warehouseman also has a lien against him for such charges and expenses whether or not the other goods have been delivered by the warehouseman. But against a person to whom a negotiable warehouse receipt is duly negotiated a warehouseman's lien is limited to charges in an amount or at a rate specified on the receipt or if no charges are so specified then to a reasonable charge for storage of the goods covered by the receipt subsequent to the date of the receipt.

(2) The warehouseman may also reserve a security interest against the bailor for a maximum amount specified on the receipt for charges other than those specified in subsection (1), such as for money advanced and interest. Such a security interest is governed by the Article on Secured Transactions (Article 9).

(3) (a) A warehouseman's lien for charges and expenses under subsection (1) or a security interest under subsection (2) is also effective against any person who so entrusted the bailor with possession of the goods that a pledge of them by him to a good faith purchaser for value would have been valid but is not effective against a person as to whom the document confers no right in the goods covered by it under Section 7—503.

(b) A warehouseman's lien on household goods for charges and expenses in relation to the goods under subsection (1) is also effective against all persons if the depositor was the legal possessor of the goods at the time of deposit. "Household goods" means furniture, furnishings and personal effects used by the depositor in a dwelling.

(4) A warehouseman loses his lien on any goods which he voluntarily delivers or which he unjustifiably refuses to deliver.

§ 7—210. **Enforcement of Warehouseman's Lien.**

(1) Except as provided in subsection (2), a warehouseman's lien may be enforced by public or private sale of the goods in bloc or in parcels, at any time or place and on any terms which are commercially reasonable, after notifying all persons known to claim an interest in the goods. Such notification must include a statement of the amount due, the nature of the proposed sale and the time and place of any public sale. The fact that a better price could have been obtained by a sale at a different time or in a different method from that selected by the warehouseman is not of itself sufficient to establish that the sale was not made in a commercially reasonable manner. If the warehouseman either sells the goods in the usual manner in any recognized market therefor, or if he sells at the price current in such market at the time of his sale, or if he has otherwise sold in conformity with commercially reasonable practices among dealers in the type of goods sold, he has sold in a commercially reasonable manner. A sale of more goods than apparently necessary to be offered to ensure satisfaction of the obligation is not commercially reasonable except in cases covered by the preceding sentence.

(2) A warehouseman's lien on goods other than goods stored by a merchant in the course of his business may be enforced only as follows:

(a) All persons known to claim an interest in the goods must be notified.

(b) The notification must be delivered in person or sent by registered or certified letter to the last known address of any person to be notified.

(c) The notification must include an itemized statement of the claim, a description of the goods subject to the lien, a demand for payment within a specified time not less than ten days after receipt of the notification, and a conspicuous statement that unless the claim is paid within the time the goods will be advertised for sale and sold by auction at a specified time and place.

(d) The sale must conform to the terms of the notification.

(e) The sale must be held at the nearest suitable place to that where the goods are held or stored.

(f) After the expiration of the time given in the notification, an advertisement of the sale must be published once a week for two weeks consecutively in a newspaper of general circulation where the sale is to be held. The advertisement must include a description of the goods, the name of the person on whose account they are being held, and the time and place of the sale. The sale must take place at least fifteen days after the first publication. If there is no newspaper of general circulation where the sale is to be held, the advertisement must be posted at least ten days before the sale in not less than six conspicuous places in the neighborhood of the proposed sale.

(3) Before any sale pursuant to this section any person claiming a right in the goods may pay the amount necessary to satisfy the lien and the reasonable expenses incurred under this section. In that event the goods must not be sold, but must be retained by the warehouseman subject to the terms of the receipt and this Article.

(4) The warehouseman may buy at any public sale pursuant to this section.

(5) A purchaser in good faith of goods sold to enforce a warehouseman's lien takes the goods free of any rights of persons against whom the lien was valid, despite noncompliance by the warehouseman with the requirements of this section.

(6) The warehouseman may satisfy his lien from the proceeds of any sale pursuant to this section but must hold the balance, if any, for delivery on demand to any person to whom he would have been bound to deliver the goods.

(7) The rights provided by this section shall be in addition to all other rights allowed by law to a creditor against his debtor.

(8) Where a lien is on goods stored by a merchant in the course of his business the lien may be enforced in accordance with either subsection (1) or (2).

(9) The warehouseman is liable for damages caused by failure to comply with the requirements for sale under this section and in case of willful violation is liable for conversion.

Part 3 Bills of Lading: Special Provisions

§ 7—301. Liability for Nonreceipt or Misdescription; "Said to Contain"; "Shipper's Load and Count"; Improper Handling.

(1) A consignee of a nonnegotiable bill who has given value in good faith or a holder to whom a negotiable bill has been duly negotiated relying in either case upon the description therein of the goods, or upon the date therein shown, may recover from the issuer damages caused by the misdating of the bill or the nonreceipt or misdescription of the goods, except to the extent that the document indicates that the issuer does not know whether any part of all of the goods in fact were received or conform to the description, as where the description is in terms of marks or labels or kind, quantity, or condition or the receipt or description is qualified by "contents or condition of contents of packages unknown", "said to contain", "shipper's weight, load and count" or the like, if such indication be true.

(2) When goods are loaded by an issuer who is a common carrier, the issuer must count the packages of goods if package freight and ascertain the kind and quantity if bulk freight. In such cases "shipper's weight, load and count" or other words indicating that the description was made by the shipper are ineffective except as to freight concealed by packages.

(3) When bulk freight is loaded by a shipper who makes available to the issuer adequate facilities for weighing such freight, an issuer who is a common carrier must ascertain the kind and quantity within a reasonable time after receiving the written request of the shipper to do so. In such cases "shipper's weight" or other words of like purport are ineffective.

(4) The issuer may by inserting in the bill the words "shipper's weight, load and count" or other words of like purport indicate that the goods were loaded by the shipper; and if such statement be true the issuer shall not be liable for damages caused by the improper loading. But their omission does not imply liability for such damages.

(5) The shipper shall be deemed to have guaranteed to the issuer the accuracy at the time of shipment of the description, marks, labels, number, kind, quantity, condition and weight, as furnished by him; and the shipper shall indemnify the issuer against damage caused by inaccuracies in such particulars. The right of the issuer to such indemnity shall in no way limit his responsibility and liability under the contract of carriage to any person other than the shipper.

§ 7—302. Through Bills of Lading and Similar Documents.

(1) The issuer of a through bill of lading or other document embodying an undertaking to be performed in part by persons acting as its agents or by connecting carriers is liable to anyone entitled to recover on the document for any breach by such other persons or by a connecting carrier of its obligation under the document but to the extent that the bill covers an undertaking to be performed overseas or in territory not contiguous to the continental United States or an undertaking including matters other than transportation this liability may be varied by agreement of the parties.

(2) Where goods covered by a through bill of lading or other document embodying an undertaking to be performed in part by persons other than the issuer are

received by any such person, he is subject with respect to his own performance while the goods are in his possession to the obligation of the issuer. His obligation is discharged by delivery of the goods to another such person pursuant to the document, and does not include liability for breach by any other such persons or by the issuer.

(3) The issuer of such through bill of lading or other document shall be entitled to recover from the connecting carrier or such other person in possession of the goods when the breach of the obligation under the document occurred, the amount it may be required to pay to anyone entitled to recover on the document therefor, as may be evidenced by any receipt, judgment, or transcript thereof, and the amount of any expense reasonably incurred by it in defending any action brought by anyone entitled to recover on the document therefor.

§ 7—303. **Diversion; Reconsignment; Change of Instructions.**

(1) Unless the bill of lading otherwise provides, the carrier may deliver the goods to a person or destination other than that stated in the bill or may otherwise dispose of the goods on instructions from

(a) the holder of a negotiable bill; or

(b) the consignor on a nonnegotiable bill notwithstanding contrary instructions from the consignee; or

(c) the consignee on a nonnegotiable bill in the absence of contrary instructions from the consignor, if the goods have arrived at the billed destination or if the consignee is in possession of the bill; or

(d) the consignee on a nonnegotiable bill if he is entitled as against the consignor to dispose of them.

(2) Unless such instructions are noted on a negotiable bill of lading, a person to whom the bill is duly negotiated can hold the bailee according to the original terms.

§ 7—304. **Bills of Lading in a Set.**

(1) Except where customary in overseas transportation, a bill of lading must not be issued in a set of parts. The issuer is liable for damages caused by violation of this subsection.

(2) Where a bill of lading is lawfully drawn in a set of parts, each of which is numbered and expressed to be valid only if the goods have not been delivered against any other part, the whole of the parts constitute one bill.

(3) Where a bill of lading is lawfully issued in a set of parts and different parts are negotiated to different persons, the title of the holder to whom the first due negotiation is made prevails as to both the document and the goods even though any later holder may have re-

ceived the goods from the carrier in good faith and discharged the carrier's obligation by surrender of his part.

(4) Any person who negotiates or transfers a single part of a bill of lading drawn in a set is liable to holders of that part as if it were the whole set.

(5) The bailee is obliged to deliver in accordance with Part 4 of this Article against the first presented part of a bill of lading lawfully drawn in a set. Such delivery discharges the bailee's obligation on the whole bill.

§ 7—305. **Destination Bills.**

(1) Instead of issuing a bill of lading to the consignor at the place of shipment a carrier may at the request of the consignor procure the bill to be issued at destination or at any other place designated in the request.

(2) Upon request of anyone entitled as against the carrier to control the goods while in transit and on surrender of any outstanding bill of lading or other receipt covering such goods, the issuer may procure a substitute bill to be issued at any place designated in the request.

§ 7—306. **Altered Bills of Lading.**

An unauthorized alteration or filling in of a blank in a bill of lading leaves the bill enforceable according to its original tenor.

§ 7—307. **Lien of Carrier.**

(1) A carrier has a lien on the goods covered by a bill of lading for charges subsequent to the date of its receipt of the goods for storage or transportation (including demurrage and terminal charges) and for expenses necessary for preservation of the goods incident to their transportation or reasonably incurred in their sale pursuant to law. But against a purchaser for value of a negotiable bill of lading a carrier's lien is limited to charges stated in the bill or the applicable tariffs, or if no charges are stated then to a reasonable charge.

(2) A lien for charges and expenses under subsection (1) on goods which the carrier was required by law to receive for transportation is effective against the consignor or any person entitled to the goods unless the carrier had notice that the consignor lacked authority to subject the goods to such charges and expenses. Any other lien under subsection (1) is effective against the consignor and any person who permitted the bailor to have control or possession of the goods unless the carrier had notice that the bailor lacked such authority.

(3) A carrier loses his lien on any goods which he voluntarily delivers or which he unjustifiably refuses to deliver.

§ 7—308. **Enforcement of Carrier's Lien.**

(1) A carrier's lien may be enforced by public or private sale of the goods, in bloc or in parcels, at any time or

place and on any terms which are commercially reasonable, after notifying all persons known to claim an interest in the goods. Such notification must include a statement of the amount due, the nature of the proposed sale and the time and place of any public sale. The fact that a better price could have been obtained by a sale at a different time or in a different method from that selected by the carrier is not of itself sufficient to establish that the sale was not made in a commercially reasonable manner. If the carrier either sells the goods in the usual manner in any recognized market therefor or if he sells at the price current in such market at the time of his sale or if he has otherwise sold in conformity with commercially reasonable practices among dealers in the type of goods sold he has sold in a commercially reasonable manner. A sale of more goods than apparently necessary to be offered to ensure satisfaction of the obligation is not commercially reasonable except in cases covered by the preceding sentence.

(2) Before any sale pursuant to this section any person claiming a right in the goods may pay the amount necessary to satisfy the lien and the reasonable expenses incurred under this section. In that event the goods must not be sold, but must be retained by the carrier subject to the terms of the bill and this Article.

(3) The carrier may buy at any public sale pursuant to this section.

(4) A purchaser in good faith of goods sold to enforce a carrier's lien takes the goods free of any rights of persons against whom the lien was valid, despite noncompliance by the carrier with the requirements of this section.

(5) The carrier may satisfy his lien from the proceeds of any sale pursuant to this section but must hold the balance, if any, for delivery on demand to any person to whom he would have been bound to deliver the goods.

(6) The rights provided by this section shall be in addition to all other rights allowed by law to a creditor against his debtor.

(7) A carrier's lien may be enforced in accordance with either subsection (1) or the procedure set forth in subsection (2) of Section 7—210.

(8) The carrier is liable for damages caused by failure to comply with the requirements for sale under this section and in case of willful violation is liable for conversion.

§ 7—309. **Duty of Care; Contractual Limitation of Carrier's Liability.**

(1) A carrier who issues a bill of lading whether negotiable or nonnegotiable must exercise the degree of care in relation to the goods which a reasonably careful man would exercise under like circumstances. This sub-

section does not repeal or change any law or rule of law which imposes liability upon a common carrier for damages not caused by its negligence.

(2) Damages may be limited by a provision that the carrier's liability shall not exceed a value stated in the document if the carrier's rates are dependent upon value and the consignor by the carrier's tariff is afforded an opportunity to declare a higher value or a value as lawfully provided in the tariff, or where no tariff is filed he is otherwise advised of such opportunity; but no such limitation is effective with respect to the carrier's liability for conversion to its own use.

(3) Reasonable provisions as to the time and manner of presenting claims and instituting actions based on the shipment may be included in a bill of lading or tariff.

Part 4 Warehouse Receipts and Bills of Lading: General Obligations

§ 7—401. **Irregularities in Issue of Receipt or Bill or Conduct of Issuer.**

The obligations imposed by this Article on an issuer apply to a document of title regardless of the fact that

 (a) the document may not comply with the requirements of this Article or of any other law or regulation regarding its issue, form or content; or

 (b) the issuer may have violated laws regulating the conduct of his business; or

 (c) the goods covered by the document were owned by the bailee at the time the document was issued; or

 (d) the person issuing the document does not come within the definition of warehouseman if it purports to be a warehouse receipt.

§ 7—402. **Duplicate Receipt or Bill; Overissue.**

Neither a duplicate nor any other document of title purporting to cover goods already represented by an outstanding document of the same issuer confers any right in the goods, except as provided in the case of bills in a set, overissue of documents for fungible goods and substitutes for lost, stolen or destroyed documents. But the issuer is liable for damages caused by his overissue or failure to identify a duplicate document as such by conspicuous notation on its face.

§ 7—403. **Obligation of Warehouseman or Carrier to Deliver; Excuse.**

(1) The bailee must deliver the goods to a person entitled under the document who complies with subsections (2) and (3), unless and to the extent that the bailee establishes any of the following:

(a) delivery of the goods to a person whose receipt was rightful as against the claimant;

(b) damage to or delay, loss or destruction of the goods for which the bailee is not liable [, but the burden of establishing negligence in such cases is on the person entitled under the document];

Note: *The brackets in (1)(b) indicate that State enactments may differ on this point without serious damage to the principle of uniformity.*

(c) previous sale or other disposition of the goods in lawful enforcement of a lien or on warehouse-man's lawful termination of storage;

(d) the exercise by a seller of his right to stop delivery pursuant to the provisions of the Article on Sales (Section 2—705);

(e) a diversion, reconsignment or other disposition pursuant to the provisions of this Article (Section 7—303) or tariff regulating such right;

(f) release, satisfaction or any other fact affording a personal defense against the claimant;

(g) any other lawful excuse.

(2) A person claiming goods covered by a document of title must satisfy the bailee's lien where the bailee so requests or where the bailee is prohibited by law from delivering the goods until the charges are paid.

(3) Unless the person claiming is one against whom the document confers no right under Sec. 7—503(1), he must surrender for cancellation or notation of partial deliveries any outstanding negotiable document covering the goods, and the bailee must cancel the document or conspicuously note the partial delivery thereon or be liable to any person to whom the document is duly negotiated.

(4) "Person entitled under the document" means holder in the case of a negotiable document, or the person to whom delivery is to be made by the terms of or pursuant to written instructions under a nonnegotiable document.

§ 7—404. **No Liability for Good Faith Delivery Pursuant to Receipt or Bill.**

A bailee who in good faith including observance of reasonable commercial standards has received goods and delivered or otherwise disposed of them according to the terms of the document of title or pursuant to this Article is not liable therefor. This rule applies even though the person from whom he received the goods had no authority to procure the document or to dispose of the goods and even though the person to whom he delivered the goods had no authority to receive them.

Part 5 Warehouse Receipts and Bills of Lading: Negotiation and Transfer

§ 7—501. **Form of Negotiation and Requirements of "Due Negotiation".**

(1) A negotiable document of title running to the order of a named person is negotiated by his indorsement and delivery. After his indorsement in blank or to bearer any person can negotiate it by delivery alone.

(2) (a) A negotiable document of title is also negotiated by delivery alone when by its original terms it runs to bearer.

(b) When a document running to the order of a named person is delivered to him the effect is the same as if the document had been negotiated.

(3) Negotiation of a negotiable document of title after it has been indorsed to a specified person requires indorsement by the special indorsee as well as delivery.

(4) A negotiable document of title is "duly negotiated" when it is negotiated in the manner stated in this section to a holder who purchases it in good faith without notice of any defense against or claim to it on the part of any person and for value, unless it is established that the negotiation is not in the regular course of business or financing or involves receiving the document in settlement or payment of a money obligation.

(5) Indorsement of a nonnegotiable document neither makes it negotiable nor adds to the transferee's rights.

(6) The naming in a negotiable bill of a person to be notified of the arrival of the goods does not limit the negotiability of the bill nor constitute notice to a purchaser thereof of any interest of such person in the goods.

§ 7—502. **Rights Acquired by Due Negotiation.**

(1) Subject to the following section and to the provisions of Section 7—205 on fungible goods, a holder to whom a negotiable document of title has been duly negotiated acquires thereby:

(a) title to the document;

(b) title to the goods;

(c) all rights accruing under the law of agency or estoppel, including rights to goods delivered to the bailee after the document was issued; and

(d) the direct obligation of the issuer to hold or deliver the goods according to the terms of the document free of any defense or claim by him except those arising under the terms of the document or under this Article. In the case of a delivery order the bailee's obligation accrues only upon acceptance and the obligation acquired by the holder is that the issuer and any indorser will procure the acceptance of the bailee.

(2) Subject to the following section, title and rights so acquired are not defeated by any stoppage of the goods represented by the document or by surrender of such goods by the bailee, and are not impaired even though the negotiation or any prior negotiation constituted a breach of duty or even though any person has been deprived of possession of the document by misrepresentation, fraud, accident, mistake, duress, loss, theft or conversion, or even though a previous sale or other transfer of the goods or document has been made to a third person.

§ 7—503. Document of Title to Goods Defeated in Certain Cases.

(1) A document of title confers no right in goods against a person who before issuance of the document had a legal interest or a perfected security interest in them and who neither

   (a) delivered or entrusted them or any document of title covering them to the bailor or his nominee with actual or apparent authority to ship, store or sell or with power to obtain delivery under this Article (Section 7—403) or with power of disposition under this Act (Sections 2—403 and 9—307) or other statute or rule of law; nor

   (b) acquiesced in the procurement by the bailor or his nominee of any document of title.

(2) Title to goods based upon an unaccepted delivery order is subject to the rights of anyone to whom a negotiable warehouse receipt or bill of lading covering the goods has been duly negotiated. Such a title may be defeated under the next section to the same extent as the rights of the issuer or a transferee from the issuer.

(3) Title to goods based upon a bill of lading issued to a freight forwarder is subject to the rights of anyone to whom a bill issued by the freight forwarder is duly negotiated; but delivery by the carrier in accordance with Part 4 of this Article pursuant to its own bill of lading discharges the carrier's obligation to deliver.

§ 7—504. Rights Acquired in the Absence of Due Negotiation; Effect of Diversion; Seller's Stoppage of Delivery.

(1) A transferee of a document, whether negotiable or nonnegotiable, to whom the document has been delivered but not duly negotiated, acquires the title and rights which his transferor had or had actual authority to convey.

(2) In the case of a nonnegotiable document, until but not after the bailee receives notification of the transfer, the rights of the transferee may be defeated

   (a) by those creditors of the transferor who could treat the sale as void under Section 2—402; or

   (b) by a buyer from the transferor in ordinary course of business if the bailee has delivered the goods to the buyer or received notification of his rights; or

   (c) as against the bailee by good faith dealings of the bailee with the transferor.

(3) A diversion or other change of shipping instructions by the consignor in a nonnegotiable bill of lading which causes the bailee not to deliver to the consignee defeats the consignee's title to the goods if they have been delivered to a buyer in ordinary course of business and in any event defeats the consignee's rights against the bailee.

(4) Delivery pursuant to a nonnegotiable document may be stopped by a seller under Section 2—705, and subject to the requirement of due notification there provided. A bailee honoring the seller's instructions is entitled to be indemnified by the seller against any resulting loss or expense.

§ 7—505. Indorser Not a Guarantor for Other Parties.

The indorsement of a document of title issued by a bailee does not make the indorser liable for any default by the bailee or by previous indorsers.

§ 7—506. Delivery Without Indorsement: Right to Compel Indorsement.

The transferee of a negotiable document of title has a specifically enforceable right to have his transferor supply any necessary indorsement but the transfer becomes a negotiation only as of the time the indorsement is supplied.

§ 7—507. Warranties on Negotiation or Transfer of Receipt or Bill.

Where a person negotiates or transfers a document of title for value otherwise than as a mere intermediary under the next following section, then unless otherwise agreed he warrants to his immediate purchaser only in addition to any warranty made in selling the goods

   (a) that the document is genuine; and

   (b) that he has no knowledge of any fact which would impair its validity or worth; and

   (c) that his negotiation or transfer is rightful and fully effective with respect to the title to the document and the goods it represents.

§ 7—508. Warranties of Collecting Bank as to Documents.

A collecting bank or other intermediary known to be entrusted with documents on behalf of another or with collection of a draft or other claim against delivery of documents warrants by such delivery of the documents only its own good faith and authority. This rule applies even though the intermediary has purchased or made advances against the claim or draft to be collected.

§ 7—509. Receipt or Bill: When Adequate Compliance With Commercial Contract.

The question whether a document is adequate to fulfill the obligations of a contract for sale or the conditions of a credit is governed by the Articles on Sales (Article 2) and on Letters of Credit (Article 5).

Part 6 Warehouse Receipts and Bills of Lading: Miscellaneous Provisions

§ 7—601. Lost and Missing Documents.

(1) If a document has been lost, stolen or destroyed, a court may order delivery of the goods or issuance of a substitute document and the bailee may without liability to any person comply with such order. If the document was negotiable the claimant must post security approved by the court to indemnify any person who may suffer loss as a result of non-surrender of the document. If the document was not negotiable, such security may be required at the discretion of the court. The court may also in its discretion order payment of the bailee's reasonable costs and counsel fees.

(2) A bailee who without court order delivers goods to a person claiming under a missing negotiable document is liable to any person injured thereby, and if the delivery is not in good faith becomes liable for conversion. Delivery in good faith is not conversion if made in accordance with a filed classification or tariff or, where no classification or tariff is filed, if the claimant posts security with the bailee in an amount at least double the value of the goods at the time of posting to indemnify any person injured by the delivery who files a notice of claim within one year after the delivery.

§ 7—602. Attachment of Goods Covered by a Negotiable Document.

Except where the document was originally issued upon delivery of the goods by a person who had no power to dispose of them, no lien attaches by virtue of any judicial process to goods in the possession of a bailee for which a negotiable document of title is outstanding unless the document be first surrendered to the bailee or its negotiation enjoined, and the bailee shall not be compelled to deliver the goods pursuant to process until the document is surrendered to him or impounded by the court. One who purchases the document for value without notice of the process or injunction takes free of the lien imposed by judicial process.

§ 7—603. Conflicting Claims; Interpleader.

If more than one person claims title or possession of the goods, the bailee is excused from delivery until he has had a reasonable time to ascertain the validity of the adverse claims or to bring an action to compel all claimants to interplead and may compel such interpleader, either in defending an action for nondelivery of the goods, or by original action, whichever is appropriate.

Article 8
INVESTMENT SECURITIES

Part 1 Short Title and General Matters

§ 8—101. Short Title.

This Article shall be known and may be cited as Uniform Commercial Code—Investment Securities.

§ 8—102. Definitions and Index of Definitions.

(1) In this Article, unless the context otherwise requires:

(a) A "certificated security" is a share, participation, or other interest in property of or an enterprise of the issuer or an obligation of the issuer which is

(i) represented by an instrument issued in bearer or registered form;

(ii) of a type commonly dealt in on securities exchanges or markets or commonly recognized in any area in which it is issued or dealt in as a medium for investment; and

(iii) either one of a class or series or by its terms divisible into a class or series of shares, participations, interests, or obligations.

(b) An "uncertificated security" is a share, participation, or other interest in property or an enterprise of the issuer or an obligation of the issuer which is

(i) not represented by an instrument and the transfer of which is registered upon books maintained for that purpose by or on behalf of the issuer;

(ii) of a type commonly dealt in on securities exchanges or markets; and

(iii) either one of a class or series or by its terms divisible into a class or series of shares, participations, interests, or obligations.

(c) A "security" is either a certificated or an uncertificated security. If a security is certificated, the terms "security" and "certificated security" may mean either the intangible interest, the instrument representing that interest, or both, as the context requires. A writing that is a certificated security is governed by this Article and not by Article 3, even though it also meets the requirements of that Article. This Article does not apply to money. If a certificated security has been retained by or surrendered to the issuer or its transfer agent for reasons other than registration of transfer, other temporary purpose, payment, exchange, or acquisition by the issuer, that security shall be treated as an uncertificated security for purposes of this Article.

(d) A certificated security is in "registered form" if

(i) it specifies a person entitled to the security or the rights it represents; and

(ii) its transfer may be registered upon books maintained for that purpose by or on behalf of the issuer, or the security so states.

(e) A certificated security is in "bearer form" if it runs to bearer according to its terms and not by reason of any indorsement.

(2) A "subsequent purchaser" is a person who takes other than by original issue.

(3) A "clearing corporation" is a corporation registered as a "clearing agency" under the federal securities laws or a corporation:

(a) at least 90 percent of whose capital stock is held by or for one or more organizations, none of which, other than a national securities exchange or association, holds in excess of 20 percent of the capital stock of the corporation, and each of which is

(i) subject to supervision or regulation pursuant to the provisions of federal or state banking laws or state insurance laws,

(ii) a broker or dealer or investment company registered under the federal securities laws, or

(iii) a national securities exchange or association registered under the federal securities laws; and

(b) any remaining capital stock of which is held by individuals who have purchased it at or prior to the time of their taking office as directors of the corporation and who have purchased only so much of the capital stock as is necessary to permit them to qualify as directors.

(4) A "custodian bank" is a bank or trust company that is supervised and examined by state or federal authority having supervision over banks and is acting as custodian for a clearing corporation.

(5) Other definitions applying to this Article or to specified Parts thereof and the sections in which they appear are:

"Adverse claim". Section 8—302.
"Bona fide purchaser". Section 8—302.

"Broker". Section 8—303.
"Debtor". Section 9—105.
"Financial intermediary". Section 8—313.
"Guarantee of the signature". Section 8—402.
"Initial transaction statement". Section 8—408.
"Instruction". Section 8—308.
"Intermediary bank". Section 4—105.
"Issuer". Section 8—201.
"Overissue". Section 8—104.
"Secured Party". Section 9—105.
"Security Agreement". Section 9—105.

(6) In addition, Article 1 contains general definitions and principles of construction and interpretation applicable throughout this Article.

Amended in 1962, 1973 and 1977.

§ 8—103. **Issuer's Lien.**

A lien upon a security in favor of an issuer thereof is valid against a purchaser only if:

(a) the security is certificated and the right of the issuer to the lien is noted conspicuously thereon; or

(b) the security is uncertificated and a notation of the right of the issuer to the lien is contained in the initial transaction statement sent to the purchaser or, if his interest is transferred to him other than by registration of transfer, pledge, or release, the initial transaction statement sent to the registered owner or the registered pledgee.

Amended in 1977.

§ 8—104. **Effect of Overissue; "Overissue".**

(1) The provisions of this Article which validate a security or compel its issue or reissue do not apply to the extent that validation, issue, or reissue would result in overissue; but if:

(a) an identical security which does not constitute an overissue is reasonably available for purchase, the person entitled to issue or validation may compel the issuer to purchase the security for him and either to deliver a certificated security or to register the transfer of an uncertificated security to him, against surrender of any certificated security he holds; or

(b) a security is not so available for purchase, the person entitled to issue or validation may recover from the issuer the price he or the last purchaser for value paid for it with interest from the date of his demand.

(2) "Overissue" means the issue of securities in excess of the amount the issuer has corporate power to issue.

Amended in 1977.

§ 8—105. **Certificated Securities Negotiable; Statements and Instructions Not Negotiable; Presumptions.**

(1) Certificated securities governed by this Article are negotiable instruments.

(2) Statements (Section 8—408), notices, or the like, sent by the issuer of uncertificated securities and instructions (Section 8—308) are neither negotiable instruments nor certificated securities.

(3) In any action on a security:

(a) unless specifically denied in the pleadings, each signature on a certificated security, in a necessary indorsement, on an initial transaction statement, or on an instruction, is admitted;

(b) if the effectiveness of a signature is put in issue, the burden of establishing it is on the party claiming under the signature, but the signature is presumed to be genuine or authorized;

(c) if signatures on a certificated security are admitted or established, production of the security entitles a holder to recover on it unless the defendant establishes a defense or a defect going to the validity of the security;

(d) if signatures on an initial transaction statement are admitted or established, the facts stated in the statement are presumed to be true as of the time of its issuance; and

(e) after it is shown that a defense or defect exists, the plaintiff has the burden of establishing that he or some person under whom he claims is a person against whom the defense or defect is ineffective (Section 8—202).

Amended in 1977.

§ 8—106. **Applicability.**

The law (including the conflict of laws rules) of the jurisdiction of organization of the issuer governs the validity of a security, the effectiveness of registration by the issuer, and the rights and duties of the issuer with respect to:

(a) registration of transfer of a certificated security;

(b) registration of transfer, pledge, or release of an uncertificated security; and

(c) sending of statements of uncertificated securities.

Amended in 1977.

§ 8—107. **Securities Transferable; Action for Price.**

(1) Unless otherwise agreed and subject to any applicable law or regulation respecting short sales, a person obligated to transfer securities may transfer any certificated security of the specified issue in bearer form or registered in the name of the transferee, or indorsed to him or in blank, or he may transfer an equivalent uncertificated security to the transferee or a person designated by the transferee.

(2) If the buyer fails to pay the price as it comes due under a contract of sale, the seller may recover the price of:

(a) certificated securities accepted by the buyer;

(b) uncertificated securities that have been transferred to the buyer or a person designated by the buyer; and

(c) other securities if efforts at their resale would be unduly burdensome or if there is no readily available market for their resale.

Amended in 1977.

§ 8—108. **Registration of Pledge and Release of Uncertificated Securities.**

A security interest in an uncertificated security may be evidenced by the registration of pledge to the secured party or a person designated by him. There can be no more than one registered pledge of an uncertificated security at any time. The registered owner of an uncertificated security is the person in whose name the security is registered, even if the security is subject to a registered pledge. The rights of a registered pledgee of an uncertificated security under this Article are terminated by the registration of release.

Added in 1977.

Part 2 Issue—Issuer

§ 8—201. **"Issuer"**

(1) With respect to obligations on or defenses to a security, "issuer" includes a person who:

(a) places or authorizes the placing of his name on a certificated security (otherwise than as authenticating trustee, registrar, transfer agent, or the like) to evidence that it represents a share, participation, or other interest in his property or in an enterprise, or to evidence his duty to perform an obligation represented by the certificated security;

(b) creates shares, participations, or other interests in his property or in an enterprise or undertakes obligations, which shares, participations, interests, or obligations are uncertificated securities;

(c) directly or indirectly creates fractional interests in his rights or property, which fractional interests are represented by certificated securities; or

(d) becomes responsible for or in place of any other person described as an issuer in this section.

(2) With respect to obligations on or defenses to a security, a guarantor is an issuer to the extent of his guaranty, whether or not his obligation is noted on a certificated security or on statements of uncertificated securities sent pursuant to Section 8—408.

(3) With respect to registration of transfer, pledge, or release (Part 4 of this Article), "issuer" means a person on whose behalf transfer books are maintained.

Amended in 1977.

§ 8—202. **Issuer's Responsibility and Defenses; Notice of Defect or Defense.**

(1) Even against a purchaser for value and without notice, the terms of a security include:

(a) if the security is certificated, those stated on the security;

(b) if the security is uncertificated, those contained in the initial transaction statement sent to such purchaser or, if his interest is transferred to him other than by registration of transfer, pledge, or release, the initial transaction statement sent to the registered owner or registered pledgee; and

(c) those made part of the security by reference, on the certificated security or in the initial transaction statement, to another instrument, indenture, or document or to a constitution, statute, ordinance, rule, regulation, order or the like, to the extent that the terms referred to do not conflict with the terms stated on the certificated security or contained in the statement. A reference under this paragraph does not of itself charge a purchaser for value with notice of a defect going to the validity of the security, even though the certificated security or statement expressly states that a person accepting it admits notice.

(2) A certificated security in the hands of a purchaser for value or an uncertificated security as to which an initial transaction statement has been sent to a purchaser for value, other than a security issued by a government or governmental agency or unit, even though issued with a defect going to its validity, is valid with respect to the purchaser if he is without notice of the particular defect unless the defect involves a violation of constitutional provisions, in which case the security is valid with respect to a subsequent purchaser for value and without notice of the defect. This subsection applies to an issuer that is a government or governmental agency or unit only if either there has been substantial compliance with the legal requirements governing the issue or the issuer has received a substantial consideration for the issue as a whole or for the particular security and a stated purpose of the issue is one for which the issuer has power to borrow money or issue the security.

(3) Except as provided in the case of certain unauthorized signatures (Section 8—205), lack of genuineness of a certificated security or an initial transaction statement is a complete defense, even against a purchaser for value and without notice.

(4) All other defenses of the issuer of a certificated or uncertificated security, including nondelivery and conditional delivery of a certificated security, are ineffective against a purchaser for value who has taken without notice of the particular defense.

(5) Nothing in this section shall be construed to affect the right of a party to a "when, as and if issued" or a "when distributed" contract to cancel the contract in the event of a material change in the character of the security that is the subject of the contract or in the plan or arrangement pursuant to which the security is to be issued or distributed.

Amended in 1977.

§ 8—203. **Staleness as Notice of Defects or Defenses.**

(1) After an act or event creating a right to immediate performance of the principal obligation represented by a certificated security or that sets a date on or after which the security is to be presented or surrendered for redemption or exchange, a purchaser is charged with notice of any defect in its issue or defense of the issuer if:

(a) the act or event is one requiring the payment of money, the delivery of certificated securities, the registration of transfer of uncertificated securities, or any of these on presentation or surrender of the certificated security, the funds or securities are available on the date set for payment or exchange, and he takes the security more than one year after that date; and

(b) the act or event is not covered by paragraph (a) and he takes the security more than 2 years after the date set for surrender or presentation or the date on which performance became due.

(2) A call that has been revoked is not within subsection (1).

Amended in 1977.

§ 8—204. **Effect of Issuer's Restrictions on Transfer.**

A restriction on transfer of a security imposed by the issuer, even if otherwise lawful, is ineffective against any person without actual knowledge of it unless:

(a) the security is certificated and the restriction is noted conspicuously thereon; or

(b) the security is uncertificated and a notation of the restriction is contained in the initial transaction statement sent to the person or, if his interest is transferred to him other than by registration of transfer, pledge, or release, the initial transaction statement sent to the registered owner or the registered pledgee.

Amended in 1977.

§ 8—205. Effect of Unauthorized Signature on Certificated Security or Initial Transaction Statement.

An unauthorized signature placed on a certificated security prior to or in the course of issue or placed on an initial transaction statement is ineffective, but the signature is effective in favor of a purchaser for value of the certificated security or a purchaser for value of an uncertificated security to whom the initial transaction statement has been sent, if the purchaser is without notice of the lack of authority and the signing has been done by:

(a) an authenticating trustee, registrar, transfer agent, or other person entrusted by the issuer with the signing of the security, of similar securities, or of initial transaction statements or the immediate preparation for signing of any of them; or

(b) an employee of the issuer, or of any of the foregoing, entrusted with responsible handling of the security or initial transaction statement.

Amended in 1977.

§ 8—206. Completion or Alteration of Certificated Security or Initial Transaction Statement.

(1) If a certificated security contains the signatures necessary to its issue or transfer but is incomplete in any other respect:

(a) any person may complete it by filling in the blanks as authorized; and

(b) even though the blanks are incorrectly filled in, the security as completed is enforceable by a purchaser who took it for value and without notice of the incorrectness.

(2) A complete certificated security that has been improperly altered, even though fraudulently, remains enforceable, but only according to its original terms.

(3) If an initial transaction statement contains the signatures necessary to its validity, but is incomplete in any other respect:

(a) any person may complete it by filling in the blanks as authorized; and

(b) even though the blanks are incorrectly filled in, the statement as completed is effective in favor of the person to whom it is sent if he purchased the security referred to therein for value and without notice of the incorrectness.

(4) A complete initial transaction statement that has been improperly altered, even though fraudulently, is effective in favor of a purchaser to whom it has been sent, but only according to its original terms.

Amended in 1977.

§ 8—207. Rights and Duties of Issuer With Respect to Registered Owners and Registered Pledgees.

(1) Prior to due presentment for registration of transfer of a certificated security in registered form, the issuer or indenture trustee may treat the registered owner as the person exclusively entitled to vote, to receive notifications, and otherwise to exercise all the rights and powers of an owner.

(2) Subject to the provisions of subsections (3), (4), and (6), the issuer or indenture trustee may treat the registered owner of an uncertificated security as the person exclusively entitled to vote, to receive notifications, and otherwise to exercise all the rights and powers of an owner.

(3) The registered owner of an uncertificated security that is subject to a registered pledge is not entitled to registration of transfer prior to the due presentment to the issuer of a release instruction. The exercise of conversion rights with respect to a convertible uncertificated security is a transfer within the meaning of this section.

(4) Upon due presentment of a transfer instruction from the registered pledgee of an uncertificated security, the issuer shall:

(a) register the transfer of the security to the new owner free of pledge, if the instruction specifies a new owner (who may be the registered pledgee) and does not specify a pledgee;

(b) register the transfer of the security to the new owner subject to the interest of the existing pledgee, if the instruction specifies a new owner and the existing pledgee; or

(c) register the release of the security from the existing pledge and register the pledge of the security to the other pledgee, if the instruction specifies the existing owner and another pledgee.

(5) Continuity of perfection of a security interest is not broken by registration of transfer under subsection (4)(b) or by registration of release and pledge under subsection (4)(c), if the security interest is assigned.

(6) If an uncertificated security is subject to a registered pledge:

(a) any uncertificated securities issued in exchange for or distributed with respect to the pledged security shall be registered subject to the pledge;

(b) any certificated securities issued in exchange for or distributed with respect to the pledged security shall be delivered to the registered pledgee; and

(c) any money paid in exchange for or in redemption of part or all of the security shall be paid to the registered pledgee.

(7) Nothing in this Article shall be construed to affect the liability of the registered owner of a security for calls, assessments, or the like.

Amended in 1977.

§ 8—208. Effect of Signature of Authenticating Trustee, Registrar, or Transfer Agent.

(1) A person placing his signature upon a certificated security or an initial transaction statement as authenticating trustee, registrar, transfer agent, or the like, warrants to a purchaser for value of the certificated security or a purchaser for value of an uncertificated security to whom the initial transaction statement has been sent, if the purchaser is without notice of the particular defect, that:

(a) the certificated security or initial transaction statement is genuine;

(b) his own participation in the issue or registration of the transfer, pledge, or release of the security is within his capacity and within the scope of the authority received by him from the issuer; and

(c) he has reasonable grounds to believe the security is in the form and within the amount the issuer is authorized to issue.

(2) Unless otherwise agreed, a person by so placing his signature does not assume responsibility for the validity of the security in other respects.

Amended in 1962 and 1977.

Part 3 Transfer

§ 8—301. Rights Acquired by Purchaser.

(1) Upon transfer of a security to a purchaser (Section 8—313), the purchaser acquires the rights in the security which his transferor had or had actual authority to convey unless the purchaser's rights are limited by Section 8—302(4).

(2) A transferee of a limited interest acquires rights only to the extent of the interest transferred. The creation or release of a security interest in a security is the transfer of a limited interest in that security.

Amended in 1977.

§ 8—302. "Bona Fide Purchaser"; "Adverse Claim"; Title Acquired by Bona Fide Purchaser.

(1) A "bona fide purchaser" is a purchaser for value in good faith and without notice of any adverse claim:

(a) who takes delivery of a certificated security in bearer form or in registered form, issued or indorsed to him or in blank;

(b) to whom the transfer, pledge, or release of an uncertificated security is registered on the books of the issuer; or

(c) to whom a security is transferred under the provisions of paragraph (c), (d)(i), or (g) of Section 8—313(1).

(2) "Adverse claim" includes a claim that a transfer was or would be wrongful or that a particular adverse person is the owner of or has an interest in the security.

(3) A bona fide purchaser in addition to acquiring the rights of a purchaser (Section 8—301) also acquires his interest in the security free of any adverse claim.

(4) Notwithstanding Section 8—301(1), the transferee of a particular certificated security who has been a party to any fraud or illegality affecting the security, or who as a prior holder of that certificated security had notice of an adverse claim, cannot improve his position by taking from a bona fide purchaser.

Amended in 1977.

§ 8—303. "Broker".

"Broker" means a person engaged for all or part of his time in the business of buying and selling securities, who in the transaction concerned acts for, buys a security from, or sells a security to, a customer. Nothing in this Article determines the capacity in which a person acts for purposes of any other statute or rule to which the person is subject.

§ 8—304. Notice to Purchaser of Adverse Claims.

(1) A purchaser (including a broker for the seller or buyer, but excluding an intermediary bank) of a certificated security is charged with notice of adverse claims if:

(a) the security, whether in bearer or registered form, has been indorsed "for collection" or "for surrender" or for some other purpose not involving transfer; or

(b) the security is in bearer form and has on it an unambiguous statement that it is the property of a person other than the transferor. The mere writing of a name on a security is not such a statement.

(2) A purchaser (including a broker for the seller or buyer, but excluding an intermediary bank) to whom the transfer, pledge, or release of an uncertificated security is registered is charged with notice of adverse claims as to which the issuer has a duty under Section 8—403(4) at the time of registration and which are noted in the initial transaction statement sent to the purchaser

or, if his interest is transferred to him other than by registration of transfer, pledge, or release, the initial transaction statement sent to the registered owner or the registered pledgee.

(3) The fact that the purchaser (including a broker for the seller or buyer) of a certificated or uncertificated security has notice that the security is held for a third person or is registered in the name of or indorsed by a fiduciary does not create a duty of inquiry into the rightfulness of the transfer or constitute constructive notice of adverse claims. However, if the purchaser (excluding an intermediary bank) has knowledge that the proceeds are being used or that the transaction is for the individual benefit of the fiduciary or otherwise in breach of duty, the purchaser is charged with notice of adverse claims.

Amended in 1977.

§ 8—305. **Staleness as Notice of Adverse Claims.**

An act or event that creates a right to immediate performance of the principal obligation represented by a certificated security or sets a date on or after which a certificated security is to be presented or surrendered for redemption or exchange does not itself constitute any notice of adverse claims except in the case of a transfer:

(a) after one year from any date set for presentment or surrender for redemption or exchange; or

(b) after 6 months from any date set for payment of money against presentation or surrender of the security if funds are available for payment on that date.

Amended in 1977.

§ 8—306. **Warranties on Presentment and Transfer of Certificated Securities; Warranties of Originators of Instructions.**

(1) A person who presents a certificated security for registration of transfer or for payment or exchange warrants to the issuer that he is entitled to the registration, payment, or exchange. But, a purchaser for value and without notice of adverse claims who receives a new, reissued, or re-registered certificated security on registration of transfer or receives an initial transaction statement confirming the registration of transfer of an equivalent uncertificated security to him warrants only that he has no knowledge of any unauthorized signature (Section 8—311) in a necessary indorsement.

(2) A person by transferring a certificated security to a purchaser for value warrants only that:

(a) his transfer is effective and rightful;

(b) the security is genuine and has not been materially altered; and

(c) he knows of no fact which might impair the validity of the security.

(3) If a certificated security is delivered by an intermediary known to be entrusted with delivery of the security on behalf of another or with collection of a draft or other claim against delivery, the intermediary by delivery warrants only his own good faith and authority, even though he has purchased or made advances against the claim to be collected against the delivery.

(4) A pledgee or other holder for security who redelivers a certificated security received, or after payment and on order of the debtor delivers that security to a third person, makes only the warranties of an intermediary under subsection (3).

(5) A person who originates an instruction warrants to the issuer that:

(a) he is an appropriate person to originate the instruction; and

(b) at the time the instruction is presented to the issuer he will be entitled to the registration of transfer, pledge, or release.

(6) A person who originates an instruction warrants to any person specially guaranteeing his signature (subsection 8—312(3)) that:

(a) he is an appropriate person to originate the instruction; and

(b) at the time the instruction is presented to the issuer

(i) he will be entitled to the registration of transfer, pledge, or release; and

(ii) the transfer, pledge, or release requested in the instruction will be registered by the issuer free from all liens, security interests, restrictions, and claims other than those specified in the instruction.

(7) A person who originates an instruction warrants to a purchaser for value and to any person guaranteeing the instruction (Section 8—312(6)) that:

(a) he is an appropriate person to originate the instruction;

(b) the uncertificated security referred to therein is valid; and

(c) at the time the instruction is presented to the issuer

(i) the transferor will be entitled to the registration of transfer, pledge, or release;

(ii) the transfer, pledge, or release requested in the instruction will be registered by the issuer free from all liens, security interests, restrictions, and claims other than those specified in the instruction; and

(iii) the requested transfer, pledge, or release will be rightful.

(8) If a secured party is the registered pledgee or the registered owner of an uncertificated security, a person who originates an instruction of release or transfer to the debtor or, after payment and on order of the debtor, a transfer instruction to a third person, warrants to the debtor or the third person only that he is an appropriate person to originate the instruction and, at the time the instruction is presented to the issuer, the transferor will be entitled to the registration of release or transfer. If a transfer instruction to a third person who is a purchaser for value is originated on order of the debtor, the debtor makes to the purchaser the warranties of paragraphs (b), (c)(ii) and (c)(iii) of subsection (7).

(9) A person who transfers an uncertificated security to a purchaser for value and does not originate an instruction in connection with the transfer warrants only that:

(a) his transfer is effective and rightful; and

(b) the uncertificated security is valid.

(10) A broker gives to his customer and to the issuer and a purchaser the applicable warranties provided in this section and has the rights and privileges of a purchaser under this section. The warranties of and in favor of the broker, acting as an agent are in addition to applicable warranties given by and in favor of his customer.

Amended in 1962 and 1977.

§ 8—307. Effect of Delivery Without Indorsement; Right to Compel Indorsement.

If a certificated security in registered form has been delivered to a purchaser without a necessary indorsement he may become a bona fide purchaser only as of the time the indorsement is supplied; but against the transferor, the transfer is complete upon delivery and the purchaser has a specifically enforceable right to have any necessary indorsement supplied.

Amended in 1977.

§ 8—308. Indorsements; Instructions.

(1) An indorsement of a certificated security in registered form is made when an appropriate person signs on it or on a separate document an assignment or transfer of the security or a power to assign or transfer it or his signature is written without more upon the back of the security.

(2) An indorsement may be in blank or special. An indorsement in blank includes an indorsement to bearer. A special indorsement specifies to whom the security is to be transferred, or who has power to transfer it. A holder may convert a blank indorsement into a special indorsement.

(3) An indorsement purporting to be only of part of a certificated security representing units intended by the issuer to be separately transferable is effective to the extent of the indorsement.

(4) An "instruction" is an order to the issuer of an uncertificated security requesting that the transfer, pledge, or release from pledge of the uncertificated security specified therein be registered.

(5) An instruction originated by an appropriate person is:

(a) a writing signed by an appropriate person; or

(b) a communication to the issuer in any form agreed upon in a writing signed by the issuer and an appropriate person.

If an instruction has been originated by an appropriate person but is incomplete in any other respect, any person may complete it as authorized and the issuer may rely on it as completed even though it has been completed incorrectly.

(6) "An appropriate person" in subsection (1) means the person specified by the certificated security or by special indorsement to be entitled to the security.

(7) "An appropriate person" in subsection (5) means:

(a) for an instruction to transfer or pledge an uncertificated security which is then not subject to a registered pledge, the registered owner; or

(b) for an instruction to transfer or release an uncertificated security which is then subject to a registered pledge, the registered pledgee.

(8) In addition to the persons designated in subsections (6) and (7), "an appropriate person" in subsections (1) and (5) includes:

(a) if the person designated is described as a fiduciary but is no longer serving in the described capacity, either that person or his successor;

(b) if the persons designated are described as more than one person as fiduciaries and one or more are no longer serving in the described capacity, the remaining fiduciary or fiduciaries, whether or not a successor has been appointed or qualified;

(c) if the person designated is an individual and is without capacity to act by virtue of death, incompetence, infancy, or otherwise, his executor, administrator, guardian, or like fiduciary;

(d) if the persons designated are described as more than one person as tenants by the entirety or with right of survivorship and by reason of death all cannot sign, the survivor or survivors;

(e) a person having power to sign under applicable law or controlling instrument; and

(f) to the extent that the person designated or any of the foregoing persons may act through an agent, his authorized agent.

(9) Unless otherwise agreed, the indorser of a certificated security by his indorsement or the originator of an instruction by his origination assumes no obligation that the security will be honored by the issuer but only the obligations provided in Section 8—306.

(10) Whether the person signing is appropriate is determined as of the date of signing and an indorsement made by or an instruction originated by him does not become unauthorized for the purposes of this Article by virtue of any subsequent change of circumstances.

(11) Failure of a fiduciary to comply with a controlling instrument or with the law of the state having jurisdiction of the fiduciary relationship, including any law requiring the fiduciary to obtain court approval of the transfer, pledge, or release, does not render his indorsement or an instruction originated by him unauthorized for the purposes of this Article.

Amended in 1962 and 1977.

§ 8—309. Effect of Indorsement Without Delivery.

An indorsement of a certificated security, whether special or in blank, does not constitute a transfer until delivery of the certificated security on which it appears or, if the indorsement is on a separate document, until delivery of both the document and the certificated security.

Amended in 1977.

§ 8—310. Indorsement of Certificated Security in Bearer Form.

An indorsement of a certificated security in bearer form may give notice of adverse claims (Section 8—304) but does not otherwise affect any right to registration the holder possesses.

Amended in 1977.

§ 8—311. Effect of Unauthorized Indorsement or Instruction.

Unless the owner or pledgee has ratified an unauthorized indorsement or instruction or is otherwise precluded from asserting its ineffectiveness:

(a) he may assert its ineffectiveness against the issuer or any purchaser, other than a purchaser for value and without notice of adverse claims, who has in good faith received a new, reissued, or re-registered certificated security on registration of transfer or received an initial transaction statement confirming the registration of transfer, pledge, or release of an equivalent uncertificated security to him; and

(b) an issuer who registers the transfer of a certificated security upon the unauthorized indorsement or who registers the transfer, pledge, or release of an uncertificated security upon the unauthorized instruction is subject to liability for improper registration (Section 8—404).

Amended in 1977.

§ 8—312. Effect of Guaranteeing Signature, Indorsement or Instruction.

(1) Any person guaranteeing a signature of an indorser of a certificated security warrants that at the time of signing:

(a) the signature was genuine;

(b) the signer was an appropriate person to indorse (Section 8—308); and

(c) the signer had legal capacity to sign.

(2) Any person guaranteeing a signature of the originator of an instruction warrants that at the time of signing:

(a) the signature was genuine;

(b) the signer was an appropriate person to originate the instruction (Section 8—308) if the person specified in the instruction as the registered owner or registered pledgee of the uncertificated security was, in fact, the registered owner or registered pledgee of the security, as to which fact the signature guarantor makes no warranty;

(c) the signer had legal capacity to sign; and

(d) the taxpayer identification number, if any, appearing on the instruction as that of the registered owner or registered pledgee was the taxpayer identification number of the signer or of the owner or pledgee for whom the signer was acting.

(3) Any person specially guaranteeing the signature of the originator of an instruction makes not only the warranties of a signature guarantor (subsection (2)) but also warrants that at the time the instruction is presented to the issuer:

(a) the person specified in the instruction as the registered owner or registered pledgee of the uncertificated security will be the registered owner or registered pledgee; and

(b) the transfer, pledge, or release of the uncertificated security requested in the instruction will be registered by the issuer free from all liens, security interests, restrictions, and claims other than those specified in the instruction.

(4) The guarantor under subsections (1) and (2) or the special guarantor under subsection (3) does not otherwise warrant the rightfulness of the particular transfer, pledge, or release.

(5) Any person guaranteeing an indorsement of a certificated security makes not only the warranties of a signature guarantor under subsection (1) but also warrants the rightfulness of the particular transfer in all respects.

(6) Any person guaranteeing an instruction requesting the transfer, pledge, or release of an uncertificated security makes not only the warranties of a special signature guarantor under subsection (3) but also warrants the rightfulness of the particular transfer, pledge, or release in all respects.

(7) No issuer may require a special guarantee of signature (subsection (3)), a guarantee of indorsement (subsection (5)), or a guarantee of instruction (subsection (6)) as a condition to registration of transfer, pledge, or release.

(8) The foregoing warranties are made to any person taking or dealing with the security in reliance on the guarantee, and the guarantor is liable to the person for any loss resulting from breach of the warranties.

Amended in 1977.

§ 8—313. When Transfer to Purchaser Occurs; Financial Intermediary as Bona Fide Purchaser; "Financial Intermediary".

(1) Transfer of a security or a limited interest (including a security interest) therein to a purchaser occurs only:

(a) at the time he or a person designated by him acquires possession of a certificated security;

(b) at the time the transfer, pledge, or release of an uncertificated security is registered to him or a person designated by him;

(c) at the time his financial intermediary acquires possession of a certificated security specially indorsed to or issued in the name of the purchaser;

(d) at the time a financial intermediary, not a clearing corporation, sends him confirmation of the purchase and also by book entry or otherwise identifies as belonging to the purchaser

(i) a specific certificated security in the financial intermediary's possession;

(ii) a quantity of securities that constitute or are part of a fungible bulk of certificated securities in the financial intermediary's possession or of uncertificated securities registered in the name of the financial intermediary; or

(iii) a quantity of securities that constitute or are part of a fungible bulk of securities shown on the account of the financial intermediary on the books of another financial intermediary;

(e) with respect to an identified certificated security to be delivered while still in the possession of a third person, not a financial intermediary, at the time that person acknowledges that he holds for the purchaser;

(f) with respect to a specific uncertificated security the pledge or transfer of which has been registered to a third person, not a financial intermediary, at the time that person acknowledges that he holds for the purchaser;

(g) at the time appropriate entries to the account of the purchaser or a person designated by him on the books of a clearing corporation are made under Section 8—320;

(h) with respect to the transfer of a security interest where the debtor has signed a security agreement containing a description of the security, at the time a written notification, which, in the case of the creation of the security interest, is signed by the debtor (which may be a copy of the security agreement) or which, in the case of the release or assignment of the security interest created pursuant to this paragraph, is signed by the secured party, is received by

(i) a financial intermediary on whose books the interest of the transferor in the security appears;

(ii) a third person, not a financial intermediary, in possession of the security, if it is certificated;

(iii) a third person, not a financial intermediary, who is the registered owner of the security, if it is uncertificated and not subject to a registered pledge; or

(iv) a third person, not a financial intermediary, who is the registered pledgee of the security, if it is uncertificated and subject to a registered pledge;

(i) with respect to the transfer of a security interest where the transferor has signed a security agreement containing a description of the security, at the time new value is given by the secured party; or

(j) with respect to the transfer of a security interest where the secured party is a financial intermediary and the security has already been transferred to the financial intermediary under paragraphs (a), (b), (c), (d), or (g), at the time the transferor has signed a security agreement containing a description of the security and value is given by the secured party.

(2) The purchaser is the owner of a security held for him by a financial intermediary, but cannot be a bona fide purchaser of a security so held except in the circumstances specified in paragraphs (c), (d)(i), and (g) of subsection (1). If a security so held is part of a fungible bulk, as in the circumstances specified in paragraphs (d)(ii) and (d)(iii) of subsection (1), the pur-

chaser is the owner of a proportionate property interest in the fungible bulk.

(3) Notice of an adverse claim received by the financial intermediary or by the purchaser after the financial intermediary takes delivery of a certificated security as a holder for value or after the transfer, pledge, or release of an uncertificated security has been registered free of the claim to a financial intermediary who has given value is not effective either as to the financial intermediary or as to the purchaser. However, as between the financial intermediary and the purchaser the purchaser may demand transfer of an equivalent security as to which no notice of adverse claim has been received.

(4) A "financial intermediary" is a bank, broker, clearing corporation, or other person (or the nominee of any of them) which in the ordinary course of its business maintains security accounts for its customers and is acting in that capacity. A financial intermediary may have a security interest in securities held in account for its customer.

Amended in 1962 and 1977.

§ 8—314. Duty to Transfer, When Completed

(1) Unless otherwise agreed, if a sale of a security is made on an exchange or otherwise through brokers:

(a) the selling customer fulfills his duty to transfer at the time he:

(i) places a certificated security in the possession of the selling broker or a person designated by the broker;

(ii) causes an uncertificated security to be registered in the name of the selling broker or a person designated by the broker;

(iii) if requested, causes an acknowledgment to be made to the selling broker that a certificated or uncertificated security is held for the broker; or

(iv) places in the possession of the selling broker or of a person designated by the broker a transfer instruction for an uncertificated security, providing the issuer does not refuse to register the requested transfer if the instruction is presented to the issuer for registration within 30 days thereafter; and

(b) the selling broker, including a correspondent broker acting for a selling customer, fulfills his duty to transfer at the time he:

(i) places a certificated security in the possession of the buying broker or a person designated by the buying broker;

(ii) causes an uncertificated security to be registered in the name of the buying broker or a person designated by the buying broker;

(iii) places in the possession of the buying broker or of a person designated by the buying broker a transfer instruction for an uncertificated security, providing the issuer does not refuse to register the requested transfer if the instruction is presented to the issuer for registration within 30 days thereafter; or

(iv) effects clearance of the sale in accordance with the rules of the exchange on which the transaction took place.

(2) Except as provided in this section or unless otherwise agreed, a transferor's duty to transfer a security under a contract of purchase is not fulfilled until he:

(a) places a certificated security in form to be negotiated by the purchaser in the possession of the purchaser or of a person designated by the purchaser;

(b) causes an uncertificated security to be registered in the name of the purchaser or a person designated by the purchaser; or

(c) if the purchaser requests, causes an acknowledgment to be made to the purchaser that a certificated or uncertificated security is held for the purchaser.

(3) Unless made on an exchange, a sale to a broker purchasing for his own account is within subsection (2) and not within subsection (1).

Amended in 1977.

§ 8—315. Action Against Transferee Based Upon Wrongful Transfer

(1) Any person against whom the transfer of a security is wrongful for any reason, including his incapacity, as against anyone except a bona fide purchaser, may:

(a) reclaim possession of the certificated security wrongfully transferred;

(b) obtain possession of any new certificated security representing all or part of the same rights;

(c) compel the origination of an instruction to transfer to him or a person designated by him an uncertificated security constituting all or part of the same rights; or

(d) have damages.

(2) If the transfer is wrongful because of an unauthorized indorsement of a certificated security, the owner may also reclaim or obtain possession of the security or a new certificated security, even from a bona fide purchaser, if the ineffectiveness of the purported indorsement can be asserted against him under the provisions of this Article on unauthorized indorsements (Section 8—311).

(3) The right to obtain or reclaim possession of a certificated security or to compel the origination of a transfer instruction may be specifically enforced and the transfer of a certificated or uncertificated security enjoined and a certificated security impounded pending the litigation.

Amended in 1977.

§ 8—316. Purchaser's Right to Requisites for Registration of Transfer, Pledge, or Release on Books

Unless otherwise agreed, the transferor of a certificated security or the transferor, pledgor, or pledgee of an uncertificated security on due demand must supply his purchaser with any proof of his authority to transfer, pledge, or release or with any other requisite necessary to obtain registration of the transfer, pledge, or release of the security; but if the transfer, pledge, or release is not for value, a transferor, pledgor, or pledgee need not do so unless the purchaser furnishes the necessary expenses. Failure within a reasonable time to comply with a demand made gives the purchaser the right to reject or rescind the transfer, pledge, or release.

Amended in 1977.

§ 8—317. Creditors' Rights

(1) Subject to the exceptions in subsections (3) and (4), no attachment or levy upon a certificated security or any share or other interest represented thereby which is outstanding is valid until the security is actually seized by the officer making the attachment or levy, but a certificated security which has been surrendered to the issuer may be reached by a creditor by legal process at the issuer's chief executive office in the United States.

(2) An uncertificated security registered in the name of the debtor may not be reached by a creditor except by legal process at the issuer's chief executive office in the United States.

(3) The interest of a debtor in a certificated security that is in the possession of a secured party not a financial intermediary or in an uncertificated security registered in the name of a secured party not a financial intermediary (or in the name of a nominee of the secured party) may be reached by a creditor by legal process upon the secured party.

(4) The interest of a debtor in a certificated security that is in the possession of or registered in the name of a financial intermediary or in an uncertificated security registered in the name of a financial intermediary may be reached by a creditor by legal process upon the financial intermediary on whose books the interest of the debtor appears.

(5) Unless otherwise provided by law, a creditor's lien upon the interest of a debtor in a security obtained pursuant to subsection (3) or (4) is not a restraint on the transfer of the security, free of the lien, to a third party for new value; but in the event of a transfer, the lien applies to the proceeds of the transfer in the hands of the secured party or financial intermediary, subject to any claims having priority.

(6) A creditor whose debtor is the owner of a security is entitled to aid from courts of appropriate jurisdiction, by injunction or otherwise, in reaching the security or in satisfying the claim by means allowed at law or in equity in regard to property that cannot readily be reached by ordinary legal process.

Amended in 1977.

§ 8—318. No Conversion by Good Faith Conduct

An agent or bailee who in good faith (including observance of reasonable commercial standards if he is in the business of buying, selling, or otherwise dealing with securities) has received certificated securities and sold, pledged, or delivered them or has sold or caused the transfer or pledge of uncertificated securities over which he had control according to the instructions of his principal, is not liable for conversion or for participation in breach of fiduciary duty although the principal had no right so to deal with the securities.

Amended in 1977.

§ 8—319. Statute of Frauds

A contract for the sale of securities is not enforceable by way of action or defense unless:

(a) there is some writing signed by the party against whom enforcement is sought or by his authorized agent or broker, sufficient to indicate that a contract has been made for sale of a stated quantity of described securities at a defined or stated price;

(b) delivery of a certificated security or transfer instruction has been accepted, or transfer of an uncertificated security has been registered and the transferee has failed to send written objection to the issuer within 10 days after receipt of the initial transaction statement confirming the registration, or payment has been made, but the contract is enforceable under this provision only to the extent of the delivery, registration, or payment;

(c) within a reasonable time a writing in confirmation of the sale or purchase and sufficient against the sender under paragraph (a) has been received by the party against whom enforcement is sought and he has failed to send written objection to its contents within 10 days after its receipt; or

(d) the party against whom enforcement is sought admits in his pleading, testimony, or otherwise in court that a contract was made for the sale of a stated quantity of described securities at a defined or stated price.

Amended in 1977.

§ 8—320. Transfer or Pledge Within Central Depository System

(1) In addition to other methods, a transfer, pledge, or release of a security or any interest therein may be effected by the making of appropriate entries on the books of a clearing corporation reducing the account of the transferor, pledgor, or pledgee and increasing the account of the transferee, pledgee, or pledgor by the amount of the obligation or the number of shares or rights transferred, pledged, or released, if the security is shown on the account of a transferor, pledgor, or pledgee on the books of the clearing corporation; is subject to the control of the clearing corporation; and

   (a) if certificated,

      (i) is in the custody of the clearing corporation, another clearing corporation, a custodian bank, or a nominee of any of them; and

      (ii) is in bearer form or indorsed in blank by an appropriate person or registered in the name of the clearing corporation, a custodian bank, or a nominee of any of them; or

   (b) if uncertificated, is registered in the name of the clearing corporation, another clearing corporation, a custodian bank, or a nominee of any of them.

(2) Under this section entries may be made with respect to like securities or interests therein as a part of a fungible bulk and may refer merely to a quantity of a particular security without reference to the name of the registered owner, certificate or bond number, or the like, and, in appropriate cases, may be on a net basis taking into account other transfers, pledges, or releases of the same security.

(3) A transfer under this section is effective (Section 8—313) and the purchaser acquires the rights of the transferor (Section 8—301). A pledge or release under this section is the transfer of a limited interest. If a pledge or the creation of a security interest is intended, the security interest is perfected at the time when both value is given by the pledgee and the appropriate entries are made (Section 8—321). A transferee or pledgee under this section may be a bona fide purchaser (Section 8—302).

(4) A transfer or pledge under this section is not a registration of transfer under Part 4.

(5) That entries made on the books of the clearing corporation as provided in subsection (1) are not appropriate does not affect the validity or effect of the entries or the liabilities or obligations of the clearing corporation to any person adversely affected thereby.

Added in 1962; amended in 1977.

§ 8—321. Enforceability, Attachment, Perfection and Termination of Security Interests

(1) A security interest in a security is enforceable and can attach only if it is transferred to the secured party or a person designated by him pursuant to a provision of Section 8—313(1).

(2) A security interest so transferred pursuant to agreement by a transferor who has rights in the security to a transferee who has given value is a perfected security interest, but a security interest that has been transferred solely under paragraph (i) of Section 8—313(1) becomes unperfected after 21 days unless, within that time, the requirements for transfer under any other provision of Section 8—313(1) are satisfied.

(3) A security interest in a security is subject to the provisions of Article 9, but:

   (a) no filing is required to perfect the security interest; and

   (b) no written security agreement signed by the debtor is necessary to make the security interest enforceable, except as provided in paragraph (h), (i), or (j) of Section 8—313(1). The secured party has the rights and duties provided under Section 9—207, to the extent they are applicable, whether or not the security is certificated, and, if certificated, whether or not it is in his possession.

(4) Unless otherwise agreed, a security interest in a security is terminated by transfer to the debtor or a person designated by him pursuant to a provision of Section 8—313(1). If a security is thus transferred, the security interest, if not terminated, becomes unperfected unless the security is certificated and is delivered to the debtor for the purpose of ultimate sale or exchange or presentation, collection, renewal, or registration of transfer. In that case, the security interest becomes unperfected after 21 days unless, within that time, the security (or securities for which it has been exchanged) is transferred to the secured party or a person designated by him pursuant to a provision of Section 8—313(1).

Added in 1977.

Part 4 Registration

§ 8—401. Duty of Issuer to Register Transfer, Pledge, or Release

(1) If a certificated security in registered form is presented to the issuer with a request to register transfer or an instruction is presented to the issuer with a request to register transfer, pledge, or release, the issuer shall register the transfer, pledge, or release as requested if:

(a) the security is indorsed or the instruction was originated by the appropriate person or persons (Section 8—308);

(b) reasonable assurance is given that those indorsements or instructions are genuine and effective (Section 8—402);

(c) the issuer has no duty as to adverse claims or has discharged the duty (Section 8—403);

(d) any applicable law relating to the collection of taxes has been complied with; and

(e) the transfer, pledge, or release is in fact rightful or is to a bona fide purchaser.

(2) If an issuer is under a duty to register a transfer, pledge, or release of a security, the issuer is also liable to the person presenting a certificated security or an instruction for registration or his principal for loss resulting from any unreasonable delay in registration or from failure or refusal to register the transfer, pledge, or release.

Amended in 1977.

§ 8—402. **Assurance that Indorsements and Instructions Are Effective**

(1) The issuer may require the following assurance that each necessary indorsement of a certificated security or each instruction (Section 8—308) is genuine and effective:

(a) in all cases, a guarantee of the signature (Section 8—312(1) or (2)) of the person indorsing a certificated security or originating an instruction including, in the case of an instruction, a warranty of the taxpayer identification number or, in the absence thereof, other reasonable assurance of identity;

(b) if the indorsement is made or the instruction is originated by an agent, appropriate assurance of authority to sign;

(c) if the indorsement is made or the instruction is originated by a fiduciary, appropriate evidence of appointment or incumbency;

(d) if there is more than one fiduciary, reasonable assurance that all who are required to sign have done so; and

(e) if the indorsement is made or the instruction is originated by a person not covered by any of the foregoing, assurance appropriate to the case corresponding as nearly as may be to the foregoing.

(2) A "guarantee of the signature" in subsection (1) means a guarantee signed by or on behalf of a person reasonably believed by the issuer to be responsible. The issuer may adopt standards with respect to responsibility if they are not manifestly unreasonable.

(3) "Appropriate evidence of appointment or incumbency" in subsection (1) means:

(a) in the case of a fiduciary appointed or qualified by a court, a certificate issued by or under the direction or supervision of that court or an officer thereof and dated within 60 days before the date of presentation for transfer, pledge, or release; or

(b) in any other case, a copy of a document showing the appointment or a certificate issued by or on behalf of a person reasonably believed by the issuer to be responsible or, in the absence of that document or certificate, other evidence reasonably deemed by the issuer to be appropriate. The issuer may adopt standards with respect to the evidence if they are not manifestly unreasonable. The issuer is not charged with notice of the contents of any document obtained pursuant to this paragraph (b) except to the extent that the contents relate directly to the appointment or incumbency.

(4) The issuer may elect to require reasonable assurance beyond that specified in this section, but if it does so and, for a purpose other than that specified in subsection (3)(b), both requires and obtains a copy of a will, trust, indenture, articles of co-partnership, by-laws, or other controlling instrument, it is charged with notice of all matters contained therein affecting the transfer, pledge, or release.

Amended in 1977.

§ 8—403. **Issuer's Duty as to Adverse Claims**

(1) An issuer to whom a certificated security is presented for registration shall inquire into adverse claims if:

(a) a written notification of an adverse claim is received at a time and in a manner affording the issuer a reasonable opportunity to act on it prior to the issuance of a new, reissued, or re-registered certificated security, and the notification identifies the claimant, the registered owner, and the issue of which the security is a part, and provides an address for communications directed to the claimant; or

(b) the issuer is charged with notice of an adverse claim from a controlling instrument it has elected to require under Section 8—402(4).

(2) The issuer may discharge any duty of inquiry by any reasonable means, including notifying an adverse claimant by registered or certified mail at the address furnished by him or, if there be no such address, at his residence or regular place of business that the certificated security has been presented for registration of transfer by a named person, and that the transfer will be registered unless within 30 days from the date of mailing the notification, either:

(a) an appropriate restraining order, injunction, or other process issues from a court of competent jurisdiction; or

(b) there is filed with the issuer an indemnity bond, sufficient in the issuer's judgment to protect the issuer and any transfer agent, registrar, or other agent of the issuer involved from any loss it or they may suffer by complying with the adverse claim.

(3) Unless an issuer is charged with notice of an adverse claim from a controlling instrument which it has elected to require under Section 8—402(4) or receives notification of an adverse claim under subsection (1), if a certificated security presented for registration is indorsed by the appropriate person or persons the issuer is under no duty to inquire into adverse claims. In particular:

(a) an issuer registering a certificated security in the name of a person who is a fiduciary or who is described as a fiduciary is not bound to inquire into the existence, extent, or correct description of the fiduciary relationship; and thereafter the issuer may assume without inquiry that the newly registered owner continues to be the fiduciary until the issuer receives written notice that the fiduciary is no longer acting as such with respect to the particular security;

(b) an issuer registering transfer on an indorsement by a fiduciary is not bound to inquire whether the transfer is made in compliance with a controlling instrument or with the law of the state having jurisdiction of the fiduciary relationship, including any law requiring the fiduciary to obtain court approval of the transfer; and

(c) the issuer is not charged with notice of the contents of any court record or file or other recorded or unrecorded document even though the document is in its possession and even though the transfer is made on the indorsement of a fiduciary to the fiduciary himself or to his nominee.

(4) An issuer is under no duty as to adverse claims with respect to an uncertificated security except:

(a) claims embodied in a restraining order, injunction, or other legal process served upon the issuer if the process was served at a time and in a manner affording the issuer a reasonable opportunity to act on it in accordance with the requirements of subsection (5);

(b) claims of which the issuer has received a written notification from the registered owner or the registered pledgee if the notification was received at a time and in a manner affording the issuer a reasonable opportunity to act on it in accordance with the requirements of subsection (5);

(c) claims (including restrictions on transfer not imposed by the issuer) to which the registration of transfer to the present registered owner was subject and were so noted in the initial transaction statement sent to him; and

(d) claims as to which an issuer is charged with notice from a controlling instrument it has elected to require under Section 8—402(4).

(5) If the issuer of an uncertificated security is under a duty as to an adverse claim, he discharges that duty by:

(a) including a notation of the claim in any statements sent with respect to the security under Sections 8—408(3), (6), and (7); and

(b) refusing to register the transfer or pledge of the security unless the nature of the claim does not preclude transfer or pledge subject thereto.

(6) If the transfer or pledge of the security is registered subject to an adverse claim, a notation of the claim must be included in the initial transaction statement and all subsequent statements sent to the transferee and pledgee under Section 8—408.

(7) Notwithstanding subsections (4) and (5), if an uncertificated security was subject to a registered pledge at the time the issuer first came under a duty as to a particular adverse claim, the issuer has no duty as to that claim if transfer of the security is requested by the registered pledgee or an appropriate person acting for the registered pledgee unless:

(a) the claim was embodied in legal process which expressly provides otherwise;

(b) the claim was asserted in a written notification from the registered pledgee;

(c) the claim was one as to which the issuer was charged with notice from a controlling instrument it required under Section 8—402(4) in connection with the pledgee's request for transfer; or

(d) the transfer requested is to the registered owner.

Amended in 1977.

§ 8—404. Liability and Non-Liability for Registration

(1) Except as provided in any law relating to the collection of taxes, the issuer is not liable to the owner, pledgee, or any other person suffering loss as a result of the registration of a transfer, pledge, or release of a security if:

(a) there were on or with a certificated security the necessary indorsements or the issuer had received an instruction originated by an appropriate person (Section 8—308); and

(b) the issuer had no duty as to adverse claims or has discharged the duty (Section 8—403).

(2) If an issuer has registered a transfer of a certificated security to a person not entitled to it, the issuer on demand shall deliver a like security to the true owner unless:

   (a) the registration was pursuant to subsection (1);

   (b) the owner is precluded from asserting any claim for registering the transfer under Section 8—405(1); or

   (c) the delivery would result in overissue, in which case the issuer's liability is governed by Section 8—104.

(3) If an issuer has improperly registered a transfer, pledge, or release of an uncertificated security, the issuer on demand from the injured party shall restore the records as to the injured party to the condition that would have obtained if the improper registration had not been made unless:

   (a) the registration was pursuant to subsection (1); or

   (b) the registration would result in overissue, in which case the issuer's liability is governed by Section 8—104.

Amended in 1977.

§ 8—405. Lost, Destroyed, and Stolen Certificated Securities

(1) If a certificated security has been lost, apparently destroyed, or wrongfully taken, and the owner fails to notify the issuer of that fact within a reasonable time after he has notice of it and the issuer registers a transfer of the security before receiving notification, the owner is precluded from asserting against the issuer any claim for registering the transfer under Section 8—404 or any claim to a new security under this section.

(2) If the owner of a certificated security claims that the security has been lost, destroyed, or wrongfully taken, the issuer shall issue a new certificated security or, at the option of the issuer, an equivalent uncertificated security in place of the original security if the owner:

   (a) so requests before the issuer has notice that the security has been acquired by a bona fide purchaser;

   (b) files with the issuer a sufficient indemnity bond; and

   (c) satisfies any other reasonable requirements imposed by the issuer.

(3) If, after the issue of a new certificated or uncertificated security, a bona fide purchaser of the original certificated security presents it for registration of transfer, the issuer shall register the transfer unless registration would result in overissue, in which event the issuer's liability is governed by Section 8—104. In addition to any rights on the indemnity bond, the issuer may recover the new certificated security from the person to whom it was issued or any person taking under him except a bona fide purchaser or may cancel the uncertificated security unless a bona fide purchaser or any person taking under a bona fide purchaser is then the registered owner or registered pledgee thereof.

Amended in 1977.

§ 8—406. Duty of Authenticating Trustee, Transfer Agent, or Registrar

(1) If a person acts as authenticating trustee, transfer agent, registrar, or other agent for an issuer in the registration of transfers of its certificated securities or in the registration of transfers, pledges, and releases of its uncertificated securities, in the issue of new securities, or in the cancellation of surrendered securities:

   (a) he is under a duty to the issuer to exercise good faith and due diligence in performing his functions; and

   (b) with regard to the particular functions he performs, he has the same obligation to the holder or owner of a certificated security or to the owner or pledgee of an uncertificated security and has the same rights and privileges as the issuer has in regard to those functions.

(2) Notice to an authenticating trustee, transfer agent, registrar or other agent is notice to the issuer with respect to the functions performed by the agent.

Amended in 1977.

§ 8—407. Exchangeability of Securities

(1) No issuer is subject to the requirements of this section unless it regularly maintains a system for issuing the class of securities involved under which both certificated and uncertificated securities are regularly issued to the category of owners, which includes the person in whose name the new security is to be registered.

(2) Upon surrender of a certificated security with all necessary indorsements and presentation of a written request by the person surrendering the security, the issuer, if he has no duty as to adverse claims or has discharged the duty (Section 8—403), shall issue to the person or a person designated by him an equivalent uncertificated security subject to all liens, restrictions, and claims that were noted on the certificated security.

(3) Upon receipt of a transfer instruction originated by an appropriate person who so requests, the issuer of an uncertificated security shall cancel the uncertificated security and issue an equivalent certificated security on which must be noted conspicuously any liens and restrictions of the issuer and any adverse claims (as to which the issuer has a duty under Section 8—403(4))

to which the uncertificated security was subject. The certificated security shall be registered in the name of and delivered to:

(a) the registered owner, if the uncertificated security was not subject to a registered pledge; or

(b) the registered pledgee, if the uncertificated security was subject to a registered pledge.

Added in 1977.

§ 8—408. Statements of Uncertificated Securities

(1) Within 2 business days after the transfer of an uncertificated security has been registered, the issuer shall send to the new registered owner and, if the security has been transferred subject to a registered pledge, to the registered pledgee a written statement containing:

(a) a description of the issue of which the uncertificated security is a part;

(b) the number of shares or units transferred;

(c) the name and address and any taxpayer identification number of the new registered owner and, if the security has been transferred subject to a registered pledge, the name and address and any taxpayer identification number of the registered pledgee;

(d) a notation of any liens and restrictions of the issuer and any adverse claims (as to which the issuer has a duty under Section 8—403(4)) to which the uncertificated security is or may be subject at the time of registration or a statement that there are none of those liens, restrictions, or adverse claims; and

(e) the date the transfer was registered.

(2) Within 2 business days after the pledge of an uncertificated security has been registered, the issuer shall send to the registered owner and the registered pledgee a written statement containing:

(a) a description of the issue of which the uncertificated security is a part;

(b) the number of shares or units pledged;

(c) the name and address and any taxpayer identification number of the registered owner and the registered pledgee;

(d) a notation of any liens and restrictions of the issuer and any adverse claims (as to which the issuer has a duty under Section 8—403(4)) to which the uncertificated security is or may be subject at the time of registration or a statement that there are none of those liens, restrictions, or adverse claims; and

(e) the date the pledge was registered.

(3) Within 2 business days after the release from pledge of an uncertificated security has been registered, the issuer shall send to the registered owner and the pledgee whose interest was released a written statement containing:

(a) a description of the issue of which the uncertificated security is a part;

(b) the number of shares or units released from pledge;

(c) the name and address and any taxpayer identification number of the registered owner and the pledgee whose interest was released;

(d) a notation of any liens and restrictions of the issuer and any adverse claims (as to which the issuer has a duty under Section 8—403(4)) to which the uncertificated security is or may be subject at the time of registration or a statement that there are none of those liens, restrictions, or adverse claims; and

(e) the date the release was registered.

(4) An "initial transaction statement" is the statement sent to:

(a) the new registered owner and, if applicable, to the registered pledgee pursuant to subsection (1);

(b) the registered pledgee pursuant to subsection (2); or

(c) the registered owner pursuant to subsection (3).

Each initial transaction statement shall be signed by or on behalf of the issuer and must be identified as "Initial Transaction Statement".

(5) Within 2 business days after the transfer of an uncertificated security has been registered, the issuer shall send to the former registered owner and the former registered pledgee, if any, a written statement containing:

(a) a description of the issue of which the uncertificated security is a part;

(b) the number of shares or units transferred;

(c) the name and address and any taxpayer identification number of the former registered owner and of any former registered pledgee; and

(d) the date the transfer was registered.

(6) At periodic intervals no less frequent than annually and at any time upon the reasonable written request of the registered owner, the issuer shall send to the registered owner of each uncertificated security a dated written statement containing:

(a) a description of the issue of which the uncertificated security is a part;

(b) the name and address and any taxpayer identification number of the registered owner;

(c) the number of shares or units of the uncertificated security registered in the name of the registered owner on the date of the statement;

(d) the name and address and any taxpayer identification number of any registered pledgee and the number of shares or units subject to the pledge; and

(e) a notation of any liens and restrictions of the issuer and any adverse claims (as to which the issuer has a duty under Section 8—403(4)) to which the uncertificated security is or may be subject or a statement that there are none of those liens, restrictions, or adverse claims.

(7) At periodic intervals no less frequent than annually and at any time upon the reasonable written request of the registered pledgee, the issuer shall send to the registered pledgee of each uncertificated security a dated written statement containing:

(a) a description of the issue of which the uncertificated security is a part;

(b) the name and address and any taxpayer identification number of the registered owner;

(c) the name and address and any taxpayer identification number of the registered pledgee;

(d) the number of shares or units subject to the pledge; and

(e) a notation of any liens and restrictions of the issuer and any adverse claims (as to which the issuer has a duty under Section 8—403(4)) to which the uncertificated security is or may be subject or a statement that there are none of those liens, restrictions, or adverse claims.

(8) If the issuer sends the statements described in subsections (6) and (7) at periodic intervals no less frequent than quarterly, the issuer is not obliged to send additional statements upon request unless the owner or pledgee requesting them pays to the issuer the reasonable cost of furnishing them.

(9) Each statement sent pursuant to this section must bear a conspicuous legend reading substantially as follows: "This statement is merely a record of the rights of the addressee as of the time of its issuance. Delivery of this statement, of itself, confers no rights on the recipient. This statement is neither a negotiable instrument nor a security."

Added in 1977.

Article 9
SECURED TRANSACTIONS; SALES OF ACCOUNTS AND CHATTEL PAPER

Note: *The adoption of this Article should be accompanied by the repeal of existing statutes dealing with conditional sales, trust re-*

ceipts, factor's liens where the factor is given a nonpossessory lien, chattel mortgages, crop mortgages, mortgages on railroad equipment, assignment of accounts and generally statutes regulating security interests in personal property.

Where the state has a retail installment selling act or small loan act, that legislation should be carefully examined to determine what changes in those acts are needed to conform them to this Article. This Article primarily sets out rules defining rights of a secured party against persons dealing with the debtor; it does not prescribe regulations and controls which may be necessary to curb abuses arising in the small loan business or in the financing of consumer purchases on credit. Accordingly there is no intention to repeal existing regulatory acts in those fields by enactment or re-enactment of Article 9. See Section 9—203(4) and the Note thereto.

Part 1 Short Title, Applicability and Definitions

§ 9—101. **Short Title.**

This Article shall be known and may be cited as Uniform Commercial Code—Secured Transactions.

§ 9—102. **Policy and Subject Matter of Article.**

(1) Except as otherwise provided in Section 9—104 on excluded transactions, this Article applies

(a) to any transaction (regardless of its form) which is intended to create a security interest in personal property or fixtures including goods, documents, instruments, general intangibles, chattel paper or accounts; and also

(b) to any sale of accounts or chattel paper.

(2) This Article applies to security interests created by contract including pledge, assignment, chattel mortgage, chattel trust, trust deed, factor's lien, equipment trust, conditional sale, trust receipt, other lien or title retention contract and lease or consignment intended as security. This Article does not apply to statutory liens except as provided in Section 9—310.

(3) The application of this Article to a security interest in a secured obligation is not affected by the fact that the obligation is itself secured by a transaction or interest to which this Article does not apply.

§ 9—103. **Perfection of Security Interest in Multiple State Transactions**

(1) Documents, instruments and ordinary goods.

(a) This subsection applies to documents and instruments and to goods other than those covered by a certificate of title described in subsection (2), mobile goods described in subsection (3), and minerals described in subsection (5).

(b) Except as otherwise provided in this subsection, perfection and the effect of perfection or non-perfection of a security interest in collateral are governed by the law of the jurisdiction where the collateral is when the last event occurs on which is based the assertion that the security interest is perfected or unperfected.

(c) If the parties to a transaction creating a purchase money security interest in goods in one jurisdiction understand at the time that the security interest attaches that the goods will be kept in another jurisdiction, then the law of the other jurisdiction governs the perfection and the effect of perfection or non-perfection of the security interest from the time it attaches until thirty days after the debtor receives possession of the goods and thereafter if the goods are taken to the other jurisdiction before the end of the thirty-day period.

(d) When collateral is brought into and kept in this state while subject to a security interest perfected under the law of the jurisdiction from which the collateral was removed, the security interest remains perfected, but if action is required by Part 3 of this Article to perfect the security interest,

> (i) if the action is not taken before the expiration of the period of perfection in the other jurisdiction or the end of four months after the collateral is brought into this state, whichever period first expires, the security interest becomes unperfected at the end of that period and is thereafter deemed to have been unperfected as against a person who became a purchaser after removal;

> (ii) if the action is taken before the expiration of the period specified in subparagraph (i), the security interest continues perfected thereafter;

> (iii) for the purpose of priority over a buyer of consumer goods (subsection (2) of Section 9—307), the period of the effectiveness of a filing in the jurisdiction from which the collateral is removed is governed by the rules with respect to perfection in subparagraphs (i) and (ii).

(2) Certificate of title.

(a) This subsection applies to goods covered by a certificate of title issued under a statute of this state or of another jurisdiction under the law of which indication of a security interest on the certificate is required as a condition of perfection.

(b) Except as otherwise provided in this subsection, perfection and the effect of perfection or non-perfection of the security interest are governed by the law (including the conflict of laws rules) of the jurisdiction issuing the certificate until four months after the goods are removed from that jurisdiction and thereafter until the goods are registered in another jurisdiction, but in any event not beyond surrender of the certificate. After the expiration of that period, the goods are not covered by the certificate of title within the meaning of this section.

(c) Except with respect to the rights of a buyer described in the next paragraph, a security interest, perfected in another jurisdiction otherwise than by notation on a certificate of title, in goods brought into this state and thereafter covered by a certificate of title issued by this state is subject to the rules stated in paragraph (d) of subsection (1).

(d) If goods are brought into this state while a security interest therein is perfected in any manner under the law of the jurisdiction from which the goods are removed and a certificate of title is issued by this state and the certificate does not show that the goods are subject to the security interest or that they may be subject to security interests not shown on the certificate, the security interest is subordinate to the rights of a buyer of the goods who is not in the business of selling goods of that kind to the extent that he gives value and receives delivery of the goods after issuance of the certificate and without knowledge of the security interest.

(3) Accounts, general intangibles and mobile goods.

(a) This subsection applies to accounts (other than an account described in subsection (5) on minerals) and general intangibles (other than uncertificated securities) and to goods which are mobile and which are of a type normally used in more than one jurisdiction, such as motor vehicles, trailers, rolling stock, airplanes, shipping containers, road building and construction machinery and commercial harvesting machinery and the like, if the goods are equipment or are inventory leased or held for lease by the debtor to others, and are not covered by a certificate of title described in subsection (2).

(b) The law (including the conflict of laws rules) of the jurisdiction in which the debtor is located governs the perfection and the effect of perfection or non-perfection of the security interest.

(c) If, however, the debtor is located in a jurisdiction which is not a part of the United States, and which does not provide for perfection of the security interest by filing or recording in that jurisdiction, the law of the jurisdiction in the United States in which the debtor has its major executive office in the United States governs the perfection and the effect of perfection or non-perfection of the security interest through filing. In the alternative, if the debtor is located in a jurisdiction which is not a part of the United States or Canada and the collateral is accounts or general intangibles for money due or to become due, the security interest may be perfected by notification to the account debtor. As used in this paragraph, "United States" includes its territories and possessions and the Commonwealth of Puerto Rico.

(d) A debtor shall be deemed located at his place of business if he has one, at his chief executive office if he has more than one place of business, otherwise at his residence. If, however, the debtor is a foreign air carrier under the Federal Aviation Act of 1958, as amended, it shall be deemed located at the designated office of the agent upon whom service of process may be made on behalf of the foreign air carrier.

(e) A security interest perfected under the law of the jurisdiction of the location of the debtor is perfected until the expiration of four months after a change of the debtor's location to another jurisdiction, or until perfection would have ceased by the law of the first jurisdiction, whichever period first expires. Unless perfected in the new jurisdiction before the end of that period, it becomes unperfected thereafter and is deemed to have been unperfected as against a person who became a purchaser after the change.

(4) Chattel paper.

The rules stated for goods in subsection (1) apply to a possessory security interest in chattel paper. The rules stated for accounts in subsection (3) apply to a nonpossessory security interest in chattel paper, but the security interest may not be perfected by notification to the account debtor.

(5) Minerals.

Perfection and the effect of perfection or non-perfection of a security interest which is created by a debtor who has an interest in minerals or the like (including oil and gas) before extraction and which attaches thereto as extracted, or which attaches to an account resulting from the sale thereof at the wellhead or minehead are governed by the law (including the conflict of laws rules) of the jurisdiction wherein the wellhead or minehead is located.

(6) Uncertificated securities.

The law (including the conflict of laws rules) of the jurisdiction of organization of the issuer governs the perfection and the effect of perfection or non-perfection of a security interest in uncertificated securities.

Amended in 1972 and 1977.

§ 9—104. **Transactions Excluded From Article.**

This Article does not apply

(a) to a security interest subject to any statute of the United States, to the extent that such statute governs the rights of parties to and third parties affected by transactions in particular types of property; or

(b) to a landlord's lien; or

(c) to a lien given by statute or other rule of law for services or materials except as provided in Section 9—310 on priority of such liens; or

(d) to a transfer of a claim for wages, salary or other compensation of an employee; or

(e) to a transfer by a government or governmental subdivision or agency; or

(f) to a sale of accounts or chattel paper as part of a sale of the business out of which they arose, or an assignment of accounts or chattel paper which is for the purpose of collection only, or a transfer of a right to payment under a contract to an assignee who is also to do the performance under the contract or a transfer of a single account to an assignee in whole or partial satisfaction of a preexisting indebtedness; or

(g) to a transfer of an interest in or claim in or under any policy of insurance, except as provided with respect to proceeds (Section 9—306) and priorities in proceeds (Section 9—312); or

(h) to a right represented by a judgment (other than a judgment taken on a right to payment which was collateral); or

(i) to any right of set-off; or

(j) except to the extent that provision is made for fixtures in Section 9—313, to the creation or transfer of an interest in or lien on real estate, including a lease or rents thereunder; or

(k) to a transfer in whole or in part of any claim arising out of tort; or

(l) to a transfer of an interest in any deposit account (subsection (1) of Section 9—105), except as provided with respect to proceeds (Section 9—306) and priorities in proceeds (Section 9—312).

Amended in 1972.

§ 9—105. **Definitions and Index of Definitions**

(1) In this Article unless the context otherwise requires:

(a) "Account debtor" means the person who is obligated on an account, chattel paper or general intangible;

(b) "Chattel paper" means a writing or writings which evidence both a monetary obligation and a security interest in or a lease of specific goods, but a charter or other contract involving the use or hire of a vessel is not chattel paper. When a transaction is evidenced both by such a security agreement or a lease and by an instrument or a series of instruments, the group of writings taken together constitutes chattel paper;

(c) "Collateral" means the property subject to a security interest, and includes accounts and chattel paper which have been sold;

(d) "Debtor" means the person who owes payment or other performance of the obligation secured, whether or not he owns or has rights in the collateral, and includes the seller of accounts or chattel paper. Where the debtor and the owner of the collateral are not the same person, the term "debtor" means the owner of the collateral in any provision of the Article dealing with the collateral, the obligor in any provision dealing with the obligation, and may include both where the context so requires;

(e) "Deposit account" means a demand, time, savings, passbook or like account maintained with a bank, savings and loan association, credit union or like organization, other than an account evidenced by a certificate of deposit;

(f) "Document" means document of title as defined in the general definitions of Article 1 (Section 1—201), and a receipt of the kind described in subsection (2) of Section 7—201;

(g) "Encumbrance" includes real estate mortgages and other liens on real estate and all other rights in real estate that are not ownership interests;

(h) "Goods" includes all things which are movable at the time the security interest attaches or which are fixtures (Section 9—313), but does not include money, documents, instruments, accounts, chattel paper, general intangibles, or minerals or the like (including oil and gas) before extraction. "Goods" also includes standing timber which is to be cut and removed under a conveyance or contract for sale, the unborn young of animals, and growing crops;

(i) "Instrument" means a negotiable instrument (defined in Section 3—104), or a certificated security (defined in Section 8—102) or any other writing which evidences a right to the payment of money and is not itself a security agreement or lease and is of a type which is in ordinary course of business transferred by delivery with any necessary indorsement or assignment;

(j) "Mortgage" means a consensual interest created by a real estate mortgage, a trust deed on real estate, or the like;

(k) An advance is made "pursuant to commitment" if the secured party has bound himself to make it, whether or not a subsequent event of default or other event not within his control has relieved or may relieve him from his obligation;

(*l*) "Security agreement" means an agreement which creates or provides for a security interest;

(m) "Secured party" means a lender, seller or other person in whose favor there is a security interest, including a person to whom accounts or chattel paper have been sold. When the holders of obligations issued under an indenture of trust, equipment trust agreement or the like are represented by a trustee or other person, the representative is the secured party;

(n) "Transmitting utility" means any person primarily engaged in the railroad, street railway or trolley bus business, the electric or electronics communications transmission business, the transmission of goods by pipeline, or the transmission or the production and transmission of electricity, steam, gas or water, or the provision of sewer service.

(2) Other definitions applying to this Article and the sections in which they appear are:
"Account". Section 9—106.
"Attach". Section 9—203.
"Construction mortgage". Section 9—313(1).
"Consumer goods". Section 9—109(1).
"Equipment". Section 9—109(2).
"Farm products". Section 9—109(3).
"Fixture". Section 9—313(1).
"Fixture filing". Section 9—313(1).
"General intangibles". Section 9—106.
"Inventory". Section 9—109(4).
"Lien creditor". Section 9—301(3).
"Proceeds". Section 9—306(1).
"Purchase money security interest". Section 9—107.
"United States". Section 9—103.

(3) The following definitions in other Articles apply to this Article:
"Check". Section 3—104.
"Contract for sale". Section 2—106.
"Holder in due course". Section 3—302.
"Note". Section 3—104.
"Sale". Section 2—106.

(4) In addition Article 1 contains general definitions and principles of construction and interpretation applicable throughout this Article.

Amended in 1966, 1972 and 1977.

§ 9—106. **Definitions: "Account"; "General Intangibles".**

"Account" means any right to payment for goods sold or leased or for services rendered which is not evidenced by an instrument or chattel paper, whether or not it has been earned by performance. "General intangibles" means any personal property (including things in action) other than goods, accounts, chattel paper, documents, instruments, and money. All rights to payment earned or unearned under a charter or other contract involving the use or hire of a vessel and all rights incident to the charter or contract are accounts.

§ 9—107. **Definitions: "Purchase Money Security Interest".**

A security interest is a "purchase money security interest" to the extent that it is

(a) taken or retained by the seller of the collateral to secure all or part of its price; or

(b) taken by a person who by making advances or incurring an obligation gives value to enable the debtor to acquire rights in or the use of collateral if such value is in fact so used.

§ 9—108. **When After-Acquired Collateral Not Security for Antecedent Debt.**

Where a secured party makes an advance, incurs an obligation, releases a perfected security interest, or otherwise gives new value which is to be secured in whole or in part by after-acquired property his security interest in the after-acquired collateral shall be deemed to be taken for new value and not as security for an antecedent debt if the debtor acquires his rights in such collateral either in the ordinary course of his business or under a contract of purchase made pursuant to the security agreement within a reasonable time after new value is given.

§ 9—109. **Classification of Goods; "Consumer Goods"; "Equipment"; "Farm Products"; "Inventory".**

Goods are

(1) "consumer goods" if they are used or bought for use primarily for personal, family or household purposes;

(2) "equipment" if they are used or bought for use primarily in business (including farming or a profession) or by a debtor who is a non-profit organization or a governmental subdivision or agency or if the goods are not included in the definitions of inventory, farm products or consumer goods;

(3) "farm products" if they are crops or livestock or supplies used or produced in farming operations or if they are products of crops or livestock in their unmanufactured states (such as ginned cotton, wool-clip, maple syrup, milk and eggs), and if they are in the possession of a debtor engaged in raising, fattening, grazing or other farming operations. If goods are farm products they are neither equipment nor inventory;

(4) "inventory" if they are held by a person who holds them for sale or lease or to be furnished under contracts of service or if he has so furnished them, or if they are raw materials, work in process or materials used or consumed in a business. Inventory of a person is not to be classified as his equipment.

§ 9—110. **Sufficiency of Description.**

For purposes of this Article any description of personal property or real estate is sufficient whether or not it is specific if it reasonably identifies what is described.

§ 9—111. **Applicability of Bulk Transfer Laws.**

The creation of a security interest is not a bulk transfer under Article 6 (see Section 6—103).

§ 9—112. **Where Collateral Is Not Owned by Debtor.**

Unless otherwise agreed, when a secured party knows that collateral is owned by a person who is not the debtor, the owner of the collateral is entitled to receive from the secured party any surplus under Section 9—502(2) or under Section 9—504(1), and is not liable for the debt or for any deficiency after resale, and he has the same right as the debtor

(a) to receive statements under Section 9—208;

(b) to receive notice of and to object to a secured party's proposal to retain the collateral in satisfaction of the indebtedness under Section 9—505;

(c) to redeem the collateral under Section 9—506;

(d) to obtain injunctive or other relief under Section 9—507(1); and

(e) to recover losses caused to him under Section 9—208(2).

§ 9—113. **Security Interests Arising Under Article on Sales or Under Article on Leases.**

A security interest arising solely under the Article on Sales (Article 2) or the Article on Leases is subject to the provisions of this Article except that to the extent that and so long as the debtor does not have or does not lawfully obtain possession of the goods

(a) no security agreement is necessary to make the security interest enforceable; and

(b) no filing is required to perfect the security interest; and

(c) the rights of the secured party on default by the debtor are governed (i) by the Article on Sales (Article 2) in the case of a security interest arising solely under such Article or (ii) by the Article on Leases (Article 2A) in the case of a security interest arising solely under such Article.

§ 9—114. **Consignment.**

(1) A person who delivers goods under a consignment which is not a security interest and who would be required to file under this Article by paragraph (3)(c) of Section 2—326 has priority over a secured party who

is or becomes a creditor of the consignee and who would have a perfected security interest in the goods if they were the property of the consignee, and also has priority with respect to identifiable cash proceeds received on or before delivery of the goods to a buyer, if

(a) the consignor complies with the filing provision of the Article on Sales with respect to consignments (paragraph (3)(c) of Section 2—326) before the consignee receives possession of the goods; and

(b) the consignor gives notification in writing to the holder of the security interest if the holder has filed a financing statement covering the same types of goods before the date of the filing made by the consignor; and

(c) the holder of the security interest receives the notification within five years before the consignee receives possession of the goods; and

(d) the notification states that the consignor expects to deliver goods on consignment to the consignee, describing the goods by item or type.

(2) In the case of a consignment which is not a security interest and in which the requirements of the preceding subsection have not been met, a person who delivers goods to another is subordinate to a person who would have a perfected security interest in the goods if they were the property of the debtor.

Part 2 Validity of Security Agreement and Rights of Parties Thereto

§ 9—201. General Validity of Security Agreement.

Except as otherwise provided by this Act a security agreement is effective according to its terms between the parties, against purchasers of the collateral and against creditors. Nothing in this Article validates any charge or practice illegal under any statute or regulation thereunder governing usury, small loans, retail installment sales, or the like, or extends the application of any such statute or regulation to any transaction not otherwise subject thereto.

§ 9—202. Title to Collateral Immaterial.

Each provision of this Article with regard to rights, obligations and remedies applies whether title to collateral is in the secured party or in the debtor.

§ 9—203. Attachment and Enforceability of Security Interest; Proceeds; Formal Requisites

(1) Subject to the provisions of Section 4—208 on the security interest of a collecting bank, Section 8—321 on security interests in securities and Section 9—113 on a security interest arising under the Article on Sales, a security interest is not enforceable against the debtor

or third parties with respect to the collateral and does not attach unless:

(a) the collateral is in the possession of the secured party pursuant to agreement, or the debtor has signed a security agreement which contains a description of the collateral and in addition, when the security interest covers crops growing or to be grown or timber to be cut, a description of the land concerned;

(b) value has been given; and

(c) the debtor has rights in the collateral.

(2) A security interest attaches when it becomes enforceable against the debtor with respect to the collateral. Attachment occurs as soon as all of the events specified in subsection (1) have taken place unless explicit agreement postpones the time of attaching.

(3) Unless otherwise agreed a security agreement gives the secured party the rights to proceeds provided by Section 9—306.

(4) A transaction, although subject to this Article, is also subject to . . . .*, and in the case of conflict between the provisions of this Article and any such statute, the provisions of such statute control. Failure to comply with any applicable statute has only the effect which is specified therein.

Amended in 1972 and 1977.

Note: *At * in subsection (4) insert reference to any local statute regulating small loans, retail installment sales and the like.*

The foregoing subsection (4) is designed to make it clear that certain transactions, although subject to this Article, must also comply with other applicable legislation.

This Article is designed to regulate all the "security" aspects of transactions within its scope. There is, however, much regulatory legislation, particularly in the consumer field, which supplements this Article and should not be repealed by its enactment. Examples are small loan acts, retail installment selling acts and the like. Such acts may provide for licensing and rate regulation and may prescribe particular forms of contract. Such provisions should remain in force despite the enactment of this Article. On the other hand if a retail installment selling act contains provisions on filing, rights on default, etc., such provisions should be repealed as inconsistent with this Article except that inconsistent provisions as to deficiencies, penalties, etc., in the Uniform Consumer Credit Code and other recent related legislation should remain because those statutes were drafted after the substantial enactment of the Article and with the intention of modifying certain provisions of this Article as to consumer credit.

§ 9—204. After-Acquired Property; Future Advances.

(1) Except as provided in subsection (2), a security agreement may provide that any or all obligations covered by the security agreement are to be secured by after-acquired collateral.

(2) No security interest attaches under an after-acquired property clause to consumer goods other than

accessions (Section 9—314) when given as additional security unless the debtor acquires rights in them within ten days after the secured party gives value.

(3) Obligations covered by a security agreement may include future advances or other value whether or not the advances or value are given pursuant to commitment (subsection (1) of Section 9—105).

§ 9—205. Use or Disposition of Collateral Without Accounting Permissible.

A security interest is not invalid or fraudulent against creditors by reason of liberty in the debtor to use, commingle or dispose of all or part of the collateral (including returned or repossessed goods) or to collect or compromise accounts or chattel paper, or to accept the return of goods or make repossessions, or to use, commingle or dispose of proceeds, or by reason of the failure of the secured party to require the debtor to account for proceeds or replace collateral. This section does not relax the requirements of possession where perfection of a security interest depends upon possession of the collateral by the secured party or by a bailee.

§ 9—206. Agreement Not to Assert Defenses Against Assignee; Modification of Sales Warranties Where Security Agreement Exists.

(1) Subject to any statute or decision which establishes a different rule for buyers or lessees of consumer goods, an agreement by a buyer or lessee that he will not assert against an assignee any claim or defense which he may have against the seller or lessor is enforceable by an assignee who takes his assignment for value, in good faith and without notice of a claim or defense, except as to defenses of a type which may be asserted against a holder in due course of a negotiable instrument under the Article on Commercial Paper (Article 3). A buyer who as part of one transaction signs both a negotiable instrument and a security agreement makes such an agreement.

(2) When a seller retains a purchase money security interest in goods the Article on Sales (Article 2) governs the sale and any disclaimer, limitation or modification of the seller's warranties.

§ 9—207. Rights and Duties When Collateral is in Secured Party's Possession.

(1) A secured party must use reasonable care in the custody and preservation of collateral in his possession. In the case of an instrument or chattel paper reasonable care includes taking necessary steps to preserve rights against prior parties unless otherwise agreed.

(2) Unless otherwise agreed, when collateral is in the secured party's possession

(a) reasonable expenses (including the cost of any insurance and payment of taxes or other charges)

incurred in the custody, preservation, use or operation of the collateral are chargeable to the debtor and are secured by the collateral;

(b) the risk of accidental loss or damage is on the debtor to the extent of any deficiency in any effective insurance coverage;

(c) the secured party may hold as additional security any increase or profits (except money) received from the collateral, but money so received, unless remitted to the debtor, shall be applied in reduction of the secured obligation;

(d) the secured party must keep the collateral identifiable but fungible collateral may be commingled;

(e) the secured party may repledge the collateral upon terms which do not impair the debtor's right to redeem it.

(3) A secured party is liable for any loss caused by his failure to meet any obligation imposed by the preceding subsections but does not lose his security interest.

(4) A secured party may use or operate the collateral for the purpose of preserving the collateral or its value or pursuant to the order of a court of appropriate jurisdiction or, except in the case of consumer goods, in the manner and to the extent provided in the security agreement.

§ 9—208. Request for Statement of Account or List of Collateral.

(1) A debtor may sign a statement indicating what he believes to be the aggregate amount of unpaid indebtedness as of a specified date and may send it to the secured party with a request that the statement be approved or corrected and returned to the debtor. When the security agreement or any other record kept by the secured party identifies the collateral a debtor may similarly request the secured party to approve or correct a list of the collateral.

(2) The secured party must comply with such a request within two weeks after receipt by sending a written correction or approval. If the secured party claims a security interest in all of a particular type of collateral owned by the debtor he may indicate that fact in his reply and need not approve or correct an itemized list of such collateral. If the secured party without reasonable excuse fails to comply he is liable for any loss caused to the debtor thereby; and if the debtor has properly included in his request a good faith statement of the obligation or a list of the collateral or both the secured party may claim a security interest only as shown in the statement against persons misled by his failure to comply. If he no longer has an interest in the obligation or collateral at the time the request is received he must disclose the name and address of any successor in in-

terest known to him and he is liable for any loss caused to the debtor as a result of failure to disclose. A successor in interest is not subject to this section until a request is received by him.

(3) A debtor is entitled to such a statement once every six months without charge. The secured party may require payment of a charge not exceeding $10 for each additional statement furnished.

Part 3 Rights of Third Parties; Perfected and Unperfected Security Interests; Rules of Priority

§ 9—301. Persons Who Take Priority Over Unperfected Security Interests; Rights of "Lien Creditor".

(1) Except as otherwise provided in subsection (2), an unperfected security interest is subordinate to the rights of

(a) persons entitled to priority under Section 9—312;

(b) a person who becomes a lien creditor before the security interest is perfected;

(c) in the case of goods, instruments, documents, and chattel paper, a person who is not a secured party and who is a transferee in bulk or other buyer not in ordinary course of business or is a buyer of farm products in ordinary course of business, to the extent that he gives value and receives delivery of the collateral without knowledge of the security interest and before it is perfected;

(d) in the case of accounts and general intangibles, a person who is not a secured party and who is a transferee to the extent that he gives value without knowledge of the security interest and before it is perfected.

(2) If the secured party files with respect to a purchase money security interest before or within ten days after the debtor receives possession of the collateral, he takes priority over the rights of a transferee in bulk or of a lien creditor which arise between the time the security interest attaches and the time of filing.

(3) A "lien creditor" means a creditor who has acquired a lien on the property involved by attachment, levy or the like and includes an assignee for benefit of creditors from the time of assignment, and a trustee in bankruptcy from the date of the filing of the petition or a receiver in equity from the time of appointment.

(4) A person who becomes a lien creditor while a security interest is perfected takes subject to the security interest only to the extent that it secures advances made before he becomes a lien creditor or within 45 days

thereafter or made without knowledge of the lien or pursuant to a commitment entered into without knowledge of the lien.

§ 9—302. When Filing Is Required to Perfect Security Interest; Security Interests to Which Filing Provisions of This Article Do Not Apply

(1) A financing statement must be filed to perfect all security interests except the following:

(a) a security interest in collateral in possession of the secured party under Section 9—305;

(b) a security interest temporarily perfected in instruments or documents without delivery under Section 9—304 or in proceeds for a 10 day period under Section 9—306;

(c) a security interest created by an assignment of a beneficial interest in a trust or a decedent's estate;

(d) a purchase money security interest in consumer goods; but filing is required for a motor vehicle required to be registered; and fixture filing is required for priority over conflicting interests in fixtures to the extent provided in Section 9—313;

(e) an assignment of accounts which does not alone or in conjunction with other assignments to the same assignee transfer a significant part of the outstanding accounts of the assignor;

(f) a security interest of a collecting bank (Section 4—208) or in securities (Section 8—321) or arising under the Article on Sales (see Section 9—113) or covered in subsection (3) of this section;

(g) an assignment for the benefit of all the creditors of the transferor, and subsequent transfers by the assignee thereunder.

(2) If a secured party assigns a perfected security interest, no filing under this Article is required in order to continue the perfected status of the security interest against creditors of and transferees from the original debtor.

(3) The filing of a financing statement otherwise required by this Article is not necessary or effective to perfect a security interest in property subject to

(a) a statute or treaty of the United States which provides for a national or international registration or a national or international certificate of title or which specifies a place of filing different from that specified in this Article for filing of the security interest; or

(b) the following statutes of this state; [list any certificate of title statute covering automobiles, trailers, mobile homes, boats, farm tractors, or the like, and any central filing statute.]; but during any period in which collateral is inventory held for sale by a person who is in the business of selling goods of that kind, the filing provisions of this Article (Part 4) apply to a security interest in that collateral created by him as debtor; or

(c) a certificate of title statute of another jurisdiction under the law of which indication of a security interest on the certificate is required as a condition of perfection (subsection (2) of Section 9—103).

(4) Compliance with a statute or treaty described in subsection (3) is equivalent to the filing of a financing statement under this Article, and a security interest in property subject to the statute or treaty can be perfected only by compliance therewith except as provided in Section 9—103 on multiple state transactions. Duration and renewal of perfection of a security interest perfected by compliance with the statute or treaty are governed by the provisions of the statute or treaty; in other respects the security interest is subject to this Article.

Amended in 1972 and 1977.

§ 9—303. When Security Interest Is Perfected; Continuity of Perfection.

(1) A security interest is perfected when it has attached and when all of the applicable steps required for perfection have been taken. Such steps are specified in Sections 9—302, 9—304, 9—305 and 9—306. If such steps are taken before the security interest attaches, it is perfected at the time when it attaches.

(2) If a security interest is originally perfected in any way permitted under this Article and is subsequently perfected in some other way under this Article, without an intermediate period when it was unperfected, the security interest shall be deemed to be perfected continuously for the purposes of this Article.

§ 9—304. Perfection of Security Interest in Instruments, Documents, and Goods Covered by Documents; Perfection by Permissive Filing; Temporary Perfection Without Filing or Transfer of Possession

(1) A security interest in chattel paper or negotiable documents may be perfected by filing. A security interest in money or instruments (other than certificated securities or instruments which constitute part of chattel paper) can be perfected only by the secured party's taking possession, except as provided in subsections (4) and (5) of this section and subsections (2) and (3) of Section 9—306 on proceeds.

(2) During the period that goods are in the possession of the issuer of a negotiable document therefor, a security interest in the goods is perfected by perfecting a security interest in the document, and any security interest in the goods otherwise perfected during such period is subject thereto.

(3) A security interest in goods in the possession of a bailee other than one who has issued a negotiable document therefor is perfected by issuance of a document in the name of the secured party or by the bailee's receipt of notification of the secured party's interest or by filing as to the goods.

(4) A security interest in instruments (other than certificated securities) or negotiable documents is perfected without filing or the taking of possession for a period of 21 days from the time it attaches to the extent that it arises for new value given under a written security agreement.

(5) A security interest remains perfected for a period of 21 days without filing where a secured party having a perfected security interest in an instrument (other than a certificated security), a negotiable document or goods in possession of a bailee other than one who has issued a negotiable document therefor

(a) makes available to the debtor the goods or documents representing the goods for the purpose of ultimate sale or exchange or for the purpose of loading, unloading, storing, shipping, transshipping, manufacturing, processing or otherwise dealing with them in a manner preliminary to their sale or exchange, but priority between conflicting security interests in the goods is subject to subsection (3) of Section 9—312; or

(b) delivers the instrument to the debtor for the purpose of ultimate sale or exchange or of presentation, collection, renewal or registration of transfer.

(6) After the 21 day period in subsections (4) and (5) perfection depends upon compliance with applicable provisions of this Article.

Amended in 1972 and 1977.

§ 9—305. When Possession by Secured Party Perfects Security Interest Without Filing

A security interest in letters of credit and advices of credit (subsection (2)(a) of Section 5—116), goods, instruments (other than certificated securities), money, negotiable documents, or chattel paper may be perfected by the secured party's taking possession of the collateral. If such collateral other than goods covered by a negotiable document is held by a bailee, the secured party is deemed to have possession from the time the bailee receives notification of the secured party's interest. A security interest is perfected by possession from the time possession is taken without a relation back and continues only so long as possession is retained, unless otherwise specified in this Article. The security interest may be otherwise perfected as provided in this Article before or after the period of possession by the secured party.

Amended in 1972 and 1977.

§ 9—306. "Proceeds"; Secured Party's Rights on Disposition of Collateral.

(1) "Proceeds" includes whatever is received upon the sale, exchange, collection or other disposition of collateral or proceeds. Insurance payable by reason of loss or damage to the collateral is proceeds, except to the extent that it is payable to a person other than a party to the security agreement. Money, checks, deposit accounts, and the like are "cash proceeds". All other proceeds are "noncash proceeds".

(2) Except where this Article otherwise provides, a security interest continues in collateral notwithstanding sale, exchange or other disposition thereof unless the disposition was authorized by the secured party in the security agreement or otherwise, and also continues in any identifiable proceeds including collections received by the debtor.

(3) The security interest in proceeds is a continuously perfected security interest if the interest in the original collateral was perfected but it ceases to be a perfected security interest and becomes unperfected ten days after receipt of the proceeds by the debtor unless

(a) a filed financing statement covers the original collateral and the proceeds are collateral in which a security interest may be perfected by filing in the office or offices where the financing statement has been filed and, if the proceeds are acquired with cash proceeds, the description of collateral in the financing statement indicates the types of property constituting the proceeds; or

(b) a filed financing statement covers the original collateral and the proceeds are identifiable cash proceeds; or

(c) the security interest in the proceeds is perfected before the expiration of the ten day period.

Except as provided in this section, a security interest in proceeds can be perfected only by the methods or under the circumstances permitted in this Article for original collateral of the same type.

(4) In the event of insolvency proceedings instituted by or against a debtor, a secured party with a perfected security interest in proceeds has a perfected security interest only in the following proceeds:

(a) in identifiable noncash proceeds and in separate deposit accounts containing only proceeds;

(b) in identifiable cash proceeds in the form of money which is neither commingled with other money nor deposited in a deposit account prior to the insolvency proceedings;

(c) in identifiable cash proceeds in the form of checks and the like which are not deposited in a deposit account prior to the insolvency proceedings; and

(d) in all cash and deposit accounts of the debtor in which proceeds have been commingled with other funds, but the perfected security interest under this paragraph (d) is

(i) subject to any right to set-off; and

(ii) limited to an amount not greater than the amount of any cash proceeds received by the debtor within ten days before the institution of the insolvency proceedings less the sum of (I) the payments to the secured party on account of cash proceeds received by the debtor during such period and (II) the cash proceeds received by the debtor during such period to which the secured party is entitled under paragraphs (a) through (c) of this subsection (4).

(5) If a sale of goods results in an account or chattel paper which is transferred by the seller to a secured party, and if the goods are returned to or are repossessed by the seller or the secured party, the following rules determine priorities:

(a) If the goods were collateral at the time of sale, for an indebtedness of the seller which is still unpaid, the original security interest attaches again to the goods and continues as a perfected security interest if it was perfected at the time when the goods were sold. If the security interest was originally perfected by a filing which is still effective, nothing further is required to continue the perfected status; in any other case, the secured party must take possession of the returned or repossessed goods or must file.

(b) An unpaid transferee of the chattel paper has a security interest in the goods against the transferor. Such security interest is prior to a security interest asserted under paragraph (a) to the extent that the transferee of the chattel paper was entitled to priority under Section 9—308.

(c) An unpaid transferee of the account has a security interest in the goods against the transferor. Such security interest is subordinate to a security interest asserted under paragraph (a).

(d) A security interest of an unpaid transferee asserted under paragraph (b) or (c) must be perfected for protection against creditors of the transferor and purchasers of the returned or repossessed goods.

§ 9—307. Protection of Buyers of Goods.

(1) A buyer in ordinary course of business (subsection (9) of Section 1—201) other than a person buying farm products from a person engaged in farming operations

takes free of a security interest created by his seller even though the security interest is perfected and even though the buyer knows of its existence [subject to the Food Security Act of 1985 (7 U.S.C. Section 1631)].

(2) In the case of consumer goods, a buyer takes free of a security interest even though perfected if he buys without knowledge of the security interest, for value and for his own personal, family or household purposes unless prior to the purchase the secured party has filed a financing statement covering such goods.

(3) A buyer other than a buyer in ordinary course of business (subsection (1) of this section) takes free of a security interest to the extent that it secures future advances made after the secured party acquires knowledge of the purchase, or more than 45 days after the purchase, whichever first occurs, unless made pursuant to a commitment entered into without knowledge of the purchase and before the expiration of the 45 day period.

§ 9—308. Purchase of Chattel Paper and Instruments.

A purchaser of chattel paper or an instrument who gives new value and takes possession of it in the ordinary course of his business has priority over a security interest in the chattel paper or instrument

(a) which is perfected under Section 9—304 (permissive filing and temporary perfection) or under Section 9—306 (perfection as to proceeds) if he acts without knowledge that the specific paper or instrument is subject to a security interest; or

(b) which is claimed merely as proceeds of inventory subject to a security interest (Section 9—306) even though he knows that the specific paper or instrument is subject to the security interest.

§ 9—309. Protection of Purchasers of Instruments, Documents and Securities

Nothing in this Article limits the rights of a holder in due course of a negotiable instrument (Section 3—302) or a holder to whom a negotiable document of title has been duly negotiated (Section 7—501) or a bona fide purchaser of a security (Section 8—302) and the holders or purchasers take priority over an earlier security interest even though perfected. Filing under this Article does not constitute notice of the security interest to such holders or purchasers.

Amended in 1977.

§ 9—310. Priority of Certain Liens Arising by Operation of Law.

When a person in the ordinary course of his business furnishes services or materials with respect to goods subject to a security interest, a lien upon goods in the possession of such person given by statute or rule of law for such materials or services takes priority over a perfected security interest unless the lien is statutory and the statute expressly provides otherwise.

§ 9—311. Alienability of Debtor's Rights: Judicial Process.

The debtor's rights in collateral may be voluntarily or involuntarily transferred (by way of sale, creation of a security interest, attachment, levy, garnishment or other judicial process) notwithstanding a provision in the security agreement prohibiting any transfer or making the transfer constitute a default.

§ 9—312. Priorities Among Conflicting Security Interests in the Same Collateral

(1) The rules of priority stated in other sections of this Part and in the following sections shall govern when applicable: Section 4—208 with respect to the security interests of collecting banks in items being collected, accompanying documents and proceeds; Section 9—103 on security interests related to other jurisdictions; Section 9—114 on consignments.

(2) A perfected security interest in crops for new value given to enable the debtor to produce the crops during the production season and given not more than three months before the crops become growing crops by planting or otherwise takes priority over an earlier perfected security interest to the extent that such earlier interest secures obligations due more than six months before the crops become growing crops by planting or otherwise, even though the person giving new value had knowledge of the earlier security interest.

(3) A perfected purchase money security interest in inventory has priority over a conflicting security interest in the same inventory and also has priority in identifiable cash proceeds received on or before the delivery of the inventory to a buyer if

(a) the purchase money security interest is perfected at the time the debtor receives possession of the inventory; and

(b) the purchase money secured party gives notification in writing to the holder of the conflicting security interest if the holder had filed a financing statement covering the same types of inventory (i) before the date of the filing made by the purchase money secured party, or (ii) before the beginning of the 21 day period where the purchase money security interest is temporarily perfected without filing or possession (subsection (5) of Section 9—304); and

(c) the holder of the conflicting security interest receives the notification within five years before the debtor receives possession of the inventory; and

(d) the notification states that the person giving the notice has or expects to acquire a purchase money security interest in inventory of the debtor, describing such inventory by item or type.

(4) A purchase money security interest in collateral other than inventory has priority over a conflicting security interest in the same collateral or its proceeds if the purchase money security interest is perfected at the time the debtor receives possession of the collateral or within ten days thereafter.

(5) In all cases not governed by other rules stated in this section (including cases of purchase money security interests which do not qualify for the special priorities set forth in subsections (3) and (4) of this section), priority between conflicting security interests in the same collateral shall be determined according to the following rules:

(a) Conflicting security interests rank according to priority in time of filing or perfection. Priority dates from the time a filing is first made covering the collateral or the time the security interest is first perfected, whichever is earlier, provided that there is no period thereafter when there is neither filing nor perfection.

(b) So long as conflicting security interests are unperfected, the first to attach has priority.

(6) For the purposes of subsection (5) a date of filing or perfection as to collateral is also a date of filing or perfection as to proceeds.

(7) If future advances are made while a security interest is perfected by filing, the taking of possession, or under Section 8—321 on securities, the security interest has the same priority for the purposes of subsection (5) with respect to the future advances as it does with respect to the first advance. If a commitment is made before or while the security interest is so perfected, the security interest has the same priority with respect to advances made pursuant thereto. In other cases a perfected security interest has priority from the date the advance is made.

Amended in 1972 and 1977.

§ 9—313. Priority of Security Interests in Fixtures.

(1) In this section and in the provisions of Part 4 of this Article referring to fixture filing, unless the context otherwise requires

(a) goods are "fixtures" when they become so related to particular real estate that an interest in them arises under real estate law

(b) a "fixture filing" is the filing in the office where a mortgage on the real estate would be filed or recorded of a financing statement covering goods which are or are to become fixtures and conforming to the requirements of subsection (5) of Section 9—402

(c) a mortgage is a "construction mortgage" to the extent that it secures an obligation incurred for the construction of an improvement on land including the acquisition cost of the land, if the recorded writing so indicates.

(2) A security interest under this Article may be created in goods which are fixtures or may continue in goods which become fixtures, but no security interest exists under this Article in ordinary building materials incorporated into an improvement on land.

(3) This Article does not prevent creation of an encumbrance upon fixtures pursuant to real estate law.

(4) A perfected security interest in fixtures has priority over the conflicting interest of an encumbrancer or owner of the real estate where

(a) the security interest is a purchase money security interest, the interest of the encumbrancer or owner arises before the goods become fixtures, the security interest is perfected by a fixture filing before the goods become fixtures or within ten days thereafter, and the debtor has an interest of record in the real estate or is in possession of the real estate; or

(b) the security interest is perfected by a fixture filing before the interest of the encumbrancer or owner is of record, the security interest has priority over any conflicting interest of a predecessor in title of the encumbrancer or owner, and the debtor has an interest of record in the real estate or is in possession of the real estate; or

(c) the fixtures are readily removable factory or office machines or readily removable replacements of domestic appliances which are consumer goods, and before the goods become fixtures the security interest is perfected by any method permitted by this Article; or

(d) the conflicting interest is a lien on the real estate obtained by legal or equitable proceedings after the security interest was perfected by any method permitted by this Article.

(5) A security interest in fixtures, whether or not perfected, has priority over the conflicting interest of an encumbrancer or owner of the real estate where

(a) the encumbrancer or owner has consented in writing to the security interest or has disclaimed an interest in the goods as fixtures; or

(b) the debtor has a right to remove the goods as against the encumbrancer or owner. If the debtor's right terminates, the priority of the security interest continues for a reasonable time.

(6) Notwithstanding paragraph (a) of subsection (4) but otherwise subject to subsections (4) and (5), a security interest in fixtures is subordinate to a construction mort-

gage recorded before the goods become fixtures if the goods become fixtures before the completion of the construction. To the extent that it is given to refinance a construction mortgage, a mortgage has this priority to the same extent as the construction mortgage.

(7) In cases not within the preceding subsections, a security interest in fixtures is subordinate to the conflicting interest of an encumbrancer or owner of the related real estate who is not the debtor.

(8) When the secured party has priority over all owners and encumbrancers of the real estate, he may, on default, subject to the provisions of Part 5, remove his collateral from the real estate but he must reimburse any encumbrancer or owner of the real estate who is not the debtor and who has not otherwise agreed for the cost of repair of any physical injury, but not for any diminution in value of the real estate caused by the absence of the goods removed or by any necessity of replacing them. A person entitled to reimbursement may refuse permission to remove until the secured party gives adequate security for the performance of this obligation.

§ 9—314. Accessions.

(1) A security interest in goods which attaches before they are installed in or affixed to other goods takes priority as to the goods installed or affixed (called in this section "accessions") over the claims of all persons to the whole except as stated in subsection (3) and subject to Section 9—315(1).

(2) A security interest which attaches to goods after they become part of a whole is valid against all persons subsequently acquiring interests in the whole except as stated in subsection (3) but is invalid against any person with an interest in the whole at the time the security interest attaches to the goods who has not in writing consented to the security interest or disclaimed an interest in the goods as part of the whole.

(3) The security interests described in subsections (1) and (2) do not take priority over

(a) a subsequent purchaser for value of any interest in the whole; or

(b) a creditor with a lien on the whole subsequently obtained by judicial proceedings; or

(c) a creditor with a prior perfected security interest in the whole to the extent that he makes subsequent advances

if the subsequent purchase is made, the lien by judicial proceedings obtained or the subsequent advance under the prior perfected security interest is made or contracted for without knowledge of the security interest and before it is perfected. A purchaser of the whole at a foreclosure sale other than the holder of a perfected

security interest purchasing at his own foreclosure sale is a subsequent purchaser within this section.

(4) When under subsections (1) or (2) and (3) a secured party has an interest in accessions which has priority over the claims of all persons who have interests in the whole, he may on default subject to the provisions of Part 5 remove his collateral from the whole but he must reimburse any encumbrancer or owner of the whole who is not the debtor and who has not otherwise agreed for the cost of repair of any physical injury but not for any diminution in value of the whole caused by the absence of the goods removed or by any necessity for replacing them. A person entitled to reimbursement may refuse permission to remove until the secured party gives adequate security for the performance of this obligation.

§ 9—315. Priority When Goods Are Commingled or Processed.

(1) If a security interest in goods was perfected and subsequently the goods or a part thereof have become part of a product or mass, the security interest continues in the product or mass if

(a) the goods are so manufactured, processed, assembled or commingled that their identity is lost in the product or mass; or

(b) a financing statement covering the original goods also covers the product into which the goods have been manufactured, processed or assembled.

In a case to which paragraph (b) applies, no separate security interest in that part of the original goods which has been manufactured, processed or assembled into the product may be claimed under Section 9—314.

(2) When under subsection (1) more than one security interest attaches to the product or mass, they rank equally according to the ratio that the cost of the goods to which each interest originally attached bears to the cost of the total product or mass.

§ 9—316. Priority Subject to Subordination.

Nothing in this Article prevents subordination by agreement by any person entitled to priority.

§ 9—317. Secured Party Not Obligated on Contract of Debtor.

The mere existence of a security interest or authority given to the debtor to dispose of or use collateral does not impose contract or tort liability upon the secured party for the debtor's acts or omissions.

§ 9—318. Defenses Against Assignee; Modification of Contract After Notification of Assignment; Term Prohibiting Assignment Ineffective; Identification and Proof of Assignment.

(1) Unless an account debtor has made an enforceable agreement not to assert defenses or claims arising out of a sale as provided in Section 9—206 the rights of an assignee are subject to

(a) all the terms of the contract between the account debtor and assignor and any defense or claim arising therefrom; and

(b) any other defense or claim of the account debtor against the assignor which accrues before the account debtor receives notification of the assignment.

(2) So far as the right to payment or a part thereof under an assigned contract has not been fully earned by performance, and notwithstanding notification of the assignment, any modification of or substitution for the contract made in good faith and in accordance with reasonable commercial standards is effective against an assignee unless the account debtor has otherwise agreed but the assignee acquires corresponding rights under the modified or substituted contract. The assignment may provide that such modification or substitution is a breach by the assignor.

(3) The account debtor is authorized to pay the assignor until the account debtor receives notification that the amount due or to become due has been assigned and that payment is to be made to the assignee. A notification which does not reasonably identify the rights assigned is ineffective. If requested by the account debtor, the assignee must seasonably furnish reasonable proof that the assignment has been made and unless he does so the account debtor may pay the assignor.

(4) A term in any contract between an account debtor and an assignor is ineffective if it prohibits assignment of an account or prohibits creation of a security interest in a general intangible for money due or to become due or requires the account debtor's consent to such assignment or security interest.

Part 4 Filing

§ 9—401. Place of Filing; Erroneous Filing; Removal of Collateral.

First Alternative Subsection (1)

(1) The proper place to file in order to perfect a security interest is as follows:

(a) when the collateral is timber to be cut or is minerals or the like (including oil and gas) or accounts subject to subsection (5) of Section 9—103, or when the financing statement is filed as a fixture filing (Section 9—313) and the collateral is goods which are or are to become fixtures, then in the office where a mortgage on the real estate would be filed or recorded;

(b) in all other cases, in the office of the [Secretary of State].

Second Alternative Subsection (1)

(1) The proper place to file in order to perfect a security interest is as follows:

(a) when the collateral is equipment used in farming operations, or farm products, or accounts or general intangibles arising from or relating to the sale of farm products by a farmer, or consumer goods, then in the office of the . . . . in the county of the debtor's residence or if the debtor is not a resident of this state then in the office of the . . . . in the county where the goods are kept, and in addition when the collateral is crops growing or to be grown in the office of the . . . . in the county where the land is located;

(b) when the collateral is timber to be cut or is minerals or the like (including oil and gas) or accounts subject to subsection (5) of Section 9—103, or when the financing statement is filed as a fixture filing (Section 9—313) and the collateral is goods which are or are to become fixtures, then in the office where a mortgage on the real estate would be filed or recorded;

(c) in all other cases, in the office of the [Secretary of State].

Third Alternative Subsection (1)

(1) The proper place to file in order to perfect a security interest is as follows:

(a) when the collateral is equipment used in farming operations, or farm products, or accounts or general intangibles arising from or relating to the sale of farm products by a farmer, or consumer goods, then in the office of the . . . . in the county of the debtor's residence or if the debtor is not a resident of this state then in the office of the . . . . in the county where the goods are kept, and in addition when the collateral is crops growing or to be grown in the office of the . . . . in the county where the land is located;

(b) when the collateral is timber to be cut or is minerals or the like (including oil and gas) or accounts subject to subsection (5) of Section 9—103, or when the financing statement is filed as a fixture filing (Section 9—313) and the collateral is goods which are or are to become fixtures, then in the office where a mortgage on the real estate would be filed or recorded;

(c) in all other cases, in the office of the [Secretary of State] and in addition, if the debtor has a place of business in only one county of this state, also in the office of . . . . of such county, or, if the debtor has no place of business in this state, but resides in the state, also in the office of . . . . of the county which he resides.

Note: *One of the three alternatives should be selected as subsection (1).*

(2) A filing which is made in good faith in an improper place or not in all of the places required by this section

is nevertheless effective with regard to any collateral as to which the filing complied with the requirements of this Article and is also effective with regard to collateral covered by the financing statement against any person who has knowledge of the contents of such financing statement.

(3) A filing which is made in the proper place in this state continues effective even though the debtor's residence or place of business or the location of the collateral or its use, whichever controlled the original filing, is thereafter changed.

Alternative Subsection (3)

[(3) A filing which is made in the proper county continues effective for four months after a change to another county of the debtor's residence or place of business or the location of the collateral, whichever controlled the original filing. It becomes ineffective thereafter unless a copy of the financing statement signed by the secured party is filed in the new county within said period. The security interest may also be perfected in the new county after the expiration of the four-month period; in such case perfection dates from the time of perfection in the new county. A change in the use of the collateral does not impair the effectiveness of the original filing.]

(4) The rules stated in Section 9—103 determine whether filing is necessary in this state.

(5) Notwithstanding the preceding subsections, and subject to subsection (3) of Section 9—302, the proper place to file in order to perfect a security interest in collateral, including fixtures, of a transmitting utility is the office of the [Secretary of State]. This filing constitutes a fixture filing (Section 9—313) as to the collateral described therein which is or is to become fixtures.

(6) For the purposes of this section, the residence of an organization is its place of business if it has one or its chief executive office if it has more than one place of business.

Note: *Subsection (6) should be used only if the state chooses the Second or Third Alternative Subsection (1).*

§ 9—402. **Formal Requisites of Financing Statement; Amendments; Mortgage as Financing Statement.**

(1) A financing statement is sufficient if it gives the names of the debtor and the secured party, is signed by the debtor, gives an address of the secured party from which information concerning the security interest may be obtained, gives a mailing address of the debtor and contains a statement indicating the types, or describing the items, of collateral. A financing statement may be filed before a security agreement is made or a security interest otherwise attaches. When the financing statement covers crops growing or to be grown, the state-

ment must also contain a description of the real estate concerned. When the financing statement covers timber to be cut or covers minerals or the like (including oil and gas) or accounts subject to subsection (5) of Section 9—103, or when the financing statement is filed as a fixture filing (Section 9—313) and the collateral is goods which are or are to become fixtures, the statement must also comply with subsection (5). A copy of the security agreement is sufficient as a financing statement if it contains the above information and is signed by the debtor. A carbon, photographic or other reproduction of a security agreement or a financing statement is sufficient as a financing statement if the security agreement so provides or if the original has been filed in this state.

(2) A financing statement which otherwise complies with subsection (1) is sufficient when it is signed by the secured party instead of the debtor if it is filed to perfect a security interest in

(a) collateral already subject to a security interest in another jurisdiction when it is brought into this state, or when the debtor's location is changed to this state. Such a financing statement must state that the collateral was brought into this state or that the debtor's location was changed to this state under such circumstances; or

(b) proceeds under Section 9—306 if the security interest in the original collateral was perfected. Such a financing statement must describe the original collateral; or

(c) collateral as to which the filing has lapsed; or

(d) collateral acquired after a change of name, identity or corporate structure of the debtor (subsection (7)).

(3) A form substantially as follows is sufficient to comply with subsection (1):

Name of debtor (or assignor) ....
Address ....
Name of secured party (or assignee) ....
Address ....
1. This financing statement covers the following types (or items) of property:
   (Describe) ....
2. (If collateral is crops) The above described crops are growing or are to be grown on:
   (Describe Real Estate) ....
3. (If applicable) The above goods are to become fixtures on *
*Where appropriate substitute either "The above timber is standing on . . . ." or "The above minerals or the like (including oil and gas) or accounts will be financed at the wellhead or minehead of the well or mine located on . . . ."
   (Describe Real Estate) ....

and this financing statement is to be filed [for record] in the real estate records. (If the debtor does not have an interest of record) The name of a record owner is ....

4. (If products of collateral are claimed) Products of the collateral are also covered.

(use ....
whichever   Signature of Debtor (or Assignor)

is   ....
applicable)   Signature of Secured Party
(or Assignee)

(4) A financing statement may be amended by filing a writing signed by both the debtor and the secured party. An amendment does not extend the period of effectiveness of a financing statement. If any amendment adds collateral, it is effective as to the added collateral only from the filing date of the amendment. In this Article, unless the context otherwise requires, the term "financing statement" means the original financing statement and any amendments.

(5) A financing statement covering timber to be cut or covering minerals or the like (including oil and gas) or accounts subject to subsection (5) of Section 9—103, or a financing statement filed as a fixture filing (Section 9—313) where the debtor is not a transmitting utility, must show that it covers this type of collateral, must recite that it is to be filed [for record] in the real estate records, and the financing statement must contain a description of the real estate [sufficient if it were contained in a mortgage of the real estate to give constructive notice of the mortgage under the law of this state]. If the debtor does not have an interest of record in the real estate, the financing statement must show the name of a record owner.

(6) A mortgage is effective as a financing statement filed as a fixture filing from the date of its recording if

(a) the goods are described in the mortgage by item or type; and

(b) the goods are or are to become fixtures related to the real estate described in the mortgage; and

(c) the mortgage complies with the requirements for a financing statement in this section other than a recital that it is to be filed in the real estate records; and

(d) the mortgage is duly recorded.

No fee with reference to the financing statement is required other than the regular recording and satisfaction fees with respect to the mortgage.

(7) A financing statement sufficiently shows the name of the debtor if it gives the individual, partnership or corporate name of the debtor, whether or not it adds other trade names or names of partners. Where the debtor so changes his name or in the case of an organization its name, identity or corporate structure that a filed financing statement becomes seriously misleading, the filing is not effective to perfect a security interest in collateral acquired by the debtor more than four months after the change, unless a new appropriate financing statement is filed before the expiration of that time. A filed financing statement remains effective with respect to collateral transferred by the debtor even though the secured party knows of or consents to the transfer.

(8) A financing statement substantially complying with the requirements of this section is effective even though it contains minor errors which are not seriously misleading.

Note: *Language in brackets is optional.*

Note: *Where the state has any special recording system for real estate other than the usual grantor-grantee index (as, for instance, a tract system or a title registration or Torrens system) local adaptations of subsection (5) and Section 9—403(7) may be necessary. See Mass.Gen.Laws Chapter 106, Section 9—409.*

§ 9—403. **What Constitutes Filing; Duration of Filing; Effect of Lapsed Filing; Duties of Filing Officer.**

(1) Presentation for filing of a financing statement and tender of the filing fee or acceptance of the statement by the filing officer constitutes filing under this Article.

2) Except as provided in subsection (6) a filed financing statement is effective for a period of five years from the date of filing. The effectiveness of a filed financing statement lapses on the expiration of the five year period unless a continuation statement is filed prior to the lapse. If a security interest perfected by filing exists at the time insolvency proceedings are commenced by or against the debtor, the security interest remains perfected until termination of the insolvency proceedings and thereafter for a period of sixty days or until expiration of the five year period, whichever occurs later. Upon lapse the security interest becomes unperfected, unless it is perfected without filing. If the security interest becomes unperfected upon lapse, it is deemed to have been unperfected as against a person who became a purchaser or lien creditor before lapse.

(3) A continuation statement may be filed by the secured party within six months prior to the expiration of the five year period specified in subsection (2). Any such continuation statement must be signed by the secured party, identify the original statement by file number and state that the original statement is still effective. A continuation statement signed by a person other than the secured party of record must be accompanied by a separate written statement of assignment signed by the

secured party of record and complying with subsection (2) of Section 9—405, including payment of the required fee. Upon timely filing of the continuation statement, the effectiveness of the original statement is continued for five years after the last date to which the filing was effective whereupon it lapses in the same manner as provided in subsection (2) unless another continuation statement is filed prior to such lapse. Succeeding continuation statements may be filed in the same manner to continue the effectiveness of the original statement. Unless a statute on disposition of public records provides otherwise, the filing officer may remove a lapsed statement from the files and destroy it immediately if he has retained a microfilm or other photographic record, or in other cases after one year after the lapse. The filing officer shall so arrange matters by physical annexation of financing statements to continuation statements or other related filings, or by other means, that if he physically destroys the financing statements of a period more than five years past, those which have been continued by a continuation statement or which are still effective under subsection (6) shall be retained.

(4) Except as provided in subsection (7) a filing officer shall mark each statement with a file number and with the date and hour of filing and shall hold the statement or a microfilm or other photographic copy thereof for public inspection. In addition the filing officer shall index the statement according to the name of the debtor and shall note in the index the file number and the address of the debtor given in the statement.

(5) The uniform fee for filing and indexing and for stamping a copy furnished by the secured party to show the date and place of filing for an original financing statement or for a continuation statement shall be $. . . . . . . if the statement is in the standard form prescribed by the [Secretary of State] and otherwise shall be $. . . . . . . , plus in each case, if the financing statement is subject to subsection (5) of Section 9—402, $. . . . . . . The uniform fee for each name more than one required to be indexed shall be $. . . . . . . The secured party may at his option show a trade name for any person and an extra uniform indexing fee of $. . . . . . . shall be paid with respect thereto.

(6) If the debtor is a transmitting utility (subsection (5) of Section 9—401) and a filed financing statement so states, it is effective until a termination statement is filed. A real estate mortgage which is effective as a fixture filing under subsection (6) of Section 9—402 remains effective as a fixture filing until the mortgage is released or satisfied of record or its effectiveness otherwise terminates as to the real estate.

(7) When a financing statement covers timber to be cut or covers minerals or the like (including oil and gas) or accounts subject to subsection (5) of Section 9—103,

or is filed as a fixture filing, [it shall be filed for record and] the filing officer shall index it under the names of the debtor and any owner of record shown on the financing statement in the same fashion as if they were the mortgagors in a mortgage of the real estate described, and, to the extent that the law of this state provides for indexing of mortgages under the name of the mortgagee, under the name of the secured party as if he were the mortgagee thereunder, or where indexing is by description in the same fashion as if the financing statement were a mortgage of the real estate described.

Note: *In states in which writings will not appear in the real estate records and indices unless actually recorded the bracketed language in subsection (7) should be used.*

§ 9—404. **Termination Statement.**

(1) If a financing statement covering consumer goods is filed on or after . . . . , then within one month or within ten days following written demand by the debtor after there is no outstanding secured obligation and no commitment to make advances, incur obligations or otherwise give value, the secured party must file with each filing officer with whom the financing statement was filed, a termination statement to the effect that he no longer claims a security interest under the financing statement, which shall be identified by file number. In other cases whenever there is no outstanding secured obligation and no commitment to make advances, incur obligations or otherwise give value, the secured party must on written demand by the debtor send the debtor, for each filing officer with whom the financing statement was filed, a termination statement to the effect that he no longer claims a security interest under the financing statement, which shall be identified by file number. A termination statement signed by a person other than the secured party of record must be accompanied by a separate written statement of assignment signed by the secured party of record complying with subsection (2) of Section 9—405, including payment of the required fee. If the affected secured party fails to file such a termination statement as required by this subsection, or to send such a termination statement within ten days after proper demand therefor, he shall be liable to the debtor for one hundred dollars, and in addition for any loss caused to the debtor by such failure.

(2) On presentation to the filing officer of such a termination statement he must note it in the index. If he has received the termination statement in duplicate, he shall return one copy of the termination statement to the secured party stamped to show the time of receipt thereof. If the filing officer has a microfilm or other photographic record of the financing statement, and of any related continuation statement, statement of assignment and statement of release, he may remove the originals from the files at any time after receipt of the ter-

mination statement, or if he has no such record, he may remove them from the files at any time after one year after receipt of the termination statement.

(3) If the termination statement is in the standard form prescribed by the [Secretary of State], the uniform fee for filing and indexing the termination statement shall be $. . . . ., and otherwise shall be $. . . . ., plus in each case an additional fee of $. . . . . . . for each name more than one against which the termination statement is required to be indexed.

Note: *The date to be inserted should be the effective date of the revised Article 9.*

§ 9—405. **Assignment of Security Interest; Duties of Filing Officer; Fees.**

(1) A financing statement may disclose an assignment of a security interest in the collateral described in the financing statement by indication in the financing statement of the name and address of the assignee or by an assignment itself or a copy thereof on the face or back of the statement. On presentation to the filing officer of such a financing statement the filing officer shall mark the same as provided in Section 9—403(4). The uniform fee for filing, indexing and furnishing filing data for a financing statement so indicating an assignment shall be $. . . . . . . if the statement is in the standard form prescribed by the [Secretary of State] and otherwise shall be $. . . . . . ., plus in each case an additional fee of $. . . . . . . for each name more than one against which the financing statement is required to be indexed.

(2) A secured party may assign of record all or part of his rights under a financing statement by the filing in the place where the original financing statement was filed of a separate written statement of assignment signed by the secured party of record and setting forth the name of the secured party of record and the debtor, the file number and the date of filing of the financing statement and the name and address of the assignee and containing a description of the collateral assigned. A copy of the assignment is sufficient as a separate statement if it complies with the preceding sentence. On presentation to the filing officer of such a separate statement, the filing officer shall mark such separate statement with the date and hour of the filing. He shall note the assignment on the index of the financing statement, or in the case of a fixture filing, or a filing covering timber to be cut, or covering minerals or the like (including oil and gas) or accounts subject to subsection (5) of Section 9—103, he shall index the assignment under the name of the assignor as grantor and, to the extent that the law of this state provides for indexing the assignment of a mortgage under the name of the assignee, he shall index the assignment of the financing statement under the name of the assignee. The uniform fee for filing, indexing and furnishing filing data about such a separate statement

of assignment shall be $. . . . . . if the statement is in the standard form prescribed by the [Secretary of State] and otherwise shall be $. . . . . ., plus in each case an additional fee of $. . . . . . for each name more than one against which the statement of assignment is required to be indexed. Notwithstanding the provisions of this subsection, an assignment of record of a security interest in a fixture contained in a mortgage effective as a fixture filing (subsection (6) of Section 9—402) may be made only by an assignment of the mortgage in the manner provided by the law of this state other than this Act.

(3) After the disclosure or filing of an assignment under this section, the assignee is the secured party of record.

§ 9—406. **Release of Collateral; Duties of Filing Officer; Fees.**

A secured party of record may by his signed statement release all or a part of any collateral described in a filed financing statement. The statement of release is sufficient if it contains a description of the collateral being released, the name and address of the debtor, the name and address of the secured party, and the file number of the financing statement. A statement of release signed by a person other than the secured party of record must be accompanied by a separate written statement of assignment signed by the secured party of record and complying with subsection (2) of Section 9—405, including payment of the required fee. Upon presentation of such a statement of release to the filing officer he shall mark the statement with the hour and date of filing and shall note the same upon the margin of the index of the filing of the financing statement. The uniform fee for filing and noting such a statement of release shall be $. . . . . . if the statement is in the standard form prescribed by the [Secretary of State] and otherwise shall be $. . . . . ., plus in each case an additional fee of $. . . . . . for each name more than one against which the statement of release is required to be indexed. Amended in 1972.

§ 9—407. **Information From Filing Officer.**

[(1) If the person filing any financing statement, termination statement, statement of assignment, or statement of release, furnishes the filing officer a copy thereof, the filing officer shall upon request note upon the copy the file number and date and hour of the filing of the original and deliver or send the copy to such person.]

[(2) Upon request of any person, the filing officer shall issue his certificate showing whether there is on file on the date and hour stated therein, any presently effective financing statement naming a particular debtor and any statement of assignment thereof and if there is, giving the date and hour of filing of each such statement and the names and addresses of each secured party therein. The uniform fee for such a certificate shall be $. . . . . . if the request for the certificate is in the standard form prescribed by the [Secretary of State] and otherwise shall be $....... Upon request the filing officer shall furnish a copy of any filed financing statement or statement of assignment for a uniform fee of $...... per page.]

Note: *This section is proposed as an optional provision to require filing officers to furnish certificates. Local law and practices should be consulted with regard to the advisability of adoption.*

§ 9—408. Financing Statements Covering Consigned or Leased Goods.

A consignor or lessor of goods may file a financing statement using the terms "consignor," "consignee," "lessor," "lessee" or the like instead of the terms specified in Section 9—402. The provisions of this Part shall apply as appropriate to such a financing statement but its filing shall not of itself be a factor in determining whether or not the consignment or lease is intended as security (Section 1—201(37)). However, if it is determined for other reasons that the consignment or lease is so intended, a security interest of the consignor or lessor which attaches to the consigned or leased goods is perfected by such filing.

Part 5 Default

§ 9—501. Default; Procedure When Security Agreement Covers Both Real and Personal Property.

(1) When a debtor is in default under a security agreement, a secured party has the rights and remedies provided in this Part and except as limited by subsection (3) those provided in the security agreement. He may reduce his claim to judgment, foreclose or otherwise enforce the security interest by any available judicial procedure. If the collateral is documents the secured party may proceed either as to the documents or as to the goods covered thereby. A secured party in possession has the rights, remedies and duties provided in Section 9—207. The rights and remedies referred to in this subsection are cumulative.

(2) After default, the debtor has the rights and remedies provided in this Part, those provided in the security agreement and those provided in Section 9—207.

(3) To the extent that they give rights to the debtor and impose duties on the secured party, the rules stated in the subsections referred to below may not be waived or varied except as provided with respect to compulsory disposition of collateral (subsection (3) of Section 9—504 and Section 9—505) and with respect to redemption of collateral (Section 9—506) but the parties may by agreement determine the standards by which the fulfillment of these rights and duties is to be measured if such standards are not manifestly unreasonable:

(a) subsection (2) of Section 9—502 and subsection (2) of Section 9—504 insofar as they require accounting for surplus proceeds of collateral;

(b) subsection (3) of Section 9—504 and subsection (1) of Section 9—505 which deal with disposition of collateral;

(c) subsection (2) of Section 9—505 which deals with acceptance of collateral as discharge of obligation;

(d) Section 9—506 which deals with redemption of collateral; and

(e) subsection (1) of Section 9—507 which deals with the secured party's liability for failure to comply with this Part.

(4) If the security agreement covers both real and personal property, the secured party may proceed under this Part as to the personal property or he may proceed as to both the real and the personal property in accordance with his rights and remedies in respect of the real property in which case the provisions of this Part do not apply.

(5) When a secured party has reduced his claim to judgment the lien of any levy which may be made upon his collateral by virture of any execution based upon the judgment shall relate back to the date of the perfection of the security interest in such collateral. A judicial sale, pursuant to such execution, is a foreclosure of the security interest by judicial procedure within the meaning of this section, and the secured party may purchase at the sale and thereafter hold the collateral free of any other requirements of this Article.

§ 9—502. Collection Rights of Secured Party.

(1) When so agreed and in any event on default the secured party is entitled to notify an account debtor or the obligor on an instrument to make payment to him whether or not the assignor was theretofore making collections on the collateral, and also to take control of any proceeds to which he is entitled under Section 9—306.

(2) A secured party who by agreement is entitled to charge back uncollected collateral or otherwise to full or limited recourse against the debtor and who undertakes to collect from the account debtors or obligors must proceed in a commercially reasonable manner and may deduct his reasonable expenses of realization from the collections. If the security agreement secures an indebtedness, the secured party must account to the debtor for any surplus, and unless otherwise agreed, the debtor is liable for any deficiency. But, if the underlying transaction was a sale of accounts or chattel paper, the debtor is entitled to any surplus or is liable for any deficiency only if the security agreement so provides.

§ 9—503. Secured Party's Right to Take Possession After Default.

Unless otherwise agreed a secured party has on default the right to take possession of the collateral. In taking possession a secured party may proceed without judicial process if this can be done without breach of the peace or may proceed by action. If the security agreement so provides the secured party may require the debtor to assemble the collateral and make it available to the secured party at a place to be designated by the secured party which is reasonably convenient to both parties. Without removal a secured party may render equipment unusable, and may dispose of collateral on the debtor's premises under Section 9—504.

§ 9—504. Secured Party's Right to Dispose of Collateral After Default; Effect of Disposition.

(1) A secured party after default may sell, lease or otherwise dispose of any or all of the collateral in its then condition or following any commercially reasonable preparation or processing. Any sale of goods is subject to the Article on Sales (Article 2). The proceeds of disposition shall be applied in the order following to

(a) the reasonable expenses of retaking, holding, preparing for sale or lease, selling, leasing and the like and, to the extent provided for in the agreement and not prohibited by law, the reasonable attorneys' fees and legal expenses incurred by the secured party;

(b) the satisfaction of indebtedness secured by the security interest under which the disposition is made;

(c) the satisfaction of indebtedness secured by any subordinate security interest in the collateral if written notification of demand therefor is received before distribution of the proceeds is completed. If requested by the secured party, the holder of a subordinate security interest must seasonably furnish reasonable proof of his interest, and unless he does so, the secured party need not comply with his demand.

(2) If the security interest secures an indebtedness, the secured party must account to the debtor for any surplus, and, unless otherwise agreed, the debtor is liable for any deficiency. But if the underlying transaction was a sale of accounts or chattel paper, the debtor is entitled to any surplus or is liable for any deficiency only if the security agreement so provides.

(3) Disposition of the collateral may be by public or private proceedings and may be made by way of one or more contracts. Sale or other disposition may be as a unit or in parcels and at any time and place and on any terms but every aspect of the disposition including the method, manner, time, place and terms must be commercially reasonable. Unless collateral is perishable or threatens to decline speedily in value or is of a type customarily sold on a recognized market, reasonable notification of the time and place of any public sale or reasonable notification of the time after which any private sale or other intended disposition is to be made shall be sent by the secured party to the debtor, if he has not signed after default a statement renouncing or modifying his right to notification of sale. In the case of consumer goods no other notification need be sent. In other cases notification shall be sent to any other secured party from whom the secured party has received (before sending his notification to the debtor or before the debtor's renunciation of his rights) written notice of a claim of an interest in the collateral. The secured party may buy at any public sale and if the collateral is of a type customarily sold in a recognized market or is of a type which is the subject of widely distributed standard price quotations he may buy at private sale.

(4) When collateral is disposed of by a secured party after default, the disposition transfers to a purchaser for value all of the debtor's rights therein, discharges the security interest under which it is made and any security interest or lien subordinate thereto. The purchaser takes free of all such rights and interests even though the secured party fails to comply with the requirements of this Part or of any judicial proceedings

(a) in the case of a public sale, if the purchaser has no knowledge of any defects in the sale and if he does not buy in collusion with the secured party, other bidders or the person conducting the sale; or

(b) in any other case, if the purchaser acts in good faith.

(5) A person who is liable to a secured party under a guaranty, indorsement, repurchase agreement or the like and who receives a transfer of collateral from the secured party or is subrogated to his rights has thereafter the rights and duties of the secured party. Such a transfer of collateral is not a sale or disposition of the collateral under this Article.

§ 9—505. Compulsory Disposition of Collateral; Acceptance of the Collateral as Discharge of Obligation.

(1) If the debtor has paid sixty per cent of the cash price in the case of a purchase money security interest in consumer goods or sixty per cent of the loan in the case of another security interest in consumer goods, and has not signed after default a statement renouncing or modifying his rights under this Part a secured party who has taken possession of collateral must dispose of it under Section 9—504 and if he fails to do so within ninety days after he takes possession the debtor at his option may recover in conversion or under Section 9—507(1) on secured party's liability.

(2) In any other case involving consumer goods or any other collateral a secured party in possession may, after default, propose to retain the collateral in satisfaction of the obligation. Written notice of such proposal shall be sent to the debtor if he has not signed after default a statement renouncing or modifying his rights under this subsection. In the case of consumer goods no other notice need be given. In other cases notice shall be sent to any other secured party from whom the secured party has received (before sending his notice to the debtor or before the debtor's renunciation of his rights) written notice of a claim of an interest in the collateral. If the secured party receives objection in writing from a person entitled to receive notification within twenty-one days after the notice was sent, the secured party must dispose of the collateral under Section 9—504. In the absence of such written objection the secured party may retain the collateral in satisfaction of the debtor's obligation. Amended in 1972.

§ 9—506. Debtor's Right to Redeem Collateral.

At any time before the secured party has disposed of collateral or entered into a contract for its disposition under Section 9—504 or before the obligation has been discharged under Section 9—505(2) the debtor or any other secured party may unless otherwise agreed in writing after default redeem the collateral by tendering fulfillment of all obligations secured by the collateral as well as the expenses reasonably incurred by the secured party in retaking, holding and preparing the collateral for disposition, in arranging for the sale, and to the extent provided in the agreement and not prohibited by law, his reasonable attorneys' fees and legal expenses.

§ 9—507. Secured Party's Liability for Failure to Comply With This Part.

(1) If it is established that the secured party is not proceeding in accordance with the provisions of this Part disposition may be ordered or restrained on appropriate terms and conditions. If the disposition has occurred the debtor or any person entitled to notification or whose security interest has been made known to the secured party prior to the disposition has a right to recover from the secured party any loss caused by a failure to comply with the provisions of this Part. If the collateral is consumer goods, the debtor has a right to recover in any event an amount not less than the credit service charge plus ten per cent of the principal amount of the debt or the time price differential plus 10 per cent of the cash price.

(2) The fact that a better price could have been obtained by a sale at a different time or in a different method from that selected by the secured party is not of itself sufficient to establish that the sale was not made in a commercially reasonable manner. If the secured party either sells the collateral in the usual manner in any recognized market therefor or if he sells at the price current in such market at the time of his sale or if he has otherwise sold in conformity with reasonable commercial practices among dealers in the type of property sold he has sold in a commercially reasonable manner. The principles stated in the two preceding sentences with respect to sales also apply as may be appropriate to other types of disposition. A disposition which has been approved in any judicial proceeding or by any bona fide creditors' committee or representative of creditors shall conclusively be deemed to be commercially reasonable, but this sentence does not indicate that any such approval must be obtained in any case nor does it indicate that any disposition not so approved is not commercially reasonable.

Article 10
EFFECTIVE DATE AND REPEALER

§ 10—101. Effective Date.

This Act shall become effective at midnight on December 31st following its enactment. It applies to transactions entered into and events occurring after that date.

§ 10—102. Specific Repealer; Provision for Transition.

(1) The following acts and all other acts and parts of acts inconsistent herewith are hereby repealed:
(Here should follow the acts to be specifically repealed including the following:

    Uniform Negotiable Instruments Act
    Uniform Warehouse Receipts Act
    Uniform Sales Act
    Uniform Bills of Lading Act
    Uniform Stock Transfer Act
    Uniform Conditional Sales Act
    Uniform Trust Receipts Act
      Also any acts regulating:
Bank collections
Bulk sales
Chattel mortgages
Conditional sales
Factor's lien acts
Farm storage of grain and similar acts
Assignment of accounts receivable)

(2) Transactions validly entered into before the effective date specified in Section 10—101 and the rights, duties and interests flowing from them remain valid thereafter and may be terminated, completed, consummated or enforced as required or permitted by any stat-

ute or other law amended or repealed by this Act as though such repeal or amendment had not occurred.

Note: *Subsection (1) should be separately prepared for each state. The foregoing is a list of statutes to be checked.*

§ 10—103. General Repealer.

Except as provided in the following section, all acts and parts of acts inconsistent with this Act are hereby repealed.

§ 10—104. Laws Not Repealed.

(1) The Article on Documents of Title (Article 7) does not repeal or modify any laws prescribing the form or contents of documents of title or the services or facilities to be afforded by bailees, or otherwise regulating bailees' businesses in respects not specifically dealt with herein; but the fact that such laws are violated does not affect the status of a document of title which otherwise complies with the definition of a document of title (Section 1—201).

[(2) This Act does not repeal . . . .*, cited as the Uniform Act for the Simplification of Fiduciary Security Transfers, and if in any respect there is any inconsistency between that Act and the Article of this Act on investment securities (Article 8) the provisions of the former Act shall control.]

Note: *At * in subsection (2) insert the statutory reference to the Uniform Act for the Simplification of Fiduciary Security Transfers if such Act has previously been enacted. If it has not been enacted, omit subsection (2).*

Article 11
(REPORTERS' DRAFT)
EFFECTIVE DATE AND
TRANSITION PROVISIONS

This material has been numbered Article 11 to distinguish it from Article 10, the transition provision of the 1962 Code, which may still remain in effect in some states to cover transition problems from pre-Code law to the original Uniform Commercial Code. Adaptation may be necessary in particular states. The terms "[old Code]" and "[new Code]" and "[old U.C.C.]" and "[new U.C.C.]" are used herein, and should be suitably changed in each state.

Note: *This draft was prepared by the Reporters and has not been passed upon by the Review Committee, the Permanent Editorial Board, the American Law Institute, or the National Conference of Commissioners on Uniform State Laws. It is submitted as a working draft which may be adapted as appropriate in each state.*

§ 11—101. Effective Date.

This Act shall become effective at 12:01 A.M. on _____ , 19___.

§ 11—102. Preservation of Old Transition Provision.

The provisions of [here insert reference to the original transition provision in the particular state] shall continue to apply to [the new U.C.C.] and for this purpose the [old U.C.C. and new U.C.C.] shall be considered one continuous statute.

§ 11—103. Transition to [New Code]—General Rule.

Transactions validly entered into after [effective date of old U.C.C.] and before [effective date of new U.C.C.], and which were subject to the provisions of [old U.C.C.] and which would be subject to this Act as amended if they had been entered into after the effective date of [new U.C.C.] and the rights, duties and interests flowing from such transactions remain valid after the latter date and may be terminated, completed, consummated or enforced as required or permitted by the [new U.C.C.]. Security interests arising out of such transactions which are perfected when [new U.C.C.] becomes effective shall remain perfected until they lapse as provided in [new U.C.C.], and may be continued as permitted by [new U.C.C.], except as stated in Section 11—105.

§ 11—104. Transition Provision on Change of Requirement of Filing.

A security interest for the perfection of which filing or the taking of possession was required under [old U.C.C.] and which attached prior to the effective date of [new U.C.C.] but was not perfected shall be deemed perfected on the effective date of [new U.C.C.] if [new U.C.C.] permits perfection without filing or authorizes filing in the office or offices where a prior ineffective filing was made.

§ 11—105. Transition Provision on Change of Place of Filing.

(1) A financing statement or continuation statement filed prior to [effective date of new U.C.C.] which shall not have lapsed prior to [the effective date of new U.C.C.] shall remain effective for the period provided in the [old Code], but not less than five years after the filing.

(2) With respect to any collateral acquired by the debtor subsequent to the effective date of [new U.C.C.], any effective financing statement or continuation statement described in this section shall apply only if the filing or filings are in the office or offices that would be appropriate to perfect the security interests in the new collateral under [new U.C.C.].

(3) The effectiveness of any financing statement or continuation statement filed prior to [effective date of new U.C.C.] may be continued by a continuation statement as permitted by [new U.C.C.], except that if [new U.C.C.] requires a filing in an office where there was no previous financing statement, a new financing statement conforming to Section 11—106 shall be filed in that office.

(4) If the record of a mortgage of real estate would have been effective as a fixture filing of goods described therein if [new U.C.C.] had been in effect on the date of recording the mortgage, the mortgage shall be deemed effective as a fixture filing as to such goods under subsection (6) of Section 9—402 of the [new U.C.C.] on the effective date of [new U.C.C.].

§ 11—106. **Required Refilings.**

(1) If a security interest is perfected or has priority when this Act takes effect as to all persons or as to certain persons without any filing or recording, and if the filing of a financing statement would be required for the perfection or priority of the security interest against those persons under [new U.C.C.], the perfection and priority rights of the security interest continue until 3 years after the effective date of [new U.C.C.]. The perfection will then lapse unless a financing statement is filed as provided in subsection (4) or unless the security interest is perfected otherwise than by filing.

(2) If a security interest is perfected when [new U.C.C.] takes effect under a law other than [U.C.C.] which requires no further filing, refiling or recording to continue its perfection, perfection continues until and will lapse 3 years after [new U.C.C.] takes effect, unless a financing statement is filed as provided in subsection (4) or unless the security interest is perfected otherwise than by filing, or unless under subsection (3) of Section 9—302 the other law continues to govern filing.

(3) If a security interest is perfected by a filing, refiling or recording under a law repealed by this Act which required further filing, refiling or recording to continue its perfection, perfection continues and will lapse on the date provided by the law so repealed for such further filing, refiling or recording unless a financing statement is filed as provided in subsection (4) or unless the security interest is perfected otherwise than by filing.

(4) A financing statement may be filed within six months before the perfection of a security interest would otherwise lapse. Any such financing statement may be signed by either the debtor or the secured party. It must identify the security agreement, statement or notice (however denominated in any statute or other law repealed or modified by this Act), state the office where and the date when the last filing, refiling or recording, if any, was made with respect thereto, and the filing number, if any, or book and page, if any, of recording and further state that the security agreement, statement or notice, however denominated, in another filing office under the [U.C.C.] or under any statute or other law repealed or modified by this Act is still effective. Section 9—401 and Section 9—103 determine the proper place to file such a financing statement. Except as specified in this subsection, the provisions of Section 9—403(3) for continuation statements apply to such a financing statement.

§ 11—107. **Transition Provisions as to Priorities.**

Except as otherwise provided in [Article 11], [old U.C.C.] shall apply to any questions of priority if the positions of the parties were fixed prior to the effective date of [new U.C.C.]. In other cases questions of priority shall be determined by [new U.C.C.].

§ 11—108. **Presumption that Rule of Law Continues Unchanged.**

Unless a change in law has clearly been made, the provisions of [new U.C.C.] shall be deemed declaratory of the meaning of the [old U.C.C.].

1978 OFFICIAL TEXT—UCC

The preceding articles and sections constitute the 1978 official text of the Uniform Commercial Code. As of January 1, 1987, the following states had adopted most of the proposed amendments of 1972, which was the year of the most recent major changes. The other states basically follow the original text plus amendments proposed in the 1960s.

1972 Amendments

States	Effective Date	States	Effective Date
Alabama	2/01/82	Nebraska	7/19/80
Alaska	7/01/83	Nevada	7/01/75
Arizona	1/01/76	New Hampshire	8/21/79
Arkansas	1/01/74	New Jersey	12/01/81
California	1/01/76	New Mexico	6/14/85
Colorado	1/01/78	New York	7/02/78
Connecticut	10/01/76	North Carolina	7/01/76
Delaware	1/01/84	North Dakota	1/01/74
Florida	1/01/80	Ohio	1/01/79
Georgia	7/01/78	Oklahoma	10/19/81
Hawaii	7/01/79	Oregon	1/01/74
Idaho	7/01/79	Pennsylvania	5/25/83
Illinois	7/01/73	Rhode Island	1/01/80
Indiana	1/01/86	South Dakota	7/01/83
Iowa	1/01/75	Tennessee	1/01/86
Kansas	1/01/76	Texas	1/01/74
Kentucky	7/01/87	Utah	7/01/77
Maine	1/01/78	Virginia	7/01/74
Maryland	1/01/81	Washington	7/01/82
Massachusetts	1/01/80	West Virginia	7/01/75
Michigan	1/01/79	Wisconsin	7/01/74
Minnesota	1/01/77	Wyoming	9/01/83
Mississippi	4/01/78		
Montana	10/01/83	District of Columbia	3/16/82

THE UNIFORM PARTNERSHIP ACT

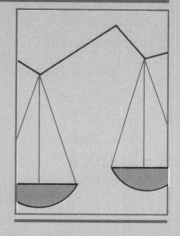

(Adopted in 49 States [all of the states except Louisiana], the District of Columbia, the Virgin Islands, and Guam. The adoptions by Alabama and Nebraska do not follow the official text in every respect, but are substantially similar, with local variations.)

The Act consists of 7 Parts as follows:

I. Preliminary Provisions

II. Nature of Partnership

III. Relations of Partners to Persons Dealing with the Partnership

IV. Relations of Partners to One Another

V. Property Rights of a Partner

VI. Dissolution and Winding Up

VII. Miscellaneous Provisions

An Act to make uniform the Law of Partnerships

Be it enacted, etc.:

Part I Preliminary Provisions

Sec. 1. Name of Act

This act may be cited as Uniform Partnership Act.

Sec. 2. Definition of Terms

In this act, "Court" includes every court and judge having jurisdiction in the case.

"Business" includes every trade, occupation, or profession.

"Person" includes individuals, partnerships, corporations, and other associations.

"Bankrupt" includes bankrupt under the Federal Bankruptcy Act or insolvent under any state insolvent act.

"Conveyance" includes every assignment, lease, mortgage, or encumbrance.

"Real property" includes land and any interest or estate in land.

Sec. 3. Interpretation of Knowledge and Notice

(1) A person has "knowledge" of a fact within the meaning of this act not only when he has actual knowledge thereof, but also when he has knowledge of such other facts as in the circumstances shows bad faith.

(2) A person has "notice" of a fact within the meaning of this act when the person who claims the benefit of the notice:

(a) States the fact to such person, or

(b) Delivers through the mail, or by other means of communication, a written statement of the fact to such person or to a proper person at his place of business or residence.

Sec. 4. Rules of Construction

(1) The rule that statutes in derogation of the common law are to be strictly construed shall have no application to this act.

(2) The law of estoppel shall apply under this act.

(3) The law of agency shall apply under this act.

(4) This act shall be so interpreted and construed as to effect its general purpose to make uniform the law of those states which enact it.

(5) This act shall not be construed so as to impair the obligations of any contract existing when the act goes into effect, nor to affect any action or proceedings begun or right accrued before this act takes effect.

Sec. 5. Rules for Cases Not Provided for in this Act.

In any case not provided for in this act the rules of law and equity, including the law merchant, shall govern.

Part II Nature of Partnership

Sec. 6. Partnership Defined

(1) A partnership is an association of two or more persons to carry on as co-owners a business for profit.

(2) But any association formed under any other statute of this state, or any statute adopted by authority, other than the authority of this state, is not a partnership under this act, unless such association would have been a partnership in this state prior to the adoption of this act; but this act shall apply to limited partnerships except in so far as the statutes relating to such partnerships are inconsistent herewith.

Sec. 7. Rules for Determining the Existence of a Partnership

In determining whether a partnership exists, these rules shall apply:

(1) Except as provided by Section 16 persons who are not partners as to each other are not partners as to third persons.

(2) Joint tenancy, tenancy in common, tenancy by the entireties, joint property, common property, or part ownership does not of itself establish a partnership, whether such co-owners do or do not share any profits made by the use of the property.

(3) The sharing of gross returns does not of itself establish a partnership, whether or not the persons sharing them have a joint or common right or interest in any property from which the returns are derived.

(4) The receipt by a person of a share of the profits of a business is prima facie evidence that he is a partner

in the business, but no such inference shall be drawn if such profits were received in payment:

(a) As a debt by installments or otherwise,

(b) As wages of an employee or rent to a landlord,

(c) As an annuity to a widow or representative of a deceased partner,

(d) As interest on a loan, though the amount of payment vary with the profits of the business.

(e) As the consideration for the sale of a good-will of a business or other property by installments or otherwise.

Sec. 8. **Partnership Property**

(1) All property originally brought into the partnership stock or subsequently acquired by purchase or otherwise, on account of the partnership, is partnership property.

(2) Unless the contrary intention appears, property acquired with partnership funds is partnership property.

(3) Any estate in real property may be acquired in the partnership name. Title so acquired can be conveyed only in the partnership name.

(4) A conveyance to a partnership in the partnership name, though without words of inheritance, passes the entire estate of the grantor unless a contrary intent appears.

Part III Relations of Partners to Persons Dealing with the Partnership

Sec. 9. **Partner Agent of Partnership as to Partnership Business**

(1) Every partner is an agent of the partnership for the purpose of its business, and the act of every partner, including the execution in the partnership name of any instrument, for apparently carrying on in the usual way the business of the partnership of which he is a member binds the partnership, unless the partner so acting has in fact no authority to act for the partnership in the particular matter, and the person with whom he is dealing has knowledge of the fact that he has no such authority.

(2) An act of a partner which is not apparently for the carrying on of the business of the partnership in the usual way does not bind the partnership unless authorized by the other partners.

(3) Unless authorized by the other partners or unless they have abandoned the business, one or more but less than all the partners have no authority to:

(a) Assign the partnership property in trust for creditors or on the assignee's promise to pay the debts of the partnership,

(b) Dispose of the good-will of the business,

(c) Do any other act which would make it impossible to carry on the ordinary business of a partnership,

(d) Confess a judgment,

(e) Submit a partnership claim or liability to arbitration or reference.

(4) No act of a partner in contravention of a restriction on authority shall bind the partnership to persons having knowledge of the restriction.

Sec. 10. **Conveyance of Real Property of the Partnership**

(1) Where title to real property is in the partnership name, any partner may convey title to such property by a conveyance executed in the partnership name; but the partnership may recover such property unless the partner's act binds the partnership under the provisions of paragraph (1) of section 9, or unless such property has been conveyed by the grantee or a person claiming through such grantee to a holder for value without knowledge that the partner, in making the conveyance, has exceeded his authority.

(2) Where title to real property is in the name of the partnership, a conveyance executed by a partner, in his own name, passes the equitable interest of the partnership, provided the act is one within the authority of the partner under the provisions of paragraph (1) of section 9.

(3) Where title to real property is in the name of one or more but not all the partners, and the record does not disclose the right of the partnership, the partners in whose name the title stands may convey title to such property, but the partnership may recover such property if the partners' act does not bind the partnership under the provisions of paragraph (1) of section 9, unless the purchaser or his assignee, is a holder for value, without knowledge.

(4) Where the title to real property is in the name of one or more or all the partners, or in a third person in trust for the partnership, a conveyance executed by a partner in the partnership name, or in his own name, passes the equitable interest of the partnership, provided the act is one within the authority of the partner under the provisions of paragraph (1) of section 9.

(5) Where the title to real property is in the names of all the partners a conveyance executed by all the partners passes all their rights in such property.

Sec. 11. **Partnership Bound by Admission of Partner**

An admission or representation made by any partner concerning partnership affairs within the scope of his authority as conferred by this act is evidence against the partnership.

Sec. 12. Partnership Charged with Knowledge of or Notice to Partner

Notice to any partner of any matter relating to partnership affairs, and the knowledge of the partner acting in the particular matter, acquired while a partner or then present to his mind, and the knowledge of any other partner who reasonably could and should have communicated it to the acting partner, operate as notice to or knowledge of the partnership, except in the case of a fraud on the partnership committed by or with the consent of that partner.

Sec. 13. Partnership Bound by Partner's Wrongful Act

Where, by any wrongful act or omission of any partner acting in the ordinary course of the business of the partnership or with the authority of his co-partners, loss or injury is caused to any person, not being a partner in the partnership, or any penalty is incurred, the partnership is liable therefor to the same extent as the partner so acting or omitting to act.

Sec. 14. Partnership Bound by Partner's Breach of Trust

The partnership is bound to make good the loss:

(a) Where one partner acting within the scope of his apparent authority receives money or property of a third person and misapplies it; and

(b) Where the partnership in the course of its business receives money or property of a third person and the money or property so received is misapplied by any partner while it is in the custody of the partnership.

Sec. 15. Nature of Partner's Liability

All partners are liable

(a) Jointly and severally for everything chargeable to the partnership under sections 13 and 14.

(b) Jointly for all other debts and obligations of the partnership; but any partner may enter into a separate obligation to perform a partnership contract.

Sec. 16. Partner by Estoppel

(1) When a person, by words spoken or written or by conduct, represents himself, or consents to another representing him to any one, as a partner in an existing partnership or with one or more persons not actual partners, he is liable to any such person to whom such representation has been made, who has, on the faith of such representation, given credit to the actual or apparent partnership, and if he has made such representation or consented to its being made in a public manner he is liable to such person, whether the representation has or has not been made or communicated to such person so giving credit by or with the knowledge of the apparent partner making the representation or consenting to its being made.

(a) When a partnership liability results, he is liable as though he were an actual member of the partnership.

(b) When no partnership liability results, he is liable jointly with the other persons, if any, so consenting to the contract or representation as to incur liability, otherwise separately.

(2) When a person has been thus represented to be a partner in an existing partnership, or with one or more persons not actual partners, he is an agent of the persons consenting to such representation to bind them to the same extent and in the same manner as though he were a partner in fact, with respect to persons who rely upon the representation. Where all the members of the existing partnership consent to the representation, a partnership act or obligation results; but in all other cases it is the joint act or obligation of the person acting and the persons consenting to the representation.

Sec. 17. Liability of Incoming Partner

A person admitted as a partner into an existing partnership is liable for all the obligations of the partnership arising before his admission as though he had been a partner when such obligations were incurred, except that this liability shall be satisfied only out of partnership property.

Part IV Relations of Partners to One Another

Sec. 18. Rules Determining Rights and Duties of Partners

The rights and duties of the partners in relation to the partnership shall be determined, subject to any agreement between them, by the following rules:

(a) Each partner shall be repaid his contributions, whether by way of capital or advances to the partnership property and share equally in the profits and surplus remaining after all liabilities, including those to partners, are satisfied; and must contribute towards the losses, whether of capital or otherwise, sustained by the partnership according to his share in the profits.

(b) The partnership must indemnify every partner in respect of payments made and personal liabilities reasonably incurred by him in the ordinary and proper conduct of its business, or for the preservation of its business or property.

(c) A partner, who in aid of the partnership makes any payment or advance beyond the amount of capital which he agreed to contribute, shall be paid interest from the date of the payment or advance.

(d) A partner shall receive interest on the capital contributed by him only from the date when repayment should be made.

(e) All partners have equal rights in the management and conduct of the partnership business.

(f) No partner is entitled to remuneration for acting in the partnership business, except that a surviving partner is entitled to reasonable compensation for his services in winding up the partnership affairs.

(g) No person can become a member of a partnership without the consent of all the partners.

(h) Any difference arising as to ordinary matters connected with the partnership business may be decided by a majority of the partners; but no act in contravention of any agreement between the partners may be done rightfully without the consent of all the partners.

Sec. 19. **Partnership Books**

The partnership books shall be kept, subject to any agreement between the partners, at the principal place of business of the partnership, and every partner shall at all times have access to and may inspect and copy any of them.

Sec. 20. **Duty of Partners to Render Information**

Partners shall render on demand true and full information of all things affecting the partnership to any partner or the legal representative of any deceased partner or partner under legal disability.

Sec. 21. **Partner Accountable as a Fiduciary**

(1) Every partner must account to the partnership for any benefit, and hold as trustee for it any profits derived by him without the consent of the other partners from any transaction connected with the formation, conduct, or liquidation of the partnership or from any use by him of its property.

(2) This section applies also to the representatives of a deceased partner engaged in the liquidation of the affairs of the partnership as the personal representatives of the last surviving partner.

Sec. 22. **Right to an Account**

Any partner shall have the right to a formal account as to partnership affairs:

(a) If he is wrongfully excluded from the partnership business or possession of its property by his co-partners,

(b) If the right exists under the terms of any agreement,

(c) As provided by section 21,

(d) Whenever other circumstances render it just and reasonable.

Sec. 23. **Continuation of Partnership Beyond Fixed Term**

(1) When a partnership for a fixed term or particular undertaking is continued after the termination of such term or particular undertaking without any express agreement, the rights and duties of the partners remain the same as they were at such termination, so far as is consistent with a partnership at will.

(2) A continuation of the business by the partners or such of them as habitually acted therein during the term, without any settlement or liquidation of the partnership affairs, is prima facie evidence of a continuation of the partnership.

Part V Property Rights of a Partner

Sec. 24. **Extent of Property Rights of a Partner**

The property rights of a partner are (1) his rights in specific partnership property, (2) his interest in the partnership, and (3) his right to participate in the management.

Sec. 25. **Nature of a Partner's Right in Specific Partnership Property**

(1) A partner is co-owner with his partners of specific partnership property holding as a tenant in partnership.

(2) The incidents of this tenancy are such that:

(a) A partner, subject to the provisions of this act and to any agreement between the partners, has an equal right with his partners to possess specific partnership property for partnership purposes; but he has no right to possess such property for any other purpose without the consent of his partners.

(b) A partner's right in specific partnership property is not assignable except in connection with the assignment of rights of all the partners in the same property.

(c) A partner's right in specific partnership property is not subject to attachment or execution, except on a claim against the partnership. When partnership property is attached for a partnership debt the partners, or any of them, or the representatives of a deceased partner, cannot claim any right under the homestead or exemption laws.

(d) On the death of a partner his right in specific partnership property vests in the surviving partner or partners, except where the deceased was the last surviving partner, when his right in such property vests in his legal representative. Such surviving partner or partners, or the legal representative of the last surviving partner, has no right to possess the partnership property for any but a partnership purpose.

(e) A partner's right in specific partnership property is not subject to dower, curtesy, or allowances to widows, heirs, or next of kin.

Sec. 26. Nature of Partner's Interest in the Partnership

A partner's interest in the partnership is his share of the profits and surplus, and the same is personal property.

Sec. 27. Assignment of Partner's Interest

(1) A conveyance by a partner of his interest in the partnership does not of itself dissolve the partnership, nor, as against the other partners in the absence of agreement, entitle the assignee, during the continuance of the partnership, to interfere in the management or administration of the partnership business or affairs, or to require any information or account of partnership transactions, or to inspect the partnership books; but it merely entitles the assignee to receive in accordance with his contract the profits to which the assigning partner would otherwise be entitled.

(2) In case of a dissolution of the partnership, the assignee is entitled to receive his assignor's interest and may require an account from the date only of the last account agreed to by all the partners.

Sec. 28. Partner's Interest Subject to Charging Order

(1) On due application to a competent court by any judgment creditor of a partner, the court which entered the judgment, order, or decree, or any other court, may charge the interest of the debtor partner with payment of the unsatisfied amount of such judgment debt with interest thereon; and may then or later appoint a receiver of his share of the profits, and of any other money due or to fall due to him in respect of the partnership, and make all other orders, directions, accounts and inquiries which the debtor partner might have made, or which the circumstances of the case may require.

(2) The interest charged may be redeemed at any time before foreclosure, or in case of a sale being directed by the court may be purchased without thereby causing a dissolution:

(a) With separate property, by any one or more of the partners, or

(b) With partnership property, by any one or more of the partners with the consent of all the partners whose interests are not so charged or sold.

(3) Nothing in this act shall be held to deprive a partner of his right, if any, under the exemption laws, as regards his interest in the partnership.

Part VI Dissolution and Winding up

Sec. 29. Dissolution Defined

The dissolution of a partnership is the change in the relation of the partners caused by any partner ceasing to be associated in the carrying on as distinguished from the winding up of the business.

Sec. 30. Partnership not Terminated by Dissolution

On dissolution the partnership is not terminated, but continues until the winding up of partnership affairs is completed.

Sec. 31. Causes of Dissolution

Dissolution is caused:

(1) Without violation of the agreement between the partners,

(a) By the termination of the definite term or particular undertaking specified in the agreement,

(b) By the express will of any partner when no definite term or particular undertaking is specified,

(c) By the express will of all the partners who have not assigned their interests or suffered them to be charged for their separate debts, either before or after the termination of any specified term or particular undertaking,

(d) By the expulsion of any partner from the business bona fide in accordance with such a power conferred by the agreement between the partners;

(2) In contravention of the agreement between the partners, where the circumstances do not permit a dissolution under any other provision of this section, by the express will of any partner at any time;

(3) By any event which makes it unlawful for the business of the partnership to be carried on or for the members to carry it on in partnership;

(4) By the death of any partner;

(5) By the bankruptcy of any partner or the partnership;

(6) By decree of court under section 32.

Sec. 32. Dissolution by Decree of Court

(1) On application by or for a partner the court shall decree a dissolution whenever:

(a) A partner has been declared a lunatic in any judicial proceeding or is shown to be of unsound mind,

(b) A partner becomes in any other way incapable of performing his part of the partnership contract,

(c) A partner has been guilty of such conduct as tends to affect prejudicially the carrying on of the business,

(d) A partner wilfully or persistently commits a breach of the partnership agreement, or otherwise so conducts himself in matters relating to the partnership business that it is not reasonably practicable to carry on the business in partnership with him,

(e) The business of the partnership can only be carried on at a loss,

(f) Other circumstances render a dissolution equitable.

(2) On the application of the purchaser of a partner's interest under sections 28 or 29 [should read 27 or 28];

(a) After the termination of the specified term or particular undertaking,

(b) At any time if the partnership was a partnership at will when the interest was assigned or when the charging order was issued.

Sec. 33. General Effect of Dissolution on Authority of Partner

Except so far as may be necessary to wind up partnership affairs or to complete transactions begun but not then finished, dissolution terminates all authority of any partner to act for the partnership,

(1) With respect to the partners,

(a) When the dissolution is not by the act, bankruptcy or death of a partner; or

(b) When the dissolution is by such act, bankruptcy or death of a partner, in cases where section 34 so requires.

(2) With respect to persons not partners, as declared in section 35.

Sec. 34. Rights of Partner to Contribution from Co-partners After Dissolution

Where the dissolution is caused by the act, death or bankruptcy of a partner, each partner is liable to his copartners for his share of any liability created by any partner acting for the partnership as if the partnership had not been dissolved unless

(a) The dissolution being by act of any partner, the partner acting for the partnership had knowledge of the dissolution, or

(b) The dissolution being by the death or bankruptcy of a partner, the partner acting for the partnership had knowledge or notice of the death or bankruptcy.

Sec. 35. Power of Partner to Bind Partnership to Third Persons After Dissolution

(1) After dissolution a partner can bind the partnership except as provided in Paragraph (3).

(a) By any act appropriate for winding up partnership affairs or completing transactions unfinished at dissolution;

(b) By any transaction which would bind the partnership if dissolution had not taken place, provided the other party to the transaction

(I) Had extended credit to the partnership prior to dissolution and had no knowledge or notice of the dissolution; or

(II) Though he had not so extended credit, had nevertheless known of the partnership prior to dissolution, and, having no knowledge or notice of dissolution, the fact of dissolution had not been advertised in a newspaper of general circulation in the place (or in each place if more than one) at which the partnership business was regularly carried on.

(2) The liability of a partner under paragraph (1b) shall be satisfied out of partnership assets alone when such partner had been prior to dissolution

(a) Unknown as a partner to the person with whom the contract is made; and

(b) So far unknown and inactive in partnership affairs that the business reputation of the partnership could not be said to have been in any degree due to his connection with it.

(3) The partnership is in no case bound by any act of a partner after dissolution

(a) Where the partnership is dissolved because it is unlawful to carry on the business, unless the act is appropriate for winding up partnership affairs; or

(b) Where the partner has become bankrupt; or

(c) Where the partner has no authority to wind up partnership affairs; except by a transaction with one who

(I) Had extended credit to the partnership prior to dissolution and had no knowledge or notice of his want of authority; or

(II) Had not extended credit to the partnership prior to dissolution, and, having no knowledge or notice of his want of authority, the fact of his want of authority has not been advertised in the manner provided for advertising the fact of dissolution in paragraph (1bII).

(4) Nothing in this section shall affect the liability under Section 16 of any person who after dissolution represents himself or consents to another representing him as a partner in a partnership engaged in carrying on business.

Sec. 36. **Effect of Dissolution on Partner's Existing Liability**

(1) The dissolution of the partnership does not of itself discharge the existing liability of any partner.

(2) A partner is discharged from any existing liability upon dissolution of the partnership by an agreement to that effect between himself, the partnership creditor and the person or partnership continuing the business; and such agreement may be inferred from the course of dealing between the creditor having knowledge of the dissolution and the person or partnership continuing the business.

(3) Where a person agrees to assume the existing obligations of a dissolved partnership, the partners whose obligations have been assumed shall be discharged from any liability to any creditor of the partnership who, knowing of the agreement, consents to a material alteration in the nature or time of payment of such obligations.

(4) The individual property of a deceased partner shall be liable for all obligations of the partnership incurred while he was a partner but subject to the prior payment of his separate debts.

Sec. 37. **Right to Wind Up**

Unless otherwise agreed the partners who have not wrongfully dissolved the partnership or the legal representative of the last surviving partner, not bankrupt, has the right to wind up the partnership affairs; provided, however, that any partner, his legal representative or his assignee, upon cause shown, may obtain winding up by the court.

Sec. 38. **Rights of Partners to Application of Partnership Property**

(1) When dissolution is caused in any way, except in contravention of the partnership agreement, each partner, as against his co-partners and all persons claiming through them in respect of their interests in the partnership, unless otherwise agreed, may have the partnership property applied to discharge its liabilities, and the surplus applied to pay in cash the net amount owing to the respective partners. But if dissolution is caused by expulsion of a partner, bona fide under the partnership agreement and if the expelled partner is discharged from all partnership liabilities, either by payment or agreement under section 36(2), he shall receive in cash only the net amount due him from the partnership.

(2) When dissolution is caused in contravention of the partnership agreement the rights of the partners shall be as follows:

(a) Each partner who has not caused dissolution wrongfully shall have,

(I) All the rights specified in paragraph (1) of this section, and

(II) The right, as against each partner who has caused the dissolution wrongfully, to damages for breach of the agreement.

(b) The partners who have not caused the dissolution wrongfully, if they all desire to continue the business in the same name, either by themselves or jointly with others, may do so, during the agreed term for the partnership and for that purpose may possess the partnership property, provided they secure the payment by bond approved by the court, or pay to any partner who has caused the dissolution wrongfully, the value of his interest in the partnership at the dissolution, less any damages recoverable under clause (2a II) of the section, and in like manner indemnify him against all present or future partnership liabilities.

(c) A partner who has caused the dissolution wrongfully shall have:

(I) If the business is not continued under the provisions of paragraph (2b) all the rights of a partner under paragraph (1), subject to clause (2a II), of this section,

(II) If the business is continued under paragraph (2b) of this section the right as against his co-partners and all claiming through them in respect of their interests in the partnership, to have the value of his interest in the partnership, less any damages caused to his co-partners by the dissolution, ascertained and paid to him in cash, or the payment secured by bond approved by the court, and to be released from all existing liabilities of the partnership; but in ascertaining the value of the partner's interest the value of the good-will of the business shall not be considered.

Sec. 39. **Rights Where Partnership is Dissolved for Fraud or Misrepresentation**

Where a partnership contract is rescinded on the ground of the fraud or misrepresentation of one of the parties thereto, the party entitled to rescind is, without prejudice to any other right, entitled,

(a) To a lien on, or right of retention of, the surplus of the partnership property after satisfying the partnership liabilities to third persons for any sum of money paid by him for the purchase of an interest in the partnership and for any capital or advances contributed by him; and

(b) To stand, after all liabilities to third persons have been satisfied, in the place of the creditors of the partnership for any payments made by him in respect of the partnership liabilities; and

(c) To be indemnified by the person guilty of the fraud or making the representation against all debts and liabilities of the partnership.

Sec. 40. **Rules for Distribution**

In settling accounts between the partners after dissolution, the following rules shall be observed, subject to any agreement to the contrary:

(a) The assets of the partnership are:

(I) The partnership property,

(II) The contributions of the partners necessary for the payment of all the liabilities specified in clause (b) of this paragraph.

(b) The liabilities of the partnership shall rank in order of payment, as follows:

(I) Those owing to creditors other than partners,

(II) Those owing to partners other than for capital and profits,

(III) Those owing to partners in respect of capital,

(IV) Those owing to partners in respect of profits.

(c) The assets shall be applied in the order of their declaration in clause (a) of this paragraph to the satisfaction of the liabilities.

(d) The partners shall contribute, as provided by section 18(a) the amount necessary to satisfy the liabilities; but if any, but not all, of the partners are insolvent, or, not being subject to process, refuse to contribute, the other partners shall contribute their share of the liabilities, and, in the relative proportions in which they share the profits, the additional amount necessary to pay the liabilities.

(e) An assignee for the benefit of creditors or any person appointed by the court shall have the right to enforce the contributions specified in clause (d) of this paragraph.

(f) Any partner or his legal representative shall have the right to enforce the contributions specified in clause (d) of this paragraph, to the extent of the amount which he has paid in excess of his share of the liability.

(g) The individual property of a deceased partner shall be liable for the contributions specified in clause (d) of this paragraph.

(h) When partnership property and the individual properties of the partners are in possession of a court for distribution, partnership creditors shall have priority on partnership property and separate creditors on individual property, saving the rights of lien or secured creditors as heretofore.

(i) Where a partner has become bankrupt or his estate is insolvent the claims against his separate property shall rank in the following order:

(I) Those owing to separate creditors,

(II) Those owing to partnership creditors,

(III) Those owing to partners by way of contribution.

Sec. 41. **Liability of Persons Continuing the Business in Certain Cases**

(1) When any new partner is admitted into an existing partnership, or when any partner retires and assigns (or the representative of the deceased partner assigns) his rights in partnership property to two or more of the partners, or to one or more of the partners and one or more third persons, if the business is continued without liquidation of the partnership affairs, creditors of the first or dissolved partnership are also creditors of the partnership so continuing the business.

(2) When all but one partner retire and assign (or the representative of a deceased partner assigns) their rights in partnership property to the remaining partner, who continues the business without liquidation of partnership affairs, either alone or with others, creditors of the dissolved partnership are also creditors of the person or partnership so continuing the business.

(3) When any partner retires or dies and the business of the dissolved partnership is continued as set forth in paragraphs (1) and (2) of this section, with the consent of the retired partners or the representative of the deceased partner, but without any assignment of his right in partnership property, rights of creditors of the dissolved partnership and of the creditors of the person or partnership continuing the business shall be as if such assignment had been made.

(4) When all the partners or their representatives assign their rights in partnership property to one or more third persons who promise to pay the debts and who continue the business of the dissolved partnership, creditors of the dissolved partnership are also creditors of the person or partnership continuing the business.

(5) When any partner wrongfully causes a dissolution and the remaining partners continue the business under the provisions of section 38(2b), either alone or with others, and without liquidation of the partnership affairs, creditors of the dissolved partnership are also creditors of the person or partnership continuing the business.

(6) When a partner is expelled and the remaining partners continue the business either alone or with others, without liquidation of the partnership affairs, creditors of the dissolved partnership are also creditors of the person or partnership continuing the business.

(7) The liability of a third person becoming a partner in the partnership continuing the business, under this

section, to the creditors of the dissolved partnership shall be satisfied out of partnership property only.

(8) When the business of a partnership after dissolution is continued under any conditions set forth in this section the creditors of the dissolved partnership, as against the separate creditors of the retiring or deceased partner or the representative of the deceased partner, have a prior right to any claim of the retired partner or the representative of the deceased partner against the person or partnership continuing the business, on account of the retired or deceased partner's interest in the dissolved partnership or on account of any consideration promised for such interest or for his right in partnership property.

(9) Nothing in this section shall be held to modify any right of creditors to set aside any assignment on the ground of fraud.

(10) The use by the person or partnership continuing the business of the partnership name, or the name of a deceased partner as part thereof, shall not of itself make the individual property of the deceased partner liable for any debts contracted by such person or partnership.

Sec. 42. **Rights of Retiring or Estate of Deceased Partner When the Business is Continued**

When any partner retires or dies, and the business is continued under any of the conditions set forth in section 41 (1, 2, 3, 5, 6), or section 38(2b) without any settlement of accounts as between him or his estate and the person or partnership continuing the business, un-less otherwise agreed, he or his legal representative as against such persons or partnership may have the value of his interest at the date of dissolution ascertained, and shall receive as an ordinary creditor an amount equal to the value of his interest in the dissolved partnership with interest, or, at his option or at the option of his legal representative, in lieu of interest, the profits attributable to the use of his right in the property of the dissolved partnership; provided that the creditors of the dissolved partnership as against the separate creditors, or the representative of the retired or deceased partner, shall have priority on any claim arising under this section, as provided by section 41(8) of this act.

Sec. 43. **Accrual of Actions**

The right to an account of his interest shall accrue to any partner, or his legal representative, as against the winding up partners or the surviving partners or the person or partnership continuing the business, at the date of dissolution, in the absence of any agreement to the contrary.

Part VII Miscellaneous Provisions

Sec. 44. **When Act Takes Effect**

This act shall take effect on the ___ day of ___ one thousand nine hundred and ___.

Sec. 45. **Legislation Repealed**

All acts or parts of acts inconsistent with this act are hereby repealed.

Appendix D

UNIFORM LIMITED PARTNERSHIP ACT

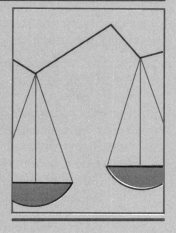

(Adopted in 13 States: Alaska, Georgia, Hawaii, Indiana, Kentucky, Maine, New Hampshire, New Mexico, New York, Pennsylvania, Tennessee, Utah, and Vermont. Also adopted in the District of Columbia, and the Virgin Islands.)

Sec. 1. **Limited Partnership Defined**

A limited partnership is a partnership formed by two or more persons under the provisions of Section 2, having as members one or more general partners and one or more limited partners. The limited partners as such shall not be bound by the obligations of the partnership.

Sec. 2. **Formation**

(1) Two or more persons desiring to form a limited partnership shall

　(a) Sign and swear to a certificate, which shall state

　　I. The name of the partnership,

　　II. The character of the business,

　　III. The location of the principal place of business,

　　IV. The name and place of residence of each member; general and limited partners being respectively designated,

　　V. The term for which the partnership is to exist,

　　VI. The amount of cash and a description of and the agreed value of the other property contributed by each limited partner,

　　VII. The additional contributions, if any, agreed to be made by each limited partner and the times at which or events on the happening of which they shall be made,

　　VIII. The time, if agreed upon, when the contribution of each limited partner is to be returned,

　　IX. The share of the profits or the other compensation by way of income which each limited partner shall receive by reason of his contribution,

　　X. The right, if given, of a limited partner to substitute an assignee as contributor in his place, and the terms and conditions of the substitution,

　　XI. The right, if given, of the partners to admit additional limited partners,

　　XII. The right, if given, of one or more of the limited partners to priority over other limited partners, as to contributions or as to compensation by way of income, and the nature of such priority,

　　XIII. The right, if given, of the remaining general partner or partners to continue the business on the death, retirement or insanity of a general partner, and

　　XIV. The right, if given, of a limited partner to demand and receive property other than cash in return for his contribution.

　(b) File for record the certificate in the office of [here designate the proper office].

(2) A limited partnership is formed if there has been substantial compliance in good faith with the requirements of paragraph (1).

Sec. 3. **Business Which May Be Carried On**

A limited partnership may carry on any business which a partnership without limited partners may carry on, except [here designate the business to be prohibited].

Sec. 4. **Character of Limited Partner's Contribution**

The contributions of a limited partner may be cash or other property, but not services.

Sec. 5. **A Name Not to Contain Surname of Limited Partner; Exceptions**

(1) The surname of a limited partner shall not appear in the partnership name, unless

　(a) It is also the surname of a general partner, or

　(b) Prior to the time when the limited partner became such the business had been carried on under a name in which his surname appeared.

(2) A limited partner whose name appears in a partnership name contrary to the provisions of paragraph (1) is liable as a general partner to partnership creditors who extend credit to the partnership without actual knowledge that he is not a general partner.

Sec. 6. **Liability for False Statements in Certificate**

If the certificate contains a false statement, one who suffers loss by reliance on such statement may hold liable any party to the certificate who knew the statement to be false.

(a) At the time he signed the certificate, or

(b) Subsequently, but within a sufficient time before the statement was relied upon to enable him to cancel or amend the certificate, or to file a petition for its cancellation or amendment as provided in Section 25(3).

Sec. 7. **Limited Partner Not Liable to Creditors**

A limited partner shall not become liable as a general partner unless, in addition to the exercise of his rights and powers as a limited partner, he takes part in the control of the business.

Sec. 8. Admission of Additional Limited Partners

After the formation of a limited partnership, additional limited partners may be admitted upon filing an amendment to the original certificate in accordance with the requirements of Section 25.

Sec. 9. Rights, Powers and Liabilities of a General Partner

(1) A general partner shall have all the rights and powers and be subject to all the restrictions and liabilities of a partner in a partnership without limited partners, except that without the written consent or ratification of the specific act by all the limited partners, a general partner or all of the general partners have no authority to

(a) Do any act in contravention of the certificate,

(b) Do any act which would make it impossible to carry on the ordinary business of the partnership,

(c) Confess a judgment against the partnership,

(d) Possess partnership property, or assign their rights in specific partnership property, for other than a partnership purpose,

(e) Admit a person as a general partner,

(f) Admit a person as a limited partner, unless the right so to do is given in the certificate,

(g) Continue the business with partnership property on the death, retirement or insanity of a general partner, unless the right so to do is given in the certificate.

Sec. 10. Rights of a Limited Partner

(1) A limited partner shall have the same rights as a general partner to

(a) Have the partnership books kept at the principal place of business of the partnership, and at all times to inspect and copy any of them.

(b) Have on demand true and full information of all things affecting the partnership, and a formal account of partnership affairs whenever circumstances render it just and reasonable, and

(c) Have dissolution and winding up by decree of court.

(2) A limited partner shall have the right to receive a share of the profits or other compensation by way of income, and to the return of his contribution as provided in Sections 15 and 16.

Sec. 11. Status of Person Erroneously Believing Himself a Limited Partner

A person who has contributed to the capital of a business conducted by a person or partnership erroneously believing that he has become a limited partner in a limited partnership, is not, by reason of his exercise of the rights of a limited partner, a general partner with the person or in the partnership carrying on the business, or bound by the obligations of such person or partnership; provided that on ascertaining the mistake he promptly renounces his interest in the profits of the business, or other compensation by way of income.

Sec. 12. One Person Both General and Limited Partner

(1) A person may be a general partner and a limited partner in the same partnership at the same time.

(2) A person who is a general, and also at the same time a limited partner, shall have all the rights and powers and be subject to all the restrictions of a general partner; except that, in respect to his contribution, he shall have the rights against the other members which he would have had if he were not also a general partner.

Sec. 13. Loans and Other Business Transactions with Limited Partner

(1) A limited partner also may loan money to and transact other business with the partnership, and, unless he is also a general partner, receive on account of resulting claims against the partnership, with general creditors, a pro rata share of the assets. No limited partner shall in respect to any such claim

(a) Receive or hold as collateral security any partnership property, or

(b) Receive from a general partner or the partnership any payment, conveyance, or release from liability, if at the time the assets of the partnership are not sufficient to discharge partnership liabilities to persons not claiming as general or limited partners,

(2) The receiving of collateral security, or a payment, conveyance, or release in violation of the provisions of paragraph (1) is a fraud on the creditors of the partnership.

Sec. 14. Relation of Limited Partners Inter Se

Where there are several limited partners the members may agree that one or more of the limited partners shall have a priority over other limited partners as to the return of their contributions, as to their compensation by way of income, or as to any other matter. If such an agreement is made it shall be stated in the certificate, and in the absence of such a statement all the limited partners shall stand upon equal footing.

Sec. 15. Compensation of Limited Partner

A limited partner may receive from the partnership the share of the profits or the compensation by way of income stipulated for in the certificate; provided, that after such payment is made, whether from the property of the partnership or that of a general partner, the partnership assets are in excess of all liabilities of the partnership except liabilities to limited partners on account of their contributions and to general partners.

Sec. 16. **Withdrawal or Reduction of Limited Partner's Contribution**

(1) A limited partner shall not receive from a general partner or out of partnership property any part of his contribution until

(a) All liabilities of the partnership, except liabilities to general partners and to limited partners on account of their contributions, have been paid or there remains property of the partnership sufficient to pay them,

(b) The consent of all members is had, unless the return of the contribution may be rightfully demanded under the provisions of paragraph (2), and

(c) The certificate is cancelled or so amended as to set forth the withdrawal or reduction.

(2) Subject to the provisions of paragraph (1) a limited partner may rightfully demand the return of his contribution

(a) On the dissolution of a partnership, or

(b) When the date specified in the certificate for its return has arrived, or

(c) After he has given six months' notice in writing to all other members, if no time is specified in the certificate either for the return of the contribution or for the dissolution of the partnership,

(3) In the absence of any statement in the certificate to the contrary or the consent of all members, a limited partner, irrespective of the nature of his contribution, has only the right to demand and receive cash in return for his contribution.

(4) A limited partner may have the partnership dissolved and its affairs wound up when

(a) He rightfully but unsuccessfully demands the return of his contribution, or

(b) The other liabilities of the partnership have not been paid, or the partnership property is insufficient for their payment as required by paragraph (1a) and the limited partner would otherwise be entitled to the return of his contribution.

Sec. 17. **Liability of Limited Partner to Partnership**

(1) A limited partner is liable to the partnership

(a) For the difference between his contribution as actually made and that stated in the certificate as having been made, and

(b) For any unpaid contribution which he agreed in the certificate to make in the future at the time and on the conditions stated in the certificate.

(2) A limited partner holds as trustee for the partnership

(a) Specific property stated in the certificate as contributed by him, but which was not contributed or which has been wrongfully returned, and

(b) Money or other property wrongfully paid or conveyed to him on account of his contribution.

(3) The liabilities of a limited partner as set forth in this section can be waived or compromised only by the consent of all members; but a waiver or compromise shall not affect the right of a creditor of a partnership who extended credit or whose claim arose after the filing and before a cancellation or amendment of the certificate, to enforce such liabilities.

(4) When a contributor has rightfully received the return in whole or in part of the capital of his contribution, he is nevertheless liable to the partnership for any sum, not in excess of such return with interest, necessary to discharge its liabilities to all creditors who extended credit or whose claims arose before such return.

Sec. 18. **Nature of Limited Partner's Interest in Partnership**

A limited partner's interest in the partnership is personal property.

Sec. 19. **Assignment of Limited Partner's Interest**

(1) A limited partner's interest is assignable.

(2) A substituted limited partner is a person admitted to all the rights of a limited partner who has died or has assigned his interest in a partnership.

(3) An assignee, who does not become a substituted limited partner, has no right to require any information or account of the partnership transactions or to inspect the partnership books; he is only entitled to receive the share of the profits or other compensation by way of income, or the return of his contribution, to which his assignor would otherwise be entitled.

(4) An assignee shall have the right to become a substituted limited partner if all the members (except the assignor) consent thereto or if the assignor, being thereunto empowered by the certificate, gives the assignee that right.

(5) An assignee becomes a substituted limited partner when the certificate is appropriately amended in accordance with Section 25.

(6) The substituted limited partner has all the rights and powers, and is subject to all the restrictions and liabilities of his assignor, except those liabilities of which he was ignorant at the time he became a limited partner and which could not be ascertained from the certificate.

(7) The substitution of the assignee as a limited partner does not release the assignor from liability to the partnership under Sections 6 and 17.

Sec. 20. Effect of Retirement, Death or Insanity of a General Partner

The retirement, death or insanity of a general partner dissolves the partnership, unless the business is continued by the remaining general partners

(a) Under a right so to do stated in the certificate, or

(b) With the consent of all members.

Sec. 21. Death of Limited Partner

(1) On the death of a limited partner his executor or administrator shall have all the rights of a limited partner for the purpose of settling his estate, and such power as the deceased had to constitute his assignee a substituted limited partner.

(2) The estate of a deceased limited partner shall be liable for all his liabilities as a limited partner.

Sec. 22. Rights of Creditors of Limited Partner

(1) On due application to a court of competent jurisdiction by any judgment creditor of a limited partner, the court may charge the interest of the indebted limited partner with payment of the unsatisfied amount of the judgment debt; and may appoint a receiver, and make all other orders, directions, and inquiries which the circumstances of the case may require.

(2) The interest may be redeemed with the separate property of any general partner, but may not be redeemed with partnership property.

(3) The remedies conferred by paragraph (1) shall not be deemed exclusive of others which may exist.

(4) Nothing in this act shall be held to deprive a limited partner of his statutory exemption.

Sec. 23. Distribution of Assets

(1) In settling accounts after dissolution the liabilities of the partnership shall be entitled to payment in the following order:

(a) Those to creditors, in the order of priority as provided by law, except those to limited partners on account of their contributions, and to general partners,

(b) Those to limited partners in respect to their share of the profits and other compensation by way of income on their contributions,

(c) Those to limited partners in respect to the capital of their contributions,

(d) Those to general partners other than for capital and profits,

(e) Those to general partners in respect to profits,

(f) Those to general partners in respect to capital.

(2) Subject to any statement in the certificate or to subsequent agreement, limited partners share in the partnership assets in respect to their claims for capital, and in respect to their claims for profits or for compensation by way of income on their contributions respectively, in proportion to the respective amounts of such claims.

Sec. 24. When Certificate Shall Be Cancelled or Amended

(1) The certificate shall be cancelled when the partnership is dissolved or all limited partners cease to be such.

(2) A certificate shall be amended when

(a) There is a change in the name of the partnership or in the amount or character of the contribution of any limited partner,

(b) A person is substituted as a limited partner,

(c) An additional limited partner is admitted,

(d) A person is admitted as a general partner,

(e) A general partner retires, dies or becomes insane, and the business is continued under Section 20,

(f) There is a change in the character of the business of the partnership,

(g) There is a false or erroneous statement in the certificate,

(h) There is a change in the time as stated in the certificate for the dissolution of the partnership or for the return of a contribution,

(i) A time is fixed for the dissolution of the partnership, or the return of a contribution, no time having been specified in the certificate, or

(j) The members desire to make a change in any other statement in the certificate in order that it shall accurately represent the agreement between them.

Sec. 25. Requirements for Amendment and for Cancellation of Certificate

(1) The writing to amend a certificate shall

(a) Conform to the requirements of Section 2(1a) as far as necessary to set forth clearly the change in the certificate which it is desired to make, and

(b) Be signed and sworn to by all members, and an amendment substituting a limited partner or adding a limited or general partner shall be signed also by the member to be substituted or added, and when a limited partner is to be substituted, the amendment shall also be signed by the assigning limited partner.

(2) The writing to cancel a certificate shall be signed by all members.

(3) A person desiring the cancellation or amendment of a certificate, if any person designated in paragraphs (1) and (2) as a person who must execute the writing refuses to do so, may petition the [here designate the proper court] to direct a cancellation or amendment thereof.

(4) If the court finds that the petitioner has a right to have the writing executed by a person who refuses to do so, it shall order the [here designate the responsible official in the office designated in Section 2] in the office where the certificate is recorded to record the cancellation or amendment of the certificate; and where the certificate is to be amended, the court shall also cause to be filed for record in said office a certified copy of its decree setting forth the amendment.

(5) A certificate is amended or cancelled when there is filed for record in the office [here designate the office designated in Section 2] where the certificate is recorded

(a) A writing in accordance with the provisions of paragraph (1), or (2) or

(b) A certified copy of the order of court in accordance with the provisions of paragraph (4).

(6) After the certificate is duly amended in accordance with this section, the amended certificate shall thereafter be for all purposes the certificate provided for by this act.

Sec. 26. **Parties to Actions**

A contributor, unless he is a general partner, is not a proper party to proceedings by or against a partnership, except where the object is to enforce a limited partner's right against or liability to the partnership.

Sec. 27. **Name of Act**

This act may be cited as The Uniform Limited Partnership Act.

Sec. 28. **Rules of Construction**

(1) The rule that statutes in derogation of the common law are to be strictly construed shall have no application to this act.

(2) This act shall be so interpreted and construed as to effect its general purpose to make uniform the law of those states which enact it.

(3) This act shall not be so construed as to impair the obligations of any contract existing when the act goes into effect, nor to affect any action or proceedings begun or right accrued before this act takes effect.

Sec. 29. **Rules for Cases Not Provided for in This Act**

In any case not provided for in this act the rules of law and equity, including the law merchant, shall govern.

Sec. 30. **Provisions for Existing Limited Partnerships**

(1) A limited partnership formed under any statute of this state prior to the adoption of this act, may become a limited partnership under this act by complying with the provisions of Section 2; provided the certificate sets forth

(a) The amount of the original contribution of each limited partner, and the time when the contribution was made, and

(b) That the property of the partnership exceeds the amount sufficient to discharge its liabilities to persons not claiming as general or limited partners by an amount greater than the sum of the contributions of its limited partners.

(2) A limited partnership formed under any statute of this state prior to the adoption of this act, until or unless it becomes a limited partnership under this act, shall continue to be governed by the provisions of [here insert proper reference to the existing limited partnership act or acts], except that such partnership shall not be renewed unless so provided in the original agreement.

Sec. 31. **Act [Acts] Repealed**

Except as affecting existing limited partnerships to the extent set forth in Section 30, the act (acts) of [here designate the existing limited partnership act or acts] is (are) hereby repealed.

REVISED UNIFORM LIMITED PARTNERSHIP ACT

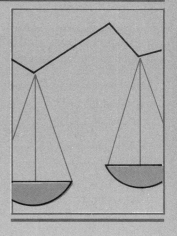

* (Adopted August 5, 1976, by the National Conference of Comissioners on Uniform State Laws, it is intended to replace the existing Uniform Limited Partnership Act (Appendix D). It has been adopted in 36 States: Alabama, Arizona, Arkansas, California, Colorado, Connecticut, Delaware, Florida, Idaho, Illinois, Iowa, Kansas, Maryland, Massachusetts, Michigan, Minnesota, Mississippi, Missouri, Montana, Nebraska, Nevada, New Jersey, North Carolina, North Dakota, Ohio, Oklahoma, Oregon, Rhode Island, South Carolina, South Dakota, Texas, Virginia, Washington, West Virginia, Wisconsin, and Wyoming.

The Act consists of 11 Articles as follows:

1. General Provisions
2. Formation; Certificate of Limited Partnership
3. Limited Partners
4. General Partners
5. Finance
6. Distributions and Withdrawal
7. Assignment of Partnership Interests
8. Dissolution
9. Foreign Limited Partnership
10. Derivative Actions
11. Miscellaneous

Article 1
GENERAL PROVISIONS

Sec. 101. **Definitions**

As used in this Act, unless the context otherwise requires:

(1) "Certificate of limited partnership" means the certificate referred to in Section 201, and the certificate as amended or restated.

(2) "Contribution" means any cash, property, services rendered, or a promissory note or other binding obligation to contribute cash or property or to perform services, which a partner contributes to a limited partnership in his capacity as a partner.

(3) "Event of withdrawal of a general partner" means an event that causes a person to cease to be a general partner as provided in Section 402.

(4) "Foreign limited partnership" means a partnership formed under the laws of any state other than this State and having as partners one or more general partners and one or more limited partners.

(5) "General partner" means a person who has been admitted to a limited partnership as a general partner in accordance with the partnership agreement and named in the certificate of limited partnership as a general partner.

(6) "Limited partner" means a person who has been admitted to a limited partnership as a limited partner in accordance with the partnership agreement.

(7) "Limited partnership" and "domestic limited partnership" mean a partnership formed by two or more persons under the laws of this State and having one or more general partners and one or more limited partners.

(8) "Partner" means a limited or general partner.

(9) "Partnership agreement" means any valid agreement, written or oral, of the partners as to the affairs of a limited partnership and the conduct of its business.

(10) "Partnership interest" means a partner's share of the profits and losses of a limited partnership and the right to receive distributions of partnership assets.

(11) "Person" means a natural person, partnership, limited partnership (domestic or foreign), trust, estate, association, or corporation.

(12) "State" means a state, territory, or possession of the United States, the District of Columbia, or the Commonwealth of Puerto Rico.

Sec. 102. **Name**

The name of each limited partnership as set forth in its certificate of limited partnership:

(1) shall contain without abbreviation the words "limited partnership";

(2) may not contain the name of a limited partner unless (i) it is also the name of a general partner or the corporate name of a corporate general partner, or (ii) the business of the limited partnership had been carried on under that name before the admission of that limited partner;

(3) may not be the same as, or deceptively similar to, the name of any corporation or limited partnership organized under the laws of this State or licensed or registered as a foreign corporation or limited partnership in this State; and

(4) may not contain the following words [here insert prohibited words].

Sec. 103. **Reservation of Name**

(a) The exclusive right to the use of a name may be reserved by:

(1) any person intending to organize a limited partnership under this Act and to adopt that name;

(2) any domestic limited partnership or any foreign limited partnership registered in this State which, in either case, intends to adopt that name;

---

*At its annual conference in August 1985, the National Conference of Commissioners on Uniform State Laws approved amendments to the "Revised Uniform Partnership Act." This printing includes these amendments.

(3) any foreign limited partnership intending to register in this State and adopt that name; and

(4) any person intending to organize a foreign limited partnership and intending to have it register in this State and adopt that name.

(b) The reservation shall be made by filing with the Secretary of State an application, executed by the applicant, to reserve a specified name. If the Secretary of State finds that the name is available for use by a domestic or foreign limited partnership, he [or she] shall reserve the name for the exclusive use of the applicant for a period of 120 days. Once having so reserved a name, the same applicant may not again reserve the same name until more than 60 days after the expiration of the last 120-day period for which that applicant reserved that name. The right to the exclusive use of a reserved name may be transferred to any other person by filing in the office of the Secretary of State a notice of the transfer, executed by the applicant for whom the name was reserved and specifying the name and address of the transferee.

Sec. 104. **Specified Office and Agent**

Each limited partnership shall continuously maintain in this State:

(1) an office, which may but need not be a place of its business in this State, at which shall be kept the records required by Section 105 to be maintained; and

(2) an agent for service of process on the limited partnership, which agent must be an individual resident of this State, a domestic corporation, or a foreign corporation authorized to do business in this State.

Sec. 105. **Records to be Kept**

(a) Each limited partnership shall keep at the office referred to in Section 104(1) the following:

(1) a current list of the full name and last known business address of each partner separately identifying the general partners (in alphabetical order) and the limited partners (in alphabetical order);

(2) a copy of the certificate of limited partnership and all certificates of amendment thereto, together with executed copies of any powers of attorney pursuant to which any certificate has been executed;

(3) copies of the limited partnership's federal, state and local income tax returns and reports, if any, for the three most recent years;

(4) copies of any then effective written partnership agreements and of any financial statements of the limited partnership for the three most recent years; and

(5) unless contained in a written partnership agreement, a writing setting out:

(i) the amount of cash and a description and statement of the agreed value of the other property or services contributed by each partner and which each partner has agreed to contribute;

(ii) the times at which or events on the happening of which any additional contributions agreed to be made by each partner are to be made;

(iii) any right of a partner to receive, or of a general partner to make, distributions to a partner which include a return of all or any part of the partner's contribution; and

(iv) any events upon the happening of which the limited partnership is to be dissolved and its affairs wound up.

(b) Records kept under this section are subject to inspection and copying at the reasonable request at the expense of any partner during ordinary business hours.

Sec. 106. **Nature of Business**

A limited partnership may carry on any business that a partnership without limited partners may carry on except [here designate prohibited activities].

Sec. 107. **Business Transactions of Partner with Partnership**

Except as provided in the partnership agreement, a partner may lend money to and transact other business with the limited partnership and, subject to other applicable law, has the same rights and obligations with respect thereto as a person who is not a partner.

Article 2
FORMATION; CERTIFICATE OF LIMITED PARTNERSHIP

Sec. 201. **Certificate of Limited Partnership**

(a) In order to form a limited partnership, a certificate of limited partnership must be executed and filed in the office of the Secretary of State. The certificate shall set forth:

(1) the name of the limited partnership;

(2) the address of the office and the name and address of the agent for service of process required to be maintained by Section 104;

(3) the name and the business address of each general partner;

(4) the latest date upon which the limited partnership is to dissolve; and

(5) any other matters the general partners determine to include therein.

(b) A limited partnership is formed at the time of the filing of the certificate of limited partnership in the office of the Secretary of State or at any later time specified in the certificate of limited partnership if, in either case, there has been substantial compliance with the requirements of this section.

Sec. 202. **Amendment to Certificate**

(a) A certificate of limited partnership is amended by filing a certificate of amendment thereto in the office of the Secretary of State. The certificate shall set forth:

(1) the name of the limited partnership;

(2) the date of filing the certificate; and

(3) the amendment to the certificate.

(b) Within 30 days after the happening of any of the following events, an amendment to a certificate of limited partnership reflecting the occurrence of the event or events shall be filed:

(1) the admission of a new general partner;

(2) the withdrawal of a general partner; or

(3) the continuation of the business under Section 801 after an event of withdrawal of a general partner.

(c) A general partner who becomes aware that any statement in a certificate of limited partnership was false when made or that any arrangements or other facts described have changed, making the certificate inaccurate in any respect, shall promptly amend the certificate.

(d) A certificate of limited partnership may be amended at any time for any other proper purpose the general partners determine.

(e) No person has any liability because an amendment to a certificate of limited partnership has not been filed to reflect the occurrence of any event referred to in subsection (b) of this section if the amendment is filed within the 30-day period specified in subsection (b).

(f) A restated certificate of limited partnership may be executed and filed in the same manner as a certificate of amendment.

Sec. 203. **Cancellation of Certificate**

A certificate of limited partnership shall be cancelled upon the dissolution and the commencement of winding up of the partnership or at any other time there are no limited partners. A certificate of cancellation shall be filed in the office of the Secretary of State and set forth:

(1) the name of the limited partnership;

(2) the date of filing of its certificate of limited partnership;

(3) the reason for filing the certificate of cancellation;

(4) the effective date (which shall be a date certain) of cancellation if it is not to be effective upon the filing of the certificate; and

(5) any other information the general partners filing the certificate determine.

Sec. 204. **Execution of Certificates**

(a) Each certificate required by this Article to be filed in the office of the Secretary of State shall be executed in the following manner:

(1) an original certificate of limited partnership must be signed by all general partners,

(2) a certificate of amendment must be signed by at least one general partner and by each other general partner designated in the certificate as a new general partner; and

(3) a certificate of cancellation must be signed by all general partners.

(b) Any person may sign a certificate by an attorney-in-fact, but a power of attorney to sign a certificate relating to the admission of a general partner must specifically describe the admission.

(c) The execution of a certificate by a general partner constitutes an affirmation under the penalties of perjury that the facts stated therein are true.

Sec. 205. **Execution by Judicial Act**

If a person required by Section 204 to execute any certificate fails or refuses to do so, any other person who is adversely affected by the failure or refusal, may petition the [designate the appropriate court] to direct the execution of the certificate. If the court finds that it is proper for the certificate to be executed and that any person so designated has failed or refused to execute the certificate, it shall order the Secretary of State to record an appropriate certificate.

Sec. 206. **Filing in Office of Secretary of State**

(a) Two signed copies of the certificate of limited partnership and of any certificates of amendment or cancellation (or of any judicial decree of amendment or cancellation) shall be delivered to the Secretary of State. A person who executes a certificate as an agent or fiduciary need not exhibit evidence of his [or her] authority as a prerequisite to filing. Unless the Secretary of State finds that any certificate does not conform to law, upon receipt of all filing fees required by law he [or she] shall:

(1) endorse on each duplicate original the word "Filed" and the day, month, and year of the filing thereof;

(2) file one duplicate original in his [or her] office; and

(3) return the other duplicate original to the person who filed it or his [or her] representative.

(b) Upon the filing of a certificate of amendment (or judicial decree of amendment) in the office of the Secretary of State, the certificate of limited partnership shall be amended as set forth therein, and upon the effective date of a certificate of cancellation (or a judicial decree thereof), the certificate of limited partnership is cancelled.

Sec. 207. **Liability for False Statement in Certificate**

If any certificate of limited partnership or certificate of amendment or cancellation contains a false statement, one who suffers loss by reliance on the statement may recover damages for the loss from:

(1) any person who executes the certificate, or causes another to execute it on his behalf, and knew, and any general partner who knew or should have known, the statement to be false at the time the certificate was executed; and

(2) any general partner who thereafter knows or should have known that any arrangement or other fact described in the certificate has changed, making the statement inaccurate in any respect within a sufficient time before the statement was relied upon reasonably to have enabled that general partner to cancel or amend the certificate, or to file a petition for its cancellation or amendment under Section 205.

Sec. 208. **Scope of Notice**

The fact that a certificate of limited partnership is on file in the office of the Secretary of State is notice that the partnership is a limited partnership and the persons designated therein as general partners are general partners, but it is not notice of any other fact.

Article 3
LIMITED PARTNERS

Sec. 301. **Admission of Additional Limited Partners**

(a) A person becomes a limited partner:

(1) at the time the limited partnership is formed; or

(2) at any later time specified in the records of the limited partnership for becoming a limited partner.

(b) After the filing of a limited partnership's original certificate of limited partnership, a person may be admitted as an additional limited partner:

(1) in the case of a person acquiring a partnership interest directly from the limited partnership, upon compliance with the partnership agreement or, if the partnership agreement does not so provide, upon the written consent of all partners; and

(2) in the case of an assignee of a partnership interest of a partner who has the power, as provided in Section 704, to grant the assignee the right to become a limited partner, upon the exercise of that power and compliance with any conditions limiting the grant or exercise of the power.

Sec. 302. **Voting**

Subject to Section 303, the partnership agreement may grant to all or to a specified group of the limited partners the right to vote (on a per capita or any other basis) upon any matter.

Sec. 303. **Liability to Third Parties**

(a) Except as provided in subsection (d), a limited partner is not liable for the obligations of a limited partnership unless he [or she] is also a general partner or, in addition to the exercise of his [or her] rights and powers as a limited partner, he [or she] participates in the control of the business. However, if the limited partner participates in the control of the business, he [or she] is liable only to persons who transact business with the limited partnership reasonably believing, based upon the limited partner's conduct, that the limited partner is a general partner.

(b) A limited partner does not participate in the control of the business within the meaning of subsection (a) solely by doing one or more of the following:

(1) being a contractor for or an agent or employee of the limited partnership or of a general partner or being an officer, director, or shareholder of a general partner that is a corporation;

(2) consulting with and advising a general partner with respect to the business of the limited partnership;

(3) acting as surety for the limited partnership or guaranteeing or assuming one or more specific obligations of the limited partnership;

(4) taking any action required or permitted by law to bring or pursue a derivative action in the right of the limited partnership;

(5) requesting or attending a meeting of partners;

(6) proposing, approving, or disapproving, by voting or otherwise, one or more of the following matters:

(i) the dissolution and winding up of the limited partnership;

(ii) the sale, exchange, lease, mortgage, pledge, or other transfer of all or substantially all of the assets of the limited partnership;

(iii) the incurrence of indebtedness by the limited partnership other than in the ordinary course of its business;

(iv) a change in the nature of the business;

(v) the admission or removal of a general partner;

(vi) the admission or removal of a limited partner;

(vii) a transaction involving an actual or potential conflict of interest between a general partner and the limited partnership or the limited partners;

(viii) an amendment to the partnership agreement or certificate of limited partnership; or

(ix) matters related to the business of the limited partnership not otherwise enumerated in this subsection (b), which the partnership agreement states in writing may be subject to the approval or disapproval of limited partners;

(7) winding up the limited partnership pursuant to Section 803; or

(8) exercising any right or power permitted to limited partners under this Act and not specifically enumerated in this subsection (b).

(c) The enumeration in subsection (b) does not mean that the possession or exercise of any other powers by a limited partner constitutes participation by him [or her] in the business of the limited partnership.

(d) A limited partner who knowingly permits his [or her] name to be used in the name of the limited partnership, except under circumstances permitted by Section 102(2), is liable to creditors who extend credit to the limited partnership without actual knowledge that the limited partner is not a general partner.

Sec. 304. **Person Erroneously Believing Himself [or Herself] Limited Partner**

(a) Except as provided in subsection (b), a person who makes a contribution to a business enterprise and erroneously but in good faith believes that he [or she] has become a limited partner in the enterprise is not a general partner in the enterprise and is not bound by its obligations by reason of making the contribution, receiving distributions from the enterprise, or exercising any rights of a limited partner, if, on ascertaining the mistake, he [or she]:

(1) causes an appropriate certificate of limited partnership or a certificate of amendment to be executed and filed; or

(2) withdraws from future equity participation in the enterprise by executing and filing in the office of the Secretary of State a certificate declaring withdrawal under this section.

(b) A person who makes a contribution of the kind described in subsection (a) is liable as a general partner to any third party who transacts business with the enterprise (i) before the person withdraws and an appropriate certificate is filed to show withdrawal, or (ii) before an appropriate certificate is filed to show that he [or she] is not a general partner, but in either case only if the third party actually believed in good faith that the person was a general partner at the time of the transaction.

Sec. 305. **Information**

Each limited partner has the right to:

(1) inspect and copy any of the partnership records required to be maintained by Section 105; and

(2) obtain from the general partners from time to time upon reasonable demand (i) true and full information regarding the state of the business and financial condition of the limited partnership, (ii) promptly after becoming available, a copy of the limited partnership's federal, state, and local income tax returns for each year, and (iii) other information regarding the affairs of the limited partnership as is just and reasonable.

Article 4
GENERAL PARTNERS

Sec. 401. **Admission of Additional General Partners**

After the filing of a limited partnership's original certificate of limited partnership, additional general partners may be admitted as provided in writing in the partnership agreement or, if the partnership agreement does not provide in writing for the admission of additional general partners, with the written consent of all partners.

Sec. 402. **Events of Withdrawal**

Except as approved by the specific written consent of all partners at the time, a person ceases to be a general partner of a limited partnership upon the happening of any of the following events:

(1) the general partner withdraws from the limited partnership as provided in Section 602;

(2) the general partner ceases to be a member of the limited partnership as provided in Section 702;

(3) the general partner is removed as a general partner in accordance with the partnership agreement;

(4) unless otherwise provided in writing in the partnership agreement, the general partner: (i) makes an assignment for the benefit of creditors; (ii) files a voluntary petition in bankruptcy; (iii) is adjudicated a bankrupt or insolvent; (iv) files a petition or answer seeking for himself [or herself] any reorganization, arrangement, composition, readjustment, liquidation, dissolution or similar relief under any statute, law, or regulation; (v) files an answer or other pleading admitting or failing to contest the material allegations of a

petition filed against him [or her] in any proceeding of this nature; or (vi) seeks, consents to, or acquiesces in the appointment of a trustee, receiver, or liquidator of the general partner or of all or any substantial part of his [or her] properties;

(5) unless otherwise provided in writing in the partnership agreement, [120] days after the commencement of any proceeding against the general partner seeking reorganization, arrangement, composition, readjustment, liquidation, dissolution or similar relief under any statute, law, or regulation, the proceeding has not been dismissed, or if within [90] days after the appointment without his [or her] consent or acquiescence of a trustee, receiver, or liquidator of the general partner or of all or any substantial part of his [or her] properties, the appointment is not vacated or stayed or within [90] days after the expiration of any such stay, the appointment is not vacated;

(6) in the case of a general partner who is a natural person,

(i) his [or her] death; or

(ii) the entry of an order by a court of competent jurisdiction adjudicating him [or her] incompetent to manage his [or her] person or his [or her] estate;

(7) in the case of a general partner who is acting as a general partner by virtue of being a trustee of a trust, the termination of the trust (but not merely the substitution of a new trustee);

(8) in the case of a general partner that is a separate partnership, the dissolution and commencement of winding up of the separate partnership;

(9) in the case of a general partner that is a corporation, the filing of a certificate of dissolution, or its equivalent, for the corporation or the revocation of its charter; or

(10) in the case of an estate, the distribution by the fiduciary of the estate's entire interest in the partnership.

Sec. 403. **General Powers and Liabilities**

(a) Except as provided in this Act or in the partnership agreement, a general partner of a limited partnership has the rights and powers and is subject to the restrictions of a partner in a partnership without limited partners.

(b) Except as provided in this Act, a general partner of a limited partnership has the liabilities of a partner in a partnership without limited partners to persons other than the partnership and the other partners. Except as provided in this Act or in the partnership agreement, a general partner of a limited partnership has the liabilities of a partner in a partnership without limited partners to the partnership and to the other partners.

Sec. 404. **Contributions by General Partner**

A general partner of a limited partnership may make contributions to the partnership and share in the profits and losses of, and in distributions from, the limited partnership as a general partner. A general partner also may make contributions to and share in profits, losses, and distributions as a limited partner. A person who is both a general partner and a limited partner has the rights and powers, and is subject to the restrictions and liabilities, of a general partner and, except as provided in the partnership agreement, also has the powers, and is subject to the restrictions, of a limited partner to the extent of his [or her] participation in the partnership as a limited partner.

Sec. 405. **Voting**

The partnership agreement may grant to all or certain identified general partners the right to vote (on a per capita or any other basis), separately or with all or any class of the limited partners, on any matter.

Article 5
FINANCE

Sec. 501. **Form of Contribution**

The contribution of a partner may be in cash, property, or services rendered, or a promissory note or other obligation to contribute cash or property or to perform services.

Sec. 502. **Liability for Contribution**

(a) A promise by a limited partner to contribute to the limited partnership is not enforceable unless set out in a writing signed by the limited partner.

(b) Except as provided in the partnership agreement, a partner is obligated to the limited partnership to perform any enforceable promise to contribute cash or property or to perform services, even if he [or she] is unable to perform because of death, disability, or any other reason. If a partner does not make the required contribution of property or services, he [or she] is obligated at the option of the limited partnership to contribute cash equal to that portion of the value, as stated in the partnership records required to be kept pursuant to Section 105, of the stated contribution which has not been made.

(c) Unless otherwise provided in the partnership agreement, the obligation of a partner to make a contribution or return money or other property paid or distributed in violation of this Act may be compromised only by consent of all partners. Notwithstanding the compromise, a creditor of a limited partnership who extends credit, or otherwise acts in reliance on that obligation after the partner signs a writing which, reflects the obligation, and before the amendment or cancellation thereof to reflect the compromise, may enforce the original obligation.

Sec. 503. **Sharing of Profits and Losses**

The profits and losses of a limited partnership shall be allocated among the partners, and among classes of partners, in the manner provided in writing in the partnership agreement. If the partnership agreement does not so provide in writing, profits and losses shall be allocated on the basis of the value, as stated in the partnership records required to be kept pursuant to Section 105, of the contributions made by each partner to the extent they have been received by the partnership and have not been returned.

Sec. 504. **Sharing of Distributions**

Distributions of cash or other assets of a limited partnership shall be allocated among the partners and among classes of partners in the manner provided in writing in the partnership agreement. If the partnership agreement does not so provide in writing, distributions shall be made on the basis of the value, as stated in the partnership records required to be kept pursuant to Section 105, of the contributions made by each partner to the extent they have been received by the partnership and have not been returned.

Article 6

DISTRIBUTIONS AND WITHDRAWAL

Sec. 601. **Interim Distributions**

Except as provided in this Article, a partner is entitled to receive distributions from a limited partnership before his [or her] withdrawal from the limited partnership and before the dissolution and winding up thereof to the extent and at the times or upon the happening of the events specified in the partnership agreement.

Sec. 602. **Withdrawal of General Partner**

A general partner may withdraw from a limited partnership at any time by giving written notice to the other partners, but if the withdrawal violates the partnership agreement, the limited partnership may recover from the withdrawing general partner damages for breach of the partnership agreement and offset the damages against the amount otherwise distributable to him [or her].

Sec. 603. **Withdrawal of Limited Partner**

A limited partner may withdraw from a limited partnership at the time or upon the happening of events specified in writing in the partnership agreement. If the agreement does not specify in writing the time or the events upon the happening of which a limited partner may withdraw or a definite time for the dissolution and winding up of the limited partnership, a limited partner may withdraw upon not less than six months' prior written notice to each general partner at his [or her] address on the books of the limited partnership at its office in this State.

Sec. 604. **Distribution Upon Withdrawal**

Except as provided in this Article, upon withdrawal any withdrawing partner is entitled to receive any distribution to which he [or she] is entitled under the partnership agreement and, if not otherwise provided in the agreement, he [or she] is entitled to receive, within a reasonable time after withdrawal, the fair value of his [or her] interest in the limited partnership as of the date of withdrawal based upon his [or her] right to share in distributions from the limited partnership.

Sec. 605. **Distribution in Kind**

Except as provided in the partnership agreement, a partner, regardless of the nature of his [or her] contribution, has no right to demand and receive any distribution from a limited partnership in any form other than cash. Except as provided in writing in the partnership agreement, a partner may not be compelled to accept a distribution of any asset in kind from a limited partnership to the extent that the percentage of the asset distributed to him [or her] exceeds a percentage of the asset which is equal to the percentage in which he [or she] shares in distributions from the limited partnership.

Sec. 606. **Right to Distribution**

At the time a partner becomes entitled to receive a distribution, he [or she] has the status of, and is entitled to all remedies available to, a creditor of the limited partnership with respect to the distribution.

Sec. 607. **Limitations on Distribution**

A partner may not receive a distribution from a limited partnership to the extent that, after giving effect to the distribution, all liabilities of the limited partnership, other than liabilities to partners on account of their partnership interests, exceed the fair value of the partnership assets.

Sec. 608. **Liability Upon Return of Contribution**

(a) If a partner has received the return of any part of his [or her] contribution without violation of the partnership agreement or this Act, he [or she] is liable to the limited partnership for a period of one year thereafter for the amount of the returned contribution, but only to the extent necessary to discharge the limited partnership's liabilities to creditors who extended credit to the limited partnership during the period the contribution was held by the partnership.

(b) If a partner has received the return of any part of his [or her] contribution in violation of the partnership agreement or this Act, he [or she] is liable to the limited partnership for a period of six years thereafter for the amount of the contribution wrongfully returned.

(c) A partner receives a return of his [or her] contribution to the extent that a distribution to him [or her] reduces his [or her] share of the fair value of the net assets of the limited partnership below the value, as set forth in the partnership records required to be kept pursuant to Section 105, of his contribution which has not been distributed to him [or her].

Article 7
ASSIGNMENT OF PARTNERSHIP INTERESTS

Sec. 701. **Nature of Partnership Interest**

A partnership interest is personal property.

Sec. 702. **Assignment of Partnership Interest**

Except as provided in the partnership agreement, a partnership interest is assignable in whole or in part. An assignment of a partnership interest does not dissolve a limited partnership or entitle the assignee to become or to exercise any rights of a partner. An assignment entitles the assignee to receive, to the extent assigned, only the distribution to which the assignor would be entitled. Except as provided in the partnership agreement, a partner ceases to be a partner upon assignment of all his [or her] partnership interest.

Sec. 703. **Rights of Creditor**

On application to a court of competent jurisdiction by any judgment creditor of a partner, the court may charge the partnership interest of the partner with payment of the unsatisfied amount of the judgment with interest. To the extent so charged, the judgment creditor has only the rights of an assignee of the partnership interest. This Act does not deprive any partner of the benefit of any exemption laws applicable to his [or her] partnership interest.

Sec. 704. **Right of Assignee to Become Limited Partner**

(a) An assignee of a partnership interest, including an assignee of a general partner, may become a limited partner if and to the extent that (i) the assignor gives the assignee that right in accordance with authority described in the partnership agreement, or (ii) all other partners consent.

(b) An assignee who has become a limited partner has, to the extent assigned, the rights and powers, and is subject to the restrictions and liabilities, of a limited partner under the partnership agreement and this Act. An assignee who becomes a limited partner also is liable for the obligations of his [or her] assignor to make and return contributions as provided in Articles 5 and 6. However, the assignee is not obligated for liabilities unknown to the assignee at the time he [or she] became a limited partner.

(c) If an assignee of a partnership interest becomes a limited partner, the assignor is not released from his [or her] liability to the limited partnership under Sections 207 and 502.

Sec. 705. **Power of Estate of Deceased or Incompetent Partner**

If a partner who is an individual dies or a court of competent jurisdiction adjudges him [or her] to be incompetent to manage his [or her] person or his [or her] property, the partner's executor, administrator, guardian, conservator, or other legal representative may exercise all the partner's rights for the purpose of settling his [or her] estate or administering his [or her] property, including any power the partner had to give an assignee the right to become a limited partner. If a partner is a corporation, trust, or other entity and is dissolved or terminated, the powers of that partner may be exercised by its legal representative or successor.

Article 8
DISSOLUTION

Sec. 801. **Nonjudicial Dissolution**

A limited partnership is dissolved and its affairs shall be wound up upon the happening of the first to occur of the following:

(1) at the time specified in the certificate of limited partnership;

(2) upon the happening of events specified in writing in the partnership agreement;

(3) written consent of all partners;

(4) an event of withdrawal of a general partner unless at the time there is at least one other general partner and the written provisions of the partnership agreement permit the business of the limited partnership to be carried on by the remaining general partner and that partner does so, but the limited partnership is not dissolved and is not required to be wound up by reason of any event of withdrawal, if, within 90 days after the withdrawal, all partners agree in writing to continue the business of the limited partnership and to the appointment of one or more additional general partners if necessary or desired; or

(5) entry of a decree of judicial dissolution under Section 802.

Sec. 802. **Judicial Dissolution**

On application by or for a partner the [designate the appropriate court] court may decree dissolution of a limited partnership whenever it is not reasonably practicable to carry on the business in conformity with the partnership agreement.

Sec. 803. **Winding Up**

Except as provided in the partnership agreement, the general partners who have not wrongfully dissolved a limited partnership or, if none, the limited partners, may wind up the limited partnership's affairs; but the [designate the appropriate court] court may wind up the limited partnership's affairs upon application of any partner, his [or her] legal representative, or assignee.

Sec. 804. **Distribution of Assets**

Upon the winding up of a limited partnership, the assets shall be distributed as follows:

(1) to creditors, including partners who are creditors, to the extent permitted by law, in satisfaction of liabilities of the limited partnership other than liabilities for distributions to partners under Section 601 or 604;

(2) except as provided in the partnership agreement, to partners and former partners in satisfaction of liabilities for distributions under Section 601 or 604; and

(3) except as provided in the partnership agreement, to partners first for the return of their contributions and secondly respecting their partnership interests, in the proportions in which the partners share in distributions.

Article 9
FOREIGN LIMITED PARTNERSHIPS

Sec. 901. **Law Governing**

Subject to the Constitution of this State, (i) the laws of the state under which a foreign limited partnership is organized govern its organization and internal affairs and the liability of its limited partners, and (ii) a foreign limited partnership may not be denied registration by reason of any difference between those laws and the laws of this State.

Sec. 902. **Registration**

Before transacting business in this State, a foreign limited partnership shall register with the Secretary of State. In order to register, a foreign limited partnership shall submit to the Secretary of State, in duplicate, an application for registration as a foreign limited partnership, signed and sworn to by a general partner and setting forth:

(1) the name of the foreign limited partnership and, if different, the name under which it proposes to register and transact business in this State;

(2) the State and date of its formation;

(3) the name and address of any agent for service of process on the foreign limited partnership whom the

foreign limited partnership elects to appoint; the agent must be an individual resident of this State, a domestic corporation, or a foreign corporation having a place of business in, and authorized to do business in, this State;

(4) a statement that the Secretary of State is appointed the agent of the foreign limited partnership for service of process if no agent has been appointed under paragraph (3) or, if appointed, the agent's authority has been revoked or if the agent cannot be found or served with the exercise of reasonable diligence;

(5) the address of the office required to be maintained in the state of its organization by the laws of that state or, if not so required, of the principal office of the foreign limited partnership;

(6) the name and business address of each general partner; and

(7) the address of the office at which is kept a list of the names and addresses of the limited partners and their capital contributions, together with an undertaking by the foreign limited partnership to keep those records until the foreign limited partnership's registration in this State is cancelled or withdrawn.

Sec. 903. **Issuance of Registration**

(a) If the Secretary of State finds that an application for registration conforms to law and all requisite fees have been paid, he [or she] shall:

(1) endorse on the application the word "Filed," and the month, day and year of the filing thereof;

(2) file in his [or her] office a duplicate original of the application; and

(3) issue a certificate of registration to transact business in this State.

(b) The certificate of registration, together with a duplicate original of the application, shall be returned to the person who filed the application or his [or her] representative.

Sec. 904. **Name**

A foreign limited partnership may register with the Secretary of State under any name, whether or not it is the name under which it is registered in its state of organization, that includes without abbreviation the words "limited partnership" and that could be registered by a domestic limited partnership.

Sec. 905. **Changes and Amendments**

If any statement in the application for registration of a foreign limited partnership was false when made or any arrangements or other facts described have changed, making the application inaccurate in any respect, the foreign limited partnership shall promptly file in the office of the Secretary of State a certificate, signed and sworn to by a general partner, correcting such statement.

Sec. 906. Cancellation of Registration

A foreign limited partnership may cancel its registration by filing with the Secretary of State a certificate of cancellation signed and sworn to by a general partner. A cancellation does not terminate the authority of the Secretary of State to accept service of process on the foreign limited partnership with respect to [claims for relief] [causes of action] arising out of the transactions of business in this State.

Sec. 907. Transaction of Business Without Registration

(a) A foreign limited partnership transacting business in this State may not maintain any action, suit, or proceeding in any court of this State until it has registered in this State.

(b) The failure of a foreign limited partnership to register in this State does not impair the validity of any contract or act of the foreign limited partnership or prevent the foreign limited partnership from defending any action, suit, or proceeding in any court of this State.

(c) A limited partner of a foreign limited partnership is not liable as a general partner of the foreign limited partnership solely by reason of having transacted business in this State without registration.

(d) A foreign limited partnership, by transacting business in this State without registration, appoints the Secretary of State as its agent for service of process with respect to [claims for relief] [causes of action] arising out of the transaction of business in this State.

Sec. 908. Action by [Appropriate Official]

The [designate the appropriate official] may bring an action to restrain a foreign limited partnership from transacting business in this State in violation of this Article.

Article 10
DERIVATIVE ACTIONS

Sec. 1001. Right of Action

A limited partner may bring an action in the right of a limited partnership to recover a judgment in its favor if general partners with authority to do so have refused to bring the action or if an effort to cause those general partners to bring the action is not likely to succeed.

Sec. 1002. Proper Plaintiff

In a derivative action, the plaintiff must be a partner at the time of bringing the action and (i) must have been a partner at the time of the transaction of which he [or she] complains or (ii) his [or her] status as a partner must have devolved upon him [or her] by operation of law or pursuant to the terms of the partnership agreement from a person who was a partner at the time of the transaction.

Sec. 1003. Pleading

In a derivative action, the complaint shall set forth with particularity the effort of the plaintiff to secure initiation of the action by a general partner or the reasons for not making the effort.

Sec. 1004. Expenses

If a derivative action is successful, in whole or in part, or if anything is received by the plaintiff as a result of a judgment, compromise or settlement of an action or claim, the court may award the plaintiff reasonable expenses, including reasonable attorney's fees, and shall direct him [or her] to remit to the limited partnership the remainder of those proceeds received by him [or her].

Article 11
MISCELLANEOUS

Sec. 1101. Construction and Application

This Act shall be so applied and construed to effectuate its general purpose to make uniform the law with respect to the subject of this Act among states enacting it.

Sec. 1102. Short Title

This Act may be cited as the Uniform Limited Partnership Act.

Sec. 1103. Severability

If any provision of this Act or its application to any person or circumstance is held invalid, the invalidity does not affect other provisions or applications of the Act which can be given effect without the invalid provision or application, and to this end the provisions of this Act are severable.

Sec. 1104. Effective Date, Extended Effective Date and Repeal

Except as set forth below, the effective date of this Act is _____ and the following acts [list existing limited partnership acts] are hereby repealed:

(1) The existing provisions for execution and filing of certificates of limited partnerships and amendments thereunder and cancellations thereof continue in effect until [specify time required to create central filing system], the extended effective date, and Sections 102, 103, 104, 105, 201, 202, 203, 204 and 206 are not effective until the extended effective date.

(2) Section 402, specifying the conditions under which a general partner ceases to be a member of a limited partnership, is not effective until the extended effective date, and the applicable provisions of existing law continue to govern until the extended effective date.

(3) Sections 501, 502 and 608 apply only to contributions and distributions made after the effective date of this Act.

(4) Section 704 applies only to assignments made after the effective date of this Act.

(5) Article 9, dealing with registration of foreign limited partnerships, is not effective until the extended effective date.

(6) Unless otherwise agreed by the partners, the applicable provisions of existing law governing allocation of profits and losses (rather than the provisions of Section 503), distributions to a withdrawing partner (rather than the provisions of Section 604), and distribution of assets upon the winding up of a limited partnership (rather than the provisions of Section 804) govern limited partnerships formed before the effective date of this Act.

Sec. 1105. **Rules for Cases Not Provided for in This Act**

In any case not provided for in this Act the provisions of the Uniform Partnership Act govern.

Sec. 1106. **Savings Clause**

The repeal of any statutory provision by this Act does not impair, or otherwise affect, the organization or the continued existence of a limited partnership existing at the effective date of this Act, nor does the repeal of any existing statutory provision by this Act impair any contract or affect any right accrued before the effective date of this Act.

THE MODEL BUSINESS CORPORATION ACT

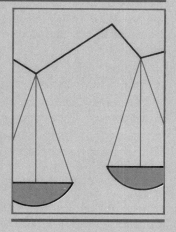

§ 1. Short Title*

This Act shall be known and may be cited as the ". . . . .† Business Corporation Act."

§ 2. Definitions

As used in this Act, unless the context otherwise requires, the term:

(a) "Corporation" or "domestic corporation" means a corporation for profit subject to the provisions of this Act, except a foreign corporation.

(b) "Foreign corporation" means a corporation for profit organized under laws other than the laws of this State for a purpose or purposes for which a corporation may be organized under this Act.

(c) "Articles of incorporation" means the original or restated articles of incorporation or articles of consolidation and all amendments thereto including articles of merger.

(d) "Shares" means the units into which the proprietary interests in a corporation are divided.

(e) "Subscriber" means one who subscribes for shares in a corporation, whether before or after incorporation.

(f) "Shareholder" means one who is a holder of record of shares in a corporation. If the articles of incorporation or the by-laws so provide, the board of directors may adopt by resolution a procedure whereby a shareholder of the corporation may certify in writing to the corporation that all or a portion of the shares registered in the name of such shareholder are held for the account of a specified person or persons. The resolution shall set forth (1) the classification of shareholder who may certify, (2) the purpose or purposes for which the certification may be made, (3) the form of certification and information to be contained therein, (4) if the certification is with respect to a record date or closing of the stock transfer books within which the certification must be received by the corporation and (5) such other provisions with respect to the procedure as are deemed necessary or desirable. Upon receipt by the corporation of a certification complying with the procedure, the persons specified in the certification shall be deemed, for the purpose or purposes set forth in the certification, to be the holders of record of the number of shares specified in place of the shareholder making the certification.

(g) "Authorized shares" means the shares of all classes which the corporation is authorized to issue.

(h) "Employee" includes officers but not directors. A director may accept duties which make him also an employee.

(i) "Distribution" means a direct or indirect transfer of money or other property (except its own shares) or incurrence of indebtedness, by a corporation to or for the benefit of any of its shareholders in respect of any of its shares, whether by dividend or by purchase, redemption or other acquisition of its shares, or otherwise.

§ 3. Purposes

Corporations may be organized under this Act for any lawful purpose or purposes, except for the purpose of banking or insurance.

§ 4. General Powers

Each corporation shall have power:

(a) To have perpetual succession by its corporate name unless a limited period of duration is stated in its articles of incorporation.

(b) To sue and be sued, complain and defend, in its corporate name.

(c) To have a corporate seal which may be altered at pleasure, and to use the same by causing it, or a facsimile thereof, to be impressed or affixed or in any other manner reproduced.

(d) To purchase, take, receive, lease, or otherwise acquire, own, hold, improve, use and otherwise deal in and with, real or personal property, or any interest therein, wherever situated.

(e) To sell, convey, mortgage, pledge, lease, exchange, transfer and otherwise dispose of all or any part of its property and assets.

(f) To lend money and use its credit to assist its employees.

(g) To purchase, take, receive, subscribe for, or otherwise acquire, own, hold, vote, use, employ, sell, mortgage, lend, pledge, or otherwise dispose of, and otherwise use and deal in and with, shares or other interests in, or obligations of, other domestic or foreign corporations, associations, partnerships or individuals, or direct or indirect obligations of the United States or of

---

*[By the Editor] The Model Business Corporation Act prepared by the Committee on Corporate Laws (Section of Corporation, Banking and Business Law) of the American Bar Association was originally patterned after the Illinois Business Corporation Act of 1933. It was first published as a complete act in 1950. In subsequent years several revisions, addenda and optional or alternative provisions were added. The Act was substantially revised and renumbered in 1969.

This Act should be distinguished from the Model Business Corporation Act promulgated in 1928 by the Commissioners on Uniform State Laws under the name "Uniform Business Corporation Act" and renamed Model Business Corporation Act in 1943. This Uniform Act was withdrawn in 1957.

The Model Business Corporation Act has been influential in the codification of corporation statutes in more than 35 states. However, there is no state that has totally adopted it in its current form. Moreover, since the Model Act itself has been substantially modified from time to time, there is considerable variation among the statutes of the states that used this Act as a model.

†Insert name of State.

any other government, state, territory, governmental district or municipality or of any instrumentality thereof.

(h) To make contracts and guarantees and incur liabilities, borrow money at such rates of interest as the corporation may determine, issue its notes, bonds, and other obligations, and secure any of its obligations by mortgage or pledge of all or any of its property, franchises and income.

(i) To lend money for its corporate purposes, invest and reinvest its funds, and take and hold real and personal property as security for the payment of funds so loaned or invested.

(j) To conduct its business, carry on its operations and have offices and exercise the powers granted by this Act, within or without this State.

(k) To elect or appoint officers and agents of the corporation, and define their duties and fix their compensation.

(l) To make and alter by-laws, not inconsistent with its articles of incorporation or with the laws of this State, for the administration and regulation of the affairs of the corporation.

(m) To make donations for the public welfare or for charitable, scientific or educational purposes.

(n) To transact any lawful business which the board of directors shall find will be in aid of governmental policy.

(o) To pay pensions and establish pension plans, pension trusts, profit sharing plans, stock bonus plans, stock option plans and other incentive plans for any or all of its directors, officers and employees.

(p) To be a promoter, partner, member, associate, or manager of any partnership, joint venture, trust or other enterprise.

(q) To have and exercise all powers necessary or convenient to effect its purposes.

§ 5. Indemnification of Directors and Officers

(a) As used in this section:

(1) "Director" means any person who is or was a director of the corporation and any person who, while a director of the corporation, is or was serving at the request of the corporation as a director, officer, partner, trustee, employee or agent of another foreign or domestic corporation, partnership, joint venture, trust, other enterprise or employee benefit plan.

(2) "Corporation" includes any domestic or foreign predecessor entity of the corporation in a merger, consolidation or other transaction in which the predecessor's existence ceased upon consummation of such transaction.

(3) "Expenses" include attorneys' fees.

(4) "Official capacity" means

(A) when used with respect to a director, the office of director in the corporation, and

(B) when used with respect to a person other than a director, as contemplated in subsection (i), the elective or appointive office in the corporation held by the officer or the employment or agency relationship undertaken by the employee or agent in behalf of the corporation,

but in each case does not include service for any other foreign or domestic corporation or any partnership, joint venture, trust, other enterprise, or employee benefit plan.

(5) "Party" includes a person who was, is, or is threatened to be made, a named defendant or respondent in a proceeding.

(6) "Proceeding" means any threatened, pending or completed action, suit or proceeding, whether civil, criminal, administrative or investigative.

(b) A corporation shall have power to indemnify any person made a party to any proceeding by reason of the fact that he is or was a director if

(1) he conducted himself in good faith; and

(2) he reasonably believed

(A) in the case of conduct in his official capacity with the corporation, that his conduct was in its best interests, and

(B) in all other cases, that his conduct was at least not opposed to its best interests; and

(3) in the case of any criminal proceeding, he had no reasonable cause to believe his conduct was unlawful.

Indemnification may be made against judgments, penalties, fines, settlements and reasonable expenses, actually incurred by the person in connection with the proceeding; except that if the proceeding was by or in the right of the corporation, indemnification may be made only against such reasonable expenses and shall not be made in respect of any proceeding in which the person shall have been adjudged to be liable to the corporation. The termination of any proceeding by judgment, order, settlement, conviction, or upon a plea of nolo contendere or its equivalent, shall not, of itself, be determinative that the person did not meet the requisite standard of conduct set forth in this subsection (b).

(c) A director shall not be indemnified under subsection (b) in respect of any proceeding charging improper personal benefit to him, whether or not involving action in his official capacity, in which he shall have been adjudged to be liable on the basis that personal benefit was improperly received by him.

(d) Unless limited by the articles of incorporation,

(1) a director who has been wholly successful, on the merits or otherwise, in the defense of any proceeding referred to in subsection (b) shall be indemnified against reasonable expenses incurred by him in connection with the proceeding; and

(2) a court of appropriate jurisdiction, upon application of a director and such notice as the court shall require, shall have authority to order indemnification in the following circumstances:

(A) if it determines a director is entitled to reimbursement under clause (1), the court shall order indemnification, in which case the director shall also be entitled to recover the expenses of securing such reimbursement; or

(B) if it determines that the director is fairly and reasonably entitled to indemnification in view of all the relevant circumstances, whether or not he has met the standard of conduct set forth in subsection (b) or has been adjudged liable in the circumstances described in subsection (c), the court may order such indemnification as the court shall deem proper, except that indemnification with respect to any proceeding by or in the right of the corporation or in which liability shall have been adjudged in the circumstances described in subsection (c) shall be limited to expenses.

A court of appropriate jurisdiction may be the same court in which the proceeding involving the director's liability took place.

(e) No indemnification under subsection (b) shall be made by the corporation unless authorized in the specific case after a determination has been made that indemnification of the director is permissible in the circumstances because he has met the standard of conduct set forth in subsection (b). Such determination shall be made:

(1) by the board of directors by a majority vote of a quorum consisting of directors not at the time parties to the proceeding; or

(2) if such a quorum cannot be obtained, then by a majority vote of a committee of the board, duly designated to act in the matter by a majority vote of the full board (in which designation directors who are parties may participate), consisting solely of two or more directors not at the time parties to the proceeding; or

(3) by special legal counsel, selected by the board of directors or a committee thereof by vote as set forth in clauses (1) or (2) of this subsection (e), or, if the requisite quorum of the full board cannot be obtained therefor and such committee cannot be established, by a majority vote of the full board (in which selection directors who are parties may participate); or

(4) by the shareholders.

Authorization of indemnification and determination as to reasonableness of expenses shall be made in the same manner as the determination that indemnification is permissible, except that if the determination that indemnification is permissible is made by special legal counsel, authorization of indemnification and determination as to reasonableness of expenses shall be made in a manner specified in clause (3) in the preceding sentence for the selection of such counsel. Shares held by directors who are parties to the proceeding shall not be voted on the subject matter under this subsection (e).

(f) Reasonable expenses incurred by a director who is a party to a proceeding may be paid or reimbursed by the corporation in advance of the final disposition of such proceeding upon receipt by the corporation of

(1) a written affirmation by the director of his good faith belief that he has met the standard of conduct necessary for indemnification by the corporation as authorized in this section, and

(2) a written undertaking by or on behalf of the director to repay such amount if it shall ultimately be determined that he has not met such standard of conduct, and after a determination that the facts then known to those making the determination would not preclude indemnification under this section. The undertaking required by clause (2) shall be an unlimited general obligation of the director but need not be secured and may be accepted without reference to financial ability to make repayment. Determinations and authorizations of payments under this subsection (f) shall be made in the manner specified in subsection (e).

(g) No provision for the corporation to indemnify or to advance expenses to a director who is made a party to a proceeding, whether contained in the articles of incorporation, the by-laws, a resolution of shareholders or directors, an agreement or otherwise (except as contemplated by subsection (j)), shall be valid unless consistent with this section or, to the extent that indemnity hereunder is limited by the articles of incorporation, consistent therewith. Nothing contained in this section shall limit the corporation's power to pay or reimburse expenses incurred by a director in connection with his appearance as a witness in a proceeding at a time when he has not been made a named defendant or respondent in the proceeding.

(h) For purposes of this section, the corporation shall be deemed to have requested a director to serve an employee benefit plan whenever the performance by him of his duties to the corporation also imposes duties on, or otherwise involves services by, him to the plan or participants or beneficiaries of the plan; excise taxes assessed on a director with respect to an employee benefit plan pursuant to applicable law shall be deemed "fines"; and action taken or omitted by him with respect to an employee benefit plan in the performance of his duties for a purpose reasonably believed by him to be in the interest of the participants and beneficiaries of the plan shall be deemed to be for a purpose which is not opposed to the best interests of the corporation.

(i) Unless limited by the articles of incorporation,

(1) an officer of the corporation shall be indemnified as and to the same extent provided in subsection (d) for a director and shall be entitled to the same extent as a director to seek indemnification pursuant to the provisions of subsection (d);

(2) a corporation shall have the power to indemnify and to advance expenses to an officer, employee or agent of the corporation to the same extent that it may indemnify and advance expenses to directors pursuant to this section; and

(3) a corporation, in addition, shall have the power to indemnify and to advance expenses to an officer, employee or agent who is not a director to such further extent, consistent with law, as may be provided by its articles of incorporation, by-laws, general or specific action of its board of directors, or contract.

(j) A corporation shall have power to purchase and maintain insurance on behalf of any person who is or was a director, officer, employee or agent of the corporation, or who, while a director, officer, employee or agent of the corporation, is or was serving at the request of the corporation as a director, officer, partner, trustee, employee or agent of another foreign or domestic corporation, partnership, joint venture, trust, other enterprise or employee benefit plan, against any liability asserted against him and incurred by him in any such capacity or arising out of his status as such, whether or not the corporation would have the power to indemnify him against such liability under the provisions of this section.

(k) Any indemnification of, or advance of expenses to, a director in accordance with this section, if arising out of a proceeding by or in the right of the corporation, shall be reported in writing to the shareholders with or before the notice of the next shareholders' meeting.

§ 6. Power of Corporation to Acquire Its Own Shares

A corporation shall have the power to acquire its own shares. All of its own shares acquired by a corporation shall, upon acquisition, constitute authorized but unissued shares, unless the articles of incorporation provide that they shall not be reissued, in which case the authorized shares shall be reduced by the number of shares acquired.

If the number of authorized shares is reduced by an acquisition, the corporation shall, not later than the time it files its next annual report under this Act with the Secretary of State, file a statement of cancellation showing the reduction in the authorized shares. The statement of cancellation shall be executed in duplicate by the corporation by its president or a vice president and by its secretary or an assistant secretary, and verified by one of the officers signing such statement, and shall set forth:

(a) The name of the corporation.

(b) The number of acquired shares cancelled, itemized by classes and series.

(c) The aggregate number of authorized shares, itemized by classes and series, after giving effect to such cancellation.

Duplicate originals of such statement shall be delivered to the Secretary of State. If the Secretary of State finds that such statement conforms to law, he shall, when all fees and franchise taxes have been paid as in this Act prescribed:

(1) Endorse on each of such duplicate originals the word "Filed", and the month, day and year of the filing thereof.

(2) File one of such duplicate originals in his office.

(3) Return the other duplicate original to the corporation or its representative.

§ 7. Defense of Ultra Vires

No act of a corporation and no conveyance or transfer of real or personal property to or by a corporation shall be invalid by reason of the fact that the corporation was without capacity or power to do such act or to make or receive such conveyance or transfer, but such lack of capacity or power may be asserted:

(a) In a proceeding by a shareholder against the corporation to enjoin the doing of any act or the transfer of real or personal property by or to the corporation. If the unauthorized act or transfer sought to be enjoined is being, or is to be, performed or made pursuant to a contract to which the corporation is a party, the court may, if all of the parties to the contract are parties to the proceeding and if it deems the same to be equitable, set aside and enjoin the performance of such contract, and in so doing may allow to the corporation or to the other parties to the contract, as the case may be, compensation for the loss or damage sustained by either of them which may result from the action of the court in setting aside and enjoining the performance of such contract, but anticipated profits to be derived from the performance of the contract shall not be awarded by the court as a loss or damage sustained.

(b) In a proceeding by the corporation, whether acting directly or through a receiver, trustee, or other legal representative, or through shareholders in a representative suit, against the incumbent or former officers or directors of the corporation.

(c) In a proceeding by the Attorney General, as provided in this Act, to dissolve the corporation, or in a proceeding by the Attorney General to enjoin the corporation from the transaction of unauthorized business.

§ 8. Corporate Name

The corporate name:

(a) Shall contain the word "corporation," "company," "incorporated" or "limited," or shall contain an abbreviation of one of such words.

(b) Shall not contain any word or phrase which indicates or implies that it is organized for any purpose other than one or more of the purposes contained in its articles of incorporation.

(c) Shall not be the same as, or deceptively similar to, the name of any domestic corporation existing under the laws of this State or any foreign corporation authorized to transact business in this State, or a name the exclusive right to which is, at the time, reserved in the manner provided in this Act, or the name of a corporation which has in effect a registration of its corporate name as provided in this Act, except that this provision shall not apply if the applicant files with the Secretary of State either of the following: (1) the written consent of such other corporation or holder of a reserved or registered name to use the same or deceptively similar name and one or more words are added to make such name distinguishable from such other name, or (2) a certified copy of a final decree of a court of competent jurisdiction establishing the prior right of the applicant to the use of such name in this State.

A corporation with which another corporation, domestic or foreign, is merged, or which is formed by the reorganization or consolidation of one or more domestic or foreign corporations or upon a sale, lease or other disposition to or exchange with, a domestic corporation of all or substantially all the assets of another corporation, domestic or foreign, including its name, may have the same name as that used in this State by any of such corporations if such other corporation was organized under the laws of, or is authorized to transact business in, this State.

§ 9. Reserved Name

The exclusive right to the use of a corporate name may be reserved by:

(a) Any person intending to organize a corporation under this Act.

(b) Any domestic corporation intending to change its name.

(c) Any foreign corporation intending to make application for a certificate of authority to transact business in this State.

(d) Any foreign corporation authorized to transact business in this State and intending to change its name.

(e) Any person intending to organize a foreign corporation and intending to have such corporation make application for a certificate of authority to transact business in this State.

The reservation shall be made by filing with the Secretary of State an application to reserve a specified corporate name, executed by the applicant. If the Secretary of State finds that the name is available for corporate use, he shall reserve the same for the exclusive use of the applicant for a period of one hundred and twenty days.

The right to the exclusive use of a specified corporate name so reserved may be transferred to any other person or corporation by filing in the office of the Secretary of State a notice of such transfer, executed by the applicant for whom the name was reserved, and specifying the name and address of the transferee.

§ 10. Registered Name

Any corporation organized and existing under the laws of any state or territory of the United States may register its corporate name under this Act, provided its corporate name is not the same as, or deceptively similar to, the name of any domestic corporation existing under the laws of this State, or the name of any foreign corporation authorized to transact business in this State, or any corporate name reserved or registered under this Act.

Such registration shall be made by:

(a) Filing with the Secretary of State (1) an application for registration executed by the corporation by an officer thereof, setting forth the name of the corporation, the state or territory under the laws of which it is incorporated, the date of its incorporation, a statement that it is carrying on or doing business, and a brief statement of the business in which it is engaged, and (2) a certificate setting forth that such corporation is in good standing under the laws of the state or territory wherein it is organized, executed by the Secretary of State of such state or territory or by such other official as may have custody of the records pertaining to corporations, and

(b) Paying to the Secretary of State a registration fee in the amount of . . . . for each month, or fraction thereof, between the date of filing such application and December 31st of the calendar year in which such application is filed.

Such registration shall be effective until the close of the calendar year in which the application for registration is filed.

§ 11. Renewal of Registered Name

A corporation which has in effect a registration of its corporate name, may renew such registration from year to year by annually filing an application for renewal setting forth the facts required to be set forth in an original application for registration and a certificate of good standing as required for the original registration and by paying a fee of . . . .
A renewal application may be filed between the first day of October and the thirty-first day of December in each year, and shall extend the registration for the following calendar year.

§ 12. Registered Office and Registered Agent

Each corporation shall have and continuously maintain in this State:

(a) A registered office which may be, but need not be, the same as its place of business.

(b) A registered agent, which agent may be either an individual resident in this State whose business office is identical with such registered office, or a domestic corporation, or a foreign corporation authorized to transact business in this State, having a business office identical with such registered office.

§ 13. Change of Registered Office or Registered Agent

A corporation may change its registered office or change its registered agent, or both, upon filing in the office of the Secretary of State a statement setting forth:

(a) The name of the corporation.

(b) The address of its then registered office.

(c) If the address of its registered office is to be changed, the address to which the registered office is to be changed.

(d) The name of its then registered agent.

(e) If its registered agent is to be changed, the name of its successor registered agent.

(f) That the address of its registered office and the address of the business office of its registered agent, as changed, will be identical.

(g) That such change was authorized by resolution duly adopted by its board of directors.

Such statement shall be executed by the corporation by its president, or a vice president, and verified by him, and delivered to the Secretary of State. If the Secretary of State finds that such statement conforms to the provisions of this Act, he shall file such statement in his office, and upon such filing the change of address of the registered office, or the appointment of a new registered agent, or both, as the case may be, shall become effective.

Any registered agent of a corporation may resign as such agent upon filing a written notice thereof, executed in duplicate, with the Secretary of State, who shall forthwith mail a copy thereof to the corporation at its registered office. The appointment of such agent shall terminate upon the expiration of thirty days after receipt of such notice by the Secretary of State.

If a registered agent changes his or its business address to another place within the same . . . . ,* he or it may change such address and the address of the registered office of any corporation of which he or it is registered agent by filing a statement as required above except that it need be signed only by the registered agent and need not be responsive to (e) or (g) and must recite that a copy of the statement has been mailed to the corporation.

§ 14. Service of Process on Corporation

The registered agent so appointed by a corporation shall be an agent of such corporation upon whom any process, notice or demand required or permitted by law to be served upon the corporation may be served.

Whenever a corporation shall fail to appoint or maintain a registered agent in this State, or whenever its registered agent cannot with reasonable diligence be found at the registered office, then the Secretary of State shall be an agent of such corporation upon whom any such process, notice, or demand may be served. Service on the Secretary of State of any such process, notice, or demand shall be made by delivering to and leaving with him, or with any clerk having charge of the corporation department of his office, duplicate copies of such process, notice or demand. In the event any such process, notice or demand is served on the Secretary of State, he shall immediately cause one of the copies thereof to be forwarded by registered mail, addressed to the corporation at its registered office. Any service so had on the Secretary of State shall be returnable in not less than thirty days.

The Secretary of State shall keep a record of all processes, notices and demands served upon him under this section, and shall record therein the time of such service and his action with reference thereto.

Nothing herein contained shall limit or affect the right to serve any process, notice or demand required or permitted by law to be served upon a corporation in any other manner now or hereafter permitted by law.

§ 15. Authorized Shares

Each corporation shall have power to create and issue the number of shares stated in its articles of incorpo-

---

*Supply designation of jurisdiction, such as county, etc., in accordance with local practice.

ration. Such shares may be divided into one or more classes with such designations, preferences, limitations, and relative rights as shall be stated in the articles of incorporation. The articles of incorporation may limit or deny the voting rights of or provide special voting rights for the shares of any class to the extent not inconsistent with the provisions of this Act.

Without limiting the authority herein contained, a corporation, when so provided in its articles of incorporation, may issue shares of preferred or special classes:

(a) Subject to the right of the corporation to redeem any of such shares at the price fixed by the articles of incorporation for the redemption thereof.

(b) Entitling the holders thereof to cumulative, noncumulative or partially cumulative dividends.

(c) Having preference over any other class or classes of shares as to the payment of dividends.

(d) Having preference in the assets of the corporation over any other class or classes of shares upon the voluntary or involuntary liquidation of the corporation.

(e) Convertible into shares of any other class or into shares of any series of the same or any other class, except a class having prior or superior rights and preferences as to dividends or distribution of assets upon liquidation.

§ 16. Issuance of Shares of Preferred or Special Classes in Series

If the articles of incorporation so provide, the shares of any preferred or special class may be divided into and issued in series. If the shares of any such class are to be issued in series, then each series shall be so designated as to distinguish the shares thereof from the shares of all other series and classes. Any or all of the series of any such class and the variations in the relative rights and preferences as between different series may be fixed and determined by the articles of incorporation, but all shares of the same class shall be identical except as to the following relative rights and preferences, as to which there may be variations between different series:

(A) The rate of dividend.

(B) Whether shares may be redeemed and, if so, the redemption price and the terms and conditions of redemption.

(C) The amount payable upon shares in the event of voluntary and involuntary liquidation.

(D) Sinking fund provisions, if any, for the redemption or purchase of shares.

(E) The terms and conditions, if any, on which shares may be converted.

(F) Voting rights, if any.

If the articles of incorporation shall expressly vest authority in the board of directors, then, to the extent that the articles of incorporation shall not have established series and fixed and determined the variations in the relative rights and preferences as between series, the board of directors shall have authority to divide any or all of such classes into series and, within the limitations set forth in this section and in the articles of incorporation, fix and determine the relative rights and preferences of the shares of any series so established.

In order for the board of directors to establish a series, where authority so to do is contained in the articles of incorporation, the board of directors shall adopt a resolution setting forth the designation of the series and fixing and determining the relative rights and preferences thereof, or so much thereof as shall not be fixed and determined by the articles of incorporation.

Prior to the issue of any shares of a series established by resolution adopted by the board of directors, the corporation shall file in the office of the Secretary of State a statement setting forth:

(a) The name of the corporation.

(b) A copy of the resolution establishing and designating the series, and fixing and determining the relative rights and preferences thereof.

(c) The date of adoption of such resolution.

(d) That such resolution was duly adopted by the board of directors.

Such statement shall be executed in duplicate by the corporation by its president or a vice president and by its secretary or an assistant secretary, and verified by one of the officers signing such statement, and shall be delivered to the Secretary of State. If the Secretary of State finds that such statement conforms to law, he shall, when all franchise taxes and fees have been paid as in this Act prescribed:

(1) Endorse on each of such duplicate originals the word "Filed," and the month, day, and year of the filing thereof.

(2) File one of such duplicate originals in his office.

(3) Return the other duplicate original to the corporation or its representative.

Upon the filing of such statement by the Secretary of State, the resolution establishing and designating the series and fixing and determining the relative rights and preferences thereof shall become effective and shall constitute an amendment of the articles of incorporation.

§ 17. Subscriptions for Shares

A subscription for shares of a corporation to be organized shall be irrevocable for a period of six months, unless otherwise provided by the terms of the subscription agreement or unless all of the subscribers consent to the revocation of such subscription.

Unless otherwise provided in the subscription agreement, subscriptions for shares, whether made before or after the organization of a corporation, shall be paid in full at such time, or in such installments and at such times, as shall be determined by the board of directors. Any call made by the board of directors for payment on subscriptions shall be uniform as to all shares of the same class or as to all shares of the same series, as the case may be. In case of default in the payment of any installment or call when such payment is due, the corporation may proceed to collect the amount due in the same manner as any debt due the corporation. The bylaws may prescribe other penalties for failure to pay installments or calls that may become due, but no penalty working a forfeiture of a subscription, or of the amounts paid thereon, shall be declared as against any subscriber unless the amount due thereon shall remain unpaid for a period of twenty days after written demand has been made therefor. If mailed, such written demand shall be deemed to be made when deposited in the United States mail in a sealed envelope addressed to the subscriber at his last post-office address known to the corporation, with postage thereon prepaid. In the event of the sale of any shares by reason of any foreefiture, the excess of proceeds realized over the amount due and unpaid on such shares shall be paid to the delinquent subscriber or to his legal representative.

§ 18. **Issuance of Shares**

Subject to any restrictions in the articles of incorporation:

(a) Shares may be issued for such consideration as shall be authorized by the board of directors establishing a price (in money or other consideration) or a minimum price or general formula or method by which the price will be determined; and

(b) Upon authorization by the board of directors, the corporation may issue its own shares in exchange for or in conversion of its outstanding shares, or distribute its own shares, pro rata to its shareholders or the shareholders of one or more classes or series, to effectuate stock dividends or splits, and any such transaction shall not require consideration; provided, that no such issuance of shares of any class or series shall be made to the holders of shares of any other class or series unless it is either expressly provided for in the articles of incorporation, or is authorized by an affirmative vote or the written consent of the holders of at least a majority of the outstanding shares of the class or series in which the distribution is to be made.

§ 19. **Payment for Shares**

The consideration for the issuance of shares may be paid, in whole or in part, in money, in other property, tangible or intangible, or in labor or services actually performed for the corporation. When payment of the consideration for which shares are to be issued shall have been received by the corporation, such shares shall be nonassessable.

Neither promissory notes nor future services shall constitute payment or part payment for the issuance of shares of a corporation.

In the absence of fraud in the transaction, the judgment of the board of directors or the shareholders, as the case may be, as to the value of the consideration received for shares shall be conclusive.

§ 20. **Stock Rights and Options**

Subject to any provisions in respect thereof set forth in its articles of incorporation, a corporation may create and issue, whether or not in connection with the issuance and sale of any of its shares or other securities, rights or options entitling the holders thereof to purchase from the corporation shares of any class or classes. Such rights or options shall be evidenced in such manner as the board of directors shall approve and, subject to the provisions of the articles of incorporation, shall set forth the terms upon which, the time or times within which and the price or prices at which such shares may be purchased from the corporation upon the exercise of any such right or option. If such rights or options are to be issued to directors, officers or employees as such of the corporation or of any subsidiary thereof, and not to the shareholders generally, their issuance shall be approved by the affirmative vote of the holders of a majority of the shares entitled to vote thereon or shall be authorized by and consistent with a plan approved or ratified by such a vote of shareholders. In the absence of fraud in the transaction, the judgment of the board of directors as to the adequacy of the consideration received for such rights or options shall be conclusive.

§ 21. **Determination of Amount of Stated Capital**

[Repealed in 1979].

§ 22. **Expenses of Organization, Reorganization and Financing**

The reasonable charges and expenses of organization or reorganization of a corporation, and the reasonable expenses of and compensation for the sale or underwriting of its shares, may be paid or allowed by such corporation out of the consideration received by it in payment for its shares without thereby rendering such shares assessable.

§ 23. Shares Represented by Certificates and Uncertified Shares

The shares of a corporation shall be represented by certificates or shall be uncertificated shares. Certificates shall be signed by the chairman or vice-chairman of the board of directors or the president or a vice president and by the treasurer or an assistant treasurer or the secretary or an assistant secretary of the corporation, and may be sealed with the seal of the corporation or a facsimile thereof. Any of or all the signatures upon a certificate may be a facsimile. In case any officer, transfer agent or registrar who has signed or whose facsimile signature has been placed upon such certificate shall have ceased to be such officer, transfer agent or registrar before such certificate is issued, it may be issued by the corporation with the same effect as if he were such officer, transfer agent or registrar at the date of its issue.

Every certificate representing shares issued by a corporation which is authorized to issue shares of more than one class shall set forth upon the face or back of the certificate, or shall state that the corporation will furnish to any shareholder upon request and without charge, a full statement of the designations, preferences, limitations, and relative rights of the shares of each class authorized to be issued, and if the corporation is authorized to issue any preferred or special class in series, the variations in the relative rights and preferences between the shares of each such series so far as the same have been fixed and determined and the authority of the board of directors to fix and determine the relative rights and preferences of subsequent series.

Each certificate representing shares shall state upon the face thereof:

(a) That the corporation is organized under the laws of this State.

(b) The name of the person to whom issued.

(c) The number and class of shares, and the designation of the series, if any, which such certificate represents.

(d) The par value of each share represented by such certificate, or a statement that the shares are without par value.

No certificate shall be issued for any share until such share is fully paid.

Unless otherwise provided by the articles of incorporation or by-laws, the board of directors of a corporation may provide by resolution that some or all of any or all classes and series of its shares shall be uncertificated shares, provided that such resolution shall not apply to shares represented by a certificate until such certificate is surrendered to the corporation. Within a reasonable time after the issuance or transfer of uncertificated shares, the corporation shall send to the registered owner thereof a written notice containing the information required to be set forth or stated on certificates pursuant to the second and third paragraphs of this section. Except as otherwise expressly provided by law, the rights and obligations of the holders of uncertificated shares and the rights and obligations of the holders of certificates representing shares of the same class and series shall be identical.

§ 24. Fractional Shares

A corporation may (1) issue fractions of a share, either represented by a certificate or uncertificated, (2) arrange for the disposition of fractional interests by those entitled thereto, (3) pay in money the fair value of fractions of a share as of a time when those entitled to receive such fractions are determined, or (4) issue scrip in registered or bearer form which shall entitle the holder to receive a certificate for a full share or an uncertificated full share upon the surrender of such scrip aggregating a full share. A certificate for a fractional share or an uncertificated fractional share shall, but scrip shall not unless otherwise provided therein, entitle the holder to exercise voting rights, to receive dividends thereon, and to participate in any of the assets of the corporation in the event of liquidation. The board of directors may cause scrip to be issued subject to the condition that it shall become void if not exchanged for certificates representing full shares or uncertificated full shares before a specified date, or subject to the condition that the shares for which scrip is exchangeable may be sold by the corporation and the proceeds thereof distributed to the holders of scrip, or subject to any other conditions which the board of directors may deem advisable.

§ 25. Liability of Subscribers and Shareholders

A holder of or subscriber to shares of a corporation shall be under no obligation to the corporation or its creditors with respect to such shares other than the obligation to pay to the corporation the full consideration for which such shares were issued or to be issued.

Any person becoming an assignee or transferee of shares or of a subscription for shares in good faith and without knowledge or notice that the full consideration therefor has not been paid shall not be personally liable to the corporation or its creditors for any unpaid portion of such consideration.

An executor, administrator, conservator, guardian, trustee, assignee for the benefit of creditors, or receiver shall not be personally liable to the corporation as a holder of or subscriber to shares of a corporation but the estate and funds in his hands shall be so liable.

No pledgee or other holder of shares as collateral security shall be personally liable as a shareholder.

§ 26. Shareholders' Preemptive Rights

The shareholders of a corporation shall have no preemptive right to acquire unissued shares of the corporation, or securities of the corporation convertible into or carrying a right to subscribe to or acquire shares, except to the extent, if any, that such right is provided in the articles of incorporation.

§ 26A. **Shareholders' Preemptive Rights [Alternative]**

Except to the extent limited or denied by this section or by the articles of incorporation, shareholders shall have a preemptive right to acquire unissued shares or securities convertible into such shares or carrying a right to subscribe to or acquire shares.

Unless otherwise provided in the articles of incorporation,

(a) No preemptive right shall exist

(1) to acquire any shares issued to directors, officers or employees pursuant to approval by the affirmative vote of the holders of a majority of the shares entitled to vote thereon or when authorized by and consistent with a plan theretofore approved by such a vote of shareholders; or

(2) to acquire any shares sold otherwise than for money.

(b) Holders of shares of any class that is preferred or limited as to dividends or assets shall not be entitled to any preemptive right.

(c) Holders of shares of common stock shall not be entitled to any preemptive right to shares of any class that is preferred or limited as to dividends or assets or to any obligations, unless convertible into shares of common stock or carrying a right to subscribe to or acquire shares of common stock.

(d) Holders of common stock without voting power shall have no preemptive right to shares of common stock with voting power.

(e) The preemptive right shall be only an opportunity to acquire shares or other securities under such terms and conditions as the board of directors may fix for the purpose of providing a fair and reasonable opportunity for the exercise of such right.

§ 27. **By-Laws**

The initial by-laws of a corporation shall be adopted by its board of directors. The power to alter, amend or repeal the by-laws or adopt new by-laws, subject to repeal or change by action of the shareholders, shall be vested in the board of directors unless reserved to the shareholders by the articles of incorporation. The by-laws may contain any provisions for the regulation and management of the affairs of the corporation not inconsistent with law or the articles of incorporation.

§ 27A. **By-Laws and Other Powers in Emergency [Optional]**

The board of directors of any corporation may adopt emergency by-laws, subject to repeal or change by action of the shareholders, which shall, notwithstanding any different provision elsewhere in this Act or in the articles of incorporation or by-laws, be operative during any emergency in the conduct of the business of the corporation resulting from an attack on the United States or any nuclear or atomic disaster. The emergency by-laws may make any provision that may be practical and necessary for the circumstances of the emergency, including provisions that:

(a) A meeting of the board of directors may be called by any officer or director in such manner and under such conditions as shall be prescribed in the emergency by-laws;

(b) The director or directors in attendance at the meeting, or any greater number fixed by the emergency by-laws, shall constitute a quorum; and

(c) The officers or other persons designated on a list approved by the board of directors before the emergency, all in such order of priority and subject to such conditions, and for such period of time (not longer than reasonably necessary after the termination of the emergency) as may be provided in the emergency by-laws or in the resolution approving the list shall, to the extent required to provide a quorum at any meeting of the board of directors, be deemed directors for such meeting.

The board of directors, either before or during any such emergency, may provide, and from time to time modify, lines of succession in the event that during such an emergency any or all officers or agents of the corporation shall for any reason be rendered incapable of discharging their duties.

The board of directors, either before or during any such emergency, may, effective in the emergency, change the head office or designate several alternative head offices or regional offices, or authorize the officers so to do.

To the extent not inconsistent with any emergency by-laws so adopted, the by-laws of the corporation shall remain in effect during any such emergency and upon its termination the emergency by-laws shall cease to be operative.

Unless otherwise provided in emergency by-laws, notice of any meeting of the board of directors during any such emergency may be given only to such of the directors as it may be feasible to reach at the time and by such means as may be feasible at the time, including publication or radio.

To the extent required to constitute a quorum at any meeting of the board of directors during any such emergency, the officers of the corporation who are present shall, unless otherwise provided in emergency by-laws, be deemed, in order of rank and within the same rank in order of seniority, directors for such meeting.

No officer, director or employee acting in accordance with any emergency by-laws shall be liable except for willful misconduct. No officer, director or employee shall be liable for any action taken by him in good faith in such an emergency in furtherance of the ordinary business affairs of the corporation even though not authorized by the by-laws then in effect.

§ 28. Meetings of Shareholders

Meetings of shareholders may be held at such place within or without this State as may be stated in or fixed in accordance with the by-laws. If no other place is stated or so fixed, meetings shall be held at the registered office of the corporation.

An annual meeting of the shareholders shall be held at such time as may be stated in or fixed in accordance with the by-laws. If the annual meeting is not held within any thirteen-month period the Court of . . . . may, on the application of any shareholder, summarily order a meeting to be held.

Special meetings of the shareholders may be called by the board of directors, the holders of not less than one-tenth of all the shares entitled to vote at the meeting, or such other persons as may be authorized in the articles of incorporation or the by-laws.

§ 29. Notice of Shareholders' Meetings

Written notice stating the place, day and hour of the meeting and, in case of a special meeting, the purpose or purposes for which the meeting is called, shall be delivered not less than ten nor more than fifty days before the date of the meeting, either personally or by mail, by or at the direction of the president, the secretary, or the officer or persons calling the meeting, to each shareholder of record entitled to vote at such meeting. If mailed, such notice shall be deemed to be delivered when deposited in the United States mail addressed to the shareholder at his address as it appears on the stock transfer books of the corporation, with postage thereon prepaid.

§ 30. Closing of Transfer Books and Fixing Record Date

For the purpose of determining shareholders entitled to notice of or to vote at any meeting of shareholders or any adjournment thereof, or entitled to receive payment of any dividend, or in order to make a determination of shareholders for any other proper purpose, the board of directors of a corporation may provide that the stock transfer books shall be closed for a stated period but not to exceed, in any case, fifty days. If the stock transfer books shall be closed for the purpose of determining shareholders entitled to notice of or to vote at a meeting of shareholders, such books shall be closed for at least ten days immediately preceding such meeting. In lieu of closing the stock transfer books, the by-laws, or in the absence of an applicable by-law the board of directors, may fix in advance a date as the record date for any such determination of shareholders, such date in any case to be not more than fifty days and, in case of a meeting of shareholders, not less than ten days prior to the date on which the particular action, requiring such determination of shareholders, is to be taken. If the stock transfer books are not closed and no record date is fixed for the determination of shareholders entitled to notice of or to vote at a meeting of shareholders, or shareholders entitled to receive payment of a dividend, the date on which notice of the meeting is mailed or the date on which the resolution of the board of directors declaring such dividend is adopted, as the case may be, shall be the record date for such determination of shareholders. When a determination of shareholders entitled to vote at any meeting of shareholders has been made as provided in this section, such determination shall apply to any adjournment thereof.

§ 31. Voting Record

The officer or agent having charge of the stock transfer books for shares of a corporation shall make a complete record of the shareholders entitled to vote at such meeting or any adjournment thereof, arranged in alphabetical order, with the address of and the number of shares held by each. Such record shall be produced and kept open at the time and place of the meeting and shall be subject to the inspection of any shareholder during the whole time of the meeting for the purposes thereof.

Failure to comply with the requirements of this section shall not affect the validity of any action taken at such meeting.

An officer or agent having charge of the stock transfer books who shall fail to prepare the record of shareholders, or produce and keep it open for inspection at the meeting, as provided in this section, shall be liable to any shareholder suffering damage on account of such failure, to the extent of such damage.

§ 32. Quorum of Shareholders

Unless otherwise provided in the articles of incorporation, a majority of the shares entitled to vote, represented in person or by proxy, shall constitute a quorum at a meeting of shareholders, but in no event shall a quorum consist of less than one-third of the shares entitled to vote at the meeting. If a quorum is present, the affirmative vote of the majority of the shares represented at the meeting and entitled to vote on the subject matter shall be the act of the shareholders, unless the vote of a greater number or voting by classes is required by this Act or the articles of incorporation or by-laws.

§ 33. Voting of Shares

Each outstanding share, regardless of class, shall be entitled to one vote on each matter submitted to a vote at a meeting of shareholders, except as may be otherwise provided in the articles of incorporation. If the articles of incorporation provide for more or less than one vote for any share, on any matter, every reference in this Act to a majority or other proportion of shares shall refer to such a majority or other proportion of votes entitled to be cast.

Shares held by another corporation if a majority of the shares entitled to vote for the election of directors of such other corporation is held by the corporation, shall not be voted at any meeting or counted in determining the total number of outstanding shares at any given time.

A shareholder may vote either in person or by proxy executed in writing by the shareholder or by his duly authorized attorney-in-fact. No proxy shall be valid after eleven months from the date of its execution, unless otherwise provided in the proxy.

[Either of the following prefatory phrases may be inserted here: "The articles of incorporation may provide that" or "Unless the articles of incorporation otherwise provide"] . . . at each election for directors every shareholder entitled to vote at such election shall have the right to vote, in person or by proxy, the number of shares owned by him for as many persons as there are directors to be elected and for whose election he has a right to vote, or to cumulate his votes by giving one candidate as many votes as the number of such directors multiplied by the number of his shares shall equal, or by distributing such votes on the same principle among any number of such candidates.

Shares standing in the name of another corporation, domestic or foreign, may be voted by such officer, agent or proxy as the by-laws of such other corporation may prescribe, or, in the absence of such provision, as the board of directors of such other corporation may determine.

Shares held by an administrator, executor, guardian or conservator may be voted by him, either in person or by proxy, without a transfer of such shares into his name. Shares standing in the name of a trustee may be voted by him, either in person or by proxy, but no trustee shall be entitled to vote shares held by him without a transfer of such shares into his name.

Shares standing in the name of a receiver may be voted by such receiver, and shares held by or under the control of a receiver may be voted by such receiver without the transfer thereof into his name if authority so to do be contained in an appropriate order of the court by which such receiver was appointed.

A shareholder whose shares are pledged shall be entitled to vote such shares until the shares have been transferred into the name of the pledgee, and thereafter the pledgee shall be entitled to vote the shares so transferred.

On and after the date on which written notice of redemption of redeemable shares has been mailed to the holders thereof and a sum sufficient to redeem such shares has been deposited with a bank or trust company with irrevocable instruction and authority to pay the redemption price to the holders thereof upon surrender of certificates therefor, such shares shall not be entitled to vote on any matter and shall not be deemed to be outstanding shares.

§ 34. Voting Trusts and Agreements Among Shareholders

Any number of shareholders of a corporation may create a voting trust for the purpose of conferring upon a trustee or trustees the right to vote or otherwise represent their shares, for a period of not to exceed ten years, by entering into a written voting trust agreement specifying the terms and conditions of the voting trust, by depositing a counterpart of the agreement with the corporation at its registered office, and by transferring their shares to such trustee or trustees for the purposes of the agreement. Such trustee or trustees shall keep a record of the holders of voting trust certificates evidencing a beneficial interest in the voting trust, giving the names and addresses of all such holders and the number and class of the shares in respect of which the voting trust certificates held by each are issued, and shall deposit a copy of such record with the corporation at its registered office. The counterpart of the voting trust agreement and the copy of such record so deposited with the corporation shall be subject to the same right of examination by a shareholder of the corporation, in person or by agent or attorney, as are the books and records of the corporation, and such counterpart and such copy of such record shall be subject to examination by any holder of record of voting trust certificates, either in person or by agent or attorney, at any reasonable time for any proper purpose.

Agreements among shareholders regarding the voting of their shares shall be valid and enforceable in accordance with their terms. Such agreements shall not be subject to the provisions of this section regarding voting trusts.

§ 35. Board of Directors

All corporate powers shall be exercised by or under authority of, and the business and affairs of a corporation shall be managed under the direction of, a board of directors except as may be otherwise provided in this

Act or the articles of incorporation. If any such provision is made in the articles of incorporation, the powers and duties conferred or imposed upon the board of directors by this Act shall be exercised or performed to such extent and by such person or persons as shall be provided in the articles of incorporation. Directors need not be residents of this State or shareholders of the corporation unless the articles of incorporation or by-laws so require. The articles of incorporation or by-laws may prescribe other qualifications for directors. The board of directors shall have authority to fix the compensation of directors unless otherwise provided in the articles of incorporation.

A director shall perform his duties as a director, including his duties as a member of any committee of the board upon which he may serve, in good faith, in a manner he reasonably believes to be in the best interests of the corporation, and with such care as an ordinarily prudent person in a like position would use under similar circumstances. In performing his duties, a director shall be entitled to rely on information, opinions, reports or statements, including financial statements and other financial data, in each case prepared or presented by:

(a) one or more officers or employees of the corporation whom the director reasonably believes to be reliable and competent in the matters presented,

(b) counsel, public accountants or other persons as to matters which the director reasonably believes to be within such person's professional or expert competence, or

(c) a committee of the board upon which he does not serve, duly designated in accordance with a provision of the articles of incorporation or the by-laws, as to matters within its designated authority, which committee the director reasonably believes to merit confidence,

but he shall not be considered to be acting in good faith if he has knowledge concerning the matter in question that would cause such reliance to be unwarranted. A person who so performs his duties shall have no liability by reason of being or having been a director of the corporation.

A director of a corporation who is present at a meeting of its board of directors at which action on any corporate matter is taken shall be presumed to have assented to the action taken unless his dissent shall be entered in the minutes of the meeting or unless he shall file his written dissent to such action with the secretary of the meeting before the adjournment thereof or shall forward such dissent by registered mail to the secretary of the corporation immediately after the adjournment of the meeting. Such right to dissent shall not apply to a director who voted in favor of such action.

§ 36. Number and Election of Directors

The board of directors of a corporation shall consist of one or more members. The number of directors shall be fixed by, or in the manner provided in, the articles of incorporation or the by-laws, except as to the number constituting the initial board of directors, which number shall be fixed by the articles of incorporation. The number of directors may be increased or decreased from time to time by amendment to, or in the manner provided in, the articles of incorporation or the by-laws, but no decrease shall have the effect of shortening the term of any incumbent director. In the absence of a by-law providing for the number of directors, the number shall be the same as that provided for in the articles of incorporation. The names and addresses of the members of the first board of directors shall be stated in the articles of incorporation. Such persons shall hold office until the first annual meeting of shareholders, and until their successors shall have been elected and qualified. At the first annual meeting of shareholders and at each annual meeting thereafter the shareholders shall elect directors to hold office until the next succeeding annual meeting, except in case of the classification of directors as permitted by this Act. Each director shall hold office for the term for which he is elected and until his successor shall have been elected and qualified.

§ 37. Classification of Directors

When the board of directors shall consist of nine or more members, in lieu of electing the whole number of directors annually, the articles of incorporation may provide that the directors be divided into either two or three classes, each class to be as nearly equal in number as possible, the term of office of directors of the first class to expire at the first annual meeting of shareholders after their election, that of the second class to expire at the second annual meeting after their election, and that of the third class, if any, to expire at the third annual meeting after their election. At each annual meeting after such classification the number of directors equal to the number of the class whose term expires at the time of such meeting shall be elected to hold office until the second succeeding annual meeting, if there be two classes, or until the third succeeding annual meeting, if there be three classes. No classification of directors shall be effective prior to the first annual meeting of shareholders.

§ 38. Vacancies

Any vacancy occurring in the board of directors may be filled by the affirmative vote of a majority of the remaining directors though less than a quorum of the board of directors. A director elected to fill a vacancy shall be elected for the unexpired term of his predecessor in office. Any directorship to be filled by reason of an increase in the number of directors may be filled by the board of directors for a term of office continuing only until the next election of directors by the shareholders.

§ 39. Removal of Directors

At a meeting of shareholders called expressly for that purpose, directors may be removed in the manner provided in this section. Any director or the entire board of directors may be removed, with or without cause, by a vote of the holders of a majority of the shares then entitled to vote at an election of directors.

In the case of a corporation having cumulative voting, if less than the entire board is to be removed, no one of the directors may be removed if the votes cast against his removal would be sufficient to elect him if then cumulatively voted at an election of the entire board of directors, or, if there be classes of directors, at an election of the class of directors of which he is a part.

Whenever the holders of the shares of any class are entitled to elect one or more directors by the provisions of the articles of incorporation, the provisions of this section shall apply, in respect to the removal of a director or directors so elected, to the vote of the holders of the outstanding shares of that class and not to the vote of the outstanding shares as a whole.

§ 40. Quorum of Directors

A majority of the number of directors fixed by or in the manner provided in the by-laws or in the absence of a by-law fixing or providing for the number of directors, then of the number stated in the articles of incorporation, shall constitute a quorum for the transaction of business unless a greater number is required by the articles of incorporation or the by-laws. The act of the majority of the directors present at a meeting at which a quorum is present shall be the act of the board of directors, unless the act of a greater number is required by the articles of incorporation or the by-laws.

§ 41. Director Conflicts of Interest

No contract or other transaction between a corporation and one or more of its directors or any other corporation, firm, association or entity in which one or more of its directors are directors or officers or are financially interested, shall be either void or voidable because of such relationship or interest or because such director or directors are present at the meeting of the board of directors or a committee thereof which authorizes, approves or ratifies such contract or transaction or because his or their votes are counted for such purpose, if:

(a) the fact of such relationship or interest is disclosed or known to the board of directors or committee which authorizes, approves or ratifies the contract or transaction by a vote or consent sufficient for the purpose without counting the votes or consents of such interested directors; or

(b) the fact of such relationship or interest is disclosed or known to the shareholders entitled to vote and they authorize, approve or ratify such contract or transaction by vote or written consent; or

(c) the contract or transaction is fair and reasonable to the corporation.

Common or interested directors may be counted in determining the presence of a quorum at a meeting of the board of directors or a committee thereof which authorizes, approves or ratifies such contract or transaction.

§ 42. Executive and Other Committees

If the articles of incorporation or the by-laws so provide, the board of directors, by resolution adopted by a majority of the full board of directors, may designate from among its members an executive committee and one or more other committees each of which, to the extent provided in such resolution or in the articles of incorporation or the by-laws of the corporation, shall have and may exercise all the authority of the board of directors, except that no such committee shall have authority to (i) authorize distributions, (ii) approve or recommend to shareholders actions or proposals required by this Act to be approved by shareholders, (iii) designate candidates for the office of director, for purposes of proxy solicitation or otherwise, or fill vacancies on the board of directors or any committee thereof, (iv) amend the by-laws, (v) approve a plan of merger not requiring shareholder approval, (vi) authorize or approve the reacquisition of shares unless pursuant to a general formula or method specified by the board of directors, or (vii) authorize or approve the issuance or sale of, or any contract to issue or sell, shares or designate the terms of a series of a class of shares, provided that the board of directors, having acted regarding general authorization for the issuance or sale of shares, or any contract therefor, and, in the case of a series, the designation thereof, may, pursuant to a general formula or method specified by the board by resolution or by adoption of a stock option or other plan, authorize a committee to fix the terms of any contract for the sale of the shares and to fix the terms upon which such shares may be issued or sold, including, without limitation, the price, the dividend rate, provisions for redemption, sinking fund, conversion, voting or preferential rights, and provisions for other features of a class of shares, or a series of a class of shares, with full power in such committee to adopt any final resolution setting forth all the terms thereof and to authorize the statement of the terms of a series for filing with the Secretary of State under this Act.

Neither the designation of any such committee, the

delegation thereto of authority, nor action by such committee pursuant to such authority shall alone constitute compliance by any member of the board of directors, not a member of the committee in question, with his responsibility to act in good faith, in a manner he reasonably believes to be in the best interests of the corporation, and with such care as an ordinarily prudent person in a like position would use under similar circumstances.

§ 43. Place and Notice of Directors' Meetings; Committee Meetings

Meetings of the board of directors, regular or special, may be held either within or without this State.

Regular meetings of the board of directors or any committee designated thereby may be held with or without notice as prescribed in the by-laws. Special meetings of the board of directors or any committee designated thereby shall be held upon such notice as is prescribed in the by-laws. Attendance of a director at a meeting shall constitute a waiver of notice of such meeting, except where a director attends a meeting for the express purpose of objecting to the transaction of any business because the meeting is not lawfully called or convened. Neither the business to be transacted at, nor the purpose of, any regular or special meeting of the board of directors or any committee designated thereby need be specified in the notice or waiver of notice of such meeting unless required by the by-laws.

Except as may be otherwise restricted by the articles of incorporation or by-laws, members of the board of directors or any committee designated thereby may participate in a meeting of such board or committee by means of a conference telephone or similar communications equipment by means of which all persons participating in the meeting can hear each other at the same time and participation by such means shall constitute presence in person at a meeting.

§ 44. Action by Directors Without a Meeting

Unless otherwise provided by the articles of incorporation or by-laws, any action required by this Act to be taken at a meeting of the directors of a corporation, or any action which may be taken at a meeting of the directors or of a committee, may be taken without a meeting if a consent in writing, setting forth the action so taken, shall be signed by all of the directors, or all of the members of the committee, as the case may be. Such consent shall have the same effect as a unanimous vote.

§ 45. Distributions to Shareholders

Subject to any restrictions in the articles of incorporation, the board of directors may authorize and the corporation may make distributions, except that no distribution may be made if, after giving effect thereto, either:

(a) the corporation would be unable to pay its debts as they become due in the usual course of its business; or

(b) the corporation's total assets would be less than the sum of its total liabilities and (unless the articles of incorporation otherwise permit) the maximum amount that then would be payable, in any liquidation, in respect of all outstanding shares having preferential rights in liquidation.

Determinations under subparagraph (b) may be based upon (i) financial statements prepared on the basis of accounting practices and principles that are reasonable in the circumstances, or (ii) a fair valuation or other method that is reasonable in the circumstances.

In the case of a purchase, redemption or other acquisition of a corporation's shares, the effect of a distribution shall be measured as of the date money or other property is transferred or debt is incurred by the corporation, or as of the date the shareholder ceases to be a shareholder of the corporation with respect to such shares, whichever is earlier. In all other cases, the effect of a distribution shall be measured as of the date of its authorization if payment occurs 120 days or less following the date of authorization, or as of the date of payment if payment occurs more than 120 days following the date of authorization.

Indebtedness of a corporation incurred or issued to a shareholder in a distribution in accordance with this Section shall be on a parity with the indebtedness of the corporation to its general unsecured creditors except to the extent subordinated by agreement.

§ 46. Distributions from Capital Surplus

[Repealed in 1979].

§ 47. Loans to Employees and Directors

A corporation shall not lend money to or use its credit to assist its directors without authorization in the particular case by its shareholders, but may lend money to and use its credit to assist any employee of the corporation or of a subsidiary, including any such employee who is a director of the corporation, if the board of directors decides that such loan or assistance may benefit the corporation.

§ 48. Liability of Directors in Certain Cases

In addition to any other liabilities, a director who votes for or assents to any distribution contrary to the provisions of this Act or contrary to any restrictions contained in the articles of incorporation, shall, unless he complies with the standard provided in this Act for the performance of the duties of directors, be liable to the corporation, jointly and severally with all other directors so voting or assenting, for the amount of such dividend which is paid or the value of such distribution in excess of the amount of such distribution which could have been made without a violation of the provisions of this Act or the restrictions in the articles of incorporation.

Any director against whom a claim shall be asserted under or pursuant to this section for the making of a distribution and who shall be held liable thereon, shall be entitled to contribution from the shareholders who accepted or received any such distribution, knowing such distribution to have been made in violation of this Act, in proportion to the amounts received by them.

Any director against whom a claim shall be asserted under or pursuant to this section shall be entitled to contribution from any other director who voted for or assented to the action upon which the claim is asserted and who did not comply with the standard provided in this Act for the performance of the duties of directors.

§ 49. Provisions Relating to Actions by Shareholders

No action shall be brought in this State by a shareholder in the right of a domestic or foreign corporation unless the plaintiff was a holder of record of shares or of voting trust certificates therefor at the time of the transaction of which he complains, or his shares or voting trust certificates thereafter devolved upon him by operation of law from a person who was a holder of record at such time.

In any action hereafter instituted in the right of any domestic or foreign corporation by the holder or holders of record of shares of such corporation or of voting trust certificates therefor, the court having jurisdiction, upon final judgment and a finding that the action was brought without reasonable cause, may require the plaintiff or plaintiffs to pay to the parties named as defendant the reasonable expenses, including fees of attorneys, incurred by them in the defense of such action.

In any action now pending or hereafter instituted or maintained in the right of any domestic or foreign corporation by the holder or holders of record of less than five per cent of the outstanding shares of any class of such corporation or of voting trust certificates therefor, unless the shares or voting trust certificates so held have a market value in excess of twenty-five thousand dollars, the corporation in whose right such action is brought shall be entitled at any time before final judgment to require the plaintiff or plaintiffs to give security for the reasonable expenses, including fees of attorneys, that may be incurred by it in connection with such action or may be incurred by other parties named as defendant for which it may become legally liable. Market value shall be determined as of the date that the plaintiff institutes the action or, in the case of an intervenor, as of the date that he becomes a party to the action. The amount of such security may from time to time be increased or decreased, in the discretion of the court, upon showing that the security provided has or may become

inadequate or is excessive. The corporation shall have recourse to such security in such amount as the court having jurisdiction shall determine upon the termination of such action, whether or not the court finds the action was brought without reasonable cause.

§ 50. Officers

The officers of a corporation shall consist of a president, one or more vice presidents as may be prescribed by the by-laws, a secretary, and a treasurer, each of whom shall be elected by the board of directors at such time and in such manner as may be prescribed by the by-laws. Such other officers and assistant officers and agents as may be deemed necessary may be elected or appointed by the board of directors or chosen in such other manner as may be prescribed by the by-laws. Any two or more offices may be held by the same person, except the offices of president and secretary.

All officers and agents of the corporation, as between themselves and the corporation, shall have such authority and perform such duties in the management of the corporation as may be provided in the by-laws, or as may be determined by resolution of the board of directors not inconsistent with the by-laws.

§ 51. Removal of Officers

Any officer or agent may be removed by the board of directors whenever in its judgment the best interests of the corporation will be served thereby, but such removal shall be without prejudice to the contract rights, if any, of the person so removed. Election or appointment of an officer or agent shall not of itself create contract rights.

§ 52. Books and Records: Financial Reports to Shareholders; Examination of Records

Each corporation shall keep correct and complete books and records of account and shall keep minutes of the proceedings of its shareholders and board of directors and shall keep at its registered office or principal place of business, or at the office of its transfer agent or registrar, a record of its shareholders, giving the names and addresses of all shareholders and the number and class of the shares held by each. Any books, records and minutes may be in written form or in any other form capable of being converted into written form within a reasonable time.

Any person who shall have been a holder of record of shares or of voting trust certificates therefor at least six months immediately preceding his demand or shall be the holder of record of, or the holder of record of voting trust certificates for, at least five percent of all the outstanding shares of the corporation, upon written demand stating the purpose thereof, shall have the right to examine, in person, or by agent or attorney, at any reasonable time or times, for any proper purpose its relevant books and records of account, minutes, and record of shareholders and to make extracts therefrom.

Any officer or agent who, or a corporation which, shall refuse to allow any such shareholder or holder of voting trust certificates, or his agent or attorney, so to examine and make extracts from its books and records of account, minutes, and record of shareholders, for any proper purpose, shall be liable to such shareholder or holder of voting trust certificates in a penalty of ten per cent of the value of the shares owned by such shareholder, or in respect of which such voting trust certificates are issued, in addition to any other damages or remedy afforded him by law. It shall be a defense to any action for penalties under this section that the person suing therefor has within two years sold or offered for sale any list of shareholders or of holders of voting trust certificates for shares of such corporation or any other corporation or has aided or abetted any person in procuring any list of shareholders or of holders of voting trust certificates for any such purpose, or has improperly used any information secured through any prior examination of the books and records of account, or minutes, or record of shareholders or of holders of voting trust certificates for shares of such corporation or any other corporation, or was not acting in good faith or for a proper purpose in making his demand.

Nothing herein contained shall impair the power of any court of competent jurisdiction, upon proof by a shareholder or holder of voting trust certificates of proper purpose, irrespective of the period of time during which such shareholder or holder of voting trust certificates shall have been a shareholder of record or a holder of record of voting trust certificates, and irrespective of the number of shares held by him or represented by voting trust certificates held by him, to compel the production for examination by such shareholder or holder of voting trust certificates of the books and records of account, minutes and record of shareholders of a corporation.

Each corporation shall furnish to its shareholders annual financial statements, including at least a balance sheet as of the end of each fiscal year and a statement of income for such fiscal year, which shall be prepared on the basis of generally accepted accounting principles, if the corporation prepares financial statements for such fiscal year on that basis for any purpose, and may be consolidated statements of the corporation and one or more of its subsidiaries. The financial statements shall be mailed by the corporation to each of its shareholders within 120 days after the close of each fiscal year and, after such mailing and upon written request, shall be mailed by the corporation to any shareholder (or holder of a voting trust certificate for its shares) to whom a copy of the most recent annual financial statements has not previously been mailed. In the case of statements

audited by a public accountant, each copy shall be accompanied by a report setting forth his opinion thereon; in other cases, each copy shall be accompanied by a statement of the president or the person in charge of the corporation's financial accounting records (1) stating his reasonable belief as to whether or not the financial statements were prepared in accordance with generally accepted accounting principles and, if not, describing the basis of presentation, and (2) describing any respects in which the financial statements were not prepared on a basis consistent with those prepared for the previous year.

§ 53. Incorporators

One or more persons, or a domestic or foreign corporation, may act as incorporator or incorporators of a corporation by signing and delivering in duplicate to the Secretary of State articles of incorporation for such corporation.

§ 54. Articles of Incorporation

The articles of incorporation shall set forth:

(a) The name of the corporation.

(b) The period of duration, which may be perpetual.

(c) The purpose or purposes for which the corporation is organized which may be stated to be, or to include, the transaction of any or all lawful business for which corporations may be incorporated under this Act.

(d) The aggregate number of shares which the corporation shall have authority to issue and, if such shares are to be divided into classes, the number of shares of each class.

(e) If the shares are to be divided into classes, the designation of each class and a statement of the preferences, limitations and relative rights in respect of the shares of each class.

(f) If the corporation is to issue the shares of any preferred or special class in series, then the designation of each series and a statement of the variations in the relative rights and preferences as between series insofar as the same are to be fixed in the articles of incorporation, and a statement of any authority to be vested in the board of directors to establish series and fix and determine the variations in the relative rights and preferences as between series.

(g) If any preemptive right is to be granted to shareholders, the provisions therefor.

(h) The address of its initial registered office, and the name of its initial registered agent at such address.

(i) The number of directors constituting the initial board of directors and the names and addresses of the persons who are to serve as directors until the first annual meeting of shareholders or until their successors be elected and qualify.

(j) The name and address of each incorporator.

In addition to provisions required therein, the articles of incorporation may also contain provisions not inconsistent with law regarding:

(1) the direction of the management of the business and the regulation of the affairs of the corporation;

(2) the definition, limitation and regulation of the powers of the corporation, the directors, and the shareholders, or any class of the shareholders, including restrictions on the transfer of shares;

(3) the par value of any authorized shares or class of shares;

(4) any provision which under this Act is required or permitted to be set forth in the by-laws.

It shall not be necessary to set forth in the articles of incorporation any of the corporate powers enumerated in this Act.

§ 55. Filing of Articles of Incorporation

Duplicate originals of the articles of incorporation shall be delivered to the Secretary of State. If the Secretary of State finds that the articles of incorporation conform to law, he shall, when all fees have been paid as in this Act prescribed:

(a) Endorse on each of such duplicate originals the word "Filed," and the month, day and year of the filing thereof.

(b) File one of such duplicate originals in his office.

(c) Issue a certificate of incorporation to which he shall affix the other duplicate original.

The certificate of incorporation, together with the duplicate original of the articles of incorporation affixed thereto by the Secretary of State, shall be returned to the incorporators or their representative.

§ 56. Effect of Issuance of Certificate of Incorporation

Upon the issuance of the certificate of incorporation, the corporate existence shall begin, and such certificate of incorporation shall be conclusive evidence that all conditions precedent required to be performed by the incorporators have been complied with and that the corporation has been incorporated under this Act, except as against this State in a proceeding to cancel or revoke the certificate of incorporation or for involuntary dissolution of the corporation.

§ 57. Organization Meeting of Directors

After the issuance of the certificate of incorporation an organization meeting of the board of directors named in the articles of incorporation shall be held, either within

or without this State, at the call of a majority of the directors named in the articles of incorporation, for the purpose of adopting by-laws, electing officers and transacting such other business as may come before the meeting. The directors calling the meeting shall give at least three days' notice thereof by mail to each director so named, stating the time and place of the meeting.

§ 58. Right to Amend Articles of Incorporation

A corporation may amend its articles of incorporation, from time to time, in any and as many respects as may be desired, so long as its articles of incorporation as amended contain only such provisions as might be lawfully contained in original articles of incorporation at the time of making such amendment, and, if a change in shares or the rights of shareholders, or an exchange, reclassification or cancellation of shares or rights of shareholders is to be made, such provisions as may be necessary to effect such change, exchange, reclassification or cancellation.

In particular, and without limitation upon such general power of amendment, a corporation may amend its articles of incorporation, from time to time, so as:

(a) To change its corporate name.

(b) To change its period of duration.

(c) To change, enlarge or diminish its corporate purposes.

(d) To increase or decrease the aggregate number of shares, or shares of any class, which the corporation has authority to issue.

(e) To provide, change or eliminate any provision with respect to the par value of any shares or class of shares.

(f) To exchange, classify, reclassify or cancel all or any part of its shares, whether issued or unissued.

(g) To change the designation of all or any part of its shares, whether issued or unissued, and to change the preferences, limitations, and the relative rights in respect of all or any part of its shares, whether issued or unissued.

(h) To change the shares of any class, whether issued or unissued [sic] into a different number of shares of the same class or into the same or a different number of shares of other classes.

(i) To create new classes of shares having rights and preferences either prior and superior or subordinate and inferior to the shares of any class then authorized, whether issued or unissued.

(j) To cancel or otherwise affect the right of the holders of the shares of any class to receive dividends which have accrued but have not been declared.

(k) To divide any preferred or special class of shares, whether issued or unissued, into series and fix and determine the designations of such series and the variations in the relative rights and preferences as between the shares of such series.

(l) To authorize the board of directors to establish, out of authorized but unissued shares, series of any preferred or special class of shares and fix and determine the relative rights and preferences of the shares of any series so established.

(m) To authorize the board of directors to fix and determine the relative rights and preferences of the authorized but unissued shares of series theretofore established in respect of which either the relative rights and preferences have not been fixed and determined or the relative rights and preferences theretofore fixed and determined are to be changed.

(n) To revoke, diminish, or enlarge the authority of the board of directors to establish series out of authorized but unissued shares of any preferred or special class and fix and determine the relative rights and preferences of the shares of any series so established.

(o) To limit, deny or grant to shareholders of any class the preemptive right to acquire additional shares of the corporation, whether then or thereafter authorized.

§ 59. Procedure to Amend Articles of Incorporation

Amendments to the articles of incorporation shall be made in the following manner:

(a) The board of directors shall adopt a resolution setting forth the proposed amendment and, if shares have been issued, directing that it be submitted to a vote at a meeting of shareholders, which may be either the annual or a special meeting. If no shares have been issued, the amendment shall be adopted by resolution of the board of directors and the provisions for adoption by shareholders shall not apply. If the corporation has only one class of shares outstanding, an amendment solely to change the number of authorized shares to effectuate a split of, or stock dividend in, the corporation's own shares, or solely to do so and to change the number of authorized shares in proportion thereto, may be adopted by the board of directors; and the provisions for adoption by shareholders shall not apply, unless otherwise provided by the articles of incorporation. The resolution may incorporate the proposed amendment in restated articles of incorporation which contain a statement that except for the designated amendment the restated articles of incorporation correctly set forth without change the corresponding provisions of the articles of incorporation as theretofore amended, and that the restated articles of incorporation together with the designated amendment supersede the original articles of incorporation and all amendments thereto.

(b) Written notice setting forth the proposed amendment or a summary of the changes to be effected thereby shall be given to each shareholder of record entitled to vote thereon within the time and in the manner provided in this Act for the giving of notice of meetings of shareholders. If the meeting be an annual meeting, the proposed amendment of such summary may be included in the notice of such annual meeting.

(c) At such meeting a vote of the shareholders entitled to vote thereon shall be taken on the proposed amendment. The proposed amendment shall be adopted upon receiving the affirmative vote of the holders of a majority of the shares entitled to vote thereon, unless any class of shares is entitled to vote thereon as a class, in which event the proposed amendment shall be adopted upon receiving the affirmative vote of the holders of a majority of the shares of each class of shares entitled to vote thereon as a class and of the total shares entitled to vote thereon.

Any number of amendments may be submitted to the shareholders, and voted upon by them, at one meeting.

§ 60. Class Voting on Amendments

The holders of the outstanding shares of a class shall be entitled to vote as a class upon a proposed amendment, whether or not entitled to vote thereon by the provisions of the articles of incorporation, if the amendment would:

(a) Increase or decrease the aggregate number of authorized shares of such class.

(b) Effect an exchange, reclassification or cancellation of all or part of the shares of such class.

(c) Effect an exchange, or create a right of exchange, of all or any part of the shares of another class into the shares of such class.

(d) Change the designations, preferences, limitations or relative rights of the shares of such class.

(e) Change the shares of such class into the same or a different number of shares of the same class or another class or classes.

(f) Create a new class of shares having rights and preferences prior and superior to the shares of such class, or increase the rights and preferences or the number of authorized shares, of any class having rights and preferences prior or superior to the shares of such class.

(g) In the case of a preferred or special class of shares, divide the shares of such class into series and fix and determine the designation of such series and the variations in the relative rights and preferences between the shares of such series, or authorize the board of directors to do so.

(h) Limit or deny any existing preemptive rights of the shares of such class.

(i) Cancel or otherwise affect dividends on the shares of such class which have accrued but have not been declared.

§ 61. Articles of Amendment

The articles of amendment shall be executed in duplicate by the corporation by its president or a vice president and by its secretary or an assistant secretary, and verified by one of the officers signing such articles, and shall set forth:

(a) The name of the corporation.

(b) The amendments so adopted.

(c) The date of the adoption of the amendment by the shareholders, or by the board of directors where no shares have been issued.

(d) The number of shares outstanding, and the number of shares entitled to vote thereon, and if the shares of any class are entitled to vote thereon as a class, the designation and number of outstanding shares entitled to vote thereon of each such class.

(e) The number of shares voted for and against such amendment, respectively, and, if the shares of any class are entitled to vote thereon as a class, the number of shares of each such class voted for and against such amendment, respectively, or if no shares have been issued, a statement to that effect.

(f) If such amendment provides for an exchange, reclassification or cancellation of issued shares, and if the manner in which the same shall be effected is not set forth in the amendment, then a statement of the manner in which the same shall be effected.

§ 62. Filing of Articles of Amendment

Duplicate originals of the articles of amendment shall be delivered to the Secretary of State. If the Secretary of State finds that the articles of amendment conform to law, he shall, when all fees and franchise taxes have been paid as in this Act prescribed:

(a) Endorse on each of such duplicate originals the word "Filed," and the month, day and year of the filing thereof.

(b) File one of such duplicate originals in his office.

(c) Issue a certificate of amendment to which he shall affix the other duplicate original.

The certificate of amendment, together with the duplicate original of the articles of amendment affixed thereto by the Secretary of State, shall be returned to the corporation or its representative.

§ 63. Effect of Certificate of Amendment

Upon the issuance of the certificate of amendment by the Secretary of State, the amendment shall become effective and the articles of incorporation shall be deemed to be amended accordingly.

No amendment shall affect any existing cause of action in favor of or against such corporation, or any pending suit to which such corporation shall be a party, or the existing rights of persons other than shareholders; and, in the event the corporate name shall be changed by amendment, no suit brought by or against such corporation under its former name shall abate for that reason.

§ 64. Restated Articles of Incorporation

A domestic corporation may at any time restate its articles of incorporation as theretofore amended, by a resolution adopted by the board of directors.

Upon the adoption of such resolution, restated articles of incorporation shall be executed in duplicate by the corporation by its president or a vice president and by its secretary or assistant secretary and verified by one of the officers signing such articles and shall set forth all of the operative provisions of the articles of incorporation as theretofore amended together with a statement that the restated articles of incorporation correctly set forth without change the corresponding provisions of the articles of incorporation as theretofore amended and that the restated articles of incorporation supersede the original articles of incorporation and all amendments thereto.

Duplicate originals of the restated articles of incorporation shall be delivered to the Secretary of State. If the Secretary of State finds that such restated articles of incorporation conform to law, he shall, when all fees and franchise taxes have been paid as in this Act prescribed:

(1) Endorse on each of such duplicate originals the word "Filed," and the month, day and year of the filing thereof.

(2) File one of such duplicate originals in his office.

(3) Issue a restated certificate of incorporation, to which he shall affix the other duplicate original.

The restated certificate of incorporation, together with the duplicate original of the restated articles of incorporation affixed thereto by the Secretary of State, shall be returned to the corporation or its representative.

Upon the issuance of the restated certificate of incorporation by the Secretary of State, the restated articles of incorporation shall become effective and shall supersede the original articles of incorporation and all amendments thereto.

§ 65. Amendment of Articles of Incorporation in Reorganization Proceedings

Whenever a plan of reorganization of a corporation has been confirmed by decree or order of a court of competent jurisdiction in proceedings for the reorganization of such corporation, pursuant to the provisions of any applicable statute of the United States relating to reorganizations of corporations, the articles of incorporation of the corporation may be amended, in the manner provided in this section, in as many respects as may be necessary to carry out the plan and put it into effect, so long as the articles of incorporation as amended contain only such provisions as might be lawfully contained in original articles of incorporation at the time of making such amendment.

In particular and without limitation upon such general power of amendment, the articles of incorporation may be amended for such purpose so as to:

(A) Change the corporate name, period of duration or corporate purposes of the corporation;

(B) Repeal, alter or amend the by-laws of the corporation;

(C) Change the aggregate number of shares or shares of any class, which the corporation has authority to issue;

(D) Change the preferences, limitations and relative rights in respect of all or any part of the shares of the corporation, and classify, reclassify or cancel all or any part thereof, whether issued or unissued;

(E) Authorize the issuance of bonds, debentures or other obligations of the corporation, whether or not convertible into shares of any class or bearing warrants or other evidences of optional rights to purchase or subscribe for shares of any class, and fix the terms and conditions thereof; and

(F) Constitute or reconstitute and classify or reclassify the board of directors of the corporation, and appoint directors and officers in place of or in addition to all or any of the directors or officers then in office.

Amendments to the articles of incorporation pursuant to this section shall be made in the following manner:

(a) Articles of amendment approved by decree or order of such court shall be executed and verified in duplicate by such person or persons as the court shall designate or appoint for the purpose, and shall set forth the name of the corporation, the amendments of the articles of incorporation approved by the court, the date of the decree or order approving the articles of amendment, the title of the proceedings in which the decree or order was entered, and a statement that such decree or order was entered by a court having jurisdiction of the proceedings for the reorganization of the corporation pursuant to the provisions of an applicable statute of the United States.

(b) Duplicate originals of the articles of amendment shall be delivered to the Secretary of State. If the Secretary of State finds that the articles of amendment conform to law, he shall, when all fees and franchise taxes have been paid as in this Act prescribed:

(1) Endorse on each of such duplicate originals the word "Filed," and the month, day and year of the filing thereof.

(2) File one of such duplicate originals in his office.

(3) Issue a certificate of amendment to which he shall affix the other duplicate original.

The certificate of amendment, together with the duplicate original of the articles of amendment affixed thereto by the Secretary of State, shall be returned to the corporation or its representative.

Upon the issuance of the certificate of amendment by the Secretary of State, the amendment shall become effective and the articles of incorporation shall be deemed to be amended accordingly, without any action thereon by the directors or shareholders of the corporation and with the same effect as if the amendments had been adopted by unanimous action of the directors and shareholders of the corporation.

§ 66. Restriction on Redemption or Purchase of Redeemable Shares

[Repealed in 1979].

§ 67. Cancellation of Redeemable Shares by Redemption or Purchase

[Repealed in 1979].

§ 68. Cancellation of Other Reacquired Shares

[Repealed in 1979].

§ 69. Reduction of Stated Capital in Certain Cases

[Repealed in 1979].

§ 70. Special Provisions Relating to Surplus and Reserves

[Repealed in 1979].

§ 71. Procedure for Merger

Any two or more domestic corporations may merge into one of such corporations pursuant to a plan of merger approved in the manner provided in this Act.

The board of directors of each corporation shall, by resolution adopted by each such board, approve a plan of merger setting forth:

(a) The names of the corporations proposing to merge, and the name of the corporation into which they propose to merge, which is hereinafter designated as the surviving corporation.

(b) The terms and conditions of the proposed merger.

(c) The manner and basis of converting the shares of each corporation into shares, obligations or other securities of the surviving corporation or of any other corporation or, in whole or in part, into cash or other property.

(d) A statement of any changes in the articles of incorporation of the surviving corporation to be effected by such merger.

(e) Such other provisions with respect to the proposed merger as are deemed necessary or desirable.

§ 72. Procedure for Consolidation

Any two or more domestic corporations may consolidate into a new corporation pursuant to a plan of consolidation approved in the manner provided in this Act.

The board of directors of each corporation shall, by a resolution adopted by each such board, approve a plan of consolidation setting forth:

(a) The names of the corporations proposing to consolidate, and the name of the new corporation into which they propose to consolidate, which is hereinafter designated as the new corporation.

(b) The terms and conditions of the proposed consolidation.

(c) The manner and basis of converting the shares of each corporation into shares, obligations or other securities of the new corporation or of any other corporation or, in whole or in part, into cash or other property.

(d) With respect to the new corporation, all of the statements required to be set forth in articles of incorporation for corporations organized under this Act.

(e) Such other provisions with respect to the proposed consolidation as are deemed necessary or desirable.

§ 72A. Procedure for Share Exchange

All the issued or all the outstanding shares of one or more classes of any domestic corporation may be acquired through the exchange of all such shares of such class or classes by another domestic or foreign corporation pursuant to a plan of exchange approved in the manner provided in this Act.

The board of directors of each corporation shall, by resolution adopted by each such board, approve a plan of exchange setting forth:

(a) The name of the corporation the shares of which are proposed to be acquired by exchange and the name of the corporation to acquire the shares of such corporation in the exchange, which is hereinafter designated as the acquiring corporation.

(b) The terms and conditions of the proposed exchange.

(c) The manner and basis of exchanging the shares to be acquired for shares, obligations or other securities of the acquiring corporation or any other corporation, or, in whole or in part, for cash or other property.

(d) Such other provisions with respect to the proposed exchange as are deemed necessary or desirable.

The procedure authorized by this section shall not be deemed to limit the power of a corporation to acquire all or part of the shares of any class or classes of a corporation through a voluntary exchange or otherwise by agreement with the shareholders.

§ 73. Approval by Shareholders

(a) The board of directors of each corporation in the case of a merger or consolidation, and the board of directors of the corporation the shares of which are to be acquired in the case of an exchange, upon approving such plan of merger, consolidation or exchange, shall, by resolution, direct that the plan be submitted to a vote at a meeting of its shareholders, which may be either an annual or a special meeting. Written notice shall be given to each shareholder of record, whether or not entitled to vote at such meeting, not less than twenty days before such meeting, in the manner provided in this Act for the giving of notice of meetings of shareholders, and, whether the meeting be an annual or a special meeting, shall state that the purpose or one of the purposes is to consider the proposed plan of merger, consolidation or exchange. A copy or a summary of the plan of merger, consolidation or exchange, as the case may be, shall be included in or enclosed with such notice.

(b) At each such meeting, a vote of the shareholders shall be taken on the proposed plan. The plan shall be approved upon receiving the affirmative vote of the holders of a majority of the shares entitled to vote thereon of each such corporation, unless any class of shares of any such corporation is entitled to vote thereon as a class, in which event, as to such corporation, the plan shall be approved upon receiving the affirmative vote of the holders of a majority of the shares of each class of shares entitled to vote thereon as a class and of the total shares entitled to vote thereon. Any class of shares of any such corporation shall be entitled to vote as a class if any such plan contains any provision which, if contained in a proposed amendment to articles of incorporation, would entitle such class of shares to vote as a class and, in the case of an exchange, if the class is included in the exchange.

(c) After such approval by a vote of the shareholders of each such corporation, and at any time prior to the filing of the articles of merger, consolidation or exchange, the merger, consolidation or exchange may be abandoned pursuant to provisions therefor, if any, set forth in the plan.

(d) (1) Notwithstanding the provisions of subsections (a) and (b), submission of a plan of merger to a vote at a meeting of shareholders of a surviving corporation shall not be required if:

(i) the articles of incorporation of the surviving corporation do not differ except in name from those of the corporation before the merger,

(ii) each holder of shares of the surviving corporation which were outstanding immediately before the effective date of the merger is to hold the same number of shares with identical rights immediately after,

(iii) the number of voting shares outstanding immediately after the merger, plus the number of voting shares issuable on conversion of other securities issued by virtue of the terms of the merger and on exercise of rights and warrants so issued, will not exceed by more than 20 percent the number of voting shares outstanding immediately before the merger, and

(iv) the number of participating shares outstanding immediately after the merger, plus the number of participating shares issuable on conversion of other securities issued by virtue of the terms of the merger and on exercise of rights and warrants so issued, will not exceed by more than 20 percent the number of participating shares outstanding immediately before the merger.

(2) As used in this subsection:

(i) "voting shares" means shares which entitle their holders to vote unconditionally in elections of directors;

(ii) "participating shares" means shares which entitle their holders to participate without limitation in distribution of earnings or surplus.

§ 74. Articles of Merger, Consolidation or Exchange

(a) Upon receiving the approvals required by Sections 71, 72 and 73, articles of merger or articles of consolidation shall be executed in duplicate by each corporation by its president or a vice president and by its secretary or an assistant secretary, and verified by one of the officers of each corporation signing such articles, and shall set forth:

(1) The plan of merger or the plan of consolidation;

(2) As to each corporation, either (i) the number of shares outstanding, and, if the shares of any class are entitled to vote as a class, the designation and number of outstanding shares of each such class, or (ii) a statement that the vote of shareholders is not required by virtue of subsection 73(d);

(3) As to each corporation the approval of whose shareholders is required, the number of shares voted for and against such plan, respectively, and, if the shares of any class are entitled to vote as a class, the number of shares of each such class voted for and against such plan, respectively.

(b) Duplicate originals of the articles of merger, consolidation or exchange shall be delivered to the Secretary of State. If the Secretary of State finds that such articles conform to law, he shall, when all fees and franchise taxes have been paid as in this Act prescribed:

(1) Endorse on each of such duplicate originals the word "Filed," and the month, day and year of the filing thereof.

(2) File one of such duplicate originals in his office.

(3) Issue a certificate of merger, consolidation or exchange to which he shall affix the other duplicate original.

(c) The certificate of merger, consolidation or exchange together with the duplicate original of the articles affixed thereto by the Secretary of State, shall be returned to the surviving, new or acquiring corporation, as the case may be, or its representative.

§ 75. Merger of Subsidiary Corporation

Any corporation owning at least ninety per cent of the outstanding shares of each class of another corporation may merge such other corporation into itself without approval by a vote of the shareholders of either corporation. Its board of directors shall, by resolution, approve a plan of merger setting forth:

(A) The name of the subsidiary corporation and the name of the corporation owning at least ninety per cent of its shares, which is hereinafter designated as the surviving corporation.

(B) The manner and basis of converting the shares of the subsidiary corporation into shares, obligations or other securities of the surviving corporation or of any other corporation or, in whole or in part, into cash or other property.

A copy of such plan of merger shall be mailed to each shareholder of record of the subsidiary corporation.

Articles of merger shall be executed in duplicate by the surviving corporation by its president or a vice president and by its secretary or an assistant secretary, and verified by one of its officers signing such articles, and shall set forth:

(a) The plan of merger;

(b) The number of outstanding shares of each class of the subsidiary corporation and the number of such shares of each class owned by the surviving corporation; and

(c) The date of the mailing to shareholders of the subsidiary corporation of a copy of the plan of merger.

On and after the thirtieth day after the mailing of a copy of the plan of merger to shareholders of the subsidiary corporation or upon the waiver thereof by the holders of all outstanding shares duplicate originals of the articles of merger shall be delivered to the Secretary of State. If the Secretary of State finds that such articles conform to law, he shall, when all fees and franchise taxes have been paid as in this Act prescribed:

(1) Endorse on each of such duplicate originals the word "Filed," and the month, day and year of the filing thereof,

(2) File one of such duplicate originals in his office, and

(3) Issue a certificate of merger to which he shall affix the other duplicate original.

The certificate of merger, together with the duplicate original of the articles of merger affixed thereto by the Secretary of State, shall be returned to the surviving corporation or its representative.

§ 76. Effect of Merger, Consolidation or Exchange

Upon the issuance of the certificate of merger or the certificate of consolidation by the Secretary of State, the merger or consolidation shall be effected.

When such merger or consolidation has been effective:

(a) The several corporations parties to the plan of merger or consolidation shall be a single corporation, which, in the case of a merger, shall be that corporation designated in the plan of merger as the surviving corporation, and, in the case of a consolidation, shall be the new corporation provided for in the plan of consolidation.

(b) The separate existence of all corporations parties to the plan of merger or consolidation, except the surviving or new corporation, shall cease.

(c) Such surviving or new corporation shall have all the rights, privileges, immunities and powers and shall be subject to all the duties and liabilities of a corporation organized under this Act.

(d) Such surviving or new corporation shall thereupon and thereafter possess all the rights, privileges, immunities, and franchises, of a public as well as of a private nature, of each of the merging or consolidating corporations; and all property, real, personal and mixed, and all debts due on whatever account, including subscriptions to shares, and all other choses in action, and all and every other interest of or belonging to or due to each of the corporations so merged or consolidated, shall be taken and deemed to be transferred to and vested in such single corporation without further act or deed; and the title to any real estate, or any interest therein, vested in any of such corporations shall not revert or be in any way impaired by reason of such merger or consolidation.

(e) Such surviving or new corporation shall thenceforth be responsible and liable for all the liabilities and obligations of each of the corporations so merged or consolidated; and any claim existing or action or proceeding pending by or against any of such corporations may be prosecuted as if such merger or consolidation had not taken place, or such surviving or new corporation may

be substituted in its place. Neither the rights of creditors nor any liens upon the property of any such corporation shall be impaired by such merger or consolidation.

(f) In the case of a merger, the articles of incorporation of the surviving corporation shall be deemed to be amended to the extent, if any, that changes in its articles of incorporation are stated in the plan of merger; and, in the case of a consolidation, the statements set forth in the articles of consolidation and which are required or permitted to be set forth in the articles of incorporation of corporations organized under this Act shall be deemed to be the original articles of incorporation of the new corporation.

§ 77. Merger, Consolidation or Exchange of Shares Between Domestic and Foreign Corporations

One or more foreign corporations and one or more domestic corporations may be merged or consolidated in the following manner, if such merger or consolidation is permitted by the laws of the state under which each such foreign corporation is organized:

(a) Each domestic corporation shall comply with the provisions of this Act with respect to the merger or consolidation, as the case may be, of domestic corporations and each foreign corporation shall comply with the applicable provisions of the laws of the state under which it is organized.

(b) If the surviving or new corporation, as the case may be, is to be governed by the laws of any state other than this State, it shall comply with the provisions of this Act with respect to foreign corporations if it is to transact business in this State, and in every case it shall file with the Secretary of State of this State:

(1) An agreement that it may be served with process in this State in any proceeding for the enforcement of any obligation of any domestic corporation which is a party to such merger or consolidation and in any proceeding for the enforcement of the rights of a dissenting shareholder of any such domestic corporation against the surviving or new corporation;

(2) An irrevocable appointment of the Secretary of State of this State as its agent to accept service of process in any such proceeding; and

(3) An agreement that it will promptly pay to the dissenting shareholders of any such domestic corporation the amount, if any, to which they shall be entitled under the provisions of this Act with respect to the rights of dissenting shareholders.

The effect of such merger or consolidation shall be the same as in the case of the merger or consolidation of domestic corporations, if the surviving or new corporation is to be governed by the laws of this State. If the surviving or new corporation is to be governed by the laws of any state other than this State, the effect of such merger or consolidation shall be the same as in the case of the merger or consolidation of domestic corporations except insofar as the laws of such other state provide otherwise.

At any time prior to the filing of the articles of merger or consolidation, the merger or consolidation may be abandoned pursuant to provisions therefor, if any, set forth in the plan of merger or consolidation.

§ 78. Sale of Assets in Regular Course of Business and Mortgage or Pledge of Assets

The sale, lease, exchange, or other disposition of all, or substantially all, the property and assets of a corporation in the usual and regular course of its business and the mortgage or pledge of any or all property and assets of a corporation whether or not in the usual and regular course of business may be made upon such terms and conditions and for such consideration, which may consist in whole or in part of cash or other property, including shares, obligations or other securities of any other corporation, domestic or foreign, as shall be authorized by its board of directors; and in any such case no authorization or consent of the shareholders shall be required.

§ 79. Sale of Assets Other Than in Regular Course of Business

A sale, lease, exchange, or other disposition of all, or substantially all, the property and assets, with or without the good will, of a corporation, if not in the usual and regular course of its business, may be made upon such terms and conditions and for such consideration, which may consist in whole or in part of cash or other property, including shares, obligations or other securities of any other corporation, domestic or foreign, as may be authorized in the following manner:

(a) The board of directors shall adopt a resolution recommending such sale, lease, exchange, or other disposition and directing the submission thereof to a vote at a meeting of shareholders, which may be either an annual or a special meeting.

(b) Written notice shall be given to each shareholder of record, whether or not entitled to vote at such meeting, not less than twenty days before such meeting, in the manner provided in this Act for the giving of notice of meetings of shareholders, and, whether the meeting be an annual or a special meeting, shall state that the purpose, or one of the purposes is to consider the proposed sale, lease, exchange, or other disposition.

(c) At such meeting the shareholders may authorize such sale, lease, exchange, or other disposition and may fix, or may authorize the board of directors to fix, any or all of the terms and conditions thereof and the con-

sideration to be received by the corporation therefor. Such authorization shall require the affirmative vote of the holders of a majority of the shares of the corporation entitled to vote thereon, unless any class of shares is entitled to vote thereon as a class, in which event such authorization shall require the affirmative vote of the holders of a majority of the shares of each class of shares entitled to vote as a class thereon and of the total shares entitled to vote thereon.

(d) After such authorization by a vote of shareholders, the board of directors nevertheless, in its discretion, may abandon such sale, lease, exchange, or other disposition of assets, subject to the rights of third parties under any contracts relating thereto, without further action or approval by shareholders.

§ 80. Right of Shareholders to Dissent and Obtain Payment for Shares

(a) Any shareholder of a corporation shall have the right to dissent from, and to obtain payment for his shares in the event of, any of the following corporate actions:

(1) Any plan of merger or consolidation to which the corporation is a party, except as provided in subsection (c);

(2) Any sale or exchange of all or substantially all of the property and assets of the corporation not made in the usual or regular course of its business, including a sale in dissolution, but not including a sale pursuant to an order of a court having jurisdiction in the premises or a sale for cash on terms requiring that all or substantially all of the net proceeds of sale be distributed to the shareholders in accordance with their respective interests within one year after the date of sale;

(3) Any plan of exchange to which the corporation is a party as the corporation the shares of which are to be acquired;

(4) Any amendment of the articles of incorporation which materially and adversely affects the rights appurtenant to the shares of the dissenting shareholder in that it:

(i) alters or abolishes a preferential right of such shares;

(ii) creates, alters or abolishes a right in respect of the redemption of such shares, including a provision respecting a sinking fund for the redemption or repurchase of such shares;

(iii) alters or abolishes a preemptive right of the holder of such shares to acquire shares or other securities;

(iv) excludes or limits the right of the holder of such shares to vote on any matter, or to cumulate his votes, except as such right may be limited by dilution through the issuance of shares or other securities with similar voting rights; or

(5) Any other corporate action taken pursuant to a shareholder vote with respect to which the articles of incorporation, the bylaws, or a resolution of the board of directors directs that dissenting shareholders shall have a right to obtain payment for their shares.

(b) (1) A record holder of shares may assert dissenters' rights as to less than all of the shares registered in his name only if he dissents with respect to all the shares beneficially owned by any one person, and discloses the name and address of the person or persons on whose behalf he dissents. In that event, his rights shall be determined as if the shares as to which he has dissented and his other shares were registered in the names of different shareholders.

(2) A beneficial owner of shares who is not the record holder may assert dissenters' rights with respect to shares held on his behalf, and shall be treated as a dissenting shareholder under the terms of this section and section 81 if he submits to the corporation at the time of or before the assertion of these rights a written consent of the record holder.

(c) The right to obtain payment under this section shall not apply to the shareholders of the surviving corporation in a merger if a vote of the shareholders of such corporation is not necessary to authorize such merger.

(d) A shareholder of a corporation who has a right under this section to obtain payment for his shares shall have no right at law or in equity to attack the validity of the corporate action that gives rise to his right to obtain payment, nor to have the action set aside or rescinded, except when the corporate action is unlawful or fraudulent with regard to the complaining shareholder or to the corporation.

§ 81. Procedures for Protection of Dissenters' Rights

(a) As used in this section:

(1) "Dissenter" means a shareholder or beneficial owner who is entitled to and does assert dissenters' rights under section 80, and who has performed every act required up to the time involved for the assertion of such rights.

(2) "Corporation" means the issuer of the shares held by the dissenter before the corporate action, or the successor by merger or consolidation of that issuer.

(3) "Fair value" of shares means their value immediately before the effectuation of the corporate action to which the dissenter objects, excluding any appreciation or depreciation in anticipation of such corporate action unless such exclusion would be inequitable.

(4) "Interest" means interest from the effective date of the corporate action until the date of payment, at the average rate currently paid by the corporation on its principal bank loans, or, if none, at such rate as is fair and equitable under all the circumstances.

(b) If a proposed corporate action which would give rise to dissenters' rights under section 80(a) is submitted to a vote at a meeting of shareholders, the notice of meeting shall notify all shareholders that they have or may have a right to dissent and obtain payment for their shares by complying with the terms of this section, and shall be accompanied by a copy of sections 80 and 81 of this Act.

(c) If the proposed corporate action is submitted to a vote at a meeting of shareholders, any shareholder who wishes to dissent and obtain payment for his shares must file with the corporation, prior to the vote, a written notice of intention to demand that he be paid fair compensation for his shares if the proposed action is effectuated, and shall refrain from voting his shares in approval of such action. A shareholder who fails in either respect shall acquire no right to payment for his shares under this section or section 80.

(d) If the proposed corporate action is approved by the required vote at a meeting of shareholders, the corporation shall mail a further notice to all shareholders who gave due notice of intention to demand payment and who refrained from voting in favor of the proposed action. If the proposed corporate action is to be taken without a vote of shareholders, the corporation shall send to all shareholders who are entitled to dissent and demand payment for their shares a notice of the adoption of the plan of corporate action. The notice shall (1) state where and when a demand for payment must be sent and certificates of certificated shares must be deposited in order to obtain payment, (2) inform holders of uncertificated shares to what extent transfer of shares will be restricted from the time that demand for payment is received, (3) supply a form for demanding payment which includes a request for certification of the date on which the shareholder, or the person on whose behalf the shareholder dissents, acquired beneficial ownership of the shares, and (4) be accompanied by a copy of sections 80 and 81 of this Act. The time set for the demand and deposit shall be not less than 30 days from the mailing of the notice.

(e) A shareholder who fails to demand payment, or fails (in the case of certificated shares) to deposit certificates, as required by a notice pursuant to subsection (d) shall have no right under this section or section 80 to receive payment for his shares. If the shares are not represented by certificates, the corporation may restrict their transfer from the time of receipt of demand for payment until effectuation of the proposed corporate action, or the release of restrictions under the terms of subsection (f). The dissenter shall retain all other rights of a shareholder until these rights are modified by effectuation of the proposed corporate action.

(f) (1) Within 60 days after the date set for demanding payment and depositing certificates, if the corporation has not effectuated the proposed corporate action and remitted payment for shares pursuant to paragraph (3), it shall return any certificates that have been deposited, and release uncertificated shares from any transfer restrictions imposed by reason of the demand for payment.

(2) When uncertificated shares have been released from transfer restrictions, and deposited certificates have been returned, the corporation may at any later time send a new notice conforming to the requirements of subsection (d), with like effect.

(3) Immediately upon effectuation of the proposed corporate action, or upon receipt of demand for payment if the corporate action has already been effectuated, the corporation shall remit to dissenters who have made demand and (if their shares are certificated) have deposited their certificates the amount which the corporation estimates to be the fair value of the shares, with interest if any has accrued. The remittance shall be accompanied by:

(i) the corporation's closing balance sheet and statement of income for a fiscal year ending not more than 16 months before the date of remittance, together with the latest available interim financial statements;

(ii) a statement of the corporation's estimate of fair value of the shares; and

(iii) a notice of the dissenter's right to demand supplemental payment, accompanied by a copy of sections 80 and 81 of this Act.

(g) (1) If the corporation fails to remit as required by subsection (f), or if the dissenter believes that the amount remitted is less than the fair value of his shares, or that the interest is not correctly determined, he may send the corporation his own estimate of the value of the shares or of the interest, and demand payment of the deficiency.

(2) If the dissenter does not file such an estimate within 30 days after the corporation's mailing of its remittance, he shall be entitled to no more than the amount remitted.

(h) (1) Within 60 days after receiving a demand for payment pursuant to subsection (g), if any such demands for payment remain unsettled, the corporation shall file in an appropriate court a petition requesting that the fair value of the shares and interest thereon be determined by the court.

(2) An appropriate court shall be a court of competent jurisdiction in the county of this state where the reg-

istered office of the corporation is located. If, in the case of a merger or consolidation or exchange of shares, the corporation is a foreign corporation without a registered office in this state, the petition shall be filed in the county where the registered office of the domestic corporation was last located.

(3) All dissenters, wherever residing, whose demands have not been settled shall be made parties to the proceeding as in an action against their shares. A copy of the petition shall be served on each such dissenter; if a dissenter is a nonresident, the copy may be served on him by registered or certified mail or by publication as provided by law.

(4) The jurisdiction of the court shall be plenary and exclusive. The court may appoint one or more persons as appraisers to receive evidence and recommend a decision on the question of fair value. The appraisers shall have such power and authority as shall be specified in the order of their appointment or in any amendment thereof. The dissenters shall be entitled to discovery in the same manner as parties in other civil suits.

(5) All dissenters who are made parties shall be entitled to judgment for the amount by which the fair value of their shares is found to exceed the amount previously remitted, with interest.

(6) If the corporation fails to file a petition as provided in paragraph (1) of this subsection, each dissenter who made a demand and who has not already settled his claim against the corporation shall be paid by the corporation the amount demanded by him, with interest, and may sue therefor in an appropriate court.

(i) (1) The costs and expenses of any proceeding under subsection (h), including the reasonable compensation and expenses of appraisers appointed by the court, shall be determined by the court and assessed against the corporation, except that any part of the costs and expenses may be apportioned and assessed as the court may deem equitable against all or some of the dissenters who are parties and whose action in demanding supplemental payment the court finds to be arbitrary, vexatious, or not in good faith.

(2) Fees and expenses of counsel and of experts for the respective parties may be assessed as the court may deem equitable against the corporation and in favor of any or all dissenters if the corporation failed to comply substantially with the requirements of this section, and may be assessed against either the corporation or a dissenter, in favor of any other party, if the court finds that the party against whom the fees and expenses are assessed acted arbitrarily, vexatiously, or not in good faith in respect to the rights provided by this Section and Section 80.

(3) If the court finds that the services of counsel for any dissenter were of substantial benefit to other dissenters

similarly situated, and should not be assessed against the corporation, it may award to these counsel reasonable fees to be paid out of the amounts awarded to the dissenters who were benefitted.

(j) (1) Notwithstanding the foregoing provisions of this section, the corporation may elect to withhold the remittance required by subsection (f) from any dissenter with respect to shares of which the dissenter (or the person on whose behalf the dissenter acts) was not the beneficial owner on the date of the first announcement to news media or to shareholders of the terms of the proposed corporate action. With respect to such shares, the corporation shall, upon effectuating the corporate action, state to each dissenter its estimate of the fair value of the shares, state the rate of interest to be used (explaining the basis thereof), and offer to pay the resulting amounts on receiving the dissenter's agreement to accept them in full satisfaction.

(2) If the dissenter believes that the amount offered is less than the fair value of the shares and interest determined according to this section, he may within 30 days after the date of mailing of the corporation's offer, mail the corporation his own estimate of fair value and interest, and demand their payment. If the dissenter fails to do so, he shall be entitled to no more than the corporation's offer.

(3) If the dissenter makes a demand as provided in paragraph (2), the provisions of subsections (h) and (i) shall apply to further proceedings on the dissenter's demand.

§ 82. Voluntary Dissolution by Incorporators

A corporation which has not commenced business and which has not issued any shares, may be voluntarily dissolved by its incorporators at any time in the following manner:

(a) Articles of dissolution shall be executed in duplicate by a majority of the incorporators, and verified by them, and shall set forth:

(1) The name of the corporation.

(2) The date of issuance of its certificate of incorporation.

(3) That none of its shares has been issued.

(4) That the corporation has not commenced business.

(5) That the amount, if any, actually paid in on subscriptions for its shares, less any part thereof disbursed for necessary expenses, has been returned to those entitled thereto.

(6) That no debts of the corporation remain unpaid.

(7) That a majority of the incorporators elect that the corporation be dissolved.

(b) Duplicate originals of the articles of dissolution shall be delivered to the Secretary of State. If the Secretary of State finds that the articles of dissolution conform to law, he shall, when all fees and franchise taxes have been paid as in this Act prescribed:

(1) Endorse on each of such duplicate originals the word "Filed," and the month, day and year of the filing thereof.

(2) File one of such duplicate originals in his office.

(3) Issue a certificate of dissolution to which he shall affix the other duplicate original.

The certificate of dissolution, together with the duplicate original of the articles of dissolution affixed thereto by the Secretary of State, shall be returned to the incorporators or their representative. Upon the issuance of such certificate of dissolution by the Secretary of State, the existence of the corporation shall cease.

§ 83. Voluntary Dissolution by Consent of Shareholders

A corporation may be voluntarily dissolved by the written consent of all of its shareholders.

Upon the execution of such written consent, a statement of intent to dissolve shall be executed in duplicate by the corporation by its president or a vice president and by its secretary or an assistant secretary, and verified by one of the officers signing such statement, which statement shall set forth:

(a) The name of the corporation.

(b) The names and respective addresses of its officers.

(c) The names and respective addresses of its directors.

(d) A copy of the written consent signed by all shareholders of the corporation.

(e) A statement that such written consent has been signed by all shareholders of the corporation or signed in their names by their attorneys thereunto duly authorized.

§ 84. Voluntary Dissolution by Act of Corporation

A corporation may be dissolved by the act of the corporation, when authorized in the following manner:

(a) The board of directors shall adopt a resolution recommending that the corporation be dissolved, and directing that the question of such dissolution be submitted to a vote at a meeting of shareholders, which may be either an annual or a special meeting.

(b) Written notice shall be given to each shareholder of record entitled to vote at such meeting within the time and in the manner provided in this Act for the giving of notice of meetings of shareholders, and, whether the meeting be an annual or special meeting, shall state that the purpose, or one of the purposes, of such meeting is to consider the advisability of dissolving the corporation.

(c) At such meeting a vote of shareholders entitled to vote thereat shall be taken on a resolution to dissolve the corporation. Such resolution shall be adopted upon receiving the affirmative vote of the holders of a majority of the shares of the corporation entitled to vote thereon, unless any class of shares is entitled to vote thereon as a class, in which event the resolution shall be adopted upon receiving the affirmative vote of the holders of a majority of the shares of each class of shares entitled to vote thereon as a class and of the total shares entitled to vote thereon.

(d) Upon the adoption of such resolution, a statement of intent to dissolve shall be executed in duplicate by the corporation by its president or a vice president and by its secretary or an assistant secretary, and verified by one of the officers signing such statement, which statement shall set forth:

(1) The name of the corporation.

(2) The names and respective addresses of its officers.

(3) The names and respective addresses of its directors.

(4) A copy of the resolution adopted by the shareholders authorizing the dissolution of the corporation.

(5) The number of shares outstanding, and, if the shares of any class are entitled to vote as a class, the designation and number of outstanding shares of each such class.

(6) The number of shares voted for and against the resolution, respectively, and, if the shares of any class are entitled to vote as a class, the number of shares of each such class voted for and against the resolution, respectively.

§ 85. Filing of Statement of Intent to Dissolve

Duplicate originals of the statement of intent to dissolve, whether by consent of shareholders or by act of the corporation, shall be delivered to the Secretary of State. If the Secretary of State finds that such statement conforms to law, he shall, when all fees and franchise taxes have been paid as in this Act prescribed:

(a) Endorse on each of such duplicate originals the word "Filed," and the month, day and year of the filing thereof.

(b) File one of such duplicate originals in his office.

(c) Return the other duplicate original to the corporation or its representative.

§ 86. Effect of Statement of Intent to Dissolve

Upon the filing by the Secretary of State of a statement of intent to dissolve, whether by consent of shareholders or by act of the corporation, the corporation shall cease to carry on its business, except insofar as may be necessary for the winding up thereof, but its corporate existence shall continue until a certificate of dissolution has been issued by the Secretary of State or until a decree dissolving the corporation has been entered by a court of competent jurisdiction as in this Act provided.

§ 87. Procedure after Filing of Statement of Intent to Dissolve

After the filing by the Secretary of State of a statement of intent to dissolve:

(a) The corporation shall immediately cause notice thereof to be mailed to each known creditor of the corporation.

(b) The corporation shall proceed to collect its assets, convey and dispose of such of its properties as are not to be distributed in kind to its shareholders, pay, satisfy and discharge its liabilities and obligations and do all other acts required to liquidate its business and affairs, and, after paying or adequately providing for the payment of all its obligations, distribute the remainder of its assets, either in cash or in kind, among its shareholders according to their respective rights and interests.

(c) The corporation, at any time during the liquidation of its business and affairs, may make application to a court of competent jurisdiction within the state and judicial subdivision in which the registered office or principal place of business of the corporation is situated, to have the liquidation continued under the supervision of the court as provided in this Act.

§ 88. Revocation of Voluntary Dissolution Proceedings by Consent of Shareholders

By the written consent of all of its shareholders, a corporation may, at any time prior to the issuance of a certificate of dissolution by the Secretary of State, revoke voluntary dissolution proceedings theretofore taken, in the following manner:

Upon the execution of such written consent, a statement of revocation of voluntary dissolution proceedings shall be executed in duplicate by the corporation by its president or a vice president and by its secretary or an assistant secretary, and verified by one of the officers signing such statement, which statement shall set forth:

(a) The name of the corporation.

(b) The names and respective addresses of its officers.

(c) The names and respective addresses of its directors.

(d) A copy of the written consent signed by all shareholders of the corporation revoking such voluntary dissolution proceedings.

(e) That such written consent has been signed by all shareholders of the corporation or signed in their names by their attorneys thereunto duly authorized.

§ 89. Revocation of Voluntary Dissolution Proceedings by Act of Corporation

By the act of the corporation, a corporation may, at any time prior to the issuance of a certificate of dissolution by the Secretary of State, revoke voluntary dissolution proceedings theretofore taken, in the following manner:

(a) The board of directors shall adopt a resolution recommending that the voluntary dissolution proceedings be revoked, and directing that the question of such revocation be submitted to a vote at a special meeting of shareholders.

(b) Written notice, stating that the purpose or one of the purposes of such meeting is to consider the advisability of revoking the voluntary dissolution proceedings, shall be given to each shareholder of record entitled to vote at such meeting within the time and in the manner provided in this Act for the giving of notice of special meetings of shareholders.

(c) At such meeting a vote of the shareholders entitled to vote thereat shall be taken on a resolution to revoke the voluntary dissolution proceedings, which shall require for its adoption the affirmative vote of the holders of a majority of the shares entitled to vote thereon.

(d) Upon the adoption of such resolution, a statement of revocation of voluntary dissolution proceedings shall be executed in duplicate by the corporation by its president or a vice president and by its secretary or an assistant secretary, and verified by one of the officers signing such statement, which statement shall set forth:

(1) The name of the corporation.

(2) The names and respective addresses of its officers.

(3) The names and respective addresses of its directors.

(4) A copy of the resolution adopted by the shareholders revoking the voluntary dissolution proceedings.

(5) The number of shares outstanding.

(6) The number of shares voted for and against the resolution, respectively.

§ 90. Filing of Statement of Revocation of Voluntary Dissolution Proceedings

Duplicate originals of the statement of revocation of voluntary dissolution proceedings, whether by consent of shareholders or by act of the corporation, shall be delivered to the Secretary of State. If the Secretary of State finds that such statement conforms to law, he shall, when all fees and franchise taxes have been paid as in this Act prescribed:

(a) Endorse on each of such duplicate originals the word "Filed," and the month, day and year of the filing thereof.

(b) File one of such duplicate originals in his office.

(c) Return the other duplicate original to the corporation or its representative.

§ 91. Effect of Statement of Revocation of Voluntary Dissolution Proceedings

Upon the filing by the Secretary of State of a statement of revocation of voluntary dissolution proceedings, whether by consent of shareholders or by act of the corporation, the revocation of the voluntary dissolution proceedings shall become effective and the corporation may again carry on its business.

§ 92. Articles of Dissolution

If voluntary dissolution proceedings have not been revoked, then when all debts, liabilities and obligations of the corporation have been paid and discharged, or adequate provision has been made therefor, and all of the remaining property and assets of the corporation have been distributed to its shareholders, articles of dissolution shall be executed in duplicate by the corporation by its president or a vice president and by its secretary or an assistant secretary, and verified by one of the officers signing such statement, which statement shall set forth:

(a) The name of the corporation.

(b) That the Secretary of State has theretofore filed a statement of intent to dissolve the corporation, and the date on which such statement was filed.

(c) That all debts, obligations and liabilities of the corporation have been paid and discharged or that adequate provision has been made therefor.

(d) That all the remaining property and assets of the corporation have been distributed among its shareholders in accordance with their respective rights and interests.

(e) That there are no suits pending against the corporation in any court, or that adequate provision has been made for the satisfaction of any judgment, order or decree which may be entered against it in any pending suit.

§ 93. Filing of Articles of Dissolution

Duplicate originals of such articles of dissolution shall be delivered to the Secretary of State. If the Secretary of State finds that such articles of dissolution conform to law, he shall, when all fees and franchise taxes have been paid as in this Act prescribed:

(a) Endorse on each of such duplicate originals the word "Filed," and the month, day and year of the filing thereof.

(b) File one of such duplicate originals in his office.

(c) Issue a certificate of dissolution to which he shall affix the other duplicate original.

The certificate of dissolution, together with the duplicate original of the articles of dissolution affixed thereto by the Secretary of State, shall be returned to the representative of the dissolved corporation. Upon the issuance of such certificate of dissolution the existence of the corporation shall cease, except for the purpose of suits, other proceedings and appropriate corporate action by shareholders, directors and officers as provided in this Act.

§ 94. Involuntary Dissolution

A corporation may be dissolved involuntarily by a decree of the . . . . court in an action filed by the Attorney General when it is established that:

(a) The corporation has failed to file its annual report within the time required by this Act, or has failed to pay its franchise tax on or before the first day of August of the year in which such franchise tax becomes due and payable; or

(b) The corporation procured its articles of incorporation through fraud; or

(c) The corporation has continued to exceed or abuse the authority conferred upon it by law; or

(d) The corporation has failed for thirty days to appoint and maintain a registered agent in this State; or

(e) The corporation has failed for thirty days after change of its registered office or registered agent to file in the office of the Secretary of State a statement of such change.

§ 95. Notification to Attorney General

The Secretary of State, on or before the last day of December of each year, shall certify to the Attorney General the names of all corporations which have failed to file their annual reports or to pay franchise taxes in accordance with the provisions of this Act, together with the facts pertinent thereto. He shall also certify, from time to time, the names of all corporations which have given other cause for dissolution as provided in this Act, together with the facts pertinent thereto. Whenever the Secretary of State shall certify the name of a corporation to the Attorney General as having given any cause for dissolution, the Secretary of State shall concurrently mail to the corporation at its registered office a notice that such certification has been made. Upon the receipt of such certification, the Attorney General shall file an action in the name of the State against such corporation for its dissolution. Every such certificate from the Secretary of State to the Attorney General pertaining to the failure of a corporation to file an annual report or pay a franchise tax shall be taken and received in all courts as prima facie evidence of the facts therein stated. If, before action is filed, the corporation shall file its annual report or pay its franchise tax, together with all penalties thereon, or shall appoint or maintain a registered agent as provided in this Act, or shall file with the Secretary of State the required statement of change of registered office or registered agent, such fact shall be forthwith certified by the Secretary of State to the Attorney General and he shall not file an action against such corporation for such cause. If, after action is filed, the corporation shall file its annual report or pay its franchise tax, together with all penalties thereon, or shall appoint or maintain a registered agent as provided in this Act, or shall file with the Secretary of State the required statement of change of registered office or registered agent, and shall pay the costs of such action, the action for such cause shall abate.

§ 96. Venue and Process

Every action for the involuntary dissolution of a corporation shall be commenced by the Attorney General either in the . . . . court of the county in which the registered office of the corporation is situated, or in the . . . . court of . . . . county. Summons shall issue and be served as in other civil actions. If process is returned not found, the Attorney General shall cause publication to be made as in other civil cases in some newspaper published in the county where the registered office of the corporation is situated, containing a notice of the pendency of such action, the title of the court, the title of the action, and the date on or after which default may be entered. The Attorney General may include in one notice the names of any number of corporations against which actions are then pending in the same court. The Attorney General shall cause a copy of such notice to be mailed to the corporation at its registered office within ten days after the first publication thereof. The certificate of the Attorney General of the mailing of such notice shall be prima facie evidence thereof. Such notice shall be published at least once each week for two successive weeks, and the first publication thereof may begin at any time after the summons has been returned. Unless a corporation shall have been served with summons, no default shall be taken against it earlier than thirty days after the first publication of such notice.

§ 97. Jurisdiction of Court to Liquidate Assets and Business of Corporation

The . . . . courts shall have full power to liquidate the assets and business of a corporation:

(a) In an action by a shareholder when it is established:

(1) That the directors are deadlocked in the management of the corporate affairs and the shareholders are unable to break the deadlock, and that irreparable injury to the corporation is being suffered or is threatened by reason thereof; or

(2) That the acts of the directors or those in control of the corporation are illegal, oppressive or fraudulent; or

(3) That the shareholders are deadlocked in voting power, and have failed, for a period which includes at least two consecutive annual meeting dates, to elect successors to directors whose terms have expired or would have expired upon the election of their successors; or

(4) That the corporate assets are being misapplied or wasted.

(b) In an action by a creditor:

(1) When the claim of the creditor has been reduced to judgment and an execution thereon returned unsatisfied and it is established that the corporation is insolvent; or

(2) When the corporation has admitted in writing that the claim of the creditor is due and owing and it is established that the corporation is insolvent.

(c) Upon application by a corporation which has filed a statement of intent to dissolve, as provided in this Act, to have its liquidation continued under the supervision of the court.

(d) When an action has been filed by the Attorney General to dissolve a corporation and it is established that liquidation of its business and affairs should precede the entry of a decree of dissolution.

Proceedings under clause (a), (b) or (c) of this section shall be brought in the county in which the registered office or the principal office of the corporation is situated.

It shall not be necessary to make shareholders parties to any such action or proceeding unless relief is sought against them personally.

§ 98. Procedure in Liquidation of Corporation by Court

In proceedings to liquidate the assets and business of a corporation the court shall have power to issue injunctions, to appoint a receiver or receivers pendente lite, with such powers and duties as the court, from time to time, may direct, and to take such other proceedings as may be requisite to preserve the corporate assets wherever situated, and carry on the business of the corporation until a full hearing can be had.

After a hearing had upon such notice as the court may direct to be given to all parties to the proceedings and to any other parties in interest designated by the court, the court may appoint a liquidating receiver or receivers with authority to collect the assets of the corporation, including all amounts owing to the corporation by subscribers on account of any unpaid portion of the consideration for the issuance of shares. Such liquidating receiver or receivers shall have authority, subject to the order of the court, to sell, convey and dispose of all or any part of the assets of the corporation wherever situated, either at public or private sale. The assets of the corporation or the proceeds resulting from a sale, conveyance or other disposition thereof shall be applied to the expenses of such liquidation and to the payment of the liabilities and obligations of the corporation, and any remaining assets or proceeds shall be distributed among its shareholders according to their respective rights and interests. The order appointing such liquidating receiver or receivers shall state their powers and duties. Such powers and duties may be increased or diminished at any time during the proceedings.

The court shall have power to allow from time to time as expenses of the liquidation compensation to the receiver or receivers and to attorneys in the proceeding, and to direct the payment thereof out of the assets of the corporation or the proceeds of any sale or disposition of such assets.

A receiver of a corporation appointed under the provisions of this section shall have authority to sue and defend in all courts in his own name as receiver of such corporation. The court appointing such receiver shall have exclusive jurisdiction of the corporation and its property, wherever situated.

§ 99. Qualifications of Receivers

A receiver shall in all cases be a natural person or a corporation authorized to act as receiver, which corporation may be a domestic corporation or a foreign corporation authorized to transact business in this State, and shall in all cases give such bond as the court may direct with such sureties as the court may require.

§ 100. Filing of Claims in Liquidation Proceedings

In proceedings to liquidate the assets and business of a corporation the court may require all creditors of the corporation to file with the clerk of the court or with the receiver, in such form as the court may prescribe, proofs under oath of their respective claims. If the court requires the filing of claims it shall fix a date, which shall be not less than four months from the date of the order, as the last day for the filing of claims, and shall prescribe the notice that shall be given to creditors and claimants of the date so fixed. Prior to the date so fixed, the court may extend the time for the filing of claims. Creditors and claimants failing to file proofs of claim on or before the date so fixed may be barred, by order of court, from participating in the distribution of the assets of the corporation.

§ 101. Discontinuance of Liquidation Proceedings

The liquidation of the assets and business of a corporation may be discontinued at any time during the liquidation proceedings when it is established that cause for liquidation no longer exists. In such event the court shall dismiss the proceedings and direct the receiver to redeliver to the corporation all its remaining property and assets.

§ 102. Decree of Involuntary Dissolution

In proceedings to liquidate the assets and business of a corporation, when the costs and expenses of such proceedings and all debts, obligations and liabilities of the corporation shall have been paid and discharged and all of its remaining property and assets distributed to its shareholders, or in case its property and assets are not sufficient to satisfy and discharge such costs, expenses, debts and obligations, all the property and assets have been applied so far as they will go to their payment, the court shall enter a decree dissolving the corporation, whereupon the existence of the corporation shall cease.

§ 103. Filing of Decree of Dissolution

In case the court shall enter a decree dissolving a corporation, it shall be the duty of the clerk of such court to cause a certified copy of the decree to be filed with the Secretary of State. No fee shall be charged by the Secretary of State for the filing thereof.

§ 104. Deposit with State Treasurer of Amount Due Certain Shareholders

Upon the voluntary or involuntary dissolution of a corporation, the portion of the assets distributable to a creditor or shareholder who is unknown or cannot be found, or who is under disability and there is no person legally competent to receive such distributive portion, shall be reduced to cash and deposited with the State Treasurer and shall be paid over to such creditor or shareholder or to his legal representative upon proof satisfactory to the State Treasurer of his right thereto.

§ 105. Survival of Remedy after Dissolution

The dissolution of a corporation either (1) by the issuance of a certificate of dissolution by the Secretary of State, or (2) by a decree of court when the court has not liquidated the assets and business of the corporation as provided in this Act, or (3) by expiration of its period of duration, shall not take away or impair any remedy available to or against such corporation, its directors, officers, or shareholders, for any right or claim existing, or any liability incurred, prior to such dissolution if action or other proceeding thereon is commenced within two years after the date of such dissolution. Any such action or proceeding by or against the corporation may be prosecuted or defended by the corporation in its corporate name. The shareholders, directors and officers shall have power to take such corporate or other action as shall be appropriate to protect such remedy, right or claim. If such corporation was dissolved by the expiration of its period of duration, such corporation may amend its articles of incorporation at any time during such period of two years so as to extend its period of duration.

§ 106. Admission of Foreign Corporation

No foreign corporation shall have the right to transact business in this State until it shall have procured a certificate of authority so to do from the Secretary of State. No foreign corporation shall be entitled to procure a certificate of authority under this Act to transact in this State any business which a corporation organized under this Act is not permitted to transact. A foreign corporation shall not be denied a certificate of authority by reason of the fact that the laws of the state or country under which such corporation is organized governing its organization and internal affairs differ from the laws of this State, and nothing in this Act contained shall be construed to authorize this State to regulate the organization or the internal affairs of such corporation.

Without excluding other activities which may not constitute transacting business in this State, a foreign corporation shall not be considered to be transacting business in this State, for the purposes of this Act, by reason of carrying on in this State any one or more of the following activities:

(a) Maintaining or defending any action or suit or any administrative or arbitration proceeding, or effecting the settlement thereof or the settlement of claims or disputes.

(b) Holding meetings of its directors or shareholders or carrying on other activities concerning its internal affairs.

(c) Maintaining bank accounts.

(d) Maintaining offices or agencies for the transfer, exchange and registration of its securities, or appointing and maintaining trustees or depositaries with relation to its securities.

(e) Effecting sales through independent contractors.

(f) Soliciting or procuring orders, whether by mail or through employees or agents or otherwise, where such orders require acceptance without this State before becoming binding contracts.

(g) Creating as borrower or lender, or acquiring, indebtedness or mortgages or other security interests in real or personal property.

(h) Securing or collecting debts or enforcing any rights in property securing the same.

(i) Transacting any business in interstate commerce.

(j) Conducting an isolated transaction completed within a period of thirty days and not in the course of a number of repeated transactions of like nature.

§ 107. Powers of Foreign Corporation

A foreign corporation which shall have received a certificate of authority under this Act shall, until a certificate of revocation or of withdrawal shall have been issued as provided in this Act, enjoy the same, but no greater, rights and privileges as a domestic corporation organized for the purposes set forth in the application pursuant to which such certificate of authority is issued; and, except as in this Act otherwise provided, shall be subject to the same duties, restrictions, penalties and liabilities now or hereafter imposed upon a domestic corporation of like character.

§ 108. Corporate Name of Foreign Corporation

No certificate of authority shall be issued to a foreign corporation unless the corporate name of such corporation:

(a) Shall contain the word "corporation," "company," "incorporated," or "limited," or shall contain an abbreviation of one of such words, or such corporation shall, for use in this State, add at the end of its name one of such words or an abbreviation thereof.

(b) Shall not contain any word or phrase which indicates or implies that it is organized for any purpose other than one or more of the purposes contained in its articles of incorporation or that it is authorized or empowered to conduct the business of banking or insurance.

(c) Shall not be the same as, or deceptively similar to, the name of any domestic corporation existing under the laws of this State or any foreign corporation authorized to transact business in this State, or a name the exclusive right to which is, at the time, reserved in the manner provided in this Act, or the name of a corporation which has in effect a registration of its name as provided in this Act except that this provision shall not apply if the foreign corporation applying for a certificate of authority files with the Secretary of State any one of the following:

(1) a resolution of its board of directors adopting a fictitious name for use in transacting business in this State which fictitious name is not deceptively similar to the name of any domestic corporation or of any foreign corporation authorized to transact business in this State or to any name reserved or registered as provided in this Act, or

(2) the written consent of such other corporation or holder of a reserved or registered name to use the same or deceptively similar name and one or more words are added to make such name distinguishable from such other name, or

(3) a certified copy of a final decree of a court of competent jurisdiction establishing the prior right of such foreign corporation to the use of such name in this State.

§ 109. Change of Name by Foreign Corporation

Whenever a foreign corporation which is authorized to transact business in this State shall change its name to one under which a certificate of authority would not be granted to it on application therefor, the certificate of authority of such corporation shall be suspended and it shall not thereafter transact any business in this State until it has changed its name to a name which is available to it under the laws of this State or has otherwise complied with the provisions of this Act.

§ 110. Application for Certificate of Authority

A foreign corporation, in order to procure a certificate of authority to transact business in this State, shall make application therefor to the Secretary of State, which application shall set forth:

(a) The name of the corporation and the state or county under the laws of which it is incorporated.

(b) If the name of the corporation does not contain the word "corporation," "company," "incorporated," or "limited," or does not contain an abbreviation of one of such words, then the name of the corporation with the word or abbreviation which it elects to add thereto for use in this State.

(c) The date of incorporation and the period of duration of the corporation.

(d) The address of the principal office of the corporation in the state or country under the laws of which it is incorporated.

(e) The address of the proposed registered office of the corporation in this State, and the name of its proposed registered agent in this State at such address.

(f) The purpose or purposes of the corporation which it proposes to pursue in the transaction of business in this State.

(g) The names and respective addresses of the directors and officers of the corporation.

(h) A statement of the aggregate number of shares which the corporation has authority to issue, itemized by classes and series, if any, within a class.

(i) A statement of the aggregate number of issued shares, itemized by class and by series, if any, within each class.

(j) An estimate, expressed in dollars, of the value of all property to be owned by the corporation for the following year, wherever located, and an estimate of the value of the property of the corporation to be located within this State during such year, and an estimate, expressed in dollars of the gross amount of business which will be transacted by the corporation during such year, and an estimate of the gross amount thereof which will be transacted by the corporation at or from places of business in this State during such year.

(k) Such additional information as may be necessary or appropriate in order to enable the Secretary of State to determine whether such corporation is entitled to a certificate of authority to transact business in this State and to determine and assess the fees and franchise taxes payable as in this Act prescribed.

Such application shall be made on forms prescribed and furnished by the Secretary of State and shall be executed in duplicate by the corporation by its president or a vice president and by its secretary or an assistant secretary, and verified by one of the officers signing such application.

§ 111. Filing of Application for Certificate of Authority

Duplicate originals of the application of the corporation for a certificate of authority shall be delivered to the Secretary of State, together with a copy of its articles of incorporation and all amendments thereto, duly authenticated by the proper officer of the state or country under the laws of which it is incorporated.

If the Secretary of State finds that such application conforms to law, he shall, when all fees and franchise taxes have been paid as in this Act prescribed:

(a) Endorse on each of such documents the word "Filed," and the month, day and year of the filing thereof.

(b) File in his office one of such duplicate originals of the application and the copy of the articles of incorporation and amendments thereto.

(c) Issue a certificate of authority to transact business in this State to which he shall affix the other duplicate original application.

The certificate of authority, together with the duplicate original of the application affixed thereto by the Secretary of State, shall be returned to the corporation or its representative.

§ 112. Effect of Certificate of Authority

Upon the issuance of a certificate of authority by the Secretary of State, the corporation shall be authorized to transact business in this State for those purposes set forth in its application, subject, however, to the right of this State to suspend or to revoke such authority as provided in this Act.

§ 113. Registered Office and Registered Agent of Foreign Corporation

Each foreign corporation authorized to transact business in this State shall have and continuously maintain in this State:

(a) A registered office which may be, but need not be, the same as its place of business in this State.

(b) A registered agent, which agent may be either an individual resident in this State whose business office is identical with such registered office, or a domestic corporation, or a foreign corporation authorized to transact business in this State, having a business office identical with such registered office.

§ 114. Change of Registered Office or Registered Agent of Foreign Corporation

A foreign corporation authorized to transact business in this State may change its registered office or change its registered agent, or both, upon filing in the office of the Secretary of State a statement setting forth:

(a) The name of the corporation.

(b) The address of its then registered office.

(c) If the address of its registered office be changed, the address to which the registered office is to be changed.

(d) The name of its then registered agent.

(e) If its registered agent be changed, the name of its successor registered agent.

(f) That the address of its registered office and the address of the business office of its registered agent, as changed, will be identical.

(g) That such change was authorized by resolution duly adopted by its board of directors.

Such statement shall be executed by the corporation by its president or a vice president, and verified by him, and delivered to the Secretary of State. If the Secretary of State finds that such statement conforms to the provisions of this Act, he shall file such statement in his office, and upon such filing the change of address of the registered office, or the appointment of a new registered agent, or both, as the case may be, shall become effective.

Any registered agent of a foreign corporation may resign as such agent upon filing a written notice thereof, executed in duplicate, with the Secretary of State, who shall forthwith mail a copy thereof to the corporation at its principal office in the state or country under the laws of which it is incorporated. The appointment of such agent shall terminate upon the expiration of thirty days after receipt of such notice by the Secretary of State.

If a registered agent changes his or its business address to another place within the same . . . .*, he or it may change such address and the address of the registered office of any corporation of which he or it is registered agent by filing a statement as required above except that it need be signed only by the registered agent and need not be responsive to (e) or (g) and must recite that a copy of the statement has been mailed to the corporation.

§ 115. Service of Process on Foreign Corporation

The registered agent so appointed by a foreign corporation authorized to transact business in this State shall be an agent of such corporation upon whom any process, notice or demand required or permitted by law to be served upon the corporation may be served.

Whenever a foreign corporation authorized to transact business in this State shall fail to appoint or maintain a registered agent in this State, or whenever any such registered agent cannot with reasonable diligence be found at the registered office, or whenever the certificate of authority of a foreign corporation shall be suspended or revoked, then the Secretary of State shall be an agent of such corporation upon whom any such process, notice, or demand may be served. Service on the Secretary of State of any such process, notice or demand shall be made by delivering to and leaving with him, or with any clerk having charge of the corporation department of his office, duplicate copies of such process, notice or demand. In the event any such process, notice or demand is served on the Secretary of State, he shall immediately cause one of such copies thereof to be forwarded by registered mail, addressed to the corporation at its principal office in the state or country under the laws of which it is incorporated. Any service so had on the Secretary of State shall be returnable in not less than thirty days.

The Secretary of State shall keep a record of all processes, notices and demands served upon him under this section, and shall record therein the time of such service and his action with reference thereto.

Nothing herein contained shall limit or affect the right to serve any process, notice or demand, required or permitted by law to be served upon a foreign corporation in any other manner now or hereafter permitted by law.

§ 116. Amendment to Articles of Incorporation of Foreign Corporation

Whenever the articles of incorporation of a foreign corporation authorized to transact business in this State are amended, such foreign corporation shall, within thirty days after such amendment becomes effective, file in the office of the Secretary of State a copy of such amend-

ment duly authenticated by the proper officer of the state or country under the laws of which it is incorporated; but the filing thereof shall not of itself enlarge or alter the purpose or purposes which such corporation is authorized to pursue in the transaction of business in this State, nor authorize such corporation to transact business in this State under any other name than the name set forth in its certificate of authority.

§ 117. Merger of Foreign Corporation Authorized to Transact Business in This State

Whenever a foreign corporation authorized to transact business in this State shall be a party to a statutory merger permitted by the laws of the state or country under the laws of which it is incorporated, and such corporation shall be the surviving corporation, it shall, within thirty days after such merger becomes effective, file with the Secretary of State a copy of the articles of merger duly authenticated by the proper officer of the state or country under the laws of which such statutory merger was effected; and it shall not be necessary for such corporation to procure either a new or amended certificate of authority to transact business in this State unless the name of such corporation be changed thereby or unless the corporation desires to pursue in this State other or additional purposes than those which it is then authorized to transact in this State.

§ 118. Amended Certificate of Authority

A foreign corporation authorized to transact business in this State shall procure an amended certificate of authority in the event it changes its corporate name, or desires to pursue in this State other or additional purposes than those set forth in its prior application for a certificate of authority, by making application therefor to the Secretary of State.

The requirements in respect to the form and contents of such application, the manner of its execution, the filing of duplicate originals thereof with the Secretary of State, the issuance of an amended certificate of authority and the effect thereof, shall be the same as in the case of an original application for a certificate of authority.

§ 119. Withdrawal of Foreign Corporation

A foreign corporation authorized to transact business in this State may withdraw from this State upon procuring from the Secretary of State a certificate of withdrawal. In order to procure such certificate of withdrawal, such foreign corporation shall deliver to the Secretary of State an application for withdrawal, which shall set forth:

(a) The name of the corporation and the state or country under the laws of which it is incorporated.

(b) That the corporation is not transacting business in this State.

---

*Supply designation of jurisdiction, such as county, etc. in accordance with local practice.

(c) That the corporation surrenders its authority to transact business in this State.

(d) That the corporation revokes the authority of its registered agent in this State to accept service of process and consents that service of process in any action, suit or proceeding based upon any cause of action arising in this State during the time the corporation was authorized to transact business in this State may thereafter be made on such corporation by service thereof on the Secretary of State.

(e) A post-office address to which the Secretary of State may mail a copy of any process against the corporation that may be served on him.

(f) A statement of the aggregate number of shares which the corporation has authority to issue, itemized by class and series, if any, within each class, as of the date of such application.

(g) A statement of the aggregate number of issued shares, itemized by class and series, if any, within each class, as of the date of such application.

(h) Such additional information as may be necessary or appropriate in order to enable the Secretary of State to determine and assess any unpaid fees or franchise taxes payable by such foreign corporation as in this Act prescribed.

The application for withdrawal shall be made on forms prescribed and furnished by the Secretary of State and shall be executed by the corporation by its president or a vice president and by its secretary or an assistant secretary, and verified by one of the officers signing the application, or, if the corporation is in the hands of a receiver or trustee, shall be executed on behalf of the corporation by such receiver or trustee and verified by him.

§ 120. Filing of Application for Withdrawal

Duplicate originals of such application for withdrawal shall be delivered to the Secretary of State. If the Secretary of State finds that such application conforms to the provisions of this Act, he shall, when all fees and franchise taxes have been paid as in this Act prescribed:

(a) Endorse on each of such duplicate originals the word "Filed," and the month, day and year of the filing thereof.

(b) File one of such duplicate originals in his office.

(c) Issue a certificate of withdrawal to which he shall affix the other duplicate original.

The certificate of withdrawal, together with the duplicate original of the application for withdrawal affixed thereto by the Secretary of State, shall be returned to the corporation or its representative. Upon the issuance of such certificate of withdrawal, the authority of the corporation to transact business in this State shall cease.

§ 121. Revocation of Certificate of Authority

The certificate of authority of a foreign corporation to transact business in this State may be revoked by the Secretary of State upon the conditions prescribed in this section when:

(a) The corporation has failed to file its annual report within the time required by this Act, or has failed to pay any fees, franchise taxes or penalties prescribed by this Act when they have become due and payable; or

(b) The corporation has failed to appoint and maintain a registered agent in this State as required by this Act; or

(c) The corporation has failed, after change of its registered office or registered agent, to file in the office of the Secretary of State a statement of such change as required by this Act; or

(d) The corporation has failed to file in the office of the Secretary of State any amendment to its articles of incorporation or any articles of merger within the time prescribed by this Act; or

(e) A misrepresentation has been made of any material matter in any application, report, affidavit, or other document submitted by such corporation pursuant to this Act.

No certificate of authority of a foreign corporation shall be revoked by the Secretary of State unless (1) he shall have given the corporation not less than sixty days' notice thereof by mail addressed to its registered office in this State, and (2) the corporation shall fail prior to revocation to file such annual report, or pay such fees, franchise taxes or penalties, or file the required statement of change of registered agent or registered office, or file such articles of amendment or articles of merger, or correct such misrepresentation.

§ 122. Issuance of Certificate of Revocation

Upon revoking any such certificate of authority, the Secretary of State shall:

(a) Issue a certificate of revocation in duplicate.

(b) File one of such certificates in his office.

(c) Mail to such corporation at its registered office in this State a notice of such revocation accompanied by one of such certificates.

Upon the issuance of such certificate of revocation, the authority of the corporation to transact business in this State shall cease.

§ 123. Application to Corporations Heretofore Authorized to Transact Business in This State

Foreign corporations which are duly authorized to transact business in this State at the time this Act takes effect, for a purpose or purposes for which a corporation might secure such authority under this Act, shall, subject to the limitations set forth in their respective certificates of authority, be entitled to all the rights and privileges applicable to foreign corporations procuring certificates of authority to transact business in this State under this Act, and from the time this Act takes effect such corporations shall be subject to all the limitations, restrictions, liabilities, and duties prescribed herein for foreign corporations procuring certificates of authority to transact business in this State under this Act.

§ 124. Transacting Business Without Certificate of Authority

No foreign corporation transacting business in this State without a certificate of authority shall be permitted to maintain any action, suit or proceeding in any court of this State, until such corporation shall have obtained a certificate of authority. Nor shall any action, suit or proceeding be maintained in any court of this State by any successor or assignee of such corporation on any right, claim or demand arising out of the transaction of business by such corporation in this State, until a certificate of authority shall have been obtained by such corporation or by a corporation which has acquired all or substantially all of its assets.

The failure of a foreign corporation to obtain a certificate of authority to transact business in this State shall not impair the validity of any contract or act of such corporation, and shall not prevent such corporation from defending any action, suit or proceeding in any court of this State.

A foreign corporation which transacts business in this State without a certificate of authority shall be liable to this State, for the years or parts thereof during which it transacted business in this State without a certificate of authority, in an amount equal to all fees and franchise taxes which would have been imposed by this Act upon such corporation had it duly applied for and received a certificate of authority to transact business in this State as required by this Act and thereafter filed all reports required by this Act, plus all penalties imposed by this Act for failure to pay such fees and franchise taxes. The Attorney General shall bring proceedings to recover all amounts due this State under the provisions of this Section.

§ 125. Annual Report of Domestic and Foreign Corporations

Each domestic corporation, and each foreign corporation authorized to transact business in this State, shall file, within the time prescribed by this Act, an annual report setting forth:

(a) The name of the corporation and the state or country under the laws of which it is incorporated.

(b) The address of the registered office of the corporation in this State, and the name of its registered agent in this State at such address, and, in case of a foreign corporation, the address of its principal office in the state or country under the laws of which it is incorporated.

(c) A brief statement of the character of the business in which the corporation is actually engaged in this State.

(d) The names and respective addresses of the directors and officers of the corporation.

(e) A statement of the aggregate number of shares which the corporation has authority to issue, itemized by class and series, if any, within each class.

(f) A statement of the aggregate number of issued shares, itemized by class and series, if any, within each class.

(g) A statement, expressed in dollars, of the value of all the property owned by the corporation, wherever located, and the value of the property of the corporation located within this State, and a statement, expressed in dollars, of the gross amount of business transacted by the corporation for the twelve months ended on the thirty-first day of December preceding the date herein provided for the filing of such report and the gross amount thereof transacted by the corporation at or from places of business in this State. If, on the thirty-first day of December preceding the time herein provided for the filing of such report, the corporation had not been in existence for a period of twelve months, or in the case of a foreign corporation had not been authorized to transact business in this State for a period of twelve months, the statement with respect to business transacted shall be furnished for the period between the date of incorporation or the date of its authorization to transact business in this State, as the case may be, and such thirty-first day of December. If all the property of the corporation is located in this State and all of its business is transacted at or from places of business in this State, then the information required by this subparagraph need not be set forth in such report.

(h) Such additional information as may be necessary or appropriate in order to enable the Secretary of State to determine and assess the proper amount of franchise taxes payable by such corporation.

Such annual report shall be made on forms prescribed and furnished by the Secretary of State, and the information therein contained shall be given as of the date of the execution of the report, except as to the information required by subparagraphs (g) and (h) which shall be given as of the close of business on the thirty-first day of December next preceding the date herein provided for the filing of such report. It shall be executed by the corporation by its president, a vice president, secretary, an assistant secretary, or treasurer, and verified by the officer executing the report, or, if the corporation is in the hands of a receiver or trustee, it shall be executed on behalf of the corporation and verified by such receiver or trustee.

§ 126. Filing of Annual Report of Domestic and Foreign Corporations

Such annual report of a domestic or foreign corporation shall be delivered to the Secretary of State between the first day of January and the first day of March of each year, except that the first annual report of a domestic or foreign corporation shall be filed between the first day of January and the first day of March of the year next succeeding the calendar year in which its certificate of incorporation or its certificate of authority, as the case may be, was issued by the Secretary of State. Proof to the satisfaction of the Secretary of State that prior to the first day of March such report was deposited in the United States mail in a sealed envelope, properly addressed, with postage prepaid, shall be deemed a compliance with this requirement. If the Secretary of State finds that such report conforms to the requirements of this Act, he shall file the same. If he finds that it does not so conform, he shall promptly return the same to the corporation for any necessary corrections, in which event the penalties hereinafter prescribed for failure to file such report within the time hereinabove provided shall not apply, if such report is corrected to conform to the requirements of this Act and returned to the Secretary of State within thirty days from the date on which it was mailed to the corporation by the Secretary of State.

§ 127. Fees, Franchise Taxes and Charges to be Collected by Secretary of State

The Secretary of State shall charge and collect in accordance with the provisions of this Act:

(a) Fees for filing documents and issuing certificates.

(b) Miscellaneous charges.

(c) License fees.

(d) Franchise taxes.

§ 128. Fees for Filing Documents and Issuing Certificates

The Secretary of State shall charge and collect for:

(a) Filing articles of incorporation and issuing a certificate of incorporation, ... dollars.

(b) Filing articles of amendment and issuing a certificate of amendment, ... dollars.

(c) Filing restated articles of incorporation, ... dollars.

(d) Filing articles of merger or consolidation and issuing a certificate of merger or consolidation, ... dollars.

(e) Filing an application to reserve a corporate name, ... dollars.

(f) Filing a notice of transfer of a reserved corporate name, ... dollars.

(g) Filing a statement of change of address of registered office or change of registered agent or both, ... dollars.

(h) Filing a statement of the establishment of a series of shares, ... dollars.

(i) Filing a statement of intent to dissolve, ... dollars.

(j) Filing a statement of revocation of voluntary dissolution proceedings, ... dollars.

(k) Filing articles of dissolution, ... dollars.

(l) Filing an application of a foreign corporation for a certificate of authority to transact business in this State and issuing a certificate of authority, ... dollars.

(m) Filing an application of a foreign corporation for an amended certificate of authority to transact business in this State and issuing an amended certificate of authority, ... dollars.

(n) Filing a copy of an amendment to the articles of incorporation of a foreign corporation holding a certificate of authority to transact business in this State, ... dollars.

(o) Filing a copy of articles of merger of a foreign corporation holding a certificate of authority to transact business in this State, ... dollars.

(p) Filing an application for withdrawal of a foreign corporation and issuing a certificate of withdrawal, ... dollars.

(q) Filing any other statement or report, except an annual report, of a domestic or foreign corporation, ... dollars.

§ 129. Miscellaneous Charges

The Secretary of State shall charge and collect:

(a) For furnishing a certified copy of any document, instrument, or paper relating to a corporation, ... cents per page and .... dollars for the certificate and affixing the seal thereto.

(b) At the time of any service of process on him as resident agent of a corporation, ... dollars, which amount may be recovered as taxable costs by the party to the suit or action causing such service to be made if such party prevails in the suit or action.

§ 130. License Fees Payable by Domestic Corporations

The Secretary of State shall charge and collect from each domestic corporation license fees, based upon the number of shares which it will have authority to issue or the increase in the number of shares which it will have authority to issue, at the time of:

(a) Filing articles of incorporation;

(b) Filing articles of amendment increasing the number of authorized shares; and

(c) Filing articles of merger or consolidation increasing the number of authorized shares which the surviving or new corporation, if a domestic corporation, will have the authority to issue above the aggregate number of shares which the constituent domestic corporations and constituent foreign corporations authorized to transact business in this State had authority to issue.

The license fees shall be at the rate of .... cents per share up to and including the first 10,000 authorized shares, ... cents per share for each authorized share in excess of 10,000 shares up to and including 100,000 shares, and .... cents per share for each authorized share in excess of 100,000 shares.

The license fees payable on an increase in the number of authorized shares shall be imposed only on the increased number of shares, and the number of previously authorized shares shall be taken into account in determining the rate applicable to the increased number of authorized shares.

§ 131. License Fees Payable by Foreign Corporations

The Secretary of State shall charge and collect from each foreign corporation license fees, based upon the proportion represented in this State of the number of shares which it has authority to issue or the increase in the number of shares which it has authority to issue, at the time of:

(a) Filing an application for a certificate of authority to transact business in this State;

(b) Filing articles of amendment which increased the number of authorized shares; and

(c) Filing articles of merger or consolidation which increased the number of authorized shares which the surviving or new corporation, if a foreign corporation, has authority to issue above the aggregate number of shares which the constituent domestic corporations and constituent foreign corporations authorized to transact business in this State had authority to issue.

The license fees shall be at the rate of .... cents per share up to and including the first 10,000 authorized shares represented in this State, ... cents per share for each authorized share in excess of 10,000 shares up to and including 100,000 shares represented in this State, and .... cents per share for each authorized share in excess of 100,000 shares represented in this State.

The license fees payable on an increase in the number of authorized shares shall be imposed only on the increased number of such shares represented in this State, and the number of previously authorized shares represented in this State shall be taken into account in determining the rate applicable to the increased number of authorized shares.

The number of authorized shares represented in this State shall be that proportion of its total authorized shares which the sum of the value of its property located in this State and the gross amount of business transacted by it at or from places of business in this State bears to the sum of the value of all of its property, wherever located, and the gross amount of its business, wherever transacted. Such proportion shall be determined from information contained in the application for a certificate of authority to transact business in this State until the filing of an annual report and thereafter from information contained in the latest annual report filed by the corporation.

§ 132. Franchise Taxes Payable by Domestic Corporations

The Secretary of State shall charge and collect from each domestic corporation an initial franchise tax at the time of filing its articles of incorporation at the rate of one-twelfth of one-half of the license fee payable by such corporation under the provisions of this Act at the time of filing its articles of incorporation, for each calendar month, or fraction thereof, between the date of the issuance of the certificate of incorporation by the Secretary of State and the first day of July of the next succeeding calendar year.

The Secretary of State shall charge and collect from each domestic corporation an annual franchise tax, payable in advance for the period from July 1 in each year to July 1 in the succeeding year, beginning July 1 in the calendar year in which such corporation is required to file its first annual report under this Act, (Alternative 1: at the rate of .... of .... per cent of the amount represented in this State of the stated capital of the corporation, as determined in accordance with accounting practices and principles that are reasonable in the circumstances, as disclosed by the latest report filed by the corporation with the Secretary of State) (Alternative 2: at the rate of .... cents per share up to and including the first 10,000 issued and outstanding shares, and .... cents per share for each issued and outstanding share in excess of 10,000 shares up to and including 100,000 shares, and .... cents per share for each issued and outstanding share in excess of 100,000 shares).

[If Alternative 2 is enacted, the following paragraph should be deleted.]

The amount represented in this State of the stated capital of the corporation shall be that proportion of its stated capital which the sum of the value of its property located in this State and the gross amount of business transacted by it at or from places of business in this State bears to the sum of the value of all of its property, wherever located, and the gross amount of its business, wherever transacted.

§ 133. Franchise Taxes Payable by Foreign Corporations

The Secretary of State shall charge and collect from each foreign corporation authorized to transact business in this State an initial franchise tax at the time of filing its application for a certificate of authority at the rate of one-twelfth of one-half of the license fee payable by such corporation under the provisions of this Act at the time of filing such application, for each month, or fraction thereof, between the date of the issuance of the certificate of authority by the Secretary of State and the first day of July of the next succeeding calendar year.

The Secretary of State shall charge and collect from each foreign corporation authorized to transact business in this State an annual franchise tax, payable in advance for the period from July 1 in each year to July 1 in the succeeding year, beginning July 1 in the calendar year in which such corporation is required to file its first annual report under this Act, (Alternative 1: at the rate of .... per cent of the amount represented in this State of the stated capital of the corporation, as determined in accordance with accounting practices and principles that are reasonable in the circumstances, as disclosed by the latest annual report filed by the corporation with the Secretary of State) (Alternative 2: at a rate of .... cents per share up to and including the first 10,000 issued and outstanding shares represented in this State, and .... cents per share for each issued and outstanding share in excess of 10,000 shares up to and including 100,000 shares represented in this State, and .... cents per share for each issued and outstanding share in excess of 100,000 shares represented in this State).

[If Alternative 2 is enacted, the following paragraph should be deleted.]

The amount represented in this State of the stated capital of the corporation shall be that proportion of its stated capital which the sum of the value of its property located in this State and the gross amount of business transacted by it at or from places of business in this State bears to the sum of the value of all of its property, wherever located, and the gross amount of its business, wherever transacted.

§ 134. Assessment and Collection of Annual Franchise Taxes

It shall be the duty of the Secretary of State to collect all annual franchise taxes and penalties imposed by, or assessed in accordance with, this Act.

Between the first day of March and the first day of June of each year, the Secretary of State shall assess against each corporation, domestic and foreign, required to file an annual report in such year, the franchise tax payable by it for the period from July 1 of such year to July 1 of the succeeding year in accordance with the provisions of this Act, and, if it has failed to file its annual report within the time prescribed by this Act, the penalty imposed by this Act upon such corporation for its failure so to do; and shall mail a written notice to each corporation against which such tax is assessed, addressed to such corporation at its registered office in this State, notifying the corporation (1) of the amount of franchise tax assessed against it for the ensuing year and the amount of penalty, if any, assessed against it for failure to file its annual report; (2) that objections, if any, to such assessment will be heard by the officer making the assessment on or before the fifteenth day of June of such year, upon receipt of a request from the corporation; and (3) that such tax and penalty shall be payable to the Secretary of State on the first day of July next succeeding the date of the notice. Failure to receive such notice shall not relieve the corporation of its obligation to pay the tax and any penalty assessed, or invalidate the assessment thereof.

The Secretary of State shall have power to hear and determine objections to any assessment of franchise tax at any time after such assessment and, after hearing, to change or modify any such assessment. In the event of any adjustment of franchise tax with respect to which a penalty has been assessed for failure to file an annual report, the penalty shall be adjusted in accordance with the provisions of this Act imposing such penalty.

All annual franchise taxes and all penalties for failure to file annual reports shall be due and payable on the first day of July of each year. If the annual franchise tax assessed against any corporation subject to the provisions of this Act, together with all penalties assessed thereon, shall not be paid to the Secretary of State on or before the thirty-first day of July of the year in which such tax is due and payable, the Secretary of State shall certify such fact to the Attorney General on or before the fifteenth day of November of such year, whereupon the Attorney General may institute an action against such corporation in the name of this State, in any court of competent jurisdiction, for the recovery of the amount of such franchise tax and penalties, together with the cost of suit, and prosecute the same to final judgment.

For the purpose of enforcing collection, all annual franchise taxes assessed in accordance with this Act, and all penalties assessed thereon and all interest and costs that shall accrue in connection with the collection thereof, shall be a prior and first lien on the real and personal property of the corporation from and including the first day of July of the year when such franchise taxes become due and payable until such taxes, penalties, interest, and costs shall have been paid.

§ 135. Penalties Imposed Upon Corporations

Each corporation, domestic or foreign, that fails or refuses to file its annual report for any year within the time prescribed by this Act shall be subject to a penalty of ten per cent of the amount of the franchise tax assessed against it for the period beginning July 1 of the year in which such report should have been filed. Such penalty shall be assessed by the Secretary of State at the time of the assessment of the franchise tax. If the amount of the franchise tax as originally assessed against such corporation be thereafter adjusted in accordance with the provisions of this Act, the amount of the penalty shall be likewise adjusted to ten per cent of the amount of the adjusted franchise tax. The amount of the franchise tax and the amount of the penalty shall be separately stated in any notice to the corporation with respect thereto.

If the franchise tax assessed in accordance with the provisions of this Act shall not be paid on or before the thirty-first day of July, it shall be deemed to be delinquent, and there shall be added a penalty of one per cent for each month or part of month that the same is delinquent, commencing with the month of August.

Each corporation, domestic or foreign, that fails or refuses to answer truthfully and fully within the time prescribed by this Act interrogatories propounded by the Secretary of State in accordance with the provisions of this Act, shall be deemed to be guilty of a misdemeanor and upon conviction thereof may be fined in any amount not exceeding five hundred dollars.

§ 136. Penalties Imposed Upon Officers and Directors

Each officer and director of a corporation, domestic or foreign, who fails or refuses within the time prescribed by this Act to answer truthfully and fully interrogatories propounded to him by the Secretary of State in accordance with the provisions of this Act, or who signs any articles, statement, report, application or other document filed with the Secretary of State which is known to such officer or director to be false in any material respect, shall be deemed to be guilty of a misdemeanor, and upon conviction thereof may be fined in any amount not exceeding .... dollars.

§ 137. Interrogatories by Secretary of State

The Secretary of State may propound to any corporation, domestic or foreign, subject to the provisions of this Act, and to any officer or director thereof, such interrogatories as may be reasonably necessary and proper to enable him to ascertain whether such corporation has complied with all the provisions of this Act applicable to such corporation. Such interrogatories shall be answered within thirty days after the mailing thereof, or within such additional time as shall be fixed by the Secretary of State, and the answers thereto shall be full and complete and shall be made in writing and under oath. If such interrogatories be directed to an individual they shall be answered by him, and if directed to a corporation they shall be answered by the president, vice president, secretary or assistant secretary thereof. The Secretary of State need not file any document to which such interrogatories relate until such interrogatories be answered as herein provided, and not then if the answers thereto disclose that such document is not in conformity with the provisions of this Act. The Secretary of State shall certify to the Attorney General, for such action as the Attorney General may deem appropriate, all interrogatories and answers thereto which disclose a violation of any of the provisions of this Act.

§ 138. Information Disclosed by Interrogatories

Interrogatories propounded by the Secretary of State and the answers thereto shall not be open to public inspection nor shall the Secretary of State disclose any facts or information obtained therefrom except insofar as his official duty may require the same to be made public or in the event such interrogatories or the answers thereto are required for evidence in any criminal proceedings or in any other action by this State.

§ 139. Powers of Secretary of State

The Secretary of State shall have the power and authority reasonably necessary to enable him to administer this Act efficiently and to perform the duties therein imposed upon him.

§ 140. Appeal from Secretary of State

If the Secretary of State shall fail to approve any articles of incorporation, amendment, merger, consolidation or dissolution, or any other document required by this Act to be approved by the Secretary of State before the same shall be filed in his office, he shall, within ten days after the delivery thereof to him, give written notice of his disapproval to the person or corporation, domestic or foreign, delivering the same, specifying the reasons therefor. From such disapproval such person or corporation may appeal to the .... court of the county in which the registered office of such corporation is, or is proposed to be, situated by filing with the clerk of such court a petition setting forth a copy of the articles or other document sought to be filed and a copy of the written disapproval thereof by the Secretary of State; whereupon the matter shall be tried de novo by the court, and the court shall either sustain the action of the Secretary of State or direct him to take such action as the court may deem proper.

If the Secretary of State shall revoke the certificate of authority to transact business in this State of any foreign corporation, pursuant to the provisions of this Act, such foreign corporation may likewise appeal to the .... court of the county where the registered office of such corporation in this State is situated, by filing with the clerk of such court a petition setting forth a copy of its certificate of authority to transact business in this State and a copy of the notice of revocation given by the Secretary of State; whereupon the matter shall be tried de novo by the court, and the court shall either sustain the action of the Secretary of State or direct him to take such action as the court may deem proper.

Appeals from all final orders and judgments entered by the .... court under this section in review of any ruling or decision of the Secretary of State may be taken as in other civil actions.

§ 141. Certificates and Certified Copies to be Received in Evidence

All certificates issued by the Secretary of State in accordance with the provisions of this Act, and all copies of documents filed in his office in accordance with the provisions of this Act when certified by him, shall be taken and received in all courts, public offices, and official bodies as prima facie evidence of the facts therein stated. A certificate by the Secretary of State under the great seal of this State, as to the existence or non-existence of the facts relating to corporations shall be taken and received in all courts, public offices, and official bodies as prima facie evidence of the existence or non-existence of the facts therein stated.

§ 142. Forms to be Furnished by Secretary of State

All reports required by this Act to be filed in the office of the Secretary of State shall be made on forms which shall be prescribed and furnished by the Secretary of State. Forms for all other documents to be filed in the office of the Secretary of State shall be furnished by the Secretary of State on request therefor, but the use thereof, unless otherwise specifically prescribed in this Act, shall not be mandatory.

§ 143. Greater Voting Requirements

Whenever, with respect to any action to be taken by the shareholders of a corporation, the articles of incorporation require the vote or concurrence of the holders of a greater proportion of the shares, or of any class or series thereof, than required by this Act with respect to such action, the provisions of the articles of incorporation shall control.

§ 144. Waiver of Notice

Whenever any notice is required to be given to any shareholder or director of a corporation under the provisions of this Act or under the provisions of the articles of incorporation or by-laws of the corporation, a waiver thereof in writing signed by the person or persons entitled to such notice, whether before or after the time stated therein, shall be equivalent to the giving of such notice.

§ 145. Action by Shareholders Without a Meeting

Any action required by this Act to be taken at a meeting of the shareholders of a corporation, or any action which may be taken at a meeting of the shareholders, may be taken without a meeting if a consent in writing, setting forth the action so taken, shall be signed by all of the shareholders entitled to vote with respect to the subject matter thereof.

Such consent shall have the same effect as a unanimous vote of shareholders, and may be stated as such in any articles or document filed with the Secretary of State under this Act.

§ 146. Unauthorized Assumption of Corporate Powers

All persons who assume to act as a corporation without authority so to do shall be jointly and severally liable for all debts and liabilities incurred or arising as a result thereof.

§ 147. Application to Existing Corporations

The provisions of this Act shall apply to all existing corporations organized under any general act of this State providing for the organization of corporations for a purpose or purposes for which a corporation might be organized under this Act, where the power has been reserved to amend, repeal or modify the act under which such corporation was organized and where such act is repealed by this Act.

§ 148. Application to Foreign and Interstate Commerce

The provisions of this Act shall apply to commerce with foreign nations and among the several states only insofar as the same may be permitted under the provisions of the Constitution of the United States.

§ 149. Reservation of Power

The ....* shall at all times have power to prescribe such regulations, provisions and limitations as it may deem advisable, which regulations, provisions and limitations shall be binding upon any and all corporations subject to the provisions of this Act, and the ....* shall have power to amend, repeal or modify this Act at pleasure.

---

*Insert name of legislative body.

§ 150. Effect of Repeal of Prior Acts

The repeal of a prior act by this Act shall not affect any right accrued or established, or any liability or penalty incurred, under the provisions of such act, prior to the repeal thereof.

§ 151. Effect of Invalidity of Part of this Act

If a court of competent jurisdiction shall adjudge to be invalid or unconstitutional any clause, sentence, paragraph, section or part of this Act, such judgment or decree shall not affect, impair, invalidate or nullify the remainder of this Act, but the effect thereof shall be confined to the clause, sentence, paragraph, section or part of this Act so adjudged to be invalid or unconstitutional.

§ 152. Exclusivity of Certain Provisions [Optional]

In circumstances to which section 45 and related sections of this Act are applicable, such provisions supersede the applicability of any other statutes of this state with respect to the legality of distributions.

§ 153. Repeal of Prior Acts
(Insert appropriate provisions) ....

———

SPECIAL COMMENTS—CLOSE CORPORATIONS

In view of the increasing importance of close corporations, both for the small family business and for the larger undertakings conducted by some small number of other corporations, this liberalizing trend has now been followed by the 1969 Amendments to the Model Act. The first sentence of section 35, providing that the business of the corporation shall be managed by a board of directors, was supplemented by a new clause "except as may be otherwise provided in the articles of incorporation." This permits the shareholders to take over and exercise the functions of the directors by appropriate provision to that effect in the articles, or to allocate functions between the directors and shareholders in such manner as may be desired. Taken with other provisions of the Model Act, which are here enumerated for convenience, this rounds out the adaptability of the Model Act for all the needs of a close corporation:

(1) By section 4(l) the by-laws may make any provision for the regulation of the affairs of the corporation that is not inconsistent with the articles or the laws of the incorporating state.

(2) By section 15 shares may be divided into several classes and the articles may limit or deny the voting rights of or provide special voting rights for the shares of any class to the extent not inconsistent with the Model Act. The narrow limits of this exception are revealed by section 33 which provides that each outstanding share, regardless of class, shall be entitled to one vote on each matter submitted to a vote at a meeting of the shareholders "except as may be otherwise provided in the articles of incorporation," thus expressly authorizing more than one vote per share or less than one vote per share, either generally or in respect to particular matters.

(3) By section 16 item (F) the shares of any preferred or special class may be issued in series and there may be variations between different series in numerous respects, including specifically the matter of voting rights, if any.

(4) By section 32 the articles may reduce a quorum of shareholders to not less than one-third of the shares entitled to vote, or leave the quorum at the standard of a majority or, as confirmed by section 143, increase the number to any desired point.

(5) By section 34 agreements among shareholders regarding the voting of their shares are made valid and enforceable in accordance with their terms without limitation in time. These could relate to the election or compensation of directors or officers or the creation of various types of securities for new financing or the conduct of business of various kinds or dividend policy or mergers and consolidations or other transactions without limit.

(6) The flexibility permitted by the revision of section 35 in the distribution or reallocation of authority among directors and stockholders has already been mentioned.

(7) Under section 36 the number of directors may be fixed by the by-laws at one or such greater number as may best serve the interests of the shareholders and that number may be increased or decreased from time to time by amendment to, or in the manner provided in, the articles or the by-laws, subject to any limiting provision adopted pursuant to law, such as an agreed requirement for a unanimous vote by directors for any such change or a requirement that amendments to the by-laws be made by shareholder vote. Similarly, under section 53, the incorporation may be effected by a single incorporator or by more as may be desired.

(8) By section 37 directors may be classified. While this relates to directors classified in such manner that the term of office of a specified proportion terminates in each year, the Model Act does not forbid the election of separate directors by separate classes of stock.

(9) Section 40 permits the articles or the by-laws to require more than a majority of the directors to constitute a quorum for the transaction of business and also permits the articles or by-laws to require the act of a greater number than a majority of those present at a meeting where a quorum is present before any specified

business may be transacted. Or a unanimous vote of all directors may be required. This may be utilized to confer a right of veto on any designated class in order to protect its special interests.

(10) By section 50 the authority and duties of the respective officers and agents of the corporation may be tailored and prescribed in the by-laws, or consistently with the by-laws, in such manner as the needs of the shareholders may indicate.

(11) By section 54 the articles may include any desired provision for the regulation of the internal affairs of the corporation, including, in particular, "any provision restricting the transfer of shares." This expressly validates agreements for prior offering of shares to the corporation or other shareholders. All such restrictions must, of course, be clearly shown on the stock certificate as required by the Uniform Commercial Code. A similarly broad provision for the contents of the by-laws is contained in section 27.

(12) By sections 60, 73 and 79, respectively, a class vote may be required for an amendment to the articles, for any merger or consolidation or for a sale of assets other than in the regular course of business.

(13) Section 143 permits the articles to require, for any particular action by the shareholders, the vote or concurrence of the holders of a greater proportion of the shares, or of any class or series thereof, than the Model Act itself requires.

(14) Section 44 permits action by directors without a meeting and section 145 permits the same for shareholders, while section 144 contains a broad provision on waiver of notice. Thus the formality of meetings may, where desired, be eliminated in whole or in part, except for the annual meeting required by section 28.

Under these provisions protection may be afforded for a great diversity of interests. By way of illustration, the shares may be divided into different classes with different voting rights and each class may be permitted to elect a different director. Or some classes may be permitted to vote on certain transactions, but not all. Even more drastically, some classes may be denied all voting rights whatever. Thus a family could provide for equal participation in the profits of the venture, but restrict the power of management to selected members. The

advantages of having a known group of business associates may be safeguarded by restrictions on the transfer of shares. Most commonly this takes the form of a requirement for *pro rata* offering to the other shareholders before selling to an outsider. Or the other shareholders may be given an option, in the event of death or a proposed transfer, to buy the stock *pro rata*. The same option may be given to the corporation. The purchase price may be fixed by any agreed formula, such as adjusted book value or some multiple of recent earnings. Or stockholder agreements may be used to assure that, at least for a limited number of years, all shares will be voted for certain directors and officers, or in a certain way on other corporate matters. Cumulative voting may be provided for, by which each shareholder has a number of votes equal to the number of his shares multiplied by the number of directors to be elected, with the privilege of casting all of his votes for a single candidate, or dividing them as he may wish. This helps minorities obtain representation on the board of directors. Thus the holder of one-fourth of the shares voting, plus one share, is sure of electing one of three directors. The preemptive right is another important protection in the case of close corporations, since it assures each stockholder a right to maintain his proportionate interest. Still more definite protection is afforded by provisions in the articles that prohibit particular transactions except with the assent of a specified percentage of all outstanding shares or of each class of shares. Much the same protection can sometimes be obtained by requiring a specially large quorum for the election of directors, or a specially large vote, or even unanimous vote, by directors for the authorization of particular transactions. Quite the opposite situation exists if one of the participants is to be an inactive investor, for whom non-voting preferred stock, with its prior right to a return from earnings, may be sufficient. But even here he may require a veto power over major transactions, such as the issuance of debt, the issuance of additional preferred shares or mergers or consolidations. Or the preferred shareholders may be given as a class the right to elect one or more of the directors, particularly in the event that dividends should be in arrears.

These possibilities are listed merely as illustrations and not in any sense as exhausting the variations permissible under the Model Act.

SELECTED PROVISIONS OF THE REVISED MODEL BUSINESS CORPORATION ACT*

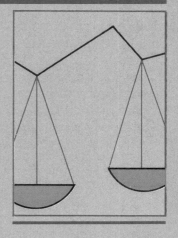

* * *

§ 2.04. Liability for Preincorporation Transactions

All persons purporting to act as or on behalf of a corporation, knowing there was no incorporation under this Act, are jointly and severally liable for all liabilities created while so acting.

* * *

§ 2.06. Bylaws

(a) The incorporators or board of directors of a corporation shall adopt initial bylaws for the corporation.

(b) The bylaws of a corporation may contain any provision for managing the business and regulating the affairs of the corporation that is not inconsistent with law or the articles of incorporation.

* * *

§ 6.21. Issuance of Shares

(a) The powers granted in this section to the board of directors may be reserved to the shareholders by the articles of incorporation.

(b) The board of directors may authorize shares to be issued for consideration consisting of any tangible or intangible property or benefit to the corporation, including cash, promissory notes, services performed, contracts for services to be performed, or other securities of the corporation.

(c) Before the corporation issues shares, the board of directors must determine that the consideration received or to be received for shares to be issued is adequate. That determination by the board of directors is conclusive insofar as the adequacy of consideration for the issuance of shares relates to whether the shares are validly issued, fully paid, and nonassessable.

(d) When the corporation receives the consideration for which the board of directors authorized the issuance of shares, the shares issued therefor are fully paid and nonassessable.

(e) The corporation may place in escrow shares issued for a contract for future services or benefits or a promissory note, or make other arrangements to restrict the transfer of the shares, and may credit distributions in respect of the shares against their purchase price, until the services are performed, the note is paid, or the benefits received. If the services are not performed, the note is not paid, or the benefits are not received, the shares escrowed or restricted and the distributions credited may be cancelled in whole or part.

* * *

---

*Reprinted with permission of the American Bar Foundation, Chicago, Illinois.

§ 7.01. Annual Meeting

(a) A corporation shall hold a meeting of shareholders annually at a time stated in or fixed in accordance with the bylaws.

(b) Annual shareholders' meetings may be held in or out of this state at the place stated in or fixed in accordance with the bylaws. If no place is stated in or fixed in accordance with the bylaws, annual meetings shall be held at the corporation's principal office.

(c) The failure to hold an annual meeting at the time stated in or fixed in accordance with a corporation's bylaws does not affect the validity of any corporate action.

* * *

§ 7.03. Court-Ordered Meeting

(a) The [name or describe] court of the county where a corporation's principal office (or, if none in this state, its registered office) is located may summarily order a meeting to be held:

(1) On application of any shareholder of the corporation entitled to participate in an annual meeting if an annual meeting was not held within the earlier of 6 months after the end of the corporation's fiscal year or 15 months after its last annual meeting; or

(2) on application of a shareholder who signed a demand for a special meeting valid under section 7.02 if:

(i) notice of the special meeting was given within 30 days after the date the demand was delivered to the corporation's secretary; or

(ii) the special meeting was not held in accordance with the notice.

(b) The court may fix the time and place of the meeting, determine the shares entitled to participate in the meeting, specify a record date for determining shareholders entitled to notice of and to vote at the meeting, prescribe the form and content of the meeting notice, fix the quorum required for specific matters to be considered at the meeting (or direct that the votes represented at the meeting constitute a quorum for action on those matters), and enter other orders necessary to accomplish the purpose or purposes of the meeting.

* * *

§ 7.27. Greater Quorum or Voting Requirements

(a) The articles of incorporation may provide for a greater quorum or voting requirement for shareholders (or voting groups of shareholders) than is provided by this Act.

(b) An amendment to the articles of incorporation that adds, changes, or deletes a greater quorum or voting requirement must meet the same quorum requirement and be adopted by the same vote and voting groups required to take action under the quorum and voting requirements then in effect or proposed to be adopted, whichever is greater.

★ ★ ★

§ 7.40. Procedure in Derivative Proceedings

(a) A person may not commence a proceeding in the right of a domestic or foreign corporation unless he was a shareholder of the corporation when the transaction complained of occurred or unless he became a shareholder through transfer by operation of law from one who was a shareholder at that time.

(b) A complaint in a proceeding brought in the right of a corporation must be verified and allege with particularity the demand made, if any, to obtain action by the board of directors and either that the demand was refused or ignored or why he did not make the demand. Whether or not a demand for action was made, if the corporation commences an investigation of the changes made in the demand or complaint, the court may stay any proceeding until the investigation is completed.

(c) A proceeding commenced under this section may not be discontinued or settled without the court's approval. If the court determines that a proposed discontinuance or settlement will substantially affect the interest of the corporation's shareholders or a class of shareholders, the court shall direct that notice be given the shareholders affected.

(d) On termination of the proceeding the court may require the plaintiff to pay any defendant's reasonable expenses (including counsel fees) incurred in defending the proceeding if it finds that the proceeding was commenced without reasonable cause.

(e) For purposes of this section, "shareholder" includes a beneficial owner whose shares are held in a voting trust or held by a nominee on his behalf.

§ 8.01. Requirement for and Duties of Board of Directors

(a) Except as provided in subsection (c), each corporation must have a board of directors.

(b) All corporate powers shall be exercised by or under the authority of, and the business and affairs of the corporation managed under the direction of, its board of directors, subject to any limitation set forth in the articles of incorporation.

(c) A corporation having 50 or fewer shareholders may dispense with or limit the authority of a board of directors by describing in its articles of incorporation who will perform some or all of the duties of a board of directors.

★ ★ ★

§ 8.03. Number and Election Of Directors

(a) A board of directors must consist of one or more individuals, with the number specified in or fixed in accordance with the articles of incorporation or bylaws.

(b) If a board of directors has power to fix or change the number of directors, the board may increase or decrease by 30 percent or less the number of directors last approved by the shareholders, but only the shareholders may increase or decrease by more than 30 percent the number of directors last approved by the shareholders.

(c) The articles of incorporation or bylaws may establish a variable range for the size of the board of directors by fixing a minimum and maximum number of directors. If a variable range is established, the number of directors may be fixed or changed from time to time, within the minimum and maximum, by the shareholders or the board of directors. After shares are issued, only the shareholders may change the range for the size of the board or change from a fixed to a variable-range size board or vice versa.

(d) Directors are elected at the first annual shareholders' meeting and at each annual meeting thereafter unless their terms are staggered under section 8.06.

§ 8.04. Election of Directors by Certain Classes of Shareholders

If the articles of incorporation authorize dividing the shares into classes, the articles may also authorize the election of all or a specified number of directors by the holders of one or more authorized classes of shares. Each class (or classes) of shares entitled to elect one or more directors is a separate voting group for purposes of the election of directors.

★ ★ ★

§ 8.08. Removal of Directors by Shareholders

(a) The shareholders may remove one or more directors with or without cause unless the articles of incorporation provide that directors may be removed only for cause.

(b) If a director is elected by a voting group of shareholders, only the shareholders of that voting group may participate in the vote to remove him.

(c) If cumulative voting is authorized, a director may not be removed if the number of votes sufficient to elect him under cumulative voting is voted against his removal. If cumulative voting is not authorized, a director may be removed only if the number of votes cast to remove him exceeds the number of votes cast not to remove him.

(d) A director may be removed by the shareholders only at a meeting called for the purpose of removing him and the meeting notice must state that the purpose, or one of the purposes, of the meeting is removal of the director.

★ ★ ★

§ 8.24. Quorum and Voting

(a) Unless the articles of incorporation or bylaws require a greater number, a quorum of a board of directors consists of:

(1) a majority of the fixed number of directors if the corporation has a fixed board size; or

(2) a majority of the number of directors prescribed, or if no number is prescribed the number in office immediately before the meeting begins, if the corporation has a variable range size board.

(b) The articles of incorporation or bylaws may authorize a quorum of a board of directors to consist of no fewer than one-third of the fixed or prescribed number of directors determined under subsection (a).

(c) If a quorum is present when a vote is taken, the affirmative vote of a majority of directors present is the act of the board of directors unless the articles of incorporation or bylaws require the vote of a greater number of directors.

(d) A director who is present at a meeting of the board of directors or a committee of the board of directors when corporate action is taken is deemed to have assented to the action taken unless: (1) he objects at the beginning of the meeting (or promptly upon his arrival) to holding it or transacting business at the meeting; (2) his dissent or abstention from the action taken is entered in the minutes of the meeting; or (3) he delivers written notice of his dissent or abstention to the presiding officer of the meeting before its adjournment or to the corporation immediately after adjournment of the meeting. The right of dissent or abstention is not available to a director who votes in favor of the action taken.

§ 8.25. Committees

(a) Unless the articles of incorporation or bylaws provide otherwise, a board of directors may create one or more committees and appoint members of the board of directors to serve on them. Each committee may have two or more members, who serve at the pleasure of the board of directors.

(b) The creation of a committee and appointment of members to it must be approved by the greater of (1) a majority of all the directors in office when the action is taken or (2) the number of directors required by the articles of incorporation or bylaws to take action under section 8.24.

(c) Sections 8.20 through 8.24, which govern meetings, action without meetings, notice and waiver of notice, and quorum and voting requirements of the board of directors, apply to committees and their members as well.

(d) To the extent specified by the board of directors or in the articles of incorporation or bylaws, each committee may exercise the authority of the board of directors under section 8.01.

(e) A committee may not, however:

(1) authorize distributions;

(2) approve or propose to shareholders action that this Act requires to be approved by shareholders;

(3) fill vacancies on the board of directors or on any of its committees;

(4) amend articles of incorporation pursuant to section 10.02;

(5) adopt, amend, or repeal bylaws;

(6) approve a plan of merger not requiring shareholder approval;

(7) authorize or approve reacquisition of shares, except according to a formula or method prescribed by the board of directors; or

(8) authorize or approve the issuance or sale or contract for sale of shares, or determine the designation and relative rights, preferences, and limitations of a class or series of shares, except that the board of directors may authorize a committee (or a senior executive officer of the corporation) to do so within limits specifically prescribed by the board of directors.

(f) The creation of, delegation of authority to, or action by a committee does not alone constitute compliance by a director with the standards of conduct described in section 8.30.

★ ★ ★

§ 8.30. General Standards for Directors

(a) A director shall discharge his duties as a director, including his duties as a member of a committee:

(1) in good faith;

(2) with the care an ordinarily prudent person in a like position would exercise under similar circumstances; and

(3) in a manner he reasonably believes to be in the best interests of the corporation.

(b) In discharging his duties a director is entitled to rely on information, opinions, reports, or statements, including financial statements and other financial data, if prepared or presented by:

(1) one or more officers or employees of the corporation whom the director reasonably believes to be reliable and competent in the matters presented;

(2) legal counsel, public accountants, or other persons as to matters the director reasonably believes are within the person's professional or expert competence; or

(3) a committee of the board of directors of which he is not a member if the director reasonably believes the committee merits confidence.

(c) A director is not acting in good faith if he has knowledge concerning the matter in question that makes reliance otherwise permitted by subsection (b) unwarranted.

(d) A director is not liable for any action taken as a director, or any failure to take any action, if he performed the duties of his office in compliance with this section.

§ 8.31. Director Conflict of Interest

(a) A conflict of interest transaction is a transaction with the corporation in which a director of the corporation has a direct or indirect interest. A conflict of interest transaction is not voidable by the corporation solely because of the director's interest in the transaction if any one of the following is true:

(1) the material facts of the transaction and the director's interest were disclosed or known to the board of directors or a committee of the board of directors and the board of directors or committee authorized, approved, or ratified the transaction;

(2) the material facts of the transaction and the director's interest were disclosed or known to the shareholders entitled to vote and they authorized, approved, or ratified the transaction; or

(3) the transaction was fair to the corporation.

(b) For purposes of this section, a director of the corporation has an indirect interest in a transaction if (1) another entity in which he has a material financial interest or in which he is a general partner is a party to the transaction or (2) another entity of which he is a director, officer, or trustee is a party to the transaction and the transaction is or should be considered by the board of directors of the corporation.

(c) For purposes of subsection (a)(1), a conflict of interest transaction is authorized, approved, or ratified if it receives the affirmative vote of a majority of the directors on the board of directors (or on the committee) who have no direct or indirect interest in the transaction, but a transaction may not be authorized, approved, or ratified under this section by a single director. If a majority of the directors who have no direct or indirect

interest in the transaction vote to authorize, approve, or ratify the transaction, a quorum is present for the purpose of taking action under this section. The presence of, or vote cast by, a director with a direct or indirect interest in the transaction does not affect the validity of any action taken under subsection (a)(1) if the transaction is otherwise authorized, approved, or ratified as provided in that subsection.

(d) For purposes of subsection (a)(2), a conflict of interest transaction is authorized, approved, or ratified if it receives the vote of a majority of the shares entitled to be counted under this subsection. Shares owned by or voted under the control of a director who has a direct or indirect interest in the transaction, and shares owned by or voted under the control of an entity described in subsection (b)(1), may not be counted in a vote of shareholders to determine whether to authorize, approve, or ratify a conflict of interest transaction under subsection (a)(2). The vote of those shares, however, shall be counted in determining whether the transaction is approved under other sections of this Act. A majority of the shares, whether or not present, that are entitled to be counted in a vote on the transaction under this subsection constitutes a quorum for the purpose of taking action under this section.

§ 8.32. Loans to Directors

(a) Except as provided by subsection (c), a corporation may not lend money to or guarantee the obligation of a director of the corporation unless:

(1) the particular loan or guarantee is approved by a majority of the votes represented by the outstanding voting shares of all classes, voting as a single voting group, except the votes of shares owned by or voted under the control of the benefited director; or

(2) the corporation's board of directors determines that the loan or guarantee benefits the corporation and either approves the specific loan or guarantee or a general plan authorizing loans and guarantees.

(b) The fact that a loan or guarantee is made in violation of this section does not affect the borrower's liability on the loan.

(c) This section does not apply to loans and guarantees authorized by statute regulating any special class of corporations.

★ ★ ★

§ 8.40. Required Officers

(a) A corporation has the officers described in its bylaws or appointed by the board of directors in accordance with the bylaws.

(b) A duly appointed officer may appoint one or more officers or assistant officers if authorized by the bylaws or the board of directors.

(c) The bylaws or the board of directors shall delegate to one of the officers responsibility for preparing minutes of the directors' and shareholders' meetings and for authenticating records of the corporation.

(d) The same individual may simultaneously hold more than one office in a corporation.

★   ★   ★

§ 8.42. Standards of Conduct for Officers

(a) An officer with discretionary authority shall discharge his duties under that authority:

(1) in good faith;

(2) with the care an ordinarily prudent person in a like position would exercise under similar circumstances; and

(3) in a manner he reasonably believes to be in the best interests of the corporation.

(b) In discharging his duties an officer is entitled to rely on information, opinions, reports, or statements, including financial statements and other financial data, if prepared or presented by:

(1) one or more officers or employees of the corporation whom the officer reasonably believes to be reliable and competent in the matters presented; or

(2) legal counsel, public accountants, or other persons as to matters the officer reasonably believes are within the person's professional or expert competence.

(c) An officer is not acting in good faith if he has knowledge concerning the matter in question that makes reliance otherwise permitted by subsection (b) unwarranted.

(d) An officer is not liable for any action taken as an officer, or any failure to take any action, if he performed the duties of his office in compliance with this section.

★   ★   ★

§ 10.02. Amendment by Board of Directors

Unless the articles of incorporation provide otherwise, a corporation's board of directors may adopt one or more amendments to the corporation's articles of incorporation without shareholder action:

(1) to extend the duration of the corporation if it was incorporated at a time when limited duration was required by law;

(2) to delete the names and addresses of the initial directors;

(3) to delete the name and address of the initial registered agent or registered office, if a statement of change is on file with the secretary of state;

(4) to change each issued and unissued authorized share of an outstanding class into a greater number of whole shares if the corporation has only shares of that class outstanding;

(5) to change the corporate name by substituting the word "corporation," "incorporated," "company," "limited," or the abbreviation "corp.," "inc.," "co.," or "ltd.," for a similar word or abbreviation in the name, or by adding, deleting, or changing a geographical attribution for the name; or

(6) to make any other change expressly permitted by this Act to be made without shareholder action.

§ 10.03. Amendment by Board of Directors and Shareholders

(a) A corporation's board of directors may propose one or more amendments to the articles of incorporation for submission to the shareholders.

(b) For the amendment to be adopted:

(1) the board of directors must recommend the amendment to the shareholders unless the board of directors determines that because of conflict of interest or other special circumstances it should make no recommendation and communicates the basis for its determination to the shareholders with the amendment; and

(2) the shareholders entitled to vote on the amendment must approve the amendment as provided in subsection (e).

(c) The board of directors may condition its submission of the proposed amendment on any basis.

(d) The corporation shall notify each shareholder, whether or not entitled to vote, of the proposed shareholders' meeting in accordance with section 7.05. The notice of meeting must also state that the purpose, or one of the purposes, of the meeting is to consider the proposed amendment and contain or be accompanied by a copy or summary of the amendment.

(e) Unless this Act, the articles of incorporation, or the board of directors (acting pursuant to subsection (c)) require a greater vote or a vote by voting groups, the amendment to be adopted must be approved by:

(1) a majority of the votes entitled to be cast on the amendment by any voting group with respect to which the amendment would create dissenters' rights; and

(2) the votes required by sections 7.25 and 7.26 by every other voting group entitled to vote on the amendment.

§ 10.04. **Voting on Amendments by Voting Groups**

(a) The holders of the outstanding shares of a class are entitled to vote as a separate voting group (if shareholder voting is otherwise required by this Act) on a proposed amendment if the amendment would:

    (1) increase or decrease the aggregate number of authorized shares of the class;

    (2) effect an exchange or reclassification of all or part of the shares of the class into shares of another class;

    (3) effect an exchange or reclassification, or create the right of exchange, of all or part of the shares of another class into shares of the class;

    (4) change the designation, rights, preferences, or limitations of all or part of the shares of the class;

    (5) change the shares of all or part of the class into a different number of shares of the same class;

    (6) create a new class of shares having rights or preferences with respect to distributions or to dissolution that are prior, superior, or substantially equal to the shares of the class;

    (7) increase the rights, preferences, or number of authorized shares of any class that, after giving effect to the amendment, have rights or preferences with respect to distributions or to dissolution that are prior, superior, or substantially equal to the shares of the class;

    (8) limit or deny an existing preemptive right of all or part of the shares of the class; or

    (9) cancel or otherwise affect rights to distributions or dividends that have accumulated but not yet been declared on all or part of the shares of the class.

(b) If a proposed amendment would affect a series of a class of shares in one or more of the ways described in subsection (a), the shares of that series are entitled to vote as a separate voting group on the proposed amendment.

(c) If a proposed amendment that entitles two or more series of shares to vote as separate voting groups under this section would affect those two or more series in the same or a substantially similar way, the shares of all the series so affected must vote together as a single voting group on the proposed amendment.

(d) A class or series of shares is entitled to the voting rights granted by this section although the articles of incorporation provide that the shares are nonvoting shares.

★   ★   ★

§ 11.01. **Merger**

(a) One or more corporations may merge into another corporation if the board of directors of each corporation adopts and its shareholders (if required by section 11.03) approve a plan of merger.

(b) The plan of merger must set forth:

    (1) the name of each corporation planning to merge and the name of the surviving corporation into which each other corporation plans to merge;

    (2) the terms and conditions of the merger; and

    (3) the manner and basis of converting the shares of each corporation into shares, obligations, or other securities of the surviving or any other corporation or into cash or other property in whole or part.

(c) The plan of merger may set forth:

    (1) amendments to the articles of incorporation of the surviving corporation; and

    (2) other provisions relating to the merger.

★   ★   ★

§ 14.07. **Unknown Claims Against Dissolved Corporation**

(a) A dissolved corporation may also publish notice of its dissolution and request that persons with claims against the corporation present them in accordance with the notice.

(b) The notice must:

    (1) be published one time in a newspaper of general circulation in the county where the dissolved corporation's principal office (or, if none in this state, its registered office) is or was last located;

    (2) describe the information that must be included in a claim and provide a mailing address where the claim may be sent; and

    (3) state that a claim against the corporation will be barred unless a proceeding to enforce the claim is commenced within five years after the publication of the notice.

(c) If the dissolved corporation publishes a newspaper notice in accordance with subsection (b), the claim of each of the following claimants is barred unless the claimant commences a proceeding to enforce the claim against the dissolved corporation within five years after the publication date of the newspaper notice:

    (1) a claimant who did not receive written notice under section 14.06;

    (2) a claimant whose claim was timely sent to the dissolved corporation but not acted on;

(3) a claimant whose claim is contingent or based on an event occurring after the effective date of dissolution.

(d) A claim may be enforced under this section:

(1) against the dissolved corporation, to the extent of its undistributed assets; or

(2) if the assets have been distributed in liquidation, against a shareholder of the dissolved corporation to the extent of his pro rata share of the claim or the corporate assets distributed to him in liquidation, whichever is less, but a shareholder's total liability for all claims under this section may not exeed the total amount of assets distributed to him.

§ 14.20. **Grounds for Administrative Dissolution**

The secretary of state may commence a proceeding under section 14.21 to administratively dissolve a corporation if:

(1) the corporation does not pay within 60 days after they are due any franchise taxes or penalties imposed by this Act or other law;

(2) the corporation does not deliver its annual report to the secretary of state within 60 days after it is due;

(3) the corporation is without a registered agent or registered office in this state for 60 days or more;

(4) the corporation does not notify the secretary of state within 60 days that its registered agent or registered office has been changed, that its registered agent has resigned, or that its registered office has been discontinued; or

(5) the corporation's period of duration stated in its articles of incorporation expires.

★　★　★

§ 14.30. **Grounds For Judicial Dissolution**

The [name or describe court or courts] may dissolve a corporation:

(1) in a proceeding by the attorney general if it is established that:

(i) the corporation obtained its articles of incorporation through fraud; or

(ii) the corporation has continued to exceed or abuse the authority conferred upon it by law;

(2) in a proceeding by a shareholder if it is established that:

(i) the directors are deadlocked in the management of the corporate affairs, the shareholders are unable to break the deadlock, and irreparable injury to the corporation is threatened or being suffered, or the business and affairs of the cor-

poration can no longer be conducted to the advantage of the shareholders generally, because of the deadlock;

(ii) the directors or those in control of the corporation have acted, are acting, or will act in a manner that is illegal, oppressive, or fraudulent;

(iii) the shareholders are deadlocked in voting power and have failed, for a period that includes at least two consecutive annual meeting dates, to elect successors to directors whose terms have expired; or

(iv) the corporate assets are being misapplied or wasted;

(3) in a proceeding by a creditor if it is established that:

(i) the creditor's claim has been reduced to judgment, the execution on the judgment returned unsatisfied, and the corporation is insolvent; or

(ii) the corporation has admitted in writing that the creditor's claim is due and owing and the corporation is insolvent; or

(4) in a proceeding by the corporation to have its voluntary dissolution continued under court supervision.

★　★　★

§ 15.01 **Authority to Transact Business Required**

(a) A foreign corporation may not transact business in this state until it obtains a certificate of authority from the secretary of state.

(b) The following activities, among others, do not constitute transacting business within the meaning of subsection (a):

(1) maintaining, defending, or settling any proceeding;

(2) holding meetings of the board of directors or shareholders or carrying on other activities concerning internal corporate affairs;

(3) maintaining bank accounts;

(4) maintaining offices or agencies for the transfer, exchange, and registration of the corporation's own securities or maintaining trustees or depositaries with respect to those securities;

(5) selling through independent contractors;

(6) soliciting or obtaining orders, whether by mail or through employees or agents or otherwise, if the orders require acceptance outside this state before they become contracts;

(7) creating or acquiring indebtedness, mortgages, and security interests in real or personal property;

(8) securing or collecting debts or enforcing mortgages and security interests in property securing the debts;

(9) owning, without more, real or personal property;

(10) conducting an isolated transaction that is completed within 30 days and that is not one in the course of repeated transactions of a like nature;

(11) transacting business in interstate commerce.

(c) The list of activities in subsection (b) is not exhaustive.

★ ★ ★

§ 16.02. **Inspection of Records by Shareholders**

(a) A shareholder of a corporation is entitled to inspect and copy, during regular business hours at the corporation's principal office, any of the records of the corporation described in section 16.01(e) if he gives the corporation written notice of his demand at least five business days before the date on which he wishes to inspect and copy.

(b) A shareholder of a corporation is entitled to inspect and copy, during regular business hours at a reasonable location specified by the corporation, any of the following records of the corporation if the shareholder meets the requirements of subsection (c) and gives the corporation written notice of his demand at least five business days before the date on which he wishes to inspect and copy:

(1) excerpts from minutes of any meeting of the board of directors, records of any action of a committee of the board of directors while acting in place of the board of directors on behalf of the corporation, minutes of any meeting of the shareholders, and records of action taken by the shareholders or board of directors without a meeting, to the extent not subject to inspection under section 16.02(a);

(2) accounting records of the corporation; and

(3) the record of shareholders.

(c) A shareholder may inspect and copy the records identified in subsection (b) only if:

(1) his demand is made in good faith and for a proper purpose;

(2) he describes with reasonable particularity his purpose and the records he desires to inspect; and

(3) the records are directly connected with his purpose.

(d) The right of inspection granted by this section may not be abolished or limited by a corporation's articles of incorporation or bylaws.

(e) This section does not affect:

(1) the right of a shareholder to inspect records under section 7.20 or, if the shareholder is in litigation with the corporation, to the same extent as any other litigant;

(2) the power of a court, independently of this Act, to compel the production of corporate records for examination.

§ 16.03. **Scope of Inspection Right**

(a) A shareholder's agent or attorney has the same inspection and copying rights as the shareholder he represents.

(b) The right to copy records under section 16.02 includes, if reasonable, the right to receive copies made by photographic, xerographic, or other means.

(c) The corporation may impose a reasonable charge, covering the costs of labor and material, for copies of any documents provided to the shareholder. The charge may not exceed the estimated cost of production or reproduction of the records.

(d) The corporation may comply with a shareholder's demand to inspect the record of shareholders under section 16.02(b)(3) by providing him with a list of its shareholders that was compiled no earlier than the date of the shareholder's demand.

★ ★ ★

§ 16.21. **Other Reports to Shareholders**

(a) If a corporation indemnifies or advances expenses to a director under section 8.51, 8.52, 8.53, or 8.54 in connection with a proceeding by or in the right of the corporation, the corporation shall report the indemnification or advance in writing to the shareholders with or before the notice of the next shareholders' meeting.

(b) If a corporation issues or authorizes the issuance of shares for promissory notes or for promises to render services in the future, the corporation shall report in writing to the shareholders the number of shares authorized or issued, and the consideration received by the corporation, with or before the notice of the next shareholders' meeting.

★ ★ ★

SPANISH EQUIVALENTS FOR IMPORTANT LEGAL TERMS IN ENGLISH

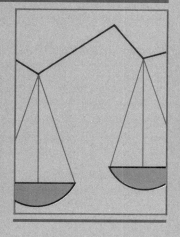

Abandoned property: bienes abandonados

Acceptance: aceptación; consentimiento; acuerdo

Acceptor: aceptante

Accession: toma de posesión; aumento; accesión

Accommodation indorser: avalista de favor

Accommodation party: firmante de favor

Accord: acuerdo; convenio; arreglo

Accord and satisfaction; transacción ejecutada

Act of state doctrine: doctrina de acto de gobierno

Administrative law: derecho administrativo

Administrative process: procedimiento o método administrativo

Administrator (-trix): administrador (-a)

Adverse possession: posesión de hecho susceptible de proscripción adquisitiva

Affirmative action: acción afirmativa

Affirmative defense: defensa afirmativa

After-acquired property: bienes adquiridos con posterioridad a un hecho dado

Agency: mandato; agencia

Agent: mandatorio; agente; representante

Agreement: convenio; acuerdo; contrato

Alien corporation: empresa extranjera

Allonge: hojas adicionales de endosos

Answer: contestación de la demande; alegato

Anticipatory breach, or anticipatory repudiation: anuncio previo de las partes de su imposibilidad de cumplir con el contrato

Appeal: apelación; recurso de apelación

Appellate jurisdiction: jurisdicción de apelaciones

Appraisal right: derecho de valuación

Abritration: arbitraje

Arson: incendio intencional

Articles of partnership: contrato social

Artisian's lien: derecho de retención que ejerce al artesano

Assault: asalto; ataque; agresión

Assignment of rights: transmisión; transferencia; cesión

Assumption of risk: no resarcimiento por exposición voluntaria al peligro

Attachment: auto judicial que autoriza el embargo; embargo

Bailee: depositario

Bailment: depósito; constitución en depósito

Bailor: depositante

Bankruptcy trustee: síndico de la quiebra

Battery: agresión; física

Bearer: portador; tenedor

Bearer instrument: documento al portador

Bequest or legacy: legado (de bienes muebles)

Bilateral contract: contrato bilateral

Bill of lading: conocimiento de embarque; carta de porte

Bill of Rights: declaración de derechos

Binder: póliza de seguro provisoria; recibo de pago a cuenta del precio

Blank indorsement: endoso en blanco

Blue Sky laws: leyes reguladoras del comercio bursátil

Bond: título de crédito; garantía; caución

Bond indenture: contrato de emisión de bonos; contrato del empréstito

Breach of contract: incumplimiento de contrato

Brief: escrito; resumen; informe

Burglary; violación de domicilio

Business judgment rule: regla de juicio comercial

Business tort: agravio comercial

Case law: ley de casos; derecho casuístico

Cashier's check: cheque de caja

Causation in fact: causalidad en realidad

Cease-and-desist order: orden para cesar y desistir

Certificate of deposit: certificado de depósito

Certified check: cheque certificado

Charitable trust: fideicomiso para fines benéficos

Chattel: bien mueble

Check: cheque

Chose in action: derecho inmaterial; derecho de acción

Civil law: derecho civil

Close corporation: sociedad de un solo accionista o de un grupo restringido de accionistas

Closed shop: taller agremiado (emplea solamente a miembros de un gremio)

Closing argument: argumento al final

Codicil: codicilo

Collateral: garantía; bien objeto de la garantía real

Comity: cortesía; cortesía entre naciones

Commercial paper: instrumentos negociables; documentos a valores commerciales

Common law: derecho consuetudinario; derecho común; ley común

Common stock: acción ordinaria

Comparative negligence: negligencia comparada

Compensatory damages: daños y perjuicios reales o compensatorios

Concurrent conditions: condiciones concurrentes

Concurrent estates: condominio

Concurrent jurisdiction: competencia concurrente de varios tribunales para entender en una misma causa

Concurring opinion: opinión concurrente

Condition: condición

Condition precedent: condición suspensiva

Condition subsequent: condición resolutoria
Confiscation: confiscación
Confusion: confusión; fusión
Conglomerate merger: fusión de firmas que operan en distintos mercados
Consent decree: acuerdo entre las partes aprobado por un tribunal
Consequential damages: daños y perjuicios indirectos
Consideration: consideración; motivo; contraprestación
Consolidation: consolidación
Constructive delivery: entrega simbólica
Constructive trust: fideicomiso creado por aplicación de la ley
Consumer-protection law: ley para proteger el consumidor
Contract: contrato
Contracts under seal: contrato formal o sellado
Contributory negligence: negligencia de la parte actora
Conversion: usurpación; conversión de valores
Copyright: derecho de autor
Corporation: sociedad anómina; corporación; persona juridica
Co-sureties: cogarantes
Counterclaim, or cross-complaint: reconvención; contrademanda
Counteroffer: contraoferta
Course of dealing: curso de transacciones
Course of performance: curso de cumplimiento
Covenant: pacto; garantía; contrato
Covenant not to sue: pacto or contrato a no demandar
Covenant of quiet enjoyment: garantía del uso y goce pacífico del inmueble
Creditors' composition agreement: concordato preventivo
Crime: crimen; delito; contravención
Criminal law: derecho penal

Cross-examination: contrainterrogatorio
Cure: cura; cuidado; derecho de remediar un vicio contractual
Customs receipts: recibos de derechos aduaneros

Damages: daños; indemnización por daños y perjuicios
Debit card: tarjeta de débito
Debtor: deudor
Debt securities: seguridades de deuda
Deceptive advertising: publicidad engañosa
Deed: escritura; título; acta translativa de domino
Defamation: difamación
Delegation of duties: delegación de obligaciones
Demand deposit: depósito a la vista
Depositions: declaración de un testigo fuera del tribunal
Derivative suit: acción judicial entablada por un accionista en nombre de la sociedad
Devise: legado; deposición testamentaria (bienes inmuebles)
Directed verdict: veredicto según orden del juez y sin participación activa del jurado
Direct examination: interrogatorio directo; primer interrogatorio
Disaffirmance: repudiación; renuncia; anulación
Discharge: descargo; liberación; cumplimiento
Disclosed principal: mandante revelado
Discovery: descubrimiento; producción de la prueba
Dissenting opinion: opinión disidente
Dissolution: disolución; terminación
Diversity of citizenship: competencia de los tribunales federales para entender en causas cuyas partes intervinientes son cuidadanos de distintos estados
Divestiture: extinción premature de derechos reales

Dividend: dividendo
Docket: orden del día; lista de causas pendientes
Domestic corporation: sociedad local
Draft: orden de pago; letrade cambio
Drawee: girado; beneficiario
Drawer: librador
Duress: coacción; violencia

Easement: servidumbre
Embezzlement: desfalco; malversación
Eminent domain: poder de expropiación
Employment discrimination: discriminación en el empleo
Entrepreneur: empresario
Environmental law: ley ambiental
Equal dignity rule: regla de dignidad egual
Equity security: tipo de participación en una sociedad
Estate: propiedad; patrimonio; derecho
Estop: impedir; prevenir
Ethical issue: cuestión ética
Exclusive jurisdiction: competencia exclusiva
Exculpatory clause: cláusula eximente
Executed contract: contrato ejecutado
Execution: ejecución; cumplimiento
Executor (-trix): albacea
Executory contract: contrato aún no completamente consumado
Executory interest: derecho futuro
Express contract: contrato expreso
Expropriation: expropiación

Federal question: caso federal
Fee simple: pleno dominio; dominio absoluto
Fee simple absolute: dominio absoluto
Fee simple defeasible: dominio sujeta a una condición resolutoria
Felony: crimen; delito grave

Fictitious payee: beneficiario ficticio
Fiduciary: fiduciaro
Firm offer: oferta en firme
Fixture: inmueble por destino, incorporación a anexación
Floating lien: gravamen continuado
Foreign corporation: sociedad extranjera; U.S. sociedad constituída en otro estado
Forgery: falso; falsificación
Formal contract: contrato formal
Franchise: privilegio; franquicia; concesión
Franchisee: persona que recibe una concesión
Franchisor: persona que vende una concesión
Fraud: fraude; dolo; engaño
Future estate; bien futuro

Garnishment: embargo de derechos
General partner: socio comanditario
General warranty deed: escritura translativa de domino con garantía de título
Gift: donación
Gift *causa mortis:* donación por causa de muerte
Gift *inter vivos:* donación entre vivos
Good faith: buena fe
Good-faith purchaser: comprador de buena fe

Holder: tenedor por contraprestación
Holder in due course: tenedor legítimo
Holographic will: testamento ológrafico
Homestead exemption laws: leyes que exceptúan las casas de familia de ejecución por duedas generales
Horizontal merger: fusión horizontal

Identification: identificación
Implied-in-fact contract: contrato implícito en realidad

Implied warranty: guarantía implícita
Implied warranty of merchantability: garantía implícita de vendibilidad
Impossibility of performance: imposibilidad de cumplir un contrato
Imposter: imposter
Incidental beneficiary: beneficiario incidental; beneficiario secundario
Incidental damages: daños incidentales
Indictment: auto de acusación; acusación
Indorsee: endorsatario
Indorsement: endoso
Indorser: endosante
Informal contract: contrato no formal; contrato verbal
Information: acusación hecha por el ministerio público
Injunction: mandamiento; orden de no innovar
Innkeeper's lien: derecho de retención que ejerce el posadero
Installment contract: contrato de pago en cuotas
Insurable interest: interés asegurable
Intended beneficiary: beneficiario destinado
Intentional tort: agravio; cuasi-delito intenciónal
International law: derecho internaciónal
Interrogatories: preguntas escritas sometidas por una parte a la otra o a un testigo
Inter vivos **trust:** fideicomiso entre vivos
Intestacy laws: leyes de la condición de morir intestado
Intestate: intestado
Investment company: compañia de inversiones
Issue: emisión

Joint tenancy: derechos conjuntos en un bien inmueble
Joint tenancy with right of survivorship: derechos conjuntos en un bien inmueble en favor del beneficiario sobreviviente

Judgment n.o.v.: juicio no obstante veredicto
Judgment rate of interest: interés de juicio
Judicial process: acto de procedimiento; proceso jurídico
Judicial review: revisión judicial
Jurisdiction: jurisdicción

Larceny: robo; hurto
Law: derecho; ley; jurisprudencia
Lease: contrato de locación; contrato de alquiler
Leasehold estate: bienes forales
Legal rate of interest: interés legal
Legatee: legatario
Less-than-freehold estate: menos de derecho de dominio absoluto
Letter of credit: carta de crédito
Levy: embargo; comiso
Libel: libelo; difamación escrita
Life estate: usufructo
Limited partner: comanditario
Limited partnership: sociedad en comandita
Liquidation: liquidación; realización
Lost property: objetos perdidos

Majority opinion: opinión de la mayoría
Maker: persona que realiza u ordena; librador
Mechanic's lien: gravamen de constructor
Mediation: mediación; intervención
Merger: fusión
Mirror-image rule: fallo de reflejo
Misdemeanor: infracción; contravención
Mislaid property: bienes extraviados
Mitigation of damages: reducción de daños
Moral hazard: riesgo moral
Mortgage: hypoteca
Motion to dismiss, or demurrer: excepción parentoria
Municipal law: derecho municipal

Mutual fund: fondo mutual

Negotiable instrument: instrumento negociable
Negotiation: negociación
Nominal damages: daños y perjuicios nominales
Novation: novación
Nuncupative will: testamento nuncupativo

Objective theory of contracts: teoria objetiva de contratos
Offer: oferta
Offeree: persona que recibe una oferta
Offeror: oferente
Order paper: instrumento o documento a la orden
Original jurisdiction: jurisdicción de primera instancia
Output contract: contrato de producción

Parol evidence rule: regla relativa a la prueba oral
Partially disclosed principal: mandante revelado en parte
Partnership: sociedad colectiva; asociación; asociación de participación
Past consideration: causa o contraprestación anterior
Patent: patente; privilegio
Pattern or practice: muestra o práctica
Payee: beneficiario de un pago
Penalty: pena; penalidad
Per capita: por cabeza
Perfection: perfeción
Performance: cumplimiento; ejecución
Personal defenses: excepciones personales
Personal property: bienes muebles
Per stirpes: por estirpe
Plea bargaining: regateo por un alegato
Pleadings: alegatos
Pledge: prenda
Police powers: poders de policia y de prevención del crimen
Policy: póliza

Positive law: derecho positivo; ley positiva
Possibility of reverter: posibilidad de reversión
Precedent: precedente
Preemptive right: derecho de prelación
Preferred stock: acciones preferidas
Premium: recompensa; prima
Presentment warranty: garantía de presentación
Price discrimination: discriminación en los precios
Principal: mandante; principal
Privity: nexo jurídico
Privity of contract: relación contractual
Probable cause: causa probable
Probate: verificación; verificación del testamento
Probate court: tribunal de sucesiones y tutelas
Proceeds: resultados; ingresos
Profit: beneficio; utilidad; lucro
Promise: promesa
Promisee: beneficiario de una promesa
Promisor: promtente
Promissory estoppel: impedimento promisorio
Promissory note: pagaré; nota de pago
Promoter: promotor; fundador
Proximate cause: causa inmediata o próxima
Proxy: apoderado; poder
Punitive, or exemplary, damages: daños y perjuicios punitivos o ejemplares

Qualified indorsement: endoso con reservas
Quasi-contract: contrato tácito o implícito
Quit-claim deed: acto de transferencia de una propiedad por finiquito, pero sin ninguna garantía sobre la validez del título transferido

Ratification: ratificación
Real defenses: defensas legitimas o legales

Real property: bienes inmuebles
Reasonable doubt: duda razonable
Rebuttal: refutación
Recognizance: promesa; compromiso; reconocimiento
Recording statutes: leyes estatales sobre registros oficiales
Redress: reparación
Reformation: rectificación; reforma; corrección
Rejoinder: dúplica; contrarréplica
Release: liberación; renuncia a un derecho
Remainder: substitución; reversión
Remedy: recurso; remedio; reparación
Replevin: acción reivindicatoria; reivindicación
Reply: réplica
Requirements contract: contrato de suministro
Rescission: rescisión
Res judicata: cosa juzgada; res judicata
Respondeat superior: responsabilidad del mandante o del maestro
Restitution: restitución
Restrictive indorsement: endoso restrictivo
Resulting trust: fideicomiso implícito
Reversion: reversión; sustitución
Revocation: revocación; derogación
Right of contribution: derecho de contribución
Right of reimbursement: derecho de reembolso
Right of subrogation: derecho de subrogación
Right-to-work law: ley de libertad de trabajo
Robbery: robo
Rule 10b-5: Regla 10b-5

Sale: venta; contrato de compreventa
Sale on approval: venta a ensayo; venta sujeta a la aprobación del comprador

Sale or return: venta con derecho de devolución

Sales contract: contrato de compraventa; boleto de compraventa

Satisfaction: satisfacción; pago

Scienter: a sabiendas

S corporation: S corporación

Secured party: acreedor garantizado

Secured transaction: transacción garantizada

Securities: volares; titulos; seguridades

Security agreement: convenio de seguridad

Security interest: interés en un bien dado en garantía que permite a quien lo detenta venderlo en caso de incumplimiento

Service mark: marca de identificación de servicios

Signature: firma; rúbrica

Slander: difamación oral; calumnia

Sovereign immunity: immunidad soberana

Special indorsement: endoso especial; endoso a la orden de una person en particular

Specific performance: ejecución precisa, según los términos del contrato

Spendthrift trust: fideicomiso para pródigos

Stale check: cheque vencido

Stare decisis: acatar las decisiones, observar los precedentes

State exemption laws: leyes que exceptúan los estados

Statutory law: derecho estatutario; derecho legislado; derecho escrito

Stock: acciones

Stock split: fraccionamiento de acciones

Stock warrant: certificado para la compra de acciones

Stop-payment order: orden de suspensión del pago de un cheque dada por el librador del mismo

Strict liability: responsabilidad uncondicional

Summary judgment: fallo sumario

Tangible property: bienes corpóreos

Tenancy at will: inguilino por tiempo indeterminado (según la voluntad del propietario)

Tenancy by sufferance: posesión por tolerancia

Tenancy by the entirety: locación conyugal conjunta

Tenancy for years: inguilino por un término fijo

Tenancy in common: specie de copropiedad indivisa

Tender: oferta de pago; oferta de ejecución

Testamentary trust: fideicomiso testamentario

Testator (-trix): testador (-a)

Third-party-beneficiary contract: contrato para el beneficio del tercero-beneficiario

Tort: agravio; cuasi-delito

Totten trust: fideicomiso creado por un depósito bancario

Trade acceptance: letra de cambio aceptada

Trademark: marca registrada

Trade name: nombre comercial; razón social

Traveler's check: cheque del viajero

Trespass to land: ingreso no authorizado a las tierras de otro

Trespass to personalty: violación de los derechos posesorios de un tercero con respecto a bienes muebles

Trust: fideicomiso; trust

Ultra vires: ultra vires; fuera de la facultad (de una sociedad anónima)

Unanimous opinion: opinión unámine

Unconscionable contract or clause: contrato leonino; cláusula leonino

Underwriter: subscriptor; asegurador

Unenforceable contract: contrato que no se puede hacer cumplir

Unilateral contract: contrato unilateral

Union shop: taller agremiado; empresa en la que todos los empleados son miembros del gremio o sindicato

Usge of trade: uso comercial

Usury: usura

Valid contract: contrato válido

Venue: lugar; sede del proceso

Vertical merger: fusión vertical de empresas

Voidable contract: contrato anulable

Void contract: contrato nulo; contrato inválido, sin fuerza legal

Voir dire: examen preliminar de un testigo a jurado por el tribunal para determinar su competencia

Voting trust: fideicomiso para ejercer el derecho de voto

Waiver: renuncia; abandono

Warranty of habitability: garantía de habitabilidad

Warranty of possession: garantía de posesión

Watered stock: acciones diluídos; capital inflado

White-collar crime: crimen administrativo

Writ of attachment: mandamiento de ejecución; mandamiento de embargo

Writ of certiorari: auto de avocación; auto de certiorari

Writ of execution: auto ejecutivo; mandamiento de ejecutión

Writ of mandamus: auto de mandamus; mandamiento; orden judicial

GLOSSARY

A

abandoned property Property over which the owner has given up dominion and control with no intention of recovering it.

abandonment In landlord-tenant law, a tenant's moving off the premises completely with no intention of returning before the end of the lease term.

acceleration clause A clause in a contract for rent, or for installment payments, which provides that all future payments will become due immediately upon the failure to tender timely payments or upon the occurrence of an event.

acceptance (1) In contract law the offeree's notification to the offeror that the offeree agrees to be bound by the terms of the offeror's proposal. Although historically the terms of acceptance had to be the mirror image of the terms of the offer, the UCC provides that even modified terms of the offer in a definite expression of acceptance constitute a contract. (2) In commercial paper law, the drawee's signed agreement to pay a draft when presented.

acceptor The person (the drawee) who accepts a draft and who engages to be primarily responsible for its payment.

accession (1) The changing (through manufacturing) of one good into a new good (*i.e.*, flour into bread). (2) The right to all that one's property produces (*i.e.*, fruit from trees) or to that which becomes added to or incorporated to that property (*i.e.*, buildings on one's land). (3) The right, upon payment for the original materials, to keep an article manufactured out of goods that were innocently converted. (see *conversion*)

accommodation party A person who signs an instrument for the purpose of lending that person's credit to another party on that instrument.

accord An agreement between two persons, one of whom has a right of action against the other, to settle a contractual obligation.

accord and satisfaction An agreement and payment (or other performance) between two parties, one of whom has a right of action against the other. After the agreement has been made and payment or other performance has been tendered, the "accord and satisfaction" is complete.

accredited investors In the context of securities offerings, "sophisticated" investors, such as banks, insurance companies, investment companies, the issuer's executive officers and directors, and persons whose income or net worth exceeds certain limits.

act of state doctrine A doctrine that provides that the judicial branch will not examine the validity of acts by a foreign nation within its own territory.

adhesion contracts Standard "form" contracts, such as those between a large retailer and a consumer, whereby the stronger party dictates the terms.

administrative agencies Governmental bodies charged with administering and implementing particular legislation. Sometimes called boards, bureaus, commissions, departments, divisions, or corporations (for example, the Federal Deposit Insurance Corporation).

administrative law A body of law created by administrative agencies such as the Securities and Exchange Commission and Federal Trade Commission in the form of rules, regulations, orders, and decisions to carry out their duties and responsibilities. This law can initially be enforced by these agencies, outside the judicial process.

administrative law judge One who presides over an administrative hearing and who has the power to administer oaths, take testimony, rule on questions of evidence, and make determinations of fact.

administrative process Procedures used by agencies in the administration of law.

administrator (-trix) One who is appointed by a court to handle the probate (disposition) of a person's estate if that person dies intestate. (see *estate, intestacy laws, will*)

adverse possession The acquisition of title to real property by occupying it, without the permission of the owner, for a period of time specified by state statutes. The occupation must be actual, open, notorious, exclusive, and in opposition to all others, including the owner.

affidavit A written or printed voluntary statement of facts, confirmed by the oath or affirmation of the party making it and made before a person having the authority to administer the oath or affirmation.

affirmative defense A response to a plaintiff's claim that attacks the plaintiff's *legal* right to bring an action, as opposed to attacking the truth of the claim. Running of the statute of limitations is an example of an affirmative defense.

after-acquired property Property of the debtor that is acquired after a security interest in the debtor's property is created.

age of majority The age (eighteen in most jurisdictions) at which a person is by law considered to be an adult for most contractual purposes; sometimes referred to as full age, legal age, majority, or adulthood.

agency A relationship between two persons where, by agreement or otherwise, one is bound by the words and acts of the other. The former is a *principal;* the latter is an *agent.*

agent A person authorized by another to act for or in place of him or her.

agreement A meeting of two or more minds. Often used as a synonym for contract.

alien corporation A corporation formed in another country but doing business in the United States is referred to within the United States as an alien corporation.

allonge A piece of paper firmly attached to a negotiable instrument, upon which transferees can make indorsements if there is no room left on the instrument itself.

alterations In landlord-tenant law, any improvements or changes that materially affect the condition of the leased property.

alternative dispute resolution (ADR) The resolution of disputes in ways other than those involved in the traditional judicial process. Mediation and arbitration are forms of ADR.

ambient standard A legal expression of the permissible amount of a pollutant allowed in the atmosphere generally. Typically, an ambient standard is measured in terms of time (for example, yearly), quantity (for example, parts per million), and community performance (that is, within a defined region).

American Arbitration Association (AAA) The major organization offering arbitration services in the United States.

annuity The right to receive fixed, periodic payments for a term of years or for life.

answer The defendant's response to the complaint. Filing of the complaint and answer are governed by rules of procedure.

antecedent claim A preexisting claim. In the law of negotiable instruments, a holder takes for value if he or she takes the instrument for an antecedent claim against any person whether or not the claim is due [UCC 3–303(b)].

anticipatory breach or **anticipatory repudiation** The assertion by a party that he or she will not perform an obligation that the party is contractually obligated to perform at a future time.

antilapse provision A clause in a life insurance policy stating that the policy will not automatically lapse if no premium payment is made on the date due. Usually, the insured has a grace period within which to pay an overdue premium.

antitrust statutes Federal and state statutes protecting trade and commerce from unlawful restraints, price discrimination, price fixing, and monopolies. The principal federal antitrust statutes are the Sherman Act (1890), the Clayton Act (1914), and the Federal Trade Commission Act (1914).

appellant The party who takes an appeal from one court to another; sometimes referred to as the petitioner.

appellee The party against whom an appeal is taken—that is, the party who opposes setting aside or reversing the judgment; sometimes referred to as the respondent.

appraisal An estimate of the value of property determined by a suitably qualified individual who has no interest in the property.

appraisal right A dissenting shareholder's right to object to an extraordinary transaction of the corporation, such as a merger or consolidation, have his or her shares appraised, and be paid the fair market value by the corporation (see Model Business Corporation Act, §§ 80–81).

appropriation In tort law, the act of making a thing one's own or exercising or making use of an object to subserve one's own interest. When the act is wrongful, a tort is committed.

arbitration The settling of a dispute by submitting it to a disinterested third party other than a court.

arbitration clause A clause in a contract that provides that in case of dispute the parties will determine their rights by arbitration rather than through the judicial system.

arson The malicious burning of another's dwelling. Some statutes have expanded this to include any real property regardless of ownership, and the destruction of property by other means, *e.g.,* explosion.

artisan's lien A possessory lien given to a person who has made improvements and added value to another person's personal property as security for payment for services performed.

assault Any word or action intended to cause the person to whom it is directed to be in fear of immediate physical harm; a reasonably believable threat. (see *battery*)

assignment The act of transferring to another all or part of one's rights under a contract.

assignment of rights See *assignment*.

assumption of risk A doctrine whereby a plaintiff may not recover for injuries or damages suffered from risks that he or she was aware of and assented to. A defense against negligence if the plaintiff has knowledge of and appreciates a danger and voluntarily exposes himself or herself to the danger.

attachment (1) In a secured transaction, the process by which a security interest in the property of another becomes enforceable. Attachment may occur upon the creditor's taking possession of the property or upon the signing of a security agreement by the person pledging the property as collateral. (2) The legal process of seizing another's property in accordance with a writ or judicial order for the purpose of securing satisfaction of a judgment yet to be rendered.

attractive nuisance doctrine A doctrine under which person who owns or controls premises that may reasonably be apprehended to be a source of danger to children is under a duty to take reasonable precautions to prevent injury to children attracted to those premises.

at-will contract In an employment context, a contract that either the employer or the employee may terminate at any time for any reason.

authorized shares That capital stock that the charter or articles of incorporation permits the corporation to sell.

automated teller machine (ATM) An electronic customer-bank communication terminal that, when activated by an access card and a personal identification number, can conduct routine banking transactions.

automatic stay A suspension of all judicial proceedings upon the occurrence of an independent event. Under the Bankruptcy Code, the moment a petition to commence bankruptcy proceedings is filed, all litigation by creditors against a debtor and the debtor's property is suspended.

award (1) As a noun, the decision rendered by an arbitrator or other extrajudicial decider of a controversy. (2) As a verb, to give or assign by sentence or judicial determination or otherwise after a careful weighing of evidence, as when a jury awards damages.

B

bailee One to whom goods are entrusted by a bailor.

bailment An agreement to entrust the goods or personal property of one person (bailor) to another (bailee) with the obligation of the bailee to return the bailed property to the bailor or dispose of the property as directed.

bailor One who entrusts goods to a bailee.

bait advertising Advertising a product (the "bait") at a very attractive price and then informing the consumer, once he or she is in the door, that the advertised product is either not available or is of poor quality; the customer is then urged to purchase a more expensive item.

bank draft A check, draft, or other order for payment of money drawn by a bank on itself (such as a cashier's check) or on another bank.

battery The unprivileged, intentional touching of another. (see *assault*)

bearer A person in possession of an instrument payable to bearer or indorsed in blank.

bequest A gift by will of personal property (from the verb—to bequeath).

beyond a reasonable doubt See *reasonable doubt*

bilateral contract A contract that includes the exchange of a promise for a promise (as compared to a unilateral contract).

bill of lading A document that serves both as evidence of the receipt of goods for shipment and as documentary evidence of title to the goods.

Bill of Rights The Bill of Rights consists of the first ten amendments to the Constitution.

binder A written, temporary insurance policy. (see *policy*)

blank indorsement One made by the mere writing of the indorser's name on the back of an instrument. Such indorsement causes an instrument, otherwise payable to order, to become payable to bearer and negotiated only by delivery.

"blue sky" laws Another name for state laws that regulate the offer and sale of securities.

bona fide occupational qualification Under Title VII of the Civil Rights Act of 1964, identifiable characteristics reasonably necessary to the normal operation of a particular business. These characteristics can include gender, national origin, and religion, but not race.

bona fide purchaser One who purchases in good faith, for value, and without notice of any defects in the seller's title to the property being sold.

bond A certificate that evidences a corporate debt. It is a security that involves no ownership interest in the issuing corporation.

bond indenture An instrument of secured indebtedness issued by a corporation.

breach of contract Failure, without legal excuse, of a promisor to perform the obligations of a contract.

brief A written summary or statement prepared by one side in a lawsuit to explain its case to the judge; a typical brief has a facts summary, a law summary, and an argument about how the law applies to the facts.

burglary The unlawful entry, usually at night, into a building with the intent to commit theft. (Some state statutes expand this to include the intent to commit any crime.)

business necessity defense A showing that an employment practice that discriminates against members of a protected class is related to job performance.

business tort A noncontractual breach of a legal duty by one party that directly results in damage or injury to another.

C

cash surrender value The amount an insurer has agreed to pay if a life insurance policy is cancelled prior to the death of the insured.

cashier's check A draft drawn by a bank on itself.

causa mortis **gift** A gift made by a donor in contemplation of his or her imminent death. If the donor does not die of that ailment, the gift is revoked.

causation in fact An act or omission without which an event would not have occurred.

cease-and-desist order An administrative or judicial order prohibiting a person or a business firm from conducting activities that an agency or a court has deemed illegal.

certificate of deposit (CD) An instrument evidencing a promissory acknowledgment by a bank of a receipt of money with an engagement to repay it.

certified check A check drawn by an individual on his or her own account but bearing a guarantee (acceptance) by a bank that the bank will pay the check regardless of whether the drawer's account contains adequate funds at the time the check is presented.

chancellor In the early King's Court, individuals petitioned the king for relief when they could not obtain an adequate remedy in a court of law. These petitions were decided by the chancellor, who was an advisor to the king.

charitable trust One in which property held by a trustee must be used for charitable purposes (advancement of health, religion, etc.).

chattel Tangible personal property.

check A draft drawn on a bank, signed by the drawer, and payable on demand.

checks and balances An arrangement of governmental powers whereby powers of one governmental branch check or balance those of other branches.

citation A citation indicates where a particular constitutional provision, statute, reported case, or article may be found; also an order for a defendant to appear in court or indicating that a person has violated a legal rule.

civil law (1) The branch of law that deals with the definition and enforcement of all private or public rights, as opposed to criminal matters. (2) A system of law derived from that of the Roman empire and based on a code rather than case law. Louisiana is the only state that has a civil law system; all others use common law.

close corporation A corporation whose shareholders are limited to a small group of persons, often including only family members. The rights of shareholders of a close corporation usually are restricted regarding transfer of shares to others.

closing argument Closing arguments are made after the plaintiff(s) and defendant(s) have rested their cases and prior to the judge's charges to the jury.

codicil A written supplement to, or modification of, a will. Codicils must be executed with the same formalities as a will.

coinsurance clause A clause in an insurance policy providing that if the owner insures the property up to a specified percentage of its value, he or she will recover any loss up to the face amount of the policy; but if the insurance is for less than the fixed percentage, the owner will be responsible for a proportionate share of the loss.

collateral Property of a debtor in which the secured party has a security interest, as security in case of nonpayment by the debtor.

collecting bank Any bank handling an item for collection, except the payor bank.

collective bargaining Negotiation between an employer and organized employees to determine and agree on employment conditions.

commercial paper Under UCC Article 3, negotiable instruments, which are signed writings by which the maker promises or drawer orders a drawee (unconditionally) to pay a certain amount of money to order or to the bearer of the paper.

common areas In landlord-tenant law, the portion of the premises over which the landlord retains control and maintenance responsibilities. Common areas may include stairs, lobbies, garages, hallways, and other areas in common use.

common law That body of law developed from custom or judicial decisions in English and American courts, not attributable to a legislature.

common stock Shares of ownership in a corporation that are lowest in priority with respect to payment of dividends and distribution of the corporation's assets upon dissolution. (see *preferred stock*)

comparative negligence A concept in tort law whereby liability for injuries resulting from negligent acts is shared by all persons who were guilty of negligence, including the injured party, on the basis of each person's proportionate carelessness.

compensatory damages A money award equivalent to the actual value of injuries or damages sustained by the aggrieved party.

complaint The pleading made by a plaintiff or a charge by the state to a judicial officer alleging wrongdoing on the part of the defendant. Thus, the plaintiff is also referred to as the complainant.

computer crime Any wrongful act that is directed against computers and computer parts, or wrongful use or abuse of computers or software.

conciliation The settlement of a dispute in an unantagonistic manner. Used before trial with a view toward avoiding trial and in labor disputes before arbitration.

concurrent conditions Conditions that must occur or be performed at the same time; they are mutually dependent. No obligations arise until these conditions are simultaneously performed.

concurrent jurisdiction Concurrent jurisdiction exists when two different courts have the power to hear a case. For example, some cases can be heard in a federal or a state court. When a case can only be tried in federal court, or only in state court, jurisdiction is "exclusive."

concurrent ownership Joint ownership.

concurring opinion An opinion, separate from that embodying the view and decision of the majority of the court, that is prepared by a judge or justice who agrees in general but wants to make or clarify a particular point or to voice disapproval of the grounds on which the decision was made (but not the decision itself).

condition A qualification, provision, or clause in a contractual agreement, the occurrence of which creates, suspends, or terminates the obligations of the contracting parties.

condition precedent A condition in a contractual agreement that must be met before the other party's obligations arise.

condition subsequent A condition in a contract that, if not met, discharges the obligation of the other party.

confusion The mixing together of goods of two or more owners so that the independent goods cannot be identified.

conglomerate mergers Mergers between firms that do not compete with each other because they are in different industries, as opposed to horizontal and vertical mergers.

consent Voluntary agreement to submit to a proposition or an act of another. A concurrence of wills.

consideration That which motivates the exchange of promises or performance in a contractual agreement. The consideration, which must be present to make the contract legally binding, must be a detriment to the promisee (something of legal value, legally sufficient, and bargained for) or a benefit to the promisor. (see *contract*)

consignment A transaction in which an owner of goods (the consignor) delivers the goods to another (the consignee) for the consignee to sell. The consignee pays the consignor for the goods when the consignee sells the goods.

consolidation A contractual and statutory process whereby two or more corporations join to become a completely new corporation. The original corporations cease to exist, and the new corporation acquires all their assets and liabilities.

constructive delivery The recognition of the act of intending that title to property be transferred to someone, even though the actual, physical delivery of the property is not made (*e.g.*, the transfer of a key to a safe constructively delivers the contents of the safe); symbolic delivery.

constructive eviction Depriving a person of the possession of rental property that he or she leases by rendering the premises unfit or unsuitable for occupancy.

constructive/implied conditions Conditions or qualifications to a promise that arise from the very nature of the promise and that the law recognizes as conditioning the promise even though not expressly stated.

constructive trust A trust created by operation of law against one who wrongfully has obtained or holds legal right to property which he should not, in equity and good conscience, hold and enjoy.

contract A set of promises constituting an agreement between parties, giving each a legal duty to the other and also the right to seek a remedy for the breach of the promises/duties owed to each. The elements of an enforceable contract are competent parties, a proper or legal purpose, consideration (an exchange of promises/ duties), and mutuality of agreement and of obligation.

contracts implied-in-law Contracts imposed upon parties by law, in the interest of justice, to prevent unjust enrichment even though the parties never intended to voluntarily enter into a contract (sometimes referred to as a quasi-contract).

contracts under seal Formal agreements in which the seal is a substitute for *consideration*. A court will not invalidate a contract under seal for lack of consideration.

contractual capacity The threshold mental capacity required by the law for a party who enters into a contract to be bound by that contract.

contributory negligence Any negligent act by a complaining party that contributed to or caused the complaining party's injuries. Contributory negligence is an absolute bar to recovery in some jurisdictions. (see *affirmative defense, comparative negligence*)

conversion The wrongful taking or retaining possession of property that belongs to another.

copyright The exclusive right of "authors" to publish, print, or sell an intellectual production for a statutory period of time. It has the same monopolistic nature as a patent or trademark, but a copyright differs from them in that it applies exclusively to works of art and literature.

corporation An association of persons created by statute as a legal entity. The law treats the corporation itself as an entity that can sue and be sued. The corporation is distinct from the individuals who comprise it (shareholders). The corporation survives the death of its investors, as the shares can usually be transferred. (see *close, domestic, and foreign corporations*)

counter-advertising New advertising that is undertaken pursuant to a Federal Trade Commission order for the purpose of correcting earlier false claims made about a product.

counterclaim A pleading by a defendant against the plaintiff in which the defendant states a claim for damages (or to defeat plaintiff's action) resulting from allegedly wrongful acts of the plaintiff.

courts of equity Courts that decide controversies and administer justice according to the rules, principles, and precedents of equity.

courts at law Under the Federal Rules of Civil Procedure, law and equity actions have been merged procedurally. In the early King's Court, however, courts of law were separate from the courts of equity, and the remedies in the two courts were also separate and distinct.

covenant of the right to convey A grantor's assurance that he or she has sufficient capacity and title to convey the estate that he or she undertakes to convey by deed.

covenant not to sue An agreement to substitute a contractual obligation for some other type of action.

covenant against encumbrances A grantor's assurance that on land conveyed there are no encumbrances—that is, that no third parties have rights to or interests in the land that would diminish its value to the grantee.

covenant of quiet enjoyment A promise by the landlord or grantor that the tenant or grantee will not be evicted or disturbed by the grantor or a person having a lien or superior title.

covenant of seisin An assurance to the purchaser that the grantor has the very estate in the quantity and quality that the grantor purports to convey.

covenant running with the land An executory promise made between a grantor and a grantee to which they and subsequent owners of the land are bound.

creditor beneficiary A creditor who has rights in a contract made by the debtor and a third person, in which the terms of the contract obligate the third person to pay the debt owed to the creditor. The creditor beneficiary can enforce the debt against either party.

creditors' composition agreement An agreement formed between a debtor and his or her creditors in which the creditors agree to accept lesser sums than those owed to them by the debtor in full satisfaction of the debts.

crime A broad term for violations of law that are punishable by the state or nation. Crimes are codified by legislatures, and their objective is the protection of the public. (see *civil law, criminal law*)

criminal law Governs and defines those actions that are crimes and that subject the convicted offender to punishment imposed by the state.

cross-complaint See counterclaim.

cure The right of a party who tenders non-conforming performance to correct his or her performance within the contract period [UCC 3–508].

D

damages Money sought as a remedy for a breach of contract action or for tortious acts.

debtor A person who owes a sum of money or other obligations to another.

decree of specific performance See *specific performance*

deed A document by which title to property (usually real property) is passed.

deed of trust An instrument or document used in some states as a security device as a type of mortgage whereby legal title to real property is transferred to a trustee to secure the repayment of a sum of money or the performance of other conditions. (see *mortgage*)

defamation Anything published or publicly spoken that causes injury to another's good name, reputation, or character. (see *slander, libel*)

default The omission or failure to perform a legal or contractual duty, to observe a promise or discharge an obligation, or to perform an agreement.

defendant The party against whom an action or suit is brought.

defense That which a defendant offers and alleges in an action or suit as a reason why the plaintiff should not recover or establish what he or she seeks.

defense of others The legally recognized privilege in which a defender may do whatever the person attacked would do to protect himself or herself. Whether one was justified and used reasonable force in the protection of another is judged on the same criteria as the privilege of self-defense.

defense of property The legally recognized privilege of a person to defend his or her property. One may only use the amount of force necessary to protect his or her property, as the use of even slightly greater force will be deemed wrongful.

delegation of duties The act of transferring to another all or part of one's duties arising under a contract.

delivery order A written order to deliver goods directed to a warehouseman, carrier, or other person who in the ordinary course of business issues warehouse receipts or bills of lading [UCC 7-102(1)(d)].

demand deposit Funds accepted by a bank subject to immediate withdrawal, in contrast to a time deposit, which requires a depositor to wait a specific time before withdrawing or pay a penalty for early withdrawal.

demurrer A pleading in which a defendant admits the facts as alleged by the plaintiff but asserts that the plaintiff's claim fails to state a cause of action (*i.e.,* has no basis in law).

***de novo* review** Reviewing a matter as if it had not been heard and no decision had been rendered before. In the context of administrative law, a court conducting a *de novo* review will not defer to the agency on questions of fact, as it normally would, but will reconsider all the evidence in forming its judgment on the issue.

depositary bank The first bank to which an item is transferred for collection even though it may also be the payor bank [UCC 4-105(a)].

deposition A generic term that refers to any written evidence verified by oath. As a legal term, it is usually limited to the testimony of a witness taken under oath, with the opportunity of cross-examination.

deregulation A reduction in the amount of regulations that governmental agencies have issued and with which businesses must comply.

derivative suit A suit by a shareholder to enforce a corporate cause of action against a third person.

devise To make a gift of real property by a will.

disaffirmance The repudiation of an obligation.

discharge The termination of one's obligation. In contract law, discharge occurs when the parties have fully performed their contractual obligations or when events, conduct of the parties, or operation of the law release the parties from further performance.

discharge in bankruptcy The release of a debtor from all debts which are provable, except those specifically excepted from discharge by statute.

disclosed principal A principal whose identity and existence as a principal is known by a third person at the time a transaction is conducted by an agent.

discovery A method by which opposing parties may obtain information from each other to prepare for trial. Generally governed by rules of procedure, but may be controlled by the court.

disparate impact discrimination In an employment context, discrimination that results from certain employer practices or procedures that, while not discriminatory on their face, have a discriminatory effect. For example, a requirement that all employees have high school diplomas is not necessarily discriminatory, but it may have the *effect* of discriminating against minority groups.

disparate-treatment discrimination In an employment context, intentional discrimination against individuals on the basis of color, gender, national origin, race, or religion.

dissenting opinion A separate opinion in which a judge or justice disagrees with the conclusion reached by the majority of the court and expounds his or her views on the case.

dissolution The formal disbanding of a partnership or corporation.

diversity of citizenship Under Article III, Section 2, of the Constitution, diversity of citizenship provides a basis for federal court jurisdiction over a lawsuit between citizens of different states.

divestiture The act of selling one or more of a company's parts, such as a subsidiary or a plant; often mandated by the courts in merger and monopolization cases.

dividend A distribution to corporate shareholders, disbursed in proportion to the number of shares held.

doctrine of commercial impracticability A doctrine under which a seller may be excused from performing a contract when (1) a contingency occurs, (2) the contingency's occurrence makes performance impracticable, and (3) the nonoccurrence of the contingency was a basic assumption on which the contract was made. Despite the fact that UCC 2-615 expressly frees only sellers under this doctrine, courts have not distinguished between buyers and sellers in applying it.

documents of title Paper exchanged in the regular course of business which evidence the right to possession of goods (*e.g.*, bills of lading, warehouse receipts, etc.).

domestic corporation In a given state, a corporation which is doing business and is organized under the laws of that state.

donee beneficiary A person not a party to a contract but to whom the benefits of a contract flow as a direct result of an intention to make a gift to that person.

draft Any instrument drawn on any person (including a bank) which orders that person to pay a certain sum of money [UCC 3–104].

drawee The person who is ordered to pay on an instrument. With a check, the bank is always the drawee.

drawer A person who initiates a draft (including a check), thereby ordering the drawee to pay.

due negotiation The transfer of a document of title in such form that the transferee becomes a holder [UCC 7-501].

dumping Selling goods in a foreign country at a price below the price charged for the same goods in the domestic market.

duress Any unlawful threat or coercion used by a person to induce another to act (or to refrain from acting) in a manner he or she otherwise would not (or would).

E

easement A nonpossessory right to use another's property in a manner established by either express or implied agreement.

electronic fund transfer A transfer of funds with the use of an electronic terminal, a telephone, a computer, or magnetic tape.

electronic fund transfer systems (EFTS) Systems used to transfer funds electronically.

embezzlement The fraudulent appropriation of money or other property by a person to whom the money or property has been entrusted.

eminent domain The power of a government to take land for public use from private citizens for a fair compensation.

employee A person who works for an employer for salary or wages.

endowment insurance A type of insurance that combines life insurance with an investment so that if the insured outlives the policy the face value is paid to him or her; if the insured does not outlive the policy, the face value is paid to his or her beneficiary.

equal dignity rule In most states, express authority given an agent must be in writing if the contract to be made on behalf of the principal is required to be in writing.

equitable principles and maxims Equitable principles and maxims are frequently involved in equity jurisdiction. They are propositions or general statements of rules of law.

equitable servitude A restriction on the use of land enforceable in a court of equity.

equity of redemption The right of a mortgagor to redeem or purchase the property, after the mortgagor has breached the mortgage agreement, prior to foreclosure proceedings.

escrow account An account that is generally held in the name of the depositor and an escrow agent and is returnable to the depositor or paid to a third person upon fulfillment of the escrow condition.

escrow agent A party who holds an escrow account, in his or her name and in the name of a depositor.

estate The extent of ownership or interest that one has in property.

estop To stop, bar, or impede.

estoppel The principle that a party's own acts prevent him or her from claiming a right to the detriment of another who was entitled to rely on those acts and did. *Agency by estoppel* arises when a principal negligently allows an agent to exercise powers not granted to the agent, thus justifying others in believing that the agent possesses the requisite agency authority.

estray statutes Laws dealing with a person's rights in property whose ownership is unknown.

eviction Depriving a person of the possession of land or rental property that he or she owns or leases.

exclusive dealing contract An agreement under which a producer of goods agrees to sell its goods exclusively through one distributor.

exclusive jurisdiction Jurisdiction is exclusive when a case can only be heard in a particular court.

exculpatory clause A contract or contract clause which releases one of the parties from liability for his or her wrongful acts.

executed contract A contract which has been completely performed by both parties.

executor (-trix) A person either expressly or by implication appointed by a testator to see that his or her will is administered appropriately. (see *testator*, *will*)

executory contract A contract that has not as yet been fully completed or performed.

executory interest A future interest held by a third person (not the grantor) which either cuts short (shifting) or begins some time after (springing) the natural termination of the preceding estate.

exemplary damages Damages above those which will compensate a victim for his or her loss, intended to solace the plaintiff for aggravations of the original wrong, or to punish the defendant for evil behavior or to make an example of the defendant. Also called punitive damages.

ex parte **contacts** In the context of administrative rulemaking, communications with an agency that are not placed in the record.

express condition A qualification or condition upon which a promise is based and which is stated in the body of the contract. (see *condition*)

express contract A contract which is either oral and/or written (as opposed to an implied contract).

express warranty A promise, ancillary to an underlying sales agreement, which is included in the written or oral terms of the sales agreement under which the promisor assures the quality, description, or performance of the goods.

extension clause A clause in a time instrument extending the instrument's date of maturity. An extension clause is the reverse of an *acceleration clause*.

F

fair trade laws State statutes which permit manufacturers or distributors of namebrand goods to fix minimum retail resale prices. These statutes are no longer valid.

federal question A federal question provides jurisdiction for federal courts. This jurisdiction arises from Article III, Section 2, of the Constitution. Federal questions may pertain to the U.S. Constitution, acts of Congress, or treaties.

federalism A form of government in which sovereign power is divided between a central governing authority and the member states of a political union. The United States has a federal form of government.

fee simple Exists when the owner or owners of property are entitled to use, possess, or dispose of that property as they choose during their lifetime, and, upon death, their interests in the property descend to their heirs.

fee simple absolute An estate or interest in land with no time, disposition, or descendibility limitations.

fee simple defeasible An estate which can be taken away (by the prior grantor) upon the occurrence or non-occurrence of a specified event.

felony A crime which carries the most severe sanctions, usually ranging from one year in a state or federal prison to the forfeiture of one's life (*i.e.*, arson, murder, rape, robbery).

felony murder At common law, the intent to commit a felony unrelated to a resulting homicide was sufficient to meet the *mens rea* requirement for murder. Because of the many new statutory felonies that pose little threat of death or bodily harm to anyone, this doctrine has been limited by courts and legislatures.

fictitious payee rule A fictitious payee is a payee on a negotiable instrument whom the maker or drawer does not intend to have an interest in the instrument. An imposter payee comes under the definition of a fictitious payee. Frequently an unscrupulous employee or agent supplies the maker or drawer, or drafts the instrument, with the name of the fictitious payee. Under the fictitious payee rule, indorsements by fictitious payees are not forgeries under negotiable instruments law [see UCC 3–405].

fiduciary relationship A relationship founded on trust or confidence reposed by one person in the integrity and fidelity of another.

financial institutions Organizations authorized to do business under state or federal laws relating to financial institutions. For example, under the Electronic Fund Transfer Act, financial institutions include banks, savings and loan associations, credit unions, and any other business entities that directly or indirectly hold accounts belonging to consumers.

firm offer A signed writing by a merchant who promises to keep an offer open. Unlike an option, no consideration need be given to make the offer irrevocable [UCC 2–205].

fixture A thing which was once personal property, but has become attached to real property in such a way that it takes on the characteristics of real property and becomes part of that real property. (see *chattel, personal property, real property*)

float time The time between the issuance of a check and the deduction of the amount of the check from the drawer's account.

floating lien A security interest retained in collateral even when the collateral changes in character, classification, or location.

foreclosure A proceeding in equity whereby a mortgagee either takes title to or forces the sale of the mortgagor's property in satisfaction of a debt.

foreign corporation In any given state, a corporation which does business in the state without being incorporated therein.

foreseeable risk In negligence law, the risk of harm or injury that a person of ordinary intelligence and prudence should reasonably have anticipated his or her negligent act or failure to act would create, whatever the actor actually believed or anticipated.

forfeiture The termination of a lease, according to its terms or the terms of a statute, when one.of the parties fails to fulfill a condition under the lease and thereby breaches it.

forgery The false or unauthorized signature of a document, or the false making of a document, with the intent to defraud. (see *fraud*)

formal contract An agreement or contract which by law requires for its validity a specific form, such as executed under seal or in the presence of witnesses or both.

franchise The Federal Trade Commission has defined a franchise as "an arrangement in which the owner of a trademark, a trade name, or a copyright licenses others, under specified conditions or limitations, to use the trademark, trade name, or copyright in purveying goods or services."

franchisee One receiving a license to use another's (the franchisor's) trademark, trade name, or copyright in the sale of goods and services.

franchisor One licensing another (the franchisee) to use his or her trademark, trade name, or copyright in the sale of goods or services.

fraud Any misrepresentation, either by misstatement or omission of a material fact, knowingly made with the intention of misrepresentation to another and on which a reasonable person would and does rely to his or her detriment.

frustration of purpose doctrine A court-created doctrine under which a party to a contract will be relieved of his or her duty to perform when the objective purpose for performance no longer exists (due to reasons beyond that party's control).

future estates A future estate is one which is not at present possessory but which will or may commence in possession in the future. Remainders and reversions are future estates.

G

garnishment A legal process whereby a creditor appropriates the debtor's property or wages which are in the hands of a third party.

generally accepted accounting principles (GAAP) The conventions, rules, and procedures necessary to define accepted accounting practices at a particular time. The sources of the principles is the Federal Accounting Standards Board.

generally accepted auditing standards (GAAS) Standards concerning an auditor's professional qualities and the judgment exercised by him or her in the performance of an examination and report. The source of the standards is the American Institute of Certified Public Accountants.

genuineness of assent Knowing and voluntary assent to the terms of a contract. If a contract is formed as a result of mistake, misrepresentation, undue influence, or duress, genuineness of assent is lacking, and the contract will be voidable.

gift Any voluntary transfer of property to another which is without consideration, past or present.

good faith Honesty in fact as well as honesty in the conduct or transaction concerned [UCC 1–201(19)].

good faith purchaser A purchaser who buys without notice of circumstance which would put a person of ordinary prudence on inquiry as to the title, or as to an impediment on the title, of a seller. Sometimes used interchangeably with a "buyer in ordinary course of business" when the seller is a merchant [UCC 1–201(9), 2–403].

grace period A span of time (usually one month) after an insurance policy premium (payment) was due, during which the policy remains in effect. (see *policy*)

grant deed A deed that simply recites words of consideration and conveyance. Under statute, a grant deed may impliedly warrant that at least the grantor has not conveyed the property's title to someone else.

grantor One who transfers property or creates a trust.

group boycott The boycott of a particular person or firm by a group of competitors; prohibited under the Sherman Act.

guaranty An agreement in which the guarantor agrees to satisfy the debt of another (the debtor), only if and when the debtor fails to repay (secondarily liable).

H

holder A person "who is in possession of a document of title or negotiable instrument or a certificated investment security drawn, issued, or indorsed to him or his order or to bearer or blank" [UCC 1–201(20)].

holder in due course A person who is a holder of an instrument who took it in good faith, for value, and without notice that the instrument is overdue or has been dishonored or that any defense or claim exists against it [UCC 3–302(1)].

holographic will A will written entirely in the signer's handwriting, usually not witnessed.

homestead exemption A law allowing a householder/head of a family to designate his or her house and adjoining land a homestead, and exempting it from liability for his or her general debts.

horizontal agreement An agreement between direct competitors to restrain competition—by fixing prices, for example.

horizontal merger A merger between two businesses which compete in the marketplace.

I

identification Proof that a thing is what it is purported or represented to be.

implied convenant of good faith A contractual promise inferred by the law according to which the parties agree to abide by their contract honestly, without malice, without intent to defraud, and without taking unconscientious advantage of each other.

implied-in-fact contract A contract formed in whole or in part from the conduct of the parties (as opposed to an express contract).

implied warranty A guarantee which the law implies either through the situation of the parties or the nature of the transaction. (see *usage of trade*, *course of dealing*)

implied warranty of habitability A presumed promise by the landlord that rented residential premises are fit for human habitation—that is, free of violations of building and sanitary codes.

implied warranty of merchantability A promise by a merchant seller of goods that they are reasonably fit for the general purpose for which they are sold, are properly packaged and labeled, and are of proper quality [UCC 2–314].

impossibility of performance A doctrine under which a party to a contract is relieved of his or her duty to perform when performance has become objectively impossible or totally impracticable (without fault of the party).

imposter One who, with the intent to deceive, pretends to be somebody else.

incidental beneficiary A person who indirectly receives, or will receive, a benefit as the result of a contract entered into by other parties. The incidental beneficiary is neither a donee beneficiary nor a creditor beneficiary and thus has no right to enforce the contract.

incidental damages Damages resulting from a breach of a contract, including all reasonable expenses incurred because of the breach [UCC 2–710 and 2–715(1)].

incontestability clause A clause in a life or health insurance policy providing that after the policy has been in force for a specified length of time—usually two or three years—the insurer cannot contest statements made in the application.

indemnification Compensation for a loss or reimburse one for expenses incurred.

independent regulatory agencies Administrative agencies that have somewhat greater protection from presidential influence. Such protection exists, for example, when their officials cannot be removed from office without cause.

indictment A charge or written accusation issued by a grand jury that a named person has committed a crime. Referred to as a "true bill."

indorsee The one to whom a negotiable instrument is transferred by indorsement.

indorsement A signature placed on an instrument or a document of title for the purpose of transferring one's ownership in the instrument or document of title [UCC 3–202].

indorser One who, being the payee or holder of a negotiable instrument, signs by indorsement on the back of it.

informal contract A contract that does not require a specified form or formality for its validity.

information A formal accusation or complaint issued in certain types of actions by a prosecuting attorney or other law officer without an indictment. The types of actions are set forth in the rules of states or the Federal Rules of Criminal Procedure.

initial order In the context of administrative law, an agency's disposition in a matter other than a rulemaking. An administrative law judge's initial order becomes final unless it is appealed.

injunction An order by a court requiring a person to act or refrain from acting in a certain manner.

innocent misrepresentation A false statement of fact or an act made in good faith which deceives and causes harm or injury to another.

in pari delicto At equal fault.

in personam jurisdiction *In personam* jurisdiction refers to the power that a court has over the "person" involved in the action.

in rem jurisdiction *In rem* jurisdiction refers to an action that is taken directly against the defendant's property. The term may be contrasted with *in personam* jurisdiction.

insider trading Purchasing or selling securities on the basis of information that has not been made available to the public.

insolvent A person is insolvent when liabilities exceed the value of his or her assets *or* when that person "either has ceased to pay his debts in the ordinary course of business or cannot pay his debts as they come due" [UCC 1–201(23)].

installment contract A contract whereby either property purchased or payments due, or both, are made periodically [UCC 2–612].

insurance A contract in which, for a stipulated consideration, one party agrees to compensate the other for loss on a specified subject by a specified peril.

intangible property A property right, usually represented by a document or certificate which has no intrinsic value, which evidences a valuable ownership interest.

integrated contract The written expression of a contract that contains the parties' entire agreement. Parol evidence is inadmissible to modify or change an integrated contract, because the parties have made the contract the final expression of their agreement.

intellectual property Property resulting from intellectual, creative processes—the products of an individual's mind.

intended beneficiary A third party for whose benefit a contract is formed; an intended beneficiary can sue the promisor directly if such a contract is breached.

intent The design, resolve, or determination with which a person acts.

intentional tort A tort in which the actor is judged to have possessed intent to do that which causes injury.

intermediary bank Any bank to which an item is transferred in the course of collection, except the depositary or payor bank [UCC 4–105(c)].

interrogatories Interrogatories are a series of written questions for which written answers are prepared and then signed under oath.

inter vivos gift A gift made by a living person which is not in contemplation of death.

inter vivos trust A trust created by the grantor (settlor) and effective during the grantor's lifetime (*i.e.*, a trust not established by a will).

intestacy laws State laws determining the division and descent of an intestate's (one who dies with no will) estate.

intestate One who has died without having created a valid will.

invitee A person who, either expressly or impliedly, is privileged to enter upon another's land. The inviter owes the invitee the duty to exercise reasonable care to protect an individual from harm (*e.g.*, a customer in a store).

irrevocable offer An offer that cannot be revoked or recalled by the offeror without liability. (see *firm offers*)

issue The first transfer, or delivery, or an instrument to a holder.

issued shares Stock which has been authorized and sold to subscribers. Such may include treasury shares. (see *authorized shares, treasury shares*)

J

joint tenancy The ownership interest of two or more co-owners of property whereby each owns an undivided portion of the property. The key feature of joint tenancy is the "right of survivorship" whereby, upon the death of one of the joint tenants, his or her interest automatically passes to the others and cannot be transferred by the will of the deceased.

joint venture A joint undertaking of a specific commercial enterprise by an association of persons. A joint venture is normally not a legal entity and is treated like a partnership for federal income tax purposes.

judgment creditor A person in whose favor a money judgment has been entered by a court of law and who has not yet been paid.

judgment n.o.v. A judgment n.o.v. is a judgment that may be entered by the court for the plaintiff (or the defendant) after there has been a jury verdict for the defendant (or plaintiff).

judgment rate of interest A rate of interest fixed by statute which is applied to a monetary judgment from the moment the judgment is awarded by a court until the judgment is paid or terminated.

judicial process A course of action pursued at least in part before a court to obtain relief; the procedures used in courts to determine controversies; the process by which judges decide cases.

judicial review The authority of a court to re-examine a previously considered dispute, especially the appeal of a lower court or the decision of an administrative agency.

jurisdiction The authority of a court to hear and decide a specific action.

jurisprudence The science or philosophy of law.

justice Justice is generally perceived as one of the primary goals of our legal system. The term refers to the ideal of being just, impartial, and fair.

justiciable A matter that is appropriate for court review. A justiciable controversy is one that is not hypothetical or academic but real and substantial.

L

laches The equitable doctrine which bars a party's right due to neglect for an unreasonable length of time to do what should have been done.

laissez-faire A doctrine advocating government restraint in the regulation of business.

landlord's lien A landlord's remedy for a tenant's failure to pay rent. Where permitted under a statute or a lease, and landlord may take and keep or sell whatever of the defaulting tenant's property is on the leased premises.

landlord-tenant relationship The legal (contractual) relationship between the lessor and the lessee of real estate.

larceny The act of taking another's personal property unlawfully. Some states classify larceny as either grand or petit, depending on the property's value.

last clear chance A doctrine under which a plaintiff may recover from a defendant for injuries or damages suffered, notwithstanding the plaintiff's own negligence, when the defendant had the opportunity—a last clear chance—to avoid harming the plaintiff through the exercise of reasonable care but failed to do so.

law Enforceable rules of conduct to be followed by citizens of a society, as pronounced by that society's government.

lease A transfer by the landlord/lessor of real or personal property to the tenant/lessee for a period of time, for a consideration (usually the payment of rent). Upon termination of the lease, the property reverts to the lessor.

leasehold estate An estate in realty held by a tenant under a lease. In every leasehold estate, the tenant has a qualified right to possess and/or use the land.

lease term The period during which a lessee may legally occupy the leased premises. The lease term does not usually include the time between the making of the lease and the tenant's entry onto the premises.

legacy A gift of personal property under a will.

legal rate of interest A rate of interest fixed by statute as either the maximum rate of interest permitted to be charged by law, or a rate of interest to be applied when the parties to a contract intend an interest rate to be paid but do not fix the rate in the contract. Even in the latter case, frequently this rate is the same as the statutory maximum rate permitted.

lessee A person who pays for the use or possession of another's property.

lessor A property owner who allows others to use his or her property in exchange for payment of rent.

less-than-freehold estate A possessory real-estate interest that gives the tenant a qualified right to exclusive possession of property for a specified period of time, such as occurs in a leasehold estate.

letter of credit A written instrument, usually issued by a bank on behalf of a customer or other person, in which the issuer promises to honor drafts or other demands for payment by third persons in accordance with the terms of the instrument [UCC 5–103(1)(a)].

levy A legal seizure of property in order to obtain money.

libel A written defamation of one's character or reputation. The press is, to a limited degree, protected from libel actions by the First Amendment.

license A revocable privilege to enter on the land of another.

licensee One whom the party in possession of real property invites onto the premises for the possessing party's benefit, such as a customer.

licensing In the context of administrative law, the granting of permission by an appropriate governmental authority to a person, firm, or corporation to pursue an occupation or conduct a business subject to regulation.

lien An encumbrance upon a property, to satisfy or protect a claim for payment of a debt.

lien creditor One whose debt or claim is secured by a lien on particular property, as distinguished from a general creditor, who has no such security.

life estate An interest in land which exists only for the duration of the life of some person, usually the holder of the estate.

limited payment life A type of life insurance for which premiums are payable for a definite period, after which the policy is fully paid.

liquidated damages An amount, stipulated in the contract, which the parties believe to be a reasonable estimation of the damages which will occur in the event of a breach.

liquidation The sale of the assets of a business or an individual for cash and the distribution of the cash received to creditors with the balance going to the owner(s).

litigant A party to a lawsuit.

long arm statute Through long arm statutes, states permit personal jurisdiction to be obtained over nonresident individuals and corporations. Individuals or corporations, however, must have certain "minimum contacts" with that state.

lost property Property which the owner has involuntarily parted with and does not know where to find or recover it.

M

mailbox rule A rule providing that an acceptance of an offer becomes effective upon dispatch (upon being placed in a mailbox), if mail is, expressly or impliedly, an authorized means of communication of the acceptance to the offeror.

majority opinion A court supported by a majority of the judges or justices involved in deciding the case.

maker One who issues a promissory note or certificate of deposit (*i.e.*, one who promises to pay a certain sum to the holder of the note or CD). (see *drawer*)

market-share test The primary measure of monopoly power. A firm's market share is the percentage of a market that the firm controls.

marshalling assets The arrangement or ranking of assets in a certain order towards the payment of debts. In equity, when two creditors have recourse to the same property of the debtor, but one has recourse to other property of the debtor, that creditor must resort first to those assets of the debtor not available to the other creditor.

mask works A series of images related to the pattern formed by the many layers of a semi-conductor chip product.

material facts Those facts to which a reasonable person would attach importance in determining his or her course of action. In regard to tender offers, for example, a fact is material if there is a substantial likelihood that a reasonable shareholder would consider it important in deciding how to vote.

mechanic's lien A statutory lien filed against the entire realty for labor, services, or materials performed in improving or repairing the realty.

mediation The settlement of a dispute by the action of a neutral third party (called a mediator).

merger A contractual process by which one corporation (the surviving corporation) acquires all the assets and liabilities of another corporation (the merged corporation). The shareholders of the merged corporation receive either payment for their shares or shares in the surviving corporation.

merges Fuses or absorbs, as when one thing or right is absorbed into another. In the context of property law, if a tenant purchases leased premises, the tenant's interest in the premises merges into the title to the property.

mirror image rule A common law rule which requires, for a valid contractual agreement, that the terms of an offeree's acceptance must adhere exactly to the terms of the offeror's offer.

mislaid property Property which the owner has voluntarily parted with, with the intention of retrieving it later, but which cannot now be found. Does not include intentionally hidden property. (see *lost property*)

mitigation of damages A doctrine which imposes on an injured party the duty to exercise reasonable diligence in attempting to minimize his or her damages after an injury has been inflicted. This is sometimes called the doctrine of "avoidable consequences." (see *damages*)

monopolies Forms of market structure in which one, or only a few, business firms dominate the total sales of a product or service.

monopoly power Under the Sherman Act, the power of fix prices, to exclude competitors, or to control the market in the relevant geographical area in question.

mortgage A written instrument giving a creditor (the mortgagee) an interest (lien) in the debtor's (mortgagor's) property as security for a debt.

mortgagee The creditor who takes the security interest under the mortgage agreement.

mortgagor The debtor who pledges collateral in a mortgage agreement.

motion to dismiss See *demurrer*.

multiple insurance coverage Insurance coverage under policies with several insurance companies, all covering the same insurable interest.

mutual assent A meeting of the minds and a manifestation of intent of the parties to a contract, whereby each party agrees to the terms and conditions in both the same sense and meaning.

mutual rescission An agreement between the parties to cancel their contract, releasing the parties from further obligations under the contract. The object of the agreement is to restore the parties to positions they would have occupied had no contract ever been made. (see *rescission*)

N

negligent misrepresentation Any manifestation by words or conduct that amounts to an untrue statement of fact made in circumstances in which a reasonable and prudent person would not have done or failed to do that which led to the misrepresentation. A representation made with an honest belief in its truth may still be negligent due to a lack of reasonable care in ascertaining the facts, in the manner of expression, or in the absence of the skill or competence required by a particular business or profession.

negotiable instruments A written and signed unconditional promise or order to pay a specified sum of money on demand or at a definite time payable to order or bearer [UCC 3–104(1)].

note See *promissory note*

novation A mutual agreement for the release of an old debt or debtor with the substitution of a new one, whereby the old debt is extinguished.

nuisance An act which interferes unlawfully with a person's possession or ability to use his or her property.

O

objective theory of contracts The view taken by American law that contracting parties shall only be bound by terms which can be actually inferred from promises made. Contract law does not examine a contracting party's subjective intent or underlying motive.

offer A proposal to do something by an offeror which creates in the offeree a legal power to bind the offeror to the terms of the proposal by accepting the offer.

offeree One to whom an offer is made.

offeror A person who makes an offer.

omnibus, or **other-driver, clause** A provision in an automobile insurance policy that protects the vehicle owner who has taken out the insurance policy and anyone who drives the vehicle with the owner's permission.

open policy An insurance policy in which the value of the object insured is left by parties to be estimated in case of loss.

option contract A contract whereby the offeror cannot revoke his or her offer for a stipulated time period, and the offeree can accept or reject during this period without fear of the offer being made to another person. The offeree must give consideration for the option (the irrevocable offer) to be enforceable.

output contract A binding agreement in which a seller agrees to deliver/sell the seller's entire output of a good (an unspecified amount at the time of agreement) to a buyer, and the buyer agrees to buy all of the goods supplied.

outstanding shares Issued shares of stock less treasury shares. (see *issued shares, treasury shares*)

P

parol evidence rule A substantive rule of contracts under which a court will not receive into evidence oral or written statements made prior to or contemporaneous with a written agreement when the court finds that the written agreement was intended by the parties to be a final, complete, and unambiguous expression of their agreement.

partial eviction Depriving a person of a portion of his or her rights in land or rental property that he or she owns or leases; may result in *constructive eviction*.

partially disclosed principal A principal whose identity is unknown by the third party, but the third party knows that the agent is or may be acting for a principal at the time the contract is made.

partnership An association of two or more persons to carry on, as co-owners, a business for profit [UPA Section 6(1)].

past consideration An act done before the contract is made, which is ordinarily by itself no consideration for a later promise to pay for the act.

patent A government grant to an inventor giving the inventor the exclusive right or privilege to make, use, or sell his or her invention for a limited time period. The word "patent" ordinarily refers to some invention and designates either the instrument by which patent rights are evidenced or the patent itself.

payee A person to whom an instrument is made payable.

payor bank A bank by which an item is payable as drawn (or is payable as accepted) [UCC 4–105(b)].

penalty A sum inserted in a contract, not as a measure of compensation for its breach, but rather as punishment for a default. The agreement as to the amount will not be enforced, and recovery will be limited to actual damages.

per capita The method of distribution of property whereby the heirs to an intestate's estate share and share alike.

perfection The method by which a secured party obtains a priority by notice that his or her security interest in the debtor's collateral is effective against the debtor's subsequent creditors. Usually accomplished by filing a financing statement at a location set out in the state statute. (see *secured party, security interest*)

periodic tendency A lease interest in land for an indefinite period where payment of rent is at fixed intervals, such as week to week, month to month, year to year.

per se **violations** Certain types of anticompetitive agreements—such as price-fixing agreements—that are considered to be so injurious to the public that there is no need to determine whether they actually injure market competition; rather, they are in themselves (*per se*) violations of the Sherman Act.

personal identification number (PIN) A number given to the holder of an access card that is used to conduct financial transactions in electronic fund transfer systems. Typically, the card will not provide access to a system without the number, which is meant to be kept secret to inhibit unauthorized use of the card.

personal property Property which is movable; any property which is not real property. (see *real property*)

per stirpes A manner of distribution of property whereby a class or group of distributees take the share which their deceased ancestor would have been entitled to (*e.g.,* A dies leaving one son, B, and two grandchildren of deceased daughter C. B takes one-half and the two grandchildren each take one-quarter).

petitioner The party who presents a petition to a court, initiates an equity proceeding, or appeals from a judgment.

piercing the corporate veil A court's act of ignoring the separate legal existence of the corporation and thereby holding the corporation's shareholders personally liable for the corporation's wrongdoings.

plea-bargaining The process by which the accused and the prosecutor in a criminal case work out a mutually satisfactory disposition of the case, subject to court approval. Usually involves the defendant pleading guilty to a lesser offense in return for a lighter sentence.

pleadings Statements by the plaintiff and the defendant which detail the facts, charges, and defenses. Modern rules simplify common law pleading, often requiring only the complaint, answer, and sometimes a reply to the answer.

pledge The bailment of personal property to a creditor as security for the payment of a debt.

point-of-sale system An electronic customer-merchant-bank communication terminal that, when activated by an access card and a personal identification number, can debit the customer's account to cover a purchase from the merchant.

police powers States possess police powers as part of their inherent sovereignty. These powers may be exercised to protect or promote the public health, safety, morals, or general welfare.

policy In insurance, the contract of indemnity against a contingent loss between the insurer and insured.

policy of comity Comity may be defined as a deference by which one nation gives effect to the laws and judicial decrees of another nation. This recognition is based primarily upon respect.

possibility of reverter A future interest in land which a grantor retains after conveying property subject to a condition subsequent.

power of attorney A document or instrument authorizing another to act as one's agent or attorney.

power of termination A future interest in land which results when a grantor conveys land subject to a condition subsequent but also conditions the reversion of the land on the affirmative retaking of possession either by the grantor or his/her heirs.

preauthorized transfer A transaction authorized in advance to recur at substantially regular intervals. The terms and procedure for preauthorized electronic transfers of funds through certain financial institutions are subject to the Electronic Fund Transfer Act.

precedent A court decision that becomes an authority for deciding subsequent cases in which identical or similar facts are presented. (see *stare decisis*)

preemptive right A shareholder's right to purchase newly issued stock of a corporation, before it is offered to any outside buyers, equal in percentage to shares presently held, enabling the shareholder to maintain proportionate ownership and voice in the corporation.

preferred stock Classes of stock which have priority over common stock both as to payment of dividends and distribution of assets upon the corporation's dissolution.

premium In insurance, the price for insurance protection for a specified period of exposure.

prenuptial agreement An agreement made by the parties to a marriage prior to the marriage. If the consideration for the agreement is the forthcoming marriage, there must be a signed writing to make the agreement enforceable.

prescription The acquiring of an easement (or profit) by continuous and open use of land owned by another for a prescribed statutory period. (see *adverse possession*)

presentment warranty A warranty impliedly made, by any person who seeks payment or acceptance of a negotiable instrument to any person who in good faith pays or accepts the instrument, that the party presenting has good title to the instrument or is authorized to obtain payment or acceptance on behalf of a person who has good title; has no knowledge that the signature of the maker or the drawer is unauthorized; and that the instrument has not been materially altered [UCC 3–417(1), 3–418].

pretrial motion A written or oral application to a court for a ruling or order, made before trial.

price discrimination Exists when two competing buyers pay two different prices for an identical product or service.

prima facie (Latin) "at first sight." Something that is considered true because, on the face of it, it appears to be true. A presumption until disproved by contrary evidence.

prima facie case A case in which the plaintiff has produced sufficient evidence of his or her conclusion that the case can go to a jury; a case in which the evidence compels the plaintiff's conclusion if the defendant produces no evidence to rebut it.

principal In agency law, a person who, by agreement or otherwise, authorizes an agent to act on his or her behalf such that the acts of the agent become binding on the principal.

privilege In tort law, the ability to act contrary to another person's right without that person having legal redress for such acts. Privilege is usually raised as a defense, such as where A attacks B, B has a privilege to fight back to reasonably protect himself or herself without B being liable for the tort of assault and battery. (see *assault, battery*)

privity of contract The relationship which exists between the promisor and promisee of a contract.

probable cause Reasonable grounds to believe the existence of facts warranting certain actions such as the search or arrest of a person.

probate The process of proving and validating a will, and the settling of all matters pertaining to administration, guardianship, and like matters.

probate court A special court, in some jurisdictions, having jurisdiction of proceedings concerning the settlement of a person's estate. (see *estate, jurisdiction, probate*)

procedural law Rules which deal with the manner of bringing an action. Sometimes referred to as adjective law as opposed to substantive law. (see *substantive law*)

proceeds In secured transactions law, whatever is received when the collateral is sold, exchanged, collected, or otherwise disposed of, such as insurance payments for destroyed or lost collateral. Money, checks, and the like are "cash proceeds," while all other proceeds received are "noncash proceeds" [UCC 9–306].

products liability The legal liability of manufacturers and sellers to buyers, users, and sometimes bystanders for injuries or damages suffered because of defects in goods purchased. Liability arises when a product has a defective condition that makes it unreasonably dangerous to the user or consumer.

profit In real property law, the right to enter upon and remove things from the property of another (*e.g.*, the right to enter onto a person's land and remove sand and gravel therefrom).

promise A declaration which binds the person who makes it (promisor) to do or forbear from a certain act. The person to whom the promise is made (promisee) has a right to expect or demand the performance of some particular thing.

promisee The person to whom a promise is made.

promisor The person who makes a promise.

promissory estoppel A doctrine which arises when there is a promise which the promisor should reasonably expect to induce action or forbearance of a definite and substantial character on the part of the promisee, and which does induce such action or forbearance in reliance thereon; such a promise is binding if injustice can be avoided only through enforcement of the promise.

promissory note A written instrument signed by a maker unconditionally promising to pay a sum certain in money to a payee or a holder on demand or on a specified date [UCC 3–104].

promoter An entrepreneur who participates in the organization of a newly formed corporation, usually by issuing a prospectus, procuring subscriptions to the stock, making contract purchases, securing a charter, and the like. Promoters generally assume substantial risks in organizing new corporations, but also stand to realize significant profits from their efforts.

protected class Persons of identifiable characteristics who historically have been victimized by discriminatory treatment for certain purposes. Depending on the context, these characteristics include age, color, gender, national origin, race, and religion.

proximate cause The "next" or "substantial" cause; in tort law, a concept used to determine whether a plaintiff's injury was the natural and forseeable result of a defendant's negligent act. If the negligent act of a defendant was the sole cause or was a substantial cause of injuries to a plaintiff, the defendant will be liable to the plaintiff.

puffing A salesperson's often exaggerated claims concerning the quality of the goods offered for sale. Such claims involve opinions rather than facts and are not considered to be legally binding promises or warranties.

punitive damages Compensation in excess of actual damages. They are awarded in order to punish the wrongdoer, and will usually be awarded only in cases involving willful or malicious misconduct. (see *exemplary damages*)

purchase-money security interest A security interest to the extent that it is: (1) taken or retained by a seller of the collateral to secure all or part of the price of the collateral; or (2) taken by a creditor who, by making advances or incurring an obligation, gives value to enable the debtor to acquire rights in or use of collateral, if such value is in fact so used [UCC 9–107].

Q

qualified indorsement An indorsement on a negotiable instrument under which the indorser disclaims to subsequent holders secondary liability on the instrument; under a qualified indorsement, however, an indorser still gives the normal transfer warranties except the qualified indorser warrants only that "he has no knowledge" that a defense of "any party is good against him . . . ." The most common qualified indorsement is "without recourse" [UCC 3–417(2)(3)].

quantum meruit Literally, "as much as he deserves"— an expression describing the extent of liability on a contract implied in law (quasi-contract). An equitable doctrine based on the concept that one who benefits from another's labor and materials should not be unjustly enriched thereby but should be required to pay a reasonable amount for the benefit received, even absent a contract.

quasi-contract An obligation or contract imposed by law, in the absence of agreement, to prevent unjust enrichment. Sometimes referred to as implied-in-law contracts (as a legal fiction) to distinguish them from implied-in-fact contracts (voluntary agreements inferred from the parties' conduct). (see *contracts implied in law*)

quasi in rem **jurisdiction** This refers to a court's jurisdiction over proceedings that are brought against the defendant personally, but it is the defendant's interest in the property that serves as the basis of the jurisdiction.

R

rate setting A form of regulation in which federal agencies determine the prices at which certain companies can sell their goods or services.

ratification The confirmation of a previous act. In contract law, the confirmation of a voidable act (that is, an act that without ratification would not be an enforceable contractual obligation). In agency law, the confirmation by one person of an act or contract performed or entered into in his or her behalf by another, who assumed, without authority, to act as his or her agent.

real property Property consisting of land and buildings thereupon, which are stationary, as opposed to personal property, which can be moved. In the absence of a contract, real property includes things growing on the land before they are severed (such as timber) as well as fixtures [UCC 2–107].

reasonable care The degree of care that a person of ordinary prudence would exercise in the same or similar circumstances.

reasonable doubt The standard used to determine the guilt or innocence of a person criminally charged. To be guilty of a crime, one must be proved guilty "beyond and to the exclusion of every reasonable doubt." A doubt that would cause prudent persons to hesitate before acting in matters important to themselves.

reasonable offeree A reasonable person in the position of the offeree.

rebuttal A rebuttal refers to evidence that is given by one party to refute evidence that has been introduced by an adverse party.

recognizance A formal obligation to do a certain act as recorded and required by a court, such as an obligation to return or reappear before a court without putting up a bail bond.

recommended order In the context of administrative law, an agency employee's recommendation to the agency of a disposition in a matter other than a rulemaking.

recording statutes Recording statutes for deeds, mortgages, etc., are enacted to provide notice to future purchasers, creditors, and encumbrancers of an existing claim.

reformation A court-ordered correction of a written instrument to cause it to reflect the true intentions of the parties.

Regulation E A set of rules issued by the Federal Reserve System's board of governors under the authority of the Electronic Fund Transfer Act to protect users of electronic fund transfer systems.

Regulation Z A set of rules promulgated by the Federal Reserve System's board of governors to implement the provisions of the Truth-in-Lending Act.

rejection An offeree's communication to an offeror that the offeree refuses to accept the terms of the proposal made by the offeror.

rejoinder In a rejoinder, the defendant's attorney answers the plaintiff's rebuttal.

release The relinquishment, concession, or giving up of a right, claim, or privilege, by the person in whom it exists or to whom it accrues, to the person against whom it might have been enforced or demanded.

remainder A future interest in property held by a person other than a grantor which occurs at the natural termination of the preceding estate. For example, G transfers real property in trust with income therefrom to A for life with the remainder to B upon A's death. B has a remainder interest. A remainder is a present right to a future interest in property and can either be vested or contingent.

remedy The term remedy refers to the rights that are given to individuals, by law or by contract, upon the happening of a particular event.

remedy at law A remedy at law is a legal remedy that is available in a court of law. Money damages are awarded as a remedy at law. This remedy is to be distinguished from a remedy in equity.

remedy in equity A remedy allowed by courts in situations where remedies at law are not appropriate. Remedies in equity are based on settled rules of fairness, justice, and honesty.

rent The compensation or fee paid, usually periodically, for the use of any property, land, buildings, equipment, and so on.

rent escalation An increase in rent during a lease term according to a lease clause.

repair and deduct A tenant's remedy for a landlord's failure to maintain leased premises. Under repair and deduct statutes or judicial recognition of a right to repair and deduct, a tenant pays for repairs and deducts the cost of the repairs from the rent.

replevin An action in equity brought to recover possession of personal property unlawfully held by another. (see *conversion*)

reply Procedurally, a plaintiff's response to a defendant's answer.

requirements contract An agreement under which a promisor promises to supply the promisee with all the goods and/or services the promisee might require from period to period. While such contracts were at one time void for indefiniteness of amount, they are now universally valid [UCC 2–306(1)].

resale price maintenance An agreement between a manufacturer and a retailer in which the manufacturer specifies the minimum retail price of its products. Such agreements are illegal *per se* under the Sherman Act.

rescission A remedy whereby the contract is cancelled and the parties are returned to the positions they occupied before the contract was made. May be done through mutual consent of the parties, by their conduct, or by the decree of a court of equity.

respondeat superior A principle of law whereby an agent or an employer is held liable for the wrongful acts committed by agents or employees while within the scope of their agency or employment.

respondent In equity practice, the party who answers a bill or other proceeding. In appellate practice, the party against whom an appeal is taken (sometimes referred to as the appellee).

restitution An equitable remedy under which a person is restored to his or her original position prior to loss or injury, or placed in the same position as if a breach had not occurred [UCC 2–718].

restrictive indorsement Any indorsement of a negotiable instrument which purports to condition or prohibit further transfer of the instrument. As against payor and intermediary banks, such indorsements are usually ineffective [UCC 3–205].

resulting trust A trust implied in law from the intentions of the parties to a given transaction. A trust in which a party holds legal title for the benefit of another, although without expressed intent to do so, because the presumption of such intent arises by operation of law.

retaliatory eviction The eviction of a tenant because of the tenant's complaints, participation in a tenant's union, or similar activity with which the landlord does not agree.

reversion A future interest under which a grantor retains a present right to a future interest in property which the grantor conveys to another; usually the residue of a life estate. The reversion is always a vested property right.

reversionary interest A right to the future enjoyment of property presently in the possession of or occupied by another. (See *reversion*.)

revocation The recall of some power, authority, or thing granted, or a destroying or making void of some will, deed, or offer that had been valid until revoked.

right of contribution In tort law, the right of a tortfeasor against whom judgment has been rendered to recover proportional shares of judgment from other joint tortfeasors whose negligence contributed to the injury and who are also liable to the plaintiff.

right of entry The right to take or resume possession of real property peaceably.

right of redemption The right to free property from the encumbrance of a foreclosure or judicial sale, or to recover the title passing thereby, by paying what is due, with all costs and interest. Includes both equity and statutory periods of redemption.

right of reimbursement The legal right of a person to be restored, repaid, or indemnified for costs, expenses, or losses incurred or expended on behalf of another.

right of subrogation The substitution of one person in the place of another giving the former the same legal rights which the latter had. Subrogation occurs most frequently in construction contracts, insurance contracts, suretyship contracts, and negotiable instrument law.

risk A specified contingency or peril.

risk management Planning to protect one's interest should some event threaten to undermine its security. In the context of insurance, transferring certain risks from the insured to the insurance company.

robbery Theft from a person, accompanied by force or fear of force. (see *assault, battery*)

rulemaking The actions undertaken by administrative agencies when formally adopting new regulations or amending old ones. Under the Administrative Procedure Act, rulemaking includes notifying the public of proposed rules or changes and receiving and considering the public's comments.

rule of reason A test by which a court balances the reasons (such as economic efficiency) for an agreement against its potentially anticompetitive effects. In antitrust litigation, most practices are analyzed under a rule of reason rather than under a *per se* rule (see *per se violations*).

S

sale The passing of title to property from the seller to the buyer for a price [UCC 2–106(1)].

sale on approval A type of conditional sale which becomes absolute only when the buyer, on trial, approves or is satisfied with the good(s) sold. Besides expressly approving the goods, approval may be inferred if the buyer keeps the goods beyond a reasonable time, or does any act with the goods which is inconsistent with the seller's ownership.

sale or return A type of conditional sale wherein title and possession pass from the seller to the buyer; however, the buyer retains the option to rescind or return the goods during a specified period even though the goods conform to the contract.

satisfaction The tender of substitute performance in return for the relinquishment of the right of action on a prior obligation. (see *accord and satisfaction*)

scienter Guilty knowledge of the defendant as to the act or omission which led to the injury or conduct complained of.

S corporation A corporation that has met certain requirements as set out by the Internal Revenue Code and thus qualifies for special income tax treatment. Essentially, an S corporation is taxed the same as a partnership while at the same time allowing the corporation's owners to enjoy the privilege of limited liability.

secondary boycott Refusal to work for, purchase from, or handle products of secondary employer with whom the union has no dispute, with the object of forcing such employer to stop doing business with the primary employer with whom the union has a labor dispute.

secured party The lender, seller, or other person in whose favor there is a security interest. (see *security interest*)

secured transaction Any transaction, regardless of its form, which is intended to create a security interest in personal property or fixtures, including goods, documents, and other intangibles [UCC 9–105].

securities Stock certificates, bonds, notes, debentures, warrants, or other documents given as evidence of an ownership interest in the corporation or as a promise of repayment by the corporation.

security agreement An agreement which creates or provides for a security interest. (see *security interest*)

security interest An interest in personal property or fixtures which secures payment or performance of an obligation [UCC 1–201(37)].

self-defense The legally recognized privilege to protect one's self or one's property against injury by another. The privilege of self-defense only protects acts which are reasonably necessary to protect one's self or one's property.

service mark A mark used in the sale or advertising of services, such as to distinguish the services of one person from the services of others. Titles, character names, and other distinctive features of radio and television programs may be registered as service marks.

shop right doctrine An employer's privilege to use an invention developed during work hours by an employee using employer's equipment and/or materials, without compensating that employee.

short-form merger A merger between a parent corporation and a subsidiary corporation when the parent corporation owns at least ninety percent of the outstanding shares of each class of stock issued by the subsidiary corporation. These mergers can be accomplished without shareholder approval of either corporation.

signature The name or mark of a person, written by that person at his or her direction. In commercial law, any name, word, or mark used with the intention to authenticate a writing constitutes a signature [UCC 1–201(39), 3–401(2)].

slander An oral defamation of one's character, reputation, business, or property rights. (see *libel*)

special indorsement An indorsement of an instrument specifying to whom or to whose order the instrument is payable [UCC 3–204(1)].

special warranty deed A deed in which the grantor only covenants to warrant and defend the title against claims and demands of the grantor and all persons claiming by, through, and under him or her.

specific performance An equitable remedy, whereby the court orders one of the parties to a contract to perform duties under the contract. Usually granted when money damages would be an inadequate remedy and the object of the contract is unique (*e.g.*, purchase and sale of real property) [UCC 2–716(1)(2)].

spendthrift trust A trust created to protect the beneficiary from spending all the money he or she is entitled to. Only a certain portion of the total amount is given to the beneficiary at any one time, and most states prohibit creditors from attaching assets of the trust.

spot zoning Granting a zoning classification to a parcel of land that is different from the classification given to other land in the immediate area.

stale check A check, other than a certified check, which is presented more than six months after its date [UCC 4–404].

standard setting In the context of administrative law, a common form of regulation by which agencies set standards with which certain businesses must comply. For example, the Occupational Safety and Health Administration may require employers to use certain equipment or procedures to ensure the health and safety of workers.

standing The requirement of standing to sue means that an individual must have a sufficient stake in a controversy in order to sue. The plaintiff must demonstrate that he or she either is injured or has been threatened with injury.

stare decisis A flexible doctrine of the courts, recognizing the value of following prior decisions (precedents) in cases similar to the one before the court—the practice by the courts of being consistent with prior decisions based on similar facts. (see *precedent*)

state-action doctrine The principle that where state regulation supplants the competitive market and regulates it intensively, federal antitrust laws do not apply. Thus, an anticompetitive arrangement that might be condemned under federal antitrust laws may be permissible under the state-action doctrine if the arrangement is expressly authorized and actively supervised by the state.

statute of limitations Statutes of the federal government and the various states setting maximum time periods during which certain actions can be brought or rights enforced. After the time period set out in the applicable statute of limitations has run, no legal action can be brought regardless of whether any cause of action ever existed. (see *laches* for equitable doctrine)

statutes of respose See *Statute of limitations*. Basically, statutes of limitations that are not dependent upon the happening of a cause of action. Statutes of respose generally begin to run at an earlier date and run for a longer time than statutes of limitations.

statutory law Laws which are enacted by a legislative body (as opposed to constitutional law, administrative law or case law).

statutory period of redemption A time period (usually set by state statute) during which a defaulted mortgage, land contract, etc., can be redeemed after foreclosure or judicial sale. (see *right of redemption*)

stock (1) The goods of a merchant kept for sale. (2) A merchant's entire property employed in business, including money, merchandise, and credit. (3) In corporation law: (a) a corporation's capital formed by subscribers' contributions or the sale of shares; (b) the aggregate of shares owned by a corporation's shareholders or the proportional share of an individual shareholder; (c) the property represented by a certificate of stock; (d) a shareholder's right to participate in the general management of a corporation and to share proportionally in its profits or earnings, or in the distribution of its assets on dissolution; (e) all corporate wealth and resources, subject to all corporate liabilities and obligations. *Stock* is distinguished from *bonds* in that stock gives a right of ownership in part of a corporation's assets and a right of interest in any surplus after payment of corporate debt; bonds represent no ownership interest.

stock warrant A certificate commonly attached to preferred stock and bonds granting one the right to buy shares of stock, usually within a set time period.

strict liability Liability regardless of fault. Under tort law, strict liability is imposed on any merchant seller who introduces into commerce any good which is unreasonably dangerous when in a defective condition.

subagent An agent appointed by one who is himself or herself an agent to perform functions the agent has undertaken for a principal. An agent appointed by an agent.

sublease A lease executed by the lessee of land to a third person, conveying the same interest which the lessee enjoys, but for a shorter term than that for which the lessee holds (as compared to assignment, in which the lessee transfers the entire unexpired term of the leasehold to a third party).

substantive law Laws which define the rights and duties of individuals with respect to each other, as opposed to procedural law which defines the manner in which these rights and duties may be enforced.

summary judgment A judgment entered by a trial court prior to trial which is based upon the valid assertion by one of the parties that there are no disputed issues of fact which would necessitate a trial.

syllogism The full logical form of a single argument, consisting of a major premise (All students are intelligent), a minor premise (John is a student), and a conclusion (Therefore, John is intelligent).

T

tenancy at sufferance The situation whereby one who, after rightfully being in possession of leased premises, continues to occupy the property after the lease has been terminated. The tenant has no estate in the land. He or she occupies only because the person entitled to evict has not done so.

tenancy at will The right of a tenant to remain in possession of land with permission of the landlord until either the tenant or the landlord chooses to terminate the tenancy.

tenancy by the entirety The joint ownership of property by husband and wife. Neither party can alienate or encumber the property without the consent of the other. It is inherited by the survivor of the two, and dissolution of marriage transforms it to a tenancy in common.

tenancy for years A non-freehold estate/lease for a specified number of years, at which time the interest reverts to the grantor.

tenancy in common Co-ownership of property whereby each party owns an undivided interest that passes to his or her heirs at death. (see *joint tenancy*)

tender A timely offer, or expression of willingness, to pay a debt or perform an obligation.

term A word or phrase in a contract, instrument, or agreement which relates to a particular matter; also a fixed period of time [UCC 1–201(42)].

testamentary trust A trust which is created by will and therefore does not take effect until the death of the testator.

testator (-trix) One who makes and executes a will. (see *will*)

third party beneficiary contract A contract between two or more parties, the performance of which is intended to directly benefit a third party, thus giving the third party a right to file suit for breach of contract against either of the original contracting parties. (see *creditor beneficiary, donee beneficiary*)

tort Civil (as opposed to criminal) wrongs not arising from a breach of contract; a breach of a legal duty owed by the defendant to the plaintiff. That breach must be the proximate cause of the harm done to plaintiff. (see *negligence, proximate cause*)

tortfeasor One who commits a personal wrong (or a tort).

totten trust A trust created by the deposit of a person's own money in his or her own name as a trustee for another. It is a tentative trust, revocable at will until the depositor dies or completes the gift in his or her lifetime by some unequivocal act or declaration.

trade acceptance A bill of exchange/draft drawn by the seller of goods on the purchaser and accepted by such purchaser or the bank of the purchaser. Once accepted, the purchaser becomes primarily liable to pay the draft [UCC 3–413(1)].

trademark A word or symbol which has become sufficiently associated with a good (common law) or has been registered with a government agency. Once established, the owner has exclusive use and has the right to bring a legal action against those who infringe upon the protection given the trademark.

trade name A name used in commercial activity to designate a particular business, or place at which a business is located, or a class of goods. Trade names can be exclusive or non-exclusive. Examples of trade names are Sears, Safeway, Firestone, and Austin Vacuum Cleaner Co.

trade secrets Information or processes that give a business an advantage over it competitors, who do not know the information or processes.

traveler's check An instrument purchased from a bank, express company, or the like, in various denominations, which can be used as cash upon a second signature by the purchaser. It has the characteristics of a cashier's check. (see *cashier's check*)

treasure trove Money or coin, gold, silver, plate, or bullion found hidden in the earth or other private place, the owner of which is unknown; literally, treasure found.

treasury shares Shares of corporate stock which have been issued as fully paid that are subsequently re-acquired by the corporation.

treble damages Damages consisting of single damages determined by a jury and tripled in amount in certain cases as required by statute.

trespasser One whom the party in possession of real property does not invite onto the property and who has no other right to be on the premises.

trespass to land At common law, the mere intentional or unintentional passing over another person's land uninvited, regardless whether any physical damage was done to the land. Today a majority of courts find trespass only in cases of intentional intrusion, negligence, or some "abnormally dangerous activity" on the part of the defendant.

trespass to personalty Any wrongful transgression or offense against the personal property of another.

trust (1) A form of business organization somewhat similar to a corporation. Originally, a device by which several corporations engaged in the same general line of business combined for their mutual advantage to eliminate competition and control the market for their products. The term trust derived from the transfer of the voting power of the corporations' shareholders to the committee or board that controlled the organization. (2) A fiduciary relationship in which title to property is held by one person (a trustee) for the benefit of another (a beneficiary).

tying arrangement A requirement in a contract between a buyer and seller whereby the buyer of a specific good is obligated to purchase additional products or services.

U

ultra vires acts Activities of a corporation's managers which are outside the scope of the power granted to the corporation by its charter or the laws of the state of incorporation.

umpire A person to whose judgment a dispute is referred when the matter has been submitted to two or more arbitrators who do not agree in their decision.

unanimous opinion A court opinion supported by all of the judges or justices involved in deciding the case.

unconscionable Grossly unfair and prohibited by public policy. An unconscionable contract or clause is one in which one party, as a result of his or her disproportionate bargaining power, is forced to accept terms that are unfairly burdensome and that unfairly benefit the dominating party. Such a contract or clause will be deemed void as against public policy.

unconscionability See *Unconscionable.*

underwriter In insurance law, the one assuming a risk in return for the payment of a premium; the insurer. In securities law, any person, banker, or syndicate that guarantees a definite sum of money to a business or government in return for the issue of stock or bonds, usually for resale purposes.

undisclosed principal A principal whose identity is unknown by a third person, and the third person has no knowledge that the agent is acting in an agency capacity at the time the contract is made. (see and compare to *disclosed* and *partially disclosed principal*)

unenforceable contract A contract having no legal effect or force in a court action.

unfair labor practices Management activities (such as interfering with employees' attempts to unionize) that are prohibited by the National Labor Relations Act and union activities (such as secondary boycotts) that are prohibited by the Taft-Hartley Act.

unilateral contract A contract under which promise of payment or performance is given in exchange for the full performance by the other party (as opposed to a promise to perform by the other party). (see *bilateral contract*)

unlawful detainer The unjustifiable retention of the possession of real property by one whose right to possession has terminated but who refuses to leave—as when a tenant holds over after the end of the lease term in spite of the landlord's demand for possession.

United States Trustee A government official who performs appointing and other administrative tasks that a bankruptcy judge would otherwise have to perform.

universal life A type of insurance that combines some aspects of term insurance with some aspects of whole life insurance.

usury Charging interest on a debt above the statutory maximum, as defined by various state statutes. A contract which includes a usurious interest rate is illegal.

V

valid contract A properly constituted contract having legal strength or force. (see *unenforceable contract*)

venue The geographical district in which the action is tried and from which the jury is selected. (see *jurisdiction*)

vertical agreements Agreements between firms at different levels in the chain of production (for example, an agreement between a manufacturer and a retailer), to fix or regulate prices or otherwise restrain competition.

vertical merger A combining of two firms, one of which purchases goods for resale from the other. If a producer or wholesaler acquires a retailer, it is a *forward* merger. If a retailer or distributor acquires its producer, it is a *backward* merger. (see *merger*)

vesting Accruing; fixing; taking effect; giving an immediate right to present or future possession.

void contract A contract having no legal force or binding effect. (see *valid contract, unenforceable contract*)

voidable contract A contract that may be legally annulled at the option of one of the parties.

W

waiver An intentional, knowing relinquishment of a legal right. (see *release*)

warehouse receipt A receipt issued by a person engaged in the business of storing goods for hire; it is a document of title [UCC 1–201(46), 7–201, 7–202].

warranty deed A deed under which the grantor guarantees to the grantee that the grantor has title to the property conveyed in the deed, that there are no encumbrances on the property other than what the grantor has represented, and that the grantee will enjoy quiet possession.

waste The abuse or destructive use of real property by one who is in rightful possession of the property but who does not have title to it. Waste does not include ordinary depreciation due to age and normal use.

watered stock Stock issued by a corporation as if fully paid for, when in fact less than par value has been paid.

whistle-blowing Telling the government or the press that one's employer is engaged in some unsafe or illegal activity.

white-collar crime White collar crime refers to nonviolent crimes committed by corporations and individuals. Embezzlement and theft are two examples of white collar crime.

whole life A life insurance policy in which the insured pays a level premium for his or her entire life and in which there is a constantly accumulating cash value against which the insured can withdraw or borrow. Sometimes referred to as straight life insurance.

will An instrument directing what is to be done with a person's property upon his or her death, made by that person and revocable during his or her lifetime. No interests pass until the testator dies. (see *testator*)

workouts A common law or bankruptcy composition with creditors whereby a debtor enters into an agreement with a creditor or creditors for a payment or plan to discharge the debtor's debt(s).

writ of attachment A writ employed to enforce obedience to an order or judgment of the court. The writ may take the form of taking or seizing property or persons to bring them under the control of the court.

writ of certiorari An order by the appellate court which is used when the court has discretion on whether to hear an appeal. If the writ is denied, the court refuses to hear the appeal and, in effect, the judgment of the lower court stands unchanged. If the writ is granted, then it has the effect of ordering the lower court to certify the record and send it up to the higher court which has used its discretion to hear the appeal.

writ of execution A writ which puts in force a court's decree or judgment.

Z

zoning The division of land of an entire city or county by legislative regulation whereby the legislature prescribes certain general or particular uses for various segments of the land, including structural and architectural design.

TABLE OF CASES

The principal cases are in bold type. Cases cited or discussed are in roman type. Cases that can also be retrieved on West Publishing's LEGAL CLERK Research Software System are indicated by a color dot. To determine which of the three versions of LEGAL CLERK a particular case appears on, please turn to the text page cited and refer to the color coded computer symbol printed with the case citation.

A red computer symbol indicates that the case appears on *Uniform Commercial Code Article 2 Sales-Version 1.0*. A black computer symbol indicates that the case is on *Government Regulation and the Legal Environment of Business-Version 1.0*. A black computer symbol with a color background identifies the case as appearing on *Contracts-Version 1.0*.

B

C

INDEX

1